The American Heritage® College Thesaurus

FIRST EDITION

The American Heritage® College Thesaurus

FIRST EDITION

Houghton Mifflin Company
Boston • New York

Visit our website: www.houghtonmifflinbooks.com

ISBN-13: 978-0-618-40219-9
ISBN-10: 0-618-40219-5
ISBN-13: 978-0-618-46029-8 (deluxe binding)
ISBN-10: 0-618-46029-2 (deluxe binding)

Library of Congress Cataloging-in-Publication Data

American heritage college thesaurus.— 1st ed.
    p. cm.
  ISBN 0-618-40219-5 — ISBN 0-618-46029-2 (deluxe bdg.)
  1. English language—Synonyms and antonyms. I. Houghton Mifflin Company.
  PE1591.A525 2004
  423'.12—dc22
                                    2004002357

Table of Contents

Editorial and Production Staff

Vice President, Publisher of Dictionaries
Margery S. Berube

Vice President, Executive Editor
Joseph P. Pickett

Editorial Project Director
David R. Pritchard

Vice President, Managing Editor
Christopher Leonesio

Assistant Project Director
Kirsten Patey Hurd

Senior Editor
Steven R. Kleinedler

Database Production Supervisor
Christopher Granniss

Associate Editor
Uchenna C. Ikonné
Patrick Taylor

Art and Production Supervisor
Margaret Anne Miles

Manufacturing Supervisor
James W. Mitchell

Contributing Editors
Erich Michael Groat
Matthew Heidenry
Robert Knippen

Editorial Production Associate
Brianne M. Lutfy

Editorial Assistance
Nicholas Durlacher
Daniel T. Harney
Hiu Ho
Ashley N. O'Bryan

Text Design
Catherine Hawkes, Cat & Mouse

Administrative Coordinator
Kevin McCarthy

Proofreaders
Kathryn Blatt
Katherine Isaacs
Julia Penelope

Pre-Press Development
Thomas Technology Solutions, Inc.

Preface

Since the publication of its first edition in 1969, *The American Heritage Dictionary* has built a reputation for authority, accessibility, and innovation in the art of lexicography. The editors of the American Heritage dictionaries are now pleased to present another first edition—*The American Heritage College Thesaurus*—prepared with the same high lexical standards and the same emphasis on the user's convenience that have become the hallmarks of American Heritage reference works.

Most people would agree that a good thesaurus is one of the most useful resources a writer can own. No one can be expected to have at immediate disposal all the word choices available in a language, and no one can count on just the right term unfailingly materializing in every situation. Whether to avoid repetition, liven up a sentence, or pin down a nuance, even gifted writers can profit from a trip to the thesaurus. At the same time, many would also agree that a typical thesaurus can be frustrating or confusing to consult. In designing *The American Heritage College Thesaurus*, we took into account the most common criticisms leveled at thesauruses by users as well as by teachers and academics.

First and foremost, we focused our synonym lists around a clear central meaning rather than, as in many thesauruses, grouping them loosely, in large numbers, under a broad category or a vaguely glossed general idea. Every sense of every entry in this Thesaurus is associated with a concisely worded definition, and the synonyms that follow are all chosen with that meaning in mind. For example, if you look up the verb **linger** in most thesauruses, you will find a single undifferentiated list of synonyms having to do generally with the idea of

remaining behind. In *The American Heritage College Thesaurus*, however, you will find two distinct senses of this verb. If the meaning you are looking for is "to continue to be in a place," you will be directed to synonyms such as *bide, tarry,* and *wait.* Or, if your meaning is "to go or move slowly so that progress is hindered," you will be directed to a different list of synonyms such as *dawdle, dilly-dally,* and *drag.* Thus the design prompts you to think first in terms of meaning; once you determine the meaning that best fits your context, the choice of an appropriate synonym—from a list that has been focused specifically around that meaning—is that much easier.

Our second goal was to provide a wide selection of current and useful synonyms without including so much extraneous material that the simple act of choosing a word becomes a chore. *The American Heritage College Thesaurus* has 20,000 headwords with more than 140,000 synonyms in all. Traditional thesauruses are often criticized for their over-long lists full of obscure and dated terminology. We have steered clear of the kind of vocabulary that is rarely if ever seen outside thesauruses themselves and concentrated instead on the terms that are most likely to fit the needs of contemporary writers. In crafting our lists, however, we have by no means restricted our synonyms only to mainstream vocabulary, since one of the main reasons writers turn to a thesaurus is in search of a colorful or striking alternative to the word they have in mind. Thus we have made a point of including a generous selection of informal, slang, and regional terms as well as numerous idioms, with each category clearly labeled, because the choice of the right level of vocabulary is an important part of selecting the best synonym.

Finally, whereas traditional thesauruses typically offer little if any guidance in choosing among the synonyms they list, we have included more than 700 core synonym paragraphs throughout the book to illustrate differences in meaning among some of the most basic and important synonyms in English. Every synonym included in the core synonym features is shown in either a sample sentence or a pertinent quotation from a well-known author. In addition, many of the paragraphs discuss the nuances of meaning and usage in greater detail. For example, the core synonym feature for **abrupt**, in the sense of "rudely informal,"

points out that while *brusque* "emphasizes rude abruptness," *gruff* "implies roughness or surliness but does not necessarily suggest rudeness."

So it is that every synonym has its own flavor, its own associations, and these subtleties go a long way toward giving our language its expressiveness. We hope that the care with which this Thesaurus was assembled will result in greater precision and more effective communication on the part of its users. To communicate with words is to make choices, and in this regard the English language contains an embarrassment of riches. We offer this book as a way of making those riches available for writers of all abilities to use.

Introduction

The American Heritage College Thesaurus is a book devoted entirely to meaning. In contrast to the old-fashioned thesaurus, which groups undifferentiated words together with an entry word with no definition, this book provides an analysis—a definition—of the meaning or meanings of each entry word in the book. Synonyms are grouped according to meaning. What, then, *is* meaning?

Meaning

The meaning of even a single word is rather more complex than one might imagine. The most obvious aspect of meaning is *denotation*, that is, the thing meant, the concept or object referred to. The denotation of the word *chair*, for example, is that it is a piece of furniture, that it has a seat, legs, a back, and often arms, and that one person can sit on it. So long as it has these features, a chair can be identified as a chair irrespective of the fact that it may be big or small, made of chrome or wood, upholstered or caned—in short, no matter what other features it may have. Furthermore, a chair is distinct from all other pieces of furniture upon which one can sit. It is different from a stool because a stool is backless and armless. It is different from a couch, on which one or more may recline, and different from a chaise longue, which has a seat long enough to support the outstretched legs of the sitter. Thus the denotation of a word includes those features that are criterial and so serve to define and distinguish.

In addition to its denotation, a word may have a *connotation*, that is, the suggestive or associative implications of an expression beyond its literal sense. Differences, as of style or expressiveness, that cause a given term to convey a denotation more— or less—formally, colorfully, humorously, or the like, constitute the connotations of the word. For example, both *mouth* and *trap* denote the opening in the body through which food is ingested. *Mouth*, however, is what might be called a neutral term; it conveys information but has no connotations. *Trap*, on the other hand, is a slang word and is often considered to be somewhat vulgar.

Words expressive of emotion frequently have connotations, but many words that are not emotive also have them. Many sets of words of identical denotation can be arranged in a spectrum of greater to lesser formality. For example, of the synonym group *transpire, happen, occur, befall, betide,* and *hap*, all meaning "to take place, come to pass," *transpire* is the most formal; *happen* and *occur* are neutral—nonconnotative; and *befall, betide,* and *hap* have a somewhat archaic flavor. All of these facts beyond the bare denotation of the terms constitute the connotations of these words. In *The American Heritage College Thesaurus* the labels *Informal, Chiefly Regional,* and *Slang* identify restrictions with respect to level or style of usage.

Synonymy and Synonyms

Given the complexity of meaning, a person searching for an alternative word must be sure that the synonym chosen is accurate and precise. Because of its emphasis on the meaning or meanings of a word, *The American Heritage College Thesaurus* is specifically designed to offer the user a choice of synonyms that lie within the denotative range of the word or sense of the word with which they correspond.

In its strict sense a *synonym* is a word with a meaning identical or very similar to that of another word. It is often said that in fact there is no such thing as an absolute synonym for any word, that is, a form that is identical in every aspect of meaning so that the two can be applied interchangeably. According to this extreme view the only true synonyms are terms having precisely the same denotation, connotation, and range of applicability. As it turns out, these so-called true synonyms are frequently technical terms and almost always concrete words coming from linguistically disparate sources. Good examples of such pairs are *celiac* (from Greek) and *abdominal* (from Latin); and *car* (from Latin) and *automobile* (from French). These meet the criteria for true synonymy: they have precisely the same denotations, connotations, and range of applicability, and they are used in identical contexts.

This view of synonymy is far too restrictive, however. In *The American Heritage College Thesaurus* synonymous terms are those having nearly identical denotations. English is rich in such words. Speakers very often have a choice from among a set of words of differing origin but the same denotation. A person may react with *anger* (from Old Norse), *wrath* (from Old English), *ire* or *fury* (both from Latin), or *choler* (from Greek). Someone's behavior might strike others as *weird* (from Old English), *odd* (from Old Norse), *unconventional* (from Latin), or *idiosyncratic* (from Greek). On a chilly evening it might feel good to don a *cloak* (from Latin), *wrap* (from Middle English), *stole* (from Greek), or *shawl* (from Persian). The reason for choosing one of these words over another is frequently stylistic: one may prefer a simpler or a more complex word; one may prefer a more formal or a less formal term. But the fact that these words share a denotation makes them synonymous and available as substitutes for words one has in mind so that one can be more precise, express oneself more colorfully, or avoid repetition. All of the terms included in the synonymies in *The American Heritage College Thesaurus* share the same denotation.

The *American Heritage College Thesaurus* is designed for quick and easy access to the best synonyms for a particular context. Concise definitions identify the central meaning shared by each group of synonyms, while a system of main entries and handy cross-references eliminates the open-ended searching associated with many thesauruses. The basic organization of the Thesaurus is given under **Overview,** below. A full description of entry elements and features follows under **Components of Entries.**

Overview

Entry Order Headwords are listed alphabetically in boldface type and are followed by an italic part-of-speech label. If a headword has more than one part of speech, each additional part of speech appears boldface and indented within the same entry. Phrasal verbs (two-word verbs consisting of a verb and an adverb or preposition) are listed in alphabetical order, also boldface and indented, directly under the base verbs:

smile *noun*
A facial expression marked by an upward curving of the lips ▸ grin, simper, smirk. *See also* **sneer.**
smile *verb*
To curve the lips upward in expressing amusement, pleasure, or happiness ▸ beam, grin, simper, smirk. *Idioms:* break into a smile, crack (*or* flash *or* give) a smile.
smile on *or* **upon** *verb*
To lend supportive approval to ▸ countenance, encourage, favor. *See also* **approve, support.**

Synonym Lists Synonyms are presented in lists following the definition to which they belong; they are introduced by the symbol ▸. There are two kinds of synonym lists in this Thesaurus.

A *main-entry list* contains all the synonyms for any particular defined sense, including any labeled synonyms and idioms relevant to that sense:

absent-minded *adjective*
So lost in thought as to be unable to remember or attend to things ▸ absent, abstracted, bemused, distracted, distrait, faraway, forgetful, inattentive, lost, oblivious, preoccupied, scatterbrained. *Slang:* spaced-out, spacy. *Idioms:* a million miles away, gathering wool, lost (*or* off) in space, out of it. *See also* **careless, detached, dreamy, negligent.**

Most of the synonyms in a main-entry list are also entered individually at their own alphabetical place in the Thesaurus as a *cross-reference list*. A cross-reference list consists of the pertinent definition along with a subset of the synonyms from the main-entry list plus a *See* cross-reference to the headword where the full list is located:

forgetful *adjective*
1. So lost in thought as to be unable to remember things ▸ abstracted, inattentive, preoccupied. *See* **absent-minded. 2.** ...

preoccupied *adjective*
... **2.** So lost in thought as to be unable to remember things ▸ abstracted, bemused, distracted. *See* **absent-minded.**

Thus no matter what word from a group you look up, you are never more than one entry away from the main-entry list with its full listing of synonyms and idioms. In many cases you may find the synonym you're looking for in the abbreviated list at the cross-reference entry itself, without turning to the main entry. Note that many of the entries in the Thesaurus contain both main-entry lists (which are generally grouped first in the entry) and cross-reference lists, as in the example for **boast** below. See the section *Cross-References* under **Components of Entries,** below, for variations in the styling of single-sense cross-reference entries.

Components of Entries

Senses and Definitions The entries in this Thesaurus are organized into defined senses, as in a dictionary. Each sense begins with a brief definition stating the meaning that is shared by the entry word and its synonyms, which are listed alphabetically after the symbol ▶. If an entry has more than one sense for any part of speech, the senses are numbered. Numbering begins again, if needed, for each new part of speech. In the entry for **boast,** the verb has two numbered senses; the noun has only one sense and is unnumbered:

> **boast** *verb*
> **1.** To talk with excessive pride ▶ bluster, brag, crow, gasconade, puff (up), swagger, swell (up), vaunt. *Informal:* blow. **Idioms:** blow one's own horn (*or* trumpet), pat oneself on the back, shoot off one's mouth (*or* face), sing one's own praises, talk big. *See also* **exaggerate, exult, strut. 2.** To have at one's disposal ▶ enjoy, have, hold. *See* **command** (3).
> **boast** *noun*
> Boastful talk or behavior ▶ boasting, brag, braggadocio, bragging, bravado, fanfaronade, gasconade, vaunt. *Informal:* blow, fish story. *Slang:* gas. *See also* **bombast.**

When an entry with only one part of speech has a single sense that is a cross-reference, the definition is omitted as unnecessary. The definition for such a sense will be found at the main entry to which the cross-reference points:

> **boaster** *noun*
> ▶ bragger, vaunter. *See* **braggart.**
>
> **braggart** *noun*
> One given to boasting ▶ blusterer, boaster, brag, braggadocio, bragger, swaggerer,

vaunter. *Informal:* blowhard. *Slang:* blower, windbag. *See also* **egotist, showoff.**

Cross-References There are two distinct types of cross-references between synonym lists. A cross-reference introduced by the word *See* leads from an abbreviated cross-reference list to the full main-entry list, as described in the section *Synonym Lists* in the **Overview** above. If the word you have looked up contains a *See* cross-reference, you know that you will find the complete list of synonyms for that sense, including all labeled terms and idioms, at the entry to which the cross-reference points. (See the example for **absent-minded** and its synonyms **forgetful** and **preoccupied** in *Synonym Lists.*)

A second kind of cross-reference, introduced by the words *See also,* leads from a main-entry list to one or more other, closely related main-entry lists elsewhere in the Thesaurus. If you have already found the right synonym for your purpose, you may not choose to follow a *See also* cross-reference. However, if you want to consider other synonyms for entries with similar but somewhat distinct meanings, the *See also* cross-references will help you broaden your search:

> **anchor** *noun*
> **1.** A device for supporting or holding in place ▶ brake, dowel, grapnel, kedge, mooring, wedge. *See also* **bond, cord, fastener, nail.**
> ...
>
> **fastener** *or* **fastening** *noun*
> A device for locking or for checking motion ▶ bar, binder, binding, buckle, catch, clamp, clasp, clip, collar, harness, hasp, hook, latch, lock, mortise, pawl, snap, vise. *See also* **anchor, bond, cord, nail.**

In addition to the *See* and *See also* cross-references, a third type of cross-reference is used to point to a core synonym paragraph. For an example of this cross-reference, see the section *Core Synonym Paragraphs* below.

Variants Variants in spelling, form, or gender identification are given after the main entry word and are boldface and preceded by an italic *or:*

> **ironic** *or* **ironical** *adjective*
> ▶ satiric, scoffing, sneering. *See* **sarcastic.** *See synonym note at* **sarcastic.**
>
> **almsman** *or* **almswoman** *noun*
> ▶ cadger, mendicant. *See* **beggar** (1).

When a single idiom can be worded in a variety of ways, the variant wordings are given parenthetically, as at **rescue:**

> **Idioms:** save by the bell, save one's bacon (*or* neck), come to the rescue of. *See also* **free, help.**

When variation exists between a verb and a phrasal verb, the variation is shown parenthetically. For example, at the entry for **design,** the synonym *map (out)* indicates that one can use either *map* or *map out* to mean "To work out and arrange the parts and details of."

Homographs and Sense Numbers   A homograph is a word that is spelled the same as another word but that differs in meaning and origin. Homographs are indicated by superscript numerals following the words to which they refer. Homograph numbers are used in headwords and cross-references to ensure that you locate the correct entry:

> **bud**[1] *noun*
> A source of further growth or development
> ► kernel, seed. *See* **germ** (2).
> **bud** *verb*
> To bear flowers ► burgeon, flower. *See* **bloom**[1] (1).
> **bud**[2] *noun*
> *Informal* A person whom one knows well, likes, and trusts ► mate. *Informal:* buddy, pal. *See* **friend** (1).

Note that cross-references that point to a particular numbered sense of an entry indicate the sense number in parentheses after the cross-reference entry word. Thus the cross-reference at the noun sense of **bud**[1], above, points to sense 2 of the noun **germ.**

Labels   All words requiring status labels are clearly tagged at the boldface entry word and in synonym lists. The usage labels *Informal* and *Slang* indicate levels of usage and styles of expression that may not be appropriate in all contexts. *Informal* generally applies to those words that are commonly used in the spoken language and in ordinary writing but that may not be appropriate in formal or official contexts. The word *buddy,* for example, carries an *Informal* label in the synonym list at **friend.** *Slang,* on the other hand, is a style of language characteristic of very casual speech. The *Slang* label appears at words and special senses of words that have an

exceptionally vivid, humorous, irreverent, or sarcastic flavor. For example, at the synonym list at **eat,** the phrasal verb *chow down* is labeled *Slang.*

The dialect label *Chiefly Regional* indicates that a term is indigenous to one or more geographic areas within the United States. For example, the words *chaw,* a synonym of *chew,* and *poorly,* a synonym of *sick,* are labeled *Chiefly Regional* because they are more commonly used in some parts of the country than in others.

Core Synonym Paragraphs   There are more than seven hundred core synonym paragraphs distributed throughout this Thesaurus. These paragraphs, located at the end of the main entry, explain the different nuances of meaning among a selected group of synonyms. Words discussed in a core synonym paragraph include a cross-reference to that paragraph.

> **frill** *noun*
> ► delight, extravagancy, indulgence. *See* **luxury** (1). *See synonym note at* **luxury.**

> **stupor** *noun*
> **1.** A deficiency in mental and physical alertness and activity ► languor, listlessness, sluggishness. *See* **lethargy** (1). *See synonym note at* **lethargy.**...

There are two kinds of synonym paragraphs. The first consists of a group of undiscriminated, alphabetically ordered words sharing a single, irreducible meaning. These synonyms are presented in illustrative examples following a core definition, as in the core synonym paragraph at **luxury,** below:

> **luxury** *noun*
> **1.** Something costly and unnecessary ► delight, extravagance, extravagancy, frill, indulgence, rarity, treat. **2.** Steady good fortune or financial security ► comfort, luxuriance, wealth. *See* **prosperity** (2).
>
> ---
> ✦ CORE SYNONYMS: *luxury, extravagance, frill.* These nouns denote something desirable and costly that is unnecessary: *the real luxury of riding in a limousine; a simple wedding without any extravagances; caviar and other culinary frills.*
> ◄ ANTONYM: *necessity*
> ---

The second kind of paragraph consists of fully discriminated synonyms ordered in a way that reflects their relationships. A brief sentence explaining the initial point of comparison of the words is given, followed by an explanation of their connotations and varying shades of meaning, along with illustrative examples, as in the paragraph at **lethargy:**

lethargy *noun*
1. A deficiency in mental and physical alertness and activity ▶ dullness, enervation, hebetude, inertness, languidness, languor, lassitude, leadenness, listlessness, slothfulness, sluggishness, stupor, torpidity, torpor. *See also* **stupidity. 2.** Lack of emotion or interest ▶ disinterest, indifference, unconcern. *See* **apathy.**

✦ CORE SYNONYMS: *lethargy, lassitude, torpor, torpidity, stupor, languor.* These nouns refer to a deficiency in mental and physical alertness and activity. *Lethargy* is a state of slug-

---

gishness, drowsy dullness, or apathy: *The war roused the nation from its lethargy. Lassitude* implies weariness or diminished energy such as might result from physical or mental strain: *"His anger had evaporated; he felt nothing but utter lassitude"* (John Galsworthy). *Torpor* and *torpidity* suggest the suspension of activity characteristic of an animal in hibernation: *"My calmness was the torpor of despair"* (Charles Brockden Brown). *Nothing could dispel the torpidity of the indifferent audience. Stupor* is often produced by the effects of alcohol or narcotics; it suggests a benumbed or dazed state of mind: *"The huge height of the buildings . . . the hubbub and endless stir . . . struck me into a kind of stupor of surprise"* (Robert Louis Stevenson). *Languor* is the indolence typical of one who is satiated by a life of luxury or pleasure: *After the banquet, I was overcome by languor.*

Core Synonym Paragraphs

Following is a list of entries in *The American Heritage College Thesaurus* that contain core synonym paragraphs. (See pages xv and xvi in the **Guide to the Thesaurus** for a description of the synonym paragraphs.) The entry word at which the paragraph appears—for example, **abandon** or **ability**—is considered the central word in that group. In addition to the associated core synonym paragraph, that entry also contains the main synonym list for that particular meaning, and every synonym treated in the paragraph is cross-referenced to that entry. Some synonyms are discussed in more than one paragraph, in which case cross-references are given to all the paragraphs that include that synonym.

abandon	aggressive	appeal	authentic
ability	agitate	appear	authorize
abrupt	agree	applaud	average
absorb	agreement	appoint	avoid
abuse	aim	approach	aware
accidental	air	appropriate	baby
accommodate	alert	area	band²
accompany	alive	argue	banish
accomplish	amateur	argument	bar
accomplishment	ambiguous	argumentative	barrage
accumulate	ambush	arouse	baseless
acknowledge	amenities	arrange	basis
actual	amiable	array	batter
adapt	amuse	arrogant	beat
advance	analyze	artificial	beautiful
adventurous	ancestor	artless	beg
advice	anger	ask	behavior
advise	angry	assemble	belief
affair	annihilate	assent	believable
affectation	announce	assistant	belittle
affecting	annoy	associate	bend
afflict	answer	attachment	beneficial
afraid	anxiety	attack	benefit
age	apology	attentive	benevolent
ageless	apparent	attribute	besiege

bet
bias
big
binge
birth
bitter
blame
blameworthy
blast
blink
block
bloom[1]
blunder
boast
bodily
book
boor
border
boring
botch
branch
brave
breach
break
breeze
bright
broach
broad-minded
brood
brush[1]
bulge
bulwark
burden[1]
burdensome
burn
business
calculate
calm
cancel
capricious
care
careful
careless
caress
carry
catch
cause
celebrate
celebrity
center
certain

character
charge
charitable
charm
chastise
cheerful
chew
choice
chronic
circumference
circumstance
citizen
claim
clean
clear
clever
cliché
climax
close
clothe
coagulate
cold
collision
combine
comfort
comfortable
comment
common
compensation
compete
complete
complex
conclude
concurrent
condemn
condescend
condition
conditional
conduct
confidence
confirm
conflict
confuse
conquest
contain
contaminate
continual
converse[1]
convert
correct
corrupt

count
country
courteous
cover
crisis
crowd
crude
cruel
crush
cry
curious
custom
damp
dark
daze
dead
deadly
debase
decay
deceive
decide
decision
decisive
decline
decrease
defeat
defect
defend
defer[1]
definite
deform
defy
deliberate
delicate
delicious
delight
demand
demote
deny
depend on
dependable
deplore
depressed
describe
desire
despise
despondent
destroy
detail
development
deviate

deviation
devote
dexterous
dialect
dictate
dictatorial
differ
difference
difficult
difficulty
diligent
dip
dirty
disadvantage
disappear
discourage
discover
disguise
disgust
dishonest
dismay
dismiss
display
dissuade
distinct
distribute
doctrine
dominant
doubt
drive
dry
dull
earn
easy
eat
eccentric
echo
economical
educate
educated
effect
effective
egotism
eject
elaborate
elevate
elevation
eliminate
embarrass
emotion
emphasis

empty	fight	heart	lethargy
enclose	figure	heavy	letter
encourage	flagrant	help	liable
endanger	flash	heritage	license
endless	flavor	hesitate	lie²
endure	flexible	hide	likeness
energetic	flirt	hinder	limit
energy	flock	hint	limp
engagement	flourish	hold	logical
enmity	flow	hollow	loose
enormous	follow	honor	loud
enrapture	foolish	humanitarian	love
entrust	forbid	idea	lucky
envy	force	idle	luxury
essential	foreign	imagination	makeshift
esteem	forgive	imitate	malign
estimate	form	immaterial	malleable
estrange	forte	importance	manipulate
ethical	found	impression	mark
even	fragile	improper	marvel
evoke	fragrance	improve	mature
exaggerate	frank	impudent	meaning
examination	frighten	incalculable	meddle
example	frown	inclination	mercy
excessive	furnish	incline	messy
exclude	futile	increase	methodical
exhaust	gaudy	indicate	mix
existence	gaze	indigenous	mixture
expect	general	injustice	model
expert	generous	innate	moderate
explain	gesture	insanity	modest
expressive	ghastly	instinctive	mood
extemporaneous	giddy	intelligence	morale
extenuate	glean	intelligent	move
extricate	glib	intense	muscular
faint	glide	intention	mysterious
fair¹	glitter	intermittent	nautical
faithful	gossip	intimidate	neat
faithless	grand	introduce	negligent
famous	graphic	introductory	new
fashion	grief	irrelevant	news
fashionable	grieve	isolate	noise
fast	guide	jerk	notice
fasten	hamper	joke	noticeable
fat	handle	judge	nurture
fateful	happen	labor	object
favorable	harass	lack	oblige
fawn	harden	last¹	obstruct
fear	haste	late	offend
fertile	healthy	latent	offensive
fidelity	heap	lazy	offer

old
opponent
opportunity
oppose
opposite
origin
outfit
overthrow
pacify
pain
part
passion
patience
pedantic
penitence
perceptible
perfect
perform
permission
persuade
pitiful
pity
pledge
poisonous
poor
possible
posture
practice
praise
predicament
predict
prevailing
prevent
primary
produce
profuse
prophesy
proportion
propose
proverb
provoke
prudence
pull
punish
pure
quality
qualm
quibble
random

range
rash[1]
recede
reciprocate
recover
refer
refrain
regard
relevant
relieve
remain
remember
repeat
replace
represent
rescue
resort
rest[1]
restrain
revere
reverse
revile
revive
rich
ridicule
right
rigid
rise
roomy
rough
rove
rude
sarcastic
satire
satisfy
scatter
secret
seduce
see
seize
send
sensuous
sentimental
series
serious
shade
shake
shapeless
sharp

sheer
shorten
shout
showy
shrewd
shy[1]
sign
silent
sleek
slow
smell
social
solitary
solitude
solve
sordid
sorrowful
sound[2]
sour
speed
spend
spirit
spontaneous
stain
standard
start
steal
steep[1]
stem
stench
still
stop
streak
stubborn
subject
submission
sufficient
superfluous
supervise
support
suppose
supposed
sure
sureness
surpass
surrender
surround
sway
taciturn

tact
task
taut
tear[1]
teem[1]
temperance
temporary
tend[2]
theoretical
thin
think
thoughtful
throw
tiny
tire
tireless
tool
touch
trial
trick
trivial
trust
turn
ugly
unctuous
understand
unfortunate
unruly
unspeakable
urgent
use
value
various
versatile
vertical
vociferous
voracious
waste
way
weak
weird
wordy
worry
wrong
young
zest

a

A-1 *adjective*

See **A-one.**

aback *adverb*

Without adequate preparation ▸ short, unawarely, unawares. *Idioms:* by surprise, off guard.

abandon *verb*

1. To give up or leave completely ▸ abdicate, cast aside, cede, demit, desert, forfeit, forgo, forsake, forswear, hand over, lay aside, lay down, leave, maroon, quit, quitclaim, relinquish, render, renounce, resign, sacrifice, surrender, throw over, waive, yield. *Idioms:* back out on, leave in the lurch, run out on, walk out on. *See also* **defect, discard, empty. 2.** To cease trying to continue ▸ break off, desist, discontinue, give up, leave off, quit, remit, stop. *Informal:* knock off, swear off. *Slang:* lay off. *Idioms:* call it a day, call it quits, have done with, throw in the towel (*or* sponge). *See also* **stop. 3.** To yield oneself unrestrainedly, as to an impulse ▸ deliver, relinquish, surrender. *Idioms:* give oneself up (*or* over). **4.** To cease consideration or treatment of ▸ give up, skip. *See* **drop** (7).

abandon *noun*

1. A complete surrender of inhibition ▸ abandonment, incontinence, unrestraint, wantonness, wildness. *See also* **enthusiasm, ease, freedom. 2.** A careless, often reckless regard for consequences ▸ blitheness, carelessness, heedlessness, thoughtlessness. *See also* **temerity.**

✦ CORE SYNONYMS: *abandon, surrender, relinquish, yield, resign, cede, waive, renounce.* These verbs mean giving something up or leaving someone or something completely. *Abandon* and *surrender* both imply no expectation of recovering what is given up; *surrender* also implies the operation of compulsion or force: *abandoned all hope for a resolution; surrendered control of the company. Relinquish* may connote regret: *can't relinquish the idea. Yield* implies giving way, as to pressure, often in the hope that such action will be temporary: *had to yield ground. Resign* suggests formal relinquishing (*resigned their claim to my land*) or acquiescence arising from hopelessness (*resigned himself to forgoing his vacation*). *Cede* connotes formal transfer, as of territory: *ceded the province to the victorious nation. Waive* implies a voluntary decision to dispense with something, such as a right: *waived all privileges.* To *renounce* is to relinquish formally and usually as a matter of principle: *renounced worldly goods.*

---

abandoned *adjective*

1. Having been given up and left alone ▸ bereft, derelict, deserted, desolate, forlorn, forsaken, jilted, lorn, marooned, outcast, rejected, relinquished. *Idioms:* left holding the bag, left in the lurch, out in the cold, out on a limb. *See also* **empty, unreserved, lonely. 2.** Lacking in moral restraint ▸ dissipated, dissolute, fast, licentious, profligate, rakish, unbridled, unconstrained, uncontrolled, ungoverned, uninhibited, unrestrained, wanton, wild. *See also* **corrupt, unscrupulous.**

abandonment *noun*

1. A giving up of a possession, claim, or right ▸ abdication, quitclaim, relinquishment, renunciation, resignation, sacrifice, surrender, waiver. **2.** The act of forsaking ▸ dereliction, desertion. **3.** An instance of defecting from or abandoning a cause ▸ disavowal, renouncement. *See* **defection. 4.** A complete surrender of inhibitions ▸ unrestraint, wantonness, wildness. *See* **abandon** (1).

abase *verb*

1. To lower the pride or dignity of ▸ degrade, demean, humiliate. *See* **humble** (1). **2.** To lower in character or quality ▸ degrade, downgrade. *See* **debase** (1). *See synonym note at* **debase. 3.** To bring disgrace on ▸ besmirch, dishonor, shame. *See* **disgrace.**

abasement *noun*

▸ degeneration, humiliation. *See* **degradation** (1).

abash *verb*

▸ chagrin, confound, discomfort. *See* **embarrass** (1). *See synonym note at* **embarrass.**

abashment *noun*

▸ chagrin, discomposure. *See* **embarrassment** (1).

abate *verb*

1. To grow or cause to grow gradually less ▸ diminish, dwindle, lessen. *See* **decrease.** *See synonym note at* **decrease. 2.** To become or cause to become less active or intense ▸ die (away, down, off, *or* out), ebb, lapse. *See* **subside** (1). **3.** To take away a quantity from another quantity ▸ discount, subtract. *See* **deduct** (1).

abatement *noun*

1. The act or process of decreasing ▸ diminishment, reduction, slowdown. *See* **decrease. 2.** The process of becoming less active or intense ▸ letup, slackening. *See* **waning. 3.** An amount deducted ▸ discount, rebate. *See* **deduction** (1).

abbé *or* **abbot** *noun*

▸ ecclesiastic, minister, parson. *See* **cleric.**

abbreviate *verb*

▸ abridge, reduce. *See* **shorten.** *See synonym note at* **shorten.**

abdicate *verb*

▸ forswear, relinquish, renounce. *See* **abandon** (1).

abdication *noun*

▸ relinquishment, resignation, waiver. *See* **abandonment** (1).

abduct *verb*

To seize and detain a person unlawfully ▸ kidnap, snatch, spirit away, take hostage. *See also* **seize, steal.**

abecedarian *noun*

▸ fledgling, neophyte, novice. *See* **beginner.**

aberrance *or* **aberrancy** *noun*
▶ aberration, deviance, irregularity. *See* **abnormality.**
aberrant *adjective*
1. Straying from a proper course or standard ▶ deviant, stray. *See* **errant** (2). 2. Departing from the normal ▶ atypical, deviant, irregular. *See* **abnormal.**
aberration *noun*
1. A departing from what is prescribed ▶ diversion, variation. *See* **deviation** (1). *See synonym note at* **deviation.** 2. The condition of being abnormal ▶ anomaly, deviation, irregularity. *See* **abnormality.**
abet *verb*
1. To give assistance to ▶ aid, assist. *See* **help** (1). 2. To help bring about ▶ cultivate, facilitate. *See* **promote** (2).
abetment *noun*
▶ aid, assistance. *See* **help** (1).
abettor *or* **abetter** *noun*
1. A person who assists someone else ▶ adjutant, deputy, helper. *See* **assistant.** 2. One who assists a lawbreaker in a wrongful or criminal act ▶ accomplice, conspirator. *See* **accessory** (1).
abeyance *noun*
The condition of being temporarily inactive ▶ dormancy, intermission, latency, quiescence, suspension, remission. *See also* **break, rest.**
abeyant *adjective*
▶ dormant, inactive, potential. *See* **latent.**
abhor *verb*
▶ abominate, execrate, loathe. *See* **hate.**
abhorrence *noun*
1. A strong feeling of hostility or dislike ▶ antipathy, aversion, loathing. *See* **hate** (1). 2. An object of extreme dislike ▶ abomination, anathema. *See* **hate** (2). 3. The feeling of despising ▶ disdain, loathing, scorn. *See* **despisal.** 4. Extreme aversion caused by something offensive ▶ loathing, nausea, queasiness. *See* **disgust.**
abhorrent *adjective*
▶ contemptible, disgusting, obnoxious. *See* **offensive** (1).
abide *verb*
1. To put up with ▶ accept, stomach, tolerate. *See* **endure** (1). *See synonym note at* **endure.** 2. To continue to be in a place ▶ bide, linger, tarry. *See* **remain** (1). *See synonym note at* **remain.** 3. To be in existence or in a certain state for an indefinitely long time ▶ continue, persist. *See* **endure** (2). 4. To have as one's domicile, usually for an extended period ▶ dwell, reside. *See* **live**[1] (2).
abide by *verb*
To act in conformity with ▶ heed, obey, observe. *See* **follow** (4).
abiding *adjective*
▶ durable, enduring, perennial. *See* **continuing** (1).
ability *noun*
1. Natural or acquired skill or talent ▶ adeptness, art, command, craft, expertise, expertness, knack, mastery, proficiency, skill, technique. *Informal:* know-how, savvy. *See also* **dexterity, talent.** 2. Physical, mental, financial, or legal power to perform ▶ capability, capacity, competence, competency, faculty, might. *See also* **energy, power.**

✦ **CORE SYNONYMS:** *ability, art, craft, expertise, knack, know-how, technique.* These nouns denote natural or acquired skill or talent: *a tricky solo passage that showcases a pianist's ability; the art of rhetoric; pottery that reveals an artist's craft; political expertise; a knack for teaching; mechanical know-how; a precise diving technique.*

---

abjuration *noun*
▶ countermand, palinode, withdrawal. *See* **retraction** (1).
abjure *verb*
1. To disavow something previously written or said irrevocably and usually formally ▶ forswear, recant, take back. *See* **retract** (1). 2. To discontinue (a habit, for example) ▶ cut out, give up, leave off. *See* **break** (1).
ablaze *adjective*
▶ afire, conflagrant. *See* **burning** (1).
able *adjective*
Having sufficient ability or resources ▶ capable, competent, good, skilled, skillful. *See also* **dexterous, expert, gifted, qualified.**
able-bodied *adjective*
1. Having good health ▶ fit, well. *See* **healthy** (1). 2. Full of vigor ▶ robust, strapping, sturdy. *See* **lusty** (1).
ablution *noun*
▶ catharsis, redemption. *See* **purification** (2).
abnegate *verb*
▶ contravene, disaffirm, disavow. *See* **deny** (1).
abnegation *noun*
▶ disaffirmation, disclaimer, rejection. *See* **denial** (1).
abnormal *adjective*
Departing from the normal ▶ aberrant, anomalistic, anomalous, atypic, atypical, deviant, divergent, irregular, preternatural, unnatural. *See also* **eccentric, unusual.**
abnormality *noun*
The condition of being abnormal ▶ aberrance, aberrancy, aberration, anomaly, deviance, deviancy, deviation, exception, irregularity, oddity, preternaturalness, unnaturalness. *See also* **defect, deformity, difference, eccentricity.**
abnormally *adverb*
▶ singularly, uncommonly, uniquely. *See* **unusually.**
abode *noun*
▶ domicile, habitation, residence. *See* **home** (1).
abolish *verb*
1. To put an end to ▶ abrogate, annihilate, annul, cancel, extinguish, invalidate, negate, nullify, set aside, vitiate, void. *Informal:* ax. *See also* **cancel, eliminate, stop, suppress.** 2. To destroy all traces of ▶ exterminate, obliterate. *See* **annihilate** (1).
abolition *or* **abolishment** *noun*
An often formal act of putting an end to ▶ abrogation,

annihilation, annulment, cancellation, defeasance, invalidation, negation, nullification, voidance. *See also* **annihilation, repeal.**

abominable *adjective*
1. So unpleasant or objectionable as to cause scorn or disgust ▸ contemptible, disgusting, obnoxious. *See* **offensive** (1). **2.** *Informal* So annoying or detestable as to deserve condemnation ▸ accursed, blasted, confounded. *See* **damned** (2).

abominate *verb*
1. To regard with utter contempt and disdain ▸ contemn, disdain, scorn. *See* **despise** (1). **2.** To feel hostility toward or strong dislike for something ▸ abhor, destest. *See* **hate.**

abomination *noun*
1. A strong feeling of hostility or dislike ▸ antipathy, aversion, loathing. *See* **hate** (1). **2.** An object of extreme dislike ▸ abhorrence, anathema, detestation. *See* **hate** (2).

aboriginal *adjective*
1. Existing, born, or produced in a land or region ▸ autochthonic, native. *See* **indigenous** (1). *See synonym note at* **indigenous.** **2.** Of, from, or within a country's own territory ▸ indigenous, national, native. *See* **domestic** (3).

abound *verb*
▸ bristle, crawl, swarm. *See* **teem**[1]. *See synonym note at* **teem**[1].

about *adverb*
1. Near to in quantity or amount ▸ almost, nearly, roughly. *See* **approximately. 2.** Toward the back ▸ around, rearward. *See* **backward.**

about-face *verb*
To turn sharply around ▸ double, double (back), reverse.

about-face *noun*
The act of changing or being changed from one position, direction, or course to the opposite ▸ inversion, transposition, turnabout. *See* **reversal** (1).

aboveboard *adjective*
1. Honest and direct, especially in speech; not lying or dissembling ▸ forthright, open, plainspoken. *See* **frank. 2.** Marked by uprightness in principle and action ▸ honorable, righteous. *See* **honest** (1).

abracadabra *noun*
1. Highly technical, often deliberately deceptive language ▸ double talk, hocus-pocus, mumbo jumbo. *See* **gibberish** (1). **2.** A word or formula believed to have magic powers ▸ charm, enchantment. *See* **spell**[2].

abrade *verb*
1. To make the skin raw by friction ▸ excoriate, irritate, rub. *See* **chafe** (1). **2.** To bring or come into abrasive contact ▸ grate, rasp. *See* **scrape** (2). **3.** To reduce gradually, as by chemical reaction, weather, or friction ▸ consume, corrode, wear (away *or* down). *See* **erode.**

abrasion *noun*
A mark or shallow cut made by contact with an object ▸ scrape, scratch, scuff, striation. *See also* **cut, furrow, impression.**

abrasive *adjective*
▸ coarse, ragged, scabrous. *See* **rough** (1).

abrasiveness *noun*
▸ coarseness, roughness, unevenness. *See* **irregularity** (1).

abridge *verb*
▸ abbreviate, reduce. *See* **shorten.** *See synonym note at* **shorten.**

abridgment *noun*
▸ brief, outline, sketch. *See* **synopsis.**

abrogate *verb*
▸ cancel, invalidate, nullify. *See* **abolish** (1).

abrogation *noun*
▸ annulment, cancellation, nullification. *See* **abolition.**

abrupt *adjective*
1. Rudely informal ▸ bluff, blunt, brief, brusque, crusty, curt, gruff, short, short-spoken. *See also* **impudent, rude. 2.** Unexpectedly sudden ▸ hurried, precipitant, precipitate, sharp, sudden, unannounced. *Idioms:* from out of nowhere (*or* the blue), without warning. *See also* **quick, rash. 3.** So sharply inclined as to be almost perpendicular ▸ sharp, sudden. *See* **steep**[1] (1). *See synonym note at* **steep**[1].

✦ **CORE SYNONYMS:** *abrupt, curt, gruff, brusque, blunt, bluff, crusty.* These adjectives mean rudely informal or discourteous. *Abrupt* and *curt* denote usually rude briefness· *an abrupt end to the conversation; a curt letter of rejection. Gruff* implies roughness or surliness but does not necessarily suggest rudeness: *a gruff reply. Brusque* emphasizes rude abruptness: *a brusque manner. Blunt* stresses utter frankness and usually a disconcerting directness: *a blunt refusal. Bluff* refers to unpolished, unceremonious manner but usually implies hearty good nature: *a bluff and courageous sailor. Crusty* suggests a rough and forbidding manner that sometimes conceals benevolence of spirit: *a crusty old gentlemen who feeds stray cats.*

---

abscond *verb*
To break loose and leave suddenly, as from confinement or a difficult situation ▸ decamp, flee. *See* **escape** (1).

abscond with *verb*
To take another's property without permission ▸ purloin, snatch, thieve. *See* **steal** (1).

absence *noun*
1. Failure to be present ▸ cut, nonappearance, nonattendance, truancy, truantry. *Informal:* hooky. *See also* **emptiness, nothingness. 2.** The condition of lacking something ▸ dearth, lack, want. *See also* **need, shortage.**

absent *adjective*
1. Not present ▸ away, elsewhere, gone, missing, nonattendant, nonexistent, off, out, truant. *Idioms:* AWOL, gone fishing, playing hooky. *See also* **empty. 2.** Lost in thought ▸ distracted, preoccupied. *See* **absent-minded.**

absent-minded *adjective*
So lost in thought as to be unable to remember or attend to things ▸ absent, abstracted, bemused, distracted, distrait, faraway, forgetful, inattentive, lost, oblivious, preoccupied, scatterbrained. *Slang:* spaced-out, spacy. *Idioms:* a million miles away, gathering wool, lost (*or* off) in space, out of it. *See also* **careless, detached, dreamy, negligent.**

absent-mindedness *noun*
▸ bemusement, daydreaming, reverie. *See* **trance** (1).

absolute *adjective*
1. Having and exercising complete political power and control ▸ absolutistic, arbitrary, autarchic, autarchical, autocratic, autocratical, despotic, dictatorial, monocratic, totalitarian, tyrannic, tyrannical, tyrannous. *See also* **influential, powerful, strong. 2.** Free from flaws or blemishes ▸ consummate, flawless, unblemished. *See* **perfect** (1). **3.** Known positively ▸ certain, sure. *See* **definite** (3). **4.** Free from extraneous elements ▸ perfect, plain, unadulterated. *See* **pure** (1). *See synonym note at* **pure. 5.** Without limitations or mitigating conditions ▸ full, unreserved. *See* **unconditional** (1). **6.** Having no reservations ▸ unconditional, unfaltering. *See* **implicit** (2). **7.** Completely such, without qualification or exception ▸ all-out, pure, sheer. *See* **utter²**.

absolutely *adverb*
1. Without question ▸ categorically, certainly, definitely, doubtless, doubtlessly, indubitably, positively, surely, undoubtedly, unquestionably. *Idioms:* beyond (*or* without) a doubt, beyond the shadow of a doubt. *See also* **considerably, really, unusually, very. 2.** To the fullest extent ▸ fully, totally, utterly. *See* **completely** (1). **3.** It is so; as you say or ask ▸ agreed, all right, assuredly. *See* **yes.**

absolution *noun*
1. The act or an instance of forgiving ▸ amnesty, excuse, pardon. *See* **forgiveness. 2.** A freeing or clearing from accusation or guilt ▸ exoneration, vindication. *See* **exculpation.**

absolutism *noun*
1. A political doctrine advocating the principle of absolute rule ▸ authoritarianism, autocracy, despotism, dictatorship, totalitarianism. *See also* **subjugation. 2.** A government in which all power is vested in a single leader or party ▸ autarchy, autocracy, despotism, dictatorship, monocracy, one-party rule, tyranny.

absolutistic *adjective*
▸ arbitrary, autocratic, despotic. *See* **absolute** (1).

absolve *verb*
1. To free from a charge of guilt ▸ acquit, exonerate, vindicate. *See* **clear** (9). **2.** To free from an obligation or duty ▸ discharge, exempt. *See* **excuse** (1).

absorb *verb*
1. To occupy the attention of ▸ consume, employ, engage, engross, immerse, involve, monopolize, occupy, preoccupy, tie up. *See also* **charm, grip. 2.** To take in and incorporate, especially mentally ▸ assimi-late, digest, drink in, grasp, imbibe, incorporate, learn, sponge up, take up. *Informal:* soak up. *See also* **know, understand. 3.** To take in moisture or liquid ▸ soak (up), sop up. *See* **drink** (3).

✦ CORE SYNONYMS: *absorb, consume, engross, monopolize, preoccupy.* These verbs mean to occupy someone's attention: *study that absorbs all her time; was consumed by fear; engrossed herself in her reading; a service monopolized by one company; was preoccupied with financial worries.*

---

absorbed *adjective*
1. Having one's thoughts fully occupied ▸ intent, preoccupied, riveted. *See* **rapt. 2.** Involved in activity or work ▸ engaged, occupied. *See* **busy** (3).

absorbent *or* **absorptive** *adjective*
Having a capacity or tendency to absorb or soak up ▸ assimilative, bibulous, imbibing, permeable, retentive, spongy.

absorption *noun*
1. The process of absorbing and incorporating ▸ assimilation, digestion, incorporation, intake, osmosis. *See also* **mastery. 2.** Total occupation of the attention or of the mind ▸ engagement, engrossment, enthrallment, immersion, involvement, preoccupation, prepossession.

absquatulate *verb*
Chiefly Regional To break loose and leave suddenly ▸ decamp, flee. *See* **escape** (1).

abstain *verb*
To hold oneself back ▸ forbear, hold off, withhold. *See* **refrain.** *See synonym note at* **refrain.**

abstain from *verb*
▸ eschew, refrain from, shun. *See* **avoid.**

abstemious *adjective*
▸ sober, spartan. *See* **temperate** (2).

abstemiousness *noun*
▸ measure, temperance. *See* **moderation** (1).

abstinence *noun*
1. The practice of refraining from use of alcoholic liquors ▸ sobriety, teetotalism. *See* **temperance** (2). **2.** Moderation or restraint of one's behavior or desires ▸ continence, self-denial, sobriety. *See* **temperance** (1). *See synonym note at* **temperance.**

abstinent *adjective*
▸ austere, self-denying. *See* **ascetic.**

abstract *adjective*
1. Existing only in concept and not in reality ▸ conceptual, hypothetical, virtual. *See* **theoretical** (2). **2.** Beyond the understanding of an average mind ▸ abstruse, esoteric, profound. *See* **deep** (2). **3.** Concerned primarily with theories rather than practical matters ▸ academic, conceptual, speculative. *See* **theoretical** (1). *See synonym note at* **theoretical.**

abstract *noun*
A shortened version or summary ▸ outline, sketch. *See* **synopsis.**

abstract *verb*
1. To remove from association with ▸ disassociate,

disengage, withdraw. *See* **detach** (1). **2.** To give a recapitulation of the salient facts of ▶ epitomize, recapitulate, summarize. *See* **review** (1).

abstracted *adjective*
▶ inattentive, preoccupied. *See* **absent-minded.**

abstraction *noun*
1. The condition of being so lost in solitary thought that one is unaware of one's surroundings ▶ bemusement, daydreaming, reverie. *See* **trance** (1). **2.** The act or process of detaching ▶ disconnection, separation, uncoupling. *See* **detachment** (1).

abstruse *adjective*
1. Beyond the understanding of an average mind ▶ abstract, esoteric, profound. *See* **deep** (2). **2.** Lacking certainty or clarity ▶ dubious, indeterminate, questionable, unclear. *See* **ambiguous** (1). *See synonym note at* **ambiguous. 3.** Not widely understood ▶ esoteric, recondite. *See* **obscure** (1).

absurd *adjective*
▶ daft, idiotic, ludicrous. *See* **foolish.** *See synonym note at* **foolish.**

absurdity *noun*
1. *Informal* Something or someone uproariously funny ▶ hoot, laugh. *See* **scream** (3). **2.** Foolish behavior ▶ folly, silliness, tomfoolery. *See* **foolishness.**

abundance *noun*
1. A great deal ▶ bounty, mass, mountain, much, plenty, plethora, profusion, wealth, world. *Informal:* barrel, heap, lot, mess, pack, peck, pile. *See also* **excess, flood. 2.** Prosperity and a sufficiency of life's necessities ▶ bounteousness, plenitude. *See* **plenty** (1).

abundant *adjective*
▶ ample, bounteous, bountiful. *See* **generous** (2). *See synonym note at* **generous.**

abundantly *adverb*
▶ much, quite, well. *See* **considerably.**

abuse *verb*
1. To treat wrongfully or harmfully ▶ exploit, ill-treat, ill-use, impose on (*or* upon), maltreat, mishandle, mistreat, misuse, oppress, persecute, use, victimize, wrong. *Idioms:* kick around, knock about (*or* around), take advantage of, treat like dirt. *See also* **injure, insult, violate. 2.** To use improperly ▶ exploit, misapply, misappropriate, mishandle, mistreat, misuse, pervert. **3.** To attack with harsh, often insulting language ▶ assail, blaspheme. *See* **revile.**

abuse *noun*
1. Improper use or handling ▶ ill-usage, misapplication, misappropriation, mishandling, misuse, perversion. *See also* **degradation. 2.** Physically harmful treatment ▶ ill-treatment, maltreatment, mishandling, mistreatment, misusage. **3.** Sustained, harshly abusive language ▶ condemnation, denunciation, invective. *See* **vituperation.**

✚ CORE SYNONYMS: *abuse, mistreat, ill-treat, maltreat.* These verbs mean to treat wrongfully or harmfully. *Abuse* applies to injurious or improper treatment: "*We abuse land because we regard it as a commodity*

belonging to us" (Aldo Leopold). *Mistreat, ill-treat,* and *maltreat* all share the sense of inflicting injury, often intentionally: "*I had seen many more patients die from being mistreated for consumption than from consumption itself*" (Earl of Lytton). *The army had orders not to ill-treat the prisoners.* "*When we misuse* [a language other than our native language], *we are in fact trying to reduce its element of foreignness. We let ourselves maltreat it as though it naturally belonged to us*" (Manchester Guardian Weekly).

---

abusive *adjective*
Of, relating to, or characterized by verbal abuse ▶ contumelious, invective, opprobrious, scurrilous, sharp-tongued, vituperative. *See also* **disdainful, impudent.**

abut *verb*
▶ border, meet, neighbor, verge. *See* **adjoin** (1).

abutting *adjective*
▶ adjacent, bordering, neighboring. *See* **adjoining.**

abysm *noun*
▶ abyss, gulf. *See* **deep** (1).

abysmal *adjective*
1. Open wide ▶ abyssal, cavernous, gaping, yawning. *See also* **broad, open. 2.** Extending far downward or inward from a surface ▶ bottomless, profound. *See* **deep** (1). **3.** Very bad ▶ appalling, dreadful, ghastly. *See* **terrible** (1).

abyss *noun*
▶ chasm, gulf. *See* **deep** (1).

abyssal *adjective*
▶ abysmal, cavernous, gaping, yawning. *See also* **broad, open.**

academic *adjective*
1. Of or relating to education ▶ pedagogic, scholastic. *See* **educational** (1). **2.** Inclined to teach or moralize excessively ▶ expository, moralizing, prescriptive. *See* **didactic** (2). **3.** Characterized by a narrow concern for book learning and formal rules ▶ bookish, literary, scholastic. *See* **pedantic.** *See synonym note at* **pedantic. 4.** Concerned primarily with theories rather than practical matters ▶ abstract, conceptual, speculative. *See* **theoretical** (1). *See synonym note at* **theoretical.**

accede *verb*
▶ agree, consent, subscribe. *See* **assent.** *See synonym note at* **assent.**

accelerate *verb*
▶ expedite, hasten, quicken. *See* **speed** (1). *See synonym note at* **speed.**

accent *noun*
1. Special attention given to something considered important ▶ accentuation, emphasis, stress, weight. *See synonym note at* **emphasis.** *See also* **importance, notice. 2.** An expressive vocal quality ▶ edge, intonation, lilt. *See* **tone** (2).

accent *or* **accentuate** *verb*
To accord emphasis to ▶ accentuate, highlight. *See* **emphasize.**

accentuation *noun*
Special attention given to something considered im-

portant ▸ accent, emphasis, stress, weight. *See also* **importance, notice.**

accept *verb*
1. To receive something offered willingly and gladly ▸ embrace, take (up), welcome. *Idioms:* receive with open arms, take (*or* fold) to one's bosom. *See also* **acquire, take. 2.** To admit to one's possession, presence, or awareness ▸ have, receive, take. *See also* **absorb. 3.** To allow admittance, as to a group ▸ admit, intromit, let in, receive, take in. *Idioms:* welcome aboard (*or* on board), take (*or* welcome) into the fold. *See also* **permit. 4.** To regard something as true or real ▸ *Slang:* buy, swallow. *See* **believe** (2). **5.** To perceive and recognize the meaning of ▸ apprehend, fathom, sense. *See* **understand** (1). **6.** To put up with ▸ stand (for), stomach, tolerate. *See* **endure** (1). **7.** To respond affirmatively; receive with agreement or compliance ▸ agree, acquiesce, consent, subscribe. *See* **assent.**

acceptable *adjective*
1. Worthy of being accepted or allowed ▸ admissible, allowable, permissible, unobjectionable, unexceptionable. *Slang:* kosher. **2.** Adequate to satisfy a need, requirement, or standard ▸ adequate, all right, average, common, decent, fair, fairish, goodish, moderate, modest, palatable, passable, popular, reasonable, respectable, satisfactory, sufficient, tolerable. *Informal:* OK, tidy. *See also* **appropriate.**

acceptance *noun*
1. The act of accepting or adopting ▸ acquiescence, adoption, agreement, assent, consent, embracement, espousal, nod, yes. *Informal:* OK. *Idioms:* stamp (*or* seal) of approval. *See also* **confirmation, permission. 2.** Favorable reception or regard ▸ acknowledgement, approbation, approval, credit, esteem, favor, recognition, regard, welcome. *See also* **praise. 3.** The capacity of enduring hardship or inconvenience without complaint ▸ resignation, tolerance. *See* **patience.**

acceptant *adjective*
▸ amenable, open-minded, responsive. *See* **receptive.**

acceptation *noun*
▸ import, sense, significance. *See* **meaning** (1). *See synonym note at* **meaning.**

accepted *adjective*
Generally approved or agreed upon ▸ admitted, conventional, customary, established, orthodox, received, recognized, sanctioned, time-honored, traditional. *See also* **common, ordinary.**

accepting *adjective*
▸ enduring, long-suffering, resigned. *See* **patient.**

access *noun*
1. The act of admitting or the state of being admitted ▸ admittance, entrance, entry. *See* **admission** (1). **2.** A sudden violent expression, as of emotion ▸ burst, eruption, explosion. *See* **outburst** (1).

access *verb*
To gain entry into a computer network or database ▸ enter, log in (*or* on). *Idioms:* gain access (*or* admittance *or* entry), get connected.

accessible *adjective*
1. Easily approached ▸ approachable, responsive, welcoming. **2.** Being within easy reach ▸ handy, nearby. *See* **convenient** (2). **3.** Available for use ▸ employable, operable, usable. *See* **open** (4).

accession *noun*
▸ addendum, augmentation. *See* **addition** (1).

accessory *noun*
1. One who assists a lawbreaker in a wrongful or criminal act ▸ abettor, accomplice, confederate, conspirator. *Idiom:* partner in crime. **2.** A subordinate element added to another entity ▸ adjunct, appendage, supplement. *See* **attachment** (1). *See synonym note at* **attachment.**

accessory *adjective*
Giving or able to give help or support ▸ assistant, contributory, subsidiary. *See* **auxiliary** (1).

accident *noun*
1. An unexpected and usually undesirable event ▸ casualty, contretemps, misadventure, mischance, misfortune, mishap, reversal, setback. *See also* **collision, disaster. 2.** An unexpected random event ▸ fluke, fortuity, happenstance. *See* **chance** (1). **3.** The random, unintended, or unpredictable element of an event or the force regarded as the cause of such an event ▸ coincidence, fortune, luck. *See* **chance** (2). **4.** A wrecking of a vehicle ▸ sideswipe, wreck. *See* **crash** (2).

accidental *adjective*
1. Occurring unexpectedly ▸ adventitious, casual, chance, contingent, fluky, fortuitous, inadvertent, incidental, odd, serendipitous, unanticipated, unexpected, unintended, unplanned. *See also* **chance, random. 2.** Not intended ▸ inadvertent, undesigned, unintended. *See* **unintentional.**

✦ **CORE SYNONYMS:** *accidental, fortuitous, contingent, incidental, adventitious.* These adjectives apply to what happens unexpectedly or unintentionally. *Accidental* primarily refers to what occurs by chance: *an accidental meeting.* It can also mean subordinate or nonessential: *"Poetry is something to which words are the accidental, not by any means the essential form"* (Frederick W. Robertson). *Fortuitous* stresses chance even more strongly: *"the happy combination of fortuitous circumstances"* (Sir Walter Scott). *Contingent* describes what is possible but uncertain because of unforeseen or uncontrollable factors: *"The results of confession were not contingent, they were certain"* (George Eliot). *Incidental* refers to a minor or unanticipated result or accompaniment: *"There is scarcely any practice which is so corrupt as not to produce some incidental good"* (Enoch Mellor). *Adventitious* applies to something acquired or added externally, sometimes by accident or chance: *"The court tries to understand 'whether the young man's misconduct was adventitious or the result of some serious flaw in his character'"* (Harry F. Rosenthal).

---

acclaim *verb*
1. To express warm approval of ▸ applaud, commend. *See* **praise** (1). *See synonym note at* **praise. 2.** To pay tribute or homage to ▸ celebrate, exalt. *See* **honor** (1).

acclaim *or* **acclamation** *noun*
An expression of warm approval ▸ accolade, celebration, kudos. *See* **praise** (1).

acclamatory *adjective*
▸ approbatory, laudatory. *See* **complimentary** (1).

acclimate *or* **acclimatize** *verb*
1. To make or become suitable to a particular situation or use ▸ adjust, fit, tailor. *See* **adapt**. **2.** To make resistant to hardship, especially through continued exposure ▸ season, toughen. *See* **harden** (1). *See synonym note at* **harden**.

acclimated *or* **acclimatized** *adjective*
▸ adapted, conditioned, inured. *See* **accustomed** (1).

acclimation *or* **acclimatization** *noun*
▸ adjustment, conditioning. *See* **adaptation** (1).

acclivity *noun*
▸ gradient, rise, slant. *See* **ascent** (2).

accolade *noun*
1. A memento received as a symbol of excellence or victory ▸ award, cup, prize, trophy. **2.** Recognition of achievement or superiority or a sign of this ▸ award, honor. *See* **distinction** (2). **3.** Something given in return for a service or accomplishment ▸ award, bonus, plum. *See* **reward** (1). **4.** An expression of admiration ▸ praise, tribute. *See* **compliment** (1). **5.** An expression of warm approval ▸ acclamation, celebration, kudos. *See* **praise** (1).

accolade *verb*
To express warm approval of ▸ applaud, commend. *See* **praise** (1).

accommodate *verb*
1. To have the room or capacity for ▸ contain, hold. **2.** To perform a service or a courteous act for ▸ favor, serve. *See* **oblige** (1). *See synonym note at* **oblige**. **3.** To provide with lodging, especially temporarily ▸ accommodate, bed (down), house. *See* **lodge** (1). **4.** To make or become suitable to a particular situation or use ▸ adjust, fit, suit. *See* **adapt**. *See synonym note at* **adapt**. **5.** To make a concession ▸ arrange, settle. *See* **compromise** (1). **6.** To bring into accord ▸ conform, integrate. *See* **harmonize** (1).

✦ **CORE SYNONYMS:** *accommodate, contain, hold.* These verbs mean to have the room or capacity for: *The bar accommodates 50 customers. The book contains some amusing passages. This pitcher holds two pints.*

---

accommodating *adjective*
▸ agreeable, complaisant. *See* **obliging**.

accommodation *noun*
1. The act or process of adapting ▸ acclimation, adjustment, conformation. *See* **adaptation** (1). **2.** A settlement of differences through mutual concession ▸ arrangement, give-and-take, settlement. *See* **compromise**.

accommodations *noun*
Steps taken in preparation for an undertaking ▸ arrangements, plans, preparations, provisions.

accompaniment *noun*
1. Something added to another for embellishment or completion ▸ add-on, complement, supplement. *See* **enhancement** (1). **2.** One that accompanies another ▸ attendant, companion. *See* **concomitant**.

accompanist *noun*
One that accompanies another ▸ associate, attendant, companion, concomitant. *See also* **associate**.

accompany *verb*
1. To be with or go with ▸ attend, chaperon, companion, company, convoy, escort. *Idioms:* go hand in hand with, hang around (*or* out) with, tag along with. *See also* **guide**. **2.** To add to or make whole ▸ augment, complete, strengthen. *See* **supplement**.

✦ **CORE SYNONYMS:** *accompany, escort, chaperon.* These verbs mean to be with or to go with another or others. *Accompany* suggests going with another on an equal basis: *She went to Europe accompanied by her colleague. Escort* stresses protective guidance: *The party chairperson escorted the candidate through the crowd. Chaperon* specifies adult supervision of young persons: *My mom helped chaperon the prom.*

---

accompanying *adjective*
▸ attendant, attending. *See* **concurrent** (1).

accomplice *noun*
▸ abbettor, conspirator. *See* **accessory** (1).

accomplish *verb*
1. To obtain a goal or objective by effort ▸ achieve, arrive at, attain, come to, fulfill, gain, get to, reach, realize. *Informal:* hit on. *Slang:* score. *Idiom:* bring to pass. *See also* **fulfill**. **2.** To succeed in doing ▸ carry out, effectuate, perform. *See* **effect** (1). **3.** To begin and carry through to completion ▸ discharge, transact. *See* **perform** (1). *See synonym note at* **perform**.

✦ **CORE SYNONYMS:** *accomplish, reach, achieve, attain, gain.* These verbs mean to obtain a goal or objective by effort. *Accomplish* and *reach* are the least specific: *accomplished the goal; reached a definitive conclusion. Achieve* suggests the application of skill or initiative: *achieved national recognition. Attain* implies the impelling force of ambition, principle, or ideals: *trying to attain self-confidence. Gain* connotes considerable effort in surmounting obstacles: *gained the workers' trust.*

---

accomplished *adjective*
Proficient as a result of practice and study ▸ finished, polished, practiced. *See also* **able, expert**.

accomplishment *noun*
1. Something that is completed or attained successfully ▸ achievement, acquirement, acquisition, arrival, attainment, coup, deed, effort, endeavor, exploit, feat, masterstroke, realization, success, successfulness, triumph, tour de force. *See also* **conquest, goal, performance**. **2.** The condition of being fulfilled ▸ culmination, fulfillment, realization. *See* **fulfillment** (1).

✦ **CORE SYNONYMS:** *achievement, exploit, feat, masterstroke, realization, triumph.* These nouns mean something completed or attained successfully: *feats of bravery; achievements of diplomacy; military exploits; a* *masterstroke of entrepreneurship; a realization of the director's vision; the triumph of winning the championship.*

accord *verb*
1. To let have as a favor, prerogative, or privilege ▸ award, concede, give, grant, vouchsafe. *See also* **yield**. 2. To come to an understanding or to terms ▸ coincide, concur. *See synonym note at* **agree**. 3. To be compatible or suitable ▸ chime, correspond, match. *See* **agree** (1). 4. To give formally or officially ▸ award, bestow, grant. *See* **confer** (2).

accord *noun*
1. The act or state of agreeing or conforming ▸ concordance, consensus, unanimity. *See* **agreement** (2). 2. Pleasing agreement, as of musical sounds ▸ concord, tune. *See* **harmony** (1). 3. An often written acceptance of terms between parties ▸ charter, contract, pact. *See* **agreement** (1). 4. A formal, usually written settlement between nations ▸ concord, convention, pact. *See* **treaty**.

accordance *noun*
1. The act or state of agreeing or conforming ▸ accord, consensus, unanimity. *See* **agreement** (2). 2. The act of conferring, as of an honor ▸ bestowal, conference, conferral. *See* **conferment**.

accordant *adjective*
1. In keeping with one's needs or expectations ▸ compatible, congenial, consonant. *See* **agreeable** (1). 2. Being in or characterized by complete agreement ▸ agreeing, consonant, like-minded. *See* **unanimous**.

accost *verb*
To approach for the purpose of speech ▸ greet, hail, salute. *See also* **encounter, interrupt, welcome**.

accouchement *noun*
▸ childbearing, delivery, labor. *See* **birth** (1).

account *noun*
1. A statement of causes or motives ▸ explanation, justification, rationale, rationalization, reason. *See also* **answer, apology, belief**. 2. A precise list of fees or charges ▸ bill, check, invoice, reckoning, statement, tally. *Informal:* damage, tab. 3. A measure of those qualities that determine merit, desirability, usefulness, or importance ▸ valuation, value, worth. *See also* **cost, importance**. 4. A recounting of past events ▸ chronicle, history, report. *See* **story** (1). 5. A feeling of deference, approval, and liking ▸ admiration, favor. *See* **esteem** (1). 6. The quality of being suitable or adaptable to an end ▸ benefit, profit, utility. *See* **use** (2).

account *verb*
To look upon in a particular way ▸ consider, deem, view. *See* **regard** (1). *See synonym note at* **regard**.

account for *verb*
To offer reasons for or a cause of ▸ explain, justify, rationalize. *See also* **clarify, resolve**.

accountability *noun*
▸ answerability, liability. *See* **responsibility** (1).

accountable *adjective*
1. Legally or officially obligated ▸ answerable, respon-

sible. *See* **liable** (1). *See synonym note at* **liable**. 2. Capable of being explained or accounted for ▸ decipherable, illustratable, interpretable. *See* **explainable**.

accouter *or* **accoutre** *verb*
▸ equip, gear, outfit. *See* **furnish** (1). *See synonym note at* **furnish**.

accouterments *or* **accoutrements** *noun*
▸ equipment, gear. *See* **outfit** (1).

accredit *verb*
1. To regard as belonging to or resulting from another ▸ ascribe, assign. *See* **attribute** (1). 2. To give authority to ▸ empower, enable, license. *See* **authorize** (1). *See synonym note at* **authorize**. 3. To accept officially ▸ approve, pass, ratify. *See* **confirm** (3).

accreditation *noun*
▸ approval, ratification, sanction. *See* **confirmation** (1).

accretion *noun*
▸ development, proliferation. *See* **buildup** (2).

accrue *verb*
▸ amass, collect, gather, pile up. *See* **accumulate**.

acculturate *verb*
To fit for companionship with others, especially in attitude or manners ▸ civilize, humanize, socialize.

acculturation *noun*
▸ acclimation, adjustment, conformation. *See* **adaptation** (1).

accumulate *verb*
To bring together so as to increase in mass or number ▸ accrue, agglomerate, aggregate, amass, assemble, build up, collect, cumulate, garner, gather, hive, heap up, mass, pile up, roll up. *See also* **assemble, increase, save**.

✚ **CORE SYNONYMS:** *accumulate, collect, assemble, amass.* These verbs mean to bring or come together so as to increase in mass or number: *Accumulate* applies to the increase of like or related things over an extended period: *They accumulated enough capital to invest. Old newspapers accumulated in the basement. Collect* frequently refers to the careful selection of like or related things that become part of an organized whole: *She collects stamps as a hobby. Tears collected in his eyes. Assemble* implies a definite and usually close relationship. With respect to persons, the term suggests convening out of common interest or purpose: *Assembling an able staff was more difficult than expected. The reporters assembled for the press conference.* With respect to things, *assemble* implies gathering and fitting together components: *The curator is assembling an interesting exhibit of Stone Age artifacts. Amass* refers to the collection or accumulation of things, often valuable things, to form an imposing quantity: *Their families had amassed great fortunes. Rocks had amassed at the bottom of the glacier.*

---

accumulation *noun*
1. A quantity accumulated ▸ aggregation, amassment, assemblage, buildup, collection, congeries, cumulation, gathering, mass. *See also* **heap**. 2. The act of accumulating ▸ agglomeration, buildup, conglomera-

tion. *See also* **increase. 3.** Matter that settles on a bottom or collects on a surface by a natural process ▸ alluvium, precipitation, sediment. *See* **deposit** (2). **4.** The result or product of building up ▸ development, proliferation. *See* **buildup** (2).

accumulative *adjective*
Increasing, as in force, by successive additions ▸ additive, cumulative.

accuracy *or* **accurateness** *noun*
1. Freedom from error ▸ correctness, definitude, exactitude, exactness, meticulousness, preciseness, precision, rightness. **2.** Correspondence with fact or truth ▸ authenticity, correctness, truth, validity. *See* **veracity.**

accurate *adjective*
1. Conforming exactly to fact ▸ actual, correct, errorless, exact, factual, faithful, precise, right, rigorous, true, veracious, veridical. *Idioms:* on the button (*or* money *or* nose), spot on. *See also* **literal, perfect, sure. 2.** Marked by attentiveness to every detail ▸ fastidious, meticulous, scrupulous. *See* **careful** (2).

accursed *adjective*
Informal So annoying or detestable as to deserve condemnation ▸ abominable, blasted, confounded. *See* **damned** (2).

accusation *noun*
A charging of someone with a misdeed ▸ arraignment, crimination, charge, denouncement, denunciation, finger-pointing, impeachment, imputation, incrimination, inculpation, indictment, recrimination.

accusatorial *or* **accusatory** *adjective*
Containing, relating to, or involving an accusation ▸ denunciative, denunciatory, incriminating, incriminatory, inculpatory. *See also* **insinuating.**

accuse *verb*
To make an accusation against ▸ arraign, blame, charge, denounce, impeach, incriminate, inculpate, indict, tax, recriminate. *Idioms:* hang (*or* pin) something on, point the finger at, put the finger on. *See also* **implicate.**

accused *noun*
A person against whom an action is brought ▸ defendant, respondent.

accuser *noun*
1. One that accuses ▸ arraigner, denouncer, indicter, recriminator. **2.** One that makes a formal complaint, especially in court ▸ claimant, complainant, plaintiff.

accustom *verb*
To make familiar through constant practice, use, or habit ▸ condition, familiarize, habituate, inure, wont. *See also* **adapt.**

accustomed *adjective*
1. Adapted to the existing environment and conditions ▸ acclimated, acclimatized, adapted, conditioned, hardened, inured, seasoned, toughened. **2.** Subject to a pattern or habit of behavior ▸ chronic, habitual, routine. **3.** In the habit ▸ habituated, used, wont. **4.** Occurring or encountered regularly ▸ commonplace, familiar, regular. *See* **common** (1).

ace *noun*
1. A person with a high degree of knowledge or skill in a particular field ▸ authority, master, proficient. *See* **expert. 2.** A key resource to be used at an opportune moment ▸ trump, trump card. *Informal:* clincher. *Idiom:* ace in the hole.

ace *adjective*
Exceptionally good of its kind ▸ first-rate, prime, splendid, tiptop. *See* **excellent.**

ace *verb*
Slang To win a victory over, as in battle or a competition ▸ conquer, surmount, vanquish. *See* **defeat** (1).

acerbic *adjective*
1. Having a sharp, unpleasant, alkaline taste ▸ acrid, harsh. *See* **bitter** (1). *See synonym note at* **bitter. 2.** Having a taste characteristic of that produced by acids ▸ sharp, tart. *See* **sour** (1). **3.** So sharp as to cause mental pain ▸ caustic, scathing, sharp, vitriolic. *See* **biting.**

acerbity *noun*
▸ acridity, causticity, mordancy, trenchancy. *See* **sarcasm.**

acetous *adjective*
▸ acerbic, tart. *See* **sour** (1).

ache *verb*
1. To be painful or sore ▸ smart, sting. *See* **hurt** (2). **2.** To experience or express compassion ▸ commiserate, condole, feel, sympathize. *Idioms:* be (*or* feel) sorry, have one's heart ache (*or* bleed) for someone, have one's heart go out to someone. *See also* **comfort, pity. 3.** To have a strong longing for ▸ covet, want, yearn. *See* **desire** (1).

ache *noun*
A sensation of physical discomfort occurring as the result of disease or injury ▸ prick, smart, soreness. *See* **pain** (1). *See synonym note at* **pain.**

achievable *adjective*
▸ practicable, viable. *See* **possible** (1).

achieve *verb*
1. To succeed in doing ▸ effectuate, implement, perform. *See* **effect** (1). **2.** To obtain a goal or objective by effort ▸ attain, gain, realize. *See* **accomplish** (1). *See synonym note at* **accomplish. 3.** To begin and carry through to completion ▸ discharge, transact. *See* **perform** (1). *See synonym note at* **perform.**

achievement *noun*
▸ deed, triumph. *See* **accomplishment** (1).

aching *or* **achy** *adjective*
▸ afflictive, hurtful, sore. *See* **painful** (1).

acicula *noun*
▸ cusp, tip. *See* **point** (1).

acicular *or* **aciculate** *or* **aciculated** *adjective*
▸ acute, cuspate, sharp. *See* **pointed** (1).

acid *or* **acidic** *adjective*
1. Having a taste characteristic of that produced by acids ▸ sharp, tart. *See* **sour** (1). *See synonym note at* **sour. 2.** So sharp as to cause mental pain ▸ caustic, scathing, sharp, vitriolic. *See* **biting.**

acidity *noun*
▸ acridity, causticity, mordancy. *See* **sarcasm.**

acidulous *adjective*
▸ sharp, tangy, tart. *See* **sour** (1). *See synonym note at* **sour.**

acknowledge *verb*
1. To admit to the reality or truth of ▸ admit, avow, concede, confess, grant, own (up). *Slang:* fess up. *Chiefly Regional:* allow. *See also* **assent. 2.** To express recognition of ▸ admit, recognize. *See also* **confirm.**

✦ CORE SYNONYMS: *acknowledge, admit, own, avow, confess, concede.* These verbs mean to admit the reality or truth of something, often reluctantly. To *acknowledge* is to accept responsibility for something one makes known: *He acknowledged his mistake. Admit* implies reluctance in acknowledging one's acts or another point of view: *"She was attracted by the frankness of a suitor who . . . admitted that he did not believe in marriage"* (Edith Wharton). *Own* stresses personal acceptance and responsibility: *She owned that she feared for the child's safety. Avow* means to assert openly and boldly: *"Old Mrs. Webb avowed that he, in the space of two hours, had worn out her pew more . . . than she had by sitting in it forty years"* (Kate Douglas Wiggin). *Confess* usually emphasizes disclosure of something damaging or inconvenient to oneself: *I have to confess that I lied to you.* To *concede* is to intellectually accept something, often against one's will: *The lawyer refused to concede that the two cases had similarities.*

---

acknowledgment *noun*
1. The act of admitting to something ▸ admission, avowal, concession, confession, recognition. **Idiom:** owning up. 2. Favorable notice, as of an achievement ▸ credit, recognition. 3. Favorable reception or regard ▸ credence, favor, regard. *See* **acceptance** (2). **4.** A being grateful ▸ gratitude, thankfulness. *See* **appreciation** (1).

acme *noun*
▸ apex, height, peak. *See* **climax** (1). *See synonym note at* **climax.**

acolyte *noun*
▸ fanatic, zealot. *See* **devotee** (1).

acquaint *verb*
1. To make known socially ▸ familiarize, introduce, present. 2. To impart information to ▸ educate, notify. *See* **inform** (1).

acquaintance *noun*
Personal knowledge derived from participation or observation ▸ conversance, experience, familiarity. *See also* **awareness.**

acquainted *adjective*
1. Having good knowledge of something ▸ conversant, familiar, versant, versed. **Idiom:** up on. *See also* **accustomed. 2.** Provided with information; made aware ▸ enlightened, instructed, knowledgeable. *See* **informed** (1).

acquiesce *verb*
1. To respond affirmatively; receive with agreement or compliance ▸ accept, agree, consent. *See* **assent.** *See synonym note at* **assent. 2.** To give up in favor of another ▸ capitulate, give in, yield. *See* **surrender** (1).

acquiescence *noun*
1. The act of accepting or adopting ▸ adoption, assent, consent. *See* **acceptance** (1). **2.** The quality or state of willingly carrying out the wishes of others ▸ complaisance, compliancy, submissiveness. *See* **obedience.**

acquiescent *adjective*
1. Submitting without objection or resistance ▸ nonresistant, resigned. *See* **passive. 2.** Disposed to accept, agree, or participate ▸ agreeable, ready. *See* **willing** (1). **3.** Willing to carry out the wishes of others ▸ complaisant, docile, submissive. *See* **obedient.**

acquirable *adjective*
▸ attainable, obtainable, procurable. *See* **available** (1).

acquire *verb*
1. To come into possession of ▸ come by, gain, procure. *See* **get** (1). **2.** To come gradually to have ▸ contract, form, incur. *See* **develop** (1). **3.** To gain knowledge or mastery of by study ▸ get, master. *See* **learn** (1).

acquirement *noun*
▸ achievement, feat, triumph. *See* **accomplishment** (1).

acquisition *noun*
1. Something completed or attained successfully ▸ achievement, attainment, feat. *See* **accomplishment** (1). **2.** Something tending to augment something else ▸ acquisition, augmentation. *See* **addition** (1).

acquisitive *adjective*
1. Having a strong urge to obtain or possess something, especially material wealth, in quantity ▸ avaricious, covetous. *See* **greedy** (1). **2.** Eager to acquire knowledge ▸ inquiring, inquisitive, questioning. *See* **curious** (2).

acquisitiveness *noun*
▸ avarice, covetousness, rapacity. *See* **greed.**

acquit *verb*
1. To free from a charge of guilt ▸ absolve, exonerate, vindicate. *See* **clear** (9). **2.** To conduct oneself in a specified way ▸ bear, behave, carry, comport. *See* **act** (1).

acquittal *noun*
▸ exoneration, vindication. *See* **exculpation.**

acreage *noun*
1. A piece of land ▸ parcel, plot, tract. *See* **lot** (1). **2.** Usually extensive real estate ▸ estate, property. *See* **land** (1).

acres *noun*
Usually extensive real estate ▸ estate, property. *See* **land** (1).

acrid *adjective*
1. Having a sharp, unpleasant, alkaline taste ▸ acerbic, harsh. *See* **bitter** (1). *See synonym note at* **bitter. 2.** So sharp as to cause mental pain ▸ caustic, sharp, vitriolic. *See* **biting.**

acridity *noun*
▸ acerbity, causticity, trenchancy. *See* **sarcasm.**

acrimonious *adjective*
▸ bitter, rancorous, virulent. *See* **resentful.**
acrimony *noun*
▸ bitterness, rancor, virulence. *See* **resentment** (1).
across *adjective*
▸ crossways, crosswise, traverse. *See* **transverse.**
act *noun*
1. Something done ▸ action, deed, doing, performance, thing, work. *See also* **accomplishment. 2.** A display of insincere behavior ▸ acting, affectation, disguise, dissemblance, dissimulation, masquerade, pretense, sham, show, simulation. *See also* **affectation, façade, pose. 3.** A short theatrical piece within a larger production ▸ sketch, skit. *See also* **satire. 4.** A characteristic behavior or performance ▸ *Slang:* routine. *See* **bit**[1] (1). **5.** The formal product of a legislative or judicial body ▸ bill, legislation. *See* **law** (2).
act *verb*
1. To conduct oneself in a specified way ▸ acquit, bear, behave, carry, comport, demean, deport, do, handle, quit. *See also* **appear. 2.** To behave insincerely or take on as a false appearance ▸ affect, assume, counterfeit, dissemble, dissimulate, fabricate, fake, feign, play-act, pose, pretend, put on, sham, simulate. *Idioms:* make believe, put on an act. *See also* **disguise, fake. 3.** To act in a specified way ▸ behave, operate, work. *See* **function** *See also* **officiate. 4.** To play the part of ▸ do, dramatize, enact, impersonate, perform, play, play-act, portray, represent. **5.** To produce on the stage ▸ dramatize, enact, perform. *See* **stage** (1).
act on *verb*
To have an impact on in a certain way ▸ incline, predispose, sway. *See* **influence** (1).
act up *verb*
1. To behave in a rowdy, improper, or unruly fashion ▸ carry on. *Informal:* horse around. *See* **misbehave. 2.** To stop working properly ▸ break down, fail. *See* **malfunction.**
acting *noun*
1. The art and occupation of an actor ▸ dramatics, stage, theater, theatrics. **2.** A display of insincere behavior ▸ disguise, masquerade, sham. *See* **act** (2).
acting *adjective*
Temporarily assuming the duties of another ▸ interim, provisional. *See* **temporary** (1). *See synonym note at* **temporary.**
action *noun*
1. Something done ▸ deed, performance, work. *See* **act** (1). **2.** The manner in which one behaves ▸ comportment, conduct, deportment. *See* **behavior** (1). **3.** The act or process of moving ▸ activity, movement, stir. *See* **motion** (1). **4.** A legal proceeding to demand justice or enforce a right ▸ case, suit. *See* **lawsuit. 5.** An encounter between opposing military forces ▸ combat, confrontation, war. *See* **battle** (1). **6.** The series of events and relationships forming the basis of a composition ▸ movement, story line. *See* **plot** (1).
activate *verb*
1. To set in motion ▸ actuate, spark, start, turn on. *See*

also **energize, provoke. 2.** To assemble, prepare, or put into operation, as for war or a similar emergency ▸ call up, ready. *See* **mobilize.**
active *adjective*
1. In action or full operation ▸ alive, functioning, going, humming, operating, operative, running, ticking, working. *Slang:* purring. *Idioms:* going full blast (*or* force *or* tilt), in high gear. *See also* **busy. 2.** Possessing, exerting, or displaying energy ▸ brisk, lively, vigorous. *See* **energetic.**
activity *noun*
1. Energetic physical action ▸ exercise, exertion. *See also* **energy. 2.** Agitated, excited activity ▸ commotion, excitement, fuss. *See* **agitation** (3). **3.** The act or process of moving ▸ action, movement, stirring. *See* **motion** (1).
actor *or* **actress** *noun*
1. A theatrical performer ▸ player, thespian, trouper. *See also* **fake, lead, mimic. 2.** One who participates ▸ participator, player, sharer. *See* **participant.**
actual *adjective*
1. Occurring or existing in act or fact ▸ existent, extant, real, true. *See also* **physical. 2.** Not counterfeit or copied ▸ genuine, real, true. *See* **authentic** (1). **3.** Conforming to fact ▸ factual, faithful, veracious. *See* **accurate** (1).

✦ **CORE SYNONYMS:** *actual, real, true, existent.* These adjectives mean not being imaginary but occurring or existing in act or fact. *Actual* means existing and not merely potential or possible: *"rocks, trees . . . the actual world"* (Henry David Thoreau). *Real* implies authenticity, genuineness, or factuality: *Don't lose the bracelet; it's made of real gold. She showed real sympathy for my predicament. True* implies consistency with fact, reality, or actuality: *"It is undesirable to believe a proposition when there is no ground whatever for supposing it true"* (Bertrand Russell). *Existent* applies to what has life or being: *Much of the beluga caviar existent in the world is found near the Caspian Sea.*

---

actuality *noun*
1. Something demonstrated to exist or known to have existed ▸ event, fact, phenomenon, reality. *Idioms:* hard (*or* cold *or* plain) fact. *See also* **information. 2.** The fact or state of existing or of being actual ▸ being, entity. *See* **existence** (1). *See synonym note at* **existence. 3.** The quality of being actual or factual ▸ fact, reality, truth. *See* **certainty** (1).
actualization *noun*
The condition of being in full force or operation ▸ being, effect, force, realization. *See also* **exercise.**
actualize *verb*
To make real or actual ▸ bring about, make happen, materialize, realize. *Idioms:* bring to pass, carry (*or* put) into effect. *See also* **effect, produce.**
actually *adverb*
1. In point of fact ▸ as a matter of fact, indeed, in fact, really. **2.** In truth ▸ genuinely, indeed, truly. *See* **really. 3.** At this moment ▸ at present, currently. *See* **now** (1).

actuate *verb*
1. To set in motion ▸ activate, start, turn on. *See also* **energize, provoke. 2.** To put into action or use ▸ apply, employ, utilize. *See* **use** (1).

acumen *noun*
▸ keenness, perceptiveness, shrewdness. *See* **discernment** (1).

acuminate *adjective*
▸ acute, cuspate, sharp. *See* **pointed** (1).

acumination *noun*
▸ cusp, tip. *See* **point** (1).

acute *adjective*
1. Having an end that tapers to a point ▸ acicular, cuspate, sharp. *See* **pointed** (1). **2.** Keenly perceptive or discerning ▸ keen, perceptive, sharp. *See* **critical** (2). **3.** Demanding immediate attention ▸ crucial, dire, pressing. *See* **urgent** (1). **4.** Mentally quick and original ▸ keen, quick-witted, sharp. *See* **clever** (1). **5.** Marked by severity or intensity ▸ gnawing, piercing. *See* **sharp** (8). **6.** Elevated in pitch ▸ piercing, shrill. *See* **high** (3).

acutely *adverb*
▸ exceedingly, extremely, highly. *See* **very.**

acuteness *noun*
▸ astuteness, selectiveness, taste. *See* **discrimination** (1).

adage *noun*
▸ aphorism, maxim, motto. *See* **proverb.** *See synonym note at* **proverb.**

adamant *adjective*
▸ bullheaded, dogged, obstinate. *See* **stubborn** (1). *See synonym note at* **stubborn.**

adapt *verb*
To make or become suitable to a particular situation or use ▸ acclimate, acclimatize, accommodate, adjust, conform, fashion, fit, remodel, shape, suit, tailor. *Idioms:* get used to, learn to live with (*or* accept). *See also* **change, convert.**

✚ **CORE SYNONYMS:** *adapt, accommodate, adjust, conform, fit, tailor.* These verbs mean to make suitable to or consistent with a particular situation or use: *adapted themselves to city life; can't accommodate myself to the new requirements; adjusting their behavior to the rules; conforming her life to accord with her moral principles; fitting the punishment to the crime; tailored the report for the needs of the committee.*

---

adaptable *adjective*
Capable of adapting or being adapted ▸ adaptive, adjustable, elastic, flexible, malleable, pliable, pliant, supple, versatile. *See also* **changeable, obedient.**

adaptation *noun*
1. The act or process of adapting ▸ acclimation, acclimatization, accommodation, acculturation, adaption, adjustment, conditioning, conformation. *See also* **change. 2.** One that is slightly different from others of the same kind or designation ▸ alteration, permutation. *See* **variation** (1).

adapted *adjective*
▸ acclimated, conditioned. *See* **accustomed** (1).

adaption *noun*
▸ accommodation, adjustment, conformation. *See* **adaptation** (1).

adaptive *adjective*
▸ adjustable, flexible, malleable. *See* **adaptable.**

add *verb*
1. To combine numbers to form a sum ▸ add up, cast, foot (up), sum (up), tot (up), total, totalize. *See also* **calculate, count. 2.** To add as a supplement or appendix ▸ annex, append. *See* **attach** (2).

add up *verb*
To come to in number or quantity ▸ number, reach, total. *See* **amount** (1).

added *adjective*
▸ extra, further, more. *See* **additional.**

addendum *noun*
▸ accession, augmentation. *See* **addition** (1).

addiction *noun*
Compulsive physiological and psychological need for a habit-forming substance ▸ craving, compulsion, dependence, drug abuse, enslavement, fixation, substance abuse. *See also* **custom.**

addition *noun*
1. Something tending to augment something else ▸ accession, acquisition, addendum, augmentation. *See also* **attachment. 2.** The act or process of adding ▸ summation, sums, totalization. *See also* **calculation. 3.** A part added to a main structure ▸ annex, wing. *See* **extension** (4).

additional *adjective*
Being an addition ▸ added, extra, fresh, further, more, new, other, supplemental, supplementary. *See also* **auxiliary.**

additionally *adverb*
In addition ▸ also, besides, further, furthermore, likewise, more, moreover, still, too, yet. *Idioms:* as well, for good measure, not to mention, on top of, to boot, to say nothing of

additive *adjective*
Increasing, as in force, by successive additions ▸ accumulative, cumulative.

additive-free *adjective*
▸ chemical-free, unadulterated. *See* **natural** (1).

addle *verb*
▸ befuddle, bewilder, confound. *See* **confuse** (1). *See synonym note at* **confuse.**

addled *or* **addlepated** *adjective*
▸ confounded, perplexed, turbid. *See* **confused** (1).

add-on *noun*
1. A part added to a main structure ▸ addition, annex, wing. *See* **extension** (4). **2.** Something added to another for embellishment or completion ▸ accompaniment, complement, supplement. *See* **enhancement** (1).

address *verb*
1. To talk to an audience formally ▸ lecture, prelect, sermonize, speak. *See also* **converse. 2.** To bring an appeal or request to the attention of ▸ appeal, apply, approach, petition. *See also* **appeal, request. 3.** To

mark a written communication with its destination ▸ direct, superscribe. *See also* **ticket**. **4.** To devote oneself or one's efforts ▸ concentrate, focus, give. *See* **apply** (1). **5.** To cause something to be conveyed to a destination ▸ consign, dispatch. *See* **send** (1). **6.** To be concerned with something ▸ consider, treat. *See* **deal** (1).

address *noun*
1. A usually formal spoken communication to an audience ▸ lecture, talk. *See* **speech** (2). **2.** Behavior that reveals one's personality or state of mind ▸ demeanor, manner, style. *See* **bearing** (2). **3.** The ability to say and do the right thing at the right time ▸ diplomacy, savoir-faire, tactfulness. *See* **tact**. *See synonym note at* **tact**. **4.** *Informal* A building or shelter where one lives ▸ domicile, habitation, residence. *See* **home** (1).

addresses *noun*
▸ moves, overture. *See* **advances**.

adduce *verb*
▸ lay, present, produce. *See* **cite** (1).

adept *adjective*
Having or demonstrating a high degree of knowledge or skill ▸ master, professional, skilled. *See* **expert**. *See synonym note at* **expert**.

adept *noun*
A person with a high degree of knowledge or skill in a particular field ▸ authority, master, proficient. *See* **expert**.

adeptness *noun*
▸ expertise, knack, proficiency. *See* **ability** (1).

adequacy *noun*
An adequate quantity ▸ enough, sufficiency.

adequate *adjective*
1. Being what is needed without being in excess ▸ competent, decent, satisfactory. *See* **sufficient** (1). *See synonym note at* **sufficient**. **2.** Adequate to satisfy a need, requirement, or standard ▸ average, decent, fair. *See* **acceptable** (2).

adhere *verb*
1. To form a tight bond ▸ cleave, cohere. *See* **bond**. **2.** To act in conformity with ▸ heed, obey, observe. *See* **follow** (4).

adherence *noun*
▸ adhesion, cohesion. *See* **bond** (3).

adherent *noun*
1. One who supports and adheres to another ▸ believer, disciple, supporter. *See* **follower** (1). **2.** One zealously devoted to a religion ▸ fanatic, zealot. *See* **devotee** (1).

adherents *noun*
The steadfast believers in a faith or cause ▸ congregation, faithful, fold. *See also* **follower, assembly**.

adhesion *noun*
▸ adherence, cohesion. *See* **bond** (3).

adhesive *adjective*
▸ gluey, gummy, tacky. *See* **sticky** (1).

ad hoc *adjective*
▸ make-do, makeshift, short-term. *See* **temporary** (2).

adieu *noun*
▸ embarkation, farewell, goodbye. *See* **departure** (1).

ad interim *adjective*
▸ interim, pro tem, provisional. *See* **temporary** (1). *See synonym note at* **temporary**.

adipose *adjective*
▸ greasy, unctuous. *See* **fatty** (1).

adjacent *adjective*
1. Not far from another in space, time, or relation ▸ near, nearby, nigh. *See* **close** (1). **2.** Sharing a common boundary ▸ abutting, bordering, neighboring. *See* **adjoining**.

adjoin *verb*
1. To be contiguous or next to ▸ abut, border, bound, butt, flank, impinge, join, meet, neighbor, touch, verge. *See also* **border**. **2.** To join one thing to another ▸ affix, fasten, secure. *See* **attach** (1).

adjoining *adjective*
Sharing a common boundary ▸ abutting, adjacent, bordering, conjoining, conterminous, contiguous, neighboring, next.

adjourn *verb*
▸ delay, postpone, suspend. *See* **defer**[1].

adjournment *noun*
▸ deferment, postponement, suspension. *See* **delay** (1).

adjudicate *or* **adjudge** *verb*
▸ decide, decree, rule. *See* **judge** (1).

adjudication *noun*
▸ edict, judgment, pronouncement. *See* **ruling**.

adjunct *noun*
▸ accessory, appendage, supplement. *See* **attachment** (1). *See synonym note at* **attachment**.

adjure *verb*
1. To make an earnest or urgent request ▸ beseech, entreat, plead. *See* **appeal** (1). **2.** To give orders to ▸ instruct, order, tell. *See* **command** (1).

adjust *verb*
1. To alter for proper or accurate functioning ▸ align, attune, calibrate, fine-tune, fix, modulate, regulate, set, temper, tweak, tune (up). *See also* **fix, tinker**. **2.** To make or become suitable to a particular situation or use ▸ acclimate, conform, reconcile. *See* **adapt**. *See synonym note at* **adapt**.

adjustable *adjective*
▸ flexible, malleable, pliable. *See* **adaptable**.

adjustment *noun*
▸ acclimation, acculturation, conformation. *See* **adaptation** (1).

adjutant *noun*
▸ aide, deputy, helper. *See* **assistant**.

ad-lib *verb*
To compose or recite without preparation ▸ fake, make up. *See* **improvise** (1).

ad-lib *noun*
Something that is improvised ▸ extemporization, impromptu, improvisation. *See also* **makeshift**.

ad-lib *adjective*
Spoken, performed, or composed with little or no

preparation or forethought ▸ impromptu, improvised. *See* **extemporaneous**. *See synonym note at* extemporaneous.

admeasure *verb*
▸ allocate, apportion, dole out. *See* **distribute** (1).

admeasurement *noun*
▸ allocation, apportionment, dispensation. *See* **distribution** (1).

administer *verb*
1. To have charge of the affairs of others ▸ administrate, captain, control, dictate, direct, dominate, govern, head, lead, manage, reign, rule, run. *Idioms:* be at the helm, be in the driver's seat, hold sway over, hold the reins. *See also* **command, supervise. 2.** To oversee the provision or execution of ▸ administrate, carry out, dispense, execute. *See also* **conduct. 3.** To provide as a remedy ▸ apply, dispense, dose, give, medicate, prescribe, treat, vaccinate. *Informal:* doctor. *See also* **cure, dress, drug. 4.** To mete out by means of some action ▸ deal, deliver, give.

administrable *adjective*
Capable of being governed ▸ controllable, governable, manageable, rulable. *See also* **loyal, obedient.**

administrant *noun*
▸ administrator, manager. *See* **executive.**

administrate *verb*
1. To have charge of the affairs of others ▸ direct, govern, rule. *See* **administer** (1). **2.** To oversee the provision or execution of ▸ carry out, dispense. *See* **administer** (2).

administration *noun*
1. The act or practice of directing ▸ direction, guidance, superintendence. *See* **management** (1). **2.** The continuous exercise of authority over a political unit ▸ control, rule. *See* **government** (1). **3.** A group of people who govern a political unit ▸ regime, state. *See* **government** (2). **4.** The act of putting into play ▸ employment, implementation, usage. *See* **exercise** (1).

administrative *adjective*
Of, for, or relating to administration or administrators ▸ directorial, executive, governmental, managerial, ministerial, organizational, supervisory.

administrator *noun*
▸ director, manager. *See* **executive.**

admirable *adjective*
Deserving honor, respect, or admiration ▸ commendable, creditable, deserving, estimable, exemplary, honorable, laudable, meritorious, praiseworthy, reputable, respectable, venerable, worthy. *See also* **choice, excellent, honest, marvelous.**

admiration *noun*
▸ account, consideration, favor. *See* **esteem** (1). *See synonym note at* **esteem.**

admire *verb*
1. To have a feeling of great awe and rapt admiration ▸ marvel, wonder. *Idioms:* be agog (*or* agape *or* awestruck). *See also* **gaze, stagger. 2.** To have a high

opinion of or regard for ▸ appreciate, esteem, respect. *See* **value** (1).

admirer *noun*
1. An ardent admirer ▸ devotee, enthusiast, fancier. *See* **fan**². **2.** A man who courts a woman ▸ courter, suitor. *See* **beau** (1).

admissible *adjective*
▸ allowable, permissible, unobjectionable. *See* **acceptable** (1).

admission *noun*
1. The act of admitting or the state of being admitted ▸ access, admittance, entrance, entrée, entry, ingress, introduction, intromission. *See also* **acceptance, permission. 2.** The act of admitting to something ▸ avowal, confession, recognition. *See* **acknowledgment** (1).

admit *verb*
1. To allow admittance, as to a group ▸ let in, receive, take in. *See* **accept** (3). **2.** To afford an opportunity for ▸ allow, let. *See* **permit** (3). **3.** To express recognition of ▸ acknowledge, recognize. *See also* **confirm. 4.** To admit to the reality or truth of ▸ concede, grant. *See* **acknowledge** (1). *See synonym note at* **acknowledge.**

admittance *noun*
▸ access, entrance, entry. *See* **admission** (1).

admitted *adjective*
▸ established, recognized, sanctioned. *See* **accepted.**

admix *verb*
▸ blend, fuse, stir. *See* **mix** (1).

admixture *noun*
▸ amalgam, blend, mix. *See* **mixture** (1). *See synonym note at* mixture.

admonish *verb*
1. To criticize for a fault or offense ▸ chide, rebuke, reprimand. *See* **chastise** (1). **2.** To notify someone of imminent danger or risk ▸ alert, caution. *See* **warn.**

admonishing *adjective*
Giving warning ▸ admonitory, cautionary, monitory, warning.

admonition *or* **admonishment** *noun*
1. Words expressive of strong disapproval ▸ lecture, reprimand, scolding. *See* **rebuke. 2.** Advice to beware, as of a person or thing ▸ alarum, caveat, monition. *See* **warning** (1).

admonitory *adjective*
Giving warning ▸ admonishing, cautionary, monitory, warning.

ado *noun*
▸ bustle, fuss, fuss. *See* **agitation** (3).

adolescence *noun*
▸ juvenility, puberty, salad days. *See* **youth** (1).

adolescent *noun*
A young person, usually between the ages of 13 and 19 ▸ teen, youth. *See* **teenager.**

adolescent *adjective*
Of or characteristic of a child, especially in immaturity ▸ immature, infantile, juvenile. *See* **childish.**

adopt *verb*
1. To take, as another's idea, and make one's own

▸ appropriate, assume, embrace, espouse, take on, take up. *See also* **act, seize. 2.** To accept officially ▸ approve, pass, ratify. *See* **confirm** (3). **3.** To be accepted or approved ▸ affiliate, clear. *See* **pass** (16).

adoption *noun*
1. The act of accepting or adopting ▸ assent, consent, espousal. *See* **acceptance** (1). **2.** An act of confirming officially ▸ approval, ratification, sanction. *See* **confirmation** (1). **3.** The act of putting into play ▸ employment, implementation, usage. *See* **exercise** (1).

adorable *adjective*
▸ delectable, enchanting, heavenly. *See* **delightful.**

adoration *noun*
1. The act of adoring, especially reverently ▸ idolization, reverence, veneration, worship. *See also* **honor, praise. 2.** An intense attachment to a person or thing ▸ devotion, fondness, worship. *See* **love** (1). **3.** A state of often extreme religious ardor ▸ piety, piousness. *See* **devotion** (1).

adore *verb*
1. To feel deep devoted love for ▸ love, worship. *Idioms:* be soft (*or* stuck *or* sweet) on. **2.** To like or enjoy enthusiastically ▸ be big on, be crazy about, be hot on, be into, be keen on, be mad about, be nuts about, be wild about, delight (in), dote on (*or* upon), love. *Slang:* eat up, get off on. **3.** To regard with the deepest respect, deference, and esteem ▸ idolize, venerate, worship. *See* **revere.** *See synonym note at* **revere. 4.** To find agreeable ▸ adore, fancy, favor. *See* **like**[1] (1).

adorn *verb*
1. To furnish with decorations ▸ bedeck, bejewel, deck (out), decorate, dress (up), embellish, emblazon, festoon, garnish, gild, ornament, trim. *Slang:* doll up, gussy up. **2.** To endow with beauty and elegance by way of a notable addition ▸ beautify, embellish, enhance, grace, set off.

adornment *noun*
Something that adorns ▸ decoration, embellishment, garnishment, garniture, ornament, ornamentation, trim, trimming.

adrift *adjective*
▸ disoriented, stray. *See* **lost** (1).

adroit *adjective*
▸ deft, facile, nimble. *See* **dexterous.** *See synonym note at* **dexterous.**

adroitness *noun*
▸ deftness, facility. *See* **dexterity** (1).

adscititious *adjective*
Not part of the real or essential nature of a thing ▸ adventitious, incidental, inessential, supervenient. *See also* **irrelevant, unnecessary.**

adulate *verb*
▸ butter up. *Informal:* soft-soap, sweet-talk. *See* **flatter** (1).

adulation *noun*
▸ blandishment, blarney. *See* **flattery.**

adulator *noun*
▸ flatterer, minion, slave. *See* **sycophant.**

adult *adjective*
▸ developed, grown, ripe. *See* **mature** (1).

adulterant *noun*
▸ impurity, poison, pollutant. *See* **contaminant.**

adulterate *verb*
1. To make impure, unclean, or inferior by contact or mixture ▸ debase, infect, pollute. *See* **contaminate** (1). *See synonym note at* **contaminate. 2.** To lessen the strength of by or as if by admixture ▸ cut, weaken. *See* **dilute.**

adulterated *adjective*
▸ alloyed, combined, polluted. *See* **impure** (2).

adulteration *noun*
▸ defilement, impurity. *See* **contamination** (1).

adulterator *noun*
▸ impurity, poison, pollutant. *See* **contaminant.**

adulterer *noun*
▸ Casanova, cheater, paramour. *See* **philanderer.**

adumbrate *verb*
1. To give an indication of something in advance ▸ augur, foretoken, portend. *See* **foreshadow. 2.** To draw up a preliminary plan or version of ▸ outline, sketch. *See* **draft** (1). **3.** To make dark or darker ▸ darken, overcast, shadow. *See* **shade** (2). **4.** To make dim ▸ blur, fog, obfuscate. *See* **obscure** (1).

advance *verb*
1. To cause to move forward or upward, as toward a goal ▸ drive, forward, foster, further, promote, propel, push. *See also* **drive, improve. 2.** To move forward ▸ come (along), get along, march, move (up), press (on), proceed, progress, push (on). *See also* **plunge. 3.** To state for consideration or debate ▸ offer, put forward, set forth. *See* **propose** (1). **4.** To raise in rank ▸ elevate, upgrade. *See* **promote** (1). **5.** To attain a higher status, rank, or condition ▸ ascend, climb, mount. *See* **rise** (6). **6.** To supply money, especially on credit ▸ discount, loan. *See* **lend. 7.** To put before another for acceptance ▸ extend, proffer. *See* **offer** (1).

advance *noun*
1. Forward movement ▸ advancement, furtherance, headway, march, procession, progress, progression, stride. *See also* **accomplishment, progress. 2.** The amount by which something is increased ▸ boost, jump. *See* **increase** (2).

advance *adjective*
Going before ▸ antecedent, anterior, earlier, precedent, preceding, previous, prior.

✤ **CORE SYNONYMS:** *advance, forward, foster, further, promote, propel.* These verbs mean to cause to move forward or upward, as toward a goal: *advance a worthy cause; forwarding their own interests; fostered friendly relations; furthering your career; efforts to promote sales; a speech that propelled the candidate to victory.*

◀ **ANTONYM:** *retard*

---

advanced *adjective*
1. Ahead of current trends or customs ▸ forward, precocious. *See* **progressive** (1). **2.** Far along in life or

time ▸ aged, elderly, senior. *See* **old** (2). **3.** Difficult to understand because of intricacy ▸ convoluted, elaborate, involved. *See* **complex** (1).

advancement *noun*
1. A progression upward in rank ▸ elevation, jump, preferment, promotion, raise, rise, upgrade. *See also* **increase**. **2.** A progression from a simple form to a more complex one ▸ advancement, progress, unfolding. *See* **development** (1). **3.** Forward movement ▸ furtherance, headway, progress. *See* **advance** (1). **4.** Steady improvement, as of an individual or society ▸ amelioration, betterment, development. *See* **progress** (1). **5.** The act of making better or the condition of being made better ▸ betterment, development, upgrade. *See* **improvement** (1).

advances *noun*
Personal approach to gain acquaintance, favor, or an agreement ▸ addresses, approach, attentions, moves, overture, proposition. *See also* **feeler, offer**.

advantage *noun*
1. A factor conducive to superiority and success ▸ handicap, head start, odds, start, toehold, vantage. *Informal:* jump. **2.** Something beneficial ▸ avail, benefit, blessing, boon, favor, gain, profit. *See also* **help, luck, patronage**. **3.** A dominating position, as in a conflict ▸ better, bulge, draw, drop, edge, leverage, superiority, upper hand, vantage, whip hand. *Informal:* inside track, jump, leg up. **4.** Something that contributes to or increases one's well-being ▸ benefit, good, interests. *See* **interest** (1). **5.** The quality of being suitable or adaptable to an end ▸ benefit, profit, utility. *See* **use** (2).

advantage *verb*
To be an advantage to ▸ benefit, serve. *See* **profit** (2).

advantageous *adjective*
1. Affording benefit or advantage ▸ favorable, helpful, propitious. *See* **beneficial**. *See synonym note at* **beneficial**. **2.** Affording profit ▸ gainful, lucrative, rewarding. *See* **profitable** (1).

advantages *noun*
▸ conveniences, resources, services. *See* **amenities** (1).

advent *noun*
The act of arriving ▸ appearance, arrival, coming. *See also* **entrance**.

adventitious *adjective*
1. Not part of the real or essential nature of a thing ▸ adscititious, incidental, inessential, supervenient. *See also* **irrelevant, unnecessary**. **2.** Occurring unexpectedly ▸ chance, fortuitous, unanticipated. *See* **accidental** (1). *See synonym note at* **accidental**.

adventure *noun*
An exciting or unusual undertaking ▸ emprise, enterprise, escapade, experience, odyssey, venture. *See also* **feat, journey, trip**.

adventure *verb*
1. To place something at risk, as in a game of chance ▸ bet, stake, wager. *See* **gamble** (2). **2.** To express at the risk of rebuff or criticism ▸ dare, hazard, presume. *See* **venture** (1).

adventurer *noun*
1. One who seeks adventure ▸ daredevil, quester, venturer. *See also* **builder**. **2.** A freelance fighter ▸ mercenary, soldier of fortune. *See also* **fighter, soldier**. **3.** One who speculates for quick profits ▸ gambler, speculator, operator.

adventuresome *adjective*
▸ daring, enterprising. *See* **adventurous** (1). *See synonym note at* **adventurous**.

adventuresomeness *noun*
▸ boldness, daredevilry, fearlessness. *See* **daring**.

adventurous *adjective*
1. Taking or willing to take risks ▸ adventuresome, audacious, bold, daredevil, daring, enterprising, venturesome, venturous. *See also* **brave, rash**[1]. **2.** Involving possible risk, loss, or injury ▸ chancy, hazardous, risky. *See* **dangerous**.

✛ CORE SYNONYMS: *adventurous, adventuresome, audacious, daredevil, daring, venturesome*. These adjectives mean inclined to undertake risks: *adventurous pioneers; an adventuresome prospector; an audacious explorer; a daredevil test pilot; daring acrobats; a venturesome investor*.

---

adventurousness *noun*
▸ audacity, boldness, daredevilry. *See* **daring**.

adversarial *adjective*
▸ antagonistic, resistant. *See* **opposing** (1).

adversary *noun*
▸ antagonist, foe, nemesis. *See* **opponent** (1).

adverse *adjective*
1. Not encouraging life or growth ▸ hostile, inhospitable, unfavorable. *See also* **severe**. **2.** Acting against or in opposition ▸ antagonistic, resistant. *See* **opposing** (1). **3.** Tending to discourage, retard, or make more difficult ▸ antagonistic, negative, untoward. *See* **unfavorable** (1). **4.** Causing harm or injury ▸ deleterious, evil, injurious. *See* **harmful**.

adversity *noun*
▸ bad luck, haplessness, unluckiness. *See* **misfortune** (1).

advert *verb*
▸ allude (to), mention, note. *See* **refer** (1). *See synonym note at* **refer**.

advertise *verb*
1. To attempt to sell or popularize by advertising or publicity ▸ market, purvey, publicize. *See* **promote** (3). **2.** To bring to public notice or make known publicly ▸ broadcast, declare, proclaim, promulgate. *See* **announce** (1). *See synonym note at* **announce**.

advertisement *noun*
▸ ballyhoo, exposure. *Slang:* hype. *See* **publicity** (1).

advertising *noun*
1. The act or profession of promoting something, as a product ▸ ballyhooing, billing, promoting, promotion, publicity, publicizing. *Informal:* plugging. **2.** Information disseminated through various media to attract public notice ▸ advertisement, ballyhoo. *Slang:* hype. *See* **publicity** (1).

advice *noun*
1. An opinion as to a decision or course of action ▸ counsel, direction, guidance, pointer, recommendation, suggestion, tip. *Idiom:* word to the wise. *See also* **command, deliberation, warning. 2.** New information, especially about recent events and happenings ▸ intelligence, report. *See* **news** (1). *See synonym note at* **news.**

━━━━━━━━━━━━━━━━━━━━━━━━━━━
✦ CORE SYNONYMS: *advice, counsel, recommendation, suggestion.* These nouns denote an opinion as to a decision or course of action: *The speaker had sound advice for the unemployed. I accepted my attorney's counsel. The committee will follow your recommendation. The teacher offered several suggestions for improving my essay.*
━━━━━━━━━━━━━━━━━━━━━━━━━━━

advisable *adjective*
Worth doing, especially for practical reasons ▸ best, desirable, expedient, politic, practicable, recommendable, well, wisest. *See also* **appropriate, sensible.**

advise *verb*
1. To give recommendations to someone about a decision or course of action ▸ counsel, direct, guide, recommend, steer. *Informal:* mentor. *Idiom:* give a piece of advice. *See also* **guide, propose, warn. 2.** To meet and exchange views to reach a decision ▸ consult, deliberate. *Informal:* powwow. *See* **confer** (1). **3.** To impart information to ▸ educate, notify. *See* **inform** (1).

━━━━━━━━━━━━━━━━━━━━━━━━━━━
✦ CORE SYNONYMS: *advise, counsel, direct, recommend.* These verbs mean to suggest a particular decision or course of action: *His friends advised him to go abroad. She will counsel her friend to be prudent. The technician directed them to read the manual. The waiter recommended that I try the halibut.*
━━━━━━━━━━━━━━━━━━━━━━━━━━━

advised *adjective*
1. Marked by careful consideration ▸ considered, studied. *See* **deliberate** (2). **2.** Provided with information; made aware ▸ educated, instructed. *See* **informed** (1).

advisement *noun*
Careful thought ▸ consideration, deliberation, study. *See also* **attention, examination, scrutiny.**

adviser *or* **advisor** *noun*
One who advises another ▸ consultant, counselor, guide, guru, mentor. *See also* **expert, lawyer.**

advisory *adjective*
Giving advice ▸ consultative, consultatory, consulting, consultive, counseling, recommendatory. *See also* **cautionary, educational.**

advisory *noun*
A report giving information ▸ bulletin, notice. *See also* **report, warning.**

advocacy *noun*
▸ backing, sponsorship. *See* **patronage** (1).

advocate *noun*
1. One that argues for or defends a cause ▸ booster, champion, defender, promoter, proponent, supporter, upholder, vindicator. *See also* **lawyer, patron, sponsor. 2.** One who represents the interests of another ▸ ambassador, deputy, proxy. *See* **representative** (2).

advocate *verb*
To aid the cause of by approving or favoring ▸ back, endorse, stand by. *See* **support** (1). *See synonym note at* **support.**

aegis *noun*
▸ backing, sponsorship. *See* **patronage** (1).

aeon *noun*
See **eon.**

aerate *verb*
To expose to circulating air ▸ air, freshen, ventilate, wind.

aerial *adjective*
1. Of or relating to air ▸ airy, atmospheric, pneumatic. **2.** Being of or at a relatively great height or altitude ▸ elevated, lofty. *See* **high** (1).

aesthetic *or* **esthetic** *adjective*
1. Relating to or appreciative of the arts ▸ artistic, creative. *Informal:* artsy, arty. **2.** Promoting culture ▸ enlightening, humanizing. *See* **cultural.**

affability *noun*
▸ agreeability, congeniality, pleasantness. *See* **amiability.**

affable *adjective*
1. Characterized by kindness and warm, unaffected courtesy ▸ courteous, gracious, hospitable. *See also* **attentive, courteous. 2.** Pleasant and friendly in disposition ▸ cordial, friendly, genial. *See* **amiable.**

affair *noun*
1. Something that concerns or involves one personally ▸ business, concern, interest, lookout. **2.** Something to be done, considered, or dealt with ▸ business, matter, thing. *See also* **business, problem, task. 3.** A social gathering, especially for pleasure ▸ celebration, gala, soiree. *See* **party** (1). **4.** An intimate sexual relationship between two people ▸ amour, love affair, romance. *See* **love** (3).

━━━━━━━━━━━━━━━━━━━━━━━━━━━
✦ CORE SYNONYMS: *affair, business, concern, lookout.* These nouns denote something that involves one personally: *I won't comment on that; it's not my affair. Please mind your own business. This situation is none of your concern. It's your lookout to file your application on time.*
━━━━━━━━━━━━━━━━━━━━━━━━━━━

affect¹ *verb*
1. To stir the emotions of ▸ get (to), strike, touch. *See* **move** (1). *See synonym note at* **move. 2.** To have an impact on in a certain way ▸ act on, impact, sway. *See* **influence** (1).

affect *noun*
A subjective mental state, such as love or hate ▸ affection, feeling. *See* **emotion.**

affect² *verb*
To behave insincerely or take on as a false appearance ▸ counterfeit, fake, feign. *See* **act** (2).

affectation *noun*
1. Behavior that is assumed rather than natural ▸ affectedness, artificiality, air, airs, mannerism, pose, pretense, simulation, theatricism. *See also* **façade, posture. 2.** A display of insincere behavior ▸ acting, pretense, show. *See* **act** (2).

✦ CORE SYNONYMS: *affectation, pose, air, airs, mannerism.* These nouns refer to personal behavior assumed for effect. An *affectation* is artificial behavior, often adopted in imitation of someone, that is perceived as being unnatural: *"His [Arthur Rubinstein's] playing stripped away . . . the affectations and exaggerations that characterized Chopin interpretation before his arrival"* (Michael Kimmelman). *Pose* denotes an attitude adopted to call favorable attention to oneself: *His humility is only a pose. Air,* meaning a distinctive but intangible quality, does not always imply sham: *The director had an air of authority.* The plural form *airs,* however, usually suggests affectation and self-importance: *The movie star was putting on airs. Mannerism* denotes an idiosyncratic trait or quirk, often one that others find obtrusive and distracting: *His mannerism of closing his eyes as he talked made it seem as if he were deep in thought.*

---

affected *adjective*
1. Not genuine or sincere ▸ feigned, insincere, phony. *See* **artificial** (2). **2.** Having concern ▸ interested, involved. *See* **concerned** (1).

affectedness *noun*
▸ airs, mannerism. *See* **affectation** (1).

affecting *adjective*
Exciting a deep, usually somber response ▸ heart-rending, impressive, moving, poignant, stirring, touching. *See also* **pitiful.**

✦ CORE SYNONYMS: *affecting, moving, stirring, poignant, touching.* These adjectives mean exciting or capable of exciting a deep, usually somber emotion. *Affecting* applies especially to what is heart-rending or bittersweet: *an affecting photo of the hostages' release. Moving* is the most general of these terms: *"A . . . widow . . . has laid her case of destitution before him in a very moving letter"* (Nathaniel Hawthorne). Something *stirring* excites strong, turbulent, but not unpleasant feelings: *a stirring speech about patriotism. Poignant* suggests the evocation of keen, painful emotion: *"Poignant grief cannot endure forever"* (W.H. Hudson). *Touching* emphasizes sympathy or tenderness: *a touching eulogy.*

---

affection *noun*
1. An intense attachment to a person or thing ▸ adoration, devotion, fondness. *See* **love** (1). *See synonym note at* **love. 2.** A subjective mental state, such as love or hate ▸ affectivity, feeling. *See* **emotion.**

affectional *or* **affective** *adjective*
Relating to, arising from, or appealing to the emotions ▸ emotional, emotive.

affectionate *adjective*
Feeling or expressing fond feelings or affection ▸ caring, devoted, doting, fond, loving, tender.

affectivity *noun*
▸ affection, feeling. *See* **emotion.**

affectless *adjective*
▸ blank, deadpan, pokerfaced. *See* **expressionless.**

affianced *adjective*
▸ betrothed, plighted. *See* **engaged** (2).

affidavit *noun*
A formal declaration of truth or fact given under oath ▸ deposition, testimony, witness.

affiliate *verb*
1. To unite or be united in a relationship ▸ combine, join, link. *See* **associate** (1). **2.** To be accepted or approved ▸ adopt, clear. *See* **pass** (16).

affiliate *noun*
1. One who is united in a relationship with another ▸ ally, partner. *See* **associate** (1). **2.** An administrative unit, as of a government or company ▸ agency, bureau. *See* **branch** (1).

affiliation *noun*
▸ alliance, connection, cooperation. *See* **association** (1).

affinity *noun*
1. The quality or state of being alike ▸ resemblance, similarity, uniformity. *See* **likeness** (1). *See synonym note at* **likeness. 2.** A natural or habitual preference for something ▸ disposition, leaning, penchant. *See* **inclination** (1).

affirm *verb*
1. To put into words positively and with conviction ▸ avow, declare, maintain. *See* **assert** (1). **2.** To accept officially ▸ approve, pass, ratify. *See* **confirm** (3). **3.** To assure the certainty or validity of ▸ authenticate, substantiate, verify. *See* **confirm** (1).

affirmation *noun*
1. The act of asserting positively or something so asserted ▸ claim, contention, declaration, statement. *See* **assertion. 2.** An act of confirming officially ▸ approval, endorsement, ratification, sanction. *See* **confirmation** (1).

affirmative *adjective*
Giving assent ▸ approving, positive. *See* **favorable** (2).

affirmative *adverb*
It is so; as you say or ask ▸ agreed, all right, assuredly. *See* **yes.**

affix *verb*
1. To join one thing to another ▸ fasten, secure. *See* **attach** (1). **2.** To ascribe the blame for a misdeed or error ▸ attribute, blame, pin. *See* **fix** (13). **3.** To add as a supplement or appendix ▸ annex, append. *See* **attach** (2).

afflict *verb*
To cause great pain or suffering to ▸ agonize, excruciate, kill, pain, plague, rack, scourge, smite, strike, torment, torture, wound. *See also* **distress, hurt, traumatize.**

✦ CORE SYNONYMS: *afflict, agonize, rack, torment, torture.* These verbs mean to bring great pain or suffering to someone: *He was afflicted with arthritis. I was agonized to see her suffering. The patient was racked with cancer. She is tormented by migraine headaches. The refugee was tortured by painful memories.*

afflicted *adjective*
▸ suffering, wretched. *See* **miserable** (1).

affliction *noun*
1. A state of physical or mental suffering ▸ agony, misery, wretchedness. *See* **distress** (1). 2. The condition of being sick ▸ affliction, illness. *See* **sickness** (1). 3. A source of persistent worry or hardship ▸ cross, tribulation. *See* **burden**¹ (1). *See synonym note at* **burden**¹. 4. A cause of suffering or harm ▸ bane, scourge. *See* **curse** (3). 5. A state of pain or anguish that tests one's resiliency and character ▸ ordeal, tribulation, visitation. *See* **trial** (1). *See synonym note at* **trial**.

afflictive *adjective*
▸ achy, hurtful, sore. *See* **painful** (1).

affluence *noun*
▸ fortune, riches, treasure. *See* **wealth** (1).

affluent *adjective*
▸ flush, moneyed, wealthy. *See* **rich** (1). *See synonym note at* **rich**.

afford *verb*
▸ make available, provide. *See* **offer** (2).

affray *noun*
▸ free-for-all, melee. *See* **fight** (1).

affright *verb*
To fill with fear ▸ horrify, scare, terrify. *See* **frighten**.

affright *noun*
A feeling of agitation in the face of trouble or danger ▸ apprehension, consternation, trepidation. *See* **fear**.

affront *verb*
1. To cause resentment or hurt by callous, rude behavior ▸ offend, outrage. *See* **insult** (1). 2. To cause anger, resentment, or hurt feelings ▸ annoy, injure, upset. *See* **offend** (1). *See synonym note at* **offend**.

affront *noun*
1. An act that offends a person's sense of pride or dignity ▸ contumely, insult. *See* **indignity**. 2. Lack of proper respect ▸ impoliteness, irreverence, rudeness. *See* **disrespect** (1).

aficionado *noun*
▸ devotee, enthusiast, fancier. *See* **fan**².

afield *adverb*
Not in the right way or on the proper course ▸ amiss, astray, awry, wrong. *See synonym note at* **wrong**.

afire *adjective*
▸ ablaze, conflagrant. *See* **burning** (1).

aflame *adjective*
▸ afire, conflagrant. *See* **burning** (1).

a fortiori *adverb*
▸ indeed, moreover, yea. *See* **even** (2).

afraid *adjective*
Filled with fear or terror ▸ aghast, alarmed, apprehensive, fearful, fearsome, frightened, funky, horrified, panicky, panic-stricken, petrified, scared, terrified, timid, timorous, tremulous. *Informal:* spooked.

Slang: chicken. *Idioms:* frightened (*or* scared) to death, scared stiff. *See also* **fearful**.

✦ **CORE SYNONYMS:** *afraid, apprehensive, fearful, frightened, scared.* These adjectives mean filled with fear or terror: *afraid of snakes; feeling apprehensive before surgery; fearful of criticism; frightened by thunder; scared of the dark.*

afresh *adverb*
▸ again, once again, over again. *See* **anew**.

after *adverb*
At a subsequent time ▸ afterwards, latterly, subsequently. *See* **later**.

after *adjective*
Following something else in time ▸ later, posterior, subsequent, ulterior. *See also* **following**.

afterlife *noun*
▸ eternity, everlasting life. *See* **immortality**.

aftermath *noun*
▸ consequence, outcome, result. *See* **effect** (1).

aftermost *adjective*
▸ hindermost, rearmost. *See* **last**¹ (2).

afterward *or* **afterwards** *adverb*
▸ after, latterly, subsequently. *See* **later**.

afterworld *noun*
▸ great beyond, heaven, hereafter. *See* **eternity** (2).

again *adverb*
▸ afresh, once again, over again. *See* **anew**.

against *adjective*
▸ disinclined, reluctant. *See* **indisposed** (1).

agape *adjective*
▸ ajar, undone, unlocked. *See* **open** (1).

age *noun*
1. Old age ▸ agedness, elderliness, maturity, old age, senectitude, senescence, seniority, years. *See also* **senility**. 2. A particular time that is notable for its distinctive characteristics ▸ day, epoch, era, period, time, times.

age *verb*
1. To grow old ▸ get along, get on. *Idiom:* advance in years. 2. To bring or come to full development ▸ develop, ripen. *See* **mature**. *See synonym note at* **mature**.

✦ **CORE SYNONYMS:** *age, period, epoch, era.* These nouns refer to a particular time notable for its distinctive characteristics. *Age* is the most general: *the Elizabethan Age; the age of Newton; the Iron Age. Period* denotes the prevalence of a specified culture, ideology, or technology (*artifacts of the pre-Columbian period*) or a distinct developmental phase (*Picasso's blue period*). *Epoch* refers to a time that is regarded as being remarkable or memorable: *"We enter on an epoch of constitutional retrogression"* (John R. Green). An *era* is a period of time notable because of new or different aspects or events: *"How many a man has dated a new era in his life from the reading of a book"* (Henry David Thoreau).

aged *adjective*
1. Brought to full flavor and richness by aging

▶ mellow, ripe. *See also* **mature. 2.** Far along in life or time ▶ advanced, elderly, senior. *See* **old** (2).

agedness *noun*

▶ maturity, seniority, years. *See* **age** (1).

ageism *noun*

Discrimination based on age ▶ discrimination, intolerance, prejudice. *See also* **hate.**

ageless *adjective*

1. Existing unchanged forever ▶ eternal, timeless. *See also* **continual, endless. 2.** Characterized by enduring excellence, appeal, and importance ▶ antique, enduring. *See* **vintage** (1).

✦ **CORE SYNONYMS:** *ageless, eternal, timeless.* These adjectives mean existing unchanged forever: *the ageless themes of love and revenge; eternal truths; timeless beauty.*

---

agency *noun*

1. That by which something is done or caused ▶ instrument, means, medium. *See* **agent** (1). **2.** An administrative unit, as of a government or company ▶ arm, bureau. *See* **branch** (1).

agenda *noun*

1. An organized list, as of procedures, activities, or events ▶ calendar, schedule, timetable. *See* **program** (1). **2.** A series, as of names or words, printed or written down ▶ register, roster, schedule. *See* **list**[1].

agent *noun*

1. That by which something is done or caused ▶ agency, channel, instrument, instrumentality, intermediary, means, mechanism, medium, organ. *See also* **go-between, representative. 2.** A person who secretly observes others to obtain information ▶ asset, operative. *See* **spy.**

age-old *adjective*

▶ ancient, antiquated, archaic. *See* **old** (1).

ages *noun*

A long time ▶ blue moon, eon, eternity, forever, long, years. *Idioms:* dog's age, coon's age, donkey's years, forever and a day, forever and ever, a month (*or* week) of Sundays.

agglomerate *verb*

▶ aggregate, amass, collect, cumulate. *See* **accumulate.**

agglomeration *noun*

1. The act of accumulating ▶ accumulation, buildup, conglomeration. **2.** A group of things gathered haphazardly ▶ drift, mass, mound. *See* **heap** (1).

aggrandize *verb*

1. To make or become greater or larger ▶ amplify, boost, enlarge. *See* **increase** (1). **2.** To raise to a high position or status ▶ elevate, magnify, uplift. *See* **exalt** (1). **3.** To make something seem greater than is actually the case ▶ hyperbolize, magnify. *See* **exaggerate** (1).

aggrandizement *noun*

1. The act of increasing or rising ▶ amplification, boost, escalation. *See* **increase** (1). **2.** The act of raising to a high position or status or the condition of being so raised ▶ apotheosis, elevation. *See* **exaltation** (1).

aggravate *verb*

1. To make greater in intensity or severity ▶ deepen, enhance, heighten. *See* **intensify. 2.** To trouble the nerves or peace of mind of, especially by repeated vexations ▶ irritate, nettle, vex. *See* **annoy** (1). *See synonym note at* **annoy.**

aggravation *noun*

1. The act of annoying or the state of being annoyed ▶ bother, irritation, vexation. *See* **annoyance** (1). **2.** Something that annoys ▶ bother, irritant, nuisance. *See* **annoyance** (2).

aggregate *noun*

1. A number or quantity obtained as a result of addition ▶ amount, sum, totality. *See* **total** (1). **2.** An amount or quantity from which nothing is left out or held back ▶ entirety, everything, total. *See* **whole** (1).

aggregate *verb*

1. To bring together so as to increase in mass or number ▶ agglomerate, collect, gather. *See* **accumulate. 2.** To come to in number or quantity ▶ number, reach, total. *See* **amount** (1).

aggregation *noun*

▶ amassment, collection, cumulation, gathering. *See* **accumulation** (1).

aggress *verb*

▶ assail, assault, storm, strike. *See* **attack** (1).

aggression *noun*

1. Hostile or warlike behavior or attitude ▶ aggressiveness, bellicoseness, belligerence, combativeness, contentiousness, hostility, militance, pugnaciousness, pugnacity, saber-rattling, truculence, truculency, warmongering. *See also* **hate. 2.** The act of attacking ▶ assault, offense, onslaught, strike. *See* **attack** (1).

aggressive *adjective*

1. Inclined to act in a way that shows hostility or an eagerness to fight ▶ bellicose, belligerent, combative, contentious, hawkish, hostile, militant, pugnacious, quarrelsome, scrappy, truculent, warlike, warmongering. **2.** Bold or confident in assertion ▶ emphatic, forceful. *See* **assertive.**

✦ **CORE SYNONYMS:** *aggressive, belligerent, bellicose, pugnacious, contentious, quarrelsome.* These adjectives mean having or showing hostility or an eagerness to fight. *Aggressive* and *belligerent* refer to a tendency to hostile behavior: *The aggressive prisoner was placed in a solitary cell. A belligerent reporter badgered the politician. Bellicose* and *pugnacious* suggest a natural disposition to fight: *"All successful newspapers are ceaselessly querulous and bellicose"* (H.L. Mencken). *A good litigator needs a pugnacious intellect. Contentious* implies chronic argumentativeness: *"His style has been described variously as abrasive and contentious, overbearing and pompous"* (Victor Merina). *Quarrelsome* suggests bad temper and a perverse readiness to bicker: *"The men gave him much room, for he was notorious as a quarrelsome person when drunk"* (Stephen Crane).

---

aggressiveness *noun*

▶ combativeness, hostility. *See* **aggression** (1).

aggressor *noun*
One who starts a hostile action ▸ assailant, assailer, assaulter, attacker, provoker. *See also* **opponent.**
aggrieve *verb*
▸ disturb, grieve, hurt. *See* **distress** (1).
aghast *adjective*
▸ fearful, frightened, scared. *See* **afraid.**
agile *adjective*
▸ agile, deft, nimble. *See* **dexterous.**
agility *or* **agileness** *noun*
The quality or state of being agile ▸ deftness, dexterity, dexterousness, nimbleness, quickness, spryness, swiftness. *See also* **energy, haste.**
aging *adjective*
▸ elderly, mature, senior. *See* **old** (2).
agitate *verb*
1. To cause to move to and fro violently ▸ churn, convulse, rock, shake, whip, worry. *See also* **disorder, disturb, upset. 2.** To impair or destroy the composure of ▸ bewilder, bother, discompose, disorient, disquiet, distract, disturb, flurry, fluster, jar, perturb, rock, ruffle, shake (up), toss, unsettle, upset. *Informal:* rattle, throw (off). *Idioms:* throw out of kilter (*or* whack). *See also* **confuse, distress, nonplus. 3.** To induce or elicit a reaction ▸ kindle, stir (up). *See* **arouse** (1).

✦ CORE SYNONYMS: *agitate, churn, convulse, rock, shake.* These verbs mean to cause to move to and fro violently: *land agitated by tremors; a storm churning the waves; buildings and streets convulsed by an explosion; a hurricane rocking trees and houses; an earthquake that shook the ground.*

---

agitated *adjective*
1. Marked by unrest or disturbance ▸ convulsed, disturbed, flustered, stormy, tempestuous, tumultuous, turbulent, restless, unsettled. *Idioms:* all shook up, all worked up, in a ferment (*or* spin *or* state *or* stir). *See also* **confused, disorderly, unruly. 2.** In a state of anxiety or uneasiness ▸ distressed, nervous, uneasy. *See* **anxious.**
agitating *adjective*
▸ bothersome, irritating, unsettling. *See* **disturbing.**
agitation *noun*
1. A condition of being agitated or disturbed; a confused or emotional situation ▸ commotion, convulsion, disorder, disturbance, ferment, helter-skelter, ruckus, scene, stir, Sturm und Drang, tempest, tumult, turbulence, turmoil, unrest, uproar. *Informal:* flap, to-do. *Slang:* hoo-ha, stink. *See also* **disorder, display, restlessness. 2.** A state of discomposure ▸ disconcertment, dither, fluster, flutter, hurry-scurry, perturbation, tumult, turmoil, twitter, upset. *Informal:* lather, stew. *Slang:* tizzy. *See also* **anxiety, confusion, worry. 3.** Agitated, excited movement and activity ▸ ado, bustle, commotion, excitement, flurry, fuss, stir, whirl, whirlpool. *Informal:* state.
agitator *noun*
One who agitates, especially politically ▸ firebrand,

fomenter, incendiary, inciter, instigator, malcontent, rabble-rouser, troublemaker. *See also* **aggressor, extremist.**
agnate *adjective*
▸ akin, allied, related. *See* **kindred.**
agnostic *noun*
▸ doubter, unbeliever. *See* **skeptic.**
ago *adjective*
▸ precedent, previous, prior. *See* **past** (1).
agog *adjective*
▸ ardent, bursting, thirsty. *See* **eager** (1).
agonize *verb*
1. To focus the attention on something moodily and at length ▸ dwell, fret, worry. *See* **brood. 2.** To cause great pain or suffering to ▸ plague, rack, torment. *See* **afflict.** *See synonym note at* **afflict.**
agonizing *adjective*
▸ excruciating, torturous. *See* **tormenting.**
agony *noun*
▸ anguish, misery, wretchedness. *See* **distress** (1).
agrarian *adjective*
▸ bucolic, pastoral, rural. *See* **country.**
agree *verb*
1. To be compatible, suitable, or in correspondence ▸ accord, belong, check, chime, comport, conform, consist, correspond, dovetail, fit, go (together), harmonize, match (up), square, tally. *Informal:* jibe. *See also* **suit. 2.** To come to an understanding or to terms ▸ accord, coincide, concur, get together, harmonize. *Idioms:* be of one mind, see eye to eye. **3.** To respond affirmatively; receive with agreement or compliance ▸ acquiesce, consent. *See* **assent.** *See synonym note at* **assent.**

✦ CORE SYNONYMS: *agree, conform, harmonize, accord, correspond, square.* These verbs all indicate a compatibility between people or things. *Agree* may indicate mere lack of incongruity or discord, although it often suggests acceptance of ideas or actions and thus accommodation: *We finally agreed on a price for the house. Conform* stresses correspondence in essence or basic characteristics, sometimes as a result of established standards: *Students are required to conform to the rules. Harmonize* implies the combination or arrangement of elements in a pleasing whole: *The print on the curtains harmonized with the striped sofa. Accord* implies harmony, unity, or consistency, as in essential nature: *"The creed [upon which America was founded] was widely seen as both progressive and universalistic: It accorded with the future, and it was open to all"* (Everett Carll Ladd). *Correspond* refers to similarity in form, nature, function, character, or structure: *The Diet in Japan corresponds to the American Congress. Square* stresses exact agreement: *The testimony of the witness squared with the plaintiff's version of the events.*

---

agreeability *noun*
▸ affability, congeniality, pleasantness. *See* **amiability.**
agreeable *adjective*
1. In keeping with one's needs or expectations ▸ accordant, compatible, concordant, conformable, con-

genial, congruous, consistent, consonant, correspondent, corresponding, harmonious. *See also* **fit, similar.**
2. Giving or affording pleasure or enjoyment ▸ enjoyable, gratifying, lovely. *See* **pleasant** (1). **3.** Pleasant
and friendly in disposition ▸ cordial, friendly, genial.
See **amiable. 4.** Disposed to accept, agree, or participate ▸ acquiescent, ready. *See* **willing** (1). **5.** Ready to do
favors for another ▸ accommodating, complaisant.
See **obliging. 6.** Giving assent ▸ approving, positive.
See **favorable** (2).

agreeableness *noun*
▸ agreeability, congeniality, pleasantness. *See* **amiability.**

agreed *adverb*
▸ affirmative, all right, assuredly. *See* **yes.**

agreeing *adjective*
▸ accordant, consonant, like-minded. *See* **unanimous.**

agreement *noun*
1. An often written acceptance of terms between
parties ▸ accord, arrangement, bargain, bond, charter,
compact, contract, convention, covenant, deal, pact,
understanding. *See also* **compromise. 2.** The act or
state of agreeing or conforming ▸ accord, accordance,
concord, concordance, chime, concert, conformance,
conformation, conformity, congruence, congruity,
consensus, consonance, correspondence, harmonization, harmony, keeping, rapport, tune, unanimity,
unanimousness, unison, unity. *Idiom:* meeting of the
minds. *See also* **understanding. 3.** A formal, usually
written settlement between nations ▸ concord, convention, pact. *See* **treaty. 4.** The act of accepting or
adopting ▸ adoption, assent, consent. *See* **acceptance**
(1).

✦ **CORE SYNONYMS:** *agreement, bargain, compact, contract, covenant, deal.* These nouns denote an acceptance, often bound in writing, of terms between
parties: *signed the purchase and sale agreement; kept
my end of the bargain and mowed the lawn; made a
compact to correspond regularly; a legally binding
contract to install new windows; a covenant for mutual
defense; ignored the requests that weren't part of the
deal.*

---

ahead *adverb*
1. Before the expected time ▸ beforehand, betimes. *See*
early. 2. Toward the front or beyond a position
▸ forth, frontward, onward. *See* **forward.**

aid *noun*
1. The act or an instance of helping ▸ abetment,
assistance. *See* **help** (1). **2.** Assistance, especially
money, food, and other necessities, given to the needy
or dispossessed ▸ handout, public assistance, welfare.
See **relief** (3). **3.** A person who assists someone else
▸ adjutant, deputy, helper. *See* **assistant.**

aid *verb*
1. To give assistance to ▸ abet, assist. *See* **help** (1). *See
synonym note at* **help. 2.** To perform a service or a
courteous act for ▸ favor, serve. *See* **oblige** (1).

aide *noun*
▸ adjutant, deputy, helper. *See* **assistant.** *See synonym
note at* **assistant.**

ail *verb*
▸ bother, trouble. *See* **worry** (1). *See synonym note at*
worry.

ailing *adjective*
▸ anemic, indisposed, unwell. *See* **sick** (1).

ailment *noun*
1. A pathological condition of mind or body ▸ disorder, malady. *See* **disease** (1). **2.** The condition of being
sick ▸ affliction, illness, malady. *See* **sickness** (1).

aim *verb*
1. To direct something, such as a weapon or a remark,
often toward a target ▸ cast, direct, head, lay, level,
point, set, train, turn, zero in. *See also* **guide. 2.** To
strive toward a goal ▸ aspire, seek. *Idioms:* go (or
grab) for the brass ring, keep one's eyes on the prize,
set one's sights on. **3.** To have in mind as a goal or
purpose ▸ design, plan, target. *See* **intend** (1). **4.** To
proceed in a specified direction ▸ head, make, set out.
See **bear** (5).

aim *noun*
1. What one intends to do or achieve ▸ end, goal,
objective. *See* **intention.** *See synonym note at* **intention. 2.** The current of thought uniting all elements of
a text or discourse ▸ drift, intent, tenor. *See* **thrust** (1).

✦ **CORE SYNONYMS:** *aim, direct, level, point, train.* These
verbs mean to turn something toward a goal or
target: *aimed the camera at the guests; directing my
eyes on the book; leveled criticism at me; pointing a
finger at the suspect; trained the gun on the intruder.*

---

aimless *adjective*
Without aim, purpose, or intent ▸ desultory,
directionless, errant, pointless, purposeless, rambling, rudderless, wandering, undirected. *See also*
erratic, futile, random.

air *noun*
1. The gaseous mixture enveloping the earth ▸ atmosphere, ether. **2.** The celestial regions as seen from the
earth ▸ firmament, heavens, sky. *Idiom:* wild blue
yonder. **3.** A natural movement or current of air
▸ blast, blow, gust. *See* **wind**[1] (1). **4.** A general impression produced by a predominant quality or characteristic ▸ ambiance, atmosphere, aura, feel, feeling,
mood, smell, tone. *Slang:* vibe, vibration. *See also*
environment, shade. 5. Behavior that reveals one's
personality or state of mind ▸ demeanor, manner,
style. *See* **bearing** (1). **6.** A pleasing succession or
arrangement of sound ▸ aria, tune. *See* **melody. 7.**
Behavior that is assumed rather than natural ▸ mannerism, pose, theatricism. *See* **affectation** (1). *See
synonym note at* **affectation.**

air *verb*
1. To expose to circulating air ▸ aerate, freshen,
ventilate, wind. **2.** To utter publicly ▸ disclose, divulge,
express, put, state, vent, ventilate, voice. *Idiom:* come
out with. *See also* **announce, say.**

✦ CORE SYNONYMS: *air, vent, express, voice.* These verbs mean to utter publically. To *air* is to show off one's feelings, beliefs, or ideas: *They aired their differences during dinner.* To *vent* is to unburden oneself of a strong pent-up emotion: *"She was jealous . . . and glad of any excuse to vent her pique"* (Edward G.E.L. Bulwer-Lytton). *Express,* a more comprehensive term, refers to both verbal and nonverbal communication: *found the precise words to express her idea; expressed his affection with a hug; "expressing emotion in the form of art"* (T.S. Eliot). *Voice* denotes the expression of outlook or viewpoint: *The lawyers voiced their satisfaction with the verdict.*

airing *noun*
1. A show that is aired on television or radio ► broadcast, program. 2. The act or an instance of expressing in words ► statement, utterance, verbalization. See **expression** (1).

airless *adjective*
1. Lacking fresh air ► close, stale, stifling, stuffy, suffocating, unventilated. See also **moldy**. 2. Lacking movement of air ► breathless, breezeless, stagnant, still, windless. *Idioms:* dead (*or* flat) calm. See also **still**.

airs *noun*
► affectedness, mannerism, pretense. See **affectation** (1). *See synonym note at* **affectation.**

airy *adjective*
1. Of or relating to air ► aerial, atmospheric, pneumatic. 2. Having little weight; not heavy ► fluffy, light, lightweight, weightless. *Idioms:* light as air (*or* a feather). See also **immaterial**. 3. Exposed to or characterized by the presence of freely circulating air or wind ► blowy, breezy, gusty, ventilated, windblown, windswept, windy. 4. Thin, fine, and light ► ethereal, gauzy, vaporous. See **sheer**² (1). *See synonym note at* **sheer**². 5. Being of or at a relatively great height or altitude ► elevated, lofty. See **high** (1). 6. Happy and free from worry or care ► blithe, buoyant, debonair. See **lighthearted** (1).

ajar *adjective*
► agape, undone, unlocked. See **open** (1).

akin *adjective*
1. Connected by or as if by kinship or common origin ► agnate, allied, related. See **kindred**. 2. Possessing the same or almost the same characteristics ► analogous, similar, uniform. See **like**².

alabaster *adjective*
► ivory, light, pale. See **fair**¹ (9).

alacrity *noun*
► expeditiousness, hurry, quickness. See **haste** (1).

à la mode *adjective*
► mod, stylish, swanky. See **fashionable.**

alarm *noun*
1. A signal that warns of imminent danger ► alarum, alert, heads up, high sign, red flag, warning. *See also* **omen.** 2. A feeling of agitation in the face of trouble or danger ► apprehension, consternation, trepidation. *See* **fear.** *See synonym note at* **fear.**

alarm *verb*
1. To fill with fear ► horrify, scare, terrify. See **frighten.**
2. To notify someone of imminent danger or risk ► alert, caution. See **warn**. 3. To deprive of courage or the power to act as a result of fear, anxiety, or disgust ► consternate, disconcert. See **dismay** (1).

alarmed *adjective*
► fearful, frightened, scared. See **afraid.**

alarming *adjective*
► appalling, dismaying, dreadful, frightening. See **fearful** (1).

alarmist *noun*
One who needlessly alarms others ► Chicken Little, panicmonger, scaremonger. *Idiom:* one who cries wolf. See also **pessimist.**

alcoholic *adjective*
Containing alcohol ► intoxicative, spirituous. See **hard** (12).

alcoholic *noun*
A person who is habitually drunk ► dipsomaniac, drunk, tippler. See **drunkard.**

alehouse *noun*
► inn, pub, saloon. See **bar** (12).

alert *adjective*
1. Vigilantly attentive ► attentive, bright-eyed, heedful, intent, observant, open-eyed, regardful, vigilant, wakeful, wary, watchful, wide-awake. *Idioms:* all ears (*or* eyes), on guard, on one's toes, on the ball, on the lookout, on the qui vive. See also **aware, wary.** 2. Mentally quick and original ► keen, quick witted, sharp. See **clever** (1).

alert *noun*
A signal that warns of imminent danger ► warning, red flag. See **alarm** (1).

alert *verb*
To notify someone of imminent danger or risk ► caution, forewarn. See **warn.**

✦ CORE SYNONYMS: *alert, heedful, watchful, vigilant.* These adjectives mean very attentive. *I remained alert to career opportunities. Please be heedful of the traffic signs. The watchful parents protected their toddler. The ranger kept a vigilant eye out for forest fires.*

alertness *noun*
The condition of being alert ► caution, vigilance, wakefulness, wariness, watchfulness. See also **care.**

alibi *noun*
Informal An explanation offered to justify an action or make it better understood ► plea, rationale. See **excuse** (1).

alien *adjective*
1. Not part of the essential nature of a thing ► foreign, extraneous, extrinsic. See also **irrelevant**. 2. From or characteristic of another place ► exotic, immigrant, strange. See **foreign** (1). *See synonym note at* **foreign.**

alien *noun*
A person coming from another country or into a new community ► expatriate, outsider, stranger. See **foreigner.**

alienate *verb*
1. To make distant, hostile, or unsympathetic ► disaffect, disunite. *See* **estrange**. *See synonym note at* **estrange**. 2. To set apart from a group ► close off, seclude, sequester. *See* **isolate** (1).

alienation *noun*
1. An interruption in friendly relations ► estrangement, fissure. *See* **breach** (1). 2. The act or process of isolating ► insulation, segregation. *See* **isolation** (1). 3. Legal transfer of ownership or title ► assignment, transfer, transferal. *See* **grant**.

alight¹ *verb*
1. To come ashore from a seacraft ► debark, disembark, land, light. 2. To come to rest on the ground ► light, set down. *See* **land** (2).

alight on *or* **upon** *verb*
To find or meet by chance ► bump into, run across, stumble on. *See* **encounter** (1).

alight² *adjective*
On fire ► afire, conflagrant. *See* **burning** (1).

align *verb*
1. To place in or form a line or lines ► dress, queue (up), range. *See* **line**. 2. To be formally associated, as by treaty ► confederate, federate. *See* **ally** (1). 3. To alter for proper functioning ► calibrate, fine-tune, tweak. *See* **adjust** (1). 4. To make even, smooth, or level ► level, smooth, straighten. *See* **even** (1). 5. To make equal ► equate, level, square. *See* **equalize** (1).

alignment *verb*
► classification, layout, positioning. *See* **arrangement** (1).

alike *adjective*
► analogous, similar, uniform. *See* **like²**.

alikeness *noun*
► resemblance, similarity, uniformity. *See* **likeness** (1).

aliment *noun*
► bread, meat, nourishment. *See* **food**.

alimentary *adjective*
► nourishing, nutritional. *See* **nutritious**.

alimentation *noun*
► bread, keep, livelihood. *See* **living**.

alimony *noun*
► bread, keep, livelihood. *See* **living**.

alive *adjective*
1. Having or exhibiting existence or life ► animate, animated, around, breathing, existent, existing, extant, live, living, subsisting, vital. *Idioms:* alive and kicking, among the living. *See also* **lively**. 2. In action or full operation ► functioning, operating, working. *See* **active** (1). 3. Full of lively activity ► bustling, crawling, swarming, teeming. *See* **busy** (1). 4. Marked by comprehension, cognizance, and perception ► cognizant, sensible, sentient. *See* **aware**.

✚ **CORE SYNONYMS:** *alive, live, living, animate, animated, vital*. These adjectives mean possessed of or exhibiting life. *Alive, live,* and *living* refer principally to organisms that are not dead: *the happiest person alive; a live canary; living plants*. *Animate* applies to living animal as distinct from living plant life: *Something animate was moving inside the box*. *Animated* suggests renewed life, vigor, or spirit: *The argument became very animated*. *Vital* refers to what is characteristic of or necessary to the continuation of life: *You must eat to maintain vital energy.*

◄ ANTONYM: *dead*

---

alky *noun*
Slang A person who is habitually drunk ► alcoholic, dipsomaniac, tippler. *See* **drunkard**.

all *adjective*
Including every constituent or individual ► entire, total, whole. *See* **complete** (1). *See synonym note at* **complete**.

all *noun*
An amount or quantity from which nothing is left out or held back ► entirety, everything, total. *See* **whole** (1).

all *adverb*
To the fullest extent ► fully, totally, utterly. *See* **completely** (1).

all-around *adjective*
1. Covering a wide scope ► all-inclusive, broad, expansive. *See* **general** (2). 2. Having many aspects, uses, or abilities ► many-sided, multifaceted. *See* **versatile** (1). *See synonym note at* **versatile**.

allay *verb*
1. To make less severe or more bearable ► alleviate, assuage, ease. *See* **relieve** (1). *See synonym note at* **relieve**. 2. To ease the anger or agitation of ► appease, mollify, soothe. *See* **pacify**.

allegation *noun*
► claim, declaration, statement. *See* **assertion**.

allege *verb*
► avow, declare, maintain. *See* **assert** (1).

alleged *adjective*
► hypothetical, presumptive, suppositional. *See* **supposed**.

allegiance *noun*
► constancy, faithfulness, loyalty, steadfastness. *See* **fidelity** (1). *See synonym note at* **fidelity**.

allegiant *adjective*
► constant, loyal, staunch. *See* **faithful** (1).

allegorize *verb*
► externalize, manifest, materialize. *See* **embody** (1).

allegory *noun*
► incarnation, manifestation, personification. *See* **embodiment** (1).

alleviate *verb*
► allay, assuage, ease. *See* **relieve** (1). *See synonym note at* **relieve**.

alleviation *noun*
► ease, mitigation, palliation. *See* **relief** (2).

alley *noun*
► path, road, route. *See* **way** (2).

alliance *noun*
1. An association for a common cause or interest ► bloc, cartel, coalition, combination, combine, confederacy, confederation, consortium, faction, federation, league, monopoly, organization, party, pool,

ring, syndicate, trust, union. *See also* **assembly, band²**, **force**, **union**. **2.** The state of being associated ▶ affiliation, connection. *See* **association** (1).

allied *adjective*
1. Closely connected by or as if by a treaty ▶ aligned, confederated, federated, unified. **2.** Connected by or as if by kinship or common origin ▶ akin, related. *See* **kindred.**

all-inclusive *adjective*
1. Covering a wide scope ▶ all-around, broad, expansive. *See* **general** (2). **2.** Characterized by attention to detail ▶ full, particular, thorough. *See* **detailed** (1).

allocate *verb*
1. To set aside or apart for a specified purpose ▶ assign, designate, earmark. *See* **appropriate** (1). *See synonym note at* **appropriate. 2.** To give out in portions or shares ▶ allot, dispense, dole out. *See* **distribute** (1).

allocation *noun*
1. The act of distributing or the condition of being distributed ▶ admeasurement, apportionment, dispensation. *See* **distribution** (1). **2.** That which is allotted ▶ allowance, ration, share. *See* **allotment** (1).

allocution *noun*
▶ lecture, talk. *See* **speech** (2).

allot *verb*
1. To give out in portions or shares ▶ allocate, apportion, dispense. *See* **distribute** (1). **2.** To set aside or apart for a specified purpose ▶ assign, set apart. *See* **appropriate** (1). *See synonym note at* **appropriate.**

allotment *noun*
1. That which is allotted ▶ allocation, allowance, apportionment, distribution, division, dole, lot, measure, part, portion, quantum, quota, ration, share, split. *Informal:* cut. *Slang:* divvy. *See also* **cut. 2.** The act of distributing or the condition of being distributed ▶ allocation, apportionment, dispensation. *See* **distribution** (1). **3.** The act or condition of being arranged ▶ categorization, distribution, positioning. *See* **arrangement** (1).

all-out *adjective*
1. Extreme in activity, strength, or effect ▶ concentrated, furious, heavy, vehement. *See* **intense** (1). **2.** Completely such, without qualification or exception ▶ absolute, pure, sheer. *See* **utter²**.

all-overs *noun*
Informal A state of nervous restlessness or agitation ▶ jumps, shivers, trembles. *See* **jitters.**

allow *verb*
1. To neither forbid nor prevent ▶ let, tolerate. *See* **permit** (1). **2.** To give one's consent to ▶ approve, authorize, sanction. *See* **permit** (2). **3.** To afford an opportunity for ▶ admit, let. *See* **permit** (3). **4.** To give out in portions or shares ▶ allocate, deal (out), dole out. *See* **distribute** (1). **5.** *Chiefly Regional* To admit to the reality or truth of ▶ concede, grant. *See* **acknowledge** (1).

allowable *adjective*
▶ admissible, permissible. *See* **acceptable** (1).

allowance *noun*
1. The approving of an action, especially when done by one in authority ▶ authorization, consent, sanction. *See* **permission. 2.** That which is allotted ▶ ration, share. *See* **allotment** (1).

alloy *noun*
Something that is produced by mixing ▶ amalgam, blend, mix. *See* **mixture** (1).

alloy *verb*
To combine into one mass or mixture ▶ blend, fuse, stir. *See* **mix** (1).

alloyed *adjective*
▶ adulterated, combined, polluted. *See* **impure** (2).

all-purpose *adjective*
▶ all-around, many-sided, multifaceted. *See* **versatile** (1).

all right *adjective*
1. Adequate to satisfy a need, requirement, or standard ▶ average, decent, moderate. *See* **acceptable** (2). **2.** Having good health ▶ fit, well. *See* **healthy** (1).

all right *adverb*
It is so; as you say or ask ▶ agreed, assuredly, aye. *See* **yes.**

all-right *adjective*
Informal Having pleasant desirable qualities ▶ bonny, enjoyable, nice. *See* **good** (1).

all-round *adjective*
1. Covering a wide scope ▶ all-inclusive, broad, expansive. *See* **general** (2). **2.** Having many aspects, uses, or abilities ▶ many-sided, multifaceted. *See* **versatile** (1).

all the same *adverb*
▶ however, nevertheless, yet. *See* **still** (1).

allude to *verb*
1. To convey an idea by indirect, subtle means ▶ insinuate, suggest. *See* **hint. 2.** To make reference to something ▶ advert, mention, note. *See* **refer** (1).

allure *verb*
1. To direct or impel to oneself by some quality or action ▶ appeal, entice, lure. *See* **attract** (1). **2.** To beguile or draw into a wrong or foolish course of action, especially a sexual act ▶ entice, lure. *See* **seduce.**

allure *noun*
The power or quality of attracting ▶ appeal, draw, enticement, lure. *See* **attraction** (1).

allurement *noun*
1. The power or quality of attracting ▶ appeal, draw, enticement, lure. *See* **attraction** (1). **2.** Something that attracts, especially with the promise of pleasure or reward ▶ bait, draw, enticement. *See* **lure** (1).

allurer *noun*
▶ charmer, tempter. *See* **seducer** (1).

alluring *adjective*
1. Tending to seduce ▶ bewitching, enticing, tempting. *See* **seductive. 2.** Arousing erotic desire ▶ enticing, sexy. *See* **desirable** (1).

allusion *noun*
▶ cue, suggestion. *See* **hint** (2).

allusive *adjective*
Tending to bring a memory, mood, or image, for example, subtly or indirectly to mind ▸ connotative, evocative, impressionistic, reminiscent, suggestive. *See also* **designative, symbolic.**

alluvion *noun*
▸ deluge, overflow, torrent. *See* **flood** (1).

alluvium *noun*
▸ accumulation, precipitation, sediment. *See* **deposit** (2).

ally *verb*
1. To be formally associated, as by treaty ▸ align, confederate, federate, league. *Idioms:* band together, join forces, team up. *See also* **combine. 2.** To unite or be united in a relationship ▸ combine, join, link. *See* **associate** (1). *See synonym note at* **associate.**

ally *noun*
One who is united in a relationship with another ▸ affiliate, partner. *See* **associate** (1).

almost *adverb*
▸ about, nearly. *See* **approximately.**

alms *noun*
▸ benefaction, contribution, offering. *See* **donation.**

almsman *or* **almswoman** *noun*
▸ cadger, mendicant. *See* **beggar** (1).

aloha *interjection*
Informal Used as a greeting ▸ good day, greetings, salutations. *See* **hello.**

alone *adverb*
1. Without the presence or aid of another ▸ single-handedly, singly, solely, solitarily, solo. *Idioms:* by oneself, all by one's lonesome. *See also* **separately. 2.** To the exclusion of anyone or anything else ▸ exclusively, only. *See* **solely** (1).

alone *adjective*
1. Set away from or lacking the company of all others ▸ companionless, lonely, isolated. *See* **solitary** (1). *See synonym note at* **solitary. 2.** Without equal or rival ▸ incomparable, singular, unparalleled. *See* **unique** (1).

aloneness *noun*
▸ isolation, loneliness. *See* **solitude.**

aloof *adjective*
1. Not friendly, sociable, or warm in manner ▸ chilly, distant, impersonal. *See* **cool** (1). **2.** Lacking interest in one's surroundings or worldly affairs ▸ disinterested, indifferent, uninvolved. *See* **detached** (1).

aloofness *noun*
1. Dissociation from one's surroundings or worldly affairs ▸ disinterest, indifference, remoteness. *See* **detachment** (2). **2.** Lack of emotion or interest ▸ disinterest, indifference, unconcern. *See* **apathy. 3.** Lack of cordiality and hospitableness ▸ inhospitableness, uncivility, unreceptiveness. *See* **inhospitality.**

already *adverb*
▸ before, previously. *See* **earlier** (1).

also *adverb*
▸ besides, furthermore, moreover. *See* **additionally.**

alter *verb*
1. To make different ▸ modify, mutate, vary. *See* change (1). **2.** To become different ▸ fluctuate, modify, turn. *See* **change** (2). **3.** To render incapable of reproducing ▸ neuter, spay. *See* **sterilize** (2). **4.** To give an inaccurate view of by representing falsely or misleadingly ▸ fudge, misrepresent, misstate, pervert. *See* **distort** (1).

alterable *adjective*
▸ fluid, unsettled, variable. *See* **changeable** (1).

alteration *noun*
1. The process or result of making or becoming different ▸ modification, mutation, variation. *See* **change** (1). **2.** One that is slightly different from others of the same kind or designation ▸ adaptation, permutation. *See* **variation** (1).

altercate *verb*
▸ dispute, fight, quarrel. *See* **argue** (1).

altercation *noun*
▸ disagreement, dispute, fight. *See* **argument** (1).

alter ego *noun*
▸ chum, intimate, mate. *See* **friend** (1).

alternate *verb*
To take turns ▸ interchange, rotate, shift.

alternate *noun*
One that can take the place of another ▸ replacement, stand-in, surrogate. *See* **substitute.**

alternation *noun*
Occurrence in successive turns ▸ interchange, rotation, shift.

alternative *noun*
1. The act, power, or right of choosing ▸ decision, discretion, option. *See* **choice** (1). *See synonym note at* **choice. 2.** One that is slightly different from others of the same kind or designation ▸ adaptation, permutation. *See* **variation** (1).

altitude *noun*
The distance of something from a given level ▸ elevation, height, loftiness, tallness. *See synonym note at* **elevation.** *See also* **ascent.**

alto *adjective*
▸ bass, contralto, deep. *See* **low** (2).

altogether *adverb*
▸ fully, totally, utterly. *See* **completely** (1).

altruism *noun*
▸ goodwill, kindheartedness, philanthropy. *See* **benevolence** (1).

altruistic *adjective*
1. Characterized by kindness and concern for others ▸ beneficent, goodhearted, kindly. *See* **benevolent** (1). **2.** Of or concerned with charity ▸ benevolent, charitable, eleemosynary, philanthropic. *See synonym note at* **charitable.**

always *adverb*
▸ endlessly, perpetually, unendingly. *See* **forever** (1).

amalgam *or* **amalgamation** *noun*
▸ admixture, blend, mix. *See* **mixture** (1). *See synonym note at* **mixture.**

amalgamate *verb*
1. To combine into one mass or mixture ▸ blend, fuse, stir. *See* **mix** (1). *See synonym note at* **mix. 2.** To unite

or be united in a relationship ▸ combine, join, link. *See* **associate** (1).

amaranthine *adjective*
▸ ceaseless, eternal. *See* **endless** (2).

amass *verb*
▸ aggregate, collect, gather. *See* **accumulate**. *See synonym note at* **accumulate**.

amassment *noun*
▸ assemblage, collection, gathering. *See* **accumulation** (1).

amateur *noun*
One lacking professional skill and ease in a particular pursuit ▸ dabbler, dilettante, layperson, nonprofessional, smatterer, uninitiate. *Informal:* duffer. *See also* **beginner, fan.**

✦ **CORE SYNONYMS:** *amateur, dabbler, dilettante.* These nouns mean one engaging in a pursuit but lacking professional skill: *a musician who is a gifted amateur, not a professional; a dabbler in the stock market; a sculptor but a mere dilettante.*

◂ **ANTONYM:** *professional*

---

amateurish *adjective*
Lacking the required professional skill ▸ crude, dilettante, dilettantish, inexpert, nonprofessional, unprofessional, unskilled, unskillful. *See also* **inefficient, unskillful.**

amativeness *noun*
1. Sexual hunger ▸ eroticism, lust, passion. *See* **desire** (2). 2. The passionate affection and desire felt by lovers for each other ▸ ardor, passion, romance. *See* **love** (2).

amatory *adjective*
▸ amorous, erogenous, sexy. *See* **erotic**.

amaze *verb*
To impress strongly by what is unexpected or unusual ▸ astonish, astound. *See* **surprise** (1).

amaze *noun*
The emotion aroused by something awe-inspiring or astounding ▸ amazement, awe, marvel. *See* **wonder** (1).

amazement *noun*
▸ astonishment, awe, marvel. *See* **wonder** (1).

amazing *adjective*
▸ astounding, staggering, unbelievable. *See* **astonishing.**

ambassador *noun*
▸ delegate, deputy, proxy. *See* **representative** (2).

ambiance *or* **ambience** *noun*
1. A general impression produced by a predominant quality or characteristic ▸ atmosphere, aura, mood. *See* **air** (4). 2. The surrounding conditions and circumstances affecting growth or development ▸ climate, surroundings. *See* **environment** (2).

ambiguity *noun*
1. An expression or term liable to more than one interpretation ▸ double-entendre, equivocality, equivocation, equivoque, tergiversation. 2. The quality or state of being imprecise or indefinite ▸ ambiguousness, equivocalness, unclearness. *See* **vagueness**.

3. The use or an instance of equivocal language ▸ euphemism, prevarication. *See* **equivocation** (1).

ambiguous *adjective*
1. Lacking certainty or clarity ▸ abstruse, borderline, chancy, clouded, cryptic, doubtful, dubious, dubitable, enigmatic, equivocal, inconclusive, indecisive, indeterminate, obscure, perplexing, problematic, questionable, recondite, uncertain, unclear, unsure, woolly. *Informal:* iffy. *Idioms:* at issue, in doubt, in question, up in the air. *See also* **indefinite, unclear.** 2. Liable to more than one interpretation ▸ ambivalent, cloudy, double-edged, equivocal, inexplicit, nebulous, obscure, two-edged, uncertain, unclear, vague.

✦ **CORE SYNONYMS:** *ambiguous, equivocal, obscure, recondite, abstruse, cryptic, enigmatic.* These adjectives mean lacking certainty or clarity. *Ambiguous* indicates the presence of two or more possible meanings: *Frustrated by ambiguous instructions, I was unable to assemble the toy.* Something *equivocal* is unclear or misleading: *"The polling had a complex and equivocal message for potential female candidates"* (David S. Broder). *Obscure* implies lack of clarity of expression: *Some say that Kafka's style is obscure and complex. Recondite* and *abstruse* connote the erudite obscurity of the scholar: *"some recondite problem in historiography"* (Walter Laqueur). *The students avoided the professor's abstruse lectures. Cryptic* suggests a sometimes deliberately puzzling terseness: *The new insurance policy is full of cryptic terms.* Something *enigmatic* is mysterious and puzzling: *The biography struggles to make sense of the artist's enigmatic life.*

---

ambiguousness *noun*
▸ ambiguity, equivocalness, unclearness. *See* **vagueness.**

ambit *noun*
1. A line around a closed figure or area ▸ circuit, perimeter. *See* **circumference**. 2. An area or set of parameters within which something or someone exists, acts, or has influence ▸ extent, realm, scope. *See* **range** (1). *See synonym note at* **range.**

ambition *noun*
1. A strong desire to achieve something ▸ ambitiousness, aspiration, emulation. *See also* **drive, enthusiasm, thirst.** 2. What one intends to do or achieve ▸ end, goal, objective. *See* **intention**. 3. A fervent hope ▸ desire, vision, wish. *See* **dream** (3).

ambitious *adjective*
Full of ambition ▸ aspiring, desirous, determined, driven, emulous, enterprising, highflying, hustling, overambitious. *Idioms:* on the fast track, on the make. *See also* **assertive, diligent.**

ambitiousness *noun*
A strong desire to achieve something ▸ ambition, aspiration, emulation. *See also* **drive, enthusiasm, thirst.**

ambivalent *adjective*
1. Liable to more than one interpretation ▸ equivocal, nebulous, vague. *See* **ambiguous** (2). 2. Experiencing

doubt ▸ hesitant, skeptical, uncertain. *See* **doubtful** (2).

amble *verb*
To walk at a leisurely pace ▸ promenade, saunter, wander. *See* **stroll**.

amble *noun*
An act of walking ▸ promenade, ramble, stroll. *See* **walk** (1).

ambrosial *adjective*
▸ delectable, savory, scrumptious. *See* **delicious** (1). *See synonym note at* **delicious**.

ambulance chaser *noun*
Slang A person who practices law ▸ attorney, jurist. *See* **lawyer**.

ambulate *verb*
▸ step, tread. *See* **walk**.

ambuscade *verb*
To attack suddenly and without warning ▸ bushwhack, surprise, waylay. *See* **ambush** (1). *See synonym note at* **ambush**.

ambuscade *noun*
An attack or stratagem for capturing or tricking an unsuspecting person ▸ ambush, trap. *See also* **deceit, trick**.

ambush

ambush *verb*
1. To attack suddenly and without warning ▸ ambuscade, bushwhack, raid, surprise, waylay. *Idioms:* lay (*or* set) a trap for, lie in wait for. *See also* **attack, catch**. **2.** To wait furtively in order to attack someone ▸ await, prowl, skulk. *See* **lurk** (1).

ambush *noun*
An attack or stratagem for capturing or tricking an unsuspecting person ▸ ambuscade, trap. *See also* **deceit, trick**.

✦ CORE SYNONYMS: *ambush, ambuscade, bushwhack, waylay*. These verbs mean to attack suddenly and without warning, especially from a concealed place: *guerrillas ambushing a platoon; highway robbers ambuscading a stagecoach; a patrol bushwhacked by poachers; a truck waylaid by robbers*.

---

ameliorate *verb*
▸ better, enhance, upgrade. *See* **improve** (1). *See synonym note at* **improve**.

amelioration *noun*
1. The act of making better or the condition of being made better ▸ betterment, development, upgrade. *See* **improvement** (1). **2.** Steady improvement, as of an individual or society ▸ advancement, betterment, development. *See* **progress** (1).

amenability *or* **amenableness** *noun*
1. The quality of willingly carrying out the wishes of others ▸ complaisance, compliancy, deference, submissiveness. *See* **obedience**. **2.** Ready acceptance of new suggestions, ideas, or opinions ▸ receptivity, responsiveness. *See* **openness** (1). **3.** The state of being responsible ▸ accountability, liability. *See* **responsibility** (1).

amenable *adjective*
1. Willing to carry out the wishes of others ▸ complaisant, docile, submissive. *See* **obedient**. **2.** Legally or officially obligated ▸ answerable, responsible. *See* **liable** (1). *See synonym note at* **liable**. **3.** Ready and willing to receive favorably, as new ideas ▸ acceptant, open-minded, responsive. *See* **receptive**. **4.** Disposed to accept, agree, or participate ▸ agreeable, ready. *See* **willing** (1).

amend *verb*
1. To advance to a more desirable state ▸ better, enhance, upgrade. *See* **improve** (1). **2.** To make right what is wrong ▸ mend, rectify, remedy. *See* **correct** (1). *See synonym note at* **correct**. **3.** To prepare a new version of ▸ emend, revamp, rework. *See* **revise** (1).

amendatory *adjective*
▸ reformative, remedial. *See* **corrective**.

amendment *noun*
1. The act of making better or the condition of being made better ▸ betterment, development, upgrade. *See* **improvement** (1). **2.** The act or process of revising ▸ emendation, rewrite. *See* **revision**.

amends *noun*
▸ damages, remuneration, reparation. *See* **compensation** (1). *See synonym note at* **compensation**.

amenities *noun*
1. Anything that increases physical comfort ▸ advantages, comforts, conveniences, facilities, resources, services. **2.** Social courtesies ▸ civility, courteousness, courtesy, graciousness, pleasantry, politeness, proprieties, urbanity. *See also* **amiability, manners, tact**.

✦ CORE SYNONYMS: *amenities, comforts, conveniences, facilities*. These nouns denote something that increases physical comfort or that facilitates work: *an apartment with amenities like air conditioning; a suite with all the comforts of home; a kitchen with modern conveniences; a school with excellent facilities*.

---

amenity *noun*
▸ congeniality, pleasantness. *See* **amiability**.

amerce *verb*
To impose a fine on ▸ fine, mulct, penalize. *See also* **punish**.

amercement *noun*
A sum of money levied as punishment for an offense ▸ fine, mulct, penalty. *See also* **punishment**.

amiability *or* **amiableness** *noun*
The quality of being pleasant and friendly ▸ affability, agreeability, agreeableness, amenity, congeniality, congenialness, cordiality, cordialness, friendliness, geniality, genialness, kindness, pleasantness, sociability, sociableness, sweetness, warmth. *See also* **amenity, benevolence**.

amiable *or* **amicable** *adjective*
Pleasant and friendly in disposition ▸ affable, agreeable, approachable, companionable, congenial, cordial, friendly, genial, good-natured, good-tempered, likeable, neighborly, pleasant, sociable, sweet, warm, warm-hearted. *See also* **benevolent, obliging, social**.

✦ CORE SYNONYMS: *amiable, cordial, genial, good-natured, sociable.* These adjectives mean pleasant and friendly in disposition: *amiable to guests; a cordial welcome; a genial guide; a good-natured roommate; enjoyed a sociable chat.*

amigo *noun*
▸ chum, intimate, mate. *See* **friend** (1).

amiss *adjective*
1. Having a defect or defects ▸ defective, blemished, faulty, flawed, imperfect. *See also* **shabby, trick.**
2. Characterized by physical confusion ▸ disordered, topsy-turvy, upside-down. *See* **confused** (2).

amiss *adverb*
Not in the right way or on the proper course ▸ afield, astray, awry, wrong. *See synonym note at* **wrong.**

amity *noun*
▸ camaraderie, companionship, fellowship. *See* **friendship.**

amnesty *noun*
▸ absolution, excuse, pardon. *See* **forgiveness.**

amoral *adjective*
▸ unconscionable, unethical, unprincipled. *See* **unscrupulous** (1).

amorist *noun*
▸ lady's man, Romeo. *See* **gallant.**

amorous *adjective*
1. Feeling or preoccupied with sexual love or desire ▸ concupiscent, lewd. *See* **lascivious** (1). **2.** Concerning or arousing sexual love or desire ▸ amatory, erogenous, sexy. *See* **erotic.**

amorousness *noun*
1. The passionate affection and desire felt by lovers for each other ▸ ardor, passion, romance. *See* **love** (2). **2.** The quality of being erotic ▸ lasciviousness, sexuality, suggestiveness. *See* **eroticism** (1).

amorphous *adjective*
▸ formless, inchoate, unshaped. *See* **shapeless.** *See synonym note at* **shapeless.**

amount *verb*
1. To come to in number or quantity ▸ add up, aggregate, come, number, reach, run, sum up, total (up). **2.** To be equal or alike ▸ constitute, correspond, equate. *See* **equal** (1).

amount *noun*
1. A number or quantity obtained as a result of addition ▸ aggregate, sum, totality. *See* **total** (1). **2.** The general sense or significance, as of an action or statement ▸ purport, substance. *See* **import** (1). **3.** A measurable whole ▸ body, bulk. *See* **quantity** (3).

amour *noun*
▸ affair, love affair, romance. *See* **love** (3).

amour-propre *noun*
1. A sense of one's own dignity or worth ▸ ego, self-regard, self-satisfaction. *See* **pride** (1). **2.** Exaggerated love for oneself or belief in one's own importance ▸ conceit, narcissism, vanity. *See* **egotism.**

ample *adjective*
1. Having plenty of room ▸ capacious, commodious,

roomy, spacious. *See synonym note at* **roomy.** *See also* **big. 2.** Of large extent or expanse ▸ extended, spacious. *See* **broad** (1). **3.** Of full measure ▸ capacious, voluminous, wide. *See* **full** (3). **4.** Characterized by abundance; as much as one needs or desires ▸ abundant, bounteous, plentiful. *See* **generous** (2). *See synonym note at* **generous. 5.** Being what is needed without being in excess ▸ competent, decent, satisfactory. *See* **sufficient** (1).

amplification *noun*
▸ aggrandizement, boost, escalation. *See* **increase** (1).

amplify *verb*
1. To make or become greater or larger ▸ aggrandize, boost, enlarge. *See* **increase** (1). **2.** To express at greater length or in greater detail ▸ develop, expand. *See* **elaborate. 3.** To increase markedly in level or intensity, especially of sound ▸ amplify, heighten, raise. *See* **elevate** (2). **4.** To make or become broader or more comprehensive ▸ dilate, enlarge, expand, widen. *See* **broaden.**

amplitude *noun*
1. Great amount or dimension ▸ magnitude, size. *See* **bulk** (2). **2.** The quality or state of being large in amount, extent, or importance ▸ bigness, greatness. *See* **size** (2).

amply *adverb*
▸ much, quite, well. *See* **considerably.**

amputate *verb*
▸ maim, mutilate. *See* **cripple** (1).

amuck *adjective*
Out of control ▸ runaway, unbridled, uncontrolled. *Idioms:* out of hand, running wild. *See also* **abandoned, loose.**

amulet *noun*
▸ mascot, talisman. *See* **charm** (1).

amuse *verb*
1. To occupy in an agreeable or pleasing way ▸ charm, cheer, divert, entertain, recreate, regale. *See also* **absorb, cheer. 2.** To give great or keen pleasure to ▸ enchant, overjoy, pleasure. *See* **delight** (1).

✦ CORE SYNONYMS: *amuse, entertain, divert, regale.* These verbs refer to actions that provide pleasure, especially as a means of passing time. *Amuse,* the least specific, implies directing attention away from serious matters: *I amused myself with a game of solitaire. Entertain* suggests acts undertaken to furnish amusement: *"They [timetables and catalogs] are much more entertaining than half the novels that are written"* (W. Somerset Maugham). *Divert* implies distraction from worrisome thought or care: *"I had neither Friends or Books to divert me"* (Richard Steele). To *regale* is to entertain with something enormously enjoyable: *"He loved to regale his friends with tales about the many memorable characters he had known as a newspaperman"* (David Rosenzweig).

---

amusement *noun*
Something that amuses, entertains, or pleases ▸ delight, disport, distraction, diversion, enjoyment, entertainment, fun, hobby, pastime, play, pleasure, rec-

reation, sport, treat. *Slang:* jollies, kicks. *See also* **gaiety.**

amusing *adjective*
1. Providing pleasure or entertainment ▸ diverting, entertaining. *See* **pleasant** (1). **2.** Causing laughter or amusement ▸ comical, humorous, laughable. *See* **funny** (1). **3.** Giving great pleasure or delight ▸ delectable, enchanting, heavenly. *See* **delightful.**

analogize *verb*
▸ compare, equate, parallel. *See* **liken.**

analogous *adjective*
▸ alike, similar, uniform. *See* **like**².

analogue *noun*
▸ correlative, counterpart. *See* **parallel.**

analogy *noun*
1. The quality or state of being alike ▸ resemblance, similarity, uniformity. *See* **likeness** (1). *See synonym note at* **likeness. 2.** Something closely analogous to something else ▸ correlative, counterpart. *See* **parallel.**

analysis *noun*
1. The separation of a whole into its parts for study ▸ anatomization, anatomy, breakdown, dissection, reduction, subdivision. **2.** The act of examining carefully or critically ▸ inspection, inquiry, scrutiny. *See* **examination** (1). **3.** A medical inquiry into a patient's state of health ▸ checkup, diagnosis. *See* **examination** (2). **4.** Exact, valid, and rational reasoning ▸ argument, rationality, reason. *See* **logic** (1).

analytical *or* **analytic** *adjective*
▸ ratiocinative, rational. *See* **logical** (1).

analyze *verb*
1. To separate into parts for study ▸ anatomize, break down, dissect, reduce, resolve, subdivide, take apart. **2.** To look at or study carefully or critically ▸ investigate, peruse, scrutinize. *See* **examine** (1).

✛ **CORE SYNONYMS:** *analyze, anatomize, dissect.* These verbs mean to separate into constituent parts for study: *analyze a chemical substance; a book that anatomizes 19th-century European history; medical students dissecting cadavers.*

anarchy *noun*
1. A lack of civil order or peace ▸ chaos, lawlessness, misrule. *See* **disorder** (2). **2.** Excessive freedom; lack of restraint ▸ licentiousness, profligacy. *See* **license** (2).

anathema *noun*
1. A denunciation invoking a wish or threat of evil or injury ▸ damnation, malediction. *See* **curse** (1). **2.** An object of extreme dislike ▸ abomination, bugbear. *See* **hate** (2).

anathematize *verb*
To invoke evil upon ▸ curse, damn, hex, imprecate. *See also* **charm.**

anatomize *verb*
▸ break down, dissect, resolve. *See* **analyze** (1). *See synonym note at* **analyze.**

anatomy *or* **anatomization** *noun*
▸ breakdown, dissection, reduction, subdivision. *See* **analysis** (1).

ancestor *noun*
1. A person from whom one is descended ▸ antecedent, ascendant, father, forebear, forefather, foremother, mother, parent, primogenitor, progenitor. **2.** One that precedes, as in time ▸ antecedent, forerunner, precursor, predecessor, progenitor, prototype.

✛ **CORE SYNONYMS:** *ancestor, forebear, forefather, progenitor.* These nouns denote a person from whom one is descended: *ancestors who were farmers; land once owned by his forebears; laws handed down from our forefathers; our progenitors' wisdom.*

◂ **ANTONYM:** *descendant*

ancestral *adjective*
Of or from one's ancestors ▸ familial, genealogical, hereditary, inherited, patrimonial.

ancestry *noun*
One's ancestors or their character or one's ancestral derivation ▸ birth, blood, bloodline, descent, derivation, extraction, family, family tree, genealogy, line, lineage, origin, parentage, pedigree, race, roots, seed, stock. *See also* **kin, progeny.**

anchor *noun*
1. A device for supporting or holding in place ▸ brake, dowel, grapnel, kedge, mooring, wedge. *See also* **bond, cord, fastener, nail. 2.** A person or group of persons whose occupation is journalism ▸ correspondent, editorialist, media. *See* **press** (1).

anchor *verb*
To make secure ▸ bind, chain, moor. *See* **fasten** (1). *See synonym note at* **fasten.**

anchorage *noun*
▸ cove, haven. *See* **harbor** (1).

anchorman *or* **anchorwoman** *noun*
▸ correspondent, editorialist, media. *See* **press** (1).

ancient *adjective*
1. Belonging to or existing in times long past ▸ age-old, antiquated, archaic. *See* **old** (1). *See synonym note at* **old. 2.** Of, existing, or occurring in a distant period ▸ primeval, primordial. *See* **early** (1).

ancient *noun*
An elderly person ▸ elder, senior citizen. *See* **senior** (2).

ancient history *noun*
▸ protohistory, time immemorial. *See* **antiquity.**

ancillary *adjective*
▸ assistant, contributory, subsidiary. *See* **auxiliary** (1).

androgynous *noun*
Being neither distinguishably masculine nor feminine ▸ degendered, epicene, genderless, gender-neutral, gender-nonspecific, sexless, ungendered. *See also* **effeminate, masculine.**

androgyny *noun*
The quality of being androgynous ▸ epicenism, gender-neutrality, sexlessness. *See also* **effeminacy, masculinity.**

anecdote *noun*
▸ fable, story, tale. *See* **yarn.**

anemic *adjective*
1. Suffering from or appearing to suffer from an

illness ▸ ailing, indisposed, unwell. *See* **sick** (1). **2.** Being weak in quality or substance ▸ bloodless, pallid. *See* **pale** (2).

anesthetic *adjective*
▸ heartless, insensitive, merciless. *See* **callous.**

anesthetize *verb*
▸ medicate, narcotize, tranquilize. *See* **drug** (1).

anew *adverb*
Once more ▸ afresh, again, once again, over again. *Idioms:* from the beginning (*or* start *or* top).

anfractuous *adjective*
1. Repeatedly curving in alternate directions ▸ convoluted, sinuous, twisting. *See* **winding** (1). **2.** Not proceeding straight to the point or object ▸ circuitous, devious, roundabout. *See* **indirect** (1).

angel *noun*
1. A pure, uncorrupted person ▸ lamb, virgin. *See* **innocent** (1). **2.** *Informal* One who assumes financial responsibility for another ▸ guarantor, underwriter. *See* **sponsor** (1). **3.** *Informal* One who supports or champions an activity, cause, or institution ▸ benefactor, sponsor. *See* **patron** (1). **4.** One who frees someone from danger ▸ deliverer, redeemer, savior. *See* **rescuer.**

angelic *or* **angelical** *adjective*
▸ pure, uncorrupted, untainted. *See* **innocent** (1).

anger *noun*
A strong feeling of displeasure or hostility ▸ animosity, choler, fury, furor, indignation, irateness, ire, outrage, rage, resentment, wrath, wrathfulness. *Informal:* dander. *See also* **enmity, hate, annoyance.**

anger *verb*
1. To cause to feel or show anger ▸ burn (up), enrage, exasperate, incense, infuriate, irritate, madden, provoke, rile. *Informal:* tee off, tick off. *Slang:* piss off, p.o.. *Idioms:* bend out of shape, gets one's dander up, gets on one's nerves, make one hot under the collar, make one's blood boil, make one's fur fly, put one's back up, rub one the wrong way. *See also* **annoy, offend. 2.** To be or become angry ▸ blow up, boil over, bristle, burn, explode, flare up, foam, fume, rage, seethe, storm. *Informal:* steam. *Idioms:* blow a fuse, blow a gasket, blow one's stack (*or* top), breathe fire, fly off the handle, foam (*or* froth) at the mouth, get hot under the collar, have a cow, hit the ceiling (*or* roof), lose one's temper, see red, throw a fit. *See also* **boil. 3.** To cause anger, resentment, or hurt feelings ▸ annoy, injure, upset. *See* **offend** (1).

✦ CORE SYNONYMS: *anger, rage, fury, ire, wrath, resentment, indignation.* These nouns denote strong feelings of marked displeasure or hostility. *Anger,* the most general, is strong displeasure: *vented my anger by denouncing the supporters of the idea. Rage* and *fury* imply intense, explosive, often destructive emotion: *smashed the glass in a fit of rage; directed his fury at the murderer. Ire* is a term for anger most frequently encountered in literature: *"The best way to escape His ire/Is, not to seem too happy"* (Robert Browning). *Wrath* applies especially to anger that seeks vengeance

or punishment: *saw the flood as a sign of the wrath of God. Resentment* refers to indignant smoldering anger generated by a sense of grievance: *deep resentment among the union employees that led to a strike. Indignation* is righteous anger at something wrongful, unjust, or evil: *"public indignation about takeovers causing people to lose their jobs"* (Allan Sloan).

---

angle¹ *verb*
To try to catch fish ▸ cast, trawl, troll. *See* **fish** (1).

angle² *noun*
1. The position from which something is observed or considered ▸ aspect, point of view, standpoint. *See* **viewpoint. 2.** *Slang* A clever, unexpected new trick or method ▸ gimmick, twist. *See* **wrinkle** (2). **3.** Something bent ▸ curvature, curve, turn. *See* **bend.**

angle *verb*
1. To move or cause to move in a bent or angular direction ▸ deflect, turn. *See* **bend** (2). **2.** To turn aside sharply from a straight course ▸ slant, veer, zigzag. *See* **swerve** (1). **3.** To alter or present material so as to favor a particular viewpoint ▸ doctor, slant. *See* **bias** (1).

angry *adjective*
Feeling or showing anger ▸ annoyed, boiling, choleric, cross, enraged, exacerbated, fuming, furious, huffy, incensed, indignant, inflamed, infuriated, irate, ireful, irritated, livid, mad, nettled, peeved, rabid, raging, seething, vexed, wrathful. *Informal:* sore. *Slang:* het up. *Idioms:* at the boiling point, bent out of shape, fit to be tied, foaming (*or* frothing) at the mouth, hot under the collar, in a rage (*or* temper), in a towering rage, seeing red, up in arms.

✦ CORE SYNONYMS: *angry, furious, indignant, infuriated, irate, ireful, livid, mad, wrathful.* These adjectives mean feeling or showing marked displeasure or hostility: *an angry retort; a furious scowl; an indignant denial; infuriated commuters who were stuck in traffic; irate protesters; ireful words; a livid disciplinarian; mad at a friend; a wrathful act.*

---

angst *noun*
▸ concern, distress, unease. *See* **anxiety** (1).

anguish *noun*
1. A state of physical or mental suffering ▸ agony, misery, wretchedness. *See* **distress** (1). **2.** Mental anguish or pain caused by loss or despair ▸ heartache, sorrow. *See* **grief.** *See synonym note at* **grief.**

anguish *verb*
1. To cause emotional suffering or painful sorrow to ▸ disturb, grieve, hurt. *See* **distress** (1). **2.** To feel, show, or express grief ▸ bemoan, mourn, sorrow. *See* **grieve** (1).

anguishing *adjective*
▸ excruciating, torturous. *See* **tormenting.**

angular *adjective*
▸ lean, skinny, slender, slim. *See* **thin** (1). *See synonym note at* **thin.**

anhydrous *adjective*
▸ moistureless, sere. *See* **dry** (1).

anima *noun*

▸ breath, soul, vitality. *See* **spirit** (2).

animal *adjective*

▸ carnal, physical, sexual. *See* **sensual** (2).

animalism *or* **animality** *noun*

▸ sexuality, voluptuousness. *See* **sensuality** (1).

animalize *verb*

▸ debase, demoralize, deprave, warp. *See* **corrupt** (1).

animate *verb*

1. To make alive ▸ enliven, quicken, vitalize, vivify. *See also* **energize, provoke. 2.** To make lively or animated ▸ brighten, enliven, light (up), perk up. **3.** To raise the spirits of ▸ buoy (up), exhilarate, inspire. *See* **elate** (1). **4.** To impart courage, inspiration, and resolution to ▸ inspire, motivate. *See* **encourage** (1). *See synonym note at* **encourage. 5.** To arouse the emotions of ▸ impassion, inspire, stir. *See* **fire** (2).

animate *adjective*

Having life ▸ live, living, vital. *See* **alive** (1). *See synonym note at* **alive.**

animated *adjective*

1. Having life ▸ live, living, vital. *See* **alive** (1). *See synonym note at* **alive. 2.** Very brisk, alert, and full of high spirits ▸ bubbly, chipper, vivacious. *See* **lively** (1). **3.** Being in or showing good spirits ▸ bright, happy, sunny. *See* **cheerful** (1).

animating *adjective*

▸ bracing, energizing, exhilarating. *See* **invigorating.**

animation *noun*

1. A lively, emphatic, eager quality or manner ▸ life, verve, vivaciousness. *See* **spirit** (1). **2.** High spirits ▸ euphoria, inspiration. *See* **elation** (1). **3.** Capacity for work or vigorous activity ▸ might, potency, power. *See* **energy.**

animosity *noun*

1. Deep-seated hatred, as between longtime opponents or rivals ▸ antagonism, hostility. *See* **enmity.** *See synonym note at* **enmity. 2.** A strong feeling of displeasure or hostility ▸ indignation, irateness, wrath. *See* **anger.**

animus *noun*

▸ antagonism, hostility, ill will. *See* **enmity.** *See synonym note at* **enmity.**

annals *noun*

A chronological record of past events ▸ archive, chronicle, historical record, history. *See also* **story.**

annex *verb*

To add as a supplement or appendix ▸ add on, append. *See* **attach** (2).

annex *noun*

A part added to a main structure ▸ annex, wing. *See* **extension** (4).

annihilate *verb*

1. To destroy all traces of ▸ abolish, blot out, clear, eradicate, erase, expunge, exterminate, extinguish, extirpate, kill, liquidate, obliterate, remove, root (out *or* up), rub out, snuff out, stamp out, uproot, wipe out. *Idioms:* do away with, make an end of, put an end to, put to bed. *See also* **abolish, overwhelm. 2.** To

kill savagely and indiscriminately ▸ butcher, slaughter, wipe out. *See* **massacre** (1). **3.** To put an end to ▸ cancel, invalidate, nullify. *See* **abolish** (1). **4.** To cause the complete ruin or wreckage of ▸ demolish, torpedo, wreck. *See* **destroy** (1).

✢ **CORE SYNONYMS:** *annihilate, exterminate, extinguish, extirpate, eradicate, obliterate.* These verbs mean to destroy all traces of: *a squadron that was annihilated in the attack; exterminated the cockroaches in the house; criticism that extinguished my enthusiasm; policies that attempt to extirpate drug abuse; scientists working to eradicate deadly diseases; a magnet that obliterated the data on the floppy disk.*

annihilation *noun*

1. Utter destruction ▸ eradication, extermination, extinction, extinguishment, extirpation, liquidation, obliteration. *See also* **defeat 2.** An often formal act of putting an end to ▸ cancellation, invalidation, nullification. *See* **abolition. 3.** The act of destroying or state of being destroyed ▸ devastation, ruin, wreck. *See* **destruction** (1).

annotation *noun*

▸ exegesis, exposition, interpretation. *See* **commentary.**

announce *verb*

1. To bring to public notice or make known publicly ▸ advertise, annunciate, blaze, blazon, broadcast, bruit, declare, herald, noise (about *or* around), proclaim, promulgate, propagate, publish, trumpet. *Idioms:* issue a statement, make public (*or* known), spread the word. *See also* **gossip, reveal, spread. 2.** To make known the presence or arrival of ▸ herald, introduce. *See* **proclaim** (1).

✢ **CORE SYNONYMS:** *announce, advertise, broadcast, declare, proclaim, promulgate, publish.* These verbs mean to bring to public notice or make known publicly: *announced a cease-fire; advertise a forthcoming concert; broadcasting their opinions; declared her political intentions; proclaiming his beliefs; promulgated a policy of nonresistance; publishing the marriage banns.*

announcement *noun*

1. The act of announcing ▸ annunciation, broadcasting, communication, declaration, notification, proclamation, promulgation, publication. **2.** Something announced or communicated ▸ annunciation, declaration, proclamation. *See* **message** (1).

annoy *verb*

1. To trouble the nerves or peace of mind of, especially by repeated vexations ▸ aggravate, bother, bug, chafe, disturb, exasperate, fret, gall, get (to), irk, irritate, molest, nettle, peeve, pester, provoke, put out, rankle, rile, ruffle, vex. *Idioms:* drive one bananas (*or* crazy *or* nuts), drive one up a wall, get in one's hair, get on one's nerves, get under one's skin, try one's patience. *See also* **agitate, distress, insult. 2.** To attack or disturb persistently ▸ harry, pester, torment. *See* **harass. 3.** To cause anger, resentment, or hurt feelings ▸ displease, injure, upset. *See* **offend** (1).

✤ CORE SYNONYMS: *annoy, irritate, bother, irk, vex, provoke, aggravate, peeve, rile.* These verbs mean to trouble a person's nerves or peace of mind, especially by repeated vexations and often evoking moderate anger: *Annoy* refers to mild disturbance caused by an act that tries one's patience: *The sound of the printer annoyed me. Irritate* is somewhat stronger: *I was irritated by their constant interruptions. Bother* implies imposition: *In the end, his complaining just bothered the supervisor. Irk* connotes a wearisome quality: *The city council's inactivity irked the community. Vex* applies to an act capable of arousing anger or perplexity: *Hecklers in the crowd vexed the speaker. Provoke* implies strong and often deliberate incitement to anger: *His behavior provoked me to reprimand the whole team. Aggravate* is a less formal equivalent: *"Threats only served to aggravate people in such cases"* (William Makepeace Thackeray). *Peeve,* also somewhat informal, suggests a querulous, resentful response to a mild disturbance: *Your flippant answers peeved me.* To *rile* is to upset and to stir up: *It riled me to have to listen to such lies.*

annoyance *noun*
1. The act of annoying or the state of being annoyed ▸ aggravation, bother, botheration, bothering, exasperation, harassment, irritation, pestering, provocation, vexation. *See also* **distress. 2.** Something that annoys ▸ aggravation, besetment, bother, irritant, irritation, nuisance, pain, peeve, pest, plague, thorn, torment, trial, vexation. *Informal.* hassle, headache. *Idioms:* pain in the neck (*or* butt), thorn in one's side.

annoyed *adjective*
▸ exacerbated, irate, peeved. *See* **angry.**

annoying *adjective*
▸ bothersome, irritating, unsettling. *See* **disturbing.**

annul *verb*
1. To put an end to ▸ cancel, invalidate, nullify. *See* **abolish** (1). **2.** To cross out or remove ▸ delete, erase, strike (out). *See* **cancel** (1).

annular *adjective*
▸ circular, globular, spherical. *See* **round** (1).

annulment *noun*
▸ cancellation, invalidation, nullification. *See* **abolition.**

annulus *noun*
▸ band, ring, wheel. *See* **circle** (1).

annunciate *verb*
▸ advertise, broadcast, declare. *See* **announce** (1).

annunciation *noun*
1. The act of announcing ▸ proclamation, publication. *See* **announcement** (1). **2.** Something announced or communicated ▸ announcement, declaration, notice. *See* **message** (1).

anoint *verb*
▸ grease, lube. *See* **oil.**

anointed *adjective*
▸ devoted, religious, sacred. *See* **divine** (2).

anomalous *or* **anomalistic** *adjective*
▸ atypical, deviant, irregular. *See* **abnormal.**

anomaly *noun*
▸ aberration, deviation, irregularity. *See* **abnormality.**

anonymity *noun*
▸ namelessness, oblivion, unimportance. *See* **obscurity** (1).

anonymous *adjective*
Having an unknown or withheld authorship or agency ▸ nameless, unacknowledged, uncredited, unidentified, unknown, unnamed, unsigned. *See also* **obscure.**

anorak *noun*
▸ jacket, overcoat, parka. *See* **coat** (1).

answer
answer *verb*
1. To speak or act in response, as to a question ▸ field, rejoin, reply, respond, retort, return, riposte. *See also* **acknowledge. 2.** To find a solution for ▸ clear up, resolve, unravel. *See* **solve** (1). *See synonym note at* **solve. 3.** To meet a need or requirement ▸ fill, fulfill, meet. *See* **satisfy** (1). *See synonym note at* **satisfy.**
answer *noun*
1. Something spoken or written in return, as to a question or demand ▸ comeback, rejoinder, repartee, reply, response, return, retort, riposte. **2.** A solution, as to a problem ▸ determination, explanation, key, resolution, result, solution. *See also* **discovery.**

✤ CORE SYNONYMS: *answer, respond, reply, retort.* These verbs mean to act in response, as to a question. *Answer, respond,* and *reply,* are the most general. *Please answer my question. Did you expect the president to respond personally to your letter? The opposing team scored three runs; the home team replied with two of their own. Respond* also denotes a reaction, either voluntary (*A bystander responded to the victim's need for help*) or involuntary (*I responded in spite of myself to the antics of the puppy*). To *retort* is to answer verbally in a quick, caustic, or witty manner: *She won the debate by retorting sharply to her opponent's questions.*

answerability *noun*
▸ accountability, liability. *See* **responsibility** (1).

answerable *adjective*
▸ accountable, responsible. *See* **liable** (1). *See synonym note at* **liable.**

antagonism *noun*
1. Deep-seated hatred, as between longtime opponents or rivals ▸ animosity, hostility. *See* **enmity.** *See synonym note at* **enmity. 2.** The act or condition of conflict ▸ contradiction, polarity. *See* **opposition** (1).

antagonist *noun*
▸ adversary, foe, nemesis. *See* **opponent** (1).

antagonistic *adjective*
1. Acting against or in opposition ▸ adverse, resistant. *See* **opposing** (1). **2.** Marked by a disposition to oppose ▸ contradictory, hostile. *See* **contrary** (1). **3.** Tending to discourage, retard, or make more

difficult ▶ adverse, negative, untoward. *See* **unfavorable** (1).

antagonize *verb*
▶ disaffect, disunite. *See* **estrange**.

ante *noun*
Something risked on an uncertain outcome ▶ pool, wager. *See* **bet** (1). *See synonym note at* **bet**.

ante *verb*
To give in common with others ▶ donate, subscribe. *See* **contribute** (1).

antecede *verb*
▶ antedate, predate. *See* **precede** (1).

antecedence *noun*
▶ priority, right of way. *See* **precedence**.

antecedent *adjective*
1. Going before ▶ anterior, earlier, preceding. *See* **advance**. 2. Just gone by or elapsed ▶ precedent, previous, prior. *See* **past** (1).

antecedent *noun*
1. That which produces an effect ▶ cause, determinant, occasion, reason. *See synonym note at* **cause**. *See also* **impact, origin, stimulus**. 2. A person from whom one is descended ▶ forebear, parent, progenitor. *See* **ancestor** (1). 3. One that precedes, as in time ▶ forerunner, precursor. *See* **ancestor** (2).

antedate *verb*
▶ antecede, predate. *See* **precede** (1).

antediluvian *adjective*
1. Belonging to or existing in times long past ▶ ancient, antiquated, archaic. *See* **old** (1). *See synonym note at* **old**. 2. Of, existing, or occurring in a distant period ▶ ancient, primeval. *See* **early** (1).

anterior *adjective*
1. Going before ▶ antecedent, earlier, preceding. *See* **advance**. 2. Just gone by or elapsed ▶ precedent, previous, prior. *See* **past** (1).

anthropic *adjective*
▶ anthropical, anthropoid. *See* **human** (1).

anthropoid *adjective*
1. Resembling a human being ▶ anthropomorphic, hominoid, humanoid. *See* **humanlike**. 2. Of or characteristic of human beings or humankind ▶ anthropic, anthropical. *See* **human** (1).

anthropomorphic *or* **anthropomorphous** *adjective*
▶ anthropoid, hominoid, humanoid. *See* **humanlike**.

antic *noun*
A mischievous act ▶ caper, joke, trick. *See* **prank**[1].

antic *adjective*
Deviating from what is conventional or customary ▶ bizarre, grotesque. *See* **eccentric**.

anticipant *adjective*
▶ anticipatory, awaiting, hopeful. *See* **expectant** (1).

anticipate *verb*
1. To know in advance ▶ divine, envision, foreknow. *See* **foresee**. 2. To look forward to confidently ▶ await, look for. *See* **expect** (1). *See synonym note at* **expect**. 3. To prohibit from occurring by advance planning or action ▶ avert, forerun, forestall. *See* **prevent**.

anticipated *adjective*
▶ expected, scheduled. *See* **due** (2).

anticipation *noun*
1. The condition of looking forward to something, especially with eagerness ▶ expectance, expectancy, expectation, high hopes, hopefulness. *See also* **desire**. 2. Something expected ▶ expectation, likelihood, promise, prospect. *See also* **chance, theory**.

anticipatory *or* **anticipative** *adjective*
▶ anticipant, awaiting, hopeful. *See* **expectant** (1).

anticlimax *noun*
▶ fiasco, letdown, washout. *See* **disappointment** (2).

antidotal *adjective*
▶ remedial, restorative. *See* **curative**.

antidote *noun*
▶ elixir, medication, remedy. *See* **cure**.

antipathetic *adjective*
1. Acting against or in opposition ▶ antagonistic, resistant. *See* **opposing** (1). 2. So objectionable as to deserve condemnation ▶ contemptible, disgusting, obnoxious. *See* **offensive** (1).

antipathy *noun*
1. Deep-seated hatred, as between longtime opponents or rivals ▶ antagonism, hostility. *See* **enmity**. *See synonym note at* **enmity**. 2. A strong feeling of hostility or dislike ▶ abhorrence, aversion, loathing. *See* **hate** (1).

antipode *or* **antipodes** *noun*
▶ antithesis, contrary. *See* **opposite**.

antipodean *or* **antipodal** *adjective*
▶ antithetical, contradictory. *See* **opposite** (1).

antiquated *adjective*
1. Of a style or method formerly in vogue ▶ antique, dated, passé. *See* **old-fashioned**. 2. Belonging to or existing in times long past ▶ ancient, antique, archaic. *See* **old** (1). *See synonym note at* **old**.

antique *adjective*
1. Of a style or method formerly in vogue ▶ dated, dowdy, passé. *See* **old-fashioned**. 2. Belonging to or existing in times long past ▶ ancient, antiquated, archaic. *See* **old** (1). *See synonym note at* **old**. 3. Characterized by enduring excellence, appeal, and importance ▶ ageless, historic. *See* **vintage** (1).

antiquity *noun*
Ancient times ▶ ancient history, distant past, prehistory, protohistory, time immemorial, time out of mind. *Idiom:* mists of time. *See also* **past**.

antiseptic *adjective*
1. Free from dirt, stain, or impurities ▶ spotless, unsoiled. *See* **clean** (1). *See synonym note at* **clean**. 2. Free or freed from microorganisms ▶ hygienic, sanitary. *See* **sterile** (1).

antiseptic *noun*
Something that purifies or cleans ▶ cathartic, cleaner. *See* **purifier**.

antithesis *noun*
1. The act or condition of conflict ▶ contradiction, polarity. *See* **opposition** (1). 2. That which is diametri-

cally opposed to another ▸ antipode, contrary. *See* **opposite.**

antithetical *adjective*
▸ antipodal, contradictory, diametric. *See* **opposite** (1). *See synonym note at* **opposite.**

antonym *noun*
▸ antithesis, contrary. *See* **opposite.**

antonymic *or* **antonymous** *adjective*
▸ antithetical, contradictory, diametric. *See* **opposite** (1).

antsy *adjective*
Slang Feeling or exhibiting nervous tension ▸ jittery, nervous. *See* **edgy.**

anxiety *noun*
1. A troubled or anxious state of mind ▸ angst, anxiousness, apprehension, care, concern, concernment, disquiet, disquietude, distress, nervousness, stress, solicitude, unease, uneasiness, worriment, worry. *See also* **agitation, fear, restlessness. 2.** An exaggerated concern ▸ complex, neurosis, phobia. *Informal:* hang-up. *See also* **obsession.**

✛ CORE SYNONYMS: *anxiety, worry, care, concern, solicitude.* These nouns refer to a troubled or anxious state of mind. *Anxiety* suggests feelings of fear and apprehension: *"Feelings of resentment and rage over this devious form of manipulation cannot surface in the child . . . . At the most, he will experience feelings of anxiety, shame, insecurity, and helplessness"* (Alice Miller). *Worry* implies persistent doubt or fear: *"Having come to a decision the lad felt a sense of relief from the worry that had haunted him for many sleepless nights"* (Edgar Rice Burroughs). *Care* denotes a state of mind burdened by heavy responsibilities: *The old man's face was worn with care. Concern* stresses serious thought combined with emotion: *"Concern for man himself and his fate must always form the chief interest of all technical endeavors"* (Albert Einstein). *Solicitude* is active and sometimes excessive concern for another's well-being: *"Animosity had given way . . . to worried solicitude for Lindbergh's safety"* (Warren Trabant).

---

anxious *adjective*
In a state of anxiety, uneasiness, or emotional distress ▸ agitated, apprehensive, concerned, distraught, distressed, disturbed, impatient, nervous, overcome, overwrought, rattled, shaken, shaken-up, solicitous, stressed, troubled, uneasy, unnerved, unsettled, upset, worried. *Informal:* stressed-out. *Slang:* het up. *Idioms:* ill at ease, on tenterhooks. *See also* **afraid, eager, edgy.**

anxiousness *noun*
▸ concern, distress, unease. *See* **anxiety** (1).

anyway *adverb*
▸ however, nevertheless, yet. *See* **still** (1).

A-one *or* **A-1** *adjective*
Informal Exceptionally good of its kind ▸ first-rate, prime, splendid, tiptop. *See* **excellent.**

apace *adverb*
▸ hastily, hurriedly, quickly, rapidly. *See* **fast.**

apart *adverb*
As a separate unit ▸ independently, singly. *See* **separately.**

apart *adjective*
Set away from or lacking the company of all others ▸ alone, isolated, solitary. *See* **solitary** (1).

apartment *noun*
An often rented living space in a building ▸ condominium, co-op, efficiency, flat, loft, pied-à-terre, rental, suite, studio, walk-up. *Informal:* condo.

apathetic *adjective*
Lacking interest ▸ blasé, detached, disinterested, impassive, incurious, indifferent, lethargic, listless, phlegmatic, supine, unconcerned, uninterested, unresponsive. *See also* **cold, cool, languid.**

apathy *noun*
Lack of emotion or interest ▸ aloofness, callousness, coldness, coolness, detachment, disinterest, impassiveness, impassivity, incuriosity, incuriousness, indifference, insensibility, insensibleness, insouciance, lassitude, lethargy, listlessness, nonchalance, phlegm, stolidity, stolidness, unconcern, uninterest, unresponsiveness.

ape *verb*
To copy the manner or expression of another, especially in an exaggerated or mocking way ▸ caricature, mock. *See* **imitate** (1). *See synonym note at* **imitate.**

ape *noun*
1. A large, ungainly, and dull-witted person ▸ lout, ox. *Informal:* lummox. *See* **oaf. 2.** One who imitates ▸ imitator, parrot. *See* **mimic.**

apéritif *noun*
▸ hors d'oeuvre, starter. *See* **appetizer.**

aperture *noun*
▸ orifice, vent. *See* **hole** (2).

apex *noun*
1. The highest point or state ▸ acme, height, peak. *See* **climax** (1). *See synonym note at* **climax. 2.** A sharp or tapered end ▸ cusp, tip. *See* **point** (1).

aphonic *adjective*
▸ inarticulate, voiceless. *See* **mute** (1).

aphorism *noun*
▸ adage, maxim, motto. *See* **proverb.** *See synonym note at* **proverb.**

aphoristic *adjective*
▸ compact, epigrammatic, pointed. *See* **pithy** (1).

aphrodisiac *adjective*
▸ amatory, erogenous, sexy. *See* **erotic.**

aping *noun*
▸ imitation, impersonation, mime. *See* **mimicry.**

apish *adjective*
▸ emulative, slavish. *See* **imitative** (1).

aplomb *noun*
1. A firm belief in one's own powers ▸ assurance, self-possession. *See* **confidence** (1). *See synonym note at* **confidence. 2.** A stable emotional state ▸ composure, coolness, equanimity, poise. *See* **balance** (2).

apocalypse *noun*
▸ disclosure, exposé, exposure. *See* **revelation.**

apocalypticist *noun*
▸ doomsayer, worrywart. *See* **pessimist** (2).
apocryphal *adjective*
1. Not true ▸ fictitious, spurious, untrue. *See false* (1).
2. Having the nature of a fable; not real ▸ fantasy, legendary. *See* **mythical.**
apogee *noun*
▸ apex, height, peak. *See* **climax** (1).
apologetic *adjective*
▸ penitent, regretful, repentant. *See* **sorry** (1).
apologia *noun*
▸ defense, justification, vindication. *See* **apology** (1).
See synonym note at **apology.**
apologize *verb*
▸ justify, maintain, vindicate. *See* **defend** (2).
apology *noun*
1. A statement that justifies or defends something, such as a past action or policy ▸ apologetic, apologia, defense, justification, plea, vindication. *See also* **explanation.** 2. A statement of acknowledgment expressing regret or asking pardon ▸ excuse, mea culpa, regrets. *See also* **acknowledgment.**

✦ CORE SYNONYMS: *apology, apologia, defense, justification.* These nouns denote a statement that justifies or defends something, such as a past action or policy: *arguments that constituted an apology for capital punishment; published an apologia expounding their version of the events; a defense based on ignorance of the circumstances; an untenable justification for police brutality.*

---

apoplexy *noun*
▸ attack, fit. *See* **seizure** (1).
apostasy *noun*
▸ disavowal, renouncement. *See* **defection.**
apostate *noun*
▸ deserter, recreant, traitor. *See* **defector.**
apostatize *verb*
▸ desert, quit, turn. *See* **defect.**
apostle *noun*
A person doing religious or charitable work in a foreign country ▸ evangelist, missionary, missioner. *See also* **cleric, representative.**
apothegm *noun*
▸ adage, maxim, motto. *See* **proverb.**
apotheosis *noun*
▸ aggrandizement, elevation. *See* **exaltation** (1).
apotheosize *verb*
▸ elevate, magnify, uplift. *See* **exalt** (1).
appall *verb*
1. To deprive of courage or the power to act as a result of fear, anxiety, or disgust ▸ consternate, disconcert. *See* **dismay** (1). *See synonym note at* **dismay.** 2. To offend the senses or feelings of ▸ nauseate, revolt, sicken. *See* **disgust** (1).
appalling *adjective*
1. Very bad ▸ awful, dreadful, horrible. *See* **terrible** (1).
2. Causing or capable of causing fear ▸ dreadful, formidable, frightful, scary. *See* **fearful** (1). 3. Shock-

ingly repellent ▸ grisly, gruesome, hideous. *See* **ghastly** (1). 4. Exceeding the bounds of morality, decency, or reason ▸ atrocious, monstrous, shocking. *See* **outrageous.**
apparatus *noun*
1. Something attached as a permanent part of something else ▸ fitting, fixture, installation. *See also* **attachment.** 2. Something, as a machine, devised for a particular function ▸ appliance, contraption, invention. *See* **device** (1). 3. Things needed for a task, journey, or other purpose ▸ equipment, gear. *See* **outfit** (1). *See synonym note at* **outfit.** 4. A small specialized mechanical device ▸ contraption, contrivance. *Slang:* gizmo. *See* **gadget.**
apparel *noun*
Articles worn to cover the body ▸ attire, clothing, garments. *See* **dress** (1).
apparel *verb*
To put clothes on ▸ attire, clothe, garb. *See* **dress** (1).
apparent *adjective*
1. Readily seen, perceived, or understood ▸ clear, clear-cut, conspicuous, crystal clear, distinct, evident, glaring, manifest, marked, noticeable, observable, obvious, patent, plain, pronounced, self-evident, unmistakable, visible. *See also* **definite, perceptible, sharp.** 2. Appearing as such but not necessarily so ▸ external, ostensible, ostensive, outward, seeming, superficial. *See also* **probable.**

✦ CORE SYNONYMS: *apparent, clear, clear-cut, distinct, evident, manifest, obvious, patent, plain.* These adjectives mean readily seen, perceived, or understood: *angry for no apparent reason; a clear danger; clear-cut evidence of tampering; distinct fingerprints; evident hostility; manifest pleasure; obvious errors; patent advantages; making my meaning plain.*

---

apparently *adverb*
On the surface ▸ evidently, externally, ostensibly, ostensively, outwardly, seemingly, superficially. *Idioms:* as far as one can tell (*or* see), on the face of it, to all appearances.
apparition *noun*
1. An immaterial supernatural being ▸ phantom, shade, specter. *See* **ghost** (1). 2. The act of coming into sight ▸ manifestation, materialization. *See* **appearance** (2).
appeal *verb*
1. To make an earnest or urgent request ▸ adjure, ask (for), beg, beseech, crave, entreat, implore, petition, plead, pray, request, seek, solicit, sue, supplicate. 2. To bring an appeal or request to the attention of ▸ address, apply, approach, petition. *See also* **appeal, request.** 3. To direct or impel to oneself by some quality or action ▸ allure, entice, lure. *See* **attract** (1).
appeal for *verb*
To ask for urgently or insistently ▸ insist on (*or* upon), require. *See* **demand** (1).
appeal *noun*
1. An earnest or urgent request ▸ application, en-

treaty, imploration, imploring, importunity, petition, plea, prayer, requisition, supplication. *See also* **question. 2.** The act of demanding ▸ behest, claim, requisition. *See* **demand** (1). **3.** The power or quality of attracting ▸ allure, enticement, lure. *See* **attraction** (1).

✤ **CORE SYNONYMS:** *appeal, beg, crave, beseech, implore, entreat.* These verbs mean to make an earnest request. *Appeal* has the broadest application: *The emcee of the marathon appealed to the listeners to make a donation. Beg* and *crave* mean to ask in a serious and sometimes humble manner, especially for something one cannot claim as a right: *I begged her to forgive me. The attorney craved the court's indulgence. Beseech* emphasizes earnestness and often implies anxiety: *Be silent, we beseech you. Implore* intensifies the sense of urgency and anxiety: *The child implored the teacher not to be angry. Entreat* pertains to persuasive pleading: *"Ask me no questions, I entreat you"* (Charles Dickens).

---

appealer *noun*
One that asks a higher authority for something, as a favor or redress ▸ appellant, petitioner, suitor.

appealing *adjective*
▸ enchanting, fetching, lovely, winsome. *See* **attractive** (1).

appear *verb*
1. To come into view ▸ come out, emerge, issue, loom, materialize, show (up), turn up. *Idioms:* come to light, make (*or* put in) an appearance, meet the eye. **2.** To give the impression of being ▸ feel, look, seem, sound. *Idioms:* have all the earmarks of being, give the idea (*or* impression) of being, strike one as being. *See also* **resemble. 3.** To come into being ▸ arise, commence, emerge. *See* **begin** (1).

✤ **CORE SYNONYMS:** *appear, emerge, issue, loom, materialize, show.* These verbs mean to come into view: *a ship appearing on the horizon; a star that emerged from behind a cloud; a diver issuing from the water; a peak that loomed through the mist; a job offer that materialized overnight; a shirtsleeve showing at the edge of the jacket.*

---

appearance *noun*
1. The way something or someone looks ▸ aspect, guise, look, looks, features, mien, semblance, stamp, visage. *See also* **face. 2.** The act of coming into sight ▸ apparition, emergence, manifestation, materialization, turning up. *Idiom:* coming into view. **3.** The act of arriving ▸ advent, arrival, coming. *See also* **entrance. 4.** The character projected or given by someone to the public ▸ image, impression. *See also* **façade.**

appease *verb*
1. To ease the anger or agitation of ▸ assuage, mollify, soothe. *See* **pacify.** *See synonym note at* **pacify. 2.** To grant or have what is demanded by a need or desire ▸ fulfill, gratify. *See* **satisfy** (2).

appellant *noun*
One that asks a higher authority for something, as a

favor or redress ▸ appealer, petitioner, suitor.

appellation *or* **appellative** *noun*
▸ cognomen, epithet, title. *See* **name** (1).

append *verb*
1. To join one thing to another ▸ affix, fasten, secure. *See* **attach** (1). **2.** To add as a supplement or appendix ▸ annex, subjoin. *See* **attach** (2).

appendage *noun*
▸ adjunct, appurtenance, supplement. *See* **attachment** (1). *See synonym note at* **attachment.**

appertain *verb*
▸ concern, pertain, relate. *See* **apply** (2).

appetence *or* **appetency** *noun*
▸ craving, longing, yearning. *See* **desire** (1).

appetite *noun*
1. A desire for food or drink ▸ hunger, ravenousness, stomach, taste, thirst. *Idioms:* a stomach for, the munchies. *See also* **voracity. 2.** A strong wanting of what promises enjoyment or pleasure ▸ craving, longing, yearning. *See* **desire** (1). **3.** Sexual hunger ▸ eroticism, lust, passion. *See* **desire** (2).

appetizer *noun*
A food or drink served before a meal ▸ amuse bouche, apéritif, hors d'oeuvre, starter, tapa. *See also* **refreshment.**

appetizing *adjective*
▸ delectable, savory, scrumptious. *See* **delicious** (1).

applaud *verb*
1. To express approval audibly, as by clapping ▸ cheer, clap, root. *Idioms:* give a big hand (*or* welcome), give an ovation, give someone a hand, put one's hands together. **2.** To express warm approval of ▸ accolade, commend. *See* **praise** (1).

✤ **CORE SYNONYMS:** *applaud, cheer, root.* These verbs mean to express approval or encouragement, especially audibly: *applauded at the end of the concert; cheered when the home team scored; rooting for the underdog in the tennis championship.*

---

applause *noun*
1. Approval expressed by clapping ▸ hand, ovation, plaudit. **2.** An expression of warm approval ▸ acclamation, celebration, kudos. *See* **praise** (1).

apple-polish *verb*
Informal To behave obsequiously or submissively ▸ grovel, kowtow. *Informal:* brownnose. *See* **fawn.** *See synonym note at* **fawn.**

apple-polisher *noun*
Informal One who flatters another in an attempt to win favor ▸ flatterer, minion, slave. *See* **sycophant.**

apple-polishing *noun*
Informal Excessive, ingratiating praise ▸ adulation, blandishment. *Informal:* soft soap. *See* **flattery.**

applesauce *noun*
Slang Something that does not have or make sense ▸ bunkum, drivel, garbage, poppycock. *See* **nonsense** (1).

appliance *noun*
▸ contraption, invention, mechanism. *See* **device** (1).

applicability *noun*
▸ application, pertinence. *See* **relevance.**

applicable *adjective*
1. Related to or affecting the matter at hand ▸ apropos, germane. *See* **relevant. 2.** In a condition to be used ▸ employable, serviceable. *See* **usable** (1).

applicant *noun*
A person who applies for or seeks something, such as a job or position ▸ aspirant, candidate, hopeful, petitioner, seeker. *See also* **competitor.**

application *noun*
1. The act of putting into play ▸ employment, implementation, usage. *See* **exercise** (1). **2.** The condition of being put to use ▸ employment, service, use. *See* **duty** (2). **3.** The relation with, or fact of being related to, the matter at hand ▸ materiality, pertinence. *See* **relevance. 4.** Steady attention and effort, as to one's occupation ▸ assiduousness, perseverance, pertinacity. *See* **diligence. 5.** An earnest or urgent request ▸ imploration, plea, supplication. *See* **appeal** (1). **6.** A document used in applying, as for a job ▸ form, paper, sheet.

apply *verb*
1. To devote oneself or one's efforts ▸ address, bend, buckle down, concentrate, dedicate, devote, direct, exert, focus, give, turn. *Idiom:* keep one's nose to the grindstone. *See also* **commit, engage. 2.** To be pertinent ▸ appertain, bear on (*or* upon), concern, pertain, refer, relate. *Idioms:* have a bearing on, have to do with. *See also* **contain. 3.** To bring an appeal or request to the attention of ▸ address, appeal, approach, petition. *See also* **appeal, request. 4.** To provide as a remedy ▸ dispense, medicate, treat. *See* **administer** (3). **5.** To put into action or use ▸ employ, exercise, utilize. *See* **use** (1). **6.** To look to when in need ▸ refer, run, turn. *See* **resort** (1). *See synonym note at* **resort. 7.** To ask for employment, acceptance, or admission ▸ petition, put in.

appoint *verb*
1. To select for an office or position ▸ assign, designate, elect, make, name, nominate, tap. *See also* **authorize, choose. 2.** To supply what is needed for some activity or purpose ▸ equip, outfit. *See* **furnish** (1). *See synonym note at* **furnish.**

✛ **CORE SYNONYMS:** *appoint, designate, name, nominate, tap.* These verbs mean to select for an office or position: *was appointed chairperson of the committee; expects to be designated leader of the opposition; a new police commissioner named by the mayor; to be nominated as her party's candidate; was tapped for fraternity membership.*

---

appointment *noun*
1. The act of appointing to an office or position ▸ assignment, designation, election, installation, naming, nomination. *See also* **confirmation. 2.** A post of employment ▸ job, spot. *See* **position** (3). **3.** An arrangement to appear at a certain time and place

▸ date, rendezvous. *See* **engagement** (1). *See synonym note at* **engagement.**

apportion *verb*
▸ allocate, deal (out), dole out. *See* **distribute** (1).

apportionment *noun*
▸ allocation, disbursement, dispensation. *See* **distribution** (1).

apposite *adjective*
▸ applicable, apropos, germane. *See* **relevant.** *See synonym note at* **relevant.**

appositeness *noun*
▸ applicability, materiality, pertinence. *See* **relevance.**

appraisal *or* **appraisement** *noun*
▸ assessment, evaluation. *See* **estimate** (1).

appraise *verb*
1. To make a judgment as to the worth or value of ▸ assay, calculate. *See* **estimate** (1). *See synonym note at* **estimate. 2.** To subject to a test of effectiveness, value, function, or other quality ▸ check, essay, try (out). *See* **test** (1).

appreciable *adjective*
1. Capable of being perceived by the senses or the mind ▸ discernible, palpable, perceivable. *See* **perceptible.** *See synonym note at* **perceptible. 2.** Capable of being readily understood ▸ comprehensible, fathomable, intelligible. *See* **understandable** (1).

appreciate *verb*
1. To have a high opinion of or regard for ▸ admire, esteem, respect. *See* **value** (1). *See synonym note at* **value. 2.** To receive pleasure from ▸ care for, savor. *See* **enjoy** (1).

appreciation *noun*
1. A being grateful ▸ acknowledgment, gratefulness, gratitude, indebtedness, thankfulness, thanks. **2.** A feeling of deference, approval, and liking ▸ admiration, favor. *See* **esteem** (1).

appreciative *adjective*
Showing or feeling gratitude ▸ grateful, thankful. *See also* **obliged.**

apprehend *verb*
1. To take into custody as a prisoner ▸ seize. *Informal:* nab, pick up. *See* **arrest** (1). **2.** To perceive directly with the intellect ▸ comprehend, fathom, grasp. *See* **know** (1). **3.** To perceive and recognize the meaning of ▸ comprehend, fathom. *See* **understand** (1). **4.** To be intuitively aware of ▸ feel, sense. *See* **perceive** (2).

apprehensible *adjective*
▸ comprehensible, fathomable, intelligible. *See* **understandable** (1).

apprehension *noun*
1. A feeling of agitation in the face of trouble or danger ▸ alarm, consternation, trepidation. *See* **fear. 2.** A seizing and holding by law ▸ seizure. *Slang:* bust, pinch. *See* **arrest** (1). **3.** Intellectual hold ▸ comprehension, grasp, grip, hold, understanding. *See also* **knowledge. 4.** A troubled or anxious state of mind ▸ concern, distress, unease. *See* **anxiety** (1).

apprehensive *adjective*
1. Filled with fear or terror ▸ fearful, frightened,

scared. *See* **afraid.** *See synonym note at* **afraid. 2.** In a state of anxiety or uneasiness ▸ distressed, nervous, uneasy. *See* **anxious.**

apprentice *noun*
1. One who is just starting to learn or do something ▸ fledgling, neophyte, novice. *See* **beginner. 2.** One who is being educated ▸ pupil, scholar, trainee. *See* **student.**

apprise *verb*
▸ advise, educate, notify. *See* **inform** (1).

approach *verb*
1. To come near in space or time ▸ close in on, converge on, gain on, near. *Idioms:* be around the corner, close the gap, come close to, come within spitting distance, draw near to (*or* nigh), stare one in the face. **2.** To attempt to equal or surpass, as in quality of amount ▸ challenge, verge on. *See* **rival** (1). **3.** To bring an appeal or request to the attention of ▸ address, appeal, apply, petition. *See also* **appeal, request. 4.** To go about the initial step in doing something ▸ begin, embark, initiate. *See* **start** (1).

approach *noun*
1. A method used for making, doing, or accomplishing something ▸ attack, blueprint, course, design, game plan, idea, layout, line, means, modus operandi, plan, procedure, process, project, schema, scheme, strategy, tack, tactic, technique. *Idiom:* course of action. *See also* **line, way. 2.** The act or fact of coming near ▸ coming, convergence, imminence, nearness. *See also* **advance, appearance. 3.** Personal approach to gain acquaintance, favor, or an agreement ▸ moves, overture. *See* **advances.**

✦ CORE SYNONYMS: *approach, blueprint, design, plan, project, scheme, strategy.* These nouns denote a method or program for making, doing, or accomplishing something: *an encouraging approach to reducing the high school dropout rate; a blueprint for reorganizing the company; social conventions of human design; has no vacation plans; an urban renewal project; a new scheme for conservation; a strategy for survival.*

approachable *adjective*
1. Easily approached ▸ accessible, responsive, welcoming. *See also* **convenient. 2.** Pleasant and friendly in disposition ▸ cordial, friendly, genial. *See* **amiable.**

approaching *adjective*
1. In the relatively near future ▸ coming, due, forthcoming, upcoming. *Idioms:* around the corner, on the horizon. *See also* **close. 2.** About to occur at any moment ▸ impending, looming. *See* **imminent.**

approaching *adverb*
Near to in quantity or amount ▸ almost, nearly, roughly. *See* **approximately.**

approbate *verb*
▸ approve, authorize, sanction. *See* **permit** (2).

approbation *noun*
1. Favorable reception or regard ▸ approval, favor, welcome. *See* **acceptance** (2). **2.** The approving of an

action, especially when done by one in authority ▸ authorization, consent, sanction. *See* **permission. 3.** An expression of warm approval ▸ acclamation, celebration, kudos. *See* **praise** (1).

approbatory *adjective*
▸ acclamatory, laudatory. *See* **complimentary** (1).

appropriate *adjective*
1. Suitable for a particular person, condition, occasion, or place ▸ apt, becoming, befitting, comely, comme il faut, correct, decent, decorous, de rigueur, felicitous, fit, fitting, nice, proper, right, respectable, seemly, tailor-made. *Idiom:* cut out for. *See also* **beneficial, opportune, relevant. 2.** Suited to one's purpose ▸ expedient, proper, suitable. *See* **convenient** (1). **3.** Consistent with prevailing or accepted standards or circumstances ▸ deserved, fitting, proper. *See* **just** (2).

appropriate *verb*
1. To set aside or apart for a specified purpose ▸ allocate, allot, assign, budget, designate, earmark, set apart, set aside. *See also* **distribute. 2.** To lay claim to or take possession of ▸ commandeer, preempt, usurp. *See* **seize** (1). **3.** To take and make one's own ▸ assume, embrace, take on. *See* **adopt** (1). **4.** To reproduce another's work without permission ▸ borrow, crib, pirate. *See* **plagiarize.**

✦ CORE SYNONYMS: *appropriate, allocate, allot, designate, earmark.* These verbs mean to set aside for a specified purpose: *appropriated funds for public education; allocated time for recreation; allotted fifty minutes for taking the test; designated a location for the new hospital; money earmarked for a vacation.*

appropriation *noun*
1. Money or other resources granted for a particular purpose ▸ budget, grant, subsidy, subvention. **2.** The act of taking possession of something ▸ expropriation, preemption, usurpation. *See* **seizure** (2).

approval *noun*
1. The approving of an action, especially when done by one in authority ▸ authorization, consent, sanction. *See* **permission. 2.** An act of confirming officially ▸ certification, ratification, sanction. *See* **confirmation** (1). **3.** Favorable reception or regard ▸ approbation, favor, welcome. *See* **acceptance** (2).

approve *verb*
1. To be favorably disposed toward ▸ countenance, favor, hold with. *Informal:* go for. *Idioms:* be in favor of, take kindly to, think highly (*or* well) of. *See also* **assent, value. 2.** To give one's consent to ▸ authorize, sanction. *See* **permit** (2). **3.** To accept officially ▸ affirm, pass, ratify. *See* **confirm** (3).

approving *adjective*
▸ agreeable, positive. *See* **favorable** (2).

approximate *verb*
1. To attempt to equal or surpass, as in quality of amount ▸ challenge, verge on. *See* **rival** (1). **2.** To calculate approximately ▸ place, reckon. *See* **estimate** (2).

approximate *adjective*
Lacking literal exactness ▸ broad, inexact, rough. *See* **loose** (3).

approximately *adverb*
Near to in quantity or amount ▸ about, almost, approaching, around, circa, nearly, practically, roughly, some. *Idioms:* for all practical purposes, for the most part, give or take a little, in all (*or* everything) but name, in the ballpark (*or* neighborhood) of, on the order of, pretty much. *See also* **fairly, usually.**

approximation *noun*
▸ estimation. *Informal:* guesstimate. *See* **estimate** (2).

appurtenance *noun*
▸ adjunct, appendage, supplement. *See* **attachment** (1). *See synonym note at* **attachment.**

apropos *adjective*
▸ applicable, germane, material. *See* **relevant.** *See synonym note at* **relevant.**

apt *adjective*
1. Suitable for a particular person, condition, occasion, or place ▸ befitting, correct, right. *See* **appropriate** (1). 2. Having or showing a tendency or likelihood ▸ disposed, prone. *See* **inclined** (1).

aptitude *noun*
1. An innate capability ▸ faculty, gift, knack. *See* **talent.** 2. The faculty of thinking, reasoning, and applying knowledge ▸ intellect, mentality, understanding. *See* **intelligence** (1).

aptness *noun*
▸ faculty, gift, knack. *See* **talent.**

aquiver *adjective*
▸ quaky, quivery, shaky. *See* **tremulous** (1).

arbiter *noun*
▸ arbitrator, referee. *See* **judge** (3). *See synonym note at* **judge.**

arbitrary *adjective*
1. Based on individual judgment or discretion ▸ discretionary, judgmental, personal, subjective, unscientific. *See also* **random.** 2. Having and exercising complete political power and control ▸ dictatorial, monocratic, totalitarian. *See* **absolute** (1). 3. Marked by whim or impulse ▸ fickle, impulsive, mercurial. *See* **capricious.** *See synonym note at* **capricious.**

arbitrate *verb*
1. To make a decision about (a controversy or dispute, for example) after deliberation, as in a court of law ▸ adjudicate, decide, rule. *See* **judge** (1). 2. To intervene between disputants in order to bring about an agreement ▸ mediate, moderate. *See also* **confer, judge.**

arbitration *noun*
▸ arrangement, give-and-take, settlement. *See* **compromise.**

arbitrator *noun*
▸ arbiter, referee. *See* **judge** (3). *See synonym note at* **judge.**

arc *verb*
To deviate from a straight line in a smooth, continu-

ous manner ▸ arch, curve, turn. *See* **bend** (1).

arc *noun*
Something bent ▸ curvature, curve, turn. *See* **bend.**

arcadian *adjective*
1. Of or relating to the countryside ▸ bucolic, pastoral, rural. *See* **country.** 2. Charmingly simple and carefree ▸ idyllic, pastoral. *See also* **fresh, still.**

arcane *adjective*
1. Difficult to explain or understand ▸ enigmatic, mystifying, puzzling. *See* **mysterious.** *See synonym note at* **mysterious.** 2. Not widely understood ▸ esoteric, recondite. *See* **obscure** (1).

arced *adjective*
▸ arched, bowed, curved, rounded. *See* **bent** (1).

arch¹ *verb*
1. To deviate from a straight line in a smooth, continuous manner ▸ arc, curve, turn. *See* **bend** (1). 2. To incline the body ▸ bend, crouch, scrunch. *See* **stoop** (1).

arch *noun*
Something bent ▸ curvature, curve, turn. *See* **bend.**

arch² *adjective*
Full of mischief or high-spirited fun ▸ frolicsome, impish, sportive. *See* **mischievous** (1).

archaic *adjective*
1. Belonging to or existing in times long past ▸ ancient, antiquated, bygone. *See* **old** (1). *See synonym note at* **old.** 2. Of a style or method formerly in vogue ▸ antique, dated, passé. *See* **old-fashioned.**

arched *adjective*
▸ bowed, curved, rounded. *See* **bent** (1).

archenemy *noun*
▸ antagonist, foe, nemesis. *See* **opponent** (1).

archetypal *or* **archetypical** *adjective*
1. Having the nature of, constituting, or serving as a type ▸ model, prototypic, representative. *See* **typical** (1). 2. Not derived from something else ▸ primary, prime. *See* **original** (1). 3. Conforming to an ultimate form of perfection or excellence ▸ exemplary, model, perfect. *See* **ideal** (1).

archetype *noun*
1. A first form from which varieties arise or imitations are made ▸ master, prototype. *See* **original** (1). 2. An ideally representative example of a type ▸ exemplar, model. *See* **epitome** (1).

archfiend *noun*
▸ beast, devil, monster. *See* **fiend** (1).

architect *noun*
▸ author, creator, inventor. *See* **originator.**

archive *noun*
1. A chronological record of past events ▸ annals, chronicle, historical record, history. *See also* **story.** 2. A place where something is deposited for safekeeping ▸ depot, storehouse, warehouse. *See* **depository.**

arciform *adjective*
▸ arched, bowed, curved, rounded. *See* **bent** (1).

arctic *adjective*
▸ chill, frigid, polar. *See* **cold** (1). *See synonym note at* **cold.**

ardent *adjective*
1. Fired with intense feeling ▸ burning, fervent, impassioned. *See* **passionate** (1). 2. Showing or having enthusiasm ▸ fervent, rabid, zealous. *See* **enthusiastic** (1). 3. Intensely desirous or interested ▸ avid, bursting. *See* **eager** (1). 4. Marked by much heat ▸ blistering, boiling, burning. *See* **hot** (1).

ardor *noun*
1. Powerful, intense emotion ▸ fervor, zeal. *See* **passion** (1). *See synonym note at* **passion**. 2. Passionate devotion to or interest in a cause or subject, for example ▸ fervor, zeal. *See* **enthusiasm** (1). 3. The passionate affection and desire felt by lovers for each other ▸ amativeness, romance. *See* **love** (2).

ardorless *adjective*
▸ cold, inhibited, undersexed. *See* **frigid** (3).

arduous *adjective*
1. Not easy to do, achieve, or master ▸ challenging, laborious, tough. *See* **difficult** (1). *See synonym note at* **difficult**. 2. Requiring great or extreme bodily, mental, or spiritual strength ▸ demanding, difficult, exacting. *See* **burdensome** (1). *See synonym note at* **burdensome**. 3. Marked by vigorous physical exertion ▸ knockabout, strenuous, tough. *See* **rough** (7).

arduously *adverb*
▸ difficultly, heavily, laboriously. *See* **hard** (2).

area *noun*
1. A sphere of activity, experience, study, or interest ▸ arena, bailiwick, circle, department, domain, field, orbit, province, realm, scene, subject, terrain, territory, world. *Slang:* bag, turf. *See also* **branch, range**. 2. A part of the earth's surface ▸ belt, district, locality, neighborhood, quarter, region, section, sector, tract, zone. *Informal:* neck of the woods. *See also* **field, territory**. 3. A particular geographic area ▸ neighborhood, vicinity. *See* **locality** (1). 4. An area in a city or town with distinctive characteristics ▸ community, district. *See* **neighborhood** (1). 5. The amount of space occupied by something ▸ extent, magnitude, proportions. *See* **size** (1).

✦ CORE SYNONYMS: *area, bailiwick, domain, field, province, realm, territory.* These nouns denote a sphere of activity, experience, study, or interest: *an expert in the area of corporate law; considers biochemistry to be her bailiwick; the domain of quantum physics; the field of comparative literature; the province of politics; the realm of constitutional law; the territory of historical research.*

arena *noun*
▸ department, domain, field, terrain. *See* **area** (1).

argot *noun*
1. A variety of a language that differs from the standard form ▸ jargon, vernacular. *See* **dialect** (1). *See synonym note at* **dialect**. 2. Specialized expressions indigenous to a particular field, subject, trade, or subculture ▸ jargon, lingo, patois. *See* **language** (2).

arguable *adjective*
▸ disputable, doubtful, questionable. *See* **debatable**.

argue *verb*
1. To engage in a quarrel ▸ altercate, bicker, brawl, broil, caterwaul, contend, dispute, fall out, feud, fight, quarrel, quibble, row, spar, spat, squabble, tiff, wrangle. *Informal:* hassle, tangle. *Idioms:* be at loggerheads, cross swords, have a brush with, have it out, have words, lock horns, mix it up. *See also* **conflict, contest, haggle**. 2. To put forth reasons for or against something, often excitedly ▸ contend, debate, dispute, moot, plead. *Idioms:* make a case for, put up an argument. *See also* **appeal, assert**. 3. To put into words positively and with conviction ▸ avow, declare, maintain. *See* **assert** (1). 4. To give grounds for believing in the existence or presence of ▸ attest, witness. *See* **indicate** (1). *See synonym note at* **indicate**. 5. To speak together and exchange ideas and opinions about ▸ converse, debate. *Informal:* kick around. *See* **discuss**.

argue into *verb*
To succeed in causing a person to act or think in a certain way ▸ bring around, convince, prevail on. *See* **persuade** (1).

✦ CORE SYNONYMS: *argue, quarrel, wrangle, squabble, bicker.* These verbs denote verbal exchange expressing conflict. To *argue* is to present reasons or facts in order to persuade someone of something: *"I am not arguing with you—I am telling you"* (James McNeill Whistler). *Quarrel* stresses hostility: *The children quarreled over whose turn it was to wash the dishes. Wrangle* refers to loud, contentious argument: *"audiences . . . who can be overheard wrangling about film facts in restaurants and coffee houses"* (Sheila Benson). *Squabble* suggests petty or trivial argument: *"The one absolutely certain way of bringing this nation to ruin . . . would be to permit it to become a tangle of squabbling nationalities"* (Theodore Roosevelt). *Bicker* connotes sharp, persistent, bad-tempered exchange: *The senators bickered about the president's tax proposal for weeks.*

argument *noun*
1. A discussion, often heated, in which a difference of opinion is expressed ▸ altercation, bicker, clash, contention, controversy, debate, difficulty, disagreement, dispute, falling out, feud, fight, fireworks, fracas, fuss, misunderstanding, polemic, quarrel, row, run-in, set-to, spat, squabble, tiff, words, wrangle. *Informal:* hassle, rhubarb, tangle. *Idiom:* war of words. *See also* **conflict, deliberation, uproar**. 2. A fact or circumstance that gives logical support to an assertion, claim, or proposal ▸ grounds, proof, wherefore. *See* **reason** (1). 3. What a speech, piece of writing, or artistic work is about ▸ matter, text, theme. *See* **subject** (1). 4. An expression of opposition ▸ exception, grievance, protestation. *See* **objection**. 5. Exact, valid, and rational reasoning ▸ analysis, rationality, reason. *See* **logic** (1).

✦ CORE SYNONYMS: *argument, dispute, controversy.* These nouns refer to a discussion, often heated, in which a difference of opinion is expressed: *Argument* stresses the advancement by each side of facts and reasons intended to persuade the other side: *Emotions are seldom swayed by argument.* *Dispute* implies animosity: *A dispute arose among union members about the terms of the new contract.* *Controversy* applies especially to major differences of opinion involving large groups of people: *The use of nuclear power is the subject of widespread controversy.*

argumentative *adjective*
Given to or characterized by arguing ► cantankerous, combative, contentious, diasagreeable, disputatious, eristic, factious, feisty, hotheaded, litigious, polemic, polemical, quarrelsome, scrappy. *Idiom:* having a chip on one's shoulder. *See also* **aggressive, ill-tempered.**

✦ CORE SYNONYMS: *argumentative, combative, contentious, disputatious, quarrelsome, scrappy.* These adjectives mean given to or fond of arguing: *an argumentative child; a combative teenager; a contentious mood; a disputatious lawyer; a quarrelsome drinker; a scrappy litigator.*

---

aria *noun*
► air, theme, tune. *See* **melody.**
arid *adjective*
1. Having little or no precipitation ► desert, droughty, rainless. *See* **dry** (2). 2. Lacking liveliness, charm, or surprise ► aseptic, colorless, pedestrian. *See* **dull** (1).
arise *verb*
1. To adopt a standing posture ► get up, rise. *See* **stand** (1). 2. To leave one's bed ► get up, roll out. *See* **rise** (2). 3. To move from a lower to a higher position ► ascend, climb, soar. *See* **rise** (3). 4. To come into being ► commence, originate. *See* **begin** (1). 5. To have as a source ► derive, emanate, originate. *See* **stem** (1). *See synonym note at* **stem.**
aristocracy *noun*
► elite, gentry, nobility. *See* **society** (1).
aristocratic *adjective*
► blue-blooded, elite, upper-class. *See* **noble** (1).
arithmetic *noun*
Arithmetic calculations ► computation, figures, numbers. *See also* **addition, calculation.**
ark *noun*
► haven, refuge, sanctuary. *See* **cover** (1).
arm *noun*
1. Something resembling or analogous to a tree branch ► division, fork, offshoot. *See* **branch** (1). *See synonym note at* **branch.** 2. An administrative unit, as of a government or company ► agency, bureau. *See* **branch** (3). 3. A part added to a main structure ► annex, wing. *See* **extension** (4).
arm *verb*
To prepare oneself for action ► fortify, ready, steel. *See* **gird** (1).
armada *noun*
A group of warships operating under one command ► fleet, flotilla.

armchair *adjective*
► academic, conceptual, speculative. *See* **theoretical** (1). *See synonym note at* **theoretical.**
armistice *noun*
► cease-fire, peace. *See* **truce.**
armpit *noun*
Slang A place known for its great filth or corruption ► cesspool, sewer. *See* **pit**[1] (3).
army *noun*
► horde, mass, throng. *See* **crowd** (1).
aroma *noun*
1. The quality of something that may be perceived by the olfactory sense ► odor, scent, smell. 2. A sweet or pleasant odor ► bouquet, perfume, scent. *See* **fragrance.** *See synonym note at* **fragrance.** 3. A distinctive yet intangible quality ► atmosphere, flavor, savor, smack. *See also* **quality.**
aromatic *adjective*
1. Having a pleasant odor ► perfumy, redolent, savory. *See* **fragrant.** 2. Having a sharp, penetrating flavor or aroma ► piquant, sharp, zesty. *See* **spicy** (1).
aromatize *verb*
To fill with a pleasant odor ► perfume, scent.
around *adverb*
1. Near to in quantity or amount ► almost, nearly, roughly. *See* **approximately.** 2. Toward the back ► about, rearward. *See* **backward.**
around *adjective*
Having life ► live, living, vital. *See* **alive** (1).
around-the-clock *adjective*
► constant, endless, everlasting. *See* **continual.**
arouse *verb*
1. To induce or elicit a reaction or emotion ► agitate, awake, awaken, kindle, raise, rouse, stir (up), waken. *See also* **provoke.** 2. To inflame the emotions of ► impassion, inspire, stir. *See* **fire** (2). 3. To cease or cause to cease sleeping ► awake, stir, waken. *See* **wake**[1].

✦ CORE SYNONYMS: *arouse, rouse, stir.* These verbs mean to induce or elicit a reaction or emotion. To *arouse* means to awaken, as from inactivity or apathy; *rouse* means the same, but more strongly implies vigorous or emotional excitement: *"In a democratic society like ours, relief must come through an aroused popular conscience that sears the conscience of the people's representatives"* (Felix Frankfurter). *"The oceangoing steamers . . . roused in him wild and painful longings"* (Arnold Bennett). To *stir* is to cause activity, strong but usually agreeable feelings, trouble, or commotion: *"It was him as stirred up th' young woman to preach last night"* (George Eliot). *"I have seldom been so . . . stirred by any piece of writing"* (Mark Twain).

---

arraign *verb*
► denounce, incriminate, inculpate, recriminate. *See* **accuse.**
arraigner *noun*
One that accuses ► accuser, denouncer, indicter, recriminator.

arraignment *noun*
▶ denouncement, imputation, incrimination. *See* **accusation.**

arrange *verb*
1. To put into a deliberate order ▶ array, codify, collocate, deploy, dispose, marshal, methodize, order, organize, range, regiment, regulate, sort, systemize, systematize. *See also* **classify, line. 2.** To plan the details or arrangements of ▶ blueprint, lay out, map (out), organize, plan, prepare, schedule, set out (*or* up), work out. *Idioms:* get (*or* put) into shape. *See also* **design, draft. 3.** To combine and adapt in order to attain a particular effect ▶ blend, integrate. *See* **harmonize (2). 4.** To bring something into a state of agreement or accord ▶ conclude, fix, negotiate, set. *See* **settle (2). 5.** To put into correct or conclusive form ▶ conclude, fix. *See* **settle (1). 6.** To make a concession ▶ accommodate, settle. *See* **compromise (1).**

✦ CORE SYNONYMS: *arrange, marshal, order, organize, sort, systematize.* These verbs mean to put things or people in a deliberate order: *arranging figures numerically; had to marshal all relevant facts for presentation; ordered the plants by genus; organized the fundraiser; sorted the sweaters by color; systematized the assorted files.*

arrangement *noun*
1. The act or condition of being arranged ▶ allotment, alignment, assortment, categorization, classification, codification, deployment, disposal, disposition, distribution, format, formation, grouping, harmonization, layout, lineup, orchestration, order, ordering, organization, positioning, ranking, sequence, setup. **2.** An often written acceptance of terms between parties ▶ accord, deal, pact. *See* **agreement (1). 3.** A settlement of differences through mutual concession ▶ accommodation, give-and-take, settlement. *See* **compromise. 4.** An organized array of individual elements and parts forming and working as a unit ▶ totality, whole. *See* **system (1).**

arrangements *noun*
Steps taken in preparation for an undertaking ▶ accommodations, plans, preparations, provisions.

arrant *adjective*
▶ all-out, pure, sheer. *See* **utter².**

array *verb*
1. To put into a deliberate order ▶ deploy, marshal, systematize. *See* **arrange (1). 2.** To dress in formal or special clothing ▶ attire, deck (out). *See* **dress up.**

array *noun*
1. An impressive or ostentatious exhibition ▶ display, manifestation, pageant, panoply, parade, pomp, show, spectacle. **2.** A number of individuals making up or considered a unit ▶ body, cluster, collection. *See* **group (1). 3.** Showy and elaborate clothing or apparel ▶ finery, regalia. *See* **attire (1).**

✦ CORE SYNONYMS: *array, display, panoply, parade, pomp.* These nouns denote an impressive or ostentatious exhibition: *an array of diamond rings; a tasteless display of wealth; a panoply of medals; a parade of knowledge and virtue; ceremonial pomp.*

arrears *or* **arrearage** *noun*
1. Something, such as money, owed by one person to another ▶ indebtedness, liability, obligation. *See* **debt** (1). **2.** A condition of owing something to another ▶ encumbrance, liability, obligation. *See* **debt** (2).

arrest *verb*
1. To take into custody as a prisoner ▶ apprehend, seize. *Informal:* nab, pick up. *Slang:* bust, collar, cuff, haul up, pinch, pull in, run in. *Idioms:* take charge (*or* hold) of. *See also* **catch, take. 2.** To prevent the occurrence or continuation of a movement, action, or operation ▶ check, immobilize. *See* **stop (2). 3.** To compel the attention, interest, or imagination of ▶ captivate, fascinate, mesmerize. *See* **grip (1).**

arrest *noun*
1. A seizing and holding by law ▶ apprehension, seizure. *Slang:* bust, collar, pickup, pinch. *See also* **catch. 2.** The state of being detained by legal authority ▶ confinement, custody, detainment. *See* **detention.**

arresting *adjective*
▶ conspicuous, outstanding, prominent. *See* **noticeable (1).** *See synonym note at* **noticeable.**

arrival *noun*
1. The act of arriving ▶ advent, appearance, coming. *See also* **entrance. 2.** One that arrives ▶ comer, newcomer, visitor. *See also* **addition, company. 3.** Something completed or attained sucessfully ▶ achievement, feat, triumph. *See* **accomplishment (1).**

arrive *verb*
1. To come to a particular place ▶ breeze in, check in, come, drop in, get in, make it, pop in, pull in, reach, roll in (*or* up), show up, turn up. *Slang:* blow in. *Idioms:* arrive (*or* come) onto the scene, make (*or* put in) an appearance, make the scene. **2.** To gain success ▶ get ahead, get on, rise, succeed. *Idioms:* go far, go places, make good, make it. **3.** To take place ▶ befall, come, occur. *See* **happen (1).**

arrive at *verb*
To reach a goal or objective ▶ achieve, attain, gain. *See* **accomplish (1).**

arrogance *noun*
The quality of being arrogant ▶ braggodocio, disdainfulness, haughtiness, hauteur, hubris, insolence, loftiness, lordliness, overbearingness, pomposity, pompousness, presumption, pride, pridefulness, priggishness, proudness, self-importance, self-satisfaction, smugness, superciliousness, superiority. *See also* **egotism, impudence.**

arrogant *adjective*
Overly convinced of one's own superiority and importance ▶ disdainful, haughty, high-and-mighty, hubristic, insolent, lofty, lordly, overbearing, overweening, prideful, priggish, proud, self-important, self-satisfied, smug, supercilious, superior. *Informal:* high-hat, snooty, swellheaded. *Idioms:* full of oneself,

on one's high horse. *See also* **dictatorial, egotistic, pompous, snobbish.**

✦ CORE SYNONYMS: *arrogant, proud, haughty, disdainful, supercilious.* These adjectives refer to one who is overly convinced of one's own superiority and importance. One who is *arrogant* is overbearing and demands excessive power or consideration: *an arrogant and pompous professor, unpopular with students and colleagues alike. Proud* can suggest justifiable self-satisfaction but often implies conceit: *"There is such a thing as a man being too proud to fight"* (Woodrow Wilson). *Haughty* suggests proud superiority, as by reason of high status: *"Her laugh was satirical, and so was the habitual expression of her arched and haughty lip"* (Charlotte Brontë). *Disdainful* emphasizes scorn or contempt: *"Nor [let] grandeur hear with a disdainful smile,/The short and simple annals of the poor"* (Thomas Gray). *Supercilious* implies haughty disdain and aloofness: *"His mother eyed me in silence with a supercilious air"* (Tobias Smollett).

---

arrogate *verb*
▸ appropriate, preempt, usurp. *See* **seize** (1). *See synonym note at* **seize.**

arrogation *noun*
▸ expropriation, usurpation. *See* **seizure** (2).

art *noun*
1. Deceitful cleverness ▸ artfulness, artifice, cleverness, craft, craftiness, cunning, deceitfulness, deviousness, disingenuousness, foxiness, guile, shrewdness, slyness, wiliness. *See also* **deceit, dishonesty, stealth. 2.** Activity pursued as a livelihood ▸ career, employment, occupation. *See* **business** (2). **3.** Natural or acquired skill or talent ▸ adeptness, expertise, mastery. *See* **ability** (1). *See synonym note at* **ability.**

artery *noun*
▸ canal, duct, vein. *See* **vessel** (2).

artful *adjective*
1. Deceitfully clever ▸ calculating, crafty, cunning, designing, double-dealing, foxy, guileful, scheming, sharp, shrewd, sly, tricky, wily. *See also* **shrewd, stealthy, underhand. 2.** Exhibiting or possessing skill and ease in performance ▸ adroit, deft, skillful. *See* **dexterous.**

artfulness *noun*
▸ artifice, craftiness, slyness. *See* **art** (1).

article *noun*
1. An individually considered portion of a whole ▸ detail, item. *See* **element** (3). **2.** Something having material existence ▸ body, item, thing. *See* **object** (1). **3.** A detail of news information ▸ feature, piece, story. *See* **item** (1).

article of faith *noun*
▸ canon, dogma, teaching. *See* **doctrine.**

articulacy *or* **articulateness** *noun*
▸ fluency, rhetoric. *See* **eloquence.**

articulate *adjective*
1. Expressed or produced in speech or by the voice ▸ spoken, verbal, vocal, voiced. *See* **oral. 2.** Fluently

persuasive and forceful ▸ silver-tongued, smooth-spoken. *See* **eloquent** (1).

articulate *verb*
1. To produce or make speech sounds ▸ enunciate, vocalize. *See* **pronounce. 2.** To put into words ▸ express, state, utter. *See* **say** (1). **3.** To bring or come together into a united whole ▸ join, unify, unite. *See* **combine** (1).

articulation *noun*
1. The act or an instance of expressing in words ▸ utterance, verbalization. *See* **expression** (1). **2.** The use of the vocal organs to produce sound or speech ▸ enunciation, utterance, vocalization. *See* **voicing.**

artifice *noun*
1. An indirect, usually cunning means of gaining an end ▸ deception, ploy, stratagem. *See* **trick** (1). *See synonym note at* **trick. 2.** Deceitful cleverness ▸ artfulness, craftiness, slyness. *See* **art** (1).

artificial *adjective*
1. Made by humans, often in imitation of something else ▸ ersatz, imitation, manmade, manufactured, mock, pretend, simulated, synthetic. *Informal:* pretend. *See also* **counterfeit, fake. 2.** Not genuine or sincere ▸ affected, contrived, feigned, insincere, phony, pretended, stagy, studied. *Slang:* phony-baloney. *See also* **pompous.**

✦ CORE SYNONYMS: *artificial, synthetic, ersatz, simulated.* These adjectives refer to what is made by humans rather than natural in origin. *Artificial* is broadest in meaning and connotation: *an artificial sweetener; artificial flowers. Synthetic* often implies the use of a chemical process to produce a substance that will look or function like the original, often with certain advantages: *synthetic rubber; a synthetic fabric.* An *ersatz* product is a transparently inferior imitation: *ersatz coffee; ersatz mink. Simulated* often refers to a fabricated substitute or imitation of a costlier substance: *simulated diamonds.*

---

artificiality *noun*
1. Lack of sincerity ▸ disingenuousness, phoniness. *See* **insincerity. 2.** Behavior that is assumed rather than natural ▸ airs, mannerism. *See* **affectation** (1).

artisan *noun*
▸ builder, constructor, manufacturer. *See* **maker** (1).

artistic *adjective*
1. Relating to or appreciative of the arts ▸ aesthetic, creative. *Informal:* artsy, arty. **2.** Characterized by or productive of new things or new ideas ▸ ingenious, innovative, original. *See* **inventive** (1).

artless *adjective*
1. Free from guile, cunning, or deceit ▸ guileless, ingenuous, innocent, naive, natural, simple, unaffected, unsophisticated, unstudied, unworldly. *See also* **frank, genuine, innocent. 2.** Of a charmingly plain and unsophisticated nature ▸ homely, homespun, natural. *See* **rustic** (1).

✦ CORE SYNONYMS: *artless, naive, simple, ingenuous, unsophisticated, natural, unaffected, guileless.* These adjectives mean free from guile, cunning, or deceit. *Artless* stresses absence of plan or purpose and suggests unconcern for or lack of awareness of the reaction produced in others: *a child of artless grace and simple goodness. Naive* sometimes connotes a credulity that impedes effective functioning in a practical world: *"this naive simple creature, with his straightforward and friendly eyes so eager to believe appearances"* (Arnold Bennett). *Simple* stresses absence of complexity, artifice, pretentiousness, or dissimulation: *"Those of highest worth and breeding are most simple in manner and attire"* (Francis Parkman). *"Among simple people she had the reputation of being a prodigy of information"* (Harriet Beecher Stowe). *Ingenuous* denotes childlike directness, simplicity, and innocence; it connotes an inability to mask one's feelings; *an ingenuous admission of responsibility. Unsophisticated* indicates absence of worldliness: *the astonishment of unsophisticated tourists at the tall buildings. Natural* stresses spontaneity that is the result of freedom from self-consciousness or inhibitions: *"When Kavanagh was present, Alice was happy, but embarrassed; Cecelia, joyous and natural"* (Henry Wadsworth Longfellow). *Unaffected* implies sincerity and lack of affectation: *"With men he can be rational and unaffected, but when he has ladies to please, every feature works"* (Jane Austen). *Guileless* signifies absence of insidious or treacherous cunning: *a guileless, disarming look.*

artlessness *noun*
The absence of guile, cunning, or deceit ▸ guilelessness, ingenuousness, innocence, naiveté, naturalness, simpleness, simplicity, unsophistication, unworldliness. *See also* **honesty.**

artsy-craftsy *adjective*
Informal Pretentiously artistic ▸ *Informal:* arty.

arty *or* **artsy** *adjective*
1. *Informal* Relating to or appreciative of the arts ▸ aesthetic, artistic, creative. **2.** *Informal* Pretentiously artistic ▸ *Informal:* artsy-craftsy.

as *conjunction*
▸ for, seeing as. *See* **because.**

ascend *verb*
1. To move upward along a surface or slope ▸ clamber, climb, go up, mount, scale, scramble. **2.** To move from a lower to a higher position ▸ arise, climb, soar. *See* **rise** (3). *See synonym note at* **rise. 3.** To attain a higher status, rank, or condition ▸ advance, climb, mount. *See* **rise** (6).

ascendance *or* **ascendancy** *noun*
▸ authority, power, supremacy. *See* **dominance** (1).

ascendant *adjective*
Exercising controlling power or influence ▸ key, predominant, reigning. *See* **dominant** (1).

ascendant *noun*
A person from whom one is descended ▸ forebear, parent, progenitor. *See* **ancestor** (1).

ascension *noun*
▸ climb, mounting. *See* **ascent** (1).

ascent *noun*
1. The act of rising or moving upward ▸ ascension,

climb, climbing, lift, mounting, rise, rising. *See also* **increase. 2.** An upward path or surface ▸ acclivity, grade, gradient, inclined plane, rise, slant, slope. *See also* **elevation, hill.**

ascertain *verb*
1. To obtain knowledge or awareness of something not known before ▸ determine, learn, unearth. *See* **discover.** *See synonym note at* **discover. 2.** To perceive and fix the identity of, especially with difficulty ▸ descry, recognize. *See* **discern** (1).

ascertainment *noun*
▸ conclusion, result, strike. *See* **discovery.**

ascetic *adjective*
Renouncing material comforts and pleasures ▸ abstinent, austere, monkish, puritan, puritanical, self-denying. *See also* **meager, temperate.**

ascribe *verb*
1. To regard as belonging to or resulting from another ▸ accredit, assign. *See* **attribute** (1). *See synonym note at* **attribute. 2.** To assign the blame for a misdeed or error ▸ attribute, blame, pin. *See* **fix** (13).

aseptic *adjective*
1. Lacking liveliness, charm, or surprise ▸ arid, colorless, pedestrian. *See* **dull** (1). **2.** Free or freed from microorganisms ▸ antiseptic, hygienic, sanitary. *See* **sterile** (1).

asepticism *noun*
▸ blandness, drabness, lifelessness. *See* **dullness** (1).

ashen *or* **ashy** *adjective*
▸ bloodless, lurid, wan. *See* **pale** (1).

ashes *noun*
The substance of the body, especially after decay or cremation ▸ clay, cremains, dust, remains.

aside *noun*
1. An instance of digressing ▸ deviation, divergence, tangent. *See* **digression. 2.** An expression of fact or opinion ▸ observation, reflection, remark. *See* **comment** (1).

asinine *adjective*
▸ daft, idiotic, ludicrous. *See* **foolish.**

ask *verb*
1. To put a question to someone ▸ cross-examine, examine, inquire, interrogate, query, question, quiz, pump. *Informal:* grill. **Idiom:** give someone the third degree. **2.** To seek an answer to a question ▸ pose, put, raise. *See also* **say. 3.** To request that someone take part in or be present at a particular occasion ▸ bid, invite, summon. **Idioms:** extend an invitation to, request the presence of. *See also* **request. 4.** To make an earnest or urgent request ▸ beseech, entreat, petition, plead. *See* **appeal** (1). **5.** To have as a need or prerequisite ▸ call for, entail, involve, necessitate. *See* **demand** (2).

✦ CORE SYNONYMS: *ask, question, inquire, query, interrogate, examine, quiz.* These verbs mean to put a question to or seek information from someone. *Ask* is the most neutral term: *The coach asked me what was wrong. Question* implies careful and continuous asking: *The prosecutor questioned the witness in great detail. Inquire* refers to a simple request for information: *The committee will inquire how it can be of help. Query* usually suggests settling a doubt: *The proofreader queried the spelling of the word. Interrogate* applies especially to official questioning: *The detectives interrogated the suspects. Examine* refers particularly to close and detailed questioning to ascertain a person's knowledge or qualifications: *Only lawyers who have been examined and certified by the bar association are admitted to practice. Quiz* denotes the informal examination of students: *The teacher quizzed the pupils on the state capitals.*

askance *adverb*
▸ doubtfully, questioningly. *See* **skeptically.**

asleep *adjective*
1. In a state of sleep ▸ snoozing, unawake. *See* **sleeping** (1). **2.** Lacking physical feeling or sensitivity ▸ inert, numb, unfeeling. *See* **dead** (2). **3.** No longer alive ▸ deceased, departed, perished. *See* **dead** (1).

aspect *noun*
1. A disposition of the facial features that conveys meaning, feeling, or mood ▸ countenance, look, visage. *See* **expression** (4). **2.** The way something or someone looks ▸ look, features, mien. *See* **appearance** (1). **3.** An outward appearance ▸ countenance, features. *See* **face** (4). **4.** The position from which something is observed or considered ▸ facet, point of view, standpoint. *See* **viewpoint.**

asperity *noun*
▸ complication, hardship, rigor. *See* **difficulty** (1).

asperse *verb*
▸ calumniate, defame, slander. *See* **malign.** *See synonym note at* **malign.**

aspersion *noun*
1. The expression of injurious, malicious statements about someone ▸ defamation, denigration, slander. *See* **libel. 2.** An act that offends a person's sense of pride or dignity ▸ contumely, insult. *See* **indignity.**

asphyxiate *verb*
▸ smother, stifle, suffocate. *See* **choke** (1).

aspirant *noun*
1. One who aspires ▸ aspirer, dreamer, hopeful, seeker. *Informal:* wannabe. **2.** A person who applies for or seeks something, such as a job or position ▸ candidate, hopeful, petitioner. *See* **applicant.**

aspiration *noun*
1. A strong desire to achieve something ▸ ambition, ambitiousness, emulation. *See also* **drive, enthusiasm, thirst. 2.** A fervent hope ▸ desire, vision, wish. *See* **dream** (3).

aspire *verb*
1. To strive toward a goal ▸ aim, seek. *Idioms:* go (*or* grab) for the brass ring, keep one's eyes on the prize, set one's sights on. **2.** To have a strong loging for ▸ dream, yearn. *See* **desire** (1).

aspirer *noun*
One who aspires ▸ aspirant, dreamer, hopeful, seeker. *Informal:* wannabe.

aspiring *adjective*
▸ determined, enterprising. *See* **ambitious.**

ass *noun*
▸ idiot, moron, simpleton. *See* **fool** (1).

assail *verb*
1. To hit heavily and repeatedly ▸ assault, batter, pummel, thresh. *See* **beat** (1). **2.** To attack with harsh, often insulting language ▸ abuse, blaspheme. *See* **revile. 3.** To set upon with violent force ▸ assault, storm, strike. *See* **attack** (1). *See synonym note at* **attack.**

assailability *noun*
▸ endangerment, susceptibility, vulnerability. *See* **exposure** (1).

assailable *adjective*
▸ attackable, helpless, unprotected. *See* **vulnerable** (1).

assailant *or* **assailer** *noun*
▸ assaulter, attacker, provoker. *See* **aggressor.**

assailment *noun*
▸ assault, offense, strike. *See* **attack** (1).

assassin *noun*
▸ killer, massacrer, slayer. *See* **murderer.**

assassinate *verb*
▸ assassinate, kill, slay. *See* **murder** (1).

assassination *noun*
▸ homicide, killing, manslaughter. *See* **murder.**

assault *noun*
The act of attacking ▸ aggression, offense, strike. *See* **attack** (1). *See synonym note at* **attack.**

assault *verb*
1. To set upon with violent force ▸ assail, storm, strike. *See* **attack** (1). **2.** To hit heavily and repeatedly ▸ assail, batter, pummel, thresh. *See* **beat** (1). **3.** To compel another to participate in or submit to a sexual act ▸ force, molest, rape, ravish, violate.

assaulter *noun*
▸ assailant, attacker, provoker. *See* **aggressor.**

assay *verb*
1. To subject to a test of effectiveness, value, function, or other quality ▸ check, essay, try (out). *See* **test** (1). **2.** To make a judgment as to the worth or value of ▸ assay, calculate. *See* **estimate** (1). *See synonym note at* **estimate. 3.** To make an attempt ▸ endeavor, strive. *See* **attempt.**

assay *noun*
A procedure that ascertains effectiveness, value, proper function, or other quality ▸ proof, trial, tryout. *See* **test** (1).

assemblage *noun*
1. A quantity accumulated ▸ aggregation, collection, gathering. *See* **accumulation** (1). **2.** A number of persons who have come or been gathered together ▸ conference, crowd, group. *Informal:* get-together. *See* **assembly** (1).

assemble *verb*
1. To come, bring, or call together ▸ call, cluster, collect, congregate, convene, convoke, forgather, gather, get together, group, muster, round up, send for, summon. *See also* **mobilize. 2.** To bring together so as to increase in mass or number ▸ collect, gather, group. *See* **accumulate.** *See synonym note at* **accumu-**

late. **3.** To create by forming, combining, or altering materials ▸ build, compose, shape. *See* **make** (1).

✦ **CORE SYNONYMS:** *assemble, convene, convoke, muster, summon.* These verbs mean to come, bring, or call together: *assembled the troops; convened a meeting; will convoke the legislature; mustering the militia; summoned a witness.*

---

assembler *noun*
▸ builder, constructor, manufacturer. *See* **maker** (1).

assembly *noun*
1. A number of persons who have come or been gathered together ▸ assemblage, body, company, conclave, conference, congregation, congress, convention, convocation, council, crowd, forum, galaxy, gathering, group, meeting, muster, rally, troop. *Informal:* get-together. *See also* **attendance, band², crowd, force. 2.** A formal assemblage of the members of a group ▸ conference, congress. *See* **convention** (1).

assent *verb*
To respond affirmatively; receive with agreement or compliance ▸ accede, accept, acquiesce, agree, concur, consent, nod, subscribe, yes. *See also* **acknowledge, agree, approve, permit.**

assent *noun*
1. The act of accepting or adopting ▸ adoption, agreement, consent. *See* **acceptance** (1). **2.** The approving of an action, especially when done by one in authority ▸ authorization, consent, sanction. *See* **permission.**

✦ **CORE SYNONYMS:** *assent, agree, accede, acquiesce, consent, concur.* These verbs denote an affirmative response to or acceptance of something, as another person's views, proposals, or actions. *Assent* implies agreement, especially as a result of deliberation: *They readily assented to our suggestion. Agree* and *accede* are related in the sense that assent has been reached after discussion or persuasion, but *accede* implies that one person or group has yielded to the other: *"It was not possible to agree to a proposal so extraordinary and unexpected"* (William Robertson). *"In an evil hour this proposal was acceded to"* (Mary E. Herbert). *Acquiesce* suggests passive assent because of inability or unwillingness to oppose: *I acquiesced in their decision despite my misgivings. Consent* implies voluntary agreement: *Our parents consented to our marriage. Concur* suggests that one has independently reached the same conclusion as another: *"I concurred with our incumbent in getting up a petition against the Reform Bill"* (George Eliot).

---

assenting *adjective*
1. Giving assent ▸ approving, positive. *See* **favorable** (2). **2.** Being in or characterized by complete agreement ▸ accordant, consonant, like-minded. *See* **unanimous.**

assert *verb*
1. To put into words positively and with conviction ▸ affirm, allege, argue, asseverate, aver, avouch, avow, claim, contend, declare, enounce, enunciate, hold, insist, maintain, profess, say, state, swear. *Idiom:* have it. *See also* **announce, confirm, stipulate, support. 2.** To defend, maintain, or insist on the recognition of ▸ demand, vindicate. *See* **claim** (1).

assertion *noun*
The act of asserting positively or something so asserted ▸ affirmation, allegation, asseveration, averment, avowal, claim, contention, declaration, profession, statement. *See also* **announcement, assumption.**

assertive *adjective*
Bold or confident in assertion ▸ aggressive, emphatic, forceful, insistent, in-your-face. *Informal:* go-ahead. *See also* **definite, dictatorial, frank.**

assess *verb*
1. To establish and apply as compulsory ▸ exact, impose, levy, put. **2.** To make a judgment as to the worth or value of ▸ appraise, calculate. *See* **estimate** (1). *See synonym note at* **estimate.**

assessed *adjective*
▸ deliberate, intentional, premeditated. *See* **calculated** (1).

assessment *noun*
1. The act or result of evaluating or appraising ▸ appraisal, evaluation. *See* **estimate** (1). **2.** A compulsory contribution that is required for the support of an authority ▸ duty, levy, tariff. *See* **tax** (1).

assessor *noun*
▸ judge, reviewer. *See* **critic** (1).

asset *noun*
1. A particularly good or beneficial quality ▸ distinction, merit. *See* **virtue** (1). **2.** A person who secretly observes others to obtain information ▸ agent, operative. *See* **spy.**

assets *noun*
1. Money or property used to produce more wealth ▸ financing, funding, stake. *See* **capital** (1). **2.** Things that have economic value ▸ capital, wealth, wherewithal. *See* **resources** (1).

asseverate *verb*
▸ avow, declare, maintain. *See* **assert** (1).

asseveration *noun*
▸ claim, declaration, statement. *See* **assertion.**

assiduity *or* **assiduousness** *noun*
▸ application, perseverance, pertinacity. *See* **diligence.**

assiduous *adjective*
▸ industrious, sedulous, studious. *See* **diligent.** *See synonym note at* **diligent.**

assign *verb*
1. To appoint and send to a particular place ▸ post, set, station. *See also* **position. 2.** To set aside or apart for a specified purpose ▸ allot, designate, earmark. *See* **appropriate** (1). **3.** To give out in portions or shares ▸ allocate, apportion, dispense. *See* **distribute** (1). **4.** To regard as belonging to or resulting from another ▸ ascribe, credit. *See* **attribute** (1). *See synonym note at* **attribute. 5.** To ascribe the blame for a misdeed or error ▸ attribute, blame, pin. *See* **fix** (13). **6.** To change the ownership of property by means of a legal

document ▸ deed, grant, sign over. *See* **transfer** (1).
7. To select for an office or position ▸ elect, name, nominate. *See* **appoint** (1).

assignation *noun*
▸ date, rendezvous. *See* **engagement** (1). *See synonym note at* **engagement**.

assignment *noun*
1. The act of distributing or the condition of being distributed ▸ allocation, apportionment, dispensation. *See* **distribution** (1). **2.** A piece of work that has been assigned ▸ chore, duty, job. *See* **task** (1). *See synonym note at* **task**. **3.** Legal transfer of ownership or title ▸ alienation, transfer, transferal. *See* **grant**. **4.** The act of appointing to an office or position ▸ designation, election, nomination. *See* **appointment** (1).

assimilate *verb*
1. To take in and incorporate, especially mentally ▸ digest, imbibe, take up. *See* **absorb** (2). **2.** To represent as similar ▸ compare, equate, parallel. *See* **liken**.

assimilation *noun*
▸ digestion, incorporation, osmosis. *See* **absorption** (1).

assimilative *adjective*
▸ absorptive, bibulous, imbibing. *See* **absorbent**.

assist *verb*
1. To give assistance to ▸ aid, boost. *See* **help** (1). *See synonym note at* **help**. **2.** To perform a service or a courteous act for ▸ favor, serve. *See* **oblige** (1).

assist *noun*
The act or an instance of helping ▸ aid, relief. *See* **help** (1).

assistance *noun*
▸ aid, relief. *See* **help** (1).

assistant *noun*
A person who assists someone else, especially a person who assumes some of the duties of a superior ▸ abettor, adjutant, aid, aide, attendant, auxiliary, coadjutant, coadjutor, deputy, help, helper, lieutenant, reliever, second, succorer. *Slang:* gofer. **Idioms:** man (*or* girl) Friday, right-hand man (*or* woman), second in command. *See also* **associate, follower, minor, subordinate**.

assistant *adjective*
Giving or able to give help or support ▸ accessory, subsidiary. *See* **auxiliary** (1).

✚ CORE SYNONYMS: *assistant, aide, coadjutant, coadjutor, helper, lieutenant, second.* These nouns denote a person who holds a position auxiliary to another and assumes some of the superior's responsibilities: *an editorial assistant; a senator's aide; the general's coadjutant; a bishop's coadjutor; a teacher's helper; a politician's lieutenant; a prizefighter's second.*

assize *noun*
▸ bill, legislation. *See* **law** (2).

associate *verb*
1. To unite or be united in a relationship ▸ amalgamate, affiliate, ally, bind, combine, conjoin, connect,

federate, incorporate, join, link, relate. *See also* **band, combine**. **2.** To be with as a companion ▸ be friendly, be intimate, consort, fall in with, fraternize, hang around, hobnob, pal (around), run (around), take up with, troop. *Slang:* hang out. **Idioms:** have relations, keep company, rub elbows (*or* shoulders). **3.** To come or bring together in one's mind or imagination ▸ bracket, connect, correlate, couple, identify, link. *See also* **equal, liken**.

associate *noun*
1. One who is united in a relationship with another ▸ affiliate, ally, cohort, colleague, compatriot, confederate, copartner, fellow, partner. *See also* **peer**[2] **2.** One who shares interests or activities with another ▸ chum, companion, comrade, crony, fellow, mate. *Informal:* bud, buddy, pal. *Slang:* sidekick. **Idiom:** partner in crime. *See also* **friend**. **3.** One that accompanies another ▸ attendant, companion. *See* **concomitant**.

✚ CORE SYNONYMS: *associate, partner, colleague, ally, confederate.* These nouns denote one who is united in a relationship, as in a venture, with another. An *associate* is the most general term: *ate lunch with her business associates every Wednesday.* A *partner* participates in a relationship in which each member has equal status: *a partner in a law firm.* A *colleague* is an associate in an occupation or profession: *a colleague and fellow professor.* An *ally* is one who associates with another, at least temporarily, in a common cause: *countries that were allies in World War II.* A *confederate* is a member of a confederacy, league, or alliance or sometimes a collaborator in a suspicious venture: *confederates in a scheme to oust the chairman.*

association *noun*
1. The state of being associated ▸ affiliation, alliance, combination, conjunction, connection, cooperation, partnership. *See also* **friendship, relation**. **2.** Something, such as a feeling or idea, associated with a specific person or thing ▸ connection, connotation, impression, suggestion. **3.** A group of people united in a relationship and having some interest, activity, or purpose in common ▸ club, league, order. *See* **union** (1). **4.** A group of athletic teams that play each other ▸ circuit, league. *See* **conference** (6).

assort *verb*
▸ categorize, class, group. *See* **classify**.

assorted *adjective*
▸ diverse, miscellaneous, sundry. *See* **various** (1). *See synonym note at* **various**.

assortment *noun*
1. A collection of various things ▸ conglomeration, gallimaufry, hodgepodge, jumble, medley, mélange, miscellany, mishmash, mixed bag, mixture, olio, patchwork, potpourri, salmagundi, variety. *Slang:* grab bag. *See also* **combination, mixture**. **2.** The act or condition of being arranged ▸ allotment, distribution, positioning. *See* **arrangement** (1).

assuage *verb*
1. To make less severe or more bearable ▸ allay,

alleviate, ease. *See* **relieve** (1). *See synonym note at* **relieve**. **2.** To ease the anger or agitation of ▶ appease, mollify, soothe. *See* **pacify**.

assuagement *noun*
▶ ease, mitigation, palliation. *See* **relief** (2).

assume *verb*
1. To take upon oneself ▶ incur, shoulder, tackle, take on, take over, undertake. *See also* **endure, take**. **2.** To take and make one's own ▶ appropriate, embrace, take on. *See* **adopt** (1). **3.** To put an article of clothing on one's person ▶ put on, slip on. *See* **don** (1). **4.** To take on as a false appearance ▶ counterfeit, fake, feign, pretend. *See* **act** (2). **5.** To consider to be true without proof ▶ posit, presume, presuppose. *See* **suppose** (1). *See synonym note at* **suppose**. **6.** To lay claim to or take possession of ▶ appropriate, preempt, usurp. *See* **seize** (1).

assumed *adjective*
Being fictitious and not real, as a name ▶ made-up, pretended, pseudonymous. *See also* **false, fictitious**.

assuming *adjective*
▶ bold, insolent, pert. *See* **impudent**.

assumption *noun*
1. Something taken to be true without proof ▶ axiom, assertion, given, lemma, postulate, postulation, premise, presumption, presupposition, speculation, supposition. *See also* **assertion, theory**. **2.** The act of taking possession of something ▶ expropriation, preemption, usurpation. *See* **seizure** (2). **3.** The state or quality of being impudent or arrogantly self-confident ▶ audacity, boldness, impertinence. *See* **impudence**.

assumptive *adjective*
1. Based on probability or presumption ▶ likely, presumable, prospective. *See* **presumptive**. **2.** Rude and disrespectful ▶ bold, insolent, pert. *See* **impudent**.

assurance *noun*
1. A declaration that one will or will not do a certain thing ▶ covenant, pledge, vow. *See* **promise** (1). **2.** The fact or condition of being without doubt ▶ assuredness, certainty, conviction. *See* **sureness** (1). *See synonym note at* **sureness**. **3.** The quality or state of being safe ▶ impenetrability, security. *See* **safety** (1). **4.** A firm belief in one's own powers ▶ aplomb, self-possession. *See* **confidence** (1). *See synonym note at* **confidence**. **5.** A tendency to expect a favorable outcome or to dwell on hopeful aspects ▶ enthusiasm, sanguinity. *See* **optimism**.

assure *verb*
1. To cause another to feel sure about something ▶ persuade, win over. *See* **convince** (1). **2.** To render certain ▶ ensure, warrant. *See* **guarantee** (2).

assured *adjective*
1. Having no doubt ▶ certain, confident, positive. *See* **sure** (1). **2.** Having a firm belief in one's own powers ▶ secure, self-confident, self-possessed. *See* **confident** (1). **3.** Expecting or suggesting a favorable outcome ▶ cheerful, sanguine. *See* **optimistic**.

assuredly *adverb*

▶ agreed, all right, aye. *See* **yes**.

assuredness *noun*
1. The fact or condition of being without doubt ▶ assurance, certainty, conviction. *See* **sureness** (1). **2.** Unwavering firmness of character, action, or will ▶ determination, purpose, resolve, will. *See* **decision** (2).

astir *adjective*
▶ bustling, crawling, swarming, teeming. *See* **busy** (2).

astonish *verb*
▶ amaze, astound. *See* **surprise** (1).

astonishing *adjective*
So remarkable as to be difficult to believe ▶ amazing, astounding, awe-inspiring, dumbfounding, fabulous, fantastic, flabbergasting, incredible, marvelous, miraculous, overwhelming, phenomenal, prodigious, staggering, stunning, stupendous, unbelievable, wonderful, wondrous. *Informal:* mind-blowing, mind-boggling. *See also* **exceptional, rare**.

astonishment *noun*
1. The emotion aroused by something awe-inspiring or astounding ▶ amazement, awe, marvel. *See* **wonder** (1). **2.** One that evokes great surprise and admiration ▶ prodigy, sensation, wonder. *See* **marvel** (1).

astound *verb*
▶ amaze, astonish. *See* **surprise** (1).

astounding *adjective*
▶ dumbfounding, staggering, unbelievable. *See* **astonishing**.

astray *adverb*
Not in the right way or on the proper course ▶ afield, amiss, awry, wrong. *See synonym note at* **wrong**.

astray *adjective*
Unable to find the correct way or place to go ▶ disoriented, stray. *See* **lost** (1).

astringent *adjective*
▶ caustic, scathing, sharp, vitriolic. *See* **biting**.

astronomical *adjective*
1. Of extraordinary size and power ▶ colossal, gigantic, mighty. *See* **enormous**. **2.** Of or relating to the heavens ▶ empyreal, supernal. *See* **heavenly** (2).

astute *adjective*
1. Having or showing a clever awareness and resourcefulness in practical matters ▶ canny, knowing, perspicacious. *See* **shrewd** (1). *See synonym note at* **shrewd**. **2.** Able to recognize small differences or draw fine distinctions ▶ discerning, discriminate, selective. *See* **discriminating** (1).

astuteness *noun*
1. Skill in perceiving, discriminating, or judging ▶ keenness, perceptiveness, shrewdness. *See* **discernment** (1). **2.** The ability to distinguish, especially to recognize small differences or draw fine distinctions ▶ acuteness, selectiveness, taste. *See* **discrimination** (1).

asylum *noun*
1. An institution that provides care and shelter ▶ hospice, shelter. *See* **home** (3). **2.** Something that physically protects, especially from danger ▶ harbor, haven, refuge. *See* **cover** (1). *See synonym note at* **cover**.

3. Protection or shelter, as from danger or hardship ▸ sanctuary, shelter. *See* **refuge** (1).

asymmetric *or* **asymmetrical** *adjective*
▸ crooked, nonuniform. *See* **irregular** (1).

asymmetry *noun*
▸ crookedness, jaggedness, unevenness. *See* **irregularity** (1).

atelier *noun*
An artist's workspace ▸ studio, workroom, workshop.

atheism *noun*
Lack of belief in God ▸ disbelief, faithlessness, godlessness, impiety, irreligion, unbelief.

atheist *noun*
One who does not believe in God ▸ heathen, infidel, non-believer, pagan.

atheistic *adjective*
Not believing in God ▸ disbelieving, faithless, godless, impious, irreligious, ungodly. *See also* **doubtful.**

athirst *adjective*
▸ avid, bursting. *See* **eager** (1).

athletic *adjective*
▸ brawny, robust, sturdy. *See* **muscular.** *See synonym note at* **muscular.**

atingle *adjective*
▸ excited, fired up, worked up. *See* **thrilled.**

atmosphere *noun*
1. The gaseous mixture enveloping the earth ▸ air, ether. 2. A general impression produced by a predominant quality or characteristic ▸ ambiance, aura, mood. *See* **air** (4). 3. The surrounding conditions and circumstances affecting growth or development ▸ climate, surroundings. *See* **environment** (2). 4. A distinctive yet intangible quality ▸ aroma, flavor, savor, smack. *See also* **quality.**

atmospheric *adjective*
Of or relating to air ▸ aerial, airy, pneumatic.

atomize *verb*
1. To reduce or become reduced to pieces or fragments ▸ crumble, decompose, fragment. *See* **disintegrate** (1). 2. To break up into tiny particles ▸ grind, mill. *See* **crush** (2).

atone *noun*
▸ expiate, pardon. *See* **purify** (1).

atonement *noun*
The act of making amends ▸ expiation, penance, reconciliation, reparation. *See also* **compensation, purification.**

atrium *noun*
▸ courtyard, enclosure, quad. *See* **court** (1).

atrocious *adjective*
1. Exceeding the bounds of morality, decency, or reason ▸ appalling, monstrous, shocking. *See* **outrageous.** 2. So objectionable as to deserve condemnation ▸ contemptible, disgusting, obnoxious. *See* **offensive** (1). 3. Extraordinarily painful or distressing ▸ excruciating, torturous. *See* **tormenting.**

atrociousness *noun*
▸ atrocity, heinousness, monstrousness. *See* **outrageousness.**

atrocity *noun*
1. The quality of being outrageous ▸ atrociousness, heinousness, monstrousness. *See* **outrageousness.**
2. A monstrous offense or evil ▸ enormity, monstrosity. *See* **outrage** (1).

atrophy *noun*
Descent to a lower level or condition ▸ decadence, decline, degeneration. *See* **deterioration** (1).

atrophy *verb*
To become lower in quality, character, or condition ▸ decline, degenerate, worsen. *See* **deteriorate** (1).

attach *verb*
1. To join one thing to another ▸ adjoin, append, affix, clamp, clip, connect, couple, fasten, fuse, fix, moor, secure. *See also* **bond, combine, join.** 2. To add as a supplement or an appendix ▸ add (on), affix, annex, append, subjoin.

attachment *noun*
1. A subordinate element added to another entity ▸ accessory, adjunct, appendage, appurtenance, supplement. *See also* **addition.** 2. The close physical union of two objects ▸ adhesion, cohesion. *See* **bond** (1). 3. An intense attachment to a person or thing ▸ devotion, fondness, liking. *See* **love** (1).

✛ CORE SYNONYMS: *attachment, appendage, appurtenance, adjunct, accessory.* These nouns denote subordinate elements added to another entity. An *attachment* adds a function to the thing to which it is connected: *The food processor has an attachment for kneading dough.* An *appendage* supplements without being essential: " . . . and the complete absence of appendages at the stern decreases hull resistance" (R.J.L. Dicker). An *appurtenance* belongs naturally as a subsidiary attribute, part, or member: *"an internationally known first-class hotel . . . equipped with such appurtenances as computers, word processors, copiers and telex"* (Oscar Millard). An *adjunct* is added as an auxiliary but is often self-sustaining: *"Intelligence analysts . . . believe that of all the countries of the Middle East, none use terrorism more effectively as an adjunct to diplomacy . . ."* (Elaine Sciolino). An *accessory* is usually nonessential but desirable: *Our new car has such accessories as air conditioning and a sunroof.*

---

attack *verb*
1. To set upon with violent force ▸ aggress, assail, assault, beset, bombard, charge, fall on (*or* upon), go at, have at, march against, rush, sail into, storm, strike. *Informal:* light into, pitch into. *Slang:* lay into, tear into. *Idioms:* gang up on, have a go at, let have it, open up on. *See also* **ambush, contend, raid.** 2. To start work on vigorously ▸ dive into, go at, plunge into, set to work, tackle, wade in (*or* into). *Idioms:* get a move on, get cracking (*or* moving), hop to it, look lively. *See also* **start.**

attack *noun*
1. The act of attacking ▸ aggression, assailment, assault, attempt, drive, offense, offensive, onrush, onset, onslaught, storming, strike. *See also* **advance, charge,**

siege. **2.** A method used for accomplishing something ▸ course, modus operandi, procedure, technique. *See* **approach** (1). **3.** A sudden and often acute manifestation of a disease ▸ apoplexy, fit. *See* **seizure** (1).

✛ CORE SYNONYMS: *attack, bombard, assail, storm, assault, beset.* These verbs mean to set upon with violent force, physically or figuratively. *Attack* applies to offensive action, especially to the onset of planned aggression: *The commandos attacked the outpost at dawn. Bombard* suggests showering with bombs or shells (*The warplanes bombarded the town*) or with words (*The celebrity was bombarded with invitations*). *Assail* implies repeated attacks: *Critics assailed the author's second novel. Storm* refers to a sudden, sweeping attempt to achieve a victory: *"After triumphantly storming the country, [the President] is obliged to storm Capitol Hill"* (The Economist). *Assault* usually implies sudden, intense violence: *Muggers often assault their victims on dark streets. Beset* suggests beleaguerment from all sides: *The fox was beset by hunters and hounds.*

---

attackable *adjective*
▸ assailable, helpless, unprotected. *See* **vulnerable** (1).
attacker *noun*
▸ assailant, assaulter, provoker. *See* **aggressor.**
attain *verb*
1. To obtain a goal or objective by effort ▸ achieve, gain, realize. *See* **accomplish** (1), *See synonym note at* **accomplish. 2.** To come into possession of ▸ come by, gain, procure. *See* **get** (1).
attainable *adjective*
1. Capable of being obtained or used ▸ acquirable, obtainable, procurable. *See* **available** (1). **2.** Capable of occurring or being done ▸ practicable, viable. *See* **possible** (1).
attainment *noun*
1. Something completed or attained successfully ▸ achievement, deed, triumph. *See* **accomplishment** (1). **2.** The condition of being fulfilled ▸ culmination, fulfillment, realization. *See* **fulfillment** (1). **3.** A quality that makes a person suitable for a particular position or task ▸ credential, endowment, qualification, skill.
attempt *verb*
To make an attempt to do or make ▸ assay, endeavor, essay, seek, strive, struggle, try (for). *Informal:* shoot for (*or* at). *Idioms:* give a whirl, go to all lengths, have a go at, have (*or* make *or* take) a shot at, have a try at, make a grab (*or* stab) at, take a crack at, try one's hand at, have (*or* take) a whack at. *See also* **aspire, presume, start.**
attempt *noun*
1. A trying to do or make something ▸ bid, crack, effort, endeavor, essay, go, offer, stab, trial, try, undertaking. *Informal:* shot, whirl. *Slang:* take. *See also* **effort. 2.** The act of attacking ▸ assault, offense, strike. *See* **attack** (1).
attend *verb*
1. To occur as a consequence ▸ ensue, follow, result. *See also* **stem. 2.** To work and care for ▸ do for,

minister to, serve, wait on (*or* upon). *See also* **help, work. 3.** To make an effort to hear something ▸ hark, hearken, heed, listen. *Idioms:* be all ears, give (*or* lend) an ear. **4.** To perceive by ear, usually attentively ▸ heed, listen. *See* **hear** (1). **5.** To be with or go with ▸ chaperon, company, escort. *See* **accompany** (1). **6.** To have the care and supervision of ▸ look after, mind, watch over. *See* **tend²** (1). *See synonym note at* **tend².**
attendance *noun*
The condition or fact of being present ▸ occurrence, presence. *See also* **existence.**
attendant *noun*
1. A person who assists someone else ▸ adjutant, aide, helper. *See* **assistant.** *See synonym note at* **assistant. 2.** One that accompanies another ▸ associate, companion. *See* **concomitant.**
attendant *adjective*
Occurring or existing at the same time ▸ accompanying, attending. *See* **concurrent** (1).
attending *adjective*
1. Occurring or existing at the same time ▸ accompanying, attendant. *See* **concurrent** (1). **2.** Occurring as a result ▸ consequent, ensuing. *See* **following** (2).
attention *noun*
1. Concentration of the mental powers on something ▸ attentiveness, concentration, consideration, contemplation, heedfulness, intentness, preoccupation, regardfulness. *See also* **alertness, care, diligence. 2.** The act of noting, observing, or taking into account ▸ heed, note, regard. *See* **notice** (1).
attentions *noun*
▸ moves, overture. *See* **advances.**
attentive *adjective*
1. Full of polite concern for the well-being of others ▸ considerate, courteous, gallant, neighborly, polite, regardful, respectful, solicitous, thoughtful. *See also* **benevolent, friendly. 2.** Giving care or attention ▸ heedful, intent, regardful. *See* **alert** (1).

✛ CORE SYNONYMS: *attentive, thoughtful, considerate, solicitous.* These adjectives mean full of polite concern for the well-being of others. *Attentive* suggests devoted, assiduous attention: *a good editor who is attentive to detail.* Although *thoughtful* and *considerate* are often used interchangeably, *thoughtful* implies a tendency to anticipate needs or wishes, whereas *considerate* stresses sensitivity to another's feelings: *a thoughtful friend who brought me soup when I was sick; considerate, quiet neighbors. Solicitous* implies deep concern that often verges on anxiety or expresses itself in exaggerated and sometimes cloying attentiveness: *was annoyed by a solicitous and meddlesome cousin.*

---

attentiveness *noun*
1. Concentration of the mental powers on something ▸ concentration, consideration. *See* **attention** (1). **2.** Thoughtful attention to others ▸ concern, regard, thoughtfulness. *See* **consideration** (1).
attenuate *verb*
1. To become diffuse ▸ rarefy, thin. **2.** To lessen or

deplete the nerve, energy, or strength of ► debilitate, weaken. *See* enervate. **3.** To lessen the strength of by or as if by admixture ► cut, weaken. *See* **dilute.**

attenuate *or* **attenuated** *adjective*
Marked by great diffusion of component particles ► rare, rarefied, thin.

attenuation *noun*
► depletion, devitalization, enfeeblement. *See* **debilitation.**

attest *verb*
1. To assure the certainty or validity of ► authenticate, corroborate, substantiate, verify. *See* **confirm** (1). **2.** To confirm formally as true, accurate, or genuine ► testify, verify, witness. *See* **certify** (1). **3.** To give grounds for believing in the existence or presence of ► argue, witness. *See* **indicate** (1). *See synonym note at* **indicate.** **4.** To give evidence or testimony under oath ► depose, swear, witness. *See* **testify** (1).

attestant *or* **attester** *or* **attestor** *noun*
One who testifies, especially in court ► deponent, testifier, witness.

attestation *noun*
► authentication, corroboration, proof, verification. *See* **confirmation** (2).

attire *noun*
1. Showy and elaborate clothing or apparel ► array, finery, frippery, regalia. *Slang:* get-up, glad-rags, Sunday best. *Idiom:* go-to-meeting clothes. **2.** Articles worn to cover the body ► apparel, clothing, garments. *See* **dress** (1).

attire *verb*
1. To put clothes on ► apparel, clothe, garb. *See* **dress** (1). **2.** To dress in formal or special clothing ► array, deck (out). *See* **dress up.**

attitude *noun*
1. A general cast of mind with regard to something ► feeling, sentiment. *See also* **idea. 2.** The way in which one is placed or arranged ► pose, position, posture. **3.** A way of holding or carrying one's body ► carriage, stance. *See* **posture** (1). *See synonym note at* **posture. 4.** A frame of mind affecting one's thoughts or behavior ► outlook, position. *See* **posture** (2).

attitudinize *verb*
1. To assume a particular position, as for a portrait ► posture, sit. *See* **pose** (1). **2.** To assume the character or appearance of ► masquerade, pose as. *See* **impersonate** (1).

attorney *noun*
► counsel, jurist. *See* **lawyer.**

attract *verb*
1. To direct or impel to oneself by some quality or action ► allure, appeal, draw, entice, lure, magnetize, take. *Informal:* pull. *Idioms:* catch one's eye, pique one's interest. *See also* **charm. 2.** To compel the attention, interest, or imagination of ► engage, fascinate, intrigue. *See* **grip** (1).

attraction *noun*
1. The power or quality of attracting ► allure, allurement, appeal, attractiveness, call, captivation, cha-

risma, charm, draw, enchantment, enticement, fascination, glamour, gravitation, lure, magnetism, witchery. *Informal:* pull. **2.** Something that attracts, especially with the promise of pleasure or reward ► bait, draw, enticement. *See* **lure** (1).

attractive *adjective*
1. Pleasing to the eye or mind ► appealing, bewitching, captivating, charismatic, charming, cute, desirable, enchanting, engaging, enticing, fascinating, fetching, glamorous, graceful, lovely, magic, magical, magnetic, pretty, sweet, taking, tempting, well-favored, winning, winsome. *See also* **delightful, seductive. 2.** Having qualities that delight the eye ► comely, gorgeous, stunning. *See* **beautiful. 3.** Pleasingly suited to the wearer ► fetching, flattering. *See* **becoming** (1).

attractiveness *noun*
► appeal, enticement, lure. *See* **attraction** (1).

attribute *verb*
1. To regard as belonging to or resulting from another ► accredit, ascribe, assign, charge, credit, refer. *See also* **accuse. 2.** To ascribe the blame for a misdeed or error ► assign, blame, pin. *See* **fix** (13).

attribute *noun*
1. An object or expression associated with and serving to identify something else ► emblem, metaphor, signifier, symbol, token. *See also* **expression, sign, term. 2.** A distinctive element ► characteristic, feature, property, trait. *See* **quality** (1). *See synonym note at* **quality.**

✦ CORE SYNONYMS: *attribute, ascribe, credit, assign, refer.* These verbs mean to regard as belonging to or resulting from another. *Attribute* and *ascribe,* often interchangeable, have the widest application: *The historian discovered a new symphony attributed to Mozart. The museum displayed an invention ascribed to the 15th century. Credit* frequently applies to an accomplishment or virtue: "*Some excellent remarks were made on immortality, but mainly borrowed from and credited to Plato*" (Oliver Wendell Holmes, Sr.). *Assign* and *refer* are often used to classify or categorize: *Program music as a genre is usually assigned to the Romantic period.* "*A person thus prepared will be able to refer any particular history he takes up to its proper place in universal history*" (Joseph Priestley).

---

attrition *noun*
► contriteness, remorse, repentance. *See* **penitence.**

attune *verb*
1. To bring into accord ► conform, integrate. *See* **harmonize** (1). **2.** To alter for proper functioning ► calibrate, fine-tune, tweak. *See* **adjust** (1).

atypical *or* **atypic** *adjective*
1. Departing from the normal ► aberrant, deviant, irregular. *See* **abnormal. 2.** Not usual or ordinary ► novel, unconventional. *See* **unusual** (1).

atypically *adverb*
► singularly, uncommonly, uniquely. *See* **unusually.**

au courant *adjective*
► current, modern, up-to-date. *See* **contemporary** (2).

auction *noun*
▸ sale, trade, transaction. *See* **deal** (1).

audacious *adjective*
1. Having or showing courage ▸ courageous, fearless, heroic. *See* **brave.** *See synonym note at* **brave. 2.** Willing to take risks ▸ daring, enterprising. *See* **adventurous** (1). *See synonym note at* **adventurous. 3.** Rude and disrespectful ▸ bold, insolent, pert. *See* **impudent.**

audacity *or* **audaciousness** *noun*
1. Willingness to take risks ▸ adventurousness, boldness, fearlessness. *See* **daring. 2.** The state or quality of being impudent or arrogantly self-confident ▸ boldness, boldness, impertinence. *See* **impudence.**

audience *noun*
1. The body of persons who admire a public personality, especially an entertainer ▸ following, public. *See also* **fan². 2.** A chance to be heard ▸ audition, hearing, listen. *Idiom:* one's day in court. **3.** One who sees something occur ▸ eyewitness, seer, viewer, witness.

audit *noun*
The act of examining carefully or critically ▸ inspection, inquiry, scrutiny. *See* **examination** (1).

audit *verb*
To look at or study carefully or critically ▸ investigation, peruse, scrutinize. *See* **examine** (1).

audition *noun*
1. A chance to be heard ▸ audience, hearing, listen. *Idiom:* one's day in court. **2.** The sense by which sound is perceived ▸ ear, hearing.

augment *verb*
1. To make or become greater or larger ▸ amplify, boost, enlarge. *See* **increase** (1). *See synonym note at* **increase. 2.** To add to or make whole ▸ complement, complete, strengthen. *See* **supplement. 3.** To achieve an increase of ▸ develop, expand. *See* **gain** (9).

augment *noun*
The act of increasing or rising ▸ amplification, boost, escalation. *See* **increase** (1).

augmentation *noun*
1. The act of increasing or rising ▸ amplification, boost, escalation. *See* **increase** (1). **2.** Something tending to augment something else ▸ accession, addendum. *See* **addition** (1).

augur *verb*
1. To tell about or make known by or as if by supernatural means ▸ divine, foretell. *See* **prophesy.** *See synonym note at* **prophesy. 2.** To give an indication of something in advance ▸ bode, foretoken, portend. *See* **foreshadow.**

augur *noun*
A person who foretells future events by or as if by supernatural means ▸ diviner, fortuneteller, soothsayer. *See* **prophet.**

augural *adjective*
▸ divinitory, oracular, sibylline. *See* **prophetic.**

augury *noun*
1. A phenomenon that serves as a sign or warning of some future good or evil ▸ portent, prognostication, sign. *See* **omen. 2.** The use of supernatural powers to influence or predict events ▸ conjuration, sorcery, witchcraft. *See* **magic** (1). **3.** Something that is foretold by or as if by supernatural means ▸ oracle, soothsaying. *See* **prophecy.**

august *adjective*
1. Impressive in size, proportion, or appearance ▸ imposing, magnificent, splendid. *See* **grand** (1). *See synonym note at* **grand. 2.** Raised to or occupying a high position or rank ▸ elevated, lofty. *See* **exalted** (1).

auld lang syne *noun*
▸ old, yesterday, yore. *See* **past** (1).

au naturel *adjective*
▸ bare, naked. *See* **nude** (1).

aura *noun*
▸ ambiance, atmosphere, mood. *See* **air** (4).

aureate *adjective*
▸ bombastic, grandiloquent, rhetorical. *See* **oratorical.**

aurora *noun*
▸ daybreak, sunrise, sunup. *See* **dawn** (1).

auspex *noun*
▸ diviner, fortuneteller, soothsayer. *See* **prophet.**

auspices *noun*
▸ backing, sponsorship. *See* **patronage** (1).

auspicious *adjective*
1. Suited for a particular purpose or occurring at a suitable time ▸ favorable, propitious, well-timed. *See* **opportune. 2.** Indicative of future success or full of promise ▸ bright, fortunate, propitious. *See* **favorable** (1). *See synonym note at* **favorable.**

austere *adjective*
1. Marked by cold and unpleasant conditions ▸ grim, severe. *See* **bleak** (1). **2.** Without addition, decoration, or qualification ▸ bare-bones, dry, plain. *See* **bare** (1). **3.** Renouncing material comforts and pleasures ▸ puritanical, self-denying. *See* **ascetic.**

austerity *noun*
▸ harshness, rigidity, stringency. *See* **severity** (1).

autarchic *or* **autarchical** *adjective*
▸ dictatorial, totalitarian, tyrannical. *See* **absolute** (1).

autarchist *noun*
▸ despot, oppressor, tyrant. *See* **dictator** (1).

autarchy *noun*
▸ despotism, dictatorship, tyranny. *See* **absolutism** (2).

authentic *adjective*
1. Not counterfeit or copied ▸ actual, bona fide, certified, confirmed, genuine, good, indubitable, legitimate, original, proved, real, tested, true, undoubted, unquestionable, verified, veritable. *Slang:* legit, kosher. *Idioms:* honest to goodness, for real, real live, sure enough, the real McCoy, the real thing, true to life. *See also* **actual, certain. 2.** Worthy of belief, as because of precision or faithfulness to an original ▸ authoritative, convincing, credible, faithful, true, trustworthy, valid. *See also* **accurate, definitive, dependable.**

✦ **CORE SYNONYMS:** *authentic, bona fide, genuine, real, true, undoubted, unquestionable.* These adjectives mean not counterfeit or copied: *an authentic painting by Corot; a bona fide transfer of property; genuine crabmeat; a real diamond; true courage; undoubted evidence; an unquestionable antique.*

◄ ANTONYM: *counterfeit*

authenticate *verb*
1. To assure the certainty or validity of ► affirm, corroborate, substantiate, verify. *See* **confirm** (1). *See synonym note at* **confirm**. **2.** To establish as true or genuine through evidence ► confirm, substantiate, validate. *See* **prove** (1).

authentication *noun*
► circumstantiation, corroboration, proof, verification. *See* **confirmation** (2).

authenticity *noun*
► correctness, truth, validity. *See* **veracity**.

author *noun*
One that creates, founds, or originates ► creator, founder, inventor. *See* **originator**.

author *verb*
To be the author of a published work or works ► compose, pen, write. *See* **publish** (2).

authoritarian *adjective*
1. Characterized by or favoring absolute obedience to authority ► autocratic, despotic, dictatorial, totalitarian, tyrannic, tyrannical. *See also* **absolute**. **2.** Given to asserting one's will or authority over others ► bossy, domineering, overbearing. *See* **dictatorial** (1). *See synonym note at* **dictatorial**.

authoritarian *noun*
1. One who imposes or favors absolute obedience to authority ► autocrat, despot, dictator, martinet, totalitarian, tyrant. **2.** An absolute ruler, especially one who is harsh and oppressive ► despot, oppressor, tyrant. *See* **dictator** (1).

authoritarianism *noun*
1. A political doctrine advocating the principle of absolute rule ► autocracy, despotism, dictatorship, totalitarianism. *See* **absolutism** (1). **2.** Absolute power, especially when exercised unjustly or cruelly ► despotism, dictatorship, totalitarianism. *See* **tyranny** (1).

authoritative *adjective*
1. Having or arising from authority ► conclusive, formal, imperial, official, ruling, sanctioned, standard, supreme. *See also* **administrative**. **2.** Exercising authority ► commanding, dominant, lordly, masterful. **3.** Worthy of belief, as because of precision or faithfulness to an original ► credible, true, valid. *See* **authentic** (2). **4.** Serving the function of deciding or settling with finality ► decisive, determinative. *See* **definitive** (1).

authority *noun*
1. The right and power to command, decide, rule, or judge ► carte blanche, command, control, domination, dominion, jurisdiction, mandate, mastery, might, omnipotence, power, prerogative, rule, sovereignty, superiority, supremacy, sway. *Informal:* muscle, say-so. **2.** The approving of an action, especially when done by one in authority ► approbation,

consent, sanction. *See* **permission**. **3.** A person with a high degree of knowledge or skill in a particular field ► master, proficient. *See* **expert**. **4.** The condition or fact of being dominant ► ascendance, power, supremacy. *See* **dominance** (1).

authorization *noun*
► approbation, consent, sanction. *See* **permission**. *See synonym note at* **permission**.

authorize *verb*
1. To give authority to ► accredit, commission, empower, enable, entitle, license, qualify. *See also* **appoint, elect, legalize**. **2.** To give one's consent to ► approve, sanction. *See* **permit** (2).

✦ CORE SYNONYMS: *authorize, accredit, commission, empower, license.* These verbs mean to give someone the authority to act: *authorized her partner to negotiate on her behalf; a representative who was accredited by his government; commissioned the real-estate agent to purchase the house; was empowered to make decisions during the president's absence; a pharmacist licensed to practice in two states.*

autochthonic *or* **authochthonal** *adjective*
► aboriginal, native. *See* **indigenous** (1).

autochthonous *adjective*
1. Existing, born, or produced in a land or region ► aboriginal, native. *See* **indigenous** (1). *See synonym note at* **indigenous**. **2.** Of, from, or within a country's own territory ► aboriginal, national, native. *See* **domestic** (3).

autocracy *noun*
1. A government in which all power is vested in a single leader or party ► dictatorship, monocracy, tyranny. *See* **absolutism** (2). **2.** A political doctrine advocating the principle of absolute rule ► authoritarianism, despotism, totalitarianism. *See* **absolutism** (1). **3.** Absolute power, especially when exercised unjustly or cruelly ► despotism, dictatorship, totalitarianism. *See* **tyranny** (1).

autocrat *noun*
1. One who imposes or favors absolute obedience to authority ► despot, dictator, tyrant. *See* **authoritarian** (1). **2.** An absolute ruler, especially one who is harsh and oppressive ► despot, oppressor, tyrant. *See* **dictator** (1).

autograph *verb*
► endorse, inscribe. *See* **sign** (1).

automatic *adjective*
1. Acting or happening without apparent forethought, prompting, or planning ► impulsive, involuntary. *See* **spontaneous** (1). *See synonym note at* **spontaneous**. **2.** Done routinely and impersonally ► mechanical, routine. *See* **perfunctory**.

autonomous *adjective*
1. Not imprisoned, enslaved, or controlled by another ► independent, self-governing, sovereign. *See* **free** (1). **2.** Free from the influence, guidance, or control of others ► autonomous, self-sufficient. *See* **independent** (1).

autonomy *noun*
1. The condition of being physically free ▸ self-government, sovereignty. *See* **freedom** (1). **2.** The capacity to manage one's own affairs, make one's own judgments, and provide for oneself ▸ self-reliance, self-sufficiency. *See* **independence** (1).

auxiliary *adjective*
1. Giving or able to give help or support ▸ accessory, aiding, ancillary, assistant, assisting, collateral, cooperating, helping, contributory, subsidiary, supporting, supportive. *See also* **minor, subordinate. 2.** Used or held in reserve ▸ backup, emergency, reserve, secondary, standby, supplemental, supplementary. *See also* **additional.**

auxiliary *noun*
A person who assists someone else ▸ aide, deputy, helper. *See* **assistant.**

avail *verb*
To be an advantage to ▸ benefit, serve. *See* **profit** (2).

avail *noun*
1. The quality of being suitable or adaptable to an end ▸ benefit, profit, utility. *See* **use** (2). **2.** Something beneficial ▸ benefit, blessing, favor. *See* **advantage** (2).

available *adjective*
1. Capable of being obtained or used ▸ acquirable, attainable, gettable, obtainable, procurable. *Idioms:* at (*or* on) hand, at one's disposal, on tap, to be had, within reach. *See also* **convenient, open, unoccupied. 2.** Not married or attached ▸ fancy-free, marriageable. *See* **single** (5).

avant-garde *noun*
The position of greatest advancement or importance ▸ cutting edge, lead, vanguard. *See* **forefront.**

avant-garde *adjective*
Ahead of current trends or customs ▸ forward, precocious. *See* **progressive** (1).

avarice *or* **avariciousness** *noun*
▸ acquisitiveness, covetousness, rapacity. *See* **greed.**

avaricious *adjective*
▸ acquisitive, covetous, grasping. *See* **greedy** (1).

avenge *verb*
To exact revenge for or from ▸ get, pay back, pay off, redress, repay, requite, vindicate. *Informal:* fix. *Idioms:* even the score, get back at, get even with, give a taste of one's own medicine, pay back in kind (*or* in one's own coin), pay off old scores, settle a score, settle (*or* square) accounts, take an eye for an eye. *See also* **punish, retaliate.**

avenging *adjective*
▸ implacable, spiteful, unforgiving. *See* **vindictive** (1).

avenue *noun*
▸ path, road, route. *See* **way** (2).

aver *verb*
▸ avow, declare, maintain. *See* **assert** (1).

average *adjective*
1. Relating to or occupying a middle position on a scale of evaluation ▸ fair, indifferent, mediocre, medium, middling, tolerable. **2.** Adequate to satisfy a need, requirement, or standard ▸ adequate, decent,
moderate. *See* **acceptable** (2). **3.** Occurring or encountered regularly ▸ commonplace, familiar, regular. *See* **common** (1). **4.** Being of no special quality or type ▸ common, mediocre, standard. *See* **ordinary** (1).

average *noun*
1. Something, as a type, number, quantity, or degree, that represents a midpoint between extremes ▸ mean, median, medium, midpoint, norm, par. *See also* **center. 2.** A regular or customary matter, condition, or course of events ▸ norm, ordinary, rule. *See* **usual.**

✤ CORE SYNONYMS: *average, medium, mediocre, fair, middling, indifferent, tolerable.* These adjectives indicate a middle position on a scale of evaluation. *Average* and *medium* apply to what is midway between extremes and imply both sufficiency and lack of distinction: *a novel of average merit; an orange of medium size. Mediocre* stresses the undistinguished aspect of what is average: *"The caliber of the students . . . has gone from mediocre to above average"* (Judy Pasternak). What is *fair* is passable but substantially below excellent: *in fair health. Middling* refers to a ranking between average and mediocre: *gave a middling performance. Indifferent* suggests neutrality: *"His home, alas, was but an indifferent attic"* (Edward Everett Hale). Something *tolerable* is merely acceptable: *prepared a tolerable meal.*

---

averageness *noun*
▸ normality, ordinariness, routineness. *See* **usualness.**

averment *noun*
▸ claim, declaration, statement. *See* **assertion.**

averse *adjective*
▸ disinclined, reluctant. *See* **indisposed** (1).

averseness *noun*
▸ aversion, opposition, reluctance. *See* **indisposition** (1).

aversion *noun*
1. A strong feeling of hostility or dislike ▸ antipathy, contempt, loathing. *See* **hate** (1). **2.** An object of extreme dislike ▸ abomination, anathema. *See* **hate** (2). **3.** The act or condition of conflict ▸ contradiction, polarity. *See* **opposition** (1). **4.** The state of not being disposed or inclined ▸ averseness, opposition, reluctance. *See* **indisposition** (1).

avert *verb*
1. To change the direction or course of ▸ deviate, divert, veer. *See* **turn** (2). **2.** To prohibit from occurring by advance planning or action ▸ anticipate, avert, forestall. *See* **prevent.** *See synonym note at* **prevent.**

avid *adjective*
1. Having an insatiable appetite for an activity or pursuit ▸ rapacious, ravenous. *See* **voracious** (1). **2.** Having a strong urge to obtain or possess something, especially material wealth, in quantity ▸ avaricious, covetous. *See* **greedy** (1). **3.** Intensely desirous or interested ▸ avid, bursting. *See* **eager** (1).

avidity *or* **avidness** *noun*
1. The quality or condition of being voracious ▸ omnivorousness, rapaciousness. *See* **voracity. 2.** Excessive desire for more than one needs or deserves

► avarice, covetousness, rapacity. *See* **greed.**

avocation *noun*
► career, employment, occupation. *See* **business** (2).

avoid *verb*
To keep away from ► abstain from, burke, bypass, circumvent, dodge, duck, elude, escape, eschew, evade, get around, lay off, refrain from, shun, stay off. *Idioms:* fight shy of, give a wide berth to, have no truck with, keep at arms length, keep (*or* stay *or* steer) clear of, keep one's distance from, let well enough alone. *See also* **evade, skirt.**

✦ CORE SYNONYMS: *avoid, escape, shun, eschew, evade, elude.* These verbs mean to keep away from persons or things. *Avoid* always involves an effort to keep away from what is considered to be a source of danger or difficulty: *avoiding strenuous exercise. Escape* can mean to get free or to remain untouched or unaffected by something unwanted: *"Let no guilty man escape, if it can be avoided"* (Ulysses S. Grant). *Shun* refers to deliberately keeping clear of what is unwelcome or undesirable: *"Family friends . . . she shunned like the plague"* (John Galsworthy). *Eschew* involves staying clear of something because to do otherwise would be unwise or morally wrong: *"Eschew evil, and do good"* (Book of Common Prayer). *Evade* implies adroit maneuvering and sometimes implies dishonesty or irresponsibility: *tried to evade jury duty.* To *elude* is to get away from artfully: *eluded their pursuers.*

---

avoidance *noun*
► bypass, circumvention. *See* **escape** (2).

avoirdupois *noun*
Informal The state or degree of being heavy ► massiveness, weightiness. *See* **heaviness.**

avouch *verb*
1. To put into words positively and with conviction ► avow, declare, maintain. *See* **assert** (1). **2.** To assure the certainty or validity of ► authenticate, corroborate, substantiate, verify. *See* **confirm** (1).

avow *verb*
1. To admit to the reality or truth of ► concede, grant. *See* **acknowledge** (1). *See synonym note at* **acknowledge. 2.** To put into words positively and with conviction ► affirm, declare, maintain. *See* **assert** (1).

avowal *noun*
1. The act of admitting to something ► admission, confession, recognition. *See* **acknowledgment** (1). **2.** The act of asserting positively or something so asserted ► claim, declaration, statement. *See* **assertion.**

await *verb*
1. To look forward to confidently ► anticipate, count on, look for. *See* **expect** (1). *See synonym note at* **expect. 2.** To wait furtively in order to attack someone ► ambush, prowl, skulk. *See* **lurk** (1).

awaiting *adjective*
► anticipatory, hopeful. *See* **expectant** (1).

awake *adjective*
1. Not in a state of sleep or unable to sleep

► unsleeping, wakeful, wide-awake. *Idiom:* tossing and turning. *See also* **restless. 2.** Marked by comprehension, cognizance, and perception ► cognizant, sensible, sentient. *See* **aware.** *See synonym note at* **aware.**

awake *or* **awaken** *verb*
1. To cease or cause to cease sleeping ► arouse, rouse, waken. *See* **wake**[1]. **2.** To induce or elicit a reaction ► kindle, stir (up). *See* **arouse** (1).

award *verb*
1. To let have as a favor, prerogative, or privilege ► accord, concede, give, grant, vouchsafe. *See also* **yield. 2.** To bestow a reward on ► guerdon, honor, reward. **3.** To give formally or officially ► accord, bestow, grant. *See* **confer** (2). **4.** To present with a gift ► endow, invest. *See* **gift. 5.** To present as a gift to a charity or cause ► bequeath, pledge. *See* **donate** (1).

award *noun*
1. A memento received as a symbol of excellence or victory ► accolade, cup, prize, trophy. *See also* **medal. 2.** Something given in return for a service or accomplishment ► accolade, bonus, plum. *See* **reward** (1). **3.** Something given to a charity or cause ► benefaction, contribution, offering. *See* **donation. 4.** Recognition of achievement or superiority or a sign of this ► accolade, honor. *See* **distinction** (2).

aware *adjective*
Marked by comprehension, cognizance, and perception ► alive, awake, cognizant, sensible, sentient, wise. *Informal:* with-it. *Slang:* hip. *Idioms:* on to, up on. *See also* **alert, informed, sensitive.**

✦ CORE SYNONYMS: *aware, cognizant, sensible, awake.* These adjectives mean marked by comprehension, cognizance, and perception. *Aware* implies knowledge gained through one's own perceptions or by means of information: *Are you aware of your opponent's hostility? I am aware that the legislation passed. Cognizant* is a formal equivalent of *aware:* *"Our research indicates that the nation's youth are cognizant of the law"* (Jerry D. Jennings). *Sensible* implies knowledge gained through intuition or intellectual perception: *"I am sensible that the mention of such a circumstance may appear trifling"* (Henry Hallam). To be *awake* is to have full consciousness of something: *"as much awake to the novelty of attention in that quarter as Elizabeth herself"* (Jane Austen).

---

awareness *noun*
The condition of being aware ► cognizance, consciousness, mindfulness, perception, realization, recognition, sense. *See also* **alertness.**

awash *adjective*
► brimful, brimming, overflowing. *See* **full** (1).

away *adjective*
► gone, missing, wanting. *See* **absent** (1).

awe *noun*
The emotion aroused by something awe-inspiring or astounding ► amazement, marvel. *See* **wonder** (1).

awe *verb*
To impress strongly by what is unexpected or unusual

▸ amaze, astonish, astound. *See* **surprise** (1).

awe-inspiring *adjective*
1. Impressive in size, proportion, or appearance ▸ imposing, magnificent, splendid. *See* **grand** (1). 2. So remarkable as to be difficult to believe ▸ astounding, staggering, unbelievable. *See* **astonishing.**

awesome *adjective*
1. *Slang* Beyond what is usual, normal, or customary ▸ extraordinary, outstanding, remarkable. *See* **exceptional** (1). 2. *Slang* Exceptionally good of its kind ▸ first-rate, prime, splendid, tiptop. *See* **excellent.** 3. Impressive in size, proportion, or appearance ▸ imposing, magnificent, splendid. *See* **grand** (1).

awful *adjective*
Very bad ▸ appalling, dreadful, ghastly. *See* **terrible** (1).

awful *adverb*
Informal To a high degree ▸ exceedingly, extremely, highly. *See* **very.**

awfully *adverb*
▸ exceedingly, extremely, highly. *See* **very.**

awkward *adjective*
1. Lacking dexterity and grace in physical movement ▸ butterfingered, cloddish, clumsy, gawky, graceless, inept, lubberly, lumpish, maladroit, stumbling, uncoordinated, ungainly, ungraceful. *Slang:* klutzy. *Idioms:* all thumbs, having two left feet. 2. Difficult to handle or manage ▸ bulky, clumsy, ungainly, unhandy, unmanageable, unwieldy. *See also* **heavy, unruly.** 3. Characterized by embarrassment and discomfort ▸ constrained, embarrassed, embarrassing, self-conscious, uncomfortable, uneasy. *Idiom:* ill at ease. *See also* **delicate, unpleasant.** 4. Clumsily lack-ing in the ability to do ▸ bumbling, clumsy, inept. *See* **unskillful** (1). 5. Characterized by inappropriateness and gracelessness, especially in expression ▸ inept, infelicitous, unhappy. *See* **unfortunate** (2).

awry *adverb*
Not in the right way or on the proper course ▸ afield, amiss, astray, wrong. *See synonym note at* **wrong.**

ax *noun*
Informal The act of dismissing or the condition of being dismissed from employment ▸ expulsion, termination. *See* **dismissal** (1).

ax *verb*
1. *Informal* To end the employment or service of ▸ drop, lay off. *See* **dismiss** (1). 2. *Informal* To put an end to ▸ annul, cancel, nullify. *See* **abolish** (1).

axial *adjective*
▸ focal, median, middle. *See* **central** (1).

axiom *noun*
1. A broad and basic rule or truth ▸ fundamental, principle. *See* **law** (3). 2. Something taken to be true without proof ▸ given, premise, presupposition. *See* **assumption** (1). 3. The principle taught by a fable or parable ▸ lesson, maxim. *See* **moral.** 4. A usually pithy and familiar statement generally accepted as wise or true ▸ adage, maxim, motto. *See* **proverb.**

axis *noun*
▸ core, focus, nucleus. *See* **center** (3).

aye *noun*
An affirmative vote or voter ▸ yea, yes.

aye *adverb*
It is so; as you say or ask ▸ agreed, all right, assuredly. *See* **yes.**

b

babble *verb*
1. To talk rapidly, incoherently, or indistinctly ▸ blather, burble, chatter, gabble, gibber, jabber, jibber-jabber, prate, prattle, rant, rave. *See also* **speak, stammer.** 2. To talk rapidly on trivial matters ▸ blab, jabber, prattle. *See* **chatter** (1). 3. To flow with or make a soft liquid sound ▸ gurgle, lap, murmur. *See* **burble** (1).

babble *noun*
1. Empty or foolish talk ▸ blarney, blather, blatherskite, double talk, drivel, gabble, gibberish, gobbledygook, jabber, jabberwocky, jargon, jibber-jabber, nonsense, prate, prattle, twaddle. *Slang:* hot air. *See also* **nonsense.** 2. Incessant and inconsequential talk ▸ drivel, patter, small talk. *See* **chatter.** 3. A soft liquid sound ▸ gurgle, lap, murmur. *See* **burble.**

babe *noun*
1. A very young child ▸ infant, newborn. *See* **baby** (1). 2. A guileless, unsophisticated person ▸ child, naive. *See* **innocent** (2). 3. *Informal* A person who is much loved ▸ beloved, honey, sweetheart. *See* **darling** (1). 4. *Slang* A person regarded as physically attractive ▸ lovely, stunner. *See* **beauty** (1).

babel *noun*
▸ clamor, din, tumult. *See* **noise** (1). *See synonym note at* **noise.**

baby *noun*
1. A very young child ▸ babe, babe in arms, bambino, cherub, infant, neonate, newborn, nursling, papoose, toddler, tot. *Informal:* preemie. *Idiom:* bundle of joy. 2. A childish or pampered person ▸ crybaby, milksop, milquetoast, mollycoddle, namby-pamby. *Informal:* softy. *Slang:* cream puff. *Idioms:* mama's boy (*or* girl). *See also* **weakling.** 3. *Informal* A person who is much loved ▸ beloved, honey, sweetheart. *See* **darling** (1).

baby *verb*

To treat indulgently ▸ cater (to), coddle, cosset, humor, indulge, mollycoddle, overindulge, pamper, spoil. *See also* **adore, defer²**.

✦ CORE SYNONYMS: *baby, pamper, indulge, humor, spoil, coddle, mollycoddle*. These verbs mean to treat someone indulgently, as by catering excessively to his or her desires or feelings. *Baby* suggests the indulgence and attention one might give to an infant: *"I should like to be made much of, and tended—yes, babied"* (Adeline D.T. Whitney). To *pamper* is to gratify appetites, tastes, or desires: *"He was pampering the poor girl's lust for singularity and self-glorification"* (Charles Kingsley). *Indulge* suggests a kindly or excessive lenience in yielding especially to wishes or impulses better left unfulfilled: *"You musn't think because I indulge you in some things that you can keep everyone waiting"* (Theodore Dreiser). *Humor* implies compliance with or accommodation to another's mood or idiosyncrasies: *"Human life is . . . but like a forward child, that must be played with and humored a little to keep it quiet till it falls asleep"* (William Temple). *Spoil* implies excessive indulgence that adversely affects the character, nature, or attitude: *"He seems to be in no danger of being spoilt by good fortune"* (George Gissing). *Coddle* and *mollycoddle* point to tender, overprotective care that often leads to weakening of character: *"I would not coddle the child"* (Samuel Johnson). *Stop mollycoddling me; I'm a grown person.*

---

babyish *adjective*

1. Of or like a baby ▸ cherubic, childlike, infantile, infantine. *Informal:* kidlike. *See also* **innocent**. 2. Of or characteristic of a child, especially in immaturity ▸ immature, infantile, juvenile. *See* **childish**.

baby-sit *verb*

▸ look after, mind, watch over. *See* **tend²** (1).

back *noun*

The part farthest from the front ▸ back end, back side, end, hind end, rear, stern, tag end, tail, tail end.

back *verb*

1. To move in a reverse direction ▸ backpedal, backtrack, back up, fall back, retreat, retrocede, retrograde, retrogress, reverse. *Idiom:* retrace one's steps. *See also* **flinch, recede, retreat**. 2. To present evidence in support of ▸ back up, bolster, buttress, corroborate, substantiate, support, sustain, vouch (for). *See also* **prove**. 3. To act as a patron to ▸ patronize, sponsor, support. *See also* **donate**. 4. To supply capital ▸ fund, subsidize. *Informal:* bankroll. *See* **finance**. 5. To aid the cause of by approving or favoring ▸ advocate, endorse, stand by. *See* **support** (1). *See synonym note at* **support**. 6. To assure the certainty or validity of ▸ authenticate, substantiate, verify. *See* **confirm** (1).

back down *or* **away** *or* **out** *verb*

1. To abandon a former position or commitment ▸ blink, retreat, walk out. *See* **renege**. 2. To move in a reverse direction ▸ backpedal, retreat, retrogress. *See* **back** (1). 3. To moderate or change a position or

course of action as a result of pressure ▸ ease off, slacken, yield. *See* **weaken** (1).

back *adjective*

1. Located in the rear ▸ hind, hinder, hindmost, hindermost, posterior, rear, rearward. 2. Far from centers of human population ▸ isolated, outlying, out-of-the-way. *See* **remote** (1). *See synonym note at* **remote** (1).

back *adverb*

Toward the back ▸ about, around. *See* **backward**.

backbite *verb*

▸ calumniate, defame, slander. *See* **malign**.

backbone *noun*

▸ bravery, fortitude, gallantry, valor. *See* **courage**.

backbreaking *adjective*

▸ arduous, crushing, laborious. *See* **burdensome** (1).

backcountry *noun*

▸ backwoods, hinterland. *See* **country** (1).

backdrop *noun*

1. The place where an action or event occurs ▸ site, stage. *See* **scene** (1). 2. The properties, objects, and accessories arranged for a dramatic presentation ▸ mise en scène, setting. *See* **scene** (2).

backer *noun*

1. One who supports or champions an activity, cause, or institution ▸ benefactor, sponsor. *See* **patron** (1). 2. One who assumes financial responsibility for another ▸ guarantor, underwriter. *See* **sponsor** (1).

backfire *verb*

1. To produce an unexpected and undesired result ▸ boomerang. *Idiom:* blow up in one's face. *See also* **fail**. 2. To release or cause to release energy suddenly and violently, especially with a loud noise ▸ burst, detonate. *See* **explode** (1).

background *noun*

1. One's previous experiences ▸ career, past, resumé. *See* **history** (2). 2. The properties, backdrops, and other objects arranged for a dramatic presentation ▸ mise en scène, set, setting. *See* **scene** (2).

backhanded *adjective*

▸ circuitous, devious, roundabout. *See* **indirect** (1).

backing *noun*

1. Aid or support given by a patron ▸ advocacy, sponsorship. *See* **patronage** (1). 2. Money or property used to produce more wealth ▸ financing, funding, stake. *See* **capital** (1). 3. An indication of commendation or approval ▸ recommendation, support. *See* **endorsement** (1). 4. That which confirms ▸ authentication, proof, verification. *See* **confirmation** (2).

backlog *noun*

▸ cache, reserve, stockpile. *See* **hoard**.

backpack *verb*

To travel about or journey on foot ▸ hike, march, tramp, trek. *See also* **journey, walk**.

backpack *noun*

A container carried on the back or around the waist ▸ kit, knapsack. *See* **pack** (1).

backpedal *verb*

▸ backtrack, retreat, retrogress. *See* **back** (1).

backset *noun*
A change from better to worse ▸ reversal, reverse, setback. *See also* **misfortune, relapse.**

backside *noun*
Informal The part of the body on which one sits ▸ posterior, rump. *Slang:* fanny. *See* **buttocks.**

backslide *verb*
To slip from a higher or better condition to a former, usually lower or poorer one ▸ lapse, regress, revert. *See* **relapse.**

backslide *or* **backsliding** *noun*
A slipping from a higher or better condition to a lower or poorer one ▸ backsliding, lapse, recidivism. *See* **relapse.**

backstairs *adjective*
▸ clandestine, covert. *See* **secret** (1).

back talk *noun*
Insolent talk ▸ mouth. *Informal:* lip, sass. *See also* **impudence.**

back-to-back *adjective*
▸ sequential, serial. *See* **consecutive.**

backtrack *verb*
▸ backpedal, retreat, retrogress. *See* **back** (1).

backup *adjective*
▸ reserve, standby, supplemental. *See* **auxiliary** (2).

backward *adjective*
1. Having only a limited ability to learn and understand ▸ dense, dull, feeble-minded, half-witted, simple, simple-minded, slow, slow-witted, thick-witted, weak-minded. *Informal:* soft. *Slang:* dim, dimwitted. *Idioms:* not playing with a full deck, soft in the head. *See also* **stupid. 2.** Behind others in progress or development ▸ lagging, underdeveloped, undeveloped. **3.** Moving or directed toward the rear ▸ rearward, retrograde, retrogressive. **4.** Economically and socially below standard ▸ disadvantaged, impoverished. *See* **depressed** (2). **5.** Exhibiting lack of education or knowledge ▸ primitive, unenlightened. *See* **ignorant** (2). **6.** Awkward or unconfident in behavior or manner ▸ bashful, demure, diffident. *See* **shy¹** (1). **7.** Clinging to obsolete ideas ▸ reactionary, unprogressive. *See also* **conservative.**

backward *adverb*
Toward the back ▸ about, around, back, backwards, rearward.

backwardness *noun*
1. An awkwardness or lack of self-confidence in the presence of others ▸ bashfulness, demureness, diffidence. *See* **shyness. 2.** The condition of being ignorant ▸ illiteracy, nescience. *See* **ignorance** (1).

backwards *adverb*
▸ about, around, rearward. *See* **backward.**

backwoods *noun*
1. A dense growth of trees and underbrush covering an area ▸ forest, timberland, woodland, woods. **2.** A remote or rural area ▸ countryside, hinterland. *See* **country** (1).

bacterium *noun*
▸ bug, microorganism, virus. *See* **germ** (1).

bad *adjective*
1. Of low or lower quality ▸ bum, coarse, common, dissatisfactory, inadequate, inferior, low-grade, low-quality, mean, mediocre, poor, second-class, second-rate, shabby, subpar, substandard, unsatisfactory. *Slang:* bush-league. *Idioms:* below par, not up to scratch (*or* snuff). *See also* **defective, shabby, shoddy, terrible. 2.** Marred by decay ▸ decayed, fly-blown, foul, overripe, putrescent, putrid, rancid, rotten, spoiled, worm-eaten, wormy. *See also* **filthy, moldy, offensive. 3.** Morally objectionable ▸ immoral, sinful. *See* **evil** (1). **4.** Not submitting to discipline or control ▸ ill-behaved, obstinate, unmanageable. *See* **unruly. 5.** Not pleasant or agreeable ▸ disagreeable, uncongenial, unsympathetic. *See* **unpleasant** (1). **6.** Bringing or predicting misfortune ▸ evil, inauspicious, sinister. *See* **fateful** (1). **7.** Causing harm or injury ▸ deleterious, destructive, evil, injurious. *See* **harmful.**

bad *noun*
Whatever is destructive or harmful ▸ badness, evil, ill, worse. *See also* **harm.**

badge *noun*
1. An emblem of honor worn on one's clothing ▸ decoration, medal, ribbon. *See* **decoration** (2). **2.** Something visible or evident that gives grounds for believing in the existence or presence of something else ▸ evidence, indication, symptom. *See* **sign** (1). *See synonym note at* **sign.**

badger *verb*
▸ harry, pester, torment. *See* **harass.** *See synonym note at* **harass.**

badinage *noun*
▸ banter, chaff, raillery. *See* **ribbing.**

badlands *noun*
▸ waste, wasteland. *See* **desert¹.**

badmouth *verb*
1. *Informal* To represent or speak of as small or insignificant ▸ deprecate, disparage, slight. *See* **belittle. 2.** *Informal* To make harmful and often untrue statements about ▸ calumniate, defame, slander. *See* **malign.**

bad name *noun*
▸ discredit, disrepute, humiliation. *See* **disgrace.**

badness *noun*
Whatever is destructive or harmful ▸ bad, evil, ill, wrong. *See also* **harm.**

bad odor *noun*
▸ discredit, disrepute, humiliation. *See* **disgrace.**

bad-tempered *adjective*
▸ cantankerous, cranky, disagreeable, grouchy, peevish. *See* **ill-tempered.**

baffle *verb*
1. To put at a loss as to what to say or do ▸ confound, mystify, nonplus, perplex. *Informal:* flummox, stick, stump, throw. *Slang:* beat. *See also* **confuse, embarrass. 2.** To prevent from accomplishing a purpose ▸ foil, stymie, thwart. *See* **frustrate** (1).

baffle *noun*
A device for slowing or stopping motion ► curb, leash, rein. *See* **brake** (1).

baffled *adjective*
► confounded, perplexed, turbid. *See* **confused** (1).

bafflement *noun*
► bewilderment, perplexity, stupor. *See* **daze**.

bag *noun*
1. A flexible container for carrying items ► pouch, sack, tote (bag). *Chiefly Regional:* croker sack, crocus sack, gunnysack, poke, tow bag, tow sack. **2.** A piece of luggage for carrying clothing ► carryon, grip, valise. *See* **suitcase**. **3.** A closeable container for carrying money and personal items ► clutch, handbag, pocketbook. *See* **purse**. **4.** *Slang* A sphere of activity, experience, study, or interest ► department, domain, field. *See* **area** (1). **5.** *Slang* Something at which a person excels ► specialty, strong point. *See* **forte**.

bag *verb*
1. To curve outward past the normal or usual limit ► balloon, jut, project. *See* **bulge** (1). **2.** To gain control of by trapping ► snare, trap. *See* **catch** (1). **3.** *Informal* To gain possession of, especially after a struggle or chase ► gain, secure, win. *See* **capture** (1). **4.** *Slang* To come into possession of ► come by, gain, procure. *See* **get** (1).

baggage *noun*
► tramp, wench, whore. *See* **slut**.

bag lady *noun*
► beggar, insolvent, tramp. *See* **pauper**.

bail¹ *noun*
1. One who posts bond ► bailsman, bondsman. **2.** Something given to guarantee the repayment of a loan or the fulfillment of an obligation ► bond, guaranty, pledge. *See* **pawn¹**.

bail² *verb*
To take a substance, as liquid, from a container by plunging the hand or a utensil into it ► ladle, scoop (up). *See* **dip** (2).

bail out *verb*
1. To catapult oneself from a disabled aircraft ► eject, jump. **2.** To leave suddenly, as from a difficult or threatening situation ► decamp, flee. *See* **escape** (1).

bailiwick *noun*
► department, domain, field. *See* **area** (1). *See synonym note at* **area**.

bailsman *noun*
One who posts bond ► bail, bondsman.

bait *noun*
1. Something that attracts, especially with the promise of pleasure or reward ► allurement, draw, enticement. *See* **lure** (1). **2.** Something that leads one into danger or entrapment ► decoy, lure. *See also* **trap, trick**.

bait *verb*
1. To arouse hope or desire without affording satisfaction ► tantalize, tease. *Idiom:* make one's mouth water. *See also* **charm**. **2.** To attack or disturb persistently ► harry, pester, torment. *See* **harass**.

bake *verb*
1. To prepare food for eating by the use of heat ► brown, roast. *See* **cook** (1). **2.** To feel or look hot ► broil, roast, swelter. *See* **burn** (3).

baked *adjective*
Slang Stupefied, intoxicated, or otherwise influenced by the taking of drugs ► high, hopped-up, lit (up). *See* **drugged**.

baker *noun*
A person who prepares food for eating ► chef, cook, culinary artist.

baking *adjective*
► blistering, boiling, burning. *See* **hot** (1).

balance *noun*
1. A stable state of opposing forces ► counterpoise, equilibrium, equipoise, poise, stasis. *See also* **equivalence, stability**. **2.** A stable emotional state ► aplomb, collectedness, composure, coolness, equanimity, imperturbability, imperturbableness, levelheadedness, nonchalance, poise, sang-froid, self-possession, steadiness, unflappability. *Slang:* cool. *See also* **calm, reserve**. **3.** Satisfying arrangement marked by even distribution of elements, as in a design ► harmony, proportion, symmetry. *See synonym note at* **proportion**. *See also* **agreement**. **4.** A remaining part ► leavings, leftover, leftovers, pickings, remainder, remains, remnant, residue, rest. *See also* **end, surplus, trace**.

balance *verb*
1. To put in balance ► counterbalance, equalize, even (out), level (off), poise, stabilize, steady. *See also* **equalize**. **2.** To act as an equalizing force to ► compensate, counteract, counterbalance, counterpoise, countervail, make up, offset, oppose, set off. *See also* **harmonize**. **3.** To rest on a narrow or insecure surface ► perch, poise, roost, teeter. *See also* **sway**. **4.** To examine in order to note similarities and differences ► contrast, counterpose, juxtapose. *See* **compare** (1). **5.** To make ineffective by applying an opposite force ► counteract, negate, offset. *See* **cancel** (2).

balanced *adjective*
1. Neither favorable nor unfavorable ► even, fifty-fifty, nip and tuck. **2.** Free from bias in judgment ► detached, impartial, just. *See* **fair¹** (1). **3.** Proceeding from or exhibiting good judgment ► commonsensical, levelheaded, prudent. *See* **sensible** (1). **4.** Characterized by or displaying symmetry, especially correspondence in scale or measure ► proportional, proportionate, regular, symmetric, symmetrical. *See also* **even, parallel**. **5.** Having components that are pleasingly combined ► concordant, congruous, harmonious, symmetrical. *See also* **pleasant**.

bald *adjective*
1. Without the usual covering ► hairless, naked, nude. *See* **bare** (3). **2.** Without addition, decoration, or qualification ► austere, plain, spare. *See* **bare** (1).

balderdash *noun*
► bunkum, drivel, garbage. *See* **nonsense** (1).

bald-faced *adjective*
► bold, insolent, pert. *See* **impudent**.

baleful *adjective*
▸ dire, ominous, unlucky. *See* **fateful** (1). *See synonym note at* **fateful.**

balk *verb*
▸ foil, stymie, thwart. *See* **frustrate** (1).

balky *adjective*
▸ antagonistic, contradictory, hostile. *See* **contrary** (1).

ball *noun*
1. A spherical object ▸ globe, orb, sphere, spheroid. *See also* **circle, drop.** 2. A party or gathering for dancing ▸ cotillion, promenade. *See* **dance.**

ballad *noun*
▸ hymn, lyrics, tune. *See* **song** (1).

balloon *verb*
1. To increase or expand suddenly, rapidly, or without control ▸ explode, mushroom, snowball. *See also* **increase.** 2. To expand from or as if from internal pressure ▸ bloat, inflate. *See* **swell** (1). 3. To curve outward past the normal or usual limit ▸ bag, jut, project. *See* **bulge** (1). *See synonym note at* **bulge.**

ballot *verb*
To cast a vote ▸ poll, vote. *Idiom:* go to the polls.

ballot *noun*
A list of candidates proposed or endorsed by a political party ▸ lineup, ticket, slate.

balloter *noun*
One who votes ▸ elector, voter. *Idiom:* member of the electorate.

ball up *verb*
1. To ruin through clumsiness or ineptness ▸ blunder, foul up, spoil. *See* **botch.** 2. To put into total disorder ▸ garble, jumble, scramble. *See* **confuse** (4).

ballyhoo *noun*
Information disseminated through various media to attract public notice ▸ advertisement, buildup. *Slang:* hype. *See* **publicity** (1).

ballyhoo *verb*
To attempt to sell or popularize by advertizing or publicity ▸ boost, publicize, talk up. *See* **promote** (3).

balm *noun*
▸ emollient, salve. *See* **ointment.**

balminess *noun*
Slang Foolish behavior ▸ folly, silliness, tomfoolery. *See* **foolishness.**

balmy *adjective*
1. Free from extremes in temperature ▸ clement, mild, moderate, temperate. *See also* **pleasant.** 2. Free from severity or violence, as in sound or movement ▸ delicate, faint, soft. *See* **gentle** (2). 3. *Slang* Displaying a lack of forethought and good sense ▸ daft, idiotic, ludicrous. *See* **foolish.**

baloney *noun*
Slang Something that does not have or make sense ▸ bunkum, drivel, garbage. *See* **nonsense** (1).

bambino *noun*
▸ babe, infant. *See* **baby** (1).

bamboozle *verb*
Informal To cause to accept something false by trickery or misrepresentation ▸ dupe, fool, hoodwink,

trick. *See* **deceive.** *See synonym note at* **deceive.**

ban *verb*
1. To refuse to allow ▸ disallow, proscribe. *See* **forbid.** *See synonym note at* **forbid.** 2. To keep from being published or transmitted ▸ stifle, suppress, withhold. *See* **censor** (2). 3. To keep from being admitted, included, or considered ▸ eliminate, keep out, rule out. *See* **exclude** (1).

ban *noun*
1. A refusal to allow ▸ prohibition, proscription. *See* **forbiddance.** 2. A denunciation invoking a wish or threat of evil or injury ▸ damnation, malediction. *See* **curse** (1).

banal *adjective*
▸ clichéd, overused, stale, tired. *See* **trite.**

banality *noun*
1. A trite expression or idea ▸ platitude, truism. *See* **cliché.** 2. The state or quality of being insipid ▸ innocuousness, vapidness, wateriness. *See* **insipidity** (1).

bananas *adjective*
Slang Afflicted with or exhibiting irrationality and mental unsoundness ▸ crazy, demented, lunatic. *See* **insane** (1).

band[1] *noun*
1. A long narrow piece, as of material ▸ bandeau, belt, cincture, cinch, fillet, girdle, riband, ribbon, sash, strap, strip, stripe, strop, swatch, swath, tape. 2. A round closed plane shape or figure ▸ hoop, ring, wheel. *See* **circle** (1). 3. A long narrow area that has a different color or marking from what surrounds it ▸ bar, line. *See* **stripe** (1).

band *verb*
1. To form a circle around ▸ circle, gird, ring. *See* **encircle** (1). 2. To mark with a line or band, as of different color or texture ▸ striate, variegate. *See* **streak.**

band[2] *noun*
1. A group of people acting together in a shared activity ▸ cohort, company, corps, party, troop, troupe, unit. *See also* **alliance, assembly, force, union.** 2. A number of individuals making up a unit ▸ collection, lot, set. *See* **group.** 3. An organized group of criminals or wrongdoers ▸ pack, ring. *See* **gang.**

band *verb*
To form a united group ▸ combine, come together, flock (together), gang (together), group, join (together), league, unite. *Idiom:* join forces. *See also* **ally, assemble, associate, combine.**

✚ CORE SYNONYMS: *band, company, corps, party, troop, troupe.* These nouns denote a group of people acting together in a shared activity or for a common purpose: *a band of laborers; a company of ballet dancers; a corps of drummers; a party of tourists; a troop of students on a field trip; a troupe of actors.*

---

bandage *verb*
▸ bind, swathe, truss. *See* **dress** (2).

bandeau *noun*
▸ band, riband, ribbon. *See* **band**[1] (1).

banderole *noun*
▸ banner, colors, pennant. *See* **flag**[1] (1).
bandit *noun*
▸ burglar, robber, stealer. *See* **thief.**
bandsman *noun*
▸ performer, virtuoso. *See* **player** (2).
bandy *verb*
1. To give and receive mutually, as words ▸ interchange, swap. *See* **exchange** (2). **2.** To speak together and exchange ideas and opinions about ▸ converse, debate. *Informal:* kick around. *See* **discuss.**
bane *noun*
1. The act of destroying or state of being destroyed ▸ devastation, ruin, wreck. *See* **destruction** (1). **2.** Anything that is injurious, destructive, or fatal ▸ canker, toxin. *See* **poison** (1). **3.** Something that causes total loss or severe impairment ▸ downfall, ruination, undoing. *See* **ruin** (1). **4.** A cause of suffering or harm ▸ affliction, scourge. *See* **curse** (3).
baneful *adjective*
▸ deleterious, evil, injurious. *See* **harmful.**
bang *verb*
1. To strike together or handle noisily ▸ clang, clap, clash, crack, crash, ding, knock, rap, slam, smack, smash, thump, thwack, whack. *See also* **hit, slap, thud. 2.** To make an explosive noise ▸ roar, thunder. *See* **blast** (1). **3.** To make a sudden, sharp noise ▸ clap, pop. *See* **crack** (2). **4.** To hit heavily and repeatedly ▸ assault, batter, pummel, thresh. *See* **beat** (1).
bang up *verb*
To injure or damage, as by abuse or heavy wear ▸ maul, rough up. *See* **batter** (1).
bang *noun*
1. A forceful movement causing a loud noise ▸ crash, slam, smash, wham. **2.** An explosive noise ▸ boom, crash. *See* **blast** (1). **3.** A sudden sharp, explosive noise ▸ clap, explosion, pop. *See* **crack** (1). **4.** A sudden heavy stroke ▸ crack, hit, swat, whack. *See* **blow**[2] (1). **5.** *Slang* A strong, pleasant feeling of excitement or stimulation ▸ lift. *Informal:* wallop. *Slang:* kick. *See* **thrill** (1).
bang *adverb*
With precision or absolute conformity ▸ exactly, precisely, squarely. *See* **directly** (3).
banish *verb*
1. To force to leave a country or place by official decree ▸ deport, exile, expatriate, expel, extradite, ostracize, transport. *See also* **eject, exclude, forbid. 2.** To rid one's mind of ▸ cast out, dispel. *See* **dismiss** (3). **3.** To direct or allow to leave ▸ cast out, expel. *See* **dismiss** (2).

✦ **CORE SYNONYMS:** *banish, exile, expatriate, deport, transport, extradite.* These verbs mean to send away from a country or state. *Banish* applies to forced departure from a country by official decree: *The spy was found guilty of treason and banished from the country. Exile* specifies voluntary or involuntary departure from one's own country because of adverse circumstances: *The royal family was exiled after the uprising. Expatriate* pertains to departure that is sometimes forced but often voluntary and may imply change of citizenship: *She was expatriated because of her political beliefs. Deport* denotes the official act of expelling an alien: *The foreigner was deported for entering the country illegally. Transport* pertains to sending a criminal abroad, usually to a penal colony: *Offenders were transported to Devil's Island. Extradite* applies to the delivery of an accused or convicted person to the state or country having jurisdiction over him or her: *The court will extradite the terrorists.*

---

banishment *noun*
▸ deportation, extradition. *See* **exile** (1).
bank[1] *noun*
A group of things gathered haphazardly ▸ drift, mass, mound. *See* **heap** (1). *See synonym note at* **heap.**
bank *verb*
To collect or pile up or onto something ▸ drift, lump. *See* **heap** (1).
bank[2] *verb*
To place money in an account ▸ deposit, invest, lay away, salt away. *Informal:* sock away. *See also* **conserve, save.**
bank on *or* **upon** *verb*
To place trust or confidence in ▸ count on (*or* upon), rely on (*or* upon). *See* **depend on** (1).
bank *noun*
A place where something is deposited for safekeeping ▸ archive, storehouse, warehouse. *See* **depository.**
bankable *adjective*
▸ gainful, lucrative, rewarding. *See* **profitable** (1).
banking *noun*
The management of money ▸ finance, investment, money management.
bankroll *verb*
Informal To supply capital ▸ back, fund. *See* **finance.**
bankroll *noun*
Informal Money or property used to produce more wealth ▸ financing, funding, stake. *See* **capital** (1).
bankrupt *verb*
1. To reduce to financial insolvency ▸ break, bust, impoverish. *See* **ruin** (3). **2.** To cause the complete ruin or wreckage of ▸ demolish, torpedo, wreck. *See* **destroy** (1).
bankrupt *noun*
An impoverished person ▸ beggar, insolvent, tramp. *See* **pauper.**
bankrupt *adjective*
1. Deprived of a quality or aspect that is desirable ▸ destitute, lacking, void. *See* **empty** (2). **2.** Having little or no money or wealth ▸ destitute, down-and-out, indigent. *See* **poor** (1).
bankruptcy *noun*
The condition of being financially insolvent ▸ failure, insolvency, ruin, ruination. *See also* **poverty.**
banned *adjective*
▸ barred, outlawed, prohibited. *See* **forbidden.**
banner *noun*
A piece of fabric used as a symbol ▸ colors, ensign, pennant. *See* **flag**[1] (1).

banner *adjective*
Exceptionally good of its kind ▸ first-rate, prime, splendid, tiptop. *See* **excellent.**

banneret *noun*
▸ banner, colors, pennant. *See* **flag**[1] (1).

banquet *noun*
A large, elaborately prepared meal ▸ feast, junket. *Informal:* feed, spread.

bantam *adjective*
▸ small, undersized. *See* **little** (1).

banter *noun*
Good-natured teasing ▸ badinage, chaff, raillery. *See* **ribbing.**

banter *verb*
To tease or mock good-humoredly ▸ chaff, josh. *Informal:* kid. *See* **joke** (2).

baptize *verb*
▸ christen, designate. *See* **name** (1).

bar *noun*
1. Something that blocks entry or passage ▸ barricade, barrier, block, blockage, bottleneck, clog, dam, encumbrance, hindrance, hurdle, impediment, obstacle, obstruction, snag, sticking point, stop, stumbling block, wall. *See also* **catch, disadvantage. 2.** A public establishment that sells alcoholic drinks and often food, often from a counter ▸ alehouse, cocktail lounge, inn, lounge, nightclub, pub, public house, roadhouse, saloon, tavern, wine bar. *Informal:* juke joint, watering hole. **3.** A straight, rigid piece of metal or other solid material ▸ shaft, stem. *See* **rod. 4.** A judicial assembly ▸ forum, tribunal. *See* **court** (2). **5.** A device for locking ▸ catch, clip, lock. *See* **fastener. 6.** A long narrow area that has a different color or marking from what surrounds it ▸ band, line, streak. *See* **stripe** (1).

bar *verb*
1. To confine within a limited area ▸ cage, coop (up), shut (in). *See* **enclose** (1). **2.** To block or fill with obstacles ▸ block, dam. *See* **obstruct** (1). *See synonym note at* **obstruct. 3.** To keep from being admitted, included, or considered ▸ eliminate, keep out, rule out. *See* **exclude** (1). **4.** To refuse to allow ▸ disallow, proscribe. *See* **forbid. 5.** To mark with a line or band, as of different color or texture ▸ striate, variegate. *See* **streak.**

✣ CORE SYNONYMS: *bar, barrier, obstacle, obstruction, block, hindrance, impediment, snag.* These nouns refer to something that blocks entry or passage or that slows progress. *Bar* and *barrier* convey that which confines or prevents exit or entry: *"Tyranny may always enter—there is no charm, no bar against it—the only bar against it is a large resolute breed of men"* (Walt Whitman). *"Literature is my Utopia . . . . No barrier of the senses shuts me out from the sweet, gracious discourse of my book friends"* (Helen Keller). *Obstacle* applies to something that literally or figuratively stands in the way of progress: *"We combat obstacles in order to get repose"* (Henry Adams). An *obstruction* makes passage or progress difficult: *A*

sandbar is an obstruction to navigation. *Block* suggests obstruction that effectively prevents all passage: *I had a mental block and couldn't remember the date.* *Hindrance* and *impediment* are applied to something that interferes with or delays passage or progress: *"an attachment that would be a hindrance to him in any honorable career"* (Thomas Hardy). *Overcrowded classrooms are an impediment to learning.* A *snag* is an unforeseen or hidden, often transitory obstacle: *Due to a snag in plans, the project was delayed.*

---

barb *noun*
1. A flippant or sarcastic remark ▸ dig, quip. *Slang:* wisecrack. *See* **crack** (5). **2.** A sharp protuberance or projection ▸ prick, prong, spine. *See* **spike** (1).

barbarian *noun*
1. An unrefined, rude person ▸ chuff, Philistine, yahoo. *See* **boor.** *See synonym note at* **boor. 2.** A perversely mean, cruel, or wicked person ▸ beast, devil, monster. *See* **fiend** (1).

barbarian *adjective*
1. Not civilized ▸ barbaric, barbarous, rude. *See* **uncivilized** (1). **2.** Lacking in delicacy or refinement ▸ indelicate, unbecoming, unrefined. *See* **coarse** (1).

barbaric *adjective*
1. Not civilized ▸ barbarian, barbarous, rude. *See* **uncivilized** (1). **2.** Lacking in delicacy or refinement ▸ indelicate, unbecoming, unrefined. *See* **coarse** (1).

barbarism *noun*
▸ malapropism, solecism. *See* **corruption** (3).

barbarity *noun*
1. The quality or condition of being cruel ▸ brutality, truculence. *See* **cruelty. 2.** A monstrous offense or evil ▸ enormity, monstrosity. *See* **outrage** (1).

barbarous *adjective*
1. Not civilized ▸ barbarian, barbaric, rude. *See* **uncivilized** (1). **2.** Inflicting suffering or pain ▸ brutal, fierce, savage. *See* **cruel** (1). *See synonym note at* **cruel.**

barbecue *verb*
▸ broil, charbroil, grill, roast. *See* **cook** (1).

barbed *adjective*
▸ brambly, bristly, prickly. *See* **thorny** (1).

bard *noun*
▸ muse, troubadour. *See* **poet.**

bare *adjective*
1. Without addition, decoration, or qualification ▸ austere, bald, bare-bones, classic, dry, plain, plain-Jane, plain vanilla, severe, simple, spare, spartan, stark, unadorned, undecorated, unvarnished, vanilla. *See also* **rustic. 2.** Just sufficient ▸ mere, scant, scanty. *See also* **insufficient, meager. 3.** Without the usual covering ▸ bald, barren, hairless, leafless, naked, nude. *See also* **open. 4.** Not wearing any clothes ▸ au naturel, naked, nude. *See* **nude** (1). **5.** Containing nothing ▸ blank, clear. *See* **empty** (1). *See synonym note at* **empty.**

bare *verb*
1. To remove the clothing or covering from ▸ denude, disrobe, divest, expose, flay, peel, strip, unclothe, uncover, undress. *See also* **skin. 2.** To make visible ▸ disclose, expose, uncover. *See* **reveal** (2).

bare-bones *adjective*
▶ austere, plain, spare. *See* **bare** (1).

barefaced *adjective*
▶ bold, insolent, pert. *See* **impudent**. *See synonym note at* **impudent**.

barely *adverb*
By a very little; almost not ▶ hardly, just, scarce, scarcely. *Idioms:* by a hair (*or* whisker), by the skin of one's teeth. *See also* **approximately, merely, only**.

bareness *noun*
1. The state of being without clothes ▶ nakedness, undress. *See* **nudity**. **2.** Total lack of ideas, meaning, or substance ▶ barrenness, hollowness. *See* **emptiness** (3).

barf *verb*
Slang To eject the contents of the stomach through the mouth ▶ retch, throw up. *Informal:* puke. *See* **vomit** (1).

bargain *noun*
1. An often written acceptance of terms between parties ▶ accord, deal, pact. *See* **agreement** (1). *See synonym note at* **agreement**. **2.** A business agreement involving goods or services ▶ sale, trade, transaction. *See* **deal** (1). **3.** Something offered or bought at a low price ▶ find. *Informal:* buy, deal. *Slang:* steal.

bargain *verb*
1. To argue about the terms, as of a sale ▶ negotiate, palter. *See* **haggle**. **2.** To enter into a formal agreement ▶ covenant, stipulate. *See* **contract** (1).

bargain for *or on verb*
To look forward to confidently ▶ await, look for. *See* **expect** (1).

bargain-basement *adjective*
▶ budget, economy, low-cost. *See* **cheap** (1).

barge in *verb*
1. To force or come in as an improper or unwanted element ▶ cut in, horn in, obtrude. *See* **intrude** (1). **2.** To interject remarks or questions into another's discourse ▶ break in, chip in, cut in. *See* **interrupt** (2).

bark *verb*
1. To make a sudden, sharp noise ▶ clap, pop. *See* **crack** (2). **2.** To speak abruptly and sharply ▶ growl, snarl. *See* **snap** (3).

bark *noun*
A sudden sharp, explosive noise ▶ bang, pop, snap. *See* **crack** (1).

barm *noun*
▶ lather, suds. *See* **foam**.

barmy *adjective*
▶ frothy, lathery, sudsy. *See* **foamy**.

barnyard *adjective*
▶ bawdy, coarse, lewd, vulgar. *See* **obscene** (1).

baronial *adjective*
▶ imposing, magnificent, splendid. *See* **grand** (1).

baroque *adjective*
1. Elaborately and heavily ornamented ▶ flamboyant, resplendent. *See* **ornate** (1). **2.** Difficult to understand because of intricacy ▶ convoluted, involved, tangled, tortuous. *See* **complex** (1).

barracks *noun*
Usually temporary living accommodations ▶ lodgings, rooms, quarters. *Slang:* crash-pad. *See also* **apartment, home**.

barrage *noun*
A concentrated outpouring, as of missiles, words, or blows ▶ bombardment, broadside, burst, cannonade, crossfire, discharge, fire, flak, fusillade, hail, rain, salvo, shower, storm, volley. *See also* **attack, blast, flood**.

barrage *verb*
To direct a barrage at ▶ blitz, bomb, bombard, cannonade, fusillade, pelt, pepper, shell, shower. *See also* **attack, overwhelm**.

✚ **CORE SYNONYMS:** *barrage, bomb, bombard, pelt, pepper, shell, shower.* These verbs mean to direct a concentrated outpouring at something or someone: *barraged the speaker with questions; bombed the village from the air; bombarded the box office with ticket orders; pelted the speaker with tomatoes; peppered the senator with protests; shelled the fortification; showered the child with gifts.*

barred *adjective*
▶ banned, outlawed, prohibited. *See* **forbidden**.

barrel *noun*
1. *Informal* A great deal ▶ bounty, mass, profusion. *See* **abundance** (1). **2.** A large vessel used to hold or store liquids ▶ basin, cask, tank. *See* **vat**.

barrel *verb*
Slang To move swiftly ▶ dash, sprint, zip. *See* **rush** (1).

barren *adjective*
1. Unable to produce offspring ▶ childless, impotent, infertile, sterile, unfruitful. **2.** Unable to support vegetation or crops ▶ dead, desert, desolate, infertile, lifeless, sterile, unfruitful, unproductive, waste. *See also* **bleak, dry**. **3.** Without the usual covering ▶ bald, naked, nude. *See* **bare** (3). **4.** Having no useful result ▶ fruitless, unsuccessful, vain. *See* **futile**. *See synonym note at* **futile**. **5.** Containing nothing ▶ clear, void. *See* **empty** (1). *See synonym note at* **empty**. **6.** Deprived of a quality or aspect that is desirable ▶ destitute, lacking, void. *See* **empty** (2).

barren *noun*
A desolate or unproductive region ▶ badlands, waste, wasteland. *See* **desert**[1].

barrenness *noun*
1. The state or condition of being unable to reproduce ▶ childlessness, fruitlessness, infertility. *See* **sterility** (2). **2.** Empty, unfilled space ▶ emptiness, vacuity. *See* **nothingness** (2). **3.** Total lack of ideas, meaning, or substance ▶ blankness, hollowness. *See* **emptiness** (3). **4.** The condition or quality of being useless or ineffective ▶ fruitlessness, uselessness, vainness. *See* **futility**.

barrens *noun*
▶ badlands, waste, wasteland. *See* **desert**[1].

barricade *noun*
1. Something that blocks entry or passage ▶ barrier,

blockage, hindrance. *See* **bar** (1). **2.** The act or a means of defending ▸ protection, safeguard, shield. *See* **defense** (1). **3.** A structure used as a defense against an attack ▸ bastion, parapet. *See* **bulwark**. *See synonym note at* **bulwark**.

barricade *verb*
To block or fill with obstacles ▸ block, dam. *See* **obstruct** (1).

barrier *noun*
1. A solid structure that encloses an area or separates one area from another ▸ partition, wall. *See also* **border, screen**. **2.** Something that blocks entry or passage ▸ barricade, blockage, hindrance. *See* **bar** (1). *See synonym note at* **bar**.

barter *noun*
1. A business agreement involving goods or services ▸ sale, trade, transaction. *See* **deal** (1). **2.** The act of exchanging ▸ interchange, switch, trade. *See* **change** (2).

barter *verb*
To give up in return for something else ▸ exchange, interchange, trade. *See* **change** (3).

basal *adjective*
1. Of or treating the most basic aspects ▸ basic, beginning. *See* **elementary** (2). **2.** Arising from or going to the root or source ▸ basic, fundamental, primary. *See* **radical** (1). **3.** Forming an essential element, as arising from the basic structure of an individual ▸ inherent, intrinsic, natural. *See* **constitutional** (1).

base¹ *noun*
1. A center of organization, supply, or activity ▸ camp, command post, complex, depot, headquarters, home, home base, home office, installation, post, station. *See also* **center**. **2.** The lowest or supporting part or structure ▸ basis, bed, bottom, cornerstone, foot, footing, foundation, ground, groundwork, pedestal, seat, stand, substratum, substructure, underpinning. *See also* **stage, support**. **3.** An underlying support, as for an argument or belief ▸ cornerstone, foundation, underpinning. *See* **basis** (1). **4.** The main part of a word to which affixes are attached ▸ root, stem. *See* **theme** (1).

base *verb*
1. To provide a basis for ▸ build, construct, establish, found, ground, model, predicate, rest, root, undergird, underpin. *See also* **depend, support**. **2.** To put in a certain position or location ▸ locate, place, situate. *See* **position**.

base² *adjective*
1. Having or proceeding from low moral standards ▸ squalid, vile. *See* **sordid**. *See synonym note at* **sordid**. **2.** Of decidedly inferior quality ▸ cheap, lousy, poor. *See* **shoddy** (1).

baseborn *adjective*
1. Born to parents who are not married to each other ▸ bastard, misbegotten. *See* **illegitimate** (1). **2.** Lacking high station or birth ▸ common, humble, unwashed. *See* **lowly** (1).

baseless *adjective*
Having no basis in fact ▸ groundless, idle, meritless, unfounded, unproved, unwarranted. *See also* **empty, false**.

✦ CORE SYNONYMS: *baseless, groundless, idle, unfounded, unwarranted*. These adjectives mean being without a basis or foundation in fact: *a baseless accusation; groundless rumors; idle gossip; unfounded suspicions; unwarranted jealousy*.

---

baselessly *adverb*
Without basis or foundation in fact ▸ groundlessly, unwarrantedly, unfoundedly.

baseness *noun*
▸ dishonesty, improbity. *Informal:* crookedness. *See* **corruption** (2).

bash *verb*
1. To deliver a sudden, sharp blow to ▸ jab, sock, whack. *See* **hit** (1). **2.** *Informal* To criticize harshly and devastatingly ▸ blast, excoriate, flay. *See* **slam** (5).

bash *noun*
1. *Informal* A sudden heavy stroke ▸ crack, hit, swat, whack. *See* **blow²** (1). **2.** *Slang* A big, exuberant party ▸ celebration. *Slang:* blowout. *See* **blast** (3). **3.** *Slang* A social gathering, especially for pleasure ▸ celebration, gala, soiree. *See* **party** (1).

bashful *adjective*
▸ backward, demure, diffident. *See* **shy¹** (1). *See synonym note at* **shy¹**.

bashfulness *noun*
▸ coyness, demureness, diffidence. *See* **shyness**.

basic *adjective*
1. Of or being an irreducible element ▸ elementary, essential, fundamental. *See* **elemental** (1). **2.** Constituting or forming part of the essence of something ▸ constitutional, fundamental. *See* **essential** (2). **3.** Of or treating the most basic aspects ▸ beginning, rudimentary. *See* **elementary** (2). **4.** Arising from or going to the root or source ▸ fundamental, primary. *See* **radical** (1).

basic *noun*
An irreducible constituent of a whole ▸ essential, fundamental. *See* **element** (1).

basically *adverb*
▸ fundamentally, underlyingly. *See* **essentially**.

basin *noun*
1. The region drained by a river system ▸ drainage basin, watershed. **2.** An area sunk below its surroundings ▸ concavity, dip, hollow. *See* **depression** (1). **3.** A large vessel used to hold or store liquids ▸ cask, tank. *See* **vat**.

basis *noun*
1. An underlying support, as for an argument, action, or belief ▸ base, cornerstone, footing, foundation, fundamental, ground, grounds, groundwork, keystone, root, rudiment, underpinning. *See also* **cause, origin, support**. **2.** A justifying fact or consideration ▸ foundation, justification, reason, warrant. *See also* **account, apology**. **3.** An established position from

which to operate or deal with others ▸ footing, standing, status, terms. *See also* **place. 4.** The lowest or supporting part or structure ▸ bottom, foot, foundation. *See* **base**[1] (2).

✦ **CORE SYNONYMS:** *basis, foundation, grounds, groundwork.* These nouns pertain to an underlying support, as for an argument, action, or belief. *Basis* is the most general term: *"Healthy scepticism is the basis of all accurate observation"* (Arthur Conan Doyle). *Foundation* often stresses firmness of support for something of relative magnitude: *"Our flagrant disregard for the law attacks the foundation of this society"* (Peter D. Relic). *Grounds* signifies a justifiable reason: *The lawyer outlined the grounds for the divorce. Groundwork* usually has the sense of a necessary preliminary: *"It* [the Universal Declaration of Human Rights] *has laid the groundwork for the world's war crimes tribunals"* (Hillary Rodham Clinton).

bask *verb*
▸ indulge, revel, wallow. *See* **luxuriate.**

basket *noun*
1. A container made of interwoven material ▸ creel, hamper, pannier. *See also* **container. 2.** The contents of a basket ▸ basketful, bushel. **3.** The goal in the game of basketball ▸ bucket, field goal, hoop, net, swish, swisher.

bass *adjective*
▸ alto, contralto, deep. *See* **low** (2).

bastard *adjective*
▸ baseborn, misbegotten. *See* **illegitimate** (1).

bastardize *verb*
▸ debase, demoralize, deprave, warp. *See* **corrupt** (1).

baste *verb*
▸ assault, batter, pummel, thresh. *See* **beat** (1). *See synonym note at* **beat** (1).

bastion *noun*
1. A position or building that has been fortified to be defended by soldiers ▸ citadel, stronghold. *See* **fort. 2.** A structure used as a defense against an attack ▸ barricade, parapet. *See* **bulwark.** *See synonym note at* **bulwark.**

bat[1] *verb*
To open and close one or both eyes rapidly ▸ twinkle, wink. *See* **blink** (1).

bat *noun*
A brief closing of the eyes ▸ flutter, wink. *See* **blink** (1).

bat[2] *noun*
Slang A drinking bout ▸ brannigan, carousal, spree. *See* **bender.**

batch *noun*
▸ body, cluster, collection. *See* **group** (1).

bate *verb*
▸ die (away, down, off, *or* out), ebb, lapse. *See* **subside** (1).

bathe *verb*
1. To make moist ▸ dampen, moisten, wash, wet. **2.** To flow against or along ▸ lap, lave, lip, wash. *See also* **flow. 3.** To rid of dirt, stains, trash, or other impurities ▸ cleanse, launder, lave. *See* **clean** (1).

bathetic *adjective*
▸ gushy, maudlin, soft. *See* **sentimental.** *See synonym note at* **sentimental.**

bathos *noun*
▸ maudlinism, treacle. *See* **sentimentality.**

baton *noun*
▸ branch, stake, twig. *See* **stick** (1).

batten *verb*
1. To make a large profit ▸ cash in, profit. *Slang:* clean up. *Idiom:* make a killing. **2.** To do or fare well ▸ boom, flourish, thrive. *See* **prosper.**

batter *verb*
1. To injure or damage, as by abuse or heavy wear ▸ bang up, knock about (*or* around), maim, mangle, manhandle, maul, mutilate, ravage, rough up, scuff, work over. *Idioms:* play (*or* wreak) havoc (on *or* with). *See also* **abuse, damage, deform. 2.** To hit heavily and repeatedly ▸ assault, bludgeon, pummel, thresh. *See* **beat** (1). *See synonym note at* **beat.**

✦ **CORE SYNONYMS:** *batter, maim, mangle, maul, mutilate.* These verbs mean to damage, injure, or disfigure as by abuse or heavy wear: *a house battered by a hurricane; a construction worker maimed in an accident; machinery that mangled the worker's fingers; a tent mauled by a hungry bear; mutilated the painting with a razor.*

battle *noun*
1. An encounter between opposing military forces ▸ action, belligerency, brush, clash, combat, conflict, confrontation, encounter, engagement, hostilities, skirmish, sortie, strife, struggle, war, warfare. *See also* **competition, conflict, fight. 2.** A vying with others for victory ▸ contest, rivalry, struggle. *See* **competition** (1).

battle *verb*
To strive in opposition ▸ clash, combat, fight. *See* **contend** (1).

battle-ax *or* **battle-axe** *noun*
1. An ugly, frightening woman, usually old ▸ crone, hag. *Slang:* biddy. *See* **witch** (2). **2.** *Informal* A person, traditionally a woman, who persistently nags or criticizes ▸ harpy, shrew. *See* **scold.**

battle cry *noun*
▸ call to arms, war cry. *See* **cry** (2).

batty *adjective*
Slang Afflicted with or exhibiting irrationality and mental unsoundness ▸ crazy, daft, off. *See* **insane** (1).

bauble *noun*
▸ knickknack, trinket. *See* **novelty** (3).

bawd *noun*
▸ courtesan, strumpet. *See* **harlot.**

bawdiness *noun*
▸ filthiness, profanity, smuttiness, vulgarness. *See* **obscenity** (1).

bawdry *noun*
▸ dirt, sleaze, smut. *See* **obscenity** (2).

bawdy *adjective*
▸ coarse, indecent, lewd, vulgar. *See* **obscene** (1).

bawl *verb*
1. To cry loudly, as an upset baby does ▸ caterwaul, holler, howl, squall, wail, yowl. *See also* **scream. 2.** To shed tears ▸ howl, sob, weep. *See* **cry** (1). **3.** To say or speak in a loud cry ▸ call, holler, yell. *See* **shout.** *See synonym note at* **shout.**

bawl out *verb*
Informal To criticize for a fault or offense ▸ chide, rebuke, reprimand. *See* **chastise** (1).

bawl *noun*
A loud, deep, prolonged sound ▸ bellow, clamor. *See* **roar** (1).

bawling *noun*
▸ blubbering, sobbing, weeping. *See* **cry** (1).

bay¹ *noun*
A body of water partly enclosed by land but having a wide outlet to the sea ▸ bight, gulf, sound. *See also* **channel, harbor, inlet.**

bay² *noun*
A long, mournful cry ▸ moan, wail, yowl. *See* **howl** (1).

bay *verb*
To utter or emit a long, mournful, plaintive sound ▸ moan, wail, yowl. *See* **howl** (1).

bayonet *verb*
▸ drill, incise, pierce, slash. *See* **cut** (1).

bazaar *noun*
▸ exposition, show. *See* **exhibition** (1).

be *verb*
To have reality or life ▸ breathe, live. *See* **exist** (1).

be into *verb*
Slang To receive pleasure from ▸ appreciate, savor. *See* **enjoy** (1).

bead *noun*
▸ driblet, droplet. *See* **drop** (1).

beak *noun*
1. The horny projection forming a bird's jaws ▸ beak, mandible, nib. **2.** *Informal* The human organ of smell ▸ proboscis. *Slang:* schnoz. *See* **nose** (1).

beam *noun*
1. A narrow line of light or other radiant energy ▸ finger, ray, shaft, stream. **2.** A sturdy horizontal structural support ▸ crossbeam, crosstie, girder, I-beam, joist, lintel, rafter, tie beam, timber, trestle, viga. *See also* **column, support.**

beam *verb*
1. To emit a bright light ▸ blaze, burn, gleam, glow, incandesce, radiate, shine. *See also* **glare, glitter, illuminate. 2.** To curve the lips upward in expressing amusement, pleasure, or happiness ▸ grin, smirk. *See* **smile.**

beamy *adjective*
▸ brilliant, incandescent, radiant. *See* **bright** (1).

bean *noun*
Slang The uppermost part of the body ▸ crown, pate. *See* **head** (1).

bear *verb*
1. To hold the weight of ▸ carry, hold (up), shoulder, support, sustain, uphold. **2.** To keep steadily in mind ▸ cherish, entertain, harbor, nourish, nurse. *See also*

ponder, think. **3.** To have as a visible characteristic ▸ carry, display, exhibit, have, possess, wear. *See also* **display, show. 4.** To give birth to ▸ bring forth, deliver, have. *Chiefly Regional:* birth. **Idioms:** be brought abed (*or* to bed) of. **5.** To proceed in a specified direction ▸ aim, go, head, make, set out, start out, strike out, turn. *Informal:* light out. *See also* **go, start, turn. 6.** To hold on one's person ▸ have, possess. *Informal:* pack. *See* **carry** (7). **7.** To move while supporting ▸ bear, haul, lug. *See* **carry** (1). *See synonym note at* **carry. 8.** To cause to come along with oneself ▸ convey, fetch. *See* **bring** (1). **9.** To conduct oneself in a specified way ▸ acquit, behave, carry, comport. *See* **act** (1). **10.** To put up with ▸ stomach, tolerate, withstand. *See* **endure** (1). *See synonym note at* **endure. 11.** To bring into existence ▸ give, provide, yield. *See* **produce** (1). *See synonym note at* **produce. 12.** To apply pressure on, against, or with ▸ press, prod, shove. *See* **push** (1).

bear on *or* **upon** *verb*
To be pertinent ▸ appertain, pertain, relate. *See* **apply** (2).

bear out *verb*
1. To assure the certainty or validity of ▸ authenticate, corroborate, substantiate, verify. *See* **confirm** (1). **2.** To establish as true or genuine through evidence ▸ confirm, document, establish, substantiate, validate. *See* **prove** (1).

bear up *verb*
To withstand stress or difficulty ▸ endure, hold up, stand up. **Idioms:** bite the bullet, grin and bear it, keep a stiff upper lip, make the best of it, take one's medicine, take it (lying down). *See also* **carry on, endure.**

bearable *adjective*
Capable of being tolerated ▸ endurable, sufferable, supportable, tolerable.

beard *verb*
▸ challenge, confront, dare. *See* **defy** (1).

bearer *noun*
▸ carrier, courier, envoy. *See* **messenger.**

bearing *noun*
1. Behavior that reveals one's personality or state of mind ▸ address, air, demeanor, manner, mien, poise, presence, style. *See also* **appearance, behavior, posture. 2.** The compass direction in which a ship or aircraft moves ▸ course, heading, vector. *See also* **direction. 3.** One's place and direction relative to one's surroundings ▸ bearings, location, orientation, position, situation, whereabouts. **4.** The relation with, or the fact of being related to, the matter at hand ▸ materiality, pertinence. *See* **relevance. 5.** The strong effect exerted by one person or thing on another ▸ impression, influence. *See* **impact** (2).

beast *noun*
▸ devil, monster, ogre. *See* **fiend** (1).

beastly *or* **beastlike** *adjective*
Similar to a beast in behavior ▸ bestial, brutish. *See also* **cruel, savage, uncivilized.**

beat *verb*

1. To hit heavily and repeatedly ▸ assail, assault, bang, baste, batter, belabor, bludgeon, buffet, club, cudgel, drub, flail, hammer, maul, pelt, pound, pummel, smash, thrash, thresh, whale. *Informal:* lambaste, lather, thump. *Slang:* clobber. *Idioms:* knock the daylights (*or* stuffing *or* tar) out of, rain blows on, tan someone's hide. *See also* **batter, hit, slap. 2.** To punish with blows or lashes ▸ birch, cane, flagellate, flay, flog, hide, horsewhip, lash, scourge, strap, thrash, whip. *Informal:* trim. *Slang:* lay into, lick. **3.** To shape, break, or flatten with repeated blows ▸ forge, hammer, pound, stamp. *See also* **even. 4.** To indicate time or rhythm ▸ count, tap (out). *Idioms:* keep time, mark time. **5.** To make rhythmic contractions, sounds, or movements ▸ drum, flutter, hammer, palpitate, pound, pulsate, pulse, tap, throb, thump, tick. **6.** To combine or process ingredients by stirring ▸ blend, cream, fold (in), mix, stir, whip, whisk. *See also* **combine, mix. 7.** To move the arms or wings up and down ▸ flutter, wave. *See* **flap** (1). **8.** To win a victory over, as in battle or a competition ▸ conquer, surmount, vanquish. *See* **defeat** (1). *See synonym note at* **defeat. 9.** *Informal* To be greater or better than ▸ exceed, excel, outshine. *See* **surpass** (1). **10.** *Informal* To put at a loss as to what to say or do ▸ confound, perplex. *Informal:* stump. *See* **baffle** (1). **11.** *Informal* To cause to accept something false, especially by trickery or misrepresentation ▸ dupe, fool, mislead, trick. *See* **deceive.**

beat down *verb*

1. To shine intensely and blindingly ▸ blaze, throb. *See* **glare** (2). **2.** To severely impair someone's spirit, health, or will ▸ overwhelm, ruin. *See* **break** (4).

beat off *verb*

To turn aside or drive away ▸ deflect, repulse, ward off. *See* **repel.**

beat *noun*

1. A stroke or blow that produces a sound ▸ bump, clunk, knock, pound, rap, smack, thud, thump, whack. *See also* **blow² 2.** An area regularly covered, as by a policeman or reporter ▸ circuit, round, rounds, route, territory. *See also* **circle. 3.** A rhythmic contraction or sound ▸ drumbeat, palpitation, pounding, pulsation, pulse, throb, throbbing, tick, ticktock. **4.** The patterned, recurring alternation of contrasting elements, such as stressed and unstressed notes in music ▸ cadence, meter, swing. *See* **rhythm.**

beat *adjective*

Informal Depleted of energy ▸ exhausted, weary, worn-out. *See* **tired** (1).

✦ CORE SYNONYMS: *beat, baste, batter, belabor, buffet, hammer, lambaste, pound, pummel, thrash.* These verbs mean to hit heavily and repeatedly with violent blows: *was mugged and beaten; basted him with a stick; was battered in the boxing ring; rioting students belabored by police officers; buffeted him with her open palm; hammered the opponent with his fists; lambasted every challenger; troops pounded with mortar fire; pummeled the bully soundly; thrashed the thief for stealing the candy.*

beatification *noun*

▸ apotheosis, elevation. *See* **exaltation** (1).

beating *noun*

1. A punishment dealt with blows or lashes ▸ caning, flagellation, flaying, flogging, hiding, lashing, pounding, thrashing, whipping. *Informal:* trimming. *Slang:* licking. **2.** The act of defeating or the condition of being defeated ▸ overthrow, trouncing, vanquishment. *See* **defeat.**

beatitude *noun*

1. A condition of well-being and good spirits ▸ blessedness, bliss, felicity. *See* **happiness. 2.** The quality of being or acting in accordance with what is holy or sacred ▸ blessedness, sanctity. *See* **holiness.**

beau *noun*

1. A man who courts a woman ▸ admirer, courter, suitor, swain, wooer. *See also* **gallant. 2.** A man who is a woman's romantic partner ▸ inamorato. *Informal:* fellow. *See* **boyfriend. 3.** A man who is vain about his clothes ▸ coxcomb, dandy, fop, peacock, swell.

beau ideal *noun*

▸ exemplar, ideal, paradigm. *See* **model.**

beautiful *adjective*

Having qualities that delight the eye ▸ attractive, beauteous, comely, exquisite, fair, good-looking, gorgeous, handsome, lovely, pretty, pulchritudinous, ravishing, sightly, statuesque, stunning. *Idiom:* easy on the eyes. *See also* **attractive, seductive.**

✦ CORE SYNONYMS: *beautiful, lovely, pretty, handsome, comely, fair.* These adjectives apply to those qualities that delight the eye. *Beautiful* is most comprehensive: *a beautiful child; a beautiful painting; a beautiful mathematical proof. Lovely* applies to what inspires emotion rather than intellectual appreciation: "*They were lovely, your eyes*" (George Seferis). What is *pretty* is beautiful in a delicate or graceful way: *a pretty face; a pretty song; a pretty room. Handsome* stresses poise and dignity of form and proportion: *We were taken to a very large, handsome paneled library.* "*She is very pretty, but not so extraordinarily handsome*" (William Makepeace Thackeray). *Comely* suggests wholesome physical attractiveness: "*Mrs. Hurd is a large woman with a big, comely, simple face*" (Ernest Hemingway). *Fair* emphasizes freshness or purity: "*In the highlands, in the country places,/Where the old plain men have rosy faces,/And the young fair maidens/Quiet eyes*" (Robert Louis Stevenson).

◂ ANTONYM: *ugly*

beautify *verb*

To endow with beauty and elegance ▸ embellish, enhance, grace, set off. *See also* **adorn.**

beauty *noun*

1. A person regarded as physically attractive ▸ Adonis (for a man), belle (for a woman), dreamboat, eyeful, goddess (for a woman), lovely, stunner, Venus (for a woman), vision. *Slang:* babe, dish, doll, fox, hotty, hunk (for a man), knockout, looker, stud (for a man).

2. A particularly good or beneficial quality ▸ asset, distinction, merit. *See* **virtue** (1).

becalm *verb*
▸ appease, mollify, soothe. *See* **pacify.**

because *conjunction*
For the reason that ▸ as, for, inasmuch as, seeing as, since. *Idioms:* on account of the fact that, in consequence of the fact that, in view of the fact that.

because of *preposition*
By the cause of ▸ as a result of, by reason of, by virtue of, due to, in consequence of, in view of, on account of, owing to, through.

beckon *verb*
▸ motion, sign, signal. *See* **gesture.**

becloud *verb*
▸ blur, fog, obfuscate. *See* **obscure** (1).

become *verb*
1. To come to be ▸ change (to *or* into), come (to be), develop (into), get (to be), grow (to be), turn (to *or* into), wax. **2.** To look good on or with ▸ enhance, flatter, suit. *Idiom:* put in the best light. **3.** To be appropriate or suitable to ▸ befit, fit, match. *See* **suit** (1).

becoming *adjective*
1. Pleasingly suited to the wearer ▸ attractive, fetching, flattering, perfect, well-suited. *See also* **attractive.** **2.** Suitable for a particular person, condition, occasion, or place ▸ befitting, correct, right. *See* **appropriate** (1).

bed *verb*
1. To go to bed ▸ *Slang:* crash, flop. *See* **retire** (2). **2.** To stay in or provide with lodging, especially temporarily ▸ board, room, house. *See* **lodge** (1). **3.** To engage in sexual relations with ▸ mate, take. *See* **sleep with.**

bed *noun*
The lowest or supporting part or structure ▸ bottom, foot, foundation. *See* **base**¹ (2).

bedaub *verb*
1. To spread with a greasy, sticky, or dirty substance ▸ dab, plaster, smudge. *See* **smear** (1). **2.** To make dirty ▸ bemire, muck up, mud. *See* **dirty** (1).

bedaze *verb*
▸ stun, stupefy. *See* **daze** (1).

bedazzle *verb*
To confuse with bright light ▸ blind, daze, dazzle.

bedeck *verb*
1. To furnish with decorations ▸ decorate, garnish, ornament. *See* **adorn** (1). **2.** To dress in formal or special clothing ▸ attire, primp. *See* **dress up.**

bedevil *verb*
▸ harry, pester, torment. *See* **harass.**

bedim *verb*
▸ blur, fog, obfuscate. *See* **obscure** (1).

bedraggled *adjective*
▸ broken-down, dilapidated, tattered. *See* **shabby** (1).

bedtime *noun*
▸ after dark, lights out. *See* **night.**

beef *noun*
1. *Informal* Solid and well-developed muscles ▸ bulk,

muscle. *See* **brawn** (1). **2.** *Slang* An expression of pain or dissatisfaction ▸ carp, whimper, whine. *See* **complaint** (1).

beef *verb*
Slang To express feelings of pain, dissatisfaction or resentment ▸ fuss, grouch, whine. *See* **complain.**

beef up *verb*
Informal To make or become greater or larger ▸ amplify, boost, enlarge. *See* **increase** (1).

beefy *adjective*
▸ brawny, robust, sturdy. *See* **muscular.**

beetle *verb*
▸ balloon, jut, project. *See* **bulge** (1).

befall *verb*
1. To take place by chance ▸ betide, chance, hap, happen. **2.** To take place ▸ come, occur, transpire. *See* **happen** (1). *See synonym note at* **happen.**

befit *verb*
1. To be suitable to or in keeping with ▸ become, fit, match. *See* **suit** (1). **2.** To be an appropriate occasion for ▸ occasion, warrant. *See* **justify** (2).

befitting *adjective*
1. Suitable for a particular person, condition, occasion, or place ▸ becoming, correct, right. *See* **appropriate** (1). **2.** Suited to one's purpose ▸ expedient, proper, suitable. *See* **convenient** (1).

befog *verb*
▸ blur, fog, obfuscate. *See* **obscure** (1).

before *adverb*
1. At a time in the past ▸ already, previously. *See* **earlier** (1). **2.** Up to this time ▸ previously, yet. *See* **earlier** (2). **3.** Until then ▸ beforehand, earlier.

beforehand *adverb*
1. At a time in the past ▸ before, previously. *See* **earlier** (1). **2.** Before the expected time ▸ ahead, betimes. *See* **early.** **3.** Until then ▸ before, earlier.

befoul *verb*
1. To make dirty ▸ bemire, muck up, mud. *See* **dirty** (1). **2.** To attack the reputation or honor of ▸ besmirch, smear, tarnish. *See* **denigrate** (1).

befuddle *verb*
1. To cause to be unclear in mind or intent ▸ addle, bewilder, confound. *See* **confuse** (1). *See synonym note at* **confuse.** **2.** To addle the mind, as with a narcotic or alcohol ▸ besot, impair, stupefy. *See* **drug** (2).

befuddlement *noun*
▸ bewilderment, perplexity, stupor. *See* **daze.**

beg *verb*
1. To ask for as charity; solicit money or favors ▸ bum, cadge. *Informal:* panhandle. *Slang:* mooch, scrounge. *Idioms:* hit someone up for, pass the cup (*or* hat), touch someone for. *See also* **freeload. 2.** To make an earnest or urgent request ▸ beseech, entreat, plead. *See* **appeal** (1). *See synonym note at* **appeal. 3.** To have as a need or prerequisite ▸ entail, involve, necessitate. *See* **demand** (2).

✦ **CORE SYNONYMS:** *beg, bum, cadge, mooch, panhandle.* These verbs mean to ask for or obtain by charity:

begging for change; bummed a ride to the stadium; cadged a meal; mooching food; homeless people forced to panhandle.

beget *verb*
1. To be the biological father of ▸ father, get, sire. **2.** To give life to ▸ propagate, spawn. *See* **breed** (1).

begetter *noun*
1. A male parent ▸ paterfamilias, patriarch, sire. *See* **father** (1). **2.** One that creates, founds, or originates ▸ author, creator, inventor. *See* **originator**.

beggar *noun*
1. One who begs habitually or for a living ▸ almsman, almswoman, cadger, mendicant. *Informal:* panhandler. *Slang:* bummer, mooch, moocher. *See also* **parasite**. **2.** An impoverished person ▸ derelict, insolvent, tramp. *See* **pauper**. **3.** One who humbly entreats ▸ petitioner, prayer, suitor, suppliant, supplicant.

beggarly *adjective*
▸ destitute, down-and-out, indigent. *See* **poor** (1).

beggary *noun*
1. The condition of being a beggar ▸ mendicancy, mendicity. **2.** The condition of being extremely poor ▸ destitution, indigence, need. *See* **poverty** (1).

begin *verb*
1. To come into being ▸ appear, arise, commence, crop up, dawn, emerge, originate, start. **Idioms:** raise (one's) head, see the light of day. *See also* **cause, stem**. **2.** To go about the initial step in doing something ▸ approach, embark, initiate. *See* **start** (1).

beginner *noun*
One who is just starting to learn or do something ▸ abecedarian, apprentice, cub, fledgling, freshman, greenhorn, initiate, learner, neophyte, newcomer, novice, novitiate, tenderfoot, tyro. *Slang:* newbie, rookie. *See also* **amateur**.

beginning *noun*
1. The act of bringing or being brought into existence ▸ commencement, conception, inauguration, inception, incipience, incipiency, initiation, introduction, invention, launch, leadoff, opening, origination, start. *Informal:* kickoff. *See also* **foundation**. **2.** The initial stage of a developmental process ▸ genesis, inception, start. *See* **birth** (2). *See synonym note at* **birth**. **3.** A point of origination ▸ provenance, root, source. *See* **origin** (1).

beginning *adjective*
1. Of or occurring at the start of something ▸ early, inaugural, inceptive, incipient, initial, initiatory, introductory, leadoff, opening, starting. *See also* **first, introductory**. **2.** Of or treating the most basic aspects ▸ basic, rudimentary. *See* **elementary** (2).

begird *verb*
▸ band, belt, gird. *See* **encircle** (1).

begrime *verb*
▸ bemire, muck up, mud. *See* **dirty** (1).

begrudge *verb*
▸ covet, envy, grudge. *See synonym note at* **envy**.

begrudging *adjective*
▸ invidious, jealous. *See* **envious**.

beguile *verb*
1. To cause to accept something false, especially by trickery or misrepresentation ▸ dupe, mislead, trick. *See* **deceive**. *See synonym note at* **deceive**. **2.** To please greatly or irresistibly ▸ bewitch, captivate, enchant. *See* **charm** (1). *See synonym note at* **charm**.

beguiling *adjective*
▸ bewitching, enticing, entrancing, tempting. *See* **seductive**.

behave *verb*
1. To conduct oneself in a specified way ▸ acquit, bear, carry, comport. *See* **act** (1). **2.** To act in a specified way ▸ operate, perform, work. *See* **function**.

behavior *noun*
1. The manner in which one behaves ▸ action, actions, comportment, conduct, deportment, form, manner, style, way, ways. *See also* **bearing, custom, manners**. **2.** The way in which something functions ▸ functioning, operation, performance, reaction, working, workings.

✦ **CORE SYNONYMS:** *behavior, conduct, deportment.* These nouns refer to the manner in which one behaves. *Behavior* is the most general: *The children were on their best behavior. Conduct* applies to actions considered from the standpoint of morality and ethics: *"Life, not the parson, teaches conduct"* (Oliver Wendell Holmes, Jr.). *Deportment* more narrowly pertains to actions measured by a prevailing code of social behavior: *"[Old Mr. Turveydrop] was not like anything in the world but a model of Deportment"* (Charles Dickens).

behemoth *noun*
One that is extremely large and powerful ▸ Goliath, monster, titan. *See* **giant**.

behemoth *adjective*
Of extraordinary size and power ▸ astronomical, colossal, gigantic, mighty. *See* **enormous**.

behest *noun*
1. An order ▸ charge, commandment, imperative. *See* **command** (1). **2.** The act of demanding ▸ appeal, claim, requisition. *See* **demand** (1).

behind *adverb*
1. So as to fall behind schedule ▸ behindhand, late, slow. **Idiom:** behind time. **2.** Not on time ▸ belatedly, tardily. *See* **late**.

behind *noun*
Informal The part of the body on which one sits ▸ posterior, rump. *Slang:* fanny. *See* **buttocks**.

behindhand *adjective*
Not on time ▸ belated, overdue. *See* **late** (1). *See synonym note at* **late**.

behindhand *adverb*
1. So as to fall behind schedule ▸ behind, late, slow. **Idiom:** behind time. **2.** Not on time ▸ belatedly, tardily. *See* **late**.

behold *verb*
▸ catch, discern, perceive. *See* **see** (1). *See synonym note at* **see**.

beholden *adjective*
▸ grateful, indebted, obligated. *See* **obliged** (1).

beholder *noun*
▸ observer, onlooker, spectator. *See* **watcher** (1).

being *noun*
1. The fact or state of existing or of being actual ▸ actuality, entity. *See* **existence** (1). *See synonym note at* **existence**. 2. The condition of being in full force or operation ▸ actualization, effect, force, realization. *See also* **exercise**. 3. One that exists independently ▸ entity, object, something. *See* **thing** (1). 4. A member of the human race ▸ human, mortal, person. *See* **human being**. 5. A basic trait or set of traits that define and establish the character of something ▸ nature, quintessence. *See* **essence** (1).

bejewel *verb*
▸ decorate, garnish, ornament. *See* **adorn** (1).

belabor *verb*
1. To hit heavily and repeatedly ▸ assault, batter, pummel, thresh. *See* **beat** (1). *See synonym note at* **beat**. 2. To discuss at great or excessive length ▸ dwell on, harp on, labor. *Idiom:* run into the ground. *See also* **elaborate, exaggerate**.

belated *adjective*
▸ behindhand, delayed, overdue. *See* **late** (1).

belatedly *adverb*
▸ behind, slow, tardily. *See* **late**.

belatedness *noun*
The quality or condition of not being on time ▸ lateness, slowness, tardiness, unpunctuality.

belay *verb*
▸ check, discontinue, immobilize. *See* **stop** (2).

belch *verb*
▸ disgorge, spew. *See* **erupt** (1).

beldam *or* **beldame** *noun*
▸ crone, hag. *Slang:* biddy. *See* **witch** (2).

beleaguer *verb*
1. To attack or disturb persistently ▸ harry, pester, torment. *See* **harass**. 2. To surround with hostile troops ▸ beset, blockade, siege. *See* **besiege** (1). *See synonym note at* **besiege**.

beleaguerment *noun*
A prolonged encirclement of an objective by hostile troops ▸ besiegement, blockade, investment, siege. *See also* **attack**.

belie *verb*
1. To give an inaccurate view of by representing falsely or misleadingly ▸ fudge, misrepresent, pervert. *See* **distort** (1). 2. To prove or show to be false ▸ discredit, disprove, rebut. *See* **refute**.

belief *noun*
1. Something believed or thought to be true ▸ conviction, estimate, estimation, feeling, idea, judgment, mind, notion, opinion, persuasion, position, sentiment, view. *See also* **assumption, deduction, posture, viewpoint**. 2. Mental acceptance of the truth or actuality of something ▸ credence, credit, faith. 3. Absolute certainty that a person or thing will not fail ▸ faith, reliance. *See* **trust** (1). 4. A statement presented

for acceptance, as by a religious group ▸ dogma, teaching. *See* **doctrine**.

✦ CORE SYNONYMS: *belief, opinion, view, sentiment, feeling, conviction, persuasion.* These nouns signify something a person believes or thinks to be true. A *belief* is a conclusion to which one subscribes strongly: *"Our belief in any particular natural law cannot have a safer basis than our unsuccessful critical attempts to refute it"* (Karl Popper). *Opinion* is applicable to a judgment based on grounds insufficient to rule out the possibility of dispute: *"A little group of willful men, representing no opinion but their own, have rendered the great Government of the United States helpless and contemptible"* (Woodrow Wilson). *View* stresses individuality of outlook: *"My view is . . . that freedom of speech means that you shall not do something to people either for the views they have or the views they express"* (Hugo L. Black). *Sentiment* and especially *feeling* stress the role of emotion as a determinant: *"If men are to be precluded from offering their sentiments on a matter which may involve the most serious and alarming consequences . . . reason is of no use to us"* (George Washington). *"There needs protection . . . against the tyranny of the prevailing opinion and feeling"* (John Stuart Mill). *Conviction* is belief that excludes doubt: *"the editor's own conviction of what, whether interesting or only important, is in the public interest"* (Walter Lippmann). *Persuasion* applies to a confidently held opinion: *"He had a strong persuasion that Likeman was wrong"* (H.G. Wells).

---

believability *noun*
▸ color, credibility, plausibility. *See* **verisimilitude**.

believable *adjective*
Worthy of being believed ▸ credible, creditable, plausible, reasonable, valid. *See also* **convincing, sound²**.

✦ CORE SYNONYMS: *believable, credible, plausible, reasonable, valid.* These adjectives mean worthy of being believed or accepted: *a believable excuse; a credible assertion; a plausible pretext; a reasonable account of the accident; a valid explanation.*

---

believe *verb*
1. To regard something as true or real ▸ accept. *Slang:* buy, swallow. *Idioms:* have no doubt about, feel certain (*or* sure) of, take for granted. 2. To have confidence in the truthfulness of ▸ credit, trust. *Idioms:* give credence to, have faith (*or* trust *or* confidence) in, take at one's word. *See also* **depend on**. 3. To have an opinion ▸ conceive, consider, deem, hold, opine, think. *Informal:* figure, judge. *Idioms:* be convinced, be of the opinion. *See also* **guess, infer, suppose**. 4. To view in a certain way ▸ feel, hold, sense, think. *See also* **perceive, regard**.

believe in *verb*
To place trust or confidence in ▸ count on (*or* upon), rely on (*or* upon). *See* **depend on** (1).

believer *noun*
1. One who supports and adheres to another ▸ adherent, cohort, disciple. *See* **follower** (1). 2. One zealously devoted to a religion ▸ fanatic, zealot. *See* **devotee** (1).

belittle *verb*

To represent or speak of as small or insignificant ▸ decry, denigrate, deprecate, depreciate, derogate, discount, disparage, downgrade, minimize, run down, slight, talk down. *Informal:* badmouth, pooh-pooh. *Slang:* put down. *Idioms:* make light (*or* little) of. *See also* **denigrate, humble, ridicule, snub.**

✦ CORE SYNONYMS: *belittle, minimize, decry, disparage, depreciate, derogate, downgrade.* These verbs mean to think, write, or speak of as being small, insignifcant, or of little importance. *Belittle* and *minimize* mean to make less important, but *minimize* strongly implies the minimum level: *He belittled the child's attempts to draw. She tried to minimize my accomplishment.* To *downgrade* is to minimize in importance or estimation: *My rival downgraded the painting, calling it decorative but superficial.* Decry *implies open denunciation or condemnation:* A staunch materialist, he decries economy. *Disparage often implies the communication of a low opinion by indirection:* Many critics disparage psychoanalysis as being a pseudoscience. *To* depreciate *is to assign a lower than customary value to someone or something:* Some musicologists depreciate Liszt's compositions. *Derogate implies a detraction that impairs:* People often derogate what they don't understand.

---

belittlement *noun*

The act or an instance of belittling ▸ denigration, deprecation, depreciation, derogation, detraction, disparagement, minimization.

belittling *adjective*

▸ deprecatory, derogatory, pejorative. *See* **disparaging.**

bell *verb*

▸ bong, chime, peal. *See* **ring²** (1).

belle *noun*

▸ lovely, stunner. *See* **beauty** (1).

bellicose *adjective*

1. Inclined to act in an aggressive or hostile way ▸ belligerent, combative, pugnacious. *See* **aggressive** (1). *See synonym note at* **aggressive. 2.** Of or inclined toward war ▸ martial, militaristic. *See* **military** (1).

bellicoseness *noun*

1. Hostile or warlike behavior or attitude ▸ belligerence, combativeness, hostility. *See* **aggression** (1). **2.** The power or will to fight ▸ belligerence, combativeness, pugnacity. *See* **fight** (2).

bellicosity *noun*

1. Warlike or hostile attitude or nature ▸ bellicoseness, belligerence, belligerency, combativeness, contentiousness, hostility, militance, militancy, pugnaciousness, pugnacity, truculence, truculency. **2.** The power or will to fight ▸ belligerence, combativeness, pugnacity. *See* **fight** (2).

belligerence *noun*

1. Hostile or warlike behavior or attitude ▸ combativeness, hostility, truculence. *See* **aggression** (1). **2.** The power or will to fight ▸ bellicosity, combativeness, pugnacity. *See* **fight** (2).

belligerency *noun*

1. An encounter between opposing military forces ▸ combat, confrontation, war. *See* **battle** (1). **2.** The power or will to fight ▸ belligerence, combativeness, pugnacity. *See* **fight** (2).

belligerent *adjective*

1. Engaged in warfare ▸ clashing, combatant, fighting, hostile, militant, warring. *Idioms:* at war, under arms. *See also* **military. 2.** Inclined to act in an aggressive or hostile way ▸ belligerent, combative, contentious. *See* **aggressive** (1). *See synonym note at* **aggressive.**

belligerent *noun*

One who engages in a combat or struggle ▸ combatant, fighter, soldier, warrior. *See also* **aggressor, soldier.**

bellow *verb*

To speak or say in a loud cry ▸ call, holler, yell. *See* **shout.** *See synonym note at* **shout.**

bellow *noun*

1. A loud, deep, prolonged sound ▸ bawl, clamor. *See* **roar** (1). **2.** A loud cry ▸ call, holler, yell. *See* **shout.**

belly *verb*

▸ balloon, jut, project. *See* **bulge** (1). *See synonym note at* **bulge.**

bellyache *verb*

Slang To express feelings of pain, dissatisfaction, or resentment ▸ fuss, grouch, whine. *See* **complain.**

complaint *noun*

Slang An expression of pain or dissatisfaction ▸ carp, whimper, whine. *See* **complaint** (1).

bellyacher *noun*

Slang A person who habitually complains or grumbles ▸ crab, grump, whiner. *See* **grouch** (1).

belong *verb*

▸ chime, correspond, match. *See* **agree** (1).

belongings *noun*

1. A thing or set of things, such as land and assets, legally possessed ▸ possessions, property. *See* **holdings. 2.** One's portable property ▸ goods, personal effects, property. *See* **effects.**

beloved *adjective*

Regarded with much love and tenderness ▸ dear, precious. *See* **darling** (1).

beloved *noun*

A person who is much loved ▸ honey, precious, sweetheart. *See* **darling** (1).

belowground *adjective*

▸ buried, subterranean. *See* **underground.**

belt *noun*

1. A part of the earth's surface ▸ district, region, zone. *See* **area** (2). **2.** *Slang* A sudden heavy stroke ▸ crack, hit, swat, whack. *See* **blow²** (1). **3.** *Slang* An act of drinking or the amount swallowed ▸ swallow, taste. *Informal:* swig. *See* **drink** (2). **4.** A long narrow piece, as of material ▸ cinch, fillet, ribbon, strap. *See* **band¹** (1). **5.** A small amount of liquor ▸ shot, sip, tot. *See* **drop** (8). **6.** A particular area used for or associated with a specific individual or activity ▸ district, region, terrain. *See* **territory** (1).

belt *verb*
1. To form a circle around ▸ band, begird, cincture, engirdle. *See* **encircle** (1). 2. *Slang* To deliver a sudden, sharp blow to ▸ jab, sock, whack. *See* **hit** (1). 3. *Slang* To take into the mouth and swallow a liquid ▸ down, sip, swill. *See* **drink** (1).

bemire *verb*
▸ bedaub, muck up, mud. *See* **dirty** (1).

bemoan *verb*
1. To express strong disapproval of ▸ condemn, denounce. *See* **deplore** (1). 2. To feel, show, or express grief ▸ anguish, mourn, sorrow. *See* **grieve** (1).

bemuse *verb*
▸ benumb, stun, stupefy. *See* **daze** (1). *See synonym note at* **daze**.

bemused *adjective*
1. So lost in thought as to be unable to remember or attend to things ▸ faraway, inattentive, preoccupied. *See* **absent-minded**. 2. Mentally uncertain ▸ confounded, perplexed, turbid. *Informal:* mixed-up. *See* **confused** (1).

bemusement *noun*
▸ abstraction, daydreaming, reverie. *See* **trance** (1).

benchmark *noun*
▸ criterion, mark, measure. *See* **standard** (1). *See synonym note at* **standard**.

bend *verb*
1. To deviate or cause to deviate from a straight line in a smooth, continuous manner ▸ arc, arch, bow, crook, curve, hook, loop, round, turn. *See also* **wave, wind²** 2. To move or cause to move in a bent or angular direction ▸ angle, deflect, flex, refract, reflect, turn, warp. *See also* **glance, swerve**. 3. To curve or yield under pressure ▸ bow, buckle, give, kink, sag, warp. *See also* **cave in, deform**. 4. To incline the body ▸ arch, crouch, scrunch. *See* **stoop** (1). 5. To devote oneself or one's efforts ▸ concentrate, focus, give. *See* **apply** (1). 6. To give an inaccurate view of by representing falsely or misleadingly ▸ fudge, misrepresent, pervert. *See* **distort** (1).

bend *noun*
Something bent or curved ▸ angle, arc, arch, bow, crescent, crook, curvature, curve, flexure, fold, hairpin, hook, horseshoe, oxbow, round, turn, turning, U-turn. *See also* **curl**.

✚ CORE SYNONYMS: *bend, crook, curve, round.* These verbs mean to deviate or to cause to deviate from a straight line in a smooth, continuous manner: *bent his knees and knelt; crooked an arm around the package; a bird that curved its talons around the branch; rounding the lips to articulate an "o."*

◂ ANTONYM: *straighten*

bendability *noun*
▸ elasticity, malleability, pliability. *See* **flexibility** (1).

bendable *adjective*
▸ ductile, flexible, plastic. *See* **malleable** (1).

bender *noun*
Slang A bout of excessive drinking ▸ bacchanal, bacchanalia, binge, brannigan, carousal, carouse, drunk, spree. *Slang:* bat, beer blast, booze, jag, souse, tear, toot. *See also* **binge, blast**.

bending *adjective*
▸ arched, bowed, curved, rounded. *See* **bent** (1).

benediction *noun*
1. A short prayer said at meals ▸ blessing, grace, thanks, thanksgiving. *See also* **prayer¹**. 2. The act of praying ▸ invocation, prayer, supplication. *See also* **appeal**.

benefaction *noun*
1. Something given to a charity or cause ▸ alms, contribution, offering. *See* **donation**. 2. A kindly act ▸ good deed, kindness. *See* **favor** (1).

benefactor *or* **benefactress** *noun*
1. One who supports or champions an activity, cause, or institution ▸ contributor, sponsor. *See* **patron** (1). 2. A person who gives to a charity or cause ▸ contributor, grantor, patron. *See* **donor**.

benefic *adjective*
▸ favorable, helpful, propitious. *See* **beneficial**.

beneficence *noun*
1. Kindly, charitable interest in others ▸ goodwill, kindheartedness, philanthropy. *See* **benevolence** (1). 2. Something given to a charity or cause ▸ benefaction, contribution, offering. *See* **donation**. 3. A kindly act ▸ good deed, kindness. *See* **favor** (1).

beneficent *adjective*
1. Characterized by kindness and concern for others ▸ goodhearted, kindly. *See* **benevolent** (1). 2. Affording benefit or advantage ▸ favorable, helpful, propitious. *See* **beneficial**.

beneficial *adjective*
Affording benefit or advantage ▸ advantageous, benefic, beneficent, benignant, constructive, contributive, favorable, fruitful, good, helpful, profitable, propitious, toward, salubrious, salutary, useful, valuable, worthwhile. *See also* **effective**.

✚ CORE SYNONYMS: *beneficial, profitable, advantageous.* These adjectives apply to what promotes a favorable result, advantage, or gain. *Beneficial* is said of what enhances well-being: *a trade agreement beneficial to all countries. Profitable* refers to what yields material gain or useful compensation: *profitable speculation on the stock market.* Something *advantageous* affords improvement in relative position or in chances of success: *found it socially advantageous to entertain often and well.*

◂ ANTONYM: *detrimental*

benefit *noun*
1. Something beneficial ▸ blessing, boon, favor. *See* **advantage** (2). 2. Something that contributes to or increases one's well-being ▸ advantage, good, interests. *See* **interest** (1). 3. The quality of being suitable or adaptable to an end ▸ avail, profit, utility. *See* **use** (2).

benefit *verb*
1. To derive advantage ▸ capitalize, gain, profit. *Idiom:*

do well. **2.** To be an advantage to ▸ avail, serve. *See* **profit** (2).

✚ CORE SYNONYMS: *benefit, capitalize, profit.* These verbs mean to derive advantage from something: *benefited from the stock split; capitalized on his adversary's blunder; profiting from her experience.*

---

benevolence *noun*
1. Kindly, charitable interest in others ▸ altruism, beneficence, benignancy, benignity, charitableness, charity, goodwill, grace, humanity, kindheartedness, kindliness, kindness, philanthropy. *Idioms:* the goodness (*or* kindness) of one's heart. *See also* **amiability, consideration, generosity. 2.** A charitable deed ▸ good turn, kindness. *See* **favor** (1).

benevolent *adjective*
1. Characterized by kindness and concern for others ▸ altruistic, beneficent, benign, benignant, good, goodhearted, helpful, kind, kindhearted, kindly. *See also* **amiable, generous, humanitarian, selfless. 2.** Of or concerned with charity ▸ altruistic, charitable, eleemosynary, philanthropic. *See synonym note at* **charitable.**

✚ CORE SYNONYMS: *benevolent, kind, kindly, kindhearted, benign.* These adjectives mean having or showing kindness and concern for others. *Benevolent* suggests charitableness and a desire to promote the welfare or happiness of others: *a benevolent contributor. Kind* and *kindly* are the least specific: *thanked her for her kind letter; a kindly gentleman. Kindhearted* especially suggests an innately kind disposition: *a kindhearted teacher. Benign* implies gentleness and mildness: *benign intentions; a benign sovereign.*

---

benighted *adjective*
▸ backward, primitive, unenlightened. *See* **ignorant** (2).

benightedness *noun*
▸ illiteracy, nescience. *See* **ignorance** (1).

benign *adjective*
1. Characterized by kindness and concern for others ▸ beneficent, goodhearted, kindly. *See* **benevolent** (1). *See synonym note at* **benevolent. 2.** Indicative of future success or full of promise ▸ bright, fortunate, propitious. *See* **favorable** (1). *See synonym note at* **favorable. 3.** Devoid of hurtful qualities ▸ innocuous, unoffensive. *See* **harmless** (1).

benignancy *noun*
▸ goodwill, kindheartedness, philanthropy. *See* **benevolence** (1).

benignant *adjective*
1. Affording benefit or advantage ▸ favorable, helpful, propitious. *See* **beneficial. 2.** Characterized by kindness and concern for others ▸ beneficent, goodhearted, kindly. *See* **benevolent** (1).

benignity *noun*
1. Kindly, charitable interest in others ▸ goodwill, kindheartedness, philanthropy. *See* **benevolence** (1). **2.** A kindly act ▸ good deed, kindness. *See* **favor** (1).

bent *adjective*
1. Deviating from a straight line ▸ angled, arced, arched, arciform, bending, bowed, crooked, curled, curved, curvilinear, curving, doubled, flexed, folded, hooked, looped, recurved, rounded, warped. *See also* **curly. 2.** Committed to or unwavering in a course of action ▸ determined, fixed. *See* **intent** (1).

bent *noun*
1. A natural or habitual preference for something ▸ disposition, leaning, penchant. *See* **inclination** (1). **2.** An innate capability ▸ faculty, gift, knack. *See* **talent. 3.** A person's customary manner of emotional response ▸ humor, nature, temperament. *See* **disposition** (1).

benumb *verb*
1. To render less sensitive ▸ desensitize, numb. *See* **deaden** (1). **2.** To dull the senses, as with a shock ▸ stun, stupefy. *See* **daze** (1). *See synonym note at* **daze. 3.** To render helpless, as by emotion ▸ numb, stun, stupefy. *See* **paralyze** (1).

benumbed *adjective*
▸ inert, numb, unfeeling. *See* **dead** (2).

bequeath *verb*
1. To convey something from one generation to the next ▸ hand down, hand on, pass (along *or* on), transmit. **2.** To give property to another after one's death ▸ devise, will. *See* **leave**[1] (1). **3.** To present as a gift to a charity or cause ▸ award, pledge. *See* **donate** (1).

bequest *noun*
1. Something bestowed voluntarily ▸ gift, present, presentation. *Slang:* freebie. *See also* **grant. 2.** Something given to a charity or cause ▸ benefaction, contribution, offering. *See* **donation.**

berate *verb*
1. To reprimand loudly or harshly ▸ bawl out, rate. *Informal:* tell off. *Idioms:* give hell to, give it to. **2.** To criticize for a fault or offense ▸ chide, rebuke, reprimand. *See* **chastise** (1). *See synonym note at* **chastise.**

berating *noun*
▸ diatribe, harangue. *See* **tirade.**

bereft *adjective*
1. Having been given up and left alone ▸ deserted, forlorn, forsaken. *See* **abandoned** (1). **2.** Deprived of a quality or aspect that is desirable ▸ destitute, lacking, void. *See* **empty** (2).

berth *noun*
A post of employment ▸ job, spot. *See* **position** (3).

berth *verb*
To provide with lodging, especially temporarily ▸ accommodate, bed (down), house. *See* **lodge** (1).

beseech *verb*
▸ beg, entreat, plead. *See* **appeal** (1). *See synonym note at* **appeal.**

beset *verb*
1. To set upon with violent force ▸ assail, assault, storm, strike. *See* **attack** (1). *See synonym note at* **attack. 2.** To surround with hostile troops ▸ blockade, siege. *See* **besiege** (1). **3.** To attack or disturb persis-

tently ▶ harry, pester, torment. *See* **harass. 4.** To shut in on all sides ▶ encircle, hedge, ring. *See* **surround** (1).

besetment *noun*
▶ bother, irritant, nuisance. *See* **annoyance** (2).

besides *adverb*
▶ also, furthermore, moreover, still. *See* **additionally.**

besiege *verb*
1. To surround with hostile troops ▶ beleaguer, beset, blockade, invest, siege. *Idiom:* lay siege to. *See also* **attack, surround. 2.** To surround and advance upon ▶ close in, envelop, hem. *See* **enclose** (2). **3.** To attack or disturb persistently ▶ harry, pester, torment. *See* **harass.**

✦ CORE SYNONYMS: *besiege, beleaguer, blockade, invest, siege.* These verbs mean to surround with hostile troops or forces: *besiege a walled city; an enclave beleaguered by enemy attack; blockaded the harbor; investing a fortress; a castle sieged by invaders.*

---

besiegement *noun*
▶ beleaguerment, blockade, investment. *See* **siege.**

besmear *verb*
1. To spread with a greasy, sticky, or dirty substance ▶ dab, smudge. *See* **smear** (1). **2.** To attack the reputation or honor of ▶ besmirch, smear, tarnish. *See* **denigrate** (1).

besmirch *verb*
1. To attack the reputation or honor of ▶ blacken, smear, tarnish. *See* **denigrate** (1). **2.** To make dirty ▶ bemire, muck up, mud. *See* **dirty** (1). **3.** To bring disgrace on ▶ abase, dishonor, shame. *See* **disgrace.**

besoil *verb*
▶ bemire, muck up, mud. *See* **dirty** (1).

besot *verb*
▶ impair, stupefy. *See* **drug** (2).

besotted *adjective*
1. Stupefied, excited, or muddled with alcoholic liquor ▶ intoxicated, sodden, tipsy. *See* **drunk. 2.** Affected with intense romantic attraction ▶ enamored, obsessed, smitten. *See* **infatuated.**

bespatter *verb*
1. To mark or soil with foreign matter ▶ discolor, spatter. *See* **stain** (1). **2.** To hurl or scatter liquid ▶ dash, spray. *See* **splash** (1). **3.** To attack the reputation or honor of ▶ besmirch, smear, tarnish. *See* **denigrate** (1). **4.** To make dirty ▶ bemire, muck up, mud. *See* **dirty** (1).

bespeak *verb*
1. To give grounds for believing in the existence or presence of ▶ attest, witness. *See* **indicate** (1). *See synonym note at* **indicate. 2.** To cause to be set aside, as for one's use, in advance ▶ engage, reserve. *See* **book** (1). *See synonym note at* **book.**

bespeckle *verb*
▶ dapple, freckle. *See* **speckle.**

bespoke *adjective*
▶ custom-made, tailor-made. *See* **custom.**

bespoken *adjective*
▶ betrothed, plighted. *See* **engaged** (2).

besprinkle *verb*
1. To scatter or release in drops or small particles ▶ dust, pepper, powder. *See* **sprinkle** (1). **2.** To mark with many small spots ▶ dapple, freckle, pepper. *See* **speckle.**

best *adjective*
1. Surpassing all others in quality, achievement, or desirability ▶ finest, first, foremost, greatest, highest, leading, nicest, optimal, optimum, preeminent, superlative, supreme, top, unsurpassed. *See also* **choice, exceptional, primary, unique. 2.** Much more than half ▶ better, biggest, greater, larger, largest, most. **3.** Worth doing, especially for practical reasons ▶ recommendable, well. *See* **advisable.**

best *noun*
1. The finest or most preferable part of something ▶ choice, cream, crème de la crème, elite, flower, pick, prize, top. *Idioms:* cream of the crop, flower of the flock, pick of the bunch (*or* crop *or* litter), top of the line, top of the heap. **2.** Friendly greetings ▶ regards, respects.

best *verb*
1. To be greater or better than ▶ exceed, excel, outshine. *See* **surpass** (1). **2.** To win a victory over, as in battle or a competition ▶ conquer, surmount, vanquish. *See* **defeat** (1).

bestain *verb*
▶ discolor, spatter. *See* **stain** (1).

bestial *adjective*
Similar to a beast in behavior ▶ beastlike, beastly, brutish. *See also* **cruel, savage, uncivilized.**

bestiality *noun*
1. Degrading, immoral acts or habits ▶ depravity, perversion, vice. *See* **corruption** (1). **2.** The quality or condition or being cruel ▶ brutality, truculence. *See* **cruelty.**

bestialize *verb*
▶ debase, demoralize, deprave, warp. *See* **corrupt** (1).

bestow *verb*
1. To give formally or officially ▶ award, grant, impart. *See* **confer** (2). **2.** To present as a gift to a charity or cause ▶ bequeath, pledge. *See* **donate** (1). **3.** To provide with lodging, especially temporarily ▶ accommodate, bed (down), house. *See* **lodge** (1).

bestowal *or* **bestowment** *noun*
▶ accordance, conferral. *See* **conferment.**

bestride *verb*
To sit or stand with a leg on each side of ▶ straddle, stride.

bet *noun*
1. Something risked on an uncertain outcome ▶ ante, kitty, pool, pot, stake, stakes, venture, wager. **2.** An undertaking depending on chance ▶ risk, speculation, wager. *See* **gamble** (1).

bet *verb*
1. To make a bet ▶ gamble, game, lay, play, wager. *Idioms:* ante (*or* pony) up, feed the pot (*or* kitty), lay odds (*or* a wager), put money on something, put up or shut up, show the color of one's money. **2.** To place

something at risk, as in a game of chance ▸ risk, stake, wager. *See* **gamble** (2). **3.** To look forward to confidently ▸ await, look for. *See* **expect** (1).

✦ CORE SYNONYMS: *bet, ante, kitty, pot, stake, wager.* These nouns denote something valuable risked on an uncertain outcome: *placed a $50 bet in the first race; raising the ante in a poker game; threw another quarter into the kitty; won the whole pot at cards; played for high stakes; laid a wager on who would win.*

---

bête noire *noun*
▸ abomination, anathema. *See* **hate** (2).

bethink *verb*
▸ recall, recollect, reminisce. *See* **remember** (1).

betide *verb*
1. To take place by chance ▸ befall, chance, hap, happen. **2.** To take place ▸ befall, come, occur. *See* **happen** (1). *See synonym note at* **happen**.

betimes *adverb*
1. Before the expected time ▸ ahead, beforehand. *See* **early**. **2.** Once in a while; at times ▸ occasionally, periodically, sometimes. *See* **intermittently**.

betoken *verb*
1. To give grounds for believing in the existence or presence of ▸ attest, witness. *See* **indicate** (1). *See synonym note at* **indicate**. **2.** To give an indication of something in advance ▸ foretell, portend, prefigure. *See* **foreshadow**.

betray *verb*
1. To be treacherous to ▸ cross up, double-cross, turn in. *Informal:* knife. *Slang:* rat (on *or* out), sell out. *Idioms:* play someone false, sell down the river, stab in the back. *See also* **abandon, disappoint, inform**. **2.** To disclose in a breach of confidence ▸ blab, divulge, expose, give away, let out, reveal, tell, uncover, unveil. *Informal:* leak, spill. *Idioms:* let slip, let the cat out of the bag, spill the beans, tell all. *See also* **reveal**. **3.** To cause to accept something false, especially by trickery or misrepresentation ▸ dupe, fool, mislead, trick. *See* **deceive**. *See synonym note at* **deceive**.

betrayal *noun*
1. An act of betraying ▸ backstabbing, double cross, double-dealing, treachery. *Slang:* sellout. *See also* **treason**. **2.** Betrayal, especially of a duty or obligation ▸ disloyalty, falseness, treachery. *See* **faithlessness** (1).

betrayer *noun*
One who betrays ▸ Benedict Arnold, double-crosser, double-dealer, Judas, quisling, snake, traitor. *Slang:* rat. *Idiom:* snake in the grass. *See also* **creep, informer, defector**.

betroth *verb*
▸ promise, vow. *See* **pledge** (1).

betrothal *noun*
The act or condition of being pledged to marry ▸ engagement, espousal, troth.

betrothed *adjective*
Pledged to marry ▸ affianced, plighted. *See* **engaged** (2).

betrothed *noun*
A person to whom one is engaged to be married ▸ fiancé, fiancée. *See* **intended**.

better[1] *adjective*
1. Of greater excellence than another ▸ finer, nicer, preferable, superior, worthier. **2.** Much more than half ▸ largest, most. *See* **best** (2).

better *adverb*
To a greater extent ▸ more.

better *noun*
1. One who stands above another in rank ▸ elder, senior, superior. *Informal:* higher-up. *See also* **chief**. **2.** A dominating position, as in a conflict ▸ edge, upper hand, vantage. *See* **advantage** (3).

better *verb*
1. To advance to a more desirable state ▸ ameliorate, enhance, upgrade. *See* **improve** (1). *See synonym note at* **improve**. **2.** To be greater or better than ▸ exceed, excel, outshine. *See* **surpass** (1).

better[2] *noun*
See **bettor**.

better half *noun*
Informal A husband or wife ▸ mate. *See* **spouse**.

betterment *noun*
1. The act of making better or the condition of being made better ▸ advancement, development, upgrade. *See* **improvement** (1). **2.** Steady improvement, as of an individual or society ▸ advancement, amelioration, development. *See* **progress** (1).

bettor *or* **better** *noun*
▸ gamester, player. *See* **gambler** (1).

between *adjective*
▸ intermediate, median, midway. *See* **middle** (1).

beveled *adjective*
▸ biased, diagonal, slanted. *See* **oblique** (1).

beverage *noun*
▸ brew, libation, refreshment. *See* **drink** (1).

bevy *noun*
1. A number of individuals making up or considered a unit ▸ body, cluster, collection. *See* **group** (1). **2.** A number of animals considered collectively ▸ drove, gaggle, herd. *See* **flock** (1). *See synonym note at* **flock**.

bewail *verb*
1. To express strong disapproval of ▸ condemn, denounce. *See* **deplore** (1). **2.** To feel, show, or express grief ▸ anguish, mourn, sorrow. *See* **grieve** (1).

beware *verb*
To be careful ▸ look out, mind, watch out. *Idioms:* be on guard, be on the lookout, keep an eye peeled, take care (*or* heed).

bewilder *verb*
1. To cause to be unclear in mind or intent ▸ addle, befuddle, confound. *See* **confuse** (1). **2.** To impair or destroy the composure of ▸ disorient, fluster, ruffle. *See* **agitate** (2). **3.** To dull the senses, as with a shock ▸ stun, stupefy. *See* **daze** (1).

bewildered *adjective*
▸ confounded, perplexed, turbid. *Informal:* mixed-up. *See* **confused** (1).

bewilderedness *noun*
▸ bafflement, perplexity, stupor. *See* **daze.**

bewilderment *noun*
1. A stunned or bewildered condition ▸ befuddle-ment, perplexity, stupor. *See* **daze. 2.** Something complex ▸ elaborateness, intricacy. *See* **complexity.**

bewitch *verb*
1. To act upon with or as if with magic ▸ enchant, mesmerize, spellbind. *See* **charm** (2). *See synonym note at* **charm. 2.** To please greatly or irresistibly ▸ beguile, captivate, enchant. *See* **charm** (1).

bewitching *adjective*
1. Pleasing to the eye or mind ▸ enchanting, fetching, lovely, winsome. *See* **attractive** (1). **2.** Tending to seduce ▸ beguiling, enticing, tempting. *See* **seductive.** **3.** Having, brought about by, or relating to supernatural powers or magic ▸ magical, wizardly. *See* **magic** (1).

bias *verb*
1. To cause to have a prejudiced view ▸ jaundice, prejudice, prepossess, turn (against), warp. *See also* **indoctrinate, influence. 2.** To alter or present material so as to favor a particular viewpoint ▸ doctor, fiddle (with), massage, skew, slant, tailor. *Informal:* angle. *See also* **distort.**

bias *noun*
1. An inclination for or against that inhibits impartial judgment ▸ one-sidedness, partiality, partisanship, preconception, prejudice, prepossession, slant, tendentiousness. **2.** A natural or habitual preference for something ▸ disposition, leaning, penchant. *See* **inclination** (1). *See synonym note at* **inclination.**

bias *adjective*
At an angle ▸ diagonal, slanted, tilted. *See* **oblique** (1).

✛ **CORE SYNONYMS:** *bias, jaundice, prejudice, warp.* These verbs mean to cause to have a prejudiced view: *His experiences biased his outlook. Dishonest leaders have jaundiced her view of politics. Lying has prejudiced the public against them. Bitterness has warped your judgment.*

---

biased *adjective*
1. Exhibiting bias ▸ discriminatory, one-sided, opinionated, partial, partisan, preconceived, predisposed, prejudiced, prejudicial, prepossessed, skewed, slanted, tendentious. *See also* **intolerant, narrow, unfair. 2.** At an angle ▸ inclined, diagonal, slanted. *See* **oblique** (1).

bibelot *noun*
▸ knickknack, trinket. *See* **novelty** (3).

bibulous *adjective*
▸ absorptive, assimilative, spongy. *See* **absorbent.**

bicker *verb*
To engage in a quarrel ▸ fight, quarrel. *See* **argue** (1). *See synonym note at* **argue.**

bicker *noun*
A heated discussion in which a difference of opinion is expressed ▸ dispute, quarrel. *See* **argument** (1).

bid *verb*
1. To request that someone take part in or be present

at a particular occasion ▸ ask, invite, summon. *Idioms:* extend an invitation to, request the presence of. *See also* **appeal, request. 2.** To give orders to ▸ instruct, order, tell. *See* **command** (1). **3.** To make an offer of ▸ offer. *Informal:* go. **4.** To strive against others for victory ▸ race, rival, vie. *See* **compete.**

bid *noun*
1. A spoken or written request for someone to take part or be present ▸ call, invitation, summons. *Informal:* invite. *See also* **request. 2.** An act of offering or the thing offered ▸ invitation, proffer. *See* **offer** (1). **3.** A trying to do or make something ▸ effort, trial. *Informal:* shot. *See* **attempt** (1).

biddable *adjective*
▸ complaisant, docile, submissive. *See* **obedient.**

bidding *noun*
▸ charge, commandment, imperative. *See* **command** (1).

biddy *noun*
▸ beldam, crone, hag. *See* **witch** (2).

bide *verb*
1. To continue to be in a place ▸ abide, linger, tarry. *See* **remain** (1). **2.** To be in existence or in a certain state for an indefinitely long time ▸ continue, persist. *See* **endure** (2).

biff *verb*
Informal To deliver a sudden, sharp blow to ▸ jab, sock, whack. *See* **hit** (1).

biff *noun*
Informal A sudden heavy stroke ▸ crack, hit, swat, whack. *See* **blow²** (1).

biform *adjective*
▸ dual, duple, twofold. *See* **double** (2).

bifurcate *verb*
▸ diverge, fork. *See* **branch.**

big *adjective*
1. Above average in amount, size, or scope ▸ biggish, considerable, extensive, good, goodly, great, healthy, king-size, large, large-scale, largish, outsize, queen-size, respectable, significant, sizable, substantial. *Informal:* tidy. *See also* **bulky, enormous, grand. 2.** Having reached full growth and development ▸ adult, ripe. *See* **mature** (1). **3.** Carrying a developing fetus within the uterus ▸ expectant, parturient. *See* **pregnant** (1). **4.** Having great significance ▸ consequential, grand, meaningful. *See* **important** (1). **5.** Willing to give of oneself and one's possessions ▸ magnanimous, unselfish. *See* **generous** (1).

✛ **CORE SYNONYMS:** *big, extensive, great, large, sizable.* These adjectives mean being notably above the average in amount, size, or scope: *The developers built a big shopping mall. The hurricane caused extensive damage. We saw a great ocean liner pull into the harbor. A large boulder blocked the road. The executive made a sizable fortune in the stock market.*

◄ **ANTONYM:** *small*

Big Brother *noun*
▸ authoritarian, oppressor, tyrant. *See* **dictator** (1).

biggest *adjective*
▸ largest, most. *See* **best** (2).

biggish *adjective*
▸ extensive, large, sizable. *See* **big** (1).

big gun *noun*
Slang An important, influential person ▸ notability, personage. *Slang:* big shot. *See* **dignitary**.

big head *or* **bigheadedness** *noun*
Informal Exaggerated love for oneself or belief in one's own importance ▸ egoism, self-importance. *Informal:* swelled head. *See* **egotism**.

bigheaded *adjective*
Informal Thinking too highly of oneself ▸ narcissistic, vain. *See* **egotistic** (1).

big-hearted *adjective*
▸ magnanimous, unselfish. *See* **generous** (1).

big-heartedness *noun*
▸ magnanimity, munificence, unselfishness. *See* **generosity**.

big house *noun*
Slang A place for the confinement of persons in lawful detention ▸ brig, penitentiary, prison. *See* **jail**.

bight *noun*
A body of water partly enclosed by land but having a wide outlet to the sea ▸ bay, gulf, sound. *See also* **channel, harbor, inlet**.

big-league *adjective*
Informal Being among the leaders in one's field ▸ big-name, blue-chip, celebrity, leading, major, major-league. *Informal:* bigtime, heavyweight. *See also* **famous, important, primary**.

big name *noun*
1. *Informal* A famous person ▸ personality, star. *See* **celebrity** (1). 2. An important, influential person ▸ notability, personage. *See* **dignitary**.

bigness *noun*
▸ amplitude, greatness. *See* **size** (2).

bigoted *adjective*
▸ close-minded, illiberal, racist. *See* **intolerant** (1).

bigotry *noun*
▸ intolerance, racism. *See* **prejudice** (1).

big shot *noun*
Slang An important, influential person ▸ notability, personage. *Slang:* big gun. *See* **dignitary**.

big-ticket *adjective*
Informal Of great value or price ▸ expensive, precious, valuable. *See* **costly**.

bigtime *or* **big-time** *adjective*
1. *Informal* Being among the leaders in one's field ▸ leading, major, major-league. *See* **big-league**. 2. *Informal* Having great significance ▸ consequential, grand, meaningful. *See* **important** (1).

big-timer *noun*
▸ notability, personage. *Slang:* big shot. *See* **dignitary**.

big wheel *noun*
1. An important, influential person ▸ notability, personage. *Slang:* big shot. *See* **dignitary**. 2. Someone who directs and supervises workers ▸ foreman, manager, supervisor. *See* **boss** (1).

bigwig *noun*
Slang An important, influential person ▸ notability, personage. *Slang:* big shot. *See* **dignitary**.

bile *noun*
▸ crankiness, prickliness, tetchiness. *See* **temper** (1).

bilge *noun*
Slang Something that does not have or make sense ▸ bunkum, drivel, garbage. *See* **nonsense** (1).

biliousness *noun*
▸ crankiness, prickliness, tetchiness. *See* **temper** (1).

bilk *verb*
To get something by deceitful trickery ▸ cozen, defraud, swindle. *See* **cheat** (1).

bilk *noun*
A person who cheats ▸ cheater, swindler, trickster. *See* **cheat** (2).

bill¹ *verb*
To present with a request or demand for payment ▸ charge, dun, invoice, solicit.

bill *noun*
1. A precise list of fees or charges ▸ check, invoice, statement. *Informal:* tab. *See* **account** (2). 2. A document that complements a public performance, presentation, or offering ▸ catalog, prospectus, syllabus. *See* **program** (2). 3. A usually public posting that conveys a message ▸ billboard, notice. *See* **sign** (2). 4. The formal product of a legislative or judicial body ▸ act, legislation. *See* **law** (2).

bill² *noun*
1. The horny projection forming a bird's jaws ▸ beak, mandible, nib. 2. The projecting rim on the front of a cap ▸ brim, eyeshade, peak, visor.

billboard *noun*
▸ bill, notice. *See* **sign** (2).

billet *noun*
A post of employment ▸ job, spot. *See* **position** (3).

billet *verb*
To stay in or provide with lodging, especially temporarily ▸ bed (down), board, room. *See* **lodge** (1).

billingsgate *noun*
▸ condemnation, denunciation, scurrility. *See* **vituperation**.

billion *noun*
Informal An indeterminately great amount or number ▸ bunch, multiplicity. *Informal:* bushel. *See* **heap** (3).

binary *adjective*
▸ dual, duple, twofold. *See* **double** (2).

bind *verb*
1. To make fast or firmly fixed, as by means of a cord or rope ▸ fasten, knot, secure, tie, tie up. 2. To apply therapeutic materials to a wound ▸ bandage, swathe. *See* **dress** (2). 3. To be morally bound to do ▸ obligate, pledge. *See* **commit** (2). 4. To unite or be united in a relationship ▸ combine, join, link. *See* **associate** (1). 5. To make secure ▸ chain, moor. *See* **fasten** (1).

bind *noun*
1. *Informal* A situation that presents difficulty, uncertainty, or perplexity ▸ issue, matter, question. *See*

problem (1). **2.** *Informal* A difficult, often embarrassing situation or condition ▸ corner, difficulty, fix. *See* **predicament.**

binder *noun*
▸ catch, clip, lock. *See* **fastener.**

binding *noun*
1. A device for locking ▸ catch, clip, lock. *See* **fastener. 2.** That which unites or binds ▸ ligature, link, tie. *See* **bond** (2).

bine *noun*
▸ offshoot, runner, sprout. *See* **shoot** (1).

binge *noun*
1. A period of uncontrolled self-indulgence ▸ debauch, fling, orgy, rampage, riot, saturnalia, splurge, spree. *Slang:* jag. *See also* **blast. 2.** A drinking bout ▸ brannigan, carousal, carouse, spree. *See* **bender.**

✦ **CORE SYNONYMS:** *binge, fling, jag, orgy, rampage, spree.* These nouns denote a period of uncontrolled self-indulgence: *a gambling binge; had one last fling before beginning a new job; a crying jag; an eating orgy; rioters on a rampage; a shopping spree.*

biome *noun*
▸ biosphere, habitat. *See* **environment** (3).

biosphere *noun*
▸ ecosphere, habitat. *See* **environment** (3).

bird *noun*
Slang One of various derisive sounds of disapproval ▸ catcall, hoot. *See* **hiss** (2).

bird *verb*
Slang To make a derisive sound of disapproval ▸ boo, hoot. *See* **hiss** (2).

birdbrained *adjective*
1. *Slang* Given to lighthearted silliness ▸ featherbrained, flighty, frivolous. *See* **giddy** (2). **2.** Lacking in intelligence ▸ dumb, idiotic, obtuse. *See* **stupid** (1).

bird-dog *verb*
Informal To keep another under surveillance by moving along behind ▸ track, trail. *Informal:* tail. *See* **follow** (3).

birth *noun*
1. The act or process of bringing forth young ▸ accouchement, birthing, childbearing, childbirth, delivery, labor, lying-in, nativity, parturition, travail. **2.** The initial stage of a developmental process ▸ beginning, commencement, dawn, embarkation, genesis, inception, nascence, nascency, onset, opening, origin, outset, spring, start. *Informal:* day one, square one. **3.** One's ancestors or ancestral derivation ▸ blood, descent, lineage. *See* **ancestry. 4.** Noble rank or status by birth ▸ blue blood, noblesse. *See* **nobility** (1).

birth *verb*
Chiefly Regional To give birth to ▸ deliver, have. *See* **bear** (4).

✦ **CORE SYNONYMS:** *birth, beginning, dawn, genesis, nascence, outset, start.* These nouns denote the initial stage of a developmental process: *the birth of a new*

nation; the beginning of a new era in technology; the dawn of civilization; the genesis of quantum mechanics; the nascence of classical sculpture; had clear objectives from the outset of the project; laid down the rules at the start of the retreat.

birthing *noun*
▸ childbearing, delivery, labor. *See* **birth** (1).

birthplace *noun*
▸ provenance, root, source. *See* **origin** (1).

birthright *noun*
1. Any special privilege accorded a firstborn ▸ heritage, inheritance, legacy, patrimony. **2.** A benefit granted to a person by law, nature, or custom ▸ freedom, perquisite, prerogative. *See* **right.** *See synonym note at* **right.**

bishop *noun*
▸ ecclesiastic, minister, parson. *See* **cleric.**

bit¹ *noun*
1. A tiny amount ▸ crumb, dab, dash, dot, dram, drop, fragment, grain, iota, jot, little, minim, mite, modicum, molecule, morsel, nip, ort, ounce, particle, pinch, scrap, scruple, shard, shred, smidgen, snip, snippet, speck, tad, tittle, trifle, whit. *See also* **flake, part, shade. 2.** A small portion of food ▸ bite, crumb, dollop, morsel, mouthful, piece, scrap, slice, sliver, swallow, taste, tidbit. *See also* **drop. 3.** A detail of news information ▸ feature, piece, story. *See* **item** (1). **4.** A rather short period ▸ interval, space, spell, time, while. *See also* **flash. 5.** *Informal* A characteristic behavior or performance ▸ *Slang:* number, routine, shtick.

bit² *noun*
A device for slowing or stopping motion ▸ curb, leash, rein. *See* **brake** (1).

bit *verb*
To control, restrict, or arrest ▸ bridle, check, curb. *See* **restrain.**

bitch *verb*
Slang To express feelings of pain, dissatisfaction, or resentment ▸ fuss, grouch, whine. *See* **complain.**

bitch *noun*
Slang An expression of pain or dissatisfaction ▸ carp, whimper, whine. *See* **complaint** (1).

bitchy *adjective*
▸ despiteful, evil, wicked. *See* **malevolent** (1).

bite *verb*
1. To seize and grind with the teeth ▸ champ, chomp, gnaw. *See* **chew.** *See synonym note at* **chew. 2.** To reduce gradually, as by chemical reaction, weather, or friction ▸ consume, corrode, wear (away *or* down). *See* **erode. 3.** To be painful ▸ ache, sting. *See* **hurt** (2).

bite *noun*
1. A cutting quality ▸ incisiveness, keenness. *See* **edge** (1). **2.** A small portion of food ▸ bit, crumb, morsel, mouthful, piece. *See* **bit¹** (2). **3.** *Informal* A light meal ▸ snack. *Informal:* nosh. *See* **refreshment** (1).

biting *adjective*
1. So sharp as to cause mental pain ▸ acerbic, acid, acidic, acrid, astringent, catty, caustic, corrosive, cut-

ting, harsh, mordacious, mordant, pungent, scathing, scorching, searing, sharp, sharp-tongued, slashing, stinging, trenchant, truculent, venomous, vitriolic, waspish, withering. *See also* **ill-tempered, resentful, sarcastic. 2.** Marked by severity or intensity ▸ gnawing, piercing. *See* **sharp** (8).

bits and pieces *noun*
▸ junk, oddments, miscellanea. *See* **odds and ends.**

bitter *adjective*
1. Having a sharp, unpleasant, alkaline taste or smell ▸ acerbic, acrid, brackish, briny, harsh, pungent. *See also* **sour. 2.** Painfully intense ▸ brutal, cruel, hard, harsh, penetrating, punishing, racking, relentless, rigorous, rough, severe, stinging, tough. *See also* **bleak, intense, sharp. 3.** Difficult to accept or bear ▸ disagreeable, distasteful, galling, indigestible, painful, unpalatable, unpleasant. *See also* **disturbing, unbearable, vexatious. 4.** Bitingly hostile ▸ acrimonious, rancorous, virulent. *See* **resentful.**

✦ CORE SYNONYMS: *bitter, acerbic, acrid, sour.* These adjectives mean having a sharp, unpleasant, alkaline taste or smell: *a bitter cough syrup; an acerbic green apple; acrid smoke; a sour lemon.*

---

bitterness *noun*
1. The quality or state of feeling bitter ▸ acrimony, rancor, virulence. *See* **resentment** (1). **2.** The use of irony to ridicule or express contempt ▸ acridity, mordancy, trenchancy. *See* **sarcasm.**

bizarre *adjective*
1. Conceived or done with no reference to reality or common sense ▸ antic, fantastic, fantastical, far-fetched, grotesque. **2.** Deviating from what is conventional or customary ▸ antic, grotesque. *See* **eccentric.** *See synonym note at* **eccentric. 3.** Very strange or strikingly unusual ▸ fantastic, outré. *See* **exotic** (2).

bizarrely *adverb*
▸ singularly, uncommonly, uniquely. *See* **unusually.**

blab *verb*
1. To disclose in a breach of confidence ▸ divulge, give away. *Informal:* spill. *See* **betray** (2). **2.** To engage in or spread gossip ▸ rumor, whisper. *See* **gossip.** *See synonym note at* **gossip. 3.** To talk rapidly on trivial matters ▸ babble, jabber, prattle. *See* **chatter** (1).

blab *noun*
1. A person habitually engaged in idle talk about others ▸ gossipmonger, taleteller, whisperer. *See* **gossip** (2). **2.** Incessant and inconsequential talk ▸ drivel, patter, small talk. *See* **chatter.**

blabber *verb*
To talk rapidly on trivial matters ▸ blab, jabber, prattle. *See* **chatter** (1).

blabber *noun*
Incessant and inconsequential talk ▸ drivel, patter, small talk. *See* **chatter.**

blabby *adjective*
Inclined to gossip ▸ gossipy, talebearing, taletelling.

black *adjective*
1. Of the darkest color ▸ blue-black, coal-black, ebon, ebony, inky, jet, jetty, onyx, pitch-black, pitchy, raven, sable, sooty. **2.** Having little or no light ▸ dark, inky, lightless, moonless, pitch-dark, starless, sunless, unlit. *See also* **shady. 3.** Having a dark color or complexion ▸ brown, brunet, dusky, swarthy. *See* **dark** (3). **4.** Covered or stained with or as if with dirt or other impurities ▸ filthy, grimy, grubby. *See* **dirty** (1). **5.** Morally objectionable ▸ immoral, sinful. *See* **evil** (1). **6.** Dark and depressing ▸ bleak, desolate, somber. *See* **gloomy** (1). **7.** Characterized by intense ill will or spite ▸ evil, vicious, wicked. *See* **malevolent** (1).

black *verb*
To make dirty ▸ bemire, muck up, mud. *See* **dirty** (1).

black out *verb*
1. To suffer temporary lack of consciousness ▸ keel over, pass out. *See* **faint. 2.** To keep from being published or transmitted ▸ stifle, suppress, withhold. *See* **censor** (2).

blackball *verb*
1. To prevent or forbid authoritatively ▸ block, turn down. *See* **veto. 2.** To keep from being admitted, included, or considered ▸ boycott, ostracize, shut out. *See* **exclude** (1). *See synonym note at* **exclude.**

blacken *verb*
1. To make dirty ▸ bemire, muck up, mud. *See* **dirty** (1). **2.** To attack the reputation or honor of ▸ besmirch, smear, tarnish. *See* **denigrate** (1).

black eye *noun*
1. A bruise surrounding the eye ▸ *Informal:* mouse. *Slang:* shiner. *See also* **bruise. 2.** A mark of discredit or disgrace ▸ blemish, spot. *See* **stain** (1).

blackjack *verb*
▸ dragoon, force. *See* **coerce** (1).

blackleg *noun*
▸ cheater, swindler, trickster. *See* **cheat** (2).

blacklist *verb*
▸ blackball, boycott, ostracize, shut out. *See* **exclude** (1). *See synonym note at* **exclude.**

black look *noun*
▸ glower, lower, scowl. *See* **frown.**

blackmail *verb*
▸ exact, squeeze, wrest. *See* **extort.**

blackout *noun*
▸ faint, fainting spell, swoon, syncope. *See synonym note at* **faint.**

black-tie *adjective*
▸ dressy, full-dress. *See* **formal** (5).

blade *noun*
The cutting part of a sharp instrument ▸ edge, knife blade, knife-edge, razor, razorblade.

blah *adjective*
1. *Informal* Lacking liveliness, charm, or surprise ▸ aseptic, colorless, pedestrian. *See* **dull** (1). **2.** *Informal* In low spirits ▸ dysphoric, gloomy, melancholy. *See* **depressed** (1). **3.** *Informal* Arousing no interest or curiosity ▸ humdrum, monotonous. *See* **boring** (1).

blahs *noun*
Informal A feeling or spell of dismally low spirits ▶ dejection, doldrums, melancholy. *See* **depression** (2).

blamable *adjective*
▶ culpable, reprehensible. *See* **blameworthy**. *See synonym note at* **blameworthy**.

blame *noun*
1. Responsibility for an error or crime ▶ blameworthiness, culpability, fault, guilt, onus. *Slang:* rap. *See also* **burden**[1], **error**, **responsibility**. **2.** The act or an instance of finding fault ▶ censure, condemnation, denunciation. *See* **criticism** (1).

blame *verb*
1. To find fault with ▶ censure, fault, reprove. *Slang:* knock. *See* **criticize** (1). **2.** To ascribe the blame for a misdeed or error ▶ attribute, lay, pin. *See* **fix** (13). **3.** To make an accusation against ▶ denounce, incriminate, inculpate. *See* **accuse**.

✚ CORE SYNONYMS: *blame, fault, guilt.* These nouns denote a sense of responsibility for an error or crime. *Blame* stresses censure or punishment for a lapse or misdeed for which one is held accountable: *The police laid the blame for the accident on the driver. Fault* is culpability for wrongdoing or failure: *It is my own fault that I wasn't prepared for the exam. Guilt* applies to willful wrongdoing and stresses moral culpability: *The prosecution presented evidence of the defendant's guilt.*

---

blamed *adjective*
Informal So annoying or detestable as to deserve condemnation ▶ accursed, blasted, confounded. *See* **damned** (2).

blameful *adjective*
▶ culpable, reprehensible. *See* **blameworthy**. *See synonym note at* **blameworthy**.

blameless *adjective*
1. Free from guilt or blame ▶ faultless, guiltless, harmless. *See* **innocent** (2). **2.** Beyond reproach ▶ faultless, unblamable. *See* **exemplary** (1).

blameworthy *adjective*
Deserving blame ▶ blamable, blameful, censurable, culpable, guilty, red-handed, reprehensible. *Idioms:* at fault, in error (*or* the wrong), to blame. *See also* **liable**.

✚ CORE SYNONYMS: *blameworthy, blamable, blameful, censurable, culpable, guilty, reprehensible.* These adjectives mean meriting reproof or punishment: *blameworthy behavior; blamable but understandable resentment; blameful impulsiveness; censurable misconduct; culpable negligence; guilty deeds; reprehensible arrogance.*

◀ ANTONYM: *blameless*

---

blanch *verb*
1. To lose normal coloration; turn pale ▶ bleach, wan. *See* **pale**. **2.** To scald (food) briefly ▶ boil, parboil. *See* **cook** (1).

bland *adjective*
1. Without definite or distinctive characteristics ▶ colorless, indistinctive, neutral. *See also* **boring**. **2.** Lacking an appetizing flavor ▶ flavorless, tasteless. *See* **flat** (2). **3.** Lacking vigor, intensity, or bite ▶ innocuous, jejune. *See* **insipid** (1). **4.** Being of no special quality or type ▶ common, mediocre. *See* **ordinary** (1).

blandish *verb*
1. To persuade or try to persuade by gentle persistent urging or flattery ▶ cajole, wheedle. *See* **coax** (1). **2.** To compliment ingratiatingly ▶ butter up. *Informal:* soft-soap, sweet-talk. *See* **flatter** (1).

blandishment *noun*
▶ adulation, blarney. *Informal:* soft soap. *See* **flattery**.

blandness *noun*
1. A lack of excitement, liveliness, or interest ▶ drabness, lifelessness, sluggishness. *See* **dullness** (1). **2.** The state or quality of being insipid ▶ innocuousness, vapidness, wateriness. *See* **insipidity** (1).

blank *adjective*
1. Containing nothing ▶ bare, vacuous. *See* **empty** (1). *See synonym note at* **empty**. **2.** Lacking expression ▶ deadpan, pokerfaced. *See* **expressionless**. **3.** Lacking intelligent thought or content ▶ empty, vacuous. *See* **vacant** (1).

blanket *noun*
A top layer of material ▶ coating, covering, overlay. *See* **coat** (2).

blanket *verb*
To extend over the surface of ▶ pave, spread. *See* **cover** (1).

blanket *adjective*
Concerned with, applicable to, or affecting the whole ▶ common, generic, universal. *See* **general** (1).

blankness *noun*
1. Total lack of ideas, meaning, or substance ▶ barrenness, hollowness. *See* **emptiness** (3). **2.** A desolate sense of loss ▶ desolation, void. *See* **emptiness** (2). **3.** Empty, unfilled space ▶ emptiness, vacuity. *See* **nothingness** (2).

blare *verb*
▶ call, holler, scream. *See* **shout**.

blaring *adjective*
▶ booming, earsplitting, roaring. *See* **loud** (1).

blarney *noun*
1. Excessive, ingratiating praise ▶ adulation, blandishment. *Informal:* soft soap. *See* **flattery**. **2.** Empty or foolish talk ▶ blather, jabber, twaddle. *See* **babble** (1).

blasé *adjective*
▶ indifferent, listless, uninterested. *See* **apathetic**.

blaspheme *verb*
1. To use profane or obscene language ▶ curse, damn, swear. *Informal:* cuss. **2.** To attack with harsh, often insulting language ▶ assail, execrate. *See* **revile**.

blasphemous *adjective*
Showing irreverence and contempt for something sacred ▶ impious, profane, sacrilegious.

blasphemy *noun*
1. An act of disrespect toward something regarded as sacred ▸ desecration, profanation, violation. *See* **sacrilege. 2.** A profane or obscene term ▸ curse, expletive. *See* **swearword.**

blast *noun*
1. An explosive noise ▸ bang, boom, crash, crump, reverberation, rumble, roar, sonic boom, thunder. *See also* **clash, crack, noise. 2.** A violent release of confined energy ▸ blowout, blowup, burst, detonation, discharge, eruption, explosion, flare-up, fulmination. *See also* **barrage. 3.** *Slang* A big, exuberant party ▸ celebration, shindig, shindy. *Informal:* wingding. *Slang:* bash, blowout. *See also* **bender, binge. 4.** A natural movement or current of air ▸ blow, gust, waft. *See* **wind**[1] (1).

blast *verb*
1. To make an explosive noise ▸ bang, boom, crash, roar, rumble, thunder. *See also* **crack. 2.** To spoil or destroy ▸ blight, corrode, corrupt, dash, nip, scorch, shrivel, wither. *See also* **destroy, ruin. 3.** To discharge a gun or firearm ▸ blast away, fire (away *or* off), pop (off), shoot (away *or* off). *Idioms:* go bang-bang, open fire, take a shot (*or* potshot). **4.** To release or cause to release energy suddenly and violently, especially with a loud noise ▸ burst, detonate. *See* **explode** (1). **5.** To criticize harshly and devastatingly ▸ bash, excoriate, flay. *See* **slam** (5).

✚ CORE SYNONYMS: *blast, blight, dash, nip, wreck.* These verbs mean to spoil, destroy, or ruin something: *actions that blasted the chance for peace; hopes blighted by ill wishes; ambitions dashed by lack of funds; plans nipped in the bud; a life wrecked by depression.*

blasted *adjective*
1. *Informal* So annoying or detestable as to deserve condemnation ▸ accursed, bloody, confounded. *See* **damned** (2). **2.** Marked by cold and unpleasant conditions ▸ grim, severe. *See* **bleak** (1).

blatancy *noun*
▸ audacity, boldness, impertinence. *See* **impudence.**

blatant *adjective*
1. Offensively loud and insistent ▸ boisterous, clamorous. *See* **vociferous.** *See synonym note at* **vociferous. 2.** Rude and disrespectful ▸ bold, insolent, pert. *See* **impudent. 3.** Easily seen through due to a lack of subtlety ▸ clear, overt, transparent. *See* **obvious** (1).

blather *noun*
1. Empty or foolish talk ▸ gibberish, jabber, twaddle. *See* **babble** (1). **2.** Something that does not have or make sense ▸ bunkum, drivel, garbage. *See* **nonsense** (1).

blather *verb*
To talk rapidly, incoherently, or indistinctly ▸ chatter, jabber, prattle. *See* **babble** (1).

blatherskite *noun*
▸ gibberish, jabber, twaddle. *See* **babble** (1).

blaze[1] *noun*
1. The visible signs of combustion ▸ conflagration, fire, flame, flare-up. **2.** An intense blinding light ▸ dazzle, flare, glare.

blaze *verb*
1. To undergo combustion; be on fire ▸ combust, flame, flare. *See* **burn** (2). **2.** To emit a bright light ▸ burn, glow. *See* **beam** (1). **3.** To shine intensely and blindingly ▸ beat down, throb. *See* **glare** (2).

blaze[2] *verb*
To bring to public notice or make known publicly ▸ advertise, broadcast, proclaim. *See* **announce** (1).

blazing *adjective*
1. Fired with intense feeling ▸ burning, fervent, impassioned. *See* **passionate** (1). **2.** On fire ▸ afire, conflagrant. *See* **burning** (1). **3.** Extremely or harshly bright ▸ blinding, glaring. *See* **brilliant** (2).

blazon *verb*
▸ advertise, broadcast, proclaim. *See* **announce** (1).

bleach *verb*
▸ blanch, wan. *See* **pale.**

bleak *adjective*
1. Marked by cold and unpleasant conditions ▸ austere, blasted, dour, exposed, forbidding, foul, grim, hard, harsh, inclement, nasty, raw, severe, stark, unsheltered, windswept. *See also* **barren, bitter, lonely. 2.** Offering little encouragement ▸ dark, depressing, dim, dismal, downbeat, discouraging, gloomy, inauspicious, pessimistic, unencouraging, unpromising, unpropitious. *See also* **doubtful, unfavorable. 3.** Dark and depressing ▸ black, desolate, somber. *See* **gloomy** (1).

blear *verb*
To make dim ▸ blur, fog, obfuscate. *See* **obscure** (1).

blear *adjective*
Not clearly perceptible ▸ dim, faint, indefinite. *See* **unclear** (1).

bleary *adjective*
1. Not clearly perceptible ▸ dim, faint, indefinite. *See* **unclear** (1). **2.** Depleted of energy ▸ exhausted, weary, worn-out. *See* **tired** (1).

bleed *verb*
1. To flow or leak out or emit something slowly ▸ exude, leach, seep. *See* **ooze. 2.** To remove a liquid by a steady, gradual process ▸ pump, strain. *See* **drain** (1).

bleep *verb*
Informal To examine and remove objectionable or improper material from a publication ▸ bowdlerize, edit, screen. *See* **censor** (1).

blemish *verb*
1. To spoil the soundness or perfection of ▸ flaw, impair. *See* **damage. 2.** To alter and spoil the natural form or appearance of ▸ disfigure, misshape, twist. *See* **deform.**

blemish *noun*
1. Something that mars the appearance or causes inadequacy or failure ▸ fault, flaw, imperfection. *See* **defect** (1). *See synonym note at* **defect. 2.** A mark of discredit or disgrace ▸ black eye, spot. *See* **stain** (1). **3.** A disfiguring abnormality of shape or form ▸ contortion, disfigurement, malformation. *See* **deformity.**

blemished *adjective*
Having a defect or defects ▸ amiss, defective, faulty, flawed, imperfect. *See also* **shabby, trick.**

blench *verb*
▸ cringe, recoil, shrink. *See* **flinch.**

blend *verb*
1. To combine into one mass or mixture ▸ alloy, fuse, stir. *See* **mix** (1). *See synonym note at* **mix. 2.** To combine and adapt in order to attain a particular effect ▸ arrange, integrate. *See* **harmonize** (2). **3.** To process ingredients by stirring ▸ mix, whip. *See* **beat** (6).

blend *noun*
1. Something produced by mixing ▸ amalgam, merger, mix. *See* **mixture** (1). *See synonym note at* **mixture. 2.** Pleasing agreement, as of musical sounds ▸ concord, tune. *See* **harmony** (1).

bless *verb*
1. To make sacred by a religious rite ▸ consecrate, hallow, sanctify. *See also* **exalt. 2.** To give over by or as if by vow to a higher purpose ▸ consecrate, dedicate. *See* **devote** (1).

blessed *adjective*
1. Regarded with particular reverence or respect, especially by a religion ▸ hallowed, sacred. *See* **holy** (1). **2.** *Informal* So annoying or detestable as to deserve condemnation ▸ accursed, blasted, confounded. *See* **damned** (2).

blessedness *noun*
1. The quality of being or acting in accordance with what is holy or sacred ▸ beatitude, sanctity. *See* **holiness. 2.** A condition of well-being and good spirits ▸ bliss, felicity. *See* **happiness.**

blessing *noun*
1. A short prayer said at meals ▸ benediction, grace, thanks, thanksgiving. *See also* **prayer**[1]. **2.** Something beneficial ▸ benefit, boon, favor. *See* **advantage** (2). **3.** An indication of commendation or approval ▸ recommendation, support. *See* **endorsement** (1).

blight *verb*
1. To spoil or destroy ▸ corrode, dash. *See* **blast** (2). *See synonym note at* **blast. 2.** To become or cause to become rotten or unsound ▸ deteriorate, rot, spoil, turn. *See* **decay.**

blight *noun*
The condition of being decayed ▸ decomposition, deterioration, rot. *See* **decay.**

blind *adjective*
1. Having little or no sight ▸ blinded, dim-sighted, eyeless, legally blind, sightless, stone-blind, unseeing, unsighted, visionless, visually impaired. **2.** Concealed from view ▸ hidden, secluded, screened, secret. *Idioms:* out of sight, out of view. *See also* **hidden. 3.** Unwilling or unable to perceive ▸ dull, insensible, obtuse, purblind, uncomprehending, undiscerning, unnoticing, unperceptive, unseeing. *See also* **ignorant. 4.** *Slang* Stupefied, excited, or muddled with alcoholic liquor ▸ intoxicated, sodden, tipsy. *See* **drunk.**

blind *verb*
To confuse with bright light ▸ bedazzle, daze, dazzle.

blind alley *noun*
A course leading nowhere ▸ cul-de-sac, dead end.

blindness *noun*
The condition of not being able to see ▸ legal blindness, sightlessness, visual impairment.

blink *verb*
1. To open and close one or both eyes rapidly ▸ bat, flutter, nictitate, twinkle, wink. **2.** To shine with intermittent gleams ▸ flash, glimmer, twinkle. *See* **glitter. 3.** To give up in favor of another ▸ capitulate, give in, yield. *See* **surrender** (1). **4.** To abandon a former position or commitment ▸ back down, retreat, walk out. *See* **renege.**

blink at *verb*
To pretend not to see ▸ connive at, disregard, ignore, overlook, pass over, wink at. *Idioms:* be blind to, close (*or* shut) one's eyes to, let go (*or* pass), look the other way, make allowances for, turn a blind eye (*or* deaf ear) to.

blink *noun*
1. A brief closing of the eyes ▸ bat, flutter, nictitation, wink. **2.** A sudden burst of light ▸ gleam, glint, spark. *See* **flash** (1). **3.** A very brief interval of time ▸ instant, second, wink. *See* **flash** (2).

✚ CORE SYNONYMS: *blink, nictitate, twinkle, wink.* These verbs mean to open and close an eye or the eyes rapidly: *a dog blinking lazily at the fire; a reptile that nictitated as it closed in on its prey; twinkled, then laughed and responded; winked conspiratorially at his friend.*

---

bliss *noun*
1. A condition of well-being and good spirits ▸ blessedness, cheerfulness, felicity. *See* **happiness. 2.** A feeling of gratification aroused by something good or desired ▸ elation, enjoyment, pleasure. *See* **delight** (1). **3.** A supremely beautiful, blissful state or experience ▸ ecstasy, paradise. *See* **heaven** (1).

blissful *adjective*
▸ delectable, enchanting, heavenly. *See* **delightful.**

blister *verb*
Slang To criticize harshly and devastatingly ▸ bash, excoriate, flay. *See* **slam** (5).

blister *noun*
1. Damage that results from burning ▸ sear, singe. *See* **burn** (1). **2.** A ridge or bump raised on the flesh, as by a lash or blow ▸ boil, pock, wart. *See* **welt** (1).

blistering *adjective*
▸ ardent, boiling, burning. *See* **hot** (1).

blithe *adjective*
1. Happy and free from worry or care ▸ buoyant, debonair, untroubled. *See* **lighthearted** (1). **2.** Lacking concern or attention ▸ mindless, unobservant, unthinking. *See* **careless** (1).

blitheness *noun*
1. A state of joyful exuberance ▸ glee, lightheartedness, mirth. *See* **merriment** (1). **2.** A careless, often

reckless regard for consequences ► abandon, carelessness, heedlessness, thoughtlessness. *See also* **temerity.**
blithesome *adjective*
► happy, jolly, jovial. *See* **cheerful** (1).
blithesomeness *noun*
► glee, lightheartedness, mirth. *See* **merriment** (1).
blitz *noun*
A swift advance or attack ► onslaught, rush. *See* **charge** (1).
blitz *verb*
To direct a barrage at ► bombard, pelt. *See* **barrage.**
blitzkrieg *noun*
► onslaught, rush. *See* **charge** (1).
bloat *verb*
► balloon, distend, inflate. *See* **swell** (1).
bloc *noun*
1. An association for a common cause or interest ► coalition, league, organization. *See also* **association.**
2. Persons as an organized body ► community, people. *See* **public** (2).
block *verb*
1. To cut off from sight ► block out, blot (out), conceal, curtain, hide, obscure, obstruct, screen, shroud, shut off (*or* out). *See also* **disguise, hide, wrap.** 2. To block or fill with obstacles ► barricade, dam. *See* **obstruct** (1). *See synonym note at* **obstruct.**
3. To plug up or block something, such as a hole or conduit ► clog, cork. *See* **fill** (2). 4. To prevent or forbid authoritatively ► stop, turn down. *See* **veto.**
block in *or* **out** *verb*
To draw up a preliminary plan or version of ► outline, sketch. *See* **draft** (1).
block *noun*
1. Something that blocks entry or passage ► barrier, blockage, hindrance. *See* **bar** (1). *See synonym note at* **bar.** 2. *Slang* The uppermost part of the body ► crown, pate. *See* **head** (1).

✚ CORE SYNONYMS: *block, hide, obscure, obstruct, screen, shroud.* These verbs mean to cut off from sight: *a tree that blocked the view; a road hidden by brush; mist that obscured the mountain peak; skyscrapers obstructing the sky; a fence that screens the alley; a face shrouded by a heavy veil.*

---

blockade *noun*
A prolonged encirclement of an objective by hostile troops ► beleaguerment, besiegement, investment, siege. *See also* **attack.**
blockade *verb*
1. To surround with hostile troops ► beset, siege. *See* **besiege** (1). *See synonym note at* **besiege.** 2. To block or fill with obstacles ► barricade, block, dam. *See* **obstruct** (1).
blockage *noun*
► barrier, dam, hindrance. *See* **bar** (1).
blockhead *noun*
► dummy, dunce, thickhead. *See* **dullard.**
blockheaded *adjective*
► dumb, idiotic, obtuse. *See* **stupid** (1).

blocky *adjective*
1. Short, heavy, and solidly built ► chunky, heavyset. *See* **stocky.** 2. Of large, often awkward size and weight ► cumbersome, heavy, oversized. *See* **bulky** (1).
blond *or* **blonde** *adjective*
► fair-haired, towheaded. *See* **fair¹** (8).
blood *noun*
1. The crime of murdering someone ► homicide, killing. *See* **murder.** 2. One's ancestors or ancestral derivation ► birth, extraction, lineage. *See* **ancestry.**
3. Noble rank or status by birth ► blue blood, noblesse. *See* **nobility** (1).
bloodbath *noun*
► bloodshed, slaughter. *See* **massacre.**
bloodcurdling *adjective*
► hair-raising, horrid, horrific, nightmarish. *See* **horrible** (1).
bloodless *adjective*
1. Lacking color ► ashen, lurid, wan. *See* **pale** (1).
2. Being weak in quality or substance ► feeble, pallid. *See* **pale** (2). 3. Lacking compassion or mercy ► heartless, insensitive, merciless. *See* **callous.**
bloodletting *noun*
► bloodshed, slaughter. *See* **massacre.**
bloodline *noun*
► descent, origin, lineage. *See* **ancestry.**
bloodshed *noun*
► bloodbath, slaughter. *See* **massacre.**
bloodstain *verb*
To cover with blood ► bloody, ensanguine, incarnadine.
bloodsucker *noun*
► leech, sponge. *Slang:* freeloader. *See* **parasite** (1).
bloodsucking *adjective*
► epizoic, parasitical. *See* **parasitic.**
bloodthirsty *adjective*
► homicidal, sanguineous, slaughterous. *See* **murderous.**
blood vessel *noun*
► canal, duct, vein. *See* **vessel** (2).
bloody *adjective*
1. Of or covered with blood ► bleeding, blood-soaked, bloodstained, gory, hemorrhaging. *See also* **ghastly.**
2. Marked by or giving rise to murder or bloodshed ► homicidal, sanguineous, slaughterous. *See* **murderous.** 3. *Informal* So annoying or detestable as to deserve condemnation ► accursed, blessed, confounded. *See* **damned** (2).
bloody *verb*
To cover with blood ► bloodstain, ensanguine, incarnadine.
bloody-minded *adjective*
► homicidal, sanguineous, slaughterous. *See* **murderous.**
bloom¹ *noun*
1. A time of vigor, youth, or peak condition ► blossom, efflorescence, florescence, flower, flush, heyday, prime, salad days. 2. The showy reproductive structure of a plant ► blossom, floret. *See* **flower** (1). 3. A

fresh rosy complexion ▸ blush, color, flush, glow. *See also* **color, complexion.**

bloom *verb*
1. To bear flowers ▸ blossom, blow, bud (out), burgeon, effloresce, flower, open (up *or* out). *Idioms:* burst into flower (*or* bloom). **2.** To grow rapidly ▸ blossom, flourish, thrive. *See also* **increase.**

✤ CORE SYNONYMS: *bloom, blossom, efflorescence, florescence, flower, flush, prime.* These nouns denote a condition or time of vigor, youth, or peak condition: *beauty in full bloom; the blossom of a great romance; the efflorescence of humanitarianism; the florescence of Greek civilization; in the flower of youthful enthusiasm; in the flush of their success; the prime of life.*

---

bloom² *noun*
A straight, rigid piece of metal or other solid material ▸ bar, shaft, stem. *See* **rod.**

bloomer *noun*
Slang A stupid, clumsy mistake ▸ bungle, fumble, solecism. *See* **blunder.**

blooming *adjective*
▸ flush, rubicund, sanguine. *See* **ruddy.**

blooper *noun*
Informal A stupid, clumsy mistake ▸ bungle, fumble, solecism. *See* **blunder.**

blossom *noun*
1. The showy reproductive structure of a plant ▸ bloom, floret. *See* **flower** (1). **2.** A time of vigor, youth, or peak condition ▸ efflorescence, prime. *See* **bloom¹** (1). *See synonym note at* **bloom¹.**

blossom *verb*
1. To bear flowers ▸ burgeon, flower. *See* **bloom¹** (1). **2.** To grow rapidly ▸ bloom, flourish, thrive. *See also* **increase.**

blot *noun*
1. A discolored mark made by smearing ▸ blotch, stain. *See* **smear** (1). **2.** A mark of discredit or disgrace ▸ blemish, spot. *See* **stain** (1). *See synonym note at* **stain.**

blot *verb*
1. To cross out or remove ▸ delete, erase, strike (out). *See* **cancel** (1). **2.** To attack the reputation or honor of ▸ besmirch, smear, tarnish. *See* **denigrate** (1). **3.** To cut off from sight ▸ conceal, hide, screen. *See* **block** (1). **4.** To bring disgrace on ▸ abase, dishonor, shame. *See* **disgrace.**

blot out *verb*
To destroy all traces of ▸ eradicate, exterminate, obliterate. *See* **annihilate** (1).

blotch *noun*
A discolored mark made by smearing ▸ smudge, stain. *See* **smear** (1).

blotch *verb*
To mark or soil with foreign matter ▸ discolor, spatter. *See* **stain** (1).

blotto *adjective*
Slang Stupefied, excited, or muddled with alcoholic liquor ▸ intoxicated, sodden, tipsy. *See* **drunk.**

blow¹ *verb*
1. To be in a state of motion, as air or wind ▸ bluster, breathe, freshen, gust, puff, rise, stir, sweep. *Idioms:* come (*or* kick *or* spring) up. **2.** To move in or on the wind ▸ drift, flap, float, flutter, fly, sail, stream, waft, wave. **3.** To come open or fly apart suddenly and violently, as from internal pressure ▸ blow out, burst, explode, pop. *Slang:* bust. **4.** To manifest strong winds and precipitation ▸ blow up, set in, squall, storm. *See also* **rain. 5.** To release or cause to release energy suddenly and violently, especially with a loud noise ▸ blow up, burst, fire. *See* **explode** (1). **6.** To breathe hard ▸ gasp, huff. *See* **pant** (1). **7.** *Informal* To talk with excessive pride ▸ bluster, vaunt. *See* **boast** (1). **8.** *Slang* To move away from a place ▸ exit, go away, retire. *See* **go** (1). **9.** *Slang* To use, consume, spend, or expend thoughtlessly or carelessly ▸ fritter away, squander, trifle away. *See* **waste** (1). *See synonym note at* **waste. 10.** *Informal* To pay for the food, drink, or entertainment of another ▸ *Informal:* stand. *Slang:* spring for. *See* **treat** (2). **11.** *Slang* To ruin through clumsiness or ineptness ▸ blunder, foul up, spoil. *See* **botch.**

blow in *verb*
Slang To come to a particular place ▸ get in, reach. *See* **arrive** (1).

blow up *verb*
1. To be or become angry ▸ fume, rage, seethe. *See* **anger** (2). **2.** To expand from or as if from internal pressure ▸ bloat, inflate. *See* **swell** (1). **3.** To make or become greater or larger ▸ amplify, boost, enlarge. *See* **increase** (1).

blow *noun*
1. A natural movement or current of air ▸ blast, gust, waft. *See* **wind¹** (1). **2.** An atmospheric disturbance characterized by strong winds and precipitation ▸ gale, tempest. *See* **storm** (1). **3.** *Informal* Boasting talk or behavior ▸ brag, vaunt. *See* **boast.**

blow² *noun*
1. A sudden heavy stroke ▸ bang, bonk, buffet, bust, chop, clout, crack, hit, jab, lick, pound, punch, slug, sock, stroke, swat, swing, swipe, thump, thwack, welt, whack, wham, whop. *Informal:* bash, biff, bop, clip, wallop. *Slang:* belt, conk, haymaker, knuckle sandwich, paste, roundhouse. *See also* **slap. 2.** Something that jars the mind or emotions ▸ jolt, surprise, trauma. *See* **shock¹** (1).

blow³ *verb*
To bear flowers ▸ burgeon, flower. *See* **bloom¹** (1).

blow-by-blow *adjective*
▸ full, particular, thorough. *See* **detailed** (1).

blower *or* **blowhard** *noun*
Slang One given to boasting ▸ bragger, vaunter. *See* **braggart.**

blowout *noun*
1. A violent release of confined energy ▸ burst, explosion. *See* **blast** (2). **2.** *Slang* A big, exuberant party ▸ celebration. *Slang:* bash. *See* **blast** (3). **3.** The act of defeating or the condition of being defeated ▸ overthrow, trouncing, vanquishment. *See* **defeat.**

blowup *noun*

1. A violent release of confined energy ▸ burst, explosion. *See* **blast** (2). **2.** A sudden violent expression, as of emotion ▸ burst, eruption, explosion. *See* **outburst** (1).

blowy *adjective*

▸ breezy, gusty. *See* **airy** (3).

blubber¹ *verb*

To shed tears ▸ howl, sob, weep. *See* **cry** (1). *See synonym note at* **cry.**

blubber² *noun*

Adipose tissue ▸ fat, lard, suet. *See also* **oil.**

blubbering *noun*

▸ bawling, sobbing, weeping. *See* **cry** (1).

bludgeon *verb*

1. To hit heavily and repeatedly ▸ assault, pummel, thresh. *See* **beat** (1). **2.** To frighten into submission or compliance ▸ browbeat, bully, cow. *See* **intimidate** (1). *See synonym note at* **intimidate.**

blue *adjective*

1. In low spirits ▸ dejected, dispirited, heavy-hearted. *See* **depressed** (1). *See synonym note at* **depressed.** **2.** Dark and depressing ▸ bleak, desolate, somber. *See* **gloomy** (1). **3.** Causing or expressing sorrow or sadness ▸ cheerless, dolorous, mournful. *See* **sorrowful** (1). **4.** Bordering on indelicacy or impropriety ▸ provocative, risqué, suggestive. *See* **racy** (1).

blue blood *noun*

1. Noble rank or status by birth ▸ birth, noblesse. *See* **nobility** (1). **2.** People of the highest social level ▸ elite, gentry, nobility. *See* **society** (1).

blue-blooded *adjective*

▸ aristocratic, elite, upper-class. *See* **noble** (1).

blue-chip *adjective*

▸ leading, major, major-league. *See* **big-league.**

bluecoat *noun*

▸ officer, trooper. *Informal:* cop. *See* **police officer.**

blue moon *noun*

▸ eon, eternity, long. *See* **ages.**

bluenose *noun*

▸ Mrs. Grundy, prig, puritan. *See* **prude.**

bluenosed *adjective*

▸ priggish, prissy, strait-laced. *See* **prudish.**

blue-pencil *verb*

Informal To examine and remove objectionable or improper material from a publication ▸ edit, expurgate, screen. *See* **censor** (1).

blueprint *noun*

1. A method used for accomplishing something ▸ course, modus operandi, procedure, technique. *See* **approach** (1). *See synonym note at* **approach.** **2.** A preliminary plan or version, as of a written work ▸ diagram, sketch. *See* **draft** (1).

blueprint *verb*

1. To form a strategy for ▸ devise, formulate, strategize. *See* **design** (1). **2.** To work out and arrange the parts and details of ▸ lay out, outline, sketch. *See* **design** (2). **3.** To plan the details or arrangements of ▸ lay out, work out. *See* **arrange** (2).

blue-ribbon *adjective*

▸ exceptional, superior, tiptop. *See* **excellent.**

blues *noun*

▸ dejection, doldrums, melancholy. *See* **depression** (2).

bluff *verb*

To cause to accept comething false by trickery or misrepresentation ▸ dupe, fool, mislead, trick. *See* **deceive.**

bluff *adjective*

Rudely informal ▸ brief, gruff. *See* **abrupt** (1). *See synonym note at* **abrupt.**

blunder *verb*

1. To move heavily or clumsily ▸ bumble, clump, flounder, galumph, hulk, lumber, lump, lurch, stump, stumble. *See also* **stagger, stumble. 2.** To proceed or perform in an unsteady, faltering manner ▸ bungle, flounder, fumble. *See* **muddle** (1). **3.** To ruin through clumsiness or ineptness ▸ ball up, foul up, spoil. *See* **botch. 4.** To make an error or mistake ▸ lapse, stumble. *See* **err** (1).

blunder *noun*

A stupid, clumsy mistake ▸ bobble, bungle, faux pas, foozle, fumble, muff, solecism, stumble. *Informal:* blooper, boner, boo-boo, fluff, no-no. *Slang:* bloomer, clinker, goof, howler. *See also* **mess, error.**

✦ CORE SYNONYMS: *blunder, bumble, flounder, lumber, lurch, stumble.* These verbs mean to move heavily or clumsily: *blundered about the dark room; flies bumbling against the screen; floundered up the muddy trail; a wagon lumbering along an unpaved road; twisted her ankle and lurched home; stumbled but regained his balance.*

---

blunderer *noun*

A clumsy, inept person ▸ botcher, bungler, dub, foozler, lubber. *Informal:* sad sack. *Slang:* klutz, screwup. *Idiom:* bull in a china shop. *See also* **boor, oaf.**

blunt *adjective*

1. Not physically sharp ▸ obtuse, edgeless, unpointed. *See* **dull** (3). **2.** Rudely informal ▸ brusque, curt, gruff. *See* **abrupt** (1). *See synonym note at* **abrupt.**

blunt *verb*

1. To make or become less sharp-edged ▸ round, turn. *See* **dull** (1). **2.** To render less sensitive ▸ desensitize, numb. *See* **deaden** (1).

blur *verb*

1. To make dim or unclear ▸ bedim, fog, obfuscate. *See* **obscure** (1). **2.** To addle the mind, as with a narcotic or alcohol ▸ impair, stupefy. *See* **drug** (2).

blurry *adjective*

▸ cloudy, dim, indistinct. *See* **unclear** (1).

blurt *verb*

▸ burst out, ejaculate. *See* **exclaim.**

blush *verb*

To become red in the face ▸ color, crimson, flush, glow, mantle, redden. *Idioms:* go red (*or* crimson *or* scarlet), turn red as a beet.

blush *noun*
A fresh rosy complexion ▸ bloom, color, flush, glow.
See also **color, complexion.**

bluster *verb*
1. To speak or say very loudly ▸ call, holler, yell. *See*
shout. 2. To talk with excessive pride ▸ brag, vaunt.
See **boast** (1). **3.** To be in a state of motion, as air or
wind ▸ breathe, gust. *See* **blow**¹ (1).

bluster *noun*
A loud, deep, prolonged sound ▸ bawl, bellow,
clamor. *See* **roar** (1).

blustery *adjective*
▸ roily, turbulent, violent. *See* **rough** (2).

board *verb*
1. To go aboard a means of transport ▸ catch, take.
Informal: hop. **2.** To stay in or provide with lodging,
especially temporarily ▸ bed (down), billet, house. *See*
lodge (1).

boards *noun*
▸ dais, podium, proscenium. *See* **stage** (1).

boast *verb*
1. To talk with excessive pride ▸ bluster, brag, crow,
gasconade, puff (up), swagger, swell (up), vaunt.
Informal: blow. *Idioms:* blow one's own horn (*or*
trumpet), pat oneself on the back, shoot off one's
mouth (*or* face), sing one's own praises, talk big. *See
also* **exaggerate, exult, strut. 2.** To have at one's
disposal ▸ enjoy, have, hold. *See* **command** (3).

boast *noun*
Boastful talk or behavior ▸ boasting, brag, braggado
cio, bragging, bravado, fanfaronade, gasconade,
vaunt. *Informal:* blow, fish story. *Slang:* gas. *See also*
bombast.

✚ CORE SYNONYMS: *boast, brag, crow, vaunt.* These verbs
mean to talk with excessive pride about oneself or
something related to oneself. *Boast* is the most
general: *"We confide* [that is, have confidence] *in our
strength, without boasting of it; we respect that of
others, without fearing it"* (Thomas Jefferson). *Brag*
implies exaggerated claims and often an air of insolent superiority: *You shouldn't brag about your grades.*
Crow stresses exultation and often loud rejoicing: *No
candidate should crow until the votes have been
counted. Vaunt* suggests ostentatiousness and lofty
extravagance of expression: *"He did not vaunt of his
new dignity, but I understood he was highly pleased
with it"* (James Boswell).

---

boaster *noun*
▸ bragger, vaunter. *See* **braggart.**

boastful *adjective*
Characterized by or given to boasting ▸ blustering,
bombastic, braggart, cocky, puffed up, swollen,
vaunting. *Idioms:* full of gas (*or* hot air). *See also*
arrogant, egotistic, pompous.

boat *noun*
A conveyance that travels over water ▸ bark, barque,
craft, vessel, watercraft, ship.

boatman *noun*
▸ mariner, navigator, seafarer. *See* **sailor.**

bob *verb*
1. To stay on top of the surface of water or stay in
mid-air ▸ hover, stay afloat. *See* **float** (1). **2.** To incline
the head or body, as in greeting, consent, courtesy,
submission, or worship ▸ curtsy, kneel. *See* **bow**¹ (1).

bode *verb*
1. To give an indication of something in advance
▸ augur, foretoken, portend. *See* **foreshadow. 2.** To
give warning signs of ▸ forewarn, portend. *See* **threat-
en** (1).

bodiless *adjective*
▸ disembodied, incorporeal, nonphysical. *See* **immaterial** (1).

bodily *adjective*
Of or relating to the body ▸ corporal, corporeal,
fleshly, incarnate, mortal, personal, physical, somatic.
See also **perceptible, physical, real.**

✚ CORE SYNONYMS: *bodily, corporal, corporeal, fleshly,
physical, somatic.* These adjectives mean of or relating
to the body: *a bodily organ; a corporal defect; corporeal
suffering; fleshly frailty; physical robustness; a somatic
symptom.*

---

body *noun*
1. The human body excluding the head and limbs
▸ midsection, torso, trunk. **2.** The physical frame of a
dead person or animal ▸ bones, cadaver, carcass,
corpse, mummy, relics, remains. *Slang:* stiff. **3.** The
physical characteristics of a person ▸ build, form,
physique. *See* **constitution** (1). **4.** A member of the
human race ▸ human, mortal, person. *See* **human
being. 5.** A number of individuals making up or
considered a unit ▸ array, cluster, collection. *See*
group (1). **6.** A group of people organized for a
particular purpose ▸ squad, team, unit. *See* **force** (5).
7. A number of persons who have come or been
gathered together ▸ conference, group. *Informal:* get-
together. *See* **assembly** (1). **8.** Something having material existence ▸ article, item, thing. *See* **object** (1).
9. A measurable whole ▸ amount, bulk. *See* **quantity**
(3). **10.** An organized array of individual elements and
parts forming and working as a unit ▸ arrangement,
totality, whole. *See* **system** (1).

body forth *verb*
To represent (an abstraction, for example) in or as if
in bodily form ▸ externalize, manifest, materialize. *See*
embody (1).

body politic *noun*
▸ country, land, nation. *See* **state** (1).

boff *or* **boffo** *or* **boffola** *noun*
Informal A dazzling, often sudden instance of success
▸ sleeper. *Informal:* smash. *See* **hit** (3).

bog *noun*
A usually low-lying area of soft waterlogged ground
and standing water ▸ fen, marsh, mire, wetland. *See*
swamp.

bog *verb*
To interfere with the progress of ▸ encumber, forestall. *See* **hinder** (1).

bog down *verb*
To interfere with the progress of ▸ dampen, obstruct. *See* **hinder.**

bogey *or* **bogeyman** *noun*
▸ phantom, shade, specter. *See* **ghost** (1).

boggle *verb*
1. To overwhelm with surprise, wonder, or bewilderment ▸ dumbfound, flabbergast. *See* **stagger** (2). **2.** To ruin through clumsiness or ineptness ▸ blunder, foul up, spoil. *See* **botch.**

bogle *noun*
▸ phantom, shade, specter. *See* **ghost** (1).

bogus *adjective*
▸ fake, fraudulent, phony. *See* **counterfeit.**

boil *verb*
1. To cook food by the use of heated water ▸ parboil, simmer, stew. *See* **cook** (1). **2.** To be in a state of turmoil or excitement ▸ bubble, burn, churn, effervesce, ferment, froth, percolate, seethe, simmer, smolder. **3.** To be or become angry ▸ boil over, fume, rage, seethe. *See* **anger** (2). **4.** To feel or look hot ▸ roast, swelter. *See* **burn** (3).

boil away *verb*
To pass off as vapor, especially when heated ▸ burn off, volatilize. *See* **evaporate** (1).

boil down *verb*
1. To reduce in complexity or scope ▸ pare (down), simplify, streamline. *Idioms:* reduce to the basics (*or* essentials *or* bare bones). *See also* **explain. 2.** To make short or shorter ▸ abbreviate, condense, reduce. *See* **shorten.**

boil *noun*
A ridge or bump raised on the flesh, as by a lash or blow ▸ blister, pock, wart. *See* **welt** (1).

boilerplate *noun*
Written material used to fill space in a publication ▸ filler. *See also* **item.**

boiling *adjective*
▸ blistering, burning, torrid. *See* **hot** (1).

boisterous *adjective*
▸ blatant, clamorous, stentorian. *See* **vociferous.** *See synonym note at* **vociferous.**

bold *adjective*
1. Willing to take risks ▸ daring, enterprising. *See* **adventurous** (1). **2.** Having or showing courage ▸ courageous, fearless, heroic. *See* **brave.** *See synonym note at* **brave. 3.** Rude and disrespectful ▸ brash, insolent, pert. *See* **impudent. 4.** Readily attracting notice ▸ conspicuous, outstanding, prominent. *See* **noticeable** (1). **5.** So sharply inclined as to be almost perpendicular ▸ abrupt, sharp, sudden. *See* **steep**[1] (1).

boldfaced *adjective*
▸ assuming, insolent, pert. *See* **impudent.**

boldness *noun*
1. Willingness to take risks ▸ audaciousness, audacity, daringness, fearlessness. *See* **daring. 2.** The state or quality of being impudent or arrogantly self-confident ▸ audacity, discourtesy, flippancy, impertinence. *See* **impudence.**

bollix up *verb*
Informal To ruin through clumsiness or ineptness ▸ blunder, foul up, spoil. *See* **botch.**

bolster *verb*
1. To make stronger or more resistant ▸ brace, reinforce, strengthen. *See* **support** (2). **2.** To support against arguments, attack, or criticism ▸ justify, maintain, vindicate. *See* **defend** (2). **3.** To present evidence in support of ▸ buttress, substantiate. *See* **back** (2).

bolt *verb*
1. To move suddenly and involuntarily ▸ jump, start. *See also* **bump, jerk. 2.** To leave hastily ▸ get out. *Slang:* scram, vamoose. *See* **run** (3). **3.** To make secure ▸ bind, chain, moor. *See* **fasten** (1). **4.** To move swiftly ▸ dash, sprint, zip. *See* **rush** (1). **5.** To swallow food or drink greedily or rapidly in large amounts ▸ englut, gobble, guzzle. *See* **gulp** (1).

bolt *noun*
1. A sudden and involuntary movement ▸ jump, start, startle. *See also* **jerk, recoil. 2.** A shaft hammered or drilled in place, used to hold together ▸ pin, spike, stud. *See* **nail.**

bomb *noun*
Slang An unsuccessful person or enterprise ▸ bust, fiasco, washout. *See* **failure** (1).

bomb *verb*
1. To direct a barrage at ▸ bombard, pelt. *See* **barrage.** *See synonym note at* **barrage. 2.** *Slang* To be unsuccessful ▸ fall short, founder, misfire. *See* **fail** (1).

bombard *verb*
1. To direct a barrage at ▸ blitz, pelt. *See* **barrage.** *See synonym note at* **barrage. 2.** To set upon with violent force ▸ assault, storm, strike. *See* **attack** (1). *See synonym note at* **attack.**

bombardment *noun*
▸ cannonade, fusillade, volley. *See* **barrage.**

bombast *noun*
Pretentious, pompous speech or writing ▸ claptrap, fire and brimstone, fustian, grandiloquence, magniloquence, orotundity, rant, turgidity. *See also* **gibberish, nonsense, oratory.**

bombastic *adjective*
1. Characterized by elevated language, such as that used in public speaking ▸ aureate, grandiloquent, rhetorical. *See* **oratorical. 2.** Characterized by or given to boasting ▸ braggart, cocky, vaunting. *See* **boastful.**

bombed *adjective*
Slang Stupefied, excited, or muddled with alcoholic liquor ▸ intoxicated, sodden, tipsy. *See* **drunk.**

bombshell *noun*
▸ jolt, surprise, trauma. *See* **shock**[1] (1).

bona fide *adjective*
▸ genuine, real, true. *Slang:* legit, kosher. *See* **authentic** (1). *See synonym note at* **authentic.**

bond *noun*
1. Something that physically confines the legs or arms ▸ ball and chain, chains, fetter, handcuffs, hobble, irons, leg irons, manacle, restraint, shackle, straitjacket, trammel. *See also* **brake, restraint. 2.** That

which unites or binds ▶ binding, cinch, girth, hitch, holdfast, knot, ligament, ligature, link, nexus, splice, tie, vinculum, yoke. *See also* **band, joint. 3.** The close physical union of two objects ▶ adherence, adhesion, attachment, cohesion. **4.** A band or fiber that is used to bind or tie ▶ cable, line, string. *See* **cord. 5.** An often written acceptance of terms between parties ▶ accord, deal, pact. *See* **agreement** (1). **6.** Something given to guarantee the repayment of a loan or the fulfillment of an obligation ▶ bail, guaranty, pledge. *See* **pawn**[1].
bond *verb*
1. To form a tight bond ▶ adhere, cleave, cling, cohere, stick. *Idioms:* hold tight (*or* fast), stick (*or* cling) tight, stick like glue (*or* a bur). *See also* **attach. 2.** To give or deposit as a pawn ▶ deposit, pledge. *See* **pawn.**
bondage *noun*
▶ enslavement, servility, thrall. *See* **slavery.**
bondservant *noun*
▶ serf, vassal. *See* **slave** (1).
bondsman *noun*
One who posts bond ▶ bail, bailsman.
bone-dry *adjective*
▶ moistureless, sere. *See* **dry** (1).
boneheaded *noun*
Informal Lacking in or showing a lack of intelligence ▶ dumb, idiotic, obtuse. *See* **stupid** (1).
boneheadedness *noun*
Informal The state of being stupid ▶ idiocy, mindlessness, obtuseness. *See* **stupidity.**
boner *noun*
Informal A stupid, clumsy mistake ▶ bungle, fumble, solecism. *See* **blunder.**
bone up *verb*
Informal To apply one's mind to the acquisition of knowledge, especially when pressed for time ▶ lucubrate, study. *Informal:* cram, grind. *Idioms:* burn the midnight oil, hit the books. *See also* **examine.**
bong *verb*
▶ ding, chime, peal. *See* **ring**[2] (1).
bonk *noun*
▶ crack, hit, swat, whack. *See* **blow**[2] (1).
bonkers *adjective*
Informal Afflicted with or exhibiting irrationality and mental unsoundness ▶ crazy, mad. *See* **insane** (1).
bonny *adjective*
▶ fine, jolly, nice. *See* **good** (1).
bonus *noun*
▶ award, bounty, plum. *See* **reward** (1).
bony *adjective*
▶ lean, skinny, slender, slim. *See* **thin** (1). *See synonym note at* **thin.**
boo *noun*
One of various derisive sounds of disapproval ▶ catcall, hoot. *See* **hiss** (2).
boo *verb*
To make a derisive sound of disapproval ▶ catcall, hoot. *See* **hiss** (2).
boob *noun*
1. *Slang* A person who is deficient in judgment and good sense ▶ idiot, imbecile, nitwit. *See* **fool** (1). **2.** *Slang* A mentally dull person ▶ dummy, dunce, thickhead. *See* **dullard.**
boobishness *noun*
Informal Foolish behavior ▶ folly, silliness, tomfoolery. *See* **foolishness.**
booby trap *noun*
▶ noose, pit. *See* **trap** (1).
boodle *noun*
1. *Slang* Money or a favor given as inducement to dishonest behavior ▶ graft. *Informal:* payoff. *See* **bribe. 2.** *Slang* Goods or property seized unlawfully ▶ booty, loot. *See* **plunder.**
boogie *verb*
Slang To move rhythmically to music, using patterns of steps or gestures ▶ foot, hoof, step. *See* **dance** (1).
book *noun*
1. A printed and bound work ▶ booklet, edition, hardcover, paperback, tome, volume. *See also* **publication. 2.** The text of a play, movie, opera, or similar work ▶ dialogue, libretto, screenplay, scenario. *See* **script** (2).
book *verb*
1. To cause to be set aside, as for one's use, in advance ▶ arrange for, bespeak, engage, reserve. *See also* **hire, lease. 2.** To place on a list or in a record or book ▶ catalog, chronicle, write down. *See* **list**[1] (1).

✦ CORE SYNONYMS: *book, bespeak, engage, reserve.* These verbs mean to cause something to be set aside in advance, as for one's use or possession: *will book a hotel room; made sure their selections were bespoken; engaged a box for the opera season; reserving a table at a restaurant.*

---

booking *noun*
A commitment, as for a performance by an entertainer ▶ date, engagement. *Slang:* gig.
bookish *adjective*
1. Devoted to study or reading ▶ scholarly, studious. *See also* **educated, intellectual, learned. 2.** Characterized by a narrow concern for book learning and formal rules ▶ academic, literary, scholastic. *See* **pedantic.** *See synonym note at* **pedantic.**
boom *verb*
1. To make a continuous deep reverberating sound ▶ growl, grumble, roll. *See* **rumble** (1). **2.** To make an explosive noise ▶ roar, thunder. *See* **blast** (1). **3.** To do or fare well ▶ batten, flourish, thrive. *See* **prosper.**
boom *noun*
An explosive noise ▶ bang, crash. *See* **blast** (1).
boomerang *verb*
To produce an unexpected and undesired result ▶ backfire, boomerang. *Idiom:* blow up in one's face. *See also* **fail.**
booming *adjective*
1. Improving, growing, or succeeding steadily ▶ prosperous, roaring, thriving. *See* **flourishing. 2.** Marked by extremely high volume and intensity of sound ▶ blaring, earsplitting, roaring. *See* **loud** (1).

boomy *adjective*
▸ prosperous, roaring, thriving. *See* **flourishing.**

boon¹ *noun*
Something beneficial ▸ benefit, blessing, favor. *See* **advantage** (2).

boon² *adjective*
Being in or showing good spirits ▸ happy, jolly, jovial. *See* **cheerful** (1).

boondocks *or* **boonies** *noun*
Slang A remote or rural area ▸ backwoods, hinterland. *See* **country** (1).

boor *noun*
An unrefined, rude person ▸ barbarian, cad, chuff, churl, Philistine, troglodyte, vulgarian, yahoo. *Informal:* caveman, slob. *See also* **blunderer, clodhopper, oaf.**

✦ CORE SYNONYMS: *boor, barbarian, churl, vulgarian, yahoo.* These nouns denote an unrefined, rude person: *listened to the boor talk about himself all night; a barbarian bewildered by the art exhibit; offended by the churl's lack of manners; refused to invite the vulgarian to the party; acted like a yahoo at the restaurant.*

---

boorish *adjective*
▸ indelicate, unbecoming, unrefined. *See* **coarse** (1).

boost *verb*
1. To increase in amount ▸ hike, jack (up), jump, raise, up. *See also* **increase. 2.** To make or become greater or larger ▸ amplify, blow up, enlarge. *See* **increase** (1). **3.** To move something to a higher position ▸ hoist, lift, raise. *See* **elevate** (1). *See synonym note at* **elevate. 4.** To give assistance to ▸ aid, assist. *See* **help** (1). **5.** To attempt to sell or popularize by advertising or publicity ▸ publicize, tout. *See* **promote** (3). **6.** *Slang* To take another's property without permission ▸ purloin, snatch. *See* **steal** (1).

boost *noun*
1. The amount by which something is increased ▸ advance, jump. *See* **increase** (2). **2.** The act of increasing or rising ▸ amplification, buildup, escalation. *See* **increase** (1). **3.** An instance of lifting or being lifted ▸ heave, hoist. *See* **lift** (1). **4.** Something that gives courage or confidence ▸ exhortation, motivation. *See* **encouragement** (1).

booster *noun*
▸ champion, defender, proponent. *See* **advocate** (1).

boot *noun*
1. *Slang* The act of dismissing or the condition of being dismissed from employment ▸ expulsion, termination. *See* **dismissal** (1). **2.** *Slang* The act of ejecting or the state of being ejected ▸ eviction, expulsion. *See* **ejection. 3.** *Slang* A strong, pleasant feeling of excitement or stimulation ▸ lift. *Informal:* wallop. *Slang:* bang. *See* **thrill** (1).

boot *verb*
1. *Slang* To end the employment or service of ▸ cashier, drop. *See* **dismiss** (1). *See synonym note at* **dismiss. 2.** *Slang* To put out by force ▸ dismiss, evict. *See* **eject** (1). **3.** *Slang* To eject the contents of the stomach

through the mouth ▸ retch, throw up. *Informal:* puke. *See* **vomit** (1).

booth *noun*
A small, often makeshift structure for the display and sale of goods ▸ counter, stand, stall. *See also* **store.**

bootleg *verb*
▸ run, sneak. *See* **smuggle.**

bootlegger *noun*
A person who engages in smuggling ▸ contrabandist, runner, smuggler. *Slang:* mule.

bootless *adjective*
▸ fruitless, unsuccessful, useless, vain. *See* **futile.** *See synonym note at* **futile.**

bootlessness *noun*
▸ fruitlessness, unprofitableness, uselessness. *See* **futility.**

bootlick *verb*
▸ grovel, kowtow, truckle. *See* **fawn.** *See synonym note at* **fawn.**

bootlicker *noun*
▸ flatterer, minion, slave. *See* **sycophant.**

booty *noun*
▸ graft, loot. *See* **plunder.**

booze *noun*
Slang A drinking bout ▸ brannigan, carousal, carouse, spree. *See* **bender.**

booze *verb*
Slang To take alcoholic liquor, especially excessively or habitually ▸ tipple. *Slang:* chug, lush. *See* **drink** (2).

boozed *or* **boozy** *adjective*
Slang Stupefied, excited, or muddled with alcoholic liquor ▸ intoxicated, sodden, tipsy. *See* **drunk.**

boozehound *or* **boozer** *noun*
Slang A person who is habitually drunk ▸ alcoholic, dipsomaniac, tippler. *See* **drunkard.**

bop *verb*
Informal To deliver a sudden, sharp blow to ▸ jab, sock, whack. *See* **hit** (1).

bop *noun*
Informal A sudden heavy stroke ▸ crack, hit, swat, whack. *See* **blow²** (1).

border *noun*
1. A line or area where something ends or abruptly changes ▸ brim, brink, curb, edge, edging, fringe, hem, limit, lip, margin, perimeter, periphery, rim, threshold, verge. *See also* **circumference. 2.** The line or area separating geopolitical units ▸ borderland, borderline, boundary, frontier, march, marchland. *See also* **limit, outskirts.**

border *verb*
1. To put or form a border on ▸ bound, edge, fringe, margin, rim, skirt, verge. **2.** To be contiguous or next to ▸ abut, bound, neighbor, verge. *See* **adjoin** (1).

border on *or* **upon** *verb*
To attempt to equal or surpass, as in quality of amount ▸ challenge, verge on. *See* **rival** (1).

✦ CORE SYNONYMS: *border, margin, edge, verge, brink, rim, brim.* These nouns refer to the line or narrow area where something ends or abruptly changes. *Border* refers either to the boundary line (*a fence along the border of the property*) or to the area immediately inside (*a frame with a wide border*). *Margin* is a border of more or less precisely definable width: *the margin of the page*. *Edge* refers to the bounding line formed by the continuous convergence of two surfaces: *sat on the edge of the chair*. *Verge* is an extreme terminating line or edge: *the sun's afterglow on the verge of the horizon*. Figuratively, it indicates a point at which something is likely to begin or to happen: *an explorer on the verge of a great discovery*. *Brink* denotes the edge of a steep place: *stood on the brink of the cliff*. In an extended sense it indicates the likelihood or imminence of a sudden change: *on the brink of falling in love*. *Rim* most often denotes the edge of something circular or curved: *a crack in the rim of the lens*. *Brim* applies to the upper edge or inner side of the rim of something shaped like a basin: *lava issuing from the brim of the crater*.

bordering *adjective*
▸ abutting, adjacent, contiguous, neighboring. *See* **adjoining.**

borderland *noun*
▸ boundary, frontier. *See* **border** (2).

borderline *noun*
The line or area separating geopolitical units ▸ borderland, frontier. *See* **border** (2).

borderline *adjective*
Lacking certainty or clarity ▸ dubious, indeterminate, questionable, unclear. *See* **ambiguous** (1).

bore¹ *verb*
1. To penetrate with a sharp edge ▸ incise, pierce, slash. *See* **cut** (1). **2.** To break, turn over, or remove (earth or sand, for example) with or as if with a tool ▸ excavate, scoop, shovel. *See* **dig** (1).

bore² *verb*
To make weary with dullness or tedium ▸ fatigue, stultify, tire, weary. *Idioms:* bore out of one's mind, bore to death (*or* distraction *or* tears), put to sleep. *See also* **annoy, tire.**

bore *noun*
Slang An unpleasant, tiresome person ▸ chump. *Slang:* pill, twit. *See* **drip** (2).

boreal *adjective*
▸ chill, frigid, polar. *See* **cold** (1).

boredom *noun*
The condition of being bored ▸ ennui, listlessness, tediousness, tedium. *Informal:* blahs, doldrums. *See also* **apathy, dullness, monotony.**

boring *adjective*
1. Arousing no interest or curiosity ▸ deadly, drear, dreary, dry, dull, humdrum, irksome, monotonous, stuffy, tedious, tiresome, uninteresting, unvaried, wearful, wearisome, weary. *Informal:* blah, ho-hum. *Slang:* draggy. *See also* **dull, insipid, trite. 2.** Being of no special quality or type ▸ common, mediocre, standard. *See* **ordinary** (1).

✦ **CORE SYNONYMS:** *boring, monotonous, tedious, irksome, tiresome, humdrum.* These adjectives refer to

that which arouses no interest or curiosity. *Boring* implies feelings of listlessness and discontent: *I had never read such a boring book*. What is *monotonous* bores because of lack of variety: "*There is nothing so desperately monotonous as the sea*" (James Russell Lowell). *Tedious* suggests dull slowness or long-windedness: *Traveling by plane avoids spending tedious days on the train*. *Irksome* describes what is demanding of time and effort and yet is dull and often unrewarding: "*I know and feel what an irksome task the writing of long letters is*" (Edmund Burke). Something *tiresome* fatigues because it seems to be interminable or to be marked by unremitting sameness: "*What a tiresome being is a man who is fond of talking*" (Benjamin Jowett). *Humdrum* refers to what is commonplace, trivial, or unexcitingly routine: *My quiet cousin led a humdrum existence*.

borough *adjective*
▸ megalopolis, metropolis, municipality. *Informal:* town. *See* **city.**

borrow *verb*
▸ appropriate, crib, pirate. *See* **plagiarize.**

bosom *noun*
The seat of a person's innermost emotions and feelings ▸ breast, heart, soul. *Idioms:* bottom of one's heart, cockles of one's heart, one's heart of hearts.

bosom *adjective*
Very closely associated ▸ close, cozy, familiar. *See* **intimate¹** (1).

boss *noun*
1. Someone who directs and supervises workers ▸ director, foreman, foreperson, forewoman, head, manager, overseer, superintendent, superior, supervisor, taskmaster, taskmistress. *Informal:* straw boss. *Slang:* big cheese, big wheel, chief. *See also* **executive. 2.** One who governs or leads ▸ chieftain, director, head, leader. *See* **chief** (1).

boss *verb*
1. To command in an arrogant manner ▸ dictate, dominate, domineer, order, rule, tyrannize. *Idioms:* boss around, lord it over, throw one's weight around. *See also* **command. 2.** To direct and watch over the work and performance of others ▸ monitor, oversee, watch over. *See* **supervise.** *See synonym note at* **supervise.**

boss *adjective*
Slang Exceptionally good of its kind ▸ first-rate, prime, splendid, tiptop. *See* **excellent.**

bossy *adjective*
▸ domineering, overassertive, overbearing. *See* **dictatorial** (1).

botch *verb*
To ruin through clumsiness or ineptness ▸ ball up, blunder, boggle, bungle, butcher, foul up, fumble, gum up, mangle, mess up, mishandle, mismanage, muddle, muff, spoil, wreck. *Informal:* bollix up, flub, muck up. *Slang:* blow, goof up, louse up, screw up, snafu. *Idioms:* make a mess (*or* muck *or* hash) of. *See also* **damage, destroy.**

botch *noun*
A confused or ruinous state ▸ ▶ foul-up, muddle, shambles. *See* **mess** (1).

✦ CORE SYNONYMS: *botch, bungle, fumble, muff.* These verbs mean to ruin through inept or clumsy handling: *botch a repair; bungle an interview; fumbled my chance to apologize; muffed the painting job.*

---

botcher *noun*
▸ bungler. *Slang:* klutz. *See* **blunderer.**

bother *noun*
1. Needless trouble ▸ botheration, fuss, pother, red tape, rigmarole. *Informal:* hassle, headache. *See also* **agitation, inconvenience. 2.** Something that annoys ▸ aggravation, irritant, nuisance. *See* **annoyance** (2).
3. The act of annoying or the state of being annoyed ▸ exasperation, irritation, vexation. *See* **annoyance** (1).

bother *verb*
1. To trouble the nerves or peace of mind of ▸ irritate, nettle, vex. *See* **annoy** (1). *See synonym note at* **annoy.**
2. To impair or destroy the composure of ▸ disorient, fluster, ruffle. *See* **agitate** (2). **3.** To cause pain, soreness, or discomfort to ▸ irritate, pain. *See* **hurt** (3). **4.** To cause anxious uneasiness in ▸ ail, trouble. *See* **worry** (1).

botheration *noun*
1. The act of annoying or the state of being annoyed ▸ bother, irritation, vexation. *See* **annoyance** (1). **2.** Needless trouble ▸ fuss, pother. *See* **bother** (1).

bothering *noun*
▸ bother, irritation, vexation. *See* **annoyance** (1).

bothersome *adjective*
▸ annoying, irritating, unsettling. *See* **disturbing.**

bottleneck *noun*
▸ barrier, blockage, hindrance. *See* **bar** (1).

bottle up *adjective*
▸ smother, stifle, suppress. *See* **repress.**

bottom *noun*
1. A side or surface that is below or under ▸ underneath, underpart, underside, undersurface. **2.** A very low or lowest level, position, or degree ▸ low, minimum, nadir, rock bottom. **3.** The lowest or supporting part or structure ▸ foot, foundation, groundwork. *See* **base**[1] (2). **4.** A point of origin or crucial factor ▸ core, focus, nucleus. *See* **center** (3). **5.** *Informal* The part of the body on which one sits ▸ posterior, rump. *Informal:* backside. *Slang:* fanny. *See* **buttocks.**

bottom *adjective*
Opposite to or farthest from the top ▸ lowermost, lowest, nethermost, undermost.

boulevard *noun*
▸ path, road, route. *See* **way** (2).

bounce *verb*
1. To reverse direction after striking something ▸ bounce back, rebound, reflect, snap back, spring back. *See also* **bend, glance. 2.** To move in a lively way ▸ skip, spring. *See* **bound**[1] (1). **3.** *Slang* To put out by force ▸ dismiss, evict. *See* **eject** (1). **4.** *Slang* To end the

employment or service of ▸ cashier, drop. *See* **dismiss** (1). *See synonym note at* **dismiss. 5.** To proceed with sudden, abrupt movements ▸ jounce, shake. *See* **bump** (1).

bounce back *verb*
1. To regain one's health ▸ improve, mend, recuperate. *See* **recover** (2). **2.** To send back the sound of ▸ reflect, reverberate. *See* **echo** (1).

bounce *noun*
1. A bouncing movement ▸ bound, hop, rebound. **2.** A sudden lively movement ▸ jump, spring. *See* **bound**[1] (2). **3.** A lively, emphatic, eager quality or manner ▸ animation, verve, vivaciousness. *See* **spirit** (1). **4.** The quality or state of being flexible ▸ elasticity, malleability, pliability. *See* **flexibility** (1). **5.** The ability to recover quickly from depression or discouragement ▸ buoyancy, elasticity, flexibility, resilience, resiliency.
6. *Slang* The act of ejecting or the state of being ejected ▸ eviction, expulsion. *See* **ejection. 7.** *Slang* The act of dismissing or the condition of being dismissed from employment ▸ expulsion, termination. *See* **dismissal** (1).

bouncy *adjective*
▸ animated, chipper, vivacious. *See* **lively** (1).

bound[1] *verb*
1. To move in a lively way ▸ bounce, hop, jump, leap, skip, skitter, spring, trip. *See also* **gambol. 2.** To place a limit on ▸ confine, fix, restrict. *See* **limit** (1).

bound *noun*
1. A bouncing movement ▸ bounce, hop, rebound.
2. A sudden lively movement ▸ bounce, hop, jump, leap, skip, spring.

bound[2] *verb*
1. To put or form a border on ▸ edge, rim. *See* **border** (1). **2.** To be contiguous or next to ▸ abut, border, meet, neighbor. *See* **adjoin** (1). **3.** To fix the limits of ▸ demarcate, limit. *See* **determine** (1).

bound *noun*
The boundary surrounding a certain area ▸ confines, end, perimeter. *See* **limits.**

bound[3] *adjective*
Being legally or morally required to do something ▸ committed, compelled, obligated. *See* **obliged** (2).

boundary *noun*
▸ borderland, frontier. *See* **border** (2).

boundless *adjective*
1. Having no ends or limits ▸ illimitable, infinite. *See* **endless** (1). *See synonym note at* **endless. 2.** Too great to be calculated ▸ immeasurable, infinite. *See* **incalculable.**

boundlessness *noun*
▸ immeasurability, limitlessness, measurelessness. *See* **infinity** (1).

bounds *noun*
▸ confines, perimeter, precincts. *See* **limits.**

bounteous *adjective*
▸ abundant, bountiful, plentiful. *See* **generous** (2).

bounteousness *noun*
1. The quality or state of being generous ▸ magna-

nimity, munificence, unselfishness. *See* **generosity.**
2. Prosperity and a sufficiency of life's necessities ► abundance, plenitude. *See* **plenty** (1).

bountiful *adjective*
1. Willing to give of oneself and one's possessions ► big-hearted, magnanimous, unselfish. *See* **generous** (1). **2.** Characterized by abundance; as much as one needs or desires ► abundant, bounteous, plentiful. *See* **generous** (2).

bountifulness *noun*
1. The quality or state of being generous ► magnanimity, munificence, unselfishness. *See* **generosity.** **2.** Prosperity and a sufficiency of life's necessities ► bounteousness, plenitude. *See* **plenty** (1).

bounty *noun*
1. Something given in return for a service or accomplishment ► award, bonus, plum. *See* **reward** (1). **2.** The quality or state of being generous ► magnanimity, munificence, unselfishness. *See* **generosity.** **3.** A great deal ► mass, profusion, wealth. *See* **abundance** (1).

bouquet *noun*
1. Cut flowers or foliage arranged or worn for display ► boutonniere, corsage, garland, lei, nosegay, posy, wreath. *See also* **flower. 2.** A sweet or pleasant odor ► aroma, perfume, scent. *See* **fragrance.** *See synonym note at* **fragrance.**

bout *noun*
1. A limited, often assigned period of activity, duty, or opportunity ► shift, stint, time. *See* **turn** (1). **2.** A test of skill or ability ► contest, match, trial. *See* **competition** (2).

boutique *noun*
A retail establishment where merchandise is sold ► emporium, outlet, shop, store.

bow¹ *verb*
1. To incline the head or body, as in greeting, consent, courtesy, submission, or worship ► bob, curtsy, genuflect, kneel, kowtow, nod, salaam. **2.** To conform to the will or judgment of another ► defer, submit, yield. *Idioms:* give ground, give way. *See also* **humor. 3.** To incline the body ► bend, crouch, scrunch. *See* **stoop** (1). **4.** To give in from or as if from a gradual loss of strength ► buckle, submit, surrender. *See* **succumb** (1). **5.** To give up in favor of another ► capitulate, give in, yield. *See* **surrender** (1). *See synonym note at* **surrender.**

bow *noun*
An inclination of the head or body, as in greeting, consent, courtesy, submission, or worship ► curtsy, genuflection, kowtow, nod, obeisance, salaam.

bow² *verb*
1. To deviate from a straight line in a smooth, continuous manner ► arch, curve, turn. *See* **bend** (1). **2.** To curve or yield under pressure ► buckle, sag. *See* **bend** (3).

bow *noun*
Something bent ► curvature, curve, turn. *See* **bend.**

bow³ *noun*
The forward part of something ► fore, front end, front side. *See* **front** (1).

bowdlerize *verb*
► edit, expurgate, sanitize. *See* **censor** (1).

bowed *adjective*
► arched, curved, rounded. *See* **bent** (1).

bowel movement *noun*
► dung, feces, waste. *See* **excrement.**

bowels *noun*
► entrails, intestines. *Informal:* guts. *See* **viscera.**

bowl *verb*
To send through the air with a motion of the hand or arm ► fling, hurl, pitch. *See* **throw** (1).

bowl over *verb*
► dumbfound, flabbergast. *See* **stagger** (2).

bowl *noun*
An act of throwing ► heave, hurl, toss. *See* **throw.**

box¹ *noun*
1. A difficult, often embarrassing situation or condition ► corner, difficulty, fix. *See* **predicament. 2.** Something wrapped or enclosed, as for transporting ► bundle, packet. *See* **package.**

box *verb*
To confine within a limited area ► cage, coop (up), shut (in). *See* **enclose** (1).

box² *verb*
1. To hit with a sharp blow, especially of the open hand ► smack, swat, whack. *See* **slap** (1). **2.** To deliver a sudden, sharp blow to ► jab, sock, whack. *See* **hit** (1).

box *noun*
A sharp blow, especially with the open hand ► smack, swat. *See* **slap** (1).

boxer *noun*
A contestant in a boxing match ► fighter, prizefighter, pugilist. *See also* **fighter.**

box office *noun*
The amount of money collected as admission, especially to a sporting event ► gate, receipts, take.

boy *noun*
1. A young male person ► boychild, lad, stripling, youth. *Informal:* junior, son. *Slang:* little shaver, nipper. *See also* **child. 2.** *Informal* A man referred to familiarly or as a member of one's group ► chap, guy. *See* **fellow** (1).

boycott *verb*
► blackball, blacklist, ostracize, shut out. *See* **exclude** (1). *See synonym note at* **exclude.**

boyfriend *noun*
A man who is a woman's romantic partner ► beau, inamorato. *Informal:* fellow, main man. *Slang:* old man. *See also* **darling, lover.**

bozo *noun*
Slang A person who is deficient in judgment and good sense ► idiot, imbecile, nitwit. *See* **fool** (1).

brace *verb*
1. To prepare oneself for action ► fortify, ready, steel. *See* **gird** (1). **2.** To make stronger or more resistant ► bolster, reinforce, strengthen. *See* **support** (2). **3.** To

make or become tense ▸ stiffen, tighten. *See* **tense.**

brace *noun*
1. A means or device that keeps something erect, stable, or secure ▸ buttress, crutch, prop. *See* **support** (1). **2.** Two items of the same kind together ▸ duet, match, pair. *See* **couple.**

bracer *noun*
Informal A medicine that restores or increases vigor ▸ energizer, stimulant. *See* **tonic.**

bracing *adjective*
▸ exhilarating, stimulating. *See* **invigorating.**

bracket *noun*
1. A division of persons or things by quality or rank ▸ league, rank, tier. *See* **class** (2). **2.** A means or device that keeps something erect, stable, or secure ▸ buttress, crutch, prop. *See* **support** (1).

bracket *verb*
1. To come or bring together in one's mind or imagination ▸ correlate, link. *See* **associate** (3). **2.** To make stronger or more resistant ▸ brace, reinforce, strengthen. *See* **support** (2).

brackish *adjective*
Containing salt ▸ briny, saline, salty.

brag *verb*
To talk with excessive pride ▸ gasconade, vaunt. *See* **boast** (1). *See synonym note at* **boast.**

brag *noun*
1. Boasting talk or behavior ▸ braggadocio, vaunt. *See* **boast. 2.** One given to boasting ▸ bragger, vaunter. *See* **braggart.**

brag *adjective*
Exceptionally good of its kind ▸ first-rate, prime, splendid, tiptop. *See* **excellent.**

braggadocio *noun*
1. The quality of being arrogant ▸ hauteur, superiority. *See* **arrogance. 2.** One given to boasting ▸ bragger, vaunter. *See* **braggart. 3.** Boasting talk or behavior ▸ brag, vaunt. *See* **boast.**

braggart *noun*
One given to boasting ▸ blusterer, boaster, brag, braggadocio, bragger, swaggerer, vaunter. *Informal:* blowhard. *Slang:* blower, windbag. *See also* **egotist, showoff.**

braggart *adjective*
Characterized by or given to boasting ▸ bombastic, cocky, vaunting. *See* **boastful.**

bragger *noun*
▸ boaster, vaunter. *See* **braggart.**

braid *verb*
To interlace strips or strands ▸ enlace, intertwine, twist. *See* **weave** (1).

braid *noun*
An open and loosely connected structure, usually interlaced, woven, or knotted ▸ lattice, net, network. *See* **web** (1).

brain *noun*
1. The seat of the faculty of intelligence and reason ▸ head, mind. *Informal:* gray matter. *See also* **imagi-** nation. **2.** A person of great mental ability ▸ intellectual, thinker. *See* **mind** (2).

braincase *noun*
▸ brainpan, cranium, skull. *See also* **head.**

brainchild *noun*
▸ contrivance, device. *See* **invention** (2).

brainless *adjective*
1. Displaying a lack of forethought and good sense ▸ fatuous, mindless, senseless. *See* **foolish. 2.** Lacking in intelligence ▸ dumb, idiotic, obtuse. *See* **stupid** (1). **3.** Lacking rational direction or purpose ▸ pointless, senseless. *See* **mindless** (1).

brainlessness *noun*
▸ idiocy, mindlessness, obtuseness. *See* **stupidity.**

brainpan *noun*
The bony framework of the head ▸ braincase, cranium, skull. *See also* **head.**

brainpower *or* **brains** *noun*
▸ intellect, mentality, understanding. *See* **intelligence** (1).

brainsick *adjective*
▸ crazy, demented, mad. *See* **insane** (1).

brainsickness *noun*
▸ dementia, derangement, lunacy. *See* **insanity** (1).

brainstorm *noun*
A sudden exciting thought ▸ inspiration, bright idea. *Informal:* brain wave. *See also* **idea.**

brainstorming *noun*
▸ cogitation, deliberation, rumination. *See* **thought** (1).

brainwash *verb*
▸ program, propagandize. *See* **indoctrinate** (2).

brainwashing *noun*
▸ disinformation, evangelism. *See* **propaganda.**

brain wave *noun*
Informal A sudden exciting thought ▸ brainstorm, bright idea, inspiration. *See also* **idea.**

brainwork *noun*
▸ cogitation, deliberation, rumination. *See* **thought** (1).

brainy *adjective*
▸ brilliant, genius, knowledgeable. *See* **intelligent** (1).

braise *verb*
▸ brown, roast, simmer. *See* **cook** (1).

brake *noun*
1. A device for slowing or stopping motion ▸ baffle, bit, bridle, checkrein, curb, damper, drag, leash, rein, restraint, snaffle. *See also* **bond, restraint. 2.** A device for supporting or holding in place ▸ dowel, grapnel, mooring. *See* **anchor** (1).

brake *verb*
To control, restrict, or arrest ▸ bridle, check, curb. *See* **restrain.**

brambly *adjective*
▸ barbed, bristly, prickly. *See* **thorny** (1).

branch *noun*
1. Something resembling or analogous to a tree branch ▸ arm, division, extension, fork, offshoot, ramification, subdivision, tributary. *See also* **division.**

2. An area of academic study that is part of a larger body of learning ▸ discipline, field, specialty. *See also* **area. 3.** An administrative unit, as of government or company ▸ affiliate, agency, arm, bureau, chapter, department, division, office, organ, section, wing. **4.** *Chiefly Regional* A small stream ▸ creek, rill. *See* **brook¹. 5.** A short straight piece of wood ▸ stake, twig. *See* **stick** (1).

branch *verb*
To separate into branches or branchlike parts ▸ bifurcate, branch out (*or* off), diverge, diversify, divide, fork, part, radiate, ramify, split, subdivide. *See also* **deviate, scatter.**

✤ CORE SYNONYMS: *branch, arm, fork, offshoot.* These nouns denote something resembling or analogous to a tree branch: *a branch of a railroad; an arm of the sea; the western fork of the river; an offshoot of a mountain range.*

brand *noun*
1. A name or other device placed on merchandise to signify its ownership or manufacture ▸ label, trademark. *See* **mark** (1). **2.** A class that is defined by the common attribute or attributes possessed by all its members ▸ ilk, mold, species. *See* **kind².**

brand *verb*
1. To cause to feel embarrassment, dishonor, and often guilt ▸ mortify, reproach, shame, stigmatize. *Idioms:* put to shame, put to the blush. *See also* **belittle, denigrate, embarrass, humble. 2.** To set off by or as if by a mark indicating ownership or manufacture ▸ identify, tag. *See* **mark** (1). *See synonym note at* **mark.**

brandish *verb*
1. To wield boldly and dramatically ▸ flourish, sweep, wave. *See synonym note at* **flourish.** *See also* **handle. 2.** To make a public and usually ostentatious show of ▸ exhibit, expose, flaunt. *See* **display** (1).

brand-new *adjective*
▸ fresh, novel, original. *See* **new** (1).

brannigan *noun*
▸ carousal, carouse, spree. *See* **bender.**

brash *adjective*
1. Characterized by unthinking boldness and haste ▸ hasty, impulsive, reckless. *See* **rash¹. 2.** Lacking sensitivity and skill in dealing with others ▸ gauche, impolitic, undiplomatic. *See* **tactless. 3.** Rude and disrespectful ▸ bold, insolent, pert. *See* **impudent.** *See synonym note at* **impudent.**

brashness *noun*
1. Foolhardy boldness or disregard of danger ▸ incautiousness, rashness, recklessness. *See* **temerity. 2.** The state or quality of being impudent or arrogantly self-confident ▸ audacity, boldness, impertinence. *See* **impudence.**

brass *noun*
Informal The state or quality of being impudent or arrogantly self-confident ▸ audacity, boldness, forwardness. *See* **impudence.**

brassbound *adjective*
▸ bullheaded, dogged, obstinate. *See* **stubborn** (1).

brass hat *noun*
Slang One who governs or leads ▸ boss, director, head, leader. *See* **chief** (1).

brass ring *noun*
Slang A person or thing worth catching ▸ *Informal:* catch. ▸ plum, prize. *See also* **treasure.**

brass-tacks *adjective*
▸ aphoristic, epigrammatic, proverbial. *See* **pithy** (1).

brassy *adjective*
Informal Rude and disrespectful ▸ bold, insolent, pert. *See* **impudent.**

brat *noun*
▸ gamin, imp, whelp. *See* **urchin.**

brattle *verb*
To make or cause to make a succession of short, sharp sounds ▸ chatter, clack, clank, clatter, rattle. *See also* **knock, shake.**

bravado *noun*
▸ brag, vaunt. *See* **boast.**

brave *adjective*
Having or showing courage ▸ audacious, bold, courageous, dashing, dauntless, doughty, fearless, fortitudinous, gallant, game, gritty, hardy, heroic, intrepid, mettlesome, nervy, plucky, spirited, stout, stouthearted, unafraid, undaunted, unflinching, valiant, valorous. *Informal:* spunky. *Slang:* gutsy, gutty. *See also* **adventurous, rash¹.**

brave *verb*
1. To confront boldly and courageously ▸ challenge, confront, dare. *See* **defy** (1). *See synonym note at* **defy. 2.** To express at the risk of rebuff or criticism ▸ dare, hazard, presume. *See* **venture** (1).

✤ CORE SYNONYMS: *brave, courageous, fearless, intrepid, bold, audacious, valiant, valorous, mettlesome, plucky, dauntless, undaunted.* These adjectives mean having or showing courage, especially under difficult or dangerous conditions. *Brave,* the least specific, is frequently associated with an innate quality: *"Familiarity with danger makes a brave man braver"* (Herman Melville). *Courageous* implies consciously rising to a specific test by drawing on a reserve of inner strength: *The courageous soldier helped the civilians escape from the enemy. Fearless* emphasizes absence of fear and resolute self-possession: *"world-class [boating] races for fearless loners willing to face the distinct possibility of being run down, dismasted, capsized, attacked by whales"* (Jo Ann Morse Ridley). *Intrepid* sometimes suggests invulnerability to fear: *Intrepid pioneers settled the American West. Bold* stresses readiness to meet danger or difficulty and often a tendency to seek it out: *"If we shrink from the hard contests where men must win at the hazard of their lives . . . then bolder and stronger peoples will pass us by"* (Theodore Roosevelt). *Audacious* implies extreme confidence and boldness: *"To demand these God-given rights is to seek black power—what I call audacious power"* (Adam Clayton Powell, Jr.). *Valiant* suggests the bravery of a hero or heroine: *"a sympathetic and detailed biography that sees Hemingway as a valiant and moral man*" (New York Times). *Valorous* applies to the deeds of heroes and heroines: "*The other hostages* [will] *never forget her calm, confident, valorous work*" (William W. Bradley). *Mettlesome* stresses spirit and love of challenge: "*her horse, whose mettlesome spirit required a better rider*" (Henry Fielding). *Plucky* emphasizes spirit and heart in the face of unfavorable odds: "*Everybody was . . . anxious to show these Belgians what England thought of their plucky little country*" (H.G. Wells). *Dauntless* refers to courage that resists subjection or intimidation: "*So faithful in love, and so dauntless in war,/There never was knight like the young Lochinvar*" (Sir Walter Scott). *Undaunted* suggests persistent courage and resolve: "*Death and sorrow will be the companions of our journey . . . . We must be united, we must be undaunted, we must be inflexible*" (Winston S. Churchill).

◄ ANTONYM: *cowardly*

bravery *noun*
▸ fortitude, gallantry, valor. *See* **courage.**

brawl *noun*
A physical conflict between two or more people ▸ free-for-all, melee. *See* **fight** (1). *See synonym note at* **fight.**

brawl *verb*
1. To exchange blows with another person ▸ fight. *Slang:* rumble. *Idioms:* duke it out, mix it up, slug it out. *See also* **wrestle. 2.** To engage in quarrel ▸ broil, caterwaul, wrangle. *See* **argue** (1).

brawn *noun*
1. Solid and well-developed muscles ▸ bulk, muscle, muscularity, physique. *Informal:* beef. *See also* **constitution. 2.** The state or quality of being physically strong ▸ potency, power, sinew. *See* **strength** (1).

brawny *adjective*
▸ athletic, robust, sturdy. *See* **muscular.** *See synonym note at* **muscular.**

bray *verb*
▸ atomize, grind, mill. *See* **crush** (2).

brazen *or* **brazenfaced** *adjective*
▸ audacious, brash, insolent. *See* **impudent.** *See synonym note at* **impudent.**

brazenness *noun*
▸ audacity, boldness, forwardness. *See* **impudence.**

breach *noun*
1. An act of breaking a law or of nonfulfillment of an obligation ▸ contravention, delinquency, dereliction, infraction, infringement, malfeasance, nonfeasance, negligence, transgression, trespass, violation. *See also* **crime. 2.** An interruption in friendly relations ▸ alienation, break, breakdown, collapse, disaffection, estrangement, falling out, fissure, rent, rift, rupture, schism, split. *See also* **argument. 3.** A partial opening caused by splitting and rupture ▸ break, cleft, fissure. *See* **crack** (2).

breach *verb*
1. To make a hole or other opening in ▸ break (through), gap, hole, perforate, pierce, punch (through), puncture. *Slang:* bust (through). *See also*

cut. **2.** To fail to fulfill a promise or conform to a regulation ▸ break, infringe. *See* **violate** (1).

✦ CORE SYNONYMS: *breach, infraction, violation, transgression, trespass, infringement.* These nouns denote an act of breaking a law or regulation, or of failing to fulfill a duty, obligation, or promise. *Breach* and *infraction* are the least specific: *Revealing the secret would be a breach of trust. Infractions of the rules will not be tolerated.* A *violation* is committed willfully and with complete lack of regard for legal, moral, or ethical considerations: *In violation of her contract, she failed to appear. Transgression* most often applies to divine or moral law: "*The children shall not be punished for the father's transgression*" (Daniel Defoe). *Trespass* implies willful intrusion on another's rights, possessions, or person: "*In the limited and confined sense* [trespass] *signifies no more than an entry on another man's ground without a lawful authority*" (William Blackstone). *Infringement* is most frequently used to denote encroachment on another's rights: "*Necessity is the plea for every infringement of human freedom*" (William Pitt the Younger).

bread *noun*
1. Material that is fit to be eaten ▸ diet, meat, nourishment. *See* **food. 2.** The means needed to support life ▸ alimony, keep, livelihood. *See* **living. 3.** *Slang* Something, such as coins or printed bills, used as a medium of exchange ▸ currency. *Slang:* dough, moola. *See* **money** (1).

bread and butter *noun*
▸ bread, keep, livelihood. *See* **living.**

breadth *noun*
The extent of something from side to side ▸ broadness, expanse, wideness, width. *See also* **distance.**

break *verb*
1. To crack or split into two or more fragments by means of force or strain ▸ crack (apart *or* open), fracture, rift, rive, shatter, shiver, smash, splinter, sunder. *Idioms:* break (*or* crack) asunder, break in two, smash to bits (*or* pieces *or* smithereens). *See also* **burst, crush, destroy, disintegrate. 2.** To break or separate into parts, sections, or branches ▸ disjoin, dissever, split up. *See* **divide** (1). **3.** To make a hole or other opening in ▸ break through, pierce, puncture. *See* **breach** (1). **4.** To severely impair someone's spirit, health, or will ▸ beat down, crush, destroy, overwhelm, ruin, shatter. **5.** To give way mentally and emotionally ▸ break down, collapse, crack, crumble, crumple, fall, fold, snap. **6.** To suddenly lose all health or strength ▸ drop, succumb. *See* **collapse** (1). **7.** To undergo partial breaking ▸ rupture, split. *See* **crack** (1). **8.** To pass into or through by overcoming resistance ▸ enter, puncture. *See* **penetrate** (1). **9.** To find the key to a code or cipher ▸ crack, decrypt, unscramble. *See* **decipher** (1). **10.** To make known ▸ disclose, divulge, transmit. *See* **communicate** (1). **11.** To be made public ▸ come out, get out, out, transpire. *Informal:* leak (out). *See also* **air, announce, appear. 12.** To stop

working properly ► act up, fail. *Slang:* conk out. *See* **malfunction. 13.** To reduce to financial insolvency ► bankrupt, bust, impoverish. *See* **ruin** (3). **14.** To lower in rank or grade ► degrade, downgrade. *See* **demote.** *See synonym note at* **demote. 15.** To fail to fulfill a promise or conform to a regulation ► contravene, infringe. *See* **violate** (1). **16.** To refuse or fail to obey ► defy, transgress. *See* **disobey.17.** To discontinue (a habit, for example) ► abjure, cut out, forswear, give up, leave off, renounce, stop. *Informal:* swear off. *Slang:* kick. *See also* **abandon. 18.** To interrupt regular activity for a short period ► recess. *Informal:* knock off. *Idioms:* take a break, take a breather, take five (*or* ten). **19.** To make an animal docile ► bust, tame. *See* **gentle** (1).

break apart *verb*
1. To break or separate into parts, sections, or branches ► disjoin, dissever, split up. *See* **divide** (1). **2.** To reduce or become reduced to pieces or fragments ► crumble, decompose, fragment. *See* **disintegrate** (1).

break away *verb*
To withdraw from an association or federation ► pull out, secede, splinter (off), withdraw. *Informal:* split (away). *See also* **quit.**

break down *verb*
1. To cause the complete ruin or wreckage of ► demolish, torpedo, wreck. *See* **destroy** (1). **2.** To stop working properly ► fail, give out. *Slang:* bust. *See* **malfunction. 3.** To separate into parts for study ► dissect, resolve, take apart. *See* **analyze** (1). **4.** To take something apart ► disassemble, dismantle, take down. **5.** To become or cause to become rotten or unsound ► deteriorate, rot, spoil, turn. *See* **decay. 6.** To reduce or become reduced to pieces or fragments ► crumble, decompose, fragment. *See* **disintegrate** (1).

break in *verb*
1. To enter forcibly or illegally ► burglarize, invade, trespass. *See also* **rob, steal. 2.** To interject remarks or questions into another's discourse ► chime in, chip in. *See* **interrupt** (2). **3.** To train to live with and be of use to people ► housebreak, tame. *See* **domesticate.**

break off *verb*
1. To bring an activity or relationship to an end suddenly ► cease, discontinue, interrupt, suspend, terminate. **2.** To cease trying to continue ► give up, quit, stop. *See* **abandon** (2). **3.** To end an association by or as if by leaving one another ► break up, part. *See* **separate** (1).

break out *verb*
1. To become manifest suddenly and in full force ► be triggered (sparked *or* touched off), burst (forth *or* out), erupt, explode, flare (up), irrupt. **2.** To break loose and leave suddenly, as from confinement or a difficult situation ► decamp, flee. *See* **escape** (1).

break up *verb*
1. To end an association by or as if by leaving one another ► divorce, part. *See* **separate** (1). **2.** To move apart and go in various directions ► disband, separate.

See **scatter** (2). **3.** *Informal* To express amusement or mirth ► guffaw, roar. *See* **laugh. 4.** To reduce or become reduced to pieces or fragments ► crumble, decompose fragment. *See* **disintegrate** (1). **5.** To break or separate into parts, sections, or branches ► disjoin, dissever, split up. *See* **divide** (1).

break *noun*
1. A cessation of continuity or regularity ► discontinuance, discontinuation, discontinuity, disruption, interruption, pause, suspension. *See also* **stop. 2.** An interval during which continuity is suspended ► hiatus, interim, lacuna. *See* **gap** (2). **3.** A pause or interval, as from work or duty ► recess, time-out. *See* **rest**[1] (1). *See synonym note at* **rest**[1]. **4.** A partial opening caused by splitting and rupture ► breach, cleft, fissure. *See* **crack** (2). **5.** The act or an instance of escaping, as from confinement or difficulty ► breakout, flight. *See* **escape** (1). **6.** A favorable or advantageous combination of circumstances ► chance, option. *See* **opportunity.** *See synonym note at* **opportunity. 7.** An interruption in friendly relations ► estrangement, fissure. *See* **breach** (2).

✦ **CORE SYNONYMS:** *break, crack, fracture, splinter, shatter, smash.* These verbs mean to crack or split into two or more fragments by means of force or strain. *Break* is the most general: *The window was broken by vandals. I broke my arm when I fell. That delicate ornament will break easily.* To *crack* is to break, often with a sharp snapping sound, without dividing into parts: *I cracked the coffeepot, but it didn't leak. The building's foundation cracked during the earthquake. Fracture* applies to a break or crack in a rigid body: *She fractured her skull in the accident. Splinter* implies splitting into long, thin, sharp pieces: *Repeated blows splintered the door.* To *shatter* is to break into many scattered pieces: *The bullet shattered the mirror upon impact. Smash* stresses force of blow or impact and suggests complete destruction: *He angrily smashed the vase against the wall.*

breakable *adjective*
► brittle, delicate, frangible. *See* **fragile** (1). *See synonym note at* **fragile.**

breakage *noun*
► destruction, impairment, wreckage. *See* **damage** (1).

breakdown *noun*
1. A sudden sharp decline in mental, emotional, or physical health ► collapse. *Informal:* crackup. *See also* **infirmity. 2.** A cessation of proper functioning ► collapse, failure, malfunction, outage. **3.** An abrupt failure ► crash, debacle, disaster. *See* **collapse** (2). **4.** The separation of a whole into its parts for study ► dissection, subdivision. *See* **analysis** (1). **5.** The condition of being decayed ► decomposition, deterioration, rot. *See* **decay. 6.** An interruption in friendly relations ► estrangement, fissure. *See* **breach** (2).

breaker *noun*
► ripple, undulation. *See* **wave** (1).

break-in *noun*
The act of entering a building or room with the

intent to commit theft ▸ breaking and entering, burglary, forced entry, trespass. *See also* **larceny.**

breakneck *adjective*
▸ brisk, express, high-speed, hurried, speedy. *See* **fast** (1).

breakout *noun*
1. The act or an instance of escaping, as from confinement or difficulty ▸ decampment, flight. *See* **escape** (1). **2.** A sudden emergence or increase ▸ burst, flare, outburst. *See* **eruption** (1).

breast *noun*
The seat of a person's innermost emotions and feelings ▸ bosom, heart, soul. *Idioms:* bottom of one's heart, cockles of one's heart, one's heart of hearts.

breastwork *noun*
▸ barricade, bastion, parapet. *See* **bulwark.** *See synonym note at* **bulwark.**

breath *noun*
1. The act or process of breathing ▸ exhalation, expiration, inhalation, inspiration, respiration, suspiration, wind. **2.** The vital principle or animating force within living beings ▸ soul, vitality. *See* **spirit** (2). **3.** A slight amount or indication ▸ hint, semblance, trace. *See* **shade** (2). **4.** A gentle wind ▸ draft, puff. *See* **breeze** (1).

breathe *verb*
1. To take a breath or breaths ▸ breathe in (*or* out), exhale, expire, inhale, inspire, respire, suspire. *Idiom:* draw breath. *See also* **pant. 2.** To tell in confidence ▸ confide, share, unbosom, whisper. *See also* **communicate, reveal, say. 3.** To have reality or life ▸ be, live. *See* **exist** (1). **4.** To be in a state of motion, as air or wind ▸ bluster, gust. *See* **blow¹** (1).

breather *noun*
▸ recess, time-out. *See* **rest¹** (1).

breathing *adjective*
▸ live, living, vital. *See* **alive** (1).

breathless *adjective*
▸ breezeless, still. *See* **airless** (2).

breech *noun*
▸ posterior, rump. *Slang:* fanny. *See* **buttocks.**

breed *verb*
1. To give life to; have offspring ▸ beget, engender, father, hatch, increase, multiply, parent, procreate, proliferate, propagate, reproduce, spawn. *See also* **produce. 2.** To raise crops or animals ▸ cultivate, propagate. *See* **grow** (1).

breed *noun*
A class that is defined by the common attribute or attributes possessed by all its members ▸ ilk, mold, species. *See* **kind².**

breeding *noun*
1. Training in the proper forms of social and personal conduct ▸ education, upbringing. *See also* **courtesy, manners. 2.** Excellent taste resulting from intellectual development ▸ cultivation, refinement. *See* **culture** (3). **3.** The process by which an organism produces others of its kind ▸ procreation, proliferation, propagation. *See* **reproduction** (3).

breeze *noun*
1. A gentle wind ▸ breath, cat's-paw, draft, eddy, puff, whiff, zephyr. *See also* **wind. 2.** *Informal* An easily accomplished task ▸ cakewalk, child's play, cinch, picnic, pushover, snap, walkaway, walkover. *Slang:* duck soup. *Idioms:* piece of cake, walk in the park. *See also* **runaway. 3.** A natural movement or current of air ▸ air, blast, blow, gust, wind, zephyr.

breeze *verb*
Informal To progress quickly and effortlessly ▸ coast, sail, skate, zip. *Informal:* romp, waltz.

✦ CORE SYNONYMS: *breeze, cinch, pushover, snap.* These nouns denote a task that is easily accomplished: *The exam was a breeze. Chopping onions is a cinch with a food processor. Winning the playoffs was no pushover. The child's card game was a snap to learn.*

---

breezeless *adjective*
▸ breathless, still. *See* **airless** (2).

breezy *adjective*
1. Exposed to or characterized by the presence of freely circulating air ▸ gusty, windy. *See* **airy** (3). **2.** Very brisk, alert, and full of high spirits ▸ animated, chipper, vivacious. *See* **lively** (1).

brew *noun*
1. The result of combining ▸ compound, merger, union. *See* **combination** (1). **2.** Any liquid that is fit for drinking ▸ beverage, refreshment. *See* **drink** (1).

brew *verb*
To be imminent ▸ hover, impend, loom. *See* **threaten** (2).

brewing *adjective*
▸ impending, looming. *See* **imminent.**

bribe *noun*
Money or a favor given as an inducement to dishonest behavior ▸ fix, graft, payola, soap, sop. *Informal:* hush money, payoff. *Slang:* boodle, grease, kickback, protection.

bribe *verb*
To give or promise a bribe to ▸ buy (off), corrupt, fix, suborn. *Informal:* pay off. *Idioms:* cross someone's palm, grease someone's palm (*or* hand), take care of.

bric-a-brac *noun*
▸ knickknack, trinket. *See* **novelty** (3).

bridal *noun*
▸ espousal, marriage, nuptials. *See* **wedding.**

bridle *noun*
A device for slowing or stopping motion ▸ curb, leash, rein. *See* **brake** (1).

bridle *verb*
To control, restrict, or arrest ▸ brake, check, curb. *See* **restrain.** *See synonym note at* **restrain.**

bridled *adjective*
▸ checked, controlled. *See* **restricted** (1).

brief *adjective*
1. Expressed in few words ▸ abbreviated, abridged, compendious, compressed, concise, condensed, crisp, curt, laconic, lean, short, succinct, summary, terse, thumbnail, trenchant. *See also* **pithy. 2.** Lasting or

existing only for a short time ▸ ephemeral, fleeting, temporary. *See* **transitory. 3.** Accomplished or experienced in very little time ▸ fast, rapid, speedy. *See* **quick** (1). **4.** Rudely informal ▸ blunt, brusque, curt. *See* **abrupt** (1).

brief *noun*
1. A shortened version or summary ▸ outline, sketch. *See* **synopsis. 2.** Something announced or communicated ▸ communication, notice, statement. *See* **message** (1).

briery *adjective*
▸ brambly, bristly, prickly. *See* **thorny** (1).

brig *noun*
▸ penitentiary, prison. *Informal:* lockup. *See* **jail.**

brigade *noun*
▸ corps, patrol, squad. *See* **detachment** (7).

brigand *noun*
▸ burglar, looter, robber. *See* **thief.**

bright *adjective*
1. Giving off or reflecting much light ▸ beaming, beamy, brilliant, effulgent, fulgent, glowing, incandescent, irradiant, lambent, lucent, luminescent, luminous, lustrous, radiant, refulgent, shining, shiny. *See also* **brilliant, glossy, sparkling. 2.** Full of color ▸ rich, vibrant, vivid. *See* **colorful** (1). **3.** Indicative of future success or full of promise ▸ auspicious, fortunate, propitious. *See* **favorable** (1). **4.** Being in or showing good spirits ▸ cheery, happy, sunny. *See* **cheerful** (1). **5.** Mentally quick and original ▸ keen, quick-witted, sharp. *See* **clever** (1). **6.** Free from clouds or mist ▸ fair, fine. *See* **clear** (2). **7.** Having or showing intelligence, often of a high order ▸ intellectual, knowledgeable. *See* **intelligent** (1). *See synonym note at* **intelligent.**

✤ CORE SYNONYMS: *bright, brilliant, radiant, lustrous, lambent, luminous, incandescent, effulgent.* These adjectives refer to what gives off or reflects much light. *Bright* is the most general: *bright sunshine; a bright blue. Brilliant* implies intense brightness and often suggests sparkling or gleaming light: *a brilliant color; a brilliant gemstone.* Something *radiant* emits or seems to emit light in rays: *a radiant sunrise; a radiant smile.* A *lustrous* object reflects an agreeable sheen: *thick, lustrous auburn hair. Lambent* applies to a soft, flickering light: *"its tranquil streets, bathed in the lambent green of budding trees"* (James C. McKinley). *Luminous* especially refers to something that glows in the dark: *My brand new watch has a luminous dial. Incandescent* stresses burning brilliance: *Flames consist of incandescent gases. Effulgent* suggests splendid radiance: *"The crocus, the snowdrop, and the effulgent daffodil are considered bright harbingers of spring"* (John Gould).

---

brighten *verb*
1. To make lively or animated ▸ animate, enliven, light (up), perk up. **2.** To become brighter ▸ illuminate, lighten. *See* **clear** (1).

bright-eyed *adjective*
▸ vigilant, wide-awake. *See* **alert** (1).

bright idea *adjective*
A sudden exciting thought ▸ brainstorm, inspiration. *Informal:* brain wave. *See also* **idea.**

brilliance *noun*
1. Exceptional brightness and clarity ▸ brilliancy, effulgence, fire, luminosity, radiance. **2.** Liveliness and vivacity of imagination ▸ brilliancy, fire, genius, inspiration. *See also* **intelligence, invention. 3.** Brilliant, showy splendor ▸ magnificence, resplendence, sparkle. *See* **glitter** (2). **4.** A height of achievement or acclaim ▸ grandness, magnificence, splendor. *See* **glory** (1).

brilliant *adjective*
1. Giving off or reflecting much light ▸ incandescent, luminous, radiant. *See* **bright** (1). *See synonym note at* **bright. 2.** Extremely or harshly bright ▸ blazing, blinding, dazzling, glaring, glary, pulsing, throbbing. *See also* **sparkling. 3.** Having a high, radiant sheen ▸ gleaming, glistening, lustrous. *See* **glossy. 4.** Marked by extraordinary beauty and splendor ▸ magnificent, resplendent, splendid. *See* **glorious** (1). **5.** Indicative of future success or full of promise ▸ bright, fortunate, propitious. *See* **favorable** (1). **6.** Having or showing intelligence, often of a high order ▸ intellectual, knowledgeable. *See* **intelligent** (1). *See synonym note at* **intelligent.**

brim *noun*
1. The projecting rim on the front of a cap ▸ peak, visor. *See* **bill^2** (2). **2.** A line or area where something ends or abruptly changes ▸ brink, fringe, margin. *See* **border** (1). *See synonym note at* **border. 3.** The greatest amount or number allowed ▸ cap, ceiling, maximum. *See* **limit** (1).

brimful *or* **brimming** *adjective*
▸ chock-full, loaded, packed. *See* **full** (1).

bring *verb*
1. To cause to come along with oneself ▸ bear, carry, convey, fetch, take (along), transport. *See also* **carry. 2.** To achieve a certain price ▸ bring in, fetch, get, go for, realize, sell for. **3.** To be the cause of ▸ generate, induce, trigger. *See* **cause.**

bring about *verb*
1. To be the cause of ▸ generate, induce, trigger. *See* **cause. 2.** To succeed in doing ▸ accomplish, achieve, carry out. *See* **effect** (1).

bring around *or* **round** *verb*
1. To succeed in causing a person to act or think in a certain way ▸ argue into, induce, talk into. *See* **persuade** (1). **2.** To cause another to feel sure about something ▸ assure, satisfy, win over. *See* **convince** (1). **3.** To cause to come back to life or consciousness ▸ restore, resuscitate, revivify. *See* **revive** (2).

bring down *verb*
To bring about the downfall of ▸ subvert, topple. *See* **overthrow** (1).

bring forth *verb*
1. To give birth to ▸ deliver, have. *See* **bear** (4). **2.** To bring into existence ▸ give, provide, yield. *See* **produce** (1).

bring in *verb*
To make as income or profit ▸ ▸ clear, gain, yield. *See* **return** (3).
bring off *verb*
To succeed in doing ▸ accomplish, achieve, carry out. *See* **effect** (1).
bring on *verb*
To be the cause of ▸ induce, trigger. *See* **cause**.
bring out *verb*
To present for circulation, exhibit, or sale ▸ issue, put out, release. *See* **publish** (1).
bring up *verb*
1. To take care of and educate a child ▸ foster, parent, raise, rear. *See also* **nurture**. **2.** To put forward a topic for discussion ▸ introduce, raise. *See* **broach**. **3.** To make reference to something ▸ allude (to), mention, note. *See* **refer** (1).
brink *noun*
▸ brim, fringe, margin. *See* **border** (1). *See synonym note at* **border**.
briny *adjective*
1. Containing salt ▸ brackish, saline, salty. **2.** Of or relating to the seas or oceans ▸ oceanic, saltwater, sea. *See* **marine** (1).
briny *noun*
A body of salt water covering a large part of the earth's surface ▸ brine, deep, main. *See* **ocean**.
brio *noun*
▸ life, verve, vivaciousness. *See* **spirit** (1).
brisk *adjective*
1. Characterized by great speed ▸ fleet, hasty, hurried, swift. *See* **fast** (1). **2.** Possessing, exerting, or displaying energy ▸ active, lively, vigorous. *See* **energetic**.
bristle *verb*
1. To be or become angry ▸ fume, rage, seethe. *See* **anger** (2). **2.** To be abundantly filled or richly supplied ▸ abound, crawl, swarm. *See* **teem**[1].
bristly *adjective*
1. Covered with sharp protuberances ▸ brambly, bristled, prickly. *See* **thorny** (1). **2.** Covered with hair ▸ furry, hirsute, shaggy. *See* **hairy** (1).
brittle *adjective*
▸ breakable, delicate, frangible. *See* **fragile** (1). *See synonym note at* **fragile**.
broach *verb*
To put forward a topic for discussion ▸ bring up, introduce, moot, put forth, raise. *See also* **name, propose, refer**.

✦ CORE SYNONYMS: *broach, introduce, moot, raise.* These verbs mean to bring forward a point, topic, or question for consideration or discussion: *broach the subject tactfully; introduce a tax bill before the legislature; an idea that was mooted before the committee; raised the problem of dropouts with the faculty.*

---

broad *adjective*
1. Of large extent or expanse ▸ ample, expansive, extended, extensive, outspread, outstretched, spacious, spread out, wide. *See also* **widespread**. **2.** Cov-

ering a wide scope ▸ all-inclusive, comprehensive, expansive. *See* **general** (2). **3.** Not narrow or intolerant ▸ liberal, open-minded, tolerant. *See* **broad-minded**. *See synonym note at* **broad-minded**. **4.** Easily seen through due to a lack of subtlety ▸ blatant, overt, transparent. *See* **obvious** (1). **5.** Offensive to accepted standards of decency ▸ bawdy, coarse, lewd, vulgar. *See* **obscene** (1). **6.** Spread out over a large area ▸ far-flung, widespread. **7.** Lacking literal exactness ▸ approximate, inexact, rough. *See* **loose** (3).
broadcast *verb*
1. To bring to public notice or make known publicly ▸ advertise, declare, herald. *See* **announce** (1). *See synonym note at* **announce**. **2.** To put seeds or young plants in soil ▸ scatter, seed, sow. *See* **plant** (1).
broadcast *noun*
A show that is aired on television or radio ▸ airing, program.
broaden *verb*
To make or become broader or more comprehensive ▸ amplify, dilate, distend, enlarge, expand, extend, spread (out), widen. *See also* **increase, lengthen, spread**.
broadening *noun*
▸ enlargement, spread. *See* **expansion**.
broad-minded *adjective*
Not narrow or intolerant; respectful of others' views ▸ accepting, broad, humanistic, liberal, open-minded, progressive, tolerant. *See also* **fair**[1], **liberal, tolerant**.

✦ CORE SYNONYMS: *broad-minded, broad, liberal, open-minded, tolerant.* These adjectives mean having or showing an inclination to respect views and beliefs that differ from one's own: *a broad-minded judge; showed broad sympathies; a liberal cleric; open-minded impartiality; a tolerant attitude.*

◂ ANTONYM: *narrow-minded*

---

broadness *noun*
The extent of something from side to side ▸ breadth, expanse, wideness, width. *See also* **distance**.
broadside *noun*
▸ cannonade, fusillade, volley. *See* **barrage**.
broad-spectrum *adjective*
▸ all-inclusive, broad, expansive. *See* **general** (2).
Brobdingnagian *adjective*
▸ behemoth, colossal, gigantic, mighty. *See* **enormous**.
broil[1] *verb*
1. To cook food by using radiant heat ▸ barbecue, charbroil, grill. *See* **cook** (1). **2.** To feel or look hot ▸ roast, swelter. *See* **burn** (3).
broil[2] *verb*
To engage in a quarrel ▸ dispute, fight, quarrel. *See* **argue** (1).
broiling *adjective*
▸ blistering, boiling, burning. *See* **hot** (1).
broke *adjective*
Informal Having little or no money or wealth ▸ destitute, down-and-out, indigent. *See* **poor** (1).

broken-down *adjective*
▶ bedraggled, dilapidated, tattered. *See* **shabby** (1).
brokenhearted *adjective*
▶ dysphoric, gloomy, melancholy, spiritless. *See* **depressed** (1).
broker *noun*
▶ intermediary, middleman. *See* **go-between**.
bromide *noun*
▶ banality, platitude. *See* **cliché**. *See synonym note at* **cliché**.
bromidic *adjective*
▶ clichéd, overused, stale, tired. *See* **trite**.
Bronx cheer *noun*
Slang One of various derisive sounds of disapproval ▶ catcall, hoot. *See* **hiss** (2).
Bronx cheer *verb*
Slang To make a derisive sound of disapproval ▶ boo, hoot. *See* **hiss** (2).
brood *verb*
To focus the attention on something moodily and at length ▶ agonize, dwell, fret, fuss, mope, worry. *Informal:* stew. **Idiom:** eat one's heart out. *See also* **ponder, sulk**.
brood *noun*
1. The offspring, as of an animal or bird, for example, that are the result of one breeding season ▶ litter, spawn, young. **2.** A person or group descended directly from the same parents or ancestors ▶ offspring, posterity, seed. *See* **progeny**. **3.** A number of animals considered collectively ▶ bevy, gaggle, litter. *See* **flock** (1). *See synonym note at* **flock**.

✦ **CORE SYNONYMS:** *brood, dwell, fret, mope, stew, worry.* These verbs mean to focus the attention on something moodily and at length: *brooding about his decline in popularity; dwelled on her defeat; fretted over the loss of his job; moping about his illness; stewing over her upcoming trial; worrying about the unpaid bills.*

---

brook¹ *noun*
A small stream ▶ arroyo, bayou, bourne, creek, feeder, rill, rivulet, runnel, tributary, watercourse. *Chiefly Regional:* branch, kill, run.
brook² *verb*
To put up with or continue despite difficulties ▶ accept, stomach, tolerate. *See* **endure** (1).
brother *noun*
▶ chum, intimate, mate. *See* **friend** (1).
brotherhood *noun*
▶ companionship, society. *See* **company** (5).
brouhaha *noun*
1. A condition of intense public interest or excitement: ▶ stir, uproar. *See* **sensation** (2). **2.** Loud and insistent utterances or noisemaking, usually expressing disapproval ▶ hullabaloo, rumpus, uproar. *See* **vociferation**. **3.** A lack of civil order or peace ▶ chaos, lawlessness, misrule. *See* **disorder** (2).
browbeat *verb*
▶ bludgeon, bully, cow. *See* **intimidate** (1). *See synonym note at* **intimidate**.

browbeater *noun*
▶ intimidator, tease, tormentor. *See* **bully**.
brown *adjective*
Having a dark color or complexion ▶ brunet, dusky, tawny. *See* **dark** (3).
brown *verb*
To prepare food for eating by the use of heat ▶ broil, grill, toast. *See* **cook** (1).
brownnose *verb*
Informal To behave obsequiously or submissively ▶ grovel, kowtow. *Informal:* apple-polish. *See* **fawn**.
brownnose *or* **brownnoser** *noun*
Informal One who flatters another or behaves obsequiously in an attempt to win favor ▶ flatterer, minion, slave. *See* **sycophant**.
brown study *noun*
▶ absent-mindedness, bemusement, reverie. *See* **trance** (1).
browse *verb*
1. To look through reading matter casually ▶ dip into, flip through, glance at (*or* over *or* through), leaf (through), look through (*or* over), riffle (through), run through, scan, skim, thumb (through). **Idioms:** pass (*or* run) one's eyes over. *See also* **examine**. **2.** To feed on vegetation ▶ crop, forage, graze, nibble (at), pasture. *See also* **chew**.
bruise *noun*
An injury that does not break the skin ▶ black-and-blue mark, contusion. *See also* **black eye, harm**.
bruise *verb*
To make a bruise or bruises on ▶ contuse. **Idioms:** beat (*or* leave) black-and-blue. *See also* **hurt**.
bruiser *noun*
Informal A person who treats others violently or roughly ▶ hoodlum, ruffian, tough. *See* **thug**.
bruit *verb*
▶ advertise, broadcast, herald. *See* **announce** (1).
brume *noun*
▶ fog, mist. *See* **haze** (1).
brunet *adjective*
▶ brown, dusky, swarthy. *See* **dark** (3).
brush¹ *noun*
1. Light and momentary contact with another person or thing ▶ flick, graze, kiss, rub, skim. **2.** An encounter between opposing military forces ▶ combat, confrontation, war. *See* **battle** (1).
brush *verb*
To make light and momentary contact with, as in passing ▶ flick, graze, kiss, rub (against *or* along), shave, skim. *See also* **caress, rub, touch**.

✦ **CORE SYNONYMS:** *brush, flick, graze, shave, skim.* These verbs mean to make light and momentary contact with something, as in passing: *Her arm brushed mine. I flicked the paper with my finger. The knife blade grazed the countertop. A taxi shaved the curb. The oar skims the pond's surface.*

---

brush² *noun*
A dense growth of shrubs ▶ brake, brushwood,

bushes, canebrake, chaparral, scrub, shrubbery, thicket, underbrush, undergrowth.

brusque *adjective*
▸ blunt, curt, gruff. *See* **abrupt** (1). *See synonym note at* **abrupt.**

brutal *adjective*
1. Painfully intense ▸ hard, harsh, severe. *See* **bitter** (2).
2. Inflicting suffering or pain ▸ barbarous, fierce, savage. *See* **cruel** (1).

brutality *noun*
▸ barbarity, truculence. *See* **cruelty.**

brutalize *verb*
▸ debase, demoralize, deprave, warp. *See* **corrupt** (1).

brute *noun*
▸ beast, devil, monster. *See* **fiend** (1).

brutish *adjective*
1. Similar to a beast in behavior ▸ beastlike, beastly. *See* **bestial** (1). **2.** Not civilized ▸ barbarian, barbaric, rude. *See* **uncivilized** (1).

bubble *noun*
1. A fantastic, impracticable plan or desire ▸ fantasy, illusion. *See* **dream** (2). **2.** A soft liquid sound ▸ gurgle, lap, murmur. *See* **burble.**

bubble *verb*
1. To form or cause to form foam ▸ fizz, lather. *See* **foam** (1). **2.** To flow with or make a soft liquid sound ▸ lap, murmur. *See* **burble** (1). **3.** To be in a state of turmoil or excitement ▸ burn, seethe. *See* **boil** (2).

bubbly *adjective*
▸ animated, chipper, vivacious. *See* **lively** (1).

buck *verb*
1. To take a stand against ▸ challenge, dispute, oppose. *See* **contest** (1). **2.** To confront boldly and courageously ▸ challenge, confront, dare. *See* **defy** (1).

buck up *verb*
To impart emotional, moral, or mental strength to ▸ hearten, nerve. *See* **encourage** (2).

bucket *verb*
To move swiftly ▸ dash, sprint, zip. *See* **rush** (1).

bucket *noun*
The goal in the game of basketball ▸ hoop, net, swish. *See* **basket** (3).

buckle *verb*
1. To fall in ▸ cave in, collapse, crumple, give, go. *Idiom:* give way. *See also* **fall. 2.** To give in from or as if from a gradual loss of strength ▸ submit, surrender. *See* **succumb** (1). **3.** To curve or yield under pressure ▸ give, sag. *See* **bend** (3). **4.** To make secure ▸ bind, chain, moor. *See* **fasten** (1).

buckle down *verb*
To devote oneself or one's efforts ▸ concentrate, focus, give. *See* **apply** (1).

buckle *noun*
A device for locking ▸ catch, clip, lock. *See* **fastener.**

buckram *adjective*
Rigidly constrained or formal; lacking grace and spontaneity ▸ starchy, stiff, stilted, wooden. *See also* **cool, forced, prudish.**

bucolic *adjective*
▸ pastoral, rural. *See* **country.** *See synonym note at* **country.**

bud¹ *noun*
A source of further growth or development ▸ kernel, seed. *See* **germ** (2).

bud *verb*
To bear flowers ▸ burgeon, flower. *See* **bloom¹** (1).

bud² *noun*
Informal A person whom one knows well, likes, and trusts ▸ mate. *Informal:* buddy, pal. *See* **friend** (1).

buddy *noun*
1. *Informal* A person whom one knows well, likes, and trusts ▸ mate. *Informal:* bud, pal. *See* **friend** (1).
2. *Informal* One who shares interests or activities with another ▸ companion, comrade. *See* **associate** (2).

budge *verb*
To move or cause to move slightly ▸ move, shift, stir.

budget *noun*
1. Money or other resources granted for a particular purpose ▸ appropriation, grant, subsidy, subvention.
2. A measurable whole ▸ amount, bulk. *See* **quantity** (3). **3.** The operating expenses of an enterprise ▸ costs, expenses. *See* **overhead.**

budget *verb*
To set aside or apart for a specified purpose ▸ assign, designate, earmark. *See* **appropriate** (1).

budget *adjective*
Low in price ▸ bargain-basement, economy, low-cost. *See* **cheap** (1).

buff¹ *verb*
To give a bright sheen or luster to ▸ burnish, glaze, polish. *See* **gloss¹** (1).

buff² *noun*
Informal An ardent devotee ▸ devotee, enthusiast, fancier. *See* **fan².**

buffet *noun*
A sudden heavy stroke ▸ crack, hit, swat, whack. *See* **blow²** (1).

buffet *verb*
To hit heavily and repeatedly ▸ assault, batter, pummel, thresh. *See* **beat** (1). *See synonym note at* **beat.**

buffoon *noun*
▸ idiot, moron, simpleton. *See* **fool** (1).

bug *noun*
1. A tiny organism usually producing disease ▸ microbe, microorganism, virus. *See* **germ** (1). **2.** The condition of being sick ▸ affliction, illness, malady. *See* **sickness** (1). **3.** Something that mars the appearance or causes inadequacy or failure ▸ fault, flaw, imperfection. *See* **defect** (1). **4.** An ardent devotee ▸ enthusiast, fanatic, fancier. *See* **fan².**

bug *verb*
1. To monitor telephone calls with a concealed device connected to the circuit ▸ tap, wiretap. **2.** To trouble the nerves or peace of mind of ▸ irritate, nettle, vex. *See* **annoy** (1).

bugbear *noun*
▸ abomination, anathema. *See* **hate** (2).

buggy *adjective*
Slang Afflicted with or exhibiting irrationality and mental unsoundness ▸ crazy, daft, off. *See* **insane** (1).

build *verb*
1. To make or form a structure ▸ carpenter, construct, erect, frame, knock together, put up, raise, rear. **2.** To create by forming, combining, or altering materials ▸ compose, produce, shape. *See* **make** (1). **3.** To make or become greater or larger ▸ amplify, boost, enlarge. *See* **increase** (1). **4.** To provide a basis for ▸ establish, ground. *See* **base**[1] (1).

build in *verb*
To construct as an integral part ▸ include, incorporate, integrate.

build up *verb*
1. To achieve an increase of ▸ develop, expand. *See* **gain** (9). **2.** To make or become greater or larger ▸ amplify, boost, enlarge. *See* **increase** (1). **3.** To bring together, so as to increase in mass or number ▸ amass, cumulate, heap up, pile up. *See* **accumulate**. **4.** To attempt to sell or popularize by advertising or publicity ▸ ballyhoo, publicize, tout. *See* **promote** (3).

build *noun*
The physical characteristics of a person ▸ body, form, physique. *See* **constitution** (1).

builder *noun*
1. A person or business that builds something ▸ carpenter, constructor, contractor, erector, mason. *See also* **maker**. **2.** A person instrumental in the growth of something, especially in its early stages ▸ contributor, producer. *See* **developer**.

building *noun*
Something built, especially for human use ▸ construction, edifice, erection, pile, structure.

building block *noun*
▸ component, piece, section. *See* **part** (1).

buildup *noun*
1. The act of accumulating ▸ accumulation, agglomeration, conglomeration. **2.** The result or product of building up ▸ accretion, accumulation, development, enlargement, growth, multiplication, proliferation, sprawl, spread. **3.** A quantity accumulated ▸ aggregation, amassment, cumulation. *See* **accumulation** (1). **4.** The act of increasing or rising ▸ boost, escalation. *See* **increase** (1). **5.** Information disseminated through various media to attract public notice ▸ advertisement. *Slang:* hype. *See* **publicity** (1).

built-in *adjective*
1. Serving as a nondetachable part of a larger unit ▸ component, constituent, incorporated, integral. **2.** Forming an essential element, as arising from the basic structure of an individual ▸ innate, intrinsic, natural. *See* **constitutional** (1).

bulge *verb*
1. To curve outward past the normal or usual limit ▸ bag, balloon, beetle, belly, jut, overhang, pouch, project, protrude, protuberate, stand out, stick out. **2.** To expand from or as if from internal pressure ▸ bloat, inflate. *See* **swell** (1).

bulge *noun*
1. A part that protrudes or extends outward ▸ knob, protrusion, protuberance. *See* **projection** (1). **2.** A dominating position, as in a conflict ▸ edge, upper hand, vantage. *See* **advantage** (3).

✦ **CORE SYNONYMS:** *bulge, balloon, belly, jut, project, protrude.* These verbs mean to curve, spread, or extend outward past the normal or usual limit: *The lawyer's wallet bulged with money. Our expenses are ballooning. The sail bellied in the wind. A pipe jutted from the side of the building. Braces can fix teeth that project from the mouth at an angle. A sconce protruded from the wall.*

---

bulk *noun*
1. Great amount or dimension ▸ amplitude, magnitude, mass, size, volume. **2.** The greatest part or portion ▸ mass, preponderance, preponderancy, weight. *See also* **center**. **3.** A measurable whole ▸ amount, body. *See* **quantity** (3). **4.** Solid and well-developed muscles ▸ muscle, physique. *See* **brawn** (1).

bulky *adjective*
1. Of large, often awkward size and weight ▸ blockish, blocky, cumbersome, cumbrous, heavy, hefty, lumpish, lumpy, massive, oversize, oversized, ponderous, voluminous. *See also* **big, heavy. 2.** Having a large body, especially in girth ▸ full-figured, heavy, hefty, hulking, hulky, husky, plus-sized, stout, sturdy. *See also* **fat, muscular, stocky. 3.** Difficult to manage ▸ ungainly, unwieldy. *See* **awkward** (2).

bull *noun*
1. *Slang* A member of a law-enforcement agency ▸ officer, trooper. *See* **police officer. 2.** *Slang* Something that does not have or make sense ▸ bunkum, drivel, garbage. *See* **nonsense** (1).

bulldoze *verb*
1. To frighten into submission or compliance ▸ browbeat, bully, cow. *See* **intimidate** (1). *See synonym note at* **intimidate. 2.** *Informal* To force one's way into a place or situation ▸ elbow, shove. *See* **muscle**.

bulldozer *noun*
▸ browbeater, tease, tormentor. *See* **bully**.

bulletin *noun*
1. Something announced or communicated ▸ announcement, notice, statement. *See* **message** (1). **2.** A detail of news or information ▸ dispatch, flash. *See* **item** (1). **3.** A report giving information ▸ advisory, notice. *See also* **report, warning**.

bullheaded *adjective*
▸ adamant, dogged, obstinate. *See* **stubborn** (1). *See synonym note at* **stubborn**.

bullheadedness *noun*
▸ doggedness, hardheadedness, rigidity. *See* **stubbornness**.

bull session *noun*
Informal Spoken exchange ▸ dialogue, discourse, talk. *See* **conversation** (1).

bully *noun*
One who is habitually cruel to smaller or weaker

people ▸ browbeater, bulldozer, hector, intimidator, persecutor, tease, tormentor. *See also* **tough.**
bully *verb*
To frighten into submission or compliance ▸ bludgeon, browbeat, cow. *See* **intimidate** (1). *See synonym note at* **intimidate.**
bully *adjective*
Informal Exceptionally good of its kind ▸ first-rate, prime, splendid, tiptop. *See* **excellent.**
bulwark *noun*
A structure used as a defense against an attack ▸ barricade, bastion, breastwork, earthwork, parapet, rampart. *See also* **base, fort.**

✚ CORE SYNONYMS: *bulwark, barricade, breastwork, earthwork, rampart, bastion, parapet.* These nouns refer literally to structures used as a defense against attack. A *bulwark* can be a mound of earth, an embankment, or a wall-like fortification. *Barricade* usually implies hasty construction to meet an imminent threat. *Breastwork* denotes a low defensive wall, especially a temporary one hurriedly built. *Earthwork* is a defensive construction of earth. A *rampart*, the main defensive structure around a guarded place, is permanent, high, and broad. A *bastion* is a projecting section of a fortification from which defenders have a wide range of view and fire. *Parapet* applies to any low fortification, typically a wall atop a rampart. Of these words, *bulwark* and *bastion* are the most frequently used to refer figuratively to something regarded as being a safeguard or a source of protection: *"The only sure bulwark of continuing liberty is a government strong enough to protect the interests of the people, and a people strong enough and well enough informed to maintain its sovereign control over its government"* (Franklin D. Roosevelt). *A free press is one of the bastions of a democracy.*

---

bum¹ *noun*
1. A self-indulgent person who spends time avoiding work or other useful activity ▸ idler, fainéant, loafer. *See* **wastrel** (2). **2.** An impoverished person ▸ beggar, insolvent, tramp. *See* **pauper.**
bum *verb*
1. To ask for as charity; solicit money or favors ▸ *Informal:* panhandle. *Slang:* mooch. *See* **beg** (1). *See synonym note at* **beg. 2.** To pass time without working or in avoiding work ▸ loaf, loiter. *See* **idle** (1).
bum out *verb*
To make sad or gloomy ▸ dishearten, dispirit, sadden. *See* **depress** (1).
bum *adjective*
Of low or lower quality ▸ inadequate, poor, unsatisfactory. *See* **bad** (1).
bum² *noun*
Informal The part of the body on which one sits ▸ posterior, rump. *Slang:* fanny. *See* **buttocks.**
bumble¹ *verb*
1. To move heavily or clumsily ▸ clump, galumph, hulk. *See* **blunder** (1). *See synonym note at* **blunder. 2.** To proceed or perform in an unsteady, faltering manner ▸ bungle, flounder, fumble. *See* **muddle** (1).

bumble² *verb*
To make a continuous low-pitched droning sound ▸ buzz, drone, whir. *See* **hum.**
bumble *noun*
A continuous low-pitched droning sound ▸ burr, buzz, drone. *See* **hum.**
bumbling *adjective*
▸ clumsy, inept. *See* **unskillful** (1).
bummer *noun*
1. *Slang* A great disappointment or regrettable fact ▸ crime, pity, shame. *Idiom:* a crying shame. **2.** *Slang* A person who spoils the enthusiasm or fun of others ▸ spoilsport. *Informal:* wet blanket. *Slang:* party pooper. *See* **killjoy. 3.** *Slang* A person who begs habitually or for a living ▸ cadger, mendicant. *See* **beggar** (1).
bump *verb*
1. To proceed with sudden, abrupt movements ▸ bounce, jar, jerk, jiggle, jolt, jounce, lurch, rattle. *See also* **shake. 2.** To come together with force ▸ crash, impact. *See* **collide** (1). **3.** To put out by force ▸ dismiss, evict. *See* **eject** (1). **4.** To lower in rank or grade ▸ degrade, downgrade. *See* **demote.**
bump into *verb*
To find or meet by chance ▸ come across, run across, stumble on. *See* **encounter** (1).
bump off *verb*
Slang To take the life of a person or persons unlawfully ▸ destroy, kill, slay. *See* **murder** (1).
bump *noun*
1. An unevenness or elevation on a surface ▸ excrescence, gnarl, growth, hump, knob, knot, lump, node, nodule, nub, outgrowth, protuberance. *See also* **projection. 2.** A small raised area of skin, as from a blow or sting ▸ bunch, knot, lump, swelling. *Informal:* boo-boo. *Slang:* goose egg. *See also* **welt. 3.** A violent forcible contact ▸ crash, impact. *See* **collision. 4.** A stroke or blow that produces a sound ▸ thud, thump. *See* **beat** (1). **5.** A natural land elevation ▸ prominence, rise. *See* **hill** (1).
bumpiness *noun*
▸ coarseness, roughness, unevenness. *See* **irregularity** (1).
bumpkin *noun*
▸ hick, rustic, yokel. *See* **clodhopper.**
bumpy *adjective*
▸ coarse, ragged, scabrous. *See* **rough** (1).
bunch *noun*
1. A number of individuals making up or considered a unit ▸ body, cluster, collection. *See* **group** (1). **2.** An indefinite amount or extent ▸ measure, portion. *See* **quantity** (2). **3.** *Informal* A small group of friends or associates ▸ coterie, group, set. *See* **circle** (3). **4.** A small raised area of skin, as from a blow or sting ▸ lump, swelling. *See* **bump** (2). **5.** An indeterminately great amount or number ▸ millions, multiplicity. *Informal:* bushel. *See* **heap** (3).
bundle *noun*
1. A number of individuals making up or considered

a unit ▸ body, cluster. *See* **group** (1). **2.** *Informal* A large sum of money ▸ mint. *Informal:* pile. *See* **fortune** (7). **3.** Something wrapped or enclosed, as for transporting ▸ box, packet. *See* **package.**

bundle *verb*
To cover completely and closely, as with clothing. ▸ envelop, roll, swathe. *See* **wrap** (1).

bundle up *verb*
To put on warm clothes ▸ wrap, wrap up.

bung *noun*
▸ cork, stop. *See* **plug** (1).

bungle *verb*
1. To proceed or perform in an unsteady, faltering manner ▸ blunder, flounder, fumble. *See* **muddle** (1). **2.** To ruin through clumsiness or ineptness ▸ blunder, foul up, spoil. *See* **botch.** *See synonym note at* **botch.**

bungle *noun*
A stupid, clumsy mistake ▸ faux pas, fumble, solecism. *See* **blunder.**

bungler *noun*
▸ botcher. *Slang:* klutz. *See* **blunderer.**

bungling *adjective*
1. Clumsily lacking in the ability to perform ▸ bumbling, clumsy, inept. *See* **unskillful** (1). **2.** Lacking the qualities, as efficiency or skill, required to produce desired results ▸ incapable, inept, unskilled. *See* **inefficient** (1).

bunk¹ *verb*
To stay in or provide with lodging, especially temporarily ▸ bed (down), board, house. *See* **lodge** (1).

bunk² *or* **bunkum** *noun*
Slang Something that does not have or make sense ▸ balderdash, drivel, garbage. *See* **nonsense** (1).

buns *noun*
Slang The part of the body on which one sits ▸ posterior, rump. *Informal:* backside. *See* **buttocks.**

Bunyanesque *adjective*
▸ behemoth, colossal, gigantic, mighty. *See* **enormous.**

buoy *verb*
1. To make stronger or more resistant ▸ bolster, reinforce, strengthen. *See* **support** (2). **2.** To raise the spirits of ▸ animate, exhilarate, inspire. *See* **elate** (1).

buoyancy *noun*
The ability to recover quickly from depression or discouragement ▸ bounce, elasticity, flexibility, resilience, resiliency.

buoyant *adjective*
▸ blithe, debonair, untroubled. *See* **lighthearted** (1).

burble *verb*
1. To flow with or make a soft liquid sound ▸ babble, bubble, gurgle, lap, murmur, purl, ripple. *See also* **trickle, wash. 2.** To talk rapidly, incoherently, or indistinctly ▸ gabble, jabber, prattle. *See* **babble** (1).

burble *noun*
A soft liquid sound ▸ babble, bubble, gurgle, lap, murmur, purl, ripple.

burden¹ *noun*
1. A source of persistent worry or hardship ▸ afflic-

tion, albatross, cross, drag, drain, millstone, onus, strain, tax, trial, tribulation, weight. *Informal:* headache, pain. **Idioms:** royal headache (*or* pain), weight (*or* load) on one's mind. *See also* **care, curse, difficulty. 2.** Something carried or transported ▸ ballast, cargo, encumbrance, freight, haul, lading, load, weight. **3.** An act or course of action that is demanded of one, as by position, custom, law, or religion ▸ charge, commitment, obligation. *See* **duty** (1).

burden *verb*
To weigh down or place a heavy load on ▸ charge, cumber, encumber, freight, lade, load, oppress, saddle, strain, tax, try, weight. *See also* **fill, hinder.**

✦ **CORE SYNONYMS:** *burden, affliction, cross, trial, tribulation.* These nouns denote a source of persistent worry or hardship: *the burden of a guilty conscience; indebtedness that is an affliction; a temper that is your cross; a troublemaker who is a trial to the teacher; suffered many tribulations in rising from poverty.*

---

burden² *noun*
1. The current of thought uniting all elements of a text or discourse ▸ drift, intent, tenor. *See* **thrust** (1). **2.** The general sense or significance, as of an action or statement ▸ purport, substance. *See* **import** (1).

burdensome *adjective*
1. Requiring great bodily, mental, or spiritual strength ▸ arduous, backbreaking, crushing, formidable, grinding, grueling, heavy, laborious, onerous, oppressive, overpowering, overtaxing, rigorous, rough, severe, taxing, toilsome, tough, trying, weighty. *See also* **difficult. 2.** Troubling to the mind or emotions ▸ bothersome, irritating, unsettling. *See* **disturbing.**

✦ **CORE SYNONYMS:** *burdensome, onerous, oppressive, arduous, grueling, rigorous.* These adjectives apply to what imposes a severe test of bodily or spiritual strength. *Burdensome* is associated with both mental and physical hardship: *The burdensome task of preparing her tax return awaited her. Onerous* connotes the figuratively heavy load imposed by something irksome or annoying: *My only onerous duty was having to clean the bathroom.* Something *oppressive* weighs one down in body or spirit: *"Old forms of government finally grow so oppressive that they must be thrown off"* (Herbert Spencer). *Arduous* and *grueling* emphasize the expenditure of sustained and often exhausting labor: *Becoming a doctor is an arduous undertaking. Digging ditches is grueling work. Rigorous* implies the imposition of severe and uncompromising demands: *"Yet out of this unflattering, rigorous realism . . . Swift made great art"* (M.D. Aeschliman).

---

bureau *noun*
▸ agency, division. *See* **branch** (3).

bureaucratic *adjective*
▸ gubernatorial, regulatory. *See* **governmental.**

burg *noun*
▸ borough, megalopolis, municipality. *See* **city.**

burgeon *verb*
1. To bear flowers ▸ blossom, flower. *See* **bloom¹** (1).

2. To make or become greater or larger ▸ amplify, boost, enlarge. *See* **increase** (1).

burgess *or* **burgher** *noun*
▸ national, subject. *See* **citizen.**

burglar *noun*
▸ bandit, robber, stealer. *See* **thief.**

burglarize *verb*
1. To enter forcibly or illegally ▸ break in, invade, trespass. *See also* **steal. 2.** To take property or possessions from someone unlawfully and usually forcibly ▸ hold up, mug, stick up. *See* **rob** (1).

burglary *noun*
1. The act of entering a building or room with the intent to commit theft ▸ break-in, breaking and entering, forced entry, trespass. **2.** The crime of taking someone else's property without consent ▸ stealing, theft, thievery. *See* **larceny.**

burial *noun*
An act of placing a body in a grave or tomb ▸ burying, entombment, inhumation, interment, sepulture. *See also* **funeral.**

buried *adjective*
1. Lying beyond what is obvious or avowed ▸ concealed, covert, hidden. *See* **ulterior** (1). **2.** Located or operating beneath the earth's surface ▸ belowground, subterranean. *See* **underground.**

burke *verb*
1. To hold something requiring an outlet in check ▸ smother, stifle, suppress. *See* **repress. 2.** To keep away from ▸ dodge, escape, evade. *See* **avoid.**

burlesque *noun*
A work that ridicules something by the use of imitation or humor ▸ farce, lampoon, parody. *See* **satire.** *See synonym note at* **satire.**

burlesque *verb*
To copy the manner or expression of another, especially in an exaggerated or mocking way ▸ caricature, mock. *See* **imitate** (1).

burly *adjective*
▸ brawny, robust, sturdy. *See* **muscular.** *See synonym note at* **muscular.**

burn *verb*
1. To undergo or cause to undergo damage by fire ▸ burn down (*or* up), carbonize, incinerate, char, scorch, sear, singe. *Slang:* torch. *Idioms:* burn to a crisp, go up in flames (*or* smoke), reduce to ashes (*or* cinders). **2.** To undergo combustion; be on fire ▸ blaze, crackle, combust, flame, flare, hiss, roar. *See also* **smolder. 3.** To feel or look hot ▸ bake, boil, broil, burn up, roast, steam, swelter. *Idiom:* be on fire. **4.** To cause to become sore or inflamed ▸ inflame, irritate, sting. **5.** To be painful or sore ▸ smart, sting. *See* **hurt** (2). **6.** To cause to feel or show anger ▸ enrage, incense, infuriate. *See* **anger** (1). **7.** To be or become angry ▸ fume, rage, seethe. *See* **anger** (2). **8.** To be in a state of turmoil or excitement ▸ bubble, seethe. *See* **boil** (2). **9.** To emit a bright light ▸ glow, radiate. *See* **beam** (1). **10.** To get something by deceitful trickery ▸ cozen, defraud, swindle. *See* **cheat** (1). **11.** *Informal* To cause

to accept something false, especially by trickery or misrepresentation ▸ dupe, fool, mislead, trick. *See* **deceive.**

burn off *verb*
To pass off as vapor, especially when heated ▸ boil away, volatilize. *See* **evaporate** (1).

burn out *verb*
To grow weary ▸ flag, wear out. *See* **tire** (2).

burn *noun*
1. Damage that results from burning ▸ blister, char, scorch, sear, singe. **2.** An act of cheating ▸ deceit, hoax, swindle. *See* **cheat** (1). **3.** A sensation of physical discomfort occurring as the result of disease or injury ▸ prick, smart, soreness. *See* **pain** (1).

✦ **CORE SYNONYMS:** *burn, scorch, singe, sear, char.* These verbs mean to undergo or cause something to undergo damage by means of fire or intense heat. *Burn,* the most general, applies to the effects of exposure to a source of heat or to something that can produce a similar effect: *burned the muffins in the oven. Scorch* involves superficial burning that discolors or damages the texture of something: *scorched the shirt with the iron. Singe* specifies superficial burning and especially the deliberate removal of projections such as feathers from a carcass before cooking: *singed my eyelashes when the fire flared up; singed the chicken before roasting it. Sear* applies to surface burning of organic tissue: *seared the lamb over high heat.* To *char* is to use fire to reduce a substance to carbon or charcoal: *wood charred by the fire.*

---

burning *adjective*
1. On fire ▸ ablaze, afire, aflame, alight, blazing, conflagrant, fiery, flaming. *Idioms:* in a blaze, in flames. **2.** Marked by much heat ▸ blistering, boiling, scorching. *See* **hot** (1). **3.** Fired with intense feeling ▸ blazing, fervent, impassioned, torrid. *See* **passionate** (1). **4.** Demanding immediate attention ▸ crucial, dire, pressing. *See* **urgent** (1).

burnish *verb*
To give a bright sheen or luster to ▸ buff, glaze, polish. *See* **gloss**[1] (1).

burnish *noun*
A surface shininess ▸ luster, polish, shine. *See* **gloss**[1] (1).

burnout *noun*
▸ fatigue, weariness. *See* **exhaustion.**

burr *noun*
A continuous low-pitched droning sound ▸ bumble, buzz, drone. *See* **hum.**

burr *verb*
To make a continuous low-pitched droning sound ▸ buzz, drone, whir. *See* **hum.**

burrow *noun*
A place used as an animal's dwelling ▸ den, hole, lair. *See also* **cave.**

burrow *verb*
To break, turn over, or remove (earth or sand, for example) with or as if with a tool ▸ excavate, scoop, shovel. *See* **dig** (1).

burst *verb*

1. To break open or fly apart suddenly, as from internal pressure ▸ blow (out), explode, pop, rupture. *Slang:* bust. *Idiom:* give way. **2.** To release or cause to release energy suddenly and violently, especially with a loud noise ▸ backfire, detonate. *See* **explode** (1). **3.** To become manifest suddenly and in full force ▸ burst forth (*or* out), erupt, explode. *See* **break** (1).

burst out *verb*

To speak suddenly or sharply, as from surprise or emotion ▸ cry, ejaculate. *See* **exclaim.**

burst *noun*

1. A violent release of confined energy ▸ blowout, explosion. *See* **blast** (2). **2.** A sudden violent expression, as of emotion ▸ access, eruption, explosion. *See* **outburst** (1). **3.** A concentrated outpouring, as of missiles, words, or blows ▸ cannonade, fusillade, volley. *See* **barrage. 4.** A sudden emergence or increase ▸ breakout, flare, outburst. *See* **eruption** (1).

bursting *adjective*

1. Completely filled ▸ brimming, loaded, packed. *See* **full** (1). **2.** Intensely desirous or interested ▸ avid, impatient. *See* **eager** (1).

bury *verb*

1. To place a corpse in or as if in a grave ▸ entomb, inhume, inter, lay, sepulcher. *Idioms:* lay (*or* put) to rest. **2.** To put or keep out of sight ▸ cache, conceal, secrete. *See* **hide**[1] (1). *See synonym note at* **hide.**

bush *noun*

▸ jungle, outback. *See* **wilderness.**

bushed *adjective*

Informal Depleted of energy ▸ exhausted, weary, worn-out. *See* **tired** (1).

bushel *noun*

1. *Informal* An indeterminately great amount or number ▸ bunch, multiplicity. *Informal:* billion. *See* **heap** (3). **2.** The contents of a basket ▸ basket, basketful.

bush-league *adjective*

Slang Of low or lower quality ▸ inadequate, poor, second-rate. *See* **bad** (1).

bushwhack *verb*

▸ ambuscade, surprise, waylay. *See* **ambush** (1). *See synonym note at* **ambush.**

business *noun*

1. Commercial, industrial, or professional activity in general ▸ commerce, enterprise, industry, trade, trading, traffic. **2.** Activity pursued as a livelihood ▸ art, avocation, calling, career, craft, employment, handicraft, job, line, métier, occupation, practice, profession, pursuit, specialty, trade, vocation, walk of life, work. *Slang:* dodge, racket. *See also* **position. 3.** A commercial organization ▸ corporation, enterprise, establishment. *See* **company** (1). **4.** The commercial transactions of customers with a supplier ▸ trade, traffic. *See* **patronage** (2). **5.** Something to be done, considered, or dealt with ▸ affair, matter, thing. *See also* **business, problem, task. 6.** Something that concerns or involves one personally ▸ affair, concern,

interest, lookout. *See synonym note at* **affair. 7.** Natural or acquired skill or talent ▸ art, craft. *See* **ability** (1).

✦ **CORE SYNONYMS:** *business, industry, commerce, trade, traffic.* These nouns apply to commercial, industrial, or professional activity in general. *Business* pertains broadly to commercial, financial, and industrial activity: *He decided to go into the oil business. Industry* entails the production and manufacture of goods or commodities, especially on a large scale: *She is a leader in the computer industry. Commerce* and *trade* refer to the exchange and distribution of goods or commodities: *Congress regulates interstate commerce. The entrepreneur was involved in the fur trade. Traffic* pertains in particular to businesses engaged in the transportation of goods or passengers: *The city renovated the docks to attract shipping traffic. Traffic* may also suggest illegal trade: *The federal agents discovered a brisk traffic in stolen goods.*

---

businesslike *adjective*

▸ earnest, sober, solemn. *See* **serious** (1).

businessperson *noun*

▸ merchant, tradesman. *See* **dealer** (1).

buss *verb*

To touch or caress with the lips, especially as a sign of passion or affection ▸ osculate, smack. *See* **kiss** (1).

buss *noun*

The act or an instance of kissing ▸ osculation, smack. *Informal:* peck. *See* **kiss** (1).

bust[1] *verb*

1. *Slang* To come open or fly apart suddenly and violently, as from internal pressure ▸ blow (out), burst, explode, pop. **2.** *Slang* To stop working properly ▸ break down, fail, give out. *See* **malfunction. 3.** To make an animal docile ▸ break, tame. *See* **gentle** (1). **4.** To reduce to financial insolvency ▸ bankrupt, break, impoverish. *See* **ruin** (3). **5.** To lower in rank or grade ▸ degrade, downgrade. *See* **demote.** *See synonym note at* **demote. 6.** To deliver a sudden, sharp blow to ▸ jab, sock, whack. *See* **hit** (1). **7.** To take into custody as a prisoner ▸ seize. *Informal:* nab, pick up. *See* **arrest** (1). **8.** *Slang* To make a hole or other opening in ▸ pierce, puncture. *See* **breach** (1).

bust *noun*

1. A person or enterprise that is unsuccessful ▸ loser, washout. *See* **failure** (1). **2.** A sudden heavy stroke ▸ crack, hit, swat. *See* **blow**[2] (1). **3.** *Slang* A seizing and holding by law ▸ apprehension, seizure. *Slang:* pinch. *See* **arrest** (1). **4.** Something that disappoints ▸ anticlimax, fiasco. *See* **disappointment** (2).

bust[2] *noun*

A work of art created by shaping a solid material ▸ figure, relief, statue. *See* **sculpture.**

busted *adjective*

▸ destitute, down-and-out, indigent. *See* **poor** (1).

bustle *verb*

To move swiftly ▸ dash, sprint, zip. *See* **rush** (1).

bustle *noun*

Agitated, excited activity ▸ commotion, excitement, fuss. *See* **agitation** (3).

bustling *adjective*
▸ crawling, swarming, teeming. *See* **busy** (2).

busy *adjective*
1. Involved in activity or work ▸ absorbed, at work, employed, engaged, occupied, taken up (with), working. *Idiom:* in the middle (of). *See also* **rapt. 2.** Full of lively activity ▸ alive, astir, bustling, crawling, hectic, humming, restless, swarming, teeming. *Informal:* hopping. *See also* **active, frantic. 3.** Excessively filled with detail ▸ cluttered, crowded, fussy, overloaded. *See also* **detailed, elaborate, ornate. 4.** Unduly interested in the affairs of others ▸ inquisitive, meddlesome, officious. *See* **curious** (1).

busy *verb*
To make busy ▸ employ, engage, occupy. *See also* **absorb, involve.**

busybody *noun*
A person who meddles or pries into the affairs of others ▸ interloper, meddler, quidnunc. *Informal:* kibitzer. *Slang:* buttinsky, nosy parker, yenta. *See also* **gossip, snoop.**

but *adverb*
Nothing more than ▸ just, merely, only, simply. *See also* **barely, solely.**

butcher *noun*
One who murders another ▸ killer, massacrer, slayer. *See* **murderer.**

butcher *verb*
1. To kill savagely and indiscriminately ▸ decimate, slaughter, wipe out. *See* **massacre** (1). **2.** To ruin through clumsiness or ineptness ▸ blunder, foul up, spoil. *See* **botch.**

butchery *noun*
▸ bloodshed, slaughter. *See* **massacre.**

butt¹ *verb*
1. To apply pressure on, against, or with ▸ press, prod, shove. *See* **push** (1). **2.** To force to move or advance with or as if with blows or pressure ▸ jolt, propel, shove, slam. *See* **drive** (2). **3.** To be contiguous or next to ▸ abut, border, bound, neighbor, touch. *See* **adjoin** (1).

butt *noun*
An act or instance of pushing ▸ press, shove, thrust. *See* **push** (1).

butt² *noun*
1. One that is fired at, attacked, or abused ▸ mark, target. **2.** An object of amusement or laughter ▸ jest, joke, laughingstock, mockery. *Idiom:* figure of fun. *See also* **fool. 3.** A focus of attention, thought, or action ▸ focus, subject, target. *See* **object** (2). **4.** A person who is easily deceived or victimized ▸ pushover, tool, victim. *See* **dupe** (1).

butt³ *noun*
1. Residual matter ▸ fragment, odds and ends, scrap, shard. *See* **end** (7). **2.** *Informal* The part of the body on which one sits ▸ posterior, rump. *Slang:* fanny. *See* **buttocks.**

butte *noun*
▸ prominence, rise. *See* **hill** (1).

butter up *verb*
▸ adulate. *Informal:* soft-soap, sweet-talk. *See* **flatter** (1).

buttery *adjective*
▸ buttery, insinuating, sugary. *See* **flattering** (1).

butt in *verb*
▸ horn in, interlope, interfere. *Informal:* kibitz. *See* **meddle** (1).

buttinsky *noun*
Slang A person who meddles or pries into the affairs of others ▸ meddler, quidnunc, snooper. *See* **busybody.**

buttocks *noun*
The part of the body on which one sits ▸ breech, derrière, fundament, hindquarters, posterior, rump, seat. *Informal:* backside, behind, bottom, bum, butt, hind end, rear, rear end. *Slang:* booty, buns, can, duff, fanny, heinie, kiester, tail, tush, tushy.

button-down *or* **buttoned-down** *adjective*
▸ conformist, orthodox, traditional. *See* **conventional** (1).

buttress *noun*
A means or device that keeps something erect, stable, or secure ▸ crutch, prop. *See* **support** (1).

buttress *verb*
1. To present evidence in support of ▸ corroborate, substantiate. *See* **back** (2). **2.** To make stronger or more resistant ▸ bolster, reinforce, strengthen. *See* **support** (2).

buxom *adjective*
▸ curvaceous, zaftig. *See* **shapely.**

buy *verb*
1. To acquire in exchange for money ▸ pay for, purchase. *Slang:* score. *See also* **get, spend. 2.** To give, offer, or promise a bribe to ▸ corrupt. *Informal:* pay off. *See* **bribe. 3.** *Slang* To regard something as true or real ▸ accept. *Slang:* swallow. *See* **believe** (1).

buy *noun*
1. Something bought or capable of being bought ▸ purchase. *See also* **effects. 2.** *Informal* Something offered or bought at a low price ▸ bargain, find. *Informal:* deal. *Slang:* steal.

buyer *noun*
▸ customer, patron, user. *See* **consumer.**

buzz *verb*
1. To make a continuous low-pitched droning sound ▸ bumble, drone, whir. *See* **hum. 2.** To communicate with someone by telephone ▸ call (up), ring (up), phone. *See* **telephone.**

buzz *noun*
1. A continuous low-pitched droning sound ▸ bumble, burr, drone. *See* **hum. 2.** A telephone communication ▸ call, ring. **3.** *Slang* A strong, pleasant feeling of excitement or stimulation ▸ lift. *Informal:* wallop. *Slang:* bang. *See* **thrill** (1).

by-and-by *noun*
Time that is yet to be ▸ future, futurity, hereafter, tomorrow. *Idiom:* time to come. *See also* **approach, possibility.**

bygone *adjective*
1. Belonging to, belonging, or occurring in times long past ▸ ancient, antiquated, archaic. *See* **old** (1). **2.** Just gone by or elapsed ▸ precedent, previous, prior. *See* **past** (1).

bylaw *noun*
▸ decree, edict, institute. *See* **law** (1).

bypass *noun*
The act, an instance, or a means of avoiding ▸ avoidance, circumvention. *See* **escape** (2).

bypass *verb*
1. To pass around but not through ▸ circumnavigate, detour, go around. *See* **skirt** (1). **2.** To keep away from

▸ abstain from, circumvent, dodge, evade, shun. *See* **avoid**.

bypast *adjective*
▸ precedent, previous, prior. *See* **past** (1).

byproduct *noun*
▸ offshoot, outgrowth, spinoff. *See* **derivative**.

bystander *noun*
▸ observer, onlooker, spectator. *See* **watcher** (1).

byword *noun*
▸ adage, maxim, motto. *See* **proverb**.

byzantine *adjective*
▸ convoluted, elaborate, involved, labyrinthine. *See* **complex** (1).

C

cabal *noun*
A secret plan to achieve an evil or an illegal end ▸ collusion, conspiracy. *See* **plot** (2).

cabal *verb*
To work out a secret plan to achieve an evil or illegal end ▸ conspire, scheme. *See* **plot** (2).

cabalistic *adjective*
1. Difficult to explain or understand ▸ enigmatic, mystifying, puzzling. *See* **mysterious. 2.** Not widely understood ▸ esoteric, recondite. *See* **obscure** (1).

cabbage *noun*
Slang Something, such as coins or printed bills, used as a medium of exchange ▸ currency. *Slang:* dough, moola. *See* **money** (1).

cabin *noun*
▸ hovel, lean-to, shack. *See* **hut**.

cable *noun*
▸ bond, line, string. *See* **cord**.

cache *noun*
1. A supply stored or hidden for possible future use ▸ backlog, reserve, stockpile. *See* **hoard. 2.** A place where something is deposited for safekeeping ▸ archive, storehouse, warehouse. *See* **depository**.

cache *verb*
1. To put or keep out of sight ▸ bury, conceal, secrete. *See* **hide**[1] (1). *See synonym note at* **hide**[1]. **2.** To have or put in a customary place ▸ keep, put, store.

cachinnate *verb*
▸ cackle, chuckle, guffaw. *See* **laugh**.

cachinnation *noun*
▸ cackle, guffaw, laughter. *See* **laugh** (1).

cackle *verb*
To express amusement or mirth ▸ cachinnate, chuckle, guffaw. *See* **laugh**.

cackle *noun*
An act of laughing ▸ giggle, guffaw, laughter. *See* **laugh** (1).

cacophonous *or* **cacophonic** *or* **cacophonical** *adjective*
▸ discordant, dissonant, inharmonic. *See* **inharmonious** (2).

cacophony *noun*
▸ clamor, din. *See* **noise** (1).

cad *noun*
▸ chuff, Philistine, yahoo. *See* **boor**.

cadaver *noun*
▸ corpse, remains. *See* **body** (2).

cadaverous *adjective*
1. Gruesomely suggestive of ghosts or death ▸ deathly, ghostly, spectral. *See* **ghastly** (2). **2.** Lacking color ▸ bloodless, lurid, wan. *See* **pale** (1). **3.** Appearing worn and exhausted ▸ emaciated, gaunt. *See* **haggard**.

cadence *noun*
▸ cadency, meter, swing. *See* **rhythm**.

cadenced *adjective*
▸ measured, metrical, rhythmic. *See* **rhythmical**.

cadency *noun*
▸ cadence, meter, swing. *See* **rhythm**.

cadge *verb*
▸ bum. *Slang:* mooch. *See* **beg** (1). *See synonym note at* **beg**.

cadger *noun*
▸ mendicant. *Informal:* panhandler. *See* **beggar** (1).

caducity *noun*
The condition of being senile ▸ anecdotage, anility, dotage, sanility. *See also* **age**.

cage *verb*
To confine within a limited area ▸ box (in), coop (up), shut (in). *See* **enclose** (1). *See synonym note at* **enclose**.

cage *noun*
An enclosure for confining an animal or bird ▸ coop, cote, crate, hutch, kennel, pound, run, stall. *See also* **pen**[2].

cagey *adjective*
▸ astute, canny, knowing, perspicacious. *See* **shrewd** (1).

caitiff *adjective*
Ignobly lacking in courage ▸ faint-hearted, pusillanimous. *Slang:* gutless. *See* **cowardly.**

caitiff *noun*
An ignoble and uncourageous person ▸ dastard, poltroon, sissy. *See* **coward.**

cajole *verb*
▸ blandish, wheedle. *See* **coax** (1).

cake *verb*
To make or become physically hard ▸ congeal, solidify. *See* **harden** (2).

cake *noun*
An irregularly shaped mass of indefinite size ▸ clod, wad. *See* **lump**[1] (1).

cakewalk *noun*
▸ rout, walkaway, walkover. *See* **runaway** (1).

calaboose *noun*
Slang A place for the confinement of persons in lawful detention ▸ brig, penitentiary, prison. *See* **jail.**

calamitous *adjective*
▸ cataclysmic, ruinous. *See* **disastrous.**

calamity *noun*
▸ cataclysm, catastrophe, tragedy. *See* **disaster** (1).

calculate *verb*
1. To ascertain by mathematics ▸ cast, cipher, compute, figure, reckon. *Idioms:* crunch numbers, do the math (*or* numbers). *See also* **add, count, measure. 2.** To make a judgment as to the worth or value of ▸ assay, judge. *See* **estimate** (1).

✦ CORE SYNONYMS: *calculate, compute, reckon, cipher, figure.* These verbs refer to the use of mathematical methods to determine a result. *Calculate,* the most comprehensive, often implies a relatively high level of abstraction or procedural complexity: *The astronomer calculated the planet's position. Compute* applies to possibly lengthy arithmetic operations: *computing fees according to time spent. Reckon, cipher,* and *figure* suggest the use of simple arithmetic: *reckoned the number of hours before her departure; had to be taught to read and to cipher; trying to figure my share of the bill.*

---

calculated *adjective*
1. Planned, weighed, or estimated in advance ▸ assessed, considered, contrived, deliberate, designed, devised, figured, formulated, intentional, predetermined, premeditated, schemed. **2.** Marked by careful consideration ▸ considered, studied. *See* **deliberate** (2).

calculating *adjective*
1. Coldly planning to achieve selfish aims ▸ conniving, designing, manipulative, scheming. **2.** Deceitfully clever ▸ foxy, tricky, wily. *See* **artful** (1).

calculation *noun*
1. The act, process, or result of calculating ▸ cast, computation, figuring, reckoning. **2.** Careful fore-

thought to avoid risk ▸ care, carefulness, wariness. *See* **caution** (1).

calendar *noun*
An organized list, as of procedures, activities, or events ▸ agenda, schedule, timetable. *See* **program** (1).

calendar *verb*
To enter on a schedule ▸ docket, program, slate, schedule. *See also* **list**[1].

calender *verb*
▸ iron, mangle, roll. *See* **press** (2).

caliber *noun*
1. Degree of excellence ▸ class, grade, quality. *See also* **degree. 2.** A level of superiority that is usually high ▸ quality, stature, value. *See* **merit** (1).

calibrate *verb*
▸ align, fine-tune, regulate. *See* **adjust** (1).

call *verb*
1. To speak or say loudly ▸ bellow, holler, yell. *See* **shout. 2.** To bring or call together ▸ convene, convoke, gather. *See* **assemble** (1). **3.** To give a name or title to ▸ christen, designate. *See* **name** (1). **4.** To describe with a word or term ▸ characterize, denominate, designate, label, name, style, tag, term, title. *See also* **describe. 5.** To communicate with someone by telephone ▸ buzz, dial, phone, ring up. *See* **telephone. 6.** To go to or seek out the company of someone in order to socialize ▸ drop by, look up, pop in. *See* **visit** (1). **7.** To tell about or make known in advance, especially by means of special knowledge ▸ forecast, prognosticate. *See* **predict.** *See synonym note at* **predict.**

call down *verb*
To criticize for a fault or offense ▸ chide, rebuke, reprimand. *See* **chastise** (1).

call for *verb*
1. To be an appropriate occasion for ▸ occasion, warrant. *See* **justify** (2). **2.** To have as a need or prerequisite ▸ entail, involve, necessitate. *See* **demand** (2). **3.** To ask for urgently or insistently ▸ insist on (*or* upon), require. *See* **demand** (1).

call forth *verb*
To bring out something latent, hidden, or unexpressed ▸ draw (out), elicit, summon. *See* **evoke.**

call off *verb*
To decide not to continue ▸ cancel. *Slang:* scrap, scratch, scrub. *See also* **defer, drop.**

call up *verb*
1. To assemble, prepare, or put into operation, as for war or a similar emergency ▸ activate, ready. *See* **mobilize. 2.** To form mental images of ▸ envision, fantasize, visualize. *See* **imagine** (1).

call *noun*
1. A loud cry ▸ holler, scream, yell. *See* **shout. 2.** A telephone communication ▸ buzz, ring. **3.** A spoken or written request for someone to take part or be present ▸ bid, invitation, summons. *Informal:* invite. *See also* **request. 4.** A basis for an action ▸ grounds, justification, occasion. *See* **cause** (2). **5.** The act of demanding ▸ appeal, claim, requisition. *See* **demand** (1). **6.** An act or an instance of going or coming to see

another ▸ stop, visitation. *See* **visit** (1). **7.** The power or quality of attracting ▸ appeal, enticement, lure. *See* **attraction** (1).

caller *noun*

A person or persons visiting one ▸ company, guest, visitant, visitor.

call girl *noun*

▸ courtesan, strumpet. *See* **harlot.**

calligraphic *adjective*

Of or relating to representation by means of writing ▸ graphic, scriptural, written.

calligraphy *noun*

▸ handwriting, longhand, penmanship. *See* **script** (1).

calling *noun*

1. An inner urge to pursue an activity or perform a service ▸ mission, vocation. *See also* **dream, duty, fate. 2.** Activity pursued as a livelihood ▸ career, employment, occupation. *See* **business** (2).

callous *adjective*

Lacking compassion or mercy ▸ anesthetic, bloodless, cold-blooded, cold-hearted, compassionless, hard, hard-boiled, hardened, hardhearted, heartless, insensate, insensible, insensitive, merciless, obdurate, pitiless, remorseless, soulless, stonyhearted, thick-skinned, uncaring, uncompassionate, unfeeling, unmerciful, unpitying, unsympathetic, untouched. *Idioms:* hard (*or* tough) as nails. *See also* **cold, severe.**

call to arms *or* **call to battle** *noun*

▸ rallying cry, war cry. *See* **cry** (2).

calm *adjective*

1. Not excited or agitated ▸ collected, composed, cool, cool-headed, detached, easygoing, even, even-tempered, imperturbable, mellow, nonchalant, peaceful, placid, poised, possessed, serene, tranquil, unflappable, unruffled. *Idiom:* cool as a cucumber. **2.** Free from disturbance, agitation, or commotion ▸ peaceful, placid, serene. *See* **still** (1). *See synonym note at* **still.**

calm *noun*

1. Lack of emotional agitation ▸ calmness, peace, peacefulness, placidity, placidness, quietude, repose, serenity, tranquillity. *Idiom:* peace of mind. *See also* **balance. 2.** An absence of motion or disturbance ▸ calmness, lull, peacefulness. *See* **stillness** (1).

calm *verb*

To ease the anger or agitation of ▸ appease, mollify, soothe. *See* **pacify.**

✤ **CORE SYNONYMS:** *calm, cool, composed, collected, unruffled, nonchalant, imperturbable, detached.* These adjectives indicate absence of excitement or agitation, especially in times of stress. *Calm* is the most general: *The calm police officer helped to prevent the crowd from panicking. Cool* usually implies merely a high degree of self-control, but it may also indicate aloofness: *"Keep strong, if possible. In any case, keep cool. Have unlimited patience"* (B.H. Liddell Hart). *"An honest hater is often a better fellow than a cool friend"* (John Stuart Blackie). *Composed* implies serenity arising from self-discipline: *The dancer was composed as she prepared for her recital. Collected* suggests self-possession: *The witness remained collected throughout the questioning. Unruffled* emphasizes calm despite circumstances that might elicit agitation: *"with contented mind and unruffled spirit"* (Anthony Trollope). *Nonchalant* describes a casual manner that may suggest, sometimes misleadingly, a lack of interest or concern: *He reacted to the news in a nonchalant manner. Imperturbable* stresses unshakable calmness usually considered as an inherent trait: *"A man . . . /Cool, and quite English, imperturbable"* (Lord Byron). *Detached* implies aloofness resulting either from lack of active concern or from resistance to emotional involvement: *He sat through the service with a detached air.*

---

calmness *noun*

1. An absence of motion or disturbance ▸ hush, lull, peacefulness. *See* **stillness** (1). **2.** Lack of emotional agitation ▸ peace, serenity. *See* **calm** (1).

calumniate *verb*

▸ asperse, defame, slander. *See* **malign.** *See synonym note at* **malign.**

calumniation *noun*

▸ defamation, denigration, slander. *See* **libel.**

calumnious *adjective*

▸ defamatory, detractive, invidious, slanderous. *See* **libelous.**

calumny *noun*

▸ defamation, denigration, slander. *See* **libel.**

camaraderie *noun*

1. The condition of being friends ▸ amity, companionship, fellowship. *See* **friendship. 2.** A pleasant association among people ▸ companionship, society. *See* **company** (5).

camouflage *verb*

1. To change or modify so as to prevent recognition of the true identity or character of ▸ dissemble, mask, veil. *See* **disguise.** *See synonym note at* **disguise. 2.** To prevent something from being known ▸ enshroud, mask. *See* **conceal** (1).

camp *noun*

▸ headquarters, installation, station. *See* **base**[1] (1).

campaign *noun*

▸ crusade, movement, push. *See* **drive** (1). *See synonym note at* **drive.**

campestral *adjective*

▸ bucolic, pastoral, rural. *See* **country.**

campiness *noun*

▸ exhibitionism, staginess, theatricality. *See* **theatricalism.**

can *noun*

1. *Slang* A place for the confinement of persons in lawful detention ▸ brig, penitentiary, prison. *See* **jail. 2.** *Slang* The part of the body on which one sits ▸ posterior, rump. *Slang:* fanny. *See* **buttocks.**

can *verb*

1. To prepare food for storage and future use ▸ jar, pickle. *See* **preserve** (1). **2.** *Slang* To end the employment or service of ▸ drop, terminate. *See* **dismiss** (1). *See synonym note at* **dismiss.**

canal *noun*
1. A tube that contains a body fluid ▸ artery, duct, vein. *See* **vessel** (2). 2. A course affording passage from one place to another ▸ path, road, route. *See* **way** (2).

canard *noun*
▸ falsehood, fib, untruth. *See* **lie²**.

cancel *verb*
1. To cross out or remove ▸ annul, blot (out), cross (off *or* out), delete, efface, erase, expunge, obliterate, rub (out), scratch (out *or* off), strike (out *or* off), undo, vacate, wipe (out), x (out). *See also* **drop, lift.** 2. To make ineffective by applying an opposite force or amount ▸ balance, compensate, counteract, counterbalance, counterpoise, countervail, negate, neutralize, nullify, offset, outweigh, redeem, set off. *See also* **abolish, balance.** 3. To decide not to continue ▸ call off. *Slang:* scrap, scratch, scrub. *See also* **defer, drop.** 4. To put an end to ▸ invalidate, nullify, void. *See* **abolish** (1).

✦ CORE SYNONYMS: *cancel, erase, expunge, efface, delete.* These verbs mean to cross out, remove, or invalidate something. To *cancel* refers to invalidating by or as if by drawing lines through something written: *canceled the postage stamp; canceled the reservation. Erase* is to wipe or rub out, literally or figuratively: *erased the equation from the blackboard; erased any hope of success. Expunge* and *efface* imply thorough removal: *expunged their names from the list; tried to efface prejudice from his mind.* To *delete* is to remove matter from a manuscript or data from a computer application: *deleted expletives from the transcript; deleted the file with one keystroke.*

---

cancellation *noun*
1. The act of erasing or the condition of being erased ▸ deletion, expunction. *See* **erasure.** 2. An often formal act of putting an end to ▸ annulment, nullification, voidance. *See* **abolition.**

candid *adjective*
▸ forthright, open, plainspoken. *See* **frank.** *See synonym note at* **frank.**

candidate *noun*
1. A person who applies for or seeks something, such as a job or position ▸ aspirant, hopeful, petitioner. *See* **applicant.** 2. One showing much promise ▸ hopeful, prospect, up-and-comer. *See* **comer** (2).

candidness *noun*
▸ frankness, openness. *See* **honesty** (1).

candy *verb*
To make superficially more acceptable or appealing ▸ sugar, sugarcoat. *See* **sweeten** (1).

cane *noun*
A long straight piece of solid material used as a support in walking ▸ staff, stave. *See* **stick** (2).

cane *verb*
To punish with blows or lashes ▸ lash, thrash, whip. *See* **beat** (2).

canker *noun*
Anything that is injurious, destructive, or fatal ▸ bane, toxin. *See* **poison** (1).

canker *verb*
1. To harm with poison ▸ envenom, infect. *See* **poison** (1). 2. To ruin morally ▸ debase, demoralize, deprave, warp. *See* **corrupt** (1).

cannonade *verb*
To direct a barrage at ▸ bombard, pelt. *See* **barrage.**

cannonade *noun*
A concentrated outpouring, as of missiles, words, or blows ▸ bombardment, fusillade, volley. *See* **barrage.**

canny *adjective*
1. Having or showing a clever awareness and resourcefulness in practical matters ▸ astute, knowing, perspicacious. *See* **shrewd** (1). 2. Careful in the use of material resources ▸ prudent, frugal. *See* **economical.**

can of worms *noun*
Informal A situation that presents difficulty, uncertainty, or perplexity ▸ case, issue, question. *See* **problem** (1).

canon *noun*
1. A principle governing affairs within or among political units ▸ decree, edict, institute. *See* **law** (1). 2. A statement presented for acceptance, as by a religious group ▸ dogma, teaching. *See* **doctrine.**

canonical *adjective*
▸ conformist, orthodox, traditional. *See* **conventional** (1).

canonization *noun*
▸ apotheosis, elevation. *See* **exaltation** (1).

canoodle *verb*
Informal To touch or stroke affectionately ▸ fondle, pet. *See* **caress.**

cant¹ *noun*
Deviation from a particular direction ▸ grade, heel. *See* **inclination** (2).

cant *verb*
To depart or cause to depart from true vertical or horizontal ▸ heel, lean. *See* **incline** (1).

cant² *noun*
1. A variety of a language that differs from the standard form ▸ jargon, vernacular. *See* **dialect** (1). *See synonym note at* **dialect.** 2. Specialized expressions indigenous to a particular field, subject, trade, or subculture ▸ jargon, lingo, patois. *See* **language** (2).

cantankerous *adjective*
1. Having or showing a bad temper ▸ cranky, grouchy, peevish. *See* **ill-tempered.** 2. Given to arguing ▸ contentious, litigious, quarrelsome. *See* **argumentative.** *See synonym note at* **argumentative.**

cantankerousness *noun*
▸ crankiness, prickliness, tetchiness. *See* **temper** (1).

canter *verb*
To move on foot at a pace faster than a walk ▸ jog, scamper, trot. *See* **run** (1).

canter *noun*
A pace faster than a trot ▸ jog, gallop, trot. *See* **run** (1).

canvass *noun*
A gathering of information or opinion from a variety of sources or individuals ▸ count, poll, survey.

canyon *noun*
▸ dale, gorge. *See* **valley.**

cap *noun*
1. Something that covers, especially to prevent contents from spilling ▸ cover, covering, lid, top. *See also* **plug. 2.** The highest point or state ▸ apex, height, peak. *See* **climax** (1). **3.** The greatest amount or number allowed ▸ brim, ceiling, maximum. *See* **limit** (1).

cap *verb*
1. To put a topping on ▸ crest, crown, tip, top, top off. *See also* **cover. 2.** To extend over the surface of ▸ pave, coat. *See* **cover** (1). **3.** To reach or bring to a climax ▸ culminate, peak. *See* **climax.**

capability *noun*
▸ capacity, competence, faculty. *See* **ability** (2).

capable *adjective*
▸ competent, good, skillful. *See* **able.**

capacious *adjective*
1. Having plenty of room ▸ ample, commodious, roomy, spacious. *See synonym note at* **roomy.** *See also* **big, broad. 2.** Of full measure ▸ ample, voluminous, wide. *See* **full** (3).

capacity *noun*
1. The ability or power to seize or attain ▸ compass, grasp, range, reach, scope. *See also* **influence. 2.** Physical, mental, financial, or legal power to perform ▸ capability, competence, faculty. *See* **ability** (2).

caper *noun*
A mischievous act ▸ antic, joke, trick. *See* **prank**[1].

caper *verb*
To leap and skip about playfully ▸ cavort, frolic, romp. *See* **gambol.**

capillary *noun*
▸ canal, duct, vein. *See* **vessel** (2).

capital *noun*
1. Money or property used to produce more wealth ▸ assets, backing, capitalization, financing, funding, grubstake, principal, resources, risk capital, stake, venture capital. *Informal:* bankroll. *See also* **funds, grant, money. 2.** The monetary resources of a government, organization, or individual ▸ finances, funds, money, moneys. **3.** Things having economic value ▸ assets, means, wealth. *See* **resources** (1).

capital *adjective*
1. Most important, influential, or significant ▸ chief, key, main, principal. *See* **primary** (1). **2.** Exceptionally good of its kind ▸ first-rate, prime, splendid, tiptop. *See* **excellent.**

capitalist *noun*
One who is occupied with or expert in large-scale financial affairs ▸ financier. *Informal:* moneyman.

capitalization *noun*
▸ financing, funding, stake. *See* **capital** (1).

capitalize *verb*
1. To supply capital ▸ fund, subsidize. *Informal:* bankroll. *See* **finance. 2.** To derive advantage ▸ gain, profit. *See* **benefit** (1). *See synonym note at* **benefit.**

capitulate *verb*
1. To give in from or as if from a gradual loss of

strength ▸ buckle, submit, surrender. *See* **succumb** (1). **2.** To give up in favor of another ▸ acquiesce, give in, yield. *See* **surrender** (1). *See synonym note at* **surrender.**

capitulation *noun*
The act of submitting or surrendering to the power of another ▸ giving up, submission, surrender. *See synonym note at* **submission.** *See also* **obedience.**

caprice *noun*
▸ impulse, notion, whim. *See* **fancy** (1).

capricious *adjective*
Marked by whim or impulse ▸ arbitrary, changeable, erratic, fickle, flighty, freakish, impulsive, inconsistent, inconstant, mercurial, shifty, temperamental, ticklish, uncertain, unpredictable, unstable, unsteady, vagrant, variable, volatile, wayward, whimsical. *See also* **changeable, spontaneous.**

✢ **CORE SYNONYMS:** *capricious, arbitrary, impulsive, whimsical.* These adjectives mean determined by whim or impulse rather than judgment or reason: *a capricious refusal; an arbitrary decision; an impulsive purchase; a whimsical remark.*

---

capsize *verb*
▸ knock over, topple. *See* **overturn** (1).

capsized *adjective*
▸ inverted, overturned. *See* **upside-down** (1).

captain *noun*
1. One who governs or leads ▸ boss, director, head, leader. *See* **chief** (1). **2.** The person in charge of a ship ▸ commander, shipmaster, skipper.

captain *verb*
To have charge of the affairs of others ▸ direct, govern, rule. *See* **administer** (1).

captious *adjective*
▸ carping, overcritical. *See* **critical** (1).

captivate *verb*
1. To please greatly or irresistibly ▸ beguile, bewitch, enchant. *See* **charm** (1). *See synonym note at* **charm. 2.** To compel the attention, interest, or imagination of ▸ capture, fascinate, mesmerize. *See* **grip** (1).

capture *verb*
1. To obtain possession or control of ▸ catch, gain, get, net, secure, take, win. *Informal:* bag. *Slang:* cop, nail. *See also* **arrest, get, seize. 2.** To seize or maintain control over by conquest ▸ conquer, overrun, subjugate. *See* **occupy** (2). **3.** To compel the attention, interest, or imagination of ▸ captivate, fascinate, mesmerize. *See* **grip** (1).

capture *noun*
The act of catching ▸ seizure, snatch. *See* **catch** (1).

carbon copy *noun*
▸ duplicate, facsimile, likeness. *See* **copy** (1).

carcass *noun*
▸ corpse, remains. *See* **body** (2).

card *noun*
1. *Informal* A person who is appealingly odd or curious ▸ eccentric, original. *Informal:* oddball. *See* **character** (7). **2.** A person whose words or actions

provoke or are intended to provoke amusement or laughter ▸ clown, comedian, jester. *See* **joker**. **3.** A document that complements a public performance, presentation, or offering ▸ catalog, prospectus, syllabus. *See* **program** (2).

cardinal *adjective*
▸ chief, key, main, principal. *See* **primary** (1).

cardsharp *noun*
▸ cheater, swindler, trickster. *See* **cheat** (2).

care *noun*
1. Cautious attentiveness ▸ carefulness, caution, gingerliness, heed, heedfulness, mindfulness, regard, wariness, watchfulness. *See also* **diligence, prudence**. **2.** The function of watching, guarding, or overseeing ▸ charge, custody, guardianship, keeping, protection, safeguard, safekeeping, superintendence, supervision, trust, tutelage, ward. *See also* **conservation, patronage**. **3.** A cause of distress or anxiety ▸ concern, stressor, trouble, worry. *See also* **anxiety, burden**[1]. **4.** A troubled or anxious state of mind ▸ concern, distress, unease. *See* **anxiety** (1). *See synonym note at* **anxiety**. **5.** Careful forethought to avoid risk ▸ calculation, carefulness, wariness. *See* **caution** (1). **6.** Attentiveness to detail ▸ fastidiousness, meticulousness, painstaking. *See* **thoroughness**. **7.** The systematic application of remedies to effect a cure ▸ regimen, rehabilitation, therapy. *See* **treatment** (1).

care *verb*
To have an objection ▸ mind, object.

care for *verb*
1. To have the care and supervision of ▸ look after, mind, watch over. *See* **tend**[2] (1). **2.** To receive pleasure from ▸ appreciate, savor. *See* **enjoy** (1).

✛ **CORE SYNONYMS:** *care, charge, custody, keeping, supervision, trust.* These nouns refer to the function of watching, guarding, or overseeing: *left the house keys in my care; has charge of all rare books in the library; had custody of his children; left the canary in the neighbors' keeping; assumed supervision of the students; documents committed to the bank's trust.*

---

careen *verb*
▸ reel, stumble, totter. *See* **stagger** (1).

career *noun*
1. Activity pursued as a livelihood ▸ calling, employment, occupation. *See* **business** (2). **2.** One's previous experiences ▸ background, past, resumé. *See* **history** (2).

carefree *adjective*
▸ blithe, debonair, light. *See* **lighthearted** (1).

careful *adjective*
1. Cautiously attentive ▸ conscious, heedful, mindful, observant, regardful, watchful. **2.** Marked by attentiveness to every detail ▸ accurate, fastidious, fussy, meticulous, painstaking, punctilious, scrupulous, solicitous. *See also* **deliberate, detailed, thorough**. **3.** Trying attentively to avoid danger, risk, or error ▸ cautious, chary, prudent. *See* **wary** (1). **4.** Kept within

sensible limits ▸ moderate, reasonable, restrained. *See* **conservative** (2).

✛ **CORE SYNONYMS:** *careful, heedful, meticulous, painstaking, scrupulous, observant, mindful, fastidious, punctilious.* These adjectives mean cautiously attentive, especially to details. *Careful* and *heedful* suggest circumspection and solicitude: *A careful examination of the gem showed it to be fake. The hikers were heedful of the danger posed by the thunderstorm.* Meticulous and *painstaking* stress extreme care: "*He had throughout been almost worryingly meticulous in his business formalities*" (Arnold Bennett). *Repairing the fine lace entailed slow and painstaking work.* Scrupulous suggests care prompted by conscience: "*Cynthia was scrupulous in her efforts to give no trouble*" (Winston Churchill). *Observant* and *mindful* imply diligence in observing a law, custom, duty, or principle: *A good driver is mindful of the speed limit. The doctor was observant of each patient's symptoms.* Fastidious implies concern, often excessive, for the requirements of taste: "*Your true lover of literature is never fastidious*" (Robert Southey). *Punctilious* specifically applies to minute details of conduct: "*The more unpopular an opinion is, the more necessary is it that the holder should be somewhat punctilious in his observance of conventionalities generally*" (Samuel Butler).

◂ **ANTONYM:** *careless*

---

carefulness *noun*
1. Careful forethought to avoid risk ▸ calculation, care, wariness. *See* **caution** (1). **2.** Attentiveness to detail ▸ fastidiousness, meticulousness, painstaking. *See* **thoroughness**. **3.** Cautious attentiveness ▸ caution, heed, mindfulness, regard. *See* **care** (1).

careless *adjective*
1. Lacking concern, attention, or regard ▸ blithe, feckless, forgetful, heedless, inadvertent, inattentive, inobservant, irresponsible, insouciant, mindless, nonchalant, reckless, thoughtless, unconcerned, unheeding, unmindful, unthinking. *See also* **apathetic, lighthearted, negligent, rash**. **2.** Marked by a lack of neatness ▸ slapdash, slipshod, sloppy. *See* **messy** (1).

✛ **CORE SYNONYMS:** *careless, heedless, thoughtless, inadvertent.* These adjectives apply to what is marked by a lack of concern, attention, or regard. *Careless* often implies negligence: "*It is natural for careless writers to run into faults they never think of*" (George Berkeley). *Heedless* often suggests recklessness: "*We have always known that heedless self-interest was bad morals; we know now that it is bad economics*" (Franklin D. Roosevelt). *Thoughtless* applies to actions taken without due consideration: "*But thoughtless follies laid him low/And stain'd his name*" (Robert Burns). *Inadvertent* implies unintentional lack of care: *With an inadvertent gesture, the child swept the vase off the table.*

◂ **ANTONYM:** *careful*

---

carelessness *noun*
A careless, often reckless disregard for consequences

▸ abandon, blitheness, heedlessness, thoughtlessness. *See also* **temerity.**

caress *verb*

To touch or handle affectionately ▸ cuddle, fondle, pat, pet, stroke. *Informal:* canoodle. *See also* **neck, snuggle.**

✚ CORE SYNONYMS: *caress, cuddle, fondle, pet.* These verbs mean to touch or handle affectionately: *caressed the baby's forehead; cuddled the kitten in his arms; fondling the dog's ears; petting her pony.*

---

caretaker *noun*

One who is legally responsible for the care and management of the person or property of an incompetent or a minor ▸ conservator, custodian, guardian, keeper. *See also* **representative.**

careworn *adjective*

▸ gaunt, wan, worn. *See* **haggard.**

cargo *noun*

▸ freight, haul, load. *See* **burden**[1] (2).

caricature *noun*

1. A false, derisive, or impudent imitation of something ▸ parody, sham, travesty. *See* **mockery** (2). **2.** A work that exposes folly by the use of humor, irony, or comic imitation ▸ burlesque, parody, spoof. *See* **satire.** *See synonym note at* **satire.**

caricature *verb*

To copy the manner or expression of another, especially in an exaggerated or mocking way ▸ burlesque, mock. *See* **imitate** (1).

caring *adjective*

▸ devoted, loving. *See* **affectionate.**

carnage *noun*

▸ bloodshed, slaughter. *See* **massacre.**

carnal *adjective*

▸ animal, sexual, voluptuous. *See* **sensual** (2).

carnality *noun*

▸ sexuality, voluptuousness. *See* **sensuality** (1).

carnival *noun*

A joyous or festive occasion ▸ festival, festivity, revels. *See* **celebration** (1).

carol *verb*

▸ chant, vocalize. *See* **sing** (1).

carol *noun*

A brief composition written or adapted for singing ▸ hymn, number, tune. *See* **song** (1).

carom *verb*

▸ graze, ricochet, skip. *See* **glance** (1).

carousal *or* **carouse** *noun*

▸ binge, drunk, spree. *See* **bender.**

carp *verb*

1. To raise unnecessary or trivial objections ▸ cavil, niggle, nitpick. *See* **quibble** (1). *See synonym note at* **quibble.** **2.** To express feelings of pain, dissatisfaction, or resentment ▸ fuss, grump, whine. *See* **complain.**

carp at *verb*

1. To scold or find fault with constantly ▸ fuss at, pick on. *See* **nag** (1). **2.** To find fault with ▸ censure, fault, reprove. *See* **criticize** (1).

carp *noun*

An expression of pain or dissatisfaction ▸ fuss, whimper, whine. *See* **complaint** (1).

carper *noun*

▸ caviler, nitpicker. *See* **critic** (2).

carpet *verb*

▸ blanket, spread. *See* **cover** (1).

carping *adjective*

▸ captious, overcritical. *See* **critical** (1).

carriage *noun*

1. The moving of persons or goods from one place to another ▸ conveyance, transit, transport. *See* **transportation** (1). **2.** A way of holding or carrying one's body ▸ pose, stance. *See* **posture** (1). *See synonym note at* **posture.**

carrier *noun*

▸ courier, envoy. *See* **messenger.**

carrot *noun*

▸ bait, draw, enticement. *See* **lure** (1).

carry *verb*

1. To move while supporting ▸ bear, cart, convey, haul, lug, pack, transport. *Informal:* tote. *Slang:* schlep. *See also* **send. 2.** To cause to come along with oneself ▸ convey, fetch. *See* **bring** (1). **3.** To serve as a conduit ▸ channel, convey, transmit. *See* **conduct** (3). **4.** To make known ▸ disclose, divulge, transmit. *See* **communicate** (1). **5.** To spread a disease to others ▸ give, spread, transmit. *See* **communicate** (4). **6.** To hold the weight of ▸ support, sustain. *See* **bear** (1). **7.** To hold on one's person ▸ bear, have, possess. *Informal:* pack. *See also* **hold. 8.** To conduct oneself in a specified way ▸ acquit, bear, comport, demean. *See* **act** (1). **9.** To proceed on a certain course or for a certain distance ▸ lead, stretch. *See* **extend** (1). **10.** To be accepted or approved ▸ affiliate, clear. *See* **pass** (16). **11.** To have as a visible characteristic ▸ display, possess. *See* **bear** (3). **12.** To have as a condition or a consequence ▸ entail, involve. **13.** To have for sale ▸ deal (in), keep, offer, stock.

carry away *verb*

To have a powerful emotional effect on someone ▸ electrify, thrill, transport. *See* **enrapture.**

carry off *verb*

1. To cause the death of ▸ cut down, destroy, finish (off). *See* **kill**[1] (1). **2.** To take another's property without permission ▸ abscond with, purloin, snatch, thieve. *See* **steal** (1).

carry on *verb*

1. To engage in (a war or campaign, for example) ▸ carry out, conduct, wage. *See also* **oppose. 2.** To control the course of an activity ▸ direct, manage, operate. *See* **conduct** (1). **3.** To involve oneself in an activity ▸ engage, partake, share. *See* **participate** (1). **4.** To put up with or continue despite difficulties ▸ keep on, persevere, soldier on. *See* **endure** (1). *See synonym note at* **endure. 5.** To express great enthusiasm ▸ enthuse, rhapsodize. *See* **rave** (1). **6.** To behave in a rowdy, improper, or unruly fashion ▸ act up. *Informal:* horse around. *See* **misbehave.**

carry out *verb*

1. To oversee the provision or execution of ▸ administrate, dispense. *See* **administer** (2). **2.** To engage in (a war or campaign, for example) ▸ carry on, conduct, wage. *See also* **oppose. 3.** To compel observance of ▸ effect, implement. *See* **enforce. 4.** To act in conformity with ▸ heed, obey, observe. *See* **follow** (4). **5.** To succeed in doing ▸ accomplish, achieve, effectuate. *See* **effect** (1). **6.** To be responsible for or guilty of an error or crime ▸ commit, do, perpetrate. *Informal:* pull off. *See also* **perform.**

carry through *verb*

To succeed in doing ▸ accomplish, achieve, effectuate. *See* **effect** (1).

✦ CORE SYNONYMS: *carry, convey, bear, transport.* These verbs mean to move while supporting. *Carry* is the most general: *The train carries baggage, mail, and passengers.* The term can also refer to conveyance through a channel or medium: *Nerve cells carry and receive nervous impulses. Convey* often implies continuous, regular movement or flow: *The assembly line conveyed the truck's components.* The word also means to serve as a medium for delivery or transmission: *A fleet of trucks will convey the produce to the market. Bear* strongly suggests the effort of supporting an important burden: *The envoy bore the sad news. Transport* is largely limited to the movement over a considerable distance: *Huge tankers are used to transport oil.*

---

cart *verb*

▸ bear, haul, lug. *See* **carry** (1).

carte blanche *noun*

▸ control, might. *See* **authority** (1).

cartel *noun*

▸ bloc, coalition, organization. *See also* **association.**

carton *noun*

▸ box, crate, packet. *See* **package.**

carve *verb*

1. To separate into parts with or as if with a sharp-edged instrument ▸ cleave, sever. *See* **cut** (2). **2.** To cut a design or inscription into a hard surface, especially for printing ▸ etch, incise. *See* **engrave** (1).

carving *noun*

▸ figure, relief, statue. *See* **sculpture.**

Casanova *noun*

1. A man amorously attentive to women ▸ Don Juan, lady's man. *See* **gallant. 2.** A man who philanders ▸ adulterer, cheater, paramour. *See* **philanderer.**

cascade *verb*

To come forth or issue in abundance ▸ gush, pour, rush. *See* **flow** (2).

cascade *noun*

Something suggestive of running water ▸ flood, stream, tide. *See* **flow.**

case *noun*

1. One that is representative of a group or class ▸ illustration, sample. *See* **example** (1). *See synonym note at* **example. 2.** Manner of being or form of existence ▸ situation, status. *See* **condition** (1). **3.** A legal proceeding to demand justice or enforce a right ▸ action, suit. *See* **lawsuit. 4.** A fact or circumstance that gives logical support to an assertion, claim, or proposal ▸ argument, point. *See* **reason** (1). **5.** A structure that supports or encloses something ▸ casing, shell. *See* **frame** (1). **6.** The material in which something is wrapped ▸ covering, packaging. *See* **wrapper. 7.** *Informal* A person who is appealingly odd or curious ▸ eccentric, original. *Informal:* oddball. *See* **character** (7). **8.** A situation that presents difficulty, uncertainty, or perplexity ▸ issue, matter, question. *See* **problem** (1). **9.** What a speech, piece of writing, or artistic work is about ▸ matter, text, theme. *See* **subject** (1).

case *verb*

Informal To look at or study carefully or critically ▸ check (out), peruse, study. *See* **examine** (1).

caseharden *verb*

▸ season, toughen. *See* **harden** (1).

cash *noun*

Something, such as coins or printed bills, used as a medium of exchange ▸ currency. *Slang:* dough, moola. *See* **money** (1).

cash in *verb*

To make a large profit ▸ batten, profit. *Slang:* clean up. *Idiom:* make a killing.

cashier *verb*

▸ discharge, drop, terminate. *See* **dismiss** (1). *See synonym note at* **dismiss.**

casing *noun*

1. A structure that supports or encloses something ▸ case, shell. *See* **frame** (1). **2.** The material in which something is wrapped ▸ covering, packaging. *See* **wrapper.**

cask *noun*

▸ basin, cistern, keg. *See* **vat.**

Cassandra *noun*

▸ apocalypticist, doomsayer, worrywart. *See* **pessimist** (2).

cast *verb*

1. To send through the air with a motion of the hand or arm ▸ fling, hurl, pitch. *See* **throw** (1). *See synonym note at* **throw. 2.** To direct something, often toward a target ▸ level, point, train. *See* **aim** (1). **3.** To send out heat, light, or energy ▸ emit, radiate. *See* **shed**[1] (1). **4.** To form a strategy for ▸ devise, formulate, strategize. *See* **design** (1). **5.** To ascertain by mathematics ▸ compute, figure, reckon. *See* **calculate** (1). **6.** To combine numbers to form a sum ▸ sum (up), total. *See* **add** (1). **7.** To try to catch fish ▸ angle, trawl, troll. *See* **fish** (1). **8.** To make a choice from a number of alternatives ▸ elect, pick (out), vote (for). *See* **choose** (1).

cast about *or* **around** *verb*

To try to find something ▸ look for, search for. *See* **seek** (1).

cast aside *verb*

To give up completely ▸ discard, forsake, quit, relinquish. *See* **abandon** (1).

cast down *verb*
To cause to descend ▸ drop, let down, take down. *See* **lower²** (1).

cast out *verb*
1. To rid one's mind of ▸ banish, dispel. *See* **dismiss** (3). **2.** To direct or allow to leave ▸ banish, expel. *See* **dismiss** (2).

cast *noun*
1. An act of throwing ▸ heave, hurl, toss. *See* **throw**. **2.** A disposition of the facial features that conveys meaning, feeling, or mood ▸ countenance, look, visage. *See* **expression** (4). **3.** A hollow device for shaping a fluid or plastic substance ▸ form, matrix, mold. **4.** A work of art created by shaping a solid material ▸ bust, figure, statue. *See* **sculpture**. **5.** The characteristic surface arrangement of a thing ▸ configuration, design, structure. *See* **form** (1). **6.** A class that is defined by the common attribute or attributes possessed by all its members ▸ ilk, mold, species. *See* **kind²**. **7.** The random, unintended, or unpredictable element of an event or the force regarded as the cause of such an event ▸ coincidence, fortune, luck. *See* **chance** (2). **8.** A natural or habitual preference for something ▸ disposition, leaning, penchant. *See* **inclination** (1). **9.** Quality of light reflected or emitted ▸ hue, shade, tint. *See* **color** (1). **10.** The act, process, or result of calculating ▸ calculation, computation, figuring, reckoning.

caste *noun*
▸ league, rank, tier. *See* **class** (2).

castigate *verb*
1. To subject one to a penalty for a wrong ▸ correct, penalize. *See* **punish**. *See synonym note at* **punish**. **2.** To criticize for a fault or offense ▸ chide, rebuke, reprimand. *See* **chastise** (1).

castigation *noun*
▸ chastisement, discipline, penalty. *See* **punishment**.

castle in the air *noun*
▸ chimera, fantasy, illusion. *See* **dream** (2).

castrate *verb*
1. To render incapable of reproducing ▸ neuter, unsex. *See* **sterilize** (2). **2.** To deprive of a limb or bodily member or its use ▸ amputate, mutilate. *See* **cripple** (1).

casual *adjective*
1. Occurring unexpectedly ▸ chance, fortuitous, inadvertent. *See* **accidental** (1). **2.** Unconstrained by rigid standards or ceremony ▸ informal, relaxed. *Informal:* laid-back. *See* **easygoing** (1). **3.** Of or suitable for ordinary days or routine occasions ▸ daily, workaday. *See* **everyday** (1).

casualness *noun*
▸ informality, naturalness. *See* **ease** (1).

casualty *noun*
1. A loss of life, or one who has lost life, usually as a result of accident, disaster, or war ▸ death, fatality, kill, loss. **2.** An unexpected and usually undesirable event ▸ mischance, misfortune, mishap. *See* **accident** (1). **3.** One that is made to suffer injury, loss, or death ▸ sufferer, wounded. *See* **victim** (1).

casuistry *noun*
▸ sophistry, speciousness, spuriousness. *See* **fallacy** (2).

catachresis *noun*
▸ malapropism, solecism. *See* **corruption** (3).

cataclysm *noun*
1. An occurrence inflicting widespread destruction and distress ▸ calamity, catastrophe, tragedy. *See* **disaster** (1). **2.** A momentous or sweeping change ▸ convulsion, upheaval. *See* **revolution** (3).

cataclysmic *adjective*
▸ calamitous, catastrophic, ruinous. *See* **disastrous**.

catacomb *noun*
▸ crypt, tomb, vault. *See* **grave¹**.

catalog *noun*
1. A series, as of names or words, printed or written down ▸ register, roll, roster. *See* **list¹**. **2.** An organized list, as of procedures, activities, or events ▸ calendar, schedule, timetable. *See* **program** (1). **3.** A document that complements a public performance, presentation, or offering ▸ card, prospectus, syllabus. *See* **program** (2).

catalog *verb*
1. To place on a list or in a record or book ▸ book, chronicle, write down. *See* **list¹** (1). **2.** To arrange according to class ▸ categorize, group. *See* **classify**.

catalyst *noun*
1. An agent that stimulates or precipitates a reaction or change ▸ ferment, leaven, leavening, reactant, yeast. **2.** Something that causes and encourages an action or response ▸ impulse, incentive. *See* **stimulus** (1).

cataract *noun*
▸ deluge, overflow, torrent. *See* **flood** (1).

catastrophe *noun*
1. An occurrence inflicting widespread destruction and distress ▸ cataclysm, fiasco, tragedy. *See* **disaster** (1). **2.** An abrupt failure ▸ crash, debacle, disaster. *See* **collapse** (2).

catastrophic *adjective*
▸ calamitous, cataclysmic, ruinous. *See* **disastrous**.

catcall *noun*
▸ boo, hoot. *See* **hiss** (2).

catcall *verb*
To make a derisive sound of disapproval ▸ boo, hoot. *See* **hiss** (2).

catch *verb*
1. To gain control of or an advantage over by or as if by trapping ▸ bag, enmesh, ensnare, ensnarl, entangle, entrap, net, snare, tangle, trammel, trap, web. *Informal:* hook. *See also* **seize, take**. **2.** To get hold of something moving ▸ clutch, grab, seize, snag, snatch. *Informal:* nab. *Idiom:* lay hands on. *See also* **grasp**. **3.** To become stuck or entangled ▸ fix, hook, lodge, snag, stick. *See also* **fix**. **4.** To obtain possession or control of ▸ net, secure, take. *See* **capture** (1). **5.** To make secure ▸ bind, chain, moor. *See* **fasten** (1). **6.** To perceive with the eyes ▸ detect, discern, perceive. *See* **see** (1). **7.** To perceive and recognize the meaning of ▸ apprehend, fathom, sense. *See* **understand** (1). **8.** To have a sudden overwhelming effect on ▸ seize, strike,

take. *See also* **move. 9.** To become affected with a disease ▸ develop, get. *See* **contract** (2). **10.** To go aboard a means of transport ▸ board, take. *Informal:* hop. **11.** *Informal* To succeed in communicating with ▸ contact, reach. *Informal:* get. **Idioms:** catch up with, get hold of, get in touch with, get through to, get to, make contact with. **12.** To deliver a sudden, sharp blow to ▸ jab, sock, whack. *See* **hit** (1).

catch up *verb*
1. To come up even with another ▸ overtake, pull alongside, pull even. *See also* **approach, equalize. 2.** To draw or be drawn in so that extrication is difficult ▸ embroil, mix up, wrap up. *See* **involve** (1). **3.** To compel the attention, interest, or imagination of ▸ captivate, fascinate, mesmerize. *See* **grip** (1).

catch *noun*
1. The act of catching, especially a sudden taking and holding ▸ capture, clutch, grab, seizure, snatch. *See also* **arrest, hold. 2.** A device for locking ▸ buckle, clip, lock. *See* **fastener. 3.** *Informal* A person or thing worth catching ▸ plum, prize. *Slang:* brass ring. **4.** *Informal* A person or thing considered exceptionally precious ▸ find, gem, pearl. *See* **treasure** (1). **5.** *Informal* A tricky or unsuspected condition ▸ hitch, rub, snag. *See also* **bar, disadvantage, trick.**

✚ CORE SYNONYMS: *catch, enmesh, ensnare, entangle, entrap, snare, tangle, trap.* These verbs mean to gain control of or an advantage over by or as if by trapping: *caught in a web of lies; enmeshed in the neighbors' dispute; ensnared an unsuspecting customer; became entangled in her own contradictions; entrapped by a convincing undercover agent; snared by false hopes; tangled by his own duplicity; trapped into incriminating himself.*

---

catching *adjective*
▸ communicable, infectious, transmittable. *See* **contagious.**

catechism *or* **catechization** *noun*
▸ exam, examination, quiz. *See* **test** (2).

catechize *verb*
1. To subject to a test of knowledge or skill ▸ examine, quiz, test. *See also* **ask. 2.** To instruct by rote or discipline ▸ drill, inculcate. *See* **indoctrinate** (1).

categorical *adjective*
▸ decided, explicit, precise. *See* **definite** (1). *See* synonym note at **definite.**

categorically *adverb*
▸ certainly, surely, unquestionably. *See* **absolutely** (1).

categorization *noun*
▸ allotment, layout, ordering. *See* **arrangement** (1).

categorize *verb*
▸ assort, class, group. *See* **classify.**

category *noun*
▸ classification, order, set. *See* **class** (1).

cater *verb*
1. To comply with the wishes or ideas of another ▸ cater to, gratify, humor, indulge. *See also* **defer²**. **2.** To treat indulgently ▸ coddle, pamper. *See* **baby.**

3. To place food before someone ▸ serve, wait on (*or* upon). *See also* **give, distribute.**

caterwaul *verb*
1. To engage in a quarrel ▸ dispute, fight, quarrel. *See* **argue** (1). **2.** To cry loudly, as an upset baby does ▸ holler, howl, wail. *See* **bawl** (1).

catharsis *noun*
1. The act or process of removing physical impurities ▸ clarification, cleaning, refinement. *See* **purification** (1). **2.** A freeing from sin, guilt, or defilement ▸ ablution, redemption. *See* **purification** (2). **3.** The act or process of discharging bodily wastes ▸ evacuation, excretion. *See* **elimination** (3).

cathartic *adjective*
Of or tending to eliminate ▸ evacuative, purgative. *See* **eliminative.**

cathartic *noun*
Something that purifies or cleans ▸ antiseptic, clarifier, cleaner. *See* **purifier.**

catholic *adjective*
▸ cosmic, global, worldwide. *See* **universal** (1).

catholicon *noun*
Something believed to cure all human disorders ▸ cure-all, elixir, panacea. *See also* **cure.**

catlike *adjective*
▸ furtive, secretive, sneaky. *See* **stealthy.**

catnap *noun*
A brief sleep ▸ doze, siesta, snooze. *See* **nap.**

catnap *verb*
To sleep for a brief period ▸ doze, nod off. *See* **nap.**

cat's cradle *noun*
▸ labyrinth, maze, web. *See* **tangle** (1).

cat's-paw *noun*
1. A person used or controlled by others ▸ puppet, stooge, tool. *See* **pawn²**. **2.** A person who is easily deceived or victimized ▸ pushover, tool, victim. *See* **dupe** (1).

catty *adjective*
▸ caustic, scathing, sharp, vitriolic. *See* **biting.**

caulking *noun*
▸ padding, stuffing. *See* **filler** (1).

cause *noun*
1. That which produces an effect ▸ antecedent, determinant, occasion, reason. *See also* **impact, origin, stimulus. 2.** A basis for an action or a decision ▸ call, grounds, justification, mainspring, motivation, motive, necessity, occasion, reason, spring, wherefore, why. *Idiom:* why and wherefore. *See also* **account, basis. 3.** A goal served with great or uncompromising dedication ▸ crusade, holy war, jihad. *See also* **drive. 4.** A legal proceeding to demand justice or enforce a right ▸ action, suit. *See* **lawsuit.**

cause *verb*
To be the cause of ▸ bring, bring about, bring on, effect, effectuate, generate, induce, ingenerate, inspire, lead to, make, occasion, precipitate, prompt, provoke, result in, secure, set off, stir (up), touch off, trigger. *Idioms:* bring to pass (*or* effect), give rise to. *See also* **begin, develop, produce, start.**

✦ CORE SYNONYMS: *cause, reason, occasion, antecedent.* These nouns refer to something that produces an effect. A *cause* is an agent or condition that permits the occurrence of an effect or leads to a result: *"He is not only dull in himself, but the cause of dullness in others"* (Samuel Foote). *Reason* refers to what explains the occurrence or nature of an effect: *There was no obvious reason for the accident. Occasion* is a situation that permits or stimulates existing causes to come into play: *"The immediate occasion of his departure . . . was the favorable opportunity . . . of migrating in a pleasant way"* (Thomas De Quincey). *Antecedent* refers to what has gone before and implies a relationship—but not necessarily a causal one—with what ensues: *Some of the antecedents of World War II lie in economic conditions in Europe following World War I.*

caustic *adjective*
▸ acid, scathing, sharp, vitriolic. *See* **biting.**

causticity *noun*
▸ acridity, mordancy, trenchancy. *See* **sarcasm.**

caution *noun*
1. Careful forethought to avoid harm or risk ▸ calculation, care, carefulness, chariness, gingerliness, precaution, wariness. **2.** Cautious attentiveness ▸ carefulness, heed, mindfulness. *See* **care** (1). **3.** The exercise of good judgment or common sense in practical matters ▸ circumspection, foresight, forethought. *See* **prudence** (1). **4.** Advice to beware, as of a person or thing ▸ alarum, caveat, monition. *See* **warning** (1). **5.** The condition of being alert ▸ vigilance, wariness, watchfulness. *See* **alertness.**

caution *verb*
To notify someone of imminent danger or risk ▸ alert, forewarn. *See* **warn.**

cautionary *adjective*
Giving warning ▸ admonishing, admonitory, monitory, warning.

cautious *adjective*
1. Trying attentively to avoid danger, risk, or error ▸ careful, chary, prudent. *See* **wary** (1). **2.** Kept within sensible limits ▸ moderate, reasonable, restrained. *See* **conservative** (2). **3.** Careful and slow in acting, moving, or deciding ▸ circumspect, measured, unhurried. *See* **deliberate** (3).

cave *noun*
A hollow beneath the earth's surface ▸ cavern, dugout, grotto, tunnel. *See also* **hole.**

cave in *verb*
1. To fall in ▸ collapse, give. *See* **buckle** (1). **2.** To suddenly lose all health or strength ▸ crack, succumb. *See* **collapse** (1).

caveat *noun*
1. Advice to beware, as of a person or thing ▸ admonition, caution, monition. *See* **warning** (1). **2.** An instance that warns or discourages prospective imitators ▸ cautionary tale, warning. *See* **example** (2).

cavern *noun*
A hollow beneath the earth's surface ▸ cave, dugout,

grotto, tunnel. *See also* **hole.**

cavernous *adjective*
1. Open wide ▸ abysmal, abyssal, gaping, yawning. *See also* **broad, open. 2.** Curving inward ▸ concave, sunken. *See* **hollow** (2).

cavil *verb*
▸ carp, niggle, nitpick. *See* **quibble** (1). *See synonym note at* **quibble.**

caviler *noun*
▸ carper, nitpicker. *See* **critic** (2).

caviling *noun*
▸ hairsplitting, niggling, nitpicking. *See* **quibbling.**

cavity *noun*
1. A space in an otherwise solid mass ▸ hollow, vacuity. *See* **hole** (1). **2.** An area sunk below its surroundings ▸ concavity, dip, hollow. *See* **depression** (1).

cavort *verb*
▸ caper, frolic, romp. *See* **gambol.**

cease *verb*
1. To bring an activity or relationship to an end suddenly ▸ break off, discontinue, interrupt, suspend, terminate. **2.** To prevent the occurrence or continuation of a movement, action, or operation ▸ stall, immobilize, tie up. *See* **stop** (2). **3.** To come to a cessation ▸ discontinue, halt, quit. *See* **stop** (1). *See synonym note at* **stop. 4.** To cease to exist ▸ depart, perish. *See* **disappear** (2). **5.** To become void, especially through passage of time or an omission ▸ expire, run out. *See* **lapse** (1).

cease *noun*
The condition of being stopped ▸ cessation, discontinuation, standstill. *See* **stop** (2).

cease-fire *noun*
▸ armistice, peace. *See* **truce.**

ceaseless *adjective*
1. Existing without interruption or end ▸ constant, endless, everlasting, perpetual. *See* **continual.** *See synonym note at* **continual. 2.** Enduring for all time ▸ amaranthine, eternal. *See* **endless** (2).

ceaselessness *noun*
▸ eternity, perpetuity. *See* **endlessness.**

cede *verb*
1. To give up or leave completely ▸ abdicate, forswear, relinquish, surrender. *See* **abandon** (1). *See synonym note at* **abandon. 2.** To change the ownership of property by means of a legal document ▸ deed, grant, sign over. *See* **transfer** (1).

ceiling *noun*
▸ brim, cap, maximum. *See* **limit** (1).

celebrate *verb*
1. To mark a day or an event with ceremonies of respect, festivity, or rejoicing ▸ commemorate, keep, observe, solemnize. *See also* **sanctify. 2.** To show joyful satisfaction in an event, especially by merrymaking ▸ feast, party, rejoice, revel. *Idioms:* beat the drum, have a ball, jump for joy, kick up one's heels, kill the fatted calf, let one's hair down, live it up, make merry, paint the town red, whoop it up. *See also*

exult, rejoice, revel. **3.** To pay tribute or homage to ► acclaim, exalt. *See* **honor** (1).

✦ CORE SYNONYMS: *celebrate, observe, keep, commemorate, solemnize.* These verbs mean to mark a day or an event with ceremonies of respect, festivity, or rejoicing. *Celebrate* often emphasizes the joy or reverence associated with an event: *We held a surprise party to celebrate her birthday. Observe* stresses compliance or respectful adherence to that which is prescribed: *observe the speed limit; observe the Sabbath. Keep* implies actions such as the discharge of a duty or the fulfillment of a promise: *keep one's word; keep personal commitments.* To *commemorate* is to honor the memory of a past event: *a ceremony that commemorated the career of a physician. Solemnize* implies dignity and gravity in the celebration of an occasion: *solemnized the funeral with a 21-gun salute.*

---

celebrated *adjective*
► famed, noted, renowned. *See* **famous.** *See synonym note at* **famous.**

celebration *noun*
1. A joyous or festive occasion ► carnival, festival, festivity, fete, fiesta, holiday, jubilee, red-letter day, revel, revels. **2.** The act of observing a day or an event with ceremonies ► commemoration, keeping, observance, solemnity, solemnization. *See also* **ceremony, memorial, praise. 3.** The act of showing joyful satisfaction in an event ► festivity, jollification, jubilation, merrymaking, pageantry, rejoicing, revelry. **4.** A social gathering, especially for pleasure ► festivity, gala, soiree. *See* **party** (1). **5.** A big, exuberant party ► *Slang:* bash, blowout. *See* **blast** (3). **6.** Joyful, exuberant activity ► gaiety, glee, mirth. *See* **merriment** (2). **7.** An expression of warm approval ► acclamation, cheer, kudos. *See* **praise** (1).

celebratory *adjective*
► festive, joyful, joyous. *See* **merry** (1).

celebrity *noun*
1. A famous person ► figure, hero, heroine, idol, legend, lion, luminary, name, notable, personage, personality, star, superstar. *Informal:* big name. *See also* **dignitary. 2.** Wide recognition for one's deeds ► notoriety, popularity, renown. *See* **fame.**

✦ CORE SYNONYMS: *celebrity, hero, luminary, name, notable, personage.* These nouns refer to a person who is famous: *a social celebrity; the heroes of science; a theatrical luminary; a big name in sports; a notable of the concert stage; a personage in the field of philosophy.*

---

celerity *noun*
► expeditiousness, hurry, quickness. *See* **haste** (1). *See synonym note at* **haste.**

celestial *adjective*
1. Of or relating to the heavens ► empyreal, supernal. *See* **heavenly** (2). **2.** Of or relating to heaven ► divine, paradisal. *See* **heavenly** (1). **3.** Of, from, like, or being a god or God ► heavenly, holy. *See* **divine** (1).

celibacy *noun*
► modesty, purity, virginity. *See* **chastity.**

celibate *adjective*
► modest, pure, virginal. *See* **chaste.**

cement *verb*
► congeal, solidify. *See* **harden** (2).

censor *verb*
1. To examine and remove objectionable or improper material from a publication ► bowdlerize, cut, edit, expurgate, sanitize, screen. *Informal:* bleep, bluepencil, red-pencil. *See also* **examine. 2.** To keep from being published or transmitted ► ban, black out, hush (up), kill, silence, stifle, suppress, withhold. *Idioms:* keep (*or* put) a lid on. *See also* **forbid, repress, silence.**

censorious *adjective*
► carping, overcritical. *See* **critical** (1).

censurable *adjective*
► culpable, reprehensible. *See* **blameworthy.** *See synonym note at* **blameworthy.**

censure *noun*
The act or an instance of finding fault ► blame, condemnation, denunciation. *See* **criticism** (1).

censure *verb*
1. To find fault with ► fault, reprove. *Slang:* knock. *See* **criticize** (1). **2.** To express strong disapproval of ► condemn, denounce. *See* **deplore** (1). *See synonym note at* **deplore. 3.** To criticize for a fault or offense ► chide, rebuke, reprimand. *See* **chastise** (1).

censurer *noun*
► caviler, nitpicker. *See* **critic** (2).

center *noun*
1. A place of concentrated activity, influence, or importance ► focus, headquarters, heart, hotbed, hub, locus, seat. **2.** A point or area equidistant from all sides of something ► median, middle, midpoint, midst, navel, omphalos. **3.** A point of origin or crucial factor ► axis, bottom, core, cynosure, focus, heart, hub, nave, nucleus, pivot, quick, root. *See also* **crisis, germ. 4.** The most central or essential part ► essence, marrow, quintessence. *See* **heart** (1).

center *verb*
To direct toward a common center ► channel, converge, focus. *See* **concentrate** (1).

center *adjective*
At, in, near, or being the center ► focal, median, middle. *See* **central** (1).

✦ CORE SYNONYMS: *center, focus, headquarters, heart, hub, seat.* These nouns refer to a place of concentrated activity, influence, or importance: *a great cultural center; the focus of research efforts; the headquarters of a multinational corporation; a town that is the heart of the colony; the hub of a steel empire; the seat of government.*

---

central *adjective*
1. At, in, near, or being the center ► axial, center, centric, equidistant, focal, inmost, innermost, medial, median, mid, middle, middlemost, midmost, nuclear. *See also* **convenient. 2.** Being at neither one extreme nor the other ► intermediate, median, midway. *See*

middle (1). **3.** Most important or influential ▸ key, pivotal. *See* **primary** (1).

centric *adjective*
▸ focal, median, middle. *See* **central** (1).

cerebral *adjective*
1. Relating to or performed by the mind ▸ intellectual, psychological. *See* **mental** (1). **2.** Appealing to or engaging the intellect ▸ sophisticated, thoughtful. *See* **intellectual** (1).

cerebrate *verb*
▸ cogitate, deliberate, reflect. *See* **think** (1). *See synonym note at* **think.**

cerebration *noun*
▸ cogitation, deliberation, rumination. *See* **thought** (1).

ceremonial *adjective*
Of or characterized by ceremony ▸ ceremonious, liturgical, ritualistic. *See* **ritual.**

ceremonial *noun*
A formal act or set of acts prescribed by ritual ▸ rite, ritual, tradition. *See* **ceremony** (1).

ceremonious *adjective*
1. Fond of or given to ceremony ▸ conventional, courtly, dignified, formal, official, punctilious, solemn, stately. *See also* **gracious, prudish, serious. 2.** Of or characterized by ceremony ▸ ceremonial, liturgical, ritualistic. *See* **ritual.**

ceremoniousness *noun*
▸ etiquette, formality, protocol. *See* **ceremony** (2).

ceremony *noun*
1. A formal act or set of acts prescribed by ritual ▸ ceremonial, custom, liturgy, observance, office, ordinance, rite, ritual, service, solemnity, tradition. **2.** Strict observance of social conventions ▸ ceremoniousness, etiquette, form, formality, protocol, punctiliousness. *See also* **custom, manners. 3.** A conventional social gesture or act without intrinsic purpose ▸ form, formality. *See* **ritual** (2).

certain *adjective*
1. Bound to happen ▸ ineluctable, inescapable, inevitable, irresistible, necessary, sure, unavoidable. *Idioms:* in the cards, sure as shooting. *See also* **fated, irrevocable, set. 2.** Established beyond a doubt ▸ conclusive, decisive, hard, inarguable, incontestable, incontrovertible, indisputable, indubitable, irrefutable, positive, sure, unassailable, undeniable, undisputable, unquestionable, unquestioned. *See also* **authentic, decided, implicit. 3.** Known positively ▸ absolute, sure. *See* **definite** (3). **4.** Certain not to fail ▸ foolproof, infallible, unerring. *See* **sure** (2). **5.** Having no doubt ▸ assured, confident, positive. *See* **sure** (1). *See synonym note at* **sure. 6.** Consisting of a number more than two or three but less than many ▸ some, few, various. *See* **several** (1).

✛ **CORE SYNONYMS:** *certain, inescapable, inevitable, sure, unavoidable.* These adjectives mean bound to happen: *soldiers who knew they faced certain death; facts that led to an inescapable conclusion; an inevitable*

result; sudden but sure retribution; an unavoidable accident.

certainly *adverb*
▸ doubtless, doubtlessly, positively, undoubtedly. *See* **absolutely** (1).

certainty *noun*
1. The quality of being actual or factual ▸ actuality, cinch, fact, reality, sure thing, truth. *Idioms:* matter of fact, the case. **2.** The fact or condition of being without doubt ▸ assuredness, certitude, conviction. *See* **sureness** (1). *See synonym note at* **sureness.**

certification *noun*
1. An assumption of responsibility, as one given by a manufacturer, for the quality, worth, or durability of a product ▸ guarantee, guaranty, surety, warrant, warranty. **2.** An act of confirming officially ▸ approval, ratification, sanction. *See* **confirmation** (1).

certify *verb*
1. To confirm formally as true, accurate, or genuine ▸ attest, swear (to), testify, verify, witness. *Idiom:* bear witness. *See also* **prove. 2.** To assume responsibility for the quality, worth, or durability of ▸ guaranty, warrant. *See* **guarantee** (1). **3.** To accept officially ▸ approve, pass, ratify. *See* **confirm** (3).

certitude *noun*
1. The fact or condition of being without doubt ▸ assuredness, certainty, conviction. *See* **sureness** (1). *See synonym note at* **sureness. 2.** A firm belief in one's own powers ▸ aplomb, self-possession. *See* **confidence** (1).

cessation *noun*
1. A concluding or terminating ▸ conclusion, ending, termination. *See* **end** (1). **2.** The act of stopping ▸ check, discontinuance, surcease. *See* **stop** (1). **3.** The condition of being stopped ▸ gridlock, standstill. *See* **stop** (2).

cesspool *or* **cesspit** *noun*
▸ gutter, sewer, sink. *See* **pit**[1] (3).

chachka *noun*
Slang A small showy article ▸ knickknack, trinket. *See* **novelty** (3).

chafe *verb*
1. To make the skin raw by friction ▸ abrade, excoriate, fret, irritate, gall, rub. *See also* **scrape. 2.** To trouble the nerves or peace of mind of ▸ irritate, nettle, vex. *See* **annoy** (1).

chaff *verb*
To tease or mock good-humoredly ▸ banter, josh. *Informal:* kid. *See* **joke** (2).

chaff *noun*
Good-natured teasing ▸ badinage, banter, raillery. *See* **ribbing.**

chagrin *noun*
Self-conscious distress ▸ abashment, discomposure. *See* **embarrassment** (1).

chagrin *verb*
1. To cause a person to be self-consciously distressed ▸ abash, discomfort. *See* **embarrass** (1). *See synonym note at* **embarrass. 2.** To cause anger, resentment, or

hurt feelings ▸ annoy, injure, upset. *See* **offend** (1).

chain *noun*

1. A band or fiber that is used to bind or tie ▸ cable, line, string. *See* **cord. 2.** A number of things placed or occurring one after the other ▸ order, procession, sequence. *See* **series.** *See synonym note at* **series.**

chain *verb*

1. To restrict the activity or free movement of ▸ fetter, handcuff, hobble. *See* **hamper**[1] (1). **2.** To make secure ▸ bind, moor. *See* **fasten** (1).

chains *noun*

▸ handcuffs, hobble, irons. *See* **bond** (1).

chalet *noun*

▸ cottage, country home, estate. *See* **villa.**

challenge *noun*

1. An act of taunting another to do something bold or rash ▸ dare, gauntlet, provocation. **2.** The act or an instance of defying ▸ disobedience, rebellion. *See* **defiance** (1). **3.** An expression of opposition ▸ exception, grievance, protestation. *See* **objection.**

challenge *verb*

1. To call on another to do something bold ▸ dare, defy. *Idiom:* throw down the gauntlet. **2.** To confront boldly and courageously ▸ brave, confront, dare. *See* **defy** (1). *See synonym note at* **defy. 3.** To attempt to equal or surpass, as in quality of amount ▸ approach, verge on. *See* **rival** (1). **4.** To express opposition ▸ except, oppose, protest. *See* **object** (1). **5.** To take a stand against ▸ buck, dispute, oppose. *See* **contest** (1). **6.** To defend, maintain, or insist on the recognition of ▸ assert, demand. *See* **claim** (1).

challenger *noun*

▸ contender, opponent, rival. *See* **competitor.**

challenging *adjective*

▸ arduous, laborious, tough. *See* **difficult** (1).

champ *verb*

To seize and grind with the teeth ▸ chomp, gnash, munch. *See* **chew.** *See synonym note at* **chew.**

champ *noun*

Informal One that wins a contest or competition ▸ champion, medalist. *See* **winner** (1).

champion *adjective*

1. Exceptionally good of its kind ▸ first-rate, prime, splendid, tiptop. *See* **excellent. 2.** Being the winner in a contest or struggle ▸ triumphant, winning. *See* **victorious.**

champion *verb*

To aid the cause of by approving or favoring ▸ back, endorse, stand by. *See* **support** (1). *See synonym note at* **support.**

champion *noun*

1. One that wins a contest or competition ▸ conqueror, medalist. *See* **winner** (1). **2.** One that argues for or defends a cause ▸ defender, proponent, upholder. *See* **advocate** (1). **3.** A person revered especially for noble courage ▸ hero, heroine, paladin. *Idiom:* knight in shining armor.

championship *noun*

▸ backing, sponsorship. *See* **patronage** (1).

chance *noun*

1. An unexpected random event ▸ accident, fluke, fortuity, hap, happenchance, happenstance, hazard. *See also* **event. 2.** The random, unintended, or unpredictable element of an event or the force regarded as the cause of such an event ▸ accident, cast, coincidence, contingency, fortuitousness, fortuity, fortune, hap, hazard, lottery, luck, serendipity. *Idiom:* luck of the draw. *See also* **fate, gamble. 3.** The likeliness of a given event occurring ▸ likelihood, odds, possibility, probability, prospects. **4.** A favorable or advantageous combination of circumstances ▸ break, option. *See* **opportunity.** *See synonym note at* **opportunity. 5.** A possibility of danger or harm ▸ gamble, hazard. *See* **risk** (1).

chance *verb*

1. To take place by chance ▸ befall, betide, hap, happen. **2.** To place something at risk, as in a game of chance ▸ bet, stake, wager. *See* **gamble** (2). **3.** To express at the risk of rebuff or criticism ▸ dare, hazard, presume. *See* **venture** (1).

chance on *or* **upon** *verb*

To find or meet by chance ▸ come across, run across, stumble on. *See* **encounter** (1).

chance *adjective*

1. Occurring unexpectedly ▸ contingent, fortuitous, inadvertent, odd. *See* **accidental** (1). **2.** Having no particular pattern, purpose, organization, or structure ▸ indiscriminate, unplanned. *See* **random.** *See synonym note at* **random.**

chancy *adjective*

1. Lacking certainty or clarity ▸ dubious, indeterminate, questionable, unclear. *See* **ambiguous** (1). **2.** Involving possible risk, loss, or injury ▸ hazardous, perilous, risky. *See* **dangerous.**

change *verb*

1. To make different ▸ alter, modify, mutate, shade, shake up, spice up, turn, vary. *See also* **adapt, renew, revise, revolutionize. 2.** To become different ▸ alter, change over, develop, evolve, fluctuate, modify, mutate, shift, turn, vacillate, vary. *See also* **convert. 3.** To give up in return for something else ▸ barter, commute, exchange, interchange, shift, substitute, switch, trade, transpose. *Informal:* swap. *See also* **reciprocate.**

change *noun*

1. The process or result of making or becoming different ▸ alteration, development, evolution, fluctuation, modification, mutation, permutation, shift, variation, vicissitude. *See also* **adaptation, renewal. 2.** The act of exchanging or substituting ▸ barter, commutation, exchange, interchange, reciprocation, reciprocity, shift, substitution, switch, trade, transposition. *Informal:* swap. **3.** The process or result of changing from one use, function, or appearance to another ▸ metamorphosis, transformation. *See* **conversion** (1). **4.** Passage from one form, state, or stage to another ▸ passage, shift, transit. *See* **transition.**

changeable *adjective*

1. Capable of or liable to change ▸ alterable, commutative, convertible, fluctuant, fluid, inconstant, kaleidoscopic, labile, modifiable, mutable, permutable, reversible, transformable, transmutable, uncertain, unsettled, unstable, unsteady, variable, variant, varying. *See also* **malleable. 2.** Changing easily, as in expression ▸ fluid, mobile, plastic. *See also* **unstable. 3.** Marked by whim or impulse ▸ fickle, impulsive, mercurial. *See* **capricious.**

changeless *adjective*
▸ constant, invariable, unfailing. *See* **unchanging.**

changelessness *noun*
The condition of being without change or variation ▸ consistency, constancy, evenness, firmness, fixedness, flatness, immutability, invariableness, invariance, permanence, regularity, sameness, steadiness, unchangingness, unfailingness, uniformity. *See also* **continuation, endlessness.**

change of heart *noun*
▸ inversion, transposition, turnabout. *See* **reversal** (1).

changeover *noun*
▸ change, mutation, shift. *See* **conversion** (1).

channel *verb*
1. To direct toward a common center ▸ center, converge, focus. *See* **concentrate** (1). **2.** To serve as a conduit ▸ convey, transmit. *See* **conduct** (3).

channel *noun*
1. A narrow body of water, usually connecting two larger bodies ▸ narrows, neck, reach, strait. *See also* **bay[1], harbor, inlet. 2.** That by which something is done or caused ▸ agency, instrument, medium. *See* **agent** (1). **3.** A long, narrow, and usually shallow depression in the ground ▸ ditch, rut, trench. *See* **furrow** (1). **4.** A course affording passage from one place to another ▸ path, road, route. *See* **way** (2).

chant *verb*
▸ carol, vocalize. *See* **sing** (1).

chaos *noun*
1. A lack of order or regular arrangement ▸ clutter, confusion, disarray. *See* **disorder** (1). **2.** The state of being messy or unkempt ▸ sloppiness, untidiness. *See* **disorderliness** (1). **3.** A lack of civil order or peace ▸ anarchy, lawlessness, misrule. *See* **disorder** (2).

chaotic *adjective*
▸ disordered, topsy-turvy, upside-down. *See* **confused** (2).

chap *noun*
Informal A man referred to familiarly or as a member of one's group ▸ boy, guy. *See* **fellow** (1).

chaperon *or* **chaperone** *verb*
▸ attend, companion, escort. *See* **accompany** (1). *See synonym note at* **accompany.**

chaperon *or* **chaperone** *noun*
A guide or companion whose purpose is to ensure propriety or restrict activity ▸ companion, escort. *See also* **guide.**

chaplain *noun*
▸ ecclesiastic, minister, parson. *See* **cleric.**

chapter *noun*
1. A particular subdivision of a written work ▸ part,

passage, section, segment. **2.** An administrative unit, as of a government or company ▸ agency, bureau. *See* **branch** (3).

char *verb*
To undergo or cause to undergo damage by or as if by fire ▸ scorch, sear, singe. *See* **burn** (1). *See synonym note at* **burn.**

char *noun*
Damage that results from burning ▸ blister, sear, singe. *See* **burn** (1).

character *noun*
1. The combination of emotional, intellectual, and moral qualities that distinguishes an individual ▸ complexion, disposition, makeup, nature, personality, temperament. *See also* **disposition, identity, psychology. 2.** Moral or ethical strength ▸ fiber, honesty, honor, integrity, principle, probity, uprightness. *See also* **good. 3.** A distinctive element ▸ characteristic, feature, trait. *See* **quality** (1). *See synonym note at* **quality. 4.** A statement attesting to personal qualifications, character, and dependability ▸ recommendation, reference, testimonial. *See also* **endorsement. 5.** Public estimation of someone ▸ name, report, reputation, repute. *Informal:* rep. *See also* **image, status. 6.** An important, influential person ▸ notability, personage. *Slang:* big shot. *See* **dignitary. 7.** A person who is appealingly odd or curious ▸ eccentric, oddity, original. *Informal:* card, case, oddball. *Slang:* flake. *See also* **crackpot. 8.** A person portrayed in fiction or drama ▸ part, persona, personage, role. **9.** A conventional mark used in a writing system ▸ figure, letter, mark, sign, symbol.

✦ CORE SYNONYMS: *character, disposition, temperament, personality, nature.* These nouns refer to the combination of emotional, intellectual, and moral qualities that distinguishes an individual. *Character* especially emphasizes moral and ethical qualities: *"Education has for its object the formation of character"* (Herbert Spencer). *Disposition* is approximately equivalent to prevailing frame of mind or spirit: *"A patronizing disposition always has its meaner side"* (George Eliot). *Temperament* applies broadly to the sum of physical, emotional, and intellectual components that affect or determine a person's actions and reactions: *"She is . . . of a serene and proud and dignified temperament"* (H.G. Wells). *Personality* is the sum of distinctive traits that give a person individuality: *possessed a cheerful and outgoing personality. Nature* denotes native or inherent qualities: *"It is my habit,—I hope I may say, my nature,—to believe the best of people"* (George W. Curtis).

---

character assassination *noun*
▸ defamation, obloquy, smear. *See* **libel.**

characteristic *adjective*
Relating to, identifying, or setting apart an individual or group ▸ distinctive, particular. *See* **special** (1).

characteristic *noun*
A distinctive element ▸ feature, trait. *See* **quality** (1).

characterization *noun*
- depiction, portrayal. *See* **representation**.

characterize *verb*
1. To describe with a word or term ▸ designate, label, name. *See* **call** (4). 2. To make noticeable or different ▸ differentiate, individualize, singularize. *See* **distinguish** (2). 3. To present a lifelike image of ▸ depict, portray, render. *See* **represent** (2).

charade *noun*
- make-believe, mask, pretense. *See* **façade** (2).

charbroil *verb*
To cook food over charcoal ▸ broil, grill. *See* **cook** (1).

charge *verb*
1. To cause to be filled, as with a particular mood or tone ▸ fill, imbue, impregnate, permeate, pervade, saturate, suffuse, transfuse. *See also* **steep²**. 2. To be morally bound to do ▸ obligate, pledge. *See* **commit** (2). 3. To place a trust upon ▸ entrust, trust. *See also* **authorize**. 4. To fill to capacity ▸ cram, load, pack. *See* **fill** (1). 5. To place a heavy load on ▸ cumber, encumber, load. *See* **burden¹**. 6. To put explosive material into a weapon ▸ load, prime, ready. 7. To give orders to ▸ instruct, order, tell. *See* **command** (1). 8. To make an accusation against ▸ blame, denounce, incriminate. *See* **accuse**. 9. To regard as belonging to or resulting from another ▸ ascribe, assign. *See* **attribute** (1). 10. To set upon with violent force ▸ assail, assault, storm, strike. *See* **attack** (1). 11. To present with a request or demand for payment ▸ invoice, solicit. *See* **bill¹**.

charge in *verb*
To force or come in as an improper or unwanted element ▸ cut in, horn in, interlope. *See* **intrude** (1).

charge with *verb*
To force another to accept a burden ▸ fasten on (*or* upon), inflict on (*or* upon), saddle with. *See* **impose on** (1).

charge *noun*
1. A swift advance or attack ▸ blitz, blitzkrieg, onslaught, raid, rush. *See also* **attack, invasion**. 2. An amount paid or to be paid for a purchase ▸ disbursement, expense, price. *See* **cost** (1). 3. A fixed amount of money charged for a service ▸ exaction, fee. *See* **toll¹** (1). 4. An act or course of action that is demanded of one, as by position, custom, law, or religion ▸ burden, commitment, obligation. *See* **duty** (1). 5. A person who relies on another for support ▸ dependent, ward. 6. The function of watching, guarding, or overseeing ▸ custody, guardianship, supervision, trust. *See* **care** (2). *See synonym note at* **care**. 7. The state of being detained by legal authority ▸ confinement, custody, detainment. *See* **detention**. 8. An order ▸ behest, commandment, imperative. *See* **command** (1). 9. The act or practice of managing ▸ command, guidance, supervision. *See* **management** (1). 10. A charging of someone with a misdeed ▸ denouncement, imputation, incrimination. *See* **accusation**. 11. An assign-

ment one is sent to carry out ▸ errand, operation. *See* **mission** (1). 12. *Slang* A stimulating or intoxicating effect ▸ *Informal:* sting, wallop. *See* **kick**.

✦ **CORE SYNONYMS:** *charge, imbue, impregnate, permeate, pervade, saturate, suffuse.* These verbs mean to cause to be filled, as with a particular mood or tone: *an atmosphere charged with excitement; poetry imbued with lyricism; a spirit impregnated with lofty ideals; optimism that permeates a group; letters pervaded with gloom; a play saturated with imagination; a heart suffused with love.*

---

chariness *noun*
- care, carefulness, wariness. *See* **caution** (1).

charisma *noun*
- appeal, draw, enticement, lure. *See* **attraction** (1).

charitable *adjective*
1. Of or concerned with charity ▸ altruistic, benevolent, eleemosynary, philanthropic. *See also* **benevolent**. 2. Not strict or severe ▸ easy, indulgent, lenient. *See* **tolerant** (1). 3. Concerned with human welfare and the remedying of social ills ▸ compassionate, humane. *See* **humanitarian**.

✦ **CORE SYNONYMS:** *charitable, benevolent, eleemosynary, philanthropic.* These adjectives mean of, concerned with, providing, or provided by charity: *a charitable foundation; a benevolent fund; eleemosynary relief; philanthropic contributions.*

---

charitableness *noun*
1. Kindly, charitable interest in others ▸ goodwill, kindheartedness, philanthropy. *See* **benevolence** (1). 2. Forbearing or lenient treatment ▸ charity, lenience, toleration. *See* **tolerance** (1).

charity *noun*
1. Something given to a charity or cause ▸ benefaction, contribution, offering. *See* **donation**. 2. Kindly, charitable interest in others ▸ goodwill, kindheartedness, philanthropy. *See* **benevolence** (1). 3. Kind, forgiving, or compassionate treatment of or disposition toward others ▸ clemency, grace. *See* **mercy**. *See synonym note at* **mercy**. 4. Forbearing or lenient treatment ▸ forbearance, lenience, toleration. *See* **tolerance** (1).

charlatan *noun*
- fraud, impostor, phony. *See* **fake** (1).

charm *verb*
1. To please greatly or irresistibly ▸ beguile, bewitch, captivate, enchant, entrance, fascinate, win over. *See also* **amuse, delight, seduce**. 2. To act upon as if with magic ▸ bewitch, enchant, ensorcell, enthrall, entrance, hypnotize, mesmerize, spell, spellbind, vamp, voodoo, witch. *See also* **enrapture**. 3. To occupy in an agreeable or pleasing way ▸ entertain, recreate, regale. *See* **amuse** (1).

charm *noun*
1. A small object worn or kept for its supposed magical power ▸ amulet, fetish, grigri, juju, mascot, obeah, periapt, phylactery, talisman. 2. The power or

quality of attracting ▸ appeal, draw, enticement, lure. *See* **attraction** (1). **3.** A word or formula believed to have magic powers ▸ abracadabra, enchantment. *See* **spell**².

✤ CORE SYNONYMS: *charm, beguile, bewitch, captivate, enchant, entrance, fascinate.* These verbs mean to attract strongly or irresistibly: *manners that charmed the old curmudgeon; delicacies that beguile even the most discerning gourmet; a performance that bewitched the audience; a novel that captivates its readers; children who enchanted their grandparents; music that entrances its listeners; a celebrity who fascinated the interviewer.*

◀ ANTONYM: *repel*

---

charmer *noun*
▸ allurer, tempter. *See* **seducer** (1).

charming *adjective*
1. Giving great pleasure or delight ▸ delectable, enchanting, heavenly. *See* **delightful. 2.** Pleasing to the eye or mind ▸ enchanting, fetching, lovely, winsome. *See* **attractive** (1).

chart *noun*
An orderly columnar display of data ▸ table, tabulation. *See also* **list**¹.

chart *verb*
1. To show graphically the direction or location of, as by using coordinates ▸ graph, lay out. *See* **plot** (1). **2.** To form a strategy for ▸ devise, formulate, strategize. *See* **design** (1)

charter *verb*
To engage the temporary use of something for a fee ▸ hire, lease, rent. *See also* **lease.**

charter *noun*
1. An often written acceptance of terms between parties ▸ accord, deal, pact. *See* **agreement** (1). **2.** A principle governing affairs within or among political units ▸ decree, edict, institute. *See* **law** (1).

chary *adjective*
1. Trying attentively to avoid danger, risk, or error ▸ cautious, circumspect, prudent. *See* **wary** (1). **2.** Careful in the use of material resources ▸ canny, frugal. *See* **economical.**

chase *verb*
1. To follow another with the intent of overtaking and capturing ▸ hunt, run after. *See* **pursue** (1). **2.** To look for and pursue game in order to capture or kill it ▸ run, stalk. *See* **hunt** (1). **3.** To attempt to gain the affection of ▸ pursue, woo. *See* **court** (2). **4.** To keep another under surveillance by moving behind ▸ heel, track, trail. *See* **follow** (3). **5.** To urge to move along ▸ herd, push, run. *See* **drive** (3).

chase *noun*
The following of another in an attempt to overtake and capture ▸ hot pursuit, hunt, pursuit.

chasm *noun*
1. Something of immeasurable and vast extent ▸ abyss, gulf. *See* **deep** (1). **2.** A space between objects or points ▸ interstice, interval, separation. *See* **gap** (1).

chaste *adjective*
Morally beyond reproach, especially in sexual conduct ▸ celibate, continent, decent, modest, moral, pure, virgin, virginal, virtuous. *Idiom:* pure as the driven snow. *See also* **innocent.**

chasten *verb*
1. To castigate for the purpose of improving ▸ chide, correct. **2.** To criticize for a fault or offense ▸ berate, rebuke, reprimand. *See* **chastise** (1).

chastise *verb*
1. To criticize for a fault or an offense ▸ admonish, berate, call down, castigate, censure, chasten, chide, dress down, jump (on *or* all over), lecture, objurgate, rap, rebuke, reprimand, reproach, reprove, scold, tax, upbraid. *Informal:* bawl out, lambaste, tell off. *Slang:* chew out. *Idioms:* blow up at, bring (*or* call *or* take) to task, call on the carpet, give hell (*or* it) to, haul (*or* rake) over the coals, jump down someone's throat, lay someone out in lavender, let someone have it. *See also* **criticize, revile, slam. 2.** To subject one to a penalty for a wrong ▸ castigate, correct, penalize. *See* **punish.** *See synonym note at* **punish.**

✤ CORE SYNONYMS: *chastise, scold, upbraid, berate, reprove, rebuke, reprimand, reproach.* These verbs mean to criticize for a fault or an offense. *Chastise* means to criticize severely: *chastised the students for talking during class. Scold* implies reproof: *parents who scolded their child for being rude. Upbraid* generally suggests a well-founded reproach, as one leveled by an authority: *upbraided by the supervisor for habitual tardiness. Berate* suggests scolding or rebuking at length: *an angry customer who berated the clerk. Reprove* usually suggests gentle criticism and constructive intent: *With a quick look, the teacher reproved the child for whispering in class. Rebuke* and *reprimand* both refer to sharp, often angry criticism: *"Some of the most heated criticism . . . has come from the Justice Department, which rarely rebukes other agencies in public"* (Howard Kurtz). *"A committee at* [the university] *asked its president to reprimand a scientist who tested gene-altered bacteria on trees"* (New York Times). *Reproach* usually refers to regretful or unhappy criticism arising from a sense of disappointment: *wrote a letter reproaching the reporter for failing to give a balanced account of the debate.*

---

chastisement *noun*
▸ castigation, correction, penalty. *See* **punishment.**

chastity *noun*
The condition of being chaste ▸ celibacy, decency, innocence, modesty, morality, purity, virginity, virtue, virtuousness.

chat *verb*
To engage in spoken exchange ▸ discourse, talk. *See* **converse**¹.

chat *noun*
1. Spoken exchange ▸ dialogue, discourse, talk. *See* **conversation** (1). **2.** Incessant and inconsequential talk ▸ drivel, patter, small talk. *See* **chatter.**

chattel *noun*
1. One's portable property ▸ goods, personal effects,

property. *See* **effects. 2.** One bound to serve another person or influence ▸ serf, vassal. *See* **slave** (1).

chatter *verb*

1. To talk rapidly and incessantly on trivial matters ▸ babble, blab, blabber, chitchat, clack, drivel, jabber, natter, palaver, patter, prate, prattle, rattle (on), run on, tattle. *Informal:* go on, ramble (on), spiel, yammer. *Slang:* chin wag, gab, gas, jaw, yak. *Idioms:* bend someone's ear, run off at the mouth, shoot the breeze (*or* bull). *See also* **speak. 2.** To talk rapidly, incoherently, or indistinctly ▸ blather, jabber, prattle. *See* **babble** (1). **3.** To make or cause to make a succession of short, sharp sounds ▸ brattle, clack, clank, clatter, rattle. *See also* **knock, shake. 4.** To engage in or spread gossip ▸ rumor, whisper. *See* **gossip.**

chatter *noun*

Incessant and usually inconsequential talk ▸ babble, blab, blabber, chat, chitchat, clack, drivel, jabber, palaver, patter, prate, prattle, small talk, tattle. *Informal:* yammer. *Slang:* gab, gas, yak. *See also* **speech.**

chatty *adjective*

1. Given to conversation ▸ garrulous, loquacious, talky. *See* **talkative. 2.** In the style of conversation ▸ colloquial, informal. *See* **conversational** (1).

chauffeur *noun*

A person who operates a motor vehicle ▸ driver, motorist, operator.

chauffeur *verb*

To run and control a motor vehicle ▸ motor, pilot, wheel. *See* **drive** (1).

chaw *verb*

Chiefly Regional To seize and grind with the teeth ▸ chomp, gnash, munch. *See* **chew.**

cheap *adjective*

1. Low in price ▸ bargain-basement, budget, dirt-cheap, economy, frugal, inexpensive, low, low-cost, low-priced. *Idiom:* for a song. *See also* **meager. 2.** Of decidedly inferior quality ▸ junky, lousy, poor. *See* **shoddy** (1). **3.** Ungenerously or pettily reluctant to spend money ▸ close-fisted, miserly, parsimonious. *See* **stingy** (1).

cheapen *verb*

1. To make less in price or value ▸ devalue, downgrade, reduce. *See* **depreciate** (1). **2.** To lower in character or quality ▸ degrade, downgrade. *See* **debase** (1).

cheapskate *noun*

▸ churl, skinflint. *Informal:* penny pincher. *See* **miser.**

cheat *verb*

1. To get money or something else from someone by deceitful trickery ▸ bilk, burn, cozen, defraud, fleece, game, gull, hoax, mulct, overcharge, rook, swindle, victimize. *Informal:* chisel, flimflam, shortchange, take, trim. *Slang:* clip, con, diddle, do, gouge, gyp, nick, rip off, scalp, scam, skin, soak, stick, sting. *Idioms:* load the dice, stack the cards (*or* deck), take someone for a ride, take someone to the cleaners. *See also* **deceive, pirate, steal. 2.** To be sexually unfaithful

to another ▸ philander. *Informal:* fool around, mess around, play around. *Slang:* two-time. **3.** To cause to accept something false, especially by trickery or misrepresentation ▸ dupe, fool, mislead, trick. *See* **deceive.**

cheat *noun*

1. An act of cheating ▸ burn, deceit, fraud, hoax, humbug, masquerade, swindle, victimization. *Informal:* flimflam. *Slang:* con, grift, gyp, scam, sting. **2.** A person who cheats ▸ bilk, blackleg, cardsharp, cheater, cozener, deceiver, defrauder, dodger, knave, masquerader, rook, sharper, swindler, trickster, victimizer. *Informal:* chiseler, crook, flimflammer. *Slang:* diddler, grifter, gyp, gypper, scammer, shill. *See also* **fake.**

cheater *noun*

1. A person who cheats ▸ bilk, swindler, trickster. *See* **cheat** (2). **2.** A man who philanders ▸ adulterer, Casanova, womanizer. *See* **philanderer.**

check *noun*

1. Something that limits or holds back ▸ circumscription, constraint, curb. *See* **restraint** (1). **2.** The act of stopping ▸ cessation, discontinuance, surcease. *See* **stop** (1). **3.** The act of examining carefully or critically ▸ inquiry, review, survey. *See* **examination** (1). **4.** A precise list of fees or charges ▸ bill, invoice, statement. *Informal:* tab. *See* **account** (2).

check *verb*

1. To prevent the occurrence or continuation of a movement, action, or operation ▸ immobilize, tie up. *See* **stop** (2). **2.** To come to a cessation ▸ desist, halt, quit. *See* **stop** (1). **3.** To control, restrict, or arrest ▸ bridle, constrain, curb. *See* **restrain.** *See synonym note at* **restrain. 4.** To prevent from accomplishing a purpose ▸ foil, stymie, thwart. *See* **frustrate** (1). **5.** To subject to a test of effectiveness, value, function, or other quality ▸ assay, essay, try (out). *See* **test** (1). **6.** To look at or study carefully or critically ▸ check out, investigate, peruse. *See* **examine** (1). **7.** To be compatible or suitable ▸ chime, correspond, match. *See* **agree** (1). **8.** To turn aside or drive away ▸ deflect, repulse, ward off. *See* **repel.**

check in *verb*

To come to a particular place ▸ get in, turn up. *Slang:* blow in. *See* **arrive** (1).

check out *verb*

Slang To cease living ▸ demise, expire, perish. *See* **die** (1).

checked *adjective*

▸ checked, controlled. *See* **restricted** (1).

checklist *noun*

▸ register, roster, schedule. *See* **list**[1].

checkmate *verb*

1. To prevent from accomplishing a purpose ▸ foil, stymie, thwart. *See* **frustrate** (1). **2.** To win a victory over, as in battle or a competition ▸ beat, surmount, vanquish. *See* **defeat** (1). *See synonym note at* **defeat.**

checkmate *noun*

The act of defeating or the condition of being

defeated ► overthrow, trouncing, vanquishment. *See* **defeat.**

checkup *noun*

1. The act of examining carefully or critically ► audit, inquiry, perusal. *See* **examination** (1). **2.** A medical inquiry into a patient's state of health ► analysis, diagnosis. *See* **examination** (2).

cheek *noun*

► flippancy, insolence, sassiness. *See* **impudence.**

cheekiness *noun*

► audacity, brashness, brazenness, impertinence. *See* **impudence.**

cheeky *adjective*

1. Rude and disrespectful; without shame ► bold, insolent, pert. *See* **impudent. 2.** Having or showing a lack of respect ► contemptuous, discourteous, impolite. *See* **disrespectful** (1).

cheer *noun*

1. A condition of well-being and good spirits ► blessedness, bliss, felicity. *See* **happiness. 2.** An expression of warm approval ► acclamation, celebration, kudos. *See* **praise** (1).

cheer *verb*

1. To give great or keen pleasure to ► enchant, overjoy, pleasure. *See* **delight** (1). **2.** To impart emotional, moral, or mental strength to ► buck up, cheer up. *See* **encourage** (2). *See synonym note at* **encourage. 3.** To impart courage, inspiration, and resolution to ► cheer on, embolden, motivate. *See* **encourage** (1). **4.** To express approval audibly, as by clapping ► applaud, clap, root. *Idioms:* give a big hand (*or* welcome), give an ovation, give someone a hand, put one's hands together. *See synonym note at* **applaud. 5.** To occupy in an agreeable or pleasing way ► entertain, recreate, regale. *See* **amuse** (1). **6.** To express warm approval of ► applaud, commend. *See* **praise** (1).

cheerful *adjective*

1. Being in or showing good spirits ► animated, blithesome, boon, bright, cheery, chipper, convivial, exhilarated, gay, glad, gleeful, happy, jocund, jolly, jovial, joyful, lighthearted, merry, mirthful, sunny. *Idiom:* on top of the world. *See also* **lighthearted, lively. 2.** Providing joy and pleasure ► festive, glad, joyous. *See* **merry** (1). **3.** Expecting or suggesting a favorable outcome ► assured, sanguine. *See* **optimistic.**

✦ **CORE SYNONYMS:** *glad, happy, cheerful, lighthearted, joyful.* These adjectives mean being in or showing good spirits. *Glad* often refers to the feeling that results from the gratification of a wish or from satisfaction with immediate circumstances: "*Some folks rail against other folks, because other folks have what some folks would be glad of*" (Henry Fielding). *Happy* applies to a pleasurable feeling of contentment: "*Ask yourself whether you are happy, and you cease to be so*" (John Stuart Mill). *Cheerful* suggests characteristic good spirits: *a cheerful volunteer.* *Lighthearted* stresses the absence of care: "*He whistles as he goes, lighthearted wretch,/Cold and yet cheerful*" (Wil-

liam Cowper). *Joyful* suggests lively, often exultant happiness: *the joyful laughter of children.*

◄ ANTONYM: *sad*

cheerfulness *noun*

1. A condition of well-being and good spirits ► blessedness, bliss, felicity. *See* **happiness. 2.** A tendency to expect a favorable outcome or to dwell on hopeful aspects ► assurance, sanguinity. *See* **optimism.**

cheering *adjective*

► heartening, likely. *See* **encouraging.**

cheerless *adjective*

1. Causing or expressing sorrow or sadness ► depressing, melancholy, mournful. *See* **sorrowful** (1). **2.** Dark and depressing ► bleak, desolate, somber. *See* **gloomy** (1).

cheery *adjective*

1. Being in or showing good spirits ► bright, happy, sunny. *See* **cheerful** (1). **2.** Providing joy and pleasure ► festive, glad, joyous. *See* **merry** (1).

cheesy *adjective*

► cheap, lousy, poor. *See* **shoddy** (1).

chef *noun*

A person who prepares food for eating ► baker, cook, culinary artist.

chef-d'oeuvre *noun*

An outstanding and ingenious work ► magnum opus, masterpiece, masterwork. *See also* **accomplishment, composition, treasure.**

chemical-free *adjective*

► additive-free, unadulterated. *See* **natural** (1).

cherish *verb*

1. To have a high opinion of or regard for ► esteem, prize, treasure. *See* **value** (1). *See synonym note at* **value. 2.** To keep steadily in mind ► nourish, nurse. *See* **bear** (2). **3.** To care enough to keep someone in mind ► remember, think about, think of.

cherub *noun*

1. A very young child ► babe, infant. *See* **baby** (1). **2.** A pure, uncorrupted person ► lamb, virgin. *See* **innocent** (1).

cherubic *adjective*

Of or like a baby ► childlike, infantile. *See* **babyish** (1).

chew *verb*

To seize and grind with the teeth ► bite, champ, chomp, chump, crump, crunch, gnash, gnaw, masticate, munch, nibble, ruminate. *Chiefly Regional:* chaw. *See also* **browse, eat.**

chew out *verb*

Slang To criticize for a fault or offense ► chide, rebuke, reprimand. *See* **chastise** (1).

chew on *or* **over** *verb*

► cogitate, deliberate, mull. *See* **ponder.**

✦ **CORE SYNONYMS:** *chew, bite, champ, chomp, gnaw.* These verbs mean to seize and tear or grind something with the teeth: *I chewed on a piece of candy. She bit into a ripe apple. The horse was champing at its bit. The cow is chomping its hay. His dog was gnawing a bone.*

chic *adjective*
1. In accordance with current fashion ▸ mod, stylish, swanky. *See* **fashionable**. **2.** Catering to, used by, or admitting only the wealthy or socially superior ▸ chichi, posh, swank. *See* **exclusive** (4).
chic *noun*
Refinement of manner, form, and style ▸ sophistication, style. *Informal:* class. *See* **elegance**.
chicanery *noun*
▸ deviousness, slyness, trickery. *See* **dishonesty** (2).
chichi *adjective*
▸ chic, posh, swank. *See* **exclusive** (4).
chick *noun*
Informal A woman ▸ *Informal:* damsel, gal, lass. *See* **girl**.
chicken *noun*
Slang An ignoble, uncourageous person ▸ dastard, milksop, sissy. *See* **coward**.
chicken *adjective*
1. *Slang* Ignobly lacking in courage ▸ faint-hearted, pusillanimous. *Slang:* gutless. *See* **cowardly**. **2.** *Slang* Filled with fear or terror ▸ fearful, frightened, scared. *See* **afraid**.
chicken feed *noun*
▸ pocket money, small change. *See* **peanuts**.
chickenhearted *adjective*
▸ faint-hearted, pusillanimous. *Slang:* gutless. *See* **cowardly**.
chickenheartedness *noun*
▸ faint-heartedness, pusillanimity. *Slang:* gutlessness. *See* **cowardice**.
chicken-livered *adjective*
▸ spineless, weak-kneed. *See* **cowardly**.
chide *verb*
1. To criticize for a fault or offense ▸ berate, rebuke, reprimand. *See* **chastise** (1). **2.** To castigate for the purpose of improving ▸ chasten, correct.
chief *noun*
1. One who governs or leads ▸ boss, captain, chieftain, commander, director, elder, emir, emperor, general, governor, head, headman, hierarch, king, kingpin, leader, lord, majesty, master, monarch, overlord, potentate, prince, queen, ringleader, ruler, sachem, sagamore, sheik, sovereign, suzerain. *Slang:* brass hat, honcho. *Idioms:* cock of the block (*or* walk). *See also* **dictator**. **2.** *Slang* Someone who directs and supervises workers ▸ foreman, manager, supervisor. *See* **boss** (1).
chief *adjective*
1. Most important, influential, or significant ▸ key, main, principal. *See* **primary** (1). *See synonym note at* **primary**. **2.** Exercising controlling power or influence ▸ key, predominant, reigning. *See* **dominant** (1).
chieftain *noun*
▸ boss, director, head, leader. *See* **chief** (1).
child *noun*
1. A young person between birth and puberty ▸ innocent, juvenile, moppet, preadolescent, preteen, tot, whelp, youngster. *Informal:* kid, young'un. *See also*

baby. **2.** One who is not yet legally of age ▸ juvenile, minor, underage person. *See also* **youth**. **3.** A guileless, unsophisticated person ▸ babe, naive. *See* **innocent** (2). **4.** A person or group descended directly from the same parents or ancestors ▸ offspring, scion, seed. *See* **progeny**.
childbirth *or* **childbearing** *noun*
▸ childbearing, labor. *See* **birth** (1).
childhood *noun*
The stage of life between birth and puberty ▸ innocence, early years, preadolescence, prepubescence. *See also* **youth**.
childish *adjective*
Of or characteristic of a child, especially in immaturity ▸ adolescent, babyish, childlike, immature, infantile, juvenile, puerile, sophomoric. *See also* **foolish**.
childless *adjective*
▸ sterile, unfruitful. *See* **barren** (1).
childlike *adjective*
1. Of or like a baby ▸ infantile, infantine. *See* **babyish** (1). **2.** Of or characteristic of a child, especially in immaturity ▸ infantile, juvenile. *See* **childish**.
child's play *noun*
▸ pushover, snap, walkover. *See* **breeze** (2).
chill *noun*
Lack of warmth ▸ chilliness, frigidity. *See* **cold**.
chill *adjective*
1. Marked by a low temperature ▸ arctic, frigid, polar. *See* **cold** (1). **2.** Not friendly, sociable, or warm in manner ▸ aloof, chilly, impersonal. *See* **cool** (1).
chill out *verb*
To take repose by ceasing work or other effort for an interval of time ▸ kick back, unbend, unwind. *See* **rest**[1] (1).
chilliness *noun*
▸ coolness, frigidity, iciness. *See* **cold**.
chilly *adjective*
1. Marked by a low temperature ▸ arctic, frigid, polar. *See* **cold** (1). *See synonym note at* **cold**. **2.** Not friendly, sociable, or warm in manner ▸ aloof, frigid, impersonal. *See* **cool** (1).
chime *verb*
1. To give forth or cause to give forth a clear resonant sound ▸ bong, knell, peal. *See* **ring**[2] (1). **2.** To be compatible or suitable ▸ check, correspond, match. *See* **agree** (1).
chime in *verb*
To interject remarks or questions into another's discourse ▸ break in, chip in, cut in. *See* **interrupt** (2).
chime *noun*
The act or state of agreeing or conforming ▸ accord, consensus, unanimity. *See* **agreement** (2).
chimera *noun*
▸ bubble, fantasy, illusion. *See* **dream** (2).
chimeric *or* **chimerical** *adjective*
1. Of, relating to, or in the nature of an illusion; lacking reality ▸ hallucinatory, illusory, phantasmagoric. *See* **illusive** (1). **2.** Existing only in the imagination ▸ fanciful, unreal. *See* **imaginary**.

chink *noun*
▶ break, cleft, fissure. *See* **crack** (2).
chintzy *adjective*
▶ flashy, garish, loud. *See* **gaudy.**
chin wag *verb*
Slang To talk rapidly and incessantly on trivial matters ▶ blab, jabber, prattle. *See* **chatter** (1).
chip *noun*
A small, thin piece of something ▶ slice, sliver, shaving. *See* **flake** (1).
chip *verb*
To come off in small, thin pieces ▶ peel, scale, shed. *See* **flake.**
chip in *verb*
1. To give in common with others ▶ donate, subscribe. *See* **contribute** (1). **2.** To interject remarks or questions into another's discourse ▶ break in, chime in, cut in. *See* **interrupt** (2). **3.** To help bring about a result ▶ participate, share. *See* **contribute** (2).
chipper *adjective*
1. Very brisk, alert, and full of high spirits ▶ animated, bubbly, vivacious. *See* **lively** (1). **2.** Being in or showing good spirits ▶ happy, jolly, jovial. *See* **cheerful** (1).
chisel *verb*
1. To get money or something else from someone by deceitful trickery ▶ bilk, defraud, swindle. *See* **cheat** (1). **2.** To cut a design or inscription into a hard surface, especially for printing ▶ etch, incise. *See* **engrave** (1).
chiseler *noun*
Informal A person who cheats ▶ cheater, swindler, trickster. *See* **cheat** (2).
chitchat *noun*
Incessant and inconsequential talk ▶ drivel, patter, small talk. *See* **chatter.**
chitchat *verb*
To talk rapidly on trivial matters ▶ blab, jabber, prattle. *See* **chatter** (1).
chivalric *adjective*
▶ chivalrous, knightly. *See* **gallant** (1).
chivalrous *adjective*
1. Characterized by elaborate but usually formal courtesy ▶ courtly, gallant, stately. *See* **gracious** (2). **2.** Respectfully attentive, especially to women ▶ gentlemanly, knightly. *See* **gallant** (1).
chivalry *or* **chilvalrousness** *noun*
Respectful attention, especially toward women ▶ gallantry. *See also* **consideration, courtesy.**
chock-full *or* **chock-a-block** *adjective*
▶ awash, fraught, jam-packed. *See* **full** (1).
choice *noun*
1. The act, power, or right of choosing ▶ alternative, decision, discretion, election, free will, option, pick, preference, selection, volition. *Informal:* druthers. *See also* **voice, will. 2.** One that is selected ▶ chosen, pick. *See* **elect. 3.** The most preferable part of something ▶ cream, elite, top. *See* **best** (1).
choice *adjective*
1. Of fine quality ▶ exceptional, fine, first-class, first-

rate, high-grade, premium, prime, select, sterling, superior, top-drawer, top-grade, top-of-the-line. *See also* **best, excellent, exceptional. 2.** Singled out in preference ▶ chosen, elect, exclusive, select. *See also* **excellent, favorite. 3.** Appealing to refined taste ▶ elegant, exquisite. *See* **delicate** (1). *See synonym note at* **delicate.**

✦ CORE SYNONYMS: *choice, alternative, option, preference, selection, election.* These nouns denote the act, power, or right of choosing. *Choice* implies broadly the freedom to choose from a set: *The store offers a wide choice of vegetables. I had no choice in the matter.* *Alternative* emphasizes choice between only two possibilities or courses of action: *"An unhappy alternative is before you, Elizabeth . . . . Your mother will never see you again if you do* not *marry Mr. Collins, and I will never see you again if you do"* (Jane Austen). *Option* often stresses a power or liberty to choose that has been granted: *The legislature outlined several tax options.* *Preference* indicates choice based on one's values, bias, or predilections: *We were offered our preference of wines.* *Selection* suggests a variety of things or persons to choose from: *The video store had a wide selection of foreign films.* *Election* especially emphasizes the use of judgment: *The university recommends careful consideration in the election of a major.*

---

choke *verb*
1. To stop breathing or to stop the breathing of ▶ asphyxiate, gag, smother, stifle, strangle, strangulate, suffocate, throttle. **2.** To hold something requiring an outlet in check ▶ smother, stifle, suppress. *See* **repress. 3.** To plug up or block something, such as a hole or conduit ▶ clog, cork. *See* **fill** (2). **4.** To block or fill with obstacles ▶ block, dam. *See* **obstruct** (1). **5.** To be unsuccessful ▶ fall short, strike out, wash out. *See* **fail** (1). **6.** To overcome opposition or uprising with overwhelming force ▶ crush, extinguish, quell. *See* **suppress** (1).
choke off *verb*
To overcome opposition or uprising with overwhelming force ▶ crush, extinguish, quell. *See* **suppress** (1).
choke *noun*
Something used to fill a hole, space, or container ▶ cork, stop. *See* **plug** (1).
choked *adjective*
▶ congested, teeming. *See* **overcrowded.**
choler *noun*
▶ indignation, irateness, wrath. *See* **anger.**
choleric *adjective*
1. Easily moved to anger ▶ irascible, quick-tempered, tetchy. *See* **testy** (1). **2.** Feeling or showing anger ▶ indignant, mad, livid. *See* **angry.**
chomp *verb*
▶ champ, gnash, munch. *See* **chew.** *See synonym note at* **chew.**
choose *verb*
1. To make a choice from a number of alternatives

► cast, cull, decide (on), elect, go with, opt (for), pick (out), select, single (out), take, vote (for), weigh, will. **2.** To have an inclination to ► desire, like, please, prefer, want, will, wish. *Idioms:* have a mind, see fit.

choosy *adjective*
► exacting, finicky. *See* **fussy** (1).

chop *verb*
To decrease, as in length or amount, by or as if by severing or excising ► crop, prune, trim, truncate. *See* **cut** (3).

chop down *verb*
To bring down, as from a shot or blow ► floor, ground, hew. *See* **drop** (6).

chop *noun*
A sudden heavy stroke ► crack, hit, swat, whack. *See* **blow²** (1).

choppiness *noun*
► bumpiness, roughness, unevenness. *See* **irregularity** (1).

chops *noun*
The opening in the body through which food is ingested ► maw. *Slang:* trap, yap. *See* **mouth** (1).

chore *noun*
1. A piece of work that has been assigned ► assignment, duty, job. *See* **task** (1). *See synonym note at* **task**. **2.** A difficult or tedious undertaking ► effort, grind, slog. *See* **task** (2).

chortle *verb*
To express amusement or mirth ► cackle, chuckle. *See* **laugh**.

chortle *noun*
An act of laughing ► cackle, chuckle, laughter. *See* **laugh** (1).

chosen *adjective*
Singled out in preference ► choice, elect, exclusive, select. *See also* **excellent, favorite**.

chosen *noun*
One that is selected ► choice, pick. *See* **elect**.

chow *noun*
Slang Material that is fit to be eaten ► foodstuff, nourishment, victuals. *See* **food**.

chow down *verb*
Slang To take food into the body as nourishment ► consume, ingest, partake. *See* **eat** (1). *See synonym note at* **eat**.

christen *verb*
► baptize, designate. *See* **name** (1).

chronic *adjective*
1. Subject to a disease or habit for a long time ► confirmed, habitual, habituated, inveterate. *See also* **stubborn**. **2.** Of long duration ► continuing, lingering, persistent, prolonged, protracted. *See also* **confirmed, continuing**. **3.** Subject to a habit or pattern of behavior ► accustomed, habitual, routine.

✤ CORE SYNONYMS: *chronic, confirmed, habitual, inveterate*. These adjectives mean having long had a habit or a disease: *a chronic complainer; a confirmed alcoholic; a habitual cheat; an inveterate smoker*.

---

chronicle *noun*
1. A chronological record of past events ► annals, archive, chronicle, historical record. **2.** A recounting of past events ► account, description, history, report. *See* **story** (1).

chronicle *verb*
To place on a list or in a record or book ► catalog, docket, write down. *See* **list¹** (1).

chronological *adjective*
► sequential, serial. *See* **consecutive**.

chubby *adjective*
► plump, pudgy, rotund. *See* **fat** (1). *See synonym note at* **fat**.

chuck *verb*
1. *Informal* To let go or get rid of as being useless or defective, for example ► dump, throw away. *Informal:* shuck (off). *See* **discard**. **2.** *Informal* To put out by force ► dismiss, evict. *See* **eject** (1). **3.** *Informal* To send through the air with a motion of the hand or arm ► heave, hurl, pitch. *See* **throw** (1). **4.** *Slang* To eject the contents of the stomach through the mouth ► retch, throw up. *Informal:* puke. *See* **vomit** (1).

chuck *noun*
An act of throwing ► fling, hurl, toss. *See* **throw**.

chuckle *verb*
To express amusement or mirth ► cackle, chortle. *See* **laugh**.

chuckle *noun*
An act of laughing ► cackle, chortle, laughter. *See* **laugh** (1).

chuff *noun*
► boor, Philistine, yahoo. *See* **boor**.

chug *or* **chugalug** *verb*
► down, imbibe, swill. *See* **drink** (2).

chum *noun*
1. A person whom one knows well, likes, and trusts ► amigo, intimate, mate. *See* **friend** (1). **2.** One who shares interests or activities with another ► companion, comrade. *See* **associate** (2).

chumminess *noun*
► camaraderie, companionship, fellowship. *See* **friendship**.

chummy *adjective*
► close, cozy, familiar. *See* **intimate¹** (1).

chump¹ *noun*
1. A mentally dumb person ► dummy, dunce, thickhead. *See* **dullard**. **2.** *Slang* An unpleasant, tiresome person ► bore. *Slang:* pill, twit. *See* **drip** (2).

chump² *verb*
To seize and grind with the teeth ► chomp, gnash, munch. *See* **chew**.

chunk *noun*
► clod, wad. *See* **lump¹** (1).

chunky *adjective*
► blocky, heavyset, squat. *See* **stocky**.

church *adjective*
Of or relating to a church or to an established religion ► churchly, ecclesiastical, religious, spiritual. *See also* **clerical, divine, holy, ritual**.

churchman *or* **churchwoman** *noun*
▸ ecclesiastic, minister, parson. *See* **cleric.**

churl *noun*
1. An unrefined, rude person ▸ chuff, Philistine, yahoo. *See* **boor.** *See synonym note at* **boor. 2.** A stingy person ▸ *Informal:* penny pincher. *Slang:* cheapskate. *See* **miser.**

churlish *adjective*
1. Lacking in delicacy or refinement ▸ indelicate, unbecoming, unrefined. *See* **coarse** (1). **2.** Having or showing a bad temper ▸ cranky, grouchy, peevish. *See* **ill-tempered.**

churn *verb*
1. To cause to move to and fro violently ▸ convulse, rock, shake. *See* **agitate** (1). *See synonym note at* **agitate. 2.** To be in a state of turmoil or excitement ▸ burn, seethe. *See* **boil** (2).

chutzpah *or* **hutzpah** *noun*
▸ audacity, boldness, impertinence. *See* **impudence.**

cinch *noun*
1. *Informal* An easily accomplished task ▸ pushover, snap, walkover. *See* **breeze** (2). *See synonym note at* **breeze. 2.** A clearly established fact ▸ actuality, sure thing. *See* **certainty** (1). **3.** A long narrow piece, as of material ▸ fillet, strap, strip, tape. *See* **band**[1] (1).

cinch *verb*
Informal To render certain ▸ assure, secure, warrant. *See* **guarantee** (2).

cincture *noun*
A long narrow piece, as of material ▸ belt, strap, strip, swath. *See* **band**[1] (1).

cincture *verb*
To form a circle around ▸ band, begird, belt, girdle. *See* **encircle** (1).

cinerarium *noun*
▸ catacomb, crypt, tomb. *See* **grave**[1].

cipher *noun*
A totally insignificant person ▸ nobody, nothing, small fry. *See* **nonentity.**

cipher *verb*
To ascertain by mathematics ▸ compute, figure, reckon. *See* **calculate** (1). *See synonym note at* **calculate.**

circa *adverb*
▸ almost, nearly, roughly. *See* **approximately.**

circle *noun*
1. A round closed plane shape or figure ▸ annulus, band, circlet, cirque, circuit, crown, disk, gyre, halo, hoop, ring, round, roundlet, wheel, wreath, zodiac. *See also* **ball, circumference, loop. 2.** A course, process, or journey that ends where it began or repeats itself ▸ circuit, cycle, orbit, round, tour, turn. **3.** A small group of friends or associates ▸ clique, coterie, crew, crowd, group, in-group, set. *Informal:* bunch, gang. *See also* **crowd, group. 4.** A sphere of activity, experience, study, or interest ▸ department, domain, field, terrain. *See* **area** (1). **5.** A circular movement around a point or about an axis ▸ circulation, gyration. *See* **revolution** (1). **6.** An area or set of param-

eters within which something or someone exists, acts, or has influence ▸ extent, realm, scope. *See* **range** (1).

circle *verb*
1. To form a circle around ▸ belt, gird, ring. *See* **encircle** (1). **2.** To shut in on all sides ▸ encircle, hedge, ring. *See* **surround** (1). *See synonym note at* **surround. 3.** To rotate on an axis or around a center ▸ twirl, whirl, wheel. *See* **turn** (1). *See synonym note at* **turn.**

circlet *noun*
▸ band, ring, wheel. *See* **circle** (1).

circuit *noun*
1. A line around a closed figure or area ▸ ambit, perimeter. *See* **circumference.** *See synonym note at* **circumference. 2.** A round closed plane shape or figure ▸ band, ring, wheel. *See* **circle** (1). **3.** A course or process that ends where it began or repeats itself ▸ cycle, orbit. *See* **circle** (2). **4.** A circular movement around a point or about an axis ▸ circulation, gyration. *See* **revolution** (1). **5.** An area regularly covered, as by a policeman or reporter ▸ round, route. *See* **beat** (2). **6.** A group of athletic teams that play each other ▸ association, league. *See* **conference** (6). **7.** The act of traveling from one place to another ▸ flight, passage, progress. *See* **journey. 8.** A length of line folded over and joined at the ends so as to form a curve or circle ▸ coil, noose, ring. *See* **loop** (1).

circuitous *adjective*
▸ anfractuous, devious, roundabout. *See* **indirect** (1).

circular *adjective*
1. Having the shape of a curve everywhere equidistant from a fixed point ▸ annular, globular, spherical. *See* **round** (1). **2.** Not proceeding straight to the point or object ▸ circuitous, devious, roundabout. *See* **indirect** (1).

circular *noun*
An announcement distributed on paper to a large number of people ▸ flier, handbill, leaflet, notice.

circulate *verb*
1. To move freely as a liquid ▸ purl, run, stream. *See* **flow** (1). **2.** To extend over a wide area ▸ disperse, disseminate, scatter. *See* **spread** (2). **3.** To become known far and wide ▸ get around, go around, spread, travel. *Idioms:* go (*or* make) the rounds.

circulation *noun*
1. A circular movement around a point or about an axis ▸ circle, gyration. *See* **revolution** (1). **2.** The passing out or spreading about of something over a wide area ▸ dispersion, scattering. *See* **distribution** (2). **3.** The act or process of publishing printed matter ▸ issue, printing, release. *See* **publication** (1).

circumference *noun*
A line around a closed figure or area ▸ ambit, circuit, compass, perimeter, periphery. *See also* **border, circle, limits.**

✦ **CORE SYNONYMS:** *circumference, circuit, compass, perimeter, periphery.* These nouns refer to a line around a closed figure or area: *the circumference of the earth; followed the circuit around the park; stayed within the*

compass of the schoolyard; the perimeter of a rectangle;
a fence around the periphery of the property.

circumlocution *noun*
▸ long-windedness, verboseness. *See* **wordiness**.

circumlocutionary *adjective*
▸ long-winded, periphrastic, verbose. *See* **wordy** (1).
See synonym note at **wordy**.

circumlocutory *adjective*
1. Not proceeding straight to the point or object
▸ circuitous, devious, roundabout. *See* **indirect** (1).
2. Using or containing an excessive number of words
▸ long-winded, periphrastic, verbose. *See* **wordy** (1).

circumnavigate *verb*
1. To pass around but not through ▸ bypass, go
around. *See* **skirt** (1). 2. To form a circle around
▸ circle, loop, orbit. *See* **encircle** (1).

circumscribe *verb*
1. To place a limit on ▸ confine, fix, restrict. *See* **limit**
(1). *See synonym note at* **limit**. 2. To fix the limits of
▸ demarcate, limit, mark. *See* **determine** (1). 3. To
form a circle around ▸ circle, ring, surround. *See*
encircle (1).

circumscribed *adjective*
▸ checked, controlled. *See* **restricted** (1).

circumscription *noun*
1. The act of limiting or condition of being limited
▸ confinement, limitation, restraint. *See* **restriction**
(1). 2. Something that limits or holds back ▸ check,
constraint, curb. *See* **restraint** (1).

circumspect *adjective*
1. Trying attentively to avoid danger, risk, or error
▸ cautious, chary, prudent. *See* **wary** (1). 2. Careful and
slow in acting, moving, or deciding ▸ cautious, measured, unhurried. *See* **deliberate** (3).

circumspection *noun*
▸ caution, foresight, forethought. *See* **prudence** (1).
See synonym note at **prudence**.

circumstance *noun*
1. Something that takes place ▸ episode, event, experience, happening, incident, occasion, occurrence,
thing. *See also* **event**. 2. One of the conditions or facts
attending an event and having some bearing on it
▸ condition, detail, fact, factor, particular. *See also*
element, quality. 3. Something significant that happens ▸ development, incident. *See* **event** (2).

✢ CORE SYNONYMS: *circumstance, occurrence, happening,
event, incident, episode.* These nouns refer to something that takes place or comes to pass.
Cirmcumstance, occurrence, and *happening* are the
most general: *"Billy had found Alice, thus bringing
about the odd circumstance of their renewing their
acquaintanceship"* (Eleanor H. Porter). *The sunrise is
an everyday occurrence. The reporter dismissed the
report as a happening of no great importance. Event
usually signifies a notable occurrence: major world
events reported on the evening news. "Great events
make me quiet and calm; it is only trifles that irritate
my nerves"* (Victoria). *Incident may apply to a minor
occurrence: a small incident blown out of proportion.*

The term may also refer to a distinct event of sharp
identity and significance: *a succession of exciting
incidents.* An *episode* is an incident in the course of a
progression or within a larger sequence: *"Happiness
was but the occasional episode in a general drama of
pain"* (Thomas Hardy).

circumstances *noun*
▸ context, setting, surroundings. *See* **conditions**.

circumstantial *adjective*
1. Characterized by attention to detail ▸ exhaustive,
particular, thorough. *See* **detailed** (1). 2. Characterized
by elaborate, usually formal courtesy ▸ courtly, gallant, stately. *See* **gracious** (2).

circumstantiate *verb*
▸ confirm, substantiate, validate. *See* **prove** (1).

circumstantiation *noun*
▸ authentication, corroboration, proof, verification.
See **confirmation** (2).

circumvent *verb*
1. To pass around but not through ▸ circumnavigate,
go around. *See* **skirt** (1). 2. To keep away from ▸ dodge,
evade, shun. *See* **avoid**.

circumvention *noun*
▸ bypass, evasion. *See* **escape** (2).

circumvolution *noun*
▸ circulation, gyration. *See* **revolution** (1).

circumvolve *verb*
▸ twirl, whirl, wheel. *See* **turn** (1).

cirque *noun*
▸ band, ring, wheel. *See* **circle** (1).

cistern *noun*
▸ basin, cask, tank. *See* **vat**.

citadel *noun*
▸ bastion, stronghold. *See* **fort**.

citation *noun*
1. The act of referring ▸ naming, referral, signification. *See* **reference** (1). 2. Recognition of achievement
or superiority or a sign of this ▸ commendation,
honor. *See* **distinction** (2). 3. A written or printed
notification of a legal infraction ▸ ticket.

cite *verb*
1. To bring forward as proof or support ▸ adduce,
invoke, lay, present, produce. *See also* **offer**. 2. To refer
to by name ▸ mention, specify. *See* **name** (2). 3. To give
a name or title to ▸ christen, designate. *See* **name** (1).

citizen *noun*
A person owing loyalty to and entitled to the protection of a given state ▸ burgess, burgher, freeman,
national, subject, taxpayer. *See also* **inhabitant**.

✢ CORE SYNONYMS: *citizen, national, subject.* These
nouns denote a person owing allegiance to a nation
or state and entitled to its protection: *an American
citizen; a Nigerian national; a French subject.*

city *noun*
A large and important town ▸ borough, megalopolis,
metropolis, municipality. *Informal:* burg, town. *See
also* **village**.

city *adjective*
Of, in, or belonging to a city ▸ civic, local, metropolitan, municipal, urban.

civic *adjective*
1. Of, representing, or carried on by people at large ▸ civil, public, societal. *See* **popular** (1). **2.** Of, in, or belonging to a city ▸ municipal, urban. *See* **city.**

civil *adjective*
1. Of, representing, or carried on by people at large ▸ civic, public, societal. *See* **popular** (1). **2.** Characterized by good manners ▸ genteel, mannerly, polite. *See* **courteous** (1). *See synonym note at* **courteous. 3.** Not religious in subject matter, form, or use ▸ non-ecclesiastical, secular, temporal. *See* **profane** (2).

civility *noun*
1. Well-mannered behavior toward others ▸ gentility, politeness. *See* **courtesy** (1). **2.** Social courtesies ▸ courteousness, pleasantry, politeness. *See* **amenities** (2).

civilization *noun*
1. The total product of human creativity and intellect ▸ culture, Kultur, society. **2.** Excellent taste resulting from intellectual development ▸ cultivation, refinement. *See* **culture** (3). **3.** Behavior patterns, traits, and products considered as an expression of a certain people or period ▸ ethos, society. *See* **culture** (2).

civilize *verb*
To fit for companionship with others, especially in attitude or manners ▸ acculturate, humanize, socialize.

civilized *adjective*
▸ cultivated, educated. *See* **cultured.**

civilizing *adjective*
▸ enlightening, humanizing. *See* **cultural.**

clabber *verb*
Chiefly Regional To change or be changed from a liquid into a soft, semisolid, or solid mass ▸ congeal, set. *See* **coagulate.**

clack *verb*
1. To make a light, sharp noise ▸ click, snap. *See also* **crackle. 2.** To make or cause to make a succession of short, sharp sounds ▸ brattle, chatter, clank, clatter, rattle. *See also* **knock, shake. 3.** To talk rapidly on trivial matters ▸ blab, jabber, prattle. *See* **chatter** (1).

clack *noun*
1. A light, sharp noise ▸ click, crackle, snap. *See also* **crack. 2.** Incessant and inconsequential talk ▸ drivel, patter, small talk. *See* **chatter.**

clad *verb*
▸ Cover, sheathe, side. *See* **face** (2).

claim *verb*
1. To defend, maintain, or insist on the recognition of ▸ assert, challenge, demand, postulate, vindicate. *Idioms:* have dibs on, lay claim to, stake a claim. **2.** To put into words positively and with conviction ▸ avow, declare, maintain. *See* **assert** (1). **3.** To ask for urgently or insistently ▸ insist on (*or* upon), require. *See* **demand** (1). *See synonym note at* **demand.**

claim *noun*
1. A legitimate or asserted right to demand some-

thing as one's due ▸ pretense, pretension, title. *Slang:* dibs. **2.** A right or legal share in something ▸ interest, portion, stake, title. *See also* **cut, right. 3.** The act of demanding ▸ appeal, requisition. *See* **demand** (1). **4.** The act of asserting positively or something so asserted ▸ averment, declaration, statement. *See* **assertion. 5.** Something, such as money, owed by one person to another ▸ indebtedness, liability, obligation. *See* **debt** (1).

✦ **CORE SYNONYMS:** *claim, pretense, pretension, title.* These nouns refer to a legitimate or asserted right to demand something as one's due: *had a legal claim to the property; makes no pretense to scholarliness; justified pretensions to the presidency; has no title to our thanks.*

---

claimant *noun*
One that makes a formal complaint, especially in court ▸ accuser, complainant, plaintiff.

clamber *verb*
▸ climb, go up, scramble. *See* **ascend** (1).

clammy *adjective*
Slightly wet ▸ damp, dank, dewy, moist. *See also* **sticky, wet.**

clamor *noun*
1. Sounds or a sound, especially when loud, confused, or disagreeable ▸ cacophony, din. *See* **noise** (1). *See synonym note at* **noise. 2.** Loud and insistent utterances or noisemaking, usually expressing disapproval ▸ hullabaloo, rumpus, uproar. *See* **vociferation. 3.** A loud, deep, prolonged sound ▸ bawl, bellow. *See* **roar** (1).

clamor *verb*
To speak or say in a loud cry ▸ call, holler, whoop. *See* **shout.**

clamorous *adjective*
1. Offensively loud and insistent ▸ boisterous, obstreperous, strident. *See* **vociferous.** *See synonym note at* **vociferous. 2.** Marked by extremely high volume and intensity of sound ▸ booming, earsplitting, roaring. *See* **loud** (1).

clamp *noun*
A device for locking ▸ catch, clip, lock. *See* **fastener.**

clamp *verb*
1. To join one thing to another ▸ append, clip, connect. *See* **attach** (1). **2.** To make secure ▸ bind, chain, moor. *See* **fasten** (1).

clampdown *noun*
Forceful subjugation, as against an uprising ▸ crackdown, lockdown, repression, suppression. *See also* **oppression, restraint.**

clan *noun*
▸ house, kindred, lineage. *See* **family** (2).

clandestine *adjective*
▸ covert, sub-rosa, undercover. *See* **secret** (1).

clandestinely *adverb*
▸ covertly, sub rosa. *See* **secretly.**

clandestinity *or* **clandestineness** *noun*
▸ concealment, secretiveness. *See* **secrecy.**

clang *verb*
▸ crash, slam, whack. *See* **bang** (1).

clang *noun*
A loud, harsh striking noise ▸ crash, smash. *See* **clash** (1).

clangor *noun*
▸ clamor, din. *See* **noise** (1).

clank *verb*
To make or cause to make a succession of short, sharp sounds ▸ brattle, chatter, clack, clatter, rattle. *See also* **knock, shake.**

clap *verb*
1. To express approval audibly, as by clapping ▸ applaud, cheer, root. *Idioms:* give a big hand (*or* welcome), give an ovation, give someone a hand, put one's hands together. **2.** To make a sudden, sharp noise ▸ snap, pop. *See* **crack** (2). **3.** To strike together noisily ▸ crash, slam, whack. *See* **bang** (1). **4.** To hit with a sharp blow, especially of the open hand ▸ smack, spank, swat, whack. *See* **slap** (1).

clap *noun*
A sudden sharp, explosive noise ▸ bang, pop, snap. *See* **crack** (1).

claptrap *noun*
1. Pretentious, pompous speech or writing ▸ fustian, grandiloquence. *See* **bombast. 2.** Something that does not have or make sense ▸ bunkum, drivel, garbage. *See* **nonsense** (1).

clarification *noun*
1. Something that serves to explain or clarify ▸ explication, illumination. *See* **explanation** (1). **2.** The act or process of removing physical impurities ▸ cleaning, refinement. *See* **purification** (1).

clarifier *noun*
▸ antiseptic, cathartic, cleaner. *See* **purifier.**

clarify *verb*
1. To make clear or clearer ▸ clear (up), define, elucidate, illuminate, illustrate, simplify. *Idioms:* shed (*or* throw) light on *or* upon. *See also* **explain, show. 2.** To remove impurities from ▸ clean, cleanse, purify, refine. *See also* **clean.**

clarity *noun*
1. The quality of being clear and easy to perceive or understand ▸ clearness, comprehensibility, distinctness, explicitness, intelligibility, legibility, limpidity, limpidness, lucidity, lucidness, pellucidity, pellucidness, perspicuity, perspicuousness, plainness, preciseness, precision, simplicity. **2.** The condition of being clean and free of contaminants ▸ cleanliness, immaculacy, taintlessness. *See* **purity** (1). **3.** The quality or condition of being visible or providing a clear view ▸ observability, visuality. *See* **visibility.**

clash *verb*
1. To strike together noisily ▸ crash, slam, whack. *See* **bang** (1). **2.** To fail to be in accord ▸ contrast, disagree, discord. *See* **conflict. 3.** To strive in opposition ▸ battle, combat, fight. *See* **contend** (1).

clash *noun*
1. A loud, harsh striking noise ▸ clang, crash, slap,

smack, smash, whack. *See also* **blow**^{2}**, crack, slam. 2.** A state of disagreement and disharmony ▸ contention, difference, discord. *See* **conflict** (1). *See synonym note at* **conflict. 3.** A discussion, often heated, in which a difference of opinion is expressed ▸ contention, fight, quarrel. *See* **argument** (1). *See synonym note at* **argument** (1). **4.** An encounter between opposing military forces ▸ combat, confrontation, war. *See* **battle** (1).

clasp *noun*
1. A device for locking ▸ catch, clip, lock. *See* **fastener. 2.** The act of embracing ▸ hug, squeeze. *See* **embrace. 3.** An act or means of holding something ▸ clench, grasp. *See* **hold** (1).

clasp *verb*
1. To put one's arms around affectionately ▸ enfold, hug. *See* **embrace** (1). **2.** To take firmly with the hand and maintain a hold on ▸ clutch, grab, grip. *See* **grasp** (1).

class *noun*
1. A subdivision of a larger group ▸ category, classification, department, division, family, genre, group, order, set. *See also* **kind. 2.** A division of persons or things by quality, rank, or grade ▸ bracket, caste, grade, hierarchy, league, level, order, range, rank, school, stratum, tier. *See also* **place. 3.** Degree of excellence ▸ caliber, grade, quality. *See also* **degree. 4.** *Informal* Refinement of manner or style ▸ chic, style, taste. *See* **elegance.**

class *verb*
To arrange according to class ▸ assort, categorize, group. *See* **classify.**

classic *adjective*
1. Having the nature of, constituting, or serving as a type ▸ model, prototypic, representative. *See* **typical** (1). **2.** Characterized by enduring excellence, appeal, and importance ▸ ageless, antique. *See* **vintage** (1). **3.** Without addition, decoration, or qualification ▸ austere, plain, simple. *See* **bare** (1).

classical *adjective*
1. Having the nature of, constituting, or serving as a type ▸ model, quintessential, typic. *See* **typical** (1). **2.** Characterized by enduring excellence, appeal, and importance ▸ ageless, antique. *See* **vintage** (1).

classification *noun*
1. The act or condition of being arranged ▸ allotment, distribution, positioning. *See* **arrangement** (1). **2.** A subdivision of a larger group ▸ category, order, set. *See* **class** (1).

classified *adjective*
▸ privileged, restricted. *See* **confidential** (3).

classify *verb*
To arrange or organize according to class ▸ assort, catalog, categorize, class, coordinate, distribute, divide, grade, group, pigeonhole, place, range, rank, rate, separate, size, sort (out), stereotype, stratify. *See also* **arrange, position.**

classy *adjective*
1. *Informal* In accordance with current fashion ▸ mod, stylish, swanky. *See* **fashionable. 2.** *Informal* Exhibit-

ing refined, tasteful beauty of manner, form, or style ► chic, exquisite, refined. *See* **elegant** (1). **3.** Catering to, used by, or admitting only the wealthy or socially superior ► chic, posh, swank. *See* **exclusive** (4).

clatter *verb*
To make or cause to make a succession of short, sharp sounds ► brattle, chatter, clack, clank, rattle. *See also* **knock, shake.**

clay *noun*
1. The soft part of the land surface of the world ► dirt, ground, soil. *See* **earth** (1). **2.** The substance of the body, especially after decay or cremation ► ashes, cremains, dust, remains.

clean *adjective*
1. Free from dirt, stain, or impurities ► antiseptic, cleanly, fresh, immaculate, scrubbed, spick-and-span, spotless, stainless, unsmirched, unsoiled, unsullied. *Idioms:* clean as a whistle, squeaky clean. *See also* **neat, sterile. 2.** Free from flaws or blemishes ► consummate, flawless, unblemished. *See* **perfect** (1). **3.** Exhibiting or possessing skill and ease in performance ► adroit, neat. *See* **dexterous. 4.** Free from evil and corruption ► uncorrupted, untainted. *See* **innocent** (1). **5.** Not lewd or obscene ► decent, inoffensive, modest, wholesome. *Informal:* G-rated. *See also* **correct, ethical. 6.** According to the rules ► fair, sporting, sportsmanlike, sportsmanly. **7.** *Slang* Free from guilt or blame ► blameless, faultless. *See* **innocent** (2).

clean *adverb*
Informal To the fullest extent ► fully, totally, utterly. *See* **completely** (1).

clean *verb*
1. To rid of dirt, stains, trash, or other impurities ► bathe, cleanse, launder, lave, rinse, wash. *See also* **scrape, refine. 2.** To remove impurities from ► clarify, cleanse, purify, refine. **3.** To make or keep an area clean and orderly ► neaten (up), spruce (up), straighten (up). *See* **tidy** (1). **4.** To make neat and trim; make presentable ► freshen (up), slick up, trim. *See* **tidy** (2).

clean out *verb*
1. To remove the contents of ► clear, evacuate. *See* **empty** (1). **2.** *Slang* To reduce to financial insolvency ► bankrupt, bust, impoverish. *See* **ruin** (3).

clean up *verb*
Slang To make a large profit ► batten, cash in, profit. *Idiom:* make a killing.

✦ CORE SYNONYMS: *clean, antiseptic, cleanly, immaculate, spotless.* These adjectives mean free from dirt, stain, or impurities: *clean clothing; antiseptic surgical instruments; a cleanly pet; an immaculate tablecloth; a spotless kitchen.*

◄ ANTONYM: *dirty*

---

cleaner *noun*
► antiseptic, cathartic, cleanser. *See* **purifier.**

cleaning *noun*
► catharsis, clarification, refinement. *See* **purification** (1).

cleanliness *noun*
► clarity, cleanness, immaculacy. *See* **purity** (1).

cleanly *adjective*
Free from dirt, stain, or impurities ► immaculate, spotless. *See* **clean** (1). *See synonym note at* **clean.**

cleanly *adverb*
In a fair, sporting manner ► correctly, fairly, properly. *See* **fair**[1] (1).

cleanness *noun*
► clarity, cleanliness, immaculacy. *See* **purity** (1).

cleanse *verb*
1. To remove impurities from ► clarify, clean, purify, refine. **2.** To free from sin, guilt, or defilement ► atone, lustrate, pardon. *See* **purify** (1). **3.** To rid of dirt, stains, trash, or other impurities ► bathe, launder, lave. *See* **clean** (1).

cleanser *noun*
► antiseptic, cathartic, cleaner. *See* **purifier.**

cleansing *noun*
► catharsis, clarification, refinement. *See* **purification** (1).

clear *adjective*
1. Free from what obscures or dims ► crystal, crystal clear, crystalline, hyaline, limpid, lucid, pellucid, see-through, translucent, transparent. *See also* **filmy, sheer. 2.** Free from clouds or mist ► bright, cloudless, fair, fine, sunny, unclouded. **3.** Free from flaws or blemishes ► consummate, flawless, unblemished. *See* **perfect** (1). **4.** Free from obstructions ► free, open, unbarred, unblocked, unhindered, unimpeded, unobstructed, unplugged. *See also* **passable. 5.** Free from extraneous elements ► perfect, plain, unadulterated. *See* **pure** (1). **6.** Readily seen, perceived, or understood ► evident, noticeable, obvious. *See* **apparent** (1). *See synonym note at* **apparent. 7.** Clearly defined; not ambiguous ► distinct, unambiguous. *See* **sharp** (3). **8.** Easily seen through due to a lack of subtlety ► blatant, overt, transparent. *See* **obvious** (1). **9.** Without any doubt ► clear-cut, definite, unquestionable. *See* **decided** (1). **10.** Clearly, fully, and emphatically expressed ► decided, explicit, precise. *See* **definite** (1). **11.** Containing nothing ► bare, vacuous. *See* **empty** (1).

clear *verb*
1. To become brighter or fairer ► brighten, clear up, kindle, illuminate, lighten. **2.** To make clear or clearer ► elucidate, illuminate. *See* **clarify** (1). **3.** To rid of obstructions ► free, open, remove, unblock. *See also* **rid. 4.** To make or keep an area clean and orderly ► neaten (up), spruce (up), straighten (up). *See* **tidy** (1). **5.** To free from an entanglement ► disengage, free, untangle. *See* **extricate. 6.** To remove the contents of ► clean out, evacuate. *See* **empty** (1). **7.** To relieve a burden ► discharge, relieve, unburden. *See* **rid. 8.** To destroy all traces of ► eradicate, liquidate, obliterate. *See* **annihilate** (1). **9.** To free from a charge or imputation of guilt ► absolve, acquit, discharge, exculpate, exonerate, justify, purge, vindicate. *Idiom:* get off the hook. *See also* **forgive. 10.** To pass by or over safely or

successfully ▶ hurdle, negotiate, surmount. **11.** To set right by giving what is due ▶ discharge, satisfy. *See* **settle** (3). **12.** To make as income or profit ▶ draw, gain, yield. *See* **return** (3). **13.** To be accepted or approved ▶ affiliate, carry. *See* **pass** (16).

clear *adverb*
Informal To the fullest extent ▶ fully, totally, utterly. *See* **completely** (1).

clear out *verb*
Informal To leave hastily ▶ bolt. *Slang:* scram, vamoose. *See* **run** (3).

clear up *verb*
To find a solution for ▶ explain, resolve, unravel. *See* **solve** (1). *See synonym note at* **solve**.

✦ CORE SYNONYMS: *clear, limpid, lucid, pellucid, transparent.* These adjectives mean free from what obscures or dims: *clear, sediment-free claret; limpid blue eyes; lucid air; a pellucid brook; transparent crystal.*

---

clearance *noun*
▶ eradication, purge. *See* **elimination** (1).

clear-cut *adjective*
1. Readily seen, perceived, or understood ▶ crystal clear, pronounced, unmistakable. *See* **apparent** (1). *See synonym note at* **apparent**. **2.** Without any doubt ▶ definite, unquestionable. *See* **decided** (1). **3.** Clearly, fully, and emphatically expressed ▶ decided, explicit, precise. *See* **definite** (1).

clearing *noun*
▶ field, meadow, pasture. *See also* **lot**.

clearness *noun*
1. The quality of being clear and easy to perceive or understand ▶ distinctness, lucidity, perspicuity, plainness. *See* **clarity** (1). **2.** The quality or condition of being visible or providing a clear view ▶ clarity, observability, visuality. *See* **visibility**.

clear-sightedness *noun*
▶ keenness, perceptiveness, shrewdness. *See* **discernment** (1).

cleavage *noun*
▶ break, cleft, fissure. *See* **crack** (2).

cleave¹ *verb*
1. To separate into parts with or as if with a sharp-edged instrument ▶ carve, sever. *See* **cut** (2). **2.** To undergo partial breaking ▶ rupture, split. *See* **crack** (1).

cleave² *verb*
To form a tight bond ▶ adhere, cohere. *See* **bond**.

cleft *noun*
▶ break, rift, fissure. *See* **crack** (2).

clemency *noun*
▶ charity, grace, mercifulness. *See* **mercy**. *See synonym note at* **mercy**.

clement *adjective*
1. Free from extremes in temperature ▶ balmy, mild, moderate, temperate. *See also* **pleasant**. **2.** Not strict or severe ▶ easy, indulgent, lenient. *See* **tolerant** (1).

clench *verb*
1. To take firmly with the hand and maintain a hold on ▶ clutch, grab, grip. *See* **grasp** (1). **2.** To move a

door, for example, in order to cover an opening ▶ close, seal, shut, slam.

clench *noun*
An act or means of holding something ▶ clasp, grasp. *See* **hold** (1).

clergyman *or* **clergywoman** *noun*
▶ ecclesiastic, minister, parson. *See* **cleric**.

cleric *noun*
A person ordained for service in a Christian church ▶ abbé, abbot, bishop, chaplain, churchman, churchwoman, clergyman, clergywoman, clerical, clerk, curate, deacon, divine, ecclesiastic, minister, monk, parson, pastor, preacher, prelate, priest, rector, vicar. *Informal:* padre, reverend.

clerical *adjective*
Of or relating to the clergy, especially in a Christian church ▶ ecclesiastical, episcopal, ministerial, pastoral, priestly, sacerdotal. *See also* **spiritual**.

clerical *noun*
A person ordained for service in a Christian church ▶ ecclesiastic, minister, parson. *See* **cleric**.

clerk *noun*
1. One who sells ▶ salesclerk, vendor. *See* **seller**. **2.** A person ordained for service in a Christian church ▶ ecclesiastic, minister, parson. *See* **cleric**.

clever *adjective*
1. Mentally quick and original ▶ acute, alert, bright, ingenious, intelligent, inventive, keen, quick, quick-thinking, quick-witted, resourceful, sharp, sharp-witted, shrewd, smart. *Idioms:* nobody's fool, on the ball (*or* beam), quick on the uptake, sharp as a tack, smart as a whip. *See also* **artful, intelligent, shrewd**. **2.** Exhibiting or employing wit or originality ▶ humorous, scintillating, smart, sparkling, witty. *See also* **funny, sarcastic**. **3.** Exhibiting or possessing skill and ease in performance ▶ deft, facile, nimble. *See* **dexterous**.

✦ CORE SYNONYMS: *clever, ingenious, shrewd.* These adjectives refer to mental adroitness or to practical ingenuity and skill. *Clever* is the most comprehensive: *"Everybody's family doctor was remarkably clever, and was understood to have immeasurable skill in the management and training of the most skittish or vicious diseases"* (George Eliot). *Ingenious* implies originality and inventiveness: *"an ingenious solution to the storage problem"* (Linda Greider). *Shrewd* emphasizes mental astuteness and practical understanding: *"a woman of shrewd intellect"* (Leslie Stephen).

---

cleverness *noun*
1. The faculty of thinking, reasoning, and applying knowledge ▶ brainpower, understanding. *See* **intelligence** (1). *See synonym note at* **intelligence**. **2.** Deceitful contrivance ▶ artfulness, slyness. *See* **art** (1). **3.** Skillfulness in the use of the hands or body ▶ deftness, prowess. *See* **dexterity** (1).

cliché *noun*
A trite expression or idea ▶ banality, bromide, com-

monplace, platitude, saw, stereotype, truism. *Idiom:* old chestnut.

✦ CORE SYNONYMS: *cliché, bromide, commonplace, platitude, truism.* These nouns denote an expression or idea that has lost its originality or force through overuse: *a short story weakened by clichés; the old bromide that we are what we eat; uttered the commonplace "welcome aboard"; a eulogy full of platitudes; a once-original thought that has become a truism.*

---

clichéd *adjective*
▸ banal, overused, stale, tired. *See* **trite.**
click *noun*
A light, sharp noise ▸ clack, crackle, snap. *See also* **crack.**
click *verb*
1. To make a light, sharp noise ▸ clack, snap. *See also* **crackle.** 2. *Slang* To turn out well ▸ go over, pan out, work out. *See* **succeed** (2). 3. *Slang* To interact with another or others in a harmonious fashion ▸ connect, harmonize. *See* **relate** (5).
client *noun*
▸ customer, patron, user. *See* **consumer.**
clientele *or* **clientage** *noun*
▸ constituency, custom. *See* **patronage** (3).
climacteric *noun*
A decisive point ▸ crossroads, juncture. *See* **crisis** (1).
climacteric *adjective*
Demanding immediate attention ▸ crucial, dire, pressing. *See* **urgent** (1).
climactic *adjective*
1. Of or constituting a climax ▸ crowning, culminating, peak. *See also* **last.** 2. Suggesting drama or a stage performance, as in emotionality or suspense ▸ melodramatic, sensational, spectacular. *See* **dramatic** (2).
climate *noun*
1. The surrounding conditions and circumstances affecting growth or development ▸ atmosphere, surroundings. *See* **environment** (2). 2. A prevailing quality, as of thought, behavior, or attitude ▸ mood, spirit, tone. *See* **temper** (3).
climax *noun*
1. The highest point or state ▸ acme, apex, apogee, cap, crest, crown, culmination, fastigium, height, meridian, peak, pinnacle, pitch, roof, summit, top, vertex, zenith. *Informal:* payoff. *See also* **crisis, face.** 2. A decisive point ▸ crossroads, juncture. *See* **crisis** (1).
climax *verb*
To reach or bring to a climax ▸ cap (off), crescendo, crest, crown, culminate, peak, top (off *or* out).

✦ CORE SYNONYMS: *climax, summit, peak, pinnacle, acme, apex, zenith.* These nouns all mean the highest point. *Climax* refers to the point of greatest strength, effect, or intensity that marks the endpoint of an ascending process: *The government's collapse was the climax of a series of constitutional crises. Summit* denotes the highest level attainable: *"This [appointment] had been the summit of Mr. Bertram's ambition"* (Sir Walter Scott). *Peak* usually refers to the

uppermost point: *"It was the peak of summer in the Berkshires"* (Saul Bellow). *Pinnacle* denotes a towering height, as of achievement: *The articulation of the theory of relativity catapulted Einstein to the pinnacle of his profession. Acme* refers to an ultimate point, as of perfection: *The artist's talents were at their acme when this work was created. Apex* is the culminating point: *The military regime represented the apex of oppression and intimidation. Zenith* is the point of highest achievement, most complete development, or greatest power: *"Chivalry was then in its zenith"* (Henry Hallam).

---

climb *verb*
1. To move upward along a suface or slope ▸ clamber, go up, mount. *See* **ascend** (1). 2. To move from a lower to a higher position ▸ ascend, lift, soar. *See* **rise** (3). *See synonym note at* **rise.** 3. To attain a higher status, rank, or condition ▸ ascend, climb, mount. *See* **rise** (6).
climb *noun*
The act of rising or moving upward ▸ lift, mounting. *See* **ascent** (1).
climbing *verb*
The act of rising or moving upward ▸ lift, mounting. *See* **ascent** (1).
clinch *verb*
1. *Slang* To put one's arms around affectionately ▸ enfold, hug. *See* **embrace** (1). 2. To make up or cause to make up one's mind ▸ determine, settle. *See* **decide** (1). 3. *Informal* To render certain ▸ ensure, warrant. *See* **guarantee** (2).
clinch *noun*
Slang The act of embracing ▸ hug, squeeze. *See* **embrace.**
clincher *noun*
Informal A key resource to be used at an opportune moment ▸ ace, trump, trump card. *Idiom:* ace in the hole.
cling *verb*
▸ cleave, cohere. *See* **bond.**
clinging *adjective*
1. Persistently holding to something ▸ fast, firm, tenacious. *See* **tight** (1). 2. Fearful of the loss of position or affection ▸ clutching, green-eyed, jealous, possessive. *See also* **envious.**
clink *noun*
Slang A place for the confinement of persons in lawful detention ▸ brig, penitentiary, prison. *See* **jail.**
clinker *noun*
1. *Informal* An unsuccessful enterprise ▸ bust, washout. *See* **failure** (1). 2. *Slang* A stupid, clumsy mistake ▸ bungle, fumble, solecism. *See* **blunder.**
clip¹ *verb*
1. To decrease, as in length or amount, by or as if by severing or excising ▸ chop, prune, trim. *See* **cut** (3). 2. *Informal* To deliver a sudden, sharp blow to ▸ jab, sock, whack. *See* **hit** (1). 3. *Slang* To get something by deceitful trickery ▸ defraud, swindle. *See* **cheat** (1).
clip *noun*
1. *Informal* Rate of motion or performance ▸ pace, speed, tempo, velocity. 2. *Informal* A sudden heavy

stroke ▸ crack, hit, swat, whack. *See* **blow²** (1).

clip² *verb*

1. To join one thing to another ▸ append, fasten, secure. *See* **attach** (1). **2.** To make secure ▸ bind, chain, moor. *See* **fasten** (1).

clip *noun*

A device for locking ▸ catch, clasp, lock. *See* **fastener**.

clippers *noun*

▸ pruner, scissors. *See* **shears**.

clique *noun*

A small group of friends or associates ▸ coterie, group, set. *See* **circle** (3).

cloaca *noun*

▸ cesspool, gutter, sewer. *See* **pit¹** (3).

cloak *noun*

1. A garment wrapped about a person ▸ shawl, stole, wrap. *See also* **scarf**. **2.** A covering that obscures or hides something ▸ cover, screen. *See* **veil** (1).

cloak *verb*

1. To cover as if with clothes ▸ drape, robe. *See* **clothe** (1). *See synonym note at* **clothe**. **2.** To surround and cover completely so as to obscure ▸ clothe, enshroud, invest. *See* **wrap** (2). **3.** To prevent something from being known ▸ enshroud, mask. *See* **conceal** (1). **4.** To change or modify so as to prevent recognition of the true identity or character of ▸ camouflage, dissemble, mask. *See* **disguise**.

cloak-and-dagger *adjective*

▸ clandestine, sub-rosa, undercover. *See* **secret** (1).

clobber *verb*

1. *Slang* To hit heavily and repeatedly ▸ assault, batter, pummel, thresh. *See* **beat** (1). **2.** *Informal* To render totally ineffective by decisive defeat ▸ crush, overcome, overpower, rout. *See* **overwhelm** (1).

clobbering *noun*

▸ overthrow, trouncing, vanquishment. *See* **defeat**.

clock *verb*

To record the speed or duration of ▸ time. *See also* **measure**.

clod *noun*

1. An irregularly shaped mass of indefinite size ▸ cake, wad. *See* **lump¹** (1). **2.** A mentally dull person ▸ dummy, dunce, thickhead. *See* **dullard**.

cloddish *adjective*

1. Lacking in or showing a lack of intelligence ▸ dumb, idiotic, obtuse. *See* **stupid** (1). **2.** Lacking desterity and grace in physical movement ▸ clumsy, gawky, graceless. *See* **awkward** (1).

cloddishness *noun*

▸ idiocy, mindlessness, obtuseness. *See* **stupidity**.

clodhopper *noun*

A clumsy, unsophisticated person ▸ bumpkin, hick, peasant, rustic, yokel. *Informal:* hillbilly. *Slang:* hayseed, rube. *See also* **boor, oaf**.

clog *noun*

Something that blocks entry or passage ▸ barrier, blockage, hindrance. *See* **bar** (1).

clog *verb*

1. To plug up or block something, such as a hole or conduit ▸ block, cork. *See* **fill** (2). **2.** To block or fill with obstacles ▸ barricade, blockade. *See* **obstruct** (1). **3.** To cause to be later or slower than expected or desired ▸ hang up, retard, stall. *See* **delay** (1).

cloister *verb*

To put into solitude ▸ isolate, seclude, sequester, sequestrate. *See also* **enclose, imprison, isolate**.

clomp *verb*

▸ clunk, whomp. *See* **thud**.

clone *verb*

1. To make a copy of ▸ imitate, replicate, reproduce. *See* **copy** (1). **2.** To copy another slavishly ▸ echo, imitate. *See* **mimic** (1).

clone *noun*

One exactly resembling another ▸ duplicate, spitting image, twin. *See* **double** (1).

close *adjective*

1. Not far from another in space, time, or relation ▸ adjacent, contiguous, immediate, near, nearby, neighboring, nigh, proximate. *Idioms:* a stone's throw, at hand, next to, within hailing (*or* spitting) distance, under one's nose, within an inch, within hailing distance. *See also* **adjoining**. **2.** Consistent with correctness, accuracy, or completeness ▸ exact, faithful, full, rigorous, strict. *See also* **careful, thorough**. **3.** Very closely associated ▸ chummy, cozy, familiar. *See* **intimate¹** (1). **4.** Indicating intimacy and mutual trust ▸ close, personal. *See* **confidential** (2). **5.** Having all parts near to each other ▸ crowded, dense, tight. *See* **thick** (2). **6.** Almost even ▸ nip and tuck, tight. *Idiom:* neck and neck. **7.** Affording little room for movement ▸ confining, cramped, snug. *See* **tight** (4). **8.** Lacking fresh air ▸ stifling, stuffy. *See* **airless** (1). **9.** Habitually untalkative ▸ reticent, silent, uncommunicative. *See* **taciturn**. **10.** Ungenerously or pettily reluctant to spend money ▸ cheap, miserly, parsimonious. *See* **stingy** (1).

close *verb*

1. To move a door, for example, in order to cover an opening ▸ clench, seal, shut, slam. **2.** To plug up or block something, such as a hole or conduit ▸ clog, cork. *See* **fill** (2). **3.** To bring or come to a natural or proper end ▸ finish, terminate. *See* **conclude** (1). *See synonym note at* **conclude**. **4.** To come together from different directions ▸ converge, join, meet, unite. *See also* **combine**. **5.** To confine within a limited area ▸ cage, coop (up), shut (in). *See* **enclose** (1).

close in *verb*

To surround and advance upon ▸ besiege, envelop, hem. *See* **enclose** (2).

close off *verb*

To set apart from a group ▸ cut off, segregate, sequester. *See* **isolate** (1).

close out *verb*

To get rid of by selling ▸ dispose of, dump, sell off, unload.

close *noun*

1. A concluding or terminating ▸ cease, completion, termination. *See* **end** (1). **2.** The last part ▸ closing, ending, epilogue. *See* **end** (2). **3.** A roofless area partially or entirely enclosed by walls or buildings ▸ courtyard, enclosure, quad. *See* **court** (1).

close *adverb*

To a point near in time, space, or relation ▸ closely, hard, near, nearby, nigh.

✦ CORE SYNONYMS: *close, immediate, near, nearby, nigh, proximate.* These adjectives mean not far from another in space, time, or relationship: *an airport close to town; her immediate family; his nearest relative; a nearby library; our nighest neighbor; the proximate neighborhood.*

◂ ANTONYM: *far*

---

closed-door *adjective*

Belonging or confined to a particular person or group as opposed to the public or the government ▸ personal, private, privy. *See also* **confidential, secret.**

close-fisted *adjective*

▸ miserly, penny-pinching. *See* **stingy** (1).

closely *adverb*

▸ near, nearby. *See* **close.**

close-minded *adjective*

▸ bigoted, hidebound, illiberal. *See* **intolerant** (1).

close-mouthed *adjective*

▸ reticent, silent, uncommunicative. *See* **taciturn.**

closeness *noun*

1. The condition of being friends ▸ camaraderie, companionship, fellowship. *See* **friendship. 2.** The condition or degree of being dense or close together ▸ compaction, density. *See* **thickness** (1).

closet *verb*

To confine within a limited area ▸ cage, confine, shut in. *See* **enclose** (1).

closing *adjective*

Coming after all others ▸ concluding, final. *See* **last**[1] (1).

closing *noun*

1. A concluding or terminating ▸ cease, completion, termination. *See* **end** (1). **2.** The last part ▸ close, ending, epilogue. *See* **end** (2).

closure *noun*

▸ cease, completion, termination. *See* **end** (1).

clot *verb*

To change or be changed from a liquid into a soft, semisolid, or solid mass ▸ congeal, set. *See* **coagulate.** *See synonym note at* **coagulate.**

clot *noun*

An irregularly shaped mass of indefinite size ▸ clod, wad. *See* **lump**[1] (1).

clothe *verb*

1. To cover as if with clothes ▸ cloak, coat, drape, jacket, mantle, robe, shawl, vest. **2.** To put clothes on ▸ apparel, costume, garb. *See* **dress** (1). **3.** To surround and cover completely so as to obscure ▸ cloak, enshroud, invest. *See* **wrap** (2).

✦ CORE SYNONYMS: *clothe, cloak, drape, mantle, robe.* These verbs mean to cover as if with clothes: *trees* *clothed in leafy splendor; mist that cloaks the mountains; a beam draped with cobwebs; a boulder mantled with moss; snow robing fields and gardens.*

---

clothing *or* **clothes** *noun*

▸ garb, garments, raiments. *See* **dress** (1).

cloud *noun*

An enormous number of persons or things gathered together ▸ horde, mass, throng. *See* **crowd** (1).

cloud *verb*

1. To make dim ▸ blur, fog, obfuscate. *See* **obscure** (1). **2.** To attack the reputation or honor of ▸ besmirch, smear, tarnish. *See* **denigrate** (1). **3.** To addle the mind, as with a narcotic or alcohol ▸ besot, impair, stupefy. *See* **drug** (2).

cloudburst *noun*

Water condensed from atmospheric vapor and falling in drops ▸ deluge, downpour, shower. *See* **rain** (2).

clouded *adjective*

1. Liable to more than one interpretation ▸ dubious, questionable, unclear. *See* **ambiguous** (1). **2.** Darkened or clouded with sediment ▸ muddy, roiled, turbid. *See* **murky** (1).

cloudiness *noun*

▸ ambiguousness, equivocalness, unclearness. *See* **vagueness.**

cloudless *adjective*

▸ fair, fine. *See* **clear** (2).

cloud nine *noun*

Informal A supremely beautiful, blissful state or experience ▸ ecstasy, paradise. *See* **heaven** (1).

cloudy *adjective*

1. Not clearly perceptible ▸ dim, faint, indefinite. *See* **unclear** (1). **2.** Darkened or clouded with sediment ▸ muddy, roiled, turbid. *See* **murky** (1). **3.** Liable to more than one interpretation ▸ equivocal, nebulous, vague. *See* **ambiguous** (2).

clout *noun*

1. A sudden heavy stroke ▸ crack, hit, swat, whack. *See* **blow**[2] (1). **2.** *Informal* Power to sway or affect based on prestige, wealth, ability, or position ▸ force, sway, weight. *See* **influence** (1).

clout *verb*

To deliver a sudden, sharp blow to ▸ jab, sock, whack. *See* **hit** (1).

clown *noun*

A person whose words or actions provoke or are intended to provoke amusement or laughter ▸ comedian, humorist, jokester. *See* **joker.**

clown *verb*

Informal To make jokes; behave playfully ▸ jest, joke, quip. *Informal:* clown (around), fool around, horse around. *Idioms:* crack wise, play the fool. *See also* **play.**

cloy *verb*

▸ engorge, surfeit. *See* **satiate.**

club *noun*

A group of people united in a relationship and having some interest, activity, or purpose in common ▸ association, league, order. *See* **union** (1).

club *verb*
To hit heavily and repeatedly ▸ assault, batter, pummel, thresh. *See* **beat** (1).

clue *noun*
1. An item of advance or inside information given as a guide to action ▸ lead, scent, steer. *See* **tip³** (1). **2.** A brief or indirect suggestion ▸ cue, suggestion. *See* **hint** (2).

clueless *adjective*
1. Without education or knowledge ▸ uncultivated, unlearned. *See* **ignorant** (1). **2.** Not aware or informed ▸ oblivious, misguided, unaware. *See* **ignorant** (3).

clump *noun*
1. An irregularly shaped mass of indefinite size ▸ clod, wad. *See* **lump¹** (1). **2.** A number of individuals making up or considered a unit ▸ body, cluster, collection. *See* **group** (1).

clump *verb*
1. To move heavily or clumsily ▸ flounder, galumph, hulk. *See* **blunder** (1). **2.** To make a dull sound by or as if by striking a surface with a heavy object ▸ clunk, whomp. *See* **thud.**

clumsy *adjective*
1. Lacking dexterity and grace in physical movement ▸ gawky, graceless. *Slang:* klutzy. *See* **awkward** (1). **2.** Difficult to manage ▸ ungainly, unwieldy. *See* **awkward** (2). **3.** Clumsily lacking in the ability to do ▸ bumbling, inept. *See* **unskillful** (1). **4.** Lacking sensitivity and skill in dealing with others ▸ gauche, impolitic, undiplomatic. *See* **tactless.**

clunk *noun*
A stroke or blow that produces a sound ▸ thud, thump. *See* **beat** (1).

clunk *verb*
To make a dull sound by or as if by striking a surface with a heavy object ▸ clomp, whomp. *See* **thud.**

clunker *noun*
Informal An unsuccessful enterprise ▸ bust, washout. *See* **failure** (1).

cluster *noun*
A number of individuals making up or considered a unit ▸ body, clump, collection. *See* **group** (1).

cluster *verb*
To come, bring, or call together ▸ convene, convoke, summon. *See* **assemble** (1).

clutch¹ *verb*
1. To take firmly with the hand and maintain a hold on ▸ clasp, grab, grip. *See* **grasp** (1). **2.** To get hold of something moving ▸ seize, snatch. *See* **catch** (2).

clutch *noun*
1. The act of catching ▸ seizure, snatch. *See* **catch** (1). **2.** An act or means of holding something ▸ clench, grasp. *See* **hold** (1). **3.** A closeable container for carrying money and personal items ▸ bag, handbag, pocketbook. *See* **purse. 4.** A decisive point ▸ crossroads, juncture. *See* **crisis** (1).

clutch² *noun*
A number of individuals making up or considered a unit ▸ body, cluster, collection. *See* **group** (1).

clutching *adjective*
Fearful of the loss of position or affection ▸ clinging, green-eyed, jealous, possessive. *See also* **envious.**

clutter *noun*
1. A lack of order or regular arrangement ▸ chaos, confusion, disarray. *See* **disorder** (1). **2.** To put out of proper order ▸ disarrange, disrupt, muddle. *See* **disorder** (1).

cluttered *adjective*
▸ crowded, fussy. *See* **busy** (3).

coach *verb*
To impart knowledge and skill to ▸ discipline, instruct. *See* **educate** (1).

coach *noun*
One who educates ▸ instructor, trainer, tutor. *See* **educator.**

coaction *noun*
▸ collaboration, teamwork. *See* **cooperation** (1).

coactive *adjective*
▸ collective, concerted, joint, synergistic. *See* **cooperative** (1).

coadjutant *noun*
▸ aide, helper. *See* **assistant.** *See synonym note at* **assistant.**

coadjutor *noun*
▸ deputy, help. *See* **assistant.** *See synonym note at* **assistant.**

coagulate *verb*
To change or be changed from a liquid into a soft, semisolid, or solid mass ▸ clot, congeal, curdle, gelatinize, jell, jelly, set, stiffen. *Chiefly Regional:* clabber. *See also* **harden.**

✚ CORE SYNONYMS: *coagulate, clot, congeal, curdle, jell, jelly, set.* These verbs mean to change or be changed from a liquid into a soft, semisolid, or solid mass: *egg white coagulating when heated; blood clotting over the wound; gravy congealing as it cools; milk that had curdled; used pectin to jell the jam; jellied consommé; allowed the aspic to set.*

---

coalesce *verb*
1. To bring or come together into a united whole ▸ join, unify, unite. *See* **combine** (1). **2.** To combine into one mass or mixture ▸ blend, fuse, stir. *See* **mix** (1). *See synonym note at* **mix.**

coalition *noun*
1. An association for a common cause or interest ▸ bloc, organization, union. *See* **alliance** (1). **2.** A bringing together into a whole ▸ consolidation, union. *See* **unification** (1).

coarse *adjective*
1. Lacking in delicacy or refinement ▸ barbarian, barbaric, boorish, churlish, common, crass, crude, gross, ill-bred, indelicate, inelegant, philistine, plebeian, rough, rude, tasteless, unbecoming, uncivilized, uncouth, uncultivated, uncultured, unpolished, unrefined, vulgar. *Informal:* tacky. *See also* **abrupt, improper, rustic. 2.** Of low or lower quality ▸ inadequate, poor, unsatisfactory. *See* **bad** (1). **3.** Offensive

to accepted standards of decency ► bawdy, indecent, lewd, vulgar. *See* **obscene** (1). **4.** Consisting of or covered with large particles ► grainy, granular, gravelly, gritty, rough, sabulous, sandy. **5.** Having a surface that is not smooth ► craggy, ragged, scabrous. *See* **rough** (1).

coarseness *noun*
1. The quality or state of being obscene ► filthiness, profanity, smuttiness, vulgarness. *See* **obscenity** (1). **2.** Lack of smoothness or regularity ► abrasiveness, roughness, unevenness. *See* **irregularity** (1).

coast *verb*
1. To move smoothly, continuously, and effortlessly ► float, slide, slither. *See* **glide** (1). *See synonym note at* **glide**. **2.** *Informal* To progress quickly and effortlessly ► skate, sail. *See* **breeze**. **3.** To ride or be pulled on a sled in the snow ► sled, sledge, sleigh-ride, slide. *Idioms:* go sledding (*or* coasting *or* sleigh-riding).

coat *noun*
1. An outer garment that has sleeves ► anorak, jacket, mackintosh, overcoat, parka, raincoat, slicker, sport coat, sport jacket, sports coat, sports jacket, suit coat, suit jacket, trench coat, windbreaker. **2.** A layer of material covering something else ► blanket, coating, covering, crust, dusting, layer, overlay, sheet. *See also* **face, finish, skin**.

coat *verb*
1. To extend over the surface of ► blanket, spread. *See* **cover** (1). **2.** To apply a surface material to ► paint, varnish. *See* **finish** (3). **3.** To cover as if with clothes ► drape, robe. *See* **clothe** (1).

coating *noun*
► blanket, covering, overlay. *See* **coat** (2).

coax *verb*
1. To persuade or try to persuade by gentle persistent urging or flattery ► blandish, cajole, honey, wheedle. *Informal:* soft-soap, sweet-talk. *See also* **flatter**. **2.** To succeed in causing a person to act or think in a certain way ► convince, prevail on, talk into. *See* **persuade** (1).

cock *noun*
► fixture, spigot. *See* **faucet**.

cock-and-bull story *noun*
► falsehood, fib, untruth. *See* **lie²**.

cockcrow *noun*
► daybreak, sunrise, sunup. *See* **dawn** (1).

cockeyed *adjective*
1. *Informal* Displaying a lack of good sense ► daft, idiotic, ludicrous. *See* **foolish**. **2.** *Informal* Stupefied, excited, or muddled with alcoholic liquor ► intoxicated, sodden, tipsy. *See* **drunk**.

cocktail lounge *noun*
► inn, pub, saloon. *See* **bar** (2).

cocky *adjective*
► bombastic, swollen, vaunting. *See* **boastful**.

coddle *verb*
1. To treat indulgently ► indulge, pamper. *See* **baby**. *See synonym note at* **baby**. **2.** To cook in hot water ► boil, simmer. *See* **cook** (1).

codify *verb*
To put into a deliberate order ► regiment, systematize. *See* **arrange** (1).

coequal *noun*
One that is very similar to another in rank or position ► colleague, equivalent, fellow. *See* **peer²**.

coequal *adjective*
Agreeing exactly in value, quantity, or effect ► identical, tantamount. *See* **equal** (1).

coequality *noun*
► equation, sameness. *See* **equivalence**.

coerce *verb*
1. To compel by threats ► blackjack, dragoon, force. *Informal:* hijack, strong-arm. *See also* **intimidate**. **2.** To cause a person or thing to act or move in spite of resistance ► compel, make, pressure. *See* **force** (1). *See synonym note at* **force**.

coercion *noun*
► might, power, strength. *See* **force** (1).

coercive *adjective*
Accomplished by force ► forced, forcible, violent. *Informal:* strong-arm.

coercively *adverb*
With force and violence ► forcibly, violently. *Idioms:* against one's will, by force, under duress.

coetaneous *adjective*
► coexistent, concurrent, synchronous. *See* **contemporary** (1).

coeval *adjective*
Belonging to the same period of time ► coexistent, concurrent, synchronous. *See* **contemporary** (1).

coeval *noun*
One of the same time or age as another ► contemporary.

coexistent *or* **coexisting** *adjective*
► concurrent, synchronous. *See* **contemporary** (1).

cogency *noun*
The power of an argument to convince or compel agreement ► force, forcefulness, justice, persuasiveness, weight. *Idiom:* sound reason. *See also* **eloquence, veracity, verisimilitude**.

cogent *adjective*
1. Serving to convince ► effective, persuasive. *See* **convincing** (1). **2.** Based on good judgment, reasoning, or evidence ► valid, well-founded. *See* **sound²** (1). *See synonym note at* **sound²**.

cogitate *verb*
1. To think or think about carefully and at length ► consider, deliberate, mull. *See* **ponder**. **2.** To use the powers of the mind ► cerebrate, deliberate, reflect. *See* **think** (1). *See synonym note at* **think**.

cogitation *noun*
► brainwork, deliberation, rumination. *See* **thought** (1).

cogitative *adjective*
► contemplative, pensive, reflective. *See* **thoughtful** (1).

cognate *adjective*
► akin, allied, related. *See* **kindred**.

cognizable *adjective*
‣ discernible, palpable, perceivable. *See* **perceptible**.

cognizance *noun*
1. The condition of being aware ‣ consciousness, perception, sense. *See* **awareness. 2.** The act of noting, observing, or taking into account ‣ heed, note, regard. *See* **notice** (1).

cognizant *adjective*
‣ alive, sensible, sentient. *See* **aware.** *See synonym note at* **aware.**

cognomen *noun*
‣ appellation, epithet, title. *See* **name** (1).

cohere *verb*
‣ cleave, stick. *See* **bond.**

coherence *noun*
‣ congruity, consistence. *See* **consistency.**

coherent *adjective*
‣ comprehensible, fathomable, intelligible. *See* **understandable** (1).

cohesion *noun*
1. The close physical union of two objects ‣ adhesion, attachment. *See* **bond** (3). **2.** Logical agreement among parts ‣ congruity, consistence, uniformity. *See* **consistency.**

cohort *noun*
1. One who is united in a relationship with another ‣ ally, partner. *See* **associate** (1). **2.** One who supports and adheres to another ‣ adherent, believer, disciple. *See* **follower** (1). **3.** A group of people acting together in a shared activity ‣ party, troop. *See* **band²** (1).

coil *verb*
To move or proceed on a repeatedly curving course ‣ snake, spiral, weave. *See* **wind²** (1).

coil *noun*
1. Something with a curled or spiral shape ‣ curlicue, spiral, twist. *See* **curl. 2.** A length of line folded over and joined at the ends so as to form a curve or circle ‣ circuit, noose, ring. *See* **loop** (1).

coin *verb*
‣ contrive, devise, dream up. *See* **invent** (1).

coincide *verb*
1. To occur at the same time ‣ concur, harmonize, synchronize. **2.** To come to an understanding or to terms ‣ accord, concur. *See* **agree** (2).

coincidence *noun*
‣ accident, fortune, luck. *See* **chance** (2).

coincident *adjective*
‣ concomitant, contemporary, simultaneous. *See* **concurrent** (1). *See synonym note at* **concurrent.**

cold *adjective*
1. Marked by a low temperature ‣ arctic, boreal, chill, chilly, cool, freezing, frigid, frosty, gelid, glacial, icy, nippy, polar, shivery, wintry. **Idioms:** bitter (*or* bitterly) cold. **2.** Lacking feeling or emotion ‣ cold-blooded, dispassionate, dry, emotionless, impassible, impassive, indifferent, insensible, insensitive, insusceptible, matter-of-fact, neutral, passionless, phlegmatic, stolid, thick-skinned, unaffected, unemotional, unmoved, unresponsive, unimpressionable,

unsusceptible. *See also* **apathetic, callous. 3.** Not friendly, sociable, or warm in manner ‣ aloof, chilly, impersonal. *See* **cool** (1). **4.** Deficient in or lacking sexual desire ‣ ardorless, inhibited, undersexed. *See* **frigid** (3). **5.** Lacking consciousness ‣ insensible, out. *See* **unconscious** (1).

cold *noun*
Lack of warmth ‣ chill, chilliness, coldness, coolness, frigidity, frigidness, frostiness, frozenness, iciness, nip, wintriness.

✛ CORE SYNONYMS: *cold, arctic, chilly, cool, frigid, frosty, gelid, glacial, icy.* These adjectives mean marked by a low or an extremely low temperature: *cold air; an arctic climate; a chilly day; cool water; a frigid room; a frosty morning; gelid seas; glacial winds; icy hands.*
◄ ANTONYM: *hot*

cold-blooded *adjective*
1. Lacking compassion or mercy ‣ heartless, insensitive, merciless. *See* **callous. 2.** Lacking feeling or emotion ‣ emotionless, impassive, stolid. *See* **cold** (2).

cold feet *noun*
Slang A feeling of agitation in the face of danger or trouble ‣ apprehension, consternation, trepidation. *See* **fear.**

cold-hearted *adjective*
‣ heartless, insensitive, merciless. *See* **callous.**

coldness *noun*
1. Lack of warmth ‣ chilliness, frigidity, iciness. *See* **cold. 2.** Lack of cordiality and hospitableness ‣ inhospitableness, uncivility, unreceptiveness. *See* **inhospitality.**

coldshoulder *verb*
Informal To slight someone deliberately ‣ shun, spurn. *See* **snub.**

cold shoulder *noun*
Informal A deliberate slight ‣ cut, shun, spurn. *See* **snub.**

collaborate *verb*
‣ concur, unite. *See* **cooperate.**

collaboration *noun*
‣ synergy, teamwork. *See* **cooperation** (1).

collaborative *adjective*
‣ collective, joint, synergistic. *See* **cooperative** (1).

collapse *verb*
1. To suddenly lose all health or strength ‣ break (down), cave in, crack, drop, give out, succumb. *Informal:* crack up. *Slang:* conk out. **Idiom:** give way. *See also* **fade, faint, tire. 2.** To undergo sudden financial failure ‣ crash, fail, go under. *Informal:* fold. **Idioms:** go bankrupt, go belly up, go broke, go bust, go down the tubes, go on the rocks, go to the wall. *See also* **fail, ruin. 3.** To give way mentally and emotionally ‣ crack, fold, snap. *See* **break** (5). **4.** To fall in ‣ cave in, give. *See* **buckle** (1). **5.** To undergo capture, defeat, or ruin ‣ fall, go down, go under, topple. *See also* **succumb, surrender.**

collapse *noun*
1. A sudden sharp decline in mental, emotional, or

physical health ▸ breakdown. *Informal:* crackup. *See also* **infirmity. 2.** An abrupt disastrous failure ▸ breakdown, catastrophe, crash, debacle, disaster, smash, smashup, wreck. *See also* **failure. 3.** A disastrous defeat or ruin ▸ fall, downfall, waterloo. *See also* **defeat. 4.** An interruption in friendly relations ▸ break, estrangement, fissure. *See* **breach** (2).

collar *noun*
1. A device for locking ▸ catch, clip, lock. *See* **fastener. 2.** *Slang* A seizing and holding by law ▸ apprehension, seizure. *Slang:* pinch. *See* **arrest** (1).

collar *verb*
To take into custody as a prisoner ▸ seize. *Informal:* nab, pick up. *See* **arrest** (1).

collate *verb*
▸ contrast, counterpose, juxtapose. *See* **compare** (1).

collateral *adjective*
1. Lying in the same plane and not intersecting ▸ parallel. *Idiom:* side by side. **2.** Giving or able to give help or support ▸ assistant, subsidiary. *See* **auxiliary** (1). **3.** Below another in standing, importance, or status ▸ secondary, subordinate. *See* **minor** (1).

collateral *noun*
Something given to guarantee the repayment of a loan or the fulfillment of an obligation ▸ security, token, warrant. *See* **pawn**[1].

collateralize *verb*
▸ deposit, pledge. *See* **pawn**[1].

collation *noun*
1. The act or state of being contrasted ▸ comparison, juxtaposition. *See* **contrast. 2.** A light meal ▸ snack. *Informal:* nosh. *See* **refreshment** (1).

colleague *noun*
1. One that is very similar to another in rank or position ▸ equivalent, fellow. *See* **peer**[2]. **2.** One who is united in a relationship with another ▸ ally, partner. *See* **associate** (1). *See synonym note at* **associate.**

collect[1] *verb*
1. To come, bring, or call together ▸ convene, convoke, group. *See* **assemble** (1). **2.** To bring together so as to increase in mass or number ▸ aggregate, amass, cumulate, gather. *See* **accumulate.** *See synonym note at* **accumulate. 3.** To bring one's emotions under control ▸ contain, control. *See* **compose** (6).

collect[2] *noun*
A formula of words used in praying ▸ litany, orison. *See* **prayer**[1] (2).

collected *adjective*
▸ composed, cool. *See* **calm** (1). *See synonym note at* **calm.**

collectedness *noun*
▸ aplomb, composure, coolness. *See* **balance** (2).

collectible *adjective*
▸ payable, receivable, unpaid. *See* **due** (1).

collection *noun*
1. A number of individuals making up or considered a unit ▸ body, cluster, party. *See* **group** (1). **2.** A quantity accumulated ▸ amassment, assemblage, gathering, mass. *See* **accumulation** (1).

collective *adjective*
▸ joint, synergistic. *See* **cooperative** (1).

collide *verb*
1. To come together with force ▸ bump, crash, knock, hit, impact, run into, slam, strike. *See also* **crash. 2.** To fail to be in accord ▸ contrast, disagree, discord. *See* **conflict. 3.** To strive in opposition ▸ clash, combat, fight. *See* **contend** (1).

collision *noun*
A violent forcible contact ▸ bump, concussion, crash, foul, hit, impact, jar, jolt, knock, percussion, shock, smash. *See also* **crash, slam.**

✦ **CORE SYNONYMS:** *collision, concussion, crash, impact, jar, jolt, shock.* These nouns denote violent forcible contact between two or more things: *the midair collision of two light planes; the concussion caused by an explosion; a crash involving two cars; the impact of a sledgehammer on pilings; felt repeated jars as the train ground to a halt; a series of jolts as the baby carriage rolled down the steps; experienced the physical shock of a sudden fall.*

---

collocate *verb*
▸ arrange, sort, systematize. *See* **arrange** (1).

collocation *noun*
▸ collocation, idiom, phrase. *See* **expression** (3).

colloquial *adjective*
▸ chatty, informal. *See* **conversational** (1).

colloquium *noun*
▸ discussion, parley, seminar. *See* **conference** (1).

colloquy *noun*
▸ dialogue, discourse, talk. *See* **conversation** (1).

collude *verb*
▸ conspire, scheme. *See* **plot** (2).

collusion *noun*
▸ cabal, conspiracy. *See* **plot** (2).

colonist *or* **colonial** *noun*
▸ colonial, pioneer. *See* **settler.**

colonize *verb*
▸ capture, overrun, subjugate. *See* **occupy** (2).

colonizer *noun*
▸ colonist, pioneer. *See* **settler.**

colony *noun*
▸ dependency, province. *See* **possession** (1).

colophon *noun*
▸ brand, label, trademark. *See* **mark** (1).

color *noun*
1. That aspect of things that is caused by differing qualities of the light reflected or emitted by them ▸ cast, hue, shade, tinge, tinct, tint, tone, undertone, wash. **2.** Something that imparts color ▸ colorant, coloring, dye, dyestuff, paint, pigment, stain, tincture. *See also* **finish. 3.** Skin tone, especially of the face ▸ coloring, complexion. **4.** A fresh rosy complexion ▸ bloom, blush, flush, glow. **5.** Appearance of truth or authenticity ▸ credibility, plausibility. *See* **verisimilitude.**

color *verb*
1. To impart color to ▸ dye, emblazon, imbue, pig-

ment, stain, tincture, tinge, tint, wash. *See also* **finish**. **2.** To become red in the face ▸ crimson, flush. *See* **blush**. **3.** To give an inaccurate view of by representing falsely or misleadingly ▸ fudge, misrepresent, pervert. *See* **distort** (1). **4.** To give a deceptively attractive appearance to ▸ gild, gloss (over), gloze (over), overlay, sugarcoat, varnish, veneer, whitewash. *Idioms:* paper over, put a good face on. *See also* **disguise, extenuate**.

colorant *noun*
▸ dye, paint, pigment. *See* **color** (2).

colorfast *adjective*
Retaining original color ▸ fast, indelible.

colorful *adjective*
1. Full of color ▸ bright, deep, fluorescent, gay, rich, vibrant, vivid. *See also* **bright**. **2.** Evoking strong mental images through distinctiveness ▸ graphic, picturesque, striking, vivid. **3.** Serving to describe ▸ graphic, representative. *See* **descriptive**. **4.** Having many different colors ▸ many-hued, polychromatic. *See* **multicolored**.

coloring *noun*
1. Something that imparts color ▸ dye, paint, pigment. *See* **color** (2). **2.** Skin tone, especially of the face ▸ color, complexion. *See also* **bloom**.

colorless *adjective*
1. Lacking color ▸ bloodless, lurid, wan. *See* **pale** (1). **2.** Lacking liveliness, charm, or surprise ▸ aseptic, deadly, pedestrian. *See* **dull** (1). *See synonym note at* **dull**. **3.** Without definite or distinctive characteristics ▸ bland, indistinctive, neutral. *See also* **boring**.

colorlessness *noun*
▸ blandness, drabness, lifelessness. *See* **dullness** (1).

colors *noun*
▸ banner, ensign, pennant. *See* **flag**¹ (1).

colossal *adjective*
▸ behemoth, gargantuan, gigantic. *See* **enormous**. *See synonym note at* **enormous**.

coltish *adjective*
▸ animated, chipper, vivacious. *See* **lively** (1).

column *noun*
1. A sturdy vertical structural support ▸ pier, pilaster, pillar, post, shaft, stud. *See also* **beam, support**. **2.** A group of people or things arranged in a row ▸ file, queue, string. *See* **line** (1).

columnist *noun*
▸ correspondent, editorialist, media. *See* **press** (1).

comatose *adjective*
▸ insensible, out. *See* **unconscious** (1).

comb *verb*
▸ forage, ransack, rummage. *See* **scour**² (1).

combat *verb*
1. To strive in opposition ▸ clash, collide, fight. *See* **contend** (1). **2.** To place in opposition or be in opposition to ▸ match, pit. *See* **oppose** (1). *See synonym note at* **oppose**.

combat *noun*
1. An encounter between opposing military forces ▸ confrontation, engagement, war. *See* **battle** (1).

2. The act or condition of conflict ▸ contradiction, polarity. *See* **opposition** (1).

combatant *noun*
One who engages in a combat or struggle ▸ belligerent, fighter, soldier, warrior. *See also* **aggressor, soldier**.

combatant *adjective*
Engaged in warfare ▸ hostile, militant. *See* **belligerent** (1).

combative *adjective*
1. Inclined to act in an aggressive or hostile way ▸ belligerent, contentious, militant. *See* **aggressive** (1). **2.** Given to arguing ▸ contentious, litigious, quarrelsome. *See* **argumentative**. *See synonym note at* **argumentative**.

combativeness *noun*
1. Hostile or warlike behavior or attitude ▸ contentiousness, militance, warmongering. *See* **aggression** (1). **2.** The power or will to fight ▸ belligerence, pugnacity. *See* **fight** (2).

combination *noun*
1. The result of combining ▸ brew, composite, compound, conjugation, entente, hybrid, incorporation, merger, unification, union, unity. *See also* **assortment, mixture**. **2.** The state of being associated ▸ alliance, conjunction. *See* **association** (1). **3.** An association for a common cause or interest ▸ bloc, coalition, organization. *See* **alliance** (1).

combine *verb*
1. To bring or come together into a united whole ▸ articulate, coalesce, compound, concrete, conjoin, conjugate, connect, consolidate, couple, integrate, join, link, marry, meld, unify, unite, wed, yoke. *See also* **mix, harmonize**. **2.** To make a part of a united whole ▸ embody, incorporate, integrate. **3.** To unite or be united in a relationship ▸ affiliate, ally, federate. *See* **associate** (1). **4.** To form a united group ▸ come together, join together, unite. *See* **band**². **5.** To work together toward a common end ▸ concur, unite. *See* **cooperate**.

combine *noun*
An association for a common cause or interest ▸ bloc, coalition, party. *See* **alliance** (1).

✦ CORE SYNONYMS: *combine, join, unite, link, connect.* These verbs mean to bring or come together into a united whole. *Combine* suggests the mixing or merging of components, often for a specific purpose: *The cook combined various ingredients.* "When bad men combine, the good must associate" (Edmund Burke). *Join* applies to the physical contact or union of at least two separate things and to the coming together of persons, as into a group: *The children joined hands. The two armies joined together to face a common enemy.* "Join the union, girls, and together say Equal Pay for Equal Work" (Susan B. Anthony). *Unite* stresses the coherence or oneness of the persons or things joined: *The volunteers united to prevent their town from flooding. The strike united the oppressed workers. Link* and *connect* imply a firm attachment in which individual components nevertheless retain their identities: *The study linked the high crime rate to unemployment. The reporter connected the police chief to the scandal.*

combined *adjective*
1. Working together toward a common end ▸ collective, joint, synergistic. *See* **cooperative** (1). 2. Mixed with other substances ▸ alloyed, diluted, polluted. *See* **impure** (2).

combust *verb*
▸ blaze, flame, flare. *See* **burn** (2).

come *verb*
1. To move forward ▸ move, proceed, progress. *See* **advance** (2). 2. To come to a particular place ▸ get in, show up, turn up. *Slang:* blow in. *See* **arrive** (1). 3. To take place ▸ befall, occur, transpire. *See* **happen** (1). 4. To have as a source ▸ derive, emanate, originate. *See* **stem** (1). 5. To have as one's home or place of origin ▸ hail, originate. *See also* **descend, stem.** 6. To come to be ▸ get (to be), grow (to be). *See* **become** (1). 7. To come to in number or quantity ▸ number, reach, total. *See* **amount** (1).

come across *verb*
1. To find or meet by chance ▸ happen on, run across, stumble on. *See* **encounter** (1). 2. *Slang* To give in common with others ▸ donate, subscribe. *See* **contribute** (1).

come around *or* **round** *verb*
1. To regain one's health ▸ convalesce, improve, recuperate. *See* **recover** (2). 2. To go to or seek out the company of someone in order to socialize ▸ drop by, look up, pop in. *See* **visit** (1).

come back *verb*
To come back to a former condition ▸ go back, reoccur, revert. *See* **return** (1).

come between *verb*
To make distant, hostile, or unsympathetic ▸ disaffect, disunite. *See* **estrange.**

come by *verb*
1. To come into possession of ▸ acquire, gain, procure. *See* **get** (1). 2. To go to or seek out the company of someone in order to socialize ▸ drop by, pop in. *See* **visit** (1).

come in *verb*
1. To come or go into a place ▸ go in, penetrate. *See* **enter** (1). 2. To complete a race or competition in a specified position ▸ finish, place, run.

come into *verb*
To receive from one who has died ▸ inherit. *Idioms:* be (*or* fall) heir to.

come on *verb*
To find or meet by chance ▸ happen on, run across, stumble on. *See* **encounter** (1).

come off *verb*
To turn out well ▸ pan out, work out. *See* **succeed** (2).

come out *verb*
1. To be made public ▸ break, get out, out, transpire. *Informal:* leak (out). *Idioms:* come out of the closet, come to light. *See also* **air, announce, appear.** 2. To come into view ▸ issue, loom, materialize. *See* **appear**

(1). 3. To make one's formal entry, as into society ▸ debut. *Idiom:* make one's bow.

come over *verb*
To go to or seek out the company of someone in order to socialize ▸ drop by, pop in. *See* **visit** (1).

come through *verb*
To exist in spite of adversity ▸ persist, pull through. *See* **survive** (1).

come to *verb*
1. To reach a goal or objective ▸ achieve, attain, gain. *See* **accomplish** (1). 2. To enter a person's mind ▸ hit, occur to. *See* **strike** (9).

come together *verb*
To form a united group ▸ join, unite. *See* **band²**.

comeback *noun*
1. A return to former prosperity or status ▸ recovery, reestablishment, restoration. *See also* **renewal, revival.** 2. Something spoken or written in return ▸ repartee, retort, riposte. *See* **answer** (1).

comedian *noun*
▸ clown, humorist, jokester. *See* **joker.**

comedic *adjective*
▸ comical, humorous, laughable. *See* **funny** (1).

comedown *noun*
▸ plunge, slide, tumble. *See* **descent** (4).

comedy *noun*
▸ funniness, ridiculousness, wittiness. *See* **humor** (1).

come-hither *adjective*
▸ bewitching, enticing, tempting. *See* **seductive.**

comely *adjective*
1. Having qualities that delight the eye ▸ attractive, gorgeous, stunning. *See* **beautiful.** *See synonym note at* **beautiful.** 2. Suitable for a particular person, condition, occasion, or place ▸ befitting, correct, right. *See* **appropriate** (1).

come-on *noun*
▸ bait, draw, enticement. *See* **lure** (1).

comer *noun*
1. One that arrives ▸ arrival, newcomer, visitor. *See also* **addition, company.** 2. One showing much promise ▸ candidate, hopeful, prospect, rising star, up-and-comer.

comestible *adjective*
Fit to be eaten ▸ eatable, edible, esculent, palatable.

comestibles *noun*
▸ fare, nourishment, victuals. *See* **food.**

comeuppance *noun*
▸ compensation, deserts, reward. *See* **due** (1).

comfort *verb*
To give support in time of grief or pain ▸ condole, console, reassure, solace, soothe, succor. *See also* **encourage, feel, help, relieve.**

comfort *noun*
1. Freedom from constraint, formality, embarrassment, or awkwardness ▸ informality, naturalness. *See* **ease** (1). 2. Steady good fortune or financial security ▸ ease, prosperousness, wealth. *See* **prosperity** (2). 3. A consoling in time of grief or pain ▸ consolation, reassurance, solace, succor. *See also* **help, pity.**

✦ CORE SYNONYMS: *comfort, console, reassure, solace.* These verbs mean to give support in time of grief or pain: *comforted the distressed child; consoling a recent widow; reassured them that everything would be all right; solaced myself with a hot cup of coffee.*

comfortable *adjective*
1. Affording pleasurable ease ▸ cozy, easeful, easy, restful, snug, soothing. *Informal:* comfy, cushy, homey, soft. 2. Being what is needed without being in excess ▸ competent, decent, satisfactory. *See* **sufficient** (1). 3. Enjoying steady good fortune or financial security ▸ well-off, well-to-do. *See* **prosperous** (1).

✦ CORE SYNONYMS: *comfortable, cozy, snug, restful.* These adjectives mean affording pleasurable ease. *Comfortable* implies the absence of sources of pain or distress: *It's important to wear comfortable shoes on the hike.* The word may also suggest peace of mind: *I felt comfortable with the decision. Cozy* suggests homey and reassuring ease: *She sat in a cozy nook near the fire. Snug* brings to mind the image of a warm, secure, compact shelter: *The children were snug in their beds. Restful* suggests a quiet conducive to tranquillity: *He spent a restful hour reading.*

◂ ANTONYM: *uncomfortable*

comfortless *adjective*
1. Causing discomfort ▸ thorny, uncomforting. *See* **uncomfortable** (1). 2. Dark and depressing ▸ bleak, desolate, somber. *See* **gloomy** (1).

comforts *noun*
▸ conveniences, resources, services. *See* **amenities** (1). *See synonym note at* **amenities.**

comfy *adjective*
Informal Affording pleasurable ease ▸ cozy, easy, snug. *See* **comfortable** (1).

comic *adjective*
Causing laughter or amusement ▸ humorous, laughable, witty. *See* **funny** (1).

comic *noun*
A person whose words or actions provoke or are intended to provoke amusement or laughter ▸ comedian, humorist, jokester. *See* **joker.**

comical *adjective*
Causing laughter or amusement ▸ amusing, droll, jocular. *See* **funny** (1).

comicalness *noun*
▸ funniness, ridiculousness, wittiness. *See* **humor** (1).

coming *adjective*
1. In the relatively near future ▸ approaching, due, forthcoming, upcoming. *Idioms:* around the corner, on the horizon. *See also* **close, imminent.** 2. Being or occurring in the time ahead ▸ later, subsequent. *See* **future.** 3. Occurring after another ▸ next, subsequent, succeeding. *See* **following** (1). 4. Showing great promise ▸ promising, up-and-coming. *Idiom:* on the way up. *See also* **encouraging.**

coming *noun*
1. The act of arriving ▸ advent, arrival, appearance.

See also **entrance.** 2. The act or fact of coming near ▸ approach, convergence, imminence, nearness. *See also* **advance, appearance.**

coming-out *noun*
The instance or occasion of being presented for the first time to society ▸ debut, presentation.

command *verb*
1. To give orders to ▸ adjure, bid, call, charge, dictate, direct, enjoin, instruct, order, summon, tell. *Idioms:* call the shots, say the word. *See also* **boss, govern.** 2. To occupy the preeminent position in ▸ control, lead, rule. *See* **dominate** (1). 3. To have at one's disposal ▸ boast, enjoy, have, hold, own, possess. *Idiom:* have at the ready. 4. To rise above, especially so as to afford a view of ▸ overlook, overshadow. *See* **dominate** (2).

command *noun*
1. An order ▸ behest, bidding, charge, commandment, dictate, dictation, direction, directive, fiat, imperative, injunction, instructions, mandate, order, word, writ. *See also* **law, ruling.** 2. The right and power to command, decide, rule, or judge ▸ control, might, sovereignty. *See* **authority** (1). 3. The act of exercising controlling power or the condition of being so controlled ▸ control, dominion, reign. *See* **domination** (1). 4. The capacity to lead others ▸ lead, leadership. 5. Natural or acquired skill or talent ▸ expertise, mastery, proficiency. *See* **ability** (1). 6. The continuous exercise of authority over a political unit ▸ control, rule. *See* **government** (1). 7. The condition or fact of being dominant ▸ authority, power, supremacy. *See* **dominance** (1).

commandeer *verb*
▸ confiscate, grab, hijack. *See* **seize** (1). *See synonym note at* **seize.**

commander *noun*
1. One who governs or leads ▸ boss, director, head, leader. *See* **chief** (1). 2. The person in charge of a ship ▸ captain, shipmaster, skipper.

commanding *adjective*
1. Exercising authority ▸ authoritative, dominant, lordly, masterful. *See also* **administrative.** 2. Exercising controlling power or influence ▸ key, predominant, reigning. *See* **dominant** (1). 3. Readily attracting notice ▸ conspicuous, outstanding, prominent. *See* **noticeable** (1).

commandment *noun*
▸ charge, directive, imperative. *See* **command** (1).

command post *noun*
▸ depot, headquarters, installation, station. *See* **base**[1] (1).

comme il faut *adjective*
▸ befitting, correct, right. *See* **appropriate** (1).

commemorate *verb*
1. To honor or keep alive the memory of ▸ memorialize. *See also* **immortalize.** 2. To mark a day or an event with ceremonies of respect, festivity, or rejoicing ▸ celebrate, keep, observe, solemnize. *See synonym note at* **celebrate.** *See also* **sanctify.**

commemoration *noun*
1. The act of observing a day or an event with ceremonies ▸ holiday, observance. *See* **celebration** (2).
2. Something, as a structure or custom, serving to honor or keep alive a memory ▸ memorial, monument, remembrance. *See also* **testimonial**.

commemorative *adjective*
Serving to honor or keep alive a memory ▸ memorial, monumental.

commence *verb*
1. To go about the initial step in doing something ▸ begin, embark, initiate. *See* **start** (1). 2. To come into being ▸ arise, originate. *See* **begin** (1).

commencement *noun*
1. The act of bringing or being brought into existence ▸ inception, initiation, start. *See* **beginning** (1). 2. The initial stage of a developmental process ▸ genesis, inception, start. *See* **birth** (2).

commend *verb*
1. To express warm approval of ▸ applaud, cheer. *See* **praise** (1). *See synonym note at* **praise**. 2. To pay a compliment to ▸ compliment, congratulate, felicitate, praise. *Idiom:* take off one's hat to. *See also* **honor**.
3. To put in the charge of another for care, use, or performance ▸ confide, delegate. *See* **entrust** (1).

commendable *adjective*
▸ deserving, laudable, worthy. *See* **admirable**.

commendation *noun*
1. An expression of warm approval ▸ acclamation, celebration, kudos. *See* **praise** (1). 2. An expression of admiration ▸ praise, tribute. *See* **compliment** (1).
3. Recognition of achievement or superiority or a sign of this ▸ award, honor. *See* **distinction** (2).

commendatory *adjective*
▸ approbatory, laudatory. *See* **complimentary** (1).

commensurate *or* **commensurable** *adjective*
▸ equivalent, proportionate. *See* **proportional** (1).

comment *noun*
1. An expression of fact or opinion ▸ aside, editorial, note, obiter dictum, observation, reflection, remark, word. *See also* **expression**. 2. Critical explanation or analysis ▸ exegesis, exposition, interpretation. *See* **commentary**.

comment *verb*
To state facts, opinions, or explanations ▸ commentate, editorialize, note, observe, opine, reflect, remark. *See also* **say**.

✦ **CORE SYNONYMS:** *comment, observation, remark.* These nouns denote an expression of fact or opinion: *made an unpleasant comment about my friend; a casual observation about the movie; an offensive personal remark.*

---

commentaries *noun*
▸ diary, reminiscences. *See* **memoir**.

commentary *noun*
Critical explanation or analysis ▸ annotation, comment, criticism, critique, exposition, exegesis, interpretation, note, notice, review. *See also* **explanation**.

commentate *verb*
▸ observe, opine, remark. *See* **comment**.

commentator *noun*
1. A person who evaluates and reports on the worth of something ▸ judge, reviewer. *See* **critic** (1). 2. A person whose occupation is journalism ▸ correspondent, editorialist. *See* **press** (1).

commerce *noun*
▸ industry, trade, traffic. *See* **business** (1). *See synonym note at* **business**.

commingle *verb*
▸ blend, fuse, stir. *See* **mix** (1).

comminute *verb*
▸ atomize, grind, mill. *See* **crush** (2).

commiserate *verb*
To experience or express compassion ▸ ache, condole, feel, sympathize. *Idioms:* be (*or* feel) sorry, have one's heart ache (*or* bleed) for someone, have one's heart go out to someone. *See also* **comfort, pity**.

commiseration *noun*
▸ compassion, empathy. *See* **pity** (1). *See synonym note at* **pity**.

commiserative *adjective*
▸ compassionate, empathetic, understanding. *See* **sympathetic**.

commission *noun*
1. An assignment one is sent to carry out ▸ errand, operation. *See* **mission** (1). 2. A document that gives permission to do something ▸ permit, warrant. *See* **license** (3).

commission *verb*
To give authority to ▸ empower, enable, license. *See* **authorize** (1). *See synonym note at* **authorize**.

commit *verb*
1. To be responsible for or guilty of an error or crime ▸ carry out, do, perpetrate. *Informal:* pull off. *See also* **perform**. 2. To be morally bound to do ▸ bind, charge, obligate, oblige, pledge. *Idiom:* be duty bound. *See also* **force, pledge**. 3. To place officially in confinement ▸ consign, institutionalize. *Informal:* send up. *See also* **imprison**. 4. To put in the charge of another for care, use, or performance ▸ confide, delegate. *See* **entrust** (1). *See synonym note at* **entrust**. 5. To assume an obligation ▸ promise, undertake. *See* **pledge** (2).

commitment *noun*
1. An act or course of action that is demanded of one, as by position, custom, law, or religion ▸ charge, imperative, obligation. *See* **duty** (1). 2. A declaration that one will or will not do a certain thing ▸ covenant, pledge, vow. *See* **promise** (1). 3. An arrangement to appear at a certain time and place ▸ date, rendezvous. *See* **engagement** (1).

committed *adjective*
1. Adhering firmly to a person, cause, duty, or faith ▸ allegiant, loyal, steadfast. *See* **faithful** (1). 2. Being legally or morally required to do something ▸ bound, compelled, obligated. *See* **obliged** (2).

commix *verb*
▸ blend, fuse, stir. *See* **mix** (1).

commixture *noun*
▶ amalgam, blend, mix. *See* **mixture** (1).
commodious *adjective*
Having plenty of room ▶ ample, capacious, roomy, spacious. *See synonym note at* **roomy.** *See also* **big, broad.**
commodity *noun*
▶ line, merchandise, ware. *See* **good** (2).
common *adjective*
1. Occurring or encountered regularly ▶ accustomed, average, commonplace, customary, daily, everyday, familiar, frequent, general, habitual, normal, ordinary, regular, routine, typical, usual, widespread, wonted. *See also* **intermittent, ordinary, prevailing. 2.** Belonging to, shared by, or applicable to all alike ▶ communal, conjoint, cooperative, general, joint, mutual, public, shared. *See also* **open. 3.** Concerned with, applicable to, or affecting the whole ▶ blanket, generic, universal. *See* **general** (1). *See synonym note at* **general. 4.** Being of no special quality or type ▶ average, mediocre, standard. *See* **ordinary** (1). **5.** Lacking high station or birth ▶ baseborn, humble, unwashed. *See* **lowly** (1). **6.** Lacking in delicacy or refinement ▶ indelicate, unbecoming, unrefined. *See* **coarse** (1). **7.** Adequate to satisfy a need, requirement, or standard ▶ average, decent, moderate. *See* **acceptable** (2). **8.** Of low or lower quality ▶ inferior, low-quality, substandard. *See* **bad** (1). **9.** Known widely and unfavorably ▶ disreputable, ill-famed, infamous. *See* **notorious** (1).
common *noun*
A tract of land set aside for public use ▶ green, lawn, park, plaza, square. *See also* **reservation.**

✦ CORE SYNONYMS: *common, ordinary, familiar.* These adjectives describe what is regularly or frequently encountered. *Common* applies to what takes place often, is widely used, or is well known: *The botanist wrote an article about the common dandelion.* The term also implies coarseness or a lack of distinction: *My wallet was stolen by a common thief. Ordinary* describes something usual that is indistinguishable from others, sometimes derogatorily: *A ballpoint pen is adequate for ordinary purposes. The critic decided to give the ordinary performance a fairly mediocre review. Familiar* applies to what is well known or quickly recognized: *Most children can recite familiar nursery rhymes.*

---

commonalty *or* **commonality** *or* **commoners** *noun*
The common people ▶ commons, crowd, hoi polloi, masses, mob, multitude, plebs, plebeians, populace, proletariat, public, rank and file, ruck, third estate. *Idioms:* the great unwashed, men (*or* women) in the street.
commonly *adverb*
▶ customarily, generally, normally. *See* **usually.**
commonplace *adjective*
1. Occurring or encountered regularly ▶ everyday, familiar, regular. *See* **common** (1). **2.** Being of no special quality or type ▶ average, mediocre, standard.

See **ordinary** (1). **3.** Without freshness or appeal because of overuse ▶ clichéd, overused, stale, tired. *See* **trite.**
commonplace *noun*
1. A trite expression or idea ▶ banality, truism. *See* **cliché.** *See synonym note at* **cliché. 2.** A regular or customary matter, condition, or course of events ▶ norm, ordinary, rule. *See* **usual.**
commons *noun*
▶ hoi polloi, masses, populace. *See* **commonalty.**
common sense *noun*
The ability to make sensible decisions ▶ judgment, mother wit, reason, sense, wisdom. *Informal:* gumption, horse sense. *See also* **discernment, prudence.**
commonsensical *or* **commonsensible** *adjective*
▶ levelheaded, prudent. *See* **sensible** (1).
commotion *noun*
1. A condition of being agitated or disturbed ▶ disturbance, turmoil, unrest. *See* **agitation** (1). **2.** Agitated, excited activity ▶ commotion, excitement, fuss. *See* **agitation** (3). **3.** A lack of civil order or peace ▶ chaos, lawlessness, misrule. *See* **disorder** (2).
communal *adjective*
1. Belonging to all alike ▶ general, mutual, public. *See* **common** (2). **2.** Of, representing, or carried on by people at large ▶ general, public, societal. *See* **popular** (1).
communalize *verb*
To place under government or group ownership or control ▶ nationalize, socialize.
communicable *adjective*
1. Capable of transmission by infection ▶ catching, infectious, taking. *See* **contagious. 2.** Disposed to be open, sociable, and talkative ▶ extroverted, gregarious. *See* **outgoing.**
communicate *verb*
1. To make known ▶ break, carry, convey, disclose, divulge, get across, impart, pass, report, reveal, tell, transmit. *See also* **air, announce, inform. 2.** To give expression to, as by gestures, facial aspects, or bodily posture ▶ convey, display. *See* **express** (3). **3.** To put into words ▶ state, utter. *See* **say** (1). **4.** To spread a disease to others ▶ carry, convey, give, infect, pass, spread, transfer, transmit. **5.** To interact with another or others in a harmonious fashion ▶ connect, harmonize. *Slang:* click. *See* **relate** (5).
communication *noun*
1. The exchange of ideas by writing, speech, or signals ▶ communion, conference, conversation, correspondence, discussion, exchange, intercommunication, interaction, intercourse, interface. *See also* **conversation, deliberation. 2.** A situation allowing exchange of ideas or messages ▶ contact, correspondence, intercommunication, touch. **3.** The act of announcing ▶ proclamation, publication. *See* **announcement** (1). **4.** Something announced or communicated ▶ announcement, notice, notification. *See* **message** (1).
communicative *adjective*
1. Disposed to be open, sociable, and talkative ▶ ex-

troverted, gregarious. *See* **outgoing. 2.** In the style of conversation ▶ colloquial, informal. *See* **conversational** (1).

communion *noun*
▶ conversation, discussion, intercourse. *See* **communication** (1).

communiqué *noun*
▶ announcement, notice, statement. *See* **message** (1).

community *noun*
1. Persons as an organized body ▶ people, society. *See* **public** (2). **2.** An area in a city or town with distinctive characteristics ▶ district, quarter. *See* **neighborhood** (1). **3.** A small group of dwellings ▶ hamlet, small town. *See* **village.**

commutation *noun*
▶ interchange, switch, trade. *See* **change** (2).

commutative *adjective*
▶ fluid, unsettled, variable. *See* **changeable** (1).

commute *verb*
▶ exchange, interchange, trade. *See* **change** (3).

comp *noun*
Informal A free ticket entitling one to transportation or admission ▶ pass. *Slang:* freebie.

compact¹ *adjective*
1. Having all parts near to each other ▶ crowded, dense, tight. *See* **thick** (2). **2.** Short, heavy, and solidly built ▶ squat, stumpy. *See* **stocky. 3.** Below average in length or size ▶ bantam, undersized. *See* **little** (1). **4.** Precisely meaningful and tersely cogent ▶ epigrammatic, pointed. *See* **pithy** (1).

compact *verb*
1. To subject to compression ▶ compress, constrict. *See* **squeeze** (1). **2.** To make smaller or narrower by binding or squeezing ▶ compress, contract, narrow. *See* **constrict** (1).

compact² *noun*
An often written acceptance of terms between parties ▶ accord, deal, pact. *See* **agreement** (1). *See synonym note at* **agreement.**

compactness *noun*
▶ compaction, density. *See* **thickness** (1).

companion *noun*
1. One who shares interests or activities with another ▶ chum, comrade. *See* **associate** (2). **2.** One that accompanies another ▶ associate, attendant. *See* **concomitant. 3.** One of a matched pair of things ▶ counterpart, duplicate. *See* **mate** (1).

companion *verb*
To be with or go with ▶ attend, chaperon, escort. *See* **accompany** (1).

companionable *adjective*
1. Enjoying company ▶ convivial, sociable. *See* **social** (1). *See synonym note at* **social. 2.** Pleasant and friendly in disposition ▶ affable, cordial, friendly, genial. *See* **amiable.**

companionless *adjective*
▶ alone, lonesome, unaccompanied. *See* **solitary** (1).

companionship *noun*
1. A pleasant association among people ▶ camarade-

rie, society. *See* **company** (5). **2.** The condition of being friends ▶ amity, chumminess, fellowship. *See* **friendship.**

company *noun*
1. A commercial organization ▶ business, concern, conglomerate, corporation, enterprise, establishment, firm, house, monopoly, multinational, partnership. *Informal:* outfit. *See also* **alliance. 2.** A number of persons who have come or been gathered together ▶ conference, congress, council. *Informal:* get-together. *See* **assembly** (1). *See synonym note at* **assembly** (1). **3.** A group of people acting together in a shared activity ▶ party, troop, unit. *See* **band²** (1). *See synonym note at* **band². 4.** A person or persons visiting one ▶ caller, guest, visitant, visitor. **5.** A pleasant association among people ▶ brotherhood, camaraderie, companionship, comradeship, fellowship, sisterhood, society. *See also* **friendship.**

company *verb*
To be with or go with ▶ attend, chaperon, escort. *See* **accompany** (1).

comparable *adjective*
1. Possessing the same or almost the same characteristics ▶ analogous, similar, uniform. *See* **like²** (1). **2.** Estimated by comparison ▶ comparative, relative.

comparative *adjective*
Estimated by comparison ▶ comparable, relative.

compare *verb*
1. To examine in order to note the similarities and differences of ▶ balance, collate, contrast, counterpoint, counterpose, juxtapose, weigh. **2.** To represent as similar ▶ analogize, equate, parallel. *See* **liken. 3.** To be equal or alike ▶ correspond, match, parallel. *See* **equal** (1).

comparison *noun*
1. The quality or state of being alike ▶ resemblance, similarity, uniformity. *See* **likeness** (1). **2.** The act or state of being contrasted ▶ collation, juxtaposition. *See* **contrast.**

compass *noun*
1. A line around a closed figure or area ▶ circuit, perimeter. *See* **circumference.** *See synonym note at* **circumference. 2.** The ability or power to seize or attain ▶ capacity, grasp, range, reach, scope. *See also* **influence. 3.** An area or set of parameters within which something or someone exists, acts, or has influence ▶ extent, realm, scope. *See* **range** (1). *See synonym note at* **range.**

compass *verb*
1. To shut in on all sides ▶ encircle, hedge, ring. *See* **surround** (1). *See synonym note at* **surround. 2.** To perceive and recognize the meaning of ▶ apprehend, follow, see. *See* **understand** (1). **3.** To perceive directly with the intellect ▶ comprehend, grasp. *See* **know** (1).

compassion *noun*
▶ commiseration, empathy. *See* **pity** (1). *See synonym note at* **pity.**

compassionate *adjective*
1. Feeling or expressing sympathy or pity ▶ commis-

erative, empathetic, understanding. *See* **sympathetic.** 2. Concerned with human welfare and the remedying of social ills ▸ charitable, humane. *See* **humanitarian.** *See synonym note at* **humanitarian.**

compassionless *adjective*
▸ heartless, insensitive, merciless. *See* **callous.**

compatible *adjective*
▸ congenial, consonant, harmonious. *See* **agreeable** (1).

compatriot *noun*
1. A person who is from one's own country ▸ countryman, countrywoman, fellow citizen, kinsman, kinswoman. 2. One who is united in a relationship with another ▸ ally, partner. *See* **associate** (1).

compeer *noun*
▸ colleague, equivalent, fellow. *See* **peer**[2].

compel *verb*
▸ coerce, make, pressure. *See* **force** (1). *See synonym note at* **force.**

compellation *noun*
▸ cognomen, epithet, title. *See* **name** (1).

compelled *adjective*
▸ bound, committed, obligated. *See* **obliged** (2).

compelling *adjective*
1. Serving to convince ▸ cogent, persuasive. *See* **convincing** (1). 2. Demanding immediate attention ▸ crucial, dire, pressing. *See* **urgent** (1).

compendious *adjective*
▸ concise, short, succinct. *See* **brief** (1).

compensate *verb*
1. To give compensation to ▸ indemnify, pay, recompense, recoup, redress, reimburse, remit, remunerate, reward, repay, requite. *See also* **settle.** 2. To act as an equalizing force to ▸ counteract, counterbalance, counterpoise. *See* **balance** (2). 3. To make ineffective by applying an opposite force ▸ negate, neutralize, outweigh. *See* **cancel** (2).

compensation *noun*
1. Something to make up for loss or damage ▸ amends, damages, indemnification, indemnity, offset, payment, quittance, recompense, recoupment, redress, reimbursement, remuneration, reparation, repayment, requital, restitution, reward, satisfaction, settlement, setoff. 2. Payment for work done ▸ earnings, pay, salary. *See* **wage.** 3. Something justly deserved ▸ comeuppance, deserts, reward. *See* **due** (1).

✦ CORE SYNONYMS: *compensation, reparation, redress, amends, restitution, indemnity.* These nouns refer to something given to make up for loss, suffering, or damage. *Compensation* is the most general term: *I received a free ticket to another concert in compensation for the concert that had been canceled. Reparation* implies recompense given to one who has suffered at the hands of another: *"reparation for our rights at home, and security against the like future violations"* (William Pitt). *Redress* involves setting an injustice right; the term may imply retaliation or punishment: *"There is no grievance that is a fit object of redress by mob law"* (Abraham Lincoln). *Amends* usually im-

plies the giving of satisfaction for a minor grievance or lesser injury: *How can I make amends for losing my temper? Restitution* is the restoration of something taken illegally: *"He attempted to enforce the restitution of the Roman lands and cities"* (George P.R. James). *Indemnity* implies repayment or reimbursement: *Homeowners demanded indemnity for the damages caused by the riot.*

compensatory *or* **compensative** *adjective*
Affording compensation ▸ reimbursable, remunerative.

compete *verb*
To strive against others for victory ▸ contend, contest, bid, emulate, play, race, rival, vie. *Idioms:* give a run for one's money, take on. *See also* **contend.**

✦ CORE SYNONYMS: *compete, contest, vie.* These verbs mean to seek to strive against others for victory: *Local hardware stores can't compete with discount outlets. I contested with other bidders for the antique. The top three students vied for the title of valedictorian.*

competence *or* **competency** *noun*
▸ capability, capacity, faculty. *See* **ability** (2).

competent *adjective*
1. Having sufficient ability or resources ▸ capable, good, skillful. *See* **able.** 2. Being what is needed without being in excess ▸ decent, satisfactory. *See* **sufficient** (1).

competition *noun*
1. A vying with others for victory or supremacy ▸ battle, contention, contest, corrivalry, race, rivalry, strife, striving, struggle, tug of war, war, warfare. *See also* **conflict.** 2. A test of skill or ability ▸ bout, contest, event, fight, game, match, meet, tournament, tourney, trial. *See also* **test, tilt.** 3. One that competes ▸ contender, opponent, rival. *See* **competitor.**

competitive *adjective*
Given to competition ▸ cutthroat, dog-eat-dog, emulous, rivalrous. *See also* **argumentative.**

competitor *noun*
One that competes ▸ challenger, competition, contender, contestant, corrival, emulator, opponent, rival. *See also* **opponent.**

complain *verb*
To express feelings of pain, dissatisfaction, or resentment ▸ carp, fuss, grouch, grumble, grump, grunt, moan, mutter, murmur, nag, repine, snivel, whimper, whine. *Informal:* crab, gripe, grouse, holler, kick, squawk, yammer. *Slang:* beef, bellyache, bitch, kvetch. *Idioms:* bitch and moan, have a bone to pick, kick up a fuss (*or* row), make a fuss (*or* stink). *See also* **object, quibble.**

complainant *noun*
One that makes a formal complaint, especially in court ▸ accuser, claimant, plaintiff.

complainer *noun*
▸ crab, grump, whiner. *See* **grouch** (1).

complaint *noun*
1. An expression of pain or dissatisfaction ▸ carp, fuss,

grievance, grouch, grumble, grunt, murmur, mutter, squawk, whimper, whine. *Informal:* gripe, grouse, yammer. *Slang:* beef, bellyache, bitch, kick, kvetch. *Idiom:* bone to pick. **2.** An expression of opposition ▸ exception, grievance, protestation. *See* **objection. 3.** A pathological condition of mind or body ▸ ailment, disorder, malady. *See* **disease** (1). **4.** The condition of being sick ▸ affliction, illness, malady. *See* **sickness** (1). **5.** An expression of opposition ▸ exception, grievance, protestation. *See* **objection.**

complaisance *noun*
▸ compliancy, deference, submissiveness. *See* **obedience.**

complaisant *adjective*
1. Ready to do favors for another ▸ agreeable, indulgent. *See* **obliging. 2.** Willing to carry out the wishes of others ▸ acquiescent, docile, submissive. *See* **obedient.**

complement *noun*
1. Something added to another for embellishment or completion ▸ add-on, accompaniment, supplement. *See* **enhancement** (1). **2.** One of a matched pair of things ▸ counterpart, duplicate. *See* **mate** (1).

complement *verb*
1. To bring to perfection or completion ▸ complete, polish, refine. *See* **perfect. 2.** To add to or make whole ▸ augment, complete, enhance, strengthen. *See* **supplement.**

complementary *or* **complemental** *adjective*
Supplying mutual needs or offsetting mutual lacks ▸ correlative, interdependent, interrelated, mutual, reciprocal, supplemental, symbiotic. *See also* **agreeable.**

complete *adjective*
1. Including every constituent or individual ▸ all, entire, full, gross, intact, integral, perfect, round, total, whole. **2.** Not shortened by omissions ▸ full-length, unabbreviated, unabridged, uncensored, uncut, unedited, unexpurgated. *See also* **continual. 3.** Having reached completion ▸ closed, concluded, consummated, done, ended, executed, finished, over, performed, terminated, through. **4.** Covering all aspects with painstaking accuracy ▸ exhaustive, full-dress. *See* **thorough** (1). **5.** Completely such, without qualification or exception ▸ all-out, pure, sheer. *See* **utter². **

complete *verb*
1. To bring or come to a natural or proper end ▸ close, finish, terminate. *See* **conclude** (1). *See synonym note at* **conclude. 2.** To bring to perfection or completion ▸ complement, polish, refine. *See* **perfect. 3.** To add to or make whole ▸ augment, complement, enrich, strengthen. *See* **supplement.**

✦ **CORE SYNONYMS:** *complete, whole, all, entire, gross, total.* These adjectives mean including every constituent or individual: *the complete vacation package included airfare, hotel, and car rental; a whole town devastated by an earthquake; all the class going on a*

field trip; entire shipments lost by the distributor; gross income; the total cost.
◂ **ANTONYM:** *partial*

---

completely *adverb*
1. To the fullest extent ▸ absolutely, all, altogether, dead, downright, entirely, flat, fully, just, perfectly, purely, quite, thoroughly, totally, utterly, well, wholly. *Informal:* clean, clear. *Idioms:* hook, line, and sinker, in toto, root and branch, through and through, to the nth degree. *See also* **absolutely, considerably, really, unusually, very. 2.** In a painstakingly complete manner ▸ comprehensively, exhaustively, intensively, thoroughly. *Idioms:* down to the ground, in and out, up and down.

completeness *noun*
The state of being entirely whole ▸ entirety, fullness, integrity, oneness, totality, wholeness.

completion *noun*
1. A concluding or terminating ▸ cease, ending, termination. *See* **end** (1). **2.** The condition of being fulfilled ▸ culmination, fulfillment, realization. *See* **fulfillment** (1).

complex *adjective*
1. Difficult to understand because of intricacy ▸ advanced, baffling, baroque, bewildering, byzantine, complicated, confounding, confusing, convoluted, crabbed, daedal, Daedalian, difficult, elaborate, entangled, inextricable, intricate, involute, involved, knotty, labyrinthine, mazy, mystifying, perplexing, puzzling, sophisticated, tangled, tortuous. *See also* **ambiguous, incomprehensible, mysterious. 2.** Consisting of two or more parts ▸ composite, compound, manifold, multiple, multiplex. *See also* **various.**

complex *noun*
1. An entity composed of interconnected parts ▸ conglomerate, group, network, syndrome, system, tissue, web. *See also* **mixture. 2.** A center of organization, supply, or activity ▸ headquarters, installation, station. *See* **base¹** (1). **3.** An exaggerated concern ▸ anxiety, neurosis, phobia. *Informal:* hang-up. *See also* **anxiety, obsession.**

✦ **CORE SYNONYMS:** *complex, complicated, intricate, involved, tangled, knotty.* These adjectives mean difficult to understand because of intricacy. *Complex* implies a combination of many associated parts: *The composer transformed a simple folk tune into a complex set of variations. Complicated* stresses elaborate relationship of parts: *The party's complicated platform confused many voters. Intricate* refers to a pattern of intertwining parts that is difficult to follow or analyze: *"No one could soar into a more intricate labyrinth of refined phraseology"* (Anthony Trollope). *Involved* stresses confusion arising from the commingling of parts and the consequent difficulty of separating them: *The movie's plot was criticized as being too involved. Tangled* strongly suggests the random twisting of many parts: *"Oh, what a tangled web we weave,/When first we practice to deceive!"* (Sir Walter Scott). *Knotty* stresses intellectual complexity leading to difficulty of solution or comprehension: *Even the professor couldn't clarify the knotty point.*

complexion *noun*
1. Skin tone, especially of the face ▸ color, coloring. *See also* **bloom, color.** 2. The combination of qualities that distinguishes an individual ▸ makeup, nature, personality. *See* **character** (1). 3. A person's customary manner of emotional response ▸ humor, nature, temperament. *See* **disposition** (1).

complexity *noun*
Something complex ▸ bewilderment, complication, elaborateness, entanglement, intricacy, perplexity. *See also* **tangle.**

compliance *or* **compliancy** *noun*
1. An act of willingly carrying out the wishes of others ▸ obedience, observance. 2. The quality or state of willingly carrying out the wishes of others ▸ complaisance, compliancy, submissiveness. *See* **obedience.**

compliant *adjective*
▸ complaisant, docile, submissive. *See* **obedient.**

complicate *verb*
To make complex, intricate, or perplexing ▸ embarrass, embroil, entangle, involve, knot, obfuscate, perplex, ravel, snarl, tangle, vex. *See also* **confuse.**

complicated *adjective*
1. Not easy to do, achieve, or master ▸ arduous, laborious, tough. *See* **difficult** (1). 2. Difficult to understand because of intricacy ▸ convoluted, elaborate, involved, labyrinthine. *See* **complex** (1). *See synonym note at* **complex.** 3. Rich in detail ▸ fancy, intricate. *See* **elaborate** (1). *See synonym note at* **elaborate.**

complication *noun*
1. Something that obstructs progress and requires great effort to overcome ▸ asperity, hardship, rigor. *See* **difficulty** (1). 2. Something complex ▸ elaborateness, intricacy. *See* **complexity.**

compliment *noun*
1. An expression of admiration or congratulation ▸ accolade, commendation, congratulations, felicitations, praise, tribute. *Informal:* congrats. *Idiom:* pat on the back. 2. An expression of warm approval ▸ acclamation, celebration, kudos. *See* **praise** (1).

compliment *verb*
1. To pay a compliment to ▸ commend, congratulate, felicitate, praise. *Idiom:* take off one's hat to. *See also* **honor.** 2. To express warm approval of ▸ applaud, commend. *See* **praise** (1). 3. To salute by raising and drinking from a glass ▸ honor, toast. *See* **drink** (4).

complimentary *adjective*
1. Serving to compliment ▸ acclamatory, approbatory, commendatory, congratulatory, encomiastic, eulogistic, laudatory. 2. Costing nothing ▸ free, gratis, gratuitous. *Idioms:* as a freebie, for free, for nothing, on the house.

comply *verb*
▸ heed, obey, observe. *See* **follow** (4).

component *noun*
A separate unit that belongs or contributes to a whole ▸ building block, piece, section. *See* **part** (1). *See synonym note at* **part.**

component *adjective*
Serving as a nondetachable part of a larger unit ▸ constituent, incorporated. *See* **built-in** (1).

comport *verb*
1. To conduct oneself in a specified way ▸ bear, behave, carry, demean. *See* **act** (1). 2. To be compatible or suitable ▸ chime, correspond, match. *See* **agree** (1).

comportment *noun*
▸ actions, conduct, deportment. *See* **behavior** (1).

compose *verb*
1. To form by artistic effort ▸ create, design, draft, indite, orchestrate, pen, produce, score, write. *See also* **invent.** 2. To create by forming, combining, or altering materials ▸ build, configure, shape. *See* **make** (1). 3. To devise and set down ▸ draft, draw up, formulate, frame. 4. To be the constituent parts of ▸ form, make up. *See also* **contain.** 5. To be the author of a published work or works ▸ author, pen, write. *See* **publish** (2). 6. To bring one's emotions under control ▸ calm down, collect, contain, control, cool, simmer down. *Idiom:* cool it. *See also* **calm.**

composed *adjective*
▸ collected, cool. *See* **calm** (1). *See synonym note at* **calm.**

composite *adjective*
Consisting of two or more parts ▸ compound, multiplex. *See* **complex** (2).

composite *noun*
1. The result of combining ▸ compound, merger, union. *See* **combination** (1). 2. Something produced by mixing ▸ amalgam, blend, mix. *See* **mixture** (1). *See synonym note at* **mixture.**

composition *noun*
1. Something that is the result of creative effort ▸ creation, invention, opus, output, piece, production, work, writing. *See also* **invention, masterpiece.** 2. A relatively brief discourse written especially as an exercise ▸ essay, paper, theme. 3. A settlement of differences through mutual concession ▸ arrangement, give-and-take, mediation, settlement. *See* **compromise.**

compos mentis *adjective*
Mentally healthy ▸ lucid, normal, rational, sane. *Idioms:* all there, in one's right mind, of sound mind. *See also* **healthy.**

composure *noun*
▸ collectedness, equanimity, sang-froid. *See* **balance** (2).

compound *verb*
To bring or come together into a united whole ▸ join, unify, unite. *See* **combine** (1).

compound *adjective*
Consisting of two or more parts ▸ composite, multiplex. *See* **complex** (2).

compound *noun*
The result of combining ▸ composite, merger, union. *See* **combination** (1).

comprehend *verb*
1. To perceive and recognize the meaning of ▸ follow, see. *See* **understand** (1). **2.** To perceive directly with the intellect ▸ apprehend, grasp. *See* **know** (1). **3.** To have as a part ▸ comprise, involve, take in. *See* **contain** (1). *See synonym note at* **contain.**

comprehensibility *noun*
▸ lucidity, perspicuity, plainness. *See* **clarity** (1).

comprehensible *adjective*
▸ appreciable, fathomable, intelligible. *See* **understandable** (1).

comprehension *noun*
Intellectual hold ▸ apprehension, grasp, grip, hold, understanding. *See also* **knowledge.**

comprehensive *adjective*
1. Covering a wide scope ▸ all-inclusive, broad, expansive. *See* **general** (2). **2.** Characterized by attention to detail ▸ full, particular, thorough. *See* **detailed** (1).

comprehensively *adverb*
▸ exhaustively, intensively, thoroughly. *See* **completely** (2).

compress *verb*
1. To subject to compression ▸ compact, constrict. *See* **squeeze** (1). **2.** To make smaller or narrower by binding or squeezing ▸ contract, narrow. *See* **constrict** (1).

compressed *adjective*
▸ crowded, dense, tight. *See* **thick** (2).

compression *noun*
▸ contraction, squeeze. *See* **constriction.**

comprise *verb*
▸ comprehend, involve, take in. *See* **contain** (1). *See synonym note at* **contain.**

compromise *noun*
A settlement of differences through mutual concession ▸ accommodation, arbitration, arrangement, composition, concession, give-and-take, mediation, settlement, tradeoff. *See also* **agreement.**

compromise *verb*
1. To make a concession ▸ accommodate, arrange, concede, settle. *Idioms:* come to an understanding, give and take, go fifty-fifty, make a deal, meet someone halfway, steer a middle course, strike a bargain. *See also* **agree, settle. 2.** To expose to possible loss or damage ▸ jeopardize, threaten. *See* **endanger.** *See synonym note at* **endanger.**

compulsion *noun*
1. Strength or energy that overcomes resistance ▸ might, power, strength. *See* **force** (1). **2.** An irrational preoccupation ▸ fetish, fixation, mania. *See* **obsession.**

compulsory *adjective*
▸ imperative, mandatory, requisite. *See* **required** (1).

compunction *noun*
1. A feeling of regret for one's sins or misdeeds ▸ contriteness, remorse, repentance. *See* **penitence.** *See synonym note at* **penitence. 2.** A feeling of uncertainty about the fitness or correctness of an action

▸ misgiving, reservation, scruple. *See* **qualm** (1). *See synonym note at* **qualm.**

compunctious *adjective*
▸ penitent, regretful, repentant. *See* **sorry** (1).

computation *noun*
1. The act, process, or result of calculating ▸ calculation, cast, figuring, reckoning. **2.** Arithmetic calculations ▸ arithmetic, figures, numbers. *See also* **addition, calculation.**

compute *verb*
▸ cipher, figure, reckon. *See* **calculate** (1). *See synonym note at* **calculate.**

comrade *noun*
1. A person whom one knows well, likes, and trusts ▸ chum, intimate, mate. *See* **friend** (1). **2.** One who shares interests or activities with another ▸ companion, fellow. *See* **associate** (2).

comradeship *noun*
1. The condition of being friends ▸ camaraderie, companionship, fellowship. *See* **friendship. 2.** A pleasant association among people ▸ companionship, society. *See* **company** (5).

con *verb*
1. *Slang* To get something by deceitful trickery ▸ bilk, defraud, swindle. *See* **cheat** (1). **2.** To look at or study carefully or critically ▸ investigate, peruse, scrutinize. *See* **examine** (1). **3.** To commit to memory ▸ learn, memorize. *Idioms:* learn by heart (*or* rote). *See also* **learn, remember.**

con *noun*
1. *Slang* An act of cheating ▸ deceit, hoax, swindle. *See* **cheat** (1). **2.** *Slang* One who commits a crime ▸ culprit, lawbreaker, offender. *See* **criminal.**

concatenation *noun*
▸ order, procession, sequence. *See* **series.**

concave *adjective*
▸ cavernous, sunken. *See* **hollow** (2).

concavity *noun*
▸ basin, dip, hollow. *See* **depression** (1).

conceal *verb*
1. To prevent something from being known ▸ camouflage, cloak, cover (up), enshroud, hide, hush (up), mask, obscure, screen, shroud, veil. *Idioms:* keep in the dark, keep under cover, keep under one's hat, keep under wraps. *See also* **block, disguise, hide[1]. 2.** To cut off from sight ▸ curtain, screen, shroud. *See* **block** (1). **3.** To put or keep out of sight ▸ bury, cache, secrete. *See* **hide[1]** (1). *See synonym note at* **hide.**

concealed *adjective*
1. Difficult or impossible to see or distinguish ▸ covert, disguised, unseen. *See* **hidden** (1). **2.** Lying beyond what is obvious or avowed ▸ buried, covert, hidden. *See* **ulterior** (1).

concealment *noun*
▸ clandestineness, secretiveness. *See* **secrecy.**

concede *verb*
1. To let have as a favor, prerogative, or privilege ▸ accord, award, give, grant, vouchsafe. *See also* **yield. 2.** To admit to the reality or truth of ▸ admit, grant.

See **acknowledge** (1). *See synonym note at* **acknowledge**. 3. To make a concession ▸ accommodate, settle. *See* **compromise** (1). 4. To give up in favor of another ▸ capitulate, give in, yield. *See* **surrender** (1).

conceit *noun*
1. Exaggerated love for oneself or belief in one's own importance ▸ narcissism, vanity. *See* **egotism**. *See synonym note at* **egotism**. 2. An impulsive turn of mind ▸ impulse, notion, whim. *See* **fancy** (1).

conceited *adjective*
▸ narcissistic, vain. *See* **egotistic** (1).

conceivable *adjective*
Capable of being anticipated, considered, or imagined ▸ earthly, imaginable, likely, mortal, possible, thinkable. *Idioms:* humanly possible, within the bounds (*or* range *or* realm) of possibility. *See also* **possible**.

conceivably *adverb*
▸ mayhap, perchance, perhaps. *See* **maybe**.

conceive *verb*
1. To form mental images of ▸ envision, fantasize, visualize. *See* **imagine** (1). 2. To form a strategy for ▸ devise, formulate, strategize. *See* **design** (1). 3. To perceive and recognize the meaning of ▸ apprehend, fathom, sense. *See* **understand** (1). 4. To have an opinion ▸ deem, hold. *See* **believe** (3).

concentrate *verb*
1. To direct toward a common center ▸ center, channel, concenter, converge, focalize, focus, hone in, zero in. *See also* **assemble**. 2. To devote oneself or one's efforts ▸ buckle down, focus, give. *See* **apply** (1).

concentrated *adjective*
1. Not diffused or dispersed ▸ exclusive, intensive, undivided, unswerving, whole. *See also* **thick**. 2. Having a high concentration of the distinguishing ingredient ▸ potent, stiff, strong. *See also* **straight**. 3. Extreme in activity, strength, or effect ▸ fierce, heavy. *See* **intense** (1).

concentration *noun*
1. Concentration of the mental powers on something ▸ attentiveness, consideration. *See* **attention** (1). 2. The act or fact of coming together ▸ confluence, conflux, convergence. *See* **junction** (1). 3. Concentrated power or force, as of effort, opinion, or emotion ▸ ferocity, pitch, vehemence. *See* **intensity**.

concept *noun*
1. That which exists in the mind as the product of careful mental activity ▸ image, notion. *See* **idea** (1). *See synonym note at* **idea**. 2. A statement presented for acceptance, as by a religious group ▸ dogma, teaching. *See* **doctrine**.

conception *noun*
1. That which exists in the mind as the product of careful mental activity ▸ image, notion. *See* **idea** (1). *See synonym note at* **idea**. 2. The act of bringing or being brought into existence ▸ inception, initiation, start. *See* **beginning** (1).

conceptual *adjective*
1. Existing only in the imagination ▸ chimerical, fanciful, unreal. *See* **imaginary**. 2. Existing only in concept and not in reality ▸ hypothetical, impractical, virtual. *See* **theoretical** (2). 3. Concerned primarily with theories rather than practical matters ▸ academic, ideological, speculative. *See* **theoretical** (1).

conceptualization *noun*
1. Abstract reasoning ▸ conjecture, philosophizing, speculation. *See* **theory** (1). 2. The act or process of thinking ▸ cogitation, deliberation, rumination. *See* **thought** (1).

conceptualize *verb*
▸ cogitate, deliberate, reflect. *See* **think** (1).

concern *verb*
1. To be pertinent ▸ appertain, pertain, relate. *See* **apply** (2). 2. To cause anxious uneasiness in ▸ bother, trouble. *See* **worry** (1).

concern *noun*
1. Something that concerns or involves one personally ▸ affair, business, interest, lookout. *See synonym note at* **affair**. 2. A cause of distress or anxiety ▸ care, stressor, trouble, worry. *See also* **anxiety, burden**[1]. 3. Thoughtful attention to others ▸ attentiveness, regard, thoughtfulness. *See* **consideration** (1). 4. Mental acquisitiveness ▸ inquisitiveness, interest, regard. *See* **curiosity** (1). 5. The quality or state of being important ▸ significance, weightiness. *See* **importance**. 6. A troubled or anxious state of mind ▸ angst, distress, unease. *See* **anxiety**. *See synonym note at* **anxiety** (1). 7. A commercial organization ▸ corporation, enterprise, establishment. *See* **company** (1). 8. A feeling of uncertainty about the fitness or correctness of an action ▸ misgiving, reservation, scruple. *See* **qualm** (1).

concerned *adjective*
1. Having concern ▸ affected, connected, engaged, interested, involved. 2. In a state of anxiety or uneasiness ▸ distressed, nervous, uneasy. *See* **anxious**. 3. Feeling or expressing sympathy or pity ▸ commiserative, compassionate, empathetic, understanding. *See* **sympathetic**.

concernment *noun*
1. The quality or state of being important ▸ significance, weightiness. *See* **importance**. 2. Mental acquisitiveness ▸ inquisitiveness, interest, regard. *See* **curiosity** (1).

concert *noun*
1. The act or state of agreeing or conforming ▸ accord, consensus, unanimity. *See* **agreement** (2). 2. Joint work toward a common end ▸ collaboration, teamwork. *See* **cooperation** (1). 3. Pleasing agreement, as of musical sounds ▸ concord, euphony, tune. *See* **harmony** (1).

concert *verb*
To work together toward a common end ▸ concur, unite. *See* **cooperate**.

concerted *adjective*
▸ collective, joint, synergistic. *See* **cooperative** (1).

concertize *verb*
To make music ▸ perform, play, render.

concession *noun*
1. The act of admitting to something ▶ admission, confession, recognition. *See* **acknowledgment** (1). 2. A settlement of differences through mutual concession ▶ give-and-take, settlement. *See* **compromise**.

conciliate *verb*
1. To reestablish friendship between ▶ make up, reconcile, reunite. 2. To ease the anger or agitation of ▶ appease, mollify, soothe. *See* **pacify**. *See synonym note at* **pacify**.

conciliation *noun*
A reestablishment of friendship or harmony ▶ rapprochement, reconcilement, reconciliation, settlement. *See also* **agreement, atonement, compromise**.

conciliatory *adjective*
▶ dovish, irenic, pacifistic. *See* **peaceable**.

concise *adjective*
▶ compendious, short, succinct. *See* **brief** (1).

conclave *noun*
1. A number of persons who have come or been gathered together ▶ conference, group. *Informal:* get-together. *See* **assembly** (1). 2. A formal assemblage of the members of a group ▶ conference, congress. *See* **convention** (1).

conclude *verb*
1. To bring or come to a natural or proper end ▶ close, complete, consummate, end, finish, play out, see through, terminate, wind up, wrap up. *See also* **abolish, stop**. 2. To bring something into a state of agreement or accord ▶ arrange, resolve, set. *See* **settle** (2). 3. To put into correct or conclusive form ▶ arrange, fix. *See* **settle** (1). 4. To make up or cause to make up one's mind ▶ determine, resolve. *See* **decide** (1). *See synonym note at* **decide**. 5. To arrive at a conclusion from evidence or reasoning ▶ deduce, gather. *See* **infer** (1).

✦ CORE SYNONYMS: *conclude, complete, close, end, finish, terminate*. These verbs mean to bring or come to a natural or proper end. *Conclude, complete,* and *finish* suggest the final stage in an undertaking: *The author concluded the article by restating the major points.* "*Nothing worth doing is completed in our lifetime*" (Reinhold Niebuhr). "*Give us the tools, and we will finish the job*" (Winston S. Churchill). *Close* applies to the ending of something ongoing or continuing: *The band closed the concert with an encore. End* emphasizes finality: *We ended the meal with fruit and cheese. Terminate* suggests reaching an established limit: *The playing of the national anthem terminated the station's broadcast for the night.* It also indicates the dissolution of a formal arrangement: *The firm terminated my contract yesterday.*

---

concluded *adjective*
▶ done, finished, through. *See* **complete** (3).

concluding *adjective*
▶ closing, final. *See* **last**[1] (1).

conclusion *noun*
1. A concluding or terminating ▶ cease, completion, termination. *See* **end** (1). 2. The last part ▶ closing, ending, epilogue. *See* **end** (2). 3. A position reached after consideration ▶ determination, resolution. *See* **decision** (1). *See synonym note at* **decision**. 4. A position arrived at by reasoning from premises ▶ deduction, inference, judgment. *See also* **belief**.

conclusive *adjective*
1. Determining or having the power to determine an outcome ▶ crucial, deciding. *See* **decisive** (1). *See synonym note at* **decisive**. 2. Serving the function of deciding or settling with finality ▶ final, ultimate. *See* **definitive** (1). 3. Having or arising from authority ▶ official, supreme. *See* **authoritative** (1). 4. Established beyond a doubt ▶ inarguable, indisputable, irrefutable. *See* **certain** (2).

conclusively *adverb*
In conclusion ▶ finally, last, lastly. *Idioms:* at last, in the end, when all is said and done.

concoct *verb*
1. To use ingenuity in making, developing, or achieving ▶ contrive, devise, dream up. *See* **invent** (1). 2. To form a strategy for ▶ formulate, plan, strategize. *See* **design** (1).

concoction *noun*
▶ brainchild, contrivance. *See* **invention** (2).

concomitant *noun*
One that accompanies another ▶ accompaniment, accompanist, associate, attendant, companion. *See also* **associate**.

concomitant *adjective*
Occurring or existing at the same time ▶ accompanying, attending, coincident. *See* **concurrent** (1). *See synonym note at* **concurrent**.

concord *noun*
1. An identity or coincidence of interests, purposes, or sympathies among the members of a group ▶ oneness, solidarity, union, unity. *See also* **alliance, union**. 2. The act or state of agreeing or conforming ▶ accord, consensus, unanimity. *See* **agreement** (2). 3. Pleasing agreement, as of musical sounds ▶ accord, tune. *See* **harmony** (1). 4. A formal, usually written settlement between nations ▶ concordat, convention, pact. *See* **treaty**.

concordance *noun*
▶ accord, consensus, unanimity. *See* **agreement** (2).

concordant *adjective*
1. Having components pleasingly combined ▶ balanced, congruous, harmonious, symmetrical. *See also* **harmonious, pleasant**. 2. In keeping with one's needs or expectations ▶ compatible, congenial, consonant. *See* **agreeable** (1). 3. Being in or characterized by complete agreement ▶ accordant, consonant, likeminded. *See* **unanimous**.

concordat *noun*
▶ accord, agreement, pact. *See* **treaty**.

concourse *noun*
1. The act or fact of coming together ▶ confluence, conflux, convergence. *See* **junction** (1). 2. An enormous number of persons or things gathered together ▶ horde, mass, throng. *See* **crowd** (1).

concrete *adjective*
1. Having physical or verifiable existence ▶ objective, substantial, tangible. *See* **real** (1). **2.** Composed of or relating to things that occupy space and can be perceived by the senses ▶ corporeal, tangible. *See* **physical** (1).
concrete *verb*
1. To bring or come together into a united whole ▶ join, unify, unite. *See* **combine** (1). **2.** To make or become physically hard ▶ firm up, set, solidify. *See* **harden** (2).
concretize *verb*
▶ externalize, manifest, materialize. *See* **embody** (1).
concupiscence *noun*
▶ eroticism, lust, passion. *See* **desire** (2).
concupiscent *adjective*
▶ amorous, lewd. *See* **lascivious** (1).
concur *verb*
1. To occur at the same time ▶ coincide, harmonize, synchronize. **2.** To come to an understanding or to terms ▶ accord, coincide. *See* **agree** (2). **3.** To work together toward a common end ▶ collaborate, unite. *See* **cooperate**. **4.** To respond affirmatively; receive with agreement or compliance ▶ agree, accede. *See* **assent**. *See synonym note at* **assent**.
concurrent *adjective*
1. Occurring or existing at the same time ▶ accompanying, attendant, attending, coexisting, coincident, concomitant, contemporary, contemporaneous, parallel, simultaneous, synchronic, synchronous. **2.** Belonging to the same period of time ▶ coexistent, synchronous. *See* **contemporary** (1).

✛ **CORE SYNONYMS:** *concurrent, contemporary, contemporaneous, simultaneous, synchronous, coincident, concomitant.* These adjectives mean occurring or existing at the same time. *Concurrent* implies parallelism in character or length of time: *The mass murderer was given three concurrent life sentences. Contemporary* is used more often of persons, *contemporaneous* of events and facts: *The composer Salieri was contemporary with Mozart. A rise in interest rates is often contemporaneous with an increase in inflation. Simultaneous* more narrowly specifies occurrence of events at the same time: *The activists organized simultaneous demonstrations in many major cities. Synchronous* refers to correspondence of events in time over a short period: *The dancers executed a series of synchronous movements. Coincident* applies to events occurring at the same time without implying a relationship: "*The resistance to the Pope's authority . . . is pretty nearly coincident with the rise of the Ottomans*" (John Henry Newman). *Concomitant* refers to coincidence in time of events so clearly related that one seems attendant on the other: *He is an adherent of Freud's theories and had a concomitant belief in the efficacy of psychoanalysis.*

---

concurrently *adverb*
At the same time ▶ simultaneously, synchronously, together. *Idioms:* all at once, all together. *See also* **together**.

concussion *noun*
▶ crash, impact. *See* **collision**. *See synonym note at* **collision**.
condemn *verb*
1. To pronounce judgment against ▶ convict, damn, doom, proscribe, sentence. *Idioms:* pass judgment (*or* sentence) on, seal someone's doom (*or* fate). *See also* **criticize, punish, slam**. **2.** To express strong disapproval of ▶ censure, denounce. *See* **deplore** (1). *See synonym note at* **deplore**.

✛ **CORE SYNONYMS:** *condemn, damn, doom, sentence.* These verbs mean to pronounce judgment against one found to be guilty or undeserving: *condemned the dissident to hard labor; damned the murderer to everlasting misery; an attempt that was doomed to failure; sentenced the traitor to life in prison.*

---

condemnable *adjective*
▶ disgraceful, shameful. *See* **deplorable** (1).
condemnation *noun*
1. Unfavorable opinion or judgment ▶ censure, disfavor, reproof. *See* **disapproval**. **2.** The act or an instance of finding fault ▶ blame, finger-pointing, reprehension. *See* **criticism** (1). **3.** Sustained, harshly abusive language ▶ denunciation, invective. *See* **vituperation**.
condemned *adjective*
Sentenced to a terrible or irrevocable punishment ▶ damned, doomed, fallen, fated, foredoomed, hellbound, lost, reprobate, sentenced. *Idiom:* gone to blazes.
condensation *noun*
1. Moisture accumulated on a surface through sweating or condensation ▶ lather, perspiration, sweat, transudation. **2.** A shortened version or summary ▶ brief, outline, sketch. *See* **synopsis**.
condense *verb*
1. To make short or shorter ▶ abridge, reduce. *See* **shorten**. **2.** To make thick or thicker, especially through evaporation or condensation ▶ inspissate, reduce, thicken. *See also* **coagulate**.
condescend *verb*
1. To bring oneself down to a level considered inappropriate to one's dignity ▶ deign, descend, lower, sink, stoop, vouchsafe. *Idioms:* come down a peg, slum it. **2.** To treat in a superciliously indulgent manner ▶ patronize. *Informal:* high-hat. *Idioms:* lord it over, queen it, speak (*or* talk) down to. *See also* **insult, snub**.

✛ **CORE SYNONYMS:** *condescend, deign, stoop.* These verbs mean to bring oneself down to a level considered inappropriate to one's dignity: *won't condescend to acknowledge his rival's greeting; didn't even deign to reply; stooped to contemptible methods to realize their ambitions.*

---

condescension *or* **condescendence** *noun*
Superciliously indulgent treatment, especially of those who are considered to be inferior ▶ haughtiness,

patronization, snobbery. *Informal:* snootiness. *See also* **arrogance.**

condiment *noun*
▸ flavor, seasoning, spice. *See* **flavoring.**

condition *noun*
1. Manner of being or form of existence ▸ case, mode, situation, state, status. **2.** Something indispensable ▸ essential, must, necessary, necessity, need, precondition, prerequisite, requirement, requisite, sine qua non. *Idiom:* be-all and end-all. *See also* **element, standard. 3.** Positioning of one individual vis-à-vis others ▸ position, rank, standing. *See* **place** (1). **4.** A state of sound readiness ▸ fettle, form, order. *See* **shape** (1). **5.** A restricting or modifying element ▸ limitation, proviso, stipulation. *See* **provision** (1). **6.** One of the conditions or facts attending an event and having some bearing on it ▸ factor, particular. *See* **circumstance** (2).

condition *verb*
To make familiar through constant practice or use ▸ habituate, inure, wont. *See* **accustom.**

✦ CORE SYNONYMS: *condition, situation, state, status.* These nouns denote the manner of being or form of existence of a person or thing: *a jogger in healthy condition; a police officer responding to a dangerous situation; an old factory in a state of disrepair; the uncertain status of the peace negotiations.*

---

conditional *adjective*
Depending on or containing a condition or conditions ▸ conditioned, contingent, dependent, provisional, provisory, relative, specified, stipulated, subject, tentative. *See also* **qualified.**

✦ CORE SYNONYMS: *conditional, contingent, dependent, relative, subject.* These adjectives mean determined or to be determined by something else: *conditional acceptance of the apology; assistance contingent on need; a water supply dependent on rainfall; the importance of a discovery as relative to its usefulness; promotion subject to merit.*

---

conditioned *adjective*
1. Depending on or containing a condition or conditions ▸ contingent, dependent, provisory, subject. *See* **conditional. 2.** Adapted to the existing environment and conditions ▸ acclimated, adapted, inured, seasoned. *See* **accustomed** (1). **3.** Not total, unlimited, or wholehearted ▸ limited, reserved, restricted. *See* **qualified** (1).

conditioning *noun*
1. The act or the process of adapting ▸ acclimation, acculturation, conformation. *See* **adaptation** (1). **2.** Repetition of an action so as to develop or maintain one's skill ▸ exercise, rehearsal. *See* **practice** (1).

conditions *noun*
Existing surroundings that affect an activity ▸ circumstances, context, environment, estate, setting, surroundings. *Slang:* scene. *See also* **air, environment.**

condolatory *adjective*
▸ compassionate, empathetic, understanding. *See* **sympathetic.**

condole *verb*
1. To experience or express compassion ▸ ache, commiserate, feel, sympathize. *Idioms:* be (*or* feel) sorry, have one's heart ache (*or* bleed) for someone, have one's heart go out to someone. *See also* **pity. 2.** To give support in time of grief or pain ▸ console, reassure, soothe. *See* **comfort.**

condolence *noun*
▸ compassion, empathy. *See* **pity** (1). *See synonym note at* **pity.**

condonable *adjective*
▸ forgivable, venial. *See* **pardonable.**

condonation *noun*
▸ amnesty, excuse, pardon. *See* **forgiveness.**

condone *verb*
▸ excuse, overlook, pardon. *See* **forgive.** *See synonym note at* **forgive.**

conduce *verb*
▸ participate, share. *See* **contribute** (2).

conducive *adjective*
Tending to contribute to a result ▸ contributive, contributory, helpful, participatory. *See also* **auxiliary.**

conduct *verb*
1. To control the course of an activity ▸ carry on, control, direct, engineer, handle, manage, operate, run, steer. *Slang:* quarterback. *See also* **administer, maneuver. 2.** To engage in (a war or campaign, for example) ▸ carry on, carry out, wage. *See also* **oppose. 3.** To serve as a conduit ▸ carry, channel, convey, mediate, pass on, transfer, transmit. *See also* **carry, send. 4.** To show the way to ▸ direct, escort, lead. *See* **guide** (1). **5.** To go through life in a certain way ▸ pass, pursue. *See* **lead** (3).

conduct *noun*
1. The manner in which one behaves ▸ comportment, deportment. *See* **behavior** (1). *See synonym note at* **behavior. 2.** The act or practice of managing ▸ oversight, stewardship, supervision. *See* **management** (1).

✦ CORE SYNONYMS: *conduct, direct, manage, control, steer.* These verbs mean to control the course of an activity. *Conduct* can apply to the guidance, authority, and responsibility of a single person: *The chairperson conducted the hearing.* It can also refer to the coordinated actions of a group: *The elections were conducted fairly. Direct* stresses regulation to assure proper planning and implementation: *The seasoned politician directed a brilliant political campaign. Manage* suggests the manipulation of a person, a group, or, often, a complex organization: *It takes skill to manage a hotel. Control* stresses regulation through restraint and also connotes domination: *Our vice president controls the firm's personnel policies. Steer* suggests guidance that controls direction or course: *I deftly steered the conversation away from politics.*

---

conductor *noun*
▸ director, escort, leader. *See* **guide** (1).

confab *noun*
Informal Spoken exchange ▸ dialogue, discourse, talk. *See* **conversation** (1).
confab *verb*
Informal To engage in spoken exchange ▸ discourse, talk. *See* **converse¹**.
confabulate *verb*
▸ discourse, talk. *See* **converse¹**.
confabulation *noun*
▸ dialogue, discourse, talk. *See* **conversation** (1).
confabulator *noun*
▸ discourser, talker. *See* **conversationalist**.
confabulatory *adjective*
▸ colloquial, informal. *See* **conversational** (1).
confederacy *noun*
▸ coalition, confederation, federation. *See* **alliance** (1).
confederate *noun*
1. One who is united in a relationship with another ▸ ally, partner. *See* **associate** (1). *See synonym note at* **associate**. **2.** One who assists a lawbreaker in a wrongful or criminal act ▸ accomplice, conspirator. *See* **accessory** (1).
confederate *verb*
To be formally associated, as by treaty ▸ align, federate. *See* **ally** (1).
confederation *noun*
1. An association for a common cause or interest ▸ coalition, league, organization. *See* **alliance** (1). **2.** A group of people united in a relationship and having some interest, activity, or purpose in common ▸ club, league, order. *See* **union** (1).
confer *verb*
1. To meet and exchange views to reach a decision ▸ advise, consult, debate, deliberate, negotiate, parley, talk. *Informal:* huddle, powwow. *See also* **converse, discuss**. **2.** To give formally or officially ▸ accord, award, bestow, give (away), grant, hand out, impart, present.
conference *noun*
1. A meeting for the exchange of views ▸ colloquium, discussion, forum, panel, parley, roundtable, seminar, summit, symposium, workshop. *Informal:* powwow. *Slang:* rap session. **2.** A number of persons who have come or been gathered together ▸ conclave, group. *Informal:* get-together. *See* **assembly** (1). **3.** A formal assemblage of the members of a group ▸ congress, convocation. *See* **convention** (1). **4.** The exchange of ideas ▸ communion, discussion, intercourse. *See* **communication** (1). **5.** An exchange of views in an attempt to reach a decision ▸ consultation, counsel, debate, parley. *See* **deliberation** (1). **6.** A group of athletic teams that play each other ▸ association, circuit, division, league, loop. *See also* **union**. **7.** The act of conferring, as of an honor ▸ accordance, conferral. *See* **conferment**.
conferment *or* **conferral** *noun*
The act of conferring, as of an honor ▸ accordance, bestowal, bestowment, conference, grant, presentation.

confess *verb*
▸ admit, concede. *See* **acknowledge** (1). *See synonym note at* **acknowledge**.
confession *noun*
1. The act of admitting to something ▸ admission, avowal, recognition. *See* **acknowledgment** (1). **2.** A system of religious belief ▸ creed, denomination. *See* **religion**.
confessor *noun*
One in whom secrets are confided ▸ confidant, confidante, intimate, repository. *See also* **friend**.
confidant *or* **confidante** *noun*
1. One in whom secrets are confided ▸ confessor, intimate, repository. **2.** A person whom one knows well, likes, and trusts ▸ chum, intimate, mate. *See* **friend** (1).
confide *verb*
1. To tell in confidence ▸ breathe, share, unbosom, whisper. *See also* **communicate, reveal, say**. **2.** To put in the charge of another for care, use, or performance ▸ commend, delegate. *See* **entrust** (1). *See synonym note at* **entrust**.
confide in *verb*
To place trust or confidence in ▸ count on (*or* upon), rely on (*or* upon). *See* **depend on** (1).
confidence *noun*
1. A firm belief in one's own powers ▸ aplomb, assurance, certitude, self-assurance, self-confidence, self-possession. *See also* **balance, courage**. **2.** Absolute certainty that a person or thing will not fail ▸ belief, faith. *See* **trust** (1). *See synonym note at* **trust**. **3.** The fact or condition of being without doubt ▸ assuredness, certainty, conviction. *See* **sureness** (1).

✛ CORE SYNONYMS: *confidence, assurance, aplomb, self-confidence, self-possession.* These nouns denote a firm belief in one's own powers, abilities, or capacities. *Confidence* is the most general: "*You gain strength, courage and confidence by every experience in which you really stop to look fear in the face*" (Eleanor Roosevelt). *Assurance* even more strongly stresses certainty and can suggest arrogance: *How can you explain an abstruse theory with such assurance? Aplomb* implies calm poise: "*It is native personality, and that alone, that endows a man to stand before presidents or generals . . . with aplomb*" (Walt Whitman). *Self-confidence* stresses trust in one's own self-sufficiency: "*The most vital quality a soldier can possess is self-confidence*" (George S. Patton). *Self-possession* implies composure arising from control over one's own reactions: "*In life courtesy and self-possession . . . are the sensible impressions of the free mind, for both arise . . . from never being swept away, whatever the emotion, into confusion or dullness*" (William Butler Yeats).

---

confident *adjective*
1. Having a firm belief in one's own powers ▸ assured, poised, secure, self-assured, self-confident, self-possessed. *See also* **brave**. **2.** Having no doubt ▸ certain, positive. *See* **sure** (1). *See synonym note at* **sure**. **3.**

Expecting or suggesting a favorable outcome ▸ cheerful, sanguine. *See* **optimistic.**

confidential *adjective*

1. Known about by very few ▸ inside, private, privy, secret. *Informal:* hush-hush. *See also* **secret. 2.** Indicating intimacy and mutual trust ▸ close, familiar, innermost, intimate, inward, personal. **3.** Of or being information available only to authorized persons ▸ classified, privileged, restricted, sensitive, top secret.

configuration *noun*

▸ cast, design, structure. *See* **form** (1). *See synonym note at* **form.**

configure *verb*

▸ build, compose, shape. *See* **make** (1).

confine *verb*

1. To place a limit on ▸ circumscribe, fix, restrict. *See* **limit** (1). *See synonym note at* **limit. 2.** To confine within a limited area ▸ cage, coop (up), shut (in). *See* **enclose** (1). **3.** To put in or as if in prison ▸ confine, incarcerate, lock (up). *See* **imprison.**

confined *adjective*

▸ checked, controlled. *See* **restricted** (1).

confinement *noun*

1. The state of being detained by legal authority ▸ custody, detainment, imprisonment. *See* **detention. 2.** The act of limiting or condition of being limited ▸ constraint, limitation, restraint. *See* **restriction** (1).

confines *noun*

▸ bounds, periphery, perimeter. *See* **limits.**

confining *adjective*

Affording little room for movement ▸ close, restrictive, snug. *See* **tight** (4).

confirm *verb*

1. To assure the certainty or validity of ▸ affirm, attest, authenticate, avouch, back (up), bear out, corroborate, declare, evidence, justify, substantiate, sustain, testify (to), validate, verify, warrant. *See also* **acknowledge, certify, legalize, prove. 2.** To make firmer in a particular conviction or habit ▸ fortify, harden, reinforce, strengthen. *See also* **back, establish. 3.** To accept officially ▸ accredit, adopt, affirm, approve, certify, endorse, pass, ratify, sanction. *See also* **accept. 4.** To establish as true or genuine through evidence ▸ authenticate, substantiate, validate. *See* **prove** (1).

✦ **CORE SYNONYMS:** *confirm, corroborate, substantiate, authenticate, validate, verify.* These verbs mean to affirm the certainty or validity of something. *Confirm* implies removal of all doubt: *"We must never make experiments to confirm our ideas, but simply to control them"* (Claude Bernard). *Corroborate* refers to supporting something by means of strengthening evidence: *The witness is expected to corroborate the plaintiff's testimony.* To *substantiate* is to establish by presenting substantial or tangible evidence: *"one of the most fully substantiated of historical facts"* (James Harvey Robinson). *Authenticate* implies the establishment of genuineness of something by the testimony of an expert: *Never purchase an antique before it has been authenticated. Validate* refers to establishing the

validity of something, such as a theory, claim, or judgment: *The divorce validated my parents' original objection to the marriage. Verify* implies proving by comparison with an original or with established fact: *The bank refused to cash the check until the signature was verified.*

---

confirmation *noun*

1. An act of confirming officially ▸ accreditation, adoption, affirmation, approval, certification, endorsement, passage, ratification, sanction, verification. *See also* **acceptance. 2.** That which confirms ▸ attestation, authentication, avouchment, backing, circumstantiation, corroboration, demonstration, documentation, evidence, justification, proof, substantiation, sustainment, testament, testimonial, testimony, validation, verification, warrant. *See also* **testimony.**

confirmed *adjective*

1. Firmly established by long standing ▸ deep-rooted, deep-seated, entrenched, established, hard-shell, incorrigible, incurable, indelible, ineradicable, ingrained, inveterate, irradicable, old-line, rooted, set, settled, vested. *See also* **firm¹, fixed. 2.** Subject to a disease or habit for a long time ▸ chronic, habitual, habituated, inveterate. *See also* **stubborn.**

confiscate *verb*

▸ appropriate, grab, snatch. *See* **seize** (1). *See synonym note at* **seize.**

confiscation *noun*

▸ expropriation, preemption, usurpation. *See* **seizure** (2).

conflagrant *adjective*

▸ afire, flaming. *See* **burning** (1).

conflagration *noun*

The visible signs of combustion ▸ blaze, fire, flame, flare-up.

conflict *noun*

1. A state of disagreement and disharmony ▸ clash, confrontation, contention, difference, difficulty, disaccord, disagreement, discord, discordance, disharmony, dissension, dissent, dissentience, dissidence, dissonance, faction, friction, inharmony, schism, strife, variance, warfare. *See also* **argument, opposition. 2.** An encounter between opposing military forces ▸ encounter, confrontation, war. *See* **battle** (1).

conflict *verb*

To fail to be in accord ▸ clash, collide, contradict, contrast, differ, disaccord, disagree, discord, diverge, jar, mismatch, oppose, vary. *Idioms:* go (*or* run) counter to.

✦ **CORE SYNONYMS:** *conflict, discord, strife, contention, dissension, clash, variance.* These nouns refer to a state of disagreement and disharmony. *Conflict* suggests antagonism of ideas or interests that often results in hostility or divisiveness: *conflict between smoking and nonsmoking factions. Discord* is a lack of harmony often marked by bickering and antipathy: *family discord. Strife* usually implies a struggle, often destructive, between rivals or factions: *political strife. Contention* suggests a dispute in the form of heated debate or quarreling: *lively contention among the candidates. Dissension* implies difference of opinion that disrupts unity within a group: *rampant dissension among the staff. Clash* involves irreconcilable ideas or interests: *a personality clash. Variance* usually suggests discrepancy or incompatibility: *actions at variance with his principles.*

conflicting *adjective*

1. Made up of parts or qualities that are disparate or otherwise markedly lacking in consistency ▸ discrepant, inconsistent. *See* **incongruous** (1). **2.** In sharp opposition ▸ contradictory, discordant, inconsistent. *See* **discrepant** (1). **3.** Devoid of harmony and accord ▸ discordant, uncongenial. *See* **inharmonious** (1). **4.** Acting against or in opposition ▸ antagonistic, resistant. *See* **opposing** (1).

confluence *noun*
▸ conflux, gathering. *See* **junction** (1).

conflux *noun*
▸ confluence, convergence. *See* **junction** (1).

conform *verb*

1. To be compatible or suitable ▸ chime, correspond, match. *See* **agree** (1). *See synonym note at* **agree**. **2.** To make or become suitable to a particular situation or use ▸ acclimate, fit. *See* **adapt**. *See synonym note at* **adapt**. **3.** To bring into accord ▸ attune, integrate. *See* **harmonize** (1). **4.** To act in conformity with ▸ heed, obey, observe. *See* **follow** (4). **5.** To make conventional ▸ standardize, stylize. *See* **conventionalize**.

conformable *adjective*

1. In keeping with one's needs or expectations ▸ compatible, congenial, harmonious. *See* **agreeable** (1). **2.** Willing to carry out the wishes of others ▸ complaisant, docile, submissive. *See* **obedient**.

conformance *noun*
▸ accord, consensus, unanimity. *See* **agreement** (2).

conformation *noun*

1. The act or process of adapting ▸ accommodation, acculturation, adjustment. *See* **adaptation** (1). **2.** The act or state of agreeing or conforming ▸ concordance, harmony, rapport. *See* **agreement** (2).

conformist *adjective*
▸ button-down, orthodox, traditional. *See* **conventional** (1).

conformity *noun*
▸ concordance, harmony, rapport. *See* **agreement** (2).

confound *verb*

1. To take one thing mistakenly for another ▸ confuse, mistake, mix up. **2.** To cause to be unclear in mind or intent ▸ befuddle, bewilder, discombobulate. *See* **confuse** (1). **3.** To cause a person to be self-consciously distressed ▸ chagrin, discomfort. *See* **embarrass** (1). **4.** To put at a loss as to what to say or do ▸ nonplus, perplex. *Informal:* stump. *See* **baffle** (1).

confounded *adjective*

1. Mentally uncertain ▸ befuddled, perplexed, turbid. *Informal:* mixed-up. *See* **confused** (1). **2.** *Informal* So

annoying or detestable as to deserve condemnation ▸ accursed, blasted, infernal. *See* **damned** (2).

confront *verb*
To meet face-to-face, especially defiantly ▸ encounter, face, front, meet. *Idiom:* stand up to. *See also* **contest, defy**.

confrontation *noun*

1. A face-to-face, usually hostile meeting ▸ duel, encounter, face-off, mano a mano, meeting, showdown. *See also* **argument, fight**. **2.** An encounter between opposing military forces ▸ combat, engagement, war. *See* **battle** (1). **3.** A state of disagreement and disharmony ▸ contention, difference, discord, strife. *See* **conflict** (1).

confuse *verb*

1. To cause to be unclear in mind or intent ▸ addle, befuddle, bewilder, confound, discombobulate, disorient, dizzy, fuddle, jumble, mix up, muddle, mystify, perplex, puzzle. *Informal:* throw. *Idioms:* make one's head reel (*or* swim *or* whirl). *See also* **agitate, complicate, daze**. **2.** To cause a person to be self-consciously distressed ▸ chagrin, discomfort. *See* **embarrass** (1). **3.** To take one thing mistakenly for another ▸ confound, mistake, mix up. **4.** To put into total disorder ▸ ball up, cross up, disorder, garble, jumble, mess up, muddle, muddy, scramble, snarl. *Slang:* snafu. *Idioms:* make a hash (*or* mess) of, play havoc with. *See also* **complicate, disorder**.

✦ CORE SYNONYMS: *confuse, addle, befuddle, discombobulate, fuddle, muddle, puzzle*. These verbs mean to cause to be unclear in mind or intent: *heavy traffic that confused the driver; problems that addle my brain; a question that befuddled even the professor; was discombobulated by all of the possibilities; a complex plot line that fuddled my comprehension; a student who was muddled by endless facts and figures; behavior that really puzzled me.*

confused *adjective*

1. Mentally uncertain ▸ addled, addlepated, baffled, befuddled, bemused, bewildered, confusional, confounded, discombobulated, disconcerted, disoriented, dizzy, dumbfounded, flustered, haywire, lost, muddle-headed, mystified, nonplused, perplexed, punch-drunk, puzzled, stuck, stumped, turbid. *Informal:* mixed-up. *Idioms:* at a loss, at sea, in a fog (*or* haze *or* state *or* tizzy). *See also* **agitated, ignorant**. **2.** Characterized by physical confusion ▸ amiss, chaotic, deranged, disarranged, disarrayed, disordered, disorganized, disrupted, disturbed, garbled, helter-skelter, higgledy-piggledy, jumbled, messy, muddled, pell-mell, scrambled, snarled, topsy-turvy, unsettled, unsystematic, upside-down, willy-nilly. *Informal:* mixed-up. *Slang:* snafu. *Idiom:* at sixes and sevens. *See also* **complex, messy**.

confusedness *noun*
▸ clutter, confusion, disarray. *See* **disorder** (1).

confusion *noun*

1. Self-conscious distress ▸ chagrin, discomposure. *See* embarrassment (1). **2.** A stunned or bewildered condition ▸ bewilderment, perplexity, stupor. *See* **daze.** **3.** A lack of order or regular arrangement ▸ clutter, lawlessness, disarray. *See* **disorder** (1). **4.** A lack of civil order or peace ▸ anarchy, lawlessness, misrule. *See* **disorder** (2). **5.** A failure to understand correctly ▸ misapprehension, misconception. *See* **misunderstanding** (1).

confusional *adjective*
▸ confounded, perplexed, turbid. *See* **confused** (1).

confute *verb*
▸ discredit, disprove, rebut. *See* **refute.**

con game *noun*
Informal An indirect, usually cunning means of gaining an end ▸ deception, ploy, stratagem. *See* **trick** (1).

congeal *verb*
1. To make or become physically hard ▸ cake, solidify. *See* **harden** (2). **2.** To change or be changed from a liquid into a semisolid or solid mass ▸ clot, set. *See* **coagulate.** *See synonym note at* **coagulate.**

congener *noun*
▸ correlative, counterpart. *See* **parallel.**

congenial *adjective*
1. Pleasant and friendly in disposition ▸ cordial, friendly, genial. *See* **amiable. 2.** Giving or affording pleasure or enjoyment ▸ agreeable, gratifying, satisfying. *See* **pleasant** (1). **3.** In keeping with one's needs or expectations ▸ compatible, consonant, harmonious. *See* **agreeable** (1).

congeniality *or* **congenialness** *noun*
▸ agreeability, friendliness, pleasantness. *See* **amiability.**

congenital *adjective*
1. Possessed at birth ▸ inborn, inherited, native. *See* **innate** (1). *See synonym note at* **innate. 2.** Forming an essential element, as arising from the basic structure of an individual ▸ basal, elemental. *See* **constitutional** (1).

congeries *noun*
▸ accumulation, aggregation, collection. *See* **accumulation** (1).

congest *verb*
▸ clog, cork. *See* **fill** (2).

congested *adjective*
▸ choked, teeming. *See* **overcrowded.**

conglomerate *noun*
1. An entity composed of interconnected parts ▸ system, tissue, web. *See* **complex** (1). **2.** A commercial organization ▸ corporation, enterprise, establishment. *See* **company** (1).

conglomeration *noun*
1. A collection of various things ▸ hodgepodge, jumble, mishmash. *See* **assortment** (1). **2.** The act of accumulating ▸ accumulation, agglomeration, buildup. *See also* **increase.**

congrats *noun*
Informal An expression of admiration or congratulation ▸ praise, tribute. *See* **compliment** (1).

congratulate *verb*
To pay a compliment to ▸ commend, compliment, felicitate, praise. *Idiom:* take off one's hat to. *See also* **honor, pride.**

congratulation *noun*
▸ praise, tribute. *See* **compliment** (1).

congratulatory *adjective*
▸ approbatory, laudatory. *See* **complimentary** (1).

congregate *verb*
▸ convene, convoke, muster. *See* **assemble** (1).

congregation *noun*
1. The steadfast believers in a faith or cause ▸ adherents, faithful, fold. *See also* **follower, assembly. 2.** A number of persons who have come or been gathered together ▸ conference, group. *Informal:* get-together. *See* **assembly** (1).

congress *noun*
1. A formal assemblage of the members of a group ▸ conference, convocation. *See* **convention** (1). **2.** A number of persons who have come or been gathered together ▸ conference, group. *Informal:* get-together. *See* **assembly** (1). **3.** A group of people united in a relationship and having some interest, activity, or purpose in common ▸ club, league, order. *See* **union** (1).

congruity *or* **congruence** *noun*
1. The act or state of agreeing or conforming ▸ concordance, harmony, rapport. *See* **agreement** (2). **2.** Logical agreement among parts ▸ coherence, consistence. *See* **consistency.**

congruous *adjective*
1. Having components that are pleasingly combined ▸ concordant, balanced, harmonious, symmetrical. *See also* **pleasant. 2.** In keeping with one's needs or expectations ▸ compatible, congenial, harmonious. *See* **agreeable** (1).

conjectural *adjective*
▸ hypothetical, presumptive, suppositional. *See* **supposed.** *See synonym note at* **supposed.**

conjecture *noun*
1. Abstract reasoning ▸ conceptualization, philosophizing, speculation. *See* **theory** (1). **2.** A judgment, estimate, or opinion arrived at by guessing ▸ guess, speculation, surmise. *See* **guess.**

conjecture *verb*
To predict or assume without sufficient information ▸ speculate, surmise. *See* **guess.**

conjectured *adjective*
▸ hypothesized, surmised, untested. *See* **untried** (1).

conjoin *verb*
1. To bring or come together into a united whole ▸ join, unify, unite. *See* **combine** (1). **2.** To unite or be united in a relationship ▸ combine, join, link. *See* **associate** (1).

conjoining *adjective*
▸ abutting, conterminous, neighboring. *See* **adjoining.**

conjoint *adjective*
▸ general, mutual, public. *See* **common** (2).

conjugal *adjective*
▸ nuptial, spousal, wedded. *See* **marital.**

conjugality *noun*
▸ coupling, matrimony, union. *See* **marriage** (1).

conjugate *verb*
▸ join, unify, unite. *See* **combine** (1).

conjugation *noun*
▸ compound, merger, union. *See* **combination** (1).

conjunction *noun*
▸ alliance, combination, connection, cooperation. *See* **association** (1).

conjuration *noun*
1. The use of skillful tricks and deceptions to produce entertainingly baffling effects ▸ legerdemain, sleight of hand. *See* **magic** (2). 2. The use of supernatural powers to influence or to predict events ▸ sorcery, witchcraft. *See* **magic** (1).

conjure *verb*
To bring out something latent, hidden, or unexpressed ▸ draw (out), elicit, summon. *See* **evoke.**

conjure up *verb*
To form mental images of ▸ envision, fantasize, visualize. *See* **imagine** (1).

conjurer *noun*
▸ enchanter, magician, sorcerer. *See* **wizard** (1).

conjuring *noun*
▸ legerdemain, sleight of hand. *See* **magic** (2).

conk *noun*
1. *Slang* The uppermost part of the body ▸ crown, pate. *See* **head** (1). 2. *Slang* A sudden heavy stroke ▸ crack, hit, swat, whack. *See* **blow²** (1).

conk *verb*
Slang To deliver a sudden, sharp blow to ▸ jab, sock, whack. *See* **hit** (1).

conk out *verb*
1. *Slang* To stop working properly ▸ break down, fail. *See* **malfunction.** 2. *Slang* To suddenly lose all health or strength ▸ give out, succumb. *See* **collapse** (1).

connatural *or* **connate** *adjective*
1. Forming an essential element, as arising from the basic structure of an individual ▸ innate, intrinsic, natural. *See* **constitutional** (1). 2. Connected by or as if by kinship or common origin ▸ akin, allied, related. *See* **kindred.** 3. Possessed at birth ▸ inborn, native. *See* **innate** (1).

connect *verb*
1. To bring or come together into a united whole ▸ join, unify, unite. *See* **combine** (1). *See synonym note at* **combine.** 2. To join one thing to another ▸ append, fix, secure. *See* **attach** (1). 3. To come or bring together in one's mind or imagination ▸ correlate, link. *See* **associate** (3). 4. To unite or be united in a relationship ▸ affiliate, federate, incorporate. *See* **associate** (1). 5. To interact with another or others in a harmonious fashion ▸ communicate. *Slang:* click. *See* **relate** (5).

connected *adjective*
▸ interested, involved. *See* **concerned** (1).

connection *noun*
1. The state of being associated ▸ alliance, conjunc-tion, cooperation. *See* **association** (1). 2. A point or position at which two or more things are joined ▸ coupling, juncture, seam. *See* **joint** (1). 3. A logical or natural association between two or more things ▸ correlation, link, relationship. *See* **relation** (1). 4. Something, such as a feeling or idea, associated with a specific person or thing ▸ association, connotation, impression, suggestion. *See also* **hint.** 5. An acquaintance who is in a position to help ▸ contact, source. *See also* **go-between.** 6. *Slang* A person who sells narcotics illegally ▸ dealer, peddler. *See* **pusher.**

conniption *or* **conniption fit** *noun*
Informal An angry outburst ▸ fit, tantrum. *See* **temper** (2).

connivance *noun*
▸ collusion, conspiracy. *See* **plot** (2).

connive *verb*
To work out a secret plan to achieve an evil or illegal end ▸ conspire, scheme. *See* **plot** (2).

connive at *verb*
To pretend not to see ▸ disregard, ignore, overlook. *See* **blink at.**

conniving *adjective*
Coldly planning to achieve selfish aims ▸ calculating, designing, manipulative, scheming. *See also* **artful.**

connoisseur *noun*
▸ authority, master, proficient. *See* **expert.**

connotation *noun*
1. Something, such as a feeling or idea, associated with a specific person or thing ▸ association, connection, impression, suggestion. *See also* **hint.** 2. Something that is conveyed or signified ▸ import, sense, significance. *See* **meaning** (1).

connotative *adjective*
Tending to bring a memory, mood, or image, for example, subtly or indirectly to mind ▸ allusive, evocative, impressionistic, reminiscent, suggestive. *See also* **designative, symbolic.**

connote *verb*
▸ denote, intend, signify. *See* **mean¹** (1).

connubial *adjective*
▸ nuptial, spousal, wedded. *See* **marital.**

connubiality *noun*
▸ conjugality, matrimony, union. *See* **marriage** (1).

conquer *verb*
1. To win a victory over, as in battle or a competition ▸ beat, surmount, vanquish. *See* **defeat** (1). *See synonym note at* **defeat.** 2. To seize or maintain control over by conquest ▸ capture, overrun, subjugate. *See* **occupy** (2).

conquering *adjective*
▸ champion, triumphant, winning. *See* **victorious.**

conqueror *noun*
1. One that conquers ▸ conquistador, master, subduer, subjugator, surmounter, vanquisher, victor, winner. 2. One that wins a contest or competition ▸ champion, medalist. *See* **winner** (1).

conquest *noun*
The act of conquering ▸ knockout, subjugation, tri-

umph, victory, win. *See also* **accomplishment, defeat.**

✦ CORE SYNONYMS: *conquest, victory, triumph.* These nouns denote the act of conquering, as by winning a war, struggle, or competition. *Conquest* connotes subduing, subjugating, or achieving control over: *"Conquest of illiteracy comes first"* (John Kenneth Galbraith). *Victory* refers especially to the final defeat of an enemy or opponent: *"Victory at all costs, victory in spite of all terror, victory however long and hard the road may be"* (Winston S. Churchill). *Triumph* denotes a victory or success that is especially noteworthy because it is decisive, significant, or spectacular: *preaching the eventual triumph of good over evil.*

---

conquistador *noun*
▸ master, victor. *See* **conqueror** (1).
consanguine *or* **consanguineous** *adjective*
▸ akin, allied, related. *See* **kindred.**
conscience *noun*
▸ grace, properness. *See* **decency** (1).
conscienceless *adjective*
▸ unconscionable, unethical, unprincipled. *See* **unscrupulous** (1).
conscientious *adjective*
1. In accordance with principles of right or good conduct ▸ principled, virtuous. *See* **ethical. 2.** Characterized by steady attention and effort ▸ assiduous, industrious, studious. *See* **diligent.** *See synonym note at* **diligent.**
conscientiousness *noun*
▸ assiduousness, perseverance, pertinacity. *See* **diligence.**
conscious *adjective*
1. Cautiously attentive ▸ heedful, mindful, observant, watchful. *See* **careful** (1). 2. Done or said on purpose ▸ intentional, purposeful, willful. *See* **deliberate** (1).
consciousness *noun*
1. The condition of being aware ▸ cognizance, perception, sense. *See* **awareness. 2.** The vital principle or animating force within living beings ▸ soul, vitality. *See* **spirit** (2).
conscript *verb*
To enroll compulsorily in military service ▸ draft, impress, induct, levy.
conscription *noun*
▸ impressment, induction, levy. *See* **draft** (2).
consecrate *verb*
1. To make sacred by a religious rite ▸ bless, hallow, sanctify. *See also* **exalt. 2.** To give over by or as if by vow to a higher purpose ▸ dedicate, sacrifice. *See* **devote** (1). *See synonym note at* **devote.**
consecrated *adjective*
1. Regarded with particular reverence or respect, especially by a religion ▸ blessed, hallowed, sacred. *See* **holy** (1). 2. In the service or worship of God or a god ▸ devoted, religious, sacred. *See* **divine** (2).
consecution *noun*
▸ order, procession, sequence. *See* **series.**

consecutive *adjective*
Following one after another in an orderly pattern or sequence ▸ back-to-back, chronological, numerical, sequent, sequential, serial, seriate, successional, successive. *Idioms:* in order, in turn. *See also* **following, gradual.**
consensual *adjective*
▸ accordant, consonant, like-minded. *See* **unanimous.**
consensus *noun*
▸ concordance, harmony, rapport. *See* **agreement** (2).
consent *verb*
1. To respond affirmatively; receive with agreement or compliance ▸ acquiesce, nod, subscribe. *See* **assent.** *See synonym note at* **assent. 2.** To give one's consent to ▸ approve, authorize, sanction. *See* **permit** (2).
consent *noun*
1. The act of accepting or adopting ▸ adoption, assent, consent. *See* **acceptance** (1). 2. The approving of an action, especially when done by one in authority ▸ authorization, license, sanction. *See* **permission.** *See synonym note at* **permission.**
consequence *noun*
1. Something brought about by a cause ▸ outcome, result, upshot. *See* **effect** (1). *See synonym note at* **effect. 2.** The quality or state of being important ▸ concernment, significance, weightiness. *See* **importance.** *See synonym note at* **importance.**
consequent *adjective*
1. Consistent with reason and intellect ▸ deducible, rational, reasonable. *See* **logical** (2). 2. Occurring as a result ▸ ensuing, resulting. *See* **following** (2).
consequential *adjective*
1. Having great significance ▸ big, grand, meaningful. *See* **important** (1). 2. Having or exercising influence ▸ important, powerful, weighty. *See* **influential. 3.** Occurring as a result ▸ consequent, ensuing, resulting. *See* **following** (2). **4.** Conveying hidden or unexpressed meaning ▸ meaningful, significant. *See* **pregnant** (2).
conservancy *noun*
▸ husbandry, preservation. *See* **conservation.**
conservation *noun*
The careful guarding of an asset ▸ conservancy, husbandry, maintenance, management, preservation, protection. *See also* **care, defense, economy.**
conservational *noun*
▸ conservative, precautionary, protective. *See* **preservative.**
conservative *adjective*
1. Favoring traditional view and values, especially as a political philosophy ▸ neoconservative, orthodox, right, rightist, right-wing, Tory, traditionalist, traditionalistic. *Informal:* neocon. *See also* **ultraconservative. 2.** Kept within sensible limits ▸ careful, cautious, discreet, guarded, moderate, modest, reasonable, restrained, temperate. **3.** Conforming to established practice or standards ▸ conformist, orthodox, traditional. *See* **conventional** (1). **4.** Tending to or capable of preserving ▸ conservational, protective. *See* **preservative.**

conservative *noun*
One with politically conservative views ▸ neo-conservative, orthodox, rightist, right-winger, Tory, traditionalist. *Informal:* neocon. *See also* **ultraconservative.**

conservator *noun*
One who is legally responsible for the care and management of the person or property of an incompetent or a minor ▸ caretaker, custodian, guardian, keeper. *See also* **representative.**

conserve *verb*
1. To protect an asset from loss or destruction ▸ husband, preserve, save. *See also* **defend. 2.** To be frugal or sparing ▸ economize, save, stint. *See* **scrimp. 3.** To prepare food for storage and future use ▸ can, cure, put up. *See* **preserve** (1).

consider *verb*
1. To receive an idea and think about it in order to form an opinion about it ▸ entertain, hear of, think about, think of. **2.** To think or think about carefully and at length ▸ cogitate, deliberate, mull. *See* **ponder. 3.** To direct the eyes on an object ▸ eye, view. *See* **look** (1). **4.** To be concerned with something ▸ address, treat. *See* **deal** (1). **5.** To look upon in a particular way ▸ account, deem, view. *See* **regard** (1). *See synonym note at* **regard. 6.** To have an opinion ▸ deem, hold. *See* **believe** (3). **7.** To have a high opinion of or regard for ▸ admire, honor, respect. *See* **value** (1). **8.** To speak together and exchange ideas and opinions about ▸ converse, debate. *Informal:* kick around. *See* **discuss.**

considerable *adjective*
1. Above average in amount, size, or scope ▸ extensive, large, sizable. *See* **big** (1). **2.** Having great significance ▸ consequential, meaningful. *See* **important** (1).

considerably *adverb*
To a considerable extent ▸ abundantly, amply, expansively, extensively, far, largely, much, quite, significantly, sizably, spaciously, substantially, well. *Idioms:* by a long shot (*or* way), by a wide margin, by far. *See also* **absolutely, completely, really, unusually, very.**

considerate *adjective*
1. Full of polite concern for the well-being of others ▸ courteous, solicitous, thoughtful. *See* **attentive** (1). *See synonym note at* **attentive. 2.** Ready to do favors for another ▸ agreeable, complaisant. *See* **obliging.**

consideration *noun*
1. Thoughtful attention to others ▸ attentiveness, concern, helpfulness, hospitality, kindness, loving kindness, regard, solicitousness, solicitude, sweetness, tenderness, thoughtfulness, warm-heartedness. *See also* **amiability, benevolence, generosity. 2.** An exchange of views in an attempt to reach a decision ▸ consultation, counsel, debate, parley. *See* **deliberation** (1). **3.** Careful thought ▸ advisement, deliberation, study. *See also* **examination, scrutiny. 4.** Concentration of the mental powers on something ▸ concentration, heedfulness. *See* **attention** (1). **5.** A feeling of deference, approval, and liking ▸ admiration, favor. *See* **esteem** (1).

considered *adjective*
1. Marked by careful consideration ▸ advised, studied. *See* **deliberate** (2). **2.** Planned, weighed, or estimated in advance ▸ deliberate, intentional, premeditated. *See* **calculated** (1).

consign *verb*
1. To put in the charge of another for care, use, or performance ▸ confide, delegate. *See* **entrust** (1). *See synonym note at* **entrust. 2.** To place officially in confinement ▸ commit, institutionalize. *Informal:* send up. *See also* **imprison. 3.** To cause something to be conveyed to a destination ▸ address, dispatch. *See* **send** (1).

consignment *noun*
▸ conveyance, shipment, transfer. *See* **delivery** (1).

consist *verb*
1. To have an inherent basis ▸ dwell, exist, inhere, lie, repose, reside, rest. *See also* **endure, live. 2.** To be compatible or suitable ▸ chime, correspond, match. *See* **agree** (1).

consistence *noun*
▸ congruity, uniformity. *See* **consistency.**

consistency *noun*
1. Logical agreement among parts ▸ coherence, cohesion, congruence, congruity, consistence, uniformity. *See also* **agreement, proportion. 2.** The condition of being without change or variation ▸ firmness, immutability. *See* **changelessness.**

consistent *adjective*
1. In keeping with one's needs or expectations ▸ compatible, congenial, harmonious. *See* **agreeable** (1). **2.** Remaining unchanged ▸ changeless, constant, same. *See* **unchanging.**

consistently *adverb*
▸ customarily, generally, normally. *See* **usually.**

consolation *noun*
▸ comfort, reassurance, solace, succor. *See also* **help, pity.**

console *verb*
▸ condole, reassure, soothe. *See* **comfort.** *See synonym note at* **comfort.**

consolidate *verb*
▸ join, unify, unite. *See* **combine** (1).

consolidated *adjective*
▸ crowded, dense, tight. *See* **thick** (2).

consolidation *noun*
▸ coalition, union. *See* **unification** (1).

consonance *noun*
1. The act or state of agreeing or conforming ▸ concordance, harmony, rapport. *See* **agreement** (2). **2.** Pleasing agreement, as of musical sounds ▸ concord, tune. *See* **harmony** (1).

consonant *adjective*
1. In keeping with one's needs or expectations ▸ compatible, congenial, harmonious. *See* **agreeable** (1). **2.** Characterized by harmony of sound ▸ musical, symphonic. *See* **harmonious** (2). **3.** Being in or characterized by complete agreement ▸ accordant, consensual, like-minded. *See* **unanimous.**

consort *noun*

A husband or wife ▸ mate, partner. *See* **spouse.**

consort *verb*

To be with as a companion ▸ fraternize, hang around, hobnob. *See* **associate** (2).

consortium *noun*

▸ coalition, federation, organization. *See* **alliance** (1).

conspicuous *adjective*

1. Readily attracting notice ▸ arresting, outstanding, prominent. *See* **noticeable** (1). *See synonym note at* **noticeable. 2.** Readily seen, perceived, or understood ▸ evident, obvious. *See* **apparent** (1).

conspiracy *noun*

▸ collusion, connivance. *See* **plot** (2).

conspirator *noun*

▸ accomplice, confederate. *See* **accessory** (1).

conspire *verb*

▸ connive, scheme. *See* **plot** (2).

constable *noun*

▸ officer, trooper. *Informal:* cop. *See* **police officer.**

constancy *noun*

1. Faithfulness or devotion to a person, cause, or obligation ▸ allegiance, faithfulness, loyalty. *See* **fidelity** (1). **2.** The condition of being without change or variation ▸ firmness, immutability. *See* **changelessness.**

constant *adjective*

1. Existing without interruption or end ▸ continuous, endless, everlasting, perpetual. *See* **continual.** *See synonym note at* **continual. 2.** Remaining unchanged ▸ changeless, invariable, unfailing. *See* **unchanging. 3.** Possessing determination or resolution ▸ resolute, steadfast, unyielding. *See* **firm**[1] (3). **4.** Adhering firmly and devotedly, as to a person, cause, or duty ▸ allegiant, loyal, staunch. *See* **faithful** (1). *See synonym note at* **faithful.**

consternate *verb*

▸ alarm, daunt, disconcert. *See* **dismay** (1).

consternation *noun*

▸ dismay, panic, trepidation. *See* **fear.** *See synonym note at* **fear.**

constituency *noun*

▸ clientage, custom. *See* **patronage** (3).

constituent *adjective*

Serving as a nondetachable part of a larger unit ▸ component, incorporated. *See* **built-in** (1).

constituent *noun*

A separate unit that belongs or contributes to a whole ▸ building block, piece, section. *See* **part** (1). *See synonym note at* **part.**

constitute *verb*

1. To be the constituent parts of ▸ compose, form, make up. *See also* **contain. 2.** To be equal or alike ▸ amount, correspond, equate. *See* **equal** (1). **3.** To put in force or cause to be by legal authority ▸ enact, legislate. *See* **establish** (3). **4.** To bring into existence formally ▸ create, establish, institute. *See* **found** (1).

constitution *noun*

1. The physical characteristics of a person ▸ body, build, figure, form, frame, habit, habitus, make, makeup, physique, shape. *See also* **character, form. 2.** The act of founding or establishing ▸ creation, establishment, institution. *See* **foundation** (1).

constitutional *adjective*

1. Forming an essential element, as arising from the basic structure of an individual ▸ basal, built-in, congenital, connate, connatural, elemental, immanent, inborn, inbred, indigenous, indwelling, ingrained, inherent, innate, intrinsic, native, natural. *Idioms:* in one's blood, runs in the family. *See also* **confirmed, elemental, innate. 2.** Constituting or forming part of the essence of something ▸ basic, fundamental. *See* **essential** (2).

constitutional *noun*

An act of walking ▸ ramble, stroll, turn. *See* **walk** (1).

constitutive *adjective*

▸ integral, vital. *See* **essential** (2).

constrain *verb*

1. To check the freedom and spontaneity of ▸ constrict, cramp, inhibit. **2.** To cause a person or thing to act or move in spite of resistance ▸ coerce, compel, pressure. *See* **force** (1). *See synonym note at* **force. 3.** To control, restrict, or arrest ▸ bridle, check, curb. *See* **restrain.**

constrained *adjective*

1. Characterized by embarrassment and discomfort ▸ uncomfortable, uneasy. *See* **awkward** (3). **2.** Tending to keep one's thoughts and emotions to oneself ▸ inhibited, restrained, self-restrained. *See* **reserved** (1). **3.** Being legally or morally required to do something ▸ bound, compelled, obligated. *See* **obliged** (2).

constraint *noun*

1. Energy that overcomes resistance ▸ might, power, strength. *See* **force** (1). **2.** The keeping of one's thoughts and emotions to oneself ▸ control, restraint, self-restraint. *See* **reserve** (2). **3.** The act of limiting or condition of being limited ▸ confinement, limitation, restraint. *See* **restriction** (1). **4.** Something that limits or holds back ▸ check, circumscription, curb. *See* **restraint** (1).

constrict *verb*

1. To make smaller or narrower by binding or squeezing ▸ compact, compress, constringe, contract, narrow, shrink, tighten. *See also* **decrease, shorten. 2.** To subject to compression ▸ compress, pinch. *See* **squeeze** (1). **3.** To check the freedom and spontaneity of ▸ constrain, cramp, inhibit. *See also* **restrain.**

constriction *noun*

The act or process of constricting ▸ compression, contraction, narrowing, shrinkage, squeeze. *See also* **decrease.**

constringe *verb*

1. To make smaller or narrower by binding or squeezing ▸ compress, contract, narrow. *See* **constrict** (1). **2.** To subject to compression ▸ compress, constrict. *See* **squeeze** (1).

construct *verb*

1. To create by forming, combining, or altering

materials ► compose, configure, shape. *See* **make** (1). **2.** To make or form a structure ► erect, raise. *See* **build** (1). **3.** To provide a basis for ► establish, ground. *See* **base**[1] (2).

construable *adjective*
► decipherable, illustratable, interpretable. *See* **explainable.**

construction *noun*
1. Something built, especially for human use ► building, edifice, erection, pile, structure. **2.** Something that serves to explain or clarify ► decipherment, illumination. *See* **explanation** (1).

constructive *adjective*
1. Producing or able to produce a desired effect ► efficient, productive. *See* **effective** (1). **2.** Affording benefit or advantage ► favorable, helpful, propitious. *See* **beneficial.**

constructor *noun*
► assembler, manufacturer. *See* **builder** (1).

construe *verb*
1. To understand in a particular way ► interpret, read, take. *Idioms:* read between the lines, see in a special light, take to mean. **2.** To make understandable ► decipher, interpret. *See* **explain** (1). *See synonym note at* **explain. 3.** To express in another language ► interpret, render. *See* **translate** (1).

construe *noun*
The act or process of translating ► crib, rendering. *See* **translation** (1).

consuetude *noun*
► form, habit, practice. *See* **custom** (1).

consul *noun*
► ambassador, deputy, proxy. *See* **representative** (2).

consult *verb*
► advise, talk. *Informal:* huddle. *See* **confer** (1).

consultant *noun*
► counselor, guide, mentor. *See* **adviser.**

consultation *noun*
► conference, counsel, debate, parley. *See* **deliberation** (1).

consulting *adjective*
► consultatory, recommendatory. *See* **advisory.**

consume *verb*
1. To engulf completely ► desolate, devastate, devour, dispatch, eat (up), ravage, swallow (up), waste. *Informal:* polish off, put away. *Idioms:* do away with, lay waste. *See also* **annihilate, destroy. 2.** To use all of ► eat up, expend, run through. *See* **exhaust** (1). **3.** To take food into the body as nourishment ► fare, ingest, partake. *See* **eat** (1). *See synonym note at* **eat. 4.** To reduce gradually, as by chemical reaction, weather, or friction ► corrode, eat (away *or* into), wear (away *or* down). *See* **erode. 5.** To be depleted ► exhaust, go, spend. *Idiom:* go down the drain. **6.** To occupy the full attention of ► engross, immerse, preoccupy. *See* **absorb** (1). *See synonym note at* **absorb.**

consumer *noun*
One who buys goods and services ► buyer, client, customer, patron, purchaser, shopper, user.

consummate *verb*
To bring or come to a natural or proper end ► close, finish, terminate. *See* **conclude** (1).

consummate *adjective*
1. Free from flaws or blemishes ► absolute, flawless, unblemished. *See* **perfect** (1). *See synonym note at* **perfect. 2.** Serving the function of deciding or settling with finality ► decisive, determinative. *See* **definitive** (1). **3.** Completely such, without qualification or exception ► all-out, pure, sheer. *See* **utter**[2].

consummation *noun*
1. A concluding or terminating ► cease, completion, termination. *See* **end** (1). **2.** The condition of being fulfilled ► culmination, fulfillment, realization. *See* **fulfillment** (1).

consumption *noun*
The act of consuming ► depletion, expenditure, usage, use, utilization. *See also* **use.**

contact *noun*
1. A coming together or touching ► contingence, taction, touch. *See also* **brush**[1], **touch. 2.** A situation allowing exchange of ideas or messages ► communication, correspondence, intercommunication, touch. *See also* **communication. 3.** An acquaintance who is in a position to help ► connection, source. **4.** One who acts as an intermediate agent between persons or groups ► intermediary, mediator, middleman. *See* **go-between.**

contact *verb*
To succeed in communicating with ► reach. *Informal:* catch, get. *Idioms:* catch up with, get hold of, get in touch with, get through to, get to.

contagion *noun*
1. Anything that is injurious, destructive, or fatal ► canker, toxin. *See* **poison** (1). **2.** One that contaminates ► impurity, poison, pollutant. *See* **contaminant.**

contagious *adjective*
Capable of transmission by infection ► catching, communicable, infectious, pestilent, pestilential, taking, transferable, transmittable, virulent.

contain *verb*
1. To have as a part ► comprehend, comprise, consist of, embody, embrace, encompass, have, include, involve, subsume, take in. **2.** To be filled by ► have, hold. *See also* **constitute. 3.** To have the room or capacity for ► accommodate, hold. *See synonym note at* **accommodate. 4.** To bring one's emotions under control ► collect, control. *See* **compose** (6). **5.** To confine within a limited area ► cage, coop (up), shut (in). *See* **enclose** (1).

✚ **CORE SYNONYMS:** *contain, include, comprise, comprehend, embrace, involve.* These verbs mean to have as a part of something larger. *Contain* is the most general: *This CD contains some of my favorite songs.* Include often implies an incomplete listing: "Through the process of amendment, interpretation and court decision I have finally been included in 'We, the people'" (Barbara C. Jordan). *Comprise* usually implies that all of the components are stated: *The book comprises 15* *chapters. Comprehend* and *embrace* usually refer to the taking in of subordinate elements: *My field of study comprehends several disciplines. This theory embraces many facets of human behavior. Involve* usually suggests inclusion as a logical consequence or necessary condition: *"Every argument involves some assumptions"* (Brooke F. Westcott).

container *noun*
An object, such as a carton, can, or jar, in which material is held or carried ► holder, receptacle, repository, vessel. *See also* **depository, package.**

contaminant *noun*
One that contaminates ► adulterant, adulterator, contagion, contamination, contaminator, disease, impurity, infection, pestilence, poison, pollutant, pollution, taint. *See also* **contamination, poison.**

contaminate *verb*
1. To make impure, unclean, or inferior by contact or mixture ► adulterate, corrupt, debase, doctor, foul, infect, load, poison, pollute, sophisticate, taint. *See also* **corrupt, dilute, dirty. 2.** To ruin morally ► debase, defile, pervert. *See* **corrupt** (1).

✚ CORE SYNONYMS: *contaminate, adulterate, debase, doctor, load.* These verbs mean to make impure, unclean, or inferior by adding foreign substances to something: *contaminated the river with industrial waste; adulterate coffee with ground acorns; silver debased with copper; doctored the wine with water; rag paper loaded with wood fiber.*

---

contaminated *adjective*
► alloyed, combined, polluted. *See* **impure** (2).

contamination *noun*
1. The state of being contaminated ► adulteration, corruption, defilement, dirtiness, foulness, impurity, infection, pollution, sophistication, uncleanliness, uncleanness, unwholesomeness. *See also* **decay, dirtiness. 2.** One that contaminates ► impurity, poison, pollutant. *See* **contaminant.**

contaminative *adjective*
► corruptive, perverting. *See* **unwholesome** (2).

contaminator *noun*
► impurity, poison, pollutant. *See* **contaminant.**

contemn *verb*
► disdain, dismiss, scorn. *See* **despise** (1). *See synonym note at* **despise.**

contemplate *verb*
1. To think or think about carefully and at length ► cogitate, deliberate, mull. *See* **ponder. 2.** To have in mind as a goal or purpose ► plan, target. *See* **intend** (1). **3.** To direct the eyes on an object ► eye, view. *See* **look** (1).

contemplation *noun*
1. An act of directing the eyes on an object ► look, regard, sight, view. *See also* **gaze, watch. 2.** The act or process of thinking ► cogitation, deliberation, rumination. *See* **thought** (1). **3.** Concentration of the mental powers on something ► concentration, consideration. *See* **attention** (1).

contemplative *adjective*
► cogitative, pensive, reflective. *See* **thoughtful** (1). *See synonym note at* **thoughtful.**

contemporaneous *adjective*
1. Belonging to the same period of time ► coexistent, concurrent, synchronous. *See* **contemporary** (1). **2.** Occurring or existing at the same time ► accompanying, coexisting. *See* **concurrent** (1). *See synonym note at* **concurrent.**

contemporary *adjective*
1. Belonging to the same period of time ► coetaneous, coeval, coexistent, concurrent, contemporaneous, synchronal, synchronic, synchronous. **2.** Characteristic of recent times or informed of what is current ► au courant, current, cutting-edge, latest, latter-day, modern, modernistic, present, recent, state-of-the-art, topical, up-to-date, up-to-the-minute, ultramodern. *See also* **fashionable, new. 3.** Existing at the same time ► attendant, attending. *See* **concurrent** (1). *See synonym note at* **concurrent. 4.** In existence now ► current, immediate. *See* **present**[1] (1).

contemporary *noun*
1. One of the same time or age as another ► coeval. **2.** A person of the present age ► modern.

contempt *noun*
1. The feeling of despising ► disdain, loathing, scorn. *See* **despisal. 2.** An attitude or behavior that is intentionally provocative or contemptuous ► despite, rebelliousness. *See* **defiance** (2). **3.** A strong feeling of hostility or dislike ► antipathy, aversion, loathing. *See* **hate** (1).

contemptible *adjective*
► abhorrent, disgusting, hateful, obnoxious. *See* **offensive** (1).

contemptuous *adjective*
1. Showing scorn and disrespect toward someone or something ► haughty, scornful, superior. *See* **disdainful** (1). **2.** Having or showing a lack of respect ► cheeky, discourteous, impolite. *See* **disrespectful** (1).

contend *verb*
1. To strive in opposition ► battle, clash, collide, combat, duel, encounter, engage, fence, fight, grapple, joust, meet, scuffle, spar, strive, struggle, take on, tilt, tussle, war, wrestle. *Idioms:* lock horns with, go to the mat with. *See also* **confront, oppose. 2.** To strive against others for victory ► race, rival, vie. *See* **compete. 3.** To engage in a quarrel ► fight, quarrel. *See* **argue** (1). **4.** To put forth reasons for or against something, often excitedly ► debate, dispute. *See* **argue** (2). **5.** To put into words positively and with conviction ► avow, declare, maintain. *See* **assert** (1).

contender *noun*
► challenger, opponent, rival. *See* **competitor.**

content *adjective*
Having achieved satisfaction, as of one's goal ► fulfilled, gratified, happy, satisfied.

content *verb*
To grant or have what is demanded by a need or desire ► fulfill, gratify. *See* **satisfy** (2).

contentedness *noun*
1. The condition of being satisfied ▶ contentment, fullfilment, gratification, satisfaction. *See also* **happiness, satiation.** 2. A condition of well-being and good spirits ▶ blessedness, bliss, felicity. *See* **happiness.**

contention *noun*
1. A discussion, often heated, in which a difference of opinion is expressed ▶ quarrel, run-in, spat. *See* **argument** (1). 2. A state of disagreement and disharmony ▶ discord, dissension, schism. *See* **conflict** (1). *See synonym note at* **conflict.** 3. A proposition to be maintained by argument ▶ proposal, proposition, thesis. *See* **theory** (2). 4. A vying with others for victory ▶ contest, rivalry, struggle. *See* **competition** (1). 5. The act of asserting positively or something so asserted ▶ claim, declaration, statement. *See* **assertion.**

contentious *adjective*
1. Given to arguing ▶ litigious, quarrelsome. *See* **argumentative.** *See synonym note at* **argumentative.** 2. Inclined to act in an aggressive or hostile way ▶ belligerent, combative, militant. *See* **aggressive** (1). *See synonym note at* **aggressive.** 3. In doubt or dispute ▶ disputable, doubtful, questionable. *See* **debatable.**

contentiousness *noun*
1. Hostile or warlike behavior or attitude ▶ aggressiveness, combativeness, militance. *See* **aggression** (1). 2. The power or will to fight ▶ belligerence, combativeness, pugnacity. *See* **fight** (2).

contentment *noun*
1. The condition of being satisfied ▶ contentedness, fullfilment, gratification, satisfaction. *See also* **happiness, satiation.** 2. A condition of well-being and good spirits ▶ blessedness, bliss, felicity. *See* **happiness.**

conterminous *adjective*
▶ bordering, contiguous, neighboring. *See* **adjoining.**

contest *noun*
1. A vying with others for victory ▶ battle, rivalry, struggle. *See* **competition** (1). 2. A test of skill or ability ▶ bout, match, trial. *See* **competition** (2).

contest *verb*
1. To take a stand against ▶ buck, challenge, dispute, oppose, resist, traverse. *Idiom:* go against. *See also* **confront, object, oppose.** 2. To strive against others for victory ▶ race, rival, vie. *See* **compete.** *See synonym note at* **compete.**

contestable *adjective*
▶ disputable, doubtful, questionable. *See* **debatable.**

contestant *noun*
▶ contender, opponent, rival. *See* **competitor.**

context *noun*
1. Existing surroundings that affect an activity ▶ circumstances, setting. *See* **conditions.** 2. The surrounding conditions and circumstances affecting growth or development ▶ climate, surroundings. *See* **environment** (2).

contexture *noun*
▶ fabric, grain, web. *See* **texture** (1).

contiguous *adjective*
1. Sharing a common boundary ▶ adjacent, bordering, neighboring. *See* **adjoining.** 2. Not far from another in space, time, or relation ▶ near, nearby, nigh. *See* **close** (1).

continence *noun*
▶ abstinence, self-denial, sobriety. *See* **temperance** (1). *See synonym note at* **temperance.**

continent *adjective*
1. Characterized by self-restraint in appetites and behavior ▶ abstemious, spartan. *See* **temperate** (2). 2. Morally beyond reproach ▶ modest, pure, virginal. *See* **chaste.**

contingence *noun*
A coming together or touching ▶ contact, taction, touch. *See also* **brush**[1], **touch.**

contingency *noun*
1. Something that may occur or be done ▶ eventuality, potentiality. *See* **possibility** (1). 2. The random, unintended, or unpredictable element of an event or the force regarded as the cause of such an event ▶ coincidence, fortune, luck. *See* **chance** (2).

contingent *adjective*
1. Having a good chance of happening or being true ▶ likely, possible. *See* **probable** (1). 2. Depending on or containing a condition or conditions ▶ dependent, provisory, tentative. *See* **conditional.** *See synonym note at* **conditional.** 3. Occurring unexpectedly ▶ chance, fortuitous, inadvertent. *See* **accidental** (1). *See synonym note at* **accidental.**

continual *adjective*
Existing or occurring without interruption or end ▶ around-the-clock, ceaseless, constant, continuous, endless, eternal, everlasting, incessant, interminable, never-ending, nonstop, ongoing, perennial, perpetual, persistent, relentless, round-the-clock, timeless, unbroken, unceasing, undying, unending, unfailing, uninterrupted, unremitting. *See also* **ageless, continuing, endless, unchanging.**

✦ **CORE SYNONYMS:** *continual, continuous, constant, ceaseless, incessant, perpetual, eternal, perennial, interminable.* These adjectives mean occurring repeatedly over a long period of time. *Continual* is chiefly restricted to what is intermittent or repeated at intervals: *The continual banging of the shutter in the wind gave me a headache. Continuous* implies lack of interruption: *The horizon is a continuous line. Constant* stresses steadiness or persistence and unvarying nature: *The constant ticking of the clock lulled him to sleep. Ceaseless* and *incessant* pertain to uninterrupted activity: *The ceaseless thunder of the surf eroded the beach. The toddler asked incessant questions. Perpetual* emphasizes both steadiness and duration: *The ambassador had a perpetual stream of visitors. Eternal* refers to what is everlasting, especially to what is seemingly without temporal beginning or end: *"That freedom can be retained only by the eternal vigilance which has always been its price"* (Elmer Davis). *Perennial* describes existence that goes on year after year, often with the suggestion of self-renewal: *The* *candidates discussed the perennial problem of urban poverty. Interminable refers to what is or seems to be endless and is often applied to something prolonged and wearisome: After an interminable delay, our flight was canceled outright.*

continually *adverb*
Without stop or interruption ▸ ceaselessly, constantly, continuously, endlessly, forever, incessantly, interminably, nonstop, perpetually, persistently, relentlessly, steadily, unceasingly, unfailingly, unremittingly. *Slang:* 24-7. *Idioms:* around (*or* round) the clock, all the time, seven days a week. *See also* **forever, usually.**

continuance *noun*
▸ continuum, persistence. *See* **continuation** (1).

continuation *noun*
1. Uninterrupted existence or succession ▸ continuance, continuity, continuum, durability, duration, endurance, permanence, persistence, persistency, survival. *See also* **endlessness, stability. 2.** A continuing after interruption ▸ renewal, resumption, resurgence, revival. *See also* **revival.**

continue *verb*
1. To begin or go on after an interruption ▸ pick up, proceed, renew, reopen, restart, resume, take up. **2.** To be in existence or in a certain state for an indefinitely long time ▸ bide, hold steady, persist. *See* **endure** (2). **3.** To proceed on a certain course or for a certain distance ▸ reach, stretch. *See* **extend** (1).

continuing *adjective*
1. Existing or remaining in the same state for an indefinitely long time ▸ abiding, durable, enduring, lasting, long-lasting, long-lived, long-standing, maintaining, old, perdurable, perennial, permanent, persevering, persistent, persisting. *See also* **continual, endless, unchanging. 2.** Of long duration ▸ lingering, persistent. *See* **chronic** (2).

continuity *noun*
▸ continuum, persistence. *See* **continuation** (1).

continuous *adjective*
▸ constant, endless, everlasting, perpetual. *See* **continual.** *See synonym note at* **continual.**

continuum *noun*
▸ continuance, persistence. *See* **continuation** (1).

contort *verb*
▸ disfigure, misshape, twist. *See* **deform.** *See synonym note at* **deform.**

contortion *noun*
▸ blemish, disfigurement, malformation. *See* **deformity.**

contour *noun*
▸ configuration, design, structure. *See* **form** (1). *See synonym note at* **form.**

contrabandist *noun*
A person who engages in smuggling ▸ bootlegger, runner, smuggler. *Slang:* mule.

contract *noun*
An often written acceptance of terms between parties ▸ compact, pact. *See* **agreement** (1). *See synonym note at* **agreement.**

contract *verb*
1. To enter into a formal agreement ▸ bargain, covenant, stipulate. *Idioms:* shake hands on, sign on the dotted line, strike a bargain. *See also* **agree, pledge, settle. 2.** To become affected with a disease ▸ catch, develop, get, incur, sicken, take. *Informal:* pick up. *Idiom:* come down with. *See also* **develop, get. 3.** To assume an obligation ▸ engage, undertake. *See* **pledge** (2). **4.** To make smaller or narrower by binding or squeezing ▸ compress, narrow, shrink. *See* **constrict** (1).

contraction *noun*
▸ compression, squeeze. *See* **constriction.**

contractor *noun*
▸ assembler, manufacturer. *See* **builder** (1).

contradict *verb*
1. To refuse to admit the truth, reality, value, or worth of ▸ contravene, disaffirm, disavow. *See* **deny** (1). *See synonym note at* **deny. 2.** To fail to be in accord ▸ contrast, disagree, discord. *See* **conflict.**

contradiction *noun*
1. The act or condition of conflict ▸ aversion, polarity. *See* **opposition** (1). **2.** A refusal to grant the truth of a statement or charge ▸ disaffirmation, disclaimer, rejection. *See* **denial** (1). **3.** That which is diametrically opposed to another ▸ antithesis, contrary. *See* **opposite.**

contradictory *adjective*
1. Diametrically opposed ▸ antithetical, contrary, diametric. *See* **opposite** (1). *See synonym note at* **opposite. 2.** Marked by a disposition to oppose ▸ antagonistic, hostile. *See* **contrary** (1). **3.** In sharp opposition ▸ conflicting, counter, inconsistent. *See* **discrepant** (1).

contradictory *noun*
That which is diametrically opposed to another ▸ antithesis, contrary. *See* **opposite.**

contradistinction *noun*
▸ contradiction, polarity. *See* **opposition** (1).

contraindicated *adjective*
▸ ill-advised, imprudent, inadvisable. *See* **unwise.**

contralto *adjective*
▸ alto, bass, deep. *See* **low** (2).

contraposition *noun*
▸ contradiction, polarity. *See* **opposition** (1).

contrapositive *noun*
▸ antithesis, contrary. *See* **opposite.**

contraption *noun*
1. Something, as a machine, devised for a particular function ▸ appliance, invention, mechanism. *See* **device** (1). **2.** A small specialized mechanical device ▸ apparatus. *Informal:* widget. *Slang:* gizmo. *See* **gadget.**

contrariness *or* **contrariety** *noun*
▸ contradiction, polarity. *See* **opposition** (1).

contrarious *adjective*
▸ antagonistic, contradictory, hostile. *See* **contrary** (1).

contrary *adjective*
1. Marked by a disposition to oppose ▸ antagonistic, balky, contradictory, contrarious, difficult, froward,

hostile, impossible, inimical, ornery, perverse, wayward. *See also* **opposing. 2.** Diametrically opposed ▸ antithetical, contradictory, diametric. *See* **opposite** (1). *See synonym note at* **opposite. 3.** Not like another in nature, quality, amount, or form ▸ contrasting, divergent, variant. *See* **different** (1).

contrary *noun*
That which is diametrically opposed to another ▸ antithesis, contrary. *See* **opposite.**

contrast *verb*
1. To fail to be in accord ▸ contradict, disagree, discord. *See* **conflict. 2.** To be unlike or dissimilar ▸ depart, diverge, vary. *See* **differ** (1). **3.** To examine in order to note similarities and differences ▸ collate, counterpose, juxtapose. *See* **compare** (1).

contrast *noun*
1. The act or state of being contrasted ▸ collation, comparison, counterpoint, juxtaposition. **2.** The condition of being unlike or dissimilar ▸ departure, discrepancy, nonconformity. *See* **difference** (1).

contrasting *adjective*
1. Not like another in nature, quality, amount, or form ▸ contrary, divergent, variant. *See* **different** (1). **2.** In sharp opposition ▸ conflicting, discordant, inconsistent. *See* **discrepant** (1). **3.** Diametrically opposed ▸ antithetical, contrary. *See* **opposite** (1).

contravene *verb*
1. To fail to fulfill a promise or conform to a regulation ▸ break, infringe. *See* **violate** (1). **2.** To refuse to admit the truth, reality, value, or worth of ▸ abnegate, disaffirm, disavow. *See* **deny** (1). *See synonym note at* **deny.**

contravention *noun*
▸ infraction, infringement, violation. *See* **breach** (1).

contretemps *noun*
▸ mischance, misfortune, reversal. *See* **accident** (1).

contribute *verb*
1. To give in common with others ▸ ante, chip in, donate, give, subscribe. *Informal:* kick in. *Slang:* come across with. *Idiom:* do one's bit. *See also* **give. 2.** To help bring about a result ▸ chip in, conduce, partake, participate, share. *Idioms:* have a hand in, take part. *See also* **advance, help, participate. 3.** To present as a gift to a charity or cause ▸ bequeath, pledge. *See* **donate** (1).

contribution *noun*
▸ benefaction, endowment, offering. *See* **donation.**

contributive *adjective*
Tending to contribute to a result ▸ conducive, contributory, helpful, participatory. *See also* **auxiliary.**

contributor *noun*
1. A person who gives to a charity or cause ▸ benefactor, giver, patron. *See* **donor. 2.** One who supports or champions an activity, cause, or institution ▸ benefactor, sponsor. *See* **patron** (1). **3.** A person instrumental in the growth of something, especially in its early stages ▸ creator, producer. *See also* **developer.**

contributory *adjective*
1. Giving or able to give help or support ▸ assistant,

subsidiary. *See* **auxiliary** (1). **2.** Tending to contribute to a result ▸ conducive, contributive, helpful, participatory.

contrite *adjective*
▸ penitent, regretful, repentant. *See* **sorry** (1).

contriteness *noun*
▸ remorse, repentance. *See* **penitence.**

contrition *noun*
▸ regret, shame. *See* **penitence.** *See synonym note at* **penitence.**

contrivance *noun*
1. Something, as a machine, devised for a particular function ▸ appliance, contraption, invention. *See* **device** (1). **2.** A small specialized mechanical device ▸ apparatus. *Informal:* widget. *Slang:* gizmo. *See* **gadget. 3.** Something invented ▸ brainchild, concoction. *See* **invention** (2).

contrive *verb*
1. To form a strategy for ▸ devise, formulate, strategize. *See* **design** (1). **2.** To use ingenuity in making, developing, or achieving ▸ concoct, devise, dream up. *See* **invent** (1).

contrived *adjective*
1. Not natural or spontaneous ▸ effortful, forced, labored, strained. *See also* **awkward, stiff. 2.** Planned, weighed, or estimated in advance ▸ deliberate, intentional, premeditated. *See* **calculated** (1).

control *verb*
1. To occupy the preeminent position in ▸ command, prevail. *See* **dominate** (1). **2.** To have charge of the affairs of others ▸ administrate, direct, manage. *See* **administer** (1). **3.** To control the functioning or outcome of ▸ determine, regulate. *See* **govern** (1). **4.** To control the course of an activity ▸ handle, run, steer. *See* **conduct** (1). *See synonym note at* **conduct. 5.** To bring one's emotions under control ▸ contain, cool. *See* **compose** (6).

control *noun*
1. The right and power to command, decide, rule, or judge ▸ carte blanche, dominion, jurisdiction, might. *See* **authority** (1). **2.** The act of exercising controlling power or the condition of being so controlled ▸ command, dominion, reign. *See* **domination** (1). **3.** The condition or fact of being dominant ▸ authority, power, supremacy. *See* **dominance** (1). **4.** The continuous exercise of authority over a political unit ▸ governance, rule. *See* **government** (1). **5.** The keeping of one's thoughts and emotions to oneself ▸ constraint, restraint, self-restraint. *See* **reserve** (2). **6.** Something that limits or holds back ▸ check, constraint, curb. *See* **restraint** (1).

controllable *adjective*
Capable of being governed ▸ administrable, governable, manageable, rulable. *See also* **loyal, obedient.**

controlled *adjective*
1. Tending to keep one's thoughts and emotions to oneself ▸ inhibited, restrained, self-restrained. *See* **reserved** (1). **2.** Kept within certain limits ▸ checked, regulated. *See* **restricted** (1).

controlling *adjective*
1. Exercising controlling power or influence ▸ key, predominant, reigning. *See* **dominant** (1). 2. Serving to restrain forcefully ▸ inhibitive, restraining, restrictive. *See* **repressive**.

controversy *noun*
▸ contention, disagreement, quarrel. *See* **argument** (1). *See synonym note at* **argument**.

controvert *verb*
▸ contravene, disaffirm, disavow. *See* **deny** (1).

contumacious *adjective*
▸ disobedient, rebellious. *See* **defiant**.

contumacy *noun*
▸ contempt, contumaciousness, despite, rebelliousness. *See* **defiance** (2).

contumelious *adjective*
1. Rude and disrespectful ▸ bold, insolent, pert. *See* **impudent**. 2. Of, relating to, or characterized by verbal abuse ▸ invective, scurrilous. *See* **abusive**.

contumely *noun*
1. An act that offends a person's sense of pride or dignity ▸ aspersion, insult. *See* **indignity**. 2. Sustained, harshly abusive language ▸ condemnation, denunciation, invective. *See* **vituperation**.

contuse *verb*
To make a bruise or bruises on ▸ bruise. *Idioms:* beat (*or* leave) black-and-blue. *See also* **hurt**.

contusion *noun*
An injury that does not break the skin ▸ black-and-blue mark, bruise. *See also* **black eye, harm, trauma**.

conundrum *noun*
▸ enigma, puzzle, riddle. *See* **mystery**.

convalesce *verb*
▸ improve, mend, recuperate. *See* **recover** (2).

convalescence *noun*
The process or period of a return to health ▸ rally, recovery, recuperation.

convene *verb*
▸ cluster, gather, muster. *See* **assemble** (1). *See synonym note at* **assemble**.

convenience *noun*
Unrestricted freedom to choose ▸ discretion, leisure, pleasure, will.

conveniences *noun*
▸ advantages, resources, services. *See* **amenities** (1). *See synonym note at* **amenities**.

convenient *adjective*
1. Suited to one's needs or purpose ▸ appropriate, befitting, expedient, fit, good, handy, meet, proper, suitable, tailor-made, useful. *See also* **beneficial, opportune**. 2. Being within easy reach ▸ accessible, handy, nearby, ready. *Idioms:* at one's fingertips, at the ready, close (*or* near) at hand, close by. *See also* **available, central, close**.

convention *noun*
1. A formal assemblage of the members of a group ▸ assembly, conclave, conference, congress, convocation, council, meeting, session, synod. 2. A number of persons who have come or been gathered together

crowd, group. *Informal:* get-together. *See* **assembly** (1). *See synonym note at* **assembly** (1). 3. An often written acceptance of terms between parties ▸ accord, deal, pact. *See* **agreement** (1). 4. A formal, usually written settlement between nations ▸ accord, concord, pact. *See* **treaty**. 5. A habitual way of behaving ▸ form, habit, practice. *See* **custom** (1). 6. Behavior patterns, traits, and products considered as an expression of a certain people or period ▸ civilization, ethos, society. *See* **culture** (2). 7. A statement presented for acceptance, as by a religious group ▸ dogma, teaching. *See* **doctrine**.

conventional *adjective*
1. Conforming to established practice or standards ▸ button-down, canonical, conformist, conservative, doctrinaire, doctrinal, establishmentarian, normal, orthodox, received, regular, standard, stereotyped, straight, time-honored, traditional, typical, usual. *Slang:* square, uncool. *See also* **common, ordinary, prevailing**. 2. Generally approved or agreed upon ▸ accepted, orthodox, received. *See* **accepted**. 3. Fond of or given to ceremony ▸ courtly, formal, stately. *See* **ceremonious** (1).

conventionalize *verb*
To make conventional ▸ conform, homogenize, normalize, regularize, standardize, stereotype, stylize, traditionalize.

converge *verb*
1. To come together from different directions ▸ close, join, meet, unite. *See also* **combine**. 2. To direct toward a common center ▸ channel, focus, hone in. *See* **concentrate** (1).

converge on *verb*
To come near in space or time ▸ close in on, gain on. *See* **approach** (1).

convergence *noun*
1. The act or fact of coming near ▸ approach, coming, imminence, nearness. *See also* **advance, appearance**. 2. The act or fact of coming together ▸ concentration, confluence, conflux. *See* **junction** (1).

conversance *noun*
Personal knowledge derived from participation or observation ▸ acquaintance, experience, familiarity. *See also* **awareness**.

conversant *adjective*
Having good knowledge of something ▸ acquainted, familiar, versant, versed. *Idiom:* up on. *See also* **accustomed, informed**.

conversation *noun*
1. Spoken exchange ▸ chat, colloquy, confabulation, converse, dialogue, discourse, discussion, heart-to-heart, interlocution, interview, pillow talk, speech, talk, tete-a-tete. *Informal:* bull session, confab, talkfest. *Slang:* gabfest, jaw, rap. *See also* **chatter, gossip**. 2. The exchange of ideas ▸ communion, discussion, intercourse. *See* **communication** (1).

conversational *adjective*
1. In the style of conversation ▸ chatty, chitchatty, colloquial, communicative, confabulatory, cozy, in-

formal. **2.** Given to conversation ▸ garrulous, loquacious, talky. *See* **talkative.**

conversationalist *or* **conversationist** *noun*
One given to or skilled at conversation ▸ confabulator, dialogist, discourser, interlocutor, talker. *See also* **speaker.**

converse[1] *verb*
1. To engage in spoken exchange ▸ buttonhole, chat, confabulate, discourse, speak, talk. *Informal:* confab, visit. *See also* **chatter, confer, say. 2.** To speak together and exchange ideas and opinions about ▸ consider, debate. *Informal:* kick around. *See* **discuss.**

converse *noun*
Spoken exchange ▸ dialogue, discourse, talk. *See* **conversation** (1).

✛ CORE SYNONYMS: *converse, speak, talk, discourse.* These verbs mean to engage in spoken exchange. *Converse* stresses interchange of thoughts and ideas: *"With thee conversing I forget all time"* (John Milton). *Speak* and *talk* are both often interchangeable and are the most general: *He ate the entire meal without once speaking to his companion. "On an occasion of this kind it becomes more than a moral duty to speak one's mind. It becomes a pleasure"* (Oscar Wilde). *I want to talk with you about vacation plans. "Let's talk sense to the American people"* (Adlai E. Stevenson). *Discourse* usually refers to formal, extended speech: *"striding through the city, stick in hand, discoursing spontaneously on the writings of Hazlitt"* (Manchester Guardian Weekly).

---

converse[2] *adjective*
Diametrically opposed ▸ antithetical, contradictory, diametric. *See* **opposite** (1).

converse *noun*
That which is diametrically opposed to another ▸ antithesis, contrary. *See* **opposite.**

conversion *noun*
1. The process or result of changing from one use, function, or appearance to another ▸ change, changeover, metamorphosis, mutation, shift, transfiguration, transformation, translation, transmogrification, transmutation, transubstantiation, turn. *See also* **change. 2.** A fundamental change in one's beliefs ▸ metanoia, rebirth. *See also* **revival.**

convert *verb*
1. To change into a different form, substance, or state ▸ denature, metamorphose, morph, mutate, reshape, transfigure, transform, translate, transmogrify, transmute, transpose, transubstantiate. *See also* **change. 2.** To cause another to feel sure about something ▸ persuade, win over. *See* **convince** (1).

✛ CORE SYNONYMS: *convert, metamorphose, transfigure, transform, transmogrify, transmute.* These verbs mean to change into a different form, substance, or state: *convert stocks into cash; misery that was metamorphosed into happiness; a gangling adolescent who was transfigured into a handsome adult; transformed the bare stage into an enchanted forest; a boom that transmogrified the sleepy town into a bustling city; impossible to transmute lead into gold.*

---

convertible *adjective*
▸ fluid, unsettled, variable. *See* **changeable** (1).

convey *verb*
1. To cause to come along with oneself ▸ bear, fetch. *See* **bring** (1). **2.** To move while supporting ▸ bear, haul, lug. *See* **carry** (1). *See synonym note at* **carry. 3.** To serve as a conduit ▸ carry, transmit. *See* **conduct** (3). **4.** To spread a disease to others ▸ give, pass, transmit. *See* **communicate** (4). **5.** To make known ▸ disclose, divulge, transmit. *See* **communicate** (1). **6.** To put into words ▸ express, state, utter. *See* **say** (1). **7.** To give expression to, as by gestures, facial aspects, or bodily posture ▸ communicate, display. *See* **express** (3). **8.** To change the ownership of property by means of a legal document ▸ deed, grant, sign over. *See* **transfer** (1). **9.** To have a particular idea ▸ denote, intend, signify. *See* **mean**[1] (1).

conveyance *noun*
1. The moving of persons or goods from one place to another ▸ carriage, transit, transport. *See* **transportation** (1). **2.** Legal transfer of ownership or title ▸ assignment, transfer, transferal. *See* **grant. 3.** The act of delivering or the condition of being delivered ▸ consignment, transfer. *See* **delivery** (1).

conveyer *noun*
▸ carrier, courier, envoy. *See* **messenger.**

convict *verb*
▸ doom, sentence. *See* **condemn** (1).

convict *noun*
One who commits a crime ▸ culprit, lawbreaker, offender. *See* **criminal.**

conviction *noun*
1. The fact or condition of being without doubt ▸ assuredness, certainty, positiveness. *See* **sureness** (1). *See synonym note at* **sureness. 2.** Something thought to be true ▸ notion, persuasion, view. *See* **belief** (1). *See synonym note at* **belief.**

convince *verb*
1. To cause another to believe or feel sure about something ▸ assure, bring around (*or* round), convert, persuade, satisfy, sell (on), turn, win over. *See also* **dispose, prove. 2.** To succeed in causing a person to act or think in a certain way ▸ coax, induce, prevail on, talk into. *See* **persuade** (1). *See synonym note at* **persuade.**

convincing *adjective*
1. Serving to convince ▸ cogent, compelling, effective, efficacious, forceful, forcible, persuasive, satisfactory, telling. *See also* **believable, definite, sound**[2]**. 2.** Worthy of belief, as because of precision or faithfulness to an original ▸ credible, true, valid. *See* **authentic** (2).

convivial *adjective*
1. Enjoying company ▸ companionable, sociable. *See* **social** (1). *See synonym note at* **social. 2.** Being in or showing good spirits ▸ happy, jolly, jovial. *See* **cheerful** (1). **3.** Providing joy and pleasure ▸ festive, joyful, joyous. *See* **merry** (1).

conviviality *noun*
▶ gaiety, merrymaking, revelry. *See* **merriment** (2).

convocation *noun*
1. A formal assemblage of the members of a group ▶ conference, congress. *See* **convention** (1). 2. A number of persons who have come or been gathered together ▶ crowd, group. *Informal:* get-together. *See* **assembly** (1).

convoke *verb*
▶ convene, muster, summon. *See* **assemble** (1). *See synonym note at* **assemble.**

convoluted *adjective*
1. Difficult to understand because of intricacy ▶ elaborate, involved, labyrinthine. *See* **complex** (1). 2. Repeatedly curving in alternate directions ▶ curvy, sinuous, twisting. *See* **winding** (1).

convoy *verb*
▶ chaperon, company, escort. *See* **accompany** (1).

convulse *verb*
▶ churn, rock, shake. *See* **agitate** (1). *See synonym note at* **agitate.**

convulsion *noun*
1. A condition of anguished struggle and disorder ▶ paroxysm, throes, spasm. 2. The condition of being agitated or disturbed ▶ commotion, turmoil, unrest. *See* **agitation** (1). 3. A sudden and often acute manifestation of a disease ▶ attack, fit. *See* **seizure** (1). 4. A momentous or sweeping change ▶ cataclysm, metamorphosis, upheaval. *See* **revolution** (3).

cook *verb*
1. To prepare food for eating by the use of heat ▶ bake, barbecue, blanch, boil, braise, broil, brown, charbroil, coddle, deep-fry, fricassee, fry, griddle, grill, pan-broil, pan-fry, parboil, poach, roast, sauté, sear, simmer, steam, stir-fry, stew, toast. 2. To give an inaccurate view of by representing falsely or misleadingly ▶ fudge, misrepresent, pervert. *See* **distort** (1).

cook up *verb*
To use ingenuity in making, developing, or achieving ▶ contrive, devise, dream up. *See* **invent** (1).

cook *noun*
A person who prepares food for eating ▶ baker, chef, culinary artist.

cooking *noun*
▶ nourishment, victuals. *See* **food.**

cool *adjective*
1. Not friendly, sociable, or warm in manner ▶ aloof, chill, chilly, detached, distant, formal, frigid, frosty, glacial, icy, impersonal, offish, remote, reserved, reticent, solitary, standoffish, unapproachable, uncommunicative, undemonstrative, withdrawn. *See also* **cold.** 2. Not excited or agitated ▶ collected, composed. *See* **calm** (1). *See synonym note at* **calm.** 3. Marked by a low temperature ▶ chill, frigid, polar. *See* **cold** (1). *See synonym note at* **cold.** 4. *Slang* Particularly excellent ▶ fantastic, sensational, superb. *See* **marvelous** (1).

cool *verb*
To bring one's emotions under control ▶ contain, control. *See* **compose** (6).

cool *noun*
Slang A stable emotional state ▶ composure, equanimity, poise. *See* **balance** (2).

cooler *noun*
Slang A place for the confinement of persons in lawful detention ▶ brig, penitentiary, prison. *See* **jail.**

cool-headed *adjective*
▶ collected, composed, cool. *See* **calm** (1).

coolness *noun*
1. Lack of warmth ▶ chilliness, frigidity. *See* **cold.** 2. A stable emotional state ▶ collectedness, composure, equanimity, sang-froid. *See* **balance** (2). 3. Lack of emotion or interest ▶ disinterest, indifference, unconcern. *See* **apathy.**

coop *noun*
1. *Slang* A place for the confinement of persons in lawful detention ▶ brig, penitentiary, prison. *See* **jail.** 2. An enclosure for confining an animal ▶ kennel, stall. *See* **cage.**

coop up *verb*
To confine within a limited area ▶ box (in), cage, shut (in). *See* **enclose** (1). *See synonym note at* **enclose.**

cooperate *verb*
To work together toward a common end ▶ collaborate, combine, concert, concur, join, unite. *Idioms:* act in concert, join forces, pull together, team up. *See also* **ally, combine.**

cooperation *noun*
1. Joint work toward a common end ▶ coaction, collaboration, concert, synergy, teamwork. *See also* **agreement, alliance.** 2. The state of being associated ▶ alliance, connection, partnership. *See* **association** (1).

cooperative *adjective*
1. Working together toward a common end ▶ coactive, collaborative, collective, combined, concerted, group, joint, synergetic, synergic, synergistic, united. 2. Belonging to, shared by, or applicable to all alike ▶ general, mutual, public. *See* **common** (2).

coordinate *verb*
1. To bring into accord ▶ conform, integrate. *See* **harmonize** (1). 2. To combine and adapt in order to attain a particular effect ▶ blend, integrate. *See* **harmonize** (2). 3. To arrange according to class ▶ categorize, class, group. *See* **classify.**

cop *noun*
Informal ▶ officer, trooper. *See* **police officer.**

cop *verb*
1. *Slang* To take another's property without permission ▶ purloin, snatch, thieve. *See* **steal** (1). *See synonym note at* **steal.** 2. *Slang* To obtain possession or control of ▶ gain, get, take, win. *See* **capture** (1).

cop out *verb*
Slang To abandon a former position or commitment ▶ back out, retreat, walk out. *See* **renege.**

copartner *noun*
▶ ally, partner. *See* **associate** (1).

cope with *verb*
▶ deal with, handle, treat.

copious *adjective*
Characterized by abundance; as much as one needs or desires ▸ abundant, bounteous, plentiful. *See* **generous** (2). *See synonym note at* **generous.**

coplanar *adjective*
▸ flush, square. *See* **even** (2).

copper *noun*
Slang A member of a law-enforcement agency ▸ officer, trooper. *See* **police officer.**

copulate *verb*
To engage in sexual relations ▸ couple, have sex, have sexual intercourse, sleep together. *Idioms:* be intimate, do it, get it on, go all the way, go to bed, make love, make whoopee, roll in the hay. *See also* **neck, philander, sleep with.**

copy *noun*
1. Something closely resembling another ▸ carbon copy, counterpart, ditto, duplicate, facsimile, image, likeness, photocopy, reduplication, replica, replication, reproduction, simulacrum. *See also* **double, parallel. 2.** An inferior substitute imitating an original ▸ ersatz, imitation, pinchbeck, reprint, simulation. *Informal:* knockoff. *See also* **counterfeit.**

copy *verb*
1. To make a copy of ▸ clone, ditto, duplicate, imitate, photocopy, replicate, reprint, reproduce, simulate. *Informal:* knock off. *See also* **counterfeit, imitate, plagiarize. 2.** To take as a model ▸ emulate, imitate, model oneself (on, upon, *or* after). *See* **follow** (5).

copycat *noun*
Informal One who imitates ▸ ape, imitator, parrot. *See* **mimic.**

coquet *verb*
▸ dally, toy, trifle. *See* **flirt** (2).

coquetry *noun*
▸ dalliance, flirtation.

coquette *noun*
A woman who is given to flirting ▸ flirt, tease. *Informal:* vamp. *See also* **seductress.**

coquettish *adjective*
▸ coy, flirtatious, flirty.

cord *noun*
A band or fiber used to bind, tie, connect, or support ▸ bond, cable, chain, cordage, fetter, guy, lace, lacing, line, noose, rope, string, thong. *See also* **band, fastener, thread.**

cordage *noun*
▸ cable, line, string. *See* **cord.**

cordial *adjective*
▸ congenial, friendly, genial. *See* **amiable.** *See synonym note at* **amiable.**

cordiality *or* **cordialness** *noun*
▸ agreeability, congeniality, pleasantness. *See* **amiability.**

cordon *verb*
▸ corral, fence (in), shut (in). *See* **enclose** (1).

core *noun*
1. A point of origin or crucial factor ▸ axis, focus, nucleus. *See* **center** (3). **2.** The most central or essential part ▸ essence, marrow, quintessence. *See* **heart** (1). *See synonym note at* **heart.**

cork *noun*
Something used to fill a hole, space, or container ▸ stopper, stop. *See* **plug** (1).

cork *verb*
To plug up or block something, such as a hole or conduit ▸ clog, plug. *See* **fill** (2).

corkscrew *verb*
▸ snake, spiral, weave. *See* **wind²** (1).

corky *adjective*
Informal Very brisk, alert, and full of high spirits ▸ animated, chipper, vivacious. *See* **lively** (1).

corner *noun*
1. A difficult, often embarrassing situation or condition ▸ deep water, difficulty, fix. *See* **predicament. 2.** Exclusive control or possession ▸ monopoly. *See also* **domination.**

cornerstone *noun*
1. The lowest or supporting part ▸ footing, foundation, groundwork. *See* **base¹** (2). **2.** An underlying support, as for an argument or belief ▸ footing, foundation, underpinning. *See* **basis** (1).

cornucopia *noun*
▸ bounteousness, plenitude. *See* **plenty** (1).

corny *adjective*
1. Without freshness or appeal because of overuse ▸ clichéd, overused, stale, tired. *See* **trite. 2.** Affectedly or extravagantly emotional ▸ gushy, maudlin, soft. *See* **sentimental.**

corollary *noun*
▸ consequence, ramification, result. *See* **effect** (1).

corporal *adjective*
▸ fleshy, physical. *See* **bodily.** *See synonym note at* **bodily.**

corporation *noun*
▸ business, enterprise. *See* **company** (1).

corporeal *adjective*
1. Of or relating to the body ▸ fleshy, physical. *See* **bodily.** *See synonym note at* **bodily. 2.** Composed of or relating to things that occupy space and can be perceived by the senses ▸ concrete, tangible. *See* **physical** (1).

corporeality *noun*
▸ palpability, physicality, tactility. *See* **tangibility.**

corps *noun*
1. A group of people acting together in a shared activity ▸ party, troop. *See* **band²** (1). *See synonym note at* **band. 2.** A group of people organized for a particular purpose ▸ squad, team, unit. *See* **force** (5). **3.** A unit of troops on special assignment ▸ brigade, patrol. *See* **detachment** (7).

corpse *noun*
▸ carcass, remains. *See* **body** (2).

corpulent *adjective*
▸ chubby, pudgy, rotund. *See* **fat** (1). *See synonym note at* **fat.**

corpus *noun*
▸ amount, bulk. *See* **quantity** (3).

corral *verb*
To confine within a limited area ▸ cordon (off), fence (in), shut (in). *See* **enclose** (1).

corral *noun*
An enclosure for livestock ▸ fold, paddock, sty. *See* **pen²** (1).

correct *verb*
1. To make right what is wrong ▸ amend, emend, fix, mend, rectify, redress, reform, remedy, repair, revise, right, straighten (up *or* out). *Idioms:* put right (*or to* rights), set right (*or to* rights). *See also* **cure, fix. 2.** To castigate for the purpose of improving ▸ chasten, chide. *See also* **chastise. 3.** To subject one to a penalty for a wrong ▸ chastise, discipline, penalize. *See* **punish.** *See synonym note at* **punish.**

correct *adjective*
1. Conforming exactly to fact ▸ errorless, exact, precise. *See* **accurate** (1). **2.** Suitable for a particular person, condition, occasion, or place ▸ befitting, proper, right. *See* **appropriate** (1).

✦ **CORE SYNONYMS:** *correct, rectify, remedy, redress, reform, revise, amend.* These verbs mean to make right what is wrong. *Correct* refers to eliminating faults, errors, or defects: *I corrected the spelling mistakes. Rectify* stresses the idea of bringing something into conformity with a standard of what is right: *The omission of her name from the list will be rectified. Remedy* involves removing or counteracting something considered a cause of harm or damage: *He took courses to remedy his abysmal ignorance. Redress* refers to setting right something considered immoral or unethical and usually involves making reparation: *The wrong is too great to be redressed. Reform* implies broad change that improves form or character: *"Let us reform our schools, and we shall find little reform needed in our prisons"* (John Ruskin). *Amend* implies improvement through alteration or correction: *"Whenever* [the people] *shall grow weary of the existing government, they can exercise their constitutional right of amending it, or their revolutionary right to dismember or overthrow it"* (Abraham Lincoln).

---

correction *noun*
▸ castigation, chastisement, penalty. *See* **punishment.**

correctional *adjective*
▸ disciplinary, penal, punitory. *See* **punishing** (1).

corrective *adjective*
Tending to correct ▸ amendatory, emendatory, reformative, reformatory, remedial, reparative. *See also* **curative.**

corrective *noun*
An agent used to restore health ▸ elixir, medication, remedy. *See* **cure.**

correctly *adverb*
▸ cleanly, fairly, properly. *See* **fair¹** (1).

correctness *noun*
1. Freedom from error ▸ exactness, precision, rightness. *See* **accuracy** (1). **2.** Correspondence with fact or truth ▸ authenticity, truth, validity. *See* **veracity. 3.** Conformity to recognized standards, as of conduct

or appearance ▸ decorum, respectability, seemliness. *See* **decency** (2).

correlate *verb*
1. To come or bring together in one's mind or imagination ▸ connect, link. *See* **associate** (3). **2.** To combine and adapt in order to attain a particular effect ▸ blend, integrate. *See* **harmonize** (2).

correlate *noun*
Something closely analogous to something else ▸ correlative, counterpart. *See* **parallel.**

correlation *noun*
▸ connection, link, relationship. *See* **relation** (1).

correlative *noun*
Something closely analogous to something else ▸ analogue, counterpart. *See* **parallel.**

correlative *adjective*
Supplying mutual needs ▸ interdependent, interrelated, reciprocal. *See* **complementary.**

correspond *verb*
1. To be compatible or suitable ▸ chime, conform, match. *See* **agree** (1). *See synonym note at* **agree. 2.** To be equal or alike ▸ compare, match, parallel. *See* **equal** (1).

correspondence *noun*
1. A situation allowing exchange of ideas or messages ▸ communication, contact, intercommunication, touch. **2.** The exchange of ideas ▸ communion, discussion, intercourse. *See* **communication** (1). **3.** A written communication directed to another ▸ epistle, missive, note. *See* **letter** (1). **4.** The act or state of agreeing or conforming ▸ concordance, harmony, rapport. *See* **agreement** (2). **5.** The quality or state of being alike ▸ resemblance, similarity, uniformity. *See* **likeness** (1).

correspondent *noun*
1. Something closely analogous to something else ▸ correlative, counterpart. *See* **parallel. 2.** A person or group of persons whose occupation is journalism ▸ anchorperson, editorialist, media. *See* **press** (1).

correspondent *adjective*
In keeping with one's needs or expectations ▸ compatible, congenial, harmonious. *See* **agreeable** (1).

corresponding *adjective*
1. In keeping with one's needs or expectations ▸ compatible, congenial, harmonious. *See* **agreeable** (1). **2.** Possessing the same or almost the same characteristics ▸ analogous, similar, uniform. *See* **like². 3.** Properly or correspondingly related in size, amount, or scale ▸ commensurate, equivalent, proportionate. *See* **proportional** (1).

corrival *noun*
▸ contender, opponent, rival. *See* **competitor.**

corrivalry *noun*
▸ contest, rivalry, struggle. *See* **competition** (1).

corroborate *verb*
1. To assure the certainty or validity of ▸ affirm, attest, testify to, verify. *See* **confirm** (1). *See synonym note at* **confirm. 2.** To present evidence in support of ▸ buttress, substantiate. *See* **back** (2). **3.** To establish as true

or genuine through evidence ▶ authenticate, document, evidence. *See* **prove** (1).

corroboration *noun*
▶ authentication, circumstantiation, proof, verification. *See* **confirmation** (2).

corrode *verb*
1. To reduce gradually, as by chemical reaction, weather, or friction ▶ consume, eat (away *or* into), wear (away *or* down). *See* **erode. 2.** To spoil or destroy ▶ blight, dash. *See* **blast** (2).

corrosive *adjective*
1. So sharp as to cause mental pain ▶ caustic, scathing, sharp, vitriolic. *See* **biting. 2.** Causing harm or injury ▶ deleterious, evil, injurious. *See* **harmful.**

corrosiveness *noun*
▶ acridity, trenchancy. *See* **sarcasm.**

corrugate *verb*
▶ curl, ripple. *See* **wave** (2).

corrupt *verb*
1. To ruin morally ▶ animalize, bastardize, bestialize, brutalize, canker, contaminate, debase, debauch, defile, demoralize, deprave, infect, pervert, poison, pollute, soil, stain, suborn, subvert, taint, vitiate, warp. *See also* **damage, debase. 2.** To make impure or unclean by contact or mixture ▶ adulterate, pollute, taint. *See* **contaminate** (1). **3.** To become or cause to become rotten or unsound ▶ deteriorate, rot, spoil, turn. *See* **decay. 4.** To spoil or destroy ▶ corrode, dash. *See* **blast** (2). **5.** To buy or promise a bribe to ▶ fix. *Informal:* pay off. *See* **bribe.**

corrupt *adjective*
1. Utterly reprehensible in nature or behavior ▶ debased, degenerate, depraved, miscreant, perverse, perverted, rotten, unhealthy, villainous. *See also* **disgraceful, evil, offensive, sordid. 2.** Open to bribery or dishonesty ▶ bribable, dishonest, dishonorable, mercenary, praetorian, profiteering, venal. *Informal:* crooked. *Idioms:* on the pad, on the take. *See also* **underhand, unscrupulous. 3.** Containing an error or errors ▶ false, inaccurate, mistaken. *See* **erroneous.**

✚ CORE SYNONYMS: *corrupt, debase, debauch, deprave, pervert, vitiate.* These verbs mean to ruin morally: *was corrupted by limitless power; debased himself by pleading with the captors; a youth debauched by drugs and drink; indulgence that depraves the moral fiber; perverted her talent by putting it to evil purposes; a proof vitiated by a serious omission.*

---

corruption *noun*
1. Degrading, immoral acts or habits ▶ bestiality, criminality, debauchery, depravity, flagitiousness, immorality, impurity, perversion, rottenness, turpitude, vice, villainousness, villainy, wickedness. *See also* **cheat, crime. 2.** Departure from what is legally, ethically, and morally correct ▶ baseness, corruptness, depravity, dishonesty, improbity, jobbery, malfeasance, venality. *Informal:* crookedness. *See also* **disobedience, evil. 3.** A misused or an incorrect term ▶ barbarism, catachresis, impropriety, malapropism,

misusage, solecism. **4.** The state of being contaminated ▶ defilement, impurity, pollution. *See* **contamination** (1).

corruptive *adjective*
1. Morally detrimental ▶ contaminative, demoralizing, perverting. *See* **unwholesome** (2). **2.** Causing harm or injury ▶ deleterious, evil, injurious. *See* **harmful.**

corruptness *noun*
▶ dishonesty, improbity. *Informal:* crookedness. *See* **corruption** (2).

corsage *noun*
▶ garland, posy. *See* **bouquet** (1).

coruscate *verb*
▶ flash, glimmer, twinkle. *See* **glitter.**

coruscation *noun*
▶ flicker, spark, twinkle. *See* **flash** (1).

cosmic *adjective*
1. So pervasive and all-inclusive as to exist in or affect the whole world ▶ global, worldwide. *See* **universal** (1). **2.** Of or relating to the heavens ▶ empyreal, supernal. *See* **heavenly** (2).

cosmopolitan *adjective*
1. Experienced in the ways of the world; lacking natural simplicity ▶ sophisticated, worldly, worldly-wise. *See also* **experienced, shrewd, suave. 2.** So pervasive and all-inclusive as to exist in or affect the whole world ▶ cosmic, global, worldwide. *See* **universal** (1).

cosmos *noun*
▶ creation, world. *See* **universe** (1).

cosset *verb*
▶ coddle, pamper. *See* **baby.**

cost *noun*
1. An amount paid or to be paid for a purchase ▶ charge, disbursement, expenditure, expense, outlay, payment, price. *Informal:* tab. *See also* **toll, wage. 2.** The expenditure at which something is obtained ▶ expense, price, sacrifice, toll. *Informal:* damage.

cost *verb*
To require a specified price ▶ go for, sell for. *Idiom:* set someone back. *See also* **demand.**

costive *adjective*
▶ close-fisted, miserly, parsimonious. *See* **stingy** (1).

costly *adjective*
Of great value or price ▶ dear, expensive, high, high-priced, inestimable, invaluable, precious, priceless, rich, valuable, worthy. *Informal:* big-ticket, pricey. *Idioms:* beyond price, of great price, worth its weight in gold. *See also* **steep**[1].

costs *noun*
▶ budget, expenses. *See* **overhead.**

costume *noun*
1. A set or style of clothing ▶ garb, guise, outfit. *See* **dress** (2). **2.** Clothes or other personal effects, such as makeup, worn to conceal one's identity ▶ guise, mask, veil. *See* **disguise** (1).

costume *verb*
To put clothes on ▶ attire, costume, garb. *See* **dress** (1).

cote *noun*
▶ coop, kennel, stall. *See* **cage**.

coterie *noun*
▶ clique, group, set. *See* **circle** (3).

cotillion *noun*
▶ ball, hop, promenade. *See* **dance**.

cottage *noun*
▶ chalet, country home. *See* **villa**.

cotton *verb*
Informal To interact with another or others in a harmonious fashion ▶ connect, harmonize. *Slang:* click. *See* **relate** (5).

couch *verb*
1. To convey in language or words of a particular form ▶ express, formulate. *See* **phrase**. 2. To be or place oneself in a prostrate or recumbent position ▶ recline, stretch (out). *See* **lie**[1] (1).

council *noun*
1. A number of persons who have come or been gathered together ▶ crowd, group. *Informal:* get-together. *See* **assembly** (1). 2. A formal assemblage of the members of a group ▶ conference, congress. *See* **convention** (1).

counsel *noun*
1. An exchange of views in an attempt to reach a decision ▶ consultation, debate, parley. *See* **deliberation** (1). 2. An opinion as to a decision or course of action ▶ guidance, recommendation. *See* **advice** (1). *See synonym note at* **advice**. 3. A person who practices law ▶ attorney, jurist. *See* **lawyer**.

counsel *verb*
To give recommendations to someone about a decision or course of action ▶ guide, recommend. *See* **advise** (1). *See synonym note at* **advise**.

counseling *adjective*
▶ consultative, consultatory, recommendatory. *See* **advisory**.

counselor *noun*
1. One who advises another ▶ consultant, mentor. *See* **adviser**. 2. A person who practices law ▶ attorney, jurist. *See* **lawyer**.

count *verb*
1. To be of significance or importance ▶ import, matter, signify, weigh. 2. To note items one by one in order to get a total ▶ enumerate, number, numerate, reckon, score, tally, tell. *See also* **add, calculate, measure**. 3. To indicate time or rhythm ▶ beat, tap. *Idioms:* keep time, mark time.

count off *verb*
To name or specify one by one ▶ list, numerate. *See* **enumerate** (1).

count on *verb*
1. To place trust or confidence in ▶ bank on (*or* upon), rely on (*or* upon). *See* **depend on** (1). 2. To look forward to confidently ▶ await, look for. *See* **expect** (1).

count out *verb*
To keep from being admitted, included, or considered ▶ eliminate, keep out, rule out. *See* **exclude** (1).

count *noun*
1. A noting of items one by one ▶ enumeration, numeration, reckoning, score, tally. *See also* **calculation, total**. 2. A gathering of information or opinion from a variety of sources or individuals ▶ canvass, poll, survey.

✤ CORE SYNONYMS: *count, import, matter, signify, weigh.* These verbs mean to be of significance or importance: *an opinion that counts; actions that import little; decisions that really matter; thoughts that signify much; considerations that weigh with her.*

---

countenance *noun*
1. The front surface of the head ▶ features, visage. *See* **face** (1). 2. A disposition of the facial features that conveys meaning, feeling, or mood ▶ face, look, visage. *See* **expression** (4). 3. An outward appearance ▶ aspect, lineaments. *See* **face** (4).

countenance *verb*
1. To lend supportive approval to ▶ encourage, favor, smile on (*or* upon). *See also* **approve, support**. 2. To be favorably disposed toward ▶ approve, favor, hold with. *Informal:* go for. *Idioms:* be in favor of, take kindly to, think highly (*or* well) of. *See also* **assent, value**.

counter *adjective*
1. Diametrically opposed ▶ antithetical, contradictory, diametric. *See* **opposite** (1). 2. In sharp opposition ▶ conflicting, discordant, inconsistent. *See* **discrepant** (1).

counter *noun*
1. A small, often makeshift structure for the display and sale of goods ▶ booth, stand, stall. *See also* **store**. 2. That which is diametrically opposed to another ▶ antithesis, contrary. *See* **opposite**.

counter *verb*
1. To return like for like, especially to return an unfriendly or hostile action with a similar one ▶ hit back, reciprocate. *See* **retaliate**. 2. To place in opposition or be in opposition to ▶ match, pit. *See* **oppose** (1). *See synonym note at* **oppose**.

counteract *verb*
1. To act as an equalizing force to ▶ compensate, counterbalance, offset. *See* **balance** (2). 2. To make ineffective by applying an opposite force ▶ negate, neutralize. *See* **cancel** (2).

counterattack *verb*
To return like for like, especially to return an unfriendly or hostile action with a similar one ▶ counter, reciprocate, retort. *See* **retaliate**.

counterattack *or* **counteraction** *noun*
The act of retaliating ▶ reciprocation, reprisal, revenge. *See* **retaliation**.

counterbalance *verb*
1. To act as an equalizing force to ▶ counteract, countervail, offset. *See* **balance** (2). 2. To put in balance ▶ equalize, stabilize. *See* **balance** (1). 3. To make ineffective by applying an opposite force ▶ counteract, negate, offset. *See* **cancel** (2).

counterblow *noun*
▸ counteraction, reciprocation, reprisal. *See* **retaliation.**

counterfactual *adjective*
▸ spurious, untrue, wrong. *See* **false** (1).

counterfeit *verb*
1. To make a fraudulent copy of ▸ fabricate, fake, falsify, forge. *See also* **copy. 2.** To take on as a false appearance ▸ fake, feign, pose. *See* **act** (2).

counterfeit *adjective*
Fraudulently or deceptively imitative ▸ bogus, ersatz, fabricated, factitious, fake, false, forged, fraudulent, phony, sham, spurious, suppositious, supposititious. *See also* **artificial.**

counterfeit *noun*
A fraudulent imitation ▸ fabrication, fake, falsification, forgery, phony, sham. *See also* **copy.**

counterfeiter *noun*
▸ fabricator, faker, falsifier, forger.

countermand *verb*
1. To disavow something previously written or said irrevocably and usually formally ▸ abjure, recant, take back. *See* **retract** (1). **2.** To take back or remove ▸ repeal, rescind, revoke. *See* **lift** (5).

countermand *noun*
A formal statement of disavowal ▸ abjuration, palinode, withdrawal. *See* **retraction** (1).

countermeasure *noun*
▸ elixir, medication, remedy. *See* **cure.**

counterpart *noun*
1. One that has the same functions and characteristics as another ▸ equivalent, opposite number, vis-à-vis. **2.** One of a matched pair of things ▸ companion, twin. *See* **mate** (1). **3.** Something closely analogous to something else ▸ analogue, correlative. *See* **parallel. 4.** Something closely resembling another ▸ duplicate, facsimile, likeness. *See* **copy** (1).

counterpoint *noun*
The act or state of being contrasted ▸ comparison, juxtaposition. *See* **contrast.**

counterpoint *verb*
To examine in order to note similarities and differences ▸ contrast, counterpose, juxtapose. *See* **compare** (1).

counterpoise *noun*
A stable state of opposing forces ▸ equilibrium, stasis. *See* **balance** (1).

counterpoise *verb*
1. To act as an equalizing force to ▸ compensate, counteract, make up, offset. *See* **balance** (2). **2.** To make ineffective by applying an opposite force ▸ counterbalance, negate, offset. *See* **cancel** (2).

counterpose *verb*
▸ contrast, counterpoint, juxtapose. *See* **compare** (1).

counterproductive *adjective*
▸ ineffective, inefficient, useless. *See* **ineffectual** (1).

countervail *verb*
1. To act as an equalizing force to ▸ counteract, counterbalance, offset. *See* **balance** (2). **2.** To make

ineffective by applying an opposite force ▸ counteract, negate, offset. *See* **cancel** (2).

countless *adjective*
▸ boundless, immeasurable, infinite. *See* **incalculable.**
See synonym note at **incalculable.**

country *adjective*
Of or relating to the countryside ▸ agrarian, arcadian, bucolic, campestral, georgic, pastoral, provincial, rural, rustic. *Informal:* hick.

country *noun*
1. A remote or rural area ▸ backcountry, backwoods, countryside, God's country, hinterland. *Informal:* sticks. *Slang:* boondocks, boonies, hicksville. *See also* **desert¹, wilderness. 2.** An organized geopolitical unit ▸ land, nation. *See* **state** (1). **3.** A particular area used for or associated with a specific individual or activity ▸ district, region, terrain. *See* **territory** (1).

✢ CORE SYNONYMS: *country, rural, bucolic, rustic, pastoral.* These adjectives mean typical of the countryside as distinguished from the city. *Country* is the most general: *I left New York City to visit my country cousins. Rural* applies to sparsely settled or agricultural country: *"I do love quiet, rural England"* (George Meredith). *Bucolic* is often used pejoratively or facetiously of country people or their manners: *"The keenest of bucolic minds felt a whispering awe at the sight of the gentry"* (George Eliot). *Rustic* frequently suggests a lack of sophistication or elegance, but it may also connote artless and pleasing simplicity: *"some rustic phrases which I had learned at the farmer's house"* (Jonathan Swift). *The hiker slept in a charming, rustic cottage. Pastoral,* which evokes the image of shepherds, sheep, and verdant countryside, suggests serenity: *The train passed through pastoral landscapes.*

---

countryman *or* **countrywoman** *noun*
A person who is from one's own country ▸ compatriot, fellow citizen, kinsman, kinswoman.

countryside *noun*
▸ backwoods, hinterland. *See* **country** (1).

coup *noun*
▸ achievement, deed, triumph. *See* **accomplishment** (1).

couple *noun*
Two items of the same kind together ▸ brace, couplet, doublet, duet, duo, dyad, match, pair, span, two, twosome, yoke. *See also* **several.**

couple *verb*
1. To join one thing to another ▸ append, fasten, secure. *See* **attach** (1). *See synonym note at* **attach** (1). **2.** To bring or come together into a united whole ▸ join, unify, unite. *See* **combine** (1). **3.** To come or bring together in one's mind or imagination ▸ correlate, link. *See* **associate** (3). **4.** To engage in sexual relations ▸ have sex, sleep together. *See* **copulate.**

couplet *noun*
▸ duet, match, pair. *See* **couple.**

coupling *noun*
▸ connection, juncture, seam. *See* **joint** (1).

courage *noun*

The quality of mind enabling one to face danger or hardship resolutely ▸ backbone, braveness, bravery, courageousness, dauntlessness, doughtiness, fearlessness, fortitude, gallantry, gameness, hardihood, hardiness, heart, heroism, intestinal fortitude, intrepidity, intrepidness, mettle, nerve, pluck, pluckiness, prowess, spine, spirit, stoutheartedness, undauntedness, valiance, valiancy, valiantness, valor. *Informal:* grit, spunk, spunkiness. *Slang:* guts, gutsiness, moxie. *See also* **daring, decision, temerity.**

courageous *adjective*

Having or showing courage ▸ audacious, fearless, heroic. *See* **brave.** *See synonym note at* **brave.**

courageousness *noun*

▸ bravery, fortitude, gallantry, valor. *See* **courage.**

courier *noun*

▸ carrier, envoy. *See* **messenger.**

course *noun*

1. A method used for accomplishing something ▸ modus operandi, procedure, technique. *See* **approach** (1). 2. A number of things placed or occurring one after the other ▸ order, procession, sequence. *See* **series.** 3. The compass direction in which a ship or aircraft moves ▸ bearing, heading, vector. 4. The spatial path along which motion or orientation is referred ▸ heading, route. *See* **direction** (1). 5. The period during which someone or something exists ▸ existence, span, term. *See* **life** (1). 6. A course affording passage from one place to another ▸ path, road, route. *See* **way** (2).

course *verb*

To move freely as a liquid ▸ run, stream. *See* **flow** (1).

court *noun*

1. A roofless area partially or entirely enclosed by walls or buildings ▸ atrium, close, courtyard, enclosure, patio, quad, quadrangle, yard. 2. A judicial assembly ▸ bar, forum, judicature, judiciary, tribunal.

court *verb*

1. To behave so as to bring on danger, for example ▸ invite, provoke, solicit, tempt. *Idiom:* ask for it. *See also* **attract, provoke.** 2. To attempt to gain the affection of ▸ chase, pursue, run after, spark, woo. *Informal:* romance. *Idiom:* make a play for. *See also* **appeal, flirt, see.**

courteous *adjective*

1. Characterized by good manners ▸ civil, genteel, gentlemanly, mannerly, polite, well-bred, well-mannered, well-spoken. *See also* **ceremonious, cultured, suave.** 2. Full of polite concern for the well-being of others ▸ considerate, solicitous, thoughtful. *See* **attentive** (1). 3. Characterized by kindness and warm, unaffected courtesy ▸ affable, gracious, hospitable. *See also* **amiable.**

✦ CORE SYNONYMS: *courteous, polite, mannerly, civil, genteel.* These adjectives mean conforming to or characterized by good manners. *Courteous* implies courtliness and dignity: *"If a man be gracious and*

courteous to strangers, it shows he is a citizen of the world" (Francis Bacon). *Polite* and *mannerly* imply consideration for others and the adherence to conventional social standards of good behavior: *"It costs nothing to be polite"* (Winston S. Churchill). *The child was scolded by the teacher for not being more mannerly. Civil* suggests only the barest observance of accepted social usages; it often means merely neither polite nor rude: *If you can't be friendly, at least be civil. Genteel,* which originally meant well-bred, now usually suggests excessive and affected refinement: *"A man, indeed, is not genteel when he gets drunk"* (James Boswell).

◂ ANTONYM: *discourteous*

courteousness *noun*

1. Well-mannered behavior toward others ▸ gentility, politeness. *See* **courtesy** (1). 2. Social courtesies ▸ civility, pleasantry, politeness. *See* **amenities** (2).

courter *noun*

▸ admirer, suitor. *See* **beau** (1).

courtesan *noun*

▸ call girl, strumpet. *See* **harlot.**

courtesy *noun*

1. Well-mannered behavior toward others ▸ civility, courteousness, genteelness, gentility, mannerliness, politeness, politesse. *See also* **consideration, manners.** 2. Social courtesies ▸ civility, pleasantry, politeness. *See* **amenities** (2). 3. A kindly act ▸ good deed, kindness. *See* **favor** (1).

courtier *noun*

▸ flatterer, minion, slave. *See* **sycophant.**

courtliness *noun*

▸ dignity, grace, urbanity. *See* **elegance.**

courtly *adjective*

1. Characterized by elaborate, usually formal courtesy ▸ chivalrous, gallant, stately. *See* **gracious** (2). 2. Fond of or given to ceremony ▸ conventional, formal, stately. *See* **ceremonious** (1). 3. Exhibiting refined, tasteful beauty of manner, form, or style ▸ graceful, refined. *See* **elegant** (1).

courtyard *noun*

▸ enclosure, quad. *See* **court** (1).

cove *noun*

▸ anchorage, haven. *See* **harbor** (1).

covenant *noun*

1. An often written acceptance of terms between parties ▸ compact, contract, pact. *See* **agreement** (1). *See synonym note at* **agreement.** 2. A declaration that one will or will not do a certain thing ▸ assurance, pledge, vow. *See* **promise** (1).

covenant *verb*

1. To enter into a formal agreement ▸ bargain, stipulate. *See* **contract** (1). 2. To guarantee by a solemn promise ▸ promise, vow. *See* **pledge** (1).

cover *verb*

1. To extend over the surface of ▸ blanket, cap, carpet, coat, overlay, overspread, pave, plate, spread. *See also* **finish.** 2. To journey over ▸ cross, go, make, traverse. *Informal:* do. *See also* **cross, journey.** 3. To prevent

something from being known ▸ enshroud, mask. *See* **conceal** (1). **4.** To put a covering of different material on ▸ clad, sheathe, side. *See* **face** (2). **5.** To change or fluctuate within limits ▸ range, vary. *See* **go** (7). **6.** To keep safe from danger, attack, or harm ▸ protect, safeguard, secure. *See* **defend** (1).

cover for *verb*
To act as a substitute ▸ cover for, fill in. *See* **substitute** (1).

cover *noun*
1. Something that physically protects, especially from danger ▸ ark, asylum, covert, coverture, harbor, haven, port, protection, refuge, retreat, safe house, sanctuary, screen, shelter. *See also* **defense, fort, hide-out. 2.** Something that covers, especially to prevent contents from spilling ▸ cap, covering, lid, top. *See also* **plug. 3.** The material in which something is wrapped ▸ covering, packaging. *See* **wrapper. 4.** A deceptive outward appearance ▸ disguise, mask, pretense. *See* **façade** (2). **5.** A covering that obscures or hides something ▸ cloak, screen. *See* **veil** (1). **6.** One that can take the place of another ▸ replacement, stand-in, surrogate. *See* **substitute.**

✦ CORE SYNONYMS: *cover, shelter, retreat, refuge, asylum, sanctuary.* These nouns refer to places affording protection, as from danger, or to the state of being protected. *Cover* suggests something that conceals: *traveled under cover of darkness. Shelter* usually implies a covered or enclosed area that protects temporarily, as from injury or attack: *built a shelter out of pine and hemlock boughs. Retreat* applies chiefly to a secluded place to which one retires for meditation, peace, or privacy: *a rural cabin that served as a weekend retreat. Refuge* suggests a place of escape from pursuit or from difficulties that beset one: *"The great advantage of a hotel is that it's a refuge from home life"* (George Bernard Shaw). *Asylum* adds to *refuge* the idea of legal protection or of immunity from arrest: *"O! receive the fugitive and prepare in time an asylum for mankind"* (Thomas Paine). *Sanctuary* denotes a sacred or inviolable place of refuge: *political refugees finding sanctuary in a monastery.*

---

coverage *noun*
The measure of how far or long something goes in space, time, or degree ▸ extension, span, stretch. *See* **extent** (1).

covering *noun*
1. Something that covers, especially to prevent contents from spilling ▸ cap, cover, lid, top. *See also* **plug. 2.** A layer of material covering something else ▸ blanket, coating, overlay. *See* **coat** (2). **3.** The material in which something is wrapped ▸ casing, packaging. *See* **wrapper.**

covert *adjective*
1. Operating in a way so as to ensure concealment and confidentiality ▸ clandestine, cloak-and-dagger, undercover. *See* **secret** (1). **2.** Lying beyond what is obvious or avowed ▸ buried, concealed, hidden. *See* **ulterior** (1). **3.** Difficult or impossible to see or distin-

guish ▸ concealed, disguised, unseen. *See* **hidden** (1).

covert *noun*
1. Something that physically protects, especially from danger ▸ harbor, haven, refuge. *See* **cover** (1). **2.** A hiding place ▸ den, hideaway, hide-out, lair.

covertly *adverb*
▸ clandestinely, sub rosa. *See* **secretly.**

covertness *noun*
▸ concealment, secretiveness. *See* **secrecy.**

covet *verb*
1. To feel envy toward or for ▸ begrudge, envy, grudge. *See synonym note at* **envy. 2.** To have a strong longing for ▸ want, yearn. *See* **desire** (1). *See synonym note at* **desire.**

covetous *adjective*
1. Resentfully or painfully desirous of another's advantages ▸ invidious, jealous. *See* **envious. 2.** Having a strong urge to obtain or possess something, especially material wealth, in quantity ▸ avaricious, hungry. *See* **greedy** (1).

covetousness *noun*
1. Resentful or painful desire for another's advantages ▸ enviousness, jealousy. *See* **envy. 2.** Excessive desire for more than one needs or deserves ▸ avarice, rapacity. *See* **greed.**

cow *verb*
▸ browbeat, bully. *See* **intimidate** (1). *See synonym note at* **intimidate.**

coward *noun*
An ignoble, uncourageous person ▸ caitiff, craven, cur, dastard, funk, milksop, milquetoast, mouse, poltroon, recreant, sissy. *Informal:* nervous Nellie, scaredy-cat. *Slang:* chicken, fraidy cat, yellow-belly. *See also* **defector, sneak, weakling.**

cowardice *noun*
Ignoble lack of courage ▸ chickenheartedness, cowardliness, cravenness, dastardliness, faint-heartedness, funk, poltroonery, pusillanimity, recreance, spinelessness, unmanliness, white feather. *Slang:* gutlessness, yellowness, yellow streak. *See also* **fear.**

cowardliness *noun*
▸ faint-heartedness, pusillanimity. *Slang:* gutlessness. *See* **cowardice.**

cowardly *adjective*
Ignobly lacking in courage ▸ caitiff, chickenhearted, chicken-livered, craven, dastardly, faint-hearted, lily-livered, pusillanimous, recreant, sissy, spineless, supine, unmanly, weak-kneed. *Slang:* chicken, gutless, wimpy, yellow, yellow-bellied. *See also* **afraid.**

cower *verb*
▸ cringe, recoil, shrink. *See* **flinch.**

coxcomb *noun*
A man who is vain about his clothes ▸ beau, dandy, fop, peacock, swell.

coy *adjective*
1. Given to flirting ▸ coquettish, flirtatious, flirty.
2. Awkward or unconfident in behavior or manner

▸ bashful, demure, diffident. *See* **shy**[1] (1). *See synonym note at* **shy**[1].

coyness *noun*

▸ bashfulness, demureness, diffidence. *See* **shyness**.

cozen *verb*

1. To cause to accept something false, especially by trickery or misrepresentation ▸ dupe, fool, mislead, trick. *See* **deceive**. 2. To get something by deceitful trickery ▸ bilk, defraud, swindle. *See* **cheat** (1).

cozener *noun*

▸ cheater, swindler, trickster. *See* **cheat** (2).

cozy *adjective*

1. Affording pleasurable ease ▸ easy, snug. *Informal:* comfy. *See* **comfortable** (1). *See synonym note at* **comfortable**. 2. Very closely associated ▸ chummy, close, familiar. *See* **intimate**[1] (1).

crab *noun*

A person who habitually complains or grumbles ▸ complainer, grump, whiner. *See* **grouch** (1).

crab *verb*

Informal To express feelings of pain, dissatisfaction, or resentment ▸ fuss, grouch, whine. *See* **complain**.

crabbed *adjective*

1. Having or showing a bad temper ▸ cranky, grouchy, peevish. *See* **ill-tempered**. 2. Difficult to understand because of intricacy ▸ convoluted, elaborate, involved, labyrinthine. *See* **complex** (1).

crabby *adjective*

▸ cranky, grouchy, peevish. *See* **ill-tempered**.

crack *verb*

1. To undergo partial breaking ▸ break, cleave, crackle, craze, fissure, fracture, rift, rupture, split. *See also* **cut, tear**[1] 2. To make a sudden, sharp noise ▸ bang, bark, clap, pop, snap. *See also* **blast, crackle, snap**. 3. To crack or split into two or more fragments by means of force or strain ▸ fracture, shatter. *See* **break** (1). *See synonym note at* **break**. 4. To strike together noisily ▸ crash, slam, whack. *See* **bang** (1). 5. To find the key to a code or cipher ▸ decrypt, unscramble. *See* **decipher** (1). 6. To suddenly lose all health or strength ▸ drop, succumb. *See* **collapse** (1). 7. To become or cause to become open ▸ free, release, unclose. *See* **open** (1).

crack up *verb*

1. *Informal* To wreck a vehicle ▸ smash, wreck. *See* **crash** (1). 2. To give way mentally and emotionally ▸ collapse, crumple, snap. *See* **break** (5). 3. *Informal* To suddenly lose all health or strength ▸ give out, succumb. *See* **collapse** (1).

crack *noun*

1. A sudden sharp, explosive noise ▸ bang, bark, clap, detonation, explosion, pop, rat-a-tat-tat, report, snap. *See also* **blast, crackle, snap**. 2. A partial opening caused by splitting and rupture ▸ breach, break, chink, cleavage, cleft, cranny, crevice, fault, fissure, fracture, niche, rift, rupture, split. *See also* **cut, hole**. 3. A sudden heavy stroke ▸ bang, hit, swat, whack. *See* **blow**[2] (1). 4. A trying to do or make something ▸ effort, trial. *Informal:* shot. *See* **attempt** (1). 5. A flippant or sarcastic remark ▸ barb, dig, jest, quip.

Slang: wisecrack. *See also* **joke**. 6. A very brief interval of time ▸ instant, second, wink. *See* **flash** (2).

crack *adjective*

Having or demonstrating a high degree of knowledge or skill ▸ master, skilled. *See* **expert**.

crackdown *noun*

Forceful subjugation, as against an uprising ▸ clampdown, lockdown, repression, suppression. *See also* **oppression, restraint**.

cracked *adjective*

1. Not closed, sealed, or fastened ▸ agape, undone, unlocked. *See* **open** (1). 2. *Informal* Afflicted with or exhibiting irrationality and mental unsoundness ▸ crazy, lunatic, mad. *See* **insane** (1).

crackerjack *adjective*

Slang Having or demonstrating a high degree of knowledge or skill ▸ adept, master, skilled. *See* **expert**.

crackerjack *noun*

Slang A person with a high degree of knowledge or skill in a particular field ▸ master, wizard. *See* **expert**.

crackle *verb*

1. To make a series of short, sharp noises ▸ crepitate, splutter, sputter. *See also* **crack, hiss, snap**. 2. To undergo partial breaking ▸ rupture, split. *See* **crack** (1). 3. To undergo combustion; be on fire ▸ combust, flare. *See* **burn** (2).

crackle *noun*

A light, sharp noise ▸ clack, click, snap. *See also* **crack, snap**.

crackpot *noun*

A person regarded as strange, eccentric, or crazy ▸ crazy, eccentric, lunatic. *Informal:* crank, loon, loony. *Slang:* cuckoo, ding-a-ling, freak, kook, nut, screwball, weirdie, weirdo. *See also* **character**.

crackup *noun*

1. *Informal* A wrecking of a vehicle ▸ sideswipe, wreck. *See* **crash** (2). 2. *Informal* A sudden sharp decline in mental, emotional, or physical health ▸ breakdown, collapse. *See also* **infirmity**.

craft *noun*

1. Natural or acquired skill or talent ▸ expertise, mastery, proficiency. *See* **ability** (1). *See synonym note at* **ability**. 2. Deceitful cleverness ▸ artfulness, slyness. *See* **art** (1). 3. Lack of straightforwardness and honesty in action ▸ deviousness, slyness, trickery. *See* **dishonesty** (2). 4. Activity pursued as a livelihood ▸ career, employment, occupation. *See* **business** (2). 5. A conveyance that travels over water ▸ bark, barque, boat, vessel, watercraft, ship. 6. The technique, style, and quality of working ▸ craftsmanship, work, workmanship. *See also* **approach**.

craftiness *noun*

1. Deceitful cleverness ▸ artfulness, cleverness, slyness. *See* **art** (1). 2. Lack of straightforwardness and honesty in action ▸ chicanery, shadiness, underhandedness. *See* **dishonesty** (2).

craftsmanship *noun*

The technique, style, and quality of working ▸ craft, work, workmanship. *See also* **approach**.

crafty *adjective*
▸ cunning, sly, wily. *See* **artful** (1).
cragged *adjective*
▸ coarse, ragged, scabrous. *See* **rough** (1).
craggy *adjective*
▸ harsh, jagged, scabrous. *See* **rough** (1).
cram *verb*
1. To move into an area or space in large numbers ▸ flock, jam, squeeze. *See* **crowd** (5). **2.** To make full; fill to capacity ▸ jam, pack. *See* **fill** (1). **3.** *Informal* To study or work hard, especially when pressed for time ▸ lucubrate, study. *Informal:* bone up, grind. **Idioms:** burn the midnight oil, hit the books. *See also* **examine.**
cramp¹ *noun*
A sensation of physical discomfort occurring as the result of disease or injury ▸ ache, pang, throe. *See* **pain** (1).
cramp² *noun*
Something that limits or holds back ▸ check, constraint, curb. *See* **restraint** (1).
cramp *verb*
To check the freedom and spontaneity of ▸ constrain, constrict, inhibit. *See also* **restrain.**
cramped *adjective*
Affording little room for movement ▸ close, crowded, restrictive. *See* **tight** (4).
cranium *noun*
The bony framework of the head ▸ braincase, brainpan, skull. *See also* **head.**
crank *noun*
1. *Informal* A person who habitually complains or grumbles ▸ crab, grump, whiner. *See* **grouch** (1). **2.** *Informal* A person regarded as strange, eccentric, or crazy ▸ lunatic. *Slang:* nut, weirdo. *See* **crackpot.**
crank up *verb*
Slang To increase markedly in level or intensity, especially of sound ▸ amplify, heighten, raise. *See* **elevate** (2).
crankiness *noun*
▸ cantankerousness, prickliness, tetchiness. *See* **temper** (1).
cranky *adjective*
1. Having or showing a bad temper ▸ bad-tempered, grouchy, peevish. *See* **ill-tempered. 2.** Deviating from what is conventional or customary ▸ bizarre, grotesque. *See* **eccentric.**
cranny *noun*
▸ break, crevice, niche. *See* **crack** (2).
crap *noun*
1. *Slang* Something that does not have or make sense ▸ bunkum, drivel, garbage. *See* **nonsense** (1). **2.** *Slang* Foul or dirty matter ▸ grime, muck. *See* **filth** (1).
crapehanger *noun*
▸ apocalypticist, doomsayer, worrywart. *See* **pessimist** (2).
crappy *adjective*
Slang Of decidedly inferior quality ▸ cheap, lousy, poor. *See* **shoddy** (1).

crapulence *noun*
1. The condition of being intoxicated with alcoholic liquor ▸ inebriation, insobriety, tipsiness. *See* **drunkenness. 2.** Unpleasant physical and mental effects following overindulgence in alcohol ▸ hangover, katzenjammer. *Informal:* head.
crapulous *or* **crapulent** *adjective*
▸ intoxicated, sodden, tipsy. *See* **drunk.**
crash *verb*
1. To wreck a vehicle ▸ rear-end, sideswipe, smash, total, wreck. *Informal:* crack up, pile up. **2.** To come together with force ▸ impact, strike. *See* **collide** (1). **3.** To strike together noisily ▸ clang, slam, whack. *See* **bang** (1). **4.** To make an explosive noise ▸ roar, thunder. *See* **blast** (1). **5.** To undergo sudden financial failure ▸ fail, go under. *See* **collapse** (2). **6.** *Slang* To go to bed ▸ bed (down). *Slang:* flop. *See* **retire** (2). **7.** To stop working properly ▸ break down, fail. *Slang:* conk out. *See* **malfunction.**
crash *noun*
1. A forceful movement causing a loud noise ▸ bang, slam, smash, wham. **2.** A wrecking of a vehicle ▸ accident, rear-ender, sideswipe, smash, smashup, wreck. *Informal:* crackup, fender-bender, pileup. **3.** A violent forcible contact ▸ bump, impact. *See* **collision.** *See synonym note at* **collision. 4.** A loud, harsh striking noise ▸ clang, smash. *See* **clash** (1). **5.** An explosive noise ▸ boom, reverberation. *See* **blast** (1). **6.** An abrupt failure ▸ debacle, disaster. *See* **collapse** (2).
crash *adjective*
Informal Designed to meet emergency needs as quickly as possible ▸ *Informal:* hurry-up, rush.
crashing *adjective*
▸ all-out, pure, sheer. *See* **utter²**.
crass *adjective*
▸ indelicate, unbecoming, unrefined. *See* **coarse** (1).
crate *noun*
1. An enclosure for confining an animal or bird ▸ coop, kennel, stall. *See* **cage. 2.** Something wrapped or enclosed, as for transporting ▸ bundle, carton, packet. *See* **package.**
crave *verb*
1. To have a greedy, obsessive desire ▸ hunger, itch, lust, thirst. *See also* **desire. 2.** To make an earnest or urgent request ▸ beseech, entreat, plead. *See* **appeal** (1). *See synonym note at* **appeal.**
craven *adjective*
Ignobly lacking in courage ▸ faint-hearted, pusillanimous. *Slang:* gutless. *See* **cowardly.**
craven *noun*
An ignoble or uncourageous person ▸ dastard, poltroon, sissy. *See* **coward.**
cravenness *noun*
▸ faint-heartedness, pusillanimity. *Slang:* gutlessness. *See* **cowardice.**
craving *noun*
▸ appetite, longing, yearning. *See* **desire** (1).
crawl *verb*
1. To move along in a crouching or prone position

► creep, sinuate, slide, snake, squiggle, squirm, undulate, waggle, wiggle, worm, wriggle, writhe. *Idiom:* go on all fours. **2.** To advance slowly ► creep, drag, inch, poke. *Idiom:* go at a snail's pace. *See also* **trudge. 3.** To be abundantly filled or richly supplied ► bristle, overflow, swarm. *See* **teem¹.** *See synonym note at* **teem¹.**

crawl *noun*
A very slow rate of speed ► creep, footpace, slow motion. *Idiom:* snail's pace.

crawling *adjective*
1. Full of lively activity ► bustling, swarming, teeming. *See* **busy** (2). **2.** Proceeding at a rate less than usual or desired ► dilatory, sluggish. *See* **slow** (1).

craze *verb*
1. To make insane ► dement, madden, unbalance. *See* **derange** (1). **2.** To undergo partial breaking ► rupture, split. *See* **crack** (1).

craze *noun*
1. The current custom ► fad, mode, vogue. *See* **fashion** (1). **2.** A subject or activity that inspires lively interest ► mania, passion. *See* **enthusiasm** (2).

craziness *noun*
1. Serious mental illness impairing a person's capacity to function normally ► dementia, disturbance, unbalance. *See* **insanity** (1). **2.** *Informal* Foolish behavior ► folly, silliness, tomfoolery. *See* **foolishness.**

crazy *adjective*
1. Afflicted with or exhibiting irrationality and mental unsoundness ► derailed, lunatic, mad. *See* **insane** (1). **2.** *Informal* Showing or having enthusiasm ► fervent, rabid, zealous. *See* **enthusiastic** (1). **3.** *Informal* Displaying a lack of good sense ► daft, idiotic, ludicrous. *See* **foolish.**

crazy *noun*
A person regarded as strange, eccentric, or crazy ► lunatic. *Slang:* nut, weirdo. *See* **crackpot.**

cream *noun*
1. A substance used on the skin to soothe or heal ► emollient, salve. *See* **ointment. 2.** The most preferable part of something ► elite, top. *See* **best** (1).

cream *verb*
1. To form or cause to form foam ► fizz, lather. *See* **foam** (1). **2.** To process ingredients by stirring ► blend, whip. *See* **beat** (6). **3.** *Slang* To render totally ineffective by decisive defeat ► crush, overcome, overpower, rout. *See* **overwhelm** (1).

creaming *noun*
► overthrow, trouncing, vanquishment. *See* **defeat.**

cream puff *noun*
1. *Slang* A childish or pampered person ► crybaby, softy. *See* **baby** (2). **2.** *Slang* A weak or ineffectual person ► pushover. *Slang:* doormat, wimp. *See* **weakling.**

crease *noun*
1. A line made by the doubling of one part over another ► crimp, pleat, wrinkle. *See* **fold** (1). **2.** An indentation or seam on the skin, especially on the face ► crinkle, furrow. *See* **wrinkle** (1).

crease *verb*
1. To bend together or form a crease ► crimp, double, pleat. *See* **fold** (1). **2.** To make irregular folds in, especially by pressing or twisting ► crimp, crinkle, rumple. *See* **wrinkle** (1).

create *verb*
1. To bring into existence ► give, provide, yield. *See* **produce** (1). **2.** To bring into existence formally ► constitute, establish, institute. *See* **found** (1). *See synonym note at* **found. 3.** To form by artistic effort ► produce, write. *See* **compose** (1).

creation *noun*
1. The act of founding or establishing ► constitution, establishment, institution. *See* **foundation** (1). **2.** The totality of all existing things ► cosmos, world. *See* **universe** (1). **3.** Something that is the result of creative effort ► piece, production, work. *See* **composition** (1). **4.** A fiction or half-truth, especially one that forms part of an ideology ► fantasy, fiction, invention. *See* **myth** (3).

creative *adjective*
1. Characterized by or productive of new things or new ideas ► ingenious, innovative, original. *See* **inventive** (1). **2.** Relating to or appreciative of the arts ► aesthetic, artistic. *Informal:* artsy, arty.

creativeness *noun*
► creativity, ingenuity, originality. *See* **invention** (1).

creativity *noun*
1. The power or ability to invent ► ingeniousness, ingenuity, originality. *See* **invention** (1). **2.** The power of the mind to form images ► inventiveness, fantasy. *See* **imagination** (1).

creator *noun*
1. One that creates, founds, or originates ► author, inventor, maker. *See* **originator. 2.** A person instrumental in the growth of something, especially in its early stages ► builder, contributor, producer. *See* **developer.**

creature *noun*
► human, mortal, person. *See* **human being.**

credence *noun*
Mental acceptance of the actuality of something ► belief, credit, faith. *See also* **trust.**

credential *noun*
A quality that makes a person suitable for a particular position or task ► attainment, endowment, qualification, skill.

credibility *or* **credibleness** *noun*
► believability, color, plausibility. *See* **verisimilitude.**

credible *adjective*
1. Worthy of being believed ► creditable, plausible. *See* **believable.** *See synonym note at* **believable. 2.** Worthy of belief, as because of precision or faithfulness to an original ► authoritative, true, valid. *See* **authentic** (2).

credit *noun*
1. Mental acceptance of the actuality of something ► belief, credence, faith. *See also* **trust. 2.** Favorable reception or regard ► acknowledgment, favor, recognition. *See* **acceptance** (2).

credit *verb*
1. To have confidence in the truthfulness of ▸ believe, trust. *Idioms:* give credence to, have faith (*or* trust *or* confidence) in, take at one's word. *See also* **depend on. 2.** To regard as belonging to or resulting from another ▸ ascribe, assign. *See* **attribute** (1). *See synonym note at* **attribute.**

creditability *or* **creditableness** *noun*
▸ believability, credibility, plausibility. *See* **verisimilitude.**

creditable *adjective*
1. Deserving honor, respect, or admiration ▸ deserving, laudable, worthy. *See* **admirable. 2.** Worthy of being believed ▸ credible, plausible, reasonable. *See* **believable.**

credo *noun*
▸ belief, dogma, teaching. *See* **doctrine.**

credulous *adjective*
▸ dupable, naive, susceptible. *See* **gullible.**

creed *noun*
1. A system of religious belief ▸ confession, denomination. *See* **religion. 2.** A statement presented for acceptance, as by a religious group ▸ dogma, teaching. *See* **doctrine.**

creek *noun*
▸ rill, watercourse. *See* **brook**[1].

creel *noun*
A container made of interwoven material ▸ basket, hamper, pannier. *See also* **container.**

creep *verb*
1. To advance slowly ▸ crawl, drag, inch, poke. *Idiom:* go at a snail's pace. *See also* **trudge. 2.** To move along in a crouching or prone position ▸ slide, slither, worm. *See* **crawl** (1). **3.** To move silently and furtively ▸ lurk, prowl. *See* **sneak** (1).

creep *noun*
1. A very slow rate of speed ▸ crawl, footpace, slow motion. *Idiom:* snail's pace. **2.** *Slang* A repulsive, despicable, or immoral person ▸ insect, jackal, lowlife, reptile, snake, weasel. *Slang:* louse, maggot, rat, skunk, sleaze, sleazebag, slimeball, toad, troll, worm. *See also* **betrayer, informer, sneak.**

creepy *adjective*
Informal Of an unnatural and usually frightening nature ▸ uncanny, unearthly. *See* **weird** (1).

crème de la crème *noun*
1. The most preferable part of something ▸ cream, elite, top. *See* **best** (1). **2.** People of the highest social level ▸ elite, gentry, nobility. *See* **society** (1).

crepitate *verb*
To make a series of short, sharp noises ▸ crackle, splutter, sputter. *See also* **crack, hiss, snap.**

crescendo *verb*
▸ culminate, peak. *See* **climax.**

crescent *noun*
▸ curvature, curve, turn. *See* **bend.**

crest *noun*
The highest point or state ▸ apex, height, peak. *See* **climax** (1).

crest *verb*
1. To put a topping on ▸ cap, crown, tip, top, top off. *See also* **cover. 2.** To reach or bring to a climax ▸ culminate, peak. *See* **climax.**

cretin *noun*
1. *Slang* A person who is deficient in judgment and good sense ▸ idiot, imbecile, nitwit. *See* **fool** (1). **2.** *Slang* A mentally dull person ▸ dummy, dunce, thickhead. *See* **dullard.**

crevice *noun*
▸ break, cleft, fissure. *See* **crack** (2).

crew *noun*
1. A group of people organized for a particular purpose ▸ squad, team, unit. *See* **force** (5). **2.** A small group of friends or associates ▸ coterie, group, set. *See* **circle** (3). **3.** An enormous number of persons or things gathered together ▸ horde, mass, throng. *See* **crowd** (1).

crib *verb*
1. To reproduce another's work without permission ▸ appropriate, pirate. *See* **plagiarize. 2.** To take another's property without permission ▸ purloin, snatch, thieve. *See* **steal** (1).

crib *noun*
The act or process of translating ▸ construe, rendering. *See* **translation** (1).

cribber *noun*
A person who reproduces another's work without permission ▸ pirate, plagiarist, plagiarizer. *See also* **forger.**

crime *noun*
1. An act that violates public law ▸ felony, illegality, malefaction, misdeed, misdemeanor, offense, tort. *See also* **breach. 2.** A wicked act or wicked behavior ▸ deviltry, diablerie, evil, evildoing, immorality, iniquity, misdeed, offense, peccancy, sin, wickedness, wrong, wrongdoing. *See also* **corruption, cruelty, outrage. 3.** A great disappointment or regrettable fact ▸ pity, shame. *Slang:* bummer. *Idiom:* a crying shame. **4.** An unjust act ▸ disservice, inequity, wrong. *See* **injustice** (1).

criminal *adjective*
1. Of, involving, or being a crime ▸ felonious, illegal, illegitimate, illicit, lawless, unlawful, wrongful. *See also* **forbidden. 2.** Contrary to accepted, especially moral conventions ▸ illicit, unlawful.

criminal *noun*
One who commits a crime ▸ convict, culprit, delinquent, desperado, felon, gangster, lawbreaker, malefactor, offender, outlaw, perpetrator, scofflaw, transgressor. *Informal:* crook, mobster. *Slang:* con, perp. *See also* **evildoer, fugitive, larcenist, thug.**

criminality *noun*
▸ depravity, perversion, vice. *See* **corruption** (1).

criminate *verb*
To cause to appear involved in or guilty of a crime or fault ▸ incriminate, implicate, inculpate. *See also* **accuse.**

crimination *noun*
▶ denouncement, imputation, incrimination. *See* **accusation.**

crimp *verb*
1. To bend together or form a crease ▶ crease, double, pleat. *See* **fold** (1). **2.** To make irregular folds in, especially by pressing or twisting ▶ crinkle, crumple, rumple. *See* **wrinkle** (1).

crimp *noun*
A line made by the doubling of one part over another ▶ pleat, wrinkle. *See* **fold** (1).

crimson *verb*
▶ color, flush. *See* **blush.**

cringe *verb*
1. To draw away or pull back in fear ▶ cower, recoil, shrink. *See* **flinch. 2.** To behave obsequiously or submissively ▶ grovel, kowtow. *Informal:* apple-polish. *See* **fawn.**

cringe *noun*
An act of drawing back in an involuntary or instinctive fashion ▶ flinch, shrink, wince. *See* **recoil.**

crinkle *verb*
1. To bend together or form a crease ▶ crease, double, pleat. *See* **fold** (1). **2.** To make irregular folds in, especially by pressing or twisting ▶ crimp, crumple, rumple. *See* **wrinkle** (1).

crinkle *noun*
1. An indentation or seam on the skin, especially on the face ▶ crow's-foot, furrow. *See* **wrinkle** (1). **2.** A line made by the doubling of one part over another ▶ crimp, pleat, wrinkle. *See* **fold** (1).

cripple *verb*
1. To deprive of a limb or bodily member or its use ▶ amputate, castrate, dismember, maim, mangle, mutilate. *See also* **batter, cut. 2.** To render powerless or motionless, as by inflicting severe injury ▶ handicap, immobilize, paralyze. *See* **disable** (1).

crisis *noun*
1. A decisive point ▶ climacteric, climax, clutch, crossroads, crunch, crux, exigence, exigency, head, juncture, pass, turning point, zero hour. *Idiom:* moment of truth. *See also* **predicament. 2.** A situation requiring immediate assistance or remedial action ▶ distress, exigency, trouble. *See* **emergency.**

✦ CORE SYNONYMS: *crisis, crossroads, exigency, head, juncture, pass.* These nouns denote a decisive or critical point: *a military crisis; government policy at the crossroads; had predicted the health-care exigency; a problem that is coming to a head; negotiations that had reached a crucial juncture; things rapidly coming to a desperate pass.*

---

crisp *adjective*
▶ concise, short, succinct. *See* **brief** (1).

crisscross *verb*
▶ crosscut, intersect. *See* **cross** (2).

criterion *noun*
▶ benchmark, mark, measure. *See* **standard** (1). *See synonym note at* **standard.**

critic *noun*
1. A person who evaluates and reports on the worth of something ▶ appraiser, assessor, commentator, judge, pundit, reviewer. **2.** A person who finds fault ▶ blamer, carper, caviler, censurer, criticizer, faultfinder, hypercritic, mudslinger, nagger, niggler, nitpicker, pettifogger, quibbler. *Informal:* Monday morning quarterback. *See also* **scold.**

critical *adjective*
1. Inclined to judge too severely ▶ captious, carping, censorious, faultfinding, hypercritical, judgmental, nagging, overcritical, reproachful. *See also* **severe. 2.** Keenly perceptive or discerning ▶ acute, discerning, discriminating, incisive, keen, penetrating, perceptive, probing, sensitive, sharp, trenchant. *See also* **careful, clever, intelligent, shrewd. 3.** Demanding immediate attention ▶ acute, dire, pressing. *See* **urgent** (1). **4.** Incapable of being dispensed with ▶ necessary, required. *See* **essential** (1).

criticism *noun*
1. The act or an instance of finding fault ▶ blame, censure, condemnation, denunciation, finger-pointing, judgment, reprehension, reprobation. *Informal:* flak, guilt trip, pan. *Slang:* knock. *See also* **disapproval, rebuke. 2.** Critical explanation or analysis ▶ critique, notice, review. *See* **commentary.**

criticize *verb*
1. To find fault with ▶ blame, carp at, censure, fault, judge, rap, reprove, scapegoat. *Informal:* guilt-trip, pan, zing. *Slang:* knock, put down. *Idioms:* find fault with, lay (*or* put) a guilt trip on, pick apart (*or* to pieces), point the finger at, speak ill of. *See also* **chastise, malign, slam. 2.** To write a critical report on ▶ critique, review. *See also* **estimate.**

criticizer *noun*
▶ caviler, nitpicker. *See* **critic** (2).

critique *noun*
Critical explanation or analysis ▶ criticism, notice, review. *See* **commentary.**

critique *verb*
To write a critical report on ▶ criticize, review. *See also* **estimate.**

croak *verb*
1. To utter in a breathless or hoarse manner ▶ pant, wheeze. *See* **gasp** (1). **2.** *Slang* To cease living ▶ drop, expire, perish. *See* **die** (1).

croaker *noun*
▶ apocalypticist, doomsayer, worrywart. *See* **pessimist** (2).

croaky or **croaking** *adjective*
▶ gruff, husky. *See* **hoarse** (1).

crocked *adjective*
Slang Stupefied, excited, or muddled with alcoholic liquor ▶ intoxicated, sodden, tipsy. *See* **drunk.**

crone *noun*
▶ beldam, hag. *Slang:* crow. *See* **witch** (2).

crony *noun*
1. A person whom one knows well, likes, and trusts ▶ chum, intimate, mate. *See* **friend** (1). **2.** One who

shares interests or activities with another ▸ companion, comrade. *See* **associate** (2).

crook *noun*
1. Something bent ▸ curvature, curve, turn. *See* **bend**. 2. *Informal* A person who cheats ▸ cheater, swindler, trickster. *See* **cheat** (2). 3. *Informal* One who commits a crime ▸ culprit, lawbreaker, offender. *See* **criminal**. 4. A fairly long straight piece of solid material used especially as a support in walking ▸ staff, stave. *See* **stick** (2).

crook *verb*
To deviate from a straight line in a smooth, continuous manner ▸ arch, curve, turn. *See* **bend** (1). *See synonym note at* **bend**.

crooked *adjective*
1. Deviating from a straight line ▸ arched, bowed, curved, rounded. *See* **bent** (1). 2. Not straight, uniform, or symmetrical ▸ asymmetric, nonuniform. *See* **irregular** (1). 3. *Informal* Open to bribery or dishonesty ▸ dishonest, mercenary, praetorian. *See* **corrupt** (2). 4. *Informal* Given to or marked by deliberate concealment or misrepresentation of the truth ▸ duplicitous, lying, mendacious. *See* **dishonest** (1).

crookedness *noun*
1. Lack of smoothness or regularity ▸ asymmetry, jaggedness, unevenness. *See* **irregularity** (1). 2. *Informal* Departure from what is legally, ethically, and morally correct ▸ baseness, dishonesty, improbity. *See* **corruption** (2). 3. *Informal* Lack of integrity ▸ deceitfulness, mendacity. *See* **dishonesty** (1).

croon *verb*
▸ chant, vocalize. *See* **sing** (1).

crooner *noun*
▸ songster, songstress, voice. *See* **vocalist**.

crop *noun*
The produce harvested from the land ▸ fruit, yield. *See* **harvest** (1).

crop *verb*
1. To decrease, as in length or amount, by or as if by severing or excising ▸ chop, prune, trim. *See* **cut** (3). 2. To collect ripe crops ▸ harvest, pick, reap. *See* **gather** (1). 3. To feed on vegetation ▸ forage, pasture. *See* **browse** (2).

crop up *verb*
To come into being ▸ arise, commence, emerge. *See* **begin** (1).

cross *noun*
A source of persistent worry or hardship ▸ affliction, tribulation. *See* **burden**[1] (1). *See synonym note at* **burden**[1].

cross *verb*
1. To go or extend across ▸ ford, pass, span, track, transit, traverse. 2. To pass through or over ▸ crisscross, crosscut, cut across, decussate, intersect. *See also* **close**. 3. To cross out or remove ▸ delete, erase, strike (out). *See* **cancel** (1). 4. *Informal* To prevent from accomplishing a purpose ▸ foil, stymie, thwart. *See* **frustrate** (1). 5. To journey over ▸ go, traverse. *See* **cover** (2).

cross up *verb*
1. To cause the complete ruin or wreckage of ▸ demolish, torpedo, wreck. *See* **destroy** (1). 2. To put into total disorder ▸ garble, jumble, scramble. *See* **confuse** (4). 3. To be treacherous to ▸ turn in. *Slang:* sell out. *See* **betray** (1).

cross *adjective*
1. Having or showing a bad temper ▸ cranky, grouchy, peevish. *See* **ill-tempered**. 2. Feeling or showing anger ▸ annoyed, irate, peeved. *See* **angry**.

crossbeam *noun*
▸ crosstie, girder, timber. *See* **beam** (2).

crosscut *verb*
▸ crisscross, intersect. *See* **cross** (2).

cross-examine *verb*
▸ interrogate, quiz. *Informal:* grill. *See* **ask** (1).

cross-examiner *noun*
▸ interrogator, investigator, questioner. *See* **inquirer**.

cross-eyed *adjective*
Marked by or affected with a squint ▸ squint-eyed, squinty, strabismal, strabismic.

crossfire *noun*
▸ cannonade, fusillade, volley. *See* **barrage**.

crossing *adjective*
Situated or lying across ▸ crossways, crosswise, traverse. *See* **transverse**.

crossing *noun*
The act of traveling from one place to another ▸ flight, passage, progress. *See* **journey**.

crossroads *noun*
1. A decisive point ▸ climax, juncture. *See* **crisis** (1). *See synonym note at* **crisis**. 2. The act or fact of coming together ▸ confluence, conflux. *See* **junction** (1).

crosstie *noun*
▸ crossbeam, girder, timber. *See* **beam** (2).

crosswise *or* **crossways** *adjective*
▸ across, traverse. *See* **transverse**.

crouch *verb*
▸ bend, huddle, scrunch. *See* **stoop** (1).

crow *verb*
1. To talk with excessive pride ▸ bluster, vaunt. *See* **boast** (1). *See synonym note at* **boast**. 2. To feel or express an uplifting joy over a success or victory ▸ glory, triumph. *See* **exult** (1).

crow *noun*
An ugly, frightening woman, usually old ▸ crone, hag. *See* **witch** (2).

crowd *noun*
1. An enormous number of persons gathered together ▸ army, cloud, concourse, crew, crush, drove, flock, gaggle, herd, horde, host, legion, mass, mob, multitude, pack, press, rout, ruck, scores, stable, swarm, throng, troop. *See also* **band**[2]**, flock, group**. 2. The common people ▸ masses, proletariat, public. *See* **commonalty**. 3. A small group of friends or associates ▸ coterie, group, set. *See* **circle** (3). 4. A number of persons who have come or been gathered together ▸ conference, group. *Informal:* get-together. *See* **assembly** (1).

crowd *verb*

1. 5. To move into an area or space in large numbers ▶ cram, crush, flock, flood, jam, pile, pour, press, squeeze, swarm, throng, troop. **2.** To apply pressure on, against, or with ▶ press, prod, shove. *See* **push** (1). **3.** To make full; fill to capacity ▶ cram, jam, mob. *See* **fill** (1).

✦ CORE SYNONYMS: *crowd, crush, flock, horde, mob, press, throng.* These nouns denote an enormous group of people gathered close to one another: *a crowd of well-wishers; a crush of autograph seekers; a flock of schoolchildren; a horde of demonstrators; a mob of hard-rock enthusiasts; a press of shoppers; throngs of tourists.*

crowded *adjective*

1. Affording little room for movement ▶ cramped, snug. *See* **tight** (4). **2.** Having all parts near to each other ▶ compressed, dense. *See* **thick** (2). **3.** Excessively filled with detail ▶ cluttered, fussy. *See* **busy** (3).

crown *noun*

1. The highest point or state ▶ apex, height, peak. *See* **climax** (1). **2.** A round closed plane shape or figure ▶ band, ring, wheel. *See* **circle** (1). **3.** The uppermost part of the body ▶ noddle, pate. *See* **head** (1).

crown *verb*

1. To put a topping on ▶ cap, crest, tip, top, top off. *See also* **cover**. **2.** To reach or bring to a climax ▶ culminate, peak. *See* **climax**.

crowning *adjective*

▶ climactic, culminating, peak. *See also* **last**.

crow's-foot *noun*

▶ crease, furrow. *See* **wrinkle** (1).

crow's nest *noun*

▶ cupola, observatory, watchtower. *See* **lookout** (2).

crucial *adjective*

1. Demanding immediate attention ▶ acute, dire, pressing. *See* **urgent** (1). **2.** Determining or having the power to determine an outcome ▶ conclusive, deciding. *See* **decisive** (1). *See synonym note at* **decisive**. **3.** Most important, influential, or significant ▶ chief, key, main, principal. *See* **primary** (1). **4.** Having great significance ▶ consequential, grand, meaningful. *See* **important** (1).

crucible *noun*

▶ ordeal, tribulation, visitation. *See* **trial** (1). *See synonym note at* **trial**.

crucify *verb*

To subject another to extreme physical cruelty, as in punishing ▶ harrow, rack, torment, torture. *Idioms:* put on the rack (*or* wheel). *See also* **punish**.

crud *noun*

Slang Foul or dirty matter ▶ grime, muck. *See* **filth** (1).

crude *adjective*

1. Being in a natural state ▶ native, raw, rough, rude, unprocessed, unrefined, virgin. *See also* **wild**. **2.** Lacking in delicacy or refinement ▶ indelicate, unbecoming, unrefined. *See* **coarse** (1). **3.** Lacking expert, careful craftsmanship ▶ homemade, primitive, unpol-

ished. *See* **rude** (1). *See synonym note at* **rude**. **4.** Not perfected, elaborated, or completed ▶ preliminary, sketchy, unpolished. *See* **rough** (10). **5.** Lacking the required professional skill ▶ nonprofessional, unskilled. *See* **amateurish**.

crude *noun*

A substance that is generally slippery, combustible, and not water soluble ▶ grease, petroleum. *See* **oil** (1).

✦ CORE SYNONYMS: *crude, native, raw, unrefined.* These adjectives mean in a natural state and not yet processed for use: *crude rubber; native iron; raw cotton; unrefined sugar.*

cruel *adjective*

1. Characterized by or inflicting suffering or pain ▶ barbarous, brutal, ferocious, fierce, grim, inhuman, inhumane, merciless, pitiless, ruthless, sadistic, savage, truculent, vicious. *See also* **fiendish, malevolent, murderous**. **2.** Painfully intense ▶ brutal, harsh, punishing. *See* **bitter** (2).

✦ CORE SYNONYMS: *cruel, fierce, ferocious, barbarous, inhuman, savage, vicious.* These adjectives mean predisposed to inflict violence, pain, or hardship, or to find satisfaction in the suffering of others: *a cruel tyrant; a fierce warrior; a ferocious attack dog; a barbarous crime; inhuman treatment of captured soldiers; a savage outburst of temper; a vicious kick.*

cruelty *noun*

The quality or condition of being cruel ▶ barbarity, bestiality, brutality, ferocity, fiendishness, fierceness, grimness, inhumanity, mercilessness, pitilessness, ruthlessness, sadism, savagery, truculence, truculency. *See also* **crime, malevolence**.

cruise *noun*

▶ flight, passage, progress. *See* **journey**.

crumb *noun*

1. A tiny amount ▶ dash, drop, smidgen. *See* **bit**[1] (1). **2.** A small portion of food ▶ dollop, morsel. *See* **bit**[1] (2).

crumble *verb*

1. To reduce or become reduced to pieces or fragments ▶ atomize, decompose, fragment. *See* **disintegrate** (1). **2.** To become or cause to become rotten or unsound ▶ deteriorate, rot, spoil, turn. *See* **decay**. *See synonym note at* **decay**. **3.** To give way mentally and emotionally ▶ crack, snap. *See* **break** (5).

crummy *adjective*

▶ cheap, lousy, poor. *See* **shoddy** (1).

crump *verb*

▶ chomp, gnash, munch. *See* **chew**.

crumple *verb*

1. To make irregular folds in, especially by pressing or twisting ▶ crimp, crinkle, rumple. *See* **wrinkle** (1). **2.** To fall in ▶ collapse, give. *See* **buckle** (1). **3.** To give way mentally and emotionally ▶ crack, crumble, snap. *See* **break** (5).

crumple *noun*

A line that is made by the doubling of one part over

another ▸ crimp, pleat, wrinkle. *See* **fold** (1).

crunch *verb*
1. To seize and grind with the teeth ▸ chomp, gnash, munch. *See* **chew. 2.** To rub together noisily ▸ gnash, grind.

crunch *noun*
A decisive point ▸ crossroads, juncture. *See* **crisis** (1).

crusade *noun*
1. An organized effort to accomplish a purpose ▸ movement, push. *See* **drive** (1). *See synonym note at* **drive. 2.** A goal served with great or uncompromising dedication ▸ cause, holy war, jihad.

crush *verb*
1. To press forcefully so as to reduce to a pulpy mass ▸ flatten, mash, mush, pulp, smash, squash. *See also* **squeeze. 2.** To break up into tiny particles ▸ atomize, bray, comminute, granulate, grind, levigate, mill, pestle, pound, powder, pulverize, smash, triturate. *See also* **break. 3.** To extract from by applying pressure ▸ express, press, squeeze. **4.** To apply pressure on, against, or with ▸ press, prod, shove. *See* **push** (1). **5.** To overcome opposition or uprising with overwhelming force ▸ choke off, extinguish, quell. *See* **suppress** (1). **6.** To cause the complete ruin or wreckage of ▸ demolish, torpedo, wreck. *See* **destroy** (1). **7.** To render totally ineffective by decisive defeat ▸ overcome, overpower, rout. *See* **overwhelm** (1). **8.** To severely impair someone's spirit, health, or will ▸ overwhelm, ruin. *See* **break** (4). **9.** To affect deeply or completely, as with emotion ▸ overcome, prostrate. *See* **overwhelm** (2). **10.** To move into an area or space in large numbers ▸ cram, jam, squeeze. *See* **crowd** (1).

crush *noun*
1. An enormous number of persons or things gathered together ▸ horde, mass, throng. *See* **crowd** (1). *See synonym note at* **crowd. 2.** An extravagant, short-lived romantic attachment ▸ *Informal:* infatuation, thing. *Idiom:* passing fancy. *See also* **love, obsession.**

✦ **CORE SYNONYMS:** *crush, mash, pulp, smash, squash.* These verbs mean to press forcefully so as to reduce to a pulpy mass: *crushed the rose geranium leaves; mashed the sweet potatoes; pulped raspberries through a sieve; smashed the bamboo stems with a hammer; squashed the wine grapes.*

crust *noun*
1. An outer layer of material ▸ blanket, coating, overlay. *See* **coat** (2). **2.** *Informal* The state or quality of being impudent or arrogantly self-confident ▸ audacity, boldness, forwardness. *See* **impudence.**

crusty *adjective*
▸ blunt, brusque, curt. *See* **abrupt** (1). *See synonym note at* **abrupt.**

crutch *noun*
▸ brace, buttress, prop. *See* **support** (1).

crux *noun*
▸ crossroads, juncture. *See* **crisis** (1).

cry *verb*
1. To shed tears ▸ bawl, blubber, howl, keen, lament,

mewl, pule, sniffle, snivel, sob, squall, wail, weep, whimper, whine, yowl. *Idioms:* cry one's eyes out, turn on the waterworks. *See also* **bawl, grieve. 2.** To speak suddenly or sharply, as from surprise or emotion ▸ burst out, ejaculate. *See* **exclaim. 3.** To speak or say very loudly ▸ call, holler, yell. *See* **shout.**

cry up *verb*
To attempt to sell or popularize by advertising or publicity ▸ ballyhoo, publicize, tout. *See* **promote** (3).

cry *noun*
1. A fit of crying ▸ bawling, blubbering, lament, lamentation, plaint, sobbing, tears, wailing, weeping, whimpering, whining. *See also* **howl. 2.** A rallying term used by proponents of a cause ▸ battle cry, call to arms, call to battle, motto, rallying cry, slogan, war cry, watchword. **3.** A loud call or utterance ▸ holler, exclamation, yell. *See* **shout. 4.** The act of demanding ▸ appeal, claim, requisition. *See* **demand** (1).

✦ **CORE SYNONYMS:** *cry, weep, wail, keen, whimper, sob, blubber.* These verbs mean to make inarticulate sounds of grief, unhappiness, or pain. *Cry* and *weep* both involve the shedding of tears; *cry* more strongly implies accompanying sound: "*She cried without trying to suppress any of the noisier manifestations of grief and confusion*" (J.D. Salinger). "*I weep for what I'm like when I'm alone*" (Theodore Roethke). *Wail* refers primarily to sustained, inarticulate mournful sound: "*The women . . . began to wail together; they mourned with shrill cries*" (Joseph Conrad). *Keen* suggests wailing and lamentation for the dead: "*It is the wild Irish women keening over their dead*" (George A. Lawrence). *Whimper* refers to low, plaintive, broken or repressed cries: *The condemned prisoner cowered and began to whimper for clemency. Sob* describes weeping or a mixture of broken speech and weeping marked by convulsive breathing or gasping: "*sobbing and crying, and wringing her hands as if her heart would break*" (Laurence Sterne). *Blubber* refers to noisy shedding of tears accompanied by broken or inarticulate speech: "*When he drew out what had been a fiddle, crushed to morsels in the greatcoat, he blubbered aloud*" (Emily Brontë).

crybaby *noun*
▸ milksop, softy. *See* **baby** (2).

crying *adjective*
Demanding immediate attention ▸ crucial, dire, pressing. *See* **urgent** (1).

crypt *noun*
▸ catacomb, gravesite, tomb. *See* **grave**[1].

cryptic *adjective*
1. Difficult to explain or understand ▸ enigmatic, inscrutable, puzzling. *See* **mysterious. 2.** Lacking certainty or clarity ▸ dubious, indeterminate, questionable, unclear. *See* **ambiguous** (1). *See synonym note at* **ambiguous.**

crystal *adjective*
▸ crystalline, limpid, lucid. *See* **clear** (1).

crystal clear *adjective*
1. Readily seen, perceived, or understood ▸ evident, noticeable, obvious. *See* **apparent** (1). **2.** Free from

what obscures ▶ see-through, translucent. *See* **clear** (1).

crystalline *adjective*
Free from what obscures ▶ crystal clear, limpid, lucid. *See* **clear** (1).

cuckoo *noun*
Slang A person regarded as strange, eccentric, or crazy ▶ lunatic. *Slang:* nut, weirdo. *See* **crackpot.**

cuckoo *adjective*
1. *Slang* Afflicted with or exhibiting irrationality and mental unsoundness ▶ crazy, lunatic, mad. *See* **insane** (1). **2.** *Slang* Showing or having enthusiasm ▶ fervent, rabid, zealous. *See* **enthusiastic** (1).

cuddle *verb*
1. To touch or handle affectionately ▶ fondle, pet. *See* **caress.** *See synonym note at* **cuddle. 2.** To lie or press close together, usually with another person or thing ▶ nestle, nuzzle. *See* **snuggle.**

cudgel *noun*
▶ assault, batter, pummel, thresh. *See* **beat** (1).

cue *noun*
A brief or indirect suggestion ▶ clue, suggestion. *See* **hint** (2).

cue in *verb*
To impart information to ▶ advise, educate, notify. *See* **inform** (1).

cuff *verb*
To hit with a sharp blow, especially of the open hand ▶ smack, spank, whack. *See* **slap** (1).

cuff *noun*
A sharp blow, especially with the open hand ▶ smack, whack. *See* **slap** (1).

cul-de-sac *noun*
A course leading nowhere ▶ blind alley, dead end.

cull *verb*
1. To make a choice from a number of alternatives ▶ elect, pick (out), vote (for). *See* **choose** (1). **2.** To collect something bit by bit ▶ garner, gather. *See* **glean** (1).

culminate *verb*
▶ cap, peak. *See* **climax.**

culminating *adjective*
▶ climactic, crowning, peak. *See also* **last.**

culmination *noun*
1. The highest point or state ▶ apex, height, peak. *See* **climax** (1). **2.** The condition of being fulfilled ▶ accomplishment, realization. *See* **fulfillment** (1).

culpability *noun*
▶ fault, guilt. *See* **blame** (1).

culpable *adjective*
▶ censurable, reprehensible. *See* **blameworthy.** *See synonym note at* **blameworthy.**

culprit *noun*
▶ convict, lawbreaker, offender. *See* **criminal.**

cult *noun*
▶ creed, faith, sect. *See* **religion.**

cultivate *verb*
1. To prepare soil for the planting of crops ▶ dig, plow, work. *See* **till. 2.** To raise crops or animals ▶ breed,

propagate. *See* **grow** (1). **3.** To help grow or develop ▶ foster, nourish. *See* **nurture.** *See synonym note at* **nurture. 4.** To help bring about ▶ encourage, facilitate. *See* **promote** (2).

cultivated *adjective*
▶ urbane, educated. *See* **cultured.**

cultivation *noun*
▶ civilization, refinement. *See* **culture** (3).

cultrate *adjective*
▶ acute, cuspate, sharp. *See* **pointed** (1).

cultural *adjective*
Promoting culture ▶ advancing, aesthetic, civilizing, cultivating, edifying, enlightening, fostering, humanizing, refining. *See also* **intellectual.**

culture *noun*
1. The total product of human creativity and intellect ▶ civilization, Kultur, society. **2.** Behavior patterns, traits, and products considered as an expression of a certain people or period ▶ civilization, convention, custom, ethos, folkways, lifestyle, mores, society, tradition. **3.** Excellent taste resulting from intellectual development ▶ breeding, civilization, cultivation, enlightenment, refinement, sophistication. *See also* **courtesy, education, elegance.**

culture *verb*
To prepare soil for the planting of crops ▶ cultivate, plow, work. *See* **till.**

cultured *adjective*
Characterized by discriminating taste and broad knowledge as a result of development or education ▶ civilized, cultivated, educated, highbrow, polished, refined, sophisticated, urbane, well bred. *See also* **courteous, delicate, suave.**

cumber *verb*
▶ encumber, saddle, tax. *See* **burden**[1].

cumbersome *or* **cumbrous** *adjective*
▶ blockish, heavy, oversized. *See* **bulky** (1).

cumshaw *noun*
▶ perquisite, tip. *See* **gratuity** (1).

cumulate *verb*
▶ accrue, amass, garner. *See* **accumulate.**

cumulation *noun*
▶ buildup, collection, congeries. *See* **accumulation** (1).

cumulative *adjective*
Increasing, as in force, by successive additions ▶ accumulative, additive.

cumulus *noun*
▶ drift, mass, mound. *See* **heap** (1).

cunning *adjective*
Deceitfully clever ▶ designing, sly, wily. *See* **artful** (1).

cunning *noun*
Deceitful cleverness ▶ artfulness, deceitfulness, slyness. *See* **art** (1).

cupidity *noun*
▶ avarice, covetousness, rapacity. *See* **greed.**

cupola *noun*
▶ crow's nest, watchtower. *See* **lookout** (2).

cur *noun*
▶ dastard, poltroon, sissy. *See* **coward.**

curate *noun*
▸ ecclesiastic, minister, parson. *See* **cleric.**

curative *adjective*
Serving to cure ▸ antidotal, healing, medicinal, remedial, restorative, therapeutic. *See also* **corrective, tonic.**

curative *noun*
▸ elixir, medication, remedy. *See* **cure.**

curatorial *adjective*
▸ conservational, precautionary, protective. *See* **preservative.**

curb *noun*
1. Something that limits or holds back ▸ check, constraint, restriction. *See* **restraint** (1). 2. A device for slowing or stopping motion ▸ baffle, leash, rein. *See* **brake** (1).

curb *verb*
To control, restrict, or arrest ▸ bridle, check, constrain. *See* **restrain.** *See synonym note at* **restrain.**

curdle *verb*
1. To change or be changed from a liquid into a soft, semisolid, or solid mass ▸ congeal, set. *See* **coagulate.** *See synonym note at* **coagulate.** 2. To become or cause to become rotten or unsound ▸ deteriorate, rot, spoil, turn. *See* **decay.**

cure *noun*
An agent used to restore health ▸ antidote, corrective, countermeasure, curative, elixir, medicament, medication, medicine, nostrum, physic, remedy, restorative, treatment. *See also* **drug.**

cure *verb*
1. To restore to health ▸ heal, rehabilitate, remedy, salve. *Informal:* doctor. *See also* **administer, fix, revive.** 2. To cause to be ready, as for use, consumption, or a special purpose ▸ fix, ready. *See* **prepare** (1). 3. To prepare food for storage and future use ▸ can, pot, put up. *See* **preserve** (1).

cure-all *noun*
Something believed to cure all human disorders ▸ catholicon, elixir, panacea. *See also* **cure.**

cureless *adjective*
▸ irremediable, irreparable. *See* **hopeless** (1).

curio *noun*
▸ knickknack, trinket. *See* **novelty** (3).

curiosity *noun*
1. Mental acquisitiveness ▸ concern, concernment, curiousness, inquisitiveness, interest, interestedness, regard. *Idiom:* thirst for knowledge. 2. Undue interest in the affairs of others ▸ curiousness, inquisitiveness, intrusiveness, meddlesomeness, prying. *Informal:* nosiness, snoopiness. 3. Anything that arouses curiosity or perplexes because it is unexplained, inexplicable, or secret ▸ enigma, puzzle, riddle, stickler. *See* **mystery.**

curious *adjective*
1. Unduly interested in the affairs of others ▸ busy, inquisitive, inquisitorial, interfering, interposing, intrusive, meddlesome, meddling, obtrusive, officious, prying. *Informal:* nosy, snoopy. 2. Eager to acquire knowledge ▸ acquisitive, inquiring, inquisitive, interested, intrigued, investigative, questioning, speculative. *See also* **eager, enthusiastic. 3.** Agreeably curious, especially in an old-fashioned or unusual way ▸ funny, odd, quaint. **4.** Causing puzzlement; perplexing ▸ odd, peculiar. *See* **funny** (3). **5.** Deviating from what is conventional or customary ▸ bizarre, grotesque. *See* **eccentric.** *See synonym note at* **eccentric.**

✦ CORE SYNONYMS: *curious, inquisitive, snoopy, nosy.* These adjectives apply to persons who are unduly interested in the affairs of other people. *Curious* most often implies an avid desire to know or learn, though it can suggest prying: *A curious child is a teacher's delight. A curious neighbor can be a nuisance. Inquisitive* frequently suggests excessive curiosity and the asking of many questions: *"Remember, no revolvers. The police are, I believe, proverbially inquisitive"* (Lord Dunsany). *Snoopy* suggests underhanded prying: *The snoopy hotel detective spied on guests in the lobby. Nosy* implies impertinent curiosity likened to that of an animal using its nose to examine or probe: *My nosy colleague went through my mail.*

---

curiously *adverb*
▸ singularly, uncommonly, uniquely. *See* **unusually.**

curiousness *noun*
1. Mental acquisitiveness ▸ inquisitiveness, interest, regard. *See* **curiosity** (1). 2. Undue interest in the affairs of others ▸ inquisitiveness. *Informal:* nosiness. *See* **curiosity** (2).

curl *verb*
1. To have or cause to have a curved or wavy surface ▸ ripple, undulate. *See* **wave** (2). 2. To move or proceed on a repeatedly curving course ▸ snake, spiral, weave. *See* **wind²** (1).

curl up *verb*
To take repose, as by sleeping or lying quietly ▸ lie (down), recline, repose, rest, stretch (out). *See also* **nap, sleep.**

curl *noun*
Something with a curled or spiral shape ▸ coil, curlicue, frizzle, kink, lock, ringlet, spiral, swirl, twist, whorl, winding. *See also* **bend.**

curly *adjective*
1. Shaped like or having curls ▸ coiled, frizzled, helical, kinky, spiral, swirly, twisted, twisty, whorled. *See also* **bent. 2.** Having a curved or ridged surface ▸ curvy, rippled. *See* **wavy.**

currency *noun*
▸ cash. *Slang:* dough, moola. *See* **money** (1).

current *adjective*
1. Characteristic of recent times or informed of what is current ▸ au courant, modern, up-to-date. *See* **contemporary** (2). 2. In existence now ▸ contemporary, existing. *See* **present¹** (1). 3. Most generally existing or encountered at a given time ▸ predominant, rampant. *See* **prevailing** (1). *See synonym note at* **prevailing.**

current *noun*
Something suggestive of running water ▸ flood,

stream, tide. *See* **flow.** *See synonym note at* **flow.**

currently *adverb*
▸ actually, at present. *See* **now** (1).

curse *noun*
1. A denunciation invoking a wish or threat of evil or injury ▸ anathema, ban, damnation, execration, hex, imprecation, malediction, oath. *Slang:* whammy. *See also* **spell². 2.** Something or someone believed to bring bad luck ▸ evil eye, hex, hoodoo, Jonah. *Informal:* jinx. **3.** A cause of suffering or harm ▸ affliction, bane, evil, ill, misery, plague, scourge, sorrow, woe. *See also* **burden¹, disaster. 4.** A profane or obscene term ▸ blasphemy, expletive. *See* **swearword.**

curse *verb*
1. To invoke evil upon ▸ anathematize, damn, hex, imprecate. *See also* **charm. 2.** To bring bad luck or evil to ▸ hex, hoodoo. *Informal:* jinx. **3.** To use profane or obscene language ▸ blaspheme, damn, curse. *Informal:* cuss. **4.** To cause great pain or suffering to ▸ plague, rack, torment. *See* **afflict.** *See synonym note at* **afflict.**

cursed *adjective*
Informal So annoying or detestable as to deserve condemnation ▸ accursed, blasted, confounded. *See* **damned** (2).

cursive *noun*
▸ handwriting, longhand, penmanship. *See* **script** (1).

cursory *adjective*
1. Lacking in intellectual depth or thoroughness ▸ one-dimensional, shallow. *See* **superficial** (1). **2.** Done routinely and impersonally ▸ automatic, mechanical. *See* **perfunctory.**

curt *adjective*
1. Rudely informal ▸ blunt, brusque, gruff. *See* **abrupt** (1). *See synonym note at* **abrupt. 2.** Expressed in few words ▸ concise, short, succinct. *See* **brief** (1).

curtail *verb*
▸ abridge, reduce. *See* **shorten.** *See synonym note at* **shorten.**

curtailment *noun*
▸ diminishment, reduction, slowdown. *See* **decrease.**

curtains *noun*
Slang The act or fact of dying ▸ demise, passing. *See* **death** (1).

curtsy *noun*
An inclination of the head or body, as in greeting, consent, courtesy, submission, or worship ▸ genuflection, obeisance. *See* **bow¹.**

curtsy *verb*
To incline the head or body, as in greeting, consent, courtesy, submission, or worship ▸ genuflect, kneel. *See* **bow¹** (1).

curvaceous *adjective*
▸ curvy, zaftig. *See* **shapely.**

curvature *noun*
▸ curve, turn. *See* **bend.**

curve *noun*
Something bent ▸ curvature, turn. *See* **bend.**

curve *verb*
1. To deviate from a straight line in a smooth, continuous manner ▸ arch, loop, turn. *See* **bend** (1). *See synonym note at* **bend. 2.** To have or cause to have a curved or wavy surface ▸ ripple, undulate. *See* **wave** (2).

curved *or* **curvilinear** *adjective*
▸ arched, bowed, rounded. *See* **bent** (1).

curving *adjective*
Having bends, curves, or angles ▸ bending, crooked, curved. *See also* **bent.**

curvy *adjective*
1. Having a full, voluptuous figure ▸ curvaceous, zaftig. *See* **shapely. 2.** Having a curved or ridged surface ▸ corrugated, rippled. *See* **wavy. 3.** Repeatedly curving in alternate directions ▸ convoluted, sinuous, twisting. *See* **winding** (1).

cushy *adjective*
Informal Affording pleasurable ease ▸ easy, snug. *Informal:* comfy. *See* **comfortable** (1).

cusp *noun*
▸ apex, tip. *See* **point** (1).

cuspate *or* **cuspated** *adjective*
▸ acute, fine, sharp. *See* **pointed** (1).

cuspidate *or* **cuspidated** *adjective*
▸ acute, fine, sharp. *See* **pointed** (1).

cuss *verb*
1. *Informal* To use profane or obscene language ▸ blaspheme, curse, damn, swear. **2.** To hurl strong deprecations, curses, or insults at ▸ *Informal:* cuss at, cuss out, mouth off at, swear at. *See also* **curse, insult, revile.**

cuss *noun*
Informal A profane or obscene term ▸ blasphemy, curse. *See* **swearword.**

custodian *noun*
One who is legally responsible for the care and management of the person or property of an incompetent or a minor ▸ caretaker, conservator, guardian, keeper. *See also* **representative.**

custody *noun*
1. The function of watching, guarding, or overseeing ▸ charge, guardianship, safekeeping, supervision. *See* **care** (2). *See synonym note at* **care. 2.** The state of being detained by legal authority ▸ confinement, detainment, ward. *See* **detention.**

custom *noun*
1. A habitual way of behaving ▸ consuetude, convention, form, habit, habitude, manner, observance, practice, praxis, precedent, routine, usage, usance, use, way, wont. *See also* **addiction, approach, behavior, fashion. 2.** Behavior patterns, traits, and products considered as an expression of a certain people or period ▸ civilization, ethos, society. *See* **culture** (2). **3.** A formal act or set of acts prescribed by ritual ▸ rite, ritual, tradition. *See* **ceremony** (1). **4.** The commercial transactions of customers with a supplier ▸ business, trade. *See* **patronage** (2). **5.** Customers or patrons collectively ▸ constituency, trade. *See* **patronage** (3).

custom *adjective*
Made according to the specifications of the buyer ▸ bespoke, custom-built, customized, custom-made, made-to-order, tailored, tailor-made. *Idiom:* made-to-measure.

✦ CORE SYNONYMS: *custom, habit, practice, usage, use, wont, habitude.* These nouns denote patterns of behavior established by continual repetition. *Custom* is behavior as established by long practice and especially by accepted conventions: *"No written law has ever been more binding than unwritten custom supported by popular opinion"* (Carrie Chapman Catt). *Habit* applies to a behavior or practice so ingrained that it is often done without conscious thought: *"Habit rules the unreflecting herd"* (William Wordsworth). *Practice* denotes an often chosen pattern of individual or group behavior: *"You will find it a very good practice always to verify your references, sir"* (Martin Joseph Routh). *Usage* refers to an accepted standard for a group that regulates individual behavior: *"laws . . . corrected, altered, and amended by acts of parliament and common usage"* (William Blackstone). *Use* and *wont* are terms for customary and distinctive practice: *"situations where the use and wont of their fathers no longer meet their necessities"* (J.A. Froude). *Habitude* refers to an individual's behaving in a certain way rather than a specific act: *"His real habitude gave life and grace/To appertainings and to ornament"* (William Shakespeare).

customarily *adverb*
▸ commonly, generally, normally. *See* **usually.**
customariness *noun*
▸ normality, ordinariness, routineness. *See* **usualness.**
customary *adjective*
1. Occurring or encountered regularly ▸ commonplace, habitual, regular. *See* **common** (1). **2.** Generally approved or agreed upon ▸ conventional, orthodox, traditional. *See* **accepted.**
custom-built *adjective*
▸ custom-made, tailor-made. *See* **custom.**
customer *noun*
▸ buyer, patron, user. *See* **consumer.**
customized *or* **custom-made** *adjective*
▸ made-to-order, tailor-made. *See* **custom.**
customs *noun*
▸ duty, levy, tariff. *See* **tax** (1).
cut *verb*
1. To penetrate with a sharp edge ▸ bayonet, bore, drill, gash, gore, gouge, hack, impale, incise, indent, knife, lacerate, lance, nick, notch, pierce, prick, punch, puncture, ream, scarify, slash, slit, spear, stab, stick, sting, transfix. *See also* **breach, crack, penetrate. 2.** To separate into parts with or as if with a sharp-edged instrument ▸ carve, cleave, dice, dissever, quarter, sever, slice, slit, snip, split. *See also* **divide. 3.** To decrease, as in length or amount, by or as if by severing or excising ▸ chop, clip, crop, cut back, cut down, lop, lower, mow, pare, prune, reap, scythe, shave, shear, sickle, skive, slash, snip, trim, truncate. *See also* **decrease, drop, shorten. 4.** To turn aside

sharply from a straight course ▸ slant, veer, zigzag. *See* **swerve** (1). **5.** To remove improper material from a publication ▸ bowdlerize, edit, expurgate. *See* **censor** (1). **6.** To lessen the strength of by or as if by admixture ▸ adulterate, weaken. *See* **dilute. 7.** To slight someone deliberately ▸ shun, spurn. *See* **snub. 8.** To fail to attend on purpose ▸ duck, shirk, truant. *Informal:* skip. *Idioms:* go AWOL, play hooky (*or* truant). *See also* **avoid.**
cut across *verb*
To pass through or over ▸ crosscut, intersect. *See* **cross** (2).
cut back *verb*
To decrease, as in length or amount, by or as if by severing or excising ▸ crop, pare, trim. *See* **cut** (3).
cut down *verb*
1. To cause the death of ▸ carry off, destroy, finish (off). *See* **kill**[1] (1). **2.** To bring down, as from a shot or blow ▸ floor, ground, hew. *See* **drop** (6). **3.** To decrease, as in length or amount, by or as if by severing or excising ▸ crop, pare, shear, trim. *See* **cut** (3).
cut in *verb*
1. To force or come in as an improper or unwanted element ▸ horn in, interlope. *See* **intrude** (1). **2.** To interject remarks or questions into another's discourse ▸ break in, chime in, chip in. *See* **interrupt** (2).
cut off *verb*
1. To set apart from a group ▸ close off, seclude, sequester. *See* **isolate** (1). **2.** To cause the death of ▸ carry off, destroy, finish (off). *See* **kill**[1] (1). **3.** To block the progress of and force to change direction ▸ head off, intercept.
cut out *verb*
1. To take the place of another against the other's will ▸ displace, supplant, usurp. *See also* **assume, occupy, seize. 2.** To discontinue (a habit, for example) ▸ abjure, give up, leave off. *See* **break** (17). **3.** *Informal* To move away from a place ▸ exit, go away, retire. *See* **go** (1).
cut up *verb*
1. *Informal* To behave in a rowdy, improper, or unruly fashion ▸ act up, carry on. *See* **misbehave. 2.** To find fault with ▸ censure, fault, reprove. *See* **criticize** (1). **3.** *Informal* To criticize harshly and devastatingly ▸ bash, excoriate, flay. *See* **slam** (5). **4.** To pull or cut into many pieces ▸ grate, slice up. *See* **shred.**
cut *adjective*
Lower than normal in strength or concentration due to admixture ▸ adulterated, watered-down. *See* **dilute.**
cut *noun*
1. An opening made by a sharp object ▸ gash, gouge, groove, incision, nick, notch, score, slash, slice, slit, split. *See also* **impression, prick, scrape. 2.** A part severed from a whole ▸ paring, piece, portion, shaving, slab, slice, sliver, snip, snippet, wedge. *See also* **flake, part. 3.** The act or process of decreasing ▸ diminishment, reduction, slowdown. *See* **decrease. 4.** *Informal* That which is allotted ▸ allowance, ration, share. *See* **allotment** (1). **5.** A deliberate slight ▸ rebuff,

snub, spurn. *Informal:* cold shoulder, go-by. **6.** Failure to be present ▸ nonappearance, truancy. *See* **absence** (1). **7.** An instance of mockery or derision ▸ insult, jeer, scoff. *See* **taunt** (1).

cut-and-dried *adjective*
▸ common, mediocre, standard. *See* **ordinary** (1).

cutback *noun*
▸ abatement, diminution, slowdown. *See* **decrease.**

cute *adjective*
1. Pleasing to the eye or mind ▸ enchanting, fetching, lovely, winsome. *See* **attractive** (1). **2.** Giving great pleasure or delight ▸ delectable, enchanting, heavenly. *See* **delightful.**

cutoff *noun*
1. The act of stopping ▸ cessation, discontinuance, surcease. *See* **stop** (1). **2.** A concluding or terminating ▸ cease, completion, termination. *See* **end** (1). **3.** The greatest amount or number allowed ▸ brim, cap, maximum. *See* **limit** (1).

cutthroat *noun*
One who murders another ▸ killer, massacrer, slayer. *See* **murderer.**

cutthroat *adjective*
1. Marked by or giving rise to murder or bloodshed ▸ homicidal, sanguineous, slaughterous. *See* **murderous. 2.** Given to competition ▸ dog-eat-dog, emulous, rivalrous. *See* **competitive.**

cutting *adjective*
▸ caustic, scathing, sharp, vitriolic. *See* **biting.**

cutting edge *noun*
▸ avant-garde, lead, vanguard. *See* **forefront.**

cutting-edge *adjective*
▸ au courant, modern, up-to-date. *See* **contemporary** (2).

cutup *noun*
▸ devil, imp, rascal. *See* **rascal.**

cycle *noun*
▸ circuit, orbit. *See* **circle** (2).

cyclic *or* **cyclical** *adjective*
▸ isochronal, recurrent. *See* **periodic.**

cyclopean *adjective*
▸ behemoth, colossal, gigantic, mighty. *See* **enormous.**

cynic *noun*
A person who expects only the worst from people ▸ misanthrope, misanthropist, pessimist. *See also* **skeptic.**

cynical *adjective*
1. Contemptuous or ironic in manner or wit ▸ ironic, sardonic, wry. *See* **sarcastic. 2.** Lacking trust or confidence ▸ doubting, suspicious, wary. *See* **distrustful** (1).

cynicism *noun*
1. The use of irony to ridicule or express contempt ▸ acridity, trenchancy. *See* **sarcasm. 2.** Lack of trust ▸ doubt, leeriness, mistrust. *See* **distrust.**

cynosure *noun*
▸ core, focus, nucleus. *See* **center** (3).

d

dab *verb*
1. To spread with a greasy, sticky, or dirty substance ▸ plaster, smudge. *See* **smear** (1). **2.** To strike lightly or gently ▸ flick, pat. *See* **tap**[1] (1).

dab *noun*
A tiny amount ▸ dash, drop, smidgen. *See* **bit**[1] (1).

dabbler *noun*
▸ dilettante, layperson, nonprofessional. *See* **amateur.** *See synonym note at* **amateur.**

dab hand *noun*
▸ authority, master, proficient. *See* **expert.**

dacha *noun*
▸ cottage, country home, estate. *See* **villa.**

dad *or* **daddy** *noun*
▸ paterfamilias, patriarch, sire. *See* **father** (1).

daedal *adjective*
▸ convoluted, elaborate, involved, labyrinthine. *See* **complex** (1).

Daedalian *adjective*
▸ byzantine, convoluted, intricate, tangled. *See* **complex** (1).

daffiness *noun*
Informal Foolish behavior ▸ folly, silliness, tomfoolery. *See* **foolishness.**

daffy *adjective*
1. *Informal* Afflicted with or exhibiting irrationality and mental unsoundness ▸ crazy, lunatic, off. *See* **insane** (1). **2.** *Informal* Displaying a lack of good sense ▸ daft, idiotic, ludicrous. *See* **foolish.**

daft *adjective*
1. Afflicted with or exhibiting irrationality and mental unsoundness ▸ crazy, dotty, moonstruck. *See* **insane** (1). **2.** Displaying a lack of good sense ▸ absurd, idiotic, ludicrous. *See* **foolish.**

daftness *noun*
▸ folly, silliness, tomfoolery, preposterousness. *See* **foolishness.**

daily *adjective*
1. Occurring or encountered regularly ▸ commonplace, everyday, regular. *See* **common** (1). **2.** Of or suitable for ordinary days or routine occasions ▸ casual, workaday. *See* **everyday** (1).

dainty *adjective*

1. Appealing to refined taste ▸ elegant, exquisite. *See* **delicate** (1). *See synonym note at* **delicate. 2.** Very difficult to please ▸ exacting, finicky. *See* **fussy** (1).

dainty *noun*

Something fine and delicious, especially a food ▸ morsel, treat. *See* **delicacy** (1).

dais *noun*

▸ boards, podium, proscenium. *See* **stage** (1).

dale *noun*

▸ canyon, gorge. *See* **valley.**

dalliance *noun*

1. The practice of flirting ▸ coquetry, flirtation. **2.** A usually brief romance entered into lightly or frivolously ▸ fling, flirtation. *See also* **love.**

dally *verb*

1. To make amorous advances without serious intentions ▸ toy, trifle. *See* **flirt** (2). **2.** To treat lightly or flippantly ▸ flirt, play, toy, trifle. *See synonym note at* **flirt. 3.** To go or move slowly so that progress is hindered ▸ dawdle, drag. *See* **delay** (2). **4.** To be irresolute in acting or doing ▸ falter, vacillate. *See* **hesitate.**

dam *verb*

To block or fill with obstacles ▸ block, clog. *See* **obstruct** (1).

dam *noun*

Something that blocks entry or passage ▸ barrier, blockage, hindrance. *See* **bar** (1).

damage *noun*

1. Harm done to property or a person ▸ breakage, destruction, deterioration, disfigurement, impairment, injury, wastage, wreckage. *See also* **decay, destruction, ruin. 2.** The action or result of inflicting loss or pain ▸ detriment, injury. *See* **harm. 3.** *Informal* A precise list of fees or charges ▸ bill, check, statement. *See* **account** (2).

damage *verb*

To spoil the soundness or perfection of ▸ blemish, detract from, disserve, flaw, harm, hurt, impair, injure, mar, prejudice, tarnish, vitiate. *See also* **abuse, batter, botch, deform.**

damages *noun*

▸ amends, remuneration, reparation. *See* **compensation** (1).

damn *verb*

1. To invoke evil upon ▸ anathematize, curse, hex, imprecate. *See also* **charm. 2.** To use profane or obscene language ▸ blaspheme, curse, swear. *Informal:* cuss. **3.** To pronounce judgment against ▸ doom, sentence. *See* **condemn** (1). *See synonym note at* **condemn.**

damn *adjective*

Informal So annoying or detestable as to deserve condemnation ▸ accursed, blasted, confounded. *See* **damned** (2).

damnation *noun*

▸ anathema, malediction. *See* **curse** (1).

damned *adjective*

1. Sentenced to terrible, irrevocable punishment

▸ doomed, lost, reprobate. *See* **condemned. 2.** *Informal* So annoying or detestable as to deserve condemnation ▸ abominable, accursed, blasted, blessed, bloody, confounded, cursed, damn, darn, execrable, infernal. *Informal:* blamed, doggone. *See also* **vexatious. 3.** Completely such, without qualification or exception ▸ all-out, pure, sheer. *See* **utter**[2].

damp *adjective*

1. Slightly wet ▸ clammy, dank, dewy, moist. *See also* **sticky, wet. 2.** Characterized by rain or drizzle ▸ drizzly, wet. *See* **rainy.**

damp *verb*

1. To cause to stop burning or giving light ▸ put out, quench, snuff out. *See* **extinguish** (1). **2.** To decrease or dull the sound of ▸ deaden, mute, stifle. *See* **muffle** (1).

✤ CORE SYNONYMS: *damp, moist, dank.* These adjectives mean slightly wet. *Damp* and *moist* both mean slightly wet, but *damp* often implies an unpleasant coldness: *a cold, damp cellar; a moist breeze. Dank* emphasizes disagreeable, often unhealthful wetness: *a dank cave.*

---

dampen *verb*

1. To make moist ▸ bathe, moisten, wash, wet. **2.** To decrease or dull the sound of ▸ deaden, mute. *See* **muffle** (1). **3.** To interfere with the progress of ▸ bog, obstruct. *See* **hinder** (1). **4.** To make sad or gloomy ▸ dishearten, dispirit, sadden. *See* **depress** (1).

damsel *noun*

Informal A woman ▸ *Informal:* chick, gal, lass. *See* **girl.**

dance *verb*

1. To move rhythmically to music, using patterns of steps or gestures ▸ foot, step. *Slang:* boogie, hoof. *Idioms:* cut a rug, foot it, get down, trip the light fantastic. **2.** To leap and skip about playfully ▸ cavort, frolic, romp. *See* **gambol.**

dance *noun*

A party or gathering for dancing ▸ ball, cotillion, formal, hoedown, masquerade, mixer, prom, promenade, rave. *Informal:* hop, sock-hop. *See also* **party.**

dancer *noun*

A person who dances, especially professionally ▸ chorine, chorus boy, chorus girl, terpsichorean. *Slang:* hoofer.

dander[1] *noun*

1. *Informal* A tendency to become angry or irritable ▸ crankiness, prickliness, tetchiness. *See* **temper** (1). **2.** *Informal* A strong feeling of displeasure or hostility ▸ choler, indignation, ire. *See* **anger.**

dander[2] *or* **dandruff** *noun*

Scaly pieces of dry shedded skin ▸ furfur, scale, scurf. *See also* **flake.**

dandy *adjective*

1. Exceptionally good of its kind ▸ first-rate, prime, splendid, tiptop. *See* **excellent. 2.** Particularly excellent ▸ fantastic, sensational, superb. *See* **marvelous** (1). **3.** Having pleasant desirable qualities ▸ bonny, enjoyable, nice. *See* **good** (1).

dandy *noun*
A man who is preoccupied with or vain about his clothes ▸ beau, coxcomb, fop, peacock, swell.

danger *noun*
Exposure to harm, loss, or injury ▸ endangerment, hazard, imperilment, jeopardy, menace, peril, pitfall, risk, sword of Damocles, threat. *See also* **trap.**

dangerous *adjective*
Involving or likely to cause risk, loss, or injury ▸ adventurous, chancy, grave, hazardous, insidious, jeopardous, menacing, parlous, perilous, risky, threatening, treacherous, unsafe, venturesome, venturous. *Slang:* dicey, hairy.

dangle *verb*
▸ sling, swing. *See* **hang** (1).

dangling *adjective*
1. Not tautly bound, held, or fastened ▸ flapping, relaxed, slack. *See* **loose** (1). *See synonym note at* **loose.**
2. Hung or appearing to be hung from a support ▸ pendulous, pensile. *See* **hanging** (1).

dangly *adjective*
▸ dangling, pendulous, pensile. *See* **hanging** (1).

dank *adjective*
Slightly wet ▸ clammy, damp, dewy, moist. *See synonym note at* **damp.** *See also* **sticky, wet.**

dapper *adjective*
▸ shipshape, tidy. *See* **neat** (1).

dapple *verb*
▸ bespeckle, freckle. *See* **speckle.**

dare *verb*
1. To call on another to do something bold ▸ challenge, defy. *Idiom:* throw down the gauntlet. 2. To express at the risk of rebuff or criticism ▸ chance, hazard, presume. *See* **venture** (1). 3. To confront boldly and courageously ▸ challenge, confront, oppose. *See* **defy** (1). *See synonym note at* **defy.**

dare *noun*
An act of taunting another to do something bold or rash ▸ challenge, gauntlet, provocation. *See also* **defiance.**

daredevil *noun*
One who seeks adventure ▸ adventurer, quester, venturer. *See also* **builder.**

daredevil *adjective*
Willing to take risks ▸ daring, enterprising. *See* **adventurous** (1). *See synonym note at* **adventurous.**

daredevilry *or* **daredeviltry** *noun*
▸ audaciousness, boldness, derring-do. *See* **daring.**

daring *noun*
Willingness to take risks ▸ adventuresomeness, adventurousness, audaciousness, audacity, boldness, daredevilry, daredeviltry, daringness, derring-do, fearlessness, venturesomeness, venturousness. *See also* **courage, temerity.**

daring *adjective*
Willing to take risks ▸ bold, enterprising. *See* **adventurous** (1). *See synonym note at* **adventurous.**

daringness *noun*
▸ adventurousness, audaciousness. *See* **daring.**

dark *adjective*
1. Deficient in brightness ▸ dim, dusky, ill-lit, murky, obscure, shadowy, shady, stygian. *See also* **shady.** 2. Having little or no light ▸ inky, pitch-dark. *See* **black** (2). 3. Having a dark color or complexion ▸ black, brown, brunet, dusky, swarthy, tawny. 4. Dark and depressing ▸ bleak, desolate, somber. *See* **gloomy** (1). 5. Bringing or predicting misfortune ▸ dire, foreboding, ominous. *See* **fateful** (1). 6. Offering little encouragement ▸ dim, pessimistic. *See* **bleak** (2). 7. Morally objectionable ▸ immoral, sinful. *See* **evil** (1).

dark *noun*
1. Absence or deficiency of light ▸ darkness, dimness, duskiness, murk, murkiness, obscureness, obscurity. *See also* **shade.** 2. The period of time between sunset and sunrise ▸ after dark, lights out. *See* **night.**

✦ CORE SYNONYMS: *dark, dim, murky, dusky, obscure, shady, shadowy.* These adjectives indicate a deficiency in brightness or light, and, by extension, a deficiency in or lack of clarity. *Dark,* the most widely applicable, can refer to insufficiency of illumination for seeing (*a dark evening*), deepness of shade or color (*dark brown*), absence of cheer (*a dark, somber mood*), or lack of rectitude (*a dark past*). *Dim* suggests lack of clarity of outline: *"life and the memory of it cramped,/dim, on a piece of Bristol board"* (Elizabeth Bishop). It can also apply to a source of light to indicate insufficiency: *"storied Windows richly dight,/Casting a dim religious light"* (John Milton). *Murky* implies darkness, often extreme, such as that produced by smoke or fog: *"The path was altogether indiscernible in the murky darkness which surrounded them"* (Sir Walter Scott). *Dusky* suggests the dimness that is characteristic of diminishing light, as at twilight: *"The dusky night rides down the sky,/And ushers in the morn"* (Henry Fielding). Also, it often refers to deepness of shade of a color: *"A dusky blush rose to her cheek"* (Edith Wharton). *Obscure* usually means unclear to the mind or senses, but it can refer to physical darkness: *the obscure rooms of a shuttered mansion. Shady* refers literally to what is sheltered from light, especially sunlight (*a shady grove of pines*) or figuratively to what is of questionable honesty (*shady business deals*). *Shadowy* also implies obstructed light (*a shadowy path*) but may suggest shifting illumination and indistinctness: *"[He] retreated from the limelight to the shadowy fringe of music history"* (Charles Sherman). It can also refer to something that seems to lack substance and is mysterious or sinister: *a shadowy figure in a black cape.*

darken *verb*
▸ adumbrate, overcast, shadow. *See* **shade** (2).

darkness *noun*
1. Absence or deficiency of light ▸ dimness, duskiness, murkiness. *See* **dark** (1). 2. The condition of being ignorant; lack of knowledge ▸ illiteracy, nescience. *See* **ignorance** (1). 3. The condition of not being able to see ▸ blindness, legal blindness, sightlessness, visual impairment.

darling *noun*
1. A person who is much loved ▸ beloved, dear, honey,

love, precious, sugar, sweet, sweetheart, truelove. *Informal:* babe, baby, honeybun, honeybunch, sweetie, sweetie-pie, sweetpea. *Idiom:* light of one's life. **2.** One liked or preferred above all others ▸ favorite, pet. *Idiom:* apple of one's eye.

darling *adjective*
1. Regarded with much love and tenderness ▸ beloved, dear, desired, loved, precious. **2.** Being favorite ▸ fair-haired, favored, pet. *See* **favorite**. **3.** *Informal* Giving great pleasure or delight ▸ delectable, enchanting, heavenly. *See* **delightful**.

darn *adjective*
Informal So annoying or detestable as to deserve condemnation ▸ accursed, blasted, confounded. *See* **damned** (2).

dart *verb*
1. To move swiftly ▸ dash, sprint, zip. *See* **rush** (1). **2.** To pass quickly and lightly through the air ▸ glide, sail, shoot. *See* **fly** (2). **3.** To send through the air with a motion of the hand or arm ▸ fling, hurl, pitch. *See* **throw** (1).

dash *verb*
1. To send through the air with a motion of the hand or arm ▸ fling, hurl, pitch. *See* **throw** (1). **2.** To hurl or scatter liquid ▸ bespatter, spray. *See* **splash** (1). **3.** To move swiftly ▸ bolt, sprint, zip. *See* **rush** (1). **4.** To spoil or destroy ▸ corrode, scorch. *See* **blast** (2). *See synonym note at* **blast**.

dash *noun*
1. A lively, emphatic, eager quality or manner ▸ life, verve, vivaciousness. *See* **spirit** (1). *See synonym note at* **spirit**. **2.** A tiny amount ▸ jot, pinch, smidgen. *See* **bit**[1] (1). **3.** A slight amount or indication ▸ hint, semblance, trace. *See* **shade** (2). **4.** A pace faster than a walk ▸ gallop, sprint. *See* **run** (1). **5.** A very small mark ▸ dot, speck. *See* **point** (2). **6.** Capacity for work or vigorous activity ▸ might, potency, power. *See* **energy**.

dashing *adjective*
1. Very brisk, alert, and full of high spirits ▸ animated, chipper, vivacious. *See* **lively** (1). **2.** In accordance with current fashion ▸ mod, stylish, swanky. *See* **fashionable**. **3.** Having or showing courage ▸ courageous, fearless, heroic. *See* **brave**.

dastard *noun*
▸ craven, poltroon, sissy. *See* **coward**.

dastardliness *noun*
▸ faint-heartedness, pusillanimity. *Slang:* gutlessness. *See* **cowardice**.

dastardly *adjective*
▸ faint-hearted, pusillanimous. *Slang:* gutless. *See* **cowardly**.

data *noun*
▸ facts, knowledge, lore. *See* **information** (1).

date *noun*
1. An arrangement to appear at a certain time and place ▸ assignation, rendezvous. *See* **engagement** (1). *See synonym note at* **engagement**. **2.** A commitment, as for a performance by an entertainer ▸ booking, engagement. *Slang:* gig.

date *verb*
To be with another person socially on a regular basis ▸ go out (with), go with, see. *Informal:* take out. *Idioms:* go steady, go together.

dated *adjective*
▸ antique, passé. *See* **old-fashioned**.

daub *verb*
To spread with a greasy, sticky, or dirty substance ▸ besmear, smudge. *See* **smear** (1).

daub *noun*
A discolored mark made by smearing ▸ blotch, stain. *See* **smear** (1).

daunt *verb*
1. To deprive of courage or the power to act as a result of fear, anxiety, or disgust ▸ consternate, disconcert. *See* **dismay** (1). *See synonym note at* **dismay**. **2.** To make less hopeful or enthusiastic ▸ dismay, dispirit. *See* **discourage** (1).

dauntless *adjective*
▸ courageous, fearless, heroic. *See* **brave**. *See synonym note at* **brave**.

dauntlessness *noun*
▸ bravery, fortitude, gallantry, valor. *See* **courage**.

dawdle *verb*
1. To go or move slowly so that progress is hindered ▸ dally, dilly-dally, drag. *See* **delay** (2). **2.** To spend (time) idly or pleasantly ▸ trifle away, waste. *See* **idle** (2). **3.** To waste time by engaging in aimless activity ▸ doodle, fiddle (around). *Informal:* fool (around). *See* **putter**.

dawdler *noun*
▸ lag, procrastinator, straggler. *See* **laggard**.

dawdling *noun*
▸ indecision, tentativeness. *See* **hesitation**.

dawn *noun*
1. The first appearance of daylight in the morning ▸ aurora, cockcrow, dawning, daybreak, morn, morning, sunrise, sunup. *Idioms:* break of day, crack of dawn. **2.** The initial stage of a developmental process ▸ genesis, inception, start. *See* **birth** (2). *See synonym note at* **birth**.

dawn *verb*
To come into being ▸ appear, commence, emerge. *See* **begin** (1).

dawn on *or* **upon** *verb*
To come as a realization ▸ register, sink in, soak in. *See also* **discover, strike, understand**.

dawning *noun*
▸ daybreak, sunrise, sunup. *See* **dawn** (1).

day *noun*
1. The period during which someone or something exists ▸ existence, span, term. *See* **life** (1). **2.** A particular time notable for its distinctive characteristics ▸ epoch, era, period. *See* **age** (2).

daybreak *noun*
▸ cockcrow, sunrise, sunup. *See* **dawn** (1).

daydream *noun*
An illusory mental image ▸ fancy, fantasy, illusion. *See* **dream** (1).

daydream *verb*
To experience dreams or daydreams ▸ fancy, hallucinate. *See* **dream** (1).

daydreamer *noun*
▸ fantasist, romantic, stargazer. *See* **dreamer** (1).

daydreaming *noun*
The condition of being so lost in solitary thought that one is unaware of one's surroundings ▸ absentmindedness, bemusement, reverie. *See* **trance** (1).

daydreaming *adjective*
Given to daydreams or reverie ▸ fanciful, musing. *See* **dreamy** (1).

daze *verb*
1. To dull the senses, as with a heavy blow, a shock, or fatigue ▸ bedaze, bemuse, benumb, bewilder, stagger, stun, stupefy. *Chiefly Regional:* maze. *Slang:* zonk. *See also* **confuse. 2.** To confuse with bright light ▸ bedazzle, blind, dazzle. **3.** To addle the mind, as with a narcotic or alcohol ▸ impair, stupefy. *See* **drug** (2).

daze *noun*
A stunned or bewildered condition ▸ bafflement, befuddlement, bewilderedness, bewilderment, confusion, discombobulation, disorientation, distraction, fog, haze, muddle, mystification, perplexity, puzzlement, stupefaction, stupor, trance.

✛ CORE SYNONYMS: *daze, bemuse, benumb, stun, stupefy.* These verbs mean to dull or paralyze the senses, as with a heavy blow, a shock, or fatigue: *dazed by the defeat; bemused by the senator's resignation; a boring performance that benumbed the audience; stunned by his sudden death; a display that stupefied all onlookers.*

---

dazed *adjective*
▸ lightheaded, reeling, spinning. *See* **dizzy** (1).

dazzle *verb*
To confuse with bright light ▸ bedazzle, blind, daze.

dazzle *noun*
An intense blinding light ▸ blaze, flare, glare.

dazzling *adjective*
1. Marked by extraordinary beauty and splendor ▸ magnificent, resplendent, splendid. *See* **glorious** (1). **2.** Extremely or harshly bright ▸ blazing, blinding, glaring. *See* **brilliant** (2).

deacon *noun*
▸ ecclesiastic, minister, parson. *See* **cleric.**

deactivate *verb*
▸ demobilize, release, separate. *See* **discharge** (4).

dead *adjective*
1. No longer alive ▸ asleep, deceased, defunct, departed, expired, extinct, gone, late, lifeless, perished. *Idioms:* at rest, dead and buried, dead as a doornail, pushing up daisies, six feet under. **2.** Lacking physical feeling or sensitivity ▸ asleep, benumbed, deadened, dull, inert, insensible, insensitive, lifeless, numb, stuporous, torpid, unfeeling, unresponsive. *See also* **unconscious. 3.** Depleted of energy ▸ exhausted, weary, worn-out. *See* **tired** (1). **4.** Completely lacking sensation or consciousness ▸ inanimate, insensate, insentient, lifeless. **5.** Unable to support vegetation

▸ sterile, unfruitful, unproductive. *See* **barren** (2). **6.** Completely such, without qualification or exception ▸ all-out, pure, sheer. *See* **utter²**.

dead *adverb*
1. To the fullest extent ▸ fully, totally, utterly. *See* **completely** (1). **2.** In a direct line ▸ straight, undeviatingly. *See* **directly** (1). **3.** With precision or absolute conformity ▸ exactly, precisely, squarely. *See* **directly** (3).

✛ CORE SYNONYMS: *dead, deceased, departed, extinct, lifeless.* These adjectives all mean no longer alive or active. *Dead* applies in general to whatever once had—but no longer has—physical life (*a dead man; a dead leaf*), function (*a dead battery*), or force or currency (*a dead issue; a dead language*). *Deceased* and *departed* refer only to nonliving humans: *attended a memorial service for a recently deceased friend; looking at pictures of departed relatives. Extinct* can refer to what has no living successors (*extinct species such as the dodo*) or to what is extinguished or inactive (*an extinct volcano*). *Lifeless* applies to what no longer has physical life (*a lifeless body*), to what does not support life (*a lifeless planet*), or to what lacks animation, spirit, or brightness (*a lifeless performance; lifeless colors*).

---

deadbeat *noun*
Slang A self-indulgent person who avoids work ▸ bum, idler, loafer. *See* **wastrel** (2).

dead duck *noun*
Slang One that is ruined or doomed ▸ dead meat, goner, toast. *See also* **through.**

deaden *verb*
1. To render less sensitive ▸ benumb, blunt, desensitize, dull, numb. *Idioms:* put to sleep, take the edge off. *See also* **drug. 2.** To decrease or dull the sound of ▸ dampen, mute. *See* **muffle** (1).

dead end *noun*
A course leading nowhere ▸ blind alley, cul-de-sac.

dead heat *noun*
An equality of scores, votes, or performances in a contest ▸ deadlock, draw, stalemate, standoff, tie.

deadliness *noun*
The quality or condition of causing death or disaster ▸ fatality, fatefulness, lethality, lethalness.

deadlock *noun*
An equality of scores, votes, or performances in a contest ▸ dead heat, draw, stalemate, standoff, tie.

deadly *adjective*
1. Causing or tending to cause death ▸ deathly, fatal, lethal, mortal, pestilent. *See also* **poisonous. 2.** Gruesomely suggestive of ghosts or death ▸ deathly, ghostly, spectral. *See* **ghastly** (2). **3.** Arousing no interest or curiosity ▸ dull, humdrum, monotonous. *See* **boring** (1). **4.** Lacking liveliness, charm, or surprise ▸ aseptic, colorless, pedestrian. *See* **dull** (1).

✛ CORE SYNONYMS: *deadly, fatal, mortal, lethal.* These adjectives apply to what causes or is likely to cause death. *Deadly* means capable of killing: *a deadly poison. Fatal* describes conditions, circumstances, or events that have caused or are destined to cause death or dire consequences: *a fatal illness. Mortal* describes a condition or action that produces death: *a mortal wound. Lethal* refers to a sure agent of death that may have been created solely for the purpose of killing: *execution by lethal injection.*

---

dead meat *noun*
Slang One that is ruined or doomed ▸ dead duck, goner, toast. *See also* **through.**

deadpan *adjective*
▸ affectless, blank, pokerfaced. *See* **expressionless.**

deafening *adjective*
▸ booming, earsplitting, roaring. *See* **loud** (1).

deal *noun*
1. A business agreement involving goods or services ▸ auction, barter, bargain, exchange, sale, trade, transaction. **2.** An often written acceptance of terms between parties ▸ accord, contract, pact. *See* **agreement** (1). *See synonym note at* **agreement. 3.** *Informal* Something offered or bought at a low price ▸ bargain, find. *Informal:* buy. *Slang:* steal. **4.** An indefinite amount or extent ▸ measure, number, portion. *See* **quantity** (2).

deal *verb*
1. To give out in portions or shares ▸ allocate, apportion, dispense. *See* **distribute** (1). *See synonym note at* **distribute. 2.** To offer for sale ▸ handle, peddle. *See* **sell** (1). **3.** To have for sale ▸ carry, keep, offer, stock. **4.** To engage in the illicit sale of narcotics ▸ peddle. *Slang:* push. *See also* **sell. 5.** To mete out by means of some action ▸ administer, deliver, give.

deal with *verb*
1. To be concerned with something ▸ address, consider, take up, treat. *Idiom:* have to do with. **2.** To behave in a specified way toward someone ▸ cope with, handle, treat.

dealer *noun*
1. A person engaged in buying and selling ▸ businessperson, entrepreneur, merchandiser, merchant, trader, tradesman, trafficker. *See also* **seller. 2.** A person who sells narcotics illegally ▸ peddler, trafficker. *See* **pusher. 3.** One who acts as an intermediate agent between persons or groups ▸ intermediary, mediator, middleman. *See* **go-between.**

dear *adjective*
1. Regarded with much love and tenderness ▸ beloved, precious. *See* **darling** (1). **2.** Of great value or price ▸ expensive, high-priced, valuable. *See* **costly.**

dear *noun*
A person who is much loved ▸ honey, precious, sweetheart. *See* **darling** (1).

dearth *noun*
The condition of lacking something ▸ absence, lack, want. *See also* **need, shortage.**

death *noun*
1. The act or fact of dying ▸ decease, demise, dissolution, end, expiration, extinction, passing, quietus, rest. *Slang:* curtains. **2.** A loss of life, or one who has lost life, usually as a result of accident, disaster, or war ▸ casualty, fatality, kill, loss. *See also* **victim.**

deathless *adjective*
▸ immortal, undying. *See also* **endless.**

deathlike *adjective*
▸ deathly, ghostly, spectral. *See* **ghastly** (2).

deathly *adjective*
1. Gruesomely suggestive of ghosts or death ▸ cadaverous, ghostly, spectral. *See* **ghastly** (2). **2.** Causing or tending to cause death ▸ fatal, lethal, mortal. *See* **deadly** (1).

debacle *noun*
1. An abrupt disastrous failure ▸ breakdown, crash, disaster. *See* **collapse** (2). **2.** An occurrence inflicting widespread destruction and distress ▸ cataclysm, catastrophe, tragedy. *See* **disaster** (1).

debar *verb*
1. To keep from being admitted, included, or considered ▸ eliminate, keep out, rule out. *See* **exclude** (1). **2.** To refuse to allow ▸ disallow, proscribe. *See* **forbid.**

debark *verb*
To come ashore from a seacraft ▸ alight, disembark, land, light.

debase *verb*
1. To lower in character or quality ▸ abase, cheapen, degrade, demean, devalue, downgrade. *See also* **belittle, humble. 2.** To make impure or inferior by contact or mixture ▸ adulterate, doctor, pollute. *See* **contaminate** (1). *See synonym note at* **contaminate. 3.** To ruin morally ▸ demoralize, deprave, warp. *See* **corrupt** (1). *See synonym note at* **corrupt. 4.** To lower the pride or dignity of ▸ degrade, demean, humiliate. *See* **humble** (1). **5.** To bring disgrace on ▸ abase, dishonor, shame. *See* **disgrace.**

debase *adjective*
Lacking scruples or principles ▸ unconscionable, unethical, unprincipled. *See* **unscrupulous** (1).

✦ **CORE SYNONYMS:** *debase, degrade, abase, demean, humble.* These verbs mean to lower in character or quality. *Debase* implies reduction in quality or value: *"debasing the moral currency"* (George Eliot). *Degrade* implies reduction to a state of shame or disgrace: *"If I pitied you for crying . . . you should spurn such pity . . . . Rise, and don't degrade yourself into an abject reptile!"* (Emily Brontë). *Abase* refers principally to loss of rank or prestige: *"Meg pardoned him, and Mrs. March's grave face relaxed . . . when she heard him declare that he would . . . abase himself like a worm before the injured damsel"* (Louisa May Alcott). *Demean* suggests lowering in social position: *"It puts him where he can make the advances without demeaning himself"* (William Dean Howells). *Humble* can refer to lowering in rank or, more often, to reducing in pride: *dreamed of humbling his opponent.*

---

debased *adjective*
1. Utterly reprehensible in nature or behavior ▸ depraved, miscreant, perverse. *See* **corrupt** (1). **2.** Mixed with other substances ▸ alloyed, combined, polluted.

See **impure** (2). **3.** Not chaste or moral ▶ corrupted, unchaste. *See* **impure** (1).

debasement *noun*
▶ degeneration, dishonor, humiliation. *See* **degradation** (1).

debatable *adjective*
In doubt or dispute ▶ arguable, contentious, contestable, contested, disputable, doubtful, exceptionable, indefinite, moot, mootable, problematic, problematical, questionable, suspect, uncertain, unconfirmed, unsettled. *Informal:* iffy.

debate *verb*
1. To put forth reasons for or against something, often excitedly ▶ contend, dispute. *See* **argue** (2). **2.** To meet and exchange views to reach a decision ▶ consult, deliberate, talk. *Informal:* huddle, powwow. *See* **confer** (1). **3.** To speak together and exchange ideas and opinions about ▶ converse, deliberate. *Informal:* kick around. *See* **discuss.**

debate *noun*
1. A discussion, often heated, in which a difference of opinion is expressed ▶ contention, fight, quarrel. *See* **argument** (1). **2.** An exchange of views in an attempt to reach a decision ▶ consultation, counsel, parley. *See* **deliberation** (1).

debauch *verb*
▶ debase, demoralize, deprave, warp. *See* **corrupt** (1). *See synonym note at* **corrupt.**

debauchee *noun*
▶ libertine, profligate. *See* **wanton** (1).

debaucher *noun*
1. A man who seduces women ▶ Don Juan, Lothario, seducer. **2.** An immoral or licentious person ▶ libertine, profligate. *See* **wanton** (1).

debauchery *noun*
▶ depravity, perversion, vice. *See* **corruption** (1).

debilitate *verb*
▶ attenuate, weaken. *See* **enervate.**

debilitated *adjective*
▶ decrepit, infirm, rundown. *See* **weak** (1). *See synonym note at* **weak.**

debilitation *noun*
The sapping away of strength or energy ▶ attenuation, depletion, devitalization, enervation, enfeeblement, impairment, impoverishment, incapacitation, weakening.

debility *noun*
▶ decrepitude, feebleness, unsubstantiality. *See* **infirmity** (1).

debit *noun*
▶ indebtedness, liability, obligation. *See* **debt** (1).

debonair *adjective*
1. Gracious and tactful in social manner ▶ smooth, suave, urbane. *See also* **courteous, cultured, sophisticated. 2.** Happy and free from worry or care ▶ blithe, buoyant, untroubled. *See* **lighthearted** (1).

debris *noun*
1. The remains of something destroyed, disintegrated, or decayed ▶ remains, rubble, wreckage. *See* **ruin** (2).

2. Items or material discarded or rejected as useless or worthless ▶ flotsam, litter, rubbish. *See* **garbage** (1).

debt *noun*
1. Something, such as money, owed by one person to another ▶ arrearage, arrears, claim, debit, due, indebtedness, liability, obligation, score. **2.** A condition of owing something to another ▶ arrearage, arrears, encumbrance, indebtedness, liability, obligation.

debunk *verb*
▶ deflate, explode, puncture. *See* **discredit** (1).

debut *noun*
The instance or occasion of being presented for the first time to society ▶ coming-out, presentation.

debut *verb*
To make one's formal entry, as into society ▶ come out. *Idiom:* make one's bow.

decadence *noun*
▶ atrophy, decline, degeneration. *See* **deterioration** (1).

decamp *verb*
▶ abscond, flee. *See* **escape** (1).

decampment *noun*
▶ breakout, flight. *See* **escape** (1).

decant *verb*
▶ empty, flow, issue. *See* **pour** (1).

decay *verb*
To become or cause to become rotten or unsound ▶ blight, break down, corrupt, crumble, curdle, decompose, deteriorate, disintegrate, fester, molder, putrefy, rot, spoil, taint, turn. *Idioms:* go bad, go to pot, go to seed.

decay *noun*
The condition of being decayed ▶ blight, breakdown, decomposition, decrepitude, deterioration, disintegration, putrefaction, putrescence, putridness, rot, rottenness, spoilage.

✣ **CORE SYNONYMS:** *decay, rot, putrefy, spoil, crumble, molder, disintegrate, decompose.* These verbs mean to become or cause something to become rotten or unsound. *Decay* can denote partial deterioration short of complete destruction: *Brush and floss regularly to prevent teeth from decaying.* *Rot* is sometimes synonymous with *decay,* but often, like *putrefy,* stresses offensiveness to the sense of smell: *The food left on the counter began to rot. Arctic cold prevented the prehistoric animal from putrefying.* *Spoil* usually refers to the process by which perishable substances become unfit for use or consumption: *Put the fish in the refrigerator before they spoil.* *Crumble* implies physical breakdown into small fragments or particles: *The ancient church had crumbled to ruins.* To *molder* is to crumble to dust: *The shawl had moldered away in the trunk. Disintegrate* refers to complete breakdown into component parts: *The sandstone façade had disintegrated from exposure to the elements. Decompose,* largely restricted to the breakdown of substances into their chemical components, also connotes rotting and putrefying, both literally and figuratively: *"trivial personalities decomposing in the eternity of print"* (Virginia Woolf).

---

decayed *adjective*
1. Marred by decay ▸ foul, overripe, putrid. *See* **bad** (2). 2. Showing signs of wear and tear or neglect ▸ broken-down, dilapidated, tattered. *See* **shabby** (1).

decaying *adjective*
▸ broken-down, dilapidated, tattered. *See* **shabby** (1).

decease *verb*
To cease living ▸ demise, expire, perish. *See* **die** (1).

decease *noun*
The act or fact of dying ▸ demise, passing. *See* **death** (1).

deceased *adjective*
▸ departed, expired, perished. *See* **dead** (1). *See synonym note at* **dead**.

deceit *noun*
1. The act or practice of deceiving ▸ cunning, deceitfulness, deception, double-dealing, duplicity, fraud, guile, shiftiness, trickery. 2. An act of cheating ▸ fraud, hoax, swindle. *See* **cheat** (1).

deceitful *adjective*
▸ duplicitous, lying, untruthful. *See* **dishonest** (1). *See synonym note at* **dishonest**.

deceitfulness *noun*
1. The act or practice of deceiving ▸ deception, duplicity, guile. *See* **deceit** (1). 2. Deceitful cleverness ▸ artfulness, cunning, slyness. *See* **art** (1). 3. Lack of integrity ▸ duplicity, mendacity. *See* **dishonesty** (1).

deceive *verb*
To cause to accept something false by trickery or misrepresentation ▸ beguile, betray, bluff, cheat, cozen, delude, double-cross, dupe, fool, hoodwink, humbug, mislead, string along, swindle, take in, trick. *Informal:* bamboozle, beat, burn, have, sucker. *Slang:* four-flush, punk, snow. *Idioms:* lead astray, play false, pull the wool over someone's eyes, put something over on, slip one over on, take for a ride. *See also* **flatter**.

✦ **CORE SYNONYMS:** *deceive, betray, mislead, beguile, delude, dupe, hoodwink, bamboozle, double-cross.* These verbs mean to cause someone to accept something false by trickery or misrepresentation. *Deceive* involves the deliberate misrepresentation of the truth: *"We are inclined to believe those whom we do not know, because they have never deceived us"* (Samuel Johnson). *Betray* implies treachery: *"When you betray somebody else, you also betray yourself"* (Isaac Bashevis Singer). *Mislead* means to lead in the wrong direction or into error of thought or action: *"My manhood, long misled by wandering fires,/Followed false lights"* (John Dryden). *Beguile* suggests deceiving by means of charm or allure: *They beguiled unwary investors with tales of overnight fortunes.* To *delude* is to mislead the mind or judgment: *The government deluded the public about the dangers of low-level radiation.* *Dupe* implies playing upon another's susceptibilities or naiveté: *The shoppers were duped by false advertising.* *Hoodwink* refers to deluding by trickery: *It is difficult to hoodwink a smart lawyer.* *Bamboozle* means to delude by the use of such tactics as hoaxing or artful persuasion: *"Perhaps if I wanted*

to be understood or to understand I would bamboozle myself into belief, but I am a reporter"* (Graham Greene). *Double-cross* implies the betrayal of a confidence or the willful breaking of a pledge: *The thief double-crossed his accomplice.*

---

deceiver *noun*
1. A person who cheats ▸ cheater, swindler, trickster. *See* **cheat** (2). 2. One who tells lies ▸ fabulist, fibber, prevaricator. *See* **liar**.

decency *noun*
1. A sense of rightness ▸ conscience, grace, properness, propriety. 2. Conformity to recognized standards, as of conduct or appearance ▸ correctness, decentness, decorousness, decorum, properness, propriety, respectability, respectableness, seemliness. 3. The condition of being chaste ▸ modesty, purity, virginity. *See* **chastity**.

decent *adjective*
1. Suitable for a particular person, condition, occasion, or place ▸ befitting, correct, right. *See* **appropriate** (1). 2. Not lewd or obscene ▸ modest, wholesome. *See* **clean** (5). 3. Being what is needed without being in excess ▸ competent, satisfactory. *See* **sufficient** (1). 4. Adequate to satisfy a need, requirement, or standard ▸ average, common, moderate. *See* **acceptable** (2). 5. Having pleasant desirable qualities ▸ bonny, enjoyable, nice. *See* **good** (1). 6. Morally beyond reproach ▸ modest, pure, virginal. *See* **chaste**. 7. *Informal* Proper in appearance ▸ modest, presentable, respectable, tasteful.

decentness *noun*
▸ decorum, respectability, seemliness. *See* **decency** (2).

deception *noun*
1. The act or practice of deceiving ▸ duplicity, guile. *See* **deceit** (1). 2. An indirect, usually cunning means of gaining an end ▸ artifice, ploy, stratagem. *See* **trick** (1).

deceptive *adjective*
1. Tending to lead one into error ▸ illusive, illusory, misleading. *See* **fallacious** (2). 2. Given to or marked by deliberate concealment or misrepresentation of the truth ▸ duplicitous, lying, mendacious. *See* **dishonest** (1). *See synonym note at* **dishonest**.

decide *verb*
1. To make up or cause to make up one's mind ▸ clinch, conclude, determine, resolve, settle. 2. To make a decision about (a controversy or dispute, for example) after deliberation, as in a court of law ▸ adjudicate, decree, rule. *See* **judge** (1). 3. To make a choice from a number of alternatives ▸ decide on, elect, pick (out), vote (for). *See* **choose** (1).

✦ **CORE SYNONYMS:** *decide, determine, settle, rule, conclude, resolve.* These verbs mean to make up or cause to make up one's mind. *Decide* is the least specific: *"If two laws conflict with each other, the courts must decide on the operation of each"* (John Marshall). *Determine* often involves somewhat narrower issues: *A jury will determine the verdict.* *Settle* stresses finality of decision: *"The lama waved a hand to show that the matter* *was finally settled in his mind"* (Rudyard Kipling). *Rule* implies that the decision is handed down by someone in authority: *The committee ruled that changes in the curriculum should be implemented.* *Conclude* suggests that a decision, opinion, or judgment has been arrived at after careful consideration: *She concluded that the criticism was unjust. Resolve* stresses the exercise of choice in making a firm decision: *I resolved to lose weight.*

decided *adjective*
1. Without any doubt ▸ clear, clear-cut, definite, distinct, pronounced, set, settled, unquestionable. **2.** Clearly, fully, and emphatically expressed ▸ clear, explicit, precise. *See* **definite** (1). **3.** Committed to or unwavering in a course of action ▸ determined, fixed, single-minded. *See* **intent** (1). **4.** Possessing determination or resolution ▸ resolute, steadfast, unyielding. *See* **firm**[1] (3).

decidedly *adverb*
▸ awfully, extremely, highly. *See* **very**.

decidedness *noun*
▸ determination, purpose, resolve, will. *See* **decision** (2).

deciding *adjective*
▸ crucial, definitive. *See* **decisive** (1).

decimate *verb*
▸ butcher, slaughter, wipe out. *See* **massacre** (1).

decimation *noun*
1. The act of destroying or the state of being destroyed ▸ devastation, ruin, wreck. *See* **destruction** (1). **2.** The savage killing of many victims ▸ bloodshed, butchery. *See* **massacre**.

decipher *verb*
1. To find the key to a code or cipher ▸ break, crack, decrypt, puzzle out, unlock, unscramble. **2.** To make understandable ▸ construe, interpret. *See* **explain** (1). **3.** To find a solution for ▸ explain, resolve, unravel. *See* **solve** (1). *See synonym note at* **solve**.

decipherable *adjective*
▸ accountable, illustratable, interpretable. *See* **explainable**.

decipherment *noun*
▸ clarification, explication, illumination. *See* **explanation** (1).

decision *noun*
1. A position reached after consideration ▸ conclusion, determination, resolution. *See also* **deduction**. **2.** Unwavering firmness of character, action, or will ▸ assuredness, decidedness, decisiveness, determination, firmness, purpose, purposefulness, resoluteness, resolution, resolve, toughness, will, willpower. *See also* **courage, drive**. **3.** The act, power, or right of choosing ▸ alternative, discretion, option. *See* **choice** (1). **4.** An authoritative or official decision ▸ edict, judgment, pronouncement. *See* **ruling**.

✛ **CORE SYNONYMS:** *decision, conclusion, determination.* These nouns denote a position, opinion, or judgment reached after consideration: *a decision unfavorable to*

the opposition; came to the conclusion not to proceed; satisfied with the panel's determination.

decisive *adjective*
1. Determining or having the power to determine an outcome ▸ conclusive, crucial, deciding, definitive, determinative. **2.** Clearly, fully, and emphatically expressed ▸ decided, explicit, precise. *See* **definite** (1). **3.** Serving the function of deciding or settling with finality ▸ conclusive, determinative. *See* **definitive** (1). **4.** Established beyond a doubt ▸ inarguable, indisputable, irrefutable. *See* **certain** (2). **5.** Possessing determination or resolution ▸ resolute, steadfast, unyielding. *See* **firm**[1] (3).

✛ **CORE SYNONYMS:** *decisive, conclusive, crucial, definitive, determinative.* These adjectives mean determining or having the power to determine an outcome: *the decisive vote; a conclusive reason; crucial experiments; a definitive verdict; the determinative battle.*

◀ **ANTONYM:** *indecisive*

decisiveness *noun*
▸ determination, purpose, resolve, will. *See* **decision** (2).

deck[1] *verb*
Slang To bring down, as from a shot or blow ▸ floor, ground, hew. *See* **drop** (6).

deck[2] *verb*
1. To dress in formal or special clothing ▸ attire, deck out, primp. *See* **dress up**. **2.** To furnish with decorations ▸ decorate, garnish, ornament. *See* **adorn** (1).

declaim *verb*
▸ harangue, orate, rave. *See* **rant** (1).

declaimer *noun*
▸ lecturer, orator, speechmaker. *See* **speaker** (1).

declamation *noun*
1. A usually formal spoken communication to an audience ▸ lecture, talk. *See* **speech** (2). **2.** The art of public speaking ▸ elocution, rhetoric. *See* **oratory**.

declamatory *adjective*
▸ bombastic, grandiloquent, rhetorical. *See* **oratorical**.

declaration *noun*
1. The act of announcing ▸ proclamation, publication. *See* **announcement** (1). **2.** Something announced or communicated ▸ announcement, declaration, notice. *See* **message** (1). **3.** The act of asserting positively or something so asserted ▸ affirmation, claim, statement. *See* **assertion**.

declare *verb*
1. To bring to public notice or make known publicly ▸ advertise, broadcast, proclaim. *See* **announce** (1). *See synonym note at* **announce**. **2.** To put into words ▸ express, state, utter. *See* **say** (1). **3.** To put into words positively and with conviction ▸ avow, contend, maintain. *See* **assert** (1). **4.** To assure the certainty or validity of ▸ authenticate, corroborate, substantiate, verify. *See* **confirm** (1).

déclassé *or* **declassed** *adjective*
‣ common, humble, unwashed. *See* **lowly** (1).

declension *noun*
‣ decline, degeneration. *See* **deterioration** (1).

declination *noun*
1. A marked loss of strength or effectiveness ‣ decline, deterioration, failure. **2.** Descent to a lower level or condition ‣ decadence, decline, degeneration. *See* **deterioration** (1).

decline *verb*
1. To be unwilling to accept, consider, or receive ‣ deny, disallow, disapprove, dismiss, pass (on), rebuff, refuse, reject, spurn, turn down, withhold. *Slang:* nix. *Idiom:* turn thumbs down on. *See also* **deprive, forbid. 2.** To become lower in price or value ‣ sag, sink, slump. *See* **fall** (7). **3.** To slope downward ‣ descend, dip. *See* **drop** (5). **4.** To lose strength or power ‣ atrophy, fail, weaken. *See* **fade** (1). **5.** To become lower in quality, character, or condition ‣ degenerate, ebb, worsen. *See* **deteriorate** (1).

decline *noun*
1. Descent to a lower level or condition ‣ decadence, declination, degeneration. *See* **deterioration** (1). **2.** A usually swift downward trend, as in prices ‣ descent, dip, downswing. *See* **fall** (3). **3.** A downward slope or distance ‣ declivity, descent. *See* **drop** (5). **4.** A marked loss of strength or effectiveness ‣ declination, deterioration, failure.

✛ CORE SYNONYMS: *decline, refuse, reject, spurn, rebuff.* These verbs all mean to be unwilling to accept, consider, or receive someone or something. To *decline* implies courtesy or politeness: *"I declined election to the National Institute of Arts and Letters . . . and now I must decline the Pulitzer Prize"* (Sinclair Lewis). *Refuse* implies determination and often brusqueness: *"The commander . . . refused to discuss questions of right"* (George Bancroft). *"I'll make him an offer he can't refuse"* (Mario Puzo). *Reject* suggests the discarding of someone or something as defective or useless; it implies categoric refusal: *"He again offered himself for enlistment and was again rejected"* (Arthur S.M. Hutchinson). To *spurn* is to reject scornfully or contemptuously: *"The more she spurns my love,/The more it grows"* (William Shakespeare). *Rebuff* pertains to blunt, often disdainful rejection: *"He had . . . gone too far in his advances, and had been rebuffed"* (Robert Louis Stevenson).

---

declivity *noun*
‣ decline, descent. *See* **drop** (5).

décolleté *adjective*
‣ low-cut, low-neck, plunging. *See* **low** (4).

decompose *verb*
1. To reduce or become reduced to pieces or fragments ‣ crumble, dissolve, fragment. *See* **disintegrate** (1). **2.** To become or cause to become rotten or unsound ‣ deteriorate, spoil, turn. *See* **decay. See** *synonym note at* decay.

decomposition *noun*
‣ blight, deterioration, rot. *See* **decay.**

decontaminate *verb*
To render free of microorganisms ‣ disinfect, irradiate, sanitize, sterilize.

decorate *verb*
‣ bedeck, garnish, ornament. *See* **adorn** (1).

decoration *noun*
1. Something that adorns ‣ embellishment, ornament, trimming. *See* **adornment.2.** An emblem of honor worn on one's clothing ‣ badge, medal, ribbon.

decorous *adjective*
‣ befitting, correct, right. *See* **appropriate** (1).

decorousness *noun*
‣ decorum, respectability, seemliness. *See* **decency** (2).

decorticate *verb*
‣ pare, strip. *See* **skin** (1).

decorum *noun*
1. Conformity to recognized standards, as of conduct or appearance ‣ respectability, seemliness. *See* **decency** (2). **2.** Socially correct behavior ‣ etiquette, propriety. *See* **manners.**

decoy *noun*
Something that leads one into danger or entrapment ‣ bait, lure. *See also* **trap, trick.**

decrease *verb*
To become or cause to become gradually less ‣ abate, diminish, drain, dwindle, ebb, lessen, lower, peter out, ratchet down, reduce, shrink, tail away, tail off, taper off, wane. *See also* **depreciate, fall, shorten, subside.**

decrease *noun*
The act or process of decreasing ‣ abatement, curtailment, cut, cutback, decrement, diminishment, diminution, drain, reduction, shrinkage, slash, slowdown, taper, tapering (off), wane, waning. *See also* **fall, waning.**

✛ CORE SYNONYMS: *decrease, lessen, reduce, dwindle, abate, diminish, subside.* These verbs mean to become or cause to become gradually less. *Decrease* and *lessen* refer to steady or gradual diminution: *Lack of success decreases confidence. His appetite lessens as his illness progresses. Reduce* emphasizes bringing down in size, degree, or intensity: *The workers reduced their wage demands. Dwindle* suggests decreasing bit by bit to a vanishing point: *Their savings dwindled away. Abate* stresses a decrease in amount or intensity and suggests a reduction of excess: *Toward evening the fire began to abate. Diminish* implies taking away or removal: *The warden's authority diminished after the revolt. Subside* implies a falling away to a more normal level: *The wild enthusiasm aroused by the team's victory did not subside for days.*

◀ ANTONYM: *increase*

---

decree *noun*
An authoritative or official decision ‣ edict, judgment, pronouncement. *See* **ruling.**

decree *verb*
1. To set forth expressly and authoritatively ‣ impose, mandate, ordain. *See* **dictate** (1). *See synonym note at*

dictate. 2. To make a decision about (a controversy or dispute, for example) after deliberation, as in a court of law ▸ adjudicate, decide, rule. *See* **judge** (1).

decrement *noun*
▸ diminishment, reduction, slowdown. *See* **decrease**.

decrepit *adjective*
1. Not physically strong ▸ feeble, frail, unsound. *See* **weak** (1). *See synonym note at* **weak. 2.** Showing signs of wear and tear or neglect ▸ broken-down, dilapidated, tattered. *See* **shabby** (1).

decrepitude *noun*
1. The condition of being infirm or physically weak ▸ feebleness, unsubstantiality. *See* **infirmity** (1). **2.** The condition of being decayed ▸ decomposition, deterioration, rot. *See* **decay**.

decriminalize *verb*
▸ legitimate, legitimatize. *See* **legalize**.

decry *verb*
1. To represent or speak of as small or insignificant ▸ deprecate, downgrade, slight. *See* **belittle**. *See synonym note at* **belittle. 2.** To express strong disapproval of ▸ condemn, denounce. *See* **deplore** (1). **3.** To have or express an unfavorable opinion of ▸ condemn, disfavor, object to. *See* **disapprove** (1).

decrypt *verb*
▸ break, crack, unscramble. *See* **decipher** (1).

decumbent *adjective*
▸ horizontal, prone, prostrate. *See* **flat** (1).

decussate *verb*
▸ crosscut, intersect. *See* **cross** (2).

dedicate *verb*
1. To give over by or as if by vow to a higher purpose ▸ consecrate, sacrifice. *See* **devote** (1). *See synonym note at* **devote. 2.** To devote oneself or one's efforts ▸ concentrate, focus, give. *See* **apply** (1).

dedicated *adjective*
▸ allegiant, loyal, staunch. *See* **faithful** (1).

deduce *verb*
▸ conclude, gather. *See* **infer** (1).

deduct *verb*
1. To take away a quantity from another quantity ▸ abate, discount, rebate, remove, subtract, take away, take off, withdraw. *Informal:* knock off. **2.** To arrive at a conclusion from evidence or reasoning ▸ deduce, gather. *See* **infer** (1).

deduction *noun*
1. An amount deducted ▸ abatement, discount, rebate, reduction. **2.** A position arrived at by reasoning from premises ▸ conclusion, inference, judgment. *See also* **belief. 3.** Exact, valid, and rational reasoning ▸ analysis, rationality, reason. *See* **logic** (1).

deed *noun*
1. Something done ▸ action, thing, work. *See* **act** (1). **2.** Something completed or attained sucessfully ▸ achievement, feat, triumph. *See* **accomplishment** (1). **3.** The fact of possessing or the legal right to possess something ▸ possession, title. *See* **ownership**.

deed *verb*
To change the ownership of property by means of a legal document ▸ assign, grant, sign over. *See* **transfer** (1).

deem *verb*
1. To have an opinion ▸ consider, hold. *See* **believe** (3). **2.** To look upon in a particular way ▸ consider, view. *See* **regard** (1). *See synonym note at* **regard**.

de-emphasize *verb*
Informal To make less emphatic or obvious ▸ play down, soft-pedal, tone down. *See also* **moderate**.

deep *adjective*
1. Extending far downward or inward from a surface ▸ abysmal, bottomless, low, profound. **2.** Beyond the understanding of an average mind ▸ abstract, abstruse, difficult, esoteric, formidable, inscrutable, profound, recondite. *Slang:* heavy. *See also* **incomprehensible. 3.** Resulting from or affecting one's innermost feelings ▸ great, heartfelt, intense, powerful, profound, strong. **4.** Being a sound produced by a relatively small frequency of vibrations ▸ alto, bass, contralto. *See* **low** (2). **5.** Full of color ▸ rich, vibrant, vivid. *See* **colorful** (1).

deep *noun*
1. Something of immeasurable and vast extent ▸ abysm, abyss, chasm, deeps, depth, depths, gulf. **2.** The body of salt water covering most of the earth's surface ▸ brine, main, sea. *See* **ocean**.

deepen *verb*
▸ aggravate, enhance, heighten. *See* **intensify**.

deep-fry *verb*
▸ brown, fry. *See* **cook** (1).

deepness *noun*
1. The extent or measurement downward from a surface ▸ depth, drop, drop-off. **2.** Intellectual penetration or range ▸ depth, profoundness, profundity, weightiness. *See also* **discernment, intelligence, wisdom**.

deep-seated *or* **deep-rooted** *adjective*
▸ entrenched, ingrained, inveterate. *See* **confirmed** (1).

deep-six *verb*
Slang To let go or get rid of as being useless or defective, for example ▸ dump, throw away. *See* **discard**.

deep water *noun*
▸ corner, difficulty, fix. *See* **predicament**.

deface *verb*
▸ disfigure, misshape, twist. *See* **deform**.

defamation *noun*
▸ aspersion, denigration, slander. *See* **libel**.

defamatory *adjective*
▸ calumnious, invidious, slanderous. *See* **libelous**.

defame *verb*
▸ defame, calumniate, slander. *See* **malign**. *See synonym note at* **malign**.

default *noun*
▸ delinquency, dereliction. *See* **failure** (2).

defeasance *noun*
▸ annulment, nullification, voidance. *See* **abolition**.

defeat *verb*
1. To win a victory over, as in battle or a competition

► beat, best, checkmate, conquer, master, outgun, outplay, overcome, prevail over, subdue, subjugate, surmount, triumph over, vanquish, worst. *Informal:* trim. *Slang:* ace, KO, lick. *Idioms:* carry (*or* win) the day, get (*or* have) the best of, get (*or* have) the better of, go someone one better. *See also* **annihilate, overwhelm. 2.** To prevent from accomplishing a purpose ► foil, stymie, thwart. *See* **frustrate** (1).

defeat *noun*
The act of defeating or the condition of being defeated ► beating, blowout, checkmate, clobbering, drubbing, overthrow, rout, thrashing, trouncing, vanquishment, waterloo. *Informal:* massacre, trimming, whipping. *Slang:* creaming, dusting, licking, shellacking.

✦ CORE SYNONYMS: *defeat, conquer, vanquish, beat, subdue, subjugate, overcome.* These verbs mean to win a victory over an adversary, as in battle or a competition. *Defeat* is the most general: "*Whether we defeat the enemy in one battle, or by degrees, the consequences will be the same*" (Thomas Paine). *Conquer* suggests decisive and often wide-scale victory: "*The Franks . . . having conquered the Gauls, established the kingdom which has taken its name from them*" (Alexander Hamilton). *Vanquish* emphasizes total mastery: *Napoleon's forces were vanquished at Waterloo. Beat* is similar to *defeat,* though less formal and often more emphatic: "*To win battles . . . you beat the soul . . . of the enemy man*" (George S. Patton). *Subdue* suggests mastery and control achieved by overpowering: "*It cost* [the Romans] *two great wars, and three great battles, to subdue that little kingdom* [Macedonia]" (Adam Smith). *Subjugate* more strongly implies reducing an opponent to submission: "*The last foreigner to subjugate England was a Norman duke in the Middle Ages named William*" (Stanley Meisler). To *overcome* is to prevail over, often by persevering: *He overcame his injury after months of physical therapy.*

defecate *verb*
To void feces ► ease oneself, have a bowel movement, move one's bowels, pass stool. *Informal:* go number two, go to the bathroom, poop. *See also* **eliminate.**

defecation *noun*
The act or process of discharging bodily wastes ► evacuation, excretion. *See* **elimination** (3).

defect *noun*
1. Something that mars the appearance or causes inadequacy or failure ► blemish, bug, failing, fault, flaw, glitch, imperfection, shortcoming, weakness. *See also* **abnormality, deformity. 2.** The condition or fact of being deficient ► deficit, inadequacy, paucity. *See* **shortage.**

defect *verb*
To abandon one's cause or party usually to join another ► apostatize, desert, disavow, forsake, quit, renegade, renounce, secede, tergiversate, turn. *Slang:* rat. *Idioms:* change sides, turn one's coat.

✦ CORE SYNONYMS: *defect, blemish, imperfection, fault, flaw.* These nouns denote something that mars the

appearance or causes inadequacy or failure. *Defect* denotes a serious functional or structural shortcoming: "*Ill breeding . . . is not a single defect, it is the result of many*" (Henry Fielding). A *blemish* mars appearance or character: "*Industry in art is a necessity—not a virtue—and any evidence of the same, in the production, is a blemish*" (James McNeill Whistler). *Imperfection* and *fault* apply more comprehensively to any deficiency or shortcoming: "*A true critic ought to dwell rather upon excellencies than imperfections*" (Joseph Addison). "*Each of us would point out to the other her most serious faults, and thereby help her to remedy them*" (Anna Howard Shaw). *Flaw* refers to an often small but always fundamental weakness: *Experiments revealed a very basic flaw in the theory.*

defection *noun*
1. An instance of defecting from or abandoning a cause ► abandonment, apostasy, disavowal, recreance, recreancy, renouncement, secession, tergiversation. **2.** Departure from one's native land to settle in another ► diaspora, transmigration. *See* **emigration.**

defective *adjective*
1. Having a defect or defects ► amiss, blemished, faulty, flawed, imperfect. *See also* **shabby, trick. 2.** Lacking an essential element ► incomplete, wanting. *See* **deficient** (1).

defector *noun*
A person who has defected ► apostate, deserter, recreant, renegade, runagate, tergiversator, traitor, turncoat. *Informal:* rat.

defend *verb*
1. To keep safe from danger, attack, or harm ► cover, guard, hedge, preserve, protect, safeguard, secure, shield, ward. **2.** To support against arguments, attack, or criticism ► apologize, bolster, justify, maintain, uphold, vindicate. *Idioms:* make a case for, speak up for, stand up for, stick up for.

✦ CORE SYNONYMS: *defend, protect, guard, preserve, shield, safeguard.* These verbs mean to make or keep safe from danger, attack, or harm. *Defend* implies repelling an attack: *defending her territory; defended his reputation. Protect* often suggests providing a barrier to discomfort, injury, or attack: *bought a dog to protect the children; wore sunglasses to protect her eyes. Guard* suggests keeping watch: *guarded the house against intruders.* To *preserve* is to take measures to maintain something in safety: *ecologists working to preserve our natural resources. Shield* suggests protecting with a piece of defensive armor: *hid the newspaper to shield me from the bad news. Safeguard* stresses protection against potential danger: *The Bill of Rights safeguards our individual liberties.*

defendable *adjective*
Capable of being defended against armed attack ► defensible, tenable. *See also* **safe.**

defendant *noun*
A person against whom an action is brought ► accused, respondent.

defender *noun*
► champion, proponent, supporter. *See* **advocate** (1).

defense *noun*

1. The act or a means of defending ▶ barricade, guard, hedge, preservation, protection, safeguard, security, shield, ward. **2.** A statement that justifies or defends something, such as a past action or policy ▶ justification, vindication. *See* **apology** (1). *See synonym note at* **apology.**

defenseless *adjective*

▶ helpless, unprotected. *See* **vulnerable** (1).

defenselessness *noun*

▶ endangerment, susceptibility, vulnerability. *See* **exposure** (1).

defensible *adjective*

1. Capable of being defended against armed attack ▶ defendable, tenable. *See also* **safe. 2.** Capable of being justified ▶ excusable, justifiable, tenable. *See also* **logical, sound²**.

defensive *adjective*

▶ precautionary, prophylactic, protective. *See* **preventive** (2).

defer¹ *verb*

To put off until a later time ▶ adjourn, delay, hold off, hold up, postpone, put off, remit, shelve, stall, stay, suspend, table, waive. *Informal:* wait. *Idioms:* put on the back burner, put on hold, keep (*or* put) on ice.

✦ CORE SYNONYMS: *defer, postpone, shelve, stay, suspend.* These verbs mean to put off until a later time: *deferred paying the bills; postponing our trip; shelved the issue; stay an execution; suspending train service.*

---

defer² *verb*

1. To conform to the will or judgment of another, especially out of respect or courtesy ▶ bow, submit, yield. *Idioms:* give ground, give way. *See also* **humor. 2.** To give up in favor of another ▶ acquiesce, capitulate, give in. *See* **surrender** (1).

deference *noun*

1. The quality or state of willingly carrying out the wishes of others ▶ complaisance, compliancy, submissiveness. *See* **obedience. 2.** Great respect or high public esteem accorded as a right or as due ▶ homage, obeisance. *See* **honor** (1). *See synonym note at* **honor.**

deferential *adjective*

Marked by courteous submission or respect ▶ duteous, dutiful, obeisant, polite, respectful, submissive, yielding.

deferment *or* **deferral** *noun*

▶ adjournment, postponement, suspension. *See* **delay** (1).

defiance *noun*

1. The act or an instance of defying ▶ challenge, disobedience, insubordination, insurgence, naughtiness, noncompliance, opposition, provocation, rebellion, resistance. **2.** An attitude or behavior that is intentionally provocative or contemptuous ▶ contempt, contumaciousness, contumacy, despite, disregard, recalcitrance, recalcitrancy, rebelliousness.

defiant *adjective*

Marked by defiance ▶ contumacious, disobedient, in-

subordinate, rebellious, recalcitrant, resistant.

deficiency *noun*

1. The condition or fact of being deficient ▶ deficit, inadequacy, paucity. *See* **shortage. 2.** The condition of being deprived of what one once had or ought to have ▶ destitution, dispossession, loss. *See* **deprivation** (1).

deficient *adjective*

1. Lacking an essential element ▶ defective, inadequate, incomplete, lacking, sketchy, wanting. **2.** Not enough to meet a demand or requirement ▶ inadequate, wanting. *See* **insufficient** (1).

deficit *noun*

▶ defect, inadequacy, paucity. *See* **shortage.**

defile *verb*

1. To make dirty ▶ bemire, muck up, mud. *See* **dirty** (1). **2.** To ruin morally ▶ debase, pervert, taint. *See* **corrupt** (1). **3.** To spoil or mar the sanctity of ▶ desecrate, profane. *See* **violate** (3). **4.** To attack the reputation or honor of ▶ besmirch, smear, tarnish. *See* **denigrate** (1).

defilement *noun*

▶ dirtiness, impurity, pollution. *See* **contamination** (1).

define *verb*

1. To make clear or clearer ▶ elucidate, illustrate. *See* **clarify** (1). **2.** To fix the limits of ▶ demarcate, limit, mark. *See* **determine** (1).

definite *adjective*

1. Clearly, fully, and emphatically expressed ▶ categorical, clear, clear-cut, decided, decisive, emphatic, explicit, express, positive, precise, ringing, specific, straightforward, strong, strongly worded, unambiguous, unequivocal. *See also* **apparent, assertive, convincing, sharp. 2.** Having distinct limits ▶ determinate, fixed, limited, precise, specific, unambiguous. *Idioms:* cast (*or* fixed *or* set) in stone. **3.** Known positively ▶ absolute, certain, positive, sure, unimpeachable. *Idioms:* beyond doubt, for certain. **4.** Without any doubt ▶ clear-cut, unquestionable. *See* **decided** (1).

✦ CORE SYNONYMS: *definite, categorical, explicit, express, specific.* These adjectives mean clearly, fully, and emphatically expressed: *a definite answer; explicit statements; a categorical refusal; my express wishes; a specific purpose.*

◀ ANTONYMS: *ambiguous, indefinite*

---

definitely *adverb*

▶ certainly, positively, surely. *See* **absolutely** (1).

definitive *adjective*

1. Serving the function of deciding or settling with finality ▶ authoritative, conclusive, consummate, decisive, determinative, final, ultimate. *See also* **authentic, complete, perfect. 2.** Determining or having the power to determine an outcome ▶ crucial, deciding. *See* **decisive** (1). *See synonym note at* **decisive.**

definitude *noun*

▶ accurateness, exactness, precision. *See* **accuracy** (1).

deflate *verb*
1. To cause to be no longer believed or valued ▸ debunk, explode, puncture. *See* **discredit** (1). **2.** To lower the pride or dignity of ▸ degrade, demean, humiliate. *See* **humble** (1).

deflect *verb*
1. To move or cause to move in a bent or angular direction ▸ refract, turn. *See* **bend** (2). **2.** To change the direction or course of ▸ deviate, divert, veer. *See* **turn** (2). **3.** To turn aside or drive away ▸ check, repulse, ward off. *See* **repel**.

deflection *noun*
An act of reflection ▸ glance, reflection, scattering. *See also* **bounce**.

deform *verb*
To alter and spoil the natural form or appearance of ▸ blemish, contort, deface, dent, disfigure, distort, injure, mar, misshape, mutilate, pit, pock, ravage, scar, twist, warp. *See also* **damage**.

✛ CORE SYNONYMS: *deform, distort, twist, contort, warp.* These verbs mean to alter and spoil the natural form or appearance of something. *Deform* refers to change that disfigures and often implies the loss of desirable qualities such as beauty: *erosion that deformed the landscape.* To *distort* is to change the physical shape of something, as by torsion or exaggeration of certain features, or to misconstrue the meaning of something: *"The human understanding is like a false mirror, which, receiving rays irregularly, distorts and discolors the nature of things"* (Francis Bacon). *Twist* applies to distortion of form or meaning: *twisted his mouth in pain; accused me of intentionally twisting her words.* *Contort* implies violent change that produces unnatural or grotesque effects: *contorted her face with rage.* *Warp* can refer to turning from a flat or straight form or from a true course or direction: *oak floorboards that had warped over the years; judgment that was warped by prejudice.*

---

deformity *noun*
A disfiguring abnormality of shape or form ▸ blemish, contortion, defacement, deformation, dent, disfigurement, distortion, malformation, pit, pock, scar, warping. *See also* **abnormality, defect**.

defraud *verb*
▸ bilk, cozen, swindle. *See* **cheat** (1).

defrauder *noun*
▸ cheater, swindler, trickster. *See* **cheat** (2).

deft *adjective*
▸ facile, nimble. *See* **dexterous**. *See synonym note at* **dexterous**.

deftness *noun*
1. Skillfulness in the use of the hands or body ▸ adroitness, facility. *See* **dexterity** (1). **2.** The quality of being agile ▸ dexterity, nimbleness, quickness. *See* **agility**.

defunct *adjective*
▸ deceased, departed, perished. *See* **dead** (1).

defy *verb*
1. To confront boldly and courageously ▸ beard, brave, buck, challenge, dare, face, front, oppose. *Idioms:* beard the lion, fly in the face of, snap one's fingers at, stand up to, thumb one's nose at. *See also* **confront, contest**. **2.** To refuse or fail to obey ▸ break, transgress. *See* **disobey**. **3.** To call on another to do something bold ▸ challenge, dare. *Idiom:* throw down the gauntlet.

✛ CORE SYNONYMS: *defy, brave, challenge, dare, face.* These verbs mean to confront boldly and courageously: *an innovator defying tradition; braving all criticism; challenged the opposition to produce proof; daring him to deny the statement; faced her accusers.*

---

degeneracy *noun*
▸ decadence, decline, degeneration. *See* **deterioration** (1).

degenerate *adjective*
Utterly reprehensible in nature or behavior ▸ depraved, miscreant, perverse. *See* **corrupt** (1).

degenerate *verb*
1. To become lower in quality, character, or condition ▸ atrophy, decline, worsen. *See* **deteriorate** (1). **2.** To lose strength or power ▸ decline, fail, weaken. *See* **fade** (1). **3.** To undergo moral deterioration ▸ fall, sink, slip. *See also* **deteriorate**.

degeneration *noun*
1. Descent to a lower level or condition ▸ decadence, decline, weakening. *See* **deterioration** (1). **2.** A lowering in or deprivation of character or self-esteem ▸ abasement, dishonor, humiliation. *See* **degradation** (1).

degradation *noun*
1. A lowering in or deprivation of character or self-esteem ▸ abasement, debasement, degeneration, disgracing, dishonor, dishonoring, humiliation, mortification. *See also* **disgrace, shame**. **2.** The act or an instance of demoting ▸ demotion, downgrade, reduction.

degrade *verb*
1. To lower in rank or grade ▸ bump, downgrade. *See* **demote**. *See synonym note at* **demote**. **2.** To lower the pride or dignity of ▸ debase, demean, humiliate. *See* **humble** (1). **3.** To lower in character or quality ▸ cheapen, downgrade. *See* **debase** (1). *See synonym note at* **debase**. **4.** To bring disgrace on ▸ abase, dishonor, shame. *See* **disgrace**.

degraded *adjective*
▸ unconscionable, unethical, unprincipled. *See* **unscrupulous** (1).

degrading *adjective*
▸ discreditable, ignominious, shameful. *See* **disgraceful** (1).

degree *noun*
1. One of the units in a course, as on an ascending or descending scale ▸ grade, interval, level, mark, peg, point, rank, rung, stage, step, unit. *Informal:* notch. **2.** Relative intensity or amount, as of a quality or attribute ▸ extent, level, magnitude, measure, proportion, range, scope. **3.** The ultimate point to which an

action, thought, discussion, or policy is carried ► end, extreme, limit. *See* **length** (3).

dehydrate *verb*
1. To make or become free of moisture ► desiccate, exsiccate, parch. *See* **dry** (1). *See synonym note at* **dry**.
2. To prepare food for storage and future use ► can, cure, put up. *See* **preserve** (1).

deific *adjective*
► celestial, heavenly, holy. *See* **divine** (1).

deification *noun*
► apotheosis, elevation. *See* **exaltation** (1).

deign *verb*
► descend, stoop, vouchsafe. *See* **condescend** (1). *See synonym note at* **condescend**.

deject *verb*
► dishearten, dispirit, sadden. *See* **depress** (1).

dejected *adjective*
1. In low spirits ► dysphoric, melancholy, spiritless. *See* **depressed** (1). *See synonym note at* **depressed**.
2. Having lost all hope ► despairing, forlorn, hopeless. *See* **despondent**.

dejection *noun*
► despondence, doldrums, melancholy. *See* **depression** (2).

delay *verb*
1. To cause to be later or slower than expected or desired ► clog, detain, hang up, hinder, hold up, impede, keep, retard, set back, slacken, slow (down *or* up), stall. *Idiom:* make late. *See also* **restrain, stop**.
2. To go or move slowly so that progress is hindered ► dally, dawdle, dilly-dally, drag, lag, linger, loiter, procrastinate, stall, tarry, trail. *Idioms:* drag one's feet (*or* heels), mark time, take one's time. *See also* **remain, wait**. **3.** To put off until a later time ► adjourn, postpone, suspend. *See* **defer**[1].

delay *noun*
1. The act of putting off or the condition of being put off ► adjournment, deferment, deferral, holdup, moratorium, postponement, procrastination, shelving, stay, suspension, tabling, waiver. *Idiom:* putting on ice. **2.** The condition or fact of being made late or slow ► detainment, holdup, lag, retardation.

delectable *adjective*
1. Giving great pleasure or delight ► enchanting, heavenly. *See* **delightful**. **2.** Highly pleasing, especially to the sense of taste ► appetizing, savory, scrumptious. *See* **delicious** (1). *See synonym note at* **delicious**.

delectation *noun*
► bliss, enjoyment, pleasure. *See* **delight** (1).

delegate *noun*
One who represents the interests of another ► ambassador, deputy, proxy. *See* **representative** (2).

delegate *verb*
To put in the charge of another for care, use, or performance ► confide, hand over. *See* **entrust** (1). *See synonym note at* **entrust**.

delete *verb*
► blot (out), erase, strike (out). *See* **cancel** (1). *See synonym note at* **cancel**.

deleterious *adjective*
► baneful, evil, injurious. *See* **harmful**.

deletion *noun*
► cancellation, expunction. *See* **erasure**.

deliberate *adjective*
1. Done or said on purpose ► conscious, intended, intentional, premeditated, purposeful, voluntary, willful, witting. **2.** Arising from or marked by careful consideration ► advised, calculated, considered, studied, studious, thought out. *See also* **sane, wary**.
3. Careful and slow in acting, moving, or deciding ► cautious, circumspect, judicious, leisurely, measured, methodic, methodical, prudent, sober, unhurried. *See also* **lethargic, slow**. **4.** Planned, weighed, or estimated in advance ► assessed, intentional, premeditated. *See* **calculated** (1).

deliberate *verb*
1. To think or think about carefully and at length ► cogitate, deliberate, mull. *See* **ponder**. **2.** To use the powers of the mind ► cogitate, conceptualize, reflect. *See* **think** (1). **3.** To meet and exchange views to reach a decision ► consult, debate, talk. *See* **confer** (1). **4.** To speak together and exchange ideas and opinions about ► converse, debate. *Informal:* kick around. *See* **discuss**.

✦ **CORE SYNONYMS:** *deliberate, intentional, voluntary, willful.* These adjectives refer to that which is done or said on purpose. *Deliberate* stresses premeditation and full awareness of the character and consequences of one's acts: *taking deliberate and decisive action. Intentional* applies to something undertaken to further a plan or realize an aim: *"I will abstain from all intentional wrongdoing and harm"* (Hippocratic Oath). *Voluntary* implies the operation of unforced choice: *"Ignorance, when it is voluntary, is criminal"* (Samuel Johnson). *Willful* implies deliberate, headstrong persistence in a self-determined course of action: *a willful waste of time.*

---

deliberation *noun*
1. An exchange of views in an attempt to reach a decision ► conference, consideration, consultation, counsel, debate, discussion, parley. **2.** Careful thought ► advisement, deliberation, study. *See also* **attention, examination, scrutiny**. **3.** The act or process of thinking ► cogitation, contemplation, rumination. *See* **thought** (1).

deliberative *adjective*
► contemplative, pensive, reflective. *See* **thoughtful** (1).

delicacy *noun*
1. Something fine and delicious, especially a food ► dainty, morsel, sweetmeat, tidbit, treat. *Informal:* goody. *See also* **luxury**. **2.** The condition of being infirm or physically weak ► decrepitude, feebleness, weakness. *See* **infirmity** (1). **3.** The ability to make or detect effects of great precision ► fineness, sensitivity. *See* **subtlety** (1). **4.** The ability to say and do the right thing at the right time ► diplomacy, savoir-faire, tactfulness. *See* **tact**.

delicate *adjective*

1. Appealing to refined taste ► choice, dainty, elegant, exquisite, fine, genteel, gentle. *See also* **cultured.** **2.** Showing sensitivity and skill in dealing with others ► diplomatic, discreet, graceful, politic, sensitive, tactful. **3.** Requiring great tact or skill ► demanding, difficult, exacting, precarious, sensitive, ticklish, touch-and-go, touchy, tricky. **4.** So slight as to be difficult to notice or appreciate ► fine, finespun, nice, precise, refined, subtle. **5.** Not physically strong ► feeble, frail, unsound. *See* **weak** (1). **6.** Easily broken or damaged ► breakable, brittle, frangible. *See* **fragile** (1). *See synonym note at* **fragile. 7.** Free from severity or violence, as in sound or movement ► balmy, faint, soft. *See* **gentle** (2). **8.** Able to make or detect effects of great precision ► nice, sensitive, subtle. *See* **fine**[1] (8).

✦ CORE SYNONYMS: *delicate, choice, dainty, elegant, exquisite, fine.* These adjectives mean appealing to refined taste: *a delicate flavor; choice exotic flowers; a dainty dish; elegant handwriting; an exquisite wine; the finest embroidery.*

delicateness *noun*
► decrepitude, feebleness. *See* **infirmity** (1).

delicious *adjective*

1. Highly pleasing, especially to the sense of taste ► ambrosial, appetizing, delectable, flavorful, heavenly, luscious, mouth-watering, palatable, savory, scrumptious, tasteful, tasty, toothsome. *Slang:* yummy. **2.** Giving great pleasure or delight ► delectable, enchanting, heavenly. *See* **delightful.**

✦ CORE SYNONYMS: *delicious, ambrosial, delectable, luscious, scrumptious, toothsome, yummy.* These adjectives mean very pleasing to the sense of taste: *a delicious pâté; ambrosial fruit salad; delectable raspberries; luscious chocolate bonbons; a scrumptious peach; a toothsome apple; yummy fudge.*

delight *noun*

1. A feeling of extreme gratification aroused by something good or desired ► bliss, delectation, ecstasy, elation, enchantment, enjoyment, glee, joy, pleasure. **2.** Something costly and unnecessary ► extravagancy, frill, indulgence. *See* **luxury** (1). **3.** Something that amuses, entertains, or pleases ► enjoyment, pleasure, treat. *See* **amusement. 4.** A condition of well-being and good spirits ► blessedness, bliss, felicity. *See* **happiness.**

delight *verb*

1. To give great or keen pleasure to ► amuse, cheer, elate, enchant, excite, gladden, gratify, overjoy, please, pleasure, thrill, tickle. *See also* **charm. 2.** To feel or take joy or pleasure ► exult, pleasure, rejoice. *See also* **enjoy, luxuriate. 3.** To like or enjoy enthusiastically, often excessively ► delight in, dote on (*or* upon), love. *Slang:* eat up, groove on. *See* **adore** (2).

✦ CORE SYNONYMS: *delight, gladden, gratify, please, tickle.* These verbs mean to give pleasure to: *a gift that*

would delight any child; was pleased by their success; praise that gladdens the spirit; progress that gratified all concerned; compliments that tickle their vanity.

delighted *adjective*
► agreeable, ready. *See* **willing** (1).

delightful *adjective*

Giving great pleasure or delight ► adorable, amusing, blissful, charming, cute, delectable, delicious, enchanting, heavenly, lovable, lovely, luscious, pleasing, pleasurable, sweet. *Informal:* darling. *See also* **attractive, pleasant.**

delimit *or* **delimitate** *verb*
► demarcate, limit, mark. *See* **determine** (1).

delineate *verb*

1. To present a lifelike image of ► depict, portray, render. *See* **represent** (2). *See synonym note at* **represent. 2.** To draw up a preliminary plan or version of ► outline, sketch. *See* **draft** (1).

delineation *noun*

1. The characteristic surface arrangement of a thing ► configuration, design, structure. *See* **form** (1). **2.** The act or process of describing in lifelike imagery ► depiction, description, portrayal. *See* **representation.**

delineative *adjective*
► graphic, representative. *See* **descriptive.**

delinquency *noun*

1. An act of breaking a law or of nonfulfillment of an obligation ► infraction, infringement, violation. *See* **breach** (1). **2.** Nonperformance of what ought to be done ► delinquency, neglect, omission. *See* **failure** (2).

delinquent *noun*
► culprit, lawbreaker, offender. *See* **criminal.**

deliquesce *verb*
► dissolve, liquefy, thaw. *See* **melt** (1).

delirious *adjective*
► fevered, frenetic, wild. *See* **frantic.**

deliver *verb*

1. To relinquish to the possession or control of another ► furnish, provide. *See* **give** (1). **2.** To mete out by means of some action ► administer, deal, give. **3.** To give birth to ► bring forth, have. *See* **bear** (4). **4.** To set free, as from danger or confinement ► recover, save. *See* **rescue.** *See synonym note at* **rescue. 5.** To yield oneself unrestrainedly, as to an impulse ► abandon, relinquish, surrender. *Idioms:* give oneself up (*or* over). **6.** To put into words ► express, state, utter. *See* **say** (1).

deliverance *noun*
► release, salvage, salvation. *See* **rescue.**

deliverer *noun*
► angel, redeemer, savior. *See* **rescuer.**

delivery *noun*

1. The act of delivering or the condition of being delivered ► consignment, conveyance, shipment, surrender, transfer, transmission, transmittal. **2.** The act or process of bringing forth young ► childbearing, labor, parturition. *See* **birth** (1). **3.** Extrication from danger or confinement ▸ deliverance, salvage, salvation. *See* **rescue.**

dell *noun*
▸ dale, gorge. *See* **valley.**

delude *verb*
▸ dupe, mislead, trick. *See* **deceive.** *See synonym note at* **deceive.**

deluge *noun*
1. An overwhelming flow of water ▸ downpour, overflow, torrent. *See* **flood** (1). **2.** Water condensed from atmospheric vapor and falling in drops ▸ cloudburst, downpour, shower. *See* **rain** (2).

deluge *verb*
1. To flow over completely ▸ engulf, overflow, submerge. *See* **flood** (1). **2.** To affect as if by an outpouring of water ▸ flood, inundate, overwhelm, swamp.

delusion *noun*
1. A phenomenon that causes a misperception ▸ hallucination, mirage. *See* **illusion** (1). **2.** A fiction or half-truth, especially one that forms part of an ideology ▸ fantasy, fiction, invention. *See* **myth** (3).

delusive *or* **delusory** *adjective*
1. Tending to lead one into error ▸ deceptive, illusive, misleading. *See* **fallacious** (2). **2.** Of, relating to, or in the nature of an illusion; lacking reality ▸ hallucinatory, illusory, phantasmagoric. *See* **illusive** (1).

deluxe *adjective*
▸ lush, luxuriant, opulent. *See* **luxurious.**

delve *verb*
1. To go into or through for the purpose of making discoveries or acquiring information ▸ inquire, investigate, probe. *See* **explore.** **2.** To break, turn over, or remove (earth or sand, for example) with or as if with a tool ▸ excavate, scoop, shovel. *See* **dig** (1).

demand *verb*
1. To ask for urgently or insistently ▸ appeal for, call for, claim, exact, importune, insist on, order, require, requisition. *Idiom:* cry out for. *See also* **urge.** **2.** To have as a need or prerequisite ▸ ask, beg, call for, entail, involve, necessitate, need, require, take, want. *See also* **lack.** **3.** To defend, maintain, or insist on the recognition of ▸ assert, vindicate. *See* **claim** (1).

demand *noun*
1. The act of demanding ▸ appeal, behest, call, claim, cry, exaction, order, requisition. **2.** Something asked for or needed ▸ desire, exigence, exigency, need, requirement, want.

✛ CORE SYNONYMS: *demand, claim, exact, require.* These verbs mean to ask for urgently or insistently: *demanding better working conditions; claiming repayment of a debt; exacted obedience from the child; tax payments required by law.*

---

demanding *adjective*
1. Requiring great tact or skill ▸ exacting, precarious, sensitive. *See* **delicate** (3). **2.** Hard to treat, manage, or cope with ▸ demanding, difficult, trying. *See* **troublesome** (2). **3.** Not easy to do, achieve, or master ▸ arduous, laborious, tough. *See* **difficult** (1). **4.** Rigorous and

unsparing in treating others ▸ harsh, stern, strict. *See* **severe** (1). **5.** Very difficult to please ▸ exacting, finicky. *See* **fussy** (1).

demarcate *verb*
▸ define, limit, mark. *See* **determine** (1).

demarcation *noun*
▸ differentiation, discernment, discretion. *See* **distinction** (1).

demean¹ *verb*
To conduct oneself in a specified way ▸ bear, carry, comport. *See* **act** (1).

demean² *verb*
1. To lower the pride or dignity of ▸ abase, degrade, humiliate. *See* **humble** (1). **2.** To lower in character or quality ▸ degrade, downgrade. *See* **debase** (1). *See synonym note at* **debase.**

demeanor *noun*
Behavior that reveals one's personality or state of mind ▸ air, manner, style. *See* **bearing** (1).

dement *verb*
▸ craze, madden, unbalance. *See* **derange** (1).

demented *adjective*
▸ crazy, lunatic, mad. *See* **insane** (1).

dementia *noun*
▸ craziness, derangement, lunacy. *See* **insanity** (1). *See synonym note at* **insanity.**

demise *noun*
The act or fact of dying ▸ dissolution, passing. *See* **death** (1).

demise *verb*
To cease living ▸ decease, expire, perish. *See* **die** (1).

demit *verb*
1. To relinquish one's engagement in or occupation with ▸ leave, quit, resign, terminate. *Idioms:* hang it up, throw in the towel. *See also* **break.** **2.** To give up or leave completely ▸ abdicate, relinquish, resign, surrender. *See* **abandon** (1).

demobilize *verb*
▸ demobilize, release, separate. *See* **discharge** (4).

democratic *adjective*
▸ general, public, societal. *See* **popular** (1).

demolish *verb*
1. To pull down or break up so that reconstruction is impossible ▸ dismantle, level, tear down. *See* **destroy** (2). *See synonym note at* **destroy.** **2.** To cause the complete ruin or wreckage of ▸ annihilate, torpedo, wreck. *See* **destroy** (1).

demolition *noun*
▸ devastation, ruin, wreck. *See* **destruction** (1).

demon *noun*
1. An intensely energetic, enthusiastic person ▸ dynamo, hustler. *Informal:* eager beaver, firebreather, go-getter, live wire. **2.** A perversely mean, cruel, or wicked person ▸ beast, monster, ogre. *See* **fiend** (1).

demonstrate *verb*
1. To demonstrate and clarify with examples ▸ evidence, exemplify, illustrate, instance. *See also* **explain, show.** **2.** To make manifest or apparent ▸ display, reveal. *See* **show** (1). **3.** To establish as true or genuine

through evidence ▸ confirm, substantiate, validate. *See* **prove** (1).

demonstration *noun*

1. An act of showing or displaying ▸ exhibition, show. *See* **display** (1). **2.** That which confirms ▸ authentication, proof, verification. *See* **confirmation** (2).

demoralize *verb*

1. To ruin morally ▸ debase, deprave, warp. *See* **corrupt** (1). **2.** To make less hopeful or enthusiastic ▸ dismay, dispirit. *See* **discourage** (1).

demoralizing *adjective*

▸ corruptive, depraving, perverting. *See* **unwholesome** (2).

demote *verb*

To lower in rank or grade ▸ break, bump, degrade, downgrade, reduce. *Slang:* bust.

✦ CORE SYNONYMS: *demote, break, bust, degrade, downgrade, reduce.* These verbs mean to lower in rank, grade, or status: *was demoted from captain to lieutenant; a noncommissioned officer broken to the ranks; a detective who was busted to uniformed traffic patrol for insubordination; a supervisor degraded to an assistant; a popular author downgraded by critical opinion to a genre writer; was reduced from a command post to a desk job.*

◂ ANTONYM: *promote*

---

demotion *noun*

The act or an instance of demoting ▸ degradation, downgrade, reduction.

demur *verb*

To express opposition ▸ except, oppose, protest. *See* **object** (1). *See synonym note at* **object.**

demur *noun*

An expression of opposition ▸ exception, grievance, protestation. *See* **objection.**

demure *adjective*

▸ bashful, diffident, modest. *See* **shy**[1] (1). *See synonym note at* **shy**[1]**.**

demureness *noun*

▸ bashfulness, diffidence. *See* **shyness.**

demystify *verb*

▸ construe, decipher, interpret. *See* **explain** (1).

den *noun*

1. A place used as an animal's dwelling ▸ burrow, hole, lair. *See also* **cave. 2.** A hiding place ▸ covert, hideaway, hide-out, lair. **3.** A place known for its great filth or corruption ▸ cesspool, gutter, sewer. *See* **pit**[1] (3).

denature *verb*

▸ mutate, transfigure, transform. *See* **convert** (1).

denial *noun*

1. A refusal to grant the truth of a statement or charge ▸ abnegation, contradiction, disaffirmance, disavowal, disaffirmation, disclaimer, negation, rejection, renunciation, repudiation, traversal. **2.** A turning down of a request ▸ disallowance, nonacceptance, refusal, rejection, turndown. *See also* **forbiddance.**

denigrate *verb*

1. To attack the reputation or honor of ▸ befoul,

besmear, besmirch, bespatter, blacken, blot, cloud, defile, dirty, smear, smudge, smut, soil, spatter, stain, sully, taint, tarnish, tear down. *Idioms:* drag through the mud (*or* dirt), give a black eye to, give someone a bad name, sling (*or* throw) mud on. *See also* **disgrace, libel, malign, slam. 2.** To represent or speak of as small or insignificant ▸ deprecate, disparage, slight. *See* **belittle.**

denigration *noun*

1. The expression of injurious, malicious statements about someone ▸ defamation, detraction, slander. *See* **libel. 2.** The act or an instance of belittling ▸ deprecation, disparagement. *See* **belittlement.**

denizen *noun*

▸ dweller, occupant, resident. *See* **inhabitant.**

denominate *verb*

1. To give a name or title to ▸ christen, designate. *See* **name** (1). **2.** To describe with a word or term ▸ designate, label, name. *See* **call** (4).

denomination *noun*

1. A system of religious belief ▸ creed, faith. *See* **religion. 2.** The word or words by which one is called and identified ▸ cognomen, epithet, title. *See* **name** (1). **3.** A class that is defined by the common attribute or attributes possessed by all its members ▸ ilk, mold, species. *See* **kind**[2].

denotation *noun*

▸ import, sense, significance. *See* **meaning** (1).

denotative *or* **denotive** *adjective*

▸ exhibitive, indicative, indicatory. *See* **designative.**

denote *verb*

1. To make known or identify, as by signs ▸ indicate, mark, specify. *See* **designate** (1). **2.** To have or convey a particular idea ▸ convey, intend, signify. *See* **mean**[1] (1).

dénouement *noun*

▸ cease, completion, termination. *See* **end** (1).

denounce *verb*

1. To express strong disapproval of ▸ condemn, reprehend. *See* **deplore** (1). *See synonym note at* **deplore. 2.** To make an accusation against ▸ blame, charge, incriminate. *See* **accuse. 3.** To have or express an unfavorable opinion of ▸ condemn, disfavor, object to. *See* **disapprove** (1).

denouncement *noun*

▸ charge, imputation, incrimination. *See* **accusation.**

denouncer *noun*

One that accuses ▸ accuser, arraigner, indicter, recriminator.

dense *adjective*

1. Having all parts near to each other ▸ crowded, packed, tight. *See* **thick** (2). **2.** Growing profusely ▸ lush, luxuriant, profuse. *See* **thick** (3). **3.** Lacking in intelligence ▸ dumb, idiotic, obtuse. *See* **stupid** (1). **4.** Having only a limited ability to learn and understand ▸ dull, simple. *See* **backward** (1).

density *noun*

1. The condition or degree of being dense or close together ▸ compaction, denseness. *See* **thickness** (1).

2. The state of being stupid ▸ idiocy, mindlessness, obtuseness. *See* **stupidity.**

dent *verb*
To alter and spoil the natural form or appearance of ▸ disfigure, misshape, twist. *See* **deform.**

dent *noun*
1. A disfiguring abnormality of shape or form ▸ contortion, disfigurement, malformation. *See* **deformity.**
2. An area sunk below its surroundings ▸ concavity, dip, hollow. *See* **depression** (1). **3.** The visible effect made on a surface by pressure ▸ indent, mark. *See* **impression** (1).

dentate *adjective*
▸ notched, serrate. *See* **saw-toothed.**

denude *verb*
▸ divest, strip, uncover. *See* **bare** (1).

denuded *adjective*
▸ destitute, lacking, void. *See* **empty** (2).

denunciation *noun*
1. The act or an instance of finding fault ▸ censure, condemnation, reprehension. *See* **criticism** (1). **2.** A charging of someone with a misdeed ▸ denouncement, imputation, incrimination. *See* **accusation.**
3. Sustained, harshly abusive language ▸ condemnation, invective. *See* **vituperation. 4.** Unfavorable opinion or judgment ▸ condemnation, disfavor, reproof. *See* **disapproval.**

denunciative *or* **denunciatory** *adjective*
▸ accusatory, incriminatory, insinuating. *See* **accusatorial.**

deny *verb*
1. To refuse to admit the truth, reality, value, or worth of ▸ abnegate, contradict, contravene, controvert, disaffirm, disavow, dismiss, dispute, gainsay, negate, negative, oppugn, renounce, traverse. *See also* **contest. 2.** To refuse to recognize or acknowledge ▸ disavow, reject, renounce. *See* **repudiate** (1). **3.** To take or keep something away from ▸ dispossess, withhold. *See* **deprive. 4.** To be unwilling to accept, consider, or receive ▸ reject, spurn. *See* **decline** (1).

✦ CORE SYNONYMS: *deny, contradict, contravene, disaffirm, gainsay, negate.* These verbs mean to refuse to admit the truth, reality, value, or worth of: *denied the rumor; contradicted the statement; contravene a conclusion; disaffirm a suggestion; trying to gainsay the evidence; negated the allegations.*

◂ ANTONYM: *affirm*

---

depart *verb*
1. To move away from a place ▸ exit, go away, retire. *See* **go** (1). **2.** To be unlike or dissimilar ▸ diverge, vary. *See* **differ** (1). **3.** To cease living ▸ demise, expire, perish. *See* **die** (1). **4.** To turn away from a prescribed course of action or conduct ▸ digress, stray. *See* **deviate** (1). *See synonym note at* **deviate. 5.** To cease to exist ▸ cease, perish. *See* **disappear** (2).

departed *adjective*
▸ deceased, expired, perished. *See* **dead** (1). *See synonym note at* **dead.**

departing *adjective*
▸ farewell, goodbye, valedictory. *See* **parting.**

department *noun*
1. An administrative unit, as of a government or company ▸ agency, bureau. *See* **branch** (3). **2.** A sphere of activity, experience, study, or interest ▸ domain, field, terrain. *See* **area** (1). **3.** A subdivision of a larger group ▸ category, order, set. *See* **class** (1).

departure *noun*
1. The act of leaving ▸ adieu, departing, egress, embarkation, embarkment, exit, exodus, farewell, going, goodbye, leave-taking, parting, retirement, valediction, withdrawal. **2.** The condition of being unlike or dissimilar ▸ contrast, discrepancy, divergence. *See* **difference** (1). **3.** A departing from what is prescribed ▸ diversion, variation. *See* **deviation** (1). **4.** The act or an example of passing out of sight ▸ dissipation, expiration, vanishment. *See* **disappearance. 5.** An instance of digressing ▸ deviation, divergence, tangent. *See* **digression.**

depend on *or* **upon** *verb*
1. To place trust or confidence in ▸ bank on (*or* upon), believe in, confide in, count on (*or* upon), reckon on (*or* upon), rely on (*or* upon), trust (in). *Idioms:* put faith in. **2.** To be determined by or contingent on something unknown, uncertain, or changeable ▸ hang on, hang upon, hinge on (*or* upon), rest on (*or* upon), revolve around, turn on, turn upon. **3.** To look forward to confidently ▸ await, look for. *See* **expect** (1).

✦ CORE SYNONYMS: *depend on, rely on, trust, reckon on.* These verbs share the meaning to place or have trust or confidence in someone or something. *Depend on* implies confidence in the help or support of another: *depends on friends for emotional support. Rely on* implies complete confidence: "*You are the only woman I can rely on to be interested in her*" (John Galsworthy). *Trust* stresses confidence arising from belief that is often based on inconclusive evidence: "*We must try to trust one another. Stay and cooperate*" (Jomo Kenyatta). *Reckon on* implies a sense of confident expectancy: "*He reckons on finding a woman as big a fool as himself*" (George Meredith).

---

dependable *adjective*
Capable of being depended on ▸ honest, reliable, responsible, solid, sound, stable, steadfast, steady, steady-going, trustworthy, trusty.

✦ CORE SYNONYMS: *dependable, reliable, responsible, trustworthy.* These adjectives mean capable of being depended on or worthy of reliance or trust: *a reliable source of information; a dependable worker; a responsible babysitter; a trustworthy report.*

---

dependence *noun*
1. The state or relation of being determined or controlled ▸ dependency, reliance. *See also* **authority, dominance, need, relation. 2.** Absolute certainty that a person or thing will not fail ▸ faith, reliance. *See* **trust** (1). *See synonym note at* **trust. 3.** Compulsive

need for a habit-forming substance ▸ compulsion, enslavement, fixation. *See* **addiction.**

dependency *noun*
1. The state or relation of being determined or controlled ▸ dependence, reliance. *See also* **authority, dominance, need, relation. 2.** An area subject to rule by an outside power ▸ colony, province. *See* **possession** (1).

dependent *adjective*
1. Subject to the authority or control of another ▸ subject, subordinate, subservient. *See also* **auxiliary. 2.** Depending on or containing a condition or conditions ▸ contingent, provisory. *See* **conditional.** *See synonym note at* **conditional.**

dependent *or* **dependant** *noun*
One who relies on another for support ▸ charge, ward.

depict *verb*
1. To present a lifelife image of ▸ delineate, portray, render. *See* **represent** (2). *See synonym note at* **represent. 2.** To perform according to one's artistic conception ▸ execute, play, render. *See* **interpret** (2).

depiction *noun*
1. The act or process of describing in lifelike imagery ▸ characterization, description, portrayal. *See* **representation. 2.** A performer's distinctive personal version of a song, dance, piece of music, or role ▸ performance, reading, rendition. *See* **interpretation** (1).

deplete *verb*
1. To use all of ▸ consume, sap, use up. *See* **exhaust** (1). *See synonym note at* **exhaust. 2.** To make or become no longer active or productive ▸ desiccate, play out, run out. *See* **dry** (2).

depletion *noun*
1. The act of consuming ▸ consumption, expenditure, usage, use, utilization. *See also* **use. 2.** The sapping away of strength or energy ▸ attenuation, devitalization, enfeeblement. *See* **debilitation.**

deplorable *adjective*
1. Worthy of severe disapproval ▸ condemnable, disgraceful, reprehensible, shameful, unfortunate, woeful, wretched. *See also* **disgraceful, offensive, miserable. 2.** Causing or expressing sorrow or sadness ▸ melancholy, mournful. *See* **sorrowful** (1).

deplore *verb*
1. To express strong disapproval of ▸ bemoan, bewail, censure, condemn, decry, denounce, reprehend, reprobate. *See also* **disapprove, condemn, hate. 2.** To feel or express sorrow for ▸ regret, repent, rue, sorrow (over). *See also* **feel, grieve.**

✦ CORE SYNONYMS: *deplore, reprehend, censure, condemn, denounce.* These verbs mean to express strong disapproval of: *Deplore* and *reprehend* imply sharp disapproval: *Somehow we had to master events, not simply deplore them* (Henry A. Kissinger); *"reprehends students who have protested apartheid"* (New York Times). *Censure* refers to open and strong expression of criticism; often it implies a formal reprimand: *"No*

man can justly censure or condemn another, because indeed no man truly knows another" (Thomas Browne). *Condemn* denotes the pronouncement of harshly adverse judgment: *"The wrongs which we seek to condemn and punish have been so calculated, so malignant and so devastating that civilization cannot tolerate their being ignored because it cannot survive their being repeated"* (Robert H. Jackson). *Denounce* implies public proclamation of condemnation or repudiation: *The press denounces the new taxation policies.*

---

deploy *verb*
▸ collocate, systematize. *See* **arrange** (1).

deployment *noun*
▸ allotment, layout, positioning. *See* **arrangement** (1).

depone *verb*
▸ depose, swear, witness. *See* **testify** (1).

deponent *noun*
One who testifies, especially in court ▸ attestant, attester, testifier, witness.

deport *verb*
1. To force to leave by official decree ▸ exile, expel. *See* **banish** (1). *See synonym note at* **banish. 2.** To conduct oneself in a specified way ▸ bear, behave, carry, demean. *See* **act** (1).

deportation *noun*
▸ banishment, extradition. *See* **exile** (1).

deportee *noun*
▸ exile, expatriate. *See* **émigré** (1).

deportment *noun*
▸ comportment, conduct. *See* **behavior** (1). *See synonym note at* **behavior.**

depose *verb*
1. To give evidence or testimony under oath ▸ depone, swear, witness. *See* **testify** (1). **2.** To bring about the downfall of ▸ subvert, topple. *See* **overthrow** (1).

deposit *verb*
1. To place money in an account ▸ lay away, salt away. *See* **bank²**. **2.** To give or deposit as a pawn ▸ collateralize, pledge. *See* **pawn¹**. **3.** To put in a certain position or location ▸ locate, place, situate. *See* **position.**

deposit *noun*
1. A partial or initial payment ▸ down payment, installment, security. **2.** Matter that settles on a bottom or collects on a surface by a natural process ▸ accumulation, alluvium, dregs, lees, precipitate, precipitation, sediment.

deposition *noun*
A formal declaration of truth or fact given under oath ▸ affidavit, testimony, witness.

depository *noun*
A place where something is deposited for safekeeping ▸ archive, bank, cache, depot, repository, safe, store, storehouse, strongbox, treasure house, treasury, vault, warehouse. *See also* **hoard.**

depot *noun*
1. A stopping place along a route for picking up or dropping off passengers ▸ station, stop, terminal, terminus. **2.** A center of organization, supply, or

activity ▸ headquarters, installation, station. *See* **base**[1] (1). **3.** A place where something is deposited for safekeeping ▸ archive, storehouse, warehouse. *See* **depository.**

deprave *verb*
▸ debase, demoralize, warp. *See* **corrupt** (1). *See synonym note at* **corrupt.**

depraved *adjective*
▸ miscreant, perverse. *See* **corrupt** (1).

depravity *noun*
1. Degrading, immoral acts or habits ▸ immorality, perversion, vice. *See* **corruption** (1). **2.** Departure from what is legally, ethically, and morally correct ▸ dishonesty, improbity. *Informal:* crookedness. *See* **corruption** (2).

deprecate *verb*
1. To have or express an unfavorable opinion of ▸ condemn, disfavor, object to. *See* **disapprove** (1). **2.** To represent or speak of as small or insignificant ▸ denigrate, disparage, slight. *See* **belittle.**

deprecation *noun*
1. The act or an instance of belittling ▸ denigration, disparagement. *See* **belittlement.** **2.** Unfavorable opinion or judgment ▸ condemnation, disfavor, reproof. *See* **disapproval.**

deprecatory *or* **deprecative** *adjective*
▸ belittling, derogatory, pejorative. *See* **disparaging.**

depreciate *verb*
1. To make less in price or value ▸ cheapen, depress, devaluate, devalue, downgrade, lessen, lower, mark down, reduce, write down. *See also* **decrease.** **2.** To become lower in price or value ▸ sag, sink, slump. *See* **fall** (7). **3.** To become lower in quality, character, or condition ▸ atrophy, degenerate, worsen. *See* **deteriorate** (1). **4.** To represent or speak of as small or insignificant ▸ deprecate, disparage, slight. *See* **belittle.** *See synonym note at* **belittle.**

depreciation *noun*
1. A lowering of price or value ▸ cheapening, depression, devaluation, lessening, markdown, reduction, shrinkage, write-down. *See also* **decrease.** **2.** A usually swift downward trend, as in prices ▸ descent, dip, downswing. *See* **fall** (3). **3.** Descent to a lower level or condition ▸ decadence, decline, degeneration. *See* **deterioration** (1). **4.** The act or an instance of belittling ▸ deprecation, disparagement. *See* **belittlement.**

depreciative *or* **depreciatory** *adjective*
▸ deprecatory, derogatory, pejorative. *See* **disparaging.**

depredate *verb*
▸ loot, plunder, ransack. *See* **sack**[2].

depress *verb*
1. To make sad or gloomy ▸ dampen, deject, dishearten, dispirit, oppress, sadden, weigh down. *Slang:* bum out. *See also* **discourage.** **2.** To cause to descend ▸ drop, let down, take down. *See* **lower**[2] (1). **3.** To make less in price or value ▸ devalue, downgrade, reduce. *See* **depreciate** (1). **4.** To apply pressure on, against, or with ▸ press, prod, shove. *See* **push** (1).

depressant *noun*
▸ hallucinogen, opiate, psychotropic. *See* **drug** (2).

depressed *adjective*
1. In low spirits ▸ blue, brokenhearted, dejected, desolate, disconsolate, discouraged, dismayed, dispirited, down, downcast, downhearted, dull, dyspeptic, dysphoric, gloomy, heartbroken, heartsick, heavy-hearted, low, melancholic, melancholy, sad, sorrowful, spiritless, tristful, unhappy, wistful. *Informal:* blah. *Idioms:* down at (*or* in) the mouth, down in the dumps. *See also* **anxious, despondent, glum, lonely.** **2.** Economically and socially below standard ▸ backward, deprived, disadvantaged, impoverished, poor, underprivileged. *See also* **poor.** **3.** Curving inward ▸ concave, sunken. *See* **hollow** (2).

✚ CORE SYNONYMS: *depressed, blue, dejected, dispirited, downcast, downhearted.* These adjectives mean affected or marked by low spirits: *depressed by the loss of his job; lonely and blue in a strange city; is dejected but trying to look cheerful; a dispirited and resigned expression on her face; looked downcast after his defeat; a downhearted patient who welcomed visitors.*

---

depressing *adjective*
1. Causing or expressing sadness, sorrow, or regret ▸ doleful, melancholy, mournful. *See* **sorrowful** (1). **2.** Offering little encouragement ▸ dim, dismal, pessimistic. *See* **bleak** (2).

depression *noun*
1. An area sunk below its surroundings ▸ basin, cavity, concavity, dent, dip, hollow, indentation, pit, recess, sag, sink, sinkhole. *See also* **hole, impression.** **2.** A feeling or spell of dismally low spirits ▸ blues, dejection, despondence, despondency, disconsolation, discouragement, disheartenment, doldrums, dolefulness, downheartedness, dumps, dysphoria, funk, gloom, glumness, heartsickness, heavy-heartedness, lowness, melancholy, mopes, mournfulness, sadness, sorrow, sorrowfulness, unhappiness, wistfulness. *Informal:* blahs. **3.** A period of decreased business activity and high unemployment ▸ downturn, recession, slowdown, slump. **4.** A lowering of price or value ▸ cheapening, markdown, reduction. *See* **depreciation** (1).

deprivation *or* **deprival** *noun*
1. The condition of being deprived of what one once had or ought to have ▸ deficiency, destitution, dispossession, divestiture, hardship, loss, penury, poverty, privation. *See also* **lack, need, poverty, seizure.** **2.** A state of prolonged anguish and privation ▸ woe, wretchedness. *See* **misery** (1).

deprive *verb*
To take or keep something away from ▸ deny, dispossess, divest, rob, strip, withhold. *See also* **decline, seize.**

deprived *adjective*
1. Economically and socially below standard ▸ disadvantaged, impoverished. *See* **depressed** (2). **2.** Deprived of a quality or aspect that is desirable ▸ desti-

tute, lacking, void, wanting. *See* **empty** (2).

depth *noun*
1. The extent or measurement downward from a surface ▸ deepness, drop, drop-off. 2. Something of immeasurable and vast extent ▸ abyss, chasm. *See* **deep** (1). 3. Concentrated power or force, as of effort, opinion, or emotion ▸ ferocity, fury, vehemence. *See* **intensity**. 4. Intellectual penetration or range ▸ deepness, profoundness, profundity, weightiness. *See also* **discernment, intelligence, wisdom.**

depths *noun*
1. Something of immeasurable and vast extent ▸ abysm, abyss, chasm. *See* **deep** (1). 2. Concentrated power or force, as of effort, opinion, or emotion ▸ ferocity, fury, vehemence. *See* **intensity**.

deputation *noun*
A diplomatic office or headquarters in a foreign country ▸ embassy, legation, mission.

deputy *noun*
1. One who represents the interests of another ▸ ambassador, delegate, proxy. *See* **representative** (2). 2. A person who assists someone else ▸ adjutant, aide, helper. *See* **assistant.**

derailed *adjective*
▸ crazy, demented, mad. *See* **insane** (1).

derange *verb*
1. To make insane ▸ craze, dement, madden, unbalance, unhinge. *Idioms:* push off (*or* over) the deep end. 2. To disturb the health or physiological functioning of ▸ disorder, turn, unsettle. *See* **upset** (1). 3. To put out of proper order ▸ disarrange, disrupt, muddle. *See* **disorder** (1).

derangement *noun*
1. Serious mental illness impairing a person's capacity to function normally ▸ dementia, lunacy. *See* **insanity** (1). 2. A lack of order or regular arrangement ▸ clutter, confusion, disarray. *See* **disorder** (1).

derelict *adjective*
1. Having been given up and left alone ▸ bereft, deserted, forlorn. *See* **abandoned** (1). 2. Lacking due care or concern ▸ lax, slack. *See* **negligent**. *See synonym note at* **negligent.**

derelict *noun*
An impoverished person ▸ beggar, insolvent, tramp. *See* **pauper.**

dereliction *noun*
1. Nonperformance of what ought to be done ▸ delinquency, neglect. *See* **failure** (2). 2. An act of breaking a law or of nonfulfillment of an obligation ▸ infraction, violation. *See* **breach** (1). 3. The act of forsaking ▸ abandonment, desertion.

deride *verb*
▸ jeer (at), lampoon, taunt. *See* **ridicule**. *See synonym note at* **ridicule.**

de rigueur *adjective*
▸ befitting, correct, right. *See* **appropriate** (1).

derision *noun*
1. Words or actions intended to evoke contemptuous laughter ▸ mockery, ridicule. *See also* **sarcasm, taunt.**

2. Loss of or damage to one's reputation ▸ discredit, disrepute, humiliation. *See* **disgrace.**

derisive *adjective*
1. Contemptuous in manner or wit ▸ satiric, scoffing, sneering. *See* **sarcastic**. 2. Tending or intending to belittle ▸ deprecatory, derogatory, pejorative. *See* **disparaging.**

derivation *noun*
1. Something derived from another ▸ offshoot, outgrowth, spinoff. *See* **derivative**. 2. A point of origination ▸ provenance, root, source. *See* **origin** (1). 3. One's ancestors or ancestral derivation ▸ blood, extraction, lineage. *See* **ancestry.**

derivational *adjective*
Stemming from an original source ▸ derivative, derived, secondary.

derivative *noun*
Something derived from another ▸ byproduct, derivation, descendant, offshoot, outgrowth, spinoff.

derivative *or* **derivate** *adjective*
1. Stemming from an original source ▸ derivational, derived, secondary. 2. Of or involving imitation ▸ emulative, slavish. *See* **imitative** (1).

derive *verb*
1. To obtain from another source ▸ draw, extract, gain, get, receive, take. 2. To arrive at through reasoning ▸ determine, educe, evolve, excogitate, work out. *See also* **decide, infer**. 3. To have as a source ▸ arise, emanate, originate. *See* **stem** (1). *See synonym note at* **stem**. 4. To have hereditary derivation ▸ issue, spring. *See* **descend** (3).

derived *adjective*
Stemming from an original source ▸ derivational, derivative, secondary.

derogate *verb*
▸ deprecate, disparage, slight. *See* **belittle**. *See synonym note at* **belittle.**

derogation *noun*
▸ deprecation, disparagement. *See* **belittlement.**

derogatory *or* **derogative** *adjective*
▸ deprecatory, derisive, pejorative. *See* **disparaging.**

derrière *noun*
▸ posterior, rump. *Slang:* fanny. *See* **buttocks.**

derring-do *noun*
▸ audaciousness, daredevilry. *See* **daring.**

descend *verb*
1. To move downward in response to gravity ▸ drop, plummet. *See* **fall** (1). 2. To slope downward ▸ decline, dip. *See* **drop** (5). 3. To have hereditary derivation ▸ come, derive, issue, spring. *Idiom:* trace one's descent. 4. To bring oneself down to a level considered inappropriate to one's dignity ▸ deign, stoop, vouchsafe. *See* **condescend** (1). 5. To become lower in quality, character, or condition ▸ atrophy, degenerate, worsen. *See* **deteriorate** (1).

descendant *noun*
1. Something derived from another ▸ offshoot, outgrowth, spinoff. *See* **derivative**. 2. A person or group descended directly from the same parents or ances-

tors ► offspring, scion, seed. *See* **progeny.**

descending *or* **descendent** *adjective*
Moving or sloping down ► downward, drooping, falling, plummeting, plunging, sinking.

descent *noun*
1. A sudden downward motion toward the ground ► dive, drop. *See* **fall** (1). **2.** A downward slope or distance ► decline, declivity. *See* **drop** (5). **3.** One's ancestors or ancestral derivation ► blood, extraction, lineage. *See* **ancestry. 4.** A sudden drop to a lower condition or status ► comedown, dip, down, downfall, downgrade, plunge, slide, tumble. **5.** A usually swift downward trend, as in prices ► decline, dip, downswing. *See* **fall** (3).

describe *verb*
1. To communicate the facts, details, or particulars of something ► detail, narrate, recite, recount, rehearse, relate, report, tell. *See also* **call, explain. 2.** To present a lifelike image of ► depict, portray, render. *See* **represent** (2).

✦ **CORE SYNONYMS:** *describe, narrate, recite, recount, rehearse, relate, report.* These verbs mean to communicate the facts, details, or particulars of something: *described the accident; narrated their travel experiences; an explorer reciting her adventures; a mercenary recounting his exploits; parents rehearsing street safety with their children; related the day's events; reported what she had seen.*

---

description *noun*
1. A recounting of past events ► account, narrative, statement. *See* **story** (1). **2.** The act or process of describing in lifelike imagery ► characterization, depiction, portrayal. *See* **representation. 3.** A class that is defined by the common attribute or attributes possessed by all its members ► ilk, mold, species. *See* **kind².**

descriptive *adjective*
Serving to describe ► colorful, delineative, graphic, representative, vivid. *See also* **eloquent, expressive.**

descry *verb*
1. To perceive and fix the identity of, especially with difficulty ► ascertain, recognize. *See* **discern** (1). **2.** To perceive with the eyes ► catch, detect, perceive. *See* **see** (1). *See synonym note at* **see. 3.** To perceive with a special effort of the senses or the mind ► detect, mark. *See* **notice.**

desecrate *verb*
► defile, pollute, profane. *See* **violate** (3).

desecration *noun*
► blasphemy, profanation, violation. *See* **sacrilege.**

desegregate *verb*
To open to all people regardless of race ► integrate.

desensitize *verb*
► dull, numb. *See* **deaden** (1).

desert¹ *noun*
A desolate or unproductive region ► badlands, barren, barrens, dust bowl, tundra, waste, wasteland. *See also* **country, wilderness.**

desert *adjective*
1. Unable to support vegetation ► sterile, unfruitful, unproductive. *See* **barren** (2). **2.** Having little or no precipitation ► arid, droughty, rainless. *See* **dry** (2).

desert³ *verb*
1. To give up or leave completely ► forsake, leave, quit. *See* **abandon** (1). **2.** To abandon one's cause or party usually to join another ► disavow, quit. *See* **defect.**

deserted *adjective*
1. Having been given up and left alone ► bereft, desolate, forsaken. *See* **abandoned** (1). **2.** Empty of people ► uninhabited, unpeopled, unpopulated. *See* **lonely** (1).

deserter *noun*
► recreant, recreant, traitor. *See* **defector.**

desertion *noun*
The act or instance of deserting ► abandonment.

deserts *noun*
1. Something, such as loss, pain, or confinement, imposed for wrongdoing ► castigation, chastisement, penalty. *See* **punishment. 2.** Something justly deserved ► comeuppance, compensation, reward. *See* **due** (1).

deserve *verb*
► gain, get, win. *See* **earn** (1). *See synonym note at* **earn.**

deserved *adjective*
► due, fitting, proper. *See* **just** (2).

deserving *adjective*
► commendable, laudable, worthy. *See* **admirable.**

desiccate *verb*
1. To make or become free of moisture ► dehydrate, exsiccate, parch. *See* **dry** (1). *See synonym note at* **dry. 2.** To make or become no longer active or productive ► deplete, play out, run out. *See* **dry** (2).

design *verb*
1. To form a strategy for ► blueprint, cast, chart, conceive, concoct, contrive, devise, formulate, frame, lay, originate, plan, predetermine, premeditate, project, scheme, strategize, work out. *Informal:* dope out. *Idiom:* lay plans. *See also* **invent, plot. 2.** To work out and arrange the parts and details of ► blueprint, draft, lay out, map (out), outline, plan, set out, sketch. *See also* **draft. 3.** To have in mind as a goal or purpose ► plan, target. *See* **intend** (1). **4.** To form by artistic effort ► produce, write. *See* **compose** (1).

design *noun*
1. An element or component in a decorative composition ► device, figure, motif, motive. *See synonym note at* **figure. 2.** What one intends to do or achieve ► end, goal, objective. *See* **intention. 3.** The characteristic surface arrangement of a thing ► configuration, contour, structure. *See* **form** (1). **4.** A method used for making, doing, or accomplishing something ► blueprint, strategy. *See* **approach** (1). *See synonym note at* **approach.**

designate *verb*
1. To make known or identify, as by signs ► denote, earmark, identify, indicate, mark, pinpoint, point out, signal, signify, specify. *See also* **mark, represent,**

show. **2.** To set aside or apart for a specified purpose ▸ assign, budget, earmark. *See* **appropriate** (1). *See synonym note at* **appropriate. 3.** To give a name or title to ▸ christen, dub. *See* **name** (1). **4.** To describe with a word or term ▸ characterize, label, name. *See* **call** (4). **5.** To select for an office or position ▸ elect, name, nominate. *See* **appoint** (1). *See synonym note at* **appoint.**

designation *noun*
1. The act of appointing to an office or position ▸ assignment, election, nomination. *See* **appointment** (1). **2.** The word or words by which one is called and identified ▸ cognomen, epithet, title. *See* **name** (1).

designative *adjective*
Serving to designate or indicate ▸ denotative, denotive, designatory, exhibitive, exhibitory, indicative, indicatory, significant. *See also* **symbolic.**

designatory *adjective*
▸ exhibitive, indicative, indicatory. *See* **designative.**

designed *adjective*
▸ deliberate, intentional, premeditated. *See* **calculated** (1).

designing *adjective*
1. Coldly planning to achieve selfish aims ▸ calculating, conniving, manipulative, scheming. *See also* **artful. 2.** Deceitfully clever ▸ cunning, wily. *See* **artful** (1).

designs *noun*
▸ collusion, conspiracy. *See* **plot** (2).

desirable *adjective*
1. Arousing erotic desire ▸ alluring, enticing, sexy. *Slang:* foxy, hot, sizzling. *Idiom:* to die for. *See also* **seductive, sensual. 2.** Pleasing to the eye or mind ▸ enchanting, fetching, lovely, winsome. *See* **attractive** (1). **3.** Worth doing, especially for practical reasons ▸ recommendable, well. *See* **advisable.**

desire *verb*
1. To have a strong longing for ▸ ache, aspire, covet, dream, hanker, hope, long, pant, pine, want, wish, yearn. *Informal:* die for, hone. *Idioms:* be dying (*or* itching) to, give the world for, set one's heart on. *See also* **lust. 2.** To have an inclination to ▸ want, wish. *See* **choose** (2).

desire *noun*
1. A strong wanting of what promises enjoyment or pleasure ▸ appetence, appetency, appetite, craving, hankering, hunger, itch, longing, lust, thirst, wish, yearning, yen. **2.** Sexual hunger ▸ amativeness, appetite, concupiscence, eroticism, erotism, itch, libidinousness, libido, lust, lustfulness, passion, prurience, pruriency, urge. *Slang:* horniness. **3.** Something asked for or needed ▸ requirement, want. *See* **demand** (2). **4.** A fervent hope ▸ aspiration, vision, wish. *See* **dream** (3).

✦ CORE SYNONYMS: *desire, covet, want, wish, yearn.* These verbs mean to have a strong longing for: *desire peace; coveted the new convertible; wanted a drink of water; got all that I wished for; yearned for a better career.*

---

desired *adjective*
▸ dear, precious. *See* **darling** (1).

desirous *adjective*
Having desire for something ▸ desiring, hankering, hungry. *See also* **voracious.**

desist *verb*
1. To come to a cessation ▸ discontinue, halt, quit. *See* **stop** (1). *See synonym note at* **stop. 2.** To cease trying continue ▸ discontinue, give up, quit, stop. *See* **abandon** (2).

desolate *adjective*
1. Empty of people ▸ uninhabited, unpeopled, unpopulated. *See* **lonely** (1). **2.** Dark and depressing ▸ bleak, dreary, somber. *See* **gloomy** (1). **3.** Having been given up and left alone ▸ bereft, deserted, forlorn. *See* **abandoned** (1). **4.** Unable to support vegetation ▸ sterile, unfruitful, unproductive. *See* **barren** (2). **5.** Dejected due to the awareness of being alone ▸ forlorn, lonesome. *See* **lonely** (2).

desolate *verb*
To engulf completely ▸ devour, ravage, waste. *See* **consume** (1).

despair *verb*
To lose all hope ▸ despond, give in, give up. *Idiom:* throw in the towel. *See also* **abandon, surrender.**

despair *noun*
Utter lack of hope ▸ desperateness, desperation, despond, despondence, despondency, discouragement, dismay, hopelessness. *See also* **depression.**

despairing *adjective*
▸ dejected, forlorn, hopeless. *See* **despondent.** *See synonym note at* **despondent.**

desperado *noun*
▸ culprit, lawbreaker, offender. *See* **criminal.**

desperate *adjective*
1. Having lost all hope ▸ dejected, forlorn, hopeless. *See* **despondent. 2.** Demanding immediate attention ▸ crucial, dire, pressing. *See* **urgent** (1). **3.** Extreme in activity, strength, or effect ▸ fierce, furious. *See* **intense** (1).

desperation *or* **desperateness** *noun*
▸ despondence, hopelessness. *See* **despair.**

despicable *or* **despisable** *adjective*
▸ contemptible, disgusting. *See* **offensive** (1).

despisal *noun*
The feeling of despising ▸ abhorrence, contempt, despite, disdain, dislike, hatred, loathing, revulsion, scorn. *See also* **disrespect, enmity, hate.**

despise *verb*
1. To regard with utter contempt ▸ abominate, contemn, disdain, dismiss, scorn, scout, sneer at, sniff at, spit on. *Idioms:* have no use for, look down on (*or* upon). *See also* **dislike, revile, snub. 2.** To regard with extreme dislike and hostility ▸ detest, loathe. *See* **hate.**

✦ CORE SYNONYMS: *despise, contemn, disdain, scorn, scout.* These verbs mean to regard with utter contempt: *despises incompetence; contemned the dictator's actions; disdained my suggestion; scorns sentimentality; scouted simplistic explanations.*

◄ ANTONYM: *esteem*

despite *noun*
1. An attitude or behavior that is intentionally provocative or contemptuous ► contempt, rebelliousness. *See* **defiance** (2). **2.** The feeling of despising ► disdain, loathing, scorn. *See* **despisal. 3.** An act that offends a person's sense of pride or dignity ► contumely, insult. *See* **indignity.**

despiteful *adjective*
► evil, wicked. *See* **malevolent** (1).

despitefulness *noun*
► maliciousness, viciousness. *See* **malevolence.**

despoil *verb*
1. To rob of goods by force, especially in time of war ► loot, plunder, ransack. *See* **sack**[2]. **2.** To spoil or mar the sanctity of ► desecrate, pollute, profane. *See* **violate** (3).

despond *verb*
To lose all hope ► despair, give in, give up. *Idiom:* throw in the towel. *See also* **abandon, surrender.**

despond *noun*
Utter lack of hope ► desperation, despondence, hopelessness. *See* **despair.**

despondence *or* **despondency** *noun*
1. Utter lack of hope ► desperation, hopelessness. *See* **despair. 2.** A feeling or spell of dismally low spirits ► dejection, doldrums, melancholy. *See* **depression** (2).

despondent *adjective*
Having lost all hope ► dejected, despairing, desperate, discouraged, forlorn, hopeless, wretched. *See also* **depressed, glum, miserable.**

✦ CORE SYNONYMS: *despondent, despairing, forlorn, hopeless.* These adjectives mean having lost all hope: *despondent about the company's failure; took a despairing view of world politics; a forlorn cause; a hopeless case.*

◄ ANTONYM: *hopeful*

despot *noun*
1. An absolute ruler, especially one who is harsh and oppressive ► authoritarian, oppressor, tyrant. *See* **dictator** (1). **2.** One who imposes or favors absolute obedience to authority ► dictator, tyrant. *See* **authoritarian** (1).

despotic *adjective*
1. Having and exercising complete political power and control ► autocratic, dictatorial, totalitarian. *See* **absolute** (1). **2.** Characterized by or favoring absolute obedience to authority ► autocratic, dictatorial, tyrannic. *See* **authoritarian** (1).

despotism *noun*
1. A government in which all power is vested in a single leader or party ► autarchy, dictatorship, monocracy, tyranny. *See* **absolutism** (2). **2.** A political

doctrine advocating the principle of absolute rule ► authoritarianism, autocracy, dictatorship, totalitarianism. *See* **absolutism** (1). **3.** Absolute power, especially when exercised unjustly or cruelly ► autocracy, dictatorship, totalitarianism. *See* **tyranny** (1).

desquamate *verb*
► peel, scale, shed. *See* **flake.**

destiny *noun*
1. The supposed power that predetermines events ► fortune, kismet, predestination. *See* **fate** (1). **2.** A personal outcome or end ► doom, fortune, lot. *See* **fate** (2).

destitute *adjective*
1. Deprived of a quality or aspect that is desirable ► barren, lacking, void. *See* **empty** (2). **2.** Having little or no money or wealth ► beggarly, down-and-out, indigent. *See* **poor** (1). *See synonym note at* **poor.**

destitution *noun*
1. The condition of being extremely poor ► beggary, indigence, need. *See* **poverty** (1). **2.** The condition of being deprived of what one once had or ought to have ► deprival, dispossession, loss. *See* **deprivation** (1).

destroy *verb*
1. To cause the complete ruin or wreckage of ► annihilate, bankrupt, break down, cross up, crush, demolish, devastate, finish, ravage, ruin, shatter, sink, smash, spoil, torpedo, undo, wash up, wrack, wreck. *Slang:* total. *Idioms:* lay waste to, put the kibosh on. *See also* **botch, damage. 2.** To pull down or break up so that reconstruction is impossible ► demolish, dismantle, dynamite, knock down, level, obliterate, pull down, pulverize, raze, tear down, wreck. **3.** To cause the death of ► cut down, dispatch, finish (off). *See* **kill**[1] (1). **4.** To take the life of a person or persons unlawfully ► assassinate, kill, slay. *See* **murder** (1). **5.** To severely impair someone's spirit, health, or will ► overwhelm, ruin. *See* **break** (4).

✦ CORE SYNONYMS: *destroy, raze, demolish, ruin, wreck.* These verbs mean to cause the complete ruin or wreckage of something or someone. *Destroy, raze,* and *demolish* can all imply reduction to ruins or even complete obliteration: "*I saw the best minds of my generation destroyed by madness*" (Allen Ginsberg); "*raze what was left of the city from the surface of the earth*" (John Lothrop Motley); *demolished the opposition's argument. Ruin* usually implies irretrievable harm but not necessarily total destruction: "*You will ruin no more lives as you ruined mine*" (Arthur Conan Doyle). To *wreck* is to ruin in or as if in a violent collision: "*The Boers had just wrecked a British military train*" (Arnold Bennett). When *wreck* is used in referring to the ruination of a person or of his or her hopes or reputation, it implies irreparable shattering: "*Coleridge, poet and philosopher wrecked in a mist of opium*" (Matthew Arnold).

destroyer *noun*
Something that causes total loss or severe impairment ► bane, downfall, undoing. *See* **ruin** (1).

destruction *noun*

1. The act of destroying or state of being destroyed ▸ annihilation, bane, decimation, demolition, devastation, havoc, pulverization, ruin, ruination, undoing, wrack, wreck, wreckage. **2.** Harm done to property or a person ▸ breakage, impairment, wreckage. *See* **damage** (1). **3.** Something that causes total loss or severe impairment ▸ bane, downfall, undoing. *See* **ruin** (1).

destructive *adjective*

▸ deleterious, evil, injurious. *See* **harmful.**

desuetude *noun*

▸ disuse, obsoletism. *See* **obsoleteness.**

desultory *adjective*

1. Without aim, purpose, or intent ▸ pointless, purposeless, rambling. *See* **aimless. 2.** Having no particular pattern, purpose, organization, or structure ▸ chance, indiscriminate, unplanned. *See* **random.** *See synonym note at* **random.**

detach *verb*

1. To remove from association with ▸ abstract, disassociate, disconnect, disengage, dissociate, separate, uncouple, withdraw. **2.** To break or separate into parts or sections ▸ disjoin, dissever, split up. *See* **divide** (1).

detached *adjective*

1. Lacking interest in one's surroundings or worldly affairs ▸ aloof, disconnected, disinterested, incurious, indifferent, remote, unconcerned, uninterested, uninvolved. **2.** Feeling or showing no strong emotional involvement ▸ disinterested, dispassionate, impersonal, indifferent, neutral. **3.** Set away from or lacking the company of all others ▸ alone, isolated, removed. *See* **solitary** (1). **4.** Lacking interest ▸ indifferent, listless, uninterested. *See* **apathetic. 5.** Not friendly, sociable, or warm in manner ▸ aloof, chilly, impersonal. *See* **cool** (1). **6.** Free from bias in judgment ▸ balanced, indifferent, nonpartisan. *See* **fair**[1] (1). **7.** Not excited or agitated ▸ collected, composed, cool. *See* **calm** (1). *See synonym note at* **calm.**

detachment *noun*

1. The act or process of detaching ▸ abstraction, disassociation, disconnection, disengagement, dissociation, separation, uncoupling, withdrawal. **2.** Dissociation from one's surroundings or worldly affairs ▸ aloofness, disinterest, distance, indifference, remoteness, unconcern, uninvolvement. **3.** The act or an instance of separating one thing from another ▸ disjunction, divorce, parting. *See* **division** (1). **4.** Lack of emotion or interest ▸ disinterest, indifference, unconcern. *See* **apathy. 5.** The quality or state of being just and unbiased ▸ disinterest, dispassion, impartiality. *See* **fairness. 6.** A group of people organized for a particular purpose ▸ squad, team, unit. *See* **force** (5). **7.** A unit of troops on special assignment ▸ brigade, corps, detail, patrol, squad.

detail *noun*

1. A small, often specialized element of a whole ▸ fine print, item, minutia, nicety, particular, singularity, specialty, technicality, trivia. *See also* **nitty-gritty. 2.** An individually considered portion of a whole ▸ article, item. *See* **element** (3). **3.** One of the conditions or facts attending an event and having some bearing on it ▸ factor, particular. *See* **circumstance** (2). **4.** A unit of troops on special assignment ▸ brigade, patrol. *See* **detachment** (7).

detail *verb*

1. To state specifically ▸ particularize, provide, specify, stipulate. *See also* **assert, designate, dictate. 2.** To communicate the facts, details, or particulars of something ▸ narrate, recount, report. *See* **describe** (1).

✦ **CORE SYNONYMS:** *detail, item, particular.* These nouns denote a small, often specialized element of a whole: *discussed the details of their trip; a shopping list with many items; furnished the particulars of the accident.*

---

detailed *adjective*

1. Characterized by attention to detail ▸ all-inclusive, blow-by-blow, circumstantial, comprehensive, elaborate, exhaustive, full, in-depth, minute, particular, thorough. **2.** Rich in detail ▸ fancy, intricate. *See* **elaborate** (1).

detain *verb*

1. To cause to be later or slower than expected or desired ▸ hang up, retard, stall. *See* **delay** (1). **2.** To keep in custody ▸ hold. **3.** To put in or as if in prison ▸ confine, incarcerate, jail. *See* **imprison.**

detainment *noun*

1. The condition or fact of being made late or slow ▸ holdup, lag, retardation. *See* **delay** (2). **2.** The state of being detained by legal authority ▸ confinement, custody, imprisonment. *See* **detention.**

detect *verb*

1. To perceive with the eyes ▸ catch, discern, perceive. *See* **see** (1). **2.** To perceive with a special effort of the senses or the mind ▸ descry, mark. *See* **notice. 3.** To obtain knowledge or awareness of something not known before ▸ determine, learn, unearth. *See* **discover. 4.** To perceive and fix the identity of, especially with difficulty ▸ ascertain, recognize. *See* **discern** (1).

detectable *adjective*

▸ discernible, noticeable, palpable, perceivable. *See* **perceptible.**

detective *noun*

A person whose work is investigating crimes or obtaining hidden evidence or information ▸ investigator, plainclothesman, sherlock, sleuth. *Informal:* eye. *Slang:* dick, gumshoe.

detention *noun*

The state of being detained by legal authority ▸ arrest, charge, confinement, custody, detainment, imprisonment, incarceration, internment, quarantine, ward.

deter *verb*

▸ discourage, disincline, divert. *See* **dissuade.** *See synonym note at* **dissuade.**

deteriorate *verb*

1. To become lower in quality, character, or condition ▸ atrophy, decline, degenerate, depreciate, descend, ebb, languish, retrograde, sink, wane, weaken, worsen. *Idioms:* go bad, go to pot, go downhill, go to seed, go to the dogs, hit the skids. *See also* **decrease, fall. 2.** To lose strength or power ▶ decline, fail, waste away, weaken. *See* **fade** (1). **3.** To become or cause to become rotten or unsound ▶ putrefy, rot, spoil, turn. *See* **decay.**

deterioration *noun*
1. Descent to a lower level or condition ▶ atrophy, decadence, declension, declination, decline, degeneracy, degeneration, depreciation, retrogradation, wane, weakening, worsening. **2.** A marked loss of strength or effectiveness ▶ declination, decline, failure. **3.** The condition of being decayed ▶ decomposition, disintegration, rot. *See* **decay. 4.** Harm done to property or a person ▶ destruction, impairment, wreckage. *See* **damage** (1).

determent *noun*
▶ deterrence, forestallment, preclusion. *See* **prevention.**

determinant *noun*
That which produces an effect ▶ antecedent, cause, occasion, reason. *See also* **impact, origin, stimulus.**

determinate *adjective*
▶ fixed, precise, specific. *See* **definite** (2).

determination *noun*
1. The act or process of ascertaining dimensions, quantity, or capacity ▶ measure, measurement, mensuration, quantification. *See also* **computation, estimation. 2.** A position reached after consideration ▶ conclusion, resolution. *See* **decision** (1). *See synonym note at* **decision. 3.** Unwavering firmness of character, action, or will ▶ assuredness, purpose, resolve, will. *See* **decision** (2). **4.** An authoritative or official decision ▶ edict, judgment, pronouncement, verdict. *See* **ruling. 5.** A solution, as to a problem ▶ explanation, resolution, solution. *See* **answer** (2). **6.** What one intends to do or achieve ▶ ambition, end, goal, objective. *See* **intention.**

determinative *adjective*
1. Serving the function of deciding or settling with finality ▶ decisive, ultimate. *See* **definitive** (1). **2.** Determining or having the power to determine an outcome ▶ crucial, deciding. *See* **decisive** (1). *See synonym note at* **decisive.**

determine *verb*
1. To fix the limits of ▶ bound, circumscribe, define, delimit, delimitate, demarcate, limit, mark (out *or* off), measure, restrict. **2.** To make a decision about (a controversy or dispute, for example) after deliberation, as in a court of law ▶ adjudicate, decide, rule. *See* **judge** (1). **3.** To set forth expressly and authoritatively ▶ impose, mandate, ordain. *See* **dictate** (1). **4.** To obtain knowledge or awareness of something not known before ▶ ascertain, learn, unearth. *See* **discover.** *See synonym note at* **discover. 5.** To make up or cause to make up one's mind ▶ conclude, settle. *See* **decide** (1). *See synonym note at* **decide. 6.** To control the functioning or outcome of ▶ control, regulate. *See*

govern (1). **7.** To arrive at through reasoning ▶ conclude, evolve. *See* **derive** (2).

determined *adjective*
1. Possessing determination or resolution ▶ resolute, steadfast, unyielding. *See* **firm**[1] (3). **2.** Committed to or unwavering in a course of action ▶ bent, fixed. *See* **intent** (1). **3.** Full of ambition ▶ aspiring, enterprising. *See* **ambitious.**

deterrence *noun*
▶ determent, forestallment, preclusion. *See* **prevention.**

deterrent *adjective*
Intended to prevent ▶ exclusive, preclusive, prohibitive. *See* **preventive.**

deterrent *noun*
Something that limits or holds back ▶ check, constraint, curb. *See* **restraint** (1).

detest *verb*
▶ abhor, despise, loathe. *See* **hate.**

detestable *adjective*
▶ contemptible, disgusting, obnoxious. *See* **offensive** (1). *See synonym note at* **offensive.**

detestation *noun*
1. A strong feeling of hostility or dislike ▶ antipathy, aversion, loathing. *See* **hate** (1). **2.** An object of extreme dislike ▶ abomination, anathema. *See* **hate** (2).

detonate *verb*
▶ blast, fire, go off. *See* **explode** (1).

detonation *noun*
1. A violent release of confined energy ▶ burst, explosion. *See* **blast** (2). **2.** A sudden sharp, explosive noise ▶ bang, pop, snap. *See* **crack** (1).

detour *verb*
▶ circumnavigate, go around. *See* **skirt** (1).

detract from *verb*
▶ flaw, impair. *See* **damage.**

detraction *noun*
1. The act or an instance of belittling ▶ deprecation, disparagement. *See* **belittlement. 2.** The expression of injurious, malicious statements about someone ▶ defamation, denigration, slander. *See* **libel.**

detractive *adjective*
1. Tending or intending to belittle ▶ deprecatory, derogatory, pejorative. *See* **disparaging. 2.** Damaging to the reputation ▶ defamatory, invidious, slanderous. *See* **libelous.**

detriment *noun*
1. The action or result of inflicting loss or pain ▶ damage, injury. *See* **harm. 2.** An unfavorable condition, circumstance, or characteristic ▶ drawback, handicap, liability. *See* **disadvantage.** *See synonym note at* **disadvantage.**

detrimental *adjective*
▶ deleterious, evil, injurious. *See* **harmful.**

de trop *adjective*
▶ excess, spare, surplus. *See* **superfluous.**

devaluate *verb*
▶ cheapen, downgrade, reduce. *See* **depreciate** (1).

devaluation *noun*
▸ cheapening, markdown, reduction. *See* **depreciation** (1).

devalue *verb*
1. To make less in price or value ▸ cheapen, downgrade, reduce. *See* **depreciate** (1). **2.** To lower in character or quality ▸ degrade, downgrade. *See* **debase** (1).

devastate *verb*
1. To engulf completely ▸ devour, ravage, waste. *See* **consume** (1). **2.** To cause the complete ruin or wreckage of ▸ annihilate, demolish, torpedo, wreck. *See* **destroy** (1).

devastation *noun*
▸ annihilation, ruin, wreck. *See* **destruction** (1).

develop *verb*
1. To come gradually to have ▸ acquire, form, grow, incur, manifest, sustain. **2.** To be disclosed gradually ▸ disentangle, evolve, unfold, unfurl, unravel. *See also* **reveal. 3.** To bring or come to full development ▸ age, ripen. *See* **mature.** *See synonym note at* **mature. 4.** To bring into existence ▸ give, provide, yield. *See* **produce** (1). **5.** To take place ▸ befall, come, occur. *See* **happen** (1). **6.** To express at greater length or in greater detail ▸ develop, expand. *See* **elaborate. 7.** To achieve an increase of ▸ build up, expand. *See* **gain** (9). **8.** To become different ▸ fluctuate, modify, turn. *See* **change** (2). **9.** To become affected with a disease ▸ catch, get. *See* **contract** (2). **10.** To make or become greater or larger ▸ amplify, boost, enlarge. *See* **increase** (1).

developed *adjective*
▸ adult, grown, ripe. *See* **mature** (1).

developer *noun*
A person instrumental in the growth of something, especially in its early stages ▸ builder, contributor, creator, innovator, pioneer, producer. *See also* **originator.**

development *noun*
1. A progression from a simple form to a more complex one ▸ advancement, blossoming, evolution, evolvement, growth, maturing, maturation, progress, unfolding. **2.** The result or product of building up ▸ accumulation, proliferation. *See* **buildup** (2). **3.** The act of making better or the condition of being made better ▸ enhancement, refinement, upgrade. *See* **improvement** (1). **4.** Steady improvement, as of an individual or society ▸ advancement, betterment, improvement. *See* **progress** (1). **5.** The process or result of making or becoming different ▸ modification, mutation, variation. *See* **change** (1). **6.** Something significant that happens ▸ circumstance, incident. *See* **event** (2). **7.** One that is slightly different from others of the same kind or designation ▸ adaptation, permutation. *See* **variation** (1).

✛ **CORE SYNONYMS:** *development, evolution, progress.* These nouns mean a progression from a simpler or lower to a more advanced, mature, or complex form

or stage: *the development of an idea into reality; the evolution of a plant from a seed; attempts made to foster social progress.*

---

deviance *or* **deviancy** *noun*
▸ aberration, deviation, irregularity. *See* **abnormality.**

deviant *adjective*
1. Departing from the normal ▸ aberrant, atypical, divergent. *See* **abnormal. 2.** Straying from a proper course or standard ▸ aberrant, stray. *See* **errant** (2).

deviant *noun*
One whose sexual behavior differs from the accepted norm ▸ deviate, pervert. *Slang:* freak.

deviate *verb*
1. To turn away from a prescribed course of action or conduct ▸ depart, digress, divagate, diverge, drift, stray, swerve, vary, veer. *Idiom:* go off on a tangent. **2.** To be unlike or dissimilar ▸ depart, diverge, vary. *See* **differ** (1). **3.** To turn aside, especially from the main subject in writing or speaking ▸ ramble, stray, wander. *See* **digress** (1). **4.** To change the direction or course of ▸ avert, divert, veer. *See* **turn** (2).

deviate *noun*
One whose sexual behavior differs from the accepted norm ▸ deviant, pervert. *Slang:* freak.

✛ **CORE SYNONYMS:** *deviate, depart, digress, diverge, stray, swerve, veer.* These verbs mean to turn away from a prescribed course of action or conduct: *deviated from the original plan; won't depart from family traditions; digressed from the main topic; opinions that diverged; strays from the truth; a gaze that never swerved; a conversation that veered away from sensitive issues.*

---

deviation *noun*
1. A departing from what is prescribed ▸ aberration, departure, divagation, divergence, divergency, diversion, variation. **2.** An instance of digressing ▸ aside, divergence, tangent. *See* **digression. 3.** The condition of being abnormal ▸ aberration, anomaly, irregularity. *See* **abnormality.**

✛ **CORE SYNONYMS:** *deviation, aberration, divergence.* These nouns mean a departure from what is prescribed or expected: *tolerates no deviation from the rules; regretted the aberrations of my adolescence; the divergence of a radical sect from accepted doctrines.*

---

device *noun*
1. Something, as a machine, that is devised for a particular function ▸ apparatus, appliance, contraption, contrivance, equipment, instrument, machine, mechanism. *See also* **gadget, tool. 2.** Something invented ▸ brainchild, contrivance. *See* **invention** (2). **3.** An indirect, usually cunning means of gaining an end ▸ deception, ploy, stratagem. *See* **trick** (1). *See synonym note at* **trick. 4.** An element or component in a decorative composition ▸ design, figure, motif, motive. *See synonym note at* **figure.**

devil *noun*
1. A perversely mean, cruel, or wicked person ▸ beast,

monster, ogre. *See* **fiend** (1). **2.** One who causes minor trouble or damage ▸ prankster, scamp. *See* **rascal**.

devilish *adjective*
1. Perversely mean, cruel, or wicked ▸ diabolical, infernal, satanic. *See* **fiendish**. **2.** Full of mischief or high-spirited fun ▸ frolicsome, impish, sportive. *See* **mischievous** (1).

devilment *noun*
▸ diablerie, high jinks, tomfoolery. *See* **mischief** (1).

deviltry *or* **devilry** *noun*
1. Annoying yet harmless, usually playful acts ▸ diablerie, high jinks, tomfoolery. *See* **mischief** (1). **2.** A wicked act or wicked behavior ▸ evil, misdeed, sin. *See* **crime** (2).

devious *adjective*
1. Marked by treachery or deceit ▸ duplicitous, shifty, sneaky. *See* **underhand**. **2.** Not proceeding straight to the point or object ▸ circuitous, oblique, roundabout. *See* **indirect** (1). **3.** Without a fixed or regular course ▸ stray, wandering. *See* **erratic** (1).

deviousness *noun*
1. Lack of straightforwardness and honesty in action ▸ chicanery, slyness, trickery. *See* **dishonesty** (2). **2.** Deceitful cleverness ▸ artfulness, slyness. *See* **art** (1).

devise *verb*
1. To use ingenuity in making, developing, or achieving ▸ contrive, dream up, hatch. *See* **invent** (1). **2.** To form a strategy for ▸ concoct, formulate, strategize. *See* **design** (1). **3.** To give property to another after one's death ▸ bequeath, will. *See* **leave**[1] (1).

devised *adjective*
▸ deliberate, premeditated. *See* **calculated** (1).

devitalization *noun*
▸ depletion, enfeeblement. *See* **debilitation**.

devitalize *verb*
▸ debilitate, weaken. *See* **enervate**.

devoid *adjective*
▸ destitute, lacking, void. *See* **empty** (2).

devoir *noun*
▸ charge, commitment, obligation. *See* **duty** (1).

devote *verb*
1. To give over by or as if by vow to a higher purpose ▸ bless, consecrate, dedicate, enshrine, hallow, pledge, sacrifice. *See also* **sanctify**. **2.** To devote oneself or one's efforts ▸ concentrate, dedicate. *See* **apply** (1).

✣ CORE SYNONYMS: *devote, dedicate, consecrate, pledge.* These verbs mean to give over by or as if by vow to a higher purpose. *Devote* implies faithfulness and loyalty: *Nurses devote themselves to the care of the sick. Dedicate* connotes a solemn, often formal commitment: *"To such a task we can dedicate our lives and our fortunes"* (Woodrow Wilson). *Consecrate* suggests sacred commitment: *His entire life is consecrated to science.* To *pledge* is to back a personal commitment by a solemn promise: *"I pledge you, I pledge myself, to a new deal for the American people"* (Franklin D. Roosevelt).

---

devoted *adjective*
1. Feeling or expressing fond feelings or affection ▸ caring, loving. *See* **affectionate**. **2.** Adhering firmly to a person, cause, duty, or faith ▸ allegiant, constant, loyal. *See* **faithful** (1). **3.** In the service or worship of God or a god ▸ consecrated, religious, sacred. *See* **divine** (2). **4.** Deeply concerned with God and the beliefs and practice of religion ▸ devout, holy, religious. *See* **pious** (1).

devotee *noun*
1. One zealously devoted to a religion ▸ acolyte, adherent, believer, disciple, enthusiast, fanatic, sectary, votary, zealot. *See also* **follower**. **2.** One who is ardently devoted ▸ enthusiast, fanatic, fancier. *See* **fan**[2].

devotion *noun*
1. A state of often extreme religious ardor ▸ adoration, devoutness, faith, faithfulness, pietism, piety, piousness, religionism, religiosity, religiousness, reverence, spirituality, zeal. *See also* **adoration**. **2.** An intense attachment to a person or thing ▸ affection, fondness, liking. *See* **love** (1). *See synonym note at* **love**. **3.** The passionate affection and desire felt by lovers for each other ▸ ardor, passion, romance. *See* **love** (2).

devotional *adjective*
Deeply concerned with God and the beliefs and practice of religion ▸ devout, holy, religious. *See* **pious** (1).

devotions *noun*
▸ litany, orison. *See* **prayer**[1] (2).

devour *verb*
1. To engulf completely ▸ dispatch, ravage, waste. *See* **consume** (1). **2.** To take food into the body as nourishment ▸ consume, ingest, partake. *See* **eat** (1). *See synonym note at* **eat**. **3.** To be avidly interested in ▸ feast on, relish. *Slang:* eat up.

devout *adjective*
1. Deeply concerned with God and the beliefs and practice of religion ▸ devoted, holy, religious. *See* **pious** (1). **2.** In the service or worship of God or a god ▸ devoted, religious, sacred. *See* **divine** (2). **3.** Feeling or showing reverence ▸ reverential, venerational, worshipful. *See* **reverent**.

devoutness *noun*
▸ piety, piousness. *See* **devotion** (1).

dexterity *noun*
1. Skillfulness in the use of the hands or body ▸ adroitness, cleverness, deftness, dexterousness, facility, grace, nimbleness, prowess, quickness, skill, sleight. *See also* **agility**. **2.** The quality of being agile ▸ deftness, nimbleness, quickness. *See* **agility**.

dexterous *adjective*
Exhibiting or possessing skill and ease in performance ▸ adroit, agile, artful, clean, clever, deft, facile, handy, neat, nimble, skillful, slick. *See also* **able, energetic, expert, fluent**.

✣ CORE SYNONYMS: *dexterous, deft, adroit, handy, nimble.* These adjectives refer to skill and ease in performance. *Dexterous* implies physical or mental agility: *dexterous fingers. Deft* suggests quickness, sureness, neatness, and lightness of touch: *deft strokes; a deft turn of phrase. Adroit* implies ease and natural skill, especially in challenging situations: *an adroit skier; an adroit negotiator. Handy* suggests a more modest aptitude, principally in manual work: *handy with tools. Nimble* stresses quickness and lightness in physical or mental performance: *nimble feet; nimble wits.*

dexterousness *noun*
1. The quality of being agile ▸ dexterity, nimbleness, quickness. *See* **agility.** 2. Skillfulness in the use of the hands or body ▸ adroitness, deftness, facility. *See* **dexterity** (1).

diablerie *noun*
1. A wicked act or wicked behavior ▸ evil, misdeed, sin. *See* **crime** (2). 2. Annoying yet harmless, usually playful acts ▸ devilment, high jinks, tomfoolery. *See* **mischief** (1).

diabolic *or* **diabolical** *adjective*
▸ devilish, infernal, satanic. *See* **fiendish.**

diagnosis *noun*
▸ analysis, probe. *See* **examination** (2).

diagonal *adjective*
▸ beveled, biased, slanted. *See* **oblique** (1).

diagram *noun*
A preliminary plan or version, as of a written work ▸ blueprint, framework, sketch. *See* **draft** (1).
diagram *verb*
To draw up a preliminary plan or version of ▸ outline, sketch. *See* **draft** (1).

dial *noun*
The marked outer surface of an instrument ▸ face, gauge, indicator.
dial *verb*
To communicate with someone by telephone ▸ call (up), ring (up), phone. *See* **telephone.**

dialect *noun*
1. A variety of a language that differs from the standard form ▸ argot, cant, jargon, lingo, patois, vernacular. 2. A system of terms used by a people sharing a history and culture ▸ tongue, vernacular. *See* **language** (1). 3. Specialized expressions indigenous to a particular field, subject, trade, or subculture ▸ jargon, lingo, patois. *See* **language** (2).

✦ CORE SYNONYMS: *dialect, vernacular, jargon, cant, argot, lingo, patois.* These nouns denote varieties of a language that differ from the standard form. *Dialect* usually applies to the vocabulary, grammar, and pronunciation characteristic of specific geographic localities or social classes. The *vernacular* is the informal everyday language spoken by a people. *Jargon* is specialized language understood only by a particular group, as one sharing an occupation or interest. *Cant* now usually refers to the specialized vocabulary of a group or trade and is often marked by the use of stock phrases. *Argot* applies especially to the language of the underworld. *Lingo* is often applied to language that is unfamiliar or difficult to understand. *Patois* is sometimes used as a synonym for *jargon* or *cant,* but it can also refer to a regional dialect that has no literary tradition.

dialogist *noun*
▸ discourser, talker. *See* **conversationalist.**

dialogue *or* **dialog** *noun*
1. Spoken exchange ▸ chat, discourse, talk. *See* **conversation** (1). 2. The text of a play, movie, opera, or similar work ▸ book, scenario, screenplay. *See* **script** (2). 3. A formal discussion of a subject, either written or spoken ▸ dissertation, essay. *See* **discourse** (1).

diametric *or* **diametrical** *adjective*
▸ antithetical, contradictory, inverse. *See* **opposite** (1).

diamond *noun*
A small sparkling decoration ▸ glitter, rhinestone, sequin, spangle.

diaphanous *adjective*
▸ ethereal, gauzy, vaporous. *See* **sheer²** (1). *See* synonym note at **sheer².**

diary *noun*
▸ commentaries, journal. *See* **memoir.**

diaspora *noun*
▸ defection, transmigration. *See* **emigration.**

diatribe *noun*
▸ harangue, jeremiad, philippic. *See* **tirade.**

dibs *noun*
Slang A legitimate or asserted right to demand something as one's due ▸ pretension, title. *See* **claim** (1).

dice *verb*
▸ cleave, sever. *See* **cut** (2).

dicey *adjective*
Slang Involving possible risk, loss, or injury ▸ chancy, hazardous, risky. *See* **dangerous.**

dick *noun*
▸ sleuth. *Informal:* eye. *Slang:* gumshoe. *See* **detective.**

dicker *verb*
▸ haggle, negotiate, palter. *See* **haggle.**

dictate *verb*
1. To set forth expressly and authoritatively ▸ decree, determine, direct, fix, impose, lay down, mandate, ordain, prescribe, rule. *Idioms:* call the shots (*or* tune), lay it on the line. *See also* **stipulate.** 2. To command in an arrogant manner ▸ domineer, rule, tyrannize. *See* **boss** (1). 3. To give orders to ▸ charge, instruct, order. *See* **command** (1). 4. To have charge of the affairs of others ▸ direct, govern, rule. *See* **administer** (1).

dictate *noun*
1. An order ▸ charge, commandment, imperative. *See* **command** (1). 2. A code or set of codes governing action or procedure, for example ▸ prescript, regulation, rubric. *See* **rule** (1).

✦ CORE SYNONYMS: *dictate, decree, impose, ordain, prescribe.* These verbs mean to set forth expressly and authoritatively: *victors dictating the terms of surrender; martial law decreed by the governor; impose obedience; a separation seemingly ordained by fate; taxes prescribed by law.*

dictated *adjective*
▶ compulsory, imperative, mandatory, requisite. *See* **required** (1).

dictation *noun*
▶ charge, commandment, imperative. *See* **command** (1).

dictator *noun*
1. An absolute ruler, especially one who is harsh and oppressive ▶ autarchist, authoritarian, autocrat, Big Brother, despot, führer, man on horseback, oligarch, oppressor, strongman, totalitarian, tyrant, usurper. **2.** One who imposes or favors absolute obedience to authority ▶ despot, martinet, tyrant. *See* **authoritarian** (1).

dictatorial *adjective*
1. Given to asserting one's will or authority over others ▶ authoritarian, bossy, dogmatic, domineering, imperious, inquisitorial, magisterial, masterful, megalomaniacal, overassertive, overbearing, overweening, peremptory. *See also* **aggressive, dominant, severe. 2.** Having and exercising complete political power and control ▶ autocratic, totalitarian, tyrannous. *See* **absolute** (1). **3.** Characterized by or favoring absolute obedience to authority ▶ despotic, tyrannic. *See* **authoritarian** (1).

✛ CORE SYNONYMS: *dictatorial, authoritarian, dogmatic, imperious, overbearing.* These adjectives mean asserting or tending to assert one's authority or to impose one's will on others. *Dictatorial* stresses the highhanded, peremptory manner characteristic of a dictator: *He ordered the staff about in his usual dictatorial manner. Authoritarian* implies the expectation of unquestioning obedience: *The authoritarian principal disciplined the unruly students. Dogmatic* suggests the imposing of one's will or opinion as though these were beyond challenge: *"When people are least sure, they are often most dogmatic"* (John Kenneth Galbraith). *Imperious* suggests the arrogant manner of one accustomed to commanding: *She dismissed my opinion with an imperious gesture. Overbearing* implies a tendency to be oppressively or rudely domineering: *The overbearing customer demanded to see the manager.*

dictatorship *noun*
1. A government in which all power is vested in a single leader or party ▶ autocracy, despotism, monocracy, tyranny. *See* **absolutism** (2). **2.** Absolute power, especially when exercised unjustly or cruelly ▶ autocracy, despotism, totalitarianism. *See* **tyranny** (1). **3.** A political doctrine advocating the principle of absolute rule ▶ authoritarianism, autocracy, despotism, totalitarianism. *See* **absolutism** (1).

diction *noun*
▶ locution, phraseology, verbalism. *See* **wording.**

dictionary *noun*
An alphabetical list of words often defined or translated ▶ glossary, lexicon, vocabulary, wordbook.

dictum *noun*
1. Something announced or communicated ▶ announcement, notice, statement. *See* **message** (1). **2.** An authoritative or official decision ▶ edict, judgment, pronouncement. *See* **ruling.**

didactic *or* **didactical** *adjective*
1. Teaching morality ▶ moralistic, moralizing, preachy. *See* **moral** (1). **2.** Inclined to teach or moralize excessively ▶ academic, expositive, expository, didactical, moralizing, preachy, prescriptive. *See also* **instructive, pedantic.**

diddle¹ *verb*
Slang To get money or something else from someone by deceitful trickery ▶ bilk, defraud, swindle. *See* **cheat** (1).

diddle² *verb*
To pass time without working or in avoiding work ▶ laze, loiter, lounge. *See* **idle** (1).

diddler *noun*
Slang A person who cheats ▶ cheater, swindler, trickster. *See* **cheat** (2).

die *verb*
1. To cease living ▶ decease, demise, depart, drop, expire, go, pass away, pass (on), perish, succumb. *Informal:* pop off. *Slang:* check out, croak, kick in, kick off. *Idioms:* bite the dust, breathe one's last, buy the farm, cash in, give up the ghost, go to one's grave, kick the bucket, meet one's end (*or* Maker), pass on to the Great Beyond, turn up one's toes. **2.** To cease to exist ▶ expire, perish. *See* **disappear** (2). **3.** To become or cause to become less active or intense ▶ abate, die away, die down, die out. *See* **subside** (1). **4.** To grow weaker in sound ▶ die away, die down, die out, quiet down. *See* **fade away** (1).

die for *verb*
Informal To have a strong longing for ▶ covet, want, yearn. *See* **desire** (1).

die-hard *adjective*
1. Firmly, often unreasonably immovable in purpose or will ▶ bullheaded, dogged, obstinate. *See* **stubborn** (1). **2.** Extremely or stubbornly conservative ▶ archconservative, old-school, reactionary. *See* **ultraconservative.**

die-hard *noun*
A person who is extremely or stubbornly conservative ▶ fossil, mossback, reactionary. *See* **ultraconservative.**

die-hardism *noun*
▶ bullheadedness, hardheadedness, rigidity. *See* **stubbornness.**

diet *noun*
▶ bread, meat, nourishment. *See* **food.**

differ *verb*
1. To be unlike or dissimilar ▶ contrast, depart, deviate, disagree, diverge, vary. *Idiom:* be at variance. **2.** To fail to be in accord ▶ contrast, disagree, discord. *See* **conflict.**

✛ CORE SYNONYMS: *differ, disagree, diverge, vary.* These verbs mean to be unlike or dissimilar: *Birds differ from mammals. Their testimony disagreed on several points. Our viewpoints diverge on the matter of foreign policy. People vary in intelligence.*

◄ ANTONYM: *agree*

difference *noun*

1. The condition of being unlike or dissimilar ► contrast, departure, disagreement, discrepancy, disparity, dissimilarity, dissimilitude, distinction, divarication, divergence, divergency, nonconformity, separateness, unlikeness, variance, variation. *See also* **abnormality, inequality. 2.** A marked lack of correspondence or agreement ► discrepancy, disparity, incongruity. *See* **gap** (3). **3.** A state of disagreement and disharmony ► clash, contention, discord. *See* **conflict** (1).

✛ CORE SYNONYMS: *difference, dissimilarity, unlikeness, divergence, variation, distinction, discrepancy.* These nouns refer to the condition of being unlike or dissimilar: *Difference* is the most general: *differences in color and size; a difference of opinion. Dissimilarity* is difference between things otherwise alike or comparable: *a dissimilarity between the twins' personalities. Unlikeness* usually implies greater and more obvious difference: *unlikeness among their teaching styles. Divergence* suggests an increasing difference: *points of divergence between British and American English. Variation* occurs between things of the same class or species; often it refers to modification of something original, prescribed, or typical: *variations in temperature; a variation in shape. Distinction* often means a difference in detail determinable only by close inspection: *the distinction between "good" and "excellent." A discrepancy* is a difference between things that should correspond or match: *a discrepancy between his words and his actions.*

different *adjective*

1. Not like another in nature, quality, amount, or form ► contrary, contrasting, disparate, dissimilar, distinct, divergent, diverse, separate, unlike, variant, various. **2.** Not the same as what was previously known or done ► fresh, novel, original. *See* **new** (1).

differentiate *verb*

1. To recognize as being different ► discern, separate. *See* **distinguish** (1). **2.** To make noticeable or different ► characterize, singularize. *See* **distinguish** (2).

differentiation *noun*

► demarcation, discretion. *See* **distinction** (1).

difficult *adjective*

1. Not easy to do, achieve, or master ► arduous, challenging, complicated, demanding, effortful, exacting, exigent, hard, laborious, serious, tall, tough, uphill. *See also* **burdensome. 2.** Causing difficulty, trouble, or discomfort ► incommodious, inconvenient, troublesome. *See also* **disturbing. 3.** Hard to treat, manage, or cope with ► difficult, trying, wicked. *See* **troublesome** (2). **4.** Marked by a disposition to oppose ► antagonistic, contradictory, hostile. *See* **contrary** (1). **5.** Difficult to understand because of intricacy ► convoluted, elaborate, involved, labyrinthine. *See* **complex** (1). **6.** Beyond the understanding of an average mind ► abstract, esoteric, profound. *See* **deep**

(2). **7.** Requiring great tact or skill ► demanding, exacting, precarious. *See* **delicate** (3).

✛ CORE SYNONYMS: *difficult, hard, arduous.* These adjectives mean requiring great physical or mental effort to do, achieve, or master. *Difficult* and *hard* are general terms and are interchangeable in many instances; however, *difficult* is often preferable where the need for skill or ingenuity is implied: *"All poetry is difficult to read,/—The sense of it is, anyhow"* (Robert Browning). *"You write with ease to show your breeding,/But easy writing's curst hard reading"* (Richard Brinsley Sheridan). *Arduous* applies to burdensome labor or sustained physical or spiritual effort: *"knowledge at which [Isaac] Newton arrived through arduous and circuitous paths"* (Thomas Macaulay).

◄ ANTONYM: *easy*

difficultly *adverb*

With effort ► arduously, heavily, laboriously. *See* **hard** (2).

difficulty *noun*

1. Something that obstructs progress and requires great effort to overcome ► asperity, complication, hardship, impediment, obstacle, obstruction, plight, problem, rigor, stumbling block, trial, trouble, vicissitude. *Idioms:* a hard (*or* tough) nut to crack, a hard (*or* tough) row to hoe, heavy sledding. *See also* **bar, distress. 2.** A difficult, often embarrassing situation or condition ► corner, fix. *See* **predicament. 3.** A state of disagreement and disharmony ► contention, difference, discord. *See* **conflict** (1). **4.** A discussion, often heated, in which a difference of opinion is expressed ► contention, dispute, quarrel. *See* **argument** (1).

✛ CORE SYNONYMS: *difficulty, hardship, obstacle, rigor, vicissitude.* These nouns denote something that requires great effort to overcome: *grappling with financial difficulties; a life of hardship; the obstacles faced in obtaining a mortgage; undergoing the rigors of prison; withstood the vicissitudes of an army career.*

diffidence *noun*

► bashfulness, demureness. *See* **shyness.**

diffident *adjective*

► bashful, demure, modest. *See* **shy**[1] (1). *See synonym note at* **shy**[1].

diffuse *verb*

To extend over a wide area ► disperse, disseminate, scatter. *See* **spread** (2).

diffuse *adjective*

1. Using or containing an excessive number of words ► long-winded, periphrastic, verbose. *See* **wordy** (1). *See synonym note at* **wordy. 2.** Marked by or given to digression ► long-winded, parenthetical, rambling. *See* **digressive.**

diffuseness *noun*

► redundancy, verboseness. *See* **wordiness.**

diffusion *noun*

1. Words or the use of words in excess of those needed for clarity or precision ► pleonasm, redundancy, verboseness. *See* **wordiness. 2.** The passing out or spreading about of something over a wide area ▸ dispersion, scattering. *See* **distribution** (2).

dig *verb*
1. To break, turn over, or remove (earth or sand, for example) with or as if with a tool ▸ bore, burrow, delve, excavate, gouge, grub, scoop, shovel, spade. **2.** To prepare soil for the planting of crops ▸ cultivate, plow, work. *See* **till**. **3.** To go into or through for the purpose of making discoveries or acquiring information ▸ delve, investigate. *See* **explore**. **4.** To find by investigation ▸ turn up, unearth. *See* **uncover** (1). **5.** To penetrate into a substance or place with force ▸ drive, stab, stick. *See* **plunge** (1). **6.** To apply pressure on, against, or with ▸ press, prod, shove. *See* **push** (1). **7.** *Slang* To perceive and recognize the meaning of ▸ apprehend, fathom, sense. *See* **understand** (1). **8.** *Slang* To receive pleasure from ▸ appreciate, savor. *See* **enjoy** (1).

dig out *or* **up** *verb*
To obtain knowledge or awareness of something not known before ▸ determine, learn, unearth. *See* **discover**.

dig *noun*
1. An act of thrusting into or against, as to attract attention ▸ jab, jog, nudge, poke, prod, punch, stab. *See also* **push**. **2.** A flippant or sarcastic remark ▸ barb, quip. *Slang:* wisecrack. *See* **crack** (5). **3.** An instance of mockery or derision ▸ cut, gibe, twit. *See* **taunt** (1).

digest *verb*
To take in and incorporate, especially mentally ▸ assimilate, imbibe, take up. *See* **absorb** (2).

digest *noun*
A shortened version or summary ▸ brief, outline, sketch. *See* **synopsis**.

digestion *noun*
▸ assimilation, incorporation, intake. *See* **absorption** (1).

dignification *noun*
▸ apotheosis, elevation. *See* **exaltation** (1).

dignified *adjective*
1. Fond of or given to ceremony ▸ courtly, formal, stately. *See* **ceremonious** (1). **2.** Characterized by careful thought and a lack of frivolity or exaggeration ▸ earnest, sedate, solemn. *See* **serious** (1). *See synonym note at* **serious**.

dignify *verb*
1. To lend dignity or honor to by an act or favor ▸ enrich, favor, grace, honor. *See also* **honor**. **2.** To raise to a high position or status ▸ elevate, magnify, uplift. *See* **exalt** (1). **3.** To cause to be eminent or recognized ▸ celebrate, exalt, honor. *See* **distinguish** (5).

dignitary *noun*
An important, influential person ▸ character, eminence, leader, lion, luminary, magnate, nabob, notability, notable, personage, worthy. *Informal:* bigfoot, big name, big-timer, heavyweight, high-up, somebody, someone, VIP. *Slang:* big gun, big shot, big wheel, bigwig, muckamuck.

dignity *noun*
1. A person's high standing among others ▸ good name, reputation. *See* **honor** (2). **2.** The quality of being dignified and serious, as in manner or bearing ▸ graveness, sobriety, solemnity. *See* **seriousness** (1). **3.** Refinement of manner, form, and style ▸ grace, refinement. *See* **elegance**.

digress *verb*
1. To turn aside, especially from the main subject in writing or speaking ▸ deviate, divagate, diverge, drift, maunder, ramble, stray, veer, wander. *Idioms:* go off at (*or* on) a tangent, go off the subject. **2.** To turn away from a prescribed course of action or conduct ▸ depart, stray. *See* **deviate** (1). *See synonym note at* **deviate**.

digression *noun*
An instance of digressing ▸ aside, departure, deviation, divagation, divergence, divergency, diversion, excursion, excursus, irrelevancy, parenthesis, rambling, straying, tangent, wandering.

digressive *adjective*
Marked by or given to digression ▸ diffuse, discursive, excursive, long-winded, meandering, parenthetic, parenthetical, rambling, tangential.

digs *noun*
Slang A building or shelter where one lives ▸ domicile, habitation, residence. *See* **home** (1).

dilapidated *adjective*
▸ broken-down, decrepit, tattered. *See* **shabby** (1).

dilate *verb*
1. To express at greater length or in greater detail ▸ develop, discourse, expand. *See* **elaborate**. **2.** To make or become broader or more comprehensive ▸ amplify, expand, widen. *See* **broaden**.

dilatory *adjective*
▸ creeping, laggard, sluggish. *See* **slow** (1). *See synonym note at* **slow**.

dilemma *noun*
▸ corner, difficulty, fix. *See* **predicament**.

dilettante *noun*
▸ dabbler, layperson, nonprofessional. *See* **amateur**. *See synonym note at* **amateur**.

dilettantish *adjective*
▸ nonprofessional, unskilled. *See* **amateurish**.

diligence *noun*
Steady attention and effort, as to one's occupation ▸ application, assiduity, assiduousness, conscientiousness, industriousness, industry, perseverance, persistence, pertinacity, sedulousness, studiousness. *Informal:* stick-to-itiveness.

diligent *adjective*
Characterized by steady attention and effort ▸ assiduous, conscientious, dogged, industrious, painstaking, persistent, pertinacious, sedulous, studious, unflagging, unremitting.

✦ **CORE SYNONYMS:** *diligent, industrious, painstaking, assiduous, sedulous.* These adjectives suggest steady attention and effort that is undertaken to accomplish something. *Diligent* indicates constant and customary work or activity: *The diligent detective pieced the clues together.* *Industrious* implies steady application that is often habitual or the result of a natural inclination: *All of the weeds were pulled by the industrious gardener.* *Painstaking* suggests constant, careful effort, often toward the achievement of a specific goal: *Piecing together the broken vase was a painstaking task.* *Assiduous* emphasizes sustained application: *Her assiduous efforts to learn French paid off.* *Sedulous* adds to *assiduous* the sense of persistent, thoroughgoing endeavor: *"the sedulous pursuit of legal and moral principles"* (Ernest van den Haag).

dilly-dallier *noun*
▸ lag, procrastinator, straggler. *See* **laggard.**

dilly-dally *verb*
1. To go or move slowly so that progress is hindered ▸ dawdle, drag, linger. *See* **delay** (2). **2.** To be irresolute in acting or doing ▸ falter, vacillate. *See* **hesitate. 3.** To shift from one attitude, interest, condition, or emotion to another ▸ swing, vacillate, waver.

dilute *verb*
To lessen the strength of by or as if by admixture ▸ adulterate, attenuate, cut, thin, water (down), weaken.

dilute *adjective*
Lower than normal in strength or concentration due to admixture ▸ adulterated, cut, thin, washy, watered-down, waterish, watery, weak.

dim *adjective*
1. Deficient in brightness ▸ dusky, murky, obscure. *See* **dark** (1). *See synonym note at* **dark. 2.** Lacking vividness or color ▸ lackluster, mat, muddy. *See* **dull** (2). **3.** Not clearly perceptible ▸ cloudy, faint, indistinct. *See* **unclear** (1). **4.** *Slang* Having only a limited ability to learn and understand ▸ dense, dull. *See* **backward** (1). **5.** Being weak in quality or substance ▸ bloodless, pallid. *See* **pale** (2). **6.** Offering little encouragement ▸ discouraging, unpromising. *See* **bleak** (2).

dim *verb*
1. To make dim ▸ blur, fog, obfuscate. *See* **obscure** (1). **2.** To addle the mind, as with a narcotic or alcohol ▸ besot, impair, stupefy. *See* **drug** (2).

dimensions *noun*
▸ extent, magnitude, proportions. *See* **size** (1).

diminish *verb*
1. To become or cause to become gradually less ▸ drain, dwindle, lessen. *See* **decrease.** *See synonym note at* **decrease. 2.** To become or cause to become less active or intense ▸ die (away, down, off, *or* out), ebb, lapse. *See* **subside** (1).

diminishment *noun*
1. The act or process of decreasing ▸ curtailment, reduction, slowdown. *See* **decrease. 2.** The process of becoming less active or intense ▸ abatement, letup, subsidence. *See* **waning.**

diminution *noun*
▸ curtailment, reduction, slowdown. *See* **decrease.**

diminutive *adjective*
▸ dwarf, miniature, minuscule. *See* **tiny.**

dimness *noun*
▸ darkness, duskiness, murkiness. *See* **dark** (1).

dimwit *noun*
▸ dummy, dunce, thickhead. *See* **dullard.**

dimwitted *adjective*
1. *Slang* Lacking in intelligence ▸ dumb, idiotic, obtuse. *See* **stupid** (1). **2.** *Slang* Having only a limited ability to learn and understand ▸ dense, dull. *See* **backward** (1).

din *noun*
▸ clamor, racket, uproar. *See* **noise** (1). *See synonym note at* **noise.**

ding *verb*
1. To strike together noisily ▸ crash, slam, whack. *See* **bang** (1). **2.** To give forth or cause to give forth a clear resonant sound ▸ bong, chime, knell, peal. *See* **ring²** (1).

ding-a-ling *noun*
Slang A person regarded as strange, eccentric, or crazy ▸ lunatic. *Informal:* loony. *Slang:* nut, weirdo. *See* **crackpot.**

ding-dong *noun*
Slang A person who is deficient in judgment and good sense ▸ idiot, imbecile, nitwit. *See* **fool** (1).

dingy *adjective*
1. Showing signs of wear and tear ▸ broken-down, dilapidated, tattered. *See* **shabby** (1). **2.** Covered with or stained by dirt ▸ black, filthy, muddy. *See* **dirty** (1).

dint *noun*
▸ indent, mark. *See* **impression** (1).

dip *verb*
1. To plunge briefly in or into a liquid ▸ douse, duck, dunk, immerge, immerse, souse, submerge, submerse. *See also* **steep², wet. 2.** To take a substance, as liquid, from a container by plunging the hand or a utensil into it ▸ bail, dredge, lade, ladle, scoop (up), spoon. **3.** To slope downward ▸ decline, descend. *See* **drop** (5). **4.** *Slang* To take another's property without permission ▸ purloin, snatch, thieve. *See* **steal** (1).

dip into *verb*
To look through reading matter casually ▸ flip through, leaf (through), skim. *See* **browse** (1).

dip *noun*
1. The act of swimming ▸ duck, dunk. *See* **plunge** (4). **2.** A usually swift downward trend, as in prices ▸ decline, descent, downswing. *See* **fall** (3). **3.** An area sunk below its surroundings ▸ concavity, dent, hollow. *See* **depression** (1). **4.** *Slang* A person who is deficient in judgment and good sense ▸ idiot, imbecile, nitwit. *See* **fool** (1). **5.** A sudden drop to a lower condition or status ▸ plunge, slide, tumble. *See* **descent** (4). **6.** *Slang* An unpleasant, tiresome person ▸ bore. *Slang:* pill, twit. *See* **drip** (2).

✛ **CORE SYNONYMS:** *dip, douse, duck, dunk.* These verbs mean to immerse briefly into a liquid: *dipped her hand into the basin; doused his head in the shower; playmates ducking each other in the pool; dunked his cookies in milk.*

diplomacy *noun*
 ▶ address, savoir-faire, tactfulness. *See* **tact.** *See synonym note at* **tact.**

diplomatic *adjective*
 1. Showing sensitivity and skill in dealing with others ▶ discreet, sensitive, tactful. *See* **delicate** (2). **2.** Characterized by elaborate, usually formal courtesy ▶ courtly, gallant, stately. *See* **gracious** (2).

dippiness *noun*
 Slang Foolish behavior ▶ folly, silliness, tomfoolery. *See* **foolishness.**

dippy *adjective*
 Slang Displaying a lack of forethought and good sense ▶ daft, idiotic, ludicrous. *See* **foolish.**

dipso *noun*
 Slang A person who is habitually drunk ▶ alcoholic, dipsomaniac, tippler. *See* **drunkard.**

dipsomaniac *noun*
 ▶ alcoholic, drunk, tippler. *See* **drunkard.**

dire *adjective*
 1. Bringing or predicting misfortune ▶ baleful, ominous, portentous, unlucky. *See* **fateful** (1). **2.** Causing or capable of causing fear ▶ appalling, scary, terrible, tremendous. *See* **fearful** (1). **3.** Demanding immediate attention ▶ compelling, crucial, pressing. *See* **urgent** (1). **4.** Having or threatening severe negative consequences ▶ grave, grievous, serious, severe. *See also* **disastrous.**

direct *verb*
 1. To have charge of the affairs of others ▶ control, govern, rule. *See* **administer** (1). **2.** To control the course of an activity ▶ handle, manage, operate. *See* **conduct** (1). *See synonym note at* **conduct. 3.** To give orders to ▶ charge, instruct, order. *See* **command** (1). **4.** To devote oneself or one's efforts ▶ concentrate, focus, give. *See* **apply** (1). **5.** To show the way to ▶ conduct, escort, lead. *See* **guide** (1). **6.** To give recommendations to someone about a decision or course of action ▶ counsel, recommend. *See* **advise** (1). *See synonym note at* **advise. 7.** To point something, often toward a target ▶ level, train, zero in. *See* **aim** (1). *See synonym note at* **aim. 8.** To mark a written communication with its destination ▶ address, superscribe. *See also* **ticket. 9.** To set forth expressly and authoritatively ▶ determine, mandate, ordain. *See* **dictate** (1). **10.** To produce on the stage ▶ dramatize, enact, perform. *See* **stage** (1).

direct *adjective*
 1. Proceeding or lying in an uninterrupted line or course ▶ linear, straight, straightforward, through, undeviating, unswerving. **2.** Marked by the absence of any intervention ▶ firsthand, immediate, primary. **3.** Of unbroken descent or lineage ▶ genealogical, hereditary, lineal, ancestral. *See also* **direct. 4.** Manifesting honesty and directness ▶ forthright, open, plainspoken. *See* **frank.**

direct *adverb*
 1. In a direct line ▶ straight, undeviatingly. *See* **directly** (1). **2.** With precision or absolute conformity

▶ exactly, precisely, squarely. *See* **directly** (3).

direction *noun*
 1. The spatial path along which motion or orientation is referred ▶ course, heading, route, way. **2.** The act or process of directing ▶ administration, guidance, leadership, supervision. *See* **management** (1). **3.** The continuous exercise of authority over a political unit ▶ control, rule. *See* **government** (1). **4.** An order ▶ charge, commandment, imperative. *See* **command** (1). **5.** An opinion as to a decision or course of action ▶ guidance, recommendation. *See* **advice** (1).

directionless *adjective*
 ▶ pointless, purposeless, rambling. *See* **aimless.**

directive *noun*
 ▶ charge, commandment, imperative. *See* **command** (1).

directly *adverb*
 1. In a direct line ▶ dead, direct, due, right, straight, straightaway, undeviatingly, unswervingly. **2.** Without intermediary ▶ firsthand, immediately. **3.** With precision or absolute conformity ▶ bang, dead, direct, exactly, fair, flush, just, plumb, precisely, right, smack, spot-on, square, squarely, straight. *Slang:* smack-dab. **4.** Without delay ▶ forthwith, instantly, straightaway. *See* **immediately** (1). **5.** In a direct, positive manner ▶ emphatically, positively. *Informal:* flat out. *See* **flatly.**

director *noun*
 1. One who governs or leads ▶ boss, chieftain, head, leader. *See* **chief** (1). **2.** Someone who directs and supervises workers ▶ foreman, manager, supervisor. *See* **boss** (1). **3.** A person having administrative or managerial authority in an organization ▶ administrator, manager. *See* **executive. 4.** Something or someone that shows the way ▶ conductor, escort, leader. *See* **guide** (1).

directorial *adjective*
 ▶ executive, managerial, organizational. *See* **administrative.**

directorship *noun*
 ▶ administration, leadership, supervision. *See* **management** (1).

directory *noun*
 ▶ register, roster, schedule. *See* **list**[1].

direful *adjective*
 1. Causing or capable of causing fear ▶ appalling, dreadful, frightful, terrible. *See* **fearful** (1). **2.** Bringing or predicting misfortune ▶ baleful, ominous, portentous. *See* **fateful** (1).

dirt *noun*
 1. The soft part of the land surface of the world ▶ clay, ground, loam, soil. *See* **earth** (1). **2.** Foul or dirty matter ▶ grime, muck. *See* **filth** (1). **3.** Something that is offensive to accepted standards of decency ▶ filth, sleaze, smut. *See* **obscenity** (2).

dirt-cheap *adjective*
 ▶ budget, economy, low-cost. *See* **cheap** (1).

dirtiness *noun*
 1. The condition or state of being dirty ▶ filth, filthiness, foulness, griminess, grubbiness, muckiness,

nastiness, smuttiness, squalor, uncleanliness, uncleanness. **2.** The state of being contaminated ▸ adulteration, defilement, impurity, pollution. *See* **contamination** (1). **3.** The quality or state of being obscene ▸ filthiness, profanity, smuttiness, vulgarness. *See* **obscenity** (1).

dirty *adjective*
1. Covered with or stained by dirt or other impurities ▸ black, dingy, filthy, foul, grimy, grubby, miry, muddy, nasty, smutty, soiled, squalid, unclean, uncleanly, vile. *Slang:* grungy. *See also* **slimy, turbid. 2.** Offensive to accepted standards of decency ▸ bawdy, coarse, lewd, vulgar. *See* **obscene** (1). **3.** Mixed with other substances ▸ alloyed, combined, polluted. *See* **impure** (2). **4.** Violently disturbed or agitated, as by storms ▸ roily, turbulent, violent. *See* **rough** (2). **5.** Not fair, right, or just ▸ discriminatory, unequal, unjust. *See* **unfair.**

dirty *verb*
1. To make dirty ▸ bedaub, befoul, begrime, bemire, besmirch, besoil, bespatter, black, blacken, defile, foul, mire, muck up, mud, muddy, slush, smudge, smutch, soil, sully. *See also* **contaminate, smear, stain. 2.** To attack the reputation or honor of ▸ besmirch, smear, tarnish. *See* **denigrate** (1).

✤ CORE SYNONYMS: *dirty, filthy, foul, squalid, grimy.* These adjectives apply to what is covered with or stained by dirt or other impurities. *Dirty* is the most general: *dirty clothes; dirty sidewalks.* Something that is *filthy* is disgustingly dirty: *filthy rags. Foul* suggests gross offensiveness, particularly to the sense of smell: *a foul stench; a foul pond. Squalid* suggests dirtiness, wretchedness, and sordidness: *lived in a squalid apartment. Grimy* describes something ingrained or smudged with dirt or soot: *grimy hands.*

◂ ANTONYM: *clean*

---

disability *noun*
▸ detriment, handicap, liability. *See* **disadvantage.**

disable *verb*
1. To render powerless or motionless, as by inflicting severe injury ▸ cripple, handicap, immobilize, impair, incapacitate, invalidate, knock out, paralyze. *Idioms:* put out of action (*or* commission). *See also* **enervate. 2.** To make incapable, as of doing a job ▸ disqualify, unfit.

disabuse *verb*
To free from false hopes or ideas ▸ disenchant, disillusion, undeceive. *Idioms:* bring down to earth, burst one's bubble, open one's eyes. *See also* **disappoint, free.**

disaccord *noun*
A state of disagreement and disharmony ▸ contention, difference, discord. *See* **conflict** (1).

disaccord *verb*
To fail to be in accord ▸ contrast, disagree, discord. *See* **conflict.**

disacknowledge *verb*
▸ disavow, reject, renounce. *See* **repudiate** (1).

disadvantage *noun*
An unfavorable condition, circumstance, or characteristic ▸ detriment, disability, downside, drawback, flaw, handicap, inconvenience, liability, minus, problem, shortcoming. *See also* **weakness.**

✤ CORE SYNONYMS: *disadvantage, detriment, drawback, handicap.* These nouns denote a condition, circumstance, or characteristic unfavorable to success: *Poor health is a disadvantage to athletes. To its detriment, the museum has no parking lot. Every job has its drawbacks. Illiteracy is a serious handicap in life.*

---

disadvantaged *adjective*
▸ deprived, impoverished. *See* **depressed** (2).

disadvantageous *adjective*
▸ antagonistic, negative, untoward. *See* **unfavorable** (1).

disaffect *verb*
▸ come between, disunite. *See* **estrange.** *See synonym note at* **estrange.**

disaffection *noun*
▸ break, estrangement, fissure. *See* **breach** (2).

disaffirm *verb*
▸ contravene, dismiss, disavow. *See* **deny** (1). *See synonym note at* **deny.**

disaffirmation *or* **disaffirmance** *noun*
▸ disavowal, disclaimer, rejection. *See* **denial** (1).

disagree *verb*
1. To be unlike or dissimilar ▸ depart, diverge, vary. *See* **differ** (1). *See synonym note at* **differ. 2.** To fail to be in accord ▸ contrast, differ, discord. *See* **conflict.**

disagreeability *noun*
▸ crankiness, prickliness, tetchiness. *See* **temper** (1).

disagreeable *adjective*
1. Not pleasant or agreeable ▸ bad, uncongenial, unsympathetic. *See* **unpleasant** (1). **2.** Having or showing a bad temper ▸ cranky, grouchy, peevish. *See* **ill-tempered. 3.** Arousing disapproval ▸ exceptionable, improper, unacceptable. *See* **objectionable. 4.** Given to arguing ▸ contentious, litigious, quarrelsome. *See* **argumentative. 5.** Difficult to accept or bear ▸ distasteful, painful, unpleasant. *See* **bitter** (3).

disagreement *noun*
1. A marked lack of correspondence or agreement ▸ discrepancy, disparity, incongruity. *See* **gap** (3). **2.** A discussion, often heated, in which a difference of opinion is expressed ▸ contention, dispute, quarrel. *See* **argument** (1). **3.** A state of disagreement and disharmony ▸ contention, difference, discord. *See* **conflict** (1). **4.** An expression of opposition ▸ exception, grievance, protestation. *See* **objection. 5.** The condition of being unlike or dissimilar ▸ contrast, discrepancy, divergence. *See* **difference** (1).

disallow *verb*
1. To refuse to allow ▸ ban, proscribe. *See* **forbid. 2.** To be unwilling to accept, consider, or receive ▸ refuse, reject, spurn. *See* **decline** (1).

disallowed *adjective*
▸ banned, outlawed, prohibited. *See* **forbidden.**

disallowance *noun*
1. A refusal to allow ▸ prohibition, proscription. *See* **forbiddance. 2.** A turning down of a request ▸ denial, nonacceptance, refusal, rejection, turndown.

disappear *verb*
1. To pass out of sight either gradually or suddenly ▸ dissipate, dissolve, ebb, evanesce, evaporate, fade, fade out, melt (away), vanish, wane. *See also* **lift. 2.** To cease to exist ▸ cease, depart, die (away *or* out), end, expire, perish. *See also* **die.**

✦ CORE SYNONYMS: *disappear, evanesce, evaporate, fade, vanish.* These verbs mean to pass out of sight or existence: *a skyscraper disappearing in the fog; time seeming to evanesce; courage evaporating; memories fading away; hope slowly vanishing.*

---

disappearance *noun*
The act or an example of passing out of sight ▸ departure, dissipation, dissolution, evanescence, evaporation, expiration, fade-out, fading, vanishment, waning.

disappoint *verb*
To cause unhappiness by failing to satisfy the hopes, desires, or expectations of ▸ discontent, discourage, disenchant, disgruntle, dishearten, disillusion, dissatisfy, dispirit, embitter, fail, frustrate, let down, sour. *Idioms:* dash someone's hopes, fall short, shatter someone's dream.

disappointing *adjective*
Disturbing because of failure to measure up to a standard or produce the desired results ▸ anticlimactic, discouraging, disheartening, inadequate, inferior, insufficient, sorry, underwhelming, unlucky, unsatisfactory, unsatisfying.

disappointment *noun*
1. Unhappiness caused by the failure of one's hopes, desires, or expectations ▸ discontent, discontentment, discouragement, disenchantment, disgruntlement, disheartenment, disillusion, disillusionment, dissatisfaction, frustration, nonfulfillment, regret, unfulfillment. 2. Something that disappoints ▸ anticlimax, bust, fiasco, letdown, washout. *Informal:* dud, fizzle, flop, lemon, nonevent. *See also* **failure.**

disapprobation *noun*
▸ condemnation, disfavor, reproof. *See* **disapproval.**

disapproval *noun*
Unfavorable opinion or judgment ▸ condemnation, denunciation, deprecation, disapprobation, disesteem, disfavor, displeasure, dissatisfaction, rejection, reproach, reproof. *See also* **dislike, objection, rebuke.**

disapprove *verb*
1. To have or express an unfavorable opinion of ▸ decry, denounce, deprecate, discountenance, disesteem, disfavor, dislike, frown on (*or* upon), object to, reject, reprobate, sniff at. *Idioms:* hold no brief for, look askance at, not go for, take a dim view of, take exception to. *See also* **condemn, deplore, disapprove, hate. 2.** To be unwilling to accept, consider, or receive ▸ refuse, reject, spurn. *See* **decline** (1).

disarrange *verb*
1. To put out of proper order ▸ clutter, disrupt, muddle. *See* **disorder** (1). **2.** To put something into a state of disarray, such as the hair or clothes ▸ dishevel, disorder, muss (up). *See* **tousle.**

disarrangement *noun*
▸ clutter, confusion, disarray. *See* **disorder** (1).

disarray *noun*
A lack of order or regular arrangement ▸ clutter, confusion, mix-up. *See* **disorder** (1).

disarray *verb*
To put out of proper order ▸ disarrange, disrupt, muddle. *See* **disorder** (1).

disassemble *verb*
To divide into component parts ▸ break down, dismantle, dismount, take apart (*or* down).

disassociate *verb*
▸ abstract, disengage, withdraw. *See* **detach** (1).

disassociation *noun*
1. The act or process of detaching ▸ disconnection, separation, uncoupling. *See* **detachment** (1). **2.** The act or an instance of separating one thing from another ▸ disjunction, divorce, parting. *See* **division** (1).

disaster *noun*
1. An occurrence inflicting widespread destruction and distress ▸ calamity, cataclysm, catastrophe, debacle, fiasco, holocaust, mishap, tragedy. **2.** An abrupt failure ▸ crash, debacle, wreck. *See* **collapse** (2).

disastrous *adjective*
Causing ruin or great destruction ▸ calamitous, cataclysmic, catastrophic, fatal, fateful, ruinous. *See also* **harmful, unfortunate.**

disavow *verb*
1. To refuse to recognize or acknowledge ▸ deny, reject, renounce. *See* **repudiate** (1). **2.** To refuse to admit the truth, reality, value, or worth of ▸ contravene, disaffirm, dispute. *See* **deny** (1). **3.** To abandon one's cause or party usually to join another ▸ desert, quit, turn. *See* **defect.**

disavowal *noun*
1. A refusal to grant the truth of a statement or charge ▸ disaffirmation, disclaimer, rejection. *See* **denial** (1). **2.** An instance of defecting from or abandoning a cause ▸ abandonment, recreance, renouncement. *See* **defection.**

disband *verb*
1. To break or separate into parts, sections, or branches ▸ disjoin, dissever, split up. *See* **divide** (1). **2.** To separate and move apart ▸ break up, disperse, split up. *See* **scatter** (2).

disbelief *noun*
1. The refusal or reluctance to believe ▸ discredit, distrust, doubt, dubiety, incredulity, incredulousness, mistrust, rejection, skepticism, unbelief. **2.** Lack of belief in God ▸ faithlessness, impiety. *See* **atheism.**

disbelieve *verb*
1. To give no credence to ▸ discredit, distrust, doubt, mistrust, question, reject. *Idiom:* take no stock in. *See*

also **repudiate. 2.** To be uncertain, disbelieving, or skeptical about ▸ query, waver. *See* **doubt** (1). **3.** To lack trust or confidence in ▸ doubt, question. *See* **distrust.**

disbelieving *adjective*
1. Refusing or reluctant to believe ▸ questioning, skeptical. *See* **incredulous. 2.** Not believing in God ▸ faithless, irreligious. *See* **atheistic.**

disburden *verb*
▸ discharge, relieve, unburden. *See* **rid.**

disburse *verb*
1. To give money as payment ▸ expend, outlay, pay. *See* **spend** (1). *See synonym note at* **spend. 2.** To give out in portions or shares ▸ allocate, deal (out), dole out. *See* **distribute** (1). *See synonym note at* **distribute.**

disbursement *noun*
1. An amount paid or to be paid for a purchase ▸ charge, expense, price. *See* **cost** (1). **2.** The act of distributing or the condition of being distributed ▸ allocation, apportionment, dispensation. *See* **distribution** (1).

disc *noun*
See **disk.**

discard *verb*
To let go or get rid of as being useless or defective, for example ▸ dispose of, dump, junk, scrap, shed, slough, throw away, throw out, toss. *Informal:* chuck (out), jettison, shuck (off). *Slang:* deep-six, ditch, eighty-six. *See also* **abandon.**

discarnate *adjective*
▸ disembodied, incorporeal, nonphysical. *See* **immaterial** (1).

discern *verb*
1. To perceive and fix the identity of, especially with difficulty ▸ ascertain, descry, detect, distinguish, find out, make out, pick out, recognize, spot. **2.** To perceive with the eyes ▸ catch, detect, perceive. *See* **see** (1). *See synonym note at* **see. 3.** To perceive with a special effort of the senses or the mind ▸ detect, mark. *See* **notice. 4.** To recognize as being different ▸ differentiate, discriminate. *See* **distinguish** (1). **5.** To obtain knowledge or awareness of something not known before ▸ determine, learn, unearth. *See* **discover.**

discernible *adjective*
1. Capable of being seen ▸ perceivable, viewable. *See* **visible** (1). **2.** Capable of being perceived by the senses or the mind ▸ appreciable, palpable, perceivable. *See* **perceptible.** *See synonym note at* **perceptible.**

discerning *adjective*
1. Keenly perceptive or discerning ▸ keen, perceptive, sharp. *See* **critical** (2). **2.** Able to recognize small differences or draw fine distinctions ▸ astute, percipient, selective. *See* **discriminating** (1).

discernment *noun*
1. Skill in perceiving, discriminating, or judging ▸ acumen, astuteness, clear-sightedness, discrimination, eye, insight, intelligence, judgment, keenness, nose, penetration, perception, perceptiveness, percipience, percipiency, perspicacity, sagaciousness, sagacity, sageness, sensitivity, sharpness, shrewdness,

wit. **2.** The act or an instance of distinguishing ▸ demarcation, differentiation. *See* **distinction** (1).

discharge *verb*
1. To relieve a burden ▸ dump, relieve, unburden. *See* **rid. 2.** To begin and carry through to completion ▸ execute, prosecute. *Informal:* pull off. *See* **perform** (1). *See synonym note at* **perform. 3.** To set at liberty ▸ emancipate, release. *See* **free** (1). **4.** To release from military duty ▸ deactivate, demobilize, muster out, release, separate. **5.** To free from an obligation or duty ▸ absolve, exempt. *See* **excuse** (1). **6.** To cause a liquid to flow in a steady stream ▸ empty, flow, issue. *See* **pour** (1). **7.** To end the employment or service of ▸ cashier, terminate. *See* **dismiss** (1). *See synonym note at* **dismiss. 8.** To free from a charge of guilt ▸ acquit, exonerate, vindicate. *See* **clear** (9). **9.** To carry out the functions, requirements, or terms of ▸ discharge, implement, perform. *See* **fulfill** (1). **10.** To set right by giving what is due ▸ clear, satisfy. *See* **settle** (3). **11.** To flow or emit something slowly ▸ exude, leach, seep. *See* **ooze.**

discharge *noun*
1. The act of beginning and carrying through to completion ▸ execution, prosecution. *See* **performance** (1). **2.** The act of dismissing or the condition of being dismissed from employment ▸ expulsion, termination. *See* **dismissal** (1). **3.** A concentrated outpouring, as of missiles, words, or blows ▸ cannonade, fusillade, volley. *See* **barrage. 4.** A violent release of confined energy ▸ burst, explosion. *See* **blast** (2).

disciple *noun*
1. One who supports and adheres to another ▸ adherent, believer, supporter. *See* **follower** (1). **2.** One zealously devoted to a religion ▸ adherent, votary. *See* **devotee** (1).

disciplinary *adjective*
▸ correctional, penal, punitory. *See* **punishing** (1).

discipline *noun*
1. Something, such as loss, pain, or confinement, imposed for wrongdoing ▸ castigation, chastisement, penalty. *See* **punishment. 2.** An area of academic study that is part of a larger body of learning ▸ branch, field, specialty. *See also* **area.**

discipline *verb*
1. To subject one to a penalty for a wrong ▸ chastise, correct, penalize. *See* **punish.** *See synonym note at* **punish. 2.** To impart knowledge and skill to ▸ coach, instruct. *See* **educate** (1). *See synonym note at* **educate.**

disclaim *verb*
▸ deny, disown, renounce. *See* **repudiate** (1).

disclaimer *noun*
▸ abnegation, contradiction, rejection, traversal. *See* **denial** (1).

disclose *verb*
1. To make visible ▸ expose, uncover. *See* **reveal** (2) **2.** To make known ▸ convey, divulge, transmit. *See* **communicate** (1). **3.** To utter publicly ▸ divulge, state, voice. *See* **air** (2).

disclosure *noun*
▸ divulgence, exposé, exposure. *See* **revelation.**
discolor *verb*
▸ bestain, spatter. *See* **stain** (1).
discombobulate *verb*
▸ befuddle, bewilder, confound. *See* **confuse** (1). *See synonym note at* **confuse.**
discombobulation *noun*
▸ bewilderment, perplexity, stupor. *See* **daze.**
discomfit *verb*
▸ chagrin, confound, discomfort. *See* **embarrass** (1). *See synonym note at* **embarrass.**
discomfiture *noun*
▸ chagrin, discomposure. *See* **embarrassment** (1).
discomfort *noun*
1. The state or quality of being inconvenient ▸ incommodiousness, incommodity, inconvenience, trouble. *See also* **bother.** 2. Something that causes difficulty, trouble, or lack of ease ▸ discommodity, incommodity, inconvenience. *See also* **annoyance.** 3. Self-conscious distress ▸ abashment, discomposure. *See* **embarrassment** (1).
discomfort *verb*
1. To cause inconvenience for ▸ incommode, put out, trouble. *See* **inconvenience.** 2. To cause a person to be self-consciously distressed ▸ chagrin, disconcert. *See* **embarrass** (1).
discommode *verb*
▸ impose on, discomfort, trouble. *See* **inconvenience.**
discommodity *noun*
Something that causes difficulty, trouble, or lack of ease ▸ discomfort, incommodity, inconvenience. *See also* **annoyance, bother.**
discompose *verb*
▸ disorient, fluster, ruffle. *See* **agitate** (2).
discomposure *noun*
▸ chagrin, discomfiture. *See* **embarrassment** (1).
disconcert *verb*
1. To cause a person to be self-consciously distressed ▸ chagrin, discomfort. *See* **embarrass** (1). *See synonym note at* **embarrass.** 2. To deprive of courage or the power to act as a result of fear, anxiety, or disgust ▸ consternate, daunt. *See* **dismay** (1). 3. To disturb the health or physiological functioning of ▸ disorder, turn, unsettle. *See* **upset** (1).
disconcertment *noun*
▸ tumult, turmoil. *Informal:* lather. *See* **agitation** (2).
disconnect *verb*
1. To break up the unity of something; separate into parts, sections, or branches ▸ disjoin, dissever, split up. *See* **divide** (1). 2. To remove from association with ▸ disassociate, disengage, withdraw. *See* **detach** (1).
disconnected *adjective*
▸ disinterested, indifferent, uninvolved. *See* **detached** (1).
disconnection *noun*
▸ abstraction, separation, uncoupling. *See* **detachment** (1).

disconsolate *adjective*
▸ dysphoric, gloomy, melancholy, spiritless. *See* **depressed** (1).
discontent *noun*
Unhappiness caused by the failure of one's hopes, desires, or expectations ▸ disillusion, letdown, regret. *See* **disappointment** (1).
discontent *verb*
To cause unhappiness by failing to satisfy the hopes, desires, or expectations of ▸ disgruntle, dissatisfy. *See* **disappoint.**
discontentment *noun*
▸ disillusion, letdown, regret. *See* **disappointment** (1).
discontinuation *or* **discontinuance** *noun*
1. The act of stopping ▸ cessation, halt, surcease. *See* **stop** (1). 2. The condition of being stopped ▸ cessation, standstill. *See* **stop** (2). 3. A cessation of continuity or regularity ▸ disruption, interruption. *See* **break** (1).
discontinue *verb*
1. To prevent the occurrence or continuation of a movement, action, or operation ▸ check, immobilize. *See* **stop** (2). 2. To bring an activity or relationship to an end suddenly ▸ break off, cease, interrupt, suspend, terminate. 3. To come to a cessation ▸ discontinue, halt. *See* **stop** (1). *See synonym note at* **stop.** 4. To cease trying continue ▸ leave off, quit, relinquish, stop. *See* **abandon** (2). 5. To cease consideration or treatment of ▸ give up, skip. *See* **drop** (7).
discontinuity *noun*
▸ disruption, interruption, pause. *See* **break** (1).
discord *noun*
A state of disagreement and disharmony ▸ clash, contention, difference. *See* **conflict** (1). *See synonym note at* **conflict.**
discord *verb*
To fail to be in accord ▸ contrast, differ, disagree. *See* **conflict.**
discordance *noun*
▸ contention, difference, discord. *See* **conflict** (1).
discordant *adjective*
1. Devoid of harmony and accord ▸ conflicting, uncongenial. *See* **inharmonious** (1). 2. Made up of parts or qualities that are disparate or otherwise markedly lacking in consistency ▸ discrepant, inconsistent. *See* **incongruous** (1). 3. Characterized by unpleasant discordance of sound ▸ dissonant, inharmonic. *See* **inharmonious** (2). 4. In sharp opposition ▸ conflicting, inconsistent. *See* **discrepant** (1).
discount *verb*
1. To take away a quantity from another quantity ▸ rebate, subtract. *See* **deduct** (1). 2. To represent or speak of as small or insignificant ▸ deprecate, disparage, slight. *See* **belittle.** 3. To supply money, especially on credit ▸ float, loan. *See* **lend.**
discount *noun*
An amount deducted ▸ abatement, rebate. *See* **deduction** (1).
discountenance *verb*
1. To have or express an unfavorable opinion of

▸ condemn, disfavor, object to. *See* **disapprove** (1).
2. To cause a person to be self-consciously distressed ▸ chagrin, discomfort. *See* **embarrass** (1).

discourage *verb*
1. To make less hopeful or enthusiastic ▸ daunt, demoralize, dishearten, dismay, dispirit, unnerve. *Idiom:* dampen the spirits of. *See also* **disillusion**.
2. To persuade a person not to do something ▸ deter, divert. *See* **dissuade**. *See synonym note at* **dissuade**.
3. To cause unhappiness by failing to satisfy the hopes, desires, or expectations of ▸ disgruntle, dissatisfy. *See* **disappoint**.

✚ CORE SYNONYMS: *discourage, dishearten, dismay, dispirit.* These verbs mean to make less hopeful or enthusiastic: *researchers who were discouraged by the problem's magnitude; apathy that disheartened the instructor; bad weather that dismayed the campers; a failure that dispirited the team.*

◂ ANTONYM: encourage

discouraged *adjective*
1. In low spirits ▸ dejected, dispirited, heavy-hearted. *See* **depressed** (1). **2.** Having lost all hope ▸ dejected, forlorn, hopeless. *See* **despondent**.

discouraging *adjective*
1. Causing or expressing sadness, sorrow, or regret ▸ depressing, melancholy, mournful. *See* **sorrowful** (1). **2.** Offering little encouragement ▸ dim, unpromising. *See* **bleak** (2). **3.** Disturbing because of failure to measure up to a standard or produce the desired results ▸ disheartening, sorry, unsatisfying. *See* **disappointing**.

discourse *noun*
1. A formal discussion of a subject, either written or spoken ▸ dialogue, disquisition, dissertation, essay, expatiation, lecture, monograph, talk, thesis, tract, treatise. *See also* **tirade**. **2.** Spoken exchange ▸ dialogue, discussion, talk. *See* **conversation** (1). **3.** The faculty, act, or product of speaking ▸ talk, utterance. *See* **speech** (1).

discourse *verb*
1. To engage in spoken exchange ▸ chat, talk. *See* **converse**[1]. *See synonym note at* **converse**[1]. **2.** To express at greater length or in greater detail ▸ develop, expand. *See* **elaborate**.

discourser *noun*
▸ interlocutor, talker. *See* **conversationalist**.

discourteous *adjective*
1. Lacking good manners ▸ disrespectful, impolite, uncivil. *See* **rude** (4). **2.** Causing displeasure, anger, or hurt feelings ▸ hurtful, impolite, rude. *See* **offensive** (2). **3.** Having or showing a lack of respect ▸ contemptuous, impertinent, impolite. *See* **disrespectful** (1).

discourtesy *noun*
▸ audacity, boldness, impertinence. *See* **impudence**.

discover *verb*
To obtain knowledge or awareness of something not known before ▸ ascertain, detect, determine, dig (up *or* out), discern, ferret out, find (out), hear, learn,

observe, realize, turn up, unearth. *Idiom:* get wind of. *See also* **discern**.

✚ CORE SYNONYMS: *discover, ascertain, determine, learn.* These verbs mean to gain knowledge or awareness of something not known before, as through observation or study: *discovered a star in a distant galaxy; ascertaining the facts; tried to determine the origins of the problem; learned the sad news from the radio.*

discovery *noun*
Something that has been discovered ▸ ascertainment, find, finding, result, strike. *See also* **deduction, invention, novelty**.

discredit *verb*
1. To cause to be no longer believed or valued ▸ debunk, deflate, explode, puncture. *Informal:* shoot down. *Idioms:* knock holes in, knock the bottom out of, shoot full of holes. **2.** To bring disgrace on ▸ abase, dishonor, shame. *See* **disgrace**. **3.** To give no credence to ▸ doubt, mistrust. *See* **disbelieve** (1).

discredit *noun*
1. Loss of or damage to one's reputation ▸ derision, disrepute, humiliation. *See* **disgrace**. **2.** The refusal or reluctance to believe ▸ incredulity, mistrust, skepticism, unbelief. *See* **disbelief** (1).

discreditable *adjective*
▸ degrading, ignominious, shameful. *See* **disgraceful** (1).

discreet *adjective*
1. Showing sensitivity and skill in dealing with others ▸ diplomatic, sensitive, tactful. *See* **delicate** (2). **2.** Kept within sensible limits ▸ moderate, reasonable, restrained. *See* **conservative** (2).

discrepancy *noun*
1. The condition of being unlike or dissimilar ▸ contrast, disagreement, divergence. *See* **difference** (1). *See synonym note at* **difference**. **2.** A marked lack of correspondence or agreement ▸ disagreement, disparity, incongruity. *See* **gap** (3).

discrepant *adjective*
1. In sharp opposition ▸ conflicting, contradictory, contrary, contrasting, counter, discordant, incompatible, incongruent, incongruous, inconsistent, opposite. *See also* **different, opposite**. **2.** Made up of parts or qualities that are disparate or otherwise markedly lacking in consistency ▸ discordant, inconsistent. *See* **incongruous** (1).

discrete *adjective*
1. Distinguished from others by nature or qualities ▸ separate, several, various. *See* **distinct** (1). *See synonym note at* **distinct**. **2.** Being or related to a distinct entity ▸ particular, singular. *See* **individual** (2).

discretely *adverb*
▸ independently, singly. *See* **separately**.

discreteness *noun*
▸ distinctiveness, particularity. *See* **individuality** (1).

discretion *noun*
1. The exercise of good judgment or common sense in practical matters ▸ circumspection, foresight, fore-

thought. *See* **prudence** (1). *See synonym note at* **prudence**. **2.** Unrestricted freedom to choose ▸ convenience, leisure, pleasure, will. **3.** The act, power, or right of choosing ▸ alternative, decision, option. *See* **choice** (1). **4.** The act or an instance of distinguishing ▸ demarcation, differentiation. *See* **distinction** (1). **5.** The ability to say and do the right thing at the right time ▸ diplomacy, savoir-faire, tactfulness. *See* **tact**.

discretionary *adjective*
1. Based on individual judgment or discretion ▸ judgmental, personal, subjective. *See* **arbitrary** (1). **2.** Not compulsory or automatic ▸ elective, permissible. *See* **optional**.

discriminate *verb*
1. To recognize as being different ▸ differentiate, discern. *See* **distinguish** (1). **2.** To make noticeable or different ▸ differentiate, individualize, singularize. *See* **distinguish** (2).

discriminate *adjective*
Able to recognize small differences or draw fine distinctions ▸ astute, discerning, selective. *See* **discriminating** (1).

discriminating *adjective*
1. Able to recognize small differences or draw fine distinctions ▸ astute, discerning, discriminate, discriminative, discriminatory, percipient, perspicacious, select, selective, subtle. *See also* **critical**. **2.** Keenly perceptive or discerning ▸ keen, perceptive, sharp. *See* **critical** (2).

discrimination *noun*
1. The ability to distinguish, especially to recognize small differences or draw fine distinctions ▸ acuteness, astuteness, percipience, percipiency, perspicacity, refinement, selectiveness, selectivity, subtlety, taste. **2.** The act or an instance of distinguishing ▸ demarcation, differentiation. *See* **distinction** (1). **3.** Skill in perceiving, discriminating, or judging ▸ keenness, perceptiveness, shrewdness. *See* **discernment** (1). **4.** Irrational suspicion or hatred of a particular group, race, or religion ▸ intolerance, racism. *See* **prejudice** (1). **5.** Lack of equality, as of opportunity, treatment, or status ▸ inequality, unfairness, unjustness. *See also* **bias**.

discriminative *adjective*
▸ astute, discerning, selective. *See* **discriminating** (1).

discriminatory *adjective*
1. Able to recognize small differences or draw fine distinctions ▸ astute, discerning, selective. *See* **discriminating** (1). **2.** Not fair, right, or just ▸ dirty, unequal, unjust. *See* **unfair**. **3.** Exhibiting bias ▸ partial, prejudiced, tendentious. *See* **biased** (1).

discursive *adjective*
▸ long-winded, parenthetical, rambling. *See* **digressive**.

discuss *verb*
To speak together and exchange ideas and opinions about ▸ argue, bandy, consider, converse, debate, deliberate, moot, parley, reason, talk over, thrash out (*or* over), thresh out (*or* over), toss around. *Informal:*

hash over, kick around, knock about (*or* around). *Slang:* rap. **Idioms:** go into a huddle, put heads together. *See also* **confer**.

discussion *noun*
1. The exchange of ideas ▸ communion, conference, intercourse. *See* **communication** (1). **2.** Spoken exchange ▸ dialogue, discourse, talk. *See* **conversation** (1). **3.** A meeting for the exchange of views ▸ colloquium, parley, seminar. *See* **conference** (1). **4.** An exchange of views in an attempt to reach a decision ▸ consultation, counsel, parley. *See* **deliberation** (1).

disdain *verb*
To regard with utter contempt ▸ dismiss, scorn. *See* **despise** (1). *See synonym note at* **despise**.

disdain *or* **disdainfulness** *noun*
1. The feeling of despising ▸ contempt, loathing, scorn. *See* **despisal**. **2.** The quality of being arrogant ▸ hauteur, loftiness, superiority. *See* **arrogance**.

disdainful *adjective*
1. Showing scorn and disrespect toward someone or something ▸ contemptuous, dismissive, disrespectful, haughty, intolerant, scornful, slighting, sneering, supercilious, superior. *Idiom:* on one's high horse. *See also* **disparaging**, **direspectful**. **2.** Overly convinced of one's own superiority and importance ▸ haughty, lofty, superior. *See* **arrogant**. *See synonym note at* **arrogant**.

disease *noun*
1. A pathological condition of mind or body ▸ ailment, complaint, disorder, ill, illness, infection, infirmity, malady, pathology, sickness. *See also* **distress**, **infirmity**. **2.** One that contaminates ▸ impurity, poison, pollutant. *See* **contaminant**.

disembark *verb*
To come ashore from a seacraft ▸ alight, debark, land, light.

disembarrass *verb*
▸ discharge, relieve, unburden. *See* **rid**.

disembodied *adjective*
▸ bodiless, incorporeal, nonphysical. *See* **immaterial** (1).

disenchant *verb*
1. To free from false hopes or ideas ▸ disillusion, undeceive. *See* **disabuse**. **2.** To cause unhappiness by failing to satisfy the hopes, desires, or expectations of ▸ disgruntle, dissatisfy. *See* **disappoint**.

disencumber *verb*
▸ discharge, relieve, unburden. *See* **rid**.

disengage *verb*
1. To free from ties or fasteners ▸ loose, release, untie. *See* **undo** (1). **2.** To break or separate into parts ▸ disjoin, dissever, split up. *See* **divide** (1). **3.** To remove from association with ▸ disassociate, disconnect, withdraw. *See* **detach** (1). **4.** To free from an entanglement ▸ free, untangle. *See* **extricate**. *See synonym note at* **extricate**.

disengagement *noun*
▸ disconnection, separation, uncoupling. *See* **detachment** (1).

disentangle *verb*
1. To free from an entanglement ▸ disengage, free, untangle. *See* **extricate**. *See synonym note at* **extricate**. 2. To be disclosed gradually ▸ unfold, unfurl, unravel. *See* **develop** (2).

disfavor *or* **disesteem** *noun*
1. Unfavorable opinion or judgment ▸ condemnation, disesteem, reproof. *See* **disapproval**. 2. Loss of or damage to one's reputation ▸ discredit, disrepute, humiliation. *See* **disgrace**.

disfavor *or* **disesteem** *verb*
To have or express an unfavorable opinion of ▸ condemn, denounce, object to. *See* **disapprove** (1).

disfavorable *adjective*
▸ ignominious, shameful. *See* **disgraceful** (1).

disfigure *verb*
▸ blemish, misshape, twist. *See* **deform**.

disfigurement *noun*
1. A disfiguring abnormality of shape or form ▸ contortion, distortion, malformation. *See* **deformity**. 2. Harm done to property or a person ▸ destruction, impairment, wreckage. *See* **damage** (1).

disgorge *verb*
▸ belch, spew. *See* **erupt** (1).

disgrace *noun*
Loss of honor, respect, or admiration ▸ bad name, bad odor, derision, discredit, disesteem, disfavor, dishonor, disrepute, humiliation, ignominy, ill repute, obloquy, odium, opprobrium, reproach, scorn, shame. *See also* **degradation, reflection, stain**.

disgrace *verb*
To bring disgrace on ▸ abase, besmirch, blot, debase, degrade, discredit, dishonor, humiliate, pillory, shame, stigmatize, sully, tarnish. *Idioms:* be a reproach to, cause to lose face, heap dishonor (*or* ignominy) on, put to shame. *See also* **denigrate, humble, ridicule**.

disgraceful *adjective*
1. Meriting or causing shame or dishonor ▸ degrading, discreditable, disfavorable, dishonorable, disreputable, humiliating, ignominious, opprobrious, reproachable, shameful. 2. Worthy of severe disapproval ▸ condemnable, shameful, unfortunate. *See* **deplorable** (1).

disgracefulness *noun*
▸ disreputableness, ignominiousness. *See* **infamy** (1).

disgruntle *verb*
▸ discontent, dissatisfy. *See* **disappoint**.

disgruntlement *noun*
▸ disillusion, letdown, regret. *See* **disappointment** (1).

disguise *verb*
To change or modify so as to prevent recognition of the true identity or character of ▸ camouflage, cloak, dissemble, dissimulate, mask, masquerade, veil.

disguise *noun*
1. Clothes or other personal effects, such as makeup, worn to conceal one's identity ▸ costume, guise, mask, masquerade, veil. *Informal:* getup. 2. A deceptive outward appearance ▸ guise, mask, pretense. *See*

façade (2). **3.** A display of insincere behavior ▸ dissemblance, masquerade, pretense, show. *See* **act** (2).

✦ CORE SYNONYMS: *disguise, camouflage, veil, dissemble, dissimulate, mask.* These verbs mean to change or modify so as to prevent recognition of the true identity or character of: *disguised her interest with nonchalance; trying to camouflage their impatience; veiled his anxiety with a smile; dissembling ill will with false solicitude; couldn't dissimulate his vanity; ambition that is masked as altruism.*

disguised *adjective*
▸ covert, imperceptible, unseen. *See* **hidden** (1).

disgust *verb*
1. To offend the senses or feelings of ▸ appall, nauseate, repel, repulse, revolt, sicken, turn off. *Slang:* gross out. *Idiom:* turn one's stomach. 2. To be very disagreeable to ▸ displease, repulse, upset. *See* **offend** (2).

disgust *noun*
Extreme aversion caused by something offensive ▸ abhorrence, loathing, nausea, queasiness, repugnance, revulsion. *See also* **hate**.

✦ CORE SYNONYMS: *disgust, nauseate, repel, revolt, sicken.* These verbs mean to offend the senses or feelings of: *a stench that disgusted us; hypocrisy that nauseated me; repelled by your arrogance; brutality that revolts my sensibilities; a fetid odor that sickened the workers.*

disgusted *adjective*
Out of patience ▸ fed up, sick, tired, weary. *Idiom:* sick and tired. *See also* **angry**.

disgusting *adjective*
1. So unpleasant or objectionable as to cause scorn or disgust ▸ contemptible, despicable, obnoxious. *See* **offensive** (1). 2. So unpleasant in flavor as to be inedible ▸ foul-tasting, unappetizing, uneatable. *See* **unpalatable** (1).

disharmonious *adjective*
▸ discordant, dissonant, inharmonic. *See* **inharmonious** (2).

disharmony *noun*
▸ contention, difference, discord. *See* **conflict** (1).

dishearten *verb*
1. To make less hopeful or enthusiastic ▸ dismay, dispirit. *See* **discourage** (1). *See synonym note at* **discourage**. 2. To deprive of courage or the power to act as a result of fear, anxiety, or disgust ▸ consternate, disconcert. *See* **dismay** (1). *See synonym note at* **dismay**. 3. To make sad or gloomy ▸ deject, dispirit, sadden. *See* **depress** (1). 4. To cause unhappiness by failing to satisfy the hopes, desires, or expectations of ▸ disgruntle, dissatisfy. *See* **disappoint**.

disheartening *adjective*
1. Causing or expressing sadness, sorrow, or regret ▸ depressing, dispiriting, mournful. *See* **sorrowful** (1). 2. Disturbing because of failure to measure up to a standard or produce the desired results ▸ discouraging, sorry, unsatisfying. *See* **disappointing**.

disheartenment *noun*
▶ dejection, doldrums, melancholy. *See* **depression** (2).

dishevel *verb*
▶ disarrange, disorder, muss (up). *See* **tousle**.

disheveled *adjective*
▶ mussy, sloppy, slovenly. *See* **messy** (1).

dishonest *adjective*
1. Given to or marked by deliberate concealment or misrepresentation of the truth ▶ ambidextrous, deceitful, deceiving, deceptive, disingenuous, double-dealing, double-faced, duplicitous, false-hearted, insincere, lying, mendacious, perfidious, two-faced, untrustworthy, untruthful. *Informal:* crooked. *See also* **hypocritical, underhand. 2.** Open to bribery or dishonesty ▶ mercenary, venal. *Informal:* crooked. *See* **corrupt** (2).

✦ CORE SYNONYMS: *dishonest, lying, untruthful, deceitful, mendacious.* These adjectives mean deliberately concealing or misrepresenting the truth. *Dishonest* is the least specific: *a dishonest business executive. Lying* conveys a blunt accusation of untruth: *a lying witness giving inconsistent testimony. Untruthful* is a softer term and suggests lack of veracity and divergence from fact: *made an untruthful statement. Deceitful* implies misleading by falsehood or by concealment of the truth: *deceitful advertising. Mendacious* is more formal than *lying* and suggests a chronic inclination toward untruth: *a mendacious and troublesome employee.*

---

dishonesty *noun*
1. Lack of integrity ▶ deceitfulness, duplicitousness, duplicity, improbity, inveracity, mendacity, untrustworthiness. *Informal:* crookedness. **2.** Lack of straightforwardness and honesty in action ▶ chicanery, craft, craftiness, deviousness, indirection, shadiness, shiftiness, slyness, sneakiness, trickery, trickiness, underhandedness, wiliness. *Informal:* crookedness. *See also* **deceit, hypocrisy, trick. 3.** Departure from what is legally, ethically, and morally correct ▶ baseness, improbity. *Informal:* crookedness. *See* **corruption** (2).

dishonor *noun*
1. Loss of or damage to one's reputation ▶ discredit, disrepute, humiliation. *See* **disgrace. 2.** A lowering in or deprivation of character or self-esteem ▶ degeneration, humiliation, mortification. *See* **degradation** (1). **3.** Lack of proper respect ▶ impoliteness, irreverence, rudeness. *See* **disrespect** (1).

dishonor *verb*
To bring disgrace on ▶ abase, blot, shame. *See* **disgrace**.

dishonorable *adjective*
1. Meriting or causing shame or dishonor ▶ discreditable, ignominious, shameful. *See* **disgraceful** (1). **2.** Open to bribery or dishonesty ▶ venal. *Informal:* crooked. *See* **corrupt** (2).

dishonorableness *noun*
▶ disreputableness, ignominiousness. *See* **infamy** (1).

disillusion *verb*
1. To free from false hopes or ideas ▶ disenchant, undeceive. *See* **disabuse. 2.** To cause unhappiness by failing to satisfy the hopes, desires, or expectations of ▶ disgruntle, dissatisfy. *See* **disappoint**.

disillusion *noun*
Unhappiness caused by the failure of one's hopes, desires, or expectations ▶ discontent, letdown, regret. *See* **disappointment** (1).

disinclination *noun*
1. An attitude or feeling of distaste or mild aversion ▶ dislike, disrelish, distaste, mislike. *See also* **disapproval, disgust, enmity, hate. 2.** The state of not being disposed or inclined ▶ aversion, opposition, reluctance. *See* **indisposition** (1).

disincline *verb*
▶ deter, discourage, divert. *See* **dissuade**.

disinclined *adjective*
▶ against, reluctant. *See* **indisposed** (1).

disinfect *verb*
To render free of microorganisms ▶ decontaminate, irradiate, sanitize, sterilize.

disinfectant *noun*
▶ antiseptic, cathartic, cleaner. *See* **purifier**.

disinfection *noun*
▶ clarity, cleanliness, immaculacy. *See* **purity** (1).

disinformation *noun*
▶ brainwashing, evangelism. *See* **propaganda**.

disingenuous *adjective*
1. Given to or marked by deliberate concealment or misrepresentation of the truth ▶ deceitful, duplicitous, mendacious. *See* **dishonest** (1). *See synonym note at* **dishonest. 2.** Marked by treachery or deceit ▶ duplicitous, shifty, sneaky. *See* **underhand**.

disingenuousness *noun*
1. Lack of sincerity ▶ artificiality, phoniness. *See* **insincerity. 2.** Deceitful cleverness ▶ artfulness, slyness. *See* **art** (1).

disintegrate *verb*
1. To reduce or become reduced to pieces or fragments ▶ atomize, break apart (down *or* up), crumble, decompose, dissolve, fragment, fragmentize. *Idioms:* fall apart (*or* to pieces), turn to dust (*or* ashes). *See also* **break, destroy, divide. 2.** To become or cause to become rotten or unsound ▶ deteriorate, spoil, turn. *See* **decay.** *See synonym note at* **decay**.

disintegration *noun*
▶ decomposition, deterioration, rot. *See* **decay**.

disinter *verb*
▶ dig (up *or* out), turn up. *See* **uncover** (1).

disinterest *noun*
1. The quality or state of being just and unbiased ▶ detachment, justice, objectivity. *See* **fairness. 2.** Lack of emotion or interest ▶ detachment, indifference, unconcern. *See* **apathy. 3.** Dissociation from one's surroundings or worldly affairs ▶ distance, indifference, remoteness. *See* **detachment** (2).

disinterested *adjective*
1. Free from bias in judgment ▶ dispassionate, impar-

tial, indifferent. *See* **fair**[1] (1). **2.** Feeling or showing no strong emotional involvement ▸ detached, dispassionate, impersonal, indifferent, neutral. **3.** Lacking interest in one's surroundings or worldly affairs ▸ aloof, indifferent, uninvolved. *See* **detached** (1). **4.** Lacking interest ▸ indifferent, listless, uninterested. *See* **apathetic.**

disinterestedness *noun*
▸ impartiality, justice, nonpartisanship. *See* **fairness.**

disinvolve *verb*
▸ disengage, free, untangle. *See* **extricate.**

disjoin *or* **disjoint** *verb*
▸ disconnect, dissever, split up. *See* **divide** (1).

disjunction *or* **disjuncture** *noun*
▸ detachment, divorce, parting. *See* **division** (1).

disk *or* **disc** *noun*
▸ band, ring, wheel. *See* **circle** (1).

dislike *verb*
1. To regard with distaste or mild aversion ▸ disrelish, mislike. *Idioms:* be averse to, be cool toward, have an aversion to (*or* distaste for), have no use for, not be crazy (*or* nuts *or* wild) about, not care for. *See also* **despise, hate. 2.** To have or express an unfavorable opinion of ▸ condemn, disfavor, object to. *See* **disapprove** (1).

dislike *noun*
1. An attitude or feeling of distaste or mild aversion ▸ disinclination, disrelish, distaste, mislike. *See also* **disapproval, disgust, enmity, hate. 2.** The feeling of despising ▸ disdain, loathing, scorn. *See* **despisal.**

dislocate *verb*
1. To alter the settled state or position of ▸ displace, disrupt. *See* **disturb** (1). **2.** To displace a bone from a socket or joint ▸ separate, throw out. *See* **slip** (7).

dislocation *noun*
▸ dislodging, movement, shift. *See* **displacement.**

disloyal *adjective*
▸ false, traitorous, treacherous. *See* **faithless** (1). *See synonym note at* **faithless.**

disloyalty *noun*
▸ infidelity, perfidy, treachery. *See* **faithlessness** (1).

dismal *adjective*
1. Causing or expressing sorrow or sadness ▸ depressing, melancholy, mournful. *See* **sorrowful** (1). **2.** Dark and depressing ▸ bleak, dismal, somber. *See* **gloomy** (1). **3.** Offering little encouragement ▸ dark, dim, pessimistic. *See* **bleak** (2).

dismantle *verb*
1. To take something apart ▸ break down, disassemble, dismount, take down. **2.** To pull down or break up so that reconstruction is impossible ▸ demolish, level, tear down. *See* **destroy** (2).

dismay *verb*
1. To deprive of courage or the power to act as a result of fear, anxiety, or disgust ▸ alarm, appall, consternate, daunt, disconcert, dishearten, dispirit, shake, shock, unnerve. *See also* **distress, frighten. 2.** To make less hopeful or enthusiastic ▸ daunt, dispirit. *See* **discourage** (1). *See synonym note at* **discourage.**

dismay *noun*
1. A feeling of agitation in the face of trouble or danger ▸ apprehension, consternation, trepidation. *See* **fear.** *See synonym note at* **fear. 2.** Utter lack of hope ▸ desperation, despondence, hopelessness. *See* **despair.**

✦ CORE SYNONYMS: *dismay, appall, daunt, dishearten, shake.* These verbs mean to deprive a person of courage or the power to act as a result of fear or anxiety. *Dismay* is the least specific: *Plummeting stock prices dismayed speculators.* *Appall* implies a sense of helplessness caused by an awareness of the enormity of something: *"for as this appalling ocean surrounds the verdant land"* (Herman Melville). *Daunt* suggests an abatement of courage: *"captains courageous, whom death could not daunt"* (Anonymous ballad). *Dishearten* implies a loss of hope or enthusiasm: *The employees were disheartened by the news of the upcoming layoffs.* To *shake* is to dismay profoundly: *"A little swift brutality shook him to the very soul"* (John Galsworthy).

dismayed *adjective*
▸ dysphoric, gloomy, melancholy, spiritless. *See* **depressed** (1).

dismaying *adjective*
▸ dreadful, unnerving, terrible. *See* **fearful** (1).

dismember *verb*
▸ amputate, mutilate. *See* **cripple** (1).

dismiss *verb*
1. To end the employment or service of ▸ cashier, discharge, drop, lay off, let go, release, terminate. *Informal:* ax, fire, pink-slip. *Slang:* boot, bounce, can, sack. *Idioms:* give someone his or her walking papers, give someone the ax (*or* gate *or* pink slip), let go, show someone the door. **2.** To direct or allow to leave ▸ banish, cast out, dispatch, drive out, excuse, expel, release, run out, send away. *Idioms:* send about one's business, send packing, show someone the door. **3.** To rid one's mind of ▸ banish, cast out, dispel, reject, repudiate, shut out. **4.** To put out by force ▸ bump, evict. *See* **eject** (1). *See synonym note at* **eject. 5.** To cease consideration or treatment of ▸ give up, skip. *See* **drop** (7). **6.** To be unwilling to accept, consider, or receive ▸ refuse, reject, spurn. *See* **decline** (1). **7.** To regard with utter contempt and disdain ▸ disdain, scorn. *See* **despise** (1). **8.** To refuse to admit the truth, reality, value, or worth of ▸ contravene, disaffirm, disavow. *See* **deny** (1).

✦ CORE SYNONYMS: *dismiss, boot, bounce, can, cashier, discharge, drop, fire, sack.* These verbs mean to end the employment or service of: *was dismissed for insubordination; was booted for being late; afraid of being bounced for union activities; wasn't canned because his uncle owns the business; will be cashiered from the army; resort workers discharged at the end of the season; was dropped for incompetence; was fired unjustly; a reporter sacked for revealing a confidential source.*

dismissal *noun*
1. The act of dismissing or the condition of being dismissed from employment ▸ discharge, expulsion, removal, termination. *Informal:* ax, pink slip. *Slang:* boot, bounce, sack. 2. The act of ejecting or the state of being ejected ▸ eviction, expulsion. *See* **ejection.**

dismissive *adjective*
1. Showing scorn and disrespect toward someone or something ▸ contemptuous, haughty, scornful. *See* **disdainful** (1). 2. Tending or intending to belittle ▸ deprecatory, pejorative. *See* **disparaging.**

dismount *verb*
To take something apart ▸ break down, disassemble, dismantle, take down.

disobedience *noun*
The act or an instance of defying ▸ challenge, rebellion. *See* **defiance** (1).

disobedient *adjective*
1. Refusing or failing to obey ▸ bad, ill-behaved, insubordinate, naughty, noncompliant, ungovernable, unmanageable. 2. Marked by defiance ▸ contumacious, rebellious. *See* **defiant.**

disobey *verb*
To refuse or fail to obey ▸ break, defy, disregard, flout, oppose, rebel, resist, transgress, violate. *Idiom:* pay no attention to. *See also* **defy.**

disorder *noun*
1. A lack of order or regular arrangement ▸ chaos, clutter, confusedness, confusion, derangement, disarrangement, disarray, disorderedness, disorderliness, disorganization, imbroglio, jumble, mess, mix-up, muddle, muss, scramble, shambles, topsy-turviness, tumble. *Slang:* snafu. 2. A lack of civil order or peace ▸ anarchy, brouhaha, chaos, commotion, confusion, disturbance, fracas, lawlessness, melee, misrule, mob rule, riot, ruckus, tumult, turmoil, unrest, uproar. 3. A condition of being agitated or disturbed ▸ commotion, disturbance, stir. *See* **agitation** (1). 4. A pathological condition of mind or body ▸ ailment, complaint, malady. *See* **disease** (1).

disorder *verb*
1. To put out of proper order ▸ clutter, derange, disarrange, disarray, disorganize, disrupt, disturb, jumble, mess up, mix up, muddle, scatter, tumble, unsettle, upset. 2. To put into total disorder ▸ garble, jumble, scramble. *See* **confuse** (4). 3. To put something into a state of disarray, such as the hair or clothes ▸ dishevel, mess (up), muss (up). *See* **tousle.** 4. To disturb the health or physiological functioning of ▸ derange, turn, unsettle. *See* **upset** (1). 5. To alter the settled state or position of ▸ displace, disrupt. *See* **disturb** (1).

disordered *adjective*
1. Characterized by physical confusion ▸ chaotic, topsy-turvy, upside-down. *See* **confused** (2). 2. Afflicted with or exhibiting irrationality and mental unsoundness ▸ crazy, off, unbalanced. *See* **insane** (1).

disorderedness *noun*
▸ clutter, confusion, disarray. *See* **disorder** (1).

disordering *noun*
▸ disruption, overthrow, upheaval. *See* **upset** (1).

disorderliness *noun*
1. The state of being messy or unkempt ▸ chaos, disorganization, messiness, sloppiness, slovenliness, topsy-turviness, untidiness. 2. A lack of order or regular arrangement ▸ clutter, confusion, disarray. *See* **disorder** (1). 3. The quality or condition of being unruly ▸ intractability, obstinacy, recalcitrance, unmanageability. *See* **unruliness.**

disorderly *adjective*
1. Upsetting civil order or peace ▸ disruptive, lawless, obstreperous, riotous, rowdy, turbulent. 2. Characterized by physical confusion ▸ disordered, topsy-turvy, upside-down. *See* **confused** (2). 3. Not submitting to discipline or control ▸ ill-behaved, obstinate, unmanageable. *See* **unruly.**

disorganization *noun*
1. A lack of order or regular arrangement ▸ clutter, confusion, disarray. *See* **disorder** (1). 2. The act or an example of upsetting ▸ disruption, overthrow, upheaval. *See* **upset** (1). 3. The state of being messy or unkempt ▸ sloppiness, untidiness. *See* **disorderliness** (1).

disorganize *verb*
1. To put out of proper order ▸ disarrange, disrupt, muddle. *See* **disorder** (1). 2. To put something into a state of disarray, such as the hair or clothes ▸ dishevel, disorder, muss (up). *See* **tousle.**

disorient *verb*
1. To impair or destroy the composure of ▸ bewilder, fluster, ruffle. *See* **agitate** (2). 2. To cause to be unclear in mind or intent ▸ befuddle, bewilder, confound. *See* **confuse** (1).

disorientation *noun*
▸ bewilderment, perplexity, stupor. *See* **daze.**

disoriented *adjective*
1. Unable to find the correct way or place to go ▸ adrift, stray. *See* **lost** (1). 2. Mentally uncertain ▸ confounded, perplexed, turbid. *Informal:* mixed-up. *See* **confused** (1).

disown *verb*
▸ deny, disclaim, renounce. *See* **repudiate** (1).

disparage *verb*
▸ denigrate, deprecate, slight. *See* **belittle.** *See synonym note at* **belittle.**

disparagement *noun*
▸ deprecation, derogation. *See* **belittlement.**

disparaging *adjective*
Tending or intending to belittle ▸ belittling, deprecative, deprecatory, depreciative, depreciatory, derisive, derogative, derogatory, detractive, dismissive, low, mocking, pejorative, slighting, uncomplimentary. *See also* **disdainful, sarcastic.**

disparate *adjective*
1. Not like another in nature, quality, amount, or form ▸ contrasting, divergent, variant. *See* **different** (1). 2. Consisting of a number of different kinds ▸ diverse, miscellaneous, sundry. *See* **various** (1).

disparity *noun*
1. The condition of being unlike or dissimilar ▶ contrast, discrepancy, divergence. *See* **difference** (1). **2.** The condition or fact of being unequal, as in age, rank, or degree ▶ disproportion, incongruity. *See* **inequality** (1). **3.** A marked lack of correspondence or agreement ▶ disagreement, disparity, incongruity. *See* **gap** (3).

dispassion *noun*
▶ disinterest, justice, nonpartisanship, objectivity. *See* **fairness.**

dispassionate *adjective*
1. Lacking feeling or emotion ▶ emotionless, impassive, stolid. *See* **cold** (2). **2.** Free from bias in judgment ▶ disinterested, impartial, indifferent, nonpartisan. *See* **fair¹** (1). *See synonym note at* **fair¹.**

dispassionately *adverb*
▶ equitably, evenhandedly, impartially, squarely. *See* **fairly** (1).

dispassionateness *noun*
▶ disinterestedness, impartialness, justice, objectivity. *See* **fairness.**

dispatch *verb*
1. To cause something to be conveyed to a destination ▶ consign, forward. *See* **send** (1). *See synonym note at* **send.** **2.** To engulf completely ▶ devour, ravage, waste. *See* **consume** (1). **3.** To cause the death of ▶ cut down, destroy, finish (off). *See* **kill¹** (1). **4.** To direct or allow to leave ▶ cast out, expel. *See* **dismiss** (2).

dispatch *noun*
1. Rapidity of movement or activity ▶ expeditiousness, hurry, quickness. *See* **haste** (1). *See synonym note at* **haste.** **2.** A detail of news or information ▶ bulletin, flash. *See* **item** (1). **3.** A written communication directed to another ▶ correspondence, missive, note. *See* **letter** (1).

dispel *verb*
1. To rid one's mind of ▶ cast out, reject. *See* **dismiss** (3). **2.** To cause to separate and go in various directions ▶ disperse, dissipate, scatter. *See synonym note at* **scatter.** *See also* **divide, separate.**

dispensable *adjective*
▶ inessential, needless, unneeded. *See* **unnecessary.**

dispensation *noun*
▶ allocation, apportionment, division. *See* **distribution** (1).

dispense *verb*
1. To give out in portions or shares ▶ allocate, deal (out), dole out. *See* **distribute** (1). *See synonym note at* **distribute.** **2.** To provide as a remedy ▶ give, medicate, treat. *See* **administer** (3). **3.** To oversee the provision or execution of ▶ carry out, execute. *See* **administer** (2). **4.** To free from an obligation or duty ▶ discharge, exempt. *See* **excuse** (1).

dispersal *noun*
▶ circulation, diffusion, scattering. *See* **distribution** (2).

disperse *verb*
1. To cause to separate and go in various directions

▶ dispel, dissipate, scatter. *See synonym note at* **scatter.** *See also* **divide, separate.** **2.** To extend over a wide area ▶ disseminate, scatter. *See* **spread** (2). **3.** To move apart and go in various directions ▶ disband, separate. *See* **scatter** (2). **4.** To disappear by or as if by rising ▶ dissipate, scatter, thin out. *See* **lift** (4).

dispersion *noun*
▶ circulation, dissemination, scattering. *See* **distribution** (2).

dispirit *verb*
1. To make less hopeful or enthusiastic ▶ dismay, unnerve. *See* **discourage** (1). *See synonym note at* **discourage.** **2.** To make sad or gloomy ▶ deject, dishearten, sadden. *See* **depress** (1). **3.** To deprive of courage or the power to act as a result of fear, anxiety, or disgust ▶ consternate, disconcert. *See* **dismay** (1). **4.** To cause unhappiness by failing to satisfy the hopes, desires, or expectations of ▶ disgruntle, dissatisfy. *See* **disappoint.**

dispirited *adjective*
▶ dysphoric, gloomy, spiritless. *See* **depressed** (1). *See synonym note at* **depressed.**

dispiriting *adjective*
Causing or expressing sorrow or sadness ▶ depressing, melancholy, mournful. *See* **sorrowful** (1).

displace *verb*
1. To substitute for or fill the place of ▶ replace, supersede, supplant, surrogate. *Idioms:* fill someone's shoes, take over from, take the reins from. *See also* **substitute.** **2.** To take the place of another against the other's will ▶ cut out, supplant, usurp. *See also* **assume, occupy, seize.** **3.** To alter the settled state or position of ▶ dislocate, disrupt. *See* **disturb** (1).

displacement *noun*
A change in normal place or position ▶ dislocation, dislodging, disturbance, move, movement, rearrangement, relocation, shift. *See also* **removal, upset.**

display *verb*
1. To make a public and usually ostentatious show of ▶ brandish, disport, exhibit, expose, flash, flaunt, parade, promenade, show (off), showcase, sport, strut, wear. **2.** To make visible ▶ disclose, expose, uncover. *See* **reveal** (2). **3.** To make manifest or apparent ▶ demonstrate, reveal. *See* **show** (1). **4.** To have as a visible characteristic ▶ exhibit, possess. *See* **bear** (3). **5.** To give expression to, as by gestures, facial aspects, or bodily posture ▶ convey, manifest. *See* **express** (3).

display *noun*
1. An act of showing or displaying ▶ demonstration, exhibit, exhibition, exposition, manifestation, presentation, show. **2.** An impressive or ostentatious exhibition ▶ show, spectacle. *See* **array** (1). *See synonym note at* **array.**

✦ CORE SYNONYMS: *display, expose, parade, flaunt.* These verbs mean to make a public and usually ostentasious show of something or someone. *Display* suggests holding up something for view in a vulgar or boorish way: *He displayed his new sports car in the driveway for all of the neighbors to see. Expose* can imply revelation of something better left concealed: *Your comment exposes your insecurity.* *Parade* usually suggests a pretentious or boastful presentation: *"He early discovered that, by parading his unhappiness before the multitude, he produced an immense sensation"* (Thomas Macaulay). *Flaunt* implies an unabashed, prideful, often arrogant display: *"Every great hostelry flaunted the flag of some foreign potentate"* (John Dos Passos).

---

displease *verb*
1. To cause anger, resentment, or hurt feelings ▸ annoy, injure, upset. *See* **offend** (1). 2. To be very disagreeable to ▸ disgust, repulse, upset. *See* **offend** (2).

displeasing *adjective*
1. Not pleasant or agreeable ▸ disagreeable, uncongenial, unsympathetic. *See* **unpleasant** (1). 2. Causing displeasure, anger, or hurt feelings ▸ hurtful, impolite, rude. *See* **offensive** (2).

displeasure *noun*
1. Unfavorable opinion or judgment ▸ condemnation, disfavor, reproof. *See* **disapproval.** 2. Extreme displeasure caused by an insult ▸ resentment, ruffled feathers, umbrage. *See* **offense** (1).

disport *verb*
1. To occupy oneself with amusement or diversion ▸ frolic, recreate. *Informal:* horse around. *See* **play** (1). 2. To make a public and usually ostentatious show of ▸ exhibit, expose, flaunt. *See* **display** (1).

disport *noun*
Something that amuses, entertains, or pleases ▸ diversion, fun, play. *See* **amusement.**

disposal *noun*
1. The act of getting rid of something useless or used up ▸ discarding, dispatching, disposition, dumping, elimination, jettison, junking, removal, riddance, scrapping, unloading. 2. The act or condition of being arranged ▸ allotment, classification, positioning. *See* **arrangement** (1).

dispose *verb*
1. To put into a deliberate order ▸ deploy, organize. *See* **arrange** (1). 2. To have an impact on in a certain way ▸ incline, predispose, sway. *See* **influence** (1).

dispose of *verb*
1. To let go or get rid of as being useless or defective, for example ▸ dump, throw away. *Informal:* chuck. *See* **discard.** 2. To get rid of by selling ▸ close out, dump, sell off, unload. 3. To put into correct or conclusive form ▸ conclude, fix. *See* **settle** (1).

disposed *adjective*
▸ apt, prone. *See* **inclined** (1).

disposition *noun*
1. A person's customary manner of emotional response ▸ bent, complexion, habit, humor, nature, temper, temperament. *See also* **mood.** 2. The combination of qualities that distinguishes an individual ▸ makeup, nature, personality. *See* **character** (1). *See synonym note at* **character.** 3. A natural or habitual preference for something ▸ leaning, penchant. *See* **inclination** (1). 4. The act or condition of being

arranged ▸ allotment, classification, positioning. *See* **arrangement** (1).

dispossess *verb*
▸ deny, divest, withhold. *See* **deprive.**

dispossession *noun*
▸ destitution, hardship, loss. *See* **deprivation** (1).

disproportion *or* **disproportionateness** *noun*
▸ disparity, imbalance, incongruity. *See* **inequality** (1).

disproportionately *adverb*
▸ excessively, extremely, overly. *See* **unduly.**

disprove *verb*
▸ belie, discredit, rebut. *See* **refute.**

disputable *adjective*
▸ arguable, doubtful, questionable. *See* **debatable.**

disputatious *adjective*
▸ contentious, litigious, quarrelsome. *See* **argumentative.** *See synonym note at* **argumentative.**

dispute *verb*
1. To put forth reasons for or against something, often excitedly ▸ debate, plead. *See* **argue** (2). 2. To engage in a quarrel ▸ fight, quarrel. *See* **argue** (1). 3. To take a stand against ▸ challenge, oppose, resist. *See* **contest** (1). 4. To refuse to admit the truth, reality, value, or worth of ▸ contravene, disaffirm, disavow. *See* **deny** (1).

dispute *noun*
1. A discussion, often heated, in which a difference of opinion is expressed ▸ contention, fight, quarrel. *See* **argument** (1). *See synonym note at* **argument.** 2. An expression of opposition ▸ exception, grievance, protestation. *See* **objection.**

disqualify *verb*
To make incapable, as of doing a job ▸ disable, unfit.

disquiet *verb*
To impair or destroy the composure of ▸ disorient, fluster, ruffle. *See* **agitate** (2).

disquiet *noun*
1. A troubled or anxious state of mind ▸ concern, distress, unease. *See* **anxiety** (1). 2. An uneasy or nervous state ▸ disquietude, uneasiness, unrest. *See* **restlessness.**

disquieting *adjective*
▸ bothersome, irritating, unsettling, vexing. *See* **disturbing.**

disquietude *noun*
1. A troubled or anxious state of mind ▸ concern, distress, unease. *See* **anxiety** (1). 2. An uneasy or nervous state ▸ edginess, uneasiness, unrest. *See* **restlessness.**

disquisition *noun*
▸ dialogue, dissertation. *See* **discourse** (1).

disregard *verb*
1. To fail to care for or give proper attention to ▸ ignore, slight. *See* **neglect** (1). 2. To fail to do or carry out ▸ ignore, let slip, overlook. *See* **neglect** (3). 3. To slight someone deliberately ▸ rebuff, spurn. *See* **snub.** 4. To pretend not to see ▸ connive at, ignore. *See* **blink at.** 5. To refuse or fail to obey ▸ defy, transgress. *See* **disobey.**

disregard *noun*
1. An act or instance of neglecting ▸ negligence, oversight. *See* **neglect** (1). 2. A lack of consideration for others' feelings ▸ inconsiderateness, unthoughtfulness. *See* **thoughtlessness** (2). 3. The act or instance of defying ▸ disobedience, noncompliance, rebellion. *See* **defiance** (1).

disregardful *adjective*
▸ inconsiderate, unthinking. *See* **thoughtless** (1).

disrelish *verb*
To regard with distaste ▸ dislike, mislike. *Idioms:* be averse to, be cool toward, have an aversion to (*or* distaste for), have no use for, not be crazy (*or* nuts *or* wild) about, not care for. *See also* **despise, disapprove, hate.**

disrelish *noun*
An attitude or feeling of distaste or mild aversion ▸ disinclination, dislike, distaste, mislike. *See also* **disapproval, disgust, enmity, hate.**

disremember *verb*
Informal To fail to remember ▸ forget. *Idioms:* draw a blank, go blank, have a senior moment, have no recollection (*or* memory).

disreputable *adjective*
▸ discreditable, ignominious, shameful. *See* **disgraceful** (1).

disreputability *or* **disreputableness** *noun*
▸ disgracefulness, ignominiousness. *See* **infamy** (1).

disrepute *noun*
▸ discredit, dishonor, humiliation. *See* **disgrace.**

disrespect *noun*
1. Lack of proper respect ▸ affront, dishonor, impoliteness, irreverence, lese majesty, rudeness. *See also* **despisal, thoughtlessness.** 2. The state or quality of being impudent or arrogantly self-confident ▸ audacity, boldness, impertinence. *See* **impudence.**

disrespectful *adjective*
1. Having or showing a lack of respect ▸ cheeky, contemptuous, discourteous, ill-bred, impertinent, impolite, impudent, insolent, insulting, irreverent, rude, sassy, scornful, unmannered, unmannerly. 2. Lacking good manners ▸ ill-bred, impolite, uncivil. *See* **rude** (4). 3. Showing scorn and disrespect toward someone or something ▸ dismissive, haughty, scornful. *See* **disdainful** (1).

disrobe *verb*
1. To remove all the clothing from ▸ strip, unclothe, undress. 2. To make bare ▸ denude, strip, unclothe. *See* **bare** (1).

disrupt *verb*
1. To break up the order or progress of ▸ disturb, interfere, interrupt, intrude, mess up, muddle, obstruct, upset. 2. To put out of proper order ▸ disarrange, jumble, muddle. *See* **disorder** (1). 3. To alter the settled state or position of ▸ displace, upset. *See* **disturb** (1).

disruption *noun*
1. The act or an example of upsetting ▸ disordering, overthrow, upheaval. *See* **upset** (1). 2. A cessation of continuity or regularity ▸ discontinuation, interruption, suspension. *See* **break** (1).

disruptive *adjective*
1. Troubling to the mind or emotions ▸ bothersome, intrusive, nettlesome. *See* **disturbing.** 2. Upsetting civil order or peace ▸ riotous, unruly. *See* **disorderly** (1).

dissatisfaction *noun*
1. Unhappiness caused by the failure of one's hopes or expectations ▸ disillusion, letdown, regret. *See* **disappointment** (1). 2. Unfavorable opinion or judgment ▸ condemnation, disfavor, reproof. *See* **disapproval.**

dissatisfactory *adjective*
▸ inferior, poor, second-rate. *See* **bad** (1).

dissatisfy *verb*
▸ disgruntle, fail. *See* **disappoint.**

dissect *verb*
▸ break down, reduce, resolve. *See* **analyze** (1). *See synonym note at* **analyze.**

dissection *noun*
▸ analysis, breakdown, subdivision. *See* **analysis** (1).

dissemblance *noun*
▸ disguise, masquerade, pretense. *See* **act** (2).

dissemble *verb*
1. To change or modify so as to prevent recognition of the true identity or character of ▸ camouflage, mask, veil. *See* **disguise.** *See synonym note at* **disguise.** 2. To take on as a false appearance ▸ fake, feign, simulate. *See* **act** (2).

disseminate *verb*
▸ disperse, distribute, scatter. *See* **spread** (2).

dissemination *noun*
▸ circulation, dispersion, scattering. *See* **distribution** (2).

dissension *noun*
1. A state of disagreement and disharmony ▸ contention, difference, discord. *See* **conflict** (1). *See synonym note at* **conflict.** 2. The condition of being divided, as in opinion ▸ dissent, disunity. *See* **division** (2).

dissent *verb*
To fail to be in accord ▸ contrast, disagree, discord. *See* **conflict.**

dissent *noun*
1. A state of disagreement and disharmony ▸ contention, difference, discord. *See* **conflict** (1). 2. The condition of being divided, as in opinion ▸ dissent, schism. *See* **division** (2).

dissenter *noun*
1. A person who dissents from the doctrine of an established church ▸ dissident, sectarian. *See* **separatist.** 2. One that opposes the purposes of another ▸ antagonist, foe, nemesis. *See* **opponent** (1). 3. Someone with unconventional opinions or approaches ▸ free-thinker, independent, maverick. *See* **rebel** (2).

dissentience *noun*
▸ contention, difference, discord. *See* **conflict** (1).

dissertation *noun*
1. A thorough, written presentation of an original

point of view ▸ thesis. **2.** A formal discussion of a subject, either written or spoken ▸ dialogue, talk. *See* **discourse** (1).

disserve *verb*
▸ flaw, impair. *See* **damage.**

disservice *noun*
▸ crime, inequity, wrong. *See* **injustice** (1).

dissever *verb*
1. To separate into parts with or as if with a sharp-edged instrument ▸ cleave, sever. *See* **cut** (2). **2.** To break or separate into parts or sections ▸ disjoin, section, split up. *See* **divide** (1).

disseverance *or* **disseverment** *noun*
▸ disjunction, divorce, parting. *See* **division** (1).

dissidence *noun*
▸ contention, difference, discord. *See* **conflict** (1).

dissident *noun*
A person who dissents from the doctrine of an established church ▸ dissenter, sectarian. *See* **separatist.**

dissident *adjective*
Devoid of harmony and accord ▸ conflicting, uncongenial. *See* **inharmonious** (1).

dissimilar *adjective*
▸ contrasting, divergent, variant. *See* **different** (1).

dissimilarity *or* **dissimilitude** *noun*
▸ contrast, discrepancy, divergence. *See* **difference** (1). *See synonym note at* **difference.**

dissimulate *verb*
1. To change or modify so as to prevent recognition of the true identity or character of ▸ dissemble, mask, veil. *See* **disguise.** *See synonym note at* **disguise. 2.** To take on as a false appearance ▸ fake, feign, put on. *See* **act** (2).

dissimulation *noun*
▸ disguise, masquerade, sham. *See* **act** (2).

dissipate *verb*
1. To cause to separate and go in various directions ▸ dispel, disperse, scatter. *See synonym note at* **scatter.** *See also* **divide, separate. 2.** To disappear by or as if by rising ▸ disperse, scatter, thin out. *See* **lift** (4). **3.** To use, consume, spend, or expend thoughtlessly or carelessly ▸ fritter away, squander, trifle away. *See* **waste** (1). *See synonym note at* **waste. 4.** To pass out of sight either gradually or suddenly ▸ dissolve, fade. *See* **disappear** (1).

dissipated *adjective*
▸ dissolute, profligate, rakish. *See* **abandoned** (2).

dissipation *noun*
▸ departure, expiration, vanishment. *See* **disappearance.**

dissipative *adjective*
▸ prodigal, profligate. *See* **extravagant** (1).

dissociate *verb*
▸ disconnect, disengage, withdraw. *See* **detach** (1).

dissociation *noun*
1. The act or process of detaching ▸ disconnection, separation, uncoupling. *See* **detachment** (1). **2.** The act or an instance of separating one thing from

another ▸ disjunction, divorce, parting. *See* **division** (1).

dissolute *adjective*
▸ licentious, profligate, rakish. *See* **abandoned** (2).

dissoluteness *noun*
▸ licentiousness, profligacy. *See* **license** (2).

dissolution *noun*
1. Excessive freedom; lack of restraint ▸ licentiousness, profligacy. *See* **license** (2). **2.** The act or fact of dying ▸ demise, passing. *See* **death** (1). **3.** The act or an example of passing out of sight ▸ dissipation, expiration, vanishment. *See* **disappearance.**

dissolve *verb*
1. To change from a solid to a liquid ▸ liquefy, thaw. *See* **melt** (1). **2.** To reduce or become reduced to pieces or fragments ▸ crumble, decompose, fragment. *See* **disintegrate** (1). **3.** To pass out of sight either gradually or suddenly ▸ dissolve, fade. *See* **disappear** (1). **4.** To make a film image disappear gradually ▸ fade out.

dissonance *noun*
▸ contention, difference, discord. *See* **conflict** (1).

dissonant *adjective*
1. Devoid of harmony and accord ▸ conflicting, dissident. *See* **inharmonious** (1). **2.** Made up of parts or qualities that are disparate or otherwise markedly lacking in consistency ▸ discrepant, inconsistent. *See* **incongruous** (1). **3.** Characterized by unpleasant discordance of sound ▸ discordant, inharmonic. *See* **inharmonious** (2).

dissuade *verb*
To persuade a person not to do something ▸ deter, discourage, disincline, divert, put off. *Idiom:* talk out of. *See also* **discourage.**

✦ **CORE SYNONYMS:** *dissuade, deter, discourage.* These verbs mean to persuade someone not to do something: *tried to dissuade her from suing; couldn't be deterred from leaving; discouraged me from accepting the offer.*

◂ **ANTONYM:** *persuade*

---

distance *noun*
1. An extent, measured or unmeasured, of linear space ▸ gap, interval, length, range, reach, space, span, stretch. *Informal:* piece, way. *See also* **extent, gap. 2.** The fact or condition of being far removed or apart ▸ farness, remoteness, separateness, separation. **3.** A wide and open area, as of land, sky, or water ▸ extent, stretch, sweep. *See* **expanse** (1). **4.** Dissociation from one's surroundings or worldly affairs ▸ disinterest, indifference, remoteness. *See* **detachment** (2).

distance *verb*
To make distant, hostile, or unsympathetic ▸ disaffect, disunite. *See* **estrange.**

distant *adjective*
1. Far from others in space, time, or relationship ▸ far, faraway, far-flung, far-off, remote, removed. *Idioms:* at a distance (*or* remove). **2.** Not friendly, sociable, or

warm in manner ▸ aloof, chilly, impersonal. *See* **cool** (1).

distaste *noun*
An attitude or feeling of mild aversion ▸ disinclination, dislike, disrelish, mislike. *See also* **disapproval, disgust, enmity, hate.**

distasteful *adjective*
1. Difficult to accept or bear ▸ disagreeable, painful, unpleasant. *See* **bitter** (3). **2.** So unpleasant in flavor as to be inedible ▸ foul-tasting, unappetizing, uneatable. *See* **unpalatable** (1).

distend *verb*
1. To make or become broader or more comprehensive ▸ amplify, expand, widen. *See* **broaden. 2.** To expand from or as if from internal pressure ▸ bloat, inflate. *See* **swell** (1).

distill *verb*
▸ dribble, trickle. *See* **drip.**

distinct *adjective*
1. Distinguished from others by nature or qualities ▸ discrete, individual, separate, several, various. *See also* **unique. 2.** Readily seen, perceived, or understood ▸ evident, noticeable, obvious. *See* **apparent** (1). *See synonym note at* **apparent. 3.** Without any doubt ▸ clear-cut, definite, unquestionable. *See* **decided** (1). **4.** Clearly defined; not ambiguous ▸ clear, unambiguous. *See* **sharp** (3). **5.** Not like another in nature, quality, amount, or form ▸ contrasting, divergent, variant. *See* **different** (1).

✦ **CORE SYNONYMS:** *distinct, discrete, separate, several.* These adjectives mean distinguished from others in nature or qualities: *12 distinct colors; a company with six discrete divisions; a problem consisting of two separate issues; performed several steps of the process.*

distinction *noun*
1. The act or an instance of distinguishing ▸ demarcation, differentiation, discernment, discretion, discrimination, separation. **2.** Recognition of achievement or superiority or a sign of this ▸ accolade, award, citation, commendation, honor, kudos, laurels, medal, prize, ribbon, trophy. *See also* **reward. 3.** The condition of being unlike or dissimilar ▸ contrast, discrepancy, divergence. *See* **difference** (1). *See synonym note at* **difference. 4.** Wide recognition for one's deeds ▸ glory, prestige, renown. *See* **fame. 5.** A particularly good or beneficial quality ▸ asset, merit. *See* **virtue** (1).

distinctive *adjective*
▸ characteristic, particular, typical. *See* **special** (1).

distinctiveness *noun*
1. The quality of being individual ▸ discreteness, particularity. *See* **individuality** (1). **2.** The set of behavioral or personal characteristics by which an individual is recognizable ▸ distinctiveness, individuality, singularity. *See* **identity** (1).

distinctness *noun*
▸ clearness, lucidity, perspicuity, plainness. *See* **clarity** (1).

distinguish *verb*
1. To recognize as being different ▸ differentiate, discern, discriminate, know, separate, single out, tell. **2.** To make noticeable or different ▸ characterize, differentiate, discriminate, identify, individualize, mark, set apart, signalize, single out, singularize. **3.** To perceive and fix the identity of, especially with difficulty ▸ ascertain, recognize. *See* **discern** (1). **4.** To perceive with a special effort of the senses or the mind ▸ detect, mark. *See* **notice.5.** To cause to be eminent or recognized ▸ dignify, elevate, ennoble, exalt, glorify, honor, praise, signalize. *See also* **celebrate, exalt, honor.**

distinguishable *adjective*
▸ appreciable, discernible, palpable, perceivable. *See* **perceptible.**

distinguished *adjective*
1. Widely known ▸ famed, noted, renowned. *See* **famous. 2.** Readily attracting notice ▸ conspicuous, outstanding, prominent. *See* **noticeable** (1).

distort *verb*
1. To give an inaccurate view of by representing falsely or misleadingly ▸ alter, belie, bend, color, cook, falsify, fudge, load, misrepresent, misstate, pervert, slant, stretch, twist, warp, wrench, wrest. *Idiom:* give a false coloring to. *See also* **bias, equivocate, lie**². **2.** To alter and spoil the natural form or appearance of ▸ disfigure, misshape, twist. *See* **deform.** *See synonym note at* **deform.**

distortion *noun*
1. A disfiguring abnormality of shape or form ▸ contortion, disfigurement, malformation. *See* **deformity. 2.** The use or an instance of equivocal language ▸ euphemism, prevarication. *See* **equivocation** (1). **3.** An untrue declaration ▸ falsehood, fib, untruth. *See* **lie**².

distract *verb*
▸ disorient, fluster, ruffle. *See* **agitate** (2).

distracted *verb*
▸ abstracted, forgetful, preoccupied. *See* **absent-minded.**

distraction *noun*
1. Something that amuses, entertains, or pleases ▸ diversion, entertainment, recreation. *See* **amusement. 2.** A stunned or bewildered condition ▸ bewilderment, perplexity, stupor. *See* **daze.**

distrait *adjective*
▸ bemused, inattentive, preoccupied. *See* **absent-minded.**

distraught *adjective*
1. In a state of anxiety or uneasiness ▸ agitated, distressed, overwrought. *See* **anxious. 2.** Afflicted with or exhibiting irrationality and mental unsoundness ▸ demented, lunatic, unsound. *See* **insane** (1).

distress *verb*
1. To cause emotional suffering or painful sorrow to ▸ aggrieve, anguish, grieve, harrow, hurt, injure, pain, traumatize, trouble, vex, wound. *See also* **afflict, agitate, annoy, offend. 2.** To cause anxious uneasi-

ness in ▶ bother, concern, trouble. *See* **worry** (1).

distress *noun*
1. A state of physical or mental suffering ▶ affliction, agony, anguish, grief, hurt, injury, misery, pain, sorrow, torment, torture, vexation, woe, wound, wretchedness. *Slang:* murder. *See also* **annoyance, difficulty. 2.** A troubled or anxious state of mind ▶ concern, disquiet, unease. *See* **anxiety** (1). **3.** A situation requiring immediate assistance or remedial action ▶ crisis, exigency, trouble. *See* **emergency. 4.** The action or result of inflicting loss or pain ▶ detriment, injury. *See* **harm.**

distressed *adjective*
▶ concerned, nervous, uneasy. *See* **anxious.**

distressing *or* **distressful** *adjective*
▶ bothersome, irritating, unsettling. *See* **disturbing.**

distribute *verb*
1. To give out in portions or shares ▶ admeasure, allocate, allot, allow, apportion, assign, deal (out), disburse, dish (out), dispense, divide, dole out, give (out), hand out, issue, measure out, mete out, parcel out, portion (out), ration (out), share. *Slang:* divvy. *See also* **appropriate. 2.** To extend or arrange over a wide area ▶ disperse, disseminate, scatter. *See* **spread** (2). **3.** To arrange according to class ▶ categorize, class, group. *See* **classify.**

✦ CORE SYNONYMS: *distribute, divide, dispense, dole out, deal, ration.* These verbs mean to give out in portions or shares. *Distribute* is the least specific: *The government distributed land to settlers. Divide* implies giving out portions, often equal, on the basis of a plan or purpose: *The estate will be divided among the heirs. Dispense* stresses the careful determination of portions, often according to measurement or weight: *The pharmacist dispensed the medication. Dole out* implies careful, usually sparing measurement of portions. It can refer to the distribution of charity: *The city doled out surplus milk to the needy.* It can also suggest lack of generosity: *The professor doled out meager praise to the students. Deal* implies orderly, equitable distribution, often piece by piece: *I dealt five cards to each player. Ration* refers to equitable division in limited portions of scarce, often necessary, items: *The government rationed fuel during the war.*

---

distribution *noun*
1. The act of distributing or the condition of being distributed ▶ admeasurement, allocation, allotment, apportionment, assignment, disbursement, dispensation, division, dishing out, doling out, meting out, portioning out, rationing out, sharing. **2.** The passing out or spreading about of something over a wide area ▶ circulation, diffusion, dispersal, dispersion, dissemination, scattering. **3.** The act or condition of being arranged ▶ allotment, layout, positioning. *See* **arrangement** (1). **4.** That which is allotted ▶ allowance, ration, share. *See* **allotment** (1).

district *noun*
1. A part of the earth's surface ▶ region, zone. *See* **area** (2). **2.** An area in a city or town with distinctive

characteristics ▶ community, quarter. *See* **neighborhood** (1). **3.** A particular area used for or associated with a specific individual or activity ▶ belt, region, terrain. *See* **territory** (1).

distrust *noun*
1. Lack of trust ▶ cynicism, doubt, leeriness, mistrust, skepticism, suspicion, wariness. **2.** A lack of conviction or certainty ▶ dubiousness, incertitude, skepticism. *See* **doubt** (1). **3.** The refusal or reluctance to believe ▶ incredulity, mistrust, skepticism, unbelief. *See* **disbelief** (1).

distrust *verb*
1. To lack trust or confidence in ▶ disbelieve, doubt, misdoubt, mistrust, question, suspect. **2.** To be uncertain, disbelieving, or skeptical about ▶ disbelieve, query, waver. *See* **doubt** (1). **3.** To give no credence to ▶ doubt, mistrust. *See* **disbelieve** (1).

distrustful *adjective*
1. Lacking trust or confidence ▶ cynical, distrusting, doubting, leery, mistrustful, skeptical, suspicious, untrusting, wary. *See also* **incredulous. 2.** Experiencing doubt ▶ hesitant, skeptical, uncertain. *See* **doubtful** (2).

distrustfully *adverb*
▶ doubtfully, questioningly. *See* **skeptically.**

distrusting *adjective*
▶ doubting, suspicious, wary. *See* **distrustful** (1).

disturb *verb*
1. To alter the settled state or position of ▶ dislocate, disorder, displace, disrupt, move, shake, shift, upset. **2.** To put out of proper order ▶ disarrange, disrupt, muddle. *See* **disorder** (1). **3.** To break up the order or progress of ▶ interfere, obstruct. *See* **disrupt** (1). **4.** To impair or destroy the composure of ▶ disorient, fluster, ruffle. *See* **agitate** (2). **5.** To trouble the nerves or peace of mind of ▶ irritate, nettle, vex. *See* **annoy** (1).

disturbance *noun*
1. A condition of being agitated or disturbed ▶ commotion, stir, tumult. *See* **agitation** (1). **2.** A change in normal place or position ▶ dislodging, movement, shift. *See* **displacement. 3.** Serious mental illness impairing a person's capacity to function normally ▶ dementia, derangement, lunacy. *See* **insanity** (1). **4.** A lack of civil order or peace ▶ anarchy, lawlessness, misrule. *See* **disorder** (2).

disturbed *adjective*
▶ agitated, distressed, overwrought. *See* **anxious.**

disturbing *adjective*
Troubling to the mind or emotions ▶ agitating, annoying, bothersome, burdensome, disquieting, disruptive, distressing, distressful, galling, intrusive, irksome, irritating, nettlesome, perturbing, plaguy, provoking, troublesome, troubling, troublous, unsettling, upsetting, vexatious, vexing, worrisome. *See also* **uncomfortable.**

disunion *noun*
1. The act or an instance of separating one thing from another ▶ disjunction, divorce, parting. *See* **division**

(1). **2.** The condition of being divided, as in opinion ► divergence, schism. *See* **division** (2).

disunite *verb*
1. To break or separate into parts or sections ► disjoin, dissever, split up. *See* **divide** (1). **2.** To make distant, hostile, or unsympathetic ► disaffect, drive away. *See* **estrange.**

disunity *noun*
► dissent, schism. *See* **division** (2).

disuse *noun*
► desuetude, obsoletism. *See* **obsoleteness.**

ditch *noun*
A long, narrow, and usually shallow depression in the ground ► channel, rut, trench. *See* **furrow** (1).

ditch *verb*
Slang To let go or get rid of as being useless or defective, for example ► dump, throw away. *Informal:* chuck. *See* **discard.**

dither *noun*
A state of discomposure ► tumult, turmoil. *Informal:* lather. *See* **agitation** (2).

dither *verb*
To be irresolute in acting or doing ► falter, vacillate. *See* **hesitate.**

dithyrambic *adjective*
► burning, fervent, impassioned, torrid. *See* **passionate** (1).

ditsiness *noun*
Slang Foolish behavior ► folly, silliness, tomfoolery. *See* **foolishness.**

ditsy *adjective*
Slang Displaying a lack of forethought and good sense ► daft, idiotic, ludicrous. *See* **foolish.**

ditto *noun*
Something closely resembling another ► duplicate, facsimile, likeness. *See* **copy** (1).

ditto *verb*
To make a copy of ► imitate, replicate, reproduce. *See* **copy** (1).

ditty *noun*
► hymn, lyrics, tune. *See* **song** (1).

ditz *noun*
Slang A person who is deficient in judgment and good sense ► idiot, imbecile, nitwit. *See* **fool** (1).

divagate *verb*
1. To turn aside, especially from the main subject in writing or speaking ► ramble, stray, wander. *See* **digress** (1). **2.** To turn away from a prescribed course of action or conduct ► digress, stray. *See* **deviate** (1).

divagation *noun*
1. An instance of digressing ► deviation, divergence, tangent. *See* **digression. 2.** A departing from what is prescribed ► abberation, variation. *See* **deviation** (1).

divarication *noun*
► contrast, discrepancy, divergence. *See* **difference** (1).

dive *verb*
1. To penetrate into a substance or place with force ► drive, stab, stick. *See* **plunge** (1). **2.** To move downward in response to gravity ► descend, drop. *See* **fall**

(1). **3.** To become lower in value or price ► drop, plummet, plunge. *See* **fall** (7).

dive into *verb*
To start work on vigorously ► go at, tackle. *See* **attack** (2).

dive *noun*
1. A sudden downward motion toward the ground ► nosedive, plunge, tumble. *See* **fall** (1). **2.** A usually swift downward trend, as in prices ► decline, descent, dip. *See* **fall** (3). **3.** *Slang* A disreputable or run-down bar or restaurant ► *Slang:* dump, honky-tonk, joint, juke house, juke joint. *Idiom:* hole in the wall.

diverge *verb*
1. To separate into branches or branchlike parts ► divide, fork. *See* **branch. 2.** To be unlike or dissimilar ► depart, disagree, vary. *See* **differ** (1). *See synonym note at* **differ. 3.** To turn away from a prescribed course of action or conduct ► digress, stray. *See* **deviate** (1). *See synonym note at* **deviate. 4.** To turn aside, especially from the main subject in writing or speaking ► ramble, stray, wander. *See* **digress** (1). **5.** To fail to be in accord ► contrast, disagree, discord. *See* **conflict.**

divergence *or* **divergency** *noun*
1. The condition of being unlike or dissimilar ► contrast, discrepancy, disparity. *See* **difference** (1). *See synonym note at* **difference. 2.** A departing from what is prescribed ► diversion, variation. *See* **deviation** (1). *See synonym note at* **deviation. 3.** An instance of digressing ► deviation, excursion, tangent. *See* **digression. 4.** The condition of being abnormal ► aberration, deviation, irregularity. *See* **abnormality. 5.** The condition of being divided, as in opinion ► discord, schism. *See* **division** (2).

divergent *adjective*
1. Departing from the normal ► aberrant, atypical. *See* **abnormal. 2.** Not like another in nature, quality, amount, or form ► contrasting, dissimilar, variant. *See* **different** (1).

divers *adjective*
1. Consisting of a number more than two or three but less than many ► some, few, various. *See* **several** (1). **2.** Consisting of many different kinds ► diverse, miscellaneous, sundry. *See* **various** (1).

diverse *adjective*
1. Not like another in nature, quality, amount, or form ► contrasting, divergent, variant. *See* **different** (1). **2.** Consisting of many different kinds ► assorted, miscellaneous, sundry. *See* **various** (1).

diversification *or* **diverseness** *noun*
► diversity, variousness. *See* **variety** (1).

diversified *adjective*
1. Consisting of many different kinds ► diverse, miscellaneous, sundry. *See* **various** (1). **2.** Not limited to a single class ► general, indefinite.

diversiform *adjective*
► crooked, nonuniform. *See* **irregular** (1).

diversify *verb*
► diverge, fork. *See* **branch.**

diversion *noun*
1. A departing from what is prescribed ▸ diversion, variation. *See* **deviation** (1). 2. Something that amuses, entertains, or pleases ▸ entertainment, pastime, recreation. *See* **amusement**. 3. An instance of digressing ▸ deviation, divergence, tangent, wandering. *See* **digression**.

diversity *noun*
▸ diverseness, heterogeneousness, variousness. *See* **variety** (1).

divert *verb*
1. To change the direction or course of ▸ deviate, shift, veer. *See* **turn** (2). 2. To persuade a person not to do something ▸ discourage, put off. *See* **dissuade**. 3. To occupy in an agreeable or pleasing way ▸ entertain, recreate, regale. *See* **amuse** (1). *See synonym note at* **amuse**.

diverting *adjective*
▸ amusing, entertaining. *See* **pleasant** (1).

divest *verb*
1. To remove the clothing or covering from ▸ expose, strip, uncover. *See* **bare** (1). 2. To take or keep something away from ▸ deny, withhold. *See* **deprive**.

divestiture *noun*
▸ destitution, dispossession, loss. *See* **deprivation** (1).

divide *verb*
1. To break up the unity of something; separate into parts, sections, or branches ▸ break, break apart (*or* up), detach, disband, disconnect, disengage, disjoin, disjoint, dissever, disunite, divorce, part, partition, section, segment, separate, split (up), uncouple. *See also* **break, cut, disintegrate, tear**[1]. 2. To separate into branches or branchlike parts ▸ diverge, fork. *See* **branch**. 3. To give out in portions or shares ▸ allocate, apportion, dispense. *See* **distribute** (1). *See synonym note at* **distribute**. 4. To arrange according to class ▸ categorize, class, separate. *See* **classify**.

divide *noun*
A space between objects or points ▸ interstice, interval, separation. *See* **gap** (1).

divination *noun*
1. Something that is foretold by or as if by supernatural means ▸ oracle, soothsaying. *See* **prophecy**. 2. The use of supernatural powers to influence or predict events ▸ conjuration, sorcery, witchcraft. *See* **magic** (1).

divine *adjective*
1. Of, from, like, or being a god or God ▸ celestial, deific, godlike, godly, heavenly, holy, supernal. 2. In the service or worship of God or a god ▸ anointed, consecrated, devoted, devout, faithful, hallowed, holy, ordained, pious, religious, sacred, sacrosanct, sanctified. *See also* **holy**. 3. Of or relating to heaven ▸ celestial, paradisal. *See* **heavenly** (1). 4. Particularly excellent ▸ fabulous, glorious, sensational. *See* **marvelous** (1).

divine *noun*
A person ordained for service in a Christian church ▸ ecclesiastic, minister, parson. *See* **cleric**.

divine *verb*
1. To tell about or make known by or as if by supernatural means ▸ auger, foretell. *See* **prophesy**. *See synonym note at* **prophesy**. 2. To know in advance ▸ anticipate, envision, foreknow. *See* **foresee**. 3. To find a solution for ▸ answer, resolve, unravel. *See* **solve** (1). *See synonym note at* **solve**.

divineness *noun*
▸ beatitude, sanctity. *See* **holiness**.

diviner *noun*
▸ augur, fortuneteller, seer, soothsayer. *See* **prophet**.

divine spark *noun*
▸ breath, soul, vitality. *See* **spirit** (2).

divinitory *adjective*
▸ augural, oracular, sibylline. *See* **prophetic**.

division *noun*
1. The act or an instance of separating one thing from another ▸ detachment, disassociation, disjunction, disjuncture, disseverance, disseverment, dissociation, disunion, divorce, divorcement, fission, fissure, parting, partition, segmentation, separation, severance, split. 2. The condition of being divided, as in opinion ▸ dissension, dissent, disunion, disunity, divergence, divergency, schism. *See also* **breach, conflict**. 3. The act of distributing or the condition of being distributed ▸ allocation, apportionment, dispensation. *See* **distribution** (1). 4. A separate unit that belongs or contributes to a whole ▸ piece, portion, section, segment. *See* **part** (1). 5. Something resembling or analogous to a tree branch ▸ arm, fork, offshoot. *See* **branch** (1). 6. An administrative unit, as of a government or company ▸ affiliate, agency, office. *See* **branch** (3). 7. A subdivision of a larger group ▸ category, order, set. *See* **class** (1). 8. A group of people organized for a particular purpose ▸ squad, team, unit. *See* **force** (5). 9. A group of athletic teams that play each other ▸ circuit, league. *See* **conference** (6). 10. That which is allotted ▸ allowance, ration, share. *See* **allotment** (1).

divorce *noun*
The act or an instance of separating one thing from another ▸ disjunction, fission, parting. *See* **division** (1).

divorce *verb*
1. To break up the unity of something ▸ disjoin, dissever, split up. *See* **divide** (1). 2. To end an association by or as if by leaving one another ▸ break up, part. *See* **separate** (1).

divorcement *noun*
▸ disjunction, dissociation, parting. *See* **division** (1).

divulge *verb*
1. To disclose in a breach of confidence ▸ give away. *Informal:* spill. *See* **betray** (2). 2. To make known ▸ disclose, impart, transmit. *See* **communicate** (1). 3. To utter publicly ▸ disclose, state, voice. *See* **air** (2).

divulgence *noun*
▸ disclosure, exposé, exposure. *See* **revelation**.

divvy *verb*
Slang To give out in portions or shares ▸ allocate,

apportion, dispense, dole out. *See* **distribute** (1).

divvy *noun*
Slang That which is allotted ▸ allowance, ration, share. *See* **allotment** (1).

dizziness *noun*
A sensation of whirling or falling ▸ giddiness, grogginess, lightheadedness, unsteadiness, vertiginousness, vertigo, wooziness.

dizzy *adjective*
1. Having a sensation of whirling or falling ▸ dazed, giddy, groggy, lightheaded, reeling, spinning, staggered, unsteady, vertiginous, woozy. **2.** Producing dizziness or vertigo ▸ dizzying, giddy, sickening, vertiginous. *See synonym note at* **giddy**. *See also* **steep**. **3.** *Slang* Given to lighthearted silliness ▸ featherbrained, flighty, frivolous. *See* **giddy** (2). **4.** Mentally uncertain ▸ confounded, perplexed, turbid. *Informal:* mixed-up. *See* **confused** (1).

dizzy *verb*
To cause to be unclear in mind or intent ▸ befuddle, bewilder, confound. *See* **confuse** (1).

dizzying *adjective*
Producing dizziness or vertigo ▸ dizzy, giddy, sickening, vertiginous. *See also* **steep**.

do *verb*
1. To begin and carry through to completion ▸ execute, prosecute. *Informal:* pull off. *See* **perform** (1). **2.** To carry out the functions, requirements, or terms of ▸ discharge, execute, implement. *See* **fulfill** (1). **3.** To conduct oneself in a specified way ▸ behave, comport, demean. *See* **act** (1). **4.** To progress or perform adequately, especially in difficult circumstances ▸ fare, fend, get by. *See* **manage** (1). **5.** To produce on the stage ▸ dramatize, enact, perform. *See* **stage** (1). **6.** To play the part of ▸ play, portray, represent. *See* **act** (4). **7.** *Informal* To journey over ▸ cross, traverse. *See* **cover** (2). **8.** To meet a need or requirement ▸ answer, serve, suffice, suit. **9.** To be responsible for or guilty of an error or crime ▸ carry out, commit, perpetrate. *Informal:* pull off. *See also* **perform**. **10.** *Informal* To spend or complete time, as a prison term ▸ put in, serve. **11.** *Slang* To get something by deceitful trickery ▸ bilk, defraud, swindle. *See* **cheat** (1). **12.** To be suitable or sufficient to fulfill a need ▸ fill, fulfill, meet. *See* **satisfy** (1). **13.** To work at, especially as a profession ▸ follow, practice, pursue. *Idiom:* hang out one's shingle. *See also* **labor**.

do for *verb*
To work and care for ▸ attend, minister to, serve, wait on (*or* upon). *See also* **help, tend², work**.

do in *verb*
1. *Slang* To make weary ▸ exhaust, wear out. *See* **tire** (1). **2.** *Slang* To take the life of a person or persons unlawfully ▸ destroy, kill, slay. *See* **murder** (1). **3.** To reduce to financial insolvency ▸ bankrupt, break, impoverish. *See* **ruin** (3).

do over *verb*
To do or perform an act again ▸ duplicate, play over, redo, repeat, replay. *See also* **copy**.

do up *verb*
To cover and tie something, as with paper and string ▸ package, wrap.

do *noun*
Informal A social gathering, especially for pleasure ▸ celebration, gala, soiree. *See* **party** (1).

doable *adjective*
▸ practicable, viable. *See* **possible** (1).

docent *noun*
▸ director, escort, leader. *See* **guide** (1).

docile *adjective*
1. Easily managed or handled ▸ domesticated, mild, tame. *See* **gentle** (3). **2.** Willing to carry out the wishes of others ▸ complaisant, compliant, submissive. *See* **obedient**. **3.** Capable of being educated ▸ educable, teachable, trainable.

docket *noun*
An organized list, as of procedures, activities, or events ▸ calendar, schedule, timetable. *See* **program** (1).

docket *verb*
1. To enter on a schedule ▸ calendar, program, slate, schedule. **2.** To place on a list or in a record or book ▸ catalog, chronicle, write down. *See* **list¹** (1).

doctor *verb*
1. *Informal* To restore to health ▸ rehabilitate, remedy. *See* **cure** (1). **2.** *Informal* To provide as a remedy ▸ dispense, medicate, treat. *See* **administer** (3). **3.** To restore to proper condition ▸ mend, overhaul, repair. *See* **fix** (1). **4.** To alter something so as to give it a false character ▸ fake, falsify. **5.** To alter or present material so as to favor a particular viewpoint ▸ skew, slant. *See* **bias** (2). **6.** To make impure or inferior by contact or mixture ▸ adulterate, debase, pollute. *See* **contaminate** (1). *See synonym note at* **contaminate**.

doctored *adjective*
▸ alloyed, combined, polluted. *See* **impure** (2).

doctrinaire *adjective*
1. Restricted in scope, outlook, or understanding ▸ insular, narrow-minded, provincial. *See* **narrow** (1). **2.** Conforming to established practice or standards ▸ conformist, orthodox, traditional. *See* **conventional** (1).

doctrinal *adjective*
▸ conformist, orthodox, traditional. *See* **conventional** (1).

doctrine *noun*
A statement presented for acceptance or belief, as by a religious or political group ▸ article of faith, belief, canon, concept, convention, credo, creed, dogma, gospel, ideology, line, opinion, orthodoxy, policy, position, precept, principle, proposition, teaching, tenet, theory, thesis. *See also* **law**.

✦ CORE SYNONYMS: *doctrine, dogma, tenet*. These nouns denote a statement presented for acceptance or belief, as by a religious or political group: *the legal doctrine of due process; church dogma; experimentation, one of the tenets of the physical sciences.*

document *verb*
▸ confirm, substantiate, validate. *See* **prove** (1).

documentation *noun*
▸ authentication, corroboration, proof, verification. *See* **confirmation** (2).

dodder *verb*
▸ reel, stumble, totter. *See* **stagger** (1).

doddering *adjective*
Relating to the mental deterioration that often accompanies old age ▸ doting, senile. *See also* **old, infirm**.

dodge *verb*
1. To keep away from ▸ circumvent, escape, evade. *See* **avoid**. 2. To avoid fulfilling or answering completely ▸ duck, hedge. *See* **evade** (1).

dodge *noun*
1. An indirect, usually cunning means of gaining an end ▸ deception, ploy, stratagem. *See* **trick** (1). *See synonym note at* **trick**. 2. *Slang* Activity pursued as a livelihood ▸ profession, pursuit, vocation. *See* **business** (2).

dodger *noun*
▸ cheater, swindler, trickster. *See* **cheat** (2).

doff *verb*
▸ cast off, take off. *See* **remove** (6).

dog *verb*
▸ track, trail. *Informal:* tail. *See* **follow** (3).

dog days *noun*
The season occurring between spring and autumn ▸ summer, summertime.

dog-eat-dog *adjective*
▸ cutthroat, emulous, rivalrous. *See* **competitive**.

dogged *adjective*
1. Firmly, often unreasonably immovable in purpose or will ▸ bullheaded, die-hard, obstinate. *See* **stubborn** (1). *See synonym note at* **stubborn**. 2. Characterized by steady attention and effort ▸ assiduous, conscientious, industrious. *See* **diligent**. *See synonym note at* **diligent**.

doggedness *noun*
▸ bullheadedness, hardheadedness, rigidity. *See* **stubbornness**.

doggone *adjective*
Informal So annoying or detestable as to deserve condemnation ▸ accursed, blasted, confounded. *See* **damned** (2).

dogma *noun*
▸ canon, teaching, tenet. *See* **doctrine**. *See synonym note at* **doctrine**.

dogmatic *adjective*
1. Restricted in scope, outlook, or understanding ▸ insular, narrow-minded, provincial. *See* **narrow** (1). 2. Given to asserting one's will or authority over others ▸ bossy, domineering, overbearing. *See* **dictatorial** (1). *See synonym note at* **dictatorial**. 3. Not tolerant of the beliefs or opinions of others ▸ close-minded, illiberal, racist. *See* **intolerant** (1).

doing *noun*
▸ action, deed, work. *See* **act** (1).

doldrums *noun*
1. A feeling or spell of dismally low spirits ▸ dejection, despondency, melancholy. *See* **depression** (2). 2. The condition of being bored ▸ listlessness, tedium. *See* **boredom**.

dole *noun*
1. *Informal* Assistance, especially money, food, and other necessities, given to the needy or dispossessed ▸ handout, public assistance, welfare. *See* **relief** (3). 2. That which is allotted ▸ allowance, ration, share. *See* **allotment** (1).

dole out *verb*
To give out in portions or shares ▸ allocate, apportion, dispense. *See* **distribute** (1). *See synonym note at* **distribute**.

doleful *adjective*
▸ depressing, melancholy, mournful. *See* **sorrowful** (1). *See synonym note at* **sorrowful**.

dolefulness *noun*
▸ dejection, doldrums, melancholy. *See* **depression** (2).

do-little *noun*
Informal A self-indulgent person who avoids work ▸ bum, idler, loafer. *See* **wastrel** (2).

doll *noun*
1. *Slang* A person regarded as physically attractive ▸ lovely, stunner. *See* **beauty** (1). 2. *Informal* A woman ▸ *Informal:* chick, damsel, gal. *See* **girl**.

doll up *verb*
1. *Slang* To dress in formal or special clothing ▸ array, attire, deck (out). *See* **dress up**. 2. *Slang* To furnish with decorations ▸ decorate, garnish, ornament. *See* **adorn** (1).

dollop *noun*
▸ crumb, morsel. *See* **bit**[1] (2).

dolorous *adjective*
▸ depressing, melancholy, mournful. *See* **sorrowful** (1).

dolt *noun*
▸ dummy, dunce, thickhead. *See* **dullard**.

doltish *adjective*
▸ dumb, idiotic, obtuse. *See* **stupid** (1).

doltishness *noun*
▸ idiocy, mindlessness, obtuseness. *See* **stupidity**.

domain *noun*
▸ department, field, terrain. *See* **area** (1). *See synonym note at* **area**.

dome *noun*
Slang The uppermost part of the body ▸ crown, pate. *See* **head** (1).

domestic *adjective*
1. Of or relating to the family or household ▸ familial, family, home, homely, homey, household, residential. 2. Trained or bred to live with and be of use to people ▸ broken (in), domesticated, housebroken, house-trained, naturalized, pet, tame. 3. Of, from, or within a country's own territory ▸ aboriginal, autochthonous, home, homegrown, indigenous, internal, national, native. *See also* **indigenous**.

domesticate *verb*
To train to live with and be of use to people ▸ break in, domesticize, gentle, housebreak, house-train, master, naturalize, tame.

domesticated *adjective*
▸ broken (in), housebroken, naturalized. *See* **domestic** (2).

domesticize *verb*
▸ break in, housebreak, tame. *See* **domesticate.**

domicile *noun*
A building or shelter where one lives ▸ abode, habitation, residence. *See* **home** (1).

domicile *verb*
1. To stay in or provide with lodging, especially temporarily ▸ bed (down), board, house. *See* **lodge** (1). **2.** To have as one's domicile, usually for an extended period ▸ dwell, reside. *See* **live**[1] (2).

dominance *noun*
1. The condition or fact of being dominant ▸ ascendance, ascendancy, authority, command, control, domination, dominion, hegemony, lead, paramountcy, power, predominance, preeminence, preponderance, preponderancy, prepotency, rule, supremacy, sway. *See also* **authority. 2.** The act of exercising controlling power or the condition of being so controlled ▸ control, mastery, reign. *See* **domination** (1).

dominant *adjective*
1. Exercising controlling power or influence ▸ ascendant, chief, commanding, controlling, dominating, dominative, governing, key, leading, main, major, paramount, predominant, preeminent, preponderant, prepotent, prevailing, primary, prime, principal, regnant, reigning, ruling, supreme. *See also* **primary. 2.** Exercising authority ▸ authoritative, commanding, lordly, masterful. *See also* **administrative.**

✦ **CORE SYNONYMS:** *dominant, predominant, preponderant, paramount, preeminent.* These adjectives mean surpassing all others in power, influence, or position. *Dominant* applies to what exercises principal control or authority or is unmistakably ascendant: *For decades, the Soviet Union was the dominant nation of eastern Europe. Predominant* often implies being uppermost at a particular time or for the time being: *"Egrets, gulls and small mammals are the predominant wildlife on the island these days"* (Dan McCoubrey). *Preponderant* implies superiority as the result of outweighing or outnumbering all others: *"No big modern war has been won without preponderant sea power"* (Samuel Eliot Morison). *Paramount* means first in importance, rank, or regard: *"My paramount object in this struggle is to save the Union"* (Abraham Lincoln). *Preeminent* suggests generally recognized supremacy: *He is the preeminent tenor of the modern era.*

dominate *verb*
1. To occupy the preeminent position in ▸ command, control, lead, predominate, preponderate, prevail, reign, rule. *Idioms:* be cock of the walk, have the

ascendancy, lord it over, reign supreme. **2.** To rise above, especially so as to afford a view of ▸ command, dwarf, overbear, overlook, overshadow, tower above (*or* over). **3.** To have charge of the affairs of others ▸ direct, govern, rule. *See* **administer** (1). **4.** To command in an arrogant manner ▸ domineer, rule, tyrannize. *See* **boss** (1). **5.** To make subservient or subordinate ▸ indenture, subjugate. *See* **enslave.**

dominating *adjective*
▸ key, predominant, reigning. *See* **dominant** (1).

domination *noun*
1. The act of exercising controlling power or the condition of being so controlled ▸ command, control, dominance, dominion, mastery, reign, repression, rule, subjugation, suppression, sway. **2.** The condition or fact of being dominant ▸ authority, power, supremacy. *See* **dominance** (1). **3.** The right and power to command, decide, rule, or judge ▸ carte blanche, might. *Informal:* say-so, muscle. *See* **authority** (1). **4.** Cruel exercise of power ▸ injustice, repression, subjugation. *See* **oppression** (1).

dominative *adjective*
▸ key, predominant, reigning. *See* **dominant** (1).

domineer *verb*
▸ dominate, rule, tyrannize. *See* **boss** (1).

domineering *adjective*
▸ bossy, dogmatic, overbearing. *See* **dictatorial** (1).

dominion *noun*
1. The right and power to command, decide, rule, or judge ▸ carte blanche, might. *Informal:* say-so, muscle. *See* **authority** (1). **2.** The fact of possessing or the legal right to possess something ▸ possession, title. *See* **ownership. 3.** The act of exercising controlling power or the condition of being so controlled ▸ command, control, reign. *See* **domination** (1). **4.** The condition or fact of being dominant ▸ authority, power, supremacy. *See* **dominance** (1).

don *verb*
1. To put an article of clothing on one's person ▸ assume, get on, pull on, put on, slip into (on). **2.** To put clothes on ▸ attire, clothe, garb. *See* **dress** (1).

donate *verb*
1. To present as a gift to a charity or cause ▸ award, bequeath, bestow, contribute, endow, give (away), grant, hand out, pledge, present, subscribe. *See also* **gift. 2.** To give in common with others ▸ give, subscribe. *See* **contribute** (1).

donation *noun*
Something given to a charity or cause ▸ alms, award, benefaction, beneficence, bequest, charity, contribution, endowment, gift, grant, gratuity, handout, largess, offering, pledge, present, subscription. *See also* **gift, gratuity, relief.**

donator *noun*
▸ benefactor, contributor, patron. *See* **donor.**

done *adjective*
1. Having reached completion ▸ concluded, finished, through. *See* **complete** (3). **2.** No longer effective, capable, or valuable ▸ done for, finished, washed-up.

See **through** (2). **3.** Having no further relationship ▸ finished, through.

done for *adjective*
▸ done, finished, washed-up. *See* **through** (2).

done in *adjective*
Slang Depleted of energy ▸ exhausted, weary, worn-out. *See* **tired** (1).

Don Juan *noun*
1. A man who seduces women ▸ debaucher, Lothario, seducer. *See also* **flirt, lecher. 2.** A man amorously attentive to women ▸ Casanova, lady's man. *See* **gallant. 3.** A man who philanders ▸ adulterer, cheater, womanizer. *See* **philanderer.**

donnish *adjective*
▸ bookish, literary, scholastic. *See* **pedantic.** *See synonym note at* **pedantic.**

donnybrook *noun*
▸ free-for-all, melee. *See* **fight** (1). *See synonym note at* **fight.**

donor *noun*
A person who gives to a charity or cause ▸ benefactor, benefactress, contributor, donator, fairy godmother, giver, grantor, humanitarian, patron, patroness, philanthropist, provider, subscriber, supplier. *Informal:* angel. *See also* **patron, sponsor.**

do-nothing *adjective*
Informal Resistant to exertion and activity ▸ idle, shiftless, slothful. *See* **lazy.**

do-nothing *noun*
Informal A self-indulgent person who avoids work ▸ bum, idler, loafer. *See* **wastrel** (2).

do-nothingism *noun*
Informal The quality or state of being lazy ▸ indolence, shiftlessness, sloth. *See* **laziness.**

doodad *or* **doohickey** *noun*
Informal A small specialized mechanical device ▸ apparatus. *Informal:* widget. *Slang:* gizmo. *See* **gadget.**

doodle *verb*
▸ dawdle (about), fiddle (around). *Informal:* fool around. *See* **putter.**

doom *noun*
A personal outcome or end ▸ destiny, fortune, lot. *See* **fate** (2).

doom *verb*
To pronounce judgment against ▸ damn, sentence. *See* **condemn** (1). *See synonym note at* **condemn.**

doomed *adjective*
▸ fated, lost, reprobate. *See* **condemned.**

doomsayer *noun*
▸ apocalypticist, worrywart. *See* **pessimist** (2).

doormat *noun*
Slang A weak or ineffectual person ▸ pushover. *Slang:* cream puff, wimp. *See* **weakling.**

dope *noun*
1. *Informal* A substance that affects the central nervous system and is often addictive ▸ narcotic, opiate, psychotropic. *See* **drug** (2). **2.** *Informal* A person who is deficient in judgment and good sense ▸ idiot, imbecile, nitwit. *See* **fool** (1). **3.** *Slang* That which is

known about a specific subject or situation ▸ facts, knowledge, lore. *See* **information** (1).

dope *verb*
Informal To administer especially a painkilling drug to someone ▸ dope up, medicate, narcotize, tranquilize. *See* **drug** (1).

dope out *verb*
1. To find a solution for ▸ clear up, resolve, unravel. *See* **solve** (1). **2.** *Informal* To form a strategy for ▸ devise, formulate, strategize. *See* **design** (1).

doped *adjective*
Informal Stupefied, intoxicated, or otherwise influenced by the taking of drugs ▸ *Slang:* high, hopped-up, lit (up). *See* **drugged.**

dopey *adjective*
1. *Slang* Lacking mental and physical alertness and activity ▸ slothful, sluggish, stuporous. *See* **lethargic** (1). **2.** *Slang* Lacking in intelligence ▸ dumb, idiotic, obtuse. *See* **stupid** (1). **3.** *Slang* Displaying a lack of forethought and good sense ▸ daft, idiotic, ludicrous. *See* **foolish.**

dopeyness *noun*
Slang Foolish behavior ▸ folly, silliness, tomfoolery. *See* **foolishness.**

dork *noun*
1. *Slang* A person who is deficient in judgment and good sense ▸ idiot, imbecile, nitwit. *See* **fool** (1). **2.** *Slang* An unpleasant, tiresome person ▸ chump. *Slang:* dweeb, nerd. *See* **drip** (2).

dormancy *noun*
▸ intermission, latency, remission, suspension. *See* **abeyance.**

dormant *adjective*
▸ abeyant, inactive, potential. *See* **latent.** *See synonym note at* **latent.**

dose *verb*
1. To administer especially a painkilling drug to someone ▸ medicate, narcotize, tranquilize. *See* **drug** (1). **2.** To provide as a remedy ▸ dispense, medicate, treat. *See* **administer** (3).

dot *noun*
1. A very small mark ▸ dash, speck. *See* **point** (2). **2.** A tiny amount ▸ dash, drop, smidgen. *See* **bit**[1] (1).

dot *verb*
To mark with many small spots ▸ dapple, freckle. *See* **speckle.**

dotage *noun*
The condition of being senile ▸ anecdotage, anility, caducity, senility. *See also* **age.**

dote on *verb*
1. To like or enjoy enthusiastically, often excessively ▸ adore, delight (in), love. *Slang:* eat up, groove on. **2.** To overindulge with affection or attention ▸ spoil. *See also* **baby, rave.**

doting *adjective*
1. Feeling or expressing fond feelings or affection ▸ caring, loving. *See* **affectionate. 2.** Relating to the mental deterioration that often accompanies old age ▸ doddering, senile. *See also* **old, infirm.**

dotty *adjective*
▸ brainsick, off, unbalanced. *See* **insane** (1).

double *adjective*
1. Consisting of two identical or similar related things, parts, or elements ▸ dual, matched, paired, twin. *See also* **equal. 2.** Composed of two parts or things ▸ biform, binary, dual, duple, duplex, duplicate, geminate, twofold, two-part, two-piece. **3.** Given to deliberate misrepresentation of the truth ▸ deceitful, double-dealing, two-faced. *See* **dishonest** (1).

double *noun*
1. One exactly resembling another ▸ clone, duplicate, image, picture, portrait, second, spitting image, twin. *Slang:* ringer. *See also* **copy. 2.** One of a matched pair of things ▸ counterpart, duplicate. *See* **mate** (1). **3.** One that can take the place of another ▸ replacement, stand-in, surrogate. *See* **substitute.**

double *verb*
1. To make or become twice as great ▸ duplicate, geminate, redouble, twin. **2.** To bend together or form a crease ▸ crimp, pleat. *See* **fold** (1). **3.** To turn sharply around ▸ about-face, double back, reverse.

double-cross *verb*
1. To be treacherous to ▸ turn in. *Slang:* sell out. *See* **betray** (1). **2.** To cause to accept something false, especially by trickery or misrepresentation ▸ dupe, mislead, trick. *See* **deceive.** *See synonym note at* **deceive.**

double cross *or* **double-cross** *noun*
An act of betraying ▸ treachery. *Slang:* sellout. *See* **betrayal** (1).

double-crosser *noun*
▸ Judas, traitor. *See* **betrayer.**

double-dealing *adjective*
Given to or marked by deliberate concealment or misrepresentation of the truth ▸ duplicitous, lying, mendacious. *See* **dishonest** (1). *See synonym note at* **dishonest.**

double-dealing *noun*
The act or practice of deceiving ▸ deception, duplicity, guile. *See* **deceit** (1).

double-edged *adjective*
▸ equivocal, nebulous, vague. *See* **ambiguous** (2).

double-entendre *noun*
▸ equivocation, tergiversation. *See* **ambiguity** (1).

double-faced *adjective*
Given to or marked by deliberate concealment or misrepresentation of the truth ▸ deceptive, double-dealing, two-faced. *See* **dishonest** (1). *See synonym note at* **dishonest.**

doublespeak *noun*
▸ hocus-pocus, mumbo jumbo. *See* **gibberish** (1).

doublet *noun*
▸ duet, match, pair. *See* **couple.**

double talk *noun*
1. Empty or foolish talk ▸ blather, jabber, twaddle. *See* **babble** (1). **2.** Highly technical, often deliberately deceptive language ▸ hocus-pocus, mumbo jumbo. *See* **gibberish** (1).

doubt *noun*
1. A lack of conviction or certainty ▸ distrust, doubtfulness, dubiety, dubiousness, incertitude, misgiving, mistrust, qualm, query, question, reservation, skepticism, suspicion, uncertainty, wonder. **2.** Lack of trust ▸ cynicism, leeriness. *See* **distrust. 3.** The refusal or reluctance to believe ▸ incredulity, mistrust, skepticism, unbelief. *See* **disbelief** (1).

doubt *verb*
1. To be uncertain, disbelieving, or skeptical about ▸ disbelieve, distrust, misdoubt, mistrust, query, question, waver, wonder. *Idiom:* have one's doubts. **2.** To lack trust or confidence in ▸ disbelieve, question. *See* **distrust. 3.** To give no credence to ▸ discredit, mistrust. *See* **disbelieve** (1).

✦ **CORE SYNONYMS:** *doubt, dubiety, uncertainty, skepticism, suspicion, mistrust.* These nouns refer to the condition of being unsure or lacking conviction about someone or something. *Doubt* and *dubiety* imply a questioning state of mind: *"Doubt is part of all religion"* (Isaac Bashevis Singer). *On this point there can be no dubiety. Uncertainty* merely denotes a lack of assurance or conviction: *I regarded my decision with growing uncertainty. Skepticism* generally suggests an instinctive or habitual tendency to question and demand proof: *"A wise skepticism is the first attribute of a good critic"* (James Russell Lowell). *Suspicion* is doubt as to the innocence, truth, integrity, honesty, or soundness of someone or something: *His furtiveness aroused my suspicions. Mistrust* denotes lack of trust or confidence, as in a person's motives, arising from suspicion: *The staff viewed the consultant's hasty recommendations with mistrust.*

---

doubter *noun*
▸ agnostic, unbeliever. *See* **skeptic.**

doubtful *adjective*
1. Not likely ▸ dubious, improbable, problematic, questionable, unapt, unlikely. **2.** Experiencing doubt ▸ ambivalent, distrustful, doubting, dubious, hesitant, irresolute, skeptical, suspicious, tentative, uncertain, undecided, unsure, vacillating, wavering. *Idiom:* in doubt. *See also* **distrustful, wary. 3.** Lacking certainty or clarity ▸ dubious, indeterminate, unclear. *See* **ambiguous** (1). **4.** In doubt or dispute ▸ disputable, questionable. *See* **debatable. 5.** Of dubious character ▸ questionable, suspicious. *See* **shady** (1).

doubtfully *adverb*
▸ askance, questioningly. *See* **skeptically.**

doubtfulness *noun*
▸ dubiousness, incertitude, skepticism. *See* **doubt** (1).

doubting *adjective*
1. Lacking trust or confidence ▸ cynical, suspicious, wary. *See* **distrustful** (1). **2.** Experiencing doubt ▸ hesitant, skeptical, uncertain. *See* **doubtful** (2).

doubting Thomas *noun*
▸ agnostic, unbeliever. *See* **skeptic.**

doubtless *adverb*
Without question ▸ certainly, doubtlessly, positively, undoubtedly. *See* **absolutely** (1).

doubtless *adjective*
Having no doubt ▸ certain, confident, positive. *See* **sure** (1).

doubtlessly *adverb*
▸ certainly, doubtless, positively, undoubtedly. *See* **absolutely** (1).

doubtlessness *noun*
▸ assuredness, certainty, confidence, conviction. *See* **sureness** (1).

dough *noun*
Slang Something, such as coins or printed bills, used as a medium of exchange ▸ currency. *Slang:* green, moola. *See* **money** (1).

doughtiness *noun*
▸ bravery, fortitude, gallantry, valor. *See* **courage**.

doughty *adjective*
▸ courageous, fearless, heroic. *See* **brave**.

doughy *adjective*
1. Yielding easily to pressure or weight ▸ mushy, pulpy, yielding. *See* **soft** (1). 2. Lacking color ▸ bloodless, lurid, wan. *See* **pale** (1).

dour *adjective*
1. Marked by cold and unpleasant conditions ▸ grim, severe. *See* **bleak** (1). 2. Broodingly and sullenly unhappy ▸ gloomy, morose, sullen. *See* **glum** (1). 3. So disagreeable as to discourage approach ▸ flinty, inhospitable, stern. *See* **forbidding** (1).

douse *verb*
1. To plunge briefly in or into a liquid ▸ dunk, submerse. *See* **dip** (1). *See synonym note at* **dip**. 2. To make thoroughly wet ▸ drench, soak, souse. *See* **wet** (1). 3. To cause to stop burning or giving light ▸ put out, snuff out. *See* **extinguish** (1).

doused *adjective*
▸ drenched, soaked, waterlogged. *See* **wet** (1).

dove *noun*
▸ angel, lamb, virgin. *See* **innocent** (1).

dovetail *verb*
1. To be the proper size and shape for something ▸ interlock, fit. *Idiom:* fit like a glove. 2. To be compatible or suitable ▸ chime, correspond, match. *See* **agree** (1).

dovish *adjective*
▸ conciliatory, nonviolent, pacifistic. *See* **peaceable**.

dowdy *adjective*
Unfashionable and lacking in stylishness ▸ frumpy, fusty. *See* **old-fashioned**.

dowel *noun*
▸ brake, grapnel, mooring. *See* **anchor** (1).

down *adjective*
1. Characterized by reduced economic activity ▸ dull, slack. *See* **slow** (2). 2. Suffering from or appearing to suffer from an illness ▸ ailing, indisposed, unwell. *See* **sick** (1). 3. In low spirits ▸ dysphoric, gloomy, melancholy, spiritless. *See* **depressed** (1).

down *noun*
1. A sudden drop to a lower condition or status ▸ plunge, slide, tumble. *See* **descent** (4). 2. A natural land elevation ▸ prominence, rise. *See* **hill** (1).

down *verb*
1. To bring down, as from a shot or blow ▸ floor, ground, hew. *See* **drop** (6). 2. *Informal* To swallow food or drink greedily or rapidly in large amounts ▸ gobble, guzzle. *See* **gulp** (1). 3. To take into the mouth and swallow a liquid ▸ gulp, sip, swill. *See* **drink** (1).

down-and-out *adjective*
Having little or no money or wealth ▸ destitute, impecunious, indigent. *See* **poor** (1).

down-and-out *noun*
An impoverished person ▸ beggar, insolvent, tramp. *See* **pauper**.

down-and-outer *noun*
▸ beggar, insolvent, tramp. *See* **pauper**.

down-at-heel *or* **down-at-the-heel** *adjective*
▸ broken-down, dilapidated, tattered. *See* **shabby** (1).

downbeat *adjective*
▸ dim, dismal, pessimistic. *See* **bleak** (2).

downcast *adjective*
▸ dysphoric, melancholy, spiritless. *See* **depressed** (1). *See synonym note at* **depressed**.

downer *noun*
▸ spoilsport. *Informal:* wet blanket. *Slang:* party pooper. *See* **killjoy**.

downfall *noun*
1. A sudden drop to a lower condition or status ▸ plunge, slide, tumble. *See* **descent** (4). 2. A disastrous defeat or ruin ▸ collapse, fall, waterloo. *See also* **defeat**. 3. Something that causes total loss or severe impairment ▸ bane, destruction, undoing. *See* **ruin** (1). 4. Water condensed from atmospheric vapor and falling in drops ▸ deluge, downpour, shower. *See* **rain** (2).

downgrade *noun*
1. The act or an instance of demoting ▸ demotion, degradation, reduction. 2. A sudden drop to a lower condition or status ▸ plunge, slide, tumble. *See* **descent** (4).

downgrade *verb*
1. To lower in rank or grade ▸ degrade, reduce. *See* **demote**. *See synonym note at* **demote**. 2. To lower in character or quality ▸ cheapen, degrade. *See* **debase** (1). 3. To represent or speak of as small or insignificant ▸ deprecate, disparage, slight. *See* **belittle**. *See synonym note at* **belittle**. 4. To make less in price or value ▸ cheapen, devalue, reduce. *See* **depreciate** (1).

downhearted *adjective*
▸ dysphoric, gloomy, spiritless. *See* **depressed** (1). *See synonym note at* **depressed**.

downheartedness *noun*
▸ dejection, doldrums, melancholy. *See* **depression** (2).

down payment *noun*
A partial or intial payment ▸ deposit, installment, security.

downpour *noun*
1. An abundant or overwhelming flow of water ▸ deluge, overflow, torrent. *See* **flood** (1). 2. Water

condensed from atmospheric vapor and falling in drops ▸ deluge, downfall, shower. *See* **rain** (2).

downright *adjective*
1. Completely such, without qualification or exception ▸ all-out, pure, sheer. *See* **utter²**. 2. Manifesting honesty and directness ▸ forthright, open, plainspoken. *See* **frank**.

downright *adverb*
To the fullest extent ▸ fully, totally, utterly. *See* **completely** (1).

downside *noun*
1. An unfavorable condition, circumstance, or characteristic ▸ drawback, handicap, liability. *See* **disadvantage**. *See synonym note at* **disadvantage**. 2. A period of decreased business activity and high unemployment ▸ downturn, recession, slump. *See* **depression**.

downswing *or* **downslide** *noun*
▸ decline, descent, downturn. *See* **fall** (3).

downtime *noun*
▸ recess, time-out. *See* **rest¹** (1).

down-to-earth *adjective*
▸ practical, pragmatic, prosaic. *See* **realistic** (1).

downtrend *noun*
▸ decline, descent, downswing. *See* **fall** (3).

downturn *noun*
1. A downward trend ▸ decline, descent, downswing. *See* **fall** (3). 2. A period of decreased business activity and high unemployment ▸ depression, recession, slowdown, slump.

downward *adjective*
▸ downward, drooping, falling. *See* **descending**.

doze *verb*
To sleep for a brief period ▸ catnap, nod off. *See* **nap**.

doze *noun*
A brief sleep ▸ siesta, snooze. *See* **nap**.

dozy *adjective*
▸ drowsy, nodding, slumberous. *See* **sleepy** (1).

drab *adjective*
1. Lacking vividness or color ▸ lackluster, mat, muddy. *See* **dull** (2). *See synonym note at* **dull**. 2. Lacking liveliness, charm, or surprise ▸ aseptic, colorless, pedestrian. *See* **dull** (1).

drabness *noun*
▸ blandness, colorlessness, lifelessness. *See* **dullness** (1).

draconian *adjective*
▸ harsh, stern, stringent. *See* **severe** (1).

draft *noun*
1. A preliminary plan or version, as of a written work ▸ blueprint, diagram, framework, layout, outline, rough, skeleton, sketch. 2. Compulsory enrollment in military service ▸ conscription, impressment, induction, levy, selective service. 3. The act of drawing or pulling a load ▸ drag, draw, tow. *See* **pull** (1). 4. An inhalation, as of a cigar, pipe, or cigarette ▸ drag, draw. *See* **pull** (2). 5. An act of drinking or the amount swallowed ▸ swallow, taste. *Informal:* swig. *See* **drink** (2). 6. A gentle wind ▸ breath, puff. *See* **breeze** (1).

draft *verb*
1. To draw up a preliminary plan or version of ▸ adumbrate, block in (*or* out), delineate, diagram, lay out, map out, outline, plan, plot, rough in (*or* out), sketch. 2. To enroll compulsorily in military service ▸ conscript, impress, induct, levy. 3. To devise and set down ▸ compose, draw up, formulate, frame. 4. To form by artistic effort ▸ produce, write. *See* **compose** (1).

drag *verb*
1. To exert force so as to move something toward the source of the force ▸ draw, haul, tug. *See* **pull** (1). *See synonym note at* **pull**. 2. To hang or cause to hang down and be pulled along behind ▸ draggle, trail, train. 3. To advance slowly ▸ crawl, creep, inch, poke. *Idiom:* go at a snail's pace. *See also* **trudge**. 4. To go or move slowly so that progress is hindered ▸ dawdle, dilly-dally, procrastinate. *See* **delay** (2).

drag *noun*
1. The act of drawing or pulling a load ▸ draft, draw, tow. *See* **pull** (1). 2. An inhalation, as of a cigar, pipe, or cigarette ▸ draft, draw. *See* **pull** (2). 3. A device for slowing or stopping motion ▸ curb, leash, rein. *See* **brake** (1). 4. Something that limits or holds back ▸ check, constraint, curb. *See* **restraint** (1). 5. A source of persistent worry or hardship ▸ cross, tribulation. *See* **burden¹** (1).

dragging *adjective*
▸ drawn-out, overlong, protracted. *See* **long¹** (2).

draggle *verb*
To hang or cause to hang down and be pulled along behind ▸ drag, trail, train. *See also* **pull**.

dragoon *verb*
▸ blackjack, force. *See* **coerce** (1).

drain *verb*
1. To remove a liquid by a steady, gradual process ▸ bleed, draw (off), drink up, evaporate, let out, milk, pump, strain, tap. 2. To cause a liquid to flow in a steady stream ▸ empty, flow, issue. *See* **pour** (1). 3. To become or cause to become gradually less ▸ diminish, dwindle, lessen. *See* **decrease**. 4. To lessen or weaken severely, as by removing something essential ▸ deplete, exhaust, impoverish, sap, use up. 5. To use all of ▸ eat up, expend, run through. *See* **exhaust** (1). *See synonym note at* **exhaust**. 6. To make weary ▸ fatigue, wear down. *See* **tire** (1). 7. To make or become free of moisture ▸ desiccate, exsiccate, parch. *See* **dry** (1).

drain *noun*
1. The act or process of decreasing ▸ reduction, slowdown. *See* **decrease**. 2. A persistent worry or hardship ▸ cross, tribulation. *See* **burden¹** (1).

drainage basin *noun*
The region drained by a river system ▸ basin, watershed.

drained *adjective*
▸ exhausted, weary, worn-out. *See* **tired** (1).

draining *adjective*
Causing fatigue ▸ exhausting, fatiguing, tiring, wearing, wearying. *See also* **burdensome**.

dram *noun*

1. A small amount of liquor ▸ shot, sip, tot. *See* **drop** (8). 2. A tiny amount ▸ dash, drop, smidgen. *See* **bit**[1] (1).

dramatic *adjective*

1. Of or relating to drama or the theater ▸ dramaturgic, dramaturgical, histrionic, histrionical, theatric, theatrical, thespian. 2. Suggesting drama or a stage performance, as in emotionality or suspense ▸ climactic, emotional, exaggerated, exciting, flamboyant, histrionic, histrionical, melodramatic, moving, sensational, spectacular, suspenseful, tense, theatric, theatrical, thrilling, vivid. *See also* **showy.**

dramatics *noun*

1. The art and occupation of an actor ▸ acting, stage, theater, theatrics. 2. Overemotional, exaggerated behavior calculated for effect ▸ histrionics, melodrama, melodramatics. *See* **theatrics** (2).

dramatize *verb*

1. To produce on the stage ▸ act (out), enact, perform. *See* **stage** (1). 2. To play the part of ▸ enact, perform, represent. *See* **act** (4).

dramaturgic *or* **dramaturgical** *adjective*

▸ histrionic, theatrical, thespian. *See* **dramatic** (1).

drape *verb*

1. To cover as if with clothes ▸ cloak, robe. *See* **clothe** (1). *See synonym note at* **clothe.** 2. To put clothes on ▸ attire, clothe, garb. *See* **dress** (1). 3. To sit or lie with the limbs spread out awkwardly ▸ spread-eagle, straddle. *See* **sprawl** (1).

draw *verb*

1. To exert force so as to move something toward the source of the force ▸ drag, haul, tug. *See* **pull** (1). *See synonym note at* **pull.** 2. To cause a liquid to flow in a steady stream ▸ decant, empty, issue. *See* **pour** (1). 3. To remove a liquid by a steady, gradual process ▸ draw off, pump, strain. *See* **drain** (1). 4. To obtain from another source ▸ extract, gain, receive. *See* **derive** (1). 5. To direct or impel to oneself by some quality or action ▸ allure, entice, lure. *See* **attract** (1). 6. To bring out something latent, hidden, or unexpressed. ▸ draw out, educe, elicit, summon. *See* **evoke.** 7. To make as income or profit ▸ clear, gain, yield. *See* **return** (3). 8. To arrive at a conclusion from evidence or reasoning ▸ deduce, gather. *See* **infer** (1). 9. To present a lifelike image of ▸ depict, portray, render. *See* **represent** (2).

draw back *verb*

To move back in the face of enemy attack or after a defeat ▸ fall back, pull out, turn back, withdraw. *See* **retreat** (4).

draw down *verb*

To use all of ▸ eat up, expend, run through. *See* **exhaust** (1).

draw in *verb*

1. To pull back in ▸ retract, withdraw. 2. To involve someone in an activity ▸ engage. *See also* **involve.** 3. To take in moisture or liquid ▸ soak (up), sop up. *See* **drink** (3).

draw into *verb*

To draw or be drawn in so that extrication is difficult ▸ embroil, mix up, wrap up. *See* **involve** (1).

draw on *verb*

To put into action or use ▸ apply, employ, utilize. *See* **use** (1).

draw out *verb*

To make or become longer ▸ extend, prolongate. *See* **lengthen.**

draw up *verb*

To devise and set down ▸ compose, draft, formulate, frame. *See also* **compose.**

draw *noun*

1. An equality of scores, votes, or performances in a contest ▸ dead heat, deadlock, stalemate, standoff, tie. 2. The act of drawing or pulling a load ▸ drag, haul, tow. *See* **pull** (1). 3. The power or quality of attracting ▸ appeal, draw, enticement, lure. *See* **attraction** (1). 4. Something that attracts, especially with the promise of pleasure or reward ▸ bait, come-on, enticement. *See* **lure** (1). 5. An inhalation, as of a cigar, pipe, or cigarette ▸ drag, puff. *See* **pull** (2). 6. A dominating position, as in a conflict ▸ edge, upper hand, vantage. *See* **advantage** (3).

drawback *noun*

▸ detriment, handicap, liability. *See* **disadvantage.** *See synonym note at* **disadvantage.**

drawing *noun*

▸ illustration, rendering. *See* **representation.**

drawn *adjective*

▸ gaunt, wan, worn. *See* **haggard.**

drawn-out *adjective*

▸ interminable, overlong, protracted. *See* **long**[1] (2).

dread *verb*

To be afraid ▸ fear. *Idioms:* break out in a cold sweat, have butterflies (in one's stomach), have knots (*or* a knot) in one's stomach, have one's heart in one's mouth, sweat blood (*or* bullets).

dread *noun*

A feeling of agitation in the face of trouble or danger ▸ apprehension, consternation, trepidation. *See* **fear.** *See synonym note at* **fear.**

dreadful *adjective*

1. Causing or capable of causing fear ▸ appalling, dire, scary, horrible. *See* **fearful** (1). 2. Very bad ▸ appalling, awful, fearful, frightful. *See* **terrible** (1). 3. Shockingly repellent ▸ grisly, gruesome, hideous. *See* **ghastly** (1).

dreadfully *adverb*

▸ awfully, exceedingly, highly. *See* **very.**

dream *noun*

1. An illusory mental image ▸ daydream, fancy, fantasy, fiction, figment, hallucination, illusion, phantasm, phantasma, phantasmagoria, phantasmagory, reverie, vision. 2. A fantastic, impracticable plan or desire ▸ bubble, castle in the air, chimera, fantasy, illusion, pipe dream, rainbow. 3. A fervent hope ▸ ambition, aspiration, desire, goal, hope, ideal, vision, wish. 4. The condition of being so lost in solitary thought that one is unaware of one's sur-

roundings ▸ absent-mindedness, bemusement, reverie. *See* **trance** (1).

dream *verb*

1. To experience dreams or daydreams ▸ daydream, fancy, fantasize, hallucinate, imagine, muse, stargaze, woolgather. *See also* **imagine.** **2.** To have a strong longing for ▸ covet, want, yearn. *See* **desire** (1).

dream up *verb*

1. To use ingenuity in making, developing, or achieving ▸ concoct, contrive, devise. *See* **invent** (1). **2.** To form mental images of ▸ envision, fantasize, visualize. *See* **imagine** (1).

dreamer *noun*

1. A person inclined to be imaginative or idealistic but impractical ▸ daydreamer, fantasist, idealist, romantic, stargazer, theorist, theorizer, utopian, visionary, wishful thinker. **2.** One who aspires ▸ aspirant, aspirer, hopeful, seeker. *Informal:* wannabe.

dreamlike *adjective*

▸ hallucinatory, illusory, phantasmagoric. *See* **illusive** (1).

dreamy *adjective*

1. Given to daydreams or reverie ▸ daydreaming, fanciful, fantasizing, moony, musing, stargazing, starry-eyed, visionary, woolgathering. **2.** *Informal* Particularly excellent ▸ fantastic, sensational, superb. *See* **marvelous** (1).

drear *adjective*

1. Arousing no interest or curiosity ▸ dull, humdrum, monotonous. *See* **boring** (1). **2.** Dark and depressing ▸ bleak, desolate, somber. *See* **gloomy** (1).

dreariness *noun*

▸ blandness, drabness, lifelessness. *See* **dullness** (1).

dreary *adjective*

1. Dark and depressing ▸ bleak, desolate, somber. *See* **gloomy** (1). **2.** Arousing no interest or curiosity ▸ dull, humdrum, monotonous. *See* **boring** (1).

dredge *verb*

▸ lade, ladle, scoop (up). *See* **dip** (2).

dregs *noun*

1. Matter that settles on a bottom or collects on a surface by a natural process ▸ accumulation, precipitation, sediment. *See* **deposit** (2). **2.** Items or material discarded or rejected as useless or worthless ▸ flotsam, litter, rubbish. *See* **garbage** (1). **3.** A person or group of persons regarded as worthless or contemptible ▸ rabble, ragtag and bobtail, vermin. *See* **riffraff.**

drench *verb*

▸ douse, soak, souse. *See* **wet** (1).

drenched *adjective*

▸ doused, soaked, waterlogged. *See* **wet** (1).

dress *verb*

1. To put clothes on ▸ apparel, attire, clothe, costume, don, drape, garb, garment, invest, outfit, robe. *Informal:* tog. *See also* **clothe.** **2.** To apply therapeutic materials to a wound ▸ bandage, bind, plaster, swathe, truss. **3.** To add fertilizer to soil ▸ fertilize, manure, top-dress. **4.** To furnish with decorations ▸ decorate, garnish, ornament. *See* **adorn** (1). **5.** To place in or

form a line or lines ▸ align, queue (up), range. *See* **line.**

dress down *verb*

To criticize for a fault or offense ▸ chide, rebuke, reprimand. *See* **chastise** (1).

dress up *verb*

To dress in formal or special clothing ▸ array, attire, bedeck, deck (out), prank, preen, primp. *Informal:* trick out (*or* up). *Slang:* doll up.

dress *noun*

1. Articles worn to cover the body ▸ apparel, attire, clothes, clothing, garb, garments, habiliments, raiment. *Informal:* duds, togs. *Slang:* threads. **2.** A set or style of clothing ▸ costume, ensemble, garb, gear, guise, habiliments, outfit, toilette, turnout, wardrobe. *Informal:* getup, rig. **3.** A one-piece skirted outer garment for women and children ▸ frock, gown, jumper, muumuu, pinafore, shift, smock.

dressy *adjective*

▸ black-tie, full-dress. *See* **formal** (5).

dribble *verb*

1. To fall or let fall in drops of liquid ▸ distill, trickle. *See* **drip.** **2.** To let saliva run from the mouth ▸ salivate, slobber. *See* **drool.**

dribble *noun*

The process or sound of dripping ▸ drip, drizzle, mizzle, trickle.

driblet *noun*

A quantity of liquid falling or resting in a spherical mass ▸ bead, droplet. *See* **drop** (1).

drift *verb*

1. To move along with or be carried away by the action of water ▸ float, wash. **2.** To move about at random, especially over a wide area ▸ gad, meander, wander. *See* **rove.** **3.** To collect or pile up or onto something ▸ hill, lump. *See* **heap** (1). **4.** To move smoothly, continuously, and effortlessly ▸ slide, slither. *See* **glide** (1). **5.** To turn away from a prescribed course of action or conduct ▸ digress, stray. *See* **deviate** (1). **6.** To move in or on the wind ▸ flap, float. *See* **blow**[1] (2). **7.** To turn aside, especially from the main subject in writing or speaking ▸ ramble, stray, wander. *See* **digress** (1).

drift *noun*

1. A group of things gathered haphazardly ▸ cumulus, mass, mound. *See* **heap** (1). **2.** Something suggestive of running water ▸ flood, stream, tide. *See* **flow.** **3.** The general sense or significance, as of an action or statement ▸ burden, purport, substance. *See* **import** (1). **4.** The current of thought uniting all elements of a text or discourse ▸ aim, intent, tenor. *See* **thrust** (1).

drifter *noun*

▸ nomad, roamer, vagabond. *See* **hobo.**

drill *noun*

Repetition of an action so as to develop or maintain one's skill ▸ exercise, rehearsal. *See* **practice** (1).

drill *verb*

1. To engage in activities in order to strengthen or condition ▸ exercise, practice, train, work out. **2.** To instruct by rote or discipline, as in a body of doctrine or belief ▸ catechize, inculcate. *See* **indoctrinate** (1). **3.** To fix (an idea, for example) in someone's mind by reemphasis and repetition ▸ drive, inculcate. *See* **instill. 4.** To penetrate with a sharp edge ▸ bayonet, incise, pierce, slash. *See* **cut** (1).

drink *verb*
1. To take into the mouth and swallow a liquid ▸ down, drink up, gulp, guzzle, imbibe, lap up, pull on, quaff, sip, slurp, sup, swill. *Informal:* swig, toss back (*or* down). *Slang:* belt. **Idiom:** wet one's whistle. **2.** To take alcoholic liquor, especially excessively or habitually ▸ guzzle, imbibe, tipple. *Informal:* nip. *Slang:* booze, chug, chugalug, lush, soak, tank up. **Idioms:** bend the elbow, hit the bottle **3.** To take in moisture or liquid ▸ absorb, draw in, imbibe, osmose, soak (up), sop up, sponge up, take up. **4.** To salute by raising and drinking from a glass ▸ compliment, honor, pledge, salute, toast.

drink in *verb*
To take in and incorporate, especially mentally ▸ digest, imbibe, take up. *See* **absorb** (2).

drink up *verb*
To remove a liquid by a steady, gradual process ▸ pump, strain. *See* **drain** (1).

drink *noun*
1. Any liquid that is fit for drinking ▸ beverage, brew, drinkable, libation, liquor, potable, potation, potion, refreshment. **2.** An act of drinking or the amount swallowed ▸ draft, potation, pull, quaff, sip, sup, swallow, swill, taste, tot. *Informal:* swig. *Slang:* belt

drinkable *noun*
▸ beverage, brew, refreshment. *See* **drink** (1).

drip *verb*
To fall or let fall in drops of liquid ▸ distill, dribble, drizzle, drop, tear, trickle, weep.

drip *noun*
1. The process or sound of dripping ▸ dribble, drizzle, mizzle, trickle. **2.** *Slang* An unpleasant, tiresome person ▸ bore, chump. *Slang:* dip, dork, dweeb, jerk, lamer, nerd, nimrod, pill, poop, schmo, schmuck, turkey, twerp, twit. *See also* **fool.**

dripping *adjective*
▸ drenched, soaked, waterlogged. *See* **wet** (1).

drippy *adjective*
Slang Affectedly or extravagantly emotional ▸ gushy, mawkish, soft. *See* **sentimental.**

drive *verb*
1. To run and control a motor vehicle ▸ chauffeur, motor, pilot, steer, taxi, wheel. *Slang:* tool. **2.** To force to move or advance with or as if with blows or pressure ▸ butt, jolt, propel, push, ram, shove, slam, thrust. *See also* **beat, hit. 3.** To urge to move along ▸ chase, herd, hustle, push, run, wrangle. *See also* **maneuver, provoke. 4.** To force to work hard ▸ push, task, tax, work. **Idiom:** crack the whip. *See also* **force. 5.** To cause to move forward or upward, as toward a goal ▸ further, propel, push. *See* **advance** (1). **6.** To exert oneself steadily, often to the point of exhaustion

▸ strain, sweat, toil. *See* **labor** (1). **7.** To penetrate into a substance or place with force ▸ dig, stab, stick. *See* **plunge** (1). **8.** To fix (an idea, for example) in someone's mind by reemphasis and repetition ▸ drill, inculcate. *See* **instill. 9.** To look for and pursue game in order to capture or kill it ▸ run, stalk. *See* **hunt** (1). **10.** To impel to action ▸ induce, press. *See* **urge.**

drive away *verb*
To make distant, hostile, or unsympathetic ▸ disaffect, disunite. *See* **estrange.**

drive out *verb*
To direct or allow to leave ▸ cast out, expel. *See* **dismiss** (2).

drive *noun*
1. An organized effort to accomplish a purpose ▸ campaign, crusade, movement, push. *See also* **cause. 2.** An aggressive readiness along with energy to undertake taxing efforts ▸ enterprise, initiative, hustle, punch. *Informal:* get-up-and-go, gumption, push. *See also* **enthusiasm. 3.** A trip in a motor vehicle ▸ jaunt, ride, run. *Informal:* spin, turn, whirl. **4.** The act of attacking ▸ assault, offense, onslaught, strike. *See* **attack** (1). **5.** A course affording passage from one place to another ▸ path, road, route. *See* **way** (2).

✦ **CORE SYNONYMS:** *drive, campaign, crusade, movement, push.* These nouns denote an organized, vigorous effort to accomplish a purpose: *a drive to sell bonds; a fund-raising campaign; a crusade for improved social services; a movement to slash costs for prescription drugs; a push to get the bill passed.*

---

drivel *verb*
1. To let saliva run from the mouth ▸ dribble, salivate, slobber. *See* **drool. 2.** To talk rapidly on trivial matters ▸ blab, jabber, prattle. *See* **chatter** (1).

drivel *noun*
1. Saliva running from the mouth ▸ drool, salivation, slaver, slobber. **2.** Something that does not have or make sense ▸ bunkum, claptrap, garbage. *See* **nonsense** (1). **3.** Empty or foolish talk ▸ blather, jabber, twaddle. *See* **babble** (1). **4.** Incessant and inconsequential talk ▸ chitchat, patter, small talk. *See* **chatter.**

driven *adjective*
▸ determined, enterprising. *See* **ambitious.**

driver *noun*
A person who operates a motor vehicle ▸ chauffeur, motorist, operator.

driving *adjective*
▸ brisk, lively, vigorous. *See* **energetic.**

drizzle *noun*
1. Water condensed from atmospheric vapor and falling in drops ▸ deluge, downpour, shower. *See* **rain** (2). **2.** The process or sound of dripping ▸ dribble, drip, mizzle, trickle.

drizzle *verb*
1. To fall in drops of water from clouds ▸ mist, precipitate, shower. *See* **rain** (2). **2.** To fall or let fall in drops of liquid ▸ dribble, trickle. *See* **drip.**

droit *noun*
▸ birthright, freedom, privilege. *See* **right**.

droll *adjective*
▸ comical, humorous, laughable. *See* **funny** (1).

drollery *or* **drollness** *noun*
▸ funniness, ridiculousness, wittiness. *See* **humor** (1).

drone[1] *noun*
1. A self-indulgent person who spends time avoiding work or other useful activity ▸ bum, idler, loafer. *See* **wastrel** (2). **2.** A person who does tedious, menial, or unpleasant work ▸ grunt, hack, menial. *See* **drudge** (1). **3.** One who works or toils tirelessly ▸ grind, grub, plodder. *See* **drudge** (2).

drone[2] *verb*
To make a continuous low-pitched droning sound ▸ bumble, buzz, whir. *See* **hum**.

drone *noun*
A continuous low-pitched droning sound ▸ bumble, burr, drone. *See* **hum**.

drool *noun*
Saliva running from the mouth ▸ drivel, salivation, slaver, slobber.

drool *verb*
To let saliva run from the mouth ▸ dribble, drivel, salivate, slaver, slobber.

drool over *verb*
Informal To make an excessive show of desire for or interest in ▸ *Informal:* ogle, slobber over. *See also* **adore, desire, lust, rave**.

droop *verb*
1. To hang limply, loosely, and carelessly ▸ flop, sag. *See* **slouch** (2). **2.** To become limp, as from loss of freshness ▸ flag, sag. *See* **wilt**. **3.** To grow weary ▸ flag, wear out. *See* **tire** (2). **4.** To go from a more erect posture to a less erect posture ▸ sink, slump. *See* **drop** (1).

drooping *adjective*
1. Not firm or stiff ▸ droopy, flaccid, floppy. *See* **limp** (1). **2.** Lacking energy and vitality ▸ languorous, listless, spiritless. *See* **languid**.

droopy *adjective*
▸ flabby, flaccid, floppy. *See* **limp** (1).

drop *noun*
1. A quantity of liquid falling or resting in a spherical mass ▸ bead, driblet, droplet, glob, globule, tear, teardrop. **2.** A sudden downward motion toward the ground ▸ descent, plunge. *See* **fall** (1). **3.** A usually swift downward trend, as in prices ▸ decline, dip, plunge. *See* **fall** (3). **4.** The extent or measurement downward from a surface ▸ deepness, depth, drop-off. **5.** A downward slope or distance ▸ decline, declivity, descent, drop-off, fall, pitch. **6.** A dominating position, as in a conflict ▸ edge, upper hand, vantage. *See* **advantage** (3). **7.** A tiny amount ▸ dash, jot, smidgen. *See* **bit**[1] (1). **8.** A small amount of liquor ▸ belt, dram, jigger, shot, sip, splash, taste, tot. *Informal:* nip, slug. *Slang:* snort.

drop *verb*
1. To go from a more erect posture to a less erect posture ▸ droop, fall, sag, sink, slump. *See also* **slouch**. **2.** To move downward in response to gravity ▸ descend, plummet. *See* **fall** (1). **3.** To come to the ground from an upright position ▸ fall over, keel over, topple. *See* **fall** (2). **4.** To become lower in value or price ▸ dive, plummet, plunge. *See* **fall** (7). **5.** To slope downward ▸ decline, descend, dip, fall, pitch, sink. **6.** To bring down, as from a shot or blow ▸ chop down, cut down, down, fell, flatten, floor, ground, hew, knock down, level, prostrate, strike down, throw. *Slang:* deck. *Idiom:* lay low. **7.** To cease consideration or treatment of ▸ abandon, discontinue, dismiss, end, forget, give over (*or* up), quit, relinquish, skip, stop, write off. *Idioms:* have done with, wash one's hands of. *See also* **abandon**. **8.** To take or leave out ▸ eliminate, exclude, let go, omit, prune, remove. *See also* **discard, remove**. **9.** To suddenly lose all health or strength ▸ crack, succumb. *See* **collapse** (1). **10.** To cease living ▸ demise, expire, perish. *See* **die** (1). **11.** To end the employment or service of ▸ cashier, terminate. *See* **dismiss** (1). *See synonym note at* **dismiss**. **12.** To cause to descend ▸ depress, let down, take down. *See* **lower**[2] (1). **13.** To fall or let fall in drops of liquid ▸ dribble, trickle. *See* **drip**.

drop by *or* **in** *verb*
To go to or seek out the company of someone in order to socialize ▸ come over, go over, pop in. *See* **visit** (1).

drop off *verb*
To sleep for a brief period ▸ doze, siesta. *See* **nap**.

droplet *noun*
▸ bead, driblet. *See* **drop** (1).

drop-off *noun*
1. The extent or measurement downward from a surface ▸ deepness, depth, drop. **2.** A usually swift downward trend ▸ decline, dip, plunge. *See* **fall** (3).

dropping *noun*
▸ dung, feces, waste. *See* **excrement**.

drossy *adjective*
▸ empty, good-for-nothing, valueless. *See* **worthless** (1).

droughty *adjective*
▸ arid, desert, rainless. *See* **dry** (2).

drove *noun*
1. An enormous number of persons gathered together ▸ horde, mass, throng. *See* **crowd** (1). **2.** A number of animals considered collectively ▸ bevy, gaggle, herd. *See* **flock** (1). *See synonym note at* **flock**.

drown *verb*
▸ engulf, overflow, submerge. *See* **flood** (1).

drowsy *adjective*
▸ dozy, nodding, slumberous. *See* **sleepy** (1).

drub *verb*
1. To hit heavily and repeatedly ▸ assault, batter, pummel, thresh. *See* **beat** (1). **2.** To render totally ineffective by decisive defeat ▸ crush, overcome, overpower, rout. *See* **overwhelm** (1). **3.** To criticize harshly and devastatingly ▸ bash, excoriate, flay, rip into. *See* **slam** (5).

drubbing *noun*
▶ overthrow, trouncing, vanquishment. *See* **defeat.**

drudge *noun*
1. A person who does tedious, menial, or unpleasant work ▶ drone, foot soldier, hack, menial, scullion, slave. *Slang:* grunt. **2.** One who works or toils tirelessly ▶ drone, grind, grub, plodder. *Informal:* workhorse.

drudge *verb*
To do tedious, difficult or menial work ▶ plod, slave. *See* **grind** (4).

drudgery *noun*
▶ toil, travail, work. *See* **labor** (1). *See synonym note at* **labor.**

drug *noun*
1. A substance used in the treatment of disease ▶ medicament, medication, medicine, pharmaceutical, pill, prescription. *See also* **cure. 2.** A substance that affects the central nervous system and is often addictive ▶ depressant, hallucinogen, narcotic, opiate, psychotropic, sedative, stimulant. *Informal:* dope. *See also* **soporific.**

drug *verb*
1. To administer especially a pain killing drug to someone ▶ anesthetize, chloroform, dose, etherize, knock out, medicate, narcotize, opiate, physic, put under, sedate, tranquilize. *Informal:* dope (up). *See also* **deaden. 2.** To addle the mind, as with a narcotic or alcohol ▶ befuddle, besot, blur, cloud, daze, dim, dull, fog, fuddle, impair, stupefy. *See also* **confuse, daze.**

drug abuse *noun*
▶ dependence, enslavement, substance abuse. *See* **addiction.**

drugged *adjective*
Stupefied, intoxicated, or otherwise influenced by the taking of drugs ▶ *Informal:* doped. *Slang:* baked, buzzed, high, hopped-up, lit (up), potted, ripped, spaced-out, stoned, tripping, turned-on, wasted, wiped-out, wired, zonked. *Idiom:* under the influence.

drum *verb*
▶ pulsate, pulse, throb. *See* **beat** (5).

drunk *adjective*
Stupefied, excited, or muddled with alcoholic liquor ▶ besotted, crapulent, crapulous, drunken, inebriate, inebriated, intoxicated, sodden, sottish, tipsy. *Informal:* cockeyed, stewed. *Slang:* blind, blotto, bombed, boozed, boozy, crocked, high, lit (up), loaded, looped, pickled, pie-eyed, pixilated, plastered, potted, sloshed, smashed, soused, sozzled, stinking, stinko, stoned, tanked, tight, zonked. *Idioms:* drunk as a skunk, half-seas over, high as a kite, in one's cups, three sheets in (*or* to) the wind.

drunk *noun*
1. A person who is habitually drunk ▶ alcoholic, dipsomaniac, tippler. *See* **drunkard. 2.** A drinking bout ▶ brannigan, carousal, carouse, spree. *See* **bender.**

drunkard *noun*
A person who is habitually drunk ▶ alcoholic, dipsomaniac, drunk, inebriate, sot, tippler, toper. *Slang:* alky, boozehound, boozer, dipso, lush, rummy, soak, souse, sponge, stiff, wino.

drunken *adjective*
▶ intoxicated, sodden, tipsy. *See* **drunk.**

drunkenness *noun*
The condition of being intoxicated with alcoholic liquor ▶ crapulence, inebriation, inebriety, insobriety, intoxication, tipsiness. *See also* **bender, binge.**

druthers *noun*
Informal The act, power, or right of choosing ▶ decision, discretion, option. *See* **choice** (1).

dry *adjective*
1. Having little or no liquid or moisture ▶ anhydrous, bone-dry, dried up, moistureless, sere, waterless. **2.** Having little or no precipitation ▶ arid, desert, droughty, parched, rainless, scorched, thirsty. *See also* **barren. 3.** Needing or desiring drink ▶ parched, thirsty. **4.** Disagreeable to the senses, especially the sense of hearing ▶ grating, jarring. *See* **harsh** (1). **5.** Having a taste characteristic of that produced by acids ▶ sharp, tart. *See* **sour** (1). *See synonym note at* **sour. 6.** Without addition, decoration, or qualification ▶ austere, plain, simple. *See* **bare** (1). **7.** Lacking feeling or emotion ▶ emotionless, impassive, stolid. *See* **cold** (2). **8.** Lacking liveliness, charm, or surprise ▶ aseptic, colorless, pedestrian. *See* **dull** (1). **9.** Arousing no interest or curiosity ▶ dull, humdrum, monotonous. *See* **boring** (1).

dry *verb*
1. To make or become free of moisture ▶ dehydrate, desiccate, drain, dry out, exsiccate, parch. **2.** To make or become physically hard ▶ congeal, solidify. *See* **harden** (2).

dry up *verb*
1. To make or become no longer fresh or shapely because of loss of moisture ▶ frizzle, mummify, pucker, sear, shrivel, wither, wizen. **2.** To make or become no longer active or productive ▶ deplete, desiccate, give out, play out, run out. *See also* **exhaust.**

✦ CORE SYNONYMS: *dry, dehydrate, desiccate, parch.* These verbs mean to make or become free of moisture: *drying the dishes; added water to eggs that were dehydrated; a factory where coconut meat is shredded and desiccated; land parched by the sun.*

◀ ANTONYM: *moisten*

---

dryness *noun*
1. A lack of excitement, liveliness, or interest ▶ blandness, drabness, lifelessness. *See* **dullness** (1). **2.** The practice of refraining from use of alcoholic liquors ▶ sobriety, teetotalism. *See* **temperance** (2).

dry run *noun*
▶ proof, trial, tryout. *See* **test** (1).

dual *adjective*
1. Consisting of two identical or similar related

things, parts, or elements ▸ double, matched, paired, twin. *See also* **equal. 2.** Composed of two parts or things ▸ biform, duple, twofold. *See* **double** (2).

dub *verb*
To give a name or title to ▸ christen, designate. *See* **name** (1).

dub *noun*
A clumsy, inept person ▸ bungler. *Slang:* klutz. *See* **blunderer.**

dubiety *noun*
1. A lack of conviction or certainty ▸ distrust, incertitude, skepticism. *See* **doubt** (1). *See synonym note at* **doubt. 2.** The refusal or reluctance to believe ▸ incredulity, mistrust, skepticism, unbelief. *See* **disbelief** (1).

dubious *adjective*
1. Experiencing doubt ▸ hesitant, skeptical, uncertain. *See* **doubtful** (2). **2.** Lacking certainty or clarity ▸ doubtful, indeterminate, questionable, unclear. *See* **ambiguous** (1). **3.** Of dubious character ▸ equivocal, questionable, suspicious. *See* **shady** (1). **4.** Not likely ▸ improbable, questionable. *See* **doubtful** (1). **5.** Refusing or reluctant to believe ▸ questioning, skeptical. *See* **incredulous.**

dubiously *adverb*
▸ doubtfully, questioningly. *See* **skeptically.**

dubiousness *noun*
▸ distrust, incertitude, skepticism. *See* **doubt** (1).

dubitable *adjective*
▸ dubious, indeterminate, questionable, unclear. *See* **ambiguous** (1).

duck *verb*
1. To avoid fulfilling or answering completely ▸ dodge, hedge. *See* **evade** (1). **2.** To keep away from ▸ dodge, evade, shun. *See* **avoid. 3.** To plunge briefly in or into a liquid ▸ dunk, submerse. *See* **dip** (1). *See synonym note at* **dip. 4.** To fail to attend on purpose ▸ shirk. *Slang:* skip. *See* **cut** (8).

duck *noun*
The act of swimming ▸ dip, dunk. *See* **plunge** (4).

duck soup *noun*
Slang An easily accomplished task ▸ pushover, snap, walkover. *See* **breeze** (2).

duct *noun*
▸ canal, capillary, vein. *See* **vessel** (2).

ductile *adjective*
1. Capable of being shaped or bent ▸ bendable, flexible, plastic. *See* **malleable** (1). *See synonym note at* **malleable. 2.** Easily altered or influenced ▸ malleable, pliable, suggestible. *See* **flexible** (3).

ductility *noun*
▸ elasticity, malleability, pliability. *See* **flexibility** (1).

dud *noun*
1. *Informal* An unsuccessful person or enterprise ▸ bust, fiasco, washout. *See* **failure** (1). **2.** *Informal* Something that disappoints ▸ anticlimax, bust, washout. *See* **disappointment** (2).

dudgeon *noun*
▸ resentment, ruffled feathers, umbrage. *See* **offense** (1).

duds *noun*
▸ apparel, clothing, garments. *See* **dress** (1).

due *adjective*
1. Owed as a debt ▸ collectible, mature, outstanding, owed, owing, payable, receivable, unpaid, unsatisfied, unsettled. **2.** Known to be about to arrive ▸ anticipated, expected, scheduled, slated. **3.** In the relatively near future ▸ approaching, coming, forthcoming, upcoming. *Idioms:* around the corner, on the horizon. *See also* **close, imminent. 4.** Consistent with prevailing or accepted standards or circumstances ▸ deserved, fitting, proper. *See* **just** (2).

due *noun*
1. Something justly deserved ▸ comeuppance, compensation, deserts, guerdon, payment, recompense, reward, satisfaction, wages. *Informal:* lumps. *Idioms:* what is coming to one, what one has coming. **2.** A benefit granted to a person by law, nature, or custom ▸ birthright, freedom, privilege. *See* **right. 3.** Something, such as money, owed by one person to another ▸ indebtedness, liability, obligation. *See* **debt** (1).

due *adverb*
In a direct line ▸ straight, undeviatingly. *See* **directly** (1).

duel *verb*
To strive in opposition ▸ clash, combat, fight. *See* **contend** (1).

duel *noun*
A face-to-face, usually hostile meeting ▸ encounter, face-off, showdown. *See* **confrontation** (1).

due process *noun*
The state, action, or principle of treating all persons equally in accordance with the law ▸ equity, justice. *See also* **fairness.**

dues *noun*
▸ exaction, fee. *See* **toll**[1] (1).

duet *noun*
▸ duo, match, pair. *See* **couple.**

due to *preposition*
▸ as a result of, on account of, owing to. *See* **because of.**

dugout *noun*
A hollow beneath the earth's surface ▸ cave, cavern, grotto, tunnel. *See also* **hole.**

dulcet *adjective*
▸ euphonic, melodic, musical. *See* **melodious.**

dulcify *verb*
▸ appease, mollify, soothe. *See* **pacify.**

dull *adjective*
1. Lacking liveliness, charm, or surprise ▸ arid, aseptic, colorless, deadly, drab, dry, earthbound, flat, flavorless, lackluster, leaden, lifeless, lusterless, matter-of-fact, pedestrian, plodding, prosaic, spiritless, sterile, stodgy, unimaginative, uninspired. *Informal:* blah. *See also* **insipid, ordinary. 2.** Lacking vividness or color ▸ dim, drab, flat, gray, lackluster, lusterless, mat, muddy, murky. *See also* **pale. 3.** Not physically sharp or keen ▸ blunt, edgeless, obtuse, unpointed, unsharpened. **4.** Arousing no interest or curiosity

▶ dry, humdrum, monotonous. *See* **boring** (1). **5.** Having only a limited ability to learn and understand ▶ simple, slow. *See* **backward** (1). **6.** Lacking physical feeling or sensitivity ▶ numb, stuporous, unresponsive. *See* **dead** (2). **7.** Unwilling or unable to perceive ▶ obtuse, unperceptive. *See* **blind** (3). **8.** In low spirits ▶ dysphoric, gloomy, melancholy, spiritless. *See* **depressed** (1). **9.** Characterized by reduced economic activity ▶ down, slack. *See* **slow** (2). **10.** Dark and depressing ▶ bleak, desolate, somber. *See* **gloomy** (1).

dull *verb*
1. To make or become less sharp-edged ▶ blunt, hebetate, round, turn. *Idiom:* take the edge off. **2.** To addle the mind, as with a narcotic or alcohol ▶ besot, impair, stupefy. *See* **drug** (2). **3.** To render less sensitive ▶ desensitize, numb. *See* **deaden** (1). **4.** To make dim ▶ blur, fog, obfuscate. *See* **obscure** (1). **5.** To decrease or dull the sound of ▶ deaden, mute. *See* **muffle** (1).

✛ CORE SYNONYMS: *dull, colorless, drab, humdrum, lackluster, pedestrian, stodgy, uninspired.* These adjectives mean lacking in liveliness, charm, or surprise: *a dull, uninteresting performance; a colorless and unimaginative person; a drab and boring job; a humdrum conversation; a lackluster life; a pedestrian movie plot; a stodgy dinner party; an uninspired lecture.*

◀ ANTONYM: *lively*

---

dullard *noun*
A mentally dull person ▶ blockhead, chump, clod, dolt, dummkopf, dummy, dunce, idiot, imbecile, moron, nincompoop, nitwit, numskull, simpleton, softhead, thickhead, woodenhead. *Informal:* bonehead, knucklehead, lamebrain, muttonhead. *Slang:* airhead, boob, cretin, dimwit, dumbbell, dumbo, fathead, half-wit, lunkhead, pinhead, simp. *See also* **drip, fool, oaf, square.**

dullness *noun*
1. A lack of excitement, liveliness, or interest ▶ asepticism, blandness, colorlessness, drabness, dreariness, dryness, familiarity, flatness, flavorlessness, insipidity, insipidness, jejuneness, lifelessness, mediocrity, routinism, sluggishness, staleness, sterileness, sterility, stodginess, tameness, tediousness, tedium, vapidity, vapidness, weariness. *See also* **monotony. 2.** A deficiency in mental and physical alertness and activity ▶ languor, listlessness, sluggishness. *See* **lethargy** (1).

dumb *adjective*
1. Lacking in intelligence ▶ doltish, idiotic, obtuse. *See* **stupid** (1). **2.** Lacking the power or faculty of speech ▶ inarticulate, voiceless. *See* **mute** (1). **3.** Temporarily unable or unwilling to speak, as from shock or fear ▶ inarticulate, mute. *See* **speechless** (1). **4.** *Informal* Lacking worth and value ▶ drossy, good-for-nothing, valueless. *See* **worthless** (1).

dumbbell *noun*
▶ dummy, moron, thickhead. *See* **dullard.**

dumbfound *verb*
▶ boggle, flabbergast. *See* **stagger** (2).

dumbfounded *adjective*
▶ confounded, perplexed, turbid. *See* **confused** (1).

dumbness *noun*
1. The avoidance of speech ▶ muteness, speechlessness. *See* **silence** (2). **2.** The state of being stupid ▶ idiocy, mindlessness, obtuseness. *See* **stupidity.**

dumbo *noun*
▶ dummy, dunce, thickhead. *See* **dullard.**

dumbstruck *adjective*
▶ inarticulate, mute. *See* **speechless** (1).

dummkopf *noun*
▶ blockhead, dunce, thickhead. *See* **dullard.**

dummy *noun*
▶ clod, dunce, thickhead. *See* **dullard.**

dump *verb*
1. To relieve a burden ▶ discharge, relieve, unburden. *See* **rid. 2.** To let go or get rid of as being useless or defective, for example ▶ dispose of, throw away. *Informal:* chuck. *See* **discard. 3.** To get rid of by selling ▶ close out, unload. *See* **dump.**

dump *noun*
Slang A disreputable or run-down bar or restaurant ▶ *Slang:* dive, honky-tonk, joint, juke house, juke joint. *Idiom:* hole in the wall.

dumping *noun*
▶ elimination, removal, riddance. *See* **disposal** (1).

dumps *noun*
▶ dejection, doldrums, melancholy. *See* **depression** (2).

dumpy *adjective*
▶ chunky, heavyset, squat. *See* **stocky.**

dun *verb*
▶ charge, invoice. *See* **bill**[1].

dunce *noun*
▶ dummy, idiot, thickhead. *See* **dullard.**

dung *noun*
▶ dropping, feces, waste. *See* **excrement.**

dunk *verb*
To plunge briefly in or into a liquid ▶ douse, submerse. *See* **dip** (1). *See synonym note at* **dip.**

dunk *noun*
The act of swimming ▶ duck, swim. *See* **plunge** (4).

duo *noun*
▶ duet, match, pair. *See* **couple.**

dupable *adjective*
▶ credulous, naive, susceptible. *See* **gullible.**

dupe *noun*
1. A person who is easily deceived or victimized ▶ butt, cat's-paw, fool, gull, lamb, pushover, tool, victim. *Informal:* sucker. *Slang:* fall guy, gudgeon, mark, monkey, patsy, pigeon, sap. **2.** A person used or controlled by others ▶ puppet, stooge, tool. *See* **pawn**[2].

dupe *verb*
To cause to accept something false, especially by trickery or misrepresentation ▶ fool, mislead, trick. *See* **deceive.** *See synonym note at* **deceive.**

duplex *or* **duple** *adjective*
▶ dual, duple, twofold. *See* **double** (2).

duplicate *noun*
1. Something closely resembling another ► ditto, facsimile, likeness. *See* **copy** (1). **2.** One exactly resembling another ► clone, spitting image, twin. *See* **double** (1). **3.** One of a matched pair of things ► counterpart, match. *See* **mate** (1).

duplicate *verb*
1. To make or become twice as great ► double, geminate, redouble, twin. **2.** To do or perform an act again ► do over, play over, redo, repeat, replay. **3.** To make a copy of ► imitate, replicate, reproduce. *See* **copy** (1).

duplicate *adjective*
Composed of two parts or things ► dual, duple, twofold. *See* **double** (2).

duplicitous *adjective*
1. Marked by treachery or deceit ► devious, shifty, sneaky. *See* **underhand**. **2.** Given to or marked by deliberate concealment or misrepresentation of the truth ► deceitful, deceptive, lying, untruthful. *See* **dishonest** (1).

duplicity *noun*
1. The act or practice of deceiving ► deception, guile. *See* **deceit** (1). **2.** Lack of integrity ► deceitfulness, mendacity. *See* **dishonesty** (1).

durability *noun*
1. Uninterrupted existence or succession ► continuance, endurance, persistence. *See* **continuation** (1). **2.** The quality or power of withstanding hardship or stress ► fortitude, stamina, toughness. *See* **endurance** (1).

durable *adjective*
► abiding, enduring, perennial. *See* **continuing** (1).

duration *noun*
1. Uninterrupted existence or succession ► continuum, persistence. *See* **continuation** (1). **2.** A specific length of time characterized by the occurrence of certain conditions or events ► span, stretch, term. *See* **period** (1). **3.** The period during which someone or something exists ► existence, span, term. *See* **life** (1).

duress *noun*
► might, power, strength. *See* **force** (1).

dusk *noun*
► eve, twilight. *See* **evening**.

duskiness *noun*
► darkness, dimness, murkiness. *See* **dark** (1).

dusky *adjective*
1. Deficient in brightness ► dim, murky, shadowy. *See* **dark** (1). *See synonym note at* **dark**. **2.** Having a dark color or complexion ► black, brunet, swarthy. *See* **dark** (3).

dust *noun*
The substance of the body, especially after decay or cremation ► ashes, clay, cremains, remains.

dust *verb*
To scatter or release in drops or small particles ► besprinkle, pepper, powder. *See* **sprinkle** (1).

dust bowl *noun*
► badlands, waste, wasteland. *See* **desert**[1].

dusting *noun*
1. An outer layer of material ► blanket, crust, overlay. *See* **coat** (2). **2.** *Slang* The act of defeating or the condition of being defeated ► overthrow, trouncing, vanquishment. *See* **defeat**.

dusty *adjective*
► powdery, pulverous, pulverulent. *See* **fine**[1] (6).

dutiful *or* **duteous** *adjective*
1. Marked by courteous submission or respect ► obeisant, polite, respectful. *See* **deferential**. **2.** Willing to carry out the wishes of others ► complaisant, docile, submissive. *See* **obedient**.

dutifulness *noun*
► compliancy, complaisance, submissiveness. *See* **obedience**.

duty *noun*
1. An act or course of action that is demanded of one, as by position, custom, law, or religion ► burden, charge, commitment, devoir, imperative, liability, must, need, obligation, onus, requirement, responsibility. **2.** The condition of being put to use ► adoption, application, employment, service, use, utilization. *See also* **exercise**. **3.** A compulsory contribution that is required for the support of an authority ► assessment, levy, tariff. *See* **tax** (1). **4.** A piece of work that has been assigned ► chore, job, office. *See* **task** (1).

dwarf *adjective*
Extremely small ► diminutive, miniature, minuscule. *See* **tiny**.

dwarf *verb*
To rise above, especially so as to afford a view of ► overlook, overshadow. *See* **dominate** (2).

dweeb *noun*
1. *Slang* An unpleasant, tiresome person ► chump. *Slang:* dork, nimrod. *See* **drip** (2). **2.** *Slang* A person who is deficient in judgment and good sense ► idiot, imbecile, nitwit. *See* **fool** (1).

dwell *verb*
1. To have as one's domicile, usually for an extended period ► abide, reside. *See* **live**[1] (2). **2.** To have an inherent basis ► exist, inhere, reside. *See* **consist** (1). **3.** To focus the attention on something moodily and at length ► fret, mope, worry. *See* **brood**. *See synonym note at* **brood**.

dwell on *verb*
To discuss at excessive length ► labor, overemphasize. *See* **belabor** (2).

dweller *noun*
► denizen, occupant, resident. *See* **inhabitant**.

dwelling *noun*
► domicile, habitation, residence. *See* **home** (1).

dwindle *verb*
► diminish, ebb, lessen. *See* **decrease**. *See synonym note at* **decrease**.

dyad *noun*
► duet, match, pair. *See* **couple**.

dye *noun*
Something that imparts color ► colorant, paint, pigment. *See* **color** (2).

dye *verb*
To impart color to ▸ dye, stain, tint. *See* **color** (1).

dyestuff *noun*
▸ dye, paint, pigment. *See* **color** (2).

dying *adjective*
▸ farewell, goodbye, valedictory. *See* **parting.**

dynamic *or* **dynamical** *adjective*
1. Possessing, exerting, or displaying energy ▸ brisk, lively, vigorous. *See* **energetic. 2.** Full of or displaying force ▸ effective, powerful, vigorous. *See* **forceful** (1).

dynamism *noun*
▸ might, potency, power. *See* **energy.**

dynamite *verb*
To pull down or break up so that reconstruction is impossible ▸ dismantle, level, tear down. *See* **destroy** (2).

dynamite *adjective*
Slang Exceptionally good of its kind ▸ first-rate, prime, splendid, tiptop. *See* **excellent.**

dynamo *noun*
An intensely energetic, enthusiastic person ▸ demon, hustler. *Informal:* eager beaver, firebreather, go-getter, live wire.

dyspeptic *adjective*
In low spirits ▸ blue, gloomy, melancholy. *See* **depressed** (1).

dysphoria *noun*
▸ dejection, doldrums, melancholy. *See* **depression** (2).

dysphoric *adjective*
▸ blue, gloomy, melancholy. *See* **depressed** (1).

e

eager *adjective*
1. Intensely desirous or interested ▸ agog, ardent, athirst, avid, bursting, impatient, keen, solicitous, thirsting, thirsty. *Informal:* raring. *Idioms:* champing at the bit, ready and willing. **2.** Disposed to accept, agree, or participate ▸ agreeable, ready. *See* **willing** (1).

eager beaver *noun*
Informal An intensely energetic, enthusiastic person ▸ demon, dynamo, hustler. *Informal:* firebreather, go-getter, live wire.

eagerness *noun*
▸ fervor, passion, zeal. *See* **enthusiasm** (1).

ear *noun*
The sense by which sound is perceived ▸ audition, hearing.

earlier *adjective*
1. Going before ▸ anterior, precedent, preceding. *See* **advance. 2.** Just gone by or elapsed ▸ precedent, previous, prior. *See* **past** (1).

earlier *adverb*
1. At a time in the past ▸ already, before, beforehand, erenow, erstwhile, formerly, once, previously. *Idioms:* ahead of time, in advance. **2.** Up to this time ▸ before, heretofore, previously, yet.

earliest *adjective*
▸ initial, original, premier. *See* **first** (1).

early *adjective*
1. Of, existing, or occurring in a distant period ▸ ancient, antediluvian, prehistoric, primal, primeval, primitive, primordial. *See also* **first. 2.** Developing, occurring, or appearing before the expected time ▸ precocious, premature, untimely. **3.** Of or occurring at the start of something ▸ initial, introductory, opening. *See* **beginning** (1).

early *adverb*
Before the expected time ▸ ahead, beforehand, betimes. *Idioms:* ahead of schedule, ahead of time, in advance, with time to spare.

earmark *verb*
1. To set aside or apart for a specified purpose ▸ assign, designate, set apart. *See* **appropriate** (1). *See synonym note at* **appropriate. 2.** To make known or identify, as by signs ▸ indicate, mark, specify. *See* **designate** (1). **3.** To attach a ticket to ▸ flag, label, mark, tag, ticket.

earmark *noun*
An identifying or descriptive slip ▸ flag, label, tag. *See* **ticket** (1).

earn *verb*
1. To acquire as a result of one's behavior or effort ▸ deserve, gain, get, merit, win. *Informal:* rate. **2.** To receive, as wages, for one's labor ▸ draw, gain, get, make, win. *Informal:* bring in, pull down, pull in, rake in. *Idiom:* earn one's keep. **3.** To make as income or profit ▸ clear, gain, yield. *See* **return** (3).

✦ CORE SYNONYMS: *earn, deserve, gain, merit, rate, win.* These verbs mean to acquire as a result of one's behavior or effort: *earns a large salary; deserves our congratulations; gained an advantage by hiring a tutor; a suggestion that merits consideration; an event that rates a mention in the news; a candidate who won wide support.*

earnest¹ *adjective*
1. Marked by careful thought and a lack of frivolity or exaggeration ▸ sober, solemn. *See* **serious** (1). *See synonym note at* **serious. 2.** Having great consequence or weight ▸ serious, severe. *See* **grave²** (1).

earnest² *noun*

Something given to guarantee the repayment of a loan or the fulfillment of an obligation ▶ collateral, token, warrant. *See* **pawn¹**.

earnestness *noun*

▶ graveness, sobriety, solemnity. *See* **seriousness** (1).

earnings *noun*

1. Payment for work done ▶ compensation, pay, salary. *See* **wage**. **2.** Something earned, won, or otherwise acquired ▶ gain, profit, return. *See also* **increase**.

earshot *noun*

Range of audibility ▶ hearing, sound. *See also* **range**.

earsplitting *adjective*

▶ booming, deafening, roaring. *See* **loud** (1). *See synonym note at* **loud**.

earth *noun*

1. The soft part of the land surface of the world ▶ clay, dirt, ground, humus, loam, sod, soil, terrain, turf. **2.** The celestial body where humans live ▶ globe, orb, planet, world. **3.** Humans as a group ▶ humanity, human race, world. *See* **humankind**.

earthbound *adjective*

1. Relating to or characteristic of the earth or of human life on earth ▶ terrestrial, worldly. *See* **earthly** (1). **2.** Lacking liveliness, charm, or surprise ▶ aseptic, colorless, pedestrian. *See* **dull** (1).

earthen *adjective*

1. Consisting of or resembling soil ▶ earthlike, earthy, terrestrial. **2.** Relating to or characteristic of the earth or of human life on earth ▶ earthbound, terrestrial, worldly. *See* **earthly** (1).

earthlike *adjective*

Consisting of or resembling soil ▶ earthen, earthy, terrestrial.

earthling *noun*

▶ human, mortal, person. *See* **human being**.

earthly *adjective*

1. Relating to or characteristic of the earth or of human life on earth ▶ earthbound, earthen, earthy, mundane, secular, sublunary, tellurian, telluric, temporal, terrene, terrestrial, worldly. *See also* **physical, profane**. **2.** Capable of being anticipated, considered, or imagined ▶ likely, possible. *See* **conceivable**.

earthquake *noun*

A shaking of the earth ▶ quake, seism, temblor, tremor. *Informal:* shake.

earth-shaking *adjective*

▶ consequential, grand, meaningful. *See* **important** (1).

earthwork *noun*

▶ barricade, bastion, parapet. *See* **bulwark**. *See synonym note at* **bulwark**.

earthy *adjective*

1. Consisting of or resembling soil ▶ earthen, earthlike, terrestrial. **2.** Relating to or characteristic of the earth or of human life on earth ▶ terrestrial, worldly. *See* **earthly** (1). **3.** Bordering on indelicacy or impropriety ▶ provocative, risqué, suggestive. *See* **racy** (1).

ease *noun*

1. Freedom from constraint, formality, embarrassment, or awkwardness ▶ casualness, comfort, easiness, informality, naturalness, poise, spontaneity, unceremoniousness, unrestraint. *See also* **abandon**. **2.** The ability to perform without apparent effort ▶ easiness, effortlessness, facileness, facility, readiness. *See also* **ability**. **3.** Reduction of pain or distress, or a cause of that reduction ▶ mitigation, palliation. *See* **relief** (2). **4.** Freedom from labor, responsibility, or strain ▶ leisure, relaxation, repose. *See* **rest** (2). **5.** Steady good fortune or financial security ▶ comfort, prosperousness, wealth. *See* **prosperity** (2).

ease *verb*

1. To reduce in tension, pressure, or rigidity ▶ let up, loose, loosen, relax, slack, slacken, untighten. **2.** To make less difficult ▶ expedite, facilitate, grease, help along. *Idioms:* clear (*or* prepare *or* smooth) the way for, grease the wheels (*or* skids) for, open the door for (*or* to). **3.** To make less severe or more bearable ▶ alleviate, lessen. *See* **relieve** (1). **4.** To become or cause to become less active or intense ▶ abate, diminish, slack off. *See* **subside** (1). **5.** To maneuver gently and slowly into place ▶ glide, slide, slip. **6.** To advance carefully and gradually ▶ edge, sidle. *See also* **crawl, sneak**.

ease off *verb*

To moderate or change a position or course of action as a result of pressure ▶ back down, slacken, yield. *See* **weaken** (1).

easeful *adjective*

▶ easy, snug. *Informal:* comfy. *See* **comfortable** (1).

easiness *noun*

1. The ability to perform without apparent effort ▶ effortlessness, facility. *See* **ease** (2). **2.** Freedom from constraint, formality, embarrassment, or awkwardness ▶ informality, naturalness. *See* **ease** (1).

easy *adjective*

1. Posing no difficulty ▶ effortless, facile, simple, smooth. *Informal:* snap. *Idioms:* easy as ABC (*or* falling off a log *or* one-two-three *or* pie), like taking candy from a baby, nothing to it. *See also* **breeze**. **2.** Requiring little effort or exertion ▶ light, moderate, undemanding. *Informal:* cushy, soft. **3.** Marked by facility of expression ▶ effortless, flowing. *See* **fluent**. **4.** Affording pleasurable ease ▶ cozy, snug. *Informal:* comfy. *See* **comfortable** (1). **5.** Enjoying steady good fortune or financial security ▶ comfortable, well-off, well-to-do. *See* **prosperous**. **6.** Unconstrained by rigid standards or ceremony ▶ informal, relaxed. *Informal:* laid-back. *See* **easygoing** (1). **7.** Not strict or severe ▶ charitable, indulgent, lenient. *See* **tolerant** (1). **8.** Easily imposed on or tricked ▶ credulous, naive, susceptible. *See* **gullible**. **9.** Not steep or abrupt ▶ gentle, moderate. *See* **gradual** (2). **10.** Sexually unrestrained ▶ fast, promiscuous, sluttish. *See* **wanton** (1).

✦ **CORE SYNONYMS:** *easy, simple, facile, effortless*. These adjectives mean posing little if any difficulty. *Easy* applies to tasks that require little effort: *"The diagnosis of disease is often easy, often difficult, and often impossible"* (Peter M. Latham). *Simple* implies a lack of complexity that facilitates understanding or performance: *"the faculty . . . of reducing his thought on any subject to the simplest and plainest terms possible"* (Baron Charnwood). *Facile* stresses readiness and fluency: *a facile speaker.* Often, though, the word implies glibness or insincerity, superficiality, or lack of care: *an explanation too facile for complex events.* *Effortless* refers to performance in which the application of great strength or skill makes the execution seem easy: *wrote effortless prose.*

easygoing *adjective*
1. Unconstrained by rigid standards or ceremony ▸ casual, easy, informal, mellow, natural, relaxed, spontaneous, unceremonious, unrestrained. *Informal:* laid-back. *See also* **loose, tolerant. 2.** Not excited or agitated ▸ cool, even-tempered. *See* **calm** (1).

easy street *noun*
Informal Steady good fortune or financial security ▸ comfort, ease, wealth. *See* **prosperity** (2).

eat *verb*
1. To take food into the body as nourishment ▸ consume, devour, ingest, partake. *Informal:* put away, tuck into. *Slang:* chow down, polish off. *See also* **chew, gulp. 2.** To have or take a meal ▸ breakfast, dine, lunch, snack, sup. **Idioms:** break bread, have (*or* take) a bite. **3.** To include as part of one's diet by nature or preference ▸ exist on, feed on, live on, subsist on. **4.** To do away with completely and destructively ▸ consume, devour, swallow (up), waste. **5.** To reduce gradually, as by chemical reaction, weather, or friction ▸ consume, corrode, wear down. *See* **erode.**

eat up *verb*
1. To engulf completely ▸ devour, ravage, waste. *See* **consume** (1). **2.** To use all of ▸ consume, expend, run through. *See* **exhaust** (1). **3.** *Slang* To be avidly interested in ▸ devour, feast on, relish. **4.** *Slang* To like or enjoy enthusiastically ▸ be into, delight (in). *See* **adore** (2).

✦ CORE SYNONYMS: *eat, consume, devour, ingest.* These verbs mean to take food into the body as nourishment by the mouth: *ate a hearty dinner; greedily consumed the sandwich; hyenas devouring their prey; whales ingesting krill.*

eatable *adjective*
Fit to be eaten ▸ comestible, edible, esculent, palatable.

eats *noun*
Slang Material that is fit to be eaten ▸ bread, meat, nourishment. *See* **food.**

ebb *verb*
1. To become or cause to become gradually less ▸ diminish, dwindle, lessen. *See* **decrease. 2.** To move back or away from a point, limit, or mark ▸ retract, retreat, retrogress. *See* **recede.** *See synonym note at* **recede. 3.** To become or cause to become less active or intense ▸ die (away, down, off, *or* out), fall, wane.

See **subside** (1). **4.** To become lower in quality, character, or condition ▸ atrophy, degenerate, worsen. *See* **deteriorate** (1). **5.** To pass out of sight either gradually or suddenly ▸ dissolve, fade. *See* **disappear** (1). **6.** To become downcast from longing or from grief ▸ pine (away), wither. *See* **languish** (1).

ebb *noun*
The process of becoming less active or intense ▸ abatement, letup, subsidence. *See* **waning.**

ebony *or* **ebon** *adjective*
▸ inky, onyx, sable. *See* **black** (1).

ebullient *adjective*
▸ animated, chipper, vivacious. *See* **lively** (1).

eccentric *adjective*
Deviating from what is conventional or customary ▸ antic, bizarre, cranky, curious, erratic, fantastic, freakish, grotesque, idiosyncratic, odd, outlandish, peculiar, quaint, queer, quirky, singular, strange, unconventional, unnatural, unorthodox, unusual, weird. *Slang:* kooky, screwball. *See also* **exotic, insane.**

eccentric *noun*
1. A person regarded as strange, eccentric, or crazy ▸ lunatic. *Slang:* nut, weirdo. *See* **crackpot. 2.** A person who is appealingly odd or curious ▸ original. *Informal:* card, oddball. *See* **character** (7).

✦ CORE SYNONYMS: *eccentric, strange, peculiar, odd, queer, quaint, outlandish, singular, curious, fantastic, bizarre, grotesque.* These adjectives describe what deviates from the usual or customary. *Eccentric* describes something that parts from a conventional or established norm or pattern: *His musical compositions were innovative but eccentric. Strange* refers especially to what is unfamiliar, unknown, or inexplicable: *All summer I traveled through strange lands. Peculiar* particularly describes what is distinct from all others: *Cloves have a peculiar aromatic odor.* Something that is *odd* or *queer* fails to accord with what is ordinary, usual, or expected; both terms can suggest strangeness or peculiarity: *I find it odd that his name is never mentioned. "Now, my suspicion is that the universe is not only queerer than we suppose, but queerer than we can suppose"* (J.B.S. Haldane). *Quaint* refers to pleasing or old-fashioned peculiarity: *"the quaint streets of New Orleans, that most foreign of American cities"* (Winston Churchill). *Outlandish* suggests alien or bizarre strangeness: *The partygoers wore outlandish costumes. Singular* describes what is unique or unparalleled; the term often suggests a quality that arouses curiosity or wonder: *Such poise is singular in one so young. Curious* suggests strangeness that excites interest: *Americans living abroad often acquire a curious hybrid accent. Fantastic* describes what seems to have slight relation to the real world because of its strangeness or extravagance: *fantastic imaginary beasts such as the unicorn. Bizarre* stresses oddness that is heightened by striking contrasts and incongruities and that shocks or fascinates: *a bizarre art nouveau façade. Grotesque* refers principally to deformity and distortion that approach the point of caricature or even absurdity: *statues of grotesque creatures.*

eccentricity *noun*
Peculiar behavior ▸ idiosyncrasy, peculiarity, quirk, quirkiness, singularity. *See also* **abnormality.**

ecclesiastic *noun*
▸ chaplain, minister, parson. *See* **cleric.**

ecclesiastical *adjective*
1. Of or relating to a church or to an established religion ▸ church, churchly, religious, spiritual. *See also* **clerical, divine, holy, ritual. 2.** Of or relating to the clergy, especially in a Christian church ▸ ministerial, pastoral. *See* **clerical.**

echelon *noun*
▸ position, rank, standing. *See* **place** (1).

echinate *adjective*
▸ brambly, bristly, prickly. *See* **thorny** (1).

echo *noun*
1. Imitative reproduction, as of the style of another ▸ imitation, reflection, reflex, repetition, reproduction. *See also* **mimicry. 2.** Repetition of sound via reflection from a surface ▸ repercussion, reverberation. **3.** One who imitates ▸ imitator, parrot. *See* **mimic. 4.** The act or process of repeating ▸ reiteration, repeat, restatement. *See* **repetition** (1).

echo *verb*
1. To send back the sound of ▸ bounce back, rebound, reecho, reflect, repeat, resound, reverberate. **2.** To copy another slavishly ▸ clone, imitate. *See* **mimic** (1).

✦ CORE SYNONYMS: *echo, reecho, reflect, resound, reverberate.* These verbs mean to send back the sound of: *a cry echoed by the canyon; a cathedral roof reechoing joyous hymns; caves that reflect the noise of footsteps; cliffs resounding the thunder of the ocean; blasting reverberated by quarry walls.*

---

echoic *adjective*
Imitating sounds ▸ imitative, mimetic, onomatopoeic, onomatopoetic.

echoism *noun*
The formation of words in imitation of sounds ▸ mimesis, onomatopoeia.

eclipse *verb*
▸ blur, fog, obfuscate. *See* **obscure** (1).

economical *adjective*
Careful in the use of material resources ▸ canny, chary, frugal, provident, prudent, saving, Scotch, sparing, thrifty. *See also* **stingy.**

✦ CORE SYNONYMS: *economical, sparing, frugal, thrifty.* These adjectives mean exercising or reflecting care in the use of resources, such as money. *Economical* emphasizes prudence, skillful management, and the avoidance of waste: *an economical shopper; an economical use of energy. Sparing* stresses restraint, as in expenditure: *a quiet librarian who was sparing of words. Frugal* implies self-denial and abstention from luxury: *a frugal diet; a frugal monk. Thrifty* suggests industry, care, and diligence in conserving means: *grew up during the Depression and learned to be thrifty.*

---

economize *verb*
To be frugal or sparing ▸ conserve, save, skimp. *See* **scrimp.**

economy *noun*
Careful use of material resources ▸ frugality, providence, prudence, thrift, thriftiness. *See also* **conservation.**

economy *adjective*
Low in price ▸ budget, dirt-cheap, low-cost. *See* **cheap** (1).

ecosystem *or* **ecosphere** *noun*
▸ biosphere, habitat. *See* **environment** (3).

ecstasy *noun*
1. A supremely beautiful, blissful state or experience ▸ bliss, paradise. *See* **heaven** (1). **2.** A feeling of gratification aroused by something good or desired ▸ bliss, enjoyment, pleasure. *See* **delight** (1).

ecumenical *adjective*
▸ cosmic, global, worldwide. *See* **universal** (1).

edacious *adjective*
1. Wanting to eat or drink more than one can reasonably consume ▸ greedy, ravenous, voracious. *See* **gluttonous** (1). **2.** Having an insatiable appetite for an activity or pursuit ▸ gluttonous, rapacious, ravenous. *See* **voracious** (1).

edacity *noun*
▸ insatiability, omnivorousness, rapaciousness. *See* **voracity.**

eddy *verb*
To move or cause to move like a rapidly rotating current of liquid ▸ swirl, whirl. *See also* **turn.**

eddy *noun*
1. A gentle wind ▸ draft, puff. *See* **breeze** (1). **2.** A rotating, often concave current of liquid ▸ maelstrom, vortex. *See* **whirlpool** (1).

edge *noun*
1. A cutting quality ▸ bite, incisiveness, keenness, sharpness, sting. **2.** The cutting part of a sharp instrument ▸ knife-edge, razorblade. *See* **blade. 3.** A line or area where something ends or abruptly changes ▸ brink, fringe, margin. *See* **border** (1). *See synonym note at* **border. 4.** The periphery of a city or town ▸ environs, suburbs. *See* **outskirts. 5.** A dominating position, as in a conflict ▸ drop, upper hand, vantage. *See* **advantage** (3). **6.** An expressive vocal quality ▸ accent, intonation, lilt. *See* **tone** (2).

edge *verb*
1. To give a sharp edge to ▸ hone, strope, whet. *See* **sharpen** (2). **2.** To put or form a border on ▸ fringe, rim. *See* **border** (1). **3.** To advance carefully and gradually ▸ ease, sidle. *See also* **crawl, sneak. 4.** To introduce or insert by subtle and artful means ▸ infiltrate, work, worm. *See* **insinuate** (1).

edginess *noun*
▸ disquietude, uneasiness, unrest. *See* **restlessness.**

edging *noun*
▸ brink, fringe, margin. *See* **border** (1).

edgy *adjective*
Feeling or exhibiting nervous tension ▸ fidgety, jittery,

jumpy, nervous, restive, restless, skittish, taut, tense, twitchy. *Slang:* antsy, hyper, uptight. *Idioms:* a bundle of nerves, all wound up, on edge. *See also* **anxious.**

edible *adjective*
Fit to be eaten ▸ comestible, eatable, esculent, palatable.

edibles *noun*
▸ fare, nourishment, victuals. *See* **food.**

edict *noun*
1. A principle governing affairs within or among political units ▸ bylaw, decree, institute. *See* **law** (1). **2.** An authoritative or official decision ▸ decree, judgment, pronouncement. *See* **ruling. 3.** Something announced or communicated ▸ announcement, declaration, notice. *See* **message** (1).

edification *noun*
1. The condition of being informed spiritually ▸ enlightenment, illumination. *See also* **education. 2.** The act, process, or art of imparting knowledge and skill ▸ pedagogy, schooling. *See* **education** (1).

edifice *noun*
Something built, especially for human use ▸ building, construction, erection, pile, structure.

edify *verb*
1. To enable one to understand, especially in a spiritual sense ▸ enlighten, illumine. *See* **illuminate** (3). **2.** To indulge in moral reflection, usually pompously ▸ moralize, pontificate, preach, sermonize. *See also* **chastise.**

edifying *adjective*
1. Promoting culture ▸ enlightening, humanizing. *See* **cultural. 2.** Serving to educate or inform ▸ enlightening, informative, instructive. *See* **educational** (2). **3.** Teaching morality ▸ moralizing, preachy. *See* **moral** (1).

edit *verb*
1. To prepare a new version of ▸ amend, revamp, rework. *See* **revise** (1). **2.** To examine and remove objectionable or improper material from a publication ▸ bowdlerize, cut, expurgate, sanitize. *See* **censor** (1).

edition *noun*
1. A printed and bound work ▸ tome, volume. *See* **book** (1). **2.** An issue of printed material offered for sale or distribution ▸ title, volume, work. *See* **publication** (2).

editor *noun*
▸ correspondent, journalist, media. *See* **press** (1).

editorial *noun*
▸ observation, reflection, remark. *See* **comment** (1).

editorialist *noun*
▸ correspondent, newshound, reporter. *See* **press** (1).

editorialize *verb*
▸ observe, opine, remark. *See* **comment.**

educable *adjective*
Capable of being educated ▸ docile, teachable, trainable. *See also* **obedient.**

educate *verb*
1. To impart knowledge and skill to ▸ coach, disci-

pline, form, instruct, school, teach, train, tutor. *See also* **indoctrinate. 2.** To impart information to ▸ advise, notify. *See* **inform** (1).

✛ CORE SYNONYMS: *educate, teach, instruct, train, school, discipline.* These verbs mean to impart knowledge or skill. *Educate* often implies formal instruction but especially stresses the development of innate capacities: *"We are educated by others . . . and this cultivation, mingling with our innate disposition, is the soil in which our desires, passions, and motives grow"* (Mary Shelley). *Teach* is the most widely applicable: *taught the child to draw; taught literature at the college. Instruct* usually suggests methodical teaching: *instructed the undergraduates in music theory. Train* suggests concentration on particular skills intended to fit a person for a desired role: *trained the vocational students to be computer technicians. School* often implies an arduous learning process: *schooled the youngster to play the viola. Discipline* usually refers to the teaching of control, especially self-control: *disciplined myself to exercise every day.*

---

educated *adjective*
1. Showing evidence of schooling, training, or experience ▸ enlightened, erudite, informed, knowledgeable, learned, lettered, literate, scholarly, schooled, trained, versed, well-read, wise. *See also* **familiar, pedantic, studious. 2.** Characterized by discriminating taste and broad knowledge as a result of development or education ▸ cultivated, polished. *See* **cultured. 3.** Provided with information; made aware ▸ enlightened, instructed, knowledgeable. *See* **informed** (1).

✛ CORE SYNONYMS: *educated, learned, scholarly, versed.* These adjectives mean showing evidence of schooling, training, or experience: *an educated population; a learned jurist; a scholarly treatise; a naturalist versed in animal behavior.*

---

education *noun*
1. The act, process, or art of imparting knowledge and skill ▸ edification, instruction, pedagogics, pedagogy, schooling, teaching, training, tuition, tutelage, tutoring. **2.** Known facts, ideas, and skills that have been imparted ▸ erudition, instruction, knowledge, learning, scholarship, science. **3.** Training in the proper forms of social and personal conduct ▸ breeding, upbringing. *See also* **courtesy, manners.**

educational *adjective*
1. Of or relating to education ▸ academic, instructional, pedagogic, pedagogical, scholastic, teaching. **2.** Serving to educate or inform ▸ edifying, educative, enlightening, illuminative, informative, instructional, instructive. *See also* **cultural.**

educative *adjective*
▸ edifying, instructive. *See* **educational** (2).

educator *noun*
One who educates ▸ coach, instructor, master, pedagogue, schoolmaster, schoolmistress, schoolteacher, teacher, trainer, tutor. *See also* **adviser.**

educe *verb*
1. To bring out something latent, hidden, or unexpressed ▸ draw (out), elicit, summon. *See* **evoke.** *See synonym note at* **evoke. 2.** To arrive at through reasoning ▸ conclude, evolve. *See* **derive** (2).

eerie *or* **eery** *adjective*
▸ freakish, uncanny, unearthly. *See* **weird** (1). *See synonym note at* **weird.**

efface *verb*
▸ delete, erase, strike (out). *See* **cancel** (1). *See synonym note at* **cancel.**

effacement *noun*
▸ deletion, expunction. *See* **erasure.**

effect *noun*
1. Something brought about by a cause ▸ aftermath, consequence, corollary, end product, event, fruit, harvest, issue, outcome, precipitate, ramification, result, resultant, sequel, sequence, sequent, upshot. *See also* **derivative. 2.** The power or capacity to produce a desired result ▸ effectiveness, effectuality, effectualness, efficaciousness, efficacy, efficiency, influence, potency. *See also* **ability. 3.** The condition of being in full force or operation ▸ actualization, being, force, realization. *See also* **exercise.**

effect *verb*
1. To succeed in doing ▸ accomplish, achieve, bring about, bring off, carry out, carry through, effectuate, execute, put through. *Informal:* swing. *See also* **accomplish, fulfill, perform, succeed. 2.** To be the cause of ▸ generate, induce, trigger. *See* **cause. 3.** To compel observance of ▸ carry out, implement. *See* **enforce. 4.** To begin and carry through to completion ▸ discharge, transact. *See* **perform** (1). *See synonym note at* **perform.**

✦ CORE SYNONYMS: *effect, consequence, result, outcome, upshot, sequel.* These nouns denote an occurrence, situation, or condition that is brought about by a cause. An *effect* is produced by the action of an agent or a cause and follows it in time: "*Every cause produces more than one effect*" (Herbert Spencer). A *consequence* has a less sharply definable relationship to its cause: "*Servitude is at once the consequence of his crime and the punishment of his guilt*" (John P. Curran). A *result* is viewed as the end product of the operation of the cause: "*Judging from the results I have seen . . . I cannot say . . . that I agree with you*" (William H. Mallock). An *outcome* more strongly implies finality and may suggest the operation of a cause over a relatively long period: *The trial's outcome might have changed if the defendant had testified.* An *upshot* is a decisive result, often of the nature of a climax: "*The upshot of the matter . . . was that she showed both of them the door*" (Robert Louis Stevenson). A *sequel* is a consequence that ensues after a lapse of time: "*Our dreams are the sequel of our waking knowledge*" (Ralph Waldo Emerson).

---

effective *adjective*
1. Producing or able to produce a desired effect ▸ constructive, effectual, efficacious, efficient, instrumental, productive. *See also* **able, beneficial. 2.** Full of

or displaying force ▸ dynamic, vigorous. *See* **forceful** (1). **3.** In effect ▸ operational, operative. *Idioms:* in force (*or* operation). *See also* **active. 4.** Serving to convince ▸ cogent, persuasive. *See* **convincing** (1).

✦ CORE SYNONYMS: *effective, effectual, efficacious, efficient.* These adjectives mean producing or capable of producing a desired effect: *an effective reprimand; an effectual complaint; an efficacious remedy; the efficient cause of the economic recovery.*

◂ ANTONYM: *ineffective*

---

effectiveness *noun*
▸ effectiveness, efficacy, potency. *See* **effect** (2).

effects *noun*
One's portable property ▸ belongings, chattel, goods, lares and penates, movables, personal effects, personal property, possessions, property, things. *Informal:* stuff. *See also* **holdings.**

effectual *adjective*
▸ efficient, productive. *See* **effective** (1). *See synonym note at* **effective.**

effectuality *or* **effectualness** *noun*
▸ effectiveness, efficacy, potency. *See* **effect** (2).

effectuate *verb*
1. To be the cause of ▸ generate, induce, trigger. *See* **cause. 2.** To succeed in doing ▸ bring off, carry out, execute. *See* **effect** (1). **3.** To compel observance of ▸ effect, implement. *See* **enforce.**

effectuation *noun*
▸ execution, prosecution. *See* **performance** (1).

effeminacy *noun*
The quality of being effeminate ▸ effeminateness, effeteness, femininity, unmanliness, womanishness. *See also* **androgyny.**

effeminate *adjective*
Having qualities traditionally attributed to a woman ▸ epicene, feminine, sissified, sissyish, unmanly, womanish. *See also* **androgynous.**

effeminateness *noun*
▸ femininity, womanishness. *See* **effeminacy.**

effervesce *verb*
1. To form or cause to form foam ▸ fizz, lather. *See* **foam** (1). **2.** To be in a state of turmoil or excitement ▸ burn, seethe. *See* **boil** (2).

effervescence *noun*
▸ lather, suds. *See* **foam.**

effervescent *adjective*
▸ animated, chipper, vivacious. *See* **lively** (1).

effete *adjective*
▸ faint, pallid, weak. *See* **pale** (2).

effeteness *noun*
▸ femininity, womanishness. *See* **effeminacy.**

efficacious *adjective*
1. Producing or able to produce a desired effect ▸ efficient, productive. *See* **effective** (1). *See synonym note at* **effective. 2.** Serving to convince ▸ cogent, persuasive. *See* **convincing** (1).

efficacy *or* **efficaciousness** *noun*
▸ effectiveness, potency. *See* **effect** (2).

efficiency *noun*
1. The power or capacity to produce a desired result ▶ effectiveness, efficacy, potency. *See* **effect** (2). **2.** The quality of being efficient ▶ productiveness, productivity. *See also* **ability, diligence. 3.** An often rented living space in a building ▶ condominium, loft, studio. *See* **apartment.**

efficient *adjective*
1. Acting effectively with minimal waste ▶ productive, streamlined, well-oiled. *See also* **diligent, methodical. 2.** Producing or able to produce a desired effect ▶ efficacious, productive. *See* **effective** (1). *See synonym note at* **effective.**

effloresce *verb*
▶ burgeon, flower. *See* **bloom**¹ (1).

efflorescence *noun*
▶ blossom, prime. *See* **bloom**¹ (1). *See synonym note at* **bloom**¹.

efflux *noun*
▶ flood, outpouring, tide. *See* **flow.**

effort *noun*
1. The use of energy to do something ▶ endeavor, exertion, pains, strain, striving, struggle, trouble, while. *Informal:* elbow grease. *See also* **diligence, labor, strength. 2.** A difficult or tedious undertaking ▶ chore, grind, slog. *See* **task** (2). **3.** A trying to do or make something ▶ trial. *Informal:* shot. *See* **attempt** (1). **4.** Something completed or attained successfully ▶ achievement, deed, feat. *See* **accomplishment** (1).

effortful *adjective*
1. Not easy to do, achieve, or master ▶ arduous, laborious, tough. *See* **difficult** (1). **2.** Not natural or spontaneous ▶ contrived, forced, labored, strained. *See also* **awkward, stiff.**

effortless *adjective*
1. Posing no difficulty ▶ simple, smooth. *See* **easy** (1). *See synonym note at* **easy. 2.** Marked by facility of expression ▶ easy, flowing. *See* **fluent.**

effortlessness *noun*
▶ easiness, facility, readiness. *See* **ease** (2).

effrontery *noun*
▶ audacity, boldness, impertinence. *See* **impudence.**

effulgence *noun*
▶ brilliancy, luminosity, radiance. *See* **brilliance** (1).

effulgent *adjective*
▶ brilliant, incandescent, radiant. *See* **bright** (1). *See synonym note at* **bright.**

effuse *verb*
▶ decant, empty, issue. *See* **pour** (1).

egghead *noun*
Informal A person of great mental ability ▶ intellectual, thinker. *See* **mind** (2).

egg on *verb*
▶ excite, prod, trigger. *See* **provoke** (1).

ego *noun*
1. Exaggerated love for oneself or belief in one's own importance ▶ conceit, narcissism, vanity. *See* **egotism. 2.** A sense of one's own dignity or worth ▶ self-regard, self-satisfaction. *See* **pride** (1).

egocentric *adjective*
1. Holding the philosophical view that the self is the center and norm of existence ▶ egoistic, egoistical, individualistic, solipsistic. **2.** Concerned only with oneself ▶ egomaniacal, selfish, self-absorbed. *See* **egotistic** (2).

egocentric *noun*
A conceited, self-centered person ▶ egomaniac, narcissist. *See* **egotist.**

egocentricity *or* **egocentrism** *noun*
▶ conceit, narcissism, vanity. *See* **egotism.**

egoism *noun*
▶ conceit, narcissism, vanity. *See* **egotism.**

egoist *noun*
▶ egomaniac, narcissist. *See* **egotist.**

egoistic *or* **egoistical** *adjective*
1. Holding the philosophical view that the self is the center and norm of existence ▶ egocentric, individualistic, solipsistic. **2.** Concerned only with oneself ▶ egomaniacal, self-absorbed. *See* **egotistic** (2). **3.** Thinking too highly of oneself ▶ narcissistic, vain. *See* **egotistic** (1).

egomania *noun*
▶ conceit, narcissism, vanity. *See* **egotism.**

egomaniac *noun*
▶ egocentric, narcissist. *See* **egotist.**

egomaniacal *adjective*
▶ egoistic, self-absorbed. *See* **egotistic** (2).

egotism *noun*
Exaggerated love for oneself or belief in one's own importance ▶ amour-propre, conceit, ego, egocentricity, egocentrism, egoism, egomania, megalomania, narcissism, pride, self-absorption, self-centeredness, self-importance, self-involvement, selfishness, vainglory, vainness, vanity. *Informal:* big head, bigheadedness, swelled head. *Slang:* ego trip. *See also* **pride, arrogance, pretentiousness.**

✦ CORE SYNONYMS: *egotism, conceit, egoism, narcissism, vanity.* These nouns denote excessive high regard for oneself: *boasting that reveals conceit; imperturbable egoism; arrogance and egotism that were obvious from her actions; narcissism that shut out everyone else; wounded his vanity by looking in the mirror.*

◀ ANTONYM: *humility*

---

egotist *noun*
A conceited, self-centered person ▶ egocentric, egoist, egomaniac, narcissist. *See also* **braggart.**

egotistic *or* **egotistical** *adjective*
1. Thinking too highly of oneself ▶ conceited, egoistic, egoistical, narcissistic, vain, vainglorious. *Informal:* bigheaded, stuck-up, swellheaded. *Idioms:* full of (*or* stuck on) oneself. *See also* **arrogant, boastful. 2.** Concerned only with oneself ▶ egocentric, egoistic, egoistical, egomaniacal, self-absorbed, self-centered, self-involved, selfish, self-seeking, self-serving. *Idiom:* wrapped up in oneself.

ego trip *noun*
▶ amour-propre, conceit, pride. *See* **egotism.**

egregious *adjective*
Conspicuously bad or offensive ▸ flagrant, glaring, gross, rank. *See synonym note at* **flagrant**. *See also* **offensive, outrageous, shameless**.

egregiousness *noun*
The quality or state of being flagrant ▸ flagrancy, glaringness, grossness, rankness. *See also* **impudence, outrageousness**.

egress *noun*
▸ embarkation, exodus, withdrawal. *See* **departure** (1).

eighty-six *verb*
▸ dump, throw away. *Informal:* chuck. *See* **discard**.

ejaculate *verb*
▸ burst out, rap out. *See* **exclaim**.

ejaculation *noun*
▸ call, exclamation, yell. *See* **shout**.

eject *verb*
1. To put out by force ▸ bump, cast out, dismiss, evict, expel, oust, throw out. *Informal:* chuck. *Slang:* boot (out), bounce, kick out. **Idioms:** give someone the boot (*or* heave-ho *or* old heave-ho), send packing, show someone the door, throw out on one's ear. *See also* **dismiss**. **2.** To catapult oneself from a disabled aircraft ▸ bail out, jump. **3.** To send forth confined matter violently ▸ disgorge, spew. *See* **erupt** (1).

✦ CORE SYNONYMS: *eject, expel, evict, dismiss, oust.* These verbs mean to put out by force. To *eject* is to throw or cast out from within: *The fire ejected yellow flames into the night sky. Expel* means to drive out or away, and it implies permanent removal: *The dean expelled the student for having cheated. Evict* most commonly refers to the expulsion of persons from property by legal process: *The apartment manager evicted the noisy tenants. Dismiss* refers to putting someone or something out of one's mind (*trying to dismiss his fears*) or, in law, to refusing to give an appeal or a complaint further consideration (*dismissed the case for lack of evidence*). *Oust* is applied chiefly to the removal of a person from a position lawfully or otherwise: *There were no grounds for ousting the prime minister.*

---

ejection *noun*
The act of ejecting or the state of being ejected ▸ dismissal, ejectment, eviction, expulsion, ouster, removal. *Slang:* boot, bounce. *See also* **dismissal, exile**.

ejectment *noun*
▸ eviction, expulsion. *See* **ejection**.

elaborate *adjective*
1. Rich in detail ▸ complicated, detailed, fancy, fussy, intricate, ornate. *See also* **busy, ornate**. **2.** Characterized by attention to detail ▸ full, particular, thorough. *See* **detailed** (1). **3.** Difficult to understand because of intricacy ▸ convoluted, entangled, involved, labyrinthine. *See* **complex** (1).

elaborate *verb*
To express at greater length or in greater detail ▸ amplify (on *or* upon), develop, dilate (on *or* upon), discourse (on *or* upon), enlarge (on *or* upon), ex-

pand (on *or* upon), expatiate (on *or* upon). **Idioms:** fill in the details, go into detail, go on and on. *See also* **belabor, explain**.

✦ CORE SYNONYMS: *elaborate, complicated, intricate, ornate.* These adjectives mean marked by richness or complexity of detail: *an elaborate lace pattern; the eye, a complicated organ; an intricate problem; an ornate candelabra.*

◂ ANTONYM: *simple*

élan *or* **élan vital** *noun*
▸ life, verve, vivaciousness. *See* **spirit** (1).

elapse *verb*
To move past in time ▸ go by, lapse, pass (away *or* by), slip (away *or* by), tick away.

elastic *adjective*
1. Capable of withstanding stress without injury ▸ flexile, resilient, supple. *See* **flexible** (1). *See synonym note at* **flexible**. **2.** Capable of adapting or being adapted ▸ malleable, pliable. *See* **adaptable**. **3.** Easily altered or influenced ▸ malleable, suggestible. *See* **flexible** (1).

elasticity *noun*
1. The quality or state of being flexible ▸ limberness, malleability, pliability. *See* **flexibility** (1). **2.** The ability to recover quickly from depression or discouragement ▸ bounce, buoyancy, flexibility, resilience, resiliency.

elate *verb*
1. To raise the spirits of ▸ animate, buoy (up), elevate, exhilarate, flush, inspire, inspirit, lift, uplift. *See also* **delight, encourage**. **2.** To give great or keen pleasure to ▸ enchant, overjoy, pleasure. *See* **delight** (1).

elated *adjective*
Feeling great delight and joy ▸ animated, elate, elevated, euphoric, exalted, exhilarated, inspired, overjoyed, uplifted. *Slang:* high, up. **Idioms:** flying (*or* riding) high, on cloud nine, on top of the world. *See also* **exultant, thrilled**.

elatedness *noun*
High spirits ▸ euphoria, inspiration. *See* **elation** (1).

elation *noun*
1. High spirits ▸ animation, elatedness, euphoria, exaltation, exhilaration, inspiration, lift, uplift. *See also* **happiness, high, merriment**. **2.** A feeling of gratification aroused by something good or desired ▸ bliss, enjoyment, pleasure. *See* **delight** (1).

elbow *verb*
1. To apply pressure on, against, or with ▸ press, prod, shove. *See* **push** (1). **2.** *Informal* To force one's way into a place or situation ▸ bulldoze, shove. *See* **muscle**.

elbow grease *noun*
Informal The use of energy to do something ▸ exertion, striving. *See* **effort** (1).

elbowroom *noun*
▸ entitlement, latitude, leeway. *See* **license** (1). *See synonym note at* **license**.

elder *noun*
1. An elderly person ▸ ancient, senior citizen. *See*

senior (2). **2.** One who stands above another in rank ▶ better, senior, superior. *Informal:* higher-up. *See also* **chief. 3.** One who governs or leads ▶ boss, director, head, leader. *See* **chief** (1).

elder *adjective*
Far along in life or time ▶ aged, elderly. *See* **old** (2).

elderliness *noun*
▶ maturity, seniority, years. *See* **age** (1).

elderly *adjective*
▶ aged, mature, senior. *See* **old** (2).

elect *verb*
1. To make a choice from a number of alternatives ▶ cast, pick (out), vote (for). *See* **choose** (1). **2.** To select for an office or position ▶ assign, name, nominate. *See* **appoint** (1). **3.** To select by vote for an office ▶ vote (in).

elect *adjective*
Singled out in preference ▶ choice, chosen, exclusive, select. *See also* **excellent, favorite.**

elect *noun*
One that is selected ▶ choice, chosen, pick, select. *See also* **best.**

election *noun*
1. The act, power, or right of choosing ▶ decision, discretion, option. *See* **choice** (1). *See synonym note at* **choice. 2.** The act of appointing to an office or position ▶ assignment, designation, nomination. *See* **appointment** (1).

elective *adjective*
▶ discretionary, possible. *See* **optional.**

elector *noun*
One who votes ▶ balloter, voter. *Idiom:* member of the electorate.

electrify *verb*
1. To cause to experience a sudden momentary shock ▶ jolt, shock. *See* **startle** (1). **2.** To have a powerful emotional effect on someone ▶ thrill, transport. *See* **enrapture.**

eleemosynary *adjective*
Of or concerned with charity ▶ altruistic, benevolent, charitable, philanthropic. *See synonym note at* **charitable.**

elegance *or* **elegancy** *noun*
Refinement of manner, form, and style ▶ chic, courtliness, dignity, elegancy, grace, polish, quality, sophistication, style, taste, tastefulness, urbanity. *Informal:* class. *See also* **attraction, culture, proportion.**

elegant *adjective*
1. Exhibiting refined, tasteful beauty of manner, form, or style ▶ chic, courtly, exquisite, graceful, refined, tasteful. *Informal:* classy. *See also* **cultured. 2.** Appealing to refined taste ▶ dainty, exquisite. *See* **delicate** (1). *See synonym note at* **delicate. 3.** Impressive in size, proportion, or appearance ▶ imposing, magnificent, splendid. *See* **grand** (1). **4.** Characterized by elaborate, usually formal courtesy ▶ courtly, gallant, stately. *See* **gracious** (2).

element *noun*
1. An irreducible constituent of a whole ▶ basic, essential, fundamental, rudiment. *Idiom:* part and parcel. *See also* **nitty-gritty. 2.** A separate unit that belongs or contributes to a whole ▶ piece, portion, section, segment. *See* **part** (1). *See synonym note at* **part. 3.** An individually considered portion of a whole ▶ article, detail, item, particular, point.

elemental *adjective*
1. Of or being an irreducible element ▶ basic, elementary, essential, fundamental, primal, primitive, ultimate, underlying. **2.** Forming an essential element, as arising from the basic structure of an individual ▶ innate, intrinsic, natural. *See* **constitutional** (1).

elementary *adjective*
1. Of or being an irreducible element ▶ basic, essential, fundamental. *See* **elemental** (1). **2.** Of or treating the most basic aspects ▶ basal, basic, beginning, rudimental, rudimentary. *See also* **constitutional.**

elephantine *adjective*
1. Of extraordinary size and power ▶ behemoth, colossal, gigantic, mighty. *See* **enormous. 2.** Lacking fluency or grace ▶ heavy-handed, labored. *See* **ponderous** (1).

elevate *verb*
1. To move something to a higher position ▶ boost, heave, hike (up), hitch up, hoist, jack (up), lift, pick up, raise, rear, take up, uphold, uplift, upraise, uprear. **2.** To increase markedly in level or intensity, especially of sound ▶ amplify, heighten, raise. *Slang:* crank up, pump up. *See also* **increase. 3.** To raise in rank ▶ advance, upgrade. *See* **promote** (1). **4.** To raise to a high position or status ▶ aggrandize, magnify, uplift. *See* **exalt** (1). **5.** To cause to be eminent or recognized ▶ dignify, exalt, honor. *See* **distinguish** (5). **6.** To raise the spirits of ▶ buoy (up), exhilarate, inspire. *See* **elate** (1).

✣ **CORE SYNONYMS:** *elevate, lift, raise, hoist, heave, boost.* These verbs mean to move something from a lower to a higher level or position. *Elevate* is often a general term (*elevated his sprained ankle*), but it more often suggests exalting, ennobling, or raising morally or intellectually: *"A generous and elevated mind is distinguished by nothing more certainly than an eminent degree of curiosity"* (Samuel Johnson). *Lift* sometimes stresses the expenditure of effort: *a trunk too heavy to lift. Raise* often implies movement to an approximately vertical position: *raised my hand so I could ask a question. Hoist* is applied principally to the lifting of heavy objects, often by mechanical means: *hoist a sunken ship.* To *heave* is to lift or raise with great effort or force: *heaved the pack onto his back. Boost* suggests upward movement effected by or as if by pushing from below: *boosted the child into the saddle.*

---

elevated *adjective*
1. Being positioned above a given level ▶ boosted, raised, uplifted, upraised. *Idiom:* on high. *See also* **higher. 2.** Abnormally increased, especially in intensity ▶ heightened, high, raised, supernormal. *Idioms:* off the charts, on the high end, over the top. *See also* **excessive. 3.** Raised to or occupying a high position

or rank ▸ august, lofty. *See* **exalted** (1). **4.** Being on a high intellectual or moral level ▸ high-minded, moral, noble, sublime. **5.** Exceedingly dignified in form, tone, or style ▸ eloquent, exalted, grand, high, high-flown, lofty, soaring, vaulting. *See also* **grandiose.** **6.** Feeling great delight and joy ▸ euphoric, overjoyed. *See* **elated. 7.** Being of or at a relatively great height or altitude ▸ aerial, lofty. *See* **high** (1). **8.** At the upper end of a degree of measure ▸ great, high, large. *See also* **exalted, extreme.**

elevation *noun*
1. The distance of something from a given level ▸ altitude, height, loftiness, tallness. *See also* **ascent.** **2.** The act of raising to a high position or status or the condition of being so raised ▸ apotheosis, dignification. *See* **exaltation** (1). **3.** A progression upward in rank ▸ promotion, upgrade. *See* **advancement** (1).

✦ CORE SYNONYMS: *elevation, altitude, height.* These nouns denote the distance of something above a point of reference such as the horizon: *a city at an elevation of 3,000 feet above sea level; flying at an altitude of 1 mile; grew to a height of 6 feet.*

---

elf *noun*
1. A creature of spirit that has supernatural powers ▸ dryad, nymph, sprite. *See* **fairy. 2.** A mischievous youngster ▸ brat, imp, whelp. *See* **urchin.**

elfish *adjective*
▸ frolicsome, impish, sportive. *See* **mischievous** (1).

elicit *verb*
▸ draw (out), educe, summon. *See* **evoke.** *See synonym note at* **evoke.**

eligibility *noun*
▸ fitness, suitability, worthiness. *See* **qualification.**

eligible *adjective*
1. Satisfying certain requirements, as for selection ▸ equal, fit, fitted, qualified, suitable, suited, up to, worthy. *See also* **appropriate. 2.** Not married or attached ▸ fancy-free, marriageable. *See* **single** (5).

eliminate *verb*
1. To get rid of, especially by banishment or execution ▸ eradicate, liquidate, purge, remove, wipe out. *Idioms:* do away with, put an end to. *See also* **annihilate, banish, kill, rid. 2.** To keep from being admitted, included, or considered ▸ blackball, keep out, rule out. *See* **exclude** (1). **3.** To take or leave out ▸ exclude, omit, prune. *See* **drop** (8). **4.** To discharge wastes from the body ▸ evacuate, excrete, expel, pass, purge, void. *See also* **defecate, urinate.**

✦ CORE SYNONYMS: *eliminate, eradicate, liquidate, purge.* These verbs mean to get rid of someone or something, especially by using drastic methods such as banishment or execution: *eliminated all opposition; eradicate guerrilla activity; liquidating traitors; purged the army of dissidents.*

---

elimination *noun*
1. The act or process of eliminating ▸ clearance,

eradication, exclusion, liquidation, purge, removal, riddance. *See also* **abolition, ejection. 2.** The act of getting rid of something useless or used up ▸ dumping, riddance. *See* **disposal** (1). **3.** The act or process of discharging bodily wastes ▸ catharsis, defecation, evacuation, excretion, purgation, urination.

eliminative *or* **eliminatory** *adjective*
Of, relating to, or tending to eliminate ▸ cathartic, emetic, evacuant, evacuative, excretory, purgative, urinary.

elite *or* **élite** *noun*
1. People of the highest social level ▸ aristocracy, gentry, nobility. *See* **society** (1). **2.** The most preferable part of something ▸ cream, crème de la crème, top. *See* **best** (1).

elite *or* **élite** *adjective*
1. Of high birth or social position ▸ blue-blooded, highborn, upper-class. *See* **noble** (1). **2.** Catering to, used by, or admitting only the wealthy or socially superior ▸ chic, posh, swank. *See* **exclusive** (4).

elitist *or* **élitist** *adjective*
Characteristic of or resembling a snob ▸ *Informal:* snooty, uppity. *See* **snobbish.**

elitist *or* **élitist** *noun*
One who despises people or things regarded as inferior, especially because of social or intellectual pretension ▸ prig, snob. *Informal:* snoot.

elixir *noun*
1. An agent used to restore health ▸ medication, nostrum, remedy. *See* **cure. 2.** Something believed to cure all human disorders ▸ catholicon, cure-all, panacea. *See also* **cure.**

ellipse *noun*
▸ egg-shape, ovoid. *See* **oval.**

ellipsoid *noun*
An egg-shaped form or figure ▸ egg-shape, ovoid. *See* **oval.**

ellipsoid *or* **ellipsoidal** *adjective*
Resembling an egg in shape ▸ elliptical, oblong. *See* **oval.**

elliptical *adjective*
▸ oblong, ovoid. *See* **oval.**

elocution *noun*
▸ declamation, rhetoric. *See* **oratory.**

elocutionary *adjective*
▸ bombastic, grandiloquent, rhetorical. *See* **oratorical.**

elongate *verb*
▸ extend, prolongate. *See* **lengthen.**

elongated *or* **elongate** *adjective*
▸ extended, lengthy, prolonged. *See* **long**[1] (1).

elongation *noun*
▸ lengthening, prolongation, stretching. *See* **extension** (1).

eloquence *noun*
Smooth or effective skill in communicating ▸ articulacy, articulateness, eloquentness, expression, expressiveness, expressivity, facility, fluency, fluidity,

glibness, rhetoric, silver tongue, volubility. *Idioms:* gift of gab

eloquent *adjective*
1. Fluently persuasive and forceful ▸ articulate, silver-tongued, smooth-spoken, voluble, well-spoken. *See also* **convincing, fluent, glib.** 2. Effectively conveying meaning, feeling, or mood ▸ meaning, significant. *See* **expressive.** *See synonym note at* **expressive.** 3. Characterized by elevated language, such as that used in public speaking ▸ bombastic, grandiloquent, rhetorical. *See* **oratorical.** 4. Exceedingly dignified in form, tone, or style ▸ exalted, grand. *See* **elevated** (5).

eloquentness *noun*
▸ articulateness, fluency, rhetoric. *See* **eloquence.**

elsewhere *adjective*
▸ away, gone, missing. *See* **absent** (1).

elucidate *verb*
1. To make clear or clearer ▸ illuminate, illustrate. *See* **clarify** (1). 2. To make understandable ▸ construe, decipher, interpret. *See* **explain** (1). *See synonym note at* **explain.**

elucidation *noun*
▸ decipherment, explication, illumination. *See* **explanation** (1).

elucidative *adjective*
▸ explicative, illustrative, interpretive. *See* **explanatory.**

elude *verb*
1. To keep away from ▸ dodge, evade, shun. *See* **avoid.** *See synonym note at* **avoid.** 2. To get away from (a pursuer) ▸ evade, slip, throw off. *See* **lose** (3). 3. To fail to be fixed by the mind, memory, or senses of ▸ escape, evade. *Idiom:* slip away from. *See also* **forget.**

elusive *adjective*
1. Inclined or intended to evade ▸ evasive, fugitive, slippery. *See also* **slick, underhand.** 2. Deliberately ambiguous or vague ▸ evasive, equivocal, indirect, misleading. *See also* **ambiguous.**

emaciated *adjective*
▸ gaunt, wan, worn. *See* **haggard.**

emanate *verb*
▸ derive, flow, originate. *See* **stem** (1). *See synonym note at* **stem.**

emancipate *verb*
▸ liberate, release. *See* **free** (1).

emancipated *adjective*
1. Able to move about at will without bounds or restraint ▸ liberated, unconfined, unrestrained. *See* **loose** (2). 2. Not imprisoned, enslaved, or controlled by another ▸ independent, self-governing, sovereign. *See* **free** (1).

emancipation *noun*
1. The state of not being in confinement or servitude ▸ freedom, liberation. *See* **liberty** (1). 2. Extrication from danger or confinement ▸ deliverance, release, salvation. *See* **rescue.**

embark *verb*
▸ begin, commence, launch. *See* **start** (1).

embarkation *noun*
1. The initial stage of a development process ▸ genesis, inception, start. *See* **birth** (2). 2. The act of leaving ▸ exit, exodus, withdrawal. *See* **departure** (1).

embarkment *noun*
▸ egress, exodus, leave-taking. *See* **departure** (1).

embarrass *verb*
1. To cause a person to be self-consciously distressed ▸ abash, chagrin, confound, confuse, discomfit, discomfort, disconcert, discountenance, faze, mortify. *Idiom:* put on the spot. *See also* **baffle, shame.** 2. To make complex, intricate, or perplexing ▸ entangle, perplex, tangle. *See* **complicate.**

✦ **CORE SYNONYMS:** *embarrass, abash, chagrin, discomfit, disconcert, faze, mortify.* These verbs mean to cause someone to feel self-conscious and uneasy: *The parents were embarrassed by their child's tantrum. I felt abashed at the extravagant praise. I will be chagrined if my confident prediction fails. He was discomfited by the sudden personal question. She is disconcerted by sarcastic remarks. They refuse to be fazed by your objections. We were mortified by the public display of vulgarity.*

---

embarrassing *adjective*
▸ uncomfortable, uneasy. *See* **awkward** (3).

embarrassment *noun*
1. Self-conscious distress ▸ abashment, chagrin, confusion, discomfiture, discomfort, discomposure, mortification. *See also* **disgrace.** 2. A condition of going or being beyond what is needed, desired, or appropriate ▸ exorbitance, extravagance, surfeit. *See* **excess** (1).

embassy *noun*
A diplomatic office or headquarters in a foreign country ▸ deputation, legation, mission.

embed *or* **imbed** *verb*
▸ entrench, ingrain, plant. *See* **fix** (4).

embellish *verb*
1. To furnish with decorations ▸ decorate, garnish, ornament. *See* **adorn** (1). 2. To endow with beauty and elegance ▸ beautify, enhance, grace, set off.

embellishment *noun*
▸ decoration, ornament, trimming. *See* **adornment.**

embezzle *verb*
▸ purloin, snatch, thieve. *See* **steal** (1).

embitter *verb*
▸ disgruntle, dissatisfy. *See* **disappoint.**

embittered *adjective*
▸ bitter, rancorous, virulent. *See* **resentful.**

embitterment *noun*
▸ bitterness, rancor, virulence. *See* **resentment** (1).

emblazon *verb*
1. To furnish with decoration ▸ decorate, garnish, ornament. *See* **adorn** (1). 2. To impart color to ▸ dye, stain, tint. *See* **color** (1).

emblem *noun*
1. An object or expression associated with and serving to identify something else ▸ attribute, metaphor,

signifier, symbol, token. *See also* **expression, sign, term. 2.** Something visible or evident that gives grounds for believing in the existence or presence of something else ▸ evidence, indication, symptom. *See* **sign** (1).

emblematic *or* **emblematical** *adjective*
▸ metaphorical, representative. *See* **symbolic** (1).

embodiment *noun*
1. A concrete entity typifying an abstraction ▸ allegory, exemplification, exteriorization, externalization, hypostasis, illustration, image, incarnation, incorporation, instantiation, manifestation, materialization, objectification, personalization, personification, prosopopeia, reification, substantiation, type, typification. *See also* **representation, symbol. 2.** One that is representative of a group or class ▸ illustration, sample. *See* **example** (1).

embody *verb*
1. To represent (an abstraction, for example) in or as if in bodily form ▸ allegorize, body forth, concretize, exteriorize, externalize, hypostatize, incarnate, instantiate, manifest, materialize, objectify, personalize, personify, reify, substantiate. *See also* **realize. 2.** To make a part of a united whole ▸ combine, incorporate, integrate. *See also* **assemble, combine. 3.** To have as a part ▸ comprise, take in. *See* **contain** (1).

embolden *verb*
▸ inspire, motivate. *See* **encourage** (1). *See synonym note at* **encourage.**

embrace *verb*
1. To put one's arms around affectionately ▸ clasp, enfold, hold, hug, press, squeeze. *Slang:* clinch. *Idioms:* give a bear hug, take in one's arms, wrap one's arms around. *See also* **grasp, snuggle. 2.** To shut in on all sides ▸ encircle, hedge, ring. *See* **surround** (1). **3.** To have as a part ▸ comprise, take in. *See* **contain** (1). *See synonym note at* **contain. 4.** To receive something given or offered willingly and gladly ▸ accept, take (up), welcome. **5.** To take and make one's own ▸ assume, espouse, take on. *See* **adopt** (1).

embrace *noun*
The act of embracing ▸ bear hug, clasp, hug, squeeze. *Slang:* clinch. *See also* **hold.**

embracement *noun*
▸ adoption, assent, espousal. *See* **acceptance** (1).

embrangle *verb*
▸ embroil, mix up, wrap up. *See* **involve** (1).

embranglement *noun*
▸ embroilment, ensnarement. *See* **entanglement** (1).

embroil *verb*
1. To draw or be drawn in so that extrication is difficult ▸ catch up, mix up, wrap up. *See* **involve** (1). **2.** To make complex, intricate, or perplexing ▸ entangle, perplex, tangle. *See* **complicate.**

embroilment *noun*
▸ embranglement, ensnarement. *See* **entanglement** (1).

embryo *noun*
▸ kernel, seed. *See* **germ** (2).

emend *verb*
1. To prepare a new version of ▸ amend, revamp, rework. *See* **revise** (1). **2.** To make right what is wrong ▸ mend, rectify, remedy. *See* **correct** (1).

emendate *verb*
▸ amend, revamp, rework. *See* **revise** (1).

emendation *noun*
▸ amendment, revisal, rewrite. *See* **revision.**

emendatory *adjective*
▸ reformative, remedial. *See* **corrective.**

emerge *verb*
1. To come into view ▸ issue, loom, materialize. *See* **appear** (1). *See synonym note at* **appear. 2.** To come into being ▸ arise, originate. *See* **begin** (1).

emergence *noun*
▸ manifestation, materialization. *See* **appearance** (2).

emergency *noun*
A situation requiring immediate assistance or remedial action ▸ crisis, distress, exigence, exigency, extremity, flash point, hot water, pinch, straits, trauma, trouble, urgency.

emergency *adjective*
Used or held in reserve ▸ reserve, supplemental. *See* **auxiliary** (2).

emergent *adjective*
Demanding immediate attention ▸ crucial, pressing. *See* **urgent** (1).

emigrant *noun*
One who emigrates ▸ migrant. *See also* **émigré, foreigner, settler.**

emigrate *verb*
To leave one's native land and settle in another ▸ immigrate (to), migrate, resettle, transmigrate. *See also* **move, settle.**

emigration *noun*
Departure from one's native land to settle in another ▸ defection, diaspora, exodus, expatriation, migration, transmigration. *Idiom:* brain drain. *See also* **immigration, exile.**

émigré *noun*
1. One forced to emigrate, usually for political reasons ▸ deportee, displaced person, DP, exile, expatriate, expellee, refugee. **2.** A person coming from another country or into a new community ▸ alien, outsider, stranger. *See* **foreigner.**

eminence *noun*
1. Wide recognition for one's deeds ▸ glory, note, renown. *See* **fame. 2.** A natural land elevation ▸ prominence, rise. *See* **hill** (1). **3.** An important, influential person ▸ notability, personage. *Slang:* big shot. *See* **dignitary.**

eminency *noun*
▸ glory, note, prestige. *See* **fame.**

eminent *adjective*
1. Widely known ▸ celebrated, notable, prominent. *See* **famous.** *See synonym note at* **famous. 2.** Readily attracting notice ▸ conspicuous, outstanding, prominent. *See* **noticeable** (1). **3.** Raised to or occupying a high position or rank ▸ elevated, lofty. *See* **exalted** (1).

eminently *adverb*
▸ exceedingly, extremely, highly. *See* **very.**

emir *noun*
▸ director, head, leader. *See* **chief** (1).

emissary *noun*
▸ ambassador, deputy, proxy. *See* **representative** (2).

emit *verb*
1. To discharge material, as vapor or fumes, usually suddenly and violently ▸ exhale, give, give forth, give off, give out, issue, let off, let out, release, send forth, throw off, vent. *See also* **erupt. 2.** To send out heat, light, or energy ▸ cast (out), radiate. *See* **shed¹** (1).

emollient *noun*
▸ balm, salve. *See* **ointment.**

emolument *noun*
▸ earnings, pay, salary. *See* **wage.**

emotion *noun*
A subjective mental state, such as love or hate ▸ affect, affection, affectivity, feeling, passion, sentiment. *See also* **passion.**

✦ CORE SYNONYMS: *emotion, feeling, passion, sentiment.* These nouns refer to complex and usually strong subjective human response. Although *emotion* and *feeling* are sometimes interchangeable, *emotion* often implies the presence of excitement or agitation: *"Poetry is not a turning loose of emotion, but an escape from emotion"* (T.S. Eliot). *Feeling* is the more general and neutral: *"Poetry is the spontaneous overflow of powerful feelings: it takes its origin from emotion recollected in tranquillity"* (William Wordsworth). *Passion* is intense, compelling emotion: *"They seemed like ungoverned children inflamed with the fiercest passions of men"* (Francis Parkman). *Sentiment* often applies to a thought or opinion arising from or influenced by emotion: *We expressed our sentiments about the government's policies.* The word can also refer to delicate, sensitive, or higher or more refined feelings: *"The mystic reverence, the religious allegiance, which are essential to a true monarchy, are imaginative sentiments that no legislature can manufacture in any people"* (Walter Bagehot).

emotional *adjective*
1. Relating to, arising from, or appealing to the emotions ▸ affectional, affective, emotive. **2.** Readily stirred by emotion ▸ feeling, sensitive. *See also* **passionate. 3.** Suggesting drama or a stage performance, as in emotionality or suspense ▸ melodramatic, sensational, spectacular. *See* **dramatic** (2).

emotionless *adjective*
▸ cold-blooded, impassive, stolid. *See* **cold** (2).

emotive *adjective*
Relating to, arising from, or appealing to the emotions ▸ affectional, affective, emotional.

empathetic *or* **empathic** *adjective*
▸ commiserative, compassionate, understanding. *See* **sympathetic.**

empathize *verb*
1. To understand or be sensitive to another's feelings or ideas ▸ sympathize, understand. *Idioms:* feel some-

one's pain, put oneself (*or* walk) in someone else's shoes. **2.** To associate or affiliate oneself closely with a person or group ▸ identify, relate, sympathize. *See also* **understand.**

empathy *noun*
1. Sympathetic, sad concern for someone in misfortune ▸ compassion, condolence. *See* **pity** (1). *See synonym note at* **pity. 2.** A very close understanding between persons ▸ sympathy, understanding.

emperor *noun*
▸ director, head, leader. *See* **chief** (1).

emphasis *noun*
Special attention given to something considered important ▸ accent, accentuation, stress, weight. *See also* **importance, notice.**

✦ CORE SYNONYMS: *emphasis, accent, stress.* These nouns mean special weight placed on something considered important: *an education with an emphasis on science; will study music with an accent on jazz; laid heavy stress on law and order.*

emphasize *verb*
To accord emphasis to ▸ accent, accentuate, feature, highlight, italicize, play up, point up, spotlight, stress, underline, underscore. *Idioms:* call attention to, lay stress on. *See also* **concentrate.**

emphatic *adjective*
1. Bold or confident in assertion ▸ forceful, insistent. *See* **assertive. 2.** Clearly, fully, and emphatically expressed ▸ decided, explicit, unambiguous. *See* **definite** (1).

emphatically *adverb*
▸ directly, positively. *Informal:* flat out. *See* **flatly.**

emplace *verb*
▸ locate, place, situate. *See* **position.**

emplacement *noun*
▸ location, point, spot. *See* **position** (1).

employ *verb*
1. To obtain the use or services of ▸ enlist, engage, hire, recruit, retain, sign (on *or* up), take on. *Idioms:* bring aboard, put on the payroll. *See also* **authorize. 2.** To make busy ▸ busy, engage, occupy. *See also* **absorb, involve. 3.** To put into action or use ▸ apply, adopt, utilize. *See* **use** (1). *See synonym note at* **use. 4.** To occupy the attention of ▸ consume, engage, immerse. *See* **absorb** (1). **5.** To direct the functioning of ▸ run, work. *See* **operate** (1).

employ *noun*
The state of being employed ▸ employment, hire, service.

employable *adjective*
1. Available for use ▸ accessible, operable, usable. *See* **open** (4). **2.** In a condition to be used ▸ applicable, serviceable. *See* **usable** (1).

employed *adjective*
1. Having a job ▸ hired, jobholding, placed, retained, wage-earning, working. *Idioms:* bringing home the bacon, gainfully employed, off the dole **2.** Involved in activity or work ▸ engaged, occupied. *See* **busy** (1).

employee *noun*
One who is employed by another ▸ help, hireling, jobholder, staffer, staff member, wage earner, worker. *Informal:* hire, hired hand, nine-to-fiver. *See also* **assistant, laborer.**

employer *noun*
One that employs persons for wages ▸ hirer.

employment *noun*
1. The act of employing for wages ▸ engagement, hire, hiring, retention. **2.** The state of being employed ▸ employ, hire, service. **3.** The act of putting into play ▸ application, implementation, usage. *See* **exercise** (1). **4.** The condition of being put to use ▸ application, service, use. *See* **duty** (2). **5.** Activity pursued as a livelihood ▸ career, handicraft, occupation. *See* **business** (2).

emporium *noun*
A retail establishment where merchandise is sold ▸ boutique, outlet, shop, store.

empower *verb*
1. To give authority to ▸ accredit, enable, license. *See* **authorize** (1). *See synonym note at* **authorize. 2.** To give the means, ability, or opportunity to do ▸ enable, permit. *Idioms:* clear the path (*or* road *or* way) for, smooth the way for. *See also* **ease, permit.**

emprise *noun*
▸ odyssey, venture. *See* **adventure.**

emptiness *noun*
1. Empty, unfilled space ▸ barrenness, vacuity. *See* **nothingness** (2). **2.** A desolate sense of loss ▸ blankness, desolation, emptiness, hollowness, vacuum, void. **3.** Total lack of ideas, meaning, or substance ▸ bareness, barrenness, blankness, hollowness, inanity, meaninglessness, vacancy, vacuity, vacuousness. *See also* **futility, insipidity.**

empty *adjective*
1. Containing nothing ▸ bare, barren, blank, clear, null, vacant, vacuous, void. *Idiom:* clean as a whistle. **2.** Deprived of a quality or aspect that is desirable ▸ bankrupt, barren, bereft, denuded, deprived, destitute, devoid, innocent, lacking, void, wanting. *Idioms:* crying out for, in want (*or* need) of. **3.** Lacking value, use, or substance ▸ otiose, vacant. *See* **hollow** (1). *See synonym note at* **hollow. 4.** Lacking intelligent thought or content ▸ blank, vacuous. *See* **vacant** (1). **5.** Lacking worth and value ▸ drossy, good-for-nothing, valueless. *See* **worthless** (1).

empty *verb*
1. To remove the contents of ▸ clean out, clear, empty out, evacuate, gut, strip, vacate, void. **2.** To cause a liquid to flow in a steady stream ▸ decant, flow, issue. *See* **pour** (1). **3.** To relieve a burden ▸ discharge, relieve, unburden. *See* **rid.**

✚ **CORE SYNONYMS:** *empty, vacant, blank, void, vacuous, bare, barren.* These adjectives mean lacking contents that could or should be present. *Empty* applies to what is wholly lacking contents or substance: *an empty room; empty promises. Vacant* refers to what is

without an occupant or incumbent, or to what is without intelligence or thought: *a vacant auditorium; a vacant stare. Blank* stresses the absence of something, especially on a surface, that would convey meaning or content: *blank pages. Void* applies to what is free from or completely destitute of discernible content: *gibberish void of all meaning. Vacuous* describes what is as devoid of substance as a vacuum is: *led a vacuous life.* Something that is *bare* lacks surface covering (*a bare head*) or detail (*the bare facts*); the word also denotes the condition of being stripped of contents or furnishings: *a bare closet. Barren* literally and figuratively stresses lack of productivity: *barren land; writing barren of insight.*

---

empty-headed *adjective*
1. Lacking intelligent thought or content ▸ empty, impassive, vacuous. *See* **vacant** (1). **2.** Given to light-hearted silliness ▸ featherbrained, flighty, frivolous. *See* **giddy** (2).

empyreal *adjective*
▸ celestial, supernal. *See* **heavenly** (2).

emulate *verb*
1. To take as a model ▸ copy, imitate. *See* **follow** (5). **2.** To strive against others for victory ▸ race, rival, vie. *See* **compete.**

emulation *noun*
1. The act, practice, or art of copying the manner or expression of another ▸ emulation, impersonation, mime. *See* **mimicry. 2.** A strong desire to achieve something ▸ ambition, ambitiousness, aspiration. *See also* **drive, enthusiasm, thirst.**

emulative *adjective*
▸ apish, slavish. *See* **imitative** (1).

emulator *noun*
▸ contender, opponent, rival. *See* **competitor.**

emulous *adjective*
1. Full of ambition ▸ determined, enterprising. *See* **ambitious. 2.** Given to competition ▸ cutthroat, dog-eat-dog, rivalrous. *See* **competitive.**

enable *verb*
1. To give the means, ability, or opportunity to do ▸ empower, permit. *Idioms:* clear the path (*or* road *or* way) for, smooth the way for. *See also* **ease, permit. 2.** To give authority to ▸ accredit, empower, license. *See* **authorize** (1).

enact *verb*
1. To put in force or cause to be by legal authority ▸ constitute, legislate. *See* **establish** (3). **2.** To play the part of ▸ perform, play, portray, represent. *See* **act** (4). **3.** To produce on the stage ▸ dramatize, perform, produce. *See* **stage** (1).

enactment *noun*
1. The formal product of a legislative or judicial body ▸ bill, legislation. *See* **law** (2). **2.** A performer's distinctive personal version of a song, dance, piece of music, or role ▸ performance, reading, rendition. *See* **interpretation** (1).

enamel *noun*
A material applied as a final coating ▸ glaze, paint, varnish. *See* **finish** (3).

enamel *verb*
To apply a coating to ▸ glaze, paint. *See* **finish** (7).

enamored *adjective*
▸ beguiled, obsessed, smitten. *See* **infatuated.**

enceinte *adjective*
▸ expectant, parturient. *See* **pregnant** (1).

enchant *verb*
1. To act upon with or as if with magic ▸ bewitch, mesmerize, spellbind. *See* **charm** (2). *See synonym note at* **charm. 2.** To please greatly or irresistibly ▸ beguile, bewitch, captivate. *See* **charm** (1). **3.** To give great or keen pleasure to ▸ amuse, overjoy, pleasure. *See* **delight** (1).

enchanter *noun*
▸ conjurer, magician, sorcerer. *See* **wizard** (1).

enchanting *adjective*
1. Pleasing to the eye or mind ▸ appealing, fetching, lovely. *See* **attractive** (1). **2.** Giving great pleasure or delight ▸ delectable, heavenly. *See* **delightful.**

enchantment *noun*
1. The power or quality of attracting ▸ appeal, draw, enticement, lure. *See* **attraction** (1). **2.** A word or formula believed to have magic powers ▸ abracadabra, charm. *See* **spell**^{2}. **3.** A feeling of extreme gratification aroused by something good or desired ▸ bliss, elation, pleasure. *See* **delight** (1).

enchantress *noun*
1. A woman who seduces or exploits men ▸ femme fatale, siren. *See* **seductress. 2.** A woman who practices magic ▸ hag, lamia, sorceress, witch. *See also* **wizard.**

encircle *verb*
1. To form a circle around ▸ band, begird, belt, cincture, circle, circumnavigate, circumscribe, gird, girdle, girt, loop, orbit, ring, surround. *See also* **turn. 2.** To shut in on all sides ▸ circle, hedge, ring. *See* **surround** (1). *See synonym note at* **surround.**

enclose *verb*
1. To confine within a limited area ▸ bar, box (in), cage, close (in), closet, confine, contain, coop (in *or* up), cordon (off), corral, fence (in), immure, impound, pen, shut (away *or* in *or* up), wall (in *or* off *or* up). *See also* **imprison, surround. 2.** To surround and advance upon ▸ besiege, close in, encompass, envelop, hedge, hem, picket. *See also* **besiege, surround.**

✚ CORE SYNONYMS: *enclose, cage, coop up, fence, pen, wall in.* These verbs mean to surround and confine within a limited area: *cattle enclosed in feedlots; was caged in the office all afternoon; was cooped up in a studio apartment; a garden fenced in by shrubbery; ships penned up in the harbor; prisoners who were walled in.*

---

enclosure *noun*
▸ courtyard, quad. *See* **court** (1).

encomiastic *adjective*
▸ approbatory, laudatory. *See* **complimentary** (1).

encomium *noun*
▸ acclamation, celebration, kudos. *See* **praise** (1).

encompass *verb*
1. To shut in on all sides ▸ encircle, hedge, ring. *See* **surround** (1). *See synonym note at* **surround. 2.** To surround and advance upon ▸ close in, envelop, hem. *See* **enclose** (2). **3.** To have as a part ▸ comprise, take in. *See* **contain** (1).

encounter *verb*
1. To find or meet by chance ▸ alight on (*or* upon), bump into, chance on (*or* upon), come across, come on (*or* upon), find, happen on (*or* upon), hit (on *or* upon), light on (*or* upon), meet, run across, run into, see, stumble on (*or* upon), tumble on. **Idiom:** meet up with. **2.** To meet face-to-face, especially defiantly ▸ confront, face, front, meet. **Idiom:** stand up to. *See also* **contest, defy. 3.** To strive in opposition ▸ battle, engage, struggle. *See* **contend** (1). **4.** To participate in or partake of personally ▸ know, undergo. *See* **experience.**

encounter *noun*
1. A face-to-face, usually hostile meeting ▸ duel, face-off, showdown. *See* **confrontation** (1). **2.** An encounter between opposing military forces ▸ combat, confrontation, war. *See* **battle** (1).

encourage *verb*
1. To impart courage, inspiration, and resolution to ▸ animate, cheer (on), embolden, inspire, inspirit, motivate. *See also* **provoke, urge. 2.** To impart emotional, moral, or mental strength to ▸ buck up, cheer (up), fortify, hearten, nerve, perk up. *See also* **comfort, energize. 3.** To lend supportive approval to ▸ countenance, favor, smile on (*or* upon). *See also* **approve, support. 4.** To help bring about ▸ cultivate, facilitate. *See* **promote** (2).

✚ CORE SYNONYMS: *encourage, animate, cheer, embolden, inspirit, motivate.* These verbs mean to impart courage, inspiration, and resolution to: *encouraged the athlete to compete; played music to animate the crowd; a visitor cheering the patient; was emboldened to sing for the guests; a pep talk that inspirited the weary team; praise that motivated us.*

◄ ANTONYM: *discourage*

---

encouragement *noun*
1. Something that gives courage or confidence ▸ boost, exhortation, inspiration, lift, motivation, stimulation. *Informal:* pep talk. **Idiom:** shot in the arm. **2.** Something that causes and encourages an action or response ▸ impulse, incentive. *See* **stimulus** (1). **3.** Aid or support given to encourage ▸ furtherance, promotion. *See* **patronage** (1).

encouraging *adjective*
Inspiring confidence or hope ▸ cheering, heartening, hopeful, likely, promising. *See also* **favorable, optimistic.**

encroach *verb*
▸ cut in, horn in, interlope. *See* **intrude** (1).

encroachment *noun*
▸ infringement, intrusion, obtrusion, transgression. *See* **trespass** (2).

encumber *verb*

1. To weigh down or place a heavy load on ▸ charge, saddle, tax. *See* **burden**[1]. **2.** To interfere with the progress of ▸ dampen, obstruct. *See* **hinder** (1).

encumbrance *noun*

1. Something that blocks entry or passage ▸ barrier, blockage, hindrance. *See* **bar** (1). **2.** A condition of owing something to another ▸ arrears, liability, obligation. *See* **debt** (2). **3.** Something carried or transported ▸ freight, load. *See* **burden**[1] (2). **4.** An excessive, unwelcome burden ▸ imposition, infliction, intrusion, obtrusion. *See also* **meddling**.

end *noun*

1. A concluding or terminating ▸ cessation, close, closing, closure, completion, conclusion, consummation, cutoff, dénouement, ending, end of the line, expiration, finis, finish, period, shutdown, stopping point, termination, terminus, wind-up, wrap-up. *See also* **stop**. **2.** The last part ▸ close, closing, conclusion, ending, envoy, epilogue, finale, finish, last, termination, wind-up, wrap-up. **3.** The part farthest from the front ▸ rear, tail, tail end. *See* **back**. **4.** The boundary surrounding a certain area ▸ bounds, confines. *See* **limits**. **5.** What one intends to do or achieve ▸ aim, goal, objective. *See* **intention**. *See synonym note at* **intention**. **6.** The ultimate point to which an action, thought, discussion, or policy is carried ▸ extreme, extremity, limit. *See* **length** (3). **7.** Residual matter ▸ butt, fragment, heel, odds and ends, ort, scrap, shard, stub. *See also* **balance**. **8.** The act or fact of dying ▸ demise, passing. *See* **death** (1). **9.** A personal outcome or end ▸ doom, fortune, lot. *See* **fate** (2).

end *verb*

1. To bring or come to a natural or proper end ▸ close, finish, terminate. *See* **conclude** (1). *See synonym note at* **conclude**. **2.** To cease to exist ▸ depart, perish. *See* **disappear** (2). **3.** To become void, especially through passage of time or an omission ▸ cease, run out. *See* **lapse** (1). **4.** To cease consideration or treatment of ▸ give up, skip. *See* **drop** (7).

endanger *verb*

To expose to danger or destruction ▸ compromise, hazard, imperil, jeopardize, menace, peril, risk, threaten. *Idioms:* lay open, put in jeopardy.

✦ CORE SYNONYMS: *endanger, compromise, imperil, jeopardize, risk*. These verbs mean to subject to danger, loss, or destruction: *driving that endangers lives; compromised his health by smoking; a forest imperiled by acid rain; strikes that jeopardized company profits; wouldn't risk her financial security.*

---

endangerment *noun*

1. Exposure to harm, loss, or injury ▸ hazard, jeopardy, peril. *See* **danger**. **2.** The condition of being laid open to something undesirable or injurious ▸ susceptibility, vulnerability. *See* **exposure** (1).

endeavor *noun*

1. A trying to do or make something ▸ effort, trial. *Informal:* shot. *See* **attempt** (1). **2.** The use of energy to do something ▸ exertion, struggle. *See* **effort** (1). **3.** Something completed or attained successfully ▸ achievement, deed, triumph. *See* **accomplishment** (1). **4.** Something undertaken, especially something requiring extensive planning and work ▸ enterprise, project, undertaking, venture. *See also* **task**.

endeavor *verb*

To make an attempt ▸ assay, strive. *See* **attempt**.

ended *adjective*

▸ concluded, finished, through. *See* **complete** (3).

endemic *adjective*

▸ autochthonic, native, regional. *See* **indigenous** (1). *See synonym note at* **indigenous**.

ending *noun*

1. A concluding or terminating ▸ cease, completion, termination. *See* **end** (1). **2.** The last part ▸ closing, conclusion, epilogue. *See* **end** (2).

endless *adjective*

1. Having no ends or limits ▸ boundless, illimitable, immeasurable, infinite, limitless, measureless, unbounded, unlimited. *See also* **incalculable**. **2.** Enduring for all time ▸ amaranthine, ceaseless, eternal, eterne, everlasting, immortal, never-ending, perpetual, sempiternal, unending. *See also* **continuing, forever, unchanging**. **3.** Existing without interruption or end ▸ constant, everlasting, perpetual. *See* **continual**.

✦ CORE SYNONYMS: *endless, boundless, eternal, illimitable, infinite, sempiternal*. These adjectives mean being having no limits or being without a beginning or end: *an endless universe; boundless ambition; eternal beauty; illimitable space; infinite wisdom; sempiternal truth.*

---

endlessly *adverb*

▸ always, perpetually, unendingly. *See* **forever** (1).

endlessness *noun*

The quality or state of having no end ▸ ceaselessness, eternality, eternalness, eternity, everlastingness, interminability, perpetuity. *See also* **infinity**.

endmost *adjective*

▸ hindermost, rearmost. *See* **last**[1] (2).

end of the line *noun*

▸ cease, completion, termination. *See* **end** (1).

endorse *verb*

1. To affix one's signature to ▸ autograph, inscribe. *See* **sign** (1). **2.** To give one's consent to ▸ approve, authorize, sanction. *See* **permit** (2). **3.** To aid the cause of by approving or favoring ▸ back, champion, stand by. *See* **support** (1). **4.** To accept officially ▸ approve, pass, ratify. *See* **confirm** (3).

endorsement *noun*

1. An indication of commendation or approval ▸ backing, blessing, recommendation, support. *Informal:* plug. *See also* **patronage, reference**. **2.** The approving of an action, especially when done by one in authority ▸ authorization, consent, sanction. *See* **permission**. **3.** An act of confirming officially ▸ approval, ratification, sanction. *See* **confirmation** (1).

endow *verb*
1. To present as a gift ▶ award, invest. *See* **gift**. 2. To present as a gift to a charity or cause ▶ bequeath, pledge. *See* **donate** (1).

endowed *adjective*
▶ natural, talented. *See* **gifted**.

endowment *noun*
1. A quality, ability, or accomplishment that makes a person suitable for a particular position or task ▶ attainment, credential, qualification, skill. *See also* **qualification**. 2. Something given to a charity or cause ▶ benefaction, contribution, offering. *See* **donation**.

end product *noun*
▶ consequence, outcome, result. *See* **effect** (1).

endue *verb*
▶ award, invest. *See* **gift**.

endurable *adjective*
▶ sufferable, tolerable. *See* **bearable**.

endurance *noun*
1. The quality or power of withstanding hardship or stress ▶ durability, fortitude, hardiness, stamina, staying power, sticking power, toughness. *See also* **courage, strength**. 2. Uninterrupted existence or succcssion ▶ persistence, survival. *See* **continuation** (1).

endure *verb*
1. To put up with or continue despite difficulties ▶ abide, accept, bear (with), brook, go on, hang on, keep on, live through, persevere, persist, sit through, soldier on, stand (for), stick out, stomach, suffer, support, sustain, swallow, take, tolerate, withstand. *Informal:* lump. *Slang:* sweat out, tough out. *Idioms:* hang in there, go the distance, keep going, keep it up, learn to live with (*or* accept), make one's peace with, never say die, resign oneself to, put up with. *See also* **deal with, survive**. 2. To be in existence or in a certain state for an indefinitely long time ▶ abide, bide, continue, go on, hold out, hold steady, keep, last, perdure, perseverate, persist, remain, stand, stay. 3. To withstand stress or difficulty ▶ hold up, stand up. *See* **bear up**.

✦ **CORE SYNONYMS:** *endure, bear, stand, abide, suffer, tolerate*. These verbs mean to put up with or withstand something, especially something difficult or painful. *Endure* specifies a continuing capacity to face pain or hardship: *"Human life is everywhere a state in which much is to be endured and little to be enjoyed"* (Samuel Johnson). *Bear* pertains broadly to the capacity to withstand: *"Those best can bear reproof who merit praise"* (Alexander Pope). *Stand* implies resoluteness of spirit: *Actors who can't stand criticism shouldn't perform in public. Abide* and *suffer* suggest the capacity to withstand patiently: *She couldn't abide fools. He suffered their insults in silence. Tolerate*, when applied to something other than pain, connotes reluctant acceptance: *"A decent . . . examination of the acts of government should be not only tolerated, but encouraged"* (William Henry Harrison).

---

enduring *adjective*
1. Existing or remaining in the same state for an indefinitely long time ▶ durable, lasting, perennial. *See* **continuing** (1). 2. Enduring or capable of enduring hardship or inconvenience without complaint ▶ long-suffering, resigned. *See* **patient**. 3. Characterized by enduring excellence, appeal, and importance ▶ ageless, antique. *See* **vintage** (1).

enemy *noun*
▶ antagonist, foe, nemesis. *See* **opponent** (1). *See synonym note at* **opponent**.

energetic *adjective*
Possessing, exerting, or displaying energy ▶ active, brisk, driving, dynamic, dynamical, enterprising, forceful, fresh, kinetic, lively, sprightly, spry, strenuous, vigorous, zippy. *Informal:* peppy, snappy. *See also* **lusty, strong**.

✦ **CORE SYNONYMS:** *energetic, active, dynamic, vigorous, lively*. These adjectives mean having or displaying energy. *Energetic* suggests sustained enthusiastic activity: *an energetic competitor. Active* means moving, doing, or functioning: *an active toddler; an active imagination; saw active service in the army. Dynamic* connotes energy and forcefulness that often inspires others: *a dynamic leader. Vigorous* implies healthy strength and robustness: *a vigorous crusader against drunk driving. Lively* suggests animated alertness: *a lively interest in politics*.

---

energetically *adverb*
▶ forcefully, powerfully, vigorously. *See* **hard** (1).

energize *verb*
To give or impart vitality and energy to ▶ exhilarate, invigorate, stimulate, vitalize. *Informal:* jazz up, jump-start, pep up. *Idioms:* light a fire under, put zip into. *See also* **fire, inspire, provoke, refresh**.

energizer *noun*
▶ restorative, stimulant. *See* **tonic**.

energizing *adjective*
▶ bracing, exhilarating, rousing. *See* **invigorating**.

energy *noun*
Capacity for work or vigorous activity ▶ animation, dash, dynamism, force, liveliness, might, potency, power, punch, sprightliness, starch, steam, strength, verve, vibrancy, vigor, vigorousness, vim, vitality. *Informal:* get-up-and-go, go, jump, pep, peppiness, snap, zip. *Idiom:* vim and vigor. *See also* **spirit**.

✦ **CORE SYNONYMS:** *energy, strength, power, might, force*. These nouns denote the capacity for work or vigorous activity. *Energy* connotes vitality and intensity: *"The same energy of character which renders a man a daring villain would have rendered him useful to society, had that society been well organized"* (Mary Wollstonecraft). *Strength* refers especially to physical, mental, or moral robustness or vigor: *"enough work to do, and strength enough to do the work"* (Rudyard Kipling). *Power* is the ability to do something and especially to produce an effect: *"I do not think the United States would come to an end if we lost our power to declare an Act of Congress void"* (Oliver Wendell Holmes, Jr.). *Might* often implies abundant or extraordinary power: *"He could defend the island* *against the whole might of the German Air Force"* (Winston S. Churchill). *Force* is the application of power or strength: *"the overthrow of our institutions by force and violence"* (Charles Evans Hughes).

enervate *verb*
To lessen or deplete the nerve, power, or vitality of ▶ attenuate, debilitate, devitalize, enfeeble, eviscerate, gut, sap, undermine, undo, unnerve, weaken. *See also* **deplete, tire.**

enervated *adjective*
1. Lacking mental and physical alertness and activity ▶ slothful, sluggish, stuporous. *See* **lethargic** (1). **2.** Not physically strong ▶ feeble, frail, infirm, unsound. *See* **weak** (1).

enervation *noun*
1. The sapping away of strength or energy ▶ depletion, devitalization, enfeeblement. *See* **debilitation. 2.** A deficiency in mental and physical alertness and activity ▶ languor, listlessness, sluggishness. *See* **lethargy** (1).

enfeeble *verb*
▶ debilitate, weaken. *See* **enervate.**

enfeeblement *noun*
▶ depletion, devitalization, incapacitation. *See* **debilitation.**

enfold *verb*
1. To cover completely and closely, as with clothing or bandages ▶ envelop, roll, swathe. *See* **wrap** (1). **2.** To surround and cover completely so as to obscure ▶ clothe, enshroud, invest. *See* **wrap** (2). **3.** To put one's arms around affectionately ▶ clasp, hug. *See* **embrace** (1).

enforce *verb*
To compel observance of ▶ carry out, effect, effectuate, execute, implement, invoke, prosecute. *Idioms:* put in force, put into action (*or* effect *or* operation).

enforcement *noun*
Carrying a law or judgment into effect ▶ execution, implementation. *See also* **effect, exercise.**

engage *verb*
1. To obtain the use or services of ▶ hire, retain. *See* **employ** (1). **2.** To cause to be set aside, as for one's use, in advance ▶ bespeak, reserve. *See* **book** (1). *See synonym note at* **book. 3.** To assume an obligation ▶ commit, undertake. *See* **pledge** (2). **4.** To occupy the attention of ▶ engross, immerse, involve. *See* **absorb** (1). **5.** To involve someone in an activity ▶ draw in. *See also* **involve. 6.** To involve oneself in an activity ▶ carry on, partake, share. *See* **participate** (1). **7.** To make busy ▶ busy, employ, occupy. *See also* **absorb, involve. 8.** To strive in opposition ▶ battle, fight, wrestle. *See* **contend** (1). **9.** To come or bring together and interlock ▶ mesh. *See also* **attach, fit**[1]. **10.** To guarantee by a solemn promise ▶ promise, vow. *See* **pledge** (1). **11.** To compel the attention, interest, or imagination of ▶ captivate, fascinate, intrigue. *See* **grip** (1).

engaged *adjective*
1. Involved in activity or work ▶ absorbed, occupied.

See **busy** (1). **2.** Pledged to marry ▶ affianced, bespoken, betrothed, intended, pledged, plighted, promised. **3.** Having concern ▶ interested, involved. *See* **concerned** (1).

engagement *noun*
1. An arrangement to appear at a certain time and place ▶ appointment, assignation, commitment, date, rendezvous, tryst. **2.** A commitment, as for a performance by an entertainer ▶ booking, date. *Slang:* gig. **3.** The act or condition of being pledged to marry ▶ betrothal, espousal, troth. **4.** The act or fact of participating ▶ involvement, partaking, participation, sharing. **5.** A declaration that one will or will not do a certain thing ▶ covenant, pledge, vow. *See* **promise** (1). **6.** Total occupation of the attention or of the mind ▶ engrossment, enthrallment, immersion. *See* **absorption** (2). **7.** The act of employing for wages ▶ employment, hire, hiring, retention. **8.** An encounter between opposing military forces ▶ combat, confrontation, war. *See* **battle** (1).

✚ CORE SYNONYMS: *engagement, appointment, assignation, date, rendezvous, tryst.* These nouns denote an arrangement to appear at a certain time and place: *a business engagement; a dental appointment; a secret assignation; a date to play tennis; a rendezvous of agents at the border; a lovers' tryst.*

engaging *adjective*
▶ enchanting, fetching, lovely, winsome. *See* **attractive** (1).

engender *verb*
1. To bring into existence ▶ give, provide, yield. *See* **produce** (1). **2.** To give life to ▶ propagate, spawn. *See* **breed** (1).

engineer *verb*
1. To use stratagems in gaining an end ▶ angle for, finesse. *See* **maneuver** (2). **2.** To control the course of an activity ▶ direct, manage, operate. *See* **conduct** (1).

englut *verb*
▶ bolt, gobble, guzzle. *See* **gulp** (1).

engorge *verb*
1. To swallow food or drink greedily or rapidly in large amounts ▶ englut, gobble. *See* **gulp** (1). **2.** To satisfy to the full or to excess ▶ cloy, sate, surfeit. *See* **satiate.**

engorgement *noun*
▶ repletion, satiety. *See* **satiation.**

engrave *verb*
1. To cut a design or inscription into a hard surface, especially for printing ▶ carve, chase, chisel, etch, grave, incise, inscribe. **2.** To produce a deep impression of ▶ etch, fix, grave, impress, imprint, inscribe, stamp. *See also* **impress.**

engross *verb*
1. To occupy the attention of ▶ consume, monopolize, preoccupy. *See* **absorb** (1). *See synonym note at* **absorb. 2.** To form letters, characters, or words on a surface with an instrument ▶ indite, pen, scribe. *See* **write** (1).

engrossed *adjective*
▸ absorbed, immersed, riveted. *See* **rapt.**

engrossment *noun*
▸ enthrallment, immersion, preoccupation, prepossession. *See* **absorption** (2).

engulf *verb*
1. To flow over completely ▸ drown, overflow, submerge. *See* **flood** (1). **2.** To affect deeply or completely, as with emotion ▸ crush, prostrate. *See* **overwhelm** (2).

enhance *verb*
1. To endow with beauty and elegance ▸ beautify, embellish, grace, set off. *See also* **adorn. 2.** To look good on or with ▸ become, flatter, suit. *Idiom:* put in the best light. **3.** To make greater in intensity or severity ▸ deepen, escalate, heighten. *See* **intensify. 4.** To add to or make whole ▸ augment, complete, strengthen. *See* **supplement. 5.** To advance to a more desirable state ▸ better, enrich, upgrade. *See* **improve** (1).

enhancement *noun*
1. Something added to another for embellishment or completion ▸ accompaniment, add-on, bells and whistles, complement, enrichment, extra, supplement. *See also* **addition, attachment. 2.** The act of making better or the condition of being made better ▸ betterment, development, upgrade. *See* **improvement** (1).

enigma *noun*
▸ conundrum, puzzle, riddle. *See* **mystery.**

enigmatic *adjective*
1. Difficult to explain or understand ▸ baffling, inscrutable, puzzling. *See* **mysterious. 2.** Lacking certainty or clarity ▸ dubious, indeterminate, questionable, unclear. *See* **ambiguous** (1). *See synonym note at* **ambiguous.**

enjoin *verb*
1. To give orders to ▸ charge, instruct, order. *See* **command** (1). **2.** To refuse to allow ▸ disallow, proscribe. *See* **forbid.** *See synonym note at* **forbid.**

enjoy *verb*
1. To receive pleasure from ▸ appreciate, care for, like, relish, savor. *Informal:* go for, go in for. *Slang:* be into, dig. *Idioms:* be big on, be crazy (*or* wild) about, be fond of, get a charge (*or* bang *or* kick) out of, have a thing about (*or* soft spot for), lap up. *See also* **like¹. 2.** To have at one's disposal ▸ have, hold. *See* **command** (3).

enjoyable *adjective*
1. Giving pleasure or entertainment ▸ gratifying, nice, pleasurable. *See* **pleasant** (1). **2.** Having pleasant desirable qualities ▸ fine, jolly, nice. *See* **good** (1).

enjoyment *noun*
1. A feeling of gratification aroused by something good or desired ▸ bliss, joy, pleasure. *See* **delight** (1). **2.** Something that amuses, entertains, or pleases ▸ diversion, entertainment, play. *See* **amusement.**

enkindle *verb*
1. To begin or cause to begin burning ▸ ignite, kindle.

See **light¹** (1). **2.** To arouse the emotions of ▸ impassion, inspire, stir. *See* **fire** (2).

enlace *verb*
▸ braid, intertwine, twist. *See* **weave** (1).

enlarge *verb*
1. To make or become greater or larger ▸ amplify, boost, grow. *See* **increase** (1). *See synonym note at* **increase. 2.** To express at greater length or in greater detail ▸ amplify (on), develop, expand (on). *See* **elaborate. 3.** To achieve an increase of ▸ develop, expand. *See* **gain** (9). **4.** To make or become broader or more comprehensive ▸ amplify, expand, widen. *See* **broaden.**

enlargement *noun*
1. The act of increasing or rising ▸ amplification, boost, escalation. *See* **increase** (1). **2.** The result or product of building up ▸ development, proliferation. *See* **buildup** (2).

enlighten *verb*
1. To enable one to understand, especially in a spiritual sense ▸ edify, illumine. *See* **illuminate** (3). **2.** To impart information to ▸ advise, educate, notify. *See* **inform** (1).

enlightened *adjective*
1. Showing evidence of schooling, training, or experience ▸ informed, lettered, literate. *See* **educated** (1). **2.** Provided with information; made aware ▸ instructed, knowledgeable. *See* **informed** (1).

enlightening *adjective*
1. Promoting culture ▸ aesthetic, humanizing. *See* **cultural. 2.** Serving to educate or inform ▸ edifying, informative, instructive. *See* **educational** (2).

enlightenment *noun*
1. The condition of being informed spiritually ▸ edification, illumination. *See also* **education. 2.** Excellent taste resulting from intellectual development ▸ cultivation, refinement. *See* **culture** (3).

enlist *verb*
1. To become a member of ▸ enroll, sign up. *See* **join** (4). **2.** To assemble, prepare, or put into operation, as for war or a similar emergency ▸ activate, ready. *See* **mobilize. 3.** To obtain the use or services of ▸ hire, retain. *See* **employ** (1).

enliven *verb*
1. To make lively or animated ▸ animate, brighten, light (up), perk up. **2.** To make alive ▸ animate, quicken, vitalize, vivify. *See also* **elate, energize, provoke.**

enlivening *adjective*
▸ bracing, energizing, exhilarating. *See* **invigorating.**

enmesh *verb*
▸ net, snare, trap. *See* **catch** (1). *See synonym note at* **catch.**

enmeshment *noun*
▸ embroilment, ensnarement. *See* **entanglement** (1).

enmity *noun*
Deep-seated hatred, as between longtime opponents or rivals ▸ animosity, animus, antagonism, antipathy, feud, hostility, ill feeling, ill will, rancor. *Idioms:* bad

blood, blood feud, hard feelings, no love lost. *See also* **despisal, hate, resentment.**

✛ CORE SYNONYMS: *enmity, hostility, antagonism, animosity, rancor, antipathy, animus.* These nouns refer to the feeling or expression of deep-seated ill will. *Enmity* is hatred such as might be felt for an enemy: *the wartime enmity of the two nations. Hostility* implies the clear expression of enmity: *"If we could read the secret history of our enemies, we should find . . . enough to disarm all hostility"* (Henry Wadsworth Longfellow). *Antagonism* is hostility that quickly results in active resistance, opposition, or contentiousness: *"the early struggles of famous authors, the notorious antagonism of publishers and editors to any new writer of exceptional promise"* (Edith Wharton). *Animosity* often triggers bitter resentment or punitive action: *overcame her animosity toward her parents. Rancor* suggests vengeful hatred and resentment: *filled with rancor after losing his job. Antipathy* is deep-seated aversion or repugnance: *an antipathy to social pretension. Animus* is distinctively personal, often based on one's prejudices or temperament: *an inexplicable animus against intellectuals.*

---

ennoble *verb*
1. To cause to be eminent or recognized ▸ dignify, exalt, honor. *See* **distinguish** (5). **2.** To raise to a high position or status ▸ elevate, magnify, uplift. *See* **exalt** (1).
ennobled *adjective*
▸ elevated, lofty. *See* **exalted** (1).
ennoblement *noun*
▸ apotheosis, elevation. *See* **exaltation** (1).
ennui *noun*
▸ listlessness, tedium. *See* **boredom.**
enormity *noun*
1. The quality of being outrageous ▸ atrocity, heinousness, monstrousness. *See* **outrageousness. 2.** A monstrous offense or evil ▸ atrocity, monstrosity. *See* **outrage** (1).
enormous *adjective*
Of extraordinary size and power ▸ astronomical, behemoth, Brobdingnagian, Bunyanesque, colossal, cyclopean, elephantine, gargantuan, giant, gigantesque, gigantic, herculean, heroic, huge, immense, jumbo, mammoth, massive, massy, mastodonic, mighty, monstrous, monumental, mountainous, prodigious, pythonic, stupendous, titanic, tremendous, vast. *Informal:* monster, walloping. *Slang:* humongous, whopping. *See also* **big, bulky, grand.**

✛ CORE SYNONYMS: *enormous, immense, huge, gigantic, colossal, mammoth, tremendous, stupendous, gargantuan, vast.* These adjectives describe what is of extraordinary size and power. *Enormous* suggests a marked excess beyond the norm in size, amount, or degree: *an enormous boulder. Immense* refers to boundless or immeasurable size or extent: *immense pleasure. Huge* especially implies greatness of size or capacity: *a huge success. Gigantic* refers to size likened to that of a giant: *a gigantic redwood tree. Colossal*

suggests a hugeness that elicits awe or taxes belief: *a colossal ancient temple. Mammoth* is applied to something of unwieldy hugeness: *"mammoth stone figures in . . . buckled eighteenth-century pumps, the very soles of which seem mountainously tall"* (Cynthia Ozick). *Tremendous* suggests awe-inspiring or fearsome size: *ate a tremendous meal. Stupendous* implies size that astounds or defies description: *"The whole thing was a stupendous, incomprehensible farce"* (W. Somerset Maugham). *Gargantuan* especially stresses greatness of capacity, as for food or pleasure: *a gargantuan appetite. Vast* refers to greatness of extent, size, area, or scope: *"Of creatures, how few vast as the whale"* (Herman Melville).

---

enormousness *noun*
The quality of being enormous ▸ hugeness, immenseness, immensity, monumentality, prodigiousness, stupendousness, tremendousness, vastness. *See also* **bulk, size.**
enough *adjective*
Being what is needed without being in excess ▸ competent, decent, satisfactory. *See* **sufficient** (1). *See synonym note at* **sufficient.**
enough *pronoun*
An adequate quantity ▸ adequacy, sufficiency.
enounce *verb*
1. To put into words positively and with conviction ▸ avow, declare. *See* **assert** (1). **2.** To produce or make speech sounds ▸ articulate, enunciate. *See* **pronounce.**
enquire *verb*
See **inquire.**
enquirer *noun*
See **inquirer.**
enquiring *adjective*
See **inquiring.**
enquiry *noun*
See **inquiry.**
enrage *verb*
▸ incense, infuriate, madden. *See* **anger** (1).
enrapture *verb*
To have a powerful emotional effect on someone ▸ carry away, electrify, excite, ravish, thrill, transport. *Slang:* send. *See also* **charm, delight.**

✛ CORE SYNONYMS: *enrapture, ravish, thrill, transport.* These verbs mean to have a powerful, agreeable, and often overwhelming emotional effect on someone: *enraptured by the music; a painting that ravished the eye; thrilled by their success; transported with joy.*

---

enraptured *adjective*
▸ enamored, obsessed, smitten. *See* **infatuated.**
enrich *verb*
1. To add to or make whole ▸ augment, complete, strengthen. *See* **supplement. 2.** To advance to a more desirable state ▸ better, enhance, upgrade. *See* **improve** (1). **3.** To lend dignity or honor to by an act or favor ▸ favor, grace, dignify, honor. *See also* **distinguish, exalt, honor. 4.** To make fertile ▸ fecundate, fertilize, pollinate. *See also* **impregnate.**

enrichment *noun*
▶ add-on, complement, supplement. *See* **enhancement** (1).

enroll *verb*
1. To place on a list or in a record or book ▶ catalog, chronicle, write down. *See* **list**[1] (1). **2.** To become a member of ▶ enlist, sign up. *See* **join** (4).

ensanguine *verb*
To cover with blood ▶ bloodstain, bloody, incarnadine.

ensconce *verb*
1. To place securely in a position or condition ▶ fix, seat. *See* **establish** (2). **2.** To put or keep out of sight ▶ bury, conceal, secrete. *See* **hide**[1] (1).

ensemble *noun*
▶ garb, guise, outfit. *See* **dress** (2).

enshrine *verb*
▶ dedicate, sacrifice. *See* **devote** (1).

enshroud *verb*
1. To surround and cover completely so as to obscure ▶ clothe, invest. *See* **wrap** (2). **2.** To prevent something from being known ▶ camouflage, mask. *See* **conceal** (1).

ensign *noun*
▶ banner, colors, pennant. *See* **flag**[1] (1).

enslave *verb*
To make subservient or subordinate ▶ dominate, enthrall, indenture, make tributary, subject, subjugate, subordinate, take captive. *See also* **defeat**.

enslavement *noun*
▶ bondage, servility, thrall. *See* **slavery**.

ensnare *verb*
▶ entangle, snare, trap. *See* **catch** (1). *See synonym note at* **catch**.

ensnarement *noun*
▶ embroilment, enmeshment, involvement. *See* **entanglement** (1).

ensnarl *verb*
1. To twist together so that separation is difficult ▶ foul, tangle. *See* **entangle** (1). **2.** To gain control of by trapping ▶ snare, trap. *See* **catch** (1).

ensue *verb*
1. To occur as a consequence ▶ attend, follow, result. *See also* **stem**. **2.** To occur after in time ▶ come next, succeed, supervene. *See* **follow** (1). *See synonym note at* **follow**.

ensuing *adjective*
1. Occurring after another ▶ next, subsequent, succeeding. *See* **following** (1). **2.** Occurring as a result ▶ attending, consequent, resulting. *See* **following** (2).

ensure *verb*
▶ assure, warrant. *See* **guarantee** (2).

entail *verb*
1. To have as a condition or a consequence ▶ carry, involve. **2.** To have as a need or prerequisite ▶ call for, involve, necessitate. *See* **demand** (2). **3.** To involve by logical necessity ▶ involve, indicate, point to. *See* **imply** (1).

entangle *verb*
1. To twist together so that separation is difficult

▶ ensnarl, foul, mat, snarl, tangle. *See also* **weave**. **2.** To make complex, intricate, or perplexing ▶ embroil, perplex, tangle. *See* **complicate**. **3.** To gain control of by trapping ▶ snare, trap. *See* **catch** (1). *See synonym note at* **catch**.

entanglement *noun*
1. The condition of being entangled or implicated ▶ embranglement, embroilment, enmeshment, ensnarement, implication, involvement. **2.** Something that is intricately and often bewilderingly complex ▶ labyrinth, maze, web. *See* **tangle** (1).

entente *noun*
1. A formal, usually written settlement between nations ▶ concord, convention, pact. *See* **treaty**. **2.** The result of combining ▶ compound, merger, union. *See* **combination** (1).

enter *verb*
1. To come or go into a place ▶ come in, go in, penetrate. *Idioms:* gain admittance (*or* entrance *or* entry), make an entrance, set foot in, walk through the door **2.** To gain entry into a computer network or database ▶ access, log in (*or* on). *Idioms:* gain access (*or* admittance *or* entry), get connected. **3.** To pass into or through by overcoming resistance ▶ break (through), puncture. *See* **penetrate** (1). **4.** To become a member of ▶ enroll, sign up. *See* **join** (4). **5.** To go about the initial step in doing something ▶ approach, embark, initiate. *See* **start** (1). **6.** To place on a list or in a record or book ▶ catalog, chronicle, write down. *See* **list**[1] (1).

enter into *verb*
To involve oneself in an activity ▶ engage, partake, share. *See* **participate** (1).

enterprise *noun*
1. Something undertaken, especially something requiring extensive planning and work ▶ endeavor, project, undertaking, venture. *See also* **task**. **2.** An exciting undertaking ▶ odyssey, venture. *See* **adventure**. **3.** A commercial organization ▶ business, corporation, establishment. *See* **company** (1). **4.** An aggressive readiness along with energy to undertake taxing efforts ▶ initiative, hustle, punch. *See* **drive** (2). **5.** Commercial, industrial, or professional activity in general ▶ industry, trade. *See* **business** (1).

enterprising *adjective*
1. Possessing, exerting, or displaying energy ▶ brisk, lively, vigorous. *See* **energetic**. **2.** Full of ambition ▶ determined, driven. *See* **ambitious**. **3.** Willing to take risks ▶ daring, venturesome. *See* **adventurous** (1).

entertain *verb*
1. To occupy in an agreeable or pleasing way ▶ charm, divert, regale. *See* **amuse** (1). *See synonym note at* **amuse**. **2.** To receive an idea and think about it in order to form an opinion about it ▶ consider, hear of, think about (of). **3.** To think or think about carefully and at length ▶ cogitate, deliberate, mull. *See* **ponder**. **4.** To keep steadily in mind ▶ nourish, nurse. *See* **bear** (2).

entertaining *adjective*
▶ amusing, diverting. *See* **pleasant** (1).

entertainment *noun*
▸ diversion, play, recreation. *See* **amusement**.

enthrall *verb*
1. To act upon with or as if with magic ▸ enchant, mesmerize, spellbind. *See* **charm** (2). **2.** To compel the attention, interest, or imagination of ▸ captivate, fascinate, mesmerize. *See* **grip** (1). **3.** To make subservient or subordinate ▸ dominate, subjugate. *See* **enslave**.

enthralling *adjective*
▸ bewitching, enticing, tempting. *See* **seductive**.

enthrallment *noun*
▸ engrossment, immersion, preoccupation, prepossession. *See* **absorption** (2).

enthuse *verb*
▸ carry on, gush, rhapsodize. *See* **rave** (1).

enthusiasm *noun*
1. Passionate devotion to or interest in a cause or subject ▸ ardency, ardor, eagerness, excitation, excitement, fanaticism, fervor, fever, fire, passion, verve, vigor, zeal, zealousness. *See also* **passion**. **2.** A subject or activity that inspires lively interest ▸ craze, fad, fancy, hobbyhorse, infatuation, mania, passion, rage. *See also* **fashion, obsession**. **3.** A tendency to expect a favorable outcome or to dwell on hopeful aspects ▸ assurance, sanguinity. *See* **optimism**.

enthusiast *noun*
1. An ardent devotee ▸ admirer, aficionado, fancier. *See* **fan²**. **2.** One zealously devoted to a religion ▸ fanatic, zealot. *See* **devotee** (1).

enthusiastic *adjective*
1. Showing or having enthusiasm ▸ ardent, exuberant, fanatic, fanatical, fervent, fervid, keen, mad, obsessive, rabid, warm, zealous. *Informal:* crazy. *Slang:* cuckoo, gung ho, nuts. *See also* **extreme, passionate**. **2.** Expecting or suggesting a favorable outcome ▸ cheerful, sanguine. *See* **optimistic**.

entice *verb*
1. To direct or impel to oneself by some quality or action ▸ appeal, lure, magnetize. *See* **attract** (1). **2.** To beguile or draw into a wrong or foolish course of action, especially a sexual act ▸ allure, lure. *See* **seduce**. *See synonym note at* **seduce**.

enticement *noun*
1. The power or quality of attracting ▸ appeal, enchantment, lure. *See* **attraction** (1). **2.** Something that attracts, especially with the promise of pleasure or reward ▸ bait, draw, magnet. *See* **lure** (1).

enticer *noun*
▸ charmer, tempter. *See* **seducer** (1).

enticing *adjective*
1. Pleasing to the eye or mind ▸ enchanting, fetching, lovely, winsome. *See* **attractive** (1). **2.** Arousing erotic desire ▸ alluring, sexy. *See* **desirable** (1). **3.** Tending to seduce ▸ bewitching, come-hither, tempting. *See* **seductive**.

entire *adjective*
1. Including every constituent or individual ▸ all, total, whole. *See* **complete** (1). *See synonym note at*

complete. **2.** In excellent condition ▸ flawless, intact, sound. *See* **good** (2).

entirely *adverb*
▸ fully, totally, utterly. *See* **completely** (1).

entirety *noun*
1. The state of being entirely whole ▸ oneness, totality. *See* **completeness**. **2.** An amount or quantity from which nothing is left out or held back ▸ all, everything, total. *See* **whole** (1).

entitle *verb*
1. To give a name or title to ▸ christen, designate. *See* **name** (1). **2.** To give authority to ▸ accredit, empower, license. *See* **authorize** (1).

entitlement *noun*
1. A benefit granted to a person by law, nature, or custom ▸ birthright, privilege. *See* **right**. **2.** Freedom from normal restraints, limitations, or regulations ▸ elbowroom, latitude, leeway. *See* **license** (1).

entity *noun*
1. One that exists independently ▸ being, object, something. *See* **thing** (1). **2.** An organized array of individual elements and parts forming and working as a unit ▸ arrangement, totality, whole. *See* **system** (1). **3.** The fact or state of existing or of being actual ▸ being, reality. *See* **existence** (1).

entomb *verb*
▸ inhume, inter. *See* **bury** (1).

entombment *noun*
▸ burying, inhumation, interment. *See* **burial**.

entourage *noun*
▸ following, suite. *See* **retinue**.

entrails *noun*
▸ bowels, intestines. *Informal:* guts. *See* **viscera**.

entrance¹ *noun*
1. The act of entering ▸ entry, incoming, ingress, ingression, penetration. **2.** The act of admitting or the state of being admitted ▸ admittance, entry, ingress. *See* **admission** (1).

entrance² *verb*
1. To act upon with or as if with magic ▸ enchant, mesmerize, spellbind. *See* **charm** (2). *See synonym note at* **charm**. **2.** To please greatly or irresistibly ▸ bewitch, captivate, enchant. *See* **charm** (1).

entrancing *adjective*
▸ bewitching, enticing, tempting. *See* **seductive**.

entrap *verb*
▸ enmesh, snare, trap. *See* **catch** (1). *See synonym note at* **catch**.

entreat *verb*
▸ beseech, implore, plead. *See* **appeal** (1). *See synonym note at* **appeal**.

entreaty *noun*
▸ imploration, plea, supplication. *See* **appeal** (1).

entrée *noun*
▸ access, admittance, entrance, entry. *See* **admission** (1).

entrench *verb*
▸ embed, ingrain, plant. *See* **fix** (4).

entrenched *adjective*
► deep-seated, established, ingrained, inveterate. *See* **confirmed** (1).
entrenchment *noun*
► infringement, intrusion, obtrusion. *See* **trespass** (2).
entrepreneur *noun*
► businessperson, merchant. *See* **dealer** (1).
entrust *verb*
1. To put in the charge of another for care, use, or performance ► commend, commit, confide, consign, delegate, give (over), hand over, relegate, remand, remit, trust, turn over. *Idioms:* give in trust (*or* charge), give (*or* put) into custody. 2. To place a trust upon ► charge, trust. *See also* **authorize**.

✦ **CORE SYNONYMS:** *entrust, confide, commit, consign, delegate.* These verbs mean to put something in the charge of another for care, use, or performance: *The task was too dangerous to be entrusted to a child. He confided her plans to her family. The troops were committed to the general's charge. The owner consigned the paintings to a dealer for sale. She delegated the assignments to the junior members of the staff.*

---

entry *noun*
1. An item inserted, as in a diary, register, or reference book ► heading, headword, insertion, item, lemma, minute, note, posting, record. 2. The act of entering ► incoming, ingress. *See* **entrance**[1] (1). 3. The act of admitting or the state of being admitted ► admittance, entrance. *See* **admission** (1).
entwine *verb*
1. To move or proceed on a repeatedly curving course ► snake, spiral, weave. *See* **wind**[2] (1). 2. To interlace strips or strands ► braid, twist. *See* **weave** (1).
enumerate *verb*
1. To name or specify one by one ► count off, inventory, itemize, list, numerate, tick off. 2. To note items one by one in order to get a total ► numerate, tally. *See* **count** (2).
enumeration *noun*
► numeration, tally. *See* **count** (1).
enunciate *verb*
1. To produce or make speech sounds ► articulate, vocalize. *See* **pronounce**. 2. To put into words positively and with conviction ► avow, declare, maintain. *See* **assert** (1).
enunciation *noun*
► articulation, utterance, vocalization. *See* **voicing**.
envelop *verb*
1. To cover completely and closely, as with clothing or bandages ► bundle, envelop, swathe. *See* **wrap** (1). 2. To surround and cover completely so as to obscure ► clothe, enshroud, invest. *See* **wrap** (2). 3. To surround and advance upon ► close in, encompass, hem. *See* **enclose** (2).
envelope *noun*
► casing, covering. *See* **wrapper**.
envenom *verb*
► canker, infect. *See* **poison** (1).

envious *adjective*
Resentfully or painfully desirous of another's advantages ► begrudging, covetous, grudging, invidious, jaundiced, jealous. *Idiom:* green with envy.
enviousness *noun*
► covetousness, jealousy. *See* **envy**.
environ *verb*
► encircle, hedge, ring. *See* **surround** (1). *See synonym note at* **surround**.
environment *noun*
1. A surrounding area ► environs, locale, locality, neighborhood, precincts, purlieu, surroundings, vicinity. *See also* **limits, outskirts**. 2. The surrounding conditions and circumstances affecting growth or development ► ambiance, atmosphere, climate, context, medium, milieu, mise en scène, surroundings, world. 3. The ecological circumstances in which organisms live ► biome, biosphere, ecosphere, ecosystem, habitat, nature, world. *See also* **habitat, universe**. 4. Existing surroundings that affect an activity ► circumstances, context. *See* **conditions**.
environs *noun*
1. A surrounding area ► locale, neighborhood. *See* **environment** (1). 2. The periphery of a city or town ► edge, suburbs. *See* **outskirts**.
envisage *verb*
► conceive, fantasize, visualize. *See* **imagine** (1).
envision *verb*
1. To form mental images of ► conceive, fantasize, visualize. *See* **imagine** (1). 2. To know in advance ► anticipate, divine, foreknow. *See* **foresee**.
envoy[1] *noun*
1. A person who carries messages or is sent on errands ► carrier, courier. *See* **messenger**. 2. One who represents the interests of another ► ambassador, deputy, proxy. *See* **representative** (2).
envoy[2] *noun*
The last part ► closing, conclusion, ending, epilogue. *See* **end** (2).
envy *noun*
Resentful or painful desire for another's advantages ► covetousness, enviousness, green-eyed monster, jaundice, jealousy. *See also* **resentment**.
envy *verb*
To feel envy toward or for ► begrudge, covet, grudge.

✦ **CORE SYNONYMS:** *envy, begrudge, covet.* These verbs mean to feel resentful or painful desire for another's advantages or possessions. *Envy,* the most general, combines discontent, resentment, and desire: *"When I peruse the conquered fame of heroes and the victories of mighty generals, I do not envy the generals"* (Walt Whitman). *Begrudge* stresses ill will and reluctance to acknowledge another's right or claim: *Why begrudge him his success? Covet* stresses a secret or culpable longing for something to which one has no right: *"We hate no people and covet no people's lands"* (Wendell L. Willkie).

---

enwrap *verb*
► clothe, enshroud, invest. *See* **wrap** (2).

eon *or* **aeon** *noun*
▸ eternity, years. *See* **ages.**
ephemeral *adjective*
▸ fleeting, temporary. *See* **transitory.**
epicene *adjective*
1. Being neither distinguishably masculine nor feminine ▸ genderless, sexless. *See* **androgynous. 2.** Having qualities traditionally attributed to a woman ▸ feminine, unmanly. *See* **effeminate.**
epicenism *noun*
The quality of being androgynous ▸ androgyny, gender-neutrality, sexlessness. *See also* **effeminacy, masculinity.**
epicure *noun*
▸ hedonist, sensualist, voluptuary. *See* **sybarite.**
epicurean *adjective*
1. Characterized by or devoted to pleasure and luxury as a lifestyle ▸ hedonic, hedonistic, sybaritic, voluptuary, voluptuous. **2.** Relating to, suggestive of, or appealing to sense gratification ▸ sensual, sensuous, sensualistic, voluptuous.
epicurean *noun*
A person devoted to pleasure and luxury ▸ hedonist, voluptuary. *See* **sybarite.**
epidemic *noun*
A sudden emergence or interruption ▸ breakout, flare, outburst. *See* **eruption** (1).
epidemic *adjective*
Most generally existing or encountered at a given time ▸ predominant, rampant. *See* **prevailing** (1).
epidermis *noun*
The tissue forming the external covering of the body ▸ integument, skin.
epigrammatic *or* **epigrammatical** *adjective*
▸ compact, pointed. *See* **pithy** (1).
epilogue *noun*
▸ closing, ending, finale. *See* **end** (2).
episcopal *adjective*
▸ ministerial, pastoral. *See* **clerical.**
episode *noun*
1. Something significant that happens ▸ development, incident. *See* **event** (2). **2.** Something that takes place ▸ incident, occurrence. *See* **circumstance** (1). *See synonym note at* **circumstance.**
epistle *noun*
▸ correspondence, missive, note. *See* **letter** (1). *See synonym note at* **letter.**
epithet *noun*
1. The word or words by which one is called and identified ▸ cognomen, namesake, title. *See* **name** (1). **2.** A profane or obscene term ▸ curse, expletive. *See* **swearword.**
epitome *noun*
1. An ideally representative example of a type ▸ archetype, exemplar, mirror, model, paragon, pattern, prototype. *See also* **model. 2.** A shortened version or summary ▸ brief, outline, sketch. *See* **synopsis.**
epitomize *verb*
1. To give a recapitulation of the salient facts of

▸ abstract, recapitulate, summarize. *See* **review** (1). **2.** To serve as an example, image, or symbol of ▸ exemplify, illustrate, typify. *See* **represent** (1).
epizoic *adjective*
▸ bloodsucking, parasitical. *See* **parasitic.**
epoch *noun*
▸ day, era, period. *See* **age** (2). *See synonym note at* **age.**
equable *adjective*
▸ constant, invariable, steady. *See* **unchanging.**
equal *adjective*
1. Agreeing exactly in value, quantity, or effect ▸ coequal, equipollent, equivalent, even, identical, same, tantamount. *Idioms:* on a par, one and the same. **2.** Free from bias in judgment ▸ evenhanded, impartial. *See* **fair**[1] (1). **3.** Satisfying certain requirements, as for selection ▸ qualified, suitable, worthy. *See* **eligible** (1).
equal *noun*
One that is very similar to another in rank or position ▸ colleague, equivalent, fellow. *See* **peer**[2].
equal *verb*
1. To be equal or alike ▸ amount, be equivalent, be tantamount, compare, constitute, correspond, match, measure up, parallel, touch. *Informal:* stack up. *Idioms:* have all the earmarks of, keep pace with. *See also* **resemble. 2.** To do or make something equal to ▸ match, meet, tie.
equality *noun*
▸ equation, sameness. *See* **equivalence.**
equalize *verb*
1. To make equal ▸ align, democratize, equate, even, level (off), square, symmetrize. *Idiom:* put in line. *See also* **conventionalize, even**[1]. **2.** To put in balance ▸ counterbalance, stabilize. *See* **balance** (1).
equanimity *noun*
▸ composure, coolness, poise. *See* **balance** (2).
equate *verb*
1. To make equal ▸ level, square. *See* **equalize** (1). **2.** To represent as similar ▸ compare, identify, parallel. *See* **liken.**
equation *noun*
▸ coequality, sameness. *See* **equivalence.**
equidistant *adjective*
▸ focal, median, middle. *See* **central** (1).
equilibrium *noun*
▸ counterpoise, equipoise, stasis. *See* **balance** (1).
equip *verb*
▸ appoint, gear, outfit. *See* **furnish** (1). *See synonym note at* **furnish.**
equipment *noun*
1. Things needed for a task, journey, or other purpose ▸ accouterments, gear. *See* **outfit** (1). *See synonym note at* **outfit. 2.** Something, as a machine, devised for a particular function ▸ appliance, contraption, invention. *See* **device** (1).
equipoise *noun*
▸ counterpoise, equilibrium, stasis. *See* **balance** (1).
equipollent *adjective*
▸ identical, tantamount. *See* **equal** (1).

equitable *adjective*
▶ evenhanded, impartial, just. *See* **fair¹** (1). *See synonym note at* **fair¹**.

equitableness *noun*
▶ dispassion, impartiality, justice, nonpartisanship. *See* **fairness.**

equitably *adverb*
▶ dispassionately, impartially, justly. *See* **fairly** (1).

equity *noun*
The state, action, or principle of treating all persons equally in accordance with the law ▶ due process, justice. *See also* **fairness.**

equivalence *noun*
The state of being equivalent ▶ coequality, equality, equation, equivalency, par, parity, sameness. *See also* **likeness, sameness.**

equivalency *noun*
▶ equation, sameness. *See* **equivalence.**

equivalent *adjective*
1. Agreeing exactly in value, quantity, or effect ▶ identical, tantamount. *See* **equal** (1). 2. Possessing the same or almost the same characteristics ▶ analogous, similar, uniform. *See* **like²**. 3. Properly or correspondingly related in size, amount, or scale ▶ commensurate, corresponding, proportionate. *See* **proportional** (1).

equivalent *noun*
1. One that is very similar to another in rank or position ▶ colleague, fellow. *See* **peer²**. 2. One that has the same functions and characteristics as another ▶ counterpart, opposite number, vis-à-vis.

equivocal *adjective*
1. Deliberately ambiguous or vague ▶ elusive, evasive, indirect, misleading. *See also* **ambiguous.** 2. Liable to more than one interpretation ▶ cloudy, nebulous, vague. *See* **ambiguous** (2). 3. Lacking certainty or clarity ▶ dubious, indeterminate, questionable, unclear. *See* **ambiguous** (1). *See synonym note at* **ambiguous.** 4. Of dubious character ▶ doubtful, questionable, suspicious. *See* **shady** (1).

equivocality *or* **equivocalness** *noun*
1. An expression or term liable to more than one interpretation ▶ equivocation, tergiversation. *See* **ambiguity** (1). 2. The quality or state of being imprecise or indefinite ▶ ambiguousness, imprecision, unclearness. *See* **vagueness.**

equivocate *verb*
1. To use evasive or deliberately vague language ▶ euphemize, fence, hedge, shuffle, tergiversate, weasel. *Informal:* pussyfoot, waffle. *Idioms:* beat about (*or* around) the bush, give one the runaround, hem and haw, mince words. *See also* **evade.** 2. To stray from truthfulness or sincerity ▶ palter, prevaricate, shuffle. *Idioms:* bend (*or* stretch) the truth. *See also* **distort, lie².**

equivocation *noun*
1. The use or an instance of equivocal language ▶ ambiguity, distortion, equivoque, euphemism, fence, hedge, misrepresentation, prevarication, shuffle, tergiversation, weasel word. *Informal:* waffle.

Idiom: hemming and hawing. *See also* **lie².** 2. An expression or term liable to more than one interpretation ▶ double-entendre, tergiversation. *See* **ambiguity** (1).

era *noun*
▶ day, epoch, period. *See* **age** (2). *See synonym note at* **age.**

eradicate *verb*
1. To destroy all traces of ▶ exterminate, liquidate, obliterate. *See* **annihilate** (1). *See synonym note at* **annihilate.** 2. To get rid of, especially by banishment or execution ▶ liquidate, purge. *See* **eliminate** (1). *See synonym note at* **eliminate.**

eradication *noun*
1. The act or process of eliminating ▶ clearance, purge. *See* **elimination** (1). 2. Utter destruction ▶ extinction, liquidation, obliteration. *See* **annihilation** (1).

erase *verb*
1. To cross out or remove ▶ delete, expunge, strike (out). *See* **cancel** (1). *See synonym note at* **cancel.** 2. To destroy all traces of ▶ eradicate, liquidate, obliterate. *See* **annihilate** (1).

erasure *noun*
The act of erasing or the condition of being erased ▶ cancellation, deletion, effacement, expunction, obliteration.

erect *adjective*
Being in a vertical or upward-pointing position ▶ raised, rampant, standing up, upraised, upreared, uprearing, upright, upstanding. *Idiom:* held high. *See* **rigid.**

erect *verb*
1. To raise upright ▶ pitch, put up, raise, rear, set up, upraise, uprear. 2. To make or form a structure ▶ construct, raise. *See* **build** (1).

erector *noun*
▶ assembler, manufacturer. *See* **builder** (1).

eristic *adjective*
▶ contentious, litigious, quarrelsome. *See* **argumentative.**

erode *verb*
To reduce gradually, as by chemical reaction, weather, or friction ▶ abrade, bite (into), consume, corrode, eat (away *or* into), gnaw (away *or* down), grind (away *or* down), wear (away *or* down). *See also* **decay, disintegrate.**

erogenous *adjective*
▶ amorous, sensual, sexual. *See* **erotic.**

erotic *adjective*
Concerning or arousing sexual love or desire ▶ amatory, amorous, aphrodisiac, erogenous, libidinal, lascivious, salacious, sensual, sensuous, sexual, sexy, spicy, steamy, suggestive. *Slang:* hot. *See also* **lascivious, desirable, obscene.**

eroticism *noun*
1. The quality of being erotic ▶ amorousness, lasciviousness, salaciousness, sensualism, sensuality, sensuousness, sexuality, sexiness, suggestiveness. *Slang:*

sizzle. *See also* **obscenity, sensuality. 2.** Sexual hunger ▸ appetite, lust, passion. *See* **desire** (2). **3.** The quality or condition of being sensual or being preoccupied with bodily desires ▸ sexuality, voluptuousness. *See* **sensuality** (1).

erotism *noun*
▸ eroticism, lust, passion. *See* **desire** (2).

err *verb*
1. To make an error or mistake ▸ blunder, lapse, miscue, mistake, slip (up), stumble, trip (up). *Informal:* fluff. *Slang:* goof (up), screw up. *Idioms:* get (*or* start) off on the wrong foot, go astray (*or* awry), take a wrong step. *See also* **blunder, botch. 2.** To violate a rule or law ▸ sin, transgress, trespass. *See* **offend** (3).

errand *noun*
▸ commission, operation, undertaking. *See* **mission** (1).

errant *adjective*
1. Traveling about, especially in search of adventure ▸ itinerant, rambling, roaming, roving, wandering. *See also* **nomadic. 2.** Straying from a proper course or standard ▸ aberrant, deviant, erring, stray. *Idioms:* far afield, wide of (*or* off) the mark. *See also* **abnormal, wrong. 3.** Without aim, purpose, or intent ▸ pointless, purposeless, rambling. *See* **aimless.**

erratic *adjective*
1. Without a fixed or regular course ▸ devious, stray, uncontrolled, unfixed, unstable, wandering, wayward. **2.** Lacking consistency or regularity in quality or performance ▸ inconsistent, patchy, variable. *See* **uneven** (1). **3.** Marked by whim or impulse ▸ fickle, impulsive, mercurial. *See* **capricious. 4.** Deviating from what is conventional or customary ▸ bizarre, grotesque. *See* **eccentric.**

erratum *noun*
▸ inaccuracy, lapse, mistake. *See* **error** (1).

erring *adjective*
▸ deviant, stray. *See* **errant** (2).

erroneous *adjective*
Containing an error or errors ▸ corrupt, fallacious, false, faulty, inaccurate, incorrect, mistaken, off, unsound, untrue, wrong. *Idioms:* all wet, in error, off base, off (*or* wide of) the mark.

error *noun*
1. An unintentional deviation from what is correct, right, or true ▸ erratum, false step, inaccuracy, incorrectness, lapse, miscue, miss, misstep, mistake, omission, oversight, slip, slip-up, trip. *See also* **blunder, defect, mess. 2.** An erroneous or false idea ▸ falsehood, falsity, untruth. *See* **fallacy** (1).

errorless *adjective*
▸ correct, exact, precise. *See* **accurate** (1).

ersatz *noun*
An inferior substitute imitating an original ▸ imitation, simulation. *See* **copy** (2).

ersatz *adjective*
1. Fraudulently or deceptively imitative ▸ fake, fraudulent, phony. *See* **counterfeit. 2.** Made by hu-

mans, often in imitation of something else ▸ manufactured, simulated. *See* **artificial** (1). *See synonym note at* **artificial.**

erstwhile *adverb*
At a time in the past ▸ before, previously. *See* **earlier** (1).

erstwhile *adjective*
Having been such previously ▸ former, onetime, past. *See* **late** (2).

eruct *verb*
▸ disgorge, spew. *See* **erupt** (1).

erudite *adjective*
▸ enlightened, lettered, scholarly. *See* **educated** (1).

erudition *noun*
▸ instruction, learning. *See* **education** (2).

erupt *verb*
1. To send forth confined matter violently: ▸ belch, disgorge, eject, eruct, expel, spew, vomit. *See also* **pour, spurt. 2.** To become manifest suddenly and in full force ▸ burst (forth *or* out), explode. *See* **break out** (1).

eruption *noun*
1. A sudden emergence or increase ▸ breakout, burst, epidemic, explosion, flare, flare-up, irruption, outbreak, outburst, paroxysm, plague, rash, surge. **2.** A sudden violent expression, as of emotion ▸ burst, gush. *See* **outburst** (1). **3.** A violent release of confined energy ▸ burst, explosion. *See* **blast** (2).

escalate *verb*
1. To make or become greater or larger ▸ amplify, boost, enlarge. *See* **increase** (1). **2.** To make greater in intensity or severity ▸ deepen, enhance, heighten. *See* **intensify.**

escalation *noun*
▸ amplification, boost, enlargement. *See* **increase** (1).

escapade *noun*
▸ odyssey, venture. *See* **adventure.**

escape *verb*
1. To break loose and leave suddenly, as from confinement or a difficult situation ▸ abscond, bail out, break out, decamp, flee, fly, get away, run away. *Informal:* make off, skip (out). *Slang:* lam. *Chiefly Regional:* absquatulate. *Idioms:* cut and run, blow (*or* fly) the coop, get clear of, give someone the slip, make a getaway, make good one's escape, take flight, take it on the lam, wriggle off the hook. **2.** To keep away from ▸ circumvent, dodge, evade. *See* **avoid.** *See synonym note at* **avoid. 3.** To fail to be fixed by the mind, memory, or senses of ▸ elude, evade. *Idiom:* slip away from. *See also* **forget.**

escape *noun*
1. The act or an instance of escaping, as from confinement or difficulty ▸ break, breakout, decampment, escapement, flight, getaway. *Slang:* lam. *See also* **rescue. 2.** The act, an instance, or a means of avoiding ▸ avoidance, bypass, circumvention, evasion. *See also* **prevention.**

escaped *adjective*
Fleeing or having fled, as from confinement or the

police ▸ fugitive, fleeing, runaway. *Idioms:* on the lam (*or* loose *or* run).

escapee *noun*
A person who flees, as from confinement or the police ▸ fugitive, outlaw, refugee, runaway. *See also* **criminal.**

escapement *noun*
▸ breakout, flight. *See* **escape** (1).

eschew *verb*
▸ circumvent, dodge, evade. *See* **avoid.** *See synonym note at* **avoid.**

escort *noun*
Something or someone that shows the way ▸ conductor, director, leader. *See* **guide** (1).

escort *verb*
1. To be with or go with ▸ attend, chaperon, company. *See* **accompany** (1). *See synonym note at* **accompany.** 2. To show the way to ▸ direct, lead. *See* **guide** (1).

esculent *adjective*
Fit to be eaten ▸ comestible, eatable, edible, palatable.

esoteric *adjective*
1. Beyond the understanding of an average mind ▸ abstract, difficult, profound. *See* **deep** (2). 2. Not widely understood ▸ arcane, recondite. *See* **obscure** (1). 3. Difficult to explain or understand ▸ enigmatic, mystical, puzzling. *See* **mysterious.** *See synonym note at* **mysterious.**

especial *adjective*
1. Beyond what is usual, normal, or customary ▸ extraordinary, outstanding, remarkable. *See* **exceptional** (1). 2. Relating to, identifying, or setting apart an individual or group ▸ characteristic, distinctive, particular. *See* **special** (1).

espial *noun*
▸ heed, note, regard. *See* **notice** (1).

espousal *noun*
1. The act or condition of being pledged to marry ▸ betrothal, engagement, troth. 2. The act or ceremony by which two people become husband and wife ▸ bridal, marriage, nuptials. *See* **wedding.** 3. The act of accepting or adopting ▸ adoption, assent, consent. *See* **acceptance** (1).

espouse *verb*
1. To join or be joined in marriage ▸ unite, wed. *See* **marry** (1). 2. To take and make one's own ▸ assume, embrace, take on. *See* **adopt** (1).

esprit *noun*
1. A lively, emphatic, eager quality or manner ▸ life, verve, vivaciousness. *See* **spirit** (1). 2. A strong sense of enthusiasm and dedication to a common goal that unites a group ▸ esprit de corps, group spirit, morale, team spirit. *See synonym note at* **morale.** *See also* **confidence, mood.**

esprit de corps *noun*
A strong sense of enthusiasm and dedication to a common goal that unites a group ▸ esprit, group spirit, morale, team spirit. *See synonym note at* **morale.** *See also* **confidence, mood, spirit.**

espy *verb*
▸ detect, discern, perceive. *See* **see** (1). *See synonym note at* **see.**

essay *noun*
1. A relatively brief discourse written especially as an exercise ▸ composition, paper, theme. 2. A procedure that ascertains effectiveness, value, proper function, or other quality ▸ proof, trial, tryout. *See* **test** (1). 3. A trying to do or make something ▸ effort, trial. *Informal:* shot. *See* **attempt** (1). 4. A formal discussion of a subject, either written or spoken ▸ dialogue, dissertation. *See* **discourse** (1).

essay *verb*
1. To make an attempt ▸ endeavor, strive. *See* **attempt.** 2. To subject to a test of effectiveness, value, function, or other quality ▸ check, evaluate, try. *See* **test** (1).

essence *noun*
1. A basic trait or set of traits that define and establish the character of something ▸ being, essentiality, grain, nature, quiddity, quintessence, sine qua non, substance, texture. *See also* **element.** 2. The most central or essential part ▸ core, marrow, quintessence. *See* **heart** (1). 3. A sweet or pleasant odor ▸ aroma, perfume, scent. *See* **fragrance.**

essential *adjective*
1. Incapable of being dispensed with ▸ critical, indispensable, necessary, needed, needful, prerequisite, required, requisite. *See also* **required.** 2. Constituting or forming part of the essence of something ▸ basic, constitutional, constitutive, fundamental, integral, quintessential, vital. *See also* **primary.** 3. Of or being an irreducible element ▸ basic, elementary, fundamental. *See* **elemental** (1).

essential *noun*
1. An irreducible constituent of a whole ▸ basic, fundamental. *See* **element** (1). 2. Something indispensable ▸ necessity, requirement. *See* **condition** (2).

✚ CORE SYNONYMS: *essential, indispensable, necessary, needful, requisite. These adjectives apply to something that is incapable of being dispensed with: funds essential to completing the project; foods indispensable to good nutrition; necessary tools and materials; provided them with all things needful; lacking the requisite qualifications.*

---

essentiality *noun*
▸ nature, quintessence. *See* **essence** (1).

essentially *adverb*
In regard to the essence of a matter ▸ basically, fundamentally, underlyingly. *Idioms:* at bottom (*or* heart *or* root), in essence, when all is said and done.

establish *verb*
1. To bring into existence formally ▸ constitute, create, institute. *See* **found** (1). *See synonym note at* **found.** 2. To place securely in a position or condition ▸ ensconce, fix, install, invest, seat, set (up), settle. 3. To put in force or cause to be by legal authority ▸ constitute, enact, institute, legislate, legitimate, make, ordain, promulgate. *See also* **confirm, legalize.**

4. To provide a basis for ▸ build, ground. *See* **base**[1] (1). **5.** To establish as true or genuine through evidence ▸ confirm, substantiate, validate. *See* **prove** (1). **6.** To control the functioning or outcome of ▸ determine, regulate. *See* **govern** (1).

established *adjective*
1. Generally approved or agreed upon ▸ conventional, customary, sanctioned. *See* **accepted. 2.** Firmly established by long standing ▸ deep-seated, ingrained, inveterate. *See* **confirmed** (1).

establishment *noun*
1. The act of founding or establishing ▸ constitution, creation, institution. *See* **foundation** (1). **2.** A commercial organization ▸ business, corporation, enterprise. *See* **company** (1).

establishmentarian *adjective*
▸ conformist, orthodox, traditional. *See* **conventional** (1).

estate *noun*
1. Usually extensive real estate ▸ acreage, property. *See* **land** (1). **2.** A thing or set of things, such as land and assets, legally possessed ▸ possessions, property. *See* **holdings. 3.** Existing surroundings that affect an activity ▸ circumstances, context. *See* **conditions. 4.** A house in the country ▸ cottage, manor. *See* **villa**.

esteem
esteem *noun*
1. A feeling of deference, approval, and liking ▸ account, admiration, appreciation, consideration, estimation, favor, honor, regard, respect. *See also* **adoration, honor. 2.** Favorable reception or regard ▸ approval, favor, welcome. *See* **acceptance** (2).
esteem *verb*
1. To have a high opinion of or regard for ▸ admire, honor, respect. *See* **value** (1). *See synonym note at* **value. 2.** To look upon in a particular way ▸ consider, deem, view. *See* **regard** (1).

✦ CORE SYNONYMS: *esteem, regard, admiration, respect.* These nouns refer to a feeling of deference, approval, and liking. *Esteem* connotes considered appraisal: *"The near-unanimity of esteem he enjoyed during his lifetime has by no means been sustained since"* (Will Crutchfield). *Regard* is the most general: *"I once thought you had a kind of regard for her"* (George Borrow). *Admiration* is a feeling of keen approbation: *"Greatness is a spiritual condition worthy to excite love, interest, and admiration"* (Matthew Arnold). *Respect* implies appreciative, often deferential regard resulting from careful assessment: *"I have a great respect for any man who makes his own way in life"* (Winston Churchill).

---

estimable *adjective*
▸ deserving, laudable, worthy. *See* **admirable**.

estimate *verb*
1. To make a judgment as to the worth or value of ▸ appraise, assay, assess, calculate, evaluate, gauge, judge, rate, size up, valuate, value, weigh. *Idiom:* take the measure of. *See also* **regard, value. 2.** To calculate

approximately ▸ approximate, place, put, reckon, set. *Informal:* guesstimate. *See also* **predict**.

estimate *noun*
1. The act or result of evaluating or appraising ▸ appraisal, appraisement, assessment, estimation, evaluation, judgment, valuation. **2.** A rough or tentative calculation ▸ approximation, estimation. *Informal:* guesstimate. **Idioms:** ballpark figure, educated guess, rough measure. *See also* **guess. 3.** Something thought to be true ▸ notion, view. *See* **belief** (1).

✦ CORE SYNONYMS: *estimate, appraise, assess, assay, evaluate, rate.* These verbs mean to form a judgment as to the worth of value of something. *Estimate* usually implies a subjective and somewhat inexact judgment: *difficult to estimate the possible results in advance. Appraise* stresses expert judgment: *appraised the works of art. Assess* implies authoritative judgment in setting a monetary value on something as a basis for taxation: *assessing real estate for investors. Assay* refers to careful examination, especially to chemical analysis of an ore: *will assay the ingot.* In extended senses *appraise, assess,* and *assay* can refer to any critical analysis: *appraised his character; will assess the impact of higher taxes; assaying the idea's merit. Evaluate* implies considered judgment in ascertaining value: *evaluating a student's thesis for content and organization. Rate* involves determining the rank or grade of someone or something in relation to others: *rated the restaurant higher than any other in the city.*

---

estimation *noun*
1. The act or result of evaluating or appraising ▸ assessment, evaluation. *See* **estimate** (1). **2.** A rough or tentative calculation ▸ approximation. *Informal:* guesstimate. *See* **estimate** (2). **3.** A feeling of deference, approval, and liking ▸ admiration, favor. *See* **esteem** (1). **4.** Something thought to be true ▸ notion, persuasion, view. *See* **belief** (1).

estrange *verb*
To make distant, hostile, or unsympathetic ▸ alienate, antagonize, come between, disaffect, distance, disunite, drive away. *Slang:* turn off. **Idioms:** set at odds, turn against one. *See also* **divide**.

✦ CORE SYNONYMS: *estrange, alienate, disaffect.* These verbs mean to make another person distant, hostile, or unsympathetic. *Estrange* and *alienate* are often used with reference to two persons whose harmonious relationship has been replaced by hostility or indifference: *Political disagreements led to quarrels that finally estranged the two friends. His persistent antagonism alienated his wife. Disaffect* usually implies discontent, ill will, and disloyalty within the membership of a group: *Colonists were disaffected by the royal governor's actions.*

---

estrangement *noun*
▸ break, falling out, fissure. *See* **breach** (2).

estuary *noun*
1. A usually narrow strip of water leading inland ▸ fjord, mouth. *See* **inlet. 2.** A relatively large natural flow of water ▸ stream, waterway. *See* **river**.

etceteras *noun*
► junk, oddments, miscellanea. *See* **odds and ends.**
etch *verb*
1. To cut a design or inscription into a hard surface, especially for printing ► carve, incise. *See* **engrave** (1).
2. To produce a deep impression of ► fix, imprint. *See* **engrave** (2).
eternal *adjective*
1. Enduring for all time ► ceaseless, perpetual. *See* **endless** (2). *See synonym note at* **endless. 2.** Existing without interruption ► constant, endless, everlasting, perpetual. *See* **continual.** *See synonym note at* **continual. 3.** Existing unchanged forever ► ageless, timeless. *See synonym note at* **ageless.** *See also* **endless.**
eternality *or* **eternalness** *noun*
► eternity, perpetuity. *See* **endlessness.**
eternalize *verb*
To cause to last endlessly ► eternize, immortalize, perpetuate. *Idioms:* cast (*or* etch *or* fix *or* set) in stone. *See also* **honor, memorialize.**
eternally *adverb*
► endlessly, perpetually, unendingly. *See* **forever** (1).
eterne *adjective*
► ceaseless, eternal. *See* **endless** (2).
eternity *noun*
1. The totality of time without beginning or end ► infinity, perpetuity, sempiternity. *See also* **forever. 2.** A place or state beyond death ► afterworld, empyrean, far shore, great beyond, happy hunting ground, heaven, hereafter, nirvana, paradise, Valhalla. **3.** Endless life after death ► afterlife, everlasting life. *See* **immortality. 4.** A long time ► eon, long. *See* **ages. 5.** The quality or state of having no end ► ceaselessness, perpetuity. *See* **endlessness.**
eternize *verb*
To cause to last endlessly ► eternalize, immortalize, perpetuate. *Idioms:* cast (*or* etch *or* fix *or* set) in stone. *See also* **honor, memorialize.**
ether *noun*
The gaseous mixture enveloping the earth ► air, atmosphere.
ethereal *adjective*
1. Thin, fine, and light ► airy, gauzy, vaporous. *See* **sheer**² (1). **2.** Having no body, form, or substance ► disembodied, incorporeal, nonphysical. *See* **immaterial** (1).
ethic *noun*
► morality, principles. *See* **ethics** (2).
ethical *adjective*
In accordance with principles of right or good conduct ► conscientious, humane, moral, principled, proper, right, righteous, rightful, right-minded, scrupulous, virtuous, upright. *See also* **frank, honest.**

✢ CORE SYNONYMS: *ethical, moral, virtuous, righteous.* These adjectives mean in accordance with principles of right or good conduct. *Ethical* stresses idealistic standards of right and wrong: *"Ours is a world of nuclear giants and ethical infants"* (Omar N. Bradley). *Moral* applies to personal character and behavior, especially sexual conduct: *"Our moral sense dictates a clearcut preference for these societies which share with us an abiding respect for individual human rights"* (Jimmy Carter). *Virtuous* implies moral excellence and loftiness of character: *"The life of the nation is secure only while the nation is honest, truthful, and virtuous"* (Frederick Douglass). *Righteous* emphasizes moral uprightness; when it is applied to actions, reactions, or impulses, it often implies justifiable outrage: *"He was . . . stirred by righteous wrath"* (John Galsworthy).

---

ethicality *or* **ethicalness** *noun*
► propriety, rectitude. *See* **ethics** (1).
ethics *noun*
1. The quality of being in accord with standards of conduct ► ethicality, ethicalness, morality, propriety, rectitude, righteousness, rightness. **2.** A set of principles of right conduct ► ethic, morality, morals, mores, principles, standards.
ethos *noun*
1. The thought processes characteristic of an individual or group ► mentality, mind, psyche. *See* **psychology. 2.** Behavior patterns, traits, and products considered as an expression of a certain people or period ► civilization, customs, mores, society. *See* **culture** (2).
etiolate *verb*
► bleach, wan. *See* **pale.**
etiquette *noun*
1. Socially correct behavior ► decorum, propriety. *See* **manners. 2.** Strict observance of social conventions ► ceremoniousness, formality, protocol. *See* **ceremony** (2).
eulogistic *adjective*
► approbatory, laudatory. *See* **complimentary** (1).
eulogize *verb*
► celebrate, exalt. *See* **honor** (1).
eulogy *noun*
► acclamation, celebration, kudos. *See* **praise** (1).
euphemism *noun*
► ambiguity, prevarication. *See* **equivocation** (1).
euphemize *verb*
► hedge, shuffle. *See* **equivocate** (1).
euphonious *or* **euphonic** *adjective*
► melodic, harmonious, sweet-sounding. *See* **melodious.**
euphoria *noun*
► animation, inspiration. *See* **elation** (1).
euphoric *adjective*
Feeling great delight and joy ► elevated, overjoyed. *See* **elated.**
evacuant *adjective*
► evacuative, purgative. *See* **eliminative.**
evacuate *verb*
1. To remove the contents of ► clean out, gut. *See* **empty** (1). **2.** To discharge wastes from the body ► excrete, void. *See* **eliminate** (4). **3.** To move back in the face of enemy attack or after a defeat ► fall back, pull out, withdraw. *See* **retreat** (4).

evacuation *noun*
1. The moving back of a military force in the face of enemy attack or after a defeat ▶ fallback, pullout, withdrawal. *See* **retreat** (1). 2. The act or process of discharging bodily wastes ▶ catharsis, excretion. *See* **elimination** (3).

evacuative *adjective*
▶ cathartic, purgative. *See* **eliminative.**

evade *verb*
1. To avoid fulfilling or answering completely ▶ dodge, duck, fence, hedge, sidestep, skirt. *Idioms:* weasel out of, wiggle (*or* wriggle *or* worm) one's way out of. *See also* **maneuver, equivocate.** 2. To keep away from ▶ circumvent, dodge, escape. *See* **avoid.** *See synonym note at* **avoid.** 3. To get away from a pursuer ▶ elude, slip, throw off. *See* **lose** (3). 4. To fail to be fixed by the mind, memory, or senses of ▶ elude, escape. *Idiom:* slip away from. *See also* **forget.**

evaluate *verb*
1. To make a judgment as to the worth or value of ▶ assay, calculate. *See* **estimate** (1). *See synonym note at* **estimate.** 2. To subject to a test of effectiveness, value, function, or other quality ▶ check, essay, try (out). *See* **test** (1).

evaluation *noun*
1. The act or result of evaluating ▶ assessment, valuation. *See* **estimate** (1). 2. A procedure that ascertains effectiveness, value, proper function, or other quality ▶ proof, trial, tryout. *See* **test** (1).

evanesce *verb*
▶ dissipate, dissolve, fade. *See* **disappear** (1). *See synonym note at* **disappear.**

evanescence *noun*
▶ dissipation, expiration, vanishment. *See* **disappearance.**

evanescent *adjective*
▶ ephemeral, fleeting, temporary. *See* **transitory.**

evangelism *noun*
▶ disinformation, indoctrination. *See* **propaganda.**

evangelist *noun*
1. A person doing religious or charitable work in a foreign country ▶ apostle, missionary, missioner. *See also* **cleric, representative.** 2. One who disseminates or engages in propaganda ▶ missionary, proselytizer. *See* **propagandist.**

evangelize *verb*
To deliver a sermon, especially as a vocation ▶ preach, sermonize. *See also* **address, moralize.**

evaporate *verb*
1. To turn into vapor, especially when heated ▶ boil away, burn off, fume, steam, sublimate, sublime, vaporize, volatilize. 2. To pass out of sight either gradually or suddenly ▶ dissolve, fade. *See* **disappear** (1). *See synonym note at* **disappear.** 3. To remove a liquid by a steady, gradual process ▶ pump, strain. *See* **drain** (1).

evaporation *noun*
▶ dissipation, expiration, vanishment. *See* **disappearance.**

evasion *noun*
▶ bypass, circumvention. *See* **escape** (2).

evasive *adjective*
1. Inclined or intended to evade ▶ elusive, fugitive, slippery. *See also* **slick, underhand.** 2. Deliberately ambiguous or vague ▶ elusive, equivocal, indirect, misleading. *See also* **ambiguous.**

eve *noun*
▶ dusk, twilight. *See* **evening.**

even *adjective*
1. Having no irregularities, roughness, or indentations ▶ flat, flush, level, mirrorlike, planar, plane, smooth, straight, unruffled, unwrinkled. *See also* **glossy.** 2. On the same plane or line ▶ coplanar, flush, in line, level, square, uniplanar. 3. Having no change or variation ▶ changeless, invariable, uniform. *See* **unchanging.** 4. Not excited or agitated ▶ collected, composed, cool. *See* **calm** (1). 5. Agreeing exactly in value, quantity, or effect ▶ equivalent, identical, tantamount. *See* **equal** (1). 6. Free from bias in judgment ▶ evenhanded, impartial. *See* **fair**[1] (1). 7. Owing or being owed nothing ▶ quit, quits, square. *Informal:* even-steven. 8. Neither favorable nor unfavorable ▶ balanced, fifty-fifty, nip and tuck. 9. Being an exact amount or number ▶ exact. *Idioms:* on the button (*or* money *or* nose). 10. Not steep or abrupt ▶ gentle, moderate. *See* **gradual** (2).

even *adverb*
1. To a more extreme degree ▶ ever more so, still, yet. 2. Not just this but also ▶ a fortiori, indeed, moreover, yea. *Idioms:* all the more, not to mention, what is more. 3. In an exact manner ▶ literally, precisely. *See* **exactly** (1).

even *verb*
1. To make even, smooth, or level ▶ align, flat, flatten, flush, level, plane, relax, roll (out), smooth, steamroll, steamroller, straighten. 2. To make equal ▶ equate, level, square. *See* **equalize** (1). 3. To put in balance ▶ equalize, stabilize. *See* **balance** (1).

✤ CORE SYNONYMS: *even, flat, level, plane, smooth, flush.* These adjectives describe surfaces without irregularities, roughness, or indentations: *Even* refers to flat surfaces in which no part is higher or lower than another: *the even surface of the mirror. Flat* applies to surfaces without curves, protuberances, or indentations: *a flat rock. Level* implies being parallel with the line of the horizon: *acres of level farmland. Plane* is a mathematical term referring to a surface containing all the straight lines connecting any two points on it: *a plane figure. Smooth* describes a surface on which the absence of irregularities can be established by sight or touch: *smooth marble. Flush* applies to a surface that is on an exact level with an adjoining one: *a door that is flush with the wall.*

---

evenhanded *adjective*
▶ equitable, impartial, nonpartisan. *See* **fair**[1] (1).

evenhandedly *adverb*
▶ equitably, impartially, justly. *See* **fairly** (1).

evenhandedness *noun*
▸ equitableness, impartiality, nonpartisanship. *See* **fairness**.

evening *noun*
The period between afternoon and nighttime ▸ dusk, eve, eventide, gloaming, nightfall, sundown, sunset, twilight. *Idiom:* close of day.

event *noun*
1. Something that takes place ▸ incident, occurrence. *See* **circumstance** (1). *See synonym note at* **circumstance**. 2. Something significant that happens ▸ circumstance, development, episode, happening, incident, news, phenomenon, occasion, occurrence, thing. *Idioms:* something to write home about, turn of events. 3. Something brought about by a cause ▸ consequence, outcome, result. *See* **effect** (1). 4. Something demonstrated to exist or known to have existed ▸ actuality, fact, phenomenon, reality. *Idioms:* hard (*or* cold *or* plain) fact. *See also* **information**. 5. A test of skill or ability ▸ bout, match, trial. *See* **competition** (2).

even-tempered *adjective*
▸ collected, composed, cool. *See* **calm** (1).

eventide *noun*
▸ eve, twilight. *See* **evening**.

eventual *adjective*
▸ coming, later. *See* **future**.

eventuality *noun*
▸ contingency, potentiality. *See* **possibility** (1).

eventually *adverb*
After a considerable length of time, usually after a delay ▸ finally. *Idiom:* at long last. *See* **ultimately** (1).

everlasting *adjective*
1. Enduring for all time ▸ ceaseless, eternal. *See* **endless** (2). 2. Existing without interruption or end ▸ constant, ongoing, perpetual. *See* **continual**.

everlastingly *adverb*
▸ endlessly, perpetually, unendingly. *See* **forever** (1).

everlastingness *noun*
1. The quality or state of having no end ▸ eternity, perpetuity. *See* **endlessness**. 2. Endless life after death ▸ afterlife, eternity. *See* **immortality**.

evermore *adverb*
▸ endlessly, perpetually, unendingly. *See* **forever** (1).

everyday *adjective*
1. Of or suitable for ordinary days or routine occasions ▸ casual, daily, quotidian, workaday, workday. *See also* **ordinary**. 2. Occurring or encountered regularly ▸ commonplace, frequent, regular. *See* **common** (1).

everyday *noun*
A regular or customary matter, condition, or course of events ▸ norm, ordinary, rule. *See* **usual**.

everything *noun*
▸ entirety, gross, total. *See* **whole** (1).

evict *verb*
▸ dismiss, oust. *See* **eject** (1). *See synonym note at* **eject**.

eviction *noun*
▸ dismissal, expulsion. *See* **ejection**.

evidence *noun*
1. That which confirms ▸ authentication, corroboration, proof, verification. *See* **confirmation** (2). 2. Something visible or evident that gives grounds for believing in the existence or presence of something else ▸ badge, indication, symptom. *See* **sign** (1).

evidence *verb*
1. To make manifest or apparent ▸ display, reveal. *See* **show** (1). 2. To establish as true or genuine through evidence ▸ confirm, substantiate, validate. *See* **prove** (1). 3. To assure the certainty or validity of ▸ authenticate, corroborate, substantiate, verify. *See* **confirm** (1). 4. To demonstrate and clarify with examples ▸ demonstrate, exemplify, illustrate, instance. *See also* **explain**.

evident *adjective*
▸ clear-cut, noticeable, obvious. *See* **apparent** (1). *See synonym note at* **apparent**.

evidently *adverb*
▸ externally, ostensibly, seemingly. *See* **apparently**.

evil *adjective*
1. Morally objectionable ▸ bad, black, dark, immoral, iniquitous, peccant, reprobate, sinful, vicious, wicked, wrong. *See also* **corrupt, sordid**. 2. Causing harm or injury ▸ deleterious, hurtful, injurious. *See* **harmful**. 3. Bringing or predicting misfortune ▸ dire, ominous, portentous. *See* **fateful** (1). 4. Characterized by intense ill will or spite ▸ evil, vicious, wicked. *See* **malevolent** (1).

evil *noun*
1. The quality or state of being morally bad or objectionable ▸ iniquity, peccancy, sin, vice, wickedness, wrong. *See also* **corruption, malevolence**. 2. A wicked act or wicked behavior ▸ deviltry, misdeed, sin. *See* **crime** (2). 3. Whatever is destructive or harmful ▸ bad, badness, ill, worse. *See also* **harm**. 4. A specific cause of suffering or harm ▸ bane, scourge. *See* **curse** (3).

evildoer *noun*
One that performs evil acts ▸ miscreant, scoundrel, sinner, villain, wrongdoer. *Informal:* baddie, bad guy. *Slang:* black hat. *See also* **criminal, fiend, rascal**.

evildoing *noun*
▸ evil, misdeed, sin. *See* **crime** (2).

evil eye *noun*
Something or someone believed to bring bad luck ▸ curse, hex, hoodoo, Jonah. *Informal:* jinx.

evince *verb*
▸ display, reveal. *See* **show** (1).

eviscerate *verb*
▸ debilitate, weaken. *See* **enervate**.

evocative *adjective*
Tending to bring a memory, mood, or image, for example, subtly or indirectly to mind ▸ allusive, connotative, impressionistic, reminiscent, suggestive. *See also* **designative, symbolic**.

evoke *verb*
To bring out something latent, hidden, or unexpressed ▸ call forth (*or* up), conjure (up), draw (out),

educe, elicit, invoke, rouse, summon (forth). *See also* **arouse, revive.**

✦ CORE SYNONYMS: *evoke, educe, elicit.* These verbs mean to call forth or bring out something latent, hidden, or unexpressed: *evoke laughter; educed significance from the event; trying to elicit the truth.*

evolution *noun*
1. A progression from a simple form to a more complex one ▸ evolvement, progress, unfolding. *See* **development** (1). 2. The process or result of making or becoming different ▸ modification, mutation, variation. *See* **change** (1).

evolve *verb*
1. To be disclosed gradually ▸ disentangle, unfold, unravel. *See* **develop** (2). 2. To become different ▸ fluctuate, modify, turn. *See* **change** (2). 3. To arrive at through reasoning ▸ conclude, determine. *See* **derive** (2).

evolvement *noun*
▸ advancement, progress, unfolding. *See* **development** (1).

exacerbate *verb*
▸ deepen, enhance, heighten. *See* **intensify.**

exact *adjective*
1. Conforming exactly to fact ▸ correct, errorless, precise. *See* **accurate** (1). 2. Strictly distinguished from others ▸ precise, very. 3. Consistent with accuracy or completeness ▸ faithful, strict. *See* **close** (2). 4. Being an exact amount or number ▸ even. *Idioms:* on the button (*or* money *or* nose).

exact *verb*
1. To obtain by coercion or intimidation ▸ blackmail, squeeze. *See* **extort.** 2. To establish and apply as compulsory ▸ assess, impose, levy, put. 3. To ask for urgently or insistently ▸ insist on (*or* upon), require. *See* **demand** (1). *See synonym note at* **demand.**

exacting *adjective*
1. Rigorous and unsparing in treating others ▸ harsh, stern, strict. *See* **severe** (1). 2. Very difficult to please ▸ demanding, finicky. *See* **fussy** (1). 3. Not easy to do, achieve, or master ▸ arduous, laborious, tough. *See* **difficult** (1). 4. Requiring great tact or skill ▸ demanding, exacting, precarious. *See* **delicate** (3).

exaction *noun*
1. The act of demanding ▸ appeal, claim, requisition. *See* **demand** (1). 2. A fixed amount of money charged for a service ▸ dues, fee. *See* **toll**[1] (1).

exactitude *noun*
1. Correspondence with fact or truth ▸ authenticity, correctness, truth, validity. *See* **veracity.** 2. Freedom from error ▸ correctness, exactness, precision. *See* **accuracy** (1).

exactly *adverb*
1. In an exact manner ▸ even, faithfully, just, literally, precisely, strictly, verbatim. *Idioms:* in all respects (*or* every respect), just so, letter for letter, to a T, to the letter, word for word. 2. With precision or absolute conformity ▸ dead, precisely, squarely. *See* **directly** (3).

exactment *noun*
▸ exaction, fee. *See* **toll**[1] (1).

exactness *noun*
1. Correspondence with fact or truth ▸ authenticity, correctness, truth, validity. *See* **veracity.** 2. Freedom from error ▸ accurateness, correctness, precision. *See* **accuracy** (1).

exaggerate *verb*
1. To make something seem greater than is actually the case ▸ aggrandize, hyperbolize, inflate, magnify, overcharge, overemphasize, overstate, puff (up). *Idioms:* blow out of proportion, lay it on thick, stretch the truth. *See also* **boast, distort.** 2. To make or become greater or larger ▸ amplify, boost, enlarge. *See* **increase** (1).

✦ CORE SYNONYMS: *exaggerate, inflate, magnify, overstate.* These verbs mean to make something seem larger or greater than it actually is: *exaggerated the size of the fish I caught; inflated his own importance; magnifying her part in their success; overstated his income on the loan application.*

◄ ANTONYM: *minimize*

exaggerated *adjective*
1. Represented as greater than is actually the case ▸ far-fetched, hyperbolic, inflated, magnified, overblown, overdrawn, overstated. *See also* **astonishing, doubtful, imaginary, outrageous.** 2. Suggesting drama or a stage performance, as in emotionality or suspense ▸ melodramatic, sensational, spectacular. *See* **dramatic** (2).

exaggeration *noun*
The act or an instance of exaggerating ▸ hyperbole, hyperbolism, overstatement, tall talk. *Informal:* fish story, tall tale. *See also* **lie**[2].

exalt *verb*
1. To raise to a high position or status ▸ aggrandize, apotheosize, dignify, elevate, ennoble, glorify, magnify, uplift. *Idioms:* put (*or* place) on a pedestal. 2. To cause to be eminent or recognized ▸ dignify, elevate, honor. *See* **distinguish** (5). 3. To pay tribute or homage to ▸ celebrate, glorify. *See* **honor** (1). 4. To honor a deity in religious worship ▸ extol, laud. *See* **praise** (3). 5. To raise in rank ▸ advance, elevate, upgrade. *See* **promote** (1).

exaltation *noun*
1. The act of raising to a high position or status or the condition of being so raised ▸ aggrandizement, apotheosis, beatification, canonization, deification, dignification, elevation, ennoblement, glorification, lionization. 2. The honoring of a deity, as in worship ▸ extolment, magnification. *See* **praise** (2). 3. High spirits ▸ euphoria, inspiration. *See* **elation** (1).

exalted *adjective*
1. Raised to or occupying a high position or rank ▸ august, elevated, ennobled, eminent, grand, high-ranking, illustrious, lofty, noble, venerable. *See also* **famous.** 2. Exceedingly dignified in form, tone, or style ▸ eloquent, grand. *See* **elevated** (5).

exam *noun*
1. A set of questions or exercises designed to determine knowledge or skill ▸ catechism, quiz. *See* **test** (2).
2. A medical inquiry into a patient's state of health ▸ analysis, diagnosis. *See* **examination** (2).

examination *noun*
1. The act of examining carefully or critically ▸ audit, analysis, check, checkup, inquest, inquisition, inquiry, inspection, investigation, perusal, probe, research, review, scrutiny, search, study, survey, view. *Informal:* going-over, once-over. **2.** A medical inquiry into a patient's state of health ▸ analysis, checkup, diagnosis, exam, probe. *Informal:* work-up. **3.** A set of questions or exercises designed to determine knowledge or skill ▸ catechism, exam, quiz. *See* **test** (2).

✚ **CORE SYNONYMS:** *examination, inquiry, inquest, inquisition, investigation, probe, research.* These nouns denote the act of examining something or someone carefully or critically, especially in the quest for knowledge, data, or truth: *an examination of the legal facts in the case; filed an inquiry about the lost shipment; holding an inquest to determine the cause of his death; an inquisition into her political activities; a criminal investigation; a probe into alleged police corruption; scientific research.*

---

examine *verb*
1. To look at or study carefully or critically ▸ analyze, audit, check (out), con, go over, inspect, investigate, peruse, pore over, research, review, scrutinize, study, survey, traverse, view. *Informal:* case. *Slang:* scope out. *Idioms:* bone up on, give the once-over (*or* a going-over), go over with a fine-tooth comb, put under a microscope. *See also* **estimate, explore, study, test.**
2. To subject to a test of effectiveness, value, function, or other quality ▸ check, essay, try (out). *See* **test** (1).
3. To subject to a test of knowledge or skill ▸ catechize, quiz, test. *See also* **ask. 4.** To put a question to someone ▸ query, question, pump. *See* **ask** (1). *See synonym note at* **ask.**

example *noun*
1. One that is representative of a group or class ▸ case, embodiment, exemplar, exemplification, exponent, illustration, instance, instantiation, representative, sample, specimen. **2.** An instance that warns or discourages prospective imitators ▸ caveat, cautionary tale, exemplar, lesson, object lesson, warning. *See also* **preventive, warning. 3.** One that is worthy of imitation or duplication ▸ exemplar, ideal, paradigm. *See* **model** (1). *See synonym note at* **model.**

✚ **CORE SYNONYMS:** *example, instance, case, illustration, sample, specimen.* These nouns refer to what is representative of or serves to explain a larger group or class. An *example* is a typically representative part that demonstrates the character of the whole: *"Of the despotism to which unrestrained military power leads we have plenty of examples from Alexander to Mao"* (Samuel Eliot Morison). An *instance* is an example that is cited to prove or to illustrate a point: *an*

instance of flagrant corruption. A *case* is an action, an occurrence, or a condition that relates specifically to something being discussed, decided, or treated: *a typical case of child neglect.* An *illustration* clarifies or explains: *a dictionary entry that provided an illustration of the word in context.* A *sample* is an actual part of something larger, presented as evidence of the quality or nature of the whole: *gave us a sample of her temper.* *Specimen* often denotes an individual, representative member of a group or class: *This poem is a fair specimen of her work.*

---

exasperate *verb*
1. To trouble the nerves or peace of mind of ▸ irritate, nettle, vex. *See* **annoy** (1). **2.** To cause to feel or show anger ▸ incense, infuriate, madden. *See* **anger** (1).

exasperation *noun*
▸ bother, irritation, vexation. *See* **annoyance** (1).

excavate *verb*
▸ burrow, scoop, shovel. *See* **dig** (1).

exceed *verb*
1. To go beyond the limits of ▸ overleap, overpass, overreach, overrun, overshoot, overstep, surpass, transcend, transgress. **2.** To be greater or better than ▸ best, excel, outshine. *See* **surpass** (1). *See synonym note at* **surpass.**

exceedingly *adverb*
▸ eminently, extremely, highly. *See* **very.**

excel *verb*
▸ exceed, outdo, outshine. *See* **surpass** (1). *See synonym note at* **surpass.**

excellence *noun*
The quality of being exceptionally good of its kind ▸ fineness, incomparability, preeminence, superbness, superiority, transcendence, virtuosity. *See also* **distinction.**

excellent *adjective*
Exceptionally good of its kind ▸ ace, banner, blue-ribbon, brag, capital, champion, dandy, fine, first-class, first-rate, prime, prize, quality, remarkable, splendid, superb, superior, terrific, tiptop, top, world-class. *Informal:* A-OK, A-one, bang-up, bully, great, jim-dandy, smashing, swell, topflight, topnotch. *Slang:* awesome, bad, boss, cool, corking, crackerjack, dynamite, hot, killer, phat, primo, tops. *Idioms:* out of this world, to die for. *See also* **best, choice, exceptional, marvelous.**

except *verb*
1. To keep from being admitted, included, or considered ▸ eliminate, keep out, rule out. *See* **exclude** (1).
2. To express opposition ▸ demur, oppose, protest. *See* **object** (1).

exception *noun*
1. An expression of opposition ▸ argument, grievance, protestation. *See* **objection. 2.** One that is excepted, especially a case not conforming to a rule ▸ anomaly, deviance, irregularity. *See* **abnormality.**

exceptionable *adjective*
1. Arousing disapproval ▸ disagreeable, improper, unacceptable. *See* **objectionable. 2.** In doubt or dispute

▸ disputable, doubtful, questionable. *See* **debatable.**

exceptional *adjective*

1. Beyond what is usual, normal, or customary ▸ especial, exquisite, extraordinary, magnificent, memorable, notable, noteworthy, outstanding, preeminent, rare, remarkable, singular, special, sublime, towering, uncommon, unprecedented, unusual. *Informal:* standout. *Slang:* awesome, out of sight. *See also* **best, excellent, noticeable, unique. 2.** Of fine quality ▸ fine, select, superior. *See* **choice** (1).

exceptionally *adverb*

1. In a manner or to a degree that is unusual ▸ singularly, uncommonly, uniquely. *See* **unusually. 2.** To a high degree ▸ extremely, highly. *See* **very.**

excess *noun*

1. A condition of going or being beyond what is needed, desired, or appropriate ▸ embarrassment, excessiveness, exorbitance, extravagance, extravagancy, extravagantness, inordinacy, inordinateness, overabundance, oversufficiency, plethora, superabundance, superfluity, superfluousness, surfeit. *Idiom:* fifth wheel. **2.** A thing, amount, or quantity beyond what is needed, desired, or appropriate ▸ overflow, oversupply, superfluity. *See* **surplus. 3.** Immoderate indulgence, as in food or drink ▸ immoderacy, immoderateness, immoderation, intemperance, overindulgence, surfeit.

excess *adjective*

Being more than is needed, desired, or appropriate ▸ extra, surplus. *See* **superfluous.** *See synonym note at* **superfluous.**

excessive *adjective*

1. Exceeding a normal or reasonable limit ▸ exorbitant, extravagant, extreme, immoderate, intemperate, inordinate, overabundant, overmuch, unbridled, undue, unrestrained. *Idioms:* out of all bounds (*or* proportion), out of control. *See also* **flagrant, outrageous. 2.** Not required, necessary, or warranted by the circumstances of the case ▸ supererogative, supererogatory, uncalled-for. *See* **wanton** (2).

✚ **CORE SYNONYMS:** *excessive, exorbitant, extravagant, immoderate, inordinate, extreme.* These adjectives mean exceeding a normal, usual, reasonable, or proper limit. *Excessive* describes a quantity, amount, or degree that is more than what is justifiable, tolerable, or desirable: *excessive drinking. Exorbitant* usually refers to a quantity or degree that far exceeds what is customary or fair: *exorbitant interest rates. Extravagant* sometimes specifies lavish or unwise expenditure (*extravagant gifts*); often it implies unbridled divergence from reason or sound judgment (*extravagant claims*). *Immoderate* denotes lack of due moderation: *immoderate enthusiasm. Inordinate* implies an overstepping of bounds imposed by authority or dictated by good sense: *inordinate demands. Extreme* suggests the utmost degree of excessiveness: *extreme danger.*

---

excessively *adverb*

▸ disproportionately, extremely, overly. *See* **unduly.**

excessiveness *noun*

▸ exorbitance, extravagance, surfeit. *See* **excess** (1).

exchange *verb*

1. To give up in return for something else ▸ exchange, interchange, trade. *See* **change** (3). **2.** To give and receive mutually, as words ▸ bandy, interchange, swap, trade. *Idiom:* give as good as one gets. *See also* **reciprocate, retaliate.**

exchange *noun*

1. The act of exchanging ▸ interchange, switch, trade. *See* **change** (2). **2.** A business agreement involving goods or services ▸ sale, trade, transaction. *See* **deal** (1). **3.** The exchange of ideas ▸ communion, discussion, intercourse. *See* **communication** (1).

excitation *noun*

▸ ardor, excitement, zeal. *See* **enthusiasm** (1).

excite *verb*

1. To stir to action or feeling ▸ egg on, prod, trigger. *See* **provoke** (1). *See synonym note at* **provoke. 2.** To have a powerful emotional effect on someone ▸ thrill, transport. *See* **enrapture. 3.** To give great or keen pleasure to ▸ enchant, overjoy, pleasure. *See* **delight** (1).

excited *adjective*

▸ atingle, fired up, worked up. *See* **thrilled.**

excitement *noun*

1. Passionate devotion to or interest in a cause or subject ▸ ardor, fervor, zeal. *See* **enthusiasm** (1). **2.** Agitated, excited activity ▸ commotion, flurry, fuss. *See* **agitation** (3).

exciting *adjective*

1. Producing or stimulating physical, mental, or emotional vigor ▸ bracing, energizing, exhilarating. *See* **invigorating. 2.** Suggesting drama or a stage performance, as in emotionality or suspense ▸ melodramatic, sensational, spectacular. *See* **dramatic** (2).

exclaim *verb*

To speak suddenly or sharply, as from surprise or emotion ▸ blurt (out), burst out, cry (out), ejaculate, rap out. *See also* **shout.**

exclamation *noun*

▸ call, holler, yell. *See* **shout.**

exclude *verb*

1. To keep from being admitted, included, or considered ▸ ban, bar, blackball, blacklist, boycott, count out, debar, eliminate, except, keep out, ostracize, reject, rule out, shut out, vote down. *See also* **banish, forbid, decline. 2.** To take or leave out ▸ eliminate, omit, prune. *See* **drop** (8).

✚ **CORE SYNONYMS:** *exclude, blackball, blacklist, boycott, ostracize, reject.* These verbs mean to keep from being admitted, included, or considered: *excluded the sensitive findings from the report; blackballed by the fraternity; blacklisted because of her political beliefs; a threat to boycott the product; ostracized following the harassment charges; rejected the proposals from the neighborhood groups.*

◀ **ANTONYM:** *admit*

exclusion *noun*
1. The act of preventing ▸ deterrence, forestallment, preclusion. *See* **prevention. 2.** The act or process of eliminating ▸ eradication, purge. *See* **elimination** (1).

exclusive *adjective*
1. Not divided among or shared with others ▸ particular, prerogative, private, single, sole. *See also* **individual. 2.** Singled out in preference ▸ choice, chosen, elect, select. *See also* **excellent, favorite. 3.** Not diffused or dispersed ▸ undivided, whole. *See* **concentrated** (1). **4.** Catering to, used by, or admitting only the wealthy or socially superior ▸ chic, chichi, classy, elite, fancy, hoity-toity, posh, selective, smart, sophisticated, swank, swanky, tony. *Informal:* ritzy. *See also* **snobbish. 5.** Intended to prevent ▸ deterrent, preclusive, prohibitive. *See* **preventive** (1).

exclusively *adverb*
▸ alone, just, only. *See* **solely** (1).

excogitate *verb*
1. To think or think about carefully and at length ▸ cogitate, deliberate, mull. *See* **ponder. 2.** To arrive at through reasoning ▸ conclude, evolve. *See* **derive** (2).

excogitation *noun*
▸ cogitation, deliberation, rumination. *See* **thought** (1).

excogitative *adjective*
▸ contemplative, pensive, reflective. *See* **thoughtful** (1).

excoriate *verb*
1. To make the skin raw by friction ▸ abrade, irritate, rub. *See* **chafe** (1). **2.** To criticize harshly and devastatingly ▸ bash, blast, flay. *See* **slam** (5).

excrement *or* **excreta** *noun*
Waste matter eliminated from the bowels ▸ bowel movement, dropping, dung, feces, filth, night soil, ordure, scat, stool, waste. *Slang:* poop.

excrete *verb*
▸ evacuate, void. *See* **eliminate** (4).

excretion *noun*
▸ evacuation, purgation. *See* **elimination** (3).

excretory *adjective*
▸ evacuative, purgative. *See* **eliminative.**

excruciate *verb*
▸ plague, rack, torment. *See* **afflict.**

excruciating *adjective*
▸ agonizing, torturous. *See* **tormenting.**

exculpate *verb*
▸ acquit, exonerate, vindicate. *See* **clear** (9).

exculpation *noun*
A freeing or clearing from accusation or guilt ▸ absolution, acquittal, exoneration, justification, remission, vindication. *See also* **forgiveness.**

excursion *noun*
1. A usually short journey taken for pleasure ▸ jaunt, junket, outing, trip. *See also* **expedition, journey. 2.** An instance of digressing ▸ deviation, divergence, tangent. *See* **digression.**

excursionist *noun*
▸ sightseer, traveler, vacationer. *See* **tourist.**

excursive *adjective*
▸ long-winded, parenthetical, rambling. *See* **digressive.**

excursus *noun*
▸ deviation, divergence, tangent. *See* **digression.**

excusable *adjective*
1. Admitting of forgiveness or pardon ▸ forgivable, venial. *See* **pardonable. 2.** Capable of being justified ▸ defensible, justifiable, tenable. *See also* **logical, sound².**

excuse *verb*
1. To free from an obligation or duty ▸ absolve, discharge, dispense, exempt, let off, release, remise, remit, relieve, spare. *Idioms:* let off the hook, make excuses for. **2.** To grant forgiveness to or for ▸ condone, overlook, pardon. *See* **forgive.** *See synonym note at* **forgive. 3.** To show to be just, right, or valid ▸ justify, rationalize, vindicate. *Idiom:* make a case for. **4.** To direct or allow to leave ▸ cast out, expel. *See* **dismiss** (2).

excuse *noun*
1. An explanation offered to justify an action or make it better understood ▸ justification, plea, pretext, rationale, rationalization. *Informal:* alibi. *See also* **account, pretense. 2.** A statement of acknowledgment expressing regret or asking pardon ▸ apology, mea culpa, regrets. *See also* **acknowledgment. 3.** The act or an instance of forgiving ▸ amnesty, condonation, pardon. *See* **forgiveness.**

exec *noun*
Informal A person having administrative or managerial authority in an organization ▸ administrator, manager. *See* **executive.**

execrable *adjective*
Informal So annoying or detestable as to deserve condemnation ▸ accursed, blasted, confounded. *See* **damned** (2).

execrate *verb*
1. To feel hostility toward or strong dislike for something ▸ abhor, detest. *See* **hate. 2.** To attack with harsh, often insulting language ▸ assail, blaspheme. *See* **revile.**

execration *noun*
1. A denunciation invoking a wish or threat of evil or injury ▸ damnation, malediction. *See* **curse** (1). **2.** An object of extreme dislike ▸ abomination, anathema. *See* **hate** (2).

execute *verb*
1. To oversee the provision or execution of ▸ carry out, dispense. *See* **administer** (2). **2.** To carry out the functions, requirements, or terms of ▸ discharge, exercise, perform. *See* **fulfill** (1). **3.** To begin and carry through to completion ▸ discharge, prosecute. *Informal:* pull off. *See* **perform** (1). *See synonym note at* **perform. 4.** To succeed in doing ▸ accomplish, achieve, carry out. *See* **effect** (1). **5.** To perform according to one's artistic conception ▸ depict, play, render. *See* **interpret** (2). **6.** To compel observance of ▸ effect, implement. *See* **enforce. 7.** To cause the death

of ▸ cut down, destroy, finish (off). *See* **kill¹** (1).
execution *noun*
1. The act of beginning and carrying through to completion ▸ effectuation, prosecution. *See* **performance** (1). **2.** Carrying a law or judgment into effect ▸ enforcement, implementation. *See also* **effect, exercise. 3.** A performer's distinctive personal version of a song, dance, piece of music, or role ▸ performance, reading, rendition. *See* **interpretation** (1).
executive *noun*
A person having administrative or managerial authority in an organization ▸ administrant, administrator, CEO, chair, chairman (of the board), chairwoman, chief executive, director, functionary, manager, middle manager, officer, official, president. *Informal:* exec, higher-up. *See also* **boss.**
executive *adjective*
Of, for, or relating to administration or administrators ▸ directorial, managerial, organizational. *See* **administrative.**
exegesis *noun*
1. Critical explanation or analysis ▸ annotation, exposition, interpretation. *See* **commentary. 2.** Something that serves to explain or clarify ▸ decipherment, explication, illumination. *See* **explanation** (1).
exegetic *adjective*
▸ explicative, illustrative, interpretive. *See* **explanatory.**
exemplar *noun*
1. One that is worthy of imitation or duplication ▸ beau ideal, ideal, paradigm. *See* **model** (1). *See synonym note at* **model. 2.** One that is representative of a group or class ▸ illustration, sample. *See* **example** (1). **3.** An instance that warns or discourages prospective imitators ▸ caveat, warning. *See* **example** (2). **4.** An ideally representative example of a type ▸ archetype, model. *See* **epitome** (1).
exemplary *adjective*
1. Beyond reproach ▸ blameless, faultless, good, lily-white, irreprehensible, irreproachable, unblamable. **2.** Deserving honor, respect, or admiration ▸ deserving, laudable, worthy. *See* **admirable. 3.** Conforming to an ultimate form of perfection or excellence ▸ model, perfect, supreme. *See* **ideal** (1).
exemplification *noun*
1. One that is representative of a group or class ▸ illustration, sample. *See* **example** (1). **2.** A concrete entity typifying an abstraction ▸ incarnation, manifestation, personification. *See* **embodiment** (1).
exemplify *verb*
1. To demonstrate and clarify with examples ▸ demonstrate, evidence, illustrate, instance. *See also* **explain, show. 2.** To serve as an example, image, or symbol of ▸ epitomize, illustrate, typify. *See* **represent** (1).
exempt *verb*
▸ discharge, let off. *See* **excuse** (1).
exemption *noun*
Temporary immunity from penalties ▸ grace, immu-

nity, reprieve, respite. *See also* **delay, forgiveness.**
exercise *noun*
1. The act of putting into play ▸ administration, adoption, application, employment, exertion, implementation, operation, play, recourse, resort, usage, use, utilization. **2.** Energetic physical action ▸ activity, exertion. **3.** Repetition of an action so as to develop or maintain one's skill ▸ conditioning, rehearsal. *See* **practice** (1). *See synonym note at* **practice.**
exercise *verb*
1. To put into action or use ▸ apply, employ, utilize. *See* **use** (1). **2.** To bring to bear steadily or forcefully, as influence ▸ exert, ply, wield. *Idiom:* throw one's weight around. **3.** To engage in activities in order to strengthen or condition ▸ drill, practice, train, work out. **4.** To carry out the functions, requirements, or terms of ▸ discharge, execute. *See* **fulfill** (1). **5.** To do or perform repeatedly so as to master ▸ go over (*or* through), run through. *See* **practice** (1).
exert *verb*
1. To bring to bear steadily or forcefully, as influence ▸ exercise, ply, wield. *Idiom:* throw one's weight around. **2.** To devote (oneself or one's efforts) ▸ concentrate, focus, give. *See* **apply** (1).
exertion *noun*
1. The act of putting into play ▸ employment, implementation, usage. *See* **exercise** (1). **2.** The use of energy to do something ▸ endeavor, struggle. *See* **effort** (1). **3.** Energetic physical action ▸ activity, exercise.
exfoliate *verb*
▸ peel, scale, shed. *See* **flake.**
exhalation *noun*
The act or process of breathing ▸ respiration, wind. *See* **breath** (1).
exhale *verb*
1. To take a breath or breaths ▸ breathe out, expire. *Idiom:* draw breath. *See* **breathe** (1). **2.** To discharge material, as vapor or fumes, usually suddenly and violently ▸ give forth, issue, release. *See* **emit** (1).
exhaust *verb*
1. To use all of ▸ consume, deplete, drain, draw down, eat up, expend, finish, play out, run through, sap, spend, use up. *Informal:* polish off. *See also* **dry. 2.** To be depleted ▸ consume, go, spend. *Idiom:* go down the drain. **3.** To make weary ▸ fatigue, wear out. *See* **tire** (1). *See synonym note at* **tire.**

✛ **CORE SYNONYMS:** *exhaust, deplete, drain.* These verbs all mean to use all of something. *Exhaust* stresses reduction to a point of uselessness: "*The resources of civilization are not yet exhausted*" (William Ewart Gladstone). *Deplete* refers to using up gradually and only hints at harmful consequences: *The campers' food supply was quickly depleted. Drain* suggests gradual drawing off and harm: *War often drains a nation's economy.*

exhausted *adjective*
▸ fatigued, weary, worn-out. *See* **tired** (1).

exhausting *adjective*
Causing fatigue ▶ draining, fatiguing, tiring, wearing, wearying. *See also* **burdensome.**

exhaustion *noun*
The condition of being extremely tired ▶ burnout, fatigue, prostration, tiredness, weariness. *See also* **debilitation, lethargy.**

exhaustive *adjective*
1. Covering all aspects with painstaking accuracy ▶ complete, full-dress. *See* **thorough** (1). **2.** Characterized by attention to detail ▶ full, particular, thorough. *See* **detailed** (1).

exhaustively *adverb*
▶ comprehensively, intensively, thoroughly. *See* **completely** (2).

exhibit *verb*
1. To make manifest or apparent ▶ demonstrate, display, reveal. *See* **show** (1). **2.** To make a public and usually ostentatious show of ▶ brandish, expose, flaunt. *See* **display** (1). **3.** To have as a visible characteristic ▶ display, possess. *See* **bear** (3).

exhibit *noun*
1. An act of showing or displaying ▶ exhibition, show. *See* **display** (1). **2.** A large public display, as of goods or works of art ▶ exposition, fair, show. *See* **exhibition** (1).

exhibition *noun*
1. A large public display, as of goods or works of art ▶ bazaar, exhibit, expo, exposition, fair, festival, installation, retrospective, salon, show. *See also* **market, display. 2.** An act of showing or displaying ▶ demonstration, show. *See* **display** (1).

exhibitionism *noun*
▶ staginess, theatricality. *See* **theatricalism.**

exhibitory *or* **exhibitive** *adjective*
▶ denotive, indicative, indicatory. *See* **designative.**

exhilarant *adjective*
▶ bracing, energizing, exhilarating. *See* **invigorating.**

exhilarate *verb*
1. To raise the spirits of ▶ buoy (up), elevate, inspire. *See* **elate** (1). **2.** To give or impart vitality and energy to someone or something ▶ invigorate, vitalize. *See* **energize.**

exhilarated *adjective*
▶ animated, happy, jovial. *See* **cheerful** (1).

exhilarating *adjective*
▶ bracing, energizing, rousing. *See* **invigorating.**

exhilaration *noun*
▶ euphoria, inspiration. *See* **elation** (1).

exhort *verb*
▶ induce, press. *See* **urge.**

exhume *verb*
▶ dig (up *or* out), turn up. *See* **uncover** (1).

exigency *or* **exigence** *noun*
1. A situation requiring immediate assistance or remedial action ▶ crisis, distress, trouble. *See* **emergency. 2.** A condition in which something necessary or desirable is required or wanted ▶ necessity, need. **3.** A decisive point ▶ crossroads, juncture. *See* **crisis** (1).

See synonym note at **crisis. 4.** Something asked for or needed ▶ need, want. *See* **demand** (2).

exigent *adjective*
1. Demanding immediate attention ▶ crucial, dire, pressing. *See* **urgent** (1). *See synonym note at* **urgent. 2.** Not easy to do, achieve, or master ▶ arduous, laborious, tough. *See* **difficult** (1).

exiguous *adjective*
▶ puny, scant, skimpy. *See* **meager** (1).

exile *noun*
1. Enforced removal from one's native country by official decree ▶ banishment, deportation, expatriation, extradition, ostracism, proscription, transportation. **2.** One who is forced to emigrate, usually for political reasons ▶ deportee, expatriate. *See* **émigré** (1). **3.** Someone who is excluded from society ▶ outsider, pariah. *See* **outcast.**

exile *verb*
To force to leave by official decree ▶ deport, expel, transport. *See* **banish** (1). *See synonym note at* **banish.**

exist *verb*
1. To have reality or life ▶ be, breathe, live, subsist. *Idioms:* be around, have one's being, walk the earth. *See also* **endure, survive. 2.** To have an inherent basis ▶ dwell, inhere, reside. *See* **consist** (1).

exist on *verb*
To include as part of one's diet by nature or preference ▶ eat, feed on, live on, subsist on.

existence *noun*
1. The fact or state of existing or of being actual ▶ actuality, being, entity, reality, substantiality, substantiveness. *See also* **certainty, fact. 2.** The period during which someone or something exists ▶ duration, span, term. *See* **life** (1). **3.** One that exists independently ▶ entity, object, something. *See* **thing** (1). **4.** The means needed to support life ▶ bread, keep, livelihood. *See* **living.**

✦ CORE SYNONYMS: *existence, actuality, being.* These nouns denote the fact or state of existing or of being actual: *laws in existence for centuries; an idea progressing from possibility to actuality; a point of view gradually coming into being.*

◀ ANTONYM: *nonexistence*

existent *adjective*
1. Occurring or existing in act or fact ▶ actual, extant, real, true. *See synonym note at* **actual.** *See also* **physical. 2.** Having life ▶ live, living, vital. *See* **alive** (1). **3.** In existence now ▶ current, present-day. *See* **present**[1] (1).

existent *noun*
One that exists independently ▶ entity, object, something. *See* **thing** (1).

existing *adjective*
1. Having life ▶ live, living, vital. *See* **alive** (1). **2.** In existence now ▶ current, present-day. *See* **present**[1] (1).

exit *noun*
The act of leaving ▶ adieu, parting, withdrawal. *See* **departure** (1).

exit *verb*
To move away from a place ▸ depart, go away, retire. *See* **go** (1).

exodus *noun*
1. Departure from one's native land to settle in another ▸ diaspora, transmigration. *See* **emigration**. 2. The act of leaving ▸ embarkation, farewell, withdrawal. *See* **departure** (1).

exonerate *verb*
▸ absolve, acquit, vindicate. *See* **clear** (9).

exoneration *noun*
▸ absolution, vindication. *See* **exculpation**.

exorbitance *noun*
▸ embarrassment, extravagance, surfeit. *See* **excess** (1).

exorbitant *adjective*
1. Exceeding a normal or reasonable limit ▸ extravagant, immoderate. *See* **excessive** (1). *See synonym note at* **excessive**. 2. Vastly exceeding a normal limit, as in cost ▸ overpriced, stiff. *See* **steep**[1] (2).

exotic *adjective*
1. From or characteristic of another place ▸ alien, immigrant, strange. *See* **foreign** (1). *See synonym note at* **foreign**. 2. Very strange or strikingly unusual ▸ bizarre, fanciful, fantastic, grotesque, outlandish, outré, strange, unorthodox. *Idioms:* from another planet (*or* outer space), off the wall. *See also* **eccentric, unusual**.

expand *verb*
1. To make or become greater or larger ▸ amplify, boost, enlarge. *See* **increase** (1). *See synonym note at* **increase**. 2. To make or become broader or more comprehensive ▸ amplify, expand, spread out, widen. *See* **broaden**. 3. To express at greater length or in greater detail ▸ develop, enlarge. *See* **elaborate**. 4. To move or arrange so as to cover a larger area ▸ extend, stretch. *See* **spread** (1). 5. To achieve an increase of ▸ develop, enlarge. *See* **gain** (9).

expandable *adjective*
▸ extendible, protractile, stretchable. *See* **extensible**.

expanse *noun*
1. A wide and open area, as of land, sky, or water ▸ distance, expansion, extent, range, reach, space, spread, stretch, sweep, tract, vista. *See also* **view**. 2. The extent of something from side to side ▸ breadth, broadness, wideness, width. *See also* **distance**.

expansible *or* **expansile** *adjective*
▸ extendible, protractile, stretchable. *See* **extensible**.

expansion *noun*
1. The process of increasing in extent or inclusiveness ▸ broadening, fanning out, extension, proliferation, spread. *See also* **distribution**. 2. The act of increasing or rising ▸ amplification, boost, escalation. *See* **increase** (1). 3. A wide and open area, as of land, sky, or water ▸ extent, stretch, sweep. *See* **expanse** (1).

expansive *adjective*
1. Of large extent or expanse ▸ extended, spacious. *See* **broad** (1). 2. Covering a wide scope ▸ all-inclusive, broad, extensive. *See* **general** (2). 3. Disposed to be open, sociable, and talkative ▸ extroverted, gregarious. *See* **outgoing**.

expansively *adverb*
▸ much, quite, well. *See* **considerably**.

expatiate *verb*
▸ develop, expand. *See* **elaborate**.

expatiation *noun*
A formal discussion of a subject, either written or spoken ▸ disquisition, dissertation. *See* **discourse** (1).

expatriate *verb*
To force to leave by official decree ▸ deport, exile, transport. *See* **banish** (1). *See synonym note at* **banish**.

expatriate *noun*
1. One forced to emigrate, usually for political reasons ▸ exile, expellee. *See* **émigré** (1). 2. A person coming from another country or into a new community ▸ alien, outsider, stranger. *See* **foreigner**.

expatriation *noun*
1. Enforced removal from one's native country by official decree ▸ deportation, extradition. *See* **exile** (1). 2. Departure from one's native land to settle in another ▸ diaspora, transmigration. *See* **emigration**.

expect *verb*
1. To look forward to confidently ▸ anticipate, await, bargain for (*or* on), bet (on), count on, depend on (*or* upon), look for, wager, wait (for). *Informal:* figure on. *See also* **foresee, intend**. 2. To oblige to do or not do by force of authority, propriety, or custom ▸ oblige, obligate, require, suppose. *See also* **must**. 3. *Informal* To consider to be true without proof ▸ posit, presume, presuppose. *See* **suppose** (1).

✦ CORE SYNONYMS: *expect, anticipate, await*. These verbs relate to the idea of looking forward to something in the future with confidence. To *expect* is to look forward to the likely occurrence or appearance of someone or something: *"We should not expect something for nothing—but we all do and call it Hope"* (Edgar W. Howe). *Anticipate* sometimes refers to taking advance action, as to forestall or prevent the occurrence of something expected or to meet a wish or request before it is articulated: *The sentinels anticipated the attack and locked the gates.* The term can also refer to having a foretaste of something expected: *The governor anticipated trouble and called in the National Guard.* To *await* is to wait expectantly and with certainty: *I am eagerly awaiting your letter.*

---

expectance *or* **expectancy** *noun*
The condition of looking forward to something, especially with eagerness ▸ anticipation, expectation, high hopes, hopefulness. *See also* **desire**.

expectant *adjective*
1. Having or marked by expectation ▸ anticipant, anticipative, anticipatory, awaiting, hopeful, hoping, looking forward to. *Idioms:* in suspense, on tenterhooks (*or* the edge of one's seat), on the lookout (*or* watch) for, with bated breath. *See also* **eager, optimistic**. 2. Carrying a developing fetus within the uterus ▸ enceinte, parturient. *See* **pregnant** (1).

expectation *noun*
1. The condition of looking forward to something, especially with eagerness ▸ anticipation, expectance, expectancy, high hopes, hopefulness. *See also* **desire.**
2. Something expected ▸ anticipation, likelihood, promise, prospect. *See also* **chance, theory.**

expected *adjective*
▸ anticipated, scheduled. *See* **due** (2).

expecting *adjective*
▸ enceinte, parturient. *See* **pregnant** (1).

expectorate *noun*
A bodily substance ejected from the mouth ▸ saliva, phlegm. *See* **spit** (1).

expectorate *verb*
To expel a small amount of saliva or mucus from the mouth ▸ hawk, spit. *See also* **drool.**

expediency *noun*
▸ make-do, stopgap. *See* **makeshift.**

expedient *adjective*
1. Suited to one's purpose ▸ proper, suitable. *See* **convenient** (1). 2. Worth doing, especially for practical reasons ▸ desirable, recommendable, well. *See* **advisable.**

expedient *noun*
Something used temporarily or reluctantly when other means are not available ▸ make-do, stopgap. *See* **makeshift.** *See synonym note at* **makeshift.**

expedite *verb*
1. To make less difficult ▸ facilitate, help along. *See* **ease** (2). 2. To increase the speed of ▸ hasten, quicken. *See* **speed** (1).

expedition *noun*
1. A journey undertaken with a specific objective ▸ grand tour, mission, odyssey, pilgrimage, quest, safari, sortie, tour, trek, voyage. 2. Rapidness of movement or activity ▸ expeditiousness, hurry, quickness. *See* **haste** (1). *See synonym note at* **haste.**

expeditious *adjective*
1. Characterized by great speed ▸ brisk, rapid, speedy. *See* **fast** (1). *See synonym note at* **fast.** 2. Accomplished or experienced in very little time ▸ fast, rapid, speedy. *See* **quick** (1).

expeditiousness *noun*
▸ alacrity, hurry, quickness. *See* **haste** (1).

expel *verb*
1. To force to leave by official decree ▸ deport, exile, transport. *See* **banish** (1). 2. To send forth confined matter violently ▸ disgorge, spew. *See* **erupt** (1). 3. To put out by force ▸ dismiss, evict. *See* **eject** (1). *See synonym note at* **eject.** 4. To direct or allow to leave ▸ cast out, release. *See* **dismiss** (2). 5. To discharge wastes from the body ▸ excrete, void. *See* **eliminate** (4).

expellee *noun*
▸ exile, expatriate. *See* **émigré** (1).

expend *verb*
1. To give money as payment ▸ disburse, outlay. *See* **spend** (1). *See synonym note at* **spend.** 2. To use all of ▸ eat up, finish, run through. *See* **exhaust** (1).

expenditure *noun*
1. An amount paid or to be paid for a purchase ▸ charge, expense, price. *See* **cost** (1). 2. The act of consuming ▸ consumption, depletion, usage, use, utilization. *See also* **use.**

expense *noun*
1. An amount paid or to be paid for a purchase ▸ charge, expenditure, price. *See* **cost** (1). 2. The expenditure at which something is obtained ▸ cost, price, sacrifice, toll. *Informal:* damage.

expenses *noun*
▸ budget, expenses. *See* **overhead.**

expensive *adjective*
▸ dear, high-priced, valuable. *See* **costly.**

experience *noun*
1. Personal knowledge derived from participation or observation ▸ acquaintance, conversance, familiarity. *See also* **awareness.** 2. An exciting undertaking ▸ odyssey, venture. *See* **adventure.** 3. Something that takes place ▸ event, incident. *See* **circumstance** (1).

experience *verb*
To participate in or partake of personally ▸ encounter, feel, go through, have, know, meet (with), pass through, sample, see, suffer, taste (of), undergo. *Idiom:* run up against.

experienced *adjective*
Skilled or knowledgeable through long practice ▸ old, practiced, seasoned, tried, versed, veteran. *Idiom:* knowing the ropes. *See also* **veteran.**

experiment *or* **experimentation** *noun*
▸ proof, trial, tryout. *See* **test** (1).

experimental *adjective*
▸ probative, trial. *See* **pilot.**

expert *noun*
A person with a high degree of knowledge or skill in a particular field ▸ ace, adept, authority, connoisseur, dab hand, master, maven, past master, professional, proficient, specialist, wizard, world-beater. *Informal:* pro, whiz. *Slang:* crackajack, crackerjack.

expert *adjective*
Having or demonstrating a high degree of knowledge or skill ▸ adept, crack, master, masterful, masterly, professional, proficient, skilled, skillful. *Informal:* pro. *Slang:* crackajack, crackerjack. *See also* **able.**

✦ CORE SYNONYMS: *expert, proficient, adept, skilled, skillful.* These adjectives mean having or demonstrating a high degree of knowledge, ability, or skill, as in a profession or field of study. *Expert* applies to one with consummate skill and command: *an expert violinist who played the sonata flawlessly. Proficient* implies an advanced degree of competence acquired through training: *is proficient in Greek and Latin. Adept* suggests a natural aptitude improved by practice: *became adept at cutting the fabric without using a pattern. Skilled* implies sound, thorough competence and often mastery, as in an art, craft, or trade: *a skilled gymnast who won an Olympic medal. Skillful* adds to *skilled* the idea of natural dexterity in performance or achievement: *is skillful in the use of the hand loom.*

expertise *or* **expertness** *noun*
► adeptness, mastery, proficiency. *See* **ability** (1). *See synonym note at* **ability**.

expiable *adjective*
► forgivable, venial. *See* **pardonable**.

expiate *verb*
► atone, lustrate, pardon. *See* **purify** (1).

expiation *noun*
The act of making amends ► atonement, penance, reconciliation, reparation. *See also* **compensation, purification.**

expiatory *adjective*
► lustrative, purificatory. *See* **purgative** (2).

expiration *noun*
1. The act or fact of dying ► demise, passing. *See* **death** (1). 2. The act or process of breathing ► exhalation, respiration. *See* **breath** (1). 3. The act or an example of passing out of sight ► dissipation, vanishment. *See* **disappearance**. 4. A concluding or terminating ► completion, termination. *See* **end** (1).

expire *verb*
1. To become void, as through passage of time or an omission ► cease, run out. *See* **lapse** (1). 2. To cease to exist ► depart. *See* **disappear** (2). 3. To cease living ► demise, depart. *See* **die** (1). 4. To take a breath or breaths ► breathe out, exhale. *See* **breathe** (1).

explain *verb*
1. To make understandable ► construe, decipher, demystify, elucidate, explicate, expound, gloss, interpret, spell out. *Idioms:* make perfectly clear, put into plain English, walk someone through. *See also* **clarify**. 2. To find a solution for ► clear up, resolve, unravel. *See* **solve** (1). *See synonym note at* **solve**. 3. To offer reasons for or a cause of ► account for, justify, rationalize. *See also* **resolve**.

explain away *verb*
To conceal or make light of a fault or offense ► gloss over, whitewash. *See* **extenuate**.

✦ **CORE SYNONYMS:** *explain, elucidate, expound, explicate, interpret, construe.* These verbs mean to make the nature or meaning of something understandable. *Explain* is the most widely applicable: *The professor explained the obscure symbols.* To *elucidate* is to throw light on something complex: *"Man's whole life and environment have been laid open and elucidated"* (Thomas Carlyle). *Expound* and *explicate* imply detailed and usually learned and lengthy exploration or analysis: *"We must never forget that it is a constitution we are expounding"* (John Marshall). *"Ordinary language philosophers tried to explicate the standards of usage"* (Jerrold J. Katz). To *interpret* is to reveal the underlying meaning of something by the application of special knowledge or insight: *"If a poet interprets a poem of his own he limits its suggestibility"* (William Butler Yeats). *Construe* involves putting a particular construction or interpretation on something: *"I take the official oath today . . . with no purpose to construe the Constitution or laws by any hypercritical rules"* (Abraham Lincoln).

---

explainable *adjective*
Capable of being explained or accounted for ► accountable, construable, decipherable, explicable, illustratable, interpretable. *See also* **justifiable, understandable.**

explanation *noun*
1. Something that serves to explain or clarify ► clarification, construction, decipherment, elucidation, exegesis, explication, exposition, gloss, illumination, illustration, interpretation, spin. 2. A statement of causes or motives ► justification, rationale, reason. *See* **account** (1). 3. A solution, as to a problem ► determination, resolution, solution. *See* **answer** (2).

explanatory *or* **explanative** *adjective*
Serving to explain ► elucidative, exegetic, explicative, expositive, expository, hermeneutic, hermeneutical, illustrative, interpretative, interpretive. *See also* **educational.**

expletive *noun*
► blasphemy, curse, oath. *See* **swearword**.

explicable *adjective*
► decipherable, illustratable, interpretable. *See* **explainable**.

explicate *verb*
► construe, decipher, interpret. *See* **explain** (1). *See synonym note at* **explain**.

explication *noun*
► decipherment, elucidation, illumination. *See* **explanation** (1).

explicative *adjective*
► elucidative, illustrative, interpretive. *See* **explanatory**.

explicit *adjective*
1. Clearly, fully, and emphatically expressed ► decided, precise, specific. *See* **definite** (1). *See synonym note at* **definite**. 2. Depicted in sharp and accurate detail ► lifelike, realistic, vivid. *See* **graphic** (1).

explicitness *noun*
► distinctness, lucidity, perspicuity, plainness. *See* **clarity** (1).

explode *verb*
1. To release or cause to release energy suddenly and violently, especially with a loud noise ► backfire, blast, blow (up), burst, detonate, fire, fulminate, go off, touch off. 2. To come open or fly apart suddenly and violently, as from internal pressure ► blow (out), burst, pop. *Slang:* bust. 3. To increase or expand suddenly, rapidly, or without control ► balloon, mushroom, snowball. *See also* **increase**. 4. To become manifest suddenly and in full force ► burst (forth *or* out), erupt. *See* **break** (1). 5. To be or become angry ► fume, rage, seethe. *See* **anger** (2). 6. To cause to be no longer believed or valued ► debunk, deflate, puncture. *See* **discredit** (1).

exploit *verb*
1. To put into action or use ► apply, employ, utilize. *See* **use** (1). 2. To treat unfairly or harmfully ► ill-treat, mistreat, wrong. *See* **abuse** (1). 3. To use improperly ► misapply, misapprriate, pervert. *See* **abuse** (2). 4. To

influence or manage shrewdly or deviously ▸ maneuver, play, use. *See* **manipulate** (1). *See synonym note at* **manipulate**.

exploit *noun*
A great deed or attainment ▸ achievement, feat. *See* **accomplishment** (1). *See synonym note at* **accomplishment**.

exploitable *adjective*
▸ dupable, naive, susceptible. *See* **gullible**.

exploration *noun*
The act or an instance of exploring or investigating ▸ investigation, probe, reconnaissance. *See also* **examination**.

explore *verb*
To go into or through for the purpose of making discoveries or acquiring information ▸ delve, dig, fathom, inquire, investigate, look into, plumb, probe, reconnoiter, scout, sound. *See also* **examine, snoop**.

explosion *noun*
1. A violent release of confined energy ▸ burst, detonation. *See* **blast** (2). **2.** A sudden emergence or increase ▸ breakout, flare, outburst. *See* **eruption** (1). **3.** A sudden sharp, explosive noise ▸ bang, pop, snap. *See* **crack** (1). **4.** A sudden violent expression, as of emotion ▸ burst, eruption, flood. *See* **outburst** (1).

exponent *noun*
▸ illustration, sample. *See* **example** (1).

expose *verb*
1. To lay open, as to something undesirable or injurious ▸ subject, leave open. *See also* **endanger**. **2.** To make visible ▸ disclose, uncover. *See* **reveal** (2). **3.** To remove the clothing or covering from ▸ denude, strip, uncover. *See* **bare** (1). **4.** To make a public and usually ostentatious show of ▸ exhibit, flash, flaunt. *See* **display** (1). *See synonym note at* **display**. **5.** To disclose in a breach of confidence ▸ divulge, give away. *Informal:* spill. *See* **betray** (2).

exposé *noun*
▸ disclosure, divulgence, exposure. *See* **revelation**.

exposed *adjective*
1. Not covered ▸ revealed, spread, uncovered. *See* **open** (2). **2.** Marked by cold and unpleasant conditions ▸ grim, severe. *See* **bleak** (1).

exposition *noun*
1. Something that serves to explain or clarify ▸ decipherment, illumination. *See* **explanation** (1). **2.** A large public display, as of goods or works of art ▸ bazaar, show. *See* **exhibition** (1). **3.** Critical explanation or analysis ▸ annotation, exegesis, interpretation. *See* **commentary**. **4.** An act of showing or displaying ▸ exhibition, show. *See* **display** (1).

expository *or* **expositive** *adjective*
1. Serving to explain ▸ illustrative, interpretive. *See* **explanatory**. **2.** Inclined to teach or moralize excessively ▸ academic, moralizing, prescriptive. *See* **didactic** (2).

expostulate *verb*
▸ except, oppose, protest. *See* **object** (1). *See synonym note at* **object**.

expostulation *noun*
▸ exception, grievance, protestation. *See* **objection**.

exposure *noun*
1. The condition of being laid open to something undesirable or injurious ▸ assailability, defenselessness, endangerment, liability, openness, pregnability, susceptibility, susceptibleness, unprotectedness, vulnerability, vulnerableness. **2.** Something disclosed, especially something not previously known or realized ▸ disclosure, divulgence, exposé. *See* **revelation**. **3.** The state of being without clothes ▸ nakedness, undress. *See* **nudity**. **4.** Information disseminated through various media to attract public notice ▸ advertisement, ballyhoo. *Slang:* hype. *See* **publicity** (1).

expound *verb*
▸ construe, decipher, interpret. *See* **explain** (1).

express *verb*
1. To put into words ▸ articulate, state, utter. *See* **say** (1). **2.** To utter publicly ▸ disclose, divulge, voice. *See* **air** (2). *See synonym note at* **air**. **3.** To give expression to, as by gestures, facial aspects, or bodily posture ▸ communicate, convey, display, manifest. *Idioms:* give sign (*or* token), make clear (*or* known *or* plain). *See also* **show**. **4.** To present a lifelike image of ▸ depict, portray, render. *See* **represent** (2). **5.** To convey in language or words of a particular form ▸ couch, formulate. *See* **phrase**. **6.** To extract from by applying pressure ▸ crush, press, squeeze. **7.** To cause something to be conveyed to a destination ▸ consign, dispatch. *See* **send** (1).

express *adjective*
1. Clearly, fully, and emphatically expressed ▸ decided, explicit, precise. *See* **definite** (1). *See synonym note at* **definite**. **2.** Relating to, identifying, or setting apart an individual or group ▸ characteristic, individual, particular. *See* **special** (1). **3.** Characterized by great speed ▸ brisk, fleet, high-speed, rapid. *See* **fast** (1).

expression *noun*
1. The act or an instance of expressing in words ▸ airing, articulation, pronunciation, statement, utterance, ventilation, verbalization, vocalization, voice. *See also* **embodiment, message, wording**. **2.** Something that takes the place of words in communicating a thought or feeling: ▸ gesture, indication, mark, sign, token. *See also* **sign**. **3.** A word or group of words forming a unit and conveying meaning ▸ collocation, idiom, locution, phrase. *See also* **proverb**. **4.** A disposition of the facial features that conveys meaning, feeling, or mood ▸ aspect, cast, countenance, face, lineaments, look, visage. *See also* **appearance, bearing**. **5.** A sound or combination of sounds that symbolizes and communicates a meaning ▸ lexeme, word. *See* **term** (1). **6.** Smooth or effective skill in communicating ▸ articulateness, fluency, rhetoric. *See* **eloquence**. **7.** The act or process of describing in lifelike imagery ▸ depiction, description, portrayal. *See* **representation**.

expressionless *adjective*
Lacking expression ▸ affectless, blank, deadpan, inex-

pressive, pokerfaced. *See also* **dull, reserved, vacant.**

expressive *adjective*
Effectively conveying meaning, feeling, or mood
▸ eloquent, meaning, meaningful, significant. *See also* **eloquent, pregnant.**

✦ CORE SYNONYMS: *expressive, eloquent, meaningful, significant.* These adjectives mean effectively conveying a feeling, idea, or mood: *an expressive gesture; an eloquent speech; a meaningful look; a significant smile.*

---

expressiveness *or* **expressivity** *noun*
▸ articulateness, fluency, volubility. *See* **eloquence.**

expressway *noun*
▸ path, road, route. *See* **way** (2).

expropriate *verb*
▸ commandeer, confiscate, snatch. *See* **seize** (1).

expropriation *noun*
▸ appropriation, preemption, usurpation. *See* **seizure** (2).

expulsion *noun*
1. The act of ejecting or the state of being ejected ▸ eviction, ouster. *See* **ejection. 2.** The act of dismissing or the condition of being dismissed from employment ▸ dismissal, termination. *See* **dismissal** (1).

expunction *noun*
▸ deletion, effacement. *See* **erasure.**

expunge *verb*
1. To cross out or remove ▸ delete, erase, strike (out). *See* **cancel** (1). *See synonym note at* **cancel. 2.** To destroy all traces of ▸ eradicate, liquidate, obliterate. *See* **annihilate** (1).

expurgate *verb*
▸ bowdlerize, edit, sanitize. *See* **censor** (1).

exquisite *adjective*
1. Appealing to refined taste ▸ elegant, gentle. *See* **delicate** (1). *See synonym note at* **delicate. 2.** Exhibiting refined, tasteful beauty of manner, form, or style ▸ graceful, refined. *See* **elegant** (1). **3.** Having qualities that delight the eye ▸ comely, gorgeous, stunning. *See* **beautiful. 4.** Beyond what is usual, normal, or customary ▸ extraordinary, outstanding, remarkable. *See* **exceptional** (1).

exsiccate *verb*
▸ dehydrate, desiccate, parch. *See* **dry** (1).

extant *adjective*
1. Occurring or existing in act or fact ▸ actual, existent, real, true. *See also* **physical. 2.** Having life ▸ live, living, vital. *See* **alive** (1).

extemporaneous *or* **extemporary** *or* **extempore** *adjective*
Spoken, performed, or composed with little or no preparation or forethought ▸ ad-lib, extemporary, extempore, impromptu, improvised, offhand, snap, spur-of-the-moment, unrehearsed. *Informal:* off-the-cuff. *See also* **spontaneous.**

✦ CORE SYNONYMS: *extemporaneous, extemporary, extempore, impromptu, offhand, unrehearsed, ad-lib.* These adjectives mean spoken, performed, done, or composed with little or no preparation or forethought. *Extemporaneous, extemporary,* and *extempore* most often apply to discourse that is delivered without the assistance of a written text, though it may have been planned in advance: *an extemporaneous address; an extemporary lecture; an extempore skit. Impromptu* even more strongly suggests happening on the spur of the moment: *an impromptu dinner. Offhand* implies not only spontaneity but also a casual or even cavalier manner: *an offhand remark.* What is *unrehearsed* is said or done without rehearsal or practice though not necessarily without forethought: *a few unrehearsed comments.* Something that is *ad-lib* is spontaneous and improvised and therefore not part of a prepared script or score: *an ad-lib joke.*

---

extemporization *noun*
Something improvised ▸ ad-lib, impromptu, improvisation. *See also* **makeshift.**

extemporize *verb*
▸ fake, make up. *See* **improvise** (1).

extend *verb*
1. To proceed on a certain course or for a certain distance ▸ carry, continue, go, reach, run, stretch. **2.** To move or arrange so as to cover a larger area ▸ expand, stretch. *See* **spread** (1). **3.** To make or become longer ▸ elongate, prolongate. *See* **lengthen. 4.** To make or become broader or more comprehensive ▸ amplify, expand, widen. *See* **broaden. 5.** To change or fluctuate within limits ▸ range, vary. *See* **go** (7). **6.** To make or become greater or larger ▸ amplify, boost, enlarge. *See* **increase** (1). *See synonym note at* **increase. 7.** To put before another for acceptance ▸ advance, proffer. *See* **offer** (1). **8.** To put forward, especially an appendage ▸ outstretch, reach, stretch (out).

extended *adjective*
1. Having great physical length ▸ elongated, lengthy, prolonged. *See* **long**[1] (1). **2.** Covering a wide scope ▸ all-inclusive, broad, expansive. *See* **general** (2). **3.** Of large extent or expanse ▸ extensive, spacious. *See* **broad** (1).

extensible *or* **extendible** *or* **extensile** *adjective*
Capable of being extended or expanded ▸ expandable, expansible, expansile, protractile, stretch, stretchable, stretchy. *See also* **malleable.**

extension *noun*
1. The act of making something longer or the condition of being made longer ▸ drawing out, elongation, lengthening, prolongation, protraction, spinning out, stretching, stringing out. **2.** The process of increasing in extent or inclusiveness ▸ enlargement, spread. *See* **expansion. 3.** An area or set of parameters within which something or someone exists, acts, or has influence ▸ ambit, realm, scope. *See* **range** (1). **4.** A part added to a main structure ▸ addition, add-on, annex, arm, wing. **5.** Something resembling or analogous to a tree branch ▸ arm, fork, offshoot. *See* **branch** (1). **6.** The measure of how far or long something goes in space, time, or degree ▸ coverage, span, stretch. *See* **extent** (1). **7.** The act of increasing or

rising ▸ amplification, boost, escalation. *See* **increase** (1).

extensive *adjective*

1. Of large extent or expanse ▸ spacious, wide. *See* **broad** (1). 2. Above average in amount, size, or scope ▸ considerable, large, sizable. *See* **big** (1). *See synonym note at* **big**. 3. Covering a wide scope ▸ all-inclusive, broad, expansive. *See* **general** (2).

extensively *adverb*

▸ much, quite, well. *See* **considerably**.

extent *noun*

1. The measure of how far or long something goes in space, time, or degree ▸ coverage, extension, length, reach, span, stretch. *See also* **depth, width**. 2. An area or set of parameters within which something or someone exists, acts, or has influence ▸ compass, realm, scope. *See* **range** (1). 3. The amount of space occupied by something ▸ area, magnitude, proportions. *See* **size** (1). 4. Relative intensity or amount, as of a quality or attribute ▸ level, magnitude, scope. *See* **degree** (2). 5. A wide and open area, as of land, sky, or water ▸ distance, stretch, sweep. *See* **expanse** (1).

extenuate *verb*

To conceal or make light of a fault or offense ▸ explain away, gloss over, gloze (over), palliate, sleek over, whitewash. *See also* **belittle, soft-pedal**.

✦ **CORE SYNONYMS:** *extenuate, gloss, gloze, palliate, whitewash.* These verbs mean to cause a fault or offense to seem less grave or less reprehensible: *couldn't extenuate the malfeasance; glossing over an unethical transaction; glozing sins and iniquities; palliate a crime; whitewashed official complicity in political extortion.*

---

exteriorization *noun*

▸ incarnation, manifestation, personification. *See* **embodiment** (1).

exteriorize *verb*

▸ externalize, manifest, materialize. *See* **embody** (1).

exterminate *verb*

▸ eradicate, liquidate, obliterate. *See* **annihilate** (1). *See synonym note at* **annihilate**.

extermination *noun*

▸ extinction, liquidation, obliteration. *See* **annihilation** (1).

external *adjective*

▸ ostensible, seeming. *See* **apparent** (2).

externalization *noun*

▸ incarnation, manifestation, personification. *See* **embodiment** (1).

externalize *verb*

▸ allegorize, manifest, materialize. *See* **embody** (1).

externally *adverb*

▸ evidently, seemingly. *See* **apparently**.

extinct *adjective*

▸ defunct, late, perished. *See* **dead** (1). *See synonym note at* **dead**.

extinction *noun*

1. Utter destruction ▸ eradication, extermination,

obliteration. *See* **annihilation** (1). 2. The act or fact of dying ▸ demise, passing. *See* **death** (1).

extinguish *verb*

1. To cause to stop burning or giving light ▸ damp, douse, put out, quench, smother, snuff out. *See also* **choke**. 2. To destroy all traces of ▸ eradicate, liquidate, obliterate. *See* **annihilate** (1). *See synonym note at* **annihilate**. 3. To overcome opposition or uprising with overwhelming force ▸ crush, put down, quell. *See* **suppress** (1). 4. To put an end to ▸ annul, invalidate, void. *See* **abolish** (1).

extinguishment *noun*

▸ extinction, liquidation, obliteration. *See* **annihilation** (1).

extirpate *verb*

▸ eradicate, liquidate, obliterate. *See* **annihilate** (1). *See synonym note at* **annihilate**.

extirpation *noun*

▸ extinction, liquidation, obliteration. *See* **annihilation** (1).

extol *verb*

1. To pay tribute or homage to ▸ celebrate, exalt. *See* **honor** (1). 2. To express warm approval of ▸ applaud, commend. *See* **praise** (1). *See synonym note at* **praise**. 3. To honor a deity in religious worship ▸ exalt, laud. *See* **praise** (3).

extolment *noun*

▸ exaltation, magnification. *See* **praise** (2).

extort *verb*

To obtain by coercion or intimidation ▸ blackmail, exact, graft, squeeze, wrench, wrest, wring. *Slang:* shake down.

extortionate *adjective*

▸ exorbitant, overpriced, stiff. *See* **steep**[1] (2).

extra *adjective*

1. Being more than is needed, desired, or appropriate ▸ excess, surplus. *See* **superfluous**. *See synonym note at* **superfluous**. 2. Being an addition ▸ added, more, new. *See* **additional**. 3. Being what remains, especially after a part has been removed ▸ leftover, remaining, stray. *Idiom:* left behind. *See also* **superfluous**.

extra *adverb*

To a high degree ▸ exceedingly, highly. *See* **very**.

extra *noun*

1. A thing, amount, or quantity beyond what is needed, desired, or appropriate ▸ overflow, oversupply, superfluity. *See* **surplus**. 2. Something added to another for embellishment or completion ▸ add-on, complement, supplement. *See* **enhancement** (1).

extract *verb*

1. To remove from a fixed position ▸ pluck, rend, wrest. *See* **pull** (2). 2. To collect something bit by bit ▸ garner, gather. *See* **glean** (1). 3. To obtain from another source ▸ draw, gain, receive. *See* **derive** (1).

extraction *noun*

▸ blood, descent, lineage. *See* **ancestry**.

extradite *verb*

▸ deport, expel. *See* **banish** (1). *See synonym note at* **banish**.

extradition *noun*
▶ deportation, proscription. *See* **exile** (1).

extramundane *adjective*
▶ metaphysical, superhuman. *See* **supernatural** (1).

extraneous *adjective*
1. Not part of the essential nature of a thing ▶ alien, foreign, extrinsic. *See also* **irrelevant. 2.** Not relevant or pertinent to the subject; not applicable ▶ immaterial, inapplicable, unconnected. *See* **irrelevant.** *See synonym note at* **irrelevant.**

extraordinarily *adverb*
▶ singularly, uncommonly, uniquely. *See* **unusually.**

extraordinary *adjective*
▶ outstanding, remarkable, uncommon. *See* **exceptional** (1).

extrasensory *adjective*
▶ metaphysical, superhuman. *See* **supernatural** (1).

extravagance *or* **extravagancy** *noun*
1. Excessive or imprudent expenditure ▶ extravagancy, lavishness, overgenerosity, prodigality, profligacy, profusion, profuseness, squander, waste, wastefulness. **2.** A condition of going or being beyond what is needed, desired, or appropriate ▶ exorbitance, inordinacy, surfeit. *See* **excess** (1). **3.** Something costly and unnecessary ▶ extravagancy, frill, indulgence. *See* **luxury** (1). *See synonym note at* **luxury.**

extravagant *adjective*
1. Characterized by excessive or imprudent spending ▶ dissipative, improvident, lavish, prodigal, profligate, profuse, spendthrift, thriftless, uneconomical, unthrifty, wasteful. *Idiom:* penny wise and pound foolish. *See also* **careless, negligent. 2.** Exceeding a normal or reasonable limit ▶ exorbitant, immoderate. *See* **excessive** (1). *See synonym note at* **excessive. 3.** Given to or marked by unrestrained abundance ▶ exuberant, lavish, opulent. *See* **profuse** (1).

extravagantly *adverb*
▶ excessively, extremely, overly. *See* **unduly.**

extravagantness *noun*
▶ exorbitance, extravagance, surfeit. *See* **excess** (1).

extraverted *adjective*
▶ extroverted, gregarious. *See* **outgoing.**

extreme *adjective*
1. Most distant or remote, as from a center ▶ farthermost, farthest, furthermost, furthest, outermost, outmost, ultimate, utmost, uttermost. *See also* **last. 2.** Greatest in quantity or highest in degree that can be attained ▶ top, ultimate, utmost. *See* **maximum. 3.** Exceeding a normal or reasonable limit ▶ extravagant, immoderate. *See* **excessive** (1). *See synonym note at* **excessive. 4.** Holding especially political views that deviate drastically from prevailing beliefs ▶ extremist, fanatic, fanatical, fire-breathing, fire-eating, fundamentalist, hard-line, lunatic, militant, rabid, radical, raving, revolutionary, ultra, wild-eyed, zealous. *Slang:* far-out. *See also* **enthusiastic, rebellious, ultraconservative, ultraliberal.**

extreme *noun*
1. The ultimate point to which an action, thought,

discussion, or policy is carried ▶ end, extremity, limit. *See* **length** (3). **2.** Either of the two points at the ends of a spectrum or range ▶ extremity, limit. *See also* **climax, low.**

extremely *adverb*
1. To a high degree ▶ exceedingly, exceptionally, highly. *See* **very. 2.** Too much ▶ excessively, overly, inordinately. *See* **unduly.**

extremist *noun*
One who holds extreme views or advocates extreme measures ▶ fanatic, fire-breather, fire-eater, fundamentalist, hard-liner, militant, radical, revolutionary, revolutionist, ultra, ultraist, zealot. *See also* **ultraconservative, ultraliberal.**

extremist *adjective*
Holding especially political views that deviate drastically from prevailing beliefs ▶ fanatical, radical, revolutionary. *See* **extreme** (4).

extremity *noun*
1. Either of the two points at the ends of a spectrum or range ▶ extreme, limit. *See also* **climax, low. 2.** A situation requiring immediate assistance ▶ crisis, distress, trouble. *See* **emergency. 3.** The ultimate point to which an action, thought, discussion, or policy is carried ▶ end, extreme, limit. *See* **length** (3).

extricate *verb*
To free from an entanglement ▶ clear, disengage, disentangle, disinvolve, free, release, untangle. *See also* **undo.**

✦ CORE SYNONYMS: *extricate, disengage, disentangle, untangle.* These verbs mean to free from an entanglement: *extricated herself from an embarrassing situation; trying to disengage his attention from the television; disentangled the oar from the water lilies; a trapped animal that untangled itself from a net.*

extrinsic *adjective*
1. Not part of the essential nature of a thing ▶ alien, extraneous, foreign. **2.** Not relevant or pertinent to the subject; not applicable ▶ immaterial, inapplicable, unconnected. *See* **irrelevant.**

extroverted *adjective*
▶ communicable, gregarious, sociable, talkative. *See* **outgoing.**

exuberant *adjective*
1. Very brisk, alert, and full of high spirits ▶ animated, chipper, vivacious. *See* **lively** (1). **2.** Given to or marked by unrestrained abundance ▶ extravagant, lavish, opulent. *See* **profuse** (1). *See synonym note at* **profuse. 3.** Showing or having enthusiasm ▶ fervent, rabid, zealous. *See* **enthusiastic** (1).

exude *verb*
▶ leach, seep. *See* **ooze.**

exult *verb*
1. To feel or express an uplifting joy over a success or victory ▶ crow, gloat, glory, jubilate, triumph. *Slang:* high-five. *See also* **boast, celebrate, rejoice. 2.** To feel or take joy or pleasure ▶ delight, pleasure, rejoice. *See also* **enjoy, luxuriate.**

exultant *adjective*
Feeling or expressing an uplifting joy over a success or victory ▸ gloating, jubilant, triumphant. *See also* **boastful.**

exultation *noun*
The act or condition of feeling an uplifting joy over a success or victory ▸ crowing, exultance, exultancy, gloating, jubilance, jubilation, triumph.

exuviate *verb*
▸ molt, slough, throw off. *See* **shed**[1] (2).

eye *noun*
1. An organ of vision ▸ eyeball, orb. *Slang:* peeper, saucer. *Idiom:* window of the soul. **2.** The faculty of seeing ▸ eyesight, optics, sight. *See* **vision** (1). **3.** Skill in perceiving, discriminating, or judging ▸ keenness, perceptiveness, shrewdness. *See* **discernment** (1). **4.** The position from which something is observed or considered ▸ aspect, point of view, standpoint. *See* **viewpoint. 5.** A length of line folded over and joined at the ends so as to form a curve or circle ▸ circuit, noose, ring. *See* **loop** (1). **6.** The most intensely active central part ▸ midst, thick. *See also* **center. 7.** *Informal* A person whose work is investigating crimes or obtaining hidden evidence or information ▸ investigator, sleuth. *Slang:* gumshoe. *See* **detective.**

eye *verb*
1. To direct the eyes on an object ▸ consider, view. *See* **look** (1). **2.** To look intently and fixedly ▸ gape, gawk, stare. *See* **gaze. 3.** To look at or on attentively or carefully ▸ observe, regard, survey. *See* **watch** (1).

eyeball *noun*
An organ of vision ▸ eye, orb. *Slang:* peeper, saucer. *Idiom:* window of the soul.

eye-catching *adjective*
▸ conspicuous, prominent. *See* **noticeable** (1).

eyeless *adjective*
▸ sightless, unseeing. *See* **blind** (1).

eyelet *noun*
1. An open space allowing passage ▸ orifice, vent. *See* **hole** (2). **2.** A length of line folded over and joined at the ends so as to form a curve or circle ▸ circuit, noose, ring. *See* **loop** (1).

eye opener *noun*
Informal Something disclosed, especially something not previously known or realized ▸ disclosure, exposé, exposure. *See* **revelation.**

eyesight *noun*
The faculty of seeing ▸ eye, optics, sight. *See* **vision** (1).

eyes-only *adjective*
▸ unmentionable, unutterable. *See* **unspeakable** (2).

eyesore *noun*
▸ monstrosity, ugliness. *See* **mess** (2).

eyewitness *noun*
Someone who sees something occur ▸ audience, seer, viewer, witness.

f

fable *noun*
1. A narrative not based on fact ▸ fiction, novel, romance, story. **2.** An entertaining and often oral account of a real or fictitious occurrence ▸ anecdote, story, tale. *See* **yarn. 3.** A traditional story or tale that has no proven factual basis ▸ legend, parable. *See* **myth** (1). **4.** An untrue declaration ▸ falsehood, fib, untruth. *See* **lie**[2].

fabled *adjective*
▸ fantasy, legendary. *See* **mythical.**

fabric *noun*
▸ fiber, grain, web. *See* **texture** (1).

fabricate *verb*
1. To use ingenuity in making, developing, or achieving ▸ contrive, devise, dream up. *See* **invent** (1). **2.** To create by forming, combining, or altering materials ▸ build, compose, shape. *See* **make** (1). **3.** To take on as a false appearance ▸ assume, fake, feign, put on. *See* **act** (2). **4.** To make a fraudulent copy of ▸ falsify, forge. *See* **counterfeit** (1).

fabricated *adjective*
▸ fantasy, legendary. *See* **mythical.**

fabrication *noun*
1. An untrue declaration ▸ falsehood, fib, untruth. *See* **lie**[2]. **2.** A fraudulent imitation ▸ forgery, sham. *See* **counterfeit. 3.** A fiction or half-truth, especially one that forms part of an ideology ▸ fantasy, fiction, invention. *See* **myth** (3).

fabricator *noun*
1. One who makes a fraudulent copy of something ▸ counterfeiter, faker, falsifier, forger. **2.** One who tells lies ▸ fabulist, fibber, prevaricator. *See* **liar.**

fabulist *noun*
▸ fabricator, fibber, prevaricator. *See* **liar.**

fabulous *adjective*
1. So remarkable as to be difficult to believe ▸ astounding, staggering, unbelievable. *See* **astonishing. 2.** Particularly excellent ▸ fantastic, glorious, spectacular. *See* **marvelous** (1). **3.** Having the nature of a fable; not real ▸ fantasy, legendary. *See* **mythical.**

façade *noun*
1. The forward outer surface of a building ▸ face, front, frontage, frontispiece, frontal. **2.** A deceptive outward appearance ▸ charade, cover, disguise, face,

false colors, front, gloss, guise, make-believe, mask, masquerade, pose, pretense, pretext, semblance, show, veneer, window-dressing. *Slang:* put-on. *See also* **affectation, act, veil.**

face *noun*

1. The front surface of the head ▶ countenance, features, lineaments, muzzle, physiognomy, visage. *Informal:* mug. *Slang:* kisser, map, pan, puss. 2. A disposition of the facial features that conveys meaning, feeling, or mood ▶ countenance, look, visage. *See* **expression** (4). 3. A contorted facial expression showing pain, contempt, or disgust ▶ grimace, moue, pout. *Informal:* mug. *See also* **frown, glare, sneer.** 4. An outward appearance ▶ aspect, countenance, features, lineaments, look, surface. 5. A deceptive outward appearance ▶ guise, mask, pretense. *See* **façade** (2). 6. The forward outer surface of a building ▶ front, frontage, frontal. *See* **façade** (1). 7. An outer surface, layer, or part of an object ▶ facet, side, surface. *See also* **back, bottom, front.** 8. The marked outer surface of an instrument ▶ dial, gauge, indicator. *See also* **front.** 9. Credit or respect in the eyes of others ▶ prestige, standing, status. *See also* **honor, pride, reputation.** 10. The state or quality of being impudent or arrogantly self-confident ▶ audacity, boldness, impertinence. *See* **impudence.**

face *verb*

1. To have the face or front turned toward ▶ front, give onto, look (on *or* upon *or* toward). *See also* **overlook.** 2. To cover with a different material ▶ clad, cover, sheathe, side, surface, veneer. *See also* **gloss¹, finish.** 3. To confront boldly and courageously ▶ challenge, confront, dare. *See* **defy** (1). *See synonym note at* **defy.** 4. To meet face-to-face, especially defiantly ▶ confront, encounter, front, meet. *Idiom:* stand up to. *See also* **contest.**

face-lift *or* **face-lifting** *noun*

▶ refurbishment, rejuvenation, renovation. *See* **renewal** (1).

face-off *noun*

▶ duel, encounter, meeting, showdown. *See* **confrontation** (1).

facet *noun*

1. An outer surface, layer, or part of an object ▶ face, side, surface. *See also* **back, bottom, front.** 2. The position from which something is observed or considered ▶ aspect, point of view, standpoint. *See* **viewpoint.**

facetious *adjective*

▶ comical, humorous, laughable. *See* **funny** (1).

facile *adjective*

1. Posing no difficulty ▶ effortless, simple. *See* **easy** (1). *See synonym note at* **easy.** 2. Marked by ease and fluency of speech that is often insincere or superficial ▶ slick, smooth-tongued. *See* **glib.** 3. Exhibiting or possessing skill and ease in performance ▶ agile, deft, nimble. *See* **dexterous.**

facileness *noun*

▶ effortlessness, facility, readiness. *See* **ease** (2).

facilitate *verb*

1. To make less difficult ▶ expedite, help along. *See* **ease** (2). 2. To help bring about ▶ cultivate, encourage. *See* **promote** (2).

facilitator *noun*

▶ intermediary, mediator, middleman. *See* **go-between.**

facilities *noun*

▶ conveniences, resources, services. *See* **amenities** (1). *See synonym note at* **amenities.**

facility *noun*

1. The ability to perform without apparent effort ▶ effortlessness, readiness. *See* **ease** (2). 2. Smooth or effective skill in communicating ▶ articulateness, fluency, volubility. *See* **eloquence.** 3. Skillfulness in the use of the hands or body ▶ deftness, prowess. *See* **dexterity** (1).

facsimile *noun*

▶ ditto, duplicate, likeness. *See* **copy** (1).

fact *noun*

1. Something demonstrated to exist or known to have existed ▶ actuality, event, phenomenon, reality. *Idioms:* hard (*or* cold *or* plain) fact. *See also* **information.** 2. The quality of being actual or factual ▶ sure thing, truth. *See* **certainty** (1). 3. One of the conditions or facts attending an event and having some bearing on it ▶ factor, particular. *See* **circumstance** (2).

faction *noun*

1. An association for a common cause or interest ▶ bloc, coalition, organization. *See* **alliance** (1). 2. A state of disagreement and disharmony ▶ clash, difference, discord. *See* **conflict** (1).

factitious *adjective*

▶ fake, fraudulent, phony. *See* **counterfeit.**

factor *noun*

1. A separate unit that belongs or contributes to a whole ▶ building block, piece, section. *See* **part** (1). *See synonym note at* **part.** 2. One of the conditions or facts attending an event and having some bearing on it ▶ condition, particular. *See* **circumstance** (2). 3. One who represents the interests of another ▶ ambassador, deputy, proxy. *See* **representative** (2).

factory *noun*

A building or complex in which an industry is located ▶ mill, plant, works.

facts *noun*

▶ data, knowledge. *See* **information** (1).

factual *adjective*

1. Conforming exactly to fact ▶ correct, exact, precise. *See* **accurate** (1). 2. Accurately representing what is depicted or described ▶ life-like, naturalistic. *See* **realistic** (2).

facultative *adjective*

▶ elective, permissible. *See* **optional.**

faculty *noun*

1. An innate capability ▶ aptitude, gift, knack. *See* **talent.** 2. Physical, mental, financial, or legal power to perform ▶ capability, capacity, competency. *See* **ability** (2).

fad *noun*

1. The current custom ▸ craze, mode, vogue. *See* **fashion** (1). **2.** A subject or activity that inspires lively interest ▸ mania, passion. *See* **enthusiasm** (2).

fade *verb*

1. To lose strength or power ▸ decline, degenerate, fail, flag, languish, sink, wane, waste away, weaken. *Informal:* fizzle (out), peter out. *See also* **decrease, deteriorate, subside, tire. 2.** To grow weaker in sound ▸ die, die away, quiet down. *See* **fade away** (1). **3.** To lose normal coloration ▸ blanch, bleach, etiolate. *See* **pale. 4.** To pass out of sight either gradually or suddenly ▸ dissolve, ebb. *See* **disappear** (1). *See synonym note at* **disappear.**

fade away *verb*

1. To grow weaker in sound ▸ die (away *or* out *or* down), fade (out), quiet (down). *See also* **silence. 2.** To disappear by or as if by rising ▸ dissipate, scatter, thin out. *See* **lift** (4).

fade out *verb*

1. To pass out of sight either gradually or suddenly ▸ dissolve, ebb. *See* **disappear** (1). **2.** To grow weaker in sound ▸ die (away *or* out *or* down), fade (away), quiet (down). *See also* **silence.**

faded *adjective*

1. Showing signs of wear and tear or neglect ▸ broken-down, dilapidated, tattered. *See* **shabby. 2.** Lacking color ▸ colorless, wan, washed out. *See* **pale** (1).

fade-out *noun*

▸ dissipation, expiration, vanishment. *See* **disappearance.**

fail *verb*

1. To go wrong or be unsuccessful ▸ choke, fall through, founder, go amiss, go astray, go awry, go wrong, miscarry, misfire, miss, strike out, wash out. *Informal:* fall down, flop, flunk. *Slang:* bomb. *Idioms:* come a cropper, fall flat, fall short, lay an egg, miss fire, miss the mark. **2.** To prove deficient or insufficient ▸ give out, run out. *Idioms:* fall short, run dry, run short. *See also* **decrease. 3.** To cause unhappiness by failing to satisfy the hopes, desires, or expectations of ▸ disgruntle, dissatisfy. *See* **disappoint. 4.** To fail to do or carry out ▸ forget, omit. *See* **neglect** (3). **5.** To lose strength or power ▸ decline, deteriorate, weaken. *See* **fade** (1). **6.** To stop working properly ▸ break down, give out. *Slang:* conk out. *See* **malfunction. 7.** To undergo sudden financial failure ▸ crash, go under. *See* **collapse** (2).

failing *noun*

1. An imperfection of character ▸ fault, shortcoming, weak point. *See* **weakness** (1). **2.** Something that mars the appearance or causes inadequacy or failure ▸ fault, flaw, imperfection. *See* **defect** (1).

fail-safe *adjective*

▸ foolproof, infallible, unerring. *See* **sure** (2).

failure *noun*

1. A person or enterprise that is unsuccessful ▸ bust, fiasco, loser, miscarriage, nonperformer, washout. *Informal:* clinker, clunker, dud, flop, lead balloon.

Slang: bomb, turkey. *See also* **collapse. 2.** Nonperformance of what ought to be done ▸ default, delinquency, dereliction, neglect, nonfeasance, omission, shirking. *See also* **negligence. 3.** A cessation of proper functioning ▸ breakdown, collapse, malfunction, outage. **4.** A marked loss of strength or effectiveness ▸ declination, decline, deterioration. **5.** The condition of being financially insolvent ▸ insolvency, ruin, ruination. *See* **bankruptcy.**

fainéant *adjective*

Resistant to exertion and activity ▸ indolent, shiftless, sluggish. *See* **lazy.** *See synonym note at* **lazy.**

fainéant *noun*

A self-indulgent person who spends time avoiding work or other useful activity ▸ bum, idler, loafer. *See* **wastrel** (2).

faint *adjective*

1. So soft as to be barely audible ▸ feeble, weak. *See also* **soft. 2.** Free from severity or violence, as in sound or movement ▸ delicate, mild, soft. *See* **gentle** (2). **3.** Of small intensity ▸ gentle, moderate, soft. *See* **light**² (2). **4.** Small in degree, especially of probability ▸ negligible, slight, slim. *See* **remote** (2). **5.** Not clearly perceptible ▸ dim, foggy, indefinite. *See* **unclear** (1). **6.** Being weak in quality or substance ▸ bloodless, pallid. *See* **pale** (2). **7.** Not physically strong ▸ feeble, frail, unsound. *See* **weak** (1).

faint *noun*

A temporary loss of consciousness ▸ blackout, fainting spell, swoon, syncope.

faint *verb*

To suffer temporary lack of consciousness ▸ black out, keel over, pass out, swoon. *Idioms:* drop (*or* faint *or* fall) dead away, see stars. *See also* **collapse.**

✦ **CORE SYNONYMS:** *faint, blackout, swoon, syncope.* These nouns denote a temporary loss of consciousness: *fell in a dead faint at the sight of the body; suffers blackouts at high altitudes; sank to the ground in a swoon; was taken to the clinic in a state of syncope.*

faint-hearted *adjective*

▸ chickenhearted, pusillanimous. *Slang:* gutless. *See* **cowardly.**

faint-heartedness *noun*

▸ chickenheartedness, pusillanimity. *Slang:* gutlessness. *See* **cowardice.**

fair¹ *adjective*

1. Free from bias in judgment ▸ balanced, detached, disinterested, dispassionate, equal, equitable, even, evenhanded, fair-minded, impartial, indifferent, just, nondiscriminatory, nonpartisan, objective, square, unbiased, unprejudiced. *Idioms:* fair and square, on the level. *See also* **broad-minded, honest, neutral. 2.** Free from clouds or mist ▸ cloudless, fine. *See* **clear** (2). **3.** Indicative of future success or full of promise ▸ bright, fortunate, propitious. *See* **favorable** (1). **4.** According to the rules ▸ clean, sporting, sportsmanly. *See* **sportsmanlike. 5.** Adequate to satisfy a need, requirement, or standard ▸ average, decent, moderate, reasonable. *See* **acceptable** (2). **6.** Relating to or occupying a middle position on a scale of evaluation ▸ mediocre, indifferent, tolerable. *See* **average** (1). *See synonym note at* **average. 7.** Having qualities that delight the eye ▸ comely, gorgeous, stunning. *See* **beautiful.** *See synonym note at* **beautiful. 8.** Having light hair ▸ blond, fair-haired, flaxen-haired, golden-haired, light-haired, towheaded. **9.** Having a light color or complexion ▸ alabaster, ivory, light, milky, pale.

fair *adverb*
1. In a fair, sporting manner ▸ cleanly, correctly, fairly, properly, sportingly. **2.** With precision or absolute conformity ▸ exactly, precisely, squarely. *See* **directly** (3).

✦ CORE SYNONYMS: *fair, just, equitable, impartial, unprejudiced, unbiased, objective, dispassionate.* These adjectives mean free from favoritism, self-interest, or preference in judgment. *Fair* is the most general: *a fair referee; a fair deal. Just* stresses conformity with what is legally or ethically right or proper: *"a just and lasting peace"* (Abraham Lincoln). *Equitable* implies justice dictated by reason, conscience, and a natural sense of what is fair: *an equitable distribution of gifts among the children. Impartial* emphasizes lack of favoritism: *"the cold neutrality of an impartial judge"* (Edmund Burke). *Unprejudiced* means without preconceived opinions or judgments: *an unprejudiced evaluation of the proposal. Unbiased* implies absence of a preference or partiality: *gave an unbiased account of her family problems. Objective* implies detachment that permits impersonal observation and judgment: *an objective jury. Dispassionate* means free from or unaffected by strong emotions: *a dispassionate reporter.*

fair² *noun*
A large public display, as of goods or works of art ▸ exposition, show. *See* **exhibition** (1).

fair-haired *adjective*
1. Having light hair ▸ blond, towheaded. *See* **fair¹** (8). **2.** Being favorite ▸ darling, favored, pet. *See* **favorite.**

fairish *adjective*
▸ average, decent, moderate. *See* **acceptable** (2).

fairly *adverb*
1. In a just or equitable manner ▸ dispassionately, equitably, evenhandedly, impartially, indifferently, justly, objectively, squarely. **2.** To some extent ▸ pretty, quite, rather. *Idioms:* in part, kind of, more or less, sort of, to a (*or* some) degree. *See also* **approximately, considerably, usually. 3.** In a fair, sporting manner ▸ cleanly, correctly. *See* **fair¹** (1). **4.** In truth ▸ genuinely, indeed, truly. *See* **really.**

fair-minded *adjective*
▸ impartial, just, nonpartisan. *See* **fair¹** (1).

fairness *or* **fair-mindedness** *noun*
The quality or state of being just and unbiased ▸ detachment, disinterest, disinterestedness, dispassion, dispassionateness, equitableness, evenhandedness, impartiality, impartialness, justice, justness, non-

partisanship, objectiveness, objectivity. *See also* **honesty.**

fair-weather *adjective*
▸ irresponsible, untrustworthy. *See* **undependable** (1).

fairy *noun*
A creature or spirit that has supernatural powers ▸ brownie, dryad, elf, goblin, hobgoblin, jinni, kelpie, leprechaun, naiad, nymph, pixie, pooka, puck, selkie, sprite, sylph.

fairy godmother *noun*
▸ benefactor, contributor, patron. *See* **donor.**

fairy tale *noun*
A traditional story or tale that has no proven factual basis ▸ folk tale, legend, parable. *See* **myth** (1).

fairy-tale *adjective*
Having the nature of a fable; not real ▸ fantasy, make-believe. *See* **mythical.**

faith *noun*
1. Mental acceptance of the actuality of something ▸ belief, credence, credit. **2.** Absolute certainty that a person or thing will not fail ▸ confidence, reliance. *See* **trust** (1). *See synonym note at* **trust. 3.** A system of religious belief ▸ creed, denomination. *See* **religion. 4.** A state of often extreme religious ardor ▸ piety, piousness. *See* **devotion** (1).

faithful *adjective*
1. Adhering firmly to a person, cause, duty, or faith ▸ allegiant, committed, constant, dedicated, devoted, fast, firm, liege, loyal, staunch, steadfast, true, true-blue. *See also* **dependable, firm¹. 2.** Worthy of belief, as because of precision or faithfulness to an original ▸ authoritative, true, valid. *See* **authentic** (2). **3.** Consistent with accuracy or completeness ▸ exact, strict. *See* **close** (2). **4.** Conforming exactly to fact ▸ correct, factual, precise. *See* **accurate** (1). **5.** In the service or worship of God or a god ▸ devoted, religious, sacred. *See* **divine** (2).

faithful *noun*
The steadfast believers in a faith or cause ▸ adherents, congregation, fold. *See also* **follower, assembly.**

✦ CORE SYNONYMS: *faithful, loyal, true, constant, fast, steadfast, staunch.* These adjectives mean adhering firmly and devotedly to someone or something that elicits or demands one's fidelity. *Faithful* and *loyal* both suggest undeviating attachment, though *loyal* applies more often to political allegiance: *a faithful employee; a loyal citizen. True* implies steadiness, sincerity, and reliability: *"I would be true, for there are those who trust me"* (Howard Arnold Walter). *Constant* stresses uniformity and invariability: *"But I am constant as the northern star"* (William Shakespeare). *Fast* suggests loyalty that is not easily deflected: *fast friends. Steadfast* strongly implies fixed, unswerving loyalty: *a steadfast ally. Staunch* even more strongly suggests unshakable attachment or allegiance: *"He lived and died a staunch loyalist"* (Harriet Beecher Stowe).

faithfully *adverb*
▸ literally, precisely. *See* **exactly** (1).

faithfulness *noun*
1. Faithfulness or devotion to a person, cause, or obligation ▶ allegiance, loyalty, steadfastness. *See* **fidelity** (1). 2. Correspondence with fact or truth ▶ authenticity, correctness, truth, validity. *See* **veracity.**

faithless *adjective*
1. Not true to duty or obligation ▶ disloyal, false, false-hearted, perfidious, recreant, traitorous, treacherous, unfaithful, untrue. *See also* **undependable.** 2. Not believing in God ▶ godless, irreligious. *See* **atheistic.**

✦ CORE SYNONYMS: *faithless, unfaithful, false, disloyal, traitorous, treacherous, perfidious.* These adjectives mean not true to duty or obligation. *Faithless* and *unfaithful* imply failure to adhere to promises, obligations, or allegiances: *was faithless to her ideals; an unfaithful spouse. False* emphasizes deceitfulness: *"To thine own self be true,/And it must follow, as the night the day,/Thou canst not then be false to any man"* (William Shakespeare). One who is *disloyal* betrays an allegiance: *disloyal staff members who exposed the senator's indiscretions. Traitorous* most commonly refers to disloyalty to a government or nation: *a traitorous double agent. Treacherous* suggests a propensity for betraying trust or faith: *"She gave the treacherous impulse time to subside"* (Henry James). *Perfidious* suggests vileness of behavior and often deceitfulness: *a perfidious assassin.*

---

faithlessness *noun*
1. Betrayal, especially of a duty or obligation ▶ betrayal, disloyalty, false-heartedness, falseness, falsity, foul play, infidelity, perfidiousness, perfidy, traitorousness, treacherousness, treachery, treason, unfaithfulness. *See also* **deceit.** 2. Lack of belief in God ▶ impiety, unbelief. *See* **atheism.**

fake
fake *noun*
1. A person who practices deceit, especially under an assumed identity ▶ charlatan, faker, fraud, humbug, impostor, mountebank, phony, pretender, quack, sham. *See also* **cheat, hypocrite, liar.** 2. A fraudulent imitation ▶ forgery, sham. *See* **counterfeit.**

fake *verb*
1. To alter something so as to give it a false character ▶ doctor, falsify. 2. To take on as a false appearance ▶ counterfeit, dissemble, feign, pretend. *See* **act** (2). 3. To make a fraudulent copy of ▶ falsify, forge. *See* **counterfeit** (1). 4. To compose or recite without preparation ▶ ad-lib, make up. *See* **improvise** (1).

fake *adjective*
Fraudulently or deceptively imitative ▶ fraudulent, phony. *See* **counterfeit.**

faker *noun*
1. One who makes a fraudulent copy of something ▶ counterfeiter, fabricator, falsifier, forger. 2. A person who practices deceit, especially under an assumed identity ▶ charlatan, fraud, impostor. *See* **fake** (1).

fall *verb*
1. To move downward in response to gravity ▶ descend, dive, drop, go down, nose-dive, pitch, plummet, plunge, sink, spill, tumble. *Idioms:* fall flat on one's face, go flying, take a fall (*or* header *or* plunge *or* spill *or* tumble). *See also* **recede, settle.** 2. To come to the ground from an upright position ▶ fall over (*or* down), keel over, tip over, topple, tumble. *See also* **buckle.** 3. To go from a more erect posture to a less erect posture ▶ sink, slump. *See* **drop** (1). 4. To slope downward ▶ decline, dip. *See* **drop** (5). 5. To undergo capture, defeat, or ruin ▶ collapse, go down, go under, topple. *See also* **succumb, surrender.** 6. To become or cause to become less active or intense ▶ abate, let up, wane. *See* **subside** (1). 7. To become lower in value or price ▶ decline, depreciate, dive, drop (off), fall off, nose-dive, plummet, plunge, sag, sink, skid, slip, slump, tumble. *Idioms:* take a sudden downtrend (*or* downturn). *See also* **collapse, decrease, deteriorate, slip.** 8. To undergo moral deterioration ▶ degenerate, sink, slip. *See also* **deteriorate.** 9. To take place ▶ befall, come, occur. *See* **happen** (1).

fall apart *verb*
1. To become reduced to pieces ▶ break down, fragment. *See* **disintegrate** (1). 2. To give way mentally and emotionally ▶ crack, crumble, snap. *See* **break** (5).

fall back *verb*
1. To move back in the face of enemy attack or after a defeat ▶ draw back, pull out, withdraw. *See* **retreat** (4). 2. To move in a reverse direction ▶ backpedal, backtrack, retreat. *See* **back** (1). 3. To slip from a higher or better condition to a former, usually lower or poorer one ▶ lapse, regress, revert. *See* **relapse.**

fall down *or* **flat** *verb*
Informal To be unsuccessful ▶ falter, strike out, wash out. *See* **fail** (1).

fall off *verb*
To become or cause to become less active or intense ▶ abate, let up, wane. *See* **subside.**

fall on *or* **upon** *verb*
To set upon with violent force ▶ assail, assault, storm, strike. *See* **attack** (1).

fall out *verb*
To quarrel ▶ fight, squabble. *See* **argue** (1).

fall short *verb*
1. To be unsuccessful ▶ founder, miscarry, wash out. *See* **fail** (1). 2. To prove insufficient ▶ give out, run short. *See* **fail** (1).

fall through *verb*
To be unsuccessful ▶ founder, miscarry, misfire. *See* **fail** (1).

fall *noun*
1. A sudden downward motion toward the ground ▶ descent, dive, drop, nosedive, pitch, plunge, spill, tumble. *Informal:* header. 2. A disastrous defeat or ruin ▶ collapse, downfall, waterloo. *See also* **defeat.** 3. A usually swift downward trend, as in prices ▶ decline, depreciation, descent, dip, dive, downslide, downswing, downtrend, downturn, drop, drop-off, nosedive, plunge, skid, slide, slump, tumble. *See also* **decrease, depreciation, depression.** 4. A downward

slope or distance ▸ decline, declivity. *See* **drop** (5).

fallacious *adjective*

1. Containing errors in reasoning ▸ false, illogical, inconsistent, invalid, irrational, self-contradictory, sophistic, specious, spurious, unsound, untenable. *See also* **baseless, foolish, unreasonable. 2.** Tending to lead one into error ▸ deceptive, delusive, delusory, illusive, illusory, insidious, misleading. *See also* **dishonest, false. 3.** Containing an error or errors ▸ false, inaccurate, mistaken. *See* **erroneous.**

fallacy *noun*

1. An erroneous or false idea ▸ error, falsehood, falsity, misapprehension, misconception, misinterpretation, misunderstanding, untruth. *See also* **error, illusion. 2.** Plausible but invalid reasoning ▸ casuistry, sophism, sophistry, speciousness, spuriousness.

fallback *noun*

▸ evacuation, pullout, withdrawal. *See* **retreat** (1).

fallen *adjective*

▸ doomed, lost, reprobate. *See* **condemned.**

fall guy *noun*

1. *Slang* One who is made an object of blame ▸ whipping boy. *Slang:* patsy. *See* **scapegoat. 2.** *Slang* A person who is easily deceived or victimized ▸ pushover, tool, victim. *See* **dupe** (1).

false *adjective*

1. Not true ▸ apocryphal, counterfactual, fictitious, specious, spurious, truthless, untrue, untruthful, wrong. *See also* **baseless, dishonest. 2.** Containing an error or errors ▸ corrupt, inaccurate, mistaken. *See* **erroneous. 3.** Containing errors in reasoning ▸ illogical, spurious, unsound. *See* **fallacious** (1). **4.** Fraudulently or deceptively imitative ▸ fake, fraudulent, phony. *See* **counterfeit. 5.** Not true to duty or obligation ▸ disloyal, traitorous, treacherous. *See* **faithless** (1). *See synonym note at* **faithless.**

false colors *noun*

▸ disguise, mask, pretense. *See* **façade** (2).

false-hearted *adjective*

1. Not true to duty or obligation ▸ disloyal, traitorous, treacherous, untrue. *See* **faithless** (1). **2.** Given to or marked by deliberate concealment or misrepresentation of the truth ▸ duplicitous, lying, mendacious. *See* **dishonest** (1). *See synonym note at* **dishonest.**

false-heartedness *noun*

▸ disloyalty, infidelity, treachery. *See* **faithlessness** (1).

falsehood *noun*

1. An untrue declaration ▸ cock-and-bull story, fib, untruth. *See* **lie².** **2.** An erroneous or false idea ▸ error, untruth. *See* **fallacy** (1). **3.** The practice of lying ▸ inveracity, perjury, untruthfulness. *See* **mendacity** (1).

false impression *noun*

▸ misapprehension, misconception. *See* **misunderstanding** (1).

falseness *noun*

▸ disloyalty, infidelity, treacherousness. *See* **faithlessness** (1).

falsification *noun*

1. A fraudulent imitation ▸ forgery, sham. *See* **coun-**

terfeit. **2.** The practice of lying ▸ inveracity, perjury. *See* **mendacity** (1).

falsifier *noun*

1. One who makes a fraudulent copy of something ▸ counterfeiter, fabricator, faker, forger. **2.** One who tells lies ▸ fabulist, fibber, prevaricator. *See* **liar.**

falsify *verb*

1. To present false information with the intention of deceiving ▸ fib, prevaricate. *See* **lie².** *See synonym note at* **lie².** **2.** To give an inaccurate view of by representing falsely or misleadingly ▸ fudge, misrepresent, pervert, stretch. *See* **distort** (1). **3.** To make a fraudulent copy of ▸ fake, forge. *See* **counterfeit** (1). **4.** To alter something so as to give it a false character ▸ fake, doctor.

falsity *noun*

1. Betrayal, especially of a duty or obligation ▸ infidelity, perfidiousness, treacherousness. *See* **faithlessness** (1). **2.** An erroneous or false idea ▸ error, misconception. *See* **fallacy** (1). **3.** An untrue declaration ▸ falsehood, fib, untruth. *See* **lie².** **4.** Lack of sincerity ▸ artificiality, disingenuousness. *See* **insincerity.**

falter *verb*

1. To be irresolute in acting or doing ▸ dilly-dally, vacillate. *See* **hesitate.** *See synonym note at* **hesitate. 2.** To walk unsteadily ▸ reel, stumble, totter. *See* **stagger** (1). **3.** To speak with involuntary repetitions or pauses ▸ sputter, stutter. *See* **stammer.**

fame *noun*

Wide recognition for one's deeds ▸ celebrity, distinction, eminence, eminency, famousness, glory, illustriousness, luster, mark, notability, note, notoriety, popularity, preeminence, prestige, renown, prominence, prominency, reputation, repute. *See also* **distinction, esteem, honor, reputation.**

famed *adjective*

▸ celebrated, eminent, noted. *See* **famous.** *See synonym note at* **famous.**

familial *adjective*

1. Of or relating to the family or household ▸ family, residential. *See* **domestic** (1). **2.** Of or from one's ancestors ▸ hereditary, inherited, genealogical. *See* **ancestral.**

familiar *adjective*

1. Having good knowledge of something ▸ acquainted, conversant, versant, versed. *Idiom:* up on. *See also* **accustomed, informed. 2.** Occurring or encountered regularly ▸ commonplace, frequent, regular. *See* **common** (1). *See synonym note at* **common. 3.** Very closely associated ▸ close, cozy, friendly. *See* **intimate¹** (1). **4.** Indicating intimacy and mutual trust ▸ close, inward, personal. *See* **confidential** (2). **5.** Rude and disrespectful ▸ bold, insolent, pert. *See* **impudent.**

familiar *noun*

A person whom one knows well, likes, and trusts ▸ chum, intimate, mate. *See* **friend** (1).

familiarity *noun*

1. Personal knowledge derived from participation or observation ▸ acquaintance, conversance, experience.

See also **awareness. 2.** The condition of being friends ▸ amity, camaraderie, companionship, fellowship. *See* **friendship. 3.** The state or quality of being impudent or arrogantly self-confident ▸ blatancy, disrespect, impertinence. *See* **impudence. 4.** A lack of excitement, liveliness, or interest ▸ blandness, drabness, lifelessness. *See* **dullness** (1).

familiarize *verb*
1. To make known socially ▸ acquaint, introduce, present. **2.** To make familiar through constant practice or use ▸ habituate, inure. *See* **accustom.**

family *noun*
1. A group of people living together as a unit ▸ house, household, ménage. **2.** A group of people sharing common ancestry ▸ clan, house, kindred, lineage, stock, tribe. *Idioms:* kith and kin, flesh and blood. **3.** One's relatives collectively ▸ kindred, kinfolk. *See* **kin. 4.** One's ancestors or one's ancestral derivation ▸ blood, descent, lineage. *See* **ancestry. 5.** A subdivision of a larger group ▸ category, order, set. *See* **class** (1).

family *adjective*
Of or relating to the family or household ▸ familial, residential. *See* **domestic** (1).

family tree *noun*
1. A written record of ancestry ▸ genealogy, pedigree. **2.** One's ancestors or ancestral derivation ▸ blood, descent, lineage. *See* **ancestry.**

famished *adjective*
▸ ravenous, starving, voracious. *See* **hungry** (1).

famous *adjective*
Widely known ▸ celebrated, distinguished, eminent, famed, glorious, great, illustrious, important, leading, legendary, notable, noted, notorious, popular, preeminent, prestigious, prominent, recognized, redoubtable, renowned, reputable, storied, well-known. *Idiom:* of note. *See also* **exalted.**

✦ CORE SYNONYMS: *famous, celebrated, eminent, famed, illustrious, notable, noted, preeminent, renowned.* These adjectives mean widely known and esteemed: *a famous actor; a celebrated musician; an eminent scholar; a famed scientist; an illustrious judge; a notable historian; a noted author; a preeminent archaeologist; a renowned painter.*

◄ ANTONYM: *obscure*

---

famousness *noun*
▸ celebrity, notoriety, renown. *See* **fame.**

fan¹ *verb*
To move or arrange so as to cover a larger area ▸ extend, stretch. *See* **spread** (1).

fan² *noun*
An ardent devotee ▸ admirer, aficionado, bug, devotee, enthusiast, fanatic, fancier, follower, groupie, hound, junkie, lover, maniac, zealot. *Informal:* buff, fiend. *Slang:* freak, nut. *See also* **follower.**

fanatic *noun*
1. One who holds extreme views or advocates extreme measures ▸ radical, revolutionist, zealot. *See*

extremist. **2.** One zealously devoted to a religion ▸ adherent, zealot. *See* **devotee** (1). **3.** An ardent devotee ▸ enthusiast, fancier, maniac. *See* **fan².**

fanatic *or* **fanatical** *adjective*
1. Holding especially political views that deviate drastically from prevailing beliefs ▸ extremist, radical, revolutionary. *See* **extreme** (4). **2.** Showing or having enthusiasm ▸ ardent, fervent, rabid, zealous. *See* **enthusiastic** (1).

fanaticism *noun*
▸ fervor, passion, zeal. *See* **enthusiasm** (1).

fancier *noun*
▸ admirer, devotee, enthusiast. *See* **fan².**

fanciful *adjective*
1. Showing invention or whimsy in design ▸ fantastic, imaginative, whimsical. *See also* **capricious, elaborate, ornate. 2.** Existing only in the imagination ▸ fantastic, make-believe, unreal. *See* **imaginary. 3.** Given to daydreams or reverie ▸ daydreaming, musing. *See* **dreamy** (1). **4.** Very strange or strikingly unusual ▸ fantastic, outré, unorthodox. *See* **exotic** (2).

fancy *noun*
1. An impulsive turn of mind ▸ caprice, conceit, freak, humor, impulse, megrim, notion, vagary, whim, whimsy. *Idiom:* bee in one's bonnet. *See also* **mood. 2.** The power of the mind to form images ▸ creativity, inventiveness. *See* **imagination** (1). *See synonym note at* **imagination. 3.** An illusory mental image ▸ daydream, fantasy, illusion. *See* **dream** (1). **4.** A desire for a particular thing or activity ▸ mind, soft spot, will. *See* **liking** (1). **5.** The passionate affection and desire felt by lovers for each other ▸ ardor, passion, romance. *See* **love** (2). **6.** A subject or activity that inspires lively interest ▸ mania, passion. *See* **enthusiasm** (2).

fancy *adjective*
1. Rich in detail ▸ detailed, intricate. *See* **elaborate** (1). **2.** Catering to, used by, or admitting only the wealthy or socially superior ▸ chic, posh, swank. *See* **exclusive** (4). **3.** Characterized by extravagant, ostentatious magnificence ▸ lush, luxuriant, opulent. *See* **luxurious.**

fancy *verb*
1. To form mental images of ▸ envision, fantasize, visualize. *See* **imagine** (1). **2.** To find agreeable ▸ adore, favor. *See* **like¹** (1). **3.** To predict or assume without sufficient information ▸ speculate, surmise. *See* **guess. 4.** To experience dreams or daydreams ▸ daydream, hallucinate. *See* **dream** (1).

fancy-free *adjective*
1. Happy and free from worry or care ▸ blithe, buoyant, debonair. *See* **lighthearted** (1). **2.** Not married or attached ▸ available, marriageable. *See* **single** (5).

fanfaronade *noun*
▸ brag, vaunt. *See* **boast.**

fanny *noun*
Slang The part of the body on which one sits ▸ posterior, rump. *Slang:* tush. *See* **buttocks.**

fantasist *noun*
▸ daydreamer, romantic, stargazer. *See* **dreamer** (1).

fantasize *verb*
1. To form mental images of ▸ envision, image, visualize. *See* **imagine** (1). 2. To experience dreams or daydreams ▸ fancy, hallucinate. *See* **dream** (1).

fantastic *adjective*
1. Showing invention or whimsy in design ▸ fanciful, imaginative, whimsical. *See also* **elaborate, ornate.** 2. Marked by whim or impulse ▸ fickle, impulsive, mercurial. *See* **capricious.** 3. Existing only in the imagination ▸ chimerical, fanciful, unreal. *See* **imaginary.** 4. Consisting or suggestive of fiction ▸ fictional, invented, made-up. *See* **fictitious** (1). 5. So remarkable as to be difficult to believe ▸ astounding, staggering, unbelievable. *See* **astonishing.** 6. Particularly excellent ▸ fabulous, glorious, terrific. *See* **marvelous** (1). 7. Deviating from what is conventional or customary ▸ bizarre, grotesque. *See* **eccentric.** *See synonym note at* **eccentric.** 8. Very strange or strikingly unusual ▸ bizarre, outré, unorthodox. *See* **exotic** (2).

fantastical *adjective*
1. Particularly excellent ▸ divine, sensational, wonderful. *See* **marvelous** (1). 2. Existing only in the imagination ▸ chimerical, fanciful, unreal. *See* **imaginary.**

fantasy *noun*
1. The power of the mind to form images ▸ creativity, mind's eye. *See* **imagination** (1). *See synonym note at* **imagination.** 2. A fiction or half-truth, especially one that forms part of an ideology ▸ delusion, fiction, invention. *See* **myth** (3). 3. A fantastic, impracticable plan or desire ▸ chimera, illusion. *See* **dream** (2). 4. An illusory mental image ▸ fancy, fiction, illusion. *See* **dream** (1).

fantasy *adjective*
Having the nature of a fable; not real ▸ fabled, legendary. *See* **mythical.**

far *adverb*
To a considerable extent ▸ much, quite, well. *See* **considerably.**

far *adjective*
Far from others in space, time, or relationship ▸ faraway, remote, removed. *See* **distant** (1).

faraway *adjective*
1. Far from others in space, time, or relationship ▸ far, remote, removed. *See* **distant** (1). 2. So lost in thought as to be forgetful ▸ distracted, inattentive, preoccupied. *See* **absent-minded.**

farce *noun*
1. A false, derisive, or impudent imitation of something ▸ caricature, sham, travesty. *See* **mockery** (2). 2. A work that exposes folly by the use of humor, irony, or comic imitation ▸ burlesque, parody, spoof. *See* **satire.**

farceur *noun*
▸ comedian, humorist, jokester. *See* **joker.**

farcical *adjective*
Causing or deserving laughter or derision ▸ laughable, ludicrous, ridiculous, risible. *See also* **foolish.**

farcicality *noun*
▸ funniness, ridiculousness, wittiness. *See* **humor** (1).

fare *verb*
1. To progress or perform adequately, especially in difficult circumstances ▸ fend, get by. *See* **manage** (1). 2. To make or go on a journey ▸ peregrinate, travel, voyage. *See* **journey.**

fare *noun*
1. Material that is fit to be eaten ▸ bread, meat, nourishment. *See* **food.** 2. A fixed amount of money charged for a service ▸ exaction, fee. *See* **toll**[1] (1).

farewell *noun*
The act of leaving ▸ embarkation, exodus, withdrawal. *See* **departure** (1).

farewell *adjective*
Of, done, given, or said on departing ▸ departing, valedictory. *See* **parting.**

farewell *interjection*
Used upon taking leave ▸ fare-thee-well. *Informal:* ciao, later. *See* **goodbye.**

far-fetched *adjective*
1. Represented as greater than is actually the case ▸ hyperbolic, inflated, overblown. *See* **exaggerated** (1). 2. Not to be believed ▸ unbelievable, unthinkable. *See* **incredible** (2).

far-flung *adjective*
1. Spread out over a large area ▸ broad, widespread. 2. Far from others in space, time, or relationship ▸ faraway, remote, removed. *See* **distant** (1).

farm *verb*
▸ cultivate, propagate. *See* **grow** (1).

farness *noun*
The fact or condition of being far removed or apart ▸ distance, remoteness, separateness, separation.

far-off *adjective*
▸ faraway, remote, removed. *See* **distant** (1).

far-out *adjective*
Slang Holding especially political views that deviate drastically from prevailing beliefs ▸ fanatical, radical, revolutionary. *See* **extreme** (4).

far-ranging *or* **far-reaching** *adjective*
▸ all-inclusive, broad, expansive. *See* **general** (2).

farsighted *adjective*
▸ imaginative, intuitive, perceptive. *See* **visionary** (1).

farsightedness *noun*
▸ innovation, inspiration, prescience. *See* **vision** (2).

farthest *or* **farthermost** *adjective*
▸ outmost, ultimate, uttermost. *See* **extreme** (1).

fascinate *verb*
1. To please greatly or irresistibly ▸ bewitch, captivate, enchant. *See* **charm** (1). *See synonym note at* **charm.** 2. To compel the attention, interest, or imagination of ▸ captivate, enthrall, mesmerize. *See* **grip** (1).

fascinating *adjective*
▸ enchanting, fetching, lovely, winsome. *See* **attractive** (1).

fascination *noun*
1. The power or quality of attracting ▸ draw, enticement, lure. *See* **attraction** (1). 2. An irrational preoccupation ▸ fetish, fixation, mania. *See* **obsession.**

fascism *noun*
▸ despotism, dictatorship, totalitarianism. *See* **tyranny** (1).

fashion *noun*
1. The current custom ▸ craze, fad, furor, mode, rage, style, trend, vogue. *Informal:* thing. *Idioms:* the in thing, the last word, the latest thing. *See also* **custom**. **2.** The approach used to do something ▸ manner, mode, style. *See* **way** (1). *See synonym note at* **way**. **3.** A distinctive way of expressing oneself ▸ manner, mode, tone. *See* **style** (1).

fashion *verb*
1. To give form to by or as if by pressing and kneading ▸ model, mold, shape. *See* **form** (1). **2.** To create by forming, combining, or altering materials ▸ build, compose, structure. *See* **make** (1). **3.** To make or become suitable to a particular situation or use ▸ adjust, fit, tailor. *See* **adapt**.

✦ CORE SYNONYMS: *fashion, style, mode, vogue*. These nouns refer to the prevailing or preferred manner of dress, adornment, behavior, or way of life at a given time. *Fashion*, the broadest term, usually refers to what accords with conventions adopted by polite society or by any culture or subculture: *a time when long hair was the fashion*. *Style* is sometimes used interchangeably with *fashion*, but like *mode* often stresses adherence to standards of elegance: *traveling in style; miniskirts that were the mode in the late sixties*. *Vogue* is applied to fashion that prevails widely and often suggests enthusiastic but short-lived acceptance: *a video game that was in vogue a few years ago*.

fashionable *adjective*
In accordance with current fashion ▸ à la mode, chic, dashing, de rigueur, mod, modish, smart, stylish, swank, swanky. *Informal:* classy, in, sharp, snappy, swish, trendy, with-it. *Slang:* funky, hip, hot, snazzy. *Idioms:* all the rage, up to the minute. *See also* **contemporary, elegant, luxurious**.

✦ CORE SYNONYMS: *fashionable, chic, dashing, in, modish, sharp, smart, stylish, swank, trendy*. These adjectives mean in accordance with the current fashion: *a fashionable restaurant; a chic dress; a dashing hat; the in place to go; modish jewelry; a sharp jacket; a smart hotel; stylish clothes; a swank apartment; a trendy neighborhood*.

fast *adjective*
1. Characterized by great speed ▸ blinding, breakneck, brisk, expeditious, express, fleet, hasty, high-speed, hurried, quick, rapid, speedy, swift. *Informal:* hell-for-leather, pedal-to-the-metal. *Idioms:* quick as a bunny (*or* wink). **2.** Accomplished or experienced in very little time ▸ brief, rapid, speedy. *See* **quick** (1). **3.** Lacking in moral restraint ▸ dissolute, licentious, profligate. *See* **abandoned** (2). **4.** Sexually unrestrained ▸ libertine, loose, promiscuous. *See* **wanton** (1). **5.** Retaining original color ▸ colorfast, indelible. **6.** Persistently holding to something ▸ firm, tenacious. *See* **tight** (1). **7.** Not easily moved or shaken ▸ solid,

stable, sure. *See* **firm**[1] (2). **8.** Adhering firmly and devotedly, as to a person, cause, or duty ▸ allegiant, constant, loyal. *See* **faithful** (1). *See synonym note at* **faithful**. **9.** Very closely associated ▸ close, cozy, familiar. *See* **intimate**[1] (1).

fast *adverb*
In a rapid way ▸ apace, hastily, hurriedly, posthaste, quick, quickly, rapidly, swiftly. *Informal:* flat out, hell-for-leather, lickety-split, pedal-to-the-metal, pronto. *Idioms:* full tilt, in a flash, in nothing flat, like a bat out of hell, like a blue streak, like a flash, like a house on fire, like a shot, like a streak, like greased lightning, like the wind, like wildfire, with dispatch.

✦ CORE SYNONYMS: *fast, rapid, swift, fleet, speedy, quick, hasty, expeditious*. These adjectives refer to something characterized by great speed. *Fast* and *rapid* are often used interchangeably, though *fast* is more often applied to the person or thing in motion, and *rapid*, to the activity or movement involved: *a fast runner; rapid strides*. *Swift* suggests smoothness and sureness of movement (*a swift current*), and *fleet*, lightness of movement (*The cheetah is the fleetest of animals*). *Speedy* refers to velocity (*a speedy train*) or to promptness or hurry (*a speedy resolution to the problem*). *Quick* most often applies to what takes little time or to what is prompt: *a quick snack; your quick reaction*. *Hasty* implies hurried action (*a hasty visit*) and often a lack of care or thought (*regretted the hasty decision*). *Expeditious* suggests rapid efficiency: *sent the package by the most expeditious means*.
◂ ANTONYM: *slow*

fasten *verb*
1. To cause to remain firmly in position or place; make secure ▸ anchor, bind, bolt, buckle, catch, chain, clamp, clip, fix, hitch, knot, lash, lock, moor, nail, pin, rivet, screw, secure, strap, tack, tie (up). *Idioms:* make fast. *See also* **support**. **2.** To join one thing to another ▸ append, fuse, secure. *See* **attach** (1). **3.** To place or set deeply ▸ entrench, ingrain, plant. *See* **fix** (4). **4.** To ascribe the blame for a misdeed or error ▸ attribute, blame, pin. *See* **fix** (13).

fasten on *or* **upon** *verb*
To force on another to accept a burden ▸ charge with, inflict on (*or* upon), saddle with. *See* **impose on** (1).

✦ CORE SYNONYMS: *fasten, anchor, fix, moor, secure*. These verbs mean to cause to remain firmly in position or place: *fastened our seat belts; anchored the television antenna to the roof; fixed the flagpole in concrete; will moor the rowboat at the dock; secured the bolt after closing the door*.

fastener *or* **fastening** *noun*
A device for locking or for checking motion ▸ bar, binder, binding, buckle, catch, clamp, clasp, clip, collar, fastening, harness, hasp, hook, latch, lock, mortise, pawl, snap, vise. *See also* **anchor, bond, cord, nail**.

fastidious *adjective*
1. Marked by attentiveness to every detail ▸ meticu-

lous, painstaking, scrupulous. *See* **careful** (2). *See synonym note at* **careful**. **2.** Very difficult to please ▸ exacting, finicky. *See* **fussy** (1).

fastidiousness *noun*
▸ carefulness, meticulousness, painstaking. *See* **thoroughness**.

fastigium *noun*
▸ apex, height, peak. *See* **climax** (1).

fastness *noun*
▸ firmness, hardness, steadiness. *See* **stability**.

fast one *noun*
Informal An indirect, usually cunning means of gaining an end ▸ deception, ploy, stratagem. *See* **trick** (1).

fat *noun*
1. Adipose tissue ▸ blubber, lard, suet. *See also* **oil**. **2.** A thing, amount, or quantity beyond what is needed, desired, or appropriate ▸ overflow, oversupply, superfluity. *See* **surplus**.

fat *adjective*
1. Having too much flesh or a full figure ▸ chubby, corpulent, fatty, flabby, fleshy, full, gross, heavy, meaty, obese, overblown, overweight, paunchy, plump, plumpish, porcine, portly, potbellied, pudgy, roly-poly, rotund, round, stout, tubby, weighty, zaftig. *Slang:* porky. *See also* **bulky, stocky**. **2.** Having the qualities of fat ▸ greasy, unctuous. *See* **fatty** (1). **3.** Affording profit ▸ gainful, lucrative, rewarding. *See* **profitable** (1). **4.** Relatively great in extent from one surface to the opposite ▸ thick. *See also* **bulky**.

✦ CORE SYNONYMS: *fat, obese, corpulent, fleshy, portly, stout, pudgy, rotund, plump, chubby*. These adjectives mean having an abundance and often an excess of flesh. *Fat* implies excessive weight and generally has negative connotations: *was getting fat and decided to exercise*. *Obese* and *corpulent* imply gross overweight: *"a woman of robust frame . . . though stout, not obese"* (Charlotte Brontë). *The dancer was corpulent but surprisingly graceful*. *Fleshy* implies a not necessarily excessive abundance of flesh: *firm, fleshy arms*. *Portly* refers to bulk combined with a stately or imposing bearing: *"a portly, rubicund man of middle age"* (Winston Churchill). *Stout* denotes a thickset, bulky figure: *a painting of stout peasants*. *Pudgy* means short and fat: *pudgy fingers*. *Rotund* suggests roundness of figure, often in a squat person: *"this pink-faced rotund specimen of prosperity"* (George Eliot). *Plump* and *chubby* apply to a pleasing fullness of figure: *a plump little toddler; chubby cheeks*.

---

fatal *adjective*
1. Causing or tending to cause death ▸ lethal, mortal, pestilent. *See* **deadly** (1). *See synonym note at* **deadly**. **2.** So critically decisive as to affect the future ▸ fateful, momentous. *See also* **decisive**. **3.** Causing ruin or destruction ▸ calamitous, cataclysmic, catastrophic. *See* **disastrous**.

fatality *noun*
1. A loss of life, or one who has lost life, usually as a result of accident, disaster, or war ▸ casualty, death,

kill, loss, statistic. *See also* **victim**. **2.** The quality or condition of causing death or disaster ▸ deadliness, fatefulness, lethality, lethalness.

fate *noun*
1. The supposed power that predetermines events ▸ destiny, fortune, kismet, luck, predestination, preordination. *See also* **chance**. **2.** A personal outcome or end ▸ destiny, doom, end, fortune, lot, luck, portion. *See also* **misfortune, ruin**.

fated *adjective*
1. Governed by fate ▸ destined, foreordained, ordained, predestined, predetermined, preordained. *See also* **certain**. **2.** Sentenced to terrible, irrevocable punishment ▸ doomed, lost, reprobate. *See* **condemned**.

fateful *adjective*
1. Bringing or predicting misfortune ▸ bad, baleful, dark, dire, direful, evil, forbidding, foreboding, grave, ill, ill-boding, ill-omened, inauspicious, looming, lowering, malign, menacing, ominous, portentous, sinister, sullen, threatening, unfavorable, unlucky, unpropitious. *See also* **unfortunate**. **2.** So critically decisive as to affect the future ▸ fatal, momentous. *See also* **decisive**. **3.** Causing ruin or destruction ▸ cataclysmic, catastrophic, ruinous. *See* **disastrous**.

✦ CORE SYNONYMS: *fateful, sinister, baleful, malign*. These adjectives mean bringing or predicting misfortune: *Fateful* applies to that which is ominously prophetic or portentous: *The fortune teller said that the remaining card represented a fateful sign of change*. *Sinister* refers to impending or lurking danger and often connotes evil: *We heard a sinister laugh from behind the door*. *Baleful* intensifies the sense of menace; it suggests a deadly, virulent, or poisonous quality: *The guard's baleful glare frightened the children*. *Malign* applies to what manifests an evil disposition, nature, influence, or intent: *"The Devil . . . with jealous leer malign/Eyed them askance"* (John Milton).

---

fatefulness *adjective*
The quality or condition of causing death or disaster ▸ deadliness, fatality, lethality, lethalness.

fatheadedness *noun*
Slang The state of being stupid ▸ idiocy, mindlessness, obtuseness. *See* **stupidity**.

father *noun*
1. A male parent ▸ begetter, paterfamilias, patriarch, sire. *Informal:* dad, daddy, pa, papa, pappy, pop. *Slang:* old boy, old man. **2.** A person from whom one is descended ▸ forebear, parent, progenitor. *See* **ancestor** (1). **3.** One that creates, founds, or originates ▸ author, creator, inventor. *See* **originator**. **4.** A first form from which varieties arise or imitations are made ▸ master, prototype. *See* **original** (1).

father *verb*
1. To be the biological father of ▸ beget, get, sire. **2.** To give life to ▸ engender, propagate, spawn. *See* **breed** (1).

fatherly *or* **fatherlike** *adjective*
Like a father, especially in caring ▸ fatherlike, paternal, patriarchal. *See also* **benevolent**.

fathom *verb*
1. To perceive and recognize the meaning of ▸ get, see. *See* **understand** (1). 2. To perceive directly with the intellect ▸ apprehend, comprehend, grasp. *See* **know** (1). 3. To go into or through for the purpose of making discoveries or acquiring information ▸ inquire, investigate, probe. *See* **explore.**

fathomable *adjective*
▸ apprehensible, comprehensible, intelligible. *See* **understandable** (1).

fatidic *or* **fatidical** *adjective*
▸ divinitory, oracular, sibylline. *See* **prophetic.**

fatigue *noun*
The condition of being extremely tired ▸ burnout, weariness. *See* **exhaustion.**

fatigue *verb*
1. To make weary ▸ drain, wear down. *See* **tire** (1). *See synonym note at* **tire.** 2. To make weary with dullness or tedium ▸ stultify, weary. *See* **bore²**.

fatigued *adjective*
▸ exhausted, weary, worn-out. *See* **tired** (1).

fatiguing *adjective*
Causing fatigue ▸ draining, exhausting, tiring, wearing, wearying. *See also* **burdensome.**

fatty *adjective*
1. Having the qualities of fat ▸ adipose, blubbery, fat, greasy, oily, oleaginous, unctuous. 2. Having too much flesh ▸ corpulent, portly. *See* **fat** (1).

fatuity *noun*
▸ folly, silliness, tomfoolery. *See* **foolishness.**

fatuous *adjective*
▸ inane, senseless, silly. *See* **foolish.** *See synonym note at* **foolish.**

fatuousness *noun*
▸ folly, silliness, tomfoolery. *See* **foolishness.**

faucet *noun*
A device that regulates the flow of a liquid ▸ cock, fixture, petcock, spigot, stopcock, tap.

fault *noun*
1. An imperfection of character ▸ failing, shortcoming, weak point. *See* **weakness** (1). 2. Something that mars the appearance or causes inadequacy or failure ▸ blemish, flaw, imperfection. *See* **defect** (1). *See synonym note at* **defect.** 3. Responsibility for an error or crime ▸ culpability, guilt. *See* **blame** (1). *See synonym note at* **blame.** 4. A partial opening caused by splitting and rupture ▸ break, cleft, fissure. *See* **crack** (2).

fault *verb*
To find fault with ▸ censure, reprove. *Slang:* knock. *See* **criticize** (1).

faultfinder *noun*
1. A person who finds fault ▸ caviler, nitpicker. *See* **critic** (2). 2. A person who habitually complains or grumbles ▸ crab, grump, whiner. *See* **grouch** (1).

faultfinding *adjective*
▸ carping, overcritical. *See* **critical** (1).

faultless *adjective*
1. Free from guilt or blame ▸ guiltless, harmless. *See* **innocent** (2). 2. Free from flaws or blemishes ▸ consummate, flawless, unblemished. *See* **perfect** (1). *See synonym note at* **perfect.** 3. Beyond reproach ▸ blameless, unblamable. *See* **exemplary** (1).

faulty *adjective*
1. Having a defect or defects ▸ amiss, blemished, defective, flawed, imperfect. *See also* **shabby, trick.** 2. Containing an error or errors ▸ false, inaccurate, mistaken. *See* **erroneous.**

faux pas *noun*
▸ bungle, fumble, solecism. *See* **blunder.**

favor *noun*
1. A kindly act ▸ benefaction, beneficence, benevolence, benignity, courtesy, good deed, good turn, grace, indulgence, kindness, kindliness, kind office, philanthropy, service. *See also* **help.** 2. Favorable reception or regard ▸ approbation, approval, welcome. *See* **acceptance** (2). 3. A feeling of deference, approval, and liking ▸ admiration, consideration. *See* **esteem** (1). 4. Preferential treatment or bias ▸ favoritism, partiality, partialness, preference. *See also* **bias, prejudice.** 5. Something beneficial ▸ blessing, gain. *See* **advantage** (2). 6. Something that causes one to remember ▸ memento, reminder. *See* **remembrance** (1).

favor *verb*
1. To show partiality toward someone ▸ prefer. *Idioms:* be partial, play favorites. *See also* **advance, baby.** 2. To be favorably disposed toward ▸ approve, countenance, hold with. *Informal:* go for. *Idioms:* be in favor of, take kindly to, think highly (*or* well) of. *See also* **assent, value.** 3. To find agreeable ▸ adore, fancy. *See* **like¹** (1). 4. To perform a service or a courteous act for ▸ accommodate, serve. *See* **oblige** (1). *See synonym note at* **oblige.** 5. To lend supportive approval to ▸ countenance, encourage, smile on (*or* upon). *See also* **support.** 6. *Chiefly Regional* To be similar to someone else in appearance ▸ look like, take after. *See* **resemble.**

favorable *adjective*
1. Indicative of future success or full of promise ▸ auspicious, benign, bright, brilliant, fair, fortunate, good, propitious. *See also* **encouraging.** 2. Giving assent ▸ affirmative, agreeable, approving, assenting, positive. 3. Affording benefit or advantage ▸ advantageous, helpful, propitious. *See* **beneficial.** 4. Suited for a particular purpose or occurring at a suitable time ▸ suitable, timely, well-timed. *See* **opportune.** 5. Giving or affording pleasure or enjoyment ▸ agreeable, gratifying, satisfying. *See* **pleasant** (1). 6. Disposed to favor one over another ▸ partial, preferential. *See also* **biased.**

✚ **CORE SYNONYMS:** *favorable, propitious, auspicious, benign.* These adjectives describe what is indicative of a successful outcome. *Favorable* can refer to what contributes in a positive way to the attainment of a goal: *a favorable review. Propitious* implies a favorable tendency or inclination: *"Miracles are propitious accidents"* (George Santayana). *Auspicious* refers to what presages good fortune: *an auspicious beginning. Benign* applies to people or things that exert a beneficial influence: *"I lingered round them, under that benign sky . . . and wondered how anyone could ever imagine unquiet slumbers, for the sleepers in that quiet earth"* (Emily Brontë).

favored *adjective*
▸ fair-haired, pet, preferred. *See* **favorite.**

favorite *noun*
1. One liked or preferred above all others ▸ darling, pet. *Idiom:* apple of one's eye. **2.** A leading contestant or sure winner ▸ front-runner, leader, number one, vanguard. *Informal:* shoo-in.

favorite *adjective*
Being a favorite ▸ darling, fair-haired, favored, pet, popular, preferred, well-liked. *See also* **select.**

favoritism *noun*
Preferential treatment or bias ▸ favor, partiality, partialness, preference. *See also* **bias, prejudice.**

fawn *verb*
To behave obsequiously or submissively ▸ bootlick, cringe, grovel, kowtow, slaver, toady, truckle. *Informal:* apple-polish, brownnose. *Slang:* suck up. *Idioms:* curry favor, dance attendance, kiss someone's feet, lick someone's boots. *See also* **flatter.**

✦ **CORE SYNONYMS:** *fawn, apple-polish, bootlick, kowtow, slaver, toady, truckle.* These verbs mean to curry favor by behaving obsequiously and submissively: *fawned on his superior; students apple-polishing the teacher; bootlicked to get a promotion; lawyers kowtowing to a judge; slavered over his rich uncle; toadying to members of the club; nobles truckling to the king.*

---

fawner *noun*
▸ flatterer, minion, slave. *See* **sycophant.**

faze *verb*
▸ chagrin, confound, discomfort. *See* **embarrass** (1). *See synonym note at* **embarrass.**

fealty *noun*
▸ allegiance, faithfulness, loyalty. *See* **fidelity** (1). *See synonym note at* **fidelity.**

fear *noun*
A feeling of agitation in the face of danger or trouble ▸ affright, alarm, apprehension, consternation, dismay, dread, fearfulness, fright, funk, horror, panic, terror, trepidation. *Slang:* cold feet. *Idiom:* fear and trembling. *See also* **anxiety, cowardice.**

fear *verb*
To be afraid ▸ dread. *Idioms:* break out in a cold sweat, have butterflies (in one's stomach), have knots (*or* a knot) in one's stomach, have one's heart in one's mouth, sweat blood (*or* bullets). *See also* **afraid, flinch.**

✦ **CORE SYNONYMS:** *fear, fright, dread, terror, horror, panic, alarm, dismay, consternation, trepidation.* These nouns denote the agitation and anxiety caused by the presence or imminence of danger. *Fear* is the most general term: *"Fear is the parent of cruelty"* (J.A. Froude). *Fright* is sudden, usually momentary, great fear: *In my fright, I forgot to lock the door. Dread* is strong fear, especially of what one is powerless to

---

avoid: *His dread of strangers kept him from socializing. Terror* is intense, overpowering fear: *"And now at the dead hour of the night, amid the dreadful silence of that old house, so strange a noise as this excited me to uncontrollable terror"* (Edgar Allan Poe). *Horror* is a combination of fear and aversion or repugnance: *Murder arouses widespread horror. Panic* is sudden frantic fear, often groundless: *The fire caused a panic among the horses. Alarm* is fright aroused by the first realization of danger: *I watched with alarm as the sky darkened. Dismay* robs one of courage or the power to act effectively: *The rumor of war caused universal dismay. Consternation* is often paralyzing, characterized by confusion and helplessness: *Consternation gripped the city as the invaders approached. Trepidation* is dread characteristically marked by trembling or hesitancy: *"They were . . . full of trepidation about things that were never likely to happen"* (John Morley).

---

fearful *adjective*
1. Causing or capable of causing fear ▸ alarming, appalling, dire, direful, dismaying, dreadful, fearsome, formidable, frightening, frightful, unnerving, redoubtable, scary, terrible. *See also* **horrible, ghastly, weird. 2.** Filled with fear or terror ▸ aghast, frightened, scared. *See* **afraid.** *See synonym note at* **afraid. 3.** Very bad ▸ abysmal, awful, dreadful, frightful. *See* **terrible** (1).

fearfulness *noun*
▸ apprehension, consternation, trepidation. *See* **fear.**

fearless *adjective*
▸ courageous, dashing, heroic. *See* **brave.** *See synonym note at* **brave.**

fearlessness *noun*
1. The quality of mind enabling one to face danger or hardship resolutely ▸ bravery, fortitude, gallantry, valor. *See* **courage. 2.** Willingness to take risks ▸ audaciousness, boldness, daringness. *See* **daring.**

fearsome *adjective*
1. Causing or capable of causing fear ▸ dreadful, formidable, frightful, scary. *See* **fearful** (1). **2.** Filled with fear or terror ▸ fearful, frightened, scared. *See* **afraid.**

feasible *adjective*
▸ practicable, viable. *See* **possible** (1). *See synonym note at* **possible.**

feast *noun*
A large, elaborately prepared meal ▸ banquet, junket. *Informal:* feed, spread.

feast *verb*
To show joyful satisfaction in an event ▸ party, rejoice, revel. *See* **celebrate** (2).

feast on *verb*
To be avidly interested in ▸ devour, relish. *Slang:* eat up.

feat *noun*
1. Something completed or attained successfully ▸ achievement, deed, triumph. *See* **accomplishment** (1). *See synonym note at* **accomplishment. 2.** A clever, dexterous act ▸ stunt, trick. *Idiom:* sleight of hand.

feather *noun*
▶ ilk, mold, species. *See* **kind**².
featherbrained *adjective*
▶ empty-headed, flighty, frivolous. *See* **giddy** (2).
feature *noun*
1. A distinctive element ▶ characteristic, property, trait. *See* **quality** (1). **2.** A detail of news information ▶ article, piece, story. *See* **item** (1).
feature *verb*
1. To accord emphasis to ▶ accentuate, highlight. *See* **emphasize**. **2.** *Informal* To form mental images of ▶ envision, fantasize, visualize. *See* **imagine** (1).
features *noun*
1. The front surface of the head ▶ countenance, visage. *See* **face** (1). **2.** An outward appearance ▶ aspect, lineaments. *See* **face** (4). **3.** The way something or someone looks ▶ aspect, look, mien. *See* **appearance** (1).
febrile *or* **febrific** *adjective*
▶ feverish, hectic, hot. *See* **feverish** (1).
feces *noun*
▶ dung, excreta, waste. *See* **excrement**.
feckless *adjective*
▶ heedless, irresponsible, unmindful. *See* **careless** (1).
fecund *adjective*
1. Capable of reproducing ▶ fertile, fruitful, productive, prolific. *See synonym note at* **fertile**. **2.** Characterized by great productivity ▶ fruitful, productive, prolific. *See* **fertile** (1).
fecundate *verb*
To make fertile ▶ enrich, fertilize, pollinate. *See also* **impregnate, pregnant**.
fecundity *noun*
1. The quality or state of being fertile ▶ fruitfulness, productiveness, richness. *See* **fertility**. **2.** The power or ability to invent ▶ creativity, ingenuity, originality. *See* **invention** (1).
federate *verb*
1. To be formally associated, as by treaty ▶ align, confederate. *See* **ally** (1). **2.** To unite or be united in a relationship ▶ combine, join, link. *See* **associate** (1).
federation *noun*
1. An association for a common cause or interest ▶ coalition, league, organization. *See* **alliance** (1). **2.** A group of people united in a relationship and having some interest, activity, or purpose in common ▶ club, league, order. *See* **union** (1).
fed up *adjective*
Out of patience ▶ disgusted, sick, tired, weary. *Idiom:* sick and tired. *See also* **angry**.
fee *noun*
1. A fixed amount of money charged for a service ▶ exaction, fare. *See* **toll**¹ (1). **2.** Payment for work done ▶ earnings, pay, salary. *See* **wage**.
feeble *adjective*
1. Not physically strong ▶ delicate, frail, unsound. *See* **weak** (1). *See synonym note at* **weak**. **2.** So soft as to be barely audible ▶ faint, weak. *See also* **soft**. **3.** Not plausible or believable ▶ flimsy, tenuous, unsubstantial. *See* **implausible**.

feeble-minded *adjective*
▶ dull, simple. *See* **backward** (1).
feebleness *noun*
▶ decrepitude, fragileness, unsubstantiality. *See* **infirmity** (1).
feed *verb*
1. To sustain a living organism with food ▶ nourish, regale. *Idiom:* wine and dine. *See also* **support**. **2.** To help bring about ▶ cultivate, facilitate. *See* **promote** (2).
feed on *verb*
To include as part of one's diet by nature or preference ▶ eat, exist on, live on, subsist on. *See also* **eat**.
feed *noun*
Informal A large, elaborately prepared meal ▶ banquet, feast, junket. *Informal:* spread.
feel *verb*
1. To bring especially the hands or fingers into contact with ▶ handle, palpate. *See* **touch** (1). *See synonym note at* **touch**. **2.** To reach about or search blindly or uncertainly ▶ fumble, grabble. *See* **grope**. **3.** To participate in or partake of personally ▶ know, undergo. *See* **experience**. **4.** To be intuitively aware of ▶ apprehend, sense. *See* **perceive** (2). **5.** To experience or express compassion ▶ ache, commiserate, condole, sympathize. *Idioms:* be (*or* feel) sorry, have one's heart ache (*or* bleed) for someone, have one's heart go out to someone. *See also* **comfort, pity**. **6.** To have a belief or impression about something ▶ believe, hold, sense, think. *See also* **believe, perceive, regard**. **7.** To give the impression of being ▶ appear, look, seem, sound. *Idioms:* have all the earmarks of being, give the idea (*or* impression) of being, strike one as being. *See also* **resemble**.
feel for *verb*
To feel pity for someone ▶ commiserate with, sympathize with. *See* **pity**.
feel out *verb*
To test the attitude of someone ▶ probe, sound (out). *Idioms:* put out feelers, run something up the flagpole, send up a trial balloon.
feel *noun*
1. A particular sensation conveyed by means of physical contact ▶ feeling, touch. *See also* **contact, brush**. **2.** The faculty or ability to perceive tactile stimulation ▶ feeling, tactility, touch. *Idiom:* sense of touch. *See also* **sensation**. **3.** An act of touching ▶ palpation, stroke. *See* **touch** (1). **4.** A general impression produced by a predominant quality or characteristic ▶ atmosphere, aura, mood. *See* **air** (4). **5.** The proper method for doing, using, or handling something ▶ knack, trick. *Informal:* hang.
feeler *noun*
Something, such as a remark, used to determine another person's attitude ▶ probe. *Idiom:* trial balloon. *See also* **advances, introduction**.
feeling *noun*
1. An intuitive awareness or sense of something ▶ foreboding, forewarning, gut reaction, hunch, idea,

impression, inkling, intuition, notion, premonition, presentiment, suspicion. *See also* **hint, instinct, qualm. 2.** A particular sensation conveyed by means of physical contact ▸ feel, touch. *See also* **contact, brush. 3.** The faculty or ability to perceive tactile stimulation ▸ feel, tactility, touch. *Idiom:* sense of touch. *See also* **sensation. 4.** An act of touching ▸ palpation, stroke. *See* **touch** (1). **5.** The capacity for or an act of responding to a stimulus ▸ sensitiveness, sensitivity. *See* **sensation** (1). **6.** A general cast of mind with regard to something ▸ attitude, sentiment. *See also* **idea. 7.** A subjective mental state, such as love or hate ▸ affection, passion. *See* **emotion.** *See synonym note at* **emotion. 8.** The quality or condition of being emotionally and intuitively sensitive ▸ sensibility, sensitiveness, sensitivity. *See also* **pity, sympathy. 9.** Something thought to be true ▸ notion, persuasion, view. *See* **belief** (1). *See synonym note at* **belief. 10.** A general impression produced by a predominant quality or characteristic ▸ atmosphere, aura, mood. *See* **air** (4).

feeling *adjective*
1. Readily stirred by emotion ▸ emotional, sensitive. *See also* **passionate. 2.** Feeling or expressing sympathy or pity ▸ commiserative, compassionate, empathetic, understanding. *See* **sympathetic.**

feign *verb*
1. To claim or allege insincerely or falsely ▸ pretend, pretext, profess, purport. **2.** To take on as a false appearance ▸ dissemble, fake, simulate. *See* **act** (2).

feigned *adjective*
▸ insincere, phony. *See* **artificial** (2).

feint *noun*
▸ deception, ploy, stratagem. *See* **trick** (1). *See synonym note at* **trick.**

feisty *adjective*
▸ contentious, litigious, quarrelsome. *See* **argumentative.**

felicitate *verb*
To pay a compliment to ▸ commend, compliment, congratulate, praise. *Idiom:* take off one's hat to. *See also* **honor.**

felicitations *noun*
▸ praise, tribute. *See* **compliment** (1).

felicitous *adjective*
▸ befitting, correct, right. *See* **appropriate** (1).

felicity *noun*
▸ blessedness, bliss, gladness. *See* **happiness.**

feline *adjective*
▸ furtive, secretive, sneaky. *See* **stealthy.**

fell *verb*
▸ floor, ground, hew. *See* **drop** (6).

fellow *noun*
1. A man referred to familiarly or as a member of one's group ▸ brother. *Informal:* boy, chap, guy, jack, lad. *Slang:* dude, hombre, homeboy. **2.** *Informal* A man who is a woman's romantic partner ▸ beau, inamorato. *See* **boyfriend. 3.** One who is united in a relationship with another ▸ ally, partner. *See* associ-

ate (1). **4.** One who shares interests or activities with another ▸ companion, comrade. *See* **associate** (2). **5.** One that is very similar to another in rank or position ▸ colleague, equivalent. *See* **peer**^{2}. **6.** One of a matched pair of things ▸ companion, match. *See* **mate** (1).

fellow citizen *noun*
A person who is from one's own country ▸ compatriot, countryman, countrywoman, kinsman, kinswoman.

fellowship *noun*
1. A pleasant association among people ▸ companionship, society. *See* **company** (5). **2.** A group of people united in a relationship and having some interest, activity, or purpose in common ▸ club, league, order. *See* **union** (1). **3.** The condition of being friends ▸ amity, camaraderie, companionship. *See* **friendship.**

felon *noun*
▸ culprit, lawbreaker, offender. *See* **criminal.**

felonious *adjective*
▸ illicit, unlawful. *See* **criminal** (1).

felony *noun*
▸ illegality, offense. *See* **crime** (1).

female *adjective*
Relating to or characteristic of women ▸ feminine, womanish, womanly.

femaleness *noun*
The quality or condition of being feminine ▸ feminineness, femininity, womanliness.

feminine *adjective*
1. Relating to or characteristic of women ▸ female, womanish, womanly. **2.** Having qualities traditionally attributed to a woman ▸ epicene, unmanly. *See* **effeminate.**

feminineness *noun*
The quality or condition of being feminine ▸ femaleness, femininity, womanliness.

femininity *noun*
1. The quality or condition of being feminine ▸ femaleness, feminineness, womanliness. **2.** The quality of being effeminate ▸ effeteness, womanishness. *See* **effeminacy.**

femme fatale *noun*
▸ enchantress, siren. *See* **seductress.**

fen *noun*
▸ marsh, mire, wetland. *See* **swamp.**

fence *verb*
1. To confine within a limited area ▸ cage, corral, shut (in). *See* **enclose** (1). *See synonym note at* **enclose. 2.** To separate with or as if with a wall ▸ partition, wall. **3.** To strive in opposition ▸ clash, combat, fight. *See* **contend** (1). **4.** To avoid fulfilling or answering completely ▸ duck, sidestep, skirt. *See* **evade** (1). **5.** To use evasive or deliberately vague language ▸ euphemize, hedge, shuffle. *See* **equivocate** (1).

fence *noun*
The use or an instance of equivocal language ▸ euphemism, prevarication. *See* **equivocation** (1).

fend *verb*
1. To turn aside or drive away ▸ deflect, repulse, ward off. *See* **repel**. 2. To progress or perform adequately, especially in difficult circumstances ▸ fare, get by. *See* **manage** (1).

fender-bender *noun*
Informal A wrecking of a vehicle ▸ sideswipe, smash-up, wreck. *See* **crash** (2).

feral *adjective*
▸ savage, undomesticated, untamed. *See* **wild** (2).

ferment *verb*
To be in a state of turmoil or excitement ▸ burn, seethe. *See* **boil** (2).

ferment *noun*
1. An agent that stimulates a reaction or change ▸ leaven, reactant, yeast. *See* **catalyst**. 2. The condition of being agitated or disturbed ▸ disturbance, turmoil, unrest. *See* **agitation** (1).

ferocious *adjective*
1. So intense as to cause extreme suffering ▸ cruel, fierce, savage, vicious. 2. Inflicting suffering or pain ▸ brutal, ruthless, pitiless. *See* **cruel** (1). *See synonym note at* **cruel**.

ferociousness *noun*
▸ ferocity, fury, vehemence. *See* **intensity**.

ferocity *noun*
1. Concentrated power or force, as of effort, opinion, or emotion ▸ depth, fury, vehemence. *See* **intensity**. 2. The quality or condition or being cruel ▸ brutality, truculence. *See* **cruelty**.

ferret *verb*
To try to find something ▸ look for, search for. *See* **seek** (1).

ferret out *verb*
To obtain knowledge or awareness of something not known before ▸ determine, learn. *See* **discover**.

fertile *adjective*
1. Characterized by great productivity ▸ fecund, fruitful, productive, prolific, rich. *See also* **inventive**. 2. Capable of reproducing ▸ fecund, fruitful, productive, prolific.

✛ CORE SYNONYMS: *fertile, fecund, fruitful, productive, prolific*. These adjectives mean characterized by great productivity: *fertile farmland; a fecund imagination; fruitful efforts; a productive meeting; a prolific writer.*

fertility *noun*
The quality or state of being fertile ▸ fecundity, fruitfulness, productiveness, productivity, prolificacy, prolificness, richness. *See also* **invention**.

fertilize *verb*
1. To add fertilizer to ▸ dress, manure, top-dress. 2. To make fertile ▸ enrich, fecundate, pollinate. *See also* **impregnate**.

fervency *noun*
▸ ardor, zeal. *See* **passion** (1).

fervent *adjective*
1. Fired with intense feeling ▸ burning, fiery, impassioned. *See* **passionate** (1). 2. Showing or having

enthusiasm ▸ ardent, rabid, zealous. *See* **enthusiastic** (1).

fervid *adjective*
1. Fired with intense feeling ▸ ardent, impassioned, torrid. *See* **passionate** (1). 2. Showing or having enthusiasm ▸ exuberant, rabid, zealous. *See* **enthusiastic** (1). 3. Characterized by hurried activity and confusion or agitation ▸ frenetic, frenzied, hectic. *See* **frantic**.

fervor *noun*
1. Powerful, intense emotion ▸ ardor, zeal. *See* **passion** (1). *See synonym note at* **passion**. 2. Passionate devotion to or interest in a cause or subject ▸ excitement, fire. *See* **enthusiasm** (1). 3. Warmth or degree of warmth ▸ hotness, torridity. *See* **heat** (1).

fess up *verb*
Slang To admit to the reality or truth of ▸ concede, grant. *See* **acknowledge** (1).

fester *verb*
▸ deteriorate, rot, spoil, turn. *See* **decay**.

festering *noun*
▸ irritation, soreness. *See* **irritation** (3).

festinate *verb*
▸ dash, sprint, zip. *See* **rush** (1).

festival *noun*
1. A joyous or festive occasion ▸ festivity, fiesta, revels. *See* **celebration** (1). 2. A large public display, as of goods or works of art ▸ exposition, show. *See* **exhibition** (1).

festive *adjective*
▸ gala, joyful, joyous. *See* **merry** (1).

festiveness *noun*
▸ gaiety, merrymaking, revelry. *See* **merriment** (2).

festivity *noun*
1. The act of showing joyful satisfaction in an event ▸ jubilation, merrymaking, rejoicing. *See* **celebration** (3). 2. A joyous or festive occasion ▸ festival, fiesta, revels. *See* **celebration** (1). 3. A social gathering, especially for pleasure ▸ affair, get-together, soiree. *See* **party** (1). 4. Joyful, exuberant activity ▸ gaiety, merrymaking, revelry. *See* **merriment** (2).

festoon *noun*
▸ decorate, garnish, ornament. *See* **adorn** (1).

fetch *verb*
1. To cause to come along with oneself ▸ convey, transport. *See* **bring** (1). 2. To achieve a certain price ▸ go for, realize, sell for. *See* **bring** (2).

fetching *adjective*
1. Pleasing to the eye or mind ▸ enchanting, enticing, lovely, winsome. *See* **attractive** (1). 2. Pleasingly suited to the wearer ▸ attractive, flattering. *See* **becoming** (1).

fete *noun*
1. A social gathering, especially for pleasure ▸ celebration, gala, soiree. *See* **party** (1). 2. A joyous or festive occasion ▸ festivity, fiesta, revels. *See* **celebration** (1).

fetid *adjective*
▸ foul, malodorous, stinking. *See* **smelly**.

fetish *noun*
1. A small object kept for its supposed magical power ▸ mascot, talisman. *See* **charm** (1). 2. An irrational

preoccupation ▸ fascination, fixation, mania. *See* **obsession.**

fetor *noun*
▸ malodor, reek, stink. *See* **stench.** *See synonym note at* **stench.**

fetter *noun*
1. Something that physically confines the legs or arms ▸ handcuffs, hobble, irons. *See* **bond** (1). **2.** A band or fiber that is used to bind or tie ▸ cable, line, string. *See* **cord.**

fetter *verb*
To restrict the activity or free movement of ▸ hamstring, handcuff, hobble. *See* **hamper**[1] (1). *See synonym note at* **hamper**[1].

fettle *noun*
▸ condition, form, order. *See* **shape** (1).

feud *noun*
1. A discussion, often heated, in which a difference of opinion is expressed ▸ contention, fight, quarrel. *See* **argument** (1). **2.** Deep-seated hatred, as between longtime opponents or rivals ▸ animosity, antagonism. *See* **enmity.**

feud *verb*
To engage in a quarrel ▸ dispute, fight, quarrel. *See* **argue** (1).

fever *noun*
▸ fervor, passion, zeal. *See* **enthusiasm** (1).

fevered *adjective*
▸ delirious, frenzied, hectic. *See* **frantic.**

feverish *adjective*
1. Having an above-normal body temperature ▸ febrific, febrile, hectic, hot, pyretic. *See also* **sick.** **2.** Fired with intense feeling ▸ ardent, fervent, flaming. *See* **passionate** (1). **3.** Characterized by hurried activity and confusion or agitation ▸ hectic, frenzied. *See* **frantic.**

few *adjective*
Consisting of a number more than two or three but less than many ▸ divers, some, various. *See* **several** (1).

few *pronoun*
A number more than two or three but less than many ▸ small number, smattering. *See* **several.**

fey *adjective*
▸ magical, witching, wizardly. *See* **magic** (1).

fiancé *or* **fiancée** *noun*
▸ betrothed, prospective spouse. *See* **intended.**

fiasco *noun*
1. An unsuccessful enterprise ▸ bust, loser, washout. *See* **failure** (1). **2.** A confused or ruinous state ▸ foul-up, muddle, shambles. *See* **mess** (1). **3.** An occurrence inflicting widespread destruction and distress ▸ cataclysm, catastrophe, tragedy. *See* **disaster** (1). **4.** Something that disappoints ▸ anticlimax, bust, washout. *See* **disappointment** (2).

fiat *noun*
▸ commandment, imperative. *See* **command** (1).

fib *noun*
An untrue declaration ▸ falsehood, inveracity, tale untruth. *See* **lie**[2]. *See synonym note at* **lie**[2].

fib *verb*
To present false information with the intention of deceiving ▸ falsify, prevaricate. *See* **lie**[2].

fibber *noun*
▸ fabulist, prevaricator. *See* **liar.**

fiber *noun*
1. A very fine continuous strand ▸ fibril, filament, microfiber, thread. *See also* **cord.** **2.** A distinctive, complex underlying pattern or structure ▸ fabric, grain, web. *See* **texture** (1). **3.** Moral or ethical strength ▸ honesty, integrity, principle. *See* **character** (2).

fibril *noun*
A very fine continuous strand ▸ fiber, filament, microfiber, thread. *See also* **cord.**

fibrous *adjective*
Containing or consisting of fibers ▸ sinewy, stringy, threadlike.

fickle *adjective*
▸ erratic, impulsive, mercurial. *See* **capricious.**

fiction *noun*
1. A narrative not based on fact ▸ fable, novel, romance, story. *See also* **yarn.** **2.** An illusory mental image ▸ fancy, fantasy, illusion. *See* **dream** (1). **3.** A half-truth, especially one that forms part of an ideology ▸ fantasy, figment, invention. *See* **myth** (3). **4.** An untrue declaration ▸ falsehood, fib, untruth. *See* **lie**[2].

fictional *adjective*
▸ fanciful, made-up. *See* **fictitious** (1).

fictitious *adjective*
1. Consisting or suggestive of fiction ▸ fantastic, fictional, fictive, invented, made-up. *See also* **imaginary.** **2.** Not true ▸ specious, untrue, wrong. *See* **false** (1).

fictive *adjective*
▸ fictional, made-up. *See* **fictitious** (1).

fiddle *verb*
1. To touch or handle something out of restlessness ▸ fidget, fool, play, toy, trifle, twiddle. *Informal:* monkey. *See also* **handle.** **2.** To waste time by engaging in aimless activity ▸ dawdle about. *Informal:* fool around. *See* **putter.** **3.** To handle something in an attempt to improve it ▸ mess, tamper. *See* **tinker** (1). **4.** To alter or present material so as to favor a particular viewpoint ▸ doctor, slant. *See* **bias** (2).

fiddle away *verb*
To spend (time) idly or pleasantly ▸ dawdle (away), trifle away, waste. *See* **idle** (2).

fiddle-faddle *noun*
▸ frivolity, nonsense, trivia. *See* **trifle** (1).

fidelity *noun*
1. Faithfulness or devotion to a person, cause, or obligation ▸ allegiance, constancy, faithfulness, fealty, loyalty, steadfastness. *See also* **attachment.** **2.** Correspondence with fact or truth ▸ authenticity, correctness, truth, validity. *See* **veracity.**

✦ CORE SYNONYMS: *fidelity, allegiance, fealty, loyalty.* These nouns denote faithfulness or devotion to a person, cause, or obligation. *Fidelity* implies the unfailing fulfillment of one's duties and obligations and strict adherence to vows or promises: *fidelity to one's spouse. Allegiance* is faithfulness considered as a duty: *"I know no South, no North, no East, no West, to which I owe any allegiance . . . . The Union, Sir, is my country"* (Henry Clay). *Fealty,* once applied to the obligation of a tenant or vassal to a feudal lord, now suggests faithfulness that one has pledged to uphold: *swore fealty to the laws of that country. Loyalty* implies a steadfast and devoted attachment that is not easily turned aside: *loyalty to a sacred oath; loyalty to one's family.*

fidget *verb*
▸ tinker, toy, twiddle. *See* **fiddle** (1).

fidgets *noun*
▸ jumps, shivers, trembles. *See* **jitters.**

fidgety *adjective*
▸ jittery, nervous, skittish. *See* **edgy.**

field *noun*
1. An area of open land ▸ clearing, meadow, pasture. *See also* **lot. 2.** An area of academic study that is part of a larger body of learning ▸ branch, discipline, specialty. **3.** A sphere of activity, experience, study, or interest ▸ department, domain, terrain. *See* **area** (1). *See synonym note at* **area.**

field *verb*
To speak or act in response ▸ rejoin, reply, riposte. *See* **answer** (1).

fiend *noun*
1. A perversely mean, cruel, or wicked person ▸ archfiend, barbarian, beast, brute, demon, devil, ghoul, hun, monster, ogre, savage, villain. *See also* **evildoer, rascal. 2.** *Informal* An ardent devotee ▸ enthusiast, fanatic, junkie. *See* **fan².**

fiendish *adjective*
Perversely mean, cruel, or wicked ▸ devilish, diabolic, diabolical, ghoulish, hellish, infernal, ogreish, satanic, villainous. *See also* **evil, fierce, malevolent.**

fierce *adjective*
1. Inflicting suffering or pain ▸ brutal, inhuman, savage. *See* **cruel** (1). *See synonym note at* **cruel. 2.** Extreme in activity, strength, or effect ▸ furious, heavy, strong. *See* **intense** (1). *See synonym note at* **intense.**

fiercely *adverb*
▸ energetically, forcefully, severely, vigorously. *See* **hard** (1).

fierceness *noun*
1. Concentrated power or force, as of effort, opinion, or emotion ▸ ferocity, fury, vehemence. *See* **intensity. 2.** The quality or condition of being cruel ▸ brutality, truculence. *See* **cruelty.**

fiery *adjective*
1. On fire ▸ ablaze, afire, conflagrant. *See* **burning** (1). **2.** Marked by much heat ▸ blistering, boiling, burning. *See* **hot** (1). **3.** Fired with intense feeling ▸ burning, fervent, impassioned, torrid. *See* **passionate** (1). **4.** Having a sharp, penetrating flavor or aroma ▸ piquant, sharp, zesty. *See* **spicy** (1).

fiesta *noun*
A joyous or festive occasion ▸ festival, festivity, revels. *See* **celebration** (1).

fifty-fifty *adjective*
Neither favorable nor unfavorable ▸ balanced, even, nip and tuck.

fight *noun*
1. A physical conflict involving two or more people ▸ affray, brawl, donnybrook, fistfight, fisticuffs, fracas, fray, free-for-all, melee, riot, row, ruction, scrap, scuffle, tumult, tussle. *Slang:* rumble, slugfest. *See also* **attack, brush¹, combat, conflict. 2.** The power or will to fight ▸ bellicoseness, bellicosity, belligerence, belligerency, combativeness, contentiousness, pugnacity, pugnaciousness, truculence, truculency. *See also* **aggression. 3.** A discussion, often heated, in which a difference of opinion is expressed ▸ contention, quarrel. *Informal:* tangle. *See* **argument** (1). **4.** A test of skill or ability ▸ bout, match, trial. *See* **competition** (2).

fight *verb*
1. To exchange blows with another person ▸ brawl. *Slang:* rumble. **Idioms:** duke it out, mix it up, slug it out. *See also* **wrestle. 2.** To engage in a quarrel ▸ dispute, quarrel. *See* **argue** (1). **3.** To strive in opposition ▸ clash, combat, spar. *See* **contend** (1). **4.** To place in opposition or be in opposition to ▸ match, pit. *See* **oppose** (1). *See synonym note at* **oppose.**

fight off *verb*
To turn aside or drive away ▸ deflect, repulse, ward off. *See* **repel.**

✦ **CORE SYNONYMS:** *fight, brawl, donnybrook, fray, free-for-all, melee, row, scuffle.* These nouns denote a physical conflict involving two or more people: *an argument that escalated into a fight; a barroom brawl; a vicious legal donnybrook; eager for the fray; a free-for-all in the schoolyard; police plunging into the melee; an angry domestic row; a scuffle between the opposing teams.*

fighter *noun*
1. One who engages in a combat or struggle ▸ belligerent, combatant, soldier, warrior. *See also* **aggressor, soldier. 2.** A contestant in a boxing match ▸ boxer, prizefighter, pugilist.

figment *noun*
1. An illusory mental image ▸ fancy, fantasy, illusion. *See* **dream** (1). **2.** A fiction or half-truth, especially one that forms part of an ideology ▸ fantasy, fiction, invention. *See* **myth** (3).

figurative *adjective*
▸ emblematical, metaphorical, representative. *See* **symbolic** (1).

figure *noun*
1. An element or component in a decorative composition ▸ design, device, motif, motive. **2.** An amount represented in numerals ▸ number, quantity. *See also* **total. 3.** The characteristic surface arrangement of a thing ▸ configuration, design, structure. *See* **form** (1). *See synonym note at* **form. 4.** A work of art created by

shaping a solid material ▸ bust, carving, statue. *See* **sculpture. 5.** A conventional mark used in a writing system ▸ letter, symbol. *See* **character** (9). **6.** A famous person ▸ luminary, personality, star. *See* **celebrity** (1). **7.** The physical characteristics of a person ▸ body, form, physique. *See* **constitution** (1).

figure *verb*
1. To ascertain by mathematics ▸ cast, cipher, compute, reckon. *See* **calculate** (1). *See synonym note at* **calculate. 2.** *Informal* To have an opinion ▸ deem, hold. *See* **believe** (3).

figure on *verb*
Informal To look forward to confidently ▸ anticipate, await, look for. *See* **expect** (1).

figure out *verb*
1. *Informal* To arrive at an answer to a mathematical problem ▸ solve, work out. *See also* **calculate. 2.** *Informal* To find a solution for ▸ explain, resolve, unravel. *See* **solve** (1). *See synonym note at* **solve.**

✤ CORE SYNONYMS: *figure, design, device, motif.* These nouns denote an element or a component in a decorative composition: *a tapestry with a floral figure; a rug with a geometric design; a brooch with a fanciful and intricate device; a scarf with a heart motif.*

---

figured *adjective*
▸ deliberate, intentional, premeditated. *See* **calculated** (1).

figures *noun*
Arithmetic calculations ▸ arithmetic, computation, numbers. *See also* **addition, calculation.**

figurine *noun*
▸ bust, carving, statue. *See* **sculpture.**

figuring *noun*
The act, process, or result of calculating ▸ calculation, cast, computation, reckoning.

filament *noun*
A very fine continuous strand ▸ fiber, fibril, microfiber, thread. *See also* **cord.**

filch *verb*
▸ pilfer, snatch, thieve. *See* **steal** (1). *See synonym note at* **steal.**

file¹ *noun*
A group of people or things that are arranged in a row ▸ column, queue, string. *See* **line** (1).

file *verb*
1. To place on a list or in a record or book ▸ catalog, chronicle, write down. *See* **list¹** (1). **2.** To place in or form a line or lines ▸ dress, queue (up), range. *See* **line.**

file² *verb*
1. To bring or come into abrasive contact ▸ abrade, rasp. *See* **scrape** (2). **2.** To give a sharp edge to ▸ grind, hone, whet. *See* **sharpen** (2).

fill *verb*
1. To make full; put as much into as can be held ▸ charge, cram, crowd, freight, heap, jam, load, mob, pack, pile, stuff, top off. *Informal:* jam-pack. **2.** To plug up or block something, such as a hole or conduit

▸ block, choke, clog, close, congest, cork, plug, seal, stop. **3.** To be suitable or sufficient to fulfill a need ▸ fulfill, meet. *See* **satisfy** (1). *See synonym note at* **satisfy. 4.** To cause to be filled, as with a particular mood ▸ permeate, suffuse. *See* **charge** (1).

fill in *verb*
1. To bring to perfection or completion ▸ complement, complete, refine. *See* **perfect. 2.** To act as a substitute ▸ cover for, serve as, stand in. *See* **substitute. 3.** To impart information to ▸ apprise, notify. *See* **inform** (1).

fill out *verb*
To bring to perfection or completion ▸ complement, complete, refine. *See* **perfect.**

fill *noun*
Material used to fill a space or container ▸ padding, stuffing. *See* **filler** (1).

filler *noun*
1. Material used to fill a space or container ▸ caulking, fill, packing, padding, stuffing, wadding. **2.** Written material used to fill space in a publication ▸ boilerplate. *See also* **item.**

fillet *noun*
▸ bandeau, ribbon, strip, stripe. *See* **band¹** (1).

fill-in *noun*
Informal One that takes the place of another ▸ alternate, replacement, surrogate. *See* **substitute.**

fill-in *adjective*
Informal Temporarily assuming the duties of another ▸ interim, provisional. *See* **temporary** (1).

filling *noun*
Something used to fill a hole, space, or container ▸ cork, stop. *See* **plug** (1).

filling *adjective*
Not readily digested because of richness ▸ heavy, rich.

fillip *noun*
▸ encouragement, impulse, incentive. *See* **stimulus** (1).

film *noun*
1. A thin outer covering ▸ membrane, sheath. *See* **skin** (2). **2.** A motion picture ▸ motion picture, movie, picture. *Slang:* flick.

filmy *adjective*
1. Thin, fine, and light ▸ ethereal, gauzy, vaporous. *See* **sheer²** (1). *See synonym note at* **sheer². 2.** Not clearly perceptible ▸ dim, faint, indefinite. *See* **unclear** (1).

filth *noun*
1. Foul or dirty matter ▸ dirt, grime, muck, mud. *Slang:* crap, crud, grunge. *See also* **slime. 2.** The condition or state of being dirty ▸ filthiness, squalor, uncleanliness. *See* **dirtiness** (1). **3.** Something that is offensive to accepted standards of decency ▸ dirt, sleaze, smut. *See* **obscenity** (2). **4.** Waste matter eliminated from the bowels ▸ dung, feces, waste. *See* **excrement.**

filthiness *noun*
1. The condition or state of being dirty ▸ foulness, squalor, uncleanliness. *See* **dirtiness** (1). **2.** The quality or state of being obscene ▸ foulness, profanity, smuttiness, vulgarness. *See* **obscenity** (1).

filthy *adjective*
1. Covered with or stained by dirt or other impurities ► grimy, soiled, unclean. *See* **dirty** (1). *See synonym note at* **dirty. 2.** Offensive to accepted standards of decency ► bawdy, coarse, lewd, vulgar. *See* **obscene** (1). **3.** So objectionable as to deserve condemnation ► abhorrent, despicable, loathsome. *See* **offensive** (1).

finagle *verb*
Informal To use stratagems in gaining an end ► engineer, finesse. *See* **maneuver** (2).

final *adjective*
1. Coming after all others ► concluding, terminal. *See* **last¹** (1). *See synonym note at* **last¹. 2.** Of or relating to a terminative condition, stage, or point ► last, latter, terminal, ultimate. *See also* **climactic. 3.** Serving the function of deciding or settling with finality ► decisive, determinative. *See* **definitive** (1).

finale *noun*
► closing, ending, epilogue. *See* **end** (2).

finalize *verb*
► arrange, conclude, fix. *See* **settle** (1).

finally *adverb*
1. In conclusion ► conclusively, last, lastly. *Idioms:* at last, in the end, when all is said and done. **2.** After a considerable length of time, usually after a delay ► eventually. *Idiom:* at long last. *See* **ultimately** (1).

finance *noun*
The management of money ► banking, investment, money management.

finance *verb*
To supply capital to or for ► back, capitalize, fund, grubstake, stake, subsidize, subvent, underwrite. *Informal:* bankroll. *Idiom:* put up money for. *See also* **patronize, support.**

finances *noun*
The monetary resources of a government, organization, or individual ► capital, funds, money (or moneys). *See also* **capital, money, resources.**

financial *adjective*
Relating to finances ► fiscal, monetary, pecuniary.

financier *noun*
One who is occupied with or expert in large-scale financial affairs ► capitalist. *Informal:* moneyman.

financing *noun*
1. Money or property used to produce more wealth ► assets, funding, stake. *See* **capital** (1). **2.** Aid or support given by a patron ► backing, sponsorship. *See* **patronage** (1).

find *verb*
1. To look for and discover ► locate, pinpoint, spot. *Informal:* scare up. *See also* **trace, uncover. 2.** To find or meet by chance ► come across, run across, stumble on. *See* **encounter** (1). **3.** To arrive at a conclusion from evidence or reasoning ► deduce, gather. *See* **infer** (1).

find out *verb*
1. To perceive and fix the identity of, especially with difficulty ► ascertain, recognize. *See* **discern** (1). **2.** To obtain knowledge or awareness of something not

known before ► ascertain, determine, learn. *See* **discover.**

find *noun*
1. Something offered or bought at a low price ► bargain. *Informal:* buy, deal. *Slang:* steal. **2.** Something that has been discovered ► conclusion, strike. *See* **discovery. 3.** Someone or something considered exceptionally precious ► pearl, plum, prize. *See* **treasure** (1).

finding *noun*
1. Something that has been discovered ► conclusion, strike. *See* **discovery. 2.** An authoritative or official decision ► edict, judgment, pronouncement. *See* **ruling.**

fine¹ *adjective*
1. Of fine quality ► exceptional, select, superior. *See* **choice** (1). **2.** Exceptionally good of its kind ► first-rate, prime, splendid, tiptop. *See* **excellent. 3.** Appealing to refined taste ► elegant, exquisite. *See* **delicate** (1). *See synonym note at* **delicate. 4.** Having pleasant desirable qualities ► bonny, enjoyable, nice. *See* **good** (1). **5.** Free from clouds or mist ► fair, sunny. *See* **clear** (2). **6.** Consisting of small particles ► dusty, powdery, pulverous, pulverulent. *See also* **minute². 7.** So slight as to be difficult to notice or appreciate ► refined, subtle. *See* **delicate** (4). **8.** Able to make or detect effects of great subtlety or precision ► delicate, nice, sensitive, subtle. *See also* **accurate. 9.** Having an end that tapers to a point ► acute, cuspate, sharp. *See* **pointed** (1).

fine² *noun*
A sum of money levied as punishment for an offense ► amercement, mulct, penalty. *See also* **punishment.**

fine *verb*
To impose a fine on ► amerce, mulct, penalize. *See also* **punish.**

fineness *noun*
1. The quality of being exceptionally good of its kind ► superbness, superiority. *See* **excellence. 2.** The ability to make or detect effects of great precision ► delicacy, sensitivity. *See* **subtlety** (1).

fine print *noun*
► particular, specialty, technicality. *See* **detail** (1).

finery *noun*
► array, frippery, regalia. *See* **attire** (1).

finespun *adjective*
► fine, refined, subtle. *See* **delicate** (4).

finesse *verb*
1. To outmaneuver an opponent ► trump. *Informal:* one-up. *See also* **deceive, outwit. 2.** To use stratagems in gaining an end ► engineer, worm. *See* **maneuver** (2). **3.** To direct the course of carefully ► jockey, navigate. *See* **maneuver** (1).

finest *noun*
► officer, trooper. *Informal:* cop. *See* **police officer.**

fine-tune *verb*
► align, calibrate, tweak. *See* **adjust** (1).

finger *verb*
1. To bring especially the hands or fingers into

contact with ▸ handle, palpate. *See* **touch** (1). *See synonym note at* **touch**. **2.** *Slang* To establish the identity of ▸ identify, know, pinpoint. *See* **place** (1).

finger *noun*
A narrow line of light or other radiant energy ▸ shaft, stream. *See* **beam** (1).

finger-pointing *noun*
1. A charging of someone with a misdeed ▸ denouncement, imputation, incrimination. *See* **accusation**. **2.** The act or an instance of finding fault ▸ censure, condemnation, denunciation. *See* **criticism** (1).

finicky *or* **finical** *adjective*
▸ exacting, fastidious. *See* **fussy** (1).

finis *noun*
▸ cease, completion, termination. *See* **end** (1).

finish *verb*
1. To complete a race or competition in a specified position ▸ come in, place, run. **2.** To bring or come to a natural or proper end ▸ close, end, terminate. *See* **conclude** (1). *See synonym note at* **conclude**. **3.** To use all of ▸ eat up, expend, run through. *See* **exhaust** (1). **4.** To cause the death of ▸ cut down, execute, dispatch. *See* **kill**[1] (1). **5.** To take the life of a person or persons unlawfully ▸ assassinate, kill, slay. *See* **murder** (1). **6.** To cause the complete ruin or wreckage of ▸ demolish, torpedo, wreck. *See* **destroy** (1). **7.** To apply a coating or surface material to ▸ enamel, glaze, lacquer, paint, plaster, polish, polyurethane, shellac, stain, surface, varnish, wax. *See also* **cover, face, gloss**[1], **smear**.

finish *noun*
1. A concluding or terminating ▸ cease, completion, termination. *See* **end** (1). **2.** The last part ▸ closing, ending, epilogue. *See* **end** (2). **3.** A final coating or material applied to a surface ▸ enamel, glaze, lacquer, paint, plaster, polish, polyurethane, shellac, stain, surface, varnish, wax. *See also* **coat, face, gloss**[1].

finished *adjective*
1. No longer effective, capable, or valuable ▸ done for, washed-up. *See* **through** (2). **2.** Having no further relationship ▸ done, through. **3.** Proficient as a result of practice and study ▸ accomplished, polished, practiced. *See also* **able, expert**. **4.** Having reached completion ▸ concluded, done, through. *See* **complete** (3).

fink *noun*
Slang One who gives incriminating information about others ▸ informant. *Slang:* snitch, squealer. *See* **informer**.

fink *verb*
Slang To give incriminating information about others, especially to the authorities ▸ tip (off). *Slang:* rat, snitch. *See* **inform** (2).

fink out *verb*
Slang To abandon a former position or commitment ▸ back down, retreat, walk out. *See* **renege**.

fire *noun*
1. The visible signs of combustion ▸ blaze, conflagration, flame, flare-up. **2.** Powerful, intense emotion ▸ ardor, zeal. *See* **passion** (1). *See synonym note at* **passion**. **3.** Passionate devotion to or interest in a cause or subject ▸ eagerness, excitement. *See* **enthusiasm** (1). **4.** Exceptional brightness and clarity ▸ effulgence, luminosity, radiance. *See* **brilliance** (1). **5.** Liveliness and vivacity of imagination ▸ brilliance, brilliancy, genius, inspiration. *See also* **intelligence, invention**. **6.** A concentrated outpouring, as of missiles, words, or blows ▸ cannonade, fusillade, volley. *See* **barrage**.

fire *verb*
1. To begin or cause to begin burning ▸ ignite, kindle. *See* **light**[1] (1). **2.** To arouse the emotions of; make ardent ▸ animate, arouse, enkindle, impassion, inflame, inspire, kindle, rouse, stir. *See also* **move**. **3.** To discharge a gun or firearm ▸ blast (away), fire away (off), pop (off), shoot (away *or* off). *Idioms:* go bang-bang, open fire, take a shot (*or* potshot). **4.** *Informal* To send through the air with a motion of the hand or arm ▸ heave, hurl, pitch. *See* **throw** (1). **5.** To release or cause to release energy suddenly and violently, especially with a loud noise ▸ burst, detonate. *See* **explode** (1). **6.** *Informal* To end the employment or service of ▸ cashier, drop. *See* **dismiss** (1). *See synonym note at* **dismiss**.

fire and brimstone *noun*
1. A place or experience of excruciating pain or punishment ▸ perdition, persecution. *See* **hell**. **2.** Pretentious, pompous speech or writing ▸ fustian, grandiloquence. *See* **bombast**.

firebrand *noun*
▸ instigator, malcontent, rabble-rouser. *See* **agitator**.

fired up *adjective*
▸ atingle, excited, worked up. *See* **thrilled**.

fireplace *noun*
An open space for holding a fire at the base of a chimney ▸ grate, hearth, ingle.

fireproof *adjective*
Resistant to catching fire or combusting ▸ fire-resistant, fire-retardant, flameproof, flame-resistant, flame-retardant, incombustible, noncombustible, nonflammable.

fireworks *noun*
▸ contention, fight, quarrel. *See* **argument** (1).

firm[1] *adjective*
1. Unyielding to pressure or force ▸ hard, incompressible, solid. **2.** Not easily moved or shaken ▸ fast, secure, solid, sound, stable, steady, strong, sturdy, substantial, sure, unshakable. *See also* **fixed, motionless**. **3.** Indicating or possessing determination or resolution ▸ constant, decided, decisive, determined, resolute, resolved, single-minded, steadfast, steady, stiff, tough, unbending, uncompromising, unflinching, unwavering, unyielding. *See also* **insistent, intent, stubborn**. **4.** Adhering firmly and devotedly, as to a person, cause, or duty ▸ loyal, steadfast, true. *See* **faithful** (1). **5.** Having no change or variation ▸ fixed, invariable, set. *See* **unchanging**. **6.** Persistently holding to something ▸ clinging, tenacious. *See* **tight** (1).

firm up *verb*

To make or become physically hard ▸ congeal, solidify. *See* **harden** (2).

firm² *noun*

A commercial organization ▸ corporation, enterprise, establishment. *See* **company** (1).

firmament *noun*

The celestial regions as seen from the earth ▸ air, heavens, sky. *Idiom:* wild blue yonder.

firmness *noun*

1. Reliability in withstanding pressure, force, or stress ▸ fastness, hardness, steadiness. *See* **stability**. **2.** Unwavering firmness of character, action, or will ▸ determination, resolve, will. *See* **decision** (2). **3.** The condition of being without change or variation ▸ constancy, immutability. *See* **changelessness**.

first *adjective*

1. Preceding all others in time ▸ earliest, inaugural, initial, maiden, original, pioneer, premier, primary, prime, primordial. *See also* **beginning**. **2.** Most important, influential, or significant ▸ chief, key, main, principal. *See* **primary** (1). **3.** Surpassing all others in quality ▸ superlative, unsurpassed. *See* **best** (1).

first-class *adjective*

1. Exceptionally good of its kind ▸ first-rate, prime, splendid, tiptop. *See* **excellent**. **2.** Of fine quality ▸ exceptional, select, superior. *See* **choice** (1).

firsthand *adjective*

Marked by the absence of any intervention ▸ direct, immediate, primary.

firsthand *adverb*

Without intermediary ▸ directly, immediately.

first-rate *adjective*

1. Exceptionally good of its kind ▸ prime, splendid, tiptop. *See* **excellent**. **2.** Of fine quality ▸ exceptional, select, superior. *See* **choice** (1).

fiscal *adjective*

Of or relating to finances ▸ financial, monetary, pecuniary.

fish *verb*

1. To try to catch fish ▸ angle, cast, go fishing, troll, trawl. *Idioms:* cast one's hook (*or* net). **2.** To try to obtain something, usually by subtleness and cunning ▸ angle, hint.

fish for *verb*

To try to find something ▸ look for, search for. *See* **seek** (1).

fish story *noun*

1. *Informal* An untrue declaration ▸ falsehood, fib, untruth. *See* **lie²**. **2.** *Informal* An instance of exaggerating ▸ hyperbolism, tall talk. *See* **exaggeration**.

fishwife *noun*

▸ harpy, shrew. *See* **scold**.

fishy *adjective*

▸ equivocal, questionable, suspicious. *See* **shady** (1).

fission *noun*

▸ disjunction, divorce, parting. *See* **division** (1).

fissure *noun*

1. A partial opening caused by splitting and rupture ▸ break, cleft, fault. *See* **crack** (2). **2.** An interruption in friendly relations ▸ break, estrangement. *See* **breach** (2). **3.** The act or an instance of separating one thing from another ▸ disjunction, divorce, parting. *See* **division** (1).

fissure *verb*

To undergo partial breaking ▸ rupture, split. *See* **crack** (1).

fistfight *or* **fisticuffs** *noun*

▸ free-for-all, melee. *See* **fight** (1).

fit¹ *verb*

1. To cause to be ready, as for use, consumption, or a special purpose ▸ fix, ready. *See* **prepare** (1). **2.** To supply what is needed for some activity or purpose ▸ equip, gear, outfit. *See* **furnish** (1). **3.** To be compatible or suitable ▸ chime, correspond, match. *See* **agree** (1). **4.** To be suitable to or in keeping with ▸ become, befit, match. *See* **suit** (1). **5.** To make or become suitable to a particular situation or use ▸ adjust, tailor. *See* **adapt**. *See synonym note at* **adapt**. **6.** To be the proper size and shape for something ▸ dovetail, interlock. *Idiom:* fit like a glove.

fit out *or* **up** *verb*

To supply what is needed for some activity or purpose ▸ equip, gear. *See* **furnish** (1).

fit *adjective*

1. Suitable for a particular person, condition, occasion, or place ▸ befitting, correct, right. *See* **appropriate** (1). **2.** Suited to one's purpose ▸ expedient, proper, suitable. *See* **convenient** (1). **3.** Satisfying certain requirements, as for selection ▸ qualified, suitable. *See* **eligible** (1). **4.** Consistent with prevailing or accepted standards or circumstances ▸ deserved, fitting, proper. *See* **just** (2). **5.** Having good health ▸ healthful, well. *See* **healthy** (1).

fit² *noun*

1. A sudden and often acute manifestation of a disease ▸ apoplexy, convulsion. *See* **seizure** (1). **2.** A sudden violent expression, as of emotion ▸ burst, eruption, explosion. *See* **outburst** (1). **3.** An angry outburst ▸ huff, passion, tantrum. *See* **temper** (2).

fitful *adjective*

▸ occasional, periodic, sporadic. *See* **intermittent**. *See synonym note at* **intermittent**.

fitfully *adverb*

▸ occasionally, periodically, sometimes. *See* **intermittently**.

fitness *noun*

1. The quality of being eligible ▸ eligibility, suitability, worthiness. *See* **qualification**. **2.** A state of sound readiness ▸ fettle, form, order. *See* **shape** (1).

fitted *adjective*

▸ qualified, suitable. *See* **eligible** (1).

fitting *adjective*

1. Suitable for a particular person, condition, occasion, or place ▸ befitting, correct, right. *See* **appropriate** (1). **2.** Consistent with prevailing or accepted standards or circumstances ▸ deserved, merited, proper. *See* **just** (2).

fitting *noun*
Something attached as a permanent part of something else ▸ apparatus, fixture, installation. *See also* **attachment.**

fix *verb*
1. To restore to proper condition or functioning ▸ doctor, fix up, mend, overhaul, patch (up), repair, revamp, right, service. *Idioms:* put right (*or* to rights), set right (*or* to rights). *See also* **cure, restore. 2.** To alter for proper functioning ▸ calibrate, regulate, set, tweak. *See* **adjust** (1). **3.** To make right what is wrong ▸ mend, rectify, remedy. *See* **correct** (1). **4.** To place or set deeply or securely ▸ embed, entrench, fasten, implant, infix, ingrain, lodge, plant, root. **5.** To place securely in a position or condition ▸ ensconce, install, seat. *See* **establish** (2). **6.** To make secure ▸ bind, chain, moor. *See* **fasten** (1). *See synonym note at* **fasten. 7.** To join one thing to another ▸ append, fasten, secure. *See* **attach** (1). **8.** To become stuck or entangled ▸ hook, lodge. *See* **catch** (3). **9.** To produce a deep impression of ▸ etch, imprint. *See* **engrave** (2). **10.** To set forth expressly and authoritatively ▸ impose, mandate, ordain. *See* **dictate** (1). **11.** To put into correct or conclusive form ▸ conclude, finalize. *See* **settle** (1). **12.** To bring something into a state of agreement or accord ▸ arrange, negotiate, rectify, set. *See* **settle** (2). **13.** To ascribe the blame for a misdeed or error ▸ affix, ascribe, assign, attribute, blame, fasten, impute, lay, pin, place. *See also* **attribute. 14.** To cause to be ready, as for use, consumption, or a special purpose ▸ cure, ready. *See* **prepare** (1). **15.** To render incapable of reproducing ▸ neuter, spay. *See* **sterilize** (2). **16.** *Informal* To exact revenge for or from ▸ pay off, vindicate. *See* **avenge. 17.** To prearrange the outcome of a contest unlawfully ▸ rig, tamper. *Idiom:* stack the deck. **18.** To control the functioning or outcome of ▸ determine, regulate. *See* **govern** (1). **19.** To buy or promise a bribe to ▸ corrupt. *Informal:* pay off. *See* **bribe. 20.** To place a limit on ▸ bound, confine, restrict. *See* **limit** (1).

fix up *verb*
1. To make new or as if new again ▸ refresh, restore, revamp. *See* **renew** (1). **2.** To restore to proper condition ▸ mend, overhaul, repair. *See* **fix** (1). **3.** To make or become physically hard ▸ congeal, solidify. *See* **harden** (2).

fix *noun*
1. Money or a favor given as inducement to dishonest behavior ▸ graft. *Informal:* payoff. *See* **bribe. 2.** A difficult, often embarrassing situation or condition ▸ corner, difficulty, hot spot. *See* **predicament.** *See synonym note at* **predicament.**

fixate *verb*
To dominate the mind or thoughts of ▸ obsess, possess, preoccupy. *See also* **absorb, grip.**

fixation *noun*
▸ fetish, mania. *See* **obsession.**

fixed *adjective*
1. Firmly in position ▸ anchored, embedded, fastened,

immobile, immovable, riveted, rooted, secured, stationary, steadfast, steady, unmovable, unmoving. *See also* **firm¹. 2.** Not moving ▸ stationary, still. *Idiom:* cast (*or* etched *or* set) in stone. *See* **motionless. 3.** Having distinct limits ▸ determinate, specific. *See* **definite** (2). **4.** Remaining unchanged ▸ constant, invariable, set. *See* **unchanging. 5.** Committed to or unwavering in a course of action ▸ determined, resolute. *See* **intent** (1).

fixture *noun*
1. Something attached as a permanent part of something else ▸ apparatus, fitting, installation. *See also* **attachment. 2.** A device that regulates the flow of a liquid ▸ cock, spigot. *See* **faucet.**

fizz *noun*
1. A mass of bubbles in or on the surface of a liquid ▸ lather, suds. *See* **foam. 2.** A sibilant sound ▸ fizzle, rustle. *See* **hiss** (1).

fizz *verb*
1. To form or cause to form foam ▸ froth, lather. *See* **foam** (1). **2.** To make a sibilant sound ▸ fizzle, swish. *See* **hiss** (1).

fizzle *verb*
1. To make a sibilant sound ▸ fizz, swish. *See* **hiss** (1). **2.** *Informal* To lose strength or power ▸ decline, flag, weaken. *See* **fade** (1).

fizzle *noun*
1. A sibilant sound ▸ fizz, rustle. *See* **hiss** (1). **2.** *Informal* Something that disappoints ▸ anticlimax, bust, washout. *See* **disappointment** (2).

fizzy *adjective*
▸ frothy, lathery, sudsy. *See* **foamy.**

fjord *noun*
▸ estuary, mouth. *See* **inlet.**

flabbergast *verb*
▸ boggle, dumbfound. *See* **stagger** (2).

flabby *adjective*
1. Having too much flesh ▸ chubby, pudgy, tubby. *See* **fat** (1). **2.** Not firm or stiff ▸ flaccid, floppy. *See* **limp** (1). *See synonym note at* **limp.**

flaccid *adjective*
▸ drooping, soft. *See* **limp** (1). *See synonym note at* **limp.**

flag¹ *noun*
1. A piece of fabric used as a symbol or emblem ▸ banderole, banner, banneret, colors, ensign, jack, oriflamme, pennant, pennon, standard, streamer. **2.** An identifying or descriptive slip ▸ earmark, label, tag. *See* **ticket** (1).

flag *verb*
1. To attach a ticket to ▸ earmark, label, mark, tag, ticket. **2.** To make bodily motions so as to convey an idea or complement speech ▸ motion, sign, signal. *See* **gesture.**

flag² *verb*
1. To become limp, as from loss of freshness ▸ droop, sag. *See* **wilt. 2.** To lose strength or power ▸ decline, weaken. *See* **fade** (1). **3.** To grow weary ▸ burn out, wear out. *See* **tire** (2).

flagellate *verb*
▸ lash, thrash, whip. *See* **beat** (2).

flagitiousness *noun*
▸ depravity, perversion, turpitude, vice. *See* **corruption** (1).

flagrancy *noun*
The quality or state of being flagrant ▸ egregiousness, glaringness, grossness, rankness. *See also* **impudence, outrageousness.**

flagrant *adjective*
Conspicuously bad or offensive ▸ egregious, glaring, gross, rank. *See also* **offensive, outrageous, shameless.**

✦ CORE SYNONYMS: *flagrant, glaring, gross, egregious, rank.* These adjectives refer to what is conspicuously bad or offensive. *Flagrant* applies to what is so offensive that it cannot escape notice: *flagrant disregard for the law.* What is *glaring* is blatantly and painfully manifest: *a glaring error; glaring contradictions. Gross* suggests a magnitude of offense or failing that cannot be condoned or forgiven: *gross ineptitude; gross injustice.* What is *egregious* is outrageously bad: *an egregious lie. Rank* implies that the term it qualifies is as indicated to an extreme, violent, or gross degree: *rank stupidity; rank treachery.*

---

flail *verb*
1. To swing about or strike at wildly ▸ thrash, thresh, toss. *See also* **stagger, sway. 2.** To beat plants to separate the grain from the straw ▸ thrash, thresh. **3.** To hit heavily and repeatedly ▸ assault, batter, pummel, thresh. *See* **beat** (1).

flair *noun*
▸ faculty, gift, knack. *See* **talent.**

flak *noun*
1. A concentrated outpouring, as of missiles, words, or blows ▸ cannonade, fusillade, volley. *See* **barrage. 2.** *Informal* The act or an instance of finding fault ▸ censure, condemnation, denunciation. *See* **criticism** (1).

flake *noun*
1. A small, thin piece of something ▸ chip, leaf, paring, scale, slice, sliver, shaving. *See also* **bit¹, cut, end. 2.** *Slang* A person who is appealingly odd or curious ▸ eccentric, original. *Informal:* oddball. *See* **character** (7).

flake *verb*
To come or fall off in small, thin pieces ▸ chip, desquamate, exfoliate, peel, scale, shed.

flamboyant *adjective*
1. Elaborately and heavily ornamented ▸ baroque, resplendent. *See* **ornate** (1). **2.** Marked by outward, often extravagant display ▸ ostentatious, splashy. *See* **showy.** *See synonym note at* **showy. 3.** Suggesting drama or a stage performance, as in emotionality or suspense ▸ melodramatic, sensational, spectacular. *See* **dramatic** (2).

flame *noun*
1. The visible signs of combustion ▸ blaze, conflagration, fire, flare-up. **2.** *Informal* A romantic interest, especially a regular sexual partner ▸ paramour, partner. *See* **lover** (1).

flame *verb*
To undergo combustion; be on fire ▸ combust, flare. *See* **burn** (2).

flameproof *or* **flame-resistant** *or* **flame-retardant** *adjective*
▸ fire-resistant, incombustible, nonflammable. *See* **fireproof.**

flaming *adjective*
1. On fire ▸ afire, conflagrant. *See* **burning** (1). **2.** Fired with intense feeling ▸ burning, fervent, impassioned, torrid. *See* **passionate** (1).

flammable *adjective*
Easily ignited ▸ combustible, ignitable, inflammable.

flank *noun*
One of two or more contrasted parts or places that is identified by its location with respect to a center ▸ hand, side.

flank *verb*
To be contiguous or next to ▸ border, join, neighbor. *See* **adjoin** (1).

flap *verb*
1. To move the arms or wings up and down ▸ beat, flitter, flop, flutter, waggle, wave. **2.** To move or cause to move about while being fixed at one edge ▸ flutter, fly, wave. **3.** To move through the air ▸ flit, flutter, sail. *See* **fly** (1). **4.** To move in or on the wind ▸ drift, waft. *See* **blow¹** (2).

flap *noun*
1. A flat, thin piece that usually hangs over something ▸ fly, skirt. **2.** A condition of being agitated or disturbed ▸ commotion, disturbance, stir. *See* **agitation** (1).

flapping *adjective*
▸ dangling, relaxed, slack. *See* **loose** (1). *See synonym note at* **loose.**

flare *verb*
1. To undergo combustion; be on fire ▸ combust, flame. *See* **burn** (2). **2.** To become manifest suddenly and in full force ▸ burst, erupt. *See* **break** (1). **3.** To shine intensely and blindingly ▸ blaze, throb. *See* **glare** (2).

flare up *verb*
To be or become angry ▸ fume, rage, seethe. *See* **anger** (2).

flare *noun*
1. An intense blinding light ▸ blaze, dazzle, glare. **2.** A sudden emergence or increase ▸ breakout, explosion, outburst. *See* **eruption** (1). *See also* **flare-up.**

flare-up *noun*
1. The visible signs of combustion ▸ blaze, conflagration, fire, flame. **2.** A sudden violent expression, as of emotion ▸ burst, eruption, explosion. *See* **outburst** (1). **3.** A violent release of confined energy ▸ burst, explosion. *See* **blast** (2). **4.** A sudden emergence or increase ▸ breakout, flare, outburst. *See* **eruption** (1).

flash *noun*
1. A sudden burst of light ▸ blink, coruscation, flicker,

glance, gleam, glimmer, glint, scintillation, spark, twinkle, wink. **2.** A very brief interval of time ▸ blink, crack, instant, minute, moment, second, trice, twinkle, twinkling, wink. *Informal:* jiff, jiffy, sec. **3.** A detail of news or information ▸ bulletin, dispatch. *See* **item** (1).

flash *verb*
1. To emit light in sudden or intermittent bursts ▸ glint, shimmer, sparkle. *See* **glitter.** *See synonym note at* **glitter. 2.** To move swiftly ▸ dash, sprint, zip. *See* **rush** (1). **3.** To make a public and usually ostentatious show of ▸ exhibit, expose, flaunt. *See* **display** (1).

✦ CORE SYNONYMS: *flash, jiffy, moment, instant, minute, second.* These nouns denote a brief interval of time. *Flash* and *jiffy* usually combine with *in a; in a flash* suggests the almost imperceptible duration of a flash of light, while *in a jiffy* means in a short space of time: *She finished the job in a flash.* "*He was on his stool in a jiffy, driving away with his pen*" (Charles Dickens). A *moment* is an indeterminately short but significant period: *I'll be with you in a moment. Instant* is a period of time almost too brief to detect; it implies haste: *He hesitated for just an instant. Minute* is often interchangeable with *moment* and *second* with *instant: The alarm will ring any minute. I'll be back in a second.*

---

flash point *noun*
▸ crisis, distress, trouble. *See* **emergency.**

flashy *adjective*
▸ garish, loud, tawdry. *See* **gaudy.** *See synonym note at* **gaudy.**

flat *adjective*
1. Lying down ▸ decumbent, horizontal, procumbent, prone, prostrate, reclining, recumbent, stretched out, supine. **2.** Lacking an appetizing flavor ▸ bland, flavorless, insipid, stale, tasteless, unsavory. **3.** Having no irregularities, roughness, or indentations ▸ flush, level. *See* **even** (1). *See synonym note at* **even. 4.** Lacking liveliness, charm, or surprise ▸ aseptic, colorless, pedestrian. *See* **dull** (1). **5.** Lacking vividness or color ▸ lackluster, mat, muddy. *See* **dull** (2). **6.** Remaining unchanged ▸ firm, invariable, fixed. *See* **unchanging. 7.** Completely such, without qualification or exception ▸ all-out, pure, sheer. *See* **utter**^{2}.

flat *adverb*
To the fullest extent ▸ fully, totally, utterly. *See* **completely** (1).

flat *verb*
To make even, smooth, or level ▸ level, smooth, straighten. *See* **even** (1).

flatfoot *noun*
Slang A member of a law-enforcement agency ▸ officer, trooper. *See* **police officer.**

flatly *adverb*
In a direct, positive manner ▸ directly, emphatically, point-blank, positively. *Informal:* flat out. *Idiom:* in no uncertain terms.

flatness *noun*
1. A lack of excitement, liveliness, or interest ▸ bland-

ness, drabness, lifelessness. *See* **dullness** (1). **2.** The condition of being without change or variation ▸ constancy, immutability. *See* **changelessness.**

flat out *adverb*
1. *Informal* In a direct, positive manner ▸ directly, emphatically, positively. *See* **flatly. 2.** In a rapid way ▸ apace, hastily, quick. *See* **fast.**

flat-out *adjective*
Informal Completely such, without qualification or exception ▸ all-out, pure, sheer. *See* **utter**^{2}.

flatten *verb*
1. To make even, smooth, or level ▸ level, smooth, straighten. *See* **even** (1). **2.** To bring down, as from a shot or blow ▸ floor, ground, hew. *See* **drop** (6).

flatter *verb*
1. To compliment excessively and ingratiatingly ▸ adulate, blandish, butter up, honey. *Informal:* softsoap, sweet-talk. *See also* **coax, deceive, fawn, seduce. 2.** To look good on or with ▸ become, enhance, suit. *Idiom:* put in the best light. *See also* **suit.**

flatterer *noun*
▸ fawner, minion, slave. *See* **sycophant.**

flattering *adjective*
1. Purposefully contrived to gain favor ▸ blandishing, buttery, cajoling, fawning, honey-tongued, ingratiating, ingratiatory, insinuating, saccharine, smoothtongued, soft-soaping, sugary, wheedling. *Informal:* brownnosing. **2.** Pleasingly suited to the wearer ▸ attractive, fetching. *See* **becoming** (1).

flattery *noun*
Excessive, ingratiating praise ▸ adulation, blandishment, blarney, oil. *Informal:* apple-polishing, soft soap, sweet talk. *Idiom:* honeyed words.

flatulent *adjective*
▸ overblown, tumescent, windy. *See* **inflated** (1).

flaunt *verb*
▸ exhibit, expose, strut. *See* **display** (1). *See synonym note at* **display.**

flavor *noun*
1. A distinctive property of a substance affecting the sense of taste ▸ relish, savor, smack, tang, taste, zest. **2.** A distinctive yet intangible quality felt to be characteristic of a given thing ▸ aroma, atmosphere, savor, smack. *See also* **quality. 3.** A substance that imparts taste ▸ condiment, seasoning, spice. *See* **flavoring.**

flavor *verb*
To impart flavor to ▸ season, spice (up), zest.

✦ CORE SYNONYMS: *flavor, relish, savor, tang, taste.* These nouns denote a distinctive property of a substance affecting the sense of taste: *the pungent flavor of garlic; the zesty relish of the salsa; the savor of rich chocolate; the fresh tang of lemonade; the salty taste of anchovies.*

---

flavorful *adjective*
▸ delectable, savory, scrumptious. *See* **delicious** (1).

flavoring *noun*
A substance that imparts taste ▸ condiment, flavor, seasoner, seasoning, spice. *See also* **zest.**

flavorless *adjective*
1. Lacking an appetizing flavor ▸ bland, insipid, taste-less. *See* **flat** (2). 2. Lacking liveliness, charm, or sur-prise ▸ aseptic, colorless, pedestrian. *See* **dull** (1).

flavorlessness *noun*
▸ blandness, drabness, lifelessness. *See* **dullness** (1).

flaw *noun*
1. Something that mars the appearance or causes inadequacy or failure ▸ fault, glitch, imperfection. *See* **defect** (1). *See synonym note at* **defect**. 2. An unfa-vorable condition, circumstance, or characteristic ▸ drawback, handicap, liability. *See* **disadvantage**. *See synonym note at* **disadvantage**.

flaw *verb*
To spoil the soundness or perfection of ▸ disserve, impair. *See* **damage**.

flawed *adjective*
Having a defect or defects ▸ amiss, blemished, defec-tive, faulty, imperfect. *See also* **shabby, trick**.

flawless *adjective*
1. Free from flaws or blemishes ▸ clear, impeccable, unblemished. *See* **perfect** (1). *See synonym note at* **perfect**. 2. In excellent condition ▸ entire, intact, sound. *See* **good** (2).

flaxen-haired *adjective*
▸ fair-haired, light-haired. *See* **fair**¹ (8).

flay *verb*
1. To criticize harshly and devastatingly ▸ bash, exco-riate, rip into. *See* **slam** (5). 2. To remove the clothing or covering from ▸ peel, strip, uncover. *See* **bare** (1). 3. To punish with blows or lashes ▸ lash, thrash, whip. *See* **beat** (2).

fleck *noun*
A very small mark ▸ dot, speck. *See* **point** (2).

fleck *verb*
To mark with many small spots ▸ dapple, freckle. *See* **speckle**.

fledgling *noun*
▸ apprentice, neophyte, novice. *See* **beginner**.

flee *verb*
▸ decamp, fly. *See* **escape** (1).

fleece *verb*
▸ bilk, defraud, swindle. *See* **cheat** (1).

fleecy *adjective*
▸ furry, hirsute, shaggy. *See* **hairy** (1).

fleer *verb*
To smile or laugh scornfully or derisively ▸ sneer, snicker, snigger. *Idiom:* curl one's lip. *See also* **gri-mace, laugh, ridicule**.

fleer *noun*
1. A facial expression or laugh conveying scorn or derision ▸ sneer, snicker, snigger. *See also* **smile**. 2. An instance of mockery or derision ▸ insult, jeer, scoff. *See* **taunt** (1).

fleet¹ *noun*
A group of warships operating under one command ▸ armada, flotilla.

fleet² *adjective*
1. Characterized by great speed ▸ brisk, quick, swift.

See **fast** (1). *See synonym note at* **fast**. 2. Lasting or existing only for a short time ▸ ephemeral, fleeting, temporary. *See* **transitory**.

fleet *verb*
To move swiftly ▸ dash, sprint, zip. *See* **rush** (1).

fleeting *adjective*
1. Lasting or existing for only a short time ▸ ephem-eral, temporary. *See* **transitory**. 2. Accomplished or experienced in very little time ▸ fast, rapid, speedy. *See* **quick** (1).

fleetness *noun*
▸ expeditiousness, hurry, quickness. *See* **haste** (1).

flesh *noun*
▸ humanity, human race, world. *See* **humankind**.

fleshless *adjective*
▸ lean, skinny, slender, slim. *See* **thin** (1). *See synonym note at* **thin**.

fleshliness *noun*
▸ sexuality, voluptuousness. *See* **sensuality** (1).

fleshly *adjective*
1. Of or relating to the human body ▸ corporal, physical. *See* **bodily**. *See synonym note at* **bodily**. 2. Relating to the desires and appetites of the body, especially sexual desire ▸ animal, sexual. *See* **sensual** (2).

fleshy *adjective*
1. Having too much flesh ▸ chubby, pudgy, tubby. *See* **fat** (1). *See synonym note at* **fat**. 2. Relating to the desires and appetites of the body, especially sexual desire ▸ physical, sexual. *See* **sensual** (2). 3. Of or relating to the body ▸ corporal, physical. *See* **bodily**.

flex *verb*
▸ deflect, turn. *See* **bend** (2).

flexibility *noun*
1. The quality or state of being flexible ▸ bendability, bounce, ductility, elasticity, flexibleness, give, limber-ness, lissomeness, litheness, malleability, malleable-ness, plasticity, pliability, pliableness, pliancy, pliant-ness, resilience, resiliency, spring, springiness, suppleness, tractableness, tractability. 2. The ability to recover quickly from depression or discouragement ▸ bounce, buoyancy, elasticity, resilience, resiliency.

flexible *adjective*
1. Capable of withstanding stress without injury ▸ elastic, flexile, plastic, resilient, springy, supple. *See also* **extensible**. 2. Having or showing bodily flexibil-ity ▸ limber, lissome, lithe, lithesome, supple. *See also* **limp**. 3. Easily altered or influenced ▸ ductile, elastic, flexile, impressionable, malleable, plastic, pliable, pli-ant, suggestible, supple. *See also* **obedient**. 4. Capable of adapting or being adapted ▸ adjustable, malleable, pliable. *See* **adaptable**. 5. Capable of being shaped, bent, or drawn out ▸ bendable, ductile, plastic. *See* **malleable** (1).

✦ **CORE SYNONYMS:** *flexible, elastic, resilient, supple*. These adjectives refer literally to what is capable of withstanding stress without injury and figuratively to what can undergo change or modification: *a flexible wire; flexible plans; an elastic rubber band; an elastic* *interpretation of the law; thin, resilient copper; a resilient temperament; supple suede; a supple mind.*

flexibleness *noun*
► elasticity, malleability, pliability. *See* **flexibility** (1).

flexile *adjective*
1. Capable of being shaped or bent ► bendable, ductile, plastic. *See* **malleable** (1). **2.** Capable of withstanding stress without injury ► elastic, resilient, supple. *See* **flexible** (1). **3.** Easily altered or influenced ► malleable, pliable, suggestible. *See* **flexible** (1).

flexuous *adjective*
1. Repeatedly curving in alternate directions ► convoluted, sinuous, twisting. *See* **winding** (1). **2.** Capable of being shaped or bent ► bendable, ductile, plastic. *See* **malleable** (1).

flexure *noun*
► curvature, curve, turn. *See* **bend**.

flick *noun*
1. Light and momentary contact with another person or thing ► graze, skim. *See* **brush**[1] (1). **2.** *Slang* A motion picture ► film, motion picture, movie, picture.

flick *verb*
1. To make light and momentary contact with, as in passing ► graze, kiss, skim. *See* **brush**[1]. *See synonym note at* **brush**[1]. **2.** To strike lightly or gently ► dab, pat. *See* **tap**[1] (1).

flicker *verb*
1. To move like a bird in flight ► flit, flitter, flutter. *See also* **flap**. **2.** To emit light in sudden or intermittent bursts ► flash, glimmer, twinkle. *See* **glitter**. **3.** To undergo partial or unsteady combustion ► smoke, sputter. *See* **smolder** (1).

flicker *noun*
A sudden burst of light ► blink, spark, twinkle. *See* **flash** (1).

flier *noun*
1. A person who flies an airplane ► aviator, pilot. **2.** An announcement distributed on paper to a large number of people ► circular, handbill, leaflet, notice.

flight *noun*
1. The act or an instance of escaping, as from confinement or difficulty ► breakout, getaway. *See* **escape** (1). **2.** A number of animals considered collectively ► bevy, gaggle, herd. *See* **flock** (1). *See synonym note at* **flock**. **3.** The act of traveling from one place to another ► passage, progress. *See* **journey**.

flighty *adjective*
1. Given to lighthearted silliness ► featherbrained, frivolous, scatterbrained. *See* **giddy** (2). **2.** Marked by whim or impulse ► fickle, impulsive, mercurial. *See* **capricious**.

flimflam *noun*
Informal An act of cheating ► deceit, hoax, swindle. *See* **cheat** (1).

flimflam *verb*
Informal To get something by deceitful trickery ► bilk, defraud, swindle. *See* **cheat** (1).

flimflammer *noun*
Informal A person who cheats ► cheater, swindler, trickster. *See* **cheat** (2).

flimsiness *noun*
► decrepitude, feebleness, unsubstantiality. *See* **infirmity** (1).

flimsy *adjective*
1. Not physically strong ► feeble, frail, unsound. *See* **weak** (1). **2.** Not plausible or believable ► improbable, inconceivable. *See* **implausible**. **3.** Being weak in quality or substance ► bloodless, pallid, watery. *See* **pale** (2).

flinch *verb*
To draw away or pull back in fear ► blench, cower, cringe, quail, recoil, shrink, shy, start, wince. *See also* **fear**.

flinch *noun*
An act of drawing back in an involuntary or instinctive fashion ► shrink, wince. *See* **recoil**.

fling *verb*
To send through the air with a motion of the hand or arm ► heave, hurl, pitch. *See* **throw** (1). *See synonym note at* **throw**.

fling *noun*
1. An act of throwing ► heave, hurl, toss. *See* **throw**. **2.** A period of uncontrolled self-indulgence ► rampage, spree. *See* **binge** (1). *See synonym note at* **binge**. **3.** *Informal* A brief trial ► crack, go, stab, try. *Informal:* shot, whack, whirl. **4.** A usually brief romance entered into lightly or frivolously ► dalliance, flirtation. *See also* **love**.

flinty *adjective*
► dour, grim. *See* **forbidding** (1).

flip *verb*
To throw a coin in order to decide something ► toss. *Idiom:* call heads or tails.

flip through *verb*
To look through reading matter casually ► dip into, leaf through, skim. *See* **browse** (1).

flip *adjective*
Informal Rude and disrespectful ► bold, insolent, pert. *See* **impudent**.

flip-flop *noun*
► inversion, transposition, turnabout. *See* **reversal** (1).

flippancy *noun*
► audacity, boldness, impertinence. *See* **impudence**.

flippant *adjective*
► bold, insolent, pert. *See* **impudent**.

flirt *verb*
1. To treat something lightly or flippantly ► dally, play, toy, trifle. **2.** To make amorous advances without serious intentions ► coquet, dally, toy, trifle. *Slang:* mash. *Idioms:* come on to, make advances, make a play for, make eyes at. *See also* **philander, seduce**.

flirt *noun*
1. A woman who is given to flirting ► coquette, tease. *Informal:* vamp. *See also* **seductress**. **2.** A man who is given to flirting ► wolf. *Slang:* masher. *See also* **philanderer, seducer**.

✛ **CORE SYNONYMS:** *flirt, dally, play, toy, trifle.* These verbs to treat something or someone lightly, casually, or flippantly: *flirted with the idea of getting a job; dallying with music; can't play with life; toyed with the problem; a person not to be trifled with.*

flirtation *noun*
1. The practice of flirting ▸ coquetry, dalliance. 2. A usually brief romance entered into lightly or frivolously ▸ dalliance, fling. *See also* **love.**

flirtatious *or* **flirty** *adjective*
Given to flirting ▸ coquettish, coy.

flit *verb*
1. To move like a bird in flight ▸ flicker, flitter, flutter. *See also* **flap. 2.** To move through the air ▸ flap, flutter, sail. *See* **fly** (1). **3.** To move swiftly ▸ dash, sprint, zip. *See* **rush** (1).

flitter *verb*
1. To move like a bird in flight ▸ flicker, flit, flutter.
2. To move through the air ▸ flit, flutter, sail. *See* **fly** (1).
3. To move the arms or wings up and down ▸ flutter, wave. *See* **flap** (1).

float *verb*
1. To stay on top of the surface of water or stay in mid-air ▸ bob, be buoyed, be buoyant, have buoyancy, hover, stay afloat. **2.** To move along with or be carried away by the action of water ▸ drift, wash. **3.** To pass quickly and lightly through the air ▸ glide, sail, shoot. *See* **fly** (2). **4.** To move smoothly, continuously, and effortlessly ▸ coast, slither. *See* **glide** (1). **5.** To move in or on the wind ▸ drift, flap. *See* **blow**[1] (2). **6.** To supply money, especially on credit ▸ discount, loan. *See* **lend.**

flock *noun*
1. A number of animals considered collectively ▸ bevy, cast, cete, covert, covey, drift, drove, exaltation, fall, flight, gaggle, gam, gang, herd, kennel, kindle, litter, murder, muster, nide, pack, pod, pride, rout, school, shrewdness, skein, skulk, sloth, sord, stable, sounder, swarm, troop, warren, watch, wisp. **2.** An enormous number of persons or things gathered together ▸ horde, mass, throng. *See* **crowd** (1).

flock *verb*
1. To move into an area or space in large numbers ▸ cram, jam, throng. *See* **crowd** (1). **2.** To form a united group ▸ join, unite. *See* **band**[2].

✛ **CORE SYNONYMS:** *flock, herd, drove, pack, gang, brood.* These nouns denote a number of animals, birds, or fish considered collectively, and some have human connotations. *Flock* is applied to a congregation of animals of one kind, especially sheep or goats herded by people, and to any congregation of wild or domesticated birds, especially when on the ground. It is also applicable to people who form the membership of a church or to people under someone's care or supervision. *Herd* is used of a number of animals, especially cattle, herded by people; or of wild animals such as antelope, elephants, and zebras; or of whales and seals. Applied to people, it is used disparagingly of a crowd or of the masses and suggests the gregarious aspect of crowd psychology. *Drove* is used of a herd or flock, as of cattle or geese, that is being moved or driven from one place to another; less often it refers to a crowd of people in movement. *Pack* is applicable to any body of animals, especially wolves, or of birds, especially grouse, and to a body of hounds trained to hunt as a unit. It also refers disparagingly to a band or group of persons. *Gang* refers to a herd, especially of buffalo or elk; to a pack of wolves or wild dogs; or to various associations of persons, especially when engaged in violent or criminal pursuits. *Brood* is applicable to offspring that are still under the care of a mother, especially the offspring of domestic or game birds or, less formally, of people. • The following related terms are used as indicated: *bevy,* a company of roe deer, larks, or quail; *cast,* the number of hawks or falcons cast off at one time, usually a pair; *cete,* a company of badgers; *covert,* a flock of coots; *covey,* a family of grouse, partridges, or other game birds; *drift,* a drove or herd, especially of hogs; *exaltation,* a flight of larks; *fall,* a family of woodcock in flight; *flight,* a flock of birds in flight; *gaggle,* a flock of geese; *gam,* a school of whales, or a social congregation of whalers, especially at sea; *kennel,* a number of hounds or dogs housed in one place or under the same ownership; *kindle,* a brood or litter, especially of kittens; *litter,* the total number of offspring produced at a single birth by a multiparous mammal; *murder,* a flock of crows; *muster,* a flock of peacocks; *nide,* a brood of pheasants; *pod,* a small herd of seals or whales; *pride,* a company of lions; *rout,* a company of people or animals in movement, especially knights or wolves; *school,* a congregation of fish or of aquatic mammals such as dolphins or porpoises; *shrewdness,* a company of apes; *skein,* a flight of wildfowl, especially geese; *skulk,* a congregation of vermin, especially foxes, or of thieves; *sloth,* a company of bears; *sord,* a flight of mallards; *sounder,* a herd of wild boar; *stable,* a number of horses housed in one place or under the same ownership; *swarm,* a colony of insects, such as ants, bees, or wasps, especially when migrating to a new nest or hive; *troop,* a number of animals, birds, or people, especially when on the move; *warren,* the inhabitants, such as rabbits, of a warren; *watch,* a flock of nightingales; and *wisp,* a flock of birds, especially of snipe.

flog *verb*
▸ lash, thrash, whip. *See* **beat** (2).

flogging *noun*
▸ lashing, thrashing, whipping. *See* **beating** (1).

flood *noun*
1. An abundant or overwhelming flow of water ▸ alluvion, cataract, deluge, downpour, freshet, inundation, overflow, spate, torrent. *See also* **abundance, excess, flow. 2.** Something suggestive of running water ▸ stream, tide. *See* **flow.** *See synonym note at* **flow. 3.** A sudden violent expression, as of emotion ▸ burst, eruption, explosion. *See* **outburst** (1).

flood *verb*
1. To flow over completely ▸ deluge, drown, engulf, flush, inundate, overflow, overwhelm, submerge, submerse. *See also* **dip, flow. 2.** To affect as if by an

outpouring of water ► deluge, inundate, overwhelm, swamp. **3.** To move into an area or space in large numbers ► cram, pour, throng. *See* **crowd** (1). **4.** To cover or fill with light ► illumine, lighten. *See* **illuminate** (1).

floor *verb*
1. To bring down, as from a shot or blow ► down, ground, hew. *See* **drop** (6). **2.** To overwhelm with surprise, wonder, or bewilderment ► dumbfound, flabbergast. *See* **stagger** (2).

floozy *noun*
► hussy, tramp, whore. *See* **slut.**

flop *verb*
1. To drop or sink heavily and noisily ► plop, plump, plunk. *See also* **fall. 2.** To hang limply, loosely, and carelessly ► droop, sag. *See* **slouch** (2). **3.** To move the arms or wings up and down ► beat, wave. *See* **flap** (1). **4.** *Informal* To be unsuccessful ► choke, founder, wash out. *See* **fail** (1). **5.** *Slang* To go to bed ► bed down. *Slang:* crash. *See* **retire** (2).

flop *noun*
1. *Informal* An unsuccessful person or enterprise ► bust, fiasco, washout. *See* **failure** (1). **2.** *Informal* Something that disappoints ► anticlimax, bust, washout. *See* **disappointment** (2).

floppy *adjective*
► droopy, flabby, flaccid. *See* **limp** (1). *See synonym note at* **limp.**

flora *noun*
The plants of an area or region ► plant life, vegetation, verdure.

florescence *noun*
► efflorescence, prime. *See* **bloom**¹ (1). *See synonym note at* **bloom**¹.

floret *noun*
► blossom, posy. *See* **flower** (1).

florid *adjective*
1. Of a healthy reddish color ► flush, rubicund, sanguine. *See* **ruddy. 2.** Elaborately and heavily ornamented ► flamboyant, resplendent. *See* **ornate** (1). **3.** Tastelessly showy ► flashy, garish, tawdry. *See* **gaudy.** *See synonym note at* **gaudy.**

flotilla *noun*
A group of warships operating under one command ► armada, fleet.

flotsam *noun*
► debris, litter, rubbish. *See* **garbage** (1).

flounce *verb*
► prance, strut, swank. *See* **strut** (1).

flounder *verb*
1. To move about in an indolent or clumsy manner ► roll about, roll around, wallow, welter. **2.** To move heavily or clumsily ► clump, galumph, hulk. *See* **blunder** (1). *See synonym note at* **blunder. 3.** To proceed or perform in an unsteady, faltering manner ► bungle, fudge, fumble. *See* **muddle** (1).

flourish *verb*
1. To wield boldly and dramatically ► brandish, sweep, wave. *See also* **handle. 2.** To grow rapidly and luxu-

riantly ► bloom, blossom, thrive. *See also* **increase. 3.** To be in one's prime ► flower, shine. *Idioms:* cut a figure, make a splash. **4.** To do or fare well ► boom, go, thrive. *See* **prosper.**

✛ CORE SYNONYMS: *flourish, brandish, sweep, wave.* These verbs mean to wield boldly and dramatically: *flourished the newly signed contract; brandish a sword; swept the magic wand across the brim of the hat; waving a baton.*

---

flourishing *adjective*
Improving, growing, or succeeding steadily ► booming, boomy, prospering, prosperous, roaring, successful, thrifty, thriving. *See also* **profuse.**

flout *verb*
► defy, transgress. *See* **disobey.**

flow *noun*
Something suggestive of running water ► cascade, current, drift, efflux, flood, flux, gush, outflow, outpour, outpouring, rush, spate, stream, surge, tide. *See also* **brook**¹, **flood, spurt.**

flow *verb*
1. To move freely as a liquid ► circulate, course, purl, ripple, run, stream, sweep. *See also* **swirl. 2.** To come forth or issue in abundance ► cascade, gush, pour, run, rush, stream, surge, well. *See also* **flood, spurt. 3.** To cause a liquid to flow in a steady stream ► decant, empty, issue. *See* **pour** (1). **4.** To have as a source ► derive, emanate, originate. *See* **stem** (1). *See synonym note at* **stem. 5.** To be abundantly filled or richly supplied ► bristle, crawl, swarm. *See* **teem**¹.

✛ CORE SYNONYMS: *flow, current, flood, flux, rush, stream, tide.* These nouns denote something suggestive of running water: *a flow of thought; the current of history; a flood of ideas; a flux of words; a rush of pity; a stream of complaints; a tide of immigration.*

---

flower *noun*
1. The showy reproductive structure of a plant ► bloom, blossom, floret, floweret, flower head, pompon, posy, spike, spray. *See also* **bouquet. 2.** A time of vigor, youth, or peak condition ► efflorescence, prime. *See* **bloom**¹ (1). *See synonym note at* **bloom**¹. **3.** The most preferable part of something ► cream, elite, top. *See* **best** (1). **4.** People of the highest social level ► elite, gentry, nobility. *See* **society** (1).

flower *verb*
1. To bear flowers ► burgeon, effloresce. *See* **bloom**¹ (1). **2.** To be in one's prime ► flourish, shine. *Idioms:* cut a figure, make a splash.

flowery *adjective*
1. Characterized by elevated language, such as that used in public speaking ► grandiloquent, rhetorical. *See* **oratorical. 2.** Elaborately and heavily ornamented ► flamboyant, resplendent. *See* **ornate** (1).

flowing *adjective*
► easy, effortless, flowing. *See* **fluent.**

flub *verb*
► blunder, foul up, spoil. *See* **botch.**

fluctuant *adjective*
▸ fluid, unsettled, variable. *See* **changeable** (1).

fluctuate *verb*
1. To become different ▸ fluctuate, modify, turn. *See* **change** (2). **2.** To move back and forth ▸ oscillate, vacillate. *See* **sway** (1). *See synonym note at* **sway.**

fluctuation *noun*
▸ modification, mutation, variation. *See* **change** (1).

fluency *noun*
▸ articulateness, facility, fluidity. *See* **eloquence.**

fluent *adjective*
Marked by facility of expression ▸ easy, effortless, flowing, fluid, graceful, smooth. *See also* **eloquent, glib.**

fluff *noun*
Informal A stupid, clumsy mistake ▸ bungle, faux pas, stumble. *See* **blunder.**

fluff *verb*
To make an error or mistake ▸ lapse, stumble. *See* **err** (1).

fluffy *adjective*
1. Having little weight; not heavy ▸ airy, light, light-weight, weightless. *Idioms:* light as air (*or* a feather). *See also* **immaterial, sheer². 2.** Of little importance or seriousness ▸ inconsequential, negligible, trifling. *See* **trivial.**

fluid *adjective*
1. Changing easily, as in expression ▸ changeable, mobile, plastic. *See also* **unstable. 2.** Marked by facility of expression ▸ effortless, flowing. *See* **fluent. 3.** Capable of or liable to change ▸ mutable, unsettled, variable. *See* **changeable** (1).

fluidity *noun*
▸ articulateness, fluency, volubility. *See* **eloquence.**

fluke *noun*
1. An unexpected random event ▸ accident, fortuity, happenstance. *See* **chance** (1). **2.** Success attained as a result of chance ▸ fortune, godsend. *See* **luck** (1).

fluky *adjective*
▸ chance, fortuitous, inadvertent. *See* **accidental** (1).

flummox *verb*
Informal To put at a loss as to what to say or do ▸ confound, perplex. *Informal:* stump. *See* **baffle** (1).

fluorescent *adjective*
▸ rich, vibrant, vivid. *See* **colorful** (1).

flunk *verb*
Informal To go wrong or be unsuccessful ▸ fall short, flop, wash out. *See* **fail** (1).

flurry *noun*
Agitated, excited activity ▸ commotion, excitement, fuss. *See* **agitation** (3).

flurry *verb*
To impair or destroy the composure of ▸ disorient, fluster, ruffle. *See* **agitate** (2).

flush *verb*
1. To become red in the face ▸ crimson, glow. *See* **blush. 2.** To raise the spirits of ▸ buoy up, exhilarate, inspire. *See* **elate** (1). **3.** To flow over completely ▸ engulf, overflow, submerge. *See* **flood** (1). **4.** To make

even, smooth, or level ▸ level, smooth, straighten. *See* **even** (1).

flush *noun*
1. A fresh rosy complexion ▸ bloom, blush, color, glow. *See also* **color, complexion. 2.** A feeling of pervasive emotional warmth ▸ glow, tingle. **3.** A time of vigor, youth, or peak condition ▸ efflorescence, prime. *See* **bloom¹** (1). *See synonym note at* **bloom¹.**

flush *adjective*
1. Of a healthy reddish color ▸ flushed, rosy, sanguine. *See* **ruddy. 2.** Possessing a large amount of money, land, or other material possessions ▸ affluent, moneyed, wealthy. *See* **rich** (1). *See synonym note at* **rich. 3.** Having no irregularities, roughness, or indentations ▸ flat, level. *See* **even** (1). *See synonym note at* **even. 4.** On the same plane or line ▸ coplanar, flat. *See* **even** (2).

flush *adverb*
With precision or absolute conformity ▸ exactly, precisely, squarely. *See* **directly** (3).

flushed *adjective*
▸ flush, rubicund, sanguine. *See* **ruddy.**

fluster *verb*
To impair or destroy the composure of ▸ disorient, disturb, ruffle. *See* **agitate** (2).

fluster *noun*
A state of discomposure ▸ tumult, turmoil. *Informal:* lather. *See* **agitation** (2).

flutter *verb*
1. To move or cause to move about while being fixed at one edge ▸ flap, fly, wave. **2.** To move through the air ▸ flit, flitter, sail. *See* **fly** (1). **3.** To move in or on the wind ▸ drift, flap. *See* **blow¹** (2). **4.** To move quickly and irregularly like a bird in flight ▸ flicker, flit, flitter. **5.** To move the arms or wings up and down ▸ beat, wave. *See* **flap** (1). **6.** To make rhythmic contractions, sounds, or movements ▸ pulsate, pulse, throb. *See* **beat** (5). **7.** To open and close the eyes rapidly ▸ twinkle, wink. *See* **blink** (1).

flutter *noun*
1. A state of discomposure ▸ tumult, turmoil. *Informal:* lather. *See* **agitation** (2). **2.** A brief closing of the eyes ▸ bat, wink. *See* **blink** (1).

flux *noun*
1. Something suggestive of running water ▸ flood, stream, tide. *See* **flow.** *See synonym note at* **flow. 2.** Passage from one form, state, or stage to another ▸ passage, shift, transit. *See* **transition.**

flux *verb*
To change from a solid to a liquid ▸ dissolve, liquefy, thaw. *See* **melt** (1).

fly *verb*
1. To move through the air with or as if with wings ▸ flap, flit, flitter, flutter, sail, wing. **2.** To move quickly or smoothly through the air ▸ dart, float, glide, sail, shoot, skim, soar. *See also* **float, plunge. 3.** To move or cause to move about while being fixed at one edge ▸ flap, flutter, wave. **4.** To move in or on the wind ▸ drift, flap. *See* **blow¹** (2). **5.** To move swiftly ▸ dash,

sprint, zip. *See* **rush** (1). **6.** To break loose and leave suddenly, as from confinement or a difficult situation ▸ decamp, flee. *See* **escape** (1).

flyblown *adjective*
▸ foul, putrid, rotten. *See* **bad** (2).

flying *adjective*
▸ fast, rapid, speedy. *See* **quick** (1).

foam *noun*
A mass of bubbles in or on the surface of a liquid ▸ barm, effervescence, fizz, froth, head, lather, spume, suds, yeast.

foam *verb*
1. To form or cause to form foam ▸ bubble, cream, effervesce, fizz, froth, lather, spume, suds, yeast. **2.** To be or become angry ▸ fume, rage, seethe. *See* **anger** (2).

foamy *adjective*
Consisting of or resembling foam ▸ barmy, fizzy, frothy, lathery, spumous, spumy, sudsy, yeasty.

fob off *verb*
To offer or put into circulation an inferior or fraudulent item ▸ foist, palm off, pass off, put off. *See also* **dump.**

focal *adjective*
▸ axial, median, middle. *See* **central** (1).

focalize *verb*
▸ channel, converge, focus. *See* **concentrate** (1).

focus *noun*
1. A place of concentrated activity, influence, or importance ▸ headquarters, heart, hub. *See* **center** (1). *See synonym note at* **center. 2.** A point of origin or crucial factor ▸ core, hub, nucleus. *See* **center** (3). **3.** A focus of attention, thought, or action ▸ butt, subject, target. *See* **object** (2).

focus *verb*
1. To direct toward a common center ▸ channel, converge, hone in. *See* **concentrate** (1). **2.** To devote oneself or one's efforts ▸ buckle down, dedicate, devote. *See* **apply** (1).

foe *noun*
▸ antagonist, enemy, nemesis. *See* **opponent** (1). *See synonym note at* **opponent.**

fog *noun*
1. A suspension in the air of tiny particles of water, dust, or smoke ▸ brume, mist. *See* **haze** (1). **2.** A stunned or bewildered condition ▸ bewilderment, perplexity, stupor. *See* **daze.**

fog *verb*
1. To make dim ▸ blur, mist, obfuscate. *See* **obscure** (1). **2.** To addle the mind, as with a narcotic or alcohol ▸ besot, impair, stupefy. *See* **drug** (2).

foggy *adjective*
▸ dim, faint, indefinite. *See* **unclear** (1).

fogy *noun*
▸ fossil, fuddy-duddy, mossback. *See* **square** (2).

foible *noun*
▸ fault, shortcoming, weak point. *See* **weakness** (1).

foil *verb*
▸ baffle, stymie, thwart. *See* **frustrate** (1).

foist *verb*
1. To offer or put into circulation an inferior or fraudulent item ▸ fob off, palm off, pass off, put off. *See also* **dump. 2.** To introduce or insert by subtle and artful means ▸ infiltrate, worm. *See* **insinuate** (1).

foist on *or* **upon** *verb*
To force another to accept a burden ▸ charge with, saddle with. *See* **impose on** (1).

fold *verb*
1. To bend together or form a crease so that one part lies over another ▸ crease, crimp, crinkle, double, plait, pleat, ply, pucker, rimple, ruck, rumple, wrinkle. **2.** *Informal* To undergo sudden financial failure ▸ fail, go under. *See* **collapse** (2). **3.** To give in from or as if from a gradual loss of strength ▸ buckle, submit, surrender. *See* **succumb** (1). **4.** To process ingredients by stirring ▸ blend, whip. *See* **beat** (6).

fold down *verb*
To give way mentally and emotionally ▸ collapse, crack, snap. *See* **break** (5).

fold *noun*
1. A line or an arrangement made by the doubling of one part over another ▸ crease, crimp, crinkle, crumple, plait, pleat, plica, plication, pucker, rimple, ruck, rumple, wrinkle. **2.** An enclosure for livestock ▸ corral, sty. *See* **pen²** (1). **3.** The steadfast believers in a faith or cause ▸ adherents, congregation, faithful. *See also* **follower, assembly. 4.** Something bent ▸ curvature, curve, turn. *See* **bend.**

folklore *noun*
▸ legend, mythology, tradition. *See* **lore** (1).

folks *noun*
▸ family, kindred. *See* **kin.**

folk tale *noun*
▸ fairy tale, legend, parable. *See* **myth** (1).

folkways *noun*
1. Behavior patterns, traits, and products considered as an expression of a certain people or a period ▸ civilization, ethos, society. *See* **culture** (2). **2.** A body of traditional beliefs and notions accumulated about a particular subject ▸ legend, mythology, tradition. *See* **lore** (1).

follow *verb*
1. To occur after in time ▸ come next, ensue, succeed, supervene. *Idioms:* follow on (*or* upon) the heels of. **2.** To occur as a consequence ▸ attend, ensue, result. *See also* **stem. 3.** To keep another under surveillance by moving along behind ▸ chase, dog, heel, shadow, tag, track, trail. *Informal:* bird-dog, tail. *See also* **hunt, pursue. 4.** To act in compliance or conformity with ▸ abide by, adhere to, carry out, comply with, conform to, heed, keep, live by, mind, obey, observe. *Idioms:* keep to the straight and narrow, toe the line (*or* mark), walk the line. **5.** To take as a model ▸ copy, emulate, imitate, model oneself (on *or* upon *or* after), pattern oneself (on *or* upon *or* after). *Idioms:* follow in the footsteps of, follow suit, follow the example of, take as a model. *See also* **imitate. 6.** To work at, especially as a profession ▸ do, practice, pursue.

Idiom: hang out one's shingle. *See also* **labor. 7.** To pay regular and close attention to ▸ monitor, observe, survey, watch. *Idioms:* have one's (*or* keep an) eye on, keep tabs on. **8.** To perceive and recognize the meaning of ▸ apprehend, fathom, sense. *See* **understand** (1).

✦ CORE SYNONYMS: *follow, succeed, ensue, result, supervene.* These verbs mean to occur after something or someone or as a consequence. *Follow,* which has the widest application, can refer to coming after in time or order, as a consequence or result, or by the operation of logic: *Night follows day. He disregarded doctor's orders, and a relapse followed. Because she decries violence, it follows that she won't carry a gun.* To *succeed* is to come next after another, especially in planned order determined by considerations such as rank, inheritance, or election: *The heir apparent succeeded to the throne. Ensue* usually applies to what is a consequence or logical development: *After the government was toppled, chaos ensued. Result* implies that what follows is caused by what has preceded: *Failure to file an income tax return can result in a fine. Supervene,* in contrast, refers to something that is often unexpected and that has little relation to what has preceded: *"A bad harvest supervened"* (Charlotte Brontë).

---

follower *noun*
1. One who supports and adheres to another ▸ adherent, believer, cohort, disciple, henchman, partisan, satellite, supporter. *See also* **pawn², student, subordinate, sycophant. 2.** An ardent devotee ▸ admirer, enthusiast, fancier. *See* **fan².**

following *adjective*
1. Occurring after another ▸ coming, ensuing, next, subsequent, succeeding, supervening. *Idioms:* coming after, in the wake of. *See also* **consecutive. 2.** Occurring as a result ▸ attending, consequent, consequential, ensuing, resulting. *See also* **logical.**

following *noun*
1. The body of persons who admire a public personality, especially an entertainer ▸ audience, public. *See also* **fan². 2.** A group of attendants or followers ▸ entourage, suite. *See* **retinue.**

folly *noun*
▸ idiocy, silliness, tomfoolery. *See* **foolishness.**

foment *verb*
▸ excite, prod, trigger. *See* **provoke** (1).

fomenter *noun*
▸ inciter, instigator, malcontent, rabble-rouser. *See* **agitator.**

fond *adjective*
▸ caring, loving. *See* **affectionate.**

fondle *verb*
▸ cuddle, pet. *See* **caress.** *See synonym note at* **caress.**

fondness *noun*
1. An intense attachment to a person or thing ▸ affection, devotion, liking. *See* **love** (1). *See synonym note at* **love. 2.** A liking for something ▸ partiality, preference, weakness. *See* **taste** (1).

font *noun*
▸ provenance, root, source. *See* **origin** (1).

food *or* **foodstuff** *noun*
Material that is fit to be eaten ▸ aliment, bread, comestibles, cooking, diet, eatables, edibles, fare, meat, nourishment, nutriment, nutrition, pabulum, provender, provisions, rations, sustenance, viands, victuals. *Slang:* chow, eats, grub, munchies.

fool *noun*
1. A person who is deficient in judgment and good sense ▸ ass, buffoon, idiot, imbecile, jackass, mooncalf, moron, nincompoop, ninny, nitwit, simpleton. *Informal:* dope, gander, goose. *Slang:* boob, bozo, cretin, ding-dong, dim bulb, dip, ditz, dork, dweeb, geek, goof, jerk, nerd, nimrod, schmo, schmuck, simp, turkey, twit. *See also* **drip, dullard, oaf, square. 2.** A person who is easily deceived or victimized ▸ pushover, tool, victim. *See* **dupe** (1).

fool *verb*
1. To cause to accept something false, especially by trickery or misrepresentation ▸ dupe, mislead, trick. *See* **deceive. 2.** To handle something in an attempt to adjust or improve it ▸ fiddle, meddle, tamper. *See* **tinker** (1). **3.** To waste time by engaging in aimless activity ▸ doodle, fiddle (around). *See* **putter. 4.** To touch or handle something out of restlessness ▸ play, toy. *Informal:* monkey. *See* **fiddle** (1).

fool around *verb*
1. *Informal* To waste time by engaging in aimless activity ▸ dawdle (about), fiddle (around). *See* **putter. 2.** *Informal* To make jokes; behave playfully ▸ jest, joke, quip. *Informal:* clown (around), horse around. *Idioms:* crack wise, play the fool. *See also* **play. 3.** *Informal* To behave in a rowdy, improper, or unruly fashion ▸ carry on. *Informal:* horse around. *See* **misbehave. 4.** *Informal* To engage in kissing, caressing, and other amorous behavior ▸ *Informal:* pet, spoon. *See* **neck. 5.** *Informal* To be sexually unfaithful to another ▸ philander. *Informal:* cheat, mess around, play around. *Slang:* two-time.

fool away *verb*
To use, consume, spend, or expend thoughtlessly or carelessly ▸ squander, trifle away. *See* **waste** (1).

foolery *noun*
▸ folly, silliness, tomfoolery. *See* **foolishness.**

foolhardiness *noun*
▸ incautiousness, rashness, recklessness. *See* **temerity.**

foolhardy *adjective*
▸ headlong, impulsive, slapdash. *See* **rash¹.** *See synonym note at* **rash¹.**

foolish *adjective*
Displaying a lack of forethought and good sense ▸ absurd, asinine, brainless, daft, fatuous, harebrained, idiotic, imbecilic, inane, insane, lunatic, ludicrous, mad, mindless, moronic, nonsensical, preposterous, ridiculous, senseless, silly, witless, zany. *Informal:* cockeyed, crazy, daffy, loony, loopy. *Slang:* balmy, dippy, ditsy, dopey, goofy, jerky, wacky. *See also* **giddy, laughable, stupid.**

+ CORE SYNONYMS: *foolish, absurd, fatuous, ludicrous, preposterous, ridiculous, silly.* These adjectives are applied to what is so devoid of wisdom or good sense as to be laughable: *a foolish expenditure of energy; an absurd idea that is bound to fail; made fatuous remarks; ludicrous criticism that was immediately dismissed; a preposterous excuse that no one believed; offered a ridiculous explanation for his tardiness; a silly argument.*

foolishness *noun*
Foolish behavior ► absurdity, daftness, fatuity, fatuousness, folly, foolery, idiocy, imbecility, inanity, insanity, ludicracy, lunacy, madness, nonsense, preposterousness, ridiculousness, senselessness, silliness, tomfoolery, zaniness. *Informal:* boobishness, craziness, daffiness, looniness, loopiness. *Slang:* balminess, dippiness, ditsiness, dopeyness, goofiness, jerkiness, wackiness. *See also* **nonsense.**

foolproof *adjective*
► fail-safe, infallible, unerring. *See* **sure** (2).

foot *noun*
The lowest or supporting part or structure ► bottom, footing, foundation. *See* **base**[1] (2).

foot *verb*
1. To go on foot ► step, tread. *See* **walk. 2.** To move rhythmically to music, using patterns of steps or gestures ► boogie, hoof, step. *See* **dance** (1). **3.** To combine numbers to form a sum ► sum (up), total. *See* **add** (1).

footfall *noun*
► footstep, gait, tread. *See* **walk** (2).

foothold *noun*
A place providing support for the foot in climbing ► footing, perch, purchase, toehold.

footing *noun*
1. The lowest or supporting part or structure ► bottom, foot, foundation. *See* **base**[1] (2). **2.** An underlying support, as for an argument or belief ► cornerstone, foundation, underpinning. *See* **basis** (1). **3.** Positioning of one individual vis-à-vis others ► position, rank, standing. *See* **place** (1). **4.** An established position from which to deal with others ► standing, terms. *See* **basis** (3). **5.** A place providing support for the foot in climbing ► foothold, perch, purchase, toehold.

footloose *adjective*
► fancy-free, marriageable. *See* **single** (5).

footpace *noun*
A very slow rate of speed ► crawl, creep, slow motion. *Idiom:* snail's pace.

footpath *noun*
► path, road, route. *See* **way** (2).

footprints *noun*
► marks, trace, trail. *See* **track** (1).

footstep *noun*
► footfall, gait, tread. *See* **walk** (2).

footstool *or* **footrest** *noun*
A stool or cushion for resting the feet ► hassock, ottoman.

foozle *noun*
► bungle, fumble, solecism. *See* **blunder.**

foozler *noun*
► bungler. *Slang:* klutz. *See* **blunderer.**

fop *noun*
A man who is preoccupied with or vain about his clothes ► beau, coxcomb, dandy, peacock, swell.

for *conjunction*
► seeing as, since. *See* **because.**

forage *verb*
1. To search through or over thoroughly ► comb, ransack, rummage. *See* **scour**[2] (1). **2.** To feed on vegetation ► crop, pasture. *See* **browse** (2).

foray *noun*
An act of invading, especially by military forces ► incursion, inroad, invasion, raid. *See also* **attack.**

foray *verb*
To enter so as to attack, plunder, destroy, or conquer ► overrun, raid. *See* **invade** (1).

forbear *verb*
1. To hold oneself back ► abstain, hold off, withhold. *See* **refrain.** *See synonym note at* **refrain. 2.** To prevent the occurrence or continuation of a movement, action, or operation ► check, discontinue, immobilize. *See* **stop** (2).

forbearance *noun*
1. The capacity of enduring hardship or inconvenience without complaint ► resignation, tolerance. *See* **patience.** *See synonym note at* **patience. 2.** Forbearing or lenient treatment ► charity, lenience, toleration. *See* **tolerance** (1).

forbearing *adjective*
1. Enduring or capable of enduring hardship or inconvenience without complaint ► enduring, long-suffering, resigned. *See* **patient. 2.** Not strict or severe ► easy, indulgent, lenient. *See* **tolerant** (1).

forbid *verb*
To refuse to allow ► ban, bar, debar, disallow, enjoin, interdict, outlaw, prohibit, proscribe, taboo. *See also* **exclude, hinder, prevent.**

+ CORE SYNONYMS: *forbid, ban, enjoin, interdict, prohibit, proscribe.* These verbs mean to refuse to allow: *laws that forbid speeding; banned smoking; was enjoined from broadcasting; interdict trafficking in drugs; rules that prohibit loitering; proscribed the importation of certain fruits.*

◄ ANTONYM: *permit*

forbiddance *noun*
A refusal to allow ► ban, disallowance, inhibition, interdiction, prohibition, proscription, taboo. *See also* **refusal, prevention.**

forbidden *adjective*
Not allowed ► banned, barred, debarred, disallowed, illicit, impermissible, interdicted, outlawed, prohibited, proscribed, taboo, verboten. *See also* **criminal, unspeakable.**

forbidding *adjective*
1. So disagreeable as to discourage approach ► dour,

flinty, grim, inhospitable, stern, unhospitable, uninviting. *See also* **cool, hostile, severe. 2.** Bringing or predicting misfortune ▸ menacing, ominous, unpropitious. *See* **fateful** (1). **3.** Marked by cold and unpleasant conditions ▸ austere, inclement, raw, stark. *See* **bleak** (1).

force *noun*

1. Strength or energy that overcomes resistance ▸ coercion, compulsion, constraint, duress, might, power, pressure, strength, violence. **2.** Capacity for work or vigorous activity ▸ might, potency, power. *See* **energy**. *See synonym note at* **energy**. **3.** The strong effect exerted by one person or thing on another ▸ bearing, impression, influence. *See* **impact** (2). **4.** The condition of being in full effect or operation ▸ actualization, being, effect, realization. *See also* **exercise. 5.** A group of people organized for a particular purpose ▸ body, corps, crew, detachment, division, gang, patrol, platoon, side, squad, squadron, team, unit. *See also* **alliance, assembly, band², union. 6.** The power of an argument to convince or compel agreement ▸ forcefulness, justice. *See* **cogency. 7.** Power to sway or affect based on prestige, wealth, ability, or position ▸ power, sway, weight. *See* **influence** (1).

force *verb*

1. To cause a person or thing to act or move in spite of resistance ▸ coerce, compel, constrain, make, obligate, oblige, pressure. *See also* **drive, urge. 2.** To compel by threats ▸ blackjack, dragoon. *See* **coerce** (1). **3.** To compel another to participate in or submit to a sexual act ▸ assault, molest, rape, ravish, violate.

✢ **CORE SYNONYMS:** *force, compel, coerce, constrain, oblige, obligate.* These verbs mean to cause a person or thing to follow a prescribed or dictated course in spite of resistance. *Force,* the most general, usually implies the exertion of physical power or the operation of circumstances that permit no options: *Tear gas forced the fugitives out of their hiding place. Compel* applies especially to an act dictated by one in authority: *Say nothing unless you're compelled to. Coerce* invariably implies the use of strength or harsh measures in securing compliance: *"The man of genius rules . . . by persuading an efficient minority to coerce an indifferent and self-indulgent majority"* (James Fitzjames Stephen). *Constrain* suggests that one is bound to a course of action by physical or moral means or by the operation of compelling circumstances: *"I will never be by violence constrained to do anything"* (Elizabeth I). *Oblige* implies the operation of authority, necessity, or moral or ethical considerations: *"Work consists of whatever a body is obliged to do"* (Mark Twain). *Obligate* applies when compliance is enforced by a legal contract or by the dictates of one's conscience or sense of propriety: *I am obligated to repay the loan.*

---

forced *adjective*

1. Accomplished by force ▸ coercive, forcible, violent. *Informal:* strong-arm. **2.** Not natural or spontaneous ▸ contrived, effortful, labored, strained. *See also* **awkward, stiff.**

forceful *adjective*

1. Full of or displaying force ▸ dynamic, dynamical, effective, forcible, hard-hitting, mighty, potent, powerful, strong, vigorous. *See also* **intense, severe. 2.** Possessing, exerting, or displaying energy ▸ brisk, lively, vigorous. *See* **energetic. 3.** Serving to convince ▸ cogent, persuasive. *See* **convincing** (1). **4.** Bold or confident in assertion ▸ emphatic, insistent. *See* **assertive.**

forcefully *adverb*

▸ energetically, powerfully, vigorously. *See* **hard** (1).

forcefulness *noun*

1. Concentrated power or force, as of effort, opinion, or emotion ▸ ferocity, fury, vehemence. *See* **intensity. 2.** The power of an argument to convince or compel agreement ▸ force, justice. *See* **cogency.**

forcible *adjective*

1. Accomplished by force ▸ coercive, forced, violent. *Informal:* strong-arm. **2.** Full of or displaying force ▸ dynamic, powerful, vigorous. *See* **forceful** (1). **3.** Serving to convince ▸ cogent, persuasive. *See* **convincing** (1).

forcibly *adverb*

1. With force and violence ▸ coercively, violently. *Idioms:* against one's will, by force, under duress. **2.** With great force, energy, or intensity ▸ forcefully, powerfully, vigorously. *See* **hard** (1).

ford *verb*

▸ pass, transit, traverse. *See* **cross** (1).

fore *noun*

1. The forward part of something ▸ forepart, front end, front side. *See* **front** (1). **2.** The position of greatest advancement or importance ▸ cutting edge, lead, vanguard. *See* **forefront.**

forearm *verb*

▸ fortify, ready, steel. *See* **gird** (1).

forebear *noun*

▸ ascendant, parent, progenitor. *See* **ancestor** (1). *See synonym note at* **ancestor.**

forebode *verb*

1. To give warning signs of impending peril ▸ forewarn, portend. *See* **threaten** (1). **2.** To tell about or make known by or as if by supernatural means ▸ divine, foretell. *See* **prophesy.**

foreboding *noun*

1. An intuitive awareness or sense of something ▸ intuition, notion, suspicion. *See* **feeling** (1). **2.** A phenomenon that serves as a sign of some future good or evil ▸ portent, prognostication, sign. *See* **omen.**

foreboding *adjective*

Bringing or predicting misfortune ▸ dire, ominous, portentous. *See* **fateful** (1).

forecast *verb*

1. To tell about or make known in advance, especially by means of special knowledge ▸ call, prognosticate. *See* **predict.** *See synonym note at* **predict. 2.** To give an indication of something in advance ▸ bode, foretell, portend. *See* **foreshadow.**

forecast *noun*
The act of predicting ▶ outlook, prognosis. *See* **prediction.**

foredoomed *adjective*
▶ doomed, lost, reprobate. *See* **condemned.**

forefather *noun*
▶ forebear, parent, progenitor. *See* **ancestor** (1). *See synonym note at* **ancestor.**

forefront *noun*
The position of greatest advancement or importance ▶ avant-garde, cutting edge, fore, front, lead, vanguard.

foregoing *adjective*
1. Next before the present one ▶ last, latter, preceding, previous. **2.** Just gone by or elapsed ▶ precedent, previous, prior. *See* **past** (1).

forehanded *adjective*
▶ cautious, chary, prudent. *See* **wary** (1).

forehandedness *noun*
▶ circumspection, foresight, forethought. *See* **prudence** (1).

foreign *adjective*
1. From or characteristic of another place or part of the world ▶ alien, exotic, expatriate, immigrant, nonnative, nonresident, strange. *See also* **distant. 2.** Not part of the essential nature of a thing ▶ alien, extraneous, extrinsic. *See also* **irrelevant.**

✦ CORE SYNONYMS: *foreign, alien, exotic, strange.* These adjectives mean from or characteristic of another place or part of the world: *a foreign accent; alien customs; exotic birds; moved to a strange city.*

---

foreigner *noun*
A person coming from another country or into a new community ▶ alien, émigré, expatriate, immigrant, newcomer, nonresident, outlander, outsider, stranger.

foreknow *verb*
▶ anticipate, divine, envision. *See* **foresee.**

foreknowledge *noun*
▶ innovation, inspiration, prescience. *See* **vision** (2).

foreman *or* **forewoman** *noun*
▶ director, manager, supervisor. *See* **boss** (1).

foremost *adjective*
1. Most important, influential, or significant ▶ chief, key, main, principal. *See* **primary** (1). *See synonym note at* **primary. 2.** Surpassing all others in quality ▶ optimum, superlative, unsurpassed. *See* **best** (1).

foremother *noun*
▶ forebear, parent, progenitor. *See* **ancestor** (1).

forenoon *noun*
The time of day from sunrise to noon ▶ before lunch, before noon, morning. *See also* **dawn.**

forepart *noun*
▶ fore, front end, front side. *See* **front** (1).

foreperson *noun*
▶ director, manager, supervisor. *See* **boss** (1).

forerun *verb*
1. To give an indication of something in advance ▶ bode, forecast, portend. *See* **foreshadow. 2.** To come, exist, or occur before in time ▶ antecede, antedate, predate. *See* **precede** (1). **3.** To prohibit from occurring by advance planning or action ▶ anticipate, avert, forestall. *See* **prevent.**

forerunner *noun*
1. One that foreshadows or prepares for something else ▶ harbinger, herald, pioneer, precursor, presager, trailblazer, vanguard. **2.** One that precedes, as in time ▶ antecedent, precursor. *See* **ancestor** (2). **3.** A first form from which varieties arise or imitations are made ▶ master, model, prototype. *See* **original** (1). **4.** A phenomenon that serves as a sign of some future good or evil ▶ portent, prognostication, sign. *See* **omen.**

foresee *verb*
To know in advance ▶ anticipate, divine, envision, foreknow, see. *See also* **expect, predict.**

foreshadow *verb*
To give an indication of something in advance ▶ adumbrate, augur, bode, betoken, forecast, forerun, foreshow, foretell, foretoken, portend, prefigure, presage, prognosticate. *See also* **mean, prophesy.**

foreshow *verb*
▶ bode, forecast, portend. *See* **foreshadow.**

foresight *noun*
1. Discernment or perception which is usually competent or creative ▶ innovation, inspiration. *See* **vision** (2). **2.** The exercise of good judgment or common sense in practical matters ▶ circumspection, discretion, forethought. *See* **prudence** (1). *See synonym note at* **prudence.**

foresighted *adjective*
▶ imaginative, intuitive, perceptive. *See* **visionary** (1).

foresightedness *noun*
▶ circumspection, foresight, forethought. *See* **prudence** (1).

forest *noun*
A dense growth of trees and underbrush covering an area ▶ backwoods, timberland, woodland, woods.

forestall *verb*
1. To prohibit from occurring by advance planning or action ▶ avert, obviate, stave off. *See* **prevent.** *See synonym note at* **prevent. 2.** To interfere with the progress of ▶ dampen, impede, obstruct. *See* **hinder** (1).

forestallment *noun*
▶ deterrence, obviation, preclusion. *See* **prevention.**

foretaste *noun*
A limited or anticipatory experience ▶ sample, sampling, taste. *See also* **glance.**

foretell *verb*
1. To tell about or make known in advance, especially by means of special knowledge ▶ forecast, project. *See* **predict.** *See synonym note at* **predict. 2.** To tell about or make known by or as if by supernatural means ▶ divine, soothsay. *See* **prophesy.** *See synonym note at* **prophesy. 3.** To give an indication of something in advance ▶ adumbrate, portend, prefigure. *See* **foreshadow.**

foreteller *noun*
▸ diviner, fortuneteller, seer, soothsayer. *See* **prophet.**

forethought *or* **forethoughtfulness** *noun*
▸ circumspection, foresight, providence. *See* **prudence** (1). *See synonym note at* **prudence.**

foretoken *verb*
To give an indication of something in advance ▸ adumbrate, portend, prefigure. *See* **foreshadow.**

foretoken *noun*
A phenomenon that serves as a sign of some future good or evil ▸ portent, prognostication, sign. *See* **omen.**

forever *adverb*
1. For all time; without end ▸ always, endlessly, eternally, everlastingly, evermore, permanently, perpetually, unendingly. *Idioms:* for ever and a day, for ever and ever, for good, for keeps, in perpetuity, till kingdom come, till Doomsday (*or* Judgment Day), till the cows come home, world without end. **2.** Without stop or interruption ▸ endlessly, nonstop, perpetually. *See* **continually.**

forever *noun*
A long time ▸ eon, eternity. *See* **ages.**

forewarn *verb*
1. To notify someone of imminent danger or risk ▸ alert, caution. *See* **warn. 2.** To give warning signs of impending peril ▸ forebode, portend. *See* **threaten** (1).

forewarning *noun*
1. An intuitive awareness or sense of something ▸ foreboding, intuition, notion. *See* **feeling** (1). **2.** A phenomenon that serves as a sign of some future good or evil ▸ portent, prognostication, sign. *See* **omen.**

foreword *noun*
▸ overture, preface, prologue. *See* **introduction** (1).

forfeit *verb*
▸ relinquish, surrender, yield. *See* **abandon** (1).

forfend *verb*
▸ anticipate, avert, obviate. *See* **prevent.**

forgather *verb*
▸ cluster, congregate, gather. *See* **assemble** (1).

forge[1] *verb*
1. To shape, break, or flatten with repeated blows ▸ hammer, pound. *See* **beat** (3). **2.** To create by forming, combining, or altering materials ▸ build, compose, shape. *See* **make** (1). **3.** To make a fraudulent copy of ▸ fake, falsify. *See* **counterfeit** (1).

forge[2] *verb*
To walk in a laborious way ▸ slog, slop, toil. *See* **trudge.**

forger *noun*
One who makes a fraudulent copy of something ▸ counterfeiter, fabricator, faker, falsifier.

forgery *noun*
▸ falsification, sham. *See* **counterfeit.**

forget *verb*
1. To fail to remember ▸ *Informal:* disremember. *Idioms:* draw a blank, go blank, have a senior moment, have no recollection (*or* memory). **2.** To fail

to do or carry out ▸ disregard, omit, overlook. *See* **neglect** (3). **3.** To cease consideration or treatment of ▸ give up, relinquish, skip. *See* **drop** (7).

forgetful *adjective*
1. So lost in thought as to be unable to remember things ▸ abstracted, inattentive, preoccupied. *See* **absent-minded. 2.** Lacking concern or attention ▸ mindless, unobservant, unthinking. *See* **careless** (1).

forgivable *adjective*
▸ condonable, venial. *See* **pardonable.**

forgive *verb*
To grant forgiveness to or for ▸ condone, excuse, let pass, overlook, pardon, remit. *Idiom:* forgive and forget. *See also* **clear, excuse.**

✚ CORE SYNONYMS: *forgive, pardon, excuse, condone.* These verbs mean to refrain from imposing punishment on an offender or demanding satisfaction for an offense. The first three can be used as conventional ways of offering apology. More strictly, to *forgive* is to grant pardon without harboring resentment: "*Children begin by loving their parents; as they grow older they judge them; sometimes they forgive them*" (Oscar Wilde). *Pardon* more strongly implies release from the liability for or penalty entailed by an offense: *After the revolution all political prisoners were pardoned.* To *excuse* is to pass over a mistake or fault without demanding punishment or redress: "*There are some acts of injustice which no national interest can excuse*" (J.A. Froude). To *condone* is to overlook an offense, usually a serious one, and often suggests tacit forgiveness: *Failure to protest the policy may imply a willingness to condone it.*

---

forgiveness *noun*
The act or an instance of forgiving ▸ absolution, amnesty, condonation, excuse, pardon, remission. *See also* **exculpation, grace.**

forgo *verb*
▸ cede, relinquish, surrender. *See* **abandon** (1).

fork *noun*
Something resembling or analogous to a tree branch ▸ arm, division, offshoot. *See* **branch** (1). *See synonym note at* **branch.**

fork *verb*
1. To separate into branches or branchlike parts ▸ diverge, part. *See* **branch. 2.** To prepare soil for the planting of crops ▸ cultivate, plow, work. *See* **till.**

fork out *or* **over** *or* **up** *verb*
Informal To give money as payment ▸ expend, outlay. *See* **spend** (1).

forlorn *adjective*
1. Dejected due to the awareness of being alone ▸ desolate, lonely, lonesome. *See* **lonely** (2). **2.** Arousing or deserving pity ▸ lamentable, poor. *See* **pitiful** (1). **3.** Having lost all hope ▸ dejected, discouraged, hopeless. *See* **despondent.** *See synonym note at* **despondent. 4.** Having been given up and left alone ▸ bereft, jilted, rejected. *See* **abandoned** (1). **5.** Empty of people ▸ uninhabited, unpeopled, unpopulated. *See* **lonely** (1).

form *noun*

1. The characteristic surface arrangement of a thing ► cast, configuration, contour, delineation, design, figure, outline, pattern, profile, shape, silhouette, structure. *See also* **arrangement, outline. 2.** A document used in applying, as for a job ► application, paper, sheet. **3.** A habitual way of behaving ► convention, habit, practice. *See* **custom** (1). **4.** The physical characteristics of a person ► body, figure, physique. *See* **constitution** (1). **5.** A conventional social gesture or act without intrinsic purpose ► ceremony, formality. *See* **ritual** (2). **6.** Strict observance of social conventions ► ceremoniousness, formality, protocol. *See* **ceremony** (2). **7.** A state of sound readiness ► fettle, fitness, order. *See* **shape** (1). **8.** A hollow device for shaping a fluid or plastic substance ► cast, matrix, mold. **9.** The manner in which one behaves ► comportment, conduct, deportment. *See* **behavior** (1). **10.** One that is slightly different from others of the same kind or designation ► adaptation, permutation. *See* **variation** (1). **11.** A regular or customary matter, condition, or course of events ► norm, ordinary, rule. *See* **usual. 12.** A class that is defined by the common attribute or attributes possessed by all its members ► ilk, mold, species. *See* **kind²**.

form *verb*

1. To give form to by or as if by pressing and kneading ► model, mold, sculpt, shape. *See also* **work. 2.** To create by forming, combining, or altering materials ► build, compose, shape. *See* **make** (1). **3.** To be the constituent parts of ► compose, make up. *See also* **contain. 4.** To impart knowledge and skill to ► discipline, instruct. *See* **educate** (1). **5.** To come gradually to have ► acquire, incur. *See* **develop** (1).

✦ CORE SYNONYMS: *form, figure, shape, configuration, contour, profile.* These nouns refer to the characterstic surface arrangement or external outline of a thing. *Form* is the outline and structure of a thing as opposed to its substance: *a brooch in the form of a lovers' knot. Figure* refers usually to form as established by bounding or enclosing lines: *The cube is a solid geometric figure. Shape* implies three-dimensional definition that indicates both outline and bulk or mass: *"He faced her, a hooded and cloaked shape"* (Joseph Conrad). *Configuration* stresses the pattern formed by the arrangement of parts within an outline: *The map shows the configuration of North America, with its mountains, rivers, and plains. Contour* refers especially to the outline of a three-dimensional figure: *I traced the contour of the bow with my finger. Profile* denotes the outline of something viewed against a background and especially the outline of the human face in side view: *The police took a photograph of the mugger's profile.*

---

formal *adjective*

1. Having or arising from authority ► official, supreme. *See* **authoritative** (1). **2.** Fond of or given to ceremony ► courtly, official, stately. *See* **ceremonious** (1). **3.** Of or characterized by ceremony ► ceremonial, liturgical, ritualistic. *See* **ritual. 4.** Not friendly, sociable, or warm in manner ► aloof, chilly, impersonal. *See* **cool** (1). **5.** Requiring elegant clothes and fine manners ► black-tie, dressy, full-dress, white-tie.

formal *noun*

A party or gathering for dancing ► ball, cotillion, promenade. *See* **dance.**

formalistic *adjective*

► bookish, literary, scholastic. *See* **pedantic.**

formality *noun*

1. Strict observance of social conventions ► ceremoniousness, form, protocol. *See* **ceremony** (2). **2.** A conventional social gesture or act without intrinsic purpose ► ceremony, form. *See* **ritual** (2).

format *noun*

1. Systematic arrangement and design ► order, organization, scheme. *See* **method** (1). **2.** The act or condition of being arranged ► allotment, layout, positioning. *See* **arrangement** (1).

formation *noun*

► grouping, lineup, positioning. *See* **arrangement** (1).

former *adjective*

1. Just gone by or elapsed ► precedent, previous, prior. *See* **past** (1). **2.** Having been such previously ► erstwhile, onetime, past. *See* **late** (2).

formerly *adverb*

► before, previously. *See* **earlier** (1).

formidable *adjective*

1. Causing or capable of causing fear ► appalling, dreadful, redoubtable, terrible. *See* **fearful** (1). **2.** Beyond the understanding of an average mind ► abstract, esoteric, profound. *See* **deep** (2). **3.** Requiring great or extreme bodily, mental, or spiritual strength ► arduous, difficult, severe. *See* **burdensome** (1).

formless *adjective*

► amorphous, unformed, unshaped. *See* **shapeless.** *See synonym note at* **shapeless.**

formula *noun*

1. A means or method of entering into or achieving something desirable ► key, route, secret. *Informal:* ticket. *See also* **trick. 2.** A broad and basic rule or truth ► axiom, principle. *See* **law** (3). **3.** The approach used to do something ► manner, mode, style. *See* **way** (1). *See synonym note at* **way.**

formulaic *adjective*

► common, mediocre, standard. *See* **ordinary** (1).

formulate *verb*

1. To devise and set down ► compose, draft, draw up, frame. *See also* **compose. 2.** To form a strategy for ► blueprint, devise, strategize. *See* **design** (1). **3.** To use ingenuity in making, developing, or achieving ► contrive, hatch, dream up. *See* **invent** (1). **4.** To convey in language or words of a particular form ► express, word. *See* **phrase.**

formulated *adjective*

► deliberate, intentional, premeditated. *See* **calculated** (1).

fornicator *noun*

► adulterer, cheater, Casanova. *See* **philanderer.**

forsake *verb*
1. To give up or leave completely ▸ desert, leave, quit. *See* **abandon** (1). **2.** To abandon one's cause or party usually to join another ▸ desert, quit, turn. *See* **defect**.

forsaken *adjective*
▸ bereft, desolate, forlorn. *See* **abandoned** (1).

forswear *verb*
1. To give up or leave completely ▸ cede, relinquish, surrender. *See* **abandon** (1). **2.** To present false information with the intention of deceiving ▸ fib, prevaricate. *See* **lie**². **3.** To discontinue (a habit, for example) ▸ abjure, give up, leave off. *See* **break** (17). **4.** To disavow something previously written or said irrevocably and usually formally ▸ recant, take back, withdraw. *See* **retract** (1).

fort *noun*
A position or building that has been fortified to be defended by soldiers ▸ bastion, citadel, fortification, fortress, redoubt, stronghold. *See also* **base**¹.

forte *noun*
Something at which a person excels ▸ long suit, métier, specialty, strength, strong point, strong suit. *Slang:* bag, thing.

✦ CORE SYNONYMS: *forte, métier, specialty, strength.* These nouns denote something at which a person is particularly skilled: *Writing fiction is her forte. The theater is his métier. The professor's specialty was the study of ancient languages. Listening to patients is one of the strengths of a good doctor.*

---

forth *adverb*
▸ ahead, onward, out. *See* **forward**.

forthcoming *adjective*
In the relatively near future ▸ approaching, coming, due, upcoming. *Idioms:* around the corner, on the horizon. *See also* **close, imminent**.

forthright *adjective*
▸ candid, open, plainspoken. *See* **frank**.

forthwith *adverb*
▸ directly, instantly, straightaway. *See* **immediately** (1).

fortification *noun*
▸ citadel, stronghold. *See* **fort**.

fortify *verb*
1. To make firmer in a particular conviction or habit ▸ confirm, harden, reinforce, strengthen. *See also* **back, establish**. **2.** To prepare oneself for action ▸ brace, ready, steel. *See* **gird** (1). **3.** To impart emotional, moral, or mental strength to ▸ hearten, nerve. *See* **encourage** (2).

fortitude *noun*
1. The quality of mind enabling one to face danger or hardship resolutely ▸ bravery, gallantry, valor. *See* **courage**. **2.** The quality or power of withstanding hardship or stress ▸ durability, stamina, toughness. *See* **endurance** (1).

fortitudinous *adjective*
▸ courageous, fearless, heroic. *See* **brave**.

fortress *noun*
▸ citadel, stronghold. *See* **fort**.

fortuitous *adjective*
1. Characterized by luck or good fortune ▸ fortunate, happy, lucky, providential. *See also* **opportune**. **2.** Occurring unexpectedly ▸ chance, contingent, fluky, inadvertent. *See* **accidental** (1). *See synonym note at* **accidental**. **3.** Suited for a particular purpose or occurring at a suitable time ▸ favorable, propitious, well-timed. *See* **opportune**.

fortuitousness *noun*
▸ coincidence, fortune, luck. *See* **chance** (2).

fortuity *noun*
1. An unexpected random event ▸ accident, fluke, happenstance. *See* **chance** (1). **2.** The random, unintended, or unpredictable element of an event or the force regarded as the cause of such an event ▸ coincidence, fortune, luck. *See* **chance** (2).

fortunate *adjective*
1. Characterized by luck or good fortune ▸ fortuitous, happy, lucky, providential. *See synonym note at* **lucky**. **2.** Indicative of future success or full of promise ▸ auspicious, bright, propitious. *See* **favorable** (1). **3.** Suited for a particular purpose or occurring at a suitable time ▸ auspicious, propitious, well-timed. *See* **opportune**.

fortunateness *noun*
▸ fortune, godsend. *See* **luck** (1).

fortune *noun*
1. The random, unintended, or unpredictable element of an event or the force regarded as the cause of such an event ▸ coincidence, fortuitousness, luck. *See* **chance** (2). **2.** The supposed power that predetermines events ▸ destiny, kismet, predestination. *See* **fate** (1). **3.** Success attained as a result of chance ▸ dumb luck, good fortune. *See* **luck** (1). **4.** A personal outcome or end ▸ doom, fortune, lot. *See* **fate** (2). **5.** Things having economic value ▸ assets, capital, means. *See* **resources** (1). **6.** A great amount of accumulated money and precious possessions ▸ pelf, riches, treasure. *See* **wealth** (1). **7.** A large sum of money ▸ mint. *Informal:* bundle, pile, pretty penny, tidy sum, wad. *Idiom:* king's ransom.

fortuneteller *noun*
▸ diviner, foreteller, seer, soothsayer. *See* **prophet**.

forum *noun*
1. A number of persons who have come or been gathered together ▸ conference, group. *Informal:* get-together. *See* **assembly** (1). **2.** A meeting for the exchange of views ▸ discussion, parley, seminar. *See* **conference** (1). **3.** A judicial assembly ▸ bar, tribunal. *See* **court** (2).

forward *verb*
1. To cause something to be conveyed to a destination ▸ consign, dispatch. *See* **send** (1). *See synonym note at* **send**. **2.** To cause to move forward or upward, as toward a goal ▸ further, propel, push. *See* **advance** (1). *See synonym note at* **advance**.

forward *adjective*
Ahead of current trends or customs ▸ advanced, precocious. *See* **progressive** (1).

forward *adverb*
Toward the front or beyond a position ► ahead, forth, frontward, out, onward. *Idiom:* in advance.
forward-looking *or* **forward-thinking** *adjective*
► forward, precocious. *See* **progressive** (1).
forwardness *noun*
► audacity, boldness, impertinence. *See* **impudence.**
fossil *noun*
1. An old-fashioned person who is reluctant to change or innovate ► fogy, fuddy-duddy, mossback. *See* **square** (2). **2.** One who is extremely or stubbornly conservative ► archconservative, reactionary. *See* **ultraconservative.**
foster *verb*
1. To help grow or develop ► cultivate, nourish, provide for. *See* **nurture.** *See synonym note at* **nurture.** **2.** To take care of and educate a child ► bring up, parent, raise, rear. **3.** To help bring about ► encourage, facilitate. *See* **promote** (2). **4.** To cause to move forward or upward, as toward a goal ► further, propel, push. *See* **advance** (1). *See synonym note at* **advance.**
foul *adjective*
1. Covered with or stained by dirt or other impurities ► grimy, soiled. *See* **dirty** (1). **2.** Having an unpleasant odor ► fetid, stinking. *See* **smelly.** **3.** Marred by decay ► decayed, putrid, rancid. *See* **bad** (2). **4.** So objectionable as to deserve condemnation ► atrocious, disgusting, loathsome. *See* **offensive** (1). **5.** Offensive to accepted standards of decency ► bawdy, coarse, lewd, vulgar. *See* **obscene** (1). **6.** Marked by cold and unpleasant conditions ► grim, severe. *See* **bleak** (1).
foul *verb*
1. To make impure or unclean by contact or mixture ► debase, poison, pollute. *See* **contaminate** (1). **2.** To make dirty ► bemire, muck up, mud. *See* **dirty** (1). **3.** To twist together so that separation is difficult ► ensnarl, tangle. *See* **entangle** (1).
foul up *verb*
To ruin through clumsiness or ineptness ► blunder, mess up, spoil. *See* **botch.**
foul *noun*
A violent forcible contact ► crash, impact. *See* **collision.**
foulness *noun*
1. The condition or state of being dirty ► filthiness, squalor, uncleanliness. *See* **dirtiness** (1). **2.** The state of being contaminated ► defilement, impurity, pollution. *See* **contamination** (1). **3.** The quality or state of being obscene ► filthiness, profanity, smuttiness, vulgarness. *See* **obscenity** (1).
foul play *noun*
1. Betrayal, especially of a duty or obligation ► disloyalty, perfidy, treacherousness. *See* **faithlessness** (1). **2.** The state of being contaminated ► defilement, impurity, pollution. *See* **contamination** (1).
foul-smelling *adjective*
► fetid, foul, stinking. *See* **smelly.**
foul-tasting *adjective*
► unappetizing, uneatable. *See* **unpalatable** (1).

foul-up *noun*
► fiasco, muddle, shambles. *See* **mess** (1).
found *verb*
1. To bring into existence formally ► constitute, create, establish, institute, organize, originate, set up, start. *See also* **start. 2.** To provide a basis for ► establish, ground. *See* **base**[1] **(1).**

✚ CORE SYNONYMS: *found, create, establish, institute, organize.* These verbs mean to bring something into existence formally and set it in operation: *founded a colony; created a trust fund; establishing a business; instituted an annual benefit concert; organizing a field trip.*

---

foundation *noun*
1. The act of founding or establishing ► constitution, creation, establishment, institution, organization, origination, start-up. *See also* **beginning. 2.** The lowest or supporting part or structure ► bottom, foot, groundwork. *See* **base**[1] **(2). 3.** An underlying support, as for an argument or belief ► cornerstone, footing, underpinning. *See* **basis** (1). *See synonym note at* **basis. 4.** A justifying fact or consideration ► justification, reason. *See* **basis** (2).
foundational *adjective*
► basic, fundamental, primary. *See* **radical** (1).
founder[1] *verb*
1. To go beneath the surface or to the bottom of a liquid ► go down, gravitate. *See* **sink** (1). **2.** To go wrong or be unsuccessful ► fall short, misfire. *See* **fail** (1).
founder[2] *noun*
One that creates, founds, or originates ► author, creator, inventor. *See* **originator.**
foundling *noun*
► ragamuffin, stray. *See* **orphan.**
fountain *or* **fount** *or* **fountainhead** *noun*
► provenance, derivation. *See* **origin** (1).
four-flush *verb*
Slang To cause to accept something false by trickery or misrepresentation ► dupe, fool, mislead, trick. *See* **deceive.**
fourth estate *noun*
► correspondent, editorialist, media. *See* **press** (1).
foxiness *noun*
► artfulness, slyness. *See* **art** (1).
foxy *adjective*
1. Deceitfully clever ► cunning, wily. *See* **artful** (1). **2.** *Slang* Arousing erotic desire ► alluring, sexy. *See* **desirable** (1).
fracas *noun*
1. A discussion, often heated, in which a difference of opinion is expressed ► contention, fight, quarrel. *See* **argument** (1). **2.** A physical conflict between two or more people ► brawl, free-for-all, melee. *See* **fight** (1). *See synonym note at* **fight. 3.** A lack of civil order or peace ► anarchy, lawlessness, misrule. *See* **disorder** (2).
fraction *noun*
► building block, piece, section. *See* **part** (1).

fractional *adjective*
‣ fragmentary, incomplete. *See* **partial** (1).
fractious *adjective*
1. Not submitting to discipline or control ‣ ill-behaved, obstinate, unmanageable. *See* **unruly**.
2. Having or showing a bad temper ‣ cranky, grouchy, peevish. *See* **ill-tempered**.
fractiousness *noun*
‣ intractability, recalcitrance, unmanageability. *See* **unruliness**.
fracture *verb*
1. To crack or split into two or more fragments by means of force or strain ‣ shatter, smash, splinter. *See* **break** (1). *See synonym note at* **break. 2.** To undergo partial breaking ‣ rupture, split. *See* **crack** (1).
fracture *noun*
A partial opening caused by splitting and rupture ‣ break, cleft, fissure. *See* **crack** (2).
fragile *adjective*
1. Easily broken or damaged ‣ breakable, brittle, delicate, frangible, friable. **2.** Not physically strong ‣ feeble, frail, unsound. *See* **weak** (1). *See synonym note at* **weak**.

✛ CORE SYNONYMS: *fragile, breakable, frangible, delicate, brittle.* These adjectives mean easily broken or damaged. *Fragile* applies to objects that are not made of strong or sturdy material and that require great care when handled: *fragile porcelain plates. Breakable* and *frangible* mean capable of being broken but do not necessarily imply inherent weakness: *breakable toys; frangible artifacts. Delicate* refers to what is so soft, tender, or fine as to be susceptible to injury: *delicate fruit. Brittle* refers to inelasticity that makes something especially likely to fracture or snap when it is subjected to pressure: *brittle bones.*

---

fragility *or* **fragileness** *noun*
‣ decrepitude, feebleness. *See* **infirmity** (1).
fragment *noun*
1. Residual matter ‣ butt, odds and ends. *See* **end** (7). **2.** A tiny amount ‣ dash, drop, smidgen. *See* **bit**[1] (1).
fragment *verb*
To reduce or become reduced to pieces or fragments ‣ crumble, decompose, dissolve. *See* **disintegrate** (1).
fragmentary *adjective*
‣ fractional, incomplete. *See* **partial** (1).
fragmentize *verb*
‣ crumble, decompose, fragment. *See* **disintegrate** (1).
fragrance *noun*
A sweet or pleasant odor ‣ aroma, bouquet, essence, perfume, redolence, scent. *See also* **smell, stench**.

✛ CORE SYNONYMS: *fragrance, aroma, bouquet, perfume, redolence, scent.* These nouns denote a pleasant or sweet odor: *the fragrance of lilacs; the aroma of sizzling bacon; the bouquet of a fine wine; the perfume of roses; the redolence of fresh coffee; the scent of newly mown hay.*

---

fragrant *adjective*
Having a pleasant odor ‣ aromatic, odoriferous,

odorous, perfumy, redolent, savory, scent-laden, sweet-smelling. *See also* **smelly**.
fraidy cat *noun*
Slang An ignoble, uncouraging person ‣ craven, milksop, sissy. *See* **coward**.
frail *adjective*
‣ delicate, feeble, unsound. *See* **weak** (1). *See synonym note at* **weak**.
frailness *noun*
‣ decrepitude, feebleness, unsubstantiality. *See* **infirmity** (1).
frailty *noun*
1. The condition of being infirm or physically weak ‣ decrepitude, unsubstantiality. *See* **infirmity** (1). **2.** An imperfection of character ‣ fault, shortcoming, weak point. *See* **weakness** (1).
frame *noun*
1. A structure that supports or encloses something ‣ case, casing, framing, framework, shell, skeleton, substructure. *See also* **form, stage, support. 2.** The physical characteristics of a person ‣ body, form, physique. *See* **constitution** (1).
frame *verb*
1. To create by forming, combining, or altering materials ‣ build, compose, shape. *See* **make** (1). **2.** To form a strategy for ‣ devise, formulate, strategize. *See* **design** (1). **3.** To devise and set down ‣ compose, draft, draw up, formulate. *See* **compose. 4.** To make or form a structure ‣ construct, erect, raise. *See* **build** (1).
frame of mind *noun*
‣ humor, temper. *See* **mood** (1).
frame of reference *noun*
‣ aspect, point of view, standpoint. *See* **viewpoint**.
framework *noun*
1. A structure that supports or encloses something ‣ case, shell. *See* **frame** (1). **2.** A preliminary plan or version, as of a written work ‣ blueprint, sketch. *See* **draft** (1).
framing *noun*
‣ case, shell. *See* **frame** (1).
franchise *noun*
‣ birthright, freedom, privilege. *See* **right**.
frangible *adjective*
‣ breakable, brittle, delicate. *See* **fragile** (1). *See synonym note at* **fragile**.
frank *adjective*
Honest and direct, especially in speech; not lying or dissembling ‣ aboveboard, candid, direct, downright, forthright, free, free-spoken, honest, ingenuous, open, outspoken, plain, plainspoken, straight, straightforward, straight-out, unreserved, upfront, vocal. *Informal:* straight-from-the-shoulder, straight-shooting. *See also* **artless, genuine, serious**.

✛ CORE SYNONYMS: *frank, candid, outspoken, straightforward, open.* These adjectives mean honest and direct, especially in speech or in revealing one's thoughts. *Frank* implies forthrightness, sometimes to the point of bluntness: *"Be calm and frank, and confess at once all that weighs on your heart"* (Emily Brontë). *Candid* often suggests refusal to evade difficult or unpleasant issues: *"Save, save, oh save me from the candid friend!"* (George Canning). *Outspoken* usually implies bold lack of reserve: *The outspoken activist protested the budget cuts. Straightforward* denotes directness of manner and expression: *"George was a straightforward soul . . . . 'See here!' he said. 'Are you engaged to anybody?'"* (Booth Tarkington). *Open* suggests freedom from all trace of reserve or secretiveness: *"I will be open and sincere with you"* (Joseph Addison).

frankness *noun*
▸ incorruptibility, integrity. *See* **honesty** (1).

frantic *adjective*
Characterized by hurried activity and confusion or agitation ▸ delirious, fervid, fevered, feverish, frenetic, frenzied, hectic, mad, wild. *See also* **anxious, busy.**

frantically *adverb*
▸ energetically, forcefully, vigorously. *See* **hard** (1).

fraternity *noun*
▸ club, league, order. *See* **union** (1).

fraternize *verb*
▸ consort, hobnob, pal around. *Slang:* hang out. *See* **associate** (2).

fraud *noun*
1. A person who practices deceit, especially under an assumed identity ▸ charlatan, impostor, quack. *See* **fake** (1). **2.** An act of cheating ▸ hoax, swindle. *See* **cheat** (1). **3.** The act or practice of deceiving ▸ deception, duplicity. *See* **deceit** (1).

fraudulent *adjective*
▸ fake, phony. *See* **counterfeit.**

fraught *adjective*
▸ brimming, loaded, packed. *See* **full** (1).

fray[1] *noun*
A physical conflict involving two or more people ▸ free-for-all, melee. *See* **fight** (1). *See synonym note at* **fight.**

fray[2] *or* **frazzle** *verb*
To wear away along the edges ▸ frazzle, tatter. *See also* **erode, shred.**

freak *noun*
1. A person or animal that is abnormally formed ▸ monster, monstrosity, mooncalf, mutant. *Idiom:* freak of nature. *See also* **deformity. 2.** An impulsive turn of mind ▸ impulse, notion, whim. *See* **fancy** (1). **3.** *Slang* An ardent devotee ▸ enthusiast, fanatic, maniac. *See* **fan**[2]**. 4.** *Slang* A person regarded as strange, eccentric, or crazy ▸ lunatic. *Slang:* nut, weirdo. *See* **crackpot. 5.** *Slang* One whose sexual behavior differs from the accepted norm ▸ deviant, deviate, pervert.

freakish *adjective*
1. Resembling a freak ▸ freaky, grotesque, monstrous. **2.** Deviating from what is conventional or customary ▸ bizarre, grotesque. *See* **eccentric. 3.** Marked by whim or impulse ▸ fickle, impulsive, mercurial. *See* **capricious. 4.** Of an unnatural and usually frightening nature ▸ uncanny, unearthly. *See* **weird** (1).

freaky *adjective*
Resembling a freak ▸ freakish, grotesque, monstrous. *See also* **eccentric, weird.**

freckle *verb*
▸ dapple, fleck. *See* **speckle.**

free *adjective*
1. Not imprisoned, enslaved, or controlled by another ▸ autonomous, emancipated, freed, independent, liberated, manumitted, released, self-governing, self-ruling, sovereign. *See also* **voluntary. 2.** Costing nothing ▸ complimentary, gratis, gratuitous. *Idioms:* as a freebie, for free, for nothing, on the house. **3.** Able to move about at will without bounds or restraint ▸ liberated, unconfined, unrestrained. *See* **loose** (2). **4.** Lacking literal exactness ▸ broad, inexact, rough. *See* **loose** (3). **5.** Free from obstructions ▸ unblocked, unobstructed. *See* **clear** (4). **6.** Manifesting honesty and directness ▸ direct, outspoken, vocal. *See* **frank. 7.** Willing to give of oneself and one's possessions ▸ big-hearted, magnanimous, unselfish. *See* **generous** (1). **8.** Not confined to few ▸ public, unrestricted. *See* **open** (3). **9.** Available for use ▸ employable, operable, usable. *See* **open** (4).

free *verb*
1. To set at liberty ▸ discharge, emancipate, liberate, loose, manumit, release. *Slang:* spring. *Idiom:* let loose. *See also* **rescue. 2.** To rid of obstructions ▸ clear, open, remove, unblock. *See also* **rid. 3.** To free from an entanglement ▸ disengage, untangle. *See* **extricate. 4.** To become or cause to become open ▸ release, unclose. *See* **open** (1).

freebie *noun*
1. *Slang* A free ticket entitling one to transportation or admission ▸ pass. *Informal:* comp. **2.** *Slang* Something bestowed voluntarily ▸ bequest, gift, present, presentation. *See also* **grant.**

freedom *noun*
1. The condition of being politically free ▸ autonomy, independence, liberty, self-determination, self-government, self-rule, sovereignty. **2.** The state of not being in confinement or servitude ▸ emancipation, liberation. *See* **liberty** (1). **3.** A benefit granted to a person by law, nature, or custom ▸ birthright, perquisite, privilege. *See* **right.**

free-for-all *noun*
▸ brawl, melee. *See* **fight** (1). *See synonym note at* **fight.**

free hand *noun*
▸ entitlement, latitude, leeway. *See* **license** (1).

freehanded *adjective*
▸ magnanimous, unselfish. *See* **generous** (1).

freehandedness *noun*
▸ magnanimity, munificence, unselfishness. *See* **generosity.**

freeload *verb*
Slang To take advantage of the generosity of others ▸ leech. *Informal:* sponge. *See also* **beg.**

freeloader *noun*
Slang One who depends on another for support

without reciprocating; ► leech, sponge. *See* **parasite** (1).

freeloading *adjective*
Slang Of or characteristic of a parasite ► bloodsucking, parasitical. *See* **parasitic.**

freely *adverb*
Of one's own free will ► by choice, spontaneously, voluntarily, willfully, willingly. *Idioms:* of one's own accord, on one's own volition.

freeman *noun*
► national, subject. *See* **citizen.**

free-spoken *adjective*
► candid, open, plainspoken. *See* **frank.**

free-thinker *noun*
► avant-gardist, independent, maverick. *See* **rebel** (2).

freeway *noun*
► path, road, route. *See* **way** (2).

freewill *adjective*
► uncompensated, unsalaried, volunteer. *See* **unpaid** (1).

free will *noun*
1. The act, power, or right of choosing ► decision, discretion, option. *See* **choice** (1). **2.** The mental faculty by which one deliberately chooses or decides ► volition, will. *See also* **spirit.**

freezing *adjective*
► chill, frigid, polar. *See* **cold** (1).

freight *noun*
1. Something carried or transported ► haul, load. *See* **burden**[1] (2). **2.** The moving of persons or goods from one place to another ► conveyance, transit, transport. *See* **transportation** (1).

freight *verb*
1. To weigh down or place a heavy load on ► encumber, saddle, tax. *See* **burden**[1]. **2.** To fill to capacity ► load, pack, pile. *See* **fill** (1).

frenetic *adjective*
► delirious, hectic, wild. *See* **frantic.**

frenzied *adjective*
► delirious, frenetic, mad. *See* **frantic.**

frenziedly *adverb*
► forcefully, frantically, vigorously. *See* **hard** (1).

frequent *adjective*
Occurring or encountered regularly ► commonplace, familiar, regular. *See* **common** (1).

frequent *verb*
To visit regularly ► hang around, haunt, repair to, resort to. *Slang:* hang out. *Idiom:* go regularly to.

frequently *adverb*
► customarily, generally, normally. *See* **usually.**

fresh *adjective*
1. Not polluted or altered by human intervention ► pristine, pure, uncontaminated, undeveloped, unpolluted, unspoiled, untouched. *See also* **pastoral. 2.** Not the same as what was previously known or done ► inventive, newfangled, original. *See* **new** (1). *See synonym note at* **new. 3.** Being an addition ► added, extra, new. *See* **additional. 4.** Free from dirt, stain, or impurities ► immaculate, spotless. *See* **clean**

(1). **5.** *Informal* Rude and disrespectful ► bold, insolent, pert. *See* **impudent. 6.** Possessing, exerting, or displaying energy ► brisk, lively, vigorous. *See* **energetic. 7.** Lacking experience and the knowledge gained from it ► inexpert, uninitiated, unpracticed. *See* **inexperienced. 8.** Being in an early period of growth or development ► immature, juvenile. *See* **young. 9.** Not sour or salted ► fresh, uncured.

freshen *verb*
1. To expose to circulating air ► aerate, air, ventilate, wind. **2.** To make neat and trim; make presentable ► clean up, slick up, trim. *See* **tidy** (2). **3.** To impart renewed energy and strength to a person ► reinvigorate, rejuvenate, revitalize. *See* **refresh** (1). **4.** To be in a state of motion, as air or wind ► bluster, gust. *See* **blow**[1] (1).

freshet *noun*
► deluge, overflow, torrent. *See* **flood** (1).

freshman *noun*
► fledgling, neophyte, novice. *See* **beginner.**

freshness *noun*
► newness, originality. *See* **novelty** (1).

fret *verb*
1. To trouble the nerves or peace of mind of ► irritate, nettle, vex. *See* **annoy** (1). **2.** To focus the attention on something moodily and at length ► dwell, fuss, worry. *See* **brood.** *See synonym note at* **brood. 3.** To make the skin raw by friction ► excoriate, irritate. *See* **chafe** (1).

fretful *adjective*
► cranky, grouchy, peevish. *See* **ill-tempered.**

friable *adjective*
► breakable, brittle, delicate. *See* **fragile** (1).

fricassee *verb*
► simmer, stew. *See* **cook** (1).

friction *noun*
► clash, difference, discord. *See* **conflict** (1).

friend *noun*
1. A person whom one knows well, likes, and trusts ► alter ego, amigo, brother, chum, comrade, confidant, confidante, crony, familiar, intimate, mate, sister, soul mate. *Informal:* bud, buddy, pal. *Slang:* sidekick. *See also* **associate. 2.** One who supports or champions an activity, cause, or institution ► benefactor, sponsor. *See* **patron** (1).

friendliness *noun*
► agreeability, congeniality, pleasantness. *See* **amiability.**

friendly *adjective*
1. Pleasant and friendly in disposition ► congenial, cordial, genial. *See* **amiable. 2.** Very closely associated ► close, cozy, familiar. *See* **intimate**[1] (1). **3.** Ready and willing to receive favorably, as new ideas ► acceptant, open-minded, responsive. *See* **receptive.**

friendship *noun*
The condition of being friends ► amity, camaraderie, chumminess, closeness, companionship, comradeship, familiarity, fellowship, intimacy. *See also* **company.**

fright *noun*
1. A feeling of agitation in the face of trouble or danger ▸ apprehension, consternation, horror, trepidation. *See* **fear**. *See synonym note at* **fear**. **2.** *Informal* An unsightly object ▸ eyesore, monstrosity. *See* **mess** (2).

frighten *verb*
To fill with fear ▸ affright, horrify, intimidate, panic, petrify, scare, scarify, startle, terrify, terrorize, unnerve. *Informal:* spook. *Idioms:* chill one to the bone, frighten (*or* scare) to death, give one the creeps (*or* heebie-jeebies), make one's blood run cold, make one's flesh crawl (*or* creep), make one's hair stand on end, put the fear of God into one, scare out of one's wits, scare silly (*or* stiff), scare the daylights out of, take one's breath away. *See also* **agitate, dismay**.

✦ CORE SYNONYMS: *frighten, scare, terrify, terrorize, startle, panic.* These verbs mean to cause a person to experience fear. *Frighten* and the less formal *scare* are the most widely applicable: *"The Count's mysterious warning frightened me at the time"* (Bram Stoker). *The angry dog scared the small child. Terrify* implies overwhelming, often paralyzing fear: *"It is the coming of death that terrifies me"* (Oscar Wilde). *Terrorize* implies intimidation and sometimes suggests deliberate coercion: *"The decent citizen was terrorized into paying public blackmail"* (Arthur Conan Doyle). *Startle* suggests a momentary shock that may cause a sudden, involuntary movement of the body: *The clap of thunder startled us. Panic* implies sudden frantic fear that often impairs self-control and rationality: *The realistic radio drama panicked the listeners who tuned in after it had begun.*

---

frightened *adjective*
▸ fearful, horrified, scared. *See* **afraid**. *See synonym note at* **afraid**.

frightening *verb*
▸ formidable, unnerving, scary. *See* **fearful** (1).

frightful *adjective*
1. Very bad ▸ appalling, dreadful, ghastly. *See* **terrible** (1). **2.** Causing or capable of causing fear ▸ frightening, scary, unnerving. *See* **fearful** (1).

frigid *adjective*
1. Marked by a low termperature ▸ freezing, frosty, icy. *See* **cold** (1). *See synonym note at* **cold**. **2.** Not friendly, sociable, or warm in manner ▸ aloof, chilly, impersonal. *See* **cool** (1). **3.** Deficient in or lacking sexual desire ▸ ardorless, cold, inhibited, passionless, undersexed, unresponsive.

frigidity *or* **frigidness** *noun*
▸ chilliness, frostiness, iciness. *See* **cold**.

frill *noun*
▸ delight, extravagancy, indulgence. *See* **luxury** (1). *See synonym note at* **luxury**.

fringe *noun*
1. A line or area where something ends or abruptly changes ▸ brink, edge, margin. *See* **border** (1). **2.** The periphery of a city or town ▸ environs, suburbs. *See* **outskirts**.

fringe *verb*
To put or form a border on ▸ edge, rim. *See* **border** (1).

frippery *noun*
1. Showy and elaborate clothing or apparel ▸ finery, regalia. *See* **attire** (1). **2.** Something or things of little importance ▸ frivolity, minutia, trivia. *See* **trifle** (1).

frisk *verb*
1. To leap and skip about playfully ▸ cavort, frolic, romp. *See* **gambol**. **2.** To examine a person or someone's personal effects in order to find something lost or concealed ▸ inspect, pat down, search. *Slang:* shake down. *Idiom:* do a body search of.

frisk *noun*
A thorough search of a place or persons ▸ search. *Slang:* shakedown.

frisky *adjective*
1. Very brisk, alert, and full of high spirits ▸ animated, chipper, vivacious. *See* **lively** (1). **2.** Full of mischief or high-spirited fun ▸ frolicsome, impish, sportive. *See* **mischievous** (1).

fritter away *verb*
▸ fool away, squander, trifle away. *See* **waste** (1). *See synonym note at* **waste**.

frivolity *noun*
▸ fiddle-faddle, minutia, trivia. *See* **trifle** (1).

frivolous *adjective*
1. Of little importance or seriousness ▸ inconsequential, negligible, trifling. *See* **trivial**. **2.** Given to lighthearted silliness ▸ featherbrained, flighty, scatterbrained. *See* **giddy** (2).

frizzle *verb*
▸ sear, shrivel, wither. *See* **dry** (1).

frock *noun*
▸ jumper, gown, shift. *See* **dress** (3).

frolic *noun*
A mischievous act ▸ caper, joke, trick. *See* **prank**[1].

frolic *verb*
1. To leap and skip about playfully ▸ cavort, frisk, romp. *See* **gambol**. **2.** To occupy oneself with amusement or diversion ▸ disport, recreate. *Informal:* horse around. *See* **play** (1). **3.** To behave riotously ▸ carouse, party, roister. *See* **revel** (1).

frolicsome *adjective*
▸ devilish, impish, sportive. *See* **mischievous** (1).

front *noun*
1. The forward part of something ▸ bow, fore, forepart, front end, front side, head. **2.** The position of greatest advancement or importance ▸ cutting edge, lead, vanguard. *See* **forefront**. **3.** The forward outer surface of a building ▸ face, frontage. *See* **façade** (1). **4.** A deceptive outward appearance ▸ guise, mask, pretense. *See* **façade** (2).

front *verb*
1. To have the face or front turned toward ▸ face, give onto, look (on *or* upon *or* toward). *See also* **overlook**. **2.** To meet face-to-face, especially defiantly ▸ confront, encounter, face, meet. *Idiom:* stand up to. *See also* **contest, defy**. **3.** To confront boldly and coura-

geously ▶ challenge, confront, dare. *See* **defy** (1).

frontage *or* frontal *noun*
▶ face, front. *See* **façade** (1).

frontier *noun*
▶ borderland, marchland. *See* **border** (2).

frontispiece *noun*
▶ face, front. *See* **façade** (1).

front-runner *noun*
A leading contestant or sure winner ▶ favorite, leader, number one, vanguard. *Informal:* shoo-in.

frontward *adverb*
▶ ahead, forth, onward. *See* **forward**.

frostiness *noun*
▶ chilliness, frigidity, wintriness. *See* **cold**.

frosty *adjective*
1. Marked by a low temperature ▶ chill, frigid, polar. *See* **cold** (1). *See synonym note at* **cold**. 2. Not friendly, sociable, or warm in manner ▶ aloof, chilly, frigid. *See* **cool** (1).

froth *noun*
1. A mass of bubbles in or on the surface of a liquid ▶ lather, suds. *See* **foam**. 2. Something or things of little importance ▶ frivolity, minutia, trivia. *See* **trifle** (1).

froth *verb*
1. To form or cause to form foam ▶ fizz, lather. *See* **foam** (1). 2. To be in a state of turmoil or excitement ▶ burn, seethe. *See* **boil** (2).

frothy *adjective*
1. Consisting of or resembling foam ▶ fizzy, lathery, sudsy. *See* **foamy**. 2. Of little importance or seriousness ▶ inconsequential, negligible, trifling. *See* **trivial**. 3. Given to lighthearted silliness ▶ featherbrained, flighty, frivolous. *See* **giddy** (2).

froward *adjective*
1. Marked by a disposition to oppose ▶ antagonistic, contradictory, hostile. *See* **contrary** (1). 2. Not submitting to discipline or control ▶ ill-behaved, obstinate, unmanageable. *See* **unruly**.

frown *verb*
To wrinkle one's brow, as in thought, puzzlement, or displeasure ▶ glower, lower, scowl. *Idioms:* knit one's brow, look black, turn one's mouth down. *See also* **glare, grimace**.

frown on *or* upon *verb*
To have or express an unfavorable opinion of ▶ condemn, disfavor, object to. *See* **disapprove** (1).

frown *noun*
The act of wrinkling the brow, as in thought, puzzlement, or displeasure ▶ black look, glower, lower, scowl. *See also* **face, glare, sneer**.

✦ CORE SYNONYMS: *frown, glower, lower, scowl.* These verbs mean to wrinkle one's brow, as in thought, puzzlement, or displeasure: *frowns when he is annoyed; glowered upon being interrupted; lowering at the noisy child; scowled at my suggestion.*

---

frowzy *adjective*
1. Marked by a lack of cleanliness or neatness ▶ disheveled, slovenly, unkempt. *See* **messy** (1). 2. Smelling of mildew or decay ▶ musty, rancid. *See* **moldy**.

frozen *adjective*
▶ stationary, still. *See* **motionless**.

frozenness *noun*
▶ chilliness, frigidity, iciness. *See* **cold**.

frugal *adjective*
1. Careful in the use of material resources ▶ prudent, thrifty. *See* **economical**. *See synonym note at* **economical**. 2. Low in price ▶ economy, inexpensive, low-cost. *See* **cheap** (1).

frugality *noun*
▶ providence, thrift. *See* **economy**.

fruit *noun*
1. The produce harvested from the land ▶ crop, yield. *See* **harvest** (1). 2. Something brought about by a cause ▶ consequence, outcome, result. *See* **effect** (1). 3. A person or group descended directly from the same parents or ancestors ▶ offspring, posterity, seed. *See* **progeny**.

fruitage *noun*
▶ fruit, yield. *See* **harvest** (1).

fruitful *adjective*
1. Capable of reproducing ▶ fertile, fecund, productive, prolific. 2. Characterized by great productivity ▶ fecund, productive, prolific. *See* **fertile** (1). *See synonym note at* **fertile**. 3. Affording benefit or advantage ▶ favorable, helpful, propitious. *See* **beneficial**.

fruitfulness *noun*
▶ fecundity, productiveness, richness. *See* **fertility**.

fruition *noun*
▶ culmination, fulfillment, realization. *See* **fulfillment** (1).

fruitless *adjective*
▶ unsuccessful, useless, vain. *See* **futile**. *See synonym note at* **futile**.

fruitlessness *noun*
1. The condition or quality of being useless or ineffective ▶ bootlessness, unprofitableness. *See* **futility**. 2. The state or condition of being unable to reproduce ▶ barrenness, infertility. *See* **sterility** (2).

fruity *adjective*
Slang Afflicted with or exhibiting irrationality and mental unsoundness ▶ crazy, lunatic. *See* **insane**.

frump *noun*
▶ spoilsport. *Informal:* wet blanket. *Slang:* party pooper. *See* **killjoy**.

frumpy *adjective*
▶ dowdy, frumpish, fusty. *See* **old-fashioned**.

frustrate *verb*
1. To prevent from accomplishing a purpose ▶ baffle, balk, check, checkmate, defeat, foil, stymie, thwart. *Informal:* cross, stump. *Idiom:* cut the ground from under. *See also* **disappoint, discourage, hinder, prevent**. 2. To cause unhappiness by failing to satisfy the hopes, desires, or expectations of ▶ discourage, dishearten, sour. *See* **disappoint**.

frustration *noun*
1. Unhappiness caused by the failure of one's hopes, desires, or expectations ▸ disillusion, letdown, regret. *See* **disappointment** (1). 2. The act of preventing ▸ deterrence, forestallment, preclusion. *See* **prevention.**

fry *verb*
▸ sauté, sear. *See* **cook** (1).

fuddle *verb*
1. To cause to be unclear in mind or intent ▸ befuddle, bewilder, confound. *See* **confuse** (1). *See synonym note at* **confuse.** 2. To addle the mind, as with a narcotic or alcohol ▸ besot, impair, stupefy. *See* **drug** (2).

fuddy-duddy *noun*
▸ fogy, fossil, mossback. *See* **square** (2).

fudge *verb*
1. To proceed or perform in an unsteady, faltering manner ▸ bungle, flounder, fumble. *See* **muddle** (1). 2. To give an inaccurate view of by representing falsely or misleadingly ▸ falsify, misrepresent, pervert. *See* **distort** (1).

fugacious *adjective*
▸ ephemeral, fleeting, temporary. *See* **transitory.**

fugitive *adjective*
1. Fleeing or having fled, as from confinement or the police ▸ escaped, fleeing, runaway. *Idioms:* on the lam (*or* loose *or* run). 2. Lasting or existing only for a short time ▸ ephemeral, fleeting, temporary. *See* **transitory.** 3. Inclined or intended to evade ▸ elusive, evasive, slippery. *See also* **slick, underhand.**

fugitive *noun*
One who flees, as from confinement or the police ▸ escapee, outlaw, refugee, runaway. *See also* **criminal.**

führer *noun*
▸ despot, totalitarian, tyrant. *See* **dictator** (1).

fulfill *verb*
1. To carry out the functions, requirements, or terms of ▸ discharge, do, execute, exercise, implement, keep, perform. *Idiom:* live up to. *See also* **effect.** 2. To begin and carry through to completion ▸ discharge, do, transact. *See* **perform** (1). *See synonym note at* **perform.** 3. To obtain or reach by persistent effort ▸ achieve, attain, reach. *See* **accomplish** (1). 4. To grant or have what is demanded by a need or desire ▸ appease, gratify. *See* **satisfy** (2). *See synonym note at* **satisfy.** 5. To be suitable or sufficient to fulfill a need ▸ fill, meet. *See* **satisfy** (1).

fulfilled *adjective*
Having achieved satisfaction, as of one's goal ▸ content, gratified, happy, satisfied.

fulfillment *noun*
1. The condition of being fulfilled ▸ accomplishment, attainment, completion, consummation, culmination, fruition, materialization, realization. *See also* **performance.** 2. The condition of being satisfied ▸ contentedness, contentment, gratification, satisfaction. *See also* **happiness, satiation.**

full *adjective*
1. Containing all that is possible; completely filled ▸ awash, brimful, brimming, bursting, charged, chockablock, chock-full, crammed, fraught, jammed, jam-packed, loaded, overflowing, packed, replete, running over, stuffed. 2. Having the appetite satisfied or overwhelmed ▸ cloyed, engorged, glutted, gorged, replete, sated, satiated, surfeited. 3. Of full measure; not narrow or restricted ▸ ample, baggy, capacious, voluminous, wide. *See also* **loose.** 4. Including every constituent or individual ▸ entire, total, whole. *See* **complete** (1). 5. Consistent with accuracy or completeness ▸ exact, strict. *See* **close** (2). 6. Characterized by attention to detail ▸ elaborate, particular, thorough. *See* **detailed** (1). 7. Having too much flesh ▸ chubby, pudgy, rotund. *See* **fat** (1). 8. Without limitations or mitigating conditions ▸ absolute, unreserved. *See* **unconditional** (1). 9. No less than; at least ▸ good, round, whole.

full-blooded *adjective*
1. Of pure breeding stock ▸ pedigreed, pureblood, purebred. *See* **thoroughbred** (1). 2. Of a healthy reddish color ▸ flushed, rosy, sanguine. *See* **ruddy.**

full-blown *adjective*
▸ adult, developed, ripe. *See* **mature** (1).

full-dress *adjective*
1. Requiring elegant clothes and fine manners ▸ black-tie, dressy. *See* **formal** (5). 2. Covering all aspects with painstaking accuracy ▸ exhaustive, thoroughgoing. *See* **thorough.**

full-fledged *or* **full-grown** *adjective*
1. Having reached full growth and development ▸ grown-up, ripe. *See* **mature** (1). 2. Completely such, without qualification or exception ▸ all-out, pure, sheer. *See* **utter**[2].

full-length *adjective*
▸ unabridged, uncensored, uncut. *See* **complete** (2).

fullness *noun*
1. The state of being entirely whole ▸ oneness, totality. *See* **completeness.** 2. The condition of being full to or beyond satisfaction ▸ fullness, repletion, satiety. *See* **satiation.**

full-strength *adjective*
▸ pure, unblended, undiluted. *See* **straight** (1).

fully *adverb*
▸ entirely, totally, utterly. *See* **completely** (1).

fulminate *verb*
To release or cause to release energy suddenly and violently, especially with a loud noise ▸ burst, detonate. *See* **explode** (1).

fulminate against *verb*
To attack with harsh, often insulting language ▸ assail, blaspheme. *See* **revile.**

fulmination *noun*
1. A long, violent, or blustering speech, usually of censure or denunciation ▸ diatribe, harangue. *See* **tirade.** 2. A violent release of confined energy ▸ burst, explosion. *See* **blast** (2).

fulsome *adjective*
▸ oleaginous, sleek, smarmy. *See* **unctuous** (1). *See synonym note at* **unctuous.**

fumble *verb*
1. To reach about or search blindly or uncertainly ▶ feel, grabble. *See* **grope**. 2. To proceed or perform in an unsteady, faltering manner ▶ bungle, flounder, limp. *See* **muddle** (1). 3. To ruin through clumsiness or ineptness ▶ blunder, foul up, spoil. *See* **botch**. *See synonym note at* **botch**.

fumble *noun*
A stupid, clumsy mistake ▶ bungle, faux pas, solecism. *See* **blunder**.

fume *noun*
Informal A condition of excited distress ▶ *Informal:* snit, sweat. *See* **state** (4).

fume *verb*
1. To be or become angry ▶ burn, rage, seethe. *See* **anger** (2). 2. To pass off as vapor, especially when heated ▶ burn off, volatilize. *See* **evaporate** (1).

fun *noun*
1. Joyful, exuberant activity ▶ gaiety, merrymaking, revelry. *See* **merriment** (2). 2. Something that amuses, entertains, or pleases ▶ diversion, pleasure, recreation. *See* **amusement**. 3. Actions taken as a joke ▶ game, jest. *See* **play** (1).

fun *adjective*
Giving or affording pleasure, enjoyment, or entertainment ▶ amusing, enjoyable, entertaining. *See* **pleasant** (1).

function *noun*
1. The proper activity of a person or thing ▶ job, purpose, role, task. *See also* **duty, position, task**. 2. One's duty or responsibility in a common effort ▶ part, piece, role, share. 3. A social gathering, especially for pleasure ▶ celebration, gala, soiree. *See* **party** (1).

function *verb*
To act or operate in a specified way ▶ act, behave, go, operate, perform, run, take, work. *See also* **officiate, substitute**.

functional *adjective*
▶ practicable, useful, utilitarian. *See* **practical** (1).

functionary *noun*
▶ administrator, manager. *See* **executive**.

functioning *noun*
The way in which something functions ▶ operation, performance. *See* **behavior** (2).

functioning *adjective*
In action or full operation ▶ alive, operating, working. *See* **active** (1).

fund *verb*
▶ back, subsidize. *Informal:* bankroll. *See* **finance**.

fundament *noun*
▶ posterior, rump. *Slang:* fanny. *See* **buttocks**.

fundamental *adjective*
1. Of or being an irreducible element ▶ basic, foundational, underlying. *See* **elemental** (1). 2. Constituting or forming part of the essence of something ▶ constitutional, quintessential, vital. *See* **essential** (2). 3. Arising from or going to the root or source ▶ elementary, primal, ultimate. *See* **radical** (1).

fundamental *noun*
1. An irreducible constituent of a whole ▶ essential, rudiment. *See* **element** (1). 2. An underlying support, as for an argument or belief ▶ cornerstone, foundation, underpinning. *See* **basis** (1). 3. A broad and basic rule or truth ▶ axiom, principle. *See* **law** (3).

fundamentalist *noun*
One who holds extreme views or advocates extreme measures ▶ fanatic, radical, revolutionist, zealot. *See* **extremist**.

fundamentalist *adjective*
Holding especially political views that deviate drastically from prevailing beliefs ▶ rabid, radical, revolutionary. *See* **extreme** (4).

fundamentally *adverb*
▶ basically, underlyingly. *See* **essentially**.

funding *noun*
▶ financing, resources, stake. *See* **capital** (1).

funds *noun*
The monetary resources of a government, organization, or individual ▶ capital, finances, money, moneys. *See also* **capital, money, resources**.

funeral *noun*
A ceremony held in connection with a burial or cremation ▶ funeral service, last rites, memorial service, obsequies, requiem. *See also* **burial**.

funereal *adjective*
▶ bleak, desolate, somber. *See* **gloomy** (1).

funk *noun*
1. Ignoble lack of courage ▶ chickenheartedness, pusillanimity. *Slang:* gutlessness. *See* **cowardice**. 2. A feeling of agitation in the face of trouble or danger ▶ apprehension, consternation, trepidation. *See* **fear**. 3. A feeling or spell of dismally low spirits ▶ dejection, doldrums, melancholy. *See* **depression** (2). 4. An ignoble, uncourageous person ▶ dastard, poltroon, sissy. *See* **coward**.

funky *adjective*
1. Filled with fear or terror ▶ frightened, scared. *See* **afraid**. 2. Smelling of mildew or decay ▶ musty, rancid. *See* **moldy**. 3. *Slang* Bordering on indelicacy or impropriety ▶ provocative, risqué, suggestive. *See* **racy** (1). 4. *Slang* In accordance with current fashion ▶ mod, stylish, swanky. *See* **fashionable**.

funniness *noun*
▶ comedy, ridiculousness, wittiness. *See* **humor** (1).

funny *adjective*
1. Causing laughter or amusement ▶ amusing, comedic, comic, comical, droll, facetious, hilarious, humorous, jocose, jocular, laughable, priceless, risible, sidesplitting, uproarious, witty, zany. *Informal:* hysterical, killing, rich. *Slang:* ripe. *Idioms:* a laugh and a half, a riot, too funny for words. *See also* **pleasant**. 2. Agreeably curious, especially in an old-fashioned or unusual way ▶ curious, odd, quaint. 3. Causing puzzlement; perplexing ▶ curious, odd, peculiar, queer, strange, weird. *See also* **shady, unusual**.

funny *noun*
Informal Words or actions intended to excite laughter

or amusement ▸ jest, quip, witticism. *See* **joke** (1).

funny business *noun*
▸ diablerie, high jinks, tomfoolery. *See* **mischief** (1).

funnyman *noun*
▸ clown, comedian, jester. *See* **joker**.

fur *noun*
The skin of an animal, sometimes including fur, hair or feathers ▸ hide, leather, pelt.

furbish *verb*
1. To give a bright sheen or luster to ▸ burnish, glaze, polish. *See* **gloss**[1] (1). **2.** To make new or as if new again ▸ refresh, restore, revamp. *See* **renew** (1).

furfur *noun*
▸ dander, dandruff, scale. *See* **scurf**.

furious *adjective*
1. Feeling or showing anger ▸ irate, livid, rabid. *See* **angry**. *See synonym note at* **angry**. **2.** Extreme in activity, strength, or effect ▸ desperate, fierce. *See* **intense** (1).

furiously *adverb*
▸ forcefully, frantically, vigorously. *See* **hard** (1).

furlough *noun*
1. A regularly scheduled period spent away from work or duty, often in recreation ▸ holiday, leave, sabbatical, vacation. *Idioms:* time (*or* day) off. *See also* **break, trip. 2.** A document that gives permission to do something ▸ permit, warrant. *See* **license** (3).

furnish *verb*
1. To supply what is needed for some activity or purpose ▸ accouter, appoint, equip, fit, fit out (*or* up), gear, outfit, rig, turn out. *See also* **adorn. 2.** To relinquish to the possession or control of another ▸ deliver, provide. *See* **give** (1). **3.** To make something readily available ▸ afford, provide, supply. *See* **offer** (2).

✚ CORE SYNONYMS: *furnish, appoint, accouter, equip, outfit.* These verbs mean to provide with what is necessary for an activity or a purpose: *furnished the team with new uniforms; a library that was appointed in leather; knights who were accoutered for battle; equip a car with snow tires; had to outfit the children for summer camp.*

---

furor *noun*
1. A strong feeling of displeasure or hostility ▸ indignation, irateness, wrath. *See* **anger. 2.** The current custom ▸ fad, mode, vogue. *See* **fashion** (1).

furrow *noun*
1. A long, narrow, and usually shallow depression in the ground ▸ channel, ditch, groove, rut, trench, trough. **2.** An indentation or seam on the skin, especially on the face ▸ crow's-foot, line. *See* **wrinkle** (1).

furry *adjective*
▸ fleecy, hirsute, shaggy. *See* **hairy** (1).

further *adjective*
Being an addition ▸ added, more, new. *See* **additional**.

further *adverb*
In addition ▸ also, furthermore, more. *See* **additionally**.

further *verb*
To cause to move forward or upward, as toward a goal ▸ drive, propel, push. *See* **advance** (1). *See synonym note at* **advance**.

furtherance *noun*
1. Forward movement ▸ headway, progress, progression. *See* **advance** (1). **2.** Aid or support given by a patron ▸ advocacy, backing, sponsorship. *See* **patronage** (1).

furthermore *adverb*
▸ also, besides, moreover. *See* **additionally**.

furthest *or* **furthermost** *adjective*
▸ outmost, uttermost. *See* **extreme** (1).

furtive *adjective*
▸ secretive, slinky, sneaky. *See* **stealthy**.

furtiveness *noun*
▸ secretiveness, sneakiness, slyness. *See* **stealth**.

fury *noun*
1. A strong feeling of displeasure or hostility ▸ indignation, irateness, wrath. *See* **anger**. *See synonym note at* **anger**. **2.** Concentrated power or force, as of effort, opinion, or emotion ▸ ferocity, vehemence, violence. *See* **intensity. 3.** A person, traditionally a woman, who persistently nags ▸ harpy, shrew. *See* **scold**.

fuse *verb*
1. To join one thing to another ▸ append, fasten, secure. *See* **attach** (1). **2.** To change from a solid to a liquid ▸ dissolve, liquefy. *See* **melt** (1). **3.** To combine into one mass or mixture ▸ blend, intermingle, stir. *See* **mix** (1). *See synonym note at* **mix**.

fusillade *noun*
A concentrated outpouring, as of missiles, words, or blows ▸ cannonade, flak, volley. *See* **barrage**.

fusillade *verb*
To direct a barrage at ▸ bombard, pelt. *See* **barrage**.

fusion *noun*
▸ amalgam, blend, mix. *See* **mixture** (1).

fuss *noun*
1. Agitated, excited activity ▸ commotion, excitement, stir. *See* **agitation** (3). **2.** A discussion, often heated, in which a difference of opinion is expressed ▸ contention, disagreement, quarrel. *See* **argument** (1). **3.** Needless trouble ▸ botheration, pother. *See* **bother** (1). **4.** An expression of pain or dissatisfaction ▸ carp, whimper, whine. *See* **complaint** (1). **5.** An expression of opposition ▸ exception, grievance, protestation. *See* **objection**.

fuss *verb*
1. To focus the attention on something moodily and at length ▸ dwell, fret, worry. *See* **brood. 2.** To express feelings of pain, dissatisfaction, or resentment ▸ carp, grump, whine. *See* **complain**.

fuss at *verb*
To scold or find fault with constantly ▸ carp at, pick on. *See* **nag** (1).

fussy *adjective*
1. Very difficult to please ▸ choosy, dainty, demanding, exacting, fastidious, finical, finicky, meticulous, nice, particular, persnickety, squeamish. *Informal:*

picky. *Idiom:* hard to please. *See also* **careful, contrary, discriminating. 2.** Excessively filled with detail ▸ cluttered, crowded. *See* **busy** (3). **3.** Marked by attentiveness to every detail ▸ fastidious, meticulous, scrupulous. *See* **careful** (2). **4.** Rich in detail ▸ fancy, intricate. *See* **elaborate** (1).

fustian *noun*
Pretentious, pompous speech or writing ▸ claptrap, grandiloquence. *See* **bombast.**

fustian *adjective*
Characterized by elevated language, such as that used in public speaking ▸ bombastic, grandiloquent, rhetorical. *See* **oratorical.**

fusty *adjective*
1. Smelling of mildew or decay ▸ musty, rancid. *See* **moldy. 2.** Of a style or method formerly in vogue ▸ antique, dated, passé. *See* **old-fashioned.**

futile *adjective*
Having no useful result ▸ barren, bootless, fruitless, pointless, profitless, unavailing, unprofitable, unsuccessful, useless, vain. *Idioms:* in vain, to no avail, to no effect. *See also* **hollow, ineffectual.**

✚ CORE SYNONYMS: *futile, barren, bootless, fruitless, unavailing, useless, vain.* These adjectives mean having no useful result or effect: *a futile effort; a barren search; bootless entreaties; fruitless labors; an unavailing attempt; a useless discussion; vain regrets.*

◂ ANTONYM: *useful*

---

futility *noun*
The condition or quality of being useless or ineffective ▸ barrenness, bootlessness, fruitlessness, pointlessness, profitlessness, unprofitableness, uselessness, vainness, vanity. *See also* **failure, ineffectuality.**

future *noun*
1. Time that is yet to be ▸ by-and-by, futurity, hereafter, tomorrow. *Idiom:* time to come. *See also* **approach, possibility. 2.** Chance of success or advancement ▸ outlook, prospects. *See also* **chance.**

future *adjective*
Being or occurring in the time ahead ▸ approaching, coming, eventual, forthcoming, later, subsequent. *Idioms:* down the road, in the cards, just around the corner, to be, to come. *See also* **coming, momentary, potential.**

futuristic *adjective*
▸ forward, precocious. *See* **progressive** (1).

futurity *noun*
Time that is yet to be ▸ by-and-by, future, hereafter, tomorrow. *Idiom:* time to come. *See also* **approach, possibility.**

fuzz *noun*
Slang A member of a law-enforcement agency ▸ officer, trooper. *See* **police officer.**

fuzzy *adjective*
1. Covered with hair ▸ furry, hirsute, shaggy. *See* **hairy** (1). **2.** Not clearly perceptible ▸ dim, faint, indefinite. *See* **unclear** (1).

g

gab *verb*
Slang To talk rapidly on trivial matters ▸ blab, jabber, prattle. *See* **chatter** (1).

gab *noun*
Slang Incessant and inconsequential talk ▸ drivel, patter, small talk. *See* **chatter.**

gabble *verb*
To talk rapidly, incoherently, or indistinctly ▸ burble, jabber, prattle. *See* **babble** (1).

gabble *noun*
Empty or foolish talk ▸ gibberish, jabber, twaddle. *See* **babble** (1).

gabby *adjective*
Slang Given to conversation ▸ garrulous, loquacious, talky. *See* **talkative.**

gabfest *noun*
Slang Spoken exchange ▸ dialogue, discourse, discussion. *See* **conversation** (1).

gad *verb*
▸ drift, meander, wander. *See* **rove.** *See synonym note at* **rove.**

gadabout *noun*
▸ nomad, roamer, vagabond. *See* **hobo.**

gadget *noun*
A small specialized mechanical device ▸ apparatus, contraption, contrivance, gimmick, jigger, thing. *Informal:* doodad, doohickey, thingamabob, thingamajig, whatchamacallit, whatsit, widget. *Slang:* gizmo. *See also* **device, novelty.**

gaffe *noun*
▸ inappropriateness, indecency, indiscretion. *See* **impropriety** (2).

gag *noun*
1. *Informal* Words or actions intended to excite laughter or amusement ▸ jest, quip, witticism. *See* **joke** (1). *See synonym note at* **joke. 2.** A mischievous act ▸ caper, joke, trick. *See* **prank**[1].

gag *verb*
1. To hold something requiring an outlet in check ▸ smother, stifle, suppress. *See* **repress. 2.** To stop breathing or stop the breathing of ▸ smother, stifle, suffocate. *See* **choke** (1).

gaga *adjective*
1. *Informal* Given to lighthearted silliness ▸ featherbrained, flighty, frivolous. *See* **giddy** (2). 2. *Informal* Afflicted with or exhibiting irrationality and mental unsoundness ▸ crazy, lunatic, off. *See* **insane** (1).

gage *noun*
▸ bond, guaranty, pledge. *See* **pawn**¹.

gaggle *noun*
1. An enormous number of persons gathered together ▸ horde, mass, throng. *See* **crowd** (1). 2. A number of animals considered collectively ▸ bevy, drove, herd. *See* **flock** (1). *See synonym note at* **flock**.

gaiety *noun*
1. A state of joyful exuberance ▸ glee, lightheartedness, mirth. *See* **merriment** (1). 2. Joyful, exuberant activity ▸ festivity, merrymaking, revelry. *See* **merriment** (2).

gain *verb*
1. To come into possession of ▸ come by, glean, procure. *See* **get** (1). 2. To obtain from another source ▸ extract, get, receive. *See* **derive** (1). 3. To obtain possession or control of ▸ get, take, win. *Slang:* cop. *See* **capture** (1). 4. To acquire as a result of one's behavior or effort ▸ deserve, get, win. *See* **earn** (1). *See synonym note at* **earn**. 5. To reach a goal or objective ▸ achieve, attain, gain. *See* **accomplish** (1). *See synonym note at* **accomplish**. 6. To receive, as wages, for one's labor ▸ get, make. *See* **earn** (2). 7. To make as income or profit ▸ clear, earn, yield. *See* **return** (3). 8. To derive advantage ▸ capitalize, profit. *See* **benefit** (1). 9. To achieve an increase of ▸ augment, build up, develop, enlarge, expand. 10. To reach a goal or objective ▸ arrive at, attain, come to, get to. *Informal:* hit on (*or* upon). 11. To regain one's health ▸ convalesce, improve, recuperate. *See* **recover** (2).

gain on *verb*
To come near in space or time ▸ close in on, near. *See* **approach** (1).

gain *noun*
1. Something earned, won, or otherwise acquired ▸ earnings, profit, return. 2. Something beneficial ▸ benefit, blessing, boon. *See* **advantage** (2).

gainful *adjective*
▸ advantageous, lucrative, rewarding. *See* **profitable** (1).

gainsay *verb*
▸ contravene, disaffirm, disavow. *See* **deny** (1). *See synonym note at* **deny**.

gait *noun*
▸ step, stride, tread. *See* **walk** (2).

gal *noun*
Informal A woman ▸ *Informal:* chick, damsel, doll. *See* **girl**.

gala *noun*
A social gathering, especially for pleasure ▸ celebration, fete, soiree. *See* **party** (1).

gala *adjective*
Providing joy and pleasure, especially in celebration ▸ festive, joyful, joyous. *See* **merry** (1).

galaxy *noun*
▸ conference, group. *Informal:* get-together. *See* **assembly** (1).

gale *noun*
▸ blow, squall, tempest. *See* **storm** (1).

gall¹ *noun*
1. The quality or state of feeling bitter ▸ bitterness, rancor, virulence. *See* **resentment** (1). 2. The state or quality of being arrogantly self-confident or impudent ▸ audacity, impertinence. *See* **impudence**.

gall² *verb*
1. To make the skin raw by friction ▸ excoriate, irritate, rub. *See* **chafe** (1). 2. To trouble the nerves or peace of mind of ▸ irritate, nettle, vex. *See* **annoy** (1).

gallant *adjective*
1. Respectfully attentive, especially to women ▸ chivalric, chivalrous, gentlemanly, knightly. 2. Having or showing courage ▸ courageous, fearless, heroic. *See* **brave**. 3. Characterized by elaborate, usually formal courtesy ▸ courtly, genteel, stately. *See* **gracious** (2). 4. Full of polite concern for the well-being of others ▸ courteous, solicitous, thoughtful. *See* **attentive** (1).

gallant *noun*
A man amorously attentive to women ▸ amorist, Casanova, Don Juan, lady's man, Lothario, Romeo. *See also* **beau**.

gallantry *noun*
1. Respectful attention, especially toward women ▸ chivalrousness, chivalry. *See also* **consideration**, **courtesy**. 2. The quality of mind enabling one to face danger or hardship resolutely ▸ bravery, fortitude, valor. *See* **courage**.

gallimaufry *noun*
▸ hodgepodge, jumble, mishmash. *See* **assortment** (1).

galling *adjective*
1. Troubling to the mind or emotions ▸ bothersome, irritating, unsettling. *See* **disturbing**. 2. Difficult to accept or bear ▸ disagreeable, painful, unpleasant. *See* **bitter** (3).

gallivant *verb*
▸ drift, meander, wander. *See* **rove**. *See synonym note at* **rove**.

gallop *verb*
To move on foot at a pace faster than a walk ▸ jog, scamper, trot. *See* **run** (1).

gallop *noun*
A pace faster than a walk ▸ jog, lope. *See* **run** (1).

galumph *verb*
▸ clump, flounder, hulk. *See* **blunder** (1).

galvanize *verb*
▸ excite, prod, trigger. *See* **provoke** (1).

gamble *verb*
1. To make a bet ▸ bet, game, lay, play, wager. *Idiom:* put one's money on something. 2. To place something at risk, as in a speculation or a game of chance ▸ bet, chance, lay (down), post, put, risk, stake, venture, wager. *Informal:* go. 3. To take a risk in the

hope of gaining advantage ▸ speculate, venture. *Idioms:* go for broke, go out on a limb, play fast and loose, stick one's neck out, take a flier, take a shot (*or* stab) in the dark, tempt fate (*or* fortune), trust to chance (*or* luck).

gamble *noun*
1. An undertaking depending on chance ▸ bet, long shot, plunge, risk, speculation, tossup, venture, wager. *Informal:* flier. *Slang:* crapshoot. *Idioms:* leap (*or* shot) in the dark, roll of the dice, toss of a coin. *See also* **attempt, try. 2.** A possibility of danger or harm ▸ chance, hazard. *See* **risk** (1).

gambler *noun*
1. One who gambles ▸ cardsharp, crapshooter, bettor, gamester, player, sharper. *Slang:* high roller. **2.** One who speculates for quick profits ▸ adventurer, operator, speculator.

gambol *verb*
To leap and skip about playfully ▸ caper, cavort, dance, frisk, frolic, rollick, romp. *See also* **bound**[1].

game *noun*
1. An object for children to play with ▸ game, toy. *See also* **amusement. 2.** A test of skill or ability ▸ bout, match, trial. *See* **competition** (2). **3.** Actions taken as a joke ▸ fun, jest. *See* **play** (1).

game *verb*
1. To make a bet ▸ bet, gamble, lay, play, wager. *Idiom:* put one's money on something. **2.** To get something by deceitful trickery ▸ cozen, defraud, swindle. *See* **cheat** (1).

game *adjective*
1. Having or showing courage ▸ courageous, fearless, heroic. *See* **brave. 2.** Disposed to accept, agree, or participate ▸ agreeable, ready. *See* **willing** (1).

gameness *noun*
▸ bravery, fortitude, gallantry, valor. *See* **courage.**

game plan *noun*
▸ course, modus operandi, procedure, technique. *See* **approach** (1).

gamesome *adjective*
▸ frolicsome, impish, sportive. *See* **mischievous** (1).

gamester *noun*
▸ cardsharp, player. *See* **gambler** (1).

gamin *or* **gamine** *noun*
▸ brat, imp, whelp. *See* **urchin.**

gamut *noun*
▸ order, procession, sequence. *See* **series.**

gamy *adjective*
▸ musty, rancid. *See* **moldy.**

gander *noun*
1. *Informal* A quick look ▸ glimpse, peek. *See* **glance** (1). **2.** *Informal* A person who is deficient in judgment and good sense ▸ idiot, imbecile, nitwit. *See* **fool** (1).

gang *noun*
1. An organized group of criminals, hoodlums, or wrongdoers ▸ band, pack, ring. *Informal:* mob. **2.** *Informal* A small group of friends or associates ▸ coterie, group, set. *See* **circle** (3). **3.** A group of people organized for a particular purpose ▸ squad, team,

unit. *See* **force** (5). **4.** A number of animals considered collectively ▸ bevy, gaggle, litter. *See* **flock** (1). *See synonym note at* **flock.**

gang *verb*
To form a united group ▸ join, unite. *See* **band**[2].

gang up on *verb*
To set upon with violent force ▸ assault, fall on, strike. *See* **attack** (1).

gangling *or* **gangly** *adjective*
Tall, thin, and awkwardly built ▸ lanky, rangy, scraggy, spindling, spindly. *See also* **thin.**

gangsta *noun*
Slang A person who treats others violently or roughly ▸ hoodlum, ruffian, tough. *See* **thug.**

gangster *noun*
▸ culprit, lawbreaker, offender. *See* **criminal.**

gap *noun*
1. A space between objects or points ▸ chasm, divide, gulf, interspace, interstice, interval, separation. *See also* **hole. 2.** An interval during which continuity is suspended ▸ break, hiatus, interlude, interim, interregnum, lacuna, lull, void. *See also* **break. 3.** A marked lack of correspondence or agreement ▸ difference, disagreement, discrepancy, disparity, imbalance, incompatibility, incongruity, inconsistency. *See also* **difference. 4.** An opening, especially in a solid structure ▸ break, perforation, rupture. *See* **breach** (1). **5.** An extent, measured or unmeasured, of linear space ▸ interval, length, stretch. *See* **distance** (1).

gap *verb*
1. To make a hole or other opening in ▸ breach, break (through), hole, perforate, pierce, puncture. **2.** To open wide ▸ gape, yawn. *See also* **open, widen.**

gape *verb*
1. To open the mouth wide with a deep breath, as when tired or bored ▸ yawn. **2.** To open wide ▸ gap, yawn. *See also* **open, widen. 3.** To look intently and fixedly ▸ eye, gawk, stare. *See* **gaze.** *See synonym note at* **gaze.**

gape *noun*
An intent fixed look ▸ gaze, stare. *See also* **look.**

gaping *adjective*
Open wide ▸ abysmal, abyssal, cavernous, yawning. *See also* **broad, open.**

garb *noun*
1. A set or style of clothing ▸ costume, guise, outfit. *See* **dress** (2). **2.** Articles worn to cover the body ▸ attire, clothing, garments. *See* **dress** (1).

garb *verb*
To put clothes on ▸ attire, clothe, don. *See* **dress** (1).

garbage *noun*
1. Items or material discarded or rejected as useless or worthless ▸ debris, dregs, flotsam, jetsam, litter, refuse, rubbish, trash, waste. *Informal:* gunk. *Idiom:* flotsam and jetsam. **2.** Something that does not have or make sense ▸ bunkum, drivel, poppycock. *See* **nonsense** (1).

garble *verb*
▸ cross up, jumble, scramble. *See* **confuse** (4).

garden *adjective*
Being of no special quality or type ▸ common, mediocre, standard. *See* **ordinary** (1).
garden *verb*
To raise crops or animals ▸ cultivate, propagate. *See* **grow** (1).
garden-variety *adjective*
▸ common, mediocre, standard. *See* **ordinary** (1).
gargantuan *adjective*
▸ behemoth, colossal, gigantic, mighty. *See* **enormous**. *See synonym note at* **enormous**.
garish *adjective*
▸ flashy, florid, loud. *See* **gaudy**. *See synonym note at* **gaudy**.
garland *noun*
▸ corsage, posy. *See* **bouquet** (1).
garment *verb*
▸ attire, clothe, garb. *See* **dress** (1).
garments *noun*
▸ attire, clothing, raiment. *See* **dress** (1).
garner *verb*
1. To collect ripe crops ▸ harvest, pick, reap. *See* **gather** (1). 2. To collect something bit by bit ▸ cull, gather, harvest. *See* **glean** (1). *See synonym note at* **glean**. 3. To bring together so as to increase in mass or number ▸ accrue, amass, collect, gather. *See* **accumulate**.
garner *noun*
The amount or quantity produced ▸ output, production, yield.
garnish *verb*
▸ decorate, festoon, ornament. *See* **adorn** (1).
garniture *or* **garnishment** *noun*
▸ decoration, embellishment, ornament. *See* **adornment**.
garrulous *adjective*
▸ chatty, loquacious, talky. *See* **talkative**.
gas *noun*
1. *Slang* Incessant and inconsequential talk ▸ drivel, patter, small talk. *See* **chatter**. 2. *Slang* Something or someone uproariously funny ▸ *Informal:* hoot, laugh. *See* **scream** (3). 3. *Slang* Boasting talk or behavior ▸ brag, vaunt. *See* **boast**.
gas *verb*
Slang To talk rapidly on trivial matters ▸ blab, jabber, prattle. *See* **chatter** (1).
gasconade *verb*
To talk with excessive pride ▸ bluster, vaunt. *See* **boast** (1).
gasconade *noun*
Boasting talk or behavior ▸ brag, vaunt. *See* **boast**.
gash *verb*
To penetrate with a sharp edge ▸ bayonet, incise, pierce, slash. *See* **cut** (1).
gash *noun*
An opening made by a sharp object ▸ incision, slash, slit. *See* **cut** (1).
gasp *verb*
1. To utter in a breathless or hoarse manner ▸ croak,

heave, pant, rasp, snort, wheeze. *See also* **shout**. 2. To breathe hard ▸ huff, puff. *See* **pant** (1).
gassy *adjective*
▸ flatulent, tumescent, windy. *See* **inflated** (1).
gate *noun*
The amount of money collected as admission, especially to a sporting event ▸ box office, take, receipts.
gatecrash *verb*
▸ cut in, horn in, interlope. *See* **intrude** (1).
gather *verb*
1. To collect ripe crops ▸ crop, garner, harvest, pick, pluck, reap. 2. To collect something bit by bit ▸ cull, garner. *See* **glean** (1). *See synonym note at* **glean**. 3. To bring together so as to increase in mass or number ▸ accumulate, aggregate, collect. *See* **accumulate**. 4. To come or bring together ▸ cluster, congregate, group. *See* **assemble** (1). 5. To arrive at a conclusion from evidence or reasoning ▸ deduce, judge. *See* **infer** (1).
gathering *noun*
1. A quantity accumulated ▸ assemblage, congeries, mass. *See* **accumulation** (1). 2. A number of persons who have come or been gathered together ▸ conference, group. *Informal:* get-together. *See* **assembly** (1). 3. The act or fact of coming together ▸ confluence, convergence, meeting. *See* **junction** (1). 4. A social gathering, especially for pleasure ▸ celebration, gala, soiree. *See* **party** (1).
gauche *adjective*
1. Lacking sensitivity and skill in dealing with others ▸ brash, impolitic, indelicate, undiplomatic. *See* **tactless**. 2. Clumsily lacking in the ability to do ▸ bumbling, clumsy, inept. *See* **unskillful** (1).
gaudy *adjective*
Tastelessly showy ▸ chintzy, flashy, florid, garish, loud, meretricious, tawdry, tinsel, vulgar. *Informal:* glitzy, tacky. *See also* **ornate, showy**.

✦ CORE SYNONYMS: *gaudy, flashy, florid, garish, loud, meretricious, tacky, tawdry.* These adjectives mean tastelessly showy: *a gaudy costume; a flashy ring; a florid polyester tie; garish colors; a loud sport shirt; a meretricious yet stylish book; tacky knickknacks; tawdry ornaments.*

gauge *noun*
1. The marked outer surface of an instrument ▸ dial, face, indicator. 2. A means by which individuals are compared and judged ▸ criterion, mark, measure. *See* **standard** (1). *See synonym note at* **standard**.
gauge *verb*
1. To ascertain the dimensions, quantity, or capacity of ▸ measure, quantify, quantitate. *Idioms:* take the dimensions (*or* measure) of. 2. To make a judgment as to the worth or value of ▸ assay, calculate. *See* **estimate** (1).
gaunt *adjective*
1. Having little flesh or fat on the body ▸ lean, skinny, slender, slim. *See* **thin** (1). *See synonym note at* **thin**. 2. Appearing worn and exhausted ▸ emaciated, wan, worn. *See* **haggard**.

gauzy *adjective*
▸ ethereal, gossamer, vaporous. *See* **sheer²** (1). *See synonym note at* **sheer²**.

gawk *noun*
A large, ungainly, and dull-witted person ▸ lout, ox. *Informal:* lummox. *See* **oaf**.

gawk *verb*
To look intently and fixedly ▸ gape, peer, stare. *See* **gaze**. *See synonym note at* **gaze**.

gawky *adjective*
▸ graceless. *Slang:* klutzy. *See* **awkward** (1).

gay *adjective*
1. Having a sexual orientation to persons of the same sex ▸ homophile, homosexual, lesbian. **2.** Being in or showing good spirits ▸ happy, jolly. *See* **cheerful** (1). **3.** Full of color ▸ rich, vibrant, vivid. *See* **colorful** (1).

gaze *verb*
To look intently and fixedly ▸ eye, gape, gawk, goggle, ogle, peer, stare. *Slang:* rubberneck. *Idioms:* gaze open-mouthed, fix rivet the eyes (on). *See also* **glare, look, watch, squint**.

gaze *noun*
An intent fixed look ▸ gape, stare. *See also* **look**.

✤ **CORE SYNONYMS:** *gaze, stare, gape, gawk, peer.* These verbs mean to look long and intently. *Gaze* is often indicative of wonder, fascination, awe, or admiration: *gazing at the stars.* Stare can indicate curiosity, boldness, insolence, or stupidity: *stared at them in disbelief. Gape* suggests a prolonged open-mouthed look reflecting amazement, awe, or lack of intelligence: *tourists gaping at the sights.* To *gawk* is to gape or stare stupidly: *Drivers gawked at the disabled truck.* To *peer* is to look narrowly, searchingly, and seemingly with difficulty: *peered at us through her glasses.*

---

gear *noun*
1. Things needed for a task, journey, or other purpose ▸ equipment, rig. *See* **outfit** (1). *See synonym note at* **outfit**. **2.** A set or style of clothing ▸ garb, guise, outfit. *See* **dress** (2).

gear *verb*
To supply what is needed for some activity or purpose ▸ equip, outfit. *See* **furnish** (1).

geek *noun*
Slang A person who is deficient in judgment and good sense ▸ idiot, imbecile, nitwit. *See* **fool** (1).

gelatinize *verb*
▸ congeal, set. *See* **coagulate**.

gelatinous *adjective*
▸ glutinous, mucilaginous, viscid. *See* **viscous**.

geld *verb*
▸ fix, neuter, spay. *See* **sterilize** (2).

gelid *adjective*
▸ boreal, frigid, glacial. *See* **cold** (1).

gelidity *or* **gelidness** *noun*
▸ chill, coolness, iciness. *See* **cold**.

gelt *noun*
Slang Something, such as coins or printed bills, used as a medium of exchange ▸ currency. *Slang:* dough, moola. *See* **money** (1).

gem *noun*
▸ find, pearl, prize. *See* **treasure** (1).

geminate *verb*
To make or become twice as great ▸ double, duplicate, redouble, twin.

geminate *adjective*
Composed of two parts or things ▸ dual, duple, twofold. *See* **double** (2).

gendarme *noun*
Slang A member of a law-enforcement agency ▸ officer, trooper. *See* **police officer**.

gender-neutral *adjective*
▸ genderless, sexless. *See* **androgynous**.

gender-neutrality *noun*
The quality of being androgynous ▸ androgyny, epicenism, sexlessness. *See also* **effeminacy, masculinity**.

genealogical *adjective*
1. Of or from one's ancestors ▸ familial, hereditary, inherited. *See* **ancestral**. **2.** Of unbroken descent or lineage ▸ direct, hereditary, lineal, natural.

genealogy *noun*
1. A written record of ancestry ▸ family tree, pedigree. **2.** One's ancestors or ancestral derivation ▸ blood, descent, lineage. *See* **ancestry**.

general *adjective*
1. Concerned with, applicable to, or affecting the whole ▸ blanket, common, generic, total, universal. **2.** Covering a wide scope ▸ all-around, all-inclusive, all-round, broad, broad-spectrum, comprehensive, expansive, extended, extensive, far-ranging, far-reaching, global, inclusive, large, overall, popular, sweeping, wide-ranging, wide-reaching, widespread. *Idiom:* across-the-board. **3.** Not limited to a single class ▸ diversified, indefinite. **4.** Belonging to, shared by, or applicable to all alike ▸ communal, mutual, public. *See* **common** (2). **5.** Of, representing, or carried on by people at large ▸ democratic, public, societal. *See* **popular** (1). **6.** Occurring or encountered regularly ▸ commonplace, frequent, regular. *See* **common** (1). **7.** Most generally existing or encountered at a given time ▸ predominant, rampant. *See* **prevailing** (1). **8.** Lacking literal exactness ▸ broad, inexact, rough. *See* **loose** (3).

general *noun*
One who governs or leads ▸ boss, director, head, leader. *See* **chief** (1).

✤ **CORE SYNONYMS:** *general, common, generic, universal.* These adjectives mean concerned with, applicable to, or affecting the whole: *the general welfare; a common enemy; generic likenesses; universal military conscription.*

◂ **ANTONYM:** *particular*

---

generally *adverb*
▸ commonly, customarily, normally, routinely. *See* **usually**.

generate *verb*
1. To bring into existence ▸ give, provide, yield. *See* **produce** (1). 2. To be the cause of ▸ bring about, induce, trigger. *See* **cause.**

generation *noun*
1. A person or group descended directly from the same parents or ancestors ▸ offspring, posterity, seed. *See* **progeny.** 2. The period during which someone or something exists ▸ existence, span, term. *See* **life** (1). 3. The process by which an organism produces others of its kind ▸ procreation, proliferation, propagation. *See* **reproduction** (3).

generative *adjective*
▸ ingenious, innovative, original. *See* **inventive** (1).

generic *adjective*
▸ blanket, common, universal. *See* **general** (1). *See synonym note at* **general.**

generosity *noun*
The quality or state of being generous ▸ bigheartedness, bounteousness, bountifulness, bounty, freehandedness, generousness, great-heartedness, large-heartedness, largess, lavishness, liberality, magnanimity, magnanimousness, munificence, openhandedness, unselfishness, unsparingness. *See also* **benevolence, consideration.**

generous *adjective*
1. Willing to give of oneself and one's possessions ▸ big, big-hearted, bountiful, free, freehanded, greathearted, handsome, large-hearted, lavish, liberal, magnanimous, munificent, openhanded, princely, prodigal, ungrudging, unselfish, unsparing, unstinting, warm-hearted. *See also* **benevolent, humanitarian, selfless.** 2. Characterized by abundance; as much as one needs or desires ▸ abounding, abundant, ample, bounteous, bountiful, copious, heavy, plenitudinous, plenteous, plentiful, substantial, voluminous. *See also* **profuse.** 3. Ready to do favors for another ▸ agreeable, complaisant. *See* **obliging.**

✛ CORE SYNONYMS: *generous, abundant, ample, copious, plenitudinous, plentiful.* These adjectives mean being fully as much as one needs or desires: *a generous serving of potatoes; the artist's abundant talent; ample space; copious provisions; a plenitudinous crop of wheat; a plentiful supply.*

◂ ANTONYM: *scant*

---

generousness *noun*
▸ magnanimity, munificence, unselfishness. *See* **generosity.**

genesis *noun*
▸ dawn, inception, start. *See* **birth** (2). *See synonym note at* **birth.**

genial *adjective*
▸ cordial, friendly, likeable. *See* **amiable.** *See synonym note at* **amiable.**

geniality *or* **genialness** *noun*
▸ agreeability, congeniality, pleasantness. *See* **amiability.**

genialness *noun*
▸ congeniality, pleasantness. *See* **amiability.**

genius *noun*
1. Liveliness and vivacity of imagination ▸ brilliance, brilliancy, fire, inspiration. *See also* **intelligence, invention.** 2. An innate capability ▸ faculty, gift, knack. *See* **talent.** 3. A person of great mental ability ▸ intellectual, thinker. *See* **mind** (2).

genius *adjective*
Having or showing intelligence, often of a high order ▸ intellectual, knowledgeable. *See* **intelligent** (1).

genocide *noun*
▸ bloodshed, slaughter. *See* **massacre.**

genre *noun*
▸ category, order, set. *See* **class** (1).

genteel *adjective*
1. Characterized by good manners ▸ mannerly, polite. *See* **courteous** (1). *See synonym note at* **courteous.** 2. Marked by excessive concern for modesty or propriety ▸ priggish, prissy, strait-laced. *See* **prudish.** 3. Characterized by elaborate, usually formal courtesy ▸ courtly, gallant, stately. *See* **gracious** (2). 4. Appealing to refined taste ▸ elegant, exquisite. *See* **delicate** (1). *See synonym note at* **delicate.**

genteelness *noun*
▸ courteousness, politeness. *See* **courtesy** (1).

gentility *noun*
1. People of the highest social level ▸ elite, gentry, nobility. *See* **society** (1). 2. Well-mannered behavior toward others ▸ civility, politeness. *See* **courtesy** (1).

gentle *adjective*
1. Of a sympathetic, considerate character ▸ compassionate, kindly, mild, sensitive, soft, softhearted, tender, tenderhearted. *See also* **attentive, sympathetic.** 2. Free from severity or violence, as in sound or movement ▸ balmy, delicate, faint, mild, moderate, slight, smooth, soothing, soft. 3. Easily managed or handled ▸ docile, domesticated, meek, mild, tame, yielding. *See also* **cooperative, obedient, obliging.** 4. Of small intensity ▸ moderate, slight, soft. *See* **light**² (2). 5. Not steep or abrupt ▸ easy, moderate. *See* **gradual** (2). 6. Appealing to refined taste ▸ elegant, exquisite. *See* **delicate** (1).

gentle *verb*
1. To make an animal docile ▸ break, bust, master, tame. 2. To train to live with and be of use to people ▸ break in, tame. *See* **domesticate.** 3. To ease the anger or agitation of ▸ appease, mollify, soothe. *See* **pacify.**

gentlemanly *adjective*
1. Characterized by good manners ▸ genteel, mannerly, polite. *See* **courteous** (1). 2. Respectfully attentive, especially to women ▸ chivalrous, knightly. *See* **gallant** (1).

gentry *noun*
▸ elite, blue blood, nobility. *See* **society** (1).

genuflect *verb*
▸ curtsy, kneel. *See* **bow**¹ (1).

genuflection *noun*
▸ curtsy, obeisance. *See* **bow**¹.

genuine *adjective*

1. Free from hypocrisy or pretense ▸ heartfelt, hearty, honest, natural, plain, real, sincere, true, unaffected, unfeigned. *See also* **artless, frank, honest, serious. 2.** Not counterfeit or copied ▸ genuine, legitimate, true. *See* **authentic** (1). *See synonym note at* **authentic. 3.** Free from extraneous elements ▸ perfect, plain, unadulterated. *See* **pure** (1).

genuinely *adverb*

▸ actually, positively, truly. *See* **really.**

genuineness *noun*

▸ authenticity, correctness, truth, validity. *See* **veracity.**

genus *noun*

▸ ilk, mold, species. *See* **kind².**

georgic *adjective*

▸ bucolic, pastoral, rural. *See* **country.**

germ *noun*

1. A tiny organism usually producing disease ▸ bacterium, bug, microbe, microorganism, parasite, pathogen, virus. **2.** A source of further growth and development ▸ bud, embryo, kernel, nucleus, seed, spark. *See also* **origin.**

germane *adjective*

▸ applicable, apropos, material. *See* **relevant.** *See synonym note at* **relevant.**

germaneness *noun*

▸ appositeness, materiality, pertinence. *See* **relevance.**

gestation *noun*

The condition of carrying a developing fetus within the uterus ▸ gravidity, gravidness, parturiency, pregnancy.

gesticulate *verb*

▸ motion, sign, signal. *See* **gesture.**

gesticulation *noun*

▸ indication, motion, signal. *See* **gesture** (1). *See synonym note at* **gesture.**

gesture *noun*

1. An expressive, meaningful bodily movement ▸ gesticulation, indication, motion, nod, sign, signal, wag, wave. *Informal:* high sign. *Idioms:* thumbs up (*or* down). **2.** Something that takes the place of words in communicating a thought or feeling ▸ indication, sign. *See* **expression** (2).

gesture *verb*

To make bodily motions so as to convey an idea or complement speech ▸ beckon, flag, gesticulate, motion, pantomime, sign, signal, signalize, wave. *Idiom:* give the high sign.

✛ CORE SYNONYMS: *gesture, gesticulation, sign, signal.* These nouns denote an expressive, meaningful bodily movement: *a gesture of approval; frantic gesticulations to get help; made a sign for silence; gave the signal to advance.*

---

get *verb*

1. To come into possession of ▸ acquire, attain, come by, gain, glean, obtain, procure, reap, receive, secure, take, win. *Informal:* land, pick up. *Slang:* bag. *See also*

obtain. **2.** To obtain from another source ▸ extract, receive. *See* **derive** (1). **3.** To acquire as a result of one's behavior or effort ▸ gain, merit, win. *See* **earn** (1). **4.** To obtain possession or control of ▸ gain, secure, win. *See* **capture** (1). **5.** To receive, as wages, for one's labor ▸ gain, make. *See* **earn** (2). **6.** To succeed in communicating with ▸ *Informal:* contact, reach. *Informal:* catch. **7.** To become affected with a disease ▸ catch, develop. *See* **contract** (2). **8.** To perceive and recognize the meaning of ▸ apprehend, fathom, sense. *See* **understand** (1). **9.** To gain knowledge or mastery of by study ▸ acquire, master. *See* **learn** (1). **10.** To be the biological father of ▸ beget, father, sire. **11.** To obtain possession or control of ▸ gain, take. *Slang:* cop. *See* **capture** (1). **12.** To stir the emotions of ▸ strike, touch. *See* **move** (1). **13.** To trouble the nerves or peace of mind of ▸ irritate, nettle, vex. *See* **annoy** (1). **14.** To come to be ▸ change (to *or* into), grow (to be). *See* **become** (1). **15.** To exact revenge for or from ▸ pay off, vindicate. *See* **avenge. 16.** To achieve a certain price ▸ fetch, realize, sell for. *See* **bring** (2).

get across *verb*

To make known ▸ disclose, divulge, transmit. *See* **communicate** (1).

get ahead *verb*

1. To gain success ▸ arrive, get on, rise, succeed. *Idioms:* go far, go places, make good, make it. **2.** To attain a higher status, rank, or condition ▸ advance, climb, mount. *See* **rise** (6).

get along *verb*

1. To grow old ▸ age, get on. **2.** To interact with another or others in a harmonious fashion ▸ connect, harmonize. *Slang:* click. *See* **relate** (5). **3.** To move forward ▸ come along, proceed, progress. *See* **advance** (2). **4.** To progress or perform adequately, especially in difficult circumstances ▸ fare, fend, get by. *See* **manage** (1).

get around *verb*

1. To become known far and wide ▸ circulate, go around, spread, travel. *Idioms:* go (*or* make) the rounds. **2.** To keep away from ▸ dodge, evade, shun. *See* **avoid.**

get away *verb*

1. To break loose and leave suddenly, as from confinement or a difficult situation ▸ decamp, flee. *See* **escape** (1). **2.** To move away from a place ▸ exit, go away, retire. *See* **go** (1).

get behind *verb*

To aid the cause of by approving or favoring ▸ back, endorse, stand by. *See* **support** (1).

get by *verb*

To progress or perform adequately, especially in difficult circumstances ▸ fare, fend, scrape by. *See* **manage** (1).

get in *verb*

To come to a particular place ▸ check in, reach. *See* **arrive** (1).

get off *verb*

1. To go about the initial step in doing something

▸ begin, embark, launch. *See* **start** (1). **2.** To move away from a place ▸ exit, go away, retire. *See* **go** (1).

get on *verb*
1. To gain success ▸ arrive, get ahead, rise, succeed. *Idioms:* go far, go places, make good, make it. **2.** To grow old ▸ age, get along. **3.** To interact with another or others in a harmonious fashion ▸ connect, harmonize. *Slang:* click. *See* **relate** (5). **4.** To put an article of clothing on one's person ▸ put on, slip on. *See* **don** (1).

get out *verb*
1. To be made public ▸ break, come out, out, transpire. *Informal:* leak (out). *See also* **air, announce, appear. 2.** To leave hastily ▸ bolt. *Slang:* scram, vamoose. *See* **run** (3).

get through *verb*
To exist in spite of adversity ▸ persist, pull through. *See* **survive** (1).

get to *verb*
1. To reach a goal or objective ▸ achieve, attain, gain. *See* **accomplish** (1). **2.** To succeed in causing a person to act or think in a certain way ▸ convince, prevail on. *See* **persuade** (1). **3.** To trouble the nerves or peace of mind of ▸ irritate, nettle, vex. *See* **annoy** (1).

get together *verb*
1. To come or bring together ▸ cluster, congregate, gather. *See* **assemble** (1). **2.** To come together by arrangement ▸ meet (up), rendezvous. **3.** To come to an understanding or to terms ▸ coincide, concur. *See* **agree** (2).

get up *verb*
1. To leave one's bed ▸ arise, roll out. *See* **rise** (2). **2.** To adopt a standing posture ▸ arise, rise. *See* **stand** (1).

get *noun*
A person or group descended directly from the same parents or ancestors ▸ offspring, posterity, seed. *See* **progeny.**

getaway *noun*
▸ breakout, flight. *See* **escape** (1).

gettable *adjective*
▸ attainable, obtainable, procurable. *See* **available** (1).

get-together *noun*
1. *Informal* A number of persons who have come or been gathered together ▸ body, conference, group. *See* **assembly** (1). **2.** A social gathering, especially for pleasure ▸ celebration, gala, soiree. *See* **party** (1). **3.** An act or an instance of going or coming to see another ▸ call, visitation. *See* **visit** (1).

getup *noun*
1. A set or style of clothing ▸ garb, guise, outfit. *See* **dress** (2). **2.** *Informal* Clothes or other personal effects, such as makeup, worn to conceal one's identity ▸ costume, mask, veil. *See* **disguise** (1).

get-up-and-go *noun*
1. *Informal* An aggressive readiness along with energy to undertake taxing efforts ▸ hustle, initiative, punch. *See* **drive** (2). **2.** *Informal* Capacity for work or vigorous activity ▸ might, potency, power. *See* **energy.**

gewgaw *noun*
▸ knickknack, trinket. *See* **novelty** (3).

ghastly *adjective*
1. Shockingly repellent ▸ appalling, dreadful, grim, grisly, gruesome, hideous, horrible, horrid, loathsome, lurid, macabre, terrifying. *See also* **fearful, offensive. 2.** Gruesomely suggestive of ghosts or death ▸ cadaverous, deadly, deathlike, deathly, ghostlike, ghostly, morbid, spectral, wraithlike. *See also* **pale, phantasmagoric, weird. 3.** Very bad ▸ appalling, awful, dreadful. *See* **terrible** (1).

✦ CORE SYNONYMS: *ghastly, grim, gruesome, grisly, macabre, lurid.* These adjectives describe what is shockingly repellent in aspect or appearance. *Ghastly* applies to what inspires shock or horror because it suggests death: *ghastly wounds. Grim* refers to what repels because of its stern or fierce aspect or its harsh, relentless nature: *the grim task of burying the earthquake victims. Gruesome* and *grisly* describe what horrifies or revolts because of its appalling crudity or utter inhumanity: *a gruesome murder; grisly jokes about cadavers. Macabre* suggests the horror of death and decay: *macabre stories about a madman. Lurid* sometimes refers to an unnatural hue suggestive of death: *The ill patient's skin had a lurid pallor.* More often, the term describes what shocks because of its terrible and ghastly nature: *lurid crimes.* It can also refer to glaring and usually unsavory sensationalism: *a lurid account of the accident.*

---

ghettoize *verb*
▸ insulate, seclude, segregate. *See* **isolate** (1).

ghost *noun*
1. An immaterial supernatural being, especially the spirit of a dead person ▸ apparition, bogey, bogeyman, bogle, eidolon, phantasm, phantasma, phantom, revenant, shade, shadow, soul, specter, spirit, visitant, wraith. *Informal:* spook. *Chiefly Regional:* haunt. *See also* **fairy. 2.** A slight amount or indication ▸ hint, semblance, trace. *See* **shade** (2).

ghostly *or* **ghostlike** *adjective*
▸ deathly, morbid, spectral. *See* **ghastly** (2).

ghoul *noun*
▸ beast, devil, monster. *See* **fiend** (1).

ghoulish *adjective*
▸ devilish, diabolical, satanic. *See* **fiendish.**

GI *noun*
▸ legionary, serviceperson, trooper. *See* **soldier** (2).

giant *noun*
One that is extraordinarily large and powerful ▸ behemoth, colossus, elephant, gargantua, Goliath, Hercules, hulk, jumbo, leviathan, mammoth, monster, ogre, titan, whale. *Slang:* whopper.

giant *adjective*
Of extraordinary size and power ▸ colossal, gargantuan, gigantic, huge. *See* **enormous.**

gibber *verb*
▸ chatter, jabber, prattle. *See* **babble** (1).

gibberish *noun*
1. Highly technical, often deliberately deceptive language ▸ abracadabra, doublespeak, double talk, gobbledygook, Greek, hocus-pocus, jabberwocky, mum-

bo jumbo. *See also* **nonsense. 2.** Empty or foolish talk ▸ blather, jabber, twaddle. *See* **babble** (1).

gibbet *verb*
To execute by suspending by the neck ▸ hang. *Informal:* string up. *Slang:* swing.

gibe *or* **jibe** *verb*
To subject to ridicule ▸ gibe at, jeer (at), lampoon, taunt. *See* **ridicule.**

gibe *noun*
An instance of mockery or derision ▸ insult, jeer, scoff. *See* **taunt** (1).

giddiness *noun*
▸ grogginess, unsteadiness, wooziness. *See* **dizziness.**

giddy *adjective*
1. Producing dizziness or vertigo ▸ dizzy, dizzying, sickening, vertiginous. *See also* **steep. 2.** Given to lighthearted silliness ▸ empty-headed, featherbrained, flighty, frivolous, frothy, harebrained, lighthearted, scatterbrained, silly. *Informal:* gaga. *Slang:* birdbrained, dizzy. *See also* **foolish, stupid. 3.** Having a sensation of whirling or falling ▸ lightheaded, reeling. *See* **dizzy** (1).

✦ CORE SYNONYMS: *giddy, dizzy, vertiginous.* These adjectives mean producing dizziness or vertigo: *a giddy precipice; a dizzy pinnacle; a vertiginous height.*

---

gift *noun*
1. Something bestowed voluntarily ▸ bequest, present, presentation. *Slang:* freebie. *See also* **grant. 2.** Something given to a charity or cause ▸ benefaction, contribution, offering. *See* **donation. 3.** An innate capability ▸ faculty, flair, knack. *See* **talent.**

gift *verb*
To present with a gift ▸ award, endow, endue, give, invest. *See also* **grant.**

gifted *adjective*
Possessing great natural ability or talent ▸ born, endowed, natural, precocious, talented. *Informal:* whiz-bang. *See also* **able, expert.**

gig *noun*
1. *Slang* A commitment, as for a performance by an entertainer ▸ booking, date, engagement. **2.** *Slang* A post of employment ▸ job, situation. *See* **position** (3).

gigantic *adjective*
▸ behemoth, colossal, gigantesque, immense. *See* **enormous.** *See synonym note at* **enormous.**

giggle *verb*
To express amusement or mirth ▸ chuckle, snicker, titter. *See* **laugh.**

giggle *noun*
An act of laughing ▸ cackle, snicker, laughter. *See* **laugh** (1).

gigolo *noun*
1. An immoral or licentious man ▸ goat, roué. *Slang:* lech. *See* **lecher. 2.** An immoral or licentious person ▸ debaucher, profligate. *See* **wanton** (1).

gild *verb*
1. To give a deceptively attractive appearance to ▸ sugarcoat, varnish, whitewash. *See* **color** (4). **2.** To

make superficially more acceptable or appealing ▸ sugar, sugarcoat. *See* **sweeten** (1). **3.** To furnish with decorations ▸ decorate, garnish, ornament. *See* **adorn** (1).

gilded *or* **gilt** *adjective*
▸ flamboyant, resplendent. *See* **ornate** (1).

gimcrack *noun*
▸ knickknack, trinket. *See* **novelty** (3).

gimmick *noun*
1. An indirect, usually cunning means of gaining an end ▸ deception, ploy, stratagem. *See* **trick** (1). **2.** A small specialized mechanical device ▸ apparatus. *Informal:* widget. *Slang:* gizmo. *See* **gadget. 3.** *Informal* A clever, unexpected new trick or method ▸ twist. *Slang:* angle, kick. *See* **wrinkle** (2). **4.** A small showy article ▸ knickknack, trinket. *See* **novelty** (3).

ginger *noun*
▸ life, verve, vivaciousness. *See* **spirit** (1).

gingerliness *noun*
1. Cautious attentiveness ▸ carefulness, caution, heed. *See* **care** (1). **2.** Careful forethought to avoid risk ▸ care, carefulness, wariness. *See* **caution** (1).

gingerly *adjective*
▸ cautious, chary, prudent. *See* **wary** (1).

gird *verb*
1. To prepare oneself for action ▸ arm, brace, forearm, fortify, ready, steel, strengthen. *Idioms:* clear the deck, gird (*or* gird up) one's loins, screw up one's courage. **2.** To form a circle around ▸ band, belt, cincture. *See* **encircle** (1).

girder *noun*
▸ crossbeam, joist, timber. *See* **beam** (2).

girdle *noun*
A long narrow piece, as of material ▸ belt, sash, ribbon, stripe. *See* **band**[1] (1).

girdle *verb*
To form a circle around ▸ band, belt, cincture, compass. *See* **encircle** (1).

girl *noun*
Informal A woman referred to informally ▸ lass. *Informal:* chick, damsel, doll, gal, missy, sis, sister. *Slang:* homegirl, momma.

girlfriend *noun*
A woman who is a man's romantic partner ▸ girl, inamorata, lady friend. *Slang:* old lady. *See also* **darling, lover.**

girt *verb*
▸ band, begird, belt, gird. *See* **encircle** (1).

gist *noun*
1. The most central or essential part ▸ essence, marrow, quintessence. *See* **heart** (1). *See synonym note at* **heart. 2.** The current of thought uniting all elements of a text or discourse ▸ drift, intent, tenor. *See* **thrust** (1).

give *verb*
1. To relinquish to the possession or control of another ▸ deliver, furnish, hand, hand in, hand over, provide, render, supply, transfer, turn over. **2.** To present as a gift to a charity or cause ▸ bestow,

contribute, donate, hand out. **3.** To give formally or officially ▸ award, bestow, grant. *See* **confer** (2). **4.** To give out in portions or shares ▸ allocate, apportion, dispense. *See* **distribute** (1). **5.** To give money as payment ▸ expend, outlay. *See* **spend** (1). **6.** To provide as a remedy ▸ dispense, give, treat. *See* **administer** (3). **7.** To mete out by means of some action ▸ administer, deal, deliver. **8.** To afford an opportunity for ▸ allow, let. *See* **permit** (3). **9.** To let have as a favor, prerogative, or privilege ▸ accord, award, concede, grant, vouchsafe. *See also* **yield**. **10.** To put in the charge of another for care, use, or performance ▸ confide, delegate. *See* **entrust** (1). **11.** To devote oneself or one's efforts ▸ concentrate, focus, turn. *See* **apply** (1). **12.** To set aside or distribute as a share ▸ allocate, measure out. *See* **allot**. **13.** To spread a disease to others ▸ convey, pass, transmit. *See* **communicate** (4). **14.** To bring into existence ▸ bring forth, provide, yield. *See* **produce** (1). **15.** To curve or yield under pressure ▸ buckle, sag. *See* **bend** (3). **16.** To fall in ▸ cave in, collapse. *See* **buckle** (1). **17.** To present with a gift ▸ award, invest. *See* **gift**.

give away *verb*
1. To disclose in a breach of confidence ▸ divulge. *Informal:* spill. *See* **betray** (2). **2.** To present as a gift to a charity or cause ▸ bequeath, pledge. *See* **donate** (1).

give back *verb*
1. To put someone in the possession of a prior position or office ▸ reappoint, reinstall, reinstate, replace, restore, return. **2.** To send, put, or carry back to a former location ▸ restore, take back. *See* **return** (2).

give forth *verb*
1. To discharge material, as vapor or fumes, usually suddenly and violently ▸ exhale, issue, release. *See* **emit** (1). **2.** To bring into existence ▸ bring forth, provide, yield. *See* **produce** (1).

give in *verb*
1. To lose all hope ▸ despair, despond, give up. *Idiom:* throw in the towel. *See also* **abandon**. **2.** To give up in favor of another ▸ capitulate, concede, yield. *See* **surrender** (1).

give off *verb*
To discharge material, as vapor or fumes, usually suddenly and violently ▸ give forth, issue, release. *See* **emit** (1).

give onto *verb*
To have the face or front turned toward ▸ face, front, look (on *or* upon *or* toward). *See also* **overlook**.

give out *verb*
1. To prove deficient or insufficient ▸ fail, run out. *Idioms:* fall short, run dry, run short. *See also* **decrease**. **2.** To discharge material, as vapor or fumes, usually suddenly and violently ▸ give forth, issue, release. *See* **emit** (1). **3.** To stop working properly ▸ break down, fail. *Slang:* conk out. *See* **malfunction**. **4.** To suddenly lose all health or strength ▸ crack, succumb. *See* **collapse** (1). **5.** To grow weary ▸ burn out, wear out. *See* **tire** (2). **6.** To make or become no

longer active or productive ▸ desiccate, play out, run out. *See* **dry** (2).

give over *verb*
1. To yield oneself unrestrainedly, as to an impulse ▸ deliver, give up, relinquish, surrender. **2.** To cease consideration or treatment of ▸ give up, relinquish, skip. *See* **drop** (7).

give up *verb*
1. To lose all hope ▸ despair, despond, give in. *Idiom:* throw in the towel. *See also* **abandon**. **2.** To cease trying to continue ▸ discontinue, leave off, quit, stop. *See* **abandon** (2). **3.** To discontinue (a habit, for example) ▸ abjure, cut out, leave off. *See* **break** (17). **4.** To cease consideration or treatment of ▸ abandon, relinquish, skip. *See* **drop** (7). **5.** To give up in favor of another ▸ capitulate, concede, yield. *See* **surrender** (1).

give *noun*
The quality or state of being flexible ▸ elasticity, malleability, pliability. *See* **flexibility** (1).

give-and-take *noun*
▸ arrangement, concession, settlement. *See* **compromise**.

given *adjective*
1. Having or showing a tendency or likelihood ▸ disposed, prone. *See* **inclined** (1). **2.** Based on probability or presumption ▸ likely, presumable, prospective. *See* **presumptive**.

given *noun*
Something taken to be true without proof ▸ axiom, premise, presupposition. *See* **assumption** (1).

giver *noun*
▸ benefactor, contributor, patron. *See* **donor**.

gizmo *noun*
Slang A small specialized mechanical device ▸ contraption, contrivance. *Informal:* doohickey. *See* **gadget**.

glacial *adjective*
1. Marked by a low temperature ▸ chill, frigid, polar. *See* **cold** (1). *See synonym note at* **cold**. **2.** Not friendly, sociable, or warm in manner ▸ aloof, chilly, frigid. *See* **cool** (1). **3.** Proceeding at a rate less than usual or desired ▸ dilatory, sluggish. *See* **slow** (1).

glad *adjective*
1. Being in or showing good spirits ▸ gleeful, happy, joyful. *See* **cheerful** (1). *See synonym note at* **cheerful**. **2.** Providing joy and pleasure ▸ festive, joyous, mirthful. *See* **merry** (1). **3.** Disposed to accept, agree, or participate ▸ amenable, delighted, eager. *See* **willing** (1).

gladden *verb*
▸ enchant, overjoy, pleasure. *See* **delight** (1). *See synonym note at* **delight**.

gladly *adverb*
▸ agreed, all right, assuredly. *See* **yes**.

gladness *noun*
1. A condition of well-being and good spirits ▸ blessedness, bliss, felicity. *See* **happiness**. **2.** A state of joyful exuberance ▸ glee, lightheartedness, mirth. *See* **merriment** (1).

gladsome *adjective*
▸ festive, joyful, joyous. *See* **merry** (1).
glamorous *adjective*
▸ enchanting, fetching, lovely, winsome. *See* **attractive** (1).
glamour *noun*
1. The power or quality of attracting ▸ appeal, draw, enticement, lure. *See* **attraction** (1). 2. Brilliant, showy splendor ▸ magnificence, resplendence, sparkle. *See* **glitter** (2).
glance *verb*
1. To strike a surface at such an angle as to be deflected ▸ carom, fly off, graze, ricochet, skim, skip. *See also* **bounce**. 2. To look briefly and quickly ▸ glimpse, peek, peep. *Idioms:* steal a glance (*or* look). *See also* **look**. 3. To emit light in sudden or intermittent bursts ▸ flash, glimmer, twinkle. *See* **glitter**. *See synonym note at* **glitter**.
glance at *or* **over** *or* **through** *verb*
To look through reading matter casually ▸ flip through, leaf (through), skim. *See* **browse** (1).
glance *noun*
1. A quick look ▸ glimpse, look, peek, peep, scan. *Informal:* gander, look-see. 2. An act of reflection ▸ deflection, reflection, scattering. *See also* **bounce**. 3. A sudden burst of light ▸ flicker, spark, twinkle. *See* **flash** (1).
glare *verb*
1. To stare fixedly and angrily ▸ glower, lower, scowl. *Idioms:* give the evil eye, look daggers. *See also* **frown**, **gaze**, **sneer**. 2. To shine intensely and blindingly ▸ beat down, blaze, flare, pulse, throb, vibrate. *See also* **beam**. 3. To be obtrusively conspicuous ▸ stand out, stick out. *Idioms:* stare someone in the face, stick out like a sore thumb.
glare *noun*
1. A fixed angry stare ▸ glower, lower, scowl. *See also* **face**, **sneer**. 2. An intense blinding light ▸ blaze, dazzle, flare. 3. Light that is reflected ▸ highlight, reflection. *See also* **flash**.
glaring *adjective*
1. Conspicuously bad or offensive ▸ egregious, flagrant, gross, rank. *See synonym note at* **flagrant**. *See also* **offensive, outrageous, shameless**. 2. Extremely or harshly bright ▸ blinding, dazzling, glary. *See* **brilliant** (2). 3. Readily seen, perceived, or understood ▸ evident, manifest, noticeable, obvious. *See* **apparent** (1).
glaringness *noun*
The quality or state of being flagrant ▸ egregiousness, flagrancy, grossness, rankness. *See also* **impudence, outrageousness**.
glary *adjective*
▸ blazing, blinding, glaring. *See* **brilliant** (2).
glassy *adjective*
1. Of or resembling glass ▸ glasslike, hyaline, vitrescent, vitreous. *See also* **translucent**. 2. Having a high, radiant sheen ▸ gleaming, glistening, lustrous. *See* **glossy**.

glaze *noun*
1. A final coating ▸ enamel, lacquer, varnish. *See* **finish** (3). 2. A surface shininess ▸ luster, polish, shine. *See* **gloss**[1] (1).
glaze *verb*
1. To apply a coating to ▸ enamel, lacquer, varnish. *See* **finish** (7). 2. To give a bright sheen or luster to ▸ burnish, polish, shine. *See* **gloss**[1] (1).
gleam *verb*
1. To shine brightly and steadily but without a flame ▸ glow, incandesce, luminesce. 2. To emit a bright light ▸ burn, glow. *See* **beam** (1). 3. To emit light in sudden or intermittent bursts ▸ flash, glimmer, twinkle. *See* **glitter**. *See synonym note at* **glitter**.
gleam *noun*
A sudden burst of light ▸ flicker, spark, twinkle. *See* **flash** (1).
gleaming *adjective*
▸ burnished, glistening, lustrous. *See* **glossy**.
glean *verb*
1. To collect something bit by bit ▸ cherry-pick, cull, extract, garner, gather, harvest, pick up. *See also* **accumulate**. 2. To come into possession of ▸ come by, gain, procure. *See* **get** (1).

✦ CORE SYNONYMS: *glean, garner, gather, harvest.* These verbs mean to collect something bit by bit: *glean information; garner compliments; gathering mushrooms; harvested rich rewards.*

---

glee *noun*
1. A state of joyful exuberance ▸ gaiety, lightheartedness, mirth. *See* **merriment** (1). 2. A feeling of gratification aroused by something good or desired ▸ bliss, enjoyment, pleasure. *See* **delight** (1). 3. A condition of well-being and good spirits ▸ blessedness, bliss, felicity. *See* **happiness**.
gleeful *adjective*
▸ happy, jolly, jovial. *See* **cheerful** (1).
gleefulness *noun*
▸ gaiety, lightheartedness, mirth. *See* **merriment** (1).
glen *noun*
▸ dale, gorge. *See* **valley**.
glib *adjective*
Marked by ease and fluency of speech that is often insincere or superficial ▸ facile, offhand, slick, smooth, smooth-talking, smooth-tongued. *See also* **eloquent, fluent, suave, talkative**.

✦ CORE SYNONYMS: *glib, slick, smooth-talking, smooth-tongued.* These adjectives mean marked by ease and fluency of speech that is often insincere or superficial: *a glib denial; a slick commercial; a smooth-talking salesperson; a smooth-tongued hypocrite.*

---

glibness *noun*
▸ articulateness, fluency, volubility. *See* **eloquence**.
glide *verb*
1. To move smoothly, continuously, and effortlessly ▸ coast, drift, float, glissade, skate, skim, slide, slip, slither, waft. 2. To maneuver gently and slowly into

place ► ease, slide, slip. *See also* **ease. 3.** To move silently and furtively ► lurk, prowl. *See* **sneak** (1). **4.** To pass quickly and lightly through the air ► dart, sail, shoot. *See* **fly** (2).

✦ **CORE SYNONYMS:** *glide, slide, slip, coast, slither.* These verbs mean to move smoothly and continuously over or as if over a slippery surface. *Glide* refers to smooth, free-flowing, seemingly effortless movement: *"four snakes gliding up and down a hollow"* (Ralph Waldo Emerson). *Slide* usually implies rapid easy movement without loss of contact with the surface: *coal that slid down a chute to the cellar. Slip* is most often applied to accidental sliding resulting in loss of balance or foothold: *slipped on a patch of ice. Coast* applies especially to downward movement resulting from the effects of gravity or momentum: *The driver let the truck coast down the incline. Slither* can mean to slip and slide, as on an uneven surface, often with friction and noise: *"The detached crystals slithered down the rock face"* (H.G. Wells). The word can also suggest the sinuous gliding motion of a reptile: *An iguana slithered across the path.*

---

glimmer *noun*
A sudden burst of light ► flicker, spark, twinkle. *See* **flash** (1).
glimmer *verb*
To emit light in sudden or intermittent bursts ► flash, gleam, twinkle. *See* **glitter.** *See synonym note at* **glitter.**
glimpse *noun*
A quick look ► peek. *Informal:* gander. *See* **glance** (1).
glimpse *verb*
To look briefly and quickly ► glance, peek, peep. *Idioms:* steal a glance (*or* look). *See also* **look.**
glint *noun*
1. A sudden burst of light ► flicker, spark, twinkle. *See* **flash** (1). **2.** Sparkling, brilliant light ► glisten, shimmer, sparkle. *See* **glitter** (1).
glint *verb*
To emit light in sudden or intermittent bursts ► flash, glimmer, twinkle. *See* **glitter.** *See synonym note at* **glitter.**
glissade *verb*
► coast, skim, slither. *See* **glide** (1).
glisten *verb*
To emit light in sudden or intermittent bursts ► flash, glimmer, twinkle. *See* **glitter.** *See synonym note at* **glitter.**
glisten *noun*
Sparkling, brilliant light ► glint, shimmer, sparkle. *See* **glitter** (1).
glistening *adjective*
1. Having a high, radiant sheen ► gleaming, lustrous, polished. *See* **glossy. 2.** Full of bright shifting or flickering light ► glinting, glittering, shimmering. *See* **sparkling** (1).
glister *verb*
To emit light in sudden or intermittent bursts ► flash, glimmer, twinkle. *See* **glitter.**

glister *noun*
Sparkling, brilliant light ► glint, shimmer, sparkle. *See* **glitter** (1).
glitch *noun*
► blemish, fault, imperfection, shortcoming. *See* **defect** (1).
glitter *noun*
1. Sparkling, brilliant light ► glint, glisten, glister, scintillation, shimmer, sparkle, twinkle. *See also* **flash. 2.** Brilliant, showy splendor ► brilliance, brilliancy, glamorousness, glamour, gorgeousness, magnificence, pageantry, pomp, resplendence, resplendency, showiness, sparkle, sumptuousness. *Informal:* glitz, razzle-dazzle. *Slang:* bling, bling bling. *See also* **array, glory. 3.** A small sparkling decoration ► diamond, rhinestone, sequin, spangle.
glitter *verb*
To emit light in sudden or intermittent bursts ► blink, coruscate, flash, flicker, glance, gleam, glimmer, glint, glisten, glister, scintillate, shimmer, spangle, sparkle, twinkle, wink. *See also* **beam.**

✦ **CORE SYNONYMS:** *glitter, sparkle, flash, gleam, glance, glint, glisten, shimmer, glimmer, twinkle, scintillate.* These verbs mean to emit light in sudden or intermittent bursts. *Glitter* and *sparkle* suggest a rapid succession of little flashes of high brilliance (*jewels glittering in the display case, crystal glasses sparkling in the candlelight*). *Flash* refers to a sudden and brilliant but short-lived outburst of light: *A bolt of lightning flashed across the horizon. Gleam* implies transient or constant light that often appears against a dark background: *"The light gleams an instant, then it's night once more"* (Samuel Beckett). *Glance* refers most often to light reflected obliquely: *Moonlight glanced off the windows of the darkened building. Glint* applies to briefly gleaming or flashing light: *Rays of sun glinted among the autumn leaves.* To *glisten* is to shine with a sparkling luster: *The snow glistened in the dawn light. Shimmer* means to shine with a soft, tremulous light: *"Everything about her shimmered and glimmered softly, as if her dress had been woven out of candlebeams"* (Edith Wharton). *Glimmer* refers to faint, fleeting light: *"On the French coast, the light/Gleams, and is gone; the cliffs of England stand,/Glimmering and vast, out in the tranquil bay"* (Matthew Arnold). To *twinkle* is to shine with quick, intermittent flashes or gleams: *"a few stars, twinkling faintly in the deep blue of the night sky"* (Hugh Walpole). *Scintillate* is applied to what flashes as if emitting sparks in a continuous stream: *"ammonium chloride . . . depositing minute scintillating crystals on the windowpanes"* (Primo Levi).

---

glitz *noun*
Informal Brilliant, showy splendor ► magnificence, resplendence, sparkle. *See* **glitter** (2).
glitzy *adjective*
Informal Tastelessly showy ► flashy, garish, loud. *See* **gaudy.**
gloaming *noun*
► eve, twilight. *See* **evening.**

gloat *verb*

1. To feel or express an uplifting joy over a success or victory ▸ glory, triumph. *See* **exult** (1). **2.** To be proud of oneself, as for an accomplishment or achievement ▸ congratulate, preen. *See* **pride.**

gloating *noun*

The act or condition of feeling an uplifting joy over a success or victory ▸ jubilance, jubilation, triumph. *See* **exultation.**

gloating *adjective*

Feeling or expressing an uplifting joy over a success or victory ▸ exultant, jubilant, triumphant. *See also* **boastful.**

glob *noun*

▸ bead, droplet. *See* **drop** (1).

global *adjective*

1. So pervasive and all-inclusive as to exist in or affect the whole world ▸ cosmic, worldwide. *See* **universal** (1). **2.** Covering a wide scope ▸ all-inclusive, broad, expansive. *See* **general** (2).

globe *noun*

1. The celestial body where humans live ▸ earth, orb, planet, world. **2.** A spherical object ▸ orb, sphere. *See* **ball** (1).

globetrotter *noun*

▸ jet-setter, traveler, vacationer. *See* **tourist.**

globular *or* **globoid** *adjective*

▸ annular, circular, spherical. *See* **round** (1).

globule *noun*

▸ bead, droplet. *See* **drop** (1).

gloom *noun*

1. Absence or deficiency of light ▸ darkness, murk, obscurity. *See* **dark** (1). **2.** A feeling or spell of dismally low spirits ▸ dejection, doldrums, melancholy. *See* **depression** (2).

gloom *verb*

1. To make dim ▸ blur, fog, obfuscate. *See* **obscure** (1). **2.** To make dark or darker ▸ darken, overcast, shadow. *See* **shade** (2).

gloomy *adjective*

1. Dark and depressing ▸ black, bleak, blue, cheerless, comfortless, dark, desolate, dismal, drear, dreary, dull, funereal, glum, joyless, murky, sepulchral, somber, stygian, tenebrific. **2.** Broodingly and sullenly unhappy ▸ morose, sour, sullen. *See* **glum** (1). **3.** In low spirits ▸ dejected, dispirited, heavy-hearted. *See* **depressed** (1). **4.** Causing or expressing sorrow ▸ cheerless, dispiriting, mournful. *See* **sorrowful** (1). **5.** Offering little encouragement ▸ dark, dismal, pessimistic. *See* **bleak** (2).

glorification *noun*

1. The act of raising to a high position or status or the condition of being so raised ▸ apotheosis, elevation. *See* **exaltation** (1). **2.** The honoring of a deity, as in worship ▸ extolment, magnification. *See* **praise** (2).

glorify *verb*

1. To raise to a high position or status ▸ elevate, magnify, uplift. *See* **exalt** (1). **2.** To pay tribute or homage to ▸ celebrate, exalt. *See* **honor** (1). **3.** To honor

a deity in religious worship ▸ extol, laud. *See* **praise** (3). **4.** To cause to be eminent or recognized ▸ dignify, exalt, honor. *See* **distinguish** (5).

glorious *adjective*

1. Marked by extraordinary beauty and splendor ▸ brilliant, dazzling, gorgeous, magnificent, proud, radiant, resplendent, shining, splendid, splendiferous, splendorous, wonderful, wondrous. *See also* **beautiful, grand, showy. 2.** Particularly excellent ▸ divine, fantastic, sensational. *See* **marvelous** (1). **3.** Widely known ▸ celebrated, illustrious, renowned. *See* **famous.**

glory *noun*

1. A height of achievement or acclaim ▸ brilliance, grandeur, grandiosity, grandness, greatness, magnificence, majesty, splendor. **2.** Wide recognition for one's deeds ▸ note, prestige, renown. *See* **fame. 3.** The honoring of a deity, as in worship ▸ extolment, magnification. *See* **praise** (2).

glory *verb*

To feel or express an uplifting joy over a success or victory ▸ crow, triumph. *See* **exult** (1).

gloss¹ *noun*

1. A surface shininess ▸ burnish, glaze, luster, polish, sheen, shine, sleekness, varnish. *See also* **finish. 2.** A deceptive outward appearance ▸ guise, mask, pretense. *See* **façade** (2).

gloss *verb*

1. To give a bright sheen or luster to ▸ buff, burnish, furbish, glaze, polish, shine, sleek, varnish. **2.** To give a deceptively attractive appearance to ▸ gild, sugarcoat, varnish. *See* **color** (4).

gloss over *verb*

1. To conceal or make light of a fault or offense ▸ explain away, whitewash. *See* **extenuate.** *See synonym note at* **extenuate. 2.** To fail to care for or give proper attention to ▸ ignore, slight. *See* **neglect** (1).

gloss² *noun*

Something that serves to explain or clarify ▸ explication, illumination. *See* **explanation** (1).

gloss *verb*

To make understandable ▸ decipher, interpret. *See* **explain** (1).

glossary *noun*

An alphabetical list of words often defined or translated ▸ dictionary, lexicon, vocabulary, wordbook.

glossy *adjective*

Having a high, radiant sheen ▸ brilliant, burnished, glassy, glazed, gleaming, glistening, lustrous, polished, shining, shiny. *See also* **sleek, sparkling.**

glow *verb*

1. To shine brightly and steadily but without a flame ▸ gleam, incandesce, luminesce. **2.** To emit a bright light ▸ burn, radiate. *See* **beam** (1). **3.** To become red in the face ▸ crimson, flush. *See* **blush.**

glow *noun*

1. A fresh rosy complexion ▸ bloom, blush, color, flush. *See also* **color, complexion. 2.** A feeling of pervasive emotional warmth ▸ flush, tingle. **3.** Electromagnetic radiation that makes vision possible ▸ lucency, luminescence. *See* **light**[1] (1).

glower *verb*

1. To wrinkle one's brow, as in thought, puzzlement, or displeasure ▸ frown, lower, scowl. *Idioms:* knit one's brow, look black, turn one's mouth down. *See synonym note at* **frown.** *See also* **grimace. 2.** To stare fixedly and angrily ▸ glare, lower, scowl. *Idioms:* give the evil eye, look daggers. *See also* **gaze, sneer.**

glower *noun*

1. A fixed angry stare ▸ glare, lower, scowl. *See also* **face, sneer. 2.** The act of wrinkling the brow, as in displeasure ▸ black look, lower, scowl. *See* **frown.**

glowing *adjective*

1. Of a healthy reddish color ▸ flushed, rosy, sanguine. *See* **ruddy. 2.** Fired with intense feeling ▸ burning, fervent, impassioned. *See* **passionate** (1). **3.** Giving off or reflecting much light ▸ brilliant, incandescent, radiant. *See* **bright** (1).

gloze *verb*

1. To conceal or make light of a fault or offense ▸ explain away, gloss over, gloze over. *See* **extenuate.** *See synonym note at* **extenuate. 2.** To give a deceptively attractive appearance to ▸ gild, sugarcoat, varnish. *See* **color** (4).

gluey *adjective*

▸ adhesive, gummy, tacky. *See* **sticky** (1).

glum *adjective*

1. Broodingly and sullenly unhappy ▸ dour, gloomy, low, moody, morose, sad, saturnine, sour, sulky, sullen, surly. *See also* **depressed, despondent, ill-tempered. 2.** Dark and depressing ▸ bleak, desolate, somber. *See* **gloomy** (1).

glumness *noun*

▸ dejection, doldrums, melancholy. *See* **depression** (2).

glut *verb*

1. To satisfy to the full or to excess ▸ engorge, surfeit. *See* **satiate. 2.** To swallow food or drink greedily or rapidly in large amounts ▸ engorge, gobble, guzzle. *See* **gulp** (1).

glut *noun*

A thing, amount, or quantity beyond what is needed, desired, or appropriate ▸ overflow, oversupply, superfluity. *See* **surplus.**

glutinous *adjective*

1. Having a heavy, gluey quality ▸ mucilaginous, viscid. *See* **viscous. 2.** Having the property of adhering ▸ adhesive, tacky. *See* **sticky** (1).

glutinousness *noun*

▸ sliminess, stickiness, thickness. *See* **viscosity.**

glutton *noun*

A person who eats or consumes immoderate amounts of food and drink ▸ hog, overeater, pig. *See also* **sybarite.**

gluttonous *adjective*

1. Wanting to eat or drink more than one can reasonably consume ▸ edacious, greedy, hoggish, piggish, ravenous, voracious. **2.** Having an insatiable appetite for an activity or pursuit ▸ rapacious, ravenous. *See* **voracious** (1). *See synonym note at* **voracious.**

gnash *verb*

1. To rub together noisily ▸ crunch, grind. **2.** To seize and grind with the teeth ▸ chomp, crunch, munch. *See* **chew.**

gnaw *verb*

1. To seize and grind with the teeth ▸ chomp, gnash, munch. *See* **chew.** *See synonym note at* **chew. 2.** To reduce gradually, as by chemical reaction, weather, or friction ▸ consume, corrode, wear (away *or* down). *See* **erode.**

gnawing *adjective*

▸ acute, gnawing, piercing. *See* **sharp** (8).

gnomic *adjective*

▸ compact, epigrammatic, pointed. *See* **pithy** (1).

go *verb*

1. To move away from a place ▸ depart, exit, get away, get off, go away, leave, pull out, quit, remove, retire, run (along *or* away), set forth (*or* off *or* out), withdraw. *Informal:* cut out, push off, shove off. *Slang:* blow, bug out (*or* off), split, take off, vamoose. *Idioms:* get going (*or* moving), hit the road, light out for the territory, make oneself scarce, make tracks, pull up stakes, take leave. **2.** To move along a particular course ▸ pass, proceed, push on, wend. *Idioms:* make (*or* wend) one's way. *See also* **advance, journey, rove. 3.** To proceed in a specified direction ▸ head, make, set out. *See* **bear** (5). **4.** To look to when in need ▸ refer, run, turn. *See* **resort** (1). *See synonym note at* **resort. 5.** To proceed on a certain course or for a certain distance ▸ reach, stretch. *See* **extend** (1). **6.** To act or operate in a specified way ▸ act, behave, work. *See synonym note at* **function. 7.** To change or fluctuate within limits ▸ cover, extend, range, run, vary. **8.** To journey over ▸ cross, traverse. *See* **cover** (2). **9.** To have a proper or suitable place ▸ belong, fit. **10.** To be depleted ▸ dry up, give out, run out. *Idioms:* go down the drain, go up in smoke. *See also* **disappear, exhaust, waste. 11.** To fall in ▸ collapse, give. *See* **buckle** (1). **12.** To cease living ▸ demise, expire, perish. *See* **die** (1). **13.** *Informal* To place something at risk, as in a game of chance ▸ bet, stake, wager. *See* **gamble** (2). **14.** *Informal* To make an offer of ▸ bid, offer. **15.** To be compatible or suitable ▸ chime, correspond, match. *See* **agree** (1).

go along *verb*

To agree to cooperate or participate ▸ *Informal:* play along.

go around *verb*

1. To become known far and wide ▸ circulate, get around, spread, travel. **2.** To pass around but not through ▸ circumnavigate, detour. *See* **skirt** (1). **3.** To rotate on an axis or around a center ▸ twirl, whirl, wheel. *See* **turn** (1).

go at *verb*

1. To start work on vigorously ▸ dive into, sail in, tackle. *See* **attack** (2). **2.** To set upon with violent force ▸ assail, assault, storm, strike. *See* **attack** (1).

go away *verb*
1. To move away from a place ▸ exit, leave, retire. *See* **go** (1). 2. To come to an end ▸ pass, pass away. *See also* **disappear.**

go back *verb*
To come back to a former condition ▸ come back, reoccur, revisit. *See* **return** (1).

go by *verb*
1. To move past in time ▸ lapse, pass away. *See* **elapse.** 2. To go to or seek out the company of someone in order to socialize ▸ drop by, look up, pop in. *See* **visit** (1).

go down *verb*
1. To undergo capture, defeat, or ruin ▸ collapse, fall, go under, topple. *See also* **succumb, surrender.** 2. To go beneath the surface or to the bottom of a liquid ▸ founder, gravitate. *See* **sink** (1). 3. To move downward in response to gravity ▸ descend, drop. *See* **fall** (1).

go for *verb*
1. To require a specified price ▸ cost, sell for. *See also* **demand.** 2. To achieve a certain price ▸ realize, sell for. *See* **bring** (2). 3. *Informal* To be favorably disposed toward ▸ favor, hold with. *See* **approve** (2). 4. *Informal* To receive pleasure from ▸ appreciate, savor. *See* **enjoy** (1).

go in *verb*
To come or go into a place ▸ come in, penetrate. *See* **enter** (1).

go off *verb*
To release or cause to release energy suddenly and violently, especially with a loud noise ▸ burst, detonate. *See* **explode** (1).

go on *verb*
1. To be in existence or in a certain state for an indefinitely long time ▸ continue, persist. *See* **endure** (2). 2. To put up with or continue despite difficulties ▸ keep on, persevere, soldier on. *See* **endure** (1). 3. *Informal* To talk rapidly on trivial matters ▸ blab, jabber, prattle. *See* **chatter** (1).

go out *verb*
To be with another person socially on a regular basis ▸ date, go with, see. *Informal:* take out. *Idioms:* go steady, go together.

go over *verb*
1. To turn out well ▸ pan out, work out. *See* **succeed** (2). 2. To look at or study carefully or critically ▸ investigate, peruse, scrutinize. *See* **examine** (1). 3. To give a recapitulation of the salient facts of ▸ abstract, recapitulate, summarize. *See* **review** (1). 4. To do or perform repeatedly so as to master ▸ exercise, run through. *See* **practice** (1). 5. To go to or seek out the company of someone in order to socialize ▸ drop by, look up, pop in. *See* **visit** (1).

go through *verb*
1. To participate in or partake of personally ▸ know, undergo. *See* **experience.** 2. To do or perform repeatedly so as to master ▸ exercise, run through. *See* **practice** (1).

go under *verb*
1. To undergo capture, defeat, or ruin ▸ collapse, fall, go down, topple. *See also* **succumb, surrender.** 2. To undergo sudden financial failure ▸ crash, fail. *See* **collapse** (2). 3. To go beneath the surface or to the bottom of a liquid ▸ founder, gravitate. *See* **sink** (1).

go up *verb*
To move upward along a slope or surface ▸ climb, mount, scramble. *See* **ascend** (1).

go with *verb*
1. To be with another person socially on a regular basis ▸ date, go out (with), see. *Informal:* take out. *Idioms:* go steady, go together. 2. To be suitable to or in keeping with ▸ become, befit, match. *See* **suit** (1). 3. To make a choice from a number of alternatives ▸ elect, pick (out), vote (for). *See* **choose** (1).

go *noun*
1. A trying to do or make something ▸ effort, trial. *Informal:* shot. *See* **attempt** (1). 2. A limited, often assigned period of activity, duty, or opportunity ▸ shift, stint, time. *See* **turn** (1). 3. *Informal* Capacity for work or vigorous activity ▸ might, potency, power. *See* **energy.**

goad *noun*
1. Something that causes an angry or resentful response ▸ incitement, trigger. *See* **provocation** (1). 2. Something that causes and encourages an action or response ▸ impulse, incentive. *See* **stimulus** (1).

goad *verb*
To stir to action or feeling ▸ excite, prod, trigger. *See* **provoke** (1).

go-ahead *adjective*
Informal Bold and confident in assertion ▸ aggressive, in-your-face. *See* **assertive.**

go-ahead *noun*
Informal The approving of an action, especially when done by one in authority ▸ authorization, consent, sanction. *See* **permission.**

goal *noun*
1. What one intends to do or achieve ▸ intent, objective. *See* **intention.** *See synonym note at* **intention.** 2. A fervent hope ▸ desire, wish. *See* **dream** (3).

goat *noun*
1. One who is made an object of blame ▸ whipping boy. *Slang:* fall guy. *See* **scapegoat.** 2. An immoral or licentious man ▸ gigolo, roué. *Slang:* lech. *See* **lecher.**

gob[1] *noun*
1. An irregularly shaped mass of indefinite size ▸ clod, wad. *See* **lump**[1] (1). 2. *Informal* An indeterminately great amount or number ▸ bunch, multiplicity. *Informal:* bushel. *See* **heap** (3).

gob[2] *noun*
Slang The opening in the body through which food is ingested ▸ chops. *Slang:* trap. *See* **mouth** (1).

gob[3] *noun*
Slang A person engaged in sailing or working on a ship ▸ mariner, navigator, seafarer. *See* **sailor.**

gobble *verb*
▸ englut, gorge, guzzle. *See* **gulp** (1).

gobbledygook *noun*
1. Highly technical, often deliberately deceptive language ▸ double talk, hocus-pocus, mumbo jumbo. *See* **gibberish** (1). 2. Empty or foolish talk ▸ blather, jabber, twaddle. *See* **babble** (1).

go-between *noun*
One who acts as an intermediate agent between persons or groups ▸ broker, contact, dealer, facilitator, interceder, intercessor, intermediary, intermediate, intermediator, mediator, middleman, negotiant, negotiator, ombudsman, troubleshooter. *See also* **agent, judge.**

go-by *noun*
▸ cut, shun, spurn. *See* **snub.**

goddess *noun*
▸ lovely, stunner. *See* **beauty** (1).

godforsaken *adjective*
▸ uninhabited, unpeopled, unpopulated. *See* **lonely** (1).

godless *adjective*
▸ disbelieving, faithless, irreligious. *See* **atheistic.**

godlessness *noun*
▸ disbelief, faithlessness, impiety. *See* **atheism.**

godlike *adjective*
▸ celestial, heavenly, holy. *See* **divine** (1).

godliness *noun*
▸ beatitude, sanctity. *See* **holiness.**

godly *adjective*
1. Deeply concerned with God and the beliefs and practice of religion ▸ devout, holy, religious. *See* **pious** (1). 2. Of, from, like, or being a god or God ▸ heavenly, holy. *See* **divine** (1).

God's country *noun*
▸ backwoods, hinterland. *See* **country** (1).

godsend *noun*
▸ fluke, fortune. *See* **luck** (1).

gofer *noun*
Slang A person who assists someone else, especially a person who assumes some of the duties of a superior ▸ aide, deputy, helper. *See* **assistant.**

go-getter *noun*
Informal An intensely energetic, enthusiastic person ▸ demon, dynamo, hustler. *Informal:* eager beaver, firebreather, live wire.

goggle *verb*
▸ gape, gawk, stare. *See* **gaze.**

going *noun*
The act of leaving ▸ embarkation, exodus, withdrawal. *See* **departure** (1).

going *adjective*
In action or full operation ▸ functioning, operating, working. *See* **active** (1).

going-over *noun*
▸ analysis, checkup, inspection, scrutiny. *See* **examination** (1).

goldbrick *verb*
▸ loiter, lounge, slack off. *See* **idle** (1).

golden ager *noun*
▸ elder, senior citizen. *See* **senior** (2).

golden-haired *adjective*
▸ blond, fair-haired. *See* **fair**[1] (8).

Goliath *noun*
▸ behemoth, monster, titan. *See* **giant.**

gone *adjective*
1. Not present ▸ away, missing, truant. *See* **absent** (1). 2. No longer in one's possession ▸ mislaid, missing. *See* **lost** (2). 3. No longer alive ▸ deceased, departed, perished. *See* **dead** (1). 4. *Slang* Affected with intense romantic attraction ▸ enamored, smitten. *See* **infatuated.** 5. *Slang* Carrying a developing fetus within the uterus ▸ expectant, parturient. *See* **pregnant** (1).

goner *noun*
Slang One that is ruined or doomed ▸ dead duck, dead meat, toast. *See also* **through.**

good *adjective*
1. Having pleasant desirable qualities ▸ bonny, dandy, decent, enjoyable, fine, jolly, nice, worthy. *Informal:* all-right. *See also* **choice, excellent.** 2. In excellent condition ▸ entire, flawless, intact, perfect, sound, unblemished, unbroken, undamaged, unharmed, unhurt, unimpaired, uninjured, unmarred, whole. 3. No less than; at least ▸ full, round, whole. 4. Giving or affording pleasure or enjoyment ▸ agreeable, gratifying, welcome. *See* **pleasant** (1). 5. Suited to one's purpose ▸ expedient, proper, suitable. *See* **convenient** (1). 6. Affording benefit or advantage ▸ favorable, helpful, propitious. *See* **beneficial.** 7. Having sufficient ability or resources ▸ capable, competent, skillful. *See* **able.** 8. Not counterfeit or copied ▸ genuine, true. *Slang:* legit, kosher. *See* **authentic** (1). 9. Above average in amount, size, or scope ▸ extensive, large, sizable. *See* **big** (1). 10. Indicative of future success or full of promise ▸ bright, fortunate, propitious. *See* **favorable** (1). 11. Beyond reproach ▸ faultless, unblamable. *See* **exemplary** (1). 12. Marked by uprightness in principle and action ▸ honorable, righteous. *See* **honest** (1). 13. Characterized by kindness and concern for others ▸ beneficent, goodhearted, kindly. *See* **benevolent** (1).

good *noun*
1. The quality or state of being morally sound ▸ goodness, morality, probity, rectitude, righteousness, rightfulness, rightness, uprightness, virtue, virtuousness. *See also* **ethic.** 2. A product or products bought and sold in commerce ▸ commodity, goods, inventory, line, merchandise, stock, ware, wares. *See also* **product.** 3. Something that contributes to or increases one's well-being ▸ advantage, benefit, interests. *See* **interest** (1).

goodbye *interjection*
Used upon taking leave ▸ farewell, fare-thee-well. *Informal:* adiós, auf Wiedersehen, au revoir, ciao, hasta mañana, later, see you, so long, take care. *Idioms:* go in peace (*or* with God), see (*or* catch) you later

goodbye *noun*
The act of leaving ▸ adieu, exit, farewell. *See* **departure** (1).

goodbye *adjective*
Of, done, given, or said on departing ▸ farewell, valedictory. *See* **parting.**

good deed *noun*
▸ grace, kindness. *See* **favor** (1).

good-for-nothing *noun*
1. *Informal* A self-indulgent person who avoids work ▸ bum, idler, loafer. *See* **wastrel** (2). 2. A person or group of people regarded as worthless or contemptible ▸ dregs, rabble, ragtag and bobtail. *See* **riffraff.**

good-for-nothing *adjective*
Lacking worth ▸ empty, valueless. *See* **worthless** (1).

goodhearted *adjective*
▸ beneficent, kindly. *See* **benevolent** (1).

goodish *adjective*
▸ average, decent, moderate. *See* **acceptable** (2).

good-looking *adjective*
▸ comely, gorgeous, stunning. *See* **beautiful.**

goodly *adjective*
▸ extensive, large, sizable. *See* **big** (1).

good name *noun*
▸ dignity, reputation. *See* **honor** (2).

good-natured *adjective*
▸ cordial, friendly, genial. *See* **amiable.** *See synonym note at* **amiable.**

goodness *noun*
▸ probity, rectitude, virtue. *See* **good** (1).

good report *noun*
▸ good name, reputation. *See* **honor** (2).

goods *noun*
1. One's portable property ▸ belongings, personal effects, property. *See* **effects.** 2. A product or products bought and sold in commerce ▸ line, merchandise, ware. *See* **good** (2).

good-tempered *adjective*
▸ cordial, friendly, genial. *See* **amiable.**

good turn *noun*
▸ grace, kindness. *See* **favor** (1).

goodwill *noun*
▸ altruism, kindheartedness, philanthropy. *See* **benevolence** (1).

goody *noun*
Informal Something fine and delicious, especially a food ▸ morsel, treat. *See* **delicacy** (1).

gooey *adjective*
1. Having the property of adhering ▸ gluey, gummy. *See* **sticky** (1). 2. *Informal* Affectedly or extravagantly emotional ▸ gushy, mawkish, soft. *See* **sentimental.**

goof *noun*
1. *Slang* A person who is deficient in judgment and good sense ▸ idiot, imbecile, nitwit. *See* **fool** (1). 2. *Slang* A stupid, clumsy mistake ▸ bungle, fumble, solecism. *See* **blunder.**

goof *verb*
Slang To pass time without working or in avoiding work ▸ bum (around), loiter, lounge. *See* **idle** (1).

goof up *verb*
1. *Slang* To ruin through clumsiness or ineptness ▸ blunder, foul up, spoil. *See* **botch.** 2. To make an error or mistake ▸ blunder, stumble. *See* **err** (1).

goofiness *noun*
Slang Foolish behavior ▸ folly, silliness, tomfoolery. *See* **foolishness.**

goofy *adjective*
Slang Displaying a lack of forethought and good sense ▸ daft, idiotic, ludicrous. *See* **foolish.**

goon *noun*
1. *Slang* A person who treats others violently or roughly ▸ hoodlum, ruffian, tough. *See* **thug.** 2. *Slang* A large, ungainly, and dull-witted person ▸ lout, ox. *Informal:* lummox. *See* **oaf.**

goose *noun*
Informal A person who is deficient in judgment and good sense ▸ idiot, imbecile, nitwit. *See* **fool** (1).

gore *verb*
▸ bayonet, incise, pierce, slash. *See* **cut** (1).

gorge *verb*
1. To satisfy to the full or excess ▸ engorge, surfeit. *See* **satiate.** 2. To swallow (food or drink) greedily or rapidly in large amounts ▸ gobble, guzzle. *See* **gulp** (1).

gorge *noun*
An elongated lowland between mountains or hills ▸ canyon, dale. *See* **valley.**

gorgeous *adjective*
1. Having qualities that delight the eye ▸ comely, good-looking, stunning. *See* **beautiful.** 2. Marked by extraordinary beauty and splendor ▸ magnificent, resplendent, splendid. *See* **glorious** (1).

gorgeousness *noun*
▸ magnificence, resplendence, sparkle. *See* **glitter** (2).

gorilla *noun*
Slang A person who treats others violently or roughly ▸ hoodlum, ruffian, tough. *See* **thug.**

gory *adjective*
1. Of or covered with blood ▸ bleeding, hemorrhaging. *See* **bloody** (1). 2. Marked by or giving rise to murder or bloodshed ▸ homicidal, sanguineous, slaughterous. *See* **murderous.**

gospel *noun*
▸ belief, dogma, teaching. *See* **doctrine.**

gossamer *or* **gossamery** *adjective*
▸ ethereal, gauzy, vaporous. *See* **sheer**^{2} (1). *See synonym note at* **sheer**^{2}.

gossip *noun*
1. Idle, often sensational and groundless talk about others ▸ gossipry, hearsay, prattle, report, rumor, scandal, slander, talebearing, talk, tattle, tittle-tattle, word. *Slang:* scuttlebutt. 2. A person habitually engaged in idle talk about others ▸ bigmouth, blab, chatterbox, gossiper, gossipmonger, newsmonger, rumormonger, scandalmonger, snoop, tabby, talebearer, taleteller, tattle, tattler, tattletale, telltale, whisperer. *Slang:* yenta. *See also* **busybody.**

gossip *verb*
To engage in or spread gossip ▸ blab, chatter, jabber, noise, prattle, rumor, talk, tattle, tittle-tattle, whisper.
Idioms: dish the dirt, spread a story, tell tales, tell tales out of school.

✦ CORE SYNONYMS: *gossip, blab, tattle.* These verbs mean to engage in or communicate idle, often sensational and groundless talk about others: *gossiping about the neighbors; can't keep a secret—he always blabs; is disliked for tattling on mischief-makers.*

---

gossiper *or* **gossipmonger** *noun*
▸ bigmouth, taleteller, whisperer. *See* **gossip** (2).

gossipry *noun*
▸ hearsay, rumor, tattle. *See* **gossip** (1).

gossipy *adjective*
Inclined to gossip ▸ blabby, talebearing, taletelling.

gouge *verb*
1. *Slang* To get money or something else from someone by deceitful trickery ▸ bilk, defraud, swindle. *See* **cheat** (1). **2.** To penetrate with a sharp edge ▸ bayonet, incise, pierce, slash. *See* **cut** (1). **3.** To break, turn over, or remove (earth or sand, for example) with or as if with a tool ▸ burrow, scoop, shovel. *See* **dig** (1).

gouge *noun*
An opening made with a sharp object ▸ groove, nick, notch. *See* **cut** (1).

govern *verb*
1. To control the functioning or outcome of ▸ control, determine, establish, fix, guide, regulate. **2.** To have charge of the affairs of others ▸ direct, manage, rule. *See* **administer** (1).

governable *adjective*
Capable of being governed ▸ administrable, controllable, manageable, rulable. *See also* **loyal, obedient.**

governance *noun*
▸ control, ministry, rule. *See* **government** (1).

governing *adjective*
▸ key, predominant, reigning. *See* **dominant** (1).

government *noun*
1. The continuous exercise of authority over a political unit ▸ administration, command, control, direction, governance, rule. *See also* **authority. 2.** A group of people who govern a political unit ▸ administration, authorities, ministry, officials, regime, state. *Idiom:* powers that be. *See also* **state. 3.** The act or process of management ▸ administration, direction, supervision. *See* **management** (1).

governmental *adjective*
1. Of or relating to government ▸ bureaucratic, gubernatorial, legislative, official, political, regulatory. **2.** Of, for, or relating to administration or administrators ▸ executive, managerial, organizational. *See* **administrative.**

governor *noun*
▸ boss, director, head, leader. *See* **chief** (1).

gown *noun*
▸ jumper, pinafore. *See* **dress** (3).

grab *verb*
1. To get hold of something moving ▸ seize, snatch. *See* **catch** (2). **2.** To take firmly with the hand and maintain a hold on ▸ clasp, clutch, grip. *See* **grasp** (1). **3.** To lay claim to or take possession of ▸ appropriate,

confiscate, snatch. *See* **seize** (1). **4.** *Informal* To compel the attention, interest, or imagination of ▸ captivate, fascinate, mesmerize. *See* **grip** (1).

grab *noun*
1. The act of catching ▸ seizure, snatch. *See* **catch** (1). **2.** The act of taking possession of something ▸ expropriation, preemption, usurpation. *See* **seizure** (2).

grab bag *noun*
Slang A collection of various things ▸ hodgepodge, jumble, mishmash. *See* **assortment** (1).

grabbiness *noun*
▸ acquisitiveness, avarice, covetousness. *See* **greed.**

grabble *verb*
▸ fumble, scrabble. *See* **grope.**

grabby *adjective*
Informal Having a strong urge to obtain or retain something, especially material wealth ▸ acquisitive, avaricious, covetous. *See* **greedy** (1).

grace *noun*
1. Refinement of manner, form, and style ▸ polish, sophistication, taste. *See* **elegance. 2.** Skillfulness in the use of the hands or body ▸ deftness, facility. *See* **dexterity** (1). **3.** A sense of rightness ▸ conscience, properness. *See* **decency** (1). **4.** Kindly, charitable interest in others ▸ goodwill, kindheartedness, philanthropy. *See* **benevolence** (1). **5.** Kind, forgiving, or compassionate treatment of or disposition toward others ▸ clemency, lenience. *See* **mercy. 6.** A kindly act ▸ good turn, kindness. *See* **favor** (1). **7.** Temporary immunity from penalties ▸ exemption, immunity, reprieve, respite. *See also* **delay. 8.** A short prayer said at meals ▸ benediction, blessing, thanks, thanksgiving. *See also* **prayer¹. 9.** The quality of being or acting in accordance with what is holy or sacred ▸ beatitude, sanctity. *See* **holiness.**

grace *verb*
1. To lend dignity or honor to by an act or favor ▸ enrich, favor, dignify, honor. *See also* **distinguish, exalt, honor. 2.** To endow with beauty and elegance ▸ beautify, embellish, enhance, set off. *See also* **adorn.**

graceful *adjective*
1. Exhibiting refined, tasteful beauty of manner, form, or style ▸ exquisite, refined. *See* **elegant** (1). **2.** Marked by facility of expression ▸ effortless, flowing. *See* **fluent. 3.** Pleasing to the eye or mind ▸ enchanting, fetching, lovely, winsome. *See* **attractive** (1). **4.** Showing sensitivity and skill in dealing with others ▸ diplomatic, sensitive, tactful. *See* **delicate** (2).

graceless *adjective*
▸ gawky. *Slang:* klutzy. *See* **awkward** (1).

gracious *adjective*
1. Characterized by kindness and warm, unaffected courtesy ▸ affable, courteous, hospitable. *See also* **amiable, attentive, courteous. 2.** Characterized by elaborate, usually formal courtesy ▸ chivalrous, circumstantial, courtly, diplomatic, elegant, gallant, genteel, stately. *See also* **ceremonious.**

graciousness *noun*
▸ civility, pleasantry, politeness. *See* **amenities** (2).

gradation *noun*
▸ hue, nuance, subtlety. *See* **shade** (1). *See synonym note at* **shade**.

gradational *adjective*
Proceeding steadily by degrees ▸ gradual, piecemeal, progressive, step-by-step. *Idioms:* one foot after another, one step at a time. *See also* **consecutive, methodical, slow**.

grade *noun*
1. One of the units in a course, as on an ascending or descending scale ▸ interval, level, step. *See* **degree** (1). **2.** Degree of excellence ▸ caliber, class, quality. **3.** A division of persons or things by quality or rank ▸ league, rank, tier. *See* **class** (2). **4.** Deviation from a particular direction ▸ cant, heel. *See* **inclination** (2). **5.** An upward path or surface ▸ gradient, rise, slant. *See* **ascent** (2).

grade *verb*
1. To evaluate and assign a grade to ▸ correct, mark, score. **2.** To arrange according to class ▸ categorize, class, group. *See* **classify**.

gradient *noun*
1. Deviation from a particular direction ▸ grade, heel. *See* **inclination** (2). **2.** An upward path or surface ▸ inclined plane, rise, slant. *See* **ascent** (2).

gradual *adjective*
1. Proceeding steadily by degrees ▸ gradational, piecemeal, progressive, step-by-step. *Idioms:* one foot after another, one step at a time. *See also* **consecutive, methodical, slow**. **2.** Not steep or abrupt ▸ easy, even, gentle, mild, moderate, steady.

gradually *adverb*
In a gradual manner ▸ by degrees, in stages, piecemeal, progressively. *Idioms:* bit by bit, inch by inch, slowly but surely, step by step.

graft *noun*
1. Money or a favor given as inducement to dishonest behavior ▸ fix. *Informal:* payoff. *See* **bribe**. **2.** Goods or property seized unlawfully ▸ booty, loot. *See* **plunder**.

graft *verb*
To obtain by coercion or intimidation ▸ blackmail, squeeze, wrest. *See* **extort**.

grain *noun*
1. A fertilized plant ovule capable of germinating ▸ kernel, pip, pit, seed. **2.** A tiny amount ▸ dash, drop, smidgen. *See* **bit**[1] (1). **3.** A distinctive, complex underlying pattern or structure ▸ fabric, fiber, web. *See* **texture** (1). **4.** A basic trait or set of traits that define and establish the character of something ▸ being, quintessence. *See* **essence** (1).

grainy *adjective*
▸ granular, gritty. *See* **coarse** (4).

grand *adjective*
1. Impressive in size, proportion, or appearance ▸ august, awe-inspiring, awesome, baronial, elegant, grandiose, great, imperial, imposing, lordly, magnific, magnificent, majestic, marvelous, noble, palatial, princely, regal, royal, splendid, stately, sublime, superb. *See also* **big, excellent, luxurious**. **2.** Exceedingly dignified in form, tone, or style ▸ eloquent, exalted. *See* **elevated** (5). **3.** Raised to or occupying a high position or rank ▸ elevated, lofty. *See* **exalted** (1). **4.** Having great significance ▸ consequential, earth-shaking, meaningful. *See* **important** (1).

✦ **CORE SYNONYMS:** *grand, magnificent, imposing, stately, majestic, august, grandiose*. These adjectives mean impressively large in size, proportion, or appearance. Both *grand* and *magnificent* apply to what is physically or aesthetically impressive. *Grand* implies dignity, sweep, or eminence: *a grand hotel lobby with marble floors*. *Magnificent* suggests splendor, sumptuousness, and grandeur: *a magnificent cathedral*. *Imposing* describes what impresses by virtue of its size, bearing, or power: *mountain peaks of imposing height*. *Stately* refers principally to what is dignified and handsome: *a stately oak*. *Majestic* suggests lofty dignity or nobility: *the majestic Alps*. *August* describes what inspires solemn reverence or awe: *the august presence of royalty*. *Grandiose* often suggests pretentiousness, affectation, or pompousness: *grandiose ideas*.

---

grandeur *noun*
▸ grandness, magnificence, splendor. *See* **glory** (1).

grandiloquence *noun*
▸ fustian, rant. *See* **bombast**.

grandiloquent *adjective*
▸ bombastic, declamatory, rhetorical. *See* **oratorical**.

grandiose *adjective*
1. Impressive in size, proportion, or appearance ▸ imposing, magnificent, splendid. *See* **grand** (1). *See synonym note at* **grand**. **2.** Characterized by an exaggerated show of dignity or self-importance ▸ hoity-toity, pretentious. *See* **pompous**.

grandioseness *noun*
▸ ostentation, pomposity, pretentiousness. *See* **pretentiousness**.

grandiosity *noun*
1. A height of achievement or acclaim ▸ grandness, magnificence, splendor. *See* **glory** (1). **2.** Boastful self-importance or display ▸ ostentation, pomposity, pretentiousness. *See* **pretentiousness**.

grandness *noun*
▸ grandeur, magnificence, splendor. *See* **glory** (1).

grant *verb*
1. To let have as a favor, prerogative, or privilege ▸ accord, award, concede, give, vouchsafe. *See also* **yield**. **2.** To give formally or officially ▸ award, bestow, impart. *See* **confer** (2). **3.** To change the ownership of property by means of a legal document ▸ assign, deed, sign over. *See* **transfer** (1). **4.** To admit to the reality or truth of ▸ admit, concede. *See* **acknowledge** (1). **5.** To present as a gift to a charity or cause ▸ bequeath, pledge. *See* **donate** (1).

grant *noun*
1. Money or other resources granted for a particular purpose ▸ appropriation, budget, subsidy, subvention. **2.** Legal transfer of ownership or title ▸ alienation, assignment, conveyance, transfer, transferal.

3. Something given to a charity or cause ▸ benefaction, contribution, offering. *See* **donation. 4.** The act of conferring, as of an honor ▸ bestowal, conference, conferral. *See* **conferment.**

grantor *noun*
▸ benefactor, contributor, patron. *See* **donor.**

granular *adjective*
▸ grainy, gritty. *See* **coarse** (4).

granulate *verb*
▸ atomize, grind, mill. *See* **crush** (2).

graph *verb*
▸ chart, lay out. *See* **plot** (1).

graphic *adjective*
1. Depicted in sharp and accurate detail ▸ explicit, lifelike, lucid, photographic, pictorial, picturesque, realistic, uncompromising, vivid. *See also* **accurate, clear, detailed. 2.** Evoking strong mental images through distinctiveness ▸ colorful, picturesque, striking, vivid. **3.** Of or relating to representation by means of writing ▸ calligraphic, scriptural, written. **4.** Of or relating to representation by drawings or pictures ▸ hieroglyphic, illustrative, photographic, pictographic, pictorial, symbolic. **5.** Serving to describe ▸ delineative, representative. *See* **descriptive.**

✛ **CORE SYNONYMS:** *graphic, lifelike, realistic, vivid.* These adjectives mean strikingly sharp and accurate in detail: *a graphic account of the battle; a lifelike portrait; a realistic description; a vivid recollection of her childhood.*

---

grapnel *noun*
▸ brake, dowel, mooring. *See* **anchor** (1).

grapple *verb*
1. To take firmly with the hand and maintain a hold on ▸ clutch, grab, grip. *See* **grasp** (1). **2.** To strive in opposition ▸ scuffle, tussle, wrestle. *See* **contend** (1).

grapple *noun*
An act or means of holding something ▸ clench, grasp. *See* **hold** (1).

grasp *verb*
1. To take firmly with the hand and maintain a hold on ▸ clasp, clench, clutch, fist, grab, grapple, grip, seize. *Idioms:* grab ahold (*or* hold) of. *See also* **handle. 2.** To perceive directly with the intellect ▸ compass, comprehend, fathom. *See* **know** (1). **3.** To perceive and recognize the meaning of ▸ apprehend, fathom, sense. *See* **understand** (1). **4.** To take in and incorporate, especially mentally ▸ assimilate, digest, imbibe, learn. *See* **absorb** (2).

grasp *noun*
1. Firm control or influence ▸ grip, handle, hold. *See also* **control, dominance. 2.** The ability or power to seize or attain ▸ capacity, compass, range, reach, scope. *See also* **influence. 3.** Intellectual hold ▸ apprehension, comprehension, grip, hold, understanding. *See also* **knowledge. 4.** An act or means of holding something ▸ clench, grip. *See* **hold** (1).

grasping *adjective*
▸ avaricious, covetous, hungry. *See* **greedy** (1).

graspingness *noun*
▸ avarice, covetousness, rapacity. *See* **greed.**

grate¹ *verb*
1. To bring or come into abrasive contact, often with a harsh sound ▸ abrade, rasp. *See* **scrape** (2). **2.** To pull or cut into many pieces ▸ cut up, slice up. *See* **shred.**

grate² *noun*
An open space for holding a fire at the base of a chimney ▸ fireplace, hearth, ingle.

grateful *adjective*
1. Showing or feeling gratitude ▸ appreciative, thankful. **2.** Giving or affording pleasure or enjoyment ▸ agreeable, pleasing, welcome. *See* **pleasant** (1). **3.** Owing something, such as gratitude, to another ▸ beholden, indebted, obligated. *See* **obliged** (1).

gratefulness *noun*
▸ gratitude, thankfulness. *See* **appreciation** (1).

gratification *noun*
The condition of being satisfied ▸ contentedness, contentment, fulfilment, satisfaction. *See also* **happiness, satiation.**

gratified *adjective*
Having achieved satisfaction, as of one's goal ▸ content, fulfilled, happy, satisfied.

gratify *verb*
1. To give great or keen pleasure to ▸ enchant, overjoy, pleasure. *See* **delight** (1). *See synonym note at* **delight. 2.** To grant or have what is demanded by a need or desire ▸ fulfill, indulge. *See* **satisfy** (2). **3.** To comply with the wishes or ideas of another ▸ cater (to), humor, indulge. *See also* **defer.**

gratifying *adjective*
▸ agreeable, satisfying, welcome. *See* **pleasant** (1).

grating *adjective*
▸ dry, jarring. *See* **harsh** (1).

gratis *adjective*
Costing nothing ▸ free, complimentary, gratuitous. *Idioms:* as a freebie, for free, for nothing, on the house.

gratitude *noun*
▸ acknowledgment, indebtedness, thankfulness. *See* **appreciation** (1).

gratuitous *adjective*
1. Costing nothing ▸ free, complimentary, gratis. *Idioms:* as a freebie, for free, for nothing, on the house. **2.** Not required, necessary, or warranted by the circumstances of the case ▸ supererogative, supererogatory, uncalled-for. *See* **wanton** (2).

gratuity *noun*
1. A material favor or gift, usually money, given in return for service ▸ baksheesh, cumshaw, largess, perquisite, tip. *Informal:* perk. *See also* **reward. 2.** Something given to a charity or cause ▸ benefaction, contribution, offering. *See* **donation.**

grave¹ *noun*
A burial place or receptacle for human remains ▸ burial chamber, burial plot, catacomb, cinerarium, crypt, gravesite, mausoleum, ossuary, sepulcher, sepulture, tomb, vault.

grave² *adjective*

1. Having great consequence or weight ▸ earnest, heavy, momentous, serious, severe, weighty. *See also* **important.** 2. Having or threatening severe negative consequences ▸ dire, grievous, serious, severe. *See also* **disastrous.** 3. Bringing or predicting misfortune ▸ dire, ominous, portentous. *See* **fateful** (1). 4. Characterized by careful thought and a lack of frivolity or exaggeration: ▸ earnest, sober, solemn. *See* **serious** (1). *See synonym note at* **serious.** 5. Involving possible risk, loss, or injury ▸ chancy, hazardous, risky. *See* **dangerous.**

grave³ *verb*

1. To cut a design or inscription into a hard surface, especially for printing ▸ etch, incise. *See* **engrave** (1). 2. To produce a deep impression of ▸ fix, imprint. *See* **engrave** (2).

gravelly *adjective*

1. Consisting of or covered with large particles ▸ granular, gritty. *See* **coarse** (4). 2. Rough, raw, or grating in sound ▸ gruff, husky. *See* **hoarse** (1).

graveness *noun*

1. The condition of being grave and of involving serious consequences ▸ gravity, momentousness, seriousness, weightiness. 2. The quality of being dignified and serious, as in manner or bearing ▸ dignity, sobriety, solemnity. *See* **seriousness** (1).

gravid *adjective*

▸ expectant, parturient. *See* **pregnant** (1).

gravidity *or* **gravidness** *noun*

The condition of carrying a developing fetus within the uterus ▸ gestation, parturiency, pregnancy.

gravitas *noun*

▸ graveness, sobriety, solemnity. *See* **seriousness** (1).

gravitate *verb*

▸ founder, go down, settle. *See* **sink** (1).

gravitation *noun*

▸ allure, draw, magnetism. *Informal:* pull. *See* **attraction** (1).

gravity *noun*

1. The condition of being grave and of involving serious consequences ▸ graveness, gravity, heaviness, momentousness, seriousness, weightiness. *See also* **severity.** 2. The quality of being dignified and serious, as in manner or bearing ▸ graveness, sobriety, solemnity. *See* **seriousness** (1).

gray *adjective*

▸ lackluster, mat, muddy. *See* **dull** (2).

gray matter *noun*

1. *Informal* The seat of the faculty of intelligence and reason ▸ brain, mind. *See also* **imagination.** 2. *Informal* The faculty of thinking, reasoning, and applying knowledge ▸ intellect, mentality, understanding. *See* **intelligence** (1).

graze¹ *verb*

1. To make light and momentary contact with, as in passing ▸ flick, kiss, skim. *See* **brush¹.** *See synonym note at* **brush¹.** 2. To strike a surface at such an angle as to be deflected ▸ fly off, ricochet. *See* **glance** (1).

graze *noun*

Light and momentary contact with another person or thing ▸ flick, skim. *See* **brush¹** (1).

graze² *verb*

To feed on vegetation ▸ crop, pasture. *See* **browse** (2).

grease *noun*

1. A substance that is generally slippery, combustible, and not water soluble ▸ lube, petroleum. *See* **oil** (1). 2. *Slang* Money or a favor given as inducement to dishonest behavior ▸ graft. *Informal:* payoff. *See* **bribe.**

grease *verb*

1. To apply oil to something ▸ anoint, lube. *See* **oil.** 2. To make less difficult ▸ facilitate, help along. *See* **ease** (2).

greasy *adjective*

▸ adipose, unctuous. *See* **fatty** (1).

great *adjective*

1. Above average in amount, size, or scope ▸ extensive, large, sizable. *See* **big** (1). *See synonym note at* **big.** 2. Impressive in size, proportion, or appearance ▸ imposing, magnificent, splendid. *See* **grand** (1). 3. *Informal* Exceptionally good of its kind ▸ first-rate, prime, splendid, tiptop. *See* **excellent.** 4. At the upper end of a degree of measure ▸ elevated, high, large. *See also* **exalted, extreme.** 5. *Informal* Particularly excellent ▸ fantastic, sensational, superb. *See* **marvelous** (1). 6. Resulting from or affecting one's innermost feelings ▸ heartfelt, strong. *See* **deep** (3). 7. Widely known ▸ eminent, noted, renowned. *See* **famous.** 8. Having great significance ▸ consequential, grand, meaningful. *See* **important** (1).

greater *adjective*

1. Being at a rank or level above another ▸ higher, senior, superior, upper. 2. Much more than half ▸ largest, most. *See* **best** (2).

great-hearted *adjective*

▸ big-hearted, magnanimous, unselfish. *See* **generous** (1).

great-heartedness *noun*

▸ magnanimity, munificence, unselfishness. *See* **generosity.**

greatly *adverb*

▸ acutely, extremely, highly. *See* **very.**

greatness *noun*

1. The quality or state of being large in amount, extent, or importance ▸ bigness, largeness. *See* **size** (2). 2. A height of achievement or acclaim ▸ grandness, magnificence, splendor. *See* **glory** (1).

greed *noun*

Excessive desire for more than one needs or deserves ▸ acquisitiveness, avarice, avariciousness, avidity, covetousness, cupidity, graspingness, hoggishness, rapacity. *Informal:* grabbiness. *See also* **voracity.**

greedy *adjective*

1. Having a strong urge to obtain or retain something, especially material wealth ▸ acquisitive, avaricious, avid, covetous, grasping, hungry. *Informal:* grabby. *See also* **egotistic, stingy.** 2. Wanting to eat or drink more than one can reasonably consume ▸ rav-

enous, voracious. *See* **gluttonous** (1). **3.** Having an insatiable appetite for an activity or pursuit ▸ rapacious, ravenous. *See* **voracious** (1).

green *noun*
1. A tract of land set aside for public use ▸ park, plaza, square. *See* **common**. **2.** *Slang* Something, such as coins or printed bills, used as a medium of exchange ▸ currency. *Slang:* dough, moola. *See* **money** (1).

green *adjective*
1. Being in an early period of growth or development ▸ immature, juvenile. *See* **young**. *See synonym note at* **young**. **2.** Lacking experience and the knowledge gained from it ▸ inexpert, uninitiated, unpracticed. *See* **inexperienced**. **3.** Having a taste characteristic of that produced by acids ▸ sharp, tart. *See* **sour** (1).

green-eyed *adjective*
1. Resentfully or painfully desirous of another's advantages ▸ invidious, jealous. *See* **envious**. **2.** Fearful of the loss of position or affection ▸ clinging, clutching, jealous, possessive.

greenhorn *noun*
▸ fledgling, neophyte, novice. *See* **beginner**.

green light *noun*
Informal The approving of an action, especially when done by one in authority ▸ authorization, consent, sanction. *See* **permission**.

greenness *noun*
1. The time of life between childhood and maturity ▸ juvenility, puberty. *See* **youth** (1). **2.** Lack of experience and the knowledge gained from it ▸ immaturity, inexpertness, rawness. *See* **inexperience**.

greet *verb*
1. To address in a friendly and respectful way ▸ hail, salute, welcome. **2.** To approach for the purpose of speech ▸ accost, hail, salute. *See also* **encounter, interrupt, welcome**.

greeting *noun*
An expression, in words or gestures, marking a meeting of persons ▸ hail, salutation, salute, welcome. *Informal:* hello.

greetings *interjection*
▸ good day, salutations. *Informal:* hey. *See* **hello**.

gregarious *adjective*
1. Disposed to be open, sociable, and talkative ▸ extroverted, unreserved. *See* **outgoing**. **2.** Enjoying company ▸ convivial, sociable. *See* **social** (1). *See synonym note at* **social**.

griddle *verb*
▸ bake, brown, toast. *See* **cook** (1).

gridlock *noun*
▸ immobilization, jam, tie-up. *See* **stop** (2).

grief *noun*
1. Mental anguish or pain caused by loss or despair ▸ anguish, heartache, heartbreak, sorrow, torment. **2.** A state of physical or mental suffering ▸ agony, misery, wretchedness. *See* **distress** (1).

✦ CORE SYNONYMS: *grief, sorrow, anguish, heartache, heartbreak*. These nouns denote mental anguish or pain caused by loss or despair. *Grief* is deep, acute personal sadness, as that arising from irreplaceable loss: *"Grief fills the room up of my absent child,/Lies in his bed, walks up and down with me"* (William Shakespeare). *Sorrow* connotes sadness caused by misfortune, affliction, or loss; it can also imply contrition: *"sorrow for his . . . children, who needed his protection, and whom he could not protect"* (James Baldwin). *Anguish* implies agonizing, excruciating mental pain: *"I pray that our heavenly Father may assuage the anguish of your bereavement"* (Abraham Lincoln). *Heartache* most often applies to sustained private sorrow: *The child's difficulties are a source of heartache to the parents. Heartbreak* is overwhelming grief: *"Better a little chiding than a great deal of heartbreak"* (Shakespeare).

◂ ANTONYM: *joy*

grievance *noun*
1. An expression of pain or dissatisfaction ▸ carp, whimper, whine. *See* **complaint** (1). **2.** An expression of opposition ▸ argument, exception, protestation. *See* **objection**.

grieve *verb*
1. To feel, show, or express grief ▸ anguish, bemoan, bewail, lament, mourn, sorrow, suffer, ululate. *See also* **cry, regret**. **2.** To cause emotional suffering or painful sorrow to ▸ disturb, hurt, trouble. *See* **distress** (1).

✦ CORE SYNONYMS: *grieve, lament, mourn, sorrow*. These verbs mean to feel, show, or express grief, sadness, or regret: *grieved over our father's death; lamenting about the decline in academic standards; mourns for lost hopes; sorrowed by the level of poverty.*

◂ ANTONYM: *rejoice*

grievous *adjective*
1. Having or threatening severe negative consequences ▸ dire, grave, serious, severe. *See also* **disastrous, fateful**. **2.** Causing or expressing sorrow or sadness ▸ depressing, melancholy, mournful. *See* **sorrowful** (1).

grift *noun*
Slang An act of cheating ▸ deceit, hoax, swindle. *See* **cheat** (1).

grifter *noun*
Slang A person who cheats ▸ cheater, swindler, trickster. *See* **cheat** (2).

grigri *noun*
▸ mascot, talisman. *See* **charm** (1).

grill *verb*
1. To cook on a gridiron ▸ barbecue, broil, charbroil. *See* **cook** (1). **2.** *Informal* To put a question to someone ▸ interrogate, quiz. *See* **ask** (1).

grim *adjective*
1. Firmly, often unreasonably immovable in purpose or will ▸ bullheaded, dogged, obstinate. *See* **stubborn** (1). **2.** So disagreeable as to discourage approach ▸ dour, flinty, stern. *See* **forbidding** (1). **3.** Marked by cold and unpleasant conditions ▸ austere, severe. *See* **bleak** (1). **4.** Shockingly repellent ▸ grisly, gruesome,

hideous. *See* **ghastly** (1). *See synonym note at* **ghastly**.
5. Inflicting suffering or pain ▸ brutal, fierce, savage. *See* **cruel** (1).

grimace *noun*
A contorted facial expression showing pain, contempt, or disgust ▸ face, moue, pout. *Informal:* mug. *See also* **frown, glare, sneer**.

grimace *verb*
To contort one's face to indicate pain, contempt, or disgust ▸ mouth, mug. *Idioms:* make a face, make faces. *See also* **frown, glare, sneer**.

grime *noun*
▸ dirt, muck. *See* **filth** (1).

griminess *noun*
▸ filthiness, foulness, squalor, uncleanliness. *See* **dirtiness** (1).

grimness *noun*
▸ bullheadedness, hardheadedness, rigidity. *See* **stubbornness**.

grimy *adjective*
▸ black, filthy, muddy. *See* **dirty** (1). *See synonym note at* **dirty**.

grin *verb*
To curve the lips upward in expressing amusement, pleasure, or happiness ▸ beam, smirk. *See* **smile**.

grin *noun*
A facial expression marked by an upward curving of the lips ▸ simper, smile, smirk. *See also* **sneer**.

grind *verb*
1. To break up into tiny particles ▸ atomize, granulate, mill. *See* **crush** (2). **2.** To reduce gradually, as by chemical reaction, weather, or friction ▸ consume, corrode, wear (away *or* down). *See* **erode**. **3.** To rub together noisily ▸ crunch, gnash. **4.** To do tedious, difficult or menial work ▸ drudge, grub, plod, slave, slog, struggle. *See also* **labor**. **5.** *Informal* To apply one's mind to the acquisition of knowledge, especially when pressed for time ▸ lucubrate, study. *Informal:* bone up, cram. *Idioms:* burn the midnight oil, hit the books. *See also* **examine**. **6.** To treat arbitrarily or cruelly ▸ trample, tyrannize. **7.** To give a sharp edge to ▸ hone, strope, whet. *See* **sharpen** (2).

grind *noun*
1. *Informal* A course of action to be followed regularly ▸ rote, rounds, track. *See* **routine** (1). **2.** One who works or toils tirelessly ▸ drone, grub, plodder. *See* **drudge** (2). **3.** Physical exertion that is usually difficult and exhausting ▸ *Informal:* toil, travail, work. *See* **labor** (1). **4.** A difficult or tedious undertaking ▸ chore, effort, slog. *See* **task** (2).

grip *verb*
1. To compel the attention, interest, or imagination of ▸ arrest, attract, captivate, capture, catch up, engage, enthrall, fascinate, hold, interest, intrigue, mesmerize, rivet, spellbind, transfix. *Informal:* grab. *Idioms:* catch one's eye, make one's mouth water, tickle one's fancy. *See also* **absorb, amuse, charm, possess**. **2.** To take firmly with the hand and maintain a hold on ▸ clutch, grab, seize. *See* **grasp** (1).

grip *noun*
1. Firm control or influence ▸ grasp, handle, hold. *See also* **control, dominance, influence**. **2.** Intellectual hold ▸ apprehension, comprehension, grasp, hold, understanding. *See also* **knowledge**. **3.** An act or means of holding something ▸ clench, grasp. *See* **hold** (1). **4.** A piece of luggage for carrying clothing ▸ carryon, valise. *See* **suitcase**.

gripe *verb*
Informal To express feelings of pain, dissatisfaction or resentment ▸ fuss, grouch, whine. *See* **complain**.

gripe *noun*
Informal An expression of pain or dissatisfaction ▸ carp, whimper, whine. *See* **complaint** (1).

griper *noun*
Informal A person who habitually complains or grumbles ▸ crab, grump, whiner. *See* **grouch** (1).

grisly *adjective*
▸ grim, gruesome, hideous. *See* **ghastly** (1). *See synonym note at* **ghastly**.

grit *noun*
Informal The quality of mind enabling one to face danger or hardship resolutely ▸ bravery, fortitude, gallantry, valor. *See* **courage**.

gritty *adjective*
1. Consisting of or covered with large particles ▸ granular, rough. *See* **coarse** (4). **2.** Having or showing courage ▸ courageous, fearless, heroic. *See* **brave**.

grizzled *adjective*
▸ aged, elderly, senior. *See* **old** (2).

grogginess *adjective*
▸ giddiness, unsteadiness, wooziness. *See* **dizziness**.

groggy *adjective*
▸ lightheaded, reeling, spinning. *See* **dizzy** (1).

groom *verb*
▸ freshen (up), slick up, trim. *See* **tidy** (2).

groove *noun*
1. A course of action to be followed regularly ▸ rote, rounds, track. *See* **routine** (1). **2.** An opening made with a sharp object ▸ incision, score, slash. *See* **cut** (1). **3.** A long, narrow, and usually shallow depression in the ground ▸ ditch, rut, trench. *See* **furrow** (1).

groove on *verb*
Slang To like or enjoy enthusiastically, often excessively ▸ adore, delight (in), dote on (*or* upon), love. *Slang:* eat up.

groovy *adjective*
▸ fantastic, sensational, superb. *See* **marvelous** (1).

grope *verb*
1. To reach about or search blindly or uncertainly ▸ feel, fumble, grabble, poke, scrabble. *See also* **seek**. **2.** *Slang* To engage in kissing, caressing, and other amorous behavior ▸ *Informal:* pet, spoon. *See* **neck**.

gross *adjective*
1. Conspicuously bad or offensive ▸ egregious, flagrant, glaring, rank. *See synonym note at* **flagrant**. *See also* **offensive, outrageous, shameless**. **2.** Lacking in delicacy or refinement ▸ indelicate, unbecoming, unrefined. *See* **coarse** (1). **3.** Offensive to accepted stan-

dards of decency ▸ bawdy, coarse, lewd, vulgar. *See* **obscene** (1). **4.** Having too much flesh ▸ chubby, pudgy, tubby. *See* **fat** (1). **5.** Including every constituent or individual ▸ entire, total, whole. *See* **complete** (1). *See synonym note at* **complete**. **6.** *Slang* So unpleasant in flavor as to be inedible ▸ foul-tasting, unappetizing, uneatable. *See* **unpalatable** (1).

gross *noun*
An amount or quantity from which nothing is left out or held back ▸ entirety, total. *See* **whole** (1).

gross *verb*
To make as income or profit ▸ clear, gain, yield. *See* **return** (3).

gross out *verb*
To offend the senses or feelings of ▸ nauseate, repulse. *See* **disgust** (1).

grossness *noun*
1. The quality or state of being flagrant ▸ egregiousness, flagrancy, glaringness, rankness. *See also* **impudence, outrageousness**. **2.** The quality or state of being obscene ▸ filthiness, profanity, smuttiness, vulgarness. *See* **obscenity** (1).

grotesque *adjective*
1. Resembling a freak ▸ freakish, monstrous. *See also* **weird**. **2.** Deviating from what is conventional or customary ▸ bizarre, freakish. *See* **eccentric**. *See synonym note at* **eccentric**. **3.** Very strange or strikingly unusual ▸ fantastic, outré. *See* **exotic** (2).

grotto *noun*
▸ cavern, tunnel. *See* **cave** (2).

grouch *noun*
1. A person who habitually complains or grumbles ▸ complainer, crab, faultfinder, growler, grumbler, grump, murmurer, mutterer, whiner. *Informal:* crank, griper, grouser. *Slang:* bellyacher, sorehead, sourpuss. *See also* **killjoy**. **2.** An expression of pain or dissatisfaction ▸ carp, whimper, whine. *See* **complaint** (1).

grouch *verb*
To express feelings of pain, dissatisfaction, or resentment ▸ fuss, grump, whine. *See* **complain**.

grouchy *adjective*
▸ cranky, disagreeable, peevish. *See* **ill-tempered**.

ground *noun*
1. The soft part of the land surface of the world ▸ clay, loam, soil. *See* **earth** (1). **2.** The lowest or supporting part or structure ▸ bottom, foot, foundation. *See* **base**[1] (2). **3.** An underlying support, as for an argument or belief ▸ cornerstone, foundation, underpinning. *See* **basis** (1).

ground *verb*
1. To bring down, as from a shot or blow ▸ chop down, floor, hew. *See* **drop** (6). **2.** To provide a basis for ▸ establish, underpin. *See* **base**[1] (1).

groundless *adjective*
▸ unfounded, unwarranted. *See* **baseless**. *See synonym note at* **baseless**.

groundlessly *adverb*
Without basis or foundation in fact ▸ baselessly, unfoundedly, unwarrantedly.

grounds *noun*
1. A basis for an action ▸ motive, reason. *See* **cause** (2). **2.** An underlying support, as for an argument or belief ▸ cornerstone, foundation, underpinning. *See* **basis** (1). *See synonym note at* **basis**. **3.** A fact or circumstance that gives logical support to an assertion, claim, or proposal ▸ proof, wherefore. *See* **reason** (1). **4.** Usually extensive real estate ▸ estate, property. *See* **land** (1).

groundwork *noun*
1. The lowest or supporting part or structure ▸ bottom, foot, foundation. *See* **base**[1] (2). **2.** An underlying support, as for an argument or belief ▸ cornerstone, foundation, underpinning. *See* **basis** (1). *See synonym note at* **basis**.

group *noun*
1. A number of individuals making up or considered to be a unit ▸ array, band, batch, bevy, body, bunch, bundle, clump, cluster, clutch, huddle, collection, knot, lot, party, set. *See also* **accumulation, system**. **2.** A number of persons who have come or have been gathered together ▸ conference, meeting. *Informal:* get-together. *See* **assembly** (1). **3.** A small group of friends or associates ▸ coterie, crowd, set. *See* **circle** (3). **4.** A subdivision of a larger group ▸ category, order, set. *See* **class** (1). **5.** An entity that is composed of interconnected parts ▸ system, tissue, web. *See* **complex** (1).

group *verb*
1. To come, bring, or call together ▸ convene, convoke, summon. *See* **assemble** (1). **2.** To form a united group ▸ join, unite. *See* **band**[2]. **3.** To arrange according to class ▸ categorize, class, sort. *See* **classify**.

group *adjective*
Working together toward a common end ▸ collective, joint, synergistic. *See* **cooperative** (1).

groupie *noun*
▸ devotee, enthusiast, fancier. *See* **fan**[2].

grouping *noun*
▸ allotment, layout, positioning. *See* **arrangement** (1).

grouse *verb*
Informal To express feelings of pain, dissatisfaction or resentment ▸ fuss, grouch, whine. *See* **complain**.

grouse *noun*
Informal An expression of pain or dissatisfaction ▸ carp, whimper, whine. *See* **complaint** (1).

grouser *noun*
Informal A person who habitually complains or grumbles ▸ crab, grump, whiner. *See* **grouch** (1).

grovel *verb*
▸ bootlick, cringe, kowtow. *Informal:* apple-polish. *See* **fawn**.

groveler *noun*
▸ flatterer, minion, slave. *See* **sycophant**.

grow *verb*
1. To raise crops or animals ▸ breed, cultivate, farm, garden, propagate, raise, tend, ranch. *See also* **nurture, plant, till**. **2.** To make or become greater or larger ▸ amplify, boost, enlarge. *See* **increase** (1). **3.** To bring

or come to full development ▸ develop, ripen. *See* **mature. 4.** To come to be ▸ come (to be), get (to be). *See* **become** (1). **5.** To come gradually to have ▸ acquire, form, incur. *See* **develop** (1).

growl *verb*
1. To make a continuous deep reverberating sound ▸ grumble, roll. *See* **rumble** (1). **2.** To speak abruptly and sharply ▸ bark, snarl. *See* **snap** (3).

growler *noun*
▸ crab, grump, whiner. *See* **grouch** (1).

grown *or* **grown-up** *adjective*
▸ big, developed, ripe. *See* **mature** (1).

growth *noun*
1. A progression from a simple form to a more complex one ▸ evolvement, progress, unfolding. *See* **development** (1). **2.** The act of increasing or rising ▸ amplification, boost, escalation. *See* **increase** (1). **3.** An unevenness or elevation on a surface ▸ lump, protuberance. *See* **bump** (1). **4.** The result or product of building up ▸ development, proliferation. *See* **buildup** (2).

grub *verb*
1. To break, turn over, or remove (earth or sand, for example) with or as if with a tool ▸ excavate, scoop, shovel. *See* **dig** (1). **2.** To do tedious, difficult or menial work ▸ plod, slave. *See* **grind** (4).

grub *noun*
1. *Slang* Material that is fit to be eaten ▸ bread, meat, nourishment. *See* **food. 2.** One who works or toils tirelessly ▸ drone, grind, plodder. *See* **drudge** (2).

grubbiness *noun*
▸ filthiness, squalor, uncleanliness. *See* **dirtiness** (1).

grubby *adjective*
▸ black, filthy, muddy. *See* **dirty** (1).

grubstake *noun*
Money or property used to produce more wealth ▸ financing, funding, stake. *See* **capital** (1).

grubstake *verb*
To supply capital ▸ fund, subsidize. *Informal:* bankroll. *See* **finance.**

grudge *verb*
To feel envy toward or for ▸ begrudge, covet, envy.

grudging *adjective*
▸ invidious, jealous. *See* **envious.**

grueling *adjective*
▸ arduous, backbreaking, laborious. *See* **burdensome** (1). *See synonym note at* **burdensome.**

gruesome *adjective*
▸ grim, grisly, hideous. *See* **ghastly** (1). *See synonym note at* **ghastly.**

gruff *adjective*
1. Rudely informal ▸ blunt, brusque, curt. *See* **abrupt** (1). *See synonym note at* **abrupt. 2.** Rough, raw, or grating in sound ▸ gravelly, husky. *See* **hoarse** (1).

grumble *verb*
1. To express feelings of dissatisfaction or resentment ▸ grunt, murmur, mutter. *See* **complain. 2.** To make a continuous deep reverberating sound ▸ growl, roll. *See* **rumble** (1).

grumble *noun*
An expression of dissatisfaction or resentment ▸ grunt, murmur, mutter. *See* **complaint.**

grumbler *noun*
▸ crab, grump, whiner. *See* **grouch** (1).

grump *noun*
1. *Informal* An expression of dissatisfaction or a circumstance regarded as a cause for such expression ▸ complaint, grievance. *Informal:* gripe. *Slang:* beef, kick. *Idiom:* bone to pick. **2.** A person who habitually complains or grumbles ▸ crab, growler, whiner. *See* **grouch** (1).

grump *verb*
To express feelings of pain, dissatisfaction, or resentment ▸ fuss, grouch, whine. *See* **complain.**

grumpy *adjective*
▸ cranky, grouchy, peevish. *See* **ill-tempered.**

grunge *noun*
Slang Foul or dirty matter ▸ grime, muck. *See* **filth** (1).

grungy *adjective*
Slang Covered with or stained by dirt ▸ black, filthy, muddy. *See* **dirty** (1).

grunt *verb*
To express feelings of dissatisfaction or resentment ▸ grumble, murmur, mutter. *See* **complain.**

grunt *noun*
1. An expression of dissatisfaction or resentment ▸ grumble, murmur, mutter. *See* **complaint. 2.** *Slang* A person who does tedious, menial, or unpleasant work ▸ drone, hack, menial. *See* **drudge** (1). **3.** *Slang* An enlisted person ▸ GI, serviceperson. *See* **soldier** (2).

guarantee *noun*
1. An assumption of responsibility, as one given by a manufacturer, for the quality, worth, or durability of a product ▸ certification, guaranty, surety, warrant, warranty. **2.** A declaration that one will or will not do a certain thing ▸ covenant, pledge, vow. *See* **promise** (1).

guarantee *verb*
1. To assume responsibility for the quality, worth, or durability of ▸ certify, guaranty, stand behind, warrant. *See also* **confirm. 2.** To render certain ▸ assure, ensure, insure, secure, warrant. *Informal:* cinch, clinch.

guarantor *noun*
▸ backer, underwriter. *See* **sponsor** (1).

guaranty *noun*
1. An assumption of responsibility, as one given by a manufacturer, for the quality, worth, or durability of a product ▸ certification, guarantee, surety, warrant, warranty. **2.** Something given to guarantee the repayment of a loan or the fulfillment of an obligation ▸ security, token, warrant. *See* **pawn**[1]. **3.** A declaration that one will or will not do a certain thing ▸ covenant, pledge, vow. *See* **promise** (1). **4.** One who assumes financial responsibility for another ▸ guarantor, underwriter. *See* **sponsor** (1).

guaranty *verb*
To assume responsibility for the quality, worth, or

durability of ▶ certify, warrant. *See* **guarantee** (1).

guard *noun*

1. One assigned to provide protection or keep watch over someone or something ▶ guardian, lookout, monitor, picket, protection, protector, sentinel, sentry, ward, watch, watchdog, watchman. *See also* **watcher. 2.** The act or a means of defending ▶ protection, safeguard, shield. *See* **defense** (1).

guard *verb*

To keep safe from danger, attack, or harm ▶ protect, safeguard, secure. *See* **defend** (1). *See synonym note at* **defend.**

guarded *adjective*

1. Kept within sensible limits ▶ moderate, reasonable, restrained. *See* **conservative** (2). **2.** Tending to keep one's thoughts and emotions to oneself ▶ inhibited, restrained, self-restrained. *See* **reserved** (1).

guardian *noun*

1. One who is legally responsible for the care and management of the person or property of an incompetent or a minor ▶ caretaker, conservator, custodian, keeper. *See also* **representative. 2.** One assigned to provide protection or keep watch over someone or something ▶ lookout, protector, sentry, ward. *See* **guard** (1).

guardianship *noun*

▶ charge, custody, superintendence, trust. *See* **care** (2).

gubernatorial *adjective*

▶ bureaucratic, regulatory. *See* **governmental.**

gudgeon *noun*

Slang A person who is easily deceived or victimized ▶ pushover, tool, victim. *See* **dupe** (1).

guerdon *noun*

1. Something given in return for a service or accomplishment ▶ award, bonus, plum. *See* **reward** (1). **2.** Something justly deserved ▶ compensation, deserts, reward. *See* **due** (1).

guerdon *verb*

To bestow a reward on ▶ award, honor, reward. *See also* **confer.**

guess *verb*

To predict or assume without sufficient information ▶ conjecture, fancy, imagine, infer, speculate, suppose, surmise, suspect, think. *See also* **believe, infer, suppose.**

guess *noun*

A judgment, estimate, or opinion arrived at by guessing ▶ conjecture, guesswork, speculation, supposition, surmise. *Informal:* guesstimate. **Idiom:** shot in the dark. *See also* **assumption, belief, estimate.**

guesstimate *verb*

Informal To calculate approximately ▶ place, reckon. *See* **estimate** (2).

guesstimate *noun*

A rough or tentative calculation ▶ approximation, estimation. *See* **estimate** (2).

guesswork *noun*

▶ conjecture, speculation, surmise. *See* **guess.**

guest *noun*

A person or persons visiting one ▶ caller, guest, visitant, visitor.

guffaw *noun*

An act of laughing ▶ cackle, laughter. *See* **laugh** (1).

guffaw *verb*

To express amusement or mirth ▶ cachinnate, cackle, chuckle. *See* **laugh.**

guidance *noun*

1. The act or practice of directing or controlling ▶ direction, leadership, supervision. *See* **management** (1). **2.** An opinion as to a decision or course of action ▶ guidance, recommendation. *See* **advice** (1).

guide *noun*

1. Something or someone that shows the way ▶ cicerone, conductor, director, docent, escort, lead, leader, pilot, shepherd, usher. **2.** One who advises another ▶ counselor, mentor. *See* **adviser.**

guide *verb*

1. To show the way to ▶ conduct, direct, escort, lead, marshal, pilot, route, shepherd, show, steer, usher. **2.** To direct the course of carefully ▶ jockey, navigate. *See* **maneuver** (1). **3.** To give recommendations to someone about a decision ▶ counsel, recommend. *See* **advise** (1). **4.** To control the functioning or outcome of ▶ determine, regulate. *See* **govern** (1).

✦ CORE SYNONYMS: *guide, lead, pilot, shepherd, steer, usher.* These verbs mean to show or conduct someone the way to a place, destination, or goal: *guided me to my seat; led the troops into battle; a teacher piloting students through the zoo; shepherding tourists to the bus; steered the applicant to the third floor; ushering a visitor out.*

---

guideline *noun*

▶ prescript, regulation, rubric. *See* **rule** (1).

guild *noun*

▶ club, league, order. *See* **union** (1).

guile *noun*

1. Deceitful cleverness ▶ artfulness, slyness. *See* **art** (1). **2.** The act or practice of deceiving ▶ deception, duplicity. *See* **deceit** (1).

guileful *adjective*

1. Deceitfully clever ▶ cunning, scheming, sly, wily. *See* **artful** (1). **2.** Marked by treachery or deceit ▶ duplicitous, shifty, sneaky. *See* **underhand.**

guileless *adjective*

▶ innocent, naive, simple. *See* **artless** (1). *See synonym note at* **artless.**

guilt *noun*

1. Responsibility for an error or crime ▶ fault, onus. *See* **blame** (1). *See synonym note at* **blame. 2.** A feeling of regret for one's sins or misdeeds ▶ contriteness, remorse, repentance. *See* **penitence.**

guiltless *adjective*

▶ blameless, faultless. *See* **innocent** (?)

guilty *adjective*

▶ culpable, reprehensible. *See* **blameworthy.** *See synonym note at* **blameworthy.**

guise *noun*

1. A deceptive outward appearance ▸ face, mask, masquerade, pretense. *See* **façade** (2). **2.** A set or style of clothing ▸ garb, toilette, outfit, wardrobe. *See* **dress** (2). **3.** The way something or someone looks ▸ aspect, look, features, mien. *See* **appearance** (1). **4.** Clothes or other personal effects, such as makeup, worn to conceal one's identity ▸ costume, mask, veil. *See* **disguise** (1).

gulf *noun*

1. A body of water partly enclosed by land but having a wide outlet to the sea ▸ bight, gulf, sound. *See also* **channel, harbor, inlet. 2.** Something of immeasurable and vast extent ▸ abysm, abyss, chasm. *See* **deep** (1). **3.** A space between objects or points ▸ interstice, interval, separation. *See* **gap** (1).

gull *noun*

A person who is easily deceived or victimized ▸ pushover, tool, victim. *See* **dupe** (1).

gull *verb*

To get something by deceitful trickery ▸ bilk, defraud, swindle. *See* **cheat** (1).

gullible *adjective*

Easily imposed on or tricked ▸ credulous, dupable, easy, exploitable, naive, simple, susceptible, susceptive, trusting.

gulp *verb*

1. To swallow food or drink greedily or rapidly in large amounts ▸ bolt, englut, engorge, glut, gobble, gorge, guzzle, ingurgitate, stuff oneself, swill. *Informal:* down, pig out, wolf (down). *Idioms:* eat like a pig (*or* hog), feed (*or* stuff) one's face, make a pig (*or* hog) of oneself. *See also* **eat, swallow. 2.** To breathe hard ▸ gasp, huff. *See* **pant** (1). **3.** To take into the mouth and swallow a liquid ▸ down, sip, slurp. *See* **drink** (1).

gulp *noun*

An act of swallowing ▸ ingestion, swallow, swig.

gummy *adjective*

▸ adhesive, gluey, tacky. *See* **sticky** (1).

gumption *noun*

1. *Informal* An aggressive readiness along with energy to undertake taxing efforts ▸ initiative, hustle, punch. *See* **drive** (2). **2.** *Informal* The ability to make sensible decisions ▸ judgment, reason, wisdom. *See* **common sense.**

gumshoe *noun*

A person whose work is investigating crimes or obtaining hidden evidence or information ▸ sleuth, investigator. *Informal:* eye. *See* **detective.**

gumshoe *verb*

Slang To move silently and furtively ▸ lurk, prowl. *See* **sneak** (1).

gum up *verb*

▸ blunder, foul up, spoil. *See* **botch.**

gun *verb*

To wound or kill with a firearm ▸ gun down, pick off, shoot. *Slang:* plug. *Idioms:* fill full of lead (*or* holes). *See also* **kill**[1], **murder.**

gun for *verb*

To follow another with the intent of overtaking and capturing ▸ chase, hunt. *See* **pursue** (1).

gung ho *adjective*

Slang Showing or having enthusiasm ▸ fervent, rabid, zealous. *See* **enthusiastic** (1).

gunk *noun*

1. *Informal* A viscous, usually offensively dirty substance ▸ muck, sludge. *See* **slime. 2.** *Informal* Items or material discarded or rejected as useless or worthless ▸ litter, trash, waste. *See* **garbage** (1).

gunsel *noun*

Slang A person who treats others violently or roughly ▸ hoodlum, ruffian, tough. *See* **thug.**

gurgle *verb*

To flow with or make a soft liquid sound ▸ babble, lap, murmur. *See* **burble** (1).

gurgle *noun*

A soft liquid sound ▸ gurgle, lap, murmur. *See* **burble.**

guru *noun*

1. One who advises another ▸ counselor, mentor. *See* **adviser. 2.** A person noted for wisdom, knowledge, and judgment ▸ pundit, scholar. *See* **sage.**

gush *verb*

1. To come forth in abundance ▸ cascade, pour, rush. *See* **flow** (2). **2.** To express great enthusiasm ▸ enthuse, rhapsodize. *See* **rave** (1).

gush *noun*

1. Something suggestive of running water ▸ flood, outpouring, tide. *See* **flow. 2.** A sudden violent expression, as of emotion ▸ burst, eruption, explosion. *See* **outburst** (1).

gushy *adjective*

▸ corny, maudlin, soft. *See* **sentimental.**

gust *noun*

1. A natural movement or current of air ▸ blast, blow, waft. *See* **wind**[1] (1). **2.** A sudden violent expression, as of emotion ▸ eruption, explosion. *See* **outburst** (1).

gust *verb*

To be in a state of motion, as air or wind ▸ bluster, puff. *See* **blow**[1] (1).

gusto *noun*

Spirited enjoyment ▸ relish, zest. *See synonym note at* **zest.** *See also* **enthusiasm.**

gusty *adjective*

▸ breezy, windy. *See* **airy** (3).

gut *adjective*

1. *Slang* Arising from one's mental or spiritual being ▸ interior, intimate. *See* **inner** (2). **2.** To remove the contents of ▸ clean out, evacuate. *See* **empty** (1).

gut *verb*

To lessen or deplete the nerve, energy, or strength of ▸ debilitate, weaken. *See* **enervate.**

gutless *adjective*

Slang Ignobly lacking in courage ▸ faint-hearted, pusillanimous. *Slang:* wimpy. *See* **cowardly.**

gutlessness *noun*

Slang Ignoble lack of courage ▸ chickenheartedness, pusillanimity. *See* **cowardice.**

gut reaction *noun*

▸ foreboding, intuition, notion, suspicion. *See* **feeling** (1).

guts *noun*

1. *Slang* The quality of mind enabling one to face danger or hardship resolutely ▸ bravery, fortitude, gallantry, valor. *See* **courage. 2.** *Informal* Internal organs of the abdomen ▸ bowels, entrails, intestines. *See* **viscera.**

gutsiness *noun*

Slang The quality of mind enabling one to face danger or hardship resolutely ▸ bravery, fortitude, gallantry, valor. *See* **courage.**

gutsy *adjective*

1. *Slang* Having or showing courage ▸ courageous, fearless, heroic. *See* **brave. 2.** Full of vigor ▸ robust, strapping, sturdy. *See* **lusty** (1).

gutter *noun*

A place known for its great flith or corruption ▸ cesspool, sewer. *See* **pit**[1] (3).

gutter *verb*

To undergo partial or unsteady combustion ▸ smoke, sputter. *See* **smolder** (1).

gutty *adjective*

▸ courageous, fearless, heroic. *See* **brave.**

guy[1] *noun*

A band or fiber used to bind, tie, connect, or support ▸ cable, line, string. *See* **cord.**

guy[2] *noun*

Informal A man referred to familiarly or as a member of one's group ▸ chap, jack. *See* **fellow** (1).

guzzle *verb*

1. To swallow food or drink greedily or rapidly in large amounts ▸ gobble, ingurgitate. *See* **gulp** (1). **2.** To take alcoholic liquor, especially excessively or habitually ▸ tipple. *Slang:* booze, lush. *See* **drink** (2). **3.** To take into the mouth and swallow a liquid ▸ down, gulp, slurp. *See* **drink** (1).

gyp *verb*

Slang To get something by deceitful trickery ▸ bilk, defraud, swindle. *See* **cheat** (1).

gyp *noun*

1. *Slang* An act of cheating ▸ deceit, hoax, swindle. *See* **cheat** (1). **2.** *Slang* A person who cheats ▸ cheater, swindler, trickster. *See* **cheat** (2).

gypper *noun*

Slang A person who cheats ▸ cheater, swindler, trickster. *See* **cheat** (2).

gypsy *noun*

▸ nomad, roamer, vagabond. *See* **hobo.**

gyrate *verb*

▸ twirl, whirl. *See* **turn** (1). *See synonym note at* **turn.**

gyration *noun*

▸ circulation, orbit. *See* **revolution** (1).

gyre *noun*

▸ band, ring, wheel. *See* **circle** (1).

h

habiliments *noun*

1. A set or style of clothing ▸ garb, guise, outfit. *See* **dress** (2). **2.** Articles worn to cover the body ▸ attire, clothing, garments. *See* **dress** (1).

habit *noun*

1. A habitual way of behaving ▸ form, practice. *See* **custom** (1). *See synonym note at* **custom. 2.** The physical characteristics of a person ▸ body, form. *See* **constitution** (1). **3.** Clothing worn by members of a religious order ▸ robe, vestment. *See also* **dress. 4.** A person's customary manner of emotional response ▸ nature, temperament. *See* **disposition** (1).

habitable *adjective*

Fit to live in ▸ inhabitable, livable.

habitat *noun*

1. The natural environment specific to an animal or plant ▸ habitation, niche, range, territory. *See also* **haunt. 2.** The ecological circumstances in which organisms live ▸ biosphere, nature. *See* **environment** (3).

habitation *noun*

1. A building or shelter where one lives ▸ domicile, lodging, residence. *See* **home** (1). **2.** The natural environment specific to an animal or plant ▸ niche, territory. *See* **habitat** (1).

habitual *adjective*

1. Subject to a habit or pattern of behavior ▸ accustomed, chronic, routine. **2.** Subject to a disease or habit for a long time ▸ chronic, confirmed, habituated, inveterate. *See also* **stubborn. 3.** Occurring or encountered regularly ▸ customary, frequent, regular. *See* **common** (1).

habitually *adverb*

▸ customarily, generally, normally. *See* **usually.**

habitualness *noun*

▸ normality, ordinariness, regularity, routineness. *See* **usualness.**

habituate *verb*

▸ condition, inure, wont. *See* **accustom.**

habituated *adjective*

1. In the habit ▸ accustomed, used, wont. **2.** Subject to a disease or habit for a long time ▸ chronic, confirmed, habitual, inveterate. *See also* **stubborn.**

habitude *noun*
▶ form, habit, practice. *See* **custom** (1). *See synonym note at* **custom.**

habitus *noun*
▶ body, form, physique. *See* **constitution** (1).

hack¹ *verb*
To penetrate with a sharp edge ▶ bayonet, incise, pierce, slash. *See* **cut** (1).

hack² *noun*
A person who does tedious, menial, or unpleasant work ▶ drone, grunt, menial. *See* **drudge** (1).

hackneyed *adjective*
▶ clichéd, overused, stale, tired. *See* **trite.**

haft *noun*
A protrusion or extension designed to be grasped by the hand ▶ handgrip, handle, hilt. *See also* **hold, knob.**

hag *noun*
1. A woman who practices magic ▶ enchantress, lamia, sorceress, witch. *See also* **wizard. 2.** An ugly, frightening woman, usually old ▶ crone. *Slang:* battle-ax, crow. *See* **witch** (2).

haggard *adjective*
Appearing worn and exhausted ▶ careworn, drawn, emaciated, gaunt, pinched, hollow-eyed, shrunken, skeletal, wan, wasted, worn. *Idiom:* skin and bones. *See also* **exhausted, thin.**

haggle *verb*
To argue about the terms, as of a sale ▶ bargain, chaffer, dicker, higgle, huckster, negotiate, palter, wrangle. *See also* **argue.**

ha-ha *noun*
Slang Words or actions intended to excite laughter or amusement ▶ jest, quip, witticism. *See* **joke** (1).

hail¹ *noun*
A concentrated outpouring, as of missiles, words, or blows ▶ cannonade, fusillade, volley. *See* **barrage.**

hail² *verb*
1. To approach for the purpose of speech ▶ accost, greet, salute. *See also* **encounter, interrupt, welcome. 2.** To address in a friendly and respectful way ▶ greet, salute, welcome. **3.** To pay tribute or homage to ▶ celebrate, exalt. *See* **honor** (1). **4.** To have as one's home or place of origin ▶ come, originate. *See also* **descend, stem.**

hail *noun*
An expression, in words or gestures, marking a meeting of persons ▶ greeting, salutation, salute, welcome. *Informal:* hello.

hair *noun*
▶ hint, semblance, trace. *See* **shade** (2).

hairless *adjective*
▶ bald, naked, nude. *See* **bare** (3).

hairline *noun*
Something suggesting the continuousness of a filament ▶ strand, thread. *See also* **thread.**

hair-raising *adjective*
▶ bloodcurdling, nightmarish. *See* **horrible** (1).

hairsplitting *noun*
▶ caviling, niggling, nitpicking. *See* **quibbling.**

hairy *adjective*
1. Covered with hair ▶ bristly, downy, fleecy, flocculent, furry, fuzzy, hirsute, pilose, pubescent, shaggy, tufted, woolly. **2.** *Slang* Involving possible risk, loss, or injury ▶ chancy, hazardous, menacing, risky. *See* **dangerous.**

halcyon *adjective*
▶ peaceful, placid, serene. *See* **still** (1).

hale *adjective*
▶ fit, well, robust. *See* **healthy** (1). *See synonym note at* **healthy.**

haleness *noun*
▶ healthiness, soundness. *See* **health** (1).

halfhearted *adjective*
Lacking warmth, interest, enthusiasm, or involvement ▶ Laodicean, lukewarm, tepid, unenthusiastic. *See also* **apathetic, cold, cool.**

half-pint *noun*
Slang A young or short person ▶ pip-squeak, runt, scrub. *See* **squirt** (2).

half-truth *noun*
▶ falsehood, fib, untruth. *See* **lie².**

half-wit *noun*
▶ dummy, imbecile, thickhead. *See* **dullard.**

half-witted *adjective*
1. Having only a limited ability to learn and understand ▶ dull, simple, slow. *See* **backward** (1). **2.** *Slang* Lacking in intelligence ▶ dumb, idiotic, obtuse. *See* **stupid** (1).

halloo *noun*
A loud cry ▶ call, holler, yell. *See* **shout.**

halloo *verb*
To speak or say in a loud cry ▶ call, holler, yell. *See* **shout.**

hallow *verb*
1. To make sacred by a religious rite ▶ bless, consecrate, sanctify. *See also* **exalt. 2.** To give over by or as if by vow to a higher purpose ▶ dedicate, sacrifice. *See* **devote** (1). **3.** To regard with the deepest respect, deference, and esteem ▶ idolize, venerate, worship. *See* **revere.**

hallowed *adjective*
1. Regarded with particular reverence or respect, especially by a religion ▶ consecrated, sacred, sacrosanct. *See* **holy** (1). **2.** In the service or worship of God or a god ▶ devoted, religious, sacred. *See* **divine** (2).

hallucinate *verb*
▶ daydream, fancy, hallucinate. *See* **dream** (1).

hallucination *noun*
1. An experience of things or events that are not real ▶ phantasmagoria, phantasmagory. *Slang:* trip. **2.** A phenomenon that causes a misperception ▶ ignis fatuus, mirage, phantasma. *See* **illusion** (1). **3.** An illusory mental image ▶ delusion, fantasy. *See* **dream** (1).

hallucinatory *adjective*
▶ dreamlike, illusory, phantasmagoric. *See* **illusive** (1).

hallucinogen *noun*
▶ narcotic, opiate, psychotropic. *See* **drug** (2).

halo *noun*
▸ band, ring, wheel. *See* **circle** (1).

halt¹ *noun*
1. The act of stopping ▸ cessation, discontinuance, surcease. *See* **stop** (1). **2.** The condition of being stopped ▸ gridlock, immobilization, standstill. *See* **stop** (2). *See synonym note at* **stop.**

halt *verb*
1. To prevent the occurrence or continuation of a movement, action, or operation ▸ check, discontinue, immobilize. *See* **stop** (2). **2.** To come to a cessation ▸ discontinue, quit. *See* **stop** (1).

halt² *verb*
1. To be irresolute in acting or doing ▸ falter, vacillate. *See* **hesitate. 2.** To walk unsteadily ▸ hitch, limp, totter. *See* **stagger** (1).

halting *adjective*
▸ indecisive, irresolute. *See* **hesitant** (1).

hamlet *noun*
▸ community, small town. *See* **village.**

hammer *verb*
1. To hit heavily and repeatedly ▸ assault, batter, pummel, thresh. *See* **beat** (1). *See synonym note at* **beat. 2.** To shape, break, or flatten with repeated blows ▸ forge, pound. *See* **beat** (3). **3.** To make rhythmic contractions, sounds, or movements ▸ pulsate, pulse, throb. *See* **beat** (5).

hamper¹ *verb*
1. To restrict the activity or free movement of ▸ chain, fetter, hamstring, handcuff, hobble, leash, manacle, shackle, tie, trammel. *Informal:* hogtie. **2.** To interfere with the progress of ▸ dampen, impede. *See* **hinder** (1). *See synonym note at* **hinder.**

✛ **CORE SYNONYMS:** *hamper, fetter, handcuff, hobble, hogtie, manacle, shackle, trammel.* These verbs mean to restrict the activity or free movement of: *a swimmer hampered by clothing; prisoners fettered by chains; handcuffed by rigid regulations; hobbled by responsibilities; leadership that refused to be hogtied; imagination manacled by fear; shackled by custom; trammeled by debts.*

---

hamper² *noun*
1. A basket normally used to contain clothes or food ▸ laundry basket, food basket, gift basket, pannier. *See also* **basket. 2.** A container made of interwoven material ▸ basket, creel. *See also* **container.**

hamstring *verb*
▸ fetter, handcuff, hobble. *See* **hamper¹** (1).

hand *noun*
1. Approval expressed by clapping ▸ applause, ovation, plaudit. **2.** The act or an instance of helping ▸ aid, assistance. *See* **help** (1). **3.** One who labors ▸ menial, toiler, worker. *See* **laborer. 4.** The position from which something is observed or considered ▸ aspect, point of view, standpoint. *See* **viewpoint. 5.** One of two or more contrasted parts or places identified by its location with respect to a center ▸ flank, side.

hand *verb*
To relinquish to the possession or control of another ▸ furnish, provide. *See* **give** (1).

hand down *verb*
1. To give property to another after one's death ▸ bequeath, will. *See* **leave¹** (1). **2.** To deliver an indictment or verdict, for example ▸ render, return.

hand in *verb*
To relinquish to the possession or control of another ▸ furnish, provide. *See* **give** (1).

hand on *verb*
To give property to another after one's death ▸ bequeath, will. *See* **leave¹** (1).

hand out *verb*
1. To give in portions or shares ▸ allot, dispense, dole out. *See* **distribute** (1). **2.** To give formally or officially ▸ award, bestow, grant. *See* **confer** (2). **3.** To present as a gift to a charity or cause ▸ bequeath, pledge. *See* **donate** (1).

hand over *verb*
1. To relinquish to the possession or control of another ▸ furnish, provide. *See* **give** (1). **2.** To put in the charge of another for care, use, or performance ▸ confide, delegate. *See* **entrust** (1). **3.** To give up or leave completely ▸ relinquish, surrender, yield. *See* **abandon** (1).

handbag *noun*
▸ bag, clutch, pocketbook. *See* **purse.**

handbill *noun*
An announcement distributed on paper to a large number of people ▸ circular, flier, leaflet, notice.

handcuff *verb*
▸ fetter, hamstring, hobble. *See* **hamper¹** (1). *See synonym note at* **hamper¹.**

handcuffs *noun*
▸ chains, manacle, irons. *See* **bond** (1).

handful *pronoun*
▸ few, small number, smattering. *See* **several.**

handicap *noun*
1. An unfavorable condition, circumstance, or characteristic ▸ detriment, drawback, liability. *See* **disadvantage.** *See synonym note at* **disadvantage. 2.** A factor conducive to superiority and success ▸ head start, vantage. *See* **advantage** (1).

handicap *verb*
To render powerless or motionless, as by inflicting severe injury ▸ cripple, immobilize, paralyze. *See* **disable** (1).

handicraft *noun*
▸ career, employment, occupation. *See* **business** (2).

handgrip *noun*
A protrusion or extension that is designed to be grasped by the hand ▸ haft, handle, hilt. *See also* **hold, knob.**

handle *verb*
1. To manipulate with the hands ▸ manipulate, ply, wield. **2.** To bring especially the hands or fingers into contact with ▸ feel, palpate. *See* **touch** (1). *See synonym note at* **touch. 3.** To behave in a specified way toward

someone ▸ cope with, treat. **4.** To control the course of an activity ▸ direct, manage, operate. *See* **conduct** (1). **5.** To conduct oneself in a specified way ▸ bear, carry, comport. *See* **act** (1). **6.** To control or to direct the functioning of ▸ run, work. *See* **operate** (1). **7.** To offer for sale ▸ deal, peddle. *See* **sell** (1).

handle *noun*
1. A protrusion or extension designed to be grasped by the hand ▸ haft, handgrip, hilt. *See also* **hold, knob**. **2.** Firm control or influence ▸ grasp, grip, hold. *See also* **control, dominance, influence**. **3.** *Slang* The word or words by which one is called and identified ▸ cognomen, epithet, title. *See* **name** (1).

✦ **CORE SYNONYMS:** *handle, manipulate, wield, ply.* These verbs mean to manipulate or operate with or as with the hands. *Handle* applies widely and suggests competence: *The lumberjack handled the ax expertly. The therapist handled every problem with sensitivity. Manipulate* connotes skillful or artful management: *The pilot confidently manipulated the controls in the cockpit.* When *manipulate* refers to people or personal affairs, it often implies deviousness or fraud in gaining an end: *I realized I'd been manipulated into helping them. Wield* implies freedom, skill, ease, and effectiveness in handling physical or figurative implements: *Ready to make kindling, she wielded a hatchet. The mayor's speechwriter wields a persuasive pen.* It also connotes effectiveness in the exercise of intangibles such as authority or influence: *The dictator wielded enormous power. Ply* suggests industry and persistence: *The hungry child was plying his knife and fork with gusto.* The term also applies to the regular and diligent engagement in a task or pursuit: *She plies the banker's trade with great success.*

hand-me-down *adjective*
▸ pre-owned, secondhand. *See* **used** (2).

handout *noun*
1. Something given to a charity or cause ▸ benefaction, contribution, offering. *See* **donation**. **2.** Assistance, especially money, food, and other necessities, given to the needy or dispossessed ▸ public assistance, welfare. *See* **relief** (3).

handsome *adjective*
1. Having qualities that delight the eye ▸ comely, gorgeous, stunning. *See* **beautiful**. *See synonym note at* **beautiful**. **2.** Willing to give of oneself and one's possessions ▸ big-hearted, magnanimous, unselfish. *See* **generous** (1).

handwriting *noun*
▸ calligraphy, longhand, penmanship. *See* **script** (1).

handy *adjective*
1. Exhibiting or possessing skill and ease in performance ▸ deft, facile, nimble. *See* **dexterous**. *See synonym note at* **dexterous**. **2.** Being within easy reach ▸ accessible, nearby. *See* **convenient** (2). **3.** Serving or capable of serving a useful purpose ▸ functional, useful, utilitarian. *See* **practical** (1). **4.** Suited to one's purpose ▸ expedient, proper, suitable. *See* **convenient** (1).

hang *verb*
1. To fasten or be fastened at one point with no support from below ▸ dangle, depend, sling, suspend, swing. *See also* **drape**. **2.** To execute by suspending by the neck ▸ gibbet. *Informal:* string up. *Slang:* swing. **3.** To remain stationary over a place or object ▸ hover, poise.

hang around *verb*
1. To visit regularly ▸ haunt, repair to. *See* **frequent**. **2.** To be with as a companion ▸ fraternize, hobnob. *Slang:* hang out. *See* **associate** (2). **3.** *Informal* To continue to be in a place ▸ bide, linger, tarry. *See* **remain** (1).

hang on *verb*
1. To be determined by or contingent on something unknown, uncertain, or changeable ▸ hinge on (*or* upon), rest on (*or* upon). *See* **depend on** (2). **2.** To put up with or continue despite difficulties ▸ keep on, persevere, soldier on. *See* **endure** (1).

hang out *verb*
1. *Slang* To visit regularly ▸ hang around, haunt, repair to. *See* **frequent**. **2.** *Slang* To be with as a companion ▸ consort, fraternize, hobnob. *See* **associate** (2).

hang over *verb*
To be imminent ▸ hover, impend, loom. *See* **threaten** (2).

hang up *verb*
To cause to be later or slower than expected or desired ▸ detain, retard, stall. *See* **delay** (1).

hang upon *verb*
To be determined by or contingent on something unknown, uncertain, or changeable ▸ hinge on (*or* upon), rest on (*or* upon). *See* **depend** (2).

hang *noun*
Informal The proper method for doing, using, or handling something ▸ feel, knack, trick.

hanger-on *noun*
▸ leech, sponge. *Slang:* freeloader. *See* **parasite** (1).

hanging *adjective*
1. Hung or appearing to be hung from a support ▸ dangling, dangly, pendent, pendulous, pensile, suspended. **2.** Not tautly bound, held, or fastened ▸ flapping, relaxed, slack. *See* **loose** (1). *See synonym note at* **loose**.

hangout *noun*
▸ meeting place. *Slang:* stamping ground, stomping ground. *See* **haunt** (1).

hangover *noun*
Unpleasant physical and mental effects following overindulgence in alcohol ▸ crapulence, katzenjammer. *Informal:* head.

hang-up *noun*
Informal An exaggerated concern ▸ anxiety, complex, neurosis, phobia. *See also* **anxiety, obsession**.

hanker *verb*
▸ covet, want, yearn. *See* **desire** (1).

hanky-panky *noun*
▸ diablerie, high jinks, tomfoolery. *See* **mischief** (1).

hap *noun*
1. The random, unintended, or unpredictable element of an event or the force regarded as the cause of such an event ▸ coincidence, fortune, luck. *See* **chance** (2). 2. An unexpected random event ▸ accident, fluke, happenstance. *See* **chance** (1).

hap *verb*
1. To take place ▸ befall, come, occur. *See* **happen** (1). 2. To take place by chance ▸ befall, betide, chance, happen.

haphazard *adjective*
▸ chance, indiscriminate, unplanned. *See* **random**. *See synonym note at* **random**.

hapless *adjective*
▸ ill-fated, ill-starred, luckless. *See* **unfortunate** (1). *See synonym note at* **unfortunate**.

haplessness *noun*
▸ adversity, haplessness, unluckiness. *See* **misfortune** (1).

happen *verb*
1. To take place ▸ arrive, befall, betide, come, come about, come off, develop, fall, hap, occur, pass, transpire. *Idiom:* come to pass. 2. To take place by chance ▸ befall, betide, chance, hap.

happen on *or* **upon** *verb*
To find or meet by chance ▸ come across, run across, stumble on. *See* **encounter** (1).

✛ **CORE SYNONYMS:** *happen, befall, betide, occur, transpire.* These verbs mean to take place or to come about: *saw an extraordinary thing happen; predicted that misery will befall humankind; woe that betides the poor soldier; was caught outdoors when the thunderstorm occurred; described the accident exactly as it transpired.*

---

happenchance *noun*
▸ accident, fluke, happenstance. *See* **chance** (1).

happening *noun*
1. Something that takes place ▸ incident, occurrence. *See* **circumstance** (1). *See synonym note at* **circumstance**. 2. Something significant that happens ▸ development, incident. *See* **event** (2).

happenstance *noun*
▸ accident, fluke, hazard. *See* **chance** (1).

happiness *noun*
A condition of supreme well-being and good spirits ▸ beatitude, blessedness, bliss, cheer, cheerfulness, contentedness, contentment, delight, felicity, gladness, glee, joy, joyfulness. *See also* **delight, elation, satisfaction**.

happy *adjective*
1. Being in or showing good spirits ▸ happy, jolly, jovial. *See* **cheerful** (1). *See synonym note at* **cheerful**. 2. Providing joy and pleasure ▸ festive, joyous, mirthful. *See* **merry** (1). 3. Having achieved satisfaction, as of one's goal ▸ content, fulfilled, gratified, satisfied. 4. Characterized by luck or good fortune ▸ fortuitous, fortunate, lucky, providential. *See synonym note at* **lucky**. *See also* **opportune**. 5. Disposed to accept,

agree, or participate ▸ agreeable, ready. *See* **willing** (1).

happy-go-lucky *adjective*
▸ blithe, buoyant, debonair. *See* **lighthearted** (1).

harangue *noun*
A long, violent, or blustering speech, usually of censure or denunciation ▸ diatribe, fulmination. *See* **tirade**.

harangue *verb*
To speak in a loud, pompous, or prolonged manner ▸ orate, rave. *See* **rant** (1).

harass *verb*
To attack or disturb persistently ▸ annoy, badger, bait, bedevil, beleaguer, besiege, beset, harrow, harry, heckle, hector, hound, importune, persecute, pester, plague, taunt, tease, torment, worry. *Informal:* hassle, needle, ride. *Slang:* rag. *See also* **insult, nag, ridicule**.

✛ **CORE SYNONYMS:** *harass, harry, hound, badger, pester, plague.* These verbs mean to attack, disturb, or trouble persistently or incessantly. *Harass* and *harry* imply systematic persecution by besieging with repeated annoyances, threats, or demands: *The landlord harassed tenants who were behind in their rent. A rude customer had harried the storekeeper. Hound* suggests unrelenting pursuit to gain a desired end: *Reporters hounded the celebrity for an interview.* To *badger* is to nag or tease persistently: *The child badgered his parents for a new bicycle.* To *pester* is to inflict a succession of petty annoyances: "*How she would have pursued and pestered me with questions and surmises*" (Charlotte Brontë). *Plague* refers to a problem likened to an epidemic disease: "*As I have no estate, I am plagued with no tenants or stewards*" (Henry Fielding).

---

harassment *noun*
▸ bother, irritation, vexation. *See* **annoyance** (1).

harbor *noun*
1. A protected area of water where ships can anchor or dock ▸ anchorage, cove, haven, lagoon, road, roadstead, port. *See also* **bay¹, channel, inlet**. 2. Something that physically protects, especially from danger ▸ haven, port, refuge. *See* **cover** (1).

harbor *verb*
1. To give refuge to ▸ haven, house, shelter, take in. *See also* **defend**. 2. To provide with lodging, especially temporarily ▸ accommodate, bed (down), house. *See* **lodge** (1). 3. To keep steadily in mind ▸ nourish, nurse. *See* **bear** (2).

harbinger *noun*
1. One that foreshadows or prepares for something else ▸ herald, precursor. *See* **forerunner** (1). 2. A phenomenon that serves as a sign of some future good or evil ▸ portent, prognostication, sign. *See* **omen**.

harborage *noun*
▸ asylum, sanctuary, shelter. *See* **refuge** (1).

hard *adjective*
1. Unyielding to pressure ▸ firm, incompressible, solid. 2. Physically toughened so as to have great endurance ▸ hard-bitten, hard-handed, hardy, rugged, tempered, tough. *Idioms:* hard (*or* tough) as

nails, hard (*or* tough) as tacks. *See also* **muscular.**
3. Not easy to do, achieve, or master ▸ arduous, laborious, tough. *See* **difficult** (1). *See synonym note at* **difficult. 4.** Conveying great physical force ▸ heavy, powerful. *See* **severe** (2). **5.** Rigorous and unsparing in treating others ▸ harsh, stern, strict. *See* **severe** (1). **6.** Marked by cold and unpleasant conditions ▸ grim, severe. *See* **bleak** (1). **7.** Painfully intense ▸ brutal, harsh, severe. *See* **bitter** (2). **8.** Lacking compassion or mercy ▸ heartless, insensitive, merciless. *See* **callous. 9.** Bitingly hostile ▸ bitter, rancorous, virulent. *See* **resentful. 10.** Established beyond a doubt ▸ inarguable, indisputable, irrefutable. *See* **certain** (2). **11.** Having or indicating an awareness of things as they really are ▸ practical, pragmatic, prosaic. *See* **realistic** (1). **12.** Containing alcohol ▸ alcoholic, intoxicating, intoxicative, spiked, spirituous, stiff, strong. **13.** Indulging in drink to an excessive degree ▸ heavy. *Informal:* two-fisted.

hard *adverb*
1. With great force, energy, or intensity ▸ all out, boldly, con brio, energetically, fervently, fiercely, forcefully, forcibly, frantically, frenziedly, furiously, lustily, powerfully, rabidly, severely, stoutly, strenuously, urgently, warmly, vigorously, wholeheartedly, zealously. *Idioms:* hammer and tongs, like all get-out, like blazes, tooth and nail, with might and main, with no holds barred. *See also* **very. 2.** With effort ▸ arduously, assiduously, difficultly, drudgingly, gruelingly, heavily, laboriously, rigorously, wearisomely. **3.** To a point near in time, space, or relation ▸ near, nearby. *See* **close**

hard-bitten *adjective*
▸ hardy, tough. *See* **hard** (2).
hard-boiled *adjective*
▸ heartless, insensitive, merciless. *See* **callous.**
harden *verb*
1. To make resistant to hardship, especially through continued exposure ▸ acclimate, acclimatize, case-harden, indurate, season, strengthen, toughen. *See also* **deaden, gird. 2.** To make or become physically hard ▸ cake, cement, concrete, congeal, dry, firm up, fix, indurate, ossify, petrify, set, solidify, stiffen, toughen. *See also* **coagulate, thicken. 3.** To make firmer in a particular conviction or habit ▸ confirm, fortify, reinforce, strengthen. *See also* **back, establish.**

✦ CORE SYNONYMS: *harden, acclimate, acclimatize, season, toughen.* These verbs mean to make resistant to hardship, especially through continued exposure: *was hardened to frontier life; is acclimated to the tropical heat; was acclimatized by long hours to overwork; became seasoned to life in prison; toughened by experience.*

---

hardened *adjective*
▸ compassionless, heartless, insensitive, merciless. *See* **callous.**
hard-fisted *adjective*
▸ close-fisted, miserly, penny-pinching. *See* **stingy** (1).

hard-handed *adjective*
▸ hardy, tough. *See* **hard** (2).
hardheaded *adjective*
1. Having or indicating an awareness of things as they really are ▸ practical, pragmatic, prosaic. *See* **realistic** (1). **2.** Firmly, often unreasonably immovable in purpose or will ▸ bullheaded, dogged, obstinate. *See* **stubborn** (1).
hardheadedness *noun*
▸ bullheadedness, doggedness, rigidity. *See* **stubbornness.**
hardhearted *adjective*
▸ heartless, insensitive, merciless. *See* **callous.**
hard-hitting *adjective*
▸ dynamic, powerful, vigorous. *See* **forceful** (1).
hardiness *noun*
▸ fortitude, stamina, toughness. *See* **endurance** (1).
hardly *adverb*
By a very little; almost not ▸ barely, just, scarce, scarcely. *Idioms:* by a hair (*or* whisker), by the skin of one's teeth. *See also* **approximately, merely, only.**
hardness *noun*
1. Reliability in withstanding pressure, force, or stress ▸ firmness, security, steadiness. *See* **stability. 2.** The fact or condition of being rigorous and unsparing ▸ harshness, rigidity, stringency. *See* **severity** (1).
hard-shell *adjective*
▸ deep-seated, entrenched, ingrained, inveterate. *See* **confirmed** (1).
hardship *noun*
1. Something that obstructs progress and requires great effort to overcome ▸ complication, impediment, rigor. *See* **difficulty** (1). *See synonym note at* **difficulty. 2.** The condition of being deprived of what one once had or ought to have ▸ destitution, dispossession, loss. *See* **deprivation** (1). **3.** A state of prolonged anguish and privation ▸ woe, wretchedness. *See* **misery** (1).
hardy *adjective*
1. Physically toughened so as to have great endurance ▸ hard-bitten, tough. *See* **hard** (2). **2.** Having or showing courage ▸ courageous, fearless, heroic. *See* **brave. 3.** Having good health ▸ fit, well. *See* **healthy** (1). *See synonym note at* **healthy. 4.** Capable of exerting considerable effort or of withstanding considerable stress or hardship ▸ sturdy, tough. *See* **strong** (2).
harebrained *adjective*
1. Displaying a lack of good sense ▸ daft, idiotic, ludicrous. *See* **foolish. 2.** Given to lighthearted silliness ▸ featherbrained, flighty, frivolous. *See* **giddy** (2).
hark *verb*
1. To make an effort to hear something ▸ attend, hearken, heed, listen. *Idioms:* give (*or* lend) an ear. **2.** To perceive by ear, usually attentively ▸ heed, listen. *See* **hear** (1).
hark back *verb*
To cause one to remember or think of ▸ recall, suggest. *Idioms:* bring to mind, put one in mind of, take one back, remind one of. *See also* **refer, remind.**

harlot *noun*

A woman who engages in sex for payment ► bawd, call girl, courtesan, harlot, scarlet woman, strumpet, tart. *Slang:* hooker, moll, working girl. *Idioms:* lady of easy virtue, lady of the night, lady of pleasure. *See also* **prostitute, slut.**

harm *noun*

The action or result of inflicting loss or pain ► damage, detriment, distress, hurt, impairment, injury, mischief, trauma. *See also* **distress, evil, offense.**

harm *verb*

To spoil the soundness or perfection of ► flaw, impair. *See* **damage.**

harmful *adjective*

Causing harm, injury, or destruction ► adverse, bad, baneful, corrosive, corruptive, damaging, deleterious, destructive, detrimental, evil, hurtful, ill, injurious, malefic, maleficent, malevolent, malign, mischievous, naughty, nocuous, noisome, noxious, pernicious, ruinous, toxic, unhealthy, unwholesome. *See also* **disastrous.**

harmless *adjective*

1. Devoid of hurtful qualities ► benign, hurtless, innocent, innocuous, inoffensive, safe, unoffensive. 2. Free from guilt or blame ► faultless, guiltless. *See* **innocent** (2).

harmonic *adjective*

► musical, symphonic. *See* **harmonious** (2).

harmonious *adjective*

1. Having components that are pleasingly combined ► balanced, concordant, congruous, symmetrical. *See also* **pleasant.** 2. Characterized by harmony of sound ► consonant, harmonic, in tune, musical, symphonic, symphonious, well-voiced. 3. Having or producing a pleasing melody or sound ► euphonic, melodic, musical. *See* **melodious.** 4. Being in or characterized by complete agreement ► accordant, consonant, likeminded. *See* **unanimous.** 5. In keeping with one's needs or expectations ► compatible, congenial, consonant. *See* **agreeable** (1).

harmonization *noun*

1. The act or state of agreeing or conforming ► concordance, harmony, rapport. *See* **agreement** (2). 2. The act or condition of being arranged ► allotment, distribution, positioning. *See* **arrangement** (1).

harmonize *verb*

1. To bring into accord ► accommodate, attune, conform, coordinate, integrate, proportion, reconcile, tune. *See also* **balance, mix.** 2. To combine and adapt in order to attain a particular effect ► arrange, blend, coordinate, correlate, integrate, mesh, orchestrate, synthesize, unify. 3. To come to an understanding or to terms ► coincide, concur. *See* **agree** (2). *See synonym note at* **agree.** 4. To be compatible or suitable ► chime, correspond, match. *See* **agree** (1). 5. To interact with another or others in a harmonious fashion ► communicate, connect. *Slang:* click. *See* **relate** (5). 6. To occur at the same time ► coincide, concur, synchronize.

harmony *noun*

1. Pleasing agreement, as of musical sounds ► accord, blend, concert, concord, consonance, euphoniousness, euphony, symphony, tune, tunefulness. 2. A relationship or an affinity between people or things in which many properties are shared ► sympathy, synch, synchronization, synchrony. 3. Satisfying arrangement marked by even distribution of elements, as in a design ► balance, proportion, symmetry. *See synonym note at* **proportion.** 4. The act or state of agreeing or conforming ► accordance, conformity, congruence. *See* **agreement** (2).

harness *noun*

A device for locking ► catch, clip, lock. *See* **fastener.**

harness *verb*

1. To put into action or use ► apply, employ, utilize. *See* **use** (1). 2. To control, restrict, or arrest ► bridle, check, curb. *See* **restrain.**

harp on *noun*

To discuss at excessive length ► dwell on, labor, overemphasize. *See* **belabor** (2).

harpy *noun*

► nag, shrew. *See* **scold.**

harridan *noun*

► harpy, shrew. *See* **scold.**

harrow *verb*

1. To subject another to extreme physical cruelty, as in punishing ► crucify, rack, torment, torture. *Idioms:* put on the rack (*or* wheel). *See also* **punish.** 2. To attack or disturb persistently ► harry, pester, torment. *See* **harass.** 3. To cause emotional suffering or painful sorrow to ► disturb, grieve, hurt. *See* **distress** (1).

harrowing *adjective*

1. Extraordinarily painful or distressing ► excruciating, torturous. *See* **tormenting.** 2. Causing great horror ► hair-raising, horrific, nightmarish. *See* **horrible** (1).

harry *verb*

1. To attack or disturb persistently ► badger, pester, torment. *See* **harass.** *See synonym note at* **harass.** 2. To enter so as to attack, plunder, destroy, or conquer ► foray, maraud. *See* **invade** (1).

harsh *adjective*

1. Disagreeable to the senses, especially the sense of hearing ► dry, grating, hoarse, jarring, rasping, raspy, raucous, rough, scratchy, shrill, squawky, strident. *See also* **vociferous, inharmonious.** 2. Having a surface that is not smooth ► coarse, ragged, scabrous. *See* **rough** (1). *See synonym note at* **rough.** 3. Painfully intense ► brutal, punishing, severe. *See* **bitter** (2). 4. Rigorous and unsparing in treating others ► demanding, stern, strict. *See* **severe** (1). 5. Marked by cold and unpleasant conditions ► grim, severe. *See* **bleak** (1). 6. So sharp as to cause mental pain ► caustic, scathing, sharp, vitriolic. *See* **biting.**

harshness *noun*

► austerity, rigidity, stringency. *See* **severity** (1).

harum-scarum *adjective*

► hasty, impulsive, reckless. *See* **rash**[1].

haruspex *noun*
▸ diviner, fortuneteller, seer, soothsayer. *See* **prophet.**

harvest *noun*
1. The produce harvested from the land ▸ crop, fruit, fruitage, vintage, yield. 2. Something brought about by a cause ▸ consequence, outcome, result. *See* **effect** (1).

harvest *verb*
1. To collect ripe crops ▸ garner, pick, reap. *See* **gather** (1). 2. To collect something bit by bit ▸ cull, pick up. *See* **glean** (1). *See synonym note at* **glean.**

hash *noun*
Informal A confused or ruinous state ▸ foul-up, muddle, shambles. *See* **mess** (1).

hash over *verb*
Informal To speak together and exchange ideas and opinions about ▸ argue, converse, debate. *See* **discuss.**

hasp *noun*
▸ catch, clip, lock. *See* **fastener.**

hassle *noun*
1. *Informal* A discussion, often heated, in which a difference of opinion is expressed ▸ dispute, fight, quarrel. *See* **argument** (1). 2. *Informal* Something that annoys ▸ bother, irritant, nuisance. *See* **annoyance** (2). 3. *Informal* Needless trouble ▸ fuss, pother. *See* **bother** (1).

hassle *verb*
1. *Informal* To engage in a quarrel ▸ dispute, fight, quarrel. *See* **argue** (1). 2. *Informal* To attack or disturb persistently ▸ harry, pester, torment. *See* **harass.**

hassock *noun*
A stool or cushion for resting the feet ▸ footrest, footstool, ottoman.

haste *noun*
1. Rapidity of movement or activity ▸ alacrity, celerity, dispatch, expedition, expeditiousness, fleetness, hurry, hustle, quickness, rapidity, rapidness, rush, speed, speediness, swiftness. 2. Careless headlong action ▸ hastiness, hurriedness, precipitance, precipitancy, precipitateness, precipitation, rashness, rush.

haste *verb*
To move swiftly ▸ dash, sprint, zip. *See* **rush** (1).

✛ CORE SYNONYMS: *haste, celerity, dispatch, expedition, hurry, speed.* These nouns denote rapidity or promptness of movement or activity: *left the room in haste; a legal system not known for celerity; advanced with all possible dispatch; cleaned up with remarkable expedition; worked without hurry; driving with excessive speed.*

---

hasten *verb*
1. To move swiftly ▸ dash, sprint, zip. *See* **rush** (1). 2. To increase the speed of ▸ expedite, quicken. *See* **speed** (1). *See synonym note at* **speed.**

hastily *adverb*
▸ hurriedly, quickly, rapidly, swiftly. *See* **fast.**

hastiness *noun*
▸ precipitance, rashness. *See* **haste** (2).

hasty *adjective*
1. Accomplished or experienced in very little time ▸ fast, rapid, speedy. *See* **quick** (1). 2. Characterized by unthinking boldness and haste ▸ brash, impulsive, reckless. *See* **rash**[1]. *See synonym note at* **rash**[1]. 3. Characterized by great speed ▸ hell-for-leather, hurried, rapid. *See* **fast** (1). *See synonym note at* **fast.**

hatch *verb*
1. To give life to ▸ engender, propagate, spawn. *See* **breed** (1). 2. To use ingenuity in making, developing, or achieving ▸ contrive, devise, dream up. *See* **invent** (1). 3. To work out a secret plan to achieve an evil or illegal end ▸ conspire, scheme. *See* **plot** (2).

hatchet man *noun*
▸ killer, massacrer, slaughterer. *See* **murderer.**

hate *verb*
To feel hostility toward or strong dislike for something ▸ abhor, abominate, detest, execrate, loathe. *Idioms:* bear antipathy (*or* malice *or* ill will) toward, be repelled (*or* repulsed *or* revolted) by, be sick of, can't stand. *See also* **despise, dislike, revile.**

hate *noun*
1. A strong feeling of hostility or dislike ▸ abhorrence, abomination, antipathy, aversion, contempt, detestation, hatred, horror, loathing, odium, rancor, repellence, repellency, repugnance, repugnancy, repulsion, revulsion. *See also* **aggression, despisal, enmity, resentment.** 2. An object of extreme dislike ▸ abhorrence, abomination, anathema, aversion, bête noire, bugbear, detestation, execration. *Informal:* horror. *See also* **annoyance.**

hateful *adjective*
1. So unpleasant or objectionable as to cause scorn or disgust ▸ despicable, mean, nasty, odious. *See* **offensive** (1). *See synonym note at* **offensive.** 2. Characterized by intense ill will or spite ▸ evil, wicked. *See* **malevolent** (1).

hatred *noun*
1. A strong feeling of hostility or dislike ▸ antipathy, aversion, loathing. *See* **hate** (1). 2. The feeling of despising ▸ disdain, loathing, scorn. *See* **despisal.**

haughtiness *noun*
1. The quality of being arrogant ▸ hauteur, superiority. *See* **arrogance.** 2. Superciliously indulgent treatment, especially of those who are considered inferior ▸ patronization, snobbery. *See* **condescension.**

haughty *adjective*
1. Overly convinced of one's own superiority and importance ▸ insolent, smug, superior. *See* **arrogant.** *See synonym note at* **arrogant.** 2. Showing scorn and disrespect toward someone or something ▸ dismissive, intolerant, scornful. *See* **disdainful** (1).

haul *verb*
1. To exert force so as to move something toward the source of the force ▸ draw, tow, tug. *See* **pull** (1). *See synonym note at* **pull.** 2. To move while supporting ▸ bear, convey, lug. *See* **carry** (1).

haul *noun*
1. The act of drawing or pulling a load ▸ drag, draw,

tow. *See* **pull** (1). **2.** Something carried or transported ► freight, load. *See* **burden**[1] (2).

hauling *noun*
► conveyance, transit. *See* **transportation** (1).

haunt *verb*
1. To come to mind continually ► obsess, torment, trouble, weigh on (*or* upon). **2.** To visit regularly ► hang around, repair to. *See* **frequent**.

haunt *noun*
1. A frequently visited place ► meeting place, rendez-vous, resort. *Slang:* hangout, stamping ground, stomping ground. *See also* **habitat**. **2.** *Chiefly Regional* An immaterial supernatural being, especially the spirit of a dead person ► phantom, shade, specter. *See* **ghost** (1).

hauteur *noun*
► haughtiness, superiority. *See* **arrogance**.

have *verb*
1. To hold on one's person ► bear, possess. *Informal:* pack. *See* **carry** (7). **2.** To have at one's disposal ► enjoy, hold, possess. *See* **command** (3). **3.** To have as a visible characteristic ► display, possess. *See* **bear** (3). **4.** To have as a part ► comprise, take in. *See* **contain** (1). **5.** To be filled by ► contain, hold. *See also* **constitute**. **6.** To admit to one's possession, presence, or awareness ► accept, receive, take. *See also* **absorb**. **7.** To participate in or partake of personally ► know, undergo. *See* **experience**. **8.** To neither forbid nor prevent ► let, tolerate. *See* **permit** (1). **9.** To organize and carry out an activity ► give, hold, stage, throw. *See also* **conduct**. **10.** To involve oneself in an activity ► engage, partake, share. *See* **participate** (1). **11.** *Informal* To cause to accept something false, especially by trickery or misrepresentation ► dupe, fool, mislead, trick. *See* **deceive**. **12.** To give birth to ► bring forth, deliver. *See* **bear** (4). **13.** To engage in sexual relations with ► mate, service. *See* **sleep with**.

have at *verb*
To set upon with violent force ► assail, assault, storm, strike. *See* **attack** (1).

haven *noun*
1. Something that physically protects, especially from danger ► asylum, harbor, refuge. *See* **cover** (1). **2.** A protected area of water where ships can anchor ► anchorage, cove. *See* **harbor** (1).

haven *verb*
To give refuge to ► harbor, house, shelter, take in. *See also* **defend**.

have-not *noun*
► beggar, insolvent, tramp. *See* **pauper**.

havoc *noun*
► devastation, ruin, wreck. *See* **destruction** (1).

hawk[1] *verb*
To travel about selling goods ► huckster, peddle, vend.

hawk[2] *verb*
To expel a small amount of saliva or mucus from the mouth ► expectorate, spit. *See also* **drool**.

hawkish *adjective*
1. Inclined to act in an aggressive or hostile way

► combative, militant, warmongering. *See* **aggressive** (1). **2.** Of or inclined toward war ► martial, militaristic. *See* **military** (1).

hayseed *noun*
Slang A clumsy, unsophisticated person ► hick, rustic, yokel. *See* **clodhopper**.

haywire *adjective*
Informal Afflicted with or exhibiting irrationality and mental unsoundness ► crazy, lunatic, mad. *See* **insane** (1).

hazard *noun*
1. An unexpected random event ► accident, fluke, happenstance. *See* **chance** (1). **2.** The random, unintended, or unpredictable element of an event or the force regarded as the cause of such an event ► coincidence, fortune, luck. *See* **chance** (2). **3.** Exposure to harm, loss, or injury ► jeopardy, peril, risk. *See* **danger**. **4.** A possibility of danger or harm ► chance, gamble. *See* **risk** (1).

hazard *verb*
1. To place something at risk, as in a game of chance ► bet, stake, wager. *See* **gamble** (2). **2.** To express at the risk of rebuff or criticism ► chance, dare, presume. *See* **venture** (1). **3.** To expose to danger or destruction ► compromise, imperil. *See* **endanger**. *See synonym note at* **endanger**.

hazardous *adjective*
► chancy, grave, risky. *See* **dangerous**.

haze *noun*
1. A suspension in the air of tiny particles of water, dust, or smoke ► brume, fog, mist, pall, smaze, smog, smudge, steam, vapor. **2.** A stunned or bewildered condition ► bewilderment, perplexity, stupor. *See* **daze**.

hazing *noun*
► inauguration, induction, installation. *See* **initiation** (2).

hazy *adjective*
1. Heavy, dark, or dense, especially with impurities ► murky, smoggy, turbid. *See also* **dirty**. **2.** Not clearly perceptible ► dim, faint, misty, indefinite. *See* **unclear** (1).

head *noun*
1. The uppermost part of the body ► crown, noddle, pate, poll. *Slang:* bean, block, conk, dome, noggin, noodle, nut. **2.** The seat of the faculty of intelligence and reason ► brain, mind. *Informal:* gray matter. *See also* **imagination**. **3.** An innate capability ► faculty, gift, knack. *See* **talent**. **4.** One who governs or leads ► boss, director, governor, leader. *See* **chief** (1). **5.** Someone who directs and supervises workers ► foreman, manager, supervisor. *See* **boss** (1). **6.** A mass of bubbles in or on the surface of a liquid ► lather, suds. *See* **foam**. **7.** A decisive point ► crossroads, juncture. *See* **crisis** (1). *See synonym note at* **crisis**. **8.** A term or terms in large type introducing a text ► header, heading, headline. **9.** The forward part of something ► fore, front end, front side. *See* **front** (1).

head *adjective*
Most important, influential, or significant ▸ chief, key, main, principal. *See* **primary** (1).
head *verb*
1. To have charge of the affairs of others ▸ direct, govern, rule. *See* **administer** (1). **2.** To direct something, often toward a target ▸ level, point, train. *See* **aim** (1). **3.** To proceed in a specified direction ▸ go, make, set out. *See* **bear** (5).
head off *verb*
1. To block the progress of and force to change direction ▸ cut off, intercept. **2.** To prohibit from occurring by advance planning or action ▸ avert, stave off, ward (off). *See* **prevent.**
headache *noun*
1. *Informal* A source of persistent worry or hardship ▸ cross, tribulation. *See* **burden**[1] (1). **2.** *Informal* Something that annoys ▸ bother, irritant, nuisance. *See* **annoyance** (2). **3.** *Informal* Needless trouble ▸ fuss, pother. *See* **bother** (1).
header *noun*
Informal A sudden downward motion toward the ground ▸ nosedive, spill, tumble. *See* **fall** (1).
heading *noun*
1. A term or terms in large type introducing a text ▸ head, header, headline. **2.** The compass direction in which a ship or aircraft moves ▸ bearing, course, vector. **3.** The spatial path along which motion or orientation is referred ▸ course, route. *See* **direction** (1). **4.** An item inserted, as in a diary, register, or reference book ▸ insertion, posting. *See* **entry** (1).
headline *noun*
1. A term or terms in large type introducing a text ▸ head, header, heading. **2.** New information, especially about recent events and happenings ▸ intelligence, report. *See* **news** (1).
headliner *noun*
▸ protagonist, star. *See* **lead** (1).
headlong *adjective*
▸ hasty, impulsive, reckless. *See* **rash**[1]. *See synonym note at* **rash**[1].
headman *noun*
▸ boss, director, head, leader. *See* **chief** (1).
headquarters *noun*
1. A center of organization, supply, or activity ▸ complex, installation, station. *See* **base**[1] (1). **2.** A place of concentrated activity, influence, or importance ▸ focus, heart, hub. *See* **center** (1). *See synonym note at* **center. 3.** *Informal* A building or shelter where one lives ▸ abode, domicile, habitation, residence. *See* **home** (1).
head start *noun*
▸ toehold, vantage. *See* **advantage** (1).
headstrong *adjective*
1. Firmly, often unreasonably immovable in purpose or will ▸ bullheaded, dogged, obstinate. *See* **stubborn** (1). *See synonym note at* **stubborn. 2.** Not submitting to discipline or control ▸ ill-behaved, obstinate, unmanageable. *See* **unruly.**

headway *noun*
1. Forward movement ▸ advancement, furtherance, progress. *See* **advance** (1). **2.** Steady improvement, as of an individual or society ▸ advancement, betterment, development. *See* **progress** (1).
headword *noun*
▸ heading, posting. *See* **entry** (1).
headwork *noun*
▸ deliberation, rumination. *See* **thought** (1).
heal *verb*
▸ rehabilitate, remedy. *See* **cure** (1).
health *noun*
1. The condition of being physically or mentally sound ▸ haleness, healthiness, heartiness, soundness, wellness, wholeness. *See also* **condition. 2.** The act of drinking to someone ▸ pledge, toast.
healthful *adjective*
1. Promoting good health ▸ healthsome, healthy, hearty, hygienic, salubrious, salutary, wholesome. *See also* **beneficial, nutritious. 2.** Having good health ▸ fit, well. *See* **healthy** (1).
healthiness *noun*
▸ haleness, soundness. *See* **health** (1).
healthsome *adjective*
▸ healthy, hygienic. *See* **healthful** (1).
healthy *adjective*
1. Having good health ▸ able-bodied, all right, fit, flourishing, hale, hardy, healthful, hearty, normal, right, robust, rosy-cheeked, sound, thriving, vigorous, well, whole, wholesome. *Idioms:* fit as a fiddle, hale and hearty, in fine fettle, in fine (*or* good) health, in fine (*or* good) shape, in the pink. *See also* **lusty, muscular, strong. 2.** Promoting good health ▸ healthsome, hygienic. *See* **healthful** (1). **3.** Above average in amount, size, or scope ▸ extensive, large, sizable. *See* **big** (1).

✦ **CORE SYNONYMS:** *healthy, sound, wholesome, hale, robust, well, hardy, vigorous.* These adjectives mean having good physical or mental health. *Healthy* stresses the absence of disease and often implies energy and strength: *The healthy athlete biked twenty miles every day. Sound* emphasizes freedom from injury, imperfection, or impairment: *"The man with the toothache thinks everyone happy whose teeth are sound"* (George Bernard Shaw). *Wholesome* suggests appealing healthiness and well-being: *"Exercise develops wholesome appetites"* (Louisa May Alcott). *Hale* stresses freedom from infirmity, especially in elderly persons, while *robust* emphasizes healthy strength and ruggedness: *"He is pretty well advanced in years, but hale, robust, and florid"* (Tobias Smollett). *Well* indicates absence of or recovery from sickness: *You should stay home from work if you're not well. Hardy* implies robust and sturdy good health: *The hardy mountaineers camped in the Alps. Vigorous* suggests healthy, active energy and strength: *"a vigorous old man, who spent half of his day on horseback"* (W.H. Hudson).

◄ **ANTONYM:** *unhealthy*

heap *noun*
1. A group of things gathered haphazardly ▸ agglomeration, bank, cumulus, drift, hill, mass, mess, mound, mountain, pile, shock, stack, tumble. *See also* **accumulation. 2.** *Informal* A great deal ▸ bounty, mass, profusion. *See* **abundance** (1). **3.** *Informal* An indeterminately great amount or number ▸ bunch, lot, multiplicity, ream. *Informal:* billion, bushel, gob, jillion, load, million, mountain, oodles, passel, peck, pile, scad, slew, ton, trillion, wad, zillion.
heap *verb*
1. To collect or pile up or onto something ▸ bank, drift, hill, load, lump, mound, pile (up *or* together), stack. *See also* **load. 2.** To fill to capacity ▸ load, pack, pile. *See* **fill** (1). **3.** To give in great abundance ▸ lavish, rain, shower. *See also* **confer, donate, give.**
heap up *verb*
To bring together so as to increase in mass or number ▸ amass, build up, pile up. *See* **accumulate.**

✦ CORE SYNONYMS: *heap, bank, mound, pile, stack.* These nouns denote a group of things gathered haphazardly: *a heap of old newspapers; a bank of thunderclouds; a mound of boulders; a pile of boxes; a stack of firewood.*

hear *verb*
1. To perceive by ear, usually attentively ▸ attend, auscultate, hark, heed, listen. *Idioms:* give (*or* lend) one's ear. **2.** To obtain knowledge or awareness of something not known before ▸ determine, learn, unearth. *See* **discover. 3.** *Informal* To perceive and recognize the meaning of ▸ follow, get, see. *See* **understand** (1).
hear of *verb*
To receive an idea and think about it in order to form an opinion about it ▸ consider, entertain, think about (of).
hearing *noun*
1. The sense by which sound is perceived ▸ audition, auditory system, ear. **2.** Range of audibility ▸ earshot, sound. *See also* **range. 3.** A chance to be heard ▸ audience, audition, listen. *Idiom:* one's day in court. **4.** The examination of evidence, charges, and claims in court ▸ court case, inquest, inquiry, trial. *See also* **examination.**
hearken *verb*
To make an effort to hear something ▸ attend, hark, heed, listen. *Idioms:* give (*or* lend) an ear.
hearsay *noun*
▸ gossipry, rumor, tattle. *See* **gossip** (1).
heart *noun*
1. The most central or essential part ▸ center, core, essence, gist, kernel, marrow, meat, nub, nucleus, pith, quintessence, root, soul, spirit, stuff, substance. *See also* **subject. 2.** The circulatory organ of the body ▸ blood pump. *Slang:* ticker. **3.** The seat of a person's innermost emotions and feelings ▸ bosom, breast, soul. *Idioms:* bottom of one's heart, cockles of one's heart, one's heart of hearts. **4.** Sympathetic, sad

concern for someone in misfortune ▸ compassion, empathy, sympathy. *See* **pity** (1). **5.** The quality of mind enabling one to face danger or hardship resolutely ▸ bravery, fortitude, gallantry, valor. *See* **courage. 6.** A place of concentrated activity, influence, or importance ▸ headquarters, hotbed, hub. *See* **center** (1). *See synonym note at* **center. 7.** A point of origin or crucial factor ▸ core, focus, nucleus. *See* **center** (3).

✦ CORE SYNONYMS: *heart, core, gist, nucleus, pith, substance.* These nouns denote the most central or essential part of something: *The negotiator addressed issues at the heart of the matter. The core of the editorial had to do with taxes. The gist of the lawyer's argument was that the evidence was inconclusive. The nucleus of the report recommended two basic changes. The scholars analyzed the pith of the essay. The committee judged the substance of the tenants' complaints.*

heartache *or* **heartbreak** *noun*
▸ anguish, sorrow. *See* **grief.** *See synonym note at* **grief.**
heartbreaking *adjective*
▸ grievous, melancholy, mournful. *See* **sorrowful** (1).
heartbroken *adjective*
▸ dysphoric, gloomy, melancholy, spiritless. *See* **depressed** (1).
hearten *verb*
▸ fortify, nerve. *See* **encourage** (2).
heartening *adjective*
▸ cheering, likely. *See* **encouraging.**
heartfelt *adjective*
1. Free from hypocrisy or pretense ▸ natural, sincere, unaffected. *See* **genuine** (1). **2.** Resulting from or affecting one's innermost feelings ▸ great, strong. *See* **deep** (3).
hearth *noun*
An open space for holding a fire at the base of a chimney ▸ fireplace, grate, ingle.
heartiness *noun*
▸ healthiness, soundness. *See* **health** (1).
heartless *adjective*
Lacking compassion or mercy ▸ cold-blooded, insensitive, merciless. *See* **callous.**
heart-rending *adjective*
1. Exciting a deep, usually somber response ▸ moving, poignant. *See* **affecting. 2.** Causing or expressing sorrow or sadness ▸ grievous, heartbreaking, rueful. *See* **sorrowful** (1).
heartsick *adjective*
▸ dysphoric, gloomy, melancholy, spiritless. *See* **depressed** (1).
heartsickness *noun*
▸ dejection, doldrums, melancholy. *See* **depression** (2).
heart-to-heart *noun*
▸ dialogue, discourse, talk. *See* **conversation** (1).
hearty *adjective*
1. Free from hypocrisy or pretense ▸ honest, sincere, unaffected. *See* **genuine** (1). **2.** Having good health

▸ fit, well. *See* **healthy** (1). **3.** Promoting good health ▸ healthy, hygienic. *See* **healthful** (1).

heat *noun*
1. Warmth or degree of warmth ▸ fervor, hotness, temperature, torridity, torridness, warmth. **2.** Powerful, intense emotion ▸ fervor, fire, warmth. *See* **passion** (1). **3.** A stage of a competition ▸ round, stage. *See also* **competition, turn. 4.** *Informal* An oppressive condition of distress ▸ strain, stress, tension. *See* **pressure** (1). **5.** *Slang* A member of a law-enforcement agency ▸ officer, trooper. *See* **police officer.**

heat up *verb*
To stir to action or feeling ▸ inflame, pique, stimulate, work up. *See* **provoke** (1).

heated *adjective*
1. Marked by much heat ▸ blistering, boiling, burning. *See* **hot** (1). **2.** Fired with intense feeling ▸ burning, fervent, impassioned, torrid. *See* **passionate** (1).

heathen *noun*
One who does not believe in God ▸ atheist, infidel, non-believer, pagan.

heathen *adjective*
Without belief in God ▸ pagan. *See also* **atheistic.**

heave *verb*
1. To move vigorously from side to side or up and down ▸ pitch, rock, roll, toss. *See also* **lurch. 2.** To move something to a higher position ▸ hoist, raise. *See* **elevate** (1). *See synonym note at* **elevate. 3.** To send through the air with a motion of the hand or arm ▸ fling, hurl, pitch. *See* **throw** (1). **4.** To utter in a breathless or hoarse manner ▸ pant, wheeze. *See* **gasp** (1). **5.** To breathe hard ▸ gasp, huff. *See* **pant** (1). **6.** *Informal* To eject the contents of the stomach through the mouth ▸ retch, throw up. *Informal:* puke. *See* **vomit** (1).

heave *noun*
1. An instance of lifting or being lifted ▸ boost, hoist. *See* **lift** (1). **2.** An act of throwing ▸ fling, hurl, toss. *See* **throw.**

heaven *noun*
1. A supremely beautiful, blissful state or experience ▸ bliss, ecstasy, Eden, nirvana, paradise, rapture, transport. *Informal:* cloud nine, seventh heaven. *See also* **delight, happiness. 2.** A place or state beyond death ▸ afterworld, great beyond, hereafter. *See* **eternity** (2).

heavenly *adjective*
1. Of or relating to heaven ▸ celestial, divine, paradisaic, paradisaical, paradisal, paradisiac, paradisiacal, supernal. **2.** Of or relating to the heavens ▸ astronomical, celestial, cosmic, empyreal, supernal. **3.** Of, from, like, or being a god or God ▸ godlike, holy. *See* **divine** (1). **4.** Giving great pleasure or delight ▸ delectable, enchanting. *See* **delightful. 5.** Highly pleasing, especially to the sense of taste ▸ delectable, savory, scrumptious. *See* **delicious** (1).

heavens *noun*
The celestial regions as seen from the earth ▸ air, firmament, sky. *Idiom:* wild blue yonder.

heavily *adverb*
▸ arduously, difficultly, laboriously. *See* **hard** (2).

heaviness *noun*
The state or degree of being heavy ▸ heftiness, mass, massiveness, ponderosity, ponderousness, weight, weightiness. *Informal:* avoirdupois. *See also* **importance.**

heavy *adjective*
1. Having relatively great weight ▸ heavyweight, hefty, leaden, massive, ponderous, weighty. **2.** Of large, often awkward size and weight ▸ cumbersome, hefty. *See* **bulky** (1). **3.** Having a large body, especially in girth ▸ husky, stout. *See* **bulky** (2). **4.** Characterized by abundance; as much as one needs or desires ▸ bounteous, plentiful. *See* **generous** (2). **5.** Extreme in activity, strength, or effect ▸ fierce, high. *See* **intense** (1). **6.** Conveying great physical force ▸ hard, powerful. *See* **severe** (2). **7.** Violently disturbed or agitated, as by storms ▸ roily, turbulent. *See* **rough** (2). **8.** Indulging in drink to an excessive degree ▸ hard. *Informal:* two-fisted. **9.** Full of or marked by dignity and seriousness ▸ serious, sober, staid. *See* **grave**² (1). **10.** Not readily digested because of richness ▸ filling, rich. **11.** Growing profusely ▸ lush, luxuriant, profuse. *See* **thick** (3). **12.** Bearing a heavy load ▸ heavy-laden, laden, loaded, weighed down. **13.** Requiring great or extreme bodily, mental, or spiritual strength ▸ backbreaking, crushing, taxing. *See* **burdensome** (1). **14.** *Slang* Beyond the understanding of an average mind ▸ abstract, esoteric, profound. *See* **deep** (2). **15.** Lacking fluency or grace ▸ heavy-handed, labored. *See* **ponderous** (1). **16.** Having too much flesh ▸ chubby, rotund. *See* **fat** (1). **17.** Having a heavy, gluey quality ▸ mucilaginous, viscid. *See* **viscous.**

heavy *noun*
Slang A mean, worthless character in a story or play ▸ bad guy, villain.

✚ CORE SYNONYMS: *heavy, weighty, hefty, massive, ponderous.* These adjectives mean having a relatively great weight. *Heavy* refers to what has great physical weight (*a heavy boulder*) and figuratively to what is burdensome or oppressive to the spirit (*heavy responsibilities*). *Weighty* literally denotes having considerable weight (*a weighty package*); figuratively, it describes what is onerous, serious, or important (*a weighty decision*). *Hefty* refers principally to physical heaviness or brawniness: *a hefty book; a tall, hefty wrestler.* *Massive* describes what is bulky, heavy, solid, and strong: *massive marble columns.* *Ponderous* refers to what has great mass and weight and usually implies unwieldiness: *ponderous prehistoric beasts.* Figuratively it describes what is complicated, involved, or lacking in grace: *a book with a ponderous plot.*

◂ ANTONYM: *light*

---

heavy-footed *adjective*
▸ heavy-handed, labored. *See* **ponderous** (1).

heavy-handed *adjective*
1. Clumsily lacking in the ability to do ▸ bumbling,

clumsy, inept. *See* **unskillful** (1). **2.** Lacking fluency or grace ▸ elephantine, labored. *See* **ponderous** (1).

heavy-hearted *adjective*
▸ dysphoric, gloomy, melancholy, spiritless. *See* **depressed** (1).

heavy-heartedness *noun*
▸ dejection, doldrums, melancholy. *See* **depression** (2).

heavy-laden *adjective*
Burdened by a weighty load ▸ heavy, laden, loaded, weighed down.

heavyset *adjective*
▸ chunky, dumpy, squat. *See* **stocky.**

heavyweight *noun*
An important, influential person ▸ notability, personage. *Slang:* big shot. *See* **dignitary.**

heavyweight *adjective*
1. Having relatively great weight ▸ hefty, ponderous. *See* **heavy** (1). **2.** *Informal* Being among the leaders in one's field ▸ leading, major, major-league. *See* **big-league.**

hebetude *noun*
▸ languor, listlessness, sluggishness. *See* **lethargy** (1).

hebetudinous *adjective*
1. Lacking mental and physical alertness and activity ▸ sluggish, stuporous, torpid. *See* **lethargic** (1). **2.** Lacking in intelligence ▸ dumb, idiotic, obtuse. *See* **stupid** (1).

hecatomb *noun*
▸ immolation, sacrifice, victim. *See* **offering** (1).

heckle *verb*
▸ harry, pester, torment. *See* **harass.**

hectic *adjective*
1. Characterized by hurried activity and by confusion or agitation ▸ frenetic, frenzied, wild. *See* **frantic.** **2.** Full of lively activity ▸ bustling, crawling, swarming. *See* **busy** (2). **3.** Having an above-normal body temperature ▸ febrile, feverish, hot. *See* **feverish** (1).

hector *noun*
One who is habitually cruel to smaller or weaker people ▸ intimidator, tormentor. *See* **bully.**

hector *verb*
1. To frighten into submission or compliance ▸ browbeat, bully, cow. *See* **intimidate** (1). **2.** To attack or disturb persistently ▸ harry, pester, torment. *See* **harass.**

hedge *verb*
1. To shut in on all sides ▸ encircle, hem, ring. *See* **surround** (1). **2.** To keep safe from danger, attack, or harm ▸ protect, safeguard, secure. *See* **defend** (1). **3.** To surround and advance upon ▸ close in, envelop, hem. *See* **enclose** (2). **4.** To use evasive or deliberately vague language ▸ fence, shuffle. *See* **equivocate** (1). **5.** To avoid fulfilling or answering completely ▸ duck, fence. *See* **evade** (1). **6.** The act or a means of defending ▸ protection, safeguard, shield. *See* **defense** (1).

hedge *noun*
The use or an instance of equivocal language ▸ euphemism, prevarication. *See* **equivocation** (1).

hedonist *noun*
▸ epicure, epicurean, sensualist, voluptuary. *See* **sybarite.**

hedonistic *or* **hedonic** *adjective*
Characterized by or devoted to pleasure and luxury as a lifestyle ▸ epicurean, sybaritic, voluptuary, voluptuous.

heebie-jeebies *noun*
Slang A state of nervous restlessness or agitation ▸ jumps, shivers, trembles. *See* **jitters.**

heed *verb*
1. To perceive by ear, usually attentively ▸ hark, listen. *See* **hear** (1). **2.** To act in conformity with ▸ adhere to, obey, observe. *See* **follow** (4). **3.** To make an effort to hear something ▸ attend, hark, hearken, listen. *Idioms:* give (*or* lend) an ear.

heed *noun*
1. Cautious attentiveness ▸ carefulness, caution, mindfulness. *See* **care** (1). **2.** The act of noting, observing, or taking into account ▸ attention, note, regard. *See* **notice** (1).

heedful *adjective*
1. Vigilantly attentive ▸ intent, vigilant. *See* **alert** (1). *See synonym note at* **alert. 2.** Cautiously attentive ▸ mindful, observant, watchful. *See* **careful** (1). *See synonym note at* **careful.**

heedfulness *noun*
1. Concentration of the mental powers on something ▸ attentiveness, concentration. *See* **attention** (1). **2.** Cautious attentiveness ▸ carefulness, caution, heed, mindfulness. *See* **care** (1).

heedless *adjective*
▸ thoughtless, unconcerned, unthinking. *See* **careless** (1). *See synonym note at* **careless.**

heedlessness *noun*
A careless, often reckless disregard for consequences ▸ abandon, blitheness, carelessness, thoughtlessness. *See also* **temerity.**

heehaw *noun*
Informal An act of laughing ▸ cackle, guffaw, laughter. *See* **laugh** (1).

heehaw *verb*
Informal To express amusement or mirth ▸ cackle, chuckle, guffaw. *See* **laugh.**

heel¹ *verb*
To keep another under surveillance by moving along behind ▸ dog, tag, trail. *See* **follow** (3).

heel² *verb*
To depart or cause to depart from true vertical or horizontal ▸ cant, lean. *See* **incline** (1).

heel *noun*
Deviation from a particular direction ▸ grade, heel. *See* **inclination** (2).

heel³ *noun*
1. The crusty end of a loaf of bread ▸ ort, scrap. *See* **end** (7). **2.** Residual matter ▸ fragment, odds and ends. *See* **end** (7).

heftiness *noun*
▸ massiveness, weightiness. *See* **heaviness.**

hefty *adjective*
1. Having relatively great weight ▸ heavyweight, ponderous. *See* **heavy** (1). *See synonym note at* **heavy.**
2. Having a large body, especially in girth ▸ husky, stout. *See* **bulky** (2). **3.** Conveying great physical force ▸ heavy, powerful. *See* **severe** (2). **4.** Of large, often awkward size and weight ▸ cumbersome, heavy, oversized. *See* **bulky** (1).

hegemony *noun*
▸ authority, power, supremacy. *See* **dominance** (1).

height *noun*
1. The distance of something from a given level ▸ altitude, elevation, loftiness, tallness. *See synonym note at* **elevation.** *See also* **ascent. 2.** The highest point or state ▸ apex, crest, peak. *See* **climax** (1). **3.** Concentrated power or force, as of effort, opinion, or emotion ▸ ferocity, pitch, vehemence. *See* **intensity.**

heighten *verb*
1. To make greater in intensity or severity ▸ deepen, enhance, step up. *See* **intensify. 2.** To increase markedly in level or intensity, especially of sound ▸ amplify, raise. *See* **elevate** (2).

heightened *adjective*
1. Extreme in activity, strength, or effect ▸ fierce, heavy. *See* **intense** (1). **2.** Abnormally increased, especially in intensity ▸ high, raised. *See* **elevated** (2).

heinous *adjective*
▸ appalling, monstrous, shocking. *See* **outrageous.**

heinousness *noun*
▸ atrocity, enormity, monstrousness. *See* **outrageousness.**

heist *verb*
1. *Slang* To take another's property without permission ▸ purloin, snatch, thieve. *See* **steal** (1). **2.** *Slang* To take property or possessions from someone unlawfully and usually forcibly ▸ hold up, mug, stick up. *See* **rob** (1).

heist *noun*
Slang The crime of taking someone else's property without consent ▸ burglary, holdup, robbery. *See* **larceny.**

hell *noun*
A place or experience of excruciating pain or punishment ▸ fire and brimstone, hellfire, inferno, living hell, perdition, persecution, torment, torture. *Idiom:* tortures of the damned. *See also* **distress, misery.**

hell *verb*
Informal To behave riotously ▸ carouse, frolic, roister. *See* **revel** (1).

hellbound *adjective*
▸ doomed, lost, reprobate. *See* **condemned.**

hellfire *noun*
▸ perdition, persecution. *See* **hell.**

hell-for-leather *adverb*
In a rapid way ▸ hastily, hurriedly, quickly, rapidly. *See* **fast.**

hell-for-leather *adjective*
Characterized by great speed ▸ breakneck, high-speed, hurried. *See* **fast** (1).

hellhole *noun*
▸ cesspool, gutter, sewer. *See* **pit**[1] (3).

hellish *adjective*
▸ devilish, diabolical, satanic. *See* **fiendish.**

hello *interjection*
Used as a greeting ▸ good day, greetings, salutations. *Informal:* aloha, hey, hey ho, hey there, hi, hi there, howdy, howdy do. *Slang:* yo, 'sup. *Idioms:* how do you do, what's up.

hello *noun*
Informal An expression, in words or gestures, marking a meeting of persons ▸ hail, greeting, salutation, salute, welcome.

helot *noun*
▸ serf, vassal. *See* **slave** (1).

helotry *noun*
▸ enslavement, servility, thrall. *See* **slavery.**

help *verb*
1. To give support or assistance to ▸ abet, aid, assist, boost, help out, relieve, succor. *Idioms:* come to the aid of, do a service, give (*or* lend) a hand, give a leg up, see someone through. *See also* **comfort, serve, support. 2.** To advance to a more desirable state ▸ better, enhance, upgrade. *See* **improve** (1). *See synonym note at* **improve. 3.** To perform a service or a courteous act for ▸ favor, serve. *See* **oblige** (1). **4.** To be an advantage to ▸ benefit, serve. *See* **profit** (2).

help along *verb*
To make less difficult ▸ expedite, facilitate. *See* **ease** (2).

help *noun*
1. The act or an instance of helping ▸ abetment, aid, assist, assistance, hand, relief, succor, support. **2.** A person who assists someone else ▸ adjutant, aide, deputy. *See* **assistant. 3.** One who is employed by another ▸ jobholder, staffer, worker. *See* **employee.**

✛ CORE SYNONYMS: *help, aid, assist, succor.* These verbs mean to give support or assistance to someone or something. *Help* and *aid,* the most general, are frequently interchangeable: *a medication that helps* (or *aids*) *the digestion. Help,* however, sometimes conveys a stronger suggestion of effectual action: *I'll help you move the piano. Assist* usually implies making a secondary contribution or acting as a subordinate: *Apprentices assisted the chef in preparing the banquet. Succor* refers to going to the relief of one in want, difficulty, or distress: *"Mr. Harding thought . . . of the worn-out, aged men he had succored"* (Anthony Trollope).

---

helper *noun*
▸ adjutant, aide, deputy. *See* **assistant.** *See synonym note at* **assistant.**

helpful *adjective*
1. Tending to contribute to a result ▸ conducive, contributive, contributory, participatory. *See also* **auxiliary. 2.** Affording benefit or advantage ▸ favorable, profitable, propitious. *See* **beneficial. 3.** Ready to do favors for another ▸ agreeable, complaisant. *See*

obliging. **4.** Characterized by kindness and concern for others ▸ beneficent, goodhearted, kindly. *See* **benevolent** (1).

helping *noun*
An individual quantity of food ▸ mess, portion. *See* **serving.**

helping *adjective*
Giving or able to give help or support ▸ accessory, contributory. *See* **auxiliary** (1).

helpless *adjective*
1. Lacking power or strength ▸ impotent, powerless, unable. **2.** Susceptible to physical or emotional injury ▸ defenseless, unprotected. *See* **vulnerable** (1). **3.** Not capable of accomplishing anything ▸ impotent, inadequate, incapable. *See* **ineffectual** (2).

helplessness *noun*
▸ impotence, inadequacy, powerlessness. *See* **ineffectuality.**

helplessly *adverb*
Without regard to desire or inclination ▸ inextricably, involuntarily, perforce, willy-nilly.

helpmate *or* **helpmeet** *noun*
A husband or wife ▸ mate, partner. *See* **spouse.**

helter-skelter *adjective*
Characterized by physical confusion ▸ disordered, topsy-turvy, upside-down. *See* **confused** (2).

helter-skelter *noun*
A condition of being agitated or disturbed ▸ commotion, disturbance, stir. *See* **agitation** (1).

hem *verb*
1. To shut in on all sides ▸ encircle, encompass, ring. *See* **surround** (1). **2.** To surround and advance upon ▸ close in, envelop, hedge. *See* **enclose** (2).

hem *noun*
A line or area where something ends or abruptly changes ▸ brink, fringe, margin. *See* **border** (1).

henchman *noun*
▸ adherent, believer, disciple. *See* **follower** (1).

henpeck *verb*
Informal To scold or find fault with constantly ▸ fuss at, pick on. *See* **nag** (1).

herald *noun*
1. One that foreshadows or prepares for something else ▸ harbinger, precursor. *See* **forerunner** (1). **2.** A person who carries messages or is sent on errands ▸ carrier, courier, envoy. *See* **messenger.**

herald *verb*
1. To make known the presence or arrival of ▸ announce, usher in. *See* **proclaim** (1). **2.** To bring to public notice or make known publicly ▸ advertise, declare, trumpet. *See* **announce** (1).

herculean *adjective*
▸ behemoth, colossal, gigantic, mighty. *See* **enormous.**

herd *verb*
To urge to move along ▸ chase, push, run. *See* **drive** (3).

herd *noun*
1. An enormous number of persons or things gath-

ered together ▸ horde, mass, throng. *See* **crowd** (1). **2.** A number of animals considered collectively ▸ bevy, gaggle, litter. *See* **flock** (1). *See synonym note at* **flock.**

hereafter *noun*
1. Time that is yet to be ▸ by-and-by, future, futurity, tomorrow. *Idiom:* time to come. *See also* **approach, possibility. 2.** A place or state that is beyond death ▸ afterworld, heaven, paradise. *See* **eternity** (2).

hereditary *adjective*
1. Possessed at birth ▸ inborn, inherited, native. *See* **innate** (1). *See synonym note at* **innate. 2.** Of unbroken descent or lineage ▸ direct, genealogical, lineal, natural. *See also* **ancestral. 3.** Of or from one's ancestors ▸ familial, inherited, genealogical. *See* **ancestral.**

heretic *noun*
▸ dissident, sectarian. *See* **separatist.**

heretofore *adverb*
▸ previously, yet. *See* **earlier** (2).

heritage *noun*
1. Something immaterial, as a style or philosophy, that is passed from one generation to another ▸ inheritance, legacy, tradition. *See also* **culture. 2.** Any special privilege accorded a firstborn ▸ birthright, inheritance, legacy, patrimony. *See also* **right.**

✛ **CORE SYNONYMS:** *heritage, inheritance, legacy, tradition.* These nouns denote something immaterial, such as a style, philosophy, or custom, that is passed from one generation to another: *a heritage of moral uprightness; a rich inheritance of storytelling; a legacy of philosophical thought; the tradition of noblesse oblige.*

---

hermeneutic *or* **hermeneutical** *adjective*
▸ explicative, illustrative, interpretive. *See* **explanatory.**

hero *noun*
1. A person revered especially for noble courage ▸ champion, heroine, paladin. *Idiom:* knight in shining armor. *See also* **winner. 2.** A famous person ▸ luminary, personality, star. *See* **celebrity** (1). *See synonym note at* **celebrity.**

heroic *adjective*
1. Having or showing courage ▸ courageous, fearless, hardy. *See* **brave. 2.** Of extraordinary size and power ▸ behemoth, colossal, gigantic, mighty. *See* **enormous.**

heroine *noun*
1. A woman revered especially for noble courage ▸ champion, hero, paladin. *Idiom:* knight in shining armor. *See also* **winner. 2.** A famous woman ▸ luminary, personality, star. *See* **celebrity** (1).

heroism *noun*
▸ bravery, fortitude, gallantry, valor. *See* **courage.**

hesitancy *noun*
▸ indecision, tentativeness. *See* **hesitation.**

hesitant *adjective*
1. Given to or exhibiting hesitation ▸ halting, hesitating, indecisive, irresolute, pendulous, shilly-shally, tentative, timid, vacillant, vacillatory, wavering. *Id-*

iom: hemming and hawing. *See also* **indisposed.**
2. Experiencing doubt ▸ irresolute, skeptical, uncertain. *See* **doubtful** (2).

hesitate *verb*
To be irresolute in acting or doing ▸ dally, dilly-dally, dither, falter, halt, pause, shilly-shally, stagger, vacillate, waver, wobble. **Idiom:** hem and haw. *See also* **delay.**

✚ CORE SYNONYMS: *hesitate, vacillate, waver, falter.* These verbs mean to be irresolute, uncertain, or indecisive. To *hesitate* is to hold back or pause because of doubt or uncertainty: *"A President either is constantly on top of events or, if he hesitates, events will soon be on top of him"* (Harry S. Truman). *Vacillate* implies going back and forth between alternative, usually conflicting courses: *She vacillated about whether to go or to stay. Waver* suggests having second thoughts about a decision: *After much wavering, he finally gave his permission.* To *falter* is to be unsteady in resolution or action: *He resolved to ask for a raise but faltered when his boss entered the room.*

---

hesitation *noun*
The act of hesitating or state of being hesitant ▸ dawdling, hesitancy, indecision, indecisiveness, irresoluteness, irresolution, pause, shilly-shally, tentativeness, timidity, timidness, to-and-fro, vacillation, wavering. **Idiom:** hemming and hawing. *See also* **delay.**

heterogeneity *or* **heterogeneousness** *noun*
▸ diversity, miscellaneousness, variousness. *See* **variety** (1).

heterogeneous *adjective*
▸ diverse, miscellaneous, sundry. *See* **various** (1). *See synonym note at* **various.**

hew *verb*
▸ cut down, floor, ground. *See* **drop** (6).

hex *noun*
1. Something or someone believed to bring bad luck ▸ curse, evil eye, hoodoo, Jonah. *Informal:* jinx. **2.** A denunciation invoking a wish or threat of evil or injury ▸ damnation, malediction. *See* **curse** (1).

hex *verb*
1. To bring bad luck or evil to ▸ curse, hoodoo. *Informal:* jinx. *See also* **afflict. 2.** To invoke evil upon ▸ anathematize, curse, damn, imprecate. *See also* **charm.**

hey *interjection*
Informal Used as a greeting ▸ good day, greetings. *See* **hello.**

heyday *noun*
▸ efflorescence, prime. *See* **bloom**[1] (1).

hi *interjection*
Informal Used as a greeting ▸ good day, salutations. *See* **hello.**

hiatus *noun*
1. An interval during which continuity is suspended ▸ break, interim, lacuna. *See* **gap** (2). **2.** A pause or interval, as from work or duty ▸ recess, time-out. *See* **rest**[1] (1).

hick *adjective*
Informal Of or relating to the countryside ▸ bucolic, pastoral, rural. *See* **country.**

hick *noun*
A clumsy, unsophisticated person ▸ bumpkin, rustic, yokel. *See* **clodhopper.**

hidden *adjective*
1. Difficult or impossible to see or distinguish ▸ camouflaged, cloaked, concealed, covert, disguised, imperceptible, indiscernible, indistinguishable, invisible, masked, obscured, secret, shrouded, unapparent, unnoticeable, unseen, veiled. *See also* **imperceptible, secret. 2.** Concealed from view ▸ blind, secluded, screened, secret. **Idioms:** out of sight, out of view. *See also* **hidden. 3.** Lying beyond what is obvious or avowed ▸ buried, concealed, covert. *See* **ulterior** (1).

hide[1] *verb*
1. To put or keep out of sight ▸ bury, cache, conceal, ensconce, occult, secrete, squirrel away. *Slang:* plant, stash. *See also* **save. 2.** To prevent something from being known ▸ enshroud, mask. *See* **conceal** (1). **3.** To cut off from sight ▸ conceal, screen. *See* **block** (1). *See synonym note at* **block.**

hide out *verb*
To shut oneself up in secrecy ▸ *Informal:* hole up. **Idioms:** go underground, lay (*or* lie) low.

✚ CORE SYNONYMS: *hide, conceal, secrete, cache, bury.* These verbs mean to keep from the sight or knowledge of others. *Hide* and *conceal* are the most general and are often used interchangeably: *I used a throw rug to hide* (or *conceal*) *the stain on the carpet. I smiled to hide* (or *conceal*) *my hurt feelings. Secrete* and *cache* involve concealment in a place unknown to others; *cache* often implies storage for later use. *The lioness secreted her cubs in the tall grass. The mountain climbers cached their provisions in a cave. Bury* implies covering over: *The pirates buried the treasure. The author buried the point of the article in a mass of details.*

---

hide[2] *noun*
The skin of an animal, sometimes including fur, hair or feathers ▸ fur, leather, pelt.

hide *verb*
To punish with blows or lashes ▸ lash, thrash, whip. *See* **beat** (2).

hideaway *noun*
A hiding place ▸ covert, den, hide-out, lair.

hidebound *adjective*
▸ close-minded, illiberal, racist. *See* **intolerant** (1).

hideous *adjective*
1. Displeasing to the eye ▸ homely, unattractive, unsightly. *See* **ugly** (1). *See synonym note at* **ugly. 2.** Shockingly repellent ▸ grisly, gruesome, macabre. *See* **ghastly** (1).

hideousness *noun*
▸ monstrosity, odiousness, unsightliness. *See* **ugliness** (1).

hide-out *noun*
A hiding place ▸ covert, den, hideaway, lair.

hiding *noun*
▶ flogging, thrashing, whipping. *See* **beating** (1).

hierarch *noun*
▶ boss, director, head, leader. *See* **chief** (1).

hierarchy *noun*
▶ league, rank, tier. *See* **class** (2).

hieroglyphic *adjective*
▶ illustrative, pictographic, pictorial. *See* **graphic** (4).

higgle *verb*
▶ haggle, negotiate, palter. *See* **haggle**.

higgledy-piggledy *adjective*
▶ disordered, topsy-turvy, upside-down. *See* **confused** (2).

high *adjective*
1. Being of or at a relatively great height or altitude ▶ aerial, airy, elevated, lofty, sky-high, soaring, tall, towering. **Idiom:** on high. **2.** At the upper end of a degree of measure ▶ elevated, great, large. *See also* **exalted, extreme. 3.** Elevated in pitch ▶ acute, high-pitched, piercing, piping, shrieky, shrill, shrilly, treble. **4.** Exceedingly dignified in form, tone, or style ▶ eloquent, grand. *See* **elevated** (5). **5.** Abnormally increased, especially in intensity ▶ heightened, raised. *See* **elevated** (2). **6.** Of great value or price ▶ expensive, high-priced, valuable. *See* **costly. 7.** Extreme in activity, strength, or effect ▶ fierce, heavy, strong. *See* **intense** (1). **8.** *Slang* Stupefied, excited, or muddled with alcoholic liquor ▶ intoxicated, sodden, tipsy. *See* **drunk. 9.** *Slang* Stupefied, intoxicated, or otherwise influenced by the taking of drugs ▶ baked, hopped-up, lit (up). *See* **drugged. 10.** Feeling great delight and joy ▶ euphoric, overjoyed. *See* **elated.**

high *noun*
Slang A strong, pleasant feeling of excitement or stimulation ▶ lift. *Informal:* wallop. *Slang:* bang. *See* **thrill** (1).

high-and-mighty *adjective*
▶ insolent, superior. *See* **arrogant.**

highball *verb*
Slang To move swiftly ▶ dash, sprint, zip. *See* **rush** (1).

highborn *adjective*
▶ blue-blooded, elite, upper-class. *See* **noble** (1).

highbred *adjective*
1. Of pure breeding stock ▶ pedigreed, pureblood, purebred. *See* **thoroughbred** (1). **2.** Of high birth or social position ▶ blue-blooded, elite, upper-class. *See* **noble** (1).

highbrow *adjective*
1. *Informal* Appealing to or engaging the intellect ▶ cerebral, thoughtful. *See* **intellectual** (1). **2.** Characterized by discriminating taste and broad knowledge as a result of development or education ▶ cultivated, educated. *See* **cultured.**

highbrow *noun*
A person of great mental ability ▶ intellectual, thinker. *See* **mind** (2)

higher *adjective*
Being at a rank or level above another ▶ greater, senior, superior, upper.

higher-up *noun*
Informal One who stands above another in rank ▶ better, elder, senior, superior. *See also* **chief.**

highest *adjective*
1. Of, being, located at, or forming the top ▶ loftiest, top, topmost, upmost, uppermost. *See also* **climactic. 2.** Surpassing all others ▶ finest, leading, optimum. *See* **best** (1).

highfalutin *or* **hifalutin** *adjective*
Informal Characterized by an exaggerated show of dignity or self-importance ▶ hoity-toity, pretentious. *See* **pompous.**

high-flown *adjective*
1. Exceedingly dignified in form, tone, or style ▶ eloquent, grand. *See* **elevated** (5). **2.** Characterized by elevated language, such as that used in public speaking ▶ bombastic, grandiloquent, rhetorical. *See* **oratorical.**

highflying *adjective*
▶ determined, driven. *See* **ambitious.**

high-grade *adjective*
▶ prime, select, superior. *See* **choice** (1).

high-hat *verb*
To treat in a superciliously indulgent manner ▶ condescend, patronize. **Idioms:** lord it over, queen it, speak (*or* talk) down to. *See also* **insult, snub.**

high-hat *adjective*
1. *Informal* Characteristic of or resembling a snob ▶ *Informal:* snooty, uppity. *See* **snobbish. 2.** *Informal* Overly convinced of one's own superiority and importance ▶ haughty, insolent. *See* **arrogant.**

high jinks *or* **hijinks** *noun*
▶ diablerie, mischievousness, tomfoolery. *See* **mischief** (1).

highlight *verb*
To accord emphasis to ▶ accentuate, feature. *See* **emphasize.**

highlight *noun*
Light that is reflected ▶ glare, reflection. *See also* **flash.**

highly *adverb*
▶ exceedingly, extremely, most. *See* **very.**

high-minded *adjective*
▶ elevated, noble. *See* **elevated** (4).

high-pitched *adjective*
▶ piercing, shrill. *See* **high** (3).

high-priced *adjective*
▶ expensive, high, valuable. *See* **costly.**

high-ranking *adjective*
▶ elevated, lofty. *See* **exalted** (1).

high sign *noun*
1. *Informal* A signal that warns of imminent danger ▶ warning, red flag. *See* **alarm** (1). **2.** *Informal* An expressive, meaningful body movement ▶ indication, signal. *See* **gesture** (1).

high-sounding *adjective*
▶ bombastic, grandiloquent, rhetorical. *See* **oratorical.**

high-speed *adjective*
▶ breakneck, express, speedy. *See* **fast** (1).

high-spirited *adjective*
▸ animated, chipper, vivacious. *See* **lively** (1).
hightail *verb*
Slang To leave hastily ▸ bolt. *Slang:* scram, vamoose. *See* **run** (3).
high-up *noun*
▸ notability, personage. *Slang:* big shot. *See* **dignitary**.
highway *noun*
▸ path, road, route. *See* **way** (2).
highwayman *noun*
▸ burglar, robber, stealer. *See* **thief**.
hijack *verb*
1. To take possession of ▸ appropriate, comandeer, snatch. *See* **seize** (1). **2.** *Informal* To compel by threats ▸ blackjack, dragoon. *See* **coerce** (1).
hike *verb*
1. To travel about or journey on foot ▸ backpack, march, tramp, trek. *See also* **journey, rove, walk**. **2.** To increase in amount ▸ boost, jack (up), jump, raise, up. **3.** To move something to a higher position ▸ hike up, hitch up, jack (up), lift, raise. *See* **elevate** (1).
hike *noun*
1. The act of increasing or rising ▸ amplification, boost, escalation. *See* **increase** (1). **2.** The amount by which something is increased ▸ boost, jump. *See* **increase** (2). **3.** An act of walking ▸ ramble, stroll. *See* **walk** (1).
hilarious *adjective*
▸ comical, humorous, laughable. *See* **funny** (1).
hilarity *noun*
▸ glee, lightheartedness, mirth. *See* **merriment** (1).
hill *noun*
1. A natural land elevation ▸ bump, butte, down, eminence, hummock, knoll, prominence, rise. *See also* **plateau**. **2.** A group of things gathered haphazardly ▸ drift, mass, mound. *See* **heap** (1).
hill *verb*
To collect or pile up or onto something ▸ drift, lump. *See* **heap** (1).
hillbilly *noun*
Informal A clumsy, unsophisticated person ▸ hick, rustic, yokel. *See* **clodhopper**.
hilt *noun*
A protrusion or extension designed to be grasped by the hand ▸ haft, handgrip, handle. *See also* **hold, knob**.
hind *adjective*
▸ posterior, rearward. *See* **back** (1).
hind end *noun*
The part farthest from the front ▸ end, tail, tail end. *See* **back**.
hinder *verb*
1. To interfere with the progress of ▸ bog (down), dampen, encumber, forestall, hamper, hold back, impede, interfere with, obstruct, retard, stem. *Idioms:* be (*or* stand *or* get) in the way of, put a damper on. *See also* **frustrate, restrain, stop**. **2.** To cause to be later or slower than expected or desired ▸ hang up, retard, stall. *See* **delay** (1).

✦ CORE SYNONYMS: *hinder, hamper, impede, obstruct*. These verbs mean to interfere with the progress of someone or something. To *hinder* is to hold back and often implies stopping or prevention: *The travelers were hindered by storms*. To *hamper* is to hinder by or as if by fastening or entangling: *His clothes hampered his efforts to swim to safety*. To *impede* is to slow by making action or movement difficult: "*Our journey was impeded by a thousand obstacles*" (Mary Shelley). *Obstruct* implies the presence of obstacles: *Competing agendas obstructed our ability to negotiate effectively*.

hindmost *or* **hindermost** *adjective*
1. Located in the rear ▸ hind, posterior. *See* **back** (1). **2.** Bringing up the rear ▸ aftermost, rearmost. *See* **last**[1] (2).
hindquarters *noun*
▸ posterior, rump. *Slang:* fanny. *See* **buttocks**.
hindrance *noun*
▸ barrier, blockage, obstacle. *See* **bar** (1). *See synonym note at* **bar**.
hinge on *or* **upon** *verb*
▸ hang on (*or* upon), rest on (*or* upon). *See* **depend on** (2).
hint *noun*
1. A subtle quality underlying or felt to underlie a situation, action, or person ▸ glimmering, implication, inkling, suspicion, undercurrent, undertone. **2.** A brief or indirect suggestion ▸ allusion, clue, cue, innuendo, insinuation, intimation, suggestion, wink. **3.** A slight amount or indication ▸ breath, semblance, trace. *See* **shade** (2). **4.** An item of advance or inside information given as a guide to action ▸ lead, scent, steer. *See* **tip**[3] (1).
hint *verb*
To convey an idea by indirect, subtle means ▸ allude to, hint at, imply, insinuate, intimate, suggest. *Idiom:* drop a hint.

✦ CORE SYNONYMS: *hint, suggest, imply, intimate, insinuate*. These verbs mean to convey thoughts or ideas by indirect, subtle means. *Hint* refers to an oblique or covert suggestion that often contains clues: *My imagination supplied the explanation you only hinted at*. *Suggest* refers to the calling of something to mind as the result of an association of ideas: "*his erect and careless attitude suggesting assurance and power*" (Joseph Conrad). To *imply* is to suggest a thought or an idea by letting it be inferred from something else, such as a statement, that is more explicit: *The effusive praise the professor heaped on one of the students seemed to imply disapproval of the rest*. *Intimate* applies to indirect, subtle expression that often reflects discretion, tact, or reserve: *She intimated that her neighbors were having marital problems*. To *insinuate* is to suggest something, usually something unpleasant, in a covert, sly, and underhanded manner: *The columnist insinuated that the candidate raised money unethically*.

hinterland *noun*
▸ backwoods, countryside. *See* **country** (1).

hip *adjective*

1. *Slang* Marked by comprehension, cognizance, and perception ▸ cognizant, sensible, sentient. *See* **aware.** 2. *Slang* In accordance with current fashion ▸ mod, stylish, swanky. *See* **fashionable.**

hire *verb*

1. To obtain the use or services of ▸ enlist, retain. *See* **employ** (1). 2. To engage the temporary use of something for a fee ▸ charter, lease, rent (out). 3. To give temporary use of in return for payment ▸ hire out, let, rent. *See* **lease** (1).

hire *noun*

1. The act of employing for wages ▸ employment, engagement, hiring, retention. 2. The state of being employed ▸ employ, employment, service. 3. Payment for work done ▸ earnings, pay, salary. *See* **wage.** 4. *Informal* One who is employed by another ▸ jobholder, staffer, worker. *See* **employee.**

hired *adjective*

▸ jobholding, working. *See* **employed** (1).

hired hand *noun*

Informal One who is employed by another ▸ jobholder, staffer, worker. *See* **employee.**

hireling *noun*

▸ jobholder, staffer, worker. *See* **employee.**

hirer *noun*

One that employs persons for wages ▸ employer.

hirsute *adjective*

▸ furry, fuzzy, shaggy. *See* **hairy** (1).

hiss *noun*

1. A sibilant sound ▸ fizz, fizzing, fizzle, fizzling, rustle, rustling, sibilant, sizzle, sizzling, swish, swishing, whiz, whizzing, whoosh, whooshing. 2. One of various derisive sounds of disapproval ▸ boo, catcall, hoot. *Slang:* bird, Bronx cheer, raspberry, razz.

hiss *verb*

1. To make a sibilant sound ▸ fizz, fizzle, rustle, sibilate, sizzle, swish, whiz, whoosh. 2. To make a derisive sound of disapproval ▸ boo, catcall, hoot. *Slang:* bird, Bronx cheer, raspberry, razz. *Idioms:* give (*or* blow) a Bronx cheer, give (*or* blow) a raspberry. 3. To undergo combustion; be on fire ▸ combust, flame, flare. *See* **burn** (2).

hissy fit *noun*

Informal An angry outburst ▸ huff, passion, tantrum. *See* **temper** (2).

historic *adjective*

1. Having great significance ▸ consequential, grand, meaningful. *See* **important** (1). 2. Characterized by enduring excellence, appeal, and importance ▸ ageless, antique. *See* **vintage** (1).

history *noun*

1. A chronological record of past events ▸ annals, archive, chronicle, historical record. *See also* **antiquity.** 2. One's previous experiences ▸ background, career, credentials, curriculum vitae, life history, past, record, resumé, vita. *See also* **accomplishment, qualification** 3. A recounting of past events ▸ chronicle, record, report. *See* **story** (1).

histrionic *or* **histrionical** *adjective*

1. Of or relating to drama or the theater ▸ dramaturgical, theatrical, thespian. *See* **dramatic** (1). 2. Suggesting drama or a stage performance, as in emotionality or suspense ▸ melodramatic, sensational, spectacular. *See* **dramatic** (2).

histrionics *noun*

▸ dramatics, melodrama, melodramatics. *See* **theatrics** (2).

hit *verb*

1. To deliver a sudden, sharp blow to ▸ bash, box, bust, catch, clout, jab, knock, pop, punch, slam, slog, slug, smash, smite, sock, strike, swat, swing at, thwack, whack, wham, whop. *Informal:* biff, bop, clip, wallop. *Slang:* belt, conk, nail, paste. *Idioms:* let fly at, let someone have it, sock it to someone. 2. To come together with force ▸ crash, impact. *See* **collide** (1). 3. To enter a person's mind ▸ come to, occur to. *See* **strike** (9). 4. To find or meet by chance ▸ come across, run across, stumble on. *See* **encounter** (1). 5. *Slang* To cause the death of ▸ cut down, destroy, finish (off). *See* **kill**[1] (1).

hit back *verb*

To return like for like, especially to return an unfriendly or hostile action with a similar one ▸ counter, reciprocate, retort. *See* **retaliate.**

hit on *verb*

Informal To obtain or reach by persistent effort ▸ achieve, attain, reach. *See* **accomplish** (1).

hit *noun*

1. A sudden heavy stroke ▸ crack, pound, swat, whack. *See* **blow**[2] (1). 2. A violent forcible contact ▸ crash, impact. *See* **collision.** 3. A dazzling, often sudden instance of success ▸ sleeper. *Informal:* knockout, smash, smash hit, ten-strike, winner, wow. *Slang:* boff, boffo, boffola. *See also* **accomplishment.** 4. *Slang* An inhalation, as of a cigar, pipe, or cigarette ▸ drag, draw, puff. *See* **pull** (2). 5. *Slang* The crime of murdering someone ▸ homicide, killing, slaying. *See* **murder.**

hitch *verb*

1. To make secure ▸ bind, chain, moor. *See* **fasten** (1). 2. To walk unsteadily ▸ halt, hobble, totter. *See* **stagger** (1).

hitch up *verb*

To move (something) to a higher position ▸ hoist, lift, raise. *See* **elevate** (1).

hitch *noun*

1. A prison term ▸ stretch, time. 2. A limited, often assigned period of activity, duty, or opportunity ▸ shift, stint, time. *See* **turn** (1). 3. *Informal* A tricky or unsuspected condition ▸ catch, rub, snag. *See also* **bar, disadvantage, trick.** 4. That which unites or binds ▸ ligature, link, tie. *See* **bond** (2).

hit man *noun*

▸ killer, massacrer, slaughterer. *See* **murderer.**

hit-or-miss *adjective*

▸ chance, indiscriminate, unplanned. *See* **random.**

hive *verb*
▶ agglomerate, amass, cumulate, pile up. *See* **accumulate.**

hoard *noun*
A supply stored or hidden for possible future use ▶ backlog, cache, inventory, nest egg, provision, reserve, reservoir, stash, stock, stockpile, store, supply, treasure. *See also* **accumulation.**

hoard *verb*
To keep for future use ▶ lay by, squirrel away, stockpile. *See* **save** (1).

hoarse *adjective*
1. Rough, raw, or grating in sound ▶ croaking, croaky, gravelly, gruff, husky, ragged, raw. **2.** Disagreeable to the senses, especially the sense of hearing ▶ grating, jarring. *See* **harsh** (1).

hoary *adjective*
▶ aged, elderly, senior. *See* **old** (2).

hoax *verb*
To get money or something else from someone by deceitful trickery ▶ defraud, swindle. *See* **cheat** (1).

hoax *noun*
An act of cheating ▶ deceit, fraud, swindle. *See* **cheat** (1).

hobble *verb*
1. To walk unsteadily ▶ halt, hitch, totter. *See* **stagger** (1). **2.** To restrict the activity or free movement of ▶ hamstring, handcuff, shackle. *See* **hamper**[1] (1). *See synonym note at* **hamper**[1].

hobble *noun*
Something that physically confines the legs or arms ▶ handcuffs, irons, shackle. *See* **bond** (1).

hobby *noun*
▶ pastime, recreation, sport. *See* **amusement.**

hobbyhorse *noun*
▶ mania, passion. *See* **enthusiasm** (2).

hobnob *verb*
▶ consort, fraternize. *Slang:* hang out. *See* **associate** (2).

hobo *noun*
One who wanders without a permanent home or livelihood ▶ drifter, gadabout, gypsy, itinerant, migrant, nomad, peregrinator, peripatetic, roamer, rover, swagman, tramp, transient, vagabond, vagrant, wanderer. *See also* **pauper.**

hock *verb*
▶ deposit, pledge. *See* **pawn**[1].

hocus-pocus *noun*
▶ double talk, jabberwocky, mumbo jumbo. *See* **gibberish** (1).

hodgepodge *noun*
▶ conglomeration, jumble, mishmash. *See* **assortment** (1).

hoggish *adjective*
▶ greedy, ravenous, voracious. *See* **gluttonous** (1).

hogtie *verb*
Informal To restrict the activity or free movement of ▶ hamstring, handcuff, hobble. *See* **hamper**[1] (1). *See synonym note at* **hamper**[1].

hogwash *noun*
▶ bunkum, claptrap, garbage. *See* **nonsense** (1).

hoi polloi *noun*
▶ masses, proletariat, public. *See* **commonalty.**

hoist *verb*
To move something to a higher position ▶ lift, raise. *See* **elevate** (1). *See synonym note at* **elevate.**

hoist *noun*
An instance of lifting or being lifted ▶ boost, heave. *See* **lift** (1).

hoity-toity *adjective*
1. Characterized by an exaggerated show of dignity or self-importance ▶ grandiose, pretentious. *See* **pompous. 2.** Catering to, used by, or admitting only the wealthy or socially superior ▶ chic, posh, swank. *See* **exclusive** (4).

hokey *adjective*
Slang Affectedly or extravagantly emotional ▶ gushy, mawkish, soft. *See* **sentimental.**

hold *verb*
1. To have and maintain in one's possession ▶ hold back, keep, keep back, reserve, retain, stick with, withhold. **2.** To hold the weight of ▶ carry, support, sustain. *See* **bear** (1). **3.** To put one's arms around affectionately ▶ enfold, hug. *See* **embrace** (1). **4.** To put in or as if in prison ▶ confine, detain, incarcerate. *See* **imprison. 5.** To compel the attention, interest, or imagination of ▶ captivate, fascinate, mesmerize. *See* **grip** (1). **6.** To be filled by ▶ contain, have. *See also* **constitute. 7.** To have the room or capacity for ▶ accommodate, contain. *See synonym note at* **accommodate. 8.** To have at one's disposal ▶ enjoy, have. *See* **command** (3). **9.** To control, restrict, or arrest ▶ bridle, check, curb. *See* **restrain. 10.** To have an opinion ▶ deem, think. *See* **believe** (3). **11.** To put into words positively and with conviction ▶ avow, declare, maintain. *See* **assert** (1). **12.** To view in a certain way ▶ believe, feel, sense, think. *See also* **perceive, regard. 13.** To prove valid under scrutiny ▶ hold up, prove out, stand up. *Informal:* wash. **14.** To organize and carry out an activity ▶ give, throw. *See* **have** (9). **15.** To seize or maintain control over by conquest ▶ capture, overrun, subjugate. *See* **occupy** (2). **16.** To make stronger or more resistant ▶ bolster, hold up, reinforce, strengthen. *See* **support** (2).

hold back *verb*
1. To interfere with the progress of ▶ dampen, obstruct. *See* **hinder** (1). **2.** To hold something requiring an outlet in check ▶ smother, stifle, suppress. *See* **repress. 3.** To control, restrict, or arrest ▶ bridle, check, curb. *See* **restrain.**

hold down *verb*
1. To hold something requiring an outlet in check ▶ smother, stifle, suppress. *See* **repress. 2.** To control, restrict, or arrest ▶ bridle, constrain, harness. *See* **restrain.**

hold in *verb*
To control, restrict, or arrest ▶ brake, check, inhibit. *See* **restrain.**

hold off *verb*
1. To put off until a later time ▸ delay, postpone, suspend. *See* **defer¹. 2.** To hold oneself back ▸ forbear, withhold. *See* **refrain.**

hold out *verb*
1. To be in existence or in a certain state for an indefinitely long time ▸ continue, persist. *See* **endure** (2). **2.** To put before another for acceptance ▸ extend, proffer. *See* **offer** (1).

hold up *verb*
1. To put off until a later time ▸ delay, postpone, suspend. *See* **defer¹. 2.** To cause to be later or slower than expected or desired ▸ hang up, retard, stall. *See* **delay** (1). **3.** To take property or possessions from someone unlawfully and usually forcibly ▸ burglarize, mug, stick up. *See* **rob** (1). **4.** To withstand stress or difficulty ▸ endure, stand up. *See* **bear. 5.** To prove valid under scrutiny ▸ prove out, stand up. *Informal:* wash.

hold with *verb*
To be favorably disposed toward ▸ approve, countenance, favor. *Informal:* go for. **Idioms:** be in favor of, take kindly to, think highly (*or* well) of. *See also* **assent, value.**

hold *noun*
1. An act or means of holding something ▸ clasp, clench, clutch, grapple, grasp, grip. **2.** Intellectual hold ▸ apprehension, comprehension, grasp, grip, understanding. *See also* **knowledge.**

✦ CORE SYNONYMS: *hold, keep, retain, withhold, reserve.* These verbs mean to have and maintain in one's possession or control. *Hold* and *keep* are the most general: *A movie must be compelling in order to hold my interest. We received a few offers but decided to keep the house. Retain* means to continue to hold, especially in the face of possible loss: *Though unhappy, he retained his sense of humor. Withhold* implies reluctance or refusal to give, grant, or allow: *The tenant withheld his rent until the owner fixed the boiler.* To *reserve* is to hold back for the future or for a special purpose: *The farmer reserved two acres for an orchard.*

---

holder *noun*
1. An object, such as a carton, can, or jar, in which material is held or carried ▸ container, receptacle, repository, vessel. *See also* **depository, package. 2.** A person who has legal title to property ▸ master, proprietor. *See* **owner.**

holdings *noun*
A thing or set of things, such as land and assets, legally possessed ▸ belongings, estate, possessions, property. *See also* **effects.**

holdup *noun*
1. The condition or fact of being made late or slow ▸ detainment, lag, retardation. *See* **delay** (2). **2.** The crime of taking someone else's property without consent ▸ burglary, robbery, thievery. *See* **larceny. 3.** The act of putting off or the condition of being put off ▸ deferment, postponement, suspension. *See* **delay** (1).

hole *noun*
1. A space in an otherwise solid mass ▸ cavity, hollow, pocket, space, vacuity, void. *See also* **crack, cut. 2.** An open space allowing passage ▸ aperture, eyelet, mouth, opening, orifice, outlet, slot, tunnel, vent. *See also* **gap, prick. 3.** A place used as an animal's dwelling ▸ burrow, den, lair. *See also* **cave. 4.** A small, roughly built dwelling ▸ hovel, shack, shanty. *See* **hut. 5.** A difficult, often embarrassing situation or condition ▸ corner, difficulty, fix. *See* **predicament.**

hole *verb*
To make a hole or other opening in ▸ perforate, pierce, puncture. *See* **breach** (1).

hole up *verb*
Informal To shut oneself up in secrecy ▸ hide out. **Idioms:** go underground, lay (*or* lie) low.

holiday *noun*
1. A regularly scheduled period spent away from work or duty, often in recreation ▸ furlough, leave, sabbatical, vacation. **Idioms:** time (*or* day) off. *See also* **break, trip. 2.** A joyous or festive occasion ▸ festivity, fiesta, revels. *See* **celebration** (1).

holier-than-thou *adjective*
Piously or overly sure of one's own righteousness ▸ moralistic, self-righteous. *See also* **arrogant, hypocritical, moral.**

holiness *noun*
The quality of being or acting in accordance with what is holy or sacred ▸ beatitude, blessedness, divineness, godliness, grace, hallowedness, inviolability, sacredness, sacrosanctity, saintliness, sanctity, venerability, venerableness. *See also* **devotion.**

holler *verb*
1. To speak or say in a loud cry ▸ call, scream, whoop. *See* **shout.** *See synonym note at* **shout. 2.** To cry loudly, as an upset baby does ▸ howl, wail, yowl. *See* **bawl** (1). **3.** *Informal* To express feelings of pain, dissatisfaction, or resentment ▸ fuss, grouch, mutter, whine. *See* **complain.**

holler *noun*
A loud cry ▸ call, scream, yell.

hollow *adjective*
1. Lacking value, use, or substance ▸ empty, idle, otiose, vacant, vain. *See also* **futile. 2.** Curving inward ▸ carved out, cavernous, concave, depressed, indented, sunken.

hollow *noun*
1. A space in an otherwise solid mass ▸ cavity, vacuity. *See* **hole** (1). **2.** An area sunk below its surroundings ▸ basin, dip, sink. *See* **depression** (1). **3.** An elongated lowland between mountains or hills ▸ dale, gorge. *See* **valley.**

✦ CORE SYNONYMS: *hollow, empty, idle, otiose, vain.* These adjectives mean lacking value, use, or substance: *hollow threats; empty pleasures; idle dreams; an otiose belief in alchemy; vain regrets.*

---

hollow-eyed *adjective*
▸ gaunt, wan, worn. *See* **haggard.**

hollowness *noun*
1. A desolate sense of loss ▸ blankness, desolation, emptiness, vacuum, void. **2.** Total lack of ideas, meaning, or substance ▸ blankness, inanity. *See* **emptiness** (3).
holocaust *noun*
1. An occurrence inflicting widespread destruction and distress ▸ cataclysm, catastrophe, tragedy. *See* **disaster** (1). **2.** The savage killing of many victims ▸ genocide, slaughter. *See* **massacre.**
holy *adjective*
1. Regarded with particular reverence or respect, especially by a religion ▸ blessed, consecrated, hallowed, inviolable, sacred, sacrosanct, sanctified, venerable, venerated, virtuous. **2.** Of, from, like, or being a god or God ▸ heavenly, supernal. *See* **divine** (1). **3.** In the service or worship of God or a god ▸ devoted, religious, sacred. *See* **divine** (2). **4.** Deeply concerned with God and the beliefs and practice of religion ▸ devout, godly, religious. *See* **pious** (1).
holy war *noun*
A goal served with great or uncompromising dedication ▸ cause, crusade, jihad. *See also* **drive.**
homage *noun*
▸ deference, obeisance, reverence. *See* **honor** (1). *See synonym note at* **honor.**
home *noun*
1. A building or shelter where one lives ▸ abode, domicile, dwelling, habitation, house, lodging, place, residence. *Informal:* address, headquarters, nest, pad. *Slang:* digs. **2.** The natural environment specific to an animal or plant ▸ habitat, habitation, niche, range, territory. **3.** An institution that provides care and shelter ▸ asylum, hospice, hospital, sanatorium, shelter. **4.** A center of organization, supply, or activity ▸ headquarters, installation, station. *See* **base**¹ (1).
home *adjective*
1. Of or relating to the family or household ▸ familial, household. *See* **domestic** (1). **2.** Of, from, or within a country's own territory ▸ homegrown, internal, native. *See* **domestic** (3).
home base *noun*
▸ headquarters, installation, station. *See* **base**¹ (1).
homegrown *adjective*
1. Of, from, or within a country's own territory ▸ internal, native. *See* **domestic** (3). **2.** Existing, born, or produced in a land or region ▸ autochthonic, native. *See* **indigenous** (1).
homeliness *noun*
▸ monstrosity, odiousness, unsightliness. *See* **ugliness** (1).
homely *adjective*
1. Displeasing to the eye ▸ plain, unattractive, unsightly. *See* **ugly** (1). **2.** Of a charmingly plain and unsophisticated nature ▸ artless, homespun, natural. *See* **rustic** (1). **3.** Of or relating to the family or household ▸ family, residential. *See* **domestic** (1). **4.** Being of no special quality or type ▸ common, mediocre, standard. *See* **ordinary** (1).

homemade *adjective*
▸ crude, primitive, unpolished. *See* **rude** (1).
home office *noun*
▸ headquarters, installation, station. *See* **base**¹ (1).
homespun *adjective*
▸ artless, homely, natural. *See* **rustic** (1).
homey *adjective*
1. *Informal* Affording pleasurable ease ▸ easy, snug. *Informal:* comfy. *See* **comfortable** (1). **2.** Of or relating to the family or household ▸ family, residential. *See* **domestic** (1).
homicidal *adjective*
▸ bloodthirsty, sanguineous. *See* **murderous.**
homicide *noun*
1. The crime of murdering someone ▸ assassination, killing. *See* **murder. 2.** One who murders another ▸ killer, massacrer, slayer. *See* **murderer.**
homily *noun*
▸ lecture, talk. *See* **speech** (2).
hominoid *adjective*
▸ anthropoid, anthropomorphic, humanoid. *See* **humanlike.**
homogenize *verb*
1. To combine into one mass or mixture ▸ blend, fuse, stir. *See* **mix** (1). **2.** To make conventional ▸ standardize, stylize. *See* **conventionalize.**
homophile *adjective*
Having a sexual orientation to members of one's own sex ▸ gay, homosexual, lesbian.
Homo sapiens *noun*
1. Humans as a group ▸ humanity, mortals, world. *See* **humankind. 2.** A member of the human race ▸ human, mortal, person. *See* **human being.**
homosexual *adjective*
Having a sexual orientation to members of one's own sex ▸ gay, homophile, lesbian.
homesteader *noun*
▸ colonist, pioneer. *See* **settler.**
honcho *noun*
Slang One who governs or leads ▸ boss, director, head, leader. *See* **chief** (1).
hone¹ *verb*
1. To give a sharp edge to ▸ edge, strope, whet. *See* **sharpen** (1). **2.** To bring to perfection or completion ▸ complement, polish, refine. *See* **perfect.**
hone in *verb*
To direct toward a common center ▸ channel, converge, focus. *See* **concentrate** (1).
hone² *verb*
Informal To have a strong longing for ▸ covet, yearn. *See* **desire** (1).
honest *adjective*
1. Marked by uprightness in principle and action ▸ aboveboard, good, honorable, incorruptible, respectable, righteous, straight, true, truthful, upright, upstanding, veracious. *Informal:* straight-shooting. *Idioms:* on the up-and-up. *See also* **ethical, innocent, moral. 2.** Manifesting honesty and directness ▸ candid, open, plainspoken. *See* **frank. 3.** Free from hy-

pocrisy or pretense ▸ natural, sincere, unaffected. *See* **genuine** (1). **4.** Capable of being depended on ▸ reliable, solid, trustworthy. *See* **dependable.**

honesty *noun*
1. The quality of being honest ▸ candidness, frankness, honor, honorableness, incorruptibility, integrity, openness, plainspokenness, reliability, righteousness, sincerity, truth, trustworthiness, upstandingness. **2.** Moral or ethical strength ▸ fiber, integrity, principle. *See* **character** (2).

honey *noun*
A person who is much loved ▸ dear, precious, sweetheart. *See* **darling** (1).

honey *verb*
1. To make superficially more acceptable or appealing ▸ sugar, sugarcoat. *See* **sweeten** (1). **2.** To compliment ingratiatingly ▸ butter up. *Informal:* soft-soap, sweet-talk. *See* **flatter** (1). **3.** To persuade or try to persuade by gentle persistent urging or flattery ▸ cajole, wheedle. *See* **coax** (1).

honeyed *adjective*
Having or suggesting the taste of sugar ▸ saccharine, sugary, sweet.

honky-tonk *noun*
Slang A disreputable or run-down bar or restaurant ▸ *Slang:* dive, dump, joint, juke house, juke joint. *Idiom:* hole in the wall.

honor *noun*
1. Great respect or high public esteem accorded as a right or as due ▸ deference, homage, obeisance, reverence, veneration. *See also* **testimonial.** **2.** A person's high standing among others ▸ dignity, good name, good report, prestige, reputation, repute, respect, status. *See also* **exaltation.** **3.** A feeling of deference, approval, and liking ▸ admiration, favor. *See* **esteem** (1). **4.** Recognition of achievement or superiority or a sign of this ▸ award, kudos. *See* **distinction** (2). **5.** The quality of being honest ▸ incorruptibility, integrity. *See* **honesty** (1). **6.** Moral or ethical strength ▸ honesty, integrity, principle. *See* **character** (2).

honor *verb*
1. To pay tribute or homage to ▸ acclaim, celebrate, eulogize, exalt, extol, glorify, hail, laud, lionize, magnify, panegyrize, praise. *Idiom:* sing someone's praises. *See also* **revere.** **2.** To lend dignity or honor to by an act or favor ▸ enrich, favor, grace, dignify. *See also* **exalt.** **3.** To bestow a reward on ▸ award, guerdon, reward. *See also* **confer.** **4.** To have a high opinion of or regard for ▸ admire, esteem, respect. *See* **value** (1). **5.** To cause to be eminent or recognized ▸ dignify, exalt, glorify. *See* **distinguish** (5). **6.** To salute by raising and drinking from a glass ▸ salute, toast. *See* **drink** (4).

✚ CORE SYNONYMS: *honor, homage, reverence, veneration, deference.* These nouns denote respect or high public esteem accorded to another as a right or as due. *Honor* is the most general term: *The hero tried to be worthy of the honor in which he was held. Homage* is often in the form of a ceremonial tribute that

conveys allegiance: *"There is no country in which so absolute a homage is paid to wealth"* (Ralph Waldo Emerson). *Reverence* is a feeling of deep respect and devotion: *"Kill reverence and you've killed the hero in man"* (Ayn Rand). *Veneration* is both the feeling and the reverential expression of respect, love, and awe: *Her veneration for her mentor never wavered. Deference* is courteous, respectful regard for another that often implies yielding to him or her: *The funeral was arranged with deference to the family of the deceased.*

honorable *adjective*
1. Deserving honor, respect, or admiration ▸ deserving, laudable, worthy. *See* **admirable. 2.** Marked by uprightness in principle and action ▸ aboveboard, righteous. *See* **honest** (1).

honorableness *noun*
▸ incorruptibility, integrity. *See* **honesty** (1).

honorarium *noun*
▸ award, bonus, plum. *See* **reward** (1).

hood *noun*
Slang A person who treats others violently or roughly ▸ hoodlum, ruffian, tough. *See* **thug.**

hoodlum *noun*
▸ hooligan, ruffian, tough. *See* **thug.**

hoodoo *noun*
Something or someone believed to bring bad luck ▸ curse, evil eye, hex, Jonah. *Informal:* jinx.

hoodoo *verb*
To bring bad luck or evil to ▸ curse, hex. *Informal:* jinx. *See also* **afflict.**

hoodwink *verb*
▸ dupe, mislead, trick. *See* **deceive.** *See synonym note at* **deceive.**

hooey *noun*
Slang Something that does not have or make sense ▸ bunkum, drivel, garbage. *See* **nonsense** (1).

hoof *verb*
1. *Slang* To move rhythmically to music, using patterns of steps or gestures ▸ boogie, foot, step. *See* **dance** (1). **2.** *Slang* To go on foot ▸ step, tread. *See* **walk.**

hoofer *noun*
Slang A person who dances, especially professionally ▸ chorine, chorus boy, chorus girl, dancer, terpsichorean.

hoo-hah *noun*
1. *Slang* A condition of intense public interest or excitement ▸ stir, uproar. *See* **sensation** (2). **2.** *Slang* A condition of being agitated or disturbed ▸ commotion, disturbance, stir. *See* **agitation** (1).

hook *noun*
1. A device for locking ▸ catch, clip, lock. *See* **fastener. 2.** Something bent ▸ curvature, curve, turn. *See* **bend.**

hook *verb*
1. To become stuck or entangled ▸ fix, lodge. *See* **catch** (3). **2.** *Informal* To gain control of by trapping ▸ snare, trap. *See* **catch** (1). **3.** To deviate from a straight line in a smooth, continuous manner ▸ arch, curve, turn. *See* **bend** (1). **4.** *Slang* To take another's property without

permission ▸ purloin, snatch, thieve. *See* **steal** (1). *See synonym note at* **steal**.

hooker *noun*
Slang A woman who engages in sex for payment ▸ courtesan, strumpet. *See* **harlot**.

hookup *noun*
▸ correlation, link, relationship. *See* **relation** (1).

hooky *noun*
Informal Failure to be present ▸ cut, truancy. *See* **absence** (1).

hooligan *noun*
▸ hoodlum, ruffian, tough. *See* **thug**.

hoop *noun*
1. A round closed plain shape or figure ▸ band, ring, wheel. *See* **circle** (1). 2. The goal in the game of basketball ▸ bucket, net, swish. *See* **basket** (3).

hoopla *noun*
Informal Information disseminated through various media to attract public notice ▸ advertisement, ballyhoo. *Slang:* hype. *See* **publicity** (1).

hoosegow *noun*
Slang A place for the confinement of persons in lawful detention ▸ brig, penitentiary, prison. *See* **jail**.

hoot *noun*
1. One of various derisive sounds of disapproval ▸ boo, catcall. *See* **hiss** (2). 2. *Informal* Something or someone uproariously funny ▸ *Informal:* joke, laugh. *See* **scream** (3).

hoot *verb*
To make a derisive sound of disapproval ▸ boo, catcall. *See* **hiss** (2).

hop *verb*
1. To move in a lively way ▸ skip, spring. *See* **bound**[1] (1). 2. *Informal* To go aboard a means of transport ▸ board, catch, take.

hop up *verb*
Slang To make greater in intensity or severity ▸ deepen, enhance, heighten. *See* **intensify**.

hop *noun*
1. A bouncing movement ▸ bounce, bound, rebound. 2. A sudden lively movement ▸ skip, spring. *See* **bound**[1] (2). 3. *Informal* A party or gathering for dancing ▸ ball, prom. *Informal:* sock-hop. *See* **dance**.

hope *verb*
To have a strong longing for ▸ covet, want, yearn. *See* **desire** (1).

hope *noun*
A fervent hope ▸ aspiration, vision, wish. *See* **dream** (3).

hopeful *adjective*
1. Inspiring confidence or hope ▸ heartening, likely. *See* **encouraging**. 2. Having or marked by expectation ▸ anticipatory, awaiting. *See* **expectant** (1).

hopeful *noun*
1. One who aspires ▸ aspirant, aspirer. *Informal:* wannabe. 2. A person who applies for or seeks something, such as a job or position ▸ aspirant, candidate, petitioner. *See* **applicant**. 3. One showing

much promise ▸ candidate, prospect, up-and-comer. *See* **comer** (2).

hopefulness *noun*
1. The condition of looking forward to something, especially with eagerness ▸ anticipation, expectance, expectancy, expectation, high hopes. *See also* **desire**. 2. A tendency to expect a favorable outcome or to dwell on hopeful aspects ▸ assurance, sanguinity. *See* **optimism**.

hopeless *adjective*
1. Offering no hope or expectation of improvement ▸ cureless, incurable, irremediable, irreparable, lost, remediless. *See also* **futile**. 2. Having lost all hope ▸ dejected, forlorn, wretched. *See* **despondent**. *See synonym note at* **despondent**.

hopelessness *noun*
▸ desperation, dismay, hopelessness. *See* **despair**.

hopped-up *adjective*
Slang Stupefied, intoxicated, or otherwise influenced by the taking of drugs ▸ baked, high, lit (up). *See* **drugged**.

hopping *adjective*
Informal Full of lively activity ▸ crawling, swarming, teeming. *See* **busy** (2).

horde *noun*
▸ host, mass, throng. *See* **crowd** (1). *See synonym note at* **flock**.

horizon *noun*
▸ range, scope. *See* **ken**.

horizontal *adjective*
▸ decumbent, prone, prostrate. *See* **flat** (1).

hornets' nest *noun*
▸ case, issue, question. *See* **problem** (1).

horn in *verb*
1. To force or come in as an improper or unwanted element ▸ barge in, cut in, interlope. *See* **intrude** (1). 2. To intervene officiously or indiscreetly in the affairs of others ▸ butt in, interfere. *See* **meddle** (1).

horniness *noun*
Slang Sexual hunger ▸ eroticism, lust, passion. *See* **desire** (2).

horrendous *adjective*
▸ appalling, awful, dreadful. *See* **terrible** (1).

horrible *adjective*
1. Causing great horror ▸ bloodcurdling, hair-raising, harrowing, horrid, horrific, horrifying, nightmarish, petrifying, terrific, terrifying. 2. Shockingly repellent ▸ grisly, gruesome, macabre. *See* **ghastly** (1). 3. Very bad ▸ appalling, awful, dreadful, wretched. *See* **terrible** (1).

horrid *adjective*
1. Causing great horror ▸ hair-raising, horrific, nightmarish. *See* **horrible** (1). 2. So objectionable as to deserve condemnation ▸ contemptible, disgusting, obnoxious. *See* **offensive** (1). 3. Shockingly repellent ▸ grisly, gruesome, macabre. *See* **ghastly** (1).

horrific *adjective*
▸ hair-raising, harrowing, nightmarish. *See* **horrible** (1).

horrified *adjective*
► fearful, frightened, scared. *See* **afraid.**

horrify *verb*
► alarm, scare, terrify. *See* **frighten.**

horror *noun*
1. A feeling of agitation in the face of trouble or danger ► apprehension, consternation, trepidation. *See* **fear.** *See synonym note at* **fear. 2.** A strong feeling of hostility or dislike ► antipathy, aversion, loathing. *See* **hate** (1). **3.** *Informal* An object of extreme dislike ► abomination, anathema. *See* **hate** (2). **4.** A monstrous offense or evil ► enormity, monstrosity. *See* **outrage** (1).

hors d'oeuvre *noun*
► apéritif, starter. *See* **appetizer.**

horse around *verb*
1. *Informal* To behave in a rowdy, improper, or unruly fashion ► act up, carry on. *See* **misbehave. 2.** *Informal* To occupy oneself with amusement or diversion ► frolic, recreate. *See* **play** (1). **3.** *Informal* To make jokes; behave playfully ► jest, joke, quip. *Informal:* clown (around), fool around. *Idioms:* crack wise, play the fool.

horseplay *noun*
► misconduct, naughtiness, wrongdoing. *See* **misbehavior.**

horse sense *noun*
Informal The ability to make sensible decisions ► judgment, reason, wisdom. *See* **common sense.**

hospice *noun*
► asylum, shelter. *See* **home** (3).

hospitable *adjective*
Characterized by kindness and warm, unaffected courtesy ► affable, courteous, gracious. *See also* **amiable, attentive, courteous.**

hospital *noun*
► hospice, shelter. *See* **home** (3).

hospitality *noun*
► concern, regard, thoughtfulness. *See* **consideration** (1).

host *noun*
► horde, mass, throng. *See* **crowd** (1).

hostage *noun*
► collateral, security, warrant. *See* **pawn**[1].

hostile *adjective*
1. Engaged in warfare ► fighting, militant. *See* **belligerent** (1). **2.** Inclined to act in an aggressive or hostile way ► belligerent, combative, contentious. *See* **aggressive** (1). **3.** Feeling or showing unfriendliness ► inimical, unfriendly. *See also* **mean**[2]. **4.** Marked by a disposition to oppose ► antagonistic, contradictory. *See* **contrary** (1). **5.** Not encouraging life or growth ► adverse, inhospitable, unfavorable. *See also* **severe.**

hostilities *noun*
► combat, confrontation, war. *See* **battle** (1).

hostility *noun*
1. Hostile or warlike behavior or attitude ► belligerence, combativeness, pugnacity. *See* **aggression** (1).
2. Deep-seated hatred, as between longtime opponents or rivals ► antagonism, animus. *See* **enmity.** *See synonym note at* **enmity.**

hot *adjective*
1. Marked by much heat ► ardent, baking, blistering, boiling, broiling, burning, fiery, heated, red-hot, roasting, scalding, scorching, searing, sizzling, sultry, sweltering, torrid, tropical, white-hot. *Idioms:* hot enough to fry an egg on, piping hot. **2.** Having an above-normal body temperature ► febrile, feverish, hectic. *See* **feverish** (1). **3.** *Informal* Of great current interest ► live, red-hot. *See also* **fashionable, important. 4.** *Slang* Particularly excellent ► fantastic, sensational, superb. *See* **marvelous** (1). **5.** *Slang* In accordance with current fashion ► mod, stylish, swanky. *See* **fashionable. 6.** Having a sharp, penetrating flavor or aroma ► piquant, sharp, zesty. *See* **spicy** (1). **7.** *Slang* Sexually attractive ► alluring, enticing. *See* **desirable** (1). **8.** *Slang* Concerning or arousing sexual love or desire ► aphrodisiac, salacious, sexy. *See* **erotic.**

hotbed *noun*
1. A place of concentrated activity, influence, or importance ► headquarters, heart, hub. *See* **center** (1). **2.** A point of origination ► provenance, root, source. *See* **origin** (1).

hot-blooded *adjective*
► burning, fervent, torrid. *See* **passionate** (1).

hotdog *noun*
Slang A person who behaves ostentatiously or performs dangerous stunts ► showoff, showboat. *See also* **braggart.**

hot-dog *verb*
Slang To behave in an ostentatious manner or perform dangerous stunts ► show off, showboat. *See also* **boast, swagger.**

hotfoot *verb*
1. *Informal* To leave hastily ► bolt. *Slang:* scram, vamoose. *See* **run** (3). **2.** *Informal* To move swiftly ► dash, sprint, zip. *See* **rush** (1).

hotheaded *adjective*
1. Characterized by unthinking boldness and haste ► hasty, impulsive, reckless. *See* **rash**[1]. **2.** Given to arguing ► contentious, litigious, quarrelsome. *See* **argumentative.** *See synonym note at* **argumentative.**

hotheadedness *noun*
► crankiness, prickliness, tetchiness. *See* **temper** (1).

hotness *noun*
► fervor, torridity. *See* **heat** (1).

hot pursuit *noun*
The following of another in an attempt to overtake and capture ► chase, hunt, pursuit.

hot spot *noun*
► corner, difficulty, fix. *See* **predicament.**

hot water *noun*
1. A situation requiring immediate assistance or remedial action ► crisis, distress, trouble. *See* **emergency. 2.** A difficult, often embarrassing situation or condition ► corner, difficulty, fix. *See* **predicament.**

hound *verb*
To attack or disturb persistently ► harry, pester,

torment. *See* **harass**. *See synonym note at* **harass**.

hound *noun*
An ardent admirer ▶ devotee, enthusiast, fancier. *See* **fan²**.

house *noun*
1. A building or shelter where one lives ▶ domicile, habitation, residence. *See* **home** (1). **2.** A group of people living together as a unit ▶ family, household, ménage. **3.** A commercial organization ▶ corporation, enterprise, establishment. *See* **company** (1). **4.** A group of people sharing common ancestry ▶ clan, kindred, lineage. *See* **family** (2).

house *verb*
1. To stay in or provide with lodging, especially temporarily ▶ accommodate, bed (down), room. *See* **lodge** (1). **2.** To have as one's domicile, usually for an extended period ▶ dwell, reside. *See* **live¹** (2). **3.** To give refuge to ▶ harbor, haven, shelter, take in. *See also* **defend**.

housebreak *verb*
▶ break in, master, tame. *See* **domesticate**.

housebreaker *noun*
▶ burglar, robber, stealer. *See* **thief**.

housebroken *adjective*
▶ broken (in), house-trained, naturalized. *See* **domestic** (2).

housecleaning *noun*
Informal A thorough or drastic reorganization ▶ overhaul, reengineering, reshuffling, shakeup. *See also* **renewal, revolution**.

household *noun*
A group of people living together as a unit ▶ family, house, ménage.

household *adjective*
Of or relating to the family or household ▶ family, residential. *See* **domestic** (1).

house of correction *noun*
▶ penitentiary, prison. *Informal:* lockup. *See* **jail**.

house-train *verb*
▶ break in, housebreak, tame. *See* **domesticate**.

house-trained *adjective*
▶ broken (in), housebroken, naturalized. *See* **domestic** (2).

housing *noun*
Dwellings in general ▶ lodging, shelter. *Idiom:* a roof over one's head. *See also* **home, hut**.

hovel *noun*
▶ cabin, lean-to, shack. *See* **hut**.

hover *verb*
1. To remain stationary over a place or object ▶ hang, poise. **2.** To stay on top of the surface of water or stay in mid-air ▶ bob, stay afloat. *See* **float** (1). **3.** To be imminent ▶ brew, impend, loom. *See* **threaten** (2).

however *adverb*
▶ all the same, nevertheless, yet. *See* **still** (1).

howl *verb*
1. To utter or emit a long, mournful, plaintive sound ▶ bay, moan, ululate, wail, yowl. **2.** To cry loudly, as an upset baby does ▶ holler, wail, yowl. *See* **bawl** (1). **3.** To

shed tears ▶ bawl, sob, weep. *See* **cry** (1). **4.** *Slang* To express amusement or mirth ▶ chuckle, guffaw, roar. *See* **laugh**. **5.** To speak or say in a loud cry ▶ call, holler, yell. *See* **shout**. *See synonym note at* **shout**.

howl *noun*
1. A long, mournful cry ▶ bay, moan, ululation, wail, yowl. **2.** A loud cry ▶ call, holler, yell. *See* **shout**. **3.** *Slang* Something or someone uproariously funny ▶ *Informal:* hoot, laugh. *See* **scream** (3). **4.** *Slang* An act of laughing ▶ cackle, roar, laughter. *See* **laugh** (1).

howler *noun*
Slang A stupid, clumsy mistake ▶ bungle, fumble, solecism. *See* **blunder**.

hub *noun*
1. A point of origin or crucial factor ▶ core, focus, nucleus. *See* **center** (3). **2.** A place of concentrated activity, influence, or importance ▶ headquarters, heart, hotbed. *See* **center** (1). *See synonym note at* **center**.

hubbub *noun*
▶ clamor, din, tumult. *See* **noise** (1). *See synonym note at* **noise**.

hubris *noun*
The quality of being arrogant ▶ hauteur, superiority. *See* **arrogance**.

huckster *verb*
1. To travel about selling goods ▶ hawk, peddle, vend. **2.** To argue about the terms, as of a sale ▶ haggle, negotiate, palter. *See* **haggle**.

huddle *verb*
1. To incline the body ▶ bend, crouch, scrunch. *See* **stoop** (1). **2.** To meet and exchange views to reach a decision ▶ consult, deliberate, talk. *Informal:* powwow. *See* **confer** (1).

huddle *noun*
A number of individuals making up a unit ▶ body, cluster, collection. *See* **group** (1).

hue *noun*
1. The aspect of things that is caused by differing qualities of the light reflected or emitted by them ▶ cast, shade, tint. *See* **color** (1). **2.** A slight variation between nearly identical entities ▶ nicety, subtlety. *See* **shade** (1).

huff *noun*
1. An angry outburst ▶ fit, passion, tantrum. *See* **temper** (2). **2.** Extreme displeasure caused by an insult ▶ resentment, ruffled feathers, umbrage. *See* **offense** (1).

huff *verb*
1. To breathe hard ▶ gasp, puff. *See* **pant** (1). **2.** To cause resentment or hurt by callous, rude behavior ▶ offend, outrage. *See* **insult** (1).

huffy *adjective*
▶ exacerbated, irate, peeved. *See* **angry**.

hug *verb*
To put one's arms around affectionately ▶ enfold, hold. *See* **embrace** (1).

hug *noun*
The act of embracing ▶ clasp, squeeze. *See* **embrace**.

huge *adjective*
▸ behemoth, colossal, gigantic, mighty. *See* **enormous**. *See synonym note at* **enormous**.

hugely *adverb*
▸ exceedingly, extremely, highly. *See* **very**.

hugeness *noun*
▸ immensity, vastness. *See* **enormousness**.

huggermugger *noun*
The habit, practice, or policy of keeping secrets ▸ concealment, secretiveness. *See* **secrecy**.

huggermugger *adjective*
Existing or operating in a way so as to ensure complete concealment and confidentiality ▸ clandestine, covert, undercover. *See* **secret** (1).

huggermugger *adverb*
In a secret way ▸ covertly, sub rosa. *See* **secretly**.

huggermuggery *noun*
▸ concealment, secretiveness. *See* **secrecy**.

hulk *noun*
1. A large, ungainly, and dull-witted person ▸ lout, ox. *Informal:* lummox. *See* **oaf**. 2. One that is extraordinarily large and powerful ▸ Goliath, monster, titan. *See* **giant**.

hulk *verb*
To move heavily or clumsily ▸ clump, galumph, lumber. *See* **blunder** (1).

hulking *or* **hulky** *adjective*
▸ hefty, husky, stout. *See* **bulky** (2).

hull *noun*
The outer covering of a fruit ▸ peel, rind, shell. *See* **skin** (3).

hull *verb*
To remove the skin of ▸ pare, strip. *See* **skin** (1).

hullabaloo *noun*
1. Sounds or a sound, especially when loud, confused, or disagreeable ▸ clamor, din. *See* **noise** (1). *See synonym note at* **noise**. 2. Loud and insistent utterances or noisemaking, usually expressing disapproval ▸ rumpus, uproar. *See* **vociferation**.

hum *verb*
To make a continuous low-pitched droning sound ▸ bombinate, bumble, burr, buzz, drone, purr, whir, whiz.

hum *noun*
A continuous low-pitched droning sound ▸ bumble, burr, buzz, buzzing, drone, humming, purr, purring, whir, whirring, whiz, whizzing.

human *adjective*
1. Of or characteristic of human beings or humankind ▸ anthropic, anthropical, anthropoid, mortal. 2. Concerned with human welfare and the remedying of social ills ▸ compassionate, humane. *See* **humanitarian**.

human *noun*
A member of the human race ▸ being, mortal, person. *See* **human being**.

human being *noun*
A member of the human race ▸ being, body, creature, earthling, Homo sapiens, human, individual, life, man, mortal, party, person, personage, self, soul, spirit.

humane *adjective*
1. Concerned with human welfare and the remedying of social ills ▸ compassionate, merciful. *See* **humanitarian**. *See synonym note at* **humanitarian**. 2. In accordance with principles of right or good conduct ▸ principled, virtuous. *See* **ethical**.

humanistic *adjective*
▸ liberal, open-minded, tolerant. *See* **broad-minded**.

humanitarian *adjective*
Concerned with human welfare and the remedying of social ills ▸ charitable, compassionate, human, humane, humanistic, merciful, philanthropic, public-spirited, social-minded. *See also* **benevolent, generous, liberal, selfless**.

humanitarian *noun*
A person who gives to a charity or cause ▸ benefactor, contributor, patron. *See* **donor**.

✤ **CORE SYNONYMS:** *humanitarian, humane, compassionate, merciful.* These adjectives mean concerned with human welfare, the remedying of social ills, and the alleviation of suffering: *released the prisoner for humanitarian reasons; a humane physician; compassionate toward impoverished people; is merciful to the repentant.*

---

humanity *noun*
1. Humans as a group ▸ men and women, mortals, world. *See* **humankind**. 2. Kindly, charitable interest in others ▸ goodwill, kindheartedness, philanthropy. *See* **benevolence** (1).

humanize *verb*
To fit for companionship with others, especially in attitude or manners ▸ acculturate, civilize, socialize.

humanizing *adjective*
▸ enlightening, humanizing. *See* **cultural**.

humankind *noun*
Humans as a group ▸ earth, flesh, Homo sapiens, human beings, humanity, human race, man, mankind, men and women, mortals, universe, world. *See also* **public**.

humanlike *or* **humanoid** *adjective*
Resembling a human being ▸ anthropoid, anthropomorphic, anthropomorphous, hominoid, manlike. *See also* **human**.

human race *noun*
▸ humanity, mortals, world. *See* **humankind**.

humble *adjective*
1. Having or expressing feelings of humility ▸ lowly, meek, modest, unambitious. *See also* **deferential**. 2. Of little distinction ▸ lowly, mean, simple. *See also* **modest**. 3. Lacking high station or birth ▸ common, ignoble, unwashed. *See* **lowly** (1).

humble *verb*
1. To lower the pride or dignity of ▸ abase, debase, deflate, degrade, demean, humiliate, lower, mortify, puncture. *Slang:* put down. *Idioms:* bring low, put in one's place, take (*or* bring) down a notch, take (*or*

bring) down a peg. *See also* **belittle, disgrace, shame.**
2. To lower in character or quality ► abase, degrade.
See **debase** (1). *See synonym note at* **debase.**

humbleness *noun*
► humility, meekness. *See* **modesty** (1).

humbug *noun*
1. A person who practices deceit, especially under an assumed identity ► charlatan, impostor, quack. *See* **fake** (1). **2.** An act of cheating ► deceit, hoax, swindle. *See* **cheat** (1).

humbug *verb*
To cause to accept something false, especially by trickery or misrepresentation ► dupe, fool, mislead, trick. *See* **deceive.**

humdrum *adjective*
1. Arousing no interest or curiosity ► dull, irksome, monotonous. *See* **boring** (1). *See synonym note at* **boring. 2.** Being of no special quality or type ► common, mediocre, standard. *See* **ordinary** (1). **3.** Lacking liveliness, charm, or surprise ► colorless, lusterless. *See* **dull** (1). *See synonym note at* **dull.**

humdrum *noun*
A tiresome lack of variety ► monotone, sameness. *See* **monotony.**

humid *adjective*
► muggy, soggy, sultry. *See* **sticky** (2).

humiliate *verb*
1. To lower the pride or dignity of ► degrade, demean, lower. *See* **humble** (1). **2.** To bring disgrace on ► abase, dishonor, shame. *See* **disgrace.**

humiliating *adjective*
► discreditable, ignominious, shameful. *See* **disgraceful** (1).

humiliation *noun*
1. A lowering in or deprivation of character or self-esteem ► degeneration, dishonor, mortification. *See* **degradation** (1). **2.** Loss of or damage to one's reputation ► discredit, disrepute, reproach. *See* **disgrace.**

humility *noun*
► humbleness, meekness, unpretentiousness. *See* **modesty** (1).

humming *adjective*
1. In action or full operation ► functioning, operating, working. *See* **active** (1). **2.** Full of lively activity ► bustling, crawling, swarming. *See* **busy** (2).

hummock *noun*
► prominence, rise. *See* **hill** (1).

humor *noun*
1. The quality of being laughable or comical ► comedy, comicality, comicalness, drollery, drollness, farcicality, funniness, humorousness, jocoseness, jocosity, jocularity, ludicrousness, ridiculousness, wit, wittiness, zaniness. **2.** A person's customary manner of emotional response ► habit, nature, temperament. *See* **disposition** (1). **3.** A temporary state of mind or feeling ► frame of mind, temper. *See* **mood** (1). *See synonym note at* **mood. 4.** An impulsive turn of mind ► impulse, notion, whim. *See* **fancy** (1).

humor *verb*
1. To comply with the wishes or ideas of another ► cater (to), gratify, indulge. *See also* **defer. 2.** To treat indulgently ► coddle, pamper, spoil. *See* **baby.** *See synonym note at* **baby.**

humorist *noun*
► clown, comedian, jester. *See* **joker.**

humorous *adjective*
1. Causing laughter or amusement ► amusing, comical, laughable. *See* **funny** (1). **2.** Exhibiting or employing wit or originality ► scintillating, witty. *See* **clever** (2).

humorousness *noun*
► comicality, funniness, ridiculousness, wittiness. *See* **humor** (1).

hump *noun*
An unevenness or elevation on a surface ► lump, protuberance. *See* **bump** (1).

hump *verb*
To incline the body ► bend, crouch, scrunch. *See* **stoop** (1).

humus *noun*
The soft part of the land surface of the world ► clay, loam, soil. *See* **earth** (1).

hunch *noun*
1. An intuitive awareness or sense of something ► idea, intuition, suspicion. *See* **feeling** (1). **2.** An irregularly shaped mass of indefinite size ► clod, wad. *See* **lump**[1] (1).

hunch *verb*
To incline the body ► bend, crouch, scrunch. *See* **stoop** (1).

hunger *noun*
1. A desire for food or drink ► stomach, taste, thirst. *See* **appetite** (1). **2.** A strong wanting of what promises enjoyment or pleasure ► craving, longing, yearning. *See* **desire** (1).

hunger *verb*
To have a greedy, obsessive desire ► crave, itch, lust, thirst. *See also* **desire.**

hungry *adjective*
1. Desiring or craving food ► famished, ravenous, starving, voracious. *Informal:* starved. **Idiom:** hungry as a wolf. **2.** Having desire for something ► desiring, desirous, hankering. *See also* **voracious. 3.** Having a strong urge to obtain or possess something, especially material wealth, in quantity ► avaricious, covetous. *See* **greedy** (1).

hunk *noun*
1. *Informal* An irregularly shaped mass of indefinite size ► clod, clump, wad. *See* **lump**[1] (1). **2.** *Slang* A person regarded as physically attractive. Used of a man ► lovely, stunner. *See* **beauty** (1).

hunker down *verb*
1. To incline the body ► bend, crouch, scrunch. *See* **stoop** (1). **2.** To sit on one's heels ► squat.

hunt *verb*
1. To look for and pursue game in order to capture or kill it ► chase (down), drive, run (down), stalk. *See*

also **track. 2.** To follow another with the intent of overtaking and capturing ▸ chase, run after. *See* **pursue** (1).

hunt down *verb*
To pursue and locate ▸ run down, track down. *See* **trace** (1).

hunt for *verb*
To try to find something ▸ look for, search for. *See* **seek** (1).

hunt *noun*
1. The following of another in an attempt to overtake and capture ▸ chase, hot pursuit, pursuit. **2.** An attempt to accomplish or attain ▸ quest, search. *See* **pursuit** (2).

hurdle *noun*
Something that blocks entry or passage ▸ barrier, blockage, hindrance. *See* **bar** (1).

hurdle *verb*
1. To pass by or over successfully ▸ clear, negotiate, surmount. **2.** To move off the ground by a muscular effort of the legs and feet ▸ spring, vault. *See* **jump** (1).

hurl *verb*
1. To send through the air with a motion of the hand or arm ▸ fling, heave, pitch. *See* **throw** (1). *See synonym* **throw. 2.** *Slang* To eject the contents of the stomach through the mouth ▸ retch, throw up. *Informal:* puke. *See* **vomit** (1).

hurl *noun*
An act of throwing ▸ fling, heave, toss. *See* **throw.**

hurried *adjective*
1. Unexpectedly sudden ▸ precipitant, precipitate, sudden. *See* **abrupt** (2). **2.** Accomplished or experienced in very little time ▸ fast, rapid, speedy. *See* **quick** (1). **3.** Characterized by great speed ▸ brisk, hasty, hell-for-leather, high-speed. *See* **fast** (1).

hurriedly *adverb*
▸ hastily, quickly, rapidly, swiftly. *See* **fast.**

hurriedness *noun*
▸ precipitance, rashness. *See* **haste** (2).

hurry *verb*
1. To move swiftly ▸ dash, sprint, zip. *See* **rush** (1). **2.** To increase the speed of ▸ hasten, quicken. *See* **speed** (1). *See synonym note at* **speed.**

hurry *noun*
Rapidity of movement or activity ▸ expeditiousness, hustle, quickness. *See* **haste** (1). *See synonym note at* **haste.**

hurry-scurry *noun*
▸ tumult, turmoil. *Informal:* lather. *See* **agitation** (2).

hurry-up *adjective*
Designed to meet emergency needs as quickly as possible ▸ *Informal:* crash, rush.

hurt *verb*
1. To cause bodily damage to a living thing ▸ injure, traumatize, wing, wound. *See also* **cut, break. 2.** To cause pain, soreness, or discomfort; be painful ▸ ache, bite, burn, smart, sting, twinge. **3.** To cause pain, soreness, or discomfort to ▸ bother, inflame, irritate, pain, pang, twinge. *See also* **afflict. 4.** To cause emo-

tional suffering or painful sorrow to ▸ disturb, grieve. *See* **distress** (1). **5.** To spoil the soundness or perfection of ▸ flaw, impair. *See* **damage. 6.** To cause anger, resentment, or hurt feelings ▸ annoy, injure, upset. *See* **offend** (1).

hurt *noun*
1. A state of physical or mental suffering ▸ agony, misery, pain. *See* **distress** (1). **2.** The action or result of inflicting loss or pain ▸ detriment, impairment, injury. *See* **harm.**

hurtful *adjective*
1. Marked by, causing, or experiencing physical pain ▸ achy, afflictive, sore. *See* **painful** (1). **2.** Causing harm or injury ▸ deleterious, evil, injurious. *See* **harmful. 3.** Causing displeasure, anger, or hurt feelings ▸ discourteous, impolite, rude. *See* **offensive** (2).

hurtle *verb*
1. To send through the air with a motion of the hand or arm ▸ heave, hurl, pitch. *See* **throw** (1). **2.** To launch with great force ▸ fire, project. *See* **shoot** (3).

hurtless *adjective*
▸ innocuous, unoffensive. *See* **harmless** (1).

husband *noun*
A male spouse ▸ consort, mate. *See* **spouse.**

husband *verb*
To protect an asset from loss or destruction ▸ conserve, preserve, save. *See also* **defend.**

husbandry *noun*
▸ conservancy, preservation. *See* **conservation.**

hush *verb*
1. To cause to become silent ▸ quiet, still. *See* **silence. 2.** To hold something requiring an outlet in check ▸ smother, stifle, suppress. *See* **repress. 3.** To prevent something from being known ▸ enshroud, mask. *See* **conceal** (1). **4.** To keep from being published or transmitted ▸ stifle, suppress, withhold. *See* **censor** (2).

hush *noun*
1. The absence of sound or noise ▸ noiselessness, quiet. *See* **silence** (1). **2.** An absence of motion or disturbance ▸ calmness, lull, peacefulness. *See* **stillness** (1).

hushed *adjective*
1. Marked by, done with, or making no sound or noise ▸ noiseless, quiet. *See* **silent** (1). **2.** Not irritating, strident, or loud ▸ quiet, subdued. *See* **soft** (2).

hush-hush *adjective*
1. *Informal* Known about by very few ▸ private, secret. *See* **confidential** (1). **2.** *Informal* Existing or operating in a way so as to ensure complete concealment and confidentiality ▸ clandestine, covert, undercover. *See* **secret** (1).

husk *noun*
The outer covering of a fruit or similar plant part ▸ rind, shell. *See* **skin** (3).

husk *verb*
To remove the skin of ▸ pare, strip. *See* **skin** (1).

husky¹ *adjective*
Rough, raw, or grating in sound ▸ gruff, ragged. *See* **hoarse** (1).

husky² *adjective*
1. Characterized by marked muscular development ▸ brawny, robust, sturdy. *See* **muscular. 2.** Having a large body, especially in girth ▸ hefty, stout. *See* **bulky** (2).

hussy *noun*
▸ jade, tramp, whore. *See* **slut.**

hustle *verb*
1. To increase the speed of ▸ hasten, quicken. *See* **speed** (1). **2.** To move swiftly ▸ dash, sprint, zip. *See* **rush** (1). **3.** To urge to move along ▸ chase, push, run. *See* **drive** (3).

hustle *noun*
1. An aggressive readiness along with energy to undertake taxing efforts ▸ enterprise, initiative, punch. *See* **drive** (2). **2.** Rapidness of movement or activity ▸ expeditiousness, hurry, quickness. *See* **haste** (1). **3.** An indirect, usually cunning means of gaining an end ▸ deception, ploy, sleight, stratagem. *See* **trick** (1).

hustler *noun*
1. An intensely energetic, enthusiastic person ▸ demon, dynamo. *Informal:* eager beaver, firebreather, go-getter, live wire. **2.** *Slang* A person who engages in sex for payment ▸ streetwalker, whore. *See* **prostitute.**

hut *noun*
A small, usually roughly built shelter ▸ cabin, hole, hovel, lean-to, shack, shanty, shed.

hutch *noun*
▸ coop, kennel, stall. *See* **cage.**

hutzpah *noun*
See **chutzpah.**

hyaline *adjective*
1. Of or resembling glass ▸ glasslike, glassy, vitreous, vitrescent. *See also* **translucent. 2.** Free from what obscures or dims ▸ crystalline, limpid, lucid. *See* **clear** (1).

hybrid *noun*
▸ compound, merger, union. *See* **combination** (1).

hygienic *adjective*
1. Promoting good health ▸ healthy, salutary. *See* **healthful** (1). **2.** Free or freed from microorganisms ▸ antiseptic, sanitary. *See* **sterile** (1).

hymeneal *adjective*
▸ nuptial, spousal, wedded. *See* **marital.**

hymn *noun*
A brief composition written or adapted for singing ▸ ballad, lyrics, tune. *See* **song** (1).

hymn *verb*
To honor a deity in religious worship ▸ extol, laud. *See* **praise** (3).

hype *noun*
Slang Information disseminated through various media to attract public notice ▸ advertisement, ballyhoo. *Informal:* hoopla. *See* **publicity** (1).

hype *verb*
Slang To attempt to sell or popularize by advertising or publicity ▸ advertise, market, publicize. *See* **promote** (3).

hyper *adjective*
Slang Feeling or exhibiting nervous tension ▸ fidgety, jittery, jumpy. *See* **edgy.**

hyperbole *or* **hyperbolism** *noun*
▸ overstatement, tall talk. *See* **exaggeration.**

hyperbolic *adjective*
▸ inflated, overblown, overstated. *See* **exaggerated** (1).

hyperbolize *verb*
▸ inflate, magnify, overcharge, overstate. *See* **exaggerate** (1).

hypercritic *noun*
▸ caviler, nitpicker. *See* **critic** (2).

hypercritical *adjective*
▸ captious, overcritical. *See* **critical** (1).

hypersensitive *adjective*
▸ thin-skinned, ticklish. *See* **oversensitive.**

hypersensitivity *adjective*
▸ ticklishness, touchiness. *See* **oversensitivity.**

hypnotic *adjective*
Inducing sleep or sedation ▸ opiate, sedative, slumberous. *See* **soporific** (1).

hypnotic *noun*
Something that induces sleep or sedation ▸ narcotic, sedative. *See* **soporific.**

hypnotic state *noun*
▸ abstraction, bemusement, daydreaming, reverie. *See* **trance** (1).

hypnotize *verb*
▸ enchant, mesmerize, spellbind. *See* **charm** (2).

hypocrisy *noun*
A show or expression of feelings or beliefs one does not actually hold or possess ▸ lip service, pharisaism, phoniness, piety, sanctimoniousness, sanctimony, tartuffery, two-facedness. *See also* **arrogance, deceit, dishonesty, faithlessness.**

hypocrite *noun*
A person who practices hypocrisy ▸ dissembler, pharisee, phony, poser, tartuffe. *See also* **liar.**

hypocritical *adjective*
Of or practicing hypocrisy ▸ Janus-faced, Pecksniffian, pharisaic, phony, pious, sanctimonious, two-faced. *See also* **arrogant, dishonest, faithless, underhand.**

hypogeal *or* **hypogean** *or* **hypogeous** *adjective*
▸ belowground, subterranean. *See* **underground.**

hypostasis *noun*
▸ incarnation, manifestation, personification. *See* **embodiment** (1).

hypostatize *verb*
▸ externalize, manifest, materialize. *See* **embody** (1).

hypothecate *verb*
▸ deposit, pledge. *See* **pawn¹.**

hypothesis *noun*
▸ contention, proposal, thesis. *See* **theory** (2).

hypothesize *verb*
To formulate as a tentative explanation ▸ speculate, theorize. *See also* **suppose.**

hypothesized *or* **hypothetical** *adjective*
1. Existing only in concept and not in reality ▶ conceptual, ideal, virtual. *See* **theoretical** (2). 2. Presumed to be true, real, or genuine, especially on inconclusive grounds ▶ presumptive, suppositional. *See* **supposed.**

See synonym note at **supposed. 3.** Not tested or proved ▶ unpracticed, untested. *See* **untried** (1).
hysterical *adjective*
Informal Causing laughter or amusement ▶ hilarious, humorous, uproarious. *See* **funny** (1).

i

I-beam *noun*
▶ crossbeam, girder, timber. *See* **beam** (2).
ice *verb*
Slang To cause the death of ▶ cut down, destroy, finish (off). *See* **kill**[1] (1).
iciness *noun*
▶ chilliness, coldness, frigidity. *See* **cold.**
icky *adjective*
Informal Not pleasant or agreeable ▶ disagreeable, uncongenial, unsympathetic. *See* **unpleasant** (1).
iconoclast *noun*
▶ free-thinker, independent, maverick. *See* **rebel** (2).
icy *adjective*
1. Marked by a low temperature ▶ chill, frigid, polar. *See* **cold** (1). *See synonym note at* **cold. 2.** Not friendly or sociable ▶ aloof, chilly, frigid. *See* **cool** (1).
idea *noun*
1. That which exists in the mind as the product of careful mental activity ▶ concept, conception, image, notion, perception, thought. *See also* **decision, estimate, understanding. 2.** Something thought to be true ▶ notion, persuasion, view. *See* **belief** (1). 3. The general sense or significance, as of an action or statement ▶ purport, substance. *See* **import** (1). 4. An intuitive awareness or sense of something ▶ hunch, intuition, suspicion. *See* **feeling** (1). 5. A method used for accomplishing something ▶ course, modus operandi, procedure, technique. *See* **approach** (1).

✦ CORE SYNONYMS: *idea, thought, notion, concept, conception.* These nouns refer to that which exists in the mind as the product of careful mental activity. *Idea* has the widest range: *"Human history is in essence a history of ideas"* (H.G. Wells). *Thought* is distinctively intellectual and stresses contemplation and reasoning: *"Language is the dress of thought"* (Samuel Johnson). *Notion* often refers to a vague, general, or even fanciful idea: *"She certainly has some notion of drawing"* (Rudyard Kipling). *Concept* and *conception* are applied to mental formulations on a broad scale: *You seem to have no concept of time. "Every succeeding scientific discovery makes greater nonsense of old-time conceptions of sovereignty"* (Anthony Eden)

ideal *adjective*
1. Conforming to an ultimate form of perfection or excellence ▶ archetypal, archetypical, exemplary, ide-

alized, model, perfect, quintessential, supreme. *See also* **excellent, perfect. 2.** Existing only in concept and not in reality ▶ conceptual, hypothetical, virtual. *See* **theoretical** (2).
ideal *noun*
1. One that is worthy of imitation or duplication ▶ exemplar, mirror, paradigm. *See* **model** (1). *See synonym note at* **model. 2.** A fervent hope ▶ desire, vision, wish. *See* **dream** (3).
idealist *noun*
▶ fantasist, romantic, stargazer. *See* **dreamer** (1).
idealistic *adjective*
Characterized by ideals that often conflict with practical considerations ▶ impractical, quixotic, romantic, starry-eyed, unrealistic, utopian, visionary. *Idiom:* having one's head in the clouds. *See also* **impossible, optimistic.**
ideate *verb*
▶ cogitate, deliberate, reflect. *See* **think** (1).
ideation *noun*
▶ deliberation, rumination. *See* **thought** (1).
identical *adjective*
1. Being one and not another; not different in nature or identity ▶ selfsame, very. *See* **same** (1). 2. Agreeing exactly in value, quantity, or effect ▶ equivalent, tantamount. *See* **equal** (1).
identicalness *noun*
The quality or condition of being exactly the same as something else ▶ identity, oneness, sameness, selfsameness. *See also* **likeness.**
identify *verb*
1. To set off by or as if by a mark indicating ownership or manufacture ▶ brand, tag. *See* **mark** (1). 2. To establish the identity of ▶ know, pinpoint. *See* **place** (1). 3. To represent as similar ▶ compare, equate, parallel. *See* **liken. 4.** To come or bring together in one's mind or imagination ▶ correlate, link. *See* **associate** (3). 5. To associate or affiliate oneself closely with a person or group ▶ empathize, relate, sympathize. *See also* **understand. 6.** To make known or identify, as by signs ▶ indicate, mark. *See* **designate** (1). 7. To make noticeable or different ▶ differentiate, individualize. *See* **distinguish** (2).
identity *noun*
1. The set of behavioral or personal characteristics by

which an individual is recognizable ▸ distinctiveness, individualism, individuality, peculiarity, selfhood, singularity, uniqueness. *See also* **character. 2.** The quality or condition of being exactly the same as something else ▸ identicalness, oneness, sameness, selfsameness. *See also* **likeness.**

ideological *adjective*
▸ academic, conceptual, speculative. *See* **theoretical** (1).

ideology *noun*
▸ dogma, teaching. *See* **doctrine.**

idiocy *noun*
1. Foolish behavior ▸ folly, silliness, tomfoolery. *See* **foolishness. 2.** The state of being stupid ▸ density, mindlessness, obtuseness. *See* **stupidity. 3.** Something that does not have or make sense ▸ bunkum, drivel, garbage. *See* **nonsense** (1).

idiom *noun*
1. Specialized expressions indigenous to a particular field, subject, trade, or subculture ▸ jargon, lingo, patois. *See* **language** (2). **2.** A word or group of words forming a unit and conveying meaning ▸ collocation, phrase. *See* **expression** (3).

idiosyncrasy *noun*
▸ peculiarity, singularity. *See* **eccentricity.**

idiosyncratic *adjective*
▸ bizarre, grotesque. *See* **eccentric.**

idiot *noun*
1. A person who is deficient in judgment and good sense ▸ jackass, moron, simpleton. *See* **fool** (1). **2.** A mentally dull person ▸ dummy, dunce, thickhead. *See* **dullard.**

idiotic *adjective*
1. Displaying a lack of forethought and good sense ▸ daft, inane, ludicrous. *See* **foolish. 2.** Lacking in intelligence ▸ dumb, dense, obtuse, softheaded. *See* **stupid** (1).

idle *adjective*
1. Marked by a lack of activity or use ▸ inactive, inert, inoperative, unemployed, unoccupied, unused, vacant. *See also* **empty, motionless, still. 2.** Resistant to exertion and activity ▸ indolent, shiftless, slothful. *See* **lazy.** *See synonym note at* **lazy. 3.** Lacking value, use, or substance ▸ empty, vacant. *See* **hollow** (1). *See synonym note at* **hollow. 4.** Having no basis in fact ▸ unfounded, unwarranted. *See* **baseless.** *See synonym note at* **baseless. 5.** Having no job ▸ jobless, unemployed, unoccupied, workless. *Idioms:* out of a job (*or* employ *or* work).

idle *verb*
1. To pass time without working or in avoiding work ▸ bum (around), laze (around), loaf (around), loiter, lounge (around), piddle (around), shirk, slack off. *Informal:* vegetate. *Slang:* diddle (around), goldbrick, goof (off). *Idioms:* kill (*or* waste) time, twiddle one's thumbs. *See also* **delay. 2.** To spend (time) idly or pleasantly ▸ dawdle (away), fiddle away, idle away, kill, trifle away, waste, while (away), wile (away). *See also* **spend. 3.** To prevent the occurrence or continu-

ation of a movement, action, or operation ▸ halt, immobilize, stall. *See* **stop** (2).

✛ CORE SYNONYMS: *idle, inactive, inert.* These adjectives mean marked by a lack of activity or use. *Idle* refers to persons who are not doing anything or are not busy: *employees idle because of the strike.* It also refers to what is not in use or operation: *idle machinery. Inactive* simply indicates absence of activity: *retired but not inactive; an inactive factory. Inert* describes things powerless to move themselves or to produce a desired effect; applied to persons, it implies lethargy or sluggishness, especially of mind or spirit: *"The Honorable Mrs. Jamieson . . . was fat and inert, and very much at the mercy of her old servants"* (Elizabeth C. Gaskell).

◂ ANTONYM: *active*

idleness *noun*
1. A lack of action or activity ▸ inaction, inertness. *See* **inaction. 2.** The quality or state of being lazy ▸ indolence, shiftlessness, sloth. *See* **laziness. 3.** The condition of being stopped ▸ immobilization, jam, tie-up. *See* **stop** (2).

idler *noun*
▸ bum, fainéant, loafer. *See* **wastrel** (2).

idol *noun*
▸ luminary, personality, star. *See* **celebrity** (1).

idolization *noun*
The act of adoring, especially reverently ▸ adoration, reverence, veneration, worship. *See also* **devotion, honor, praise.**

idolize *verb*
1. To regard with the deepest respect, deference, and esteem ▸ venerate, worship. *See* **revere.** *See synonym note at* **revere. 2.** To make an extravagant show of appreciation or desire for ▸ gush over, rave (about), rhapsodize. *See* **drool.**

idyllic *adjective*
Charmingly simple and carefree ▸ arcadian, pastoral. *See also* **country, fresh, still.**

i.e. *adverb*
▸ specifically, videlicet. *See* **namely.**

iffy *adjective*
1. *Informal* Lacking certainty or clarity ▸ dubious, indeterminate, questionable, unclear. *See* **ambiguous** (1). **2.** *Informal* In doubt or dispute ▸ disputable, doubtful, questionable. *See* **debatable.**

ignis fatuus *noun*
▸ hallucination, mirage, phantasma. *See* **illusion** (1).

ignite *verb*
▸ enkindle, fire, kindle. *See* **light**[1] (1).

ignoble *adjective*
1. Having or proceeding from low moral standards ▸ squalid, vile. *See* **sordid.** *See synonym note at* **sordid. 2.** Lacking high station or birth ▸ common, humble, unwashed. *See* **lowly** (1).

ignominious *adjective*
▸ discreditable, disfavorable, shameful. *See* **disgraceful** (1).

ignominiousness *noun*
▸ disreputableness, shamefulness. *See* **infamy** (1).
ignominy *noun*
▸ discredit, disrepute, humiliation. *See* **disgrace**.
ignorance *noun*
1. The condition of being ignorant; lack of knowledge or learning ▸ backwardness, benightedness, darkness, illiteracy, illiterateness, nescience, unintelligence. *See also* **inexperience, stupidity**. 2. The condition of being uninformed or unaware ▸ innocence, nescience, obliviousness, unawareness, unconsciousness, unfamiliarity. *See also* **artlessness, misunderstanding**.
ignorant *adjective*
1. Without education or knowledge ▸ clueless, illiterate, lowbrow, nescient, uncultivated, uneducated, uninstructed, unlearned, unlettered, unread, unscholarly, unschooled, unstudious, untaught, untutored. *Idiom:* in the dark. *See also* **artless, backward, inexperienced**. 2. Exhibiting lack of education or knowledge ▸ backward, benighted, primitive, unenlightened, uninformed. *See also* **dumb, stupid**. 3. Not aware or informed ▸ clueless, ill-informed, innocent, misguided, misinformed, oblivious, unacquainted, unaware, unconscious, unenlightened, unfamiliar, unilluminated, uninformed, unknowing, unwitting. *Idiom:* in the dark. *See also* **blind, confused**.
ignore *verb*
1. To slight someone deliberately ▸ shun, spurn, slight. *See* **snub**. 2. To pretend not to see ▸ disregard, overlook. *See* **blink at**. 3. To fail to care for or give proper attention to ▸ gloss over, slight. *See* **neglect** (1). 4. To fail to do or carry out ▸ disregard, omit, overlook. *See* **neglect** (3).
ilk *noun*
▸ genus, mold, species. *See* **kind²**.
ill *adjective*
1. Suffering from or appearing to suffer from an illness ▸ ailing, indisposed, unwell. *See* **sick** (1). 2. Causing harm or injury ▸ deleterious, evil, injurious. *See* **harmful**. 3. Bringing or predicting misfortune ▸ evil, ominous, unlucky. *See* **fateful** (1).
ill *noun*
1. Whatever is destructive or harmful ▸ bad, badness, evil, worse. *See also* **harm**. 2. A pathological condition of mind or body ▸ ailment, disorder, malady. *See* **disease** (1). 3. A cause of suffering or harm ▸ bane, scourge. *See* **curse** (3).
ill-advised *adjective*
▸ ill-considered, imprudent, inadvisable. *See* **unwise**.
ill-behaved *adjective*
▸ intractable, obstinate, unmanageable. *See* **unruly**.
ill-boding *adjective*
▸ bad, ominous, portentous. *See* **fateful** (1).
ill-bred *adjective*
1. Lacking in delicacy or refinement ▸ unbecoming, unrefined *See* **coarse** (1). 2. Lacking good manners ▸ disrespectful, impolite, uncivil. *See* **rude** (4). 3. Having or showing a lack of respect ▸ contemptuous, discourteous. *See* **disrespectful** (1).

ill-chosen *adjective*
▸ inept, infelicitous, unhappy. *See* **unfortunate** (2).
ill-considered *adjective*
1. Characterized by unthinking boldness and haste ▸ hasty, impulsive, reckless. *See* **rash¹**. 2. Not wise ▸ ill-advised, imprudent, inadvisable. *See* **unwise**.
illegal *adjective*
1. Prohibited by law ▸ illegitimate, illicit, lawless, outlawed, unlawful, wrongful. *Idiom:* against the law. *See also* **forbidden**. 2. Of, involving, or being a crime ▸ illicit, unlawful. *See* **criminal** (1).
illegality *noun*
1. The state or quality of being illegal ▸ illegitimacy, illicitness, lawlessness, unlawfulness. 2. An act that violates public law ▸ felony, offense. *See* **crime** (1).
illegitimacy *noun*
The state or quality of being illegal ▸ illegality, illicitness, lawlessness, unlawfulness.
illegitimate *adjective*
1. Born to parents who are not married to each other ▸ baseborn, bastard, misbegotten, natural, spurious, unlawful. *Idiom:* born out of wedlock. 2. Prohibited by law ▸ illicit, unlawful. *See* **illegal** (1). 3. Of, involving, or being a crime ▸ illicit, unlawful. *See* **criminal** (1).
ill-fated *adjective*
▸ hapless, ill-starred, luckless. *See* **unfortunate** (1). *See synonym note at* **unfortunate**.
ill-favored *adjective*
1. Displeasing to the eye ▸ homely, unattractive, unsightly. *See* **ugly** (1). *See synonym note at* **ugly**. 2. Arousing disapproval ▸ exceptionable, improper, unacceptable. *See* **objectionable**.
illiberal *adjective*
▸ close-minded, narrow-minded, puritanical. *See* **intolerant** (1).
illicit *adjective*
1. Contrary to accepted, especially moral conventions ▸ criminal, unlawful. 2. Prohibited by law ▸ outlawed, unlawful. *See* **illegal** (1). 3. Not allowed ▸ banned, outlawed, prohibited. *See* **forbidden**. 4. Of, involving, or being a crime ▸ illegal, unlawful. *See* **criminal** (1).
illicitness *noun*
The state or quality of being illegal ▸ illegality, illegitimacy, lawlessness, unlawfulness.
illimitable *adjective*
▸ boundless, incalculable, infinite. *See* **endless** (1). *See synonym note at* **endless**.
illiteracy *noun*
▸ benightedness, nescience. *See* **ignorance** (1).
illiterate *adjective*
▸ lowbrow, uncultivated, unlearned. *See* **ignorant** (1).
illiterateness *noun*
▸ illiteracy, nescience. *See* **ignorance** (1).
ill mannered *adjective*
Lacking good manners ▸ disrespectful, impolite, uncivil. *See* **rude** (4).
illness *noun*
1. The condition of being sick ▸ affliction, indisposi-

tion. *See* **sickness** (1). **2.** A pathological condition of mind or body ▸ ailment, disorder, malady. *See* **disease** (1).

illogical *adjective*
1. Not governed by or predicated on reason ▸ irrational, unreasonable, unreasoned. *Idioms:* out of bounds, without rhyme or reason. *See also* **foolish. 2.** Containing errors in reasoning ▸ invalid, spurious, unsound. *See* **fallacious** (1).

illogicality *or* **illogicalness** *noun*
The absence of reason ▸ irrationality, unreason, unreasonableness. *See also* **fallacy, foolishness.**

ill-omened *adjective*
▸ bad, ominous, portentous. *See* **fateful** (1).

ill repute *noun*
▸ discredit, disrepute, humiliation. *See* **disgrace.**

ill-starred *adjective*
▸ hapless, ill-fated, luckless. *See* **unfortunate** (1). *See synonym note at* **unfortunate.**

ill-suited *adjective*
▸ inapt, malapropos, unbecoming. *See* **improper** (2).

ill-tempered *adjective*
Having or showing a bad temper ▸ bad-tempered, cantankerous, churlish, crabbed, cranky, cross, curmudgeonly, disagreeable, fractious, fretful, grouchy, grumpy, ill humored, ill-natured, irascible, irritable, nasty, peevish, petulant, querulous, short-tempered, snappish, snappy, splenetic, surly, testy, ugly, waspish. *Informal:* crabby, mean. *Slang:* snarky. *Idiom:* out of sorts. *See also* **abrupt, argumentative, testy.**

ill-timed *adjective*
1. Not occurring at a favorable time ▸ inconvenient, inopportune, untimely. *See also* **fateful. 2.** Not suitable for or characteristic of the season ▸ mistimed, untimely. *See* **unseasonable.**

ill-treat *verb*
▸ ill-use, mishandle, mistreat. *See* **abuse** (1). *See synonym note at* **abuse.**

ill-treatment *noun*
▸ mishandling, mistreatment. *See* **abuse** (2).

illume *verb*
1. To cover or fill with light ▸ illumine, lighten. *See* **illuminate** (1). **2.** To enable one to understand, especially in a spiritual sense ▸ edify, enlighten. *See* **illuminate** (3).

illuminate *verb*
1. To cover or fill with light ▸ flood, illume, illumine, light (up), lighten. *See also* **beam. 2.** To make clear or clearer ▸ elucidate, illustrate. *See* **clarify** (1). **3.** To enable one to understand, especially in a spiritual or intellectual sense ▸ edify, enlighten, illume, illumine. *Idioms:* make plain, remove the scales from someone's eyes, shed (*or* throw) light upon. *See also* **explain. 4.** To become brighter ▸ brighten, lighten. *See* **clear** (1).

illumination *noun*
1. The act of physically illuminating or the condition of being filled with light ▸ light, lighting. *See also* **brilliance. 2.** Electromagnetic radiation that makes vision possible ▸ lucency, luminescence. *See* **light**[1] (1). **3.** The condition of being informed spiritually ▸ edification, enlightenment. *See also* **education. 4.** Something that serves to explain or clarify ▸ decipherment, explication. *See* **explanation** (1).

illuminative *adjective*
▸ edifying, enlightening, informative. *See* **educational** (2).

illumine *verb*
1. To cover or fill with light ▸ illume, lighten. *See* **illuminate** (1). **2.** To enable one to understand, especially in a spiritual sense ▸ edify, enlighten. *See* **illuminate** (3).

ill-usage *noun*
▸ misappropriation, misuse, perversion. *See* **abuse** (1).

ill-use *verb*
▸ maltreat, mishandle, misuse. *See* **abuse** (1).

illusion *noun*
1. A phenomenon that causes a misperception ▸ delusion, hallucination, ignis fatuus, mirage, phantasm, phantasma, phantasmagoria, phantasmagory, will-o'-the-wisp. **2.** An illusory mental image ▸ fantasy, reverie, vision. *See* **dream** (1). **3.** The use of skillful tricks and deceptions to produce entertainingly baffling effects ▸ legerdemain, sleight of hand. *See* **magic** (2). **4.** A fantastic, impracticable plan or desire ▸ chimera, fantasy, pipe dream. *See* **dream** (2).

illusive *or* **illusory** *adjective*
1. Of, relating to, or in the nature of an illusion; lacking reality ▸ chimeric, chimerical, delusive, delusory, dreamlike, hallucinatory, phantasmagoric, phantasmal, phantasmic, unreal, visionary. *See also* **imaginary. 2.** Tending to lead one into error ▸ deceptive, delusive, misleading. *See* **fallacious** (2).

illustratable *adjective*
▸ decipherable, explicable, interpretable. *See* **explainable.**

illustrate *verb*
1. To demonstrate and clarify with examples ▸ demonstrate, evidence, exemplify, instance. *See also* **explain, show. 2.** To serve as an example, image, or symbol of ▸ exemplify, symbolize, typify. *See* **represent** (1). **3.** To make clear or clearer ▸ define, elucidate. *See* **clarify** (1).

illustration *noun*
1. Something that serves to explain or clarify ▸ decipherment, explication, illumination. *See* **explanation** (1). **2.** One that is representative of a group or class ▸ case, sample. *See* **example** (1). *See synonym note at* **example. 3.** The act or process of describing in lifelike imagery ▸ delineation, drawing, rendering. *See* **representation. 4.** A concrete entity typifying an abstraction ▸ incarnation, manifestation, personification. *See* **embodiment** (1).

illustrative *adjective*
1. Serving to explain ▸ explicative, interpretive. *See* **explanatory. 2.** Of or relating to representation by drawings or pictures ▸ pictographic, pictorial. *See* **graphic** (4).

illustrious *adjective*
1. Widely known ▸ celebrated, noted, renowned. *See* **famous.** *See synonym note at* **famous. 2.** Raised to or occupying a high position or rank ▸ elevated, lofty. *See* **exalted** (1).
illustriousness *noun*
▸ glory, note, prestige. *See* **fame.**
ill will *noun*
1. Deep-seated hatred, as between longtime opponents or rivals ▸ antagonism, hostility. *See* **enmity. 2.** A desire to harm others or to see others suffer ▸ maliciousness, viciousness. *See* **malevolence.**
image *noun*
1. An image caused by reflection ▸ likeness, reflection. **2.** Something closely resembling another ▸ ditto, facsimile, likeness. *See* **copy** (1). **3.** One exactly resembling another ▸ clone, spitting image, twin. *See* **double** (1). **4.** The character projected or given by someone to the public ▸ appearance, impression. *See also* **façade. 5.** That which exists in the mind as the product of careful mental activity ▸ conception, notion. *See* **idea** (1). **6.** A concrete entity typifying an abstraction ▸ incarnation, manifestation, personification. *See* **embodiment** (1).
image *verb*
1. To present a lifelike image of ▸ depict, portray, render. *See* **represent** (2). **2.** To copy another slavishly ▸ clone, imitate. *See* **mimic** (1). **3.** To send back or form an image of ▸ mirror, reflect. **4.** To form mental images of ▸ envision, fantasize, visualize. *See* **imagine** (1).
imaginable *adjective*
▸ earthly, likely, possible. *See* **conceivable.**
imaginary *adjective*
Existing only in the imagination ▸ chimeric, chimerical, conceptual, fanciful, fantastic, fantastical, invented, make-believe, notional, unreal, visionary. *Idiom:* pie in the sky. *See also* **fictitious, illusive, mythical.**
imagination *noun*
1. The power of the mind to form images ▸ creativity, inventiveness, fancy, fantasy, imaginativeness, mind's eye. *See also* **invention. 2.** Discernment or perception which is usually competent or creative ▸ inspiration, prescience. *See* **vision** (2).

✦ CORE SYNONYMS: *imagination, fancy, fantasy.* These nouns refer to the power of the mind to form images, especially of what is not present to the senses. *Imagination* is the most broadly applicable: *"In the world of words, the imagination is one of the forces of nature"* (Wallace Stevens). *Fancy* especially suggests mental invention that is whimsical, capricious, or playful and that is characteristically well removed from reality: *"All power of fancy over reason is a degree of insanity"* (Samuel Johnson). *Fantasy* is applied principally to elaborate or extravagant fancy as a product of the imagination given free rein: *"The poet is in command of his fantasy, while it is exactly the*

mark of the neurotic that he is possessed by his fantasy" (Lionel Trilling).

---

imaginative *adjective*
1. Showing invention or whimsy in design ▸ fanciful, fantastic, whimsical. *See also* **capricious, elaborate, ornate. 2.** Characterized by foresight or vision ▸ intuitive, perceptive. *See* **visionary** (1).
imaginativeness *noun*
▸ creativity, fantasy. *See* **imagination** (1).
imagine *verb*
1. To form mental images of ▸ call up, conceive, conjure up, dream up, envisage, envision, fancy, fantasize, image, make up, picture, see, think, vision, visualize. *Informal:* feature. *See also* **invent. 2.** To predict or assume without sufficient information ▸ speculate, surmise. *See* **guess. 3.** To consider to be true without proof ▸ posit, presume, presuppose. *See* **suppose** (1). **4.** To experience dreams or daydreams ▸ fancy, hallucinate. *See* **dream** (1).
imbalance *noun*
1. A marked lack of correspondence or agreement ▸ discrepancy, disparity, incongruity. *See* **gap** (3). **2.** The condition or fact of being unequal, as in age, rank, or degree ▸ disproportion, incongruity. *See* **inequality** (1).
imbecile *noun*
1. A person who is deficient in judgment and good sense ▸ idiot, moron, nincompoop. *See* **fool** (1). **2.** A mentally dull person ▸ dummy, idiot, thickhead. *See* **dullard.**
imbecilic *adjective*
1. Displaying a lack of forethought and good sense ▸ daft, idiotic, ludicrous. *See* **foolish. 2.** Lacking in intelligence ▸ dumb, idiotic, obtuse. *See* **stupid** (1).
imbecility *noun*
1. Foolish behavior ▸ folly, silliness, tomfoolery. *See* **foolishness. 2.** The state of being stupid ▸ idiocy, mindlessness, obtuseness. *See* **stupidity.**
imbed *verb*
See **embed.**
imbibe *verb*
1. To take into the mouth and swallow a liquid ▸ down, sip, swill. *See* **drink** (1). **2.** To take alcoholic liquor, especially excessively or habitually ▸ tipple. *Slang:* booze, lush. *See* **drink** (2). **3.** To take in moisture or liquid ▸ absorb, sponge up. *See* **drink** (3). **4.** To take in and incorporate, especially mentally ▸ assimilate, digest, take up. *Informal:* soak (up). *See* **absorb** (2).
imbibing *adjective*
▸ absorptive, permeable, spongy. *See* **absorbent.**
imbroglio *noun*
1. A lack of order ▸ clutter, confusion, disarray. *See* **disorder** (1). **2.** Something that is intricately and often bewilderingly complex ▸ labyrinth, maze, web. *See* **tangle** (1).
imbue *verb*
1. To cause to be filled, as with a particular mood or tone ▸ permeate, suffuse. *See* **charge** (1). *See synonym*

note at **charge. 2.** To impart color to ▸ dye, stain, tint. See **color** (1).

imitate *verb*

1. To copy the manner or expression of another, especially in an exaggerated or mocking way ▸ ape, burlesque, caricature, impersonate, mimic, mock, parody, simulate, travesty. *Idioms:* do a takeoff on, do (*or* make) like. *See also* **act, impersonate. 2.** To take as a model ▸ copy, emulate. *See* **follow** (5). **3.** To copy another slavishly ▸ clone, image. *See* **mimic** (1). **4.** To make a copy of ▸ replicate, reproduce. *See* **copy** (1).

✛ CORE SYNONYMS: *imitate, mimic, ape, parody, simulate.* These verbs mean to copy the manner or expression of another, especially in an exaggerated or mocking way. To *imitate* is the most general: *The student made the class laugh by imitating the stern principal.* To *mimic* is to make a close imitation, often with an intent to ridicule: *"fresh carved cedar, mimicking a glade/Of palm and plaintain"* (John Keats). To *ape* is to follow another's lead slavishly but often with an absurd result: *"Those* [superior] *states of mind do not come from aping an alien culture"* (John Russell). To *parody* is either to imitate with comic effect or to attempt a serious imitation and fail: *"All these peculiarities* [of Samuel Johnson's literary style] *have been imitated by his admirers and parodied by his assailants"* (Thomas Macaulay). To *simulate* is to feign or falsely assume the appearance or character of something: *"I . . . lay there simulating death"* (W.H. Hudson).

---

imitation *noun*

1. The act, practice, or art of copying the manner or expression of another ▸ emulation, impersonation, mime. *See* **mimicry. 2.** Imitative reproduction, as of the style of another ▸ reflection, repetition. *See* **echo** (1). **3.** A work that exposes folly by the use of humor, irony, or comic imitation ▸ burlesque, parody, spoof. *See* **satire. 4.** An inferior substitute imitating an original ▸ ersatz, simulation. *See* **copy** (2).

imitation *adjective*
Made by humans, often in imitation of something else ▸ simulated, synthetic. *See* **artificial** (1).

imitative *adjective*

1. Of or involving imitation ▸ apish, derivative, emulative, mimetic, slavish. *See also* **counterfeit. 2.** Imitating sounds ▸ echoic, mimetic, onomatopoeic, onomatopoetic.

imitator *noun*
▸ ape, echo, parrot. *See* **mimic.**

immaculacy *or* **immaculateness** *noun*
▸ clarity, cleanliness. *See* **purity** (1).

immaculate *adjective*
▸ antiseptic, spotless. *See* **clean** (1). *See synonym note at* **clean.**

immanent *adjective*
▸ innate, intrinsic, natural. *See* **constitutional** (1).

immaterial *adjective*

1. Having no body, form, or substance ▸ bodiless, discarnate, disembodied, ethereal, impalpable, incorporeal, insubstantial, intangible, metaphysical, nonphysical, spiritual, unbodied, uncorporal, unsubstantial. *See also* **supernatural. 2.** Not relevant or pertinent to the subject; not applicable ▸ extraneous, inapplicable, unconnected. *See* **irrelevant.** *See synonym note at* **irrelevant.**

✛ CORE SYNONYMS: *immaterial, incorporeal, insubstantial, metaphysical, spiritual.* These adjectives mean lacking material body, form, or substance: *immaterial apparitions; an incorporeal spirit; insubstantial victories; metaphysical forces; spiritual beings.*

---

immature *adjective*

1. Being in an early period of growth or development ▸ fresh, juvenile. *See* **young.** *See synonym note at* **young. 2.** Of or characteristic of a child, especially in immaturity ▸ childlike, infantile, juvenile. *See* **childish. 3.** Lacking experience and the knowledge gained from it ▸ inexpert, uninitiated, unpracticed. *See* **inexperienced.**

immaturity *noun*
▸ greenness, inexpertness, rawness. *See* **inexperience.**

immeasurable *adjective*

1. Too great to be calculated ▸ boundless, infinite. *See* **incalculable.** *See synonym note at* **incalculable. 2.** Having no ends or limits ▸ boundless, infinite. *See* **endless** (1).

immeasurability *or* **immeasurableness** *noun*
▸ boundlessness, limitlessness, measurelessness. *See* **infinity** (1).

immediate *adjective*

1. Occurring at once ▸ instant, instantaneous. *See also* **fast, quick. 2.** Not far from another in space, time, or relation ▸ near, nearby, nigh. *See* **close** (1). *See synonym note at* **close. 3.** Marked by the absence of any intervention ▸ direct, firsthand, primary. **4.** In existence now ▸ current, present-day. *See* **present**[1] (1).

immediately *adverb*

1. Without delay ▸ ASAP, directly, forthwith, instant, instantly, now, promptly, right away, right off, straightaway, straight off. *Informal:* lickety-split, PDQ, yesterday. *Slang:* pronto. *Idioms:* at once, before you can say Jack Sprat (*or* Jack Robinson), first off, in the blink of an eye, like a shot, on the double, this instant (*or* minute *or* second). *See also* **fast. 2.** Without intermediary ▸ directly, firsthand.

immemorial *adjective*
▸ ancient, bygone, timeworn. *See* **old** (1).

immense *adjective*
▸ behemoth, colossal, gigantic, mighty. *See* **enormous.** *See synonym note at* **enormous.**

immensity *or* **immenseness** *noun*
▸ hugeness, vastness. *See* **enormousness.**

immerge *verb*
▸ dunk, immerse, submerse. *See* **dip** (1).

immerse *verb*

1. To plunge briefly in or into a liquid ▸ dunk, submerse. *See* **dip** (1). **2.** To occupy the full attention of ▸ consume, engross, preoccupy. *See* **absorb** (1).

immersed *adjective*
▸ absorbed, engrossed, intent. *See* **rapt.**

immersion *noun*
▸ engrossment, enthrallment, involvement, prepossession. *See* **absorption** (2).

immigrant *noun*
1. One who immigrates ▸ migrant. *See also* **émigré, settler.** 2. A person coming from another country or into a new community ▸ alien, outsider, stranger. *See* **foreigner.**

immigrant *adjective*
From or characteristic of another place ▸ alien, exotic, strange. *See* **foreign** (1).

immigrate *verb*
To leave one's native land and settle in another ▸ emigrate (from), migrate, resettle, transmigrate. *See also* **move, settle.**

immigration *noun*
Settling in a country to which one is not native ▸ migration, transmigration. *See also* **emigration.**

imminence *noun*
The act or fact of coming near ▸ approach, coming, convergence, nearness. *See also* **advance, appearance.**

imminent *adjective*
About to occur at any moment ▸ at hand, approaching, brewing, impending, in store, looming, proximate. *Idioms:* around the corner, in the offing, in the wind, on the horizon. *See also* **close, coming.**

immobile *adjective*
1. Firmly in position ▸ stationary, steadfast, unmoving. *See* **fixed** (1). 2. Not moving ▸ stationary, still. *See* **motionless.**

immobilization *noun*
▸ gridlock, jam, tie-up. *See* **stop** (2).

immobilize *verb*
1. To render powerless or motionless, as by inflicting severe injury ▸ handicap, impair, paralyze. *See* **disable** (1). 2. To prevent the occurrence or continuation of a movement, action, or operation ▸ halt, idle, stall. *See* **stop** (2).

immoderate *adjective*
▸ extravagant, unbridled. *See* **excessive** (1). *See synonym note at* **excessive.**

immoderation *or* **immoderacy** *noun*
▸ overindulgence, surfeit. *See* **excess** (3).

immodest *adjective*
▸ indecent, indelicate. *See* **improper** (1).

immolate *verb*
To offer as a sacrifice ▸ sacrifice, victimize.

immolation *noun*
▸ hecatomb, sacrifice, victim. *See* **offering** (1).

immoral *adjective*
1. Morally objectionable ▸ bad, sinful. *See* **evil** (1). 2. Not chaste or moral ▸ debased, uncleanly. *See* **impure** (1).

immorality *noun*
1. A wicked act or wicked behavior ▸ evil, misdeed, sin. *See* **crime** (2). 2. Degrading, immoral acts or habits

▸ depravity, perversion, vice. *See* **corruption** (1).

immortal *adjective*
1. Not being subject to death ▸ deathless, undying. 2. Enduring for all time ▸ ceaseless, eternal. *See* **endless** (2).

immortality *noun*
Endless life after death ▸ afterlife, deathlessness, eternal life, eternity, everlasting life, everlastingness, life eternal, life everlasting. *See also* **endlessness, eternity.**

immortalize *verb*
To cause to last endlessly ▸ eternalize, eternize, perpetuate. *Idioms:* cast (*or* etch *or* fix *or* set) in stone. *See also* **honor, memorialize.**

immovable *adjective*
▸ stationary, steadfast, unmoving. *See* **fixed** (1).

immune *adjective*
1. Having the capacity to withstand ▸ impervious, insusceptible, unsusceptible. *See* **resistant** (1). 2. Affording protection ▸ impenetrable, invulnerable, unconquerable. *See* **safe** (2).

immunity *noun*
1. The capacity to withstand ▸ imperviousness, insusceptibility, resistance, unsusceptibility. *See also* **endurance, stability.** 2. Temporary immunity from penalties ▸ exemption, grace, reprieve, respite. *See also* **delay.** 3. The quality or state of being safe ▸ impenetrability, security. *See* **safety** (1).

immure *verb*
1. To confine within a limited area ▸ cage, shut (in), wall (up). *See* **enclose** (1). 2. To put in or as if in prison ▸ confine, incarcerate, jail. *See* **imprison.**

immutability *noun*
▸ constancy, regularity, sameness. *See* **changelessness.**

immutable *adjective*
1. Incapable of changing or being modified ▸ inalterable, inconvertible, inflexible, invariable, ironclad, rigid, unalterable, unchangeable, unmodifiable. *See also* **continuing, firm, fixed.** 2. Remaining unchanged ▸ changeless, invariable, unfailing. *See* **unchanging.**

imp *noun*
1. One who causes minor trouble or damage ▸ prankster, scamp. *See* **rascal.** 2. A mischievous youngster ▸ brat, gamin, whelp. *See* **urchin.**

impact *noun*
1. A violent forcible contact ▸ crash, knock. *See* **collision.** *See synonym note at* **collision.** 2. The strong effect exerted by one person or thing on another ▸ bearing, force, impression, influence, repercussion, reverberation. *See also* **cause, effect, stimulus.**

impact *verb*
1. To come together with force ▸ crash, strike. *See* **collide** (1). 2. To have an impact on in a certain way ▸ affect, sway. *See* **influence** (1).

impair *verb*
1. To spoil the soundness or perfection of ▸ flaw, mar. *See* **damage.** 2. To addle the mind, as with a narcotic or alcohol ▸ besot, stupefy. *See* **drug** (2). 3. To render

powerless or motionless, as by inflicting severe injury ▸ handicap, immobilize, paralyze. *See* **disable** (1).

impairment *noun*
1. Harm done to property or a person ▸ destruction, injury, wreckage. *See* **damage** (1). 2. The sapping away of strength or energy ▸ depletion, devitalization, enfeeblement. *See* **debilitation**. 3. The action or result of inflicting loss or pain ▸ detriment, injury. *See* **harm**.

impale *verb*
▸ bayonet, incise, pierce, slash. *See* **cut** (1).

impalpable *adjective*
1. Incapable of being apprehended by the mind or the senses ▸ imponderable, indiscernible. *See* **imperceptible** (1). 2. Having no body, form, or substance ▸ disembodied, incorporeal, nonphysical. *See* **immaterial** (1).

impart *verb*
1. To make known ▸ disclose, divulge, transmit. *See* **communicate** (1). 2. To give formally or officially ▸ award, bestow, grant. *See* **confer** (2).

impartial *adjective*
1. Free from bias in judgment ▸ equitable, nonpartisan, objective. *See* **fair**[1] (1). *See synonym note at* **fair**[1]. 2. Not inclining toward or actively taking either side in a matter under dispute ▸ nonaligned, unbiased. *See* **neutral** (1).

impartially *adverb*
▸ equitably, evenhandedly, objectively. *See* **fairly** (1).

impartiality *or* **impartialness** *noun*
▸ justice, nonpartisanship, objectivity. *See* **fairness**.

impassable *adjective*
Incapable of being negotiated or overcome ▸ insuperable, insurmountable, unconquerable. *See also* **impossible, invincible**.

impasse *noun*
▸ corner, difficulty, fix. *See* **predicament**.

impassible *adjective*
▸ insensitive, unimpressionable, unsusceptible. *See* **cold** (2).

impassion *verb*
▸ animate, inspire, stir. *See* **fire** (2).

impassioned *adjective*
▸ burning, fervent, torrid. *See* **passionate** (1).

impassive *adjective*
1. Lacking interest ▸ indifferent, listless, uninterested. *See* **apathetic**. 2. Lacking feeling or emotion ▸ emotionless, indifferent, stolid. *See* **cold** (2). 3. Lacking intelligent thought or content ▸ empty, vacuous. *See* **vacant** (1).

impassivity *or* **impassiveness** *noun*
▸ disinterest, indifference, unconcern. *See* **apathy**.

impatient *adjective*
1. Being unable or unwilling to endure irritation or opposition, for example ▸ intolerant, unforbearing, unindulgent. *See also* **ill-tempered, intolerant**. 2. Intensely desirous or interested ▸ avid, bursting. *See* **eager** (1). 3. In a state of anxiety or uneasiness ▸ distressed, nervous, uneasy. *See* **anxious**.

impeach *verb*
▸ charge, denounce, incriminate. *See* **accuse**.

impeachment *noun*
▸ denouncement, imputation, incrimination. *See* **accusation**.

impeccable *adjective*
▸ consummate, flawless, unblemished. *See* **perfect** (1). *See synonym note at* **perfect**.

impecuniosity *or* **impecuniousness** *noun*
▸ destitution, indigence, need. *See* **poverty** (1).

impecunious *adjective*
▸ destitute, down-and-out, indigent. *See* **poor** (1). *See synonym note at* **poor**.

impede *verb*
1. To interfere with the progress of ▸ dampen, encumber, obstruct. *See* **hinder** (1). *See synonym note at* **hinder**. 2. To cause to be later or slower than expected or desired ▸ hang up, retard, stall. *See* **delay** (1).

impediment *noun*
1. Something that blocks entry or passage ▸ barrier, blockage, hindrance. *See* **bar** (1). *See synonym note at* **bar**. 2. Something that obstructs progress and requires great effort to overcome ▸ complication, hardship, rigor. *See* **difficulty** (1).

impel *verb*
▸ excite, prod, trigger. *See* **provoke** (1).

impelled *adjective*
▸ committed, compelled, obligated. *See* **obliged** (2).

impend *verb*
To be imminent ▸ hover, loom, menace. *See* **threaten** (2).

impending *adjective*
▸ brewing, proximate. *See* **imminent**.

impenetrability *noun*
▸ immunity, security. *See* **safety** (1).

impenetrable *adjective*
1. Incapable of being grasped by the intellect or understanding ▸ unfathomable, unintelligible. *See* **incomprehensible**. 2. Affording protection ▸ immune, invulnerable, unconquerable. *See* **safe** (2). 3. Difficult to explain or understand ▸ confounding, inscrutable, occult. *See* **mysterious**.

impenitent *adjective*
Devoid of remorse ▸ remorseless, unrepentant.

imperative *adjective*
1. Demanding immediate attention ▸ crucial, dire, pressing. *See* **urgent** (1). *See synonym note at* **urgent**. 2. Imposed on one by authority, command, or convention ▸ compulsory, mandatory, requisite. *See* **required** (1).

imperative *noun*
1. An act or course of action that is demanded of one, as by position, custom, law, or religion ▸ charge, commitment, obligation. *See* **duty** (1). 2. An order ▸ charge, commandment, injunction. *See* **command** (1).

imperceptible *adjective*
1. Incapable of being apprehended by the mind or the senses ▸ impalpable, imponderable, inappreciable,

indiscernible, indistinguishable, insensible, intangible, invisible, subtle, unnoticeable, unobservable. *See also* **ambiguous, remote, unclear. 2.** So small as not to be discernible ► infinitesimal, microscopic. *See also* **tiny. 3.** Difficult or impossible to see or distinguish ► covert, disguised, unseen. *See* **hidden** (1).

imperfect *adjective*
1. Having a defect or defects ► amiss, blemished, defective, faulty, flawed. *See also* **shabby, trick. 2.** Not perfected, elaborated, or completed ► preliminary, sketchy, unpolished. *See* **rough** (10).

imperfection *noun*
► fault, glitch, weakness. *See* **defect** (1). *See synonym note at* **defect.**

imperial *adjective*
1. Having or arising from authority ► official, supreme. *See* **authoritative** (1). **2.** Impressive in size, proportion, or appearance ► imposing, magnificent, splendid. *See* **grand** (1).

imperil *verb*
► jeopardize, threaten. *See* **endanger.** *See synonym note at* **endanger.**

imperilment *noun*
► endangerment, hazard, jeopardy, risk. *See* **danger.**

imperious *adjective*
► bossy, domineering, overbearing. *See* **dictatorial** (1). *See synonym note at* **dictatorial.**

impermanent *adjective*
► make-do, makeshift, short-term. *See* **temporary** (2).

impermissible *adjective*
► banned, outlawed, prohibited. *See* **forbidden.**

impersonal *adjective*
1. Feeling or showing no strong emotional involvement ► detached, disinterested, dispassionate, indifferent, neutral. **2.** Not friendly, sociable, or warm in manner ► aloof, chilly, distant. *See* **cool** (1).

impersonate *verb*
1. To assume the character or appearance of ► attitudinize, masquerade, pass for, pose as, posture. *Idiom:* pass oneself off as. **2.** To play the part of ► do, play, portray, represent. *See* **act** (4). **3.** To copy the manner or expression of another, especially in an exaggerated or mocking way ► caricature, mock. *See* **imitate** (1).

impersonation *noun*
1. A work, such as a novel, play, or dramatic speech, that exposes folly by the use of humor, irony, or comic imitation ► burlesque, parody, spoof. *See* **satire. 2.** The act, practice, or art of copying the manner or expression of another ► imitation, mime. *See* **mimicry.**

impersonator *noun*
► ape, imitator, parrot. *See* **mimic.**

impertinence *noun*
► audacity, boldness, incivility. *See* **impudence.**

impertinent *adjective*
1. Rude and disrespectful; without shame ► bold, insolent, pert. *See* **impudent. 2.** Having or showing a lack of respect ► contemptuous, discourteous, impolite. *See* **disrespectful** (1). **3.** Causing displeasure, an-

ger, or hurt feelings ► hurtful, insulting, rude. *See* **offensive** (2). **4.** Not relevant or pertinent to the subject; not applicable ► immaterial, inapplicable, unconnected. *See* **irrelevant.** *See synonym note at* **irrelevant.**

imperturbability *or* **imperturbableness** *noun*
► equanimity, nonchalance, sang-froid, unflappability. *See* **balance** (2).

imperturbable *adjective*
► collected, composed, cool. *See* **calm** (1). *See synonym note at* **calm.**

impervious *adjective*
► immune, insusceptible, unsusceptible. *See* **resistant** (1).

imperviousness *noun*
The capacity to withstand ► immunity, insusceptibility, resistance, unsusceptibility. *See also* **endurance, stability.**

impetuous *adjective*
► hasty, impulsive, reckless. *See* **rash[1].** *See synonym note at* **rash[1].**

impetus *noun*
► catalyst, impulse, incentive. *See* **stimulus** (1).

impiety *noun*
1. Lack of belief in God ► disbelief, irreligion. *See* **atheism. 2.** An act of disrespect toward something regarded as sacred ► desecration, profanation, violation. *See* **sacrilege.**

impinge *verb*
► border, neighbor, touch. *See* **adjoin** (1).

impingement *noun*
► infringement, intrusion, obtrusion. *See* **trespass** (2).

impious *adjective*
1. Showing irreverence and contempt for something sacred ► blasphemous, profane, sacrilegious. **2.** Not believing in God ► disbelieving, faithless, irreligious. *See* **atheistic.**

impish *adjective*
► frolicsome, gamesome, sportive. *See* **mischievous** (1).

impishness *noun*
► diablerie, high jinks, tomfoolery. *See* **mischief** (1).

implacability *or* **implacableness** *noun*
► bullheadedness, hardheadedness, rigidity. *See* **stubbornness.**

implacable *adjective*
1. Firmly, often unreasonably immovable in purpose or will ► bullheaded, dogged, obstinate. *See* **stubborn** (1). **2.** Disposed to seek revenge ► avenging, spiteful, unforgiving. *See* **vindictive** (1).

implant *verb*
1. To fix (an idea, for example) in someone's mind by reemphasis and repetition ► drive, inculcate. *See* **instill. 2.** To place or set deeply or securely ► entrench, ingrain, plant. *See* **fix** (4). **3.** To put or set into, between, or among another or other things ► infuse, insert, interpose. *See* **introduce** (2).

implausible *adjective*
Not plausible or believable ► feeble, flimsy, improb-

able, inconceivable, incredible, insubstantial, lame, shaky, tenuous, thin, unbelievable, unconceivable, unconvincing, unlikely, unsubstantial, weak. *Idiom:* beyond belief. *See also* **doubtful, fallacious, impossible.**

implement *verb*
1. To put into action or use ▸ apply, employ, utilize. *See* **use** (1). **2.** To carry out the functions, requirements, or terms of ▸ discharge, execute, perform. *See* **fulfill** (1). **3.** To compel observance of ▸ effect, invoke. *See* **enforce.**

implement *noun*
A device used to do work or perform a task ▸ instrument, tool, utensil. *See synonym note at* **tool.** *See also* **agent, device, gadget.**

implementation *noun*
1. The act of putting into play ▸ employment, operation, usage. *See* **exercise** (1). **2.** Carrying a law or judgment into effect ▸ enforcement, execution. *See also* **effect.**

implicate *verb*
1. To cause to appear involved in or guilty of a crime or fault ▸ criminate, incriminate, inculpate. *See also* **accuse. 2.** To involve by logical necessity ▸ involve, indicate, point to. *See* **imply** (1). **3.** To draw or be drawn in so that extrication is difficult ▸ embroil, mix up, wrap up. *See* **involve** (1).

implicating *adjective*
▸ incriminating, insinuatory, suggestive. *See* **insinuating** (1).

implication *noun*
1. A subtle quality underlying or felt to underlie a situation, action, or person ▸ inkling, suspicion. *See* **hint** (1). **2.** The condition of being entangled or implicated ▸ embroilment, ensnarement. *See* **entanglement** (1).

implicit *adjective*
1. Conveyed indirectly without words or speech ▸ hinted, implied, inferred, insinuated, suggested, tacit, unarticulated, understood, unexpressed, unsaid, unspoken, unstated, unuttered, unvocalized, wordless. *Idiom:* taken for granted. *See also* **constitutional, silent. 2.** Having no reservations ▸ absolute, unconditional, undoubting, unfaltering, unhesitating, unquestioning, unreserved, wholehearted. *Idiom:* without reservations. *See also* **definite, sure.**

implied *adjective*
▸ inferred, tacit, unspoken. *See* **implicit** (1).

imploration *noun*
▸ entreaty, plea, supplication. *See* **appeal** (1).

implore *verb*
▸ beseech, entreat, plead. *See* **appeal** (1). *See synonym note at* **appeal.**

imply *verb*
1. To involve by logical necessity ▸ entail, implicate, involve, lead to, point to, suggest. *See also* **demand, mean, suppose. 2.** To convey an idea by indirect, subtle means ▸ insinuate, suggest. *See* **hint.** *See synonym note at* **hint.**

impolite *adjective*
1. Lacking good manners ▸ disrespectful, ill-bred, uncivil. *See* **rude** (4). **2.** Causing displeasure, anger, or hurt feelings ▸ hurtful, insulting, rude. *See* **offensive** (2). **3.** Having or showing a lack of respect ▸ contemptuous, discourteous, scornful. *See* **disrespectful** (1).

impoliteness *noun*
▸ affront, irreverence, rudeness. *See* **disrespect** (1).

impolitic *adjective*
1. Not wise ▸ ill-considered, impractical. *See* **unwise. 2.** Lacking sensitivity and skill in dealing with others ▸ gauche, insensitive, undiplomatic. *See* **tactless.**

imponderable *adjective*
▸ impalpable, indiscernible. *See* **imperceptible** (1).

import *verb*
1. To have or convey a particular idea ▸ denote, intend, signify. *See* **mean**[1] (1). **2.** To be of significance ▸ matter, weigh. *See* **count** (1). *See synonym note at* **count.**

import *noun*
1. The general sense or significance, as of an action or statement ▸ amount, burden, drift, gist, idea, purport, substance, tenor. *Idioms:* sum and substance, sum total. *See also* **heart, thrust. 2.** Something that is conveyed or signified ▸ point, sense, significance. *See* **meaning** (1). *See synonym note at* **meaning. 3.** The quality or state of being important ▸ concernment, significance, weightiness. *See* **importance.** *See synonym note at* **importance.**

importance *noun*
The quality or state of being important ▸ concern, concernment, consequence, import, magnitude, moment, significance, significancy, weight, weightiness. *See also* **import, meaning.**

✦ CORE SYNONYMS: *importance, consequence, moment, significance, import, weight.* These nouns refer to the quality or state of being important, influential, or worthy of note or esteem. *Importance* is the most general term: *the importance of a proper diet.* *Consequence* is especially applicable to persons or things of notable rank or position (*scholars of consequence*) and to what is important because of its possible outcome, result, or effect (*tax laws of consequence to investors*). *Moment* implies importance or consequence that is readily apparent: *making decisions of great moment.* *Significance* and *import* refer to the quality of something, often not obvious, that gives it special meaning or value: *an event of real significance; works of great social import.* *Weight* suggests a personal evaluation or judgment of importance: *"The popular faction at Rome . . . was led by men of weight"* (J.A. Froude).

◂ ANTONYM: *unimportant*

---

important *adjective*
1. Having great significance ▸ big, consequential, considerable, crucial, earth-shaking, grand, great, historic, key, large, material, meaningful, momentous, monumental, significant, substantial, worldshaking. *Informal:* bigtime. *See also* **big-league, critical, essential, primary. 2.** Having or exercising

influence ▸ powerful, weighty. *See* **influential. 3.** Widely known ▸ celebrated, noted, renowned. *See* **famous.**

importunate *adjective*
Firm or obstinate, as in making a demand or maintaining a stand ▸ importune, insistent, persistent, urgent. *See also* **firm, stubborn.**

importune *verb*
1. To attack or disturb persistently ▸ harry, pester, torment. *See* **harass. 2.** To ask for urgently or insistently ▸ insist on (*or* upon), require. *See* **demand** (1).

importune *adjective*
Firm or obstinate, as in making a demand or maintaining a stand ▸ importunate, insistent, persistent, urgent. *See also* **firm, stubborn.**

impose *verb*
1. To establish and apply as compulsory ▸ assess, exact, levy, put. *See also* **bill, demand. 2.** To set forth expressly and authoritatively ▸ determine, mandate, ordain. *See* **dictate** (1). *See synonym note at* **dictate. 3.** To cause to undergo or bear (something unwelcome or damaging, for example) ▸ play, wreak. *See* **inflict.**

impose on *or* **upon** *verb*
1. To force another to accept a burden ▸ charge with, fasten on (*or* upon), foist on (*or* upon), inflict on (*or* upon), lay on (*or* upon), put on (*or* upon), saddle with, tax with, yoke with. *Informal:* stick with. *Idiom:* weight down with. **2.** To treat unfairly ▸ exploit, mistreat. *See* **abuse** (1). **3.** To cause inconvenience for ▸ incommode, put out, trouble. *See* **inconvenience.**

imposing *adjective*
▸ awesome, magnificent, splendid. *See* **grand** (1). *See synonym note at* **grand.**

imposition *noun*
An excessive, unwelcome burden ▸ encumbrance, infliction, intrusion, obtrusion. *See also* **burden, meddling.**

impossible *adjective*
1. Not capable of happening or being done ▸ impracticable, impractical, infeasible, unachievable, unattainable, unimaginable, unobtainable, unrealizable, unthinkable, unworkable. *Idioms:* beyond the bounds of possiblity (*or* reason), hardly possible, out of the question. *See also* **implausible, incredible, insuperable, foolish. 2.** So unpleasant or painful as not to be endured ▸ insufferable, intolerable, unendurable. *See* **unbearable. 3.** Marked by a disposition to oppose ▸ antagonistic, contradictory, hostile. *See* **contrary** (1).

impost *noun*
▸ duty, levy, tariff. *See* **tax** (1).

impostor *noun*
▸ charlatan, pretender, quack. *See* **fake** (1).

imposture *noun*
▸ deception, ploy, stratagem. *See* **trick** (1).

impotence *noun*
1. The condition or state of being incapable of accomplishing anything ▸ helplessness, ineffective-

ness. *See* **ineffectuality. 2.** The state or condition of being unable to reproduce ▸ fruitlessness, infertility. *See* **sterility** (2).

impotent *adjective*
1. Lacking power or strength ▸ helpless, powerless, unable. **2.** Not capable of accomplishing anything ▸ inadequate, incapable. *See* **ineffectual** (2). **3.** Unable to produce offspring ▸ sterile, unfruitful. *See* **barren** (1).

impound *verb*
1. To confine within a limited area ▸ cage, pen, shut (in). *See* **enclose** (1). **2.** To take possession of ▸ confiscate, expropriate, grab. *See* **seize** (1).

impoundment *noun*
▸ expropriation, preemption, usurpation. *See* **seizure** (2).

impoverish *verb*
▸ bankrupt, break, pauperize. *See* **ruin** (3).

impoverished *adjective*
1. Having little or no money or wealth ▸ destitute, down-and-out, indigent. *See* **poor** (1). *See synonym note at* **poor. 2.** Economically and socially below standard ▸ disadvantaged, poor. *See* **depressed** (2).

impoverishment *noun*
1. The condition of being extremely poor ▸ destitution, indigence, need. *See* **poverty** (1). **2.** The sapping away of strength or energy ▸ depletion, devitalization, enfeeblement. *See* **debilitation.**

impracticable *adjective*
1. Not capable of happening or being done ▸ impractical, unattainable, unworkable. *See* **impossible** (1). **2.** Incapable of being used or availed of to advantage ▸ unserviceable, unusable. *See* **unworkable** (1).

impractical *adjective*
1. Not capable of happening or being done ▸ impracticable, unattainable, unworkable. *See* **impossible** (1). **2.** Characterized by ideals that often conflict with practical considerations ▸ romantic, unrealistic, utopian. *See* **idealistic. 3.** Lacking the qualities, as efficiency or skill, required to produce desired results ▸ incapable, inept, unskilled. *See* **inefficient** (1). **4.** Not wise ▸ ill-considered, impolitic. *See* **unwise. 5.** Existing only in concept and not in reality ▸ conceptual, hypothetical, virtual. *See* **theoretical** (2). **6.** Concerned primarily with theories rather than practical matters ▸ academic, conceptual, speculative. *See* **theoretical** (1).

imprecate *verb*
To invoke evil upon ▸ anathematize, curse, damn, hex. *See also* **charm.**

imprecation *noun*
▸ damnation, malediction. *See* **curse** (1).

imprecise *adjective*
1. Lacking precise limits ▸ inexact, undetermined. *See* **indefinite** (1). **2.** Lacking literal exactness ▸ broad, inexact, rough. *See* **loose** (3).

imprecision *noun*
▸ ambiguousness, equivocalness, unclearness. *See* **vagueness.**

impregnability *noun*
▸ impenetrability, security. *See* **safety** (1).
impregnable *adjective*
▸ impenetrable, invulnerable, unconquerable. *See* **safe** (2).
impregnate *verb*
1. To cause to be filled, as with a particular mood ▸ permeate, suffuse. *See* **charge** (1). *See synonym note at* **charge. 2.** To make pregnant ▸ inseminate. *Slang:* knock up. *Idioms:* get (*or* put) in a family way, get with child. *See also* **fertilize.**
impress¹ *verb*
1. To stir the emotions of ▸ get (to), strike, touch. *See* **move** (1). *See synonym note at* **move. 2.** To fix (an idea, for example) in someone's mind by reemphasis and repetition ▸ drill, inculcate. *See* **instill. 3.** To produce a deep impression of ▸ fix, imprint. *See* **engrave** (2). **4.** To enter a person's mind ▸ hit, occur to. *See* **strike** (9).
impress *noun*
The visible effect made on a surface by pressure ▸ indent, mark. *See* **impression** (1). *See synonym note at* **impression.**
impress² *verb*
To enroll compulsorily in military service ▸ conscript, draft, induct, levy.
impressible *adjective*
▸ impressionable, responsive. *See* **sensitive** (1)
impression *noun*
1. The visible effect made on a surface by pressure ▸ dent, dint, impress, imprint, indent, indentation, mark, print, stamp. *See also* **depression. 2.** The character projected or given by someone to the public ▸ appearance, image. *See also* **façade. 3.** Something, such as a feeling or idea, associated with a specific person or thing ▸ association, connection, connotation, suggestion. **4.** The strong effect exerted by one person or thing on another ▸ force, influence. *See* **impact** (2). **5.** An intuitive awareness or sense of something ▸ hunch, idea, intuition. *See* **feeling** (1). **6.** The capacity for or an act of responding to a stimulus ▸ feeling, sensitivity. *See* **sensation** (1). **7.** The act, practice, or art of copying the manner or expression of another ▸ imitation, impersonation. *See* **mimicry.**

✦ CORE SYNONYMS: *impression, impress, imprint, print, stamp.* These nouns denote a visible effect made on a surface by pressure: *an impression of a notary's seal on wax; the impress of bare feet in the sand; a medal with the imprint of a bald eagle; the print of automobile tires in the tar; a gold ingot with the refiner's stamp.*

---

impressionable *adjective*
1. Easily altered or influenced ▸ malleable, pliable, suggestible. *See* **flexible** (3). **2.** Able to receive and respond to external stimuli ▸ impressible, responsive. *See* **sensitive** (1).
impressionistic *adjective*
Tending to bring a memory, mood, or image, for example, subtly or indirectly to mind ▸ allusive, connotative, evocative, reminiscent, suggestive. *See also* **designative, symbolic.**
impressive *adjective*
1. Exciting a deep, usually somber response ▸ moving, poignant. *See* **affecting. 2.** Readily attracting notice ▸ conspicuous, outstanding, prominent. *See* **noticeable** (1).
impressment *noun*
▸ conscription, induction, levy. *See* **draft** (2).
imprimatur *noun*
▸ authorization, consent, sanction. *See* **permission.**
imprint *verb*
To produce a deep impression of ▸ fix, impress. *See* **engrave** (2).
imprint *noun*
1. The visible effect made on a surface by pressure ▸ impress, mark. *See* **impression** (1). *See synonym note at* **impression. 2.** A name or other device placed on merchandise to signify its ownership or manufacture ▸ label, trademark. *See* **mark** (1).
imprison *verb*
To put in or as if in prison ▸ confine, detain, hold, immure, incarcerate, intern, jail, lock (away *or* in *or* up), shut (away *or* in *or* up). *Informal:* put away. *Idioms:* clap in jail (*or* prison *or* irons), put behind bars, throw in the cooler (*or* slammer). *See also* **enclose, restrain.**
imprisonment *noun*
▸ confinement, custody, detainment. *See* **detention.**
improbable *adjective*
1. Not likely ▸ dubious, questionable. *See* **doubtful** (1). **2.** Not plausible or believable ▸ flimsy, inconceivable. *See* **implausible.**
improbity *noun*
1. Departure from what is legally, ethically, and morally correct ▸ dishonesty, malfeasance. *Informal:* crookedness. *See* **corruption** (2). **2.** Lack of integrity ▸ deceitfulness, mendacity. *See* **dishonesty** (1).
impromptu *adjective*
Spoken, performed, or composed with little or no preparation or forethought ▸ extemporary, improvised. *See* **extemporaneous.** *See synonym note at* **extemporaneous.**
impromptu *noun*
Something improvised ▸ ad-lib, extemporization, improvisation. *See also* **makeshift.**
improper *adjective*
1. Not in keeping with conventional mores ▸ immodest, indecent, indecorous, indelicate, indiscreet, naughty, risqué, unbecoming, unbefitting, unjudicious, ungentlemanly, unladylike, unseemly, untoward. *Idiom:* out of line. *See also* **abandoned, foolish, rude, wrong 2.** Not suited to circumstances ▸ ill-fitted, ill-suited, inappropriate, inapt, incongruous, incorrect, inept, infelicitous, malapropos, mismatched, unapt, unbecoming, unbefitting, unfit, unfitting, unseemly, unsuitable, unsuited. *Idioms:* out of line (*or* place). *See also* **deficient, inadequate. 3.**

Arousing disapproval ▸ disagreeable, exceptionable, unacceptable. *See* **objectionable**.

✛ CORE SYNONYMS: *improper, unbecoming, unseemly, indelicate, indecent, indecorous*. These adjectives mean not in keeping with conventional mores or accepted standards of what is right or proper. *Improper* often refers to unethical conduct, a breach of etiquette, or morally offensive behavior: *improper business practices; improper behavior at the dinner table*. *Unbecoming* suggests what is beneath the standard implied by one's character or position: *language unbecoming to an officer*. What is *unseemly* or *indelicate* is in gross violation of good taste; *indelicate* especially suggests immodesty, coarseness, or tactlessness: *an unseemly use of profanity; an indelicate suggestion*. *Indecent* refers to what is morally offensive or harmful: *an earthy but not indecent story*. *Indecorous* implies violation of societal manners: *an indecorous remark about overeating*.

improperness *noun*
▸ indecency, unseemliness. *See* **impropriety** (1).
impropriety *noun*
1. The condition of being improper ▸ improperness, inappropriateness, incongruity, incorrectness, indecency, indecorousness, indiscretion, unbecomingness, unfitness, unseemliness, unsuitability, unsuitableness. *See also* **impudence**. 2. An improper act or statement ▸ gaffe, gaucherie, indecency, indecorum, indelicacy, indiscretion, solecism. *See also* **blunder, breach**. 3. A misused or incorrect term ▸ malapropism, solecism. *See* **corruption** (3).
improve *verb*
1. To advance to a more desirable state ▸ ameliorate, amend, better, enhance, enrich, help, meliorate, upgrade. *See also* **correct, renew**. 2. To regain one's health ▸ convalesce, recuperate. *See* **recover** (2).

✛ CORE SYNONYMS: *improve, better, help, ameliorate*. These verbs mean to advance to a more desirable, valuable, or excellent state. *Improve* and *better,* the most general terms, are often interchangeable: *You can improve* (or *better*) *your mind through study; I got a haircut to improve* (or *better*) *my appearance*. *Help* usually implies limited relief or change: *Gargling helps a sore throat*. To *ameliorate* is to improve circumstances that demand change: *Volunteers were able to ameliorate conditions in the refugee camp*.

improvement *noun*
1. The act of making better or the condition of being made better ▸ advancement, amelioration, amendment, betterment, development, enhancement, melioration, refinement, rehabilitation, upgrade. *See also* **change, revision**. 2. Steady improvement, as of an individual or a society ▸ amelioration, betterment, development, melioration, progress.
improvident *adjective*
1. Characterized by excessive or imprudent spending ▸ thriftless, uneconomical, unthrifty. *See* **extravagant** (1). 2. Characterized by unthinking boldness and haste ▸ hasty, impulsive, reckless. *See* **rash**[1].

improvisation *noun*
Something improvised ▸ ad-lib, extemporization, impromptu. *See also* **makeshift**.
improvise *verb*
1. To compose or recite without preparation ▸ ad-lib, extemporize, fake, make up. *Idioms:* make it up as one goes along, play by ear, speak off the cuff, think on one's feet, wing it. *See also* **invent**. 2. To make or provide from available materials ▸ cobble together, jerry-rig, jury-rig, rig up, slap together, throw together. *Idiom:* make do with. *See also* **invent**.
improvised *adjective*
▸ ad-lib, impromptu, unrehearsed. *See* **extemporaneous**.
imprudent *adjective*
▸ ill-considered, impractical. *See* **unwise**.
impudence *noun*
The state or quality of being impudent or arrogantly self-confident ▸ assumption, audaciousness, audacity, blatancy, boldness, brashness, brazenness, cheek, cheekiness, chutzpah, discourtesy, disrespect, effrontery, face, familiarity, flippancy, forwardness, gall, impertinence, impudency, incivility, insolence, nerve, nerviness, overconfidence, pertness, presumptuousness, pushiness, rudeness, sassiness, sauciness, shamelessness. *Informal:* brass, brassiness, crust, sauce, uppishness, uppityness. *See also* **back talk, flagrancy**.
impudent *adjective*
Rude and disrespectful; without shame ▸ assuming, assumptive, audacious, bald-faced, barefaced, blatant, bold, boldfaced, brash, brazen, brazenfaced, cheeky, contumelious, familiar, flippant, forward, impertinent, insolent, malapert, nervy, overconfident, pert, presuming, presumptuous, pushy, sassy, saucy, shameless, smart, snippy, unabashed, unblushing. *Informal:* brassy, flip, fresh, smart-alecky, snippety, uppish, uppity. *Slang:* snotty, wise. *See also* **disrespectful, flagrant, offensive, rude**.

✛ CORE SYNONYMS: *impudent, shameless, brazen, barefaced, brash, unblushing*. These adjectives apply to that which rudely and disrespectfully defies social or moral proprieties and is marked by a bold lack of shame. *Impudent* suggests offensive boldness or effrontery: *an impudent student; an impudent misrepresentation*. *Shameless* implies a lack of modesty, sense of decency, or regard for others' rights or feelings: *a shameless liar; a shameless accusation*. *Brazen* suggests flagrant, insolent audacity: *a brazen impostor; brazen arrogance*. *Barefaced* specifies undisguised brazenness: *a barefaced hypocrite; a barefaced lie*. *Brash* stresses impetuousness, lack of tact, and often crass indifference to consequences or to considerations of decency: *a brash newcomer; brash demands*. *Unblushing* implies an inappropriate lack of shame or embarrassment: *an unblushing apologist; unblushing obsequiousness*.

---

impulse *noun*
1. Something that causes and encourages an action or

response ▸ goad, incentive. *See* **stimulus** (1). **2.** An impulsive turn of mind ▸ caprice, notion, whim. *See* **fancy** (1).

impulsive *adjective*
1. Characterized by unthinking boldness and haste ▸ hasty, impetuous, reckless. *See* **rash**[1]. **2.** Acting or happening without apparent forethought, prompting, or planning ▸ automatic, involuntary. *See* **spontaneous** (1). *See synonym note at* **spontaneous**. **3.** Marked by whim or impulse ▸ fickle, flighty, mercurial. *See* **capricious**. *See synonym note at* **capricious**.

impulsivity *noun*
▸ automaticity, impulsiveness, reflexivity. *See* **spontaneity** (1).

impure *adjective*
1. Not chaste or moral ▸ corrupted, debased, debauched, defiled, immoral, unchaste, unclean, uncleanly, unvirtuous. *See also* **evil, improper, obscene**. **2.** Mixed with other substances ▸ adulterated, alloyed, blended, combined, contaminated, corrupted, cut, debased, diluted, dirty, doctored, infected, loaded, mixed, polluted, sophisticated, sullied, tainted, tampered with, vitiated. *See also* **dirty**.

impurity *noun*
1. The state of being contaminated ▸ defilement, pollution. *See* **contamination** (1). **2.** One that contaminates ▸ adulterant, poison, pollutant. *See* **contaminant**. **3.** Degrading, immoral acts or habits ▸ depravity, perversion, turpitude, vice. *See* **corruption** (1).

imputation *noun*
1. An implied criticism ▸ reflection, slur. *See also* **crack, libel**. **2.** A charging of someone with a misdeed ▸ denouncement, impeachment, incrimination. *See* **accusation**.

impute *verb*
▸ attribute, blame, pin. *See* **fix** (13).

in *adjective*
Informal In accordance with current fashion ▸ mod, stylish, swanky. *See* **fashionable**.

inability *noun*
Lack of ability or capacity ▸ incapability, incapacity, incompetence, incompetency, inefficiency, ineptitude, ineptness, powerlessness. *See also* **disadvantage, futility, ineffectuality**.

inaccessible *adjective*
1. Unable to be reached ▸ inapproachable, unapproachable, unattainable, unavailable, unobtainable, unreachable. *Idioms:* beyond reach, out of reach, out of the way. *See also* **distant, remote**. **2.** Not accessible or handy ▸ inconvenient, unhandy. *Idioms:* beyond reach, out of reach, out of the way. *See also* **awkward**. **3.** Not friendly, sociable, or warm in manner ▸ aloof, chilly, impersonal. *See* **cool** (1).

inaccuracy *noun*
▸ erratum, lapse, mistake. *See* **error** (1).

inaccurate *adjective*
▸ false, incorrect, mistaken. *See* **erroneous**.

inaction *noun*
A lack of action or activity ▸ idleness, inactivity, inertness, inoperativeness, lifelessness, sedentariness, stagnation, vegetation. *See also* **abeyance, laziness, stillness**.

inactive *adjective*
1. Marked by a lack of activity or use ▸ inert, unemployed, unused. *See* **idle** (1). *See synonym note at* **idle**. **2.** Present but not evident or active ▸ dormant, possible, potential. *See* **latent**.

inactivity *noun*
▸ inaction, inertness. *See* **inaction**.

inadequacy *noun*
1. The condition or state of being incapable of accomplishing anything ▸ helplessness, ineffectiveness. *See* **ineffectuality**. **2.** The condition or fact of being deficient ▸ deficit, insufficiency, paucity. *See* **shortage**.

inadequate *adjective*
1. Not enough to meet a demand or requirement ▸ short, wanting. *See* **insufficient** (1). **2.** Lacking an essential element ▸ incomplete, wanting. *See* **deficient** (1). **3.** Of low or lower quality ▸ low-grade, poor, unsatisfactory. *See* **bad** (1). **4.** Lacking the qualities, as efficiency or skill, required to produce desired results ▸ incapable, inept, unskilled. *See* **inefficient** (1). **5.** Not capable of accomplishing anything ▸ impotent, incapable. *See* **ineffectual** (2). **6.** Disturbing because of failure to measure up to a standard or produce the desired results ▸ discouraging, sorry, unsatisfying. *See* **disappointing**.

inadmissible *adjective*
▸ exceptionable, improper, unacceptable. *See* **objectionable**.

inadvertent *adjective*
1. Not intended ▸ accidental, undesigned, unintended. *See* **unintentional**. **2.** Lacking concern or attention ▸ forgetful, heedless, thoughtless. *See* **careless** (1). *See synonym note at* **careless**. **3.** Occurring unexpectedly ▸ chance, contingent, fortuitous. *See* **accidental** (1).

inadvisable *adjective*
▸ ill-considered, impolitic. *See* **unwise**.

inalterable *adjective*
▸ inflexible, invariable, unalterable. *See* **immutable** (1).

inane *adjective*
1. Lacking intelligent thought or content ▸ empty, vacuous. *See* **vacant** (1). **2.** Displaying a lack of good sense ▸ daft, idiotic, ludicrous. *See* **foolish**.

inanimate *adjective*
Completely lacking sensation or consciousness ▸ dead, insensate, insentient, lifeless. *See also* **dead**.

inanity *noun*
1. Total lack of ideas, meaning, or substance ▸ blankness, hollowness. *See* **emptiness** (3). **2.** Foolish behavior ▸ folly, silliness, tomfoolery. *See* **foolishness**.

inapplicable *adjective*
▸ immaterial, unconnected. *See* **irrelevant**.

inapposite *adjective*
▸ immaterial, inapplicable, unconnected. *See* **irrelevant**. *See synonym note at* **irrelevant**.

inappreciable *adjective*
▸ imponderable, indiscernible, subtle. *See* **imperceptible** (1).

inapproachable *adjective*
▸ unavailable, unreachable. *See* **inaccessible** (1).

inappropriate *adjective*
1. Not suited to circumstances ▸ inapt, malapropos, unbecoming. *See* **improper** (2). 2. Characterized by inappropriateness and gracelessness, especially in expression ▸ inept, infelicitous, unhappy. *See* **unfortunate** (2).

inappropriateness *noun*
▸ improperness, indecency, unseemliness. *See* **impropriety** (1).

inapt *adjective*
1. Not suited to circumstances ▸ ill-fitted, malapropos, unbecoming. *See* **improper** (2). 2. Lacking the qualities, as efficiency or skill, required to produce desired results ▸ incapable, inept, unskilled. *See* **inefficient** (1).

inarguable *adjective*
▸ incontestable, indisputable, irrefutable. *See* **certain** (2).

inarticulate *adjective*
1. Lacking the power or faculty of speech ▸ aphonic, voiceless. *See* **mute** (1). 2. Temporarily unable or unwilling to speak, as from shock or fear ▸ dumbstruck, mute. *See* **speechless** (1).

inasmuch as *conjunction*
▸ for, seeing as. *See* **because**.

inattentive *adjective*
1. So lost in thought as to be forgetful ▸ bemused, faraway, preoccupied. *See* **absent-minded**. 2. Lacking concern or attention ▸ heedless, thoughtless, unmindful. *See* **careless** (1).

inaudible *adjective*
▸ noiseless, quiet. *See* **silent** (1).

inaugural *noun*
The act or process of formally admitting a person to membership or office ▸ induction, installation. *See* **initiation** (2).

inaugural *adjective*
1. Preceding all others ▸ initial, original, premier. *See* **first** (1). 2. Of or occurring at the start of something ▸ initial, introductory, opening. *See* **beginning** (1).

inaugurate *verb*
1. To admit formally into membership or office, as with ritual ▸ induct, instate. *See* **initiate** (2). 2. To go about the initial step in doing something ▸ begin, commence, initiate. *See* **start** (1).

inauguration *noun*
1. The act or process of formally admitting a person to membership or office ▸ induction, instatement. *See* **initiation** (2). 2. The act of bringing or being brought into existence ▸ inception, initiation, start. *See* **beginning** (1).

inauspicious *adjective*
1. Bringing or predicting misfortune ▸ bad, evil, ill, portentous. *See* **fateful** (1). 2. Offering little encouragement ▸ dark, dismal, pessimistic. *See* **bleak** (2).

in-between *adjective*
▸ intermediate, median, midway. *See* **middle** (1).

inborn *adjective*
1. Possessed at birth ▸ inherited, native. *See* **innate** (1). *See synonym note at* **innate**. 2. Forming an essential element, as arising from the basic structure of an individual ▸ innate, intrinsic, natural. *See* **constitutional** (1). 3. Derived from or prompted by a natural tendency or impulse ▸ intuitive, visceral. *See* **instinctive** (1).

inbred *adjective*
▸ innate, intrinsic, natural. *See* **constitutional** (1).

incalculable *adjective*
Too great to be calculated ▸ boundless, countless, immeasurable, incomputable, inestimable, infinite, innumerable, measureless, uncountable, unfathomable. *See also* **endless**.

✦ CORE SYNONYMS: *incalculable, countless, immeasurable, incomputable, inestimable, infinite, innumerable, measureless.* These adjectives apply to that which is too great to be calculated or reckoned: *incalculable riches; countless hours; an immeasurable distance; an incomputable amount; jewels of inestimable value; an infinite number of reasons; innumerable difficulties; measureless power.*

incandesce *verb*
1. To shine brightly and steadily but without a flame ▸ gleam, glow, luminesce. 2. To emit a bright light ▸ burn, glow. *See* **beam** (1).

incandescent *adjective*
▸ brilliant, luminous, radiant. *See* **bright** (1). *See synonym note at* **bright**.

incantation *noun*
▸ abracadabra, enchantment. *See* **spell²**.

incapability *noun*
1. Lack of ability or capacity ▸ incapacity, incompetency. *See* **inability**. 2. The condition or state of being incapable of accomplishing anything ▸ helplessness, ineffectiveness. *See* **ineffectuality**.

incapable *adjective*
1. Lacking the qualities, as efficiency or skill, required to produce desired results ▸ incompetent, inept, unskilled. *See* **inefficient** (1). 2. Not capable of accomplishing anything ▸ impotent, inadequate. *See* **ineffectual** (2).

incapacitate *verb*
▸ handicap, immobilize, paralyze. *See* **disable** (1).

incapacitation *noun*
▸ depletion, devitalization, enfeeblement. *See* **debilitation**.

incapacity *noun*
▸ incompetence, ineptitude. *See* **inability**.

incarcerate *verb*
▸ confine, intern, jail. *See* **imprison**.

incarceration *noun*
► confinement, custody, detainment. *See* **detention.**
incarnate *verb*
To represent (an abstraction, for example) in or as if in bodily form ► externalize, manifest, materialize. *See* **embody** (1).
incarnate *adjective*
Of or relating to the body ► corporal, physical. *See* **bodily.**
incarnation *noun*
► image, manifestation, personification. *See* **embodiment** (1).
incautious *adjective*
► hasty, impulsive, reckless. *See* **rash**[1].
incautiousness *noun*
► brashness, rashness, recklessness. *See* **temerity.**
incendiary *noun*
► instigator, malcontent, rabble-rouser. *See* **agitator.**
incense *verb*
► enrage, infuriate, madden. *See* **anger** (1).
incentive *noun*
► catalyst, impulse, incentive. *See* **stimulus** (1).
inception *noun*
1. The act of bringing or being brought into existence ► initiation, start. *See* **beginning** (1). 2. The initial stage of a developmental process ► genesis, nascency, start. *See* **birth** (2).
inceptive *adjective*
► initial, introductory, opening. *See* **beginning** (1).
incertitude *noun*
► dubiousness, misgiving, skepticism. *See* **doubt** (1).
incessant *adjective*
► constant, endless, everlasting, perpetual. *See* **continual.** *See synonym note at* **continual.**
inch *verb*
To advance slowly ► crawl, creep, drag, poke. *Idiom:* go at a snail's pace. *See also* **trudge.**
inchoate *adjective*
► amorphous, formless, unshaped. *See* **shapeless.**
incident *noun*
1. Something that takes place ► episode, occurrence. *See* **circumstance** (1). *See synonym note at* **circumstance.** 2. Something significant that happens ► development, happening. *See* **event** (2).
incidental *adjective*
1. Not part of the real or essential nature of a thing ► adscititious, adventitious, inessential, supervenient. *See also* **irrelevant, unnecessary.** 2. Occurring unexpectedly ► fluky, fortuitous, serendipitous. *See* **accidental** (1). *See synonym note at* **accidental.**
incidentals *noun*
► junk, oddments, miscellanea. *See* **odds and ends.**
incinerate *verb*
► scorch, sear, singe. *See* **burn** (1).
incipience *or* **incipiency** *noun*
The act of bringing or being brought into existence ► inception, initiation, start. *See* **beginning** (1).
incipient *adjective*
► initial, introductory, opening. *See* **beginning** (1).

incise *verb*
1. To penetrate with a sharp edge ► bayonet, gore, pierce, slash. *See* **cut** (1). 2. To cut a design or inscription into a hard surface, especially for printing ► chisel, etch. *See* **engrave** (1).
incision *noun*
► gash, slash, slit. *See* **cut** (1).
incisive *adjective*
► keen, penetrating, sharp. *See* **critical** (2).
incisiveness *noun*
► bite, keenness. *See* **edge** (1).
incite *verb*
► excite, prod, trigger. *See* **provoke** (1). *See synonym note at* **provoke.**
incitement *or* **incitation** *noun*
► goad, stimulus, trigger. *See* **provocation** (1).
inciter *noun*
► instigator, malcontent, rabble-rouser. *See* **agitator.**
incivility *noun*
1. The state or quality of being impudent or arrogantly self-confident ► audacity, boldness, impertinence. *See* **impudence.** 2. An act that offends a person's sense of pride or dignity ► contumely, insult. *See* **indignity.**
inclement *adjective*
► grim, severe. *See* **bleak** (1).
inclination *noun*
1. A natural or habitual preference for something ► affinity, bent, bias, cast, disposition, leaning, partiality, penchant, predilection, predisposition, prejudice, proclivity, proneness, propensity, tendency, trend, urge, turn. *See also* **fancy, liking, love.** 2. Deviation from a particular direction ► cant, grade, gradient, heel, incline, lean, list, rake, slant, slope, tilt, tip. *See also* **bend, hill.**

✦ CORE SYNONYMS: *inclination, bias, leaning, partiality, penchant, predilection, prejudice, proclivity, propensity.* These nouns denote a natural or habitual preference for something: *an inclination to indulge in sweets; a pro-American bias; conservative leanings; a partiality for liberal-minded friends; a penchant for exotic foods; a predilection for classical composers; a prejudice in favor of the underprivileged; a proclivity for self-assertiveness; a propensity for exaggeration.*

---

incline *verb*
1. To depart or cause to depart from true vertical or horizontal ► cant, heel, lean, list, rake, slant, slope, tilt, tip. *See also* **bend, turn.** 2. To have a tendency or inclination ► lean, skew, trend. *See* **tend**[1]. 3. To have an impact on in a certain way ► act on, predispose, sway. *See* **influence** (1).
incline *noun*
Deviation from a particular direction ► grade, heel. *See* **inclination** (2).

✦ CORE SYNONYMS: *incline, lean, slant, slope, tilt, tip.* These verbs mean to depart or cause to depart from true vertical or horizontal: *inclined her head toward the speaker; leaned against the railing; rays of light slanting through the window; a driveway that slopes downhill; tilted his hat at a rakish angle; tipped her chair against the wall.*

inclined *adjective*
1. Having or showing a tendency or likelihood ▶ apt, disposed, given, liable, likely, predisposed, prone, tending, wont. 2. At an angle ▶ biased, diagonal, slanted. *See* **oblique** (1).

inclined plane *noun*
▶ gradient, rise, slant. *See* **ascent** (2).

include *verb*
1. To have as a part ▶ comprise, take in. *See* **contain** (1). *See synonym note at* **contain.** 2. To construct as an integral part ▶ build in, incorporate, integrate.

inclusive *adjective*
▶ all-around, broad, expansive. *See* **general** (2).

incombustible *adjective*
▶ fire-resistant, flameproof, flame-resistant. *See* **fireproof.**

income *noun*
▶ bread, keep, livelihood. *See* **living.**

incoming *noun*
▶ entry, ingress. *See* **entrance**[1] (1).

incommode *verb*
▶ discommode, put out, trouble. *See* **inconvenience.**

incommodious *adjective*
Causing difficulty, trouble, or discomfort ▶ difficult, inconvenient, troublesome. *See also* **awkward, disturbing.**

incommodiousness *noun*
The state or quality of being inconvenient ▶ discomfort, incommodity, inconvenience, trouble. *See also* **bother.**

incommodity *noun*
1. The state or quality of being inconvenient ▶ discomfort, incommodiousness, inconvenience, trouble. *See also* **bother.** 2. Something that causes difficulty, trouble, or lack of ease ▶ discomfort, discommodity, inconvenience. *See also* **annoyance.**

incommunicative *adjective*
▶ reticent, silent, uncommunicative. *See* **taciturn.**

incomparability *noun*
▶ superbness, superiority. *See* **excellence.**

incomparable *adjective*
▶ singular, unparalleled. *See* **unique** (1).

incompatibility *noun*
▶ discrepancy, disparity, incongruity. *See* **gap** (3).

incompatible *adjective*
1. Made up of parts or qualities that are disparate or otherwise markedly lacking in consistency ▶ discrepant, inconsistent. *See* **incongruous** (1). 2. In sharp opposition ▶ conflicting, discordant, inconsistent. *See* **discrepant** (1). 3. Diametrically opposed ▶ antithetical, contradictory, diametric. *See* **opposite** (1).

incompetence *or* **incompetency** *noun*
▶ incapacity, ineptitude, powerlessness. *See* **inability.**

incompetent *adjective*
▶ incapable, inept, unskilled. *See* **inefficient** (1).

incomplete *adjective*
1. Lacking an essential element ▶ inadequate, wanting. *See* **deficient** (1). 2. Not total ▶ fragmentary, unfinished. *See* **partial** (1). 3. Not perfected, elaborated, or completed ▶ preliminary, sketchy, unpolished. *See* **rough** (10).

incompliance *or* **incompliancy** *noun*
▶ bullheadedness, hardheadedness, rigidity. *See* **stubbornness.**

incompliant *adjective*
▶ bullheaded, dogged, obstinate. *See* **stubborn** (1).

incomprehensible *adjective*
Incapable of being grasped by the intellect or understanding ▶ impenetrable, inscrutable, uncomprehensible, unfathomable, unintelligible. *See also* **complex, deep, mysterious.**

incompressible *adjective*
Unyielding to pressure ▶ firm, hard, solid.

incomputable *adjective*
▶ countless, immeasurable, infinite. *See* **incalculable.** *See synonym note at* **incalculable.**

inconceivable *adjective*
1. Not to be believed ▶ unbelievable, unthinkable. *See* **incredible** (2). 2. Not plausible or believable ▶ improbable, thin. *See* **implausible.**

inconclusive *adjective*
▶ dubious, indeterminate, questionable, unclear. *See* **ambiguous** (1).

incongruent *adjective*
1. Made up of parts or qualities that are disparate or otherwise markedly lacking in consistency ▶ discrepant, inconsistent. *See* **incongruous** (1). 2. In sharp opposition ▶ conflicting, discordant, inconsistent. *See* **discrepant** (1).

incongruity *noun*
1. A marked lapse of correspondence or agreement ▶ discrepancy, disparity. *See* **gap** (3). 2. The condition or fact of being unequal, as in age, rank, or degree ▶ disproportion, imbalance. *See* **inequality** (1). 3. The condition of being improper ▶ inappropriateness, unseemliness. *See* **impropriety** (1).

incongruous *adjective*
1. Made up of parts or qualities that are disparate or otherwise markedly lacking in consistency ▶ conflicting, discordant, discrepant, dissonant, incompatible, incongruent, inconsistent, inconsonant, irregular, jarring, mismatched. *See also* **inharmonious, opposite.** 2. In sharp opposition ▶ conflicting, discordant, inconsistent. *See* **discrepant** (1). 3. Not suited to circumstances ▶ inapt, malapropos, unbecoming. *See* **improper** (2).

inconsequence *noun*
▶ frivolity, insignificance, minutia. *See* **trifle** (1).

inconsequent *or* **inconsequential** *adjective*
▶ frivolous, negligible, trifling. *See* **trivial.**

inconsiderable *adjective*
▶ inconsequential, negligible, trifling. *See* **trivial.**

inconsiderableness *noun*
▶ frivolity, minutia, trivia. *See* **trifle** (1).

inconsiderate *adjective*
▶ disregardful, tactless, unthinking, unthoughtful. *See* **thoughtless** (1).

inconsideration *or* **inconsiderateness** *noun*
▶ disregard, unthoughtfulness. *See* **thoughtlessness** (2).

inconsistency *noun*
1. A marked lack of correspondence or agreement ▶ discrepancy, disparity, incongruity. *See* **gap** (3).
2. The quality or condition of being erratic and undependable ▶ insecurity, unstableness, unsteadiness. *See* **instability.**

inconsistent *adjective*
1. Lacking consistency or regularity in quality or performance ▶ erratic, patchy, variable. *See* **uneven** (1). 2. Containing errors in reasoning ▶ false, illogical, spurious. *See* **fallacious** (1). 3. Marked by whim or impulse ▶ fickle, impulsive, mercurial. *See* **capricious.** 4. In sharp opposition ▶ conflicting, discordant, opposite. *See* **discrepant** (1). 5. Made up of parts or qualities that are disparate or otherwise markedly lacking in consistency ▶ discrepant, mismatched. *See* **incongruous** (1).

inconsonant *adjective*
1. Devoid of harmony or accord ▶ conflicting, dissident, uncongenial. *See* **inharmonious** (1). 2. Made up of parts or qualities that are disparate or otherwise markedly lacking in consistency ▶ discrepant, inconsistent. *See* **incongruous** (1).

inconspicuous *adjective*
Not readily noticed or seen ▶ obscure, unassuming, unconspicuous, undistinguished, unnoticeable, unobtrusive. *Idioms:* having (*or* keeping) a low profile *See also* **hidden, modest, secluded.**

inconstant *adjective*
1. Capable of or liable to change ▶ fluid, unsettled, variable. *See* **changeable** (1). 2. Marked by whim or impulse ▶ fickle, impulsive, mercurial. *See* **capricious.**

incontestable *adjective*
▶ inarguable, indisputable, irrefutable. *See* **certain** (2).

incontinence *noun*
▶ abandonment, unrestraint, wantonness. *See* **abandon** (1).

incontrovertible *adjective*
▶ inarguable, indisputable, irrefutable. *See* **certain** (2).

inconvenience *noun*
1. The state or quality of being inconvenient ▶ discomfort, incommodiousness, incommodity, trouble. *See also* **bother.** 2. Something that causes difficulty, trouble, or lack of ease ▶ discomfort, discommodity, incommodity. *See also* **annoyance. 3.** An unfavorable condition, circumstance, or characteristic ▶ drawback, handicap, minus. *See* **disadvantage.**

inconvenience *verb*
To cause inconvenience for ▶ discomfort, discommode, impose on (*or* upon), incommode, put out, trouble. *See also* **annoy.**

inconvenient *adjective*
1. Not accessible or handy ▶ inaccessible, unhandy.

Idioms: beyond reach, out of reach, out of the way. *See also* **awkward, remote. 2.** Causing difficulty, trouble, or discomfort ▶ difficult, incommodious, troublesome. *See also* **disturbing. 3.** Not occurring at a favorable time ▶ ill-timed, inopportune, mistimed, untimely. *See also* **fateful.**

incorporate *verb*
1. To construct as an integral part ▶ build, include, integrate. 2. To make a part of a united whole ▶ combine, embody, integrate. 3. To take in and incorporate, especially mentally ▶ assimilate, digest, grasp. *See* **absorb** (2). 4. To unite or be united in a relationship ▶ combine, join, link. *See* **associate** (1).

incorporated *adjective*
▶ constituent, integral. *See* **built-in** (1).

incorporation *noun*
1. The process of incorporating ▶ assimilation, digestion, intake. *See* **absorption** (1). 2. The result of combining ▶ compound, merger, union. *See* **combination** (1). 3. A concrete entity typifying an abstraction ▶ incarnation, manifestation, personification. *See* **embodiment** (1).

incorporeal *adjective*
▶ disembodied, intangible, nonphysical. *See* **immaterial** (1). *See synonym note at* **immaterial.**

incorrect *adjective*
1. Containing an error or errors ▶ false, inaccurate, mistaken. *See* **erroneous. 2.** Not suited to circumstances ▶ inapt, malapropos, unbecoming. *See* **improper** (2).

incorrectness *noun*
1. An unintentional deviation from what is correct, right, or true ▶ inaccuracy, lapse, mistake. *See* **error** (1). 2. The condition of being improper ▶ inappropriateness, unseemliness. *See* **impropriety** (1).

incorrigible *adjective*
▶ deep-seated, entrenched, ingrained, inveterate. *See* **confirmed** (1).

incorruptibility *noun*
▶ candidness, integrity. *See* **honesty** (1).

incorruptible *adjective*
▶ honorable, righteous. *See* **honest** (1).

increase *verb*
1. To make or become greater or larger ▶ aggrandize, amplify, augment, blow up, boost, build, build up, burgeon, develop, enlarge, escalate, exaggerate, expand, extend, grow, magnify, mount, multiply, proliferate, ratchet up, rise, rocket, run up, skyrocket, snowball, soar, step up, surge, swell, upsurge, wax. *Informal:* beef up. *See also* **advance, broaden, elevate, raise. 2.** To give life to ▶ engender, propagate, spawn. *See* **breed** (1).

increase *noun*
1. The act of increasing or rising ▶ aggrandizement, amplification, augment, augmentation, boost, buildup, burgeoning, enlargement, escalation, expansion, extension, growth, hike, jump, magnification, multiplication, proliferation, raise, rise, snowballing, soaring, swell, upsurge, upswing, upturn. *See also*

advancement, progress. **2.** The amount by which something is increased ▸ advance, boost, hike, increment, jump, raise, rise.

✛ CORE SYNONYMS: *increase, expand, enlarge, extend, augment, multiply.* These verbs mean to make or become greater or larger. *Increase* sometimes suggests steady growth: *The mayor's political influence rapidly increased. "No machines will increase the possibilities of life. They only increase the possibilities of idleness"* (John Ruskin). To *expand* is to increase in size, area, volume, bulk, or range: *He inhaled deeply, expanding his chest. "Work expands so as to fill the time available for its completion"* (C. Northcote Parkinson). *Enlarge* refers to expansion in size, extent, capacity, or scope: *The landowner enlarged her property by repeated purchases. My knowledge of literature has enlarged considerably since I joined a reading group.* To *extend* is to lengthen in space or time or to broaden in range: *The transit authority extended the subway line to the next town. The baseball season extends into October. Augment* usually applies to what is already developed or well under way: *She augmented her collection of books each month. His depression augments with each visit to the hospital.* To *multiply* is to increase in number, especially by propagation or procreation: *"As for my cats, they multiplied"* (Daniel Defoe). *"May thy days be multiplied!"* (Sir Walter Scott).

◂ ANTONYM: *decrease*

---

incredible *adjective*
1. Not plausible or believable ▸ improbable, inconceivable. *See* **implausible.2.** Not to be believed ▸ farfetched, inconceivable, unbelievable, unimaginable, unthinkable. *Idioms:* beyond belief, contrary to all reason. *See also* **doubtful, outrageous. 3.** So remarkable as to be difficult to believe ▸ astounding, staggering, unbelievable. *See* **astonishing.**
incredibly *adverb*
▸ singularly, uncommonly, uniquely. *See* **unusually.**
incredulity *noun*
▸ dubiety, mistrust, skepticism, unbelief. *See* **disbelief** (1).
incredulous *adjective*
Refusing or reluctant to believe ▸ disbelieving, dubious, questioning, skeptical, unbelieving, unconvinced. *See also* **distrustful, doubtful.**
incredulousness *noun*
▸ incredulity, mistrust, skepticism, unbelief. *See* **disbelief** (1).
increment *noun*
▸ boost, jump. *See* **increase** (2).
incriminate *verb*
1. To cause to appear involved in or guilty of a crime or fault ▸ criminate, implicate, inculpate. *See also* **accuse. 2.** To make an accusation against ▸ denounce, inculpate, indict. *See* **accuse.**
incriminating *adjective*
1. Containing, relating to, or involving an accusation ▸ denunciative, incriminatory. *See* **accusatorial.**
2. Provoking a change of outlook and especially gradual doubt and suspicion ▸ implicating,

insinuatory, suggestive. *See* **insinuating** (1).
incrimination *noun*
▸ denouncement, imputation, inculpation. *See* **accusation.**
incriminatory *adjective*
▸ denunciative, inculpatory. *See* **accusatorial.**
inculcate *verb*
1. To fix (an idea, for example) in someone's mind by reemphasis and repetition ▸ drive, ingrain. *See* **instill.**
2. To instruct by rote or discipline, as in a body of doctrine or belief ▸ catechize, drill. *See* **indoctrinate** (1).
inculpable *adjective*
▸ faultless, guiltless, harmless. *See* **innocent** (2).
inculpate *verb*
1. To cause to appear involved in or guilty of a crime or fault ▸ criminate, implicate, incriminate. *See also* **accuse. 2.** To make an accusation against ▸ charge, denounce, incriminate. *See* **accuse.**
inculpation *noun*
▸ denouncement, imputation, incrimination. *See* **accusation.**
inculpatory *adjective*
▸ denunciative, incriminatory. *See* **accusatorial.**
incumbency *noun*
The holding of a position ▸ occupancy, occupation, tenure. *See also* **period.**
incur *verb*
1. To take upon oneself ▸ shoulder, take on. *See* **assume** (1). **2.** To come gradually to have ▸ acquire, form. *See* **develop** (1). **3.** To become affected with a disease ▸ develop, get. *See* **contract** (2).
incurable *adjective*
1. Offering no hope or expectation of improvement ▸ irremediable, irreparable. *See* **hopeless** (1). **2.** Firmly established by long standing ▸ deep-seated, entrenched, ingrained, inveterate. *See* **confirmed** (1).
incuriosity *noun*
▸ disinterest, indifference, unconcern. *See* **apathy.**
incurious *adjective*
1. Lacking interest in one's surroundings or worldly affairs ▸ disinterested, indifferent, uninvolved. *See* **detached** (1). **2.** Lacking interest ▸ indifferent, listless, uninterested. *See* **apathetic.**
incuriousness *noun*
▸ detachment, impassivity, listlessness. *See* **apathy.**
incursion *noun*
An act of invading, especially by military forces ▸ foray, inroad, invasion, raid. *See also* **attack.**
indebted *adjective*
▸ beholden, grateful, obligated. *See* **obliged** (1).
indebtedness *noun*
1. A condition of owing something to another ▸ encumbrance, liability, obligation. *See* **debt** (2). **2.** Something, such as money, owed by one person to another ▸ due, liability, obligation. *See* **debt** (1).
indecency *noun*
1. The condition of being improper ▸ inappropriateness, unseemliness. *See* **impropriety** (1). **2.** An im-

proper act or statement ▸ indiscretion, indecorum. *See* **impropriety** (2).

indecent *adjective*
1. Not in keeping with conventional mores ▸ immodest, indelicate. *See* **improper** (1). *See synonym note at* **improper**. 2. Offensive to accepted standards of decency ▸ bawdy, coarse, lewd, profane, vulgar. *See* **obscene** (1).

indecision *noun*
▸ dawdling, tentativeness. *See* **hesitation**.

indecisive *adjective*
1. Given to or exhibiting hesitation ▸ halting, irresolute. *See* **hesitant** (1). 2. Lacking certainty or clarity ▸ dubious, indeterminate, questionable, unclear. *See* **ambiguous** (1).

indecisiveness *noun*
▸ dawdling, indecision, tentativeness, timidity. *See* **hesitation**.

indecorous *adjective*
▸ indecent, indelicate. *See* **improper** (1). *See synonym note at* **improper**.

indecorum *noun*
1. An improper act or statement ▸ impropriety, indecency, indelicacy. 2. An improper act or statement ▸ indiscretion, indecency. *See* **impropriety** (2).

indeed *adverb*
1. In truth ▸ actually, positively, truly. *See* **really**. 2. In point of fact ▸ actually, really. 3. Not just this but also ▸ moreover, yea. *See* **even** (2). 4. It is so; as you say or ask ▸ agreed, all right, assuredly. *See* **yes**.

indefatigable *adjective*
▸ inexhaustible, unflagging, untiring. *See* **tireless**. *See synonym note at* **tireless**.

indefectible *adjective*
▸ consummate, faultless, flawless, unblemished. *See* **perfect** (1).

indefensible *adjective*
▸ unforgivable, unjustifiable, unpardonable. *See* **inexcusable**.

indefinable *adjective*
▸ indescribable, inexpressible, undescribable. *See* **unspeakable** (1). *See synonym note at* **unspeakable**.

indefinite *adjective*
1. Lacking precise limits ▸ imprecise, indeterminate, inexact, undefined, undetermined. *See also* **endless, incalculable**. 2. Marked by lack of firm decision or commitment; of questionable outcome ▸ open, uncertain, undecided, undetermined, unresolved, unsettled, unspecified, unsure, vague. *Idiom:* up in the air. *See also* **ambiguous**. 3. Not clearly perceptible ▸ dim, faint, vague. *See* **unclear** (1). 4. In doubt or dispute ▸ disputable, doubtful, questionable. *See* **debatable**. 5. Not limited to a single class ▸ diversified, general.

indefiniteness *noun*
▸ ambiguousness, equivocalness, unclearness. *See* **vagueness**.

indelible *adjective*
1. Retaining original color ▸ colorfast, fast. 2. Firmly

established by long standing ▸ deep-seated, entrenched, ingrained, inveterate. *See* **confirmed** (1).

indelicacy *noun*
▸ inappropriateness, indiscretion, indecency. *See* **impropriety** (2).

indelicate *adjective*
1. Not in keeping with conventional mores ▸ indecent, unbecoming. *See* **improper** (1). *See synonym note at* **improper**. 2. Lacking in delicacy or refinement ▸ common, unbecoming, unrefined. *See* **coarse** (1). 3. Lacking sensitivity and skill in dealing with others ▸ gauche, impolitic, undiplomatic. *See* **tactless**.

indemnification *noun*
▸ amends, remuneration, reparation. *See* **compensation** (1).

indemnify *verb*
▸ pay, recompense, remunerate. *See* **compensate** (1).

indemnity *noun*
▸ amends, remuneration, reparation. *See* **compensation** (1). *See synonym note at* **compensation**.

indent *noun*
The visible effect made on a surface by pressure ▸ impress, mark. *See* **impression** (1).

indent *verb*
To penetrate with a sharp edge ▸ bayonet, incise, pierce, slash. *See* **cut** (1).

indentation *noun*
1. The visible effect made on a surface by pressure ▸ indent, mark. *See* **impression** (1). 2. An area sunk below its surroundings ▸ basin, dip, sink. *See* **depression** (1).

indented *adjective*
▸ concave, sunken. *See* **hollow** (2).

indenture *verb*
▸ dominate, subjugate. *See* **enslave**.

independence *noun*
1. The capacity to manage one's own affairs, make one's own judgments, and provide for oneself ▸ autonomy, self-containment, self-determination, self-reliance, self-sufficiency. 2. The condition of being politically free ▸ autonomy, sovereignty. *See* **freedom** (1).

independent *adjective*
1. Free from the influence, guidance, or control of others ▸ autonomous, individualistic, self-contained, self-determined, self-directed, self-reliant, self-sufficient. 2. Able to support oneself financially ▸ self-sufficient, self-supporting. 3. Not imprisoned, enslaved, or controlled by another ▸ autonomous, self-governing, sovereign. *See* **free** (1).

independent *noun*
Someone with unconventional opinions or approaches ▸ free-thinker, maverick. *See* **rebel** (2).

independently *adverb*
▸ apart, singly. *See* **separately**.

in-depth *adjective*
▸ full, particular, thorough. *See* **detailed** (1).

indiscreet *adjective*
1. Not in keeping with conventional mores ▸ indecent,

indelicate. *See* **improper** (1). **2.** Not wise ▸ ill-advised, imprudent, inadvisable. *See* **unwise.**

indescribable *adjective*
▸ incommunicable, inexpressible, undescribable. *See* **unspeakable** (1). *See synonym note at* **unspeakable.**

indeterminate *adjective*
1. Lacking certainty or clarity ▸ dubious, inconclusive, questionable, unclear. *See* **ambiguous** (1). **2.** Lacking precise limits ▸ inexact, undetermined. *See* **indefinite** (1).

index *noun*
1. Something visible or evident that gives grounds for believing in something else ▸ evidence, indication, symptom. *See* **sign** (1). **2.** A series, as of names or words, printed or written down ▸ register, roster, schedule. *See* **list**¹.

indicate *verb*
1. To give grounds for believing in the existence or presence of ▸ argue, attest, bespeak, betoken, mark, point to, testify, witness. **2.** To lead to by logical inference ▸ imply, point to, suggest. **3.** To make known or identify, as by signs ▸ denote, mark, specify. *See* **designate** (1). **4.** To give a precise indication of, as on a register or scale ▸ mark, register. *See* **show** (3). **5.** To have or convey a particular idea ▸ denote, intend, signify. *See* **mean**¹ (1).

✦ CORE SYNONYMS: *indicate, argue, attest, bespeak, betoken, testify, witness.* These verbs mean to give grounds for supposing or inferring the existence or presence of something: *a fever indicating illness; a shabby house that argues poverty; paintings that attest the artist's genius; disorder that bespeaks negligence; melting snows that betoken spring floods; a comment testifying ignorance; a stunned silence that witnessed his shock.*

---

indication *noun*
1. Something that takes the place of words in communicating a thought or feeling ▸ gesture, sign. *See* **expression** (2). **2.** An expressive, meaningful bodily movement ▸ gesticulation, signal. *See* **gesture** (1). **3.** Something visible or evident that gives grounds for believing in the existence or presence of something else ▸ evidence, index, symptom. *See* **sign** (1).

indicative *adjective*
▸ denotive, exhibitive, indicatory. *See* **designative.**

indicator *noun*
1. Something visible or evident that gives grounds for believing in the existence or presence of something else ▸ indication, manifestation, symptom. *See* **sign** (1). **2.** The marked outer surface of an instrument ▸ dial, face, gauge.

indicatory *adjective*
▸ denotive, exhibitive, significant. *See* **designative.**

indict *verb*
▸ charge, denounce, incriminate. *See* **accuse.**

indicter *or* **indictor** *noun*
One that accuses ▸ accuser, arraigner, denouncer, recriminator.

indictment *noun*
▸ denouncement, imputation, incrimination. *See* **accusation.**

indifference *noun*
1. Lack of emotion or interest ▸ disinterest, impassivity, unconcern. *See* **apathy. 2.** Dissociation from one's surroundings or worldly affairs ▸ disinterest, remoteness, unconcern. *See* **detachment** (2). **3.** Something or things of little importance ▸ frivolity, inconsequence, trivia. *See* **trifle** (1).

indifferent *adjective*
1. Free from bias in judgment ▸ disinterested, dispassionate, unprejudiced. *See* **fair**¹ (1). **2.** Lacking feeling or emotion ▸ emotionless, impassive, stolid. *See* **cold** (2). **3.** Lacking interest ▸ incurious, listless, uninterested. *See* **apathetic. 4.** Lacking interest in one's surroundings or worldly affairs ▸ disinterested, remote, uninvolved. *See* **detached** (1). **5.** Being of no special quality or type ▸ common, mediocre, standard. *See* **ordinary** (1). **6.** Relating to or occupying a middle position on a scale of evaluation ▸ mediocre, fair. *See* **average** (1). *See synonym note at* **average.**

indifferently *adverb*
▸ dispassionately, equitably, justly. *See* **fairly** (1).

indigence *noun*
▸ destitution, impecuniosity, need. *See* **poverty** (1).

indigenous *adjective*
1. Existing, born, or produced in a land or region ▸ aboriginal, autochthonal, autochthonic, autochthonous, endemic, homegrown, local, native, regional. *Idiom:* native to the soil. **2.** Forming an essential element, as arising from the basic structure of an individual ▸ innate, intrinsic, natural. *See* **constitutional** (1). **3.** Of, from, or within a country's own territory ▸ aboriginal, native. *See* **domestic** (3).

✦ CORE SYNONYMS: *indigenous, native, endemic, autochthonous, aboriginal.* These adjectives mean existing, born, or produced in a specific land, region, or country. *Indigenous* specifies that something or someone is from a particular place rather than coming or being brought in from elsewhere: *an indigenous crop; the Ainu, a people indigenous to the northernmost islands of Japan. Native* implies birth or origin in the specified place: *a native New Yorker; the native North American sugar maple.* Something *endemic* is prevalent in or peculiar to a particular locality or people: *endemic disease. Autochthonous* applies to what is native and unchanged by outside sources: *autochthonous folk melodies. Aboriginal* describes what has existed from the beginning; it is often applied to the earliest known inhabitants of a place: *the aboriginal population; aboriginal nature.*

---

indigent *adjective*
Having little or no money or wealth ▸ destitute, down-and-out, impoverished. *See* **poor** (1). *See synonym note at* **poor.**

indigent *noun*
An impoverished person ▸ beggar, insolvent, tramp. *See* **pauper.**

indigestible *adjective*
► disagreeable, painful, unpleasant. *See* **bitter** (3).

indignant *adjective*
► exacerbated, irate, peeved. *See* **angry**. *See synonym note at* **angry**.

indignation *noun*
► choler, irateness, wrath. *See* **anger**. *See synonym note at* **anger**.

indignity *noun*
An act that offends a person's sense of pride or dignity ► affront, aspersion, contumely, despite, incivility, insult, offense, outrage, putdown, slight. *Idioms:* backhanded (*or* lefthanded) compliment, kick in the teeth, slap in the face. *See also* **injustice, outrage, snub, vituperation.**

indirect *adjective*
1. Not proceeding straight to the point or object ► anfractuous, backhanded, circuitous, circular, circumlocutory, curving, devious, meandering, oblique, out-of-the-way, rambling, roundabout, tortuous, twisting, wandering, winding, zigzag. *See also* **digressive.** 2. Deliberately ambiguous or vague ► elusive, equivocal, evasive, misleading. *See also* **ambiguous.** 3. Marked by treachery or deceit ► duplicitous, shifty, sneaky. *See* **underhand.**

indirection *noun*
► deviousness, slyness, trickery. *See* **dishonesty** (2).

indiscernible *adjective*
1. Incapable of being apprehended by the mind or the senses ► imponderable, unobservable. *See* **imperceptible** (1). 2. Difficult or impossible to see or distinguish ► covert, disguised, unseen. *See* **hidden** (1).

indiscreet *adjective*
► ill-considered, impolitic. *See* **unwise.**

indiscretion *noun*
1. The condition or being improper ► inappropriateness, unseemliness. *See* **impropriety** (1). 2. An improper act or statement ► gaffe, indecency. *See* **impropriety** (2).

indiscriminate *adjective*
► chance, haphazard, unplanned. *See* **random.**

indispensable *adjective*
► critical, necessary, required. *See* **essential** (1). *See synonym note at* **essential.**

indisposed *adjective*
1. Not inclined or willing to do or undertake ► against, averse, disinclined, loath, opposed, reluctant, resistant, unwilling. *Idioms:* not feeling like, not in the mood. *See also* **hesitant, wary.** 2. Suffering from or appearing to suffer from an illness ► ailing, ill, unwell. *See* **sick** (1).

indisposition *noun*
1. The state of not being disposed or inclined ► averseness, aversion, disinclination, opposition, reluctance, resistance, unwillingness. *See also* **objection.** 2. The condition of being sick ► affliction, illness, malady. *See* **sickness** (1).

indisputable *adjective*
► inarguable, incontestable, irrefutable. *See* **certain** (2).

indistinct *adjective*
► dim, faint, indefinite. *See* **unclear** (1).

indistinctive *adjective*
Without definite or distinctive characteristics ► bland, colorless, netural. *See also* **boring.**

indistinguishable *adjective*
1. Incapable of being apprehended by the mind or the senses ► imponderable, indiscernible. *See* **imperceptible** (1). 2. Difficult or impossible to see or distinguish ► covert, disguised, unseen. *See* **hidden** (1).

indite *verb*
1. To form by artistic effort ► produce, write. *See* **compose** (1). 2. To form letters, characters, or words on a surface with an instrument ► pen, scribe. *See* **write** (1).

individual *adjective*
1. Belonging to, relating to, or affecting a particular person ► personal, private. 2. Being or related to a distinct entity ► discrete, lone, particular, separate, single, singular, sole. 3. Relating to, identifying, or setting apart an individual or group ► characteristic, distinctive, particular. *See* **special** (1). 4. Distinguished from others by nature or qualities ► separate, several, various. *See* **distinct** (1). *See synonym note at* **distinct.**
individual *noun*
1. A member of the human race ► human, mortal, person. *See* **human being.** 2. One that exists independently ► entity, object, something. *See* **thing** (1).

individualism *noun*
► distinctiveness, individuality, selfhood. *See* **identity** (1).

individualistic *adjective*
1. Holding the philosophical view that the self is the center and norm of existence ► egocentric, egoistic, egoistical, solipsistic. 2. Free from the influence, guidance, or control of others ► autonomous, self-sufficient. *See* **independent** (1).

individuality *noun*
1. The quality of being individual ► discreteness, distinctiveness, particularity, separateness, singularity. *See also* **novelty, uniqueness.** 2. The set of behavioral or personal characteristics by which an individual is recognizable ► distinctiveness, selfhood. *See* **identity** (1).

individualize *verb*
► differentiate, identify, singularize. *See* **distinguish** (2).

individually *adverb*
► independently, singly. *See* **separately.**

indocile *adjective*
► ill-behaved, obstinate, unmanageable. *See* **unruly.**

indocility *noun*
► intractability, recalcitrance, unmanageability. *See* **unruliness.**

indoctrinate *verb*
1. To instruct by rote or discipline, as in a body of doctrine or belief ► catechize, drill, inculcate. *Idioms:* beat (*or* drum *or* pound) something into someone's head, put someone through his or her paces. *See also*

educate, practice. **2.** To teach to accept a system of thought uncritically ► brainwash, program, propagandize. *See also* **bias, influence.**

indoctrination *noun*
► disinformation, evangelism. *See* **propaganda.**

indolence *noun*
► idleness, shiftlessness, sloth. *See* **laziness.**

indolent *adjective*
► idle, shiftless, slothful. *See* **lazy.** *See synonym note at* **lazy.**

indomitable *adjective*
Incapable of being conquered or subjugated ► invincible, unbeatable, unconquerable, undefeatable. *See also* **insuperable, safe.**

indubitability *noun*
► assuredness, certainty, conviction. *See* **sureness** (1).

indubitable *adjective*
1. Established beyond a doubt ► inarguable, indisputable, irrefutable. *See* **certain** (2). **2.** Not counterfeit or copied ► genuine, true. *Slang:* legit, kosher. *See* **authentic** (1).

indubitably *adverb*
1. It is so; as you say or ask ► agreed, all right, assuredly. *See* **yes. 2.** Without question ► certainly, definitely, positively. *See* **absolutely** (1).

induce *verb*
1. To succeed in causing a person to act or think in a certain way ► convince, prevail on, talk into. *See* **persuade** (1). *See synonym note at* **persuade. 2.** To be the cause of ► generate, inspire, trigger. *See* **cause. 3.** To impel to action ► drive, press. *See* **urge.**

inducement *noun*
1. Something that causes and encourages an action or response ► impulse, incentive. *See* **stimulus** (1). **2.** Something that attracts, especially with the promise of pleasure or reward ► bait, draw, enticement. *See* **lure** (1).

induct *verb*
1. To admit formally into membership or office, as with ritual ► inaugurate, instate. *See* **initiate** (2). **2.** To enroll compulsorily in military service ► conscript, draft, impress, levy.

induction *noun*
1. The act or process of formally admitting a person to membership or office ► inauguration, installation. *See* **initiation** (2). **2.** Compulsory enrollment in military service ► impressment, levy. *See* **draft** (2). **3.** A short section of preliminary remarks ► overture, preface, prologue. *See* **introduction** (1). **4.** Exact, valid, and rational reasoning ► analysis, rationality, reason. *See* **logic** (1).

inductive *adjective*
► prefatory, preparatory. *See* **introductory** (1).

indulge *verb*
1. To comply with the wishes or ideas of another ► cater (to), gratify, humor. *See also* **defer. 2.** To treat indulgently ► coddle, pamper, spoil. *See* **baby.** *See synonym note at* **baby. 3.** To grant or have what is demanded by a need or desire ► fulfill, gratify. *See*

satisfy (2). **4.** To take extravagant pleasure ► bask, revel, wallow. *See* **luxuriate. 5.** To involve oneself in an activity ► engage, partake, share. *See* **participate** (1). **6.** To perform a service or a courteous act for ► favor, serve. *See* **oblige** (1). *See synonym note at* **oblige.**

indulgence *noun*
1. Forbearing or lenient treatment ► charity, lenience, toleration. *See* **tolerance** (1). **2.** A kindly act ► good turn, kindness. *See* **favor** (1). **3.** Excessive freedom; lack of restraint ► licentiousness, profligacy. *See* **license** (2). **4.** Something costly and unnecessary ► extravagancy, frill, treat. *See* **luxury** (1).

indulgent *adjective*
1. Ready to do favors for another ► agreeable, complaisant. *See* **obliging. 2.** Not strict or severe ► easy, forbearing, lenient. *See* **tolerant** (1).

indurate *verb*
1. To make or become physically hard ► congeal, solidify. *See* **harden** (2). **2.** To make resistant to hardship, especially through continued exposure ► season, toughen. *See* **harden** (1).

industrious *adjective*
► assiduous, conscientious, studious. *See* **diligent.** *See synonym note at* **diligent.**

industriousness *noun*
► assiduousness, perseverance, pertinacity. *See* **diligence.**

industry *noun*
1. Commercial, industrial, or professional activity in general ► commerce, trade. *See* **business** (1). *See synonym note at* **business. 2.** Steady attention and effort, as to one's occupation ► assiduousness, perseverance, pertinacity. *See* **diligence.**

indwelling *adjective*
► innate, intrinsic, natural. *See* **constitutional** (1).

inebriate *adjective*
Stupefied, excited, or muddled with alcoholic liquor ► intoxicated, sodden, tipsy. *See* **drunk.**

inebriate *noun*
A person who is habitually drunk ► alcoholic, dipsomaniac, tippler. *See* **drunkard.**

inebriated *adjective*
► intoxicated, sodden, tipsy. *See* **drunk.**

inebriation *or* **inebriety** *noun*
► insobriety, intoxication, tipsiness. *See* **drunkenness.**

inedible *adjective*
► unappetizing, uneatable. *See* **unpalatable** (1).

ineffable *adjective*
► indescribable, inexpressible, undescribable. *See* **unspeakable** (1). *See synonym note at* **unspeakable.**

ineffective *adjective*
1. Not having the desired effect ► counterproductive, useless. *See* **ineffectual** (1). **2.** Not capable of accomplishing anything ► impotent, inadequate, incapable. *See* **ineffectual** (2).

ineffectiveness *noun*
► helplessness, inefficacy. *See* **ineffectuality.**

ineffectual *adjective*
1. Not having the desired effect ► counterproductive,

inefficacious, inefficient, useless. *Idioms:* all wind, to no avail. **2.** Not capable of accomplishing anything ▸ helpless, impotent, inadequate, incapable, ineffective, inefficient, insufficient, lame, powerless, unable, useless, weak. *See also* **inefficient, futile.**

ineffectuality *noun*
The condition or state of being incapable of accomplishing anything ▸ helplessness, impotence, inadequacy, incapability, ineffectiveness, ineffectualness, inefficacy, insufficiency, powerlessness, uselessness. *See also* **futility, inability.**

inefficacious *adjective*
▸ inefficient, useless. *See* **ineffectual** (1).

inefficacy *noun*
▸ helplessness, ineffectiveness. *See* **ineffectuality.**

inefficiency *noun*
▸ incapacity, incompetency. *See* **inability.**

inefficient *adjective*
1. Lacking the qualities, as efficiency or skill, required to produce desired results ▸ bungling, impractical, inadequate, inapt, incapable, incompetent, inept, inexpert, unable, unequal, unfit, unqualified, unskilled, unskillful, unworkmanlike. *See also* **amateurish, improper. 2.** Not having the desired effect ▸ ineffective, useless. *See* **ineffectual** (1).

inelastic *adjective*
▸ inflexible, stiff, unyielding. *See* **rigid** (1). *See synonym note at* **rigid.**

inelegant *adjective*
▸ indelicate, tasteless, unbecoming. *See* **coarse** (1).

ineluctable *adjective*
▸ inevitable, sure, unavoidable. *See* **certain** (1).

inept *adjective*
1. Not suited to circumstances ▸ ill-suited, inapt, malapropos, unbecoming. *See* **improper** (2). **2.** Characterized by inappropriateness and gracelessness, especially in expression ▸ awkward, infelicitous, unhappy. *See* **unfortunate** (2). **3.** Lacking the qualities, as efficiency or skill, required to produce desired results ▸ incapable, incompetent, inexpert. *See* **inefficient** (1). **4.** Clumsily lacking in the ability to do ▸ bumbling, clumsy. *See* **unskillful** (1). **5.** Lacking dexterity and grace in physical movement ▸ gawky, graceless. *See* **awkward** (1).

ineptitude *noun*
▸ incapacity, incompetency. *See* **inability.**

inequality *noun*
1. The condition or fact of being unequal, as in age, rank, or degree ▸ disparity, disproportion, disproportionateness, imbalance, incongruity. *See also* **difference. 2.** Lack of equality, as of opportunity, treatment, or status ▸ discrimination, unfairness, unjustness. *See also* **bias. 3.** Lack of smoothness or regularity ▸ asymmetry, crookedness, unevenness. *See* **irregularity** (1).

inequitable *adjective*
▸ discriminatory, unequal, unjust. *See* **unfair.**

inequity *noun*
1. Lack of justice ▸ iniquity, wrong. *See* **injustice** (2).

2. An unjust act ▸ disservice, offense, wrong. *See* **injustice** (1).

ineradicable *adjective*
▸ deep-seated, entrenched, ingrained, inveterate. *See* **confirmed** (1).

inert *adjective*
1. Marked by a lack of creativity or use ▸ unemployed, unused. *See* **idle** (1). *See synonym note at* **idle. 2.** Lacking physical feeling or sensitivity ▸ insensible, numb, unfeeling. *See* **dead** (2). **3.** Lacking mental and physical alertness and activity ▸ slothful, sluggish, stuporous. *See* **lethargic** (1).

inertness *noun*
1. A lack of action or activity ▸ inaction, inoperativeness. *See* **inaction. 2.** A deficiency in mental and physical alertness and activity ▸ languor, listlessness, sluggishness. *See* **lethargy** (1).

inescapable *adjective*
▸ inevitable, sure, unavoidable. *See* **certain** (1). *See synonym note at* **certain.**

inessential *adjective*
1. Not part of the real or essential nature of a thing ▸ adscititious, adventitious, incidental, supervenient. *See also* **irrelevant. 2.** Not necessary ▸ dispensable, needless, unneeded. *See* **unnecessary.**

inestimable *adjective*
1. Too great to be calculated ▸ immeasurable, infinite. *See* **incalculable.** *See synonym note at* **incalculable. 2.** Of great value or price ▸ expensive, precious, valuable. *See* **costly.**

inevitable *adjective*
▸ inescapable, sure, unavoidable. *See* **certain** (1). *See synonym note at* **certain.**

inexact *adjective*
1. Lacking precise limits ▸ imprecise, undetermined. *See* **indefinite** (1). **2.** Lacking literal exactness ▸ broad, imprecise, rough. *See* **loose** (3).

inexcusable *adjective*
Impossible to excuse, pardon, or justify ▸ indefensible, inexpiable, irremissible, unforgivable, unjustifiable, unpardonable, unwarrantable. *See also* **evil, deplorable.**

inexhaustibility *or* **inexhaustibleness** *noun*
▸ immeasurability, limitlessness, measurelessness. *See* **infinity** (1).

inexhaustible *adjective*
▸ indefatigable, unflagging, untiring. *See* **tireless.**

inexorability *or* **inexorableness** *noun*
▸ bullheadedness, hardheadedness, rigidity. *See* **stubbornness.**

inexorable *adjective*
▸ bullheaded, dogged, obstinate. *See* **stubborn** (1). *See synonym note at* **stubborn.**

inexpedient *adjective*
▸ ill-considered, impolitic. *See* **unwise.**

inexpensive *adjective*
▸ budget, economy, low-cost. *See* **cheap** (1).

inexperience *noun*
Lack of experience and the knowledge gained from it

▸ greenness, immaturity, inexpertness, newness, rawness. *See also* **artlessness, ignorance.**

inexperienced *adjective*
Lacking experience and the knowledge gained from it ▸ fresh, green, immature, inexpert, new, raw, unconversant, uninitiate, uninitiated, unpracticed, unseasoned, untried, unversed. *Idiom:* wet behind the ears. *See also* **artless, ignorant.**

inexpert *adjective*
1. Lacking the qualities, as efficiency or skill, required to produce desired results ▸ incapable, inept, unskilled. *See* **inefficient** (1). **2.** Lacking experience and the knowledge gained from it ▸ uninitiated, unpracticed. *See* **inexperienced.**

inexpertness *noun*
▸ immaturity, newness, rawness. *See* **inexperience.**

inexpiable *adjective*
▸ unforgivable, unjustifiable, unpardonable. *See* **inexcusable.**

inexplicable *adjective*
That cannot be explained ▸ unaccountable, unexplainable. *See also* **mysterious.**

inexplicit *adjective*
▸ equivocal, nebulous, vague. *See* **ambiguous** (2).

inexpressible *adjective*
▸ indescribable, ineffable, undescribable. *See* **unspeakable** (1). *See synonym note at* **unspeakable.**

inexpressive *adjective*
▸ affectless, deadpan, pokerfaced. *See* **expressionless.**

inextricable *adjective*
▸ convoluted, elaborate, involved, labyrinthine. *See* **complex** (1).

infallible *adjective*
▸ foolproof, secure, unerring. *See* **sure** (2).

infamous *adjective*
1. Known widely and unfavorably ▸ common, ill-famed. *See* **notorious** (1). **2.** So objectionable as to deserve condemnation ▸ contemptible, disgusting, obnoxious. *See* **offensive** (1).

infamousness *noun*
▸ infamy, notoriousness. *See* **notoriety** (1).

infamy *noun*
1. The condition of being infamous ▸ disgracefulness, dishonorableness, disreputability, disreputableness, ignominiousness, shamefulness. **2.** Unfavorable, usually unsavory renown ▸ infamousness, notoriousness. *See* **notoriety** (1).

infant *noun*
A very young child ▸ babe, newborn. *See* **baby** (1).

infant *adjective*
Being in an early period of growth or development ▸ immature, juvenile. *See* **young.**

infantile *adjective*
1. Of or like a baby ▸ childlike, infantine. *See* **babyish** (1). **2.** Of or characteristic of a child, especially in immaturity ▸ childlike, immature, juvenile. *See* **childish.**

infantine *adjective*
Of or like a baby ▸ childlike, infantine. *See* **babyish** (1).

infatuated *or* **infatuate** *adjective*
Affected with intense romantic attraction ▸ beguiled, besotted, captivated, charmed, enamored, enraptured, obsessed, smitten, spellbound, taken. *Slang:* gone. *Idioms:* crazy (*or* mad *or* nuts *or* wild) about, cuckoo over, hung up on.

infatuation *noun*
1. An extravagant, short-lived romantic attachment ▸ *Informal:* crush, thing. *Idiom:* passing fancy. *See also* **love. 2.** An irrational preoccupation ▸ fetish, fixation, mania. *See* **obsession. 3.** A subject or activity that inspires lively interest ▸ mania, passion. *See* **enthusiasm** (2).

infeasible *adjective*
▸ impractical, unattainable, unworkable. *See* **impossible** (1).

infect *verb*
1. To harm with poison ▸ envenom, intoxicate. *See* **poison** (1). **2.** To make impure or unclean by contact or mixture ▸ adulterate, poison, pollute. *See* **contaminate** (1). **3.** To ruin morally ▸ debase, defile, taint. *See* **corrupt** (1). **4.** To spread a disease to others ▸ convey, pass, transmit. *See* **communicate** (4).

infection *noun*
1. The state of being contaminated ▸ defilement, impurity, pollution. *See* **contamination** (1). **2.** One that contaminates ▸ impurity, poison, pollutant. *See* **contaminant. 3.** A pathological condition of mind or body ▸ ailment, disorder, malady. *See* **disease** (1).

infectious *adjective*
▸ communicable, pestilent, transmittable. *See* **contagious.**

infelicitous *adjective*
1. Characterized by inappropriateness and gracelessness, especially in expression ▸ inept, unhappy. *See* **unfortunate** (2). **2.** Not suited to circumstances ▸ inapt, malapropos, unbecoming. *See* **improper** (2).

infer *verb*
1. To arrive at a conclusion from evidence or reasoning ▸ conclude, deduce, deduct, draw, find, gather, judge, reason, understand. *See also* **believe, derive, suppose. 2.** To predict or assume without sufficient information ▸ speculate, surmise. *See* **guess.**

inference *noun*
A position arrived at by reasoning from premises ▸ conclusion, deduction, judgment. *See also* **belief.**

inferential *adjective*
▸ hypothetical, presumptive, suppositional. *See* **supposed.**

inferior *adjective*
1. Below another in standing, importance, or status ▸ junior, low, secondary. *See* **minor** (1). **2.** Of low or lower quality ▸ low-grade, second-rate, shabby. *See* **bad** (1). **3.** Disturbing because of failure to measure up to a standard or produce the desired results ▸ discouraging, sorry, unsatisfying. *See* **disappointing.**

inferior *noun*
One belonging to a lower class or rank ▸ junior, secondary, underling. *See* **subordinate.**

infernal *adjective*
1. Perversely mean, cruel, or wicked ▸ devilish, diabolical, hellish. *See* **fiendish. 2.** *Informal* So annoying or detestable as to deserve condemnation ▸ accursed, blasted, confounded. *See* **damned** (2).

inferred *adjective*
▸ hinted, tacit, unspoken. *See* **implicit** (1).

infertile *adjective*
1. Unable to support vegetation ▸ sterile, unfruitful, unproductive. *See* **barren** (2). **2.** Unable to produce offspring ▸ sterile, unfruitful. *See* **barren** (1).

infertility *noun*
▸ barrenness, fruitlessness, impotence. *See* **sterility** (2).

infidel *noun*
One who does not believe in God ▸ atheist, heathen, non-believer, pagan.

infidelity *noun*
▸ disloyalty, perfidy, treachery, unfaithfulness. *See* **faithlessness** (1).

infiltrate *verb*
▸ edge, work, worm. *See* **insinuate** (1).

infinite *adjective*
1. Having no ends or limits ▸ illimitable, limitless. *See* **endless** (1). *See synonym note at* **endless. 2.** Too great to be calculated ▸ immeasurable, innumerable. *See* **incalculable.** *See synonym note at* **incalculable.**

infiniteness *noun*
▸ immeasurability, limitlessness, measurelessness. *See* **infinity** (1).

infinitesimal *adjective*
So small as not to be discernible ▸ imperceptible, microscopic. *See also* **tiny.**

infinity *noun*
1. The state or quality of being infinite ▸ boundlessness, immeasurability, immeasurableness, inexhaustibility, inexhaustibleness, infiniteness, infinitude, limitlessness, measurelessness, unboundedness, unlimitedness. *See also* **endlessness. 2.** The totality of time without beginning or end ▸ eternity, perpetuity, sempiternity. *See also* **forever.**

infirm *adjective*
1. Not physically strong ▸ feeble, frail, unsound. *See* **weak** (1). *See synonym note at* **weak. 2.** Lacking stability ▸ shaky, tottering, unsteady. *See* **insecure** (2).

infirmity *noun*
1. The condition of being infirm or physically weak ▸ debility, decrepitude, delicacy, delicateness, feebleness, flimsiness, fragileness, fragility, frailness, frailty, insubstantiality, puniness, unsoundness, unsubstantiality, weakliness, weakness. *See also* **breakdown. 2.** A pathological condition of mind or body ▸ ailment, disorder, malady. *See* **disease** (1). **3.** The condition of being sick ▸ affliction, illness. *See* **sickness** (1). **4.** An imperfection of character ▸ fault, shortcoming, weak point. *See* **weakness** (1).

infix *verb*
▸ entrench, ingrain, plant. *See* **fix** (4).

inflame *verb*
1. To stir to action or feeling ▸ excite, prod, trigger. *See*

provoke (1). **2.** To cause pain, soreness, or discomfort to ▸ irritate, pain. *See* **hurt** (3). **3.** To arouse the emotions of ▸ impassion, inspire, stir. *See* **fire** (2).

inflamed *adjective*
▸ achy, hurtful, sore. *See* **painful** (1).

inflammation *noun*
▸ irritation, soreness. *See* **irritation** (3).

inflate *verb*
1. To make something seem greater than is actually the case ▸ hyperbolize, magnify, overcharge. *See* **exaggerate** (3). **2.** To expand from or as if from internal pressure ▸ bloat, tumesce. *See* **swell** (1).

inflated *adjective*
1. Filled up with or as if with something insubstantial ▸ flatulent, gassy, overblown, tumescent, tumid, turgid, windy. **2.** Represented as greater than is actually the case ▸ magnified, overblown, outrageous. *See* **exaggerated** (1). **3.** Characterized by elevated language, such as that used in public speaking ▸ bombastic, grandiloquent, rhetorical. *See* **oratorical. 4.** Expanded from or as if from internal pressure ▸ bloated, tumescent. *See* **swollen** (1).

inflection *noun*
▸ edge, intonation, lilt. *See* **tone** (2).

inflexibility *or* **inflexibleness** *noun*
▸ hardheadedness, rigidity. *See* **stubbornness.**

inflexible *adjective*
1. Not changing shape or bending ▸ inelastic, stiff, unyielding. *See* **rigid** (1). *See synonym note at* **rigid. 2.** Incapable of changing or being modified ▸ inalterable, invariable, unalterable. *See* **immutable** (1). **3.** Firmly, often unreasonably immovable in purpose or will ▸ bullheaded, dogged, obstinate. *See* **stubborn** (1). *See synonym note at* **stubborn. 4.** Restricted in scope, outlook, or understanding ▸ insular, narrow-minded, provincial. *See* **narrow** (1).

inflict *verb*
To cause to undergo or bear (something unwelcome or damaging, for example) ▸ bring, impose, play, visit, wreak.

inflict on *or* **upon** *verb*
To force another to accept a burden ▸ charge with, foist on (*or* upon), saddle with. *See* **impose on** (1).

infliction *noun*
1. An excessive, unwelcome burden ▸ encumbrance, imposition, intrusion, obtrusion. *See also* **burden, meddling. 2.** Something, such as loss, pain, or confinement, imposed for wrongdoing ▸ castigation, chastisement, penalty. *See* **punishment.**

influence *noun*
1. Power to sway or affect based on prestige, wealth, ability, or position ▸ force, leverage, power, sway, weight. *Informal:* clout, muscle. *Slang:* pull. **2.** The power or capacity to produce a desired result ▸ effectiveness, efficacy, potency. *See* **effect** (2). **3.** The strong effect exerted by one person or thing on another ▸ impression, repercussion. *See* **impact** (2).

influence *verb*
1. To have an impact on in a certain way ▸ act on,

affect, dispose, impact, incline, lead (into), predispose, sway, work on. *See also* **bias, change, persuade.** **2.** To stir the emotions of ▸ get (to), strike, touch. *See* **move** (1). *See synonym note at* **move.**

influential *adjective*
Having or exercising influence ▸ consequential, guiding, important, powerful, seminal, weighty. *See also* **dominant, famous, important, primary.**

infold *verb*
▸ clothe, enshroud, invest. *See* **wrap** (2).

inform *verb*
1. To impart information to ▸ acquaint, advise, apprise, cue in, educate, enlighten, fill in, notify, tell. *Idiom:* break the news. *See also* **communicate, describe, reveal, say. 2.** To give incriminating information about others, especially to the authorities ▸ report, talk, tattle, tell, tip (off). *Slang:* fink, rat, sing, snitch, squeal, stool. *Idioms:* blow the whistle, drop a dime on, name names, put the finger on. *See also* **accuse, betray, implicate.**

informal *adjective*
1. Unconstrained by rigid standards or ceremony ▸ unceremonious, relaxed. *Informal:* laid-back. *See* **easygoing** (1). **2.** In the style of conversation ▸ chatty, colloquial. *See* **conversational** (1).

informality *noun*
▸ casualness, naturalness. *See* **ease** (1).

informant *noun*
▸ tattler. *Slang:* snitch, squealer. *See* **informer.**

information *noun*
1. That which is known about a specific subject or situation ▸ data, facts, intelligence, knowledge, lore. ▸ info, low-down. *Slang:* dope, poop. *See also* **education, knowledge. 2.** New information, especially about recent events and happenings ▸ intelligence, report. *See* **news** (1).

informative *adjective*
▸ edifying, enlightening, instructive. *See* **educational** (2).

informed *adjective*
1. Provided with information; made aware ▸ acquainted, advised, educated, enlightened, instructed, knowing, knowledgeable, up on. *Idioms:* in the know, up to date. *See also* **aware, familiar. 2.** Showing evidence of schooling, training, or experience ▸ lettered, literate. *See* **educated** (1).

informer *noun*
One who gives incriminating information about others ▸ informant, mole, source, talebearer, tattler, tattletale, telltale, whistleblower. *Informal:* rat, tipster. *Slang:* canary, finger, fink, nark, snitch, snitcher, squealer, stoolie, stool pigeon. *See also* **betrayer, gossip.**

infraction *noun*
▸ infraction, infringement, violation. *See* **breach** (1). *See synonym note at* **breach.**

infrequent *adjective*
Rarely occurring or appearing ▸ occasional, rare, scarce, sporadic, uncommon, unusual. *Idioms:* few

and far between, like a snowball in summer, once in a lifetime. *See also* **intermittent, unique.**

infrequently *adverb*
At rare intervals ▸ inhabitually, little, occasionally, rarely, seldom, sporadically, uncommonly. *Idioms:* hardly (*or* scarcely) ever, once in a blue moon, when the spirit moves.

infringe *verb*
▸ break, contravene, overstep. *See* **violate** (1).

infringement *noun*
1. An act of breaking a law or of nonfulfillment of an obligation ▸ infraction, violation. *See* **breach** (1). *See synonym note at* **breach. 2.** An advance beyond proper or legal limits ▸ intrusion, obtrusion, transgression. *See* **trespass** (2).

infuriate *verb*
▸ incense, irritate, madden. *See* **anger** (1).

infuriated *adjective*
Feeling or showing anger ▸ irate, livid, rabid. *See* **angry.** *See synonym note at* **angry.**

infuse *verb*
1. To cause something to become thoroughly wet or saturated by immersion in a liquid ▸ soak, saturate, souse. *See* **steep**². **2.** To put or set into, between, or among another or other things ▸ implant, insert, interpose. *See* **introduce** (2).

ingenerate *verb*
▸ generate, induce, trigger. *See* **cause.**

ingenious *adjective*
1. Characterized by or productive of new things or new ideas ▸ creative, innovative, original. *See* **inventive** (1). **2.** Mentally quick and original ▸ keen, quick-witted, sharp. *See* **clever** (1). *See synonym note at* **clever.**

ingénue *noun*
▸ babe, child, naive. *See* **innocent** (2).

ingenuity *or* **ingeniousness** *noun*
▸ creativity, inventiveness, originality. *See* **invention** (1).

ingenuous *adjective*
1. Free from guile, cunning, or deceit ▸ innocent, naive, simple. *See* **artless** (1). *See synonym note at* **artless. 2.** Manifesting honesty and directness ▸ candid, open, plainspoken. *See* **frank.**

ingest *verb*
1. To cause to pass from the mouth into the stomach ▸ swallow, take. *See also* **drink, gulp. 2.** To take food into the body as nourishment ▸ consume, fare, partake. *See* **eat** (1). *See synonym note at* **eat.**

ingestion *noun*
An act of swallowing ▸ gulp, swallow, swig.

ingle *noun*
An open space for holding a fire at the base of a chimney ▸ fireplace, grate, hearth.

ingrain *verb*
1. To place or set deeply or securely ▸ entrench, implant, plant. *See* **fix** (4). **2.** To fix (an idea, for example) in someone's mind by reemphasis and repetition ▸ drive, inculcate. *See* **instill.**

ingrained *adjective*
1. Firmly established by long standing ▸ deep-seated, entrenched, established, inveterate. *See* **confirmed** (1). 2. Forming an essential element, as arising from the basic structure of an individual ▸ innate, intrinsic, natural. *See* **constitutional** (1).

ingratiating *adjective*
▸ buttery, insinuating, sugary. *See* **flattering** (1).

ingredient *noun*
▸ building block, piece, section. *See* **part** (1). *See synonym note at* **part.**

ingress *noun*
1. The act of entering ▸ incoming, penetration. *See* **entrance**[1] (1). 2. The act of admitting or the state of being admitted ▸ admittance, entrance, entry. *See* **admission** (1).

ingression *noun*
1. The state of being allowed entry ▸ access, entrance, entry. *See* **admission** (1). 2. The act of entering ▸ incoming, penetration. *See* **entrance**[1] (1).

in-group *noun*
▸ coterie, group, set. *See* **circle** (3).

ingurgitate *verb*
▸ engorge, gobble, guzzle. *See* **gulp** (1).

inhabit *verb*
To live in a place, as does a people ▸ occupy, people, populate. *See also* **live, settle.**

inhabitable *adjective*
Fit to live in ▸ habitable, livable.

inhabitant *noun*
One who resides in a place, especially on a permanent basis ▸ denizen, dweller, native, occupant, resident, tenant, townsman, townswoman, villager. *Informal:* local. *See also* **citizen.**

inhalation *noun*
▸ inspiration, respiration, wind. *See* **breath** (1).

inhale *verb*
▸ breathe in, inpire. *Idiom:* draw breath. *See* **breathe** (1).

inharmonic *or* **inharmonical** *adjective*
▸ discordant, dissonant, untuneful. *See* **inharmonious** (2).

inharmonious *adjective*
1. Devoid of harmony and accord ▸ conflicting, differing, disagreeing, discordant, dissident, dissonant, inconsonant, uncongenial, unharmonious. *Idioms:* at odds, at opposite poles, at sixes and sevens, at war, out of accord. *See also* **discrepant, incongruous.** 2. Characterized by unpleasant discordance of sound ▸ cacophonous, discordant, disharmonious, dissonant, inharmonic, tuneless, unharmonious, unmelodious, unmusical, untuneful. *See also* **harsh.**

inharmony *noun*
▸ clash, difference, discord. *See* **conflict** (1).

inhere *verb*
▸ exist, lie, reside. *See* **consist** (1).

inherent *adjective*
1. Forming an essential element, as arising from the basic structure of an individual ▸ innate, intrinsic, natural. *See* **constitutional** (1). 2. Derived from or prompted by a natural tendency or impulse ▸ inborn, intuitive, visceral. *See* **instinctive** (1).

inherit *verb*
To receive from one who has died ▸ come into. *Idioms:* be fall heir to.

inheritance *noun*
1. Any special privilege that is accorded a firstborn ▸ birthright, heritage, legacy, patrimony. *See also* **right.** 2. Something immaterial, as a style or philosophy, that is passed from one generation to another ▸ heritage, legacy, tradition. *See synonym note at* **heritage.**

inherited *adjective*
1. Of or from one's ancestors ▸ familial, hereditary, genealogical. *See* **ancestral.** 2. Possessed at birth ▸ inborn, native. *See* **innate** (1).

inhibit *verb*
1. To check the freedom and spontaneity of ▸ constrain, constrict, cramp. 2. To control, restrict, or arrest ▸ bridle, check, curb. *See* **restrain.** *See synonym note at* **restrain.**

inhibited *adjective*
1. Tending to keep one's thoughts and emotions to oneself ▸ introverted, restrained, self-restrained. *See* **reserved** (1). 2. Deficient in or lacking sexual desire ▸ cold, passionless, undersexed. *See* **frigid** (3).

inhibition *noun*
1. A refusal to allow ▸ prohibition, proscription. *See* **forbiddance.** 2. Something that limits or holds back ▸ check, constraint, curb. *See* **restraint** (1).

inhibitive *or* **inhibitory** *adjective*
▸ controlling, restraining, suppressive. *See* **repressive.**

inhospitable *adjective*
1. Not encouraging life or growth ▸ adverse, hostile, unfavorable. *See also* **severe.** 2. So disagreeable as to discourage approach ▸ dour, flinty, stern. *See* **forbidding** (1).

inhospitality *noun*
Lack of cordiality and hospitableness ▸ aloofness, coldness, inhospitableness, uncivility, uncongeniality, unfriendliness, ungraciousness, unreceptiveness, unwelcome, unwelcomeness.

inhuman *adjective*
1. Characterized by or inflicting suffering or pain ▸ brutal, fierce, savage. *See* **cruel** (1). *See synonym note at* **cruel.** 2. Exceeding the bounds of morality, decency, or reason ▸ appalling, intolerable, shocking. *See* **outrageous.**

inhumane *adjective*
▸ brutal, fierce, savage. *See* **cruel** (1). *See synonym note at* **cruel.**

inhumanity *noun*
1. The quality or condition or being cruel ▸ brutality, truculence. *See* **cruelty.** 2. A monstrous offense or evil ▸ enormity, monstrosity. *See* **outrage** (1).

inhumation *noun*
▸ entombment, interment, sepulture. *See* **burial.**

inhume *verb*
▶ entomb, inter. *See* **bury** (1).

inimical *adjective*
1. Feeling or showing unfriendliness ▶ hostile, unfriendly. *See also* **mean²**. 2. Marked by a disposition to oppose ▶ antagonistic, contradictory, hostile. *See* **contrary** (1).

iniquitous *adjective*
▶ immoral, sinful. *See* **evil** (1).

iniquity *noun*
1. The quality or sate of being morally bad or objectionable ▶ peccancy, wickedness. *See* **evil** (1). 2. Lack of justice ▶ unfairness, wrong. *See* **injustice** (2). 3. A wicked act or wicked behavior ▶ evil, misdeed, sin. *See* **crime** (2).

initial *adjective*
1. Of or occurring at the start of something ▶ early, introductory, opening. *See* **beginning** (1). 2. Preceding all others ▶ earliest, original, premier. *See* **first** (1).

initiate *verb*
1. To go about the initial step in doing something ▶ begin, embark, institute. *See* **start** (1). 2. To admit formally into membership or office, as with ritual ▶ inaugurate, induct, install, instate, invest. *See also* **admit, indoctrinate.**

initiate *noun*
One who is just starting to learn or do something ▶ fledgling, neophyte, novice. *See* **beginner.**

initiation *noun*
1. The act of bringing or being brought into existence ▶ inception, start. *See* **beginning** (1). 2. The act or process of formally admitting a person to membership or office ▶ hazing, inaugural, inauguration, induction, installation, instatement, investiture. *See also* **admission.**

initiative *noun*
▶ enterprise, hustle, punch. *See* **drive** (2).

initiatory *adjective*
▶ initial, introductory, opening. *See* **beginning** (1).

inject *verb*
▶ infuse, insert, interpose. *See* **introduce** (2).

injudicious *adjective*
▶ ill-advised, imprudent, inadvisable. *See* **unwise.**

injunction *noun*
▶ charge, commandment, imperative. *See* **command** (1).

injure *verb*
1. To cause bodily damage to a living thing ▶ hurt, traumatize, wing, wound. *See also* **cut, break.** 2. To spoil the soundness or perfection of ▶ hurt, impair, mar. *See* **damage.** 3. To cause emotional suffering or painful sorrow to ▶ disturb, grieve, hurt. *See* **distress** (1). 4. To cause anger, resentment, or hurt feelings ▶ annoy, hurt, upset. *See* **offend** (1). 5. To alter and spoil the natural form or appearance of ▶ disfigure, misshape, twist. *See* **deform.**

injurious *adjective*
1. Causing harm or injury ▶ deleterious, evil, malevolent. *See* **harmful.** 2. Damaging to the reputation ▶ defamatory, invidious, slanderous. *See* **libelous.**

injury *noun*
1. The action or result of inflicting loss or pain ▶ detriment, mischief. *See* **harm.** 2. An unjust act ▶ disservice, inequity, wrong. *See* **injustice** (1). *See synonym note at* **injustice.** 3. Harm done to property or a person ▶ destruction, impairment, wreckage. *See* **damage** (1).

injustice *noun*
1. An unjust act ▶ crime, disservice, inequity, injury, malpractice, offense, outrage, raw deal, wrong. *See also* **breach, crime, indignity.** 2. Lack of justice ▶ inequity, iniquity, unfairness, unjustness, wrong. *See also* **favoritism, inequality, prejudice.** 3. Cruel exercise of power ▶ domination, repression, subjugation. *See* **oppression** (1).

✦ CORE SYNONYMS: *injustice, injury, wrong.* These nouns denote acts or conditions that cause people to suffer hardship or loss undeservedly. An *injustice* is a violation of a person's rights; the term can also refer to unfair treatment of another or others: *"Injustice anywhere is a threat to justice everywhere"* (Martin Luther King, Jr.). An *injury* is an injustice for which legal redress is available: *The court awarded the plaintiff compensation for the injury to his property.* *Wrong* is now more emphatic than *injustice* and in a legal sense refers to what violates the rights of an individual or adversely affects the public welfare: *"The age of chivalry is never past, so long as there is a wrong left unredressed on earth"* (Charles Kingsley).

---

inkhorn *adjective*
▶ bookish, literary, scholastic. *See* **pedantic.**

inkling *noun*
1. A subtle quality underlying or felt to underlie a situation, action, or person ▶ implication, suspicion. *See* **hint** (1). 2. An intuitive awareness or sense of something ▶ hunch, idea, impression. *See* **feeling** (1).

inky *adjective*
▶ dark, unlit. *See* **black** (2).

inlet *noun*
A usually narrow stretch of water leading inland ▶ estuary, fjord, mouth. *See also* **bay¹, channel, harbor.**

inlying *adjective*
Located inside or farther in ▶ inner, inside, interior, internal. *See also* **central, secluded.**

inmost *adjective*
▶ focal, median, middle. *See* **central** (1).

inn *noun*
▶ alehouse, pub, saloon. *See* **bar** (2).

innate *adjective*
1. Possessed at birth ▶ congenital, connate, connatural, hereditary, inborn, inherited, native. *See also* **essential.** 2. Forming an essential element, as arising from the basic structure of an individual ▶ inborn, intrinsic, natural. *See* **constitutional** (1). 3. Derived from or prompted by a natural tendency or impulse ▶ inborn, inherent, intuitive, visceral. *See* **instinctive** (1).

✦ CORE SYNONYMS: *innate, inborn, congenital, hereditary.* These adjectives mean existing in a person or thing from birth or origin. Something that is *innate* seems essential to the nature, character, or constitution: *innate common sense. Inborn* strongly implies that something has been present since birth: *inborn intelligence. Congenital* is applied principally to characteristics, especially defects, acquired during fetal development: *a congenital disease.* It is also used figuratively of characteristics or people with characteristics that are so deep-seated as to appear natural: *a congenital pessimism; a congenital liar. Hereditary* refers to what is transmitted by biological heredity (*a hereditary heart anomaly*) or by tradition: *"that ignorance and superstitiousness hereditary to all sailors"* (Herman Melville).

inner *adjective*
1. Located inside or farther in ▸ inlying, inside, interior, internal. *See also* **central, secluded. 2.** Arising from one's mental or spiritual being ▸ interior, internal, intimate, inward, visceral. *Slang:* gut. *See also* **constitutional, essential, personal.**

innermost *adjective*
1. At, in, near, or being the center ▸ focal, median, middle. *See* **central** (1). **2.** Indicating intimacy and mutual trust ▸ close, familiar, personal. *See* **confidential** (2).

innerving *adjective*
▸ bracing, energizing, exhilarating. *See* **invigorating.**

inning *noun*
▸ shift, stint, time. *See* **turn** (1).

innocence *noun*
1. The condition of being chaste ▸ modesty, purity, virginity. *See* **chastity. 2.** The condition of being uninformed or unaware ▸ nescience, unawareness. *See* **ignorance** (2). **3.** The stage of life between birth and puberty ▸ childhood, early years, preadolescence, prepubescence. *See also* **youth. 4.** The absence of guile, cunning, or deceit ▸ ingenuousness, naiveté. *See* **artlessness.**

innocent *adjective*
1. Free from evil and corruption ▸ angelic, angelical, clean, lily-white, pure, sinless, unblemished, uncorrupted, undefiled, unstained, unsullied, untainted, virginal. *Idiom:* pure as the driven snow. *See also* **clean, ethical, inexperienced, moral. 2.** Free from guilt or blame ▸ blameless, faultless, guiltless, harmless, inculpable, irreproachable, lily-white, unblamable, unoffending. *Slang:* clean. *Idioms:* above suspicion, in the clear. *See also* **honest. 3.** Devoid of hurtful qualities ▸ innocuous, unoffensive. *See* **harmless** (1). **4.** Free from guile, cunning, or deceit ▸ naive, simple. *See* **artless** (1). **5.** Not aware or informed ▸ oblivious, misguided, unaware. *See* **ignorant** (3). **6.** Deprived of a quality or aspect that is desirable ▸ destitute, lacking, void. *See* **empty** (2).

innocent *noun*
1. A pure, uncorrupted person ▸ angel, cherub, dove, lamb, virgin. **2.** A guileless, unsophisticated person ▸ babe, child, ingénue, naive. *Idioms:* babe in the woods, pure heart, simple soul. *See also* **fool. 3.** A young person between birth and puberty ▸ juvenile, tot, youngster. *See* **child** (1).

innocuous *adjective*
1. Devoid of hurtful qualities ▸ benign, unoffensive. *See* **harmless** (1). **2.** Lacking vigor, intensity, or bite ▸ bland, jejune. *See* **insipid** (1).

innocuousness *noun*
▸ banality, vapidness, wateriness. *See* **insipidity** (1).

innovate *verb*
▸ originate, pioneer. *See* **introduce** (1).

innovation *noun*
1. A new and unusual thing ▸ novelty. *Idioms:* the latest craze (*or* fashion *or* thing), the in thing, whole new ball of wax. **2.** Something invented ▸ contrivance, device. *See* **invention** (2). **3.** Discernment or perception which is usually competent or creative ▸ inspiration, prescience. *See* **vision** (2).

innovative *adjective*
1. Characterized by or productive of new things or new ideas ▸ creative, ingenious, original, resourceful. *See* **inventive** (1). **2.** Not the same as what was previously known or done ▸ fresh, novel, original. *See* **new** (1).

innovativeness *noun*
▸ newness, originality. *See* **novelty** (1).

innovator *noun*
▸ contributor, creator, producer. *See* **developer.**

innuendo *noun*
▸ insinuation, intimation, suggestion. *See* **hint** (2).

innumerable *adjective*
▸ boundless, immeasurable, infinite. *See* **incalculable.** *See synonym note at* **incalculable.**

inobservant *adjective*
▸ heedless, inattentive, thoughtless. *See* **careless** (1).

inobtrusive *adjective*
▸ quiet, subdued. *See* **modest** (1).

inoffensive *adjective*
1. Devoid of hurtful qualities ▸ innocuous, unoffensive. *See* **harmless** (1). **2.** Not lewd or obscene ▸ modest, wholesome. *See* **clean** (5). **3.** Lacking vigor, intensity, or bite ▸ bland, jejune. *See* **insipid** (1).

inoperative *adjective*
▸ inert, unemployed, unused. *See* **idle** (1).

inoperativeness *noun*
▸ inaction, inertness. *See* **inaction.**

inopportune *adjective*
1. Not occurring at a favorable time ▸ ill-timed, inconvenient, untimely. *See also* **fateful. 2.** Not suitable for or characteristic of the season ▸ ill-timed, untimely. *See* **unseasonable.**

inordinacy *noun*
▸ exorbitance, extravagance, surfeit. *See* **excess** (1).

inordinate *adjective*
▸ extravagant, immoderate. *See* **excessive** (1). *See synonym note at* **excessive.**

inordinately *adverb*
▸ excessively, extremely, overly. *See* **unduly.**

inordinateness *noun*
▶ exorbitance, extravagance, surfeit. *See* **excess** (1).

input *noun*
The right or chance to express an opinion or participate in a decision ▶ say, suffrage, voice, vote. *Informal:* say-so.

inquest *noun*
1. The examination of evidence, charges, and claims in court ▶ court case, hearing, inquiry, trial. 2. The act of examining carefully or critically ▶ inquest, investigation, study. *See* **examination** (1). *See synonym note at* **examination.**

inquietude *noun*
▶ disquietude, uneasiness, unrest. *See* **restlessness.**

inquire *or* **enquire** *verb*
1. To put a question to someone ▶ query, question, pump. *See* **ask** (1). *See synonym note at* **ask.** 2. To go into or through for the purpose of making discoveries or acquiring information ▶ investigate, probe. *See* **explore.**

inquirer *or* **enquirer** *noun*
One who inquires ▶ cross-examiner, inquisitor, interrogator, interviewer, investigator, prober, querier, quester, questioner, researcher. *See also* **busybody.**

inquiring *or* **enquiring** *adjective*
▶ acquisitive, questioning. *See* **curious** (2).

inquiry *or* **enquiry** *noun*
1. A request for data ▶ interrogation, query, question, questioning. *See also* **demand, problem.** 2. The act of examining carefully or critically ▶ inquest, investigation, study. *See* **examination** (1). *See synonym note at* **examination.** 3. The examination of evidence, charges, and claims in court ▶ court case, hearing, inquest, trial.

inquisition *noun*
▶ inquest, investigation, study. *See* **examination** (1). *See synonym note at* **examination.**

inquisitive *adjective*
1. Unduly interested in the affairs of others ▶ inquisitorial, meddlesome, officious. *See* **curious** (1). *See synonym note at* **curious.** 2. Eager to acquire knowledge ▶ acquisitive, questioning. *See* **curious** (2).

inquisitiveness *noun*
1. Undue interest in the affairs of others ▶ curiousness. *Informal:* nosiness. *See* **curiosity** (2). 2. Mental acquisitiveness ▶ curiousness, interest, regard. *See* **curiosity** (1).

inquisitor *noun*
▶ interrogator, investigator, questioner. *See* **inquirer.**

inquisitorial *adjective*
1. Unduly interested in the affairs of others ▶ inquisitive, meddlesome, officious. *See* **curious** (1). 2. Given to asserting one's will or authority over others ▶ bossy, domineering, overbearing. *See* **dictatorial** (1).

inroad *noun*
An act of invading, especially by military forces ▶ foray, incursion, invasion, raid. *See also* **attack.**

insalubrious *adjective*
1. Not sustaining or promoting health ▶ unhealthy,
unhygienic. *See* **unwholesome** (1). 2. Characterized by preoccupation with unwholesome thoughts or feelings ▶ sick, unhealthy. *See* **morbid** (1).

insane *adjective*
1. Afflicted with or exhibiting irrationality and mental unsoundness ▶ brainsick, certifiable, crazed, crazy, daft, demented, derailed, disordered, distraught, dotty, lunatic, mad, maniac, maniacal, mentally ill, moonstruck, non compos mentis, off, sick, touched, unsound, wrong. *Informal:* bonkers, cracked, daffy, gaga, haywire, loony, unhinged. *Slang:* bananas, bats, batty, buggy, cuckoo, fruity, loco, nuts, nutty, psycho, screwy, unbalanced, wacko, wacky, whack. **Idioms:** around the bend, bereft of reason, crazy as a loon, having a screw loose, mad as a hatter (*or* March hare), not all there, not playing with a full deck, nutty as a fruitcake, off one's nut (*or* rocker), off (*or* out of) one's head, off the wall, out of one's mind (*or* gourd *or* senses *or* tree *or* wits), sick (*or* soft) in the head, stark raving mad, of unsound mind. 2. Displaying a lack of good sense ▶ daft, idiotic, ludicrous. *See* **foolish.**

insaneness *noun*
▶ dementia, derangement, lunacy. *See* **insanity** (1).

insanity *noun*
1. Serious mental illness impairing a person's capacity to function normally ▶ brainsickness, craziness, dementia, derangement, disturbance, insaneness, lunacy, madness, mania, mental illness, psychopathy, unbalance. 2. Foolish behavior ▶ folly, silliness, tomfoolery. *See* **foolishness.**

✦ CORE SYNONYMS: *insanity, lunacy, madness, mania, dementia.* These nouns denote conditions of serious mental illness or disorder. *Insanity* is a grave, often prolonged condition that prevents a person from being held legally responsible for his or her actions: *was judged not guilty for reasons of insanity. Lunacy* often denotes derangement relieved intermittently by periods of clear-mindedness: *yelled wildly in a moment of utter lunacy. Madness* often stresses the violent aspect of mental illness: *a story about obsession and madness. Mania* refers principally to the excited, or manic, phase of bipolar disorder: *prescribed drugs to control the patient's periods of mania. Dementia* implies mental deterioration brought on by an organic brain disorder: *underwent progressive stages of dementia.*

---

insatiable *adjective*
▶ gluttonous, rapacious, ravenous. *See* **voracious** (1).

insatiability *noun*
▶ avidness, omnivorousness, rapaciousness. *See* **voracity.**

inscribe *verb*
1. To form letters, characters, or words on a surface with an instrument ▶ indite, pen, scribe. *See* **write** (1). 2. To cut a design or inscription into a hard surface, especially for printing ▶ etch, incise. *See* **engrave** (1). 3. To place on a list or in a record or book ▶ catalog, chronicle, write down. *See* **list**[1] (1). 4. To affix one's

signature to ▸ endorse, subscribe. *See* **sign** (1). **5.** To produce a deep impression of ▸ fix, imprint. *See* **engrave** (2).

inscrutable *adjective*
1. Incapable of being grasped by the intellect or understanding ▸ unfathomable, unintelligible. *See* **incomprehensible. 2.** Beyond the understanding of an average mind ▸ abstract, esoteric, profound. *See* **deep** (2). **3.** Difficult to explain or understand ▸ enigmatic, esoteric, puzzling. *See* **mysterious.** *See synonym note at* **mysterious.**

insecure *adjective*
1. Inadequately protected ▸ ill-protected, unattended, undefended, unfortified, unguarded, unprotected, unsafe, unshielded. *See also* **open, vulnerable. 2.** Lacking stability ▸ infirm, precarious, rickety, shaky, teetering, tottering, tottery, unstable, unsteady, unsure, wavering, weak, wiggly, wobbly. *See also* **weak.**

insecurity *or* **insecureness** *noun*
▸ inconsistency, unstableness, unsteadiness. *See* **instability.**

inseminate *verb*
To make pregnant ▸ impregnate. *Slang:* knock up. *Idioms:* get (*or* put) in a family way, get with child. *See also* **fertilize.**

insensate *adjective*
1. Completely lacking sensation or consciousness ▸ dead, inanimate, insentient, lifeless. *See also* **dead. 2.** Lacking compassion or mercy ▸ heartless, insensitive, merciless. *See* **callous. 3.** Displaying a lack of forethought and good sense ▸ brainless, fatuous, silly. *See* **foolish.**

insensibility *or* **insensibleness** *noun*
▸ disinterest, indifference, unconcern. *See* **apathy.**

insensible *adjective*
1. Incapable of being apprehended by the mind or the senses ▸ imponderable, indiscernible. *See* **imperceptible** (1). **2.** Lacking consciousness ▸ comatose, out. *See* **unconscious** (1). **3.** Lacking physical feeling or sensitivity ▸ inert, numb, unfeeling. *See* **dead** (2). **4.** Lacking feeling or emotion ▸ emotionless, impassive, stolid. *See* **cold** (2). **5.** Lacking compassion or mercy ▸ heartless, insensitive, merciless. *See* **callous. 6.** Unwilling or unable to perceive ▸ obtuse, unperceptive. *See* **blind** (3).

insensitive *adjective*
1. Lacking physical feeling or sensitivity ▸ inert, numb, unfeeling. *See* **dead** (2). **2.** Lacking feeling or emotion ▸ emotionless, impassive, stolid. *See* **cold** (2). **3.** Lacking compassion or mercy ▸ heartless, insensate, merciless. *See* **callous. 4.** Lacking sensitivity and skill in dealing with others ▸ gauche, impolitic, undiplomatic. *See* **tactless. 5.** Devoid of consideration for others' feelings ▸ inconsiderate, unthinking, unthoughtful. *See* **thoughtless** (1).

insensitivity *noun*
▸ disregard, unthoughtfulness. *See* **thoughtlessness** (2).

insentient *adjective*
Completely lacking sensation or consciousness ▸ dead, inanimate, insensate, lifeless. *See also* **dead.**

insert *verb*
1. To put or set into, between, or among another or other things ▸ infuse, inject, interpose. *See* **introduce** (2). *See synonym note at* **introduce. 2.** To place on a list or in a record or book ▸ catalog, chronicle, write down. *See* **list**[1] (1).

insertion *noun*
▸ heading, posting. *See* **entry** (1).

inside *adjective*
1. Located inside or farther in ▸ inlying, inner, interior, internal. *See also* **central, secluded. 2.** Known about by very few ▸ private, secret. *See* **confidential** (1).

insides *noun*
▸ bowels, entrails, intestines. *See* **viscera.**

inside track *noun*
Informal A dominating position, as in a conflict ▸ edge, upper hand, vantage. *See* **advantage** (3).

insidious *adjective*
1. Tending to lead one into error ▸ deceptive, illusive, misleading. *See* **fallacious** (2). **2.** Involving possible risk, loss, or injury ▸ chancy, hazardous, risky. *See* **dangerous.**

insight *noun*
1. The power to discern the true nature of a person or situation ▸ intuitiveness, intuition, sixth sense. *See* **instinct** (2). **2.** Deep, thorough, or mature understanding ▸ profundity, sagacity, sapience. *See* **wisdom** (1). **3.** Skill in perceiving, discriminating, or judging ▸ keenness, perceptiveness, shrewdness. *See* **discernment** (1).

insightful *adjective*
▸ imaginative, inspired, intuitive, perceptive. *See* **visionary** (1).

insignificance *noun*
1. Something or things of little importance ▸ frivolity, inconsequence, minutia. *See* **trifle** (1). **2.** The quality or state of being little known ▸ namelessness, oblivion, unimportance. *See* **obscurity** (1).

insignificant *adjective*
1. Of little importance or seriousness ▸ inconsequential, negligible, trifling. *See* **trivial. 2.** Not widely known ▸ little-known, unheard-of. *See* **obscure** (2).

insincere *adjective*
1. Not genuine or sincere ▸ feigned, phony. *See* **artificial** (2). **2.** Given to or marked by deliberate concealment or misrepresentation of the truth ▸ deceitful, disingenuous, mendacious. *See* **dishonest** (1). *See synonym note at* **dishonest.**

insincerity *noun*
Lack of sincerity ▸ ambidexterity, artificiality, disingenuousness, falsity, phoniness, pretense. *See also* **dishonesty, hypocrisy.**

insinuate *verb*
1. To introduce or insert by subtle and artful means ▸ edge, foist, infiltrate, wind, work, worm. *See also*

maneuver. **2.** To convey an idea by indirect, subtle means ▸ imply, suggest. *See* **hint.** *See synonym note at* **hint.**

insinuating *adjective*
1. Provoking a change of outlook and especially gradual doubt and suspicion ▸ implicating, incriminating, insinuative, insinuatory, suggestive. **2.** Purposefully contrived to gain favor ▸ buttery, ingratiating, sugary. *See* **flattering** (1).

insinuation *noun*
▸ innuendo, intimation, suggestion. *See* **hint** (2).

insinuative *or* **insinuatory** *adjective*
▸ implicating, suggestive. *See* **insinuating** (1).

insipid *adjective*
1. Lacking vigor, intensity, or bite ▸ bland, innocuous, inoffensive, jejune, milk-and-water, namby-pamby, vapid, washy, watered down, waterish, watery, whitebread. *Informal:* wishy-washy. *See also* **dull, harmless, trite. 2.** Lacking an appetizing flavor ▸ bland, flavorless, tasteless. *See* **flat** (2).

insipidity *or* **insipidness** *noun*
1. The state or quality of being insipid ▸ banality, blandness, innocuousness, jejuneness, vapidity, vapidness, washiness, wateriness. *Informal:* wishy-washiness. *See also* **emptiness. 2.** A lack of excitement, liveliness, or interest ▸ blandness, drabness, lifelessness. *See* **dullness** (1).

insist *verb*
1. To take and maintain a stand obstinately ▸ be resolute, carry on, persevere, persist. *Idioms:* make (*or* take) a stand, not take no for an answer, stand firm (*or* tall), stick to one's guns, hold (*or* stand) one's ground. *See also* **carry on, continue, endure. 2.** To put into words positively and with conviction ▸ avow, declare, maintain. *See* **assert** (1).

insist on *or* **upon** *verb*
To ask for urgently or insistently ▸ claim (*or* upon), require. *See* **demand** (1).

insistence *or* **insistency** *noun*
1. The state or quality of being insistent ▸ perseverance, persistence, persistency. *See also* **decision. 2.** Urgent solicitation ▸ persuasion, pressing, urging. *See also* **demand.**

insistent *adjective*
1. Firm or obstinate, as in making a demand or maintaining a stand ▸ importunate, importune, persistent, urgent. *See also* **firm, stubborn. 2.** Bold or confident in assertion ▸ emphatic, forceful. *See* **assertive.**

insobriety *noun*
▸ inebriation, intoxication, tipsiness. *See* **drunkenness.**

insolence *noun*
1. The quality of being arrogant ▸ hauteur, loftiness, superiority. *See* **arrogance. 2.** The state or quality of being impudent or arrogantly self-confident ▸ audacity, boldness, impertinence. *See* **impudence.**

insolent *adjective*
1. Overly convinced of one's own superiority and importance ▸ haughty, superior. *See* **arrogant. 2.** Rude and disrespectful ▸ bold, brazen, pert. *See* **impudent. 3.** Having or showing a lack of respect ▸ contemptuous, discourteous, impolite. *See* **disrespectful** (1).

insolvency *noun*
▸ ruin, ruination. *See* **bankruptcy.**

insolvent *noun*
An impoverished person ▸ beggar, derelict, tramp. *See* **pauper.**

insolvent *adjective*
Having little or no money or wealth ▸ destitute, down-and-out, indigent. *See* **poor** (1).

insouciant *adjective*
▸ heedless, nonchalant, unconcerned. *See* **careless** (1).

inspect *verb*
1. To look at or study carefully or critically ▸ investigate, peruse, scrutinize. *See* **examine** (1). **2.** To examine a person or someone's personal effects in order to find something lost or concealed ▸ frisk, pat down, search. *Slang:* shake down. *Idiom:* do a body search of.

inspection *noun*
▸ analysis, inquiry, scrutiny. *See* **examination** (1).

inspiration *noun*
1. Liveliness and vivacity of imagination ▸ brilliance, brilliancy, fire, genius. *See also* **intelligence, invention. 2.** Something that gives courage or confidence ▸ boost, exhortation, motivation. *See* **encouragement** (1). **3.** A sudden exciting thought ▸ brainstorm, bright idea. *Informal:* brain wave. *See also* **idea. 4.** The act or process of breathing ▸ respiration, wind. *See* **breath** (1). **5.** High spirits ▸ euphoria, exhilaration. *See* **elation** (1). **6.** Discernment or perception which is usually competent or creative ▸ farsightedness, prescience. *See* **vision** (2).

inspire *verb*
1. To arouse the emotions of ▸ impassion, inflame, stir. *See* **fire** (2). **2.** To raise the spirits of ▸ buoy (up), exhilarate, lift. *See* **elate** (1). **3.** To impart courage, inspiration, and resolution to ▸ animate, motivate. *See* **encourage** (1). **4.** To stir to action or feeling ▸ excite, prod, trigger. *See* **provoke** (1). **5.** To be the cause of ▸ generate, induce, trigger. *See* **cause. 6.** To take a breath or breaths ▸ breathe in, inhale. *See* **breathe** (1).

inspired *adjective*
▸ imaginative, intuitive, perceptive. *See* **visionary** (1).

inspirit *verb*
1. To impart courage, inspiration, and resolution to ▸ inspire, motivate. *See* **encourage** (1). *See synonym note at* **encourage. 2.** To raise the spirits of ▸ buoy (up), exhilarate, inspire. *See* **elate** (1).

inspissate *verb*
To make thick or thicker, especially through evaporation or condensation ▸ condense, reduce, thicken. *See also* **coagulate.**

instability *noun*
The quality or condition of being erratic and undependable ▸ flightiness, inconsistency, inconstancy, insecureness, insecurity, irregularity, precariousness,

shakiness, unpredictability, unreliability, unstableness, unsteadiness, unsureness. *See also* **change.**

install *verb*

1. To put in a certain position or location ▸ locate, place, situate. *See* **position. 2.** To admit formally into membership or office, as with ritual ▸ induct, instate. *See* **initiate** (2). **3.** To place securely in a position or condition ▸ fix, seat. *See* **establish** (2).

installation *noun*

1. Something attached as a permanent part of something else ▸ apparatus, fitting, fixture. *See also* **attachment. 2.** A large public display of works of art ▸ exposition, show. *See* **exhibition** (1). **3.** The act or process of formally admitting a person to membership or office ▸ inauguration, induction. *See* **initiation** (2). **4.** A center of organization, supply, or activity ▸ headquarters, post, station. *See* **base**[1] (1).

installment *noun*

A partial or intial payment ▸ deposit, down payment, security.

instance *noun*

1. One that is representative of a group or class ▸ illustration, sample. *See* **example** (1). *See synonym note at* **example. 2.** A legal proceeding to demand justice or enforce a right ▸ action, suit. *See* **lawsuit.**

instance *verb*

1. To demonstrate and clarify with examples ▸ demonstrate, evidence, exemplify, illustrate. *See also* **explain, show. 2.** To refer to by name ▸ mention, specify. *See* **name** (2).

instant *noun*

1. A very brief interval of time ▸ minute, second, wink. *See* **flash** (2). *See synonym note at* **flash. 2.** The general point at which an event occurs ▸ juncture, moment. *See* **occasion** (1).

instant *adjective*

1. Occurring at once ▸ immediate, instantaneous. *Idioms:* on-the-spot, split-second. *See also* **fast, quick. 2.** Demanding immediate attention ▸ crucial, dire, pressing. *See* **urgent** (1).

instant *adverb*

Without delay ▸ forthwith, instantly, straightaway. *See* **immediately** (1).

instantaneous *adjective*

Occurring at once ▸ immediate, instant. *Idioms:* on-the-spot, split-second. *See also* **fast, quick.**

instantiate *verb*

▸ externalize, manifest, materialize. *See* **embody** (1).

instantiation *noun*

1. One that is representative of a group or class ▸ illustration, representative, sample. *See* **example** (1). **2.** A concrete entity typifying an abstraction ▸ incarnation, manifestation, personification. *See* **embodiment** (1).

instantly *adverb*

▸ forthwith, promptly, straightaway. *See* **immediately** (1).

instate *verb*

▸ inaugurate, induct, instate. *See* **initiate** (2).

instatement *noun*

▸ inauguration, induction, installation. *See* **initiation** (2).

instigate *verb*

▸ excite, prod, trigger. *See* **provoke** (1).

instigation *noun*

▸ incitement, stimulus, trigger. *See* **provocation** (1).

instigator *noun*

▸ inciter, malcontent, rabble-rouser. *See* **agitator.**

instill *verb*

To fix (an idea, for example) in someone's mind by reemphasis and repetition ▸ beat into, drill, drive, implant, impress, inculcate, ingrain, pound. *Idioms:* drum (*or* hammer *or* knock) into one's head. *See also* **indoctrinate, teach.**

instinct *noun*

1. An innate capability ▸ faculty, gift, knack. *See* **talent.2.** The power to discern the true nature of a person or situation ▸ insight, intuitiveness, intuition, penetration, sense, sixth sense. *See also* **feeling, inclination.**

instinctive *adjective*

1. Derived from or prompted by a natural tendency or impulse ▸ inborn, inherent, innate, instinctual, intuitive, unlearned, untaught, visceral. *See also* **constitutional. 2.** Acting or happening without apparent forethought, prompting, or planning ▸ impulsive, involuntary. *See* **spontaneous** (1). *See synonym note at* **spontaneous.**

✦ CORE SYNONYMS: *instinctive, instinctual, intuitive, visceral.* These adjectives mean derived from or prompted by a natural tendency or impulse: *an instinctive fear of snakes; instinctual behavior; an intuitive perception; visceral revulsion.*

instinctual *adjective*

▸ inborn, intuitive, visceral. *See* **instinctive** (1). *See synonym note at* **instinctive.**

institute *verb*

1. To bring into existence formally ▸ constitute, establish, originate. *See* **found** (1). *See synonym note at* **found. 2.** To go about the initial step in doing something ▸ begin, embark, initiate. *See* **start** (1). **3.** To put in force or cause to be by legal authority ▸ enact, legislate. *See* **establish** (3).

institute *noun*

A principle governing affairs within or among political units ▸ decree, edict, ordinance. *See* **law** (1).

institution *noun*

▸ constitution, creation, establishment. *See* **foundation** (1).

institutionalize *verb*

To place officially in confinement ▸ commit, consign. *Informal:* send up. *See also* **imprison.**

instruct *verb*

1. To impart knowledge and skill to ▸ discipline, teach. *See* **educate** (1). *See synonym note at* **educate. 2.** To give orders to ▸ charge, direct, order. *See* **command** (1).

instructed *adjective*
▸ advised, educated, knowledgeable. *See* **informed** (1).

instruction *noun*
1. The act, process, or art of imparting knowledge and skill ▸ pedagogy, schooling. *See* **education** (1). 2. Known facts, ideas, and skill that have been imparted ▸ erudition, learning. *See* **education** (2). 3. An order ▸ charge, commandment, imperative. *See* **command** (1).

instructional *adjective*
1. Serving to educate or inform ▸ informative, instructive. *See* **educational** (2). 2. Of or relating to education ▸ pedagogic, scholastic, teaching. *See* **educational** (1).

instructive *adjective*
Serving to educate or inform ▸ edifying, informative, instructional. *See* **educational** (2).

instructor *noun*
▸ coach, trainer, tutor. *See* **educator**.

instrument *noun*
1. A device used to do work or perform a task ▸ implement, tool, utensil. *See synonym note at* **tool**. *See also* **gadget**. 2. Something, as a machine, devised for a particular function ▸ appliance, contraption, invention. *See* **device** (1). 3. That by which something is done or caused ▸ agency, means, medium. *See* **agent** (1). 4. A person used or controlled by others ▸ puppet, stooge, tool. *See* **pawn**².

instrumental *adjective*
▸ efficient, productive. *See* **effective** (1).

instrumentalist *noun*
▸ performer, virtuoso. *See* **player** (2).

instrumentality *noun*
▸ agency, means, medium. *See* **agent** (1).

insubordinate *adjective*
1. Not submitting to discipline or control ▸ obstinate, unmanageable. *See* **unruly**. 2. Marked by defiance ▸ disobedient, rebellious. *See* **defiant**.

insubordination *noun*
▸ disobedience, noncompliance, rebellion. *See* **defiance** (1).

insubstantial *adjective*
1. Having no body, form, or substance ▸ disembodied, incorporeal, nonphysical. *See* **immaterial** (1). *See synonym note at* **immaterial**. 2. Not plausible or believable ▸ feeble, flimsy, tenuous. *See* **implausible**. 3. Not physically strong ▸ feeble, frail, unsound. *See* **weak** (1). 4. Conspicuously deficient in quantity, fullness, or extent ▸ puny, scant, skimpy. *See* **meager** (1).

insubstantiality *noun*
▸ debility, feebleness, weakness. *See* **infirmity** (1).

insufferable *adjective*
▸ intolerable, unacceptable, unendurable. *See* **unbearable**.

insufficiency *noun*
1. The condition or fact of being deficient ▸ deficit, inadequacy, paucity. *See* **shortage**. 2. The condition or state of being incapable of accomplishing anything ▸ helplessness, ineffectiveness. *See* **ineffectuality**.

insufficient *adjective*
1. Not enough to meet a demand or requirement ▸ deficient, inadequate, scarce, short, shy, under, wanting. *Idioms:* at a premium, in short supply, on the short end. *See also* **deficient, inefficient, meager**. 2. Not capable of accomplishing anything ▸ impotent, inadequate, incapable. *See* **ineffectual** (2). 3. Disturbing because of failure to measure up to a standard or produce the desired results ▸ discouraging, sorry, unsatisfying. *See* **disappointing**.

insular *adjective*
1. Far from centers of human population ▸ isolated, removed, secluded. *See* **remote** (1). 2. Restricted in scope, outlook, or understanding ▸ inflexible, narrow-minded, provincial. *See* **narrow** (1).

insulate *verb*
▸ close off, seclude, sequester. *See* **isolate** (1). *See synonym note at* **isolate**.

insulation *noun*
▸ alienation, segregation. *See* **isolation** (1).

insult *verb*
1. To cause resentment or hurt by callous, rude behavior ▸ affront, huff, miff, offend, outrage, pique. *Informal:* badmouth, slam. *Slang:* dis, put down. *Idioms:* add insult to injury, call names, give offense, hurt someone's feelings, step on someone's toes. *See also* **revile, ridicule, snub**. 2. To cause anger, resentment, or hurt feelings ▸ annoy, injure, upset. *See* **offend** (1). *See synonym note at* **offend**.

insult *noun*
1. An act that offends a person's sense of pride or dignity ▸ contumely, putdown. *See* **indignity**. 2. An instance of mockery or derision ▸ fleer, jeer, scoff. *See* **taunt** (1).

insulting *adjective*
1. So unpleasant or objectionable as to cause scorn or disgust ▸ hurtful, impolite, rude. *See* **offensive** (2). 2. Having or showing a lack of respect ▸ contemptuous, discourteous, impolite. *See* **disrespectful** (1).

insuperable *adjective*
Incapable of being negotiated or overcome ▸ impassable, insurmountable, unconquerable. *See also* **impossible, invincible**.

insupportable *adjective*
▸ insufferable, intolerable, unendurable. *See* **unbearable**.

insure *verb*
▸ assure, secure, warrant. *See* **guarantee** (2).

insurgence *noun*
1. Organized opposition intended to change or overthrow existing authority ▸ mutiny, revolt, uprising. *See* **rebellion** (1). 2. The act or an instance of defying ▸ disobedience, rebellion. *See* **defiance** (1).

insurgency *noun*
▸ mutiny, revolt, uprising. *See* **rebellion** (1).

insurgent *adjective*
Participating in open revolt against a government or ruling authority ▸ mutinous, revolutionary. *See* **rebellious** (1).

insurgent *noun*
A person who rebels ▶ insurrectionist, revolutionist, transgressor. *See* **rebel** (1).

insurmountable *adjective*
Incapable of being negotiated or overcome ▶ impassable, insuperable, unconquerable. *See also* **impossible, invincible.**

insurrection *noun*
▶ mutiny, revolt, uprising. *See* **rebellion** (1).

insurrectionary *or* **insurrectionist** *noun*
▶ insurgent, revolutionist, transgressor. *See* **rebel** (1).

insusceptibility *noun*
The capacity to withstand ▶ immunity, imperviousness, resistance, unsusceptibility. *See also* **endurance, stability.**

insusceptible *adjective*
1. Lacking feeling or emotion ▶ impassive, insensitive, unimpressionable. *See* **cold** (2). **2.** Having the capacity to withstand ▶ immune, impervious, repellent. *See* **resistant** (1).

intact *adjective*
1. Including every constituent or individual ▶ entire, total, whole. *See* **complete** (1). **2.** In excellent condition ▶ flawless, perfect, sound. *See* **good** (2).

intake *noun*
▶ assimilation, incorporation, osmosis. *See* **absorption** (1).

intangible *adjective*
1. Incapable of being apprehended by the mind or the senses ▶ imponderable, indiscernible. *See* **imperceptible** (1). **2.** Having no body, form, or substance ▶ disembodied, incorporeal, nonphysical. *See* **immaterial** (1).

integral *adjective*
1. Constituting or forming part of the essence of something ▶ constitutional, fundamental. *See* **essential** (2). **2.** Including every constituent or individual ▶ entire, total, whole. *See* **complete** (1). **3.** Serving as a nondetachable part of a larger unit ▶ constituent, incorporated. *See* **built-in** (1).

integral *noun*
An organized array of individual elements and parts forming and working as a unit ▶ arrangement, totality, whole. *See* **system** (1).

integrate *verb*
1. To bring or come together into a united whole ▶ join, unify, unite. *See* **combine** (1). **2.** To combine and adapt in order to attain a particular effect ▶ blend, correlate. *See* **harmonize** (2). **3.** To bring into accord ▶ conform, proportion. *See* **harmonize** (1). **4.** To construct as an integral part ▶ build in, include, incorporate. **5.** To make a part of a united whole ▶ combine, embody, incorporate. **6.** To open to all people regardless of race ▶ desegregate.

integrity *noun*
1. Moral or ethical strength ▶ honesty, honor, principle. *See* **character** (2). **2.** The quality of being honest ▶ incorruptibility, reliability. *See* **honesty** (1). **3.** The condition of being free from defects or flaws ▶ solid-

ity, strength. *See* **soundness** (1). **4.** The state of being entirely whole ▶ oneness, totality. *See* **completeness.**

integument *noun*
The tissue forming the external covering of the body ▶ epidermis, skin.

intellect *noun*
1. The faculty of thinking, reasoning, and applying knowledge ▶ mentality, understanding. *See* **intelligence** (1). *See synonym note at* **intelligence. 2.** A person of great mental ability ▶ brain, thinker. *See* **mind** (2).

intellection *noun*
▶ cogitation, deliberation, rumination. *See* **thought** (1).

intellective *adjective*
▶ cerebral, psychic, psychological. *See* **mental** (1).

intellectual *adjective*
1. Appealing to or engaging the intellect ▶ cerebral, mental, sophisticated, thoughtful. *Informal:* egg-headed, highbrow. *Slang:* pointy-headed. *See also* **complex, educated. 2.** Relating to or performed by the mind ▶ psychic, psychological. *See* **mental** (1). **3.** Having or showing intelligence, often of a high order ▶ genius, knowledgeable. *See* **intelligent** (1). *See synonym note at* **intelligent.**

intellectual *noun*
A person of great mental ability ▶ genius, thinker. *See* **mind** (2).

intelligence *noun*
1. The faculty of thinking, reasoning, and applying knowledge ▶ aptitude, brainpower, brains, brightness, cleverness, intellect, mentality, mind, quick-wittedness, sense, smartness, understanding, wit. *Informal:* eggheadedness, gray matter. *Slang:* smarts. *Idioms:* intellectual (*or* mental) grasp, mental aptitude (*or* capacity), power of the mind (*or* thought). *See also* **common sense. 2.** That which is known about a specific subject or situation ▶ facts, knowledge, lore. *See* **information** (1). **3.** New information, especially about recent events and happenings ▶ headline, report. *See* **news** (1). *See synonym note at* **news. 4.** Skill in perceiving, discriminating, or judging ▶ keenness, perceptiveness, shrewdness. *See* **discernment** (1). **5.** Deep, thorough, or mature understanding ▶ profundity, sagacity. *See* **wisdom** (1).

✦ **CORE SYNONYMS:** *intelligence, mind, intellect, brain, wit.* These nouns denote the faculty of thinking, reasoning, and acquiring and applying knowledge. *Intelligence* implies solving problems, learning from experience, and reasoning abstractly: *"The world of the future will be an ever more demanding struggle against the limitations of our intelligence"* (Norbert Wiener). *Mind* refers broadly to the capacities for thought, perception, memory, and decision: *"No passion so effectually robs the mind of all its powers of acting and reasoning as fear"* (Edmund Burke). *Intellect* stresses knowing, thinking, and understanding: *"Opinion is ultimately determined by the feelings, and not by the intellect"* (Herbert Spencer). *Brains* suggests strength of intellect: *We racked our brains to find a solution.* *Wit* stresses quickness of intelligence or facility of comprehension: *"There is no such whetstone, to sharpen a good wit and encourage a will to learning, as is praise"* (Roger Ascham).

intelligent *adjective*

1. Having or showing intelligence, often of a high order ▸ bright, brilliant, genius, intellectual, knowing, knowledgeable, smart. *Informal:* brainy. *See also* **critical, shrewd, wise. 2.** Mentally quick and original ▸ keen, quick-witted, sharp. *See* **clever** (1). **3.** Consistent with reason and intellect ▸ deducible, rational, reasonable. *See* **logical** (2).

✦ CORE SYNONYMS: *intelligent, bright, brilliant, knowing, smart, intellectual.* These adjectives mean having or showing intelligence, often of a high order. *Intelligent* usually implies the ability to cope with new problems and to use the power of reasoning and inference effectively: *The intelligent math students excelled in calculus. Bright* implies quickness or ease in learning: *The bright child learned the alphabet quickly. Brilliant* suggests unusually impressive mental acuteness: *"The dullard's envy of brilliant men is always assuaged by the suspicion that they will come to a bad end"* (Max Beerbohm). *Knowing* implies the possession of knowledge, information, or understanding: *Knowing collectors bought all the auctioned paintings. Smart* refers to quick intelligence and often a ready capability for taking care of one's own interests: *Smart lawyers can effectively manipulate juries. Intellectual* implies the capacity to grasp difficult or abstract concepts: *Dinner at the philosopher's house was noted for its intellectual conversations.*

---

intelligibility *noun*

▸ distinctness, lucidity, perspicuity, plainness. *See* **clarity** (1).

intelligible *adjective*

▸ comprehensible, fathomable, unambiguous. *See* **understandable** (1).

intemperance *noun*

▸ overindulgence, surfeit. *See* **excess** (3).

intemperate *adjective*

▸ extravagant, immoderate. *See* **excessive** (1).

intend *verb*

1. To have in mind as a goal or purpose ▸ aim, contemplate, design, mean, plan, project, propose, purpose, target. *Chiefly Regional:* mind. *Idioms:* be fixing to, have one's heart set on, set one's sights on. *See also* **aim, decide, expect. 2.** To have or convey a particular idea ▸ denote, signify. *See* **mean¹** (1).

intended *adjective*

1. Done or said on purpose ▸ intentional, purposeful, willful. *See* **deliberate** (1). **2.** Pledged to marry ▸ betrothed, plighted. *See* **engaged** (2).

intended *noun*

Informal A person to whom one is engaged to be married ▸ betrothed, bride-to-be, fiancé, fiancée, future husband, future wife, husband-to-be, prospective spouse.

intense *adjective*

1. Extreme in activity, strength, or effect ▸ all-out, concentrated, desperate, fierce, furious, heavy, heightened, high, intensive, overpowering, overwhelming, strong, terrible, vehement, violent. *See also* **forceful, severe, sharp. 2.** Resulting from or affecting one's innermost feelings ▸ heartfelt, strong. *See* **deep** (3).

✦ CORE SYNONYMS: *intense, fierce, overpowering, vehement, violent.* These adjectives mean extreme in activity, strength, or effect: *intense fear; fierce pride; an overpowering stench; vehement dislike; violent rage.*

---

intensely *adverb*

▸ exceedingly, extremely, highly. *See* **very.**

intensify *verb*

To make greater in intensity or severity ▸ aggravate, deepen, enhance, escalate, exacerbate, heighten, redouble, sharpen, step up. *Slang:* hop up. *Idioms:* add fuel to the fire (*or* flame). *See also* **emphasize, increase, support.**

intensity *noun*

Concentrated power or force, as of effort, opinion, or emotion ▸ concentration, depth, depths, ferociousness, ferocity, fever pitch, fierceness, forcefulness, fury, height, pitch, severity, strain, vehemence, vehemency, violence. *See also* **force, passion, strength.**

intensive *adjective*

1. Extreme in activity, strength, or effect ▸ fierce, heavy. *See* **intense** (1). **2.** Not diffused or dispersed ▸ undivided, whole. *See* **concentrated** (1).

intensively *adverb*

▸ comprehensively, exhaustively, thoroughly. *See* **completely** (2).

intent *noun*

1. What one intends to do or achieve ▸ end, goal, objective. *See* **intention.** *See synonym note at* **intention. 2.** The current of thought uniting all elements of a text or discourse ▸ drift, gist, tenor. *See* **thrust** (1). **3.** Something that is conveyed or signified ▸ import, sense, significance. *See* **meaning** (1).

intent *adjective*

1. Committed to or unwavering in a course of action ▸ bent, decided, determined, fixed, resolute, resolved, set, single-minded, unhesitating. *See also* **firm¹, insistent, stubborn. 2.** Vigilantly attentive ▸ heedful, vigilant. *See* **alert** (1). **3.** Having one's thoughts fully occupied ▸ absorbed, preoccupied, riveted. *See* **rapt.**

intention *noun*

What one intends to do or achieve ▸ aim, ambition, design, determination, end, goal, intent, mark, meaning, object, objective, point, projection, purpose, target, view, why. *Idioms:* end in view, why and wherefore. *See also* **approach, dream, mission.**

✦ CORE SYNONYMS: *intention, intent, purpose, goal, end, aim, object, objective.* These nouns refer to what one intends or plans to do or achieve. *Intention* simply signifies a course of action that one proposes to follow: *It is my intention to take a vacation next month. Intent* more strongly implies deliberateness: *The executor complied with the testator's intent. Purpose* strengthens the idea of resolution or determination: "*His purpose was to discover how long these guests intended to stay*" (Joseph Conrad). *Goal* may suggest an idealistic or long-term purpose: *The college's goal was to raise ten million dollars for a new library. End* suggests a long-range goal: *The candidate wanted to win and pursued every means to achieve that end. Aim* stresses the direction one's efforts take in pursuit of an end: *The aim of most students is to graduate.* An *object* is an end that one tries to carry out: *The object of chess is to checkmate your opponent's king. Objective* often implies that the end or goal can be reached: *The report outlines the committee's objectives.*

intentional *adjective*
  1. Done or said on purpose ▸ conscious, purposeful, willful. *See* **deliberate** (1). *See synonym note at* **deliberate. 2.** Planned, weighed, or estimated in advance ▸ deliberate, considered, premeditated. *See* **calculated** (1).
inter *verb*
  ▸ inhume, sepulcher. *See* **bury** (1).
interaction *noun*
  ▸ communion, discussion, intercourse. *See* **communication** (1).
interceder *or* **intercessor** *noun*
  ▸ broker, intermediary, mediator, middleman. *See* **go-between.**
intercept *verb*
  To block the progress of and force to change direction ▸ cut off, head off.
interchange *verb*
  1. To give up in return for something else ▸ exchange, interchange, substitute, trade. *See* **change** (3). **2.** To give and receive mutually, as words ▸ bandy, swap. *See* **exchange** (2). **3.** To take turns ▸ alternate, rotate, shift.
interchange *noun*
  1. Occurrence in successive turns ▸ alternation, rotation, shift. **2.** The act of exchanging ▸ exchange, switch, trade. *See* **change** (2).
intercommunication *noun*
  1. A situation allowing exchange of ideas or messages ▸ communication, correspondence, contact, touch. *See also* **communication. 2.** The exchange of ideas ▸ communion, discussion, intercourse. *See* **communication** (1).
interconnection *noun*
  ▸ correlation, link, relationship. *See* **relation** (1).
intercourse *noun*
  ▸ communion, discussion, exchange. *See* **communication** (1).
interdependence *noun*
  ▸ correlation, link, relationship. *See* **relation** (1).
interdependent *adjective*
  ▸ correlative, interrelated, reciprocal. *See* **complementary.**

interdict *verb*
  To refuse to allow ▸ disallow, proscribe. *See* **forbid.** *See synonym note at* **forbid.**
interdict *noun*
  A coercive measure intended to ensure compliance or conformity ▸ interdiction, penalty, sanction. *See also* **restriction, punishment.**
interdiction *noun*
  1. A coercive measure intended to ensure compliance or conformity ▸ interdict, penalty, sanction. *See also* **restriction, punishment. 2.** A refusal to allow ▸ prohibition, proscription. *See* **forbiddance.**
interdictive *adjective*
  ▸ deterrent, preclusive, prohibitive. *See* **preventive** (1).
interest *noun*
  1. Something that contributes to or increases one's well-being ▸ advantage, benefit, good, interests, profit, use. *See also* **advantage. 2.** A right or legal share in something ▸ claim, portion, stake, title. *See also* **cut, right. 3.** Something that concerns or involves one personally ▸ affair, business, concern, lookout. **4.** Mental acquisitiveness ▸ inquisitiveness, regard. *See* **curiosity** (1).
interest *verb*
  To compel the attention, interest, or imagination of ▸ engage, fascinate, intrigue. *See* **grip** (1).
interested *adjective*
  1. Having concern ▸ engaged, involved. *See* **concerned** (1). **2.** Eager to acquire knowledge ▸ acquisitive, questioning. *See* **curious** (2).
interestedness *noun*
  ▸ inquisitiveness, interest, regard. *See* **curiosity** (1).
interface *noun*
  ▸ communion, discussion, intercourse. *See* **communication** (1).
interfere *verb*
  1. To intervene officiously or indiscreetly in the affairs of others ▸ butt in, horn in. *See* **meddle** (1). *See synonym note at* **meddle. 2.** To break up the order or progress of ▸ interruption, obstruct. *See* **disrupt** (1).
interfere with *verb*
  To interfere with the progress of ▸ dampen, obstruct. *See* **hinder** (1).
interference *noun*
  ▸ interfering, intrusion, obtrusion. *See* **meddling.**
interfering *adjective*
  ▸ inquisitive, meddlesome, officious. *See* **curious** (1).
interim *noun*
  An interval during which continuity is suspended ▸ hiatus, interlude, lacuna. *See* **gap** (2).
interim *adjective*
  1. Intended, used, or present for a limited time ▸ provisional, short-term. *See* **temporary** (2). **2.** Temporarily assuming the duties of another ▸ acting, provisional. *See* **temporary** (1). *See synonym note at* **temporary.**
interior *adjective*
  1. Located inside or farther in ▸ inlying, inner, inside, internal. *See also* **central, secluded. 2.** Arising from

one's mental or spiritual being ▶ internal, visceral. *See* **inner** (2).

interject *verb*

▶ infuse, insert, interpose. *See* **introduce** (2). *See synonym note at* **introduce.**

interlace *verb*

▶ braid, intertwine, twist. *See* **weave** (1).

interlard *verb*

▶ infuse, insert, interpose. *See* **introduce** (2).

interlock *verb*

To be the proper size and shape for something ▶ dovetail, fit. *Idiom:* fit like a glove.

interlocution *noun*

▶ dialogue, discourse, talk. *See* **conversation** (1).

interlocutor *noun*

▶ discourser, talker. *See* **conversationalist.**

interlope *verb*

1. To intervene officiously or indiscreetly in the affairs of others ▶ butt in, horn in, interfere. *See* **meddle** (1). 2. To force or come in as an improper or unwanted element ▶ cut in, horn in, interlope. *See* **intrude** (1).

interloper *noun*

▶ meddler, quidnunc, snooper. *See* **busybody.**

interlude *noun*

▶ hiatus, interim, lacuna. *See* **gap** (2).

intermeddle *verb*

▶ butt in, horn in, interfere. *See* **meddle** (1).

intermediary *noun*

1. One who acts as an intermediate agent between persons or groups ▶ broker, mediator, middleman. *See* **go-between. 2.** That by which something is done or caused ▶ agency, means, medium. *See* **agent** (1).

intermediary *adjective*

Being at neither one extreme nor the other ▶ intermediate, median, midway. *See* **middle** (1).

intermediate *noun*

One who acts as an intermediate agent between persons or groups ▶ intermediary, mediator, middleman. *See* **go-between.**

intermediate *adjective*

Being at neither one extreme nor the other ▶ between, median, midway. *See* **middle** (1).

intermediator *noun*

▶ broker, intermediary, mediator, middleman. *See* **go-between.**

interment *noun*

▶ entombment, inhumation, sepulture. *See* **burial.**

interminability *noun*

▶ eternity, perpetuity. *See* **endlessness.**

interminable *adjective*

1. Existing without interruption or end ▶ constant, endless, everlasting, perpetual. *See* **continual.** *See synonym note at* **continual. 2.** Extending tediously beyond a standard duration ▶ drawn-out, overlong, protracted. *See* **long**[1] (2).

intermingle *verb*

▶ blend, fuse, stir. *See* **mix** (1).

intermission *noun*

1. The condition of being temporarily inactive ▶ dor-

mancy, latency, quiescence, suspension. *See* **abeyance. 2.** A pause or interval, as from work or duty ▶ recess, time-out. *See* **rest**[1] (1). *See synonym note at* **rest**[1].

intermittent *adjective*

Happening or appearing now and then ▶ fitful, irregular, occasional, periodic, periodical, sporadic. *Informal:* on-again, off-again. *Idioms:* here and there, on and off. *See also* **infrequent.**

✦ CORE SYNONYMS: *intermittent, periodic, sporadic, occasional, fitful.* These adjectives all mean recurring or reappearing now and then. *Intermittent* describes something that stops and starts at intervals: *intermittent rain showers.* Something *periodic* occurs at regular or at least generally predictable intervals: *periodic feelings of anxiety. Sporadic* implies scattered, irregular, unpredictable, or isolated instances: *sporadic bombing raids.* What is *occasional* happens at random and irregularly: *occasional outbursts of temper.* Something *fitful* occurs in spells and often abruptly: *fitful bursts of energy.*

---

intermittently *adverb*

Once in a while; at times ▶ betimes, fitfully, occasionally, periodically, sometimes, sporadically. *Idioms:* ever and again (*or* anon), now and again (*or* then).

intermix *verb*

▶ blend, fuse, stir. *See* **mix** (1).

intern *verb*

▶ confine, incarcerate, jail. *See* **imprison.**

internal *adjective*

1. Located inside or farther in ▶ inlying, inner, inside, interior. *See also* **central, secluded. 2.** Arising from one's mental or spiritual being ▶ inward, visceral. *See* **inner** (2). **3.** Of, from, or within a country's own territory ▶ homegrown, native. *See* **domestic** (3).

internment *noun*

▶ confinement, custody, detainment. *See* **detention.**

interpolate *verb*

▶ infuse, insert, interpose. *See* **introduce** (2). *See synonym note at* **introduce.**

interpose *verb*

▶ infuse, insert, interpolate. *See* **introduce** (2). *See synonym note at* **introduce.**

interpret *verb*

1. To understand in a particular way ▶ construe, read, take. *Idioms:* read between the lines, see in a special light, take to mean. *See also* **understand. 2.** To perform according to one's artistic conception ▶ depict, execute, play, present, render, represent. *See also* **act. 3.** To make understandable ▶ decipher, explicate. *See* **explain** (1). *See synonym note at* **explain. 4.** To express in another language ▶ construe, render. *See* **translate** (1).

interpretable *adjective*

▶ accountable, decipherable, illustratable. *See* **explainable.**

interpretation *noun*

1. A performer's distinctive personal version of a song, dance, piece of music, or role ▶ depiction,

enactment, execution, performance, portrayal, presentation, reading, realization, rendering, rendition, representation. **2.** Something that serves to explain or clarify ▸ decipherment, explication, illumination. *See* **explanation** (1). **3.** Critical explanation or analysis ▸ annotation, exegesis, exposition. *See* **commentary. 4.** The act or process of translating ▸ crib, rendering. *See* **translation** (1).

interpretive *or* **interpretative** *adjective*
▸ explicative, expositive, illustrative. *See* **explanatory.**

interregnum *noun*
An interval during which continuity is suspended ▸ hiatus, interim, lacuna. *See* **gap** (2).

interrelated *adjective*
▸ correlative, interdependent, reciprocal. *See* **complementary.**

interrelationship *noun*
▸ correlation, link, relationship. *See* **relation** (1).

interrogate *verb*
▸ cross-examine, inquire, quiz. *See* **ask** (1). *See synonym note at* **ask.**

interrogation *noun*
A request for data ▸ inquiry, query, question, questioning. *See also* **demand, problem.**

interrogator *or* **interrogater** *noun*
One who inquires ▸ investigator, prober, questioner. *See* **inquirer.**

interrupt *verb*
1. To stop suddenly, as a conversation, activity, or relationship ▸ break off, cease, discontinue, suspend, terminate. **2.** To interject remarks or questions into another's discourse ▸ barge in, break in, chime in, chip in, cut in. *Idioms:* break one's train of thought, talk out of turn. *See also* **intrude, meddle. 3.** To break up the order or progress of ▸ interfere, obstruct. *See* **disrupt** (1). **4.** To stop for an indefinite period ▸ pause, suspend. *Idioms:* put on hold (*or* on ice). *See also* **rest.**

interruption *noun*
▸ discontinuation, disruption, suspension. *See* **break** (1).

intersect *verb*
▸ crisscross, crosscut. *See* **cross** (2).

interstice *or* **interspace** *noun*
▸ divide, interval, separation. *See* **gap** (1).

intertwine *verb*
▸ braid, entwine, twist. *See* **weave** (1).

interval *noun*
1. A space between objects or points ▸ divide, separation. *See* **gap** (1). **2.** A rather short period ▸ time, while. *See* **bit**[1] (4). **3.** One of the units in a course, as on an ascending or descending scale ▸ grade, level, step. *See* **degree** (1). **4.** An extent, measured or unmeasured, of linear space ▸ gap, length, stretch. *See* **distance** (1).

intervention *noun*
▸ interfering, intrusion, obtrusion. *See* **meddling.**

interview *noun*
▸ dialogue, discourse, talk. *See* **conversation** (1).

intestinal fortitude *noun*
▸ bravery, fortitude, gallantry, valor. *See* **courage.**

intestines *noun*
▸ bowels, entrails. *Informal:* insides. *See* **viscera.**

intimacy *noun*
▸ camaraderie, companionship, fellowship. *See* **friendship.**

intimate[1] *adjective*
1. Very closely associated ▸ bosom, chummy, close, cozy, familiar, fast, friendly, near. *Informal:* solid, thick. *Slang:* tight. *Idioms:* buddy-buddy with, hand in glove with. *See also* **faithful. 2.** Arising from one's mental or spiritual being ▸ internal, inward. *See* **inner** (2). **3.** Indicating intimacy and mutual trust ▸ close, familiar, personal. *See* **confidential** (2).

intimate *noun*
1. A person whom one knows well, likes, and trusts ▸ chum, comrade, mate. *See* **friend** (1). **2.** One in whom secrets are confided ▸ confessor, confidant, confidante, repository.

intimate[2] *verb*
To convey an idea by indirect, subtle means ▸ imply, insinuate, suggest. *See* **hint.** *See synonym note at* **hint.**

intimation *noun*
1. A brief or indirect suggestion ▸ cue, suggestion. *See* **hint** (2). **2.** A slight amount or indication ▸ hint, semblance, trace. *See* **shade** (2).

intimidate *verb*
1. To frighten into submission, compliance, or acquiescence ▸ bludgeon, browbeat, bulldoze, bully, bullyrag, cow, hector, lean on, menace, push around, threaten. *Informal:* strong-arm. *Idioms:* flex one's muscles, put the screws (*or* squeeze) on, threaten with bodily harm, turn the heat on, twist someone's arm. *See also* **coerce, harass. 2.** To fill with fear ▸ horrify, scare, terrify. *See* **frighten.**

✛ **CORE SYNONYMS:** *intimidate, browbeat, bulldoze, cow, bully, bludgeon.* These verbs all mean to frighten into submission, compliance, or acquiescence. *Intimidate* implies the presence or operation of a fear-inspiring force: "*It* [atomic energy] *may intimidate the human race into bringing order into its international affairs*" (Albert Einstein). *Browbeat* suggests the persistent application of highhanded, disdainful, or imperious tactics: *browbeating a witness. Bulldoze* connotes the leveling of all spirit of opposition: *was bulldozed into hiring an unacceptable candidate. Cow* implies bringing out an abject state of timorousness and often demoralization: *a dog that was cowed by abuse.* To *bully* is to intimidate through blustering, domineering, or threatening behavior: *workers who were bullied into accepting a poor contract. Bludgeon* suggests the use of grossly aggressive or combative methods: *had to be bludgeoned into fulfilling his duties.*

---

intimidation *noun*
An expression of the intent to hurt or punish another ▸ menace, threat.

intimidator *noun*
▸ browbeater, tease, tormentor. *See* **bully.**

intolerable *adjective*
1. So unpleasant or painful as not to be endured or tolerated ▶ insufferable, insupportable, unendurable. *See* **unbearable. 2.** Exceeding the bounds of morality, decency, or reason ▶ appalling, monstrous, shocking. *See* **outrageous.**

intolerance *noun*
▶ discrimination, racism. *See* **prejudice** (1).

intolerant *adjective*
1. Not tolerant of the beliefs or opinions of others ▶ bigoted, close-minded, dogmatic, hidebound, illiberal, judgmental, narrow-minded, opinionated, puritanical. *See also* **biased, narrow, stubborn. 2.** Being unable or unwilling to endure irritation or opposition, for example ▶ impatient, unforbearing, unindulgent. *See also* **ill-tempered, intolerant. 3.** Showing scorn and disrespect toward someone or something ▶ dismissive, haughty, scornful. *See* **disdainful** (1).

intonation *noun*
▶ edge, inflection, lilt. *See* **tone** (2).

intone *verb*
▶ chant, vocalize. *See* **sing** (1).

intoxicate *verb*
▶ envenom, infect. *See* **poison** (1).

intoxicated *adjective*
▶ besotted, sodden, tipsy. *See* **drunk.**

intoxicating *adjective*
1. Containing alcohol ▶ alcoholic, spirituous. *See* **hard** (12). 2. Producing or stimulating physical, mental, or emotional vigor ▶ bracing, energizing, exhilarating. *See* **invigorating.**

intoxication *noun*
▶ inebriation, insobriety, tipsiness. *See* **drunkenness.**

intoxicative *adjective*
▶ alcoholic, spirituous. *See* **hard** (12).

intractability *or* **intractableness** *noun*
▶ indocility, recalcitrance, unmanageability. *See* **unruliness.**

intractable *adjective*
▶ ill-behaved, obstinate, unmanageable. *See* **unruly.** *See synonym note at* **unruly.**

intransigence *or* **intransigency** *noun*
▶ bullheadedness, hardheadedness, rigidity. *See* **stubbornness.**

intransigent *adjective*
▶ bullheaded, dogged, obstinate. *See* **stubborn** (1).

intrepid *adjective*
▶ courageous, fearless, heroic. *See* **brave.** *See synonym note at* **brave.**

intrepidity *or* **intrepidness** *noun*
▶ bravery, fortitude, gallantry, valor. *See* **courage.**

intricacy *noun*
▶ elaborateness, perplexity. *See* **complexity.**

intricate *adjective*
1. Rich in detail ▶ fancy, detailed. *See* **elaborate** (1). *See synonym note at* **elaborate. 2.** Difficult to understand because of intricacy ▶ convoluted, elaborate, involved. *See* **complex** (1). *See synonym note at* **complex.**

intrigue *noun*
A secret plan to achieve an evil or illegal end ▶ collusion, conspiracy. *See* **plot** (2).

intrigue *verb*
1. To work out a secret plan to achieve an evil or illegal end ▶ conspire, scheme. *See* **plot** (2). 2. To compel the attention, interest, or imagination of ▶ captivate, engage, fascinate. *See* **grip** (1).

intrigued *adjective*
▶ acquisitive, questioning. *See* **curious** (2).

intrinsic *adjective*
▶ elemental, inborn, innate, natural. *See* **constitutional** (1).

introduce *verb*
1. To bring into currency, use, fashion, or practice ▶ innovate, launch, originate, pioneer, popularize, put forward, usher in. *Idiom:* start the ball rolling. *See also* **found, start. 2.** To put or set into, between, or among another or other things ▶ implant, infuse, inject, insert, interject, interlard, interpolate, interpose, put in, stick in, throw in. *See also* **attach, fix. 3.** To begin something with preliminary or prefatory material ▶ lead, precede, preface, ring in, usher in. *Idioms:* pave the way, ring up the curtain. *See also* **start. 4.** To make known socially ▶ acquaint, familiarize, present. **5.** To make known the presence or arrival of ▶ announce, herald. *See* **proclaim** (1). **6.** To put forward a topic for discussion ▶ bring up, raise. *See* **broach.** *See synonym note at* **broach.**

✛ CORE SYNONYMS: *introduce, insert, interject, interpolate, interpose.* These verbs mean to put or set a person or thing into, between, or among others: *introduce suspense into a novel; insert a letter into an envelope; interject a comment into a conversation; interpolated a transitional passage into the text; interposed himself between the scrapping boys.*

introduction *noun*
1. A short section of preliminary remarks ▶ foreword, induction, lead-in, overture, preamble, preface, prelude, prolegomenon, prologue. **2.** The act of admitting or the state of being admitted ▶ admittance, entrance, entry. *See* **admission** (1). **3.** The act of bringing or being brought into existence ▶ inception, initiation, start. *See* **beginning** (1).

introductory *adjective*
1. Serving to introduce or prepare for something ▶ inductive, prefatory, preliminary, preparatory. **2.** Of or occurring at the start of something ▶ early, initial, opening. *See* **beginning** (1).

✛ CORE SYNONYMS: *introductory, prefatory, preliminary, preparatory.* These adjectives mean serving to introduce or prepare for something: *introductory remarks; an author's prefatory notes; a preliminary investigation; preparatory steps.*

intromission *noun*
The act of admitting or the state of being admitted ▶ admittance, entry, introduction. *See* **admission** (1).

intromit *verb*
► let in, receive, take in. *See* **accept** (3).

introversion *noun*
► remoteness, taciturny, uncommunicativeness. *See* **reserve** (2).

introverted *adjective*
1. Awkward or unconfident in behavior or manner ► bashful, demure, diffident. *See* **shy**[1] (1). *See synonym note at* **shy**[1]. **2.** Tending to keep one's thoughts and one's emotions to oneself ► inhibited, restrained, self-restrained. *See* **reserved** (1).

intrude *verb*
1. To force or come in as an improper or unwanted element ► barge in, charge in, cut in, encroach, gatecrash, horn in, interlope, obtrude, trespass. *See also* **interrupt, meddle. 2.** To break up the order or progress of ► interfere, obstruct. *See* **disrupt** (1).

intrusion *noun*
1. The act or an instance of interfering or intruding ► interfering, obtrusion. *See* **meddling. 2.** An advance beyond proper or legal limits ► infringement, obtrusion, transgression. *See* **trespass** (2). **3.** An excessive, unwelcome burden ► encumbrance, imposition, infliction, obtrusion. *See also* **burden.**

intrusive *adjective*
1. Troubling to the mind or emotions ► bothersome, irritating, unsettling. *See* **disturbing. 2.** Unduly interested in the affairs of others ► inquisitive, meddlesome, officious. *See* **curious** (1).

intuit *verb*
► feel, sense. *See* **perceive** (2).

intuition *noun*
1. An intuitive awareness or sense of something ► hunch, impression, suspicion. *See* **feeling** (1). **2.** The power to discern the true nature of a person or situation ► insight, intuitiveness, sixth sense. *See* **instinct** (2).

intuitive *adjective*
1. Derived from or prompted by a natural tendency or impulse ► inborn, visceral. *See* **instinctive** (1). *See synonym note at* **instinctive. 2.** Characterized by foresight or vision ► imaginative, perceptive. *See* **visionary** (1).

intuitiveness *noun*
► insight, intuition, sense. *See* **instinct** (2).

inundate *verb*
1. To affect as if by an outpouring of water ► deluge, flood, overwhelm, swamp. **2.** To flow over completely ► engulf, overflow, submerge. *See* **flood** (1).

inundation *noun*
► deluge, overflow, torrent. *See* **flood** (1).

inure *verb*
► habituate, wont. *See* **accustom.**

inured *adjective*
► acclimated, adapted, conditioned. *See* **accustomed** (1).

invade *verb*
1. To enter so as to attack, plunder, destroy, or conquer ► foray, harry, maraud, overrun, raid. *Idioms:*
enter by force, take by storm. *See also* **attack, sack. 2.** To seize or maintain control over by conquest ► capture, overrun, subjugate. *See* **occupy** (2). **3.** To enter forcibly or illegally ► break in, burglarize, trespass. *See also* **rob, steal.**

invalid *adjective*
► false, illogical, unsound. *See* **fallacious** (1).

invalidate *verb*
1. To put an end to ► cancel, nullify, void. *See* **abolish** (1). **2.** To render powerless or motionless, as by inflicting severe injury ► handicap, immobilize, paralyze. *See* **disable** (1).

invalidation *noun*
► annulment, negation, nullification, voidance. *See* **abolition.**

invaluable *adjective*
► expensive, precious, valuable. *See* **costly.**

invariable *adjective*
1. Having no change or variation ► changeless, constant, unvarying. *See* **unchanging. 2.** Incapable of changing or being modified ► inflexible, ironclad, unalterable. *See* **immutable** (1).

invariant *adjective*
► changeless, constant, unvarying. *See* **unchanging.**

invasion *noun*
An act of invading, especially by military forces ► foray, incursion, inroad, raid. *See also* **attack.**

invective *noun*
Sustained, harshly abusive language ► condemnation, denunciation. *See* **vituperation.**

invective *adjective*
Of, relating to, or characterized by verbal abuse ► contumelious, scurrilous. *See* **abusive.**

inveigh *verb*
► except, oppose, protest. *See* **object** (1).

inveigle *verb*
► allure, entice, lure. *See* **seduce.** *See synonym note at* **seduce.**

inveiglement *noun*
► bait, draw, enticement. *See* **lure** (1).

inveigler *noun*
► charmer, tempter. *See* **seducer** (1).

invent *verb*
1. To use ingenuity in making, developing, or achieving ► coin, concoct, contrive, devise, dream up, fabricate, formulate, hatch, make up, mint, think up. *Informal:* cook up. **Idiom:** come up with. *See also* **design, introduce, produce, make. 2.** To present false information with the intention of deceiving ► fib, prevaricate. *See* **lie**[2].

invented *adjective*
► fictional, made-up. *See* **fictitious** (1).

invention *noun*
1. The power or ability to invent ► creativeness, creativity, fecundity, ingeniousness, ingenuity, inventiveness, originality, resourcefulness. *See also* **ability, brilliance, imagination. 2.** Something invented ► brainchild, concoction, contrivance, device, innovation, origination. *See also* **device, discovery, novelty.**

3. A fiction or half-truth, especially one that forms part of an ideology ▶ fantasy, fiction, figment. *See* **myth** (3). **4.** Something that is the result of creative effort ▶ piece, production, work. *See* **composition** (1). **5.** The act of bringing or being brought into existence ▶ inception, initiation, start. *See* **beginning** (1). **6.** An untrue declaration ▶ falsehood, fib, untruth. *See* **lie²**.

inventive *adjective*
1. Characterized by or productive of new things or new ideas ▶ artistic, creative, generative, ingenious, innovative, original, resourceful, seminal. *See also* **fertile, visionary. 2.** Not the same as what was previously known or done ▶ fresh, novel, original. *See* **new** (1). **3.** Mentally quick and original ▶ ingenious, quick-thinking, resourceful. *See* **clever** (1).

inventiveness *noun*
▶ creativity, ingenuity, originality. *See* **invention** (1).

inventor *noun*
▶ author, creator, maker. *See* **originator.**

inventory *noun*
1. A supply stored or hidden for possible future use ▶ cache, reserve, stockpile. *See* **hoard. 2.** A product or products bought and sold in commerce ▶ line, merchandise, ware. *See* **good** (2). **3.** A series, as of names or words, printed or written down ▶ register, roster, schedule. *See* **list¹.**

inventory *verb*
To name or specify one by one ▶ list, tick off. *See* **enumerate** (1).

inveracity *noun*
1. The practice of lying ▶ perjury, untruthfulness. *See* **mendacity** (1). **2.** An untrue declaration ▶ falsehood, fib, untruth. *See* **lie².**

inverse *noun*
That which is diametrically opposed to another ▶ antithesis, contrary. *See* **opposite.**

inverse *adjective*
Diametrically opposed ▶ antithetical, contradictory, diametric. *See* **opposite.**

inversion *noun*
▶ about-face, transposition, turnabout. *See* **reversal** (1).

invert *verb*
1. To change to the opposite position, direction, or course ▶ transpose, turn (about, around, over, *or* round). *See* **reverse** (1). *See synonym note at* **reverse. 2.** To turn or cause to turn from a vertical or horizontal position ▶ knock over, topple. *See* **overturn** (1).

inverted *adjective*
▶ capsized, overturned. *See* **upside-down** (1).

invest *verb*
1. To admit formally into membership or office, as with ritual ▶ induct, instate. *See* **initiate** (2). **2.** To present with a gift ▶ award, give. *See* **gift. 3.** To put clothes on ▶ attire, clothe, garb. *See* **dress** (1). **4.** To surround and cover completely so as to obscure ▶ clothe, enshroud. *See* **wrap** (2). **5.** To surround with hostile troops ▶ beset, blockade, siege. *See* **besiege** (1).

See synonym note at **besiege. 6.** To place money in an account ▶ lay away, salt away. *See* **bank². 7.** To place securely in a position or condition ▶ fix, seat. *See* **establish** (2).

investigate *verb*
1. To look at or study carefully or critically ▶ inspect, peruse, scrutinize. *See* **examine** (1). **2.** To go into or through for the purpose of making discoveries or acquiring information ▶ inquire, probe. *See* **explore.**

investigation *noun*
1. The act or an instance of exploring or investigating ▶ exploration, probe, reconnaissance. **2.** The act of examining carefully or critically ▶ inspection, inquiry, scrutiny. *See* **examination** (1). *See synonym note at* **examination.**

investigative *adjective*
▶ acquisitive, questioning. *See* **curious** (2).

investigator *noun*
1. A person whose work is investigating crimes or obtaining hidden evidence or information ▶ sleuth. *Informal:* eye. *Slang:* gumshoe. *See* **detective. 2.** One who inquires ▶ interrogator, questioner. *See* **inquirer.**

investiture *noun*
▶ inauguration, induction, installation. *See* **initiation** (2).

investment *noun*
1. The management of money ▶ banking, finance, money management. **2.** A prolonged encirclement of an objective by hostile troops ▶ beleaguerment, besiegement, blockade, siege. *See also* **attack.**

inveterate *adjective*
1. Firmly established by long standing ▶ deep-seated, entrenched, ingrained, settled. *See* **confirmed** (1). **2.** Subject to a disease or habit for a long time ▶ chronic, confirmed, habitual, habituated. *See also* **stubborn.**

invidious *adjective*
1. Damaging to the reputation ▶ defamatory, injurious, slanderous. *See* **libelous. 2.** Resentfully or painfully desirous of another's advantages ▶ jaundiced, jealous. *See* **envious.**

invigorate *verb*
▶ exhilarate, vitalize. *See* **energize.**

invigorating *adjective*
Producing or stimulating physical, mental, or emotional vigor ▶ animating, bracing, energizing, enlivening, exciting, exhilarant, exhilarating, innerving, intoxicating, quickening, refreshing, reinvigorating, renewing, restorative, roborant, rousing, stimulating, tonic, vitalizing, vivifying. *See also* **curative, pleasant.**

invincible *adjective*
Incapable of being conquered or subjugated ▶ indomitable, unbeatable, unconquerable, undefeatable. *See also* **safe.**

inviolability *noun*
1. The quality or condition of being safe from assault, trespass, or violation ▶ sacredness, sacrosanctity, sanctity. **2.** The quality of being or acting in accordance

with what is holy or sacred ▶ beatitude, sanctity. *See* **holiness.**

inviolable *adjective*
1. Affording protection ▶ impenetrable, invulnerable, unconquerable. *See* **safe** (2). **2.** Regarded with particular reverence or respect ▶ consecrated, hallowed, sacred. *See* **holy** (1).

invisible *adjective*
1. Incapable of being apprehended by the mind or the senses ▶ imponderable, indiscernible. *See* **imperceptible** (1). **2.** Difficult or impossible to see or distinguish ▶ covert, disguised, unseen. *See* **hidden** (1).

invitation *noun*
1. A spoken or written request for someone to take part or be present ▶ call, bid, summons. *Informal:* invite. *See also* **request. 2.** Something that attracts, especially with the promise of pleasure or reward ▶ bait, draw, enticement. *See* **lure** (1). **3.** An act of offering or the thing offered ▶ bid, proffer. *See* **offer** (1).

invite *verb*
1. To request that someone take part in or be present at a particular occasion ▶ ask, bid, summon. *Idioms:* extend an invitation to, request the presence of. *See also* **appeal, request. 2.** To behave so as to bring on danger, for example ▶ provoke, tempt. *See* **court** (1).

invite *noun*
Informal A spoken or written request for someone to take part or be present ▶ call, bid, invitation, summons. *See also* **request.**

inviting *adjective*
▶ bewitching, enticing, tempting. *See* **seductive.**

invocation *noun*
The act of praying ▶ benediction, prayer, supplication. *See also* **appeal.**

invoice *noun*
1. A precise list of fees or charges ▶ bill, check, statement. *Informal:* tab. *See* **account** (2). **2.** A series, as of names or words, printed or written down ▶ register, roster, schedule. *See* **list**[1].

invoice *verb*
To present with a request or demand for payment ▶ charge, solicit. *See* **bill**[1].

invoke *verb*
1. To compel observance of ▶ effect, implement. *See* **enforce. 2.** To offer a reverent petition to God or a god ▶ pray, supplicate. *See also* **appeal. 3.** To bring forward as proof or support ▶ adduce, present, produce. *See* **cite** (1). **4.** To bring out something latent, hidden, or unexpressed ▶ draw (out), elicit, summon. *See* **evoke.**

involuntarily *adverb*
1. Without regard to desire or inclination ▶ perforce, willy-nilly. *See* **helplessly. 2.** Without apparent forethought, prompting, or planning ▶ automatically, impulsively. *See* **spontaneously** (1).

involuntary *adjective*
1. Acting or happening without apparent forethought ▶ automatic, impulsive, reflex. *See* **spontaneous** (1).

See synonym note at **spontaneous. 2.** Not intended ▶ inadvertent, undesigned. *See* **unintentional.**

involute *adjective*
▶ convoluted, elaborate, involved, labyrinthine. *See* **complex** (1).

involve *verb*
1. To draw in so that extrication is difficult ▶ catch up, draw into, embrangle, embroil, implicate, mix up, suck, wrap up. *See also* **catch. 2.** To have as a part ▶ comprise, take in. *See* **contain** (1). *See synonym note at* **contain. 3.** To have as a condition or a consequence ▶ carry, entail. **4.** To have as a need or prerequisite ▶ entail, necessitate, require. *See* **demand** (2). **5.** To involve by logical necessity ▶ involve, indicate, point to. *See* **imply** (1). **6.** To occupy the attention of ▶ consume, engage, occupy. *See* **absorb** (1). **7.** To make complex, intricate, or perplexing ▶ entangle, perplex, tangle. *See* **complicate.**

involved *adjective*
1. Difficult to understand because of intricacy ▶ convoluted, elaborate, involute, labyrinthine. *See* **complex** (1). *See synonym note at* **complex. 2.** Having concern ▶ engaged, interested. *See* **concerned** (1).

involvement *noun*
1. The act or fact of participating ▶ engagement, partaking, participation, sharing. **2.** The condition of being entangled or implicated ▶ embroilment, implication. *See* **entanglement** (1). **3.** Total occupation of the attention or of the mind ▶ engagement, engrossment, enthrallment, immersion. *See* **absorption** (2).

invulnerability *noun*
▶ impenetrability, security. *See* **safety** (1).

invulnerable *adjective*
▶ impenetrable, unconquerable. *See* **safe** (2).

inward *adjective*
1. Arising from one's mental or spiritual being ▶ internal, visceral. *See* **inner** (2). **2.** Indicating intimacy and mutual trust ▶ close, familiar. *See* **confidential** (2).

in-your-face *adjective*
▶ aggressive, forceful, insistent. *See* **assertive.**

iota *noun*
▶ dash, drop, smidgen. *See* **bit**[1] (1).

irascibility *or* **irascibleness** *noun*
▶ crankiness, prickliness, tetchiness. *See* **temper** (1).

irascible *adjective*
1. Having or showing a bad temper ▶ cranky, grouchy, peevish. *See* **ill-tempered. 2.** Easily moved to anger ▶ choleric, quick-tempered, tetchy. *See* **testy** (1).

irate *adjective*
▶ cross, livid, rabid. *See* **angry.** *See synonym note at* **angry.**

irateness *noun*
▶ indignation, rage, wrath. *See* **anger.**

ire *noun*
▶ indignation, rage, wrath. *See* **anger.** *See synonym note at* **anger.**

ireful *adjective*
▶ enraged, infuriated, seething. *See* **angry.** *See synonym note at* **angry.**

irenic *adjective*
▸ conciliatory, pacifistic. *See* **peaceable.**

irk *verb*
▸ irritate, nettle, vex. *See* **annoy** (1). *See synonym note at* **annoy.**

irksome *adjective*
1. Troubling to the mind or emotions ▸ bothersome, irritating, unsettling. *See* **disturbing. 2.** Arousing no interest or curiosity ▸ dull, humdrum, monotonous. *See* **boring** (1). *See synonym note at* **boring.**

iron *adjective*
1. Full of vigor ▸ robust, strapping, sturdy. *See* **lusty** (1). **2.** Firmly, often unreasonably immovable in purpose or will ▸ bullheaded, dogged, obstinate. *See* **stubborn** (1). *See synonym note at* **stubborn.**

iron *verb*
To smooth by applying heat and pressure ▸ calender, roll. *See* **press** (2).

ironbound *adjective*
▸ coarse, ragged, scabrous. *See* **rough** (1).

ironclad *adjective*
▸ inflexible, invariable, unalterable. *See* **immutable** (1).

ironic *or* **ironical** *adjective*
▸ satiric, scoffing, sneering. *See* **sarcastic.** *See synonym note at* **sarcastic.**

irons *noun*
▸ chains, handcuffs, shackle. *See* **bond** (1).

irony *noun*
▸ acerbity, mordancy, trenchancy. *See* **sarcasm.**

irradiant *adjective*
▸ brilliant, incandescent, radiant. *See* **bright** (1).

irradiate *verb*
1. To send out heat, light, or energy ▸ cast (out), emit, radiate. *See* **shed**[1] (1). **2.** To render free of microorganisms ▸ decontaminate, disinfect, sanitize, sterilize.

irradicable *adjective*
▸ deep-seated, entrenched, ingrained, inveterate. *See* **confirmed** (1).

irrational *adjective*
1. Not governed by or predicated on reason ▸ illogical, unreasonable, unreasoned. *Idioms:* out of bounds, without rhyme or reason. *See also* **foolish. 2.** Containing errors in reasoning ▸ illogical, spurious, unsound. *See* **fallacious** (1).

irrationality *noun*
The absence of reason ▸ illogicality, illogicalness, unreason, unreasonableness. *See also* **fallacy, foolishness.**

irrefutable *adjective*
▸ inarguable, indisputable, sure. *See* **certain** (2).

irregular *adjective*
1. Not straight, uniform, or symmetrical ▸ asymmetric, asymmetrical, crooked, diversiform, nonuniform, variform. *See also* **uneven, rough. 2.** Departing from the normal ▸ aberrant, atypical, divergent. *See* **abnormal. 3.** Made up of parts or qualities that are disparate or otherwise markedly lacking in consistency ▸ discrepant, inconsistent. *See* **incongruous** (1). **4.**

Happening or appearing now and then ▸ occasional, periodic, sporadic. *See* **intermittent.**

irregularity *noun*
1. Lack of smoothness or regularity ▸ abrasiveness, asymmetry, bumpiness, choppiness, coarseness, crookedness, inequality, jaggedness, pockedness, raggedness, roughness, unevenness, ununiformity. **2.** The condition of being abnormal ▸ aberration, anomaly, deviation. *See* **abnormality.**

irrelevancy *noun*
▸ deviation, divergence, tangent. *See* **digression.**

irrelevant *adjective*
Not relevant or pertinent to the subject; not applicable ▸ extraneous, extrinsic, immaterial, impertinent, inapplicable, inapposite, unconnected, ungermane, unrelated. *Idioms:* beside the point, neither here nor there, off the subject (*or* topic), out of place. *See also* **digressive, trivial.**

✚ CORE SYNONYMS: *irrelevant, extraneous, immaterial, impertinent.* These adjectives mean not pertinent to the subject under consideration: *an irrelevant comment; a question extraneous to the discussion; an objection that is immaterial; mentioned several impertinent facts.*

◄ ANTONYM: *relevant*

---

irreligion *noun*
▸ disbelief, faithlessness, impiety. *See* **atheism.**

irreligious *adjective*
▸ disbelieving, faithless, impious. *See* **atheistic.**

irremediable *adjective*
▸ incurable, irreparable. *See* **hopeless** (1).

irremissible *adjective*
▸ unforgivable, unpardonable. *See* **inexcusable.**

irreparable *adjective*
▸ incurable, irremediable. *See* **hopeless** (1).

irreprehensible *adjective*
▸ faultless, unblamable. *See* **exemplary** (1).

irreproachable *adjective*
1. Beyond reproach ▸ faultless, unblamable. *See* **exemplary** (1). **2.** Free from guilt or blame ▸ faultless, guiltless, harmless. *See* **innocent** (2).

irresistible *adjective*
▸ inevitable, sure, unavoidable. *See* **certain** (1).

irresolute *adjective*
1. Given to or exhibiting hesitation ▸ indecisive, pendulous. *See* **hesitant** (1). **2.** Experiencing doubt ▸ hesitant, skeptical, uncertain. *See* **doubtful** (2).

irresolution *or* **irresoluteness** *noun*
▸ indecision, tentativeness. *See* **hesitation.**

irresponsible *adjective*
1. Lacking concern, attention, or regard ▸ feckless, heedless, unmindful. *See* **careless** (1). **2.** Not to be depended on ▸ fair-weather, untrustworthy. *See* **undependable** (1).

irretrievable *adjective*
That cannot be revoked or undone ▸ irreversible, irrevocable, unalterable. *Idiom:* beyond recall. *See also* **immutable, unchangeable.**

irreverence *noun*
> impoliteness, rudeness. *See* **disrespect** (1).

irreverent *adjective*
> contemptuous, discourteous, impolite. *See* **disrespectful** (1).

irreversible *adjective*
That cannot be revoked or undone > irretrievable, irrevocable, unalterable. *Idiom:* beyond recall. *See also* **immutable, unchangeable.**

irrevocable *adjective*
That cannot be revoked or undone > irretrievable, irreversible, unalterable. *Idiom:* beyond recall. *See also* **immutable, unchangeable.**

irritability *noun*
> crankiness, petulance, prickliness, tetchiness. *See* **temper** (1).

irritable *adjective*
> cranky, grouchy, peevish. *See* **ill-tempered.**

irritant *noun*
> bother, nuisance, plague. *See* **annoyance** (2).

irritate *verb*
1. To trouble the nerves or peace of mind of > bother, nettle, vex. *See* **annoy** (1). *See synonym note at* **annoy.**
2. To make the skin raw by friction > abrade, excoriate, rub. *See* **chafe** (1). 3. To cause pain, soreness, or discomfort to > inflame, pain. *See* **hurt** (3). 4. To cause to feel or show anger > incense, infuriate, madden. *See* **anger** (1).

irritated *adjective*
> annoyed, cross, irate. *See* **angry.**

irritating *adjective*
1. Troubling to the mind or emotions > bothersome, distressful, unsettling. *See* **disturbing.** 2. Marked by or causing pain > inflamed, raw, stinging. *See* **painful** (1).

irritation *noun*
1. The act of annoying or the state of being annoyed > bother, exasperation, vexation. *See* **annoyance** (1). 2. Something that annoys > bother, nuisance, vexation. *See* **annoyance** (2). 3. An instance of being irritated, as in a part of the body > festering, inflammation, rankling, redness, sensitiveness, soreness, tenderness. *See also* **bump, disease, pain.**

isochronal *or* **isochronous** *adjective*
> cyclical, recurrent. *See* **periodic.**

isolate *verb*
1. To set apart or cut off from others > alienate, close off, cut off, ghettoize, insulate, seclude, segregate, separate, sequester, sequestrate, set apart. *See also* **exclude.** 2. To put into solitude > cloister, seclude, sequester, sequestrate. *See also* **enclose, imprison.**

isolate *adjective*
Set away from or lacking the company of all others > alone, apart, removed. *See* **solitary** (1).

✦ CORE SYNONYMS: *isolate, insulate, seclude, segregate, sequester.* These verbs mean to set apart or cut off from others: *a mountain that isolated the village from larger towns; insulated herself from the chaos surround-*

ing her; a celebrity who was secluded from public scrutiny; segregated the infectious patients in a special ward; sequestering a jury during its deliberations.

isolated *adjective*
1. Set away from or lacking the company of all others > alone, detached, removed. *See* **solitary** (1). 2. Far from centers of human population > lonely, outlying, secluded. *See* **remote** (1).

isolation *noun*
1. The act or process of isolating > alienation, insulation, segregation, separation, sequestration. *See also* **breach.** 2. The act of secluding or the state of being secluded > reclusion, separateness, sequestration. *See* **seclusion** (1). 3. The quality or state of being alone > aloneness, loneliness. *See* **solitude.** *See synonym note at* **solitude.**

issue *noun*
1. The act or process of publishing printed matter > printing, release. *See* **publication** (1). 2. Something brought about by a cause > consequence, outcome, result. *See* **effect** (1). 3. A person or group descended directly from the same parents or ancestors > offspring, posterity, seed. *See* **progeny.** 4. A situation that presents difficulty, uncertainty, or perplexity > case, matter, question. *See* **problem** (1).

issue *verb*
1. To cause a liquid to flow in a steady stream > decant, empty, flow. *See* **pour** (1). 2. To discharge material, as vapor or fumes, usually suddenly and violently > give forth, give out, release. *See* **emit** (1). 3. To give out in portions or shares > allocate, apportion, dispense. *See* **distribute** (1). 4. To come into view > loom, materialize, show up. *See* **appear** (1). *See synonym note at* **appear.** 5. To have hereditary derivation > come, spring. *See* **descend** (3). 6. To present for circulation, exhibit, or sale > bring out, put out, release. *See* **publish** (1). 7. To have as a source > derive, emanate, originate. *See* **stem** (1). *See synonym note at* **stem.**

italicize *verb*
> accentuate, highlight. *See* **emphasize.**

itch *noun*
1. A strong wanting of what promises enjoyment or pleasure > craving, longing, yearning. *See* **desire** (1). 2. Sexual hunger > eroticism, lust, passion. *See* **desire** (2).

itch *verb*
To have a greedy, obsessive desire > crave, hunger, lust, thirst. *See also* **desire.**

item *noun*
1. A detail of news or information > article, bit, bulletin, dispatch, feature, flash, news flash, notice, paragraph, piece, squib, story, write up. *See also* **message, news, story.** 2. An individually considered portion of a whole > detail, particular. *See* **element** (3). 3. A small, often specialized element of a whole > particular, specialty, technicality. *See* **detail** (1). *See synonym note at* **detail.** 4. Something having material existence > article, body, thing. *See* **object** (1). 5. An

item inserted, as in a diary, register, or reference book ▸ heading, posting. *See* **entry** (1).

item *adverb*
In addition ▸ besides, furthermore, more. *See* **additionally.**

itemize *verb*
▸ list, tick off. *See* **enumerate** (1).

iterate *verb*
1. To state again ▸ reiterate, restate, retell. *See* **repeat** (1). *See synonym note at* **repeat. 2.** To happen again or repeatedly ▸ reappear, recur, reoccur, repeat.

iteration *noun*
▸ reiteration, repeat, restatement. *See* **repetition** (1).

iterative *adjective*
Characterized by repetition ▸ reiterative, repetitious, repetitive. *See also* **boring, superfluous, wordy.**

itinerant *adjective*
1. Moving from one area to another in search of work ▸ migrant, migratory. 2. Leading the life of a person without a fixed domicile; moving from place to place ▸ traveling, vagabond. *See* **nomadic. 3.** Traveling about, especially in search of adventure ▸ rambling, roving. *See* **errant** (1).

iterant *noun*
One who wanders without a permanent home or livelihood ▸ nomad, roamer, vagabond. *See* **hobo.**

ivory *adjective*
▸ alabaster, light, pale. *See* **fair¹** (9).

ivory-tower *adjective*
▸ academic, conceptual, speculative. *See* **theoretical** (1).

j

jab *verb*
1. To apply pressure on, against, or with ▸ press, prod, shove. *See* **push** (1). **2.** To pass into or through by overcoming resistance ▸ poke, puncture. *See* **penetrate** (1). **3.** To deliver a sudden, sharp blow to ▸ bash, sock, whack. *See* **hit** (1).

jab *noun*
1. An act of thrusting into or against, as to attract attention ▸ nudge, poke, prod. *See* **dig** (1). **2.** A sudden heavy stroke ▸ crack, hit, swat, whack. *See* **blow²** (1).

jabber *verb*
1. To talk rapidly, incoherently, or indistinctly ▸ chatter, gibber, prattle. *See* **babble** (1). **2.** To talk rapidly on trivial matters ▸ blab, natter, prattle. *See* **chatter** (1). **3.** To engage in or spread gossip ▸ rumor, whisper. *See* **gossip. 4.** To speak or utter indistinctly, as by lowering the voice or partially closing the mouth ▸ murmur, whisper. *See* **mutter** (1).

jabber *noun*
1. Empty or foolish talk ▸ blather, gibberish, twaddle. *See* **babble** (1). **2.** Incessant and inconsequential talk ▸ drivel, patter, small talk. *See* **chatter.**

jabberwocky *noun*
1. Highly technical, often deliberately deceptive language ▸ double talk, hocus-pocus, mumbo jumbo. *See* **gibberish** (1). **2.** Empty or foolish talk ▸ blather, jabber, twaddle. *See* **babble** (1).

jack *noun*
1. A piece of fabric used as a symbol ▸ banner, colors, pennant. *See* **flag¹** (1). **2.** *Slang* Something, such as coins or printed bills, used as a medium of exchange ▸ currency. *Slang:* dough, moola. *See* **money** (1). **3.** *Informal* A man referred to familiarly or as a member of one's group ▸ chap, guy. *See* **fellow** (1).

jack *verb*
1. To increase in amount ▸ boost, hike, jack up, jump, raise, up. **2.** To move something to a higher position ▸ hike (up), jack up, raise. *See* **elevate** (1).

Jack *noun*
▸ mariner, navigator, seafarer. *See* **sailor.**

jackass *noun*
▸ idiot, moron, simpleton. *See* **fool** (1).

jacket *noun*
1. An outer garment that has sleeves ▸ slicker, sportcoat, windbreaker. *See* **coat** (1). **2.** The material in which something is wrapped ▸ casing, covering. *See* **wrapper.**

jacket *verb*
To cover as if with clothes ▸ drape, robe. *See* **clothe** (1).

Jack-tar *noun*
▸ mariner, navigator, seafarer. *See* **sailor.**

jade *noun*
A person, typically a woman, who is sexually promiscuous ▸ tramp, wench. *See* **slut.**

jade *verb*
To make weary ▸ fatigue, wear out. *See* **tire** (1). *See synonym note at* **tire.**

jaded *adjective*
▸ exhausted, weary, worn-out. *See* **tired** (1).

jag¹ *noun*
1. *Slang* A drinking bout ▸ brannigan, carousal, carouse, spree. *See* **bender. 2.** *Slang* A period of uncontrolled self-indulgence ▸ rampage, spree. *See* **binge** (1). *See synonym note at* **binge.**

jag² *noun*
A sharp protuberance or projection ▸ prick, prong, spine. *See* **spike** (1).

jagged *adjective*
▶ coarse, ragged, scabrous. *See* **rough** (1). *See synonym note at* **rough.**

jaggedness *noun*
▶ coarseness, roughness, unevenness. *See* **irregularity** (1).

jail *noun*
A place for the confinement of persons in lawful detention ▶ brig, house of correction, keep, penitentiary, prison. *Informal:* lockup, pen. *Slang:* big house, calaboose, can, clink, cooler, coop, hoosegow, joint, jug, pokey, slammer, stir.

jail *verb*
To put in or as if in prison ▶ confine, incarcerate, lock (up). *See* **imprison.**

jailer *noun*
A guard or keeper of a prison ▶ turnkey, warden. *Slang:* screw. *See also* **guard, police officer.**

jam *verb*
1. To move into an area or space in large numbers ▶ cram, press, squeeze. *See* **crowd** (1). **2.** To fill to capacity ▶ load, pack, stuff. *See* **fill** (1). **3.** To apply pressure on, against, or with ▶ press, prod, shove. *See* **push** (1).

jam *noun*
1. The condition of being stopped ▶ immobilization, standstill, tie-up. *See* **stop** (2). **2.** A difficult, often embarrassing situation or condition ▶ corner, difficulty, fix. *See* **predicament.** *See synonym note at* **predicament. 3.** An act or instance of pushing ▶ press, shove, thrust. *See* **push** (1).

jam-pack *verb*
Informal To fill to capacity ▶ cram, jam, stuff. *See* **fill** (1).

Janus-faced *adjective*
▶ Pecksniffian, phony, two-faced. *See* **hypocritical.**

jape *noun*
▶ jest, quip, witticism. *See* **joke** (1).

jar *verb*
1. To fail to be in accord ▶ contrast, disagree, discord. *See* **conflict. 2.** To impair or destroy the composure of ▶ disorient, fluster, ruffle. *See* **agitate** (2). **3.** To cause to move to and fro with short, jerky movements ▶ jiggle, joggle, shake. **4.** To proceed with sudden, abrupt movements ▶ bounce, jounce, shake. *See* **bump** (1).

jar *noun*
A violent forcible contact ▶ crash, impact. *See* **collision.** *See synonym note at* **collision.**

jargon *noun*
1. Empty or foolish talk ▶ blather, jabber, twaddle. *See* **babble** (1). **2.** A variety of a language that differs from the standard form ▶ argot, vernacular. *See* **dialect** (1). *See synonym note at* **dialect. 3.** Specialized expressions indigenous to a particular field, subject, trade, or subculture ▶ argot, lingo, patois. *See* **language** (2).

jarring *adjective*
1. Disagreeable to the senses, especially the sense of hearing ▶ grating, hoarse. *See* **harsh** (1). **2.** Made up of parts or qualities that are disparate or otherwise markedly lacking in consistency ▶ discrepant, inconsistent. *See* **incongruous** (1).

jaundice *verb*
To cause to have a prejudiced view ▶ prejudice, warp. *See* **bias** (1). *See synonym note at* **bias.**

jaundice *noun*
Resentful or painful desire for another's advantages ▶ enviousness, jealousy. *See* **envy.**

jaundiced *adjective*
▶ invidious, jealous. *See* **envious.**

jaunt *noun*
1. A usually short journey taken for pleasure ▶ excursion, junket, outing, trip. *See also* **excursion, journey. 2.** A trip in a motor vehicle ▶ ride, run. *See* **drive** (3).

jaunt *verb*
To make or go on a journey ▶ peregrinate, travel, voyage. *See* **journey.**

jaunty *adjective*
▶ animated, chipper, vivacious. *See* **lively** (1).

jaw *verb*
Slang To talk rapidly on trivial matters ▶ blab, jabber, prattle. *See* **chatter** (1).

jaw *noun*
Slang Spoken exchange ▶ dialogue, discourse, discussion. *See* **conversation** (1).

jazz up *verb*
Informal To give or impart vitality and energy to ▶ invigorate, vitalize. *See* **energize.**

jealous *adjective*
1. Fearful of the loss of position or affection ▶ clinging, clutching, green-eyed, possessive. *See also* **envious. 2.** Resentfully or painfully desirous of another's advantages ▶ invidious, jaundiced. *See* **envious.**

jealousy *noun*
▶ enviousness, jaundice. *See* **envy.**

jeer *verb*
To subject to ridicule ▶ laugh at, lampoon, taunt. *See* **ridicule.**

jeer *noun*
An instance of mockery or derision ▶ cut, insult, scoff. *See* **taunt** (1).

jeering *adjective*
▶ satiric, scoffing, sneering. *See* **sarcastic.**

jejune *adjective*
▶ bland, vapid. *See* **insipid** (1).

jejuneness *noun*
1. The state or quality of being insipid ▶ innocuousness, vapidness. *See* **insipidity** (1). **2.** A lack of excitement, liveliness, or interest ▶ blandness, drabness, lifelessness. *See* **dullness** (1).

jell *or* **jelly** *verb*
▶ congeal, set. *See* **coagulate.** *See synonym note at* **coagulate.**

jellyfish *noun*
Informal A weak or an ineffectual person ▶ pushover. *Slang:* wimp. *See* **weakling.**

jeopardize *verb*
▶ imperil, threaten. *See* **endanger.** *See synonym note at* **endanger.**

jeopardous *adjective*
▸ chancy, hazardous, risky. *See* **dangerous.**

jeopardy *noun*
▸ hazard, peril, risk. *See* **danger.**

jeremiad *noun*
▸ diatribe, harangue. *See* **tirade.**

jerk *verb*
1. To move or cause to move with a sudden abrupt motion ▸ lurch, snap, twitch, wrench, yank. *See also* **move. 2.** To proceed with sudden, abrupt movements ▸ jounce, shake. *See* **bump** (1). **3.** An act of drawing back in an involuntary or instinctive fashion ▸ flinch, shrink, wince. *See* **recoil.**

jerk *noun*
1. A sudden motion, such as a pull ▸ lurch, snap, tug, twitch, wrench, yank. *See also* **pull. 2.** A nervous shaking of the body ▸ quiver, shake, twitch. *See* **tremor** (2). **3.** *Slang* A person who is deficient in judgment and good sense ▸ idiot, imbecile, nitwit. *See* **fool** (1). **4.** *Slang* An unpleasant, tiresome person ▸ chump. *Slang:* schmuck, twit. *See* **drip** (2).

✦ CORE SYNONYMS: *jerk, snap, twitch, wrench, yank.* These verbs mean to move with a sudden abrupt motion: *jerked the rope twice to pull it taut; snapped the lock shut; was twitching her mouth nervously; wrenched the stick out of his hand; yanked the door open abruptly.*

---

jerkiness *noun*
Slang Foolish behavior ▸ folly, silliness, tomfoolery. *See* **foolishness.**

jerky *adjective*
1. Marked by or affected with tremors ▸ quaky, quivery, shaky. *See* **tremulous** (1). **2.** *Slang* Displaying a lack of forethought and good sense ▸ daft, idiotic, ludicrous. *See* **foolish.**

jerry-rig *verb*
▸ rig up, throw together. *See* **improvise** (2).

jest *noun*
1. An object of amusement or laughter ▸ butt, joke, laughingstock, mockery. *Idiom:* figure of fun. *See also* **fool. 2.** Actions taken as a joke ▸ fun, game. *See* **play** (1). **3.** Words or actions intended to excite laughter or amusement ▸ gag, quip, witticism. *See* **joke** (1). *See synonym note at* **joke. 4.** A flippant or sarcastic remark ▸ barb, quip. *Slang:* wisecrack. *See* **crack** (5).

jest *verb*
1. *Informal* To make jokes; behave playfully ▸ joke, quip. *Informal:* clown (around), fool around, horse around. *Idioms:* crack wise, play the fool. *See also* **play. 2.** To subject to ridicule ▸ jeer (at), lampoon, taunt. *See* **ridicule.**

jester *noun*
▸ clown, comedian, humorist. *See* **joker.**

jet¹ *adjective*
Of the darkest color ▸ ebony, inky, onyx. *See* **black** (1).

jet² *noun*
A sudden swift stream of ejected liquid ▸ spout, spray, spurt, squirt. *See also* **flow.**

jet *verb*
To eject or be ejected in a sudden thin, swift stream ▸ spout, spray, spurt, squirt. *See also* **erupt, flow.**

jetsam *noun*
▸ debris, litter, rubbish. *See* **garbage** (1).

jet-setter *noun*
▸ globetrotter, traveler, vacationer. *See* **tourist.**

jettison *verb*
Informal To let go or get rid of as being useless or defective, for example ▸ dump, throw away. *Informal:* chuck. *See* **discard.**

jettison *noun*
The act of getting rid of something useless or used up ▸ elimination, riddance. *See* **disposal** (1).

jetty *adjective*
▸ ebony, inky, jet. *See* **black** (1).

jibber-jabber *verb*
To talk rapidly, incoherently, or indistinctly ▸ gabble, jabber, prattle. *See* **babble** (1).

jibber-jabber *noun*
Empty or foolish talk ▸ blather, gibberish, twaddle. *See* **babble** (1).

jibe¹ *verb*
Informal To be compatible, suitable, or in correspondence ▸ chime, correspond, match. *See* **agree** (1).

jibe² *verb*
See **gibe.**

jiffy *or* **jiff** *noun*
Informal A very brief interval of time ▸ instant, second, wink. *See* **flash** (2). *See synonym note at* **flash.**

jig *noun*
▸ deception, ploy, stratagem. *See* **trick** (1). *See synonym note at* **trick.**

jigger *noun*
1. A small amount of liquor ▸ shot, sip, tot. *See* **drop** (8). **2.** A small specialized mechanical device ▸ apparatus. *Informal:* widget. *Slang:* gizmo. *See* **gadget.**

jiggle *verb*
1. To cause to move to and fro with short, jerky movements ▸ jar, joggle, shake. **2.** To proceed with sudden, abrupt movements ▸ bounce, jounce, shake. *See* **bump** (1).

jihad *noun*
A goal served with great or uncompromising dedication ▸ cause, crusade. *See also* **drive.**

jillion *noun*
Informal An indeterminately great amount or number ▸ bunch, multiplicity. *See* **heap** (3).

jilted *adjective*
▸ deserted, forsaken, rejected. *See* **abandoned** (1).

jim-jams *noun*
Slang A state of nervous restlessness or agitation ▸ jumps, shivers, trembles. *See* **jitters.**

jingle *noun*
▸ hymn, lyrics, tune. *See* **song** (1).

jinx *noun*
Informal Something or someone believed to bring bad luck ▸ curse, evil eye, hex, hoodoo, Jonah.

jinx *verb*
Informal To bring bad luck or evil to ► curse, hex, hoodoo.

jitters *noun*
A state of nervous restlessness or agitation ► fidgets, jumps, shivers, trembles. *Informal:* all-overs, shakes. *Slang:* heebie-jeebies, jim-jams, whim-whams, willies.

jittery *adjective*
► fidgety, nervous. *See* **edgy.**

jive *verb*
Slang To tease or mock good-humoredly ► chaff, josh. *Informal:* kid. *See* **joke** (2).

job *noun*
1. Activity pursued as a livelihood ► career, employment, occupation. *See* **business** (2). 2. A post of employment ► billet, situation. *See* **position** (3). 3. A piece of work that has been assigned ► chore, duty, project. *See* **task** (1). *See synonym note at* **task.** 4. The proper activity of a person or thing ► purpose, role, task. *See* **function** (1). 5. *Informal* A difficult or tedious undertaking ► effort, grind, slog. *See* **task** (2).

jobbery *noun*
► dishonesty, improbity. *See* **corruption** (2).

jobholder *noun*
► hireling, staffer, worker. *See* **employee.**

jobholding *adjective*
► hired, working. *See* **employed** (1).

jobless *adjective*
Having no job ► idle, unemployed, unoccupied, workless. *Idioms:* out of (a job *or* employ *or* work).

jockey *verb*
1. To direct the course of carefully ► finesse, navigate. *See* **maneuver** (1). 2. To use stratagems in gaining an end ► engineer, finesse. *See* **maneuver** (2).

jocose *adjective*
► comical, humorous, laughable. *See* **funny** (1).

jocosity *or* **jocoseness** *noun*
1. A state of joyful exuberance ► glee, lightheartedness, mirth. *See* **merriment** (1). 2. The quality of being laughable or comical ► funniness, ridiculousness, wittiness. *See* **humor** (1).

jocular *adjective*
► comical, humorous, laughable. *See* **funny** (1).

jocularity *noun*
1. The quality of being laughable or comical ► funniness, ridiculousness, wittiness. *See* **humor** (1). 2. A state of joyful exuberance ► glee, lightheartedness, mirth. *See* **merriment** (1).

jocund *adjective*
► happy, jolly, jovial. *See* **cheerful** (1).

jocundity *noun*
► glee, lightheartedness, mirth. *See* **merriment** (1).

jog *verb*
1. To apply pressure on, against, or with ► press, prod, shove. *See* **push** (1). 2. To move on foot at a pace faster than a walk ► lope, scamper, trot. *See* **run** (1).

jog *noun*
1. An act of thrusting into or against, as to attract attention ► nudge, poke, prod. *See* **dig** (1). 2. A pace faster than a walk ► lope, trot. *See* **run** (1).

joggle *verb*
To cause to move to and fro with short, jerky movements ► jar, jiggle, shake.

join *verb*
1. To be contiguous to or next to ► meet, neighbor, touch. *See* **adjoin** (1). 2. To bring or come together into a united whole ► connect, unify, unite. *See* **combine** (1). *See synonym note at* **combine.** 3. To unite or be united in a relationship ► combine, connect, link. *See* **associate** (1). 4. To become a member of ► enlist, enroll, enter, muster in, sign up. *Informal:* sign on. 5. To form a united group ► group, unite. *See* **band²**. 6. To come together from different directions ► close, converge, meet, unite. 7. To work together toward a common end ► concur, unite. *See* **cooperate.** 8. To involve oneself in an activity ► engage, partake, share. *See* **participate** (1).

join *noun*
A point or position at which two or more things are joined ► coupling, juncture, seam. *See* **joint** (1).

joint *noun*
1. A point or position at which two or more things are joined ► connection, coupling, join, junction, juncture, seam, union. 2. *Slang* A disreputable or run-down bar or restaurant ► *Slang:* dive, dump, honky-tonk, juke house, juke joint. *Idiom:* hole in the wall. 3. *Slang* A place for the confinement of persons in lawful detention ► brig, penitentiary, prison. *See* **jail.**

joint *adjective*
1. Belonging to, shared by, or applicable to all alike ► general, mutual, public. *See* **common** (2). 2. Working together toward a common end ► collective, synergistic. *See* **cooperative** (1).

jointly *adverb*
In, into, or as a single body ► together. *Idioms:* as one, in one breath, in the same breath, in unison, with one accord, with one voice.

joist *noun*
► crossbeam, girder, timber. *See* **beam** (2).

joke *noun*
1. Words intended to excite laughter or amusement ► gag, jape, jest, one-liner, quip, sally, witticism. *Informal:* funny, knee-slapper, rib-tickler, zinger. *Slang:* ha-ha. *See also* **crack, taunt.** 2. A mischievous act ► caper, gag, trick. *See* **prank¹**. 3. *Informal* Something or someone uproariously funny ► *Informal:* hoot, laugh. *See* **scream** (3). 4. An object of amusement or laughter ► butt, jest, laughingstock, mockery. *Idiom:* figure of fun. *See also* **fool.**

joke *verb*
1. *Informal* To make jokes; behave playfully ► jest, quip. *Informal:* clown (around), fool around, horse around. *Idioms:* crack wise, play the fool. *See also* **play.** 2. To tease or mock good-humoredly ► banter, chaff, josh. *Informal:* kid, rib, ride. *Slang:* jive, rag, razz. *Idiom:* pull (someone's) leg.

+ CORE SYNONYMS: *joke, jest, witticism, quip, gag.* These nouns refer to something that is said or done in order to evoke laughter or amusement. *Joke* especially denotes an amusing story with a punch line at the end: *told jokes at the party. Jest* suggests frolicsome humor: *amusing jests that defused the tense situation.* A *witticism* is a witty, usually cleverly phrased remark: *a speech full of witticisms.* A *quip* is a clever, pointed, often sarcastic remark: *responded to the tough questions with quips. Gag* is principally applicable to a broadly comic remark or to comic by-play in a theatrical routine: *one of the most memorable gags in the history of vaudeville.*

joker *noun*
A person whose words or actions provoke or are intended to provoke amusement or laughter ▸ clown, comedian, comic, farceur, funnyman, humorist, jester, jokester, quipster, wag, wit, zany. *Informal:* card. *See also* **smart aleck.**
jokester *noun*
▸ clown, comedian, jester. *See* **joker.**
jollification *noun*
▸ jubilation, merrymaking, rejoicing. *See* **celebration** (3).
jollies *noun*
1. *Slang* Something that amuses, entertains, or pleases ▸ enjoyment, entertainment, sport. *See* **amusement.**
2. *Slang* A strong, pleasant feeling of excitement or stimulation ▸ lift. *Slang:* bang. *See* **thrill** (1).
jolliness *noun*
▸ glee, lightheartedness, mirth. *See* **merriment** (1).
jollity *noun*
1. A state of joyful exuberance ▸ glee, lightheartedness, joviality. *See* **merriment** (1). **2.** Joyful, exuberant activity ▸ gaiety, merrymaking, revelry. *See* **merriment** (2).
jolly *adjective*
1. Being in or showing good spirits ▸ happy, jolly, jovial. *See* **cheerful** (1). **2.** Having pleasant desirable qualities ▸ bonny, enjoyable, nice. *See* **good** (1).
jolt *verb*
1. To cause to experience a sudden momentary shock ▸ electrify, shock. *See* **startle** (1). **2.** To proceed with sudden, abrupt movements ▸ bounce, jounce, shake. *See* **bump** (1). **3.** To force to move or advance with or as if with blows or pressure ▸ butt, shove, slam. *See* **drive** (2).
jolt *noun*
1. A violent forcible contact ▸ crash, impact. *See* **collision.** *See synonym note at* **collision. 2.** Something that jars the mind or emotions ▸ blow, surprise, trauma. *See* **shock**[1] (1).
jongleur *noun*
▸ minstrel, troubadour. *See* **poet.**
josh *verb*
▸ banter, chaff. *Informal:* kid. *See* **joke** (2).
jostle *verb*
To apply pressure on, against, or with ▸ press, prod, shove. *See* **push** (1).

jostle *noun*
An act or instance of pushing ▸ press, shove, thrust. *See* **push** (1).
jot *noun*
▸ dash, drop, smidgen. *See* **bit**[1] (1).
jounce *noun*
▸ bounce, jar, shake. *See* **bump** (1).
journal *noun*
▸ commentaries, diary, reminiscences. *See* **memoir.**
journalist *noun*
▸ correspondent, editorialist, media. *See* **press** (1).
journey *noun*
The act of traveling from one place to another ▸ circuit, crossing, cruise, flight, odyssey, passage, peregrination, progress, transit, travel, traversal, trip, voyage, wayfaring. *See also* **expedition, trip.**
journey *verb*
To make or go on a journey ▸ fare, jaunt, pass, peregrinate, sightsee, tour, travel, trek, trip, voyage. *Idioms:* hit the road, see the country (*or* world). *See also* **hike, migrate, rove.**
joust *noun*
Any competition or test of opposing wills likened to the sport in which knights fought with lances ▸ tilt, tournament, tourney. *See also* **battle, competition.**
joust *verb*
To strive in opposition ▸ clash, combat, fight. *See* **contend** (1).
jovial *adjective*
▸ happy, jolly, jovial. *See* **cheerful** (1).
joviality *noun*
▸ glee, lightheartedness, mirth. *See* **merriment** (1).
joy *noun*
1. A feeling of gratification aroused by something good or desired ▸ bliss, enjoyment, pleasure. *See* **delight** (1). **2.** A condition of well-being and good spirits ▸ blessedness, bliss, felicity. *See* **happiness.**
joyful *adjective*
1. Providing joy and pleasure ▸ festive, joyous, mirthful. *See* **merry** (1). **2.** Being in or showing good spirits ▸ gleeful, happy, lighthearted. *See* **cheerful** (1). *See synonym note at* **cheerful.**
joyfulness *noun*
▸ blessedness, bliss, felicity. *See* **happiness.**
joyless *adjective*
1. Causing or expressing sorrow or sadness ▸ depressing, melancholy, mournful. *See* **sorrowful** (1). **2.** Dark and depressing ▸ bleak, desolate, somber. *See* **gloomy** (1).
joyous *adjective*
▸ convivial, festive, mirthful. *See* **merry** (1).
jubilance *noun*
▸ crowing, jubilation, triumph. *See* **exultation.**
jubilant *adjective*
Feeling or expressing an uplifting joy over a success or victory ▸ exultant, gloating, triumphant. *See also* **boastful.**
jubilate *verb*
▸ glory, triumph. *See* **exult** (1).

jubilation *noun*
1. The act or condition of feeling an uplifting joy over a success or victory ▸ jubilance, triumph. *See* **exultation. 2.** The act of showing joyful satisfaction in an event ▸ festivity, merrymaking, rejoicing. *See* **celebration** (3).

jubilee *noun*
▸ festival, festivity, revels. *See* **celebration** (1).

Judas *noun*
▸ double-crosser, traitor. *See* **betrayer.**

judge *verb*
1. To make a decision about (a controversy or dispute, for example) after deliberation, as in a court of law ▸ adjudge, adjudicate, arbitrate, decide, decree, determine, referee, rule, umpire. *Idiom:* sit in judgment. *See also* **hear. 2.** To arrive at a conclusion from evidence or reasoning ▸ deduce, gather. *See* **infer** (1). **3.** To make a judgment as to the worth or value of ▸ assay, calculate. *See* **estimate** (1). **4.** *Informal* To have an opinion ▸ deem, hold. *See* **believe** (3). **5.** To find fault with ▸ censure, fault, reprove. *Slang:* knock. *See* **criticize** (1).

judge *noun*
1. A person who evaluates and reports on the worth of something ▸ commentator, reviewer. *See* **critic** (1). **2.** A public official who decides cases brought before a court of law in order to administer justice ▸ jurist, jurisprudent, justice, justice of the peace, magistrate. *See also* **go-between. 3.** A person, usually appointed, who decides the issues of, decides the results of, or supervises the conduct of a competition or conflict ▸ arbiter, arbitrator, referee, umpire. *Informal:* ref, ump.

✦ CORE SYNONYMS: *judge, arbitrator, arbiter, referee, umpire.* These nouns denotes a person who decides the issues or results, or supervises the conduct, of a competition or conflict. *judge* is one capable of making rational, dispassionate, and wise decisions: *In this case, the jury members are the judges of the truth.* An *arbitrator* is either appointed or derives authority from the consent of the disputants: *An experienced arbitrator mediated the contract dispute.* An *arbiter* is one whose opinion or judgment is recognized as being unassailable or binding: *The critic considered himself an arbiter of fine literature.* A *referee* is an attorney appointed by a court to investigate and report on a case: *The referee handled many bankruptcy cases each month.* An *umpire* is a person appointed to settle an issue that arbitrators are unable to resolve: *The umpire studied complex tax cases.* In sports *referee* and *umpire* refer to officials who enforce the rules and settle points at issue.

---

judgment *noun*
1. A position arrived at by reasoning from premises ▸ conclusion, deduction, inference. *See also* **belief. 2.** The ability to make sensible decisions ▸ reason, sense, wisdom. *See* **common sense. 3.** The act or result of evaluating or appraising ▸ assessment, evaluation. *See estimate* (1). **4.** An authoritative or official decision

▸ decree, edict, pronouncement. *See* **ruling. 5.** Something thought to be true ▸ notion, persuasion, view. *See* **belief** (1). **6.** The act or an instance of finding fault ▸ censure, condemnation, denunciation. *See* **criticism** (1). **7.** Skill in perceiving, discriminating, or judging ▸ keenness, perceptiveness, shrewdness. *See* **discernment** (1).

judgmental *adjective*
1. Based on individual judgment or discretion ▸ personal, subjective. *See* **arbitrary** (1). **2.** Not tolerant of the beliefs or opinions of others ▸ close-minded, illiberal, racist. *See* **intolerant** (1). **3.** Inclined to judge too severely ▸ carping, overcritical. *See* **critical** (1).

judiciary *or* **judicature** *noun*
▸ forum, tribunal. *See* **court** (2).

judicious *adjective*
1. Proceeding from or exhibiting good judgment ▸ commonsensical, levelheaded, prudent. *See* **sensible** (1). **2.** Careful and slow in acting, moving, or deciding ▸ circumspect, measured, unhurried. *See* **deliberate** (3).

jug *noun*
Slang A place for the confinement of persons in lawful detention ▸ brig, penitentiary, prison. *See* **jail.**

juju *noun*
▸ mascot, talisman. *See* **charm** (1).

jumble *verb*
1. To put into total disorder ▸ garble, mess up, scramble. *See* **confuse** (4). **2.** To put out of proper order ▸ disarrange, disrupt, muddle. *See* **disorder** (1). **3.** To mix together so as to change the order of arrangement ▸ reconfigure, scramble. *See* **shuffle** (1). **4.** To cause to be unclear in mind or intent ▸ befuddle, bewilder, confound. *See* **confuse** (1).

jumble *noun*
1. A collection of various things ▸ conglomeration, hodgepodge, mishmash. *See* **assortment** (1). **2.** A lack of order or regular arrangement ▸ clutter, confusion, disarray. *See* **disorder** (1).

jumbled *adjective*
▸ disordered, topsy-turvy, upside-down. *See* **confused** (2).

jumbo *noun*
One that is extraordinarily large and powerful ▸ Goliath, monster, titan. *See* **giant.**

jumbo *adjective*
Of extraordinary size and power ▸ behemoth, colossal, gigantic, mighty. *See* **enormous.**

jump *verb*
1. To move off the ground by a muscular effort of the legs and feet ▸ hurdle, leap, pounce, spring, vault. *See also* **plunge. 2.** To move in a lively way ▸ skip, spring. *See* **bound**[1] (1). **3.** To move suddenly and involuntarily ▸ bolt, start. *See also* **bump, jerk. 4.** To catapult oneself from a disabled aircraft ▸ bail out, eject. **5.** To increase in amount ▸ boost, hike, jack (up), raise, up. **6.** To raise in rank ▸ elevate, upgrade. *See* **promote** (1).

jump on *verb*
To criticize for a fault or offense ▸ chide, rebuke,

reprimand, reproach, upbraid. *See* **chastise** (1).

jump up *verb*
To adopt a standing posture ► arise, rise. *See* **stand** (1).

jump *noun*
1. The act of jumping ► leap, pounce, spring, vault. *See also* **fall**. **2.** A sudden lively movement ► bounce, spring. *See* **bound¹** (2). **3.** A sudden and involuntary movement ► bolt, start, startle. *See also* **jerk, recoil**. **4.** *Informal* A dominating position, as in a conflict ► edge, upper hand. *See* **advantage** (3). **5.** The act of increasing or rising ► amplification, boost. *See* **increase** (1). **6.** The amount by which something is increased ► boost, hike. *See* **increase** (2). **7.** A progression upward in rank ► promotion, upgrade. *See* **advancement** (1). **8.** *Informal* Capacity for work or vigorous activity ► might, potency, power. *See* **energy**.

jumper *noun*
► frock, gown, shift. *See* **dress** (3).

jumpiness *noun*
► disquietude, uneasiness, unrest. *See* **restlessness**.

jumps
jumps *noun*
► fidgets, shivers, trembles. *See* **jitters**.

jump-start *verb*
Informal To give or impart vitality and energy to ► invigorate, vitalize. *See* **energize**.

jumpy *adjective*
► jittery, nervous. *See* **edgy**.

junction *noun*
1. The act or fact of coming together ► concentration, concourse, confluence, conflux, convergence, crossroads, gathering, meeting, terminal. *See also* **unification**. **2.** A point or position at which two or more things are joined ► coupling, juncture, seam. *See* **joint** (1).

juncture *noun*
1. A point or position at which two or more things are joined ► connection, coupling, joint, junction, seam, union. **2.** A decisive point ► crossroads, head. *See* **crisis** (1). *See synonym note at* **crisis**. **3.** The general point at which an event occurs ► instant, moment. *See* **occasion** (1).

jungle *noun*
1. An uninhabited region that is left in its natural state ► bush, outback. *See* **wilderness**. **2.** Something that is intricately and often bewilderingly complex ► labyrinth, maze, web. *See* **tangle** (1).

junior *adjective*
Below another in standing, importance, or status ► inferior, low, secondary. *See* **minor** (1).

junior *noun*
One belonging to a lower class or rank ► inferior, secondary. *See* **subordinate**.

junk *verb*
To let go or get rid of as being useless or defective, for example ► dump, throw away. *Informal:* chuck. *See* **discard**.

junk *noun*
Articles too small or numerous to be specified ► incidentals, miscellanea, oddments, things. *See* **odds and ends**.

junk *adjective*
Not sustaining or promoting health ► unhealthy, unhygienic, unsalutary. *See* **unwholesome** (1).

junket *noun*
1. A large, elaborately prepared meal ► banquet, feast, junket. *Informal:* feed, spread. **2.** A usually short journey taken for pleasure ► excursion, jaunt, outing, trip. *See also* **excursion, journey**.

junkie *noun*
► devotee, enthusiast, fancier. *See* **fan²**.

junky *noun*
► cheap, lousy, poor. *See* **shoddy** (1).

jurisdiction *noun*
► mandate, might. *Informal:* say-so, muscle. *See* **authority** (1).

jurisprudent *noun*
A public official who decides cases brought before a court of law in order to administer justice ► judge, jurist, justice, justice of the peace, magistrate. *See also* **judge**.

jurist *noun*
1. A public official who decides cases brought before a court of law in order to administer justice ► judge, jurisprudent, justice, justice of the peace, magistrate. *See also* **judge**. **2.** A person who practices law ► attorney, counsel. *See* **lawyer**.

jury-rig *verb*
► rig up, throw together. *See* **improvise** (2).

just *adjective*
1. Free from bias in judgment ► impartial, objective, unbiased. *See* **fair¹** (1). *See synonym note at* **fair¹**. **2.** Consistent with prevailing or accepted standards or circumstances ► appropriate, deserved, due, fit, fitting, merited, proper, right, rightful, suitable. *See also* **relevant**. **3.** Within, allowed by, or sanctioned by the law ► legal, permitted, valid. *See* **lawful**. **4.** Based on good judgment, reasoning, or evidence ► valid, well-founded. *See* **sound²** (1).

just *adverb*
1. In an exact manner ► literally, precisely. *See* **exactly** (1). **2.** With precision or absolute conformity ► exactly, precisely, squarely. *See* **directly** (3). **3.** To the fullest extent ► fully, totally, utterly. *See* **completely** (1). **4.** Not long ago ► newly, recently. *See* **lately**. **5.** By a very little; almost not ► barely, hardly, scarce, scarcely. *Idioms:* by a hair (*or* whisker), by the skin of one's teeth. *See also* **approximately, merely, only**. **6.** Nothing more than ► but, merely, only, simply. *See also* **barely, solely**. **7.** To the exclusion of anyone or anything else ► exclusively, only. *See* **solely** (1).

justice *noun*
1. The quality or state of being just and unbiased ► impartiality, nonpartisanship, objectivity. *See* **fairness**. **2.** The state, action, or principle of treating all persons equally in accordance with the law ► due process, equitableness, equity. *See also* **legality**. **3.** A public official who decides cases brought before a

court of law in order to administer justice ▸ judge, jurisprudent, jurist, justice of the peace, magistrate. *See also* **judge. 4.** The power of an argument to convince or compel agreement ▸ force, persuasiveness. *See* **cogency.**

justice of the peace *noun*
A public official who decides cases brought before a court of law in order to administer justice ▸ judge, jurist, jurisprudent, justice, magistrate. *See also* **judge.**

justifiable *adjective*
Capable of being justified ▸ defensible, excusable, tenable. *See also* **logical, sound².**

justification *noun*
1. A statement that justifies or defends something, such as a past action or policy ▸ defense, vindication. *See* **apology** (1). *See synonym note at* **apology. 2.** A statement of causes or motives ▸ explanation, rationale, rationalization, reason. *See* **account** (1). **3.** A justifying fact or consideration ▸ foundation, reason. *See* **basis** (2). **4.** A basis for an action ▸ call, grounds, occasion. *See* **cause** (2). **5.** That which confirms ▸ authentication, corroboration, proof, verification. *See* **confirmation** (2). **6.** An explanation offered to justify an action or make it better understood ▸ pretext, rationale. *See* **excuse** (1). **7.** A freeing or clearing from accusation or guilt ▸ exoneration, vindication. *See* **exculpation.**

justify *verb*
1. To show to be just, right, or valid ▸ excuse, rationalize, vindicate. *Idiom:* make a case for. **2.** To be an appropriate occasion for ▸ call for, befit, occasion, warrant. *See also* **suit. 3.** To assure the certainty or validity of ▸ authenticate, corroborate, substantiate, verify. *See* **confirm** (1). **4.** To support against arguments, attack, or criticism ▸ maintain, vindicate. *See* **defend** (2). **5.** To offer reasons for or a cause of ▸ account for, explain, rationalize. *See also* **clarify,**

resolve. **6.** To free from a charge of guilt ▸ acquit, exonerate, vindicate. *See* **clear** (9). **7.** To establish as true or genuine through evidence ▸ confirm, substantiate, validate. *See* **prove** (1).

justly *adverb*
▸ equitably, evenhandedly, impartially. *See* **fairly** (1).

justness *noun*
▸ impartialness, nonpartisanship, objectiveness. *See* **fairness.**

jut *verb*
To curve outward past the normal or usual limit ▸ overhang, project, protrude. *See* **bulge** (1). *See synonym note at* **bulge.**

jut *noun*
A part that protrudes or extends outward ▸ knob, protrusion, protuberance. *See* **projection** (1).

juvenescence *noun*
▸ juvenility, puberty, salad days. *See* **youth** (1).

juvenile *adjective*
1. Being in an early period of growth or development ▸ immature, youthful. *See* **young.** *See synonym note at* **young. 2.** Of or characteristic of a child, especially in immaturity ▸ childlike, immature, infantile. *See* **childish.**

juvenile *noun*
1. A young person between birth and puberty ▸ tot, youngster. *See* **child** (1). **2.** One who is not yet legally of age ▸ child, minor, underage person. *See also* **child, youth.**

juvenile delinquent *noun*
▸ brat, imp, whelp. *See* **urchin.**

juvenility *noun*
▸ adolescence, puberty, salad days. *See* **youth** (1).

juxtapose *verb*
▸ contrast, counterpose, weigh. *See* **compare** (1).

juxtaposition *noun*
▸ comparison, counterpoint. *See* **contrast.**

k

kaleidoscopic *adjective*
▸ fluid, transformable, unsettled, variable. *See* **changeable** (1).

kaput *adjective*
Informal No longer effective, capable, or valuable ▸ done for, finished, washed-up. *See* **through** (2).

katzenjammer *noun*
1. Unpleasant physical and mental effects following overindulgence in alcohol ▸ crapulence, hangover. *Informal:* head. **2.** Loud and insistent utterances or noisemaking, usually expressing disapproval ▸ hullabaloo, rumpus, uproar. *See* **vociferation.**

keel *verb*
▸ roll, seesaw, yaw. *See* **lurch** (1).

keel over *verb*
1. To lose consciousness temporarily ▸ black out, faint, pass out, swoon. *Idioms:* drop (*or* faint) dead away, see stars. **2.** To come to the ground from an upright position ▸ topple, tumble. *See* **fall** (2).

keen¹ *adjective*
1. Having a fine edge, as for cutting ▸ honed, whetted. *See* **sharp** (1). **2.** Mentally quick and original ▸ bright, quick-witted, sharp. *See* **clever** (1). **3.** Keenly perceptive or discerning ▸ incisive, penetrating, sharp. *See*

critical (2). **4.** Showing or having enthusiasm ▸ fervent, rabid, zealous. *See* **enthusiastic** (1). **5.** Intensely desirous or interested ▸ avid, bursting. *See* **eager** (1). **6.** *Slang* Particularly excellent ▸ fantastic, sensational, superb. *See* **marvelous** (1). **7.** Having an end that tapers to a point ▸ acute, cuspate, sharp. *See* **pointed** (1).

keen² *verb*
To shed tears ▸ howl, sob, weep. *See* **cry** (1). *See synonym note at* **cry.**

keenness *noun*
1. A cutting quality ▸ incisiveness, sharpness. *See* **edge** (1). **2.** Skill in perceiving, discriminating, or judging ▸ insight, perceptiveness, shrewdness. *See* **discernment** (1).

keep *verb*
1. To have and maintain in one's possession ▸ reserve, retain. *See* **hold** (1). *See synonym note at* **hold. 2.** To have for sale ▸ carry, deal (in), offer, stock. **3.** To supply with the necessities of life ▸ maintain, provide for, support. *Idiom:* take care of. *See also* **nourish. 4.** To have or put in a customary place ▸ cache, put, store. **5.** To remain fresh and unspoiled ▸ last. **6.** To persevere in some condition, action, or belief ▸ keep to, maintain, retain, stay with, stick to, stick with, sustain. **7.** To be in existence or in a certain state for an indefinitely long time ▸ go on, persist, remain, stay. *See* **endure** (2). **8.** To control, restrict, or arrest ▸ bridle, check, curb. *See* **restrain. 9.** To hold oneself back ▸ forbear, hold off, withhold. *See* **refrain. 10.** To hold or store for future use ▸ lay aside, salt away, set by. *See* **save** (1). **11.** To carry out the functions, requirements, or terms of ▸ discharge, execute, implement. *See* **fulfill** (1). **12.** To act in conformity with ▸ heed, obey, observe. *See* **follow** (4). **13.** To mark a day or an event with ceremonies of respect, festivity, or rejoicing ▸ celebrate, commemorate, observe, solemnize. *See synonym note at* **celebrate.** *See also* **sanctify. 14.** To cause to be later or slower than expected or desired ▸ hang up, retard, stall. *See* **delay** (1).

keep back *verb*
1. To have and maintain in one's possession ▸ reserve, retain. *See* **hold** (1). **2.** To hold something requiring an outlet in check ▸ smother, stifle, suppress. *See* **repress. 3.** To control, restrict, or arrest ▸ hold in, pull in, rein (back, in, *or* up). *See* **restrain. 4.** To control, restrict, or arrest ▸ bridle, check, curb. *See* **restrain.**

keep off *verb*
To turn aside or drive away ▸ deflect, repulse, ward off. *See* **repel.**

keep on *verb*
To put up with or continue despite difficulties ▸ go on, persevere, soldier on. *See* **endure** (1).

keep out *verb*
To keep from being admitted, included, or considered ▸ eliminate, exclude, rule out. *See* **exclude** (1).

keep up *verb*
To keep in a condition of good repair, efficiency, or use ▸ maintain, preserve, sustain.

keep *noun*
1. The means needed to support life ▸ alimony, bread, livelihood. *See* **living. 2.** A place for the confinement of persons in lawful detention ▸ penitentiary, prison. *Informal:* lockup. *See* **jail.**

keeper *noun*
One who is legally responsible for the care and management of the person or property of an incompetent or a minor ▸ caretaker, conservator, custodian, guardian. *See also* **representative.**

keeping *noun*
1. The function of watching, guarding, or overseeing ▸ charge, custody, guardianship. *See* **care** (2). *See synonym note at* **care. 2.** The act or state of agreeing or conforming ▸ concordance, harmony, rapport. *See* **agreement** (2). **3.** The act of observing a day or an event with ceremonies ▸ fiesta, holiday, observance. *See* **celebration** (2).

keepsake *noun*
▸ memento, reminder. *See* **remembrance** (1).

keg *noun*
▸ barrel, cask, tank. *See* **vat.**

ken *noun*
The extent of one's perception, understanding, knowledge, or vision ▸ horizon, purview, range, reach, scope. *See also* **awareness, area.**

kennel *noun*
1. An enclosure used for confining an animal or bird ▸ coop, stall. *See* **cage. 2.** A number of animals considered collectively ▸ litter, pack. *See* **flock** (1). *See synonym note at* **flock.**

kernel *noun*
1. A fertilized plant ovule capable of germinating ▸ grain, pip, pit, seed. **2.** A source of further growth and development ▸ nucleus, seed. *See* **germ** (2). **3.** The most central or essential part ▸ essence, marrow, quintessence. *See* **heart** (1).

key *noun*
1. A means or method of entering into or achieving something that is desirable ▸ formula, route, secret. *Informal:* ticket. *See also* **trick. 2.** A solution, as to a problem ▸ explanation, resolution, solution. *See* **answer** (2).

key *adjective*
1. Most important, influential, or significant ▸ central, main, pivotal. *See* **primary** (1). **2.** Exercising controlling power or influence ▸ chief, predominant, reigning. *See* **dominant** (1). **3.** Having great significance ▸ consequential, grand, meaningful. *See* **important** (1).

keystone *noun*
▸ cornerstone, foundation, underpinning. *See* **basis** (1).

kibitz *verb*
Informal To intervene officiously or indiscreetly in the affairs of others ▸ horn in, interlope, interfere. *See* **meddle** (1).

kibitzer *noun*
Informal A person who meddles or pries into the

affairs of others ▸ meddler, quidnunc, snooper. *See* **busybody.**

kick *verb*
1. *Informal* To express feelings of pain, dissatisfaction or resentment ▸ fuss, grouch, whine. *See* **complain.** **2.** *Informal* To express opposition ▸ except, oppose, protest. *See* **object** (1). **3.** *Slang* To discontinue (a habit, for example) ▸ abjure, give up, leave off. *See* **break** (17).

kick around *verb*
Informal To speak together and exchange ideas and opinions about ▸ converse, debate. *Informal:* knock about (around). *See* **discuss.**

kick back *verb*
To take repose by ceasing work or other effort for an interval of time ▸ chill out, unbend, unwind. *See* **rest¹** (1).

kick in *verb*
1. *Informal* To give in common with others ▸ donate, subscribe. *See* **contribute** (1). **2.** *Slang* To cease living ▸ demise, expire, perish. *See* **die** (1).

kick off *verb*
1. *Informal* To go about the initial step in doing something ▸ inaugurate, embark, launch. *See* **start** (1). **2.** *Slang* To cease living ▸ demise, expire, perish. *See* **die** (1).

kick out *verb*
To put out by force ▸ dismiss, evict. *See* **eject** (1).

kick *noun*
1. *Slang* The act of expressing strong or reasoned opposition ▸ challenge, protest, remonstrance. *See* **objection. 2.** *Slang* A stimulating or intoxicating effect ▸ charge, potency. *Informal:* punch, sting, wallop. **3.** *Slang* A strong, pleasant feeling of excitement or stimulation ▸ lift. *Informal:* wallop. *Slang:* bang. *See* **thrill** (1). **4.** *Slang* A temporary concentration of interest ▸ *Slang:* trip. **5.** *Slang* A clever, unexpected new trick or method ▸ twist. *Slang:* angle. *See* **wrinkle** (2). **6.** *Slang* An expression of pain or dissatisfaction ▸ carp, whimper, whine. *See* **complaint** (1).

kickback *noun*
▸ fix, graft. *Informal:* payoff. *See* **bribe.**

kicker *noun*
▸ twist. *Slang:* angle, kick. *See* **wrinkle** (2).

kickoff *noun*
Informal The act of bringing or being brought into existence ▸ inception, initiation, start. *See* **beginning** (1).

kicks *noun*
Slang Something that amuses, entertains, or pleases ▸ diversion, entertainment, sport. *See* **amusement.**

kid *noun*
1. *Informal* A young person between birth and puberty ▸ juvenile, tot, youngster. *See* **child** (1). **2.** *Informal* A young person, usually between the ages of 13 and 19 ▸ adolescent, juvenile, youth. *See* **teenager.**

kid *verb*
Informal To tease or mock good-humoredly ▸ chaff, josh. *Informal:* kid. *See* **joke** (2).

kidlike *noun*
Informal Of or like a baby ▸ childlike, infantile. *See* **babyish** (1).

kidnap *verb*
To seize and detain a person unlawfully ▸ abduct, snatch, spirit away, take hostage. *See also* **seize, steal.**

kids *noun*
Informal Young people collectively ▸ young, youth.

kill¹ *verb*
1. To cause the death of ▸ carry off, cut down, cut off, destroy, dispatch, execute, finish (off), slay. *Slang:* hit, ice, rub out, waste, wipe out, zap. *Idioms:* put an end to, put to death, put to sleep, take the life of. *See also* **massacre. 2.** To take the life of a person or persons unlawfully ▸ assassinate, slay. *See* **murder** (1). **3.** To destroy all traces of ▸ eradicate, liquidate, obliterate. *See* **annihilate** (1). **4.** To spend (time) idly or pleasantly ▸ trifle away, waste. *See* **idle** (2). **5.** To keep from being published or transmitted ▸ stifle, suppress, withhold. *See* **censor** (2). **6.** To cause great pain or suffering to ▸ plague, rack, torment. *See* **afflict.**

kill *noun*
A loss of life, or one who has lost life, usually as a result of accident, disaster, or war ▸ casualty, death, fatality, loss. *See also* **victim.**

kill² *noun*
A small stream ▸ rill, watercourse. *See* **brook¹.**

killer *noun*
▸ assassin, massacrer, slayer. *See* **murderer.**

killing *noun*
The crime of murdering someone ▸ homicide, manslaughter. *See* **murder.**

killing *adjective*
Causing laughter or amusement ▸ hilarious, laughable, priceless. *See* **funny** (1).

killjoy *noun*
One who spoils the enthusiasm or fun of others ▸ frump, spoilsport. *Informal:* stick-in-the-mud, wet blanket. *Slang:* bummer, downer, party pooper, pill. *Idiom:* dog in the manger. *See also* **grouch, square.**

kilter *noun*
▸ fettle, form, order. *See* **shape** (1).

kin *noun*
One's relatives collectively ▸ family, folks, kindred, kinfolk, kith and kin, people. *See also* **relative.**

kin *adjective*
1. Connected by or as if by kinship or common origin ▸ akin, allied, related. *See* **kindred. 2.** Possessing the same or almost the same characteristics ▸ analogous, similar, uniform. *See* **like².**

kind¹ *adjective*
Characterized by kindness and concern for others ▸ beneficent, goodhearted, kindly. *See* **benevolent** (1). *See synonym note at* **benevolent.**

kind² *noun*
A class that is defined by the common attribute or attributes possessed by all its members ▸ brand, breed, cast, denomination, description, feather, form, genus, ilk, lot, manner, mold, nature, order, persua-

sion, sort, species, stamp, stripe, type, variety. *See also* **class.**

kindhearted *adjective*
▸ beneficent, goodhearted, kindly. *See* **benevolent** (1). *See synonym note at* **benevolent.**

kindheartedness *noun*
▸ goodwill, humanity, philanthropy. *See* **benevolence** (1).

kindle *verb*
1. To begin or cause to begin burning ▸ fire, ignite. *See* **light**[1] (1). **2.** To arouse the emotions of ▸ impassion, inspire, stir. *See* **fire** (2). **3.** To induce or elicit a reaction ▸ awaken, stir (up). *See* **arouse** (1). **4.** To become brighter ▸ illuminate, lighten. *See* **clear** (1).

kindliness *noun*
1. Kindly, charitable interest in others ▸ goodwill, kindheartedness, philanthropy. *See* **benevolence** (1). **2.** A kindly act ▸ good deed, kindness. *See* **favor** (1).

kindly *adjective*
1. Charcaterized by kindness and concern for others ▸ beneficent, goodhearted. *See* **benevolent** (1). **2.** Of a sympathetic, considerate character ▸ compassionate, softhearted, tender, tenderhearted. *See* **gentle** (1).

kindness *noun*
1. Kindly, charitable interest in others ▸ goodwill, kindheartedness, philanthropy. *See* **benevolence** (1). **2.** The quality of being pleasant and friendly ▸ agreeability, congeniality, pleasantness. *See* **amiability. 3.** A kindly act ▸ good deed, kindness. *See* **favor** (1). **4.** Thoughtful attention to others ▸ concern, regard, thoughtfulness. *See* **consideration** (1).

kind office *noun*
▸ good deed, kindness. *See* **favor** (1).

kindred *noun*
1. A group of people sharing common ancestry ▸ clan, lineage, tribe. *See* **family** (2). **2.** One's relatives collectively ▸ family, kinfolk. *See* **kin.**

kindred *adjective*
Connected by or as if by kinship or common origin ▸ agnate, akin, allied, cognate, connate, connatural, consanguine, consanguineous, kin, related. *See also* **ancestral.**

kinetic *adjective*
▸ brisk, lively, vigorous. *See* **energetic.**

kinfolk *or* **kinfolks** *noun*
▸ family, kindred. *See* **kin.**

king *noun*
▸ boss, director, head, leader. *See* **chief** (1).

kink *noun*
Something with a curled or spiral shape ▸ curlicue, spiral, twist. *See* **curl.**

kink *verb*
To curve or yield under pressure ▸ buckle, sag. *See* **bend** (3).

kinsman *or* **kinswoman** *noun*
1. A person connected to another person by blood or marriage ▸ relation, relative. *See also* **ancestry, family, kin. 2.** A person who is from one's own country

▸ compatriot, countryman, countrywoman, fellow citizen, kinswoman.

kismet *noun*
▸ destiny, fortune, predestination. *See* **fate** (1).

kiss *verb*
1. To touch or caress with the lips, especially as a sign of passion or affection ▸ buss, osculate, smack. *Informal:* peck. *Slang:* lock lips, make out, smooch, suck face, swap spit. *See also* **neck. 2.** To make light and momentary contact with, as in passing ▸ graze, skim. *See* **brush**[1].

kiss *noun*
1. The act or an instance of kissing ▸ buss, osculation, smack, smacker. *Informal:* peck. *Slang:* smooch. **2.** Light and momentary contact with another person or thing ▸ graze, skim. *See* **brush**[1] (1).

kisser *noun*
1. *Slang* The front surface of the head ▸ countenance, visage. *See* **face** (1). **2.** *Slang* The opening in the body through which food is ingested ▸ chops. *Slang:* trap. *See* **mouth** (1).

kit *noun*
1. A container carried on the back or around the waist ▸ backpack, knapsack. *See* **pack** (1). **2.** A container or piece of luggage for carrying clothing and other items ▸ carryon, grip, valise. *See* **suitcase.**

kith and kin *noun*
▸ family, kindred. *See* **kin.**

kitty *noun*
▸ ante, pot, wager. *See* **bet** (1). *See synonym note at* **bet.**

klutz *noun*
1. *Informal* A large, ungainly, and dull-witted person ▸ lout, ox. *Informal:* lummox. *See* **oaf. 2.** *Slang* A clumsy, inept person ▸ bungler. *Slang:* screwup. *See* **blunderer.**

klutzy *adjective*
Slang Lacking dexterity and grace in physical movement ▸ gawky, graceless. *See* **awkward** (1).

knack *noun*
1. The proper method for doing, using, or handling something ▸ feel, trick. *Informal:* hang. **2.** Natural or acquired skill or talent ▸ command, mastery, proficiency. *See* **ability** (1). *See synonym note at* **ability. 3.** An innate capability ▸ faculty, gift, instinct. *See* **talent.**

knapsack *noun*
▸ backpack, kit. *See* **pack** (1).

knave *noun*
▸ cheater, swindler, trickster. *See* **cheat** (2).

knead *verb*
1. To handle in a way so as to mix, form, and shape ▸ manipulate, squeeze, work. **2.** To move over or along with pressure ▸ manipulate, massage, press, work. *See* **rub** (2).

kneel *verb*
▸ curtsy, genuflect. *See* **bow**[1] (1).

knee-slapper *noun*
Informal Words or actions intended to excite laughter or amusement ▸ jest, quip, witticism. *See* **joke** (1).

knell *verb*
▸ bong, chime, peal. *See* **ring²** (1).

knickknack *noun*
▸ bauble, trinket. *See* **novelty** (3).

knife *verb*
1. To penetrate with a sharp edge ▸ bayonet, incise, pierce, slash. *See* **cut** (1). **2.** *Informal* To be treacherous to ▸ turn in. *Slang:* sell out. *See* **betray** (1).

knifelike *adjective*
▸ acute, gnawing, piercing. *See* **sharp** (8).

knightly *adjective*
▸ chivalrous, gentlemanly. *See* **gallant** (1).

knob *noun*
1. A part that protrudes or extends outward ▸ bulge, protrusion, protuberance. *See* **projection** (1). **2.** An unevenness or elevation on a surface ▸ lump, protuberance. *See* **bump** (1).

knock *verb*
1. To deliver a sudden, sharp blow to ▸ jab, sock, whack. *See* **hit** (1). **2.** To strike together noisily ▸ crack, slam, thump. *See* **bang** (1). **3.** To come together with force ▸ crash, impact. *See* **collide** (1). **4.** *Slang* To find fault with ▸ censure, fault, reprove. *See* **criticize** (1).

knock about *or* **around** *verb*
1. To be rough or brutal with ▸ rough up, slap around. *See* **manhandle** (1). **2.** To injure or damage, as by abuse or heavy wear ▸ maul, rough up. *See* **batter** (1). **3.** *Informal* To speak together and exchange ideas and opinions about ▸ converse, debate. *Informal:* kick around. *See* **discuss**.

knock down *verb*
1. To bring down, as from a shot or blow ▸ floor, ground, hew. *See* **drop** (6). **2.** To pull down or break up so that reconstruction is impossible ▸ dismantle, level, tear down. *See* **destroy** (2).

knock off *verb*
1. *Informal* To take away a quantity from another ▸ discount, subtract. *See* **deduct** (1). **2.** *Slang* To take the life of a person or persons unlawfully ▸ kill, slay. *See* **murder** (1). **3.** *Slang* To take property or possessions from someone unlawfully and usually forcibly ▸ mug, stick up. *See* **rob** (1). **4.** *Informal* To make a copy of ▸ imitate, replicate. *See* **copy** (1). **5.** To cease an activity ▸ discontinue, quit. *See* **abandon** (2).

knock out *verb*
1. To render powerless or motionless, as by inflicting severe injury ▸ handicap, immobilize, paralyze. *See* **disable** (1). **2.** *Informal* To make weary ▸ exhaust, wear out. *See* **tire** (1). **3.** To administer especially a painkilling drug to someone ▸ medicate, narcotize, tranquilize. *See* **drug** (1).

knock over *verb*
To turn or cause to turn from a vertical or horizontal position ▸ capsize, topple. *See* **overturn** (1).

knock together *verb*
To make or form a structure ▸ erect, raise. *See* **build** (1).

knock *noun*
1. The sound made by a light blow ▸ rap, rapping, tap,
tapping. **2.** A violent forcible contact ▸ crash, impact. *See* **collision**. **3.** A stroke or blow that produces a sound ▸ thud, thump. *See* **beat** (1). **4.** The act or an instance of finding fault ▸ censure, condemnation, denunciation. *See* **criticism** (1).

knockabout *adjective*
▸ arduous, strenuous, tough. *See* **rough** (7).

knocked-out *adjective*
Informal Depleted of energy ▸ exhausted, weary, worn-out. *See* **tired** (1).

knocked-up *adjective*
Slang Carrying a developing fetus within the uterus ▸ expectant, parturient. *See* **pregnant** (1).

knockoff *noun*
▸ imitation, simulation. *See* **copy** (2).

knockout *noun*
1. *Slang* A person regarded as physically attractive ▸ lovely, stunner. *See* **beauty** (1). **2.** The act of conquering ▸ triumph, victory. *See* **conquest**. **3.** *Informal* A dazzling, often sudden instance of success ▸ winner. *Informal:* smash. *See* **hit** (3).

knoll *noun*
▸ prominence, rise. *See* **hill** (1).

knot *noun*
1. That which unites or binds ▸ ligature, link, tie. *See* **bond** (2). **2.** A number of individuals making up or considered as a unit ▸ body, cluster, collection. *See* **group** (1). **3.** Something that is intricately and often bewilderingly complex ▸ labyrinth, maze, web. *See* **tangle** (1). **4.** An unevenness or elevation on a surface ▸ lump, protuberance. *See* **bump** (1). **5.** A small raised area of skin, as from a blow or sting ▸ lump, swelling. *See* **bump** (2). **6.** A part that protrudes or extends outward ▸ knob, protrusion, protuberance. *See* **projection** (1).

knot *verb*
1. To make fast or firmly fixed, as by means of a cord or rope ▸ bind, fasten, secure, tie, tie up. **2.** To make secure ▸ bind, chain, moor. *See* **fasten** (1). **3.** To make complex, intricate, or perplexing ▸ entangle, perplex, tangle. *See* **complicate**.

knotty *adjective*
▸ convoluted, elaborate, involved, labyrinthine. *See* **complex** (1). *See synonym note at* **complex**.

know *verb*
1. To perceive directly with the intellect ▸ apprehend, compass, comprehend, fathom, grasp. *Idioms:* be sure, be certain. *See also* **understand**. **2.** To be acquainted with ▸ know of, know about. *Idioms:* be acquainted with, be aware of. **3.** To participate in or partake of personally ▸ encounter, undergo. *See* **experience**. **4.** To undergo an emotional reaction ▸ experience, feel, have, savor, taste. **5.** To perceive to be identical with something held in the memory ▸ recognize. **6.** To recognize as being different ▸ differentiate, discriminate, single out. *See* **distinguish** (1). **7.** To establish the identity of ▸ identify, pinpoint. *See* **place** (1).

knowable *adjective*
► comprehensible, fathomable, intelligible. *See* **understandable** (1).

know-how *noun*
Informal Natural or acquired facility in a specific activity ► command, expertise, knack. *See* **ability** (1). *See synonym note at* **ability.**

knowing *adjective*
1. Having or showing intelligence, often of a high order ► intellectual, knowledgeable. *See* **intelligent** (1). *See synonym note at* **intelligent. 2.** Having deep knowledge and understanding ► sagacious, sage, sapient, wise. **3.** Cleverly aware and resourceful in practical matters ► astute, canny. *See* **shrewd** (1).

know-it-all *noun*
Informal One who is obnoxiously self-assertive and arrogant ► *Slang:* wisecracker, wise guy. *See* **smart aleck.**

knowledge *noun*
1. The sum of what has been perceived, discovered, or inferred ► lore, understanding, wisdom. *See also* **actuality. 2.** Known facts, ideas, and skill that have been imparted ► instruction, learning. *See* **education** (2). **3.** That which is known about a specific subject or situation ► facts, lore. *See* **information** (1).

knowledgeable *adjective*
1. Provided with information; made aware ► educated, instructed. *See* **informed** (1). **2.** Having or showing intelligence, often of a high order ► genius, intellectual. *See* **intelligent** (1). **3.** Showing evidence of schooling, training, or experience ► lettered, literate, versed. *See* **educated** (1).

knuckleheaded *adjective*
Informal Lacking in or showing a lack of intelligence ► dumb, idiotic, obtuse. *See* **stupid** (1).

KO *verb*
Slang To win a victory over, as in battle or a competition ► conquer, surmount, vanquish. *See* **defeat** (1).

kook *noun*
Slang A person regarded as strange, eccentric, or crazy ► lunatic. *Informal:* loony. *Slang:* nut, weirdo. *See* **crackpot.**

kooky *adjective*
Slang Deviating from what is conventional or customary ► bizarre, grotesque. *See* **eccentric.**

kosher *adjective*
1. *Slang* Worthy of being accepted or allowed ► allowable, permissible. *See* **acceptable** (1). **2.** *Slang* Not counterfeit or copied ► genuine, true. *Slang:* legit. *See* **authentic** (1).

kowtow *verb*
1. To behave obsequiously or submissively ► cringe, grovel. *Informal:* apple-polish. *See* **fawn.** *See synonym note at* **fawn. 2.** To incline the head or body, as in greeting, consent, courtesy, submission, or worship ► curtsy, kneel. *See* **bow**[1] (1).

kowtow *noun*
An inclination of the head or body, as in greeting, consent, courtesy, submission, or worship ► genuflection, obeisance. *See* **bow**[1].

kudos *noun*
1. Recognition of achievement or superiority or a sign of this ► award, honor. *See* **distinction** (2). **2.** An expression of warm approval ► acclamation, celebration, laudation. *See* **praise** (1).

Kultur *noun*
The total product of human creativity and intellect ► civilization, culture, society.

kvetch *verb*
Slang To express feelings of pain, dissatisfaction, or resentment ► fuss, grouch, whine. *See* **complain.**

kvetch *noun*
Slang An expression of pain or dissatisfaction ► carp, whimper, whine. *See* **complaint** (1).

L

label *noun*
1. An identifying or descriptive slip ► flag, tab, tag. *See* **ticket** (1). **2.** A name or other device placed on merchandise to signify its ownership or manufacture ► imprint, trademark. *See* **mark** (1).

label *verb*
1. To attach a ticket to ► earmark, flag, mark, tag, ticket. **2.** To set off by or as if by a mark indicating ownership or manufacture ► identify, tag. *See* **mark** (1). *See synonym note at* **mark. 3.** To describe with a word or term ► characterize, designate, name. *See* **call** (4).

labile *adjective*
► fluid, unsettled, variable. *See* **changeable** (1).

labor *noun*
1. Physical exertion that is usually difficult and exhausting ► drudgery, moil, toil, travail, work. *Informal:* grind, sweat. *Idiom:* sweat of one's brow. **2.** The act or process of bringing forth young ► childbearing, delivery, parturition. *See* **birth** (1).

labor *verb*
1. To exert oneself steadily, often to the point of exhaustion ► drive, moil, slave, strain, strive, sweat, toil, travail, tug, work. *Idioms:* bend over backward,

break one's back (*or* neck), break (*or* bust) one's butt, bust a gut. *See also* **grind. 2.** To discuss at excessive length ▸ dwell on, harp on, overemphasize. *See* **belabor** (2).

✦ **CORE SYNONYMS:** *labor, work, toil, drudgery, travail.* These nouns refer to physical exertion that is usually difficult and exhausting. *Labor* and *work* are the most general: "*Which of us . . . is to do the hard and dirty work for the rest—and for what pay?*" (John Ruskin); "*garner the fruits of their own labors*" (Roger Casement). *Toil* applies principally to strenuous, fatiguing labor: "*I have nothing to offer but blood, toil, tears and sweat*" (Winston S. Churchill). *Drudgery* suggests dull, wearisome, or monotonous work: "*the drudgery of penning definitions and marking quotations for transcription*" (Thomas Macaulay). *Travail* connotes arduous work involving pain or suffering: "*prisoners of the splendor and travail of the earth*" (Henry Beston).

---

labored *adjective*
1. Not natural or spontaneous ▸ contrived, effortful, forced, strained. *See also* **awkward, stiff. 2.** Lacking fluency or grace ▸ heavy-handed, leaden. *See* **ponderous** (1).

laborer *noun*
One who labors ▸ day laborer, hand, menial, operative, roustabout, toiler, wage slave, worker, working girl, workingman, workingwoman, workman, workwoman. *See also* **employee.**

laborious *adjective*
1. Requiring great or extreme bodily, mental, or spiritual strength ▸ backbreaking, grueling, weighty. *See* **burdensome** (1). **2.** Not easy to do, achieve, or master ▸ arduous, complicated, tough. *See* **difficult** (1).

laboriously *adverb*
▸ arduously, difficultly, heavily. *See* **hard** (2).

labyrinth *noun*
▸ imbroglio, maze, web. *See* **tangle** (1).

labyrinthine *adjective*
▸ convoluted, elaborate, involved, tangled. *See* **complex** (1).

lace *noun*
1. A band or fiber used to bind, tie, connect, or support ▸ cable, line, string. *See* **cord. 2.** An open and loosely connected structure, usually interlaced, woven, or knotted ▸ lattice, net, network. *See* **web** (1).

lacerate *verb*
1. To criticize harshly and devastatingly ▸ bash, excoriate, flay. *See* **slam** (5). **2.** To penetrate with a sharp edge ▸ bayonet, incise, pierce, slash. *See* **cut** (1).

laceration *noun*
Marked tissue damage, especially when produced by physical injury ▸ lesion, trauma, traumatism, wound. *See also* **harm.**

lachrymose *adjective*
▸ teary, weepy. *See* **tearful.**

lacing *noun*
1. A band or fiber that is used to bind, tie, connect, or

---

support ▸ cable, line, string. *See* **cord. 2.** An open and loosely connected structure, usually interlaced, woven, or knotted ▸ lattice, net, network. *See* **web** (1).

lack *verb*
To be without what is needed, required, or essential ▸ need, require, want. *See also* **demand.**

lack *noun*
1. The condition of lacking something ▸ absence, dearth, want. *See also* **need. 2.** The condition or fact of being deficient ▸ deficit, inadequacy, paucity. *See* **shortage.**

✦ **CORE SYNONYMS:** *lack, want, need.* These verbs mean to be without something, especially something that is necessary or desirable. *Lack* emphasizes the absence of something: *I lack the money to buy new shoes. The plant died because it lacked moisture. Want* and *need* stress the urgent necessity for filling a void or remedying an inadequacy: "*Her pens were uniformly bad and wanted fixing*" (Bret Harte). *The garden needs care.*

---

lackadaisical *adjective*
▸ languorous, listless, spiritless. *See* **languid.**

lackey *noun*
▸ flatterer, minion, slave. *See* **sycophant.**

lacking *adjective*
1. Missing an essential element ▸ incomplete, wanting. *See* **deficient** (1). **2.** Deprived of a quality or aspect that is desirable ▸ destitute, void, wanting. *See* **empty** (2).

lackluster *adjective*
1. Lacking vividness or color ▸ gray, mat, muddy. *See* **dull** (2). **2.** Lacking liveliness, charm, or surprise ▸ aseptic, colorless, pedestrian. *See* **dull** (1).

laconic *adjective*
1. Expressed in few words ▸ concise, short, succinct. *See* **brief** (1). **2.** Habitually untalkative ▸ reticent, silent, uncommunicative. *See* **taciturn.** *See synonym note at* **taciturn.**

lacquer *noun*
A final coating ▸ glaze, paint, varnish. *See* **finish** (3).

lacquer *verb*
To apply a coating to ▸ glaze, paint, varnish. *See* **finish** (7).

lacuna *noun*
▸ break, hiatus, lull. *See* **gap** (2).

lad *noun*
Informal A man referred to familiarly or as a member of one's group ▸ chap, guy. *See* **fellow** (1).

laden *adjective*
Burdened by a weighty load ▸ heavy, heavy-laden, loaded, weighed down.

ladle *verb*
▸ bail, dredge, scoop (up). *See* **dip** (2).

lady-killer *noun*
▸ Casanova, womanizer. *See* **philanderer.**

lady's man *noun*
1. A man amorously attentive to women ▸ Casanova, Don Juan. *See* **gallant. 2.** A man who philanders

▸ adulterer, Casanova, womanizer. *See* **philanderer.**

lag *verb*
To go or move slowly so that progress is hindered ▸ dawdle, dilly-dally, drag. *See* **delay** (2).

lag *noun*
1. The condition or fact of being made late or slow ▸ holdup, retardation. *See* **delay** (2). 2. One that lags ▸ dawdler, procrastinator, straggler. *See* **laggard.**

laggard *adjective*
Proceeding at a rate less than usual or desired ▸ dilatory, sluggish. *See* **slow** (1). *See synonym note at* **slow.**

laggard *or* **lagger** *noun*
One that lags ▸ dawdler, dilly-dallier, lag, lingerer, loiterer, poke, procrastinator, snail, straggler, tarrier. *Informal:* slowpoke.

lagging *adjective*
▸ underdeveloped, undeveloped. *See* **backward** (2).

laid-back *adjective*
Informal Unconstrained by rigid standards or ceremony ▸ casual, relaxed. *See* **easygoing** (1).

laid up *adjective*
Informal Suffering from an illness ▸ ailing, indisposed, unwell. *See* **sick** (1).

lair *noun*
1. A place used as an animal's dwelling ▸ burrow, den, hole. *See also* **cave.** 2. A hiding place ▸ covert, den, hideaway, hide-out.

lam *verb*
Slang To break loose and leave suddenly, as from confinement or a difficult situation ▸ decamp, flee. *See* **escape** (1).

lam *noun*
Slang The act or an instance of escaping, as from confinement ▸ breakout, flight. *See* **escape** (1).

lamb *noun*
1. A pure, uncorrupted person ▸ angel, virgin. *See* **innocent** (1). 2. A person who is easily deceived or victimized ▸ pushover, tool, victim. *See* **dupe** (1).

lambaste *verb*
1. *Informal* To hit heavily and repeatedly ▸ assault, batter, pummel, thresh. *See* **beat** (1). *See synonym note at* **beat.** 2. *Informal* To criticize for a fault or offense ▸ chide, rebuke, reprimand. *See* **chastise** (1). 3. *Informal* To criticize harshly and devastatingly ▸ bash, excoriate, flay. *See* **slam** (5).

lambency *noun*
▸ lucency, luminescence. *See* **light**[1] (1).

lambent *adjective*
▸ brilliant, incandescent, radiant. *See* **bright** (1). *See synonym note at* **bright.**

lame *adjective*
1. Not capable of accomplishing anything ▸ impotent, inadequate, incapable. *See* **ineffectual** (2). 2. Not plausible or believable ▸ flimsy, tenuous, unsubstantial. *See* **implausible.**

lamebrained *adjective*
Informal Lacking in or showing a lack of intelligence ▸ dumb, idiotic, obtuse. *See* **stupid** (1).

lament *verb*
1. To feel, show, or express grief ▸ anguish, mourn, sorrow. *See* **grieve** (1). *See synonym note at* **grieve.** 2. To shed tears ▸ howl, sob, weep. *See* **cry** (1).

lament *noun*
A fit of crying ▸ blubbering, sobbing, weeping. *See* **cry** (1).

lamentable *adjective*
1. Causing or expressing sadness, sorrow, or regret ▸ depressing, lugubrious, mournful. *See* **sorrowful** (1). 2. Arousing or deserving pity ▸ forlorn, poor. *See* **pitiful** (1). *See synonym note at* **pitiful.**

lamentation *noun*
▸ blubbering, sobbing, weeping. *See* **cry** (1).

lamia *noun*
A woman who practices magic ▸ enchantress, hag, sorceress, witch. *See also* **wizard.**

lamina *noun*
▸ membrane, sheath. *See* **skin** (2).

lampoon *noun*
A work that exposes folly by the use of humor, irony, or comic imitation ▸ burlesque, parody, spoof. *See* **satire.** *See synonym note at* **satire.**

lampoon *verb*
To subject to ridicule ▸ deride, jeer (at), taunt. *See* **ridicule.**

lance *verb*
▸ bayonet, incise, pierce, slash. *See* **cut** (1).

land *noun*
1. Usually extensive real estate ▸ acreage, acres, estate, grounds, lands, manor, property. 2. An organized geopolitical unit ▸ country, nation. *See* **state** (1).

land *verb*
1. To come ashore from a seacraft ▸ alight, debark, disembark, light. 2. To come to rest on the ground ▸ alight, light, set down, settle, touch down. 3. *Informal* To come into possession of ▸ come by, gain, procure. *See* **get** (1).

landscape *noun*
▸ panorama, perspective, vista. *See* **view** (2).

lane *noun*
▸ path, road, route. *See* **way** (2).

language *noun*
1. A system of terms used by a people sharing a history and culture ▸ dialect, mother tongue, speech, tongue, vernacular. 2. Specialized expressions indigenous to a particular field, subject, trade, or subculture ▸ argot, cant, dialect, idiom, jargon, lexicon, lingo, parlance, patois, terminology, vernacular, vocabulary.

languid *adjective*
Lacking energy and vitality ▸ drooping, flagging, lackadaisical, languorous, leaden, limp, listless, lymphatic, sleepy, spiritless, unspirited. *See also* **apathetic, lazy, slow, weak.**

languidness *noun*
▸ languor, listlessness, sluggishness. *See* **lethargy** (1).

languish *verb*
1. To become downcast from longing or grief ▸ ebb,

pine (away), shrivel, waste (away), wither. **2.** To lose strength or power ▸ decline, fail, weaken. *See* **fade** (1). **3.** To become lower in quality, character, or condition ▸ atrophy, degenerate, worsen. *See* **deteriorate** (1).

languor *noun*
▸ dullness, listlessness, sluggishness. *See* **lethargy** (1). *See synonym note at* **lethargy.**

languorous *adjective*
▸ lackadaisical, listless, spiritless. *See* **languid.**

lank *adjective*
▸ lean, skinny, slender, slim. *See* **thin** (1). *See synonym note at* **thin.**

lanky *adjective*
1. Tall, thin, and awkwardly built ▸ rangy, spindling, spindly. *See* **gangling. 2.** Having little flesh or fat on the body ▸ lean, skinny, slender, slim. *See* **thin** (1). *See synonym note at* **thin.**

lap *verb*
1. To flow against or along ▸ bathe, lave, lip, wash. *See also* **flow. 2.** To make the sound of moving or disturbed water ▸ splash, swash, wash. *See also* **swish. 3.** To flow with or make a soft liquid sound ▸ babble, gurgle, murmur. *See* **burble** (1).

lap up *verb*
To take into the mouth and swallow a liquid ▸ down, sip, slurp. *See* **drink** (1).

lap *noun*
A soft liquid sound ▸ babble, gurgle, murmur. *See* **burble.**

lapse *verb*
1. To become void, especially through passage of time or an omission ▸ cease, end, expire, run out, terminate. **2.** To slip from a higher or better condition to a former, usually lower or poorer one ▸ backslide, regress, revert. *See* **relapse. 3.** To become or cause to become less active or intense ▸ die (away, down, off, *or* out), ebb, wane. *See* **subside** (1). **4.** To move past in time ▸ go by, slip away. *See* **elapse. 5.** To make an error or mistake ▸ miscue, stumble. *See* **err** (1).

lapse *noun*
1. An unintentional deviation from what is correct, right, or true ▸ inaccuracy, incorrectness, mistake. *See* **error** (1). **2.** A slipping from a higher or better condition to a lower or poorer one ▸ backsliding, recidivism. *See* **relapse.**

lapsed *adjective*
▸ precedent, previous, prior. *See* **past** (1).

larcenist *or* **larcener** *noun*
▸ burglar, looter, robber. *See* **thief.**

larcenous *adjective*
▸ light-fingered, sticky-fingered, thieving. *See* **thievish.**

larceny *noun*
The crime of taking someone else's property without consent ▸ banditry, brigandage, burglary, holdup, looting, pilferage, purloining, robbery, steal, stealing, theft, thievery. *Slang:* heist, rip-off, stickup.

lard *noun*
Adipose tissue ▸ blubber, fat, suet. *See also* **oil.**

lares and penates *noun*
▸ goods, personal effects, property. *See* **effects.**

large *adjective*
1. Above average in amount, size, or scope ▸ extensive, significant, sizable. *See* **big** (1). *See synonym note at* **big. 2.** Covering a wide scope ▸ all-inclusive, broad, expansive. *See* **general** (2). **3.** Having great significance ▸ consequential, grand, meaningful. *See* **important** (1). **4.** At the upper end of a degree of measure ▸ elevated, great, high. *See also* **exalted, extreme.**

large-hearted *adjective*
▸ big-hearted, magnanimous, unselfish. *See* **generous** (1).

large-heartedness *noun*
▸ magnanimity, munificence, unselfishness. *See* **generosity.**

largely *adverb*
▸ much, quite, well. *See* **considerably.**

largeness *noun*
▸ bigness, greatness. *See* **size** (2).

larger *adjective*
▸ largest, most. *See* **best** (2).

large-scale *adjective*
▸ extensive, significant, sizable. *See* **big** (1).

largess *noun*
1. A material favor or gift, usually money, given in return for service ▸ perquisite, tip. *See* **gratuity** (1). **2.** The quality or state of being generous ▸ magnanimity, munificence, unselfishness. *See* **generosity. 3.** Something given to a charity or cause ▸ benefaction, contribution, offering. *See* **donation.**

largest *adjective*
▸ biggest, most. *See* **best** (2).

largish *adjective*
▸ extensive, respectable, sizable. *See* **big** (1).

lark *noun*
▸ caper, joke, trick. *See* **prank**[1].

larkish *adjective*
▸ frolicsome, impish, sportive. *See* **mischievous** (1).

lascivious *adjective*
1. Feeling or preoccupied with sexual love or desire ▸ amorous, concupiscent, lecherous, lewd, libidinous, lubricious, lustful, lusty, passionate, prurient, sexy. *See also* **obscene, wanton. 2.** Concerning or arousing sexual love or desire ▸ erogenous, libidinal, salacious. *See* **erotic.**

lash *verb*
1. To punish with blows or lashes ▸ flog, thrash, whip. *See* **beat** (2). **2.** To make secure ▸ bind, chain, moor. *See* **fasten** (1). **3.** To criticize harshly and devastatingly ▸ bash, excoriate, flay. *See* **slam** (5).

lashing *noun*
▸ flogging, thrashing, whipping. *See* **beating** (1).

lass *noun*
Informal A woman ▸ *Informal:* chick, damsel, gal. *See* **girl.**

lassitude *noun*
1. A deficiency in mental and physical alertness and activity ▸ languor, listlessness, sluggishness. *See* **leth-**

argy (1). *See synonym note at* **lethargy. 2.** Lack of emotion or interest ▸ disinterest, indifference, unconcern. *See* **apathy.**

last¹ *adjective*
1. Coming after all others ▸ closing, concluding, final, terminal, ultimate. **2.** Bringing up the rear ▸ aftermost, endmost, hindermost, hindmost, lattermost, rearmost, tail. *See also* **extreme. 3.** Next before the present one ▸ foregoing, latter, preceding, previous. *See also* **past. 4.** Of or relating to a terminative condition, stage, or point ▸ final, latter, terminal, ultimate. *See also* **climactic.**

last *adverb*
In conclusion ▸ conclusively, finally, lastly, ultimately. *Idioms:* at last, in the end, when all is said and done.

last *noun*
The last part ▸ closing, conclusion, ending, epilogue. *See* **end** (2).

✦ **CORE SYNONYMS:** *last, final, terminal, ultimate.* These adjectives mean coming after all others in chronology or sequence. *Last* applies to what comes at the end of a series: *the last day of the month.* Something *final* stresses the definitiveness and decisiveness of the conclusion: *"I believe that unarmed truth and unconditional love will have the final word in reality"* (Martin Luther King, Jr.). *Terminal* applies to what marks or forms a limit or boundary, as in space, time, or development: *The railroad chose as its terminal city a town with a large harbor. Ultimate* applies to what concludes a series, process, or progression, to what constitutes a final result or objective, and to what is most distant or remote, as in time: *the ultimate sonata of that opus; our ultimate goal; the ultimate effect.*

◂ **ANTONYM:** *first*

---

last² *verb*
1. To remain fresh and unspoiled ▸ keep. **2.** To be in existence or in a certain state for an indefinitely long time ▸ continue, persist. *See* **endure** (2). **3.** To exist in spite of adversity ▸ come through, pull through. *See* **survive** (1).

lasting *adjective*
▸ durable, enduring, perennial. *See* **continuing** (1).

lastly *adverb*
In conclusion ▸ conclusively, finally, last. *Idioms:* at last, in the end, when all is said and done.

last rites *noun*
▸ funeral service, memorial service, requiem. *See* **funeral.**

latch *noun*
▸ catch, clip, lock. *See* **fastener.**

late *adjective*
1. Coming or occurring after the correct, usual, or expected time; not on time ▸ behindhand, belated, delayed, overdue, slow, tardy. **2.** Having been such previously ▸ erstwhile, former, old, once, onetime, past, previous, quondam, sometime, whilom. **3.** No longer alive ▸ deceased, departed, perished. *See* **dead** (1).

late *adverb*
Not on time ▸ behind, behindhand, belatedly, slow, tardily. *Idiom:* behind time.

✦ **CORE SYNONYMS:** *late, behindhand, overdue, tardy.* These adjectives mean not arriving, occurring, acting, or done at the scheduled, expected, or usual time: *late for the plane; behindhand with her car payments; an overdue bus; tardy in making his dental appointment.*

◂ **ANTONYM:** *prompt*

---

lately *adverb*
Not long ago ▸ freshly, just (now), lately, latterly, newly, recently. *Idioms:* of late, only a moment (*or* while) ago.

latency *noun*
▸ dormancy, intermission, quiescence, suspension. *See* **abeyance.**

lateness *noun*
The quality or condition of not being on time ▸ belatedness, slowness, tardiness, unpunctuality.

latent *adjective*
Present but not evident or active ▸ abeyant, dormant, hibernating, inactive, lurking, possible, potential, quiescent, sleeping, smoldering, torpid. *See also* **hidden, implicit.**

✦ **CORE SYNONYMS:** *latent, dormant, quiescent.* These adjectives mean present or in existence but not evident or active. What is *latent* is present but not evident: *latent ability. Dormant* evokes the idea of sleep: *a dormant volcano. Quiescent* sometimes—but not always—suggests temporary inactivity: *"For a time, he* [the whale] *lay quiescent"* (Herman Melville).

---

later *adjective*
1. Following something else in time ▸ after, posterior, subsequent, ulterior. *See also* **following. 2.** Being or occurring in the time ahead ▸ coming, subsequent. *See* **future.**

later *adverb*
At a subsequent time ▸ after, afterward, afterwards, latterly, next, subsequently, ulteriorly. *Idioms:* after a while, by and by, later on.

later *interjection*
Used upon taking leave ▸ farewell. *Informal:* see you, so long. *See* **goodbye.**

latest *adjective*
▸ current, modern, up-to-date. *See* **contemporary** (2).

lather *noun*
1. Moisture accumulated on a surface through sweating or condensation ▸ condensation, perspiration, sweat, transudation. **2.** Bubbles on the surface of a liquid ▸ froth, suds. *See* **foam. 3.** *Informal* A state of discomposure ▸ tumult, turmoil. *See* **agitation** (2).

lather *verb*
1. To excrete moisture through a porous skin or layer ▸ perspire, sweat, transude. **2.** To form or cause to form foam ▸ fizz, froth. *See* **foam** (1). **3.** *Informal* To hit heavily and repeatedly ▸ assault, batter, pummel, thresh. *See* **beat** (1).

lathery *adjective*
▸ fizzy, frothy, sudsy. *See* **foamy.**

latitude *noun*
▸ entitlement, free hand, leeway. *See* **license** (1). *See synonym note at* **license.**

latter *adjective*
1. Of or relating to a terminative condition, stage, or point ▸ final, last, terminal, ultimate. *See also* **climactic.** 2. Next before the present one ▸ foregoing, last, preceding, previous. *See also* **past.**

latter-day *adjective*
▸ current, modern, recent. *See* **contemporary** (2).

latterly *adverb*
1. At a subsequent time ▸ afterwards, next, subsequently. *See* **later.** 2. Not long ago ▸ newly, recently. *See* **lately.**

lattermost *adjective*
▸ hindermost, rearmost. *See* **last**[1] (2).

lattice *noun*
▸ lacing, net, network. *See* **web** (1).

laud *verb*
1. To pay tribute or homage to ▸ celebrate, exalt. *See* **honor** (1). 2. To express warm approval of ▸ applaud, commend. *See* **praise** (1). *See synonym note at* **praise.** 3. To honor a deity in religious worship ▸ extol, magnify. *See* **praise** (3).

laud *noun*
An expression of warm approval ▸ acclamation, celebration, kudos. *See* **praise** (1).

laudable *adjective*
▸ commendable, deserving, worthy. *See* **admirable.**

laudation *noun*
1. An expression of warm approval ▸ acclamation, celebration, kudos. *See* **praise** (1). 2. The honoring of a deity, as in worship ▸ extolment, magnification. *See* **praise** (2).

laudatory *adjective*
▸ approbatory, commendatory. *See* **complimentary** (1).

laugh *verb*
To express amusement or mirth by smiling and emitting inarticulate sounds ▸ cachinnate, cackle, chortle, chuckle, giggle, guffaw, roar, snicker, snigger, tee-hee, titter. *Informal:* break up, heehaw, yuk. *Slang:* howl. *Idioms:* be in stitches, die laughing, laugh one's head off, roll in the aisles, split one's sides.

laugh at *verb*
To subject to ridicule ▸ jeer (at), lampoon, taunt. *See* **ridicule.**

laugh *noun*
1. An act of laughing ▸ cachinnation, cackle, chortle, chuckle, giggle, guffaw, laughter, roar, snicker, snigger, tee-hee, titter. *Informal:* heehaw, yuk. *Slang:* howl. 2. *Informal* One that is uproariously funny ▸ absurdity. *Informal:* hoot. *See* **scream** (3).

laughable *adjective*
1. Causing or deserving laughter or derision ▸ farcical, ludicrous, ridiculous, risible. *See also* **foolish.** 2. Caus-

ing laughter or amusement ▸ amusing, comical, humorous. *See* **funny** (1).

laughingstock *noun*
An object of amusement or laughter ▸ butt, jest, joke, mockery. *Idiom:* figure of fun.

laughter *noun*
▸ cachinnation, cackle, guffaw. *See* **laugh** (1).

launch *verb*
1. To send through the air with a motion of the hand or arm ▸ heave, hurl, pitch. *See* **throw** (1). 2. To go about the initial step in doing something ▸ begin, embark, initiate. *See* **start** (1). 3. To bring into currency, use, fashion, or practice ▸ originate, pioneer. *See* **introduce** (1).

launch *noun*
1. An act of throwing ▸ fling, hurl, toss. *See* **throw.** 2. The act of bringing or being brought into existence ▸ inception, initiation, start. *See* **beginning** (1).

launder *verb*
▸ bathe, cleanse, lave. *See* **clean** (1).

laurels *noun*
▸ award, commendation, honor. *See* **distinction** (2).

lavation *noun*
▸ clarification, cleaning, refinement. *See* **purification** (1).

lave *verb*
1. To flow against or along ▸ bathe, lap, lip, wash. *See also* **flow.** 2. To rid of dirt, stains, trash, or other impurities ▸ bathe, cleanse, lave. *See* **clean** (1).

lavish *adjective*
1. Characterized by extravagant, ostentatious magnificence ▸ lush, luxuriant, opulent. *See* **luxurious.** 2. Characterized by excessive or imprudent spending ▸ prodigal, profligate. *See* **extravagant** (1). 3. Given to or marked by unrestrained abundance ▸ exuberant, luxuriant, opulent. *See* **profuse** (1). *See synonym note at* **profuse.** 4. Willing to give of oneself and one's possessions ▸ big-hearted, magnanimous, unselfish. *See* **generous** (1).

lavish *verb*
To give in great abundance ▸ heap, rain, shower. *See also* **confer, donate, give.**

lavishness *noun*
1. Excessive or imprudent expenditure ▸ squander, wastefulness. *See* **extravagance** (1). 2. The quality or state of being generous ▸ magnanimity, munificence, unselfishness. *See* **generosity.**

law *noun*
1. A principle governing affairs within or among political units ▸ bylaw, canon, charter, edict, institute, ordinance, precept, prescription, regulation, rule, tenet. *See also* **doctrine.** 2. The formal product of a legislative or judicial body ▸ act, assize, bill, enactment, legislation, lex, measure, statute. *See also* **command, ruling.** 3. A broad and basic rule or truth ▸ axiom, formula, fundamental, maxim, principle, theorem, truism, universal. 4. A code or set of codes governing action or procedure, for example ▸ prescript, regulation, rubric. *See* **rule** (1). 5. *Informal* A

member of a law-enforcement agency ▸ officer, trooper. *See* **police officer.**

law *verb*
To institute or subject to legal proceedings ▸ litigate, prosecute, sue. *Idioms:* bring suit, haul (*or* drag) into court.

lawbreaker *noun*
▸ culprit, gangster, offender. *See* **criminal.**

lawful *adjective*
Within, allowed by, or sanctioned by the law ▸ authorized, just, legal, legitimate, licit, permitted, rightful, valid, warranted. *Slang:* legit. *See also* **acceptable.**

lawfulness *noun*
▸ legitimacy, licitness, validity. *See* **legality.**

lawless *adjective*
1. Prohibited by law ▸ illicit, outlawed, unlawful. *See* **illegal** (1). 2. Of, involving, or being a crime ▸ illicit, unlawful. *See* **criminal** (1). 3. Not submitting to discipline or control ▸ ill-behaved, obstinate, unmanageable. *See* **unruly.** 4. Upsetting civil order or peace ▸ disruptive, riotous. *See* **disorderly** (1).

lawlessness *noun*
1. The state or quality of being illegal ▸ illegality, illegitimacy, illicitness, unlawfulness. 2. A lack of civil order or peace ▸ anarchy, chaos. *See* **disorder** (2). 3. The quality or condition of being unruly ▸ intractability, recalcitrance. *See* **unruliness.**

lawn *noun*
▸ park, plaza, square. *See* **common.**

lawsuit *noun*
A legal proceeding to demand justice or enforce a right ▸ action, case, cause, instance, litigation, suit.

lawyer *noun*
A person who practices law ▸ attorney, counsel, counselor, jurist, pettifogger. *Slang:* ambulance chaser, legal eagle.

lax *adjective*
1. Not strict or severe ▸ easy, indulgent, lenient. *See* **tolerant** (1). 2. Lacking due care or concern ▸ derelict, slack. *See* **negligent.** *See synonym note at* **negligent.** 3. Not tautly bound, held, or fastened ▸ flapping, relaxed, slack. *See* **loose** (1). *See synonym note at* **loose.**

laxity *or* **laxness** *noun*
1. The state or quality of being negligent ▸ remissness, slackness. *See* **negligence.** 2. Excessive freedom; lack of restraint ▸ licentiousness, profligacy. *See* **license** (2).

lay¹ *verb*
1. To put in a certain position or location ▸ locate, place, situate. *See* **position.** 2. To place a corpse in or as if in a grave ▸ inhume, inter. *See* **bury** (1). 3. To arrange tableware upon a table in preparation for a meal ▸ set, spread. 4. To form a strategy for ▸ devise, formulate, strategize. *See* **design** (1). 5. To bring forward as proof or support ▸ adduce, present, produce. *See* **cite** (1). 6. To direct something, often toward a target ▸ level, point, train. *See* **aim** (1). 7. To ascribe the blame for a misdeed or error ▸ attribute, blame, pin. *See* **fix** (13). 8. To place something at risk, as in a game of chance ▸ bet, stake, wager. *See* **gamble** (2). 9. To

make a bet ▸ bet, gamble, game, play, wager. *Idiom:* put one's money on something.

lay away *verb*
1. To keep for future use ▸ lay aside (*or* by *or* in *or* up), put by, salt away, set by. *See* **save** (1). 2. To place money in an account ▸ deposit, salt away. *See* **bank²**.

lay down *verb*
1. To give up completely ▸ cede, relinquish, surrender. *See* **abandon** (1). 2. To set forth expressly and authoritatively ▸ impose, mandate, ordain. *See* **dictate** (1).

lay for *verb*
Informal To wait furtively in order to attack someone ▸ ambush, prowl, skulk. *See* **lurk** (1).

lay into *verb*
1. *Slang* To punish with blows or lashes ▸ lash, thrash, whip. *See* **beat** (2). 2. *Slang* To set upon with violent force ▸ assail, assault, storm, strike. *See* **attack** (1).

lay off *verb*
1. *Slang* To cease trying to continue ▸ give up, leave off, quit. *See* **abandon** (2). 2. To end the employment or service of ▸ cashier, terminate. *See* **dismiss** (1).

lay on *or* **upon** *verb*
To force another to accept a burden ▸ charge with, inflict on (*or* upon), saddle with. *See* **impose on** (1).

lay out *verb*
1. To plan the details or arrangements of ▸ arrange, prepare, schedule, work out. 2. To work out and arrange the parts or details of ▸ blueprint, map (out), plan. *See* **design** (2). 3. To show graphically the direction or location of, as by using coordinates ▸ graph, plan. *See* **plot** (1). 4. To give money as payment ▸ expend, outlay. *See* **spend** (1). 5. To draw up a preliminary plan or version of ▸ outline, sketch. *See* **draft** (1).

lay² *adjective*
Not religious in subject matter, form, or use ▸ nonecclesiastical, secular, temporal. *See* **profane** (2).

layabout *noun*
Informal A self-indulgent person who avoids work ▸ bum, idler, loafer. *See* **wastrel** (2).

layer *noun*
An outer layer of material ▸ blanket, coating, overlay. *See* **coat** (2).

layout *noun*
1. A method used for accomplishing something ▸ course, modus operandi, procedure, technique. *See* **approach** (1). 2. The act or condition of being arranged ▸ allotment, orchestration, positioning. *See* **arrangement** (1). 3. A preliminary plan or version, as of a written work ▸ blueprint, sketch. *See* **draft** (1).

layperson *noun*
▸ dabbler, dilettante, nonprofessional. *See* **amateur.**

laze *verb*
▸ bum (around), loiter, lounge. *See* **idle** (1).

laziness *noun*
The quality or state of being lazy ▸ fainéance, fainéancy, idleness, indolence, otioseness, otiosity, shiftlessness, sloth, slothfulness, sluggardness, sluggishness. *Informal:* do-nothingism.

lazy *adjective*
Resistant to exertion and activity ▸ fainéant, idle, indolent, otiose, shiftless, slothful, sluggard, sluggish. *Informal:* do-nothing. **Idiom:** bone lazy.

✦ CORE SYNONYMS: *lazy, fainéant, idle, indolent, slothful.* These adjectives mean resistant to exertion, work, and activity: *too lazy to wash the dishes; fainéant aristocrats; an idle drifter; an indolent hanger-on; slothful employees.*

---

lazybones *noun*
Informal A self-indulgent person who avoids work ▸ bum, idler, loafer. *See* **wastrel** (2).

leach *verb*
▸ exude, seep. *See* **ooze.**

lead *verb*
1. To show the way to ▸ direct, escort, marshal. *See* **guide** (1). *See synonym note at* **guide.** 2. To have charge of the affairs of others ▸ direct, govern, rule. *See* **administer** (1). 3. To go through life in a certain way ▸ conduct, live, pass, pursue, spend. 4. To begin something with preliminary or prefatory material ▸ precede, preface. *See* **introduce** (3). 5. To have an impact on in a certain way ▸ incline, predispose, sway. *See* **influence** (1). 6. To occupy the preeminent position in ▸ control, prevail. *See* **dominate** (1).

lead off *verb*
To go about the initial step in doing something ▸ begin, embark, initiate. *See* **start** (1).

lead to *verb*
1. To be the cause of ▸ generate, induce, trigger. *See* **cause.** 2. To involve by logical necessity ▸ involve, indicate, point to. *See* **imply** (1).

lead *noun*
1. The main performer in a theatrical production ▸ headliner, leading lady, leading man, prima donna, principal, protagonist, star, starlet. 2. Something or someone that shows the way ▸ director, escort, leader. *See* **guide** (1). 3. The position of greatest advancement or importance ▸ cutting edge, fore, vanguard. *See* **forefront.** 4. An item of advance or inside information given as a guide to action ▸ clue, pointer, scent. *See* **tip³** (1). 5. The act or process of managing or directing ▸ administration, direction, guidance, supervision. *See* **management** (1). 6. The condition or fact of being dominant ▸ authority, power, supremacy. *See* **dominance** (1).

lead balloon *noun*
Informal An unsuccessful enterprise ▸ bust, fiasco. *See* **failure** (1).

leaden *adjective*
1. Lacking energy and vitality ▸ languorous, listless, spiritless. *See* **languid.** 2. Lacking liveliness, charm, or surprise ▸ aseptic, colorless, pedestrian. *See* **dull** (1). 3. Lacking fluency or grace ▸ heavy-handed, labored. *See* **ponderous** (1). 4. Having relatively great weight ▸ hefty, ponderous. *See* **heavy** (1).

leadenness *noun*
▸ languor, listlessness, sluggishness. *See* **lethargy** (1).

leader *noun*
1. A leading contestant or sure winner ▸ favorite, front-runner, number one, vanguard. *Informal:* shoo-in. 2. Something or someone that shows the way ▸ director, escort. *See* **guide** (1). 3. One who governs or leads ▸ boss, director, head, ruler. *See* **chief** (1). 4. An important, influential person ▸ notability, personage. *Slang:* big shot. *See* **dignitary.**

leadership *noun*
1. The capacity to lead others ▸ command, lead. 2. The act or process of managing or directing ▸ direction, guidance, supervision. *See* **management** (1).

lead-in *noun*
▸ overture, preface, prologue. *See* **introduction** (1).

leading *adjective*
1. Most important, influential, or significant ▸ chief, key, main, principal. *See* **primary** (1). *See synonym note at* **primary.** 2. Widely known ▸ notorious, popular, well-known. *See* **famous.** 3. Surpassing all others in quality ▸ optimum, superlative, unsurpassed. *See* **best** (1). 4. Being among the leaders in one's field ▸ blue-chip, major, major-league. *See* **big-league.** 5. Exercising controlling power or influence ▸ key, predominant, reigning. *See* **dominant** (1).

leadoff *noun*
The act of bringing or being brought into existence ▸ inception, initiation, start. *See* **beginning** (1).

leadoff *adjective*
Of or occurring at the start of something ▸ initial, introductory, opening. *See* **beginning** (1).

leaf *noun*
A small, thin piece of something ▸ chip, sliver, shaving. *See* **flake** (1).

leaf *verb*
To look through reading matter casually ▸ flip through, riffle (through), scan. *See* **browse** (1).

leafless *adjective*
▸ bald, barren, naked. *See* **bare** (3).

leaflet *noun*
An announcement distributed on paper to a large number of people ▸ circular, flier, handbill, notice.

league *noun*
1. An association for a common cause or interest ▸ coalition, federation, union. *See* **alliance** (1). 2. A group of people united in a relationship and having some interest, activity, or purpose in common ▸ club, fellowship, order. *See* **union** (1). 3. A group of athletic teams that play each other ▸ circuit, division. *See* **conference** (6). 4. A division of persons or things by quality or rank ▸ grade, rank, tier. *See* **class** (2).

league *verb*
1. To be formally associated, as by treaty ▸ confederate, federate. *See* **ally** (1). 2. To form a united group ▸ join, unite. *See* **band²**.

leak *verb*
1. *Informal* To be made public ▸ break, come out, get out, out, transpire. *Informal:* leak out. *See also* **air, announce, appear.** 2. To flow or emit something slowly ▸ exude, leach, seep. *See* **ooze.** 3. *Informal* To

disclose in a breach of confidence ▸ divulge, give away. *Informal:* spill. *See* **betray** (2).

lean¹ *verb*
1. To depart or cause to depart from true vertical or horizontal ▸ heel, rake. *See* **incline** (1). *See synonym note at* **incline. 2.** To have a tendency or inclination ▸ incline, slant, trend. *See* **tend¹.**

lean *noun*
Deviation from a particular direction ▸ grade, heel. *See* **inclination** (2).

lean² *adjective*
1. Having little flesh or fat on the body ▸ skinny, slender, slim. *See* **thin** (1). *See synonym note at* **thin. 2.** Expressed in few words ▸ concise, short, succinct. *See* **brief** (1). **3.** Characterized by an economy of artistic expression ▸ spare, taut. *See* **tight** (3).

leaning *noun*
A natural or habitual preference for something ▸ cast, disposition, penchant. *See* **inclination** (1). *See synonym note at* **inclination.**

leaning *adjective*
At an angle ▸ diagonal, slanted, tilted. *See* **oblique** (1).

lean-to *noun*
▸ cabin, hovel, shack. *See* **hut.**

leap *verb*
1. To move off the ground by a muscular effort of the legs and feet ▸ spring, vault. *See* **jump** (1). **2.** To move in a lively way ▸ skip, spring. *See* **bound¹** (1).

leap *noun*
1. The act of jumping ▸ jump, pounce, spring, vault. *See also* **fall. 2.** A sudden lively movement ▸ jump, spring. *See* **bound¹** (2).

learn *verb*
1. To gain knowledge or mastery of by study ▸ acquire, get, master. *Informal:* pick up. **2.** To commit to memory ▸ con, memorize. *Idioms:* learn by heart (*or* rote). *See also* **remember. 3.** To take in and incorporate, especially mentally ▸ assimilate, digest, grasp. *See* **absorb** (2). **4.** To obtain knowledge or awareness of something not known before ▸ determine, hear, unearth. *See* **discover.** *See synonym note at* **discover.**

learned *adjective*
▸ informed, lettered, literate. *See* **educated** (1). *See synonym note at* **educated.**

learner *noun*
1. One who is being educated ▸ apprentice, pupil, scholar. *See* **student. 2.** One who is just starting to learn or do something ▸ fledgling, neophyte, novice. *See* **beginner.**

learning *noun*
▸ instruction, knowledge. *See* **education** (2).

lease *verb*
1. To give temporary use of in return for payment ▸ hire (out), let (out), rent (out), sublet. **2.** To engage the temporary use of something for a fee ▸ charter, hire, rent.

leash *verb*
To restrict the activity or free movement of ▸ fetter, handcuff, hobble. *See* **hamper¹** (1).

leash *noun*
A device for slowing or stopping motion ▸ curb, rein, restraint. *See* **brake** (1).

least *adjective*
▸ littlest, smallest. *See* **minimal.**

leather *noun*
The skin of an animal, sometimes including fur, hair, or feathers ▸ fur, hide, pelt.

leave¹ *verb*
1. To give property to another after one's death ▸ bequeath, devise, hand down, hand on, pass (along *or* on), transmit, will. *See also* **donate, give. 2.** To relinquish one's engagement in or occupation with ▸ demit, quit, resign, terminate. *Idioms:* hang it up, throw in the towel. *See also* **break. 3.** To move away from a place ▸ exit, go away, retire. *See* **go** (1). **4.** To give up or leave completely ▸ desert, forsake, quit. *See* **abandon** (1).

leave off *verb*
1. To come to a cessation ▸ discontinue, halt, quit. *See* **stop** (1). **2.** To cease trying to continue ▸ desist, give up, quit, stop. *See* **abandon** (2). **3.** To discontinue (a habit, for example) ▸ abjure, give up, renounce. *See* **break** (17).

leave² *noun*
1. A regularly scheduled period spent away from work or duty, often in recreation ▸ furlough, holiday, sabbatical, vacation. *Idioms:* time (*or* day) off. *See also* **break, trip. 2.** The approving of an action, especially when done by one in authority ▸ authorization, consent, sanction. *See* **permission.** *See synonym note at* **permission.**

leaven *or* **leavening** *noun*
▸ leavening, reactant, yeast. *See* **catalyst.**

leave-taking *noun*
▸ embarkation, exit, exodus, withdrawal. *See* **departure** (1).

leavings *noun*
▸ leftover, remainder, remnant, rest. *See* **balance** (4).

lecher *noun*
An immoral or licentious man ▸ gigolo, goat, roué, satyr. *Informal:* dirty old man. *Slang:* lech. *See also* **philanderer, wanton.**

lecherous *adjective*
▸ concupiscent, lewd. *See* **lascivious** (1).

lecture *noun*
1. A usually formal spoken communication to an audience ▸ homily, talk. *See* **speech** (2). **2.** Words expressive of strong disapproval ▸ admonition, reprimand, scolding. *See* **rebuke. 3.** A formal discussion of a subject, either written or spoken ▸ dialogue, dissertation. *See* **discourse** (1).

lecture *verb*
1. To talk to an audience formally ▸ address, prelect, sermonize, speak. *See also* **converse. 2.** To criticize for a fault or offense ▸ chide, rebuke, reprimand. *See* **chastise** (1).

lecturer *noun*
▸ declaimer, speechmaker. *See* **speaker** (1).

leech *noun*
One who depends on another for support without reciprocating ▸ bloodsucker, sponge. *Slang:* freeloader. *See* **parasite** (1).

leech *verb*
To take advantage of the generosity of others ▸ *Informal:* sponge. *Slang:* freeload. *See also* **beg.**

leeriness *noun*
▸ doubt, mistrust, suspicion. *See* **distrust.**

leery *adjective*
▸ doubting, suspicious, wary. *See* **distrustful** (1).

lees *noun*
▸ accumulation, precipitation, sediment. *See* **deposit** (2).

leeway *noun*
▸ entitlement, latitude, margin. *See* **license** (1). *See synonym note at* **license.**

left *adjective*
▸ leftist, liberalistic, progressive. *See* **liberal** (1).

left-handed *adjective*
▸ disingenuous, underhanded. *See* **underhand.**

leftist *noun*
One with politically liberal views ▸ liberalist, progressive. *See* **liberal.**

leftist *adjective*
Favoring civil liberties and social reform, especially as a political philosophy ▸ left, left-wing. *See* **liberal** (1).

leftover *adjective*
Being what remains, especially after a part has been removed ▸ extra, remaining, residual, stray. *Idiom:* left behind. *See also* **superfluous.**

leftover *noun*
1. A remaining part ▸ remainder, remains, remnant. *See* **balance** (4). 2. A thing, amount, or quantity beyond what is needed, desired, or appropriate ▸ overflow, oversupply, superfluity. *See* **surplus.**

leftovers *noun*
▸ leftover, remainder, remains. *See* **balance** (4).

left-wing *adjective*
▸ leftist, liberalistic, progressive. *See* **liberal** (1).

left-winger *noun*
▸ leftist, liberalist, progressive. *See* **liberal.**

legacy *noun*
1. Something immaterial, as a style or philosophy, that is passed from one generation to another ▸ heritage, inheritance, tradition. *See synonym note at* **heritage.** 2. Any special privilege accorded a firstborn ▸ birthright, heritage, inheritance, patrimony. *See also* **right.**

legal *adjective*
▸ licit, permitted, valid. *See* **lawful.**

legality *noun*
The state or quality of being within the law ▸ lawfulness, legitimacy, legitimateness, licitness, permissibility, rightfulness, soundness, validity. *See also* **justice.**

legalize *verb*
To make lawful ▸ decriminalize, legitimate, legitimatize, legitimize, warrant. *See also* **authorize, confirm, permit.**

legation *noun*
A diplomatic office or headquarters in a foreign country ▸ deputation, embassy, mission.

legend *noun*
1. A traditional story or tale that has no proven factual basis ▸ fairy tale, parable. *See* **myth** (1). 2. A body of traditional beliefs and notions accumulated about a particular subject ▸ folkways, mythology, tradition. *See* **lore** (1). 3. A famous person ▸ luminary, personality, star. *See* **celebrity** (1).

legendary *adjective*
1. Having the nature of a fable; not real ▸ fabled, fabulous, fairy tale. *See* **mythical.** 2. Widely known ▸ celebrated, illustrious, storied. *See* **famous.**

legerdemain *noun*
▸ illusion, sleight of hand. *See* **magic** (2).

legibility *noun*
▸ distinctness, lucidity, perspicuity, plainness. *See* **clarity** (1).

legion *noun*
An enormous number of persons or things gathered together ▸ horde, mass, throng. *See* **crowd** (1).

legion *adjective*
Amounting to or consisting of a large, indefinite number ▸ myriad, numerous. *See* **many.**

legionnaire *or* **legionary** *noun*
▸ GI, militiaman, serviceperson. *See* **soldier** (2).

legislate *verb*
▸ enact, ordain. *See* **establish** (3).

legislation *noun*
▸ bill, enactment. *See* **law** (2).

legislative *adjective*
▸ bureaucratic, regulatory. *See* **governmental.**

legit *adjective*
1. *Slang* Not counterfeit or copied ▸ real, true. *Slang:* kosher. *See* **authentic** (1). 2. *Slang* Within, allowed by, or sanctioned by the law ▸ legal, permitted, valid. *See* **lawful.**

legitimacy *or* **legitimateness** *noun*
▸ lawfulness, licitness, rightfulness, validity. *See* **legality.**

legitimate *adjective*
1. Not counterfeit or copied ▸ genuine, true. *Slang:* legit, kosher. *See* **authentic** (1). 2. Within, allowed by, or sanctioned by the law ▸ legal, permitted, valid. *See* **lawful.** 3. Being so legitimately ▸ rightful, true.

legitimate *verb*
1. To make lawful ▸ decriminalize, legitimatize. *See* **legalize.** 2. To put in force or cause to be by legal authority ▸ enact, legislate. *See* **establish** (3).

legitimize *or* **legitimatize** *verb*
▸ decriminalize, warrant. *See* **legalize.**

legman *noun*
▸ correspondent, editorialist, media. *See* **press** (1).

leisure *noun*
1. Unrestricted freedom to choose ▸ convenience, discretion, pleasure, will. 2. Freedom from labor, responsibility, or strain ▸ ease, relaxation, repose. *See* **rest** (2).

leisurely *adjective*
▸ circumspect, measured, unhurried. *See* **deliberate** (3).

lemma *noun*
1. Something taken to be true without proof ▸ axiom, given. *See* **assumption** (1). 2. An item inserted, as in a reference book ▸ heading, posting. *See* **entry** (1).

lend *verb*
To supply money, especially on credit ▸ advance, discount, float, loan. *Idiom:* extend credit to.

length *noun*
1. The measure of how far or long something goes in space, time, or degree ▸ coverage, span, stretch. *See* **extent** (1). 2. An extent, measured or unmeasured, of linear space ▸ interval, range, stretch. *See* **distance** (1). 3. The ultimate point to which an action, thought, discussion, or policy is carried ▸ degree, end, extreme, extremity, limit.

lengthen *verb*
To make or become longer ▸ draw out, elongate, extend, prolong, prolongate, protract, spin (out), stretch (out), string out. *See also* **broaden, increase.**

lengthening *noun*
▸ drawing out, prolongation, stretching. *See* **extension** (1).

lengthy *adjective*
1. Having great physical length ▸ elongated, extended, prolonged. *See* **long**[1] (1). 2. Extending tediously beyond a standard duration ▸ drawn-out, overlong, protracted. *See* **long**[1] (2).

lenience *or* **leniency** *noun*
1. Kind, forgiving, or compassionate treatment of or disposition toward others ▸ clemency, grace. *See* **mercy.** 2. Forbearing or lenient treatment ▸ charity, forbearance, toleration. *See* **tolerance** (1).

lenient *adjective*
▸ easy, indulgent, lax. *See* **tolerant** (1).

lese majesty *noun*
1. Willful violation of allegiance to one's country ▸ sedition, seditiousness, traitorousness, treason. *See also* **faithlessness.** 2. Lack of proper respect ▸ impoliteness, irreverence, rudeness. *See* **disrespect** (1).

lesion *noun*
Marked tissue damage, especially when produced by physical injury ▸ laceration, trauma, traumatism, wound. *See also* **harm.**

lessen *verb*
1. To grow or cause to grow gradually less ▸ diminish, dwindle, ebb. *See* **decrease.** *See synonym note at* **decrease.** 2. To make less severe or more bearable ▸ alleviate, ease. *See* **relieve** (1). 3. To make less in price or value ▸ devalue, downgrade, reduce. *See* **depreciate** (1).

lesser *adjective*
▸ junior, low, secondary. *See* **minor** (1).

lesson *noun*
1. The principle taught by a fable or parable ▸ axiom, maxim. *See* **moral.** 2. An instance that warns or discourages prospective imitators ▸ caveat, warning. *See* **example** (2).

let *verb*
1. To give one's consent to ▸ approve, authorize, sanction. *See* **permit** (2). 2. To afford an opportunity for ▸ allow, give. *See* **permit** (3). 3. To neither forbid nor prevent ▸ allow, tolerate. *See* **permit** (1). 4. To give temporary use of in return for payment ▸ rent (out), sublet. *See* **lease** (1).

let down *verb*
1. To cause unhappiness by failing to satisfy the hopes, desires, or expectations of ▸ disgruntle, dissatisfy. *See* **disappoint.** 2. To cause to descend ▸ depress, drop, take down. *See* **lower**[2] (1).

let go *verb*
1. To end the employment or service of ▸ cashier, terminate. *See* **dismiss** (1). 2. To take or leave out ▸ exclude, omit, prune. *See* **drop** (8).

let in *verb*
To allow admittance, as to a group ▸ receive, take in. *See* **accept** (3).

let off *verb*
1. To discharge material, as vapor or fumes, usually suddenly and violently ▸ give forth, issue, release. *See* **emit** (1). 2. To free from an obligation or duty ▸ discharge, exempt. *See* **excuse** (1).

let out *verb*
1. To discharge material, as vapor or fumes, usually suddenly and violently ▸ give forth, issue, release. *See* **emit** (1). 2. To remove a liquid by a steady, gradual process ▸ pump, strain. *See* **drain** (1). 3. To disclose in a breach of confidence ▸ divulge, give away. *Informal:* spill. *See* **betray** (2). 4. To give temporary use of in return for payment ▸ rent, sublet. *See* **lease** (1).

let up *verb*
1. To become or cause to become less active or intense ▸ ebb, lapse. *See* **subside** (1). 2. To reduce in tension, pressure, or rigidity ▸ loosen, slacken. *See* **ease** (1).

letdown *noun*
▸ anticlimax, bust, washout. *See* **disappointment** (2).

lethal *adjective*
▸ deathly, fatal, mortal. *See* **deadly** (1). *See synonym note at* **deadly.**

lethality *or* **lethalness** *noun*
The quality or condition of causing death or disaster ▸ deadliness, fatality, fatefulness.

lethargic *adjective*
1. Lacking mental and physical alertness and activity ▸ enervated, hebetudinous, inert, slothful, sluggish, stupid, stuporous, torpid. *Slang:* dopey. *See also* **dull, languid.** 2. Lacking interest ▸ indifferent, listless, uninterested. *See* **apathetic.**

lethargy *noun*
1. A deficiency in mental and physical alertness and activity ▸ dullness, enervation, hebetude, inertness, languidness, languor, lassitude, leadenness, listlessness, slothfulness, sluggishness, stupor, torpidity, torpor. *See also* **stupidity.** 2. Lack of emotion or interest ▸ disinterest, indifference, unconcern. *See* **apathy.**

✦ **CORE SYNONYMS:** *lethargy, lassitude, torpor, torpidity, stupor, languor.* These nouns refer to a deficiency in mental and physical alertness and activity. *Lethargy* is a state of sluggishness, drowsy dullness, or apathy: *The war roused the nation from its lethargy. Lassitude* implies weariness or diminished energy such as might result from physical or mental strain: *"His anger had evaporated; he felt nothing but utter lassitude"* (John Galsworthy). *Torpor* and *torpidity* suggest the suspension of activity characteristic of an animal in hibernation: *"My calmness was the torpor of despair"* (Charles Brockden Brown). *Nothing could dispel the torpidity of the indifferent audience. Stupor* is often produced by the effects of alcohol or narcotics; it suggests a benumbed or dazed state of mind: *"The huge height of the buildings . . . the hubbub and endless stir . . . struck me into a kind of stupor of surprise"* (Robert Louis Stevenson). *Languor* is the indolence typical of one who is satiated by a life of luxury or pleasure: *After the banquet, I was overcome by languor.*

letter *noun*
1. A written communication that is directed to another ▸ correspondence, dispatch, epistle, line, memo, memorandum, message, missive, note. **2.** A conventional mark used in a writing system ▸ figure, symbol. *See* **character** (9).

✦ **CORE SYNONYMS:** *letter, epistle, memorandum, missive, note.* These nouns denote a written communication that is directed to another: *received a letter of complaint; the Epistles of the New Testament; a company memorandum about the vacation policy; a missive of condolence; a thank-you note.*

lettered *adjective*
▸ erudite, literate, scholarly. *See* **educated** (1).
lettuce *noun*
Slang Something, such as coins or printed bills, used as a medium of exchange ▸ currency. *Slang:* dough, moola. *See* **money** (1).
letup *noun*
The process of becoming less active or intense ▸ abatement, ebb, subsidence. *See* **waning.**
level *noun*
1. One of the units in a course, as on an ascending or descending scale ▸ interval, mark, step. *See* **degree** (1). **2.** Relative intensity or amount, as of a quality or attribute ▸ extent, magnitude, scope. *See* **degree** (2). **3.** Positioning of one individual vis-à-vis others ▸ position, rank, standing. *See* **place** (1). **4.** A division of persons or things by quality or rank ▸ league, rank, tier. *See* **class** (2).
level *adjective*
1. Having no irregularities, roughness, or indentations ▸ flush, planar. *See* **even** (1). *See synonym note at* **even. 2.** On the same plane or line ▸ coplanar, flat. *See* **even** (2).
level *verb*
1. To make even, smooth, or level ▸ smooth, straighten. *See* **even** (1). **2.** To pull down or break up

so that reconstruction is impossible ▸ dismantle, pulverize, tear down. *See* **destroy** (2). **3.** To bring down, as from a shot or blow ▸ floor, ground, hew. *See* **drop** (6). **4.** To make equal ▸ equate, even, square. *See* **equalize** (1). **5.** To put in balance ▸ equalize, stabilize. *See* **balance** (1). **6.** To direct something, often toward a target ▸ direct, point, train. *See* **aim** (1). *See synonym note at* **aim.**
levelheaded *adjective*
▸ commonsensical, prudent. *See* **sensible** (1).
levelheadedness *adjective*
▸ collectedness, equanimity, poise. *See* **balance** (2).
leverage *noun*
1. Power to sway or affect based on prestige, wealth, ability, or position ▸ force, sway, weight. *See* **influence** (1). **2.** A dominating position, as in a conflict ▸ edge, upper hand, vantage. *See* **advantage** (3).
leviathan *noun*
▸ Goliath, monster, titan. *See* **giant.**
levity *noun*
▸ frivolity, minutia, trivia. *See* **trifle** (1).
levy *verb*
1. To establish and apply as compulsory ▸ assess, exact, impose, put. **2.** To enroll compulsorily in military service ▸ conscript, draft, impress, induct.
levy *noun*
1. A compulsory contribution that is required for the support of an authority ▸ duty, impost, tariff. *See* **tax** (1). **2.** Compulsory enrollment in military service ▸ induction, selective service. *See* **draft** (2).
lewd *adjective*
1. Feeling or preoccupied with sexual love or desire ▸ concupiscent, lustful. *See* **lascivious** (1). **2.** Offensive to accepted standards of decency ▸ bawdy, coarse, indecent, vulgar. *See* **obscene** (1).
lewdness *noun*
▸ filthiness, profanity, smuttiness, vulgarness. *See* **obscenity** (1).
lex *noun*
▸ bill, legislation. *See* **law** (2).
lexeme *noun*
▸ expression, locution, word. *See* **term** (1).
lexical *adjective*
Relating to, consisting of, or having the nature of words ▸ linguistic, verbal, wordy.
lexicon *noun*
1. An alphabetical list of words often defined or translated ▸ dictionary, glossary, vocabulary, wordbook. **2.** All the words of a language ▸ vocabulary, word-hoard. **3.** Specialized expressions indigenous to a particular field, subject, trade, or subculture ▸ jargon, lingo, patois. *See* **language** (2).
liability *noun*
1. A condition of owing something to another ▸ arrears, encumbrance, obligation. *See* **debt** (2). **2.** The condition of being laid open to something undesirable or injurious ▸ endangerment, susceptibility, vulnerability. *See* **exposure** (1). **3.** Something, such as money, owed by one person to another ▸ indebted-

ness, obligation, score. *See* **debt** (1). **4.** The state of being responsible ▸ accountability, answerability. *See* **responsibility** (1). **5.** An act or course of action that is demanded of one, as by position, custom, law, or religion ▸ charge, commitment, obligation. *See* **duty** (1). **6.** An unfavorable condition, circumstance, or characteristic ▸ drawback, handicap, minus. *See* **disadvantage.**

liable *adjective*
1. Legally or officially obligated ▸ accountable, amenable, answerable, responsible. *See also* **obligated.**
2. Tending to incur ▸ open, prone, subject, susceptible, susceptive, vulnerable. *See also* **helpless. 3.** Having or showing a tendency or likelihood ▸ disposed, prone. *See* **inclined** (1).

✦ CORE SYNONYMS: *liable, responsible, answerable, accountable, amenable.* These adjectives mean legally or officialy obliged to answer, as for one's actions, to an authority that may impose a penalty for failure. *Liable* may refer to a legal obligation, as to pay damages or to perform jury duty: *Wage earners are liable to income tax. Responsible* often implies the satisfactory performance of duties or the trustworthy care for or disposition of possessions: *"I am responsible for the ship's safety"* (Robert Louis Stevenson). *Answerable* suggests a moral or legal responsibility subject to review by a higher authority: *The court held the parents answerable for their minor child's acts of vandalism. Accountable* especially emphasizes giving an account of one's discharge of a responsibility: *"The liberal philosophy holds that enduring governments must be accountable to someone beside themselves"* (Walter Lippmann). *Amenable* implies being subject to the control of an authority and therefore the absence of complete autonomy: *"There is no constitutional tribunal to which* [the king] *is amenable"* (Alexander Hamilton).

---

liaison *noun*
▸ amour, love affair, romance. *See* **love** (3).

liar *noun*
One who tells lies ▸ deceiver, dissimulator, fabricator, fabulist, false witness, falsifier, fibber, perjurer, prevaricator. *Informal:* storyteller. *See also* **hypocrite.**

libation *noun*
▸ beverage, brew, refreshment. *See* **drink** (1).

libel *noun*
The expression of injurious, malicious statements about someone ▸ aspersion, badmouthing, calumniation, calumny, character assassination, defamation, denigration, detraction, mudslinging, obloquy, scandal, slander, smear, smear campaign, traducement, vilification. *See also* **belittlement, vituperation.**

libel *verb*
To make harmful and often untrue statements about ▸ calumniate, defame, slander. *See* **malign.** *See synonym note at* **malign.**

libelous *adjective*
Damaging to the reputation ▸ calumnious, defamatory, detractive, injurious, invidious, scandalous, slanderous. *See also* **derogatory.**

liberal *adjective*
1. Favoring civil liberties and social reform, especially as a political philosophy ▸ left, leftist, left-wing, liberalistic, neoliberal, progressive, reformist, reform-minded, Whiggish. *See also* **ultraliberal. 2.** Not narrow or intolerant ▸ broad, open-minded, tolerant. *See* **broad-minded.** *See synonym note at* **broad-minded.**
3. Willing to give of oneself and one's possessions ▸ big-hearted, magnanimous, unselfish. *See* **generous** (1).

liberal *noun*
One with politically liberal views ▸ leftist, left-winger, liberalist, neoliberal, progressive, Whig. *See also* **ultraliberal.**

liberality *noun*
▸ magnanimity, munificence, unselfishness. *See* **generosity.**

liberate *verb*
▸ emancipate, release. *See* **free** (1).

liberated *adjective*
▸ free, unconfined, unrestrained. *See* **loose** (2).

liberation *noun*
1. The state of not being in confinement or servitude ▸ emancipation, freedom. *See* **liberty** (1). **2.** Extrication from danger or confinement ▸ deliverance, release, salvation. *See* **rescue.**

liberator *noun*
▸ deliverer, redeemer, savior. *See* **rescuer.**

libertine *noun*
An immoral or licentious person ▸ debaucher, profligate. *See* **wanton** (1).

libertine *adjective*
Sexually unrestrained ▸ fast, loose, promiscuous. *See* **wanton** (1).

libertinism *noun*
▸ licentiousness, profligacy. *See* **license** (2).

liberty *noun*
1. The state of not being in confinement or servitude ▸ emancipation, freedom, liberation, manumission.
2. The condition of being politically free ▸ autonomy, sovereignty. *See* **freedom** (1). **3.** Freedom from normal restraints or regulations ▸ entitlement, prerogative, privilege. *See* **license** (1).

libidinous *or* **libidinal** *adjective*
▸ concupiscent, lewd. *See* **lascivious** (1).

libido *or* **libidinousness** *noun*
▸ eroticism, lust, passion. *See* **desire** (2).

libretto *noun*
▸ dialogue, scenario, text. *See* **script** (2).

license *noun*
1. Freedom from normal restraints, limitations, or regulations ▸ elbowroom, entitlement, free hand, latitude, leeway, liberty, margin, play, privilege, room, scope. *See also* **right. 2.** Excessive freedom; lack of restraint ▸ anarchy, dissoluteness, dissolution, indulgence, laxity, laxness, libertinism, licentiousness, profligacy, slackness. *See also* **abandon, excess. 3.** A document that gives permission to do something ▸ commission, furlough, passport, permit, ticket, visa,

warrant. **4.** The approving of an action, especially when done by one in authority ▸ authorization, consent, sanction. *See* **permission.**

license *verb*

1. To give authority to ▸ accredit, empower, enable. *See* **authorize** (1). *See synonym note at* **authorize. 2.** To give one's consent to ▸ approve, authorize, sanction. *See* **permit** (2).

✦ **CORE SYNONYMS:** *license, elbowroom, latitude, leeway, margin, play, room, scope.* These nouns denote freedom from normal restraints, limitations, or regulations: *had license to do as they pleased; needed elbowroom to negotiate effectively; no latitude allowed in conduct; allowed the chef leeway in choosing the menu; no margin for error; imagination given full play; room for improvement; permitting their talents free scope.*

licentious *adjective*
▸ dissolute, rakish, unbridled. *See* **abandoned** (2).
licentiousness *noun*
▸ dissolution, profligacy. *See* **license** (2).
licit *adjective*
▸ legal, permitted, valid. *See* **lawful.**
licitness *noun*
▸ legitimacy, rightfulness, validity. *See* **legality.**
lick *verb*
1. *Slang* To punish with blows or lashes ▸ lash, thrash, whip. *See* **beat** (2). **2.** *Slang* To win a victory over, as in battle or a competition ▸ conquer, surmount, vanquish. *See* **defeat** (1).
lick *noun*
A sudden heavy stroke ▸ crack, hit, swat, whack. *See* **blow²** (1).
lickety-split *adverb*
1. In a rapid way ▸ hurriedly, posthaste, pronto, quickly. *See* **fast** (1). **2.** *Informal* Without delay ▸ forthwith, instantly, straightaway. *See* **immediately** (1).
licking *noun*
1. *Slang* A punishment dealt with blows or lashes ▸ lashing, thrashing, whipping. *See* **beating** (1). **2.** *Slang* The act of defeating or the condition of being defeated ▸ overthrow, trouncing, vanquishment. *See* **defeat.**
lid *noun*
1. Something that covers, especially to prevent contents from spilling ▸ cap, cover, covering, top. *See also* **plug. 2.** The greatest amount or number allowed ▸ brim, cap, maximum. *See* **limit** (1).
lie¹ *verb*
1. To be or place oneself in a prostrate or recumbent position ▸ couch, lie down, recline, repose, stretch (out). **2.** To take repose, as by sleeping or lying quietly ▸ curl up, recline, repose, rest, stretch (out). *See also* **nap, sleep. 3.** To have an inherent basis ▸ exist, reside. *See* **consist** (1).
lie² *noun*
An untrue declaration ▸ bald-faced lie, barefaced lie, canard, cock-and-bull story, distortion, fable, fabri-

cation, falsehood, falsity, fib, fiction, half-truth, invention, inveracity, mendacity, misrepresentation, misstatement, prevarication, story, tale, untruth, white lie. *Informal:* fish story, tall tale. *Slang:* whopper.
lie *verb*
To present false information with the intention of deceiving ▸ falsify, fib, forswear, invent, make up, perjure, prevaricate. *Idioms:* lie like a trooper, like through one's teeth, speak with a forked tongue. *See also* **act, distort.**

✦ **CORE SYNONYMS:** *lie, falsify, fib, prevaricate.* These verbs mean to present false information with the intention of deceiving someone: *a witness who lied under oath; a scoundrel who falsified evidence; fibbed to escape being scolded; didn't prevaricate but answered honestly.*

liege *adjective*
▸ allegiant, loyal, staunch. *See* **faithful** (1).
lieu *noun*
The function or position customarily occupied by another ▸ place, stead.
lieutenant *noun*
1. A person who assists someone else ▸ aide, deputy, helper. *See* **assistant.** *See synonym note at* **assistant. 2.** One who represents the interests of another ▸ ambassador, deputy, proxy. *See* **representative** (2).
life *noun*
1. The period during which someone or something exists ▸ course, day, days, duration, existence, generation, lifetime, span, term, time. *See also* **age. 2.** A lively, emphatic, eager quality or manner ▸ animation, verve, vivaciousness. *See* **spirit** (1). **3.** A member of the human race ▸ mortal, person. *See* **human being.**
life force *noun*
▸ breath, soul, vitality. *See* **spirit** (2).
lifeless *adjective*
1. No longer alive ▸ deceased, departed, perished. *See* **dead** (1). *See synonym note at* **dead. 2.** Completely lacking sensation or consciousness ▸ dead, inanimate, insensate, insentient. **3.** Lacking physical feeling or sensitivity ▸ inert, numb, unfeeling. *See* **dead** (2). **4.** Unable to support vegetation ▸ sterile, unfruitful, unproductive. *See* **barren** (2). **5.** Lacking liveliness, charm, or surprise ▸ aseptic, colorless, pedestrian. *See* **dull** (1). **6.** Lacking intelligent thought or content ▸ empty, vacuous. *See* **vacant** (1).
lifelessness *noun*
1. A lack of excitement, liveliness, or interest ▸ blandness, drabness, flatness. *See* **dullness** (1). **2.** A lack of action or activity ▸ inaction, inertness. *See* **inaction.**
lifelike *adjective*
1. Accurately representing what is depicted or described ▸ naturalistic, true-life. *See* **realistic** (2). **2.** Depicted in sharp and accurate detail ▸ explicit, realistic, vivid. *See* **graphic** (1). *See synonym note at* **graphic.**
lifesaver *noun*
▸ deliverer, redeemer, savior. *See* **rescuer.**

lifestyle *noun*
▸ civilization, ethos, society. *See* **culture** (2).
lifetime *noun*
▸ existence, span, term. *See* **life** (1).
lift *verb*
1. To move something to a higher position ▸ pick up, raise. *See* **elevate** (1). *See synonym note at* **elevate**. 2. To move from a lower to a higher position ▸ ascend, climb, soar. *See* **rise** (3). 3. To rise up in flight ▸ lift off, take off. 4. To disappear by or as if by rising ▸ disperse, dissipate, fade away, scatter, thin out, withdraw. *See also* **disappear**. 5. To take back or remove ▸ countermand, overturn, pull, quash, recall, repeal, rescind, reverse, revoke. *See also* **abolish, retract**. 6. To raise the spirits of ▸ buoy (up), exhilarate, inspire. *See* **elate** (1). 7. *Informal* To take another's property without permission ▸ filch, pilfer. *See* **steal** (1). *See synonym note at* **steal**. 8. *Informal* To reproduce another's work without permission ▸ appropriate, crib, pirate. *See* **plagiarize**.
lift *noun*
1. An instance of lifting or being lifted ▸ boost, heave, hoist, uplift, upthrust. 2. The act of rising or moving upward ▸ ascension, mounting. *See* **ascent** (1). 3. High spirits ▸ euphoria, inspiration. *See* **elation** (1). 4. A strong, pleasant feeling of excitement or stimulation ▸ *Informal:* wallop. *Slang:* bang, kick. *See* **thrill** (1). 5. Something that gives courage or confidence ▸ boost, exhortation, motivation. *See* **encouragement** (1).
liftoff *noun*
The act of rising in flight ▸ takeoff.
ligament *or* **ligature** *noun*
▸ binding, link, tie. *See* **bond** (2).
light¹ *noun*
1. Electromagnetic radiation that makes vision possible ▸ glow, illumination, lambency, lucency, luminescence. *See also* **flash**. 2. The act of physically illuminating or the condition of being filled with light ▸ illumination, lighting. *See also* **brilliance**. 3. The position from which something is observed or considered ▸ aspect, respect, standpoint. *See* **viewpoint**.
light *verb*
1. To begin or cause to begin burning ▸ enkindle, fire, ignite, kindle, touch off. *Slang:* torch. *Idioms:* burst into flame, catch fire (*or* on fire), set fire to, set afire (*or* on fire). *See also* **burn**. 2. To cover or fill with light ▸ illumine, lighten. *See* **illuminate** (1). 3. To make lively or animated ▸ animate, brighten, enliven, light up, perk up.
light *adjective*
Having a light color or complexion ▸ alabaster, ivory, pale. *See* **fair¹** (9).
light² *adjective*
1. Having little weight; not heavy ▸ airy, fluffy, lightweight, weightless. *Idioms:* light as air (*or* a feather). *See also* **immaterial, sheer²** 2. Of small intensity ▸ faint, gentle, moderate, modest, slight, soft. *See also*

imperceptible. 3. Requiring little effort or exertion ▸ easy, moderate, undemanding. *Informal:* cushy, soft. 4. Of little importance or seriousness ▸ inconsequential, negligible, trifling. *See* **trivial**. 5. Happy and free from worry or care ▸ blithe, buoyant, debonair. *See* **lighthearted** (1). 6. Sexually unrestrained ▸ fast, loose, promiscuous. *See* **wanton** (1).
light *verb*
1. To come ashore from a seacraft ▸ alight, debark, disembark, land. 2. To come to rest on the ground ▸ alight, set down. *See* **land** (2).
light into *verb*
1. *Informal* To set upon with violent force ▸ assail, assault, storm, strike. *See* **attack** (1). 2. *Informal* To criticize harshly and devastatingly ▸ bash, excoriate, flay. *See* **slam** (5).
light on *or* **upon** *verb*
To find or meet by chance ▸ come across, run across, stumble on. *See* **encounter** (1).
light out *verb*
Informal To proceed in a specified direction ▸ head, make, set out. *See* **bear** (5).
lighten¹ *verb*
1. To cover or fill with light ▸ illume, illumine. *See* **illuminate** (1). 2. To become brighter ▸ brighten, illuminate. *See* **clear** (1).
lighten² *verb*
To make less severe or more bearable ▸ alleviate, ease, lessen. *See* **relieve** (1). *See synonym note at* **relieve**.
light-fingered *adjective*
▸ sticky-fingered, thieving. *See* **thievish**.
light-haired *adjective*
▸ blond, fair-haired. *See* **fair¹** (8).
lightheaded *adjective*
▸ dazed, groggy, reeling. *See* **dizzy** (1).
lightheadedness *noun*
▸ grogginess, unsteadiness, vertigo, wooziness. *See* **dizziness**.
lighthearted *adjective*
1. Happy and free from worry or care ▸ airy, blithe, buoyant, carefree, debonair, fancy-free, happy-go-lucky, light, untroubled. *Idioms:* free and easy, without a care in the world. *See also* **careless, lively, merry**. 2. Being in or showing good spirits ▸ happy, jolly, jovial. *See* **cheerful** (1). *See synonym note at* **cheerful**. 3. Given to lighthearted silliness ▸ featherbrained, flighty, frivolous. *See* **giddy** (2).
lightheartedness *noun*
▸ glee, joviality, mirth. *See* **merriment** (1).
lighting *noun*
The act of physically illuminating or the condition of being filled with light ▸ illumination, light. *See also* **brilliance**.
lightness *noun*
▸ frivolity, levity, trivia. *See* **trifle** (1).
lights out *noun*
▸ after dark, dark. *See* **night**.
lightweight *adjective*
1. Having little weight; not heavy ▸ airy, fluffy, light,

weightless. *Idioms:* light as air (*or* a feather). *See also* **immaterial, sheer².** **2.** Of little importance or seriousness ▸ inconsequential, negligible, trifling. *See* **trivial.**

lightweight *noun*
A totally insignificant person ▸ nobody, nothing, small fry. *See* **nonentity.**

like¹ *verb*
1. To find agreeable ▸ adore, fancy, favor, love, take to. *Idioms:* take a fancy (*or* liking *or* shine) to. *See also* **value.** **2.** To receive pleasure from ▸ appreciate, savor. *See* **enjoy** (1). **3.** To have an inclination to ▸ want, wish. *See* **choose** (2).

like² *adjective*
Possessing the same or almost the same characteristics ▸ akin, alike, analogous, comparable, corresponding, equivalent, kin, matching, parallel, resembling, similar, uniform. *See also* **equal.**

likeable *adjective*
▸ cordial, friendly, genial. *See* **amiable.**

likelihood *noun*
1. The likeliness of a given event occurring ▸ odds, possibility, probability. *See* **chance** (3). **2.** Something expected ▸ anticipation, expectation, promise, prospect. *See also* **theory.**

likely *adjective*
1. Having a good chance of happening or being true ▸ contingent, possible. *See* **probable** (1). **2.** Based on probability or presumption ▸ assumptive, presumable, prospective. *See* **presumptive.** **3.** Capable of being anticipated, considered, or imagined ▸ earthly, imaginable, possible. *See* **conceivable.** **4.** Inspiring confidence or hope ▸ heartening, hopeful. *See* **encouraging.** **5.** Having or showing a tendency or likelihood ▸ disposed, prone. *See* **inclined** (1).

likely *adverb*
More likely than not ▸ believably, presumably. *See* **probably.**

like-minded *adjective*
▸ accordant, consonant, unified. *See* **unanimous.**

liken *verb*
To represent as similar ▸ analogize, assimilate, compare, equate, identify, match, parallel, relate. *See also* **associate.**

likeness *noun*
1. The quality or state of being alike ▸ affinity, alikeness, analogy, comparison, correspondence, parallelism, resemblance, similarity, similitude, uniformity, uniformness. *See also* **agreement, sameness.** **2.** Something closely resembling another ▸ ditto, facsimile, replica. *See* **copy** (1). **3.** An image caused by reflection ▸ image, reflection. *See also* **copy.**

✦ CORE SYNONYMS: *likeness, similarity, similitude, resemblance, analogy, affinity.* These nouns denote the quality or state of being alike. *Likeness* implies close agreement: *The forgery was renowned for its likeness to the original. Similarity* and *similitude* suggest agreement only in some respects or to some degree: *They were drawn to each other by similarity of interests.* "*A striking similitude between the brother and sister now*

first arrested my attention" (Edgar Allan Poe). *Resemblance* refers to similarity in external or superficial details: "*The child . . . bore a remarkable resemblance to her grandfather*" (Lytton Strachey). *Analogy* is similarity, as of properties or functions, between things that are otherwise not comparable: *The operation of a computer presents an interesting analogy to the working of the human brain. Affinity* is likeness deriving from kinship or from the possession of shared properties or sympathies: *Being an orphan, she felt an affinity with other parentless children.*

---

likewise *adverb*
In addition ▸ also, besides, too. *See* **additionally.**

likewise *adjective*
In a similar manner ▸ similarly, so. *Idioms:* by the same token, in like fashion, in like manner, in the same way.

liking *noun*
1. A desire for a particular thing or activity ▸ fancy, mind, pleasure, soft spot, will. *See also* **inclination, taste.** **2.** An intense attachment to a person or thing ▸ affection, devotion, fondness. *See* **love** (1).

Lilliputian *adjective*
▸ dwarf, miniature, minuscule. *See* **tiny.**

lilt *noun*
▸ edge, intonation, inflection. *See* **tone** (2).

lily-livered *adjective*
▸ faint-hearted, pusillanimous. *Slang:* gutless. *See* **cowardly.**

lily-white *adjective*
1. Beyond reproach ▸ faultless, unblamable. *See* **exemplary** (1). **2.** Free from evil and corruption ▸ pure, uncorrupted. *See* **innocent** (1). **3.** Free from guilt or blame ▸ faultless, guiltless. *See* **innocent** (2).

limber *adjective*
▸ lissome, lithe, supple. *See* **flexible** (2).

limberness *noun*
▸ elasticity, malleability, pliability. *See* **flexibility** (1).

limit *noun*
1. The greatest amount or number allowed ▸ brim, cap, ceiling, cutoff, lid, limitation, maximum. *See also* **allotment, maximum.** **2.** Either of the two points at the ends of a spectrum or range ▸ extreme, extremity. *See also* **climax, low.** **3.** The boundary surrounding a certain area ▸ bounds, confines, perimeter. *See* **limits.** **4.** Something that limits or holds back ▸ check, constraint, curb. *See* **restraint** (1). **5.** The ultimate point to which an action, thought, discussion, or policy is carried ▸ end, extreme. *See* **length** (3). **6.** A line or area where something ends or abruptly changes ▸ brink, fringe, margin. *See* **border** (1).

limit *verb*
1. To place a limit on ▸ bound, circumscribe, confine, fix, restrict, set. *See also* **restrain.** **2.** To fix the limits of ▸ define, demarcate, mark. *See* **determine** (1).

✦ CORE SYNONYMS: *limit, restrict, confine, circumscribe.* These verbs mean to establish or keep within specified limits. *Limit* refers principally to the establishment of a maximum beyond which a person or thing cannot or may not go: *The Constitution limits the President's term of office to four years.* To *restrict* is to keep within prescribed limits, as of choice or action: *The sale of alcoholic beverages is restricted to those over 21. Confine* suggests imprisonment, restraint, or impediment: *The children were confined to the nursery. Circumscribe* connotes an encircling or surrounding line that confines, especially narrowly: *"A man . . . should not circumscribe his activity by any inflexible fence of rigid rules"* (John Stuart Blackie).

limitation *noun*
   1. The act of limiting or condition of being limited ▶ confinement, constraint, restraint. *See* **restriction** (1). **2.** Something that limits or holds back ▶ check, constraint, curb. *See* **restraint** (1). **3.** The greatest amount or number that is allowed ▶ brim, cap, maximum. *See* **limit** (1). **4.** A restricting or modifying element ▶ condition, proviso, stipulation. *See* **provision** (1).

limited *adjective*
   1. Kept within certain limits ▶ checked, controlled. *See* **restricted** (1). **2.** Having distinct limits ▶ fixed, specific. *See* **definite** (2). **3.** Restricted in scope, outlook, or understanding ▶ insular, narrow-minded, provincial. *See* **narrow** (1). **4.** Not total, unlimited, or wholehearted ▶ conditioned, reserved, restricted. *See* **qualified** (1). **5.** Confined to a particular location or site ▶ bounded, regional. *See* **local** (1).

limitless *adjective*
   ▶ illimitable, infinite. *See* **endless** (1).

limitlessness *noun*
   ▶ immeasurability, inexhaustibility, measurelessness. *See* **infinity** (1).

limits *noun*
   The boundary surrounding a certain area ▶ bound, bounds, confines, end, limit, perimeter, periphery, precincts. *See also* **border, circumference, outskirts.**

limn *verb*
   ▶ depict, portray, render. *See* **represent** (2). *See synonym note at* **represent.**

limp *verb*
   1. To walk unsteadily ▶ halt, hobble, totter. *See* **stagger** (1). **2.** To proceed or perform in an unsteady, faltering manner ▶ bungle, flounder, fumble. *See* **muddle** (1).

limp *adjective*
   1. Not firm or stiff ▶ drooping, droopy, flabby, flaccid, floppy, soft. *See also* **flexible, loose, malleable. 2.** Lacking energy and vitality ▶ languorous, listless, spiritless. *See* **languid.**

✤ **CORE SYNONYMS:** *limp, flabby, flaccid, floppy.* These adjectives mean lacking in stiffness or firmness: *a limp shirt collar; flabby, wrinkled flesh; flaccid cheeks; a floppy hat brim.*

◄ **ANTONYM:** *firm*

limpid *adjective*
   ▶ crystalline, hyaline, lucid. *See* **clear** (1). *See synonym note at* **clear.**

limpidity *or* **limpidness** *noun*
   ▶ distinctness, lucidity, perspicuity, plainness. *See* **clarity** (1).

line *noun*
   1. A group of people or things arranged in a row ▶ column, file, queue, rank, row, string, tier. *See also* **series. 2.** An indentation or seam on the skin, especially on the face ▶ crease, crow's-foot, furrow. *See* **wrinkle** (1). **3.** A method used for accomplishing something ▶ course, modus operandi, procedure, technique. *See* **approach** (1). **4.** A statement presented for belief, as by a religious group ▶ position, principle, tenet. *See* **doctrine. 5.** Activity pursued as a livelihood ▶ career, employment, occupation. *See* **business** (2). **6.** A product or products bought and sold in commerce ▶ commodity, merchandise, ware. *See* **good** (2). **7.** One's ancestors or ancestral derivation ▶ blood, descent, lineage. *See* **ancestry. 8.** A band or fiber that is used to bind or tie ▶ cable, rope, string. *See* **cord. 9.** A long narrow area that has a different color or marking from what surrounds it ▶ bar, streak. *See* **stripe** (1). **10.** A written communication directed to another ▶ correspondence, missive, note. *See* **letter** (1).

line *verb*
   1. To place in or form a line or lines ▶ align, dress, file, line up, queue (up), range. *See also* **arrange. 2.** To mark with a line or band, as of different color or texture ▶ striate, variegate. *See* **streak.**

lineage *noun*
   1. One's ancestral derivation ▶ bloodline, origin. *See* **ancestry. 2.** A group of people sharing common ancestry ▶ clan, house, kindred. *See* **family** (2).

lineal *adjective*
   Of unbroken descent or lineage ▶ direct, genealogical, hereditary, natural. *See also* **ancestral.**

lineaments *noun*
   1. The front surface of the head ▶ countenance, features, visage. *See* **face** (1). **2.** A disposition of the facial features that conveys meaning, feeling, or mood ▶ countenance, look, visage. *See* **expression** (4). **3.** An outward appearance ▶ aspect, features. *See* **face** (4).

linear *adjective*
   ▶ straight, unswerving. *See* **direct** (1).

lineup *noun*
   1. The act or condition of being arranged ▶ classification, layout, positioning. *See* **arrangement** (1). **2.** An organized list, as of procedures, activities, or events ▶ calendar, schedule, timetable. *See* **program** (1). **3.** A list of candidates proposed or endorsed by a political party ▶ ballot, slate, ticket.

linger *verb*
   1. To continue to be in a place ▶ bide, tarry, wait. *See* **remain** (1). *See synonym note at* **remain. 2.** To go or move slowly so that progress is hindered ▶ dawdle, dilly-dally, drag. *See* **delay** (2).

lingerer *noun*
   ▶ lag, procrastinator, straggler. *See* **laggard.**

lingering *adjective*
   ▶ continuing, persistent. *See* **chronic** (2).

lingo *noun*
1. A variety of a language that differs from the standard form ▸ jargon, vernacular. *See* **dialect** (1). *See synonym note at* **dialect**. **2.** Specialized expressions indigenous to a particular field, subject, trade, or subculture ▸ jargon, lexicon, patois. *See* **language** (2).
linguistic *adjective*
Relating to, consisting of, or having the nature of words ▸ lexical, verbal, wordy.
liniment *noun*
▸ emollient, salve. *See* **ointment**.
link *noun*
1. That which unites or binds ▸ ligature, nexus, tie. *See* **bond** (2). **2.** A logical or natural association between two or more things ▸ correlation, relationship. *See* **relation** (1).
link *verb*
1. To unite or be united in a relationship ▸ combine, connect, join. *See* **associate** (1). **2.** To bring or come together into a united whole ▸ join, unify, unite. *See* **combine** (1). *See synonym note at* **combine**. **3.** To come or bring together in one's mind or imagination ▸ correlate, identify. *See* **associate** (3).
linkage *noun*
▸ correlation, link, relationship. *See* **relation** (1).
lintel *noun*
▸ crossbeam, girder, timber. *See* **beam** (2).
lion *noun*
1. An important, influential person ▸ notability, personage. *Slang:* big shot. *See* **dignitary**. **2.** A famous person ▸ luminary, personality, star. *See* **celebrity** (1).
lionization *noun*
▸ apotheosis, elevation. *See* **exaltation** (1).
lip *noun*
1. *Informal* Insolent talk ▸ back talk, mouth. *Informal:* sass. *See also* **impudence**. **2.** A line or area where something ends or abruptly changes ▸ brink, fringe, margin. *See* **border** (1). **3.** A part that protrudes or extends outward ▸ knob, protrusion, protuberance. *See* **projection** (1).
lip *verb*
To flow against or along ▸ bathe, lap, lave, wash. *See also* **flow**.
lip service *noun*
▸ phoniness, sanctimoniousness, sanctimony. *See* **hypocrisy**.
liquefy *verb*
▸ dissolve, flux, thaw. *See* **melt** (1).
liquidate *verb*
1. To set right by giving what is due ▸ discharge, satisfy. *See* **settle** (3). **2.** To destroy all traces of ▸ eradicate, expunge, obliterate. *See* **annihilate** (1). **3.** To get rid of, especially by banishment or execution ▸ purge, wipe out. *See* **eliminate** (1). *See synonym note at* **eliminate**. **4.** To take the life of a person or persons unlawfully ▸ assassinate, kill, slay. *See* **murder** (1).
liquidation *noun*
1. The act or process of eliminating ▸ eradication, purge. *See* **elimination** (1). **2.** Utter destruction ▸ ex-
termination, extinction, obliteration. *See* **annihilation** (1). **3.** The crime of murdering someone ▸ homicide, killing. *See* **murder**. **4.** The savage killing of many victims ▸ bloodshed, butchery. *See* **massacre**.
liquor *noun*
▸ beverage, brew, refreshment. *See* **drink** (1).
lissome *adjective*
▸ limber, lithe, supple. *See* **flexible** (2).
lissomeness *noun*
▸ elasticity, malleability, pliability. *See* **flexibility** (1).
list¹ *noun*
A series, as of names or words, printed or written down ▸ agenda, catalog, checklist, directory, index, inventory, invoice, listing, manifest, register, roll, roster, schedule, table.
list *verb*
1. To place on a list or in a record or book ▸ book, catalog, chronicle, docket, enroll, enter, file, inscribe, insert, log, minute, post, record, register, set down, tabulate, write down. *See also* **schedule**. **2.** To name or specify one by one ▸ inventory, tick off. *See* **enumerate** (1).
list² *noun*
Deviation from a particular direction ▸ grade, heel. *See* **inclination** (2).
list *verb*
To depart or cause to depart from true vertical or horizontal ▸ heel, lean. *See* **incline** (1).
listen *verb*
1. To make an effort to hear something ▸ attend, hark, hearken, heed. *Idioms:* give (*or* lend) an ear. **2.** To perceive by ear, usually attentively ▸ hark, heed. *See* **hear** (1).
listen *noun*
A chance to be heard ▸ audience, audition, hearing.
listing *noun*
▸ register, roster, schedule. *See* **list¹**.
listless *adjective*
1. Lacking energy and vitality ▸ languorous, limp, spiritless. *See* **languid**. **2.** Lacking interest ▸ indifferent, lethargic, uninterested. *See* **apathetic**.
listlessness *noun*
1. A deficiency in mental and physical alertness and activity ▸ dullness, languor, sluggishness. *See* **lethargy** (1). **2.** Lack of emotion or interest ▸ disinterest, indifference, unconcern. *See* **apathy**. **3.** The condition of being bored ▸ ennui, tedium. *See* **boredom**.
lit *adjective*
1. *Slang* Stupefied, excited, or muddled with alcoholic liquor ▸ besotted, drunken, inebriated. *See* **drunk**. **2.** *Slang* Stupefied, intoxicated, or otherwise influenced by the taking of drugs ▸ *Slang:* high, hopped-up, stoned. *See* **drugged**.
litany *noun*
▸ devotions, orison. *See* **prayer¹** (2).
literal *adjective*
1. Employing the very same words as another ▸ undeviating, unvarnished, verbal, verbatim, word-for-word. *Idiom:* to the letter. *See also* **accurate**. **2.**

Marked by a narrow concern for book learning and formal rules ▶ bookish, scholastic. *See* **pedantic.**

literally *adverb*
▶ faithfully, precisely. *See* **exactly** (1).

literary *adjective*
▶ bookish, donnish, scholastic. *See* **pedantic.**

literate *adjective*
▶ enlightened, informed, lettered. *See* **educated** (1).

lithe *or* **lithesome** *adjective*
▶ limber, lissome, supple. *See* **flexible** (2).

litheness *noun*
▶ elasticity, malleability, pliability. *See* **flexibility** (1).

litigate *verb*
To institute or subject to legal proceedings ▶ law, prosecute, sue. *Idioms:* bring suit, haul (*or* drag) into court.

litigation *noun*
▶ action, suit. *See* **lawsuit.**

litigious *adjective*
▶ contentious, quarrelsome. *See* **argumentative.**

litter *noun*
1. The offspring, as of an animal or bird, for example, that are the result of one breeding season ▶ brood, young. *See also* **progeny. 2.** A number of animals considered collectively ▶ bevy, gaggle, herd. *See* **flock** (1). *See synonym note at* **flock. 3.** Items or material discarded or rejected as useless or worthless ▶ rubbish, trash, waste. *See* **garbage** (1).

little *adjective*
1. Below average in amount, length, size, or scope ▶ bantam, compact, petite, runty, short, small, smallish, undersized. *See also* **stocky, tiny. 2.** Of little importance or seriousness ▶ inconsequential, negligible, trifling. *See* **trivial. 3.** Restricted in scope, outlook, or understanding ▶ insular, narrow-minded, provincial. *See* **narrow** (1).

little *adverb*
At rare intervals ▶ rarely, seldom. *See* **infrequently.**

little *noun*
A tiny amount ▶ dash, drop, smidgen. *See* **bit**[1] (1).

little-known *adjective*
▶ insignificant, unheard-of. *See* **obscure** (2).

littlest *adjective*
▶ least, smallest. *See* **minimal.**

liturgical *adjective*
▶ ceremonial, formal, ritualistic. *See* **ritual.**

liturgy *noun*
▶ rite, ritual, tradition. *See* **ceremony** (1).

livable *adjective*
Fit to live in ▶ habitable, inhabitable.

live[1] *verb*
1. To have reality or life ▶ breathe, subsist. *See* **exist** (1). **2.** To have as one's domicile, usually for an extended period ▶ abide, domicile, dwell, house, reside, stay. *See also* **inhabit. 3.** To go through life in a certain way ▶ conduct, pass, pursue. *See* **lead** (3).

live by *verb*
To act in conformity with ▶ heed, obey, observe. *See* **follow** (4).

live on *verb*
To include as part of one's diet by nature or preference ▶ eat, exist on, feed on, subsist on.

live through *verb*
To put up with ▶ stick out, tolerate, withstand. *See* **endure** (1).

live[2] *adjective*
1. Having life ▶ animate, living, vital. *See* **alive** (1). *See synonym note at* **alive. 2.** *Informal* Of great current interest ▶ red-hot, hot. *See also* **fashionable, important.**

livelihood *noun*
▶ bread, keep, maintenance. *See* **living.**

liveliness *noun*
1. A lively, emphatic, eager quality or manner ▶ life, verve, vivaciousness. *See* **spirit** (1). **2.** Capacity for work or vigorous activity ▶ force, potency, power. *See* **energy.**

lively *adjective*
1. Very brisk, alert, and full of high spirits ▶ animated, bouncy, breezy, bubbly, chipper, coltish, dashing, ebullient, effervescent, exuberant, frisky, high-spirited, jaunty, perky, pert, sassy, sparkling, sparkly, spirited, vibrant, vivacious. *Informal:* corky, peppy, snappy. *Idioms:* bright-eyed and bushy-tailed, full of life. *See also* **enthusiastic, passionate. 2.** Possessing, exerting, or displaying energy ▶ brisk, dynamic, vigorous. *See* **energetic.**

live wire *noun*
Informal An intensely energetic, enthusiastic person ▶ demon, dynamo, hustler. *Informal:* eager beaver, firebreather, go-getter.

livid *adjective*
1. Lacking color ▶ bloodless, lurid, wan. *See* **pale** (1). **2.** Feeling or showing anger ▶ irate, livid, rabid. *See* **angry.** *See synonym note at* **angry.**

living *adjective*
Having life ▶ breathing, live, vital. *See* **alive** (1). *See synonym note at* **alive.**

living *noun*
The means needed to support life ▶ alimentation, alimony, bread, bread and butter, existence, income, keep, livelihood, maintenance, subsistence, support, sustenance, upkeep.

living hell *noun*
▶ perdition, persecution. *See* **hell.**

load *noun*
1. Something carried or transported ▶ encumbrance, haul. *See* **burden**[1] (2). **2.** *Informal* An indeterminately great amount or number ▶ bunch, multiplicity. *Informal:* bushel. *See* **heap** (3).

load *verb*
1. To weigh down or place a heavy load on ▶ encumber, saddle, tax. *See* **burden**[1]. **2.** To fill to capacity ▶ charge, heap, pack. *See* **fill** (1). **3.** To put explosive material into a weapon ▶ charge, prime, ready. **4.** To give an inaccurate view of by representing falsely or misleadingly ▶ fudge, misrepresent, pervert. *See* **distort** (1). **5.** To make impure or inferior by contact or

mixture ▸ adulterate, debase, doctor. *See* **contaminate** (1). *See synonym note at* **contaminate. 6.** To collect or pile up or onto something ▸ drift, lump, mound. *See* **heap** (1).

loaded *adjective*

1. Burdened by a weighty load ▸ heavy, heavy-laden, laden, weighed down. **2.** Mixed with other substances ▸ alloyed, combined, polluted. *See* **impure** (2). **3.** *Slang* Stupefied, excited, or muddled with alcoholic liquor ▸ intoxicated, sodden, tipsy. *See* **drunk. 4.** *Slang* Possessing a large amount of money, land, or other material possessions ▸ affluent, moneyed, wealthy. *See* **rich** (1). *See synonym note at* **rich.**

loaf *verb*

▸ loiter, lounge, slack off. *See* **idle** (1).

loafer *noun*

▸ bum, idler, ne'er-do-well. *See* **wastrel** (2).

loam *noun*

▸ clay, soil. *See* **earth** (1).

loan *verb*

▸ discount, float. *See* **lend.**

loath *adjective*

▸ disinclined, reluctant. *See* **indisposed** (1).

loathe *verb*

▸ abominate, despise, execrate. *See* **hate.**

loathing *noun*

1. A strong feeling of hostility or dislike ▸ antipathy, aversion, horror. *See* **hate** (1). **2.** The feeling of despising ▸ disdain, hatred, scorn. *See* **despisal. 3.** Extreme aversion caused by something offensive ▸ abhorrence, queasiness, revulsion. *See* **disgust.**

loathsome *adjective*

1. So unpleasant or objectionable as to cause scorn or disgust ▸ contemptible, disgusting, obnoxious. *See* **offensive** (1). **2.** Shockingly repellent ▸ grisly, gruesome, macabre. *See* **ghastly** (1).

loathsomeness *noun*

▸ monstrosity, odiousness, unsightliness. *See* **ugliness** (1).

lob *verb*

To send through the air with a motion of the hand or arm ▸ heave, hurl, pitch. *See* **throw** (1).

lob *noun*

An act of throwing ▸ fling, hurl, toss. *See* **throw.**

local *adjective*

1. Confined to a particular location or site ▸ bounded, limited, localized, on-site, regional. **2.** Of, in, or belonging to a city ▸ municipal, urban. *See* **city. 3.** Restricted in scope, outlook, or understanding ▸ insular, narrow-minded, provincial. *See* **narrow** (1). **4.** Existing, born, or produced in a land or region ▸ autochthonic, native. *See* **indigenous** (1).

local *noun*

Informal One who resides in a place ▸ denizen, occupant, resident. *See* **inhabitant.**

locale *noun*

1. A surrounding area ▸ environs, neighborhood. *See* **environment** (1). **2.** A particular geographic area ▸ neighborhood, vicinity. *See* **locality** (1). **3.** The place

where an action or event occurs ▸ site, stage. *See* **scene** (1).

locality *noun*

1. A particular geographic area ▸ area, locale, location, neighborhood, place, vicinity. *See also* **position, scene. 2.** A part of the earth's surface ▸ district, region, zone. *See* **area** (2). **3.** A surrounding area ▸ locale, neighborhood. *See* **environment** (1).

localized *adjective*

▸ bounded, limited. *See* **local** (1).

locate *verb*

1. To look for and discover ▸ find, pinpoint, spot. *Informal:* scare up. *See also* **trace, uncover. 2.** To move to a place and reside there ▸ relocate, settle. **Idioms:** fix one's residence, make one's home, put down roots, take up residence. *See also* **emigrate, live¹, move. 3.** To put in a certain position or location ▸ install, place, situate. *See* **position.**

location *noun*

1. A particular geographic area ▸ neighborhood, vicinity. *See* **locality** (1). **2.** One's place and direction relative to one's surroundings ▸ orientation, position. *See* **bearing** (3). **3.** The place where a person or thing is located ▸ locus, point, spot. *See* **position** (1).

lock¹ *noun*

A device for locking ▸ catch, clip, latch. *See* **fastener.**

lock *verb*

To make secure ▸ bolt, clamp, lash. *See* **fasten** (1).

lock away *or* **in** *or* **up** *verb* To put in or as if in prison ▸ incarcerate, jail, shut (away). *See* **imprison.**

lock² *noun*

Something with a curled or spiral shape ▸ coil, ringlet, twist. *See* **curl.**

lockup *noun*

Informal A place for the confinement of persons in lawful detention ▸ penitentiary, prison. *Informal:* pen. *See* **jail.**

loco *adjective*

Slang Afflicted with or exhibiting irrationality and mental unsoundness ▸ crazy, lunatic, mad. *See* **insane** (1).

locus *noun*

1. The place where a person or thing is located ▸ location, point, spot. *See* **position** (1). **2.** A place of concentrated activity, influence, or importance ▸ headquarters, heart, hub. *See* **center** (1).

locution *noun*

1. A sound or combination of sounds that symbolizes and communicates a meaning ▸ lexeme, word. *See* **term** (1). **2.** A word or group of words forming a unit and conveying meaning ▸ collocation, phrase. *See* **expression** (3). **3.** Choice of words and the way in which they are used ▸ phraseology, verbalism. *See* **wording.**

lodge *verb*

1. To stay in or provide with lodging, especially temporarily ▸ accommodate, bed (down), berth, bestow, billet, board, bunk, domicile, harbor, house, put up, quarter, room, sojourn, stay, visit. *See also* **live¹.**

2. To become stuck or entangled ▸ fix, hook. *See* **catch** (3). **3.** To place or set deeply or securely ▸ entrench, ingrain, plant. *See* **fix** (4).

lodging *noun*
1. Dwellings in general ▸ housing, shelter. *Idiom:* a roof over one's head. *See also* **hut**. **2.** A building or shelter where one lives ▸ domicile, habitation, residence. *See* **home** (1).

lodgings *noun*
Usually temporary living accommodations ▸ barracks, quarters, rooms. *Slang:* crash-pad. *See also* **apartment, home.**

loftiest *adjective*
Of, being, located at, or forming the top ▸ highest, top, topmost, upmost, uppermost. *See also* **climactic.**

loftiness *noun*
1. The distance of something from a given level ▸ altitude, height, loftiness, tallness. *See also* **ascent**. **2.** The quality of being arrogant ▸ hauteur, proudness, superiority. *See* **arrogance**. **3.** Boastful selfimportance or display ▸ ostentation, pomposity. *See* **pretentiousness.**

lofty *adjective*
1. Being of or at a relatively great height or altitude ▸ elevated, towering. *See* **high** (1). **2.** Exceedingly dignified in form, tone, or style ▸ eloquent, grand. *See* **elevated** (5). **3.** Raised to or occupying a high position or rank ▸ august, elevated, high-ranking. *See* **exalted** (1). **4.** Overly convinced of one's own superiority and importance ▸ insolent, proud, superior. *See* **arrogant.**

log *verb*
To place on a list or in a record or book ▸ catalog, chronicle, write down. *See* **list¹** (1).

log in *or* **on** *verb*
To gain entry into a computer network or database ▸ access, enter. *Idioms:* gain access (*or* admittance *or* entry), get connected.

logic *noun*
1. Exact, valid, and rational reasoning ▸ analysis, argument, deduction, induction, ratiocination, rationality, reason. **2.** What is sound or reasonable ▸ rationality, reason. *See* **sense** (1).

logical *adjective*
1. Able to reason validly ▸ analytic, analytical, ratiocinative, rational. *See also* **sensible**. **2.** Consistent with reason and intellect ▸ consequent, deducible, intelligent, rational, reasonable. *See also* **sound².**

✚ **CORE SYNONYMS:** *logical, analytic, ratiocinative, rational.* These adjectives mean capable of or showing correct and valid reasoning: *a logical mind; an analytic thinker; the ratiocinative process; a rational being.*

◂ **ANTONYM:** *illogical*

---

loiter *verb*
1. To go or move slowly so that progress is hindered ▸ dawdle, dilly-dally, drag. *See* **delay** (2). **2.** To pass time without working or in avoiding work ▸ loaf, lounge. *See* **idle** (1).

loiterer *noun*
▸ lag, procrastinator, straggler. *See* **laggard.**

loll *verb*
1. To take on or move with an awkward, slovenly posture ▸ slouch, slump. *See also* **bow¹, stoop**. **2.** To hang limply, loosely, and carelessly ▸ flop, sag. *See* **slouch** (2). **3.** To sit or lie with the limbs spread out awkwardly ▸ spread-eagle, straddle. *See* **sprawl** (1).

lone *adjective*
1. Alone in a given category ▸ one, only, particular, separate, single, singular, sole, solitary, unique. *Idioms:* all by one's lonesome, first and last, one and only. **2.** Set away from or lacking the company of all others ▸ alone, isolated, unaccompanied. *See* **solitary** (1). **3.** Not married or attached ▸ fancy-free, marriageable. *See* **single** (5). **4.** Being or related to a distinct entity ▸ particular, singular. *See* **individual** (2).

loneliness *noun*
▸ isolation, seclusion. *See* **solitude.**

lonely *or* **lonesome** *adjective*
1. Empty of people ▸ deserted, desolate, forlorn, godforsaken, uninhabited, unfrequented, unpeopled, unpopulated, vacant. **2.** Dejected due to the awareness of being alone ▸ desolate, forlorn, lorn. *See also* **depressed, miserable**. **3.** Set apart from or lacking the company of all others ▸ alone, companionless, isolated. *See* **solitary** (1). *See synonym note at* **solitary. 4.** Far from centers of human population ▸ outlying, removed, secluded. *See* **remote** (1).

long¹ *adjective*
1. Having great physical length ▸ elongate, elongated, extended, lengthy, outstretched, prolonged, stretching. **2.** Extending tediously beyond a standard duration ▸ dragging, drawn-out, interminable, lengthy, long-drawn-out, overlong, prolonged, protracted, sustained, unending.

long *noun*
A long time ▸ eon, eternity. *See* **ages.**

long² *verb*
To have a strong longing for ▸ covet, want, yearn. *See* **desire** (1).

longanimity *noun*
▸ resignation, tolerance. *See* **patience.**

long-drawn-out *adjective*
▸ drawn-out, overlong, protracted. *See* **long¹** (2).

long green *noun*
Slang Something, such as coins or printed bills, used as a medium of exchange ▸ currency. *Slang:* dough, moola. *See* **money** (1).

longhand *noun*
▸ cursive, handwriting, penmanship. *See* **script** (1).

longing *noun*
▸ craving, hunger, yearning. *See* **desire** (1).

long-lasting *or* **long-lived** *or* **long-standing** *adjective*
▸ durable, enduring, perennial. *See* **continuing** (1).

long-suffering *adjective*
Enduring or capable of enduring hardship or inconvenience without complaint ▸ enduring, resigned. *See* **patient.**

long-suffering *noun*
The capacity of enduring hardship or inconvenience without complaint ▸ resignation, tolerance. *See* **patience**. *See synonym note at* **patience**.

long suit *noun*
▸ specialty, strong point. *See* **forte**.

long-winded *adjective*
1. Using or containing an excessive number of words ▸ periphrastic, verbose. *See* **wordy** (1). *See synonym note at* **wordy**. 2. Marked by or given to digression ▸ diffuse, parenthetical, rambling. *See* **digressive**.

long-windedness *noun*
▸ redundancy, verboseness. *See* **wordiness**.

look *verb*
1. To direct the eyes on an object ▸ consider, contemplate, eye, view. *Idioms:* clap (*or* lay *or* set) one's eyes on. *See also* **gaze, glimpse, survey, watch**. 2. To give the impression of being ▸ appear, feel, seem, sound. *Idioms:* have all the earmarks of being, give the idea (*or* impression) of being, strike one as being. *See also* **resemble**.

look after *verb*
To have the care and supervision of ▸ care for, mind, watch over. *See* **tend²** (1).

look for *verb*
1. To look forward to confidently ▸ await, wager. *See* **expect** (1). 2. To try to find something ▸ cast about, search for. *See* **seek** (1).

look in *verb*
To go to or seek out the company of someone in order to socialize ▸ call, look up. *See* **visit** (1).

look into *verb*
To go into or through for the purpose of making discoveries or acquiring information ▸ inquire, investigate. *See* **explore**.

look on *or* **toward** *verb*
To have the face or front turned toward ▸ face, front, give onto. *See also* **overlook**.

look out *verb*
To be careful ▸ beware, mind, watch out. *Idioms:* be on guard, be on the lookout, keep an eye peeled, take care (*or* heed).

look over *verb*
1. To look through reading matter casually ▸ flip through, leaf (through), skim. *See* **browse** (1). 2. To view broadly or from a height ▸ overlook, scan, survey.

look through *verb*
To look through reading matter casually ▸ flip through, leaf (through), skim. *See* **browse** (1).

look up *verb*
To go to or seek out the company of someone in order to socialize ▸ call, come by. *See* **visit** (1).

look upon *verb*
1. To look upon in a particular way ▸ consider, deem, view. *See* **regard** (1). 2. To have the face or front turned toward ▸ face, front, give onto. *See also* **overlook**.

look *noun*
1. An act of directing the eyes on an object ▸ contemplation, regard, sight, view. *See also* **gaze, watch**. 2. A disposition of the facial features that conveys meaning, feeling, or mood ▸ countenance, face, visage. *See* **expression** (4). 3. An outward appearance ▸ aspect, surface. *See* **face** (4). 4. The way something or someone looks ▸ aspect, features, mien. *See* **appearance** (1). 5. A quick look ▸ glimpse, peek. *See* **glance** (1).

looker *noun*
Slang A person regarded as physically attractive ▸ lovely, stunner. *See* **beauty** (1).

looker-on *noun*
▸ observer, onlooker, spectator. *See* **watcher** (1).

look-in *noun*
▸ call, stop, visitation. *See* **visit** (1).

lookout *noun*
1. The act of carefully watching ▸ monitoring, stakeout, surveillance, vigil, vigilance, watch. *Idiom:* watch and ward. *See also* **watch**. 2. A high structure or place commanding a wide view ▸ crow's nest, cupola, observation post, observatory, outlook, overlook, post, vista, watchtower. 3. One assigned to provide protection or keep watch over someone or something ▸ guardian, protector, ward. *See* **guard** (1). 4. That which is or can be seen ▸ panorama, perspective, vista. *See* **view** (2). 5. Something that concerns or involves one personally ▸ affair, business, concern, interest. *See synonym note at* **affair**.

looks *noun*
▸ aspect, features, mien. *See* **appearance** (1).

loom *verb*
1. To come into view ▸ issue, materialize, show up. *See* **appear** (1). *See synonym note at* **appear**. 2. To be imminent ▸ hover, impend, menace. *See* **threaten** (2).

looming *adjective*
1. Bringing or predicting misfortune ▸ bad, ominous, portentous. *See* **fateful** (1). 2. About to occur at any moment ▸ brewing, impending. *See* **imminent**.

loon *noun*
Informal A person regarded as strange, eccentric, or crazy ▸ lunatic. *Slang:* nut, weirdo. *See* **crackpot**.

looniness *noun*
Informal Foolish behavior ▸ folly, silliness, tomfoolery. *See* **foolishness**.

loony *adjective*
1. *Informal* Displaying a lack of good sense ▸ daft, idiotic, ludicrous. *See* **foolish**. 2. *Informal* Afflicted with or exhibiting irrationality and mental unsoundness ▸ crazy, lunatic, mad. *See* **insane** (1).

loony *noun*
Informal A person regarded as strange, eccentric, or crazy ▸ lunatic. *Slang:* nut, weirdo. *See* **crackpot**.

loop *noun*
1. A length of line folded over and joined at the ends so as to form a curve or circle ▸ circuit, coil, eye, eyelet, noose, ring, ringlet. *See also* **circle**. 2. A group of athletic teams that play each other ▸ circuit, league. *See* **conference** (6).

loop *verb*
1. To form a circle around ▸ circle, orbit, ring. *See*

encircle (1). **2.** To deviate from a straight line in a smooth, continuous manner ▸ arch, curve, turn. *See* **bend** (1).

looped *adjective*
Slang Stupefied, excited, or muddled with alcoholic liquor ▸ intoxicated, sodden, tipsy. *See* **drunk.**

loopiness *noun*
Informal Foolish behavior ▸ folly, silliness, tomfoolery. *See* **foolishness.**

loopy *adjective*
Informal Displaying a lack of forethought and good sense ▸ daft, idiotic, ludicrous. *See* **foolish.**

loose *adjective*
1. Not tautly bound, held, or fastened ▸ dangling, flapping, hanging, lax, relaxed, slack, unbound, unfastened. *See also* **limp. 2.** Able to move about at will without bounds or restraint ▸ emancipated, free, liberated, unbridled, unchained, unchecked, unconfined, unfettered, unhindered, unrestrained, untrammeled. *Idioms:* at large, at liberty, free as a bird, on the loose. *See also* **clear. 3.** Lacking literal exactness ▸ approximate, broad, free, general, imprecise, inexact, rough. **4.** Sexually unrestrained ▸ fast, promiscuous, sluttish. *See* **wanton** (1).

loose *verb*
1. To set at liberty ▸ emancipate, release. *See* **free** (1). **2.** To free from ties or fasteners ▸ loosen, release, untie. *See* **undo** (1). **3.** To launch with great force ▸ hurtle, project, propel. *See* **shoot** (3). **4.** To reduce in tension, pressure, or rigidity ▸ let up, slacken. *See* **ease** (1).

✦ CORE SYNONYMS: *loose, lax, slack.* These adjectives mean not tautly bound, held, or fastened: *loose reins; a lax rope; slack sails.*

◂ ANTONYM: *tight*

---

loosen *verb*
1. To free from ties or fasteners ▸ loose, release, untie. *See* **undo** (1). **2.** To reduce in tension, pressure, or rigidity ▸ let up, slacken. *See* **ease** (1).

loot *noun*
Goods or property seized unlawfully ▸ booty, pillage. *See* **plunder.**

loot *verb*
To rob of goods by force, especially in time of war ▸ despoil, plunder, ransack. *See* **sack²**.

looter *noun*
▸ burglar, looter, robber. *See* **thief.**

looting *noun*
▸ stealing, theft, thievery. *See* **larceny.**

lop¹ *verb*
To decrease, as in length or amount, by or as if by severing or excising ▸ chop, prune, trim. *See* **cut** (3).

lop² *verb*
To hang limply and loosely ▸ droop, flop, sag. *See* **slouch** (2).

lope *verb*
To move on foot at a pace faster than a walk ▸ jog, scamper, trot. *See* **run** (1).

lope *noun*
A pace faster than a walk ▸ jog, trot. *See* **run** (1).

loquacious *adjective*
▸ garrulous, talky, voluble. *See* **talkative.**

lord *noun*
▸ boss, director, head, leader. *See* **chief** (1).

lordliness *noun*
▸ hauteur, proudness, superiority. *See* **arrogance.**

lordly *adjective*
1. Exercising authority ▸ authoritative, commanding, dominant, masterful. *See also* **administrative. 2.** Impressive in size, proportion, or appearance ▸ imposing, magnificent, splendid. *See* **grand** (1). **3.** Overly convinced of one's own superiority and importance ▸ insolent, proud, superior. *See* **arrogant.** *See synonym note at* **arrogant.**

lore *noun*
1. A body of traditional beliefs and notions accumulated about a particular subject ▸ folklore, folkways, legend, myth, mythology, mythos, tradition, superstition. **2.** The sum of what has been perceived, discovered, or inferred ▸ knowledge, understanding, wisdom. *See also* **actuality. 3.** That which is known about a specific subject or situation ▸ data, facts. *See* **information** (1).

lorn *adjective*
1. Having been given up and left alone ▸ bereft, deserted, forsaken. *See* **abandoned** (1). **2.** Dejected due to the awareness of being alone ▸ forlorn, lonely, lonesome. *See* **lonely** (2).

lose *verb*
1. To be unable to find ▸ mislay, misplace, miss. *Idioms:* have something go missing **2.** To fail to take advantage of ▸ miss, pass up, relinquish, squander, waste. *Idioms:* let slip, let slip through one's fingers, lose out on. *See also* **neglect. 3.** To get away from a pursuer ▸ elude, evade, outrun, shake off, slip, throw off. *Slang:* shake. *Idioms:* give someone the shake (*or* slip).

loser *noun*
1. One that fails ▸ bust, fiasco, washout. *See* **failure** (1). **2.** One living under very unhappy circumstances ▸ miserable, wretch. *See* **unfortunate.**

loss *noun*
1. The act or an instance of losing something ▸ losing, mislaying, misplacement, missing. **2.** A loss of life, or one who has lost life, usually as a result of accident, disaster, or war ▸ casualty, death, fatality, kill. *See also* **victim. 3.** A sad or tragic deprivation ▸ waste. **4.** The condition of being deprived of what one once had or ought to have ▸ destitution, dispossession, hardship. *See* **deprivation** (1).

lost *adjective*
1. Unable to find the correct way or place to go ▸ adrift, astray, disoriented, stray. *Idiom:* wandering in the wilderness. **2.** No longer in one's possession ▸ gone, mislaid, misplaced, missing, vanished. *Idiom:* gone missing. *See also* **absent. 3.** So involved in thought as to be forgetful ▸ bemused, faraway, pre-

occupied. *See* **absent-minded**. **4.** Mentally uncertain ▸ confounded, perplexed, turbid. *Informal:* mixed-up. *See* **confused** (1). **5.** Sentenced to terrible, irrevocable punishment ▸ doomed, fated. *See* **condemned**. **6.** Offering no hope or expectation of improvement ▸ irremediable, irreparable. *See* **hopeless** (1).

lot *noun*
1. A piece of land ▸ acreage, parcel, patch, plat, plot, tract. *See also* **field**. **2.** That which is allotted ▸ allowance, ration, share. *See* **allotment** (1). **3.** A personal outcome or end ▸ destiny, fortune, luck. *See* **fate** (2). **4.** A number of individuals making up or considered a unit ▸ body, cluster, collection. *See* **group** (1). **5.** A class that is defined by the common attribute or attributes possessed by all its members ▸ ilk, mold, species. *See* **kind**². **6.** *Informal* A great deal ▸ bounty, mass, profusion. *See* **abundance** (1). **7.** An indeterminately great amount or number ▸ bunch, multiplicity. *Informal:* bushel. *See* **heap** (3). **8.** *Informal* An indefinite amount or extent ▸ deal, quantity.

Lothario *noun*
1. A man who seduces women ▸ debaucher, Don Juan, seducer. *See also* **flirt, lecher, philanderer**. **2.** A man who is amorously attentive to women ▸ Casanova, lady's man. *See* **gallant**.

lotion *noun*
▸ emollient, salve. *See* **ointment**.

lottery *noun*
▸ coincidence, fortune, luck. *See* **chance** (2).

loud *adjective*
1. Marked by extremely high volume and intensity of sound ▸ blaring, booming, clamorous, deafening, earsplitting, noisy, piercing, roaring, shrill, stentorian, strident, thunderous. **2.** Tastelessly showy ▸ flashy, florid, garish. *See* **gaudy**. *See synonym note at* **gaudy**.

✦ CORE SYNONYMS: *loud, earsplitting, stentorian, strident.* These adjectives mean marked by or producing great volume and often disagreeable intensity of sound: *loud trumpets; earsplitting shrieks; stentorian tones; strident, screeching brakes.*

◀ ANTONYM: *soft*

loudmouthed *adjective*
▸ boisterous, clamorous. *See* **vociferous**.

lounge *verb*
1. To pass time without working or in avoiding work ▸ loiter, piddle. *See* **idle** (1). **2.** To take repose by ceasing work or other effort for an interval of time ▸ kick back, unbend, unwind. *See* **rest**¹ (1). **3.** To sit or lie with the limbs spread out awkwardly ▸ spread-eagle, straddle. *See* **sprawl** (1).

lounge *noun*
A public establishment that sells alcoholic drinks and often food, often from a counter ▸ inn, pub, saloon. *See* **bar** (2).

lounger *noun*
Informal A self-indulgent person who avoids work ▸ bum, idler, loafer. *See* **wastrel** (2).

louse *noun*
Slang A repulsive, despicable, or immoral person ▸ lowlife. *Slang:* maggot. *See* **creep** (2).

louse up *verb*
Slang To ruin through clumsiness or ineptness ▸ blunder, foul up, spoil. *See* **botch**.

lousy *adjective*
1. So objectionable as to deserve condemnation ▸ contemptible, disgusting, obnoxious. *See* **offensive** (1). **2.** Of decidedly inferior quality ▸ cheap, paltry, poor. *See* **shoddy** (1). **3.** Very bad ▸ appalling, rotten, wretched. *See* **terrible** (1).

lout *noun*
▸ ape, ox. *Informal:* lummox. *See* **oaf**.

lovable *adjective*
▸ delectable, enchanting, heavenly. *See* **delightful**.

love *noun*
1. An intense attachment to a person or thing ▸ adoration, affection, attachment, devotion, fondness, heart, liking, love affair, loyalties, passion, romance, tenderness, worship. *See also* **inclination**. **2.** The passionate affection and desire felt by lovers for each other ▸ amativeness, amorousness, ardor, devotion, fancy, passion, romance. *See also* **desire**. **3.** An intimate sexual relationship between two people ▸ affair, amour, liaison, love affair, romance. **4.** A person who is much loved ▸ honey, precious, sweetheart. *See* **darling** (1).

love *verb*
1. To feel deep devoted love for ▸ adore, worship. *Idioms:* be soft (*or* stuck *or* sweet) on. **2.** To like or enjoy enthusiastically ▸ be into, delight (in). *See* **adore** (2). **3.** To find agreeable ▸ adore, fancy. *See* **like**¹ (1).

✦ CORE SYNONYMS: *love, affection, devotion, fondness.* These nouns denote feelings of warm personal attachment or strong attraction to another person. *Love* is the most intense: *marrying for love. Affection* is a less ardent and more unvarying feeling of tender regard: *parental affection. Devotion* is earnest, affectionate dedication and implies selflessness: *teachers admired for their devotion to children. Fondness* is strong liking or affection: *a fondness for small animals.*

love affair *noun*
1. An intimate sexual relationship between two people ▸ amour, liaison, romance. *See* **love** (3). **2.** An intense attachment to a person or thing ▸ adoration, fondness, passion. *See* **love** (1).

loved *adjective*
▸ dear, precious. *See* **darling** (1).

lovely *adjective*
1. Pleasing to the eye or mind ▸ enchanting, fetching, pretty, winsome. *See* **attractive** (1). **2.** Having qualities that delight the eye ▸ comely, gorgeous, stunning. *See* **beautiful**. *See synonym note at* **beautiful**. **3.** Giving or affording pleasure or enjoyment ▸ agreeable, enjoyable, pleasurable. *See* **pleasant** (1).

lovely *noun*
A person who is regarded as physically attractive ► dreamboat, stunner. *See* **beauty** (1).

lover *noun*
1. A romantic interest, especially a regular sexual partner ► heartthrob, paramour, partner, steady. *Informal:* flame, significant other. *Slang:* main squeeze, squeeze. *See also* **boyfriend, darling, girlfriend. 2.** An ardent devotee ► admirer, enthusiast, fancier. *See* **fan².**

loving *adjective*
1. Feeling or expressing fond feelings or affection ► caring, devoted. *See* **affectionate. 2.** Feeling or expressing sympathy or pity ► commiserative, empathetic, understanding. *See* **sympathetic.**

low *adjective*
1. Extending far downward or inward from a surface ► abysmal, bottomless. *See* **deep** (1). **2.** Being a sound produced by a relatively small frequency of vibrations ► alto, bass, contralto, deep, low-pitched. **3.** Not irritating, strident, or loud ► quiet, subdued. *See* **soft** (2). **4.** Cut to reveal the wearer's neck, chest, and back ► décolleté, low-cut, low-neck, low-necked, plunging. **5.** Below another in standing, importance, or status ► junior, minor-league, secondary. *See* **minor** (1). **6.** So objectionable as to deserve condemnation ► contemptible, disgusting, obnoxious. *See* **offensive** (1). **7.** Having or proceeding from low moral standards ► squalid, vile. *See* **sordid.** *See synonym note at* **sordid. 8.** Tending or intending to belittle ► deprecatory, derogatory, pejorative. *See* **disparaging. 9.** In low spirits ► dysphoric, gloomy, melancholy, spiritless. *See* **depressed** (1). **10.** Suffering from or appearing to suffer from an illness ► ailing, indisposed, unwell. *See* **sick** (1). **11.** Low in price ► budget, economy, inexpensive. *See* **cheap** (1).

low *noun*
A very low or lowest level, position, or degree ► bottom, minimum, nadir, rock bottom.

lowborn *adjective*
► common, humble, unwashed. *See* **lowly** (1).

lowbrow *adjective*
► uncultivated, uneducated, unlearned. *See* **ignorant** (1).

low-cost *adjective*
► budget, economy, inexpensive. *See* **cheap** (1).

low-cut *adjective*
► décolleté, low-neck, plunging. *See* **low** (4).

low-down *adjective*
Having or proceeding from low moral standards ► ignoble, squalid, vile. *See* **sordid.**

low-down *noun*
Informal That which is known about a specific subject or situation ► facts, knowledge, lore. *See* **information** (1).

lower¹ *verb*
1. To wrinkle one's brow, as in thought, puzzlement, or displeasure ► frown, glower, scowl. *Idioms:* knit one's brow, look black, turn one's mouth down. *See*

synonym note at **frown.** *See also* **grimace. 2.** To stare fixedly and angrily ► glare, glower, scowl. *Idioms:* give the evil eye, look daggers. *See also* **gaze, sneer. 3.** To be imminent ► hover, impend, loom. *See* **threaten** (2).

lower *noun*
1. The act of wrinkling the brow, as in displeasure ► black look, glower, scowl. *See* **frown. 2.** A fixed angry stare ► glare, glower, scowl. *See also* **face, sneer.**

lower² *verb*
1. To cause to descend ► cast down, depress, drop, let down, sink, take down. **2.** To decrease, as in length or amount, by or as if by severing or excising ► chop, prune, trim. *See* **cut** (3). **3.** To make less in price or value ► cheapen, devalue, reduce. *See* **depreciate** (1). **4.** To bring oneself down to a level considered inappropriate to one's dignity ► deign, descend, stoop. *See* **condescend** (1). **5.** To lower the pride or dignity of ► degrade, demean, humiliate. *See* **humble** (1). **6.** To become or cause to become gradually less ► diminish, dwindle, ebb. *See* **decrease.**

lower *adjective*
Below another in standing, importance, or status ► junior, low, secondary. *See* **minor** (1).

lowering *adjective*
► bad, ominous, portentous. *See* **fateful** (1).

lowest *or* **lowermost** *adjective*
Opposite to or farthest from the top ► bottom, nethermost, undermost.

low-grade *adjective*
► inferior, mediocre, substandard. *See* **bad** (1).

low-key *or* **low-keyed** *adjective*
► hushed, quiet, subdued. *See* **soft** (2).

lowland *noun*
► dale, gorge. *See* **valley.**

lowlife *noun*
► weasel. *Slang:* louse, maggot. *See* **creep** (2).

lowliness *noun*
► humility, meekness. *See* **modesty** (1).

lowly *adjective*
1. Lacking high station or birth ► baseborn, common, déclassé, declassed, humble, ignoble, lowborn, low-ranking, mean, plebeian, unwashed, vulgar. *See also* **poor. 2.** Having or expressing feelings of humility ► humble, meek, modest, unambitious. *See also* **deferential. 3.** Of little distinction ► humble, mean, simple. *See also* **modest.**

low-necked *or* **low-neck** *adjective*
► décolleté, low-neck, plunging. *See* **low** (4).

lowness *noun*
► dejection, doldrums, melancholy. *See* **depression** (2).

low-pitched *adjective*
► bass, contralto, deep. *See* **low** (2).

low-priced *adjective*
► budget, economy, low-cost. *See* **cheap** (1).

low-quality *adjective*
► common, inferior, substandard. *See* **bad** (1).

low-ranking *adjective*
► common, humble, unwashed. *See* **lowly** (1).

loyal *adjective*
▶ staunch, steadfast, true. *See* **faithful** (1). *See synonym note at* **faithful.**

loyalties *noun*
▶ affection, attachment, devotion. *See* **love** (1).

loyalty *noun*
▶ allegiance, faithfulness, fealty. *See* **fidelity** (1). *See synonym note at* **fidelity.**

lube *noun*
A substance that is generally slippery, combustible, and not water soluble ▶ grease, petroleum. *See* **oil** (1).
lube *verb*
To apply oil to something ▶ anoint, grease, lubricate. *See* **oil.**

lubricant *noun*
▶ grease, petroleum. *See* **oil** (1).

lubricate *verb*
▶ grease, lube. *See* **oil.**

lubricious *adjective*
1. So smooth and glassy as to offer insecure hold or footing ▶ slippery, slithery. *See* **slick** (1). **2.** Marked by treachery or deceit ▶ duplicitous, shifty, sneaky. *See* **underhand. 3.** Feeling or preoccupied with sexual love or desire ▶ concupiscent, lewd, lusty. *See* **lascivious** (1).

lucency *noun*
▶ illumination, luminescence. *See* **light**[1] (1).

lucent *adjective*
▶ brilliant, incandescent, radiant. *See* **bright** (1).

lucid *adjective*
1. Mentally healthy ▶ compos mentis, normal, rational, sane. *Idioms:* all there, in one's right mind, of sound mind. *See also* **healthy. 2.** Free from what obscures ▶ crystalline, limpid, transparent. *See* **clear** (1). *See synonym note at* **clear. 3.** Depicted in sharp and accurate detail ▶ explicit, realistic, vivid. *See* **graphic** (1). **4.** Capable of being readily understood ▶ comprehensible, fathomable, intelligible. *See* **understandable** (1).

lucidity *or* **lucidness** *noun*
1. The quality of being clear and easy to perceive ▶ distinctness, legibility, perspicuity, plainness. *See* **clarity** (1). **2.** A healthy mental state ▶ mind, rationality, reason. *See* **sanity.**

luck *noun*
1. Success attained as a result of chance ▶ dumb luck, fluke, fortunateness, fortune, godsend, good fortune (*or* luck), luckiness. *Idioms:* gift from above (*or* heaven *or* on high), stroke of luck. **2.** The random, unintended, or unpredictable element of an event or the force regarded as the cause of such an event ▶ coincidence, fortune, serendipity. *See* **chance** (2). **3.** The supposed power that predetermines events ▶ fortune, kismet, predestination. *See* **fate** (1). **4.** A personal outcome or end ▶ doom, fortune, lot. *See* **fate** (2).

luckless *adjective*
▶ ill-fated, ill-starred, star-crossed. *See* **unfortunate** (1). *See synonym note at* **unfortunate.**

lucky *adjective*
Characterized by luck or good fortune ▶ fortuitous, fortunate, happy, providential. *See also* **opportune.**

✦ **CORE SYNONYMS:** *lucky, fortunate, happy, providential.* These adjectives mean characterized by luck or good fortune: *a lucky guess; a fortunate omen; a happy outcome; a providential recovery.*

◀ **ANTONYM:** *unlucky*

---

lucrative *adjective*
▶ gainful, remunerative, rewarding. *See* **profitable** (1).

lucre *noun*
▶ currency. *Slang:* dough, moola. *See* **money** (1).

lucubrate *verb*
To apply one's mind to the acquisition of knowledge, especially when pressed for time ▶ study. *Informal:* bone up, cram, grind. *Idioms:* burn the midnight oil, hit the books. *See also* **examine.**

ludicracy *noun*
▶ folly, silliness, tomfoolery. *See* **foolishness.**

ludicrous *adjective*
1. Causing or deserving laughter or derision ▶ farcical, laughable, ridiculous, risible. **2.** Displaying a lack of good sense ▶ daft, idiotic, imbecilic. *See* **foolish.** *See synonym note at* **foolish.**

ludicrousness *noun*
▶ funniness, ridiculousness, wittiness. *See* **humor** (1).

lug[1] *noun*
Slang A large, ungainly, and dull-witted person ▶ lout, ox. *Informal:* lummox. *See* **oaf.**

lug[2] *verb*
1. To move while supporting ▶ bear, haul. *See* **carry** (1). **2.** To exert force so as to move something toward the source of the force ▶ drag, tug. *See* **pull** (1).

lugubrious *adjective*
▶ depressing, melancholy, mournful. *See* **sorrowful** (1).

lukewarm *adjective*
Lacking warmth, interest, enthusiasm, or involvement ▶ halfhearted, Laodicean, tepid, unenthusiastic. *See also* **apathetic, cold, cool.**

lull *verb*
To ease the anger or agitation of ▶ appease, mollify, soothe. *See* **pacify.**

lull *noun*
1. An absence of motion or disturbance ▶ peace, serenity. *See* **stillness** (1). **2.** An interval when continuity is suspended ▶ break, interlude. *See* **gap** (2).

lumber *verb*
▶ clump, galumph, hulk. *See* **blunder** (1). *See synonym note at* **blunder.**

luminary *noun*
1. A famous person ▶ idol, personality, star. *See* **celebrity** (1). *See synonym note at* **celebrity. 2.** An important, influential person ▶ notability, personage. *Slang:* big shot. *See* **dignitary.**

luminesce *verb*
To shine brightly and steadily but without a flame ▶ gleam, glow, incandesce. *See also* **beam.**

luminescence *noun*
▸ illumination, lucency. *See* **light¹** (1).

luminosity *noun*
▸ effulgence, fire, radiance. *See* **brilliance** (1).

luminous *or* **luminescent** *adjective*
▸ brilliant, incandescent, radiant. *See* **bright** (1). *See synonym note at* **bright**.

lummox *noun*
Informal A large, ungainly, and dull-witted person ▸ lout, ox. *Slang:* goon. *See* **oaf**.

lump¹ *noun*
1. An irregularly shaped mass of indefinite size ▸ cake, chunk, clod, clot, clump, gob, hunch, nugget, slab, wad. *Informal:* hunk. **2.** An unevenness or elevation on a surface ▸ hump, protuberance. *See* **bump** (1). **3.** A small raised area of skin, as from a blow or sting ▸ bunch, swelling. *See* **bump** (2). **4.** A large, ungainly, and dull-witted person ▸ lout, ox. *Informal:* lummox. *See* **oaf**.

lump *verb*
1. To collect or pile up or onto something ▸ drift, hill. *See* **heap** (1). **2.** To move heavily or clumsily ▸ clump, galumph, hulk. *See* **blunder** (1).

lump² *verb*
Informal To put up with ▸ stomach, tolerate, withstand. *See* **endure** (1).

lumpenproletariat *noun*
▸ dregs, rabble, ragtag and bobtail. *See* **riffraff**.

lumpish *adjective*
1. Lacking dexterity and grace in physical movement ▸ gawky, graceless. *Slang:* klutzy. *See* **awkward** (1). **2.** Of large, often awkward size and weight ▸ cumbersome, heavy, oversized. *See* **bulky** (1).

lumps *noun*
Informal Something justly deserved ▸ compensation, deserts, reward. *See* **due** (1).

lumpy *adjective*
▸ cumbersome, heavy, oversized. *See* **bulky** (1).

lunacy *noun*
1. Serious mental illness impairing a person's capacity to function normally ▸ dementia, derangement. *See* **insanity** (1). *See synonym note at* **insanity**. **2.** Foolish behavior ▸ folly, silliness, tomfoolery. *See* **foolishness**.

lunatic *adjective*
1. Afflicted with or exhibiting irrationality and mental unsoundness ▸ crazy, derailed, mad. *See* **insane** (1). **2.** Displaying a lack of good sense ▸ daft, idiotic, ludicrous. *See* **foolish**. **3.** Holding especially political views that deviate drastically from prevailing beliefs ▸ extremist, radical, revolutionary. *See* **extreme** (4).

lunatic *noun*
A person regarded as strange, eccentric, or crazy ▸ crazy. *Slang:* nut, weirdo. *See* **crackpot**.

lunge *verb*
▸ drive, stab, stick. *See* **plunge** (1).

lunkheaded *adjective*
Slang Lacking in or showing a lack of intelligence ▸ dumb, idiotic, obtuse. *See* **stupid** (1).

lurch *verb*
1. To lean suddenly, unsteadily, and erratically from the vertical axis ▸ keel, pitch, roll, seesaw, yaw. *See also* **incline, sway, toss**. **2.** To move or cause to move with a sudden abrupt motion ▸ jerk, snap, twitch, wrench, yank. *See also* **move**. **3.** To move heavily or clumsily ▸ flounder, stumble. *See* **blunder** (1). *See synonym note at* **blunder**. **4.** To walk unsteadily ▸ reel, stumble, totter. *See* **stagger** (1). **5.** To proceed with sudden, abrupt movements ▸ jolt, shake. *See* **bump** (1).

lurch *noun*
A sudden motion, such as a pull ▸ tug, wrench. *See* **jerk** (1).

lure *noun*
1. Something that attracts, especially with the promise of pleasure or reward ▸ allurement, attraction, bait, carrot, come-on, draw, enticement, inducement, inveiglement, invitation, magnet, seduction, temptation. **2.** Something that leads one into danger or entrapment ▸ bait, decoy. *See also* **trap, trick**. **3.** The power or quality of attracting ▸ appeal, magnetism. *Informal:* pull. *See* **attraction** (1).

lure *verb*
1. To beguile or draw into a wrong or foolish course of action, especially a sexual act ▸ entice, tempt. *See* **seduce**. *See synonym note at* **seduce**. **2.** To direct or impel to oneself by some quality or action ▸ entice, magnetize. *See* **attract** (1).

lurer *noun*
▸ charmer, tempter. *See* **seducer** (1).

lurid *adjective*
1. Shockingly repellent ▸ grisly, gruesome, hideous. *See* **ghastly** (1). *See synonym note at* **ghastly**. **2.** Lacking color ▸ bloodless, cadaverous, wan. *See* **pale** (1).

luring *adjective*
▸ bewitching, enticing, tempting. *See* **seductive**.

lurk *verb*
1. To wait furtively in order to attack someone ▸ ambush, await, prowl, skulk. *Informal:* lay for. *Idioms:* lay wait for, lie in wait for. *See also* **ambush**. **2.** To move silently and furtively ▸ creep, prowl, slink. *See* **sneak** (1).

luscious *adjective*
1. Highly pleasing, especially to the sense of taste ▸ delectable, scrumptious. *See* **delicious** (1). *See synonym note at* **delicious**. **2.** Giving great pleasure or delight ▸ enchanting, heavenly. *See* **delightful**.

lush¹ *adjective*
1. Growing profusely ▸ dense, luxuriant, profuse. *See* **thick** (3). **2.** Given to or marked by unrestrained abundance ▸ exuberant, lavish, opulent. *See* **profuse** (1). *See synonym note at* **profuse**. **3.** Characterized by extravagant, ostentatious magnificence ▸ lavish, luxuriant, opulent. *See* **luxurious**.

lush² *noun*
Slang A person who is habitually drunk ▸ alcoholic, dipsomaniac, tippler. *See* **drunkard**.

lush *verb*
Slang To take alcoholic liquor, especially excessively

or habitually ▸ tipple. *Slang:* booze, chugalug. *See* **drink** (2).

lust *noun*
1. A strong wanting of what promises enjoyment or pleasure ▸ craving, longing, yearning. *See* **desire** (1). 2. Sexual hunger ▸ libido, passion. *See* **desire** (2).

lust *verb*
To have a greedy, obsessive desire ▸ crave, hunger, itch, thirst.

luster *noun*
1. A surface shininess ▸ glaze, polish, shine. *See* **gloss**[1] (1). 2. Wide recognition of one's deeds ▸ glory, note, prestige. *See* **fame.**

lusterless *adjective*
1. Lacking vividness or color ▸ lackluster, mat, muddy. *See* **dull** (2). 2. Lacking liveliness, charm, or surprise ▸ aseptic, colorless, pedestrian. *See* **dull** (1).

lustful *adjective*
▸ concupiscent, lewd. *See* **lascivious** (1).

lustfulness *noun*
▸ eroticism, libido, passion. *See* **desire** (2).

lustral *adjective*
▸ expiatory, lustrative, purificatory. *See* **purgative** (2).

lustrate *verb*
▸ atone, cleanse, pardon. *See* **purify** (1).

lustration *noun*
▸ ablution, pardoning, redemption. *See* **purification** (2).

lustrative *adjective*
▸ expiatory, lustral, purificatory. *See* **purgative** (2).

lustrous *adjective*
1. Having a high, radiant sheen ▸ gleaming, glistening, polished. *See* **glossy.** 2. Giving off or reflecting much light ▸ brilliant, incandescent, radiant. *See* **bright** (1). *See synonym note at* **bright.**

lusty *adjective*
1. Full of vigor ▸ able-bodied, gutsy, iron, red-blooded, robust, strapping, sturdy, vigorous, vital. *See also* **energetic, healthy.** 2. Feeling or preoccupied with sexual love or desire ▸ concupiscent, lewd. *See* **lascivious** (1).

luxuriance *noun*
▸ comfort, luxury, wealth. *See* **prosperity** (2).

luxuriant *adjective*
1. Growing profusely ▸ lush, profuse. *See* **thick** (3).

2. Given to or marked by unrestrained abundance ▸ exuberant, opulent. *See* **profuse** (1). *See synonym note at* **profuse.** 3. Marked by extravagant magnificence ▸ lavish, lush, opulent. *See* **luxurious.**

luxuriate *verb*
To take extravagant pleasure ▸ bask, indulge, revel, roll, rollick, splurge, wallow. *See also* **enjoy.**

luxurious *adjective*
Characterized by extravagant, ostentatious magnificence ▸ deluxe, fancy, lavish, lush, luxuriant, opulent, palatial, plush, plushy, rich, ritzy, sumptuous. *See also* **exclusive, glorious, sybaritic.**

luxury *noun*
1. Something costly and unnecessary ▸ delight, extravagance, extravagancy, frill, indulgence, rarity, treat. 2. Steady good fortune or financial security ▸ comfort, luxuriance, wealth. *See* **prosperity** (2).

✦ CORE SYNONYMS: *luxury, extravagance, frill.* These nouns denote something desirable and costly that is unnecessary: *the real luxury of riding in a limousine; a simple wedding without any extravagances; caviar and other culinary frills.*

◄ ANTONYM: *necessity*

lying *adjective*
Given to or marked by deliberate concealment or misrepresentation of the truth ▸ duplicitous, mendacious, untruthful. *See* **dishonest** (1). *See synonym note at* **dishonest.**

lying *noun*
The practice of lying ▸ inveracity, perjury. *See* **mendacity** (1).

lying-in *noun*
▸ childbearing, delivery, labor. *See* **birth** (1).

lymphatic *adjective*
▸ languorous, listless, spiritless. *See* **languid.**

lyric or **lyrical** *adjective*
Relating to the characteristics of poetry ▸ poetic, poetical. *See also* **melodious, rhythmical.**

lyricism *noun*
A creation or experience having beauty suggestive of poetry ▸ poem, poetry.

lyrics *noun*
▸ hymn, jingle, tune. *See* **song** (1).

m

macabre *adjective*
1. Characterized by preoccupation with thoughts or feelings that are unwholesome ▸ insalubrious, sick, unhealthy. *See* **morbid** (1). 2. Shockingly repellent ▸ appalling, grisly, gruesome, hideous, horrid, terri-

fying. *See* **ghastly** (1). *See synonym note at* **ghastly.**

macerate *verb*
▸ soak, saturate, souse. *See* **steep**[2].

machinate *verb*
▸ conspire, scheme. *See* **plot** (2).

machination *noun*
▶ collusion, conspiracy. *See* **plot** (2).

machine *noun*
1. An organized array of individual elements and parts forming and working as a unit ▶ arrangement, totality, whole. *See* **system** (1). **2.** Something devised for a particular function ▶ apparatus, contraption, mechanism. *See* **device** (1).

machismo *noun*
▶ maleness, manliness, virility. *See* **masculinity**.

macho *adjective*
▶ male, mannish, masculine. *See* **manly**.

mackintosh *noun*
▶ anorak, overcoat, raincoat. *See* **coat** (1).

macrocosm *noun*
▶ creation, world. *See* **universe** (1).

mad *adjective*
1. Feeling or showing anger ▶ indignant, irate, vexed. *See* **angry**. *See synonym note at* **angry**. **2.** Afflicted with or exhibiting irrationality and mental unsoundness ▶ crazy, derailed, lunatic. *See* **insane** (1). **3.** Displaying a lack of good sense ▶ daft, idiotic, ludicrous. *See* **foolish**. **4.** Showing or having enthusiasm ▶ fervent, rabid, zealous. *See* **enthusiastic** (1). **5.** Characterized by hurried activity and confusion or agitation ▶ delirious, frenzied, wild. *See* **frantic**.

madcap *adjective*
▶ foolhardy, harum-scarum, hotheaded, slapdash. *See* **rash**[1].

madden *verb*
1. To cause to feel or show anger ▶ enrage, incense, infuriate. *See* **anger** (1). **2.** To make insane ▶ craze, dement, unbalance. *See* **derange** (1).

made-to-order *adjective*
▶ custom-made, tailor-made. *See* **custom**.

made-up *adjective*
1. Consisting or suggestive of fiction ▶ fictional, invented. *See* **fictitious** (1). **2.** Being fictitious and not real, as a name ▶ assumed, pretended, pseudonymous. *See also* **false**.

madness *noun*
1. Serious mental illness impairing a person's capacity to function normally ▶ dementia, derangement, lunacy. *See* **insanity** (1). *See synonym note at* **insanity**. **2.** Foolish behavior ▶ folly, silliness, tomfoolery. *See* **foolishness**.

maelstrom *noun*
▶ eddy, swirl, vortex. *See* **whirlpool** (1).

magic *noun*
1. The use of supernatural powers to influence or predict events ▶ augury, black art, black magic, conjuration, divination, hoodoo, incantation, necromancy, occultism, sorcery, sortilege, thaumaturgy, theurgy, witchcraft, witchery, witching, wizardry. *See also* **prediction**. **2.** The use of skillful tricks and deceptions to produce entertainingly baffling effects ▶ conjuration, conjuring, illusion, legerdemain, prestidigitation, sleight of hand, trickery. **3.** A word or formula that is believed to have magic powers ▶ abracadabra, enchantment, incantation. *See* **spell**[2].

magic *or* **magical** *adjective*
1. Having, brought about by, or relating to supernatural powers or magic ▶ bewitching, enchanted, fey, spellbinding, talismanic, thaumaturgic, thaumaturgical, theurgic, theurgical, witching, wizardly. *See also* **mysterious, supernatural**. **2.** Pleasing to the eye or mind ▶ bewitching, enchanting, fetching. *See* **attractive** (1).

magician *noun*
▶ conjurer, enchanter, necromancer, sorcerer. *See* **wizard** (1).

magisterial *adjective*
▶ bossy, domineering, imperious, overbearing. *See* **dictatorial** (1).

magistrate *noun*
A public official who decides cases brought before a court of law in order to administer justice ▶ judge, jurist, jurisprudent, justice, justice of the peace. *See also* **judge**.

magnanimity *noun*
▶ large-heartedness, munificence, unselfishness. *See* **generosity**.

magnanimous *adjective*
▶ big-hearted, unselfish. *See* **generous** (1).

magnanimousness *noun*
▶ magnanimity, munificence, unselfishness. *See* **generosity**.

magnate *noun*
▶ notability, personage. *Slang:* big shot, big wheel. *See* **dignitary**.

magnet *noun*
▶ bait, draw, enticement. *See* **lure** (1).

magnetic *adjective*
▶ enchanting, fetching, lovely, winsome. *See* **attractive** (1).

magnetism *noun*
▶ enticement, lure. *Informal:* pull. *See* **attraction** (1).

magnetize *verb*
▶ entice, lure. *Informal:* pull. *See* **attract** (1).

magnific *adjective*
▶ imposing, marvelous, splendid. *See* **grand** (1).

magnification *noun*
1. The honoring of a deity, as in worship ▶ extolment, laudation. *See* **praise** (2). **2.** The act of increasing or rising ▶ amplification, boost, escalation. *See* **increase** (1).

magnificence *noun*
1. Brilliant, showy splendor ▶ brilliance, resplendence, sparkle. *See* **glitter** (2). **2.** A height of achievement or acclaim ▶ grandeur, grandness, splendor. *See* **glory** (1).

magnificent *adjective*
1. Marked by extraordinary beauty and splendor ▶ brilliant, resplendent, splendid. *See* **glorious** (1). **2.** Impressive in size, proportion, or appearance ▶ august, grandiose, splendid. *See* **grand** (1). *See synonym note at* **grand**. **3.** Beyond what is usual, normal, or customary ▶ extraordinary, outstanding, remarkable. *See* **exceptional** (1).

magnified *adjective*
▸ inflated, overblown, overstated. *See* **exaggerated** (1).

magnify *verb*
1. To make or become greater or larger ▸ amplify, boost, enlarge. *See* **increase** (1). 2. To make something seem greater than is actually the case ▸ inflate, overcharge. *See* **exaggerate** (1). 3. To pay tribute or homage to ▸ celebrate, exalt. *See* **honor** (1). 4. To honor a deity in religious worship ▸ extol, laud. *See* **praise** (3). 5. To raise to a high position or status ▸ elevate, glorify, uplift. *See* **exalt** (1).

magniloquence *noun*
▸ fustian, grandiloquence. *See* **bombast.**

magniloquent *adjective*
▸ bombastic, grandiloquent, rhetorical. *See* **oratorical.**

magnitude *noun*
1. Great amount or dimension ▸ amplitude, size. *See* **bulk** (1). 2. The quality or state of being large in amount, extent, or importance ▸ bigness, greatness. *See* **size** (2). 3. Relative intensity or amount, as of a quality or attribute ▸ extent, level, scope. *See* **degree** (2). 4. The amount of space occupied by something ▸ extent, measure, proportions. *See* **size** (1). 5. The quality or state of being important ▸ concernment, significance, weightiness. *See* **importance.**

magnum opus *noun*
An outstanding and ingenious work ▸ chef-d'oeuvre, masterpiece, masterwork. *See also* **accomplishment, composition, treasure.**

maiden *adjective*
▸ initial, original, premier. *See* **first** (1).

mail *verb*
▸ consign, dispatch. *See* **send** (1).

maim *verb*
1. To deprive of a limb or bodily member or its use ▸ amputate, mutilate. *See* **cripple** (1). 2. To injure or damage, as by abuse or heavy wear ▸ maul, rough up. *See* **batter** (1). *See synonym note at* **batter.**

main *adjective*
1. Most important, influential, or significant ▸ chief, key, principal. *See* **primary** (1). *See synonym note at* **primary.** 2. Exercising controlling power or influence ▸ key, predominant, reigning. *See* **dominant** (1).

main *noun*
The body of salt water covering most of the earth's surface ▸ brine, deep, sea. *See* **ocean.**

mainly *adverb*
▸ customarily, generally, normally. *See* **usually.**

mainspring *noun*
▸ call, grounds, motive. *See* **cause** (2).

maintain *verb*
1. To keep in a condition of good repair, efficiency, or use ▸ keep up, preserve, sustain. 2. To persevere in some condition, action, or belief ▸ retain, stay with, sustain. *See* **keep** (6). 3. To supply with the necessities of life ▸ keep, provide for, support. *See also* **nourish.** 4. To support against arguments, attack, or criticism

▸ justify, vindicate. *See* **defend** (2). 5. To put into words positively and with conviction ▸ avow, declare, profess. *See* **assert** (1).

maintenance *noun*
1. The work of keeping something in proper condition ▸ preservation, repairs, reparation, sustenance, upkeep. *See also* **care.** 2. The means needed to support life ▸ bread, keep, livelihood. *See* **living.** 3. The careful guarding of an asset ▸ husbandry, preservation. *See* **conservation.**

majestic *adjective*
▸ imposing, magnificent, splendid. *See* **grand** (1). *See synonym note at* **grand.**

majesty *noun*
1. A height of achievement or acclaim ▸ grandness, magnificence, splendor. *See* **glory** (1). 2. One who governs or leads ▸ boss, director, head, leader. *See* **chief** (1).

major *adjective*
1. Being among the leaders in one's field ▸ blue-chip, major, major-league. *See* **big-league.** 2. Most important, influential, or significant ▸ chief, key, main, principal. *See* **primary** (1). 3. Exercising controlling power or influence ▸ key, predominant, reigning. *See* **dominant** (1).

major-league *adjective*
▸ blue-chip, leading, major. *See* **big-league.**

make *verb*
1. To create by forming, combining, or altering materials ▸ assemble, build, compose, configure, construct, fabricate, fashion, forge, form, frame, manufacture, mold, pattern, produce, put together, shape, structure. *See also* **arrange, design, invent.** 2. To bring into existence ▸ give, provide, yield. *See* **produce** (1). 3. To be the cause of ▸ generate, induce, trigger. *See* **cause.** 4. To cause a person or thing to act or move in spite of resistance ▸ coerce, compel, pressure. *See* **force** (1). 5. To cause to be ready, as for use, consumption, or a special purpose ▸ fix, ready. *See* **prepare** (1). 6. To put in force or cause to be by legal authority ▸ enact, legislate. *See* **establish** (3). 7. To journey over ▸ go, traverse. *See* **cover** (2). 8. To proceed in a specified direction ▸ go, head, set out. *See* **bear** (5). 9. To receive, as wages, for one's labor ▸ gain, get. *See* **earn** (2). 10. To select for an office or position ▸ elect, name, nominate. *See* **appoint** (1).

make off *verb*
Informal To break loose and leave suddenly, as from confinement or a difficult situation ▸ decamp, flee. *See* **escape** (1).

make out *verb*
1. To perceive and fix the identity of, especially with difficulty ▸ ascertain, recognize. *See* **discern** (1). 2. To perceive and recognize the meaning of ▸ apprehend, fathom, sense. *See* **understand** (1). 3. *Informal* To progress or perform adequately, especially in difficult circumstances ▸ fare, fend, get by. *See* **manage** (1). 4. *Slang* To engage in kissing, caressing, and other amorous behavior ▸ *Informal:* pet, spoon. *See* **neck.**

make over *verb*
To change the ownership of property by means of a legal document ▸ deed, sign over. *See* **transfer** (1).

make up *verb*
1. To reestablish friendship between ▸ conciliate, reconcile, reunite. *See also* **pacify. 2.** To use ingenuity in making, developing, or achieving ▸ contrive, devise, dream up. *See* **invent** (1). **3.** To compose or recite without preparation ▸ ad-lib, fake. *See* **improvise** (1). **4.** To act as an equalizing force to ▸ counteract, counterbalance, offset. *See* **balance** (2). **5.** To be the constituent parts of ▸ compose, form. *See also* **contain. 6.** To form mental images of ▸ envision, fantasize, visualize. *See* **imagine** (1). **7.** To present false information with the intention of deceiving ▸ fib, prevaricate. *See* **lie²**. **8.** To get back ▸ regain, repossess, retrieve. *See* **recover** (1).

make *noun*
The physical characteristics of a person ▸ body, form, physique. *See* **constitution** (1).

make-believe *noun*
A deceptive outward appearance ▸ charade, mask, pretense. *See* **façade** (2).

make-believe *adjective*
1. Having the nature of a fable; not real ▸ fantasy, legendary. *See* **mythical. 2.** Existing only in the imagination ▸ chimerical, fanciful, unreal. *See* **imaginary.**

make-do *noun*
Something used temporarily or reluctantly when other means are not available ▸ expedient, stopgap. *See* **makeshift.**

make-do *adjective*
Intended, used, or present for a limited time ▸ interim, short-term. *See* **temporary** (2).

maker *noun*
1. One that makes or assembles something ▸ artificer, artisan, assembler, craftsman, craftsperson, craftswoman, fabricator, manufacturer, modeler, producer. *See also* **builder. 2.** One that creates, founds, or originates ▸ author, creator, inventor. *See* **originator.**

makeshift *noun*
Something that is used temporarily or reluctantly when other means are not available ▸ expediency, expedient, make-do, resort, shift, stopgap. *See also* **substitute.**

makeshift *adjective*
Intended, used, or present for a limited time ▸ interim, provisional, short-term. *See* **temporary** (2).

✛ CORE SYNONYMS: *makeshift, expedient, resort, stopgap.* These nouns denote something used temporarily or reluctantly as a substitute when other means fail or are not available: *lacked a cane but used a stick as a makeshift; exhausted every expedient before filing suit; will use force only as a last resort; a crate serving as a stopgap for a chair.*

---

makeup *or* **make-up** *noun*
1. The combination of emotional, intellectual, and moral qualities that distinguishes an individual ▸ nature, personality, temperament. *See* **character** (1). **2.** The physical characteristics of a person ▸ body, form, physique. *See* **constitution** (1).

makings *noun*
Indication of future success or development ▸ possibility, potential, promise, prospects. *See also* **material.**

maladroit *adjective*
1. Lacking dexterity and grace in physical movement ▸ gawky, graceless. *Slang:* klutzy. *See* **awkward** (1). **2.** Clumsily lacking in the ability to do ▸ bumbling, clumsy, inept. *See* **unskillful** (1). **3.** Lacking sensitivity and skill in dealing with others ▸ gauche, impolitic, undiplomatic. *See* **tactless.**

malady *noun*
1. A pathological condition of mind or body ▸ ailment, disorder, pathology. *See* **disease** (1). **2.** The condition of being sick ▸ affliction, illness, poor health. *See* **sickness** (1).

malaise *noun*
▸ bug, complaint, malady. *See* **sickness** (1).

malapert *adjective*
▸ bold, insolent, pert. *See* **impudent.**

malapropism *noun*
▸ barbarism, solecism. *See* **corruption** (3).

malapropos *adjective*
▸ inapt, unapt, unbecoming. *See* **improper** (2).

malarkey *noun*
Slang Something that does not have or make sense ▸ bunkum, drivel, garbage. *See* **nonsense** (1).

malcontent *noun*
▸ instigator, malcontent, rabble-rouser. *See* **agitator.**

male *adjective*
▸ macho, mannish, masculine. *See* **manly.**

malediction *noun*
▸ damnation, hex. *See* **curse** (1).

malefaction *noun*
▸ illegality, offense. *See* **crime** (1).

malefactor *noun*
▸ culprit, lawbreaker, offender. *See* **criminal.**

maleficent *or* **malefic** *adjective*
▸ deleterious, evil, injurious. *See* **harmful.**

maleness *noun*
▸ machismo, manliness, virility. *See* **masculinity.**

malevolence *noun*
A desire to harm others or to see others suffer ▸ despitefulness, ill will, malice, maliciousness, malignancy, malignity, meanness, nastiness, poisonousness, spite, spitefulness, venomousness, viciousness, vindictiveness. *See also* **cruelty, evil, hate.**

malevolent *adjective*
1. Characterized by intense ill will or spite ▸ black, despiteful, evil, evil-minded, hateful, ill-natured, malicious, malign, malignant, mean, nasty, poisonous, rancorous, spiteful, venomous, vicious, vindictive, wicked. *Slang:* bitchy. *See also* **cruel, fiendish, ill-tempered. 2.** Causing harm or injury ▸ deleterious, evil, injurious. *See* **harmful.**

malfeasance *noun*
1. Departure from what is legally, ethically, and

morally correct ▸ dishonesty, improbity. *Informal:* crookedness. *See* **corruption** (2). **2.** An act of breaking a law or of nonfulfillment of an obligation ▸ infraction, infringement, violation. *See* **breach** (1).

malformation *noun*
▸ contortion, disfigurement, warping. *See* **deformity**.

malfunction *verb*
To become unusable or stop working properly ▸ act up, break (down), crash, fail, give out. *Slang:* bust, conk out, crap out, poop out. *Idioms:* get out of whack (*or* kilter), go haywire, go on the blink (*or* fritz). *See also* **collapse, fail**.

malfunction *noun*
A cessation of proper functioning ▸ breakdown, collapse, failure, outage.

malice *or* **maliciousness** *noun*
▸ venomousness, viciousness. *See* **malevolence**.

malicious *adjective*
▸ evil, wicked. *See* **malevolent** (1).

malign *verb*
To make harmful and often untrue statements about ▸ asperse, backbite, calumniate, defame, libel, slander, slur, tear down, traduce, vilify. *Informal:* badmouth. *Idioms:* cast aspersions on, give someone a bad name, speak evil of. *See also* **belittle, denigrate, slam**.

malign *adjective*
1. Bringing or predicting misfortune ▸ dire, foreboding, ominous. *See* **fateful** (1). *See synonym note at* **fateful**. **2.** Characterized by intense ill will or spite ▸ evil, wicked. *See* **malevolent** (1). **3.** Causing harm or injury ▸ deleterious, evil, injurious. *See* **harmful**.

✦ **CORE SYNONYMS:** *malign, defame, traduce, vilify, asperse, slander, calumniate, libel.* These verbs mean to make evil, harmful, often untrue statements about another. *Malign* stresses malicious intent: *"Have I not taken your part when you were maligned?"* (Thackeray). *Defame* suggests damage to reputation through misrepresentation: *The plaintiff had been defamed and had legitimate grounds for a lawsuit. Traduce* connotes the resulting humiliation or disgrace: *"My character was traduced by Captain Hawkins . . . even the ship's company cried out shame"* (Frederick Marryat). *Vilify* pertains to open, deliberate, vicious defamation: *"One who belongs to the most vilified and persecuted minority in history is not likely to be insensible to the freedoms guaranteed by our Constitution"* (Felix Frankfurter). To *asperse* is to spread unfavorable charges or insinuations against: *"Who could be so base as to asperse the character of a family so harmless as ours?"* (Oliver Goldsmith). *Slander* and *calumniate* apply to oral expression: *He slandered his political opponent. She calumniated and ridiculed her former employer. Libel* involves the communication of written or pictorial material: *The celebrity sued the tabloid that libeled her.*

---

malignancy *noun*
▸ venomousness, viciousness. *See* **malevolence**.

malignant *adjective*
1. Characterized by intense ill will or spite ▸ evil, hateful. *See* **malevolent** (1). **2.** Capable of injuring or

killing by poison ▸ noxious, toxic, venomous. *See* **poisonous** (1).

malignity *noun*
▸ maliciousness, spitefulness. *See* **malevolence**.

malleability *or* **malleableness** *noun*
▸ elasticity, plasticity, pliability. *See* **flexibility** (1).

malleable *adjective*
1. Capable of being shaped, bent, or drawn out, as by hammering or pressure ▸ bendable, ductile, flexible, flexile, flexuous, moldable, plastic, pliable, pliant, supple, tractable, workable. *See also* **changeable, extensible**. **2.** Easily altered or influenced ▸ elastic, pliable, suggestible. *See* **flexible** (3). **3.** Capable of adapting or being adapted ▸ elastic, flexible, pliable. *See* **adaptable**.

✦ **CORE SYNONYMS:** *malleable, ductile, plastic, pliable, pliant.* These adjectives mean capable of being shaped, bent, or drawn out: *malleable metals such as gold and silver; ductile copper; a plastic substance such as wax; soaked the leather to make it pliable; pliant molten glass.*

---

malodor *noun*
▸ fetor, reek, stink. *See* **stench**. *See synonym note at* **stench**.

malodorous *adjective*
▸ fetid, foul, stinking. *See* **smelly**.

malpractice *noun*
▸ disservice, inequity, wrong. *See* **injustice** (1).

maltreat *verb*
▸ ill-treat, misuse, wrong. *See* **abuse** (1). *See synonym note at* **abuse**.

maltreatment *noun*
▸ mishandling, mistreatment. *See* **abuse** (2).

mammoth *noun*
One that is extraordinarily large and powerful ▸ Goliath, monster, titan. *See* **giant**.

mammoth *adjective*
Of extraordinary size and power ▸ behemoth, colossal, gigantic, mighty. *See* **enormous**. *See synonym note at* **enormous**.

man *noun*
1. A member of the human race ▸ human, mortal, person. *See* **human being**. **2.** Humans as a group ▸ humanity, mortals, world. *See* **humankind**. **3.** *Slang* A member of a law-enforcement agency ▸ officer, trooper. *Informal:* cop. *See* **police officer**.

manacle *noun*
Something that physically confines the legs or arms ▸ handcuffs, hobble, irons. *See* **bond** (1).

manacle *verb*
To restrict the activity or free movement of ▸ fetter, handcuff, hobble. *See* **hamper**¹ (1). *See synonym note at* **hamper**¹.

manage *verb*
1. To progress or perform adequately, especially in difficult circumstances ▸ do, fare, fend, get along, get by, muddle through, scrape by, shift, squeak by. *Informal:* make out. *Idioms:* make do, make shift,

make the best of it. *See also* **endure. 2.** To direct the functioning of ▸ run, work. *See* **operate** (1). **3.** To control the course of an activity ▸ direct, handle, operate. *See* **conduct** (1). *See synonym note at* **conduct. 4.** To have charge of the affairs of others ▸ direct, govern, rule. *See* **administer** (1).

manageable *adjective*
Capable of being governed ▸ administrable, controllable, governable, rulable. *See also* **loyal, obedient.**

management *noun*
1. The act or practice of directing or controlling ▸ administration, charge, conduct, direction, directorship, guidance, government, lead, leadership, oversight, stewardship, superintendence, supervision. *See also* **domination, duty. 2.** The careful guarding of an asset ▸ husbandry, preservation. *See* **conservation.**

manager *noun*
1. A person having administrative or managerial authority in an organization ▸ administrator, functionary. *See* **executive. 2.** Someone who directs and supervises workers ▸ foreman, head, supervisor. *See* **boss** (1).

managerial *adjective*
▸ executive, governmental, organizational. *See* **administrative.**

mandate *noun*
1. An order ▸ charge, commandment, imperative. *See* **command** (1). **2.** The right and power to command, decide, rule, or judge ▸ control, might. *Informal:* say-so, muscle. *See* **authority** (1). **3.** An area subject to rule by an outside power ▸ dependency, province. *See* **possession** (1).

mandate *verb*
To set forth expressly and authoritatively ▸ impose, ordain, rule. *See* **dictate** (1).

mandatory *adjective*
▸ compulsory, imperative, requisite. *See* **required** (1).

maneuver *noun*
1. A method of deploying troops and equipment in combat ▸ battle plan, plan of attack, stratagem, strategy, tactic. **2.** An action calculated to achieve an end ▸ measure, move, procedure, step, tactic. **3.** An indirect, usually cunning means of gaining an end ▸ deception, ploy, stratagem. *See* **trick** (1).

maneuver *verb*
1. To direct the course of carefully ▸ finesse, guide, jockey, navigate, pilot, steer. *Idiom:* back and fill. *See also* **drive, operate. 2.** To use stratagems in gaining an end ▸ angle for, engineer, finesse, jockey, worm. *Informal:* finagle, wangle. *Idioms:* pull strings (*or* wires). *See also* **plot. 3.** To go or cause to go from one place to another ▸ shift, transfer. *See* **move** (2). **4.** To influence or manage shrewdly or deviously ▸ exploit, use. *See* **manipulate** (1). *See synonym note at* **manipulate.**

manful *adjective*
▸ male, mannish, masculine. *See* **manly.**

mangle¹ *verb*
1. To injure or damage, as by abuse or heavy wear

▸ maul, rough up. *See* **batter** (1). *See synonym note at* **batter. 2.** To deprive of a limb or bodily member or its use ▸ amputate, mutilate. *See* **cripple** (1). **3.** To ruin through clumsiness or ineptness ▸ blunder, foul up, spoil. *See* **botch.**

mangle² *verb*
To smooth by applying heat or pressure ▸ calender, iron, roll. *See* **press** (2).

mangy *adjective*
▸ broken-down, dilapidated, tattered. *See* **shabby** (1).

manhandle *verb*
1. To be rough or brutal with ▸ knock about (*or* around), rough up, slap around. *Slang:* mess up. *See also* **abuse, beat, hit. 2.** To injure or damage, as by abuse or heavy wear ▸ maul, rough up. *See* **batter** (1).

manhood *noun*
▸ maleness, manliness, virility. *See* **masculinity.**

mania *noun*
1. A subject or activity that inspires lively interest ▸ hobbyhorse, passion. *See* **enthusiasm** (2). **2.** An irrational preoccupation ▸ fetish, fixation. *See* **obsession. 3.** Serious mental illness impairing a person's capacity to function normally ▸ dementia, derangement, lunacy. *See* **insanity** (1). *See synonym note at* **insanity.**

maniac *noun*
▸ enthusiast, fanatic, zealot. *See* **fan².**

maniacal *or* **maniac** *adjective*
▸ demented, lunatic, mad. *See* **insane** (1).

manifest *verb*
1. To make manifest or apparent ▸ display, reveal. *See* **show** (1). **2.** To come gradually to have ▸ acquire, form, incur. *See* **develop** (1). **3.** To give expression to, as by gestures, facial aspects, or bodily posture ▸ convey, display. *See* **express** (3). **4.** To represent (an abstraction, for example) in or as if in bodily form ▸ externalize, incarnate, materialize. *See* **embody** (1).

manifest *noun*
A series, as of names or words, printed or written down ▸ register, roster, schedule. *See* **list¹.**

manifest *adjective*
Readily seen, perceived, or understood ▸ evident, noticeable, obvious. *See* **apparent** (1). *See synonym note at* **apparent.**

manifestation *noun*
1. An act of showing or displaying ▸ exhibition, show. *See* **display** (1). **2.** Something visible or evident that gives grounds for believing in the existence or presence of something else ▸ evidence, indication, symptom. *See* **sign** (1). **3.** A concrete entity typifying an abstraction ▸ incarnation, instantiation, personification. *See* **embodiment** (1). **4.** The act of coming into sight ▸ emergence, materialization. *See* **appearance** (2). **5.** An impressive or ostentatious exhibition ▸ display, spectacle. *See* **array** (1).

manifesto *noun*
▸ announcement, declaration, proclamation. *See* **message** (1).

manifold *adjective*
▸ compound, multiplex. *See* **complex** (2).

manipulate *verb*

1. To influence or manage in a shrewd or devious manner ▸ exploit, maneuver, play, use. *Idioms:* pull strings, wheel and deal. *See also* **plot, wangle. 2.** To use with or as if with the hands ▸ handle, ply, wield. *See synonym note at* **handle. 3.** To handle in a way so as to mix, form, and shape ▸ knead, squeeze, work. **4.** To move over or along with pressure ▸ knead, press, work. *See* **rub** (2). **5.** To bring especially the hands or fingers into contact with ▸ handle, palpate. *See* **touch** (1).

✦ CORE SYNONYMS: *manipulate, exploit, maneuver.* These verbs mean to influence, manage, use, or control to one's advantage by artful or indirect means: *manipulated me into helping him; exploits natural resources; maneuvered me out of one job and into another.*

manipulation *noun*

▸ feeling, palpation, stroke. *See* **touch** (1).

manipulative *adjective*

Coldly planning to achieve aims that are selfish ▸ calculating, conniving, designing, scheming. *See also* **artful.**

mankind *noun*

▸ humanity, mortals, world. *See* **humankind.**

manlike *adjective*

1. Having qualities traditionally attributed to a man ▸ male, mannish, masculine. *See* **manly. 2.** Resembling a human being ▸ anthropoid, anthropomorphic, humanoid. *See* **humanlike.**

manliness *noun*

▸ maleness, manhood, virility. *See* **masculinity.**

manly *adjective*

Having qualities that are traditionally attributed to a man ▸ macho, male, manful, manlike, mannish, masculine, virile.

manmade *adjective*

▸ simulated, synthetic. *See* **artificial** (1).

manner *noun*

1. The approach used to do something ▸ fashion, mode, style. *See* **way** (1). *See synonym note at* **way. 2.** Behavior that reveals one's personality or state of mind ▸ demeanor, mien, style. *See* **bearing** (1). **3.** A habitual way of behaving ▸ form, habit, practice. *See* **custom** (1). **4.** A distinctive way of expressing oneself ▸ mode, tone. *See* **style** (1). **5.** A class that is defined by the common attribute or attributes possessed by all its members ▸ ilk, mold, species. *See* **kind²**. **6.** The manner in which one behaves ▸ comportment, conduct, deportment. *See* **behavior** (1).

mannered *adjective*

1. Artificially genteel ▸ affected, artificial, precious. *Informal:* la-di-da. **2.** Marked by excessive concern for modesty or propriety ▸ priggish, prissy, strait-laced. *See* **prudish.**

mannerism *noun*

▸ airs, pose. *See* **affectation** (1). *See synonym note at* **affectation.**

mannerliness *noun*

▸ gentility, politeness. *See* **courtesy** (1).

mannerly *adjective*

▸ genteel, polite. *See* **courteous** (1). *See synonym note at* **courteous.**

manners *noun*

Socially correct behavior ▸ decorum, etiquette, good behavior, good form, mores, proprieties, propriety, p's and q's, refinement. *See also* **courtesy.**

mannish *adjective*

▸ male, masculine. *See* **manly.**

mannishness *noun*

▸ maleness, manliness, virility. *See* **masculinity.**

man on horseback *noun*

▸ despot, oppressor, tyrant. *See* **dictator** (1).

manor *noun*

1. A house in the country ▸ cottage, country home, estate. *See* **villa. 2.** Usually extensive real estate ▸ estate, property. *See* **land** (1).

manslaughter *noun*

▸ assassination, homicide, killing. *See* **murder.**

manslayer *noun*

▸ killer, massacrer, slayer. *See* **murderer.**

mantic *adjective*

▸ divinitory, oracular, sibylline. *See* **prophetic.**

mantle *verb*

1. To cover as if with clothes ▸ drape, robe. *See* **clothe** (1). *See synonym note at* **clothe. 2.** To become red in the face ▸ crimson, flush. *See* **blush.**

mantle *noun*

A covering that obscures or hides something ▸ cover, screen. *See* **veil** (1).

manufacture *verb*

To create by forming, combining, or altering materials ▸ compose, fashion, shape. *See* **make** (1).

manufacture *noun*

Something produced by human effort ▸ produce, product, production, work. *See also* **composition, good.**

manufactured *adjective*

▸ simulated, synthetic. *See* **artificial** (1).

manufacturer *noun*

▸ artisan, constructor, manufacturer. *See* **maker** (1).

manumission *noun*

▸ emancipation, freedom. *See* **liberty** (1).

manumit *verb*

▸ emancipate, release. *See* **free** (1).

manumitted *adjective*

▸ emancipated, independent, sovereign. *See* **free** (1).

manuscript *noun*

▸ dialogue, play, scenario. *See* **script** (2).

many *adjective*

Amounting to or consisting of a large, indefinite number ▸ legion, multitudinous, myriad, numerous. *Informal:* umpteen. **Idiom:** quite a few. *See also* **abundance, generous, heap, incalcuable.**

many-colored *or* **many-hued** *adjective*

▸ colorful, many-hued, polychromatic. *See* **multicolored.**

many-sided *adjective*
▶ all-purpose, multifaceted, protean. *See* **versatile** (1). *See synonym note at* **versatile.**

map *verb*
1. To show graphically the direction or location of, as by using coordinates ▶ graph, lay out. *See* **plot** (1). **2.** To plan the details or arrangements of ▶ blueprint, work out. *See* **arrange** (2). **3.** To work out and arrange the parts and details of ▶ blueprint, lay out, sketch. *See* **design** (2).

map out *verb*
To draw up a preliminary plan or version of ▶ outline, sketch. *See* **draft** (1).

map *noun*
Slang The front surface of the head ▶ countenance, visage. *See* **face** (1).

mar *verb*
1. To spoil the soundness or perfection of ▶ flaw, impair. *See* **damage. 2.** To alter and spoil the natural form or appearance of ▶ disfigure, misshape, twist. *See* **deform.**

maraud *verb*
▶ harry, raid. *See* **invade** (1).

marbles *noun*
Slang A healthy mental state ▶ lucidity, rationality, reason. *See* **sanity.**

march¹ *verb*
1. To travel about or journey on foot ▶ backpack, hike, tramp, trek. *See also* **journey, walk, rove. 2.** To move forward ▶ proceed, progress. *See* **advance** (2).

march *noun*
1. Forward movement ▶ furtherance, headway, progress. *See* **advance** (1). **2.** An act of walking ▶ hike, ramble. *See* **walk** (1).

march² *or* **marchland** *noun*
The line or area separating geopolitical units ▶ borderland, frontier. *See* **border** (2).

margin *noun*
1. A line or area where something ends or abruptly changes ▶ brink, fringe, periphery. *See* **border** (1). *See synonym note at* **border. 2.** Freedom from normal restraints, limitations, or regulations ▶ entitlement, latitude, leeway. *See* **license** (1). *See synonym note at* **license.**

margin *verb*
To put or form a border on ▶ edge, rim. *See* **border** (1).

marinate *verb*
▶ soak, saturate, souse. *See* **steep².**

marine *adjective*
1. Of or relating to the seas or oceans ▶ briny, maritime, oceangoing, oceanic, pelagic, saltwater, salty, sea, seafaring, seagoing, seawater, thalassic. **2.** Of or relating to sea navigation ▶ maritime, nautical, naval, navigational. *See synonym note at* **nautical.**

mariner *noun*
▶ boatman, navigator, seafarer. *See* **sailor.**

marital *adjective*
Of, relating to, or typical of marriage ▶ conjugal, connubial, hymeneal, married, matrimonial, nuptial, spousal, wedded.

maritime *adjective*
1. Of or relating to sea navigation ▶ marine, nautical, naval, navigational. *See synonym note at* **nautical. 2.** Of or relating to the seas or oceans ▶ oceanic, saltwater, sea. *See* **marine** (1).

mark *noun*
1. A name or other device placed on an article to signify its ownership, manufacture, or origin ▶ brand, colophon, imprint, label, monogram, trademark. *See also* **symbol. 2.** The visible effect made on a surface by pressure ▶ indent, print. *See* **impression** (1). **3.** A conventional mark used in a writing system ▶ figure, symbol. *See* **character** (9). **4.** Something visible or evident that gives grounds for believing in the existence or presence of something else ▶ evidence, indication, symptom. *See* **sign** (1). *See synonym note at* **sign. 5.** Something that takes the place of words in communicating a thought or feeling ▶ indication, sign. *See* **expression** (2). **6.** A distinctive element ▶ characteristic, feature, trait. *See* **quality** (1). **7.** A means by which individuals are compared and judged ▶ criterion, gauge, measure. *See* **standard** (1). **8.** Wide recognition for one's deeds ▶ glory, note, prestige. *See* **fame. 9.** The act of noting, observing, or taking into account ▶ heed, note, regard. *See* **notice** (1). **10.** One that is fired at, attacked, or abused ▶ butt, target. **11.** What one intends to do or achieve ▶ end, goal, objective. *See* **intention. 12.** *Slang* A person who is easily deceived or victimized ▶ pushover, tool, victim. *See* **dupe** (1). **13.** One of the units in a course, as on an ascending or descending scale ▶ interval, level, step. *See* **degree** (1).

mark *verb*
1. To set off by or as if by a mark indicating ownership or manufacture ▶ brand, identify, label, tag, trademark. **2.** To attach a ticket to ▶ earmark, flag, label, tag, ticket. **3.** To evaluate and assign a grade to ▶ correct, grade, score. **4.** To make known or identify, as by signs ▶ indicate, pinpoint, specify. *See* **designate** (1). **5.** To give a precise indication of, as on a register or scale ▶ indicate, register. *See* **show** (3). **6.** To make a target of ▶ target. *Idioms:* draw (*or* get) a bead on, get in one's sights. **7.** To give grounds for believing in the existence or presence of ▶ attest, witness. *See* **indicate** (1). **8.** To make noticeable or different ▶ differentiate, individualize, singularize. *See* **distinguish** (2). **9.** To fix the limits of ▶ demarcate, limit, measure. *See* **determine** (1). **10.** To perceive with a special effort of the senses or the mind ▶ detect, note, recognize. *See* **notice.**

mark down *verb*
To become or make less in price or value ▶ depress, devalue, reduce. *See* **depreciate** (1).

✦ **CORE SYNONYMS:** *mark, brand, label, tag.* These verbs mean to set off by or as if by a mark indicating ownership or manufacture: *marked the parts as they* *left the assembly line; brands cattle; labeled the boxes with the company logo; tagged suitcases.*

markdown *noun*
▶ cheapening, devaluation, reduction. *See* **depreciation** (1).

marked *adjective*
▶ conspicuous, outstanding, prominent. *See* **noticeable** (1). *See synonym note at* **noticeable**.

market *verb*
1. To offer for sale ▶ handle, peddle. *See* **sell** (1). **2.** To attempt to sell or popularize by advertising or publicity ▶ advertise, publicize, purvey. *See* **promote** (3).

marketability *or* **marketableness** *noun*
Market appeal ▶ salability, salableness, sell.

marks *noun*
▶ footmarks, footprints, trail. *See* **track** (1).

maroon *verb*
▶ desert, forsake, leave. *See* **abandon** (1).

marooned *adjective*
▶ deserted, forsaken, outcast. *See* **abandoned** (1).

marriage *noun*
1. The state of being married ▶ conjugality, coupling, connubiality, holy matrimony, matrimony, union, wedded bliss, wedlock. *See also* **union**. **2.** The act or ceremony by which two people become husband and wife ▶ bridal, espousal, nuptials. *See* **wedding**.

marriageable *adjective*
▶ available, eligible, unattached. *See* **single** (5).

married *adjective*
▶ nuptial, spousal, wedded. *See* **marital**.

marrow *noun*
▶ essence, kernel, quintessence. *See* **heart** (1).

marrowy *adjective*
▶ aphoristic, epigrammatic, pointed. *See* **pithy** (1).

marry *verb*
1. To join or be joined in marriage ▶ espouse, mate, unite, wed. *Slang:* get hitched, get hooked. *Idioms:* join in matrimony, join together, lead to the altar, take the plunge, tie the knot. **2.** To bring or come together into a united whole ▶ join, unify, unite. *See* **combine** (1).

marsh *noun*
▶ bog, mire, wetland. *See* **swamp**.

marshal *verb*
1. To assemble, prepare, or put into operation, as for war or a similar emergency ▶ activate, ready. *See* **mobilize**. **2.** To put into a deliberate order ▶ deploy, organize, systematize. *See* **arrange** (1). *See synonym note at* **arrange**. **3.** To show the way to ▶ direct, escort, lead. *See* **guide** (1).

marshal *noun*
A member of a law-enforcement agency ▶ officer, trooper. *Informal:* cop. *See* **police officer**.

marshland *noun*
▶ fen, mire, wetland. *See* **swamp**.

martial *adjective*
1. Relating to armed service ▶ enlisted, soldierly. *See* **military** (2). **2.** Of or inclined toward war ▶ bellicose, militaristic. *See* **military** (1).

martinet *noun*
▶ despot, dictator, tyrant. *See* **authoritarian** (1).

martyr *noun*
▶ casualty, sufferer, wounded. *See* **victim** (1).

marvel *noun*
1. One that evokes great surprise and admiration ▶ astonishment, miracle, phenomenon, prodigy, sensation, stunner, surprise, wonder, wonderment. *Idioms:* one for the books, eighth wonder of the world. *See also* **display**. **2.** The emotion aroused by something awe-inspiring or astounding ▶ amazement, awe. *See* **wonder** (1).

marvel *verb*
To have a feeling of great awe and rapt admiration ▶ admire, wonder. *Idioms:* be agog (*or* agape *or* awestruck). *See also* **gaze, stagger**.

✦ CORE SYNONYMS: *marvel, miracle, phenomenon, prodigy, sensation, wonder.* These nouns denote one that evokes great surprise, admiration, or amazement: *a marvel of modern technology; a miracle of culinary art; a phenomenon of medical science; a musical prodigy; the theatrical sensation of the season; saw the wonders of Prague.*

marvelous *adjective*
1. Particularly excellent ▶ dandy, divine, fabulous, fantastic, fantastical, glorious, sensational, spectacular, splendid, superb, terrific, wonderful. *Informal:* dreamy, great, ripping, super, swell, tremendous. *Slang:* cool, groovy, hot, keen, neat, nifty, phat. *Idiom:* out of this world. *See also* **excellent, exceptional**. **2.** So remarkable as to be difficult to believe ▶ astounding, staggering, unbelievable. *See* **astonishing**. **3.** Impressive in size, proportion, or appearance ▶ imposing, magnificent, splendid. *See* **grand** (1).

mascot *noun*
▶ amulet, talisman. *See* **charm** (1).

masculine *adjective*
▶ male, mannish, virile. *See* **manly**.

masculinity *adjective*
The quality of being masculine ▶ machismo, maleness, manhood, manliness, mannishness, virility.

mash *verb*
1. To press forcefully so as to reduce to a pulpy mass ▶ mush, squash. *See* **crush** (1). *See synonym note at* **crush**. **2.** *Slang* To make amorous advances without serious intentions ▶ dally, toy, trifle. *See* **flirt** (2).

masher *noun*
Slang A man who is given to flirting ▶ flirt, wolf. *See also* **philanderer, seducer**.

mask *noun*
1. A deceptive outward appearance ▶ guise, pretense, show. *See* **façade** (2). **2.** Clothes or other personal effects, such as makeup, worn to conceal one's identity ▶ costume, guise, veil. *See* **disguise** (1).

mask *verb*
1. To prevent something from being known ▶ enshroud, veil. *See* **conceal** (1). **2.** To change or modify so as to prevent recognition of the true identity or

character of ▸ dissemble, dissimulate, veil. *See* **disguise.** *See synonym note at* **disguise.**

masquerade *noun*
1. A deceptive outward appearance ▸ front, gloss, guise, mask. *See* **façade** (2). **2.** A party or gathering for dancing ▸ ball, cotillion, promenade. *See* **dance. 3.** A display of insincere behavior ▸ disguise, pretense, sham, show. *See* **act** (2). **4.** An act of cheating ▸ deceit, hoax, swindle. *See* **cheat** (1). **5.** Clothes or other personal effects, such as makeup, worn to conceal one's identity ▸ costume, mask, veil. *See* **disguise** (1).

masquerade *verb*
1. To change or modify so as to prevent recognition of the true identity or character of ▸ dissemble, mask, veil. *See* **disguise. 2.** To assume the character or appearance of ▸ attitudinize, pose as. *See* **impersonate** (1).

masquerader *noun*
▸ cheater, swindler, trickster. *See* **cheat** (2).

mass *noun*
1. The greatest part or portion ▸ bulk, preponderance, preponderancy, weight. *See also* **center. 2.** Great amount or dimension ▸ magnitude, size. *See* **bulk** (1). **3.** The state or degree of being heavy ▸ massiveness, weightiness. *See* **heaviness. 4.** Something having material existence ▸ body, item, thing. *See* **object** (1). **5.** A quantity accumulated ▸ aggregation, amassment, cumulation. *See* **accumulation** (1). **6.** A group of things gathered haphazardly ▸ drift, hill, mound. *See* **heap** (1). **7.** A great deal ▸ bounty, profusion, wealth. *See* **abundance** (1). **8.** An enormous number of persons or things gathered together ▸ horde, host, throng. *See* **crowd** (1).

mass *verb*
To bring together so as to increase in mass or number ▸ build up, hive, pile up. *See* **accumulate.**

massacre *noun*
The savage killing of many victims ▸ bloodbath, bloodletting, bloodshed, butchering, butchery, carnage, decimation, genocide, holocaust, liquidation, mass murder, slaughter. *See also* **murder.**

massacre *verb*
1. To kill savagely and indiscriminately ▸ annihilate, butcher, decimate, kill off, slaughter, wipe out. *See also* **kill. 2.** *Informal* To render totally ineffective by decisive defeat ▸ crush, overcome, rout. *See* **overwhelm** (1).

massage *verb*
1. To alter or present material so as to favor a particular viewpoint ▸ doctor, slant. *See* **bias** (2). **2.** To move over or along with pressure ▸ manipulate, press, work. *See* **rub** (2).

masses *noun*
▸ crowd, proletariat, public. *See* **commonalty.**

massive *adjective*
1. Of large, often awkward size and weight ▸ cumbersome, heavy, oversized. *See* **bulky** (1). **2.** Having relatively great weight ▸ hefty, ponderous. *See* **heavy** (1). *See synonym note at* **heavy. 3.** Of extraordinary size

and power ▸ behemoth, colossal, gigantic, mighty. *See* **enormous.**

massiveness *noun*
▸ heftiness, weightiness. *See* **heaviness.**

massy *adjective*
▸ behemoth, colossal, gigantic, mighty. *See* **enormous.**

master *noun*
1. One who governs or leads ▸ boss, director, head, leader. *See* **chief** (1). **2.** A person who has legal title to property ▸ holder, proprietor. *See* **owner. 3.** One that conquers ▸ conquistador, victor. *See* **conqueror** (1). **4.** A person with a high degree of knowledge or skill in a particular field ▸ authority, proficient. *See* **expert. 5.** A first form from which varieties arise or imitations are made ▸ father, prototype. *See* **original** (1). **6.** One who educates ▸ instructor, trainer, tutor. *See* **educator.**

master *adjective*
Having or demonstrating a high degree of knowledge or skill ▸ professional, skilled. *See* **expert.**

master *verb*
1. To gain knowledge or mastery of by study ▸ acquire, get. *See* **learn** (1). **2.** To win a victory over, as in battle or a competition ▸ conquer, surmount, vanquish. *See* **defeat** (1). **3.** To train to live with and be of use to people ▸ break in, tame. *See* **domesticate. 4.** To make an animal docile ▸ bust, tame. *See* **gentle** (1).

masterful *adjective*
1. Having or demonstrating a high degree of knowledge or skill ▸ professional, proficient, skilled. *See* **expert. 2.** Exercising authority ▸ authoritative, commanding, dominant, lordly. *See also* **administrative. 3.** Given to asserting one's will or authority over others ▸ bossy, domineering, imperious, overbearing. *See* **dictatorial** (1).

masterly *adjective*
▸ adept, professional, skilled. *See* **expert.**

mastermind *noun*
▸ intellectual, thinker. *See* **mind** (2).

masterpiece *or* **masterwork** *noun*
An outstanding and ingenious work ▸ chef-d'oeuvre, magnum opus. *See also* **accomplishment, composition, treasure.**

masterstroke *noun*
▸ exploit, feat. *See* **accomplishment** (1). *See synonym note at* **accomplishment.**

mastery *noun*
1. Natural or acquired talent or skill ▸ command, expertise, knack. *See* **ability** (1). **2.** The right and power to command, decide, rule, or judge ▸ control, might. *See* **authority** (1). **3.** The act of exercising controlling power or the condition of being so controlled ▸ control, dominion, reign. *See* **domination** (1).

masticate *verb*
▸ chomp, gnash, munch. *See* **chew.**

mastodonic *adjective*
▸ behemoth, colossal, gigantic. *See* **enormous.**

mat¹ *verb*

To twist together so that separation is difficult ▸ foul, tangle. *See* **entangle** (1).

mat² *or* **matte** *adjective*

Lacking vividness or color ▸ lackluster, lusterless, muddy. *See* **dull** (2).

match *noun*

1. One of a matched pair of things ▸ counterpart, duplicate. *See* **mate** (1). **2.** Something closely analogous to something else ▸ correlative, counterpart. *See* **parallel**. **3.** One that is very similar to another in rank or position ▸ colleague, equivalent, fellow. *See* **peer²**. **4.** Two items of the same kind together ▸ duet, duo, pair. *See* **couple**. **5.** A test of skill or ability ▸ bout, contest, trial. *See* **competition** (2).

match *verb*

1. To do or make something equal to ▸ equal, meet, tie. **2.** To be equal or alike ▸ correspond, parallel, touch. *See* **equal** (1). **3.** To be compatible or suitable ▸ chime, correspond, harmonize. *See* **agree** (1). **4.** To be similar especially in appearance ▸ be like, look like. *See* **resemble**. **5.** To be suitable to or in keeping with ▸ become, befit, fit. *See* **suit** (1). **6.** To place in opposition or be in opposition to ▸ match, pit. *See* **oppose** (1). **7.** To represent as similar ▸ compare, equate, parallel. *See* **liken**.

matched *adjective*

Consisting of two identical or similar related things, parts, or elements ▸ double, dual, paired, twin. *See also* **double, equal**.

matchless *adjective*

▸ incomparable, singular, unparalleled. *See* **unique** (1).

matchlessness *noun*

▸ oneness, singleness, singularity. *See* **uniqueness** (1).

mate *noun*

1. One of a matched pair of things ▸ companion, complement, counterpart, double, duplicate, fellow, match, twin. **2.** A husband or wife ▸ consort, partner. *See* **spouse**. **3.** One who shares interests or activities with another ▸ companion, comrade. *See* **associate** (2). **4.** A person whom one knows well, likes, and trusts ▸ chum, comrade, intimate. *See* **friend** (1).

mate *verb*

1. To join or be joined in marriage ▸ espouse, wed. *See* **marry** (1). **2.** To engage in sexual relations with ▸ bed, copulate with. *See* **sleep with**.

materfamilias *noun*

▸ matriarch. *Informal:* mama, mom. *See* **mother** (1).

material *noun*

1. That from which things are or can be made ▸ matter, medium, stuff, substance. *Idiom:* grist for one's mill. **2.** Things needed for a task, journey, or other purpose ▸ equipment, gear. *See* **outfit** (1). *See synonym note at* **outfit**. **3.** A person considered to have qualities suitable for a particular activity ▸ stuff, timber. *See also* **comer, potential**.

material *adjective*

1. Composed of or relating to things that occupy space and can be perceived by the senses ▸ corporeal, tangible. *See* **physical** (1). **2.** Of or preoccupied with that which is material rather than spiritual or intellectual ▸ materialistic, sensual. *See also* **earthly, greedy, superficial**. **3.** Related to or affecting the matter at hand ▸ apropos, germane. *See* **relevant**. *See synonym note at* **relevant**. **4.** Having great significance ▸ consequential, grand, meaningful. *See* **important** (1).

materialistic *adjective*

Of or preoccupied with that which is material rather than spiritual or intellectual ▸ material, sensual. *See also* **earthly, greedy, superficial**.

materiality *noun*

1. That which occupies space and can be perceived by the senses ▸ matter, substance. *See also* **element, object, thing**. **2.** The relation with, or fact of being related to, the matter at hand ▸ appositeness, pertinence. *See* **relevance**.

materialization *noun*

1. The condition of being fulfilled ▸ culmination, realization. *See* **fulfillment** (1). **2.** A concrete entity typifying an abstraction ▸ incarnation, manifestation, personification. *See* **embodiment** (1). **3.** The act of coming into sight ▸ emergence, manifestation. *See* **appearance** (2).

materialize *verb*

1. To make real or actual ▸ actualize, bring about, make happen, realize. *Idioms:* bring to pass, carry (*or* put) into effect. *See also* **effect, produce**. **2.** To come into view ▸ emerge, loom, show up. *See* **appear** (1). *See synonym note at* **appear**. **3.** To represent (an abstraction, for example) in or as if in bodily form ▸ externalize, manifest, objectify. *See* **embody** (1).

materiel *or* **matériel** *noun*

▸ equipment, gear. *See* **outfit** (1).

matriarch *noun*

▸ materfamilias. *Informal:* mama, mom. *See* **mother** (1).

matrimonial *adjective*

▸ nuptial, spousal, wedded. *See* **marital**.

matrimony *noun*

▸ conjugality, matrimony, union. *See* **marriage** (1).

matrix *noun*

A hollow device for shaping a fluid or plastic substance ▸ cast, form, mold.

matter *noun*

1. That which occupies space and can be perceived by the senses ▸ materiality, substance. *See also* **element, object, thing**. **2.** That from which things are or can be made ▸ stuff, substance. *See* **material** (1). **3.** What a speech, piece of writing, or artistic work is about ▸ text, theme. *See* **subject** (1). *See synonym note at* **subject**. **4.** Something to be done, considered, or dealt with ▸ affair, business, thing. *See also* **business, task**. **5.** A situation that presents difficulty, uncertainty, or perplexity ▸ case, issue, question. *See* **problem** (1).

matter *verb*

To be of significance ▸ signify, weigh. *See* **count** (1). *See synonym note at* **count**.

matter-of-fact *adjective*
1. Lacking liveliness, charm, or surprise ▶ aseptic, colorless, pedestrian. *See* **dull** (1). **2.** Having or indicating an awareness of things as they really are ▶ practical, pragmatic, prosaic. *See* **realistic** (1). **3.** Lacking feeling or emotion ▶ emotionless, impassive, stolid. *See* **cold** (2).

maturate *verb*
▶ age, develop, ripen. *See* **mature.**

maturation *noun*
▶ evolvement, progress. *See* **development** (1).

mature *adjective*
1. Having reached full growth and development ▶ adult, advanced, big, developed, evolved, full-blown, full-fledged, full-grown, full-size, grown, grown-up, matured, older, ripe. *Idioms:* in full bloom, in one's prime, of age. *See also* **aged. 2.** Far along in life or time ▶ aged, elderly, senior. *See* **old** (2). **3.** Owed as a debt ▶ collectible, payable, unpaid. *See* **due** (1).

mature *verb*
To bring or come to full development ▶ age, develop, grow (up), maturate, mellow, ripen. *Idioms:* come of age, reach adulthood. *See also* **age.**

✦ CORE SYNONYMS: *mature, age, develop, ripen.* These verbs mean to bring or come to full development or maximum excellence: *maturing the wines in vats; aged the brandy for 100 years; developed the flavor slowly; fruits that were ripened on the vine.*

---

maturity *noun*
▶ agedness, seniority, years. *See* **age** (1).

maudlin *adjective*
▶ gushy, mawkish, soft. *See* **sentimental.** *See synonym note at* **sentimental.**

maudlinism *noun*
▶ bathos, treacle. *See* **sentimentality.**

maul *verb*
1. To injure or damage, as by abuse ▶ maim, rough up. *See* **batter** (1). *See synonym note at* **batter. 2.** To hit heavily and repeatedly ▶ assault, pummel, thresh. *See* **beat** (1).

maunder *noun*
To turn aside, especially from the main subject in writing or speaking ▶ ramble, stray, wander. *See* **digress** (1).

maunder *verb*
To speak or utter indistinctly, as by lowering the voice or partially closing the mouth ▶ jabber, murmur, whisper. *See* **mutter** (1).

mausoleum *noun*
▶ catacomb, crypt, tomb. *See* **grave¹.**

maven *noun*
▶ authority, master, proficient. *See* **expert.**

maverick *noun*
▶ free-thinker, independent, original. *See* **rebel** (2).

maw *noun*
The opening in the body through which food is ingested ▶ chops. *Slang:* trap, yap. *See* **mouth** (1).

mawkish *adjective*
▶ gushy, maudlin, soft. *See* **sentimental.** *See synonym note at* **sentimental.**

mawkishness *noun*
▶ bathos, treacle. *See* **sentimentality.**

maxim *noun*
1. A usually pithy and familiar statement generally accepted as wise or true ▶ adage, byword, motto. *See* **proverb.** *See synonym note at* **proverb. 2.** The principle taught by a fable or parable ▶ lesson, principle. *See* **moral. 3.** A broad and basic rule or truth ▶ axiom, truism. *See* **law** (3).

maximal *adjective*
▶ topmost, uttermost. *See* **maximum.**

maximum *noun*
1. The greatest quantity or highest degree attainable ▶ outside, top, ultimate, utmost, uttermost. *Slang:* max. *Idioms:* daddy of them all, the last word, ne plus ultra. *See also* **climax. 2.** The greatest amount or number allowed ▶ brim, cap, limitation. *See* **limit** (1).

maximum *adjective*
Greatest in quantity or highest in degree that can be attained ▶ extreme, greatest, highest, maximal, peak, top, topmost, transcendent, ultimate, unsurpassable, utmost. *Slang:* max, tops. *See also* **best.**

maybe *or* **mayhap** *adverb*
Possibly but not certainly ▶ conceivably, feasibly, perchance, perhaps, possibly. *See also* **probably.**

maze *noun*
Something that is intricately and often bewilderingly complex ▶ labyrinth, morass, web. *See* **tangle** (1).

maze *verb*
Chiefly Regional To dull the senses, as with a shock ▶ stun, stupefy. *See* **daze** (1).

mea culpa *noun*
A statement of acknowledgment expressing regret or asking pardon ▶ apology, excuse, regrets. *See also* **acknowledgment.**

meadow *noun*
▶ clearing, field, pasture. *See also* **lot.**

meager *adjective*
1. Conspicuously deficient in quantity, fullness, or extent ▶ exiguous, insubstantial, poor, puny, scant, scanty, scrimpy, skimpy, spare, sparse, spartan, stingy, thin. *Slang:* measly. *Idioms:* in short supply, scraping the bottom of the barrel. *See also* **insufficient, little, trivial. 2.** Having little flesh or fat on the body ▶ lean, skinny, slim. *See* **thin** (1). *See synonym note at* **thin.**

mean¹ *verb*
1. To have or convey a particular idea ▶ connote, convey, denote, import, intend, indicate, signify, spell. *Idioms:* add up to, come down to. *See also* **communicate, imply, represent. 2.** To have in mind as a goal or purpose ▶ design, plan, target. *See* **intend** (1).

mean² *adjective*
1. Characterized by intense ill will or spite ▶ evil, wicked. *See* **malevolent** (1). **2.** Having or proceeding from low moral standards ▶ squalid, vile. *See* **sordid.** *See synonym note at* **sordid. 3.** Ungenerously or pettily

reluctant to spend money ▸ close-fisted, miserly. *See* **stingy** (1). **4.** Of low or lower quality ▸ inferior, substandard. *See* **bad** (1). **5.** Of little distinction ▸ humble, lowly, simple. *See also* **modest. 6.** Lacking high station or birth ▸ common, humble. *See* **lowly** (1). **7.** So objectionable as to deserve condemnation ▸ contemptible, disgusting, obnoxious. *See* **offensive** (1). **8.** *Informal* Having or showing a bad temper ▸ cranky, grouchy, peevish. *See* **ill-tempered. 9.** *Slang* Hard to treat, manage, or cope with ▸ demanding, difficult, trying. *See* **troublesome** (2).

mean³ *noun*
Something that represents a midpoint between extremes ▸ medium, norm. *See* **average** (1).

mean *adjective*
Being at neither one extreme nor the other ▸ intermediate, median, midway. *See* **middle** (1).

meander *verb*
1. To move or proceed on a repeatedly curving course ▸ snake, spiral, weave. *See* **wind²** (1). **2.** To move about at random, especially over a wide area ▸ drift, gad, wander. *See* **rove.** *See synonym note at* **rove.**

meandering *adjective*
1. Marked by or given to digression ▸ long-winded, parenthetical, rambling. *See* **digressive. 2.** Not proceeding straight to the point or object ▸ circuitous, devious, roundabout. *See* **indirect** (1). **3.** Repeatedly curving in alternate directions ▸ convoluted, sinuous, twisting. *See* **winding** (1).

meaning *noun*
1. Something that is conveyed or signified ▸ acceptation, connotation, denotation, import, intent, message, point, purport, sense, significance, significancy, signification, value. *See also* **feeling, idea, import, thrust. 2.** What one intends to do or achieve ▸ end, goal, objective. *See* **intention.**

meaning *adjective*
Effectively conveying meaning, feeling, or mood ▸ eloquent, significant. *See* **expressive.**

✦ **CORE SYNONYMS:** *meaning, acceptation, import, sense, significance, signification.* These nouns refer to the idea conveyed by something, such as a word, action, gesture, or situation: *Synonyms are words with the same or nearly the same meaning. In one of its acceptations, "value" is a technical term in music. The import of his statement is ambiguous. The term "anthropometry" has only one sense. The significance of a green traffic light is widely understood. Linguists have determined the hieroglyphics' signification.*

---

meaningful *adjective*
1. Effectively conveying meaning, feeling, or mood ▸ eloquent, significant. *See* **expressive.** *See synonym note at* **expressive. 2.** Conveying hidden or unexpressed meaning ▸ consequential, significant. *See* **pregnant** (2). **3.** Having great significance ▸ consequential, grand, significant. *See* **important** (1).

meaningless *adjective*
▸ pointless, senseless. *See* **mindless** (1).

meaninglessness *noun*
▸ blankness, hollowness. *See* **emptiness** (3).

meanness *noun*
1. A desire to harm others or to see others suffer ▸ maliciousness, viciousness. *See* **malevolence. 2.** *Informal* A tendency to become angry or irritable ▸ crankiness, prickliness, tetchiness. *See* **temper** (1).

means *noun*
1. That by which something is done or caused ▸ agency, instrument, medium. *See* **agent** (1). **2.** Things that have economic value ▸ assets, capital, wealth. *See* **resources** (1). **3.** A method used for accomplishing something ▸ course, modus operandi, procedure, technique. *See* **approach** (1).

measly *adjective*
1. *Slang* Conspicuously deficient in quantity, fullness, or extent ▸ puny, scant, skimpy. *See* **meager** (1). **2.** *Slang* Of little importance or seriousness ▸ inconsequential, negligible, trifling. *See* **trivial.**

measure *verb*
1. To ascertain the dimensions, quantity, or capacity of ▸ gauge, quantify, quantitate. *Idioms:* take the dimensions (*or* measure) of. *See also* **estimate. 2.** To fix the limits of ▸ demarcate, limit, mark. *See* **determine** (1).

measure out *verb*
To give out in portions or shares ▸ allocate, apportion, dispense. *See* **distribute** (1).

measure up *verb*
To be equal or alike ▸ correspond, match, parallel. *See* **equal** (1).

measure *noun*
1. The act or process of ascertaining dimensions, quantity, or capacity ▸ determination, measurement, mensuration, quantification. *See also* **computation, estimation. 2.** The amount of space occupied by something ▸ extent, magnitude, proportions. *See* **size** (1). **3.** Relative intensity or amount, as of a quality or attribute ▸ extent, magnitude, scope. *See* **degree** (2). **4.** A means by which individuals are compared and judged ▸ criterion, mark, norm. *See* **standard** (1). *See synonym note at* **standard. 5.** That which is allotted ▸ allowance, ration, share. *See* **allotment** (1). **6.** Avoidance of extremes of opinion, feeling, or personal conduct ▸ abstemiousness, sobriety, temperance. *See* **moderation** (1). **7.** An action that is calculated to achieve an end ▸ maneuver, move, procedure, step, tactic. **8.** The formal product of a legislative or judicial body ▸ bill, enactment, legislation. *See* **law** (2). **9.** The patterned, recurring alternation of contrasting elements, such as stressed and unstressed notes in music ▸ cadence, meter, swing. *See* **rhythm. 10.** An indefinite amount or extent ▸ number, portion. *See* **quantity** (2).

measured *adjective*
1. Careful and slow in acting, moving, or deciding ▸ circumspect, leisurely, unhurried. *See* **deliberate** (3). **2.** Marked by a regular rhythm ▸ cadenced, metrical, rhythmic. *See* **rhythmical.**

measureless *adjective*
1. Too great to be calculated ▸ immeasurable, infinite. *See* **incalculable**. *See synonym note at* **incalculable**.
2. Having no ends or limits ▸ illimitable, infinite. *See* **endless** (1).

measurelessness *noun*
▸ immeasurability, limitlessness, unlimitedness. *See* **infinity** (1).

measurement *noun*
The act or process of ascertaining dimensions, quantity, or capacity ▸ determination, measure, mensuration, quantification. *See also* **calculation, estimation**.

measurements *noun*
▸ extent, magnitude, proportions. *See* **size** (1).

meat *noun*
1. Material that is fit to be eaten ▸ bread, foodstuff, nourishment. *See* **food**. 2. The most central or essential part ▸ essence, marrow, quintessence. *See* **heart** (1).

meatball *or* **meathead** *noun*
Slang A large, ungainly, and dull-witted person ▸ lout, ox. *Informal:* lummox. *See* **oaf**.

meaty *adjective*
1. Conveying hidden or unexpressed meaning ▸ consequential, significant. *See* **pregnant** (2). 2. Having too much flesh ▸ chubby, pudgy, rotund. *See* **fat** (1).

mechanical *adjective*
▸ automatic, cursory, routine. *See* **perfunctory**.

mechanism *noun*
1. That by which something is done or caused ▸ agency, instrument, means, medium. *See* **agent** (1).
2. Something, as a machine, devised for a particular function ▸ appliance, contraption, invention. *See* **device** (1).

medal *noun*
1. An emblem of honor worn on one's clothing ▸ badge, decoration, ribbon. *See* **decoration** (2). 2. Recognition of achievement or superiority or a sign of this ▸ award, honor. *See* **distinction** (2).

medalist *noun*
▸ champion, titleholder. *See* **winner** (1).

meddle *verb*
1. To intervene officiously or indiscreetly in the affairs of others ▸ butt in, horn in, interfere, interlope, intermeddle, obtrude. *Informal:* kibitz. **Idioms:** poke (*or* stick) one's nose in, stick one's oar in. *See also* **interrupt, snoop**. 2. To handle something in an attempt to adjust or improve it ▸ fool, fiddle, tamper. *See* **tinker** (1).

✦ **CORE SYNONYMS:** *meddle, interfere, obtrude*. These verbs mean to intervene officiously or indiscreetly in the affairs of others. *Meddle* stresses unwanted, unwarranted, or unnecessary intrusion: "*wholly unacquainted with the world in which they are so fond of meddling*" (Edmund Burke). *Interfere* implies action that seriously hampers, hinders, or frustrates: "*Romantics of all ages can recall occasions when lust interfered with reason*" (Christine Gorman). To *obtrude* is to impose oneself or one's ideas on others

with undue insistence or without invitation: *He tried to obtrude his schemes on the members of the council.*

meddler *noun*
▸ interloper, quidnunc, snooper. *See* **busybody**.

meddling *noun*
The act or an instance of interfering or intruding ▸ interference, interfering, interrupting, intervention, intruding, intrusion, obtrusion, prying, snooping.

meddling *or* **meddlesome** *adjective*
Unduly interested in the affairs of others ▸ inquisitive, intrusive, officious. *See* **curious** (1).

media *noun*
▸ fourth estate, mass media. *See* **press** (1).

median *noun*
1. A point or area equidistant from all sides ▸ middle, midpoint, midst. *See* **center** (2). 2. Something that represents a midpoint between extremes ▸ mean, norm. *See* **average** (1).

median *or* **medial** *adjective*
1. At, in, near, or being the center ▸ focal, innermost, middle. *See* **central** (1). 2. Being at neither one extreme nor the other ▸ intermediate, medial, midway. *See* **middle** (1).

mediate *verb*
1. To intervene between disputants in order to bring about an agreement ▸ arbitrate, moderate. *See also* **confer, judge**. 2. To serve as a conduit ▸ convey, transmit. *See* **conduct** (3).

mediation *noun*
▸ arrangement, give-and-take, settlement. *See* **compromise**.

mediator *noun*
▸ intermediary, negotiator. *See* **go-between**.

medicament *noun*
1. An agent used to restore health ▸ elixir, medication, remedy. *See* **cure**. 2. A substance used in treating disease ▸ medication, medicine. *See* **drug** (1).

medicate *verb*
1. To administer especially a painkilling drug to someone ▸ narcotize, tranquilize. *See* **drug** (1). 2. To provide as a remedy ▸ dispense, give, treat. *See* **administer** (3).

medication *noun*
1. An agent used to restore health ▸ elixir, medicine, remedy. *See* **cure**. 2. A substance used in the treatment of disease ▸ medicament, medicine, pharmaceutical. *See* **drug** (1).

medicinal *adjective*
▸ remedial, restorative. *See* **curative**.

medicine *noun*
1. An agent used to restore health ▸ elixir, medication, remedy. *See* **cure**. 2. A substance used in the treatment of disease ▸ medicament, medication, pharmaceutical. *See* **drug** (1).

mediocre *adjective*
1. Being of no special quality or type ▸ common, homely, standard. *See* **ordinary** (1). 2. Of low or lower quality ▸ inferior, low-quality, substandard. *See* **bad** (1). 3. Relating to or occupying a middle position on

a scale of evaluation ▸ fair, tolerable. *See* **average** (1). *See synonym note at* **average.**

mediocrity *noun*
▸ blandness, drabness, lifelessness. *See* **dullness** (1).

meditate *verb*
▸ cogitate, deliberate, mull. *See* **ponder.**

meditation *noun*
▸ cogitation, deliberation, rumination. *See* **thought** (1).

meditative *adjective*
▸ contemplative, pensive, reflective. *See* **thoughtful** (1). *See synonym note at* **thoughtful.**

medium *noun*
1. Something that represents a midpoint between extremes ▸ median, norm. *See* **average** (1). 2. That by which something is done or caused ▸ agency, means, mechanism. *See* **agent** (1). 3. The surrounding conditions and circumstances affecting growth or development ▸ climate, surroundings. *See* **environment** (2). 4. That from which things are or can be made ▸ stuff, substance. *See* **material** (1).

medium *adjective*
Relating to or occupying a middle position on a scale of evaluation ▸ mediocre, fair. *See* **average** (1). *See synonym note at* **average.**

medley *noun*
▸ hodgepodge, jumble, mishmash. *See* **assortment** (1).

meek *adjective*
1. Having or expressing feelings of humility ▸ humble, lowly, modest, unambitious. *See also* **deferential.** 2. Easily managed or handled ▸ domesticated, mild, tame. *See* **gentle** (3).

meekness *noun*
▸ humbleness, humility. *See* **modesty** (1).

meet[1] *verb*
1. To come together face-to-face, especially defiantly ▸ confront, encounter, face, front. *Idiom:* stand up to. *See also* **contest, defy.** 2. To come together by arrangement ▸ meet up, get together, rendezvous. *See also* **assemble.** 3. To come together from different directions ▸ close, converge, join, unite. *See also* **combine.** 4. To be contiguous or next to ▸ butt, join, neighbor, touch. *See* **adjoin** (1). 5. To participate in or partake of personally ▸ go through, meet with, undergo. *See* **experience.** 6. To do or make something equal to ▸ equal, match, tie. 7. To be suitable or sufficient to fulfill a need ▸ fill, fulfill. *See* **satisfy** (1). *See synonym note at* **satisfy.** 8. To strive in opposition ▸ battle, fight, wrestle. *See* **contend** (1). 9. To find or meet by chance ▸ come across, run across, stumble on. *See* **encounter** (1).

meet *noun*
A test of skill or ability ▸ bout, match, trial. *See* **competition** (2).

meet[2] *adjective*
Suited to one's needs or purpose ▸ expedient, proper, suitable. *See* **convenient** (1).

meeting *noun*
1. The act or fact of coming together ▸ confluence, convergence, gathering. *See* **junction** (1). 2. A number of persons who have come or been gathered together ▸ conference, group. *Informal:* get-together. *See* **assembly** (1). 3. A formal assemblage of the members of a group ▸ conference, congress. *See* **convention** (1). 4. A face-to-face, usually hostile meeting ▸ duel, face-off, showdown. *See* **confrontation** (1).

megalomania *noun*
▸ egoism, self-importance. *Informal:* big head. *See also* **egotism.**

megalomaniacal *adjective*
▸ bossy, domineering, overbearing. *See* **dictatorial** (1).

megalopolis *noun*
▸ borough, metropolis, municipality. *See* **city.**

megrim *noun*
▸ impulse, notion, whim. *See* **fancy** (1).

melancholic *adjective*
▸ dejected, dispirited, sad. *See* **depressed** (1).

melancholy *noun*
A feeling or spell of dismally low spirits ▸ dejection, doldrums, funk. *See* **depression** (2).

melancholy *adjective*
1. In low spirits ▸ dejected, downhearted, sad. *See* **depressed** (1). 2. Causing or expressing sorrow or sadness ▸ depressing, doleful, mournful. *See* **sorrowful** (1). *See synonym note at* **sorrowful.**

mélange *noun*
▸ hodgepodge, jumble, mishmash. *See* **assortment** (1).

meld *verb*
▸ join, unify, unite. *See* **combine** (1).

melee *noun*
1. A physical conflict involving two or more people ▸ free-for-all, riot. *See* **fight** (1). *See synonym note at* **fight.** 2. A lack of civil order or peace ▸ anarchy, lawlessness, misrule. *See* **disorder** (2).

meliorate *verb*
▸ better, enhance, upgrade. *See* **improve** (1). *See synonym note at* **improve.**

melioration *noun*
1. The act of making better or the condition of being made better ▸ betterment, development, upgrade. *See* **improvement** (1). 2. Steady improvement, as of an individual or society ▸ advancement, betterment, development. *See* **progress** (1).

mellifluous *adjective*
▸ euphonic, melodic, musical. *See* **melodious.**

mellow *adjective*
1. Brought to full flavor and richness by aging ▸ aged, ripe. *See also* **mature.** 2. Having or producing a full, deep, or rich sound ▸ resounding, sonorous, vibrant. *See* **resonant.** 3. Not excited or agitated ▸ even-tempered, imperturbable, nonchalant. *See* **calm** (1). 4. Unconstrained by rigid standards or ceremony ▸ casual, easy, relaxed. *See* **easygoing** (1).

mellow *verb*
To bring or come to full development ▸ develop, ripen. *See* **mature.**

mellow out *verb*
To take repose by ceasing work or other effort for an

interval of time ▸ kick back, unbend, unwind. *See* **rest**[1] (1).

melodious *or* **melodic** *adjective*
Having or producing a pleasing melody or sound ▸ dulcet, euphonic, euphonious, harmonious, mellifluous, melodic, musical, silvery, sweet-sounding, tuneful. *See also* **harmonious, pleasant.**

melodrama *or* **melodramatics** *noun*
▸ dramatics, histrionics, melodramatics. *See* **theatrics** (2).

melodramatic *adjective*
▸ histrionic, sensational, spectacular. *See* **dramatic** (2).

melody *noun*
A pleasing succession or arrangement of sound ▸ air, aria, strain, theme, tune. *See also* **song.**

melt *verb*
1. To change from a solid to a liquid ▸ deliquesce, dissolve, flux, fuse, liquefy, run, thaw. 2. To disappear gradually ▸ dissolve, fade, vanish. *See* **disappear** (1).

member *noun*
▸ building block, piece, section. *See* **part** (1).

membrane *noun*
▸ lamina, sheath. *See* **skin** (2).

memento *noun*
▸ favor, reminder. *See* **remembrance** (1).

memo *noun*
1. *Informal* A brief note written as an aid to the memory ▸ notation, reminder. *See* **note** (1). 2. A written communication directed to another ▸ correspondence, missive, note. *See* **letter** (1).

memoir *noun*
A personal narrative or record of experiences ▸ autobiography, commentaries, diary, journal, reminiscences. *See also* **memory, story.**

memorable *adjective*
▸ extraordinary, noteworthy, special. *See* **exceptional** (1).

memorandum *noun*
1. A brief record written as an aid to the memory ▸ notation, reminder. *See* **note** (1). 2. A written communication directed to another ▸ correspondence, missive, note. *See* **letter** (1). *See synonym note at* **letter.**

memorial *noun*
Something, as a structure or custom, serving to honor or keep alive a memory ▸ commemoration, monument, remembrance. *See also* **testimonial.**

memorial *adjective*
Serving to honor or keep alive a memory ▸ commemorative, monumental.

memorialize *verb*
To honor or keep alive the memory of ▸ commemorate. *See also* **immortalize.**

memorize *verb*
To commit to memory ▸ con, learn. *Idioms:* learn by heart (*or* rote). *See also* **learn, remember.**

memory *noun*
1. The power of retaining and recalling past experience ▸ recall, recollection, remembrance, reminiscence, retention. *Idiom:* power of recall. 2. An act or instance of remembering ▸ mental image, recollection, remembrance, reminiscence. *See also* **idea.**

menace *noun*
1. An expression of the intent to hurt or punish another ▸ intimidation, threat. 2. Exposure to harm, loss, or injury ▸ hazard, jeopardy, peril, risk. *See* **danger.**

menace *verb*
1. To frighten into submission or compliance ▸ browbeat, bully, cow. *See* **intimidate** (1). 2. To expose to possible loss or damage ▸ jeopardize, threaten. *See* **endanger.** 3. To be imminent ▸ hover, impend, loom. *See* **threaten** (2).

menacing *adjective*
1. Bringing or predicting misfortune ▸ bad, ominous, portentous. *See* **fateful** (1). 2. Involving possible risk, loss, or injury ▸ chancy, hazardous, risky. *See* **dangerous.**

ménage *noun*
A group of people living together as a unit ▸ family, house, household.

mend *verb*
1. To restore to proper condition ▸ doctor, overhaul, repair. *See* **fix** (1). 2. To make right what is wrong ▸ rectify, remedy. *See* **correct** (1). 3. To regain one's health ▸ convalesce, improve, recuperate. *See* **recover** (2).

mendacious *adjective*
▸ duplicitous, lying, untruthful. *See* **dishonest** (1). *See synonym note at* **dishonest.**

mendacity *noun*
1. The practice of lying ▸ falsehood, falsification, inveracity, lying, perjury, prevarication, truthlessness, untruthfulness. *See also* **deceit.** 2. Lack of integrity ▸ deceitfulness, shadiness. *See* **dishonesty** (1). 3. An untrue declaration ▸ falsehood, fib, untruth. *See* **lie**[2].

mendicancy *or* **mendicity** *noun*
The condition of being a beggar ▸ beggary, mendicity. *See also* **poverty.**

mendicant *noun*
One who begs habitually or for a living ▸ cadger. *See* **beggar** (1).

mendicant *adjective*
Having little or no money or wealth ▸ destitute, down-and-out, indigent. *See* **poor** (1).

menial *adjective*
Excessively eager to serve or obey ▸ obsequious, subservient. *See* **servile.**

menial *noun*
1. A person who does tedious, menial, or unpleasant work ▸ grunt, hack, scullion. *See* **drudge** (1). 2. One who labors ▸ hand, toiler, worker. *See* **laborer.**

mensuration *noun*
The act or process of ascertaining dimensions, quantity, or capacity ▸ determination, measure, measurement, quantification. *See also* **computation, estimation.**

mental *adjective*
1. Relating to or performed by the mind ▸ cerebral,

intellective, intellectual, psychic, psychical, psychological, reasoning, thinking. *See also* **arbitrary.** 2. Appealing to or engaging the intellect ▸ sophisticated, thoughtful. *See* **intellectual** (1).

mental illness *noun*
▸ dementia, derangement, lunacy. *See* **insanity** (1).

mental image *noun*
An act or instance of remembering ▸ memory, recollection, remembrance, reminiscence. *See also* **idea.**

mentality *noun*
1. The thought processes characteristic of an individual or group ▸ ethos, mind, psyche. *See* **psychology.** 2. The faculty of thinking, reasoning, and applying knowledge ▸ intellect, understanding. *See* **intelligence** (1).

mentally ill *adjective*
▸ crazy, lunatic, mad. *See* **insane** (1).

mention *verb*
1. To make reference to something ▸ allude (to), note, point out. *See* **refer** (1). *See synonym note at* **refer.** 2. To refer to by name ▸ cite, specify. *See* **name** (2).

mentor *noun*
One who advises another ▸ consultant, counselor. *See* **adviser.**

mentor *verb*
Informal To give recommendations to someone about a decision or course of action ▸ counsel, guide, recommend. *See* **advise** (1).

mephitic *or* **mephitical** *adjective*
1. Capable of injuring or killing by poison ▸ noxious, toxic, venomous. *See* **poisonous** (1). *See synonym note at* **poisonous.** 2. Having an unpleasant odor ▸ foul, stinking. *See* **smelly.**

mercenary *noun*
A freelance fighter ▸ adventurer, soldier of fortune. *See also* **fighter, soldier.**

mercenary *adjective*
Open to bribery or dishonesty ▸ venal. *Informal:* crooked. *See* **corrupt** (2).

merchandise *noun*
A product or products bought and sold in commerce ▸ line, stock, ware. *See* **good** (2).

merchandise *verb*
To offer for sale ▸ handle, peddle. *See* **sell** (1).

merchandiser *noun*
▸ merchant, tradesman. *See* **dealer** (1).

merchant *noun*
A person engaged in buying and selling ▸ trader, tradesman. *See* **dealer** (1).

merchant *verb*
To offer for sale ▸ handle, peddle. *See* **sell** (1).

merciful *adjective*
1. Concerned with human welfare and the remedying of social ills ▸ compassionate, humane. *See* **humanitarian.** *See synonym note at* **humanitarian.** 2. Not strict or severe ▸ easy, indulgent, lenient. *See* **tolerant** (1).

mercifulness *noun*
▸ clemency, grace. *See* **mercy.**

merciless *adjective*
1. Lacking compassion or mercy ▸ heartless, insensitive, pitiless. *See* **callous.** 2. Inflicting suffering or pain ▸ brutal, fierce, savage. *See* **cruel** (1).

mercurial *adjective*
▸ fickle, impulsive, shifty. *See* **capricious.**

mercy *noun*
Kind, forgiving, or compassionate treatment of or disposition toward others ▸ charity, clemency, grace, lenience, leniency, lenity, mercifulness. *See also* **pity.**

✦ **CORE SYNONYMS:** *mercy, leniency, lenity, clemency, charity.* These nouns mean humane and kind, sympathetic, or forgiving treatment of or disposition toward others. *Mercy* is compassionate forbearance: "*We hand folks over to God's mercy, and show none ourselves*" (George Eliot). *Leniency* and *lenity* imply mildness, gentleness, and often a tendency to reduce punishment: "*When you have gone too far to recede, do not sue* [appeal] *to me for leniency*" (Charles Dickens). "*His Majesty gave many marks of his great lenity, often . . . endeavoring to extenuate your crimes*" (Jonathan Swift). *Clemency* is mercy shown by someone with judicial authority: *The judge believed in clemency for youthful offenders. Charity* is goodwill and benevolence in judging others: "*But how shall we expect charity towards others, when we are uncharitable to ourselves?*" (Thomas Browne).

---

mere *adjective*
Just sufficient ▸ bare, scant, scanty. *See also* **insufficient, meager.**

merely *adverb*
Nothing more than ▸ but, just, only, simply. *See also* **barely, solely.**

meretricious *adjective*
Tastelessly showy ▸ flashy, garish, loud. *See* **gaudy.** *See synonym note at* **gaudy.**

merge *verb*
▸ blend, fuse, stir. *See* **mix** (1). *See synonym note at* **mix.**

merger *noun*
1. The result of combining ▸ compound, merger, union. *See* **combination** (1). 2. Something produced by mixing ▸ amalgam, blend, mix. *See* **mixture** (1).

meridian *noun*
▸ apex, height, peak. *See* **climax** (1).

merit *noun*
1. A level of superiority that is usually high ▸ caliber, quality, stature, value, virtue, worth. *See also* **advantage.** 2. A particularly good or beneficial quality ▸ asset, distinction. *See* **virtue** (1). 3. The quality of being suitable or adaptable to an end ▸ benefit, profit, utility. *See* **use** (2).

merit *verb*
To acquire as a result of one's behavior or one's effort ▸ gain, get, win. *See* **earn** (1). *See synonym note at* **earn.**

merited *adjective*
▸ deserved, fitting, proper. *See* **just** (2).

meritless *adjective*
▸ unfounded, unwarranted. *See* **baseless.**

meritorious *adjective*
▸ deserving, laudable, worthy. *See* **admirable.**

merriment *noun*
1. A state of joyful exuberance ▸ blitheness, gaiety, gladness, glee, gleefulness, hilarity, jocoseness, jocosity, jocularity, jocundity, jolliness, jollity, joviality, lightheartedness, merriness, mirth, mirthfulness. *See also* **elation. 2.** Joyful, exuberant activity ▸ celebration, conviviality, festiveness, festivity, fun, gaiety, jollity, merrymaking, revelry, revels. *See also* **blast, celebration, party.**

merriness *noun*
▸ glee, lightheartedness, mirth. *See* **merriment** (1).

merry *adjective*
1. Providing joy and pleasure, especially in celebration ▸ celebratory, cheerful, cheery, convivial, festive, gala, glad, gladsome, happy, joyful, joyous, mirthful, pleasing. *See also* **lighthearted. 2.** Being in or showing good spirits ▸ happy, jolly, jovial. *See* **cheerful** (1).

merrymaking *noun*
1. The act of showing joyful satisfaction in an event ▸ jubilation, rejoicing, revelry. *See* **celebration** (3). **2.** Joyful, exuberant activity ▸ gaiety, jollity, revelry. *See* **merriment** (2).

mesa *noun*
A natural, flat land elevation ▸ plateau, table. *See also* **hill.**

mesh *noun*
1. An open and loosely connected structure, usually interlaced, woven, or knotted ▸ lattice, net. *See* **web** (1). **2.** Something that is intricately and often bewilderingly complex ▸ maze, web. *See* **tangle** (1).

mesh *verb*
1. To come or bring together and interlock ▸ engage. *See also* **attach, fit**[1]. **2.** To combine and adapt in order to attain a particular effect ▸ blend, integrate. *See* **harmonize** (2).

mesmerize *verb*
1. To act upon with or as if with magic ▸ bewitch, enchant, spellbind. *See* **charm** (2). **2.** To compel the attention, interest, or imagination of ▸ captivate, fascinate, transfix. *See* **grip** (1).

mess *noun*
1. A confused or ruinous state ▸ botch, fiasco, foul-up, mix-up, muddle, shambles. *Informal:* hash. *Slang:* screwup, snafu. *See also* **blunder. 2.** An unsightly object ▸ disaster, eyesore, monstrosity, ugliness. *Informal:* fright, sight, ugly. *Idiom:* something the cat dragged in. **3.** A group of things gathered haphazardly ▸ drift, mass, mound. *See* **heap** (1). **4.** A lack of order or regular arrangement ▸ clutter, confusion, disarray. *See* **disorder** (1). **5.** A difficult, often embarrassing situation or condition ▸ corner, difficulty, fix. *See* **predicament. 6.** An individual quantity of food ▸ helping, portion. *See* **serving. 7.** *Informal* A great deal ▸ bounty, mass, profusion. *See* **abundance** (1).

mess *verb*
1. To handle something in an attempt to adjust or improve it ▸ fiddle, fool. *Informal:* monkey. *See* **tinker** (1). **2.** To put something into a state of disarray, such as the hair or clothes ▸ dishevel, disorder, muss (up). *See* **tousle.**

mess around *verb*
1. *Informal* To be sexually unfaithful to another ▸ philander. *Informal:* cheat, fool around, play around. *Slang:* two-time. **2.** *Informal* To waste time by engaging in aimless activity ▸ dawdle (about), fiddle (around). *See* **putter. 3.** To handle something in an attempt to adjust or improve it ▸ fiddle, fool. *Informal:* monkey. *See* **tinker.**

mess up *verb*
1. To ruin through clumsiness or ineptness ▸ blunder, foul up, spoil. *See* **botch. 2.** To put into total disorder ▸ garble, jumble, scramble. *See* **confuse** (4). **3.** To put out of proper order ▸ disarrange, disrupt, muddle. *See* **disorder** (1). **4.** To be rough or brutal with ▸ slap around, rough up. *See* **manhandle** (1). **5.** To break up the order or progress of ▸ interfere, obstruct. *See* **disrupt** (1).

message *noun*
1. Something announced or communicated ▸ announcement, annunciation, brief, bulletin, communication, communiqué, declaration, dictum, edict, manifesto, notice, notification, proclamation, pronouncement, statement, word. **2.** Something that is conveyed or signified ▸ import, sense, significance. *See* **meaning** (1). **3.** A written communication directed to another ▸ correspondence, missive, note. *See* **letter** (1).

messenger *noun*
A person who carries messages or is sent on errands ▸ bearer, carrier, conveyer, courier, envoy, errand boy, errand girl, herald, runner. *Slang:* gofer. *See also* **agent, representative.**

messiness *noun*
▸ sloppiness, untidiness. *See* **disorderliness** (1).

messy *adjective*
1. Marked by a lack of cleanliness or neatness ▸ careless, disheveled, frowzy, mussy, slapdash, slipshod, sloppy, slovenly, unkempt, untidy. **2.** Lacking regular or logical order ▸ disorderly, unsystematic.

✦ **CORE SYNONYMS:** *messy, sloppy, slovenly, unkempt, slipshod.* These adjectives mean marked by lack of cleanliness or neatness. *Messy* indicates that which is disorderly: *a messy desk.* *Sloppy* evokes the idea of careless spilling, spotting, or splashing; it suggests slackness, untidiness, or diffuseness: *a sloppy kitchen; sloppy dress;* "*I do not see how the sloppiest reasoner can evade that*" (H.G. Wells). *Slovenly* implies habitual negligence and a lack of system or thoroughness: *a slovenly appearance; slovenly inaccuracies.* *Unkempt* stresses dishevelment resulting from a neglectful lack of proper maintenance: "*an unwashed brow, an unkempt head of hair*" (Sir Walter Scott). *Slipshod* suggests inattention to detail and a general absence of meticulousness: "*the new owners' camp . . . a slipshod and slovenly affair, tent half stretched, dishes unwashed*" (Jack London).

metamorphose *verb*
1. To change into a different form or state ▸ mutate, transform. *See* **convert** (1). *See synonym note at* **convert**. 2. To bring about a radical change in ▸ revolutionize, transform. *See also* **change, overhaul**.

metamorphosis *noun*
1. The process or result of changing from one use, function, or appearance to another ▸ change, mutation, transformation. *See* **conversion** (1). 2. A momentous or sweeping change ▸ cataclysm, convulsion, upheaval. *See* **revolution** (3).

metanoia *noun*
A fundamental change in one's beliefs ▸ conversion, rebirth, regeneration. *See also* **revival**.

metaphor *noun*
An object or expression associated with and serving to identify something else ▸ attribute, emblem, signifier, symbol, token. *See also* **expression, sign, term**.

metaphorical *or* **metaphoric** *adjective*
▸ emblematical, figurative, representative. *See* **symbolic** (1).

metaphrase *noun*
The act or process of translating ▸ crib, rendering. *See* **translation** (1).

metaphrase *verb*
To express in another language ▸ interpret, render. *See* **translate** (1).

metaphysical *adjective*
1. Having no body, form, or substance ▸ disembodied, incorporeal, nonphysical. *See* **immaterial** (1). *See synonym note at* **immaterial**. 2. Of or relating to existence outside the natural world ▸ extramundane, superhuman. *See* **supernatural** (1)

mete *verb*
▸ allocate, apportion, dispense. *See* **distribute** (1).

meter *noun*
▸ cadence, measure, swing. *See* **rhythm**.

method *noun*
1. Systematic arrangement and design ▸ format, order, orderliness, organization, pattern, plan, process, scheme, system, systematization, systemization. *See also* **arrangement, form**. 2. The approach used to do something ▸ manner, mode, style. *See* **way** (1). *See synonym note at* **way**. 3. A course of action to be followed regularly ▸ rote, rounds, track. *See* **routine** (1).

methodical *or* **methodic** *adjective*
1. Arranged or proceeding in a set, systematized pattern ▸ arranged, neat, ordered, orderly, organized, regular, regulated, structured, systematic, systematical. *See also* **neat, symmetrical**. 2. Careful and slow in acting, moving, or deciding ▸ circumspect, measured, unhurried. *See* **deliberate** (3).

✦ **CORE SYNONYMS:** *methodical, orderly, systematic.* These adjectives mean arranged or proceeding in a set, systematized pattern. *Methodical* stresses adherence to a logically and carefully planned succession of steps: *methodical instructions for assembly. Orderly* especially implies correct or customary procedure or proper or harmonious arrangement: *an orderly evacuation of the burning building; orderly and symmetrical rows. Systematic* emphasizes observance of a coordinated and orderly set of procedures constituting part of a complex but unitary whole: *systematic research into antigens to combat immune disorders.*

---

methodize *verb*
▸ order, organize, systematize. *See* **arrange** (1).

meticulous *adjective*
1. Marked by attentiveness to every detail ▸ fastidious, painstaking, scrupulous. *See* **careful** (2). *See synonym note at* **careful**. 2. Very difficult to please ▸ exacting, finicky. *See* **fussy** (1).

meticulousness *noun*
1. Freedom from error ▸ accurateness, exactitude, precision. *See* **accuracy** (1). 2. Attentiveness to detail ▸ fastidiousness, pains, painstaking. *See* **thoroughness**.

métier *noun*
1. Activity pursued as a livelihood ▸ career, employment, occupation. *See* **business** (2). 2. Something at which a person excels ▸ specialty, strong point. *See* **forte**. *See synonym note at* **forte**.

metrical *adjective*
▸ cadenced, measured, rhythmic. *See* **rhythmical**.

metropolis *noun*
▸ borough, megalopolis, municipality. *See* **city**.

metropolitan *adjective*
▸ civic, municipal, urban. *See* **city**.

mettle *noun*
▸ bravery, fortitude, gallantry, valor. *See* **courage**.

mettlesome *adjective*
▸ courageous, fearless, heroic. *See* **brave**. *See synonym note at* **brave**.

mewl *verb*
▸ howl, sob, weep. *See* **cry** (1).

miasmic *adjective*
▸ noxious, toxic, venomous. *See* **poisonous** (1).

microbe *or* **microorganism** *noun*
▸ bug, parasite, virus. *See* **germ** (1).

microscopic *adjective*
1. So small as not to be discernible ▸ imperceptible, infinitesimal. 2. Extremely small ▸ dwarf, miniature, minuscule. *See* **tiny**.

micturate *verb*
▸ make water, pass water. *See* **urinate**.

mid *adjective*
1. Being at neither one extreme nor the other ▸ intermediate, median, midway. *See* **middle** (1). 2. At, in, near, or being the center ▸ focal, median, middle. *See* **central** (1).

middle *adjective*
1. Being at neither one extreme nor the other ▸ between, central, in-between, intermediary, intermediate, mean, medial, median, mid, middle-of-the-road, midway. *See also* **neutral**. 2. At, in, near, or being the center ▸ focal, median, midmost. *See* **central** (1).

middle *noun*
A point or an area that is equidistant from all sides

▸ median, midpoint, midst. *See* **center** (2).

middleman *noun*
▸ intermediary, mediator. *See* **go-between**.

middlemost *adjective*
▸ focal, median, middle. *See* **central** (1).

middle-of-the-road *adjective*
▸ intermediate, median, midway. *See* **middle** (1).

middling *adjective*
1. Being of no special quality or type ▸ common, mediocre, standard. *See* **ordinary** (1). **2.** Relating to or occupying a middle position on a scale of evaluation ▸ mediocre, fair. *See* **average** (1). *See synonym note at* **average**.

midget *adjective*
▸ dwarf, miniature, minuscule. *See* **tiny**.

midmost *adjective*
▸ focal, median, middle. *See* **central** (1).

midpoint *noun*
1. Something that represents a halfway point between extremes ▸ mean, medium, norm. *See* **average** (1). **2.** A point or area equidistant from all sides of something ▸ median, middle, midst. *See* **center** (2).

midst *noun*
1. The most intensely active central part ▸ eye, thick. *See also* **center**. **2.** A point or area equidistant from all sides ▸ median, middle, midpoint. *See* **center** (2).

midway *adjective*
▸ intermediate, median, middle-of-the-road. *See* **middle** (1).

mien *noun*
1. Behavior that reveals one's personality or state of mind ▸ demeanor, manner, style. *See* **bearing** (1). **2.** The way something or someone looks ▸ look, features, semblance. *See* **appearance** (1).

miff *verb*
1. To cause resentment or hurt by callous, rude behavior ▸ offend, outrage. *See* **insult** (1). **2.** To cause anger, resentment, or hurt feelings ▸ annoy, injure, upset. *See* **offend** (1).

miff *noun*
Extreme displeasure caused by an insult ▸ resentment, ruffled feathers, umbrage. *See* **offense** (1).

might *noun*
1. Physical, mental, financial, or legal power to perform ▸ capability, competence, faculty. *See* **ability** (2). **2.** The right and power to command, decide, rule, or judge ▸ dominion, jurisdiction, omnipotence. *See* **authority** (1). **3.** The state or quality of being physically strong ▸ potency, power. *See* **strength** (1). **4.** Capacity for work or vigorous activity ▸ force, potency, power. *See* **energy**. *See synonym note at* **energy**. **5.** Energy that overcomes resistance ▸ coercion, power, strength. *See* **force** (1).

mighty *adjective*
1. Full of or displaying force ▸ potent, powerful, vigorous. *See* **forceful** (1). **2.** Having great physical strength ▸ potent, powerful, strong. *See also* **energetic, muscular**. **3.** Of extraordinary size and power ▸ behemoth, colossal, gigantic, titanic. *See* **enormous**.

mighty *adverb*
Informal To a high degree ▸ exceedingly, extremely, highly. *See* **very**.

migrant *noun*
1. One who migrates ▸ emigrant, immigrant, transmigrant. *See also* **émigré, foreigner, settler**. **2.** One who wanders without a permanent home or livelihood ▸ nomad, roamer, vagabond. *See* **hobo**.

migrant *adjective*
1. Moving from one area to another in search of work ▸ itinerant, migratory. **2.** Moving from one habitat to another on a seasonal basis ▸ migrational, transient. *See* **migratory** (1).

migrate *verb*
1. To leave one's native land and settle in another ▸ emigrate (from), immigrate (to), resettle, transmigrate. *See also* **move, settle**. **2.** To change habitat seasonally ▸ transmigrate.

migration *noun*
1. Settling in a country to which one is not native ▸ immigration, transmigration. **2.** Departure from one's native land to settle in another ▸ diaspora, transmigration. *See* **emigration**.

migrational *adjective*
▸ migrational, seasonal, transient. *See* **migratory** (1).

migratory *adjective*
1. Moving from one habitat to another on a seasonal basis ▸ migrant, migrational, seasonal, transient, transmigratory. *See also* **mobile, nomadic**. **2.** Moving from one area to another in search of work ▸ itinerant, migrant.

mild *adjective*
1. Free from extremes in temperature ▸ balmy, clement, moderate, temperate. *See also* **pleasant**. **2.** Of a sympathetic, considerate character ▸ kindly, softhearted, tender, tenderhearted. *See* **gentle** (1). **3.** Easily managed or handled ▸ domesticated, meek, tame. *See* **gentle** (3). **4.** Free from severity or violence, as in sound or movement ▸ delicate, faint, soft. *See* **gentle** (2). **5.** Not steep or abrupt ▸ easy, moderate. *See* **gradual** (2).

mildewed *adjective*
▸ musty, rancid. *See* **moldy**.

milieu *noun*
▸ climate, surroundings. *See* **environment** (2).

militance *noun*
▸ belligerence, combativeness, hostility. *See* **aggression** (1).

militant *adjective*
1. Engaged in warfare ▸ hostile, warring. *See* **belligerent** (1). **2.** Inclined to act in an aggressive or hostile way ▸ belligerent, combative, hostile. *See* **aggressive** (1). **3.** Holding especially political views that deviate drastically from prevailing beliefs ▸ fanatical, radical, revolutionary. *See* **extreme** (4).

militant *noun*
One who holds extreme views or advocates extreme measures ▸ radical, revolutionist, zealot. *See* **extremist**.

militaristic *adjective*
▸ martial, warlike. *See* **military** (1).

militarize *verb*
▸ call up, ready. *See* **mobilize**.

military *adjective*
1. Of or inclined toward war ▸ bellicose, chauvinistic, hawkish, jingoistic, martial, militaristic, warlike, warmongering. *See also* **aggressive**. **2.** Relating to armed service ▸ barracks, enlisted, martial, regimental, soldierly. *Idiom:* in uniform.

militiaman *noun*
▸ legionary, serviceperson, trooper. *See* **soldier** (2).

milk *verb*
▸ bleed, pump, strain. *See* **drain** (1).

milksop *noun*
1. A childish or pampered person ▸ milquetoast, mollycoddle. *See* **baby** (2). **2.** An ignoble, uncourageous person ▸ dastard, poltroon, sissy. *See* **coward**.

milky *adjective*
▸ ivory, light. *See* **fair**¹ (9).

mill *noun*
A building or complex in which an industry is located ▸ factory, plant, works.

mill *verb*
To break up into tiny particles ▸ atomize, grind, pound. *See* **crush** (2).

million *noun*
Informal An indeterminately great amount or number ▸ bunch, multiplicity. *See* **heap** (3).

millstone *noun*
▸ cross, tribulation. *See* **burden**¹ (1).

milquetoast *noun*
1. A childish or pampered person ▸ milksop, mollycoddle. *See* **baby** (2). **2.** An ignoble, uncourageous person ▸ dastard, poltroon, sissy. *See* **coward**.

mime *noun*
1. The act, practice, or art of copying the manner or expression of another ▸ imitation, impersonation, impression. *See* **mimicry**. **2.** One who imitates ▸ imitator, parrot. *See* **mimic**.

mimesis *noun*
The formation of words in imitation of sounds ▸ echoism, onomatopoeia.

mimetic *adjective*
1. Imitating sounds ▸ echoic, imitative, onomatopoeic, onomatopoetic. **2.** Of or involving imitation ▸ emulative, slavish. *See* **imitative** (1).

mimic *verb*
1. To copy another slavishly ▸ clone, echo, image, imitate, mirror, parrot, reflect, repeat. *See also* **copy**. **2.** To be similar especially in appearance ▸ be like, look like. *See* **resemble**. **3.** To copy the manner or expression of another, especially in an exaggerated or mocking way ▸ caricature, mock. *See* **imitate** (1). *See synonym note at* **imitate**.

mimic *noun*
One who imitates ▸ ape, echo, imitator, impersonator, mime, parrot. *Informal:* copycat.

mimicry *noun*
The act, practice, or art of copying the manner or expression of another ▸ aping, copying, echoing, emulation, imitation, impersonation, impression, mime, mirroring, parroting. *See also* **mockery**.

mincing *adjective*
▸ priggish, prissy, strait-laced. *See* **prudish**.

mind *noun*
1. The seat of the faculty of intelligence and reason ▸ brain, head. *Informal:* gray matter. *See also* **imagination**. **2.** A person of great mental ability ▸ brain, genius, highbrow, intellect, intellectual, mastermind, thinker. *Informal:* egghead, whiz. *Slang:* brainiac, pointy-head. *See also* **expert, sage**. **3.** The faculty of thinking, reasoning, and applying knowledge ▸ intellect, understanding. *See* **intelligence** (1). *See synonym note at* **intelligence**. **4.** The thought processes characteristic of an individual or group ▸ ethos, mentality, psyche. *See* **psychology**. **5.** Something thought to be true ▸ notion, persuasion, view. *See* **belief** (1). **6.** A desire for a particular thing or activity ▸ fancy, soft spot, will. *See* **liking** (1). **7.** A healthy mental state ▸ lucidity, rationality, reason. *See* **sanity**.

mind *verb*
1. To be careful ▸ beware, look out, watch out. *Idioms:* be on guard, be on the lookout, keep an eye peeled, take care (*or* heed). **2.** To renew an image or thought in the mind ▸ recall, recollect, reminisce. *See* **remember** (1). **3.** To perceive with a special effort of the senses or the mind ▸ detect, mark. *See* **notice**. **4.** To act in conformity with ▸ heed, obey, observe. *See* **follow** (4). **5.** To have an objection ▸ care, object. *See* **care**. **6.** To have the care and supervision of ▸ look after, minister to, watch over. *See* **tend**² (1). *See synonym note at* **tend**².

mind-boggling *or* **mind-blowing** *adjective*
Informal So remarkable as to be difficult to believe ▸ astounding, staggering, unbelievable. *See* **astonishing**.

minded *adjective*
▸ agreeable, ready. *See* **willing** (1).

mindful *adjective*
▸ heedful, observant, watchful. *See* **careful** (1). *See synonym note at* **careful**.

mindfulness *noun*
▸ carefulness, caution, heed, regard. *See* **care** (1).

mindless *adjective*
1. Lacking rational direction or purpose ▸ brainless, meaningless, pointless, purposeless, senseless. *Idiom:* without rhyme or reason. *See also* **boring, perfunctory, vacant**. **2.** Displaying a lack of forethought and good sense ▸ brainless, fatuous, silly. *See* **foolish**. **3.** Lacking in intelligence ▸ dumb, idiotic, obtuse. *See* **stupid** (1). **4.** Lacking concern or attention ▸ heedless, unconcerned. *See* **careless** (1).

mindlessness *noun*
▸ idiocy, imbecility, obtuseness. *See* **stupidity**.

mindset *or* **mind-set** *noun*
1. The thought processes characteristic of an indi-

vidual or group ▸ ethos, mentality, mind. *See* **psychology. 2.** A temporary state of mind or feeling ▸ humor, temper. *See* **mood** (1). **3.** A frame of mind affecting one's thoughts or behavior ▸ outlook, position. *See* **posture** (2).

mind's eye *noun*
▸ creativity, fantasy. *See* **imagination** (1).

mingle *verb*
1. To take part in social activities ▸ mix, socialize. **2.** To combine into one mass or mixture ▸ blend, fuse, stir. *See* **mix** (1). *See synonym note at* **mix.**

miniature *or* **mini** *adjective*
▸ dwarf, midget, minuscule. *See* **tiny.**

minim *noun*
▸ dash, drop, smidgen. *See* **bit**[1] (1).

minimal *adjective*
Comprising the least possible ▸ least, littlest, minimum, minutest, slightest, smallest, tiniest. *See also* **trivial.**

minimization *noun*
▸ deprecation, disparagement. *See* **belittlement.**

minimize *verb*
▸ deprecate, disparage, slight. *See* **belittle.** *See synonym note at* **belittle.**

minimum *adjective*
Comprising the least possible ▸ least, smallest. *See* **minimal.**

minimum *noun*
A very low or lowest level, position, or degree ▸ bottom, low, nadir, rock bottom.

minion *noun*
▸ bootlicker, fawner, toady. *See* **sycophant.**

minister *noun*
1. A person who is ordained for service in a Christian church ▸ ecclesiastic, monk, parson. *See* **cleric. 2.** A person who represents the interests of another ▸ ambassador, deputy, proxy, steward. *See* **representative** (2).

minister to *verb*
1. To work and care for ▸ attend, do for, serve, wait on (*or* upon). *See also* **help, work. 2.** To have the care and supervision of ▸ look after, mind, watch over. *See* **tend**[2] (1). *See synonym note at* **tend**[2].

ministerial *adjective*
1. Of or relating to the clergy, especially in a Christian church ▸ ecclesiastical, pastoral. *See* **clerical. 2.** Of, for, or relating to administration or administrators ▸ executive, managerial, organizational. *See* **administrative.**

ministry *noun*
▸ administration, authorities, state. *See* **government** (2).

minor *adjective*
1. Below another in standing, importance, or status ▸ collateral, inferior, junior, lesser, little known, low, lower, minor-league, petty, secondary, second-class, slight, small, subaltern, subordinate, under. *Informal:* smalltime. *See also* **auxiliary, trivial. 2.** Not yet a legal adult ▸ underage.

minor *noun*
One who is not yet legally of age ▸ child, juvenile, underage person. *See also* **child, youth.**

minor-league *adjective*
▸ junior, low, secondary. *See* **minor** (1).

minstrel *noun*
▸ muse, troubadour. *See* **poet.**

mint *noun*
▸ *Informal:* bundle, pile. *See* **fortune** (7).

mint *verb*
To use ingenuity in making, developing, or achieving ▸ contrive, devise, dream up. *See* **invent** (1).

minus *noun*
▸ drawback, handicap, liability. *See* **disadvantage.**

minuscule *adjective*
▸ dwarf, miniature, wee. *See* **tiny.**

minute[1] *noun*
1. A very brief time ▸ blink, instant. *See* **flash** (2). *See synonym note at* **flash. 2.** An item inserted, as in a diary, register, or reference book ▸ heading, posting. *See* **entry** (1).

minute *verb*
To place on a list or in a record or book ▸ catalog, chronicle, write down. *See* **list**[1] (1).

minute[2] *adjective*
1. Extremely small ▸ dwarf, miniature, minuscule. *See* **tiny. 2.** Characterized by attention to detail ▸ full, particular, thorough. *See* **detailed** (1).

minutia *noun*
1. Something or things of little importance ▸ frivolity, nonsense, trivia. *See* **trifle** (1). **2.** A small, often specialized element of a whole ▸ particular, specialty, technicality. *See* **detail** (1).

minx *noun*
▸ brat, imp, whelp. *See* **urchin.**

miracle *noun*
1. An event inexplicable by the laws of nature ▸ wonder. *Idiom:* act of God. **2.** One that evokes great surprise and admiration ▸ prodigy, sensation, wonder. *See* **marvel** (1). *See synonym note at* **marvel.**

miraculous *adjective*
1. Of or relating to existence outside the natural world ▸ metaphysical, superhuman. *See* **supernatural** (1). **2.** So remarkable as to be difficult to believe ▸ astounding, unbelievable. *See* **astonishing.**

mirage *noun*
▸ delusion, hallucination, phantasma. *See* **illusion** (1).

mire *noun*
1. A usually low-lying area of soft waterlogged ground and standing water ▸ marsh, wetland. *See* **swamp. 2.** A viscous, usually offensively dirty substance ▸ muck, sludge. *See* **slime.**

mire *verb*
To make dirty ▸ bemire, muck up, mud. *See* **dirty** (1).

mirror *noun*
1. One that is worthy of imitation or duplication ▸ exemplar, ideal, paradigm. *See* **model** (1). **2.** An ideally representative example of a type ▸ archetype, model. *See* **epitome** (1).

mirror *verb*
1. To send back or form an image of ▸ image, reflect.
2. To copy another slavishly ▸ clone, imitate. *See* **mimic** (1).

mirth *noun*
▸ glee, joviality, lightheartedness. *See* **merriment** (1).

mirthful *adjective*
1. Being in or showing good spirits ▸ bright, happy, sunny. *See* **cheerful** (1). 2. Providing joy and pleasure ▸ festive, glad, joyful. *See* **merry** (1).

mirthfulness *noun*
▸ gaiety, glee, jolliness. *See* **merriment** (1).

miry *adjective*
1. Of, relating to, or covered with slime ▸ mucky, oozy. *See* **slimy**. 2. Covered or soiled with mud ▸ filthy, muddy. *See* **dirty** (1).

misadventure *noun*
▸ mischance, misfortune, mishap. *See* **accident** (1).

misanthrope *or* **misanthropist** *noun*
A person who expects only the worst from people ▸ cynic, pessimist. *See also* **skeptic**.

misapplication *noun*
▸ misappropriation, misuse, perversion. *See* **abuse** (1).

misapply *verb*
▸ misappropriate, mishandle, pervert. *See* **abuse** (2).

misapprehend *verb*
▸ misconceive, mistake. *See* **misunderstand**.

misapprehension *noun*
1. A failure to understand correctly ▸ confusion, misconception. *See* **misunderstanding** (1). 2. An erroneous or false idea ▸ error, falsehood, falsity. *See* **fallacy** (1).

misappropriate *verb*
▸ misapply, mishandle, pervert. *See* **abuse** (2).

misappropriation *noun*
▸ ill-usage, mishandling, misuse, perversion. *See* **abuse** (1).

misbegotten *adjective*
▸ baseborn, bastard, natural. *See* **illegitimate** (1).

misbehave *verb*
To behave in a rowdy, improper, or unruly fashion ▸ act up, be naughty, carry on. *Informal:* cut up, fool around, horse around. *See also* **offend**.

misbehavior *noun*
Improper, often rude behavior ▸ bad manners, horseplay, misconduct, misdoing, naughtiness, wrongdoing. *See also* **crime, impropriety**.

miscalculate *verb*
To count or calculate wrongly ▸ miscount, misestimate, misjudge, misreckon, overestimate, underestimate. *See also* **err, misunderstand**.

miscalculation *noun*
A wrong calculation ▸ misestimate, misestimation, misjudgment, misreckoning, overestimation, underestimation. *See also* **error, misunderstanding**.

miscarriage *noun*
▸ bust, fiasco. *See* **failure** (1).

miscarry *verb*
▸ fall short, founder, misfire. *See* **fail** (1).

miscellanea *noun*
▸ incidentals, junk, oddments. *See* **odds and ends**.

miscellaneous *adjective*
▸ diverse, heterogeneous, sundry. *See* **various** (1). *See synonym note at* **various**.

miscellaneousness *noun*
▸ diversity, heterogeneousness, variousness. *See* **variety** (1).

miscellany *noun*
▸ hodgepodge, jumble, mishmash. *See* **assortment** (1).

mischance *noun*
▸ misadventure, misfortune, mishap. *See* **accident** (1).

mischief *noun*
1. Annoying yet harmless, usually playful acts ▸ devilment, devilry, deviltry, diablerie, high jinks, impishness, mischief-making, mischievousness, playfulness, prankishness, pranks, rascality, roguery, roguishness, tomfoolery, tricks. *Informal:* shenanigans. *Slang:* funny business, hanky-panky, monkey business.
2. One who causes minor trouble or damage ▸ prankster, scamp. *See* **rascal**. 3. The action or result of inflicting loss or pain ▸ detriment, injury. *See* **harm**.

mischievous *adjective*
1. Full of mischief or high-spirited fun ▸ arch, devilish, elfish, frisky, frolicsome, gamesome, impish, larkish, playful, prankish, puckish, rascally, roguish, sportful, sportive, trickish, waggish. *See also* **lively**.
2. Causing harm or injury ▸ deleterious, evil, injurious. *See* **harmful**.

mischievousness *noun*
▸ diablerie, high jinks, tomfoolery. *See* **mischief** (1).

misconceive *verb*
▸ misapprehend, mistake. *See* **misunderstand**.

misconception *noun*
1. A failure to understand correctly ▸ misapprehension, mistake. *See* **misunderstanding** (1). 2. An erroneous or false idea ▸ error, falsehood. *See* **fallacy** (1).

misconduct *noun*
▸ horseplay, wrongdoing. *See* **misbehavior**.

misconstrue *verb*
▸ misconceive, mistake. *See* **misunderstand**.

miscount *verb*
▸ misestimate, misjudge, underestimate. *See* **miscalculate**.

miscreant *adjective*
Utterly reprehensible in reputation or behavior ▸ depraved, perverse. *See* **corrupt** (1).

miscreant *noun*
One that performs evil acts ▸ scoundrel, villain. *See* **evildoer**.

miscue *noun*
An unintentional deviation from what is correct, right, or true ▸ inaccuracy, lapse, mistake. *See* **error** (1).

miscue *verb*
To make an error or mistake ▸ blunder, stumble. *See* **err** (1).

misdeed *noun*
1. A wicked act or wicked behavior ▸ evil, offense, sin.

See **crime** (2). **2.** An act that violates public law ▸ illegality, offense. See **crime** (1).

misdemeanor *noun*
▸ illegality, offense. See **crime** (1).

misdoing *noun*
▸ naughtiness, wrongdoing. See **misbehavior.**

misdoubt *verb*
1. To be uncertain, disbelieving, or skeptical about ▸ disbelieve, query, waver. See **doubt** (1). **2.** To lack trust or confidence in ▸ disbelieve, question. See **distrust.**

mise en scène *noun*
1. The properties, backdrops, and other objects arranged for a dramatic presentation ▸ backdrop, set, setting. See **scene** (2). **2.** The surrounding conditions and circumstances affecting growth or development ▸ climate, surroundings. See **environment** (2).

miser *noun*
. A stingy person ▸ churl, niggard, pinchpenny, Scrooge, skinflint. *Informal:* penny pincher. *Slang:* cheapskate, piker, stiff, tightwad.

miserable *adjective*
1. Very uncomfortable or unhappy ▸ afflicted, agonized, anguished, suffering, woebegone, woeful, wretched. *See also* **depressed, despondent, glum.** **2.** Of decidedly inferior quality ▸ cheap, lousy, poor. See **shoddy** (1).

miserable *noun*
A person living under very unhappy circumstances ▸ loser, wretch. See **unfortunate.**

miserly *adjective*
▸ close-fisted, parsimonious, penny-pinching. See **stingy** (1).

misery *noun*
1. A state of prolonged anguish and privation ▸ deprival, deprivation, hardship, misfortune, suffering, woe, wretchedness. *See also* **hell, poverty. 2.** A state of physical or mental suffering ▸ agony, torment, wretchedness. See **distress** (1). **3.** *Informal* A sensation of physical discomfort occurring as the result of disease or injury ▸ prick, smart, soreness. See **pain** (1). **4.** A cause of suffering or harm ▸ bane, scourge. See **curse** (3).

misestimate *verb*
1. To make a mistake in judging ▸ misjudge, mistake, prejudge. *See also* **misunderstand, suppose. 2.** To count or calculate wrongly ▸ misjudge, underestimate. See **miscalculate.**

misestimate *or* **misestimation** *noun*
A wrong calculation ▸ misjudgment, misreckoning. See **miscalculation.**

misfire *verb*
▸ fall short, miscarry, wash out. See **fail** (1).

misfortune *noun*
1. Bad fortune ▸ adversity, bad luck, haplessness, hard luck, ill luck, unfortunateness, unluckiness, untowardness. *See also* **predicament. 2.** An unexpected and usually undesirable event ▸ misadventure, mischance, mishap. See **accident** (1). **3.** A state of prolonged anguish and privation ▸ woe, wretchedness. See **misery** (1).

misgiving *noun*
1. A feeling of uncertainty about the fitness or correctness of an action ▸ compunction, reservation, scruple. See **qualm** (1). *See synonym note at* **qualm.** **2.** A lack of conviction or certainty ▸ dubiousness, incertitude, skepticism. See **doubt** (1).

misguided *adjective*
▸ oblivious, misinformed, unaware. See **ignorant** (3).

mishandle *verb*
1. To use improperly ▸ misappropriate, misuse, pervert. See **abuse** (2). **2.** To treat unfairly or harmfully ▸ ill-use, mistreat, wrong. See **abuse** (1). **3.** To ruin through clumsiness or ineptness ▸ blunder, foul up, spoil. See **botch. 4.** To treat unfairly or harmfully ▸ ill-treat, mistreat, wrong. See **abuse** (1).

mishandling *noun*
1. Physically harmful treatment ▸ ill-treatment, mistreatment. See **abuse** (2). **2.** Improper use or handling ▸ misappropriation, misuse, perversion. See **abuse** (1).

mishap *noun*
1. An unexpected and usually undesirable event ▸ contretemps, misadventure, mischance. See **accident** (1). **2.** An occurrence inflicting widespread destruction and distress ▸ cataclysm, catastrophe, tragedy. See **disaster** (1).

mishear *verb*
▸ misconceive, mistake. See **misunderstand.**

mishmash *noun*
▸ hodgepodge, jumble, miscellany. See **assortment** (1).

misinformed *adjective*
▸ oblivious, misguided, unaware. See **ignorant** (3).

misinterpret *verb*
▸ misconceive, mistake. See **misunderstand.**

misinterpretation *noun*
1. A failure to understand correctly ▸ misapprehension, misconception. See **misunderstanding** (1). **2.** An erroneous or false idea ▸ error, falsehood, misconception. See **fallacy** (1).

misjudge *verb*
1. To make a mistake in judging ▸ misestimate, mistake, prejudge. *See also* **misunderstand, suppose. 2.** To count or calculate wrongly ▸ miscount, underestimate. See **miscalculate.**

misjudgment *noun*
▸ misestimate, misestimation, misreckoning. See **miscalculation.**

mislaid *adjective*
▸ gone, missing. See **lost** (2).

mislay *verb*
To be unable to find ▸ lose, misplace, miss. ***Idioms:*** have something go missing

mislead *verb*
▸ dupe, fool, trick. See **deceive.** *See synonym note at* **deceive.**

misleading *adjective*
1. Deliberately ambiguous or vague ▸ elusive, equivocal, evasive, indirect. *See also* **ambiguous. 2.** Tending

to lead one into error ▸ deceptive, illusive, illusory. *See* **fallacious** (2).

mislike *verb*
To regard with distaste ▸ dislike, disrelish. **Idioms:** be averse to, be cool toward, have an aversion to (*or* distaste for), have no use for, not be crazy (*or* nuts *or* wild) about, not care for. *See also* **despise, disapprove, hate.**

mislike *noun*
An attitude or feeling of distaste or mild aversion ▸ disinclination, dislike, disrelish, distaste. *See also* **disapproval, disgust, enmity, hate.**

mismanage *verb*
▸ blunder, foul up, spoil. *See* **botch.**

mismatch *verb*
▸ contrast, disagree, discord. *See* **conflict.**

mismatched *adjective*
1. Made up of parts or qualities that are disparate or otherwise markedly lacking in consistency ▸ discrepant, inconsistent. *See* **incongruous** (1). **2.** Not suited to circumstances ▸ inapt, malapropos, unbecoming. *See* **improper** (2).

misplace *verb*
To be unable to find ▸ lose, mislay, miss. **Idioms:** have something go missing

misplaced *adjective*
▸ mislaid, missing. *See* **lost** (2).

misplacement *noun*
▸ mislaying, missing. *See* **loss** (1).

misread *verb*
▸ misconceive, mistake. *See* **misunderstand.**

misreckon *verb*
▸ miscount, misjudge, underestimate. *See* **miscalculate.**

misreckoning *noun*
▸ misestimate, misestimation, misjudgment. *See* **miscalculation.**

misrepresent *verb*
▸ belie, fudge, pervert. *See* **distort** (1).

misrepresentation *noun*
1. An untrue declaration ▸ falsehood, fib, untruth. *See* **lie²**. **2.** The use or an instance of equivocal language ▸ euphemism, prevarication. *See* **equivocation** (1).

misrule *noun*
A lack of civil order or peace ▸ anarchy, lawlessness, turmoil. *See* **disorder** (2).

miss *verb*
1. To be unsuccessful ▸ fall short, strike out, wash out. *See* **fail** (1). **2.** To fail to take advantage of ▸ pass up, squander. *See* **lose** (2). **3.** To be unable to find ▸ lose, mislay, misplace. **Idioms:** have something go missing

miss *noun*
An unintentional deviation from what is correct, right, or true ▸ inaccuracy, lapse, mistake. *See* **error** (1).

misshape *verb*
▸ disfigure, distort, twist. *See* **deform.**

missing *adjective*
1. Not present ▸ away, gone, nonattendant. *See* **absent**

(1). **2.** No longer in one's possession ▸ mislaid, misplaced. *See* **lost** (2).

mission *noun*
1. An assignment one is sent to carry out ▸ charge, commission, errand, operation, undertaking. *See also* **adventure, intention, task. 2.** A diplomatic office or headquarters in a foreign country ▸ deputation, embassy, legation. **3.** An inner urge to pursue an activity or perform a service ▸ calling, vocation. *See also* **dream, duty, fate. 4.** A journey undertaken with a specific objective ▸ pilgrimage, tour. *See* **expedition** (1).

missionary *or* **missioner** *noun*
1. A person doing religious or charitable work in a foreign country ▸ apostle, evangelist. *See also* **cleric, representative. 2.** One who disseminates or engages in propaganda ▸ evangelist, proselytizer. *See* **propagandist.**

missive *noun*
▸ correspondence, epistle, note. *See* **letter** (1). *See synonym note at* **letter.**

misstate *verb*
▸ fudge, misrepresent, pervert. *See* **distort** (1).

misstatement *noun*
▸ falsehood, fib, untruth. *See* **lie²**.

misstep *noun*
▸ inaccuracy, lapse, mistake. *See* **error** (1).

missy *noun*
Informal A woman ▸ *Informal:* chick, damsel, gal. *See* **girl.**

mist *noun*
1. A suspension in the air of tiny particles of water, dust, or smoke ▸ brume, fog. *See* **haze** (1). **2.** Water condensed from atmospheric vapor and falling in drops ▸ deluge, downpour, shower. *See* **rain** (2).

mist *verb*
1. To make dim ▸ blur, fog, obfuscate. *See* **obscure** (1). **2.** To fall in drops of water from clouds ▸ drizzle, precipitate, shower. *See* **rain** (2).

mistake *noun*
1. An unintentional deviation from what is correct, right, or true ▸ inaccuracy, lapse, miscue, oversight. *See* **error** (1). **2.** A failure to understand correctly ▸ misapprehension, misconception. *See* **misunderstanding** (1).

mistake *verb*
1. To take one thing mistakenly for another ▸ confound, confuse, mix up. **2.** To make a mistake in judging ▸ misestimate, misjudge, prejudge. *See also* **suppose. 3.** To make an error or mistake ▸ blunder, stumble. *See* **err** (1). **4.** To understand incorrectly ▸ misapprehend, misconceive. *See* **misunderstand.**

mistaken *adjective*
▸ false, inaccurate, unsound. *See* **erroneous.**

mistimed *adjective*
▸ ill-timed, untimely. *See* **unseasonable.**

mistreat *verb*
1. To treat wrongfully or harmfully ▸ ill-treat, mishandle, wrong. *See* **abuse** (1). *See synonym note at*

abuse. **2.** To use improperly ▸ misappropriate, misuse, pervert. *See* **abuse** (2).

mistreatment *noun*

▸ mishandling, misusage. *See* **abuse** (2).

mistrust *noun*

1. Lack of trust ▸ cynicism, leeriness. *See* **distrust. 2.** A lack of conviction or certainty ▸ dubiousness, incertitude, skepticism. *See* **doubt** (1). *See synonym note at* **doubt. 3.** The refusal or reluctance to believe ▸ incredulity, skepticism, unbelief. *See* **disbelief** (1).

mistrust *verb*

1. To lack trust or confidence in ▸ disbelieve, question. *See* **distrust. 2.** To be uncertain, disbelieving, or skeptical about ▸ disbelieve, query, waver. *See* **doubt** (1). **3.** To give no credence to ▸ doubt, question. *See* **disbelieve** (1).

mistrustful *adjective*

▸ doubting, suspicious, wary. *See* **distrustful** (1).

mistrustfully *adverb*

▸ doubtfully, questioningly. *See* **skeptically.**

misty *adjective*

1. Not clearly perceptible ▸ dim, faint, indefinite. *See* **unclear** (1). **2.** Affectedly or extravagantly emotional ▸ gushy, maudlin, soft. *See* **sentimental. 3.** Characterized by rain or drizzle ▸ drizzly, wet. *See* **rainy.**

misunderstand *verb*

To understand incorrectly ▸ misapprehend, misconceive, misconstrue, mishear, misinterpret, misread, mistake. *Idioms:* get something wrong, get the wrong idea, miss the point. *See also* **confuse, miscalculate.**

misunderstanding *noun*

1. A failure to understand correctly ▸ confusion, false impression, misapprehension, misconception, misinterpretation, mistake. *See also* **miscalculation. 2.** An erroneous or false idea ▸ error, falsehood, misconception. *See* **fallacy** (1). **3.** A discussion, often heated, in which a difference of opinion is expressed ▸ contention, disagreement, quarrel. *See* **argument** (1).

misusage *noun*

1. Physically harmful treatment ▸ mishandling, mistreatment. *See* **abuse** (2). **2.** A misused or incorrect term ▸ malapropism, solecism. *See* **corruption** (3).

misuse *noun*

Improper use or handling ▸ misappropriation, mishandling, perversion. *See* **abuse** (1).

misuse *verb*

1. To use improperly ▸ misapply, misappropriate, pervert. *See* **abuse** (2). **2.** To treat unfairly or harmfully ▸ ill-treat, mishandle, mistreat. *See* **abuse** (1).

mite *noun*

▸ dash, drop, smidgen. *See* **bit¹** (1).

mitigate *verb*

▸ alleviate, ease, lessen. *See* **relieve** (1). *See synonym note at* **relieve.**

mitigation *noun*

▸ alleviation, ease, palliation. *See* **relief** (2).

mix *verb*

1. To combine into one mass or mixture ▸ admix, alloy, amalgamate, blend, coalesce, commingle, com-

mix, fuse, homogenize, intermingle, intermix, merge, mingle, stir. *See also* **combine. 2.** To take part in social activities ▸ mingle, socialize. **3.** To process ingredients by stirring ▸ blend, whip. *See* **beat** (6).

mix up *verb*

1. To take one thing mistakenly for another ▸ confound, confuse, mistake. **2.** To cause to be unclear in mind or intent ▸ befuddle, bewilder, confound. *See* **confuse** (1). **3.** To put out of proper order ▸ disarrange, disrupt, muddle. *See* **disorder** (1). **4.** To draw or be drawn in so that extrication is difficult ▸ catch up, embroil, wrap up. *See* **involve** (1).

mix *noun*

Something produced by mixing ▸ amalgam, blend, fusion. *See* **mixture** (1).

✦ CORE SYNONYMS: *mix, blend, mingle, merge, amalgamate, coalesce, fuse.* These verbs mean to put into or come together in one mass so that constituent parts or elements are diffused or commingled. *Mix* is the least specific: *The cook mixed eggs, flour, and sugar. Greed and charity don't mix.* To *blend* is to mix intimately and harmoniously so that the components lose their original definition: *The clerk blended the hot chocolate with coffee. Snow-covered mountains blended into the clouds. Mingle* implies combination without loss of individual characteristics: *"Respect was mingled with surprise"* (Sir Walter Scott). *"His companions mingled freely and joyously with the natives"* (Washington Irving). *Merge* and *amalgamate* imply resultant homogeneity: *Tradition and innovation are merged in this new composition. Twilight merged into night. "The four sentences of the original are amalgamated into two"* (William Minto). *Coalesce* implies a slow merging: *Indigenous peoples and immigrants coalesced into the present-day population. Fuse* emphasizes an enduring union, as that formed by heating metals: *"He diffuses a tone and spirit of unity, that blends, and (as it were) fuses, each into each"* (Samuel Taylor Coleridge).

mixed *adjective*

1. Consisting of a number of different kinds ▸ diverse, miscellaneous, sundry. *See* **various** (1). *See synonym note at* **various. 2.** Mixed with other substances ▸ alloyed, combined, polluted. *See* **impure** (2).

mixed bag *noun*

▸ hodgepodge, jumble, mishmash. *See* **assortment** (1).

mixed-up *adjective*

1. *Informal* Characterized by physical confusion ▸ disordered, topsy-turvy, upside-down. *See* **confused** (2). **2.** *Informal* Mentally uncertain ▸ confounded, disoriented, perplexed, turbid. *See* **confused** (1).

mixture *noun*

1. Something produced by mixing ▸ admixture, alloy, amalgam, amalgamation, blend, commixture, composite, fusion, merger, mix. *See also* **combination, unification. 2.** A collection of various things ▸ hodgepodge, jumble, mishmash. *See* **assortment** (1).

✦ CORE SYNONYMS: *mixture, blend, amalgam, admixture, composite.* These nouns refer to a combination that are produced by mixing. *Mixture* has the widest application: *She routinely drank a mixture of tea and honey. "He showed a curious mixture of eagerness and terror"* (Francis Parkman). *Blend* and *amalgam* imply that the original components have lost their distinctness: *The novel is a fascinating blend of romance and realism. The comedian's act was an amalgam of incisive wit and unceasing good humor.* *Admixture* suggests that one of the components is dissimilar to the others: *The chemist concocted a perfume containing an essential oil with a large admixture of alcohol.* A *composite* has components that may retain part of their identities: *a musical suite that is a composite of operatic themes.*

mix-up *noun*
1. A lack of order or regular arrangement ▸ clutter, confusion, disarray. *See* **disorder** (1). 2. A confused or ruinous state ▸ foul-up, muddle, shambles. *See* **mess** (1).

mizzle *noun*
1. The process or sound of dripping ▸ dribble, drip, drizzle, trickle. 2. Water condensed from atmospheric vapor and falling in drops ▸ deluge, downpour, shower. *See* **rain** (2).

mizzle *verb*
To fall in drops of water from clouds ▸ drizzle, precipitate, shower. *See* **rain** (2).

moan *noun*
A long, mournful cry ▸ bay, ululation, wail. *See* **howl** (1).

moan *verb*
1. To utter or emit a long, mournful, plaintive sound ▸ bay, wail, yowl. *See* **howl** (1). 2. To express feelings of pain, dissatisfaction, or resentment ▸ fuss, grouch, whine. *See* **complain.**

mob *noun*
1. *Informal* An organized group of criminals, hoodlums, or wrongdoers ▸ band, gang, pack, ring. 2. An enormous number of persons or things gathered together ▸ horde, mass, throng. *See* **crowd** (1). *See synonym note at* **crowd.** 3. The common people ▸ masses, proletariat, public. *See* **commonalty.**

mob *verb*
To fill to capacity ▸ crowd, jam, pack. *See* **fill** (1).

mobile *adjective*
1. Capable of moving or being moved from place to place ▸ movable, moving, portable, transportable, traveling, unstationary. *See also* **loose, migrant.** 2. Changing easily, as in expression ▸ changeable, fluid, plastic. *See also* **changeable, unstable.**

mobilization *noun*
▸ prearrangement, readiness. *See* **preparation.**

mobilize *verb*
To assemble, prepare, or put into operation, as for war or a similar emergency ▸ activate, call up, enlist, marshal, militarize, muster, organize, rally, ready. *Idioms:* call to action, call out the troops. *See also* **assemble, energize, provoke.**

mobster *noun*
▸ culprit, lawbreaker, offender. *See* **criminal.**

mock *verb*
1. To subject to ridicule ▸ jeer (at), lampoon, taunt. *See* **ridicule.** *See synonym note at* **ridicule.** 2. To copy the manner or expression of another, especially in an exaggerated or mocking way ▸ caricature, mimic. *See* **imitate** (1).

mock *adjective*
Made by humans, often in imitation of something else ▸ simulated, synthetic. *See* **artificial** (1).

mockery *noun*
1. Words or actions intended to evoke contemptuous laughter ▸ derision, ridicule. *See also* **sarcasm, taunt.** 2. A false, derisive, or impudent imitation of something ▸ caricature, farce, parody, sham, travesty. *See also* **counterfeit, satire.** 3. An object of amusement or laughter ▸ butt, jest, joke, laughingstock. *Idiom:* figure of fun. *See also* **fool.**

mocking *adjective*
1. Contemptuous or ironic in manner or wit ▸ satiric, scoffing, sneering. *See* **sarcastic.** 2. Tending or intending to belittle ▸ deprecatory, derogatory, pejorative. *See* **disparaging.**

mod *adjective*
▸ chic, stylish, swanky. *See* **fashionable.**

mode *noun*
1. The approach used to do something ▸ manner, method, style. *See* **way** (1). *See synonym note at* **way.** 2. A distinctive way of expressing oneself ▸ manner, tone. *See* **style** (1). 3. Manner of being or form of existence ▸ situation, status. *See* **condition** (1). 4. The current custom ▸ craze, fad, vogue. *See* **fashion** (1). *See synonym note at* **fashion.**

model *noun*
1. One that is worthy of imitation or duplication ▸ beau ideal, example, exemplar, ideal, mirror, nonpareil, paradigm, paragon, pattern, precedent, role model, standard. *Idioms:* man among men, woman among women. *See also* **celebrity.** 2. A first form from which varieties arise or imitations are made ▸ master, prototype. *See* **original** (1). 3. An ideally representative example of a type ▸ archetype, mirror. *See* **epitome** (1).

model *verb*
1. To take as a model ▸ copy, imitate, pattern oneself (on, upon, *or* after). *See* **follow** (5). 2. To give form to by or as if by pressing and kneading ▸ fashion, mold, shape. *See* **form** (1). 3. To provide a basis for ▸ establish, ground. *See* **base**[1] (1). 4. To assume a particular position, as for a portrait ▸ posture, sit. *See* **pose** (1).

model *adjective*
1. Having the nature of, constituting, or serving as a type ▸ archetypical, prototypic, representative. *See* **typical** (1). 2. Conforming to an ultimate form of perfection or excellence ▸ exemplary, perfect, supreme. *See* **ideal** (1).

✦ **CORE SYNONYMS:** *model, exemplar, ideal, example, standard, pattern.* These nouns refer to someone or something worthy of imitation or duplication. *Model* and *exemplar* connote that which perfectly or most appropriately represents something or someone, by being either very worthy or truly representative: *"Our fellow countryman is a model of a man"* (Charles Dickens). *"He is indeed the perfect exemplar of all nobleness"* (Jane Porter). An *ideal* is a sometimes unattainable standard of perfection: *"Religion is the vision of . . . something which is the ultimate ideal, and the hopeless quest"* (Alfred North Whitehead). An *example* can refer to something that is worthy of imitation but can also indicate something that serves as a deterrent or warning: *"Our Government is the potent, the omnipresent teacher. For good or for ill, it teaches the whole people by its example"* (Louis D. Brandeis). A *standard* is an established criterion or recognized level of excellence: *"It wouldn't be quite fair to test him by our standards"* (William Dean Howells). A *pattern* serves as a model, plan, or guide in the creation of something: *"I will be the pattern of all patience"* (William Shakespeare).

moderate *verb*
1. To make or become less severe or extreme ▸ mute, play down, qualify, soften, subdue, tame, temper, tone down. *See also* **decrease, relieve. 2.** To become or cause to become less active or intense ▸ ebb, lapse. *See* **subside** (1). **3.** To intervene between disputants in order to bring about an agreement ▸ arbitrate, mediate. *See also* **confer, judge.**
moderate *adjective*
1. Kept within sensible limits ▸ modest, reasonable, restrained. *See* **conservative** (2). **2.** Adequate to satisfy a need, requirement, or standard ▸ modest, popular, reasonable. *See* **acceptable** (2). **3.** Not steep or abrupt ▸ easy, gentle. *See* **gradual** (2). **4.** Of small intensity ▸ gentle, slight, soft. *See* **light**[2] (2). **5.** Free from extremes in temperature ▸ balmy, clement, mild, temperate. *See also* **pleasant. 6.** Requiring little effort or exertion ▸ easy, light, undemanding. *Informal:* cushy, soft. **7.** Free from severity or violence, as in sound or movement ▸ delicate, faint, soft. *See* **gentle** (2).

✦ **CORE SYNONYMS:** *moderate, qualify, temper.* These verbs mean to make or become less severe or extreme: *moderated the severity of his rebuke; qualified her criticism; admiration tempered with fear.*

◂ ANTONYM: *intensify*

moderateness *noun*
▸ measure, temperance. *See* **moderation** (1).
moderation *noun*
1. Avoidance of extremes of opinion, feeling, or personal conduct ▸ abstemiousness, measure, moderateness, sobriety, temperance. *See also* **prudence, restraint. 2.** The process of becoming less active or less intense ▸ abatement, letup, subsidence. *See* **waning.**
modern *adjective*
Characteristic of recent times or informed of what is current ▸ current, recent. *See* **contemporary** (2).
modern *noun*
A person of the present age ▸ contemporary.

modernize *verb*
To make modern in appearance or style ▸ streamline, update. **Idiom:** bring up to date. *See also* **improve, renew.**
modest *adjective*
1. Not showy or obtrusive, as in appearance, style, or behavior ▸ inobtrusive, plain, quiet, restrained, simple, subdued, tasteful, unassuming, unobtrusive, unostentatious, unpretentious. *See also* **appropriate, inconspicuous, reserved. 2.** Having or expressing feelings of humility ▸ humble, lowly, meek, unambitious. *See also* **deferential. 3.** Awkward or unconfident in behavior or manner ▸ bashful, demure, diffident. *See* **shy**[1] (1). *See synonym note at* **shy**[1]. **4.** Morally beyond reproach ▸ decent, pure, virginal. *See* **chaste. 5.** Not lewd or obscene ▸ decent, wholesome. *See* **clean** (5). **6.** Of small intensity ▸ gentle, moderate, soft. *See* **light**[2] (2). **7.** Kept within sensible limits ▸ moderate, reasonable, restrained. *See* **conservative** (2). **8.** Adequate to satisfy a need, requirement, or standard ▸ moderate, popular, reasonable. *See* **acceptable** (2). **9.** Proper in appearance ▸ presentable, respectable. *See* **decent** (7).

✦ **CORE SYNONYMS:** *modest, plain, simple, unostentatious, unpretentious.* These adjectives mean not showy, obtrusive, or ostentatious: *a modest cottage; a plain hairstyle; a simple dark suit; an unostentatious office; an unpretentious country church.*

modesty *noun*
1. Lack of vanity or self-importance ▸ humbleness, humility, lowliness, meekness, unassumingness, unpretentiousness. **2.** Lack of ostentation or pretension ▸ inobtrusiveness, plainness, quietness, restraint, simpleness, simplicity, tastefulness, unassumingness, unobtrusiveness, unostentatiousness, unpretentiousness. **3.** An awkwardness or lack of self-confidence in the presence of others ▸ bashfulness, demureness, diffidence. *See* **shyness. 4.** The condition of being chaste ▸ innocence, virginity. *See* **chastity.**
modicum *noun*
▸ dash, drop, smidgen. *See* **bit**[1] (1).
modifiable *adjective*
▸ fluid, unsettled, variable. *See* **changeable** (1).
modification *noun*
1. The process or result of making or becoming different ▸ alteration, mutation, variation. *See* **change** (1). **2.** One that is slightly different from others of the same kind or designation ▸ adaptation, permutation. *See* **variation** (1).
modified *adjective*
▸ limited, reserved, restricted. *See* **qualified** (1).
modify *verb*
1. To make different ▸ alter, mutate, vary. *See* **change** (1). **2.** To become different ▸ fluctuate, modify, turn. *See* **change** (2).
modish *adjective*
▸ mod, stylish, swanky. *See* **fashionable.** *See synonym note at* **fashionable.**

modulate *verb*
► calibrate, temper, tweak. *See* **adjust** (1).

modus operandi *noun*
1. A method that is used for accomplishing something ► course, procedure, technique. *See* **approach** (1). **2.** The approach that is used to do something ► manner, mode, style. *See* **way** (1). *See synonym note at* **way.**

moil *verb*
To exert oneself steadily, often to the point of exhaustion ► strain, sweat, toil. *See* **labor** (1).

moil *noun*
Physical exertion that is usually difficult and exhausting ► toil, travail, work. *See* **labor** (1).

moist *adjective*
Slightly wet ► clammy, damp, dank, dewy. *See synonym note at* **damp.** *See also* **sticky, wet.**

moisten *verb*
To make moist ► bathe, dampen, wash, wet.

moistureless *adjective*
► anhydrous, sere. *See* **dry** (1).

mold *noun*
1. A hollow device for shaping a fluid or plastic substance ► cast, form, matrix. **2.** A class that is defined by the common attribute or attributes possessed by all its members ► ilk, order, species. *See* **kind²**.

mold *verb*
1. To create by forming, combining, or altering materials ► build, compose, shape. *See* **make** (1). **2.** To give form to by or as if by pressing and kneading ► fashion, model, shape. *See* **form** (1).

moldable *adjective*
► bendable, ductile, plastic. *See* **malleable** (1).

molder *verb*
► rot, spoil, turn. *See* **decay.** *See synonym note at* **decay.**

moldy *or* **moldering** *adjective*
Smelling of mildew or decay ► frowzy, funky, fusty, gamy, mildewed, musty, rancid, rank, rotten, stale. *See also* **airless, bad, smelly.**

mole *noun*
► tattler. *Slang:* snitch, squealer. *See* **informer.**

molecule *noun*
► dash, drop, smidgen. *See* **bit¹** (1).

molest *verb*
1. To trouble the nerves or peace of mind, especially by repeated vexations ► irritate, nettle, vex. *See* **annoy** (1). **2.** To compel another to participate in or submit to a sexual act ► assault, force, rape, ravish, violate.

moll *noun*
Slang A woman who engages in sex for payment ► courtesan, strumpet. *See* **harlot.**

mollify *verb*
► appease, placate, soothe. *See* **pacify.** *See synonym note at* **pacify.**

mollycoddle *noun*
A child or pampered person ► milksop, softy. *See* **baby** (2).

mollycoddle *verb*
To treat indulgently ► coddle, humor, pamper. *See* **baby.** *See synonym note at* **baby.**

molt *verb*
► exuviate, slough, throw off. *See* **shed¹** (2).

mom *or* **mommy** *noun*
Informal A female parent ► matriarch. *Informal:* ma, mama. *See* **mother** (1).

moment *noun*
1. A very brief interval of time ► instant, second, wink. *See* **flash** (2). *See synonym note at* **flash. 2.** The general point at which an event occurs ► instant, point. *See* **occasion** (1). **3.** The quality or state of being important ► concernment, significance, weightiness. *See* **importance.** *See synonym note at* **importance.**

momentary *adjective*
► ephemeral, fleeting, temporary. *See* **transitory.**

momentous *adjective*
1. Having great consequence or weight ► serious, severe, weighty. *See* **grave²** (1). **2.** So critically decisive as to affect the future ► fatal, fateful. *See also* **decisive. 3.** Having great significance ► consequential, grand, meaningful. *See* **important** (1).

momentousness *noun*
The condition of being grave and of involving serious consequences ► graveness, gravity, heaviness, seriousness, weightiness. *See also* **severity.**

momma *noun*
1. *Informal* A female parent ► matriarch. *Informal:* mama, mom. *See* **mother** (1). **2.** *Slang* A woman ► *Informal:* chick, damsel, gal. *See* **girl.**

monarch *noun*
► boss, director, head, leader. *See* **chief** (1).

Monday morning quarterback *noun*
Informal A person who finds fault ► caviler, nitpicker. *See* **critic** (2).

monetary *adjective*
Of or relating to finances ► financial, fiscal, pecuniary.

money *noun*
1. Something, such as coins or printed bills, used as a medium of exchange ► bills, cash, coin, currency, greenbacks, lucre, notes. *Informal:* bucks, wampum. *Slang:* bread, cabbage, dough, gelt, green, jack, juice, lettuce, long green, mazuma, moola, roll, scratch, shekels. **2.** The monetary resources of a government, organization, or individual ► capital, finances, funds. *See also* **capital, resources. 3.** A great amount of accumulated money and precious possessions ► fortune, riches, treasure. *See* **wealth** (1).

moneyed *adjective*
► flush, wealthy. *See* **rich** (1). *See synonym note at* **rich.**

moneymaking *adjective*
► gainful, lucrative, rewarding. *See* **profitable** (1).

moneyman *noun*
One who is occupied with or expert in large-scale financial affairs ► capitalist, financier.

money management *noun*
The management of money ► banking, finance, investment.

moniker *or* **monicker** *noun*
Slang The word or words by which one is called and identified ▸ cognomen, epithet, title. *See* **name** (1).

monition *noun*
▸ admonition, caution, caveat. *See* **warning** (1).

monitor *verb*
1. To pay regular and close attention to ▸ follow, observe, survey, watch. *Idioms:* have one's (*or* keep an) eye on, keep tabs on. **2.** To direct and watch over the work and performance of others ▸ boss, overlook. *See* **supervise**. **3.** To maintain or keep in order ▸ patrol, regulate. *See* **police** (1).

monitor *noun*
One assigned to provide protection or keep watch over someone or something ▸ guardian, protector, ward. *See* **guard** (1).

monitory *adjective*
Giving warning ▸ admonishing, admonitory, cautionary, warning.

monk *noun*
▸ ecclesiastic, minister, parson. *See* **cleric**.

monkey *noun*
Slang A person who is easily deceived or victimized ▸ pushover, tool, victim. *See* **dupe** (1).

monkey *verb*
1. *Informal* To handle something in an attempt to adjust or improve it ▸ fiddle, fool, meddle, tamper. *See* **tinker** (1). **2.** *Informal* To touch or handle something out of restlessness ▸ fidget, fool, play, toy. *See* **fiddle** (1).

monkey business *noun*
▸ diablerie, high jinks, tomfoolery. *See* **mischief** (1).

monkeyshine *noun*
Slang A mischievous act ▸ caper, joke, trick. *See* **prank**[1].

monocracy *noun*
▸ autocracy, despotism, dictatorship, tyranny. *See* **absolutism** (2).

monocratic *adjective*
▸ autocratic, dictatorial, tyrannical, tyrannous. *See* **absolute** (1).

monogram *noun*
▸ brand, label, trademark. *See* **mark** (1).

monograph *noun*
▸ essay, treatise. *See* **discourse** (1).

monopolize *verb*
▸ consume, engross, preoccupy. *See* **absorb** (1). *See synonym note at* **absorb**.

monopoly *noun*
1. Exclusive control or possession ▸ corner. *See also* **domination**. **2.** An association for a common cause or interest ▸ cartel, pool, syndicate. *See* **alliance** (1). **3.** A commercial organization ▸ corporation, enterprise, establishment. *See* **company** (1).

monotonous *adjective*
▸ dull, humdrum, weariful. *See* **boring** (1). *See synonym note at* **boring**.

monotony *or* **monotonousness** *or* **monotone** *noun*
A tiresome lack of variety ▸ humdrum, invariability, repetition, repititiousness, repetitiveness, sameness, tedium, tediousness. *See also* **boredom, dullness, routine.**

monster *noun*
1. A person or animal that is abnormally formed ▸ freak, monstrosity, mooncalf, mutant. *Idiom:* freak of nature. *See also* **deformity**. **2.** One that is extraordinarily large and powerful ▸ Goliath, leviathan, titan. *See* **giant**. **3.** A perversely mean, cruel, or wicked person ▸ beast, devil, ogre. *See* **fiend** (1).

monster *adjective*
Informal Of extraordinary size and power ▸ behemoth, colossal, gigantic, mighty. *See* **enormous**.

monstrosity *noun*
1. An unsightly object ▸ eyesore, ugliness. *See* **mess** (2). **2.** A monstrous offense or evil ▸ enormity, inhumanity. *See* **outrage** (1). **3.** A person or animal that is abnormally formed ▸ freak, monster, mooncalf, mutant. *Idiom:* freak of nature. *See also* **deformity**. **4.** The quality or condition of being ugly ▸ hideousness, odiousness, unsightliness. *See* **ugliness** (1).

monstrous *adjective*
1. Exceeding the bounds of morality, decency, or reason ▸ appalling, intolerable, shocking. *See* **outrageous**. **2.** Of extraordinary size and power ▸ behemoth, colossal, gigantic, mighty. *See* **enormous**. **3.** Resembling a freak ▸ freakish, freaky, grotesque. *See also* **eccentric, weird**. **4.** Displeasing to the eye ▸ homely, unattractive, unsightly. *See* **ugly** (1).

monstrousness *noun*
1. The quality of being outrageous ▸ atrocity, heinousness, scandalousness. *See* **outrageousness**. **2.** The quality or condition of being ugly ▸ monstrosity, odiousness, unsightliness. *See* **ugliness** (1).

monument *noun*
Something, as a structure or custom, serving to honor or keep alive a memory ▸ commemoration, memorial, remembrance. *See also* **testimonial**.

monumental *adjective*
1. Of extraordinary size and power ▸ behemoth, colossal, gigantic, mighty. *See* **enormous**. **2.** Having great significance ▸ consequential, grand, meaningful. *See* **important** (1). **3.** Serving to honor or keep alive a memory ▸ commemorative, memorial.

monumentality *noun*
▸ hugeness, immensity. *See* **enormousness**.

mooch *verb*
1. *Slang* To ask for as charity; solicit money or favors ▸ cadge. *Informal:* panhandle. *See* **beg** (1). *See synonym note at* **beg**. **2.** To take another's property without permission ▸ purloin, snatch, thieve. *See* **steal** (1).

moocher *noun*
Slang One who begs habitually or for a living ▸ cadger, mendicant. *See* **beggar** (1).

mood *noun*
1. A temporary state of mind or feeling ▸ frame of mind, humor, mindset, spirits, state of mind, temper, vein. *See also* **disposition, posture**. **2.** A general impression produced by a predominant quality or

characteristic ▸ ambiance, atmosphere, aura. *See* **air** (4). **3.** A prevailing quality, as of thought, behavior, or attitude ▸ climate, spirit, tone. *See* **temper** (3).

✦ CORE SYNONYMS: *mood, humor, temper*. These nouns refer to a temporary state of mind or feeling. *Mood* is the most inclusive: *"I was in no mood to laugh and talk with strangers"* (Mary Shelley). *Humor* often implies a state of mind resulting from one's characteristic disposition or temperament: *"All which had been done . . . was the effect not of humor, but of system"* (Edmund Burke). *Temper* most often refers to irritability or intense anger: *"The nation was in such a temper that the smallest spark might raise a flame"* (Thomas Macaulay).

---

moody *adjective*
1. Given to changeable emotional states, especially of anger or gloom ▸ temperamental. *See also* **capricious, testy. 2.** Broodingly and sullenly unhappy ▸ gloomy, morose, sullen. *See* **glum** (1).

moola *or* **moolah** *noun*
Slang Something, such as coins or printed bills, used as a medium of exchange ▸ currency. *Slang:* dough, green. *See* **money** (1).

mooncalf *noun*
1. A person who is deficient in judgment and good sense ▸ idiot, moron, simpleton. *See* **fool** (1). **2.** A person or animal that is abnormally formed ▸ freak, monster, monstrosity, mutant. *Idiom:* freak of nature. *See also* **deformity.**

moonstruck *or* **moonstricken** *adjective*
▸ crazy, lunatic, mad. *See* **insane** (1).

moony *adjective*
▸ daydreaming, fanciful, musing. *See* **dreamy** (1).

moor[1] *verb*
1. To join one thing to another ▸ append, fasten, secure. *See* **attach** (1). **2.** To make secure ▸ bind, chain. *See* **fasten** (1). *See synonym note at* **fasten.**

moor[2] *noun*
A usually low-lying area of soft waterlogged ground and standing water ▸ marsh, mire, wetland. *See* **swamp.**

mooring *noun*
▸ dowel, grapnel, wedge. *See* **anchor** (1).

moot *verb*
1. To put forward a topic for discussion ▸ introduce, raise. *See* **broach.** *See synonym note at* **broach. 2.** To speak together and exchange ideas and opinions about ▸ talk over, toss around. *Informal:* kick around. *See* **discuss. 3.** To put forth reasons for or against something, often excitedly ▸ debate, dispute. *See* **argue** (2).

moot *adjective*
1. In doubt or dispute ▸ disputable, doubtful, questionable. *See* **debatable. 2.** Concerned primarily with theories rather than practical matters ▸ academic, conceptual, speculative. *See* **theoretical** (1).

mope *verb*
1. To focus the attention on something moodily and

at length ▸ dwell, fret, worry. *See* **brood.** *See synonym note at* **brood. 2.** To be sullenly aloof or withdrawn, as in silent resentment or protest ▸ pet, pout, sulk. *See also* **brood.**

mopes *noun*
▸ dejection, doldrums, melancholy. *See* **depression** (2).

moppet *noun*
▸ juvenile, tot, youngster. *See* **child** (1).

moral *adjective*
1. Teaching morality ▸ didactic, didactical, edifying, moralistic, moralizing, preachy. **2.** In accordance with principles of right or good conduct ▸ principled, virtuous. *See* **ethical.** *See synonym note at* **ethical. 3.** Being on a high intellectual or moral level ▸ elevated, noble. *See* **elevated** (4). **4.** Morally beyond reproach ▸ modest, pure, virginal. *See* **chaste.**

moral *noun*
The principle taught by a fable or parable ▸ axiom, lesson, maxim, principle. *See also* **idea, law, meaning.**

morale *noun*
A strong sense of enthusiasm and dedication to a common goal that unites a group ▸ esprit, esprit de corps, group spirit, team spirit. *See also* **confidence, mood, spirit.**

✦ CORE SYNONYMS: *morale, esprit, esprit de corps*. These nouns denote a strong sense of enthusiasm and dedication to a common goal that unites a group: *the high morale of the troops; the esprit of an orchestra; the esprit de corps of the swim team.*

---

moralistic *adjective*
1. Teaching morality ▸ moralizing, preachy. *See* **moral** (1). **2.** Piously or overly sure of one's own righteousness ▸ holier-than-thou, self-righteous. *See also* **arrogant, hypocritical, moral.**

morality *noun*
1. The quality or state of being morally sound ▸ probity, virtue. *See* **good** (1). **2.** The condition of being chaste ▸ modesty, purity, virginity. *See* **chastity. 3.** The quality of conforming to standards of conduct ▸ ethicality, propriety. *See* **ethics** (1). **4.** A set of principles of right conduct ▸ principles, standards. *See* **ethics** (2).

moralize *verb*
To indulge in moral reflection, usually pompously ▸ edify, pontificate, preach, sermonize. *See also* **chastise.**

moralizing *adjective*
1. Teaching morality ▸ didactic, preachy. *See* **moral** (1). **2.** Inclined to teach or moralize excessively ▸ academic, expository, prescriptive. *See* **didactic** (2).

morals *noun*
▸ morality, principles. *See* **ethics** (2).

morass *noun*
1. A usually low-lying area of soft waterlogged ground and standing water ▸ marsh, mire, wetland. *See* **swamp. 2.** Something that is intricately and often

bewilderingly complex ▸ labyrinth, maze, web. *See* **tangle** (1).

moratorium *noun*
▸ deferment, postponement, suspension. *See* **delay** (1).

morbid *adjective*
1. Characterized by preoccupation with unwholesome thoughts or feelings ▸ insalubrious, macabre, sick, unhealthy, unwholesome. *See also* **abnormal. 2.** Gruesomely suggestive of ghosts or death ▸ cadaverous, deathlike, ghostly. *See* **ghastly** (2).

mordacity *or* **mordancy** *noun*
▸ acridity, trenchancy. *See* **sarcasm.**

mordant *or* **mordacious** *adjective*
▸ caustic, scathing, sharp, vitriolic. *See* **biting.**

more *adjective*
Being an addition ▸ added, extra, further, new. *See* **additional.**

more *adverb*
1. To a greater extent ▸ better. **2.** In addition ▸ also, besides, further, too. *See* **additionally.**

moreover *adverb*
1. In addition ▸ also, besides, furthermore. *See* **additionally. 2.** Not just this but also ▸ indeed, yea. *See* **even** (2).

mores *noun*
1. Socially correct behavior ▸ etiquette, propriety. *See* **manners. 2.** Behavior patterns, traits, and products considered as an expression of a certain people or period ▸ civilization, ethos, society. *See* **culture** (2). **3.** A set of principles of right conduct ▸ morality, principles. *See* **ethics** (2).

morn *noun*
▸ daybreak, sunrise, sunup. *See* **dawn** (1).

morning *noun*
1. The time of day from sunrise to noon ▸ before lunch, before noon, forenoon. **2.** The first appearance of daylight ▸ daybreak, sunrise, sunup. *See* **dawn** (1).

moron *noun*
1. A person who is deficient in judgment and good sense ▸ imbecile, nitwit, simpleton. *See* **fool** (1). **2.** A mentally dull person ▸ dummy, idiot, thickhead. *See* **dullard.**

moronic *adjective*
1. Displaying a lack of forethought and good sense ▸ daft, idiotic, ludicrous. *See* **foolish. 2.** Lacking in intelligence ▸ dumb, idiotic, obtuse. *See* **stupid** (1).

morose *adjective*
▸ gloomy, moody, sullen. *See* **glum** (1).

morph *verb*
▸ mutate, transfigure, transform. *See* **convert** (1).

morsel *noun*
1. A small portion of food ▸ crumb, scrap. *See* **bit**[1] (2). **2.** Something fine and delicious, especially a food ▸ dainty, treat. *See* **delicacy** (1). **3.** A tiny amount ▸ dash, drop, smidgen. *See* **bit**[1] (1).

mortal *adjective*
1. Of or characteristic of human beings or humankind ▸ anthropical, anthropoid. *See* **human** (1). **2.**

Causing or tending to cause death ▸ fatal, lethal, pestilent. *See* **deadly** (1). *See synonym note at* **deadly. 3.** Capable of being anticipated, considered, or imagined ▸ earthly, likely, possible. *See* **conceivable. 4.** Of or relating to the body ▸ corporal, physical. *See* **bodily.**

mortal *noun*
A member of the human race ▸ human, person. *See* **human being.**

mortgage *verb*
▸ deposit, pledge. *See* **pawn**[1].

mortification *noun*
1. A lowering in or degradation of character or self-esteem ▸ degeneration, dishonor, humiliation. *See* **degradation** (1). **2.** Self-conscious distress ▸ abashment, discomposure. *See* **embarrassment** (1).

mortify *verb*
1. To cause to feel embarrassment, dishonor, and often guilt ▸ brand, reproach, shame, stigmatize. *See also* **belittle, denigrate. 2.** To cause a person to be self-consciously distressed ▸ chagrin, discomfort. *See* **embarrass** (1). *See synonym note at* **embarrass. 3.** To lower the pride or dignity of ▸ degrade, demean, humiliate. *See* **humble** (1).

mortise *noun*
▸ catch, clip, lock. *See* **fastener.**

mosey *verb*
Informal To walk at a leisurely pace ▸ promenade, saunter, wander. *See* **stroll.**

mossback *noun*
1. One who is extremely or stubbornly conservative ▸ archconservative, die-hard, reactionary. *See* **ultraconservative. 2.** An old-fashioned person who is reluctant to change or innovate ▸ fossil, fuddy-duddy. *See* **square** (2).

mossbacked *adjective*
▸ old-line, reactionary, standpat. *See* **ultraconservative.**

most *adjective*
Much more than half ▸ biggest, largest. *See* **best** (2).

most *adverb*
To a high degree ▸ exceedingly, extremely, highly. *See* **very.**

mostly *adverb*
▸ customarily, generally, normally. *See* **usually.**

mother *noun*
1. A female parent ▸ materfamilias, matriarch. *Informal:* ma, mama, mammy, mom, momma, mommy, mum, mummy. *Slang:* old lady. **2.** A person from whom one is descended ▸ forebear, parent, progenitor. *See* **ancestor** (1). **3.** A point of origination ▸ provenance, root, source. *See* **origin** (1).

motif *noun*
An element or component in a decorative composition ▸ design, device, figure, motive. *See synonym note at* **figure.**

motion *noun*
1. The act or process of moving ▸ action, activity, move, movement, moving, stir, stirring. *See also*

change. **2.** An expressive, meaningful bodily movement ▸ indication, signal. *See* **gesture** (1). **3.** Something that is put forward for consideration ▸ proposition, submission, suggestion. *See* **proposal** (1).

motion *verb*
To make bodily motions so as to convey an idea or complement speech ▸ gesticulate, sign, signal. *See* **gesture.**

motionless *adjective*
Not moving ▸ at rest, fixed, frozen, halted, immobile, paralyzed, resting, rigid, static, stationary, still, stock-still, transfixed, unmoving. *Idioms:* at a dead calm, at a quiet stop, at a standstill, at a deadlock. *See also* **dormant, fixed, inactive.**

motivate *verb*
1. To stir to action or feeling ▸ excite, prod, trigger. *See* **provoke** (1). **2.** To impart courage, inspiration, and resolution to ▸ inspire, inspirit. *See* **encourage** (1). *See synonym note at* **encourage.**

motivation *noun*
1. Something that encourages ▸ encouragement, inspiration, stimulation. **2.** Something that causes and encourages an action or response ▸ impulse, incentive. *See* **stimulus** (1). **3.** A basis for an action ▸ motive, reason. *See* **cause** (2).

motive *noun*
1. A basis for an action ▸ motivation, reason. *See* **cause** (2). **2.** An element or component in a decorative composition ▸ design, device, figure, motif.

motivic *adjective*
Of, constituting, or relating to a theme or themes ▸ thematic, topical.

motley *adjective*
1. Consisting of a number of different kinds ▸ diverse, miscellaneous, sundry. *See* **various** (1). **2.** Having many different colors ▸ colorful, polychromatic. *See* **multicolored.**

motor *verb*
▸ pilot, wheel. *See* **drive** (1).

motorist *noun*
A person who operates a motor vehicle ▸ chauffeur, driver, operator.

mottle *verb*
▸ dapple, freckle. *See* **speckle.**

mottled *adjective*
▸ colorful, motley, polychromatic. *See* **multicolored.**

motto *noun*
1. A usually pithy and familiar statement generally accepted as wise or true ▸ adage, maxim, saying. *See* **proverb.** *See synonym note at* **proverb.** **2.** A rallying term used by proponents of a cause ▸ call to arms, war cry. *See* **cry** (2).

moue *noun*
A contorted facial expression showing pain, contempt, or disgust ▸ face, pout. *Informal:* mug. *See also* **frown, glare, sneer.**

mound *noun*
A group of things gathered haphazardly ▸ drift, mass, mountain. *See* **heap** (1). *See synonym note at* **heap.**

mound *verb*
To collect or pile up or onto something ▸ drift, lump. *See* **heap** (1).

mount *verb*
1. To move upward along a surface or slope ▸ climb, go up, scramble. *See* **ascend** (1). **2.** To move from a lower to a higher position ▸ ascend, climb, soar. *See* **rise** (3). **3.** To make or become greater or larger ▸ amplify, boost, enlarge. *See* **increase** (1). **4.** To attain a higher status, rank, or condition ▸ advance, climb, progress. *See* **rise** (6). *See synonym note at* **rise. 5.** To produce on the stage ▸ dramatize, enact, produce. *See* **stage** (1).

mountain *noun*
1. A group of things gathered haphazardly ▸ drift, mass, pile. *See* **heap** (1). *See synonym note at* **heap. 2.** An indeterminately great amount or number ▸ bunch, multiplicity. *Informal:* bushel. *See* **heap** (3). **3.** A great deal ▸ mass, profusion, wealth. *See* **abundance** (1).

mountainous *adjective*
▸ behemoth, colossal, gigantic, mighty. *See* **enormous.**

mountebank *noun*
▸ charlatan, fraud, impostor. *See* **fake** (1).

mounting *noun*
▸ lift, rise. *See* **ascent** (1).

mourn *verb*
▸ anguish, bewail, sorrow. *See* **grieve** (1). *See synonym note at* **grieve.**

mournful *adjective*
▸ depressing, dispiriting, melancholy. *See* **sorrowful** (1).

mournfulness *noun*
▸ dejection, doldrums, melancholy. *See* **depression** (2).

mouse *noun*
1. *Slang* A bruise surrounding the eye ▸ black eye. *Slang:* shiner. *See also* **bruise. 2.** An ignoble, uncourageous person ▸ dastard, poltroon, sissy. *See* **coward.**

mouse *verb*
To move silently and furtively ▸ lurk, prowl. *See* **sneak** (1).

mouth *noun*
1. The opening in the body through which food is ingested ▸ chops, maw. *Slang:* gob, hole, jaws, kisser, pie hole, puss, smacker, trap, yap. **2.** A person who speaks on behalf of another or others ▸ mouth, spokesperson. *See* **speaker** (2). **3.** An open space allowing passage ▸ orifice, vent. *See* **hole** (2). **4.** A usually narrow stretch of water leading inland ▸ estuary, fjord. *See* **inlet. 5.** Insolent talk ▸ back talk. *Informal:* lip, sass. *See also* **impudence.**

mouth *verb*
1. To contort one's face to indicate pain, contempt, or disgust ▸ grimace, mug. *Idioms:* make a face, make faces. *See also* **frown, glare, sneer. 2.** To speak in a

loud, pompous, or prolonged manner ▸ orate, rave.
See **rant** (1).

mouthful *noun*

▸ crumb, morsel. *See* **bit¹** (2).

mouthpiece *noun*

Informal A person who speaks on behalf of another
or others ▸ mouth, spokesperson. *See* **speaker** (2).

mouth-watering *adjective*

▸ delectable, savory, scrumptious. *See* **delicious** (1).

movable *adjective*

▸ moving, portable, transportable. *See* **mobile** (1).

movables *noun*

▸ goods, personal effects, property. *See* **effects.**

move *verb*

1. To stir the emotions of ▸ affect, get (to), impress,
influence, strike, touch. *Idioms:* hit (*or* touch) a soft
spot, touch a chord, tug at one's heartstrings. *See also*
disturb, encourage. 2. To go or cause to go from one
place to another ▸ maneuver, remove, shift, transfer,
travel. *See also* **go, journey. 3.** To change one's residence or place of business, for example ▸ relocate,
remove, transfer. *Idiom:* pull up stakes. *See also*
emigrate, settle. 4. To move or cause to move slightly
▸ budge, shift, stir. **5.** To succeed in causing a person
to act or think in a certain way ▸ convince, prevail on.
See **persuade** (1). **6.** To alter the settled state or
position of ▸ displace, disrupt. *See* **disturb** (1). **7.** To
move forward ▸ come along, proceed, progress. *See*
advance (2). **8.** To stir to action or feeling ▸ excite,
prod, trigger. *See* **provoke** (1). **9.** To state for consideration or debate ▸ offer, put forward, set forth. *See*
propose (1).

move apart *verb*

To separate and go in various directions ▸ disperse,
split up. *See* **scatter** (2).

move *noun*

1. The act or process of moving ▸ action, movement,
stir. *See* **motion** (1). **2.** The act of moving from one
place to another ▸ relocation, remotion, removal.
Idioms: change of address (*or* residence). *See also*
departure. 3. An action calculated to achieve an end
▸ maneuver, measure, procedure, step, tactic. **4.** Passage from one form, state, or stage to another
▸ passage, shift, transit. *See* **transition. 5.** A change in
normal place or position ▸ dislodging, movement,
shift. *See* **displacement.**

✦ CORE SYNONYMS: *move, affect, influence, impress,
touch, strike.* These verbs mean to stir the emotions
or a person or group. *Move* suggests a profound
emotional effect: *The account of her experiences moved
us to tears.* To *affect* is to act upon a person's
emotions: *Adverse criticism of the book didn't affect the
author. Influence* implies some control over the thinking, actions, and emotions of another: *"Humanity is
profoundly influenced by what you do"* (Pope John
Paul II). To *impress* is to produce a marked, often
enduring effect: *"The Tibetan landscape particularly
impressed him"* (Doris Kerns Quinn). *Touch* usually
means to arouse a tender response: *"The tributes [to*

the two deceased musicians] *were fitting and touching"* (Daniel Cariaga). *Strike* implies keenness or
force of mental response: *I was struck by the sudden
change in his appearance.*

movement *noun*

1. The act or process of moving ▸ action, move, stir.
See **motion** (1). **2.** A change in normal place or
position ▸ dislodging, move, shift. *See* **displacement.**
3. An organized effort to accomplish a purpose
▸ campaign, crusade. *See* **drive** (1). *See synonym note at*
drive. 4. The series of events and relationships forming the basis of a composition ▸ action, story line. *See*
plot (1).

moves *noun*

▸ approach, overture. *See* **advances.**

movie *noun*

A motion picture ▸ film, motion picture, picture.
Slang: flick.

moving *adjective*

1. Capable of moving or being moved from place to
place ▸ movable, transportable. *See* **mobile** (1). **2.** Exciting a deep, usually somber response ▸ poignant,
touching. *See* **affecting.** *See synonym note at* **affecting. 3.** Suggesting drama or a stage performance, as in
emotionality or suspense ▸ melodramatic, sensational, spectacular. *See* **dramatic** (2).

mow *verb*

▸ chop, prune, trim. *See* **cut** (3).

moxie *noun*

Slang The quality of mind enabling one to face
danger or hardship resolutely ▸ bravery, fortitude,
valor. *See* **courage.**

Mrs. Grundy *noun*

▸ bluenose, priss, puritan. *See* **prude.**

much *noun*

A great deal ▸ mass, profusion, wealth. *See* **abundance** (1).

much *adverb*

To a considerable extent ▸ far, quite, well. *See* **considerably.**

muchness *noun*

▸ bounteousness, plenitude. *See* **plenty** (1).

mucilaginous *adjective*

1. Having a heavy, gluey quality ▸ gelatinous, syrupy,
viscid. *See* **viscous. 2.** Having the property of adhering ▸ adhesive, gluey. *See* **sticky** (1).

muck *noun*

1. A viscous, usually offensively dirty substance
▸ mire, sludge. *See* **slime. 2.** Foul or dirty matter ▸ dirt,
grime. *See* **filth** (1).

muck up *verb*

1. *Informal* To ruin through clumsiness or ineptness
▸ blunder, foul up, spoil. *See* **botch. 2.** To make dirty
▸ bemire, bespatter, mud, muck. *See* **dirty** (1).

muckamuck *noun*

Slang An important, influential person ▸ notability,
personage. *Slang:* big shot. *See* **dignitary.**

muckiness *noun*

▸ filthiness, squalor, uncleanliness. *See* **dirtiness** (1).

mucky *adjective*
▸ miry, oozy, sludgy. *See* **slimy.**

mucro *or* **mucronation** *noun*
▸ cusp, tip. *See* **point** (1).

mucronate *adjective*
▸ acute, cuspate, sharp. *See* **pointed** (1).

mud *verb*
To make dirty ▸ bemire, muck up, slush. *See* **dirty** (1).

mud *noun*
Foul or dirty matter ▸ grime, muck. *See* **filth** (1).

muddle *verb*
1. To proceed or perform in an unsteady, faltering manner ▸ blunder, bumble, bungle, flounder, fudge, fumble, limp, shuffle, stagger, stumble. **2.** To put out of proper order ▸ disarrange, disrupt, mix up. *See* **disorder** (1). **3.** To put into total disorder ▸ garble, jumble, scramble. *See* **confuse** (4). **4.** To cause to be unclear in mind or intent ▸ befuddle, bewilder, confound. *See* **confuse** (1). *See synonym note at* **confuse. 5.** To ruin through clumsiness or ineptness ▸ blunder, foul up, spoil. *See* **botch. 6.** To break up the order or progress of ▸ interfere, obstruct. *See* **disrupt** (1).

muddle through *verb*
To progress or perform adequately, especially in difficult circumstances ▸ fare, fend, get by. *See* **manage** (1).

muddle *noun*
1. A lack of order or regular arrangement ▸ clutter, confusion, disarray. *See* **disorder** (1). **2.** A confused or ruinous state ▸ foul-up, mix-up, shambles. *See* **mess** (1). **3.** A stunned or bewildered condition ▸ bewilderment, perplexity, stupor. *See* **daze.**

muddled *adjective*
▸ disordered, topsy-turvy, upside-down. *See* **confused** (2).

muddle-headed *adjective*
▸ confounded, perplexed, turbid. *Informal:* mixed-up. *See* **confused** (1).

muddy *adjective*
1. Covered or soiled with mud ▸ filthy, miry. *See* **dirty** (1). **2.** Darkened or clouded with sediment ▸ cloudy, roiled, turbid. *See* **murky** (1). **3.** Lacking vividness or color ▸ lackluster, mat, murky. *See* **dull** (2).

muddy *verb*
1. To make dirty ▸ bemire, muck up, mud. *See* **dirty** (1). **2.** To put into total disorder ▸ garble, mess up, scramble. *See* **confuse** (4).

mudslinger *noun*
▸ caviler, nitpicker. *See* **critic** (2).

mudslinging *noun*
▸ calumny, defamation, slander. *See* **libel.**

muff *verb*
To ruin through clumsiness or ineptness ▸ blunder, foul up, mishandle, spoil. *See* **botch.** *See synonym note at* **botch.**

muff *noun*
A stupid, clumsy mistake ▸ bungle, fumble, solecism. *See* **blunder.**

muffle *verb*
1. To decrease or dull the sound of ▸ damp (down), dampen, deaden, dull, mute, stifle. *See also* **decrease, silence, soften. 2.** To hold something requiring an outlet in check ▸ smother, stifle, suppress. *See* **repress.**

mug *noun*
1. *Informal* A contorted facial expression showing pain, contempt, or disgust ▸ face, grimace, moue, pout. *See also* **frown, glare, sneer. 2.** *Informal* The front surface of the head ▸ countenance, features, visage. *See* **face** (1). **3.** A person who treats others violently or roughly ▸ hoodlum, ruffian, tough. *See* **thug.**

mug *verb*
1. To contort one's face to indicate pain, contempt, or disgust ▸ grimace, mouth. *Idioms:* make a face, make faces. *See also* **frown, glare, sneer. 2.** To take property or possessions from someone unlawfully and usually forcibly ▸ hold up, stick up. *See* **rob** (1).

muggy *adjective*
▸ humid, soggy, sultry. *See* **sticky** (2).

mulct *noun*
A sum of money levied as punishment for an offense ▸ amercement, fine, penalty. *See also* **punishment.**

mulct *verb*
1. To impose a fine on ▸ amerce, fine, penalize. *See also* **punish. 2.** To get something by deceitful trickery ▸ bilk, defraud, swindle. *See* **cheat** (1).

mule *noun*
Slang A person who engages in smuggling ▸ bootlegger, contrabandist, runner, smuggler.

mulish *adjective*
▸ bullheaded, dogged, obstinate. *See* **stubborn** (1). *See synonym note at* **stubborn.**

mulishness *noun*
▸ bullheadedness, hardheadedness, rigidity. *See* **stubbornness.**

mull *verb*
▸ cogitate, deliberate, ruminate. *See* **ponder.**

multicolored *adjective*
Having many different colors ▸ colorful, many-colored, many-hued, motley, mottled, pied, polychromatic, polychrome, polychromic, polychromous, varicolored, variegated, versicolor, versicolored. *Idiom:* of all the colors in the rainbow. *See also* **bright, colorful.**

multifaceted *adjective*
▸ all-around, many-sided, various. *See* **versatile** (1). *See synonym note at* **versatile.**

multifarious *adjective*
▸ diverse, miscellaneous, sundry. *See* **various** (1).

multifariousness *noun*
▸ diversity, heterogeneousness, variousness. *See* **variety** (1).

multiform *adjective*
▸ diverse, miscellaneous, sundry. *See* **various** (1).

multiformity *noun*
▸ diversity, heterogeneousness, variousness. *See* **variety** (1).

multinational *noun*
▸ corporation, enterprise, establishment. *See* **company** (1).

multiple *or* **multiplex** *adjective*
▸ compound, multiplex. *See* **complex** (2).

multiplication *noun*
1. The act of increasing or rising ▸ amplification, boost, escalation. *See* **increase** (1). **2.** The result or product of building up ▸ development, proliferation. *See* **buildup** (2). **3.** The process by which an organism produces others of its kind ▸ procreation, proliferation, propagation. *See* **reproduction** (3).

multiplicity *noun*
1. The quality of being made of many different elements, forms, kinds, or individuals ▸ diversity, heterogeneousness, variousness. *See* **variety** (1). **2.** An indeterminately great amount or number ▸ bunch, ream. *Informal:* bushel. *See* **heap** (3).

multiply *verb*
1. To make or become greater or larger ▸ amplify, boost, enlarge. *See* **increase** (1). *See synonym note at* **increase**. **2.** To give life to ▸ engender, propagate, spawn. *See* **breed** (1).

multipurpose *or* **multitalented** *adjective*
▸ all-purpose, many-sided, multifaceted. *See* **versatile** (1).

multitude *noun*
1. An enormous number of persons or things gathered together ▸ horde, mass, throng. *See* **crowd** (1). **2.** The common people ▸ masses, proletariat, public. *See* **commonalty**.

multitudinous *adjective*
▸ legion, myriad, numerous. *See* **many**.

mum *adjective*
▸ inarticulate, mute. *See* **speechless** (1).

mumble *verb*
To speak or utter indistinctly, as by lowering the voice or partially closing the mouth ▸ murmur, whisper. *See* **mutter** (1).

mumble *noun*
A low, indistinct, and often continuous sound ▸ sigh, susurration, whisper. *See* **murmur** (1).

mumbo jumbo *noun*
▸ abracadabra, doublespeak, hocus-pocus. *See* **gibberish** (1).

mummery *noun*
▸ ceremony, form, formality. *See* **ritual** (2).

mummify *verb*
▸ sear, shrivel, wither. *See* **dry** (1).

mummy *noun*
▸ corpse, remains. *See* **body** (2).

munch *verb*
▸ chomp, gnash, gnaw. *See* **chew**.

mundane *adjective*
1. Relating to or characteristic of the earth or of human life on earth ▸ terrestrial, worldly. *See* **earthly** (1). **2.** Being of no special quality or type ▸ boring, commonplace, humdrum, unremarkable. *See* **ordinary** (1).

municipal *adjective*
▸ civic, metropolitan, urban. *See* **city**.

municipality *noun*
▸ borough, megalopolis, metropolis. *See* **city**.

munificence *noun*
▸ magnanimity, openhandedness, unselfishness. *See* **generosity**.

munificent *adjective*
▸ big-hearted, magnanimous, unselfish. *See* **generous** (1).

murder *noun*
The crime of murdering someone ▸ assassination, blood, homicide, killing, liquidation, manslaughter, slaying. *Slang:* hit, rubout, wipeout.

murder *verb*
1. To take the life of a person or persons unlawfully ▸ assassinate, destroy, finish (off), kill, liquidate, slay. *Informal:* put away. *Slang:* bump off, do in, ice, snuff, knock off, off, pop off, rub out, snuff out, take out, waste, wipe out, zap. **Idiom:** do away with. *See also* **massacre**. **2.** To render totally ineffective by decisive defeat ▸ crush, overpower, rout. *See* **overwhelm** (1).

murderer *noun*
One who murders another ▸ assassin, butcher, cutthroat, exterminator, homicide, killer, liquidator, manslayer, massacrer, murderess, slaughterer, slayer, triggerman. *Slang:* axman, hatchet man, hired gun, hit man.

murderous *adjective*
Marked by or giving rise to murder or bloodshed ▸ bloodthirsty, bloody, bloody-minded, cutthroat, death-dealing, homicidal, gory, killing, man-killing, sanguinary, sanguineous, slaughterous. *See also* **deadly, fierce**.

murk *or* **murkiness** *noun*
▸ darkness, murkiness, obscurity. *See* **dark** (1).

murky *adjective*
1. Darkened or clouded with sediment ▸ clouded, cloudy, muddy, roiled, roily, sedimentary, turbid, unsettled. **2.** Heavy, dark, or dense, especially with impurities ▸ hazy, smoggy, turbid. *See also* **dirty**. **3.** Deficient in brightness ▸ dim, obscure, shadowy. *See* **dark** (1). *See synonym note at* **dark**. **4.** Lacking vividness or color ▸ lackluster, mat, muddy. *See* **dull** (2).

murmur *noun*
1. A low, indistinct, and often continuous sound ▸ mumble, rustle, sigh, sough, susurration, susurrus, whisper. *See also* **hum**. **2.** A soft liquid sound ▸ babble, gurgle, lap. *See* **burble**. **3.** An expression of dissatisfaction or resentment ▸ grumble, grunt, mutter. *See* **complaint**.

murmur *verb*
1. To make a low, continuous, and indistinct sound ▸ rustle, sigh, sough, whisper. *See also* **hum**. **2.** To express feelings of dissatisfaction or resentment ▸ grumble, grunt, mutter. *See* **complain**. **3.** To speak or utter indistinctly, as by lowering the voice or partially

closing the mouth ▸ jabber, whisper. *See* **mutter** (1).
4. To flow with or make a soft liquid sound ▸ gurgle, lap, ripple. *See* **burble** (1).

murmurer *noun*
▸ crab, grump, whiner. *See* **grouch** (1).

muscle *noun*
1. The state or quality of being physically strong ▸ potency, power. *See* **strength** (1). **2.** *Informal* Power to sway or affect based on prestige, wealth, ability, or position ▸ force, sway, weight. *See* **influence** (1). **3.** Solid and well-developed muscles ▸ bulk, physique. *See* **brawn** (1). **4.** *Informal* The right and power to command, decide, rule, or judge ▸ control, might, sovereignty. *See* **authority** (1).

muscle *verb*
Informal To force one's way into a place or situation ▸ bulldoze, elbow, push, shoulder, shove. *See also* **push.**

muscular *adjective*
Characterized by marked muscular development ▸ athletic, beefy, brawny, burly, husky, rugged, robust, sinewy, strapping, sturdy. *Slang:* built. *See also* **healthy, rugged, strong.**

✦ CORE SYNONYMS: *muscular, athletic, brawny, burly, sinewy.* These adjectives mean strong and powerfully built: *a muscular build; an athletic swimmer; brawny arms; a burly lumberjack; a lean and sinewy frame.*

muscularity *noun*
▸ bulk, muscle, physique. *See* **brawn** (1).

muse¹ *verb*
1. To experience dreams or daydreams ▸ fancy, hallucinate. *See* **dream** (1). **2.** To think or think about carefully and at length ▸ cogitate, deliberate, mull. *See* **ponder.**

muse *noun*
The condition of being so lost in solitary thought that one is unaware of one's surroundings ▸ absent-mindedness, bemusement, reverie. *See* **trance** (1).

muse² *noun*
One who writes poetry ▸ bard, troubadour. *See* **poet.**

mush *verb*
To press forcefully so as to reduce to a pulpy mass ▸ mash, squash. *See* **crush** (1).

mush *or* **mushiness** *noun*
Informal The quality or condition of being affectedly or overly emotional ▸ bathos, treacle. *See* **sentimentality.**

mushroom *verb*
To increase or expand suddenly, rapidly, or without control ▸ balloon, explode, snowball. *See also* **increase.**

mushy *adjective*
1. Yielding easily to pressure or weight ▸ doughy, pulpy, yielding. *See* **soft** (1). **2.** *Informal* Affectedly or extravagantly emotional ▸ gushy, mawkish, soft. *See* **sentimental.**

musical *adjective*
1. Characterized by harmony of sound ▸ consonant, symphonic. *See* **harmonious** (2). **2.** Having or producing a pleasing melody or sound ▸ euphonic, melodic, sweet-sounding. *See* **melodious.**

musician *noun*
▸ performer, virtuoso. *See* **player** (2).

musing *noun*
▸ cogitation, deliberation, rumination. *See* **thought** (1).

muskeg *noun*
▸ marsh, mire, wetland. *See* **swamp.**

muss *verb*
To put something into a state of disarray, such as the hair or clothes ▸ dishevel, disorder, mess (up). *See* **tousle.**

muss *noun*
A lack of order or regular arrangement ▸ clutter, confusion, disarray. *See* **disorder** (1).

mussy *adjective*
▸ disheveled, sloppy, slovenly. *See* **messy** (1).

must *verb*
To be required to do ▸ be compelled, be obliged, need, ought, should. *Idioms:* have got to, have to.

must *noun*
1. An act or course of action that is demanded of one, as by position, custom, law, or religion ▸ charge, commitment, obligation. *See* **duty** (1). **2.** Something indispensable ▸ necessity, requirement. *See* **condition** (2).

muster *verb*
1. To assemble, prepare, or put into operation, as for war or a similar emergency ▸ activate, ready. *See* **mobilize.** **2.** To bring or call together ▸ convene, convoke, summon. *See* **assemble** (1). *See synonym note at* **assemble.**

muster in *verb*
To become a member of ▸ enroll, sign up. *See* **join** (4).

muster out *verb*
To release from military duty ▸ demobilize, release, separate. *See* **discharge** (4).

muster *noun*
A number of persons who have come or been gathered together ▸ conference, group. *Informal:* get-together. *See* **assembly** (1).

musty *adjective*
1. Smelling of mildew or decay ▸ frowzy, rancid. *See* **moldy.** **2.** Without freshness or appeal because of overuse ▸ clichéd, overused, stale, tired. *See* **trite.**

mutable *adjective*
▸ fluid, unsettled, variable. *See* **changeable** (1).

mutant *noun*
A person or animal that is abnormally formed ▸ freak, monster, monstrosity, mooncalf. *Idiom:* freak of nature. *See also* **deformity.**

mutate *verb*
1. To make different ▸ alter, modify, vary. *See* **change** (1). **2.** To become different ▸ fluctuate, modify, turn. *See* **change** (2). **3.** To change into a different form, substance, or state ▸ transform, transmute, transpose. *See* **convert** (1).

mutation *noun*
1. The process or result of making or becoming different ▸ alteration, modification, variation. *See* **change** (1). 2. The process or result of changing from one use, function, or appearance to another ▸ change, metamorphosis, transformation. *See* **conversion** (1).

mute *adjective*
1. Lacking the power or faculty of speech ▸ aphonic, dumb, inarticulate, silent, speechless, tongueless, tongue-tied, voiceless, wordless. 2. Temporarily unable or unwilling to speak, as from shock or fear ▸ inarticulate, silent. *See* **speechless** (1).

mute *verb*
1. To decrease or dull the sound of ▸ deaden, stifle. *See* **muffle** (1). 2. To make or become less severe or extreme ▸ soften, tame. *See* **moderate** (1).

muteness *noun*
▸ dumbness, speechlessness. *See* **silence** (2).

mutilate *verb*
1. To deprive of a limb or bodily member or its use ▸ amputate, maim. *See* **cripple** (1). 2. To injure or damage, as by abuse or heavy wear ▸ maul, rough up. *See* **batter** (1). *See synonym note at* **batter.** 3. To alter and spoil the natural form or appearance of ▸ disfigure, misshape, twist. *See* **deform.**

mutineer *noun*
▸ insurrectionist, revolutionist, transgressor. *See* **rebel** (1).

mutinous *adjective*
▸ insurgent, revolutionary, subversive. *See* **rebellious** (1).

mutiny *noun*
Organized opposition intended to change or overthrow existing authority ▸ revolt, uprising. *See* **rebellion** (1).

mutiny *verb*
To vehemently defy and break allegiance with ▸ rebel, revolt, rise (up). *See also* **defect, defy.**

mutter *verb*
1. To speak or utter indistinctly, as by lowering the voice or partially closing the mouth ▸ jabber, maunder, mumble, murmur, whisper. *Idioms:* speak under one's breath, talk to one's self. 2. To express feelings of dissatisfaction or resentment ▸ grumble, grunt, murmur. *See* **complain.**

mutter *noun*
An expression of dissatisfaction or resentment ▸ grumble, grunt, murmur. *See* **complaint.**

mutterer *noun*
▸ crab, grump, whiner. *See* **grouch** (1).

muttonheaded *adjective*
Informal Lacking in or showing a lack of intelligence ▸ dumb, idiotic, obtuse. *See* **stupid** (1).

mutual *adjective*
1. Directed and received by each toward the other ▸ exchanged, give-and-take, reciprocal, reciprocative, requited, shared, two-sided. *See also* **cooperative.** 2. Belonging to, shared by, or applicable to all alike ▸ communal, general, public. *See* **common** (2). 3. Supplying mutual needs ▸ correlative, interrelated, reciprocal. *See* **complementary.**

muumuu *noun*
▸ jumper, gown, shift. *See* **dress** (3).

muzzle *verb*
To hold something requiring an outlet in check ▸ smother, stifle, suppress. *See* **repress.**

muzzle *noun*
The front of the head ▸ countenance, visage. *See* **face** (1).

myriad *adjective*
▸ legion, multitudinous, numerous. *See* **many.**

mysterious *adjective*
Difficult to explain or understand ▸ arcane, baffling, cabalistic, confounding, cryptic, enigmatic, esoteric, impenetrable, inexplicable, inscrutable, mystic, mystical, mystifying, occult, perplexing, puzzling, unaccountable. *See also* **funny, obscure, secret, weird.**

✦ CORE SYNONYMS: *mysterious, esoteric, arcane, occult, inscrutable.* These adjectives mean difficult to explain or understand. Something *mysterious* arouses wonder and inquisitiveness: *"The sea lies all about us . . . . In its mysterious past it encompasses all the dim origins of life"* (Rachel Carson). What is *esoteric* is mysterious because only a select group knows and understands it: *a compilation of esoteric philosophical essays.* Arcane applies to what is hidden from general knowledge: *arcane economic theories.* Occult suggests knowledge reputedly gained only by secret, magical, or supernatural means: *an occult rite.* Something that is *inscrutable* cannot be fathomed by means of investigation or scrutiny: *"It is not for me to attempt to fathom the inscrutable workings of Providence"* (Earl of Birkenhead).

mystery *noun*
Anything that arouses curiosity or perplexes because it is unexplained, inexplicable, or secret ▸ brainteaser, conundrum, curiousity, enigma, perplexity, puzzle, puzzler, question mark, riddle, stickler, weirdness.

mystical *or* **mystic** *adjective*
1. Difficult to explain or understand ▸ enigmatic, inscrutable, puzzling. *See* **mysterious.** 2. Of or relating to existence outside the natural world ▸ metaphysical, superhuman. *See* **supernatural** (1).

mystification *noun*
▸ bewilderment, perplexity, stupor. *See* **daze.**

mystify *verb*
1. To cause to be unclear in mind or intent ▸ befuddle, confound. *See* **confuse** (1). 2. To put at a loss as to what to do ▸ confound, perplex. *See* **baffle** (1).

mystifying *adjective*
▸ baffling, inscrutable, puzzling. *See* **mysterious.**

myth *noun*
1. A traditional story or tale that has no proven factual basis ▸ fable, fairy tale, folk tale, just-so story, legend, parable. *See also* **fiction, story, yarn.** 2. A body of traditional beliefs and notions accumulated about a particular subject ▸ legend, mythology, tradition. *See* **lore** (1). 3. A fiction or half-truth, especially one

that forms part of an ideology ▸ creation, delusion, fabrication, fantasy, fiction, figment, invention. *See also* **lie²**.

mythical *or* **mythic** *adjective*
Having the nature of a fable; not real ▸ apocryphal, fabled, fabricated, fabulous, fairy-tale, fantasy, legendary, make-believe, mythologic, mythological. *See also* **fanciful, fictitious, imaginary.**

mythological *or* **mythologic** *adjective*
▸ fantasy, legendary. *See* **mythical.**

mythology *or* **mythos** *noun*
▸ legend, mythos, tradition. *See* **lore** (1).

n

nab *verb*
1. *Informal* To take into custody as a prisoner ▸ apprehend, seize. *Slang:* bust. *See* **arrest** (1). **2.** *Informal* To get hold of something moving ▸ seize, snatch. *See* **catch** (2).

nabob *noun*
▸ notability, personage. *Slang:* big shot. *See* **dignitary.**

nadir *noun*
A very low or lowest level, position, or degree ▸ bottom, low, minimum, rock bottom.

nag *verb*
1. To scold or find fault with constantly ▸ carp at, fuss at, niggle, peck at, pick at. *Informal:* henpeck. *See also* **annoy, harass, quibble. 2.** To express feelings of pain, dissatisfaction or resentment ▸ fuss, grouch, whine. *See* **complain.**

nag *noun*
A person, traditionally a woman, who persistently nags ▸ harpy, shrew. *See* **scold.**

nagging *adjective*
1. Marked by, causing, or experiencing physical pain ▸ achy, hurtful, sore. *See* **painful** (1). **2.** Inclined to judge too severely ▸ carping, overcritical. *See* **critical** (1).

nail *verb*
1. *Slang* To gain possession of, especially after a struggle or chase ▸ catch, get, secure, win. *See* **capture** (1). **2.** *Slang* To deliver a sudden, sharp blow to ▸ jab, sock, whack. *See* **hit** (1). **3.** To make secure ▸ bind, chain, moor. *See* **fasten** (1).

nail *noun*
A bolt or shaft hammered or drilled in place, used to support or hold together ▸ bolt, peg, pin, rivet, screw, spike, stud, tack. *See also* **anchor, cord, fastener.**

naive *adjective*
1. Free from guile, cunning, or deceit ▸ innocent, simple. *See* **artless** (1). *See synonym note at* **artless. 2.** Easily imposed on or tricked ▸ dupable, exploitable, susceptible. *See* **gullible. 3.** Lacking in intellectual depth or thoroughness ▸ one-dimensional, shallow. *See* **superficial** (1).

naive *noun*
A guileless, unsophisticated person ▸ babe, child. *See* **innocent** (2).

naiveté *noun*
▸ ingenuousness, simplicity. *See* **artlessness.**

naked *adjective*
1. Not wearing any clothes ▸ bare, unclad. *See* **nude** (1). **2.** Without the usual covering ▸ bald, hairless, nude. *See* **bare** (3).

nakedness *noun*
▸ bareness, undress. *See* **nudity.**

namby-pamby *adjective*
1. Lacking vigor, intensity, or bite ▸ bland, jejune. *See* **insipid** (1). **2.** Affectedly or extravagantly emotional ▸ gushy, mawkish, soft. *See* **sentimental.**

namby-pamby *noun*
A childish or pampered person ▸ crybaby, milksop. *See* **baby** (2).

name *noun*
1. The word or words by which one is called and identified ▸ appellation, appellative, cognomen, compellation, denomination, designation, epithet, namesake, nickname, pet name, sobriquet, style, tag, title. *Slang:* handle, moniker. **2.** Public estimation of someone ▸ character, report, reputation, repute. *Informal:* rep. *See also* **image, place. 3.** A famous person ▸ luminary, personality, star. *See* **celebrity** (1). *See synonym note at* **celebrity.**

name *verb*
1. To give a name or title to ▸ baptize, call, christen, denominate, designate, dub, entitle, nickname, style, term, title. *Idiom:* give a handle to. *See also* **call. 2.** To refer to by name ▸ cite, instance, mention, point to, refer to, single out, specify. **3.** To describe with a word or term ▸ designate, label, term. *See* **call** (4). **4.** To select for an office or position ▸ elect, designate, nominate. *See* **appoint** (1). *See synonym note at* **appoint.**

nameless *adjective*
1. Not known or not widely known by name ▸ obscure, unheard-of, unknown. **2.** Having an unknown authorship or agency ▸ unacknowledged, uncredited, unnamed. *See* **anonymous.**

namelessness *noun*
▸ anonymity, oblivion, unimportance. *See* **obscurity** (1).

namely *adverb*
That is to say ▸ i.e., particularly, scilicet, specifically,

videlicet, viz. *Idioms:* by way of explanation, in other words, strictly speaking, to wit.

namesake *noun*
▸ cognomen, epithet, title. *See* **name** (1).

nap *noun*
A brief sleep ▸ catnap, doze, power nap, siesta, snooze. *Informal:* forty winks. *See also* **rest, sleep.**

nap *verb*
To sleep for a brief period ▸ catnap, doze (off), drop off, nod (off), snooze. *Idioms:* catch (*or* grab *or* take) forty winks, get some shuteye. *See also* **rest, sleep.**

narc *noun*
Slang A member of a law-enforcement agency ▸ officer, trooper. *See* **police officer.**

narcissism *or* **narcism** *noun*
▸ conceit, megalomania, vanity. *See* **egotism.** *See synonym note at* **egotism.**

narcissist *noun*
▸ egoist, egomaniac. *See* **egotist.**

narcissistic *adjective*
▸ conceited, vain. *See* **egotistic** (1).

narcotic *noun*
1. A substance that affects the central nervous system and is often addictive ▸ hallucinogen, opiate, psychotropic. *See* **drug** (2). 2. Something that induces sleep or sedation ▸ opiate, sedative. *See* **soporific.**

narcotic *adjective*
Inducing sleep or sedation ▸ opiate, sedative, slumberous. *See* **soporific** (1).

narcotize *verb*
▸ medicate, tranquilize. *See* **drug** (1).

nark *noun*
Slang One who gives incriminating information ▸ informant. *Slang:* snitch, squealer. *See* **informer.**

narrate *verb*
▸ detail, recount, report. *See* **describe** (1). *See synonym note at* **describe.**

narrative *or* **narration** *noun*
▸ chronicle, description, report. *See* **story** (1).

narrow *adjective*
1. Restricted in scope, outlook, or understanding ▸ doctrinaire, dogmatic, inflexible, insular, limited, little, local, narrow-minded, parochial, petty, provincial, small, small-minded, small-town. 2. Affording little room for movement ▸ close, confining, restrictive. *See* **tight** (4). 3. Having the restricted outlook often characteristic of geographic isolation ▸ insular, limited, local, narrow-minded, parochial, provincial, small-town. 4. Small in degree, especially of probability ▸ slight, slim. *See* **remote** (2).

narrow *verb*
To make smaller or narrower by binding or squeezing ▸ compress, contract. *See* **constrict** (1).

narrow-minded *adjective*
1. Not tolerant of the beliefs or opinions of others ▸ close-minded, illiberal, racist. *See* **intolerant** (1). 2. Restricted in scope, outlook, or understanding ▸ insular, petty, provincial. *See* **narrow** (1).

nascence *or* **nascency** *noun*
▸ genesis, inception, start. *See* **birth** (2). *See synonym note at* **birth.**

nastiness *noun*
1. A desire to harm others or to see others suffer ▸ maliciousness, viciousness. *See* **malevolence.** 2. The condition or state of being dirty ▸ filthiness, squalor, uncleanliness. *See* **dirtiness** (1). 3. The quality or state of being obscene ▸ filthiness, profanity, smuttiness, vulgarness. *See* **obscenity** (1).

nasty *adjective*
1. Covered with or stained by dirt ▸ filthy, foul, grimy. *See* **dirty** (1). 2. So objectionable as to deserve condemnation ▸ abhorrent, foul, repellent. *See* **offensive** (1). 3. Offensive to accepted standards of decency ▸ bawdy, coarse, lewd, vulgar. *See* **obscene** (1). 4. Characterized by intense ill will or spite ▸ evil, wicked. *See* **malevolent** (1). 5. Having or showing a bad temper ▸ cranky, grouchy, peevish. *See* **ill-tempered.** 6. So objectionable as to elicit despisal or deserve condemnation ▸ abhorrent, abominable, antipathetic, contemptible, despicable, despisable, detestable, disgusting, filthy, foul, infamous, loathsome, lousy, low, mean, nefarious, obnoxious, odious, repugnant, rotten, shabby, vile, wretched. 7. Marked by cold and unpleasant conditions ▸ grim, severe. *See* **bleak** (1).

nation *noun*
▸ body politic, country, land. *See* **state** (1).

national *adjective*
1. Of, representing, or carried on by people at large ▸ general, public, societal. *See* **popular** (1). 2. Of, from, or within a country's own territory ▸ homegrown, internal, native. *See* **domestic** (3).

national *noun*
A person owing loyalty to and entitled to the protection of a given state ▸ burgher, subject. *See* **citizen.** *See synonym note at* **citizen.**

nationalize *verb*
To place under government or group ownership or control ▸ communalize, socialize.

native *adjective*
1. Possessed at birth ▸ inborn, inherited. *See* **innate** (1). 2. Forming an essential element, as arising from the basic structure of an individual ▸ innate, intrinsic, natural. *See* **constitutional** (1). 3. Existing, born, or produced in a land or region ▸ autochthonic, homegrown. *See* **indigenous** (1). *See synonym note at* **indigenous.** 4. Not cultivated ▸ natural, rough, uncultivated. *See* **wild** (1). 5. Being in a natural state ▸ raw, unrefined. *See* **crude** (1). *See synonym note at* **crude.** 6. Of, from, or within a country's own territory ▸ homegrown, internal. *See* **domestic** (3).

native *noun*
One who resides in a place ▸ denizen, occupant, resident. *See* **inhabitant.**

nativity *noun*
▸ childbearing, delivery, labor. *See* **birth** (1).

natter *verb*
▸ blab, jabber, prattle. *See* **chatter** (1).

natty *adjective*
▸ shipshape, tidy. *See* **neat** (1).
natural *adjective*
1. Produced by nature; not artificial or manmade ▸ additive-free, chemical-free, organic, unadulterated, unprocessed, unsynthetic. *Idiom:* pure as the driven snow. *See also* **authentic, pure. 2.** Not cultivated ▸ native, rough, uncultivated. *See* **wild** (1). **3.** Forming an essential element, as arising from the basic structure of an individual ▸ innate, intrinsic, native. *See* **constitutional** (1). **4.** Acting or happening without apparent forethought, prompting, or planning ▸ impulsive, involuntary. *See* **spontaneous** (1). *See synonym note at* **spontaneous. 5.** Free from hypocrisy or pretense ▸ honest, sincere, unaffected. *See* **genuine** (1). **6.** Free from guile, cunning, or deceit ▸ innocent, naive, simple. *See* **artless** (1). *See synonym note at* **artless. 7.** Possessing great natural ability or talent ▸ endowed, talented. *See* **gifted. 8.** Unconstrained by rigid standards or ceremony ▸ informal, relaxed. *Informal:* laid-back. *See* **easygoing** (1). **9.** Of a charmingly plain and unsophisticated nature ▸ artless, homespun, unadorned. *See* **rustic** (1). **10.** Accurately representing what is depicted or described ▸ factual, true-life. *See* **realistic** (2). **11.** Born to parents who are not married to each other ▸ bastard, misbegotten. *See* **illegitimate** (1). **12.** Of unbroken descent or lineage ▸ direct, genealogical, hereditary, lineal. *See also* **ancestral.**
naturalistic *adjective*
▸ factual, lifelike, true-life. *See* **realistic** (2).
naturalize *verb*
▸ break in, master, tame. *See* **domesticate.**
naturalized *adjective*
▸ broken (in), housebroken, pet, tame. *See* **domestic** (2).
naturally *adverb*
1. In an expected or customary manner ▸ customarily, generally, normally. *See* **usually. 2.** It is so; as you say or ask ▸ agreed, all right, assuredly. *See* **yes.**
naturalness *noun*
1. Freedom from constraint, formality, embarrassment, or awkwardness ▸ informality, unceremoniousness. *See* **ease** (1). **2.** The absence of guile, cunning, or deceit ▸ ingenuousness, naiveté. *See* **artlessness.**
nature *noun*
1. The totality of all existing things ▸ creation, world. *See* **universe** (1). **2.** A class that is defined by the common attribute or attributes possessed by all its members ▸ ilk, mold, species. *See* **kind**[2]**. 3.** The combination of qualities that distinguishes an individual ▸ makeup, personality, temperament. *See* **character** (1). *See synonym note at* **character. 4.** A basic trait or set of traits that define and establish the character of something ▸ being, quintessence. *See* **essence** (1). **5.** A person's customary manner of emotional response ▸ bent, humor, temperament. *See* **disposition** (1). **6.** The ecological circumstances in which organisms live ▸ biosphere, habitat. *See* **environment** (3).

naughtiness *noun*
1. Improper, often rude behavior ▸ misconduct, misdoing, wrongdoing. *See* **misbehavior. 2.** The act or instance of defying ▸ disobedience, noncompliance, rebellion. *See* **defiance** (1).
naughty *adjective*
1. Not submitting to discipline or control ▸ ill-behaved, obstinate, unmanageable. *See* **unruly. 2.** Causing harm or injury ▸ deleterious, evil, injurious. *See* **harmful. 3.** Not in keeping with conventional mores ▸ indecent, indelicate. *See* **improper** (1).
nausea *noun*
▸ abhorrence, loathing, queasiness. *See* **disgust.**
nauseate *verb*
▸ appall, revolt, sicken. *See* **disgust** (1). *See synonym note at* **disgust.**
nauseating *adjective*
1. So unpleasant or objectionable as to cause scorn or disgust ▸ contemptible, disgusting, obnoxious. *See* **offensive** (1). **2.** So unpleasant in flavor as to be inedible ▸ distasteful, unappetizing, uneatable. *See* **unpalatable** (1).
nautical *adjective*
▸ marine, maritime, naval, navigational. *See also* **marine.**

✤ CORE SYNONYMS: *nautical, marine, maritime, naval, navigational.* These adjectives mean of or relating to the sea, ships, shipping, sailors, or navigation: *nautical charts; marine insurance; maritime law; a naval officer; navigational hazards.*

naval *adjective*
Of or relating to sea navigation ▸ marine, maritime, nautical, navigational. *See synonym note at* **nautical.** *See also* **marine.**
nave *noun*
▸ core, focus, nucleus. *See* **center** (3).
navel *noun*
▸ median, middle, midpoint. *See* **center** (2).
navigable *adjective*
▸ negotiable, passable, traversable. *See* **passable** (1).
navigate *verb*
▸ jockey, steer. *See* **maneuver** (1).
navigational *adjective*
Of or relating to sea navigation ▸ marine, maritime, nautical, naval. *See synonym note at* **nautical.** *See also* **marine.**
navigator *noun*
▸ boatman, mariner, seafarer. *See* **sailor.**
nay *adverb*
Not so ▸ not. *Informal:* nope. *See* **no.**
nay *noun*
1. A negative response ▸ refusal, rejection. *See* **no** (1). **2.** A negative vote or voter ▸ no.
near *adverb*
To a point near in time, space, or relation ▸ closely, nearby. *See* **close.**
near *adjective*
1. Not far from another in space, time, or relation

▸ immediate, nearby, nigh. *See* **close** (1). *See synonym note at* **close.** **2.** Very closely associated ▸ close, cozy, familiar. *See* **intimate**[1] (1).

near *verb*
To come near in space or time ▸ close in on, gain on. *See* **approach** (1).

nearby *adjective*
1. Not far from another in space, time, or relation ▸ near, neighboring, nigh. *See* **close** (1). *See synonym note at* **close.** **2.** Being within easy reach ▸ handy, ready. *See* **convenient** (2).

nearby *adverb*
To a point near in time, space, or relation ▸ closely, near. *See* **close.**

nearly *adverb*
▸ almost, circa, roughly. *See* **approximately.**

nearness *noun*
The act or fact of coming near ▸ approach, coming, convergence, imminence. *See also* **advance, appearance.**

neat *adjective*
1. In good order or clean condition ▸ dapper, natty, orderly, prim, shipshape, snug, spick-and-span, spruce, taut, tidy, trig, trim, well-groomed, well-kept, well-ordered. *Idioms:* in apple pie order, in good order, neat as a pin. *See also* **clean, methodical.** **2.** Exhibiting or possessing skill and ease in performance ▸ adroit, clean. *See* **dexterous.** **3.** Not diluted or mixed with other substances ▸ pure, unblended. *See* **straight** (1). **4.** *Slang* Particularly excellent ▸ fantastic, sensational, superb. *See* **marvelous** (1). **5.** Arranged or proceeding in a set, systematized pattern ▸ orderly, regular, systematic. *See* **methodical** (1).

✦ CORE SYNONYMS: *neat, tidy, trim, shipshape, spick-and-span.* These adjectives mean in good order or clean condition: *Neat* is the most general: *a neat room; neat hair. Tidy* emphasizes precise arrangement and order: *"When she saw me come in tidy and well dressed, she even smiled"* (Charlotte Brontë). *Trim* stresses especially smart appearance: *"A trim little sailboat was dancing out at her moorings"* (Herman Melville). *Shipshape* evokes meticulous order: *"We'll try to make this barn a little more shipshape"* (Rudyard Kipling). *Spick-and-span* suggests the immaculate freshness of something new: *"young men in spick-and-span uniforms"* (Edith Wharton).

---

neaten *verb*
1. To make or keep an area clean and orderly ▸ clean (up), spruce (up), straighten (up). *See* **tidy** (1). **2.** To make neat and trim; make presentable ▸ freshen (up), slick up, trim. *See* **tidy** (2).

neb *noun*
▸ cusp, tip. *See* **point** (1).

nebbish *noun*
▸ nobody, nothing, small fry. *See* **nonentity.**

nebulous *adjective*
▸ equivocal, two-edged, vague. *See* **ambiguous** (2).

nebulousness *noun*
▸ ambiguousness, unclearness. *See* **vagueness.**

necessary *adjective*
1. Imposed on one by authority, command, or convention ▸ imperative, mandatory, requisite. *See* **required** (1). **2.** Incapable of being dispensed with ▸ indispensable, required. *See* **essential** (1). *See synonym note at* **essential.** **3.** Bound to happen ▸ inevitable, sure, unavoidable. *See* **certain** (1).

necessary *noun*
Something indispensable ▸ necessity, prerequisite, requirement. *See* **condition** (2).

necessitate *verb*
▸ entail, involve, require. *See* **demand** (2).

necessitous *adjective*
▸ destitute, down-and-out, indigent. *See* **poor** (1).

necessity *noun*
1. A basis for an action ▸ call, justification, occasion. *See* **cause** (2). **2.** Something indispensable ▸ essential, prerequisite, requirement. *See* **condition** (2). **3.** A condition in which something necessary or desirable is required or wanted ▸ exigence, exigency, need.

neck *verb*
Informal To engage in kissing, caressing, and other amorous behavior ▸ *Informal:* fool around, pet, spoon. *Slang:* grope, make out. *Idioms:* bill and coo, play kissy (*or* sucky) face, play post office. *See also* **caress, copulate, kiss, snuggle.**

neck *noun*
A narrow body of water ▸ narrows, strait. *See* **channel.**

neck of the woods *noun*
Informal A part of the earth's surface ▸ district, region, zone. *See* **area** (2).

necromancer *noun*
▸ enchanter, magician, sorcerer. *See* **wizard** (1).

need *noun*
1. A condition in which something necessary or desirable is required or wanted ▸ exigence, exigency, necessity. **2.** Something indispensable ▸ necessity, prerequisite, requirement. *See* **condition** (2). **3.** Something asked for or needed ▸ requirement, want. *See* **demand** (2). **4.** An act or course of action that is demanded of one, as by position, custom, law, or religion ▸ charge, commitment, obligation. *See* **duty** (1). **5.** The condition of being extremely poor ▸ destitution, indigence, penury. *See* **poverty** (1).

need *verb*
1. To be required to do ▸ be obliged, ought, should. *See* **must.** **2.** To have as a need or prerequisite ▸ entail, involve, necessitate. *See* **demand** (2). **3.** To be without what is needed, required, or essential ▸ lack, require, want. *See synonym note at* **lack.** *See also* **demand.**

needful *adjective*
▸ critical, necessary, required. *See* **essential** (1). *See synonym note at* **essential.**

neediness *noun*
▸ destitution, indigence, need. *See* **poverty** (1).

needle *noun*
A sharp protuberance or projection ▸ prick, prong, spine. *See* **spike** (1).

needle *verb*
Informal To attack or disturb persistently ► harry, pester, torment. *See* **harass.**

needless *adjective*
► inessential, nonessential, unneeded. *See* **unnecessary.**

needy *adjective*
► destitute, down-and-out, indigent. *See* **poor** (1). *See synonym note at* **poor.**

ne'er-do-well *noun*
► bum, idler, loafer. *See* **wastrel** (1).

nefarious *adjective*
► contemptible, disgusting, obnoxious. *See* **offensive** (1).

negate *verb*
1. To make ineffective by applying an opposite force ► counteract, neutralize. *See* **cancel** (2). **2.** To put an end to ► annul, nullify, void. *See* **abolish** (1). **3.** To refuse to admit the truth, reality, value, or worth of ► contravene, disaffirm, disavow. *See* **deny** (1). *See synonym note at* **deny.**

negation *noun*
1. An often formal act of putting an end to ► annulment, invalidation, nullification. *See* **abolition. 2.** A refusal to grant the truth of a statement or charge ► contradiction, disaffirmation, disclaimer, rejection. *See* **denial** (1).

negative *adjective*
Tending to discourage, retard, or make more difficult ► antagonistic, disadvantageous, untoward. *See* **unfavorable** (1).

negative *verb*
1. To prevent or forbid authoritatively ► block, turn down. *See* **veto. 2.** To refuse to admit the truth, reality, value, or worth of ► contravene, disaffirm, disavow. *See* **deny** (1).

neglect *verb*
1. To fail to care for or give proper attention to ► be lax about, disregard, gloss over, ignore, let slide, let slip, pass over, slight. *Idioms:* lose sight (*or* track) of, lie down on the job, turn a blind eye to. **2.** To slight someone deliberately ► shun, spurn, slight. *See* **snub.3.** To fail to do or carry out ► disregard, fail (to do something), forget, ignore, omit, overlook, shirk. *Idioms:* leave undone, let slide, let slip, pass over.

neglect *noun*
1. An act or instance of neglecting ► disregard, negligence, omission, oversight, slight. *See also* **error, negligence. 2.** Nonperformance of what ought to be done ► delinquency, dereliction. *See* **failure** (2).

neglectful *adjective*
► lax, slack. *See* **negligent.** *See synonym note at* **negligent.**

negligence *noun*
1. The state or the quality of being negligent ► carelessness, forgetfulness, heedlessness, inattentiveness, laxity, laxness, remissness, slackness, sloppiness, thoughtlessness. *See also* **abandon, apathy, failure. 2.** An act or instance of neglecting ► disregard, over-

sight. *See* **neglect** (1). **3.** An act of breaking a law or of nonfulfillment of an obligation ► infraction, infringement, violation. *See* **breach** (1).

negligent *adjective*
Guilty of neglect; lacking due care or concern ► derelict, lax, neglectful, remiss, slack, slipshod, sloppy, unconcerned. *See also* **careless.**

✦ CORE SYNONYMS: *negligent, derelict, lax, neglectful, remiss, slack.* These adjectives mean guilty of a lack of due care or concern: *an accident caused by a negligent driver; was derelict in his civic responsibilities; lax in attending classes; neglectful of her own financial security; remiss of you not to pay your bill; slack in maintaining discipline.*

---

negligibility *or* **negligibleness** *noun*
► frivolity, minutia, trivia. *See* **trifle** (1).

negligible *adjective*
1. Of little importance or seriousness ► inconsequential, insignificant, trifling. *See* **trivial. 2.** Small in degree, especially of probability ► slight, slim. *See* **remote** (2).

negotiable *adjective*
► navigable, passable. *See* **passable** (1).

negotiant *noun*
► broker, intermediary, mediator, middleman. *See* **go-between.**

negotiate *verb*
1. To argue about the terms, as of a sale ► haggle, palter. *See* **haggle. 2.** To bring something into a state of agreement or accord ► arrange, fix, set. *See* **settle** (2). **3.** To meet and exchange views to reach a decision ► consult, deliberate, talk. *Informal:* huddle, powwow. *See* **confer** (1). **4.** To pass by or over successfully ► clear, hurdle, surmount.

negotiation *noun*
The act or process of dealing with another to reach an agreement ► parley, talk. *See also* **conversation.**

negotiator *noun*
► broker, intermediary, mediator, middleman. *See* **go-between.**

neighbor *verb*
► border, bound, meet, touch. *See* **adjoin** (1).

neighborhood *noun*
1. An area in a city or town with distinctive characteristics ► area, community, district, quarter, quarters, ward. *Slang:* 'hood. **2.** A part of the earth's surface ► district, region, zone. *See* **area** (2). **3.** A surrounding area ► locale, surroundings. *See* **environment** (1). **4.** A particular geographic area ► locale, vicinity. *See* **locality** (1). **5.** *Informal* Approximate size or amount ► range, vicinity.

neighboring *adjective*
1. Sharing a common boundary ► bordering, conterminous, contiguous. *See* **adjoining. 2.** Not far from another in space, time, or relation ► near, nearby, nigh. *See* **close** (1).

neighborly *adjective*
1. Pleasant and friendly in disposition ► congenial,

cordial, genial. *See* **amiable. 2.** Full of polite concern for the well-being of others ▸ courteous, solicitous, thoughtful. *See* **attentive** (1). *See synonym note at* **attentive.**

nemesis *noun*
▸ antagonist, foe, resister. *See* **opponent** (1).

neonate *noun*
▸ babe, newborn. *See* **baby** (1).

neophyte *noun*
1. One who is just starting to learn or do something ▸ fledgling, freshman, novice. *See* **beginner. 2.** An entrant who has not yet taken the final vows of a religious order ▸ novice, novitiate, postulant.

nerd *noun*
1. *Slang* A person who is deficient in judgment and good sense ▸ idiot, imbecile, nitwit. *See* **fool** (1). **2.** *Slang* An unpleasant, tiresome person ▸ bore. *Slang:* dweeb, turkey. *See* **drip** (2).

nerve *noun*
1. The quality of mind enabling one to face danger or hardship resolutely ▸ bravery, fortitude, gallantry, valor. *See* **courage. 2.** The state or quality of being impudent or arrogantly self-confident ▸ audacity, boldness, impertinence. *See* **impudence.**

nerve *verb*
To impart emotional, moral, or mental strength to ▸ hearten, buck up. *See* **encourage** (2).

nerviness *noun*
▸ audacity, boldness, brashness, impertinence. *See* **impudence.**

nervous *adjective*
1. In a state of anxiety or uneasiness ▸ distressed, overwrought, uneasy. *See* **anxious. 2.** Feeling or exhibiting nervous tension ▸ jittery, skittish. *See* **edgy.**

nervousness *noun*
1. A troubled or anxious state of mind ▸ concern, distress, unease. *See* **anxiety** (1). **2.** An uneasy or nervous state ▸ disquietude, uneasiness, unrest. *See* **restlessness.**

nervy *adjective*
1. Rude and disrespectful; without shame ▸ bold, insolent, pert. *See* **impudent. 2.** Having or showing courage ▸ courageous, fearless, heroic. *See* **brave.**

nescience *noun*
1. The condition of being uninformed or unaware ▸ innocence, unawareness. *See* **ignorance** (2). **2.** the condition or being ignorant; lack of knowledge or learning ▸ illiteracy, unintelligence. *See* **ignorance** (1).

nescient *adjective*
▸ lowbrow, uncultivated, unlearned. *See* **ignorant** (1).

nest *noun*
Informal A building or shelter where one lives ▸ domicile, habitation, residence. *See* **home** (1).

nest egg *noun*
▸ cache, reserve, stockpile. *See* **hoard.**

nestle *verb*
▸ cuddle, nuzzle, snug. *See* **snuggle.**

net¹ *noun*
1. An open and loosely connected structure, usually interlaced, woven, or knotted ▸ lattice, mesh, network. *See* **web** (1). **2.** The goal in the game of basketball ▸ bucket, hoop, swish. *See* **basket** (3).

net *verb*
1. To obtain possession or control of ▸ gain, get, take, win. *See* **capture** (1). **2.** To gain control of by trapping ▸ snare, trap. *See* **catch** (1).

net² *verb*
To make as income or profit ▸ clear, gain, yield. *See* **return** (3).

nethermost *adjective*
▸ lowest, undermost. *See* **bottom.**

netting *noun*
▸ lattice, net, network. *See* **web** (1).

nettle *verb*
▸ bother, irritate, vex. *See* **annoy** (1).

nettlesome *adjective*
1. Full of irritating difficulties or controversies ▸ prickly, spiny, thorny. *See also* **complex, delicate, disturbing, troublesome. 2.** Troubling to the mind or emotions ▸ bothersome, irritating, unsettling. *See* **disturbing.**

network *noun*
1. An open and loosely connected structure, usually interlaced, woven, or knotted ▸ lattice, mesh, net. *See* **web** (1). **2.** An entity composed of interconnected parts ▸ system, tissue, web. *See* **complex** (1).

neurosis *noun*
An exaggerated concern ▸ anxiety, complex, phobia. *Informal:* hang-up. *See also* **anxiety, obsession.**

neuter *adjective*
Not inclining toward or actively taking either side in a matter under dispute ▸ nonaligned, unbiased. *See* **neutral** (1).

neuter *verb*
To render incapable of reproducing ▸ castrate, spay. *See* **sterilize** (2).

neutral *adjective*
1. Not inclining toward or actively taking either side in a matter that is under dispute ▸ impartial, neuter, nonaligned, nonpartisan, unbiased, uncommitted, uninvolved, unprejudiced. *Idiom:* on the fence. *See also* **fair, receptive. 2.** Lacking feeling or emotion ▸ emotionless, impassive, stolid. *See* **cold** (2). **3.** Without definite or distinctive characteristics ▸ bland, colorless, indistinctive. *See also* **boring.**

neutralize *verb*
▸ counteract, negate, offset. *See* **cancel** (2).

never-ending *adjective*
1. Enduring for all time ▸ ceaseless, eternal. *See* **endless** (2). **2.** Existing without interruption or end ▸ constant, endless, everlasting, perpetual. *See* **continual.**

nevertheless *adverb*
▸ however, nonetheless, yet. *See* **still** (1).

new *adjective*
1. Not the same as what was previously known or done ▸ brand-new, different, fresh, innovative, inventive, newfangled, novel, original, unfamiliar, unprec-

edented. *See also* **contemporary, progressive. 2.** In existence now ▸ current, present-day. *See* **present**[1] (1). **3.** Being an addition ▸ added, extra, fresh, more. *See* **additional. 4.** Lacking experience and the knowledge gained from it ▸ inexpert, uninitiated, unpracticed. *See* **inexperienced.**

✦ CORE SYNONYMS: *new, fresh, novel, newfangled, original.* These adjectives describe what has existed for only a short time, has only lately come into use, or has only recently arrived at a state or position, as of prominence: *New* is the most general: *a new movie; a new friend. "It is time for a new generation of leadership, to cope with new problems and new opportunities"* (John F. Kennedy). Something *fresh* has qualities of newness such as briskness, brightness, or purity: *fresh footprints in the snow; fresh hope of discovering a vaccine. Novel* applies to the new and strikingly unusual: *"His sermons were considered bold in thought and novel in language"* (Edith Wharton). *Newfangled* suggests that something is needlessly novel: *"the newfangled doctrine of utility"* (John Galt). Something that is *original* is novel and the first of its kind: *"The science of pure mathematics, in its modern development, may claim to be the most original creation of the human spirit"* (Alfred North Whitehead).

---

newborn *noun*
▸ babe, infant. *See* **baby** (1).
newcomer *noun*
1. A person coming from another country or into a new territory ▸ alien, outsider, stranger. *See* **foreigner. 2.** One that arrives ▸ arrival, comer, visitor. *See also* **addition, company. 3.** One who is just starting to learn or do something ▸ fledgling, neophyte, novice. *See* **beginner.**
newfangled *adjective*
▸ fresh, novel, original. *See* **new** (1). *See synonym note* at **new.**
newfangledness *noun*
▸ newness, originality. *See* **novelty** (1).
newly *adverb*
▸ just (now), recently. *See* **lately.**
newness *noun*
1. The quality of being novel ▸ freshness, originality. *See* **novelty** (1). **2.** Lack of experience and the knowledge gained from it ▸ immaturity, inexpertness, rawness. *See* **inexperience.**
news *noun*
1. New information, especially about recent events and happenings ▸ advice, headline, information, intelligence, report, tidings, word. *Informal:* scoop. *See also* **notice. 2.** Something significant that happens ▸ development, incident. *See* **event** (2).

✦ CORE SYNONYMS: *news, advice, intelligence, tidings, word.* These nouns denote new information about recent events and happenings: *just heard the good news; sent advice that the loan was approved; a source of intelligence about the war; tidings of victory; received word of his death.*

newscaster *noun*
▸ correspondent, editorialist, media. *See* **press** (1).
news flash *noun*
▸ bulletin, dispatch, story. *See* **item** (1).
newshound *noun*
▸ correspondent, editorialist, media. *See* **press** (1).
newsmonger *noun*
▸ gossipmonger, taleteller, whisperer. *See* **gossip** (2).
newspaperman *or* **newspaperwoman** *noun*
▸ correspondent, editorialist, media. *See* **press** (1).
newsperson *noun*
▸ correspondent, editorialist, media. *See* **press** (1).
next *adjective*
1. Sharing a common boundary ▸ adjacent, conterminous, neighboring. *See* **adjoining. 2.** Occurring after another ▸ ensuing, subsequent, succeeding. *See* **following** (1).
next *adverb*
At a subsequent time ▸ afterwards, latterly, subsequently. *See* **later.**
nexus *noun*
▸ ligature, link, tie. *See* **bond** (2).
nib *noun*
▸ cusp, tip. *See* **point** (1).
nibble *verb*
1. To seize and grind with the teeth ▸ chomp, gnash, munch. *See* **chew. 2.** To feed on vegetation ▸ crop, pasture. *See* **browse** (2).
nice *adjective*
1. Giving or affording pleasure or enjoyment ▸ agreeable, favorable, gratifying. *See* **pleasant** (1). **2.** Having pleasant desirable qualities ▸ enjoyable, jolly, fine. *See* **good** (1). **3.** Suitable for a particular person, condition, occasion, or place ▸ befitting, correct, right. *See* **appropriate** (1). **4.** Very difficult to please ▸ exacting, finicky. *See* **fussy** (1). **5.** Able to make or detect effects of great precision ▸ delicate, sensitive, subtle. *See* **fine**[1] (8). **6.** So slight as to be difficult to notice or appreciate ▸ refined, subtle. *See* **delicate** (4).
nicety *noun*
1. A small, often specialized element of a whole ▸ particular, specialty, technicality. *See* **detail** (1). **2.** A slight variation between nearly identical entities ▸ hue, subtlety. *See* **shade** (1). **3.** A conventional social gesture or act without intrinsic purpose ▸ ceremony, form, formality. *See* **ritual** (2).
niche *noun*
1. The proper or designated location ▸ place. **2.** A partial opening caused by splitting and rupture ▸ break, cranny, crevice. *See* **crack** (2). **3.** The ecological circumstances in which organisms live ▸ biosphere, habitat. *See* **environment** (3). **4.** The natural environment that is specific to an animal or plant ▸ habitation, territory. *See* **habitat** (1).
nick *verb*
1. *Slang* To get money or something else from someone by deceitful trickery ▸ bilk, defraud, swindle. *See* **cheat** (1). **2.** To penetrate with a sharp edge ▸ bayonet, incise, pierce, slash. *See* **cut** (1).

nick *noun*
1. An opening made with a sharp object ▸ groove, notch, slit. *See* **cut** (1). **2.** A small mark or hole made by a sharp, pointed object ▸ notch, puncture. *See* **prick** (1).

nickname *noun*
The word or words by which one is called ▸ cognomen, epithet, title. *See* **name** (1).

nickname *verb*
To give a name or title to ▸ christen, designate. *See* **name** (1).

nictitate *verb*
▸ bat, flutter, wink. *See* **blink** (1). *See synonym note at* **blink.**

nictitation *noun*
▸ bat, wink. *See* **blink** (1).

nifty *adjective*
▸ fantastic, sensational, superb. *See* **marvelous** (1).

niggard *noun*
A stingy person ▸ churl. *Informal:* penny pincher. *See* **miser.**

niggard *adjective*
Ungenerously or pettily reluctant to spend money ▸ close-fisted, miserly, parsimonious. *See* **stingy** (1).

niggardly *adjective*
▸ close-fisted, miserly, parsimonious. *See* **stingy** (1).

niggle *verb*
1. To raise unnecessary or trivial objections ▸ carp, cavil, nitpick. *See* **quibble** (1). *See synonym note at* **quibble.** **2.** To scold or find fault with constantly ▸ fuss at, pick on. *See* **nag** (1).

niggler *noun*
▸ caviler, nitpicker. *See* **critic** (2).

niggling *adjective*
Of little importance or seriousness ▸ inconsequential, negligible, trifling. *See* **trivial.**

niggling *noun*
The act of making trivial objections or distinctions ▸ caviling, hairsplitting, nitpicking. *See* **quibbling.**

nigh *adverb*
To a point near in time, space, or relation ▸ closely, nearby. *See* **close.**

nigh *adjective*
Not far from another in space, time, or relation ▸ near, nearby, proximate. *See* **close** (1). *See synonym note at* **close.**

night *noun*
The period of time between sunset and sunrise ▸ after dark, after dinner, bedtime, dark, lights out, nighttime. *Idioms:* dark of night, hours of darkness, witching hours. *See also* **evening.**

night *adjective*
Of or occurring during the night ▸ nightly, nocturnal.

nightclub *noun*
▸ inn, pub, saloon. *See* **bar** (2).

nightfall *noun*
▸ eve, twilight. *See* **evening.**

nightly *adjective*
Of or occurring during the night ▸ night, nocturnal.

nightmarish *adjective*
▸ hair-raising, horrific, petrifying. *See* **horrible** (1).

night soil *noun*
▸ dung, feces, waste. *See* **excrement.**

nighttime *noun*
▸ after dark, lights out. *See* **night.**

nihility *noun*
▸ nonexistence, nullity. *See* **nothingness** (1).

nil *noun*
▸ null. *Informal:* zero. *See* **nothing** (1).

nimble *adjective*
▸ agile, deft, facile. *See* **dexterous.** *See synonym note at* **dexterous.**

nimbleness *noun*
1. The quality of being agile ▸ deftness, dexterity, quickness. *See* **agility.** **2.** Skillfulness in the use of the hands or body ▸ deftness, facility. *See* **dexterity** (1).

nimrod *noun*
▸ chump. *Slang:* dork, twerp. *See* **drip** (2).

nincompoop *noun*
1. A person who is deficient in judgment and good sense ▸ idiot, moron, simpleton. *See* **fool** (1). **2.** A mentally dull person ▸ dummy, dunce, thickhead. *See* **dullard.**

ninny *noun*
▸ idiot, moron, simpleton. *See* **fool** (1).

nip¹ *verb*
1. To try to bite something quickly or eagerly ▸ snap, snatch, strike. **2.** To spoil or destroy ▸ corrode, dash. *See* **blast** (2). *See synonym note at* **blast.** **3.** *Slang* To take another's property without permission ▸ purloin, snatch, thieve. *See* **steal** (1).

nip *noun*
Lack of warmth ▸ chilliness, frigidity. *See* **cold.**

nip² *noun*
Informal A small amount of liquor ▸ shot, sip, tot. *See* **drop** (8).

nip *verb*
1. *Informal* To take alcoholic liquor, especially excessively or habitually ▸ tipple. *Slang:* booze, lush. *See* **drink** (2). **2.** A tiny amount ▸ dash, drop, smidgen. *See* **bit¹** (1).

nip and tuck *adjective*
1. Almost even ▸ tight. *Idiom:* neck and neck. **2.** Neither favorable nor unfavorable ▸ balanced, even, fifty-fifty.

nippy *adjective*
▸ chill, frigid, polar. *See* **cold** (1).

nitpick *verb*
▸ cavil, niggle, squabble. *See* **quibble** (1). *See synonym note at* **quibble.**

nitpicker *noun*
▸ caviler, quibbler. *See* **critic** (2).

nitpicking *noun*
▸ caviling, hairsplitting, niggling. *See* **quibbling.**

nitty-gritty *noun*
Informal Practical or basic details ▸ brass tacks, details, nuts and bolts, practicalities, specifics. *See also* **detail, heart, element.**

nitwit *noun*
1. A person who is deficient in judgment and good sense ▸ idiot, moron, simpleton. *See* **fool** (1). **2.** A mentally dull person ▸ dummy, idiot, thickhead. *See* **dullard.**

nix *noun*
Slang No thing; not anything ▸ null. *Informal:* zero. *See* **nothing** (1).

nix *adverb*
Slang Not so ▸ not. *Informal:* nope. *See* **no.**

nix *verb*
1. *Slang* To prevent or forbid authoritatively ▸ blackball, turn down. *See* **veto.** **2.** *Slang* To be unwilling to accept, consider, or receive ▸ refuse, reject, spurn. *See* **decline** (1).

no *adverb*
Not so ▸ nay, not. *Informal:* nope, noway. *Slang:* negative, nix. **Idioms:** by no means, absolutely not, not at all, not on your life, nothing doing.

no *noun*
1. A negative response ▸ nay, naysay, refusal, rejection, thumbs-down. *Slang:* no go. *See also* **refusal.** **2.** A negative vote or voter ▸ nay.

no-account *adjective*
▸ drossy, good-for-nothing, valueless. *See* **worthless** (1).

nobility *noun*
1. Noble rank or status by birth ▸ birth, blood, blue blood, high blood, noble blood, noblesse, royalty. *See also* **ancestry, status.** **2.** People of the highest social level ▸ blue blood, elite, gentry, upper class. *See* **society** (1).

noble *adjective*
1. Of high birth or social position ▸ aristocratic, blue-blooded, elite, gentle, highborn, highbred, imperial, patrician, regal, royal, thoroughbred, titled, upper-class, wellborn. *Informal:* upper-crust. **2.** Being on a high intellectual or moral level ▸ elevated, moral. *See* **elevated** (4). **3.** Impressive in size, proportion, or appearance ▸ imposing, magnificent, splendid. *See* **grand** (1). **4.** Raised to or occupying a high position or rank ▸ elevated, lofty. *See* **exalted** (1).

noblesse *noun*
▸ blue blood, royalty. *See* **nobility** (1).

nobody *pronoun*
No person ▸ none, not anybody, not one, no one. **Idioms:** no one at all, not a soul.

nobody *noun*
A totally insignificant person ▸ nebbish, nothing, small fry. *See* **nonentity.**

nocturnal *adjective*
Of or occurring during the night ▸ night, nightly.

nod *verb*
1. To respond affirmatively; receive with agreement or compliance ▸ acquiesce, subscribe. *See* **assent.** **2.** To sleep for a brief period ▸ doze, siesta. *See* **nap.** **3.** To incline the head or body, as in greeting, consent, courtesy, submission, or worship ▸ curtsy, kneel. *See* **bow**[1] (1).

nod *noun*
1. An inclination of the head or body, as in greeting, consent, courtesy, submission, or worship ▸ genuflection, obeisance. *See* **bow**[1]. **2.** An expressive, meaningful bodily movement ▸ indication, signal. *See* **gesture** (1). **3.** The approving of an action, especially when done by one in authority ▸ authorization, consent, sanction. *See* **permission. 4.** The act of accepting or adopting ▸ assent, consent. *See* **acceptance** (1).

nodding *adjective*
▸ drowsy, slumberous, somnolent. *See* **sleepy** (1).

noddle *noun*
▸ crown, pate. *See* **head** (1).

node *or* **nodule** *noun*
▸ lump, protuberance. *See* **bump** (1).

noggin *noun*
Slang The uppermost part of the body ▸ crown, pate. *See* **head** (1).

no-good *adjective*
Lacking worth and value ▸ good-for-nothing, valueless. *See* **worthless** (1).

no-good *noun*
Informal A self-indulgent person who avoids work ▸ bum, idler, loafer. *See* **wastrel** (2).

noise *noun*
1. Sounds or a sound, especially when loud, confused, or disagreeable ▸ babel, cacophony, clamor, clangor, din, hubbub, hullabaloo, pandemonium, racket, row, rumpus, tumult, uproar. **Idiom:** hue and cry. *See also* **disorder, senstation. 2.** Vibrations detected by the ear ▸ sonance, sound. *See also* **tone.**

noise *verb*
1. To bring to public notice or make known publicly ▸ broadcast, declare, proclaim, promulgate. *See* **announce** (1). **2.** To engage in or spread gossip ▸ rumor, whisper. *See* **gossip.**

✦ CORE SYNONYMS: *noise, din, racket, uproar, pandemonium, hullabaloo, hubbub, clamor, babel.* These nouns refer to loud, confused, or disagreeable sound or sounds. *Noise* is the least specific: *deafened by the noise in the subway.* A *din* is a jumble of loud, usually discordant sounds: *the din of the factory. Racket* is loud, distressing noise: *the racket made by trucks rolling along cobblestone streets. Uproar, pandemonium,* and *hullabaloo* imply disorderly tumult together with loud, bewildering sound: *"The evening uproar of the howling monkeys burst out"* (W.H. Hudson); *"a pandemonium of dancing and whooping, drumming and feasting"* (Francis Parkman); *a tremendous hullabaloo in the agitated crowd. Hubbub* emphasizes turbulent activity and concomitant din: *the hubbub of bettors, speculators, tipsters, and touts. Clamor* is loud, usually sustained noise, as of a public outcry of dissatisfaction: *"not in the clamor of the crowded street"* (Henry Wadsworth Longfellow); *a debate that was interrupted by a clamor of opposition. Babel* stresses confusion of vocal sounds arising from simultaneous utterance and random mixture of languages: *guests chattering in a babel of tongues at the diplomatic reception.*

noiseless *adjective*
▶ hushed, inaudible, quiet. *See* **silent** (1). *See synonym note at* **silent.**

noiselessness *noun*
▶ hush, quiet. *See* **silence** (1).

noisome *adjective*
1. Having an unpleasant odor ▶ fetid, foul, stinking. *See* **smelly. 2.** Causing harm or injury ▶ deleterious, evil, injurious. *See* **harmful.**

noisy *adjective*
▶ booming, earsplitting, roaring. *See* **loud** (1).

nomad *noun*
▶ gypsy, roamer, vagabond. *See* **hobo.**

nomadic *adjective*
Leading the life of a person without a fixed domicile; moving from place to place ▶ drifting, itinerant, peripatetic, roaming, roving, traveling, vagabond, vagrant, wayfaring, wandering. *See also* **migratory, mobile.**

nominate *verb*
▶ elect, name, tap. *See* **appoint** (1). *See synonym note at* **appoint.**

nomination *noun*
1. The act of appointing to an office or position ▶ assignment, election, installation. *See* **appointment** (1). **2.** Something that is put forward for consideration ▶ proposition, submission, suggestion. *See* **proposal** (1).

nonaligned *adjective*
▶ neuter, unbiased. *See* **neutral** (1).

nonappearance *noun*
▶ cut, truancy. *See* **absence** (1).

nonassertive *adjective*
▶ bashful, demure, diffident. *See* **shy¹** (1).

nonattendance *noun*
▶ nonappearance, truancy. *See* **absence** (1).

nonattendant *adjective*
▶ away, elsewhere, truant. *See* **absent** (1).

nonbeing *noun*
▶ nonexistence, nullity. *See* **nothingness** (1).

nonbeliever *noun*
▶ agnostic, unbeliever. *See* **skeptic.**

nonchalance *noun*
1. A stable emotional state ▶ coolness, imperturbability, sang-froid, unflappability. *See* **balance** (2). **2.** Lack of emotion or interest ▶ disinterest, indifference, unconcern. *See* **apathy.**

nonchalant *adjective*
1. Not excited or agitated ▶ collected, composed, cool. *See* **calm** (1). *See synonym note at* **calm. 2.** Lacking concern or attention ▶ heedless, insouciant, unconcerned. *See* **careless** (1).

noncombustible *adjective*
▶ fire-resistant, flameproof. *See* **fireproof.**

noncommittal *adjective*
▶ inhibited, restrained, self-restrained. *See* **reserved** (1).

noncompliance *noun*
▶ disobedience, insurgence, rebellion. *See* **defiance** (1).

noncompliant *adjective*
▶ insubordinate, recalcitrant, unmanageable. *See* **unruly.**

non compos mentis *adjective*
▶ crazy, lunatic, mad. *See* **insane** (1).

nonconformist *noun*
1. Someone who dissents from the doctrine of an established church ▶ dissident, sectarian. *See* **separatist. 2.** Someone with unconventional opinions or approaches ▶ free-thinker, independent, maverick. *See* **rebel** (2).

nonconformity *noun*
▶ contrast, discrepancy, divergence. *See* **difference** (1).

nondescript *adjective*
▶ common, mediocre, standard. *See* **ordinary** (1).

nondiscriminatory *adjective*
▶ balanced, detached, unbiased, unprejudiced. *See* **fair¹** (1).

none *pronoun*
▶ not anybody, no one. *See* **nobody.**

nonentity *noun*
1. A totally insignificant person ▶ cipher, lightweight, menial, nebbish, no-account, nobody, nonperson, nothing, obscurity, scrub, small fry, whipper-snapper. *Informal:* pip-squeak, squirt, zero. *Slang:* punk, shrimp, small fish, twerp, zilch. **Idioms:** small potatoes, small fish in a big pond. *See also* **drip, fool, squirt. 2.** The condition of not existing ▶ nonexistence, nullity. *See* **nothingness** (1).

nonessential *adjective*
▶ inessential, needless, unneeded. *See* **unnecessary.**

nonesuch *noun*
A person or thing so excellent as to have no equal or match ▶ nonpareil, paragon, phoenix. *See also* **best, celebrity, model.**

nonetheless *adverb*
▶ however, nevertheless, yet. *See* **still** (1).

nonevent *noun*
▶ anticlimax, bust, washout. *See* **disappointment** (2).

nonexistence *noun*
▶ nilhility, nullity. *See* **nothingness** (1).

nonexistent *adjective*
▶ gone, missing, truant. *See* **absent** (1).

nonfeasance *noun*
1. Nonperformance of what ought to be done ▶ delinquency, dereliction. *See* **failure** (2). **2.** An act of breaking a law or of nonfulfillment of an obligation ▶ infraction, infringement, violation. *See* **breach** (1).

nonflammable *adjective*
▶ fire-resistant, flameproof, incombustible. *See* **fireproof.**

nonnative *adjective*
▶ alien, exotic, strange. *See* **foreign** (1).

no-nonsense *adjective*
1. Characterized by careful thought and a lack of frivolity or exaggeration ▶ earnest, sober, solemn. *See* **serious** (1). **2.** Serving or capable of serving a useful purpose ▶ functional, useful, utilitarian. *See* **practical** (1).

nonpareil *adjective*
Without equal or rival ▸ incomparable, singular, un-paralleled. *See* **unique** (1).

nonpareil *noun*
1. A person or thing so excellent as to have no equal or match ▸ nonesuch, paragon, phoenix. *See also* **best, celebrity, model. 2.** One that is worthy of imitation or duplication ▸ exemplar, ideal, paradigm. *See* **model** (1).

nonpartisan *adjective*
1. Not inclining toward or actively taking either side in a matter under dispute ▸ nonaligned, unbiased. *See* **neutral** (1). **2.** Free from bias in judgment ▸ impartial, just, objective. *See* **fair¹** (1).

nonpartisanship *noun*
▸ equitableness, impartiality, objectivity. *See* **fairness.**

nonperformer *noun*
▸ bust, loser. *See* **failure** (1).

nonphysical *adjective*
▸ disembodied, incorporeal, unbodied. *See* **immaterial** (1).

nonplus *verb*
▸ confound, perplex. *Informal:* stump. *See* **baffle** (1).

nonprofessional *noun*
One lacking professional skill ▸ dabbler, dilettante, layperson. *See* **amateur.**

nonprofessional *adjective*
Lacking the required professional skill ▸ dilettante, unskilled. *See* **amateurish.**

nonresident *noun*
A person coming from another country or into a new community ▸ alien, outsider, stranger. *See* **foreigner.**

nonresident *adjective*
From or characteristic of another place ▸ alien, exotic, strange. *See* **foreign** (1).

nonresistant *adjective*
▸ acquiescent, resigned. *See* **passive.**

nonsense *noun*
1. Something that does not have or make sense ▸ balderdash, blather, bunkum, claptrap, drivel, foolishness, garbage, hogwash, idiocy, piffle, poppycock, rigmarole, rot, rubbish, senselessness, silliness, tomfoolery, trash, twaddle. *Informal:* tommyrot. *Slang:* applesauce, baloney, bilge, bull, bunk, crap, hooey, malarkey. *See also* **emptiness, gibberish. 2.** Empty or foolish talk ▸ blather, jabber, twaddle. *See* **babble** (1). *See* **3.** Foolish behavior ▸ folly, silliness, tomfoolery. *See* **foolishness. 4.** Something or things of little importance ▸ frivolity, minutia, trivia. *See* **trifle** (1).

nonsensical *adjective*
▸ daft, idiotic, ludicrous. *See* **foolish.**

nonstop *adjective*
Existing without interruption or end ▸ constant, endless, everlasting, perpetual. *See* **continual.**

nonstop *adverb*
Without stop or interruption ▸ endlessly, forever, perpetually. *See* **continually.**

nonuniform *adjective*
▸ asymmetric, crooked. *See* **irregular** (1).

nonviolent *adjective*
▸ conciliatory, dovish, pacifistic. *See* **peaceable.**

noodle *noun*
Slang The uppermost part of the body ▸ crown, pate. *See* **head** (1).

no one *pronoun*
▸ none, not anybody. *See* **nobody.**

noose *noun*
1. A length of line folded over and joined at the ends so as to form a curve or circle ▸ circuit, eye, ring. *See* **loop** (1). **2.** A band or fiber user to tie, connect, or support ▸ cable, rope, string. *See* **cord. 3.** A device or stratagem for catching or tricking a person or animal ▸ booby trap, pit, snare. *See* **trap** (1).

nope *adverb*
▸ not. *Informal:* noway. *See* **no.**

norm *noun*
1. A regular or customary matter, condition, or course of events ▸ commonplace, ordinary, rule. *See* **usual. 2.** Something that represents a midpoint between extremes ▸ mean, par. *See* **average** (1). **3.** A means by which individuals are compared and judged ▸ criterion, mark, measure. *See* **standard** (1).

normal *adjective*
1. Occurring or encountered regularly ▸ commonplace, familiar, regular. *See* **common** (1). **2.** Mentally healthy ▸ compos mentis, lucid, rational, sane. *Idioms:* all there, in one's right mind, of sound mind. *See also* **healthy. 3.** Conforming to established standards ▸ conformist, orthodox, traditional. *See* **conventional** (1). **4.** Having good health ▸ fit, well. *See* **healthy** (1).

normalcy *or* **normality** *noun*
▸ normality, ordinariness, routineness. *See* **usualness.**

normalize *verb*
▸ standardize, stylize. *See* **conventionalize.**

normally *adverb*
▸ customarily, generally, naturally. *See* **usually.**

nose *noun*
1. The human organ of smell ▸ proboscis. *Informal:* beak, snoot. *Slang:* honker, nozzle, schnoz, schnozzle, smeller, sniffer, snout. **2.** The sense by which odors are perceived ▸ olfaction, scent, smell. **3.** Skill in perceiving, discriminating, or judging ▸ keenness, perceptiveness, shrewdness. *See* **discernment** (1).

nose *verb*
1. To perceive with the olfactory sense ▸ sniff, whiff. *See* **smell** (1). **2.** *Informal* To look into or inquire about curiously, inquisitively, or in a meddlesome fashion ▸ poke, pry, snoop. *Informal:* sniff about (*or* around). *Idiom:* stick one's nose into. *See also* **meddle.**

nose out *verb*
To pursue and locate ▸ hunt down, run down. *See* **trace** (1).

nosedive *noun*
1. A sudden downward motion toward the ground ▸ dive, plunge, tumble. *See* **fall** (1). **2.** A usually swift downward trend, as in prices ▸ decline, dip, downswing. *See* **fall** (3).

nose-dive *verb*
1. To move downward in response to gravity ▸ drop, plunge, tumble. *See* **fall** (1). 2. To become lower in value or price ▸ dive, drop, plummet. *See* **fall** (7).

nosegay *noun*
▸ corsage, posy. *See* **bouquet** (1).

nosey *adjective*
See **nosy**.

nosh *noun*
Informal A light meal ▸ snack. *Informal:* bite. *See* **refreshment** (1).

nosiness *noun*
▸ inquisitiveness. *Informal:* snoopiness. *See* **curiosity** (2).

nostrum *noun*
▸ elixir, medication, remedy. *See* **cure**.

nosy *or* **nosey** *adjective*
▸ inquisitive, meddlesome, officious. *See* **curious** (1). *See synonym note at* **curious**.

not *adverb*
▸ nay. *Informal:* nope. *See* **no**.

notability *noun*
1. Wide recognition for one's deeds ▸ glory, note, prestige. *See* **fame**. 2. An important, influential person ▸ eminence, personage. *See* **dignitary**.

notable *adjective*
1. Widely known ▸ celebrated, noted, renowned. *See* **famous**. *See synonym note at* **famous**. 2. Beyond what is usual, normal, or customary ▸ extraordinary, outstanding, remarkable. *See* **exceptional** (1).

notable *noun*
1. An important, influential person ▸ eminence, personage. *Slang:* big shot. *See* **dignitary**. 2. A famous person ▸ luminary, personality, star. *See* **celebrity** (1). *See synonym note at* **celebrity**.

notably *adverb*
▸ exceedingly, extremely, highly. *See* **very**.

notation *noun*
▸ memorandum, reminder. *See* **note** (1).

notch *noun*
1. An opening made with a sharp object ▸ gouge, slash, slit. *See* **cut** (1). 2. *Informal* One of the units in a course, as on an ascending or descending scale ▸ degree, grade, level, peg, point, rung, stage, step. 3. *Informal* One of the units in a course, as on an ascending or descending scale ▸ interval, level, step. *See* **degree** (1). 4. A small mark or hole made by a sharp, pointed object ▸ nick, puncture. *See* **prick** (1).

notch *verb*
1. *Informal* To gain a point or points in a game or contest ▸ post, score, tally. *Idioms:* make a goal (*or* point). 2. To penetrate with a sharp edge ▸ bayonet, incise, pierce, slash. *See* **cut** (1).

notched *adjective*
▸ dentate, serrate. *See* **saw-toothed**.

note *noun*
1. A brief record that is written as an aid to the memory ▸ jotting, memorandum, notation, reminder. *Informal:* memo. 2. A written communica-

tion directed to another ▸ correspondence, epistle, missive. *See* **letter** (1). *See synonym note at* **letter**. 3. An expression of fact or opinion ▸ observation, reflection, remark. *See* **comment** (1). 4. Critical explanation or analysis ▸ exegesis, exposition, interpretation. *See* **commentary**. 5. Something visible or evident that gives grounds for believing in the existence or presence of something else ▸ evidence, indication, symptom. *See* **sign** (1). *See synonym note at* **sign**. 6. Wide recognition for one's deeds ▸ glory, prestige, renown. *See* **fame**. 7. The act of noting, observing, or taking into account ▸ heed, mark, regard. *See* **notice** (1). 8. An item inserted, as in a diary, register, or reference book ▸ heading, posting. *See* **entry** (1).

note *verb*
1. To perceive with a special effort of the senses or the mind ▸ detect, mark. *See* **notice**. *See synonym note at* **notice**. 2. To state facts, opinions, or explanations ▸ observe, opine, remark. *See* **comment**. 3. To make reference to something ▸ allude (to), mention, point out. *See* **refer** (1). *See synonym note at* **refer**.

noted *adjective*
▸ celebrated, prominent, renowned. *See* **famous**. *See synonym note at* **famous**.

noteworthy *adjective*
▸ extraordinary, outstanding, remarkable. *See* **exceptional** (1).

nothing *noun*
1. No thing; not anything ▸ nil, null. *Informal:* zero. *Slang:* diddly-squat, goose egg, nix, squat, zilch. 2. A totally insignificant person ▸ nobody, scrub, small fry. *See* **nonentity**. 3. The condition of not existing ▸ nonexistence, nullity. *See* **nothingness** (1).

nothing *adjective*
Informal Lacking worth and value ▸ drossy, good-for-nothing, valueless. *See* **worthless** (1).

nothingness *noun*
1. The condition of not existing ▸ nihility, nonbeing, nonentity, nonexistence, nonsubsistence, nothing, nullity. 2. Empty, unfilled space ▸ barrenness, blankness, emptiness, vacancy, vacuity, vacuum, void. *See also* **deep**.

notice *noun*
1. The act of noting, observing, or taking into account ▸ attention, cognizance, espial, heed, looking, mark, note, observance, observation, regard, remark, seeing, viewing, watching, witnessing. 2. A usually public posting that conveys a message ▸ billboard, placard. *See* **sign** (2). 3. Something announced or communicated ▸ announcement, bulletin, notification. *See* **message** (1). 4. Critical explanation or analysis ▸ criticism, critique, review. *See* **commentary**. 5. An announcement distributed on paper to a large number of people ▸ circular, flier, handbill, leaflet. 6. A report giving information ▸ advisory, bulletin. *See also* **report, warning**. 7. A detail of news or information ▸ bulletin, dispatch. *See* **item** (1).

notice *verb*
To perceive with a special effort of the senses or the

mind ► descry, detect, discern, distinguish, mark, mind, note, observe, recognize, remark, see. *See also* **discover, see.**

✦ **CORE SYNONYMS:** *notice, note, remark, observe.* These verbs mean to perceive with a special effort of the senses or the mind. *Notice, note,* and *remark* suggest close, detailed observation, and *note* in particular implies making a careful, systematic mental recording: *I notice that you're out of sorts. Be careful to note that we turn left at the museum. "Their assemblies afforded me daily opportunities of remarking characters and manners"* (Samuel Johnson). *Observe* emphasizes careful, closely directed attention: *"I saw the pots . . . and observed that they did not crack at all"* (Daniel Defoe).

---

noticeable *adjective*
1. Readily attracting notice ► arresting, bold, commanding, conspicuous, distinguished, eminent, eye-catching, impressive, marked, observable, outstanding, pointed, prominent, pronounced, remarkable, salient, signal, striking, undisguised. *Idiom:* sticking out like a sore thumb. *See also* **exceptional, obvious.**
2. Readily seen, perceived, or understood ► evident, observable, obvious. *See* **apparent** (1). **3.** Capable of being perceived by the senses or the mind ► discernible, palpable, perceivable. *See* **perceptible.** *See synonym note at* **perceptible.**

✦ **CORE SYNONYMS:** *noticeable, observable, marked, conspicuous, prominent, outstanding, salient, remarkable, arresting, striking.* These adjectives mean readily attracting notice. *Noticeable* and *observable* both refer to something that can be readily noticed or observed: *"His long, feminine eyelashes were very noticeable"* (Joseph Conrad). *The prowler's movements were observable from the window.* What is *marked* is emphatically evident: *a marked limp; a marked success. Conspicuous* applies to what is immediately apparent and noteworthy: *a conspicuous stain. "Conspicuous consumption of valuable goods is a means of reputability to the gentleman of leisure"* (Thorstein Veblen). *Prominent* and *outstanding* connote a standing out, especially among others of a kind: *the most prominent mountain in the range; the century's outstanding figures.* What is *salient* is so prominent and consequential that it seems to leap out and claim the attention: *"Defenders of the pit bull always seem to miss the salient point that it is the ferocity of the bite, not the number of bites, that has made the dog so feared today"* (Sports Illustrated). *Remarkable* describes what elicits comment because it is unusual or extraordinary: *"This story of Mongolian conquests is surely the most remarkable in all history"* (H.G. Wells). *Arresting* applies to what attracts and holds the attention: *one of Ellington's most arresting compositions. Striking* describes something that seizes the attention and produces a vivid impression on the sight or the mind: *The child bears a striking resemblance to his uncle.*

---

notification *noun*
1. Something that is announced or communicated ► announcement, notice, statement. *See* **message** (1). **2.** The act of announcing ► proclamation, publication. *See* **announcement** (1).

notify *verb*
► acquaint, apprise, fill in. *See* **inform** (1).

notion *noun*
1. Something thought to be true ► conviction, persuasion, view. *See* **belief** (1). **2.** That which exists in the mind as the product of careful mental activity ► conception, image. *See* **idea** (1). *See synonym note at* **idea.** **3.** An impulsive turn of mind ► conceit, impulse, whim. *See* **fancy** (1). **4.** An intuitive awareness or sense of something ► idea, impression, intuition. *See* **feeling** (1).

notional *adjective*
1. Existing only in the imagination ► chimerical, fanciful, unreal. *See* **imaginary.** **2.** Existing only in concept and not in reality ► conceptual, hypothetical, virtual. *See* **theoretical** (2).

notoriety *noun*
1. Unfavorable, usually unsavory renown ► disrepute, ill fame, ill repute, infamousness, infamy, notoriousness. **2.** Wide recognition for one's deeds ► popularity, renown, repute. *See* **fame.**

notorious *adjective*
1. Known widely and unfavorably ► common, disreputable, ill-famed, ill-reputed, infamous. *See also* **evil, shady. 2.** Widely known ► noted, popular, well-known. *See* **famous.**

notoriousness *noun*
► infamy, infamousness. *See* **notoriety** (1).

nourish *verb*
1. To sustain a living organism with food ► feed, regale. *Idiom:* wine and dine. *See also* **support. 2.** To help grow or develop ► foster, nurse. *See* **nurture. 3.** To keep steadily in mind ► harbor, nurse. *See* **bear** (2). **4.** To help bring about ► cultivate, facilitate. *See* **promote** (2).

nourishing *adjective*
► alimentary, nutritional. *See* **nutritious.**

nourishment *noun*
► bread, fare, nutriment. *See* **food.**

novel *adjective*
1. Not the same as what was previously known or done ► fresh, innovative, original. *See* **new** (1). *See synonym note at* **new. 2.** Not usual or ordinary ► atypic, atypical, unconventional. *See* **unusual** (1).

novel *noun*
A narrative not based on fact ► fiction, fable, romance, story. *See also* **yarn.**

novelty *noun*
1. The quality of being novel ► freshness, imaginativeness, innovativeness, newfangledness, newness, originality, rareness, rarity, recentness, strangeness, uncommonness, uniqueness, unusualness. **2.** A new and unusual thing ► innovation. *Idioms:* the latest craze (*or* fashion *or* thing), the in thing, whole new ball of wax. **3.** A small showy article ► bauble, bibelot, bric-a-brac, curio, gewgaw, gimcrack, gimmick, knick-

knack, toy, trifle, trinket, whatnot. *Slang:* chachka. *See also* **gadget, remembrance.**

novice *noun*
1. One who is just starting to learn or do something ▸ fledgling, neophyte, newcomer. *See* **beginner. 2.** An entrant who has not yet taken the final vows of a religious order ▸ neophyte, novitiate, postulant.

novitiate *noun*
1. An entrant who has not yet taken the final vows of a religious order ▸ neophyte, novice, postulant. **2.** One who is just starting to learn or do something ▸ fledgling, neophyte, novice. *See* **beginner.**

now *adverb*
1. At this moment ▸ actually, at present, currently. *Idioms:* even (*or* just *or* right) now, at this instant (*or* moment *or* time), here and now. *See also* **soon. 2.** Without delay ▸ forthwith, instantly, straightaway. *See* **immediately** (1). **3.** At the present; these days ▸ nowadays, today. *Idioms:* in our time, in this day and age.

now *noun*
The current time ▸ nowadays, present, today. *Idioms:* modern times, the here and now, the present age (*or* day *or* time).

now *adjective*
In existence now ▸ current, present-day. *See* **present¹** (1).

nowadays *adverb*
At the present; these days ▸ now, today. *Idioms:* in our time, in this day and age.

nowadays *noun*
The current time ▸ present, today. *See* **now.**

noway *adverb*
▸ not. *Informal:* nope. *See* **no.**

noxious *adjective*
1. Capable of injuring or killing by poision ▸ malignant, toxic, venomous. *See* **poisonous** (1). **2.** Causing harm or injury ▸ deleterious, evil, injurious. *See* **harmful.**

nozzle *noun*
Slang The human organ of smell ▸ proboscis. *Informal:* snoot. *See* **nose** (1).

nuance *noun*
▸ gradation, hue, subtlety. *See* **shade** (1). *See synonym note at* **shade.**

nub *noun*
1. An unevenness or elevation on a surface ▸ lump, protuberance. *See* **bump** (1). **2.** The most essential part ▸ essence, marrow, quintessence. *See* **heart** (1).

nuclear *adjective*
▸ focal, median, middle. *See* **central** (1).

nucleus *noun*
1. A source of further growth and development ▸ kernel, seed. *See* **germ** (2). **2.** A point of origin or crucial factor ▸ core, focus, root. *See* **center** (3). **3.** The most central or essential part ▸ essence, marrow, quintessence. *See* **heart** (1). *See synonym note at* **heart.**

nude *adjective*
1. Not wearing any clothes ▸ au naturel, bare, dis-robed, exposed, naked, stripped, unclad, unclothed, undraped, undressed. *Idioms:* buck naked, in one's birthday suit, in the (*or* altogether *or* buff *or* raw), naked as a jaybird, stark naked, without a stitch. **2.** Without the usual covering ▸ bald, hairless, naked. *See* **bare** (3).

nudeness *noun*
▸ nakedness, undress. *See* **nudity.**

nudge *verb*
To apply pressure on, against, or with ▸ press, prod, shove. *See* **push** (1).

nudge *noun*
An act of thrusting into or against, as to attract attention ▸ jab, poke, prod. *See* **dig** (1).

nudity *noun*
The state of being without clothes ▸ bareness, exposure, nakedness, nudeness, undress.

nugatory *adjective*
▸ inconsequential, negligible, trifling. *See* **trivial.**

nugget *noun*
▸ clod, wad. *See* **lump¹** (1).

nuisance *noun*
▸ bother, irritant, torment. *See* **annoyance** (2).

null *noun*
No thing; not anything ▸ nil. *Informal:* zero. *See* **nothing** (1).

null *adjective*
Containing nothing ▸ bare, vacant, vacuous. *See* **empty** (1).

nullification *noun*
▸ annulment, invalidation, negation. *See* **abolition.**

nullify *verb*
1. To put an end to ▸ annul, negate, void. *See* **abolish** (1). **2.** To make ineffective by applying an opposite force ▸ negate, neutralize. *See* **cancel** (2).

nullity *noun*
▸ nonexistence, nothing. *See* **nothingness** (1).

numb *adjective*
Lacking physical feeling or sensitivity ▸ inert, lifeless, unfeeling. *See* **dead** (2).

numb *verb*
1. To render less sensitive ▸ benumb, desensitize. *See* **deaden** (1). **2.** To render helpless, as by emotion ▸ stun, stupefy. *See* **paralyze** (1).

number *noun*
1. An amount represented in numerals ▸ figure, quantity. *See also* **total. 2.** A brief composition written or adapted for singing ▸ hymn, lyrics, tune. *See* **song** (1). **3.** *Slang* A characteristic behavior or performance ▸ act. *See* **bit¹** (5). **4.** An indefinite amount or extent ▸ measure, portion. *See* **quantity** (2).

number *verb*
1. To note items one by one in order to get a total ▸ numerate, tally. *See* **count** (2). **2.** To come to in number or quantity ▸ add up, reach, total. *See* **amount** (1).

number one *noun*
A leading contestant or sure winner ▸ favorite, front-runner, leader, vanguard. *Informal:* shoo-in.

number one *adjective*
Most important, influential, or significant ▸ chief, key, main, principal. *See* **primary** (1).

numbers *noun*
Arithmetic calculations ▸ arithmetic, computation, figures. *See also* **addition, calculation.**

numerate *verb*
1. To note items one by one in order to get a total ▸ score, tally. *See* **count** (2). **2.** To name or specify one by one ▸ list, tick off. *See* **enumerate** (1).

numeration *noun*
▸ enumeration, tally. *See* **count** (1).

numerical *adjective*
▸ sequential, serial. *See* **consecutive.**

numerous *adjective*
▸ legion, multitudinous, myriad. *See* **many.**

numinous *adjective*
▸ metaphysical, superhuman. *See* **supernatural** (1).

numskull *noun*
▸ dummy, dunce, thickhead. *See* **dullard.**

nuptial *adjective*
▸ connubial, spousal, wedded. *See* **marital.**

nuptials *noun*
▸ espousal, marriage, spousals. *See* **wedding.**

nurse *verb*
1. To help grow or develop ▸ foster, nourish. *See* **nurture.** *See synonym note at* **nurture. 2.** To keep steadily in mind ▸ harbor, nourish. *See* **bear** (2).

nursling *noun*
▸ baby, infant. *See* **baby** (1).

nurture *verb*
1. To help grow or develop ▸ cultivate, foster, nourish, nurse, provide for, sustain, tend. *See also* **grow, rear²,**

tend². **2.** To help bring about ▸ cultivate, facilitate. *See* **promote** (2).

✚ CORE SYNONYMS: *nurture, cultivate, foster, nurse.* These verbs mean to promote and sustain the growth and development of someone or something: *nurturing hopes; cultivating tolerance; foster friendly relations; nursed the fledgling business.*

---

nut *noun*
1. *Slang* A person who is regarded as strange, eccentric, or crazy ▸ lunatic. *Informal:* loony. *Slang:* cuckoo, weirdo. *See* **crackpot. 2.** *Slang* An ardent devotee ▸ enthusiast, fanatic, junkie. *See* **fan². 3.** *Slang* The uppermost part of the body ▸ crown, pate. *See* **head** (1).

nutrient *adjective*
▸ alimentary, nutritional. *See* **nutritious.**

nutrition *or* **nutriment** *noun*
▸ bread, meat, nourishment. *See* **food.**

nutritious *or* **nutritional** *or* **nutritive** *adjective*
Providing nourishment ▸ alimentary, nourishing, nutrient. *See also* **healthful.**

nuts *adjective*
1. *Slang* Afflicted with or exhibiting irrationality and mental unsoundness ▸ crazy, lunatic, mad. *See* **insane** (1). **2.** *Slang* Showing or having enthusiasm ▸ fervent, rabid, zealous. *See* **enthusiastic** (1).

nutty *adjective*
Slang Afflicted with or exhibiting irrationality and mental unsoundness ▸ brainsick, demented, off. *See* **insane** (1).

nuzzle *verb*
▸ cuddle, nestle, snug. *See* **snuggle.**

O

oaf *noun*
A large, ungainly, and dull-witted person ▸ ape, bear, gawk, hulk, lout, lump, ox. *Informal:* lummox. *Slang:* goon, klutz, lug, meatball, meathead, palooka, schlep, schlub. *See also* **blunderer, dullard, fool.**

oath *noun*
1. A profane or obscene term ▸ curse, expletive. *See* **swearword. 2.** A denunciation invoking a wish or threat of evil or injury ▸ damnation, malediction. *See* **curse** (1). **3.** A declaration that one will or will not do a certain thing ▸ covenant, pledge, vow. *See* **promise** (1).

obduracy *or* **obdurateness** *noun*
▸ bullheadedness, hardheadedness, rigidity. *See* **stubbornness.**

obdurate *adjective*
1. Lacking compassion or mercy ▸ heartless, insensi-

tive, merciless. *See* **callous. 2.** Firmly, often unreasonably immovable in purpose or will ▸ bullheaded, dogged, obstinate. *See* **stubborn** (1). *See synonym note at* **stubborn.**

obeah *noun*
▸ mascot, talisman. *See* **charm** (1).

obedience *noun*
The quality, state, or act of willingly carrying out the wishes of others ▸ acquiescence, amenability, amenableness, complaisance, compliance, compliancy, deference, dutifulness, observance, submission, submissiveness, tractability, tractableness. *See also* **loyalty.**

obedient *adjective*
Willing to carry out the wishes of others ▸ acquiescent, amenable, biddable, complaisant, compliant, conformable, docile, duteous, dutiful, pliant, submis-

sive, supple, tractable. *See also* **deferential, loyal, passive.**

obeisance *noun*
1. An inclination of the head or body, as in greeting, consent, courtesy, submission, or worship ► genuflection, nod. *See* **bow**[1]. 2. Great respect or high public esteem accorded as a right or as due ► deference, homage. *See* **honor** (1). *See synonym note at* **honor.**

obeisant *adjective*
► duteous, dutiful. *See* **deferential.**

obese *adjective*
► corpulent, overweight, rotund. *See* **fat** (1). *See synonym note at* **fat.**

obey *verb*
► heed, live by, observe. *See* **follow** (4).

obfuscate *verb*
1. To make dim ► blur, fog, shadow. *See* **obscure** (1). 2. To make complex, intricate, or perplexing ► entangle, perplex, tangle. *See* **complicate.**

obiter dictum *noun*
► observation, reflection, remark. *See* **comment** (1).

object *noun*
1. Something having material existence ► article, body, item, mass, something, thing. *Informal:* thingamabob, thingamajig, thingy. *See also* **gadget.** 2. A focus of attention, thought, or action ► butt, focus, receiver, recipient, subject, target. 3. One that exists independently ► being, entity. *See* **thing** (1). 4. What one intends to do or achieve ► goal, objective. *See* **intention.** *See synonym note at* **intention.**

object *verb*
1. To express opposition, often by argument ► challenge, demur, except, expostulate, inveigh, oppose, protest, remonstrate, speak up. *Informal:* kick, squawk. *See also* **argue, complain, contest, quibble.** 2. To have an objection ► care, mind. *See* **care.**

object to *verb*
To have or express an unfavorable opinion of ► condemn, disfavor, reprobate. *See* **disapprove** (1).

✚ CORE SYNONYMS: *object, protest, demur, remonstrate, expostulate.* These verbs mean to express opposition to something, usually by presenting arguments against it. *Object* implies the expression of disapproval or distaste: *"Freedom of the press in Britain is freedom to print such of the proprietor's prejudices as the advertisers don't object to"* (Hannen Swaffer). *Protest* suggests strong opposition, usually forthrightly expressed: *The citizens protested against the tax hike.* To *demur* is to raise an objection that may delay decision or action: *We proposed a revote, but the president demurred.* *Remonstrate* implies the presentation of objections, complaints, or reproof: *"The people of Connecticut . . . remonstrated against the bill"* (George Bancroft). To *expostulate* is to express objection in the form of earnest reasoning: *The teacher expostulated with them regarding their bad behavior.*

---

objectification *noun*
► incarnation, manifestation, personification. *See* **embodiment** (1).

objectify *verb*
► externalize, manifest, materialize, substantiate. *See* **embody** (1).

objection *noun*
An expression of opposition ► argument, challenge, complaint, demur, demurral, disagreement, dispute, exception, expostulation, fuss, grievance, problem, protest, protestation, remonstrance, remonstration. *Slang:* kick.

objectionable *adjective*
Arousing disapproval ► disagreeable, exceptionable, ill-favored, improper, inadmissible, unacceptable, undesirable, unsuitable, unwanted, unwelcome. *See also* **deplorable, offensive.**

objective *adjective*
1. Composed of or relating to things that occupy space and can be perceived by the senses ► corporeal, tangible. *See* **physical** (1). 2. Having physical or verifiable existence ► substantial, tangible. *See* **real** (1). 3. Free from bias in judgment ► impartial, nonpartisan, unprejudiced. *See* **fair**[1] (1). *See synonym note at* **fair**[1]. 4. Having or indicating an awareness of things as they really are ► practical, pragmatic, prosaic. *See* **realistic** (1).

objective *noun*
What one intends to do or achieve ► end, goal, object. *See* **intention.** *See synonym note at* **intention.**

objectively *adverb*
► equitably, impartially, justly. *See* **fairly** (1).

objectivity *or* **objectiveness** *noun*
► detachment, impartiality, nonpartisanship. *See* **fairness.**

object lesson *noun*
► caveat, warning. *See* **example** (2).

objurgate *verb*
► chide, rebuke, reprimand. *See* **chastise** (1).

oblation *noun*
► immolation, sacrifice, victim. *See* **offering** (1).

obligate *verb*
1. To oblige to do or not do by force of authority, propriety, or custom ► expect, oblige, require, suppose. *See also* **must.** 2. To cause a person or thing to act or move in spite of resistance ► coerce, compel, pressure. *See* **force** (1). *See synonym note at* **force.** 3. To be morally bound to do ► bind, pledge. *See* **commit** (2).

obligated *adjective*
1. Owing something, such as gratitude, to another ► beholden, indebted, thankful. *See* **obliged** (1). 2. Being legally or morally required to do something ► bound, committed, compelled. *See* **obliged** (2).

obligation *noun*
1. An act or course of action that is demanded of one, as by position, custom, law, or religion ► charge, commitment, onus. *See* **duty** (1). 2. Something, such as money, owed by one person to another ► indebtedness, liability, score. *See* **debt** (1). 3. A condition of owing something to another ► encumbrance, indebtedness, liability. *See* **debt** (2).

obligatory *adjective*
▸ imperative, mandatory, necessary, requisite. *See* **required** (1).

oblige *verb*
1. To perform a service or courteous act for ▸ accommodate, aid, assist, favor, help, indulge, serve. **2.** To cause to do or not do by force of authority, propriety, or custom ▸ expect, obligate, require, suppose. *See also* **must. 3.** To cause a person or thing to act or move in spite of resistance ▸ coerce, compel, pressure. *See* **force** (1). *See synonym note at* **force. 4.** To be morally bound to do ▸ charge, obligate, pledge. *See* **commit** (2).

✤ CORE SYNONYMS: *oblige, accommodate, favor, indulge.* These verbs mean to perform a service or a courteous act for: *obliged me by keeping the matter quiet; accommodating her by lending her money; favor an audience with an encore; indulged the twins by allowing them to stay up late.*

---

obliged *adjective*
1. Owing something, such as gratitude, to another ▸ beholden, grateful, indebted, obligated, thankful. *Idiom:* in someone's debt. **2.** Being legally or morally required to do something ▸ bound, committed, compelled, constrained, impelled, obligated, pledged, required, sworn. *Idioms:* duty (*or* honor) bound, under obligation (*or* contract *or* oath). *See also* **liable.**

obliging *adjective*
Ready to do favors for another ▸ accommodating, agreeable, complaisant, considerate, generous, helpful, indulgent. *See also* **amiable, obedient, willing.**

oblique *adjective*
1. At an angle ▸ angled, askew, aslant, beveled, bias, biased, canted, diagonal, inclined, leaning, listing, pitched, raked, skewed, slanted, slanting, sloped, sloping, tilted. *See also* **transverse. 2.** Not proceeding straight to the point or object ▸ circuitous, devious, tortuous. *See* **indirect** (1).

obliterate *verb*
1. To destroy all traces of ▸ eradicate, liquidate, remove. *See* **annihilate** (1). *See synonym note at* **annihilate. 2.** To cross out or remove ▸ delete, erase, strike (out). *See* **cancel** (1). **3.** To pull down or break up so that reconstruction is impossible ▸ dismantle, level, tear down. *See* **destroy** (2).

obliteration *noun*
1. Utter destruction ▸ extermination, extinction, liquidation. *See* **annihilation** (1). **2.** The act of erasing or the condition of being erased ▸ deletion, expunction. *See* **erasure.**

oblivion *noun*
▸ anonymity, namelessness, unimportance. *See* **obscurity** (1).

oblivious *adjective*
1. So lost in thought as to be unable to remember ▸ abstracted, faraway, forgetful. *See* **absent-minded. 2.** Not aware or informed ▸ clueless, unaware, unconscious. *See* **ignorant** (3).

obliviousness *noun*
▸ nescience, unawareness. *See* **ignorance** (2).

oblong *adjective*
▸ elliptical, ovoid. *See* **oval.**

obloquy *noun*
1. Sustained, harshly abusive language ▸ abuse, billingsgate, invective. *See* **vituperation. 2.** Loss of or damage to one's reputation ▸ discredit, disrepute, humiliation. *See* **disgrace. 3.** The expression of injurious, malicious statements about someone ▸ defamation, denigration, slander. *See* **libel.**

obnoxious *adjective*
▸ contemptible, disgusting, repugnant. *See* **offensive** (1).

obscene *adjective*
1. Offensive to accepted standards of decency ▸ barnyard, bawdy, broad, coarse, dirty, filthy, foul, gross, indecent, lewd, nasty, profane, ribald, scatologic, scatological, scurrilous, smutty, vulgar. *Slang:* raunchy. *See also* **erotic, racy. 2.** Exceeding the bounds of morality, decency, or reason ▸ appalling, monstrous, shocking. *See* **outrageous.**

obscenity *noun*
1. The quality or state of being obscene ▸ bawdiness, coarseness, dirtiness, filthiness, foulness, grossness, indecentness, lewdness, nastiness, profaneness, profanity, scurrility, scurrilousness, smuttiness, vulgarity, vulgarness. *Slang:* raunch, raunchiness. **2.** Something that is offensive to accepted standards of decency ▸ bawdry, dirt, filth, pornography, profanity, ribaldry, scatology, sleaze, smut, vulgarity. *Slang:* porn, raunch. *See also* **impropriety. 3.** A profane or obscene term ▸ curse, expletive. *See* **swearword.**

obscure *adjective*
1. Not widely understood ▸ abstruse, arcane, cabalistic, esoteric, occult, recondite. *See also* **mysterious. 2.** Not widely known ▸ insignificant, little-known, undistinguished, unheard-of, unknown. *See also* **anonymous, remote. 3.** Deficient in brightness ▸ dim, murky, shadowy. *See* **dark** (1). *See synonym note at* **dark. 4.** Not clearly perceptible ▸ dim, faint, indefinite. *See* **unclear** (1). **5.** Not readily noticed or seen ▸ unnoticeable, unobtrusive. *See* **inconspicuous. 6.** Liable to more than one interpretation ▸ equivocal, nebulous, vague. *See* **ambiguous** (2). **7.** Lacking certainty or clarity ▸ dubious, indeterminate, questionable, unclear. *See* **ambiguous** (1). *See synonym note at* **ambiguous.**

obscure *verb*
1. To make dim or unclear ▸ adumbrate, becloud, bedim, befog, blear, blur, cloud, dim, dull, eclipse, fog, gloom, mist, obfuscate, overcast, overshadow, shadow. *See also* **shade. 2.** To cut off from sight ▸ conceal, hide, screen. *See* **block** (1). *See synonym note at* **block. 3.** To prevent something from being known ▸ enshroud, mask. *See* **conceal** (1).

obscured *adjective*
1. Lying beyond what is obvious or avowed ▸ concealed, covert, hidden. *See* **ulterior** (1). **2.** Difficult or

impossible to see or distinguish ▸ covert, disguised, unseen. *See* **hidden** (1).

obscurity *noun*
1. The quality or state of being little known ▸ anonymity, insignificance, namelessness, oblivion, obscureness, unimportance. 2. Absence or deficiency of light ▸ darkness, dimness, murkiness, obscureness. *See* **dark** (1). 3. The quality or state of being imprecise or indefinite ▸ ambiguousness, equivocalness, unclearness. *See* **vagueness**.

obsequies *noun*
▸ funeral service, memorial service, requiem. *See* **funeral**.

obsequious *adjective*
▸ menial, subservient. *See* **servile**.

observable *adjective*
1. Readily seen, perceived, or understood ▸ evident, noticeable, obvious. *See* **apparent** (1). *See synonym note at* **apparent**. 2. Capable of being perceived by the senses or the mind ▸ discernible, palpable, perceivable. *See* **perceptible**. 3. Readily attracting notice ▸ conspicuous, outstanding, prominent. *See* **noticeable** (1). *See synonym note at* **noticeable**. 4. Capable of being seen ▸ perceivable, viewable. *See* **visible** (1).

observance *noun*
1. The act of observing, often for an extended time ▸ observation, scrutiny, watch, watching. 2. The act of noting, observing, or taking into account ▸ heed, note, regard. *See* **notice** (1). 3. The act of observing a day or an event with ceremonies ▸ fiesta, holiday, solemnity. *See* **celebration** (2). 4. A formal act or set of acts prescribed by ritual ▸ rite, ritual, tradition. *See* **ceremony** (1). 5. The quality or state of willingly carrying out the wishes of others ▸ compliancy, complaisance, submissiveness. *See* **obedience**. 6. A habitual way of behaving ▸ form, habit, practice. *See* **custom** (1).

observant *adjective*
1. Vigilantly attentive ▸ vigilant, wide-awake. *See* **alert** (1). 2. Cautiously attentive ▸ heedful, mindful, watchful. *See* **careful** (1). *See synonym note at* **careful**.

observation *noun*
1. The act of observing, often for an extended time ▸ observance, scrutiny, watch, watching. 2. The act of noting, observing, or taking into account ▸ heed, note, regard. *See* **notice** (1). 3. An expression of fact or opinion ▸ note, reflection, remark. *See* **comment** (1). *See synonym note at* **comment**.

observatory *noun*
▸ crow's nest, overlook, watchtower. *See* **lookout** (2).

observe *verb*
1. To perceive with a special effort of the senses or the mind ▸ detect, mark. *See* **notice**. *See synonym note at* **notice**. 2. To look at or on attentively or carefully ▸ eye, regard, survey. *See* **watch** (1). 3. To state facts, opinions, or explanations ▸ editorialize, opine, remark. *See* **comment**. 4. To act in conformity with ▸ heed, live by, obey. *See* **follow** (4). 5. To mark a day or an event with ceremonies of respect, festivity, or

rejoicing ▸ celebrate, commemorate, keep, solemnize. *See synonym note at* **celebrate**. *See also* **sanctify**. 6. To obtain knowledge or awareness of something not known before ▸ determine, learn, unearth. *See* **discover**. 7. To pay regular and close attention to ▸ follow, monitor, survey, watch. *Idioms:* have one's (*or* keep an) eye on, keep tabs on.

observer *noun*
▸ beholder, onlooker, spectator. *See* **watcher** (1).

obsess *verb*
1. To come to mind continually ▸ haunt, torment, trouble, weigh on (*or* upon). 2. To dominate the mind or thoughts of ▸ fixate, possess, preoccupy. *See also* **absorb, grip**.

obsessed *adjective*
▸ enamored, enraptured, smitten. *See* **infatuated**.

obsession *noun*
An irrational preoccupation ▸ compulsion, fascination, fetish, fixation, infatuation, mania. *Informal:* thing. *Idiom:* bee in one's bonnet. *See also* **complex, enthusiasm**.

obsessive *adjective*
1. Showing or having enthusiasm ▸ fervent, rabid, zealous. *See* **enthusiastic** (1). 2. Having an insatiable appetite for an activity or pursuit ▸ gluttonous, rapacious, ravenous. *See* **voracious** (1).

obsessiveness *noun*
▸ avidness, omnivorousness, rapaciousness. *See* **voracity**.

obsolescent *adjective*
▸ outdated, outmoded. *See* **obsolete**.

obsolete *adjective*
No longer in use ▸ obsolescent, outdated, outmoded, out-of-date, superannuated, superseded. *Idioms:* in mothballs, on the shelf. *See also* **old-fashioned**.

obsoleteness *noun*
The quality or state of being obsolete ▸ desuetude, disuse, obsoletism, outdatedness, outmodedness.

obstacle *noun*
1. Something that blocks entry or passage ▸ barrier, blockage, hindrance. *See* **bar** (1). *See synonym note at* **bar**. 2. Something that obstructs progress and requires great effort to overcome ▸ complication, hardship, rigor. *See* **difficulty** (1). *See synonym note at* **difficulty**.

obstinacy *noun*
1. The quality or condition of being unruly ▸ intractability, recalcitrance, unmanageability. *See* **unruliness**. 2. The quality or state of being stubbornly inflexible ▸ bullheadedness, hardheadedness, rigidity. *See* **stubbornness**.

obstinate *adjective*
1. Not submitting to discipline or control ▸ ill-behaved, recalcitrant, unmanageable. *See* **unruly**. 2. Difficult to alleviate or cure ▸ persistent, pertinacious, stubborn. 3. Firmly, often unreasonably immovable in purpose or will ▸ bullheaded, dogged, obdurate. *See* **stubborn** (1). *See synonym note at* **stubborn**.

obstinateness *noun*
1. The quality or state of being stubbornly inflexible ▸ bullheadedness, hardheadedness, rigidity. *See* **stubbornness. 2.** The quality or condition of being unruly ▸ intractability, recalcitrance, unmanageability. *See* **unruliness.**

obstreperous *adjective*
1. Not submitting to discipline or control ▸ ill-behaved, obstinate, unmanageable. *See* **unruly. 2.** Offensively loud and insistent ▸ boisterous, clamorous. *See* **vociferous. 3.** Upsetting civil order or peace ▸ disruptive, unruly. *See* **disorderly** (1).

obstreperousness *noun*
▸ intractability, recalcitrance, unmanageability. *See* **unruliness.**

obstruct *verb*
1. To block or fill with obstacles ▸ bar, barricade, block, blockade, choke, clog, dam. *Idioms:* close (*or* cut) off. **2.** To interfere with the progress of ▸ dampen, retard. *See* **hinder** (1). *See synonym note at* **hinder. 3.** To cut off from sight ▸ conceal, hide, screen. *See* **block** (1). *See synonym note at* **block. 4.** To break up the order or progress of ▸ interfere, upset. *See* **disrupt** (1).

✦ CORE SYNONYMS: *obstruct, block, dam, bar.* These verbs mean to block or fill with obstacles. *Obstruct* is the most general: *A building obstructed our view of the mountains. Block* refers to complete obstruction that prevents progress, passage, or action: *"Do not block the way of inquiry"* (Charles S. Peirce). *Dam* suggests obstruction of the flow, progress, or release of something: *She dammed the brook to form a pool. He dammed up his emotions.* To *bar* is to prevent entry or exit or prohibit a course of action: *The legislature passed laws that bar price fixing.*

obstruction *noun*
1. Something that blocks entry or passage ▸ barrier, blockage, hindrance. *See* **bar** (1). *See synonym note at* **bar. 2.** Something that obstructs progress and requires great effort to overcome ▸ complication, hardship, rigor. *See* **difficulty** (1).

obtain *verb*
▸ come by, gain, procure. *See* **get** (1).

obtainable *adjective*
▸ acquirable, attainable, procurable. *See* **available** (1).

obtrude *verb*
1. To force or come in as an improper or unwanted element ▸ cut in, horn in, interlope. *See* **intrude** (1). **2.** To intervene officiously or indiscreetly in the affairs of others ▸ butt in, horn in, interfere. *See* **meddle** (1). *See synonym note at* **meddle.**

obtrusion *noun*
1. The act or an instance of interfering or intruding ▸ interfering, intrusion. *See* **meddling. 2.** An advance beyond proper or legal limits ▸ infringement, intrusion, transgression. *See* **trespass** (2). **3.** An excessive, unwelcome burden ▸ encumbrance, imposition, infliction, intrusion. *See also* **burden.**

obtrusive *adjective*
▸ inquisitive, meddlesome, officious, prying. *See* **curious** (1).

obtuse *adjective*
1. Lacking in or showing a lack of intelligence ▸ dumb, idiotic, unintelligent. *See* **stupid** (1). **2.** Unwilling or unable to perceive ▸ insensible, unperceptive. *See* **blind** (3). **3.** Not physically sharp or keen ▸ blunt, edgeless, unpointed. *See* **dull** (3).

obtuseness *noun*
▸ density, idiocy, mindlessness. *See* **stupidity.**

obviate *verb*
▸ anticipate, avert, forestall. *See* **prevent.** *See synonym note at* **prevent.**

obviation *noun*
▸ deterrence, forestallment, preclusion. *See* **prevention.**

obvious *adjective*
1. Easily seen through due to a lack of subtlety ▸ blatant, broad, clear, overt, patent, plain, transparent, undisguised, unmistakable, unsubtle. *Idiom:* sticking out like a sore thumb. **2.** Readily seen, perceived, or understood ▸ evident, noticeable, unmistakable. *See* **apparent** (1). *See synonym note at* **apparent.**

occasion *noun*
1. The general point at which an event occurs ▸ instant, juncture, moment, point, stage, time. *Idiom:* point in time. *See also* **period. 2.** That which produces an effect ▸ antecedent, cause, determinant, reason. *See synonym note at* **cause.** *See also* **impact, origin, stimulus. 3.** Something that takes place ▸ incident, occurrence. *See* **circumstance** (1). **4.** Something significant that happens ▸ development, incident. *See* **event** (2). **5.** A favorable or advantageous combination of circumstances ▸ chance, option. *See* **opportunity.** *See synonym note at* **opportunity. 6.** A basis for an action ▸ call, justification, reason. *See* **cause** (2). **7.** A social gathering, especially for pleasure ▸ celebration, gala, soiree. *See* **party** (1).

occasion *verb*
1. To be the cause of ▸ generate, induce, trigger. *See* **cause. 2.** To be an appropriate occasion for ▸ call for, warrant. *See* **justify** (2).

occasional *adjective*
1. Happening or appearing now and then ▸ fitful, periodic, sporadic. *See* **intermittent.** *See synonym note at* **intermittent. 2.** Rarely occurring or appearing ▸ uncommon, unusual. *See* **infrequent.**

occasionally *adverb*
1. Once in a while; at times ▸ betimes, periodically, sometimes. *See* **intermittently. 2.** At rare intervals ▸ rarely, seldom. *See* **infrequently.**

occult *adjective*
1. Difficult to explain or understand ▸ enigmatic, esoteric, mystifying. *See* **mysterious.** *See synonym note at* **mysterious. 2.** Not widely understood ▸ esoteric, recondite. *See* **obscure** (1).

occult *verb*
To put or keep out of sight ▸ bury, conceal, secrete. *See* **hide**[1] (1).

occupancy *noun*
The holding of something, such as a position ▸ incumbency, occupation, tenure. *See also* **period.**

occupant *noun*
▸ denizen, dweller, resident. *See* **inhabitant.**

occupation *noun*
1. Activity pursued as a livelihood ▸ career, employment, vocation. *See* **business** (2). 2. The holding of something, such as a position ▸ incumbency, occupancy, tenure. *See also* **period.**

occupied *adjective*
▸ engaged, absorbed. *See* **busy** (1).

occupy *verb*
1. To live in a place, as does a people ▸ inhabit, people, populate. *See also* **live, settle.** 2. To seize or maintain control over by conquest ▸ capture, colonize, conquer, hold, invade, overrun, seize, subjugate, take over. *Idiom:* take possession of. *See also* **control.** 3. To make busy ▸ busy, employ, engage. 4. To occupy the attention of ▸ consume, engage, involve. *See* **absorb** (1).

occur *verb*
To take place ▸ befall, come, transpire. *See* **happen** (1). *See synonym note at* **happen.**

occur to *verb*
To enter a person's mind ▸ hit, occur to. *See* **strike** (9).

occurrence *noun*
1. The condition or fact of being present ▸ attendance, presence. *See also* **existence.** 2. Something that takes place ▸ incident, occasion. *See* **circumstance** (1). *See synonym note at* **circumstance.** 3. Something significant that happens ▸ incident, news. *See* **event** (2).

ocean *noun*
A body of salt water covering a large part of the earth's surface ▸ brine, briny, deep, high seas, main, sea.

oceanic *adjective*
▸ maritime, sea, thalassic. *See* **marine** (1).

ocular *adjective*
Serving, resulting from, or relating to the sense of sight ▸ optic, optical, seeing, visual.

odd *adjective*
1. Agreeably curious, especially in an old-fashioned or unusual way ▸ curious, funny, quaint. 2. Deviating from what is conventional or customary ▸ bizarre, grotesque. *See* **eccentric.** *See synonym note at* **eccentric.** 3. Causing puzzlement; perplexing ▸ curious, peculiar. *See* **funny** (3). 4. Occurring unexpectedly ▸ chance, contingent, fluky. *See* **accidental** (1).

oddball *noun*
Informal A person who is appealingly odd or curious ▸ eccentric, oddity, original. *See* **character** (7).

oddity *noun*
1. The state or quality of being odd ▸ anomaly, peculiarity, singularity. *See* **abnormality.** 2. A person who is appealingly odd or curious ▸ eccentric, original. *Informal:* oddball. *See* **character** (7).

oddly *adverb*
▸ singularly, uncommonly, uniquely. *See* **unusually.**

oddments *noun*
▸ incidentals, junk, miscellanea. *See* **odds and ends.**

odds *noun*
1. The likeliness of a given event occurring ▸ likelihood, possibility, probability. *See* **chance** (3). 2. A factor conducive to superiority and success ▸ head start, vantage. *See* **advantage** (1).

odds and ends *noun*
1. Articles too small or numerous to be specified ▸ bits and pieces, etceteras, incidentals, junk, miscellanea, oddments, sundries, things. 2. Residual matter ▸ fragment, shard. *See* **end** (7).

odious *adjective*
▸ abhorrent, detestable, loathsome. *See* **offensive** (1). *See synonym note at* **offensive.**

odiousness *noun*
▸ monstrosity, plainness, unsightliness. *See* **ugliness** (1).

odium *noun*
1. Loss of honor, respect, or admiration ▸ discredit, disrepute, humiliation. *See* **disgrace.** 2. A strong feeling of hostility or dislike ▸ antipathy, contempt, loathing. *See* **hate** (1).

odor *noun*
1. The quality of something that may be perceived by smelling ▸ aroma, scent, smell. 2. A visible sign or mark of the passage of someone or something ▸ scent, trace, trail. *See* **track** (1).

odorous *or* **odoriferous** *adjective*
1. Having a pleasant odor ▸ aromatic, redolent, scent-laden. *See* **fragrant.** 2. Having an unpleasant odor ▸ foul-smelling, malodorous, stinking. *See* **smelly.**

odyssey *noun*
1. An exciting or unusual undertaking ▸ enterprise, venture. *See* **adventure.** 2. A journey that is undertaken with a specific objective ▸ mission, pilgrimage, quest. *See* **expedition** (1). 3. The act of traveling from one place to another ▸ flight, passage, progress. *See* **journey.**

off *adjective*
1. Characterized by reduced economic activity ▸ dull, slack. *See* **slow** (2). 2. Not present ▸ away, elsewhere, gone. *See* **absent** (1). 3. Containing an error or errors ▸ false, inaccurate, mistaken. *See* **erroneous.** 4. Afflicted with or exhibiting irrationality and mental unsoundness ▸ crazy, disordered, unbalanced. *See* **insane** (1).

off *verb*
Slang To take the life of a person or persons unlawfully ▸ destroy, kill, slay. *See* **murder** (1).

offbeat *adjective*
Slang Not usual or ordinary ▸ atypical, novel, unconventional. *See* **unusual** (1).

off-color *adjective*
1. Bordering on indelicacy or impropriety ▸ provocative, risqué, suggestive. *See* **racy** (1). 2. Suffering from or appearing to suffer from an illness ▸ ailing, ill, in-

disposed, unhealthy, unwell. *See* **sick** (1).

offend *verb*

1. To cause anger, resentment, or hurt feelings in ▶ affront, anger, annoy, chagrin, displease, hurt, injure, insult, miff, outrage, pique, provoke, put out, scandalize, upset, wound, wrong. *See also* **anger, annoy, stagger. 2.** To be very disagreeable or displeasing to ▶ disgust, displease, put off, repel, repulse, upset. *Slang:* turn off. *Idioms:* give offense to, not set right (*or* well) with. **3.** To violate a rule or law ▶ err, sin, transgress, trespass. *Idioms:* break the law (*or* rules), go astray. **4.** To cause resentment or hurt by callous, rude behavior ▶ affront, outrage. *See* **insult** (1).

✦ **CORE SYNONYMS:** *offend, insult, affront, outrage.* These verbs mean to cause someone to feel anger, resentment, humiliation, or hurt. To *offend* is to cause displeasure, wounded feelings, or repugnance in another: *"He often offended men who might have been useful friends"* (John Lothrop Motley). *Insult* implies gross insensitivity, insolence, or contemptuous rudeness: *"I . . . refused to stay any longer in the room with him, because he had insulted me"* (Anthony Trollope). To *affront* is to insult openly, usually intentionally: *"He continued to belabor the poor woman in a studied effort to affront his hated chieftain"* (Edgar Rice Burroughs). *Outrage* implies the flagrant violation of a person's integrity, pride, or sense of right and decency: *"Agnes . . . was outraged by what seemed to her Rose's callousness"* (Mrs. Humphry Ward).

offender *noun*

▶ culprit, lawbreaker, perpetrator. *See* **criminal.**

offense *noun*

1. Extreme displeasure caused by an insult or slight ▶ bad feelings, displeasure, dudgeon, huff, hurt, miff, pique, resentment, ruffled feathers, umbrage. *See also* **anger. 2.** An act that offends a person's sense of pride or dignity ▶ contumely, insult. *See* **indignity. 3.** A wicked act or wicked behavior ▶ evil, misdeed, sin. *See* **crime** (2). **4.** An unjust act ▶ disservice, inequity, wrong. *See* **injustice** (1). **5.** An act that violates public law ▶ illegality, tort. *See* **crime** (1). **6.** The act of attacking ▶ assault, onslaught, strike. *See* **attack** (1).

offensive *adjective*

1. So unpleasant or objectionable as to cause scorn or disgust ▶ abhorrent, abominable, antipathetic, atrocious, contemptible, despicable, despisable, detestable, disgusting, filthy, foul, hateful, horrid, infamous, loathsome, lousy, low, mean, nasty, nauseating, nefarious, obnoxious, odious, repellent, repugnant, repulsive, revolting, rotten, shabby, sickening, stomach-churning, ugly, unwholesome, vile, wretched. *See also* **bad, deplorable, disgraceful, obscene. 2.** Causing displeasure, anger, or hurt feelings ▶ discourteous, displeasing, hurtful, impertinent, impolite, insulting, rude, uncivil. *See also* **impudent, objectionable. 3.** Not pleasant or agreeable ▶ disagreeable, uncongenial, unsympathetic. *See* **unpleasant** (1).

offensive *noun*

The act of attacking ▶ assault, strike. *See* **attack** (1).

✦ **CORE SYNONYMS:** *offensive, hateful, detestable, odious, repellent.* These often interchangeable adjectives describe a person or thing that is so unpleasant or objectionable as to cause scorn or disgust. *Offensive* applies to what offends or excites displeasure: *an offensive suggestion. Hateful* refers to what evokes hatred or deep animosity: *"No vice is universally as hateful as ingratitude"* (Joseph Priestley). *Detestable* applies to what arouses abhorrence or scorn: *detestable crimes against humanity.* Something *odious* is the object of disgust, aversion, or intense displeasure: *"a kind of slimy stuff . . . of a most nauseous, odious smell"* (Daniel Defoe). Something *repellent* arouses repugnance or disgust: *repellent criminal behavior.*

offer *verb*

1. To put before another for acceptance ▶ advance, extend, hold out, present, proffer, put forward, put up, render, submit, tender, turn in, volunteer. *Idioms:* come forward with, hand to on a silver plate (*or* platter), lay before, lay at someone's feet. *See also* **donate. 2.** To make something readily available ▶ afford, furnish, make available, present, provide, render, supply. *Idioms:* place (*or* put) at one's disposal. *See also* **allow. 3.** To have for sale ▶ carry, deal (in), keep, stock. **4.** To make an offer of ▶ bid. *Informal:* go. **5.** To state for consideration or debate ▶ advance, put forward, set forth. *See* **propose** (1).

offer *noun*

1. An act of offering or the thing offered ▶ bid, invitation, presentation, proffer, tender. *See also* **proposal. 2.** A trying to do or make something ▶ effort, trial. *Informal:* shot. *See* **attempt** (1).

✦ **CORE SYNONYMS:** *offer, proffer, tender, present.* These verbs mean to put before another for acceptance or rejection. *Offer* is the basic general term in this group: *offered us some tea; a store that offered sizable discounts. Proffer* implies voluntary action motivated especially by courtesy or generosity: *"Mr. van der Luyden . . . proffered to Newland low-voiced congratulations"* (Edith Wharton). To *tender* is to offer formally: *tendered her respects; tendered my resignation. Present* suggests formality and often a measure of ceremony: *"A footman entered, and presented . . . some mail on a silver tray"* (Winston Churchill).

offering *noun*

1. Something, especially a slain animal or group of animals, presented to a deity as an act of worship ▶ hecatomb, immolation, oblation, sacrifice, victim. **2.** Something given to a charity or cause ▶ benefaction, contribution, gratuity. *See* **donation.**

offhand *adjective*

1. Spoken, performed, or composed with little or no preparation or forethought ▶ impromptu, improvised. *See* **extemporaneous.** *See synonym note at* **extemporaneous. 2.** Marked by ease and fluency of speech that is often insincere or superficial ▶ slick, smooth-talking, smooth-tongued. *See* **glib.**

office *noun*
1. An administrative unit, as of a government or company ▸ agency, bureau. *See* **branch** (3). **2.** A piece of work that has been assigned ▸ chore, duty, job. *See* **task** (1). **3.** A post of employment ▸ job, spot. *See* **position** (3). **4.** A formal act or set of acts prescribed by ritual ▸ rite, ritual, tradition. *See* **ceremony** (1).

officer *noun*
1. A person having administrative or managerial authority in an organization ▸ administrator, manager. *See* **executive. 2.** A member of a law-enforcement agency ▸ bluecoat, trooper. *Informal:* cop. *See* **police officer.**

official *adjective*
1. Having or arising from authority ▸ formal, supreme. *See* **authoritative** (1). **2.** Fond of or given to ceremony ▸ courtly, formal, stately. *See* **ceremonious** (1). **3.** Of or relating to government ▸ bureaucratic, regulatory. *See* **governmental.**

official *noun*
A person having administrative or managerial authority in an organization ▸ administrator, manager. *See* **executive.**

officiate *verb*
To peform assigned or official duties ▸ act as, function as, serve as.

officious *adjective*
Unduly interested in the affairs of others ▸ inquisitive, meddlesome, obtrusive. *See* **curious** (1).

offish *adjective*
▸ aloof, chilly, impersonal. *See* **cool** (1).

offset *noun*
Something to make up for loss or damage ▸ amends, remuneration, reparation. *See* **compensation** (1).

offset *verb*
1. To act as an equalizing force to ▸ counteract, counterbalance, oppose. *See* **balance** (2). **2.** To make ineffective by applying an opposite force ▸ counteract, negate, neutralize. *See* **cancel** (2).

offshoot *noun*
1. Something resembling or analogous to a tree branch ▸ arm, fork, offshoot. *See* **branch** (1). *See synonym note at* **branch. 2.** Something derived from another ▸ byproduct, outgrowth, spinoff. *See* **derivative. 3.** A young stemlike growth arising from a plant ▸ runner, sprout. *See* **shoot** (1).

offspring *noun*
▸ child, issue, seed. *See* **progeny.**

off-the-cuff *adjective*
▸ ad-lib, impromptu, spur-of-the-moment. *See* **extemporaneous.**

often *adverb*
▸ customarily, generally, normally. *See* **usually.**

ogle *verb*
1. To look intently and fixedly ▸ gawk, peer, stare. *See* **gaze. 2.** *Informal* To make an excessive show of desire for or interest in ▸ *Informal:* drool over, slobber over. *See also* **adore, desire, lust, rave.**

ogre *noun*
▸ beast, devil, monster. *See* **fiend** (1).

ogreish *adjective*
▸ devilish, diabolical, satanic. *See* **fiendish.**

oil *noun*
1. A substance that is generally slippery, combustible, and not water-soluble ▸ crude, grease, lube, lubricant, petroleum, unction. *See also* **fat, ointment, slime. 2.** Excessive, ingratiating praise ▸ adulation, blandishment. *Informal:* soft soap. *See* **flattery.**

oil *verb*
To apply oil to something ▸ anoint, grease, lube, lubricate. *See also* **smear.**

oily *adjective*
1. Having the qualities of fat ▸ greasy, unctuous. *See* **fatty** (1). **2.** Affectedly and self-servingly earnest ▸ oleaginous, smarmy. *See* **unctuous** (1). *See synonym note at* **unctuous. 3.** So smooth and glassy as to offer insecure hold or footing ▸ slippery, slithery. *See* **slick** (1).

ointment *noun*
A substance used on the skin to soothe or heal ▸ balm, cream, emollient, liniment, lotion, salve, unction, unguent.

OK *or* **okay** *noun*
1. *Informal* The approving of an action, especially when done by one in authority ▸ authorization, consent, sanction. *See* **permission. 2.** *Informal* The act of accepting or adopting ▸ adoption, assent, consent. *See* **acceptance** (1).

OK *or* **okay** *verb*
Informal To give one's consent to ▸ allow, authorize. *See* **permit** (2).

OK *or* **okay** *adverb*
Informal It is so; as you say or ask ▸ agreed, all right, assuredly. *See* **yes.**

OK *or* **okay** *adjective*
Informal Adequate to satisfy a need, requirement, or standard ▸ decent, moderate. *See* **acceptable** (2).

old *adjective*
1. Belonging to, existing, or occurring in times long past ▸ age-old, ancient, antediluvian, antiquated, antique, archaic, bygone, of yore, olden, old-time, timeworn, venerable. *Idioms:* old as Methuselah (*or* the hills *or* time). *See also* **early, shabby. 2.** Far along in life or time ▸ advanced, aged, aging, elder, elderly, grizzled, hoary, mature, older, senescent, senior. *Idioms:* getting along (*or* on) in years, long in the tooth, no spring chicken, over the hill. *See also* **senile. 3.** Existing in the same state for an indefinitely long time ▸ durable, enduring, perennial. *See* **continuing** (1). **4.** Having been such previously ▸ former, onetime, past. *See* **late** (2). **5.** Of a style or method formerly in vogue ▸ antique, dated, passé. *See* **old-fashioned. 6.** Skilled or knowledgeable through long practice ▸ practiced, seasoned. *See* **experienced.**

old *noun*
The time before the present ▸ yore, yesterday. *See* **past** (1).

✦ **CORE SYNONYMS:** *old, ancient, archaic, antediluvian, antique, antiquated.* These adjectives describe what belongs to or dates from an earlier time or period. *Old* is the most general term: *old lace; an old saying.* *Ancient* pertains to the distant past: *"the hills,/Rock-ribbed, and ancient as the sun"* (William Cullen Bryant). *Archaic* implies a very remote, often primitive period: *an archaic Greek bronze of the seventh century* BC. *Antediluvian* applies to what is extremely outdated: *"a branch of one of your antediluvian families"* (William Congreve). *Antique* is applied to what is especially appreciated or valued because of its age: *antique furniture; an antique vase.* *Antiquated* describes what is out of date, no longer fashionable, or discredited: *"No idea is so antiquated that it was not once modern. No idea is so modern that it will not someday be antiquated"* (Ellen Glasgow).

---

old age *noun*
▸ agedness, elderliness, senescence. *See* **age** (1).

old boy *noun*
▸ begetter, patriarch, sire. *See* **father** (1).

olden *adjective*
▸ ancient, antiquated, archaic. *See* **old** (1).

older *adjective*
▸ aged, elderly, senior. *See* **old** (2).

old-fashioned *adjective*
Of a style or method formerly in vogue ▸ antiquated, antique, archaic, dated, dowdy, frumpish, frumpy, fusty, old, old-time, out, outdated, outmoded, out-of-date, passé, unfashionable. *Idioms:* old hat, old school. *See also* **obsolete, trite, vintage.**

old hand *noun*
One who has had long experience in a given activity or capacity ▸ past master, vet, veteran. *Informal:* old-timer. *See also* **expert.**

old lady *noun*
1. *Slang* A female parent ▸ materfamilias, matriarch. *See* **mother** (1). **2.** *Slang* A woman who is a man's romantic partner ▸ girl, inamorata. *See* **girlfriend.**

old-line *adjective*
1. Extremely or stubbornly conservative ▸ moss-backed, reactionary, standpat. *See* **ultraconservative.** **2.** Firmly established by long standing ▸ entrenched, ingrained, inveterate. *See* **confirmed** (1).

old maid *noun*
Informal One who is excessively concerned with being proper, modest, or righteous ▸ Mrs. Grundy, prig, puritan. *See* **prude.**

old man *noun*
1. *Slang* A male parent ▸ begetter, patriarch, sire. *See* **father** (1). **2.** *Slang* A man who is a woman's romantic partner ▸ beau, inamorato. *See* **boyfriend.**

oldster *noun*
Informal An elderly person ▸ elder, senior citizen. *See* **senior** (2).

old-time *adjective*
1. Belonging to or existing in times long past ▸ ancient, antiquated, archaic. *See* **old** (1). **2.** Of a style or method formerly in vogue ▸ antique, dated, passé. *See* **old-fashioned.**

old-timer *noun*
1. *Informal* One who has had long experience in a given activity or capacity ▸ old hand, past master, vet, veteran. *See also* **expert. 2.** *Informal* An elderly person ▸ elder, senior citizen. *See* **senior** (2).

oleaginous *adjective*
1. Having the qualities of fat ▸ greasy, unctuous. *See* **fatty** (1). **2.** Affectedly and self-servingly earnest ▸ oily, smarmy. *See* **unctuous** (1). *See synonym note at* **unctuous.**

olfaction *noun*
The sense by which odors are perceived ▸ nose, scent, smell.

oligarch *noun*
▸ despot, oppressor, tyrant. *See* **dictator** (1).

olio *noun*
▸ hodgepodge, jumble, mishmash. *See* **assortment** (1).

omen *noun*
A phenomenon that serves as a sign or warning of some future good or evil ▸ augury, foreboding, forerunner, foreshadowing, foretoken, forewarning, harbinger, portent, prefigurement, presage, prognostic, prognostication, sign, thundercloud, warning. *Idioms:* writing (*or* handwriting) on the wall. *See also* **prediction, sign, threat.**

ominous *adjective*
▸ dire, portentous, unlucky. *See* **fateful** (1).

omission *noun*
1. Nonperformance of what ought to be done ▸ dereliction, neglect. *See* **failure** (2). **2.** An act or instance of neglecting ▸ negligence, oversight. *See* **neglect** (1). **3.** An unintentional deviation from what is correct, right, or true ▸ lapse, mistake. *See* **error** (1).

omit *verb*
1. To take or leave out ▸ eliminate, exclude, prune. *See* **drop** (8). **2.** To fail to do or carry out ▸ ignore, let slide, overlook. *See* **neglect** (3).

omnipotence *noun*
▸ jurisdiction, might. *Informal:* say-so, muscle. *See* **authority** (1).

omnipresent *adjective*
Ever present in all places ▸ ubiquitous, universal. *See also* **rampant.**

omnivorous *adjective*
▸ gluttonous, rapacious, ravenous. *See* **voracious** (1).

omnivorousness *noun*
▸ avidity, insatiability, rapaciousness. *See* **voracity.**

omphalos *noun*
▸ middle, midpoint, midst. *See* **center** (2).

once *adverb*
At a time in the past ▸ before, previously. *See* **earlier** (1).

once *adjective*
Having been such previously ▸ former, onetime, past. *See* **late** (2).

once again *adverb*
▸ afresh, again, over again. *See* **anew.**

once-over *noun*
▸ inspection, inquiry, scrutiny. *See* **examination** (1).

one *adjective*
► only, single, solitary. *See* **lone** (1).

one-dimensional *adjective*
► cursory, shallow, skin-deep, uncritical. *See* **superficial** (1).

one-liner *noun*
► jest, quip, witticism. *See* **joke** (1).

oneness *noun*
1. The condition of being one ► singleness, singularity, unity. 2. An identity or coincidence of interests, purposes, or sympathies among the members of a group ► concord, solidarity, union, unity. *See also* **alliance, union**. 3. The quality or condition of being exactly the same as something else ► identicalness, identity, sameness, selfsameness. *See also* **likeness**. 4. The quality or condition of being unique ► matchlessness, singleness, singularity. *See* **uniqueness** (1). 5. The state of being entirely whole ► entirety, totality. *See* **completeness**.

onerous *adjective*
► arduous, oppressive, rough. *See* **burdensome** (1). *See synonym note at* **burdensome**.

one-sided *adjective*
► partial, prejudiced, tendentious. *See* **biased** (1).

one-sidedness *noun*
► partiality, prejudice. *See* **bias** (1).

onetime *adjective*
► former, once, past. *See* **late** (2).

one-up *verb*
Informal To outmaneuver an opponent ► finesse, trump. *See also* **deceive, maneuver, outwit**.

ongoing *adjective*
► constant, endless, everlasting, perpetual. *See* **continual**.

onlooker *noun*
► beholder, observer, spectator. *See* **watcher** (1).

only *adjective*
1. Alone in a given category ► one, single, solitary. *See* **lone** (1). 2. Without equal or rival ► incomparable, singular, unparalleled. *See* **unique** (1).

only *adverb*
1. Nothing more than ► but, just, merely, simply. *See also* **barely**. 2. To the exclusion of anyone or anything else ► exclusively, just. *See* **solely** (1).

onomatopoeia *noun*
The formation of words in imitation of sounds ► echoism, mimesis.

onomatopoetic *or* **onomatopoeic** *adjective*
Imitating sounds ► echoic, imitative, mimetic.

onrush *noun*
► assault, strike. *See* **attack** (1).

onset *noun*
1. The act of attacking ► onslaught, strike. *See* **attack** (1). 2. The initial stage of a developmental process ► genesis, inception, start. *See* **birth** (2).

onslaught *noun*
1. The act of attacking ► assault, strike. *See* **attack** (1). 2. A long, violent, or blustering speech, usually of censure or denunciation ► diatribe, harangue. *See*

tirade. 3. A swift advance or attack ► raid, rush. *See* **charge** (1).

onus *noun*
1. A source of persistent worry or hardship ► cross, tribulation. *See* **burden**[1] (1). 2. A mark of discredit or disgrace ► blemish, spot. *See* **stain** (1). 3. Responsibility for an error or crime ► fault, guilt. *See* **blame** (1). 4. An act or course of action that is demanded of one, as by position, custom, law, or religion ► charge, commitment, obligation. *See* **duty** (1).

onward *adverb*
► ahead, forth, out. *See* **forward**.

onyx *adjective*
► ebony, inky, jet. *See* **black** (1).

oodles *noun*
Informal An indeterminately great amount or number ► bunch, multiplicity. *Informal:* bushel. *See* **heap** (3).

oomph *noun*
► life, verve, vivaciousness. *See* **spirit** (1).

ooze *verb*
To flow or leak out or emit something slowly ► bleed, discharge, exude, leach, leak, percolate, seep, sweat, transpire, transude, weep. *See also* **drip, flow**.

ooze *noun*
A viscous, usually offensively dirty substance ► muck, sludge. *See* **slime**.

oozy *adjective*
► miry, mucky, slushy. *See* **slimy**.

open *adjective*
1. Not closed, sealed, or fastened ► agape, ajar, cracked, unbuttoned, unbuckled, unclosed, undone, unlaced, unlocked, untied, unzipped, wide. *See also* **loose, yawning**. 2. Not covered ► exposed, revealed, spread, unconcealed, uncovered, unfurled, unprotected, unrolled, unsheltered. *See also* **apparent, perceptible**. 3. Not restricted or confined to few ► free, nonexclusive, open-door, public, unrestricted. *See also* **common**. 4. Available for use or occupation ► accessible, employable, free, operable, operative, practicable, unfilled, uninhabited, unoccupied, unreserved, usable, utilizable, vacant, vacated. *See also* **available, empty**. 5. Free from obstructions ► unblocked, unobstructed. *See* **clear** (4). 6. Tending to incur ► prone, subject, vulnerable. *See* **liable** (2). 7. Ready and willing to receive favorably, as new ideas ► acceptant, open-minded, responsive. *See* **receptive**. 8. Marked by lack of firm decision or commitment; of questionable outcome ► uncertain, undetermined. *See* **indefinite** (2). 9. Manifesting honesty and directness ► candid, ingenuous, plainspoken. *See* **frank**. *See synonym note at* **frank**.

open *verb*
1. To become or cause to become open ► crack, free, release, throw wide, unbutton, unbuckle, unclose, undo, unfasten, unlace, unlock, untie, unzip. *See also* **reveal, undo**. 2. To rid of obstructions ► clear, free, remove, unblock. *See also* **rid**. 3. To move or arrange so as to cover a larger area ► extend, stretch. *See*

spread (1). **4.** To go about the initial step in doing something ▸ begin, embark, initiate. *See* **start** (1).

open-door *adjective*
▸ public, unrestricted. *See* **open** (3).

open-eyed *adjective*
▸ vigilant, wide-awake. *See* **alert** (1).

openhanded *adjective*
▸ big-hearted, magnanimous, unselfish. *See* **generous** (1).

openhandedness *noun*
▸ magnanimity, munificence, unselfishness. *See* **generosity.**

opening *noun*
1. An open space allowing passage ▸ orifice, vent. *See* **hole** (2). **2.** The initial stage of a developmental process ▸ genesis, inception, start. *See* **birth** (2). **3.** The act of bringing or being brought into existence ▸ inception, initiation, start. *See* **beginning** (1). **4.** A favorable or advantageous combination of circumstances ▸ chance, option. *See* **opportunity.** *See synonym note at* **opportunity.**

opening *adjective*
Of or occurring at the start of something ▸ initial, introductory, starting. *See* **beginning** (1).

open-minded *adjective*
1. Ready and willing to receive favorably, as new ideas ▸ acceptant, responsive. *See* **receptive. 2.** Not narrow or intolerant ▸ humanistic, liberal, tolerant. *See* **broad-minded.** *See synonym note at* **broad-minded.**

open-mindedness *noun*
▸ receptivity, responsiveness. *See* **openness** (1).

openness *noun*
1. Ready acceptance of new suggestions, ideas, or opinions ▸ amenability, amenableness, open-mindedness, receptiveness, receptivity, responsiveness. *See also* **acceptance. 2.** The condition of being laid open to something undesirable or injurious ▸ endangerment, susceptibility, vulnerability. *See* **exposure** (1). **3.** The quality of being honest ▸ incorruptibility, integrity. *See* **honesty** (1).

operable *adjective*
▸ employable, operative, usable. *See* **open** (4).

operate *verb*
1. To control or direct the functioning of ▸ employ, handle, manage, run, use, utilize, wield, work. *See also* **administer, drive, maneuver. 2.** To control the course of an activity ▸ direct, manage, steer. *See* **conduct** (1). **3.** To act in a specified way ▸ behave, perform, work. *See* **function.**

operating *adjective*
▸ functioning, operative, working. *See* **active** (1).

operation *noun*
1. The way in which something functions ▸ functioning, performance. *See* **behavior** (2). **2.** The act of putting into play ▸ employment, implementation, usage. *See* **exercise** (1). **3.** An assignment one is sent to carry out ▸ errand, undertaking. *See* **mission** (1).

operational *adjective*
1. In effect ▸ effective, operative. *Idioms:* in force (*or* operation). **2.** In a condition to be used ▸ applicable, serviceable. *See* **usable** (1).

operative *adjective*
1. In effect ▸ effective, operational. *Idioms:* in force (*or* operation). **2.** Available for use ▸ employable, operable, usable. *See* **open** (4). **3.** In action or full operation ▸ functioning, operating, working. *See* **active** (1).

operative *noun*
1. One who labors ▸ menial, toiler, worker. *See* **laborer. 2.** A person who secretly observes others to obtain information ▸ agent, asset. *See* **spy.**

operator *noun*
1. A person who operates a motor vehicle ▸ chauffeur, driver, motorist. **2.** One who speculates for quick profits ▸ adventurer, gambler, speculator.

opiate *noun*
1. A substance that affects the central nervous system and is often addictive ▸ hallucinogen, narcotic, psychotropic. *See* **drug** (2). **2.** Something that induces sleep or sedation ▸ narcotic, sedative. *See* **soporific.**

opiate *adjective*
Inducing sleep or sedation ▸ hypnotic, sedative, slumberous. *See* **soporific** (1).

opiate *verb*
To administer especially a painkilling drug to someone ▸ medicate, narcotize, tranquilize. *See* **drug** (1).

opine *verb*
1. To have an opinion ▸ deem, hold. *See* **believe** (3). **2.** To state facts, opinions, or explanations ▸ observe, reflect, remark. *See* **comment.**

opinion *noun*
1. Something believed or thought to be true ▸ notion, persuasion, view. *See* **belief** (1). *See synonym note at* **belief. 2.** An authoritative or official decision ▸ edict, judgment, pronouncement. *See* **ruling. 3.** A statement presented for acceptance, as by a religious group ▸ dogma, teaching. *See* **doctrine.**

opinionated *adjective*
1. Not tolerant of the beliefs or opinions of others ▸ close-minded, illiberal, racist. *See* **intolerant** (1). **2.** Exhibiting bias ▸ partial, prejudiced, tendentious. *See* **biased** (1).

opponent *noun*
1. One that opposes the purposes or interests of another ▸ adversary, antagonist, archenemy, dissenter, enemy, foe, nemesis, opposer, opposition, oppositionist, resister. **2.** One that competes ▸ competition, contender, rival. *See* **competitor.**

✦ **CORE SYNONYMS:** *enemy, foe, opponent.* These nouns denote one who is hostile to or opposes the purposes or interests of another: *betrayed by enemies; a foe of fascism; a political opponent.*

---

opportune *adjective*
Suited for a particular purpose or occurring at a suitable time ▸ auspicious, favorable, fortuitous, fortunate, propitious, prosperous, seasonable, timely, well-timed. *See also* **appropriate, convenient.**

opportunity *noun*
A favorable or advantageous combination of circumstances ▸ break, chance, occasion, opening, option. *Informal:* shot. *See also* **turn.**

✣ CORE SYNONYMS: *opportunity, occasion, opening, chance, break.* These nouns refer to a favorable or advantageous circumstance or combination of circumstances. *Opportunity* is an auspicious state of affairs or a suitable time: *"If you prepare yourself . . . you will be able to grasp opportunity for broader experience when it appears"* (Eleanor Roosevelt). *Occasion* suggests the proper time for action: *an auspicious occasion; an occasion for celebration.* An *opening* is an opportunity affording a good possibility of success: *waited patiently for her opening, then exposed the report's inconsistency. Chance* often implies an opportunity that arises through luck or accident: *a chance for us to chat; no chance of losing.* A *break* is an often sudden piece of luck, especially good luck: *got his first big break in Hollywood.*

oppose *verb*
1. To place in opposition or be in opposition to ▸ combat, counter, fight, match, pit, play off, resist, stand against, withstand. *Idioms:* bump heads with, meet head-on, mount (*or* offer) resistance, put up a fight, set (*or* be) at odds, set (*or* be) at someone's throat, stand up to. *See also* **contend. 2.** To confront boldly and courageously ▸ challenge, confront, dare. *See* **defy** (1). **3.** To take a stand against ▸ challenge, dispute, resist. *See* **contest** (1). **4.** To fail to be in accord ▸ contrast, disagree, discord. *See* **conflict. 5.** To act as an equalizing force to ▸ counteract, counterbalance, offset. *See* **balance** (2). **6.** To express opposition ▸ demur, except, expostulate, protest. *See* **object** (1). **7.** To refuse or fail to obey ▸ defy, disregard, transgress. *See* **disobey.**

✣ CORE SYNONYMS: *oppose, fight, combat, resist, withstand.* These verbs mean to place someone or something in opposition to another. *Oppose* has the widest application: *The community opposed the building of a nuclear power plant. "The idea is inconsistent with our constitutional theory and has been stubbornly opposed . . . since the early days of the Republic"* (E.B. White). *Fight* and *combat* suggest vigor and aggressiveness: *"All my life I have fought against prejudice and intolerance"* (Harry S. Truman). *"We are not afraid . . . to tolerate any error so long as reason is left free to combat it"* (Thomas Jefferson). To *resist* is to strive to fend off or offset the actions, effects, or force of: *"Pardon was freely extended to all who had resisted the invasion"* (John R. Green). *Withstand* often implies successful resistance: *"Neither the southern provinces, nor Sicily, could have withstood his power"* (Henry Hallam).

opposed *adjective*
1. Acting against or in opposition ▸ antagonistic, resistant. *See* **opposing** (1). **2.** Not inclined or willing to do or undertake ▸ disinclined, reluctant. *See* **indisposed** (1).

opposer *noun*
▸ antagonist, foe, nemesis. *See* **opponent** (1).

opposing *adjective*
1. Acting against or in opposition ▸ adversarial, adverse, antagonistic, antipathetic, conflicting, countervailing, opposed, oppositional, resistant, unfavorable. *Idioms:* at odds, in opposition to. *See also* **contrary, hostile. 2.** Diametrically opposed ▸ antithetical, contradictory, diametric. *See* **opposite** (1).

opposite *adjective*
1. Diametrically opposed ▸ antipodal, antipodean, antithetical, antonymic, antonymous, contradictory, contrary, contrasting, converse, counter, diametric, diametrical, incompatible, inverse, irreconcilable, opposing, polar, reverse. **2.** In sharp opposition ▸ conflicting, discordant, inconsistent. *See* **discrepant** (1).

opposite *noun*
That which is diametrically opposed to another ▸ antipode, antipodes, antithesis, antonym, contradiction, contradictory, contrapositive, contrary, converse, counter, inverse, reverse.

✣ CORE SYNONYMS: *opposite, contrary, antithetical, contradictory.* These adjectives mean marked by a natural or innate and irreconcilable opposition. Two things that are altogether different are *opposite: Antonyms are words of opposite meaning. "It is said that opposite characters make a union happiest"* (Charles Reade). *Contrary* stresses extreme divergence: *Democrats and Republicans often hold contrary opinions. Antithetical* emphasizes diametrical opposition: *engaged in practices entirely antithetical to their professed beliefs. Contradictory* implies denial or inconsistency: *"contradictory attributes of unjust justice and loving vindictiveness"* (John Morley).

opposite number *noun*
One that has the same functions and characteristics as another ▸ counterpart, equivalent, vis-à-vis.

opposition *noun*
1. The act or condition of conflict ▸ antagonism, antithesis, aversion, combat, contradiction, contradistinction, contraposition, contrariety, contrariness, polarity. *See also* **conflict, enmity. 2.** The act of resisting ▸ renitence, renitency, resistance. **3.** A clandestine organization of freedom fighters in an oppressed land ▸ resistance, underground. **4.** One that opposes the purposes of another ▸ antagonist, foe, nemesis. *See* **opponent** (1). **5.** The state of not being disposed or inclined ▸ aversion, disinclination, reluctance. *See* **indisposition** (1).

oppositional *adjective*
▸ antagonistic, resistant. *See* **opposing** (1).

oppositionist *noun*
▸ antagonist, foe, nemesis. *See* **opponent** (1).

oppress *verb*
1. To treat improperly or unjustly ▸ mistreat, persecute, wrong. *See* **abuse** (1). **2.** To make sad or gloomy ▸ dishearten, dispirit, sadden. *See* **depress** (1). **3.** To weigh down or place a heavy load on ▸ encumber, saddle, tax. *See* **burden**[1].

oppression *noun*
1. Cruel exercise of power ▸ domination, injustice, persecution, repression, subjugation. *See also* **cruelty, slavery. 2.** Absolute power, especially when exercised unjustly or cruelly ▸ despotism, dictatorship, totalitarianism. *See* **tyranny** (1).

oppressive *adjective*
▸ demanding, severe, taxing. *See* **burdensome** (1). *See synonym note at* **burdensome.**

oppressor *noun*
▸ authoritarian, despot, tyrant. *See* **dictator** (1).

opprobrious *adjective*
1. Of, relating to, or characterized by verbal abuse ▸ contumelious, invective, scurrilous. *See* **abusive. 2.** Meriting or causing shame or dishonor ▸ discreditable, ignominious, shameful. *See* **disgraceful** (1).

opprobrium *noun*
1. Loss of or damage to one's reputation ▸ discredit, disrepute, humiliation. *See* **disgrace. 2.** Words expressive of strong disapproval ▸ admonition, reprimand, scolding. *See* **rebuke.**

oppugn *verb*
▸ contravene, disaffirm, disavow. *See* **deny** (1).

opt *verb*
▸ elect, opt for, pick (out), vote (for). *See* **choose** (1).

optic *or* **optical** *adjective*
Serving, resulting from, or relating to the sense of sight ▸ ocular, seeing, visual.

optics *noun*
▸ eyesight, seeing, sight. *See* **vision** (1).

optimal *adjective*
▸ optimum, superlative, unsurpassed. *See* **best** (1).

optimism *noun*
A tendency to expect a favorable outcome or to dwell on hopeful aspects ▸ assurance, cheerfulness, enthusiasm, hopefulness, sanguineness, sanguinity. *See also* **sureness.**

optimist *noun*
One who expects a favorable outcome or dwells on hopeful aspects ▸ Pollyanna, positivist. *See also* **dreamer.**

optimistic *adjective*
Expecting or suggesting a favorable outcome ▸ assured, cheerful, confident, enthusiastic, Panglossian, positive, roseate, rose-colored, rosy, sanguine, upbeat. *Idioms:* looking on the bright side, looking through rose-colored glasses. *See also* **encouraging, idealistic.**

optimum *adjective*
▸ superlative, unsurpassed. *See* **best** (1).

option *noun*
1. The act, power, or right of choosing ▸ decision, discretion, preference. *See* **choice** (1). *See synonym note at* **choice. 2.** A favorable or advantageous combination of circumstances ▸ chance, opening. *See* **opportunity.**

optional *adjective*
Not compulsory or automatic ▸ discretionary, elective, facultative, noncompulsory, nonobligatory, permissible, possible. *See also* **voluntary.**

opulence *noun*
▸ fortune, riches, treasure. *See* **wealth** (1).

opulent *adjective*
1. Characterized by extravagant, ostentatious magnificence ▸ lush, luxuriant, palatial. *See* **luxurious. 2.** Given to or marked by unrestrained abundance ▸ exuberant, lavish, superabundant. *See* **profuse** (1).

opus *noun*
1. Something that is the result of creative effort ▸ piece, production, work. *See* **composition** (1). **2.** An issue of printed material offered for sale or distribution ▸ title, volume, work. *See* **publication** (2).

oracle *noun*
1. Something that is foretold by or as if by supernatural means ▸ augury, soothsaying. *See* **prophecy. 2.** A person who foretells future events by or as if by supernatural means ▸ fortuneteller, seer, soothsayer. *See* **prophet.**

oracular *adjective*
▸ divinitory, mantic, sibylline. *See* **prophetic.**

oral *adjective*
Expressed or produced in speech or by the voice ▸ articulate, phonetic, phonic, pronounced, spoken, unwritten, uttered, verbal, vocal, voiced, word-of-mouth.

orate *verb*
▸ harangue, mouth, rave. *See* **rant** (1).

oration *noun*
▸ lecture, talk. *See* **speech** (2).

orator *noun*
▸ lecturer, speechmaker. *See* **speaker** (1).

oratorical *adjective*
Characterized by elevated language, such as that used in public speaking ▸ aureate, bombastic, declamatory, elocutionary, eloquent, flowery, fustian, grandiloquent, high-flown, high-sounding, inflated, magniloquent, orotund, overblown, rhetorical, sonorous.

oratory *noun*
The art of public speaking ▸ declamation, elocution, rhetoric, speech. *See also* **bombast, eloquence.**

orb *noun*
1. A spherical object ▸ globe, sphere. *See* **ball** (1). **2.** The celestial body where humans live ▸ earth, globe, planet, world. **3.** An organ of vision ▸ eye, eyeball. *Slang:* peeper, saucer. *Idiom:* window of the soul.

orbicular *adjective*
▸ circular, globular, spherical. *See* **round** (1).

orbit *noun*
1. A course or process that ends where it began or repeats itself ▸ circuit, cycle. *See* **circle** (2). **2.** A sphere of activity, experience, study, or interest ▸ department, domain, field, terrain. *See* **area** (1). **3.** An area or set of parameters within which something or someone exists, acts, or has influence ▸ extent, realm, scope. *See* **range** (1). *See synonym note at* **range. 4.** A circular movement around a point or about an axis ▸ circulation, gyration. *See* **revolution** (1).

orbit *verb*
1. To rotate on an axis or around a center ▸ twirl,

N
P

whirl, wheel. *See* **turn** (1). **2.** To form a circle around ► compass, loop, ring. *See* **encircle** (1).

orchestrate *verb*
1. To form by artistic effort ► produce, write. *See* **compose** (1). **2.** To combine and adapt to attain a particular effect ► blend, integrate. *See* **harmonize** (2).

ordain *verb*
1. To set forth expressly and authoratatively ► impose, mandate, rule. *See* **dictate** (1). *See synonym note at* **dictate**. **2.** To put in force or cause to be by legal authority ► enact, legislate. *See* **establish** (3).

ordained *adjective*
► devoted, religious, sacred. *See* **divine** (2).

ordeal *noun*
► affliction, tribulation, visitation. *See* **trial** (1). *See synonym note at* **trial**.

order *noun*
1. The act or condition of being arranged ► allotment, layout, positioning. *See* **arrangement** (1). **2.** The act of demanding ► appeal, claim, requisition. *See* **demand** (1). **3.** Systematic arrangement and design ► format, organization, scheme. *See* **method** (1). **4.** A state of sound readiness ► condition, fettle, form. *See* **shape** (1). **5.** A number of things placed or occurring one after the other ► course, procession, sequence. *See* **series**. **6.** An order ► charge, commandment, imperative. *See* **command** (1). **7.** A group of people united in a relationship and having some interest, activity, or purpose in common ► club, league, society. *See* **union** (1). **8.** A class that is defined by the common attribute or attributes possessed by all its members ► ilk, mold, species. *See* **kind²**. **9.** A subdivision of a larger group ► category, classification, set. *See* **class** (1). **10.** A division of persons or things by quality or rank ► league, rank, tier. *See* **class** (2).

order *verb*
1. To give orders to ► charge, instruct, tell. *See* **command** (1). **2.** To command in an arrogant manner ► domineer, rule, tyrannize. *See* **boss** (1). **3.** To put into a deliberate order ► methodize, organize, systematize. *See* **arrange** (1). *See synonym note at* **arrange**. **4.** To ask for urgently or insistently ► insist on (*or* upon), require. *See* **demand** (1).

orderliness *noun*
► order, organization, scheme. *See* **method** (1).

orderly *adjective*
1. In good order or clean condition ► shipshape, tidy. *See* **neat** (1). **2.** Arranged or proceeding in a set, systematized pattern ► regular, systematic. *See* **methodical**. *See synonym note at* **methodical** (1).

orders of the day *noun*
► calendar, schedule, timetable. *See* **program** (1).

ordinance *noun*
1. A principle governing affairs within or among political units ► decree, edict, institute. *See* **law** (1). **2.** A formal act or set of acts prescribed by ritual ► rite, ritual, tradition. *See* **ceremony** (1).

ordinarily *adverb*
► customarily, generally, normally. *See* **usually**.

ordinariness *noun*
► normality, regularity, routineness. *See* **usualness**.

ordinary *adjective*
1. Being of no special quality or type ► average, bland, boring, common, commonplace, cut-and-dried, formulaic, garden, garden-variety, homely, humdrum, indifferent, mediocre, middling, mundane, nondescript, plain, routine, run-of-the-mill, so-so, standard, stock, undistinguished, unexceptional, unremarkable, white-bread. *Informal:* ho-hum. *Idioms:* fair-to-middling, no great shakes. *See also* **acceptable, humble, modest**. **2.** Occurring or encountered regularly ► commonplace, frequent, regular. *See* **common** (1). *See synonym note at* **common**.

ordinary *noun*
A regular or customary matter, condition, or course of events ► commonplace, norm, rule. *See* **usual**.

ordure *noun*
► dung, feces, waste. *See* **excrement**.

organ *noun*
1. An administrative unit, as of a government or company ► agency, bureau. *See* **branch** (3). **2.** That by which something is done or caused ► agency, means, medium. *See* **agent** (1). **3.** An issue of printed material offered for sale or distribution ► title, volume, work. *See* **publication** (2).

organic *adjective*
► additive-free, unadulterated. *See* **natural** (1).

organization *noun*
1. The act of founding or establishing ► constitution, establishment, institution. *See* **foundation** (1). **2.** The act or condition of being arranged ► allotment, layout, positioning. *See* **arrangement** (1). **3.** Systematic arrangement and design ► order, pattern, scheme. *See* **method** (1). **4.** A group of people united in a relationship and having some interest, activity, or purpose in common ► club, league, order. *See* **union** (1). **5.** An association for a common cause or interest ► coalition, federation, league. *See* **alliance** (1). **6.** An organized array of individual elements and parts forming and working as a unit ► arrangement, totality, whole. *See* **system** (1).

organizational *adjective*
► executive, managerial, ministerial. *See* **administrative**.

organize *verb*
1. To put into a deliberate order ► order, methodize, systematize. *See* **arrange** (1). *See synonym note at* **arrange**. **2.** To plan the details or arrangements of ► blueprint, work out. *See* **arrange** (2). **3.** To assemble, prepare, or put into operation, as for war or a similar emergency ► activate, ready. *See* **mobilize**. **4.** To bring into existence formally ► constitute, establish, institute. *See* **found** (1). *See synonym note at* **found**.

organized *adjective*
► orderly, regular, systematic. *See* **methodical** (1).

orgy *noun*
► rampage, spree. *See* **binge** (1). *See synonym note at* **binge**.

orientation *noun*
▸ location, position. *See* **bearing** (3).

orifice *noun*
▸ aperture, vent. *See* **hole** (2).

oriflamme *noun*
▸ banner, colors, pennant. *See* **flag**[1] (1).

origin *noun*
1. A point of origination ▸ beginning, birthplace, cradle, derivation, font, fount, fountain, fountainhead, hotbed, mother, parent, provenance, provenience, rise, root, rootstock, source, spring, well, wellspring. *See also* **germ**. **2.** The initial stage of a developmental process ▸ genesis, inception, start. *See* **birth** (2). **3.** One's ancestors or ancestral derivation ▸ blood, extraction, lineage. *See* **ancestry**.

✦ **CORE SYNONYMS:** *origin, source, root*. These nouns signify the point at which something originates. *Origin* is the point at which something comes into existence: *The origins of some words are unknown.* When *origin* refers to people, it means parentage or ancestry: *"He came . . . of mixed French and Scottish origin"* (Charlotte Brontë). *Source* signifies the point at which something springs into being or from which it derives or is obtained: *"The mysterious . . . is the source of all true art and science"* (Albert Einstein). *Root* often denotes what is considered the fundamental cause of or basic reason for something: *"Lack of money is the root of all evil"* (George Bernard Shaw).

---

original *adjective*
1. Not derived from something else ▸ archetypal, archetypical, primary, prime, primitive, pristine, prototypic, prototypical, seminal. *See also* **elemental**. **2.** Preceding all others ▸ earliest, initial, premier. *See* **first** (1). **3.** Arising from or going to the root or source ▸ basic, fundamental, primary. *See* **radical** (1). **4.** Not counterfeit or copied ▸ genuine, true. *Slang:* legit, kosher. *See* **authentic** (1). **5.** Not the same as what was previously known or done ▸ fresh, innovative, novel. *See* **new** (1). *See synonym note at* **new**. **6.** Characterized by or productive of new things or new ideas ▸ creative, ingenious, innovative. *See* **inventive** (1).

original *noun*
1. A first form from which varieties arise or imitations are made ▸ archetype, father, forerunner, master, model, paradigm, pattern, protoplast, prototype, standard. **2.** A person who is appealingly odd or curious ▸ eccentric, oddity. *Informal:* oddball. *See* **character** (7). **3.** Someone with unconventional opinions or approaches ▸ free-thinker, independent, maverick. *See* **rebel** (2).

originality *noun*
1. The quality of being novel ▸ newness, uniqueness. *See* **novelty** (1). **2.** The power or ability to invent ▸ creativity, ingenuity, inventiveness. *See* **invention** (1).

originate *verb*
1. To bring into existence ▸ give, provide, yield. *See* **produce** (1). **2.** To form a strategy for ▸ devise, formulate, strategize. *See* **design** (1). **3.** To bring into exis-

tence formally ▸ constitute, establish, institute. *See* **found** (1). **4.** To bring into currency, use, fashion, or practice ▸ launch, pioneer. *See* **introduce** (1). **5.** To come into being ▸ arise, commence. *See* **begin** (1). **6.** To have as a source ▸ derive, emanate, upspring. *See* **stem** (1). *See synonym note at* **stem**. **7.** To have as one's home or place of origin ▸ hail, come. *See also* **descend**.

origination *noun*
1. The act of bringing or being brought into existence ▸ inception, initiation, start. *See* **beginning** (1). **2.** The act of founding or establishing ▸ constitution, establishment, institution. *See* **foundation** (1). **3.** Something invented ▸ contrivance, device. *See* **invention** (2).

originator *noun*
One that creates, founds, or originates ▸ architect, author, begetter, creator, father, framer, founder, initiator, inventor, maker, parent, patriarch, prime mover. *See also* **developer**.

orison *noun*
▸ litany, rogations. *See* **prayer**[1] (2).

ornament *noun*
Something that adorns ▸ decoration, embellishment, garnishment. *See* **adornment**.

ornament *verb*
To furnish with decorations ▸ decorate, garnish, gild. *See* **adorn** (1).

ornamentation *noun*
▸ decoration, embellishment, ornament. *See* **adornment**.

ornate *adjective*
1. Elaborately and heavily ornamented ▸ baroque, decorated, flamboyant, florid, flowery, gilded, gilt, jeweled, ornamented, ostentatious, resplendent, rococo. *See also* **gaudy, showy**. **2.** Rich in detail ▸ complicated, intricate. *See* **elaborate** (1). *See synonym note at* **elaborate**.

orneriness *noun*
▸ crankiness, prickliness, tetchiness. *See* **temper** (1).

ornery *adjective*
▸ antagonistic, contradictory, hostile. *See* **contrary** (1).

orotund *adjective*
1. Characterized by elevated language, such as that used in public speaking ▸ bombastic, grandiloquent, rhetorical. *See* **oratorical**. **2.** Having or producing a full, deep, or rich sound ▸ resounding, sonorous, vibrant. *See* **resonant**.

orotundity *noun*
▸ fustian, grandiloquence. *See* **bombast**.

orphan *noun*
A child or young animal without parents ▸ foundling, ragamuffin, stray, waif.

ort *noun*
1. Residual matter ▸ fragment, odds and ends. *See* **end** (7). **2.** A tiny amount ▸ dash, drop, smidgen. *See* **bit**[1] (1).

orthodox *adjective*
1. Conforming to established standards ▸ conformist,

traditional. *See* **conventional** (1). **2.** Generally approved or agreed upon ▶ accepted, conventional, sanctioned. *See* **accepted**. **3.** Favoring traditional views and values, especially as a political philosophy ▶ right-wing, traditionalist. *See* **conservative** (1).

orthodox *noun*
One with politically conservative views ▶ rightist, traditionalist. *See* **conservative**.

orthodoxy *noun*
▶ dogma, teaching. *See* **doctrine**.

oscillate *verb*
▶ swing, vacillate, waggle. *See* **sway** (1). *See synonym note at* **sway**.

osculate *verb*
▶ buss, smack. *See* **kiss** (1).

osculation *noun*
▶ buss, smack. *Informal:* peck. *See* **kiss** (1).

osmose *verb*
▶ absorb, draw in, sop up. *See* **drink** (3).

osmosis *noun*
▶ assimilation, digestion, intake. *See* **absorption** (1).

ossify *verb*
▶ congeal, solidify. *See* **harden** (2).

ossuary *noun*
▶ catacomb, crypt, tomb. *See* **grave**¹.

ostensible *or* **ostensive** *adjective*
▶ external, seeming. *See* **apparent** (2).

ostensibly *or* **ostensively** *adverb*
▶ evidently, externally, seemingly. *See* **apparently**.

ostentation *noun*
▶ grandiosity, loftiness, pomposity. *See* **pretentiousness**.

ostentatious *adjective*
1. Marked by outward, often extravagant display ▶ flamboyant, splashy. *See* **showy**. *See synonym note at* **showy**. **2.** Elaborately and heavily ornamented ▶ flamboyant, resplendent. *See* **ornate** (1).

ostracism *noun*
▶ deportation, extradition. *See* **exile** (1).

ostracize *verb*
1. To keep from being admitted, included, or considered ▶ blacklist, boycott, shut out. *See* **exclude** (1). *See synonym note at* **exclude**. **2.** To force to leave by official decree ▶ deport, exile, transport. *See* **banish** (1).

other *adjective*
▶ added, extra, more, new. *See* **additional**.

otherworldly *adjective*
1. Of or relating to existence outside the natural world ▶ metaphysical, superhuman. *See* **supernatural** (1). **2.** Of an unnatural and usually frightening nature ▶ uncanny, unearthly. *See* **weird** (1).

otiose *adjective*
1. Lacking value, use, or substance ▶ empty, vacant. *See* **hollow** (1). *See synonym note at* **hollow**. **2.** Resistant to exertion and activity ▶ idle, shiftless, slothful. *See* **lazy**.

otiosity *or* **otioseness** *noun*
▶ indolence, shiftlessness, sloth. *See* **laziness**.

ottoman *noun*
A stool or cushion for resting the feet ▶ footrest, footstool, hassock.

ought *verb*
▶ be compelled, need, ought. *See* **must**.

ounce *noun*
▶ dash, drop, smidgen. *See* **bit**¹ (1).

oust *verb*
▶ dismiss, evict. *See* **eject** (1). *See synonym note at* **eject**.

ouster *noun*
▶ eviction, expulsion. *See* **ejection**.

out *verb*
To be made public ▶ break, come out, get out, transpire. *Informal:* leak (out). *See also* **air, announce, appear**.

out *adjective*
1. Not present ▶ away, elsewhere, nonexistent, truant. *See* **absent** (1). **2.** Of a style or method formerly in vogue ▶ antique, dated, passé. *See* **old-fashioned**. **3.** Lacking consciousness ▶ comatose, insensible. *See* **unconscious** (1).

out *adverb*
Toward the front or beyond a position ▶ ahead, forth, onward. *See* **forward**.

outage *noun*
A cessation of proper functioning ▶ breakdown, collapse, failure, malfunction.

out-and-out *adjective*
▶ all-out, pure, sheer. *See* **utter**².

outback *noun*
▶ bush, jungle. *See* **wilderness**.

outbreak *noun*
1. A sudden emergence or increase ▶ breakout, flare, outburst. *See* **eruption** (1). **2.** A sudden violent expression, as of emotion ▶ burst, eruption, explosion. *See* **outburst** (1).

outburst *noun*
1. A sudden violent expression, as of emotion ▶ access, blowup, burst, dambreak, damburst, eruption, explosion, fit, flare-up, flood, gush, gust, outbreak, outpouring, paroxysm, torrent. **2.** A sudden emergence or increase ▶ breakout, flare, paroxysm. *See* **eruption** (1).

outcast *noun*
Someone excluded from society ▶ exile, outsider, pariah, persona non grata, reject, untouchable. *See also* **fugitive**.

outcast *adjective*
Having been given up and left alone ▶ forlorn, rejected, relinquished. *See* **abandoned** (1).

outcome *noun*
▶ consequence, end product, result. *See* **effect** (1). *See synonym note at* **effect**.

outcry *noun*
1. A loud cry ▶ call, holler, yell. *See* **shout**. **2.** Loud and insistent utterances or noisemaking, usually expressing disapproval ▶ hullabaloo, rumpus, uproar. *See* **vociferation**.

outdated *adjective*
 1. Of a style or method formerly in vogue ▸ antique, dated, passé. *See* **old-fashioned. 2.** No longer in use ▸ obsolescent, outmoded. *See* **obsolete.**

outdo *verb*
 ▸ exceed, excel, outshine. *See* **surpass** (1). *See synonym note at* **surpass.**

outdoors *noun*
 ▸ bush, jungle. *See* **wilderness.**

outermost *adjective*
 ▸ farthest, outmost, ultimate. *See* **extreme** (1).

outfit *noun*
 1. Things needed for a task, journey, or other purpose ▸ accouterments, apparatus, equipment, gear, material, materiel, paraphernalia, rig, tackle, turnout. **2.** A set or style of clothing ▸ garb, guise, outfit. *See* **dress** (2). **3.** *Informal* A commercial organization ▸ corporation, enterprise, establishment. *See* **company** (1).

outfit *verb*
 1. To supply what is needed for some activity or purpose ▸ equip, gear. *See* **furnish** (1). *See synonym note at* **furnish. 2.** To put clothes on ▸ attire, clothe, garb. *See* **dress** (1).

✚ CORE SYNONYMS: *outfit, apparatus, equipment, gear, materiel, paraphernalia.* These nouns denote the materials needed for a task, journey, or other purpose: *an explorer's outfit; laboratory apparatus; hiking equipment; skiing gear; naval materiel; a beekeeper's paraphernalia.*

---

outflow *noun*
 ▸ flood, gush, outpouring. *See* **flow.**

outfox *verb*
 ▸ outsmart, outthink, overreach. *See* **outwit.**

outgoing *adjective*
 Disposed to be open, sociable, and talkative ▸ communicable, communicative, expansive, extraverted, extroverted, gregarious, unreserved. *See also* **friendly, social, talkative.**

outgrowth *noun*
 1. Something derived from another ▸ byproduct, offshoot, spinoff. *See* **derivative. 2.** An unevenness or elevation on a surface ▸ lump, protuberance. *See* **bump** (1).

outgun *verb*
 ▸ conquer, surmount, vanquish. *See* **defeat** (1).

outing *noun*
 A usually short journey taken for pleasure ▸ excursion, jaunt, junket, trip. *See also* **excursion, journey.**

outlander *noun*
 ▸ alien, outsider, stranger. *See* **foreigner.**

outlandish *adjective*
 1. Deviating from what is conventional or customary ▸ bizarre, grotesque. *See* **eccentric.** *See synonym note at* **eccentric. 2.** Very strange or strikingly unusual ▸ fantastic, outré, unorthodox. *See* **exotic** (2).

outlast *verb*
 To live, exist, or remain longer than ▸ outlive, outwear, survive. *See also* **survive.**

outlaw *verb*
 To refuse to allow ▸ disallow, proscribe. *See* **forbid.**

outlaw *noun*
 1. One who flees, as from confinement or the police ▸ escapee, fugitive, refugee, runaway. *See also* **criminal. 2.** One who commits a crime ▸ culprit, lawbreaker, offender. *See* **criminal.**

outlawed *adjective*
 ▸ illegitimate, illicit, unlawful. *See* **illegal** (1).

outlay *noun*
 1. An amount paid or to be paid for a purchase ▸ charge, expense, price. *See* **cost** (1). **2.** The operating expenses of an enterprise ▸ costs, expenses. *See* **overhead.**

outlay *verb*
 To give money as payment ▸ expend, give. *See* **spend** (1).

outlet *noun*
 1. A socket connected to a power supply ▸ plug, electric socket, socket, terminal, wall socket. **2.** A retail establishment where merchandise is sold ▸ boutique, emporium, shop, store. **3.** An open space allowing passage ▸ orifice, vent. *See* **hole** (2).

outline *noun*
 1. The characteristic surface arrangement of a thing ▸ configuration, design, structure. *See* **form** (1). **2.** A preliminary plan or version, as of a written work ▸ blueprint, sketch. *See* **draft** (1). **3.** A shortened version or summary ▸ brief, sketch. *See* **synopsis.**

outline *verb*
 1. To draw up a preliminary plan or version of ▸ delineate, sketch. *See* **draft** (1). **2.** To work out and arrange the parts and details of ▸ blueprint, lay out, sketch. *See* **design** (2).

outlive *verb*
 To live, exist, or remain longer than ▸ outlast, outwear, survive. *See also* **survive.**

outlook *noun*
 1. The position from which something is observed or considered ▸ aspect, point of view, standpoint. *See* **viewpoint. 2.** A frame of mind affecting one's thoughts or behavior ▸ attitude, position. *See* **posture** (2). **3.** Chance of success or advancement ▸ future, prospects. *See also* **chance. 4.** The act of predicting ▸ forecast, prognosis. *See* **prediction. 5.** A high structure or place commanding a wide view ▸ crow's nest, observatory, watchtower. *See* **lookout** (2). **6.** That which is or can be seen ▸ panorama, perspective, vista. *See* **view** (2).

outlying *adjective*
 ▸ isolated, out-of-the-way, removed. *See* **remote** (1).

outmaneuver *verb*
 ▸ outsmart, outthink, overreach. *See* **outwit.**

outmatch *verb*
 ▸ exceed, excel, outshine. *See* **surpass** (1).

outmoded *adjective*
 1. Of a style or method formerly in vogue ▸ antique, dated, passé. *See* **old-fashioned. 2.** No longer in use ▸ outdated, superseded. *See* **obsolete.**

outmost *adjective*
▸ farthest, outermost, ultimate. *See* **extreme** (1).

out-of-date *adjective*
1. Of a style or method formerly in vogue ▸ antique, dated, passé. *See* **old-fashioned. 2.** No longer in use ▸ outdated, outmoded. *See* **obsolete.**

out of sight *adjective*
Slang Beyond what is usual, normal, or customary ▸ extraordinary, outstanding, remarkable. *See* **exceptional** (1).

out-of-the-way *adjective*
1. Far from centers of human population ▸ outlying, removed, secluded. *See* **remote** (1). **2.** Not proceeding straight to the point or object ▸ circuitous, devious, roundabout. *See* **indirect** (1).

outpace *verb*
▸ outrun, overtake. *See* **pass** (2).

outplay *verb*
▸ conquer, surmount, vanquish. *See* **defeat** (1).

outpour *noun*
Something suggestive of running water ▸ gush, outflow, surge. *See* **flow.**

outpouring *noun*
1. Something suggestive of running water ▸ flood, rush, surge. *See* **flow. 2.** A sudden violent expression, as of emotion ▸ burst, eruption, explosion. *See* **outburst** (1).

output *noun*
1. The amount or quantity produced ▸ garner, production, yield. **2.** Something that is the result of creative effort ▸ piece, production, work. *See* **composition** (1).

outrage *noun*
1. A monstrous offense or evil ▸ atrocity, barbarity, enormity, horror, inhumanity, monstrosity. *See also* **crime. 2.** An unjust act ▸ disservice, inequity, wrong. *See* **injustice** (1). **3.** An act that offends a person's sense of pride or dignity ▸ contumely, insult. *See* **indignity. 4.** A strong feeling of displeasure or hostility ▸ indignation, rage, wrath. *See* **anger.**

outrage *verb*
1. To cause resentment or hurt by callous, rude behavior ▸ offend, pique. *See* **insult** (1). **2.** To cause anger, resentment, or hurt feelings ▸ annoy, injure, upset. *See* **offend** (1). *See synonym note at* **offend.**

outrageous *adjective*
Exceeding the bounds of morality, decency, or reason ▸ appalling, atrocious, heinous, inhuman, intolerable, monstrous, obscene, preposterous, reprehensible, ridiculous, scandalous, shocking, unconscionable, unreasonable, unspeakable, wanton. *Idioms:* beyond the pale, out of bounds, out of sight. *See also* **eccentric, excessive, flagrant, offensive, shameful.**

outrageousness *noun*
The quality or state of being outrageous ▸ atrociousness, atrocity, enormity, heinousness, monstrousness, scandalousness. *See also* **flagrancy.**

outré *adjective*
▸ bizarre, fantastic, unorthodox. *See* **exotic** (2).

outright *adjective*
▸ all-out, pure, sheer. *See* **utter².**

outrun *verb*
1. To catch up with and move past ▸ outpace, overtake. *See* **pass** (2). **2.** To get away from a pursuer ▸ evade, slip, throw off. *See* **lose** (3). **3.** To be greater or better than ▸ exceed, excel, outshine, transcend. *See* **surpass** (1).

outset *noun*
▸ genesis, inception, start. *See* **birth** (2). *See synonym note at* **birth.**

outshine *verb*
▸ exceed, excel, transcend. *See* **surpass** (1).

outside *noun*
The greatest quantity or highest degree attainable ▸ ultimate, utmost. *See* **maximum** (1).

outside *adjective*
Small in degree, especially of probability ▸ negligible, slight, slim. *See* **remote** (2).

outsider *noun*
1. A person coming from another country or into another community ▸ alien, immigrant, stranger. *See* **foreigner. 2.** Someone excluded from society ▸ exile, pariah. *See* **outcast.**

outsize *adjective*
▸ extensive, large, sizable. *See* **big** (1).

outskirts *noun*
The periphery of a city or town ▸ city limits, edge, environs, exurbs, fringe, skirts, suburbs, town line. *See also* **border, limits.**

outsmart *verb*
▸ outfox, outthink, overreach. *See* **outwit.**

outspoken *adjective*
▸ forthright, free-spoken, unreserved. *See* **frank.** *See synonym note at* **frank.**

outstanding *adjective*
1. Readily attracting notice ▸ conspicuous, pointed, prominent. *See* **noticeable** (1). *See synonym note at* **noticeable. 2.** Beyond what is usual, normal, or customary ▸ extraordinary, remarkable. *See* **exceptional** (1). **3.** Owed as a debt ▸ collectible, payable, unpaid. *See* **due** (1).

outstretch *verb*
1. To put forward, especially an appendage ▸ extend, reach, stretch (out). **2.** To move or arrange so as to cover a larger area ▸ extend, stretch. *See* **spread** (1).

outstretched *adjective*
▸ extended, lengthy, prolonged. *See* **long¹** (1).

outstrip *verb*
1. To be greater or better than ▸ exceed, excel, outshine. *See* **surpass** (1). *See synonym note at* **surpass. 2.** To catch up with and move past ▸ outrun, overtake. *See* **pass** (2).

outthink *verb*
▸ outsmart, overreach, take in. *See* **outwit.**

outward *adjective*
▸ ostensible, seeming. *See* **apparent** (2).

outwardly *adverb*
▸ evidently, externally, seemingly. *See* **apparently.**

outwear *verb*
To live, exist, or remain longer than ▸ outlast, outlive, survive. *See also* **survive.**

outweigh *verb*
▸ counteract, negate, offset. *See* **cancel** (2).

outwit *verb*
To get the better of by cleverness or cunning ▸ outfox, outguess, outmaneuver, outsmart, outthink, overreach, second-guess, take in. *Idioms:* get the better of, put one over on. *See also* **baffle, confuse, deceive.**

oval *adjective*
Resembling an egg in shape ▸ egg-shaped, ellipsoidal, elliptical, oblong, ovate, oviform, ovoid, ovoidal.

oval *noun*
An egg-shaped form or figure ▸ egg-shape, ellipse, ellipsoid, ovoid.

ovate *adjective*
▸ elliptical, ovoid. *See* **oval.**

ovation *noun*
1. Approval expressed by clapping ▸ applause, hand, plaudit. **2.** A formal token of appreciation and admiration for a person's high achievements ▸ salute, tribute. *See* **testimonial** (2).

over *noun*
▸ concluded, done, through. *See* **complete** (3).

overabundance *noun*
▸ exorbitance, extravagance, surfeit. *See* **excess** (1).

overabundant *adjective*
▸ extravagant, immoderate. *See* **excessive** (1).

over again *adverb*
▸ afresh, again, once again. *See* **anew.**

overage *noun*
▸ overflow, oversupply, superfluity. *See* **surplus.**

overall *adjective*
▸ all-inclusive, broad, expansive. *See* **general** (2).

overambitious *adjective*
▸ determined, driven. *See* **ambitious.**

overbear *verb*
▸ command, overlook, overshadow. *See* **dominate** (2).

overbearing *adjective*
1. Overly convinced of one's own superiority and importance ▸ insolent, proud, superior. *See* **arrogant.** *See synonym note at* **arrogant. 2.** Given to asserting one's will or authority over others ▸ bossy, domineering, peremptory. *See* **dictatorial** (1). *See synonym note at* **dictatorial.**

overbearingness *noun*
▸ hauteur, superiority. *See* **arrogance.**

overblown *adjective*
1. Characterized by elevated language, such as that used in public speaking ▸ bombastic, grandiloquent, rhetorical. *See* **oratorical. 2.** Filled up with or as if with something insubstantial ▸ tumescent, windy. *See* **inflated** (1). **3.** Having too much flesh ▸ chubby, overweight, tubby. *See* **fat** (1). **4.** Represented as greater than is actually the case ▸ hyperbolic, inflated, magnified. *See* **exaggerated** (1).

overcast *verb*
1. To make dim or unclear ▸ blur, fog, obfuscate. *See*

obscure (1). **2.** To make dark or darker ▸ darken, gloom, shadow. *See* **shade** (2).

overcharge *verb*
1. To get something by deceitful trickery ▸ bilk, defraud, swindle. *See* **cheat** (1). **2.** To make something seem greater than is actually the case ▸ inflate, magnify, overstate. *See* **exaggerate** (1).

overcoat *noun*
▸ anorak, parka, windbreaker. *See* **coat** (1).

overcome *verb*
1. To affect deeply or completely, as with emotion ▸ crush, prostrate. *See* **overwhelm** (2). **2.** To render totally ineffective by decisive defeat ▸ crush, overpower, rout. *See* **overwhelm** (1). **3.** To win a victory over, as in battle or a competition ▸ conquer, surmount. *See* **defeat** (1). *See synonym note at* **defeat.**

overcome *adjective*
In a state of anxiety, uneasiness, or distress ▸ agitated, distressed, overwrought. *See* **anxious.**

overconfidence *noun*
▸ audacity, boldness, forwardness. *See* **impudence.**

overconfident *adjective*
▸ bold, insolent, pert. *See* **impudent.**

overcritical *adjective*
▸ carping, judgmental. *See* **critical** (1).

overcrowded *adjective*
Filled beyond capacity ▸ choked, congested, overflowing, overpopulated, swarming, teeming. *See also* **full, tight.**

overdo *verb*
To do, use, or stress something to excess ▸ overindulge, overreach, overwork, stretch, strain. *Idioms:* bite off more than one can chew, carry too far (*or* to extremes), do to death, go overboard (*or* too far *or* to extremes), kill oneself, knock oneself out. *See also* **exaggerate, exceed.**

overdrawn *adjective*
▸ far-fetched, overstated. *See* **exaggerated** (1).

overdue *adjective*
▸ behind, delayed, overdue. *See* **late** (1). *See synonym note at* **late.**

overeater *noun*
One who eats or consumes immoderate amounts of food and drink ▸ glutton, hog, pig. *See also* **sybarite.**

overemphasize *verb*
1. To discuss at great or excessive length ▸ dwell on, harp on, labor. *See* **belabor** (2). **2.** To make something seem greater than is actually the case ▸ inflate, magnify, overcharge. *See* **exaggerate** (2).

overestimate *verb*
▸ miscount, misestimate, misjudge. *See* **miscalculate.**

overflow *verb*
1. To flow over completely ▸ engulf, inundate, submerge. *See* **flood** (1). **2.** To be abundantly filled or richly supplied ▸ bristle, crawl, swarm. *See* **teem**[1]. *See synonym note at* **teem**[1].

overflow *noun*
1. An overwhelming flow of water ▸ deluge, down-

pour, torrent. *See* **flood** (1). **2.** A thing, amount, or quantity beyond what is needed, desired, or appropriate ▸ oversupply, superfluity. *See* **surplus.**

overflowing *adjective*
1. Completely filled ▸ awash, brimful, loaded. *See* **full** (1). **2.** Filled beyond capacity ▸ choked, congested, teeming. *See* **overcrowded.**

overgenerosity *noun*
▸ prodigality, squander, wastefulness. *See* **extravagance** (1).

overgrown *adjective*
▸ lush, luxuriant, profuse. *See* **thick** (3).

overhang *verb*
1. To curve outward past the normal or usual limit ▸ balloon, jut, project. *See* **bulge** (1). **2.** To be imminent ▸ hover, impend, loom. *See* **threaten** (2).

overhang *noun*
A part that protrudes or extends outward ▸ knob, protrusion, protuberance. *See* **projection** (1).

overhaul *verb*
1. To reorganize thoroughly or drastically ▸ reconfigure, reengineer, reshuffle, shake up. *Idioms:* clean house, make a clean sweep. *See also* **renew, restore. 2.** To restore to proper condition ▸ mend, patch, repair. *See* **fix** (1). **3.** To catch up with and move past ▸ outrun, overtake. *See* **pass** (2).

overhaul *noun*
A thorough or drastic reorganization ▸ reengineering, reshuffling, shakeup. *Informal:* housecleaning. *Idiom:* clean sweep. *See also* **renewal, revolution.**

overhead *noun*
The operating expenses of an enterprise ▸ budget, costs, expenses, operating costs, operating expenses, outlay.

overindulge *verb*
1. To treat indulgently ▸ coddle, indulge, pamper. *See* **baby. 2.** To do, use, or stress something to excess ▸ overreach, strain. *See* **overdo.**

overindulgence *noun*
▸ immoderacy, surfeit. *See* **excess** (3).

overjoy *verb*
▸ enchant, gladden, pleasure. *See* **delight** (1).

overjoyed *adjective*
▸ euphoric, overjoyed. *See* **elated.**

overlay *verb*
1. To extend over the surface of ▸ blanket, spread. *See* **cover** (1). **2.** To give a deceptively attractive appearance to ▸ gild, sugarcoat, varnish. *See* **color** (4).

overlay *noun*
An outer layer of material ▸ blanket, coating, layer. *See* **coat** (2).

overleap *verb*
▸ overstep, surpass. *See* **exceed** (1).

overlong *adjective*
▸ drawn-out, long-drawn-out, protracted. *See* **long¹** (2).

overlook *verb*
1. To view broadly or from a height ▸ look over, scan, survey. *See also* **look. 2.** To direct and watch over the

work and performance of others ▸ boss, monitor. *See* **supervise.** *See synonym note at* **supervise. 3.** To rise above, especially so as to afford a view of ▸ overbear, overshadow. *See* **dominate** (2). **4.** To fail to do or carry out ▸ disregard, omit, pass over. *See* **neglect** (3). **5.** To grant forgiveness to or for ▸ condone, excuse, pardon. *See* **forgive. 6.** To pretend not to see ▸ disregard, ignore. *See* **blink at.**

overlook *noun*
A high structure or place commanding a wide view ▸ crow's nest, observatory, watchtower. *See* **lookout** (2).

overlord *noun*
▸ boss, director, head, leader. *See* **chief** (1).

overly *adverb*
▸ excessively, extremely, inordinately. *See* **unduly.**

overmuch *adjective*
Exceeding a normal or reasonable limit ▸ extravagant, immoderate. *See* **excessive** (1).

overmuch *adverb*
Too much ▸ excessively, extremely, overly. *See* **unduly.**

overmuch *noun*
A thing, amount, or quantity beyond what is needed, desired, or appropriate ▸ overflow, oversupply, superfluity. *See* **surplus.**

overpass *verb*
▸ overstep, surpass. *See* **exceed** (1).

overpopulated *adjective*
▸ congested, teeming. *See* **overcrowded.**

overpower *verb*
1. To render totally ineffective by decisive defeat ▸ crush, overcome, rout. *See* **overwhelm** (1). **2.** To affect deeply or completely, as with emotion ▸ crush, prostrate. *See* **overwhelm** (2).

overpowering *adjective*
1. Extreme in activity, strength, or effect ▸ fierce, heavy, terrible. *See* **intense** (1). *See synonym note at* **intense. 2.** Having an unpleasant odor ▸ foul-smelling, malodorous, stinking. *See* **smelly.**

overpriced *adjective*
▸ exorbitant, sky-high, stiff. *See* **steep¹** (2).

overreach *verb*
1. To go beyond the limits of ▸ overstep, surpass. *See* **exceed** (1). **2.** To get the better of by cleverness or cunning ▸ outsmart, outthink. *See* **outwit. 3.** To do, use, or stress something to excess ▸ overindulge, strain. *See* **overdo.**

overrefined *adjective*
▸ priggish, prissy, strait-laced. *See* **prudish.**

overripe *adjective*
▸ decayed, putrid, rotten. *See* **bad** (2).

overrun *verb*
1. To enter so as to attack, plunder, destroy, or conquer ▸ foray, raid. *See* **invade** (1). **2.** To go beyond the limits of ▸ overstep, surpass. *See* **exceed** (1). **3.** To seize or maintain control over by conquest ▸ capture, invade, subjugate. *See* **occupy** (2).

overrun *noun*
A thing, amount, or quantity beyond what is needed,

desired, or appropriate ▸ overflow, oversupply, superfluity. *See* **surplus.**

oversee *verb*
▸ boss, monitor. *See* **supervise.** *See synonym note at* **supervise.**

overseer *noun*
▸ foreman, manager, supervisor. *See* **boss** (1).

oversensitive *adjective*
Quick to take offense or become angry or upset ▸ hypersensitive, sensitive, thin-skinned, ticklish, touchy. *See also* **ill-tempered.**

oversensitivity *adjective*
Quickness to take offense ▸ hypersensitivity, sensitivity, ticklishness, touchiness. *Idiom:* thin skin. *See also* **temper.**

overshadow *verb*
1. To make dim or unclear ▸ blur, fog, obfuscate. *See* **obscure** (1). **2.** To make dark or darker ▸ darken, overcast, shadow. *See* **shade** (2). **3.** To rise above, especially so as to afford a view of ▸ overlook, tower above. *See* **dominate** (2).

overshoot *verb*
▸ overstep, surpass. *See* **exceed** (1).

oversight *noun*
1. An act or instance of neglecting ▸ negligence, omission. *See* **neglect** (1). **2.** The act or process of managing or directing ▸ administration, direction, leadership. *See* **management** (1). **3.** An unintentional deviation from what is correct, right, or true ▸ inaccuracy, lapse, mistake. *See* **error** (1).

oversize *or* **oversized** *adjective*
▸ cumbersome, heavy, voluminous. *See* **bulky** (1).

overspread *verb*
▸ blanket, coat. *See* **cover** (1).

overstate *verb*
▸ inflate, magnify, overcharge. *See* **exaggerate** (1).

overstated *adjective*
▸ inflated, magnified, overblown. *See* **exaggerated** (1).

overstatement *noun*
▸ hyperbolism, tall talk. *See* **exaggeration.**

overstep *verb*
1. To go beyond the limits of ▸ overrun, surpass. *See* **exceed** (1). **2.** To fail to fulfill a promise or conform to a regulation ▸ break, infringe. *See* **violate** (1).

overstock *noun*
▸ overflow, oversupply, superfluity. *See* **surplus.**

oversufficiency *noun*
▸ exorbitance, extravagance, surfeit. *See* **excess** (1).

oversupply *noun*
▸ overflow, overmuch, superfluity. *See* **surplus.**

overt *adjective*
▸ blatant, patent, transparent. *See* **obvious** (1).

overtake *verb*
1. To come up even with another ▸ catch (up), pull alongside, pull even. *See also* **approach, equalize. 2.** To catch up with and move past ▸ overhaul, outrun. *See* **pass** (2).

overthrow *verb*
1. To bring about the downfall of ▸ bring down,

depose, overturn, subvert, topple, tumble, unhorse, upset. *See also* **defeat. 2.** To turn or cause to turn from a vertical or horizontal position ▸ knock over, topple. *See* **overturn** (1).

overthrow *noun*
1. The act of defeating or the condition of being defeated ▸ beating, trouncing, vanquishment. *See* **defeat. 2.** The act or an example of upsetting ▸ disruption, overturn, upheaval. *See* **upset** (1).

✚ CORE SYNONYMS: *overthrow, overturn, subvert, topple, upset.* These verbs mean to cause the downfall, destruction, abolition, or undoing of: *overthrow an empire; overturn existing institutions; subverting civil order; toppled the government; upset all our plans.*

---

overture *noun*
1. A short section of preliminary remarks ▸ foreword, preface, prologue. *See* **introduction** (1). **2.** Personal approach to gain acquaintance, favor, or an agreement ▸ moves, proposition. *See* **advances.**

overturn *verb*
1. To turn or cause to turn from a vertical or horizontal position ▸ capsize, invert, knock over, overthrow, tip over, topple, turn over, upend, upset, upturn. **2.** To bring about the downfall of ▸ subvert, topple. *See* **overthrow** (1). *See synonym note at* **overthrow. 3.** To take back or remove ▸ repeal, rescind, revoke. *See* **lift** (5).

overturn *noun*
The act or an example of upsetting ▸ disruption, overthrow, upheaval. *See* **upset** (1).

overturned *adjective*
▸ capsized, inverted. *See* **upside-down** (1).

overused *adjective*
▸ clichéd, hackneyed, stale, tired. *See* **trite.**

overview *noun*
A general or comprehensive view or treatment ▸ survey. *See also* **synopsis.**

overweening *adjective*
1. Overly convinced of one's own superiority and importance ▸ insolent, superior. *See* **arrogant. 2.** Given to asserting one's will or authority over others ▸ bossy, domineering, overbearing. *See* **dictatorial** (1).

overweight *adjective*
▸ corpulent, obese, tubby. *See* **fat** (1).

overwhelm *verb*
1. To render totally ineffective by decisive defeat ▸ crush, drub, overcome, overpower, rout, smash, steamroller, thrash, trounce. *Informal:* clobber, massacre, wallop, whip. *Slang:* cream, murder, shellac, skunk, smear. *Idioms:* clean someone's clock, eat someone alive, eat someone's lunch, kick someone's butt, take to the cleaners. *See also* **annihilate, defeat. 2.** To affect deeply or completely, as with emotion ▸ crush, engulf, overcome, overpower, pierce, prostrate. *See also* **daze, stagger. 3.** To affect as if by an outpouring of water ▸ deluge, flood, inundate, swamp. **4.** To flow over completely ▸ engulf, overflow,

submerge. *See* **flood** (1). **5.** To severely impair some-one's spirit, health, or will ▸ crush, ruin. *See* **break** (4).

overwhelming *adjective*
1. Extreme in activity, strength, or effect ▸ fierce, heavy, terrible. *See* **intense** (1). **2.** So remarkable as to be difficult to believe ▸ astounding, staggering, unbelievable. *See* **astonishing.**

overwork *verb*
▸ overreach, strain. *See* **overdo.**

overworked *adjective*
▸ clichéd, overused, stale, tired. *See* **trite.**

overwrought *adjective*
▸ distressed, nervous, uneasy. *See* **anxious.**

oviform *adjective*
▸ elliptical, ovoid. *See* **oval.**

ovoid *noun*
An egg-shaped form or figure ▸ egg-shape, ellipsoid. *See* **oval.**

ovoid or **ovoidal** *adjective*
Resembling an egg in shape ▸ elliptical, oblong. *See* **oval.**

owed or **owing** *adjective*
▸ collectible, payable, unpaid. *See* **due** (1).

owing to *preposition*
▸ as a result of, on account of, through. *See* **because of.**

own *verb*
1. To have at one's disposal ▸ enjoy, have, hold. *See* **command** (3). **2.** To admit to the reality or truth of ▸ concede, grant, own up. *See* **acknowledge** (1). *See synonym note at* **acknowledge.**

owner *noun*
A person who has legal title to property ▸ holder, landlady, landlord, master, possessor, proprietor, titleholder.

ownership *noun*
The fact of possessing or the legal right to possess something ▸ deed, dominion, possession, proprietorship, title.

ox *noun*
▸ gawk, lout. *Informal:* lummox. *See* **oaf.**

p

pa *noun*
Informal A male parent ▸ sire. *Informal:* dad, papa. *See synonym note at* **father** (1).

pabulum *noun*
▸ fare, nourishment, sustenance. *See* **food.**

pace *noun*
1. Rate of motion or performance ▸ speed, tempo, velocity. *Informal:* clip. **2.** A manner of walking ▸ gait, stride, tread. *See* **walk** (2).

pace *verb*
To go on foot ▸ step, tread. *See* **walk.**

pacific or **pacifical** *adjective*
1. Inclined or disposed to peace; not quarrelsome or unruly ▸ conciliatory, dovish, pacifist. *See* **peaceable.**
2. Free from disturbance, agitation, or commotion ▸ peaceful, placid, serene. *See* **still** (1). *See synonym note at* **still.**

pacifist or **pacifistic** *adjective*
▸ conciliatory, dovish, nonviolent. *See* **peaceable.**

pacify *verb*
To ease the anger or agitation of ▸ allay, appease, assuage, becalm, calm (down), conciliate, dulcify, gentle, lull, mollify, placate, propitiate, quiet, settle, soften, soothe, still, sweeten, tranquilize. *Idiom:* pour oil on troubled water. *See also* **moderate, satiate.**

✦ **CORE SYNONYMS:** *pacify, mollify, conciliate, appease, placate.* These verbs refer to easing another's anger, belligerence, discontent, or agitation. To *pacify* is to

restore calm to or establish peace in: *"The explanation . . . was merely an invention framed to pacify his guests"* (Charlotte Brontë). *An army was required in order to pacify the islands. Mollify* stresses the soothing of hostile feelings: *The therapist mollified the angry teenager by speaking gently. Conciliate* implies winning over, often by reasoning and with mutual concessions: *"A wise government knows how to enforce with temper or to conciliate with dignity"* (George Grenville). *Appease* and *placate* suggest satisfying claims or demands or tempering antagonism, often by granting concessions: *I appeased my friend's anger with a compliment. A sincere apology placated the indignant customer.*

pack *noun*
1. A container carried on the back or around the waist ▸ backpack, belly pack, daypack, fanny pack, haversack, kit, knapsack, rucksack, waist pack. **2.** An organized group of criminals, hoodlums, or wrong-doers ▸ band, gang, ring. *Informal:* mob. **3.** An enormous number of persons or things gathered together ▸ horde, mass, throng. *See* **crowd** (1). **4.** A number of animals considered collectively ▸ bevy, gaggle, litter. *See* **flock** (1). *See synonym note at* **flock. 5.** *Informal* A great deal ▸ mass, profusion. *See* **abundance** (1).

pack *verb*
1. To fill to capacity ▸ cram, load, stuff. *See* **fill** (1). **2.** To move while supporting ▸ bear, convey, lug. *See* **carry** (1). **3.** *Informal* To hold on one's person ▸ bear, have, possess. *See* **carry** (7).

package *verb*
To cover and tie something, as with paper and string ▸ do up, wrap.

package *noun*
Something wrapped or enclosed, as for transporting ▸ box, bundle, carton, crate, mailer, packet, parcel, tin. *See also* **container.**

packaging *noun*
▸ casing, covering. *See* **wrapper.**

packed *adjective*
1. Completely filled ▸ brimming, loaded, overflowing. *See* **full** (1). 2. Having all parts near to each other ▸ crowded, dense, tight. *See* **thick** (2).

packet *noun*
▸ bundle, carton, parcel. *See* **package.**

packing *noun*
▸ padding, stuffing. *See* **filler** (1).

pact *noun*
1. An often written acceptance of terms between parties ▸ accord, deal, understanding. *See* **agreement** (1). 2. A formal, usually written settlement between nations ▸ concord, convention, entente. *See* **treaty.**

pad *noun*
Informal A building or shelter where one lives ▸ domicile, habitation, residence. *See* **home** (1).

padding *noun*
▸ packing, stuffing. *See* **filler** (1).

paddock *noun*
▸ corral, fold. *See* **pen²** (1).

padre *noun*
Informal A person ordained for service in a Christian church ▸ ecclesiastic, minister, parson. *See* **cleric.**

paean *noun*
▸ acclamation, celebration, kudos. *See* **praise** (1).

pagan *noun*
1. One who does not believe in God ▸ atheist, heathen, infidel, non-believer. 2. A person devoted to pleasure and luxury ▸ hedonist, sensualist, voluptuary. *See* **sybarite.**

pagan *adjective*
Without belief in God ▸ heathen. *See also* **atheistic.**

pageant *noun*
▸ display, spectacle. *See* **array** (1).

pageantry *noun*
1. The act of showing joyful satisfaction in an event ▸ jubilation, merrymaking, rejoicing. *See* **celebration** (3). 2. Brilliant, showy splendor ▸ magnificence, resplendence, sparkle. *See* **glitter** (2).

pain *noun*
1. A sensation of physical discomfort occurring as the result of disease or injury ▸ ache, burn, cramp, crick, gripes, pang, prick, prickle, shoot, smart, soreness, spasm, stab, sting, stitch, throe, twinge. *Informal:* misery. *See also* **harm.** 2. A state of physical or mental suffering ▸ agony, misery, wretchedness. *See* **distress** (1). 3. Something that annoys ▸ bother, irritant, nuisance. *See* **annoyance** (2). 4. A source of persistent worry or hardship ▸ cross, tribulation. *See* **burden¹** (1).

pain *verb*
1. To cause great pain or suffering to ▸ plague, rack, strike. *See* **afflict.** 2. To cause emotional suffering or painful sorrow to ▸ disturb, grieve, hurt. *See* **distress** (1). 3. To cause pain, soreness, or discomfort to ▸ bother, inflame. *See* **hurt** (3).

✛ CORE SYNONYMS: *pain, ache, pang, smart, stitch, throe, twinge.* These nouns denote a sensation of severe physical discomfort: *abdominal pain; aches in my leg; the pangs of a cramped muscle; aspirin that alleviated the smart; a stitch in my side; the throes of dying; a twinge of arthritis.*

painful *adjective*
1. Marked by, causing, or experiencing physical pain ▸ aching, achy, afflictive, hurtful, inflamed, irritating, nagging, raw, smarting, sore, stabbing, stinging, tender. *See also* **grievous, tormenting, uncomfortable.** 2. Difficult to accept or bear ▸ disagreeable, galling, unpleasant. *See* **bitter** (3).

pains *noun*
1. Attentiveness to detail ▸ fastidiousness, meticulousness, painstaking. *See* **thoroughness.** 2. The use of energy to do something ▸ exertion, struggle. *See* **effort** (1).

painstaking *adjective*
1. Marked by attentiveness to every detail ▸ fastidious, meticulous, scrupulous. *See* **careful** (2). *See synonym note at* **careful.** 2. Characterized by steady attention and effort ▸ assiduous, persistent. *See* **diligent.** *See synonym note at* **diligent.**

painstaking *noun*
Attentiveness to detail ▸ fastidiousness, meticulousness, pains. *See* **thoroughness.**

paint *noun*
1. A final coating ▸ glaze, stain, varnish. *See* **finish** (3). 2. Something that imparts color ▸ colorant, dye, pigment. *See* **color** (2).

paint *verb*
To apply a coating or surface material to ▸ glaze, stain, varnish. *See* **finish** (7).

pair *noun*
▸ duet, match, twosome. *See* **couple.**

paired *adjective*
Consisting of two identical or similar related things, parts, or elements ▸ double, dual, matched, twin. *See also* **equal.**

pal *noun*
1. *Informal* A person whom one knows well, likes, and trusts ▸ amigo. *Informal:* bud, buddy. *See* **friend** (1). 2. *Informal* A person who shares interests or activities with another ▸ companion, comrade. *See* **associate** (2).

pal *verb*
To be with as a companion ▸ fraternize, hobnob, pal around. *Slang:* hang out. *See* **associate** (2).

paladin *noun*
A person revered especially for noble courage

▶ champion, hero, heroine. *Idiom:* knight in shining armor. *See also* **winner.**

palatable *adjective*
1. Fit to be eaten ▶ comestible, eatable, edible, esculent. 2. Highly pleasing, especially to the sense of taste ▶ delectable, savory, scrumptious. *See* **delicious** (1). 3. Adequate to satisfy a need, requirement, or standard ▶ fair, sufficient, tolerable. *See* **acceptable** (2).

palatial *adjective*
1. Characterized by extravagant, ostentatious magnificence ▶ lush, luxuriant, opulent. *See* **luxurious.** 2. Impressive in size, proportion, or appearance ▶ imposing, magnificent, splendid. *See* **grand** (1).

palaver *noun*
Incessant and inconsequential talk ▶ drivel, patter, small talk. *See* **chatter.**

palaver *verb*
To talk rapidly on trivial matters ▶ blab, jabber, prattle. *See* **chatter** (1).

pale *adjective*
1. Lacking color ▶ ashen, ashy, bloodless, cadaverous, colorless, doughy, etiolated, faded, livid, lurid, pallid, pastel, pasty, sallow, wan, washed out, waxen, waxy, whey-faced. *Idioms:* green about the gills, white as a sheet. *See also* **dull, haggard, sick.** 2. Being weak in quality or substance ▶ anemic, bloodless, dim, effete, faint, flimsy, pallid, sickly, thin, waterish, watery, weak. *See also* **insipid, weak.** 3. Having a light color or complexion ▶ alabaster, ivory, light. *See* **fair**¹ (9).

pale *verb*
To lose normal coloration; turn pale ▶ blanch, bleach, etiolate, fade, peak, sallow, wan, wash out, whiten.

palinode *noun*
▶ abjuration, countermand, withdrawal. *See* **retraction** (1).

palliate *verb*
1. To conceal or make light of a fault or offense ▶ explain away, palliate, sleek over. *See* **extenuate.** *See synonym note at* **extenuate.** 2. To make less severe or more bearable ▶ alleviate, ease, lessen. *See* **relieve** (1). *See synonym note at* **relieve.**

palliation *noun*
▶ ease, mitigation, succor. *See* **relief** (2).

pallid *adjective*
1. Lacking color ▶ bloodless, lurid, wan. *See* **pale** (1). 2. Being weak in quality or substance ▶ bloodless, faint. *See* **pale** (2).

palmist *noun*
▶ diviner, fortuneteller, seer, soothsayer. *See* **prophet.**

palm off *verb*
To offer or put into circulation an inferior or fraudulent item ▶ foist, fob off, pass off, put off. *See also* **dump.**

palpability *noun*
▶ corporeality, physicality, tactility. *See* **tangibility.**

palpable *adjective*
1. Discernible by touch ▶ tactile, tangible, touchable. 2. Composed of or relating to things that occupy

space and can be perceived by the senses ▶ corporeal, tangible. *See* **physical** (1). 3. Capable of being perceived by the senses or the mind ▶ discernible, perceivable, sensible. *See* **perceptible.** *See synonym note at* **perceptible.**

palpate *verb*
▶ feel, handle, stroke. *See* **touch** (1). *See synonym note at* **touch.**

palpation *noun*
▶ feeling, manipulation, stroke. *See* **touch** (1).

palpitate *verb*
▶ pulsate, pulse, throb. *See* **beat** (5).

palpitation *noun*
▶ pulsation, pulse, throb. *See* **beat** (3).

palter *verb*
1. To stray from truthfulness or sincerity ▶ prevaricate, shuffle. *See* **equivocate** (2). 2. To argue about the terms, as of a sale ▶ haggle, negotiate. *See* **haggle.**

paltriness *noun*
▶ frivolity, minutia, trivia. *See* **trifle** (1).

paltry *adjective*
1. Of little importance or seriousness ▶ inconsequential, negligible, trifling. *See* **trivial.** *See synonym note at* **trivial.** 2. Of decidedly inferior quality ▶ cheap, lousy, poor. *See* **shoddy** (1).

pamper *verb*
▶ coddle, indulge, spoil. *See* **baby.** *See synonym note at* **baby.**

pamphleteer *noun*
▶ evangelist, missionary, proselytizer. *See* **propagandist.**

pan *noun*
1. *Slang* The front surface of the head ▶ countenance, visage. *See* **face** (1). 2. *Informal* The act or an instance of finding fault ▶ censure, condemnation, denunciation. *See* **criticism** (1).

pan *verb*
Informal To find fault with ▶ censure, fault, reprove. *Slang:* knock. *See* **criticize** (1).

pan out *verb*
To turn out well ▶ go over, work out. *See* **succeed** (2).

panacea *noun*
Something believed to cure all human disorders ▶ catholicon, cure-all, elixir. *See also* **cure.**

pan-broil *verb*
▶ broil, brown, fry. *See* **cook** (1).

pandemic *adjective*
1. So pervasive and all-inclusive as to exist in or affect the whole world ▶ cosmic, global, worldwide. *See* **universal** (1). 2. Most generally existing or encountered at a given time ▶ predominant, rampant. *See* **prevailing** (1).

pandemonium *noun*
▶ clamor, din, uproar. *See* **noise** (1). *See synonym note at* **noise.**

panegyric *noun*
▶ acclamation, celebration, kudos. *See* **praise** (1).

panegyrize *verb*
▶ celebrate, exalt. *See* **honor** (1).

panel *noun*
► discussion, parley, seminar. *See* **conference** (1).

pan-fry *verb*
► parboil, simmer, stew. *See* **cook** (1).

pang *noun*
A sensation of physical discomfort occurring as the result of disease or injury ► prick, smart, soreness. *See* **pain** (1). *See synonym note at* **pain**.

pang *verb*
To cause pain, soreness, or discomfort to ► irritate, pain. *See* **hurt** (3).

Panglossian *adjective*
► cheerful, sanguine. *See* **optimistic**.

panhandle *verb*
Informal To ask for as charity; solicit money or favors ► cadge. *Slang:* mooch. *See* **beg** (1). *See synonym note at* **beg**.

panhandler *noun*
Informal One who begs habitually or for a living ► cadger, mendicant. *See* **beggar** (1).

panic *noun*
1. A feeling of agitation in the face of trouble or danger ► apprehension, consternation, trepidation. *See* **fear**. *See synonym note at* **fear**. **2.** *Slang* Something or someone uproariously funny ► *Informal:* hoot, laugh. *See* **scream** (3).

panic *verb*
To fill with fear ► horrify, scare, terrify. *See* **frighten**. *See synonym note at* **frighten**.

panicky *or* **panic-stricken** *adjective*
► fearful, frightened, scared. *See* **afraid**.

panicmonger *noun*
One who needlessly alarms others ► alarmist, Chicken Little, scaremonger. **Idiom:** one who cries wolf. *See also* **pessimist**.

panoply *noun*
► display, spectacle. *See* **array** (1). *See synonym note at* **array**.

panorama *noun*
► landscape, perspective, vista. *See* **view** (2).

pant *verb*
1. To breathe hard ► blow, gasp, gulp, heave, huff, puff, wheeze. **Idioms:** suck air (*or* wind). *See also* **breathe**. **2.** To utter in a breathless or hoarse manner ► heave, wheeze. *See* **gasp** (1). **3.** To have a strong longing for ► covet, want, yearn. *See* **desire** (1).

pantomime *verb*
► motion, sign, signal. *See* **gesture**.

pantywaist *noun*
Slang A weak or ineffectual person ► pushover. *Slang:* doormat, wimp. *See* **weakling**.

papa *noun*
Informal A male parent ► sire. *Informal:* dad, pa. *See synonym note at* **father** (1).

paper *noun*
1. Something that is the result of creative effort ► composition, essay, theme. **2.** A document used in applying, as for a job ► application, form, sheet. **3.** An issue of printed material offered for sale or distribu-

tion ► title, volume, work. *See* **publication** (2).

papoose *noun*
► babe, infant. *See* **baby** (1).

pappy¹ *adjective*
Yielding easily to pressure or weight ► mushy, pulpy, yielding. *See* **soft** (1).

pappy² *noun*
Informal A male parent ► sire. *Informal:* dad, papa. *See synonym note at* **father** (1).

par *noun*
1. Something that represents a midpoint between extremes ► medium, norm. *See* **average** (1). **2.** The state of being equivalent ► equation, sameness. *See* **equivalence**.

parable *noun*
► fairy tale, folk tale, legend. *See* **myth** (1).

parade *noun*
1. A formal military inspection ► review. **2.** An impressive or ostentatious exhibition ► display, spectacle. *See* **array** (1). *See synonym note at* **array**.

parade *verb*
To make a public and usually ostentatious show of ► exhibit, expose, flaunt. *See* **display** (1). *See synonym note at* **display**.

paradigm *noun*
1. One that is worthy of imitation or duplication ► exemplar, ideal, nonpareil. *See* **model** (1). **2.** A first form from which varieties arise or imitations are made ► master, prototype. *See* **original** (1).

paradigmatic *adjective*
► model, prototypic, representative. *See* **typical** (1).

paradisaic *or* **paradisaical** *adjective*
► divine, paradisal. *See* **heavenly** (1).

paradisal *adjective*
► divine, supernal. *See* **heavenly** (1).

paradise *noun*
1. A supremely beautiful, blissful state or experience ► ecstasy, rapture. *See* **heaven** (1). **2.** A place or state beyond death ► afterworld, heaven, hereafter. *See* **eternity** (2).

paradisiac *or* **paradisiacal** *adjective*
► divine, paradisal. *See* **heavenly** (1).

paragon *noun*
1. A person or thing so excellent as to have no equal or match ► nonesuch, nonpareil, phoenix. *See also* **best, celebrity**. **2.** One that is worthy of imitation or duplication ► exemplar, ideal, paradigm. *See* **model** (1). **3.** An ideally representative example of a type ► archetype, model. *See* **epitome** (1).

paragraph *noun*
► feature, piece, story. *See* **item** (1).

parallel *adjective*
1. Lying in the same plane and not intersecting ► collateral. **Idiom:** side by side. **2.** Possessing the same or almost the same characteristics ► analogous, similar, uniform. *See* **like²**. **3.** Existing at the same time ► attendant, attending. *See* **concurrent** (1).

parallel *noun*
Something closely analogous to something else ► ana-

logue, analogy, congener, correlate, correlative, correspondent, counterpart, match. *See also* **copy,
likeness.**

parallel *verb*
1. To be equal or alike ▸ correspond, match, touch. *See*
equal (1). **2.** To represent as similar ▸ compare, equate,
identify. *See* **liken.**

parallelism *noun*
▸ resemblance, similarity, uniformity. *See* **likeness** (1).

paralyze *verb*
1. To render helpless, as by emotion ▸ benumb, numb,
petrify, stun, stupefy, wither. *Idioms:* strike dumb (*or*
speechless). *See also* **daze, stagger. 2.** To render powerless or motionless, as by inflicting severe injury
▸ handicap, immobilize, impair. *See* **disable** (1).

paralyzed *adjective*
▸ stationary, still. *See* **motionless.**

paramount *adjective*
1. Most important, influential, or significant ▸ chief,
key, main, principal. *See* **primary** (1). **2.** Exercising
controlling power or influence ▸ key, predominant,
reigning. *See* **dominant** (1). *See synonym note at*
dominant.

paramountcy *noun*
▸ authority, power, supremacy. *See* **dominance** (1).

paramour *noun*
1. A romantic interest, especially a regular sexual
partner ▸ partner. *Informal:* significant other. *See*
lover (1). **2.** A man who philanders ▸ adulterer,
Casanova. *See* **philanderer.**

paranormal *adjective*
▸ extrasensory, metaphysical, superhuman. *See* **supernatural** (1).

parapet *noun*
▸ barricade, bastion, rampart. *See* **bulwark.** *See synonym note at* **bulwark.**

paraphernalia *noun*
▸ equipment, gear. *See* **outfit** (1). *See synonym note at*
outfit.

paraphrase *noun*
A restating of something in other, especially simpler,
words ▸ rendering, rendition, restatement, translation, version. *See also* **summary, synopsis.**

paraphrase *verb*
To express the meaning of in other, especially simpler,
words ▸ rehash, render, rephrase, restate, reword,
translate. *See also* **review.**

parasite *noun*
1. One who depends on another for support without
reciprocating ▸ bloodsucker, hanger-on, leech,
sponge, sponger. *Slang:* freeloader. *See also* **beggar,
sycophant. 2.** A tiny organism usually producing
disease ▸ microbe, microorganism, virus. *See* **germ**
(1).

parasitic *or* **parasitical** *adjective*
Of or characteristic of a parasite ▸ bloodsucking,
epizoic. *Slang:* freeloading.

parboil *verb*
▸ blanch, boil. *See* **cook** (1).

parcel *noun*
1. A piece of land ▸ acreage, plot, tract. *See* **lot** (1).
2. Something wrapped or enclosed, as for transporting ▸ bundle, carton, packet. *See* **package.**

parcel out *verb*
To give out in portions or shares ▸ allocate, apportion, dispense. *See* **distribute** (1).

parch *verb*
▸ dehydrate, desiccate, exsiccate. *See* **dry** (1). *See synonym note at* **dry.**

parched *adjective*
1. Needing or desiring drink ▸ dry, thirsty. **2.** Having
little or no precipitation ▸ desert, droughty, rainless.
See **dry** (2).

pardon *verb*
1. To grant forgiveness to or for ▸ condone, excuse,
overlook. *See* **forgive.** *See synonym note at* **forgive.**
2. To free from sin, guilt, or defilement ▸ atone,
cleanse, lustrate. *See* **purify** (1).

pardon *noun*
The act or an instance of forgiving ▸ amnesty, excuse,
remission. *See* **forgiveness.**

pardonable *adjective*
Admitting of forgiveness or pardon ▸ condonable,
excusable, expiable, forgivable, remissible, understandable, venial. *See also* **acceptable, justifiable.**

pardoning *noun*
▸ ablution, redemption. *See* **purification** (2).

pare *verb*
1. To remove the skin of ▸ decorticate, strip. *See* **skin**
(1). **2.** To decrease, as in length or amount, by or as if
by severing or excising ▸ chop, prune, trim. *See* **cut** (3).
3. To reduce in complexity or scope ▸ boil down,
simplify, streamline. *Idioms:* reduce to the basics (*or*
essentials *or* bare bones). *See also* **explain.**

parent *noun*
1. A person from whom one is descended ▸ antecedent, forebear, progenitor. *See* **ancestor** (1). **2.** One
that creates, founds, or originates ▸ author, creator,
inventor. *See* **originator. 3.** A point of origination
▸ provenance, root, source. *See* **origin** (1).

parent *verb*
1. To take care of and educate a child ▸ bring up,
foster, raise, rear. *See also* **nurture. 2.** To give life to
▸ engender, propagate, spawn. *See* **breed** (1).

parentage *noun*
▸ blood, extraction, lineage. *See* **ancestry.**

parenthesis *noun*
▸ deviation, divergence, tangent. *See* **digression.**

parenthetic *or* **parenthetical** *adjective*
▸ long-winded, meandering, rambling. *See* **digressive.**

pariah *noun*
▸ exile, outsider. *See* **outcast.**

parity *noun*
▸ equation, sameness. *See* **equivalence.**

park *noun*
1. A tract of land set aside for public use ▸ green,
plaza, square. *See* **common. 2.** Public land kept for a

special purpose ▶ preserve, reserve, reservation, sanctuary.

parka *noun*

▶ anorak, overcoat, windbreaker. *See* **coat** (1).

parlance *noun*

1. Choice of words and the way they are used ▶ locution, phraseology, verbalism. *See* **wording. 2.** Specialized expressions indigenous to a particular field, subject, trade, or subculture ▶ jargon, lingo, patois. *See* **language** (2).

parley *noun*

1. The act or process of dealing with another to reach an agreement ▶ negotiation, talk. *See also* **conversation. 2.** An exchange of views in an attempt to reach a decision ▶ consultation, counsel, debate. *See* **deliberation** (1). **3.** A meeting for the exchange of views ▶ discussion, forum, seminar. *See* **conference** (1).

parley *verb*

1. To meet and exchange views to reach a decision ▶ consult, deliberate, talk. *Informal:* huddle, powwow. *See* **confer** (1). **2.** To speak together and exchange ideas and opinions about ▶ converse, debate. *Informal:* kick around. *See* **discuss.**

parlous *adjective*

▶ chancy, hazardous, risky. *See* **dangerous.**

parochial *adjective*

▶ insular, narrow-minded, provincial. *See* **narrow** (1).

parody *noun*

1. A work that exposes folly by the use of humor, irony, or comic imitation ▶ burlesque, lampoon, spoof. *See* **satire.** *See synonym note at* **satire. 2.** A false, derisive, or impudent imitation of something ▶ farce, sham, travesty. *See* **mockery** (2).

parody *verb*

To copy the manner or expression of another, especially in an exaggerated or mocking way ▶ caricature, mock. *See* **imitate** (1). *See synonym note at* **imitate.**

paroxysm *noun*

1. A condition of anguished struggle and disorder ▶ convulsion, throes. **2.** A sudden and often acute manifestation of a disease ▶ apoplexy, fit. *See* **seizure** (1). **3.** A sudden violent expression, as of emotion ▶ burst, eruption, explosion. *See* **outburst** (1). **4.** A sudden emergence or increase ▶ breakout, flare, outburst. *See* **eruption** (1). **5.** A nervous shaking of the body ▶ quiver, shiver, tic. *See* **tremor** (2).

parrot *noun*

One who imitates ▶ imitator, mime. *See* **mimic.**

parrot *verb*

To copy another slavishly ▶ clone, imitate. *See* **mimic** (1).

parry *verb*

▶ deflect, repulse, ward off. *See* **repel.**

parsimonious *adjective*

▶ close-fisted, miserly, tight. *See* **stingy** (1).

parson *noun*

▶ ecclesiastic, minister, preacher. *See* **cleric.**

part *noun*

1. A separate unit that belongs or contributes to a whole ▶ building block, component, constituent, division, element, factor, fraction, ingredient, member, percentage, piece, portion, section, sector, segment, subdivision. *See also* **bit¹, cut, element. 2.** One's duty or responsibility in a common effort ▶ function, piece, role, share. *See also* **function. 3.** A particular subdivision of a written work ▶ chapter, passage, section, segment. **4.** The position from which something is observed or considered ▶ aspect, point of view, standpoint. *See* **viewpoint. 5.** A person portrayed in fiction or drama ▶ character, persona, personage, role. **6.** That which is allotted ▶ allowance, ration, share. *See* **allotment** (1).

part *verb*

1. To break up the unity of something ▶ disjoin, dissever, split up. *See* **divide** (1). **2.** To end an association by or as if by leaving one another ▶ break up, divorce. *See* **separate** (1). **3.** To separate into branches or branchlike parts ▶ diverge, fork. *See* **branch.**

part *adjective*

Not total ▶ fragmentary, incomplete. *See* **partial** (1).

✚ **CORE SYNONYMS:** *part, component, constituent, element, factor, ingredient.* These nouns denote one of the separate units that belong or contribute to a whole: *protein, an important part of a balanced diet; jealousy, a component of his character; melody and harmony, two of the constituents of a musical composition; the grammatical elements of a sentence; ambition as a key factor in her success; humor, an effective ingredient of a speech.*

partake *verb*

1. To help bring about a result ▶ participate, share. *See* **contribute** (2). **2.** To involve oneself in an activity ▶ engage, indulge, share. *See* **participate** (1). **3.** To take food into the body as nourishment ▶ consume, fare, ingest. *See* **eat** (1). *See synonym note at* **eat.**

partial *adjective*

1. Not total ▶ fractional, fragmentary, incomplete, part, unfinished. *See also* **rough. 2.** Disposed to favor one over another ▶ favorable, preferential. **3.** Exhibiting bias ▶ one-sided, prejudiced. *See* **biased** (1).

partiality *noun*

1. Preferential treatment or bias ▶ favor, favoritism, partialness, preference. *See also* **prejudice. 2.** An inclination for or against that inhibits impartial judgment ▶ one-sidedness, prejudice. *See* **bias** (1). **3.** A liking for something ▶ fondness, preference, weakness. *See* **taste** (1). **4.** A natural or habitual preference for something ▶ disposition, leaning, penchant. *See* **inclination** (1). *See synonym note at* **inclination.**

partialness *noun*

Preferential treatment or bias ▶ favor, favoritism, partiality, preference. *See also* **bias, prejudice.**

participant *noun*

One who participates ▶ actor, partaker, participator, party, player, sharer. *See also* **associate.**

participate *verb*

1. To involve oneself in an activity ▶ carry on, engage, enter into, have, indulge, join (in), partake. *Idioms:* have a hand in, take part. *See also* **contribute. 2.** To help bring about a result ▸ chip in, share. *See* **contribute** (2).

participation *noun*
The act or fact of participating ▸ engagement, involvement, partaking, sharing.

participatory *adjective*
Tending to contribute to a result ▸ conducive, contributive, contributory, helpful. *See also* **auxiliary.**

particle *noun*
▸ dash, drop, smidgen. *See* **bit**¹ (1).

particular *adjective*
1. Being or related to a distinct entity ▸ discrete, singular. *See* **individual** (2). **2.** Relating to, identifying, or setting apart an individual or group ▸ characteristic, individual, specific. *See* **special** (1). **3.** Alone in a given category ▸ only, single, solitary. *See* **lone** (1). **4.** Characterized by attention to detail ▸ full, circumstantial, thorough. *See* **detailed** (1). **5.** Very difficult to please ▸ exacting, finicky. *See* **fussy** (1). **6.** Not divided among or shared with others ▸ prerogative, sole. *See* **exclusive** (1).

particular *noun*
1. An individually considered portion of a whole ▸ detail, item. *See* **element** (3). **2.** A small, often specialized element of a whole ▸ nicety, specialty, technicality. *See* **detail** (1). *See synonym note at* **detail. 3.** One of the conditions or facts attending an event and having some bearing on it ▸ condition, factor. *See* **circumstance** (2).

particularity *noun*
▸ distinctiveness, singularity. *See* **individuality** (1).

particularize *verb*
To state specifically ▸ detail, provide, specify, stipulate. *See also* **assert, describe, designate, dictate.**

particularly *adverb*
1. That is to say ▸ specifically, videlicet. *See* **namely. 2.** To a high degree ▸ exceedingly, extremely, highly. *See* **very.**

parting *noun*
1. The act or an instance of separating one thing from another ▸ disjunction, divorce, segmentation. *See* **division** (1). **2.** The act of leaving ▸ embarkation, exodus, withdrawal. *See* **departure** (1).

parting *adjective*
Of, done, given, or said on departing ▸ departing, dying, farewell, goodbye, leaving, valedictory. *See also* **last.**

partisan *noun*
One who supports and adheres to another ▸ adherent, believer, disciple. *See* **follower** (1).

partisan *adjective*
Exhibiting bias ▸ partial, prejudiced, tendentious. *See* **biased** (1).

partisanship *noun*
▸ partiality, prejudice. *See* **bias** (1).

partition *noun*
1. A solid structure that encloses an area or separates one area from another ▸ barrier, wall. *See also* **border, screen. 2.** The act or an instance of separating one thing from another ▸ disjunction, divorce, parting. *See* **division** (1).

partition *verb*
1. To separate with or as if with a wall ▸ fence, wall. *See also* **enclose. 2.** To break or separate into parts or sections ▸ disjoin, segment, split up. *See* **divide** (1).

partner *noun*
1. One who is united in a relationship with another ▸ ally, colleague. *See* **associate** (1). *See synonym note at* **associate. 2.** A husband or wife ▸ consort, mate. *See* **spouse. 3.** A romantic interest, especially a regular sexual partner ▸ paramour. *Informal:* significant other. *See* **lover** (1).

partnership *noun*
1. The state of being associated ▸ alliance, connection, cooperation. *See* **association** (1). **2.** A commercial organization ▸ corporation, enterprise, establishment. *See* **company** (1).

parturiency *noun*
The condition of carrying a developing fetus within the uterus ▸ gestation, gravidity, gravidness, pregnancy.

parturient *adjective*
▸ expectant, gestating. *See* **pregnant** (1).

parturition *noun*
▸ childbearing, delivery, labor. *See* **birth** (1).

party *noun*
1. A social gathering, especially for pleasure ▸ affair, celebration, festivity, fete, function, gala, gathering, get-together, occasion, social, soiree, tea. *Informal:* do. *Slang:* bash. *See also* **blast, celebration, dance. 2.** A group of people acting together in a shared activity ▸ company, troop. *See* **band**² (1). *See synonym note at* **band. 3.** An association for a common cause or interest ▸ bloc, coalition, organization. *See* **alliance** (1). **4.** One who participates ▸ actor, player, sharer. *See* **participant. 5.** A member of the human race ▸ human, mortal, person. *See* **human being. 6.** A number of individuals making up or considered a unit ▸ body, cluster, collection. *See* **group** (1).

party *verb*
1. To show joyful satisfaction in an event ▸ feast, rejoice, revel. *See* **celebrate** (2). **2.** To behave riotously ▸ carouse, frolic, roister. *See* **revel** (1).

party pooper *noun*
Slang One who spoils the enthusiasm or fun of others ▸ spoilsport. *Slang:* downer, pill. *See* **killjoy.**

pass *verb*
1. To move along a particular course ▸ go, proceed, push on, wend. *Idioms:* make (*or* wend) one's way. *See also* **advance, rove. 2.** To catch up with and move past ▸ outpace, outrun, outstrip, overhaul, overtake. *See also* **overtake. 3.** To make or go on a journey ▸ peregrinate, travel, voyage. *See* **journey. 4.** To be greater or better than ▸ exceed, excel, outshine. *See* **surpass** (1). **5.** To go or extend across ▸ track, transit, traverse. *See* **cross** (1). **6.** To move past in time ▸ lapse,

pass away, pass by, slip away. *See* **elapse. 7.** To use time in a particular way ▸ put in, spend. *See also* **idle. 8.** To make known ▸ disclose, divulge, transmit. *See* **communicate** (1). **9.** To spread a disease to others ▸ convey, infect, transmit. *See* **communicate** (4). **10.** To come as by lot or inheritance ▸ devolve, fall. **11.** To give property to another after one's death ▸ bequeath, will. *See* **leave**[1] (1). **12.** To come to an end ▸ go away, pass away. **13.** To cease living ▸ demise, expire, perish. *See* **die** (1). **14.** To take place ▸ befall, come, occur. *See* **happen** (1). **15.** To go through life in a certain way ▸ conduct, pursue. *See* **lead** (3). **16.** To be accepted or approved ▸ adopt, affiliate, carry, clear. *Informal:* sign off. **17.** To accept officially ▸ approve, endorse, ratify. *See* **confirm** (3). **18.** To penetrate into a substance or place with force ▸ drive, stab, stick. *See* **plunge** (1). **19.** To be unwilling to accept, consider, or receive ▸ refuse, reject, spurn. *See* **decline** (1).

pass away *verb*
1. To come to an end ▸ go away, pass. **2.** To cease living ▸ demise, expire, perish. *See* **die** (1).

pass for *verb*
To assume the character or appearance of ▸ masquerade, pose as. *See* **impersonate** (1).

pass off *verb*
To offer or put into circulation an inferior or fraudulent item ▸ foist, fob off, palm off, put off. *See also* **dump.**

pass on *verb*
1. To serve as a conduit ▸ carry, transmit. *See* **conduct** (3). **2.** To cease living ▸ demise, expire, perish. *See* **die** (1).

pass out *verb*
To suffer temporary lack of consciousness ▸ black out, faint, keel over, swoon. *Idioms:* drop (*or* faint *or* fall) dead away, see stars. *See also* **collapse.**

pass over *verb*
1. To pretend not to see ▸ disregard, ignore. *See* **blink at. 2.** To fail to do or carry out ▸ ignore, omit, overlook. *See* **neglect** (3).

pass through *verb*
To participate in or partake of personally ▸ know, undergo. *See* **experience.**

pass up *verb*
To fail to take advantage of ▸ miss, squander. *See* **lose** (2).

pass *noun*
1. A free ticket entitling one to transportation or admission ▸ *Informal:* comp. *Slang:* freebie. **2.** A course affording passage from one place to another ▸ path, road, route. *See* **way** (2). **3.** A decisive point ▸ crossroads, juncture. *See* **crisis** (1). *See synonym note at* **crisis.**

passable *adjective*
1. Capable of being passed, traversed, or crossed ▸ navigable, negotiable, penetrable, surmountable, traversable. *See also* **clear. 2.** Adequate to satisfy a need, requirement, or standard ▸ average, decent, moderate. *See* **acceptable** (2).

passage *noun*
1. Passage from one form, state, or stage to another ▸ change, shift, transit. *See* **transition. 2.** A particular subdivision of a written work ▸ chapter, part, section, segment. **3.** An act of confirming officially ▸ approval, ratification, sanction. *See* **confirmation** (1). **4.** The act of traveling from one place to another ▸ flight, odyssey, progress. *See* **journey. 5.** A course affording passage from one place to another ▸ path, road, route. *See* **way** (2).

passageway *noun*
▸ path, road, route. *See* **way** (2).

passé *adjective*
▸ antique, dated, outmoded. *See* **old-fashioned.**

passel *noun*
Informal An indeterminately great amount or number ▸ bunch. *Informal:* bushel. *See* **heap** (3).

passing *adjective*
Lasting or existing only for a short time ▸ ephemeral, fleeting, temporary. *See* **transitory.**

passing *noun*
The act or fact of dying ▸ demise, extinction. *See* **death** (1).

passion *noun*
1. Powerful, intense emotion ▸ ardor, fervency, fervor, fire, heat, warmth, zeal. *Slang:* sizzle. *See also* **intensity. 2.** Passionate devotion to or interest in a cause or subject ▸ fervor, fire, zeal. *See* **enthusiasm** (1). **3.** A subjective mental state, such as love or hate ▸ affection, feeling. *See* **emotion.** *See synonym note at* **emotion. 4.** The passionate affection and desire felt by lovers for each other ▸ ardor, devotion, romance. *See* **love** (2). **5.** Sexual hunger ▸ eroticism, lust, urge. *See* **desire** (2). **6.** An intense attachment to a person or thing ▸ adoration, fondness, love affair. *See* **love** (1). **7.** A subject or activity that inspires lively interest ▸ mania, rage. *See* **enthusiasm** (2). **8.** An angry outburst ▸ fit, huff, tantrum. *See* **temper** (2). **9.** A subjective mental state, such as love or hate ▸ affect, feeling. *See* **emotion.** *See synonym note at* **emotion.**

✦ **CORE SYNONYMS:** *passion, fervor, fire, zeal, ardor.* These nouns denote powerful, intense emotion. *Passion* is a deep, overwhelming emotion: *"There is not a passion so strongly rooted in the human heart as envy"* (Richard Brinsley Sheridan). The term may signify sexual desire or anger: *"He flew into a violent passion and abused me mercilessly"* (H.G. Wells). *Fervor* is great warmth and intensity of feeling: *"The union of the mathematician with the poet, fervor with measure, passion with correctness, this surely is the ideal"* (William James). *Fire* is burning passion: *"In our youth our hearts were touched with fire"* (Oliver Wendell Holmes, Jr.). *Zeal* is strong, enthusiastic devotion to a cause, ideal, or goal and tireless diligence in its furtherance: *"Laurie [resolved], with a glow of philanthropic zeal, to found and endow an institution for . . . women with artistic tendencies"* (Louisa May Alcott). *Ardor* is fiery intensity of feeling: *"the furious ardor of my zeal repressed"* (Charles Churchill).

passionate *adjective*
1. Fired with intense feeling ▸ ardent, blazing, burning, dithyrambic, fervent, fervid, feverish, fiery, flaming, glowing, heated, hot-blooded, impassioned, perfervid, red-hot, scorching, torrid. *See also* **enthusiastic, lively. 2.** Feeling or preoccupied with sexual love or desire ▸ concupiscent, lewd. *See* **lascivious** (1).

passionless *adjective*
1. Deficient in or lacking sexual desire ▸ cold, inhibited, undersexed. *See* **frigid** (3). **2.** Lacking feeling or emotion ▸ emotionless, impassive, stolid. *See* **cold** (2).

passive *adjective*
Submitting without objection or resistance ▸ acquiescent, nonresistant, resigned, submissive, yielding. *See also* **obedient.**

passport *noun*
▸ permit, warrant. *See* **license** (3).

past *adjective*
1. Just gone by or elapsed ▸ ago, antecedent, anterior, bygone, bypast, earlier, foregoing, former, lapsed, precedent, preceding, previous, prior. *See also* **last, old. 2.** Having been such previously ▸ former, once, onetime. *See* **late** (2).

past *noun*
1. The time before the present ▸ auld lang syne, old, yesterday, yesteryear, yore. *Idioms:* bygone days, days gone by, days of yore, long ago, the good old days, the old (*or* olden) days, water under the bridge. *See also* **antiquity. 2.** One's previous experiences ▸ background, career, resumé. *See* **history** (2).

paste *verb*
Slang To deliver a sudden, sharp blow to ▸ jab, sock, whack. *See* **hit** (1).

paste *noun*
Slang A sudden heavy stroke ▸ crack, hit, swat, whack. *See* **blow²** (1).

pastel *adjective*
▸ bloodless, lurid, wan. *See* **pale** (1).

pastime *noun*
▸ hobby, sport, recreation. *See* **amusement.**

past master *noun*
1. One who has had long experience in a given activity or capacity ▸ old hand, vet, veteran. *Informal:* old-timer. **2.** A person with a high degree of knowledge or skill in a particular field ▸ authority, master, proficient. *See* **expert.**

pastor *noun*
▸ ecclesiastic, minister, parson. *See* **cleric.**

pastoral *adjective*
1. Of or relating to the countryside ▸ bucolic, rural. *See* **country.** *See synonym note at* **country. 2.** Charmingly simple and carefree ▸ arcadian, idyllic. *See also* **fresh, still. 3.** Of or relating to the clergy, especially in a Christian church ▸ ministerial, priestly. *See* **clerical.**

pasture *noun*
An area of open land ▸ clearing, field, meadow. *See also* **lot.**

pasture *verb*
To feed on vegetation ▸ crop, forage. *See* **browse** (2).

pasty *adjective*
▸ bloodless, lurid, wan. *See* **pale** (1).

pat *verb*
1. To touch or handle affectionately ▸ fondle, pet. *See* **caress. 2.** To strike lightly or gently ▸ dab, flick. *See* **tap¹** (1).

pat down *verb*
To examine a person or someone's personal effects in order to find something lost or concealed ▸ frisk, inspect, search. *Slang:* shake down. *Idiom:* do a body search of.

patch *verb*
To restore to proper condition or functioning ▸ mend, overhaul, repair. *See* **fix** (1).

patch *noun*
A piece of land ▸ acreage, plot, tract. *See* **lot** (1).

patchwork *noun*
▸ hodgepodge, jumble, mishmash. *See* **assortment** (1).

patchy *adjective*
▸ inconsistent, spotty, variable. *See* **uneven** (1).

pate *noun*
▸ crown, poll. *See* **head** (1).

patent *adjective*
1. Readily seen, perceived, or understood ▸ evident, noticeable, obvious. *See* **apparent** (1). *See synonym note at* **apparent. 2.** Easily seen through due to a lack of subtlety ▸ blatant, overt, transparent. *See* **obvious** (1).

paterfamilias *noun*
▸ begetter, patriarch, sire. *See* **father** (1).

paternal *adjective*
Like a father, especially in caring ▸ fatherlike, fatherly, patriarchal. *See also* **benevolent.**

path *noun*
1. A course affording passage from one place to another ▸ channel, road, route. *See* **way** (2). **2.** The approach used to do something ▸ manner, mode, style. *See* **way** (1). *See synonym note at* **way.**

pathetic *adjective*
1. Arousing or deserving pity ▸ forlorn, lamentable, poor, sorry. *See* **pitiful** (1). *See synonym note at* **pitiful. 2.** Very bad ▸ appalling, awful, dreadful. *See* **terrible** (1).

pathogen *noun*
▸ bug, microorganism, virus. *See* **germ** (1).

pathology *noun*
▸ ailment, disorder, malady. *See* **disease** (1).

patience *noun*
The capacity of enduring hardship or inconvenience without complaint ▸ acceptance, forbearance, longanimity, long-suffering, resignation, stoicism, sufferance, tolerance. *See also* **endurance, tolerance.**

✦ CORE SYNONYMS: *patience, long-suffering, resignation, forbearance.* These nouns denote the capacity to endure hardship, difficulty, or inconvenience without complaint. *Patience* emphasizes calmness, self-control, and the willingness or ability to tolerate delay: *Our patience will achieve more than our force* (Edmund Burke). *Long-suffering* is long and patient endurance, as of wrong or provocation: *The general, a man not known for docility and long-suffering, flew into a rage. Resignation* implies acceptance of or submission to something trying, as out of despair or necessity: *I undertook the job with an air of resignation. Forbearance* denotes restraint, as in retaliating, demanding what is due, or voicing disapproval: *"It is the mutual duty of all to practice Christian forbearance, love, and charity towards each other"* (Patrick Henry).

◄ ANTONYM: *impatience*

patient *adjective*
Enduring or capable of enduring hardship or inconvenience without complaint ► accepting, enduring, forbearing, long-suffering, resigned, stoic, tolerant. *See also* **passive.**

patio *noun*
► courtyard, enclosure, quad. *See* **court** (1).

patois *noun*
1. A variety of a language that differs from the standard form ► jargon, vernacular. *See* **dialect** (1). *See synonym note at* **dialect. 2.** Specialized expressions indigenous to a particular field, subject, trade, or subculture ► jargon, lingo, terminology. *See* **language** (2).

patriarch *noun*
1. One that creates, founds, or originates ► author, creator, inventor. *See* **originator. 2.** A male parent ► begetter, paterfamilias, sire. *See* **father** (1).

patriarchal *adjective*
Like a father, especially in caring ► fatherlike, fatherly, paternal. *See also* **benevolent.**

patrician *adjective*
► blue-blooded, elite, upper-class. *See* **noble** (1).

patriciate *noun*
► elite, gentry, nobility. *See* **society** (1).

patrimonial *adjective*
► hereditary, inherited, genealogical. *See* **ancestral.**

patrimony *noun*
Any special privilege accorded a firstborn ► birthright, heritage, inheritance, legacy. *See also* **right.**

patrol *verb*
To maintain or keep in order with or as if with police ► monitor, regulate. *See* **police** (1).

patrol *noun*
1. A group of people organized for a particular purpose ► squad, team, unit. *See* **force** (5). **2.** A unit of troops on special assignment ► brigade, corps, squad. *See* **detachment** (7).

patrolman *or* **patrolwoman** *noun*
► officer, trooper. *Informal:* cop. *See* **police officer.**

patron *noun*
1. One who supports or champions an activity, cause, or institution ► backer, benefactor, benefactress, contributor, friend, philanthropist, sponsor, supporter. *Informal:* angel. *See also* **advocate, follower. 2.** One who buys goods and services ► client, customer, user. *See* **consumer. 3.** A person who gives to a charity or cause ► benefactor, contributor, humanitarian. *See* **donor.**

patronage *noun*
1. Aid or support given by a patron ► advocacy, aegis, auspices, backing, championship, encouragement, financing, furtherance, patronization, promotion, sponsorship. *See also* **donation, help. 2.** The commercial transactions of customers with a supplier ► business, custom, trade, traffic. *See also* **business, deal. 3.** Customers or patrons collectively ► clientage, clientele, constituency, custom, trade. **4.** The political appointments or jobs that are at the disposal of those in power ► pork, spoils.

patroness *noun*
► benefactor, contributor, patron. *See* **donor.**

patronization *noun*
1. Aid or support given by a patron ► backing, sponsorship. *See* **patronage** (1). **2.** Superciliously indulgent treatment, especially of those considered inferior ► haughtiness, snobbery. *See* **condescension.**

patronize *verb*
1. To act as a patron to ► back, sponsor, support. *See also* **donate, finance, support. 2.** To treat in a superciliously indulgent manner ► condescend. *Informal:* high-hat. *Idioms:* lord it over, queen it, speak (*or* talk) down to. *See also* **insult, snub.**

patsy *noun*
1. *Slang* A person who is easily deceived or victimized ► pushover, tool, victim. *See* **dupe** (1). **2.** *Slang* One who is made an object of blame ► whipping boy. *Slang:* fall guy. *See* **scapegoat.**

patter *verb*
To talk rapidly on trivial matters ► blab, jabber, prattle. *See* **chatter** (1).

patter *noun*
Incessant and inconsequential talk ► drivel, prattle, small talk. *See* **chatter.**

pattern *noun*
1. One that is worthy of imitation or duplication ► exemplar, ideal, paradigm. *See* **model** (1). *See synonym note at* **model. 2.** The surface arrangement of a thing ► configuration, figure, shape. *See* **form** (1). **3.** Systematic arrangement and design ► order, organization, scheme. *See* **method** (1). **4.** A first form from which varieties arise or imitations are made ► master, prototype. *See* **original** (1). **5.** An ideally representative example of a type ► archetype, model. *See* **epitome** (1). **6.** A regular or customary matter, condition, or course of events ► norm, ordinary, rule. *See* **usual.**

pattern *verb*
1. To take as a model ► copy, emulate, imitate. *See* **follow** (5). **2.** To create by forming, combining, or altering materials ► build, compose, shape. *See* **make** (1).

paucity *noun*
► deficit, inadequacy, scantness. *See* **shortage.**

paunchy *adjective*
► chubby, pudgy, rotund. *See* **fat** (1).

pauper *noun*
An impoverished person ► bankrupt, beggar, bum, derelict, down-and-out, down-and-outer, have-not,

indigent, insolvent, tramp, vagabond. *Slang:* bag lady, skell. *See also* **beggar, hobo.**

pauperism *noun*
► destitution, indigence, need. *See* **poverty** (1).

pauperize *verb*
► bankrupt, break, impoverish. *See* **ruin** (3).

pause *verb*
1. To stop for an indefinite period ► interrupt, suspend. *Idiom:* put on hold. *See also* **rest. 2.** To continue to be in a place ► bide, linger, tarry. *See* **remain** (1). **3.** To be irresolute in acting or doing ► falter, vacillate. *See* **hesitate.**

pause *noun*
1. A cessation of continuity or regularity ► discontinuation, disruption, interruption. *See* **break** (1). **2.** The act of hesitating or state of being hesitant ► indecision, tentativeness. *See* **hesitation.**

pave *verb*
► blanket, spread. *See* **cover** (1).

pawl *noun*
► catch, clip, lock. *See* **fastener.**

pawn¹ *noun*
Something given to guarantee the repayment of a loan or the fulfillment of an obligation ► bail, bond, collateral, earnest, gage, guaranty, hostage, pledge, recognizance, security, token, warrant, warranty. *See also* **guarantee, promise.**

pawn *verb*
To give or deposit as a pawn ► bond, collateralize, deposit, hypothecate, mortgage, pledge. *Slang:* hock.

pawn² *noun*
A person who is used or controlled by others ► cat's-paw, dupe, instrument, puppet, stooge, tool. *See also* **dupe.**

pay *verb*
1. To give compensation to ► indemnify, recompense, remunerate. *See* **compensate** (1). **2.** To give money as payment ► expend, outlay. *See* **spend** (1). **3.** To set right by giving what is due ► discharge, satisfy. *See* **settle** (3). **4.** To make as income or profit ► clear, gain, yield. *See* **return** (3).

pay back *verb*
To exact revenge for or from ► pay off, vindicate. *See* **avenge.**

pay off *verb*
1. To exact revenge for or from ► pay back, vindicate. *See* **avenge. 2.** *Informal* To give, offer, or promise a bribe to ► corrupt, fix. *See* **bribe.**

pay *noun*
Payment for work done ► earnings, emolument, salary. *See* **wage.**

payable *adjective*
► collectible, outstanding, unpaid. *See* **due** (1).

payment *noun*
1. Something to make up for loss or damage ► amends, remuneration, reparation. *See* **compensation** (1). **2.** An amount paid or to be paid for a purchase ► charge, expense, price. *See* **cost** (1). **3.** Something, such as loss, pain, or confinement,

imposed for wrongdoing ► castigation, chastisement, penalty. *See* **punishment. 4.** Something justly deserved ► compensation, deserts, reward. *See* **due** (1). **5.** Payment for work done ► earnings, pay, salary. *See* **wage.**

payoff *noun*
1. *Informal* The highest point or state ► apex, height, peak. *See* **climax** (1). **2.** *Informal* Money or a favor given as inducement to dishonest behavior ► graft. *Slang:* boodle. *See* **bribe.**

payola *noun*
► fix, graft. *Informal:* payoff. *See* **bribe.**

PDQ *adverb*
Informal Without delay ► instantly, straightaway. *See* **immediately** (1).

peace *noun*
1. Lack of emotional agitation ► quietude, serenity. *See* **calm** (1). **2.** An absence of motion or disturbance ► calmness, lull, tranquility. *See* **stillness** (1). **3.** A temporary cessation of hostilities ► armistice, cease-fire. *See* **truce.**

peaceable *adjective*
Inclined or disposed to peace; not quarrelsome or unruly ► conciliatory, dovish, irenic, nonviolent, pacific, pacifical, pacifist, pacifistic, peaceful. *See also* **amiable.**

peaceful *adjective*
1. Not excited or agitated ► placid, serene, tranquil. *See* **calm** (1). **2.** Free from disturbance, agitation, or commotion ► peaceful, placid, serene. *See* **still** (1). *See synonym note at* **still. 3.** Inclined or disposed to peace; not quarrelsome or unruly ► conciliatory, dovish, pacifist. *See* **peaceable.**

peacefulness *noun*
1. Lack of emotional agitation ► peace, serenity. *See* **calm** (1). **2.** An absence of motion or disturbance ► calmness, lull, placidity. *See* **stillness** (1).

peace officer *noun*
► marshal, officer, trooper. *Informal:* cop. *See* **police officer.**

peacock *verb*
To walk with pompous bearing ► prance, strut, swank. *See* **strut** (1).

peacock *noun*
A man who is vain about his clothes ► beau, coxcomb, dandy, fop, swell.

peak¹ *noun*
1. The projecting rim on the front of a cap ► brim, visor. *See* **bill²** (2). **2.** The highest point or state ► apex, height, pinnacle. *See* **climax** (1). *See synonym note at* **climax.**

peak *verb*
To reach or bring to a climax ► cap, culminate. *See* **climax.**

peak *adjective*
1. Of or constituting a climax ► climactic, crowning, culminating. *See also* **last. 2.** Greatest in quantity or highest in degree that can be attained ► top, ultimate, utmost. *See* **maximum.**

peak² *verb*
To lose normal coloration; turn pale ▸ bleach, wan. *See* **pale.**

peaked *adjective*
▸ ailing, indisposed, unwell. *See* **sick** (1).

peal *verb*
▸ bong, chime, strike. *See* **ring²** (1).

peanuts *noun*
Informal A small or trifling amount of money ▸ pocket money, small change. *Slang:* chicken feed, two bits.

pearl *noun*
▸ find, pearl, prize. *See* **treasure** (1).

peasant *noun*
▸ hick, rustic, yokel. *See* **clodhopper.**

peccancy *noun*
1. A wicked act or wicked behavior ▸ evil, misdeed, sin. *See* **crime** (2). **2.** The quality or sate of being morally bad or objectionable ▸ iniquity, wickedness. *See* **evil** (1).

peccant *adjective*
▸ immoral, sinful. *See* **evil** (1).

peck¹ *verb*
To touch or caress with the lips, especially as a sign of passion or affection ▸ osculate, smack. *See* **kiss** (1).

peck at *verb*
To scold or find fault with constantly ▸ fuss at, pick on. *See* **nag** (1).

peck *noun*
Informal The act or an instance of kissing ▸ osculation, smack. *See* **kiss** (1).

peck² *noun*
1. *Informal* A great deal ▸ bounty, mass, profusion. *See* **abundance** (1). **2.** *Informal* An indeterminately great amount or number ▸ bunch, multiplicity. *Informal:* bushel. *See* **heap** (3).

Pecksniffian *adjective*
▸ pharisaic, phony, sanctimonious. *See* **hypocritical.**

peculiar *adjective*
1. Deviating from what is conventional or customary ▸ bizarre, grotesque. *See* **eccentric.** *See synonym note at* **eccentric. 2.** Causing puzzlement; perplexing ▸ curious, odd. *See* **funny** (3). **3.** Relating to, identifying, or setting apart an individual or group ▸ characteristic, individual, particular. *See* **special** (1).

peculiarity *noun*
1. A distinctive element ▸ characteristic, feature, trait. *See* **quality** (1). **2.** Peculiar behavior ▸ idiosyncrasy, quirk. *See* **eccentricity. 3.** The set of behavioral or personal characteristics by which an individual is recognizable ▸ distinctiveness, individuality, singularity. *See* **identity** (1).

peculiarly *adverb*
▸ singularly, uncommonly, uniquely. *See* **unusually.**

pecuniary *adjective*
Of or relating to finances ▸ financial, fiscal, monetary.

pedagogic *or* **pedagogical** *adjective*
1. Characterized by a narrow concern for book learning and formal rules ▸ bookish, literary, scholas-

tic. *See* **pedantic. 2.** Of or relating to education ▸ academic, scholastic, teaching. *See* **educational** (1).

pedagogue *noun*
▸ instructor, trainer, tutor. *See* **educator.**

pedagogy *or* **pedagogics** *noun*
▸ edification, schooling. *See* **education** (1).

pedantic *adjective*
Characterized by a narrow concern for book learning and formal rules ▸ academic, bookish, donnish, formalistic, inkhorn, literal, literary, pedagogic, pedantical, purist, scholastic. *See also* **educated.**

✦ **CORE SYNONYMS:** *pedantic, academic, bookish, donnish, scholastic.* These adjectives mean marked by a narrow, often tiresome focus on or display of learning and especially its trivial aspects: *a pedantic writing style; an academic insistence on precision; a bookish vocabulary; donnish refinement of speech; scholastic and excessively subtle reasoning.*

peddle *verb*
1. To travel about selling goods ▸ hawk, huckster, vend. **2.** To offer for sale ▸ handle, retail. *See* **sell** (1). **3.** To engage in the illicit sale of narcotics ▸ deal. *Slang:* push.

peddler *noun*
1. One who sells ▸ salesclerk, vendor. *See* **seller. 2.** A person who sells narcotics illegally ▸ dealer, trafficker. *See* **pusher.**

pedestal *noun*
▸ footing, foundation, groundwork. *See* **base¹** (2).

pedestrian *adjective*
▸ aseptic, colorless, lusterless. *See* **dull** (1). *See synonym note at* **dull.**

pedigree *noun*
1. One's ancestors or ancestral derivation ▸ blood, extraction, lineage. *See* **ancestry. 2.** A written record of ancestry ▸ family tree, genealogy.

pedigreed *adjective*
▸ pureblood, purebred. *See* **thoroughbred** (1).

pee *verb*
Informal To excrete urine ▸ make water, micturate. *See* **urinate.**

peek *verb*
To look briefly and quickly ▸ glance, glimpse, peep. *Idioms:* steal a glance (or look). *See also* **look.**

peek *noun*
A quick look ▸ glimpse, peep. *See* **glance** (1).

peel *noun*
The outer covering of a fruit ▸ rind, shell. *See* **skin** (3).

peel *verb*
1. To remove the skin of ▸ pare, strip. *See* **skin** (1). **2.** To remove the clothing or covering from ▸ flay, strip, uncover. *See* **bare** (1). **3.** To come off in small, thin pieces ▸ chip, scale, shed. *See* **flake.**

peep *verb*
To look briefly and quickly ▸ glance, glimpse, peek. *Idioms:* steal a glance (or look). *See also* **look.**

peep *noun*
A quick look ▸ glimpse, peek. *See* **glance** (1).

peer¹ *verb*
To look intently and fixedly ▸ gape, gawk, stare. *See* **gaze.** *See synonym note at* **gaze.**

peer² *noun*
One that is very similar to another in rank or position ▸ coequal, colleague, compeer, equal, equivalent, fellow, match, rival. *See also* **associate, parallel.**

peerless *adjective*
▸ incomparable, singular, unparalleled. *See* **unique** (1).

peerlessness *noun*
▸ oneness, singleness, singularity. *See* **uniqueness** (1).

peeve *verb*
To trouble the nerves or peace of mind of ▸ irritate, nettle, vex. *See* **annoy** (1). *See synonym note at* **annoy.**

peeve *noun*
Something that annoys ▸ bother, irritant, nuisance. *See* **annoyance** (2).

peevish *adjective*
▸ cranky, grouchy, snappish. *See* **ill-tempered.**

peevishness *noun*
▸ crankiness, prickliness, tetchiness. *See* **temper** (1).

peewee *adjective*
Informal Extremely small ▸ dwarf, miniature, minuscule. *See* **tiny.**

peg *noun*
1. One of the units in a course, as on an ascending or descending scale ▸ interval, level, step. *See* **degree** (1). **2.** A shaft hammered or drilled in place, used to hold together ▸ pin, spike, stud. *See* **nail. 3.** Something that is used to fill a hole, space, or container ▸ cork, stop. *See* **plug** (1). **4.** An act of throwing ▸ fling, hurl, toss. *See* **throw.**

peg *verb*
To send through the air with a motion of the hand or arm ▸ heave, hurl, pitch. *See* **throw** (1).

pejorative *adjective*
▸ deprecatory, derogatory, slighting. *See* **disparaging.**

pelagic *adjective*
▸ oceanic, sea, thalassic. *See* **marine** (1).

pelf *noun*
▸ fortune, riches, treasure. *See* **wealth** (1).

pellucid *adjective*
▸ crystalline, limpid, lucid. *See* **clear** (1). *See synonym note at* **clear.**

pellucidity *or* **pellucidness** *noun*
▸ distinctness, legibility, perspicuity, plainness. *See* **clarity** (1).

pelt¹ *noun*
The skin of an animal, sometimes including fur, hair or feathers ▸ fur, hide, leather.

pelt² *verb*
1. To move swiftly ▸ dash, sprint, zip. *See* **rush** (1). **2.** To send through the air with a motion of the hand or arm ▸ heave, hurl, pitch. *See* **throw** (1). **3.** To direct a barrage at ▸ bombard, shell. *See* **barrage.** *See synonym note at* **barrage. 4.** To hit heavily and repeatedly ▸ assault, batter, pummel, thresh. *See* **beat** (1).

pen¹ *verb*
1. To be the author of a published work or works

▸ author, compose, write. *See* **publish** (2). **2.** To form by artistic effort ▸ produce, write. *See* **compose** (1). **3.** To form letters, characters, or words on a surface with an instrument ▸ inscribe, scribe. *See* **write** (1).

pen² *noun*
1. An enclosure for livestock ▸ corral, fold, paddock, sty, yard. *See also* **cage. 2.** *Informal* A place for the confinement of persons in lawful detention ▸ penitentiary, prison. *Informal:* lockup. *See* **jail.**

pen *verb*
To confine within a limited area ▸ cage, coop (up), shut (in). *See* **enclose** (1). *See synonym note at* **enclose.**

penal *adjective*
▸ disciplinary, punitive, punitory. *See* **punishing** (1).

penalize *verb*
1. To subject one to a penalty for a wrong ▸ chastise, correct, discipline. *See* **punish.** *See synonym note at* **punish. 2.** To impose a fine on ▸ amerce, fine, mulct.

penalty *noun*
1. A coercive measure intended to ensure compliance or conformity ▸ interdict, interdiction, sanction. *See also* **forbiddance, restriction. 2.** Something, such as loss, pain, or confinement, imposed for wrongdoing ▸ castigation, chastisement, discipline. *See* **punishment. 3.** A sum of money levied as punishment for an offense ▸ amercement, fine, mulct.

penance *noun*
1. The act of making amends ▸ atonement, expiation, reconciliation, reparation. *See also* **compensation, purification. 2.** Something, such as loss, pain, or confinement, imposed for wrongdoing ▸ castigation, chastisement, discipline. *See* **punishment.**

penchant *noun*
▸ bias, disposition, leaning. *See* **inclination** (1). *See synonym note at* **inclination.**

pendent *adjective*
▸ dangling, pendulous, pensile. *See* **hanging** (1).

pendulous *adjective*
1. Hung or appearing to be hung from a support ▸ dangling, pensile. *See* **hanging** (1). **2.** Given to or exhibiting hesitation ▸ indecisive, irresolute. *See* **hesitant** (1).

penetrable *adjective*
▸ negotiable, passable, traversable. *See* **passable** (1).

penetrate *verb*
1. To pass into or through by overcoming resistance ▸ break (through), enter, jab, perforate, pierce, poke, punch, puncture. *See also* **cut. 2.** To come or go into a place ▸ come in, go in. *See* **enter** (1).

penetrating *adjective*
1. Having the quality or tendency to pervade or permeate ▸ permeating, pervading, pervasive, suffusive. *See also* **general, prevailing, recurrent. 2.** Keenly perceptive or discerning ▸ incisive, perceptive, probing. *See* **critical** (2). **3.** Painfully intense ▸ brutal, harsh, severe. *See* **bitter** (2).

penetration *noun*
1. Skill in perceiving, discriminating, or judging

▶ keenness, perceptiveness, shrewdness. *See* **discernment** (1). **2.** The power to discern the true nature of a person or situation ▶ intuitiveness, intuition. *See* **instinct** (2). **3.** The act of entering ▶ incoming, ingress. *See* **entrance**[1] (1).

penitence *or* **penitency** *noun*
A feeling of regret for one's sins or misdeeds ▶ attrition, compunction, contriteness, contrition, guilt, regret, remorse, remorsefulness, repentance, rue, self-reproach, shame.

✦ CORE SYNONYMS: *penitence, compunction, contrition, remorse, repentance.* These nouns denote a feeling of regret for one's sins or misdeeds: *showed no penitence; ended the relationship without compunction; pangs of contrition; tears of remorse; sincere repentance.*

---

penitent *adjective*
▶ contrite, regretful, repentant. *See* **sorry** (1).

penitentiary *noun*
▶ brig, prison. *Informal:* lockup. *See* **jail**.

penmanship *noun*
▶ calligraphy, cursive, handwriting. *See* **script** (1).

pennant *noun*
▶ banner, colors, ensign. *See* **flag**[1] (1).

penniless *adjective*
▶ destitute, down-and-out, indigent. *See* **poor** (1). *See synonym note at* **poor.**

pennilessness *noun*
▶ destitution, indigence, need. *See* **poverty** (1).

pennon *noun*
▶ banner, colors, pennant. *See* **flag**[1] (1).

penny pincher *noun*
▶ churl. *Slang:* stiff, tightwad. *See* **miser.**

penny-pinching *adjective*
▶ close-fisted, miserly, parsimonious. *See* **stingy** (1).

pensile *adjective*
▶ dangling, pendent, pendulous. *See* **hanging** (1).

pension *verb*
To withdraw or remove from business or active life ▶ retire, step down, superannuate. *Idioms:* call it quits, hang up one's spurs, put out to pasture, turn in one's badge. *See also* **dismiss, quit.**

pensive *adjective*
▶ contemplative, meditative, reflective. *See* **thoughtful** (1). *See synonym note at* **thoughtful.**

penumbra *noun*
Comparative darkness that results from the blocking of light rays ▶ shade, shadiness, shadow, umbra. *See also* **dark, twilight.**

penurious *adjective*
1. Ungenerously or pettily reluctant to spend money ▶ close-fisted, miserly, parsimonious. *See* **stingy** (1). **2.** Having little or no money or wealth ▶ destitute, down-and-out, indigent. *See* **poor** (1).

penuriousness *noun*
▶ destitution, indigence, need. *See* **poverty** (1).

penury *noun*
1. The condition of being extremely poor ▶ destitution, indigence, need. *See* **poverty** (1). **2.** The condi-

tion of being deprived of what one once had or ought to have ▶ destitution, dispossession, loss. *See* **deprivation** (1).

people *noun*
1. Persons as an organized body ▶ community, society. *See* **public** (2). **2.** One's relatives collectively ▶ family, kindred. *See* **kin.**

people *verb*
To live in a place, as does a people ▶ inhabit, occupy, populate. *See also* **live, settle.**

pep *noun*
1. A lively, emphatic, eager quality or manner ▶ life, verve, vivaciousness. *See* **spirit** (1). **2.** *Informal* Capacity for work or vigorous activity ▶ might, potency, power. *See* **energy.**

pep up *verb*
Informal To give or impart vitality and energy to ▶ invigorate, vitalize. *See* **energize.**

pepper *verb*
1. To mark with many small spots ▶ dapple, freckle. *See* **speckle.** **2.** To direct a barrage at ▶ bombard, pelt. *See* **barrage.** *See synonym note at* **barrage.** **3.** To scatter or release in drops or small particles ▶ besprinkle, dust, powder. *See* **sprinkle** (1).

peppery *adjective*
1. Easily moved to anger ▶ irascible, quick-tempered, tetchy. *See* **testy** (1). **2.** Having a sharp, penetrating flavor or aroma ▶ piquant, sharp, zesty. *See* **spicy** (1).

peppiness *noun*
1. A lively, emphatic, eager quality or manner ▶ life, verve, vivaciousness. *See* **spirit** (1). **2.** *Informal* Capacity for work or vigorous activity ▶ might, potency, power. *See* **energy.**

peppy *adjective*
1. *Informal* Possessing, exerting, or displaying energy ▶ brisk, lively, vigorous. *See* **energetic.** **2.** *Informal* Very brisk, alert, and full of high spirits ▶ animated, chipper, vivacious. *See* **lively** (1).

pep talk *noun*
Informal Something that gives courage or confidence ▶ boost, exhortation, motivation. *See* **encouragement** (1).

perambulate *verb*
▶ promenade, saunter, wander. *See* **stroll.**

perambulation *noun*
▶ promenade, ramble, stroll. *See* **walk** (1).

perceivable *adjective*
▶ discernible, palpable, sensible. *See* **perceptible.**

perceive *verb*
1. To perceive with the eyes ▶ catch, discern, spot. *See* **see** (1). *See synonym note at* **see.** **2.** To be intuitively aware of ▶ apprehend, feel, intuit, sense. *Idioms:* feel in one's bones, get vibrations. *See also* **understand.**

percentage *noun*
▶ building block, piece, section. *See* **part** (1).

perceptibility *noun*
▶ clarity, observability, visuality. *See* **visibility.**

perceptible *adjective*
Capable of being perceived by the senses or the mind

▸ appreciable, cognizable, detectable, discernible, distinguishable, noticeable, observable, palpable, perceivable, ponderable, recognizable, sensible. *See also* **apparent, physical, understandable.**

✛ CORE SYNONYMS: *perceptible, palpable, appreciable, noticeable, discernible.* These adjectives apply to what is capable of being perceived by the senses or the mind. *Perceptible* is the least specific: *She noticed a perceptible pause in the flow of his speech. Palpable* applies both to what is perceptible by means of the sense of touch and to what is readily perceived by the mind: *"The advantages Mr. Falkland possessed . . . are palpable"* (William Godwin). What is *appreciable* is capable of being estimated or measured: *The firm was accused of dumping appreciable amounts of noxious waste into the harbor. Noticeable* means easily observed: *There are noticeable shadows under your eyes. Discernible* means distinguishable, especially by the faculty of vision or the intellect: *The mediator found no discernible progress in the contract negotiations.*

perception *noun*
1. The condition of being aware ▸ cognizance, consciousness, sense. *See* **awareness. 2.** That which exists in the mind as the product of careful mental activity ▸ conception, notion. *See* **idea** (1). **3.** The capacity for or an act of responding to a stimulus ▸ feeling, sensitivity. *See* **sensation** (1). **4.** Skill in perceiving, discriminating, or judging ▸ keenness, perceptiveness, shrewdness. *See* **discernment** (1).

perceptive *adjective*
1. Keenly perceptive or discerning ▸ penetrating, sensitive, sharp. *See* **critical** (2). **2.** Characterized by foresight or vision ▸ imaginative, intuitive. *See* **visionary** (1).

perceptiveness *noun*
▸ keenness, sagacity, shrewdness. *See* **discernment** (1).

perch *verb*
To rest on a narrow or insecure surface ▸ poise, roost. *See* **balance** (3).

perch *noun*
A place providing support for the foot in climbing ▸ foothold, footing, purchase, toehold.

perchance *adverb*
▸ conceivably, mayhap, perhaps. *See* **maybe.**

percipience *or* **percipiency** *noun*
1. Skill in perceiving, discriminating, or judging ▸ keenness, perceptiveness, shrewdness. *See* **discernment** (1). **2.** The ability to distinguish, especially to recognize small differences or draw fine distinctions ▸ acuteness, selectiveness, taste. *See* **discrimination** (1).

percipient *adjective*
▸ astute, discerning, selective, subtle. *See* **discriminating** (1).

percolate *verb*
1. To flow or leak out or emit something slowly ▸ exude, leach, seep. *See* **ooze. 2.** To be in a state of turmoil or excitement ▸ burn, seethe. *See* **boil** (2).

percussion *noun*
▸ crash, impact. *See* **collision.**

perdition *noun*
▸ living hell, persecution. *See* **hell.**

perdurable *adjective*
▸ durable, enduring, perennial. *See* **continuing** (1).

perdure *verb*
▸ continue, persist. *See* **endure** (2).

peregrinate *verb*
1. To make or go on a journey ▸ pass, travel, voyage. *See* **journey. 2.** To move about at random, especially over a wide area ▸ drift, meander, wander. *See* **rove.**

peregrination *noun*
▸ flight, passage, progress. *See* **journey.**

peregrinator *noun*
▸ nomad, roamer, vagabond. *See* **hobo.**

peremptory *adjective*
▸ bossy, domineering, overbearing. *See* **dictatorial** (1).

perennial *adjective*
1. Existing in the same state for an indefinitely long time ▸ durable, enduring, lasting. *See* **continuing** (1). **2.** Existing without interruption or end ▸ constant, endless, everlasting, perpetual. *See* **continual.** *See synonym note at* **continual.**

perfect *adjective*
1. Free from flaws or blemishes ▸ absolute, clean, clear, consummate, faultless, flawless, impeccable, indefectible, regular, unblemished, unflawed, unmarked. *Idiom:* in mint condition. **2.** In excellent condition ▸ flawless, intact, sound. *See* **good** (2). **3.** Conforming to an ultimate form of perfection or excellence ▸ exemplary, model, supreme. *See* **ideal** (1). **4.** Completely such, without qualification or exception ▸ all-out, pure, sheer. *See* **utter**^{2}. **5.** Including every constituent or individual ▸ entire, total, whole. *See* **complete** (1). **6.** Free from extraneous elements ▸ genuine, plain, unadulterated. *See* **pure** (1).

perfect *verb*
To bring to perfection or completion ▸ complement, complete, fill in (*or* out), hone, polish, refine, round off (*or* out), smooth. *Idiom:* smooth off the rough edges. *See also* **climax, complete, satisfy.**

✛ CORE SYNONYMS: *perfect, consummate, faultless, flawless, impeccable.* These adjectives mean completely free from flaws or blemishes: *a perfect diamond; a consummate performer; faultless logic; a flawless instrumental technique; speaks impeccable Russian.*

perfection *noun*
▸ solidity, strength. *See* **soundness** (1).

perfectly *adverb*
▸ fully, totally, utterly. *See* **completely** (1).

perfervid *adjective*
▸ burning, fervent, impassioned, torrid. *See* **passionate** (1).

perfidious *adjective*
1. Not true to duty or obligation ▸ disloyal, traitorous, treacherous. *See* **faithless** (1). *See synonym note at* **faithless. 2.** Given to or marked by deliberate concealment or misrepresentation of the truth ▸ duplicitous, lying, untruthful. *See* **dishonest** (1).

perfidy *or* **perfidiousness** *noun*
1. Betrayal, especially of a duty or obligation ► disloyalty, infidelity, treachery. *See* **faithlessness** (1). 2. Willful betrayal of fidelity, confidence, or trust ► treacherousness, treachery, treason.

perforate *verb*
1. To make a hole or other opening in ► pierce, puncture. *See* **breach** (1). 2. To pass into or through by overcoming resistance ► break (through), puncture. *See* **penetrate** (1).

perforation *noun*
► nick, puncture, stab. *See* **prick** (1).

perforce *adverb*
► involuntarily, willy-nilly. *See* **helplessly.**

perform *verb*
1. To begin and carry through to completion ► accomplish, achieve, discharge, do, effect, execute, fulfill, prosecute, transact. *Informal:* pull off. *See also* **accomplish, effect.** 2. To act in a specified way ► behave, operate, work. *See* **function.** 3. To carry out the functions, requirements, or terms of ► discharge, execute, implement. *See* **fulfill** (1). 4. To play the part of ► do, play, portray. *See* **act** (4). 5. To produce on the stage ► dramatize, enact, produce. *See* **stage** (1). 6. To make music ► concertize, play, render.

✦ CORE SYNONYMS: *perform, execute, accomplish, achieve, effect, fulfill, discharge.* These verbs mean to begin and carry through to completion. To *perform* is to carry out an action, undertaking, or procedure, often with great skill or care. *The ship's captain performed the wedding ceremony. Laser experiments are performed regularly in the laboratory. Execute* implies performing a task or putting something into effect in accordance with a plan or design: *"To execute laws is a royal office; to execute orders is not to be a king"* (Edmund Burke). *Accomplish* connotes the successful completion of something, often of something that requires tenacity or talent: *"Make one brave push and see what can be accomplished in a week"* (Robert Louis Stevenson). To *achieve* is to accomplish something, often something significant, especially despite difficulty: *"Some are born great . . . Some achieve greatness . . . And some have greatness thrust upon them"* (William Shakespeare). *Effect* suggests the power of an agent to bring about a desired result: *The prescribed antibiotics didn't effect a complete cure.* To *fulfill* is to live up to expectations or satisfy demands, wishes, or requirements: *All their desires could not be fulfilled.* To *discharge* an obligation or duty is to perform all the steps necessary for its fulfillment: *"I have found it impossible . . . to discharge my duties as King as I would wish to do"* (Edward VIII).

---

performance *noun*
1. The act of beginning and carrying through to completion ► discharge, effectuation, execution, prosecution, transaction. *See also* **accomplishment, fulfillment.** 2. Something done ► action, deed, work. *See* **act** (1). 3. A performer's distinctive personal version of a song, dance, piece of music, or role ► depiction, reading, rendition. *See* **interpretation** (1). 4. The way

in which something functions ► functioning, operation. *See* **behavior** (2).

performer *noun*
► musician, virtuoso. *See* **player** (2).

perfume *noun*
A sweet or pleasant odor ► aroma, bouquet, scent. *See* **fragrance.** *See synonym note at* **fragrance.**

perfume *verb*
To fill with a pleasant odor ► aromatize, scent.

perfumy *adjective*
► aromatic, redolent, savory. *See* **fragrant.**

perfunctory *adjective*
Done routinely and impersonally ► automatic, cursory, mechanical, routine. *See also* **apathetic, careless.**

perhaps *adverb*
► conceivably, perchance, possibly. *See* **maybe.**

periapt *noun*
► mascot, talisman. *See* **charm** (1).

peril *noun*
Exposure to harm, loss, or injury ► hazard, jeopardy, risk. *See* **danger.**

peril *verb*
To expose to possible loss or damage ► jeopardize, threaten. *See* **endanger.**

perilous *adjective*
► chancy, hazardous, risky. *See* **dangerous.**

perimeter *noun*
1. A line around a closed figure or area ► circuit, compass. *See* **circumference.** *See synonym note at* **circumference.** 2. A line or area where something ends or abruptly changes ► brink, fringe, margin. *See* **border** (1). 3. The boundary surrounding a certain area ► bounds, confines. *See* **limits.**

period *noun*
1. A specific length of time characterized by the occurrence of certain conditions or events ► duration, season, session, space, span, stretch, term, time. *See also* **bit**[1]. 2. An interval regarded as a distinct evolutionary or developmental unit ► phase, stage. *See also* **degree.** 3. A particular time notable for its distinctive characteristics ► epoch, era, times. *See* **age** (2). *See synonym note at* **age.** 4. A concluding or terminating ► cease, completion, termination. *See* **end** (1).

periodic *or* **periodical** *adjective*
1. Happening or appearing at regular intervals ► cyclic, cyclical, isochronal, isochronous. *Idiom:* like clockwork. *See also* **recurrent.** 2. Happening or appearing now and then ► fitful, occasional, sporadic. *See* **intermittent.** *See synonym note at* **intermittent.**

periodically *adverb*
► occasionally, sometimes, sporadically. *See* **intermittently.**

peripatetic *adjective*
Leading the life of a person without a fixed domicile; moving from place to place ► traveling, vagabond. *See* **nomadic.**

peripatetic *noun*
One who wanders without a permanent home or

livelihood ▸ nomad, roamer, vagabond. *See* **hobo.**

periphery *noun*
1. A line around a closed figure or area ▸ circuit, perimeter. *See* **circumference.** *See synonym note at* **circumference. 2.** A line or area where something ends or abruptly changes ▸ brink, fringe, margin. *See* **border** (1). **3.** The boundary surrounding a certain area ▸ bounds, confines. *See* **limits.**

periphrastic *adjective*
▸ long-winded, prolix, verbose. *See* **wordy** (1).

perish *verb*
1. To cease living ▸ demise, expire, succumb. *See* **die** (1). **2.** To cease to exist ▸ depart, expire. *See* **disappear** (2).

perjure *verb*
▸ fib, prevaricate. *See* **lie².**

perjurer *noun*
▸ fabulist, fibber, prevaricator. *See* **liar.**

perjury *noun*
▸ inveracity, lying, untruthfulness. *See* **mendacity** (1).

perk *noun*
Informal A material favor or gift, usually money, given in return for service ▸ largess, perquisite, tip. *See* **gratuity** (1).

perk up *verb*
1. To make lively or animated ▸ animate, brighten, enliven, light (up). **2.** To impart emotional, moral, or mental strength to ▸ hearten, nerve. *See* **encourage** (2). **3.** To regain one's health ▸ convalesce, improve, recuperate. *See* **recover** (2).

perky *adjective*
▸ animated, chipper, vivacious. *See* **lively** (1).

permanence *noun*
1. The condition of being without change or variation ▸ constancy, immutability. *See* **changelessness. 2.** Uninterrupted existence or succession ▸ endurability, persistence. *See* **continuation** (1).

permanent *adjective*
1. Existing or remaining in the same state for an indefinitely long time ▸ durable, enduring. *See* **continuing** (1). **2.** Having no change or variation; remaining unchanged ▸ changeless, immutable, unvarying. *See* **unchanging.**

permanently *adverb*
▸ endlessly, perpetually, unendingly. *See* **forever** (1).

permeable *adjective*
▸ assimilative, imbibing, retentive. *See* **absorbent.**

permeate *verb*
▸ imbue, suffuse. *See* **charge** (1). *See synonym note at* **charge.**

permissibility *noun*
▸ legitimacy, licitness, validity. *See* **legality.**

permissible *adjective*
1. Worthy of being accepted or allowed ▸ admissible, allowable. *See* **acceptable** (1). **2.** Not compulsory or automatic ▸ elective, possible. *See* **optional.**

permission *noun*
The approving of an action, especially when done by one in authority ▸ allowance, approbation, approval, assent, authority, authorization, consent, endorsement, imprimatur, leave, license, nod, permit, rubber stamp, sanction, thumbs-up. *Informal:* go-ahead, green light, OK. *Idiom:* seal of approval. *See also* **acceptance, admission.**

✚ CORE SYNONYMS: *permission, authorization, consent, leave, license, sanction.* These nouns denote the approving of an action, especially when granted by one in authority: *was refused permission to smoke; seeking authorization to begin construction; gave their consent to the marriage; will ask leave to respond to the speaker; was given license to depart; gave sanction to the project.*

◀ ANTONYM: *prohibition*

---

permissive *adjective*
▸ easy, indulgent, lenient. *See* **tolerant** (1).

permissiveness *noun*
▸ charity, lenience, toleration. *See* **tolerance** (1).

permit *verb*
1. To neither forbid nor prevent ▸ allow, have, let, suffer, tolerate. **2.** To give one's consent to ▸ allow, approbate, approve, authorize, consent, endorse, let, license, sanction. *Informal:* OK. *See also* **assent, grant, legalize. 3.** To afford an opportunity for ▸ admit, allow, give, let. **4.** To give the means, ability, or opportunity to do ▸ empower, enable. *Idioms:* clear the path (*or* road *or* way) for, smooth the way for. *See also* **ease, permit.**

permit *noun*
1. The approving of an action, especially when done by one in authority ▸ authorization, consent, sanction. *See* **permission. 2.** A document that gives permission to do something ▸ commission, permit, warrant. *See* **license** (3).

permitted *adjective*
▸ legal, licit, valid. *See* **lawful.**

permutable *adjective*
▸ fluid, unsettled, variable. *See* **changeable** (1).

permutation *noun*
1. The process or result of making or becoming different ▸ modification, mutation, variation. *See* **change** (1). **2.** One that is slightly different from others of the same kind or designation ▸ adaptation, form. *See* **variation** (1).

pernicious *adjective*
1. Capable of injuring or killing by poison ▸ noxious, toxic, venomous. *See* **poisonous** (1). **2.** Causing harm or injury ▸ deleterious, evil, injurious. *See* **harmful.**

perorate *verb*
▸ harangue, orate, rave. *See* **rant** (1).

perp *noun*
Slang One who commits a crime ▸ culprit, lawbreaker, offender. *See* **criminal.**

perpendicular *adjective*
▸ on end, standing, upright. *See* **vertical.** *See synonym note at* **vertical.**

perpetrate *verb*
To be responsible for or guilty of an error or crime

▸ carry out, commit, do. *Informal:* pull off. *See also* **perform.**

perpetrator *noun*
▸ culprit, lawbreaker, offender. *See* **criminal.**

perpetual *adjective*
1. Enduring for all time ▸ ceaseless, eternal. *See* **endless** (2). **2.** Existing without interruption or end ▸ constant, endless, everlasting, unceasing. *See* **continual.** *See synonym note at* **continual.**

perpetually *adverb*
▸ endlessly, evermore, unendingly. *See* **forever** (1).

perpetuate *verb*
To cause to last endlessly ▸ eternalize, eternize, immortalize. *Idioms:* cast (*or* etch *or* fix *or* set) in stone. *See also* **honor, memorialize.**

perpetuity *noun*
1. The totality of time without beginning or end ▸ eternity, infinity, sempiternity. *See also* **forever.** **2.** The quality or state of having no end ▸ eternity, interminability. *See* **endlessness.**

perplex *verb*
1. To cause to be unclear in mind or intent ▸ befuddle, bewilder, confound. *See* **confuse** (1). **2.** To make complex, intricate, or perplexing ▸ entangle, obfuscate, tangle. *See* **complicate.** **3.** To put at a loss as to what to say or do ▸ confound, nonplus. *Informal:* stump. *See* **baffle** (1).

perplexed *adjective*
▸ confounded, disoriented, turbid. *Informal:* mixed up. *See* **confused** (1).

perplexing *adjective*
▸ dubious, indeterminate, questionable, unclear. *See* **ambiguous** (1).

perplexity *noun*
1. A stunned or bewildered condition ▸ bewilderment, muddle, stupor. *See* **daze.** **2.** Anything that arouses curiosity or perplexes because it is unexplained, inexplicable, or secret ▸ enigma, puzzle, riddle. *See* **mystery.** **3.** Something complex ▸ elaborateness, intricacy. *See* **complexity.**

perquisite *noun*
1. A material favor or gift, usually money, given in return for service ▸ largess, tip. *See* **gratuity** (1). **2.** A benefit granted to a person by law, nature, or custom ▸ birthright, due. *See* **right.** *See synonym note at* **right.**

persecute *verb*
1. To treat wrongfully or harmfully ▸ exploit, ill-treat, maltreat. *See* **abuse** (1). **2.** To attack or disturb persistently ▸ harry, plague, torment. *See* **harass.**

persecution *noun*
1. A place or experience of excruciating pain ▸ living hell, perdition. *See* **hell.** **2.** Cruel exercise of power ▸ injustice, repression, subjugation. *See* **oppression** (1).

perseverance *noun*
1. The state or quality of being insistent ▸ insistence, insistency, persistence, persistency. *See also* **decision.** **2.** Steady attention and effort, as to one's occupation ▸ assiduousness, industry, pertinacity. *See* **diligence.**

perseverate *verb*
▸ continue, persist. *See* **endure** (2).

persevere *verb*
1. To put up with or continue despite difficulties ▸ keep on, persist, soldier on. *See* **endure** (1). **2.** To take and maintain a stand obstinately ▸ carry on, persist. *See* **insist** (1). **3.** To exist in spite of adversity ▸ persist, pull through. *See* **survive** (1).

persist *verb*
1. To take and maintain a stand obstinately ▸ carry on, persevere. *See* **insist** (1). **2.** To put up with or continue despite difficulties ▸ keep on, persevere, soldier on. *See* **endure** (1). **3.** To exist in spite of adversity ▸ get through, pull through. *See* **survive** (1). **4.** To be in existence or in a certain state for an indefinitely long time ▸ continue, perseverate. *See* **endure** (2).

persistence *or* **persistency** *noun*
1. The state or quality of being insistent ▸ insistence, insistency, perseverance. *See also* **decision.** **2.** Uninterrupted existence or succession ▸ continuum, endurance. *See* **continuation** (1). **3.** Steady attention and effort, as to one's occupation ▸ assiduousness, perseverance, pertinacity. *See* **diligence.**

persistent *adjective*
1. Firm or obstinate, as in making a demand or maintaining a stand ▸ importunate, importune, insistent, urgent. *See also* **firm, stubborn. 2.** Difficult to alleviate or cure ▸ obstinate, pertinacious, stubborn. **3.** Existing without interruption or end ▸ constant, endless, everlasting, perpetual. *See* **continual. 4.** Existing in the same state for an indefinitely long time ▸ durable, enduring, perennial. *See* **continuing** (1). **5.** Of long duration ▸ lingering, prolonged. *See* **chronic** (2). **6.** Characterized by steady attention and effort ▸ assiduous, conscientious, industrious. *See* **diligent.** *See synonym note at* **diligent.**

persnickety *adjective*
▸ exacting, finicky. *See* **fussy** (1).

person *noun*
▸ human, mortal. *See* **human being.**

persona *noun*
A person portrayed in fiction or drama ▸ character, part, personage, role.

personage *noun*
1. A person portrayed in fiction or drama ▸ character, part, persona, role. **2.** A member of the human race ▸ human, person. *See* **human being. 3.** An important, influential person ▸ luminary, notability. *Slang:* big shot. *See* **dignitary. 4.** A famous person ▸ luminary, personality, star. *See* **celebrity** (1). *See synonym note at* **celebrity.**

personal *adjective*
1. Belonging to, relating to, or affecting a particular person ▸ individual, private. **2.** Belonging or confined to a particular person or group as opposed to the public or the government ▸ closed-door, private, privy. *See also* **secret. 3.** Based on individual judgment or discretion ▸ judgmental, subjective. *See* **arbitrary** (1). **4.** Indicating intimacy and mutual trust

▸ close, familiar. *See* **confidential** (2). **5.** Of or relating to the body ▸ corporal, physical. *See* **bodily.**

personal effects *noun*
▸ belongings, goods, property. *See* **effects.**

personality *noun*
1. The combination of qualities that distinguishes an individual ▸ makeup, nature, temperament. *See* **character** (1). *See synonym note at* **character. 2.** A famous person ▸ luminary, notable, star. *See* **celebrity** (1).

personalization *noun*
▸ incarnation, manifestation, personification. *See* **embodiment** (1).

personalize *verb*
▸ externalize, manifest, materialize. *See* **embody** (1).

personal property *noun*
▸ goods, personal effects, property. *See* **effects.**

persona non grata *noun*
▸ exile, pariah. *See* **outcast.**

personification *noun*
▸ incarnation, manifestation, type. *See* **embodiment** (1).

personify *verb*
1. To represent (an abstraction, for example) in or as if in bodily form ▸ externalize, manifest, materialize. *See* **embody** (1). **2.** To serve as an example, image, or symbol of ▸ exemplify, illustrate, typify. *See* **represent** (1).

perspective *noun*
1. That which is or can be seen ▸ panorama, vista. *See* **view** (2). **2.** The position from which something is observed or considered ▸ aspect, point of view, standpoint. *See* **viewpoint. 3.** A frame of mind affecting one's thoughts or behavior ▸ outlook, position. *See* **posture** (2).

perspicacious *adjective*
1. Having or showing a clever awareness and resourcefulness in practical matters ▸ canny, knowing, street-smart. *See* **shrewd** (1). *See synonym note at* **shrewd. 2.** Able to recognize small differences or draw fine distinctions ▸ astute, discerning, selective. *See* **discriminating** (1).

perspicacity *noun*
1. Skill in perceiving, discriminating, or judging ▸ keenness, perceptiveness, shrewdness. *See* **discernment** (1). **2.** The ability to distinguish, especially to recognize small differences or draw fine distinctions ▸ acuteness, selectiveness, taste. *See* **discrimination** (1).

perspicuity *or* **perspicuousness** *noun*
▸ distinctness, legibility, lucidity, plainness. *See* **clarity** (1).

perspiration *noun*
Moisture accumulated on a surface through sweating or condensation ▸ condensation, lather, sweat, transudation.

perspire *verb*
To excrete moisture through a porous skin or layer ▸ lather, sweat, transude.

perspiring *adjective*
Producing or covered with sweat ▸ sudoriferous,

sweaty, sweating. *See also* **damp, sticky.**

persuade *verb*
1. To succeed in causing a person to act or think in a certain way ▸ argue into, bring around (*or* round), coax, convince, get to, induce, move, prevail on (*or* upon), sell (on), talk into. *See also* **coax, influence. 2.** To cause another to feel sure about something ▸ convert, win over. *See* **convince** (1).

✛ CORE SYNONYMS: *persuade, induce, prevail on, convince.* These verbs mean to succeed in causing a person to act or think in a certain way. *Persuade* means to win someone over, as by reasoning or personal forcefulness: *Nothing can persuade me to change my mind.* To *induce* is to lead, as to a course of action, by means of influence or persuasion: *"Pray what could induce him to commit so rash an action?"* (Oliver Goldsmith). One *prevails on* (or *upon*) somebody who resists: *"He had prevailed upon the king to spare them"* (Daniel Defoe). To *convince* is to persuade by the use of argument or evidence: *The sales clerk convinced me that the car was worth the price.*

persuasion *noun*
1. Urgent solicitation ▸ insistence, insistency, pressing, urging. *See also* **demand. 2.** Something thought to be true ▸ notion, sentiment, view. *See* **belief** (1). *See synonym note at* **belief. 3.** A system of religious belief ▸ creed, denomination. *See* **religion. 4.** *Informal* A class that is defined by the common attribute or attributes possessed by all its members ▸ ilk, mold, species. *See* **kind².**

persuasive *adjective*
▸ cogent, satisfactory. *See* **convincing** (1).

persuasiveness *noun*
▸ force, justice. *See* **cogency.**

pert *adjective*
1. Very brisk, alert, and full of high spirits ▸ animated, chipper, vivacious. *See* **lively** (1). **2.** Rude and disrespectful ▸ bold, insolent, pushy. *See* **impudent.**

pertain *verb*
▸ appertain, concern, relate. *See* **apply** (2).

pertinacious *adjective*
1. Difficult to alleviate or cure ▸ obstinate, persistent, stubborn. **2.** Firmly, often unreasonably immovable in purpose or will ▸ bullheaded, dogged, obstinate. *See* **stubborn** (1). *See synonym note at* **stubborn. 3.** Characterized by steady attention and effort ▸ assiduous, conscientious, industrious. *See* **diligent.** *See synonym note at* **diligent.**

pertinacity *or* **pertinaciousness** *noun*
1. The quality or state of being immovable in purpose or will ▸ bullheadedness, hardheadedness, rigidity. *See* **stubbornness. 2.** Steady attention and effort, as to one's occupation ▸ assiduousness, perseverance. *See* **diligence.**

pertinence *or* **pertinency** *noun*
▸ appositeness, materiality. *See* **relevance.**

pertinent *adjective*
▸ apropos, germane, material. *See* **relevant.** *See synonym note at* **relevant.**

pertness *noun*
1. A lively, emphatic, eager quality or manner ▸ life, verve, vivaciousness. *See* **spirit** (1). 2. The state or quality of being impudent or arrogantly self-confident ▸ audacity, boldness, forwardness. *See* **impudence.**

perturb *verb*
▸ disorient, fluster, ruffle. *See* **agitate** (2).

perturbation *noun*
▸ tumult, turmoil. *Informal:* lather. *See* **agitation** (2).

perturbing *adjective*
▸ bothersome, irritating, unsettling. *See* **disturbing.**

perusal *noun*
▸ check, review, survey. *See* **examination** (1).

peruse *verb*
▸ investigate, review, scrutinize. *See* **examine** (1).

pervade *verb*
▸ permeate, suffuse. *See* **charge** (1). *See synonym note at* **charge.**

pervasive *adjective*
Having the quality or tendency to pervade or permeate ▸ penetrating, permeating, pervading, suffusive. *See also* **general, prevailing, recurrent.**

perverse *adjective*
1. Utterly reprehensible in nature or behavior ▸ depraved, miscreant. *See* **corrupt** (1). 2. Marked by a disposition to oppose ▸ antagonistic, contradictory, hostile. *See* **contrary** (1). 3. Firmly, often unreasonably immovable in purpose or will ▸ bullheaded, dogged, obstinate. *See* **stubborn** (1).

perversion *noun*
1. Improper use or handling ▸ misappropriation, misuse. *See* **abuse** (1). 2. Degrading, immoral acts or habits ▸ depravity, immorality, vice. *See* **corruption** (1).

perversity *or* **perverseness** *noun*
▸ bullheadedness, hardheadedness, rigidity. *See* **stubbornness.**

pervert *verb*
1. To ruin morally ▸ debase, demoralize, deprave, warp. *See* **corrupt** (1). *See synonym note at* **corrupt.** 2. To use improperly ▸ misappropriate, mishandle, misuse. *See* **abuse** (2). 3. To give an inaccurate view of by representing falsely or misleadingly ▸ fudge, misrepresent, misstate. *See* **distort** (1).

pervert *noun*
One whose sexual behavior differs from the accepted norm ▸ deviant, deviate. *Slang:* freak.

perverted *adjective*
▸ depraved, miscreant, perverse. *See* **corrupt** (1).

pesky *adjective*
Informal Hard to treat, manage, or cope with ▸ demanding, difficult, trying. *See* **troublesome** (2).

pessimist *noun*
1. A person who expects only the worst from people ▸ cynic, misanthrope, misanthropist. *See also* **skeptic.** 2. A prophet of misfortune or disaster ▸ apocalypticist, Cassandra, crapehanger, croaker, doomsayer, worrywart.

pessimistic *adjective*
▸ dismal, gloomy, inauspicious. *See* **bleak** (2).

pest *noun*
▸ bother, irritant, nuisance. *See* **annoyance** (2).

pester *verb*
1. To attack or disturb persistently ▸ harry, plague, torment. *See* **harass.** *See synonym note at* **harass.** 2. To trouble the nerves or peace of mind of ▸ irritate, nettle, vex. *See* **annoy** (1).

pestering *noun*
▸ botheration, irritation, vexation. *See* **annoyance** (1).

pestilence *noun*
▸ impurity, poison, pollutant. *See* **contaminant.**

pestilent *or* **pestilential** *adjective*
1. Capable of injuring or killing by poison ▸ noxious, toxic, venomous. *See* **poisonous** (1). *See synonym note at* **poisonous.** 2. Capable of transmission by infection ▸ communicable, infectious, transmittable. *See* **contagious.** 3. Causing or tending to cause death ▸ fatal, lethal, mortal. *See* **deadly** (1).

pestle *verb*
▸ atomize, grind, mill. *See* **crush** (2).

pet¹ *noun*
One liked or preferred above all others ▸ darling, favorite. *Idiom:* apple of one's eye.

pet *adjective*
1. Being favorite ▸ fair-haired, favored, preferred. *See* **favorite.** 2. Trained or bred to live with and be of use to people ▸ broken (in), housebroken, naturalized. *See* **domestic** (2).

pet *verb*
1. To touch or handle affectionately ▸ fondle, pat. *See* **caress.** *See synonym note at* **caress.** 2. *Informal* To engage in kissing, caressing, and other amorous behavior ▸ *Informal:* fool around, spoon. *See* **neck.**

pet² *verb*
To be sullenly aloof or withdrawn, as in silent resentment or protest ▸ mope, pout, sulk. *See also* **brood.**

petcock *noun*
▸ fixture, spigot. *See* **faucet.**

peter out *verb*
1. To become or cause to become gradually less ▸ abate, diminish, ebb. *See* **decrease.** 2. *Informal* To lose strength or power ▸ decline, fail, weaken. *See* **fade** (1).

petite *adjective*
▸ bantam, petite, undersized. *See* **little** (1).

petition *verb*
1. To bring an appeal or request to the attention of ▸ address, appeal, apply, approach. *See also* **request.** 2. To make an earnest or urgent request ▸ beseech, entreat, plead. *See* **appeal** (1). 3. To ask for employment, acceptance, or admission ▸ apply, put in.

petition *noun*
An earnest or urgent request ▸ imploration, plea, supplication. *See* **appeal** (1).

petitioner *noun*
1. One that asks a higher authority for something, as

a favor or redress ► appealer, appellant, suitor. **2.** A person who applies for or seeks something, such as a job or position ► candidate, hopeful, seeker. *See* **applicant.**

pet name *noun*
► cognomen, epithet, title. *See* **name** (1).

petrified *adjective*
► fearful, frightened, scared. *See* **afraid.**

petrify *verb*
1. To make or become physically hard ► congeal, solidify. *See* **harden** (2). **2.** To render helpless, as by emotion ► numb, stun, stupefy. *See* **paralyze** (1). **3.** To fill with fear ► horrify, terrify. *See* **frighten.**

petroleum *noun*
► grease, lubricant. *See* **oil** (1).

pettifog *verb*
► cavil, niggle, nitpick. *See* **quibble** (1). *See synonym note at* **quibble.**

pettifogger *noun*
1. A person who finds fault ► caviler, nitpicker. *See* **critic** (2). **2.** A person who practices law ► attorney, jurist. *See* **lawyer.**

pettifoggery *noun*
► caviling, hairsplitting, nitpicking. *See* **quibbling.**

pettiness *noun*
► frivolity, minutia, triviality. *See* **trifle** (1).

petty *adjective*
1. Of little importance or seriousness ► inconsequential, paltry, trifling. *See* **trivial.** *See synonym note at* **trivial. 2.** Restricted in scope, outlook, or understanding ► insular, narrow-minded, provincial. *See* **narrow** (1). **3.** Ungenerously or pettily reluctant to spend money ► close-fisted, miserly, parsimonious. *See* **stingy** (1). **4.** Below another in standing, importance, or status ► junior, low, secondary. *See* **minor** (1).

petulance *noun*
► crankiness, prickliness, tetchiness. *See* **temper** (1).

petulant *adjective*
► cranky, grouchy, peevish. *See* **ill-tempered.**

phantasm *or* **phantasma** *noun*
1. An immaterial supernatural being, especially the spirit of a dead person ► phantom, shade, specter. *See* **ghost** (1). **2.** An illusory mental image ► fancy, fantasy, illusion. *See* **dream** (1). **3.** A phenomenon that causes a misperception ► hallucination, mirage. *See* **illusion** (1).

phantasmagoria *or* **phantasmagory** *noun*
1. An illusory mental image ► fancy, fantasy, illusion. *See* **dream** (1). **2.** A phenomenon that causes a misperception ► hallucination, mirage, phantasma. *See* **illusion** (1). **3.** An experience of things or events that are not real ► hallucination. *Slang:* trip.

phantasmagoric *adjective*
► hallucinatory, illusory, unreal. *See* **illusive** (1).

phantasmal *or* **phantasmic** *adjective*
► hallucinatory, illusory, phantasmagoric. *See* **illusive** (1).

phantom *noun*
► apparition, shade, specter. *See* **ghost** (1).

pharisaic *adjective*
► holier-than-thou, phony, sanctimonious. *See* **hypocritical.**

pharisaism *noun*
► phoniness, sanctimoniousness, sanctimony. *See* **hypocrisy.**

pharisee *noun*
► dissembler, phony, tartuffe. *See* **hypocrite.**

pharmaceutical *noun*
► medicament, medication, medicine. *See* **drug** (1).

phase *noun*
1. An interval regarded as a distinct evolutionary or developmental unit ► period, stage. *See also* **degree. 2.** The position from which something is observed or considered ► aspect, respect, standpoint. *See* **viewpoint.**

phenomenal *adjective*
1. Composed of or relating to things that occupy space and can be perceived by the senses ► corporeal, tangible. *See* **physical** (1). **2.** So remarkable as to be difficult to believe ► astounding, staggering, unbelievable. *See* **astonishing.**

phenomenon *noun*
1. Something demonstrated to exist or known to have existed ► actuality, event, fact, reality. *Idioms:* hard (*or* cold *or* plain) fact. *See also* **information. 2.** One that evokes great surprise and admiration ► prodigy, sensation, wonder. *See* **marvel** (1). *See synonym note at* **marvel. 3.** Something significant that happens ► development, incident. *See* **event** (2).

phenomenonally *adverb*
► singularly, uncommonly, uniquely. *See* **unusually.**

philander *verb*
To be sexually unfaithful to another ► *Informal:* cheat, fool around, mess around, play around. *Slang:* two-time.

philanderer *noun*
A man who philanders ► adulterer, Casanova, cheater, Don Juan, fornicator, lady's man, paramour, womanizer. *Slang:* lady-killer, wolf. *Idioms:* man on the make, skirt chaser. *See also* **flirt, seducer, wanton.**

philanthropic *adjective*
1. Of or concerned with charity ► altruistic, benevolent, charitable, eleemosynary. *See synonym note at* **charitable. 2.** Concerned with human welfare and the remedying of social ills ► compassionate, humane. *See* **humanitarian.**

philanthropist *noun*
1. One who supports or champions an activity, cause, or institution ► benefactor, sponsor. *See* **patron** (1). **2.** A person who gives to a charity or cause ► benefactor, contributor, patron. *See* **donor.**

philanthropy *noun*
1. Kindly, charitable interest in others ► altruism, goodwill, kindheartedness. *See* **benevolence** (1). **2.** A kindly act ► benevolence, good deed, kindliness. *See* **favor** (1).

philippic *noun*
► diatribe, harangue. *See* **tirade.**

Philistine *noun*
An unrefined, rude person ▶ chuff, vulgarian, yahoo. *See* **boor.**

philistine *adjective*
Lacking in delicacy or refinement ▶ indelicate, unbecoming, unrefined. *See* **coarse** (1).

philosopher *noun*
A person who seeks truth by thinking ▶ reasoner, theorist, thinker.

philosophizing *noun*
▶ conceptualization, conjecture, speculation. *See* **theory** (1).

philosophy *noun*
▶ outlook, position. *See* **posture** (2).

phlegm *noun*
1. A bodily substance ejected from the mouth ▶ saliva, phlegm. *See* **spit** (1). **2.** Lack of emotion or interest ▶ disinterest, indifference, unconcern. *See* **apathy.**

phlegmatic *adjective*
1. Lacking interest ▶ indifferent, listless, uninterested. *See* **apathetic. 2.** Lacking feeling or emotion ▶ emotionless, impassive, stolid. *See* **cold** (2).

phobia *noun*
An exaggerated concern ▶ anxiety, complex, neurosis. *Informal:* hang-up. *See also* **anxiety, obsession.**

phoenix *noun*
A person or thing so excellent as to have no equal or match ▶ nonesuch, nonpareil, paragon. *See also* **best, celebrity, model.**

phonate *verb*
▶ articulate, enunciate, vocalize. *See* **pronounce.**

phone *verb*
▶ buzz, call (up), ring (up). *See* **telephone.**

phoniness *noun*
1. Lack of sincerity ▶ artificiality, disingenuousness. *See* **insincerity. 2.** A show or expression of feelings or beliefs one does not actually hold or possess ▶ sanctimoniousness, sanctimony, two-facedness. *See* **hypocrisy.**

phony *adjective*
1. Fraudulently or deceptively imitative ▶ fake, fraudulent. *See* **counterfeit. 2.** Not genuine or sincere ▶ feigned, insincere. *See* **artificial** (2). **3.** Of or practicing hypocrisy ▶ Pecksniffian, pharisaic, two-faced. *See* **hypocritical.**

phony *noun*
1. A fraudulent imitation ▶ forgery, sham. *See* **counterfeit. 2.** A person who practices deceit, especially under an assumed identity ▶ charlatan, fraud, impostor. *See* **fake** (1). **3.** A person who practices hypocrisy ▶ dissembler, poser, tartuffe. *See* **hypocrite.**

photocopy *noun*
Something closely resembling another ▶ ditto, facsimile, likeness. *See* **copy** (1).

photocopy *verb*
To make a copy of ▶ imitate, replicate, reproduce. *See* **copy** (1).

photographic *adjective*
1. Of or relating to representation by drawings or pictures ▶ illustrative, pictographic, pictorial. *See* **graphic** (4). **2.** Depicted in sharp and accurate detail ▶ explicit, realistic, vivid. *See* **graphic** (1).

phrase *noun*
1. A word or group of words forming a unit and conveying meaning ▶ collocation, idiom, phrase. *See* **expression** (3). **2.** Choice of words and the way in which they are used ▶ locution, phraseology, verbalism. *See* **wording.**

phrase *verb*
To convey in language or words of a particular form ▶ couch, express, formulate, put, word. *Idiom:* put into words. *See also* **say.**

phraseology *or* **phrasing** *noun*
▶ locution, parlance, verbalism. *See* **wording.**

phylactery *noun*
▶ mascot, talisman. *See* **charm** (1).

physic *noun*
An agent used to restore health ▶ elixir, medication, remedy. *See* **cure.**

physic *verb*
To administer especially a painkilling drug to someone ▶ medicate, narcotize, tranquilize. *See* **drug** (1).

physical *adjective*
1. Composed of or relating to things that occupy space and can be perceived by the senses ▶ concrete, corporeal, material, objective, palpable, phenomenal, sensible, solid, substantial, tangible. *See also* **perceptible, real. 2.** Of or relating to the body ▶ corporal, somatic. *See* **bodily.** *See synonym note at* **bodily. 3.** Relating to the desires and appetites of the body, especially sexual desire ▶ animal, sexual. *See* **sensual** (?).

physicality *noun*
1. The quality or condition of being sensual ▶ sexuality, voluptuousness. *See* **sensuality** (1). **2.** The quality or condition of being discernible by touch ▶ corporeality, palpability, tactility. *See* **tangibility.**

physiognomy *noun*
▶ countenance, visage. *See* **face** (1).

physique *noun*
1. The physical characteristics of a person ▶ body, form, shape. *See* **constitution** (1). **2.** Solid and well-developed muscles ▶ bulk, muscle. *See* **brawn** (1).

picayune *adjective*
Of little importance ▶ inconsequential, negligible, trifling. *See* **trivial.** *See synonym note at* **trivial.**

picayune *noun*
Something or things of little importance ▶ frivolity, minutia, trivia. *See* **trifle** (1).

pick *verb*
1. To make a choice from a number of alternatives ▶ elect, go with, pick out, vote (for). *See* **choose** (1). **2.** To collect ripe crops ▶ harvest, pluck, reap. *See* **gather** (1). **3.** To remove from a fixed position ▶ pluck, rend, wrest. *See* **pull** (2).

pick at *or* **pick on** *verb*
To scold or find fault with constantly ▶ carp at, fuss at. *See* **nag** (1).

pick off *verb*
To wound or kill with a firearm ▸ gun (down), shoot. *Slang:* plug. *Idioms:* fill full of lead (*or* holes). *See also* **kill¹, murder.**

pick out *verb*
To perceive and fix the identity of, especially with difficulty ▸ ascertain, recognize. *See* **discern** (1).

pick up *verb*
1. To move something to a higher position ▸ hoist, lift, raise. *See* **elevate** (1). **2.** To collect something bit by bit ▸ garner, gather. *See* **glean** (1). **3.** *Informal* To come into possession of ▸ come by, gain, procure. *See* **get** (1). **4.** *Informal* To gain knowledge or mastery of by study ▸ acquire, get. *See* **learn** (1). **5.** To take into custody as a prisoner ▸ seize. *Informal:* nab. *Slang:* bust. *See* **arrest** (1). **6.** To begin or go on after an interruption ▸ restart, resume. *See* **continue** (1). **7.** *Informal* To become affected with a disease ▸ develop, get. *See* **contract** (2).

pick *noun*
1. The most preferable part of something ▸ cream, elite, top. *See* **best** (1). **2.** One that is selected ▸ chosen, select. *See* **elect**. **3.** The act, power, or right of choosing ▸ decision, discretion, option. *See* **choice** (1).

picket *noun*
One assigned to provide protection or keep watch over ▸ guardian, protector. *See* **guard** (1).

picket *verb*
1. To cease working in support of demands made upon an employer ▸ strike, walk out. *Idioms:* go on strike, stop work. **2.** To surround and advance upon ▸ close in, envelop, hem. *See* **enclose** (2).

pickings *noun*
▸ remainder, remains, remnant. *See* **balance** (4).

pickle *noun*
Informal A difficult, often embarrassing situation or condition ▸ corner, difficulty, fix. *See* **predicament**. *See synonym note at* **predicament**.

pickle *verb*
1. To cause something to become thoroughly wet or saturated by immersion in a liquid ▸ saturate, soak, souse. *See* **steep²**. **2.** To prepare food for storage and future use ▸ can, pot, put up. *See* **preserve** (1).

pickled *adjective*
Slang Stupefied, excited, or muddled with alcoholic liquor ▸ intoxicated, sodden, tipsy. *See* **drunk**.

pick-me-up *noun*
Informal A medicine that restores or increases vigor ▸ energizer, stimulant. *See* **tonic**.

pickpocket *noun*
▸ burglar, looter, robber. *See* **thief**.

pickup *noun*
Slang A seizing and holding by law ▸ apprehension, seizure. *Slang:* bust. *See* **arrest** (1).

picky *adjective*
Informal Very difficult to please ▸ exacting, finicky. *See* **fussy** (1).

pictographic *adjective*
▸ illustrative, photographic, pictorial. *See* **graphic** (4).

pictorial *adjective*
1. Of or relating to representation by drawings or pictures ▸ illustrative, pictographic. *See* **graphic** (4). **2.** Depicted in sharp and accurate detail ▸ explicit, realistic, vivid. *See* **graphic** (1).

picture *noun*
1. One exactly resembling another ▸ clone, spitting image, twin. *See* **double** (1). **2.** That which is or can be seen ▸ panorama, perspective, vista. *See* **view** (2).

picture *verb*
1. To form mental images of ▸ envision, fantasize, visualize. *See* **imagine** (1). **2.** To present a lifelike image of ▸ depict, portray, render. *See* **represent** (2). *See synonym note at* **represent**.

picturesque *adjective*
1. Evoking strong mental images through distinctiveness ▸ colorful, graphic, striking, vivid. **2.** Depicted in sharp and accurate detail ▸ explicit, realistic, vivid. *See* **graphic** (1).

piddle *verb*
▸ loiter, lounge, slack off. *See* **idle** (1).

piddling *adjective*
▸ inconsequential, negligible, trifling. *See* **trivial**.

piece *noun*
1. A separate unit that belongs or contributes to a whole ▸ building block, element, section. *See* **part** (1). **2.** One's duty or responsibility in a common effort ▸ function, part, role, share. **3.** A part severed from a whole ▸ portion, section. *See* **cut** (2). **4.** A small portion of food ▸ crumb, morsel. *See* **bit¹** (2). **5.** Something that is the result of creative effort ▸ creation, production, work. *See* **composition** (1). **6.** A detail of news information ▸ article, feature, story. *See* **item** (1). **7.** *Informal* An extent, measured or unmeasured, of linear space ▸ interval, length, stretch. *See* **distance** (1). **8.** A brief composition written or adapted for singing ▸ hymn, lyrics, tune. *See* **song** (1).

piecemeal *adjective*
Proceeding steadily by degrees ▸ gradational, gradual, progressive, step-by-step. *Idioms:* one foot after another, one step at a time. *See also* **consecutive, methodical, slow.**

piecemeal *adverb*
In a gradual manner ▸ by degrees, progressively. *See* **gradually**.

pie-eyed *adjective*
Slang Stupefied, excited, or muddled with alcoholic liquor ▸ intoxicated, sodden, tipsy. *See* **drunk**.

pie hole *noun*
Slang The opening in the body through which food is ingested ▸ chops. *Slang:* trap. *See* **mouth** (1).

pier *noun*
▸ pillar, post. *See* **column** (1).

pierce *verb*
1. To penetrate with a sharp edge ▸ bayonet, incise, knife, slash. *See* **cut** (1). **2.** To make a hole or other opening in ▸ perforate, puncture. *See* **breach** (1). **3.** To pass into or through by overcoming resistance ▸ break (through), puncture. *See* **penetrate** (1). **4.** To affect

deeply or completely, as with emotion ▸ crush, prostrate. *See* **overwhelm** (2).

piercing *adjective*
1. Marked by severity or intensity ▸ gnawing, shooting. *See* **sharp** (8). 2. Elevated in pitch ▸ acute, shrill. *See* **high** (3). 3. Marked by extremely high volume and intensity of sound ▸ booming, earsplitting, noisy. *See* **loud** (1).

pietism *noun*
▸ faith, piousness. *See* **devotion** (1).

pietistic *or* **pietistical** *adjective*
▸ devout, holy, religious. *See* **pious** (1).

piety *noun*
1. A state of often extreme religious ardor ▸ faith, piousness. *See* **devotion** (1). 2. A show or expression of feelings or beliefs one does not actually hold or possess ▸ phoniness, sanctimony. *See* **hypocrisy**.

piffle *noun*
▸ bunkum, drivel, garbage. *See* **nonsense** (1).

pig *noun*
A person who eats or consumes immoderate amounts of food and drink ▸ glutton, hog, overeater. *See also* **sybarite**.

pig out *verb*
Slang To swallow food or drink greedily or rapidly in large amounts ▸ gobble, ingurgitate. *See* **gulp** (1).

pigeon *noun*
Slang A person who is easily deceived or victimized ▸ pushover, tool, victim. *See* **dupe** (1).

pigeonhole *verb*
▸ categorize, class, group. *See* **classify**.

piggish *adjective*
▸ greedy, ravenous, voracious. *See* **gluttonous** (1).

pigheaded *adjective*
▸ bullheaded, dogged, obstinate. *See* **stubborn** (1). *See synonym note at* **stubborn**.

pigheadedness *noun*
▸ bullheadedness, hardheadedness, rigidity. *See* **stubbornness**.

pigment *noun*
Something that imparts color ▸ colorant, dye, paint. *See* **color** (2).

pigment *verb*
To impart color to ▸ dye, stain, tint. *See* **color** (1).

pilaster *noun*
▸ pillar, post. *See* **column** (1).

pile *noun*
1. A group of things gathered haphazardly ▸ drift, mass, mountain. *See* **heap** (1). *See synonym note at* **heap**. 2. *Informal* An indeterminately great amount or number ▸ bunch, multiplicity. *Informal:* bushel. *See* **heap** (3). *See synonym note at* **heap**. 3. *Informal* A great deal ▸ bounty, mass, profusion. *See* **abundance** (1). 4. *Informal* A large sum of money ▸ bundle, mint. *See* **fortune** (7). 5. Something built, especially for human use ▸ building, construction, edifice, erection, structure.

pile *verb*
1. To collect or pile up or onto something ▸ drift,

lump. *See* **heap** (1). 2. To fill to capacity ▸ charge, load, pack. *See* **fill** (1). 3. To move into an area or space in large numbers ▸ cram, press, squeeze. *See* **crowd** (1).

pile up *verb*
1. To bring together so as to increase in mass or number ▸ accrue, amass, cumulate, hive. *See* **accumulate**. 2. *Informal* To wreck a vehicle ▸ smash, wreck. *See* **crash** (1).

pileup *noun*
Informal A wrecking of a vehicle ▸ sideswipe, smashup, wreck. *See* **crash** (2).

pilfer *verb*
▸ purloin, snatch, thieve. *See* **steal** (1). *See synonym note at* **steal**.

pilferage *noun*
▸ stealing, theft, thievery. *See* **larceny**.

pilferer *noun*
▸ burglar, robber, stealer. *See* **thief**.

pilgrimage *noun*
▸ mission, tour, voyage. *See* **expedition** (1).

pill *noun*
1. *Slang* An unpleasant, tiresome person ▸ chump. *Slang:* dweeb, twit. *See* **drip** (2). 2. *Slang* One who spoils the enthusiasm or fun of others ▸ spoilsport. *Informal:* wet blanket. *Slang:* party pooper. *See* **killjoy**. 3. A substance that is used in the treatment of disease ▸ medication, medicine, pharmaceutical. *See* **drug** (1).

pillage *verb*
To rob of goods by force, especially in time of war ▸ loot, plunder, ransack. *See* **sack**².

pillage *noun*
Goods or property seized unlawfully ▸ booty, loot. *See* **plunder**.

pillar *noun*
▸ pilaster, post. *See* **column** (1).

pillory *verb*
▸ abase, dishonor, shame. *See* **disgrace**.

pillow talk *noun*
▸ dialogue, discourse, talk. *See* **conversation** (1).

pilose *adjective*
▸ furry, hirsute, shaggy. *See* **hairy** (1).

pilot *noun*
1. A person who flies an airplane ▸ aviator, flier. 2. Something or someone that shows the way ▸ director, escort, leader. *See* **guide** (1).

pilot *verb*
1. To run and control a motor vehicle ▸ chauffeur, motor, wheel. *See* **drive** (1). 2. To direct the course of carefully ▸ jockey, navigate. *See* **maneuver** (1). 3. To show the way to ▸ direct, escort, lead. *See* **guide** (1). *See synonym note at* **guide**.

pilot *adjective*
Serving as a tentative model for future experiment or development ▸ experimental, probationary, probative, test, trial. *See also* **introductory**.

pin *noun*
A bolt or shaft that is hammered or drilled in place, used to support or hold together ▸ bolt, spike, stud. *See* **nail**.

pin *verb*

1. To ascribe the blame for a misdeed or error ▶ attribute, blame, place. *See* **fix** (13). 2. To make secure ▶ bind, chain, moor. *See* **fasten** (1).

pinafore *noun*

▶ jumper, gown, shift. *See* **dress** (3).

pinch *verb*

1. To be severely sparing in order to economize ▶ scrape, skimp, stint. *See* **scrimp**. 2. *Slang* To take another's property without permission ▶ purloin, snatch, thieve. *See* **steal** (1). *See synonym note at* **steal**. 3. To take into custody as a prisoner ▶ seize. *Informal:* apprehend, nab. *See* **arrest** (1). 4. To subject to compression ▶ compress, constrict. *See* **squeeze** (1).

pinch *noun*

1. *Slang* A seizing and holding by law ▶ apprehension, seizure. *Slang:* bust. *See* **arrest** (1). 2. A situation requiring immediate assistance or remedial action ▶ crisis, distress, trouble. *See* **emergency**. 3. A tiny amount ▶ dash, drop, smidgen. *See* **bit¹** (1). 4. A difficult, often embarrassing situation or condition ▶ corner, difficulty, fix. *See* **predicament**.

pinchbeck *noun*

▶ imitation, simulation. *See* **copy** (2).

pinch-hit *verb*

Informal To act as a substitute ▶ cover for, fill in. *See* **substitute** (1).

pinch hitter *noun*

▶ alternate, replacement, surrogate. *See* **substitute**.

pinching *adjective*

▶ close-fisted, miserly, parsimonious, petty. *See* **stingy** (1).

pinchpenny *noun*

▶ churl, Scrooge. *Informal:* penny pincher. *See* **miser**.

pine *verb*

1. To have a strong longing for ▶ covet, want, yearn. *See* **desire** (1). 2. To become downcast from longing or grief ▶ ebb, pine away, wither. *See* **languish** (1).

pinheaded *adjective*

Slang Lacking in or showing a lack of intelligence ▶ dumb, idiotic, mindless, obtuse. *See* **stupid** (1).

pinheadedness *noun*

Slang The state of being stupid ▶ idiocy, mindlessness, obtuseness. *See* **stupidity**.

pink-slip *verb*

Informal To end the employment or service of ▶ cashier, drop. *See* **dismiss** (1).

pinnacle *noun*

▶ apex, culmination, peak. *See* **climax** (1). *See synonym note at* **climax**.

pinpoint *verb*

1. To look for and discover ▶ find, locate, spot. *Informal:* scare up. *See also* **trace, uncover**. 2. To establish the identity of ▶ identify, know, recognize. *See* **place** (1). 3. To make known or identify, as by signs ▶ indicate, mark, specify. *See* **designate** (1).

pinpoint *noun*

A very small mark ▶ dot, speck. *See* **point** (2).

pintsize *or* **pintsized** *adjective*

Informal Extremely small ▶ dwarf, miniature, minuscule. *See* **tiny**.

pioneer *noun*

1. A person instrumental in the growth of something, especially in its early stages ▶ contributor, creator, producer. *See* **developer**. 2. One that foreshadows or prepares for something else ▶ herald, precursor. *See* **forerunner** (1). 3. One who settles in a new region ▶ colonist, homesteader. *See* **settler**.

pioneer *verb*

To bring into currency, use, fashion, or practice ▶ originate, pioneer. *See* **introduce** (1).

pioneer *adjective*

Preceding all others ▶ initial, premier. *See* **first** (1).

pious *adjective*

1. Deeply concerned with God and the beliefs and practice of religion ▶ devoted, devotional, devout, godly, holy, pietistic, pietistical, prayerful, religious, saintlike, saintly, zealous. *See also* **faithful, righteous, spiritual**. 2. In the service or worship of God or a god ▶ devoted, religious, sacred. *See* **divine** (2). 3. Feeling or showing reverence ▶ reverential, venerational, worshipful. *See* **reverent**. 4. Of or practicing hypocrisy ▶ pharisaic, phony, sanctimonious. *See* **hypocritical**.

piousness *noun*

▶ adoration, piety, reverence. *See* **devotion** (1).

pip *noun*

A fertilized plant ovule capable of germinating ▶ grain, kernel, pit, seed.

pipe dream *noun*

▶ chimera, fantasy, illusion. *See* **dream** (2).

piping *adjective*

▶ piercing, shrill. *See* **high** (3).

pip-squeak *noun*

1. *Informal* A totally insignificant person ▶ nobody, nothing, small fry. *See* **nonentity**. 2. *Informal* A small or young person ▶ pup, runt, scrub. *See* **squirt** (2).

piquant *adjective*

▶ peppery, sharp, zesty. *See* **spicy** (1).

pique *noun*

Extreme displeasure caused by an insult ▶ resentment, ruffled feathers, umbrage. *See* **offense** (1).

pique *verb*

1. To cause resentment or hurt by callous, rude behavior ▶ offend, outrage. *See* **insult** (1). 2. To stir to action or feeling ▶ excite, prod, trigger. *See* **provoke** (1). 3. To cause anger, resentment, or hurt feelings ▶ annoy, injure, upset. *See* **offend** (1). 4. To be proud of oneself, as for an accomplishment or achievement ▶ gloat, preen. *See* **pride**.

pirate *noun*

One who reproduces another's work without permission ▶ cribber, plagiarist, plagiarizer. *See also* **forger**.

pirate *verb*

To reproduce another's work without permission ▶ appropriate, borrow, crib. *See* **plagiarize**.

pit¹ *noun*

1. An area sunk below its surroundings ▶ basin, dip.

See **depression** (1). **2.** A disfiguring abnormality of shape or form ▸ contortion, malformation. *See* **deformity. 3.** A place known for its great filth or corruption ▸ cesspit, cesspool, cloaca, den, gutter, hellhole, septic tank, sewer, sink, sump. *Slang:* armpit. **4.** A device or stratagem for catching or tricking a person or animal ▸ booby trap, noose. *See* **trap** (1).

pit *verb*
1. To place in opposition or be in opposition to ▸ match, play off. *See* **oppose** (1). **2.** To alter and spoil the natural form or appearance of ▸ disfigure, misshape, twist. *See* **deform.**

pit² *noun*
A fertilized plant ovule capable of germinating ▸ grain, kernel, pip, seed.

pitch *verb*
1. To move vigorously from side to side or up and down ▸ heave, rock, roll, toss. **2.** To send through the air with a motion of the hand or arm ▸ heave, hurl, pelt. *See* **throw** (1). *See synonym note at* **throw. 3.** To raise upright ▸ put up, raise. *See* **erect** (1). **4.** To move downward in response to gravity ▸ drop, plunge, tumble. *See* **fall** (1). **5.** To lean suddenly, unsteadily, and erratically from the vertical axis ▸ roll, seesaw, yaw. *See* **lurch** (1). **6.** To slope downward ▸ decline, dip. *See* **drop** (5). **7.** *Informal* To attempt to sell or popularize by advertising or publicity ▸ advertise, publicize, talk up. *See* **promote** (3).

pitch into *verb*
Informal To set upon with violent force ▸ assail, assault, storm, strike. *See* **attack** (1).

pitch *noun*
1. An act of throwing ▸ fling, hurl, toss. *See* **throw. 2.** A sudden downward motion toward the ground ▸ dive, nosedive, plunge. *See* **fall** (1). **3.** A downward slope or distance ▸ declivity, descent. *See* **drop** (5). **4.** Concentrated power or force, as of effort, opinion, or emotion ▸ ferocity, fury, vehemence. *See* **intensity. 5.** *Informal* Information that is disseminated through various media to attract public notice ▸ advertisement, ballyhoo. *Slang:* hype. *See* **publicity** (1). **6.** The highest point or state ▸ apex, height, peak. *See* **climax** (1). **7.** An expressive vocal quality ▸ edge, intonation, lilt. *See* **tone** (2).

pitch-black *or* **pitch-dark** *or* **pitchy** *adjective*
▸ ebony, inky, jet. *See* **black** (1).

piteous *adjective*
▸ forlorn, lamentable, poor. *See* **pitiful** (1). *See synonym note at* **pitiful.**

pitfall *noun*
1. A device or stratagem for catching or tricking a person or animal ▸ booby trap, noose, pit. *See* **trap** (1). **2.** Exposure to harm, loss, or injury ▸ hazard, menace, peril. *See* **danger.**

pith *noun*
▸ essence, marrow, quintessence. *See* **heart** (1). *See synonym note at* **heart.**

pithy *adjective*
1. Precisely meaningful and tersely cogent ▸ aphoris-

tic, compact, epigrammatic, epigrammatical, gnomic, marrowy, pointed, proverbial, pungent, sententious, succinct. *Informal:* brass-tacks. *Idioms:* down to brass tacks (*or* the nitty-gritty), short and sweet, to the point. *See also* **brief, critical. 2.** Conveying hidden or unexpressed meaning ▸ consequential, significant. *See* **pregnant** (2).

pitiable *adjective*
▸ forlorn, lamentable, poor. *See* **pitiful** (1). *See synonym note at* **pitiful.**

pitiful *adjective*
1. Arousing or deserving pity ▸ forlorn, lamentable, pathetic, piteous, pitiable, poor, rueful, ruthful, sorry. *See also* **affecting, deplorable. 2.** Very bad ▸ appalling, awful, dreadful, horrendous, wretched. *See* **terrible** (1).

✦ CORE SYNONYMS: *pitiful, pitiable, pathetic, piteous, lamentable.* These adjectives describe what inspires or deserves pity. *Pitiful* and *pitiable* apply to what is touchingly sad: *"She told a most pitiful story"* (Samuel Butler). *"The emperor had been in a state of pitiable vacillation"* (William Hickling Prescott). Something *pathetic* elicits sympathetic sadness and compassion: *"a most earnest . . . entreaty, addressed to you in the most pathetic tones of the voice so dear to you"* (Charles Dickens). Sometimes these three terms connote contemptuous pity, as for what is hopelessly inept or inadequate: *"To be guided by second-hand conjecture is pitiful"* (Jane Austen). *"That cold accretion called the world, which, so terrible in the mass, is so unformidable, even pitiable, in its units"* (Thomas Hardy). *The state government took over schools with pathetic academic standards.* Piteous applies to what cries out for pity: *"They . . . made piteous lamentation to us to save them"* (Daniel Defoe). *Lamentable* suggests the evocation of pity mixed with sorrow: *"Tell thou the lamentable tale of me,/And send the hearers weeping to their beds"* (William Shakespeare).

---

pitiless *adjective*
1. Lacking compassion or mercy ▸ heartless, insensitive, merciless. *See* **callous. 2.** Inflicting suffering or pain ▸ brutal, fierce, savage. *See* **cruel** (1).

pity *noun*
1. Sympathetic, sad concern for someone in misfortune ▸ commiseration, compassion, condolence, empathy, heart, softheartedness, sympathy. *See also* **mercy. 2.** A great disappointment or regrettable fact ▸ crime, shame. *Slang:* bummer. *Idiom:* a crying shame.

pity *verb*
To feel pity for someone ▸ ache for, bleed for, commiserate with, feel for, sympathize with. *Idioms:* feel sorry for, have pity on, take pity on. *See also* **comfort, feel.**

✦ CORE SYNONYMS: *pity, compassion, commiseration, sympathy, condolence, empathy.* These nouns signify sympathetic, sad concern aroused by the misfortune, affliction, or suffering of another. *Pity* often implies a feeling of sorrow that inclines one to help or to show mercy: *He felt pity for the outcast. Compassion* denotes deep awareness of the suffering of another and the wish to relieve it: *"Compassion is not weakness, and concern for the unfortunate is not socialism"* (Hubert H. Humphrey). *Commiseration* signifies the expression of pity or sorrow: *My advisors expressed their commiseration over the failure of the experiment. Sympathy* denotes the act of or capacity for sharing in the sorrows or troubles of another: *"They had little sympathy to spare for their unfortunate enemies"* (William Hickling Prescott). *Condolence* is a formal, conventional expression of pity, usually to relatives upon a death: *The minister extended her condolences to the bereaved family. Empathy* is an identification with and understanding of another's situation, feelings, and motives: *Having changed schools several times as a child, I feel empathy for the transfer students.*

pitying *adjective*
▸ commiserative, compassionate, empathetic, understanding. *See* **sympathetic.**

pivot *verb*
1. To turn or cause to turn in place, as on a hinge or fixed point, tracing an arclike path ▸ slue, swing, swivel, wheel. **2.** To rotate on an axis or around a center ▸ twirl, whirl, wheel. *See* **turn** (1). *See synonym note at* **turn.**

pivot *noun*
A point of origin or crucial factor ▸ core, focus, nucleus. *See* **center** (3).

pivotal *adjective*
▸ central, key. *See* **primary** (1).

pixilated *adjective*
Slang Stupefied, excited, or muddled with alcoholic liquor ▸ intoxicated, sodden, tipsy. *See* **drunk.**

placard *noun*
▸ billboard, notice. *See* **sign** (2).

placate *verb*
▸ appease, mollify, soothe. *See* **pacify.** *See synonym note at* **pacify.**

place *noun*
1. Positioning of one individual vis-à-vis others ▸ condition, echelon, footing, level, position, rank, situation, standing, station, status. *See also* **class. 2.** The function or position customarily occupied by another ▸ lieu, stead. **3.** The proper or designated location ▸ niche. **4.** The place where a person or thing is located ▸ location, point, spot. *See* **position** (1). **5.** A building or shelter where one lives ▸ domicile, habitation, residence. *See* **home** (1). **6.** A particular geographic area ▸ neighborhood, vicinity. *See* **locality** (1). **7.** A post of employment ▸ job, situation. *See* **position** (3).

place *verb*
1. To establish the identity of ▸ identify, know, pinpoint, recognize. *Slang:* finger. **Idiom:** put one's finger on. *See also* **discern. 2.** To put in a certain position or location ▸ locate, situate, stick. *See* **position. 3.** To arrange according to class ▸ categorize, class, group. *See* **classify. 4.** To calculate approximately ▸ approximate, reckon. *See* **estimate** (2). **5.** To

ascribe the blame for a misdeed or error ▸ attribute, blame, pin. *See* **fix** (13). **6.** To complete a race or competition in a specified position ▸ come in, finish, run.

placement *noun*
1. The act or condition of being arranged ▸ allotment, distribution, organization. *See* **arrangement** (1). **2.** The place where a person or thing is located ▸ location, point, spot. *See* **position** (1).

placid *adjective*
1. Not excited or agitated ▸ peaceful, serene, tranquil. *See* **calm** (1). **2.** Free from disturbance, agitation, or commotion ▸ peaceful, quiet, serene. *See* **still** (1). *See synonym note at* **still.**

placidity *or* **placidness** *noun*
1. Lack of emotional agitation ▸ peace, serenity. *See* **calm** (1). **2.** An absence of motion or disturbance ▸ calmness, lull, peacefulness. *See* **stillness** (1).

plagiarist *or* **plagiarizer** *noun*
One who reproduces another's work without permission ▸ cribber, pirate. *See also* **forger.**

plagiarize *verb*
To reproduce another's work without permission ▸ appropriate, borrow, crib, pirate, poach. *Informal:* lift. *See also* **adopt, copy, counterfeit.**

plague *noun*
1. A cause of suffering or harm ▸ bane, scourge. *See* **curse** (3). **2.** A sudden emergence or increase ▸ breakout, flare, outburst. *See* **eruption** (1). **3.** Something that annoys ▸ bother, irritant, nuisance. *See* **annoyance** (2).

plague *verb*
1. To attack or disturb persistently ▸ harry, pester, torment. *See* **harass.** *See synonym note at* **harass. 2.** To cause great pain or suffering to ▸ agonize, rack, strike. *See* **afflict.**

plaguy *adjective*
▸ bothersome, galling, irritating, unsettling. *See* **disturbing.**

plain *adjective*
1. Readily seen, perceived, or understood ▸ evident, noticeable, obvious. *See* **apparent** (1). *See synonym note at* **apparent. 2.** Easily seen through due to a lack of subtlety ▸ blatant, overt, transparent. *See* **obvious** (1). **3.** Not showy or obtrusive ▸ inobtrusive, quiet, subdued. *See* **modest** (1). *See synonym note at* **modest. 4.** Without addition, decoration, or qualification ▸ austere, bare-bones, vanilla. *See* **bare** (1). **5.** Honest and direct ▸ candid, forthright, upfront. *See* **frank. 6.** Free from hypocrisy or pretense ▸ natural, sincere, unaffected. *See* **genuine** (1). **7.** Free from extraneous elements ▸ perfect, simple, unadulterated. *See* **pure** (1). **8.** Not diluted or mixed with other substances ▸ pure, unblended, undiluted. *See* **straight** (1). **9.** Being of no special quality or type ▸ common, mediocre, standard. *See* **ordinary** (1). **10.** Displeasing to the eye ▸ homely, unattractive, unsightly. *See* **ugly** (1). **11.** Completely such, without qualification or exception ▸ all-out, pure, sheer. *See* **utter**[2].

plainclothesman *noun*
▸ detective, sleuth. *Slang:* gumshoe. *See* **detective**.

plain-Jane *adjective*
▸ austere, plain, unadorned. *See* **bare** (1).

plainness *noun*
1. The quality of being clear and easy to perceive ▸ distinctness, legibility, lucidness, perspicuity. *See* **clarity** (1). **2.** Lack of ostentation or pretension ▸ inobtrusiveness, simpleness, simplicity. *See* **modesty** (2). **3.** The quality or condition of being ugly ▸ odiousness, unsightliness. *See* **ugliness** (1).

plainspoken *adjective*
▸ candid, ingenuous, open. *See* **frank**.

plainspokenness *noun*
▸ incorruptibility, integrity. *See* **honesty** (1).

plaint *noun*
▸ blubbering, sobbing, weeping. *See* **cry** (1).

plaintiff *noun*
One that makes a formal complaint, especially in court ▸ accuser, claimant, complainant.

plaintive *adjective*
▸ doleful, melancholy, mournful. *See* **sorrowful** (1).

plait *verb*
1. To bend together or form a crease ▸ crimp, double, pleat. *See* **fold** (1). **2.** To interlace strips or strands ▸ braid, intertwine, twist. *See* **weave** (1).

plait *noun*
A line made by the doubling of one part over another ▸ crimp, pleat, wrinkle. *See* **fold** (1).

plan *noun*
1. A method used for accomplishing something ▸ procedure, technique. *See* **approach** (1). *See synonym note at* **approach**. **2.** Systematic arrangement and design ▸ order, scheme. *See* **method** (1).

plan *verb*
1. To work out and arrange the parts and details of ▸ blueprint, map out, outline. *See* **design** (2). **2.** To have in mind as a goal or purpose ▸ design, target. *See* **intend** (1). **3.** To set the time for an event or occasion ▸ schedule, set, time. **4.** To plan the details or arrangements of ▸ lay out, work out. *See* **arrange** (2). **5.** To form a strategy for ▸ contrive, devise, strategize. *See* **design** (1). **6.** To show graphically the direction or location of, as by using coordinates ▸ graph, lay out. *See* **plot** (1). **7.** To draw up a preliminary plan or version of ▸ outline, sketch. *See* **draft** (1).

planar *adjective*
▸ flush, level. *See* **even** (1).

plane *adjective*
Having no irregularities, roughness, or indentations ▸ flush, level, smooth. *See* **even** (1). *See synonym note at* **even**.

plane *verb*
To make even, smooth, or level ▸ level, smooth, straighten. *See* **even** (1).

planet *noun*
The celestial body where humans live ▸ earth, globe, orb, world.

planetary *adjective*
▸ cosmic, global, worldwide. *See* **universal** (1).

plangent *adjective*
▸ resounding, sonorous, vibrant. *See* **resonant**.

plans *noun*
Steps taken in preparation for an undertaking ▸ accommodations, arrangements, preparations, provisions.

plant *verb*
1. To put seeds or young plants in soil ▸ broadcast, pot, root, scatter, seed, set (out), sow, transplant. *See also* **grow, till**. **2.** To place or set deeply or securely ▸ entrench, ingrain, lodge. *See* **fix** (4). **3.** *Slang* To put or keep out of sight ▸ bury, conceal, secrete. *See* **hide**[1] (1).

plant *noun*
A building or complex in which an industry is located ▸ factory, mill, works.

plant life *noun*
The plants of an area or region ▸ flora, vegetation, verdure.

plaster *noun*
A final coating ▸ glaze, surface, varnish. *See* **finish** (3).

plaster *verb*
1. To spread with a greasy, sticky, or dirty substance ▸ dab, smudge. *See* **smear** (1). **2.** To apply a coating to ▸ glaze, surface, varnish. *See* **finish** (7). **3.** To apply therapeutic materials to a wound ▸ bandage, swathe. *See* **dress** (2).

plastered *adjective*
Slang Stupefied, excited, or muddled with alcoholic liquor ▸ intoxicated, sodden, tipsy. *See* **drunk**.

plastic *adjective*
1. Capable of being shaped or bent ▸ bendable, ductile, pliable. *See* **malleable** (1). *See synonym note at* **malleable**. **2.** Changing easily, as in expression ▸ changeable, fluid, mobile. *See also* **changeable, unstable**. **3.** Easily altered or influenced ▸ malleable, pliable, suggestible. *See* **flexible** (3). **4.** Capable of withstanding stress without injury ▸ elastic, resilient, supple. *See* **flexible** (1).

plasticity *noun*
▸ elasticity, malleability, pliability. *See* **flexibility** (1).

plat *noun*
▸ acreage, plot, tract. *See* **lot** (1).

plate *verb*
▸ blanket, pave. *See* **cover** (1).

plateau *noun*
A natural, flat land elevation ▸ mesa, table. *See also* **hill**.

platform *noun*
A temporary framework with a floor, used by laborers ▸ scaffold, scaffolding, stage, staging.

platitude *noun*
▸ banality, truism. *See* **cliché**. *See synonym note at* **cliché**.

platitudinal *or* **platitudinous** *adjective*
▸ clichéd, overused, stale, tired. *See* **trite**.

platoon *noun*
▸ squad, team, unit. *See* **force** (5).

plaudit *noun*
1. An expression of warm approval ▸ acclaim, acclamation, celebration, kudos. *See* **praise** (1). **2.** Approval that is expressed by clapping ▸ applause, hand, ovation.

plausibility *noun*
▸ believability, credibility, plausibleness. *See* **verisimilitude.**

plausible *or* **plausibleness** *adjective*
▸ creditable, reasonable. *See* **believable.** *See synonym note at* **believable.**

play *verb*
1. To occupy oneself with amusement or diversion ▸ disport, frolic, recreate, sport. *Informal:* horse around. *See also* **gambol, idle, joke. 2.** To make a bet ▸ bet, gamble, game, lay, wager. *Idiom:* put one's money on something. **3.** To touch or handle something out of restlessness ▸ fool, toy, trifle. *Informal:* monkey. *See* **fiddle** (1). **4.** To treat lightly or flippantly ▸ dally, flirt, toy, trifle. *See synonym note at* **flirt. 5.** To play the part of ▸ impersonate, perform, portray, represent. *See* **act** (4). **6.** To make music ▸ concertize, perform, render. **7.** To perform according to one's artistic conception ▸ depict, present, render. *See* **interpret** (2). **8.** To be performed ▸ run, show. **9.** To influence or manage shrewdly or deviously ▸ maneuver, use. *See* **manipulate** (1). **10.** To cause to undergo or bear (something unwelcome or damaging, for example) ▸ impose, wreak. *See* **inflict. 11.** To strive against others for victory ▸ contend, race, rival, vie. *See* **compete.**

play around *verb*
1. *Informal* To be sexually unfaithful to another ▸ philander. *Informal:* cheat, fool around, mess around. *Slang:* two-time. **2.** *Informal* To waste time by engaging in aimless activity ▸ dawdle (about), fiddle (around), fool. *See* **putter.**

play down *verb*
1. *Informal* To make less emphatic or obvious ▸ de-emphasize, soft-pedal, tone down. **2.** To make or become less severe or extreme ▸ soften, tame. *See* **moderate** (1).

play off *verb*
To place in opposition or be in opposition to ▸ match, pit.

play out *verb*
1. To cause a line to become longer and less taut ▸ uncoil, unreel, unroll. *See* **unwind** (1). **2.** To come to a natural or proper end ▸ close, end, finish. *See* **conclude** (1). **3.** To use all of ▸ eat up, expend, run through. *See* **exhaust** (1). **4.** To make or become no longer active or productive ▸ desiccate, give out, run out. *See* **dry** (2).

play over *verb*
To do or perform an act again ▸ duplicate, do over, redo, repeat, replay. *See also* **copy.**

play up *verb*
To accord emphasis to ▸ accentuate, highlight. *See* **emphasize.**

play *noun*
1. Actions that are taken as a joke ▸ fun, game, jest, sport. *Idioms:* fun and games, in fun. **2.** Something that amuses, entertains, or pleases ▸ diversion, fun, pleasure. *See* **amusement. 3.** The act of putting into play ▸ employment, implementation, usage. *See* **exercise** (1). **4.** Freedom from normal restraints, limitations, or regulations ▸ entitlement, latitude, leeway. *See* **license** (1). *See synonym note at* **license. 5.** The text of a play, movie, opera, or similar work ▸ dialogue, libretto, scenario. *See* **script** (2).

play-act *verb*
1. To play the part of ▸ perform, portray, represent. *See* **act** (4). **2.** To take on as a false appearance ▸ dissemble, feign, pretend. *See* **act** (2).

play-acting *noun*
▸ histrionics, melodramatics. *See* **theatrics** (2).

playbill *noun*
▸ catalog, prospectus, syllabus. *See* **program** (2).

player *noun*
1. A theatrical performer ▸ actor, actress, thespian, trouper. *See also* **fake, lead, mimic. 2.** One who plays a musical instrument ▸ bandsman, instrumentalist, musician, performer, virtuosa, virtuoso. *See also* **vocalist. 3.** One who participates ▸ actor, participator, sharer. *See* **participant. 4.** One who gambles ▸ bettor, gamester. *See* **gambler** (1).

playful *adjective*
▸ frolicsome, impish, sportive. *See* **mischievous** (1).

plaything *noun*
An object for children to play with ▸ game, toy. *See also* **amusement.**

plaza *noun*
▸ green, park, square. *See* **common.**

plea *noun*
1. An earnest or urgent request ▸ entreaty, imploration, supplication. *See* **appeal** (1). **2.** An explanation offered to justify an action or make it better understood ▸ pretext, rationale. *See* **excuse** (1). **3.** A statement that justifies or defends something, such as a past action or policy ▸ defense, vindication. *See* **apology** (1).

pleach *verb*
▸ braid, intertwine, twist. *See* **weave** (1).

plead *verb*
1. To make an earnest or urgent request ▸ beseech, entreat, implore. *See* **appeal** (1). **2.** To put forth reasons for or against something, often excitedly ▸ debate, dispute. *See* **argue** (2).

pleasant *adjective*
1. Giving or affording pleasure, enjoyment, or entertainment ▸ agreeable, amusing, congenial, diverting, enjoyable, entertaining, favorable, fun, good, grateful, gratifying, lovely, nice, pleasing, pleasurable, satisfying, welcome. *Idiom:* not half bad. *See also* **attractive, delightful, invigorating. 2.** Pleasant and friendly in disposition ▸ cordial, friendly, genial, likeable. *See* **amiable.**

pleasantness *noun*
▸ congeniality, friendliness. *See* **amiability**.

pleasantry *noun*
▸ civility, graciousness, politeness. *See* **amenities** (2).

please *verb*
1. To give great or keen pleasure to ▸ enchant, overjoy, pleasure. *See* **delight** (1). *See synonym note at* **delight**. 2. To meet a need or requirement ▸ do, suit. *See* **satisfy** (1). 3. To have an inclination to ▸ want, wish. *See* **choose** (2).

pleased *adjective*
▸ agreeable, ready. *See* **willing** (1).

pleasing *adjective*
1. Giving or affording pleasure or enjoyment ▸ agreeable, enjoyable, satisfying. *See* **pleasant** (1). 2. Providing joy and pleasure ▸ festive, glad, joyful. *See* **merry** (1). 3. Giving great pleasure or delight ▸ delectable, enchanting, heavenly. *See* **delightful**.

pleasurable *adjective*
1. Giving or affording pleasure or enjoyment ▸ congenial, favorable, gratifying. *See* **pleasant** (1). 2. Giving great pleasure or delight ▸ delectable, enchanting, heavenly. *See* **delightful**.

pleasure *noun*
1. A feeling of gratification aroused by something good or desired ▸ bliss, enjoyment, joy. *See* **delight** (1). 2. A desire for a particular thing or activity ▸ mind, soft spot, will. *See* **liking** (1). 3. Something that amuses, entertains, or pleases ▸ diversion, entertainment, fun. *See* **amusement**. 4. Unrestricted freedom to choose ▸ convenience, discretion, leisure, will.

pleasure *verb*
1. To feel or take joy or pleasure ▸ delight, exult, rejoice. *See also* **enjoy**, **luxuriate**. 2. To give great or keen pleasure to ▸ amuse, gladden, overjoy. *See* **delight** (1).

pleat *noun*
A line made by the doubling of one part over another ▸ crimp, wrinkle. *See* **fold** (1).

pleat *verb*
To bend together or form a crease ▸ crimp, double. *See* **fold** (1).

plebeian *adjective*
1. Lacking high station or birth ▸ common, humble, unwashed. *See* **lowly** (1). 2. Lacking in delicacy or refinement ▸ indelicate, unbecoming, unrefined. *See* **coarse** (1).

plebeians *or* **plebs** *noun*
▸ masses, proletariat, public. *See* **commonalty**.

pledge *noun*
1. A declaration that one will or will not do a certain thing ▸ covenant, oath, vow. *See* **promise** (1). 2. Something given to guarantee the repayment of a loan or the fulfillment of an obligation ▸ security, token, warrant. *See* **pawn**[1]. 3. The act of drinking to someone ▸ health, toast. 4. Something given to a charity or cause ▸ contribution, offering. *See* **donation**.

pledge *verb*
1. To guarantee by a solemn promise ▸ betroth,

covenant, engage, plight, promise, swear, troth, vow. *Idioms:* cross one's heart and hope to die, give one's word of honor. *See also* **confirm**, **contract**, **guarantee**. 2. To assume an obligation ▸ commit, contract, engage, promise, undertake. 3. To give over by or as if by vow to a higher purpose ▸ dedicate, sacrifice. *See* **devote** (1). *See synonym note at* **devote**. 4. To be morally bound to do ▸ bind, obligate. *See* **commit** (2). 5. To give or deposit as a pawn ▸ collateralize, deposit. *See* **pawn**[1]. 6. To salute by raising and drinking from a glass ▸ honor, toast. *See* **drink** (4). 7. To present as a gift to a charity or cause ▸ bequeath, give away. *See* **donate** (1).

✦ CORE SYNONYMS: *pledge, promise, swear, vow.* These verbs mean to guarantee solemnly that one will follow a particular course of action: *pledged to uphold the law; promises to write soon; swore to get revenge; vowed to fight to the finish.*

---

plenitude *or* **plenteousness** *noun*
▸ bounteousness, plenitude. *See* **plenty** (1).

plenitudinous *or* **plenteous** *or* **plentiful** *adjective*
Characterized by abundance; as much as one needs or desires ▸ abundant, bounteous. *See* **generous** (2). *See synonym note at* **generous**.

plenty *noun*
1. Prosperity and a sufficiency of life's necessities ▸ abundance, ampleness, bounteousness, bountifulness, copiousness, cornucopia, horn of plenty, muchness, plenitude, plenteousness, plentifulness. 2. A great deal ▸ mass, profusion, wealth. *See* **abundance** (1).

pleonasm *noun*
▸ circumlocution, redundancy, verboseness. *See* **wordiness**.

pleonastic *adjective*
▸ long-winded, periphrastic, verbose. *See* **wordy** (1).

plethora *noun*
1. A condition of going or being beyond what is needed, desired, or appropriate ▸ exorbitance, extravagance, surfeit. *See* **excess** (1). 2. A great deal ▸ mass, profusion, wealth. *See* **abundance** (1).

pliability *or* **pliableness** *noun*
▸ bendability, elasticity, malleability, pliancy. *See* **flexibility** (1).

pliable *adjective*
1. Capable of being shaped or bent ▸ bendable, ductile, plastic. *See* **malleable** (1). *See synonym note at* **malleable**. 2. Capable of adapting or being adapted ▸ elastic, flexible, malleable. *See* **adaptable**. 3. Easily altered or influenced ▸ malleable, pliant, suggestible. *See* **flexible** (3).

pliancy *or* **pliantness** *noun*
▸ elasticity, malleability, pliability. *See* **flexibility** (1).

pliant *adjective*
1. Capable of being shaped or bent ▸ bendable, ductile, plastic. *See* **malleable** (1). *See synonym note at* **malleable**. 2. Capable of adapting or being adapted ▸ elastic, flexible, malleable, pliable. *See* **adaptable**.

3. Easily altered or influenced ▸ malleable, pliable, suggestible. *See* **flexible** (3). **4.** Willing to carry out the wishes of others ▸ complaisant, compliant, submissive. *See* **obedient.**

plica *or* **plication** *noun*
▸ crimp, pleat, wrinkle. *See* **fold** (1).

plight¹ *noun*
1. A difficult, often embarrassing situation or condition ▸ corner, difficulty, fix. *See* **predicament.** *See synonym note at* **predicament. 2.** Something that obstructs progress and requires great effort to overcome ▸ complication, hardship, rigor. *See* **difficulty** (1).

plight² *verb*
To guarantee by a solemn promise ▸ promise, vow. *See* **pledge** (1).

plight *noun*
A declaration that one will or will not do a certain thing ▸ covenant, pledge, vow. *See* **promise** (1).

plighted *adjective*
▸ betrothed, promised. *See* **engaged** (2).

plod *verb*
1. To walk in a laborious way ▸ slog, slop, toil. *See* **trudge. 2.** To do tedious, difficult or menial work ▸ drudge, slave. *See* **grind** (4).

plodder *noun*
▸ drone, grind, grub. *See* **drudge** (2).

plodding *adjective*
1. Lacking fluency or grace ▸ elephantine, labored, leaden. *See* **ponderous** (1). **2.** Lacking liveliness, charm, or surprise ▸ aseptic, colorless, pedestrian. *See* **dull** (1). **3.** Proceeding at a rate less than usual or desired ▸ dilatory, sluggish. *See* **slow** (1).

plop *verb*
To drop or sink heavily and noisily ▸ flop, plump, plunk. *See also* **fall.**

plot *noun*
1. The series of events and relationships forming the basis of a composition ▸ action, movement, scenario, story, story line. **2.** A secret plan to achieve an evil or illegal end ▸ cabal, collusion, connivance, conspiracy, designs, intrigue, machination, scheme. *See also* **trick. 3.** A piece of land ▸ acreage, patch, tract. *See* **lot** (1).

plot *verb*
1. To show graphically the direction or location of, as by using coordinates ▸ chart, graph, lay out, map (out), plan. **2.** To work out a secret plan to achieve an evil or illegal end ▸ cabal, collude, connive, conspire, hatch, intrigue, machinate, scheme. *See also* **design. 3.** To draw up a preliminary plan or version of ▸ outline, sketch. *See* **draft** (1).

plow *verb*
▸ cultivate, turn (over), work. *See* **till.**

ploy *noun*
▸ deception, maneuver, stratagem. *See* **trick** (1).

pluck *or* **pluckiness** *verb*
1. To remove from a fixed position ▸ pick, rend, wrest. *See* **pull** (2). **2.** To collect ripe crops ▸ harvest, pick, reap. *See* **gather** (1).

pluck *noun*
The quality of mind enabling one to face danger or hardship resolutely ▸ bravery, fortitude, gallantry, valor. *See* **courage.**

plucky *adjective*
▸ courageous, fearless, heroic. *See* **brave.** *See synonym note at* **brave.**

plug *noun*
1. Something used to fill a hole, space, or container ▸ bung, choke, cork, filling, peg, spigot, spile, stop, stopper, stopple, tap, wad. *See also* **cover. 2.** A socket connected to a power supply ▸ plug, socket. *See* **outlet** (1). **3.** Information disseminated through various media to attract public notice ▸ advertisement, ballyhoo. *Slang:* hype. *See* **publicity** (1). **4.** *Informal* An indication of commendation or approval ▸ recommendation, support. *See* **endorsement** (1).

plug *verb*
1. To plug up or block something, such as a hole or conduit ▸ clog, cork. *See* **fill** (2). **2.** *Slang* To wound or kill with a firearm ▸ gun (down), pick off, shoot. *Idioms:* fill full of lead (*or* holes). *See also* **kill¹, murder. 3.** *Informal* To attempt to sell or popularize by advertising or publicity ▸ advertise, publicize, talk up. *See* **promote** (3).

plug-ugly *noun*
Slang A person who treats others violently or roughly, especially for hire ▸ hoodlum, ruffian, tough. *Informal:* bruiser. *See* **thug.**

plum *noun*
1. Something given in return for a service or accomplishment ▸ award, bonus, premium. *See* **reward** (1). **2.** A person or thing worth catching ▸ prize. *Informal:* catch. *Slang:* brass ring. **3.** Someone or something considered exceptionally precious ▸ find, pearl, prize. *See* **treasure** (1).

plumb *adjective*
At right angles to the horizon or to level ground ▸ on end, upright. *See* **vertical.** *See synonym note at* **vertical.**

plumb *adverb*
With precision or absolute conformity ▸ smack, squarely, straight. *Slang:* smack-dab. *See* **directly** (3).

plumb *verb*
To go into or through for the purpose of making discoveries or acquiring information ▸ inquire, investigate, probe. *See* **explore.**

plume *verb*
▸ congratulate, gloat, preen. *See* **pride.**

plummet *verb*
1. To become lower in value or price ▸ dive, drop, tumble. *See* **fall** (7). **2.** To move downward in response to gravity ▸ descend, drop. *See* **fall** (1).

plump¹ *or* **plumpish** *adjective*
Having too much flesh ▸ chubby, pudgy, rotund. *See* **fat** (1). *See synonym note at* **fat.**

plump² *verb*
To drop or sink heavily and noisily ▸ flop, plop, plunk. *See also* **fall.**

plump for *verb*
To aid the cause of by approving or favoring ▶ back, endorse, stand by. *See* **support** (1).

plunder *noun*
Goods or property seized unlawfully ▶ booty, graft, loot, pillage, prize, spoils. *Slang:* boodle, swag.

plunder *verb*
To rob of goods by force, especially in time of war ▶ loot, pillage, ransack. *See* **sack²**.

plunge *verb*
1. To penetrate into a substance or place with force ▶ dig, dive, drive, lunge, pass, ram, run, sink, stab, stick, strike, thrust. *See also* **cut. 2.** To move downward in response to gravity ▶ drop, spill, topple. *See* **fall** (1). **3.** To become lower in value or price ▶ dive, drop, plummet. *See* **fall** (7).

plunge into *verb*
To start work on vigorously ▶ go at, tackle. *See* **attack** (2).

plunge *noun*
1. A sudden downward motion toward the ground ▶ dive, nosedive, tumble. *See* **fall** (1). **2.** A sudden drop to a lower condition or status ▶ dip, slide, tumble. *See* **descent** (4). **3.** A usually swift downward trend, as in prices ▶ decline, dip, downtrend. *See* **fall** (3). **4.** The act of swimming ▶ dip, duck, dunk, swim. **5.** An undertaking depending on chance ▶ risk, speculation, wager. *See* **gamble** (1).

plunging *adjective*
1. Cut to reveal the wearer's neck, chest, and back ▶ décolleté, low-cut, low-neck. *See* **low** (4). **2.** Moving or sloping down ▶ downward, falling, sinking. *See* **descending.**

plunk *verb*
1. To drop or sink heavily and noisily ▶ flop, plop, plump. *See also* **fall. 2.** To make a dull sound by or as if by striking a surface with a heavy object ▶ clunk, whomp. *See* **thud.**

plush *or* **plushy** *adjective*
▶ lush, luxuriant, opulent. *See* **luxurious.**

ply¹ *verb*
To bend together or form a crease ▶ crimp, double, pleat. *See* **fold** (1).

ply² *verb*
1. To use with or as if with the hands ▶ handle, manipulate, wield. *See synonym note at* **handle. 2.** To bring to bear steadily or forcefully, as influence ▶ exercise, exert, wield. *Idiom:* throw one's weight around.

pneuma *noun*
▶ anima, soul, vitality. *See* **spirit** (2).

pneumatic *adjective*
Of or relating to air ▶ aerial, airy, atmospheric.

poach¹ *verb*
To prepare food for eating by the use of heat ▶ boil, coddle, simmer. *See* **cook** (1).

poach² *noun*
To reproduce another's work without permission ▶ appropriate, crib, pirate. *See* **plagiarize.**

pock *verb*
To alter and spoil the natural form or appearance of ▶ disfigure, misshape, twist. *See* **deform.**

pock *noun*
1. A disfiguring abnormality of shape or form ▶ contortion, disfigurement, malformation. *See* **deformity. 2.** A ridge or bump raised on the flesh, as by a lash or blow ▶ blister, boil, wart. *See* **welt** (1).

pocket *noun*
▶ hollow, vacuity. *See* **hole** (1).

pocketbook *noun*
▶ bag, clutch, handbag. *See* **purse.**

pocket money *noun*
▶ small change. *Slang:* two bits. *See* **peanuts.**

podium *noun*
▶ dais, pulpit, proscenium. *See* **stage** (1).

poem *noun*
1. A poetic work or poetic works ▶ poesy, poetry, rhyme, song, verse. **2.** A creation or experience having beauty suggestive of poetry ▶ lyricism, poetry.

poesy *noun*
▶ poetry, verse. *See* **poem** (1).

poet *noun*
A writer of poetry ▶ bard, jongleur, minstrel, muse, poetess, rhymer, rhymester, troubadour, versifier.

poetess *noun*
A woman who writes poetry ▶ muse, troubadour. *See* **poet.**

poetic *or* **poetical** *adjective*
Relating to the characteristics of poetry ▶ lyric, lyrical, poetical. *See also* **melodious, rhythmical.**

poetry *noun*
1. A poetic work or poetic works ▶ poesy, verse. *See* **poem** (1). **2.** A creation or experience having beauty suggestive of poetry ▶ lyricism, poem.

poignant *adjective*
▶ impressive, moving, touching. *See* **affecting.** *See synonym note at* **affecting.**

point *noun*
1. A sharp or tapered end ▶ acicula, acumination, apex, cusp, mucro, mucronation, neb, nib, tip. *See also* **spike. 2.** A very small mark ▶ dash, dot, fleck, pinpoint, speck, speckle, spot. *See also* **impression. 3.** The place where a person or thing is located ▶ location, place, spot. *See* **position** (1). **4.** One of the units in a course, as on an ascending or descending scale ▶ interval, level, step. *See* **degree** (1). **5.** What one intends to do or achieve ▶ end, goal, objective. *See* **intention. 6.** What a speech, piece of writing, or artistic work is about ▶ text, theme. *See* **subject** (1). **7.** Something that is conveyed or signified ▶ import, sense, significance. *See* **meaning** (1). **8.** The general point at which an event occurs ▶ instant, moment. *See* **occasion** (1). **9.** A fact or circumstance that gives logical support to an assertion, claim, or proposal ▶ argument, case. *See* **reason** (1). **10.** An individually considered portion of a whole ▶ detail, item. *See* **element** (3). **11.** The quality of being suitable or adaptable to an end ▶ benefit, profit, utility. *See* **use** (2).

point *verb*
To direct something, often toward a target ▸ level, set, train. *See* **aim** (1). *See synonym note at* **aim.**

point out *verb*
1. To make known or identify, as by signs ▸ indicate, mark, specify. *See* **designate** (1). **2.** To make reference to something ▸ allude (to), mention, note. *See* **refer** (1).

point to *verb*
1. To give grounds for believing in the existence or presence of ▸ attest, witness. *See* **indicate** (1). **2.** To involve by logical necessity ▸ involve, indicate, lead to. *See* **imply** (1). **3.** To refer to by name ▸ mention, specify. *See* **name** (2).

point up *verb*
To accord emphasis to ▸ accentuate, highlight. *See* **emphasize.**

point-blank *adverb*
▸ directly, positively. *Informal:* flat out. *See* **flatly.**

pointed *adjective*
1. Having an end that tapers to a point ▸ acicular, aciculate, aciculated, acuminate, acute, barbed, cultrate, cuspate, cuspated, cuspidate, cuspidated, fine, keen, mucronate, pointy, pronged, spiked, spined, sharp, tined. *See also* **sharp, thorny. 2.** Precisely meaningful and tersely cogent ▸ compact, epigrammatic. *See* **pithy** (1). **3.** Readily attracting notice ▸ conspicuous, outstanding, prominent. *See* **noticeable** (1).

pointer *noun*
1. An item of advance or inside information given as a guide to action ▸ lead, scent, steer. *See* **tip³** (1). **2.** An opinion as to a decision or course of action ▸ counsel, recommendation. *See* **advice** (1).

pointless *adjective*
1. Without aim, purpose, or intent ▸ desultory, purposeless, rambling. *See* **aimless. 2.** Lacking rational direction or purpose ▸ brainless, senseless. *See* **mindless** (1). **3.** Having no useful result ▸ fruitless, unsuccessful, useless, vain. *See* **futile.**

pointlessness *noun*
▸ barrenness, fruitlessness, unprofitableness. *See* **futility.**

point of view *noun*
▸ aspect, standpoint, vantage. *See* **viewpoint.**

pointy *adjective*
▸ acute, cuspate, sharp. *See* **pointed** (1).

poise *verb*
1. To rest on a narrow or insecure surface ▸ perch, roost. *See* **balance** (3). **2.** To remain stationary over a place or object ▸ hang, hover. **3.** To put in balance ▸ equalize, stabilize. *See* **balance** (1).

poise *noun*
1. A stable emotional state ▸ aplomb, composure, steadiness. *See* **balance** (2). **2.** A stable state of opposing forces ▸ counterpoise, equilibrium, stasis. *See* **balance** (1). **3.** Freedom from constraint, formality, embarrassment, or awkwardness ▸ informality, naturalness. *See* **ease** (1). **4.** Behavior that reveals one's

personality or state of mind ▸ demeanor, demeanor, mien. *See* **bearing** (1).

poised *adjective*
1. Not excited or agitated ▸ composed, serene, tranquil. *See* **calm** (1). **2.** Having a firm belief in one's own powers ▸ secure, self-confident, self-possessed. *See* **confident** (1).

poison *noun*
1. Anything that is injurious, destructive, or fatal ▸ bane, canker, contagion, toxicant, toxin, venom, virus. **2.** One that contaminates ▸ impurity, infection, pollutant. *See* **contaminant.**

poison *verb*
1. To harm with poison ▸ canker, envenom, infect, intoxicate. *See also* **hurt. 2.** To make impure or unclean by contact or mixture ▸ debase, foul, pollute. *See* **contaminate** (1). **3.** To ruin morally ▸ debase, demoralize, deprave, warp. *See* **corrupt** (1).

poison *adjective*
Capable of injuring or killing by poison ▸ noxious, toxic, venomous. *See* **poisonous** (1).

poisonous *adjective*
1. Capable of injuring or killing by poison ▸ malignant, mephitic, mephitical, miasmic, noxious, pernicious, pestiferous, pestilent, pestilential, poison, toxic, toxicant, venomous, virulent. *See also* **deadly, harmful. 2.** Characterized by intense ill will or spite ▸ evil, wicked. *See* **malevolent** (1). **3.** Morally detrimental ▸ corruptive, demoralizing, perverting. *See* **unwholesome** (2).

✚ **CORE SYNONYMS:** *poisonous, mephitic, pestilent, pestilential, toxic, venomous, virulent.* These adjectives mean having the destructive or fatal effect of a poison: *a poisonous snake; a mephitic vapor; a pestilent agitator; pestilential jungle mists; toxic fumes; venomous jealousy; a virulent form of cancer.*

---

poisonousness *noun*
▸ maliciousness, spitefulness. *See* **malevolence.**

poke¹ *verb*
1. To apply pressure on, against, or with ▸ press, nudge, shove. *See* **push** (1). **2.** To pass into or through by overcoming resistance ▸ break (through), puncture. *See* **penetrate** (1). **3.** To look into or inquire about curiously, inquisitively, or in a meddlesome fashion ▸ pry, snoop. *Informal:* nose (around), sniff about (*or* around). *Idiom:* stick one's nose into. *See also* **meddle. 4.** To reach about or search blindly or uncertainly ▸ fumble, grabble. *See* **grope. 5.** To go or move slowly so that progress is hindered ▸ dawdle, dilly-dally, drag. *See* **delay** (2). **6.** To advance slowly ▸ crawl, creep, drag, inch. *Idiom:* go at a snail's pace. *See also* **trudge.**

poke *noun*
1. An act of thrusting into or against, as to attract attention ▸ jab, poke, prod. *See* **dig** (1). **2.** One that lags ▸ lag, procrastinator, straggler. *See* **laggard.**

poke² *noun*
Chiefly Regional A flexible container that is used for

carrying items ▸ pouch, sack, tote. *See* **bag** (1).

pokerfaced *adjective*
▸ blank, deadpan, pokerfaced. *See* **expressionless**.

pokey *noun*
Slang A place for the confinement of persons in lawful detention ▸ brig, penitentiary, prison. *See* **jail**.

poky *adjective*
▸ laggard, sluggish, tardy. *See* **slow** (1).

polar *adjective*
1. Marked by a low temperature ▸ chill, frigid, icy. *See* **cold** (1). **2.** Diametrically opposed ▸ antithetical, contradictory, diametric. *See* **opposite** (1).

polarity *noun*
▸ contradiction, contrariness. *See* **opposition** (1).

pole *noun*
▸ cane, staff, stave. *See* **stick** (2).

polemic *noun*
A discussion, often heated, in which a difference of opinion is expressed ▸ contention, fight, quarrel. *See* **argument** (1).

polemic *or* **polemical** *adjective*
Given to arguing ▸ contentious, litigious, quarrelsome. *See* **argumentative**.

police *verb*
1. To maintain or keep in order with or as if with police ▸ monitor, patrol, regulate, secure. *Idioms:* keep the peace, keep watch, pound a beat. *See also* **defend**. **2.** To make or keep an area clean and orderly ▸ neaten (up), spruce (up), straighten (up). *See* **tidy** (1).

policeman *or* **policewoman** *noun*
▸ officer, trooper. *Informal:* cop. *See* **police officer**.

police officer *noun*
A member of a law-enforcement agency ▸ bluecoat, constable, finest, marshal, officer, patrolman, patrolwoman, peace officer, policeman, policewoman, sheriff, trooper. *Informal:* cop, law. *Slang:* bull, copper, flatfoot, fuzz, gendarme, heat, man, narc. *See also* **detective**.

policy *noun*
▸ dogma, teaching. *See* **doctrine**.

polish *verb*
1. To apply a coating to ▸ glaze, stain, varnish. *See* **finish** (7). **2.** To give a bright sheen or luster to ▸ burnish, furbish, glaze. *See* **gloss**[1] (1). **3.** To bring to perfection or completion ▸ complement, refine, smooth. *See* **perfect**. **4.** To improve by making minor changes or additions ▸ remodel, retouch, touch up. *See also* **fix, renew**.

polish off *verb*
1. *Informal* To use all of ▸ eat up, expend, run through. *See* **exhaust** (1). **2.** *Informal* To engulf completely ▸ devour, ravage, waste. *See* **consume** (1). **3.** *Slang* To take food into the body as nourishment ▸ consume, ingest, partake. *See* **eat** (1). *See synonym note at* **eat**.

polish *noun*
1. A final coating ▸ glaze, stain, varnish. *See* **finish** (3). **2.** A surface shininess ▸ luster, sheen, shine. *See* **gloss**[1]

(1). **3.** Refinement of manner, form, and style ▸ grace, sophistication, taste. *See* **elegance**.

polished *adjective*
1. Having a high, radiant sheen ▸ gleaming, glistening, lustrous. *See* **glossy**. **2.** Characterized by discriminating taste and broad knowledge as a result of development or education ▸ cultivated, educated. *See* **cultured**. **3.** Proficient as a result of practice and study ▸ accomplished, finished, practiced. *See also* **able, expert**.

polite *adjective*
1. Full of polite concern for the well-being of others ▸ courteous, solicitous, thoughtful. *See* **attentive** (1). **2.** Characterized by good manners ▸ genteel, mannerly. *See* **courteous** (1). *See synonym note at* **courteous**. **3.** Marked by courteous submission or respect ▸ dutiful, obeisant. *See* **deferential**.

politeness *noun*
1. Well-mannered behavior toward others ▸ civility, gentility. *See* **courtesy** (1). **2.** Social courtesies ▸ civility, pleasantry, urbanity. *See* **amenities** (2).

politesse *noun*
▸ gentility, mannerliness. *See* **courtesy** (1).

politic *adjective*
1. Showing sensitivity and skill in dealing with others ▸ diplomatic, sensitive, tactful. *See* **delicate** (2). **2.** Worth doing, especially for practical reasons ▸ recommendable, well. *See* **advisable**.

political *adjective*
▸ bureaucratic, regulatory. *See* **governmental**.

polity *noun*
▸ country, land, nation. *See* **state** (1).

poll *noun*
1. A gathering of information or opinion from a variety of sources or individuals ▸ count, poll, survey. **2.** The uppermost part of the body ▸ crown, pate. *See* **head** (1).

poll *verb*
To cast a vote ▸ ballot, vote. *Idiom:* go to the polls.

pollinate *verb*
To make fertile ▸ enrich, fecundate, fertilize. *See also* **impregnate, pregnant**.

pollutant *noun*
▸ impurity, poison, taint. *See* **contaminant**.

pollute *verb*
1. To make impure or unclean by contact or mixture ▸ debase, foul, poison. *See* **contaminate** (1). **2.** To ruin morally ▸ debase, defile, pervert. *See* **corrupt** (1). **3.** To spoil or mar the sanctity of ▸ desecrate, profane. *See* **violate** (3).

polluted *adjective*
▸ alloyed, combined, tainted. *See* **impure** (2).

pollution *noun*
1. The state of being contaminated ▸ defilement, impurity. *See* **contamination** (1). **2.** One that contaminates ▸ impurity, poison, pollutant. *See* **contaminant**.

Pollyanna *noun*
One who expects a favorable outcome or dwells on

hopeful aspects ► optimist, positivist. *See also* **dreamer.**

poltroon *noun*
► dastard, craven, sissy. *See* **coward.**

polychromatic *or* **polychrome** *adjective*
Having many different colors ► colorful, many-hued, motley. *See* **multicolored.**

polysyllabic *adjective*
Having many syllables ► sesquipedal, sesquipedalian.

polyurethane *noun*
A final coating ► lacquer, shellac, varnish. *See* **finish** (3).

polyurethane *verb*
To apply a coating to ► lacquer, shellac, varnish. *See* **finish** (7).

pomp *noun*
1. An impressive or ostentatious exhibition ► display, spectacle. *See* **array** (1). *See synonym note at* **array.**
2. Brilliant, showy splendor ► magnificence, resplendence, sparkle. *See* **glitter** (2).

pomposity *or* **pompousness** *noun*
1. Boastful self-importance or display ► loftiness, ostentation, pretentiousness. *See* **pretentiousness.**
2. The quality of being arrogant ► hauteur, loftiness, superiority. *See* **arrogance.**

pompous *adjective*
Characterized by an exaggerated show of dignity or self-importance ► grandiose, hoity-toity, pontifical, pretentious, puffed-up, puffy, self-important. *Informal:* highfalutin. *See also* **arrogant, boastful, snobbish.**

ponder *verb*
To think or think about carefully and at length ► chew on (*or* over), cogitate, consider, contemplate, deliberate, entertain, excogitate, meditate, mull, muse, reflect, revolve, ruminate, study, think, think out, think over, think through, turn over, weigh. *Idioms:* cudgel one's brains, put on one's thinking cap, rack one's brain. *See also* **brood, think.**

ponderable *adjective*
► discernible, palpable, perceivable. *See* **perceptible.**

pondering *noun*
► cogitation, deliberation, rumination. *See* **thought** (1).

ponderosity *or* **ponderousness** *noun*
► massiveness, weightiness. *See* **heaviness.**

ponderous *adjective*
1. Lacking fluency or grace ► elephantine, ham-handed, heavy, heavy-footed, heavy-handed, labored, leaden, lumbering, plodding. *See also* **awkward.**
2. Having relatively great weight ► hefty, massive. *See* **heavy** (1). *See synonym note at* **heavy.** **3.** Of large, often awkward size and weight ► cumbersome, heavy, oversized. *See* **bulky** (1).

pontifical *adjective*
► hoity-toity, pretentious. *See* **pompous.**

pontificate *verb*
To indulge in moral reflection, usually pompously ► edify, moralize, preach, sermonize. *See also* **chastise.**

pony *noun*
► crib, rendering. *See* **translation** (1).

pool *noun*
1. An association for a common cause or interest ► cartel, trust. *See* **alliance** (1). **2.** Something risked on an uncertain outcome ► ante, wager. *See* **bet** (1).

poop¹ *verb*
Slang To make weary ► exhaust, fatigue. *See* **tire** (1).

poop out *verb*
1. *Slang* To grow weary ► flag, wear out. *See* **tire** (2).
2. *Slang* To stop working properly ► break down, fail, give out. *See* **malfunction.**

poop² *noun*
Slang An unpleasant, tiresome person ► bore. *Slang:* pill, twit. *See* **drip** (2).

poop³ *verb*
To void feces ► move one's bowels, pass stool. *See* **defecate.**

poop *noun*
Slang Waste matter eliminated from the bowels ► dung, feces, waste. *See* **excrement.**

pooped *adjective*
Slang Depleted of energy ► exhausted, weary, worn-out. *See* **tired** (1).

poor *adjective*
1. Having little or no money or wealth ► bankrupt, beggarly, busted, destitute, down-and-out, impecunious, impoverished, indigent, insolvent, mendicant, necessitous, needy, penniless, penurious, poverty-stricken. *Informal:* broke, strapped. *Idioms:* flat stone broke, hard up, on one's uppers, on welfare. **2.** Of low or lower quality ► inadequate, unsatisfactory. *See* **bad** (1). **3.** Of decidedly inferior quality ► cheap, lousy, worthless. *See* **shoddy** (1). **4.** Conspicuously deficient in quantity, fullness, or extent ► puny, scant, skimpy. *See* **meager** (1). **5.** Arousing or deserving pity ► lamentable, rueful. *See* **pitiful** (1). **6.** Economically and socially below standard ► disadvantaged, impoverished. *See* **depressed** (2).

✦ CORE SYNONYMS: *poor, indigent, needy, impecunious, penniless, impoverished, poverty-stricken, destitute.* These adjectives mean having little or no money or wealth. *Poor* is the most general: *"Resolve not to be poor: whatever you have, spend less. Poverty is a great enemy to human happiness"* (Samuel Johnson). *Indigent* and *needy* refer to one in need or want: *indigent people living on the street; distributed food to needy families. Impecunious* and *penniless* mean having little or no money: *"Certainly an impecunious Subaltern was not a catch"* (Rudyard Kipling). *Poor investments left him penniless.* A person or place that is *impoverished* has been reduced to poverty: *an impoverished, third-world country. Poverty-stricken* means suffering from poverty and miserably poor: *refugees living in poverty-stricken camps. Destitute* means lacking any means of subsistence: *tenants left destitute by the fire.*

---

poorly *adjective*
Chiefly Regional Suffering from an illness ► ailing, indisposed, unwell. *See* **sick** (1).

poorness *noun*
▸ destitution, impoverishment, indigence, need. *See* **poverty** (1).
pop¹ *verb*
1. To come open or fly apart suddenly and violently, as from internal pressure ▸ blow (out), burst, explode. *Slang:* bust. **2.** To make a sudden, sharp noise ▸ clap, snap. *See* **crack** (2). **3.** To discharge a gun or firearm ▸ blast (away), fire (away *or* off), pop off, shoot (away *or* off). *Idioms:* go bang-bang, open fire, take a shot (*or* potshot). **4.** To deliver a sudden, sharp blow to ▸ jab, sock, whack. *See* **hit** (1).
pop in *verb*
To go to or seek out the company of someone in order to socialize ▸ drop by, go by. *See* **visit** (1).
pop off *verb*
Informal To cease living ▸ demise, expire, perish. *See* **die** (1).
pop *noun*
A sudden sharp, explosive noise ▸ bang, clap, snap. *See* **crack** (1).
pop² *noun*
Informal A male parent ▸ begetter, patriarch, sire. *See* **father** (1).
poppycock *noun*
▸ bunkum, drivel, garbage. *See* **nonsense** (1).
populace *noun*
▸ masses, proletariat, public. *See* **commonalty.**
popular *adjective*
1. Of, representing, or carried on by people at large ▸ civic, civil, communal, democratic, general, national, public, social, societal. *See also* **common.** **2.** Widely known ▸ famed, notorious, well-known. *See* **famous. 3.** Being favorite ▸ fair-haired, favored, pet. *See* **favorite. 4.** Adequate to satisfy a need, requirement, or standard ▸ moderate, modest, reasonable. *See* **acceptable** (2). **5.** Most generally existing or encountered at a given time ▸ predominant, rampant. *See* **prevailing** (1). **6.** Covering a wide scope ▸ all-inclusive, broad, expansive. *See* **general** (2).
popularize *verb*
1. To attempt to sell or popularize by advertising or publicity ▸ advertise, ballyhoo, build up. *See* **promote** (3). **2.** To bring into currency, use, fashion, or practice ▸ originate, pioneer. *See* **introduce** (1).
popularity *noun*
▸ celebrity, notoriety, renown. *See* **fame.**
populate *verb*
To live in a place, as does a people ▸ inhabit, occupy, people. *See also* **live, settle.**
porcine *adjective*
▸ chubby, pudgy, tubby. *See* **fat** (1).
pork *noun*
The political appointments or jobs that are at the disposal of those in power ▸ patronage, spoils.
porky *adjective*
Slang Having too much flesh or a full figure ▸ chubby, pudgy, rotund. *See* **fat** (1).

pornography *noun*
▸ dirt, sleaze, smut. *See* **obscenity** (2).
port *noun*
1. A protected area of water where ships can anchor ▸ anchorage, haven. *See* **harbor** (1). **2.** Something that physically protects, especially from danger ▸ harbor, haven, refuge. *See* **cover** (1).
portable *adjective*
▸ moving, transportable. *See* **mobile** (1).
portend *verb*
1. To give an indication of something in advance ▸ adumbrate, prefigure, presage. *See* **foreshadow. 2.** To tell about or make known in advance, especially by means of special knowledge ▸ forecast, prognosticate. *See* **predict. 3.** To give warning signs of ▸ forebode, forewarn. *See* **threaten** (1).
portent *noun*
▸ harbinger, prognostication, sign. *See* **omen.**
portentous *adjective*
▸ dire, ominous, unlucky. *See* **fateful** (1).
portion *noun*
1. A separate unit that belongs or contributes to a whole ▸ building block, piece, section. *See* **part** (1). **2.** An indefinite amount or extent ▸ measure, number. *See* **quantity** (2). **3.** A part severed from a whole ▸ piece, section. *See* **cut** (2). **4.** That which is allotted ▸ allowance, ration, share. *See* **allotment** (1). **5.** An individual quantity of food ▸ helping, mess. *See* **serving. 6.** A right or legal share in something ▸ claim, interest, stake, title. *See also* **right. 7.** That which is inevitably destined ▸ destiny, fate, fortune, kismet, lot, predestination. **8.** A personal outcome or end ▸ doom, fortune, lot. *See* **fate** (2).
portion *verb*
To give out in portions or shares ▸ allocate, apportion, dispense. *See* **distribute** (1).
portly *adjective*
▸ chubby, pudgy, stout. *See* **fat** (1). *See synonym note at* **fat.**
portrait *noun*
▸ clone, spitting image, twin. *See* **double** (1).
portray *verb*
1. To present a lifelike image of ▸ characterize, portray, render. *See* **represent** (2). *See synonym note at* **represent. 2.** To play the part of ▸ do, impersonate, play, represent. *See* **act** (4).
portrayal *noun*
1. The act or process of describing in lifelike imagery ▸ depiction, description, expression, rendering. *See* **representation. 2.** A performer's distinctive personal version of a song, dance, piece of music, or role ▸ enactment, performance, reading, rendition. *See* **interpretation** (1).
pose *verb*
1. To assume a particular position, as for a portrait ▸ attitudinize, model, posture, sit. *Idiom:* strike an attitude. **2.** To seek an answer to a question ▸ ask, put, raise. *See also* **say. 3.** To take on as a false appearance ▸ fake, feign, pretend. *See* **act** (2). **4.** To state for

consideration or debate ▸ offer, put forward, set forth. *See* **propose** (1). *See synonym note at* **propose**.

pose as *verb*

To assume the character or appearance of ▸ attitudinize, masquerade. *See* **impersonate** (1).

pose *noun*

1. The way in which one is placed or arranged ▸ attitude, position, posture. **2.** A way of holding or carrying one's body ▸ carriage, stance. *See* **posture** (1). *See synonym note at* **posture**. **3.** Behavior that is assumed rather than natural ▸ airs, mannerism. *See* **affectation** (1). *See synonym note at* **affectation**. **4.** A deceptive outward appearance ▸ front, guise. *See* **façade** (2).

poser *noun*

▸ dissembler, phony, tartuffe. *See* **hypocrite**.

posh *adjective*

▸ chic, hoity-toity, swank. *See* **exclusive** (4).

posit *verb*

▸ postulate, presume, presuppose. *See* **suppose** (1). *See synonym note at* **suppose**.

position *noun*

1. The place where a person or thing is located ▸ emplacement, location, locus, place, placement, point, site, situation, spot. **2.** The way in which one is placed or arranged ▸ attitude, pose, posture. **3.** A post of employment ▸ appointment, berth, billet, job, office, place, situation, slot, spot, work. *Slang:* gig. *See also* **business**. **4.** One's place and direction relative to one's surroundings ▸ location, orientation. *See* **bearing** (3). **5.** The position from which something is considered ▸ perspective, point of view. *See* **viewpoint**. **6.** A frame of mind affecting one's thoughts or behavior ▸ outlook, philosophy. *See* **posture** (2). **7.** Something thought to be true ▸ notion, persuasion, view. *See* **belief** (1). **8.** Positioning of one individual vis-à-vis others ▸ echelon, rank, standing. *See* **place** (1). **9.** A statement presented for acceptance, as by a religious group ▸ dogma, teaching. *See* **doctrine**.

position *verb*

To put in a certain position or location ▸ base, deposit, emplace, install, lay, locate, place, put, set, site, situate, spot, stick. *See also* **station**.

positioning *noun*

▸ format, layout, sequence. *See* **arrangement** (1).

positive *adjective*

1. Giving assent ▸ approving, assenting. *See* **favorable** (2). **2.** Clearly, fully, and emphatically expressed ▸ decided, explicit, precise. *See* **definite** (1). **3.** Established beyond a doubt ▸ inarguable, indisputable, irrefutable. *See* **certain** (2). **4.** Known positively ▸ absolute, sure. *See* **definite** (3). **5.** Having no doubt ▸ certain, confident. *See* **sure** (1). *See synonym note at* **sure**. **6.** *Informal* Completely such, without qualification or exception ▸ all-out, pure, sheer. *See* **utter**[2]. **7.** Expecting or suggesting a favorable outcome ▸ cheerful, sanguine. *See* **optimistic**.

positively *adverb*

1. In a direct, positive manner ▸ directly, emphatically.

Informal: flat out. *See* **flatly**. **2.** Without question ▸ certainly, doubtless, doubtlessly, undoubtedly. *See* **absolutely** (1). **3.** In truth ▸ genuinely, truly, veritably. *See* **really**.

positivity *or* **positiveness** *noun*

▸ assuredness, certainty, confidence, conviction. *See* **sureness** (1).

possess *verb*

1. To have at one's disposal ▸ enjoy, have, hold. *See* **command** (3). **2.** To hold on one's person ▸ bear, have. *Informal:* pack. *See* **carry** (7). **3.** To have as a visible characteristic ▸ display, wear. *See* **bear** (3). **4.** To dominate the mind or thoughts of ▸ fixate, obsess, preoccupy. *See also* **absorb, grip**.

possessed *adjective*

▸ collected, composed, cool. *See* **calm** (1).

possession *noun*

1. An area subject to rule by an outside power ▸ colony, dependency, mandate, protectorate, province, satellite, settlement, territory. **2.** The fact of possessing or the legal right to possess something ▸ deed, title. *See* **ownership**.

possessions *noun*

1. A thing or set of things, such as land and assets, legally possessed ▸ belongings, property. *See* **holdings**. **2.** One's portable property ▸ goods, personal effects, property. *See* **effects**.

possessive *adjective*

Fearful of the loss of position or affection ▸ clinging, clutching, green-eyed, jealous. *See also* **envious**.

possessor *noun*

▸ master, proprietor. *See* **owner**.

possibility *noun*

1. Something that may occur or be done ▸ contingency, eventuality, potential, potentiality. *See also* **expectation**. **2.** Indication of future success or development ▸ makings, potential, promise, prospects. *See also* **material**. **3.** The likeliness of a given event occurring ▸ likelihood, odds, probability. *See* **chance** (3).

possible *adjective*

1. Capable of occurring or being done ▸ achievable, attainable, doable, feasible, performable, practicable, viable, workable. *Idiom:* within reach. **2.** Present but not evident or active ▸ dormant, inactive, potential. *See* **latent**. **3.** Having a chance of happening or being true ▸ likely, potential. *See* **probable** (1). **4.** Capable of being anticipated, considered, or imagined ▸ earthly, imaginable, likely. *See* **conceivable**. **5.** Not compulsory or automatic ▸ elective, permissible. *See* **optional**.

✦ CORE SYNONYMS: *possible, workable, practicable, feasible, viable.* These adjectives mean capable of occurring or being done. *Possible* indicates that something may happen, exist, be true, or be realizable: *"I made out a list of questions and possible answers"* (Mary Roberts Rinehart). *Workable* is used of something that can be put into effective operation: *If the scheme is workable, how will you implement it?* Something that is *practicable* is capable of being effected, done, or put into practice: *"As soon as it was practicable, he would conclude his business"* (George Eliot). *Feasible* refers to what can be accomplished, brought about, or carried out: *Making cars by hand is possible but not economically feasible. Viable* implies having the capacity for continuing effectiveness or success: *"How viable are the ancient legends as vehicles for modern literary themes?"* (Richard Kain).

◄ ANTONYM: *impossible*

---

possibly *adverb*
► conceivably, perchance, perhaps. *See* **maybe.**
post[1] *verb*
To gain a point or points in a game or contest ► score, tally. *Informal:* notch. **Idioms:** make a goal (*or* point).
post[2] *noun*
1. A center of organization, supply, or activity ► headquarters, installation, station. *See* **base**[1] (1). **2.** A sturdy vertical structural support ► pillar, shaft. *See* **column** (1). **3.** A high structure or place commanding a wide view ► crow's nest, observatory, watchtower. *See* **lookout** (2).
post *verb*
1. To appoint and send to a particular place ► assign, set, station. *See also* **position. 2.** To place something at risk, as in a game of chance ► bet, stake, wager. *See* **gamble** (2).
post[3] *verb*
1. To place on a list or in a record or book ► catalog, chronicle, write down. *See* **list**[1] (1). **2.** To cause something to be conveyed to a destination ► consign, dispatch. *See* **send** (1).
poster *noun*
► billboard, notice. *See* **sign** (2).
posterior *adjective*
1. Located in the rear ► hind, hindmost. *See* **back** (1). **2.** Following something else in time ► after, later, subsequent, ulterior. *See also* **following.**
posterior *noun*
The part of the body on which one sits ► fundament, rump. *Informal:* backside. *See* **buttocks.**
posterity *noun*
► brood, offspring, seed. *See* **progeny** (1).
posthaste *adverb*
► apace, hastily, pronto, quickly. *See* **fast.**
posting *noun*
► heading, record. *See* **entry** (1).
postpone *verb*
► delay, hold off, suspend. *See* **defer**[1]. *See synonym note at* **defer**[1].
postponement *noun*
► deferment, holdup, suspension. *See* **delay** (1).
postulant *noun*
An entrant who has not yet taken the final vows of a religious order ► neophyte, novice, novitiate.
postulate *verb*
1. To consider to be true without proof ► posit, presume, presuppose. *See* **suppose** (1). *See synonym note at* **suppose. 2.** To defend, maintain, or insist on

the recognition of ► assert, demand. *See* **claim** (1).
postulate *or* **postulation** *noun*
Something taken to be true without proof ► given, premise, presupposition. *See* **assumption** (1).
postulated *adjective*
► conceptual, hypothetical, virtual. *See* **theoretical** (2).
posture *noun*
1. A way of holding or carrying one's body ► attitude, carriage, pose, stance. *See also* **bearing. 2.** A frame of mind affecting one's thoughts or behavior ► attitude, mindset, outlook, perspective, philosophy, position, stance. *See also* **mood, viewpoint. 3.** The way in which one is placed or arranged ► attitude, pose, position.
posture *verb*
1. To assume a particular position, as for a portrait ► model, sit. *See* **pose** (1). **2.** To assume the character or appearance of ► masquerade, pose as. *See* **impersonate** (1).

✚ CORE SYNONYMS: *posture, attitude, carriage, pose, stance.* These nouns denote a way of holding or carrying one's bony: *a model's erect posture; an attitude of prayer; the monarch's dignified carriage; an activist who struck a defiant pose; an athlete's alert stance.*

---

posy *noun*
1. Cut flowers or foliage arranged or worn for display ► corsage, nosegay. *See* **bouquet** (1). **2.** The showy reproductive structure of a plant ► blossom, floret. *See* **flower** (1).
pot *noun*
Something risked on an uncertain outcome ► pool, wager. *See* **bet** (1). *See synonym note at* **bet.**
pot *verb*
1. To put seeds or young plants in soil ► broadcast, seed, sow. *See* **plant** (1). **2.** To prepare food for storage and future use ► can, cure, put up. *See* **preserve** (1).
potable *noun*
► beverage, brew, refreshment. *See* **drink** (1).
potation *noun*
1. An act of drinking or the amount swallowed ► swallow, taste. *Informal:* swig. *See* **drink** (2). **2.** Any liquid that is fit for drinking ► brew, refreshment. *See* **drink** (1).
potbellied *adjective*
► chubby, pudgy, rotund. *See* **fat** (1).
potency *noun*
1. The state or quality of being physically strong ► power, sinew. *See* **strength** (1). **2.** Capacity for work or vigorous activity ► force, might, power. *See* **energy. 3.** The power or capacity to produce a desired result ► effectiveness, efficacy, influence. *See* **effect** (2). **4.** *Slang* A stimulating or intoxicating effect ► *Informal:* sting, wallop. *See* **kick.**
potent *adjective*
1. Having a high concentration of the distinguishing ingredient ► concentrated, stiff, strong. *See also* **straight. 2.** Having great physical strength ► mighty, powerful, strong. *See also* **energetic, muscular. 3.** Full

of or displaying force ▸ powerful, strong, vigorous. *See* **forceful** (1).

potentate *noun*
▸ boss, director, head, leader. *See* **chief** (1).

potential *noun*
1. Indication of future success or development ▸ makings, possibility, promise, prospects. *See also* **material**. 2. Something that may occur or be done ▸ contingency, eventuality, potentiality. *See* **possibility** (1).

potential *adjective*
1. Present but not evident or active ▸ dormant, inactive, possible. *See* **latent**. 2. Having a good chance of happening or being true ▸ likely, possible. *See* **probable** (1).

potentiality *noun*
▸ contingency, eventuality. *See* **possibility** (1).

pother *noun*
▸ fuss, rigmarole. *See* **bother** (1).

potion *noun*
▸ beverage, brew, refreshment. *See* **drink** (1).

potpourri *noun*
▸ hodgepodge, jumble, mishmash. *See* **assortment** (1).

potted *adjective*
1. *Slang* Stupefied, excited, or muddled with alcoholic liquor ▸ intoxicated, sodden, tipsy. *See* **drunk**. 2. *Slang* Stupefied, intoxicated, or otherwise influenced by the taking of drugs ▸ high, hopped-up, lit (up). *See* **drugged**.

pouch *verb*
To curve outward past the normal or usual limit ▸ balloon, jut, project. *See* **bulge** (1).

pouch *noun*
A flexible container for carrying items ▸ sack, tote. *See* **bag** (1).

pounce *verb*
To move off the ground by a muscular effort of the legs and feet ▸ spring, vault. *See* **jump** (1).

pounce *noun*
The act of jumping ▸ jump, pounce, leap, spring. *See also* **fall**.

pound¹ *verb*
1. To hit heavily and repeatedly ▸ assault, batter, pummel, thresh. *See* **beat** (1). *See synonym note at* **beat**. 2. To shape, break, or flatten with repeated blows ▸ hammer, stamp. *See* **beat** (3). 3. To make rhythmic contractions, sounds, or movements ▸ pulsate, pulse, throb. *See* **beat** (5). 4. To fix (an idea, for example) in someone's mind by reemphasis and repetition ▸ drive, inculcate. *See* **instill**. 5. To break up into tiny particles ▸ atomize, grind, mill. *See* **crush** (2).

pound *noun*
1. A sudden heavy stroke ▸ crack, hit, swat, whack. *See* **blow²** (1). 2. A stroke or blow that produces a sound ▸ thud, thump. *See* **beat** (1).

pound² *noun*
An enclosure for confining an animal or bird ▸ coop, kennel, stall. *See* **cage**.

pour *verb*
1. To cause a liquid to flow in a steady stream

▸ decant, discharge, drain, draw (off), effuse, empty, flow, issue, run. 2. To come forth in abundance ▸ gush, run, rush. *See* **flow** (2). 3. To fall in drops of water from clouds ▸ drizzle, precipitate, shower. *See* **rain** (2). 4. To move into an area or space in large numbers ▸ cram, flood, throng. *See* **crowd** (1).

pour *noun*
Water condensed from atmospheric vapor and falling in drops ▸ deluge, downpour, shower. *See* **rain** (2).

pout *verb*
To be sullenly aloof or withdrawn, as in silent resentment or protest ▸ mope, pet, sulk. *See also* **brood**.

pout *noun*
A contorted facial expression showing pain, contempt, or disgust ▸ face, grimace, moue. *Informal:* mug. *See also* **frown, glare, sneer**.

poverty *noun*
1. The condition of being extremely poor ▸ beggary, destitution, impecuniosity, impecuniousness, impoverishment, indigence, need, neediness, pauperism, pennilessness, penuriousness, penury, poorness, privation, straits, want. *See also* **bankruptcy, beggary**. 2. The condition or fact of being deficient ▸ deficit, inadequacy, paucity. *See* **shortage**. 3. The condition of being deprived of what one once had or ought to have ▸ destitution, dispossession, loss. *See* **deprivation** (1).

poverty-stricken *adjective*
▸ destitute, down-and-out, indigent. *See* **poor** (1). *See synonym note at* **poor**.

powder *verb*
1. To break up into tiny particles ▸ atomize, grind, mill. *See* **crush** (2). 2. To scatter or release in drops or small particles ▸ besprinkle, dust, pepper. *See* **sprinkle** (1).

powdery *adjective*
▸ dusty, pulverous, pulverulent. *See* **fine¹** (6).

power *noun*
1. Capacity for work or vigorous activity ▸ might, potency, vigor. *See* **energy**. *See synonym note at* **energy**. 2. The state or quality of being physically strong ▸ potency, sinew. *See* **strength** (1). 3. The right and power to command, decide, rule, or judge ▸ control, might. *See* **authority** (1). 4. Power to sway or affect based on prestige, wealth, ability, or position ▸ force, sway, weight. *See* **influence** (1). 5. Energy that overcomes resistance ▸ might, pressure, strength. *See* **force** (1). 6. The condition or fact of being dominant ▸ authority, hegemony, supremacy. *See* **dominance** (1).

powerful *adjective*
1. Having great physical strength ▸ mighty, potent, strong. *See also* **energetic, muscular**. 2. Full of or displaying force ▸ hard-hitting, strong, vigorous. *See* **forceful** (1). 3. Resulting from or affecting one's innermost feelings ▸ heartfelt, strong. *See* **deep** (3). 4. Conveying great physical force ▸ hard, heavy. *See* **severe**

(2). **5.** Having or exercising influence ▸ important, weighty. *See* **influential.**

powerfully *adverb*
▸ energetically, forcefully, vigorously. *See* **hard** (1).

powerfulness *noun*
▸ potency, power, sinew. *See* **strength** (1).

powerless *adjective*
1. Lacking power or strength ▸ helpless, impotent, unable. **2.** Not capable of accomplishing anything ▸ impotent, inadequate, incapable. *See* **ineffectual** (2).

powerlessness *noun*
1. Lack of ability or capacity ▸ incapacity, incompetency. *See* **inability. 2.** The condition or state of being incapable of accomplishing anything ▸ helplessness, ineffectiveness. *See* **ineffectuality.**

powwow *noun*
Informal A meeting for the exchange of views ▸ discussion, parley, seminar. *See* **conference** (1).

powwow *verb*
To meet and exchange views to reach a decision ▸ consult, deliberate, talk. *Informal:* huddle. *See* **confer** (1).

practicable *adjective*
1. Capable of occurring or being done ▸ doable, viable. *See* **possible** (1). *See synonym note at* **possible. 2.** Serving or capable of serving a useful purpose ▸ functional, useful, utilitarian. *See* **practical** (1). **3.** Available for use ▸ employable, operable, usable. *See* **open** (4). **4.** Worth doing, especially for practical reasons ▸ recommendable, well. *See* **advisable.**

practical *adjective*
1. Serving or capable of serving a useful purpose ▸ functional, handy, no-nonsense, practicable, serviceable, useful, utilitarian. *See also* **beneficial, usable. 2.** Having or indicating an awareness of things as they really are ▸ pragmatic, prosaic. *See* **realistic** (1).

practicality *noun*
▸ benefit, profit, utility. *See* **use** (2).

practical joke *noun*
▸ caper, joke, trick. *See* **prank**[1].

practically *adverb*
▸ almost, nearly, roughly. *See* **approximately.**

practice *verb*
1. To do or perform repeatedly so as to master ▸ exercise, go over (through), rehearse, run through, walk through. *See also* **indoctrinate. 2.** To work at, especially as a profession ▸ do, follow, pursue. *Idiom:* hang out one's shingle. *See also* **labor. 3.** To engage in activities in order to strengthen or condition ▸ drill, exercise, train, work out. **4.** To put into action or use ▸ apply, employ, utilize. *See* **use** (1).

practice *noun*
1. Repetition of an action so as to develop or maintain one's skill ▸ conditioning, drill, exercise, regimen, rehearsal, routine, study, training, workout. **2.** A habitual way of behaving ▸ form, habit, routine. *See* **custom** (1). *See synonym note at* **custom. 3.** Activity pursued as a livelihood ▸ profession, pursuit, vocation. *See* **business** (2).

✦ CORE SYNONYMS: *practice, exercise, rehearse.* These verbs mean to do repeatedly so as to master: *practice the shot put; exercising one's wits; rehearsed the play for 14 days.*

practiced *adjective*
1. Proficient as a result of practice and study ▸ accomplished, finished, polished. *See also* **able, expert. 2.** Skilled or knowledgeable through long practice ▸ old, seasoned. *See* **experienced.**

praetorian *adjective*
▸ dishonest, mercenary, venal. *See* **corrupt** (2).

pragmatic *or* **pragmatical** *adjective*
▸ practical, prosaic. *See* **realistic** (1).

praise *noun*
1. An expression of warm approval ▸ acclaim, acclamation, accolade, applause, approbation, celebration, cheer, commendation, compliment, encomium, eulogy, kudos, laud, laudation, paean, panegyric, plaudit. *See also* **applause, exaltation. 2.** The honoring of a deity, as in worship ▸ exaltation, extolment, glory, glorification, laudation, magnification, prostration. *See also* **adoration, honor. 3.** An expression of admiration ▸ accolades, commendation, tribute. *See* **compliment** (1).

praise *verb*
1. To express warm approval of ▸ acclaim, accolade, applaud, cheer, commend, compliment, extol, laud. **2.** To pay a compliment to ▸ commend, compliment, congratulate, felicitate. *Idiom:* take off one's hat to. **3.** To honor a deity in religious worship ▸ exalt, extol, glorify, hymn, laud, magnify. *See also* **revere. 4.** To pay tribute or homage to ▸ celebrate, exalt. *See* **honor** (1). **5.** To cause to be eminent or recognized ▸ dignify, exalt, honor. *See* **distinguish** (5).

✦ CORE SYNONYMS: *praise, acclaim, commend, extol, laud.* These verbs mean to express approval or admiration. To *praise* is to voice approbation, commendation, or esteem: *"She was enthusiastically praising the beauties of Gothic architecture"* (Francis Marion Crawford). *Acclaim* usually implies hearty approbation warmly and publicly expressed: *The film was highly acclaimed by many critics. Commend* suggests moderate or restrained approval, as that accorded by a superior: *The judge commended the jury for their hard work. Extol* suggests exaltation or glorification: *"that sign of old age, extolling the past at the expense of the present"* (Sydney Smith). *Laud* connotes respectful or lofty, often inordinate praise: *"aspirations which are lauded up to the skies"* (Charles Kingsley).

praiseworthy *adjective*
▸ deserving, laudable, worthy. *See* **admirable.**

prance *verb*
▸ flounce, strut, swank. *See* **strut** (1).

prank[1] *noun*
A mischievous act ▸ antic, caper, frolic, gag, joke, lark, practical joke, trick. *Informal:* shenanigan. *Slang:* monkeyshine, put-on. *See also* **mischief.**

prank² *verb*
To dress in formal or special clothing ▸ attire, deck (out), preen. *See* **dress up.**

prankish *adjective*
▸ frolicsome, impish, sportive. *See* **mischievous** (1).

prankishness *or* **pranks** *noun*
▸ diablerie, high jinks, tomfoolery. *See* **mischief** (1).

prankster *noun*
▸ devil, imp, scamp. *See* **rascal.**

prate *verb*
1. To talk rapidly, incoherently, or indistinctly ▸ chatter, jabber, prattle. *See* **babble** (1). **2.** To talk rapidly on trivial matters ▸ blab, jabber, prattle. *See* **chatter** (1).

prate *noun*
1. Empty or foolish talk ▸ gibberish, jabber, twaddle. *See* **babble** (1). **2.** Incessant and inconsequential talk ▸ drivel, patter, small talk. *See* **chatter.**

prattle *verb*
1. To talk rapidly, incoherently, or indistinctly ▸ blather, chatter, jabber. *See* **babble** (1). **2.** To talk rapidly on trivial matters ▸ blab, jabber, prattle. *See* **chatter** (1). **3.** To engage in or spread gossip ▸ rumor, whisper. *See* **gossip.**

prattle *noun*
1. Empty or foolish talk ▸ gibberish, jabber, twaddle. *See* **babble** (1). **2.** Incessant and inconsequential talk ▸ drivel, patter, small talk. *See* **chatter. 3.** Idle, often sensational and groundless talk about others ▸ hearsay, rumor, tattle. *See* **gossip** (1).

praxis *noun*
▸ form, habit, practice. *See* **custom** (1).

pray *verb*
1. To offer a reverent petition to God or a god ▸ invoke, supplicate. **2.** To make an earnest or urgent request ▸ beseech, entreat, plead. *See* **appeal** (1).

prayer¹ *noun*
1. The act of praying ▸ benediction, invocation, supplication. **2.** A formula of words used in praying ▸ collect, devotions, litany, orison, rogations. *See also* **grace. 3.** An earnest or urgent request ▸ entreaty, imploration, supplication. *See* **appeal** (1).

prayer² *noun*
One who humbly entreats ▸ beggar, petitioner, suitor, suppliant, supplicant.

prayerful *adjective*
▸ devout, holy, religious. *See* **pious** (1).

preach *verb*
1. To deliver a sermon, especially as a vocation ▸ evangelize, sermonize. *See also* **address. 2.** To indulge in moral reflection, usually pompously ▸ edify, moralize, pontificate, sermonize. *See also* **chastise.**

preacher *noun*
▸ ecclesiastic, minister, parson. *See* **cleric.**

preachy *adjective*
1. Inclined to moralize excessively ▸ academic, prescriptive. *See* **didactic** (2). **2.** Teaching morality ▸ moralistic, moralizing. *See* **moral** (1).

preadolescence *noun*
The stage of life between birth and puberty ▸ childhood, early years, innocence, prepubescence. *See also* **youth.**

preadolescent *noun*
▸ juvenile, tot, youngster. *See* **child** (1).

preamble *noun*
▸ overture, preface, prologue. *See* **introduction** (1).

prearrangement *noun*
▸ mobilization, readiness. *See* **preparation.**

precarious *adjective*
1. Lacking stability ▸ shaky, unsteady. *See* **insecure** (2). **2.** Requiring great tact or skill ▸ demanding, exacting, specific. *See* **delicate** (3).

precariousness *noun*
▸ insecurity, unstableness, unsteadiness. *See* **instability.**

precaution *noun*
1. Careful forethought to avoid risk ▸ care, carefulness, wariness. *See* **caution** (1). **2.** The exercise of good judgment or common sense in practical matters ▸ circumspection, foresight, forethought. *See* **prudence** (1).

precautionary *adjective*
1. Defending against disease ▸ defensive, prophylactic, protective. *See* **preventive** (2). **2.** Tending to or capable of preserving ▸ conservational, protective. *See* **preservative.**

precede *verb*
1. To come, exist, or occur before in time ▸ antecede, antedate, forerun, predate, preexist. **2.** To begin something with preliminary or prefatory material ▸ lead, preface. *See* **introduce** (3).

precedence *noun*
The act, condition, or right of preceding or coming before ▸ antecedence, precedency, precession, priority, right of way.

precedent *noun*
1. One that is worthy of imitation or duplication ▸ example, exemplar, paradigm. *See* **model** (1). **2.** A habitual way of behaving ▸ form, habit, practice. *See* **custom** (1).

precedent *adjective*
1. Going before ▸ anterior, earlier, preceding. *See* **advance** (0). **2.** Just gone by or elapsed ▸ ago, previous, prior. *See* **past** (1).

preceding *adjective*
1. Next before the present one ▸ foregoing, last, latter, previous. **2.** Going before ▸ anterior, earlier, precedent. *See* **advance** (0). **3.** Just gone by or elapsed ▸ lapsed, previous, prior. *See* **past** (1).

precept *noun*
1. A principle governing affairs within or among political units ▸ decree, edict, institute. *See* **law** (1). **2.** A statement presented for acceptance, as by a religious group ▸ dogma, teaching. *See* **doctrine.**

precession *noun*
▸ priority, right of way. *See* **precedence.**

precincts *noun*
1. The boundary surrounding a certain area ▸ bounds, confines, perimeter. *See* **limits. 2.** A sur-

rounding area ▸ locale, neighborhood. *See* **environment** (1).

precious *adjective*
1. Of great value or price ▸ expensive, invaluable, valuable. *See* **costly**. **2.** Regarded with much love and tenderness ▸ dear, loved. *See* **darling** (1).

precious *noun*
A person who is much loved ▸ dear, honey, sweetheart. *See* **darling** (1).

precipitance *or* **precipitancy** *noun*
▸ hastiness, rashness. *See* **haste** (2).

precipitant *adjective*
1. Characterized by unthinking boldness and haste ▸ hasty, impulsive, reckless. *See* **rash**[1]. **2.** Unexpectedly sudden ▸ hurried, precipitate, sudden. *See* **abrupt** (2).

precipitate *verb*
1. To put down, especially in layers, by a natural process ▸ deposit. **2.** To be the cause of ▸ bring on, generate, induce, trigger. *See* **cause**. **3.** To fall in drops of water from clouds ▸ drizzle, spatter, shower. *See* **rain** (2).

precipitate *adjective*
1. Characterized by unthinking boldness and haste ▸ hasty, impulsive, reckless. *See* **rash**[1]. *See synonym note at* **rash**[1]. **2.** Unexpectedly sudden ▸ hurried, precipitant, sudden. *See* **abrupt** (2).

precipitate *noun*
1. Matter that settles on a bottom or collects on a surface by a natural process ▸ accumulation, dregs, sediment. *See* **deposit** (2). **2.** Something brought about by a cause ▸ consequence, outcome, result. *See* **effect** (1).

precipitateness *noun*
▸ precipitance, rashness. *See* **haste** (2).

precipitation *noun*
1. Careless headlong action ▸ hastiness, rashness. *See* **haste** (2). **2.** Matter that settles on a bottom or collects on a surface by a natural process ▸ accumulation, dregs, sediment. *See* **deposit** (2). **3.** Water condensed from atmospheric vapor and falling in drops ▸ deluge, downpour, shower. *See* **rain** (2).

precipitous *adjective*
▸ abrupt, sharp, sudden. *See* **steep**[1] (1). *See synonym note at* **steep**[1].

precise *adjective*
1. Clearly, fully, and emphatically expressed ▸ decided, explicit, specific. *See* **definite** (1). **2.** Having distinct limits ▸ fixed, specific. *See* **definite** (2). **3.** Conforming exactly to fact ▸ correct, exact, faithful. *See* **accurate** (1). **4.** Strictly distinguished from others ▸ exact, very. **5.** So slight as to be difficult to notice or appreciate ▸ refined, subtle. *See* **delicate** (4).

precisely *adverb*
1. In an exact manner ▸ literally, verbatim. *See* **exactly** (1). **2.** With precision or absolute conformity ▸ exactly, just, squarely. *See* **directly** (3).

precision *or* **preciseness** *noun*
1. Freedom from error ▸ accurateness, exactitude, rightness. *See* **accuracy** (1). **2.** The quality of being

clear and easy to perceive ▸ distinctness, legibility, perspicuity, plainness. *See* **clarity** (1).

preclude *verb*
▸ anticipate, avert, obviate. *See* **prevent**. *See synonym note at* **prevent**.

preclusion *noun*
▸ deterrence, forestallment, prohibition. *See* **prevention**.

preclusive *adjective*
▸ deterrent, interdictive, prohibitive. *See* **preventive** (1).

precocious *adjective*
1. Developing, occurring, or appearing before the expected time ▸ early, premature, untimely. **2.** Ahead of current trends or customs ▸ advanced, forward. *See* **progressive** (1). **3.** Possessing great natural ability or talent ▸ endowed, talented. *See* **gifted**.

preconception *noun*
▸ partiality, prejudice. *See* **bias** (1).

precondition *noun*
1. Something indispensable ▸ necessity, prerequisite, requirement. *See* **condition** (2). **2.** A restricting or modifying element ▸ condition, proviso, stipulation. *See* **provision** (1).

precursor *noun*
1. One that foreshadows or prepares for something else ▸ harbinger, herald. *See* **forerunner** (1). **2.** One that precedes, as in time ▸ antecedent, predecessor. *See* **ancestor** (2).

predate *verb*
▸ antecede, antedate, preexist. *See* **precede** (1).

predecessor *noun*
▸ forerunner, precursor. *See* **ancestor** (2).

predestination *noun*
▸ destiny, fortune, kismet. *See* **fate** (1).

predetermine *verb*
▸ contrive, devise, premeditate. *See* **design** (1).

predetermined *adjective*
▸ deliberate, intentional, premeditated. *See* **calculated** (1).

predicament *noun*
A difficult, often embarrassing situation or condition ▸ box, corner, deep water, difficulty, dilemma, Dutch, fix, hole, hot spot, hot water, impasse, jam, mess, pinch, plight, quagmire, quandary, scrape, soup, straits, tightrope, trouble. *Informal:* bind, pickle, spot. *Idiom:* pretty kettle of fish. *See also* **crisis, difficulty, entanglement**.

✦ CORE SYNONYMS: *predicament, plight, quandary, jam, fix, pickle.* These nouns refer to a situation from which it is difficult to free oneself. A *predicament* is a problematic situation about which one does not know what to do: "*Werner finds himself suddenly in a most awkward predicament*" (Thomas Carlyle). A *plight* is a bad or unfortunate situation: *The report examined the plight of homeless people.* A *quandary* is a state of perplexity, especially about what course of action to take: "*Having captured our men, we were in a quandary how to keep them*" (Theodore Roosevelt).

Jam and *fix* are less formal terms that refer to predicaments from which it is difficult to escape: *kids who were in a jam with the authorities; "If we get left on this wreck we are in a fix"* (Mark Twain). An informal term, a *pickle* is a disagreeable, embarrassing, or troublesome predicament: *"I could see no way out of the pickle I was in"* (Robert Louis Stevenson).

predicate *verb*
▶ establish, ground. *See* **base¹** (1).

predict *verb*
To tell about or make known in advance, especially by means of special knowledge ▶ call, forecast, foretell, portend, presage, prognosticate, project. *See also* **foresee, foreshadow, prophesy.**

✢ CORE SYNONYMS: *predict, call, forecast, foretell, prognosticate.* These verbs mean to tell about or make known something in advance of its occurrence, especially by means of special knowledge or inference: *predict an eclipse; couldn't call the outcome of the game; forecasting the weather; foretold events that would happen; prognosticating a rebellion.*

prediction *noun*
The act of predicting ▶ forecast, outlook, prescience, prevision, prognosis, prognostication, projection. *See also* **omen, prophecy.**

predictive *adjective*
Of or relating to prediction ▶ prescient, previsionary, prognostic, prognosticative. *See also* **prophetic.**

predilection *noun*
▶ disposition, leaning, penchant. *See* **inclination** (1). *See synonym note at* **inclination.**

predispose *verb*
▶ incline, act on, sway. *See* **influence** (1).

predisposed *adjective*
▶ disposed, prone. *See* **inclined** (1).

predisposition *noun*
▶ disposition, leaning, penchant. *See* **inclination** (1).

predominance *noun*
▶ authority, power, supremacy. *See* **dominance** (1).

predominant *adjective*
1. Exercising controlling power or influence ▶ key, leading, reigning. *See* **dominant** (1). *See synonym note at* **dominant.** 2. Most generally existing or encountered at a given time ▶ current, rampant. *See* **prevailing** (1).

predominate *verb*
▶ control, lead, prevail. *See* **dominate** (1).

preeminence *noun*
1. The condition or fact of being dominant ▶ authority, power, supremacy. *See* **dominance** (1). 2. Wide recognition for one's deeds ▶ glory, note, prestige. *See* **fame.** 3. The quality of being exceptionally good of its kind ▶ superbness, superiority. *See* **excellence.**

preeminent *adjective*
1. Beyond what is usual, normal, or customary ▶ extraordinary, outstanding, remarkable. *See* **exceptional** (1). 2. Widely known ▶ celebrated, noted, renowned. *See* **famous.** *See synonym note at* **famous.**

3. Surpassing all others in quality ▶ optimum, superlative, unsurpassed. *See* **best** (1). 4. Exercising controlling power or influence ▶ key, predominant, reigning. *See* **dominant** (1). *See synonym note at* **dominant.**

preempt *verb*
▶ appropriate, assume, usurp. *See* **seize** (1). *See synonym note at* **seize.**

preemption *noun*
▶ expropriation, grab, usurpation. *See* **seizure** (2).

preen *verb*
1. To be proud of oneself, as for an accomplishment or achievement ▶ gloat, plume. *See* **pride.** 2. To dress in formal or special clothing ▶ attire, deck (out). *See* **dress up.**

preexist *verb*
▶ antecede, antedate, predate. *See* **precede** (1).

preface *noun*
A short section of preliminary remarks ▶ overture, preamble, prologue. *See* **introduction** (1).

preface *verb*
To begin something with preliminary or prefatory material ▶ lead, precede. *See* **introduce** (3).

prefatory *adjective*
▶ inductive, preliminary, preparatory. *See* **introductory** (1). *See synonym note at* **introductory.**

prefer *verb*
1. To show partiality toward someone ▶ favor. *Idioms:* be partial, play favorites. *See also* **advance, baby.** 2. To have an inclination to ▶ want, wish. *See* **choose** (2).

preferable *adjective*
Of greater excellence than another ▶ better, superior.

preference *noun*
1. Preferential treatment or bias ▶ favor, favoritism, partiality, partialness. *See also* **bias, prejudice.** 2. The act, power, or right of choosing ▶ decision, discretion, option. *See* **choice** (1). *See synonym note at* **choice.** 3. A liking for something ▶ appetite, partiality, weakness. *See* **taste** (1).

preferential *adjective*
1. Disposed to favor one over another ▶ favorable, partial. *See also* **biased.** 2. Not fair, right, or just ▶ discriminatory, unequal, unjust. *See* **unfair.**

preferment *noun*
▶ promotion, upgrade. *See* **advancement** (1).

preferred *adjective*
▶ fair-haired, favored, well-liked. *See* **favorite.**

prefigure *verb*
▶ adumbrate, foretell, portend. *See* **foreshadow.**

prefigurement *noun*
▶ portent, prognostication, sign. *See* **omen.**

pregnability *noun*
▶ endangerment, susceptibility, vulnerability. *See* **exposure** (1).

pregnable *adjective*
▶ helpless, unprotected. *See* **vulnerable** (1).

pregnancy *noun*
The condition of carrying a developing fetus within the uterus ▶ gestation, gravidity, gravidness, parturiency.

pregnant *adjective*
1. Carrying a developing fetus within the uterus ▸ big, enceinte, expectant, expecting, gestating, gravid, parturient. *Slang:* gone, knocked-up, preggers, preggo. *Idioms:* having a bun in the oven, in a family way, with child. 2. Conveying hidden or unexpressed meaning ▸ consequential, meaningful, meaty, pithy, significant, suggestive, weighty. *See also* **important.**

prehistoric *adjective*
Of, existing, or occurring in a distant period ▸ ancient, primeval, primordial. *See* **early** (1).

prehistory *noun*
▸ ancient times, protohistory, time immemorial. *See* **antiquity.**

prejudge *verb*
To make a mistake in judging ▸ misestimate, misjudge, mistake. *See also* **misunderstand, suppose.**

prejudice *noun*
1. Irrational suspicion or hatred of a particular group, race, or religion ▸ bigotry, discrimination, intolerance. *See also* **hate.** 2. An inclination for or against that inhibits impartial judgment ▸ partiality, one-sidedness. *See* **bias** (1). 3. A natural or habitual preference for something ▸ disposition, leaning, penchant. *See* **inclination** (1). *See synonym note at* **inclination.**

prejudice *verb*
1. To cause to have a prejudiced view ▸ jaundice, warp. *See* **bias** (1). 2. To spoil the soundness or perfection of ▸ flaw, impair. *See* **damage.**

prejudiced *or* **prejudicial** *adjective*
▸ partial, skewed, tendentious. *See* **biased** (1). *See synonym note at* **bias.**

prelate *noun*
▸ ecclesiastic, minister, parson. *See* **cleric.**

prelect *verb*
To talk to an audience formally ▸ lecture, sermonize, speak. *See also* **converse.**

prelection *noun*
▸ lecture, talk. *See* **speech** (2).

preliminary *adjective*
1. Serving to introduce or prepare for something ▸ prefatory, preparatory. *See* **introductory** (1). *See synonym note at* **introductory.** 2. Not perfected, elaborated, or completed ▸ crude, sketchy, unpolished. *See* **rough** (10).

prelude *noun*
▸ overture, preface, prologue. *See* **introduction** (1).

premature *adjective*
Developing, occurring, or appearing before the expected time ▸ early, precocious, untimely.

premeditate *verb*
▸ contrive, devise, predetermine. *See* **design** (1).

premeditated *adjective*
1. Planned or estimated in advance ▸ deliberate, intentional. *See* **calculated** (1). 2. Done or said on purpose ▸ purposeful, willful. *See* **deliberate** (1).

premier *adjective*
1. Most important, influential, or significant ▸ chief, key, main, principal. *See* **primary** (1). 2. Preceding all others ▸ initial, original, prime. *See* **first** (1).

premise *noun*
Something taken to be true without proof ▸ axiom, given, presupposition. *See* **assumption** (1).

premise *verb*
To consider to be true without proof ▸ posit, presume, presuppose. *See* **suppose** (1).

premium *noun*
Something given in return for a service or accomplishment ▸ award, bonus, plum. *See* **reward** (1).

premium *adjective*
Of fine quality ▸ exceptional, select, superior. *See* **choice** (1).

premonition *noun*
▸ hunch, idea, intuition. *See* **feeling** (1).

preoccupation *noun*
1. Total occupation of the attention or of the mind ▸ engrossment, enthrallment, prepossession. *See* **absorption** (2). 2. Concentration of the mental powers on something ▸ concentration, consideration. *See* **attention** (1).

preoccupied *adjective*
1. Having one's thoughts fully occupied ▸ absorbed, intent, riveted. *See* **rapt.** 2. So lost in thought as to be forgetful ▸ abstracted, bemused, distracted. *See* **absent-minded.**

preoccupy *verb*
1. To occupy the attention of ▸ consume, immerse, monopolize. *See* **absorb** (1). *See synonym note at* **absorb.** 2. To dominate the mind or thoughts of ▸ fixate, obsess, possess. *See also* **grip.**

pre-owned *adjective*
▸ hand-me-down, secondhand. *See* **used** (2).

prep *verb*
▸ cure, fix, ready. *See* **prepare** (1).

preparation *noun*
The condition of being made ready beforehand ▸ mobilization, prearrangement, preparedness, readiness. *Idiom:* made ready.

preparations *noun*
Steps that are taken in preparation for an undertaking ▸ accommodations, arrangements, plans, provisions.

preparatory *adjective*
▸ prefatory, preliminary. *See* **introductory** (1). *See synonym note at* **introductory.**

prepare *verb*
1. To cause to be ready, as for use, consumption, or a special purpose ▸ cure, fit, fix, make, prime, ready. *Informal:* prep. 2. To plan the details or arrangements of ▸ schedule, work out. *See* **arrange** (2). *See synonym note at* **arrange.**

preparedness *noun*
▸ mobilization, readiness. *See* **preparation.**

preponderance *or* **preponderancy** *noun*
1. The condition or fact of being dominant ▸ authority, power, supremacy. *See* **dominance** (1). 2. The

greatest part or portion ▸ bulk, mass, weight. *See also* center.

preponderant *adjective*
Exercising controlling power or influence ▸ key, predominant, reigning. *See* **dominant** (1). *See synonym note at* **dominant.**

preponderate *verb*
▸ control, lead, prevail. *See* **dominate** (1).

prepossess *verb*
▸ prejudice, warp. *See* **bias** (1).

prepossessed *adjective*
▸ partial, prejudiced, tendentious. *See* **biased** (1).

prepossession *noun*
1. An inclination for or against that inhibits impartial judgment ▸ partiality, prejudice. *See* **bias** (1). **2.** Total occupation of the attention or of the mind ▸ engrossment, enthrallment, immersion, preoccupation. *See* **absorption** (2).

preposterous *adjective*
1. Displaying a lack of good sense ▸ daft, idiotic, ludicrous. *See* **foolish.** *See synonym note at* **foolish.** **2.** Exceeding the bounds of morality, decency, or reason ▸ appalling, monstrous, shocking. *See* **outrageous.**

preposterousness *noun*
▸ folly, silliness, tomfoolery. *See* **foolishness.**

prepotency *noun*
▸ authority, power, supremacy. *See* **dominance** (1).

prepotent *adjective*
▸ key, predominant, reigning. *See* **dominant** (1).

prepubescence *noun*
The stage of life between birth and puberty ▸ childhood, early years, innocence, preadolescence. *See also* **youth.**

prerequisite *noun*
1. A benefit granted to a person by law, nature, or custom ▸ birthright, freedom, privilege. *See* **right. 2.** A restricting or modifying element ▸ condition, proviso, stipulation. *See* **provision** (1). **3.** Something indispensable ▸ necessity, precondition, requirement. *See* **condition** (2).

prerequisite *adjective*
Incapable of being dispensed with ▸ necessary, required. *See* **essential** (1).

prerogative *noun*
1. A benefit granted to a person by law, nature, or custom ▸ birthright, freedom, privilege. *See* **right.** *See synonym note at* **right. 2.** The right and power to command, decide, rule, or judge ▸ control, might. *Informal:* say-so. *See* **authority** (1).

prerogative *adjective*
Not divided among or shared with others ▸ particular, sole. *See* **exclusive** (1).

presage *noun*
A phenomenon that serves as a sign of some future good or evil ▸ portent, prognostication, sign. *See* **omen.**

presage *verb*
1. To give an indication of something in advance ▸ adumbrate, foretell, portend, prefigure. *See* **foreshadow. 2.** To tell about or make known in advance, especially by means of special knowledge ▸ forecast, prognosticate. *See* **predict.**

presager *noun*
▸ herald, precursor. *See* **forerunner** (1).

prescience *noun*
1. Discernment or perception which is usually competent or creative ▸ innovation, inspiration. *See* **vision** (2). **2.** The act of predicting ▸ outlook, prognosis. *See* **prediction.**

prescient *adjective*
1. Characterized by foresight or vision ▸ imaginative, intuitive. *See* **visionary** (1). **2.** Of or relating to prediction ▸ previsionary, prognosticative. *See* **predictive.**

prescribe *verb*
1. To set forth expressly and authoritatively ▸ impose, mandate, ordain. *See* **dictate** (1). *See synonym note at* **dictate. 2.** To provide as a remedy ▸ dispense, medicate, treat. *See* **administer** (3).

prescribed *adjective*
▸ imperative, mandatory, requisite. *See* **required** (1).

prescript *noun*
▸ guideline, regulation, rubric. *See* **rule** (1).

prescription *noun*
1. A principle governing affairs within or among political units ▸ decree, edict, institute. *See* **law** (1). **2.** A substance used in the treatment of disease ▸ medication, medicine, pharmaceutical. *See* **drug** (1).

prescriptive *adjective*
▸ academic, moralizing. *See* **didactic** (2).

presence *noun*
1. The condition or fact of being present ▸ attendance, occurrence. *See also* **existence. 2.** Behavior that reveals one's personality or state of mind ▸ demeanor, manner, style. *See* **bearing** (1).

present¹ *noun*
The current time ▸ nowadays, today. *See* **now.**

present *adjective*
1. In existence now ▸ contemporary, current, existent, existing, immediate, new, now, present-day. **2.** Characteristic of recent times or informed of what is current ▸ current, modern, up-to-date. *See* **contemporary** (2).

present *verb*
To present as a gift to a charity or cause ▸ bequeath, pledge. *See* **donate** (1).

present² *verb*
1. To make known socially ▸ acquaint, familiarize, introduce. **2.** To produce on the stage ▸ act (out), enact, perform. *See* **stage** (1). **3.** To give formally or officially ▸ award, bestow, grant. *See* **confer** (2). **4.** To bring forward as proof or support ▸ adduce, lay, produce. *See* **cite** (1). **5.** To put before another for acceptance ▸ extend, proffer. *See* **offer** (1). *See synonym note at* **offer. 6.** To make something readily available ▸ make available, provide. *See* **offer** (2). **7.** To perform according to one's artistic conception ▸ depict, play, render. *See* **interpret** (2).

present *noun*
1. Something bestowed voluntarily ▸ bequest, gift, presentation. *Slang:* freebie. *See also* **grant**. 2. Something given to a charity or cause ▸ benefaction, contribution, offering. *See* **donation**.

presentable *adjective*
▸ modest, respectable. *See* **decent** (7).

presentation *noun*
1. The act of conferring, as of an honor ▸ bestowal, conference, conferral. *See* **conferment**. 2. Something bestowed voluntarily ▸ bequest, gift, present. *Slang:* freebie. *See also* **grant**. 3. The instance or occasion of being presented for the first time to society ▸ coming-out, debut. 4. An act of offering or the thing offered ▸ invitation, proffer. *See* **offer** (1). 5. An act of showing or displaying ▸ exhibition, show. *See* **display** (1). 6. A performer's distinctive personal version of a song, dance, piece of music, or role ▸ performance, reading, rendition. *See* **interpretation** (1).

present-day *adjective*
▸ current, new. *See* **present¹** (1).

presentiment *noun*
▸ hunch, idea, intuition. *See* **feeling** (1).

preservation *noun*
1. The careful guarding of an asset ▸ husbandry, management. *See* **conservation**. 2. The act or a means of defending ▸ protection, safeguard, shield. *See* **defense** (1). 3. The work of keeping something in proper condition ▸ repairs, upkeep. *See* **maintenance** (1).

preservative *adjective*
Tending to or capable of preserving ▸ conservational, conservative, curatorial, precautionary, protective.

preserve *verb*
1. To prepare food for storage and future use ▸ brine, can, conserve, cure, dehydrate, dry, freeze, jerk, keep, kipper, pickle, pot, put up, refrigerate, salt, season, smoke, souse. 2. To protect an asset from loss or destruction ▸ conserve, husband, save. *See also* **defend**. 3. To keep in a condition of good repair, efficiency, or use ▸ keep up, maintain, sustain. 4. To keep safe from danger, attack, or harm ▸ protect, safeguard, secure. *See* **defend** (1). *See synonym note at* **defend**.

preserve *noun*
Public land kept for a special purpose ▸ park, reservation, reserve, sanctuary. *See also* **common**.

press *verb*
1. To extract from by applying pressure ▸ crush, express, squeeze. 2. To smooth by applying heat or pressure ▸ calender, iron, mangle, roll. *See also* **even**. 3. To apply pressure on, against, or with ▸ elbow, prod, shove. *See* **push** (1). 4. To impel to action ▸ exhort, induce. *See* **urge**. 5. To move into an area or space in large numbers ▸ cram, jam, squeeze. *See* **crowd** (1). 6. To put one's arms around affectionately ▸ enfold, hug. *See* **embrace** (1). 7. To move forward ▸ come along, proceed, progress. *See* **advance** (2). 8. To move over or along with pressure ▸ manipulate, work. *See* **rub** (2). 9. To bring especially the hands or fingers

into contact with ▸ handle, palpate. *See* **touch** (1).

press *noun*
1. A person or group of persons whose occupation is journalism ▸ anchor, anchorman, anchorperson, anchorwoman, columnist, commentator, correspondent, editor, editorialist, fourth estate, journalist, mass media, media, newscaster, newshound, newsman, newspaperman, newspaperwoman, newsperson, newswoman, reporter, stringer. *Informal:* legman. 2. An enormous number of persons or things that are gathered together ▸ horde, mass, throng. *See* **crowd** (1). *See synonym note at* **crowd**. 3. An act or instance of pushing ▸ jostle, shove, thrust. *See* **push** (1).

pressing *adjective*
Demanding immediate attention ▸ acute, crucial, dire. *See* **urgent** (1). *See synonym note at* **urgent**.

pressing *noun*
Urgent solicitation ▸ insistence, insistency, persuasion, urging. *See also* **demand**.

pressure *noun*
1. An oppressive condition of distress ▸ strain, stress, tautness, tenseness, tension. *Informal:* heat. *See also* **anxiety**. 2. Energy that overcomes resistance ▸ might, power, strength. *See* **force** (1).

pressure *verb*
To cause a person or thing to act or move in spite of resistance ▸ coerce, compel, make. *See* **force** (1).

prestidigitation *noun*
▸ legerdemain, sleight of hand. *See* **magic** (2).

prestidigitator *noun*
▸ enchanter, magician, sorcerer. *See* **wizard** (1).

prestige *noun*
1. Credit or respect in the eyes of others ▸ standing, status. *See* **face** (9). 2. A person's high standing among others ▸ good name, reputation. *See* **honor** (2). 3. Wide recognition for one's deeds ▸ glory, note, renown. *See* **fame**.

prestigious *adjective*
▸ celebrated, noted, renowned. *See* **famous**.

presumable *adjective*
▸ assumptive, likely, probable. *See* **presumptive**.

presume *verb*
1. To consider to be true without proof ▸ assume, posit, presuppose. *See* **suppose** (1). *See synonym note at* **suppose**. 2. To express at the risk of rebuff or criticism ▸ dare, hazard, pretend. *See* **venture** (1). 3. To take advantage of unfairly ▸ abuse, exploit, impose, use.

presuming *adjective*
▸ bold, insolent, pert. *See* **impudent**.

presumption *noun*
1. The quality of being arrogant ▸ hauteur, superiority. *See* **arrogance**. 2. Something taken to be true without proof ▸ assertion, postulate, postulation, supposition. *See* **assumption** (1).

presumptive *adjective*
Based on probability or presumption ▸ assumptive, given, likely, presumable, probable, prospective, sup-

posable. *Idiom:* taken for granted. *See also* **due, supposed.**

presumptuous *adjective*
▸ bold, insolent, pert. *See* **impudent.**

presumptuousness *noun*
▸ audacity, boldness, forwardness. *See* **impudence.**

presuppose *verb*
▸ assume, posit, presume. *See* **suppose** (1). *See synonym note at* **suppose.**

presupposition *noun*
▸ given, postulate, premise, supposition. *See* **assumption** (1).

preteen *noun*
▸ juvenile, tot, youngster. *See* **child** (1).

pretend *verb*
1. To take on a false appearance ▸ dissemble, fake, feign. *See* **act** (2). 2. To claim or allege insincerely or falsely ▸ feign, pretext, profess, purport. 3. To express at the risk of rebuff or criticism ▸ dare, hazard, presume. *See* **venture** (1).

pretend *adjective*
Informal Made by humans, often in imitation of something else ▸ manmade, simulated. *See* **artificial** (1).

pretended *adjective*
1. Being fictitious and not real, as a name ▸ assumed, made-up, pseudonymous. *See also* **false, fictitious.** 2. Not genuine or sincere ▸ feigned, insincere, phony. *See* **artificial** (2).

pretender *noun*
▸ charlatan, impostor, phony. *See* **fake** (1).

pretense *noun*
1. A professed but feigned reason or excuse ▸ pretension, pretext. *See also* **excuse.** 2. A display of insincere behavior ▸ dissemblance, sham, show, simulation. *See* **act** (2). 3. Behavior that is assumed rather than natural ▸ airs, mannerism. *See* **affectation** (1). 4. A deceptive outward appearance ▸ guise, mask, semblance. *See* **façade** (2). 5. Lack of sincerity ▸ artificiality, disingenuousness. *See* **insincerity.** 6. A legitimate or asserted right to demand something as one's due ▸ pretension, title. *See* **claim** (1). *See synonym note at* **claim.**

pretension *noun*
1. A professed but feigned reason or excuse ▸ pretense, pretext. *See also* **excuse.** 2. A legitimate or asserted right to demand something as one's due ▸ pretense, title. *See* **claim** (1). *See synonym note at* **claim.** 3. Boastful self-importance or display ▸ grandiosity, ostentation. *See* **pretentiousness.**

pretentious *adjective*
1. Characterized by an exaggerated show of dignity or self-importance ▸ hoity-toity, puffed-up. *See* **pompous.** 2. Marked by outward, often extravagant display ▸ flamboyant, splashy. *See* **showy.** *See synonym note at* **showy.**

pretentiousness *noun*
Boastful self-importance or display ▸ grandioseness, grandiosity, loftiness, ostentation, pomposity, pom-

pousness, pretension. *See also* **arrogance, egotism.**

preternatural *adjective*
1. Departing from the normal ▸ aberrant, atypical, divergent. *See* **abnormal.** 2. Greatly exceeding or departing from the normal course of nature ▸ supernatural, unnatural. 3. Of or relating to existence outside the natural world ▸ metaphysical, superhuman. *See* **supernatural** (1).

preternaturalness *noun*
▸ aberration, deviance, irregularity. *See* **abnormality.**

pretext *noun*
1. A professed but feigned reason or excuse ▸ pretense, pretension. 2. An explanation offered to justify an action or make it better understood ▸ plea, rationale. *See* **excuse** (1). 3. A deceptive outward appearance ▸ face, mask, pretense. *See* **façade** (2).

pretext *verb*
To claim or allege insincerely or falsely ▸ feign, pretend, profess, purport.

pretty *adjective*
1. Pleasing to the eye or mind ▸ enchanting, fetching, lovely, winsome. *See* **attractive** (1). 2. Having qualities that delight the eye ▸ comely, gorgeous, stunning. *See* **beautiful.** *See synonym note at* **beautiful.**

pretty *adverb*
To some extent ▸ quite, rather. *See* **fairly** (2).

pretty penny *noun*
Informal A large sum of money ▸ mint. *Informal:* pile. *See* **fortune** (7).

prevail *verb*
To occupy the preeminent position in ▸ control, reign. *See* **dominate** (1).

prevail on *or* **upon** *verb*
To succeed in causing a person to act or think in a certain way ▸ convince, talk into. *See* **persuade** (1). *See synonym note at* **persuade.**

prevail over *verb*
To win a victory over, as in battle or a competition ▸ conquer, surmount, vanquish. *See* **defeat** (1).

prevailing *adjective*
1. Most generally existing or encountered at a given time ▸ current, epidemic, general, pandemic, popular, predominant, prevalent, rampant, regnant, reigning, rife, ruling, widespread. *See also* **common, pervasive.** 2. Exercising controlling power or influence ▸ key, predominant, reigning. *See* **dominant** (1).

✚ **CORE SYNONYMS:** *prevailing, prevalent, current.* These adjectives denote what exists or is encountered generally at a given time. *Prevailing* applies to what is most frequent or common at a certain time or in a certain place: *took a poll to find the prevailing opinion. Prevalent* suggests widespread existence or occurrence but does not imply predominance: *a belief that was prevalent in the Middle Ages. Current* often stresses the present time and is frequently applied to what is subject to frequent change: *current psychoanalytic theories.*

prevalence *noun*
▸ normality, ordinariness, routineness. *See* **usualness.**
prevalent *adjective*
▸ current, predominant, rampant. *See* **prevailing** (1).
See synonym note at **prevailing.**
prevaricate *verb*
1. To stray from truthfulness or sincerity ▸ palter, shuffle. *See* **equivocate** (2). **2.** To present false information with the intention of deceiving ▸ fib, forswear. *See* **lie²**. *See synonym note at* **lie.**
prevarication *noun*
1. The use or an instance of equivocal language ▸ euphemism, misrepresentation. *See* **equivocation** (1). **2.** An untrue declaration ▸ falsehood, fib, untruth. *See* **lie²**. **3.** The practice of lying ▸ inveracity, perjury, untruthfulness. *See* **mendacity** (1).
prevaricator *noun*
▸ fabulist, faker, fibber. *See* **liar.**
prevent *verb*
To prohibit from occurring by advance planning or action ▸ anticipate, avert, forerun, forestall, forfend, head off, obviate, preclude, prohibit, rule out, stave off, ward (off). *Idioms:* nip in the bud. *See also* **forbid, frustrate, stop.**

✦ CORE SYNONYMS: *prevent, preclude, avert, obviate, forestall.* These verbs mean to stop or hinder something from happening, especially by advance planning or action. *Prevent* implies anticipatory counteraction: *"The surest way to prevent war is not to fear it"* (John Randolph). To *preclude* is to exclude the possibility of an event or action: *"a tranquillity which . . . his wife's presence would have precluded"* (John Henry Newman). To *avert* is to ward off something about to happen: *The pilot's quick thinking averted an accident. Obviate* implies that something, such as a difficulty, has been anticipated and disposed of effectively: *"the objections . . . having . . . been obviated in the preceding chapter"* (Joseph Butler). *Forestall* usually suggests anticipatory measures taken to counteract, neutralize, or nullify the effects of something: *We installed an alarm system to forestall break-ins.*

---

prevention *noun*
The act of preventing ▸ determent, deterrence, exclusion, forestallment, frustration, obviation, preclusion, prohibition. *See also* **forbiddance, stop.**
preventive *or* **preventative** *adjective*
1. Intended to prevent ▸ deterrent, exclusive, interdictive, preclusive, prohibitive, proscriptive. **2.** Defending against disease ▸ defensive, precautionary, prophylactic, protective.
previous *adjective*
1. Next before the present one ▸ foregoing, last, latter, preceding. **2.** Going before ▸ anterior, earlier, preceding. *See* **advance.** **3.** Just gone by or elapsed ▸ ago, lapsed, prior. *See* **past** (1). **4.** Having been such previously ▸ former, onetime, past. *See* **late** (2).
previously *adverb*
1. At a time in the past ▸ before, once. *See* **earlier** (1). **2.** Up to this time ▸ heretofore, yet. *See* **earlier** (2).

prevision *noun*
▸ outlook, prognosis. *See* **prediction.**
previsionary *adjective*
▸ prescient, prognostic. *See* **predictive.**
prey *noun*
▸ casualty, sufferer, wounded. *See* **victim** (1).
price *noun*
1. An amount paid or to be paid for a purchase ▸ charge, expense. *See* **cost** (1). **2.** The expenditure at which something is obtained ▸ cost, price, sacrifice, toll. *Informal:* damage.
priceless *adjective*
1. Of great value or price ▸ expensive, precious, valuable. *See* **costly.** **2.** Causing laughter or amusement ▸ hilarious, humorous, sidesplitting. *See* **funny** (1).
pricey *adjective*
Informal Of great value or price ▸ expensive, precious, valuable. *See* **costly.**
prick *noun*
1. A small mark or hole made by a sharp, pointed object ▸ nick, notch, perforation, puncture, stab. *See also* **cut, scrape.** **2.** A sensation of physical discomfort occurring as the result of disease or injury ▸ pang, smart, soreness. *See* **pain** (1). **3.** A sharp protuberance or projection ▸ prickle, prong, spine. *See* **spike** (1).
prick *verb*
1. To stir to action or feeling ▸ excite, prod, trigger. *See* **provoke** (1). **2.** To penetrate with a sharp edge ▸ bayonet, incise, pierce, slash. *See* **cut** (1).
prickle *noun*
1. A sharp protuberance or projection ▸ prick, prong, spine. *See* **spike** (1). **2.** A sensation of physical discomfort occurring as the result of disease or injury ▸ prick, smart, soreness. *See* **pain** (1).
prickliness *noun*
▸ crankiness, petulance, tetchiness. *See* **temper** (1).
prickly *adjective*
1. Covered with sharp protuberances ▸ brambly, bristly, echinate. *See* **thorny** (1). **2.** Full of irritating difficulties or controversies ▸ nettlesome, spiny, thorny. *See also* **complex, delicate, disturbing, troublesome.**
pricky *adjective*
▸ brambly, bristly, prickly. *See* **thorny** (1).
pride *noun*
1. A sense of one's own dignity or worth ▸ amourpropre, ego, proudness, self-contentment, self-esteem, self-regard, self-respect, self-satisfaction. **2.** The quality of being arrogant ▸ hauteur, superiority. *See* **arrogance. 3.** Exaggerated love for oneself or belief in one's own importance ▸ conceit, narcissism, vanity. *See* **egotism. 4.** A number of animals considered collectively ▸ bevy, gaggle, herd. *See* **flock** (1). *See synonym note at* **flock.**
pride *verb*
To be proud of oneself, as for an accomplishment or achievement ▸ gloat, pique, plume, preen.
prideful *adjective*
1. Overly convinced of one's own superiority and

importance ▸ insolent, superior. *See* **arrogant.**
2. Properly valuing oneself, one's honor, or one's dignity ▸ self-content, self-respecting, self-satisfied. *See* **proud** (1).

pridefulness *noun*
▸ hauteur, superiority. *See* **arrogance.**

prier *or* **pryer** *noun*
A person who snoops ▸ pry, snoop, snooper. *See also* **busybody.**

priest *noun*
▸ ecclesiastic, minister, parson. *See* **cleric.**

priestly *adjective*
▸ ministerial, pastoral. *See* **clerical.**

prig *noun*
1. One who despises people or things regarded as inferior, especially because of social or intellectual pretension ▸ elitist, snob. *Informal:* snoot. **2.** One who is excessively concerned with being proper, modest, or righteous ▸ Mrs. Grundy, priss, puritan. *See* **prude.**

priggish *adjective*
1. Marked by excessive concern for modesty or propriety ▸ genteel, prissy, strait-laced. *See* **prudish.**
2. Overly convinced of one's own superiority and importance ▸ insolent, proud, superior. *See* **arrogant.**

prim *adjective*
1. Marked by excessive concern for modesty or propriety ▸ priggish, prissy, strait-laced. *See* **prudish.**
2. In good order or clean condition ▸ shipshape, tidy. *See* **neat** (1).

prima donna *noun*
▸ protagonist, star. *See* **lead** (1).

primal *adjective*
1. Of, existing, or occurring in a distant period ▸ primeval, primordial. *See* **early** (1). **2.** Of or being an irreducible element ▸ basic, fundamental, primitive. *See* **elemental** (1).

primary *adjective*
1. Most important, influential, or significant ▸ capital, cardinal, central, chief, crucial, first, foremost, head, key, leading, main, major, number one, paramount, pivotal, premier, prime, principal, staple, top, vital. *See also* **elemental, essential, important. 2.** Preceding all others ▸ initial, original, premier. *See* **first** (1). **3.** Not derived from something else ▸ archetypal, primary. *See* **original** (1). **4.** Arising from or going to the root or source ▸ basic, fundamental. *See* **radical** (1). **5.** Marked by the absence of any intervention ▸ direct, firsthand, immediate. **6.** Exercising controlling power or influence ▸ key, predominant, reigning. *See* **dominant** (1).

✦ CORE SYNONYMS: *primary, chief, principal, main, leading, foremost, prime.* These adjectives refer to what is first in importance, influence, or significance. *Primary* stresses first in the sense of origin, sequence, or development: *primary school.* It can also mean first in the sense of "fundamental": *the primary function of this machine. Chief* applies to a person of the highest authority: *a chief magistrate.* Used figuratively, *chief* implies maximum importance or value: *my chief joy.*

Principal applies to someone or something of the first order in power or significance: *their principal source of entertainment. Main* applies to what exceeds others in extent, size, or importance: *the main building on the campus. Leading* suggests personal magnetism, a record of achievement, or capacity for influencing others: *one of the leading physicians of the city. Foremost* emphasizes the sense of having forged ahead of others: *the foremost research scientist of the day. Prime* applies to what is first in comparison with others and to what is of the best quality: *a theory of prime significance; a prime Burgundy.*

prime *adjective*
1. Of fine quality ▸ exceptional, select, superior. *See* **choice** (1). **2.** Exceptionally good of its kind ▸ first-rate, splendid, tiptop. *See* **excellent. 3.** Most important, influential, or significant ▸ chief, key, main, principal. *See* **primary** (1). *See synonym note at* **primary. 4.** Preceding all others ▸ initial, original, premier. *See* **first** (1). **5.** Not derived from something else ▸ archetypal, primary. *See* **original** (1). **6.** Exercising controlling power or influence ▸ key, predominant, reigning. *See* **dominant** (1).

prime *noun*
A time of vigor, youth, or peak condition ▸ efflorescence, flush. *See* **bloom**[1] (1). *See synonym note at* **bloom**[1].

prime *verb*
1. To cause to be ready, as for use, consumption, or a special purpose ▸ fix, ready. *See* **prepare** (1). **2.** To put explosive material into a weapon ▸ charge, load, ready.

primeval *adjective*
▸ ancient, primordial. *See* **early** (1).

primitive *adjective*
1. Not derived from something else ▸ archetypal, primary. *See* **original** (1). **2.** Of or being an irreducible element ▸ basic, elementary, fundamental. *See* **elemental** (1). **3.** Of, existing, or occurring in a distant period ▸ ancient, primeval. *See* **early** (1). **4.** Exhibiting lack of education or knowledge ▸ benighted, unenlightened. *See* **ignorant** (2). **5.** Lacking expert, careful craftsmanship ▸ crude, raw, unpolished. *See* **rude** (1). *See synonym note at* **rude. 6.** Not civilized ▸ barbarian, barbaric, rude. *See* **uncivilized** (1). **7.** Arising from or going to the root or source ▸ basic, fundamental, primary. *See* **radical** (1).

primogenitor *noun*
▸ forebear, parent, progenitor. *See* **ancestor** (1).

primordial *adjective*
1. Preceeding all others in time ▸ initial, original, premier. *See* **first** (1). **2.** Of, existing, or occurring in a distant period ▸ ancient, primeval. *See* **early** (1).

primp *verb*
▸ attire, deck (out), preen. *See* **dress up.**

prince *noun*
▸ boss, director, head, leader. *See* **chief** (1).

princely *adjective*
1. Impressive in size, proportion, or appearance ▸ imposing, magnificent, splendid. *See* **grand** (1). **2.** Will-

ing to give of oneself and one's possessions ▸ big-hearted, magnanimous, unselfish. *See* **generous** (1).

principal *adjective*

1. Most important, influential, or significant ▸ chief, key, main. *See* **primary** (1). *See synonym note at* **primary**. **2.** Exercising controlling power or influence ▸ key, predominant, reigning. *See* **dominant** (1).

principal *noun*

1. The main performer in a theatrical production ▸ protagonist, star. *See* **lead** (1). **2.** Money or property used to produce more wealth ▸ financing, funding, stake. *See* **capital** (1).

principle *noun*

1. A broad and basic rule or truth ▸ axiom, fundamental. *See* **law** (3). **2.** Moral or ethical strength ▸ honesty, integrity, probity. *See* **character** (2). **3.** A statement presented for acceptance, as by a religious group ▸ dogma, teaching. *See* **doctrine**. **4.** The principle taught by a fable or parable ▸ axiom, maxim. *See* **moral**.

principled *adjective*

▸ humane, virtuous. *See* **ethical**.

principles *noun*

▸ morality, standards. *See* **ethics** (2).

print *noun*

1. The visible effect made on a surface by pressure ▸ indent, mark. *See* **impression** (1). *See synonym note at* **impression**. **2.** A visible sign or mark of the passage of someone or something ▸ scent, trace, trail. *See* **track** (1).

print *verb*

To present for circulation, exhibit, or sale ▸ bring out, issue, release. *See* **publish** (1).

printing *noun*

1. The act or process of publishing printed matter ▸ issue, release. *See* **publication** (1). **2.** The entire number of copies of a publication printed from a single typesetting ▸ impression.

prior *adjective*

1. Going before ▸ anterior, earlier, preceding. *See* **advance**. **2.** Just gone by or elapsed ▸ ago, lapsed, previous. *See* **past** (1).

priority *noun*

▸ antecedence, right of way. *See* **precedence**.

prison *noun*

▸ brig, penitentiary. *Informal:* lockup. *See* **jail**.

priss *noun*

▸ Mrs. Grundy, prig, puritan. *See* **prude**.

prissy *adjective*

▸ priggish, proper, strait-laced. *See* **prudish**.

pristine *adjective*

1. Not polluted or altered by human intervention ▸ pure, unpolluted, unspoiled. *See* **fresh** (1). **2.** Not derived from something else ▸ archetypal, primary. *See* **original** (1).

privacy *noun*

▸ isolation, loneliness. *See* **solitude**.

private *adjective*

1. Belonging to, relating to, or affecting a particular person ▸ individual, personal. **2.** Belonging or confined to a particular person or group as opposed to the public or the government ▸ closed-door, personal, privy. *See also* **secret**. **3.** Known about by very few ▸ inside, secret. *See* **confidential** (1). **4.** Not divided among or shared with others ▸ particular, sole. *See* **exclusive** (1).

privation *noun*

1. The condition of being extremely poor ▸ destitution, indigence, need. *See* **poverty** (1). **2.** The condition of being deprived of what one once had or ought to have ▸ destitution, dispossession, loss. *See* **deprivation** (1).

privilege *noun*

1. A benefit granted to a person by law, nature, or custom ▸ birthright, freedom, prerogative. *See* **right**. *See synonym note at* **right**. **2.** Freedom from normal restraints, limitations, or regulations ▸ entitlement, latitude, leeway. *See* **license** (1).

privileged *adjective*

▸ classified, restricted. *See* **confidential** (3).

privy *adjective*

1. Belonging or confined to a particular person or group as opposed to the public or the government ▸ closed-door, personal, private. *See also* **secret**. **2.** Known about by very few ▸ private, secret. *See* **confidential** (1).

prize[1] *noun*

1. A memento received as a symbol of excellence or victory ▸ accolade, cup, award, trophy. *See also* **medal**. **2.** A person or thing worth catching ▸ *Informal:* catch. ▸ plum. *Slang:* brass ring. **3.** Someone or something considered exceptionally precious ▸ find, pearl, plum. *See* **treasure** (1). **4.** The most preferable part of something ▸ cream, elite, top. *See* **best** (1). **5.** Something given in return for a service or accomplishment ▸ award, bonus, plum. *See* **reward** (1). **6.** Recognition of achievement or superiority or a sign of this ▸ award, honor. *See* **distinction** (2).

prize *verb*

To a high regard for or opinion of ▸ cherish, regard, treasure. *See* **value** (1). *See synonym note at* **value**.

prize *adjective*

Exceptionally good of its kind ▸ first-rate, prime, splendid, tiptop. *See* **excellent**.

prize[2] *noun*

Goods or property seized unlawfully ▸ booty, loot. *See* **plunder**.

prizefighter *noun*

A contestant in a boxing match ▸ boxer, fighter, pugilist. *See also* **fighter**.

prizewinner *noun*

▸ champion, medalist. *See* **winner** (1).

pro *noun*

1. *Informal* A person with a high degree of knowledge or skill in a particular field ▸ authority, master, proficient. *See* **expert**. **2.** *Slang* A person who engages in sex for payment ▸ streetwalker, whore. *See* **prostitute**.

pro *adjective*
Informal Having or demonstrating a high degree of knowledge or skill ► master, skilled. *See* **expert.**

probability *noun*
► odds, possibility, prospects. *See* **chance** (3).

probable *adjective*
1. Having a good chance of happening or being true ► contingent, likely, possible, potential. *Idiom:* in the cards. *See also* **believable, inclined, liable. 2.** Based on probability or presumption ► assumptive, likely, prospective. *See* **presumptive.**

probably *adverb*
More likely than not ► believably, likely, presumably, reasonably, seemingly. *Idioms:* all things being equal, in all likelihood (*or* probability). *See also* **maybe.**

probationary *or* **probative** *adjective*
► experimental, trial. *See* **pilot.**

probe *noun*
1. The act or an instance of exploring or investigating ► exploration, investigation, reconnaissance. **2.** Something, as a remark, used to determine another person's attitude ► feeler. *Idiom:* trial balloon. *See also* **advances, introduction. 3.** The act of examining carefully or critically ► inquest, investigation, study. *See* **examination** (1). *See synonym note at* **examination. 4.** A medical inquiry into a patient's state of health ► analysis, diagnosis. *See* **examination** (2).

probe *verb*
1. To test the attitude of ► feel out, sound (out). *Idioms:* put out feelers, run something up the flagpole, send up a trial balloon. **2.** To go into or through for the purpose of making discoveries or acquiring information ► inquire, investigate, reconnoiter. *See* **explore.**

prober *noun*
► inquisitor, interrogator, questioner. *See* **inquirer.**

probing *adjective*
► incisive, penetrating, perceptive. *See* **critical** (2).

probity *noun*
1. The quality or state of being morally sound ► goodness, virtue. *See* **good** (1). **2.** Moral or ethical strength ► honesty, integrity, principle. *See* **character** (2).

problem *noun*
1. A situation that presents difficulty, uncertainty, or perplexity ► case, hornets' nest, issue, matter, question. *Informal:* bind, can of worms, tight spot. *See also* **predicament. 2.** Something that obstructs progress and requires great effort to overcome ► complication, hardship, rigor. *See* **difficulty** (1). **3.** *Informal* A feeling of uncertainty about the fitness or correctness of an action ► misgiving, reservation, scruple. *See* **qualm** (1). **4.** An unfavorable condition, circumstance, or characteristic ► drawback, handicap, minus. *See* **disadvantage.**

problematic *adjective*
1. In doubt or dispute ► disputable, doubtful, questionable. *See* **debatable. 2.** Lacking certainty or clarity ► dubious, indeterminate, questionable, unclear. *See* **ambiguous** (1). **3.** Not likely ► dubious, questionable. *See* **doubtful** (1).

pro bono *adjective*
► uncompensated, unsalaried, volunteer. *See* **unpaid** (1).

proboscis *noun*
► *Slang:* honker, schnoz, snout. *See* **nose** (1).

procedure *noun*
1. An action calculated to achieve an end ► maneuver, measure, move, step, tactic. **2.** A method used for accomplishing something ► course, modus operandi, technique. *See* **approach** (1).

proceed *verb*
1. To move along a particular course ► go, pass, push on, wend. *Idioms:* make (*or* wend) one's way. *See also* **hike, journey, rove. 2.** To move forward ► come along, move, progress. *See* **advance** (2). **3.** To have as a source ► derive, emanate, originate. *See* **stem** (1). *See synonym note at* **stem. 4.** To begin or go on after an interruption ► restart, resume. *See* **continue** (1).

process *noun*
1. A method used for accomplishing something ► course, modus operandi, technique. *See* **approach** (1). **2.** Systematic arrangement and design ► order, organization, scheme. *See* **method** (1).

procession *noun*
1. A number of things placed or occurring one after the other ► order, progression, sequence. *See* **series. 2.** Forward movement ► furtherance, headway, progress. *See* **advance** (1).

proclaim *verb*
1. To make known the presence or arrival of ► announce, herald, introduce, usher in. **2.** To bring to public notice or make known publicly ► advertise, broadcast, declare. *See* **announce** (1). *See synonym note at* **announce. 3.** To make manifest or apparent ► display, reveal. *See* **show** (1).

proclamation *noun*
1. The act of announcing ► annunciation, publication. *See* **announcement** (1). **2.** Something that is announced or communicated ► announcement, declaration, statement. *See* **message** (1).

proclivity *noun*
► disposition, leaning, penchant. *See* **inclination** (1). *See synonym note at* **inclination.**

procrastinate *verb*
► dawdle, dilly-dally, drag. *See* **delay** (2).

procrastination *noun*
► deferment, postponement, suspension. *See* **delay** (1).

procrastinator *noun*
► dawdler, lag, straggler. *See* **laggard.**

procreant *adjective*
Of or relating to reproduction ► generative, procreative, reproductive.

procreate *verb*
► engender, propagate, spawn. *See* **breed** (1).

procreation *noun*
▸ breeding, proliferation, propagation. *See* **reproduction** (3).

procreative *adjective*
Of or relating to reproduction ▸ generative, procreant, reproductive.

procumbent *adjective*
▸ horizontal, prone, prostrate. *See* **flat** (1).

procurable *adjective*
▸ acquirable, attainable, obtainable. *See* **available** (1).

procure *verb*
▸ come by, gain, take. *See* **get** (1).

prod *verb*
1. To apply pressure on, against, or with ▸ press, poke, shove. *See* **push** (1). **2.** To stir to action or feeling ▸ excite, spur, trigger. *See* **provoke** (1).

prod *noun*
1. Something that causes and encourages an action or response ▸ impulse, incentive. *See* **stimulus** (1). **2.** An act of thrusting into or against, as to attract attention ▸ nudge, poke, stab. *See* **dig** (1). **3.** Something that causes an angry or resentful response ▸ incitement, stimulus, trigger. *See* **provocation** (1).

prodigal *adjective*
1. Characterized by excessive or imprudent spending ▸ dissipative, profligate. *See* **extravagant** (1). **2.** Given to or marked by unrestrained abundance ▸ exuberant, lavish, opulent. *See* **profuse** (1). *See synonym note at* **profuse**. **3.** Willing to give of oneself and one's possessions ▸ big-hearted, magnanimous, unselfish. *See* **generous** (1).

prodigal *noun*
A person who spends money or resources wastefully ▸ profligate, spendthrift. *See* **wastrel** (1).

prodigality *noun*
▸ lavishness, squander, wastefulness. *See* **extravagance** (1).

prodigious *adjective*
1. Of extraordinary size and power ▸ behemoth, colossal, gigantic, mighty. *See* **enormous**. **2.** So remarkable as to be difficult to believe ▸ astounding, staggering, unbelievable. *See* **astonishing**.

prodigiousness *noun*
▸ immensity, vastness. *See* **enormousness**.

prodigy *noun*
▸ astonishment, sensation, wonder. *See* **marvel** (1). *See synonym note at* **marvel**.

produce *verb*
1. To bring into existence ▸ bear, bring forth, create, develop, engender, generate, give, give forth, make, originate, provide, spawn, yield. *Idioms:* give birth (*or* rise) to. *See also* **breed, give, offer**. **2.** To bring (a product or idea, for example) into being ▸ develop, generate. **3.** To make as income or profit ▸ clear, gain, yield. *See* **return** (3). **4.** To form by artistic effort ▸ create, write. *See* **compose** (1). **5.** To create by forming, combining, or altering materials ▸ build, compose, shape. *See* **make** (1). **6.** To bring forward as proof or support ▸ adduce, present. *See* **cite** (1). **7.** To

produce on the stage ▸ dramatize, enact, perform. *See* **stage** (1).

produce *noun*
Something produced by human effort ▸ product, production, manufacture, work. *See also* **composition, good**.

✛ CORE SYNONYMS: *produce, bear, yield*. These verbs mean to bring forth as a product: *a mine that produces gold; a seed that finally bore fruit; a plant that yields a medicinal oil.*

---

producer *noun*
1. One that makes or assembles something ▸ builder, constructor, manufacturer. *See* **maker** (1). **2.** A person instrumental in the growth of something, especially in its early stages ▸ contributor, creator. *See* **developer**.

product *noun*
Something produced by human effort ▸ produce, production, manufacture, work. *See also* **composition, good**.

production *noun*
1. Something produced by human effort ▸ produce, product, manufacture, work. *See also* **good**. **2.** The amount or quantity produced ▸ garner, output, yield. **3.** Something that is the result of creative effort ▸ creation, piece, work. *See* **composition** (1).

productive *adjective*
1. Producing or able to produce a desired effect ▸ efficient, instrumental. *See* **effective** (1). **2.** Capable of reproducing ▸ fertile, fecund, fruitful, prolific. *See synonym note at* **fertile**. **3.** Characterized by great productivity ▸ fecund, fruitful, prolific. *See* **fertile** (1). **4.** Acting effectively with minimal waste ▸ efficient, streamlined, well-oiled. *See also* **diligent, methodical**.

productivity *or* **productiveness** *noun*
1. The quality or state of being fertile ▸ fecundity, fruitfulness, prolificacy. *See* **fertility**. **2.** The quality of being efficient ▸ efficiency. *See also* **ability, diligence**.

profanation *noun*
▸ desecration, impiety, violation. *See* **sacrilege**.

profane *adjective*
1. Showing irreverence and contempt for something sacred ▸ blasphemous, impious, sacrilegious. **2.** Not religious in subject matter, form, or use ▸ civil, lay, nonecclesiastical, nonreligious, nonspiritual, secular, temporal, worldly. *See also* **earthly**. **3.** Offensive to accepted standards of decency ▸ bawdy, coarse, lewd, vulgar. *See* **obscene** (1).

profane *verb*
To spoil or mar the sanctity of ▸ desecrate, pollute. *See* **violate** (3).

profaneness *noun*
▸ filthiness, vulgarness. *See* **obscenity** (1).

profanity *noun*
1. The quality or state of being obscene ▸ filthiness, scurrility, smuttiness, vulgarness. *See* **obscenity** (1). **2.** Something that is offensive to accepted standards of decency ▸ dirt, sleaze, smut. *See* **obscenity** (2). **3.** A

profane or obscene term ▸ curse, expletive. *See* **swear-word**.

profess *verb*
1. To claim or allege insincerely or falsely ▸ feign, pretend, pretext, purport. 2. To put into words positively and with conviction ▸ avow, declare, maintain. *See* **assert** (1).

profession *noun*
1. Activity pursued as a livelihood ▸ career, employment, occupation. *See* **business** (2). 2. A system of religious belief ▸ creed, denomination. *See* **religion**. 3. The act of asserting positively or something so asserted ▸ claim, declaration, statement. *See* **assertion**.

professional *adjective*
Having or demonstrating a high degree of knowledge or skill ▸ master, skilled. *See* **expert**.

professional *noun*
A person with a high degree of knowledge or skill in a particular field ▸ authority, master, proficient. *See* **expert**.

proffer *verb*
1. To put before another for acceptance ▸ extend, put forward. *See* **offer** (1). *See synonym note at* **offer**. 2. To state for consideration or debate ▸ offer, put forward, set forth. *See* **propose** (1).

proffer *noun*
An act of offering or the thing offered ▸ invitation, presentation. *See* **offer** (1).

proficiency *noun*
▸ command, expertise, mastery. *See* **ability** (1).

proficient *adjective*
Having or demonstrating a high degree of knowledge or skill ▸ adept, skilled. *See* **expert**. *See synonym note at* **expert**.

proficient *noun*
A person with a high degree of knowledge or skill in a particular field ▸ ace, authority, master. *See* **expert**.

profile *noun*
▸ configuration, design, structure. *See* **form** (1). *See synonym note at* **form**.

profit *noun*
1. Something earned, won, or otherwise acquired ▸ earnings, gain, return. *See also* **increase**. 2. Something beneficial ▸ benefit, blessing, favor. *See* **advantage** (2). 3. Something that contributes to or increases one's well-being ▸ benefit, good, interests. *See* **interest** (1). 4. The quality of being suitable or adaptable to an end ▸ benefit, usefulness, utility. *See* **use** (2).

profit *verb*
1. To make a large profit ▸ batten, cash in. *Slang:* clean up. *Idiom:* make a killing. 2. To be an advantage to ▸ advantage, avail, benefit, help, serve. *Idioms:* do someone good, serve someone well, stand someone in good stead. 3. To derive advantage ▸ capitalize, gain. *See* **benefit** (1). *See synonym note at* **benefit**.

profitable *adjective*
1. Affording profit ▸ advantageous, bankable, fat, gainful, lucrative, moneymaking, remunerative, re-warding. 2. Affording benefit or advantage ▸ favorable, helpful, propitious. *See* **beneficial**. *See synonym note at* **beneficial**.

profitless *adjective*
▸ fruitless, unsuccessful, useless, vain. *See* **futile**.

profitlessness *noun*
▸ fruitlessness, uselessness, vainness. *See* **futility**.

profligacy *noun*
1. Excessive freedom; lack of restraint ▸ dissolution, licentiousness. *See* **license** (2). 2. Excessive or imprudent expenditure ▸ prodigality, squander, wastefulness. *See* **extravagance** (1).

profligate *adjective*
1. Lacking in moral restraint ▸ dissolute, licentious, wanton. *See* **abandoned** (2). 2. Characterized by excessive or imprudent spending ▸ prodigal, thriftless. *See* **extravagant** (1).

profligate *noun*
1. An immoral or licentious person ▸ debaucher, libertine. *See* **wanton** (1). 2. A person who spends money or resources wastefully ▸ prodigal, spendthrift. *See* **wastrel** (1).

profound *adjective*
1. Extending far downward or inward from a surface ▸ abysmal, bottomless. *See* **deep** (1). 2. Resulting from or affecting one's innermost feelings ▸ heartfelt, strong. *See* **deep** (3). 3. Beyond the understanding of an average mind ▸ abstract, esoteric, recondite. *See* **deep** (2).

profoundness *noun*
Intellectual penetration or range ▸ deepness, depth, profundity, weightiness. *See also* **discernment, intelligence, wisdom**.

profundity *noun*
1. Intellectual penetration or range ▸ deepness, depth, profoundness, weightiness. *See also* **discernment, intelligence**. 2. Deep, thorough, or mature understanding ▸ insight, sagacity. *See* **wisdom** (1).

profuse *adjective*
1. Given to or marked by unrestrained abundance ▸ extravagant, exuberant, lavish, lush, luxuriant, opulent, prodigal, riotous, superabundant. *See also* **generous**. 2. Growing profusely ▸ lush, luxuriant, rank. *See* **thick** (3). 3. Characterized by excessive or imprudent spending ▸ prodigal, profligate. *See* **extravagant** (1).

✦ CORE SYNONYMS: *profuse, exuberant, lavish, lush, luxuriant, prodigal, riotous.* These adjectives mean given to or marked by unrestrained abundance: *profuse apologies; an exuberant growth of moss; lavish praise; lush vegetation; luxuriant hair; a prodigal party giver; an artist's riotous use of color.*

◂ ANTONYM: *spare*

---

profuseness *noun*
▸ prodigality, squander, wastefulness. *See* **extravagance** (1).

profusion *noun*
1. Excessive or imprudent expenditure ▸ prodigality,

squander, wastefulness. *See* **extravagance** (1). **2.** A great deal ▸ mass, mountain, wealth. *See* **abundance** (1).

progenitor *noun*
1. A person from whom one is descended ▸ ascendant, forebear, parent. *See* **ancestor** (1). *See synonym note at* **ancestor. 2.** One that precedes, as in time ▸ forerunner, precursor. *See* **ancestor** (2).

progeny *noun*
A person or group descended directly from the same parents or ancestors ▸ brood, child, children, descendant, fruit, generation, get, issue, offspring, posterity, scion, seed, spawn. *See also* **ancestry, family.**

prognosis *noun*
▸ outlook, prevision. *See* **prediction.**

prognostic *adjective*
Of or relating to prediction ▸ prescient, prognosticative. *See* **predictive.**

prognostic *noun*
A phenomenon that serves as a sign of some future good or evil ▸ portent, prognostication, sign. *See* **omen.**

prognosticate *verb*
1. To tell about or make known in advance, especially by means of special knowledge ▸ forecast, portend. *See* **predict.** *See synonym note at* **predict. 2.** To give an indication of something in advance ▸ bode, foretell, prefigure. *See* **foreshadow.**

prognostication *noun*
1. The act of predicting ▸ outlook, prognosis. *See* **prediction. 2.** A phenomenon that serves as a sign of some future good or evil ▸ portent, prefigurement, sign. *See* **omen.**

prognosticative *adjective*
▸ prescient, previsionary. *See* **predictive.**

prognosticator *noun*
▸ diviner, fortuneteller, oracle, seer, soothsayer. *See* **prophet.**

program *noun*
1. An organized list, as of procedures, activities, or events ▸ agenda, calendar, catalog, docket, lineup, orders of the day, schedule, timetable. *See also* **approach, list¹ 2.** A document that complements a public performance, presentation, or offering ▸ bill, card, catalog, playbill, prospectus, syllabus. **3.** A show that is aired on television or radio ▸ airing, broadcast.

program *verb*
1. To enter on a schedule ▸ calendar, docket, schedule, slate. *See also* **list¹, post³. 2.** To teach to accept a system of thought uncritically ▸ brainwash, propagandize. *See* **indoctrinate** (2).

progress *noun*
1. Steady improvement, as of an individual or society ▸ advancement, amelioration, betterment, development, headway, improvement, melioration. *See also* **improvement. 2.** Forward movement ▸ advancement, headway, stride. *See* **advance** (1). **3.** A progression from a simple form to a more complex one ▸ evolvement, growth, unfolding. *See* **development** (1). **4.** The

act of traveling from one place to another ▸ passage, transit. *See* **journey.**

progress *verb*
1. To move forward ▸ come along, move, proceed. *See* **advance** (2). **2.** To attain a higher status, rank, or condition ▸ advance, climb, mount. *See* **rise** (6).

progression *noun*
1. Forward movement ▸ advancement, furtherance, headway. *See* **advance** (1). **2.** A number of things placed or occurring one after the other ▸ order, procession, sequence. *See* **series.** *See synonym note at* **series. 3.** Passage from one form, state, or stage to another ▸ passage, shift, transit. *See* **transition.**

progressive *adjective*
1. Ahead of current trends or customs ▸ advanced, avant-garde, forward, forward-looking, forward-thinking, futuristic, precocious, revolutionary. *Idiom:* ahead of the times. *See also* **inventive, new. 2.** Not narrow or intolerant ▸ liberal, open-minded, tolerant. *See* **broad-minded. 3.** Favoring civil liberties and social reform, especially as a political philosophy ▸ leftist, liberalistic. *See* **liberal** (1). **4.** Proceeding steadily by degrees ▸ gradational, gradual, piecemeal, step-by-step. *Idioms:* one foot after another, one step at a time. *See also* **consecutive, methodical, slow.**

progressive *noun*
One with politically liberal views ▸ left-winger, liberalist. *See* **liberal.**

prohibit *verb*
1. To refuse to allow ▸ disallow, proscribe. *See* **forbid.** *See synonym note at* **forbid. 2.** To prohibit from occurring by advance planning or action ▸ anticipate, avert, obviate. *See* **prevent.**

prohibited *adjective*
▸ banned, outlawed, taboo. *See* **forbidden.**

prohibition *noun*
1. A refusal to allow ▸ ban, proscription. *See* **forbiddance. 2.** The act of preventing ▸ deterrence, forestallment, preclusion. *See* **prevention.**

prohibitive *adjective*
▸ deterrent, preclusive, proscriptive. *See* **preventive** (1).

project *noun*
1. Something undertaken, especially something requiring extensive planning and work ▸ endeavor, enterprise, undertaking, venture. **2.** A piece of work that has been assigned ▸ chore, duty, job. *See* **task** (1). **3.** A method used for accomplishing something ▸ course, modus operandi, procedure, technique. *See* **approach** (1). *See synonym note at* **approach.**

project *verb*
1. To curve outward past the normal or usual limit ▸ balloon, jut, protrude. *See* **bulge** (1). *See synonym note at* **bulge. 2.** To launch with great force ▸ hurtle, propel. *See* **shoot** (3). **3.** To send out heat, light, or energy ▸ emit, radiate. *See* **shed¹** (1). **4.** To form a strategy for ▸ devise, formulate, strategize. *See* **design** (1). **5.** To have in mind as a goal or purpose ▸ design, plan, target. *See* **intend** (1). **6.** To tell about or make

known in advance, especially by means of special knowledge ▸ forecast, prognosticate. *See* **predict.**

projection *noun*
1. A part that protrudes or extends outward ▸ bulb, bulge, jut, knob, knot, lip, overhang, protrusion, protuberance, salient. *See also* **bump.** 2. The act of predicting ▸ outlook, prognosis. *See* **prediction.** 3. What one intends to do or achieve ▸ end, goal, objective. *See* **intention.**

prolegomenon *noun*
▸ overture, preface, prologue. *See* **introduction** (1).

proletariat *noun*
▸ masses, multitude, public. *See* **commonalty.**

proliferate *verb*
1. To give life to ▸ engender, propagate, spawn. *See* **breed** (1). 2. To make or become greater or larger ▸ amplify, boost, enlarge. *See* **increase** (1).

proliferation *noun*
1. The process by which an organism produces others of its kind ▸ breeding, procreation, propagation. *See* **reproduction** (3). 2. The act of increasing or rising ▸ amplification, boost, escalation. *See* **increase** (1). 3. The result or product of building up ▸ development, multiplication. *See* **buildup** (2). 4. The process of increasing in extent or inclusiveness ▸ enlargement, spread. *See* **expansion.**

prolific *adjective*
1. Capable of reproducing ▸ fertile, fecund, fruitful, productive. *See synonym note at* **fertile.** 2. Characterized by great productivity ▸ fecund, fruitful, productive. *See* **fertile** (1).

prolificacy *or* **prolificness** *noun*
▸ fecundity, fruitfulness, productiveness. *See* **fertility.**

prolix *adjective*
▸ long-winded, periphrastic, verbose. *See* **wordy** (1). *See synonym note at* **wordy.**

prolixity *noun*
▸ pleonasm, redundancy, verboseness. *See* **wordiness.**

prologue *noun*
▸ overture, preface, prelude. *See* **introduction** (1).

prolong *or* **prolongate** *verb*
▸ elongate, extend, string out. *See* **lengthen.**

prolongation *noun*
▸ lengthening, protraction, stretching. *See* **extension** (1).

prolonged *adjective*
1. Of long duration ▸ lingering, persistent. *See* **chronic** (2). 2. Having great physical length ▸ extended, lengthy, stretching. *See* **long¹** (1). 3. Extending tediously beyond a standard duration ▸ drawn-out, overlong, protracted. *See* **long¹** (2).

prom *noun*
▸ ball, cotillion, hop, promenade. *See* **dance.**

promenade *noun*
1. An act of walking ▸ ramble, stroll. *See* **walk** (1). 2. A party or gathering for dancing ▸ ball, cotillion, prom. *See* **dance.**

promenade *verb*
1. To walk at a leisurely pace ▸ amble, saunter, wan-

der. *See* **stroll.** 2. To make a public and usually ostentatious show of ▸ exhibit, expose, flaunt. *See* **display** (1).

prominence *noun*
1. Wide recognition for one's deeds ▸ glory, note, prestige. *See* **fame.** 2. A natural land elevation ▸ eminence, rise. *See* **hill** (1).

prominency *noun*
▸ glory, note, prestige. *See* **fame.**

prominent *adjective*
1. Readily attracting notice ▸ conspicuous, outstanding, striking. *See* **noticeable** (1). *See synonym note at* **noticeable.** 2. Widely known ▸ celebrated, noted, renowned. *See* **famous.**

promiscuous *adjective*
▸ fast, loose, sluttish. *See* **wanton** (1).

promise *noun*
1. A declaration that one will or will not do a certain thing ▸ assurance, commitment, covenant, engagement, guarantee, guaranty, oath, pledge, plight, solemn word, vow, warrant, word, word of honor. *See also* **pawn¹.** 2. Indication of future success or development ▸ makings, possibility, potential, prospects. *See also* **material.** 3. Something expected ▸ anticipation, expectation, likelihood, prospect. *See also* **chance, theory.**

promise *verb*
1. To assume an obligation ▸ engage, undertake. *See* **pledge** (2). *See synonym note at* **pledge.** 2. To guarantee by a solemn promise ▸ betroth, vow. *See* **pledge** (1).

promised *adjective*
▸ betrothed, plighted. *See* **engaged** (2).

promising *adjective*
1. Showing great promise ▸ coming, up-and-coming. *Idiom:* on the way up. 2. Inspiring confidence or hope ▸ heartening, likely. *See* **encouraging.**

promote *verb*
1. To raise in rank ▸ advance, elevate, exalt, jump, raise, up, upgrade. *Idioms:* kick upstairs, move up. 2. To help bring about ▸ abet, cultivate, encourage, facilitate, feed, foster, nourish, nurture. *See also* **support.** 3. To attempt to sell or popularize by advertising or publicity ▸ advertise, ballyhoo, boost, build up, cry up, market, popularize, publicize, puff (up), purvey, sell, talk up, tout. *Informal:* pitch, plug. *Slang:* hype, push. *Idioms:* beat the drum for, make a plug for. *See also* **emphasize.** 4. To cause to move forward or upward, as toward a goal ▸ drive, propel, push. *See* **advance** (1). *See synonym note at* **advance.**

promotion *noun*
1. A progression upward in rank ▸ elevation, upgrade. *See* **advancement** (1). 2. Aid or support given by a patron ▸ backing, sponsorship. *See* **patronage** (1). 3. Information disseminated through various media to attract public notice ▸ advertisement, ballyhoo. *Slang:* hype. *See* **publicity** (1). 4. The act or profession of promoting something ▸ billing, publicity. *See* **advertising** (1).

prompt *adjective*
Occurring, acting, or performed exactly at the time appointed ▸ punctual, timely.

prompt *verb*
1. To stir to action or feeling ▸ excite, prod, trigger. *See* **provoke** (1). 2. To be the cause of ▸ generate, induce, trigger. *See* **cause.**

promptly *adverb*
1. Without delay ▸ forthwith, instantly, straightaway. *See* **immediately** (1). 2. In the near future ▸ imminently, quickly. *See* **soon.**

promulgate *verb*
1. To bring to public notice or make known publicly ▸ advertise, proclaim. *See* **announce** (1). *See synonym note at* **announce.** 2. To put in force or cause to be by legal authority ▸ enact, legislate. *See* **establish** (3).

promulgation *noun*
▸ proclamation, publication. *See* **announcement** (1).

prone *adjective*
1. Lying down ▸ horizontal, procumbent, prostrate. *See* **flat** (1). 2. Having or showing a tendency or likelihood ▸ disposed, tending. *See* **inclined** (1). 3. Tending to incur ▸ subject, susceptible, vulnerable. *See* **liable** (2).

proneness *noun*
▸ disposition, leaning, penchant. *See* **inclination** (1).

prong *noun*
▸ prick, snag, spine. *See* **spike** (1).

pronounce *verb*
To produce or make speech sounds ▸ articulate, enounce, enunciate, phonate, say, sound, utter, vocalize, voice. *See also* **say.**

pronounced *adjective*
1. Readily seen, perceived, or understood ▸ evident, noticeable, obvious. *See* **apparent** (1). 2. Readily attracting notice ▸ conspicuous, outstanding, prominent. *See* **noticeable** (1). 3. Without any doubt ▸ clearcut, definite, unquestionable. *See* **decided** (1). 4. Expressed or produced in speech or by the voice ▸ spoken, verbal, vocal, voiced. *See* **oral.**

pronouncement *noun*
1. An authoritative or official decision ▸ edict, judgment, resolution. *See* **ruling.** 2. Something announced or communicated ▸ announcement, declaration, statement. *See* **message** (1).

pronto *adverb*
1. In a rapid way ▸ lickety-split, posthaste, rapidly, swiftly. *See* **fast.** 2. *Slang* Without delay ▸ forthwith, instantly, straightaway. *See* **immediately** (1). 3. *Informal* In the near future ▸ imminently, quickly. *See* **soon.**

pronunciation *noun*
1. Something that takes the place of words in communicating a thought or feeling ▸ statement, utterance, verbalization. *See* **expression** (1). 2. The use of the vocal organs to produce sound or speech ▸ enunciation, utterance, vocalization. *See* **voicing.**

proof *noun*
1. That which confirms ▸ authentication, corrobora-

tion, substantiation, verification. *See* **confirmation** (2). 2. A fact or circumstance that gives logical support to an assertion, claim, or proposal ▸ grounds, wherefore. *See* **reason** (1). 3. A procedure that ascertains effectiveness, value, proper function, or other quality ▸ experiment, trial, tryout. *See* **test** (1).

proof *adjective*
Having the capacity to withstand ▸ impervious, insusceptible, unsusceptible. *See* **resistant** (1).

prop *noun*
A means or device that keeps something erect, stable, or secure ▸ buttress, crutch. *See* **support** (1).

prop *verb*
To make stronger or more resistant ▸ bolster, prop up, reinforce, strengthen. *See* **support** (2).

propaganda *noun*
The systematic widespread promotion of a particular doctrine or idea ▸ brainwashing, disinformation, evangelism, indoctrination, propagandism, proselytism. *See also* **advertising, publicity.**

propagandist *noun*
One who disseminates or engages in propaganda ▸ brainwasher, disseminator, evangelist, indoctrinator, missionary, missioner, pamphleteer, proselytizer. *See also* **advocate.**

propagandize *verb*
▸ brainwash, program. *See* **indoctrinate** (2).

propagate *verb*
1. To raise crops or animals ▸ cultivate, garden. *See* **grow** (1). 2. To give life to ▸ engender, proliferate, spawn. *See* **breed** (1). 3. To bring to public notice or make known publicly ▸ advertise, broadcast, promulgate. *See* **announce** (1).

propagation *noun*
▸ breeding, procreation. *See* **reproduction** (3).

propel *verb*
1. To launch with great force ▸ hurtle, project. *See* **shoot** (3). 2. To force to move or advance with or as if with blows or pressure ▸ butt, shove, slam. *See* **drive** (2). 3. To cause to move forward or upward, as toward a goal ▸ drive, forward, push. *See* **advance** (1). *See synonym note at* **advance.** 4. To stir to action or feeling ▸ excite, prod, trigger. *See* **provoke** (1).

propensity *noun*
▸ disposition, leaning, penchant. *See* **inclination** (1). *See synonym note at* **inclination.**

proper *adjective*
1. Suitable for a particular person, condition, occasion, or place ▸ befitting, correct, right. *See* **appropriate** (1). 2. Suited to one's purpose ▸ expedient, suitable. *See* **convenient** (1). 3. Consistent with prevailing or accepted standards or circumstances ▸ deserved, fitting, merited. *See* **just** (2). 4. In accordance with principles of right or good conduct ▸ principled, virtuous. *See* **ethical.** 5. Marked by excessive concern for modesty or propriety ▸ priggish, prissy, straitlaced. *See* **prudish.**

properly *adverb*
▸ cleanly, correctly, fairly. *See* **fair**[1] (1).

properness *noun*
1. Conformity to recognized standards, as of conduct or appearance ▸ decorum, respectability, seemliness. *See* **decency** (2). **2.** A sense of rightness ▸ grace, propriety. *See* **decency** (1).

property *noun*
1. One's portable property ▸ goods, personal effects, things. *See* **effects. 2.** A thing or set of things, such as land and assets, legally possessed ▸ estate, possessions. *See* **holdings. 3.** Usually extensive real estate ▸ estate, grounds. *See* **land** (1). **4.** A distinctive element ▸ characteristic, feature, trait. *See* **quality** (1). *See synonym note at* **quality.**

prophecy *noun*
Something that is foretold by or as if by supernatural means ▸ augury, divination, oracle, soothsaying, vaticination, vision. *See also* **omen, prediction.**

prophesier *noun*
▸ fortuneteller, seer, soothsayer. *See* **prophet.**

prophesy *verb*
To tell about or make known by or as if by supernatural means ▸ augur, divine, forebode, foretell, soothsay, vaticinate. *See also* **foreshadow, predict.**

✛ CORE SYNONYMS: *prophesy, augur, divine, foretell, prophesy, vaticinate. These verbs mean to tell about something beforehand by or as if by supernatural means: prophesying a stock-market boom; augured a scandal; divined the enemy's victory; foretelling the future; atrocities vaticinated by the antifascists.*

---

prophet *noun*
A person who foretells future events by or as if by supernatural means ▸ augur, auspex, diviner, foreteller, fortuneteller, haruspex, oracle, palmist, prognosticator, prophesier, prophetess, seer, sibyl, soothsayer, vaticinator.

prophetess *noun*
A woman who foretells future events by or as if by supernatural means ▸ diviner, fortuneteller, soothsayer. *See* **prophet.**

prophetic *or* **prophetical** *adjective*
Of or relating to the foretelling of events by or as if by supernatural means ▸ augural, divinitory, fatidic, fatidical, mantic, oracular, sibylline, vatic, vatical, vaticinal, visionary. *See also* **predictive.**

prophylactic *adjective*
▸ defensive, defensive, prophylactic. *See* **preventive** (2).

propitiate *verb*
▸ appease, mollify, soothe. *See* **pacify.**

propitious *adjective*
1. Affording benefit or advantage ▸ favorable, helpful, profitable. *See* **beneficial. 2.** Suited for a particular purpose or occurring at a suitable time ▸ favorable, well-timed. *See* **opportune. 3.** Indicative of future success or full of promise ▸ auspicious, bright, fortunate. *See* **favorable** (1). *See synonym note at* **favorable.**

proponent *noun*
▸ champion, defender, supporter. *See* **advocate** (1).

proportion *noun*
1. Satisfying arrangement marked by even distribution of elements, as in a design ▸ balance, harmony, symmetry. *See also* **agreement. 2.** Relative intensity or amount, as of a quality or attribute ▸ extent, magnitude, scope. *See* **degree** (2).

proportion *verb*
To bring into accord ▸ conform, integrate. *See* **harmonize** (1).

✛ CORE SYNONYMS: *proportion, harmony, symmetry, balance. These nouns mean an aesthetic or satisfying arrangement marked by proper distribution of elements, as in design. Proportion is the agreeable relation of parts within a whole: a house with rooms of gracious proportion. Harmony is the pleasing interaction or appropriate combination of elements: the harmony of your facial features. Symmetry and balance both imply an arrangement of parts on either side of a dividing line, but symmetry frequently emphasizes mirror-image correspondence of parts, while balance often suggests dissimilar parts that offset each other harmoniously: flowers planted in perfect symmetry around the pool; "In all perfectly beautiful objects, there is found the opposition of one part to another, and a reciprocal balance"* (John Ruskin).

---

proportional *or* **proportionate** *adjective*
1. Properly or correspondingly related in size, amount, or scale ▸ commensurable, commensurate, corresponding, equivalent. *Idiom:* in proportion. *See also* **equal. 2.** Characterized by or displaying symmetry, especially correspondence in scale or measure ▸ balanced, regular, symmetric, symmetrical. *See also* **even, parallel.**

proportions *noun*
▸ extent, magnitude, volume. *See* **size** (1).

proposal *noun*
1. Something that is put forward for consideration ▸ motion, nomination, proposition, submission, suggestion. **2.** Something offered ▸ bid, offer, proffer, tender. **3.** A proposition maintained by argument or empirical evidence ▸ contention, hypothesis, thesis. *See* **theory** (2).

propose *verb*
1. To state for consideration or debate ▸ advance, move, offer, pose, proffer, propound, put forward, set forth, submit, suggest, throw out. *See also* **broach, name, offer, refer. 2.** To have in mind as a goal or purpose ▸ contemplate, design, plan, target. *See* **intend** (1).

✛ CORE SYNONYMS: *propose, pose, propound, submit. These verbs mean to state for consideration or debate: proposes a solution; posed many questions; propound a theory; submits a plan.*

---

proposition *noun*
1. Something that is put forward for consideration ▸ motion, submission, suggestion. *See* **proposal** (1). **2.** Personal approach to gain acquaintance, favor, or an agreement ▸ moves, overture. *See* **advances. 3.** A

statement presented for acceptance, as by a religious group ▸ dogma, teaching. *See* **doctrine.**

propound *verb*
▸ offer, put forward, set forth. *See* **propose** (1). *See synonym note at* **propose.**

proprieties *noun*
▸ civility, pleasantry, politeness. *See* **amenities** (2).

proprietor *noun*
▸ master, possessor. *See* **owner.**

proprietorship *noun*
▸ possession, title. *See* **ownership.**

propriety *noun*
1. Conformity to recognized standards, as of conduct or appearance ▸ decorum, respectability, seemliness. *See* **decency** (2). **2.** The quality of conforming to standards of conduct ▸ ethicality, rectitude. *See* **ethics** (1). **3.** Socially correct behavior ▸ etiquette, mores. *See* **manners. 4.** A sense of rightness ▸ grace, properness. *See* **decency** (1).

prosaic *adjective*
1. Having or indicating an awareness of things as they really are ▸ practical, pragmatic. *See* **realistic** (1). **2.** Lacking liveliness, charm, or surprise ▸ aseptic, colorless, pedestrian. *See* **dull** (1).

proscenium *noun*
▸ dais, podium, rostrum. *See* **stage** (1).

proscribe *verb*
1. To refuse to allow ▸ disallow, prohibit. *See* **forbid.** *See synonym note at* **forbid. 2.** To pronounce judgment against ▸ doom, sentence. *See* **condemn** (1).

proscription *noun*
1. A refusal to allow ▸ prohibition, taboo. *See* **forbiddance. 2.** Enforced removal from one's native country by official decree ▸ deportation, extradition. *See* **exile** (1).

proscriptive *adjective*
▸ deterrent, preclusive, prohibitive. *See* **preventive** (1).

prosecute *verb*
1. To institute or subject to legal proceedings ▸ law, litigate, sue. *Idioms:* bring suit, haul (*or* drag) into court. **2.** To begin and carry through to completion ▸ discharge, execute. *Informal:* pull off. *See* **perform** (1). **3.** To compel observance of ▸ effect, implement. *See* **enforce.**

prosecution *noun*
1. The act of beginning and carrying through to completion ▸ execution, transaction. *See* **performance** (1). **2.** An attempt to accomplish or attain ▸ hunt, quest, search. *See* **pursuit** (2).

proselytism *noun*
▸ disinformation, evangelism. *See* **propaganda.**

proselytizer *noun*
▸ evangelist, missionary, pamphleteer. *See* **propagandist.**

prosopopeia *noun*
▸ incarnation, manifestation, personification. *See* **embodiment** (1).

prospect *noun*
1. Something expected ▸ anticipation, expectation,

likelihood, promise. *See also* **chance, theory. 2.** That which is or can be seen ▸ panorama, perspective, vista. *See* **view** (2).

prospect *adjective*
One showing much promise ▸ candidate, hopeful, up-and-comer. *See* **comer** (2).

prospective *adjective*
▸ assumptive, likely, probable. *See* **presumptive.**

prospects *noun*
1. Chance of success or advancement ▸ outlook, future. **2.** Indication of future success or development ▸ makings, possibility, potential, promise. *See also* **material. 3.** The likeliness of a given event occurring ▸ odds, possibility, probability. *See* **chance** (3).

prospectus *noun*
▸ catalog, playbill, syllabus. *See* **program** (2).

prosper *verb*
To do or fare well ▸ batten, boom, flourish, go, thrive. *Slang:* score. *Idioms:* do right for oneself, get (*or* go) somewhere, go great guns, go strong. *See also* **succeed.**

prospering *adjective*
▸ prosperous, roaring, thriving. *See* **flourishing.**

prosperity *noun*
1. A state of health, happiness, and prospering ▸ weal, welfare, well-being. *See also* **condition, happiness. 2.** Steady good fortune or financial security ▸ comfort, ease, luxuriance, luxury, prosperousness, wealth. *Informal:* easy street. *Idioms:* comfortable (*or* easy) circumstances, the good life. *See also* **success, wealth.**

prosperous *adjective*
1. Enjoying steady good fortune or financial security ▸ comfortable, easy, successful, well-heeled, well-off, well-to-do. *Informal:* well-fixed. *Idioms:* comfortably off, in clover, on easy street, on top of the world. *See also* **rich. 2.** Improving, growing, or succeeding steadily ▸ prospering, roaring, thriving. *See* **flourishing. 3.** Suited for a particular purpose or occurring at a suitable time ▸ favorable, propitious, well-timed. *See* **opportune.**

prosperousness *noun*
▸ comfort, ease, wealth. *See* **prosperity** (2).

prostitute *noun*
A person who engages in sex for payment ▸ sex worker, streetwalker, whore. *Slang:* hustler, pro. *See also* **harlot, slut.**

prostrate *verb*
1. To bring down, as from a shot or blow ▸ floor, ground, hew. *See* **drop** (6). **2.** To affect deeply or completely, as with emotion ▸ crush, prostrate. *See* **overwhelm** (2).

prostrate *adjective*
Lying down ▸ horizontal, procumbent, prone. *See* **flat** (1).

prostration *noun*
1. The honoring of a deity, as in worship ▸ extolment, magnification. *See* **praise** (2). **2.** The condition of being extremely tired ▸ burnout, weariness. *See* **exhaustion.**

protagonist *noun*
▶ headliner, star. *See* **lead** (1).

protean *adjective*
▶ all-round, many-sided, multifaceted, various. *See* **versatile** (1).

protect *verb*
▶ preserve, safeguard, secure. *See* **defend** (1). *See synonym note at* **defend**.

protection *noun*
1. The act or a means of defending ▶ barricade, safeguard, shield. *See* **defense** (1). 2. Something that physically protects, especially from danger ▶ harbor, haven, refuge. *See* **cover** (1). 3. The function of watching, guarding, or overseeing ▶ charge, custody, safeguard. *See* **care** (2). 4. The careful guarding of an asset ▶ husbandry, preservation. *See* **conservation**. 5. Money or a favor given as inducement to dishonest behavior ▶ graft. *Informal:* payoff. *See* **bribe**. 6. One assigned to provide protection or keep watch over someone or something ▶ guardian, protector, ward. *See* **guard** (1).

protective *adjective*
1. Tending to or capable of preserving ▶ conservational, precautionary. *See* **preservative**. 2. Defending against disease ▶ defensive, prophylactic. *See* **preventive** (2).

protector *noun*
▶ guardian, picket, ward. *See* **guard** (1).

protectorate *noun*
▶ dependency, province. *See* **possession** (1).

pro tem *adjective*
▶ interim, provisional. *See* **temporary** (1).

protest *verb*
To express opposition ▶ except, oppose, remonstrate. *See* **object** (1). *See synonym note at* **object**.

protest *or* **protestation** *noun*
An expression of opposition ▶ exception, grievance, protestation. *See* **objection**.

protocol *noun*
▶ ceremoniousness, formality, punctiliousness. *See* **ceremony** (2).

protohistory *noun*
▶ ancient history, protohistory, time immemorial. *See* **antiquity**.

protoplast *noun*
▶ master, prototype. *See* **original** (1).

prototypal *adjective*
▶ model, prototypic, representative. *See* **typical** (1).

prototype *noun*
1. A first form from which varieties arise or imitations are made ▶ master, paradigm. *See* **original** (1). 2. One that precedes, as in time ▶ forerunner, precursor. *See* **ancestor** (2). 3. An ideally representative example of a type ▶ archetype, model. *See* **epitome** (1).

prototypical *or* **prototypic** *adjective*
1. Having the nature of, constituting, or serving as a type ▶ archetypical, model, representative. *See* **typical** (1). 2. Not derived from something else ▶ archetypal, primary. *See* **original** (1).

protract *verb*
▶ draw out, elongate, prolongate. *See* **lengthen**.

protracted *adjective*
1. Of long duration ▶ lingering, persistent. *See* **chronic** (2). 2. Extending tediously beyond a standard duration ▶ drawn-out, overlong, prolonged. *See* **long**[1] (2).

protractile *adjective*
▶ extendible, stretch, stretchable. *See* **extensible**.

protraction *noun*
▶ lengthening, prolongation, stretching. *See* **extension** (1).

protrude *verb*
▶ balloon, jut, project. *See* **bulge** (1). *See synonym note at* **bulge**.

protrusion *noun*
▶ knob, lip, protuberance. *See* **projection** (1).

protuberance *noun*
1. A part that protrudes or extends outward ▶ knob, protrusion, salient. *See* **projection** (1). 2. An unevenness or elevation on a surface ▶ lump, outgrowth. *See* **bump** (1).

protuberate *verb*
▶ balloon, jut, project. *See* **bulge** (1).

proud *adjective*
1. Properly valuing oneself, one's honor, or one's dignity ▶ prideful, self-content, self-regarding, self-respecting, self-satisfied. 2. Overly convinced of one's own superiority and importance ▶ haughty, insolent, supercilious. *See* **arrogant**. *See synonym note at* **arrogant**. 3. Marked by extraordinary beauty and splendor ▶ magnificent, splendid. *See* **glorious** (1).

proudness *noun*
1. The quality of being arrogant ▶ hauteur, superiority. *See* **arrogance**. 2. A sense of one's own dignity or worth ▶ ego, self-contentment, self-satisfaction. *See* **pride** (1).

prove *verb*
1. To establish as true or genuine through evidence ▶ authenticate, bear out, circumstantiate, confirm, corroborate, demonstrate, document, establish, evidence, justify, show, substantiate, sustain, validate, verify. *See also* **back, confirm, defend, show**. 2. To subject to a test of effectiveness, value, function, or other quality ▶ check, essay, try (out). *See* **test** (1).

prove out *verb*
To prove valid under scrutiny ▶ hold up, stand up. *Informal:* wash. *Idioms:* hold water, pass muster, ring true.

provenance *noun*
▶ mother, root, source. *See* **origin** (1).

provender *noun*
▶ fare, nourishment, victuals. *See* **food**.

provenience *noun*
▶ provenance, root, source. *See* **origin** (1).

proverb *noun*
A usually pithy and familiar statement generally accepted as wise or true ▶ adage, aphorism, apothegm, axiom, byword, maxim, motto, saw, saying. *See also* **doctrine, expression**.

✦ CORE SYNONYMS: *proverb, saying, maxim, adage, saw, motto, aphorism.* These nouns refer to concise verbal expressions setting forth wisdom or a truth. *Proverb* refers to an old and popular expression that illustrates something such as a basic truth or a practical precept: *"Slow and steady wins the race" is a proverb to live by.* A *saying* is an often repeated and familiar expression: *a collection of philosophical sayings.* *Maxim* denotes particularly an expression of a general truth or a rule of conduct: *"For a wise man, he seemed to me . . . to be governed too much by general maxims"* (Edmund Burke). *Adage* applies to a saying that has gained credit through long use: *a gift that gave no credence to the adage, "Good things come in small packages."* *Saw* often refers to a familiar saying that has become trite through frequent repetition: *old saws that gave little comfort to the losing team.* A *motto* expresses the aims, character, or guiding principles of a person, group, or institution: *"Exuberance over taste" is my motto.* *Aphorism*, denoting a concise expression of a truth or principle, implies depth of content and stylistic distinction: *Few writers have coined more aphorisms than Benjamin Franklin.*

proverbial *adjective*
▸ compact, epigrammatic, pointed. *See* **pithy** (1).
provide *verb*
1. To make something readily available ▸ make available, supply. *See* **offer** (2). **2.** To relinquish to the possession or control of another ▸ furnish, render. *See* **give** (1). **3.** To bring into existence ▸ bear, give, yield. *See* **produce** (1).
provide for *verb*
1. To supply with the necessities of life ▸ keep, maintain, support. *See also* **nourish**. **2.** To help grow or develop ▸ foster, nourish. *See* **nurture**. **3.** To state specifically ▸ detail, particularize, specify, stipulate. *See also* **assert, describe, designate, dictate**.
providence *noun*
1. Careful use of material resources ▸ frugality, thrift. *See* **economy**. **2.** The exercise of good judgment or common sense in practical matters ▸ circumspection, foresight, forethought. *See* **prudence** (1).
provident *adjective*
▸ frugal, saving, thrifty. *See* **economical**.
providential *adjective*
Characterized by luck or good fortune ▸ fortuitous, fortunate, happy, lucky. *See synonym note at* **lucky**. *See also* **opportune**.
provider *noun*
▸ benefactor, contributor, patron. *See* **donor**.
province *noun*
1. An area subject to rule by an outside power ▸ dependency, satellite. *See* **possession** (1). **2.** A sphere of activity, experience, study, or interest ▸ department, domain, field, terrain. *See* **area** (1). *See synonym note at* **area**.
provincial *adjective*
1. Of or relating to the countryside ▸ bucolic, pastoral, rural. *See* **country**. **2.** Restricted in scope, outlook, or

understanding ▸ insular, narrow-minded, small-town. *See* **narrow** (1).
provision *noun*
1. A restricting or modifying element ▸ condition, limitation, qualification, precondition, prerequisite, proviso, reservation, specification, stipulation, term. *Informal:* string. *See also* **restriction**. **2.** A supply stored or hidden for possible future use ▸ cache, reserve, stockpile. *See* **hoard**.
provisional *adjective*
1. Intended, used, or present for a limited time ▸ interim, short-term. *See* **temporary** (2). **2.** Temporarily assuming the duties of another ▸ interim, substitute. *See* **temporary** (1). *See synonym note at* **temporary**. **3.** Depending on or containing a condition or conditions ▸ dependent, provisory, tentative. *See* **conditional**.
provisions *noun*
1. Steps taken in preparation for an undertaking ▸ arrangements, accommodations, plans, preparations. **2.** Material that is fit to be eaten ▸ fare, nourishment, victuals. *See* **food**.
proviso *noun*
▸ condition, qualification, stipulation. *See* **provision** (1).
provisory *adjective*
▸ contingent, provisional, tentative. *See* **conditional**.
provocation *noun*
1. Something that causes others to feel angry or resentful ▸ goad, incitation, incitement, instigation, prod, stimulus, trigger. **2.** An act of taunting another to do something bold or rash ▸ challenge, dare, gauntlet. **3.** The act of annoying or the state of being annoyed ▸ bother, irritation, vexation. *See* **annoyance** (1). **4.** The act or instance of defying ▸ disobedience, noncompliance, rebellion. *See* **defiance** (1).
provocative *adjective*
▸ earthy, risqué, suggestive. *See* **racy** (1).
provoke *verb*
1. To stir to action or feeling ▸ egg on, excite, foment, galvanize, goad, heat up, impel, incent, incentivize, incite, inflame, inspire, instigate, motivate, move, pique, prick, prod, prompt, propel, set off, spark, spur, stimulate, touch off, trigger, work up. *See also* **arouse, energize, move, urge**. **2.** To cause to feel or show anger ▸ incense, infuriate, madden. *See* **anger** (1). **3.** To trouble the nerves or peace of mind of ▸ irritate, nettle, vex. *See* **annoy** (1). *See synonym note at* **annoy**. **4.** To be the cause of ▸ generate, induce, trigger. *See* **cause**. **5.** To behave so as to bring on danger, for example ▸ invite, tempt. *See* **court** (1). **6.** To cause anger, resentment, or hurt feelings ▸ annoy, injure, upset. *See* **offend** (1).

✦ CORE SYNONYMS: *provoke, incite, excite, stimulate.* These verbs mean to stir someone to action or feeling. *Provoke* often merely states the consequences produced: *"Let my presumption not provoke thy wrath"* (William Shakespeare). *"A situation which in the country would have provoked meetings"* (John

Galsworthy). To *incite* is to provoke and urge on: *Members of the opposition incited the insurrection.* *Excite* implies a strong or emotional reaction: *The movie will fail; the plot excites little interest or curiosity.* *Stimulate* suggests renewed vigor of action as if by spurring or goading: *"Our vigilance was stimulated by our finding traces of a large . . . encampment"* (Francis Parkman).

provoker *noun*
▸ assailant, assaulter, attacker. *See* **aggressor.**

provoking *adjective*
▸ bothersome, irritating, unsettling. *See* **disturbing.**

prowess *noun*
1. Skillfulness in the use of the hands or body ▸ deftness, facility. *See* **dexterity** (1). 2. The quality of mind enabling one to face danger or hardship resolutely ▸ bravery, fortitude, gallantry, valor. *See* **courage.**

prowl *verb*
1. To move silently and furtively ▸ creep, lurk, skulk. *See* **sneak** (1). 2. To wait furtively in order to attack someone ▸ ambush, lay for, skulk. *See* **lurk** (1).

prowler *noun*
One who behaves in a stealthy, furtive way ▸ skulker, sneak, sneaker, weasel. *See also* **creep, betrayer.**

proximate *adjective*
1. Not far from another in space, time, or relation ▸ near, nearby, nigh. *See* **close** (1). *See synonym note at* **close.** 2. About to occur at any moment ▸ brewing, impending. *See* **imminent.**

proxy *noun*
1. One who represents the interests of another ▸ ambassador, deputy, steward. *See* **representative** (2). 2. One that can take the place of another ▸ replacement, stand-in, surrogate. *See* **substitute.**

prude *noun*
One excessively concerned with being proper, modest, or righteous ▸ bluenose, Mrs. Grundy, prig, priss, puritan, schoolmarm, Victorian. *Informal:* old maid. *See also* **square.**

prudence *noun*
1. The exercise of good judgment or common sense in practical matters ▸ caution, circumspection, discretion, forehandedness, foresight, foresightedness, forethought, forethoughtfulness, precaution, providence. *See also* **care, caution, common sense.** 2. Careful use of material resources ▸ providence, thrift. *See* **economy.**

✦ CORE SYNONYMS: *prudence, discretion, foresight, forethought, circumspection.* These nouns refer to the exercise of good judgment, common sense, and caution in the conduct of practical matters. *Prudence* is the most comprehensive: *"She had been forced into prudence in her youth, she learned romance as she grew older"* (Jane Austen). *Discretion* suggests wise self-restraint, as in resisting a rash impulse: *"The better part of valor is discretion"* (William Shakespeare). *Foresight* implies the ability to foresee and make provision for what may happen: *She had the foresight to make backups of her computer files.* *Forethought* suggests advance consideration of future eventualities: *The empty refrigerator indicated a lack of forethought.* *Circumspection* implies discretion, as out of concern for moral or social repercussions: *"The necessity of the times, more than ever, calls for our utmost circumspection"* (Samuel Adams).

prudent *adjective*
1. Proceeding from or exhibiting good judgment ▸ commonsensical, levelheaded. *See* **sensible** (1). 2. Careful in the use of material resources ▸ chary, frugal. *See* **economical. 3.** Trying attentively to avoid danger, risk, or error ▸ cautious, chary. *See* **wary** (1). 4. Careful and slow in acting, moving, or deciding ▸ measured, unhurried. *See* **deliberate** (3).

prudish *adjective*
Marked by excessive concern for modesty or propriety ▸ bluenosed, genteel, mannered, mincing, overnice, overrefined, priggish, prim, prissy, proper, puritanical, schoolmarmish, strait-laced, stuffy, Victorian. *Informal:* old-maidish. **Idiom:** prim and proper. *See also* **ceremonious, fussy, stiff.**

prune *verb*
1. To decrease, as in length or amount, by or as if by severing or excising ▸ chop, reap, trim. *See* **cut** (3). 2. To take or leave out ▸ eliminate, exclude, omit. *See* **drop** (8).

pruner *noun*
▸ clippers, cutters, scissors. *See* **shears.**

prurience *or* **pruriency** *noun*
▸ eroticism, lust, passion. *See* **desire** (2).

prurient *adjective*
▸ concupiscent, lewd. *See* **lascivious** (1).

pry *verb*
To look into or inquire about curiously, inquisitively, or in a meddlesome fashion ▸ poke, snoop. *Informal:* nose (around), sniff about (*or* around). **Idiom:** stick one's nose into. *See also* **meddle.**

pry *noun*
A person who snoops ▸ prier, pryer, snoop, snooper. *See also* **busybody.**

pryer *noun*
See **prier.**

prying *adjective*
Unduly interested in the affairs of others ▸ inquisitive, meddlesome, officious. *See* **curious** (1).

prying *noun*
Undue interest in the affairs of others ▸ inquisitiveness. *Informal:* nosiness. *See* **curiosity** (2).

p's and q's *noun*
▸ etiquette, propriety. *See* **manners.**

pseudonymous *adjective*
Being fictitious and not real, as a name ▸ assumed, made-up, pretended. *See also* **false, fictitious.**

psyche *noun*
1. The vital principle or animating force within living beings ▸ soul, vitality. *See* **spirit** (2). 2. The thought processes characteristic of an individual or group ▸ ethos, mentality, mind. *See* **psychology.**

psyched *adjective*
Informal Feeling a very strong emotion ▸ excited, fired up, worked up. *See* **thrilled.**

psychic *adjective*
▸ cerebral, intellectual, psychological. *See* **mental** (1).

psycho *adjective*
Slang Afflicted with or exhibiting irrationality and mental unsoundness ▸ crazy, demented, off. *See* **insane** (1).

psychological *adjective*
▸ cerebral, intellectual, psychic. *See* **mental** (1).

psychology *noun*
The thought processes characteristic of an individual or group ▸ ethos, mentality, mind, mindset, psyche. *Idiom:* what makes someone tick. *See also* **character, identity.**

psychopathy *noun*
▸ dementia, derangement, lunacy. *See* **insanity** (1).

psychotropic *noun*
▸ hallucinogen, narcotic, opiate. *See* **drug** (2).

pub *noun*
▸ inn, lounge, saloon. *See* **bar** (2).

puberty *or* **pubescence** *noun*
▸ adolescence, juvenility, salad days. *See* **youth** (1).

public *adjective*
1. Of, representing, or carried on by people at large ▸ civic, general, societal. *See* **popular** (1). 2. Belonging to, shared by, or applicable to all alike ▸ general, mutual, shared. *See* **common** (2). 3. Not confined to few ▸ free, unrestricted. *See* **open** (3).

public *noun*
1. The common people ▸ masses, proletariat, third estate. *See* **commonalty.** 2. Persons as an organized body ▸ bloc, community, people, society. *See also* **circle.** 3. The body of persons who admire a public personality, especially an entertainer ▸ audience, following. *See also* **fan².**

public assistance *noun*
▸ aid, handout, welfare. *See* **relief** (3).

publication *noun*
1. The act or process of publishing printed matter ▸ circulation, issue, printing, publishing, release. 2. An issue of printed material offered for sale or distribution ▸ edition, opus, organ, paper, title, volume, work. *See also* **advisory, book.** 3. The act of announcing ▸ annunciation, proclamation. *See* **announcement** (1).

public house *noun*
▸ inn, pub, saloon. *See* **bar** (2).

publicity *noun*
1. Information disseminated through various media to attract public notice ▸ advertisement, advertising, ballyhoo, buildup, exposure, promotion, puff, puffery. *Informal:* hoopla, pitch, plug. *Slang:* hype. *See also* **propaganda.** 2. The act or profession of promoting something ▸ billing, promotion. *See* **advertising** (1).

publicize *verb*
▸ advertise, boost, talk up. *See* **promote** (3).

publish *verb*
1. To present for circulation, exhibit, or sale ▸ bring out, issue, print, put out, release, run off. *See also* **spread.** 2. To be the author of a published work or works ▸ author, compose, pen, write. *See also* **compose, write.** 3. To bring to public notice or make known publicly ▸ advertise, broadcast, proclaim, promulgate. *See* **announce** (1). *See synonym note at* **announce.**

publishing *noun*
▸ issue, printing, release. *See* **publication** (1).

pucker *noun*
A line made by the doubling of one part over another ▸ crimp, pleat, wrinkle. *See* **fold** (1).

pucker *verb*
1. To bend together or form a crease ▸ crimp, double, pleat. *See* **fold** (1). 2. To make or become no longer fresh or shapely because of loss of moisture ▸ sear, shrivel, wither. *See* **dry** (1).

puckish *adjective*
▸ frolicsome, impish, sportive. *See* **mischievous** (1).

pudgy *adjective*
▸ chubby, portly, stout. *See* **fat** (1). *See synonym note at* **fat.**

puerile *adjective*
1. Of or characteristic of a child, especially in immaturity ▸ immature, infantile, juvenile. *See* **childish.** 2. Being in an early period of growth or development ▸ immature, juvenile. *See* **young.** *See synonym note at* **young.**

puff *noun*
1. An inhalation, as of a cigar, pipe, or cigarette ▸ drag, draw. *See* **pull** (2). 2. Information disseminated through various media to attract public notice ▸ advertisement, ballyhoo. *Slang:* hype. *See* **publicity** (1). 3. A gentle wind ▸ draft, zephyr. *See* **breeze** (1).

puff *verb*
1. To be in a state of motion, as air or wind ▸ bluster, gust. *See* **blow¹** (1). 2. To breathe hard ▸ gasp, huff. *See* **pant** (1). 3. To expand from or as if from internal pressure ▸ bloat, inflate. *See* **swell** (1). 4. To attempt to sell or promote by advertising or publicity ▸ ballyhoo, boost, talk up. *See* **promote** (3). 5. To talk with excessive pride ▸ gasconade, vaunt. *See* **boast** (1). 6. To make something seem greater than is actually the case ▸ hyperbolize, magnify. *See* **exaggerate** (1).

puffed-up *or* **puffy** *adjective*
▸ hoity-toity, pretentious. *See* **pompous.**

puffery *noun*
▸ advertisement, ballyhoo. *Slang:* hype. *See* **publicity** (1).

pugilist *noun*
A contestant in a boxing match ▸ boxer, fighter, prizefighter. *See also* **fighter.**

pugnacious *adjective*
▸ belligerent, combative, hostile. *See* **aggressive** (1). *See synonym note at* **aggressive.**

pugnacity *or* **pugnaciousness** *noun*
1. Hostile or warlike behavior or attitude ▸ conten-

tiousness, militance, truculence. *See* **aggression** (1). **2.** The power or will to fight ▸ belligerence, combativeness, contentiousness. *See* **fight** (2).

puke *verb*
Informal To eject the contents of the stomach through the mouth ▸ retch, throw up. *Slang:* heave. *See* **vomit** (1).

pulchritudinous *adjective*
▸ comely, gorgeous, stunning. *See* **beautiful.**

pule *verb*
▸ weep, whimper, whine. *See* **cry** (1).

pull *verb*
1. To exert force so as to move something toward the source of the force ▸ drag, draw, haul, lug, tow, tug, yank. *See also* **trail. 2.** To remove from a fixed position ▸ extract, pick, pluck, rend, tear, wrench, wrest, yank. *See also* **remove. 3.** *Informal* To direct or impel to oneself by some quality or action ▸ allure, draw. *See* **attract** (1). **4.** To take back or remove ▸ repeal, rescind, revoke. *See* **lift** (5).

pull back *verb*
To move back in the face of enemy attack or after a defeat ▸ draw back, pull out, withdraw. *See* **retreat** (4).

pull down *verb*
1. To pull down or break up so that reconstruction is impossible ▸ dismantle, level, tear down. *See* **destroy** (2). **2.** *Informal* To receive, as wages, for one's labor ▸ get, make. *See* **earn** (2).

pull in *verb*
1. To come to a particular place ▸ get in, reach, turn up. *See* **arrive** (1). **2.** To control, restrict, or arrest ▸ bridle, check, curb. *See* **restrain. 3.** *Informal* To receive, as wages, for one's labor ▸ get, make. *See* **earn** (2).

pull off *verb*
1. *Informal* To be responsible for or guilty of an error or crime ▸ carry out, commit, do, perpetrate. **2.** *Informal* To begin and carry through to completion ▸ execute, prosecute. *See* **perform** (1).

pull on *verb*
1. To put an article of clothing on one's person ▸ put on, slip on. *See* **don** (1). **2.** To take into the mouth and swallow a liquid ▸ down, sip, swill. *See* **drink** (1).

pull out *verb*
1. To move away from a place ▸ exit, go away, retire. *See* **go** (1). **2.** To move back in the face of enemy attack or after a defeat ▸ draw back, fall back, withdraw. *See* **retreat** (4). **3.** To withdraw from an association or federation ▸ break off, secede, splinter (off), withdraw. *Informal:* split (away). *See also* **quit.**

pull through *verb*
To exist in spite of adversity ▸ persist, ride out. *See* **survive** (1).

pull *noun*
1. The act of drawing or pulling a load ▸ draft, drag, draw, haul, tow, traction, yank. *See also* **jerk. 2.** An inhalation, as of a cigar, pipe, or cigarette ▸ draft, drag, draw, puff. *Slang:* hit. **3.** An act of drinking or the amount swallowed ▸ swallow, taste. *Informal:*

swig. *See* **drink** (2). **4.** *Informal* Power to sway or affect based on prestige, wealth, ability, or position ▸ force, sway, weight. *See* **influence** (1). **5.** *Informal* The power or quality of attracting ▸ allure, draw, enchantment. *See* **attraction** (1).

✛ CORE SYNONYMS: *pull, drag, draw, haul, tow, tug.* These verbs mean to exert force so as to move something toward the source of the force: *pull a sled up a hill; drag furniture across the floor; drew up a chair; hauls wood from the forest; a car that tows a trailer; tugged at the oars.*

◂ ANTONYM: *push*

---

pullback *noun*
▸ fallback, pullout, withdrawal. *See* **retreat** (1).

pullout *noun*
▸ evacuation, fallback, withdrawal. *See* **retreat** (1).

pullulate *verb*
▸ bristle, crawl, swarm. *See* **teem**[1].

pulp *verb*
▸ mush, squash. *See* **crush** (1). *See synonym note at* **crush.**

pulpit *noun*
▸ dais, podium, proscenium. *See* **stage** (1).

pulpy *or* **pulpous** *adjective*
▸ mushy, spongy, yielding. *See* **soft** (1).

pulsate *verb*
▸ drum, pulse, throb. *See* **beat** (5).

pulsation *noun*
▸ pulse, throb. *See* **beat** (3).

pulse *noun*
A rhythmic contraction or sound ▸ pulsation, throb. *See* **beat** (3).

pulse *verb*
1. To make rhythmic contractions, sounds, or movements ▸ drum, pulsate, throb. *See* **beat** (5). **2.** To shine intensely and blindingly ▸ blaze, throb. *See* **glare** (2).

pulverize *verb*
1. To break up into tiny particles ▸ atomize, grind, mill. *See* **crush** (2). **2.** To pull down or break up so that reconstruction is impossible ▸ dismantle, level, tear down. *See* **destroy** (2).

pulverous *or* **pulverulent** *adjective*
▸ dusty, powdery. *See* **fine**[1] (6).

pummel *verb*
▸ assault, batter, thresh. *See* **beat** (1). *See synonym note at* **beat.**

pump *verb*
1. To remove a liquid by a steady, gradual process ▸ bleed, strain. *See* **drain** (1). **2.** To put a question to someone ▸ interrogate, quiz. *Informal:* grill. *See* **ask** (1).

pump up *verb*
Slang To increase markedly in level or intensity, especially of sound ▸ amplify, heighten, raise. *See* **elevate** (2).

punch *verb*
1. To deliver a sudden, sharp blow to ▸ jab, sock, whack. *See* **hit** (1). **2.** To pass into or through by

overcoming resistance ▸ break (through), puncture. *See* **penetrate** (1). **3.** To penetrate with a sharp edge ▸ bayonet, incise, pierce, slash. *See* **cut** (1). **4.** To make a hole or other opening in ▸ perforate, pierce, puncture. *See* **breach** (1).

punch *noun*
1. A sudden heavy stroke ▸ crack, hit, swat, whack. *See* **blow²** (1). **2.** An act of thrusting into or against, as to attract attention ▸ nudge, poke, prod. *See* **dig** (1). **3.** Capacity for work or vigorous activity ▸ might, potency, power. *See* **energy**. **4.** An aggressive readiness along with energy to undertake taxing efforts ▸ enterprise, initiative, hustle. *See* **drive** (2). **5.** *Slang* A stimulating or intoxicating effect ▸ *Informal:* sting, wallop. *See* **kick**.

punch-drunk *adjective*
▸ confounded, perplexed, turbid. *Informal:* mixed-up. *See* **confused** (1).

punctilious *adjective*
1. Marked by attentiveness to every detail ▸ fastidious, meticulous, painstaking, scrupulous. *See* **careful** (2). *See synonym note at* **careful**. **2.** Fond of or given to ceremony ▸ courtly, formal, stately. *See* **ceremonious** (1).

punctiliousness *noun*
1. Attentiveness to detail ▸ fastidiousness, meticulousness, painstaking. *See* **thoroughness**. **2.** Strict observance of social conventions ▸ ceremoniousness, formality, protocol. *See* **ceremony** (2).

punctual *adjective*
Occurring, acting, or performed exactly at the time appointed ▸ prompt, timely. **Idioms:** on the dot (*or* nose), on schedule, on time.

puncture *verb*
1. To make a hole or other opening in ▸ perforate, pierce. *See* **breach** (1). **2.** To pass into or through by overcoming resistance ▸ break (through), punch. *See* **penetrate** (1). **3.** To cause to be no longer believed or valued ▸ deflate, explode. *Informal:* shoot down. *See* **discredit** (1). **4.** To lower the pride or dignity of ▸ degrade, demean, humiliate. *See* **humble** (1). **5.** To penetrate with a sharp edge ▸ bayonet, incise, pierce, slash. *See* **cut** (1).

puncture *noun*
A small mark or hole made by a sharp, pointed object ▸ nick, perforation. *See* **prick** (1).

pundit *noun*
1. A person noted for wisdom, knowledge, and judgment ▸ guru, scholar. *See* **sage**. **2.** A person who evaluates and reports on the worth of something ▸ judge, reviewer. *See* **critic** (1).

pungent *adjective*
1. Having a sharp, penetrating flavor or aroma ▸ piquant, sharp, zesty. *See* **spicy** (1). **2.** Precisely meaningful and tersely cogent ▸ epigrammatic, pointed. *See* **pithy** (1). **3.** So sharp as to cause mental pain ▸ caustic, scathing, sharp, vitriolic. *See* **biting**. **4.** Having a sharp, unpleasant, alkaline taste ▸ acrid, harsh. *See* **bitter** (1).

puniness *noun*
▸ decrepitude, feebleness, weakliness. *See* **infirmity** (1).

punish *verb*
To subject one to a penalty for a wrong ▸ castigate, chastise, correct, discipline, penalize, sentence. *See also* **chastise, condemn, fine²**.

✛ CORE SYNONYMS: *punish, correct, chastise, discipline, castigate, penalize.* These verbs mean to subject a person to something negative for an offense, sin, or fault. *Punish* is the least specific: *The principal punished the students who were caught cheating.* To *correct* is to punish so that the offender will mend his or her ways: *Regulations formerly permitted prison wardens to correct unruly inmates.* *Chastise* implies either corporal punishment or a verbal rebuke as a means of effecting improvement in behavior: *I chastised the bully by giving him a thrashing. The sarcastic child was roundly chastised for insolence.* *Discipline* stresses punishment inflicted by an authority in order to control or to eliminate unacceptable conduct: *The worker was disciplined for insubordination.* *Castigate* means to censure or criticize severely, often in public: *The judge castigated the attorney for badgering the witness.* *Penalize* usually implies the forfeiture of money or of a privilege or gain because rules or regulations have been broken: *Those who file their income-tax returns late will be penalized.*

---

punishing *adjective*
1. Inflicting or aiming to inflict punishment ▸ correctional, disciplinary, penal, punitive, punitory. **2.** Painfully intense ▸ brutal, harsh, severe. *See* **bitter** (2).

punishment *noun*
Something, such as loss, pain, or confinement, imposed for wrongdoing ▸ castigation, chastisement, correction, deserts, discipline, infliction, payment, penalty, penance, rap, retribution, sentence. *See also* **fine, ruling**.

punitive *or* **punitory** *adjective*
▸ disciplinary, penal, punitory. *See* **punishing** (1).

punk *noun*
1. *Slang* A person who treats others violently or roughly ▸ hoodlum, ruffian, tough. *See* **thug**. **2.** *Informal* A totally insignificant person ▸ nobody, nothing, small fry. *See* **nonentity**. **3.** *Slang* A small or young person ▸ pip-squeak, runt, scrub. *See* **squirt** (2).

punk *verb*
Slang To cause to accept something false by trickery or misrepresentation ▸ dupe, fool, hoodwink. *See* **deceive**.

puny *adjective*
1. Not physically strong ▸ feeble, frail, unsound. *See* **weak** (1). **2.** Conspicuously deficient in quantity, fullness, or extent ▸ poor, scant, skimpy. *See* **meager** (1).

pup *noun*
▸ pip-squeak, runt, scrub. *See* **squirt** (2).

pupil *noun*
▸ apprentice, learner, scholar. *See* **student**.

puppet *noun*
▸ stooge, tool. *See* **pawn²**.

puppy *noun*
▶ pip-squeak, runt, scrub. *See* **squirt** (2).
purblind *adjective*
▶ obtuse, unperceptive. *See* **blind** (3).
purchase *verb*
To acquire in exchange for money ▶ pay for, purchase. *Slang:* score. *See* **buy** (1).
purchase *noun*
1. Something bought or capable of being bought ▶ buy. *See also* **effects**. 2. A place providing support for the foot in climbing ▶ foothold, footing, perch, toehold.
purchaser *noun*
▶ customer, patron, user. *See* **consumer**.
pure *adjective*
1. Free from extraneous elements ▶ absolute, clear, genuine, perfect, plain, sheer, simple, unadulterated, undiluted, unmixed. *See also* **perfect**. 2. Not diluted or mixed with other substances ▶ unblended, undiluted. *See* **straight** (1). 3. Not polluted or altered by human intervention ▶ pristine, undeveloped, unspoiled. *See* **fresh** (1). 4. Completely such, without qualification or exception ▶ all-out, downright, sheer. *See* **utter²**. 5. Free from evil and corruption ▶ uncorrupted, untainted. *See* **innocent** (1). 6. Morally beyond reproach ▶ modest, moral, virginal. *See* **chaste**.

✢ CORE SYNONYMS: *pure, absolute, sheer, simple, unadulterated*. These adjectives mean free of extraneous elements: *pure gold; absolute oxygen; sheer alcohol; a simple substance; unadulterated coffee*.

---

pureblood *or* **pureblooded** *adjective*
▶ full-blooded, pedigreed, purebred. *See* **thoroughbred** (1).
purebred *adjective*
▶ highbred, pedigreed, pureblood. *See* **thoroughbred** (1).
purely *adverb*
▶ fully, totally, utterly. *See* **completely** (1).
pureness *noun*
▶ clarity, cleanliness, immaculacy. *See* **purity** (1).
purgation *noun*
1. A freeing from sin, guilt, or defilement ▶ ablution, redemption. *See* **purification** (2). 2. The act or process of discharging bodily wastes ▶ evacuation, excretion. *See* **elimination** (3).
purgative *noun*
Something that purifies or cleans ▶ antiseptic, cathartic, cleaner. *See* **purifier**.
purgative *or* **purgatorial** *adjective*
1. Of, relating to, or tending to eliminate ▶ evacuative, urinal. *See* **eliminative**. 2. Serving to purify of sin ▶ expiatory, lustral, lustrative, purificatory.
purge *verb*
1. To free from sin, guilt, or defilement ▶ expiate, lustrate, pardon. *See* **purify** (1). 2. To free from a charge of guilt ▶ acquit, exonerate, vindicate. *See* **clear** (9). 3. To get rid of, especially by banishment or execution ▶ liquidate, wipe out. *See* **eliminate** (1). *See*

synonym note at **eliminate**. 4. To discharge wastes from the body ▶ excrete, void. *See* **eliminate** (4).
purge *noun*
The act or process of eliminating ▶ eradication, removal. *See* **elimination** (1).
purification *noun*
1. The act or process of removing physical impurities ▶ catharsis, clarification, cleaning, cleansing, lavation, refinement. 2. A freeing from sin, guilt, or defilement ▶ ablution, catharsis, lustration, pardoning, purgation, redemption. *See also* **atonement**.
purificatory *adjective*
▶ expiatory, lustrative, purgatorial. *See* **purgative** (2).
purifier *noun*
Something that purifies or cleans ▶ antiseptic, cathartic, clarifier, cleaner, cleanser, disinfectant, purgative, refiner, refinery.
purify *verb*
1. To free from sin, guilt, or defilement ▶ atone, cleanse, expiate, lustrate, pardon, purge, redeem. 2. To remove impurities from ▶ clarify, clean, cleanse, refine. *See also* **clean**.
purist *adjective*
▶ bookish, literary, scholastic. *See* **pedantic**.
puritan *noun*
One excessively concerned with being proper, modest, or righteous ▶ Mrs. Grundy, priss, schoolmarm. *See* **prude**.
puritan *adjective*
Renouncing material comforts and pleasures ▶ austere, self-denying. *See* **ascetic**.
puritanical *adjective*
1. Not tolerant of the beliefs or opinions of others ▶ close-minded, illiberal, racist. *See* **intolerant** (1). 2. Marked by excessive concern for modesty or propriety ▶ priggish, prissy, strait-laced. *See* **prudish**. 3. Renouncing material comforts and pleasures ▶ austere, self-denying. *See* **ascetic**.
purity *noun*
1. The condition of being clean and free of contaminants ▶ clarity, cleanliness, cleanness, disinfection, immaculacy, immaculateness, pureness, taintlessness. *See also* **sterility**. 2. The condition of being chaste ▶ modesty, morality, virginity. *See* **chastity**.
purl *verb*
1. To move freely as a liquid ▶ circulate, run, stream. *See* **flow** (1). 2. To flow with or make a soft liquid sound ▶ gurgle, lap, ripple. *See* **burble** (1).
purl *noun*
A soft liquid sound ▶ gurgle, lap, murmur. *See* **burble**.
purlieu *noun*
▶ locale, surroundings. *See* **environment** (1).
purloin *verb*
▶ carry off, snatch, thieve. *See* **steal** (1). *See synonym note at* **steal**.
purloiner *noun*
▶ burglar, robber, stealer. *See* **thief**.
purport *noun*
1. Something that is conveyed or signified ▶ import,

sense, significance. *See* **meaning** (1). **2.** The general sense or significance, as of an action or statement ▸ burden, substance. *See* **import** (1). **3.** The current of thought uniting all elements of a text or discourse ▸ drift, intent, tenor. *See* **thrust** (1).

purport *verb*
To claim or allege insincerely or falsely ▸ feign, pretend, pretext, profess.

purported *adjective*
▸ hypothetical, presumptive, suppositional. *See* **supposed.**

purpose *noun*
1. The proper activity of a person or thing ▸ job, role, task. *See* **function** (1). **2.** What one intends to do or achieve ▸ end, goal, objective. *See* **intention.** *See synonym note at* **intention. 3.** Unwavering firmness of character, action, or will ▸ determination, resolve, will. *See* **decision** (2).

purpose *verb*
To have in mind as a goal or purpose ▸ design, plan, target. *See* **intend** (1).

purposeful *adjective*
▸ intentional, premeditated, willful. *See* **deliberate** (1).

purposefulness *noun*
▸ determination, purpose, resolve, will. *See* **decision** (2).

purposeless *adjective*
1. Without aim, purpose, or intent ▸ desultory, pointless, rambling. *See* **aimless. 2.** Lacking rational direction or purpose ▸ pointless, senseless. *See* **mindless** (1).

purr *verb*
To make a continuous low-pitched droning sound ▸ buzz, drone, whir. *See* **hum.**

purr *noun*
A continuous low-pitched droning sound ▸ bumble, burr, drone. *See* **hum.**

purring *adjective*
Slang In action or full operation ▸ functioning, operating, working. *See* **active** (1).

purse *noun*
A closeable container for carrying money and personal items ▸ bag, clutch, handbag, pocketbook, reticule.

pursuance *noun*
▸ hunt, quest, search. *See* **pursuit** (2).

pursue *verb*
1. To follow another with the intent of overtaking and capturing ▸ chase (down), gun for, hunt, run after. *Idioms:* be (*or* go) in pursuit, give chase. *See also* **follow, seek. 2.** To work at, especially as a profession ▸ do, follow, practice. *Idiom:* hang out one's shingle. *See also* **labor. 3.** To go through life in a certain way ▸ conduct, pass. *See* **lead** (3). **4.** To attempt to gain the affection of ▸ chase, woo. *See* **court** (2).

pursuing *noun*
▸ hunt, quest, search. *See* **pursuit** (2).

pursuit *noun*
1. The following of another in an attempt to overtake and capture ▸ chase, hot pursuit, hunt. **2.** An attempt to accomplish or attain ▸ hunt, prosecution, pursuance, pursuing, quest, search. *See also* **expedition, exploration. 3.** Activity pursued as a livelihood ▸ practice, profession, vocation. *See* **business** (2).

purvey *verb*
▸ advertise, market, sell. *See* **promote** (3).

purview *noun*
1. An area or set of parameters within which something or someone exists, acts, or has influence ▸ extent, realm, scope. *See* **range** (1). *See synonym note at* **range. 2.** The extent of one's perception, understanding, knowledge, or vision ▸ range, scope. *See* **ken.**

push *verb*
1. To apply pressure on, against, or with ▸ bear (down), butt, crowd, crush, depress, dig, elbow, jab, jam, jog, jostle, nudge, poke, press, prod, ram, shoulder, shove, thrust. **2.** To cause to move forward or upward, as toward a goal ▸ drive, forward, propel. *See* **advance** (1). **3.** To move forward ▸ come along, proceed, progress. *See* **advance** (2). **4.** To force to move or advance with or as if with blows or pressure ▸ butt, shove, slam. *See* **drive** (2). *See synonym note at* **drive. 5.** *Informal* To force one's way into a place or situation ▸ elbow, shove. *See* **muscle. 6.** *Slang* To attempt to sell or popularize by advertising or publicity ▸ advertise, publicize, talk up. *See* **promote** (3). **7.** *Slang* To engage in the illicit sale of narcotics ▸ deal, peddle. *See also* **sell. 8.** To force to work hard ▸ drive, task, tax, work. *Idiom:* crack the whip. *See also* **force. 9.** To urge to move along ▸ chase, herd, run. *See* **drive** (3).

push off *verb*
Informal To move away from a place ▸ exit, go away, retire. *See* **go** (1).

push on *verb*
To move along a particular course ▸ go, pass, proceed, wend. *Idioms:* make (*or* wend) one's way. *See also* **advance, journey, rove.**

push *noun*
1. An act or instance of pushing ▸ butt, jam, jostle, press, shove, thrust. *See also* **dig. 2.** An organized effort to accomplish a purpose ▸ crusade, movement. *See* **drive** (1). **3.** Something that causes and encourages an action or response ▸ impulse, incentive. *See* **stimulus** (1). **4.** *Informal* An aggressive readiness along with energy to undertake taxing efforts ▸ initiative, hustle, punch. *See* **drive** (2).

pusher *noun*
Slang A person who sells narcotics illegally ▸ dealer, peddler, trafficker. *Slang:* connection.

pushiness *noun*
▸ audacity, boldness, forwardness. *See* **impudence.**

pushover *noun*
1. A person who is easily deceived or victimized ▸ butt, tool, victim. *See* **dupe** (1). **2.** A weak or ineffectual person ▸ *Slang:* cream puff, wimp. *See* **weakling. 3.** *Informal* An easily accomplished task ▸ cinch, snap, walkover. *See* **breeze** (2). *See synonym note at* **breeze.**

pushy *adjective*
▸ bold, insolent, pert. *See* **impudent.**

pusillanimity *noun*
▸ faint-heartedness, funk. *Slang:* gutlessness. *See* **cowardice.**

pusillanimous *adjective*
▸ faint-hearted, dastardly. *Slang:* gutless. *See* **cowardly.**

puss *noun*
1. *Slang* The opening in the body through which food is ingested ▸ chops, maw. *Slang:* trap. *See* **mouth** (1). 2. *Slang* The front surface of the head ▸ countenance, visage. *See* **face** (1).

pussyfoot *verb*
1. To move silently and furtively ▸ lurk, prowl. *See* **sneak** (1). 2. *Informal* To use evasive or deliberately vague language ▸ hedge, shuffle. *See* **equivocate** (1).

put *verb*
1. To put in a certain position or location ▸ locate, place, situate. *See* **position.** 2. To calculate approximately ▸ place, reckon. *See* **estimate** (2). 3. To establish and apply as compulsory ▸ assess, exact, impose, levy. 4. To place something at risk, as in a game of chance ▸ bet, stake, wager. *See* **gamble** (2). 5. To seek an answer to a question ▸ ask, pose, raise. *See also* **say.** 6. To utter publicly ▸ disclose, divulge, voice. *See* **air** (2). 7. To express in another language ▸ interpret, render. *See* **translate** (1). 8. To convey in language or words of a particular form ▸ express, formulate. *See* **phrase.** 9. To have or put in a customary place ▸ cache, keep, store.

put away *verb*
1. *Informal* To engulf completely ▸ devour, ravage, waste. *See* **consume** (1). 2. *Informal* To take the life of a person or persons unlawfully ▸ assassinate, kill, slay. *See* **murder** (1). 3. To put in or as if in prison ▸ confine, incarcerate, lock (up). *See* **imprison.** 4. *Informal* To take food into the body as nourishment ▸ consume, devour, ingest, partake. *See* **eat** (1). *See synonym note at* **eat.**

put by *verb*
To keep for future use ▸ lay aside, salt away, store. *See* **save** (1).

put down *verb*
1. To overcome opposition or uprising with overwhelming force ▸ crush, extinguish, quell. *See* **suppress** (1). 2. *Slang* To lower the pride or dignity of ▸ degrade, demean, humiliate. *See* **humble** (1). 3. *Slang* To represent or speak of as small or insignificant ▸ deprecate, disparage, slight. *See* **belittle.** 4. *Slang* To find fault with ▸ censure, fault, reprove. *Slang:* knock. *See* **criticize** (1).

put forth *verb*
To put forward a topic for discussion ▸ introduce, raise. *See* **broach.**

put forward *verb*
1. To state for consideration or debate ▸ offer, pose, set forth. *See* **propose** (1). 2. To put before another for acceptance ▸ extend, proffer. *See* **offer** (1).

put in *verb*
1. To ask for employment, acceptance, or admission ▸ apply, petition. 2. To spend or complete time, as a prison term ▸ serve. *Informal:* do. 3. To use time in a particular way ▸ pass, spend. *See also* **idle.** 4. To put or set into, between, or among another or other things ▸ infuse, insert, interpose. *See* **introduce** (2).

put off *verb*
1. To offer or put into circulation an inferior or fraudulent item ▸ foist, fob off, palm off, pass off. *See also* **dump.** 2. To put off until a later time ▸ delay, postpone, suspend. *See* **defer¹.** 3. To be very disagreeable to ▸ displease, repulse, upset. *See* **offend** (2). 4. To persuade a person not to do something ▸ discourage, divert. *See* **dissuade.**

put on *verb*
1. To put an article of clothing on one's person ▸ pull on, slip on. *See* **don** (1). 2. To take on as a false appearance ▸ assume, fake, feign, simulate. *See* **act** (2). 3. To produce on the stage ▸ dramatize, enact, perform. *See* **stage** (1). 4. To force another to accept a burden ▸ charge with, inflict on (*or* upon), saddle with. *See* **impose on** (1).

put out *verb*
1. To cause to stop burning or giving light ▸ quench, snuff out. *See* **extinguish** (1). 2. To present for circulation, exhibit, or sale ▸ bring out, issue, release. *See* **publish** (1). 3. To cause inconvenience for ▸ incommode, trouble. *See* **inconvenience.** 4. To trouble the nerves or peace of mind of ▸ irritate, nettle, vex. *See* **annoy** (1). 5. To cause anger, resentment, or hurt feelings ▸ annoy, injure, upset. *See* **offend** (1).

put through *verb*
To succeed in doing ▸ bring off, carry out, execute. *See* **effect** (1).

put together *verb*
To create by forming, combining, or altering materials ▸ build, compose, shape. *See* **make** (1).

put up *verb*
1. To raise upright ▸ pitch, raise. *See* **erect** (1). 2. To make or form a structure ▸ erect, raise. *See* **build** (1). 3. To prepare food for storage and future use ▸ can, cure, pickle. *See* **preserve** (1). 4. To provide with lodging, especially temporarily ▸ accommodate, bed (down), house. *See* **lodge** (1). 5. To put before another for acceptance ▸ extend, proffer. *See* **offer** (1).

putative *adjective*
▸ hypothetical, presumptive, suppositional. *See* **supposed.** *See synonym note at* **supposed.**

putdown *noun*
1. A deliberate slight or affront ▸ cut, shun, spurn. *See* **snub.** 2. An act that offends a person's sense of pride or dignity ▸ contumely, insult. *See* **indignity.**

put-on *noun*
1. A deceptive outward appearance ▸ guise, pretense, show. *See* **façade** (2). 2. *Slang* A mischievous act ▸ caper, joke, trick. *See* **prank¹.**

putrefaction *or* **putrescence** *noun*
▸ decomposition, deterioration, rot. *See* **decay.**

putrefy *verb*
▸ deteriorate, spoil, turn. *See* **decay.** *See synonym note at* **decay.**
putrid *or* **putrescent** *adjective*
▸ foul, rotten. *See* **bad** (2).
putridness *noun*
▸ decomposition, deterioration, rot. *See* **decay.**
putter *verb*
To waste time by engaging in aimless activity ▸ dawdle (about), doodle, fiddle (around), fool. *Informal:* fool around, mess around, play around. *Slang:* screw around (*or* off). *See also* **delay, idle.**
puzzle *verb*
To cause to be unclear in mind or intent ▸ befuddle, bewilder, confound. *See* **confuse** (1). *See synonym note at* **confuse.**
puzzle out *verb*
To find the key to a code or cipher ▸ crack, unscramble. *See* **decipher** (1).

puzzle *noun*
Anything that arouses curiosity or perplexes because it is unexplained, inexplicable, or secret ▸ enigma, perplexity, riddle. *See* **mystery.**
puzzled *adjective*
▸ confounded, perplexed, turbid. *Informal:* mixed-up. *See* **confused** (1).
puzzlement *noun*
▸ bewilderment, perplexity, stupor. *See* **daze.**
puzzler *noun*
▸ enigma, perplexity, riddle. *See* **mystery.**
puzzling *adjective*
▸ arcane, cryptic, inscrutable. *See* **mysterious.**
pygmy *adjective*
▸ dwarf, miniature, minuscule. *See* **tiny.**
pyretic *adjective*
▸ feverish, hectic, hot. *See* **feverish** (1).
pythonic *adjective*
▸ behemoth, colossal, mighty. *See* **enormous.**

q

quack *noun*
▸ charlatan, impostor, phony. *See* **fake** (1).
quad *or* **quadrangle** *noun*
▸ courtyard, enclosure. *See* **court** (1).
quaff *verb*
To take into the mouth and swallow a liquid ▸ down, sip, swill. *See* **drink** (1).
quaff *noun*
An act of drinking or the amount swallowed ▸ swallow, taste. *Informal:* swig. *See* **drink** (2).
quag *noun*
▸ marsh, mire, wetland. *See* **swamp.**
quaggy *adjective*
▸ mushy, pulpy, yielding. *See* **soft** (1).
quagmire *noun*
1. A usually low-lying area of soft waterlogged ground and standing water ▸ marsh, mire, wetland. *See* **swamp.** 2. A difficult, often embarrassing situation or condition ▸ corner, fix. *See* **predicament.**
quail *verb*
▸ cringe, recoil, shrink. *See* **flinch.**
quaint *adjective*
1. Agreeably curious, especially in an old-fashioned or unusual way ▸ curious, funny, odd. 2. Deviating from what is conventional or customary ▸ bizarre, grotesque. *See* **eccentric.**
quake *verb*
1. To move back and forth ▸ swing, vacillate, waggle. *See* **sway** (1). 2. To move to and fro in short, jerky movements ▸ quiver, tremble, twitter. *See* **shake** (1). *See synonym note at* **shake.**

quake *noun*
1. A shaking of the earth ▸ carthquake, seism, temblor, tremor. *Informal:* shake. 2. A nervous shaking of the body ▸ quiver, shake, shudder, twitch. *See* **tremor** (2).
quaking *or* **quaky** *adjective*
▸ quivering, shivering, trembling. *See* **tremulous** (1).
qualification *noun*
1. The quality or state of being eligible ▸ correctness, eligibility, fitness, suitability, suitableness, worthiness. 2. A quality that makes a person suitable for a particular position or task ▸ attainment, credential, endowment, skill. 3. The act or process of ascertaining dimensions, quantity, or capacity ▸ determination, measure, measurement, mensuration. *See also* **computation, estimation.** 4. A restricting or modifying element ▸ condition, proviso, stipulation. *See* **provision** (1).
qualified *adjective*
1. Not total, unlimited, or wholehearted ▸ conditioned, limited, modified, reserved, restricted. 2. Satisfying certain requirements, as for selection ▸ equal, suitable. *See* **eligible** (1).
qualify *verb*
1. To give authority to ▸ accredit, empower, license. *See* **authorize** (1). 2. To make or become less severe or extreme ▸ soften, tame. *See* **moderate** (1). *See synonym note at* **moderate.**
quality *noun*
1. A distinctive element ▸ attribute, character, characteristic, feature, mark, peculiarity, property, savor,

trait. *See also* **essence**. **2.** A level of superiority that is usually high ▸ stature, value. *See* **merit** (1). **3.** Refinement of manner, form, and style ▸ grace, refinement, sophistication. *See* **elegance**. **4.** Degree of excellence ▸ caliber, class, grade. *See also* **degree**. **5.** People of the highest social level ▸ elite, gentry, nobility. *See* **society** (1).

quality *adjective*
Exceptionally good of its kind ▸ first-rate, prime, splendid, tiptop. *See* **excellent**.

✦ CORE SYNONYMS: *quality, property, attribute, character, trait.* These nouns signify an element that distinguishes or identifies someone or something: *explained the qualities of noble gases; tested the resilient property of rubber; knew the attributes of a fine wine; liked the rural character of the ranch; had positive traits such as kindness and generosity.*

---

qualm *noun*
1. A feeling of uncertainty about the fitness or correctness of an action ▸ compunction, concern, misgiving, reservation, scruple, worry. *Informal:* problem, trouble. **2.** A lack of conviction or certainty ▸ dubiousness, incertitude, skepticism. *See* **doubt** (1).

✦ CORE SYNONYMS: *qualm, scruple, compunction, misgiving.* These nouns denote a feeling of uncertainty about the fitness or correctness of an action. *Qualm* is a disturbing feeling of uneasiness and self-doubt: *"an ignorant ruffianly gaucho, who . . . would . . . fight, steal, and do other naughty things without a qualm"* (W.H. Hudson). *Scruple* is an uneasy feeling arising from conscience or principle about a course of action: *"My father's old-fashioned notions boggled a little at first to this arrangement . . . but his scruples were in the end overruled"* (John Galt). *Compunction* implies a prick or twinge of conscience aroused by wrongdoing or the prospect of wrongdoing: *stole the money without compunction. Misgiving* suggests often sudden apprehension: *had misgivings about quitting his job.*

---

quandary *noun*
▸ corner, difficulty, fix. *See* **predicament**. *See synonym note at* **predicament**.

quantify *or* **quantitate** *verb*
To ascertain the dimensions, quantity, or capacity of ▸ gauge, measure. *Idioms:* take the dimensions (*or* measure) of. *See also* **estimate**.

quantity *noun*
1. An amount represented in numerals ▸ figure, number. *See also* **total**. **2.** An indefinite amount or extent ▸ bunch, deal, measure, number, portion. **3.** A measurable whole ▸ amount, body, budget, bulk, corpus, quantum. *See also* **hoard**.

quantum *noun*
1. That which is allotted ▸ allowance, ration, share. *See* **allotment** (1). **2.** A measurable whole ▸ amount, bulk. *See* **quantity** (3).

quarantine *noun*
▸ confinement, custody, detainment. *See* **detention**.

quarrel *noun*
A discussion, often heated, in which a difference of opinion is expressed ▸ contention, fight, run-in. *See* **argument** (1).

quarrel *verb*
To engage in a quarrel ▸ dispute, fight. *See* **argue** (1). *See synonym note at* **argue**.

quarrelsome *adjective*
1. Given to arguing ▸ contentious, litigious. *See* **argumentative**. *See synonym note at* **argumentative**. **2.** Inclined to act in an aggressive or hostile way ▸ bellicose, belligerent, truculent. *See* **aggressive** (1). *See synonym note at* **aggressive**.

quarry *noun*
▸ casualty, sufferer, wounded. *See* **victim** (1).

quarter *noun*
1. One of four equal parts of something ▸ one-fourth, quartern. **2.** A coin equal to one-fourth of the dollar of the United States and Canada ▸ two bits, quarter-dollar. **3.** A part of the earth's surface ▸ district, region, zone. *See* **area** (2). **4.** An area in a city or town with distinctive characteristics ▸ community, district. *See* **neighborhood** (1).

quarter *verb*
1. To stay in or provide with lodging, especially temporarily ▸ accommodate, billet, house. *See* **lodge** (1). **2.** To separate into parts with or as if with a sharp-edged instrument ▸ cleave, sever. *See* **cut** (2).

quarterback *verb*
▸ direct, manage, operate. *See* **conduct** (1).

quartern *noun*
One of four equal parts of something ▸ one-fourth, quarter.

quarters *noun*
1. Usually temporary living accommodations ▸ barracks, lodgings, rooms. *Slang:* crash-pad. *See also* **apartment, home**. **2.** An area in a city or town with distinctive characteristics ▸ community, district. *See* **neighborhood** (1).

quash *verb*
1. To overcome opposition or uprising with overwhelming force ▸ crush, extinguish, quell. *See* **suppress** (1). **2.** To take back or remove ▸ repeal, rescind, revoke. *See* **lift** (5).

quaver *verb*
1. To move to and fro in short, jerky movements ▸ quiver, tremble, twitter. *See* **shake** (1). **2.** A nervous shaking of the body ▸ jerk, quake, tic. *See* **tremor** (2).

queasiness *noun*
▸ abhorrence, loathing, revulsion. *See* **disgust**.

queasy *adjective*
▸ ailing, indisposed, unwell. *See* **sick** (1).

queen *noun*
▸ leader, monarch, ruler. *See* **chief** (1).

queer *adjective*
1. Deviating from what is conventional or customary ▸ bizarre, grotesque. *See* **eccentric**. *See synonym note at* **eccentric**. **2.** Causing puzzlement; perplexing ▸ odd, peculiar. *See* **funny** (3).

quell *verb*
1. To overcome opposition or uprising with overwhelming force ▸ crush, extinguish, squash. *See* **suppress** (1). 2. To make less severe or more bearable ▸ alleviate, ease, lessen. *See* **relieve** (1).

quench *verb*
1. To cause to stop burning or giving light ▸ put out, snuff out. *See* **extinguish** (1). 2. To hold something requiring an outlet in check ▸ smother, stifle, suppress. *See* **repress**. 3. To overcome opposition or uprising with overwhelming force ▸ crush, extinguish, quell. *See* **suppress** (1).

querier *noun*
▸ inquisitor, interrogator, questioner. *See* **inquirer**.

querulous *adjective*
▸ cranky, grouchy, peevish. *See* **ill-tempered**.

query *noun*
1. A request for data ▸ inquiry, interrogation, question, questioning. *See also* **demand, problem**. 2. A lack of conviction or certainty ▸ dubiousness, incertitude, skepticism. *See* **doubt** (1).

query *verb*
1. To put a question to someone ▸ inquire, question, pump. *See* **ask** (1). *See synonym note at* **ask**. 2. To be uncertain, disbelieving, or skeptical about ▸ disbelieve, mistrust, waver. *See* **doubt** (1).

quest *noun*
1. An attempt to accomplish or attain ▸ hunt, search. *See* **pursuit** (2). 2. A journey undertaken with a specific objective ▸ pilgrimage, tour, voyage. *See* **expedition** (1).

quest *verb*
To try to find something ▸ cast about, hunt, look, search, seek.

quester *noun*
1. One who seeks adventure ▸ adventurer, daredevil, venturer. *See also* **builder**. 2. One who inquires ▸ inquisitor, questioner. *See* **inquirer**.

question *noun*
1. A request for data ▸ inquiry, interrogation, query, questioning. *See also* **demand, problem**. 2. A situation that presents difficulty, uncertainty, or perplexity ▸ case, issue, matter. *See* **problem** (1). 3. A lack of conviction or certainty ▸ dubiousness, incertitude, skepticism. *See* **doubt** (1).

question *verb*
1. To put a question to someone ▸ inquire, query, pump. *See* **ask** (1). *See synonym note at* **ask**. 2. To be uncertain, disbelieving, or skeptical about ▸ disbelieve, query, waver. *See* **doubt** (1). 3. To lack trust or confidence in ▸ disbelieve, suspect. *See* **distrust**. 4. To give no credence to ▸ doubt, mistrust. *See* **disbelieve** (1).

questionable *adjective*
1. In doubt or dispute ▸ disputable, doubtful. *See* **debatable**. 2. Lacking certainty or clarity ▸ dubious, indeterminate, obscure, unclear. *See* **ambiguous** (1). 3. Not likely ▸ dubious, improbable. *See* **doubtful** (1).

4. Of dubious character ▸ equivocal, suspect, uncertain. *See* **shady** (1).

questioner *noun*
▸ inquisitor, interrogator, querier. *See* **inquirer**.

questioning *adjective*
1. Eager to acquire knowledge ▸ acquisitive, speculative. *See* **curious** (2). 2. Refusing or reluctant to believe ▸ dubious, skeptical. *See* **incredulous**.

questioning *noun*
A request for data ▸ inquiry, interrogation, query, question. *See also* **demand, problem**.

questioningly *adverb*
▸ doubtfully, suspiciously. *See* **skeptically**.

queue *noun*
A group of people or things arranged in a row ▸ file, rank, string. *See* **line** (1).

queue *verb*
To place in or form a line or lines ▸ align, dress, range. *See* **line**.

quibble *verb*
1. To raise unnecessary or trivial objections ▸ carp, cavil, niggle, nitpick, pettifog, squabble. *Idiom:* pick to pieces. *See also* **complain, nag, object**. 2. To engage in a quarrel ▸ dispute, fight, quarrel. *See* **argue** (1).

✦ **CORE SYNONYMS:** *quibble, carp, cavil, niggle, nitpick, pettifog*. These verbs mean to raise petty or frivolous objections or complaints: *quibbling about minor details; a critic who constantly carped; caviling about the price of coffee; an editor who niggled about commas; tried to stop nitpicking all the time; pettifogging about trivialities*.

quibbler *noun*
▸ caviler, nitpicker. *See* **critic** (2).

quibbling *noun*
The act of making trivial objections or distinctions ▸ caviling, hairsplitting, niggling, nitpicking, pettifoggery, trichoschistism.

quick *adjective*
1. Accomplished or experienced in very little time ▸ brief, expeditious, fast, fleeting, flying, hasty, hurried, rapid, short, speedy, swift. *See also* **instant, little, transitory**. 2. Characterized by great speed ▸ brisk, expeditious, rapid, rapid. *See* **fast** (1). *See synonym note at* **fast**. 3. Mentally quick and original ▸ keen, quick-witted, sharp. *See* **clever** (1).

quick *noun*
A point of origin or crucial factor ▸ core, focus, nucleus. *See* **center** (3).

quick *adverb*
In a rapid way ▸ hastily, hurriedly, rapidly, swiftly. *See* **fast**.

quicken *verb*
1. To increase the speed of ▸ hasten, speed up. *See* **speed** (1). *See synonym note at* **speed**. 2. To make alive ▸ animate, enliven, vitalize, vivify. *See also* **elate, energize, provoke**.

quickening *adjective*
▸ bracing, energizing, exhilarating. *See* **invigorating**.

quickly *adverb*
1. In a rapid way ▸ apace, posthaste, rapidly, swiftly. *See* **fast. 2.** In the near future ▸ imminently, promptly. *See* **soon.**

quickness *noun*
1. Rapidness of movement or activity ▸ expeditiousness, hurry, rapidity. *See* **haste** (1). **2.** The quality of being agile ▸ dexterity, quickness, swiftness. *See* **agility. 3.** Skillfulness in the use of the hands or body ▸ deftness, facility. *See* **dexterity** (1).

quick-tempered *adjective*
▸ irascible, short-tempered, tetchy. *See* **testy** (1).

quick-witted *adjective*
▸ keen, quick, sharp. *See* **clever** (1).

quiddity *noun*
▸ nature, quintessence. *See* **essence** (1).

quidnunc *noun*
▸ meddler, prier, snooper. *See* **busybody.**

quiescence *noun*
▸ dormancy, intermission, latency, suspension. *See* **abeyance.**

quiescent *adjective*
▸ dormant, inactive, potential. *See* **latent.** *See synonym note at* **latent.**

quiet *adjective*
1. Marked by, done with, or making no sound or noise ▸ noiseless, soundless. *See* **silent** (1). *See synonym note at* **silent. 2.** Not irritating, strident, or loud ▸ hushed, subdued. *See* **soft** (2). **3.** Free from disturbance, agitation, or commotion ▸ peaceful, placid, serene. *See* **still** (1). **4.** Not showy or obtrusive ▸ inobtrusive, plain, subdued. *See* **modest** (1). **5.** Habitually untalkative ▸ reticent, silent, uncommunicative. *See* **taciturn.**

quiet *noun*
1. The absence of sound or noise ▸ noiselessness, soundlessness. *See* **silence** (1). **2.** An absence of motion or disturbance ▸ calmness, lull, peacefulness. *See* **stillness** (1).

quiet *verb*
1. To cause to become silent ▸ hush, still. *See* **silence. 2.** To ease the anger or agitation of ▸ appease, mollify, soothe. *See* **pacify.**

quiet down *verb*
To grow weaker in sound ▸ die (out), fade (away, out *or* down). *See* **fade away** (1).

quieten *verb*
▸ quiet, still. *See* **silence.**

quietness *noun*
1. The absence of sound or noise ▸ noiselessness, quiet. *See* **silence** (1). **2.** An absence of motion or disturbance ▸ calmness, lull, peacefulness. *See* **stillness** (1). **3.** Lack of ostentation or pretension ▸ plainness, simpleness, simplicity, unobtrusiveness. *See* **modesty** (2).

quietude *noun*
▸ peace, serenity. *See* **calm** (1).

quietus *noun*
▸ demise, passing. *See* **death** (1).

quill *noun*
▸ prick, prong, spine. *See* **spike** (1).

quintessence *noun*
1. The most central or essential part ▸ essence, marrow, soul. *See* **heart** (1). **2.** A basic trait or set of traits that define and establish the character of something ▸ nature, quiddity. *See* **essence** (1).

quintessential *adjective*
1. Having the nature of, constituting, or serving as a type ▸ model, prototypic, representative. *See* **typical** (1). **2.** Constituting or forming part of the essence of something ▸ constitutional, fundamental. *See* **essential** (2). **3.** Conforming to an ultimate form of perfection or excellence ▸ exemplary, model, perfect. *See* **ideal** (1).

quip *noun*
1. Words or actions intended to excite laughter or amusement ▸ gag, jest, witticism. *See* **joke** (1). *See synonym note at* **joke. 2.** A flippant or sarcastic remark ▸ barb, dig. *Slang:* wisecrack. *See* **crack** (5).

joke *verb*
Informal To make jokes; behave playfully ▸ jest, joke. *Informal:* clown (around), fool around, horse around. *Idioms:* crack wise, play the fool. *See also* **play.**

quipster *noun*
▸ clown, comedian, jester. *See* **joker.**

quirk *or* **quirkiness** *noun*
▸ peculiarity, singularity. *See* **eccentricity.**

quirky *adjective*
▸ bizarre, grotesque. *See* **eccentric.**

quit *verb*
1. To relinquish one's engagement in or occupation with ▸ demit, leave, resign, terminate. *Idioms:* hang it up, throw in the towel. *See also* **break, retire. 2.** To move away from a place ▸ exit, go away, retire. *See* **go** (1). **3.** To give up or leave completely ▸ desert, forsake, leave. *See* **abandon** (1). **4.** To cease trying to continue ▸ desist, give up, stop. *See* **abandon** (2). **5.** To come to a cessation ▸ discontinue, halt. *See* **stop** (1). *See synonym note at* **stop. 6.** To conduct oneself in a specified way ▸ acquit, bear, behave, carry. *See* **act** (1). **7.** To abandon one's cause or party usually to join another ▸ desert, forsake, turn. *See* **defect. 8.** To cease consideration or treatment of ▸ give up, relinquish, skip. *See* **drop** (7).

quit *adjective*
Owing or being owed nothing ▸ even, quits, square. *Informal:* even-steven.

quitclaim *noun*
A giving up of a possession, claim, or right ▸ abdication, relinquishment, surrender. *See* **abandonment** (1).

quitclaim *verb*
▸ abdicate, cede, relinquish, surrender. *See* **abandon** (1).

quite *adverb*
1. To the fullest extent ▸ fully, totally, utterly. *See* **completely** (1). **2.** To a considerable extent ▸ much,

significantly, well. *See* **considerably. 3.** To some extent ▸ pretty, rather. *See* **fairly** (2).

quits *adjective*
Owing or being owed nothing ▸ even, quit, square. *Informal:* even-steven.

quittance *noun*
▸ amends, reparation. *See* **compensation** (1).

quiver *verb*
To move to and fro in short, jerky movements ▸ quake, tremble, twitter. *See* **shake** (1). *See synonym note at* **shake.**

quiver *noun*
A nervous shaking of the body ▸ quake, shake, twitch. *See* **tremor** (2).

quivering *or* **quivery** *adjective*
▸ jerky, quaky, shaky. *See* **tremulous** (1).

quixotic *adjective*
▸ romantic, unrealistic, utopian. *See* **idealistic.**

quiz *verb*
1. To put a question to someone ▸ inquire, question, pump. *See* **ask** (1). *See synonym note at* **ask. 2.** To subject to a test of knowledge or skill ▸ catechize, examine, quiz. *See also* **ask.**

quiz *noun*
A set of questions or exercises designed to determine knowledge or skill ▸ catechization, exam, examination. *See* **test** (2).

quondam *adjective*
▸ former, onetime, past. *See* **late** (2).

quota *noun*
▸ allowance, ration, share. *See* **allotment** (1).

quote-unquote *adjective*
▸ hypothetical, presumptive, suppositional. *See* **supposed.**

quotidian *adjective*
▸ casual, workaday. *See* **everyday** (1).

r

rabble *noun*
▸ dregs, good for-nothings, ragtag and bobtail. *See* **riffraff.**

rabble-rouser *noun*
▸ instigator, malcontent, troublemaker. *See* **agitator.**

rabid *adjective*
1. Showing or having enthusiasm ▸ fervent, mad, zealous. *See* **enthusiastic** (1). **2.** Holding especially political views that deviate drastically from prevailing beliefs ▸ fanatical, radical, revolutionary. *See* **extreme** (4). **3.** Feeling or showing anger ▸ furious, irate, livid. *See* **angry.**

race¹ *noun*
One's ancestors or their character or one's ancestral derivation ▸ extraction, line, origin. *See* **ancestry.**

race² *noun*
A vying with others for victory ▸ contest, rivalry, struggle. *See* **competition** (1).

race *verb*
1. To move swiftly ▸ dash, sprint, zip. *See* **rush** (1). **2.** To strive against others for victory ▸ contend, rival, vie. *See* **compete.**

racism *noun*
Discrimination based on race ▸ discrimination, intolerance, prejudice. *See also* **hate.**

racist *adjective*
▸ bigoted, discriminatory, prejudiced. *See also* **intolerant.**

rack *verb*
1. To cause great pain or suffering to ▸ plague, scourge, strike. *See* **afflict.** *See synonym note at* **afflict. 2.** To subject another to extreme physical cruelty, as in

punishing ▸ crucify, harrow, torment, torture. *Idioms:* put on the rack (*or* wheel). *See also* **punish.**

racket *noun*
1. Sounds or a sound, especially when loud, confused, or disagreeable ▸ clamor, din. *See* **noise** (1). *See synonym note at* **noise. 2.** *Slang* Activity pursued as a livelihood ▸ career, employment, occupation. *See* **business** (2).

racy *adjective*
1. Bordering on indelicacy or impropriety ▸ blue, earthy, off-color, provocative, risqué, salty, scabrous, spicy, suggestive. *Slang:* funky. *See also* **erotic, obscene, rude. 2.** Having a sharp, penetrating flavor or aroma ▸ piquant, pungent, seasoned, zesty. *See* **spicy** (1).

raddle *verb*
▸ braid, intertwine, twist. *See* **weave** (1).

radiance *noun*
▸ effulgence, fire, luminosity. *See* **brilliance** (1).

radiant *adjective*
1. Giving off or reflecting much light ▸ brilliant, incandescent, luminous. *See* **bright** (1). *See synonym note at* **bright. 2.** Marked by extraordinary beauty and splendor ▸ magnificent, resplendent, splendid. *See* **glorious** (1).

radiate *verb*
1. To emit a bright light ▸ burn, glow. *See* **beam** (1). **2.** To send out heat, light, or energy ▸ emit, throw (out). *See* **shed¹** (1). **3.** To extend over a wide area ▸ disperse, disseminate, scatter. *See* **spread** (2). **4.** To separate into branches or branchlike parts ▸ diverge, fork. *See* **branch.**

radical *adjective*
1. Arising from or going to the root or source ▸ basal, basic, foundational, fundamental, original, primary, primitive, underlying. *See also* **deep, elemental, first, original. 2.** Holding especially political views that deviate drastically from prevailing beliefs ▸ fanatical, lunatic, revolutionary. *See* **extreme** (4).

radical *noun*
1. One who holds extreme views or advocates extreme measures ▸ fanatic, revolutionist, zealot. *See* **extremist. 2.** The main part of a word to which affixes are attached ▸ root, stem. *See* **theme** (1).

rafter *noun*
▸ crossbeam, girder, timber. *See* **beam** (2).

rag *verb*
1. *Slang* To tease or mock good-humoredly ▸ josh. *Informal:* kid. *See* **joke** (2). **2.** *Slang* To attack or disturb persistently ▸ harry, pester. *See* **harass.**

ragamuffin *noun*
1. A person wearing ragged or tattered clothing ▸ tatterdemalion. *See also* **hobo. 2.** A child or young animal without parents ▸ foundling, stray. *See* **orphan.**

rage *noun*
1. A strong feeling of displeasure or hostility ▸ indignation, irateness, wrath. *See* **anger.** *See synonym note at* **anger. 2.** A subject or activity that inspires lively interest ▸ mania, passion. *See* **enthusiasm** (2). **3.** The current custom ▸ fad, mode, vogue. *See* **fashion** (1).

rage *verb*
To be or become angry ▸ burn, fume, seethe. *See* **anger** (2).

ragged *adjective*
1. Showing signs of wear and tear or neglect ▸ broken-down, dilapidated, tattered. *See* **shabby** (1). **2.** Having a surface that is not smooth ▸ coarse, jagged, scabrous. *See* **rough** (1). **3.** Rough, raw, or grating in sound ▸ gruff, husky. *See* **hoarse** (1).

raggedness *noun*
▸ crookedness, jaggedness, unevenness. *See* **irregularity** (1).

raggedy *adjective*
▸ broken-down, dilapidated, tattered. *See* **shabby** (1).

raging *adjective*
▸ roily, turbulent, violent. *See* **rough** (2).

rags *noun*
Torn and ragged clothing ▸ shreds, tatters.

ragtag and bobtail *noun*
▸ dregs, rabble. *See* **riffraff.**

raid *noun*
1. An act of invading, especially by military forces ▸ foray, incursion, inroad, invasion. *See also* **attack. 2.** A swift advance or attack ▸ onslaught, rush. *See* **charge** (1).

raid *verb*
1. To enter so as to attack, plunder, destroy, or conquer ▸ overrun, maraud. *See* **invade** (1). **2.** To attack suddenly and without warning ▸ bushwhack, waylay. *See* **ambush** (1).

rail¹ *noun*
A string of railroad cars led by a locomotive ▸ railroad train, railway, train. *Informal:* choo-choo, choo-choo train.

rail² *verb*
▸ assail, blaspheme, spit on. *See* **revile.** *See synonym note at* **revile.**

railing *noun*
▸ abuse, condemnation. *See* **vituperation.**

raillery *noun*
▸ badinage, banter, chaff. *See* **ribbing.**

railway *noun*
A string of railroad cars led by a locomotive ▸ rail, railroad train, train. *Informal:* choo-choo, choo-choo train.

raiment *noun*
▸ attire, clothing, garments. *See* **dress** (1).

rain *verb*
1. To give in great abundance ▸ heap, lavish, shower. *See also* **confer, donate, give. 2.** To fall in drops of water from clouds ▸ drizzle, mist, mizzle, pour, precipitate, shower, spatter, spit, sprinkle, teem. *Idioms:* come down in buckets (*or* sheets *or* torrents), rain cats and dogs. *See also* **splash, storm.**

rain *noun*
1. A concentrated outpouring, as of missiles, words, or blows ▸ cannonade, fusillade, volley. *See* **barrage. 2.** Water condensed from atmospheric vapor and falling in drops ▸ cloudburst, deluge, downfall, downpour, drizzle, mist, mizzle, pour, precipitation, rainfall, shower, spit, sprinkle, torrent. *See also* **storm.**

raincoat *noun*
▸ jacket, mackintosh, slicker. *See* **coat** (1).

rainfall *noun*
▸ deluge, downpour, shower. *See* **rain** (2).

rainless *adjective*
▸ desert, droughty, scorched. *See* **dry** (2).

rainy *adjective*
Characterized by rain or drizzle ▸ damp, drizzly, misty, soft, wet. *See also* **stormy.**

raise *verb*
1. To move something to a higher position ▸ hoist, lift. *See* **elevate** (1). *See synonym note at* **elevate. 2.** To raise upright ▸ put up, rear. *See* **erect** (1). **3.** To make or form a structure ▸ construct, erect. *See* **build** (1). **4.** To increase in amount ▸ boost, hike, jack (up), jump, up. *See also* **increase. 5.** To increase markedly in level or intensity, especially of sound ▸ amplify, heighten. *See* **elevate** (2). **6.** To raise in rank ▸ elevate, upgrade. *See* **promote** (1). **7.** To raise crops or animals ▸ cultivate, propagate. *See* **grow** (1). **8.** To take care of and educate a child ▸ bring up, rear. **9.** To seek an answer to a question ▸ ask, pose, put. *See also* **say. 10.** To put forward a topic for discussion ▸ introduce, put forth. *See* **broach.** *See synonym note at* **broach. 11.** To induce or elicit a reaction ▸ kindle, stir (up). *See* **arouse** (1).

raise *noun*
1. The act of increasing or rising ▸ amplification,

boost, escalation. *See* **increase** (1). **2.** The amount by which something is increased ▸ boost, jump. *See* **increase** (2). **3.** A progression upward in rank ▸ promotion, upgrade. *See* **advancement** (1).

raised *adjective*
1. Being positioned above a given level ▸ boosted, raised. *See* **elevated** (1). **2.** Directed or pointed upward ▸ rampant, upstanding. *See* **erect**. **3.** Abnormally increased, especially in intensity ▸ high, supernormal. *See* **elevated** (2).

rake¹ *noun*
An immoral or licentious person ▸ debaucher, profligate. *See* **wanton** (2).

rake² *verb*
To depart or cause to depart from true vertical or horizontal ▸ heel, lean. *See* **incline** (1).

rake *noun*
Deviation from a particular direction ▸ grade, heel. *See* **inclination** (2).

rake³ *verb*
To prepare soil for the planting of crops ▸ cultivate, plow, work. *See* **till**.

rakehell *noun*
▸ debaucher, profligate. *See* **wanton** (2).

rakish *adjective*
▸ licentious, profligate, unbridled. *See* **abandoned** (2).

rally *verb*
1. To assemble, prepare, or put into operation, as for war or a similar emergency ▸ activate, ready. *See* **mobilize**. **2.** To regain one's health ▸ convalesce, improve, recuperate. *See* **recover** (2).

rally *noun*
1. A number of persons who have come or been gathered together ▸ conference, group. *Informal:* gettogether. *See* **assembly** (1). **2.** The process or period of a return to health ▸ convalescence, recovery, recuperation.

rallying cry *noun*
▸ call to arms, war cry. *See* **cry** (2).

ram *verb*
1. To penetrate into a substance or place with force ▸ drive, stab, stick. *See* **plunge** (1). **2.** To force to move or advance with or as if with blows or pressure ▸ butt, shove, slam. *See* **drive** (2). **3.** To apply pressure on, against, or with ▸ press, prod, shove. *See* **push** (1).

ramble *verb*
1. To move about at random, especially over a wide area ▸ drift, meander, wander. *See* **rove**. *See synonym note at* **rove**. **2.** To walk at a leisurely pace ▸ promenade, saunter, wander. *See* **stroll**. **3.** To turn aside, especially from the main subject in writing or speaking ▸ diverge, stray, wander. *See* **digress** (1).

ramble on *verb*
Informal To talk rapidly on trivial matters ▸ blab, jabber, prattle. *See* **chatter** (1).

ramble *noun*
An act of walking ▸ hike, stroll. *See* **walk** (1).

rambling *adjective*
1. Marked by or given to digression ▸ long-winded,

parenthetical, tangential. *See* **digressive**. **2.** Without aim, purpose, or intent ▸ pointless, purposeless, wandering. *See* **aimless**. **3.** Traveling about, especially in search of adventure ▸ itinerant, roving. *See* **errant** (1). **4.** Not proceeding straight to the point or object ▸ circuitous, devious, roundabout. *See* **indirect** (1).

ramification *noun*
1. Something brought about by a cause ▸ consequence, outcome, result. *See* **effect** (1). **2.** Something resembling or analogous to a tree branch ▸ arm, fork, offshoot. *See* **branch** (1).

ramify *verb*
▸ diverge, fork. *See* **branch**.

rampage *noun*
▸ fling, spree. *See* **binge** (1). *See synonym note at* **binge**.

rampant *adjective*
1. Most generally existing or encountered at a given time ▸ current, predominant, rife. *See* **prevailing** (1). **2.** Directed or pointed upward ▸ raised, upstanding. *See* **erect**.

rampart *noun*
▸ barricade, bastion, parapet. *See* **bulwark**. *See synonym note at* **bulwark**.

ramshackle *adjective*
▸ broken-down, dilapidated, tattered. *See* **shabby** (1).

ranch *verb*
▸ cultivate, propagate. *See* **grow** (1).

rancid *adjective*
1. Smelling of mildew or decay ▸ musty, rotten. *See* **moldy**. **2.** Marred by decay ▸ foul, putrid, rotten. *See* **bad** (2).

rancor *noun*
1. The quality or state of feeling bitter ▸ acrimony, bitterness, virulence. *See* **resentment** (1). **2.** A strong feeling of hostility or dislike ▸ antipathy, aversion, loathing. *See* **hate** (1). **3.** Deep-seated hatred, as between longtime opponents or rivals ▸ animosity, antagonism, ill will. *See* **enmity**. *See synonym note at* **enmity**.

rancorous *adjective*
▸ bitter, rancorous, virulent. *See* **resentful**.

rancorousness *noun*
▸ bitterness, rancor, virulence. *See* **resentment** (1).

random *adjective*
Having no particular pattern, purpose, organization, or structure ▸ chance, desultory, haphazard, hit-or-miss, indiscriminate, spot, unplanned, unpredictable. *See also* **confused, spontaneous**.

✦ CORE SYNONYMS: *random, chance, haphazard, desultory*. These adjectives apply to what is determined not by deliberation but by accident. *Random* implies the absence of a specific pattern or objective: *took a random guess. Chance* stresses lack of premeditation: *a chance meeting with a friend. Haphazard* implies a carelessness or a willful leaving to chance: *a haphazard plan of action. Desultory* suggests a shifting about from one thing to another that reflects a lack of method: *a desultory conversation.*

R and R *noun*
Informal Freedom from labor, responsibility, or strain ▸ leisure, relaxation, repose. *See* **rest** (2).

range *noun*
1. An area or set of parameters within which something or someone exists, acts, or has influence ▸ ambit, circle, compass, extension, extent, orbit, purview, reach, realm, scope, spectrum, sphere, sweep, swing, territory. *See also* **area, beat, limit.** **2.** The extent of one's perception, understanding, knowledge, or vision ▸ horizon, scope. *See* **ken. 3.** The ability or power to seize or attain ▸ capacity, compass, grasp, reach, scope. *See also* **influence. 4.** A division of persons or things by quality or rank ▸ league, rank, tier. *See* **class** (2). **5.** Approximate size or amount ▸ *Informal:* neighborhood. ▸ vicinity. **6.** A number of things placed or occurring one after the other ▸ order, procession, sequence. *See* **series. 7.** Relative intensity or amount, as of a quality or attribute ▸ extent, magnitude, scope. *See* **degree** (2). **8.** The natural environment specific to an animal or plant ▸ habitation, territory. *See* **habitat** (1). **9.** A wide and open area, as of land, sky, or water ▸ extent, stretch, sweep. *See* **expanse** (1). **10.** An extent, measured or unmeasured, of linear space ▸ interval, length, stretch. *See* **distance** (1).

range *verb*
1. To put into a deliberate order ▸ deploy, systematize. *See* **arrange** (1). **2.** To place in or form a line or lines ▸ dress, file, queue (up). *See* **line. 3.** To arrange according to class ▸ categorize, class, group. *See* **classify. 4.** To change or fluctuate within limits ▸ cover, vary. *See* **go** (7). **5.** To move about at random, especially over a wide area ▸ drift, meander, wander. *See* **rove.** *See synonym note at* **rove.**

✦ CORE SYNONYMS: *range, ambit, compass, orbit, purview, reach, scope, sweep.* These nouns denote an area within which something or someone exists, acts, or has influence: *the range of a nuclear missile; the ambit of municipal legislation; information within the compass of the article; countries within the political orbit of a world power; regulations under the government's purview; outside the reach of the law; issues within the scope of an investigation; outside the sweep of federal authority.*

---

rangy *adjective*
▸ spindling, spindly. *See* **gangling.**

rank¹ *noun*
1. Positioning of one individual vis-à-vis others ▸ level, position, standing. *See* **place** (1). **2.** A division of persons or things by quality or rank ▸ league, order, tier. *See* **class** (2). **3.** A group of people or things arranged in a row ▸ file, queue, string. *See* **line** (1). **4.** One of the units in a course, as on an ascending or descending scale ▸ interval, level, step. *See* **degree** (1).

rank *verb*
To arrange according to class ▸ categorize, class, group. *See* **classify.**

rank² *adjective*
1. Conspicuously bad or offensive ▸ egregious, flagrant, glaring, gross. *See synonym note at* **flagrant.** *See also* **offensive, outrageous, shameless. 2.** Growing profusely ▸ lush, luxuriant, profuse. *See* **thick** (3). **3.** Smelling of mildew or decay ▸ musty, rancid. *See* **moldy.**

rank and file *noun*
▸ masses, proletariat, public. *See* **commonalty.**

ranking *noun*
▸ format, layout, ordering, positioning. *See* **arrangement** (1).

rankle *verb*
▸ irritate, nettle, vex. *See* **annoy** (1).

rankness *noun*
The quality or state of being flagrant ▸ egregiousness, flagrancy, glaringness, grossness. *See also* **impudence, outrageousness.**

ransack *verb*
1. To search through or over thoroughly ▸ forage, rummage, search. *See* **scour²** (1). **2.** To rob of goods by force, especially in time of war ▸ loot, plunder, ravage. *See* **sack².**

rant *verb*
1. To speak in a loud, pompous, or prolonged manner ▸ declaim, harangue, mouth (off), orate, perorate, rave. *See also* **revile. 2.** To talk rapidly, incoherently, or indistinctly ▸ gibber, jabber. *See* **babble** (1).

rant *noun*
Pretentious, pompous speech or writing ▸ fustian, grandiloquence. *See* **bombast.**

rap¹ *verb*
1. To strike together noisily ▸ crack, knock, whack. *See* **bang** (1). **2.** To strike lightly or gently ▸ flick, pat. *See* **tap¹** (1). **3.** To criticize for a fault or offense ▸ chide, rebuke, reprimand. *See* **chastise** (1). **4.** To find fault with ▸ censure, fault, reprove. *Slang:* knock. *See* **criticize** (1).

rap out *verb*
To speak suddenly or sharply, as from surprise or emotion ▸ burst out, ejaculate. *See* **exclaim.**

rap *noun*
1. The sound made by a light blow ▸ knock, rapping, tap, tapping. *See also* **beat. 2.** Words expressive of strong disapproval ▸ admonition, reprimand, scolding. *See* **rebuke. 3.** A stroke or blow that produces a sound ▸ thud, thump. *See* **beat** (1). **4.** Something, such as loss, pain, or confinement, imposed for wrongdoing ▸ castigation, chastisement, penalty. *See* **punishment. 5.** *Slang* Responsibility for an error or crime ▸ fault, guilt. *See* **blame** (1).

rap² *noun*
1. *Slang* An exchanging of views ▸ conference, discussion, ventilation. **2.** *Slang* Spoken exchange ▸ dialogue, discourse, discussion. *See* **conversation** (1).

rap *verb*
Slang To speak together and exchange ideas and opinions about ▸ converse, debate. *Informal:* kick around. *See* **discuss.**

rapacious *adjective*
▶ gluttonous, greedy, ravenous. *See* **voracious** (1). *See synonym note at* **voracious**.

rapaciousness *noun*
▶ edacity, omnivorousness, ravenousness. *See* **voracity**.

rapacity *noun*
1. The quality or condition of being voracious ▶ omnivorousness, rapaciousness. *See* **voracity**. 2. Excessive desire for more than one needs or deserves ▶ avarice, covetousness. *See* **greed**.

rape *verb*
1. To compel another to participate in or submit to a sexual act ▶ assault, force, molest, ravish, violate. 2. To rob of goods by force, especially in time of war ▶ loot, plunder, ransack. *See* **sack²**.

rapid *adjective*
1. Characterized by great speed ▶ expeditious, quick, speedy. *See* **fast** (1). *See synonym note at* **fast**. 2. Accomplished or experienced in very little time ▶ fast, fleeting, speedy. *See* **quick** (1).

rapidity *noun*
▶ expeditiousness, hurry, quickness. *See* **haste** (1).

rapidly *adverb*
▶ hastily, hurriedly, quickly, swiftly. *See* **fast**.

rapidness *noun*
▶ expeditiousness, hurry, quickness. *See* **haste** (1).

rapport *noun*
▶ concordance, harmony, unison. *See* **agreement** (2).

rapprochement *noun*
A reestablishment of friendship or harmony ▶ conciliation, reconcilement, reconciliation, settlement. *See also* **agreement, atonement, compromise**.

rap session *noun*
Slang A meeting for the exchange of views ▶ discussion, parley, seminar. *See* **conference** (1).

rapt *adjective*
Having one's thoughts fully occupied ▶ absorbed, engrossed, immersed, intent, preoccupied, riveted. *Idioms:* wrapped (*or* caught) up in. *See also* **busy**.

rapture *noun*
▶ ecstasy, paradise. *See* **heaven** (1).

rare *adjective*
1. Rarely occurring or appearing ▶ uncommon, unusual. *See* **infrequent**. 2. Beyond what is usual, normal, or customary ▶ extraordinary, outstanding, remarkable. *See* **exceptional** (1). 3. Marked by great diffusion of component particles ▶ attenuate, attenuated, rarefied, thin.

rarefied *adjective*
Marked by great diffusion of component particles ▶ attenuate, attenuated, rare, thin.

rarefy *verb*
To become diffuse ▶ attenuate, thin.

rarely *adverb*
▶ little, occasionally, seldom. *See* **infrequently**.

raring *adjective*
Informal Intensely desirous or interested ▶ avid, bursting. *See* **eager** (1).

rarity *noun*
1. The quality of being novel ▶ newness, originality. *See* **novelty** (1). 2. Something costly and unnecessary ▶ extravagancy, frill, indulgence. *See* **luxury** (1).

rascal *noun*
One who causes minor trouble or damage ▶ devil, imp, mischief, mischief-maker, prankster, rogue, scamp, scoundrel. *Informal:* cutup, scalawag. *See also* **agitator, evildoer, urchin**.

rascality *noun*
▶ diablerie, high jinks, tomfoolery. *See* **mischief** (1).

rascally *adjective*
▶ frolicsome, impish, sportive. *See* **mischievous** (1).

rash¹ *adjective*
Characterized by unthinking boldness and haste ▶ brash, foolhardy, harum-scarum, hasty, headlong, hotheaded, ill-considered, impetuous, improvident, impulsive, incautious, madcap, precipitant, precipitate, reckless, slapdash, temerarious, unconsidered. *See also* **abrupt, callous, spontaneous, unwise**.

✦ CORE SYNONYMS: *rash, reckless, precipitate, foolhardy, temerarious, impetuous, hasty, headlong*. These adjectives describe unthinking boldness, haste, or lack of deliberation. *Rash* implies haste, impetuousness, and insufficient consideration: *"Take calculated risks. That is quite different from being rash"* (George S. Patton). *Reckless* suggests wild carelessness and disregard for consequences: *"conceiving measures to protect the fur-bearing animals from reckless slaughter"* (Getrude Atherton). *Precipitate* connotes headlong haste without due deliberation: *"destroyed in a precipitate burning of his papers a few days before his death"* (James Boswell). *Foolhardy* implies injudicious or imprudent boldness: *a foolhardy attempt to wrest the gun from the mugger*. *Temerarious* suggests reckless presumption: *"this temerarious foeman who dared intervene between himself* [the elephant] *and his intended victim"* (Edgar Rice Burroughs).*Impetuous* suggests forceful impulsiveness or impatience: *"[a race driver who was] flamboyant, impetuous, disdainful of death"* (Jim Murray). *Hasty* and *headlong* both stress hurried, often reckless action: *"Hasty marriage seldom proveth well"* (William Shakespeare). *"In his headlong flight down the circular staircase, . . .* [he] *had pitched forward violently, struck his head against the door to the east veranda, and probably broken his neck"* (Mary Roberts Rinehart).

---

rash² *noun*
A sudden emergence or increase ▶ breakout, flare, outburst. *See* **eruption** (1).

rashness *noun*
1. Careless headlong action ▶ precipitance, rush. *See* **haste** (2). 2. Foolhardy boldness or disregard of danger ▶ brashness, recklessness. *See* **temerity**.

rasp *verb*
1. To bring into abrasive contact ▶ grate, scratch. *See* **scrape** (2). 2. To utter in a breathless or hoarse manner ▶ pant, wheeze. *See* **gasp** (1).

raspberry *noun*
Slang One of various derisive sounds of disapproval

▸ catcall, hoot. *Slang:* Bronx cheer. *See* **hiss** (2).

raspberry *verb*
Slang To make a derisive sound of disapproval ▸ boo, hoot. *See* **hiss** (2).

rasping *adjective*
▸ grating, jarring. *See* **harsh** (1).

raspy *or* **rasping** *adjective*
▸ grating, jarring. *See* **harsh** (1).

rat *noun*
1. *Informal* One who betrays ▸ Judas, traitor. *See* **betrayer**. **2.** *Informal* One who gives incriminating information about others ▸ informant. *Slang:* snitch, squealer. *See* **informer**. **3.** *Informal* A person who has defected ▸ deserter, recreant, traitor. *See* **defector**. **4.** *Slang* A repulsive, despicable, or immoral person ▸ *Slang:* louse, maggot. *See* **creep** (2).

rat *verb*
1. *Slang* To abandon one's cause or party usually to join another ▸ desert, quit, turn. *See* **defect**. **2.** *Slang* To be treacherous to ▸ turn in. *Slang:* sell out. *See* **betray** (1). **3.** *Slang* To give incriminating information about others, especially to the authorities ▸ tip (off). *Slang:* fink, snitch. *See* **inform** (2).

rat-a-tat-tat *noun*
▸ bang, pop, snap. *See* **crack** (1).

rate *verb*
1. To make a judgment as to the worth or value of ▸ assay, calculate. *See* **estimate** (1). *See synonym note at* **estimate**. **2.** To arrange according to class ▸ categorize, class, group. *See* **classify**. **3.** *Informal* To acquire as a result of one's behavior or effort ▸ gain, get, win. *See* **earn** (1). *See synonym note at* **earn**.

rate *noun*
A fixed amount of money charged for a service ▸ exaction, fee. *See* **toll**[1] (1).

rather *adverb*
▸ pretty, quite. *See* **fairly** (2).

ratification *noun*
▸ approval, certification, sanction. *See* **confirmation** (1).

ratify *verb*
▸ approve, pass, sanction. *See* **confirm** (3).

ratiocinate *verb*
▸ cogitate, deliberate, reflect. *See* **think** (1).

ratiocination *noun*
▸ analysis, rationality, reason. *See* **logic** (1).

ratiocinative *adjective*
▸ analytic, analytical, rational. *See* **logical** (1). *See synonym note at* **logical**.

ration *noun*
That which is allotted ▸ allowance, share. *See* **allotment** (1).

ration *verb*
To give out in portions or shares ▸ allocate, apportion, dispense. *See* **distribute** (1). *See synonym note at* **distribute**.

rational *adjective*
1. Able to reason validly ▸ analytic, analytical, ratiocinative. *See* **logical** (1). *See synonym note at* **logical**.

2. Proceeding from or exhibiting good judgment ▸ commonsensical, levelheaded, prudent. *See* **sensible** (1). **3.** Mentally healthy ▸ compos mentis, lucid, normal, sane. *Idioms:* all there, in one's right mind, of sound mind. *See also* **healthy**. **4.** Consistent with reason and intellect ▸ intelligent, reasonable. *See* **logical** (2).

rationale *noun*
1. A statement of causes or motives ▸ explanation, rationalization, reason. *See* **account** (1). **2.** An explanation offered to justify an action or make it better understood ▸ plea, pretext, rationalization. *See* **excuse** (1).

rationality *noun*
1. What is sound or reasonable ▸ logic, reason. *See* **sense** (1). **2.** Exact, valid, and rational reasoning ▸ analysis, ratiocination, reason. *See* **logic** (1). **3.** A healthy mental state ▸ lucidity, mind, reason. *See* **sanity**.

rationalization *noun*
1. A statement of causes or motives ▸ explanation, justification, rationale, reason. *See* **account** (1). **2.** An explanation offered to justify an action or make it better understood ▸ pretext, rationale. *See* **excuse** (1).

rationalize *verb*
1. To show to be just, right, or valid ▸ excuse, justify, vindicate. *Idiom:* make a case for. **2.** To offer reasons for or a cause of ▸ account for, explain, justify. *See also* **clarify, resolve**.

rationalness *noun*
▸ rationality, reason. *See* **sense** (1).

rations *noun*
▸ bread, meat, nourishment. *See* **food**.

rattle *verb*
1. To make or cause to make a succession of short, sharp sounds ▸ brattle, chatter, clack, clank, clatter. *See also* **knock, shake**. **2.** To talk rapidly on trivial matters ▸ blab, jabber, prattle. *See* **chatter** (1). **3.** *Informal* To impair or destroy the composure of ▸ rock, ruffle, shake (up). *See* **agitate** (2). **4.** To proceed with sudden, abrupt movements ▸ bounce, jounce, shake. *See* **bump** (1).

ratty *adjective*
▸ broken-down, dilapidated, tattered. *See* **shabby** (1).

raucous *adjective*
▸ grating, jarring. *See* **harsh** (1).

raunch *noun*
1. *Slang* The quality or state of being obscene ▸ filthiness, obscenity, profaneness, profanity. *See* **obscenity** (1). **2.** *Slang* Something that is offensive to accepted standards of decency ▸ dirt, sleaze, smut. *See* **obscenity** (2).

raunchiness *noun*
Slang The quality or state of being obscene ▸ filthiness, obscenity, profaneness, profanity. *See* **obscenity** (1).

raunchy *adjective*
Slang Offensive to accepted standards of decency ▸ bawdy, coarse, lewd, vulgar. *See* **obscene** (1).

ravage *verb*

1. To engulf completely ▸ devour, waste. *See* **consume** (1). 2. To rob of goods by force, especially in time of war ▸ loot, plunder, ransack. *See* **sack²**. 3. To injure or damage, as by abuse or heavy wear ▸ maul, rough up. *See* **batter** (1). 4. To alter and spoil the natural form or appearance of ▸ disfigure, misshape, twist. *See* **deform**. 5. To cause the complete ruin or wreckage of ▸ demolish, torpedo, wreck. *See* **destroy** (1).

rave *verb*

1. To express great enthusiasm ▸ carry on, enthuse, gush, rhapsodize. *Informal:* boom. *Idiom:* wax poetic. *See also* **adore, drool**. 2. To speak in a loud, pompous, or prolonged manner ▸ harangue, orate. *See* **rant** (1). 3. To talk rapidly, incoherently, or indistinctly ▸ gibber, jabber. *See* **babble** (1).

ravel *verb*

▸ entangle, perplex, tangle. *See* **complicate**.

ravenous *adjective*

1. Desiring or craving food ▸ famished, starving. *See* **hungry** (1). 2. Wanting to eat or drink more than one can reasonably consume ▸ greedy, voracious. *See* **gluttonous** (1). 3. Having an insatiable appetite for an activity or pursuit ▸ rapacious, unappeasable. *See* **voracious** (1). *See synonym note at* **voracious**.

ravenousness *noun*

▸ avidity, omnivorousness, rapaciousness. *See* **voracity**.

ravish *verb*

1. To compel another to participate in or submit to a sexual act ▸ assault, force, molest, rape, violate. 2. To have a powerful emotional effect on someone ▸ thrill, transport. *See* **enrapture**. *See synonym note at* **enrapture**.

ravishing *adjective*

▸ comely, gorgeous, stunning. *See* **beautiful**.

raw *adjective*

1. Not cooked ▸ uncooked. 2. Being in a natural state ▸ rough, unrefined. *See* **crude** (1). *See synonym note at* **crude**. 3. Lacking expert, careful craftsmanship ▸ crude, primitive, unpolished. *See* **rude** (1). *See synonym note at* **rude**. 4. Lacking experience and the knowledge gained from it ▸ inexpert, uninitiated, unpracticed. *See* **inexperienced**. 5. Marked by, causing, or experiencing physical pain ▸ achy, hurtful, sore. *See* **painful** (1). 6. Marked by cold and unpleasant conditions ▸ grim, severe. *See* **bleak** (1). 7. Rough or grating in sound ▸ gruff, husky. *See* **hoarse** (1).

rawboned *adjective*

▸ lean, skinny, slender, slim. *See* **thin** (1). *See synonym note at* **thin**.

raw deal *noun*

▸ disservice, inequity, wrong. *See* **injustice** (1).

rawness *noun*

▸ greenness, immaturity, inexpertness. *See* **inexperience**.

ray *noun*

▸ shaft, stream. *See* **beam** (1).

raze *verb*

▸ dismantle, level, tear down. *See* **destroy** (2). *See synonym note at* **destroy**.

razz *noun*

Slang One of various derisive sounds of disapproval ▸ catcall, hoot. *See* **hiss** (2).

razz *verb*

1. *Slang* To tease or mock good-humoredly ▸ chaff, josh. *Informal:* kid. *See* **joke** (2). 2. *Slang* To make a derisive sound of disapproval ▸ boo, hoot. *See* **hiss** (2).

razzle-dazzle *noun*

Informal Brilliant, showy splendor ▸ brilliance, resplendence, sparkle. *See* **glitter** (2).

reach *verb*

1. To put forward, especially an appendage ▸ extend, outstretch, stretch (out). 2. To reach a goal or objective ▸ achieve, attain, gain. *See* **accomplish** (1). *See synonym note at* **accomplish**. 3. To succeed in communicating with ▸ contact. *Informal:* catch, get. *Idioms:* catch up with, get hold of, get in touch with, get through to, get to, make contact with. *See also* **find, relate**. 4. To proceed on a certain course or for a certain distance ▸ lead, stretch. *See* **extend** (1). 5. To come to a particular place ▸ get in. *Slang:* blow in. *See* **arrive** (1). 6. To come to in number or quantity ▸ number, run, total. *See* **amount** (1).

reach *noun*

1. The measure of how far or long something goes in space, time, or degree ▸ coverage, span, stretch. *See* **extent** (1). 2. The ability or power to seize or attain ▸ capacity, compass, grasp, range, scope. *See also* **influence**. 3. The extent of one's perception, understanding, knowledge, or vision ▸ range, scope. *See* **ken**. 4. An area or set of parameters within which something or someone exists, acts, or has influence ▸ extent, realm, scope. *See* **range** (1). *See synonym note at* **range**. 5. A wide and open area, as of land, sky, or water ▸ extent, stretch, sweep. *See* **expanse** (1). 6. An extent, measured or unmeasured, of linear space ▸ interval, length, stretch. *See* **distance** (1).

react *verb*

To act in return to something, as a stimulus ▸ counter, respond. *Idiom:* act in response. *See also* **retaliate**.

reactant *noun*

▸ ferment, leaven, yeast. *See* **catalyst**.

reaction *noun*

1. An action elicited by a stimulus ▸ response, retroaction. *See also* **retaliation**. 2. The way in which something functions ▸ functioning, performance. *See* **behavior** (2).

reactionary *adjective*

1. Extremely or stubbornly conservative ▸ mossbacked, old-line, standpat. *See* **ultraconservative**. 2. Clinging to obsolete ideas ▸ backward, unprogressive.

reactionary *noun*

One who is extremely or stubbornly conservative ▸ archconservative, fossil, die-hard. *See* **ultraconservative**.

reactivate *verb*
▸ rekindle, resuscitate, revitalize. *See* **revive** (1).
reactivation *noun*
▸ rebirth, renaissance, renewal. *See* **revival** (1).
read *verb*
1. To perceive and recognize the meaning of ▸ apprehend, fathom, sense. *See* **understand** (1). 2. To understand in a particular way ▸ construe, interpret, take. *Idioms:* read between the lines, see in a special light, take to mean. 3. To give a precise indication of, as on a register or scale ▸ mark, register. *See* **show** (3).
readiness *noun*
1. The condition of being made ready beforehand ▸ mobilization, prearrangement. *See* **preparation**.
2. The ability to perform without apparent effort ▸ effortlessness, facility. *See* **ease** (2).
reading *noun*
▸ performance, rendition. *See* **interpretation** (1).
ready *adjective*
1. In a state of preparedness ▸ prepared, set. *Informal:* go. *Slang:* together. *Idioms:* all set, in working order, on deck. 2. Disposed to accept, agree, or participate ▸ agreeable, pleased. *See* **willing** (1). 3. Being within easy reach ▸ handy, nearby. *See* **convenient** (2).
ready *verb*
1. To prepare oneself for action ▸ brace, fortify, steel. *See* **gird** (1). 2. To cause to be ready, as for use, consumption, or a special purpose ▸ fix, ready. *See* **prepare** (1). 3. To assemble, prepare, or put into operation, as for war or a similar emergency ▸ activate, organize. *See* **mobilize**.
real *adjective*
1. Having physical or verifiable existence ▸ concrete, objective, solid, substantial, substantive, tangible. *See also* **physical**. 2. Occurring or existing in act or fact ▸ actual, extant, existent, true. *See synonym note at* **actual**. *See also* **physical**. 3. Not counterfeit or copied ▸ original, true. *Slang:* kosher. *See* **authentic** (1). *See synonym note at* **authentic**. 4. Free from hypocrisy or pretense ▸ honest, sincere, unaffected. *See* **genuine** (1).
realistic *adjective*
1. Having or indicating an awareness of how things really are or what should be done ▸ down-to-earth, hard, hardheaded, matter-of-fact, objective, practical, pragmatic, pragmatical, prosaic, sober, straight, tough-minded, unromantic. *See also* **appropriate, frank, genuine**. 2. Accurately representing what is depicted or described ▸ factual, lifelike, natural, naturalistic, true, true-life, truthful. *See also* **accurate**. 3. Depicted in sharp and accurate detail ▸ explicit, vivid. *See* **graphic** (1). *See synonym note at* **graphic**.
reality *noun*
1. The fact or state of existing or of being actual ▸ being, entity. *See* **existence** (1). 2. The quality of being actual or factual ▸ actuality, fact, truth. *See* **certainty** (1). 3. Something demonstrated to exist or known to have existed ▸ actuality, event, fact, phenomenon. *Idioms:* hard (*or* cold *or* plain) fact. *See also* **information**.

realization *noun*
1. The condition of being fulfilled ▸ culmination, fulfillment, materialization. *See* **fulfillment** (1).
2. Something completed or attained successfully ▸ achievement, deed, triumph. *See* **accomplishment** (1). *See synonym note at* **accomplishment**. 3. The condition of being in full force or operation ▸ actualization, being, effect, force. *See also* **exercise**. 4. A performer's distinctive personal version of a song, dance, piece of music, or role ▸ performance, reading, rendition. *See* **interpretation** (1).
realize *verb*
1. To make real or actual ▸ actualize, bring about, make happen, materialize. *Idioms:* bring to pass, carry (*or* put) into effect. *See also* **effect, produce**. 2. To obtain or reach by persistent effort ▸ achieve, attain, reach. *See* **accomplish** (1). 3. To make as income or profit ▸ clear, gain, yield. *See* **return** (3). 4. To achieve a certain price ▸ go for, sell for. *See* **bring** (2). 5. To obtain knowledge or awareness of something not known before ▸ determine, learn, unearth. *See* **discover**.
really *adverb*
In truth or fact ▸ actually, fairly, genuinely, indeed, positively, truly, truthfully, verily, veritably. *Idioms:* as a matter of fact, beyond (*or* without) a doubt, beyond a reasonable (*or* shadow of a) doubt, for fair (*or* real *or* sure *or* true), in point of fact. *See also* **absolutely, completely, considerably, unusually, very**.
realm *noun*
1. An area or set of parameters within which something or someone exists, acts, or has influence ▸ extent, orbit, scope. *See* **range** (1). 2. A sphere of activity, experience, study, or interest ▸ department, domain, field, terrain. *See* **area** (1). *See synonym note at* **area**.
realness *noun*
▸ authenticity, correctness, truth, validity. *See* **veracity**.
ream *noun*
An indeterminately great amount or number ▸ bunch, multiplicity. *Informal:* bushel. *See* **heap** (3).
ream *verb*
To penetrate with a sharp edge ▸ bayonet, incise, pierce, slash. *See* **cut** (1).
reanimate *verb*
▸ rekindle, resuscitate, revitalize. *See* **revive** (1).
reap *verb*
1. To collect ripe crops ▸ harvest, pick, pluck. *See* **gather** (1). 2. To make as income or profit ▸ clear, gain, yield. *See* **return** (3). 3. To decrease, as in length or amount, by or as if by severing or excising ▸ chop, prune, trim. *See* **cut** (3). 4. To come into possession of ▸ come by, gain, procure. *See* **get** (1).
reappear *verb*
To happen again or repeatedly ▸ iterate, recur, reoccur, repeat.
reappearance *noun*
▸ reiteration, repeat, restatement. *See* **repetition** (1).

rear¹ *noun*
1. The part farthest from the front ▸ end, hind end, tail. *See* **back. 2.** The part or area farthest from the front ▸ back, rearward. **3.** *Informal* The part of the body on which one sits ▸ posterior, rump. *Slang:* fanny. *See* **buttocks.**
rear *adjective*
Located in the rear ▸ hind, posterior. *See* **back** (1).
rear² *verb*
1. To take care of and educate a child ▸ bring up, foster, parent, raise. *See also* **nurture. 2.** To raise upright ▸ put up, raise. *See* **erect** (1). **3.** To move something to a higher position ▸ hoist, lift, raise. *See* **elevate** (1). **4.** To make or form a structure ▸ erect, knock together. *See* **build** (1).
rear-end *verb*
▸ smash, total, wreck. *See* **crash** (1).
rear-guard *adjective*
▸ mossbacked, reactionary, standpat. *See* **ultraconservative.**
rearmost *adjective*
▸ hindermost, tail. *See* **last¹** (2).
rearrange *verb*
▸ reconfigure, scramble. *See* **shuffle** (1).
rearrangement *noun*
▸ dislodging, movement, shift. *See* **displacement.**
rearward *adverb*
Toward the back ▸ about, around. *See* **backward.**
rearward *adjective*
1. Moving or directed toward the rear ▸ retrograde, retrogressive. *See* **backward** (3). **2.** Located in rear ▸ hind, posterior. *See* **back** (1).
reason *noun*
1. A fact or circumstance that gives logical support to an assertion, claim, or proposal ▸ argument, case, grounds, point, proof, wherefore, why. *Idiom:* why and wherefore. *See also* **account, explanation. 2.** A basis for an action ▸ grounds, motive, spring. *See* **cause** (2). **3.** That which produces an effect ▸ antecedent, cause, determinant, occasion. *See synonym note at* **cause.** *See also* **impact, origin, stimulus. 4.** A justifying fact or consideration ▸ justification, warrant. *See* **basis** (2). **5.** A statement of causes or motives ▸ explanation, justification, rationale. *See* **account** (1). **6.** Exact, valid, and rational reasoning ▸ analysis, ratiocination, rationality. *See* **logic** (1). **7.** What is sound or reasonable ▸ logic, rationality. *See* **sense** (1). **8.** A healthy mental state ▸ lucidity, rationality, saneness. *See* **sanity. 9.** The ability to make sensible decisions ▸ judgment, sense, wisdom. *See* **common sense.**
reason *verb*
1. To arrive at (a conclusion) from evidence or reasoning ▸ conclude, gather. *See* **infer** (1). **2.** To speak together and exchange ideas and opinions about ▸ argue, deliberate, thrash out (*or* over). *See* **discuss. 3.** To use the powers of the mind ▸ cogitate, deliberate, reflect. *See* **think** (1). *See synonym note at* **think.**
reasonable *adjective*
1. Consistent with reason and intellect ▸ consequent,

deducible, rational. *See* **logical** (2). **2.** Proceeding from or exhibiting good judgment ▸ commonsensical, levelheaded, prudent. *See* **sensible** (1). **3.** Kept within sensible limits ▸ moderate, restrained, temperate. *See* **conservative** (2). **4.** Worthy of being believed ▸ creditable, plausible. *See* **believable.** *See synonym note at* **believable. 5.** Adequate to satisfy a need, requirement, or standard ▸ moderate, modest, popular. *See* **acceptable** (2).
reasoning *noun*
▸ philosophizing, speculation. *See* **theory** (1).
reasoner *noun*
A person who seeks truth by thinking ▸ philosopher, theorist, thinker.
reassume *verb*
▸ reoccupy, repossess, retake. *See* **resume** (1).
reassurance *noun*
A consoling in time of grief or pain ▸ comfort, consolation, solace, succor. *See also* **help, pity.**
reassure *verb*
▸ condole, console, soothe. *See* **comfort.** *See synonym note at* **comfort.**
reawaken *verb*
▸ rekindle, resuscitate, revitalize. *See* **revive** (1).
rebate *noun*
An amount deducted ▸ abatement, reduction. *See* **deduction** (1).
rebate *verb*
1. To take away a quantity from another quantity ▸ discount, subtract. *See* **deduct** (1). **2.** To grow or cause to grow gradually less ▸ diminish, dwindle, ebb. *See* **decrease.**
rebel *verb*
1. To vehemently defy and break allegiance with ▸ mutiny, revolt, rise (up). *See also* **defect, defy. 2.** To refuse or fail to obey ▸ defy, transgress. *See* **disobey.**
rebel *noun*
1. A person who rebels ▸ insurgent, insurrectionary, insurrectionist, mutineer, revolutionary, revolutionist, subversive, transgressor. *See also* **separatist. 2.** Someone with unconventional opinions or approaches ▸ avant-gardist, dissenter, free-thinker, iconoclast, independent, maverick, nonconformist, original, rule-breaker, visionary.
rebellion *noun*
1. Organized opposition intended to change or overthrow existing authority ▸ insurgence, insurgency, insurrection, mutiny, revolt, revolution, sedition, uprising. *See also* **competition, battle. 2.** The act or an instance of defying ▸ disobedience, provocation. *See* **defiance** (1).
rebellious *adjective*
1. Participating in open revolt against a government or ruling authority ▸ insurgent, insurrectionary, mutinous, revolutionary, seditionary, subversive. **2.** Marked by defiance ▸ disobedient, insubordinate. *See* **defiant.**
rebelliousness *noun*
▸ contempt, despite, rebelliousness. *See* **defiance** (2).

rebirth *noun*
1. A fundamental change in one's beliefs ▸ conversion, metanoia, regeneration. 2. The act of reviving or condition of being revived ▸ reactivation, renaissance, renewal. *See* **revival** (1).

rebound *verb*
1. To spring back or up after colliding with something ▸ bounce (back), bound, hop. 2. To jerk backward, as a gun upon firing ▸ recoil. 3. To send back the sound of ▸ reflect, reverberate. *See* **echo** (1). 4. To reverse direction after striking something ▸ bounce, reflect, snap back, spring back. *See also* **bend, glance.**

rebound *noun*
A bouncing movement ▸ bounce, bound, hop.

rebuff *noun*
A deliberate slight or affront ▸ cut, shun, spurn. *See* **snub.**

rebuff *verb*
1. To slight someone deliberately ▸ shun, spurn. *See* **snub.** 2. To be unwilling to accept, consider, or receive ▸ refuse, reject. *See* **decline** (1). *See synonym note at* **decline.** 3. To turn aside or drive away ▸ deflect, repulse, ward off. *See* **repel.**

rebuild *verb*
▸ recondition, reconstruct, rejuvenate, restitute. *See* **restore** (3).

rebuke *verb*
To criticize for a fault or offense ▸ chide, dress down, reprimand. *See* **chastise** (1). *See synonym note at* **chastise.**

rebuke *noun*
Words expressive of strong disapproval ▸ admonishment, admonition, berating, chiding, dressing-down, lecture, opprobrium, remonstrance, reprimand, reproach, reproof, reproval, scolding, slap, upbraiding. *Informal:* tongue-lashing. *Slang:* chewing-out, rap, slam. *Idiom:* trip to the woodshed. *See also* **criticism, snub, vituperation.**

rebut *verb*
▸ belie, discredit, disprove. *See* **refute.**

recalcitrance *or* **recalcitrancy** *noun*
1. An attitude or behavior that is intentionally provocative or contemptuous ▸ despite, rebelliousness. *See* **defiance** (2). 2. The quality or condition of being unruly ▸ intractability, obstinacy, unmanageability. *See* **unruliness.**

recalcitrant *adjective*
1. Marked by defiance ▸ contumacious, rebellious. *See* **defiant.** 2. Not submitting to discipline or control ▸ ill-behaved, obstinate, unmanageable. *See* **unruly.** *See synonym note at* **unruly.**

recall *verb*
1. To cause one to remember or think of ▸ hark back, suggest. *Idioms:* bring to mind, put one in mind of, take one back, remind one of. *See also* **refer, remind.** 2. To renew an image or thought in the mind ▸ recollect, reminisce. *See* **remember** (1). *See synonym note at* **remember.** 3. To take back or remove ▸ repeal, rescind, revoke. *See* **lift** (5). 4. To disavow something

previously written or said irrevocably and usually formally ▸ abjure, recant, take back. *See* **retract** (1).

recall *noun*
1. The power of retaining and recalling past experience ▸ recollection, remembrance, reminiscence. *See* **memory** (1). 2. The act of reversing or annulling ▸ rescission, reversal, revocation. *See* **repeal.**

recant *verb*
▸ abjure, recall, take back. *See* **retract** (1).

recantation *noun*
▸ abjuration, palinode, withdrawal. *See* **retraction** (1).

recap *verb*
1. *Informal* To give a recapitulation of the salient facts of ▸ abstract, recapitulate, summarize. *See* **review** (1). 2. *Informal* To state again ▸ reiterate, restate, retell. *See* **repeat** (1).

recap *noun*
A review of the essential points or consequences of something: ▸ rundown, wrap-up. *See* **summary.**

recapitulate *verb*
1. To give a summary of the salient facts of ▸ abstract, go over, summarize. *See* **review** (1). 2. To state again ▸ reiterate, restate, retell. *See* **repeat** (1).

recapitulation *noun*
▸ rundown, summing-up, wrap-up. *See* **summary.**

recede *verb*
To move back or away from a point, limit, or mark ▸ ebb, retract, retreat, retrocede, retrograde, retrogress, step back. *See also* **back, wane, withdraw.**

✦ **CORE SYNONYMS:** *recede, ebb, retract, retreat, retrograde.* To move back or away from a point, limit, or mark: *a hairline that had receded; waters that ebb at low tide; a turtle that retracted into its shell; an army that retreated to avoid defeat; academic standards that have retrograded.*

---

receipts *noun*
The amount of money collected as admission ▸ box office, gate, take.

receivable *adjective*
▸ collectible, payable, unpaid. *See* **due** (1).

receive *verb*
1. To admit to one's possession, presence, or awareness ▸ accept, have, take. *See also* **absorb.** 2. To allow admittance, as to a group ▸ admit, let in, take in. *See* **accept** (3). 3. To come into possession of ▸ come by, gain, procure. *See* **get** (1). 4. To obtain from another source ▸ extract, gain. *See* **derive** (1).

received *adjective*
1. Generally approved or agreed upon ▸ conventional, orthodox, recognized. *See* **accepted.** 2. Conforming to established practice or standards ▸ conformist, orthodox, traditional. *See* **conventional** (1).

receiver *noun*
▸ focus, subject, target. *See* **object** (2).

recension *noun*
▸ amendment, emendation, rewrite. *See* **revision.**

recent *adjective*
▸ current, modern, present. *See* **contemporary** (2).

recently *adverb*
▸ just (now), newly. *See* **lately.**
receptacle *noun*
An object, such as a carton, can, or jar, in which material is held or carried ▸ container, holder, repository, vessel. *See also* **depository, package.**
receptive *adjective*
Ready and willing to receive favorably, as new ideas ▸ acceptant, amenable, friendly, open, open-minded, responsive. *See also* **alert, attentive, fair, neutral.**
receptivity *or* **receptiveness** *noun*
▸ open-mindedness, responsiveness. *See* **openness** (1).
recess *noun*
1. A pause or interval, as from work or duty ▸ break, time-out. *See* **rest**[1] (1). *See synonym note at* **rest**[1]. 2. An area sunk below its surroundings ▸ basin, dip, sink. *See* **depression** (1).
recess *verb*
To interrupt regular activity for a short period ▸ break. *Idioms:* take a break, take a breather, take five (*or* ten).
recession *noun*
A period of decreased business activity and high unemployment ▸ depression, downturn, slowdown, slump.
recidivism *noun*
▸ backsliding, lapse, recidivism. *See* **relapse.**
recipient *noun*
▸ focus, subject, target. *See* **object** (2).
reciprocal *adjective*
1. Having the same relationship each to the other ▸ reciprocative, requited. *See* **mutual** (1). 2. Supplying mutual needs ▸ correlative, interrelated, supplemental. *See* **complementary.**
reciprocate *verb*
1. To give or take mutually ▸ requite, return. *Idiom:* respond in kind. *See also* **exchange, respond.** 2. To return like for like, especially to return an unfriendly or hostile action with a similar one ▸ counter, hit back, retort. *See* **retaliate.**

✚ CORE SYNONYMS: *reciprocate, requite, return.* These verbs mean to give or take mutually: *doesn't reciprocate favors; consideration requited with disregard; return a compliment.*

---

reciprocation *noun*
1. The act of retaliating ▸ counteraction, counterblow, reprisal. *See* **retaliation.** 2. The act of exchanging ▸ interchange, switch, trade. *See* **change** (2).
reciprocative *adjective*
▸ reciprocal, requited, shared. *See* **mutual** (1).
reciprocity *noun*
▸ interchange, switch, trade. *See* **change** (2).
recite *verb*
▸ narrate, recount, report. *See* **describe** (1). *See synonym note at* **describe.**
reckless *adjective*
1. Lacking concern or regard ▸ heedless, thoughtless, unconcerned. *See* **careless** (1). 2. Characterized by

unthinking boldness and haste ▸ brash, hasty, impetuous. *See* **rash**[1]. *See synonym note at* **rash**[1]. 3. Not required, necessary, or warranted by the circumstances of the case ▸ supererogative, supererogatory, uncalled-for. *See* **wanton** (1).
recklessness *noun*
▸ brashness, incautiousness, rashness. *See* **temerity.**
reckon *verb*
1. To note items one by one in order to get a total ▸ numerate, tally. *See* **count** (2). 2. To ascertain by mathematics ▸ cipher, compute, figure. *See* **calculate** (1). *See synonym note at* **calculate.** 3. To calculate approximately ▸ place, put. *See* **estimate** (2). 4. To look upon in a particular way ▸ consider, deem, view. *See* **regard** (1). *See synonym note at* **regard.** 5. *Informal* To consider to be true without proof ▸ posit, presume, presuppose. *See* **suppose** (1).
reckon on *or* **upon** *verb*
To place trust or confidence in ▸ count on (*or* upon), rely on (*or* upon). *See* **depend on** (1). *See synonym note at* **depend on.**
reckoning *noun*
1. A noting of items one by one ▸ numeration, tally. *See* **count** (1). 2. The act, process, or result of calculating ▸ calculation, cast, computation, figuring. 3. A precise list of fees or charges ▸ bill, invoice, statement. *Informal:* tab. *See* **account** (2).
reclaim *verb*
1. To bring back to a previous normal condition ▸ recondition, reconstruct, rejuvenate. *See* **restore** (3). 2. To set free, as from danger or confinement ▸ recover, save, salvage. *See* **rescue.** *See synonym note at* **rescue.**
re-claim *verb*
▸ reassume, reoccupy, repossess. *See* **resume** (1).
recline *verb*
1. To be or place oneself in a prostrate or recumbent position ▸ repose, stretch (out). *See* **lie**[1] (1). 2. To take repose, as by sleeping or lying quietly ▸ curl up, lie (down), repose, rest, stretch (out). *See also* **nap, sleep.**
reclining *adjective*
▸ horizontal, prone, prostrate. *See* **flat** (1).
reclusion *noun*
▸ isolation, retirement, sequestration. *See* **seclusion** (1).
reclusive *or* **recluse** *adjective*
▸ alone, companionless, isolated. *See* **solitary** (1).
recognition *noun*
1. Favorable reception or regard ▸ acknowledgment, approval, credit. *See* **acceptance** (2). 2. The act of admitting to something ▸ admission, avowal, confession. *See* **acknowledgment** (1).
recognizable *adjective*
▸ discernible, palpable, perceivable. *See* **perceptible.**
recognizance *noun*
▸ security, token, warrant. *See* **pawn**[1].
recognize *verb*
1. To establish the identity of ▸ identify, know, pin-

point. *See* **place** (1). **2.** To express recognition of ▸ acknowledge, admit. *See also* **confirm**. **3.** To perceive with a special effort of the senses or the mind ▸ detect, mark. *See* **notice**. **4.** To perceive and fix the identity of, especially with difficulty ▸ ascertain, spot. *See* **discern** (1).

recognized *adjective*
1. Generally approved or agreed upon ▸ accepted, conventional, orthodox. *See* **accepted**. **2.** Widely known ▸ celebrated, noted, well-known. *See* **famous**.

recoil *verb*
To draw away or pull back in fear ▸ cringe, quail, shrink. *See* **flinch**.

recoil *noun*
An act of drawing back in an involuntary or instinctive fashion ▸ cringe, flinch, jerk (back), shrink, wince. *See also* **start**.

recollect *verb*
▸ recall, reminisce, retain. *See* **remember** (1). *See synonym note at* **remember**.

recollection *noun*
1. The power of retaining and recalling past experience ▸ remembrance, reminiscence. *See* **memory** (1). **2.** An act or instance of remembering ▸ memory, mental image, remembrance, reminiscence. *See also* **idea**.

recommend *verb*
1. To aid the cause of by approving or favoring ▸ back, endorse, stand by. *See* **support** (1). **2.** To give recommendations to someone about a decision or course of action ▸ counsel, direct. *See* **advise** (1). *See synonym note at* **advise**.

recommendable *adjective*
▸ expedient, well. *See* **advisable**.

recommendation *noun*
1. An indication of commendation or approval ▸ backing, support. *See* **endorsement** (1). **2.** A statement attesting to personal qualifications, character, and dependability ▸ character, reference, testimonial. *See also* **endorsement**. **3.** An opinion as to a decision or course of action ▸ guidance, recommendation. *See* **advice** (1). *See synonym note at* **advice**.

recommendatory *adjective*
▸ consultatory, consulting. *See* **advisory**.

recompense *verb*
To give compensation to ▸ indemnify, pay, remunerate. *See* **compensate** (1).

recompense *noun*
1. Something to make up for loss or damage ▸ amends, remuneration, reparation. *See* **compensation** (1). **2.** Something justly deserved ▸ compensation, deserts, reward. *See* **due** (1). **3.** Payment for work done ▸ earnings, pay, salary. *See* **wage**.

reconcile *verb*
1. To reestablish friendship between ▸ conciliate, make up, reunite. *See also* **pacify**. **2.** To bring something into a state of agreement or accord ▸ arrange, set. *See* **settle** (2). **3.** To bring oneself to accept ▸ resign. *Idiom:* get used to. **4.** To make or become suitable to a particular situation or use ▸ acclimate, acclimatize, accommodate, adapt, adjust, conform, fashion, fit, square, suit, tailor. **5.** To bring into accord ▸ conform, integrate. *See* **harmonize** (1).

reconcilement *noun*
A reestablishment of friendship or harmony ▸ conciliation, rapprochement, reconciliation, settlement. *See also* **agreement, atonement, compromise**.

reconciliation *noun*
1. A reestablishment of friendship or harmony ▸ conciliation, rapprochement, reconcilement, settlement. *See also* **agreement, atonement, compromise**. **2.** The act of making amends ▸ atonement, expiation, penance, reparation. *See also* **compensation, purification**.

recondite *adjective*
1. Beyond the understanding of an average mind ▸ abstract, esoteric, profound. *See* **deep** (2). **2.** Lacking certainty or clarity ▸ dubious, indeterminate, questionable, unclear. *See* **ambiguous** (1). *See synonym note at* **ambiguous**. **3.** Not widely understood ▸ arcane, esoteric. *See* **obscure** (1).

recondition *verb*
1. To bring back to a previous normal condition ▸ rebuild, reconstruct, rejuvenate. *See* **restore** (3). **2.** To make new or as if new again ▸ refresh, restore, revamp. *See* **renew** (1).

reconfigure *verb*
1. To mix together so as to change the order of arrangement ▸ rearrange, scramble. *See* **shuffle** (1). **2.** To reorganize thoroughly ▸ reengineer, reshuffle. *See* **overhaul** (1).

reconnaissance *noun*
The act or an instance of exploring or investigating ▸ exploration, investigation, probe. *See also* **examination**.

reconnoiter *verb*
▸ inquire, investigate, probe. *See* **explore**.

reconsider *verb*
To consider again, especially with the possibility of change ▸ reevaluate, reexamine, rethink, reweigh, review. *See also* **consider, doubt**.

reconstruct *verb*
▸ rebuild, recondition, rejuvenate, restitute. *See* **restore** (3).

record *verb*
1. To place on a list or in a record or book ▸ catalog, chronicle, write down. *See* **list**[1] (1). **2.** To give a precise indication of, as on a register or scale ▸ mark, register. *See* **show** (3).

record *noun*
1. An item inserted, as in a diary, register, or reference book ▸ heading, posting. *See* **entry** (1). **2.** A recounting of past events ▸ chronicle, history, report. *See* **story** (1). **3.** One's previous experiences ▸ career, past, resumé. *See* **history** (2). **4.** A mark or remnant that indicates the former presence of something ▸ remains, trace, vestige. *See* **trace** (1).

recount *verb*
▸ detail, narrate, report. *See* **describe** (1). *See synonym note at* **desire.**

recoup *verb*
1. To get back ▸ repossess, retrieve. *See* **recover** (1). *See synonym note at* **recover.** 2. To give compensation to ▸ indemnify, pay, recompense. *See* **compensate** (1).

recoup *noun*
The act of getting back or regaining ▸ recovery, repossession, retrieval.

recoupment *noun*
▸ amends, remuneration, reparation. *See* **compensation** (1).

recourse *noun*
1. That to which one turns for help when in desperation ▸ refuge, resort, resource. *See also* **help, support.** 2. The act of putting into play ▸ employment, implementation, usage. *See* **exercise** (1).

recover *verb*
1. To get back ▸ make up, recoup, regain, repossess, retrieve. 2. To regain one's health ▸ bounce back, come around (*or* round), convalesce, gain, get better, get well, improve, mend, perk up, rally, recuperate. *Idiom:* be on the mend. *See also* **revive.** 3. To set free, as from danger or confinement ▸ reclaim, save. *See* **rescue.**

✦ CORE SYNONYMS: *recover, regain, recoup, retrieve.* These verbs mean to get back something lost or taken away. *Recover* is the least specific: *The police recovered the stolen car.* "*In a few days Mr. Barnstaple had recovered strength of body and mind*" (H.G. Wells). *Regain* suggests success in recovering something that has been taken from one: "*hopeful to regain/Thy Love*" (John Milton). To *recoup* is to get back the equivalent of something lost: *earned enough profit to recoup her expenses. Retrieve* pertains to the effortful recovery of something (*retrieved the ball*) or to the making good of something gone awry: "*By a brilliant coup he has retrieved . . . a rather serious loss*" (Samuel Butler).

---

recovery *noun*
1. The act of getting back or regaining ▸ recoup, repossession, retrieval. 2. The process or period of a return to health ▸ convalescence, rally, recuperation. 3. A return to former prosperity or status ▸ comeback, reestablishment, restoration. *See also* **renewal, revival.**

recreance *or* **recreancy** *noun*
▸ abandonment, disavowal, renouncement. *See* **defection.**

recreant *adjective*
1. Not true to duty or obligation ▸ disloyal, traitorous, treacherous. *See* **faithless** (1). 2. Ignobly lacking in courage ▸ faint-hearted, pusillanimous. *Slang:* gutless. *See* **cowardly.**

recreant *noun*
1. A person who has defected ▸ deserter, renegade, traitor. *See* **defector.** 2. An ignoble, uncourageous person ▸ dastard, poltroon, sissy. *See* **coward.**

recreate *verb*
1. To occupy in an agreeable or pleasing way ▸ divert, entertain, regale. *See* **amuse** (1). 2. To occupy oneself with amusement or diversion ▸ frolic, sport. *Informal:* horse around. *See* **play** (1).

re-create *verb*
▸ refresh, restore, revamp. *See* **renew** (1).

recreation *noun*
▸ distraction, entertainment, fun. *See* **amusement.**

recriminate *verb*
▸ charge, denounce, incriminate. *See* **accuse.**

recrimination *noun*
▸ denouncement, incrimination. *See* **accusation.**

recriminator *noun*
One that accuses ▸ accuser, arraigner, denouncer, indicter.

recrudesce *verb*
▸ recur, reoccur, revert. *See* **return** (1).

recruit *verb*
▸ hire, retain. *See* **employ** (1).

rectify *verb*
1. To make right what is wrong ▸ mend, remedy. *See* **correct** (1). *See synonym note at* **correct.** 2. To bring something into a state of agreement or accord ▸ arrange, set. *See* **settle** (2).

rectitude *noun*
1. The quality or state of being morally sound ▸ probity, virtue. *See* **good** (1). 2. The quality of conforming to accepted standards of conduct ▸ ethicality, morality. *See* **ethics** (1).

rector *noun*
▸ ecclesiastic, minister, parson. *See* **cleric.**

recumbent *adjective*
▸ horizontal, prone, prostrate. *See* **flat** (1).

recuperate *verb*
▸ convalesce, improve, rally. *See* **recover** (2).

recuperation *noun*
The process or period of a return to health ▸ convalescence, rally, recovery.

recur *verb*
1. To happen again or repeatedly ▸ iterate, reappear, reoccur, repeat. 2. To come back to a former condition ▸ recrudesce, reoccur, revert. *See* **return** (1).

recurrence *noun*
▸ echo, reappearance, reoccurrence. *See* **repetition** (1).

recurrent *adjective*
Happening or appearing consistently or repeatedly ▸ regular, repeating, repetitive. *See also* **periodic, pervasive, thematic.**

redaction *noun*
▸ amendment, recension, rewrite. *See* **revision.**

red-blooded *adjective*
▸ robust, strapping, sturdy. *See* **lusty** (1).

redden *verb*
▸ crimson, flush. *See* **blush.**

redecorate *verb*
▸ refresh, restore, revamp. *See* **renew** (1).

redeem *verb*
1. To set free, as from danger or confinement ▸ re-

cover, save. *See* **rescue.** *See synonym note at* **rescue.**
2. To make ineffective by applying an opposite force
▶ counteract, negate, offset. *See* **cancel** (2). **3.** To free
from sin, guilt, or defilement ▶ expiate, lustrate,
pardon. *See* **purify** (1).

redeemer *noun*
▶ deliverer, liberator, savior. *See* **rescuer.**

redemption *noun*
▶ ablution, catharsis. *See* **purification** (2).

red-hot *adjective*
1. Marked by much heat ▶ blistering, boiling, burning. *See* **hot** (1). **2.** Fired with intense feeling ▶ burning,
fervent, impassioned, torrid. *See* **passionate** (1). **3.** *Informal* Of great current interest ▶ hot, live. *See also*
fashionable, important.

redo *verb*
To do or perform an act again ▶ do over, duplicate,
play over, repeat, replay. *See also* **copy.**

redolence *noun*
▶ aroma, perfume, scent. *See* **fragrance.** *See synonym
note at* **fragrance.**

redolent *adjective*
1. Having a pleasant odor ▶ aromatic, perfumy, savory. *See* **fragrant. 2.** Having a sharp, penetrating
flavor or aroma ▶ piquant, sharp, zesty. *See* **spicy** (1).

redouble *verb*
1. To make or become twice as great ▶ double,
duplicate, geminate, twin. **2.** To make greater in
intensity or severity ▶ deepen, enhance, heighten. *See*
intensify.

redoubt *noun*
▶ citadel, stronghold. *See* **fort.**

redoubtable *adjective*
1. Causing or capable of causing fear ▶ formidable,
frightful, scary, unnerving. *See* **fearful** (1). **2.** Widely
known ▶ celebrated, notable, noted, renowned. *See*
famous.

red-pencil *verb*
Informal To examine and remove objectionable or
improper material from a publication ▶ bowdlerize,
edit, expurgate. *See* **censor** (1).

redraft *verb*
To prepare a new version of something ▶ amend,
revamp, rework. *See* **revise** (1).

redraft *noun*
The act or process of revising ▶ amendment, emendation, rewrite. *See* **revision.**

redress *verb*
1. To make right what is wrong ▶ mend, rectify,
remedy. *See* **correct** (1). *See synonym note at* **correct.**
2. To exact revenge for or from ▶ pay off, vindicate.
See **avenge. 3.** To give compensation to ▶ indemnify,
pay, recompense. *See* **compensate** (1).

redress *noun*
Something to make up for loss or damage ▶ amends,
remuneration, reparation. *See* **compensation** (1). *See
synonym note at* **compensation.**

red tape *noun*
▶ fuss, pother. *See* **bother** (1).

reduce *verb*
1. To grow or cause to grow gradually less ▶ diminish,
dwindle, lessen. *See* **decrease.** *See synonym note at*
decrease. 2. To make short or shorter ▶ abridge,
curtail. *See* **shorten. 3.** To lower in rank or grade
▶ degrade, downgrade. *See* **demote.** *See synonym note
at* **demote. 4.** To become or make less in price or
value ▶ devalue, downgrade, reduce. *See* **depreciate**
(1). **5.** To lose body weight, as by dieting ▶ slim
(down), thin (down), trim down. *Idioms:* get the
weight off, lose weight, shed some pounds. **6.** To
separate into parts for study ▶ break down, dissect,
resolve. *See* **analyze** (1). **7.** To make thick or thicker,
especially through evaporation or condensation
▶ condense, inspissate, thicken. *See also* **coagulate.**

reduction *noun*
1. The act or process of decreasing ▶ diminishment,
shrinkage, slowdown. *See* **decrease. 2.** The act or an
instance of demoting ▶ demotion, degradation,
downgrade. **3.** A lowering of price or value ▶ cheapening, markdown, shrinkage. *See* **depreciation** (1).
4. An amount deducted ▶ abatement, rebate. *See*
deduction (1). **5.** The separation of a whole into its
parts for study ▶ breakdown, dissection, subdivision.
See **analysis** (1).

redundancy *or* **redundance** *noun*
▶ pleonasm, prolixity, verboseness. *See* **wordiness.**

redundant *adjective*
1. Using or containing an excessive number of words
▶ long-winded, periphrastic, verbose. *See* **wordy** (1).
2. Being more than is needed, desired, or appropriate
▶ excess, surplus. *See* **superfluous.**

reduplication *noun*
▶ ditto, facsimile, likeness. *See* **copy** (1).

reecho *verb*
▶ reflect, repeat, reverberate. *See* **echo** (1). *See synonym
note at* **echo.**

reek *verb*
To have or give off a foul odor ▶ smell, stink. *Idiom:*
stink to high heaven.

reek *noun*
A strong, foul odor ▶ malodor, stink. *See* **stench.** *See
synonym note at* **stench.**

reeking *or* **reeky** *adjective*
▶ fetid, foul, stinking. *See* **smelly.**

reel *verb*
1. To walk unsteadily ▶ careen, stumble, totter. *See*
stagger (1). **2.** To have the sensation of turning in
circles ▶ spin, swim, swirl, whirl. *Idiom:* go round and
round. **3.** To rotate on an axis or around a center
▶ twirl, whirl, wheel. *See* **turn** (1).

reeling *adjective*
▶ lightheaded, spinning, unsteady. *See* **dizzy** (1).

reengineer *verb*
▶ reconfigure, reshuffle, shake up. *See* **overhaul** (1).

reengineering *noun*
A thourough or drastic reorganization ▶ overhaul,
reshuffling, shakeup. *Informal:* housecleaning. *See
also* **renewal, revolution.**

reestablish *verb*

To bring back into existence or use ► reinstate, reintroduce, renew, restore, return, revive. *See also* **restore.**

reestablishment *noun*

A return to former prosperity or status ► comeback, recovery, restoration. *See also* **renewal, revival.**

reevaluate *verb*

► reexamine, rethink, review. *See* **reconsider.**

ref *noun*

Informal A person, usually appointed, who decides the issues of, decides the results of, or supervises the conduct of a competition or conflict ► arbiter, umpire. *See* **judge** (3).

refer *verb*

1. To make reference to something ► advert, allude (to), bring up, mention, note, point to (*or* out), touch (on *or* upon). *Idioms:* call (*or* direct) attention to. *See also* **cite, designate, propose, recall. 2.** To direct a person elsewhere for help or information ► send, transfer, turn over. **3.** To regard as belonging to or resulting from another ► ascribe, assign. *See* **attribute** (1). *See synonym note at* **attribute. 4.** To be pertinent ► appertain, pertain, relate. *See* **apply** (2). **5.** To look to when in need ► apply, run, turn. *See* **resort** (1). *See synonym note at* **resort.**

refer to *verb*

To refer to by name ► mention, point to, specify. *See* **name** (2).

✦ **CORE SYNONYMS:** *refer, advert, mention, note.* These verbs mean to make reference to something. *The article referred to the mayor's indiscretion. In therapy, he adverted to childhood experiences. She often mentions her friends from college. Please note that your grade will depend on your attendance in class.*

---

referee *noun*

A person, usually appointed, who decides the issues of, decides the results of, or supervises the conduct of a competition or conflict ► arbitrator, umpire. *See* **judge** (3). *See synonym note at* **judge.**

referee *verb*

To make a decision about (a controversy or dispute, for example) after deliberation, as in a court of law ► adjudicate, decide, rule. *See* **judge** (1).

reference *noun*

1. The act of referring ► citation, naming, pointing out, referral, signification, signifying. *See also* **meaning, sign. 2.** An object referred to ► referent, signified. *See also* **meaning. 3.** A statement attesting to personal qualifications, character, and dependability ► character, recommendation, testimonial. *See also* **endorsement.**

referent *noun*

An object referred to ► reference, signified. *See also* **meaning.**

referral *noun*

The act of referring ► naming, signification. *See* **reference** (1).

refine *verb*

1. To remove impurities from ► clarify, clean, cleanse, purify. *See also* **clean. 2.** To bring to perfection or completion ► complete, polish, round off, smooth. *See* **perfect.**

refined *adjective*

1. Exhibiting refined, tasteful beauty of manner, form, or style ► exquisite, graceful. **2.** Characterized by discriminating taste and broad knowledge as a result of development or education ► cultivated, educated. *See* **cultured. 3.** So slight as to be difficult to notice or appreciate ► precise, subtle. *See* **delicate** (4).

refinement *noun*

1. The act or process of removing physical impurities ► clarification, cleaning, lavation. *See* **purification** (1). **2.** Refinement of manner, form, and style ► grace, polish, sophistication. *See* **elegance. 3.** Excellent taste resulting from intellectual development ► cultivation, enlightenment. *See* **culture** (3). **4.** The ability to distinguish, especially to recognize small differences or draw fine distinctions ► acuteness, selectiveness, taste. *See* **discrimination** (1). **5.** Socially correct behavior ► etiquette, propriety. *See* **manners. 6.** The act of making better or the condition of being made better ► enhancement, rehabilitation, upgrade. *See* **improvement** (1).

refinery *or* **refiner** *noun*

► antiseptic, clarifier, cleanser. *See* **purifier.**

refining *adjective*

► enlightening, humanizing. *See* **cultural.**

reflect *verb*

1. To send back the sound of ► repeat, reverberate. *See* **echo** (1). *See synonym note at* **echo. 2.** To send back or form an image of ► image, mirror. *See also* **represent. 3.** To copy another slavishly ► clone, imitate. *See* **mimic** (1). **4.** To think or think about carefully and at length ► cogitate, deliberate, mull. *See* **ponder. 5.** To use the powers of the mind ► cogitate, deliberate, reason. *See* **think** (1). *See synonym note at* **think. 6.** To state facts, opinions, or explanations ► observe, opine, remark. *See* **comment. 7.** To move or cause to move in a bent or angular direction ► deflect, turn. *See* **bend** (2). **8.** To reverse direction after striking something ► bound (back), rebound, snap back, spring back. *See also* **bend, glance.**

reflection *noun*

1. An image caused by reflection ► image, likeness. *See also* **copy. 2.** Light that is reflected ► glare, highlight. *See also* **flash. 3.** An act of reflection ► deflection, glance, scattering. *See also* **bounce. 4.** Imitative reproduction, as of the style of another ► repetition, reflex. *See* **echo** (1). **5.** The act or process of thinking ► cogitation, deliberation, rumination. *See* **thought** (1). **6.** An implied criticism ► imputation, slur. *See also* **crack, libel. 7.** An expression of fact or opinion ► note, observation, remark. *See* **comment** (1).

reflective *adjective*

► contemplative, pensive, ruminative. *See* **thoughtful** (1). *See synonym note at* **thoughtful.**

reflex *adjective*
Acting or happening without apparent forethought, prompting, or planning ▸ impulsive, involuntary. *See* **spontaneous** (1).

reflex *noun*
Imitative reproduction, as of the style of another ▸ reflection, repetition. *See* **echo** (1).

reflexive *adjective*
▸ impulsive, involuntary. *See* **spontaneous** (1).

reform *verb*
▸ mend, rectify, remedy. *See* **correct** (1). *See synonym note at* **correct.**

reformative *or* **reformatory** *adjective*
▸ amendatory, remedial. *See* **corrective.**

refract *verb*
▸ deflect, turn. *See* **bend** (2).

refractoriness *noun*
The quality or condition of being unruly ▸ intractability, obstinacy, unmanageability. *See* **unruliness.**

refractory *adjective*
▸ ill-behaved, obstinate, unmanageable. *See* **unruly.** *See synonym note at* **unruly.**

refrain *verb*
To hold oneself back ▸ abstain, forbear, hold off, keep, withhold. *Informal:* sit out. *See also* **avoid, hesitate.**

refrain from *verb*
To keep away from ▸ eschew, obstain from, shun. *See* **avoid.**

✛ **CORE SYNONYMS:** *refrain, abstain, forbear.* These verbs mean to hold oneself back from doing or saying something: *refrained from commenting; abstained from smoking; can't forbear criticizing them.*

---

refresh *verb*
1. To impart renewed energy and strength to a person ▸ freshen, reinvigorate, rejuvenate, renew, restore, revitalize, revivify. *See also* **energize.** 2. To make new or as if new again ▸ re-create, restore, revamp. *See* **renew** (1).

refreshing *adjective*
▸ bracing, energizing, exhilarating. *See* **invigorating.**

refreshment *noun*
1. A light meal ▸ collation, snack. *Informal:* bite, nosh. *Slang:* munchies. *See also* **appetizer.** 2. Any liquid that is fit for drinking ▸ beverage, liquor. *See* **drink** (1).

refuge *noun*
1. Protection or shelter, as from danger or hardship ▸ asylum, harborage, safety, sanctuary, shelter. *Idiom:* safe haven. *See also* **defense.** 2. Something that physically protects, especially from danger ▸ harbor, haven, sanctuary. *See* **cover** (1). *See synonym note at* **cover.** 3. That to which one turns for help when in desperation ▸ recourse, resort, resource. *See also* **help, support.**

refugee *noun*
1. One who flees, as from confinement or the police ▸ escapee, fugitive, outlaw, runaway. *See also* **criminal.** 2. One forced to emigrate, usually for political reasons ▸ deportee, expatriate. *See* **émigré** (1).

refulgent *adjective*
▸ brilliant, incandescent, radiant. *See* **bright** (1).

refund *verb*
To give back, especially money ▸ reimburse, repay, restitute. *See also* **compensate, return.**

refund *noun*
A quantity of money that is returned ▸ reimbursement, repayment. *See also* **deduction, return.**

refurbish *verb*
▸ refresh, restore, revamp. *See* **renew** (1).

refurbishment *noun*
▸ refurbishment, rejuvenation, renovation. *See* **renewal** (1).

refusal *noun*
1. A negative response ▸ nay, rejection. *See* **no** (1). 2. A turning down of a request ▸ denial, disallowance, nonacceptance, rejection, turndown. *See also* **forbiddance.**

refuse[1] *verb*
To be unwilling to accept, consider, or receive ▸ deny, reject, spurn. *See* **decline** (1). *See synonym note at* **decline.**

refuse[2] *noun*
Items or material discarded or rejected as useless or worthless ▸ debris, litter, rubbish. *See* **garbage** (1).

refute *verb*
To prove or show to be false ▸ belie, confute, disprove, rebut. *See also* **cancel, discredit, repudiate.**

regain *verb*
▸ recoup, repossess, retrieve. *See* **recover** (1). *See synonym note at* **recover.**

regal *adjective*
1. Impressive in size, proportion, or appearance ▸ imposing, magnificent, splendid. *See* **grand** (1). 2. Of high birth or social position ▸ blue-blooded, elite, upper-class. *See* **noble** (1).

regale *verb*
1. To occupy in an agreeable or pleasing way ▸ divert, entertain, recreate. *See* **amuse** (1). *See synonym note at* **amuse.** 2. To sustain with food ▸ feed, nourish. *Idiom:* wine and dine. *See also* **support.**

regalia *noun*
▸ array, finery, frippery. *See* **attire** (1).

regard *verb*
1. To look upon in a particular way ▸ account, consider, deem, esteem, look upon, reckon, see, think of, view. *See also* **believe.** 2. To look at or on attentively or carefully ▸ eye, observe, survey. *See* **watch** (1). 3. To have a high opinion of ▸ admire, esteem, respect. *See* **value** (1).

regard *noun*
1. An act of directing the eyes on an object ▸ contemplation, look, sight, view. *See also* **gaze, watch.** 2. Thoughtful attention to others ▸ concern, solicitude, thoughtfulness. *See* **consideration** (1). 3. Cautious attentiveness ▸ caution, heed, mindfulness, wariness. *See* **care** (1). 4. Mental acquisitiveness ▸ inquisitiveness, interest. *See* **curiosity** (1). 5. The act of noting, observing, or taking into account ▸ heed,

note, remark. *See* **notice** (1). **6.** A feeling of deference, approval, and liking ▸ admiration, favor. *See* **esteem** (1). *See synonym note at* **esteem**. **7.** Favorable reception or regard ▸ approval, favor, welcome. *See* **acceptance** (2). **8.** The position from which something is observed or considered ▸ aspect, respect, standpoint. *See* **viewpoint**.

✦ **CORE SYNONYMS:** *regard, consider, deem, account, reckon.* These verbs refer to look upon or hold an opinions in a particular way. *Regard* often implies a personal attitude: *I regard your apology as genuine.* *Consider* suggests objective reflection and reasoning: *He considers success to be of little importance. Deem* is more subjective, emphasizing judgment rather than contemplation: *The faculty deemed the essay to be acceptable. Account* and *reckon* in this sense are literary and imply calculated judgment: *"I account no man to be a philosopher who attempts to do more"* (John Henry Newman). *"I cannot reckon you as an admirer"* (Nathaniel Hawthorne).

regardful *adjective*
1. Vigilantly attentive ▸ intent, vigilant. *See* **alert** (1). **2.** Cautiously attentive ▸ heedful, mindful, watchful. *See* **careful** (1). **3.** Full of polite concern for the well-being of others ▸ courteous, solicitous, thoughtful. *See* **attentive** (1). *See synonym note at* **attentive**.

regardfulness *noun*
▸ attentiveness, concentration, consideration. *See* **attention** (1).

regards *noun*
Friendly greetings or acknowledgment ▸ best, greetings, respects. *See also* **hello**.

regenerate *verb*
▸ restore, resuscitate, revivify. *See* **revive** (2).

regeneration *noun*
A fundamental change in one's beliefs ▸ conversion, metanoia, rebirth. *See also* **revival**.

regime *noun*
▸ administration, authorities, state. *See* **government** (2).

regimen *noun*
1. The systematic application of remedies to effect a cure ▸ care, rehabilitation, therapy. *See* **treatment** (1). **2.** Repetition of an action so as to develop or maintain one's skill ▸ exercise, rehearsal. *See* **practice** (1).

regiment *verb*
▸ organize, systematize. *See* **arrange** (1).

region *noun*
1. A part of the earth's surface ▸ district, zone. *See* **area** (2). **2.** A particular area used for or associated with a specific individual or activity ▸ belt, district, terrain. *See* **territory** (1).

regional *adjective*
1. Relating to or restricted to a particular territory ▸ sectional, territorial. *See also* **local**. **2.** Existing, born, or produced in a land or region ▸ autochthonic, native. *See* **indigenous** (1). **3.** Confined to a particular location or site ▸ bounded, limited. *See* **local** (1).

register *noun*
A series, as of names or words, printed or written down ▸ catalog, roll, roster. *See* **list**[1].

register *verb*
1. To place on a list or in a record or book ▸ catalog, chronicle, write down. *See* **list**[1] (1). **2.** To give a precise indication of, as on a register or scale ▸ mark, record. *See* **show** (3). **3.** To come as a realization ▸ dawn on (*or* upon), sink in, soak in. *See also* **discover, strike, understand**.

regnant *adjective*
1. Exercising controlling power or influence ▸ key, predominant, reigning. *See* **dominant** (1). **2.** Most generally existing or encountered at a given time ▸ predominant, rampant. *See* **prevailing** (1).

regress *verb*
▸ fall back, lapse, revert. *See* **relapse**.

regression *noun*
▸ backsliding, lapse, recidivism. *See* **relapse**.

regret *verb*
To feel or express sorrow for ▸ deplore, repent, rue, sorrow (over). *See also* **feel, grieve**.

regret *noun*
1. Unhappiness caused by the failure of one's hopes, desires, or expectations ▸ disillusion, letdown, frustration. *See* **disappointment** (1). **2.** A feeling of regret for one's sins or misdeeds ▸ contriteness, remorse, repentance. *See* **penitence**.

regretful *adjective*
▸ penitent, repentant, rueful. *See* **sorry** (1).

regrets *noun*
A statement of acknowledgment expressing regret or asking pardon ▸ apology, excuse, mea culpa. *See also* **acknowledgment**.

regrettable *adjective*
▸ depressing, lamentable, mournful. *See* **sorrowful** (1).

regular *adjective*
1. Occurring or encountered regularly ▸ commonplace, frequent, routine. *See* **common** (1). **2.** Characterized by or displaying symmetry, especially correspondence in scale or measure ▸ balanced, proportional, proportionate, symmetric, symmetrical. *See also* **even, parallel**. **3.** Free from flaws or blemishes ▸ clean, flawless, unblemished. *See* **perfect** (1). **4.** Arranged or proceeding in a set, systematized pattern ▸ orderly, organized, systematic. *See* **methodical** (1). **5.** Having no change or variation ▸ constant, same, steady. *See* **unchanging**. **6.** Conforming to established standards ▸ conformist, orthodox, traditional. *See* **conventional** (1). **7.** Happening or appearing consistently or repeatedly ▸ recurrent, repeating, repetitive. *See also* **periodic, pervasive, thematic**.

regularity *noun*
1. The quality or condition of being usual ▸ normality, ordinariness, routineness. *See* **usualness**. **2.** The condition of being without change or variation ▸ constancy, immutability. *See* **changelessness**.

regularize *verb*
▸ standardize, stylize. *See* **conventionalize**.

regularly *adverb*
▸ customarily, generally, normally. *See* **usually**.

regulate *verb*
1. To control the functioning or outcome of ▸ determine, fix. *See* **govern** (1). 2. To alter for proper functioning ▸ attune, calibrate, fine-tune, set. *See* **adjust** (1). 3. To put into a deliberate order ▸ deploy, organize, systematize. *See* **arrange** (1). 4. To maintain or keep in order with or as if with police ▸ monitor, patrol. *See* **police** (1).

regulated *adjective*
▸ checked, controlled. *See* **restricted** (1).

regulation *noun*
1. A principle governing affairs within or among political units ▸ decree, edict, institute. *See* **law** (1). 2. A code or set of codes governing action or procedure, for example ▸ guideline, prescript, rubric. *See* **rule** (1).

regulatory *adjective*
▸ bureaucratic, legislative. *See* **governmental**.

rehab *noun*
Informal The systematic application of remedies to effect a cure ▸ regimen, rehabilitation, therapy. *See* **treatment** (1).

rehabilitate *verb*
1. To bring back to a previous normal condition ▸ recondition, reconstruct, rejuvenate. *See* **restore** (3). 2. To restore to health ▸ heal, remedy. *See* **cure** (1).

rehabilitation *noun*
1. The systematic application of remedies to effect a cure ▸ care, regimen, therapy. *See* **treatment** (1). 2. The act of making better or the condition of being made better ▸ enhancement, refinement, upgrade. *See* **improvement** (1).

rehash *verb*
▸ reword, translate. *See* **paraphrase**.

rehearsal *noun*
▸ exercise, regimen. *See* **practice** (1).

rehearse *verb*
1. To do or perform repeatedly so as to master ▸ exercise, run through. *See* **practice** (1). *See synonym note at* **practice**. 2. To communicate the facts, details, or particulars of something ▸ narrate, recount, report. *See* **describe** (1). *See synonym note at* **describe**.

reification *noun*
▸ incarnation, manifestation, personification. *See* **embodiment** (1).

reify *verb*
▸ externalize, manifest, materialize. *See* **embody** (1).

reign *noun*
The act of exercising controlling power or the condition of being so controlled ▸ control, dominion, rule. *See* **domination** (1).

reign *verb*
1. To have charge of the affairs of others ▸ direct, govern, rule. *See* **administer** (1). 2. To occupy the preeminent position in ▸ control, prevail. *See* **dominate** (1).

reigning *adjective*
1. Exercising controlling power or influence ▸ key,

predominant, principal. *See* **dominant** (1). 2. Most generally existing or encountered at a given time ▸ predominant, rampant. *See* **prevailing** (1).

reimbursable *adjective*
Affording compensation ▸ compensative, compensatory, remunerative.

reimburse *verb*
1. To give back, especially money ▸ refund, repay, restitute. *See also* **compensate, return**. 2. To give compensation to ▸ indemnify, pay, recompense. *See* **compensate** (1).

reimbursement *noun*
1. Something to make up for loss or damage ▸ amends, remuneration, reparation. *See* **compensation** (1). 2. A quantity of money that is returned ▸ refund, repayment. *See also* **deduction, return**.

rein *verb*
To control, restrict, or arrest ▸ bridle, check, curb. *See* **restrain**.

rein *noun*
A device for slowing or stopping motion ▸ curb, leash, restraint. *See* **brake** (1).

reinforce *verb*
1. To make stronger or more resistant ▸ bolster, buttress, strengthen. *See* **support** (2). 2. To add to or make whole ▸ augment, complete. *See* **supplement**. 3. To make firmer in a particular conviction or habit ▸ confirm, fortify, harden, strengthen. *See also* **back, establish**.

reinforcement *noun*
▸ buttress, crutch, prop. *See* **support** (1).

reinstall *verb*
To put someone in the possession of a prior position or office ▸ give back, reappoint, reinstate, replace, restore, return.

reinstate *verb*
1. To bring back into existence or use ▸ reestablish, reintroduce, renew, restore, return, revive. 2. To put someone in the possession of a prior position or office ▸ give back, reappoint, reinstall, replace, restore, return. 3. To bring back to a previous normal condition ▸ recondition, reconstruct, rejuvenate. *See* **restore** (3).

reintroduce *verb*
To bring back into existence or use ▸ reestablish, reinstate, renew, restore, return, revive. *See also* **restore**.

reinvigorate *verb*
▸ freshen, rejuvenate, revitalize. *See* **refresh** (1).

reinvigorating *adjective*
▸ bracing, energizing, exhilarating. *See* **invigorating**.

reiterate *verb*
▸ iterate, restate, retell. *See* **repeat** (1). *See synonym note at* **repeat**.

reiteration *noun*
▸ echo, repeat, restatement. *See* **repetition** (1).

reiterative *adjective*
Characterized by repetition ▸ iterative, repetitious, repetitive. *See also* **boring, superfluous, wordy**.

reject *verb*

1. To be unwilling to accept, consider, or receive ▸ refuse, spurn. *See* **decline** (1). *See synonym note at* **decline. 2.** To refuse to recognize or acknowledge ▸ deny, disown, renounce. *See* **repudiate** (1). **3.** To keep from being admitted, included, or considered ▸ bar, eliminate, banish. *See* **exclude** (1). *See synonym note at* **exclude. 4.** To rid one's mind of ▸ cast out, dispel. *See* **dismiss** (3). **5.** To have or express an unfavorable opinion of ▸ condemn, disfavor, object to. *See* **disapprove** (1). **6.** To give no credence to ▸ doubt, mistrust. *See* **disbelieve** (1).

reject *noun*

Someone excluded from society ▸ exile, pariah. *See* **outcast.**

rejected *adjective*

1. Having been given up and left alone ▸ forsaken, outcast, relinquished. *See* **abandoned** (1). **2.** Not welcome or wanted ▸ uninvited, unwanted. *See* **unwelcome** (1).

rejection *noun*

1. A negative response ▸ refusal, thumbs-down. *See* **no** (1). **2.** A refusal to grant the truth of a statement or charge ▸ disaffirmation, disclaimer, renunciation. *See* **denial** (1). **3.** A turning down of a request ▸ denial, disallowance, nonacceptance, refusal, turndown. *See also* **forbiddance. 4.** The refusal or reluctance to believe ▸ incredulity, mistrust, skepticism, unbelief. *See* **disbelief** (1). **5.** Unfavorable opinion or judgment ▸ condemnation, disfavor, reproof. *See* **disapproval.**

rejoice *verb*

1. To feel or take joy or pleasure ▸ delight, exult, pleasure. *See also* **enjoy, luxuriate. 2.** To show joyful satisfaction in an event ▸ feast, party, revel. *See* **celebrate** (2).

rejoicing *noun*

▸ jubilation, merrymaking, revelry. *See* **celebration** (3).

rejoin *verb*

▸ reply, respond, retort. *See* **answer** (1).

rejoinder *noun*

▸ reply, retort, return. *See* **answer** (1).

rejuvenate *verb*

1. To impart renewed energy and strength to a person ▸ reinvigorate, revitalize. *See* **refresh** (1). **2.** To bring back to a previous normal condition ▸ recondition, reconstruct, renovate. *See* **restore** (3). **3.** To make new or as if new again ▸ refresh, restore, revamp. *See* **renew** (1).

rejuvenation *noun*

▸ refurbishment, regeneration, renovation. *See* **renewal** (1).

rekindle *verb*

▸ reawaken, resuscitate, revitalize. *See* **revive** (1). *See synonym note at* **revive.**

relapse *verb*

To slip from a higher or better condition to a former, usually lower or poorer one ▸ backslide, fall back, lapse, regress, retrogress, revert. *See also* **deteriorate.**

relapse *noun*

A slipping from a higher or better condition to a former, usually lower or poorer one ▸ backslide, backsliding, lapse, recidivation, recidivism, regression, retrogradation, retrogression. *See also* **deterioration, reverse.**

relate *verb*

1. To communicate the facts, details, or particulars of something ▸ narrate, recount, report. *See* **describe** (1). *See synonym note at* **describe. 2.** To be pertinent ▸ appertain, pertain, refer. *See* **apply** (2). **3.** To unite or be united in a relationship ▸ combine, join, link. *See* **associate** (1). **4.** To associate or affiliate oneself closely with a person or group ▸ empathize, identify, sympathize. *See also* **understand. 5.** To interact with another or others in a harmonious fashion ▸ communicate, connect, get along (on), harmonize. *Informal:* cotton (to). *Slang:* click. *Idioms:* be in synch, be on the same wavelength, hit it off, make a good fit (*or* match). *See also* **agree. 6.** To represent as similar ▸ compare, equate, parallel. *See* **liken.**

related *adjective*

▸ akin, allied, connate. *See* **kindred.**

relation *noun*

1. A logical or natural association between two or more things ▸ connection, correlation, interconnection, interdependence, interrelationship, link, linkage, relationship, tie-in. *Informal:* hookup. *See also* **bond, relevance. 2.** A person connected to another person by blood or marriage ▸ kinsman, kinswoman, relative. *See also* **ancestry, family, kin.**

relationship *noun*

▸ correlation, link, tie-in. *See* **relation** (1).

relative *adjective*

1. Estimated by comparison ▸ comparable, comparative. **2.** Depending on or containing a condition or conditions ▸ contingent, dependent, provisory. *See* **conditional.** *See synonym note at* **conditional.**

relative *noun*

A person connected to another person by blood or marriage ▸ kinsman, kinswoman, relation. *See also* **ancestry, family, kin.**

relax *verb*

1. To reduce in tension, pressure, or rigidity ▸ let up, loosen, slacken. *See* **ease** (1). **2.** To take repose by ceasing work or other effort for an interval of time ▸ kick back, unbend, unwind. *See* **rest**[1] (1). **3.** To make even, smooth, or level ▸ level, smooth. *See* **even** (1).

relaxation *noun*

▸ leisure, relaxation, repose. *See* **rest**[1] (2).

relaxed *adjective*

1. Not tautly bound, held, or fastened ▸ flapping, slack, unbound. *See* **loose** (1). **2.** Unconstrained by rigid standards or ceremony ▸ informal, casual. *Informal:* laid-back. *See* **easygoing** (1).

release *verb*

1. To set at liberty ▸ emancipate, liberate. *See* **free** (1). **2.** To discharge material, as vapor or fumes, usually suddenly and violently ▸ give forth, issue, send forth.

See **emit** (1). **3.** To relieve a burden ▸ discharge, relieve, unburden. *See* **rid. 4.** To end the employment or service of ▸ cashier, terminate. *See* **dismiss** (1). **5.** To release from military duty ▸ demobilize, release, separate. *See* **discharge** (4). **6.** To free from an entanglement ▸ disengage, free, untangle. *See* **extricate. 7.** To become or cause to become open ▸ free, unclose. *See* **open** (1). **8.** To direct or allow to leave ▸ cast out, expel. *See* **dismiss** (2). **9.** To free from an obligation or duty ▸ discharge, exempt. *See* **excuse** (1). **10.** To present for circulation, exhibit, or sale ▸ bring out, issue, put out. *See* **publish** (1). **11.** To free from ties or fasteners ▸ loose, slip, untie. *See* **undo** (1).

release *noun*
1. The act or process of publishing printed matter ▸ issue, printing. *See* **publication** (1). **2.** Extrication from danger or confinement ▸ deliverance, liberation, salvation. *See* **rescue.**

relegate *verb*
▸ confide, delegate. *See* **entrust** (1).

relent *verb*
▸ ease off, slacken, yield. *See* **weaken** (1).

relentless *adjective*
1. Firmly, often unreasonably immovable in purpose or will ▸ bullheaded, dogged, obstinate. *See* **stubborn** (1). **2.** Existing without interruption or end ▸ constant, endless, everlasting, perpetual. *See* **continual. 3.** Painfully intense ▸ brutal, harsh, severe. *See* **bitter** (2).

relentlessness *noun*
▸ bullheadedness, hardheadedness, rigidity. *See* **stubbornness.**

relevance *or* **relevancy** *noun*
The relation with, or fact of being related to, the matter at hand ▸ applicability, application, appositeness, bearing, germaneness, materiality, pertinence, pertinency, relevancy. *See also* **importance, influence, interest.**

relevant *adjective*
Related to or affecting the matter at hand ▸ applicable, apposite, apropos, germane, material, pertinent. *Idiom:* to the point. *See also* **influential, important.**

✤ CORE SYNONYMS: *relevant, pertinent, germane, material, apposite, apropos.* These adjectives describe what relates to and has a direct bearing on the matter at hand. Something *relevant* is connected with a subject or issue: *performed experiments relevant to her research. Pertinent* suggests a logical, precise relevance: *assigned pertinent articles for the class to read. Germane* implies close kinship and appropriateness: *"He asks questions that are germane and central to the issue"* (Marlin Fitzwater). Something *material* is not only relevant but also crucial to a matter: *reiterated the material facts of the lawsuit. Apposite* implies a striking appropriateness and pertinence: *used apposite verbal images in the paper.* Something *apropos* is both to the point and opportune: *an apropos comment that concisely answered my question.*

◂ ANTONYM: *irrelevant*

---

reliability *noun*
1. The quality of being honest ▸ incorruptibility, integrity. *See* **honesty** (1). **2.** Correspondence with fact or truth ▸ authenticity, correctness, truth, validity. *See* **veracity.**

reliable *adjective*
▸ honest, responsible, trustworthy. *See* **dependable.** *See synonym note at* **dependable.**

reliance *noun*
1. Absolute certainty that a person or thing will not fail ▸ confidence, faith. *See* **trust** (1). *See synonym note at* **trust. 2.** The state or relation of being determined or controlled ▸ dependence, dependency. *See also* **authority, dominance, need, relation.**

relic *noun*
1. A mark or remnant that indicates the former presence of something ▸ remains, trace, vestige. *See* **trace** (1). **2.** Something that causes one to remember ▸ memento, reminder. *See* **remembrance** (1).

relics *noun*
▸ corpse, remains. *See* **body** (2).

relief *noun*
1. The act or an instance of helping ▸ aid, assistance. *See* **help** (1). **2.** Reduction of pain or distress, or a cause of that reduction ▸ alleviation, assuagement, ease, mitigation, palliation, succor. *See also* **comfort, decrease, waning. 3.** Assistance, especially money, food, and other necessities, given to the needy or dispossessed ▸ aid, handout, public assistance, welfare. *Informal:* dole. *See also* **donation. 4.** One that can take the place of another ▸ alternate, proxy, replacement. *See* **substitute. 5.** A work of art created by shaping a solid material ▸ carving, cast, figure. *See* **sculpture.**

relieve *verb*
1. To make less severe or more bearable ▸ allay, alleviate, assuage, ease, lessen, lighten, mitigate, palliate, quell. *See also* **comfort, help. 2.** To relieve a burden ▸ discharge, release, unburden. *See* **rid. 3.** To give assistance to ▸ aid, assist. *See* **help** (1). **4.** To free from an obligation or duty ▸ discharge, exempt. *See* **excuse** (1). **5.** To free from a specific duty by acting as a substitute ▸ spell, take over. *See also* **substitute.**

✤ CORE SYNONYMS: *relieve, allay, alleviate, assuage, lighten, mitigate, palliate.* These verbs mean to make something less severe or more bearable. To *relieve* is to make more endurable something causing discomfort or distress: *"that misery which he strives in vain to relieve"* (Henry David Thoreau). *Allay* suggests at least temporary relief from what is burdensome or painful: *"This music crept by me upon the waters,/Allaying both their fury and my passion/With its sweet air"* (William Shakespeare). *Alleviate* connotes temporary lessening of distress without removal of its cause: *"No arguments shall be wanting on my part that can alleviate so severe a misfortune"* (Jane Austen). To *assuage* is to soothe or make milder: *assuaged his guilt by confessing to the crime. Lighten* signifies to make less heavy or oppressive: *legislation that would lighten the taxpayer's burden. Mitigate* and *palliate* connote moderating the force or intensity of something that causes suffering: *"I . . . prayed to the Lord to mitigate a calamity"* (John Galt). *"Men turn to him in the hour of distress, as of all statesmen the most fitted to palliate it"* (William E.H. Lecky).

reliever *noun*
▸ adjutant, deputy, helper. *See* **assistant.**

religion *noun*
A system of religious belief, worship or ritual ▸ confession, creed, cult, denomination, faith, persuasion, profession, sect. *See also* **devotion, doctrine.**

religiosity *or* **religionism** *noun*
▸ piety, reverence. *See* **devotion** (1).

religious *adjective*
1. Deeply concerned with God and the beliefs and practice of religion ▸ devout, holy, saintly. *See* **pious** (1). **2.** In the service or worship of God or a god ▸ devoted, pious, sacred. *See* **divine** (2). **3.** Of or relating to a church or to an established religion ▸ church, churchly, ecclesiastical, spiritual. *See also* **clerical, divine, holy, ritual.**

religiousness *noun*
▸ piety, piousness. *See* **devotion** (1).

relinquish *verb*
1. To give up or leave completely ▸ surrender, quit, yield. *See* **abandon** (1). *See synonym note at* **abandon.** **2.** To yield oneself unrestrainedly, as to an impulse ▸ abandon, deliver, surrender. *Idioms:* give oneself up (*or* over). **3.** To cease consideration or treatment of ▸ give up, quit, skip. *See* **drop** (7). **4.** To fail to take advantage of ▸ miss, pass up. *See* **lose** (2).

relinquished *adjective*
▸ deserted, outcast, rejected. *See* **abandoned** (1).

relinquishment *noun*
▸ abdication, resignation, surrender. *See* **abandonment** (1).

relish *noun*
1. A liking for something ▸ partiality, preference, weakness. *See* **taste** (1). **2.** Spirited enjoyment ▸ gusto, zest. *See synonym note at* **zest.** *See also* **enthusiasm. 3.** A distinctive property affecting the sense of taste ▸ tang, taste, zest. *See* **flavor** (1). *See synonym note at* **flavor.**

relish *verb*
1. To receive pleasure from ▸ appreciate, savor. *See* **enjoy** (1). **2.** To be avidly interested in ▸ devour, feast on. *Slang:* eat up.

relocate *verb*
1. To change one's residence or place of business, for example ▸ move, remove, transfer. *Idiom:* pull up stakes. *See also* **emigrate, go. 2.** To move to a place and reside there ▸ locate, settle. *Idioms:* fix one's residence, make one's home, put down roots, take up residence. *See also* **live¹.**

relocation *noun*
1. The act of moving from one place to another ▸ move, remotion, removal. *Idioms:* change of address (*or* residence). *See also* **departure. 2.** A change

in normal place or position ▸ dislodging, movement, shift. *See* **displacement.**

reluctance *noun*
▸ aversion, opposition. *See* **indisposition** (1).

reluctant *adjective*
▸ disinclined, unwilling. *See* **indisposed** (1).

rely on *or* upon *verb*
▸ count on (*or* upon), trust in. *See* **depend on** (1). *See synonym note at* **depend on.**

remain *verb*
1. To continue to be in a place ▸ abide, bide, linger, pause, stay, tarry, wait. *Informal:* hang around, stick around. *Idioms:* cool one's heels (*or* jets), stay put. *See also* **delay. 2.** To be in existence or in a certain state for an indefinitely long time ▸ continue, persist. *See* **endure** (2).

✦ **CORE SYNONYMS:** *remain, stay, wait, abide, tarry, linger.* These verbs mean to continue to be in a given place. *Remain* often implies continuing or being left after others have gone: *I remained at the end of the meeting to talk to the speaker. Stay* often suggests that the person involved is a guest or visitor: *"Must you go? Can't you stay?"* (Charles J. Vaughan). *Wait* suggests remaining in readiness, anticipation, or expectation: *"Your father is waiting for me to take a walk with him"* (Booth Tarkington). *Abide* implies continuing for a lengthy period: *"Abide with me"* (Henry Francis Lyte). *Tarry* and *linger* both imply a delayed departure, but *linger* more strongly suggests reluctance to leave: *"She was not anxious but puzzled that her husband tarried"* (Eden Phillpotts). *"I alone sit lingering here"* (Henry Vaughan).

remainder *noun*
1. A remaining part ▸ leavings, leftover, remains. *See* **balance** (4). **2.** A mark or remnant that indicates the former presence of something ▸ remains, trace, vestige. *See* **trace** (1).

remaining *adjective*
Being what remains, especially after a part has been removed ▸ extra, leftover, stray. *Idiom:* left behind. *See also* **superfluous.**

remains *noun*
1. A remaining part ▸ leavings, leftover, remainder, remnant. *See* **balance** (4). **2.** A mark or remnant that indicates the former presence of something ▸ record, trace, vestige. *See* **trace** (1). **3.** The physical frame of a dead person or animal ▸ cadaver, corpse, remains. *See* **body** (2). **4.** The substance of the body, especially after decay or cremation ▸ ashes, clay, cremains, dust. **5.** The remains of something destroyed, disintegrated, or decayed ▸ debris, rubble, wreck, wreckage. *See* **ruin** (2).

remand *verb*
▸ confide, delegate. *See* **entrust** (1).

remark *verb*
1. To state facts, opinions, or explanations ▸ observe, opine, reflect. *See* **comment. 2.** To perceive with a special effort of the senses or the mind ▸ detect, mark. *See* **notice.** *See synonym note at* **notice.**

remark *noun*
1. The act of noting, observing, or taking into account ▸ heed, note, regard. *See* **notice** (1). **2.** An expression of fact or opinion ▸ observation, reflection, word. *See* **comment** (1). *See synonym note at* **comment.**

remarkable *adjective*
1. Readily attracting notice ▸ conspicuous, outstanding, prominent. *See* **noticeable** (1). *See synonym note at* **noticeable. 2.** Beyond what is usual, normal, or customary ▸ extraordinary, outstanding. *See* **exceptional** (1). **3.** Exceptionally good of its kind ▸ first-rate, prime, splendid, tiptop. *See* **excellent.**

remarkably *adverb*
▸ singularly, uncommonly, uniquely. *See* **unusually.**

remedial *adjective*
1. Serving to cure ▸ medicinal, restorative. *See* **curative. 2.** Tending to correct ▸ amendatory, reformative. *See* **corrective.**

remedy *noun*
An agent used to restore health ▸ antidote, elixir, medication. *See* **cure.**

remedy *verb*
1. To restore to health ▸ rehabilitate, salve. *See* **cure** (1). **2.** To make right what is wrong ▸ mend, rectify. *See* **correct** (1). *See synonym note at* **correct.**

remember *verb*
1. To renew an image or thought in the mind ▸ bethink, mind, recall, recollect, remind oneself, reminisce, retain, retrieve, revive. *Idiom:* bring to mind. *See also* **imagine, memorize, think. 2.** To care enough to keep someone in mind ▸ cherish, think about, think of.

✢ CORE SYNONYMS: *remember, recall, recollect, reminisce.* These verbs mean to bring an image or a thought back to the mind: *can't remember his name; recalling her kindness; recollected the events leading to the accident; reminisced about playing soccer in college.*

◂ ANTONYM: *forget*

---

remembrance *noun*
1. Something that causes one to remember ▸ favor, forget-me-not, keepsake, memento, relic, reminder, souvenir, token, trophy. *See also* **memorial, novelty. 2.** An act or instance of remembering ▸ memory, mental image, recollection, reminiscence. *See also* **idea. 3.** The power of retaining and recalling past experience ▸ recollection, reminiscence. *See* **memory** (1). **4.** Something, as a structure or custom, serving to honor or keep alive a memory ▸ commemoration, memorial, monument. *See also* **testimonial.**

remind *noun*
To cause to remember ▸ bring back to. *Idiom:* make think of. *See also* **recall, suggest.**

reminder *noun*
1. Something that causes one to remember ▸ memento, token. *See* **remembrance** (1). **2.** A brief record written as an aid to the memory ▸ memorandum, notation. *See* **note** (1).

reminisce *verb*
▸ recall, recollect, retain. *See* **remember** (1). *See synonym note at* **remember.**

reminiscence *noun*
1. An act or instance of remembering ▸ memory, mental image, recollection, remembrance. *See also* **idea. 2.** The power of retaining and recalling past experience ▸ recall, remembrance. *See* **memory** (1).

reminiscences *noun*
▸ commentaries, diary. *See* **memoir.**

reminiscent *adjective*
Tending to bring a memory, mood, or image, for example, subtly or indirectly to mind ▸ allusive, connotative, evocative, impressionistic, suggestive. *See also* **designative, symbolic.**

remise *verb*
▸ discharge, exempt. *See* **excuse** (1).

remiss *adjective*
▸ lax, slack. *See* **negligent.** *See synonym note at* **negligent.**

remissible *adjective*
▸ forgivable, venial. *See* **pardonable.**

remission *noun*
1. The process of becoming less active or intense ▸ abatement, letup, subsidence. *See* **waning. 2.** The condition of being temporarily inactive ▸ dormancy, latency, suspension. *See* **abeyance. 3.** The act or an instance of forgiving ▸ amnesty, excuse, pardon. *See* **forgiveness. 4.** A freeing or clearing from accusation or guilt ▸ exoneration, vindication. *See* **exculpation.**

remissness *noun*
▸ laxness, slackness. *See* **negligence.**

remit *verb*
1. To grant forgiveness to or for ▸ excuse, overlook, pardon. *See* **forgive. 2.** To become or cause to become less active or intense ▸ die (away, down, off, *or* out), ebb, lapse. *See* **subside** (1). **3.** To cease trying to continue ▸ give up, quit, stop. *See* **abandon** (2). **4.** To put off until a later time ▸ delay, postpone, suspend. *See* **defer**[1]. **5.** To give compensation to ▸ indemnify, pay, recompense. *See* **compensate** (1). **6.** To put in the charge of another for care, use, or performance ▸ confide, delegate. *See* **entrust** (1). **7.** To free from an obligation or duty ▸ discharge, exempt. *See* **excuse** (1).

remnant *noun*
1. A remaining part ▸ leavings, leftover, remainder, residue. *See* **balance** (4). **2.** A mark or remnant that indicates the former presence of something ▸ remains, trace, vestige. *See* **trace** (1).

remodel *verb*
▸ adjust, shape, tailor. *See* **adapt.**

remonstrance *noun*
1. An expression of opposition ▸ exception, grievance, protestation. *See* **objection. 2.** Words expressive of strong disapproval ▸ admonition, reprimand, scolding. *See* **rebuke.**

remonstrate *verb*
▸ except, oppose, protest. *See* **object** (1). *See synonym note at* **object.**

remonstration *noun*
▶ exception, grievance, protestation. *See* **objection.**

remorse *noun*
▶ contrition, regret, repentance. *See* **penitence.** *See synonym note at* **penitence.**

remorseful *adjective*
▶ penitent, regretful, repentant. *See* **sorry** (1).

remorsefulness *noun*
▶ contriteness, regret, repentance. *See* **penitence.**

remorseless *adjective*
1. Lacking compassion or mercy ▶ heartless, insensitive, merciless. *See* **callous. 2.** Firmly, often unreasonably immovable in purpose or will ▶ bullheaded, dogged, obstinate. *See* **stubborn** (1). **3.** Devoid of remorse ▶ impenitent, unrepentant.

remorselessness *noun*
▶ bullheadedness, hardheadedness, rigidity. *See* **stubbornness.**

remote *adjective*
1. Far from centers of human population ▶ back, insular, isolated, lonely, lonesome, outlying, out-of-the-way, removed, secluded, solitary. *Slang:* backwater. *Idioms:* centrally isolated, off the beaten path (*or* track). *See also* **inaccessible, lonely, obscure. 2.** Small in degree, especially of probability ▶ faint, narrow, negligible, outside, slender, slight, slim. *See also* **doubtful, tiny. 3.** Far from others in space, time, or relationship ▶ faraway, far-flung, removed. *See* **distant** (1). **4.** Not friendly, sociable, or warm in manner ▶ aloof, chilly, impersonal. *See* **cool** (1). **5.** Lacking interest in one's surroundings or in worldly affairs ▶ disinterested, indifferent, uninvolved. *See* **detached** (1).

remoteness *noun*
1. The fact or condition of being far removed or apart ▶ distance, farness, separateness, separation. **2.** Dissociation from one's surroundings or in worldly affairs ▶ disinterest, indifference, unconcern. *See* **detachment** (2).

remotion *noun*
The act of moving from one place to another ▶ move, relocation, removal. *Idioms:* change of address (*or* residence). *See also* **departure.**

removal *noun*
1. The act of moving from one place to another ▶ move, relocation, remotion. *Idioms:* change of address (*or* residence). *See also* **departure. 2.** The moving back of a military force in the face of enemy attack or after a defeat ▶ fallback, pullout, withdrawal. *See* **retreat** (1). **3.** The act or process of eliminating ▶ eradication, purge. *See* **elimination** (1). **4.** The act of getting rid of something useless or used up ▶ elimination, riddance. *See* **disposal** (1). **5.** The act of ejecting or the state of being ejected ▶ eviction, expulsion. *See* **ejection.**

remove *verb*
1. To move something from a position occupied ▶ carry (off *or* away), pick out, pluck out, rip out, take, take away, take off, take out, tear out, uproot,

withdraw. *Idioms:* pluck (*or* pull) out by the roots. *See also* **carry, drop, pull. 2.** To move back in the face of enemy attack or after a defeat ▶ draw back, pull out, withdraw. *See* **retreat** (4). **3.** To go or cause to go from one place to another ▶ shift, transfer. *See* **move** (2). **4.** To move away from a place ▶ depart, go away, retire. *See* **go** (1). **5.** To change one's residence or place of business, for example ▶ move, relocate, transfer. *Idiom:* pull up stakes. *See also* **emigrate, go. 6.** To take from one's own person ▶ cast off, doff, pull off, slip off, slough off, take off. *Idioms:* slip (*or* step) out of. **7.** To rid of obstructions ▶ clear, free, open, unblock. *See also* **rid. 8.** To get rid of, especially by banishment or execution ▶ liquidate, purge. *See* **eliminate** (1). **9.** To take away a quantity from another quantity ▶ discount, subtract. *See* **deduct** (1).

removed *adjective*
1. Far from others in space, time, or relationship ▶ faraway, far-flung, remote. *See* **distant** (1). **2.** Far from centers of human population ▶ isolated, outlying, secluded. *See* **remote** (1). **3.** Set away from or lacking the company of all others ▶ alone, isolated, lone. *See* **solitary** (1).

remunerate *verb*
▶ indemnify, pay, recompense. *See* **compensate** (1).

remuneration *noun*
1. Payment for work done ▶ earnings, pay, salary. *See* **wage. 2.** Something to make up for loss or damage ▶ amends, quittance, reparation. *See* **compensation** (1).

remunerative *adjective*
1. Affording compensation ▶ compensative, compensatory, reimbursable. **2.** Affording profit ▶ gainful, lucrative, rewarding. *See* **profitable** (1).

renaissance *noun*
▶ rebirth, renewal, resurgence. *See* **revival** (1).

renascence *noun*
▶ rebirth, renaissance, renewal. *See* **revival** (1).

rend *verb*
1. To separate or pull apart by force ▶ rip, rive, split. *See* **tear**[1] (1). *See synonym note at* **tear. 2.** To remove from a fixed position ▶ pluck, wrench, wrest. *See* **pull** (2).

render *verb*
1. To give up or leave completely ▶ abdicate, relinquish, surrender. *See* **abandon** (1). **2.** To make music ▶ concertize, perform, play. **3.** To present a lifelike image of ▶ depict, describe, render. *See* **represent** (2). **4.** To perform according to one's artistic conception ▶ depict, play, represent. *See* **interpret** (2). **5.** To express in another language ▶ interpret, transcribe. *See* **translate** (1). **6.** To express the meaning of in other, especially simpler, words ▶ reword, translate. *See* **paraphrase. 7.** To deliver an indictment or verdict, for example ▶ hand down, return. **8.** To put before another for acceptance ▶ extend, proffer. *See* **offer** (1). **9.** To make something readily available ▶ make available, provide. *See* **offer** (2). **10.** To relinquish to the

possession or control of another ▸ furnish, provide. See **give** (1).

rendering *noun*
1. A performer's distinctive personal version of a song, dance, piece of music, or role ▸ performance, reading, rendition. See **interpretation** (1). 2. A restating of something in other, especially simpler, words ▸ restatement, translation. See **paraphrase**. 3. The act or process of translating ▸ crib, transliteration. See **translation** (1). 4. The act or process of describing in lifelike imagery ▸ delineation, drawing, illustration. See **representation**.

rendezvous *noun*
1. An arrangement to appear at a certain time and place ▸ date, tryst. See **engagement** (1). See *synonym note at* **engagement**. 2. A frequently visited place ▸ meeting place. *Slang:* hangout, stamping ground. See **haunt** (1).

rendezvous *verb*
To come together by arrangement ▸ get together, meet (up). See also **assemble**.

rendition *noun*
1. A performer's distinctive personal version of a song, dance, piece of music, or role ▸ performance, reading, representation. See **interpretation** (1). 2. A restating of something in other, especially simpler, words ▸ restatement, translation. See **paraphrase**.

renege *verb*
To abandon a former position or commitment ▸ back down (*or* away *or* out), blink, retreat, skip out, walk out. *Slang:* cop out, fink out. *Idioms:* beat a (hasty) retreat, cut and run. See also **abandon, escape, retreat, surrender**.

renegade *noun*
A person who has defected ▸ deserter, recreant, traitor. See **defector**.

renegade *verb*
To abandon one's cause or party usually to join another ▸ desert, quit, turn. See **defect**.

renew *verb*
1. To make new or as if new again ▸ do over, fix up, furbish, recondition, re-create, redecorate, redo, refresh, refurbish, regenerate, rejuvenate, renovate, restore, revamp, smarten up, spruce up. *Idioms:* give a facelift to, give a new look to. See also **fix¹, modernize, overhaul, restore, streamline**. 2. To begin or go on after an interruption ▸ restart, resume. See **continue** (1). 3. To impart renewed energy and strength to a person ▸ reinvigorate, rejuvenate, revitalize. See **refresh** (1). 4. To rouse from a state of inactivity or quiescence ▸ rekindle, resuscitate, revitalize. See **revive** (1). 5. To bring back into existence or use ▸ reestablish, reinstate, reintroduce, restore, return, revive. See also **restore**.

renewal *noun*
1. The act of making new or as if new again ▸ face-lift, facelifting, furbishment, reconditioning, redecorating, refurbishment, regeneration, rejuvenation, renovation, restoration, revampment. 2. A continuing

after interruption ▸ continuation, resumption, resurgence, revival. 3. The act of reviving or condition of being revived ▸ rebirth, renaissance, resurgence. See **revival** (1). 4. A return to former prosperity or status ▸ recovery, reestablishment, revival. See **comeback**.

renewing *adjective*
▸ bracing, energizing, exhilarating. See **invigorating**.

renounce *verb*
1. To give up or leave completely ▸ abdicate, relinquish, surrender. See **abandon** (1). See *synonym note at* **abandon**. 2. To refuse to recognize or acknowledge ▸ deny, disown, reject. See **repudiate** (1). 3. To refuse to admit the truth, reality, value, or worth of ▸ contravene, disaffirm, disavow. See **deny** (1). 4. To abandon one's cause or party usually to join another ▸ desert, quit, turn. See **defect**. 5. To discontinue (a habit, for example) ▸ abjure, give up, leave off. See **break** (17).

renouncement *noun*
▸ abandonment, disavowal, secession. See **defection**.

renovate *verb*
1. To bring back to a previous normal condition ▸ recondition, reconstruct, rejuvenate. See **restore** (3). 2. To make new or as if new again ▸ refresh, restore, revamp. See **renew** (1). 3. To rouse from a state of inactivity or quiescence ▸ rekindle, resuscitate, revitalize. See **revive** (1).

renovation *noun*
▸ refurbishment, rejuvenation, restoration. See **renewal** (1).

renown *noun*
1. Wide recognition for one's deeds ▸ glory, note, prestige. See **fame**. 2. Wide recognition for one's deeds ▸ celebrity, fame, famousness, notoriety, popularity, reputation, repute.

renowned *adjective*
▸ celebrated, noted, redoubtable. See **famous**. See *synonym note at* **famous**.

rent¹ *verb*
1. To engage the temporary use of something for a fee ▸ charter, hire, lease. 2. To give temporary use of in return for payment ▸ let (out), sublet. See **lease** (1).

rent² *noun*
1. A hole made by tearing ▸ rip, run, tear. See also **crack**. 2. An interruption in friendly relations ▸ break, fissure. See **breach** (2).

renunciation *noun*
1. A giving up of a possession, claim, or right ▸ abdication, relinquishment, surrender. See **abandonment** (1). 2. A refusal to grant the truth of a statement or charge ▸ disaffirmation, disclaimer, rejection. See **denial** (1).

reoccupy *verb*
▸ reassume, repossess, retake. See **resume** (1).

reoccur *verb*
1. To happen again or repeatedly ▸ iterate, reappear, recur, repeat. 2. To come back to a former condition ▸ recrudesce, recur, revert. See **return** (1).

reoccurrence *noun*
▸ reiteration, repeat, restatement. See **repetition** (1).

reopen *verb*
▸ restart, resume. *See* **continue** (1).
reorder *verb*
▸ reconfigure, scramble. *See* **shuffle** (1).
rep *noun*
Informal Public estimation of someone ▸ character, name, report, reputation, repute. *See also* **image, place.**
repair¹ *verb*
1. To restore to proper condition or functioning ▸ mend, overhaul, patch. *See* **fix** (1). **2.** To make right what is wrong ▸ mend, rectify, remedy. *See* **correct** (1).
repair *noun*
A state of sound readiness ▸ fettle, form, order. *See* **shape** (1).
repair² *verb*
1. To look to when in need ▸ refer, run, turn. *See* **resort** (1). **2.** To visit regularly ▸ hang around, haunt. *See* **frequent.**
repairs *noun*
▸ preservation, upkeep. *See* **maintenance** (1).
reparation *noun*
1. Something to make up for loss or damage ▸ amends, remuneration, restitution. *See* **compensation** (1). *See synonym note at* **compensation. 2.** The work of keeping something in proper condition ▸ repairs, upkeep. *See* **maintenance** (1). **3.** The act of making amends ▸ atonement, expiation, penance, reconciliation. *See also* **compensation, purification.**
reparative *adjective*
▸ reformative, remedial. *See* **corrective.**
repartee *noun*
▸ comeback, retort, riposte. *See* **answer** (1).
repay *verb*
1. To exact revenge for or from ▸ pay off, vindicate. *See* **avenge. 2.** To give back, especially money ▸ refund, reimburse, restitute. *See also* **compensate, return. 3.** To give compensation to ▸ indemnify, pay, recompense. *See* **compensate** (1). **4.** To make as income or profit ▸ clear, gain, yield. *See* **return** (3).
repayment *noun*
1. Something to make up for loss or damage ▸ amends, remuneration, reparation. *See* **compensation** (1). **2.** A quantity of money that is returned ▸ refund, reimbursement. *See also* **deduction, return.**
repeal *verb*
To take back or remove ▸ recall, rescind, revoke. *See* **lift** (5).
repeal *noun*
The act of reversing or annulling ▸ recall, rescindment, rescission, retraction, reversal, revocation. *See also* **abolition.**
repeat *verb*
1. To state again ▸ iterate, recapitulate, reiterate, restate, retell, reutter. *Informal:* recap. *See also* **say, tell. 2.** To send back the sound of ▸ reflect, reverberate. *See* **echo** (1). **3.** To copy another slavishly ▸ clone, imitate. *See* **mimic** (1). **4.** To do or perform an act again ▸ do over, duplicate, play over, redo, replay. *See*

also **copy. 5.** To happen again or repeatedly ▸ iterate, reappear, recur, reoccur.
repeat *noun*
The act or process of repeating ▸ reiteration, restatement. *See* **repetition** (1).

✦ **CORE SYNONYMS:** *repeat, iterate, reiterate, restate.* These verbs mean to state again: *repeated the warning; iterate a demand; reiterated the question; restated the obvious.*

---

repel *verb*
1. To turn aside or drive away ▸ beat off, check, deflect, fend (off), fight off, keep off, parry, rebuff, repulse, resist, stave off, ward off, withstand. *See also* **suppress. 2.** To offend the senses or feelings of ▸ appall, revolt, sicken. *See* **disgust** (1). *See synonym note at* **disgust. 3.** To be very disagreeable to ▸ displease, repulse, upset. *See* **offend** (2).
repellence *or* **repellency** *noun*
▸ antipathy, aversion, loathing. *See* **hate** (1).
repellent *adjective*
1. So objectionable as to cause scorn ▸ contemptible, disgusting, obnoxious. *See* **offensive** (1). *See synonym note at* **offensive. 2.** Having the capacity to withstand ▸ impervious, insusceptible, unsusceptible. *See* **resistant** (1).
repent *verb*
To feel or express sorrow for ▸ deplore, regret, rue, sorrow (over). *See also* **feel, grieve.**
repentance *noun*
▸ contriteness, remorse, rue. *See* **penitence.** *See synonym note at* **penitence.**
repentant *adjective*
▸ penitent, regretful, rueful. *See* **sorry** (1).
repercussion *noun*
1. The strong effect exerted by one person or thing on another ▸ impression, influence. *See* **impact** (2). **2.** Repetition of sound via reflection from a surface ▸ echo, reverberation.
repetition *noun*
1. The act or process of repeating ▸ echo, iteration, reappearance, recurrence, reiteration, reoccurrence, repeat, restatement, return. *See also* **reproduction. 2.** A tiresome lack of variety ▸ humdrum, sameness. *See* **monotony. 3.** Imitative reproduction, as of the style of another ▸ reflection, reflex. *See* **echo** (1).
repetitious *adjective*
Characterized by repetition ▸ iterative, reiterative, repetitive. *See also* **boring, superfluous, wordy.**
repetitive *adjective*
1. Characterized by repetition ▸ iterative, reiterative, repetitious. *See also* **boring, superfluous, wordy. 2.** Happening or appearing consistently or repeatedly ▸ recurrent, regular, repeating. *See also* **periodic, pervasive, thematic.**
rephrase *verb*
▸ reword, translate. *See* **paraphrase.**
repine *verb*
▸ fuss, grouch, whine. *See* **complain.**

replace *verb*

1. To put someone in the possession of a prior position or office ▸ give back, reappoint, reinstall, reinstate, restore, return. **2.** To send, put, or carry back to a former location ▸ give back, restore, take back. *See* **return** (2). **3.** To substitute for or fill the place of ▸ displace, supersede, supplant, surrogate. *Idioms:* fill someone's shoes, take over from, take the reins from. *See also* **substitute.**

✚ **CORE SYNONYMS:** *replace, supplant, supersede.* These verbs mean to substitute for or fill the place of another. To *replace* is to be or to furnish an equivalent or substitute, especially for one that has been lost, depleted, worn out, or discharged: *"A conspiracy was carefully engineered to replace the Directory by three Consuls"* (H.G. Wells). *Supplant* often suggests the use of intrigue or underhanded tactics to take another's place: *"The rivaling poor Jones, and supplanting him in her affections, added another spur to his pursuit"* (Henry Fielding). To *supersede* is to replace one person or thing by another held to be more valuable or useful, or less antiquated: *"In our island the Latin appears never to have superseded the old Gaelic speech"* (Thomas Macaulay).

replacement *noun*

▸ alternate, proxy, surrogate. *See* **substitute.**

replay *verb*

To do or perform an act again ▸ do over, duplicate, play over, redo, repeat. *See also* **copy.**

replete *adjective*

1. Completely filled ▸ brimming, loaded, packed. *See* **full** (1). **2.** Having the appetite satisfied ▸ engorged, sated, satiated. *See* **full** (2).

repletion *noun*

▸ fullness, satiety. *See* **satiation.**

replica *noun*

▸ ditto, facsimile, likeness. *See* **copy** (1).

replicate *verb*

▸ imitate, reproduce. *See* **copy** (1).

replication *noun*

▸ ditto, facsimile, likeness. *See* **copy** (1).

reply *verb*

To speak or act in response ▸ respond, retort, riposte. *See* **answer** (1). *See synonym note at* **answer.**

reply *noun*

Something spoken or written in return ▸ repartee, retort, riposte. *See* **answer** (1).

report *noun*

1. A recounting of past events ▸ account, history, statement. *See* **story** (1). **2.** New information, especially about recent events and happenings ▸ intelligence, word. *See* **news** (1). **3.** Public estimation of someone ▸ character, name, reputation, repute. *Informal:* rep. *See also* **image, place. 4.** Idle, often sensational and groundless talk about others ▸ hearsay, rumor, tattle. *See* **gossip** (1). **5.** A sudden sharp, explosive noise ▸ bang, pop, snap. *See* **crack** (1).

report *verb*

1. To communicate the facts, details, or particulars of

something ▸ narrate, recount, relate. *See* **describe** (1). *See synonym note at* **describe. 2.** To make known ▸ disclose, divulge, transmit. *See* **communicate** (1). **3.** To give incriminating information about others, especially to the authorities ▸ tip (off). *Slang:* rat, snitch. *See* **inform** (2).

repose *noun*

1. Freedom from labor, responsibility, or strain ▸ ease, leisure, relaxation. *See* **rest**[1] (2). **2.** Lack of emotional agitation ▸ peace, serenity, tranquillity. *See* **calm** (1).

repose *verb*

1. To be or place oneself in a prostrate or recumbent position ▸ recline, stretch (out). *See* **lie**[1] (1). **2.** To take repose, as by sleeping or lying quietly ▸ curl up, lie (down), recline, rest (1), stretch (out). *See also* **nap, sleep. 3.** To have an inherent basis ▸ exist, inhere, reside. *See* **consist** (1).

repository *noun*

1. A place where something is deposited for safekeeping ▸ archive, storehouse, warehouse. *See* **depository. 2.** One in whom secrets are confided ▸ confessor, confidant, confidante, intimate. **3.** An object, such as a carton, can, or jar, in which material is held or carried ▸ container, holder, receptacle, vessel. *See also* **depository, package.**

repossess *verb*

1. To get back ▸ regain, retrieve. *See* **recover** (1). **2.** To occupy or take again ▸ reassume, reoccupy, retake. *See* **resume** (1).

repossession *noun*

The act of getting back or regaining ▸ recoup, recovery, retrieval.

reprehend *verb*

▸ condemn, denounce. *See* **deplore** (1). *See synonym note at* **deplore.**

reprehensible *adjective*

1. Deserving blame ▸ culpable, guilty. *See* **blameworthy.** *See synonym note at* **blameworthy. 2.** Worthy of severe disapproval ▸ disgraceful, shameful, unfortunate. *See* **deplorable** (1). **3.** Exceeding the bounds of morality, decency, or reason ▸ appalling, monstrous, shocking. *See* **outrageous.**

reprehension *noun*

▸ censure, condemnation, denunciation. *See* **criticism** (1).

represent *verb*

1. To serve as an example, image, or symbol of ▸ epitomize, exemplify, illustrate, personify, stand for, symbolize, typify. *See also* **designate, embody, equal, mean. 2.** To present a lifelike image of ▸ characterize, delineate, depict, describe, draw, express, illustrate, image, limn, picture, portray, render, show. *See also* **act, interpret. 3.** To serve as an official delegate of ▸ act (as *or* for), answer for, speak for, stand for. *Idioms:* be spokesperson (*or* representative) for, be the voice of. *See also* **substitute. 4.** To play the part of ▸ impersonate, play, portray. *See* **act** (4). **5.** To perform according to one's artistic conception ▸ depict, play, render. *See* **interpret** (2).

✦ CORE SYNONYMS: *represent, delineate, depict, limn, picture, portray.* These verbs mean to render or present a lifelike image of: *a statue representing a king; cave paintings that delineate hunters; a cartoon depicting a sea monster; the personality of a great leader limned in words; a landscape pictured in soft colors; a book portraying life in the Middle Ages.*

representation *noun*
1. The act or process of describing in lifelike imagery ▸ characterization, delineation, depiction, description, drawing, expression, illustration, portrayal, rendering. **2.** A performer's distinctive personal version of a song, dance, piece of music, or role ▸ performance, reading, rendition. *See* **interpretation** (1).

representational *adjective*
▸ emblematical, figurative, metaphorical. *See* **symbolic** (1).

representative *noun*
1. One that is representative of a group or class ▸ illustration, sample. *See* **example** (1). **2.** One who represents the interests of another ▸ advocate, ambassador, consul, delegate, deputy, emissary, envoy, factor, lieutenant, minister, proxy, steward. *See also* **agent, speaker, substitute.**

representative *adjective*
1. Serving as a symbol ▸ emblematical, representative. *See* **symbolic** (1). **2.** Serving to describe ▸ graphic, vivid. *See* **descriptive**. **3.** Having the nature of, constituting, or serving as a type ▸ model, prototypic, quintessential. *See* **typical** (1).

repress *verb*
To hold something requiring an outlet in check ▸ bottle up, burke, choke (back), gag, hold back, hold down, hold in, hush (up), keep back (*or* in), muffle, muzzle, quench, smother, squelch, stifle, strangle, subdue, suppress, throttle. *Informal:* sit on (*or* upon). *Idiom:* keep in check. *See also* **censor, hinder, restrain, suppress.**

repression *noun*
1. Forceful subjugation, as against an uprising ▸ clampdown, crackdown, lockdown, suppression. *See also* **restraint. 2.** The act of exercising controlling power or the condition of being so controlled ▸ control, dominion, reign. *See* **domination** (1). **3.** Cruel exercise of power ▸ injustice, persecution, subjugation. *See* **oppression** (1).

repressive *adjective*
Serving to restrain forcefully ▸ inhibitive, inhibitory, restraining, restrictive, stifling, suppressive. *See also* **absolute, authoritarian.**

reprieve *noun*
▸ exemption, grace, immunity, respite. *See also* **delay.**

reprimand *verb*
To criticize for a fault or offense ▸ chide, rebuke, scold. *See* **chastise** (1). *See synonym note at* **chastise.**

reprimand *noun*
Words expressive of strong disapproval ▸ admonition, lecture, scolding. *See* **rebuke.**

reprint *noun*
Something closely resembling another ▸ imitation, simulation. *See* **copy** (2).

reprint *verb*
To make a copy of ▸ imitate, replicate, reproduce. *See* **copy** (1).

reprisal *noun*
▸ counteraction, reciprocation, retribution. *See* **retaliation.**

reproach *verb*
1. To criticize for a fault or offense ▸ admonish, chide, dress down, rebuke, reprimand. *See* **chastise** (1). *See synonym note at* **chastise. 2.** To cause to feel embarrassment, dishonor, and often guilt ▸ brand, mortify, shame, stigmatize. *Idioms:* put to shame, put to the blush. *See also* **belittle, denigrate, embarrass, humble.**

reproach *noun*
1. Words expressive of strong disapproval ▸ admonition, reprimand, scolding. *See* **rebuke. 2.** Loss of or damage to one's reputation ▸ discredit, disrepute, humiliation. *See* **disgrace. 3.** Unfavorable opinion or judgment ▸ condemnation, disfavor, reproof. *See* **disapproval.**

reproachable *adjective*
▸ discreditable, ignominious, shameful. *See* **disgraceful** (1).

reproachful *adjective*
▸ carping, overcritical. *See* **critical** (1).

reprobate *adjective*
1. Morally objectionable ▸ immoral, sinful. *See* **evil** (1). **2.** Sentenced to terrible, irrevocable punishment ▸ damned, doomed, lost. *See* **condemned. 3.** Sexually unrestrained ▸ fast, promiscuous, sluttish. *See* **wanton** (1).

reprobate *verb*
1. To express strong disapproval of ▸ condemn, denounce. *See* **deplore** (1). **2.** To have or express an unfavorable opinion of ▸ condemn, disfavor, object to. *See* **disapprove** (1).

reprobate *noun*
An immoral or licentious person ▸ libertine, profligate. *See* **wanton** (1).

reprobation *noun*
▸ censure, condemnation, denunciation. *See* **criticism** (1).

reproduce *verb*
1. To make a copy of ▸ imitate, replicate. *See* **copy** (1). **2.** To give life to ▸ engender, propagate, spawn. *See* **breed** (1).

reproduction *noun*
1. Something closely resembling another ▸ ditto, facsimile, likeness. *See* **copy** (1). **2.** Imitative reproduction, as of the style of another ▸ imitation, reflection. *See* **echo** (1). **3.** The process by which an organism produces others of its kind ▸ breeding, generation, multiplication, procreation, proliferation, propagation, spawning.

reproductive *adjective*
Of or relating to reproduction ▸ generative, procreant, procreative.

reproof *noun*
1. Words expressive of strong disapproval ▸ admonition, reprimand, scolding. *See* **rebuke. 2.** Unfavorable opinion or judgment ▸ condemnation, disfavor, reproach. *See* **disapproval.**

reproval *noun*
▸ admonition, reprimand, scolding. *See* **rebuke.**

reprove *verb*
1. To criticize for a fault or offense ▸ chide, rebuke, reprimand. *See* **chastise** (1). *See synonym note at* **chastise. 2.** To find fault with ▸ censure, fault. *Slang:* knock. *See* **criticize** (1).

reptile *noun*
▸ weasel. *Slang:* louse, maggot. *See* **creep** (2).

repudiate *verb*
1. To refuse to recognize or acknowledge ▸ deny, disacknowledge, disavow, disclaim, disown, reject, renounce. *Idioms:* turn one's back on, turn up one's nose at. *See also* **deny, disbelieve, retract. 2.** To rid one's mind of ▸ cast out, dispel. *See* **dismiss** (3).

repudiation *noun*
▸ disaffirmation, disclaimer, rejection. *See* **denial** (1).

repugnance *noun*
1. A strong feeling of hostility or dislike ▸ antipathy, aversion, loathing. *See* **hate** (1). **2.** Extreme aversion caused by something offensive ▸ abhorrence, loathing, queasiness. *See* **disgust.**

repugnancy *noun*
▸ antipathy, aversion, loathing. *See* **hate** (1).

repugnant *adjective*
▸ contemptible, disgusting, obnoxious. *See* **offensive** (1).

repulse *verb*
1. To turn aside or drive away ▸ deflect, resist, ward off. *See* **repel. 2.** To be very disagreeable to ▸ displease, revolt, upset. *See* **offend** (2). **3.** To offend the senses or feelings of ▸ appall, revolt, sicken. *See* **disgust** (1).

repulsion *noun*
▸ antipathy, aversion, loathing. *See* **hate** (1).

repulsive *adjective*
1. So unpleasant or objectionable as to cause scorn or disgust ▸ contemptible, disgusting, obnoxious. *See* **offensive** (1). **2.** So unpleasant in flavor as to be inedible ▸ distasteful, unappetizing, uneatable. *See* **unpalatable** (1).

repulsiveness *noun*
▸ monstrosity, odiousness, unsightliness. *See* **ugliness** (1).

reputable *adjective*
1. Deserving honor, respect, or admiration ▸ deserving, laudable, worthy. *See* **admirable. 2.** Widely known ▸ celebrated, noted, popular. *See* **famous.**

reputation *noun*
1. Public estimation of someone ▸ character, name, report, repute. *Informal:* rep. *See also* **image, place. 2.** Wide recognition for one's deeds ▸ celebrity, noto-

riety, renown. *See* **fame. 3.** A person's high standing among others ▸ good name, repute. *See* **honor** (2).

repute
  repute *noun*
  1. Public estimation of someone ▸ character, name, report, reputation. *Informal:* rep. *See also* **image, place. 2.** Wide recognition for one's deeds ▸ celebrity, notoriety, renown. *See* **fame. 3.** A person's high standing among others ▸ good name, reputation. *See* **honor** (2).

reputed *adjective*
▸ alleged, conjectural, presumed. *See* **supposed.** *See synonym note at* **supposed.**

request *verb*
▸ ask (for), seek, solicit. *See* **appeal** (1).

requiem *noun*
▸ funeral service, memorial service, obsequies. *See* **funeral.**

require *verb*
1. To have as a need or prerequisite ▸ entail, involve, necessitate. *See* **demand** (2). **2.** To be without what is needed, required, or essential ▸ lack, need, want. *See also* **demand. 3.** To ask for urgently or insistently ▸ insist on (*or* importune), order. *See* **demand** (1). *See synonym note at* **demand. 4.** To oblige to do or not do by force of authority, propriety, or custom ▸ expect, oblige, obligate, suppose. *See also* **must.**

required *adjective*
1. Imposed on one by authority, command, or convention ▸ compulsory, dictated, imperative, mandatory, necessary, obligatory, prescribed, requisite. **2.** Incapable of being dispensed with ▸ necessary, requisite. *See* **essential** (1). **3.** Being legally or morally required to do something ▸ committed, compelled, obligated. *See* **obliged** (2).

requirement *noun*
1. Manner of being or form of existence ▸ necessity, prerequisite, sine qua non. *See* **condition** (2). **2.** Something asked for or needed ▸ exigence, want. *See* **demand** (2). **3.** An act or course of action that is demanded of one, as by position, custom, law, or religion ▸ charge, commitment, obligation. *See* **duty** (1).

requisite *adjective*
1. Incapable of being dispensed with ▸ necessary, required. *See* **essential** (1). *See synonym note at* **essential. 2.** Imposed on one by authority, command, or convention ▸ imperative, mandatory, obligatory. *See* **required** (1).

requisite *noun*
Something indispensable ▸ necessity, precondition, requirement. *See* **condition** (2).

requisition *noun*
1. The act of demanding ▸ appeal, claim, exaction. *See* **demand** (1). **2.** An earnest or urgent request ▸ imploration, plea, supplication. *See* **appeal** (1).

requisition *verb*
To ask for urgently or insistently ▸ insist on (*or* upon), require. *See* **demand** (1).

requital *noun*

1. Something to make up for loss or damage ▸ amends, remuneration, reparation. *See* **compensation** (1). **2.** The act of retaliating ▸ counteraction, reciprocation, reprisal. *See* **retaliation.**

requite *verb*

1. To give compensation to ▸ indemnify, pay, recompense. *See* **compensate** (1). **2.** To give or take mutually ▸ reciprocate, return. *Idiom:* respond in kind. *See synonym note at* **reciprocate. 3.** To exact revenge for or from ▸ pay off, vindicate. *See* **avenge. 4.** To return like for like, especially to return an unfriendly or hostile action with a similar one ▸ counter, reciprocate, retort. *See* **retaliate.**

requited *adjective*

▸ reciprocal, reciprocative, shared. *See* **mutual** (1).

rescind *verb*

▸ recall, repeal, revoke. *See* **lift** (5).

rescission *noun*

▸ recall, reversal, revocation. *See* **repeal.**

rescue *verb*

To set free, as from danger or confinement ▸ bail out, deliver, reclaim, recover, redeem, salvage, save. *Idioms:* save by the bell, save one's bacon (*or* neck), come to the rescue of. *See also* **free, help.**

rescue *noun*

Extrication from danger or confinement ▸ deliverance, delivery, emancipation, freeing, liberation, release, salvage, salvation, saving. *See also* **freedom.**

✚ CORE SYNONYMS: *rescue, save, reclaim, redeem, deliver.* These verbs mean to set free a person or thing from danger, evil, confinement, or servitude. *Rescue* and *save* are the most general, although *rescue* often implies saving from immediate harm or danger by direct action *The curator rescued a rare manuscript from a fire. The smallpox vaccine has saved many lives. Reclaim* can mean to bring a person back, as from error to virtue or to right or proper conduct: *"To reclaim me from this course of life was the sole cause of his journey to London"* (Henry Fielding). To *redeem* is to free someone from captivity or the consequences of sin or error; the term can imply the expenditure of money or effort: *The price for redeeming the hostages was extortionate. Deliver* applies to liberating people from something such as misery, peril, error, or evil: *"consigned to a state of wretchedness from which no human efforts will deliver them"* (George Washington).

---

rescuer *noun*

One who frees someone from danger or confinement ▸ angel, deliverer, liberator, lifesaver, redeemer, savior. *See also* **guard, patron.**

research *noun*

The act of examining carefully or critically ▸ analysis, investigation, study. *See* **examination** (1). *See synonym note at* **examination.**

research *verb*

To look at or study carefully or critically ▸ analyze, investigate, scrutinize. *See* **examine** (1).

researcher *noun*

▸ inquisitor, interrogator, questioner. *See* **inquirer.**

resemblance *noun*

▸ alikeness, similarity, uniformity. *See* **likeness** (1). *See synonym note at* **likeness.**

resemble *verb*

To be similar especially in appearance ▸ be like, look like, match, mimic, take after. *Chiefly Regional:* favor. *Idioms:* be a dead ringer for, be like as two peas in a pod, be the spitting (*or* spit and) image of. *See also* **agree, appear, equal.**

resentful *adjective*

Bitingly hostile ▸ acrimonious, bitter, embittered, hard, rancorous, virulent. *See also* **angry, hostile.**

resentfulness *noun*

▸ bitterness, rancor, virulence. *See* **resentment** (1).

resentment *noun*

1. The quality or state of feeling bitter ▸ acrimony, bitterness, embitterment, gall, rancor, rancorousness, resentfulness, virulence, virulency. *See also* **enmity, hate. 2.** Extreme displeasure caused by an insult ▸ huff, ruffled feathers, umbrage. *See* **offense** (1). **3.** A strong feeling of displeasure or hostility ▸ animosity, wrath. *See* **anger.** *See synonym note at* **anger.**

reservation *noun*

1. A restricting or modifying element ▸ condition, proviso, stipulation. *See* **provision** (1). **2.** A feeling of uncertainty about the fitness or correctness of an action ▸ misgiving, scruple, worry. *See* **qualm** (1). **3.** Public land kept for a special purpose ▸ park, preserve, reserve, sanctuary. *See also* **common. 4.** A lack of conviction or certainty ▸ dubiousness, incertitude, skepticism. *See* **doubt** (1).

reserve *verb*

1. To have and maintain in one's possession ▸ keep, retain. *See* **hold** (1). *See synonym note at* **hold. 2.** To cause to be set aside, as for one's use, in advance ▸ bespeak, engage. *See* **book** (1). *See synonym note at* **book.**

reserve *noun*

1. A supply stored or hidden for possible future use ▸ cache, provision, stockpile. *See* **hoard. 2.** The keeping of one's thoughts and emotions to oneself ▸ constraint, control, guardedness, introversion, remoteness, reservedness, restraint, reticence, self-control, self-restraint, taciturnity, uncommunicativeness, unresponsiveness. *See also* **balance, inhospitality, silence. 3.** Public land kept for a special purpose ▸ park, preserve, reservation, sanctuary. *See also* **common.**

reserve *adjective*

Used or held in reserve ▸ backup, standby, supplemental. *See* **auxiliary** (2).

reserved *adjective*

1. Tending to keep one's thoughts and emotions to oneself ▸ constrained, controlled, guarded, inhibited, introverted, noncommittal, remote, restrained, self-controlled, self-restrained, unresponsive. **2.** Not total, unlimited, or wholehearted ▸ limited, modified, restricted. *See* **qualified** (1). **3.** Not friendly, sociable, or

warm in manner ▸ aloof, chilly, impersonal. *See* **cool** (1). **4.** Habitually untalkative ▸ reticent, silent, uncommunicative. *See* **taciturn.** *See synonym note at* **taciturn.**

reservoir *noun*
▸ cache, reserve, stockpile. *See* **hoard.**

resettle *verb*
To leave one's native land and settle in another ▸ emigrate (from), immigrate (to), migrate, transmigrate. *See also* **move, settle.**

reshape *verb*
▸ mutate, transfigure, transform. *See* **convert** (1).

reshuffle *verb*
▸ reconfigure, reengineer. *See* **overhaul** (1).

reshuffling *noun*
A thorough or drastic reorganization ▸ overhaul, reengineering, shakeup. *Informal:* housecleaning. *See also* **renewal, revolution.**

reside *verb*
1. To have as one's domicile, usually for an extended period ▸ dwell, stay. *See* **live**[1] (2). **2.** To have an inherent basis ▸ exist, inhere, rest. *See* **consist** (1).

residence *noun*
▸ domicile, dwelling, place. *See* **home** (1).

resident *noun*
▸ denizen, occupant, tenant. *See* **inhabitant.**

residential *adjective*
▸ family, homey, household. *See* **domestic** (1).

residual *adjective*
Being what remains, especially after a part has been removed ▸ extra, leftover, remaining, stray. *Idiom:* left behind. *See also* **superfluous.**

residue *noun*
▸ leftover, remainder, remains, remnant. *See* **balance** (4).

resign *verb*
1. To bring oneself to accept ▸ reconcile. *Idiom:* get used to. **2.** To relinquish one's engagement in or occupation with ▸ demit, leave, quit, terminate. *Idioms:* hang it up, throw in the towel. *See also* **break. 3.** To give up or leave completely ▸ abdicate, relinquish, surrender. *See* **abandon** (1). *See synonym note at* **abandon.**

resignation *noun*
1. A giving up of a possession, claim, or right ▸ abdication, relinquishment, surrender. *See* **abandonment** (1). **2.** The capacity of enduring hardship or inconvenience without complaint ▸ longanimity, tolerance. *See* **patience.** *See synonym note at* **patience.**

resigned *adjective*
1. Submitting without objection or resistance ▸ nonresistant, yielding. *See* **passive. 2.** Enduring or capable of enduring hardship or inconvenience without complaint ▸ enduring, long-suffering. *See* **patient.**

resilience *or* **resiliency** *noun*
1. The quality or state of being flexible ▸ elasticity, malleability, pliability. *See* **flexibility** (1). **2.** The ability to recover quickly from depression or discouragement ▸ bounce, buoyancy, elasticity, flexibility, resiliency.

resilient *adjective*
▸ elastic, flexile, supple. *See* **flexible** (1). *See synonym note at* **flexible.**

resist *verb*
1. To place in opposition or be in opposition to ▸ counter, fight, withstand. *See* **oppose** (1). *See synonym note at* **oppose. 2.** To take a stand against ▸ buck, challenge, contest, dispute, oppose, traverse. **3.** To turn aside or drive away ▸ deflect, repulse, ward off. *See* **repel. 4.** To refuse or fail to obey ▸ defy, transgress. *See* **disobey.**

resistance *noun*
1. The act or an instance of defying ▸ disobedience, rebellion. *See* **defiance** (1). **2.** The capacity to withstand ▸ immunity, imperviousness, insusceptibility, unsusceptibility. *See also* **endurance, stability. 3.** A clandestine organization of freedom fighters in an oppressed land ▸ opposition, underground. **4.** The state of not being disposed or inclined ▸ aversion, opposition, reluctance. *See* **indisposition** (1).

resistant *adjective*
1. Having the capacity to withstand ▸ immune, impervious, insusceptible, proof, repellent, resisting, resistive, unsusceptible. *See also* **defiant, stable, strong, stubborn. 2.** Acting against or in opposition ▸ antagonistic, unfavorable. *See* **opposing** (1). **3.** Not inclined or willing to do or undertake ▸ disinclined, reluctant. *See* **indisposed** (1).

resister *noun*
▸ antagonist, foe, nemesis. *See* **opponent** (1).

resisting *adjective*
▸ impervious, insusceptible, unsusceptible. *See* **resistant** (1).

resistive *adjective*
Having the capacity to withstand ▸ immune, repellent, unsusceptible. *See* **resistant** (1).

resolute *adjective*
1. Possessing determination or resolution ▸ constant, steadfast, unyielding. *See* **firm**[1] (3). **2.** Committed to or unwavering in a course of action ▸ determined, fixed. *See* **intent** (1).

resoluteness *noun*
▸ determination, purpose, resolve, will. *See* **decision** (2).

resolution *noun*
1. Unwavering firmness of character, action, or will ▸ determination, purpose, resolve, will. *See* **decision** (2). **2.** A position reached after consideration ▸ conclusion, determination. *See* **decision** (1). **3.** A solution, as to a problem ▸ explanation, solution, result. *See* **answer** (2). **4.** An authoritative or official decision ▸ edict, judgment, pronouncement. *See* **ruling.**

resolve *verb*
1. To make up or cause to make up one's mind ▸ determine, settle. *See* **decide** (1). *See synonym note at* **decide. 2.** To separate into parts for study ▸ break down, dissect, reduce. *See* **analyze** (1). **3.** To find a

solution for ▸ clear up, explain, unravel. *See* **solve** (1). *See synonym note at* **solve. 4.** To bring something into a state of agreement or accord ▸ arrange, set. *See* **settle** (2).

resolve *noun*
Unwavering firmness of character, action, or will ▸ determination, purpose, will. *See* **decision** (2).

resonance *noun*
▸ edge, intonation, inflection. *See* **tone** (2).

resonant *adjective*
1. Having or producing a full, deep, or rich sound ▸ mellow, orotund, plangent, resounding, ringing, rotund, round, sonorous, vibrant. *See also* **loud. 2.** Tending to bring a memory, mood, or image, for example, subtly or indirectly to mind ▸ allusive, connotative, evocative, impressionistic, reminiscent, resonant. *See also* **designative, symbolic.**

resort *verb*
1. To look to when in need ▸ apply, go, refer, repair, run, turn. *Idioms:* fall back on (*or* upon), have recourse to. **2.** To visit regularly ▸ hang around, haunt. *See* **frequent.**

resort *noun*
1. A frequently visited place ▸ meeting place. *Slang:* hangout, stamping ground. *See* **haunt** (1). **2.** That to which one turns for help when in desperation ▸ recourse, refuge, resource. *See also* **help, support. 3.** The act of putting into play ▸ employment, implementation, usage. *See* **exercise** (1). **4.** Something used temporarily or reluctantly when other means are not available ▸ make-do, stopgap. *See* **makeshift.** *See synonym note at* **makeshift.**

✦ CORE SYNONYMS: *resort, apply, go, refer, turn.* These verbs mean to look to or fall back on someone or something when in need: *resorted to corporal punishment; apply to a bank for a loan; goes to her friends for comfort; referred to his notes to refresh his memory; turns to his parents for support.*

---

resound *verb*
1. To send back the sound of ▸ reflect, repeat, reverberate. *See* **echo** (1). *See synonym note at* **echo. 2.** To make a continuous deep reverberating sound ▸ growl, grumble, roll. *See* **rumble** (1).

resounding *adjective*
▸ orotund, sonorous, vibrant. *See* **resonant.**

resource *noun*
That to which one turns for help when in desperation ▸ recourse, refuge, resort. *See also* **help, support.**

resourceful *adjective*
1. Mentally quick and original ▸ ingenious, inventive, quick-thinking. *See* **clever** (1). **2.** Characterized by or productive of new things or new ideas ▸ ingenious, innovative, original. *See* **inventive** (1).

resourcefulness *noun*
▸ creativity, ingenuity, originality. *See* **invention** (1).

resources *noun*
1. Things, such as money, property, or goods, having economic value ▸ assets, capital, fortune, means,

wealth, wherewithal. *See also* **funds, money. 2.** Money or property used to produce more wealth ▸ financing, funding, stake. *See* **capital** (1). **3.** Anything that increases physical comfort ▸ conveniences, facilities, services. *See* **amenities** (1).

respect *verb*
To have a high opinion of ▸ admire, honor, regard. *See* **value** (1).

respect *noun*
1. A feeling of deference, approval, and liking ▸ admiration, favor. *See* **esteem** (1). *See synonym note at* **esteem. 2.** A person's high standing among others ▸ good name, reputation. *See* **honor** (2). **3.** The particular angle from which something is considered ▸ angle, aspect, facet, frame of reference, hand, light, phase, regard, side.

respectability *or* **respectableness** *noun*
▸ decorum, seemliness. *See* **decency** (2).

respectable *adjective*
1. Deserving honor, respect, or admiration ▸ deserving, laudable, worthy. *See* **admirable. 2.** Marked by uprightness in principle and action ▸ honorable, righteous. *See* **honest** (1). **3.** Suitable for a particular person, condition, occasion, or place ▸ befitting, correct, right. *See* **appropriate** (1). **4.** Adequate to satisfy a need, requirement, or standard ▸ average, decent, moderate. *See* **acceptable** (2). **5.** Above average in amount, size, or scope ▸ extensive, large, sizable. *See* **big** (1). **6.** Proper in appearance ▸ modest, tasteful. *See* **decent** (7).

respectful *adjective*
1. Full of polite concern for the well-being of others ▸ courteous, solicitous, thoughtful. *See* **attentive** (1). **2.** Marked by courteous submission or respect ▸ dutiful, obeisant. *See* **deferential.**

respects *noun*
▸ best, greetings. *See* **regards.**

respiration *noun*
▸ exhalation, inhalation. *See* **breath** (1).

respire *verb*
▸ exhale, inhale. *See* **breathe** (1).

respite *noun*
1. A pause or interval, as from work or duty ▸ recess, time-out. *See* **rest**[1] (1). *See synonym note at* **rest**[1]. **2.** Temporary immunity from penalties ▸ exemption, grace, immunity, reprieve. *See also* **delay.**

resplendence *or* **resplendency** *noun*
▸ brilliance, magnificence, sparkle. *See* **glitter** (2).

resplendent *adjective*
1. Marked by extraordinary beauty and splendor ▸ brilliant, magnificent, splendid. *See* **glorious** (1). **2.** Elaborately and heavily ornamented ▸ flamboyant, ostentatious. *See* **ornate** (1). **3.** Full of bright shifting or flickering light ▸ glinting, glittering, shimmering. *See* **sparkling** (1).

respond *verb*
1. To speak or act in response, as to a question ▸ reply, retort, riposte. *See* **answer** (1). *See synonym note at* **answer. 2.** To act in return to something, as a stim-

ulus ▸ counter, react. *Idiom:* act in response. *See also* **retaliate**.

respondent *noun*
A person against whom an action is brought ▸ accused, defendant.

response *noun*
1. Something spoken or written in return ▸ repartee, retort, riposte. *See* **answer** (1). 2. An action elicited by a stimulus ▸ reaction, retroaction. *See also* **retaliation**.

responsibility *noun*
1. The state of being responsible ▸ accountability, amenability, amenableness, answerability, liability. *See also* **blame, burden**[1]. 2. An act or course of action that is demanded of one, as by position, custom, law, or religion ▸ charge, commitment, obligation. *See* **duty** (1).

responsible *adjective*
1. Legally or officially obligated ▸ accountable, answerable. *See* **liable** (1). *See synonym note at* **liable**. 2. Capable of being depended on ▸ reliable, stable, trustworthy. *See* **dependable**. *See synonym note at* **dependable**.

responsive *adjective*
1. Able to receive and respond to external stimuli ▸ impressionable, sentient. *See* **sensitive** (1). 2. Ready and willing to receive favorably, as new ideas ▸ acceptant, open-minded. *See* **receptive**. 3. Easily approached ▸ accessible, approachable, welcoming. *See also* **convenient**.

responsiveness *noun*
▸ open-mindedness, receptivity. *See* **openness** (1).

rest[1] *noun*
1. A pause or interval, as from work or duty ▸ break, breathing spell, downtime, hiatus, intermission, recess, respite, time-out. *Informal:* breather. *See also* **abeyance, gap, stop**. 2. Freedom from labor, responsibility, or strain ▸ ease, leisure, relaxation, repose, time-out. *Informal:* R and R. *See also* **calm, inaction, sleep**. 3. The act or fact of dying ▸ demise, passing. *See* **death** (1).

rest *verb*
1. To take repose by ceasing work or other effort for an interval of time ▸ chill out, kick back, lounge, mellow out, relax, sit back, unbend, unwind. *Idioms:* lead (*or* live) the life of Riley, put one's feet up, take a load off one's feet, take it easy. 2. To take repose, as by sleeping or lying quietly ▸ curl up, lie (down), recline, repose, stretch (out). *See also* **nap, sleep**. 3. To have an inherent basis ▸ exist, inhere, reside. *See* **consist** (1). 4. To provide a basis for ▸ establish, ground. *See* **base**[1] (1). 5. To be in a certain position; have a location ▸ be located, be situated, sit, stand.

rest on *or* **upon** *verb*
To be determined by or contingent on something unknown, uncertain, or changeable ▸ hinge on (*or* upon), revolve around. *See* **depend on** (2).

⊕ CORE SYNONYMS: *rest, break, intermission, recess, respite.* These nouns denote a pause or interval, as from

work, duty, or action: *needed a rest after a long morning at work; took an hourlong break for dinner; a concert with a 15-minute intermission; the legislature's summer recess; toiling without respite.*

rest[2] *noun*
A remaining part ▸ remainder, remains, remnant. *See* **balance** (4).

restart *verb*
▸ proceed, resume. *See* **continue** (1).

restate *verb*
1. To state again ▸ iterate, reiterate, retell. *See* **repeat** (1). *See synonym note at* **repeat**. 2. To express the meaning of in other, especially simpler, words ▸ reword, translate. *See* **paraphrase**.

restatement *noun*
1. The act or process of repeating ▸ reiteration, repeat. *See* **repetition** (1). 2. A restating of something in other, especially simpler, words ▸ rendering, translation. *See* **paraphrase**.

restful *adjective*
▸ easy, snug. *Informal:* comfy. *See* **comfortable** (1). *See synonym note at* **comfortable**.

restitute *verb*
1. To bring back to a previous normal condition ▸ recondition, reconstruct, rejuvenate. *See* **restore** (3). 2. To give back, especially money ▸ reimburse, refund, repay. *See also* **compensate, return**. 3. To send, put, or carry back to a former location ▸ give back, restore, take back. *See* **return** (2).

restitution *noun*
▸ amends, remuneration, reparation. *See* **compensation** (1). *See synonym note at* **compensation**.

restive *adjective*
▸ jittery, nervous. *See* **edgy**.

restiveness *noun*
▸ disquietude, uneasiness, unrest. *See* **restlessness**.

restless *adjective*
1. Affording no quiet, repose, or rest ▸ uneasy, unquiet, unsettled. *See also* **wakeful**. 2. Feeling or exhibiting nervous tension ▸ jittery, tense. *See* **edgy**. 3. Full of lively activity ▸ bustling, crawling, swarming. *See* **busy** (2).

restlessness *noun*
An uneasy or nervous state ▸ disquiet, disquietude, edginess, inquietude, jumpiness, nervousness, restiveness, skittishness, tenseness, twitchiness, unease, uneasiness, unrest. *See also* **agitation, anxiety, excitement**.

restoration *noun*
1. The act of making new or as if new again ▸ refurbishment, rejuvenation, renovation. *See* **renewal** (1). 2. A return to former prosperity or status ▸ comeback, reestablishment, renewal. *See also* **renewal, revival**. 3. The act of reviving or condition of being revived ▸ rebirth, renaissance, renewal. *See* **revival** (1).

restorative *adjective*
1. Serving to cure ▸ medicinal, remedial. *See* **curative**. 2. Producing or stimulating physical, mental,

or emotional vigor ▶ bracing, energizing, exhilarating. *See* **invigorating.**

restorative *noun*

1. A medicine that restores or increases vigor ▶ energizer, stimulant. *See* **tonic. 2.** An agent used to restore health ▶ elixir, medication, remedy. *See* **cure.**

restore *verb*

1. To bring back into existence or use ▶ reestablish, reinstate, reintroduce, renew, return, revive. **2.** To cause to come back to life or consciousness ▶ regenerate, resuscitate, revivify. *See* **revive** (2). **3.** To bring back to a previous normal condition ▶ rebuild, reclaim, recondition, reconstruct, rehabilitate, reinstate, rejuvenate, renovate, restitute. **4.** To put someone in the possession of a prior position or office ▶ give back, reinstate, replace, return. **5.** To make new or as if new again ▶ refresh, renovate, revamp. *See* **renew** (1). **6.** To impart renewed energy and strength to a person ▶ reinvigorate, rejuvenate, revitalize. *See* **refresh** (1). **7.** To send, put, or carry back to a former location ▶ give back, restitute, take back. *See* **return** (2).

restrain *verb*

To control, restrict, or arrest ▶ bit, bottle (up), brake, bridle, check, constrain, curb, harness, hold, hold back, hold down, hold in, inhibit, keep, keep back, pull in, rein (back, in, *or* up). *Idioms:* hold in leash, keep in check, keep under control, keep within bounds, put a lid on. *See also* **hinder, limit, repress, stop.**

✦ **CORE SYNONYMS:** *restrain, curb, check, bridle, inhibit.* These verbs mean to restrict, or arrest, or keep under control. *Restrain* implies restriction or limitation, as on one's freedom of action: *"a wise and frugal government, which shall restrain men from injuring one another"* (Thomas Jefferson). To *curb* is to restrain as if with reins: *"You might curb your magnanimity"* (John Keats). *Check* implies arresting or stopping, often suddenly or forcibly: *"a light to guide, a rod/To check the erring"* (William Wordsworth). To *bridle* is often to hold in or govern one's emotions or passions: *I tried with all my might to bridle my resentment. Inhibit* usually connotes a check on one's actions, thoughts, or emotions: *A fear of strangers inhibited his ability to travel.*

---

restrained *adjective*

1. Kept within sensible limits ▶ moderate, reasonable, temperate. *See* **conservative** (2). **2.** Not showy or obtrusive ▶ inobtrusive, quiet, subdued. *See* **modest** (1). **3.** Tending to keep one's thoughts and emotions to oneself ▶ guarded, inhibited, self-controlled. *See* **reserved** (1). **4.** Kept within certain limits ▶ checked, controlled, restricted. *See* **restricted** (1).

restraint *noun*

1. Something that limits or holds back ▶ check, circumscription, constraint, control, cramp, curb, deterrent, drag, inhibition, limit, limitation, restriction, stay, stricture. **2.** The act of limiting or condition of being limited ▶ confinement, constraint, limita-

tion. *See* **restriction** (1). **3.** A device for slowing or stopping motion ▶ curb, leash, rein. *See* **brake** (1). **4.** Something that physically confines the legs or arms ▶ handcuffs, hobble, irons. *See* **bond** (1). **5.** The keeping of one's thoughts and emotions to oneself ▶ constraint, control, self-restraint. *See* **reserve** (2). **6.** Lack of ostentation or pretension ▶ plainness, simpleness, simplicity. *See* **modesty** (2).

restrict *verb*

1. To place a limit on ▶ confine, fix, set. *See* **limit** (1). *See synonym note at* **limit. 2.** To fix the limits of ▶ demarcate, limit, mark. *See* **determine** (1).

restricted *adjective*

1. Kept within certain limits ▶ bridled, checked, circumscribed, confined, controlled, held back, limited, regulated, reined in, restrained. *See also* **local. 2.** Not total, unlimited, or wholehearted ▶ limited, modified, reserved. *See* **qualified** (1). **3.** Of or being information available only to authorized persons ▶ privileged, top secret. *See* **confidential** (3).

restriction *noun*

1. The act of limiting or condition of being limited ▶ circumscription, confinement, constraint, limitation, restraint, stranglehold, throttlehold. *See also* **provision. 2.** Something that limits or holds back ▶ check, constraint, curb. *See* **restraint** (1).

restrictive *adjective*

1. Serving to restrain forcefully ▶ inhibitive, restraining, suppressive. *See* **repressive. 2.** Affording little room for movement ▶ close, confining, snug. *See* **tight** (4).

restyle *verb*

▶ amend, revamp, rework. *See* **revise** (1).

result *verb*

To occur as a consequence ▶ attend, ensue, follow. *See* **follow.**

result in *verb*

To be the cause of ▶ generate, induce, trigger. *See* **cause.**

result *noun*

1. Something brought about by a cause ▶ consequence, outcome, upshot. *See* **effect** (1). *See synonym note at* **effect. 2.** A solution, as to a problem ▶ explanation, solution. *See* **answer** (2). **3.** Something that has been discovered ▶ conclusion, strike. *See* **discovery.**

resultant *noun*

▶ consequence, outcome, result. *See* **effect** (1).

resume *verb*

1. To occupy or take again ▶ reassume, re-claim, reoccupy, repossess, retake, take back. **2.** To begin or go on after an interruption ▶ pick up, restart. *See* **continue** (1).

resumé *verb*

▶ background, past, vita. *See* **history** (2).

resumption *noun*

A continuing after interruption ▶ continuation, renewal, resurgence, revival.

resurgence *noun*

1. A continuing after interruption ▶ continuation,

renewal, resumption, revival. **2.** The act of reviving or condition of being revived ▶ rebirth, renaissance, renewal. *See* **revival** (1).

resurrect *verb*
▶ rekindle, resuscitate, revitalize. *See* **revive** (1).

resurrection *noun*
▶ rebirth, renaissance, renewal. *See* **revival** (1).

resuscitate *verb*
1. To cause to come back to life or consciousness ▶ restore, revivify. *See* **revive** (2). **2.** To rouse from a state of inactivity or quiescence ▶ rekindle, resurrect, revitalize. *See* **revive** (1). *See synonym note at* **revive**.

resuscitation *noun*
▶ rebirth, renaissance, renewal. *See* **revival** (1).

retail *verb*
▶ handle, peddle. *See* **sell** (1).

retailer *noun*
▶ salesclerk, vendor. *See* **seller**.

retain *verb*
1. To have and maintain in one's possession ▶ keep, reserve. *See* **hold** (1). *See synonym note at* **hold**. **2.** To persevere in some condition, action, or belief ▶ maintain, stay with, sustain. *See* **keep** (6). **3.** To renew an image or thought in the mind ▶ recall, recollect, reminisce. *See* **remember** (1). **4.** To obtain the use or services of ▶ hire, recruit. *See* **employ** (1).

retained *adjective*
▶ jobholding, working. *See* **employed** (1).

retake *verb*
▶ reassume, reoccupy, repossess. *See* **resume** (1).

retaliate *verb*
To return like for like, especially to return an unfriendly or hostile action with a similar one ▶ counter, counterattack, hit back, reciprocate, requite, retort, strike back. *See also* **avenge, exchange**.

retaliation *noun*
The act of retaliating ▶ counteraction, counterattack, counterblow, reciprocation, reprisal, requital, retribution, revenge, tit for tat, vengeance. *Idioms:* an eye for an eye, a tooth for a tooth, like for like, measure for measure.

retard *verb*
1. To cause to be later or slower than expected or desired ▶ hang up, keep, stall. *See* **delay** (1). **2.** To interfere with the progress of ▶ dampen, obstruct. *See* **hinder** (1).

retardation *noun*
▶ detainment, holdup, lag. *See* **delay** (2).

retch *verb*
▶ spit up, throw up. *Informal:* puke. *See* **vomit** (1).

retell *verb*
▶ iterate, reiterate, restate. *See* **repeat** (1).

retention *noun*
1. The act of employing for wages ▶ employment, engagement, hire, hiring. **2.** The power of retaining and recalling past experience ▶ recollection, remembrance. *See* **memory** (1).

retentive *adjective*
▶ absorptive, imbibing, spongy. *See* **absorbent**.

rethink *verb*
▶ reexamine, reweigh, review. *See* **reconsider**.

reticence *noun*
1. The keeping of one's thoughts and emotions to oneself ▶ constraint, restraint, self-restraint. *See* **reserve** (2). **2.** Reserve in speech, behavior, or dress ▶ demureness, diffidence, modesty, self-effacement.

reticent *adjective*
1. Habitually untalkative ▶ close-mouthed, silent, uncommunicative. *See* **taciturn**. *See synonym note at* **taciturn**. **2.** Not friendly, sociable, or warm in manner ▶ aloof, chilly, impersonal. *See* **cool** (1).

retinue *noun*
A group of attendants or followers ▶ entourage, following, suite, train. *See also* **circle, follower, public**.

retire *verb*
1. To move away from a place ▶ exit, go away, leave. *See* **go** (1). **2.** To go to bed ▶ bed (down). *Informal:* turn in. *Slang:* crash, flop. *Idioms:* call it a night, go beddy-bye (*or* night-night), hit the hay (*or* sack). *See also* **sleep**. **3.** To withdraw or remove from business or active life ▶ pension (off), step down, superannuate. *Idioms:* call it quits, hang up one's spurs, put out to pasture, turn in one's badge. *See also* **dismiss, quit**. **4.** To move back in the face of enemy attack or after a defeat ▶ draw back, pull out, withdraw. *See* **retreat** (4).

retirement *noun*
1. The act of secluding or the state of being secluded ▶ isolation, reclusion, sequestration. *See* **seclusion** (1). **2.** The moving back of a military force in the face of enemy attack or after a defeat ▶ fallback, pullout, withdrawal. *See* **retreat** (1). **3.** The quality or state of being alone ▶ isolation, loneliness, privacy. *See* **solitude**. *See synonym note at* **solitude**. **4.** The act of leaving ▶ egress, leave-taking, withdrawal. *See* **departure** (1).

retiring *adjective*
▶ bashful, demure, diffident. *See* **shy**[1] (1).

retiringness *noun*
▶ bashfulness, demureness, diffidence. *See* **shyness**.

retort
retort *verb*
1. To speak or act in response, as to a question ▶ reply, respond, riposte. *See* **answer** (1). *See synonym note at* **answer**. **2.** To return like for like, especially to return an unfriendly or hostile action with a similar one ▶ counter, reciprocate, strike back. *See* **retaliate**.

retort *noun*
Something spoken or written in return ▶ comeback, repartee, riposte. *See* **answer** (1).

retouch *verb*
To improve by making minor changes or additions ▶ polish, remodel, touch up. *See also* **fix, renew**.

retract *verb*
1. To disavow something previously written or said irrevocably and usually formally ▶ abjure, countermand, forswear, recall, recant, take back, unsay, withdraw. *See also* **lift**. **2.** To pull back in ▶ draw in,

withdraw. **3.** To move back or away from a point, limit, or mark ▸ retreat, retrogress. *See* **recede.** *See synonym note at* **recede.**

retraction *noun*
1. A formal statement of disavowal ▸ abjuration, countermand, palinode, recantation, retractation, withdrawal. **2.** The act of reversing or annulling ▸ recall, reversal, revocation. *See* **repeal.**

retreat *noun*
1. The moving back of a military force in the face of enemy attack or after a defeat ▸ evacuation, fallback, pullback, pullout, removal, retirement, withdrawal. *See also* **escape. 2.** Something that physically protects, especially from danger ▸ asylum, refuge, sanctuary. *See* **cover** (1). *See synonym note at* **cover. 3.** The quality or state of being alone ▸ isolation, loneliness. *See* **solitude.**

retreat *verb*
1. To move back or away from a point, limit, or mark ▸ retract, retrogress. *See* **recede.** *See synonym note at* **recede. 2.** To move in a reverse direction ▸ backpedal, retrogress, reverse. *See* **back** (1). **3.** To abandon a former position or commitment ▸ blink, skip out, walk out. *See* **renege.4.** To move back in the face of enemy attack or after a defeat ▸ draw back, evacuate, fall back, pull back, pull out, remove, retire, turn back, withdraw. *Idioms:* beat a retreat, give ground (or way). *See also* **escape.**

retribution *noun*
1. The act of retaliating ▸ counteraction, reciprocation, reprisal. *See* **retaliation. 2.** Something, such as loss, pain, or confinement, imposed for wrongdoing ▸ castigation, chastisement, penalty. *See* **punishment.**

retrieval *noun*
The act of getting back or regaining ▸ recoup, recovery, repossession.

retrieve *verb*
1. To get back ▸ regain, repossess. *See* **recover** (1). *See synonym note at* **recover. 2.** To rouse from a state of inactivity or quiescence ▸ rekindle, resuscitate, revitalize. *See* **revive** (1). **3.** To renew an image or thought in the mind ▸ recall, recollect, reminisce. *See* **remember** (1).

retroaction *noun*
An action elicited by a stimulus ▸ reaction, response. *See also* **retaliation.**

retrocede *verb*
1. To move back or away from a point, limit, or mark ▸ ebb, retract, retreat. *See* **recede. 2.** To move in a reverse direction ▸ backtrack, retreat, retrogress. *See* **back** (1).

retrogradation *noun*
1. A return to a former, usually worse condition ▸ backsliding, lapse, recidivism. *See* **relapse. 2.** Descent to a lower level or condition ▸ decadence, decline, degeneration. *See* **deterioration** (1).

retrograde *adjective*
Moving or directed toward the rear ▸ rearward, retrogressive. *See* **backward** (3).

retrograde *verb*
1. To move in a reverse direction ▸ backpedal, retreat. *See* **back** (1). **2.** To move back or away from a point, limit, or mark ▸ ebb, retract, retreat. *See* **recede.** *See synonym note at* **recede. 3.** To become lower in quality, character, or condition ▸ atrophy, degenerate, worsen. *See* **deteriorate** (1).

retrogress *verb*
1. To slip from a higher or better condition to a former, usually lower or poorer one ▸ lapse, regress, revert. *See* **relapse. 2.** To move in a reverse direction ▸ back up, retreat. *See* **back** (1). **3.** To move back or away from a point, limit, or mark ▸ ebb, retract, retreat. *See* **recede.**

retrogression *noun*
▸ backsliding, lapse, recidivism. *See* **relapse.**

retrogressive *adjective*
▸ rearward, retrograde. *See* **backward** (3).

retrospective *noun*
▸ exposition, show. *See* **exhibition** (1).

return *verb*
1. To come back to a former condition or place ▸ come back, go back, recrudesce, recur, reoccur, revert, revisit, turn back. *See also* **relapse. 2.** To send, put, or carry back to a former location ▸ give back, replace, restitute, restore, take back. *See also* **refund. 3.** To make as income or profit ▸ bring in, clear, draw, earn, gain, gross, net, pay, produce, realize, reap, repay, yield. *Idioms: Informal* rake in. **4.** To bring back into existence or use ▸ reestablish, reinstate, reintroduce, renew, restore, revive. *See also* **restore. 5.** To speak or act in response, as to a question ▸ reply, respond, riposte. *See* **answer** (1). **6.** To give or take mutually ▸ reciprocate, requite. *Idiom:* respond in kind. *See synonym note at* **reciprocate.** *See also* **exchange, respond. 7.** To deliver an indictment or verdict, for example ▸ hand down, render. **8.** To put someone in the possession of a prior position or office ▸ give back, reappoint, reinstall, reinstate, replace, restore.

return *noun*
1. The act or process of repeating ▸ reiteration, repeat, restatement. *See* **repetition** (1). **2.** Something that is earned, won, or otherwise acquired ▸ earnings, gain, profit. *See also* **increase. 3.** Something that is spoken or written in return ▸ repartee, retort, riposte. *See* **answer** (1).

reunite *verb*
To reestablish friendship between ▸ conciliate, make up, reconcile. *See also* **pacify.**

reutter *verb*
▸ reiterate, restate, retell. *See* **repeat** (1).

revamp *verb*
1. To restore to proper condition ▸ mend, overhaul, repair. *See* **fix** (1). **2.** To make new or as if new again ▸ refresh, rejuvenate, restore. *See* **renew** (1). **3.** To prepare a new version of ▸ amend, edit, rework. *See* **revise** (1).

revampment *noun*
▸ refurbishment, rejuvenation, renovation. *See* **renewal** (1).

reveal *verb*
1. To disclose in a breach of confidence ▸ divulge, give away. *Informal:* spill. *See* **betray** (2). **2.** To make visible or known ▸ bare, disclose, display, expose, show, unclothe, uncover, unmask, unveil. *Idioms:* bring to light (*or* view), lay open (*or* bare), make plain (*or* public). *See also* **announce, display. 3.** To make manifest or apparent ▸ display, proclaim. *See* **show** (1). **4.** To make known ▸ disclose, divulge, transmit. *See* **communicate** (1).

revel *verb*
1. To behave riotously ▸ carouse, frolic, party, riot, roister, romp. *Informal:* hell (around). *Idioms:* blow off steam, cut loose, kick over the traces, kick up one's heels, let go, let loose, make merry, make whoopee, paint the town red, raise Cain (*or* the devil *or* hell), whoop it up. *See also* **celebrate. 2.** To take extravagant pleasure ▸ bask, indulge, wallow. *See* **luxuriate. 3.** To show joyful satisfaction in an event ▸ feast, party, rejoice. *See* **celebrate** (2).

revel *noun*
A joyous or festive occasion ▸ festivity, fiesta, holiday. *See* **celebration** (1).

revelation *noun*
Something disclosed, especially something not previously known or realized ▸ apocalypse, disclosure, divulgence, exposé, exposure. *Informal:* eye opener. *See also* **acknowledgment, news.**

revelry *noun*
1. The act of showing joyful satisfaction in an event ▸ jubilation, merrymaking, rejoicing. *See* **celebration** (3). **2.** Joyful, exuberant activity ▸ gaiety, jollity, merrymaking. *See* **merriment** (2).

revels
revels *noun*
1. A joyous or festive occasion ▸ festivity, fiesta, holiday. *See* **celebration** (1). **2.** Joyful, exuberant activity ▸ festivity, gaiety, merrymaking. *See* **merriment** (2).

revenant *noun*
▸ phantom, shade, specter. *See* **ghost** (1).

revenge *noun*
1. The act of retaliating ▸ counteraction, reciprocation, reprisal. *See* **retaliation. 2.** The quality or condition of being vindictive ▸ spite, spitefulness, vengefulness, vindictiveness. *See also* **resentment.**

revengeful *adjective*
▸ avenging, spiteful, unforgiving. *See* **vindictive** (1).

reverberate *verb*
▸ reflect, repeat, resound. *See* **echo** (1). *See synonym note at* **echo.**

reverberation *noun*
1. Repetition of sound via reflection from a surface ▸ echo, repercussion. **2.** An explosive noise ▸ boom, crash. *See* **blast** (1). **3.** The strong effect exerted by one person or thing on another ▸ impression, influence. *See* **impact** (2).

revere *verb*
To regard with deep respect, deference, and esteem ▸ adore, hallow, idolize, reverence, venerate, worship. *See also* **distinguish, praise, honor, value.**

✛ CORE SYNONYMS: *revere, worship, venerate, adore, idolize.* These verbs mean to regard with deep respect, deference, and esteem. *Revere* suggests awe coupled with profound honor: *"At least one third of the population . . . reveres every sort of holy man"* (Rudyard Kipling). *Worship* implies reverent love and homage rendered to God or a god: *The ancient Egyptians worshiped a number of gods.* In a more general sense *worship* connotes an often uncritical devotion: *"She had worshiped intellect"* (Charles Kingsley). *Venerate* connotes reverence accorded by virtue, especially of dignity or age: *"I venerate the memory of my grandfather"* (Horace Walpole). To *adore* is to worship with deep, often rapturous love: *The students adored their caring teacher.* Idolize implies worship like that accorded an object of religious devotion: *He idolizes his wife.*

reverence *noun*
1. The act of adoring, especially reverently ▸ adoration, idolization, veneration, worship. *See also* **devotion, honor, praise. 2.** A state of often extreme religious ardor ▸ piety, piousness. *See* **devotion** (1). **3.** Great respect or high public esteem accorded as a right or as due ▸ homage, obeisance. *See* **honor** (1). *See synonym note at* **honor.**

reverence *verb*
To regard with the deepest respect, deference, and esteem ▸ idolize, venerate, worship. *See* **revere.**

reverend *noun*
Informal A person ordained for service in a Christian church ▸ ecclesiastic, minister, parson. *See* **cleric.**

reverent *adjective*
Feeling or showing reverence ▸ devout, pious, reverential, venerational, worshipful. *See also* **deferential.**

reverential *adjective*
▸ pious, venerational, worshipful. *See* **reverent.**

reverie *noun*
1. The condition of being so lost in solitary thought that one is unaware of one's surroundings ▸ absentmindedness, bemusement, study. *See* **trance** (1). **2.** An illusory mental image ▸ fancy, fantasy, illusion. *See* **dream** (1).

reversal *noun*
1. The act of changing or being changed from one position, direction, or course to the opposite ▸ aboutface, change of heart, flip-flop, inversion, transposition, turnabout, turnaround, U-turn. **2.** A change from better to worse ▸ backset, reverse, setback. *See also* **misfortune, relapse. 3.** An unexpected and usually undesirable event ▸ contretemps, mischance, mishap. *See* **accident** (1). **4.** The act of reversing or annulling ▸ recall, rescission, revocation. *See* **repeal.**

reverse *adjective*
Diametrically opposed ▸ antithetical, contradictory, diametric. *See* **opposite** (1).

reverse *noun*
1. That which is diametrically opposed to another ▸ antithesis, contrary. *See* **opposite. 2.** A change from better to worse ▸ backset, reversal, setback. *See also* **misfortune, relapse.**

reverse *verb*
1. To change to the opposite position, direction, or course ▸ flip-flop, invert, transpose, turn (about, around, over, *or* round,). **2.** To move in a reverse direction ▸ backpedal, retreat. *See* **back** (1). **3.** To turn sharply around ▸ about-face, double (back). **4.** To take back or remove ▸ repeal, rescind, revoke. *See* **lift** (5).

✦ CORE SYNONYMS: *reverse, invert, transpose.* These verbs mean to change to the opposite position, direction, or course. *Reverse* implies a complete turning about to a contrary position: *reversed the placement of the sofa and chairs.* To *invert* is basically to turn something upside down or inside out, but the term may imply placing something in a reverse order: *inverted the glass; invert subject and verb to form an interrogative. Transpose* applies to altering position in a sequence by reversing or changing the order: *often misspells* receive *by transposing the e and the i.*

reversible *adjective*
▸ fluid, unsettled, variable. *See* **changeable** (1).

reversion *noun*
▸ backsliding, lapse, recidivism. *See* **relapse.**

revert *verb*
1. To come back to a former condition ▸ recrudesce, recur, reoccur. *See* **return** (1). **2.** To slip from a higher or better condition to a former, usually lower or poorer one ▸ lapse, regress. *See* **relapse.**

review *verb*
1. To give a recapitulation of the salient facts of ▸ abstract, epitomize, go over, recapitulate, run down, run through, summarize, sum up, synopsize, wrap up. *Informal:* recap. *See also* **paraphrase. 2.** To consider again, especially with the possibility of change ▸ reexamine, rethink. *See* **reconsider. 3.** To write a critical report on ▸ criticize, critique. *See also* **comment, estimate. 4.** To look at or study carefully or critically ▸ investigate, scrutinize. *See* **examine** (1).

review *noun*
1. The act of examining carefully or critically ▸ audit, checkup, survey. *See* **examination** (1). **2.** Critical explanation or analysis ▸ criticism, critique, notice. *See* **commentary. 3.** A formal military inspection ▸ parade.

reviewer *noun*
▸ judge, pundit. *See* **critic** (1).

revile *verb*
To attack with harsh, often insulting language ▸ abuse, assail, blaspheme, execrate, fulminate against, rail (at), spit on, vilify, vituperate (against). *Idioms:* call names, vent one's spleen at. *See also* **chastise, despise, dislike, hate.**

✦ CORE SYNONYMS: *revile, vituperate, rail.* These verbs mean to attack with harsh, often insulting language.

Revile and *vituperate* stress the use of disparaging or abusive language: *critics who reviled the novel as unsophisticated pulp.* "*The incensed priests . . . continued to raise their voices, vituperating each other in bad Latin*" (Sir Walter Scott). *Rail* suggests bitter, harsh, or denunciatory language: "*Why rail at fate? The mischief is your own*" (John Greenleaf Whittier).

revilement *or* **reviling** *noun*
▸ condemnation, invective. *See* **vituperation.**

revisal *noun*
▸ amendment, emendation, rewrite. *See* **revision.**

revise *verb*
1. To prepare a new version of ▸ amend, edit, emend, emendate, redraft, restyle, revamp, rework, rewrite, work over. *See also* **change. 2.** To make right what is wrong ▸ amend, redress. *See* **correct** (1). *See synonym note at* **correct.**

revision *noun*
The act or process of revising ▸ amendment, emendation, recension, redaction, redraft, revisal, rewrite. *See also* **improvement.**

revisit *verb*
▸ go back, reoccur, revert. *See* **return** (1).

revitalization *noun*
▸ rebirth, renaissance, renewal. *See* **revival** (1).

revitalize *verb*
1. To impart renewed energy and strength to a person ▸ reinvigorate, rejuvenate, revivify. *See* **refresh** (1). **2.** To rouse from a state of inactivity or quiescence ▸ rekindle, resuscitate, revivify. *See* **revive** (1).

revival *noun*
1. The act of reviving or condition of being revived ▸ reactivation, rebirth, renaissance, renascence, renewal, restoration, resurgence, resurrection, resuscitation, revitalization, revivification. *See also* **comeback, renewal. 2.** A continuing after interruption ▸ continuation, renewal, resumption, resurgence. **3.** A return to former prosperity or status ▸ recovery, restoration, renewal. *See* **comeback.**

revive *verb*
1. To rouse from a state of inactivity or quiescence ▸ reactivate, reanimate, reawaken, rekindle, renew, renovate, resurrect, resuscitate, retrieve, revitalize, revivify. *See also* **refresh. 2.** To cause to come back to life or consciousness ▸ bring around (*or* round), regenerate, restore, resuscitate, revivify. *See also* **cure, evoke, recover. 3.** To bring back into existence or use ▸ reestablish, reinstate, reintroduce, renew, restore, return. *See also* **restore. 4.** To renew an image or thought in the mind ▸ recall, recollect, reminisce. *See* **remember** (1).

✦ CORE SYNONYMS: *revive, rekindle, resuscitate, revivify.* These verbs mean to rouse from a state of inactivity or quiescence: *rains that revive lawns; rekindled an old romance after twenty years apart; resuscitating old hopes; a celebration that revivified our spirits.*

revivification *noun*
▸ rebirth, renaissance, renewal. *See* **revival** (1).

revivify *verb*

1. To cause to come back to life or consciousness ► restore, resuscitate. *See* **revive** (2). **2.** To impart renewed energy and strength to a person ► reinvigorate, rejuvenate, revitalize. *See* **refresh** (1). **3.** To rouse from a state of inactivity or quiescence ► rekindle, resurrect, resuscitate. *See* **revive** (1). *See synonym note at* **revive.**

revocation *noun*

► recall, rescission, reversal. *See* **repeal.**

revoke *verb*

► repeal, rescind, reverse. *See* **lift** (5).

revolt *verb*

1. To vehemently defy and break allegiance with ► mutiny, rebel, rise (up). *See also* **defect, defy. 2.** To offend the senses or feelings of ► appall, nauseate, repel, sicken. *See* **disgust** (1). *See synonym note at* **disgust.**

revolt *noun*

Organized opposition intended to change or overthrow existing authority ► mutiny, uprising. *See* **rebellion** (1).

revolting *adjective*

► contemptible, disgusting, obnoxious. *See* **offensive** (1).

revolution *noun*

1. A circular movement around a point or about an axis ► circle, circuit, circulation, circumvolution, gyration, orbit, rotation, spin, swirl, turn, twirl, wheel, whirl. **2.** Organized opposition intended to change or overthrow existing authority ► mutiny, revolt, sedition. *See* **rebellion** (1). **3.** A momentous or sweeping change ► cataclysm, convulsion, metamorphosis, transformation, upheaval. *See also* **change, shakeup.**

revolutionary *adjective*

1. Participating in open revolt against a government or ruling authority ► mutinous, subversive. *See* **rebellious** (1). **2.** Holding especially political views that deviate drastically from prevailing beliefs ► fanatical, radical, zealous. *See* **extreme** (4). **3.** Ahead of current trends or customs ► forward, precocious. *See* **progressive** (1).

revolutionary *or* **revolutionist** *noun*

1. A person who rebels ► insurrectionist, transgressor. *See* **rebel** (1). **2.** One who holds extreme views or advocates extreme measures ► radical, revolutionist, zealot. *See* **extremist.**

revolutionize *verb*

To bring about a radical change in ► metamorphose, transform. *See also* **change, overhaul.**

revolve *verb*

1. To rotate on an axis or around a center ► twirl, whirl, wheel. *See* **turn** (1). *See synonym note at* **turn. 2.** To think or think about carefully and at length ► cogitate, deliberate, mull. *See* **ponder.**

revolve around *verb*

To be determined by or contingent on something unknown, uncertain, or changeable ► hinge on (*or* upon), rest on (*or* upon). *See* **depend on** (2).

revulsion *noun*

1. A strong feeling of hostility or dislike ► antipathy, aversion, loathing. *See* **hate** (1). **2.** The feeling of despising ► disdain, loathing, scorn. *See* **despisal. 3.** Extreme aversion caused by something offensive ► abhorrence, loathing, queasiness. *See* **disgust.**

reward *noun*

1. Something given in return for a service or accomplishment ► accolade, award, bonus, bounty, guerdon, honorarium, plum, premium, prize. *Idioms:* token of appreciation (*or* esteem). *See also* **distinction, gratuity, trophy. 2.** Something justly deserved ► compensation, deserts, recompense. *See* **due** (1). **3.** Something to make up for loss or damage ► amends, remuneration, reparation. *See* **compensation** (1).

reward *verb*

1. To bestow a reward on ► award, guerdon, honor. *See also* **confer. 2.** To give compensation to ► indemnify, pay, recompense. *See* **compensate** (1).

rewarding *adjective*

► gainful, lucrative, moneymaking. *See* **profitable** (1).

reword *verb*

► render, translate. *See* **paraphrase.**

rework *verb*

► amend, revamp, rewrite. *See* **revise** (1).

rewrite *verb*

To prepare a new version of ► amend, revamp, rework. *See* **revise** (1).

rewrite *noun*

The act or process of revising ► amendment, emendation, revisal. *See* **revision.**

rhapsodize *verb*

1. To express great enthusiasm ► enthuse, gush. *See* **rave** (1). **2.** To make an extravagant show of appreciation or desire for ► enthuse, gush over, rave (about). *See* **drool.**

rhetoric *noun*

1. The art of public speaking ► elocution, speech. *See* **oratory. 2.** Smooth or effective skill in communicating ► articulateness, fluency, glibness. *See* **eloquence.**

rhetorical *adjective*

► bombastic, grandiloquent, orotund. *See* **oratorical.**

rhetorician *noun*

► lecturer, speechmaker. *See* **speaker** (1).

rhinestone *noun*

A small sparkling decoration ► diamond, glitter, sequin, spangle.

rhubarb *noun*

Informal A discussion, often heated, in which a difference of opinion is expressed ► dispute, fight, quarrel. *See* **argument** (1).

rhyme *noun*

► poetry, verse. *See* **poem** (1).

rhymer *or* **rhymester** *noun*

► muse, troubadour. *See* **poet.**

rhythm *noun*

The patterned, recurring alternation of contrasting elements, such as stressed and unstressed notes in music ▸ beat, cadence, cadency, measure, meter, swing. *See also* **beat.**

rhythmical *or* **rhythmic** *adjective*
Marked by a regular rhythm ▸ cadenced, measured, metrical. *See also* **poetic.**

rib *verb*
Informal To tease or mock good-humoredly ▸ chaff, josh. *Informal:* kid. *See* **joke** (2).

ribald *adjective*
▸ bawdy, coarse, lewd, vulgar. *See* **obscene** (1).

ribaldry *noun*
▸ dirt, sleaze, smut. *See* **obscenity** (2).

riband *noun*
▸ bandeau, cinch, ribbon, sash. *See* **band**[1] (1).

ribbing *noun*
Informal Good-natured teasing ▸ badinage, banter, chaff, joking, kidding, raillery, taunt, teasing. *See also* **taunt.**

ribbon *noun*
1. A long narrow piece, as of material ▸ bandeau, riband, sash, strip. *See* **band**[1] (1). **2.** An emblem of honor worn on one's clothing ▸ badge, decoration, medal. *See* **decoration** (2). **3.** Recognition of achievement or superiority or a sign of this ▸ award, honor. *See* **distinction** (2).

rib-tickler *noun*
Informal Words or actions intended to excite laughter or amusement ▸ jest, quip, witticism. *See* **joke** (1).

rich *adjective*
1. Possessing a large amount of money, land, or other material possessions ▸ affluent, flush, moneyed, wealthy. *Slang:* loaded. *Idioms:* having money to burn, in the money, made of money, rolling in money. *See also* **luxurious, prosperous. 2.** Characterized by extravagant, ostentatious magnificence ▸ lush, luxuriant, opulent. *See* **luxurious. 3.** Of great value or price ▸ expensive, precious, valuable. *See* **costly. 4.** Characterized by great productivity ▸ fecund, fruitful, productive, prolific. *See* **fertile** (1). **5.** Not readily digested because of richness ▸ filling, heavy. **6.** Full of color ▸ bright, vibrant, vivid. *See* **colorful** (1). **7.** Causing laughter or amusement ▸ comical, humorous, laughable. *See* **funny** (1).

✢ **CORE SYNONYMS:** *rich, affluent, flush, loaded, moneyed, wealthy.* These adjectives mean having an abundant supply of money, property, or possessions of value: *a rich executive; an affluent banker; a speculator flush with cash; not merely rich but loaded; moneyed heirs; wealthy corporations.*

◂ **ANTONYM:** *poor*

riches *noun*
▸ fortune, pelf, treasure. *See* **wealth** (1).

richness *noun*
▸ fecundity, fruitfulness, productiveness. *See* **fertility.**

ricketiness *noun*
▸ wiggling, wobbliness. *See* **unsteadiness** (1).

rickety *adjective*
▸ shaky, unsteady. *See* **insecure** (2).

ricochet *verb*
▸ graze, skim, skip. *See* **glance** (1). *See also* **bounce.**

rid *verb*
To relieve a burden ▸ clear, disburden, discharge, disembarrass, disencumber, dump, empty, release, relieve, shake off, throw off, unburden, unlade, unload. *Slang:* shake. *See also* **clear, eliminate.**

riddance *noun*
1. The act of getting rid of something useless or used up ▸ elimination, removal. *See* **disposal** (1). **2.** The act or process of eliminating ▸ eradication, purge. *See* **elimination** (1).

riddle *noun*
▸ enigma, puzzle, stickler. *See* **mystery.**

ride *verb*
1. *Informal* To tease or mock good-humoredly ▸ chaff, josh. *Informal:* kid. *See* **joke** (2). **2.** *Informal* To attack or disturb persistently ▸ harry, pester, torment. *See* **harass.**

ride out *verb*
To exist in spite of adversity ▸ persist, pull through. *See* **survive** (1).

ride *noun*
A trip in a motor vehicle ▸ jaunt, run. *See* **drive** (3).

ridicule *noun*
Words or actions intended to evoke contemptuous laughter ▸ derision, mockery. *See also* **sarcasm, taunt.**

ridicule *verb*
To subject to ridicule ▸ deride, gibe (at), jeer (at), jest (at), lampoon, laugh at, mock (at), pillory, scoff (at), scout (at), sneer at, taunt, twit. *Idioms:* make a laughingstock out of, make fun (*or* sport) of, poke fun at, thumb one's nose at. *See also* **belittle, denigrate, disgrace.**

✢ **CORE SYNONYMS:** *ridicule, mock, taunt, twit, deride.* These verbs refer to making another the object of conemptuous laughter. *Ridicule* implies purposeful disparagement: "*My father discouraged me by ridiculing my performances*" (Benjamin Franklin). To *mock* is to poke fun at someone, often by mimicking and caricaturing speech or actions: "*Seldom he smiles, and smiles in such a sort/As if he mock'd himself, and scorn'd his spirit*" (William Shakespeare). *Taunt* suggests mocking, insulting, or scornful reproach: "*taunting him with want of courage to leap into the great pit*" (Daniel Defoe). To *twit* is to taunt by calling attention to something embarrassing: "*The schoolmaster was twitted about the lady who threw him over*" (J.M. Barrie). *Deride* implies scorn and contempt: "*Was all the world in a conspiracy to deride his failure?*" (Edith Wharton).

ridiculous *adjective*
1. Causing or deserving laughter or derision ▸ farcical, laughable, ludicrous, risible. **2.** Exceeding the bounds of morality, decency, or reason ▸ appalling, monstrous, shocking. *See* **outrageous. 3.** Displaying a lack of good sense ▸ daft, fatuous, harebrained, idiotic, ludicrous, preposterous. *See* **foolish.** *See synonym note at* **foolish.**

ridiculousness *noun*
1. The quality of being laughable or comical ▸ funniness, jocosity. *See* **humor** (1). 2. Foolish behavior ▸ folly, silliness, tomfoolery. *See* **foolishness.**

rife *adjective*
▸ predominant, rampant. *See* **prevailing** (1).

riffle *verb*
1. To mix together so as to change the order of arrangement ▸ reconfigure, scramble. *See* **shuffle** (1). 2. To look through reading matter casually ▸ flip through, leaf (through). *See* **browse** (1).

riffraff *noun*
A person or group of persons regarded as worthless or contemptible ▸ dregs, good-for-nothing, lumpenproletariat, rabble, ragtag and bobtail, trash, vermin. *Slang:* scum. *Idioms:* scum of the earth, tag and rag, the great unwashed. *See also* **nonentity.**

rift *noun*
1. A partial opening caused by splitting and rupture ▸ break, cleft, fissure. *See* **crack** (2). 2. An interruption in friendly relations ▸ break, fissure. *See* **breach** (2).

rift *verb*
1. To crack or split into two or more fragments by means of force or strain ▸ shatter, smash, splinter. *See* **break** (1). 2. To undergo partial breaking ▸ rupture, split. *See* **crack** (1).

rig *verb*
1. To supply what is needed for some activity or purpose ▸ equip, gear, outfit. *See* **furnish** (1). 2. To prearrange the outcome of a contest ▸ fix, tamper. *Idiom:* stack the deck.

rig up *verb*
To make or provide from available materials ▸ juryrig, throw together. *See* **improvise** (2).

rig *noun*
1. Things needed for a task, journey, or other purpose ▸ equipment, gear. *See* **outfit** (1). 2. *Informal* A set or style of clothing ▸ garb, guise, outfit. *See* **dress** (2).

rigamarole *noun*
See **rigmarole.**

right *adjective*
1. In accordance with principles of right or good conduct ▸ principled, virtuous. *See* **ethical.** 2. Consistent with prevailing or accepted standards or circumstances ▸ deserved, fitting, proper. *See* **just** (2). 3. Conforming exactly to fact ▸ correct, exact, precise. *See* **accurate** (1). 4. Conforming to accepted standards ▸ becoming, befitting, comely, comme il faut, correct, decent, decorous, de rigueur, nice, proper, respectable, seemly. 5. Suitable for a particular person, condition, occasion, or place ▸ befitting, correct, proper. *See* **appropriate** (1). 6. Having good health ▸ fit, well. *See* **healthy** (1). 7. Favoring traditional views and values, especially as a political philosophy ▸ right-wing, traditionalist. *See* **conservative** (1).

right *noun*
A benefit granted to a person by law, nature, or custom ▸ birthright, civil liberty, droit, due, entitlement, franchise, freedom, perquisite, prerogative, privilege. *See also* **authority, claim, permission.**

right *adverb*
1. In a direct line ▸ straight, undeviatingly. *See* **directly** (1). 2. With precision or absolute conformity ▸ exactly, precisely, squarely. *See* **directly** (3). 3. It is so; as you say or ask ▸ agreed, all right, assuredly. *See* **yes.**

right *verb*
1. To restore to proper condition ▸ mend, overhaul, repair. *See* **fix** (1). 2. To make right what is wrong ▸ mend, rectify, remedy. *See* **correct** (1).

✦ CORE SYNONYMS: *right, privilege, prerogative, perquisite, birthright.* These nouns apply to a benefit granted to a person by law, nature, or custom. *Right* refers to a legally, morally, or traditionally just claim: *"I'm a champion for the Rights of Woman"* (Maria Edgeworth). *"An unconditional right to say what one pleases about public affairs is what I consider to be the minimum guarantee of the First Amendment"* (Hugo L. Black). *Privilege* usually suggests a right not enjoyed by everyone: *Use of the company jet was a privilege reserved for the top executives.* *Prerogative* denotes an exclusive right or privilege, as one based on custom, law, or office: *It is my prerogative to change my mind.* A *perquisite* is a privilege or advantage accorded to one by virtue of one's position or the needs of one's employment: *"The wardrobe of her niece was the perquisite of her [maid]"* (Tobias Smollett). A *birthright* is a right to which one is entitled by birth: *Many view gainful employment as a birthright.*

---

right away *adverb*
▸ forthwith, instantly, straightaway. *See* **immediately** (1).

righteous *adjective*
1. Marked by uprightness in principle and action ▸ honorable, upright. *See* **honest** (1). 2. In accordance with principles of right or good conduct ▸ principled, virtuous. *See* **ethical.** *See synonym note at* **ethical.**

righteousness *noun*
1. The quality or state of being morally sound ▸ probity, virtue. *See* **good** (1). 2. The quality of conforming to accepted standards of conduct ▸ ethicality, morality. *See* **ethics** (1). 3. The quality of being honest ▸ incorruptibility, integrity. *See* **honesty** (1).

rightful *adjective*
1. In accordance with principles of right or good conduct ▸ ethical, moral, principled, proper, right, righteous, right-minded, virtuous. 2. Consistent with prevailing or accepted standards or circumstances ▸ deserved, fitting, proper. *See* **just** (2). 3. Being so legitimately ▸ legitimate, true. 4. Within, allowed by, or sanctioned by the law ▸ legal, permitted, valid. *See* **lawful.**

rightfulness *noun*
1. The quality or state of being morally sound ▸ goodness, probity, virtue. *See* **good** (1). 2. The state or quality of being within the law ▸ legitimacy, licitness, validity. *See* **legality.**

rightist *noun*
One with politically conservative views ▸ orthodox, traditionalist. *See* **conservative.**
rightist *adjective*
Favoring traditional views and values, especially as a political philosophy ▸ orthodox, traditionalist. *See* **conservative** (1).
right-minded *adjective*
▸ principled, virtuous. *See* **ethical.**
rightness *noun*
1. The quality or state of being morally sound ▸ probity, virtue. *See* **good** (1). **2.** The quality of conforming to accepted standards of conduct ▸ ethicality, morality. *See* **ethics** (1). **3.** Freedom from error ▸ correctness, exactness, precision. *See* **accuracy** (1).
right off *adverb*
▸ instantly, straightaway. *See* **immediately** (1).
right of way *noun*
▸ precession, priority. *See* **precedence.**
right on *adverb*
Slang It is so; as you say or ask ▸ agreed, all right, assuredly. *See* **yes.**
right-wing *adjective*
▸ orthodox, traditionalist. *See* **conservative** (1).
right-winger *noun*
▸ rightist, traditionalist. *See* **conservative.**
rigid *adjective*
1. Not changing shape or bending ▸ inelastic, inflexible, stiff, unbending, unyielding. *See also* **firm**[1], **taut.** **2.** Incapable of changing or being modified ▸ inflexible, invariable, unalterable. *See* **immutable** (1). **3.** Rigorous and unsparing in treating others ▸ harsh, stern, strict. *See* **severe** (1). **4.** Firmly, often unreasonably immovable in purpose or will ▸ bullheaded, dogged, obstinate. *See* **stubborn** (1). **5.** Not moving ▸ stationary, still. *See* **motionless.**

✦ CORE SYNONYMS: *rigid, inflexible, stiff, inelastic.* These adjectives describe what is very firm and does not easily bend or give way. *Rigid* and *inflexible* apply to what cannot be bent without damage or deformation (*a table of rigid plastic; an inflexible knife blade*); figuratively they describe what does not relent or yield: *"under the dictates of a rigid disciplinarian"* (Thomas B. Aldrich). *Stiff* refers to what can be flexed only with difficulty (*a brush with stiff bristles*); with reference to persons it often suggests a lack of ease, cold formality, or fixity, as of purpose: *"stiff in opinions"* (John Dryden). *"In religion the law is written, and inflexible, never to do evil"* (Oliver Goldsmith). *Inelastic* refers largely to what will not stretch and spring back without marked physical change: *inelastic construction materials.*

◂ ANTONYM: *flexible*

---

rigidity *or* **rigidness** *noun*
1. The quality or state of being stubbornly inflexible ▸ bullheadedness, hardheadedness, renacity. *See* **stubbornness. 2.** The fact or condition of being rigorous and unsparing ▸ harshness, sternness, stringency. *See* **severity** (1).

rigmarole *or* **rigamarole** *noun*
1. Something that does not have or make sense ▸ bunkum, drivel, garbage. *See* **nonsense** (1). **2.** Needless trouble ▸ fuss, pother. *See* **bother** (1).
rigor *noun*
1. The fact or condition of being rigorous and unsparing ▸ harshness, rigidity, stringency. *See* **severity** (1). **2.** Something that obstructs progress and requires great effort to overcome ▸ complication, hardship, impediment. *See* **difficulty** (1). *See synonym note at* **difficulty.**
rigorous *adjective*
1. Requiring great or extreme bodily, mental, or spiritual strength ▸ arduous, grueling, laborious. *See* **burdensome** (1). *See synonym note at* **burdensome. 2.** Consistent with accuracy or completeness ▸ exact, strict. *See* **close** (2). **3.** Conforming exactly to fact ▸ correct, exact, precise. *See* **accurate** (1). **4.** Strict and unsparing in treating others ▸ harsh, stern, tough. *See* **severe** (1). **5.** Painfully intense ▸ brutal, harsh, severe. *See* **bitter** (2).
rigorousness *noun*
▸ harshness, rigidity, stringency. *See* **severity** (1).
rile *verb*
1. To trouble the nerves or peace of mind of ▸ irritate, nettle, vex. *See* **annoy** (1). *See synonym note at* **annoy. 2.** To cause to feel or show anger ▸ incense, infuriate, madden. *See* **anger** (1).
rim *noun*
A line or area where something ends or abruptly changes ▸ brink, fringe, margin. *See* **border** (1). *See synonym note at* **border.**
rim *verb*
To put or form a border on ▸ edge, margin. *See* **border** (1).
rimple *noun*
A line made by the doubling of one part over another ▸ crimp, pleat, wrinkle. *See* **fold** (1).
rimple *verb*
1. To bend together or form a crease ▸ crimp, double, pleat. *See* **fold** (1). **2.** To make irregular folds in, especially by pressing or twisting ▸ crimp, crinkle, rumple. *See* **wrinkle** (1).
rind *noun*
▸ peel, zest. *See* **skin** (3).
ring[1] *noun*
1. A round closed plane shape or figure ▸ band, hoop, wheel. *See* **circle** (1). **2.** A length of line folded over and joined at the ends so as to form a curve or circle ▸ circuit, noose, ringlet. *See* **loop** (1). **3.** An association for a common cause or interest ▸ bloc, coalition, party. *See* **alliance** (1). **4.** An organized group of criminals, hoodlums, or wrongdoers ▸ band, gang, pack. *Informal:* mob.
ring *verb*
1. To form a circle around ▸ compass, girt, loop, orbit. *See* **encircle** (1). **2.** To shut in on all sides ▸ beset, encircle, hedge. *See* **surround** (1). *See synonym note at* **surround.**

ring in *verb*
To begin something with preliminary or prefatory material ▸ lead, preface. *See* **introduce** (3).

ring² *verb*
1. To give forth or cause to give forth a clear resonant sound ▸ bell, bong, chime, ding, knell, peal, sound, strike, toll. **2.** To communicate with someone by telephone ▸ call (up), dial, phone, ring up. *See* **telephone.**

ring *noun*
A telephone communication ▸ buzz, call.

ringer *noun*
1. *Slang* One exactly resembling another ▸ clone, spitting image, twin. *See* **double** (1). **2.** *Informal* One that takes the place of another ▸ alternate, replacement, surrogate. *See* **substitute.**

ringing *adjective*
1. Having or producing a full, deep, or rich sound ▸ resounding, sonorous, vibrant. *See* **resonant.** **2.** Clearly, fully, and emphatically expressed ▸ decided, explicit, precise. *See* **definite** (1).

ringleader *noun*
▸ boss, director, head, leader. *See* **chief** (1).

ringlet *noun*
▸ circuit, eyelet, ring. *See* **loop** (1).

rinky-dink *adjective*
Slang Of little importance or seriousness ▸ inconsequential, negligible, trifling. *See* **trivial.**

rinse *verb*
▸ cleanse, launder, lave. *See* **clean** (1).

riot *noun*
1. A lack of civil order or peace ▸ anarchy, lawlessness, misrule. *See* **disorder** (2). **2.** A physical conflict between two or more people ▸ free-for-all, melee. *See* **fight** (1). **3.** A period of uncontrolled self-indulgence ▸ rampage, spree. *See* **binge** (1). **4.** *Slang* Something or someone uproariously funny ▸ *Informal:* hoot, laugh. *See* **scream** (3).

riot *verb*
To behave riotously ▸ carouse, frolic, roister. *See* **revel** (1).

riot away *verb*
To use, consume, spend, or expend thoughtlessly or carelessly ▸ fritter away, squander, trifle away. *See* **waste** (1).

riotous *adjective*
1. Upsetting civil order or peace ▸ disruptive, unruly. *See* **disorderly** (1). **2.** Given to or marked by unrestrained abundance ▸ exuberant, lavish, opulent. *See* **profuse** (1). *See synonym note at* **profuse.**

rip *verb*
1. To separate or pull apart by force ▸ rend, rive, split. *See* **tear¹** (1). *See synonym note at* **tear. 2.** *Informal* To move swiftly ▸ dash, sprint, zip. *See* **rush** (1).

rip into *verb*
To criticize harshly and devastatingly ▸ bash, excoriate, flay. *See* **slam** (5).

rip off *verb*
1. *Slang* To take another's property without permis-

sion ▸ purloin, snatch, thieve. *See* **steal** (1). **2.** *Slang* To get something by deceitful trickery ▸ bilk, defraud, swindle. *See* **cheat** (1).

rip up *verb*
To pull or cut into many pieces ▸ grate, slice up. *See* **shred.**

rip *noun*
A hole made by tearing ▸ rent, run, tear. *See also* **crack.**

rip² *noun*
An immoral or licentious person ▸ debaucher, profligate. *See* **wanton** (1).

ripe *adjective*
1. Having reached full growth and development ▸ developed, grown. *See* **mature** (1). **2.** Brought to full flavor and richness by aging ▸ aged, mellow. *See also* **mature.**

ripen *verb*
▸ age, develop, mellow. *See* **mature.** *See synonym note at* **mature.**

rip-off *noun*
Slang The crime of taking someone else's property without consent ▸ stealing, theft, thievery. *See* **larceny.**

riposte *noun*
Something spoken or written in return ▸ comeback, repartee, retort. *See* **answer** (1).

riposte *verb*
To speak or act in response ▸ rejoin, reply, respond. *See* **answer** (1).

ripped *adjective*
Slang Stupefied, intoxicated, or otherwise influenced by the taking of drugs ▸ high, hopped-up, lit (up). *See* **drugged.**

ripping *adjective*
▸ fantastic, sensational, superb. *See* **marvelous** (1).

ripple *verb*
1. To have or cause to have a curved or wavy surface ▸ curl, undulate. *See* **wave** (1). **2.** To flow with or make a soft liquid sound ▸ babble, gurgle, murmur. *See* **burble** (1). **3.** To move freely as a liquid ▸ purl, run, stream. *See* **flow** (1).

ripple *noun*
1. A ridge or swell of water, or a shape suggestive of such a swell ▸ breaker, undulation. *See* **wave** (1). **2.** A soft liquid sound ▸ gurgle, lap, murmur. *See* **burble.**

rippled *adjective*
▸ curvy, sinusoidal. *See* **wavy.**

rise *verb*
1. To adopt a standing posture ▸ arise, get up. *Idiom:* get to one's feet. *See* **stand** (1). **2.** To leave one's bed ▸ arise, get up, roll out. *Informal:* turn out. *Slang:* hit the deck. *Idioms:* jump (*or* leap *or* pile *or* spring) out of bed, rise and shine. *See also* **wake¹ 3.** To move from a lower to a higher position ▸ arise, ascend, climb, lift, mount, soar, tower. *See also* **ascend, soar. 4.** To make or become greater or larger ▸ amplify, boost, enlarge. *See* **increase** (1). **5.** To have as a source ▸ derive, emanate, originate. *See* **stem** (1). *See synonym note at*

stem. **6.** To attain a higher status, rank, or condition ► advance, ascend, climb, get ahead, mount, progress. *Idiom:* go up the ladder. *See also* **advance. 7.** To gain success ► arrive, get ahead, get on, succeed. *Idioms:* go far, go places, make good, make it. **8.** To refuse allegiance to and oppose by force a government or ruling authority ► mutiny, rebel, revolt, rise up. *See also* **defect, defy. 9.** To be in a state of motion, as air or wind ► bluster, gust. *See* **blow**[1] (1).

rise *noun*
1. The act of rising or moving upward ► lift, mounting. *See* **ascent** (1). **2.** An upward path or surface ► acclivity, rise, slant. *See* **ascent** (2). **3.** A natural land elevation ► knoll, prominence. *See* **hill** (1). **4.** The act of increasing or rising ► amplification, boost, escalation. *See* **increase** (1). **5.** The amount by which something is increased ► boost, jump. *See* **increase** (2). **6.** A progression upward in rank ► promotion, upgrade. *See* **advancement** (1). **7.** A point of origination ► provenance, root, source. *See* **origin** (1).

✦ CORE SYNONYMS: *rise, ascend, climb, soar, tower, mount.* These verbs mean to move upward from a lower to a higher position. *Rise* has the widest range of application: *We rose at dawn. The sun rises early in the summer. Prices rise and fall. Ascend* frequently suggests a gradual step-by-step rise: *The plane took off and ascended steadily until it was out of sight. Climb* connotes steady, often effortful progress, as against gravity: *"You climb up through the little grades and then get to the top"* (John Updike). *Soar* implies effortless ascent to a great height: *A lone condor soared above the Andean peaks.* To *tower* is to attain a height or prominence exceeding one's surroundings: *"the tall Lombardy poplar . . . towering high above all other trees"* (W.H. Hudson). *Mount* connotes a progressive climb to a higher level: *Our expenses mounted fearfully.*

◄ ANTONYM: *descend*

---

risible *adjective*
1. Causing laughter or amusement ► comical, humorous, laughable. *See* **funny** (1). **2.** Causing or deserving laughter or derision ► farcical, laughable, ludicrous, ridiculous. *See also* **foolish.**

rising *noun*
► ascension, mounting. *See* **ascent** (1).

rising star *noun*
► candidate, hopeful, prospect. *See* **comer** (2).

risk *noun*
1. A possibility of danger or harm ► chance, gamble, hazard. *Informal:* shaky ground, thin ice. **2.** Exposure to harm, loss, or injury ► hazard, jeopardy, peril. *See* **danger. 3.** An undertaking depending on chance ► speculation, wager. *See* **gamble** (1).

risk *verb*
1. To expose to possible loss or damage ► imperil, jeopardize, threaten. *See* **endanger.** *See synonym note at* **endanger. 2.** To place something at risk, as in a game of chance ► bet, stake, wager. *See* **gamble** (2). **3.** To express at the risk of rebuff or criticism

► dare, hazard, presume. *See* **venture** (1).

risk capital *noun*
► financing, funding, stake. *See* **capital** (1).

risky *adjective*
► chancy, hazardous, perilous. *See* **dangerous.**

risqué *adjective*
1. Bordering on indelicacy or impropriety ► provocative, scabrous, suggestive. *See* **racy** (1). **2.** Not in keeping with conventional mores ► immodest, indelicate. *See* **improper** (1). *See synonym note at* **improper.**

rite *noun*
► ceremonial, ritual, tradition. *See* **ceremony** (1).

ritual *noun*
1. A formal act or set of acts prescribed by ritual ► rite, service, tradition. *See* **ceremony** (1). **2.** A conventional social gesture or act without intrinsic purpose ► ceremony, form, formality, mummery, nicety. *See also* **custom, manners.**

ritual *adjective*
Of or characterized by ceremony ► ceremonial, ceremonious, formal, liturgical, ritualistic. *See also* **ceremonious, spiritual.**

ritualistic *adjective*
► ceremonial, formal, liturgical. *See* **ritual.**

ritzy *adjective*
1. *Informal* Catering to only the wealthy or socially superior ► chic, posh, swank. *See* **exclusive** (4). **2.** Characterized by extravagant, ostentatious magnificence ► luxuriant, opulent. *See* **luxurious.**

rival *noun*
1. One that competes ► competition, contender, opponent. *See* **competitor. 2.** One that is very similar to another in rank or position ► colleague, equivalent, fellow. *See* **peer**[2].

rival *verb*
1. To attempt to equal or surpass, as in quality or amount ► approach, approximate, border on (*or* upon), challenge, verge on. **2.** To strive against others for victory ► contend, race, vie. *See* **compete.**

rivalrous *adjective*
► cutthroat, dog-eat-dog, emulous. *See* **competitive.**

rivalry *noun*
► battle, contest, struggle. *See* **competition** (1).

rive *verb*
1. To separate or pull apart by force ► rend, rip, split. *See* **tear**[1] (1). **2.** To crack or split into two or more fragments by means of force or strain ► shatter, smash, splinter. *See* **break** (1).

river *noun*
A relatively large natural flow of water ► estuary, stream, tributary, watercourse, waterway. *See also* **brook**[1].

rivet *noun*
A shaft hammered or drilled in place, used to hold together ► pin, spike, stud. *See* **nail.**

rivet *verb*
1. To make secure ► anchor, fix, secure. *See* **fasten** (1). **2.** To compel the attention, interest, or imagination of ► captivate, fascinate, mesmerize. *See* **grip** (1).

riveted *adjective*
▶ absorbed, engrossed, intent. *See* **rapt.**

road *noun*
▶ channel, path, route. *See* **way** (2).

roam *verb*
▶ drift, meander, wander. *See* **rove.** *See synonym note at* **rove.**

roamer *noun*
▶ nomad, tramp, vagabond. *See* **hobo.**

roaming *adjective*
▶ itinerant, roving. *See* **errant** (1).

roar *verb*
1. To speak or say in a loud cry ▶ call, holler, yell. *See* **shout.** *See synonym note at* **shout.** 2. To express amusement or mirth ▶ chuckle, guffaw. *See* **laugh.** 3. To make an explosive noise ▶ bang, thunder. *See* **blast** (1). 4. To undergo combustion; be on fire ▶ crackle, hiss. *See* **burn** (2).

roar *noun*
1. A loud, deep, prolonged sound ▶ bawl, bellow, bluster, clamor, roll, rumble. 2. An explosive noise ▶ boom, crash. *See* **blast** (1). 3. A loud cry ▶ call, holler, yell. *See* **shout.** 4. An act of laughing ▶ cackle, guffaw, laughter. *See* **laugh** (1).

roaring *adjective*
1. Marked by extremely high volume and intensity of sound ▶ booming, earsplitting, noisy. *See* **loud** (1). 2. Improving, growing, or succeeding steadily ▶ prosperous, successful, thriving. *See* **flourishing.**

roast *verb*
1. To cook with dry heat ▶ barbecue, broil. *See* **cook** (1). 2. To feel or look hot ▶ broil, swelter. *See* **burn** (3). 3. *Informal* To criticize harshly and devastatingly ▶ bash, excoriate, flay. *See* **slam** (5).

roasting *adjective*
▶ blistering, boiling, burning. *See* **hot** (1).

rob *verb*
1. To take property or possessions from someone unlawfully and usually forcibly ▶ burglarize, hold up, mug, stick up. *Slang:* heist, knock off. *See also* **sack, steal.** 2. To take or keep something away from ▶ deny, withhold. *See* **deprive.**

robber *noun*
▶ burglar, looter, stealer. *See* **thief.**

robbery *noun*
▶ stealing, theft, thievery. *See* **larceny.**

robe *noun*
Clothing worn by members of a religious order ▶ habit, vestment.

robe *verb*
To cover as if with clothes ▶ coat, drape. *See* **clothe** (1). *See synonym note at* **clothe.**

roborant *adjective*
Producing or stimulating physical, mental, or emotional vigor ▶ energizing, exhilarating, stimulating. *See* **invigorating.**

roborant *noun*
A medicine that restores or increases vigor ▶ energizer, stimulant. *See* **tonic.**

robust *adjective*
1. Full of vigor ▶ red-blooded, strapping, sturdy. *See* **lusty** (1). 2. Characterized by marked muscular development ▶ brawny, rugged, sturdy. *See* **muscular.** 3. Having good health ▶ fit, well. *See* **healthy** (1). *See synonym note at* **healthy.**

rock *verb*
1. To move vigorously from side to side or up and down ▶ heave, pitch, roll, toss. *See also* **lurch.** 2. To move back and forth ▶ swing, vacillate, waggle. *See* **sway** (1). *See synonym note at* **sway.** 3. To cause to move to and fro violently ▶ churn, convulse, shake. *See* **agitate** (1). *See synonym note at* **agitate.** 4. To impair or destroy the composure of ▶ disorient, fluster, ruffle. *See* **agitate** (2).

rock bottom *noun*
A very low or lowest level, position, or degree ▶ bottom, low, minimum, nadir.

rocket *verb*
1. To move swiftly ▶ dash, sprint, zip. *See* **rush** (1). 2. To rise abruptly and precipitously ▶ sky, skyrocket. *See* **soar** (1).

rococo *adjective*
▶ flamboyant, resplendent. *See* **ornate** (1).

rod *noun*
A straight, rigid piece of metal or other solid material ▶ bar, bloom, shaft, stem. *See also* **stick.**

rogations *noun*
▶ litany, orison. *See* **prayer**[1] (2).

roger *adverb*
▶ agreed, all right, assuredly. *See* **yes.**

rogue *noun*
▶ devil, prankster, scamp. *See* **rascal.**

roguery *noun*
▶ diablerie, high jinks, tomfoolery. *See* **mischief** (1).

roguish *adjective*
▶ frolicsome, impish, sportive. *See* **mischievous** (1).

roguishness *noun*
▶ diablerie, high jinks, tomfoolery. *See* **mischief** (1).

roiled *or* **roily** *adjective*
1. Darkened or clouded with sediment ▶ cloudy, muddy, turbid. *See* **murky** (1). 2. Violently disturbed or agitated, as by storms ▶ stormy, turbulent, violent. *See* **rough** (2).

roister *verb*
▶ carouse, frolic, riot. *See* **revel** (1).

role *noun*
1. One's duty or responsibility in a common effort ▶ function, part, piece, share. 2. The proper activity of a person or thing ▶ job, purpose, task. *See* **function** (1). 3. A person portrayed in fiction or drama ▶ character, part, persona, personage.

role model *noun*
▶ exemplar, ideal, paradigm. *See* **model.**

roll *verb*
1. To cover completely and closely, as with clothing or bandages ▶ bundle, envelop, swathe. *See* **wrap** (1). 2. To move vigorously from side to side or up and down ▶ heave, pitch, rock, toss. *See also* **lurch.** 3. To send

through the air with a motion of the hand or arm ▸ heave, hurl, pitch. *See* **throw** (1). **4.** To lean suddenly, unsteadily, and erratically from the vertical axis ▸ pitch, seesaw, yaw. *See* **lurch** (1). **5.** To make a continuous deep reverberating sound ▸ growl, grumble. *See* **rumble** (1). **6.** To take extravagant pleasure ▸ indulge, revel, wallow. *See* **luxuriate.** **7.** To smooth by applying heat and pressure ▸ calender, iron. *See* **press** (2). **8.** To be abundantly filled or richly supplied ▸ bristle, crawl, swarm. *See* **teem**[1].

roll about *or* **around** *verb*
To move about in an indolent or clumsy manner ▸ flounder, roll around, wallow, welter.

roll out *verb*
1. To leave one's bed ▸ arise, get up. *See* **rise** (2). **2.** To make even, smooth, or level ▸ level, smooth, straighten. *See* **even** (1).

roll up *verb*
To bring together so as to increase in mass or number ▸ accrue, amass, cumulate, pile up. *See* **accumulate.**

roll *noun*
1. A series, as of names or words, printed or written down ▸ register, roster, schedule. *See* **list**[1]. **2.** A loud, deep, prolonged sound ▸ bawl, bellow, rumble. *See* **roar** (1). **3.** An act of throwing ▸ fling, hurl, toss. *See* **throw.**

rollick *verb*
1. To leap and skip about playfully ▸ cavort, frolic, romp. *See* **gambol.** **2.** To take extravagant pleasure ▸ indulge, revel, wallow. *See* **luxuriate.**

roly-poly *adjective*
▸ chubby, pudgy, stout. *See* **fat** (1).

romance *noun*
1. An intimate sexual relationship between two people ▸ amour, love affair, passion. *See* **love** (3). **2.** The passionate affection and desire felt by lovers for each other ▸ ardor, devotion, passion. *See* **love** (2). **3.** An intense attachment to a person or thing ▸ adoration, fondness, love affair. *See* **love** (1). **4.** A narrative not based on fact ▸ fable, fiction, novel, story. *See also* **yarn.**

romance *verb*
Informal To attempt to gain the affection of ▸ chase, woo. *See* **court** (2).

romantic *adjective*
1. Affectedly or extravagantly emotional ▸ gushy, mawkish, soft. *See* **sentimental.** *See synonym note at* **sentimental.** **2.** Characterized by ideals that often conflict with practical considerations ▸ quixotic, unrealistic, utopian. *See* **idealistic.**

romantic *noun*
A person inclined to be imaginative or idealistic but impractical ▸ fantasist, idealist, stargazer. *See* **dreamer** (1).

Romeo *noun*
▸ Casanova, lady's man. *See* **gallant.**

romp *verb*
1. To leap and skip about playfully ▸ cavort, frolic, rollick. *See* **gambol.** **2.** To behave riotously ▸ carouse,

frolic, roister. *See* **revel** (1). **3.** *Informal* To progress quickly and effortlessly ▸ coast, sail. *See* **breeze.**

romp *noun*
Slang An easy victory ▸ walkaway, walkover. *See* **runaway** (1).

roof *noun*
▸ apex, height, peak. *See* **climax** (1).

rook *noun*
A person who cheats ▸ cheater, swindler, trickster. *See* **cheat** (2).

rook *verb*
To get something by deceitful trickery ▸ bilk, defraud, swindle. *See* **cheat** (1).

rookie *noun*
Slang A person who is just starting to learn or do something ▸ fledgling, neophyte, novice. *See* **beginner.**

room *noun*
Freedom from normal restraints, limitations, or regulations ▸ entitlement, latitude, leeway. *See* **license** (1). *See synonym note at* **license.**

room *verb*
To stay in or provide with lodging, especially temporarily ▸ accommodate, bed (down), house. *See* **lodge** (1).

roomy *adjective*
Having plenty of room ▸ ample, capacious, commodious, spacious. *See also* **big, broad.**

✛ CORE SYNONYMS: *roomy, ample, capacious, commodious, spacious.* These adjectives mean having plenty of room: *roomy pockets; an ample kitchen; a capacious purse; a commodious harbor; a spacious apartment.*

---

roost *verb*
▸ perch, poise. *See* **balance** (3).

root[1] *noun*
1. The most central or essential part ▸ essence, marrow, quintessence. *See* **heart** (1). **2.** An underlying support, as for an argument or belief ▸ cornerstone, foundation, underpinning. *See* **basis** (1). **3.** A point of origination ▸ mother, provenance, source. *See* **origin** (1). *See synonym note at* **origin.** **4.** A point of origin or crucial factor ▸ core, focus, nucleus. *See* **center** (3). **5.** The main part of a word to which affixes are attached ▸ base, stem. *See* **theme** (1).

root *verb*
1. To place or set deeply or securely ▸ entrench, ingrain, plant. *See* **fix** (4). **2.** To provide a basis for ▸ establish, ground. *See* **base**[1] (1). **3.** To destroy all traces of ▸ eradicate, liquidate, obliterate. *See* **annihilate** (1). **4.** To put seeds or young plants in soil ▸ broadcast, seed, sow. *See* **plant** (1).

root[2] *verb*
To express approval audibly, as by clapping ▸ applaud, cheer, clap. *Idioms:* give a big hand (*or* welcome), give an ovation, give someone a hand, put one's hands together. *See synonym note at* **applaud.**

rooted *adjective*
1. Firmly in position ▸ anchored, immovable, station-

ary. *See* **fixed** (1). **2.** Firmly established by long standing ► deep-seated, entrenched, ingrained. *See* **confirmed** (1).

roots *noun*
► blood, extraction, lineage. *See* **ancestry.**

rootstock *noun*
► provenance, root, source. *See* **origin** (1).

rope *noun*
► cable, line, string. *See* **cord.**

roseate *or* **rose-colored** *adjective*
► cheerful, sanguine. *See* **optimistic.**

roster *noun*
► register, roll, schedule. *See* **list**[1].

rostrum *noun*
► dais, podium, proscenium. *See* **stage** (1).

rosy *adjective*
1. Of a healthy reddish color ► blooming, flushed, glowing. *See* **ruddy. 2.** Expecting or suggesting a favorable outcome ► cheerful, sanguine. *See* **optimistic.**

rot *verb*
To become or cause to become rotten or unsound ► deteriorate, spoil, turn. *See* **decay.** *See synonym note at* **decay.**

rot *noun*
1. The condition of being decayed ► decomposition, deterioration, putrefaction. *See* **decay. 2.** Something that does not have or make sense ► bunkum, claptrap, garbage. *See* **nonsense** (1).

rotate *verb*
1. To rotate on an axis or around a center ► twirl, whirl, wheel. *See* **turn** (1). *See synonym note at* **turn. 2.** To take turns ► alternate, interchange, shift.

rotation *noun*
1. A circular movement around a point or about an axis ► circulation, gyration. *See* **revolution** (1). **2.** Occurrence in successive turns ► alternation, interchange, shift.

rote *noun*
► rut, rounds, track. *See* **routine** (1).

rotten *adjective*
1. Marred by decay ► foul, putrid. *See* **bad** (2). **2.** Smelling of mildew or decay ► musty, rancid. *See* **moldy. 3.** Utterly reprehensible in nature or behavior ► depraved, miscreant, perverse. *See* **corrupt** (1). **4.** So objectionable as to deserve condemnation ► contemptible, disgusting, obnoxious. *See* **offensive** (1). **5.** Of decidedly inferior quality ► cheap, lousy, poor. *See* **shoddy** (1). **6.** *Informal* Lacking worth and value ► drossy, good-for-nothing, valueless. *See* **worthless** (1). **7.** Very bad ► appalling, awful, dreadful. *See* **terrible** (1).

rottenness *noun*
► decomposition, deterioration, rot. *See* **decay.**

rotund *adjective*
1. Having too much flesh ► chubby, obese, stout. *See* **fat** (1). *See synonym note at* **fat. 2.** Having or producing a full, deep, or rich sound ► resounding, sonorous, vibrant. *See* **resonant.**

roué *noun*
► gigolo, satyr. *Slang:* lech. *See* **lecher.**

rough *adjective*
1. Having a surface that is not smooth ► abrasive, bumpy, coarse, cragged, craggy, harsh, ironbound, jagged, ragged, rugged, scabrous, scraggy, scratchy, uneven. **2.** Violently disturbed or agitated, as by storms ► blustery, dirty, heavy, raging, roiled, roily, rugged, stormy, tempestuous, tumultuous, turbulent, ugly, violent, wild. *See also* **intense. 3.** Consisting of or covered with large particles ► granular, gritty. *See* **coarse** (4). **4.** Requiring great or extreme bodily, mental, or spiritual strength ► backbreaking, difficult, trying. *See* **burdensome** (1). **5.** Painfully intense ► brutal, harsh, severe. *See* **bitter** (2). **6.** Lacking in delicacy or refinement ► indelicate, unbecoming, unrefined. *See* **coarse** (1). **7.** Marked by vigorous physical exertion ► arduous, knockabout, rough-and-tumble, rugged, strenuous, tough. *See also* **burdensome, difficult. 8.** Disagreeable to the senses, especially the sense of hearing ► grating, jarring. *See* **harsh** (1). **9.** Not cultivated ► native, natural, uncultivated. *See* **wild** (1). **10.** Not perfected, elaborated, or completed ► crude, imperfect, incomplete, preliminary, sketchy, tentative, unfinished, unperfected, unpolished. **11.** Lacking expert, careful craftsmanship ► crude, primitive, unpolished. *See* **rude** (1). *See synonym note at* **rude. 12.** Being in a natural state ► raw, unrefined. *See* **crude** (1). **13.** Lacking literal exactness ► broad, free, inexact. *See* **loose** (3).

rough in *or* **out** *verb*
To draw up a preliminary plan or version of ► outline, sketch. *See* **draft** (1).

rough up *verb*
1. To injure or damage, as by abuse or heavy wear ► mangle, maul. *See* **batter** (1). **2.** To be rough or brutal with ► knock about (*or* around), slap around. *See* **manhandle** (1).

rough *noun*
A preliminary plan or version, as of a written work ► blueprint, sketch. *See* **draft** (1).

✛ CORE SYNONYMS: *rough, harsh, jagged, rugged, scabrous, uneven.* These adjectives mean having a surface that is not smooth. *Rough* describes something that to the sight or touch has inequalities, as projections or ridges: *rough bark; rough, chapped hands.* Something *harsh* is unpleasantly rough, discordant, or grating: *harsh, scratchy burlap. Jagged* refers to an edge or surface with irregular projections and indentations: *a jagged piece of glass. Rugged* can apply to land surfaces characterized by irregular, often steep rises and slopes: *rugged countryside. Scabrous* means rough and scaly to the touch: *granular, scabrous skin. Uneven* describes lines or surfaces of which some parts are not level with others: *uneven ground; uneven handwriting.*

---

rough-and-tumble *adjective*
► arduous, knockabout, strenuous, tough. *See* **rough** (7).

roughly *adverb*
- almost, nearly, some. *See* **approximately**.

roughneck *noun*
- hoodlum, ruffian, tough. *See* **thug**.

roughness *noun*
- coarseness, raggedness, unevenness. *See* **irregularity** (1).

round *adjective*
1. Having the shape of a curve everywhere equidistant from a fixed point ▸ annular, circular, globoid, globular, orbicular, spheric, spherical. 2. Having too much flesh ▸ chubby, pudgy, stout. *See* **fat** (1). 3. Having or producing a full, deep, or rich sound ▸ resounding, sonorous, vibrant. *See* **resonant**. 4. Including every constituent or individual ▸ entire, total, whole. *See* **complete** (1). 5. No less than; at least ▸ full, good, whole.

round *noun*
1. Something bent ▸ curvature, curve, turn. *See* **bend**. 2. A stage of a competition ▸ heat, stage. *See also* **competition, turn**. 3. A course or process that ends where it began or repeats itself ▸ cycle, orbit. *See* **circle** (2). 4. A number of things placed or occurring one after the other ▸ order, procession, sequence. *See* **series**. 5. An area regularly covered, as by a policeman or reporter ▸ circuit, route. *See* **beat** (2). 6. A round closed plane shape or figure ▸ band, ring, wheel. *See* **circle** (1).

round *verb*
1. To deviate from a straight line in a smooth, continuous manner ▸ arch, curve, turn. *See* **bend** (1). *See synonym note at* **bend**. 2. To make or become less sharp-edged ▸ hebetate, turn. *See* **dull** (1).

round off *verb*
To bring to perfection or completion ▸ complete, refine, round out. *See* **perfect**.

round up *verb*
To bring together ▸ cluster, gather, muster. *See* **assemble** (1).

roundabout *adjective*
- circuitous, devious, oblique. *See* **indirect** (1).

rounded *adjective*
- arched, bowed, curved. *See* **bent** (1).

rounder *noun*
- debaucher, libertine, profligate. *See* **wanton** (1).

roundlet *noun*
- band, ring, wheel. *See* **circle** (1).

rounds *noun*
- rote, rut, track. *See* **routine** (1).

roundtable *noun*
- discussion, parley, seminar. *See* **conference** (1).

round-the-clock *adjective*
- constant, endless, perpetual. *See* **continual**.

rouse *verb*
1. To cease or cause to cease sleeping ▸ awake, stir, waken. *See* **wake**[1]. 2. To induce or elicit a reaction ▸ kindle, stir (up). *See* **arouse** (1). *See synonym note at* **arouse**. 3. To arouse the emotions of ▸ impassion, inspire, stir. *See* **fire** (2). 4. To bring out something latent, hidden, or unexpressed ▸ draw (out), elicit, summon. *See* **evoke**.

rousing *adjective*
- bracing, energizing, enlivening. *See* **invigorating**.

roustabout *noun*
- menial, toiler, worker. *See* **laborer**.

rout *noun*
1. The act of defeating or the condition of being defeated ▸ overthrow, trouncing, vanquishment. *See* **defeat**. 2. An easy victory ▸ walkaway, walkover. *See* **runaway** (1). 3. An enormous number of persons or things gathered together ▸ horde, mass, throng. *See* **crowd** (1). 4. A number of animals considered collectively ▸ bevy, gaggle, herd. *See* **flock** (1). *See synonym note at* **flock**.

rout *verb*
To render totally ineffective by decisive defeat ▸ crush, overcome, overpower. *See* **overwhelm** (1).

route *noun*
1. A course affording passage from one place to another ▸ path, road, thoroughfare. *See* **way** (1). 2. An area regularly covered, as by a policeman or reporter ▸ round, territory. *See* **beat** (2). 3. A means or method of entering into or achieving something desirable ▸ formula, key, secret. *Informal:* ticket. *See also* **ticket**. 4. The spatial path along which motion or orientation is referred ▸ course, heading. *See* **direction** (1).

route *verb*
1. To cause something to be conveyed to a destination ▸ consign, dispatch. *See* **send** (1). *See synonym note at* **send**. 2. To show the way to ▸ direct, escort, lead. *See* **guide** (1).

routine *noun*
1. A course of action to be followed regularly ▸ method, rote, rounds, rut, track, treadmill. *Informal:* grind. *Slang:* groove. 2. A regular or customary matter, condition, or course of events ▸ norm, ordinary, rule. *See* **usual**. 3. *Slang* A characteristic behavior or performance ▸ act. *See* **bit**[1] (5). 4. A habitual way of behaving ▸ form, habit, practice. *See* **custom** (1). 5. Repetition of an action so as to develop or maintain one's skill ▸ exercise, rehearsal. *See* **practice** (1).

routine *adjective*
1. Subject to a habit or pattern of behavior ▸ accustomed, chronic, habitual. 2. Done routinely and impersonally ▸ automatic, mechanical. *See* **perfunctory**. 3. Occurring or encountered regularly ▸ commonplace, frequent, regular. *See* **common** (1). 4. Being of no special quality or type ▸ common, mediocre, standard. *See* **ordinary** (1).

routinely *adverb*
- customarily, generally, normally. *See* **usually**.

routineness *noun*
- normality, ordinariness, regularity. *See* **usualness**.

routinism *noun*
- blandness, drabness, lifelessness. *See* **dullness** (1).

rove *verb*
To move about at random, especially over a wide area

► drift, gad, gallivant, meander, peregrinate, ramble, range, roam, stray, traipse, tramp, wander. *See also* **hike, journey, walk.**

✦ CORE SYNONYMS: *rove, roam, wander, ramble, range, meander, stray, gallivant, gad.* These verbs mean to move about at random or without destination or purpose, especially over a wide area. *Rove* and *roam* emphasize freedom of movement, often over a wide area: *"For ten long years I roved about, living first in one capital, then another"* (Charlotte Brontë). *"Herds of horses and cattle roamed at will over the plain"* (George W. Cable). *Wander* and *ramble* stress the absence of a fixed course or goal: *wandered down the hall lost in thought.* *"They would go off together, rambling along the river"* (John Galsworthy). *Range* suggests wandering in all directions: *"a large hunting party known to be ranging the prairie"* (Francis Parkman). *Meander* suggests leisurely wandering over an irregular or winding course: *"He meandered to and fro . . . observing the manners and customs of Hillport society"* (Arnold Bennett). *Stray* refers to deviation from a proper course: *"I ask pardon, I am straying from the question"* (Oliver Goldsmith). *Gallivant* refers to wandering in search of pleasure: *gallivanted all over the city during our visit.* *Gad* suggests restlessness: *gadded about unaccompanied in foreign places.*

---

rover *noun*
► nomad, roamer, vagabond. *See* **hobo.**

roving *adjective*
► itinerant, wandering. *See* **errant** (1).

row¹ *noun*
A group of people or things arranged in a row ► file, queue, string. *See* **line** (1).

row² *noun*
1. A discussion, often heated, in which a difference of opinion is expressed ► contention, quarrel. *Informal:* rhubarb. *See* **argument** (1). **2.** A physical conflict between two or more people ► free-for-all, melee. *See* **fight** (1). *See synonym note at* **fight. 3.** Sounds or a sound, especially when loud, confused, or disagreeable ► clamor, din. *See* **noise** (1).

row *verb*
To engage in a quarrel ► dispute, fight, quarrel. *See* **argue** (1).

rowdy *noun*
A person who treats others violently or roughly ► hoodlum, ruffian, tough. *See* **thug.**

rowdy *adjective*
Upsetting civil order or peace ► disruptive, unruly. *See* **disorderly** (1).

royal *adjective*
1. Impressive in size, proportion, or appearance ► imposing, magnificent, splendid. *See* **grand** (1). **2.** Of high birth or social position ► blue-blooded, elite, upper-class. *See* **noble** (1).

royalty *noun*
► blue blood, noblesse. *See* **nobility** (1).

rub *verb*
1. To make the skin raw by friction ► abrade, excoriate, irritate. *See* **chafe** (1). **2.** To move over or along

with pressure ► knead, manipulate, massage, press, rub down, stroke, work (over). *See also* **brush¹, touch. 3.** To cross out or remove ► delete, erase, strike (out). *See* **cancel** (1).

rub against *or* **along** *verb*
To make light and momentary contact with, as in passing ► graze, kiss, skim. *See* **brush¹.**

rub away *or* **off** *verb*
To remove an outer layer or something adherent from an object by friction ► scour, scrape, scrub.

rub out *verb*
1. To destroy all traces of ► eradicate, liquidate, obliterate. *See* **annihilate** (1). **2.** *Slang* To take the life of a person or persons unlawfully ► destroy, kill, slay. *See* **murder** (1).

rub *noun*
1. *Informal* A tricky or unsuspected condition ► catch, hitch, snag. *See also* **bar, disadvantage, trick. 2.** Light and momentary contact with another person or thing ► graze, skim. *See* **brush¹** (1).

rubber stamp *noun*
► authorization, consent, sanction. *See* **permission.**

rubbish *noun*
1. Items or material discarded or rejected as useless or worthless ► litter, trash, waste. *See* **garbage** (1). **2.** Something that does not have or make sense ► bunkum, drivel, garbage. *See* **nonsense** (1).

rubble *noun*
► debris, remains, wreckage. *See* **ruin** (2).

rube *noun*
Slang A clumsy, unsophisticated person ► hick, rustic, yokel. *See* **clodhopper.**

rubicund *adjective*
► blooming, flushed, rosy. *See* **ruddy.**

rubric *noun*
► guideline, prescript, regulation. *See* **rule** (1).

ruck¹ *noun*
1. An enormous number of persons or things gathered together ► horde, mass, throng. *See* **crowd** (1). **2.** The common people ► masses, proletariat, public. *See* **commonalty.**

ruck² *verb*
To bend together or form a crease ► crimp, double, pleat. *See* **fold** (1).

ruck *noun*
A line made by the doubling of one part over another ► crimp, pleat, wrinkle. *See* **fold** (1).

ruckus *noun*
► anarchy, lawlessness, misrule. *See* **disorder** (2).

ruction *noun*
► free-for-all, melee. *See* **fight** (1).

rudderless *adjective*
► pointless, purposeless, rambling. *See* **aimless.**

ruddy *adjective*
Of a healthy reddish color ► blooming, blushing, florid, flush, flushed, full-blooded, glowing, red, rosy, rubicund, sanguine.

rude *adjective*
1. Lacking expert, careful craftsmanship ► crude,

homemade, primitive, raw, rough, rough-hewn, unpolished. *See also* **shoddy. 2.** Not civilized ▸ barbarian, barbaric, savage. *See* **uncivilized** (1). **3.** Lacking in delicacy or refinement ▸ boorish, unbecoming, unrefined. *See* **coarse** (1). **4.** Lacking good manners ▸ discourteous, disrespectful, foul-mouthed, ill-bred, ill-mannered, impolite, rugged, uncivil, ungracious, unmannered, unmannerly, unpolished. *See also* **disrespectful, tactless, thoughtless. 5.** Characterized by unpleasant discordance of sound ▸ cacophonous, discordant, disharmonious, dissonant, inharmonic, inharmonious, unharmonious, unmusical. **6.** Causing displeasure, anger, or hurt feelings ▸ hurtful, impolite, insulting. *See* **offensive** (2). **7.** Being in a natural state ▸ raw, unrefined. *See* **crude** (1). **8.** Having or showing a lack of respect ▸ contemptuous, discourteous, impolite. *See* **disrespectful** (1).

✦ CORE SYNONYMS: *rude, crude, primitive, raw, rough.* These adjectives mean lacking expert or careful craftmanship: *a rude hut; a crude drawing; primitive kitchen facilities; a raw wooden canoe; a rough sketch.*

rudeness *noun*
1. The state or quality of being impudent ▸ audacity, boldness, forwardness. *See* **impudence. 2.** Lack of proper respect ▸ impoliteness, irreverence. *See* **disrespect** (1).

rudiment *noun*
1. An underlying support, as for an argument or belief ▸ cornerstone, foundation, underpinning. *See* **basis** (1). **2.** An irreducible constituent of a whole ▸ essential, fundamental. *See* **element** (1).

rudimentary *adjective*
▸ basic, beginning, rudimentary. *See* **elementary** (2).

rue *verb*
To feel or express sorrow for ▸ deplore, regret, repent, sorrow (over). *See also* **feel, grieve.**

rue *noun*
A feeling of regret for one's sins or misdeeds ▸ contriteness, remorse, repentance. *See* **penitence.**

rueful *adjective*
1. Arousing or deserving pity ▸ lamentable, poor. *See* **pitiful** (1). **2.** Causing or expressing sorrow or sadness ▸ depressing, grievous, mournful. *See* **sorrowful** (1). **3.** Feeling or expressing sympathy, pity, or regret ▸ penitent, regretful, repentant. *See* **sorry** (1).

ruffian *noun*
▸ hoodlum, hooligan, tough. *See* **thug.**

ruffle *verb*
1. To impair or destroy the composure of ▸ disorient, fluster, jar. *See* **agitate** (2). **2.** To trouble the nerves or peace of mind of ▸ irritate, nettle, vex. *See* **annoy** (1).

ruffled feathers *noun*
▸ huff, resentment, umbrage. *See* **offense** (1).

rugged *adjective*
1. Having a surface that is not smooth ▸ coarse, ragged, scabrous. *See* **rough** (1). *See synonym note at* **rough. 2.** Characterized by marked muscular development ▸ brawny, robust, sturdy. *See* **muscular.**

3. Physically toughened so as to have great endurance ▸ hardy, tough. *See* **hard** (2). **4.** Violently disturbed or agitated, as by storms ▸ roily, turbulent, violent. *See* **rough** (2). **5.** Marked by vigorous physical exertion ▸ knockabout, strenuous, tough. *See* **rough** (7).

ruin *noun*
1. Something that causes total loss or severe impairment ▸ bane, destroyer, destruction, downfall, ruination, undoing, wrecker. *See also* **breakdown, curse. 2.** The remains of something destroyed, disintegrated, or decayed ▸ debris, remains, rubble, wrack, wreck, wreckage. *See also* **trace. 3.** The act of destroying or state of being destroyed ▸ devastation, undoing, wreck. *See* **destruction** (1). **4.** The condition of being financially insolvent ▸ failure, insolvency. *See* **bankruptcy.**

ruin *verb*
1. To cause the complete ruin or wreckage of ▸ demolish, torpedo, wreck. *See* **destroy** (1). *See synonym note at* **destroy. 2.** To severely impair (someone's spirit, health, or will) ▸ overwhelm, shatter. *See* **break** (4). **3.** To reduce to financial insolvency ▸ bankrupt, break, bust, do in, impoverish, pauperize. *Slang:* clean out.

ruination *noun*
1. The act of destroying or state of being destroyed ▸ devastation, ruin, wreck. *See* **destruction** (1). **2.** Something that causes total loss or severe impairment ▸ bane, downfall, undoing. *See* **ruin** (1). **3.** The condition of being financially insolvent ▸ insolvency, ruin. *See* **bankruptcy.**

ruinous *adjective*
1. Causing ruin or great destruction ▸ calamitous, cataclysmic, catastrophic. *See* **disastrous. 2.** Showing signs of wear and tear or neglect ▸ broken-down, dilapidated, tattered. *See* **shabby** (1). **3.** Causing harm or injury ▸ deleterious, evil, injurious. *See* **harmful.**

rulable *adjective*
Capable of being governed ▸ administrable, controllable, governable, manageable. *See also* **loyal, obedient.**

rule *noun*
1. A code or set of codes governing action or procedure, for example ▸ dictate, guideline, law, prescript, regulation, rubric. *See also* **standard. 2.** The act of exercising controlling power or the condition of being so controlled ▸ control, dominion, reign. *See* **domination** (1). **3.** The right and power to command, decide, rule, or judge ▸ dominion, jurisdiction, might. *See* **authority** (1). **4.** The continuous exercise of authority over a political unit ▸ control, governance. *See* **government** (1). **5.** A principle governing affairs within or among political units ▸ decree, edict. *See* **law** (1). **6.** A regular or customary matter, condition, or course of events ▸ commonplace, norm. *See* **usual. 7.** The condition or fact of being dominant ▸ authority, power, supremacy. *See* **dominance** (1).

rule *verb*
1. To have charge of the affairs of others ▸ direct,

govern, manage. *See* **administer** (1). **2.** To command in an arrogant manner ▸ domineer, order, tyrannize. *See* **boss** (1). **3.** To occupy the preeminent position in ▸ control, prevail. *See* **dominate** (1). **4.** To make a decision about (a controversy or dispute, for example) after deliberation, as in a court of law ▸ adjudicate, decide. *See* **judge** (1). *See synonym note at* **decide.**

rule out *verb*
1. To prohibit from occurring by advance planning or action ▸ anticipate, avert, obviate. *See* **prevent. 2.** To set forth expressly and authoritatively ▸ impose, mandate, ordain. *See* **dictate** (1). **3.** To keep from being admitted, included, or considered ▸ eliminate, keep out, vote down. *See* **exclude** (1).

ruler *noun*
▸ boss, director, head, leader. *See* **chief** (1).

ruling *adjective*
1. Exercising controlling power or influence ▸ key, predominant, reigning. *See* **dominant** (1). **2.** Most generally existing or encountered at a given time ▸ prevalent, reigning. *See* **prevailing** (1).

ruling *noun*
An authoritative or official decision, especially one made by a court ▸ adjudication, decision, dictum, decree, determination, edict, finding, judgment, opinion, pronouncement, resolution, sentence, verdict. *See also* **command, law.**

rumble *verb*
1. To make a continuous deep reverberating sound ▸ boom, growl, grumble, resound, roll. **2.** To make an explosive noise ▸ roar, thunder. *See* **blast** (1). **3.** *Slang* To exchange blows with another person ▸ fight. *Idioms:* duke it out, mix it up, slug it out. *See also* **wrestle.**

rumble *noun*
1. A loud, deep, prolonged sound ▸ bawl, bellow, clamor. *See* **roar** (1). **2.** An explosive noise ▸ boom, crash. *See* **blast** (1). **3.** *Slang* A physical conflict between two or more people ▸ free-for-all, melee. *See* **fight** (1).

ruminate *verb*
1. To think or think about carefully and at length ▸ cogitate, deliberate, mull. *See* **ponder. 2.** To seize and grind with the teeth ▸ chomp, gnash, munch. *See* **chew.**

rumination *noun*
▸ cogitation, deliberation, reflection. *See* **thought** (1).

ruminative *adjective*
▸ contemplative, pensive, reflective. *See* **thoughtful** (1).

rummage *verb*
▸ comb, forage, search. *See* **scour**² (1).

rummy¹ *noun*
Slang A person who is habitually drunk ▸ alcoholic, dipsomaniac, tippler. *See* **drunkard.**

rumor *noun*
Idle, often sensational and groundless talk about others ▸ hearsay, scandal, tattle. *See* **gossip** (1).

rumor *verb*
To engage in or spread gossip ▸ chatter, whisper. *See* **gossip.**

rumormonger *noun*
▸ gossipmonger, taleteller, whisperer. *See* **gossip** (2).

rump *noun*
▸ posterior, seat. *Slang:* fanny. *See* **buttocks.**

rumple *verb*
1. To bend together or form a crease ▸ crimp, double, pleat. *See* **fold** (1). **2.** To put something into a state of disarray, such as the hair or clothes ▸ dishevel, disorder, mess (up). *See* **tousle.**

rumple *noun*
A line made by the doubling of one part over another ▸ crimp, pleat, wrinkle. *See* **fold** (1).

rumpus *noun*
1. Sounds or a sound, especially when loud, confused, or disagreeable ▸ clamor, din. *See* **noise** (1). **2.** Loud and insistent utterances or noisemaking, usually expressing disapproval ▸ hullabaloo, uproar. *See* **vociferation.**

run *verb*
1. To move on foot at a pace faster than a walk ▸ canter, gallop, jog, lope, scamper, scurry, scuttle, shin, sprint, trot. *See also* **bound**¹, **rush. 2.** To move swiftly ▸ dash, sprint, zip. *See* **rush** (1). **3.** To leave hastily ▸ bolt, get out. *Informal:* clear out, get, hotfoot, skedaddle. *Slang:* hightail, scram, take off, vamoose. *Idioms:* beat it, hightail it, hotfoot it, make tracks, take a powder. **4.** To move or proceed away from a place ▸ depart, exit, get away, get off, go, go away, leave, pull out, quit, retire, run along, withdraw. *Informal:* cut out, push off, shove off. *Slang:* blow, split, take off. **5.** To be with as a companion ▸ fraternize, run around. *Slang:* hang out. *See* **associate** (2). **6.** To look to when in need ▸ refer, run, turn. *See* **resort** (1). **7.** To complete a race or competition in a specified position ▸ come in, finish, place. **8.** To move freely as a liquid ▸ purl, ripple, stream. *See* **flow** (1). **9.** To cause a liquid to flow in a steady stream ▸ decant, empty, issue. *See* **pour** (1). **10.** To come forth in abundance ▸ gush, rush. *See* **flow** (2). **11.** To change from a solid to a liquid ▸ liquefy, thaw. *See* **melt** (1). **12.** To proceed on a certain course or for a certain distance ▸ lead, reach. *See* **extend** (1). **13.** To change or fluctuate within limits ▸ range, vary. *See* **go** (7). **14.** To be performed ▸ play, show. **15.** To urge to move along ▸ chase, push, wrangle. *See* **drive** (3). **16.** To look for and pursue game in order to capture or kill it ▸ chase, stalk. *See* **hunt** (1). **17.** To act or operate in a specified way ▸ operate, perform, work. *See* **function. 18.** To direct the functioning of ▸ manage, work. *See* **operate** (1). **19.** To import or export secretly and illegally ▸ bootleg, sneak. *See* **smuggle. 20.** To separate or pull apart by force ▸ rip, rive, split. *See* **tear**¹ (1). **21.** To penetrate into a substance or place with force ▸ drive, stab, stick. *See* **plunge** (1). **22.** To control the course of an activity ▸ direct, manage, operate. *See* **conduct** (1). **23.** To have charge of the affairs of others ▸ direct,

govern, rule. *See* **administer** (1). **24.** To come to in number or quantity ▸ number, reach, total. *See* **amount** (1).

run across *verb*

To find or meet by chance ▸ come across, happen on, stumble on. *See* **encounter** (1).

run after *verb*

1. To follow another with the intent of overtaking and capturing ▸ chase, hunt. *See* **pursue** (1). **2.** To attempt to gain the affection of ▸ chase, woo. *See* **court** (2).

run along *or* **away** *verb*

To move away from a place ▸ exit, go away, retire. *See* **go** (1).

run away *verb*

To break loose and leave suddenly, as from confinement or a difficult situation ▸ decamp, flee. *See* **escape** (1).

run down *verb*

1. To pursue and locate ▸ hunt down, track down. *See* **trace** (1). **2.** To represent or speak of as small or insignificant ▸ deprecate, disparage, slight. *See* **belittle**. **3.** To give a recapitulation of the salient facts of ▸ abstract, recapitulate, summarize. *See* **review** (1).

run in *verb*

1. *Slang* To take into custody as a prisoner ▸ apprehend, seize. *See* **arrest** (1). **2.** To go to or seek out the company of someone in order to socialize ▸ drop by, pop in. *See* **visit** (1).

run into *verb*

1. To find or meet by chance ▸ come across, happen on, stumble on. *See* **encounter** (1). **2.** To come together with force ▸ bump, strike. *See* **collide** (1).

run off *verb*

To present for circulation, exhibit, or sale ▸ bring out, issue, release. *See* **publish** (1).

run on *verb*

To talk rapidly on trivial matters ▸ blab, jabber, prattle. *See* **chatter** (1).

run out *verb*

1. To make or become no longer active or productive ▸ deplete, desiccate, play out. *See* **dry** (2). **2.** To prove deficient or insufficient ▸ fail, give out. *Idioms:* fall short, run dry, run short. *See also* **decrease**. **3.** To become void, especially through passage of time or an omission ▸ cease, end. *See* **lapse** (1). **4.** To direct or allow to leave ▸ cast out, expel. *See* **dismiss** (2).

run through *verb*

1. To use all of ▸ eat up, expend, finish. *See* **exhaust** (1). **2.** To give a recapitulation of the salient facts of ▸ abstract, recapitulate, summarize. *See* **review** (1). **3.** To look through reading matter casually ▸ flip through, leaf (through), skim. *See* **browse** (1). **4.** To do or perform repeatedly so as to master ▸ exercise, rehearse. *See* **practice** (1).

run up *verb*

To make or become greater or larger ▸ amplify, boost, enlarge. *See* **increase** (1).

run *noun*

1. A pace faster than a walk ▸ canter, dash, gallop, jog,

lope, sprint, trot. *See also* **hike, walk**. **2.** A trip in a motor vehicle ▸ jaunt, ride. *See* **drive** (3). **3.** A small stream ▸ rill, watercourse. *See* **brook**[1]. **4.** A length of torn or unraveled stitches in knitted fabric ▸ rent, rip, tear. **5.** A number of things placed or occurring one after the other ▸ order, procession, sequence. *See* **series**. **6.** An enclosure for confining an animal or bird ▸ coop, kennel, stall. *See* **cage**.

runagate *noun*

▸ deserter, recreant, traitor. *See* **defector**.

runaway *noun*

1. An easy victory ▸ cakewalk, rout, walkaway, walkover. *Slang:* romp. *Idiom:* clean sweep. *See also* **breeze, defeat**. **2.** One who flees, as from confinement or the police ▸ escapee, fugitive, outlaw, refugee. *See also* **criminal**.

runaway *adjective*

1. Fleeing or having fled, as from confinement or the police ▸ escaped, fugitive, fleeing. *Idioms:* on the lam (*or* loose *or* run). **2.** Out of control ▸ amuck, unbridled, uncontrolled. *Idioms:* out of hand, running wild. *See also* **abandoned, loose**.

rundown *noun*

A review of the essential points or consequences of something: ▸ recap, wrap-up. *See* **summary**.

rundown *adjective*

1. Depleted of energy ▸ exhausted, weary, worn-out. *See* **tired** (1). **2.** Showing signs of wear and tear or neglect ▸ broken-down, dilapidated, ramshackle. *See* **shabby** (1). **3.** Not physically strong ▸ feeble, frail, unsound. *See* **weak** (1).

rung *noun*

▸ interval, level, step. *See* **degree** (1).

run-in *noun*

▸ contention, quarrel. *Informal:* tangle. *See* **argument** (1).

runner *noun*

1. A person who carries messages or is sent on errands ▸ carrier, courier, envoy. *See* **messenger**. **2.** A person who engages in smuggling ▸ bootlegger, contrabandist, smuggler. *Slang:* mule. **3.** A young stemlike growth arising from a plant ▸ offshoot, sprout. *See* **shoot** (1).

running *adjective*

▸ functioning, operating, ticking, working. *See* **active** (1).

run-of-the-mill *adjective*

▸ common, mediocre, standard. *See* **ordinary** (1).

runt *noun*

Slang A young or short person ▸ pip-squeak, scrub, small fry. *See* **squirt** (2).

run-through *noun*

▸ rundown, sum, wrap-up. *See* **summary**.

runty *adjective*

▸ bantam, petite, undersized. *See* **little** (1).

rupture *noun*

1. An opening, especially in a solid structure ▸ breach, break, gap, hole, perforation. **2.** An interruption in friendly relations ▸ break, fissure, rift. *See* **breach** (2).

rupture *verb*
To undergo partial breaking ▸ fissure, split. *See* **crack** (1).

rural *adjective*
▸ bucolic, pastoral. *See* **country**. *See synonym note at* **country**.

ruse *noun*
▸ deception, ploy, stratagem. *See* **trick** (1). *See synonym note at* **trick**.

rush *verb*
1. To move swiftly ▸ bolt, bucket, bustle, dart, dash, festinate, flash, fleet, flit, fly, haste, hasten, hurry, hustle, pelt, race, rocket, run, sail, sally, scoot, scour, shoot, speed, sprint, tear, trot, whirl, whisk, whiz, wing, zing, zip, zoom. *Informal:* rip. *Slang:* barrel, highball. *Idioms:* get a move on, get cracking, go like lightning, go like the wind, hotfoot it, make haste, make time, make tracks, run like the wind, shake a leg, step (*or* jump) on it. *See also* **run**. **2.** To come forth in abundance ▸ gush, pour, run. *See* **flow** (2). **3.** To set upon with violent force ▸ assail, assault, storm, strike. *See* **attack** (1).

rush *noun*
1. Careless headlong action ▸ precipitance, rashness. *See* **haste** (2). **2.** A swift advance or attack ▸ onslaught, raid. *See* **charge** (1). **3.** Something suggestive of running water ▸ flood, stream, tide. *See* **flow**. *See synonym note at* **flow**. **4.** Rapidness of movement or activity ▸ expeditiousness, hurry, quickness. *See* **haste** (1).

rush *adjective*
Informal: Designed to meet emergency needs as

quickly as possible ▸ *Informal:* crash, hurry-up.

rustic *adjective*
1. Of a charmingly plain and unsophisticated nature ▸ artless, homely, homespun, natural, simple, unadorned, unpolished. *See also* **coarse**. **2.** Of or relating to the countryside ▸ bucolic, pastoral, rural. *See* **country**. *See synonym note at* **country**.

rustic *noun*
A clumsy, unsophisticated person ▸ hick, peasant, yokel. *See* **clodhopper**.

rustle *noun*
1. A sibilant sound ▸ fizzle, sibilant. *See* **hiss** (1). **2.** A low, indistinct, and often continuous sound ▸ sigh, susurration, whisper. *See* **murmur** (1).

rustle *verb*
1. To make a sibilant sound ▸ fizzle, swish. *See* **hiss** (1). **2.** To make a low, continuous, and indistinct sound ▸ murmur, sigh, sough, whisper. *See also* **burble, hum**.

rut *noun*
1. A long, narrow, and usually shallow depression in the ground ▸ ditch, groove, trench. *See* **furrow** (1). **2.** A course of action to be followed regularly ▸ rote, rounds, track. *See* **routine** (1).

ruthful *adjective*
▸ lamentable, poor. *See* **pitiful** (1).

ruthless *adjective*
1. Lacking scruples or principles ▸ unconscionable, unethical, unprincipled. *See* **unscrupulous** (1). **2.** Inflicting suffering or pain ▸ brutal, fierce, savage. *See* **cruel** (1).

S

sabbatical *noun*
A regularly scheduled period spent away from work or duty, often in recreation ▸ furlough, holiday, leave, vacation. *Idioms:* time (*or* day) off. *See also* **break, trip**.

saber-rattling *noun*
▸ combativeness, pugnacity, warmongering. *See* **aggression** (1).

sable *adjective*
▸ ebony, inky, jet. *See* **black** (1).

sabotage *noun*
Treacherous action to defeat or do harm to an endeavor ▸ subversion, undermining. *See also* **defeat, destruction**.

sabotage *verb*
To damage, destroy, or defeat by sabotage ▸ subvert, undermine. *See also* **destroy, disorder**.

sabulous *adjective*
▸ granular, gritty. *See* **coarse** (4).

saccharine *adjective*
1. Having or suggesting the taste of sugar ▸ honeyed, sugary, sweet. **2.** Purposefully contrived to gain favor ▸ buttery, insinuating, sugary. *See* **flattering** (1).

sacerdotal *adjective*
▸ ministerial, pastoral. *See* **clerical**.

sachem *noun*
▸ boss, director, head, leader. *See* **chief** (1).

sack¹ *noun*
1. A flexible container for carrying items ▸ pouch, tote. *Chiefly Regional:* poke. *See* **bag** (1). **2.** *Slang* The act of dismissing or the condition of being dismissed from employment ▸ expulsion, termination. *See* **dismissal** (1).

sack *verb*
Slang To end the employment or service of ▸ drop, let go. *See* **dismiss** (1). *See synonym note at* **dismiss**.

sack out *verb*
Slang To be asleep ▸ sleep, slumber. *Idioms:* be in the

land of Nod, catch some shuteye, catch (*or* cop) some z's, saw logs (*or* wood), sleep like a log (*or* baby *or* rock *or* top), sleep tight. *See also* **nap, rest.**

sack² *verb*
To rob of goods by force, especially in time of war ▸ depredate, despoil, loot, pillage, plunder, ransack, rape, ravage, strip. *See also* **attack, invade.**

sacrarium *noun*
A sacred or holy place ▸ sanctorium, sanctuary, sanctum, shrine.

sacred *adjective*
1. In the service or worship of God or a god ▸ devoted, religious, sanctified. *See* **divine** (2). **2.** Regarded with particular reverence or respect ▸ consecrated, hallowed, sacrosanct. *See* **holy** (1). **3.** That may not be spoken of ▸ unmentionable, unutterable. *See* **unspeakable** (2).

sacredness *noun*
▸ beatitude, sanctity. *See* **holiness.**

sacrifice *noun*
1. Something offered to a deity as part of a religious rite ▸ immolation, oblation. *See* **offering** (1). **2.** A giving up of a possession, claim, or right ▸ relinquishment, renunciation, surrender. *See* **abandonment** (1). **3.** The expenditure at which something is obtained ▸ cost, expense, price, toll. *Informal:* damage.

sacrifice *verb*
1. To offer as a sacrifice ▸ immolate, victimize. **2.** To give up completely ▸ forfeit, relinquish, surrender. *See* **abandon** (1). **3.** To give over by or as if by vow to a higher purpose ▸ dedicate, enshrine, hallow. *See* **devote** (1).

sacrilege *noun*
An act of disrespect or impiety toward something regarded as sacred ▸ blasphemy, desecration, impiety, profanation, violation.

sacrilegious *adjective*
Showing irreverence and contempt for something sacred ▸ blasphemous, impious, profane.

sacrosanct *adjective*
1. Regarding with particular reverence or respect, especially by a religion ▸ consecrated, hallowed, sacred. *See* **holy** (1). **2.** In the service or worship of God or a god ▸ devoted, religious, sacred. *See* **divine** (2).

sacrosanctity *noun*
▸ beatitude, sanctity. *See* **holiness.**

sad *adjective*
1. In low spirits ▸ dejected, dispirited, heavy-hearted. *See* **depressed** (1). **2.** Causing or expressing sadness, sorrow, or regret ▸ depressing, dismal, melancholy. *See* **sorrowful** (1). *See synonym note at* **sorrowful.**

sadden *verb*
▸ dishearten, dispirit, weigh down. *See* **depress** (1).

saddle *verb*
To weigh down or place a heavy load on ▸ encumber, lade, tax. *See* **burden¹.**

saddle with *verb*
To force another to accept a burden ▸ charge with, inflict on (*or* upon), tax with. *See* **impose on** (1).

sadism *noun*
▸ brutality, truculence. *See* **cruelty.**

sadistic *adjective*
▸ brutal, inhuman, vicious. *See* **cruel** (1).

sadness *noun*
▸ dejection, doldrums, melancholy. *See* **depression** (2).

safari *noun*
▸ pilgrimage, tour, voyage. *See* **expedition** (1).

safe *adjective*
1. Free from danger, injury, or the threat of harm ▸ unharmed, unhurt, uninjured, unscathed. *Idioms:* out of danger, out of harm's way, safe and sound. *See also* **good, healthy. 2.** Affording protection ▸ defended, guarded, immune, impenetrable, impregnable, invulnerable, secure, unassailable, unconquerable. *See also* **invincible. 3.** Devoid of hurtful qualities ▸ innocuous, unoffensive. *See* **harmless** (1).

safe *noun*
A place where something is deposited for safekeeping ▸ archive, storehouse, warehouse. *See* **depository.**

safeguard *noun*
1. The act or a means of defending ▸ protection, security, shield. *See* **defense** (1). **2.** The function of watching, guarding, or overseeing ▸ custody, guardianship, safekeeping. *See* **care** (2).

safeguard *verb*
To keep safe from danger, attack, or harm ▸ preserve, protect, secure. *See* **defend** (1). *See synonym note at* **defend.**

safe house *noun*
▸ asylum, haven, refuge. *See* **cover** (1).

safekeeping *noun*
▸ custody, guardianship, trust. *See* **care** (2).

safeness *noun*
▸ impenetrability, security. *See* **safety** (1).

safety *noun*
1. The quality or state of being safe ▸ assurance, immunity, impenetrability, impregnability, invulnerability, safeness, security, unassailability, unconquerability. *See also* **defense. 2.** Protection or shelter, as from danger or hardship ▸ asylum, sanctuary, shelter. *See* **refuge** (1).

sag *verb*
1. To become limp, as from loss of freshness ▸ flag, wither. *See* **wilt. 2.** To hang limply, loosely, and carelessly ▸ flop, wilt. *See* **slouch** (2). **3.** To decline in value or quantity ▸ drop off, slip. *See* **fall** (7). **4.** To curve or yield under pressure ▸ buckle, warp. *See* **bend** (3). **5.** To go from a more erect posture to a less erect posture ▸ sink, slump. *See* **drop** (1).

sag *noun*
An area sunk below its surroundings ▸ basin, dip, sink. *See* **depression** (1).

saga *verb*
▸ chronicle, history, narrative. *See* **story** (1).

sagacious *adjective*
1. Possessing deep knowledge and understanding ▸ knowing, sage, sapient, wise. **2.** Proceeding from or

exhibiting good judgment ▸ commonsensical, level-headed, prudent. *See* **sensible** (1). **3.** Having or showing a clever awareness and resourcefulness in practical matters ▸ astute, canny, perspicacious. *See* **shrewd** (1). *See synonym note at* **shrewd.**

sagacity *or* **sagaciousness** *noun*
1. Skill in perceiving, discriminating, or judging ▸ keenness, perceptiveness, shrewdness. *See* **discernment** (1). **2.** Deep, thorough, or mature understanding ▸ profundity, sapience. *See* **wisdom** (1).

sagamore *noun*
▸ boss, director, head, leader. *See* **chief** (1).

sage *noun*
A person noted for wisdom, knowledge, and judgment ▸ guru, pundit, savant, scholar, wise man, wise woman. *See also* **expert, mind.**

sage *adjective*
1. Possessing deep knowledge and understanding ▸ knowing, sagacious, sapient, wise. **2.** Proceeding from or showing good judgment ▸ balanced, commonsensical, levelheaded, prudent, sane. *See* **sensible** (1).

sageness *noun*
1. Skill in perceiving, discriminating, or judging ▸ keenness, perceptiveness, shrewdness. *See* **discernment** (1). **2.** Deep, thorough, or mature understanding ▸ profundity, sapience. *See* **wisdom** (1).

sail *verb*
1. To move swiftly ▸ dash, sprint, zip. *See* **rush** (1). **2.** To move through the air ▸ flit, flutter, wing. *See* **fly** (1). **3.** To pass quickly and lightly through the air ▸ dart, glide, shoot. *See* **fly** (2). **4.** To move in or on the wind ▸ drift, flap. *See* **blow**[1] (2). **5.** *Informal* To progress quickly and effortlessly ▸ coast, zip. *See* **breeze.**

sail into *verb*
To set upon with violent force ▸ assail, assault, storm, strike. *See* **attack** (1).

sailor *noun*
A person engaged in sailing or working on a ship ▸ boatman, Jack, Jack-tar, mariner, navigator, sea dog, seafarer, seaman. *Informal:* salt, tar. *Slang:* gob.

saintliness *noun*
▸ beatitude, sanctity. *See* **holiness.**

saintly *adjective*
▸ devout, holy, religious. *See* **pious** (1).

salaam *verb*
To incline the head or body, as in greeting, consent, courtesy, submission, or worship ▸ curtsy, kneel. *See* **bow**[1] (1).

salaam *noun*
An inclination of the head or body, as in greeting, consent, courtesy, submission, or worship ▸ genuflection, obeisance. *See* **bow**[1].

salability *or* **salableness** *noun*
Market appeal ▸ marketability, sell.

salacious *adjective*
▸ amorous, erogenous, libidinal. *See* **erotic.**

salad days *noun*
▸ juvenility, puberty, youthfulness. *See* **youth** (1).

salary *noun*
▸ earnings, pay, recompense. *See* **wage.**

sale *noun*
▸ exchange, trade, transaction. *See* **deal** (1).

salesclerk *or* **salesperson** *noun*
▸ clerk, vendor. *See* **seller.**

salesman *or* **saleswoman** *noun*
▸ salesclerk, vendor. *See* **seller.**

salient *adjective*
Readily attracting notice ▸ conspicuous, outstanding. *See* **noticeable** (1). *See synonym note at* **noticeable.**

salient *noun*
A part that protrudes or extends outward ▸ knob, protrusion, protuberance. *See* **projection** (1).

saline *adjective*
Containing salt ▸ brackish, briny, salty.

saliva *noun*
▸ expectorate, phlegm. *See* **spit** (1).

salivate *verb*
▸ dribble, slobber. *See* **drool.**

salivation *noun*
Saliva running from the mouth ▸ drivel, drool, slaver, slobber.

sallow *adjective*
Lacking color ▸ bloodless, lurid, wan. *See* **pale** (1).

sallow *verb*
To lose normal coloration; turn pale ▸ bleach, wan. *See* **pale.**

sally *verb*
To move swiftly ▸ dash, sprint, zip. *See* **rush** (1).

sally *noun*
Words or actions intended to excite laughter or amusement ▸ jest, quip, witticism. *See* **joke** (1).

salmagundi *noun*
▸ hodgepodge, jumble, mishmash. *See* **assortment** (1).

salon *noun*
A large public display of art ▸ exhibit, fair, exposition, show. *See* **exhibition** (1).

saloon *noun*
▸ inn, pub, tavern. *See* **bar** (2).

salt *noun*
Informal A person engaged in sailing or working on a ship ▸ mariner, navigator, seafarer. *See* **sailor.**

salt *verb*
To prepare food for storage and future use ▸ can, cure, put up. *See* **preserve** (1).

salt away *verb*
1. To keep for future use ▸ lay aside, put by, store. *See* **save** (1). **2.** To place money in an account ▸ deposit, lay away. *See* **bank**[2].

salty *adjective*
1. Containing salt ▸ brackish, briny, saline. **2.** Of or relating to the seas or oceans ▸ oceanic, saltwater, sea. *See* **marine** (1). **3.** Bordering on indelicacy or impropriety ▸ provocative, risqué, suggestive. *See* **racy** (1).

salutary *or* **salubrious** *adjective*
1. Affording benefit or advantage ▸ favorable, helpful, propitious. *See* **beneficial. 2.** Promoting good health ▸ healthsome, wholesome. *See* **healthful** (1).

salutation *noun*
An expression, in words or gestures, marking a meeting of persons ▶ hail, greeting, salute, welcome. *Informal:* hello.

salutations *interjection*
▶ good day, greetings. *Informal:* hey there. *See* **hello.**

salute *verb*
1. To address in a friendly and respectful way ▶ greet, hail, welcome. **2.** To approach for the purpose of speech ▶ accost, greet, hail. *See also* **encounter, interrupt, welcome. 3.** To salute by raising and drinking from a glass ▶ honor, toast. *See* **drink** (4).

salute *noun*
1. An expression, in words or gestures, marking a meeting of persons ▶ hail, greeting, salutation, welcome. *Informal:* hello. **2.** A formal token of appreciation and admiration for a person's high achievements ▶ ovation, tribute. *See* **testimonial** (2).

salvage *noun*
Extrication from danger or confinement ▶ deliverance, freeing, salvation. *See* **rescue.**

salvage *verb*
To set free, as from danger or confinement ▶ recover, save. *See* **rescue.**

salvation *noun*
▶ deliverance, release, saving. *See* **rescue.**

salve *noun*
A substance used on the skin to soothe or heal ▶ emollient, liniment. *See* **ointment.**

salve *verb*
To restore to health ▶ rehabilitate, remedy. *See* **cure** (1).

salvo *noun*
1. A concentrated outpouring, as of missiles, words, or blows ▶ cannonade, fusillade, volley. *See* **barrage. 2.** A formal token of appreciation and admiration for a person's high achievements ▶ salute, tribute. *See* **testimonial** (2).

same *adjective*
1. Being the one and not another; not different in nature or identity ▶ identical, selfsame, very. *See also* **like². 2.** Agreeing exactly in value, quantity, or effect ▶ identical, tantamount. *See* **equal** (1). **3.** Having no change or variation ▶ changeless, constant, unvarying. *See* **unchanging.**

sameness *noun*
1. The quality or condition of being exactly the same as something else ▶ identicalness, identity, oneness, selfsameness. *See also* **likeness. 2.** The state of being equivalent ▶ equality, parity. *See* **equivalence. 3.** A tiresome lack of variety ▶ humdrum, tedium. *See* **monotony. 4.** The condition of being without change or variation ▶ constancy, immutability. *See* **changelessness.**

sample *noun*
1. One that is representative of a group or class ▶ illustration, specimen. *See* **example** (1). *See synonym note at* **example. 2.** A limited or anticipatory experience ▶ foretaste, sampling, taste. *See also* **glance.**

sample *verb*
To participate in or partake of personally ▶ know, undergo. *See* **experience.**

sanctified *adjective*
1. In the service or worship of God or a god ▶ devoted, religious, sacred. *See* **divine** (2). **2.** Regarding with particular reverence or respect, especially by a religion ▶ consecrated, hallowed, sacred. *See* **holy** (1).

sanctify *verb*
To make sacred by a religious rite ▶ bless, consecrate, hallow. *See also* **exalt.**

sanctimonious *adjective*
▶ phony, pious, self-righteous, two-faced. *See* **hypocritical.**

sanctimony *or* **sanctimoniousness** *noun*
▶ phoniness, piety. *See* **hypocrisy.**

sanction *noun*
1. A coercive measure intended to ensure compliance or conformity ▶ interdict, interdiction, penalty. *See also* **forbiddance, restraint, punishment. 2.** The approving of an action, especially when done by one in authority ▶ authorization, consent. *See* **permission.** *See synonym note at* **permission. 3.** An act of confirming officially ▶ approval, ratification, verification. *See* **confirmation** (1).

sanction *verb*
1. To give one's consent to ▶ approve, authorize, license. *See* **permit** (2). **2.** To accept officially ▶ approve, pass, ratify. *See* **confirm** (3).

sanctioned *adjective*
1. Generally approved or agreed upon ▶ orthodox, received, recognized. *See* **accepted. 2.** Having or arising from authority ▶ conclusive, official, standard. *See* **authoritative** (1).

sanctity *noun*
▶ beatitude, venerability. *See* **holiness.**

sanctorium *noun*
A sacred or holy place ▶ sacrarium, sanctuary, sanctum, shrine.

sanctuary *noun*
1. A sacred or holy place ▶ sacrarium, sanctorium, sanctum, shrine. **2.** Public land kept for a special purpose ▶ park, preserve, reserve, reservation. *See also* **common. 3.** Something that physically protects, especially from danger ▶ harbor, haven, refuge. *See* **cover** (1). *See synonym note at* **cover. 4.** Protection or shelter, as from danger or hardship ▶ asylum, shelter. *See* **refuge** (1).

sanctum *noun*
A sacred or holy place ▶ sacrarium, sanctorium, sanctuary, shrine.

sandy *adjective*
▶ granular, gritty. *See* **coarse** (4).

sane *adjective*
1. Mentally healthy ▶ compos mentis, lucid, normal, rational. *Idioms:* all there, in one's right mind, of sound mind. *See also* **healthy. 2.** Proceeding from or exhibiting good judgment ▶ commonsensical, levelheaded, prudent. *See* **sensible** (1).

saneness *noun*
▸ lucidity, rationality, reason. *See* **sanity.**

sang-froid *noun*
▸ composure, imperturbability, nonchalance, unflappability. *See* **balance** (2).

sanguinary *adjective*
▸ homicidal, sanguineous. *See* **murderous.**

sanguine *adjective*
1. Of a healthy reddish color ▸ blooming, flushed, rosy. *See* **ruddy. 2.** Expecting or suggesting a favorable outcome ▸ cheerful, rosy. *See* **optimistic.**

sanguineous *adjective*
▸ bloodthirsty, cutthroat, slaughterous. *See* **murderous.**

sanguinity *or* **sanguineness** *noun*
▸ enthusiasm, hopefulness. *See* **optimism.**

sanitary *adjective*
▸ antiseptic, hygienic, sanitized. *See* **sterile** (1).

sanitize *verb*
1. To render free of microorganisms ▸ decontaminate, disinfect, irradiate, sterilize. *See also* **clean. 2.** To remove objectionable material from a publication ▸ bowdlerize, expurgate, screen. *See* **censor** (1).

sanitized *adjective*
▸ antiseptic, hygienic, sanitary. *See* **sterile** (1).

sanity *noun*
A healthy mental state ▸ lucidity, lucidness, mind, rationality, reason, saneness, sense (*or* senses), soundness, wits. *Slang:* marbles.

sap[1] *noun*
Slang A person who is easily deceived or victimized ▸ pushover, tool, victim. *See* **dupe** (1).

sap[2] *verb*
1. To lessen or deplete the nerve, energy, or strength of ▸ debilitate, weaken. *See* **enervate. 2.** To use all of ▸ eat up, expend, run through. *See* **exhaust** (1).

sapience *noun*
▸ insight, profundity, sagacity. *See* **wisdom** (1).

sapient *adjective*
1. Possessing deep knowledge and understanding ▸ knowing, sagacious, sage, wise. **2.** Proceeding from or exhibiting good judgment ▸ commonsensical, levelheaded, prudent. *See* **sensible** (1).

sappiness *noun*
Slang The quality or condition of being affectedly or overly emotional ▸ bathos, sentimentalism. *See* **sentimentality.**

sappy *adjective*
Slang Affectedly or extravagantly emotional ▸ gushy, mawkish, soft. *See* **sentimental.**

sarcasm *noun*
The use of irony to ridicule or express contempt ▸ acerbity, acidity, acridity, bitterness, causticity, corrosiveness, cynicism, irony, mordacity, mordancy, trenchancy. *See also* **mockery, ridicule.**

sarcastic *adjective*
Contemptuous or ironic in manner or wit ▸ cynical, derisive, ironic, ironical, jeering, mocking, sardonic, satiric, satirical, scoffing, sneering, snide, wry. *See also* **biting.**

✦ **CORE SYNONYMS:** *sarcastic, ironic, satirical, sardonic.* These adjectives mean contemptuous or ironic in manner or wit. *Sarcastic* suggests sharp taunting and ridicule that wounds: "*a deserved reputation for sarcastic, acerbic and uninhibited polemics*" (Burke Marshall). *Ironic* implies a subtler form of mockery in which an intended meaning is conveyed obliquely: "*a man of eccentric charm, ironic humor, and—above all—profound literary genius*" (Jonathan Kirsch). *Satirical* implies exposure, especially of vice or folly, to ridicule: "*on the surface a satirical look at commercial radio, but also a study of the misuse of telecommunications*" (Richard Harrington). *Sardonic* is associated with scorn, derision, mockery, and often cynicism: "*He was proud, sardonic, harsh to inferiority of every description*" (Charlotte Brontë).

sardonic *adjective*
▸ satiric, scoffing, sneering. *See* **sarcastic.** *See synonym note at* **sarcastic.**

sash *noun*
▸ belt, ribbon, stripe. *See* **band**[1] (1).

sashay *verb*
▸ prance, strut, swank. *See* **strut** (1).

sass *verb*
Informal To utter an impertinent rejoinder ▸ talk back, talk up. *Informal:* sauce. *Idioms:* give someone lip (*or* mouth *or* sass).

sass *noun*
Informal Insolent talk ▸ back talk, mouth. *Informal:* lip. *See also* **impudence, taunt.**

sassiness *noun*
▸ audacity, boldness, forwardness. *See* **impudence.**

sassy *adjective*
1. Rude and disrespectful; without shame ▸ bold, insolent, pert. *See* **impudent. 2.** Very brisk, alert, and full of high spirits ▸ animated, chipper, vivacious. *See* **lively** (1).

satanic *adjective*
▸ devilish, diabolical, infernal. *See* **fiendish.**

satchel *noun*
▸ carryon, grip, valise. *See* **suitcase.**

sate *verb*
▸ engorge, glut, surfeit. *See* **satiate.**

satellite *noun*
1. One who supports and adheres to another ▸ adherent, believer, disciple. *See* **follower** (1). **2.** An area subject to rule by an outside power ▸ dependency, province. *See* **possession** (1).

satiate *verb*
To satisfy to the full or to excess ▸ cloy, engorge, glut, gorge, sate, surfeit. *See also* **pacify, relieve, satisfy.**

satiation *or* **satiety** *noun*
The condition of being full to or beyond satisfaction ▸ engorgement, fullness, repletion, surfeit. *See also* **fulfillment.**

satiny *adjective*
Smooth and lustrous as if polished ▸ silken, silky,

sleek. *See synonym note at* **sleek**. *See also* **even, glossy, slick.**

satire *noun*

A work, such as a novel, play, or dramatic speech, that exposes folly by the use of humor, irony, or comic imitation ▸ burlesque, caricature, farce, imitation, impersonation, lampoon, parody, spoof. *Informal:* send-up, takeoff.

✦ CORE SYNONYMS: *satire, caricature, burlesque, parody, lampoon.* These nouns denote artistic forms that expose folly by the use of humor, irony, or comic imitation. *Satire* is a written work that usually involves ridiculing follies and vices: *She employs satire in her poetry.* A *caricature* grossly exaggerates a distinctive or striking feature with intent to ridicule: *He drew a caricature of the politician. Burlesque,* which usually denotes a dramatic work, suggests outlandish mimicry and broad comedy to provoke laughter: *We went to see a burlesque at the theater. Parody* employs the manner and style of a well-known work or writer for a ludicrous effect: *She wrote a parody of a famous novel.* A *lampoon* is a malicious but broadly humorous satire: *The lampoon was written by a standup comic.*

---

satirical *or* **satiric** *adjective*

▸ satiric, scoffing, sneering. *See* **sarcastic**. *See synonym note at* **sarcastic.**

satisfaction *noun*

1. The condition of being satisfied ▸ contentendness, contentment, fullfilment, gratification. *See also* **happiness, satiation. 2.** Something to make up for loss or damage ▸ amends, remuneration, reparation. *See* **compensation** (1). **3.** Something justly deserved ▸ compensation, deserts, reward. *See* **due** (1).

satisfactory *adjective*

1. Being what is needed without being in excess ▸ competent, decent. *See* **sufficient** (1). **2.** Adequate to satisfy a need, requirement, or standard ▸ average, decent, moderate. *See* **acceptable** (2). **3.** Serving to convince ▸ cogent, persuasive. *See* **convincing** (1).

satisfied *adjective*

Having achieved satisfaction, as of one's goal ▸ content, fulfilled, gratified, happy.

satisfy *verb*

1. To be suitable or sufficient to fulfill a need, demand, or purpose ▸ answer, do, fill, fulfill, meet, please, serve, suffice, suit. *Idioms:* fill the bill, pass muster. **2.** To grant or have what is demanded by a need or desire ▸ appease, content, fulfill, gratify, indulge. *See also* **delight, pacify, relieve, satiate. 3.** To cause another to feel sure about something ▸ persuade, win over. *See* **convince** (1). **4.** To set right by giving what is due ▸ discharge, square. *See* **settle** (3).

✦ CORE SYNONYMS: *satisfy, answer, fill, fulfill, meet.* These verbs mean to be suitable or sufficient to fulfill a need, demand, or purpose: *satisfied all requirements; answered our needs; fills a purpose; fulfilled their aspirations; met her obligations.*

---

satisfying *adjective*

▸ agreeable, enjoyable, welcome. *See* **pleasant** (1).

saturate *verb*

1. To cause to be filled, as with a particular mood ▸ permeate, suffuse. *See* **charge** (1). *See synonym note at* **charge. 2.** To make thoroughly wet ▸ drench, soak, souse. *See* **wet** (1).

saturated *adjective*

▸ drenched, soaked, waterlogged. *See* **wet** (1).

saturnine *adjective*

▸ gloomy, morose, sullen. *See* **glum** (1).

satyr *noun*

▸ gigolo, roué. *Slang:* lech. *See* **lecher.**

sauce *noun*

Informal The state or quality of being impudent or arrogantly self-confident ▸ audacity, boldness, forwardness. *See* **impudence.**

sauce *verb*

Informal To utter an impertinent rejoinder ▸ talk back, talk up. *Informal:* sass. **Idiom:** give someone lip.

saucebox *noun*

Informal One who is obnoxiously self-assertive and arrogant ▸ *Informal:* know-it-all, smarty-pants. *See* **smart aleck.**

sauciness *noun*

▸ audacity, boldness, forwardness. *See* **Impudence.**

saucy *adjective*

▸ bold, insolent, pert. *See* **impudent.**

saunter *verb*

To walk at a leisurely pace ▸ amble, promenade, wander. *See* **stroll.**

saunter *noun*

An act of walking ▸ amble, stroll. *See* **walk** (1).

sauté *verb*

▸ fry, pan-fry, stir-fry. *See* **cook** (1).

savage *adjective*

1. Not domesticated ▸ feral, undomesticated, untamed. *See* **wild** (2). **2.** Not civilized ▸ barbarian, barbaric, rude. *See* **uncivilized** (1). **3.** Inflicting suffering or pain ▸ brutal, fierce, vicious. *See* **cruel** (1). *See synonym note at* **cruel.**

savage *noun*

A perversely mean, cruel, or wicked person ▸ beast, devil, monster. *See* **fiend** (1).

savagery *noun*

▸ brutality, truculence. *See* **cruelty.**

savant *noun*

▸ guru, scholar. *See* **sage.**

save *verb*

1. To keep or accumulate for future use ▸ hoard, keep, lay aside (*or* away *or* by), lay in (up), put by, salt away, save up, set aside, set by, squirrel away, stockpile, store (up), stow, treasure, warehouse. *Informal:* sock away. *Slang:* stash. *See also* **accumulate, bank², hide¹. 2.** To be frugal or sparing ▸ conserve, economize, pinch, skimp. *See* **scrimp. 3.** To set free, as from danger or confinement ▸ recover, redeem. *See* **rescue**. *See synonym note at* **rescue. 4.** To protect an asset from loss or destruction ▶ conserve, husband, preserve. *See also* **defend.**

saving *adjective*
▶ chary, frugal. *See* **economical.**

savior *noun*
▶ deliverer, lifesaver, redeemer. *See* **rescuer.**

savoir-faire *noun*
▶ diplomacy, sensitivity, tactfulness. *See* **tact.** *See synonym note at* **tact.**

savor *noun*
1. A distinctive property affecting the sense of taste ▶ tang, taste, zest. *See* **flavor** (1). *See synonym note at* **flavor. 2.** A distinctive yet intangible quality ▶ aroma, atmosphere, flavor, smack. **3.** A distinctive element ▶ characteristic, feature, trait. *See* **quality** (1).

savor *verb*
1. To have a particular flavor or suggestion of something ▶ smack, smell, suggest, taste. *See also* **hint. 2.** To receive pleasure from ▶ appreciate, relish. *See* **enjoy** (1). **3.** To undergo an emotional reaction ▶ experience, feel, have, know, taste.

savory *adjective*
1. Highly pleasing, especially to the sense of taste ▶ delectable, palatable, scrumptious. *See* **delicious** (1). **2.** Having a pleasant odor ▶ aromatic, perfumy, redolent. *See* **fragrant. 3.** Having a sharp, penetrating flavor or aroma ▶ fiery, piquant, sharp, zesty. *See* **spicy** (1).

savvy *adjective*
Informal Having or showing a clever awareness and resourcefulness in practical matters ▶ canny, knowing, perspicacious. *See* **shrewd** (1).

savvy *noun*
Informal Natural or acquired skill or talent ▶ command, knack. *Informal:* know-how. *See* **ability** (1).

savvy *verb*
Informal To perceive and recognize the meaning of ▶ apprehend, fathom, sense. *See* **understand** (1).

saw *noun*
1. A usually pithy and familiar statement generally accepted as wise or true ▶ adage, maxim, motto. *See* **proverb.** *See synonym note at* **proverb. 2.** A trite expression or idea ▶ banality, truism. *See* **cliché.**

saw-toothed *adjective*
Having a notched edge like a saw ▶ dentate, notched, serrate, serrated, toothed. *See also* **rough.**

say *verb*
1. To put into words ▶ articulate, communicate, convey, declare, deliver, express, state, talk, tell, utter, vent, verbalize, vocalize, voice. *Idioms:* give tongue (*or* vent *or* voice) to. *See also* **air, believe, describe, speak. 2.** To produce or make speech sounds ▶ enounce, enunciate. *See* **pronounce. 3.** To put into words positively and with conviction ▶ avow, declare, maintain. *See* **assert** (1).

say *noun*
The right or chance to express an opinion or participate in a decision ▶ input, suffrage, voice, vote. *Informal:* say-so.

saying *noun*
1. A usually pithy and familiar statement generally accepted as wise or true ▶ adage, maxim, motto. *See* **proverb.** *See synonym note at* **proverb. 2.** Something said ▶ statement, utterance, word. *See also* **language, speech. 3.** The use of the vocal organs to produce sound or speech ▶ enunciation, utterance, vocalization. *See* **voicing.**

say-so *noun*
1. *Informal* The right or chance to express an opinion or participate in a decision: ▶ input, say, suffrage, voice, vote. **2.** *Informal* The right and power to command, decide, rule, or judge ▶ control, might, sovereignty. *See* **authority** (1).

scabrous *adjective*
1. Having a surface that is not smooth ▶ coarse, ragged, rugged. *See* **rough** (1). *See synonym note at* **rough. 2.** Bordering on indelicacy or impropriety ▶ provocative, risqué, suggestive. *See* **racy** (1).

scad *noun*
Informal An indeterminately great amount or number ▶ bunch, multiplicity. *Informal:* bushel. *See* **heap** (3).

scaffolding *or* **scaffold** *noun*
A temporary framework with a floor, used by laborers ▶ platform, stage, staging. *See also* **base¹.**

scalawag *noun*
▶ imp, prankster, scamp. *See* **rascal.**

scalding *adjective*
▶ blistering, boiling, burning. *See* **hot** (1).

scale¹ *noun*
1. A small, thin piece of something ▶ chip, sliver, shaving. *See* **flake** (1). **2.** Scaly pieces of dry shedded skin ▶ dander, dandruff, furfur, scurf. *See also* **flake.**

scale *verb*
1. To remove the skin of ▶ pare, strip. *See* **skin** (1). **2.** To come off in small, thin pieces ▶ chip, peel, shed. *See* **flake.**

scale² *verb*
To move upward along a surface or slope ▶ climb, go up, scramble. *See* **ascend** (1).

scale *noun*
A number of things placed or occurring one after the other ▶ order, procession, sequence. *See* **series.**

scalp *verb*
Slang To get money or something else from someone by deceitful trickery ▶ bilk, defraud. *See* **cheat** (1).

scam *verb*
Slang To get money or something else from someone by deceitful trickery ▶ bilk, defraud. *See* **cheat** (1).

scam *noun*
Slang An act of cheating ▶ deceit, hoax, swindle. *See* **cheat** (1).

scammer *noun*
Slang A person who cheats ▶ cheater, swindler, trickster. *See* **cheat** (2).

scamp *noun*
1. One who causes minor trouble or damage ▶ prank-

ster, rogue. *See* **rascal. 2.** A mischievous youngster ▸ brat, imp, whelp. *See* **urchin.**

scamper *verb*
▸ scurry, shin, sprint. *See* **run** (1).

scan *verb*
1. To view broadly or from a height ▸ look over, overlook, survey. *See also* **look. 2.** To look through reading matter casually ▸ flip through, leaf (through), skim. *See* **browse** (1).

scan *noun*
A quick look ▸ glimpse, peek. *See* **glance** (1).

scandal *noun*
1. The expression of injurious, malicious statements about someone ▸ defamation, denigration, slander. *See* **libel. 2.** Idle, often sensational and groundless talk about others ▸ hearsay, rumor, tattle. *See* **gossip** (1).

scandalize *verb*
▸ outrage, provoke, shock. *See* **offend** (1).

scandalmonger *noun*
▸ gossipmonger, taleteller, whisperer. *See* **gossip** (2).

scandalous *adjective*
1. Exceeding the bounds of morality, decency, or reason ▸ appalling, monstrous, shocking. *See* **outrageous. 2.** Damaging to the reputation ▸ defamatory, invidious, slanderous. *See* **libelous.**

scandalousness *noun*
▸ atrocity, heinousness, monstrousness. *See* **outrageousness.**

scant *adjective*
1. Just sufficient ▸ bare, mere, scanty. *See also* **insufficient. 2.** Conspicuously deficient in quantity, fullness, or extent ▸ puny, skimpy, sparse. *See* **meager** (1).

scantiness *or* **scantness** *noun*
▸ deficit, inadequacy, paucity. *See* **shortage.**

scanty *adjective*
1. Just sufficient ▸ bare, mere, scant. *See also* **insufficient. 2.** Conspicuously deficient in quantity, fullness, or extent ▸ spartan, skimpy, sparse. *See* **meager** (1).

scapegoat *noun*
One who is made an object of blame ▸ goat, whipping boy. *Slang:* fall guy, patsy. *See also* **dupe, victim.**

scapegoat *verb*
To find fault with ▸ fault, reprove. *Slang:* knock. *See* **criticize** (1).

scar *verb*
To alter and spoil the natural form or appearance of ▸ disfigure, misshape, twist. *See* **deform.**

scar *noun*
A disfiguring abnormality of shape or form ▸ contortion, disfigurement, malformation. *See* **deformity.**

scarce *adjective*
1. Not enough to meet a demand or requirement ▸ inadequate, wanting. *See* **insufficient** (1). **2.** Rarely occurring or appearing ▸ uncommon, unusual. *See* **infrequent.**

scarce *adverb*
By a very little; almost not ▸ barely, hardly, just, scarcely. *Idioms:* by a hair (*or* whisker), by the skin of one's teeth. *See also* **approximately, merely, only.**

scarcely *adverb*
By a very little; almost not ▸ barely, hardly, just, scarce. *Idioms:* by a hair (*or* whisker), by the skin of one's teeth. *See also* **approximately, merely, only.**

scarcity *or* **scarceness** *noun*
▸ deficit, inadequacy, paucity. *See* **shortage.**

scare *verb*
To fill with fear ▸ horrify, startle, terrify. *See* **frighten.** *See synonym note at* **frighten.**

scare up *verb*
To look for and discover ▸ find, locate, pinpoint, spot. *See also* **trace, uncover.**

scared *adjective*
▸ fearful, frightened, terrified. *See* **afraid.** *See synonym note at* **afraid.**

scaredy-cat *noun*
Informal An ignoble, uncourageous person ▸ dastard, poltroon, sissy. *See* **coward.**

scaremonger *noun*
One who needlessly alarms others ▸ alarmist, Chicken Little, panicmonger. *Idiom:* one who cries wolf. *See also* **pessimist.**

scarf *noun*
A long piece of cloth worn about the head, neck, or shoulders ▸ ascot, cravat, fichu, headscarf, kerchief, muffler, rebozo. *See also* **wrap.**

scarify[1] *verb*
1. To criticize harshly and devastatingly ▸ bash, excoriate, flay. *See* **slam** (5). **2.** To penetrate with a sharp edge ▸ bayonet, incise, pierce, slash. *See* **cut** (1).

scarify[2] *verb*
To fill with fear ▸ horrify, scare, terrify. *See* **frighten.**

scarlet woman *noun*
▸ courtesan, strumpet. *See* **harlot.**

scary *adjective*
▸ fearsome, formidable, frightening, redoubtable. *See* **fearful** (1).

scat *noun*
▸ dung, feces, waste. *See* **excrement.**

scathe *verb*
▸ bash, excoriate, flay. *See* **slam** (5).

scathing *adjective*
▸ caustic, mordant, sharp, vitriolic. *See* **biting.**

scatological *or* **scatologic** *adjective*
▸ bawdy, coarse, lewd, vulgar. *See* **obscene** (1).

scatology *noun*
▸ dirt, sleaze, smut. *See* **obscenity** (2).

scatter *verb*
1. To cause to separate and go in various directions ▸ dispel, disperse, dissipate. *See also* **divide, separate. 2.** To move apart and go in various directions ▸ break up, disband, disperse, move apart, separate, split up. *See also* **branch, divide. 3.** To extend over a wide area ▸ splay, stretch, unfurl. *See* **spread** (2). **4.** To put out of proper order ▸ disarrange, disrupt, muddle. *See* **disorder** (1). **5.** To disappear by or as if by rising ▸ dissipate, thin out, withdraw. *See* **lift** (4). **6.** To put seeds or young plants in soil ▸ broadcast, seed, sow. *See* **plant** (1).

✦ CORE SYNONYMS: *scatter, disperse, dissipate, dispel.* These verbs mean to cause a mass or aggregate to separate and go in various directions. *Scatter* refers to loose or haphazard distribution of components: *"the scattered driftwood, bleached and dry"* (Celia Laighton Thaxter). *Disperse* implies the complete breaking up of the mass or aggregate: *"only a few industrious Scots perhaps, who indeed are dispersed over the face of the whole earth"* (George Chapman). *Dissipate* suggests a reduction to nothing: *"The main of life is composed . . . of meteorous pleasures which dance before us and are dissipated"* (Samuel Johnson). *Dispel* suggests driving away or off by or as if by scattering: *"But he . . . with high words . . . gently raised/Their fainting courage, and dispelled their fears"* (John Milton).

scatterbrained *adjective*
1. Given to lighthearted silliness ▸ featherbrained, flighty, frivolous. *See* **giddy** (2). **2.** So lost in thought as to be forgetful ▸ bemused, inattentive, preoccupied. *See* **absent-minded.**

scattergood *noun*
▸ profligate, spendthrift. *See* **wastrel** (1).

scattering *noun*
1. The passing out or spreading about of something over a wide area ▸ circulation, dispersion, dissemination. *See* **distribution** (2). **2.** An act of reflection ▸ deflection, glance, reflection. *See also* **bounce.**

scenario *noun*
1. The text of a play, movie, opera, or similar work ▸ dialogue, screenplay, text. *See* **script** (2). **2.** The series of events and relationships forming the basis of a composition ▸ action, story line. *See* **plot** (1).

scene *noun*
1. The place where an action or event occurs ▸ backdrop, locale, setting, site, stage. *See also* **environment, locality. 2.** The properties, objects, and accessories arranged for a dramatic presentation ▸ backdrop, background, mise en scène, props, scenery, set, setting, staging. *See also* **stage. 3.** That which is or can be seen ▸ panorama, perspective, vista. *See* **view** (2). **4.** A sphere of activity, experience, study, or interest ▸ department, field, terrain. *See* **area** (1). **5.** A confused or emotional situation ▸ disturbance, tumult, uproar. *See* **agitation** (1). **6.** *Slang* Existing surroundings that affect an activity ▸ circumstances, context. *See* **conditions.**

scenery *noun*
1. The properties, objects, and accessories arranged for a dramatic presentation ▸ mise en scène, set, setting. *See* **scene** (2). **2.** That which is or can be seen ▸ panorama, perspective, vista. *See* **view** (2).

scent *noun*
1. The quality of something that may be perceived by the olfactory sense ▸ aroma, odor, smell. **2.** The sense by which odors are perceived ▸ nose, olfaction, smell. **3.** A sweet or pleasant odor ▸ aroma, perfume, redolence. *See* **fragrance.** *See synonym note at* **fragrance. 4.** A visible sign or mark of the passage of someone or something ▸ trace, trail. *See* **track** (1). **5.** An item of

advance or inside information given as a guide to action ▸ lead, pointer, steer. *See* **tip³** (1).

scent *verb*
1. To perceive with the olfactory sense ▸ sniff, whiff. *See* **smell** (1). **2.** To fill with a pleasant odor ▸ aromatize, perfume.

schedule *noun*
1. A series, as of names or words, printed or written down ▸ register, roll, roster. *See* **list¹. 2.** An organized list, as of procedures, activities, or events ▸ calendar, lineup, timetable. *See* **program** (1).

schedule *verb*
1. To enter on a schedule ▸ calendar, docket, program, slate. *See also* **list¹. 2.** To set the time for an event or occasion ▸ plan, set, time. **3.** To plan the details or arrangements of ▸ lay out, organize, work out. *See* **arrange** (2).

scheduled *adjective*
▸ expected, slated. *See* **due** (2).

schema *noun*
▸ course, modus operandi, procedure, technique. *See* **approach** (1).

scheme *noun*
1. A method used for accomplishing something ▸ course, modus operandi, procedure, technique. *See* **approach** (1). *See synonym note at* **approach. 2.** A secret plan to achieve an evil or illegal end ▸ collusion, conspiracy. *See* **plot** (2). **3.** Systematic arrangement and design ▸ order, organization, pattern. *See* **method** (1).

scheme *verb*
1. To work out a secret plan to achieve an evil or illegal end ▸ collude, conspire. *See* **plot** (2). **2.** To form a strategy for ▸ devise, formulate, strategize. *See* **design** (1).

schemed *adjective*
▸ deliberate, intentional, premeditated. *See* **calculated** (1).

scheming *adjective*
1. Coldly planning to achieve selfish aims ▸ calculating, conniving, designing, manipulative. **2.** Deceitfully clever ▸ cunning, sharp, sly, wily. *See* **artful** (1).

schism *noun*
1. An interruption in friendly relations ▸ break, estrangement, split. *See* **breach** (2). **2.** A state of disagreement and disharmony ▸ clash, difference, discord. *See* **conflict** (1). **3.** The condition of being divided, as in opinion ▸ divergence, split. *See* **division** (2).

schismatic *noun*
▸ dissident, sectarian. *See* **separatist.**

schlep *verb*
1. *Slang* To move while supporting ▸ bear, haul, lug. *See* **carry** (1). **2.** *Slang* To walk in a laborious way ▸ plod, tramp. *See* **trudge.**

schlep *noun*
Slang A large, ungainly, and dull-witted person ▸ lout, ox. *Informal:* lummox. *See* **oaf.**

schlocky *adjective*
Slang Of decidedly inferior quality ▶ cheap, lousy, poor. *See* **shoddy** (1).

schmaltz *or* **schmaltziness** *noun*
Informal The quality or condition of being affectedly or overly emotional ▶ bathos, treacle. *See* **sentimentality**.

schmaltzy *adjective*
Informal Affectedly or extravagantly emotional ▶ gushy, mawkish, soft. *See* **sentimental**.

schmo *noun*
1. *Slang* A person who is deficient in judgment and good sense ▶ jackass, ninny, simpleton. *See* **fool** (1). 2. *Slang* An unpleasant, tiresome person ▶ chump. *Slang:* pill, twit. *See* **drip** (2).

schmuck *noun*
1. *Slang* A person who is deficient in judgment and good sense ▶ idiot, imbecile, nitwit. *See* **fool** (1). 2. *Slang* An unpleasant, tiresome person ▶ chump. *Slang:* pill, twit. *See* **drip** (2).

schnoz *or* **schnozzle** *noun*
Slang The human organ of smell ▶ proboscis. *Informal:* beak. *See* **nose** (1).

scholar *noun*
1. A person noted for wisdom, knowledge, and judgment ▶ guru, savant. *See* **sage**. 2. One who is being educated ▶ apprentice, pupil. *See* **student**.

scholarly *adjective*
1. Devoted to study or reading ▶ bookish, studious. *See also* **intellectual**. 2. Showing evidence of schooling, training, or experience ▶ informed, lettered, literate. *See* **educated** (1). *See synonym note at* **educated**.

scholarship *noun*
▶ instruction, learning. *See* **education** (2).

scholastic *adjective*
1. Characterized by a narrow concern for book learning and formal rules ▶ bookish, literary, purist. *See* **pedantic**. *See synonym note at* **pedantic**. 2. Of or relating to education ▶ academic, instructional, teaching. *See* **educational** (1).

school *verb*
To impart knowledge and skill to ▶ discipline, instruct. *See* **educate** (1). *See synonym note at* **educate**.

school *noun*
1. A division of persons or things by quality or rank ▶ league, rank, tier. *See* **class** (2). 2. A number of animals considered collectively ▶ bevy, gaggle, herd. *See* **flock** (1). *See synonym note at* **flock**.

schooling *noun*
▶ pedagogy, training. *See* **education** (1).

schoolmaster *or* **schoolmistress** *noun*
▶ instructor, trainer, tutor. *See* **educator**.

schoolteacher *noun*
▶ instructor, trainer, tutor. *See* **educator**.

science *noun*
▶ instruction, learning. *See* **education** (2).

scilicet *adverb*
▶ specifically, videlicet. *See* **namely**.

scintillate *verb*
▶ flash, glimmer, twinkle. *See* **glitter**. *See synonym note at* **glitter**.

scintillating *adjective*
1. Exhibiting or employing wit or originality ▶ smart, witty. *See* **clever** (2). 2. Full of bright shifting or flickering light ▶ glinting, glittering, shimmering. *See* **sparkling** (1).

scintillation *noun*
1. Sparkling, brilliant light ▶ glisten, shimmer, sparkle. *See* **glitter** (1). 2. A sudden burst of light ▶ flicker, spark, twinkle. *See* **flash** (1).

scion *noun*
▶ child, offspring, seed. *See* **progeny**.

scissors *noun*
▶ clippers, cutters, pruner. *See* **shears**.

scoff *verb*
To subject to ridicule ▶ jeer (at), lampoon, taunt. *See* **ridicule**.

scoff *noun*
An instance of mockery or derision ▶ insult, jeer, twit. *See* **taunt** (1).

scoffing *adjective*
▶ satiric, sardonic, sneering. *See* **sarcastic**.

scofflaw *noun*
▶ culprit, lawbreaker, offender. *See* **criminal**.

scold *verb*
To criticize for a fault or offense ▶ chide, rebuke, reprimand. *See* **chastise** (1). *See synonym note at* **chastise**.

scold *noun*
A person, traditionally a woman, who persistently nags or criticizes ▶ fishwife, fury, harpy, harridan, nag, shrew, termagant, virago, vixen. *Informal:* battle-ax. *See also* **critic, grouch**.

scolding *noun*
▶ admonition, reprimand, reproof. *See* **rebuke**.

scoop *noun*
New information, especially about recent events and happenings ▶ intelligence, report. *See* **news** (1).

scoop *verb*
1. To break, turn over, or remove (earth or sand, for example) with or as if with a tool ▶ excavate, gouge, shovel. *See* **dig** (1). 2. To take a substance, as liquid, from a container by plunging the hand or a utensil into it ▶ bail, ladle, scoop up. *See* **dip** (2).

scoot *verb*
▶ dash, sprint, zip. *See* **rush** (1).

scope *noun*
1. The extent of one's perception, understanding, knowledge, or vision ▶ range, reach. *See* **ken**. 2. The ability or power to seize or attain ▶ capacity, compass, grasp, range, reach. *See also* **influence**. 3. Freedom from normal restraints, limitations, or regulations ▶ entitlement, latitude, leeway. *See* **license** (1). *See synonym note at* **license**. 4. An area or set of parameters within which something or someone exists, acts, or has influence ▶ circle, realm, territory. *See* **range** (1). *See synonym note at* **range**. 5. Relative intensity or

amount, as of a quality or attribute ▸ extent, level, magnitude. *See* **degree** (2).

scope out *verb*

Slang To examine carefully or critically ▸ inspect, survey, view. *See* **examine** (1).

scorch *verb*

1. To undergo or cause to undergo damage by or as if by fire ▸ sear, singe. *See* **burn** (1). *See synonym note at* **burn. 2.** To criticize harshly and devastatingly ▸ bash, excoriate, flay. *See* **slam** (5). **3.** To spoil or destroy ▸ corrode, dash. *See* **blast** (2).

scorch *noun*

Damage that results from burning ▸ blister, sear, singe. *See* **burn** (1).

scorched *adjective*

▸ desert, droughty, rainless. *See* **dry** (2).

scorching *adjective*

1. Marked by much heat ▸ blistering, boiling, burning. *See* **hot** (1). **2.** Fired with intense feeling ▸ burning, fervent, impassioned. *See* **passionate** (1). **3.** So sharp as to cause mental pain ▸ caustic, scathing, sharp, vitriolic. *See* **biting.**

score *noun*

1. A noting of items one by one ▸ numeration, tally. *See* **count** (1). **2.** An opening made with a sharp object ▸ groove, notch, slit. *See* **cut** (1). **3.** Something, such as money, owed by one person to another ▸ indebtedness, liability, obligation. *See* **debt** (1).

score *verb*

1. To gain a point or points in a game or contest ▸ post, tally. *Informal:* notch. *Idioms:* make a goal (*or* point). **2.** To evaluate and assign a grade to ▸ correct, grade, mark. **3.** To criticize harshly and devastatingly ▸ bash, excoriate, flay. *See* **slam** (5). **4.** To reach a goal or objective ▸ achieve, attain, gain. *See* **accomplish** (1). **5.** To form by artistic effort ▸ produce, write. *See* **compose** (1). **6.** To note items one by one in order to get a total ▸ numerate, tally. *See* **count** (2). **7.** *Slang* To do or fare well ▸ boom, flourish, thrive. *See* **prosper. 8.** *Slang* To acquire in exchange for money ▸ pay for, purchase. *See* **buy** (1).

scores *noun*

▸ horde, mass, throng. *See* **crowd** (1).

scorn *noun*

1. The feeling of despising ▸ disdain, loathing, revulsion. *See* **despisal. 2.** Loss of or damage to one's reputation ▸ discredit, disrepute, humiliation. *See* **disgrace.**

scorn *verb*

To regard with utter contempt and disdain ▸ disdain, dismiss. *See* **despise** (1). *See synonym note at* **depise.**

scornful *adjective*

1. Showing scorn and disrespect toward someone or something ▸ dismissive, haughty, sneering. *See* **disdainful** (1). **2.** Having or showing a lack of respect ▸ contemptuous, discourteous, impolite. *See* **disrespectful** (1).

Scotch *adjective*

▸ chary, frugal, thrifty. *See* **economical.**

scoundrel *noun*

1. One that performs evil acts ▸ miscreant, villain. *See* **evildoer. 2.** One who causes minor trouble or damage ▸ prankster, scamp. *See* **rascal.**

scour[1] *verb*

To remove an outer layer or something adherent from an object by friction ▸ rub away (off), scrape, scrub.

scour[2] *verb*

1. To search through or over thoroughly ▸ comb, forage, ransack, rummage, search. *Slang:* shake down. *Idioms:* beat the bushes, leave no stone unturned, look (*or* search) high and low, look (*or* search) up and down, turn inside out, turn upside down. *See also* **examine, explore, seek. 2.** To move swiftly ▸ dash, sprint, zip. *See* **rush** (1).

scourge *noun*

A cause of suffering or harm ▸ bane, sorrow. *See* **curse** (3).

scourge *verb*

1. To punish with blows or lashes ▸ lash, thrash, whip. *See* **beat** (2). **2.** To cause great pain or suffering to ▸ plague, rack, torment. *See* **afflict. 3.** To criticize harshly and devastatingly ▸ bash, excoriate, flay. *See* **slam** (5).

scout[1] *verb*

To go into or through for the purpose of making discoveries or acquiring information ▸ inquire, investigate, probe. *See* **explore.**

scout[2] *verb*

1. To regard with utter contempt and disdain ▸ disdain, scorn. *See* **despise** (1). *See synonym note at* **despise. 2.** To subject to ridicule ▸ jeer (at), lampoon, scout at, taunt. *See* **ridicule.**

scowl *verb*

1. To wrinkle one's brow, as in thought, puzzlement, or displeasure ▸ frown, glower, lower. *Idioms:* knit one's brow, look black, turn one's mouth down. *See synonym note at* **frown.** *See also* **grimace. 2.** To stare fixedly and angrily ▸ glare, glower, lower. *Idioms:* give the evil eye, look daggers. *See also* **gaze, sneer.**

scowl *noun*

1. The act of wrinkling the brow, as in displeasure ▸ black look, glower, lower. *See* **frown. 2.** A fixed angry stare ▸ glare, glower, lower. *See also* **face, sneer.**

scrabble *verb*

▸ fumble, grabble. *See* **grope.**

scraggy *adjective*

▸ coarse, jagged, scabrous. *See* **rough** (1).

scram *verb*

Slang To leave hastily ▸ bolt. *Slang:* hightail, vamoose. *See* **run** (3).

scramble *verb*

1. To move upward along a surface or slope ▸ clamber, mount, scale. *See* **ascend** (1). **2.** To put into total disorder ▸ garble, jumble, mess up. *See* **confuse** (4). **3.** To mix together so as to change the order of arrangement ▸ rearrange, reconfigure, reorder. *See* **shuffle** (1).

scramble *noun*
A lack of order or regular arrangement ► clutter, confusion, disarray. *See* **disorder** (1).

scrap¹ *noun*
1. A tiny amount ► dash, drop, smidgen. *See* **bit¹** (1). **2.** A small portion of food ► crumb, morsel, tidbit. *See* **bit¹** (2). **3.** Residual matter ► fragment, odds and ends, shard. *See* **end** (7).

scrap *verb*
1. To let go or get rid of as being useless or defective, for example ► dump, throw away. *Informal:* chuck. *See* **discard**. **2.** *Slang* To decide not to continue ► call off, cancel. *Slang:* scratch, scrub. *See also* **defer, drop.**

scrap² *noun*
A physical conflict involving two or more people ► free-for-all, melee. *See* **fight** (1).

scrape *verb*
1. To remove an outer layer or something adherent from an object by friction ► rub away (off), scour, scrub. **2.** To bring or come into abrasive contact, often with a harsh sound ► abrade, file, grate, rasp, scratch. *See also* **chafe**. **3.** To be severely sparing in order to economize ► pinch, skimp, stint. *See* **scrimp.**

scrape *noun*
1. A mark or shallow cut made by contact with an object ► abrasion, scratch, scuff, striation. *See also* **cut, furrow, impression**. **2.** A difficult, often embarrassing situation or condition ► corner, difficulty, fix. *See* **predicament**.

scrappy *adjective*
1. Given to arguing ► contentious, quarrelsome. *See* **argumentative**. *See synonym note at* **argumentative**. **2.** Inclined to act in an aggressive or hostile way ► combative, pugnacious. *See* **aggressive** (1).

scratch *verb*
1. To bring or come into abrasive contact ► grate, rasp. *See* **scrape** (2). **2.** To cross out or remove ► delete, erase, strike (out). *See* **cancel** (1). **3.** *Slang* To decide not to continue ► call off, cancel. *Slang:* scrap, scrub. *See also* **defer, drop.**

scratch *noun*
1. A mark or shallow cut made by contact with an object ► abrasion, scrape, scuff, striation. *See also* **cut, furrow, impression**. **2.** *Slang* Something, such as coins or printed bills, used as a medium of exchange ► currency. *Slang:* dough, moola. *See* **money** (1).

scratchy *adjective*
1. Disagreeable to the senses, especially the sense of hearing ► grating, jarring. *See* **harsh** (1). **2.** Having a surface that is not smooth ► coarse, ragged, scabrous. *See* **rough** (1).

scrawny *adjective*
► lean, skinny, slim. *See* **thin** (1). *See synonym note at* **thin**.

screak *noun*
A long, loud, piercing cry, as of fright ► scream, screech, shriek. *See also* **howl**.

screak *verb*
To utter a long, loud, piercing cry, as of fright

► scream, screech, shriek, shrill. *See also* **howl**.

scream *verb*
1. To utter a long loud piercing cry, as in fright ► screak, screech, shriek, shrill. *See also* **howl**. **2.** To speak or say in a loud cry ► call, holler, yell. *See* **shout**.

scream *noun*
1. A long loud piercing cry, as of fright ► screak, screech, shriek. *See also* **howl**. **2.** A loud call or cry ► call, holler, yell. *See* **shout**. **3.** *Informal* Something or someone uproariously funny or absurd ► absurdity. *Informal:* hoot, joke, laugh. *Slang:* gas, howl, panic, riot. *Idiom:* a laugh a minute. *See also* **foolishness**.

screech *noun*
1. A long, loud, piercing cry, as of fright ► screak, scream, shriek. *See also* **howl**. **2.** A loud call or cry ► call, holler, yell. *See* **shout**.

screech *verb*
1. To utter a long loud piercing cry, as in fright ► screak, scream, shriek, shrill. *See also* **howl**. **2.** To speak or say in a loud cry ► call, holler, yell. *See* **shout**.

screed *noun*
► diatribe, harangue. *See* **tirade**.

screen *verb*
1. To cut off from sight ► curtain, hide, shroud. *See* **block** (1). *See synonym note at* **block**. **2.** To prevent something from being known ► cover up, enshroud, mask. *See* **conceal** (1). **3.** To shelter, especially from light ► shade, shadow. **4.** To remove improper material from a publication ► bowdlerize, edit, expurgate. *See* **censor** (1).

screen *noun*
1. Something that physically protects, especially from danger ► harbor, haven, refuge. *See* **cover** (1). **2.** A covering that obscures or hides something ► cloak, mantle. *See* **veil** (1).

screened *adjective*
Concealed from view ► blind, hidden, secluded, secret. *Idioms:* out of sight, out of view. *See also* **hidden**.

screenplay *noun*
► book, dialogue, scenario. *See* **script** (2).

screw *verb*
To make secure ► bind, chain, moor. *See* **fasten** (1).

screw around *or* **off** *verb*
Slang To waste time by engaging in aimless activity ► dawdle (about), fiddle (around). *See* **putter**.

screw up *verb*
1. *Slang* To ruin through clumsiness or ineptness ► blunder, foul up, spoil. *See* **botch**. **2.** To make an error or mistake ► blunder, stumble. *See* **err** (1).

screw *noun*
A shaft hammered or drilled in place, used to hold together ► pin, spike, stud. *See* **nail**.

screwball *noun*
Slang A person regarded as strange, eccentric, or crazy ► lunatic. *Informal:* loony. *Slang:* nut, weirdo. *See* **crackpot**.

screwball *adjective*
Slang Deviating from what is conventional or cus-

tomary ▸ bizarre, quirky, strange. *See* **eccentric.**

screwup *noun*
1. *Slang* A clumsy, inept person ▸ bungler. *Slang:* klutz. *See* **blunderer. 2.** *Slang* A confused or ruinous state ▸ foul-up, muddle, shambles. *See* **mess** (1).

screwy *adjective*
Slang Afflicted with or exhibiting irrationality and mental unsoundness ▸ crazy, lunatic, mad. *See* **insane** (1).

scribble *verb*
▸ indite, pen, scribe. *See* **write** (1).

scrimp *verb*
To be frugal or sparing ▸ conserve, economize, pinch, save, scrape, skimp, spare, stint. *Idioms:* pinch pennies, tighten one's belt.

scrimpy *adjective*
▸ puny, scant, skimpy. *See* **meager** (1).

script *noun*
1. Writing done with the hand ▸ calligraphy, cursive, handwriting, longhand, penmanship. **2.** The text of a play, movie, opera, or similar work ▸ book, dialogue, libretto, manuscript, play, screenplay, scenario.

scriptural *adjective*
Of or relating to representation by means of writing ▸ calligraphic, graphic, written.

Scrooge *noun*
▸ churl, skinflint. *Informal:* penny pincher. *See* **miser.**

scrounge *verb*
Slang To ask for as charity ▸ *Informal:* panhandle. *Slang:* mooch. *See* **beg** (1).

scrub *verb*
1. To remove an outer layer or something adherent from an object by friction ▸ rub away (*or* off), scour, scrape. **2.** *Slang* To decide not to continue ▸ call off, cancel. *Slang:* scrap, scratch. *See also* **defer, drop.**

scrub *noun*
1. A totally insignificant person ▸ no-account, nobody, nothing. *See* **nonentity. 2.** *Informal* A small or young person ▸ pip-squeak, runt, small fry. *See* **squirt** (2).

scrubby *adjective*
▸ broken-down, dilapidated, tattered. *See* **shabby** (1).

scruffy *adjective*
▸ mangy, ragged, seedy. *See* **shabby** (1).

scrumptious *adjective*
▸ delectable, savory, tasteful. *See* **delicious** (1). *See synonym note at* **delicious.**

scrunch *verb*
▸ bend, crouch, hunch. *See* **stoop** (1).

scruple *noun*
1. A feeling of uncertainty about the fitness or correctness of an action ▸ misgiving, reservation, worry. *See* **qualm** (1). *See synonym note at* **qualm. 2.** A tiny amount ▸ dash, drop, smidgen. *See* **bit**[1] (1).

scrupulous *adjective*
1. Marked by attentiveness to every detail ▸ fastidious, meticulous, painstaking. *See* **careful** (2). *See synonym note at* **careful. 2.** In accordance with principles of

right or good conduct ▸ principled, virtuous. *See* **ethical.**

scrupulousness *noun*
▸ fastidiousness, meticulousness, painstaking. *See* **thoroughness.**

scrutinize *verb*
1. To look at or study carefully or critically ▸ investigate, peruse, survey. *See* **examine** (1). **2.** To look at or on attentively or carefully ▸ eye, observe, regard. *See* **watch** (1).

scrutiny *noun*
1. The act of observing, often for an extended time ▸ observance, observation, watch, watching. **2.** The act of examining carefully or critically ▸ analysis, inquiry, study. *See* **examination** (1).

scuff *verb*
1. To walk in a laborious way ▸ scuffle, shamble, shuffle. *See* **trudge. 2.** To injure or damage, as by abuse or heavy wear ▸ bang up, maul, rough up. *See* **batter** (1).

scuff *noun*
A mark or shallow cut made by contact with an object ▸ abrasion, scrape, scratch, striation. *See also* **cut, furrow, impression.**

scuffle *verb*
1. To strive in opposition ▸ grapple, tussle, wrestle. *See* **contend** (1). **2.** To walk in a laborious way ▸ scuff, shamble, shuffle. *See* **trudge.**

scuffle *noun*
A physical conflict between two or more people ▸ free-for-all, melee. *See* **fight** (1). *See synonym note at* **fight.**

scullion *noun*
▸ grunt, hack, menial. *See* **drudge** (1).

sculpt *verb*
▸ model, mold, shape. *See* **form** (1).

sculpture *noun*
A work of art created by shaping a solid material ▸ bust, carving, cast, figure, figurine, relief, statue, statuette. *See also* **form.**

scum *noun*
Slang A person or group of persons regarded as worthless or contemptible ▸ dregs, rabble, ragtag and bobtail. *See* **riffraff.**

scurf *noun*
Scaly pieces of dry shedded skin ▸ dander, dandruff, furfur, scale. *See also* **flake.**

scurrility *or* **scurrilousness** *noun*
1. The quality or state of being obscene ▸ filthiness, profanity, smuttiness, vulgarness. *See* **obscenity** (1). **2.** Sustained, harshly abusive language ▸ denunciation, invective. *See* **vituperation.**

scurrilous *adjective*
1. Of, relating to, or characterized by verbal abuse ▸ contumelious, invective, vituperative. *See* **abusive. 2.** Offensive to accepted standards of decency ▸ bawdy, coarse, lewd, vulgar. *See* **obscene** (1).

scurry *verb*
▸ scamper, shin. *See* **run** (1).

scuttle *verb*
▶ scurry, sprint. *See* **run** (1).

scuttlebutt *noun*
Slang Idle, often sensational and groundless talk about others ▶ hearsay, rumor, tattle. *See* **gossip** (1).

scythe *verb*
▶ chop, prune, trim. *See* **cut** (3).

sea *noun*
A body of salt water covering a large part of the earth's surface ▶ brine, deep, main. *See* **ocean.**

sea *adjective*
Of or relating to the seas or oceans ▶ oceanic, thalassic. *See* **marine** (1).

sea dog *noun*
▶ mariner, navigator. *See* **sailor.**

seafarer *noun*
▶ navigator, seaman. *See* **sailor.**

seal *verb*
1. To move a door, for example, in order to cover an opening ▶ close, clench, shut, slam. **2.** To plug up or block something, such as a hole or conduit ▶ clog, cork. *See* **fill** (2).

seam *noun*
▶ coupling, juncture. *See* **joint** (1).

seaman *noun*
▶ mariner, navigator, seafarer. *See* **sailor.**

seamy *adjective*
▶ ignoble, squalid, vile. *See* **sordid.**

sear *verb*
1. To undergo or cause to undergo damage by or as if by fire ▶ scorch, singe. *See* **burn** (1). *See synonym note at* **burn. 2.** To make or become no longer fresh or shapely because of loss of moisture ▶ mummify, shrivel, wither. *See* **dry** (1). **3.** To cook by sudden application of intense dry heat ▶ broil, brown, pan-fry, parboil. *See* **cook** (1).

sear *noun*
Damage that results from burning ▶ blister, singe. *See* **burn** (1).

search *verb*
1. To look through or over thoroughly ▶ comb, forage, rummage. *See* **scour**² (1). **2.** To examine a person or someone's personal effects in order to find something lost or concealed ▶ frisk, inspect, pat down. *Slang:* shake down. **Idiom:** do a body search of.

search for *verb*
To try to find something ▶ cast about, look for. *See* **seek** (1).

search *noun*
1. A thorough search of a place or persons ▶ body search, frisk, patdown. *Slang:* shakedown. **2.** An attempt to accomplish or attain ▶ hunt, quest. *See* **pursuit** (2). **3.** The act of examining carefully or critically ▶ inquiry, perusal, study. *See* **examination** (1).

searing *adjective*
1. Marked by much heat ▶ blistering, boiling, burning. *See* **hot** (1). **2.** So sharp as to cause mental pain ▶ caustic, scathing, sharp, vitriolic. *See* **biting.**

season *noun*
A specific length of time characterized by the occurrence of certain conditions or events ▶ span, stretch, term. *See* **period** (1).

season *verb*
1. To impart flavor to ▶ flavor, spice (up), zest. **2.** To make resistant to hardship, especially through continued exposure ▶ indurate, toughen. *See* **harden** (1). *See synonym note at* **harden.**

seasonable *adjective*
▶ favorable, propitious, well-timed. *See* **opportune.**

seasonal *adjective*
▶ migrational, transient, transmigratory. *See* **migratory** (1).

seasoned *adjective*
1. Skilled or knowledgeable through long practice ▶ practiced, versed. *See* **experienced. 2.** Having a sharp, penetrating flavor or aroma ▶ piquant, sharp, zesty. *See* **spicy** (1).

seasoning *or* **seasoner** *noun*
▶ condiment, flavor, spice. *See* **flavoring.**

seat *noun*
1. The lowest or supporting part or structure ▶ bottom, foot, foundation. *See* **base**¹ (2). **2.** A place of concentrated activity, influence, or importance ▶ headquarters, heart, hub. *See* **center** (1). *See synonym note at* **center. 3.** The part of the body on which one sits ▶ posterior, rump. *Slang:* fanny. *See* **buttocks.**

seat *verb*
To place securely in a position or condition ▶ fix, invest. *See* **establish** (2).

sec *noun*
Informal A very brief interval of time ▶ instant, second, wink. *See* **flash** (2).

secede *verb*
1. To break away or withdraw from an association or federation ▶ break away, pull out, splinter (off), withdraw. *Informal:* split (away). *See also* **quit. 2.** To abandon one's cause or party usually to join another ▶ desert, quit, turn. *See* **defect.**

secession *noun*
▶ abandonment, disavowal, renunciation. *See* **defection.**

seclude *verb*
1. To put into solitude ▶ cloister, isolate, sequester, sequestrate. *See also* **enclose, imprison. 2.** To set apart from a group ▶ close off, cut off, set apart. *See* **isolate** (1). *See synonym note at* **isolate.**

secluded *adjective*
1. Far from centers of human population ▶ isolated, lonely, outlying. *See* **remote** (1). **2.** Concealed from view ▶ blind, hidden, screened, secret. *Idioms:* out of sight, out of view. *See also* **hidden.**

seclusion *noun*
1. The act of secluding or the state of being secluded ▶ isolation, reclusion, retirement, separateness, sequestration. **2.** The quality or state of being alone ▶ isolation, loneliness. *See* **solitude.** *See synonym note at* **solitude.**

second¹ *noun*

A very brief interval of time ▸ instant, minute, wink. *See* **flash** (2). *See synonym note at* **flash**.

second² *noun*

1. One exactly resembling another ▸ clone, spitting image, twin. *See* **double** (1). **2.** A person who assists someone else, especially a person who assumes some of the duties of a superior ▸ aide, deputy, helper. *See* **assistant**. *See synonym note at* **assistant**.

secondary *adjective*

1. Below another in standing, importance, or status ▸ junior, low, subaltern. *See* **minor** (1). **2.** Used or held in reserve ▸ reserve, standby, supplemental. *See* **auxiliary** (2). **3.** Stemming from an original source ▸ derivational, derivative, derived.

secondary *noun*

One belonging to a lower class or rank ▸ inferior, junior. *See* **subordinate**.

second-class *adjective*

1. Of low or lower quality ▸ common, inferior. *See* **bad** (1). **2.** Below another in standing, importance, or status ▸ junior, low. *See* **minor** (1).

second fiddle *noun*

▸ inferior, junior, secondary. *See* **subordinate**.

secondhand *adjective*

▸ hand-me-down, pre-owned. *See* **used** (2).

second-rate *adjective*

▸ common, inferior, low-grade. *See* **bad** (1).

secrecy *noun*

The habit, practice, or policy of keeping secrets ▸ clandestineness, clandestinity, concealment, covertness, huggermugger, huggermuggery, secretiveness, secretness. *See also* **stealth**.

secret *adjective*

1. Operating in a way so as to ensure concealment and confidentiality ▸ backstairs, clandestine, cloak-and-dagger, covert, huggermugger, sub-rosa, undercover. *Informal:* hush-hush. *Idiom:* under wraps. *See also* **artful**. **2.** Known about by very few ▸ inside, private. *See* **confidential** (1). **3.** Difficult or impossible to see or distinguish ▸ covert, disguised, unseen. *See* **hidden** (1). **4.** Concealed from view ▸ blind, hidden, screened, secluded. *Idioms:* out of sight, out of view. *See also* **hidden**.

secret *noun*

A means or method of entering into or achieving something desirable ▸ formula, key, route. *Informal:* ticket. *See also* **trick**.

✚ **CORE SYNONYMS:** *secret, stealthy, covert, clandestine, furtive, surreptitious, underhand.* These adjectives mean operating or designed so as to ensure concealment and confidentiality. *Secret* is the most general: *a desk with a secret compartment; secret negotiations. Stealthy* suggests quiet, cautious deceptiveness intended to escape notice: *heard stealthy footsteps on the stairs. Covert* describes something that is concealed or disguised: *protested covert actions undertaken by the CIA. Clandestine* implies stealth and secrecy for the concealment of an often illegal or improper purpose:

clandestine intelligence operations. Furtive suggests the slyness, shiftiness, and evasiveness of a thief: *a menacing and furtive look to his eye.* Something *surreptitious* is stealthy, furtive, and often unseemly or unethical: *the surreptitious mobilization of troops preparing for a sneak attack. Underhand* implies unfairness, deceit, or slyness as well as secrecy: *achieved success by underhand methods.*

---

secrete *verb*

▸ bury, cache, conceal. *See* **hide¹** (1). *See synonym note at* **hide¹**.

secretive *adjective*

▸ furtive, slinky, sneaky. *See* **stealthy**.

secretiveness *noun*

1. The habit, practice, or policy of keeping secrets ▸ concealment, huggermuggery. *See* **secrecy**. **2.** The act of proceeding slowly so as to escape observation ▸ sneakiness, slyness. *See* **stealth**.

secretly *adverb*

In a secret way ▸ clandestinely, covertly, huggermugger, sub rosa. *Idioms:* behind closed doors, by stealth, on the q.t., on the sly, under cover.

secretness *noun*

The habit, practice, or policy of keeping secrets ▸ concealment, secretiveness. *See* **secrecy**.

sect *noun*

▸ creed, denomination. *See* **religion**.

sectarian *noun*

▸ dissident, heretic. *See* **separatist**.

sectary *noun*

1. One zealously devoted to a religion ▸ fanatic, zealot. *See* **devotee** (1). **2.** A person who dissents from the doctrine of an established church ▸ dissident, sectarian. *See* **separatist**.

section *noun*

1. A separate unit that belongs or contributes to a whole ▸ building block, piece, segment. *See* **part** (1). **2.** A particular subdivision of a written work ▸ chapter, part, passage, segment. **3.** A part of the earth's surface ▸ district, locality, quarter. *See* **area** (2). **4.** An administrative unit, as of a government or company ▸ agency, bureau. *See* **branch** (3).

section *verb*

To break or separate into parts or sections ▸ break up, dissever, split up. *See* **divide** (1).

sectional *adjective*

Relating to or restricted to a particular territory ▸ regional, territorial. *See also* **local**.

sector *noun*

1. A part of the earth's surface ▸ district, locality. *See* **area** (2). **2.** A separate unit that belongs or contributes to a whole ▸ piece, section. *See* **part** (1).

secular *adjective*

1. Relating to or characteristic of the earth or of human life on earth ▸ terrestrial, worldly. *See* **earthly** (1). **2.** Not religious in subject matter, form, or use ▸ nonecclesiastical, temporal, worldly. *See* **profane** (2).

secure *adjective*

1. Affording protection ▸ impenetrable, invulnerable,

unconquerable. *See* **safe** (2). **2.** Having a firm belief in one's own powers ▸ assured, self-confident, self-possessed. *See* **confident** (1). **3.** Not easily moved or shaken ▸ solid, stable, sure. *See* **firm**[1] (2). **4.** Persistently holding to something ▸ clinging, tenacious. *See* **tight** (1). **5.** Certain not to fail ▸ foolproof, infallible, unerring. *See* **sure** (2).

secure *verb*

1. To keep safe from danger, attack, or harm ▸ protect, safeguard, shield. *See* **defend** (1). **2.** To maintain or keep in order with or as if with police ▸ monitor, patrol. *See* **police** (1). **3.** To make secure ▸ anchor, fix, moor. *See* **fasten** (1). *See synonym note at* **fasten. 4.** To join one thing to another ▸ affix, append, moor. *See* **attach** (1). **5.** To make fast or firmly fixed, as by means of a cord or rope ▸ bind, fasten, knot, tie, tie up. **6.** To render certain ▸ ensure, warrant. *See* **guarantee** (2). **7.** To come into possession of ▸ come by, gain, procure. *See* **get** (1). **8.** To obtain control of after a struggle ▸ catch, net, take. *See* **capture** (1). **9.** To be the cause of ▸ generate, induce, trigger. *See* **cause.**

security *noun*

1. The quality or state of being safe ▸ impenetrability, safeness. *See* **safety** (1). **2.** Reliability in withstanding pressure, force, or stress ▸ firmness, hardness, steadiness. *See* **stability. 3.** The act or a means of defending ▸ protection, safeguard, shield. *See* **defense** (1). **4.** Something given to guarantee the repayment of a loan or the fulfillment of an obligation ▸ collateral, token, warrant. *See* **pawn**[1]. **5.** A partial or initial payment ▸ deposit, down payment, installment.

sedate[1] *adjective*

Characterized by careful thought and a lack of frivolity or exaggeration ▸ earnest, sober, solemn. *See* **serious** (1). *See synonym note at* **serious.**

sedate[2] *verb*

To administer especially a painkilling drug to someone ▸ dose, medicate, narcotize, tranquilize. *See* **drug** (1).

sedateness *noun*

▸ graveness, sobriety, solemnity. *See* **seriousness** (1).

sedative *adjective*

Inducing sleep or sedation ▸ opiate, sleepy, slumberous. *See* **soporific** (1).

sedative *noun*

1. Something that induces sleep or sedation ▸ narcotic, tranquilizer. *See* **soporific. 2.** A substance that affects the central nervous system and is often addictive ▸ narcotic, opiate, psychotropic. *See* **drug** (2).

sediment *noun*

▸ accumulation, dregs, precipitation. *See* **deposit** (2).

sedimentary *adjective*

▸ muddy, roiled, turbid. *See* **murky** (1).

sedition *noun*

1. Willful violation of allegiance to one's country ▸ lese majesty, seditiousness, traitorousness, treason. *See also* **faithlessness. 2.** Organized opposition intended to change or overthrow existing authority ▸ mutiny, revolt. *See* **rebellion** (1).

seditious *adjective*

Involving or constituting treason ▸ traitorous, treasonable, treasonous. *See also* **faithless.**

seditiousness *noun*

Willful violation of allegiance to one's country ▸ lese majesty, sedition, traitorousness, treason. *See also* **faithlessness.**

seduce *verb*

To beguile or lure into a wrong or foolish course of action, especially a sexual act ▸ allure, entice, inveigle, lure, tempt. *Idiom:* lead astray. *See also* **charm, corrupt, flirt, philander.**

✤ **CORE SYNONYMS:** *seduce, lure, entice, inveigle, tempt.* These verbs mean to lead or attempt to lead into a wrong or foolish course. To *seduce* is to entice away and usually suggests the overcoming of moral resistance: *"The French King attempted by splendid offers to seduce him from the cause of the Republic"* (Thomas Macaulay). *Lure* suggests the use of something that attracts like bait: *Industry often lures scientists from universities by offering them huge salaries.* To *entice* is to draw on skillfully, as by arousing hopes or desires: *The teacher tried to entice the shy child into entering the classroom. Inveigle* implies winning over by coaxing, flattery, or artful talk: *He inveigled a friend into becoming his law partner. Tempt* implies an encouragement or an attraction to do something, especially something immoral, unwise, or contrary to one's better judgment: *I am tempted to tell him what I really think of him.*

---

seducer *noun*

1. A person who beguiles or seduces ▸ allurer, beguiler, charmer, enticer, inveigler, lurer, tempter. **2.** A man who seduces women ▸ debaucher, Don Juan, Lothario. *See also* **flirt, lecher, philanderer.**

seduction *noun*

▸ bait, draw, enticement. *See* **lure** (1).

seductive *adjective*

Tending to seduce ▸ alluring, beguiling, bewitching, come-hither, enthralling, enticing, entrancing, inviting, luring, sexy, siren, tantalizing, tempting, witching. *See also* **attractive, beautiful.**

seductress *noun*

A woman who seduces or exploits men ▸ enchantress, femme fatale, siren, temptress. *Informal:* vamp, witch. *See also* **flirt.**

sedulous *adjective*

▸ assiduous, industrious, studious. *See* **diligent.** *See synonym note at* **diligent.**

sedulousness *noun*

▸ assiduousness, perseverance, pertinacity. *See* **diligence.**

see *verb*

1. To perceive with the eyes ▸ behold, catch, descry, detect, discern, espy, perceive, spot, spy. *Idioms:* cast one's eyes on, catch sight of, get a load of, get a look at, lay (*or* clap) eyes on. *See also* **glimpse, look. 2.** To perceive with a special effort of the senses or the mind ▸ detect, mark. *See* **notice. 3.** To look at or on attentively or carefully ▸ eye, observe, regard. *See* **watch** (1). **4.** To form mental images of ▸ envision, fantasize, visualize. *See* **imagine** (1). **5.** To perceive and recognize the meaning of ▸ apprehend, fathom, sense. *See* **understand** (1). **6.** To look upon in a particular way ▸ consider, deem, view. *See* **regard** (1). **7.** To know in advance ▸ anticipate, envision, foreknow. *See* **foresee**. **8.** To participate in or partake of personally ▸ know, undergo. *See* **experience**. **9.** To be with another person socially on a regular basis ▸ date, go out (with), go with. *Informal:* take out. *Idioms:* go steady, go together. **10.** To go to or seek out the company of someone in order to socialize ▸ come over, look up. *See* **visit** (1). **11.** To find or meet by chance ▸ come across, run across, stumble on. *See* **encounter** (1).

see through *verb*
To bring to an end ▸ close, complete, finish. *See* **conclude** (1).

see to *verb*
To have the care and supervision of ▸ look after, mind, watch over. *See* **tend²** (1).

✦ **CORE SYNONYMS:** *see, behold, descry, espy, perceive, discern.* These verbs refer to being or becoming visually aware of something. *See,* the most general, can mean merely to use the faculty of sight but more often implies recognition, understanding, or appreciation: *"If I have seen further (than . . . Descartes) it is by standing upon the shoulders of Giants"* (Isaac Newton). *Behold* implies gazing at or looking intently upon what is seen: *"My heart leaps up when I behold/A rainbow in the sky"* (William Wordsworth). *Descry* and *espy* both stress acuteness of sight that permits the detection of something distant or obscure: *"the lighthouse, which can be descried from a distance"* (Michael Strauss). *"espied the misspelled Latin word in* [the] *letter"* (Los Angeles Times). *Perceive* and *discern* both imply not only visual recognition but also mental comprehension; *perceive* is especially associated with insight, and *discern,* with the ability to distinguish, discriminate, and make judgments: *"I plainly perceive* [that] *some objections remain"* (Edmund Burke). *"Your sense of humor would discern the hollowness beneath all the pomp and ceremony"* (Edna Ferber).

---

seeable *adjective*
▸ observable, perceivable, viewable. *See* **visible** (1).

seed *noun*
1. A fertilized plant ovule capable of germinating ▸ grain, kernel, pip, pit. **2.** A source of further growth and development ▸ kernel, nucleus. *See* **germ** (2). **3.** A person or group descended directly from the same parents or ancestors ▸ offspring, issue, posterity. *See* **progeny**. **4.** One's ancestors or ancestral derivation ▸ blood, extraction, lineage. *See* **ancestry**.

seed *verb*
To put seeds or young plants in soil ▸ broadcast, scatter, sow. *See* **plant** (1).

seedtime *noun*
The season of the year during which the weather becomes warmer and plants revive ▸ spring, springtide, springtime.

seedy *adjective*
▸ broken-down, dilapidated, tatty. *See* **shabby** (1).

seeing *noun*
The faculty of seeing ▸ optics, sight. *See* **vision** (1).

seeing *adjective*
Serving, resulting from, or relating to the sense of sight ▸ ocular, optic, optical, visual.

seek *verb*
1. To try to find something ▸ cast about (*or* around), ferret (around), fish for, hunt for, look for, search for, sniff about (*or* around). *See also* **pursue, scour²**. **2.** To strive toward a goal ▸ aspire, seek. *Idioms:* go (*or* grab) for the brass ring, keep one's eyes on the prize, set one's sights on. **3.** To make an earnest or urgent request ▸ ask (for), plead, seek. *See* **appeal** (1). **4.** To make an attempt ▸ endeavor, strive. *See* **attempt**.

seeker *noun*
1. A person who applies for or seeks something, such as a job or position ▸ candidate, hopeful, petitioner. *See* **applicant**. **2.** One who aspires ▸ aspirant, aspirer, dreamer, hopeful. *Informal:* wannabe.

seem *verb*
To give the impression of being ▸ appear, feel, look, sound. *Idioms:* have all the earmarks of being, give the idea (*or* impression) of being, strike one as being. *See also* **resemble**.

seeming *adjective*
Appearing as such but not necessarily so ▸ ostensible, outward. *See* **apparent** (2).

seemingly *adverb*
▸ evidently, externally, seemingly. *See* **apparently**.

seemliness *noun*
▸ decorum, respectability. *See* **decency** (2).

seemly *adjective*
▸ befitting, correct, right. *See* **appropriate** (1).

seep *verb*
▸ exude, leach. *See* **ooze**.

seer *noun*
1. Someone who sees something occur ▸ audience, eyewitness, viewer, witness. **2.** A person who foretells future events by or as if by supernatural means ▸ diviner, fortuneteller, soothsayer. *See* **prophet**.

seesaw *verb*
▸ pitch, roll, yaw. *See* **lurch** (1).

seethe *verb*
1. To be in a state of turmoil or excitement ▸ burn, froth. *See* **boil** (2). **2.** To be or become angry ▸ burn, fume, rage. *See* **anger** (2).

see-through *adjective*
▸ crystalline, limpid, lucid. *See* **clear** (1).

segment *noun*
1. A separate unit that belongs or contributes to a whole ▸ building block, piece, section. *See* **part** (1). **2.** A particular subdivision of a written work ▸ chapter, part, passage, section.

segment *verb*
To break or separate into parts or sections ▸ disjoin,

dissever, separate, split up. *See* **divide** (1).

segmentation *noun*
▶ disjunction, divorce, parting, severance. *See* **division** (1).

segregate *verb*
▶ close off, seclude, sequester. *See* **isolate** (1). *See synonym note at* **isolate**.

segregation *noun*
▶ separation, sequestration. *See* **isolation** (1).

seism *noun*
A shaking of the earth ▶ earthquake, quake, temblor, tremor. *Informal:* shake.

seize *verb*
1. To lay claim to or take possession of ▶ appropriate, arrogate, assume, commandeer, confiscate, expropriate, grab, hijack, impound, preempt, take, snatch, usurp. *Idiom:* help oneself to. *See also* **steal**. 2. To take firmly with the hand and maintain a hold on ▶ clench, clutch, grip. *See* **grasp** (1). 3. To get hold of something moving ▶ grab, snatch. *See* **catch** (2). 4. To take into custody as a prisoner ▶ apprehend. *Informal:* pick up. *See* **arrest** (1). 5. To seize or maintain control over by conquest ▶ capture, overrun, subjugate. *See* **occupy** (2). 6. To have a sudden overwhelming effect on ▶ catch, strike, take. *See also* **move**.

✦ CORE SYNONYMS: *seize, appropriate, arrogate, commandeer, confiscate, preempt, usurp.* These verbs mean to lay claim to or take possession of something: *seized hidden contraband; appropriated the family car; arrogated the chair at the head of the table; commandeered a plane for the escape; confiscating stolen property; preempted the glory for themselves; usurped the throne.*

---

seizure *noun*
1. A sudden and often acute manifestation of a disease ▶ apoplexy, attack, convulsion, fit, paroxysm. *Informal:* spell. 2. The act of taking possession of something ▶ appropriation, arrogation, assumption, commandeering, confiscation, expropriation, grab, hijacking, impoundment, preemption, seizing, snatch, taking, usurpation. *See also* **larceny**. 3. The act of catching ▶ capture, snatch. *See* **catch** (1). 4. A seizing and holding by law ▶ apprehension. *Slang:* pickup, pinch. *See* **arrest** (1).

seldom *adverb*
▶ occasionally, rarely, uncommonly. *See* **infrequently**.

select *verb*
To make a choice from a number of alternatives ▶ elect, pick (out), vote (for). *See* **choose** (1).

select *adjective*
1. Singled out in preference ▶ choice, chosen, elect, exclusive. *See also* **excellent, favorite**. 2. Of fine quality ▶ exceptional, fine, superior. *See* **choice** (1). 3. Able to recognize small differences or draw fine distinctions ▶ astute, discerning, perspicacious. *See* **discriminating** (1).

select *noun*
One that is selected ▶ chosen, choice. *See* **elect**.

selection *noun*
▶ decision, discretion, option. *See* **choice** (1). *See synonym note at* **choice**.

selective *adjective*
1. Able to recognize small differences or draw fine distinctions ▶ astute, discerning, percipient. *See* **discriminating** (1). 2. Catering to, used by, or admitting only the wealthy or socially superior ▶ chic, posh, swank. *See* **exclusive** (4).

selective service *noun*
▶ conscription, induction, levy. *See* **draft** (2).

selectivity *or* **selectiveness** *noun*
▶ acuteness, refinement, taste. *See* **discrimination** (1).

self *noun*
▶ human, person. *See* **human being**.

self-absorbed *adjective*
▶ egomaniacal, selfish. *See* **egotistic** (2).

self-absorption *noun*
▶ conceit, narcissism, vanity. *See* **egotism**.

self-assurance *noun*
▶ aplomb, self-possession. *See* **confidence** (1).

self-assured *adjective*
▶ secure, self-possessed. *See* **confident** (1).

self-centered *adjective*
▶ egomaniacal, self-absorbed. *See* **egotistic** (2).

self-centeredness *noun*
▶ conceit, narcissism, vanity. *See* **egotism**.

self-confidence *noun*
▶ assurance, certitude, self-possession. *See* **confidence** (1). *See synonym note at* **confidence**.

self-confident *adjective*
▶ secure, self-possessed. *See* **confident** (1).

self-conscious *adjective*
▶ uncomfortable, uneasy. *See* **awkward** (3).

self-contained *adjective*
▶ autonomous, self-sufficient. *See* **independent** (1).

self-containment *noun*
▶ self-reliance, self-sufficiency. *See* **independence** (1).

self-content *adjective*
▶ prideful, self-respecting, self-satisfied. *See* **proud** (1).

self-contentment *noun*
▶ ego, self-regard, self-satisfaction. *See* **pride** (1).

self-contradictory *adjective*
▶ false, illogical, unsound. *See* **fallacious** (1).

self-control *noun*
▶ constraint, restraint, self-restraint. *See* **reserve** (2).

self-controlled *adjective*
▶ inhibited, restrained, self-restrained. *See* **reserved** (1).

self-denial *noun*
▶ abstinence, continence, sobriety. *See* **temperance** (1). *See synonym note at* **temperance**.

self-denying *adjective*
1. Without concern for oneself ▶ self-forgetful, unselfish. *See* **selfless**. 2. Renouncing material comforts and pleasures ▶ austere, puritanical. *See* **ascetic**.

self-determination *noun*
1. The capacity to manage one's own affairs, make one's own judgments, and provide for oneself ▶ self-

reliance, self-sufficiency. *See* **independence** (1). **2.** The condition of being politically free ▸ autonomy, sovereignty. *See* **freedom** (1).

self-determined *adjective*
▸ autonomous, self-sufficient. *See* **independent** (1).

self-directed *adjective*
▸ autonomous, self-sufficient. *See* **independent** (1).

self-effacement *noun*
▸ bashfulness, demureness, diffidence. *See* **shyness**.

self-effacing *adjective*
▸ bashful, demure, diffident. *See* **shy**¹ (1).

self-esteem *noun*
▸ ego, self-regard, self-satisfaction. *See* **pride** (1).

self-evident *adjective*
▸ clear, manifest, obvious. *See* **apparent** (1).

self-forgetful *or* **self-forgetting** *adjective*
▸ self-denying, unselfish. *See* **selfless**.

self-governing *adjective*
▸ independent, self-ruling, sovereign. *See* **free** (1).

self-government *noun*
▸ autonomy, sovereignty. *See* **freedom** (1).

selfhood *noun*
▸ distinctiveness, individuality, singularity. *See* **identity** (1).

self-importance *noun*
1. The quality of being arrogant ▸ hauteur, insolence, superiority. *See* **arrogance**. **2.** Exaggerated love for oneself or belief in one's own importance ▸ conceit, narcissism, vanity. *See* **egotism**.

self-important *adjective*
1. Characterized by an exaggerated show of dignity or self-importance ▸ hoity-toity, pretentious. *See* **pompous**. **2.** Overly convinced of one's own superiority and importance ▸ insolent, superior. *See* **arrogant**.

self-involved *adjective*
▸ egomaniacal, self-absorbed. *See* **egotistic** (2).

self-involvement *noun*
▸ conceit, narcissism, vanity. *See* **egotism**.

selfish *adjective*
▸ egomaniacal, self-absorbed. *See* **egotistic** (2).

selfishness *noun*
▸ conceit, narcissism, vanity. *See* **egotism**.

selfless *adjective*
Without concern for oneself ▸ self-denying, self-forgetful, self-forgetting, self-sacrificing, unselfish. *See also* **benevolent, generous, humanitarian**.

self-possessed *adjective*
▸ assured, secure, self-assured. *See* **confident** (1).

self-possession *noun*
1. A firm belief in one's own powers ▸ assurance, certitude. *See* **confidence** (1). *See synonym note at* **confidence**. **2.** A stable emotional state ▸ composure, equanimity, poise, steadiness. *See* **balance** (2).

self-regard *noun*
▸ ego, self-contentment, self-satisfaction. *See* **pride** (1).

self-reliance *noun*
▸ autonomy, self-sufficiency. *See* **independence** (1).

self-reliant *adjective*
▸ autonomous, self-sufficient. *See* **independent** (1).

self-reproach *noun*
▸ contriteness, remorse, repentance. *See* **penitence**.

self-respect *noun*
▸ ego, self-regard, self-satisfaction. *See* **pride** (1).

self-respecting *adjective*
▸ self-content, self-satisfied. *See* **proud** (1).

self-restrained *adjective*
▸ controlled, noncommittal, unresponsive. *See* **reserved** (1).

self-restraint *noun*
▸ constraint, control. *See* **reserve** (2).

self-righteous *adjective*
Piously or overly sure of one's own righteousness ▸ holier-than-thou, moralistic. *See also* **arrogant, hypocritical, moral**.

self-rule *noun*
▸ autonomy, sovereignty. *See* **freedom** (1).

self-ruling *adjective*
▸ autonomous, independent, self-governing, sovereign. *See* **free** (1).

self-sacrificing *adjective*
▸ self-denying, unselfish. *See* **selfless**.

selfsame *adjective*
▸ identical, very. *See* **same** (1).

selfsameness *noun*
The quality or condition of being exactly the same as something else ▸ identicalness, identity, oneness, sameness. *See also* **likeness**.

self-satisfaction *noun*
1. The quality of being arrogant ▸ pride, self-importance, smugness. *See* **arrogance**. **2.** A sense of one's own dignity or worth ▸ ego, self-regard, self-respect. *See* **pride** (1).

self-satisfied *noun*
1. Overly convinced of one's own superiority and importance ▸ self-important, smug, superior. *See* **arrogant**. **2.** Properly valuing oneself, one's honor, or one's dignity ▸ self-content, self-respecting. *See* **proud** (1).

self-seeking *adjective*
▸ egomaniacal, self-absorbed. *See* **egotistic** (2).

self-serving *adjective*
▸ self-involved, selfish. *See* **egotistic** (2).

self-sufficiency *noun*
▸ autonomy, self-reliance. *See* **independence** (1).

self-sufficient *adjective*
1. Free from the influence, guidance, or control of others ▸ autonomous, self-reliant. *See* **independent** (1). **2.** Able to support oneself financially ▸ independent, self-supporting.

self-supporting *adjective*
Able to support oneself financially ▸ independent, self-sufficient. *Idiom:* on one's own.

sell *verb*
1. To offer for sale ▸ deal (in), handle, market, merchandise, merchant, peddle, retail, trade (in), vend. *Idioms:* put up for sale, put on the block. *See also* **carry, offer**. **2.** To attempt to sell or popularize by advertising or publicity ▸ advertise, publicize, talk up.

See **promote** (3). **3.** To succeed in causing a person to act or think in a certain way ▸ convince, prevail on. *See* **persuade** (1). **4.** To cause another to feel sure about something ▸ bring around, persuade, sell on, win over. *See* **convince** (1).

sell for *verb*

1. To achieve a certain price ▸ go for, realize. *See* **bring** (2). **2.** To require a specified price ▸ cost, go for. *Idiom:* set someone back. *See also* **demand.**

sell off *or* **out** *verb*

To get rid of by selling ▸ close out, dispose of, dump, unload.

sell *noun*

Slang Market appeal ▸ marketability, marketableness, salability, salableness.

seller *noun*

One who sells ▸ clerk, peddler, retailer, salesclerk, salesman, salesperson, saleswoman, vendor. *See also* **dealer.**

sellout *noun*

Slang An act of betraying ▸ double cross, treachery. *See* **betrayal** (1).

semblance *noun*

1. A deceptive outward appearance ▸ face, mask, pretense. *See* **façade** (2). **2.** A slight amount or indication ▸ hint, suggestion, trace. *See* **shade** (2). **3.** The way something or someone looks ▸ look, features, mien. *See* **appearance** (1).

seminal *adjective*

1. Not derived from something else ▸ archetypal, primary, prototypical. *See* **original** (1). **2.** Having or exercising influence ▸ important, powerful, weighty. *See* **influential. 3.** Characterized by or productive of new things or new ideas ▸ ingenious, innovative, original. *See* **inventive** (1).

seminar *noun*

▸ discussion, parley, symposium. *See* **conference** (1).

sempiternal *adjective*

▸ ceaseless, eternal, limitless. *See* **endless** (2). *See synonym note at* **endless.**

sempiternity *noun*

The totality of time without beginning or end ▸ eternity, infinity, perpetuity. *See also* **forever.**

send *verb*

1. To cause something to be conveyed to a destination ▸ address, consign, dispatch, express, forward, mail, post, route, ship, transmit. *See also* **convey, pass. 2.** To direct or allow to leave ▸ dismiss, send away. *Idioms:* send about one's business, send packing, show someone the door. **3.** To direct a person elsewhere for help or information ▸ refer, transfer, turn over. **4.** *Slang* To have a powerful emotional effect on someone ▸ thrill, transport. *See* **enrapture.**

send away *verb*

To direct or allow to leave ▸ cast out, expel. *See* **dismiss** (2).

send for *verb*

To bring or call together ▸ convene, muster, summon. *See* **assemble** (1).

send forth *verb*

1. To discharge material, as vapor or fumes, usually suddenly and violently ▸ give forth, issue, release. *See* **emit** (1). **2.** To send out heat, light, or energy ▸ emit, radiate. *See* **shed**[1] (1).

send up *verb*

Informal To place officially in confinement ▸ consign, institutionalize. *See* **commit.**

✦ CORE SYNONYMS: *send, dispatch, forward, route, ship, transmit.* These verbs mean to cause to go or be taken to a destination: *sent the package by parcel post; dispatched a union representative to the factory; forwards the mail to their new address; routed the soldiers through New York; shipped his books to his dormitory; transmits money by cable.*

---

send-up *noun*

Informal A work, such as a novel, play, or dramatic speech, that exposes folly by the use of humor, irony, or comic imitation ▸ burlesque, parody, spoof. *See* **satire.**

senescence *or* **senectitude** *noun*

▸ elderliness, seniority, years. *See* **age** (1).

senescent *adjective*

▸ elderly, mature, senior. *See* **old** (2).

senile *adjective*

Relating to the mental deterioration that often accompanies old age ▸ doddering, doting. *See also* **old, infirm.**

senility *noun*

The condition of being senile ▸ anecdotage, anility, caducity, dotage. *See also* **age.**

senior *adjective*

1. Being at a rank or level above another ▸ greater, higher, superior, upper. **2.** Far along in life or time ▸ aged, elderly, mature. *See* **old** (2).

senior *noun*

1. One who stands above another in rank ▸ better, elder, superior. *Informal:* higher-up. *See also* **chief. 2.** An elderly person ▸ ancient, elder, golden ager, senior citizen. *Informal:* oldster, old-timer.

senior citizen *noun*

▸ elder, golden ager. *See* **senior** (2).

seniority *noun*

▸ maturity, senescence, years. *See* **age** (1).

sensation *noun*

1. The capacity for or an act of responding to a stimulus ▸ feeling, impression, perception, sense, sensibility, sensitiveness, sensitivity. *See also* **awareness, emotion. 2.** A condition of intense public interest or excitement ▸ ado, brouhaha, bustle, stir, uproar. *Informal:* to-do. *Slang:* hoo-hah. *See also* **agitation. 3.** One that evokes great surprise and admiration ▸ phenomenon, prodigy, wonder. *See* **marvel** (1). *See synonym note at* **marvel.**

sensational *adjective*

1. Of or relating to sensation or the senses ▸ sensitive, sensorial, sensory, sensual, sensuous. **2.** Suggesting drama or a stage performance, as in emotionality or suspense ▸ histrionic, melodramatic, spectacular. *See* **dramatic** (2). **3.** Particularly excellent ▸ fabulous, glorious, superb. *See* **marvelous** (1).

sense *noun*
1. What is sound or reasonable ▸ logic, rationality, rationalness, reason, reasonableness. **2.** The ability to make sensible decisions ▸ judgment, reason, wisdom. *See* **common sense**. **3.** A healthy mental state ▸ lucidity, reason, wits. *See* **sanity**. **4.** The capacity for or an act of responding to a stimulus ▸ feeling, sensitivity. *See* **sensation** (1). **5.** The condition of being aware ▸ cognizance, consciousness, perception. *See* **awareness**. **6.** The faculty of thinking, reasoning, and applying knowledge ▸ intellect, mentality, understanding. *See* **intelligence** (1). **7.** Something that is conveyed or signified ▸ import, point, significance. *See* **meaning** (1). *See synonym note at* **meaning**.

sense *verb*
1. To be intuitively aware of ▸ apprehend, feel. *See* **perceive** (2). **2.** To view in a certain way ▸ believe, hold, think. *See also* **believe, regard**. **3.** To perceive and recognize the meaning of ▸ apprehend, fathom, take in. *See* **understand** (1).

senseless *adjective*
1. Lacking rational direction or purpose ▸ pointless, purposeless. *See* **mindless** (1). **2.** Displaying a lack of forethought and good sense ▸ brainless, fatuous, mindless. *See* **foolish**. **3.** Lacking consciousness ▸ insensible, out. *See* **unconscious** (1).

senselessness *noun*
1. Foolish behavior ▸ folly, silliness, tomfoolery. *See* **foolishness**. **2.** Something that does not have or make sense ▸ bunkum, claptrap, garbage. *See* **nonsense** (1).

sensibility *noun*
1. The quality or condition of being emotionally and intuitively sensitive ▸ feeling, sensibility, sensitiveness. *See also* **pity, sympathy**. **2.** The capacity for or an act of responding to a stimulus ▸ feeling, sensitivity. *See* **sensation** (1).

sensible *adjective*
1. Proceeding from or exhibiting good judgment and prudence ▸ balanced, commonsensible, commonsensical, judicious, levelheaded, prudent, rational, reasonable, sagacious, sage, sane, sapient, sober, sound, well-founded, well-grounded, wise. *See also* **advisable, logical**. **2.** Composed of or relating to things that occupy space and can be perceived by the senses ▸ corporeal, tangible. *See* **physical** (1). **3.** Capable of being perceived by the senses or the mind ▸ discernible, palpable, perceivable. *See* **perceptible**. **4.** Able to receive and respond to external stimuli ▸ impressionable, responsive. *See* **sensitive** (1). **5.** Marked by comprehension, cognizance, and perception ▸ alive, cognizant, sentient. *See* **aware**. *See synonym note at* **aware**.

sensitive *adjective*
1. Able to receive and respond to external stimuli ▸ impressible, impressionable, responsive, sensible, sentient, susceptible, susceptive. *See also* **aware**. **2.** Of or relating to sensation or the senses ▸ sensorial, sensory. *See* **sensational** (1). **3.** Keenly perceptive or discerning ▸ incisive, keen, perceptive. *See* **critical** (2). **4.** Readily stirred by emotion ▸ emotional, feeling. *See also* **passionate**. **5.** Quick to take offense or become angry or upset ▸ thin-skinned, ticklish. *See* **oversensitive**. **6.** Showing sensitivity and skill in dealing with others ▸ diplomatic, politic, tactful. *See* **delicate** (2). **7.** Requiring great tact or skill ▸ demanding, exacting, precarious. *See* **delicate** (3). **8.** Able to make or detect effects of great precision ▸ delicate, nice, subtle. *See* **fine**[1] (8). **9.** Of or being information available only to authorized persons ▸ privileged, restricted. *See* **confidential** (3). **10.** Of a sympathetic, considerate character ▸ kindly, softhearted, tender. *See* **gentle** (1).

sensitiveness *noun*
1. The quality or condition of being emotionally and intuitively sensitive ▸ feeling, sensibility, sensitivity. *See also* **pity, sympathy**. **2.** The capacity for or an act of responding to a stimulus ▸ feeling, sensibility, sensitivity. *See* **sensation** (1).

sensitivity *noun*
1. The quality or condition of being emotionally and intuitively sensitive ▸ feeling, sensibility, sensitiveness. *See also* **pity, sympathy**. **2.** The capacity for or an act of responding to a stimulus ▸ feeling, sense. *See* **sensation** (1). **3.** The ability to make or detect effects of great precision ▸ fineness, niceness. *See* **subtlety** (1). **4.** Skill in perceiving, discriminating, or judging ▸ keenness, perceptiveness, shrewdness. *See* **discernment** (1). **5.** The ability to say and do the right thing at the right time ▸ diplomacy, savoir-faire, tactfulness. *See* **tact**. **6.** Quickness to take offense ▸ ticklishness, touchiness. *See* **oversensitivity**.

sensory *or* **sensorial** *adjective*
▸ sensorial, sensuous. *See* **sensational** (1).

sensual *adjective*
1. Relating to, suggestive of, or appealing to sense gratification ▸ epicurean, sensuous, sensualistic, voluptuous. *See synonym note at* **sensuous**. *See also* **sybaritic**. **2.** Relating to the desires and appetites of the body, especially sexual desire ▸ animal, carnal, fleshly, fleshy, physical, sexual, sexy, voluptuous. **3.** Concerning or arousing sexual love or desire ▸ amorous, erogenous, sexy. *See* **erotic**. **4.** Of or relating to sensation or the senses ▸ sensorial, sensory. *See* **sensational** (1). **5.** Of or preoccupied with material rather than spiritual or intellectual things ▸ material, materialistic. *See also* **earthly, greedy, superficial**.

sensualism *noun*
1. The quality or condition of being sensuous ▸ sensuality, sensuousness, voluptuousness. **2.** The quality of being erotic ▸ lasciviousness, sexuality, suggestiveness. *See* **eroticism** (1).

sensualist *noun*
▸ hedonist, pagan, voluptuary. *See* **sybarite**.

sensualistic *adjective*
Relating to, suggestive of, or appealing to sense

gratification ► epicurean, sensual, sensuous, voluptuous. *See synonym note at* **sensuous**. *See also* **sybaritic.**

sensuality *noun*

1. The quality or condition of being sensual or being preoccupied with bodily desires ► animalism, animality, carnality, eroticism, fleshliness, physicality, sexiness, sexuality, suggestiveness, voluptuousness. *See also* **desire**. 2. The quality or condition of being sensuous ► sensuousness, sensualism, voluptuousness. 3. The quality of being erotic ► lasciviousness, sexuality, suggestiveness. *See* **eroticism** (1).

sensuous *adjective*

1. Relating to, suggestive of, or appealing to sense gratification ► epicurean, sensual, sensualistic, voluptuous. *See also* **sybaritic**. 2. Concerning or arousing sexual love or desire ► aphrodisiac, salacious, sexy. *See* **erotic**. 3. Of or relating to sensation or the senses ► sensorial, sensory. *See* **sensational** (1).

✦ CORE SYNONYMS: *sensuous, sensual, voluptuous*. These adjectives mean of, given to, or furnishing gratification of the senses. *Sensuous* usually applies to the senses involved in aesthetic enjoyment, as of art or music: *"The sensuous joy from all things fair/His strenuous bent of soul repressed"* (John Greenleaf Whittier). *Sensual* more often applies to the physical senses or appetites, particularly those associated with sexual pleasure: *"Of music Dr. Johnson used to say that it was the only sensual pleasure without vice"* (William Seward). *Voluptuous* principally implies abandoning oneself to pleasures, especially sensual pleasures: *"Lucullus . . . returned to Rome to lounge away the remainder of his days in voluptuous magnificence"* (J.A. Froude).

---

sensuousness *noun*

1. The quality or condition of being sensuous ► sensualism, sensuality, voluptuousness. 2. The quality of being erotic ► lasciviousness, sexuality, suggestiveness. *See* **eroticism** (1).

sentence *noun*

An authoritative or official decision ► edict, judgment, pronouncement. *See* **ruling**.

sentence *verb*

1. To pronounce judgment against ► convict, doom. *See* **condemn** (1). *See synonym note at* **condemn**. 2. To subject one to a penalty for a wrong ► chastise, correct, penalize. *See* **punish**.

sentenced *adjective*

► doomed, lost, reprobate. *See* **condemned**.

sententious *adjective*

► epigrammatic, pointed, succinct. *See* **pithy** (1).

sentient *adjective*

1. Marked by comprehension, cognizance, and perception ► awake, cognizant, sensible. *See* **aware**. 2. Able to receive and respond to external stimuli ► impressionable, responsive, susceptible. *See* **sensitive** (1).

sentiment *noun*

1. A general cast of mind with regard to something

► attitude, feeling. *See also* **idea**. 2. Something thought to be true ► notion, persuasion, view. *See* **belief** (1). *See synonym note at* **belief**. 3. A subjective mental state, such as love or hate ► affection, feeling. *See* **emotion**. *See synonym note at* **emotion**. 4. The quality or condition of being affectedly or overly emotional ► bathos, treacle. *See* **sentimentality**.

sentimental *adjective*

Affectedly or extravagantly emotional ► bathetic, corny, gushy, maudlin, mawkish, misty, misty-eyed, namby-pamby, romantic, romanticized, slushy, sobby, soft, soppy, syrupy, treacly. *Informal:* gooey, mushy, schmaltzy, sloppy, soft-boiled, soupy. *Slang:* drippy, hokey, sappy, tear-jerking.

✦ CORE SYNONYMS: *sentimental, bathetic, maudlin, mawkish, romantic, slushy, soppy*. These adjectives mean affectedly or extravagantly emotional: *a sentimental card; a bathetic novel; maudlin expressions of sympathy; mawkish sentiment; a romantic adolescent; slushy poetry; a soppy letter*.

---

sentimentality *or* **sentimentalism** *noun*

The quality or condition of being affectedly or overly emotional ► bathos, corniness, maudlinism, mawkishness, romanticism, sentiment, treacle. *Informal:* mush, mushiness, sloppiness, schmaltz, schmaltziness. *Slang:* hokiness, sappiness.

sentry *or* **sentinel** *noun*

► lookout, ward, watchdog. *See* **guard** (1).

separate *verb*

1. To end an association by or as if by leaving one another ► break off, break up, divorce, part. *Informal:* split (up). *Idioms:* call it quits, come to a parting of the ways, part company. 2. To set apart one kind or type from others ► sift, sort, winnow. *Idiom:* separate the sheep from the goats. 3. To set apart from a group ► close off, seclude, sequester. *See* **isolate** (1). 4. To move apart in different directions ► break up, disperse, split up. *See* **scatter** (2). 5. To remove from association with ► disassociate, disengage, withdraw. *See* **detach** (1). 6. To break up the unity of something ► disunite, partition, split (up). *See* **divide** (1). 7. To arrange according to class ► assort, categorize, divide. *See* **classify**. 8. To recognize as being different ► differentiate, discriminate. *See* **distinguish** (1). 9. To displace a bone from a socket or joint ► dislocate, throw out. *See* **slip** (7). 10. To release from military duty ► demobilize, release, separate. *See* **discharge** (4).

separate *adjective*

1. Being or related to a distinct entity ► particular, singular. *See* **individual** (2). 2. Not like another in nature, quality, amount, or form ► contrasting, divergent, variant. *See* **different** (1). 3. Alone in a given category ► only, single, solitary. *See* **lone** (1). 4. Distinguished from others by nature or qualities ► discrete, several, various. *See* **distinct** (1). *See synonym note at* **distinct**.

separately *adverb*

As a separate unit ► apart, discretely, independently,

individually, singly. *Idioms:* one at a time, one by one. *See also* **alone.**

separateness *noun*
1. The quality of being individual ▸ distinctiveness, particularity. *See* **individuality** (1). 2. The condition of being unlike or dissimilar ▸ contrast, discrepancy, divergence. *See* **difference** (1). 3. The act of secluding or the state of being secluded ▸ isolation, retirement, sequestration. *See* **seclusion** (1).

separation *noun*
1. The act or an instance of separating one thing from another ▸ disjunction, divorce, parting. *See* **division** (1). 2. The act or process of detaching ▸ disconnection, disengagement, uncoupling. *See* **detachment** (1). 3. The act or an instance of distinguishing ▸ demarcation, differentiation. *See* **distinction** (1). 4. The act or process of isolating ▸ insulation, segregation. *See* **isolation** (1). 5. A space between objects or points ▸ interstice, interval. *See* **gap** (1).

separatist *or* **separationist** *noun*
A person who dissents from the doctrine of an established church ▸ dissenter, dissident, heretic, nonconformist, schismatic, sectarian, sectary. *See also* **rebel.**

sepulcher *noun*
A burial place or receptacle for human remains ▸ catacomb, crypt, tomb. *See* **grave**[1].

sepulcher *verb*
To place a corpse in or as if in a grave ▸ inhume, inter. *See* **bury** (1).

sepulture *noun*
1. A burial place or receptacle for human remains ▸ catacomb, crypt, tomb. *See* **grave**[1]. 2. An act of placing a body in a grave or tomb ▸ entombment, inhumation, interment. *See* **burial.**

sequel *noun*
▸ consequence, outcome, upshot. *See* **effect** (1). *See synonym note at* **effect.**

sequence *noun*
1. A number of things placed or occurring one after the other ▸ order, procession, succession. *See* **series.** *See synonym note at* **series.** 2. The act or condition of being arranged ▸ allotment, layout, positioning. *See* **arrangement** (1). 3. Something brought about by a cause ▸ outcome, result, upshot. *See* **effect** (1).

sequent *adjective*
Following one after another in an orderly pattern ▸ sequential, serial. *See* **consecutive.**

sequent *noun*
Something brought about by a cause ▸ consequence, outcome, result. *See* **effect** (1).

sequential *adjective*
▸ back-to-back, serial. *See* **consecutive.**

sequester *or* **sequestrate** *verb*
1. To put into solitude ▸ cloister, seclude. *See also* **imprison.** 2. To set apart from a group ▸ alienate, set off. *See* **isolate** (1). *See synonym note at* **isolate.**

sequestration *noun*
1. The act or process of isolating ▸ alienation, segregation. *See* **isolation** (1). 2. The act of secluding or the state of being secluded ▸ reclusion, retirement. *See* **seclusion** (1).

sequin *noun*
A small sparkling decoration ▸ diamond, glitter, rhinestone, spangle.

sere *adjective*
▸ anhydrous, moistureless. *See* **dry** (1).

serendipitous *adjective*
▸ chance, fortuitous, inadvertent, unplanned. *See* **accidental** (1).

serendipity *noun*
▸ coincidence, fortune, luck. *See* **chance** (2).

serene *adjective*
1. Not excited or agitated ▸ peaceful, placid, tranquil. *See* **calm** (1). 2. Free from disturbance, agitation, or commotion ▸ peaceful, placid. *See* **still** (1). *See synonym note at* **still.**

serenity *noun*
1. Lack of emotional agitation ▸ peace, quietude. *See* **calm** (1). 2. An absence of motion or disturbance ▸ calmness, lull, peacefulness. *See* **stillness** (1).

serf *noun*
▸ bondservant, vassal. *See* **slave** (1).

serfdom *noun*
▸ enslavement, servility, thrall. *See* **slavery.**

serial *or* **seriate** *adjective*
▸ sequential, successive. *See* **consecutive.**

series *noun*
A number of things placed or occurring one after the other ▸ chain, concatenation, consecution, course, gamut, order, procession, progression, range, round, run, scale, sequence, string, succession, suite, train. *Informal:* streak. *See also* **group, line.**

✦ CORE SYNONYMS: *series, succession, progression, sequence, chain, train, string.* These nouns denote a number of things placed or occurring one after the other. *Series* refers to like, related, or identical things arranged or occurring in order: *a series of days; a series of facts.* In a *succession* the elements follow each other, generally in order of time and without interruption: *a succession of failures.* A *progression* reveals a definite pattern of advance: *a geometric progression.* In a *sequence* elements are ordered in a way that indicates a causal, temporal, numerical, or logical relationship or a recurrent pattern: *a natural sequence of ideas.* In a *chain* the elements are closely linked or connected: *the chain of command; a chain of proof.* *Train* can apply to a procession or to a sequence of ideas or events: *a train of mourners; my train of thought.* A *string* consists of similar or uniform elements likened to objects threaded on a long cord: *a string of islands; a string of questions.*

---

serious *adjective*
1. Characterized by careful thought and a lack of frivolity or exaggeration ▸ businesslike, dignified, earnest, grave, no-nonsense, sedate, sober, sobersided, solemn, somber, staid. *Idiom:* in earnest. *See also* **ceremonious, forbidding, frank, severe.** 2.

Having or threatening severe negative consequences ▸ dire, grave, grievous, severe. *See also* **disastrous, fateful. 3.** Having great consequence or weight ▸ severe, weighty. *See* **grave²** (1). **4.** Not easy to do, achieve, or master ▸ arduous, laborious, tough. *See* **difficult** (1).

✦ CORE SYNONYMS: *serious, sober, grave, solemn, earnest, sedate, staid.* These adjectives mean characterized by careful thought and a lack of frivolity or exaggeration. *Serious* implies a concern with responsibility and work as opposed to play: *serious students of music. Sober* emphasizes circumspection and self-restraint: *"My sober mind was no longer intoxicated by the fumes of politics"* (Edward Gibbon). *Grave* suggests the dignity and somberness associated with weighty matters: *"a quiet, grave man, busied in charts, exact in sums, master of the art of tactics"* (Walter Bagehot). *Solemn* often adds to *grave* the suggestion of impressiveness: *the judge's solemn tone as she handed down her decision. Earnest* implies sincerity and intensity of purpose: *disputants who showed an earnest desire to reach an equitable solution. Sedate* implies a composed, dignified manner: *"One of those calm, quiet, sedate natures, to whom the temptations of turbulent nerves or vehement passions are things utterly incomprehensible"* (Harriet Beecher Stowe). *Staid* emphasizes dignity and an often strait-laced observance of propriety: *"a grave and staid God-fearing man"* (Tennyson).

---

seriousness *noun*
1. The quality of being dignified and serious, as in manner or bearing ▸ dignity, earnestness, graveness, gravitas, gravity, sedateness, sobersidedness, sobriety, solemnness, solemnity, somberness, staidness. *See also* **ceremony, severity. 2.** The condition of being grave and of involving serious consequences ▸ graveness, gravity, heaviness, momentousness, weightiness. *See also* **severity.**
sermon *noun*
▸ lecture, talk. *See* **speech** (2).
sermonize *verb*
1. To deliver a sermon, especially as a vocation ▸ evangelize, preach. *See also* **address. 2.** To indulge in moral reflection, usually pompously ▸ edify, moralize, pontificate, preach. *See also* **chastise. 3.** To talk to an audience formally ▸ lecture, prelect, speak. *See also* **converse.**
serpentine *adjective*
▸ convoluted, sinuous, twisting. *See* **winding** (1).
serrated *or* **serrate** *adjective*
▸ notched, toothed. *See* **saw-toothed.**
servant *noun*
▸ serf, vassal. *See* **slave** (1).
serve *verb*
1. To work and care for ▸ attend, do for, minister to, wait on (*or* upon). *See also* **help, tend², work. 2.** To place food before someone ▸ wait on (*or* upon). *See also* **give, distribute. 3.** To spend or complete time, as a prison term ▸ put in. *Informal:* do. **4.** To meet a need or requirement ▸ answer, do, suffice. *See* **satisfy** (1).

5. To be an advantage to ▸ benefit, help. *See* **profit** (2).
6. To perform a service or a courteous act for ▸ favor, help. *See* **oblige** (1).
service *noun*
1. The condition of being put to use ▸ application, employment, use. *See* **duty** (2). **2.** A formal act or set of acts prescribed by ritual ▸ rite, ritual, tradition. *See* **ceremony** (1). **3.** A kindly act ▸ good turn, kindness. *See* **favor** (1). **4.** The state of being employed ▸ employ, employment, hire.
service *verb*
1. To restore to proper condition or functioning ▸ mend, revamp. *See* **fix** (1). **2.** *Slang* To engage in sexual relations with ▸ bed, mate. *See* **sleep with.**
serviceable *adjective*
1. In a condition to be used ▸ applicable, operational. *See* **usable** (1). **2.** Serving or capable of serving a useful purpose ▸ functional, useful, utilitarian. *See* **practical** (1).
serviceman *or* **servicewoman** *noun*
▸ legionary, serviceperson, trooper. *See* **soldier** (2).
services *noun*
▸ conveniences, facilities, resources. *See* **amenities** (1).
servile *adjective*
Excessively eager to serve or obey ▸ bootlicking, cringing, fawning, grovelling, menial, obsequious, slavish, subservient, sycophantic, toadying. *See also* **humble, lowly, unctuous.**
servility *or* **servileness** *noun*
▸ enslavement, serfdom, thrall. *See* **slavery.**
serving *noun*
An individual quantity of food ▸ bowlful, helping, mess, plateful, portion. *See also* **allotment.**
servitude *noun*
▸ enslavement, servility, thrall. *See* **slavery.**
sesquipedalian *or* **sesquipedal** *adjective*
Having many syllables ▸ polysyllabic.
session *noun*
1. A formal assemblage of the members of a group ▸ assembly, conference, council. *See* **convention** (1). **2.** A specific length of time characterized by the occurrence of certain conditions or events ▸ span, stretch, term. *See* **period** (1).
set¹ *verb*
1. To put in a certain position or location ▸ locate, stick, situate. *See* **position. 2.** To alter for proper functioning ▸ calibrate, attune, tweak. *See* **adjust** (1). **3.** To arrange tableware upon a table in preparation for a meal ▸ lay, spread. **4.** To set the time for an event or occasion ▸ plan, schedule, time. *See also* **arrange. 5.** To bring something into a state of agreement or accord ▸ arrange, fix, negotiate. *See* **settle** (2). **6.** To appoint and send to a particular place ▸ assign, post, station. *See also* **position. 7.** To calculate approximately ▸ place, reckon. *See* **estimate** (2). **8.** To direct something, often toward a target ▸ level, point, train. *See* **aim** (1). **9.** To change or be changed from a liquid into a semisolid or solid mass ▸ congeal, curdle. *See* **coagulate.** *See synonym note at* **coagulate. 10.** To

make or become physically hard ► congeal, solidify. *See* **harden** (2). **11.** To place a limit on ► confine, fix, restrict. *See* **limit** (1).

set about *verb*
To go about the initial step in doing something ► begin, embark, initiate. *See* **start** (1).

set apart *verb*
1. To make noticeable or different ► differentiate, individualize, singularize. *See* **distinguish** (2). **2.** To set apart from a group ► close off, seclude, sequester. *See* **isolate** (1). *See synonym note at* **isolate. 3.** To set aside or apart for a specified purpose ► assign, designate, earmark. *See* **appropriate** (1).

set aside *verb*
1. To put an end to ► annul, nullify, void. *See* **abolish** (1). **2.** To keep for future use ► put by, salt away, store. *See* **save** (1). **3.** To set aside or apart for a specified purpose ► assign, designate, earmark. *See* **appropriate** (1).

set back *verb*
To cause to be later or slower than expected or desired ► hang up, retard, stall. *See* **delay** (1).

set by *verb*
To keep for future use ► put by, salt away, store. *See* **save** (1).

set down *verb*
1. To place on a list or in a record or book ► catalog, chronicle, write down. *See* **list¹** (1). **2.** To come to rest on the ground ► light, settle. *See* **land** (2).

set forth *verb*
1. To state for consideration or debate ► offer, put forward, suggest. *See* **propose** (1). **2.** To move away from a place ► depart, go away, retire. *See* **go** (1).

set in *verb*
To manifest strong winds and precipitation ► blow (up), squall, storm. *See also* **rain.**

set off *verb*
1. To be the cause of ► generate, induce, trigger. *See* **cause. 2.** To stir to action or feeling ► excite, prod, trigger. *See* **provoke** (1). **3.** To endow with beauty and elegance ► beautify, embellish, enhance, grace. *See also* **adorn. 4.** To act as an equalizing force to ► counteract, counterbalance, offset. *See* **balance** (2). **5.** To make ineffective by applying an opposite force ► counteract, negate, offset. *See* **cancel** (2). **6.** To move away from a place ► depart, go away, retire. *See* **go** (1).

set out *verb*
1. To go about the initial step in doing something ► approach, embark, initiate. *See* **start** (1). **2.** To plan the details or arrangements of ► lay out, organize, schedule. *See* **arrange** (2). **3.** To proceed in a specified direction ► head, make, turn. *See* **bear** (5). **4.** To put seeds or young plants in soil ► broadcast, seed, sow. *See* **plant** (1). **5.** To work out and arrange the parts and details of ► blueprint, lay out, sketch. *See* **design** (2). **6.** To move away from a place ► exit, go away, retire. *See* **go** (1).

set to *verb*
To go about the initial step in doing something

► begin, embark, initiate, launch. *See* **start** (1).

set up *verb*
1. To raise upright ► put up, raise. *See* **erect** (1). **2.** To bring into existence formally ► constitute, establish, institute. *See* **found** (1). **3.** *Informal* To pay for the food, drink, or entertainment of another ► *Informal:* stand. *Slang:* spring for. *See* **treat** (2). **4.** To place securely in a position or condition ► fix, seat. *See* **establish** (2).

set *adjective*
1. Firmly established by long standing ► deep-seated, entrenched, ingrained, inveterate. *See* **confirmed** (1). **2.** Remaining unchanged ► constant, fixed, uniform. *See* **unchanging. 3.** Without any doubt ► clear-cut, definite, unquestionable. *See* **decided** (1). **4.** Relating to, identifying, or setting apart an individual or group ► characteristic, individual, particular. *See* **special** (1). **5.** Committed to a course of action ► bent, decided, determined. *See* **intent** (1). **6.** In a state of preparedness ► prepared, ready. *Informal:* go. *Slang:* together.

set² *noun*
1. A number of individuals making up or considered a unit ► body, cluster, collection. *See* **group** (1). **2.** A subdivision of a larger group ► category, classification, order. *See* **class** (1). **3.** A small group of friends or associates ► coterie, group. *See* **circle** (3). **4.** The properties, backdrops, and other objects arranged for a dramatic presentation ► mise en scène, setting. *See* **scene** (2).

setback *noun*
1. A change from better to worse ► backset, reverse, reversal. *See also* **misfortune, relapse. 2.** An unexpected and usually undesirable event ► contretemps, mishap, reversal. *See* **accident** (1).

setoff *noun*
► amends, remuneration, reparation. *See* **compensation** (1).

setting *noun*
1. The place where an action or event occurs ► site, stage. *See* **scene** (1). **2.** The properties, backdrops, and other objects arranged for a dramatic presentation ► mise en scène, set. *See* **scene** (2). **3.** Existing surroundings that affect an activity ► circumstances, surroundings. *See* **conditions.**

settle *verb*
1. To put into correct or conclusive form ► arrange, conclude, dispose of, finalize, fix. *See also* **conclude. 2.** To bring something into a state of agreement or accord ► arrange, conclude, fix, negotiate, reconcile, rectify, resolve, set, settle upon, smooth over, straighten out. *See also* **compromise, decide, judge. 3.** To set right by giving what is due ► clear, discharge, liquidate, pay (off *or* up), satisfy, square. *See also* **satisfy. 4.** To move to a place and reside there ► locate, relocate. *Idioms:* fix one's residence, make one's home, put down roots, take up residence. *See also* **emigrate, live¹, move. 5.** To place securely in a position or condition ► fix, seat. *See* **establish** (2). **6.** To ease the anger or agitation of ► appease, mollify,

soothe. *See* **pacify. 7.** To go beneath the surface or to the bottom of a liquid ▸ founder, gravitate. *See* **sink** (1). **8.** To come to rest on the ground ▸ light, set down, touch down. *See* **land** (2). **9.** To make up or cause to make up one's mind ▸ determine, resolve. *See* **decide** (1). *See synonym note at* **decide.**

settled *adjective*
1. Firmly established by long standing ▸ deep-seated, entrenched, ingrained, inveterate. *See* **confirmed** (1). **2.** Without any doubt ▸ clear-cut, definite, unquestionable. *See* **decided** (1).

settlement *noun*
1. A reestablishment of friendship or harmony ▸ conciliation, rapprochement, reconcilement, reconciliation. *See also* **agreement, atonement, compromise. 2.** A reconciling of differences through mutual concession ▸ arrangement, give-and-take, tradeoff. *See* **compromise. 3.** Something to make up for loss or damage ▸ payment, reimbursement. *See* **compensation** (1). **4.** A small group of dwellings ▸ hamlet, small town. *See* **village. 5.** An area subject to rule by an outside power ▸ dependency, province. *See* **possession** (1).

settler *noun*
One who settles in a new region ▸ colonial, colonist, colonizer, homesteader, pioneer.

setup *noun*
▸ classification, layout, positioning. *See* **arrangement** (1).

seventh heaven *noun*
Informal A supremely beautiful, blissful state or experience ▸ ecstasy, paradise. *See* **heaven** (1).

sever *verb*
▸ cleave, split. *See* **cut** (2).

several *adjective*
1. Consisting of a number more than two or three but less than many ▸ certain, divers, few, some, sundry, various. **2.** Distinguished from others by nature or qualities ▸ discrete, separate, various. *See* **distinct** (1). *See synonym note at* **distinct.**

several *pronoun*
A number more than two or three but less than many ▸ few, handful, small number, some, smattering, sprinkling. *See also* **couple.**

severance *noun*
▸ disjunction, divorce, parting. *See* **division** (1).

severe *adjective*
1. Rigorous and unsparing in treating others ▸ demanding, draconian, exacting, hard, harsh, rigid, rigorous, stern, strict, stringent, tough, uncompromising, unyielding. *See also* **cruel, firm¹, forbidding, stubborn. 2.** Conveying great physical force ▸ hard, heavy, hefty, powerful. *See also* **forceful, intense. 3.** Having or threatening severe negative consequences ▸ dire, grave, grievous, serious. *See also* **disastrous, fateful. 4.** Marked by cold and unpleasant conditions ▸ grim, stark. *See* **bleak** (1). **5.** Without addition, decoration, or qualification ▸ bare-bones, dry, simple. *See* **bare** (1). **6.** Painfully intense ▸ brutal,

harsh, rough. *See* **bitter** (2). **7.** Having great consequence or weight ▸ serious, weighty. *See* **grave²** (1). **8.** Requiring great or extreme bodily, mental, or spiritual strength ▸ demanding, difficult, exacting. *See* **burdensome** (1).

severity *noun*
1. The fact or condition of being rigorous and unsparing ▸ austerity, hardness, harshness, rigidity, rigidness, rigor, rigorousness, sternness, strictness, stringency, toughness. *See also* **cruelty, seriousness, stubbornness. 2.** Concentrated power or force, as of effort, opinion, or emotion ▸ ferocity, fury, vehemence. *See* **intensity.**

sewer *noun*
▸ cesspool, gutter. *See* **pit¹** (3).

sexiness *noun*
1. The quality or condition of being sensual ▸ sexuality, voluptuousness. *See* **sensuality** (1). **2.** The quality of being erotic ▸ lasciviousness, suggestiveness. *See* **eroticism** (1).

sexism *noun*
Discrimination based on gender ▸ discrimination, intolerance, prejudice. *See also* **hate.**

sexist *adjective*
▸ bigoted, discriminatory, prejudiced. *See also* **intolerant.**

sexless *adjective*
▸ epicene, genderless. *See* **androgynous.**

sexlessness *noun*
The quality of being androgynous ▸ androgyny, epicenism, gender-neutrality. *See also* **effeminacy, masculinity.**

sexual *adjective*
1. Concerning or arousing sexual love or desire ▸ amorous, erogenous, sexy. *See* **erotic. 2.** Relating to the desires and appetites of the body, especially sexual desire ▸ physical, voluptuous. *See* **sensual** (2). **3.** Employed in reproduction ▸ reproductive.

sexuality *noun*
1. The quality or condition of being sensual or being preoccupied with bodily desires ▸ animality, voluptuousness. *See* **sensuality** (1). **2.** The quality of being erotic ▸ lasciviousness, suggestiveness. *See* **eroticism** (1).

sexy *adjective*
1. Arousing erotic desire ▸ alluring, enticing. *See* **desirable** (1). **2.** Relating to the desires and appetites of the body, especially sexual desire ▸ physical, sexual. *See* **sensual** (2). **3.** Concerning or arousing sexual love or desire ▸ erogenous, sensual. *See* **erotic. 4.** Feeling or preoccupied with sexual love or desire ▸ concupiscent, lewd. *See* **lascivious** (1). **5.** Tending to seduce ▸ bewitching, enticing, tempting. *See* **seductive.**

shabby *adjective*
1. Showing signs of wear and tear or neglect ▸ bedraggled, broken-down, decayed, decaying, decrepit, deteriorated, dilapidated, dingy, down-at-heel, faded, frayed, mangy, ragged, raggedy, ramshackle, ruinous,

rundown, scrubby, scruffy, seedy, shoddy, sleazy, tatterdemalion, tattered, tatty, threadbare, tumbledown, worn, worn-out. *Informal:* tacky. *Slang:* ratty. *Idioms:* all the worse for wear, gone to pot (*or* seed), past cure (*or* hope). *See also* **miserable, shoddy, terrible. 2.** Of low or lower quality ▸ inferior, low-quality, substandard. *See* **bad** (1). **3.** So objectionable as to deserve condemnation ▸ contemptible, disgusting, obnoxious. *See* **offensive** (1).

shack *noun*
▸ hovel, lean-to, shanty. *See* **hut.**

shackle *noun*
Something that physically confines the legs or arms ▸ handcuffs, hobble, irons. *See* **bond** (1).

shackle *verb*
To restrict the activity or free movement of ▸ fetter, handcuff, hobble. *See* **hamper**[1] (1). *See synonym note at* **hamper**[1].

shade *noun*
1. A slight variation between nearly identical entities ▸ gradation, hue, nicety, nuance, subtlety. **2.** A slight amount or indication ▸ breath, dash, ghost, hair, hint, intimation, semblance, shadow, soupçon, streak, suggestion, suspicion, taste, tinge, touch, trace, whiff, whisper. *Informal:* whisker. *See also* **bit**[1]. **3.** Comparative darkness that results from the blocking of light rays ▸ penumbra, shadiness, shadow, umbra. *See also* **dark, twilight. 4.** Quality of light reflected or emitted ▸ hue, tinge, tint. *See* **color** (1). **5.** An immaterial supernatural being, especially the spirit of a dead person ▸ apparition, phantom, specter. *See* **ghost** (1).

shade *verb*
1. To shelter, especially from light ▸ screen, shadow. **2.** To make dark or darker ▸ adumbrate, darken, gloom, overcast, overshadow, shadow. *See also* **obscure. 3.** To make a slight reduction in a price ▸ shave, trim. **4.** To make different ▸ alter, modify, turn. *See* **change** (1).

✦ **CORE SYNONYMS:** *shade, nuance, gradation.* These nouns denote a slight variation or differentiation between nearly identical entities: *subtle shades of meaning; sensitive to delicate nuances of style; gradations of feeling from infatuation to deep affection.*

---

shaded *adjective*
Full of or affording shade ▸ shadowy, umbrageous. *See* **shady** (2).

shadiness *noun*
1. Comparative darkness that results from the blocking of light rays ▸ penumbra, shade, shadow, umbra. *See also* **dark, twilight. 2.** Lack of straightforwardness and honesty in action ▸ deviousness, slyness, trickery. *See* **dishonesty** (2).

shadow *noun*
1. Comparative darkness that results from the blocking of light rays ▸ penumbra, shade, shadiness, umbra. *See also* **dark, twilight. 2.** An immaterial supernatural being, especially the spirit of a dead person ▸ phantom, shade, specter. *See* **ghost** (1). **3.** An agent

assigned to observe and report on another ▸ watcher. *Informal:* tail. *See also* **detective. 4.** A slight amount or indication ▸ hint, semblance, suggestion, trace. *See* **shade** (2).

shadow *verb*
1. To shelter, especially from light ▸ screen, shade. **2.** To make dim ▸ blur, fog, obfuscate. *See* **obscure** (1). **3.** To make dark or darker ▸ darken, gloom, overcast. *See* **shade** (2). **4.** To keep another under surveillance by moving behind ▸ track, trail. *Informal:* tail. *See* **follow** (3).

shadowy *adjective*
1. Full of or affording shade ▸ shaded, umbrageous. *See* **shady** (2). **2.** Deficient in brightness ▸ dim, dusky, unlit. *See* **dark** (1). *See synonym note at* **dark. 3.** Not clearly perceptible ▸ dim, faint, indefinite. *See* **unclear** (1).

shady *adjective*
1. Of doubtful honesty or character ▸ doubtful, dubious, equivocal, left-handed, questionable, suspect, suspicious, uncertain, untrustworthy. *Informal:* fishy. *See also* **dishonest, illegal, underhand. 2.** Full of or affording shade ▸ dappled, leafy, shaded, shadowy, umbrageous. *See also* **gloomy. 3.** Deficient in brightness ▸ dusky, obscure, shadowy. *See* **dark** (1). *See synonym note at* **dark.**

shaft *noun*
1. A narrow line of light or other radiant energy ▸ ray, stream. *See* **beam** (1). **2.** A straight, rigid piece of metal or other solid material ▸ bar, stem. *See* **rod. 3.** A sturdy vertical structural support ▸ pillar, post. *See* **column** (1).

shaggy *adjective*
▸ furry, fuzzy, woolly. *See* **hairy** (1).

shake *verb*
1. To move to and fro in short, jerky movements ▸ quake, quaver, quiver, shiver, shudder, switch, tremble, twitter, vibrate. *See also* **bump. 2.** To cause to move to and fro with short, jerky movements ▸ jar, jiggle, joggle. **3.** To cause to move to and fro violently ▸ churn, convulse, rock. *See* **agitate** (1). *See synonym note at* **agitate. 4.** To move back and forth ▸ oscillate, undulate, vacillate. *See* **sway** (1). *See synonym note at* **sway. 5.** To alter the settled state or position of ▸ displace, disrupt. *See* **disturb** (1). **6.** *Slang* To relieve a burden ▸ discharge, relieve, unburden. *See* **rid. 7.** To deprive of courage or the power to act as a result of fear, anxiety, or disgust ▸ consternate, disconcert. *See* **dismay** (1). *See synonym note at* **dismay. 8.** *Slang* To get away from a pursuer ▸ elude, slip, throw off. *See* **lose** (3).

shake down *verb*
1. *Slang* To obtain by coercion or intimidation ▸ squeeze, wrench. *See* **extort. 2.** *Slang* To examine a person or someone's personal effects in order to find something lost or concealed ▸ frisk, inspect, pat down, search. *Idiom:* do a body search of.

shake off *verb*
1. To relieve a burden ▸ clear, release, unburden. *See*

rid. 2. To get away from a pursuer ▸ evade, slip, throw off. *See* **lose** (3).

shake up *verb*
1. To reorganize thoroughly ▸ reconfigure, reshuffle. *See* **overhaul** (1). **2.** To impair or destroy the composure of ▸ disturb, upset. *See* **agitate** (2).

shake *noun*
1. A nervous shaking of the body ▸ quiver, shiver, twitch. *See* **tremor** (2). **2.** *Informal* A shaking of the earth ▸ earthquake, quake, seism, temblor, tremor.

✤ **CORE SYNONYMS:** *shake, tremble, quake, quiver, shiver, shudder.* These verbs mean to move to and fro in short, jerky movements. *Shake* is the most general: *The floor shook when I walked heavily across the room.* *Tremble* implies quick, rather slight movement, as from excitement, weakness, or anger: *The speaker trembled as he denounced his opponents.* *Quake* refers to more violent movement, as that caused by shock or upheaval: *I was so scared that my legs began to quake.* *Quiver* suggests a slight, rapid, tremulous movement: *"Her lip quivered like that of a child about to cry"* (Booth Tarkington). *Shiver* involves rapid trembling, as of a person experiencing a chill: *"as I in hoary winter night stood shivering in the snow"* (Robert Southwell). *Shudder* applies chiefly to convulsive shaking caused by fear, horror, or revulsion: *"She starts like one that spies an adder/ . . . The fear whereof doth make him shake and shudder"* (William Shakespeare).

---

shakedown *noun*
1. *Slang* A thorough search of a place or persons ▸ frisk, search. **2.** A procedure that ascertains effectiveness, value, proper function, or other quality ▸ proof, trial, tryout. *See* **test** (1).

shaken *or* **shaken-up** *adjective*
▸ agitated, distressed, overwrought. *See* **anxious**.

shakes *noun*
Informal a state of nervous restlessness or agitation ▸ jumps, shivers, trembles. *See* **jitters**.

shakeup *noun*
A thorough or drastic reorganization ▸ overhaul, reengineering, reshuffling. *Informal:* housecleaning. *See also* **renewal, revolution**.

shakiness *noun*
▸ insecurity, unstableness, unsteadiness. *See* **instability**.

shaky *adjective*
1. Marked by or affected with tremors ▸ quaky, quivery, shivery. *See* **tremulous** (1). **2.** Lacking stability ▸ precarious, unsteady. *See* **insecure** (2). **3.** Not plausible or believable ▸ improbable, inconceivable. *See* **implausible**.

shallow *adjective*
▸ cursory, one-dimensional, sketchy. *See* **superficial** (1).

sham *noun*
1. A fraudulent imitation ▸ forgery, phony. *See* **counterfeit**. **2.** A person who practices deceit, especially under an assumed identity ▸ charlatan, fraud, pre-

tender. *See* **fake** (1). **3.** A false, derisive, or impudent imitation of something ▸ farce, parody, travesty. *See* **mockery** (2). **4.** A display of insincere behavior ▸ dissemblance, pretense, show, simulation. *See* **act** (2).

sham *adjective*
Fraudulently or deceptively imitative ▸ fake, fraudulent, phony. *See* **counterfeit**.

sham *verb*
To take on as a false appearance ▸ counterfeit, dissemble, fake, fabricate. *See* **act** (2).

shamble *verb*
▸ scuff, scuffle, shuffle. *See* **trudge**.

shambles *noun*
1. A confused or ruinous state ▸ foul-up, muddle. *See* **mess** (1). **2.** A lack of order or regular arrangement ▸ clutter, confusion, disarray. *See* **disorder** (1).

shame *noun*
1. A great disappointment or regrettable fact ▸ crime, pity. *Slang:* bummer. *Idiom:* a crying shame. **2.** Loss of or damage to one's reputation ▸ discredit, disrepute, humiliation. *See* **disgrace**. **3.** A feeling of regret for one's sins or misdeeds ▸ contriteness, remorse, repentance. *See* **penitence**.

shame *verb*
1. To cause to feel embarrassment, dishonor, and often guilt ▸ brand, mortify, reproach, stigmatize. *Idioms:* put to shame, put to the blush. *See also* **belittle, denigrate, embarrass, humble. 2.** To bring disgrace on ▸ abase, dishonor, sully. *See* **disgrace**.

shameful *adjective*
1. Meriting or causing shame or dishonor ▸ discreditable, ignominious, reproachable. *See* **disgraceful** (1). **2.** Worthy of severe disapproval ▸ condemnable, reprehensible, unfortunate. *See* **deplorable** (1).

shamefulness *noun*
▸ disreputableness, ignominiousness. *See* **infamy** (1).

shameless *adjective*
1. Rude and disrespectful ▸ bold, insolent, pert. *See* **impudent**. *See synonym note at* **impudent. 2.** Lacking scruples or principles ▸ unconscionable, unethical, unprincipled. *See* **unscrupulous** (1).

shamelessness *noun*
▸ audacity, boldness, forwardness. *See* **impudence**.

shanty *noun*
▸ hovel, lean-to, shack. *See* **hut**.

shape *noun*
1. A state of sound readiness ▸ condition, fettle, fitness, form, kilter, order, repair, trim. **2.** The surface arrangement of a thing ▸ configuration, outline, pattern. *See* **form** (1). *See synonym note at* **form. 3.** The physical characteristics of a person ▸ body, form, physique. *See* **constitution** (1).

shape *verb*
1. To give form to by or as if by pressing and kneading ▸ fashion, model, mold. *See* **form** (1). **2.** To create by forming, combining, or altering materials ▸ build, compose, shape. *See* **make** (1). **3.** To make or become suitable to a particular situation or use ▸ adjust, fashion, tailor. *See* **adapt**.

shapeless *adjective*
Having no distinct shape ▸ amorphous, formless, inchoate, unformed, unshaped, unstructured.

✦ **CORE SYNONYMS:** *shapeless, amorphous, formless, unformed, unshaped.* These adjectives mean having no distinct shape: *a mass of shapeless slag; an amorphous cloud; an aggregate of formless particles; an unformed lump of clay; unshaped dough.*

---

shapely *adjective*
Having a full, voluptuous figure ▸ bosomy, buxom, curvaceous, curvy, full-bosomed, full-figured, well-developed, well-endowed, zaftig. *Informal:* built. *Slang:* stacked.

shard *noun*
1. Residual matter ▸ fragment, odds and ends. *See* **end** (7). **2.** A tiny amount ▸ dash, drop, smidgen. *See* **bit**[1] (1).

share *noun*
1. One's duty or responsibility in a common effort ▸ function, part, piece, role. *See also* **function.** **2.** That which is allotted ▸ allowance, ration. *See* **allotment** (1).

share *verb*
1. To give out in portions or shares ▸ allocate, apportion, dispense. *See* **distribute** (1). **2.** To tell in confidence ▸ breathe, confide, unbosom, whisper. *See also* **communicate, reveal, say.** **3.** To help bring about a result ▸ chip in, participate. *See* **contribute** (2).

shared *adjective*
1. Belonging to, shared by, or applicable to all alike ▸ general, mutual, public. *See* **common** (2). **2.** Having the same relationship each to the other ▸ requited, reciprocative. *See* **mutual** (1).

sharing *noun*
1. The act or fact of participating ▸ engagement, involvement, partaking, participation. **2.** The act of distributing or the condition of being distributed ▸ allocation, apportionment, dispensation. *See* **distribution** (1).

sharp *adjective*
1. Having a fine edge, as for cutting ▸ honed, keen, keen-edged, knife-edged, razor-edged, razor-sharp, sharpened, whetted. **2.** Having an end that tapers to a point ▸ acute, cuspate, fine. *See* **pointed** (1). **3.** Clearly defined; not ambiguous ▸ clear, distinct, unambiguous, unequivocal, unmistakable, well-defined. *See also* **apparent, definite.** **4.** Mentally quick and original ▸ keen, quick-witted, smart. *See* **clever** (1). **5.** Keenly perceptive or discerning ▸ incisive, keen, penetrating. *See* **critical** (2). **6.** Deceitfully clever ▸ cunning, sly, wily. *See* **artful** (1). **7.** So sharp as to cause mental pain ▸ caustic, scathing, slashing, vitriolic. *See* **biting.** **8.** Marked by pain that is severe or intense ▸ acute, biting, gnawing, knifelike, piercing, shooting, stabbing, throbbing. *See also* **bitter, intense, severe.** **9.** Unexpectedly sudden ▸ precipitate, sudden. *See* **abrupt** (2). **10.** *Informal* In accordance with current fashion ▸ mod, stylish, swanky. *See* **fashionable.**

11. Having a taste characteristic of that produced by acids ▸ acerbic, tart. *See* **sour** (1). **12.** Having a sharp, penetrating flavor or aroma ▸ piquant, redolent, zesty. *See* **spicy** (1). **13.** So sharply inclined as to be almost perpendicular ▸ abrupt, sudden. *See* **steep**[1] (1).

✦ **CORE SYNONYMS:** *sharp, keen, acute.* These adjectives all apply literally to fine edges, points, or tips. Figuratively they indicate mental alertness and clarity of comprehension. *Sharp* suggests quickness and astuteness: *"a young man of sharp and active intellect"* (John Henry Newman). *Keen* implies clearheadedness and acuity: *a journalist with a keen mind and quick wits. Acute* suggests penetrating perception or discernment: *an acute observer of national politics.*

---

sharpen *verb*
1. To give a sharp edge to ▸ edge, file, grind, hone, strop, whet. *Idioms:* make sharp, put an edge on. **2.** To make greater in intensity or severity ▸ deepen, enhance, heighten. *See* **intensify.**

sharper *noun*
▸ cheater, swindler, trickster. *See* **cheat** (2).

sharpness *noun*
1. A cutting quality ▸ incisiveness, keenness. *See* **edge** (1). **2.** Skill in perceiving, discriminating, or judging ▸ keenness, perceptiveness, shrewdness. *See* **discernment** (1).

sharp-tongued *adjective*
1. So sharp as to cause mental pain ▸ caustic, scathing, sharp, vitriolic. *See* **biting.** **2.** Of, relating to, or characterized by verbal abuse ▸ contumelious, invective, scurrilous. *See* **abusive.**

sharp-witted *adjective*
▸ keen, quick-witted, sharp. *See* **clever** (1).

shatter *verb*
1. To crack or split into two or more fragments by means of force or strain ▸ rive, smash, splinter. *See* **break** (1). *See synonym note at* **break.** **2.** To cause the complete ruin or wreckage of ▸ demolish, torpedo, wreck. *See* **destroy** (1). **3.** To severely impair someone's spirit, health, or will ▸ overwhelm, ruin. *See* **break** (4).

shave *verb*
1. To make light and momentary contact with, as in passing ▸ graze, kiss, skim. *See* **brush**[1]. *See synonym note at* **brush**[1]. **2.** To make a slight reduction in a price ▸ shade, trim. **3.** To decrease, as in length or amount, by or as if by severing or excising ▸ chop, prune, trim. *See* **cut** (3).

shaving *noun*
▸ chip, slice, sliver. *See* **flake** (1).

shawl *noun*
A garment wrapped about a person ▸ cloak, stole, wrap. *See also* **scarf.**

shawl *verb*
To cover as if with clothes ▸ drape, robe. *See* **clothe** (1).

shear *verb*
▸ chop, prune, trim. *See* **cut** (3).

shears *noun*

An implement used for cutting or pruning ▸ clippers, cutters, loppers, nippers, pruner, scissors, snips, snippers.

sheath *or* **sheathing** *noun*

▸ membrane, sheet. *See* **skin** (2).

sheathe *verb*

▸ clad, cover, side. *See* **face** (2).

shed¹ *verb*

1. To send out heat, light, or energy ▸ cast (out), emit, irradiate, project, radiate, send forth (out), throw (out). *See also* **emit**. **2.** To cast off by a natural process ▸ exuviate, molt, slough, throw off. **3.** To come off in small, thin pieces ▸ chip, peel, scale. *See* **flake**. **4.** To let go or get rid of as being useless or defective, for example ▸ dump, throw away. *Informal:* chuck. *See* **discard**.

shed² *noun*

A small, usually roughly built shelter ▸ cabin, shack, shanty. *See* **hut**.

sheen *noun*

▸ luster, polish, shine. *See* **gloss¹** (1).

sheer¹ *verb*

To turn aside sharply from a straight course ▸ slant, veer, zigzag. *See* **swerve** (1).

sheer² *adjective*

1. Thin, fine, and light ▸ airy, diaphanous, ethereal, filmy, gauzy, gossamer, gossamery, transparent, vaporous, vapory. **2.** Completely such, without qualification or exception ▸ all-out, pure, total. *See* **utter²**. **3.** Free from extraneous elements ▸ perfect, plain, unadulterated. *See* **pure** (1). *See synonym note at* **pure**. **4.** So sharply inclined as to be almost perpendicular ▸ sharp, sudden. *See* **steep¹** (1). *See synonym note at* **steep¹**.

✦ **CORE SYNONYMS:** *sheer, airy, diaphanous, ethereal, filmy, gauzy, gossamer, transparent, vaporous. These adjectives mean so thin, fine, and light as to suggest air or a thin film: sheer silk stockings; airy curtains blowing at the window; a diaphanous veil; ethereal mist; the filmy wings of a moth; gauzy clouds in the sky; a gown of gossamer fabric; transparent chiffon; vaporous shadows at dusk.*

---

sheet *noun*

1. A thin outer covering ▸ membrane, sheath. *See* **skin** (2). **2.** A thin layer of material covering something else ▸ covering, overlay. *See* **coat** (2). **3.** A document used in applying, as for a job ▸ application, form, paper.

sheik *noun*

▸ boss, director, head, leader. *See* **chief** (1).

shell *noun*

1. A structure that supports or encloses something ▸ case, skeleton. *See* **frame** (1). **2.** The outer covering of a fruit ▸ peel, rind. *See* **skin** (3).

shell *verb*

1. To direct a barrage at ▸ bombard, pelt. *See* **barrage**. *See synonym note at* **barrage**. **2.** To remove the skin of ▸ pare, strip. *See* **skin** (1).

shell out *verb*

Informal To give money as payment ▸ expend, outlay. *See* **spend** (1).

shellac *verb*

1. To apply a coating to ▸ lacquer, stain, varnish. *See* **finish** (7). **2.** *Slang* To render totally ineffective by decisive defeat ▸ crush, overcome, overpower, rout. *See* **overwhelm** (1).

shellac *noun*

A final coating ▸ lacquer, stain, varnish. *See* **finish** (3).

shellacking *noun*

▸ overthrow, trouncing, vanquishment. *See* **defeat**.

shelter *noun*

1. Dwellings in general ▸ housing, lodging. **Idiom:** a roof over one's head. *See also* **home, hut**. **2.** Something that physically protects, especially from danger ▸ harbor, haven, refuge. *See* **cover** (1). *See synonym note at* **cover**. **3.** Protection or shelter, as from danger or hardship ▸ asylum, sanctuary. *See* **refuge** (1). **4.** An institution that provides care and shelter ▸ hospice, hospital. *See* **home** (3).

shelter *verb*

To give refuge to ▸ harbor, haven, house, take in. *See also* **defend**.

shelve *verb*

▸ delay, postpone, suspend. *See* **defer¹**. *See synonym note at* **defer¹**.

shenanigan *noun*

1. *Informal* An indirect, usually cunning means of gaining an end ▸ deception, ploy, stratagem. *See* **trick** (1). **2.** *Informal* A mischievous act ▸ caper, joke, trick. *See* **prank¹**.

shenanigans *noun*

Informal Annoying yet harmless, usually playful acts ▸ diablerie, high jinks, tomfoolery. *See* **mischief** (1).

shepherd *noun*

Something or someone that shows the way ▸ director, escort, leader. *See* **guide** (1).

shepherd *verb*

To show the way to ▸ direct, escort, lead. *See* **guide** (1). *See synonym note at* **guide**.

sheriff *noun*

▸ officer, trooper. *Informal:* cop. *See* **police officer**.

sherlock *noun*

▸ sleuth. *Informal:* eye. *Slang:* gumshoe. *See* **detective**.

shield *noun*

The act or a means of defending ▸ protection, safeguard, ward. *See* **defense** (1).

shield *verb*

To keep safe from danger, attack, or harm ▸ protect, secure. *See* **defend** (1). *See synonym note at* **defend**.

shift *verb*

1. To move or cause to move slightly ▸ budge, move, stir. **2.** To take turns ▸ alternate, interchange, rotate. **3.** To alter the settled state or position of ▸ displace, disrupt. *See* **disturb** (1). **4.** To go or cause to go from one place to another ▸ maneuver, transfer. *See* **move** (2). **5.** To change the direction or course of ▸ deviate, divert, veer. *See* **turn** (2). **6.** To give up in return for

something else ▸ exchange, trade. *See* **change** (3).
shift *noun*
1. Occurrence in successive turns ▸ alternation, interchange, shift. 2. An often sudden change or departure, as in a trend ▸ tack, turn, twist. *See also* **deviation**. 3. The act of exchanging ▸ exchange, interchange, switch. *See* **change** (2). 4. The process or result of making or becoming different ▸ modification, mutation, variation. *See* **change** (1). 5. A limited, often assigned period of activity, duty, or opportunity ▸ stint, time, watch. *See* **turn** (1). 6. Something used temporarily or reluctantly when other means are not available ▸ expedient, make-do, stopgap. *See* **makeshift**. 7. A change in normal place or position ▸ dislodging, movement, rearrangement. *See* **displacement**. 8. The process or result of changing from one use, function, or appearance to another ▸ change, mutation, transformation. *See* **conversion** (1). 9. Passage from one form, state, or stage to another ▸ change, passage, transit. *See* **transition**. 10. A one-piece skirted outer garment for women and children ▸ jumper, gown. *See* **dress** (3).
shiftiness *noun*
1. The act or practice of deceiving ▸ deception, duplicity, guile. *See* **deceit** (1). 2. Lack of straightforwardness and honesty in action ▸ deviousness, slyness, trickery. *See* **dishonesty** (2).
shiftless *adjective*
▸ idle, indolent, slothful. *See* **lazy**.
shiftlessness *noun*
▸ idleness, indolence, sloth. *See* **laziness**.
shifty *adjective*
1. Marked by treachery or deceit ▸ devious, duplicitous, sneaky. *See* **underhand**. 2. Marked by whim or impulse ▸ fickle, impulsive, mercurial. *See* **capricious**.
shill *noun*
Slang A person who cheats ▸ cheater, swindler, trickster. *See* **cheat** (2).
shilly-shally *verb*
To be irresolute in acting or doing ▸ falter, vacillate. *See* **hesitate** (1).
shilly-shally *adjective*
Given to or exhibiting hesitation ▸ indecisive, irresolute. *See* **hesitant**.
shilly-shally *noun*
The act of hesitating or state of being hesitant ▸ indecision, tentativeness. *See* **hesitation**.
shimmer *verb*
To emit light in sudden or intermittent bursts ▸ flash, glimmer, twinkle. *See* **glitter**. *See synonym note at* **glitter**.
shimmer *noun*
Sparkling, brilliant light ▸ glint, glisten, sparkle. *See* **glitter** (1).
shin *verb*
▸ scamper, scurry, sprint. *See* **run** (1).
shindig *or* **shindy** *noun*
A big, exuberant party ▸ *Slang:* bash, blowout. *See* **blast** (3).

shine *verb*
1. To emit a bright light ▸ burn, glow. *See* **beam** (1). 2. To give a bright sheen or luster to ▸ burnish, glaze, polish. *See* **gloss¹** (1). 3. To be in one's prime ▸ flourish, flower. *Idioms:* cut a figure, make a splash.
shine *noun*
A surface shininess ▸ luster, polish, sheen. *See* **gloss¹** (1).
shiner *noun*
Slang A bruise surrounding the eye ▸ black eye. *Informal:* mouse. *See also* **bruise**.
shining *adjective*
1. Giving off or reflecting much light ▸ brilliant, incandescent, radiant. *See* **bright** (1). 2. Having a high, radiant sheen ▸ gleaming, glistening, lustrous. *See* **glossy**. 3. Marked by extraordinary beauty and splendor ▸ magnificent, resplendent, splendid. *See* **glorious** (1).
shiny *adjective*
1. Giving off or reflecting much light ▸ brilliant, incandescent, radiant. *See* **bright** (1). 2. Having a high, radiant sheen ▸ gleaming, glistening, lustrous. *See* **glossy**.
ship *noun*
A conveyance that travels over water ▸ bark, barque, boat, craft, vessel, watercraft.
ship *verb*
To cause something to be conveyed to a destination ▸ consign, dispatch. *See* **send** (1). *See synonym note at* **send**.
shipment *noun*
▸ conveyance, surrender, transfer. *See* **delivery** (1).
shipping *noun*
▸ conveyance, transit, transport. *See* **transportation** (1).
shipshape *adjective*
▸ prim, tidy. *See* **neat** (1). *See synonym note at* **neat**.
shipwreck *verb*
To damage, disable, or destroy a seacraft ▸ run aground, sink, wreck.
shirk *verb*
1. To fail to do or carry out ▸ disregard, omit, overlook. *See* **neglect** (3). 2. To pass time without working or in avoiding work ▸ loiter, lounge. *See* **idle** (1). 3. To fail to attend on purpose ▸ duck, truant. *Slang:* skip. *See* **cut** (8).
shirker *noun*
▸ idler, loafer, ne'er-do-well. *See* **wastrel** (2).
shirking *noun*
▸ delinquency, dereliction. *See* **failure** (2).
shiver¹ *verb*
To move to and fro in short, jerky movements ▸ quiver, tremble, twitter. *See* **shake** (1). *See synonym note at* **shake**.
shiver *noun*
A nervous shaking of the body ▸ quiver, shake, twitch. *See* **tremor** (2).
shiver² *verb*
To crack or split into two or more fragments by

means of force or strain ▸ shatter, smash, splinter. *See* **break** (1).

shivering *adjective*
▸ quaking, quivering, trembling. *See* **tremulous** (1).

shivers *noun*
▸ fidgets, jumps, trembles. *See* **jitters.**

shivery *adjective*
1. Marked by or affected with tremors ▸ quaky, quivery, shaky. *See* **tremulous** (1). **2.** Marked by a low temperature ▸ chill, frigid, polar. *See* **cold** (1).

shock¹ *noun*
1. Something that stuns or jars the mind ▸ blow, bombshell, jolt, rude awakening, surprise, trauma, wake-up call. *Idiom:* bolt from the blue. **2.** A violent forcible contact ▸ crash, impact. *See* **collision.** *See synonym note at* **collision.**

shock *verb*
1. To deprive of courage or the power to act as a result of fear, anxiety, or disgust ▸ consternate, disconcert. *See* **dismay** (1). **2.** To cause to experience a sudden momentary shock ▸ electrify, jolt. *See* **startle** (1). **3.** To overwhelm with surprise, wonder, or bewilderment ▸ dumbfound, flabbergast. *See* **stagger** (2).

shock² *noun*
A group of things gathered haphazardly ▸ drift, mass, mound. *See* **heap** (1).

shocking *adjective*
1. Exceeding the bounds of morality, decency, or reason ▸ appalling, monstrous, reprehensible. *See* **outrageous. 2.** Very bad ▸ appalling, awful, dreadful, wretched. *See* **terrible** (1). **3.** Exceeding the bounds of morality, decency, or reason ▸ atrocious, monstrous, preposterous. *See* **outrageous.**

shoddy *adjective*
1. Of decidedly inferior quality ▸ base, cheap, junky, lousy, miserable, paltry, poor, rotten, sleazy, sorry, trashy, worthless. *Informal:* cheesy. *Slang:* crappy, crummy, schlocky, stinko. *See also* **bad, rude, terrible. 2.** Showing signs of wear and tear or neglect ▸ broken-down, dilapidated, tattered. *See* **shabby** (1).

shoo-in *noun*
Informal A leading contestant or sure winner ▸ favorite, front-runner, leader, number one, vanguard.

shoot *verb*
1. To wound or kill with a firearm ▸ gun (down), pick off. *Slang:* plug. *Idioms:* fill full of lead (*or* holes). *See also* **kill¹, murder. 2.** To discharge a gun or firearm ▸ blast (away), fire (away *or* off), pop (off), shoot away (off). *Idioms:* go bang-bang, open fire, take a shot (*or* potshot). **3.** To launch with great force ▸ fire, hurtle, loose, project, propel. *Idiom:* let fly. **4.** To send through the air with a motion of the hand or arm ▸ heave, hurl, pitch. *See* **throw** (1). **5.** To move swiftly ▸ dash, hasten, sprint, zip. *See* **rush** (1). **6.** To pass quickly and lightly through the air ▸ dart, glide, sail, soar. *See* **fly** (2).

shoot down *verb*
To cause to be no longer believed or valued ▸ deflate, explode, puncture. *See* **discredit** (1).

shoot for *or* **at** *verb*
To make an attempt ▸ endeavor, strive. *See* **attempt.**

shoot up *verb*
Informal To rise abruptly and precipitously ▸ rocket, sky, skyrocket. *See* **soar** (1).

shoot *noun*
1. A young stemlike growth arising from a plant ▸ bine, offshoot, runner, sprig, sprout, sucker, tendril. **2.** A sensation of physical discomfort occurring as the result of disease or injury ▸ ache, pang, throe. *See* **pain** (1).

shooting *adjective*
▸ acute, gnawing, piercing. *See* **sharp** (8).

shop *noun*
A retail establishment where merchandise is sold ▸ boutique, emporium, outlet, store.

shopper *noun*
▸ customer, patron, user. *See* **consumer.**

shopworn *adjective*
▸ clichéd, overused, stale, tired. *See* **trite.**

shore *noun*
A means or device that keeps something erect, stable, or secure ▸ buttress, crutch, reinforcement. *See* **support** (1).

shore *verb*
To make stronger or more resistant ▸ bolster, reinforce, shore up, strengthen. *See* **support** (2).

short *adjective*
1. Below average in length or size ▸ bantam, undersized. *See* **little** (1). **2.** Lasting or existing only for a short time ▸ ephemeral, fleeting, temporary. *See* **transitory. 3.** Accomplished or experienced in very little time ▸ fast, rapid, speedy. *See* **quick** (1). **4.** Expressed in few words ▸ concise, curt, succinct. *See* **brief** (1). **5.** Rudely informal ▸ blunt, brusque, gruff. *See* **abrupt** (1). **6.** Not enough to meet a demand or requirement ▸ inadequate, wanting. *See* **insufficient** (1).

short *adverb*
Without adequate preparation ▸ aback, unawarely, unawares. *Idioms:* by surprise, off guard.

shortage *noun*
The condition or fact of being deficient ▸ defect, deficit, deficiency, inadequacy, insufficiency, lack, paucity, poverty, scantiness, scantness, scant supply, scarceness, scarcity, shortcoming, shortfall, underage. *See also* **absence, need.**

shortchange *verb*
Informal To get money or something else from someone by deceitful trickery ▸ bilk, defraud, swindle. *See* **cheat** (1).

shortcoming *noun*
1. The condition or fact of being deficient ▸ deficit, inadequacy, paucity. *See* **shortage. 2.** Something that mars the appearance or causes inadequacy or failure ▸ fault, glitch, imperfection. *See* **defect** (1). **3.** An imperfection of character ▸ fault, frailty, weak point. *See* **weakness** (1). **4.** An unfavorable condition, circumstance, or characteristic ▸ drawback, handicap, minus. *See* **disadvantage.**

shorten *verb*

To make short or shorter ▸ abbreviate, abridge, boil down, condense, curtail, reduce, shrink, truncate. *See also* **constrict, cut, decrease.**

✚ CORE SYNONYMS: *shorten, abbreviate, abridge, curtail, truncate.* These verbs mean to make short or shorter: *vices that will shorten your life; abbreviated the speech; abridging the citizens' rights; curtailed their visit; truncated the conversation.*

◂ ANTONYM: *lengthen*

---

shortfall *noun*

▸ deficit, inadequacy, paucity. *See* **shortage.**

short fuse *noun*

Slang A tendency to become angry or irritable ▸ crankiness, prickliness, tetchiness. *See* **temper** (1).

short-handed *adjective*

Having fewer workers or participants than are needed ▸ short-staffed, undermanned, understaffed.

short-lived *adjective*

▸ ephemeral, fleeting, temporary. *See* **transitory.**

short-range *adjective*

1. Intended, used, or present for a limited time ▸ interim, provisional, short-term. *See* **temporary** (2). 2. Designed or implemented so as to gain a temporary limited advantage ▸ tactical.

short-spoken *adjective*

▸ blunt, brusque, curt. *See* **abrupt** (1).

short-staffed *adjective*

Having fewer workers or participants than are needed ▸ short-handed, undermanned, understaffed.

short-tempered *adjective*

1. Easily moved to anger ▸ irascible, quick-tempered, tetchy. *See* **testy** (1). 2. Having or showing a bad temper ▸ cranky, grouchy, peevish. *See* **ill-tempered.**

short-term *adjective*

▸ interim, provisional. *See* **temporary** (2).

shorty *noun*

Informal A young or short person ▸ pip-squeak, runt, scrub. *See* **squirt** (2).

shot *noun*

1. *Informal* A brief trial ▸ crack, go, stab, try. *Informal:* fling, whack, whirl. 2. *Informal* A trying to do or make something ▸ effort, trial. *See* **attempt** (1). 3. *Informal* A favorable or advantageous combination of circumstances ▸ chance, option. *See* **opportunity.** 4. A small amount of liquor ▸ dram, sip, tot. *See* **drop** (8).

should *verb*

▸ be compelled, need, ought. *See* **must.**

shoulder *verb*

1. To take upon oneself ▸ tackle, take on. *See* **assume** (1). 2. To hold the weight of ▸ support, sustain. *See* **bear** (1). 3. To apply pressure on, against, or with ▸ press, prod, shove. *See* **push** (1). 4. *Informal* To force one's way into a place or situation ▸ elbow, shove. *See* **muscle.**

shout *verb*

To speak or say in a loud cry ▸ bawl, bellow, blare, bluster, call (out), clamor, cry (out), halloo, holler, howl, roar, scream, screech, shriek, squawk, vociferate, wail, whoop, yell. *See also* **exclaim, howl, yelp.**

shout *noun*

A loud call or cry ▸ bellow, call, cry, ejaculation, exclamation, halloo, holler, howl, outcry, roar, scream, screech, shriek, squawk, wail, yell. *See also* **vociferation, yelp.**

✚ CORE SYNONYMS: *shout, bawl, bellow, holler, howl, roar, whoop, yell.* These verbs mean to speak or say in a loud, strong cry: *fans shouting their approval; bawled out orders; bellows with rage; hollered a warning; howling with pain; a crowd roaring its disapproval; children whooping at play; troops yelling as they attacked.*

---

shove *verb*

1. To force to move or advance with or as if with blows or pressure ▸ butt, ram, slam. *See* **drive** (2). 2. To apply pressure on, against, or with ▸ dig, press, prod. *See* **push** (1). 3. *Informal* To force one's way into a place or situation ▸ elbow, shoulder. *See* **muscle.**

shove off *verb*

Informal To move away from a place ▸ exit, go away, retire. *See* **go** (1).

shove *noun*

An act or instance of pushing ▸ jostle, press, thrust. *See* **push** (1).

shovel *verb*

▸ excavate, gouge, scoop. *See* **dig** (1).

show *verb*

1. To make manifest or apparent ▸ demonstrate, display, evidence, evince, exhibit, manifest, proclaim, reveal. *See also* **clarify, explain.** 2. To establish as true or genuine through evidence ▸ confirm, substantiate, validate. *See* **prove** (1). 3. To give a precise indication of, as on a register or scale ▸ indicate, mark, read, record, register. 4. To make visible ▸ disclose, expose, uncover. *See* **reveal** (2). 5. To come into view ▸ issue, loom, materialize. *See* **appear** (1). *See synonym note at* **appear.** 6. To present a lifelike image of ▸ depict, portray, render. *See* **represent** (2). 7. To make a public and usually ostentatious show of ▸ exhibit, expose, flaunt. *See* **display** (1). 8. To show the way to ▸ direct, escort, lead. *See* **guide** (1). 9. To be performed ▸ play, run.

show off *verb*

1. To make a public and usually ostentatious show of ▸ flash, flaunt, parade. *See* **display** (1). 2. To behave in an ostentatious manner or perform dangerous stunts ▸ *Slang:* hot-dog, showboat. *See also* **boast, swagger.**

show up *verb*

To come to a particular place ▸ check in, reach, turn up. *See* **arrive** (1).

show *noun*

1. An act of showing or displaying ▸ exhibition, manifestation. *See* **display** (1). 2. A deceptive outward appearance ▸ disguise, mask. *See* **façade** (2). 3. A display of insincere behavior ▸ masquerade, pretense, simulation. *See* **act** (2). 4. An impressive or ostenta-

tious exhibition ▸ display, spectacle. *See* **array** (1). **5.** A large public display, as of goods or works of art ▸ exposition, festival. *See* **exhibition** (1).

showboat *noun*
A person who behaves in an ostentatious manner or performs dangerous stunts ▸ *Slang:* hotdog, showoff. *See also* **braggart.**

showboat *verb*
To behave in an ostentatious manner or perform dangerous stunts ▸ *Slang:* hot-dog, show off. *See also* **boast, swagger.**

showcase *verb*
▸ exhibit, expose, flaunt. *See* **display** (1).

showdown *noun*
▸ duel, face-off, meeting. *See* **confrontation** (1).

shower *noun*
1. A concentrated outpouring, as of missiles, words, or blows ▸ cannonade, fusillade, volley. *See* **barrage.** *See synonym note at* **barrage. 2.** Water condensed from atmospheric vapor and falling in drops ▸ deluge, downpour, sprinkle. *See* **rain** (2).

shower *verb*
1. To give in great abundance ▸ heap, lavish, rain. *See also* **confer, donate, give. 2.** To direct a barrage at ▸ bombard, pelt. *See* **barrage. 3.** To fall in drops of water from clouds ▸ precipitate, spit. *See* **rain** (2).

showiness *noun*
▸ brilliance, resplendence, sparkle. *See* **glitter** (2).

showoff *noun*
A person who behaves in an ostentatious manner or performs dangerous stunts ▸ *Slang:* hotdog, showboat. *See also* **braggart.**

showy *adjective*
Marked by outward, often extravagant display ▸ flamboyant, ostentatious, pretentious, splashy, splurgy. *See also* **gaudy, ornate.**

✦ **CORE SYNONYMS:** *showy, flamboyant, ostentatious, pretentious, splashy.* These adjectives mean marked by outward, often extravagant display: *a showy rhinestone bracelet; an entertainer's flamboyant personality; an ostentatious sable coat; a pretentious scholarly edition; a splashy advertising campaign.*

---

shred *noun*
A tiny amount ▸ dash, drop, smidgen. *See* **bit**[1] (1).

shred *verb*
To pull or cut into many pieces ▸ cut up, grate, rip up, slice up, tear up.

shreds *noun*
Torn and ragged clothing ▸ rags, tatters.

shrew *noun*
▸ harpy, nag. *See* **scold.**

shrewd *adjective*
1. Having or showing a clever awareness and resourcefulness in practical matters ▸ astute, cagey, canny, knowing, perspicacious, sagacious, slick, smart, street-smart, wise. *Informal:* savvy. *See also* **sophisticated. 2.** Deceitfully clever ▸ cunning, sly,

wily. *See* **artful** (1). **3.** Mentally quick and original ▸ keen, quick-witted, sharp. *See* **clever** (1). *See synonym note at* **clever.**

✦ **CORE SYNONYMS:** *shrewd, sagacious, astute, perspicacious.* These adjectives mean having or showing a clever awareness, sound judgment, and resourcefulness, especially in practical matters. *Shrewd* suggests a sharp intelligence, hardheadedness, and often an intuitive grasp of practical considerations: *"He was too shrewd to go along with them upon a road which could lead only to their overthrow"* (J.A. Froude). *Sagacious* connotes prudence, discernment, and farsightedness: *"He was observant and thoughtful, and given to asking sagacious questions"* (John Galt). *Astute* suggests shrewdness, especially with regard to one's own interests: *An astute tenant always reads the small print in a lease. Perspicacious* implies penetration and clear-sightedness: *She is much too perspicacious to be taken in by such a spurious argument.*

---

shrewdness *noun*
1. Skill in perceiving, discriminating, or judging ▸ keenness, perceptiveness, sharpness. *See* **discernment** (1). **2.** Deceitful cleverness ▸ craftiness, cunning, slyness. *See* **art** (1).

shriek *noun*
1. A long, loud, piercing cry, as of fright ▸ screak, scream, screech. *See also* **howl. 2.** A loud call or cry ▸ bellow, scream, yell. *See* **shout.**

shriek *verb*
1. To utter a long loud piercing cry, as in fright ▸ screak, scream, screech, shrill. *See also* **howl. 2.** To speak or say in a loud cry ▸ call, holler, yell. *See* **shout.**

shrieky *adjective*
▸ piercing, shrill. *See* **high** (3).

shrill *adjective*
1. Elevated in pitch ▸ piercing, treble. *See* **high** (3). **2.** Disagreeable to the senses, especially the sense of hearing ▸ grating, jarring. *See* **harsh** (1). **3.** Marked by extremely high volume and intensity of sound ▸ booming, earsplitting, noisy. *See* **loud** (1).

shrill *verb*
To utter a long, loud, piercing cry, as of fright ▸ screak, scream, screech, shriek. *See also* **howl.**

shrilly *adjective*
▸ piercing, treble. *See* **high** (3).

shrimp *noun*
1. *Slang* A totally insignificant person ▸ nobody, nothing, small fry. *See* **nonentity. 2.** *Informal* A small or young person ▸ pip-squeak, runt, scrub. *See* **squirt** (2).

shrine *noun*
A sacred or holy place ▸ sacrarium, sanctorium, sanctuary, sanctum.

shrink *verb*
1. To make smaller or narrower by binding or squeezing ▸ compress, contract, narrow. *See* **constrict** (1). **2.** To draw away or pull back in fear ▸ cringe, recoil, wince. *See* **flinch. 3.** To become or cause to become gradually less ▸ diminish, dwindle, lessen. *See*

decrease. **4.** To make short or shorter ▸ abridge, reduce. *See* **shorten.**

shrink *noun*
An act of drawing back in an involuntary or instinctive fashion ▸ flinch, wince. *See* **recoil.**

shrinkage *noun*
1. The act or process of constricting ▸ compression, contraction. *See* **constriction. 2.** The act or process of decreasing ▸ diminishment, reduction, slowdown. *See* **decrease. 3.** A lowering of price or value ▸ markdown, reduction. *See* **depreciation** (1).

shrivel *verb*
1. To make or become no longer fresh or shapely because of loss of moisture ▸ mummify, sear, wither. *See* **dry** (1). **2.** To spoil or destroy ▸ corrode, dash. *See* **blast** (2). **3.** To become downcast from longing or grief ▸ ebb, wither. *See* **languish** (1).

shroud *verb*
1. To cut off from sight ▸ conceal, hide, screen. *See* **block** (1). *See synonym note at* **block. 2.** To surround and cover completely so as to obscure ▸ clothe, invest. *See* **wrap** (2). **3.** To prevent something from being known ▸ enshroud, mask. *See* **conceal** (1).

shroud *noun*
1. A cloth or garment in which a corpse is buried ▸ cerecloth, cerement, cerements, grave clothes, winding sheet. **2.** A covering that obscures or hides something ▸ cover, screen. *See* **veil** (1).

shrubbery *noun*
▸ bushes, thicket, undergrowth. *See* **brush²**.

shrunken *adjective*
▸ emaciated, wan, worn. *See* **haggard.**

shuck *verb*
1. *Informal* To let go or get rid of as being useless or defective, for example ▸ dump, throw away. *Informal:* chuck. *See* **discard. 2.** To remove the skin of ▸ pare, strip. *See* **skin** (1).

shudder *verb*
To move to and fro in short, jerky movements ▸ quiver, tremble, twitter. *See* **shake** (1). *See synonym note at* **shake.**

shudder *noun*
A nervous shaking of the body ▸ quiver, shake, twitch. *See* **tremor** (2).

shuddering *adjective*
▸ quaking, quivering, shaking. *See* **tremulous** (1).

shuffle *verb*
1. To mix together so as to change the order of arrangement ▸ jumble, rearrange, reconfigure, reorder, riffle, scramble. *Informal:* rejigger. **2.** To walk in a laborious way ▸ scuffle, shamble. *See* **trudge. 3.** To proceed or perform in an unsteady, faltering manner ▸ bungle, flounder, fumble. *See* **muddle** (1). **4.** To use evasive or deliberately vague language ▸ hedge, weasel. *See* **equivocate** (1). **5.** To stray from truthfulness or sincerity ▸ palter, prevaricate. *See* **equivocate** (2).

shuffle *noun*
The use or an instance of equivocal language ▸ euphemism, prevarication. *See* **equivocation** (1).

shun *verb*
1. To keep away from ▸ circumvent, escape, evade. *See* **avoid.** *See synonym note at* **avoid. 2.** To slight someone deliberately ▸ rebuff, spurn. *See* **snub.**

shunt *verb*
▸ deviate, divert, veer. *See* **turn** (2).

shush *verb*
▸ quiet, still. *See* **silence.**

shut *verb*
To move a door, for example, in order to cover an opening ▸ close, clench, seal, slam.

shut away *or* **in** *or* **up** *verb* **1.** To confine within a limited area ▸ cage, coop (in *or* up), fence (in). *See* **enclose** (1). **2.** To put in or as if in prison ▸ confine, incarcerate, lock (up). *See* **imprison.**

shut off *or* **out** *verb*
To cut off from sight ▸ conceal, screen. *See* **block** (1).

shut out *verb*
1. To keep from being admitted, included, or considered ▸ eliminate, rule out. *See* **exclude** (1). **2.** To rid one's mind of ▸ cast out, dispel. *See* **dismiss** (3).

shut up *verb*
1. To enclose so as to hinder or prohibit escape ▸ closet, confine, imprison. **2.** To cause to become silent ▸ quiet, still. *See* **silence.**

shutdown *noun*
▸ cease, completion, termination. *See* **end** (1).

shuteye *noun*
Slang The natural recurring condition of suspended consciousness by which the body rests ▸ sleep, slumber. *Idiom:* land of Nod. *See also* **nap, rest.**

shy¹ *adjective*
1. Awkward or unconfident in the presence of others ▸ backward, bashful, coy, demure, diffident, introverted, modest, nonassertive, retiring, self-effacing, timid, unassuming. *See also* **cool, reserved, taciturn. 2.** Not enough to meet a demand or requirement ▸ inadequate, short. *See* **insufficient** (1).

shy *verb*
To draw away or pull back in fear ▸ cringe, recoil, shrink. *See* **flinch.**

✦ **CORE SYNONYMS:** *shy, bashful, diffident, modest, coy, demure.* These adjectives mean awkward, reticent, or unconfident in the presence of others. One who is *shy* draws back from others, either because of a withdrawn nature or out of timidity: *"The poor man was shy and hated society"* (George Bernard Shaw). *Bashful* suggests self-consciousness or awkwardness in the presence of others: *"I never laughed, being bashful./Lowering my head, I looked at the wall"* (Ezra Pound). *Diffident* implies lack of self-confidence: *He was too diffident to express his opinion. Modest* is associated with an unassertive nature and absence of vanity or pretension: *Despite her fame she remained a modest, unassuming person. Coy* usually implies feigned, often flirtatious shyness: *"yielded with coy submission"* (John Milton). *Demure* often denotes an affected shyness or modesty: *Her assistant nodded in agreement, flashing a demure smile.*

shy² *verb*

To send through the air with a motion of the hand or arm ▸ heave, hurl, pitch. *See* **throw** (1).

shy *noun*

An act of throwing ▸ fling, hurl, toss. *See* **throw**.

shyness *noun*

An awkwardness or lack of self-confidence in the presence of others ▸ backwardness, bashfulness, coyness, demureness, diffidence, modesty, retiringness, self-effacement, timidity, timidness. *See also* **reserve**.

sibilant *noun*

▸ fizzle, rustle. *See* **hiss** (1).

sibilate *verb*

▸ fizzle, swish. *See* **hiss** (1).

sibyl *noun*

▸ diviner, fortuneteller, soothsayer. *See* **prophet**.

sibylline *adjective*

▸ divinitory, oracular, vatic. *See* **prophetic**.

sick *adjective*

1. Suffering from or appearing to suffer from an illness ▸ ailing, anemic, down, ill, indisposed, low, nauseated, nauseous, off-color, peaked, queasy, sickly, unhealthy, unwell. *Informal:* laid up. *Chiefly Regional:* poorly. *Idioms:* green around the gills, under the weather. *See also* **feverish, infirm, pale, weak. 2.** Characterized by preoccupation with unwholesome thoughts or feelings ▸ insalubrious, unhealthy. *See* **morbid** (1). **3.** Out of patience ▸ disgusted, fed up, tired, weary. *Idiom:* sick and tired. *See also* **angry. 4.** Afflicted with or exhibiting irrationality and mental unsoundness ▸ crazy, lunatic, mad. *See* **insane** (1).

sicken *verb*

1. To become affected with a disease ▸ develop, get. *See* **contract** (2). **2.** To offend the senses or feelings of ▸ appall, revolt, turn off. *See* **disgust** (1). *See synonym note at* **disgust**.

sickening *adjective*

1. So unpleasant or objectionable as to cause scorn or disgust ▸ contemptible, disgusting, obnoxious. *See* **offensive** (1). **2.** So unpleasant in flavor as to be inedible ▸ distasteful, unappetizing, uneatable. *See* **unpalatable** (1). **3.** Producing dizziness or vertigo ▸ dizzy, dizzying, giddy, vertiginous. *See also* **steep**.

sickle *verb*

▸ chop, prune, trim. *See* **cut** (3).

sickly *adjective*

1. Suffering from or appearing to suffer from an illness ▸ ailing, indisposed, unwell. *See* **sick** (1). **2.** Being weak in quality or substance ▸ bloodless, pallid. *See* **pale** (2).

sickness *noun*

1. The condition of being sick ▸ affliction, ailment, bug, complaint, failing health, ill health, illness, indisposition, infirmity, malady, malaise, poor health, unhealthiness. *See also* **distress. 2.** A pathological condition of mind or body ▸ ailment, disorder, malady. *See* **disease** (1).

side *noun*

1. An outer surface, layer, or part of an object ▸ face,

facet, surface. *See also* **back, bottom, front. 2.** One of two or more contrasted parts or places identified by its location with respect to a center ▸ flank, hand. **3.** The position from which something is observed or considered ▸ aspect, respect, standpoint. *See* **viewpoint. 4.** A group of people organized for a particular purpose, especially in a contest ▸ squad, team. *See* **force** (5).

side *verb*

To cover with a different material ▸ clad, cover, sheathe. *See* **face** (2).

side with *verb*

To aid the cause of by approving or favoring ▸ back, endorse, stand by. *See* **support** (1).

sidekick *noun*

1. *Slang* A person whom one knows well, likes, and trusts ▸ *Informal:* bud, buddy, pal. *See* **friend** (1). **2.** *Slang* One who shares interests or activities with another ▸ companion, comrade, fellow. *See* **associate** (2).

sidesplitting *adjective*

▸ comical, humorous, laughable. *See* **funny** (1).

sidestep *verb*

▸ duck, hedge. *See* **evade** (1).

sideswipe *verb*

To wreck a vehicle ▸ rear-end, smash, wreck. *See* **crash** (1).

sideswipe *noun*

A wrecking of a vehicle ▸ smash, wreck. *See* **crash** (2).

sidle *verb*

To advance carefully and gradually ▸ ease, edge. *See also* **crawl, sneak**.

siege *noun*

A prolonged encirclement of an objective by hostile troops ▸ beleaguerment, besiegement, blockade, investment. *See also* **attack**.

siege *verb*

To surround with hostile troops ▸ beset, blockade. *See* **besiege** (1). *See synonym note at* **besiege**.

siesta *noun*

▸ doze, snooze. *See* **nap**.

sift *verb*

To set apart one kind or type from others ▸ separate, sort, winnow. *Idiom:* separate the sheep from the goats.

sigh *verb*

To make a low, continuous, and indistinct sound ▸ murmur, rustle, sough, whisper. *See also* **burble, hum**.

sigh *noun*

A low, indistinct, and often continuous sound ▸ sough, susurration, whisper. *See* **murmur** (1).

sight *noun*

1. An act of directing the eyes on an object ▸ contemplation, look, regard, view. *See also* **gaze, watch. 2.** The faculty of seeing ▸ eyesight, optics. *See* **vision** (1). **3.** That which is or can be seen ▸ panorama, perspective, vista. *See* **view** (2). **4.** *Informal* An unsightly object ▸ eyesore, monstrosity. *See* **mess** (2).

sightless *adjective*
▸ eyeless, unseeing. *See* **blind** (1).

sightlessness *noun*
The condition of not being able to see ▸ blindness, darkness, legal blindness, visual impairment.

sightly *adjective*
▸ comely, gorgeous, stunning. *See* **beautiful.**

sightseer *noun*
▸ excursionist, traveler, vacationer. *See* **tourist.**

sign *noun*
1. Something visible or evident that gives grounds for believing in the existence or presence of something else ▸ badge, emblem, evidence, index, indication, indicator, mark, manifestation, note, signification, stamp, symbol, symptom, token, witness. *See also* **hint, symbol, trace, track. 2.** A usually public posting that conveys a message ▸ bill, billboard, notice, placard, poster. **3.** Something that takes the place of words in communicating a thought or feeling ▸ indication, token. *See* **expression** (2). **4.** An expressive, meaningful bodily movement ▸ indication, signal. *See* **gesture** (1). *See synonym note at* **gesture. 5.** A conventional mark used in a writing system ▸ figure, symbol. *See* **character** (9). **6.** A phenomenon that serves as a sign of some future good or evil ▸ portent, prognostication, warning. *See* **omen.**

sign *verb*
1. To affix one's signature to ▸ autograph, endorse, inscribe, subscribe, undersign. *Idioms:* put one's John Hancock on, set one's hand to. **2.** To make bodily motions so as to convey an idea or complement speech ▸ gesticulate, motion, signal. *See* **gesture. 3.** To obtain the use or services of ▸ hire, retain. *See* **employ** (1).

sign on *verb*
Informal To become a member of ▸ enlist, enroll. *See* **join** (4).

sign over *verb*
To change the ownership of property by means of a legal document ▸ deed, grant. *See* **transfer** (1).

sign up *verb*
To become a member of ▸ enroll, muster in. *See* **join** (4).

✚ CORE SYNONYMS: *sign, symbol, emblem, badge, mark, token, symptom, note.* These nouns denote something visible or evident that gives grounds for believing in the existence or presence of something else. *Sign* is the most general: *"The exile of Gaveston was the sign of the barons' triumph"* (John R. Green). *Symbol* and *emblem* often refer to something associated with and standing for, representing, or identifying something else: *"There was One whose suffering changed an instrument of torture, degradation and shame, into a symbol of glory, honor, and immortal life"* (Harriet Beecher Stowe); *"a bed of sweet-scented lillies, the emblem of France"* (Amy Steedman). *Badge* usually refers to something that is worn as an insignia of membership, is an emblem of achievement, or is a characteristic sign: *a sheriff's badge. "Sweet mercy is nobility's true badge"* (William Shakespeare). *Mark*

can refer to a visible trace or impression (*a laundry mark*) or to an indication of a distinctive trait or characteristic: *Intolerance is the mark of a bigot. Token* usually refers to evidence or proof of something intangible: *sent flowers as a token of her affection. Symptom* suggests outward evidence of a process or condition, especially an adverse condition: *bad weather that showed no symptoms of improving anytime soon. Note* applies to the sign of a particular quality or feature: *"the eternal note of sadness"* (Matthew Arnold).

signal *noun*
An expressive, meaningful bodily movement ▸ indication, sign. *See* **gesture** (1). *See synonym note at* **gesture.**

signal *adjective*
Readily attracting notice ▸ conspicuous, outstanding, prominent. *See* **noticeable** (1).

signal *verb*
1. To make bodily motions so as to convey an idea or complement speech ▸ motion, sign. *See* **gesture. 2.** To make known or identify, as by signs ▸ indicate, mark, specify. *See* **designate** (1).

signalize *verb*
1. To make noticeable or different ▸ differentiate, individualize, singularize. *See* **distinguish** (2). **2.** To cause to be eminent or recognized ▸ dignify, exalt, honor. *See* **distinguish** (5). **3.** To make bodily motions so as to convey an idea or complement speech ▸ motion, sign, signal. *See* **gesture.**

significance *or* **significancy** *noun*
1. The quality or state of being important ▸ concernment, weightiness. *See* **importance.** *See synonym note at* **importance. 2.** Something that is conveyed or signified ▸ import, point, sense. *See* **meaning** (1). *See synonym note at* **meaning.**

significant *adjective*
1. Effectively conveying meaning, feeling, or mood ▸ eloquent, meaningful. *See* **expressive.** *See synonym note at* **expressive. 2.** Conveying hidden or unexpressed meaning ▸ consequential, pithy. *See* **pregnant** (2). **3.** Having great significance ▸ consequential, grand, meaningful. *See* **important** (1). **4.** Above average in amount, size, or scope ▸ extensive, large, sizable. *See* **big** (1). **5.** Serving to designate or indicate ▸ denotive, exhibitive, indicatory. *See* **designative.**

significantly *adverb*
▸ much, quite, well. *See* **considerably.**

signification *noun*
1. Something that is conveyed or signified ▸ import, sense, significance. *See* **meaning** (1). *See synonym note at* **meaning. 2.** Something visible or evident that gives grounds for believing in the existence or presence of something else ▸ evidence, indication, symptom. *See* **sign** (1). **3.** The act of referring ▸ naming, referral. *See* **reference** (1).

signifier *noun*
An object or expression associated with and serving to identify something else ▸ attribute, emblem, meta-

phor, symbol, token. *See also* **expression, sign, term.**

signify *verb*

1. To have or convey a particular idea ▸ denote, intend. *See* **mean**[1] (1). 2. To be of significance ▸ matter, weigh. *See* **count** (1). *See synonym note at* **count.** 3. To make known or identify, as by signs ▸ indicate, mark, specify. *See* **designate** (1).

sign off *verb*

▸ affiliate, clear. *See* **pass** (16).

silence *noun*

1. The absence of sound or noise ▸ hush, noiselessness, quiet, quietness, soundlessness, still, stillness. *See also* **calm, stillness.** 2. The avoidance of speech ▸ dumbness, muteness, speechlessness, wordlessness. *See also* **reserve.**

silence *verb*

1. To cause to become silent ▸ hush, quiet, quieten, shush, shut up, still. *See also* **repress, suppress.** 2. To keep from being published or transmitted ▸ ban, suppress, withhold. *See* **censor** (2).

silent *adjective*

1. Marked by, done with, or making no sound or noise ▸ hushed, inaudible, noiseless, quiet, soundless, still. 2. Not voiced or expressed ▸ tacit, undeclared, unexpressed, unsaid, unspoken, unuttered, unvoiced, wordless. *See also* **implicit, ulterior.** 3. Habitually untalkative ▸ reticent, tightlipped, uncommunicative. *See* **taciturn.** *See synonym note at* **taciturn.** 4. Temporarily unable or unwilling to speak, as from shock or fear ▸ inarticulate, mute. *See* **speechless** (1). 5. Lacking the power or faculty of speech ▸ inarticulate, voiceless. *See* **mute** (1).

✤ CORE SYNONYMS: *silent, still, quiet, noiseless, soundless.* These adjectives mean marked by, done with, or making no sound or noise. *Silent* can suggest a profound hush: *"I like the silent church before the service begins"* (Ralph Waldo Emerson). *Still* implies lack of motion or disturbance and often connotes rest or tranquillity: *"But after tempest . . . /There came a day as still as heaven"* (Tennyson). *Quiet* suggests the absence of bustle, tumult, or agitation: *"life being very short, and the quiet hours of it few"* (John Ruskin). *Noiseless* and *soundless* imply the absence of disturbing sound: *"th' inaudible and noiseless foot of time"* (William Shakespeare); *"the soundless footsteps on the grass"* (John Galsworthy).

---

silhouette *noun*

▸ configuration, design, structure. *See* **form** (1).

silky *or* **silken** *adjective*

Smooth and lustrous as if polished ▸ satiny, sleek. *See synonym note at* **sleek.** *See also* **even, glossy, slick.**

silliness *noun*

1. Foolish behavior ▸ folly, ridiculousness, tomfoolery. *See* **foolishness.** 2. Something that does not have or make sense ▸ bunkum, claptrap, garbage. *See* **nonsense** (1).

silly *adjective*

1. Displaying a lack of good sense ▸ fatuous, inane, senseless. *See* **foolish.** *See synonym note at* **foolish.**

2. Given to lighthearted silliness ▸ featherbrained, flighty, frivolous. *See* **giddy** (2).

silver-tongued *adjective*

▸ articulate, smooth-spoken. *See* **eloquent** (1).

similar *adjective*

▸ analogous, equivalent, uniform. *See* **like**[2].

similarity *noun*

▸ resemblance, similitude, uniformity. *See* **likeness** (1). *See synonym note at* **likeness.**

similarly *adjective*

In a similar manner ▸ likewise, so. *Idioms:* by the same token, in like fashion, in like manner, in the same way.

similitude *noun*

▸ resemblance, similarity, uniformity. *See* **likeness** (1). *See synonym note at* **likeness.**

simmer *verb*

1. To cook in a liquid just at or below boiling point ▸ boil, coddle, fricassee, stew. *See* **cook** (1). 2. To be in a state of turmoil or excitement ▸ burn, seethe. *See* **boil** (2).

simmer down *verb*

To bring one's emotions under control ▸ contain, control. *See* **compose** (6).

simper *verb*

To curve the lips upward in expressing amusement, pleasure, or happiness ▸ grin, smirk. *See* **smile.**

simper *noun*

A facial expression marked by an upward curving of the lips ▸ grin, smile, smirk. *See also* **sneer.**

simple *adjective*

1. Free from extraneous elements ▸ perfect, plain, unadulterated. *See* **pure** (1). *See synonym note at* **pure.** 2. Posing no difficulty ▸ effortless. *Informal:* snap. *See* **easy** (1). *See synonym note at* **easy.** 3. Without addition, decoration, or qualification ▸ bald, spare, plain. *See* **bare** (1). 4. Not showy or obtrusive ▸ inobtrusive, quiet, subdued. *See* **modest** (1). *See synonym note at* **modest.** 5. Having only a limited ability to learn and understand ▸ dull, slow, slow-witted. *See* **backward** (1). 6. Free from guile, cunning, or deceit ▸ innocent, naive. *See* **artless** (1). *See synonym note at* **artless.** 7. Of little distinction ▸ humble, lowly, mean. *See also* **modest.** 8. Of a charmingly plain and unsophisticated nature ▸ homely, homespun, natural. *See* **rustic** (1). 9. Easily imposed on or tricked ▸ dupable, naive, susceptible. *See* **gullible.**

simple *noun*

A peson who is deficient in judgment and good sense ▸ jackass, ninny, simpleton. *See* **fool** (1).

simple-minded *adjective*

▸ dull, slow, slow-witted. *See* **backward** (1).

simpleness *noun*

1. Lack of ostentation or pretension ▸ plainness, restraint, simplicity. *See* **modesty** (2). 2. The absence of guile, cunning, or deceit ▸ ingenuousness, naiveté. *See* **artlessness.**

simpleton *noun*

1. A person who is deficient in judgment and good

sense ► idiot, imbecile, nitwit. *See* **fool** (1). **2.** A mentally dull person ► dummy, imbecile, thickhead. *See* **dullard.**

simplex *noun*
► root, stem. *See* **theme** (1).

simplicity *noun*
1. Lack of ostentation or pretension ► plainness, simpleness, tastefulness. *See* **modesty** (2). **2.** The quality of being clear and easy to perceive ► distinctness, legibility, perspicuity, plainness. *See* **clarity** (1). **3.** The state of being stupid ► idiocy, mindlessness, obtuseness. *See* **stupidity. 4.** The absence of guile, cunning, or deceit ► ingenuousness, naiveté. *See* **artlessness.**

simplify *verb*
1. To reduce in complexity or scope ► boil down, pare (down), streamline. *Idioms:* reduce to the basics (*or* essentials *or* bare bones). *See also* **explain. 2.** To make clear or clearer ► elucidate, illustrate. *See* **clarify** (1).

simply *adverb*
Nothing more than ► but, just, merely, only. *See also* **barely, solely.**

simulacrum *noun*
► ditto, facsimile, likeness. *See* **copy** (1).

simulate *verb*
1. To make a copy of ► imitate, replicate, reproduce. *See* **copy** (1). **2.** To take on as a false appearance ► counterfeit, fake, feign. *See* **act** (2). **3.** To copy the manner or expression of another, especially in an exaggerated or mocking way ► caricature, mock. *See* **imitate** (1). *See synonym note at* **imitate.**

simulated *adjective*
► manmade, synthetic. *See* **artificial** (1). *See synonym note at* **artificial.**

simulation *noun*
1. An inferior substitute imitating an original ► imitation, reprint. *See* **copy** (2). **2.** A display of insincere behavior ► dissemblance, masquerade, pretense, sham. *See* **act** (2). **3.** Behavior that is assumed rather than natural ► airs, mannerism. *See* **affectation** (1).

simultaneous *adjective*
► attendant, attending, concomitant. *See* **concurrent** (1). *See synonym note at* **concurrent.**

simultaneously *adverb*
At the same time ► concurrently, synchronously, together. *Idioms:* all at once, all together.

sin *noun*
1. The quality or sate of being morally bad or objectionable ► iniquity, wickedness. *See* **evil** (1). **2.** A wicked act or wicked behavior ► evil, misdeed, peccancy. *See* **crime** (2).

sin *verb*
To violate a rule or law ► err, transgress, trespass. *See* **offend** (3).

since *conjunction*
► for, seeing as. *See* **because.**

sincere *adjective*
► honest, unaffected, unfeigned. *See* **genuine** (1).

sincerity *noun*
► incorruptibility, integrity. *See* **honesty** (1).

sine qua non *noun*
1. Something indispensable ► necessity, prerequisite, requirement. *See* **condition** (2). **2.** A basic trait or set of traits that define and establish the character of something ► being, nature, quintessence. *See* **essence** (1).

sinew *noun*
► brawn, potency, power. *See* **strength** (1).

sinewy *adjective*
1. Characterized by marked muscular development ► brawny, robust, sturdy. *See* **muscular.** *See synonym note at* **muscular. 2.** Containing or consisting of fibers ► fibrous, stringy, threadlike.

sinful *adjective*
► immoral, reprobate. *See* **evil** (1).

sing *verb*
1. To utter words or sounds in musical tones ► carol, chant, croon, intone, trill, vocalize, warble. *Slang:* belt (out). **2.** *Slang* To give incriminating information about others, especially to the authorities ► tip (off). *Slang:* rat, snitch. *See* **inform** (2).

singe *verb*
To undergo or cause to undergo damage by or as if by fire ► scorch, sear. *See* **burn** (1). *See synonym note at* **burn.**

singe *noun*
Damage that results from burning ► blister, sear. *See* **burn** (1).

singer *noun*
► songster, songstress, voice. *See* **vocalist.**

single *adjective*
1. Apart from or lacking the company of all others ► alone, companionless, lonely. *See* **solitary** (1). **2.** Alone in a given category ► only, particular, solitary. *See* **lone** (1). **3.** Being or related to a distinct entity ► particular, singular. *See* **individual** (2). **4.** Not divided among or shared with others ► particular, sole. *See* **exclusive** (1). **5.** Not married or involved in a committed relationship ► available, eligible, fancy-free, footloose, lone, marriageable, nubile, sole, spouseless, unattached, unmarried, unwed. *Idioms:* footloose and fancy-free, in the market.

single *verb*
To make a choice from a number of alternatives ► elect, pick (out), single out, vote (for). *See* **choose** (1).

single out *verb*
1. To refer to by name ► mention, specify. *See* **name** (2). **2.** To recognize as being different ► differentiate, discriminate. *See* **distinguish** (1). **3.** To make noticeable or different ► differentiate, individualize, singularize. *See* **distinguish** (2).

single-handedly *adverb*
► solitarily, solo. *See* **alone** (1).

single-minded *adjective*
1. Committed to or unwavering in a course of action ► bent, fixed, unhesitating. *See* **intent** (1). **2.** Possessing determination or resolution ► resolute, steadfast, unyielding. *See* **firm**[1] (3).

singleness *noun*
1. The condition of being one ▸ oneness, singularity, unity. *See also* **completeness. 2.** The quality or state of being alone ▸ isolation, loneliness. *See* **solitude. 3.** The quality or condition of being unique ▸ oneness, peerlessness, singularity. *See* **uniqueness** (1).

singly *adverb*
1. Without the presence or aid of another ▸ solitarily, solo. *See* **alone** (1). **2.** As a separate unit ▸ independently, individually. *See* **separately.**

singular *adjective*
1. Being or related to a distinct entity ▸ particular, sole. *See* **individual** (2). **2.** Alone in a given category ▸ only, single, solitary. *See* **lone** (1). **3.** Without equal or rival ▸ incomparable, unparalleled. *See* **unique** (1). **4.** Beyond what is usual, normal, or customary ▸ extraordinary, outstanding, remarkable. *See* **exceptional** (1). **5.** Deviating from what is conventional or customary ▸ bizarre, grotesque. *See* **eccentric.** *See synonym note at* **eccentric.**

singularity *noun*
1. The condition of being one ▸ oneness, singleness, unity. *See also* **completeness. 2.** A small, often specialized element of a whole ▸ particular, specialty, technicality. *See* **detail** (1). **3.** The quality of being individual ▸ distinctiveness, particularity. *See* **individuality** (1). **4.** The quality or condition of being unique ▸ matchlessness, oneness, singleness. *See* **uniqueness** (1). **5.** The set of behavioral or personal characteristics by which an individual is recognizable ▸ distinctiveness, individuality, selfhood. *See* **identity** (1). **6.** Peculiar behavior ▸ peculiarity, quirk. *See* **eccentricity.**

singularize *verb*
▸ differentiate, individualize. *See* **distinguish** (2).

singularly *adverb*
▸ exceptionally, uncommonly, uniquely. *See* **unusually.**

sinister *adjective*
▸ baleful, dire, malign. *See* **fateful** (1). *See synonym note at* **fateful.**

sink *verb*
1. To go beneath the surface or to the bottom of a liquid ▸ founder, go down, go under, gravitate, settle, submerge, submerse, subside. **2.** To move downward in response to gravity ▸ descend, drop, plummet. *See* **fall** (1). **3.** To go from a more erect posture to a less erect posture ▸ droop, slump. *See* **drop** (1). **4.** To slope downward ▸ decline, dip. *See* **drop** (5). **5.** To become lower in quality, character, or condition ▸ atrophy, degenerate, worsen. *See* **deteriorate** (1). **6.** To bring oneself down to a level considered inappropriate to one's dignity ▸ deign, descend, stoop. *See* **condescend** (1). **7.** To undergo moral deterioration ▸ degenerate, fall, slip. *See also* **deteriorate. 8.** To cause the complete ruin or wreckage of ▸ demolish, torpedo, wreck. *See* **destroy** (1). **9.** To damage, disable, or destroy a seacraft ▸ run aground, shipwreck, wreck. **10.** To become lower in value or price ▸ dive, drop, plummet. *See* **fall**

(7). **11.** To lose strength or power ▸ decline, fail, weaken. *See* **fade** (1). **12.** To penetrate into a substance or place with force ▸ drive, stab, stick. *See* **plunge** (1). **13.** To cause to descend ▸ drop, let down, take down. *See* **lower**^{2} (1).

sink in *verb*
To come as a realization ▸ dawn on (*or* upon), register, soak in. *See also* **discover, strike, understand.**

sink *noun*
1. An area sunk below its surroundings ▸ basin, dip, hollow. *See* **depression** (1). **2.** A place known for its great filth or corruption ▸ cesspool, gutter, sewer. *See* **pit**^{1} (3).

sinkhole *noun*
▸ basin, dip, indentation. *See* **depression** (1).

sinless *adjective*
▸ pure, uncorrupted, untainted. *See* **innocent** (1).

sinner *noun*
▸ scoundrel, villain. *See* **evildoer.**

sinuate *verb*
▸ creep, slither, worm. *See* **crawl** (1).

sinuous *adjective*
▸ convoluted, meandrous, twisting. *See* **winding** (1).

sip *verb*
To take into the mouth and swallow a liquid ▸ imbibe, lap up, swill. *See* **drink** (1).

sip *noun*
1. An act of drinking or the amount swallowed ▸ swallow, taste. *Informal:* swig. *See* **drink** (2). **2.** A small amount of liquor ▸ dram, shot, tot. *See* **drop** (8).

sire *noun*
A male parent ▸ begetter, paterfamilias, patriarch. *See* **father** (1).

sire *verb*
1. To be the biological father of ▸ beget, father, get. **2.** To give life to ▸ engender, propagate, spawn. *See* **breed** (1).

siren *noun*
A woman who seduces or exploits men ▸ femme fatale, temptress. *See* **seductress.**

siren *adjective*
Tending to seduce ▸ bewitching, enticing, tempting. *See* **seductive.**

sis *noun*
Informal A woman ▸ *Informal:* chick, damsel, gal. *See* **girl.**

sissified *adjective*
▸ feminine, unmanly. *See* **effeminate.**

sissy *adjective*
Ignobly lacking in courage ▸ faint-hearted, pusillanimous. *Slang:* gutless. *See* **cowardly.**

sissy *noun*
An ignoble, uncourageous person ▸ dastard, poltroon, recreant. *See* **coward.**

sissyish *adjective*
▸ feminine, unmanly. *See* **effeminate.**

sister *noun*
1. A woman whom one knows well, likes, and trusts

► confidante, comrade, intimate. *See* **friend** (1). **2.** *Informal* A woman ► *Informal:* chick, damsel, gal. *See* **girl.**

sisterhood *noun*
► companionship, society. *See* **company** (5).

sit *verb*
1. To assume a position resting on the buttocks with the torso upright ► be seated, seat oneself, sit down. *Informal:* park oneself. *Idioms:* take a load off (one's feet), take a seat. *See also* **squat. 2.** To assume a particular position, as for a portrait ► model, posture. *See* **pose** (1). **3.** To be in a certain position; have a location ► be located, be situated, rest, stand.

sit back *verb*
To take repose by ceasing work or other effort for an interval of time ► kick back, unbend, unwind. *See* **rest¹** (1).

sit on *or* **upon** *verb*
To hold something requiring an outlet in check ► smother, stifle, suppress. *See* **repress.**

sit out *verb*
To hold oneself back ► forbear, hold off, withhold. *See* **refrain.**

sit through *verb*
To put up with ► stick out, tolerate, withstand. *See* **endure** (1).

site *noun*
1. The place where a person or thing is located ► location, point, spot. *See* **position** (1). **2.** The place where an action or event occurs ► locale, setting. *See* **scene** (1).

site *verb*
To put in a certain position or location ► locate, place, situate. *See* **position.**

situate *verb*
► locate, place, spot. *See* **position.**

situation *noun*
1. One's place and direction relative to one's surroundings ► orientation, position. *See* **bearing** (3). **2.** The place where a person or thing is located ► location, point, spot. *See* **position** (1). **3.** Positioning of one individual vis-à-vis others ► position, rank, standing. *See* **place** (1). **4.** Manner of being or form of existence ► case, state, status. *See* **condition** (1). *See synonym note at* **condition. 5.** A post of employment ► job, situation. *See* **position** (3).

sixth sense *noun*
► insight, intuitiveness, intuition. *See* **instinct** (2).

sizable *adjective*
► extensive, large, substantial. *See* **big** (1). *See synonym note at* **big.**

sizableness *noun*
► bigness, greatness. *See* **size** (2).

sizably *adverb*
► much, quite, well. *See* **considerably.**

size *noun*
1. The amount of space occupied by something ► area, dimensions, extent, magnitude, measure, measurements, proportions, volume. *See also* **range.**

2. The quality or state of being large in amount, extent, or importance ► amplitude, bigness, greatness, largeness, magnitude, sizableness, voluminousness. *See also* **enormousness, heaviness. 3.** Great amount or dimension ► magnitude, mass. *See* **bulk** (1).

size *verb*
To arrange according to class ► categorize, class, group. *See* **classify.**

size up *verb*
To make a judgment as to the worth or value of ► assay, calculate. *See* **estimate** (1).

sizzle *verb*
To make a sibilant sound ► fizzle, swish. *See* **hiss** (1).

sizzle *noun*
1. A sibilant sound ► fizzle, rustle. *See* **hiss** (1). **2.** *Slang* Powerful, intense emotion ► fervor, fire, warmth. *See* **passion** (1). **3.** *Slang* The quality of being erotic ► sexiness, suggestiveness. *See* **eroticism** (1).

sizzling *adjective*
1. Marked by much heat ► blistering, boiling, burning. *See* **hot** (1). **2.** *Slang* Arousing erotic desire ► alluring, enticing. *See* **desirable** (1).

skate *verb*
1. To move smoothly, continuously, and effortlessly ► coast, slide, slip. *See* **glide** (1). **2.** *Informal* To progress quickly and effortlessly ► coast, sail. *See* **breeze.**

skedaddle *verb*
Informal To leave hastily ► bolt. *Slang:* scram, vamoose. *See* **run** (3).

skein *noun*
► labyrinth, maze, web. *See* **tangle** (1).

skeletal *adjective*
► gaunt, wan, worn. *See* **haggard.**

skeleton *noun*
1. A preliminary plan or version, as of a written work ► blueprint, sketch. *See* **draft** (1). **2.** A structure that supports or encloses something ► case, shell. *See* **frame** (1).

skell *noun*
► beggar, insolvent, tramp. *See* **pauper.**

skeptic *noun*
One who habitually or instinctively doubts or questions ► agnostic, doubter, doubting Thomas, nonbeliever, unbeliever.

skeptical *adjective*
1. Experiencing doubt ► hesitant, tentative, uncertain. *See* **doubtful** (2). **2.** Refusing or reluctant to believe ► questioning, unbelieving. *See* **incredulous. 3.** Lacking trust or confidence ► doubting, suspicious, wary. *See* **distrustful** (1).

skeptically *adverb*
With skepticism ► askance, distrustfully, distrustingly, doubtfully, doubtingly, dubiously, leerily, mistrustfully, questioningly, suspiciously, untrustingly. *Idioms:* with a grain of salt, with reservations.

skepticism *noun*
1. A lack conviction or certainty ► dubiousness, incertitude, reservation. *See* **doubt** (1). *See synonym note at* **doubt. 2.** Lack of trust ► cynicism, leeriness. *See*

distrust. **3.** The refusal or reluctance to believe ▸ incredulity, mistrust, rejection, unbelief. *See* **disbelief** (1).

sketch *noun*
1. A preliminary plan or version, as of a written work ▸ blueprint, outline. *See* **draft** (1). **2.** A short theatrical piece within a larger production ▸ act, skit. *See also* **satire**. **3.** A shortened version or summary ▸ brief, outline. *See* **synopsis**.

sketch *verb*
1. To draw up a preliminary plan or version of ▸ outline, plan. *See* **draft** (1). **2.** To work out and arrange the parts and details of ▸ blueprint, lay out, set out. *See* **design** (2).

sketchy *adjective*
1. Not perfected, elaborated, or completed ▸ preliminary, tentative, unpolished. *See* **rough** (10). **2.** Lacking in intellectual depth or thoroughness ▸ one-dimensional, shallow. *See* **superficial** (1). **3.** Lacking an essential element ▸ incomplete, wanting. *See* **deficient** (1).

skew *verb*
1. To turn aside sharply from a straight course ▸ slant, veer, zigzag. *See* **swerve** (1). **2.** To alter or present material so as to favor a particular viewpoint ▸ doctor, slant. *See* **bias** (2). **3.** To have a tendency or inclination ▸ incline, lean, trend. *See* **tend**[1].

skid *noun*
A usually swift downward trend, as in prices ▸ decline, dip, plunge. *See* **fall** (3).

skid *verb*
1. To lose one's balance and fall or almost fall ▸ slip, trip. *See* **stumble** (1). **2.** To become lower in value or price ▸ dive, drop, tumble. *See* **fall** (7).

skill *noun*
1. Natural or acquired facility in a specific activity ▸ craft, knack, proficiency. *See* **ability** (1). **2.** Skillfulness in the use of the hands or body ▸ deftness, facility. *See* **dexterity** (1). **3.** A quality that makes a person suitable for a particular position or task ▸ attainment, credential, endowment, qualification.

skilled *adjective*
1. Having sufficent ability or resources ▸ capable, competent, skillful. *See* **able**. **2.** Having or demonstrating a high degree of knowledge or skill ▸ master, professional. *See* **expert**. *See synonym note at* **expert**.

skillful *adjective*
1. Having sufficient ability or resources ▸ capable, competent, skilled. *See* **able**. **2.** Having or demonstrating a high degree of knowledge or skill ▸ master, professional. *See* **expert**. *See synonym note at* **expert**. **3.** Exhibiting or possessing skill and ease in performance ▸ deft, facile, nimble. *See* **dexterous**.

skim *verb*
1. To strike a surface at such an angle as to be deflected ▸ graze, ricochet, skip. *See* **glance** (1). *See also* **bounce**. **2.** To make light and momentary contact with, as in passing ▸ graze, kiss. *See* **brush**[1]. *See synonym note at* **brush**[1]. **3.** To pass quickly and lightly

through the air ▸ glide, sail, shoot. *See* **fly** (2). **4.** To move smoothly, continuously, and effortlessly ▸ coast, slip. *See* **glide** (1). **5.** To look through reading matter casually ▸ flip through, leaf (through), scan. *See* **browse** (1).

skim *noun*
Light and momentary contact with another person or thing ▸ graze, rub. *See* **brush**[1] (1).

skimp *verb*
▸ save, scrape, stint. *See* **scrimp**.

skimpy *adjective*
▸ puny, scant, sparse. *See* **meager** (1).

skin *noun*
1. The tissue forming the external covering of the body ▸ epidermis, integument. **2.** A thin outer covering of an object ▸ film, lamina, membrane, sheath, sheathing, sheet. *See also* **coat**. **3.** The outer covering of a fruit or similar plant part ▸ hull, husk, peel, rind, shell, zest.

skin *verb*
1. To remove the skin of ▸ decorticate, hull, husk, pare, peel, scale, shell, shuck, strip. **2.** *Slang* To get something by deceitful trickery ▸ bilk, defraud, swindle. *See* **cheat** (1).

skin-deep *adjective*
▸ cursory, naive, one-dimensional, shallow. *See* **superficial** (1).

skinflint *noun*
▸ churl, Scrooge. *Informal:* penny pincher. *See* **miser**.

skinny *adjective*
▸ lean, slender, slim. *See* **thin** (1). *See synonym note at* **thin**.

skip *verb*
1. To move in a lively way ▸ bounce, hop. *See* **bound**[1] (1). **2.** To strike a surface at such an angle as to be deflected ▸ graze, ricochet, skim. *See* **glance** (1). *See also* **bounce**. **3.** To cease consideration or treatment of ▸ give up, relinquish, stop. *See* **drop** (7). **4.** *Informal* To break loose and leave suddenly, as from confinement or a difficult situation ▸ decamp, flee. *See* **escape** (1). **5.** *Informal* To fail to attend on purpose ▸ duck, shirk. *Idiom:* go AWOL. *See also* **cut** (8).

skip out *verb*
To abandon a former position or commitment ▸ blink, retreat, walk out. *See* **renege**.

skip *noun*
A sudden lively movement ▸ bounce, spring. *See* **bound**[1].

skipper *noun*
▸ captain, commander, shipmaster.

skirmish *noun*
▸ brush, clash, confrontation. *See* **battle** (1).

skirt *verb*
1. To pass around but not through ▸ bypass, circumnavigate, circumvent, detour, go around. *See also* **avoid**. **2.** To avoid fulfilling or answering completely ▸ duck, hedge. *See* **evade** (1).

skirts *noun*
▸ edge, environs, suburbs. *See* **outskirts**.

skit *noun*

A short theatrical piece within a larger production ▸ act, sketch. *See also* **satire.**

skitter *verb*

▸ skip, spring. *See* **bound**[1] (1).

skittish *adjective*

▸ jittery, nervous. *See* **edgy.**

skulk *verb*

1. To move silently and furtively ▸ creep, lurk, prowl. *See* **sneak** (1). **2.** To wait furtively in order to attack someone ▸ ambush, lay for, prowl. *See* **lurk** (1).

skull *noun*

The bony framework of the head ▸ braincase, brainpan, cranium. *See also* **head.**

skunk *verb*

Slang To render totally ineffective by decisive defeat ▸ crush, overcome, rout. *See* **overwhelm** (1).

skunk *noun*

Slang A repulsive, despicable, or immoral person ▸ *Slang:* louse, maggot. *See* **creep** (2).

sky *noun*

The celestial regions as seen from the earth ▸ air, firmament, heavens. *Idiom:* wild blue yonder.

sky *verb*

To rise abruptly and precipitously ▸ rocket, skyrocket. *See* **soar** (1).

sky-high *adjective*

1. Being of or at a relatively great height or altitude ▸ elevated, lofty. *See* **high** (1). **2.** Vastly exceeding a normal limit, as in cost ▸ exorbitant, overpriced. *See* **steep**[1] (2).

skyrocket *verb*

▸ rocket, sky. *Informal:* shoot up. *See* **soar** (1).

slab *noun*

1. An irregularly shaped mass of indefinite size ▸ clod, wad. *See* **lump**[1] (1). **2.** A part severed from a whole ▸ portion, section. *See* **cut** (2).

slack *adjective*

1. Characterized by reduced economic activity ▸ dull, soft. *See* **slow** (2). **2.** Not tautly bound, held, or fastened ▸ flapping, relaxed, unbound. *See* **loose** (1). *See synonym note at* **loose.** **3.** Lacking due care or concern ▸ lax, remiss. *See* **negligent.** *See synonym note at* **negligent.**

slack *verb*

1. To reduce in tension, pressure, or rigidity ▸ let up, loosen. *See* **ease** (1). **2.** To avoid the fulfillment of ▸ disregard, neglect, shirk. *Idiom:* let slide.

slack off *verb*

1. To become or cause to become less active or intense ▸ abate, moderate. *See* **subside** (1). **2.** To pass time without working or in avoiding work ▸ loiter, lounge. *See* **idle** (1).

slacken *verb*

1. To reduce in tension, pressure, or rigidity ▸ let up, loosen. *See* **ease** (1). **2.** To become or cause to become less active or intense ▸ die (away, down, off, *or* out), ebb, lapse. *See* **subside** (1). **3.** To moderate or change a position or course of action as a result of pressure ▸ ease off, soften, yield. *See* **weaken** (1). **4.** To cause to be later or slower than expected or desired ▸ hang up, retard, stall. *See* **delay** (1).

slackening *noun*

▸ abatement, letup, subsidence. *See* **waning.**

slacker *noun*

▸ bum, idler, loafer. *See* **wastrel** (2).

slackness *noun*

1. The state or quality of being negligent ▸ laxness, remissness. *See* **negligence. 2.** Excessive freedom; lack of restraint ▸ licentiousness, profligacy. *See* **license** (2).

slam *verb*

1. To strike together noisily ▸ crash, knock, whack. *See* **bang** (1). **2.** To deliver a sudden, sharp blow to ▸ jab, sock, whack. *See* **hit** (1). **3.** To come together with force ▸ impact, strike. *See* **collide** (1). **4.** To move a door, for example, in order to cover an opening ▸ close, clench, seal, shut. **5.** *Slang* To criticize harshly and devastatingly ▸ blast, blister, drub, excoriate, flay, lacerate, lash, rip into, scarify, scathe, scorch, score, scourge, slap, slash, tear into, wither. *Informal:* bash, cut up, lambaste, light into, roast. *Slang:* trash. *Idioms:* burn someone's ears, crawl (*or* jump) all over someone, jump down someone's throat, let someone have it, pin someone's ears back, put someone on the griddle, put someone on the hot seat, rake over the coals, read the riot act to. *See also* **chastise, criticize, malign. 6.** To force to move or advance with or as if with blows or pressure ▸ butt, shove, thrust. *See* **drive** (2).

slam *noun*

1. A forceful movement causing a loud noise ▸ bang, crash, smash, wham. **2.** Words expressive of strong disapproval ▸ admonition, reprimand, scolding. *See* **rebuke.**

slammer *noun*

Slang A place for the confinement of persons in lawful detention ▸ brig, penitentiary, prison. *See* **jail.**

slander *noun*

1. The expression of injurious, malicious statements about someone ▸ defamation, denigration, smear. *See* **libel. 2.** Idle, often sensational and groundless talk about others ▸ hearsay, rumor, tattle. *See* **gossip** (1).

slander *verb*

To make harmful and often untrue statements about ▸ calumniate, defame, slur. *See* **malign.** *See synonym note at* **malign.**

slanderous *adjective*

▸ defamatory, invidious, scandalous. *See* **libelous.**

slant *verb*

1. To depart or cause to depart from true vertical or horizontal ▸ heel, lean. *See* **incline** (1). *See synonym note at* **incline. 2.** To have a tendency or inclination ▸ lean, slant. *See* **tend**[1] (2). **3.** To alter or present material so as to favor a particular viewpoint ▸ doctor, skew. *See* **bias** (2). **4.** To turn aside sharply from a straight course ▸ cut, veer, zigzag. *See* **swerve** (1). **5.** To give an inaccurate view of by representing falsely or misleadingly ▸ fudge, misrepresent, pervert. *See* **distort** (1).

slant *noun*

1. An upward path or surface ▸ gradient, inclined plane, rise. *See* **ascent** (2). **2.** Deviation from a particular direction ▸ grade, heel. *See* **inclination** (2). **3.** The position from which something is observed or considered ▸ aspect, point of view, standpoint. *See* **viewpoint. 4.** An inclination for or against that inhibits impartial judgment ▸ partiality, prejudice. *See* **bias** (1).

slanted *adjective*

1. At an angle ▸ biased, diagonal, inclined. *See* **oblique** (1). **2.** Exhibiting bias ▸ partial, prejudiced, tendentious. *See* **biased** (1).

slanting *adjective*

▸ biased, diagonal, inclined. *See* **oblique** (1).

slap *noun*

1. A sharp blow, especially with the open hand ▸ box, cuff, smack, smacker, spank, swat, whack. *Informal:* spat. *See also* **blow²**. **2.** A loud, harsh striking noise ▸ clang, smash. *See* **clash** (1). **3.** Words expressive of strong disapproval ▸ admonition, reprimand, scolding. *See* **rebuke.**

slap *verb*

1. To hit with a sharp blow, especially of the open hand ▸ box, clap, cuff, smack, spank, swat, whack. *Informal:* spat. *See also* **beat, hit. 2.** To criticize harshly and devastatingly ▸ excoriate, flay. *Informal:* bash. *See* **slam** (5).

slap around *verb*

To be rough or brutal with ▸ knock about (*or* around), rough up. *See* **manhandle** (1).

slapdash *adjective*

1. Marked by a lack of neatness ▸ careless, slipshod, sloppy. *See* **messy** (1). **2.** Characterized by unthinking boldness and haste ▸ brash, hasty, impetuous. *See* **rash¹.**

slash *verb*

1. To penetrate with a sharp edge ▸ bayonet, incise, pierce, stab. *See* **cut** (1). **2.** To criticize harshly and devastatingly ▸ excoriate, flay. *Informal:* bash. *See* **slam** (5). **3.** To decrease, as in length or amount, by or as if by severing or excising ▸ chop, prune, trim. *See* **cut** (3).

slash *noun*

1. An opening made with a sharp object ▸ gash, slice, slit. *See* **cut** (1). **2.** The act or process of decreasing ▸ curtailment, diminishment, reduction. *See* **decrease.**

slashing *adjective*

▸ caustic, scathing, sharp, vitriolic. *See* **biting.**

slate *noun*

A list of candidates proposed or endorsed by a political party ▸ ballot, lineup, ticket.

slate *verb*

To enter on a schedule ▸ calendar, docket, program, schedule. *See also* **list¹, post³.**

slated *adjective*

▸ expected, scheduled. *See* **due** (2).

slattern *noun*

▸ hussy, tramp, whore. *See* **slut.**

slaughter *noun*

The savage killing of many victims ▸ bloodshed, butchery. *See* **massacre.**

slaughter *verb*

To kill savagely and indiscriminately ▸ annihilate, butcher, decimate. *See* **massacre** (1).

slaughterer *noun*

▸ killer, massacrer, slayer. *See* **murderer.**

slaughterous *adjective*

▸ homicidal, gory, sanguineous. *See* **murderous.**

slave *noun*

1. One bound to serve another person or influence ▸ bondservant, chattel, helot, serf, servant, vassal. *See also* **subordinate. 2.** A person who does tedious, menial, or unpleasant work ▸ grunt, hack, menial. *See* **drudge** (1). **3.** One who flatters another or behaves obsequiously in an attempt to win favor ▸ flatterer, minion. *See* **sycophant.**

slave *verb*

1. To do tedious, difficult or menial work ▸ plod, slog. *See* **grind** (4). **2.** To exert oneself steadily, often to the point of exhaustion ▸ strain, sweat, toil. *See* **labor** (1).

slaver *verb*

1. To let saliva run from the mouth ▸ salivate, slobber. *See* **drool. 2.** To behave obsequiously or submissively ▸ grovel, kowtow. *Informal:* apple-polish. *See* **fawn.** *See synonym note at* **fawn.**

slaver *noun*

Saliva running from the mouth ▸ drivel, drool, salivation, slobber.

slavery *noun*

A state of subjugation to an owner or master ▸ bondage, enslavement, helotry, involuntary servitude, serfdom, servileness, servility, servitude, thrall, thralldom, villeinage, yoke.

slavish *adjective*

1. Excessively eager to serve or obey ▸ obsequious, subservient. *See* **servile. 2.** Of or involving imitation ▸ emulative, mimetic. *See* **imitative** (1).

slay *verb*

1. To cause the death of ▸ cut down, destroy, finish (off). *See* **kill¹** (1). **2.** To take the life of a person or persons unlawfully ▸ assassinate, kill, liquidate. *See* **murder** (1).

slayer *noun*

▸ killer, massacrer, slaughterer. *See* **murderer.**

sleaze *noun*

▸ dirt, smut, vulgarity. *See* **obscenity** (2).

sleazy *adjective*

1. Showing signs of wear and tear or neglect ▸ broken-down, dilapidated, tattered. *See* **shabby** (1). **2.** Of decidedly inferior quality ▸ cheap, lousy, poor. *See* **shoddy** (1).

sled *or* **sledge** *verb*

To ride or be pulled on a sled in the snow ▸ coast, sleigh-ride, slide. *Idioms:* go sledding (*or* coasting *or* sleigh-riding).

sleek *adjective*

1. Smooth and lustrous as if polished ▸ satiny, silken,

silky. *See also* **even, glossy, slick. 2.** Having slender and graceful lines ▸ streamlined, trim. **3.** Affectedly and self-servingly earnest ▸ oleaginous, smarmy. *See* **unctuous** (1).

sleek *verb*
To give a bright sheen or luster to ▸ burnish, glaze, polish. *See* **gloss¹** (1).

sleek over *verb*
To conceal or make light of a fault or offense ▸ gloss over, whitewash. *See* **extenuate.**

✦ CORE SYNONYMS: *sleek, satiny, silken, silky.* These adjectives mean having a surface that is smooth and lustrous as if polished: *sleek black fur; satiny gardenia petals; silken butterfly wings; silky skin.*

---

sleekness *noun*
▸ luster, polish, shine. *See* **gloss¹** (1).

sleep *noun*
The natural recurring condition of suspended consciousness by which the body rests ▸ dreamland, slumber. *Slang:* shuteye, z's. *Idioms:* land of Nod, the arms of Morpheus. *See also* **nap, rest.**

sleep *verb*
To be asleep ▸ slumber. *Slang:* sack out. *Idioms:* be in the land of Nod, catch some shuteye, catch (*or* cop) some z's, saw logs (*or* wood), sleep like a log (*or* baby *or* rock *or* top), sleep tight. *See also* **nap, rest.**

sleep with *verb*
To engage in sexual relations with ▸ bed, copulate with, have, lie with, mate, service, take. *Idioms:* be intimate with, get it on with, go all the way with, go to bed with, have intercourse with, have sex with, make love with, roll in the hay with. *See also* **copulate.**

sleeper *noun*
▸ *Informal:* knockout, smash. *See* **hit** (3).

sleeping *adjective*
1. In a state of sleep ▸ asleep, snoozing, unawake. *Slang:* conked out, sacked out, zonked. *Idioms:* catching (*or* copping) some z's, dead to the world, fast (*or* sound) asleep, in a sound (*or* wakeless) sleep, in the arms of Morpheus, in the land of Nod, out like a light, sawing logs (*or* wood). **2.** Present but not evident or active ▸ dormant, inactive, potential. *See* **latent.**

sleepless *adjective*
Marked by an absence of sleep ▸ slumberless, wakeful. *See also* **wakeful.**

sleepwalking *noun*
▸ absent-mindedness, bemusement, reverie. *See* **trance** (1).

sleepy *adjective*
1. Ready for or needing sleep ▸ dozy, drowsy, nodding, slumberous, slumbery, somnolent, soporific. **2.** Inducing sleep or sedation ▸ narcotic, sedative, somniferous. *See* **soporific** (1). **3.** Lacking energy and vitality ▸ languorous, listless, spiritless. *See* **languid.**

sleight *noun*
1. Skillfulness in the use of the hands or body

▸ deftness, facility. *See* **dexterity** (1). **2.** An indirect, usually cunning means of gaining an end ▸ deception, ploy, stratagem. *See* **trick** (1).

sleight of hand *noun*
▸ legerdemain, trickery. *See* **magic** (2).

slender *adjective*
1. Having little flesh or fat on the body ▸ lean, skinny, slim. *See* **thin** (1). *See synonym note at* **thin. 2.** Small in degree, especially of probability ▸ slight, slim. *See* **remote** (2).

sleuth *noun*
▸ investigator. *Slang:* gumshoe. *See* **detective.**

slew *or* **slue** *noun*
Informal An indeterminately great amount or number ▸ bunch, multiplicity. *Informal:* bushel. *See* **heap** (3).

slice *noun*
1. An opening made with a sharp object ▸ gash, slash, slit. *See* **cut** (1). **2.** A part severed from a whole ▸ portion, section. *See* **cut** (2). **3.** A small, thin piece of something ▸ chip, sliver, shaving. *See* **flake** (1). **4.** A small portion of food ▸ crumb, morsel. *See* **bit¹** (2).

slice *verb*
To separate into parts with or as if with a sharp-edged instrument ▸ cleave, sever. *See* **cut** (2).

slice up *verb*
To pull or cut into many pieces ▸ grate, rip up. *See* **shred.**

slick *adjective*
1. So smooth and glassy as to offer insecure hold or footing ▸ lubricious, oily, slippery, slithery. *Idiom:* slippery as an eel. *See also* **sleek. 2.** Exhibiting or possessing skill and ease in performance ▸ deft, facile, nimble. *See* **dexterous. 3.** Having or showing a clever awareness and resourcefulness in practical matters ▸ canny, knowing, perspicacious. *See* **shrewd** (1). **4.** Marked by ease and fluency of speech that is often insincere or superficial ▸ facile, smooth-tongued. *See* **glib.** *See synonym note at* **glib.**

slick up *verb*
To make neat and trim; make presentable ▸ freshen (up), neaten up, trim. *See* **tidy** (2).

slicker *noun*
▸ mackintosh, raincoat, trench coat. *See* **coat** (1).

slide *verb*
1. To ride or be pulled on a sled in the snow ▸ coast, sled, sledge, sleigh-ride. *Idioms:* go sledding (*or* coasting *or* sleigh-riding). **2.** To maneuver gently and slowly into place ▸ ease, glide, slip. *See also* **ease. 3.** To move smoothly, continuously, and effortlessly ▸ coast, slip. *See* **glide** (1). *See synonym note at* **glide. 4.** To move silently and furtively ▸ lurk, prowl. *See* **sneak** (1). **5.** To move along in a crouching or prone position ▸ creep, slither, worm. *See* **crawl** (1). **6.** To lose one's balance and fall or almost fall ▸ skid, slip. *See* **stumble** (1).

slide *noun*
1. A usually swift downward trend, as in prices ▸ decline, dip, plunge. *See* **fall** (3). **2.** A sudden drop to

a lower condition or status ► dip, plunge, tumble. *See* **descent** (4).

slight *adjective*
1. Of small intensity ► gentle, moderate, soft. *See* **light²** (2). **2.** Small in degree, especially of probability ► negligible, slim. *See* **remote** (2). **3.** Below another in standing, importance, or status ► junior, low, secondary. *See* **minor** (1). **4.** Free from severity or violence, as in sound or movement ► delicate, faint, soft. *See* **gentle** (2).

slight *verb*
1. To represent or speak of as small or insignificant ► deprecate, disparage, run down. *See* **belittle**. **2.** To ignore someone deliberately ► cut, spurn, shun. *See* **snub**. **3.** To fail to care for or give proper attention to ► ignore, let slip. *See* **neglect** (1).

slight *noun*
1. An act or instance of neglecting ► negligence, oversight. *See* **neglect** (1). **2.** An act that offends a person's sense of pride or dignity ► contumely, insult. *See* **indignity**.

slighting *adjective*
1. Tending or intending to belittle ► deprecatory, derogatory, pejorative. *See* **disparaging**. **2.** Showing scorn and disrespect toward someone or something ► dismissive, haughty, scornful. *See* **disdainful** (1).

slim *adjective*
1. Having little flesh or fat on the body ► lean, skinny, slender. *See* **thin** (1). *See synonym note at* **thin**. **2.** Small in degree, especially of probability ► negligible, slight. *See* **remote** (2).

slim *verb*
To lose body weight, as by dieting ► reduce, slim down, thin, trim down. *Idioms:* get the weight off, lose weight, shed some pounds.

slime *noun*
A viscous, usually dirty substance ► mire, muck, ooze, slop, sludge, slush. *Informal:* goo, gunk. *Slang:* goop. *See also* **oil**.

slimy *adjective*
Relating to or covered with slime ► miry, mucky, oozy, sludgy, slushy. *Informal:* gooey, gunky. *Slang:* goopy. *See also* **fatty**.

sling *noun*
An act of throwing ► fling, hurl, toss. *See* **throw**.

sling *verb*
1. To send through the air with a motion of the hand or arm ► fling, heave, launch. *See* **throw** (1). **2.** To fasten or be fastened at one point with no support from below ► dangle, swing. *See* **hang** (1).

slink *verb*
► creep, lurk, prowl. *See* **sneak** (1).

slinkiness *noun*
► secretiveness, sneakiness, slyness. *See* **stealth**.

slinky *adjective*
► furtive, secretive, sneaky. *See* **stealthy**.

slip *verb*
1. To move smoothly, continuously, and effortlessly ► coast, slide. *See* **glide** (1). *See synonym note at* **glide**.
2. To move silently and furtively ► lurk, prowl. *See* **sneak** (1). **3.** To lose one's balance and fall or almost fall ► skid, trip. *See* **stumble** (1). **4.** To maneuver gently and slowly into place ► ease, glide, slide. *See also* **ease**. **5.** To free from ties or fasteners ► loose, release, untie. *See* **undo** (1). **6.** To get away from a pursuer ► evade, shake off, throw off. *See* **lose** (3). **7.** To displace a bone from a socket or joint ► dislocate, separate, throw out. *Idiom:* throw out of joint. **8.** To become lower in value or price ► drop off, plummet, sag. *See* **fall** (7). **9.** To make an error or mistake ► lapse, stumble. *See* **err** (1). **10.** To undergo moral deterioration ► degenerate, fall, sink. *See also* **deteriorate**. **11.** To move past in time ► lapse, slip away, slip by, tick away. *See* **elapse**.

slip into *or* **on** *verb*
To put an article of clothing on one's person ► pull on, put on. *See* **don** (1).

slip *noun*
1. A minor mistake ► lapse, slip-up. *Informal:* fluff. **2.** An unintentional deviation from what is correct, right, or true ► lapse, mistake. *See* **error** (1).

slippery *adjective*
1. Inclined or intended to evade ► elusive, evasive, fugitive. *See also* **underhand**. **2.** So smooth and glassy as to offer insecure hold or footing ► oily, slithery. *See* **slick** (1).

slipshod *adjective*
1. Marked by a lack of cleanliness or neatness ► sloppy, slovenly, untidy. *See* **messy** (1). *See synonym note at* **messy**. **2.** Lacking due care or concern ► lax, slack. *See* **negligent**.

slip-up *noun*
1. A minor mistake ► lapse, slip. *Informal:* fluff. **2.** An unintentional deviation from what is correct, right, or true ► inaccuracy, lapse, mistake. *See* **error** (1).

slit *noun*
An opening made with a sharp object ► gash, incision, slash. *See* **cut** (1).

slit *verb*
1. To penetrate with a sharp edge ► bayonet, incise, pierce, slash. *See* **cut** (1). **2.** To separate into parts with or as if with a sharp-edged instrument ► cleave, sever. *See* **cut** (2).

slither *verb*
1. To lose one's balance and fall or almost fall ► skid, slip. *See* **stumble** (1). **2.** To move along in a crouching or prone position ► creep, snake, worm. *See* **crawl** (1). **3.** To move smoothly, continuously, and effortlessly ► coast, slip. *See* **glide** (1). *See synonym note at* **glide**.

slithery *adjective*
► lubricious, slippery, slithery. *See* **slick** (1).

sliver *noun*
1. A small, thin piece of something ► chip, slice, shaving. *See* **flake** (1). **2.** A small portion of food ► crumb, morsel. *See* **bit¹** (2). **3.** A part severed from a whole ► portion, section. *See* **cut** (2).

slob *noun*
Informal An unrefined, rude person ► chuff, Philistine, yahoo. *See* **boor**.

slobber *noun*
Saliva running from the mouth ▸ drivel, drool, salivation, slaver.

slobber *verb*
To let saliva run from the mouth ▸ salivate, slaver. See **drool.**

slobber over *verb*
Informal To make an excessive show of desire for or interest in ▸ *Informal:* drool over, ogle. *See also* **adore, desire, lust, rave.**

slog *verb*
1. To walk in a laborious way ▸ plod, slop, toil. *See* **trudge. 2.** To do tedious, difficult or menial work ▸ plod, slave. *See* **grind** (4). **3.** To deliver a sudden, sharp blow to ▸ jab, sock, whack. *See* **hit** (1).

slog *noun*
A difficult or tedious undertaking ▸ chore, effort, grind. *See* **task** (2).

slogan *noun*
▸ call to arms, motto, war cry. *See* **cry** (2).

slop *noun*
A viscous, usually offensively dirty substance ▸ ooze, sludge. *See* **slime.**

slop *verb*
1. To hurl or scatter liquid ▸ bespatter, spray. *See* **splash** (1). **2.** To walk in a laborious way ▸ plod, slog, toil. *See* **trudge.**

slope *verb*
To depart or cause to depart from true vertical or horizontal ▸ heel, lean. *See* **incline** (1). *See synonym note at* **incline.**

slope *noun*
1. Deviation from a particular direction ▸ grade, heel. *See* **inclination** (2). **2.** An upward path or surface ▸ gradient, inclined plane, rise. *See* **ascent** (2).

sloppiness *noun*
1. The state of being messy or unkempt ▸ messiness, untidiness. *See* **disorderliness** (1). **2.** *Informal* The quality or condition of being affectedly or overly emotional ▸ bathos, mawkishness, treacle. *See* **sentimentality.**

sloppy *adjective*
1. Marked by a lack of cleanliness ▸ slipshod, slovenly, untidy. *See* **messy** (1). *See synonym note at* **messy. 2.** *Informal* Affectedly or extravagantly emotional ▸ gushy, mawkish, soft. *See* **sentimental. 3.** Lacking due care or concern ▸ lax, slack. *See* **negligent.**

slosh *verb*
▸ bespatter, spray. *See* **splash** (1).

sloshed *adjective*
Slang Stupefied, excited, or muddled with alcoholic liquor ▸ intoxicated, sodden, tipsy. *See* **drunk.**

slot *noun*
1. A post of employment ▸ job, situation. *See* **position** (3). **2.** An open space allowing passage ▸ orifice, vent. *See* **hole** (2).

sloth *noun*
1. The quality or state of being lazy ▸ idleness, indolence, shiftlessness. *See* **laziness. 2.** *Informal* A

self-indulgent person who avoids work ▸ bum, idler, loafer. *See* **wastrel** (2).

slothful *adjective*
1. Resistant to exertion and activity ▸ idle, shiftless, sluggish. *See* **lazy.** *See synonym note at* **lazy. 2.** Lacking mental and physical alertness and activity ▸ inert, sluggish, stuporous. *See* **lethargic** (1).

slothfulness *noun*
1. The quality or state of being lazy ▸ indolence, shiftlessness, sloth. *See* **laziness. 2.** A deficiency in mental and physical alertness and activity ▸ languor, listlessness, sluggishness. *See* **lethargy** (1).

slouch *verb*
1. To take on or move with an awkward, slovenly posture ▸ loll, slump. *See also* **bow¹, stoop. 2.** To hang limply and loosely ▸ droop, flop, loll, lop, sag, wilt.

slouch *noun*
Slang A self-indulgent person who avoids work ▸ bum, idler, loafer. *See* **wastrel** (2).

slough¹ *noun*
A usually low-lying area of soft waterlogged ground and standing water ▸ marsh, mire, wetland. *See* **swamp.**

slough² *verb*
1. To cast off by a natural process ▸ exuviate, molt, throw off. *See* **shed¹** (2). **2.** To let go or get rid of as being useless or defective, for example ▸ dump, throw away. *Informal:* chuck. *See* **discard.**

slovenliness *noun*
▸ sloppiness, untidiness. *See* **disorderliness** (1).

slovenly *adjective*
▸ slipshod, sloppy, untidy. *See* **messy** (1). *See synonym note at* **messy.**

slow *adjective*
1. Proceeding at a rate less than usual or desired ▸ crawling, creeping, delaying, dilatory, glacial, laggard, laboring, plodding, procrastinating, slow-footed, slow-going, slow-paced, sluggish, snaillike, tardy. *Informal:* poky. *Idiom:* slow as molasses in January. *See also* **deliberate, languid, lethargic. 2.** Characterized by reduced economic activity ▸ down, dull, off, slack, sluggish, soft, stagnant. **3.** Not on time ▸ behind, overdue. *See* **late** (1). **4.** Having only a limited ability to learn and understand ▸ dull, simple. *See* **backward** (1).

slow *adverb*
Behind schedule ▸ behind, behindhand. *See* **late.**

slow *verb*
To cause to be later or slower than expected or desired ▸ hang up, retard, stall. *See* **delay** (1).

✛ **CORE SYNONYMS:** *slow, dilatory, sluggish, laggard.* These adjectives mean proceeding at a rate less than usual or desired. *Slow* is the least specific: *a slow bus; a slow heartbeat; slow to anger. Dilatory* implies lack of promptness caused by delay, procrastination, or indifference: *paid a late fee because I was dilatory in paying the bill. Sluggish* suggests a lack of movement, activity, or progress: *was sluggish after eating the heavy lunch; sluggish growth. Laggard* implies hanging back or falling behind: *"the horses' laggard pace"* (Rudyard Kipling).

◄ ANTONYM: *fast*

---

slowdown *noun*
1. A period of decreased business activity and high unemployment ► depression, downturn, recession, slump. **2.** The act or process or decreasing ► curtailment, diminishment, reduction. *See* **decrease.**

slow-going *or* **slow-footed** *adjective*
► dilatory, laggard, sluggish. *See* **slow** (1).

slow motion *noun*
A very slow rate of speed ► crawl, creep, footpace. *Idiom:* snail's pace.

slowness *noun*
The quality or condition of not being on time ► belatedness, lateness, tardiness, unpunctuality.

slow-paced *adjective*
► dilatory, laggard, sluggish. *See* **slow** (1).

slowpoke *noun*
Informal One that lags ► lag, procrastinator, straggler. *See* **laggard.**

slow-witted *adjective*
► dull, simple, slow. *See* **backward** (1).

sludge *noun*
► muck, ooze, slush. *See* **slime.**

sludgy *adjective*
► miry, mucky, oozy. *See* **slimy.**

slue *or* **slew** *verb*
1. To turn or cause to turn in place, as on a hinge or fixed point, tracing an arclike path ► pivot, swing, swivel, wheel. *See also* **turn. 2.** To turn aside sharply from a straight course ► slant, veer, zigzag. *See* **swerve** (1).

slug[1] *noun*
Informal A small amount of liquor ► shot, sip, tot. *See* **drop** (8).

slug[2] *noun*
Informal A self-indulgent person who avoids work ► bum, idler, loafer. *See* **wastrel** (2).

slug[3] *verb*
To deliver a sudden, sharp blow to ► jab, sock, whack. *See* **hit** (1).

slug *noun*
A sudden heavy stroke ► crack, hit, swat, whack. *See* **blow**[2] (1).

slugabed *noun*
Slang A self-indulgent person who avoids work ► bum, idler, loafer. *See* **wastrel** (2).

slugfest *noun*
Slang A physical conflict involving two or more people ► free-for-all, melee. *See* **fight** (1).

sluggard *noun*
A self-indulgent person who avoids work or other useful activity ► bum, idler, loafer. *See* **wastrel** (2).

sluggard *adjective*
Resistant to exertion and activity ► idle, shiftless, slothful. *See* **lazy.**

sluggardness *noun*
► indolence, shiftlessness, sloth. *See* **laziness.**

sluggish *adjective*
1. Characterized by reduced economic activity ► dull, slack. *See* **slow** (2). **2.** Lacking mental and physical alertness and activity ► inert, stuporous, torpid. *See* **lethargic** (1). **3.** Resistant to exertion and activity ► idle, shiftless, slothful. *See* **lazy. 4.** Proceeding at a rate less than usual or desired ► laggard, slow-going. *See* **slow** (1). *See synonym note at* **slow.**

sluggishness *noun*
1. A deficiency in mental and physical alertness and activity ► languor, listlessness, torpidity. *See* **lethargy** (1). **2.** The quality or state of being lazy ► indolence, shiftlessness, sloth. *See* **laziness. 3.** A lack of excitement, liveliness, or interest ► blandness, drabness, lifelessness. *See* **dullness** (1).

slumber *verb*
To be asleep ► sleep. *Slang:* sack out. *Idioms:* be in the land of Nod, catch some shuteye, catch (*or* cop) some z's, saw logs (*or* wood), sleep like a log (*or* baby *or* rock *or* top), sleep tight. *See also* **nap, rest.**

slumber *noun*
The natural recurring condition of suspended consciousness by which the body rests ► dreamland, sleep. *Slang:* shuteye, z's. *Idioms:* land of Nod, the arms of Morpheus. *See also* **nap, rest.**

slumberless *adjective*
Marked by an absence of sleep ► sleepless, wakeful.

slumberous *or* **slumbrous** *adjective*
1. Ready for or needing sleep ► drowsy, nodding. *See* **sleepy** (1). **2.** Inducing sleep or sedation ► opiate, sedative, somnolent. *See* **soporific** (1).

slumbery *adjective*
► dozy, drowsy, nodding. *See* **sleepy** (1).

slump *verb*
1. To take on or move with an awkward, slovenly posture ► loll, slouch. *See also* **bow**[1], **stoop. 2.** To go from a more erect posture to a less erect posture ► sag, sink. *See* **drop** (1). **3.** To become lower in value or price ► dive, drop, plummet. *See* **fall** (7).

slump *noun*
1. A period of decreased business activity and high unemployment ► depression, downturn, recession, slowdown. **2.** A usually swift downward trend, as in prices ► decline, dip, plunge. *See* **fall** (3).

slur *verb*
To make harmful and often untrue statements about ► calumniate, defame, slander. *See* **malign.**

slur *noun*
An implied criticism ► imputation, reflection. *See also* **crack, libel.**

slurp *verb*
► down, gulp, quaff. *See* **drink** (1).

slush *noun*
A viscous, usually offensively dirty substance ► muck, sludge. *See* **slime.**

slush *verb*
To make dirty ► bemire, muck up, mud. *See* **dirty** (1).

slushy *adjective*
1. Of, relating to, or covered with slime ► mucky, oozy.

See **slimy. 2.** Affectedly or extravagantly emotional ▸ gushy, mawkish, soft. *See* **sentimental.** *See synonym note at* **sentimental.**

slut *noun*
A person, typically a woman, who is sexually promiscuous ▸ baggage, hussy, jade, slattern, tart, tramp, wanton, wench, whore. *Slang:* floozy. *See also* **harlot, prostitute.**

sluttish *adjective*
▸ fast, loose, trampy. *See* **wanton** (1).

sly *adjective*
1. Deceitfully clever ▸ cunning, tricky, wily. *See* **artful** (1). **2.** Trickily secret ▸ furtive, secretive, sneaky. *See* **stealthy.**

slyness *noun*
1. Deceitful cleverness ▸ cunning, wiliness. *See* **art** (1). **2.** Lack of straightforwardness and honesty in action ▸ deviousness, shadiness, trickery. *See* **dishonesty** (2). **3.** The act of proceeding slowly so as to escape observation ▸ secretiveness, sneakiness, surreptitiousness. *See* **stealth.**

smack¹ *verb*
1. To touch or caress with the lips, especially as a sign of passion or affection ▸ buss, osculate. *See* **kiss** (1). **2.** To hit with a sharp blow, especially of the open hand ▸ spank, swat, whack. *See* **slap** (1). **3.** To strike together noisily ▸ crash, slam, whack. *See* **bang** (1).

smack *noun*
1. The act or an instance of kissing ▸ buss, osculation. *Informal:* peck. *See* **kiss** (1). **2.** A sharp blow, especially with the open hand ▸ spank, swat, whack. *See* **slap** (1). **3.** A loud, harsh striking noise ▸ clang, smash. *See* **clash** (1). **4.** A stroke or blow that produces a sound ▸ thud, thump. *See* **beat** (1).

smack *adverb*
With precision or absolute conformity ▸ exactly, precisely, squarely. *See* **directly** (3).

smack² *noun*
1. A distinctive yet intangible quality ▸ aroma, atmosphere, flavor, savor. *See also* **quality. 2.** A distnctive property of a substance affecting the sense of taste ▸ relish, savor, tang. *See* **flavor** (1).

smack *verb*
To have a particular flavor or suggestion of something ▸ savor, smell, suggest, taste. *See also* **hint.**

smack-dab *adverb*
▸ exactly, precisely, squarely. *See* **directly** (3).

smacker *noun*
1. The act or an instance of kissing ▸ osculation, smack. *Informal:* peck. *See* **kiss** (1). **2.** *Slang* The opening in the body through which food is ingested ▸ chops. *Slang:* yap. *See* **mouth** (1). **3.** A sharp blow, especially with the open hand ▸ smack, swat, whack. *See* **slap** (1).

small *adjective*
1. Below average in amount, length, size, or scope ▸ bantam, petite, smallish. *See* **little** (1). **2.** Of little importance or seriousness ▸ inconsequential, negligible, trifling. *See* **trivial. 3.** Below another in stand-

ing, importance, or status ▸ junior, low, secondary. *See* **minor** (1). **4.** Restricted in scope, outlook, or understanding ▸ insular, narrow-minded, provincial. *See* **narrow** (1). **5.** Not irritating, strident, or loud ▸ quiet, subdued. *See* **soft** (2).

small change *noun*
1. *Informal* A small or trifling amount of money ▸ pocket money, small change. *See* **peanuts. 2.** Something or things of little importance ▸ fiddle-faddle, frivolity. *Informal:* small potatoes. *See* **trifle** (1).

smallest *adjective*
▸ least, tiniest. *See* **minimal.**

small fry *noun*
1. A totally insignificant person ▸ nobody, nothing, scrub. *See* **nonentity. 2.** *Informal* A small or young person ▸ pip-squeak, runt, scrub. *See* **squirt** (2).

smallish *adjective*
▸ bantam, petite, undersized. *See* **little** (1).

small-minded *adjective*
1. Restricted in scope, outlook, or understanding ▸ insular, narrow-minded, provincial. *See* **narrow** (1). **2.** Of little importance or seriousness ▸ inconsequential, negligible, trifling. *See* **trivial.**

smallness *noun*
▸ frivolity, minutia, trivia. *See* **trifle** (1).

small potatoes *noun*
Informal Something or things of little importance ▸ fiddle-faddle, frivolity, small change. *See* **trifle** (1).

small talk *noun*
▸ drivel, patter, prattle. *See* **chatter.**

smalltime *or* **small-time** *adjective*
Informal Below another in standing, importance, or status ▸ junior, low, secondary. *See* **minor** (1).

small-town *adjective*
▸ insular, narrow-minded, provincial. *See* **narrow** (1).

smarmy *adjective*
▸ oleaginous, sleek. *See* **unctuous** (1). *See synonym note at* **unctuous.**

smart *adjective*
1. Having or showing intelligence, often of a high order ▸ intellectual, knowledgeable. *See* **intelligent** (1). *See synonym note at* **intelligent. 2.** Mentally quick and original ▸ keen, quick-witted, sharp. *See* **clever** (1). **3.** Exhibiting or employing wit or originality ▸ scintillating, witty. *See* **clever** (2). **4.** Rude and disrespectful ▸ bold, insolent, pert. *See* **impudent. 5.** Having or showing a clever awareness and resourcefulness in practical matters ▸ canny, knowing, perspicacious. *See* **shrewd** (1). **6.** In accordance with current fashion ▸ mod, stylish, swanky. *See* **fashionable.** *See synonym note at* **fashionable. 7.** Catering to, used by, or admitting only the wealthy or socially superior ▸ chic, posh, swank. *See* **exclusive** (4).

smart *verb*
To be painful or sore ▸ ache, sting. *See* **hurt** (2).

smart *noun*
A sensation of physical discomfort occurring as the result of disease or injury ▸ crick, pang, soreness. *See* **pain** (1). *See synonym note at* **pain.**

smart aleck *noun*
Informal One who is obnoxiously self-assertive and arrogant ▸ *Informal:* know-it-all, saucebox, smarty, smarty-pants, wisenheimer. *Slang:* wiseacre, wisecracker, wise guy. *See also* **boaster, joker.**

smart-alecky *adjective*
Informal Rude and disrespectful ▸ bold, insolent, pert. *See* **impudent.**

smarten *verb*
▸ refresh, restore, revamp. *See* **renew** (1).

smarting *adjective*
▸ achy, hurtful, sore. *See* **painful** (1).

smarts *noun*
▸ intellect, understanding. *See* **intelligence** (1).

smarty *or* **smarty-pants** *noun*
Informal One who is obnoxiously self-assertive and arrogant ▸ *Informal:* know-it-all, wisenheimer. *See* **smart aleck.**

smash *verb*
1. To crack or split into two or more fragments by means of force or strain ▸ shatter, splinter, sunder. *See* **break** (1). *See synonym note at* **break. 2.** To strike together noisily ▸ crash, slam, whack. *See* **bang** (1). 3. To wreck a vehicle ▸ sideswipe, wreck. *See* **crash** (1). **4.** To deliver a sudden, sharp blow to ▸ jab, sock, whack. *See* **hit** (1). **5.** To hit heavily and repeatedly ▸ assault, batter, pummel, thresh. *See* **beat** (1). **6.** To cause the complete ruin or wreckage of ▸ demolish, torpedo, wreck. *See* **destroy** (1). **7.** To render totally ineffective by decisive defeat ▸ crush, overcome, overpower, rout. *See* **overwhelm** (1). **8.** To press forcefully so as to reduce to a pulpy mass ▸ mush, squash. *See* **crush** (1). *See synonym note at* **crush. 9.** To break up into tiny particles ▸ atomize, grind, pulverize. *See* **crush** (2).

smash *noun*
1. A forceful movement causing a loud noise ▸ bang, crash, slam, wham. **2.** A loud, harsh striking noise ▸ clang, whack. *See* **clash** (1). **3.** An abrupt failure ▸ crash, debacle, disaster. *See* **collapse** (2). **4.** A violent forcible contact ▸ crash, impact. *See* **collision. 5.** A wrecking of a vehicle ▸ sideswipe, wreck. *See* **crash** (2). **6.** *Informal* A dazzling, often sudden instance of success ▸ sleeper. *Informal:* ten-strike. *See* **hit** (3).

smashed *adjective*
Slang Stupefied, excited, or muddled with alcoholic liquor ▸ intoxicated, sodden, tipsy. *See* **drunk.**

smash hit *noun*
Informal A dazzling, often sudden instance of success ▸ sleeper. *Informal:* smash. *See* **hit** (3).

smashup *noun*
1. An abrupt failure ▸ crash, debacle, disaster. *See* **collapse** (2). **2.** A wrecking of a vehicle ▸ sideswipe, wreck. *See* **crash** (2).

smatterer *noun*
▸ dilettante, layperson, nonprofessional. *See* **amateur.**

smear *verb*
1. To spread with a greasy, sticky, or dirty substance ▸ bedaub, besmear, dab, daub, plaster, smirch,

smudge. *See also* **dirty, finish, oil, stain. 2.** To attack the reputation or honor of ▸ besmirch, defile, tarnish. *See* **denigrate** (1). **3.** *Slang* To render totally ineffective by decisive defeat ▸ crush, overcome, overpower, rout. *See* **overwhelm** (1).

smear *noun*
1. A discolored mark made by smearing or soiling ▸ blot, blotch, daub, smirch, smudge, smutch, splotch, spot, stain. **2.** The expression of malicious statements about someone ▸ defamation, mudslinging, obloquy. *See* **libel.**

smell *verb*
1. To perceive with the olfactory sense ▸ nose, scent, sniff, snuff, whiff. *Idioms:* catch (*or* get) a whiff of. *See also* **breathe. 2.** To have or give off a foul odor ▸ reek, stink. *Idiom:* stink to high heaven. **3.** To have a particular flavor or suggestion of something ▸ savor, smack, suggest, taste. *See also* **hint.**

smell out *verb*
To folllow the traces of, as in hunting ▸ sniff out, trace, track (down), trail. *Idiom:* be hot on the trail of. *See also* **hunt.**

smell *noun*
1. The sense by which odors are perceived ▸ nose, olfaction, scent. **2.** The quality of something that may be perceived by smelling ▸ aroma, odor, scent. *See also* **fragrance, stench. 3.** A general impression that is produced by a predominant quality or characteristic ▸ atmosphere, aura, mood. *See* **air** (4).

✦ **CORE SYNONYMS:** *smell, aroma, odor, scent.* These nouns denote a quality that can be perceived by the olfactory sense: *the smell of gas; the aroma of frying onions; hospital odors; the scent of pine needles.*

---

smelly *adjective*
Informal Having an unpleasant odor ▸ fetid, foul, foul-smelling, malodorous, mephitic, mephitical, noisome, odoriferous, odorous, overpowering, reeking, reeky, stinking. *See also* **bad, fragrant, moldy, offensive.**

smidgen *noun*
▸ dash, drop, pinch. *See* **bit**[1] (1).

smile *noun*
A facial expression marked by an upward curving of the lips ▸ grin, simper, smirk. *See also* **sneer.**

smile *verb*
To curve the lips upward in expressing amusement, pleasure, or happiness ▸ beam, grin, simper, smirk. *Idioms:* break into a smile, crack (*or* flash *or* give) a smile.

smile on *or* **upon** *verb*
To lend supportive approval to ▸ countenance, encourage, favor. *See also* **approve, support.**

smirch *verb*
To spread with a greasy, sticky, or dirty substance ▸ dab, smudge. *See* **smear** (1).

smirch *noun*
A discolored mark made by smearing ▸ blotch, stain. *See* **smear** (1).

smirk *verb*
To curve the lips upward in expressing amusement, pleasure, or happiness ▸ grin, simper. *See* **smile**.

smirk *noun*
A facial expression marked by an upward curving of the lips ▸ grin, simper, smile. *See also* **sneer**.

smite *verb*
1. To deliver a sudden, sharp blow to ▸ jab, sock, whack. *See* **hit** (1). **2.** To cause great pain or suffering to ▸ plague, rack, torment. *See* **afflict**.

smitten *adjective*
▸ enamored, obsessed, spellbound. *See* **infatuated**.

smock *noun*
▸ frock, jumper, gown. *See* **dress** (3).

smog *noun*
▸ fog, mist. *See* **haze** (1).

smoggy *adjective*
Heavy, dark, or dense, especially with impurities ▸ hazy, murky, turbid. *See also* **dirty**.

smoke *verb*
▸ flicker, gutter, sputter. *See* **smolder** (1).

smolder *verb*
1. To undergo partial or unsteady combustion ▸ flicker, gutter, smoke, sputter. *See also* **burn. 2.** To be in a state of turmoil or excitement ▸ burn, seethe. *See* **boil** (2).

smooch *noun*
Slang The act or an instance of kissing ▸ osculation, smack. *Informal:* peck. *See* **kiss** (1).

smooch *verb*
Slang To touch or caress with the lips, especially as a sign of passion or affection ▸ osculate, smack. *See* **kiss** (1).

smooth *adjective*
1. Having no irregularities, roughness, or indentations ▸ flush, level. *See* **even** (1). *See synonym note at* **even. 2.** Free from severity or violence, as in sound or movement ▸ delicate, faint, soft. *See* **gentle** (2). **3.** Posing no difficulty ▸ effortless, simple. *See* **easy** (1). **4.** Gracious and tactful in social manner ▸ debonair, suave, urbane. *See also* **courteous, cultured, sophisticated. 5.** Marked by facility of expression ▸ effortless, flowing. *See* **fluent. 6.** Marked by ease and fluency of speech that is often insincere or superficial ▸ slick, smooth-tongued. *See* **glib**.

smooth *verb*
1. To make even, smooth, or level ▸ level, straighten. *See* **even** (1). **2.** To bring to perfection or completion ▸ complete, polish, refine. *See* **perfect**.

smooth over *verb*
To bring something into a state of agreement or accord ▸ arrange, negotiate, set. *See* **settle** (2).

smooth-spoken *adjective*
▸ articulate, well-spoken. *See* **eloquent** (1).

smooth-talking *or* **smooth-tongued** *adjective*
▸ offhand, slick, talkative. *See* **glib**. *See synonym note at* **glib**.

smother *verb*
1. To stop breathing or stop the breathing of ▸ as-phyxiate, stifle, suffocate. *See* **choke** (1). **2.** To hold something requiring an outlet in check ▸ muffle, stifle, suppress. *See* **repress. 3.** To cause to stop burning or giving light ▸ put out, snuff out. *See* **extinguish** (1).

smudge *verb*
1. To make dirty ▸ bemire, muck up, mud. *See* **dirty** (1). **2.** To spread with a greasy, sticky, or dirty substance ▸ dab, smirch. *See* **smear** (1). **3.** To attack the reputation or honor of ▸ besmirch, smear, tarnish. *See* **denigrate** (1).

smudge *noun*
1. A discolored mark made by smearing ▸ blotch, stain. *See* **smear** (1). **2.** A suspension in the air of tiny particles of water, dust, or smoke ▸ brume, mist, pall. *See* **haze** (1).

smug *adjective*
▸ haughty, insolent, superior. *See* **arrogant**.

smuggle *verb*
To bring in or take out secretly and illegally ▸ bootleg, run, sneak, spirit. *Idiom:* run contraband.

smuggler *noun*
A person who engages in smuggling ▸ bootlegger, contrabandist, runner. *Slang:* mule.

smut *noun*
Something that is offensive to accepted standards of decency ▸ dirt, sleaze, vulgarity. *See* **obscenity** (2).

smut *verb*
1. To mark or soil with foreign matter ▸ discolor, spatter. *See* **stain** (1). **2.** To attack the reputation or honor of ▸ besmirch, smear, tarnish. *See* **denigrate** (1).

smutch *verb*
To make dirty ▸ bemire, muck up, mud. *See* **dirty** (1).

smutch *noun*
A discolored mark made by smearing ▸ blotch, stain. *See* **smear** (1).

smuttiness *noun*
1. The condition or state of being dirty ▸ filthiness, squalor, uncleanliness. *See* **dirtiness** (1). **2.** The quality or state of being obscene ▸ filthiness, profanity, scurrility, vulgarness. *See* **obscenity** (1).

smutty *adjective*
1. Covered with or stained by dirt ▸ black, filthy, muddy. *See* **dirty** (1). **2.** Offensive to accepted standards of decency ▸ bawdy, coarse, lewd, vulgar. *See* **obscene** (1).

snack *noun*
A light meal ▸ collation. *Informal:* nosh. *See* **refreshment** (1).

snack *verb*
To have or take a meal ▸ breakfast, lunch. *See* **eat** (2).

snaffle *noun*
▸ curb, leash, rein. *See* **brake** (1).

snafu *noun*
1. *Slang* A confused or ruinous state ▸ foul-up, muddle, shambles. *See* **mess** (1). **2.** *Slang* A lack of order or regular arrangement ▸ clutter, confusion, disarray. *See* **disorder** (1).

snafu *verb*
1. *Slang* To put into total disorder ▸ garble, jumble, scramble. *See* **confuse** (4). 2. *Slang* To ruin through clumsiness or ineptness ▸ blunder, foul up, spoil. *See* **botch.**

snafu *adjective*
Slang Characterized by physical confusion ▸ disordered, topsy-turvy, upside-down. *See* **confused** (2).

snag *noun*
1. Something that blocks entry or passage ▸ barrier, blockage, hindrance. *See* **bar** (1). *See synonym note at* **bar.** 2. *Informal* A tricky or unsuspected condition ▸ catch, hitch, rub. *See also* **disadvantage, trick.** 3. A sharp protuberance or projection ▸ prick, prong, spine. *See* **spike** (1).

snag *verb*
1. To get hold of something moving ▸ seize, snatch. *See* **catch** (2). 2. To become stuck or entangled ▸ hook, lodge. *See* **catch** (3).

snail *noun*
▸ lag, procrastinator, straggler. *See* **laggard.**

snake *verb*
1. To move along in a crouching or prone position ▸ creep, slither, worm. *See* **crawl** (1). 2. To move or proceed on a repeatedly curving course ▸ coil, spiral, weave. *See* **wind²** (1). 3. To move silently and furtively ▸ lurk, prowl. *See* **sneak** (1).

snake *noun*
1. One who betrays another ▸ double-crosser, traitor. *See* **betrayer.** 2. A repulsive, despicable, or immoral person ▸ *Slang:* louse, maggot. *See* **creep** (2).

snaky *adjective*
▸ convoluted, sinuous, twisting. *See* **winding** (1)

snap *verb*
1. To make a light, sharp noise ▸ clack, click. *See also* **crackle.** 2. To try to bite something quickly or eagerly ▸ nip, snatch, strike. 3. To speak abruptly and sharply ▸ bark, growl, snarl. *Idioms:* bite someone's head off, snap someone's head (*or* nose) off. *See also* **chastise, revile, say, shout.** 4. To move or cause to move with a sudden abrupt motion ▸ jerk, lurch, twitch, wrench, yank. *See synonym note at* **jerk.** *See also* **move.** 5. To make a sudden, sharp noise ▸ clap, pop. *See* **crack** (2). 6. To give way mentally and emotionally ▸ collapse, crack, fold. *See* **break** (5).

snap back *verb*
To reverse direction after striking something ▸ bounce (back), rebound, reflect, spring back. *See also* **bend, glance.**

snap *noun*
1. A light, sharp noise ▸ clack, click, crackle. 2. A sudden sharp, explosive noise ▸ bang, pop, rat-a-tat. *See* **crack** (1). 3. A sudden motion, such as a pull ▸ tug, wrench. *See* **jerk** (1). 4. A device for locking ▸ catch, clip, lock. *See* **fastener.** 5. *Informal* Capacity for work or vigorous activity ▸ might, potency, power. *See* **energy.** 6. *Informal* An easily accomplished task ▸ cinch, pushover, walkover. *See* **breeze** (2). *See synonym note at* **breeze.**

snap *adjective*
1. Spoken, performed, or composed with little or no preparation or forethought ▸ impromptu, improvised. *See* **extemporaneous.** 2. *Informal* Posing no difficulty ▸ effortless, simple. *See* **easy** (1).

snappish *adjective*
▸ cranky, grouchy, peevish. *See* **ill-tempered.**

snappy *adjective*
1. *Informal* Very brisk, alert, and full of high spirits ▸ effervescent, high-spirited, perky. *See* **lively** (1). 2. *Informal* Possessing, exerting, or displaying energy ▸ brisk, lively, vigorous. *See* **energetic.** 3. *Informal* In accordance with current fashion ▸ mod, stylish, swanky. *See* **fashionable.** 4. Having or showing a bad temper ▸ cranky, grouchy, peevish. *See* **ill-tempered.**

snare *noun*
A device or stratagem for catching or tricking a person or animal ▸ booby trap, noose, pit. *See* **trap** (1).

snare *verb*
To gain control of by trapping ▸ net, trap. *See* **catch** (1). *See synonym note at* **catch.**

snarl¹ *verb*
To speak abruptly and sharply ▸ bark, growl. *See* **snap** (3).

snarl² *noun*
Something that is intricately and often bewilderingly complex ▸ labyrinth, maze, web. *See* **tangle** (1).

snarl *verb*
1. To twist together so that separation is difficult ▸ foul, tangle. *See* **entangle** (1). 2. To make complex, intricate, or perplexing ▸ entangle, perplex, tangle. *See* **complicate.** 3. To put into total disorder ▸ garble, jumble, scramble. *See* **confuse** (1).

snatch *verb*
1. To try to bite something quickly or eagerly ▸ nip, snap, strike. 2. To seize and detain a person unlawfully ▸ abduct, kidnap, spirit away, take hostage. 3. To get hold of something moving ▸ grab, seize. *See* **catch** (2). 4. To take possession of ▸ confiscate, expropriate, grab. *See* **seize** (1). 5. To take another's property without permission ▸ purloin, spirit away, thieve. *See* **steal** (1).

snatch *noun*
1. The act of catching ▸ capture, seizure. *See* **catch** (1). 2. The act of taking possession of something ▸ expropriation, preemption, usurpation. *See* **seizure** (2).

snazzy *adjective*
Slang In accordance with current fashion ▸ mod, stylish, swanky. *See* **fashionable.**

sneak *verb*
1. To move silently and furtively ▸ creep, glide, lurk, mouse, prowl, pussyfoot, skulk, slide, slink, slip, snake, steal. *Slang:* gumshoe. *See also* **lay¹.** 2. To bring in or take out secretly and illegally ▸ bootleg, run. *See* **smuggle.**

sneak *or* **sneaker** *noun*
A person who behaves in a stealthy, furtive way ▸ prowler, skulker, sneaker, weasel. *See also* **creep, betrayer.**

sneakiness *noun*
1. The act of proceeding slowly so as to escape observation ▸ secretiveness, slyness. *See* **stealth. 2.** Lack of straightforwardness and honesty in action ▸ deviousness, slyness, trickery. *See* **dishonesty** (2).

sneaking *adjective*
▸ furtive, secretive, sneaky. *See* **stealthy.**

sneaky *adjective*
1. Trickily secret ▸ furtive, secretive, slinky. *See* **stealthy. 2.** Marked by treachery or deceit ▸ duplicitous, shifty, unscrupulous. *See* **underhand.**

sneer *noun*
A facial expression or laugh conveying scorn or derision ▸ fleer, snicker, snigger. *See also* **face, grimace, laugh, smile.**

sneer *verb*
To smile or laugh scornfully or derisively ▸ fleer, snicker, snigger. *Idiom:* curl one's lip. *See also* **grimace, laugh, smile.**

sneer at *verb*
1. To regard with utter contempt and disdain ▸ disdain, scorn. *See* **despise** (1). **2.** To subject to ridicule ▸ jeer (at), lampoon, taunt. *See* **ridicule.**

sneering *adjective*
1. Contemptuous or ironic in manner or wit ▸ satiric, scoffing, snide. *See* **sarcastic. 2.** Showing scorn and disrespect toward someone or something ▸ dismissive, haughty, scornful. *See* **disdainful** (1).

snicker *verb*
1. To smile or laugh scornfully or derisively ▸ fleer, sneer, snigger. *Idiom:* curl one's lip. *See also* **grimace, smile. 2.** To express amusement or mirth ▸ chuckle, giggle, titter. *See* **laugh.**

snicker *noun*
1. A facial expression or laugh conveying scorn or derision ▸ fleer, sneer, snigger. *See also* **smile. 2.** An act of laughing ▸ giggle, laughter, snigger. *See* **laugh** (1).

snide *adjective*
▸ satiric, scoffing, sneering. *See* **sarcastic.**

sniff *verb*
1. To breathe audibly through the nose ▸ sniffle, snort, snuff, snuffle. **2.** To perceive with the olfactory sense ▸ scent, whiff. *See* **smell** (1).

sniff about *or* **around** *verb*
1. *Informal* To look into or inquire about curiously, inquisitively, or in a meddlesome fashion ▸ poke, pry, snoop. *Informal:* nose (around). *Idioms:* stick one's nose into. *See also* **meddle. 2.** To try to find something ▸ look for, search for. *See* **seek** (1).

sniff at *verb*
1. To have or express an unfavorable opinion of ▸ condemn, disfavor, object to. *See* **disapprove** (1). **2.** To regard with utter contempt and disdain ▸ disdain, scorn. *See* **despise** (1).

sniff out *verb*
To folllow the traces of, as in hunting ▸ smell out, trace, track (down), trail. *See also* **hunt.**

sniffle *verb*
1. To breathe audibly through the nose ▸ sniff, snort,

snuff, snuffle. **2.** To shed tears ▸ howl, sob, weep. *See* **cry** (1).

snigger *noun*
1. A facial expression or laugh conveying scorn or derision ▸ fleer, sneer, snicker. *See also* **smile. 2.** An act of laughing ▸ giggle, laughter, snicker. *See* **laugh** (1).

snigger *verb*
1. To smile or laugh scornfully or derisively ▸ fleer, sneer, snicker. *Idiom:* curl one's lip. *See also* **grimace, smile. 2.** To express amusement or mirth ▸ giggle, snicker, titter. *See* **laugh.**

snip *noun*
1. A part severed from a whole ▸ slab, slice, sliver. *See* **cut** (2). **2.** A tiny amount ▸ dash, drop. *See* **bit**[1] (1).

snip *verb*
1. To separate into parts with or as if with a sharp-edged instrument ▸ cleave, sever. *See* **cut** (2). **2.** To decrease, as in length or amount, by or as if by severing or excising ▸ chop, prune, trim. *See* **cut** (3).

snippet *noun*
1. A part severed from a whole ▸ slab, sliver, slice. *See* **cut** (2). **2.** A tiny amount ▸ dash, drop, smidgen. *See* **bit**[1] (1).

snippety *or* **snippy** *adjective*
Informal Rude and disrespectful ▸ bold, insolent, pert. *See* **impudent.**

snit *noun*
Informal A condition of excited distress ▸ fume. *Informal:* sweat, swivet. *See* **state** (4).

snitch *or* **snitcher** *verb*
1. *Slang* To take another's property without permission ▸ purloin, snatch, thieve. *See* **steal** (1). *See synonym note at* **steal. 2.** *Slang* To give incriminating information about others, especially to the authorities ▸ report. *Slang:* rat, squeal. *See* **inform** (2).

snitch *noun*
Slang One who gives incriminating information about others ▸ informant. *Slang:* fink, squealer. *See* **informer.**

snivel *verb*
1. To express feelings of pain, dissatisfaction, or resentment ▸ fuss, grouch, whine. *See* **complain. 2.** To shed tears ▸ howl, sob, weep. *See* **cry** (1).

snob *noun*
One who despises people or things regarded as inferior, especially because of social or intellectual pretension ▸ elitist, prig. *Informal:* snoot.

snobbery *noun*
▸ condescendence, haughtiness, patronization. *See* **condescension.**

snobbish *or* **snobby** *adjective*
Characteristic of or resembling a snob ▸ elitist. *Informal:* high-hat, snooty, stuck-up, uppish, uppity. *See also* **arrogant, pompous.**

snoop *verb*
To look into or inquire about curiously, inquisitively, or in a meddlesome fashion ▸ poke, pry. *Informal:* nose (around), sniff about (*or* around). *Idiom:* stick one's nose into. *See also* **meddle.**

snoop *or* **snooper** *noun*
1. A person who snoops ▸ prier, pryer, pry. *See also* **busybody**. 2. A person habitually engaged in idle talk about others ▸ gossipmonger, taleteller, whisperer. *See* **gossip** (2).

snoopiness *noun*
▸ inquisitiveness. *Informal:* nosiness. *See* **curiosity** (2).

snoopy *adjective*
▸ inquisitive, meddlesome, officious. *See* **curious** (1). *See synonym note at* **curious**.

snoot *noun*
1. *Informal* One who despises people or things regarded as inferior, especially because of social or intellectual pretension ▸ elitist, prig, snob. 2. *Informal* The human organ of smell ▸ proboscis. *Slang:* schnoz. *See* **nose** (1).

snootiness *noun*
Informal Superciliously indulgent treatment, especially of those considered inferior ▸ haughtiness, patronization, snobbery. *See* **condescension** (1).

snooty *adjective*
1. *Informal* Characteristic of or resembling a snob ▸ elitist. *Informal:* high-hat, uppity. *See* **snobbish**. 2. *Informal* Overly convinced of one's own superiority and importance ▸ haughty, insolent. *See* **arrogant**.

snooze *verb*
To sleep for a brief period ▸ doze, nod off. *See* **nap**.

snooze *noun*
A brief sleep ▸ doze, siesta. *See* **nap**.

snort *noun*
Slang A small amount of liquor ▸ shot, sip, tot. *See* **drop** (8).

snort *verb*
1. To breathe audibly through the nose ▸ sniff, sniffle, snuff, snuffle. 2. To utter in a breathless or hoarse manner ▸ pant, wheeze. *See* **gasp** (1).

snotty *adjective*
Slang Rude and disrespectful; without shame ▸ impertinent, saucy, snippy. *See* **impudent**.

snout *noun*
Slang The human organ of smell ▸ proboscis. *Informal:* snoot. *See* **nose** (1).

snow *verb*
Slang To cause to accept something false by trickery or misrepresentation ▸ dupe, fool, hoodwink. *See* **deceive**.

snowball *verb*
1. To increase or expand suddenly, rapidly, or without control ▸ balloon, explode, mushroom. 2. To make or become greater or larger ▸ amplify, boost, enlarge. *See* **increase** (1).

snow job *noun*
Slang An indirect, usually cunning means of gaining an end ▸ deception, ploy, stratagem. *See* **trick** (1).

snub *verb*
To slight someone deliberately ▸ cut, disregard, ignore, neglect, rebuff, shun, slight, spurn. *Informal:* coldshoulder. *Idioms:* give someone the cold shoulder, give someone the go-by, turn one's back on, turn

up one's nose at, close (*or* shut) the door on. *See also* **belittle, blackball, neglect**.

snub *noun*
A deliberate slight or affront ▸ cut, putdown, rebuff, spurning. *Informal:* cold shoulder, go-by. *See also* **rebuke**.

snuff *verb*
1. To breathe audibly through the nose ▸ sniff, sniffle, snort, snuffle. 2. To perceive with the olfactory sense ▸ sniff, whiff. *See* **smell** (1).

snuff out *verb*
1. To cause to stop burning or giving light ▸ put out, smother. *See* **extinguish** (1). 2. To destroy all traces of ▸ eradicate, liquidate, obliterate. *See* **annihilate** (1). 3. *Slang* To take the life of a person or persons unlawfully ▸ destroy, kill, slay. *See* **murder** (1).

snuffle *verb*
To breathe audibly through the nose ▸ sniff, sniffle, snort, snuff.

snug *adjective*
1. Affording pleasurable ease ▸ easy, restful. *Informal:* comfy. *See* **comfortable** (1). *See synonym note at* **comfortable**. 2. In good order or clean condition ▸ shipshape, tidy. *See* **neat** (1). 3. Affording little room for movement ▸ close, confining, narrow. *See* **tight** (4).

snug *verb*
To lie or press close together, usually with another person or thing ▸ nestle, nuzzle. *See* **snuggle**.

snuggle *verb*
To lie or press close together, usually with another person or thing ▸ cuddle, nestle, nuzzle, snug. *See also* **embrace, neck**.

so *adjective*
In a similar manner ▸ likewise, similarly. *Idioms:* by the same token, in like fashion, in like manner, in the same way.

soak *verb*
1. To make thoroughly wet ▸ drench, saturate, souse. *See* **wet** (1). 2. To cause something to become thoroughly wet or saturated by immersion in a liquid ▸ soak, suffuse. *See* **steep**². 3. To take in moisture or liquid ▸ absorb, sop up. *See* **drink** (3). 4. *Slang* To take alcoholic liquor, especially excessively or habitually ▸ tipple. *Slang:* booze, lush. *See* **drink** (2). 5. *Slang* To get something by deceitful trickery ▸ bilk, defraud, swindle. *See* **cheat** (1).

soak in *verb*
To come as a realization ▸ dawn on (*or* upon), register, sink in. *See also* **discover, strike, understand**.

soak up *verb*
To take in and incorporate, especially mentally ▸ digest, imbibe, take up. *See* **absorb** (2).

soak *noun*
Slang A person who is habitually drunk ▸ alcoholic, dipsomaniac, tippler. *See* **drunkard**.

soaked *or* **soaking** *adjective*
▸ drenched, saturated, waterlogged. *See* **wet** (1).

soar *verb*
1. To rise steeply and abruptly ▸ rocket, sky, skyrocket.

Informal: shoot up. **2.** To move from a lower to a higher position ▸ ascend, climb, lift. *See* **rise** (3). *See synonym note at* **rise. 3.** To make or become greater or larger ▸ amplify, boost, enlarge. *See* **increase** (1). **4.** To pass quickly and lightly through the air ▸ glide, sail, shoot. *See* **fly** (2).

soaring *adjective*
1. Being of or at a relatively great height ▸ elevated, lofty. *See* **high** (1). **2.** Exceedingly dignified in form, tone, or style ▸ eloquent, grand. *See* **elevated** (5).

sob *verb*
▸ howl, snivel, weep. *See* **cry** (1). *See synonym note at* **cry.**

sobbing *noun*
▸ blubbering, plaint, weeping. *See* **cry** (1).

sobby *adjective*
▸ gushy, mawkish, soft. *See* **sentimental.**

sober *adjective*
1. Characterized by self-restraint in appetites and behavior ▸ abstemious, continent, spartan. *See* **temperate** (2). **2.** Having or indicating an awareness of things as they really are ▸ practical, pragmatic, prosaic. *See* **realistic** (1). **3.** Proceeding from or exhibiting good judgment ▸ commonsensical, levelheaded, prudent. *See* **sensible** (1). **4.** Characterized by careful thought and a lack of frivolity or exaggeration ▸ earnest, sedate, solemn. *See* **serious** (1). *See synonym note at* **serious. 5.** Careful and slow in acting, moving, or deciding ▸ circumspect, measured, unhurried. *See* **deliberate** (3).

soberness *noun*
▸ sobriety, teetotalism. *See* **temperance** (2).

sobersided *adjective*
▸ earnest, sober, solemn. *See* **serious** (1).

sobersidedness *noun*
▸ graveness, sobriety, solemnity. *See* **seriousness** (1).

sobriety *noun*
1. The practice of refraining from use of alcoholic liquors ▸ abstinence, teetotalism. *See* **temperance** (2). **2.** Moderation or restraint of one's behavior or desires ▸ abstinence, self-denial. *See* **temperance** (1). *See synonym note at* **temperance. 3.** The quality of being dignified and serious, as in manner or bearing ▸ graveness, sobersidedness, solemnity. *See* **seriousness** (1). **4.** Avoidance of extremes of opinion, feeling, or personal conduct ▸ abstemiousness, measure. *See* **moderation** (1).

sobriquet *noun*
▸ cognomen, epithet, title. *See* **name** (1).

so-called *adjective*
▸ hypothetical, suppositional. *See* **supposed.**

sociability *noun*
▸ agreeability, congeniality, pleasantness. *See* **amiability.**

sociable *adjective*
1. Enjoying company ▸ companionable, convivial. *See* **social** (1). *See synonym note at* **social. 2.** Pleasant and friendly in disposition ▸ cordial, friendly, genial. *See* **amiable.** *See synonym note at* **amiable.**

sociableness *noun*
▸ agreeability, congeniality, pleasantness. *See* **amiability.**

social *adjective*
1. Enjoying company ▸ companionable, convivial, gregarious, sociable. *See also* **amiable, outgoing, talkative. 2.** Of, representing, or carried on by people at large ▸ general, public, societal. *See* **popular** (1).

social *noun*
A social gathering, especially for pleasure ▸ celebration, gala, soiree. *See* **party** (1).

✦ **CORE SYNONYMS:** *social, companionable, convivial, gregarious, sociable.* These adjectives refer to those who enjoy the company of others: *a friendly social gathering; a companionable pet; a cheery, convivial disposition; a gregarious person who avoids solitude; a sociable conversation.*

◄ **ANTONYM:** *antisocial*

---

socialize *verb*
1. To take part in social activities ▸ mingle, mix. **2.** To place under government or group ownership or control ▸ communalize, nationalize. **3.** To fit for companionship with others, especially in attitude or manners ▸ acculturate, civilize, humanize.

societal *adjective*
▸ general, public, social. *See* **popular** (1).

society *noun*
1. People of the highest social level ▸ aristocracy, blue blood, crème de la crème, elite, flower, gentility, gentry, high society, jet set, nobility, patriciate, quality, smart set, upper class, who's who. *Informal:* upper crust. **2.** Persons as an organized body ▸ community, people. *See* **public** (2). **3.** A group of people united in a relationship and having some interest, activity, or purpose in common ▸ club, league, order. *See* **union** (1). **4.** A pleasant association among people ▸ companionship, sisterhood. *See* **company** (5). **5.** The total product of human creativity and intellect ▸ civilization, culture, Kultur. **6.** Behavior patterns, traits, and products considered as an expression of a certain people or period ▸ civilization, ethos, tradition. *See* **culture** (2).

sock *verb*
To deliver a sudden, sharp blow to ▸ jab, punch, whack. *See* **hit** (1).

sock *noun*
A sudden heavy stroke ▸ crack, hit, whack. *See* **blow²** (1).

sock away *verb*
1. *Informal* To keep for future use ▸ put by, stockpile, store. *See* **save** (1). **2.** *Informal* To place money in an account ▸ deposit, salt away. *See* **bank²**.

socket *noun*
▸ plug, terminal. *See* **outlet** (1).

sock-hop *noun*
▸ ball, prom, hop. *See* **dance.**

sod *noun*
▸ ground, soil. *See* **earth** (1).

sodden *adjective*

1. Covered with or full of liquid ► drenched, soaked, waterlogged. *See* **wet** (1). **2.** Stupefied, excited, or muddled with alcoholic liquor ► besotted, intoxicated, tipsy. *See* **drunk.**

sodden *verb*

To make thoroughly wet ► drench, soak, souse. *See* **wet** (1).

soft *adjective*

1. Yielding easily to pressure or weight ► doughy, mushy, pappy, pulpous, pulpy, quaggy, spongy, squashy, squishy, yielding. *Informal:* squooshy. **2.** Not irritating, strident, or loud ► hushed, low, low-key, low-keyed, muffled, muted, quiet, small, subdued, whispery. *See also* **faint, low. 3.** Not firm or stiff ► droopy, flaccid, floppy. *See* **limp** (1). **4.** Free from severity or violence, as in sound or movement ► delicate, faint, soothing. *See* **gentle** (2). **5.** Of small intensity ► gentle, moderate, slight. *See* **light²** (2). **6.** Of a sympathetic, considerate character ► kindly, softhearted, tender, tenderhearted. *See* **gentle** (1). **7.** Not strict or severe ► easy, indulgent, lenient. *See* **tolerant** (1). **8.** Affectedly or extravagantly emotional ► gushy, mawkish, soppy. *See* **sentimental. 9.** Characterized by reduced economic activity ► dull, slack. *See* **slow** (2). **10.** *Informal* Affording pleasurable ease ► easy, snug. *Informal:* comfy. *See* **comfortable** (1). **11.** Characterized by rain or drizzle ► drizzly, wet. *See* **rainy.**

soften *verb*

1. To moderate or change a position or course of action as a result of pressure ► ease off, slacken, yield. *See* **weaken** (1). **2.** To make or become less severe or extreme ► qualify, tame. *See* **moderate** (1). **3.** To ease the anger or agitation of ► appease, mollify, soothe. *See* **pacify.**

softhead *noun*

1. A person who is deficient in judgment and good sense ► idiot, moron, nincompoop. *See* **fool** (1). **2.** A mentally dull person ► dummy, imbecile, moron. *See* **dullard.**

softheaded *adjective*

► dumb, idiotic, obtuse. *See* **stupid** (1).

softheadedness *noun*

► idiocy, mindlessness, obtuseness. *See* **stupidity.**

softhearted *adjective*

1. Of a sympathetic, considerate character ► kindly, sensitive, tender, tenderhearted. *See* **gentle** (1). **2.** Feeling or expressing sympathy or pity ► commiserative, compassionate, empathetic, understanding. *See* **sympathetic.**

soft-pedal *verb*

Informal To make less emphatic or obvious ► de-emphasize, play down, tone down. *See also* **moderate.**

soft soap *noun*

Informal Excessive, ingratiating praise ► adulation, blandishment. *Informal:* apple-polishing. *See* **flattery.**

soft-soap *verb*

1. *Informal* To persuade or try to persuade by gentle persistent urging or flattery ► cajole, wheedle. *See* **coax** (1). **2.** *Informal* To compliment ingratiatingly ► adulate, butter up. *Informal:* sweet-talk. *See* **flatter** (1).

soft spot *noun*

► mind, pleasure, will. *See* **liking** (1).

softy *noun*

1. *Informal* A childish or pampered person ► crybaby, milksop. *See* **baby** (2). **2.** *Informal* A weak or ineffectual person ► pushover. *Slang:* doormat, wimp. *See* **weakling.**

soggy *adjective*

1. Covered with or full of liquid ► drenched, soaked, waterlogged. *See* **wet** (1). **2.** Damp and warm ► humid, muggy. *See* **sticky** (2).

soil *noun*

The soft part of the land surface of the world ► clay, loam, soil. *See* **earth** (1).

soil *verb*

1. To make dirty ► bemire, muck up, muddy. *See* **dirty** (1). **2.** To attack the reputation or honor of ► besmirch, smear, tarnish. *See* **denigrate** (1). **3.** To ruin morally ► debase, defile, pollute. *See* **corrupt** (1).

soiled *adjective*

► filthy, muddy. *See* **dirty** (1).

soiree *or* **soireé** *noun*

► celebration, gala, social. *See* **party** (1).

sojourn *verb*

To remain as a guest or lodger ► sojourn, stay. *See* **lodge** (1).

sojourn *noun*

A remaining in a place as a guest or lodger ► stay, stop, stopover, visit.

sojourner *noun*

► traveler, vacationer, visitor. *See* **tourist.**

solace *noun*

A consoling in time of grief or pain ► comfort, consolation, reassurance, succor. *See also* **help, pity.**

solace *verb*

To give hope to in time of grief or pain ► condole, reassure, soothe. *See* **comfort.** *See synonym note at* **comfort.**

soldier *noun*

1. One who engages in a combat or struggle ► belligerent, combatant, fighter, warrior. *See also* **aggressor. 2.** An enlisted person ► GI, legionnaire, legionary, military man, military woman, militiaman, serviceman, serviceperson, servicewoman, trooper. *Slang:* GI Jane, GI Joe, grunt. *See also* **mercenary.**

soldier *verb*

To put up with or continue despite difficulties ► keep on, persevere, persist, soldier on. *See* **endure** (1).

soldierly *adjective*

► enlisted, martial. *See* **military** (2).

soldier of fortune *noun*

A freelance fighter ► adventurer, mercenary. *See also* **fighter, soldier.**

sole *adjective*

1. Alone in a given category ► only, single, solitary. *See*

lone (1). **2.** Not divided among or shared with others ▸ particular, single. *See* **exclusive** (1). **3.** Not married or attached ▸ fancy-free, marriageable. *See* **single** (5). **4.** Being or related to a distinct entity ▸ particular, singular. *See* **individual** (2).

solecism *noun*
1. A misused or incorrect term ▸ malapropism, misusage. *See* **corruption** (3). **2.** A stupid, clumsy mistake ▸ bungle, fumble, stumble. *See* **blunder. 3.** An improper act or statement ▸ indiscretion, indecency. *See* **impropriety** (2).

solely *adverb*
1. To the exclusion of anyone or anything else ▸ alone, exclusively, just, only. *See also* **completely, merely. 2.** Without the presence or aid of another ▸ solitarily, solo. *See* **alone** (1).

solemn *adjective*
1. Characterized by careful thought and a lack of frivolity or exaggeration ▸ earnest, sober, somber. *See* **serious** (1). *See synonym note at* **serious. 2.** Fond of or given to ceremony ▸ courtly, formal, stately. *See* **ceremonious** (1).

solemnity *noun*
1. The quality of being dignified and serious, as in manner or bearing ▸ graveness, sobriety, staidness. *See* **seriousness** (1). **2.** A formal act or set of acts prescribed by ritual ▸ rite, ritual, tradition. *See* **ceremony** (1). **3.** The act of observing a day or an event with ceremonies ▸ fiesta, holiday, observance. *See* **celebration** (2).

solemnization *noun*
▸ fiesta, holiday, jubilee, observance. *See* **celebration** (2).

solemnize *verb*
To mark a day or an event with ceremonies of respect, festivity, or rejoicing ▸ celebrate, commemorate, keep, observe. *See synonym note at* **celebrate.** *See also* **sanctify.**

solemnness *noun*
▸ graveness, sobriety, solemnity. *See* **seriousness** (1).

solicit *verb*
1. To make an earnest or urgent request ▸ ask (for), plead, seek. *See* **appeal** (1). **2.** To behave so as to bring on danger, for example ▸ provoke, tempt. *See* **court** (1). **3.** To present with a request or demand for payment ▸ charge, invoice. *See* **bill**[1].

solicitous *adjective*
1. In a state of anxiety or uneasiness ▸ distressed, nervous, uneasy. *See* **anxious. 2.** Intensely desirous or interested ▸ avid, bursting. *See* **eager** (1). **3.** Full of polite concern for the well-being of others ▸ courteous, respectful, thoughtful. *See* **attentive** (1). *See synonym note at* **attentive. 4.** Marked by attentiveness to every detail ▸ fastidious, meticulous, scrupulous. *See* **careful** (2).

solicitude *noun*
1. A troubled or anxious state of mind ▸ concern, distress, unease. *See* **anxiety** (1). *See synonym note at* **anxiety. 2.** Thoughtful attention to others ▸ concern,

regard, thoughtfulness. *See* **consideration** (1).

solid *adjective*
1. Unyielding to pressure ▸ firm, hard, incompressible. **2.** Not easily moved or shaken ▸ secure, stable, sure. *See* **firm**[1] (2). **3.** Based on good judgment, reasoning, or evidence ▸ valid, well-founded. *See* **sound**[2] (1). **4.** Capable of being depended on ▸ reliable, stable, trustworthy. *See* **dependable. 5.** Composed of or relating to things that occupy space and can be perceived by the senses ▸ corporeal, tangible. *See* **physical** (1). **6.** Being in or characterized by complete agreement ▸ accordant, consonant, like-minded. *See* **unanimous. 7.** Very closely associated ▸ close, cozy, familiar. *See* **intimate**[1] (1). **8.** Having physical or verifiable existence ▸ objective, substantial, tangible. *See* **real** (1).

solidarity *noun*
An identity or coincidence of interests, purposes, or sympathies among the members of a group ▸ concord, oneness, union, unity. *See also* **alliance, union.**

solidify *verb*
▸ congeal, toughen. *See* **harden** (2).

solidity *noun*
1. The quality, condition, or degree of being thick ▸ compactness, density, thickness. **2.** Reliability in withstanding pressure, force, or stress ▸ firmness, hardness, steadiness. *See* **stability.**

solipsistic *adjective*
Holding the philosophical view that the self is the center and norm of existence ▸ egocentric, egoistic, egoistical, individualistic.

solitarily *adverb*
▸ single-handedly, solo. *See* **alone** (1).

solitariness *noun*
▸ isolation, loneliness. *See* **solitude.**

solitary *adjective*
1. Set away from or lacking the company of all others ▸ alone, apart, cloistered, companionless, detached, friendless, isolate, isolated, lone, lonely, lonesome, recluse, reclusive, removed, sequestered, single, unaccompanied. *Idiom:* by one's lonesome. *See also* **abandoned, lonely. 2.** Far from centers of human population ▸ outlying, removed, secluded. *See* **remote** (1). **3.** Not friendly, sociable, or warm in manner ▸ aloof, chilly, impersonal. *See* **cool** (1). **4.** Alone in a given category ▸ only, single, unique. *See* **lone** (1).

✦ CORE SYNONYMS: *solitary, alone, lonely, lonesome.* These adjectives describe lack of companionship. *Solitary* often stresses physical isolation that is self-imposed: *I thoroughly enjoyed my solitary dinner. Alone* emphasizes being apart from others but does not necessarily imply unhappiness: *"I am never less alone, than when I am alone"* (James Howell). *Lonely* often connotes painful awareness of being alone: *"'No doubt they are dead,' she thought, and felt . . . sadder and . . . lonelier for the thought"* (Ouida). *Lonesome* emphasizes a plaintive desire for companionship: *"You must keep up your spirits, mother, and not be lonesome because I'm not at home"* (Charles Dickens).

solitude *noun*
The quality or state of being alone ► aloneness, isolation, loneliness, privacy, retirement, retreat, seclusion, singleness, solitariness. *See also* **calm, stillness.**

✦ CORE SYNONYMS: *solitude, isolation, seclusion, retirement.* These nouns denote the quality or state of being alone. *Solitude* implies the absence of all others: *"The worst solitude is to be destitute of sincere friendship"* (Francis Bacon). *"I love tranquil solitude"* (Percy Bysshe Shelley). *Isolation* emphasizes total separation or detachment from others: *"the isolation of Crusoe, depicted by Defoe's genius"* (Winston Churchill). *Seclusion* suggests removal, though not necessarily complete inaccessibility; the term often connotes a withdrawal from social contact: *enjoyed my walk in the seclusion of the woods. Retirement* suggests a withdrawal or retreat from active life, as for serenity or privacy: *"an elegant sufficiency, content,/Retirement, rural quiet, friendship, books"* (James Thomson).

---

solemn word *noun*
► covenant, pledge, vow. *See* **promise** (1).
solo *adverb*
► single-handedly, solitarily. *See* **alone** (1).
solution *noun*
► explanation, resolution. *See* **answer** (2).
solve *verb*
1. To find a solution for ► answer, clear up, decipher, divine, explain, reason out, resolve, think out (*or* through), unravel, untangle. *Informal:* dope out, figure out. *Idioms:* get to the bottom of, hit on the answer (*or* solution), put two and two together. *See also* **analyze, decipher. 2.** To arrive at an answer to a mathematical problem ► work out. *Informal:* figure out. *See also* **calculate.**

✦ CORE SYNONYMS: *solve, decipher, resolve, unravel.* These verbs mean to find a solution: *solve a riddle; can't decipher your handwriting; resolve a problem; unravel a mystery.*

---

somatic *adjective*
► corporal, physical. *See* **bodily.** *See synonym note at* **bodily.**
somber *adjective*
1. Dark and depressing ► bleak, desolate, glum. *See* **gloomy** (1). **2.** Characterized by careful thought and a lack of frivolity or exaggeration ► earnest, sedate, solemn. *See* **serious** (1). *See synonym note at* **serious.**
some *adjective*
Consisting of a number more than two or three but less than many ► few, various. *See* **several** (1).
some *adverb*
Near to in quantity or amount ► almost, nearly, roughly. *See* **approximately.**
some *pronoun*
A number more than two or three but less than many ► few, small number, smattering. *See* **several.**
somebody *or* **someone** *noun*
► notability, personage. *Slang:* big shot. *See* **dignitary.**

something *noun*
1. One that exists independently ► being, entity, object. *See* **thing** (1). **2.** Something having material existence ► body, item, thing. *See* **object** (1).
sometime *adjective*
► former, onetime, past. *See* **late** (2).
sometimes *adverb*
► occasionally, periodically, sporadically. *See* **intermittently.**
somnifacient *adjective*
Inducing sleep or sedation ► narcotic, sedative, sleepy. *See* **soporific** (1).
somnifacient *noun*
Something that induces sleep or sedation ► narcotic, sedative. *See* **soporific.**
somniferous *or* **somnific** *adjective*
► narcotic, sedative, tranquilizing. *See* **soporific** (1).
somnolent *adjective*
1. Ready for or needing sleep ► drowsy, nodding. *See* **sleepy** (1). **2.** Inducing sleep or sedation ► narcotic, sedative, somniferous. *See* **soporific** (1).
sonance *noun*
Vibrations detected by the ear ► noise, sound. *See also* **tone.**
song *noun*
1. A brief composition written or adapted for singing ► ballad, carol, ditty, hymn, jingle, lyrics, number, piece, tune. *See also* **melody. 2.** A poetic work or poetic works ► poetry, verse. *See* **poem** (1).
sonorous *adjective*
1. Having or producing a full, deep, or rich sound ► resounding, ringing, vibrant. *See* **resonant. 2.** Characterized by elevated language, such as that used in public speaking ► bombastic, grandiloquent, rhetorical. *See* **oratorical.**
soon *adverb*
In the near future ► before long, by and by, imminently, presently, promptly, quickly, shortly, without delay. *Informal:* pronto. *Idioms:* before long, in a bit (*or* jiffy *or* minute *or* moment), in short order. *See also* **immediately.**
soothe *verb*
1. To ease the anger or agitation of ► appease, mollify, placate. *See* **pacify. 2.** To give hope to in time of grief or pain ► condole, console, reassure, solace. *See* **comfort.**
soothing *adjective*
1. Affording pleasurable ease ► easy, snug. *Informal:* comfy. *See* **comfortable** (1). **2.** Free from severity or violence, as in sound or movement ► delicate, faint, soft. *See* **gentle** (2).
soothsay *verb*
► divine, foretell. *See* **prophesy.**
soothsayer *noun*
► diviner, fortuneteller, seer. *See* **prophet.**
soothsaying *noun*
► oracle, vaticination. *See* **prophecy.**
sooty *adjective*
► ebony, inky, jet. *See* **black** (1).

sop *verb*
To make thoroughly wet ▸ drench, soak. *See* **wet** (1).
sop up *verb*
To take in moisture or liquid ▸ soak (up), sponge up. *See* **drink** (3).
sop *noun*
Money or a favor given as inducement to dishonest behavior ▸ graft. *Informal:* payoff. *See* **bribe.**
sophism *noun*
▸ casuistry, sophistry, spuriousness. *See* **fallacy** (1).
sophistic *adjective*
▸ false, illogical, spurious, unsound. *See* **fallacious** (1).
sophisticate *verb*
▸ adulterate, debase, doctor. *See* **contaminate** (1).
sophisticated *adjective*
1. Experienced in the ways of the world; lacking natural simplicity ▸ cosmopolitan, worldly, worldly-wise. *See also* **experienced, shrewd, suave. 2.** Characterized by discriminating taste and broad knowledge as a result of development or education ▸ cultivated, educated, urbane. *See* **cultured. 3.** Appealing to or engaging the intellect ▸ cerebral, thoughtful. *See* **intellectual** (1). **4.** Difficult to understand because of intricacy ▸ elaborate, involved. *See* **complex** (1). **5.** Mixed with other substances ▸ alloyed, combined, polluted. *See* **impure** (2). **6.** Catering to, used by, or admitting only the wealthy or socially superior ▸ chic, posh, swank. *See* **exclusive** (4).
sophistication *noun*
1. Refinement of manner, form, and style ▸ urbanity, refinement, taste. *See* **elegance. 2.** Excellent taste resulting from intellectual development ▸ cultivation, enlightenment. *See* **culture** (3). **3.** The state of being contaminated ▸ defilement, impurity, pollution. *See* **contamination** (1).
sophistry *noun*
▸ casuistry, speciousness, spuriousness. *See* **fallacy** (2).
sophomoric *adjective*
▸ immature, infantile, juvenile. *See* **childish.**
soporific *adjective*
1. Inducing sleep or sedation ▸ hypnotic, narcotic, opiate, sedative, sleepy, slumberous, somnifacient, somniferous, somnific, somnolent, stupefacient, tranquilizing. **2.** Ready for or needing sleep ▸ drowsy, nodding. *See* **sleepy** (1).
soporific *noun*
Something that induces sleep or sedation ▸ hypnotic, narcotic, opiate, sedative, somnifacient, stupefacient, tranquilizer. *See also* **drug.**
sopping *adjective*
▸ drenched, soaked, waterlogged. *See* **wet** (1).
soppy *adjective*
1. Covered with or full of liquid ▸ drenched, soaked, waterlogged. *See* **wet** (1). **2.** Affectedly or extravagantly emotional ▸ gushy, mawkish, soft. *See* **sentimental.** *See synonym note at* **sentimental.**
sorcerer *noun*
One who practices sorcery or magic ▸ enchanter, magician, warlock. *See* **wizard** (1).

sorceress *noun*
A woman who practices magic ▸ enchantress, hag, lamia, witch. *See also* **wizard.**
sorcery *noun*
▸ conjuration, witchcraft. *See* **magic** (1).
sordid *adjective*
Having or proceeding from low moral standards ▸ base, ignoble, low, low-down, mean, seamy, squalid, vile. *See also* **corrupt, disgraceful.**

✦ CORE SYNONYMS: *sordid, mean, low, base, ignoble.* These adjectives mean lacking in dignity or falling short of moral standards. *Sordid* suggests foul, repulsive degradation: *"It is through art . . . that we can shield ourselves from the sordid perils of actual existence"* (Oscar Wilde). *Mean* suggests pettiness or spite: *"Never ascribe to an opponent motives meaner than your own"* (J.M. Barrie). Something *low* violates standards of morality, ethics, or propriety: *low cunning; a low trick. Base* suggests a contemptible, mean-spirited, or selfish lack of human decency: *"that liberal obedience, without which your army would be a base rabble"* (Edmund Burke). *Ignoble* means lacking noble qualities, such as elevated moral character: *"For my part I think it a less evil that some criminals should escape than that the government should play an ignoble part"* (Oliver Wendell Holmes, Jr.).

---

sore *adjective*
1. Marked by, causing, or experiencing physical pain ▸ achy, hurtful, smarting. *See* **painful** (1). **2.** *Informal* Feeling or showing anger ▸ choleric, indignant, mad. *See* **angry.**
sorehead *noun*
Slang A person who habitually complains or grumbles ▸ crab, grump, whiner. *See* **grouch** (1).
soreness *noun*
1. A sensation of physical discomfort occurring as the result of disease or injury ▸ prick, smart, throe. *See* **pain** (1). **2.** An instance of being irritated, as in a part of the body ▸ irritation, tenderness. *See* **irritation** (3).
sorority *noun*
▸ club, league, order. *See* **union** (1).
sorrow *noun*
1. Mental anguish or pain caused by loss or despair ▸ heartache, heartbreak. *See* **grief.** *See synonym note at* **grief. 2.** A cause of suffering or harm ▸ bane, scourge. *See* **curse** (3). **3.** A feeling or spell of dismally low spirits ▸ dejection, doldrums, melancholy. *See* **depression** (2). **4.** A state of physical or mental suffering ▸ agony, misery, wretchedness. *See* **distress** (1).
sorrow *verb*
1. To feel or express sorrow for ▸ deplore, regret, repent, rue. *See also* **feel. 2.** To feel, show, or express grief ▸ anguish, mourn. *See* **grieve** (1). *See synonym note at* **grieve.**
sorrowful *adjective*
1. Causing or expressing sadness, sorrow, or regret ▸ blue, cheerless, deplorable, depressing, discouraging, disheartening, dismal, dispiriting, doleful, dolor-

ous, gloomy, grievous, heartbreaking, heart-rending, joyless, lamentable, lugubrious, melancholy, mournful, plaintive, regrettable, rueful, sad, saddening, woebegone, woeful. *See also* **affecting, gloomy, pitiful.** **2.** In low spirits ▸ dejected, dispirited, heavy-hearted. *See* **depressed** (1).

✦ CORE SYNONYMS: *sorrowful, sad, melancholy, doleful, woebegone.* These adjectives mean causing or expressing sadness, sorrow, or regret. *Sorrowful* applies to emotional pain as that resulting from loss: *sorrowful mourners at the funeral. Sad* is the most general term: *"Better by far you should forget and smile/Than that you should remember and be sad"* (Christina Rossetti). *Melancholy* can refer to lingering or habitual somberness or sadness: *a melancholy poet's gloomy introspection. Doleful* describes what is mournful or morose: *the doleful expression of a reprimanded child. Woebegone* suggests grief or wretchedness, especially as reflected in a person's appearance: *"His sorrow . . . made him look . . . haggard and . . . woebegone"* (George du Maurier).

sorry *adjective*
1. Feeling or expressing sympathy, pity, or regret ▸ apologetic, compunctious, contrite, penitent, penitential, regretful, remorseful, repentant, rueful. *Idiom:* down on one's knees. **2.** Disturbing because of failure to measure up to a standard or produce the desired results ▸ discouraging, unsatisfying. *See* **disappointing. 3.** Arousing or deserving pity ▸ lamentable, poor. *See* **pitiful** (1). **4.** Of decidedly inferior quality ▸ cheap, lousy, poor. *See* **shoddy** (1).

sort *noun*
A class that is defined by the common attribute or attributes possessed by all its members ▸ ilk, mold, species. *See* **kind².**

sort *verb*
1. To set apart one kind or type from others ▸ separate, sift, winnow. *Idiom:* separate the sheep from the goats. **2.** To arrange according to class ▸ categorize, class, group. *See* **classify. 3.** To put into a deliberate order ▸ deploy, marshal, organize. *See* **arrange** (1).

sortie *noun*
1. An encounter between opposing military forces ▸ brush, confrontation, skirmish. *See* **battle** (1). **2.** A journey undertaken with a specific objective ▸ pilgrimage, tour, voyage. *See* **expedition** (1).

sortilege *noun*
▸ conjuration, sorcery, witchcraft. *See* **magic** (1).

so-so *adjective*
▸ common, mediocre, middling. *See* **ordinary** (1).

sot *noun*
▸ alcoholic, dipsomaniac, tippler. *See* **drunkard.**

sottish *adjective*
▸ intoxicated, sodden, tipsy. *See* **drunk.**

sough *noun*
A low, indistinct, and often continuous sound ▸ sigh, susurration, whisper. *See* **murmur** (1).

sough *verb*
To make a low, continuous, and indistinct sound

▸ murmur, rustle, sigh, whisper. *See also* **burble, hum.**

soul *noun*
1. The seat of a person's innermost emotions and feelings ▸ bosom, breast, heart. *Idioms:* bottom of one's heart, cockles of one's heart, one's heart of hearts. **2.** The vital principle or animating force within living beings ▸ divine spark, vitality. *See* **spirit** (2). **3.** An immaterial supernatural being, especially the spirit of a dead person ▸ phantom, shade, specter. *See* **ghost** (1). **4.** A member of the human race ▸ human, person. *See* **human being. 5.** The most central or essential part ▸ essence, marrow, quintessence. *See* **heart** (1).

soulless *adjective*
▸ heartless, insensitive, merciless. *See* **callous.**

soul mate *noun*
▸ chum, comrade, mate. *See* **friend** (1).

sound¹ *noun*
1. Vibrations detected by the ear ▸ noise, sonance. *See also* **noise, tone. 2.** Range of audibility ▸ earshot, hearing. *See also* **range.**

sound *verb*
1. To give the impression of being ▸ appear, feel, look, seem. *Idioms:* have all the earmarks of being, give the idea (*or* impression) of being, strike one as being. *See also* **resemble. 2.** To produce or make speech sounds ▸ enunciate, vocalize. *See* **pronounce. 3.** To go into or through for the purpose of making discoveries or acquiring information ▸ inquire, investigate, probe. *See* **explore. 4.** To give forth or cause to give forth a clear resonant sound ▸ bong, chime, peal. *See* **ring²** (1).

sound² *adjective*
1. Based on good judgment, reasoning, or evidence ▸ cogent, just, solid, tight, valid, well-considered, well-founded, well-grounded. *See also* **convincing, logical. 2.** In excellent condition ▸ flawless, intact, unblemished. *See* **good** (2). **3.** Having good health ▸ fit, well. *See* **healthy** (1). *See synonym note at* **healthy. 4.** Not easily moved or shaken ▸ secure, solid, stable. *See* **firm¹** (2). **5.** Capable of being depended on ▸ reliable, solid, trustworthy. *See* **dependable. 6.** Proceeding from or exhibiting good judgment ▸ commonsensical, levelheaded, prudent. *See* **sensible** (1).

✦ CORE SYNONYMS: *sound, valid, cogent.* These adjectives describe assertions, arguments, conclusions, reasons, or intellectual processes that are based on good judgment, reasoning, or evidence. What is *sound* is free from logical flaws or is based on valid reasoning: *a sound theory; sound principles.* What is *valid* is based on or borne out by truth or fact or has legal force: *a valid excuse; a valid claim.* Something *cogent* is both sound and compelling: *cogent testimony; a cogent explanation.*

sound³ *verb*
To test the attitude of someone ▸ feel (out), probe, sound out. *Idioms:* put out feelers, run something up the flagpole, send up a trial balloon.

sound⁴ *noun*
A body of water partly enclosed by land but having a wide outlet to the sea ▸ bay, bight, gulf. *See also* **channel, harbor, inlet.**

soundless *adjective*
▸ hushed, noiseless, quiet. *See* **silent** (1). *See synonym note at* **silent.**

soundlessness *noun*
▸ noiselessness, quiet. *See* **silence** (1).

soundness *noun*
1. The condition of being free from defects or flaws ▸ flawlessness, intactness, integrity, perfection, wholeness. *Idiom:* mint condition. **2.** The condition of being physically or mentally sound ▸ healthiness, wellness. *See* **health** (1). **3.** A healthy mental state ▸ lucidity, rationality, reason. *See* **sanity. 4.** Reliability in withstanding pressure, force, or stress ▸ firmness, hardness, steadiness. *See* **stability. 5.** The state or quality of being within the law ▸ legitimacy, licitness, validity. *See* **legality.**

soup *noun*
▸ corner, difficulty, fix. *See* **predicament.**

soupçon *noun*
▸ hint, semblance, trace. *See* **shade** (2).

soupy *adjective*
Informal Affectedly or extravagantly emotional ▸ gushy, mawkish, soft. *See* **sentimental.**

sour *adjective*
1. Having a taste characteristic of that produced by acids ▸ acerbic, acetous, acid, acidic, acidulous, dry, green, sharp, tangy, tart, unripe, vinegary. **2.** Broodingly and sullenly unhappy ▸ gloomy, morose, sullen. *See* **glum** (1). **3.** Having a sharp, unpleasant, alkaline taste ▸ acrid, harsh, pungent. *See* **bitter** (1). *See synonym note at* **bitter.**

sour *verb*
To cause unhappiness by failing to satisfy the hopes, desires, or expectations of ▸ disgruntle, embitter, let down. *See* **disappoint.**

✦ CORE SYNONYMS: *sour, acid, acidic, acidulous, dry, tart.* These adjectives mean having a taste characteristic of that produced by an acid: *sour cider; acid, unripe grapes; mildly acidic yogurt; an acidulous tomato; dry white wine; tart cherries.*

---

source *noun*
1. A point of origination ▸ provenance, root, spring. *See* **origin** (1). *See synonym note at* **origin. 2.** An acquaintance who is in a position to help ▸ connection, contact. **3.** One who gives incriminating information about others ▸ mole. *Slang:* snitch, squealer. *See* **informer.**

sourpuss *noun*
Slang A person who habitually complains or grumbles ▸ crab, grump, whiner. *See* **grouch** (1).

souse *verb*
1. To plunge briefly in or into a liquid ▸ dunk, submerse. *See* **dip** (1). **2.** To make thoroughly wet ▸ drench, soak, sop. *See* **wet** (1). **3.** To cause something to become thoroughly wet or saturated by immersion in a liquid ▸ soak, saturate. *See* **steep².**

souse *noun*
1. *Slang* A person who is habitually drunk ▸ alcoholic, dipsomaniac, tippler. *See* **drunkard. 2.** *Slang* A drinking bout ▸ brannigan, carousal, carouse, spree. *See* **bender.**

soused *adjective*
Slang Stupefied, excited, or muddled with alcoholic liquor ▸ intoxicated, sodden, tipsy. *See* **drunk.**

souvenir *noun*
▸ memento, reminder. *See* **remembrance** (1).

sovereign *adjective*
Not imprisoned, enslaved, or controlled by another ▸ autonomous, independent, self-governing. *See* **free** (1).

sovereign *noun*
One who governs or leads ▸ boss, director, head, leader. *See* **chief** (1).

sovereignty *noun*
1. The right and power to command, decide, rule, or judge ▸ control, dominion, might. *See* **authority** (1). **2.** The condition of being politically free ▸ autonomy, self-government. *See* **freedom** (1).

sow *verb*
▸ pot, seed, transplant. *See* **plant** (1).

sozzled *noun*
Slang Stupefied, excited, or muddled with alcoholic liquor ▸ intoxicated, sodden, tipsy. *See* **drunk.**

space *noun*
1. An extent, measured or unmeasured, of linear space ▸ interval, length, stretch. *See* **distance** (1). **2.** A wide and open area, as of land, sky, or water ▸ extent, stretch, sweep. *See* **expanse** (1). **3.** A rather short period ▸ interval, while. *See* **bit¹** (4). **4.** A specific length of time characterized by the occurrence of certain conditions or events ▸ span, stretch, term. *See* **period** (1). **5.** A space in an otherwise solid mass ▸ hollow, vacuity. *See* **hole** (1).

spaced-out *adjective*
1. *Slang* Stupefied, intoxicated, or otherwise influenced by the taking of drugs ▸ high, hopped-up, lit (up). *See* **drugged. 2.** *Slang* So lost in thought as to be inattentive ▸ bemused, distracted, preoccupied. *See* **absent-minded.**

spacious *adjective*
1. Having plenty of room ▸ ample, capacious, commodious, roomy. *See synonym note at* **roomy.** *See also* **big. 2.** Of large extent or expanse ▸ extended, wide. *See* **broad** (1).

spade *verb*
1. To break, turn over, or remove (earth or sand, for example) with or as if with a tool ▸ excavate, scoop, shovel. *See* **dig** (1). **2.** To prepare soil for the planting of crops ▸ cultivate, plow, work. *See* **till.**

span¹ *noun*
1. The measure of how far or long something goes in space, time, or degree ▸ coverage, stretch. *See* **extent** (1). **2.** The period during which someone or some-

thing exists ▸ existence, generation, term. *See* **life** (1).
3. A specific length of time characterized by the occurrence of certain conditions or events ▸ season, stretch, term. *See* **period** (1). **4.** An extent, measured or unmeasured, of linear space ▸ interval, length, stretch. *See* **distance** (1).

span *verb*
To go or extend across ▸ pass, transit, traverse. *See* **cross** (1).

span² *noun*
Two items of the same kind together ▸ duet, match, pair. *See* **couple.**

spangle *noun*
A small sparkling decoration ▸ diamond, glitter, rhinestone, sequin.

spangle *verb*
To emit light in sudden or intermittent bursts ▸ flash, glimmer, twinkle. *See* **glitter.**

spank *verb*
To hit with a sharp blow, especially of the open hand ▸ smack, swat, whack. *See* **slap** (1).

spank *noun*
A sharp blow, especially with the open hand ▸ swat, whack. *See* **slap** (1).

spar *verb*
1. To strive in opposition ▸ clash, combat, fight. *See* **contend** (1). **2.** To engage in a quarrel ▸ dispute, fight. *See* **argue** (1).

spare *verb*
1. To free from an obligation or duty ▸ discharge, exempt. *See* **excuse** (1). **2.** To be frugal or sparing ▸ save, skimp, stint. *See* **scrimp.**

spare *adjective*
1. Being more than is needed, desired, or appropriate ▸ excess, surplus. *See* **superfluous.** *See synonym note at* **superfluous. 2.** Conspicuously deficient in quantity, fullness, or extent ▸ puny, scant, skimpy. *See* **meager** (1). **3.** Without addition, decoration, or qualification ▸ austere, bare-bones, spartan. *See* **bare** (1). **4.** Having little flesh or fat on the body ▸ lean, skinny, slender, slim. *See* **thin** (1). *See synonym note at* **thin. 5.** Characterized by an economy of artistic expression ▸ minimalist, taut. *See* **tight** (3).

sparing *adjective*
▸ canny, chary, frugal. *See* **economical.** *See synonym note at* **economical.**

spark¹ *noun*
1. A sudden burst of light ▸ flicker, glance, twinkle. *See* **flash** (1). **2.** A source of further growth and development ▸ kernel, seed. *See* **germ** (2).

spark *verb*
1. To set in motion ▸ activate, actuate, start, turn on. *See also* **energize, provoke. 2.** To stir to action or feeling ▸ excite, prod, trigger. *See* **provoke** (1).

spark² *verb*
To attempt to gain the affection of ▸ chase, woo. *See* **court** (2).

sparkle *verb*
To emit light in sudden or intermittent bursts ▸ flash,

glimmer, twinkle. *See* **glitter.** *See synonym note at* **glitter.**

sparkle *noun*
1. A lively, emphatic, eager quality or manner ▸ life, verve, vivaciousness. *See* **spirit** (1). **2.** Sparkling, brilliant light ▸ glint, glisten, shimmer. *See* **glitter** (1). **3.** Brilliant, showy splendor ▸ brilliance, magnificence, resplendence. *See* **glitter** (2).

sparkling *adjective*
1. Full of bright shifting or flickering light ▸ coruscating, flashing, gleaming, glinting, glistening, glittering, resplendent, scintillating, shimmering, twinkling, twinkly. *See also* **bright, brilliant, glossy. 2.** Very brisk, alert, and full of high spirits ▸ animated, chipper, vivacious. *See* **lively** (1). **3.** Exhibiting or employing wit or originality ▸ scintillating, witty. *See* **clever** (2).

sparkly *adjective*
▸ animated, chipper, vivacious. *See* **lively** (1).

sparse *adjective*
▸ puny, scant, skimpy. *See* **meager** (1).

spartan *adjective*
1. Without addition, decoration, or qualification ▸ austere, bare-bones, spare. *See* **bare** (1). **2.** Conspicuously deficient in quantity, fullness, or extent ▸ puny, scant, skimpy. *See* **meager** (1). **3.** Characterized by self-restraint in appetites and behavior ▸ abstemious, continent, sober. *See* **temperate** (2).

spasm *noun*
1. A sensation of physical discomfort occurring as the result of disease or injury ▸ ache, pang, throe. *See* **pain** (1). **2.** A nervous shaking of the body ▸ quiver, shake, twitch. *See* **tremor** (2).

spasmodic *adjective*
▸ inconsistent, patchy, variable. *See* **uneven** (1).

spat *noun*
1. A discussion, often heated, in which a difference of opinion is expressed ▸ fight, quarrel. *Informal:* tangle. *See* **argument** (1). **2.** *Informal* A sharp blow, especially with the open hand ▸ smack, whack. *See* **slap** (1).

spat *verb*
1. To engage in a quarrel ▸ dispute, fight, quarrel. *See* **argue** (1). **2.** *Informal* To hit with a sharp blow, especially of the open hand ▸ smack, spank, swat, whack. *See* **slap** (1).

spate *noun*
1. An abundant or overwhelming flow of water ▸ deluge, overflow, torrent. *See* **flood** (1). **2.** Something suggestive of running water ▸ flood, stream, tide. *See* **flow.**

spatter *verb*
1. To hurl or scatter liquid ▸ bespatter, spray. *See* **splash** (1). **2.** To mark or soil with foreign matter ▸ discolor, spot. *See* **stain** (1). **3.** To attack the reputation or honor of ▸ besmirch, smear, tarnish. *See* **denigrate** (1). **4.** To fall in drops of water from clouds ▸ drizzle, precipitate, shower. *See* **rain** (2).

spawn *verb*
1. To give life to ▸ engender, propagate, reproduce. *See*

breed (1). **2.** To bring into existence ▸ give, provide, yield. *See* **produce** (1).

spawn *noun*
1. A person or group descended directly from the same parents or ancestors ▸ offspring, posterity, seed. *See* **progeny. 2.** The offspring, as of an animal or bird, for example, that are the result of one breeding season ▸ brood, litter, young.

spawning *noun*
▸ breeding, procreation, propagation. *See* **reproduction** (3).

spay *verb*
▸ fix, neuter, spay. *See* **sterilize** (2).

speak *verb*
1. To express oneself in speech ▸ talk, verbalize, vocalize. *Idioms:* bend someone's ear, open one's mouth (*or* lips), put in (*or* into) words, wag one's tongue. *See also* **babble, chatter, say. 2.** To direct speech to ▸ address, talk. **3.** To talk to an audience formally ▸ lecture, prelect, sermonize. **4.** To engage in spoken exchange ▸ discourse, talk. *See* **converse**[1]. *See synonym note at* **converse**[1].

speak for *verb*
To serve as an official delegate of ▸ act (as *or* for), answer for, represent, stand for. *Idioms:* be spokesperson (*or* representative) for, be the voice of. *See also* **substitute.**

speak up *verb*
To express opposition, often by argument ▸ except, oppose, remonstrate. *See* **object** (1).

speaker *noun*
1. One who delivers a public speech ▸ declaimer, lecturer, orator, rhetorician, speechifier, speechmaker. **2.** A person who speaks on behalf of another or others ▸ mouth, spokesman, spokesperson, spokeswoman. *Informal:* mouthpiece. *See also* **representative.**

spear *verb*
▸ bayonet, incise, pierce, slash. *See* **cut** (1).

special *adjective*
1. Relating to, identifying, or setting apart an individual or group ▸ characteristic, distinctive, distinguishing, especial, express, individual, particular, peculiar, set, specific, typical, vintage. *See also* **definite, distinct. 2.** Beyond what is usual, normal, or customary ▸ extraordinary, remarkable. *See* **exceptional** (1).

specialist *noun*
▸ authority, master, proficient. *See* **expert.**

specialty *noun*
1. Something at which a person excels ▸ long suit, strong point. *See* **forte.** *See synonym note at* **forte. 2.** A small, often specialized element of a whole ▸ particular, singularity, technicality. *See* **detail** (1). **3.** An area of academic study that is part of a larger body of learning ▸ branch, discipline, field. *See also* **area. 4.** Activity pursued as a livelihood ▸ profession, pursuit, vocation. *See* **business** (2).

species *noun*
▸ ilk, mold, sort. *See* **kind**[2].

specific *adjective*
1. Clearly, fully, and emphatically expressed ▸ decided, explicit, precise. *See* **definite** (1). *See synonym note at* **definite. 2.** Having distinct limits ▸ fixed, precise. *See* **definite** (2). **3.** Relating to, identifying, or setting apart an individual or group ▸ characteristic, individual, particular. *See* **special** (1).

specifically *adverb*
▸ i.e., videlicet. *See* **namely.**

specification *noun*
▸ condition, limitation, proviso, stipulation. *See* **provision** (1).

specify *verb*
1. To state specifically ▸ detail, particularize, provide, stipulate. *See also* **assert, describe, dictate. 2.** To make known or identify, as by signs ▸ indicate, mark, signify. *See* **designate** (1). **3.** To refer to by name ▸ mention, point to. *See* **name** (2).

specimen *noun*
▸ illustration, sample. *See* **example** (1). *See synonym note at* **example.**

specious *adjective*
1. Containing errors in reasoning ▸ false, illogical, unsound. *See* **fallacious** (1). **2.** Not true ▸ spurious, untrue, wrong. *See* **false** (1).

speciousness *noun*
▸ casuistry, sophism, spuriousness. *See* **fallacy** (2).

speck *noun*
1. A very small mark ▸ dot, pinpoint. *See* **point** (2). **2.** A tiny amount ▸ dash, drop, smidgen. *See* **bit**[1] (1).

speck *verb*
To mark with many small spots ▸ dapple, freckle. *See* **speckle.**

speckle *verb*
To mark with many small spots ▸ bespeckle, besprinkle, dapple, dot, fleck, freckle, mottle, pepper, speck, spot, sprinkle, stipple. *See also* **streak.**

speckle *noun*
A very small mark ▸ dot, pinpoint. *See* **point** (2).

spectacle *noun*
1. An impressive or ostentatious exhibition ▸ display, show. *See* **array** (1). **2.** That which is or can be seen ▸ panorama, perspective, vista. *See* **view** (2).

spectacular *adjective*
1. Suggesting drama or a stage performance, as in emotionality or suspense ▸ melodramatic, sensational, showy. *See* **dramatic** (2). **2.** Particularly excellent ▸ fabulous, glorious, sensational. *See* **marvelous** (1).

spectator *noun*
▸ beholder, observer, onlooker. *See* **watcher** (1).

specter *noun*
▸ phantom, shade, spirit. *See* **ghost** (1).

spectral *adjective*
▸ deathly, ghostly, wraithlike. *See* **ghastly** (2).

spectrum *noun*
▸ extent, realm, scope. *See* **range** (1).

speculate *verb*
1. To use the powers of the mind ▸ cogitate, deliber-

ate, reflect. *See* **think** (1). **2.** To predict or assume without sufficient information ▸ conjecture, surmise. *See* **guess. 3.** To formulate as a tentative explanation ▸ hypothesize, theorize. *See also* **suppose. 4.** To take a risk in the hope of gaining advantage ▸ venture. *See* **gamble** (3).

speculation *noun*
1. The act or process of thinking ▸ cogitation, deliberation, rumination. *See* **thought** (1). **2.** A judgment, estimate, or opinion arrived at by guessing ▸ conjecture, guess, surmise. *See* **guess. 3.** Abstract reasoning ▸ conceptualization, philosophizing, theorization. *See* **theory** (1). **4.** An undertaking depending on chance ▸ risk, wager. *See* **gamble** (1). **5.** Something taken to be true without proof ▸ axiom, given, presupposition. *See* **assumption** (1).

speculative *adjective*
1. Of, characterized by, or disposed to thought ▸ contemplative, pensive, reflective. *See* **thoughtful** (1). **2.** Concerned primarily with theories rather than practical matters ▸ academic, conceptual, impractical. *See* **theoretical** (1). *See synonym note at* **theoretical. 3.** Eager to acquire knowledge ▸ acquisitive, questioning. *See* **curious** (2).

speculator *noun*
One who speculates for quick profits ▸ adventurer, gambler, operator.

speech *noun*
1. The faculty, act, or product of speaking ▸ discourse, talk, utterance, verbalization, vocalization. *See also* **babble, chatter, expression. 2.** A usually formal spoken communication to an audience ▸ address, allocution, declamation, homily, lecture, oration, prelection, sermon, talk. *See also* **discourse, tirade. 3.** Spoken exchange ▸ dialogue, discourse, talk. *See* **conversation** (1). **4.** A system of terms used by a people sharing a history and culture ▸ tongue, vernacular. *See* **language** (1). **5.** The art of public speaking ▸ elocution, rhetoric. *See* **oratory.**

speechifier *noun*
▸ lecturer, speechmaker. *See* **speaker** (1).

speechless *adjective*
1. Temporarily unable or unwilling to speak, as from shock or fear ▸ dumb, dumbstruck, inarticulate, mum, mute, silent, tongue-tied, voiceless, wordless. **2.** Lacking the power or faculty of speech ▸ inarticulate, voiceless. *See* **mute** (1).

speechlessness *noun*
▸ muteness, wordlessness. *See* **silence** (2).

speechmaker *noun*
▸ lecturer, rhetorician. *See* **speaker** (1).

speed *verb*
1. To increase the speed of ▸ accelerate, expedite, hasten, hurry, hustle, quicken, speed up, step up. **2.** To move swiftly ▸ dash, hustle, rocket, sprint, zip. *See* **rush** (1).

speed *noun*
1. Rate of motion or performance ▸ pace, tempo, velocity. *Informal:* clip. **2.** Rapidness of movement or

activity ▸ expeditiousness, hurry, quickness. *See* **haste** (1). *See synonym note at* **haste.**

✦ **CORE SYNONYMS:** *speed, hurry, hasten, quicken, accelerate.* These verbs mean to proceed or cause to proceed rapidly or more rapidly. *Speed* refers to swift motion or action: *The train sped through the countryside. Postal workers labored overtime to speed delivery of the holiday mail. Hurry* implies a markedly faster rate than usual, often with concomitant confusion or commotion: *Hurry, or you'll miss the plane! Don't let anyone hurry you into making a decision. Hasten* suggests urgency and often eager or rash swiftness: *My doctor hastened to reassure me that the tests were negative. His off-color jokes only hastened his dismissal. Quicken* and especially *accelerate* refer to increase in rate of activity, growth, or progress: *The skater's breathing quickened as he neared the end of his routine. The runner quickened her pace as she drew near the finish line. The economic expansion has continued but is no longer accelerating. Heat greatly accelerates the deterioration of perishable foods.*

speediness *noun*
▸ expeditiousness, hurry, quickness. *See* **haste** (1).

speedy *adjective*
1. Marked by great speed ▸ quick, swift. *See* **fast** (1). *See synonym note at* **fast. 2.** Done or experienced in very little time ▸ fast, rapid, swift. *See* **quick** (1).

spell[1] *verb*
To have or convey a particular idea ▸ denote, intend, signify. *See* **mean**[1] (1).

spell out *verb*
To make understandable ▸ decipher, interpret. *See* **explain** (1).

spell[2] *noun*
A word or formula believed to have magic powers ▸ abracadabra, charm, enchantment, incantation, magic. *See also* **curse.**

spell *verb*
To act upon with or as if with magic ▸ enchant, mesmerize, spellbind. *See* **charm** (2).

spell[3] *noun*
1. A rather short period ▸ interval, while. *See* **bit**[1] (4). **2.** A limited, often assigned period of activity, duty, or opportunity ▸ shift, stint, time. *See* **turn** (1). **3.** A sudden and often acute manifestation of a disease ▸ apoplexy, fit. *See* **seizure** (1).

spell *verb*
To free from a specific duty by acting as a substitute ▸ relieve, take over. *See also* **substitute.**

spellbind *verb*
1. To act upon with or as if with magic ▸ bewitch, enchant, mesmerize. *See* **charm** (2). **2.** To compel the attention, interest, or imagination of ▸ captivate, fascinate, mesmerize. *See* **grip** (1).

spend *verb*
1. To give money as payment ▸ disburse, expend, give, lay out, outlay, pay (out). *Informal:* fork out (*or* over *or* up), shell out. *See also* **waste. 2.** To use time in a particular way ▸ pass, put in. *See also* **idle. 3.** To be

depleted ▸ consume, exhaust, go. *Idiom:* go down the drain. **4.** To use all of ▸ eat up, expend, run through. *See* **exhaust** (1). **5.** To go through life in a certain way ▸ conduct, pass, pursue. *See* **lead** (3).

✦ CORE SYNONYMS: *spend, disburse, expend.* These verbs mean to pay or give out money or an equivalent: *spent eight dollars for a movie ticket; disbursed funds from the account; expended all her energy teaching the class.*

◂ ANTONYM: *save*

---

spendthrift *noun*
A person who spends money or resources wastefully ▸ profligate, scattergood. *See* **wastrel** (1).
spendthrift *adjective*
Characterized by excessive or imprudent spending ▸ prodigal, profligate. *See* **extravagant** (1).
spent *adjective*
▸ exhausted, weary, worn-out. *See* **tired** (1).
spew *verb*
1. To send forth (confined matter) violently ▸ disgorge, expel. *See* **erupt** (1). **2.** *Slang* To eject the contents of the stomach through the mouth ▸ retch, throw up. *See* **vomit** (1).
sphere *noun*
1. An area or set of parameters within which something or someone exists, acts, or has influence ▸ extent, realm, scope. *See* **range** (1). **2.** A spherical object ▸ globe, orb. *See* **ball** (1).
spherical *or* **spheric** *adjective*
▸ circular, globular. *See* **round** (1).
spheroid *noun*
▸ orb, sphere. *See* **ball** (1).
spice *noun*
A substance that imparts taste ▸ condiment, flavor, seasoning. *See* **flavoring**.
spice *verb*
To impart flavor to ▸ flavor, season.
spice up *verb*
To make different ▸ modify, mutate, vary. *See* **change** (1).
spick-and-span *adjective*
1. In good order or clean condition ▸ shipshape, tidy. *See* **neat** (1). *See synonym note at* **neat**. **2.** Free from dirt, stain, or impurities ▸ immaculate, spotless. *See* **clean** (1).
spicy *adjective*
1. Having a sharp, penetrating flavor or aroma ▸ aromatic, fiery, hot, peppery, piquant, pungent, racy, redolent, savory, seasoned, sharp, zesty. *See also* **delicious**. **2.** Bordering on indelicacy or impropriety ▸ provocative, risqué, suggestive. *See* **racy** (1). **3.** Concerning or arousing sexual love or desire ▸ erogenous, sensual. *See* **erotic**.
spiel *verb*
▸ blab, jabber, prattle. *See* **chatter** (1).
spigot *noun*
1. A device that regulates the flow of a liquid ▸ fixture, petcock. *See* **faucet**. **2.** Something used to fill a hole,

space, or container ▸ cork, stop. *See* **plug** (1).
spike *noun*
1. A sharp protuberance or projection ▸ barb, jag, needle, prick, prickle, prong, quill, snag, spine, spinule, spur, sticker, thorn, tine, tooth. *See also* **point**. **2.** A bolt or shaft hammered or drilled in place, used to support or hold together ▸ bolt, pin, stud. *See* **nail**.
spiky *adjective*
▸ brambly, bristly, prickly. *See* **thorny** (1).
spile *noun*
▸ cork, stop. *See* **plug** (1).
spill *verb*
1. To move downward in response to gravity ▸ drop, plunge, tumble. *See* **fall** (1). **2.** To grow or extend over a wide area ▸ radiate, sprawl. *See* **spread** (2). **3.** *Informal* To disclose in a breach of confidence ▸ divulge, give away. *See* **betray** (2).
spill *noun*
A sudden downward motion toward the ground ▸ dive, nosedive, plunge. *See* **fall** (1).
spin *verb*
1. To rotate on an axis or around a center ▸ twirl, whirl, wheel. *See* **turn** (1). *See synonym note at* **turn**. **2.** To have the sensation of turning in circles ▸ reel, swim, swirl, whirl. *Idiom:* go round and round. **3.** To make or become longer ▸ elongate, prolong, spin out. *See* **lengthen**.
spin *noun*
1. *Informal* A trip in a motor vehicle ▸ jaunt, ride. *See* **drive** (3). **2.** A circular movement around a point or about an axis ▸ circulation, gyration. *See* **revolution** (1). **3.** Something that serves to explain or clarify ▸ decipherment, explication, illumination. *See* **explanation** (1).
spindling *or* **spindly** *adjective*
▸ gangly, lanky, rangy. *See* **gangling**.
spine *noun*
1. A sharp protuberance or projection ▸ prick, prong, snag. *See* **spike** (1). **2.** The quality of mind enabling one to face danger or hardship resolutely ▸ bravery, fortitude, mettle. *See* **courage**.
spineless *adjective*
▸ faint-hearted, pusillanimous. *Slang:* gutless. *See* **cowardly**.
spinning *adjective*
▸ dazed, lightheaded, reeling. *See* **dizzy** (1).
spinoff *noun*
▸ byproduct, offshoot, outgrowth. *See* **derivative**.
spinule *noun*
▸ prick, prong, spine. *See* **spike** (1).
spiny *adjective*
1. Covered with sharp protuberances ▸ brambly, bristly, prickly. *See* **thorny** (1). **2.** Full of irritating difficulties or controversies ▸ nettlesome, prickly, thorny. *See also* **complex, delicate, disturbing, troublesome**.
spiral *verb*
To move or proceed on a repeatedly curving course ▸ coil, snake, weave. *See* **wind²** (1).

spiral *noun*
Something with a curled or spiral shape ▸ curlicue, ringlet, twist. *See* **curl.**

spiral *adjective*
Shaped like or having curls ▸ coiled, swirly, twisted. *See* **curly** (1).

spirit *noun*
1. A lively, emphatic, eager quality or manner ▸ animation, bounce, brio, dash, élan, esprit, life, liveliness, pertness, sparkle, verve, vigor, vim, vivaciousness, vivacity, zing, zip. *Informal:* ginger, pep, peppiness. *Slang:* oomph. *See also* **energy. 2.** The vital principle or animating force within living beings ▸ anima, breath, consciousness, divine spark, élan vital, life force, pneuma, psyche, soul, vital force, vitality. **3.** An immaterial supernatural being, especially the spirit of a dead person ▸ phantom, shade, specter. *See* **ghost** (1). **4.** A member of the human race ▸ human, person. *See* **human being. 5.** The most central or essential part ▸ essence, marrow, quintessence. *See* **heart** (1). **6.** The quality of mind enabling one to face danger or hardship resolutely ▸ bravery, fortitude, gallantry, valor. *See* **courage. 7.** A prevailing quality, as of thought, behavior, or attitude ▸ climate, mood, tone. *See* **temper** (3).

spirit *verb*
To bring in or take out secretly and illegally ▸ bootleg, run. *See* **smuggle.**

spirit away *verb*
1. To seize and detain a person unlawfully ▸ abduct, kidnap, snatch, take hostage. *See also* **seize, steal. 2.** To take another's property without permission ▸ purloin, snatch, thieve. *See* **steal** (1).

✦ CORE SYNONYMS: *spirit, dash, verve, vigor, vim.* These nouns denote a lively, emphatic, eager quality or manner: *a cheerleading cry that showed real spirit; played the piano with dash; painted with verve; intellectual vigor; arguing with their usual vim.*

---

spirited *adjective*
1. Very brisk, alert, and full of high spirits ▸ animated, chipper, vivacious. *See* **lively** (1). **2.** Having or showing courage ▸ bold, gritty, nervy. *See* **brave.**

spiritless *adjective*
1. Lacking energy and vitality ▸ lackadaisical, languorous, listless. *See* **languid. 2.** In low spirits ▸ dysphoric, gloomy, melancholy, unhappy. *See* **depressed** (1). **3.** Lacking liveliness, charm, or surprise ▸ aseptic, colorless, pedestrian. *See* **dull** (1).

spirits *noun*
▸ humor, temper. *See* **mood** (1).

spiritual *adjective*
1. Of or relating to a church or to an established religion ▸ church, churchly, ecclesiastical, religious. *See also* **clerical, divine, holy, ritual. 2.** Having no body, form, or substance ▸ disembodied, incorporeal, nonphysical. *See* **immaterial** (1). *See synonym note at* **immaterial. 3.** Of or relating to existence outside the natural world ▸ metaphysical, superhuman. *See* **supernatural** (1).

spirituality *noun*
▸ faith, piety, reverence. *See* **devotion** (1).

spirituous *adjective*
▸ intoxicative, stiff. *See* **hard** (12).

spit *noun*
1. Saliva or other liquid ejected from the mouth ▸ expectorate, mucus, phlegm, saliva, spittle, sputum. *See also* **drool. 2.** Water condensed from atmospheric vapor and falling in drops ▸ deluge, downpour, shower. *See* **rain** (2).

spit *verb*
1. To expel a small amount of saliva or mucus from the mouth ▸ expectorate, hawk. *See also* **drool. 2.** To fall in drops of water from clouds ▸ drizzle, precipitate, shower. *See* **rain** (2).

spit up *verb*
To eject the contents of the stomach through the mouth ▸ retch, throw up. *Informal:* puke. *See* **vomit** (1).

spite *noun*
1. The quality or condition of being vindictive ▸ revenge, spitefulness, vengefulness, vindictiveness. *See also* **resentment. 2.** A desire to harm others or to see others suffer ▸ venomousness, viciousness. *See* **malevolence.**

spiteful *adjective*
1. Characterized by intense ill will or spite ▸ evil, wicked. *See* **malevolent** (1). **2.** Disposed to seek revenge ▸ avenging, unforgiving. *See* **vindictive** (1).

spitefulness *noun*
1. The quality or condition of being vindictive ▸ revenge, spite, vengefulness, vindictiveness. *See also* **resentment. 2.** A desire to harm others or to see others suffer ▸ maliciousness, viciousness. *See* **malevolence.**

spitting image *noun*
▸ clone, image, twin. *See* **double** (1).

spittle *noun*
▸ expectorate, phlegm. *See* **spit** (1).

splash *verb*
1. To hurl or scatter liquid ▸ bespatter, dash, slop, slosh, spatter, splatter, spray, sprinkle, swash. *See also* **rain, squirt. 2.** To make the sound of moving or disturbed water ▸ lap, swash, wash. *See also* **burble, swish.**

splash *noun*
A small amount of liquor ▸ shot, sip, taste, tot. *See* **drop** (8).

splashy *adjective*
▸ flamboyant, ostentatious, pretentious. *See* **showy.** *See synonym note at* **showy.**

splatter *verb*
1. To hurl or scatter liquid ▸ bespatter, spray. *See* **splash** (1). **2.** To mark or soil with foreign matter ▸ discolor, spatter. *See* **stain** (1).

splay *verb*
▸ extend, stretch. *See* **spread** (1).

spleen *noun*
▸ crankiness, prickliness, tetchiness. *See* **temper** (1).

splendid *adjective*
1. Marked by extraordinary beauty and splendor ▸ brilliant, magnificent, resplendent. *See* **glorious** (1). 2. Impressive in size, proportion, or appearance ▸ imposing, magnificent, superb. *See* **grand** (1). 3. Exceptionally good of its kind ▸ first-rate, prime, tiptop. *See* **excellent**. 4. Particularly excellent ▸ fabulous, glorious, sensational. *See* **marvelous** (1).

splendor *noun*
▸ grandeur, greatness, magnificence. *See* **glory** (1).

splendorous *or* **splendrous** *adjective*
▸ magnificent, resplendent, splendid. *See* **glorious** (1).

splenetic *adjective*
▸ cranky, grouchy, peevish. *See* **ill-tempered**.

splice *verb*
▸ braid, intertwine, twist. *See* **weave** (1).

splinter *verb*
1. To withdraw from an association or federation ▸ pull out, secede, splinter off, withdraw. *Informal:* split (away). *See also* **quit**. 2. To crack or split into two or more fragments by means of force or strain ▸ shatter, smash, sunder. *See* **break** (1). *See synonym note at* **break**.

split *verb*
1. To separate into parts with or as if with a sharp-edged instrument ▸ cleave, sever. *See* **cut** (2). 2. To undergo partial breaking ▸ rupture, fracture. *See* **crack** (1). 3. To separate or pull apart by force ▸ rend, rip, rive. *See* **tear**[1] (1). *See synonym note at* **tear**. 4. To break or separate into parts or sections ▸ disjoin, dissever, partition. *See* **divide** (1). 5. *Informal* To withdraw from an association or federation ▸ pull out, secede, splinter (off), withdraw. *Informal:* split (away). *See also* **quit**. 6. *Informal* To end an association by or as if by leaving one another ▸ break up, part, split up. *See* **separate** (1). 7. *Slang* To move away from a place ▸ exit, go away, retire. *See* **go** (1). 8. To separate into branches or branchlike parts ▸ diverge, fork. *See* **branch**.

split up *verb*
To move apart and go in various directions ▸ disband, separate. *See* **scatter** (2).

split *noun*
1. The act or an instance of separating one thing from another ▸ disjunction, divorce, parting. *See* **division** (1). 2. An opening made with a sharp object ▸ gash, slash, slit. *See* **cut** (1). 3. A partial opening caused by splitting and rupture ▸ break, cleft, fissure. *See* **crack** (2). 4. An interruption in friendly relations ▸ break, estrangement, fissure. *See* **breach** (2). 5. That which is allotted ▸ allowance, ration, share. *See* **allotment** (1).

splotch *noun*
A discolored mark made by smearing ▸ blotch, stain. *See* **smear** (1).

splotch *verb*
To mark or soil with foreign matter ▸ discolor, spatter. *See* **stain** (1).

splurge *noun*
A period of uncontrolled self-indulgence ▸ fling, rampage, spree. *See* **binge** (1).

splurge *verb*
1. To take extravagant pleasure ▸ bask, revel, wallow. *See* **luxuriate**. 2. To use, consume, spend, or expend thoughtlessly or carelessly ▸ fritter away, squander, trifle away. *See* **waste** (1). *See synonym note at* **waste**.

splurgy *adjective*
▸ flamboyant, splashy. *See* **showy**.

splutter *verb*
1. To make a series of short, sharp noises ▸ crackle, crepitate, sputter. *See also* **crack, hiss, snap**. 2. To speak with involuntary repetitions or pauses ▸ sputter, stutter. *See* **stammer**.

spoil *verb*
1. To become or cause to become rotten or unsound ▸ deteriorate, rot, turn. *See* **decay**. *See synonym note at* **decay**. 2. To cause the complete ruin or wreckage of ▸ demolish, torpedo, wreck. *See* **destroy** (1). 3. To ruin through clumsiness or ineptness ▸ blunder, foul up, wreck. *See* **botch**. 4. To treat indulgently ▸ coddle, indulge, pamper. *See* **baby**. *See synonym note at* **baby**. 5. To overindulge with affection or attention ▸ dote on. *See also* **rave**.

spoilage *noun*
▸ decomposition, deterioration, rot. *See* **decay**.

spoiled *adjective*
▸ decayed, putrid, rotten. *See* **bad** (2).

spoils *noun*
1. The political appointments or jobs that are at the disposal of those in power ▸ patronage, pork. 2. Goods or property seized unlawfully ▸ booty, loot. *See* **plunder**.

spoilsport *noun*
▸ *Informal:* stick-in-the-mud, wet blanket. *Slang:* party pooper. *See* **killjoy**.

spoken *adjective*
▸ spoken, verbal, vocal, voiced. *See* **oral**.

spokesman *or* **spokeswoman** *noun*
▸ mouth, spokesperson. *See* **speaker** (2).

sponge *noun*
1. One who depends on another for support without reciprocating ▸ bloodsucker, leech. *Slang:* freeloader. *See* **parasite** (1). 2. *Slang* A person who is habitually drunk ▸ alcoholic, tippler. *See* **drunkard**.

sponge *verb*
Informal To take advantage of the generosity of others ▸ leech. *Slang:* freeload. *See also* **beg**.

sponge up *verb*
1. To take in moisture or liquid ▸ soak (up), sop up. *See* **drink** (3). 2. To take in and incorporate, especially mentally ▸ assimilate, take up. *Informal:* soak (up). *See* **absorb** (2).

spongy *adjective*
1. Yielding easily to pressure or weight ▸ mushy, pulpy, yielding. *See* **soft** (1). 2. Having a capacity or tendency to absorb or soak up ▸ absorptive, imbibing, permeable. *See* **absorbent**.

sponsor *noun*
1. One who assumes financial responsibility for another ▸ backer, guarantor, guaranty, surety, underwriter. *Informal:* angel. *See also* **advocate, donor.**
2. One who supports or champions an activity, cause, or institution ▸ benefactor, supporter. *See* **patron** (1).
sponsor *verb*
To act as a patron to ▸ back, patronize, support. *See also* **donate, finance, support.**
sponsorship *noun*
▸ backing, financing. *See* **patronage** (1).
spontaneity *noun*
1. The absence of forethought, prompting, or planning in action ▸ automaticity, impulsiveness, impulsivity, instinctiveness, involuntariness, reflexiveness, reflexivity. *See also* **improvisation, temerity.** 2. Freedom from constraint, formality, embarrassment, or awkwardness ▸ informality, naturalness. *See* **ease** (1).
spontaneous *adjective*
1. Acting or happening without apparent forethought, prompting, or planning ▸ automatic, impulsive, instinctive, involuntary, natural, reflex, reflexive, unplanned, unpremeditated, unprompted, unrehearsed. *See also* **extemporaneous, instinctive, rash[1], unintentional.** 2. Of or relating to free exercise of the will ▸ willful, uncompelled. *See* **voluntary** (1). 3. Unconstrained by rigid standards or ceremony ▸ informal, relaxed. *Informal:* laid-back. *See* **easygoing** (1).

✛ CORE SYNONYMS: *spontaneous, impulsive, instinctive, involuntary, automatic.* These adjectives mean acting, reacting, or happening without apparent forethought, prompting, or planning. *Spontaneous* applies to what arises naturally rather than resulting from external constraint or stimulus: *"The highest and best form of efficiency is the spontaneous cooperation of a free people"* (Woodrow Wilson). *Impulsive* refers to the operation of a sudden urge or feeling not governed by reason: *Buying a car was an impulsive act that he immediately regretted. Instinctive* implies behavior that is a natural consequence of membership in a species. The term also applies to what reflects or comes about as a result of a natural inclination or innate impulse: *Helping people in an emergency seems as instinctive as breathing. Involuntary* refers to what is not subject to the control of the will: *"People drew in their breath with involuntary surprise and suspense"* (Harriet Beecher Stowe). *Automatic* implies an unvarying mechanical response or reaction: *She accepted the subpoena with an automatic "thank you."*

---

spontaneously *adverb*
1. Without apparent forethought, prompting, or planning ▸ automatically, impulsively, instinctively, involuntarily, reflexively. 2. Of one's own free will ▸ by choice, freely, voluntarily, willfully, willingly. *Idioms:* of one's own accord, on one's own volition.
spoof *noun*
▸ burlesque, parody. *See* **satire.**
spook *noun*
1. *Informal* An immaterial supernatural being, especially the spirit of a dead person ▸ phantom, shade, specter. *See* **ghost** (1). 2. *Informal* A person who secretly observes others to obtain information ▸ agent, operative. *See* **spy.**
spook *verb*
Informal To fill with fear ▸ horrify, scare, terrify. *See* **frighten.**
spooked *adjective*
Informal Filled with fear or terror ▸ fearful, frightened, scared. *See* **afraid.**
spooky *adjective*
Informal Of an unnatural and usually frightening nature ▸ uncanny, unearthly. *See* **weird** (1).
spoon *verb*
1. To take a substance, as liquid, from a container by plunging the hand or a utensil into it ▸ ladle, scoop (up). *See* **dip** (2). 2. *Informal* To engage in kissing, caressing, and other amorous behavior ▸ *Informal:* fool around, pet. *See* **neck.**
spoor *noun*
▸ scent, trace, trail. *See* **track** (1).
sporadic *adjective*
1. Happening or appearing now and then ▸ fitful, occasional, periodic. *See* **intermittent.** *See synonym note at* **intermittent.** 2. Rarely occurring or appearing ▸ occasional, unusual. *See* **infrequent.**
sporadically *adverb*
1. Once in a while; at times ▸ occasionally, periodically, sometimes. *See* **intermittently.** 2. At rare intervals ▸ occasionally, rarely. *See* **infrequently.**
sport *noun*
1. Something that amuses, entertains, or pleases ▸ diversion, fun, recreation. *See* **amusement.** 2. Actions taken as a joke ▸ game, jest. *See* **play** (1).
sport *verb*
1. To occupy oneself with amusement or diversion ▸ frolic, recreate. *Informal:* horse around. *See* **play** (1). 2. To make a public and usually ostentatious show of ▸ exhibit, expose, flaunt. *See* **display** (1).
sport coat *or* **sports coat** *or* **sport jacket** *or* **sports jacket** *noun*
▸ jacket, suit coat, windbreaker. *See* **coat** (1).
sporting *adjective*
According to the rules ▸ clean, fair, sportsmanlike, sportsmanly.
sportingly *adverb*
▸ cleanly, correctly, properly. *See* **fair[1]** (1).
sportive *adjective*
▸ frolicsome, impish, rascally. *See* **mischievous** (1).
sportsmanlike *or* **sportsmanly** *adjective*
According to the rules ▸ clean, fair, sporting.
spot *noun*
1. A very small mark ▸ dot, speck. *See* **point** (2). 2. A mark of discredit or disgrace ▸ blemish, onus. *See* **stain** (1). 3. The place where a person or thing is located ▸ location, point, site. *See* **position** (1). 4. A post of employment ▸ job, situation. *See* **position** (3). 5. *Informal* A difficult, often embarrassing situation or condition ▸ corner, difficulty, fix. *See* **predicament.**

6. A discolored mark made by smearing ▸ blotch, stain. *See* **smear** (1).

spot *verb*
1. To mark or soil with foreign matter ▸ blotch, discolor, splatter. *See* **stain** (1). **2.** To put in a certain position or location ▸ locate, place, situate. *See* **position. 3.** To perceive with the eyes ▸ catch, discern, perceive. *See* **see** (1). **4.** To perceive and fix the identity of, especially with difficulty ▸ ascertain, recognize. *See* **discern** (1). **5.** To look for and discover ▸ find, locate, pinpoint. *Informal:* scare up. *See also* **trace, uncover. 6.** To mark with many small spots ▸ dapple, freckle. *See* **speckle.**

spot *adjective*
Having no particular pattern, purpose, organization, or structure ▸ chance, indiscriminate, unplanned. *See* **random.**

spotless *adjective*
▸ immaculate, unsoiled. *See* **clean** (1). *See synonym note at* **clean.**

spotlight *verb*
▸ accentuate, highlight. *See* **emphasize.**

spotty *adjective*
▸ inconsistent, patchy, variable. *See* **uneven** (1).

spousal *adjective*
▸ connubial, matrimonial, wedded. *See* **marital.**

spousals *noun*
▸ espousal, marriage, nuptials. *See* **wedding.**

spouse *noun*
A person who is married to another ▸ consort, helpmate, helpmeet, husband, mate, partner, wife. *Informal:* better half, hubby, missis, other half. *Slang:* old lady, old man. *See also* **lover.**

spouseless *adjective*
▸ fancy-free, marriageable. *See* **single** (5).

spout *verb*
To eject or be ejected in a sudden thin, swift stream ▸ jet, spray, spurt, squirt. *See also* **erupt, flow.**

spout *noun*
A sudden swift stream of ejected liquid ▸ jet, spray, spurt, squirt. *See also* **flow.**

sprain *verb*
To injure a bodily part by twisting ▸ strain, twist, turn, wrench. *See also* **hurt.**

sprawl *verb*
1. To sit or lie with the limbs spread out awkwardly ▸ drape, loll, lounge, spread-eagle, straddle. *See also* **lie¹, slouch. 2.** To grow or extend over a wide area ▸ radiate, scatter. *See* **spread** (2).

sprawl *noun*
The result or product of building up ▸ development, proliferation. *See* **buildup** (2).

spray *noun*
A sudden swift stream of ejected liquid ▸ jet, spout, spurt, squirt. *See also* **flow.**

spray *verb*
1. To eject or be ejected in a sudden thin, swift stream ▸ jet, spout, spurt, squirt. *See also* **erupt, flow. 2.** To

hurl or scatter liquid ▸ bespatter, splatter. *See* **splash** (1).

spread *verb*
1. To move or arrange so as to cover a larger area ▸ expand, extend, fan (out), open (out *or* up), outstretch, splay, stretch, unfold, unfurl, unroll. **2.** To extend or distribute over a wide area ▸ circulate, diffuse, disperse, disseminate, distribute, radiate, scatter, spill, sprawl, straggle, strew. *See also* **distribute. 3.** To extend over the surface of ▸ blanket, pave. *See* **cover** (1). **4.** To spread a disease to others ▸ convey, pass, transmit. *See* **communicate** (4). **5.** To become known far and wide ▸ circulate, get around, go around, travel. *Idioms:* go (*or* make) the rounds. **6.** To arrange tableware upon a table in preparation for a meal ▸ lay, set. **7.** To make or become broader or more comprehensive ▸ amplify, expand, widen. *See* **broaden.**

spread *noun*
1. The process of increasing in extent or inclusiveness ▸ enlargement, proliferation. *See* **expansion. 2.** A wide and open area, as of land, sky, or water ▸ extent, stretch, sweep. *See* **expanse** (1). **3.** The result or product of building up ▸ development, proliferation. *See* **buildup** (2). **4.** *Informal* A large, elaborately prepared meal ▸ banquet, feast, junket. *Informal:* feed.

spread *adjective*
Not covered ▸ revealed, uncovered. *See* **open** (2).

spread-eagle *verb*
▸ loll, straddle. *See* **sprawl** (1).

spree *noun*
1. A drinking bout ▸ brannigan, carousal, carouse. *See* **bender. 2.** A period of uncontrolled self-indulgence ▸ rampage, riot. *See* **binge** (1). *See synonym note at* **binge.**

sprig *noun*
▸ offshoot, runner, sprout. *See* **shoot** (1).

sprightliness *noun*
▸ might, potency, power. *See* **energy.**

sprightly *adjective*
▸ brisk, lively, vigorous. *See* **energetic.**

spring *verb*
1. To move off the ground by a muscular effort of the legs and feet ▸ leap, vault. *See* **jump** (1). **2.** To move in a lively way ▸ skip, trip. *See* **bound¹** (1). **3.** To have as a source ▸ derive, emanate, originate. *See* **stem** (1). *See synonym note at* **stem. 4.** To have hereditary derivation ▸ derive, issue. *See* **descend** (3). **5.** *Slang* To set at liberty ▸ emancipate, release. *See* **free** (1).

spring back *verb*
To reverse direction after striking something ▸ bounce (back), rebound, reflect, snap back. *See also* **bend, glance.**

spring for *verb*
Informal To pay for the food, drink, or entertainment of another ▸ *Informal:* set up, stand. *See* **treat** (2).

spring *noun*
1. The act of jumping ▸ jump, pounce, leap, vault. *See also* **fall. 2.** A sudden lively movement ▸ jump, skip.

See **bound**[1] (2). **3.** The quality or state of being flexible ► elasticity, malleability, pliability. *See* **flexibility** (1). **4.** A point of origination ► provenance, root, source. *See* **origin** (1). **5.** A basis for an action ► motive, reason. *See* **cause** (2). **6.** The initial stage of a developmental process ► genesis, inception, start. *See* **birth** (2). **7.** The season of the year during which the weather becomes warmer and plants revive ► seedtime, springtide, springtime. **8.** *Informal* The time of life between childhood and maturity ► juvenility, puberty, salad days. *See* **youth** (1).

springiness *noun*
► elasticity, malleability, pliability. *See* **flexibility** (1).

springtide *noun*
The season of the year during which the weather becomes warmer and plants revive ► seedtime, spring, springtime.

springtime *noun*
1. The season of the year during which the weather becomes warmer and plants revive ► seedtime, spring, springtide. **2.** *Informal* The time of life between childhood and maturity ► juvenility, puberty, salad days. *See* **youth** (1).

springy *adjective*
► elastic, resilient, supple. *See* **flexible** (1).

sprinkle *verb*
1. To scatter or release in drops or small particles ► besprinkle, dust, pepper, powder. *See also* **spread**. **2.** To hurl or scatter liquid ► bespatter, spray. *See* **splash** (1). **3.** To mark with many small spots ► dapple, freckle, mottle. *See* **speckle**. **4.** To fall in drops of water from clouds ► drizzle, precipitate, shower. *See* **rain** (2).

sprinkle *noun*
Water condensed from atmospheric vapor and falling in drops ► drizzle, shower. *See* **rain** (2).

sprint *verb*
1. To move on foot at a pace faster than a walk ► scamper, scurry, shin. *See* **run** (1). **2.** To move swiftly ► dash, speed, zip. *See* **rush** (1).

sprint *noun*
A pace that is faster than a walk ► dash, gallop. *See* **run** (1).

sprite *noun*
► elf, goblin, nymph. *See* **fairy**.

sprout *noun*
► runner, sprig, sprout. *See* **shoot** (1).

spruce *adjective*
In good order or clean condition ► shipshape, tidy. *See* **neat** (1).

spruce *verb*
1. To make new or as if new again ► refresh, restore, revamp. *See* **renew** (1). **2.** To make or keep an area clean and orderly ► clean (up), neaten (up), straighten (up). *See* **tidy** (1). **3.** To make neat and trim; make presentable ► freshen (up), slick up, trim. *See* **tidy** (2).

spry *adjective*
► brisk, lively, vigorous. *See* **energetic**.

spryness *noun*
► dexterity, nimbleness, quickness. *See* **agility**.

spume *noun*
A mass of bubbles in or on the surface of a liquid ► lather, suds. *See* **foam**.

spume *verb*
To form or cause to form foam ► fizz, lather. *See* **foam** (1).

spumous *or* **spumy** *adjective*
► frothy, lathery, sudsy. *See* **foamy**.

spunk *or* **spunkiness** *noun*
Informal The quality of mind enabling one to face danger or hardship resolutely ► bravery, fortitude, gallantry, valor. *See* **courage**.

spunky *adjective*
► courageous, fearless, heroic. *See* **brave**.

spur *noun*
1. Something that causes and encourages an action or response ► impulse, incentive. *See* **stimulus** (1). **2.** A sharp protuberance or projection ► prick, prong, spine. *See* **spike** (1).

spur *verb*
To stir to action or feeling ► excite, prod, trigger. *See* **provoke** (1).

spurious *adjective*
1. Fraudulently or deceptively imitative ► fake, fraudulent, phony. *See* **counterfeit**. **2.** Containing errors in reasoning ► false, illogical, unsound. *See* **fallacious** (1). **3.** Not true ► untrue, wrong. *See* **false** (1). **4.** Born to parents who are not married to each other ► bastard, misbegotten. *See* **illegitimate** (1).

spuriousness *noun*
► casuistry, sophistry, speciousness. *See* **fallacy** (2).

spurn *verb*
1. To be unwilling to accept, consider, or receive ► refuse, reject. *See* **decline** (1). *See synonym note at* **decline**. **2.** To slight someone deliberately ► cut, shun. *See* **snub**.

spur-of-the-moment *adjective*
► ad-lib, impromptu, improvised. *See* **extemporaneous**.

spurt *noun*
A sudden swift stream of ejected liquid ► jet, spout, spray, squirt. *See also* **flow**.

spurt *verb*
To eject or be ejected in a sudden thin, swift stream ► jet, spout, spray, squirt. *See also* **erupt, flow**.

sputter *verb*
1. To make a series of short, sharp noises ► crackle, crepitate, splutter. *See also* **crack, hiss, snap**. **2.** To speak with involuntary repetitions or pauses ► falter, stutter. *See* **stammer**. **3.** To undergo partial or unsteady combustion ► flicker, smoke. *See* **smolder** (1).

sputum *noun*
► saliva, phlegm. *See* **spit** (1).

spy *noun*
A person who secretly observes others to obtain information ► agent, asset, fifth columnist, operative, secret agent, undercover agent. *Informal:* spook.

spy *verb*
To perceive with the eyes ▸ catch, discern, perceive. *See* **see** (1).

squabble *verb*
1. To engage in a quarrel ▸ dispute, fight, quarrel. *See* **argue** (1). *See synonym note at* **argue. 2.** To raise unnecessary or trivial objections ▸ cavil, niggle, nit-pick. *See* **quibble** (1).

squabble *noun*
A discussion, often heated, in which a difference of opinion is expressed ▸ fight, quarrel. *See* **argument** (1).

squad *noun*
1. A group of people organized for a particular reason ▸ corps, team, unit. *See* **force** (5). **2.** A unit of troops on special assignment ▸ brigade, patrol. *See* **detachment** (7).

squadron *noun*
▸ squad, team, unit. *See* **force** (5).

squalid *adjective*
1. Heavily soiled; very dirty or unclean ▸ filthy, foul, nasty, vile. **2.** Having or proceeding from low moral standards ▸ seamy, vile. *See* **sordid. 3.** Covered with or stained by dirt or other impurities ▸ dingy, grimy, soiled. *See* **dirty** (1). *See synonym note at* **dirty.**

squall¹ *verb*
1. To cry loudly, as an upset baby does ▸ howl, wail, yowl. *See* **bawl** (1). **2.** To shed tears ▸ howl, sob, weep. *See* **cry** (1).

squall² *noun*
An atmospheric disturbance characterized by strong winds and precipitation ▸ blow, tempest. *See* **storm** (1).

squall *verb*
To manifest strong winds and precipitation ▸ blow (up), set in, storm. *See also* **rain.**

squalor *noun*
▸ filthiness, grubbiness, uncleanliness. *See* **dirtiness** (1).

squander *verb*
1. To use, consume, spend, or expend thoughtlessly or carelessly ▸ fritter away, riot away, trifle away. *See* **waste** (1). *See synonym note at* **waste. 2.** To fail to take advantage of ▸ miss, pass up. *See* **lose** (2).

squander *noun*
Excessive or imprudent expenditure ▸ prodigality, wastefulness. *See* **extravagance** (1).

square *noun*
1. A tract of land set aside for public use ▸ lawn, park, plaza. *See* **common. 2.** *Slang* An old-fashioned person who is reluctant to change or innovate ▸ fogy, fossil, fuddy-duddy, mossback. *Informal:* stick-in-the-mud, stuffed shirt. *See also* **drip, dullard, fool.**

square *adjective*
1. Free from bias in judgment ▸ equitable, nonpartisan, objective. *See* **fair¹** (1). **2.** Owing or being owed nothing ▸ even, quit, quits. *Informal:* even-steven. **3.** *Slang* Conforming to established standards ▸ conformist, orthodox, traditional. *See* **conventional** (1).

4. On the same plane or line ▸ coplanar, flat. *See* **even** (2).

square *verb*
1. To make equal ▸ equate, even, level. *See* **equalize** (1). **2.** To be compatible or suitable ▸ chime, correspond, match. *See* **agree** (1). *See synonym note at* **agree. 3.** To set right by giving what is due ▸ discharge, satisfy. *See* **settle** (3).

square *adverb*
With precision or absolute conformity ▸ exactly, precisely, right. *See* **directly** (3).

squarely *adverb*
1. With precision or absolute conformity ▸ exactly, precisely, straight. *See* **directly** (3). **2.** In a just or equitable manner ▸ equitably, impartially, justly. *See* **fairly** (1).

squash *verb*
1. To press forcefully so as to reduce to a pulpy mass ▸ mush, smash. *See* **crush** (1). *See synonym note at* **crush. 2.** To overcome opposition or uprising with overwhelming force ▸ crush, extinguish, quell. *See* **suppress** (1).

squashy *adjective*
▸ mushy, pulpy, yielding. *See* **soft** (1).

squat *verb*
To bend or lower the body ▸ bend, crouch, scrunch. *See* **stoop** (1).

squat *adjective*
Short, heavy, and solidly built ▸ chunky, heavyset. *See* **stocky.**

squawk *verb*
1. To utter a loud cry ▸ scream, screech, yell. *See* **shout. 2.** *Informal* To express opposition ▸ except, oppose, protest. *See* **object** (1). **3.** *Informal* To express feelings of pain, dissatisfaction or resentment ▸ fuss, grouch, whine. *See* **complain.**

squawk *noun*
1. A loud cry ▸ call, shriek, yell. *See* **shout. 2.** An expression of pain or dissatisfaction ▸ carp, whimper, whine. *See* **complaint** (1).

squawky *adjective*
▸ grating, jarring. *See* **harsh** (1).

squeal *verb*
1. To utter a shrill, short cry ▸ yap, yawp, yelp, yip. *See also* **cry, shout. 2.** *Slang* To give incriminating information about others, especially to the authorities ▸ tip (off). *Slang:* rat, snitch. *See* **inform** (2).

squeal *noun*
A shrill, short cry ▸ yap, yawp, yelp, yip.

squealer *noun*
Slang One who gives incriminating information about others ▸ informant. *Slang:* snitch, stoolie. *See* **informer.**

squeamish *adjective*
▸ exacting, finicky. *See* **fussy** (1).

squeeze *verb*
1. To subject to compression ▸ compact, compress, constrict, constringe, pinch. *See also* **crush, wrench. 2.** To extract from by applying pressure ▸ crush,

express, press. **3.** To handle in a way so as to mix, form, and shape ▸ knead, manipulate, work. **4.** To put one's arms around affectionately ▸ enfold, hug. *See* **embrace** (1). **5.** To obtain by coercion or intimidation ▸ blackmail, wrest. *See* **extort. 6.** To move into an area or space in large numbers ▸ cram, jam, press. *See* **crowd** (1).

squeeze *noun*
1. The act or process of constricting ▸ contraction, narrowing. *See* **constriction. 2.** The act of embracing ▸ clasp, hug. *See* **embrace.**

squelch *verb*
1. To overcome opposition or uprising with overwhelming force ▸ crush, extinguish, quell. *See* **suppress** (1). **2.** To hold something requiring an outlet in check ▸ smother, stifle, suppress. *See* **repress.**

squib *noun*
▸ feature, piece, story. *See* **item** (1).

squiggle *verb*
▸ creep, wiggle, worm. *See* **crawl** (1).

squinch *verb*
To peer with the eyes partly closed ▸ squint. *Idiom:* screw up one's eyes. *See also* **gaze, glimpse.**

squint *verb*
1. To peer with the eyes partly closed ▸ squinch. *Idiom:* screw up one's eyes. *See also* **gaze, glimpse. 2.** To have a tendency or inclination ▸ incline, lean, slant. *See* **tend**[1].

squint-eyed *or* **squinty** *adjective*
Marked by or affected with a squint ▸ cross-eyed, strabismal, strabismic.

squirm *verb*
1. To twist agitatedly, as in pain, struggle, or embarrassment ▸ toss, twist, writhe. *See also* **shake. 2.** To move along in a crouching or prone position ▸ creep, wiggle, worm. *See* **crawl** (1).

squirrel away *verb*
1. To put or keep out of sight ▸ bury, conceal, secrete. *See* **hide**[1] (1). **2.** To store for future use ▸ put by, salt away. *See* **save** (1).

squirt *verb*
To eject or be ejected in a sudden thin, swift stream ▸ jet, spout, spray, spurt. *See also* **erupt, flow.**

squirt *noun*
1. A sudden swift stream of ejected liquid ▸ jet, spout, spurt, spray. *See also* **flow. 2.** *Informal* A small or young person ▸ pup, puppy, scrub, small fry. *Informal:* pip-squeak, shorty *Slang:* half-pint, punk, runt, shrimp. **3.** *Informal* A totally insignificant person ▸ nobody, nothing, small fry. *See* **nonentity.**

squishy *adjective*
▸ mushy, pulpy, yielding. *See* **soft** (1).

stab *verb*
1. To penetrate into a substance or place with force ▸ drive, ram, stick. *See* **plunge** (1). **2.** To penetrate with a sharp edge ▸ bayonet, incise, pierce, slash. *See* **cut** (1).

stab *noun*
1. A small mark or hole made by a sharp, pointed object ▸ nick, puncture. *See* **prick** (1). **2.** An act of

thrusting into or against, as to attract attention ▸ nudge, poke, prod. *See* **dig** (1). **3.** A sensation of physical discomfort occurring as the result of disease or injury ▸ prick, smart, soreness. *See* **pain** (1). **4.** A trying to do or make something ▸ effort, trial. *Informal:* shot. *See* **attempt** (1).

stabbing *adjective*
1. Marked by pain that is severe or intense ▸ acute, gnawing, piercing. *See* **sharp** (8). **2.** Marked by, causing, or experiencing physical pain ▸ achy, hurtful, sore. *See* **painful** (1).

stability *noun*
Reliability in withstanding pressure, force, or stress ▸ fastness, firmness, hardness, security, solidity, soundness, stableness, steadiness, strength, sturdiness, sureness. *See also* **balance.**

stabilize *verb*
1. To make stronger or more resistant ▸ brace, reinforce, strengthen. *See* **support** (2). **2.** To put in balance ▸ equalize, steady. *See* **balance** (1).

stable *adjective*
1. Not easily moved or shaken ▸ solid, strong, sure. *See* **firm**[1] (2). **2.** Capable of being depended on ▸ reliable, solid, trustworthy. *See* **dependable.**

stable *noun*
1. An enormous number of persons or things gathered together ▸ horde, mass, throng. *See* **crowd** (1). **2.** A number of animals considered collectively ▸ bevy, gaggle, herd. *See* **flock** (1). *See synonym note at* **flock.**

stableness *noun*
▸ firmness, hardness, steadiness. *See* **stability.**

stack *noun*
A group of things gathered haphazardly ▸ drift, mass, mound. *See* **heap** (1). *See synonym note at* **heap.**

stack *verb*
To collect or pile up or onto something ▸ drift, lump. *See* **heap** (1).

stack up *verb*
Informal To be equal or alike ▸ compare, match, measure up. *See* **equal** (1).

staff *noun*
▸ cane, pole, stave. *See* **stick** (2).

staffer *noun*
▸ jobholder, wage earner, worker. *See* **employee.**

stage *noun*
1. A raised platform on which theatrical performances or speeches are given ▸ boards, dais, podium, proscenium, pulpit, rostrum, soapbox. **2.** The art and occupation of an actor ▸ acting, dramatics, theater, theatrics. **3.** A temporary framework with a floor, used by laborers ▸ platform, scaffold, scaffolding, staging. *See also* **base**[1]. **4.** The place where an action or event occurs ▸ setting, site. *See* **scene** (1). **5.** One of the units in a course, as on an ascending or descending scale ▸ interval, level, step. *See* **degree** (1). **6.** An interval regarded as a distinct evolutionary or developmental unit ▸ period, phase. **7.** A stage of a competition ▸ heat, round. *See also* **competition, turn. 8.** The general point at which an event occurs ▸ in-

stant, juncture, moment. *See* **occasion** (1).

stage *verb*
1. To produce on the stage ▸ act (out), direct, do, dramatize, enact, give, mount, perform, present, produce, put on. *See also* **conduct**. **2.** To organize and carry out an activity ▸ give, hold. *See* **have** (9).

stagger *verb*
1. To walk unsteadily ▸ careen, dodder, falter, halt, hitch, hobble, limp, lurch, reel, stumble, sway, teeter, totter, weave, wobble. *See also* **blunder, sway, trudge**. **2.** To overwhelm with surprise, wonder, or bewilderment ▸ boggle, bowl over, dumbfound, flabbergast, floor, shock, stun. *Idioms:* be thunderstruck at, strike dumb (*or* speechless), take someone's breath away. *See also* **startle, surprise**. **3.** To proceed or perform in an unsteady, faltering manner ▸ bungle, flounder, fumble. *See* **muddle** (1). **4.** To be irresolute in acting or doing ▸ falter, vacillate. *See* **hesitate**. **5.** To dull the senses, as with a shock ▸ stun, stupefy. *See* **daze** (1).

staggering *adjective*
▸ astounding, stunning, unbelievable. *See* **astonishing**.

staginess *noun*
▸ campiness, exhibitionism, theatricality. *See* **theatricalism**.

stagnant *adjective*
1. Characterized by reduced economic activity ▸ down, dull, slack. *See* **slow** (2). **2.** Lacking movement of air ▸ breezeless, still. *See* **airless** (2).

stagnation *noun*
▸ inaction, inertness. *See* **inaction**.

staid *adjective*
▸ earnest, sober, solemn. *See* **serious** (1). *See synonym note at* **serious**.

staidness *noun*
▸ graveness, sobriety, solemnity. *See* **seriousness** (1).

stain *verb*
1. To mark or soil with foreign matter ▸ bespatter, bestain, blotch, discolor, smut, spatter, splatter, splotch, spot. *See also* **dirty, smear**. **2.** To attack the reputation or honor of ▸ besmirch, smear, tarnish. *See* **denigrate** (1). **3.** To ruin morally ▸ debase, demoralize, deprave. *See* **corrupt** (1). **4.** To impart color to ▸ dye, imbue, tint. *See* **color** (1). **5.** To apply a coating to ▸ lacquer, paint, varnish. *See* **finish** (7).

stain *noun*
1. A mark of discredit or disgrace ▸ black eye, blemish, blot, onus, spot, stigma, taint, tarnish. *Idioms:* a blot on one's name (*or* escutcheon). *See also* **disgrace, reflection**. **2.** A discolored mark made by smearing ▸ blotch, spot. *See* **smear** (1). **3.** Something that imparts color ▸ colorant, dye, pigment. *See* **color** (2). **4.** A final coating ▸ lacquer, paint, varnish. *See* **finish** (3).

✦ **CORE SYNONYMS:** *stain, blot, stigma, taint.* These nouns denote a mark of discredit or disgrace, as on one's good name: *a stain on his honor; the blot of* treason; the stigma of ignominious defeat; the taint of vice.

stainless *adjective*
Free from dirt, stain, or impurities ▸ immaculate, spotless. *See* **clean** (1).

stake *noun*
1. A right or legal share in something ▸ claim, interest, portion, title. *See also* **cut, right**. **2.** Something risked on an uncertain outcome ▸ pool, wager. *See* **bet** (1). *See synonym note at* **bet**. **3.** Money or property used to produce more wealth ▸ assets, financing, funding. *See* **capital** (1). **4.** A short straight piece of wood ▸ branch, twig. *See* **stick** (1).

stake *verb*
1. To place something at risk, as in a game of chance ▸ bet, risk, wager. *See* **gamble** (2). **2.** To supply capital ▸ fund, subsidize, underwrite. *Informal:* bankroll. *See* **finance**.

stakeout *noun*
▸ monitoring, vigilance, watch. *See* **lookout** (1).

stale *adjective*
1. Lacking an appetizing flavor ▸ bland, insipid, tasteless. *See* **flat** (2). **2.** Lacking fresh air ▸ stuffy, suffocating. *See* **airless** (1). **3.** Without freshness or appeal because of overuse ▸ clichéd, overused, shopworn, tired. *See* **trite**. **4.** Smelling of mildew or decay ▸ musty, rancid. *See* **moldy**.

stalemate *noun*
An equality of scores, votes, or performances in a contest ▸ dead heat, deadlock, draw, standoff, tie.

staleness *noun*
▸ blandness, drabness, lifelessness. *See* **dullness** (1).

stalk¹ *noun*
The main ascending part of a plant, which supports the other parts ▸ stem, stock, trunk. *See also* **shoot**.

stalk² *verb*
To look for and pursue game in order to capture or kill it ▸ drive, run. *See* **hunt** (1).

stall¹ *verb*
1. To prevent the occurrence or continuation of a movement, action, or operation ▸ check, discontinue, immobilize. *See* **stop** (2). **2.** To come to a cessation ▸ discontinue, leave off, quit. *See* **stop** (1).

stall *noun*
1. A small, often makeshift structure for the display and sale of goods ▸ booth, counter, stand. *See also* **store**. **2.** An enclosure for confining an animal or bird ▸ coop, hutch, kennel. *See* **cage**.

stall² *verb*
1. To cause to be later or slower than expected or desired ▸ hang up, keep, retard. *See* **detain** (1). **2.** To put off until a later time ▸ delay, postpone, suspend. *See* **defer¹**. **3.** To go or move slowly so that progress is hindered ▸ dawdle, dilly-dally, drag. *See* **delay** (2).

stalwart *adjective*
▸ hardy, sturdy, tough. *See* **strong** (2).

stamina *noun*
▸ fortitude, staying power, toughness. *See* **endurance** (1).

stammer *verb*

To speak with involuntary repetitions or pauses; speak hesitatingly or clumsily ► falter, splutter, sputter, stumble, stutter. *See also* **babble, chatter, hesitate.**

stammer *noun*

A way of speaking marked by involuntary repetitions and pauses ► stammering, stutter, stuttering.

stamp *verb*

1. To step on heavily and repeatedly so as to crush, injure, or destroy ► stomp, tramp, trample, tread, tromp. *See also* **crush. 2.** To walk in a laborious way ► stomp, tramp, trample. *See* **trudge. 3.** To produce a deep impression of ► fix, imprint. *See* **engrave** (2). **4.** To shape, break, or flatten with repeated blows ► hammer, pound. *See* **beat** (3).

stamp out *verb*

To destroy all traces of ► eradicate, liquidate, obliterate. *See* **annihilate** (1).

stamp *noun*

1. The visible effect made on a surface by pressure ► indent, mark. *See* **impression** (1). *See synonym note at* **impression. 2.** Something visible or evident that gives grounds for believing in the existence or presence of something else ► evidence, indication, symptom. *See* **sign** (1). **3.** A class that is defined by the common attribute or attributes possessed by all its members ► ilk, mold, species. *See* **kind²**. **4.** The way something or someone looks ► look, features, mien. *See* **appearance** (1).

stamping ground *noun*

Slang A frequently visited place ► meeting place. *Slang:* hangout, stomping ground. *See* **haunt** (1).

stance *noun*

1. A way of holding or carrying one's body ► carriage, pose. *See* **posture** (1). *See synonym note at* **posture. 2.** A frame of mind affecting one's thoughts or behavior ► outlook, position. *See* **posture** (2).

stand *verb*

1. To adopt a standing posture ► arise, get up, jump up, rise, stand up, uprise. *Idioms:* get (*or* jump *or* leap *or* spring) to one's feet, take one's feet. **2.** To be in a certain position; have a location ► be located, be situated, rest, sit. **3.** To be in a certain state for an indefinitely long time ► continue, remain. *See* **endure** (2). **4.** To put up with ► stand for, stomach, tolerate, withstand. *See* **endure** (1). *See synonym note at* **endure. 5.** *Informal* To pay for the food, drink, or entertainment of another ► *Informal:* set up. *Slang:* spring for. *See* **treat** (2).

stand against *verb*

To be in opposition to ► fight, resist. *See* **oppose** (1).

stand behind *verb*

1. To aid the cause of by approving or favoring ► back, endorse, recommend. *See* **support** (1). **2.** To assume responsibility for the quality, worth, or durability of ► certify, warrant. *See* **guarantee** (1).

stand by *verb*

To aid the cause of by approving or favoring ► advocate, endorse, get behind, uphold. *See* **support** (1).

stand for *verb*

1. To serve as an official delegate of ► act (as *or* for), answer for, represent, speak for. *Idioms:* be spokesperson (*or* representative) for, be the voice of. *See also* **substitute. 2.** To serve as an example, image, or symbol of ► exemplify, illustrate, typify. *See* **represent** (1).

stand in *verb*

To act as a substitute ► cover for, fill in. *See* **substitute** (1).

stand out *verb*

1. To be obtrusively conspicuous ► glare, stick out. *Idioms:* stare someone in the face, stick out like a sore thumb. **2.** To curve outward past the normal or usual limit ► balloon, jut, project. *See* **bulge** (1).

stand up *verb*

1. To prove valid under scrutiny ► hold up, prove out. *Informal:* wash. *Idioms:* hold water, pass muster, ring true. **2.** To withstand stress or difficulty ► endure, hold up. *See* **bear.**

stand *noun*

1. A small, often makeshift structure for the display and sale of goods ► booth, counter, stall. *See also* **store. 2.** The lowest or supporting part or structure ► bottom, foot, foundation. *See* **base¹** (2). **3.** The position from which something is considered ► perspective, point of view. *See* **viewpoint.**

standard *noun*

1. A means by which individuals are compared and judged ► benchmark, criterion, gauge, mark, measure, norm, test, touchstone, yardstick. *See also* **condition, law, rule. 2.** A piece of fabric used as a symbol ► banner, colors, pennant. *See* **flag¹** (1). **3.** One that is worthy of imitation or duplication ► exemplar, ideal, paradigm. *See* **model** (1). *See synonym note at* **model. 4.** A first form from which varieties arise or imitations are made ► master, prototype. *See* **original** (1).

standard *adjective*

1. Having or arising from authority ► official, imperial, supreme. *See* **authoritative** (1). **2.** Being of no special quality or type ► common, mediocre, nondescript. *See* **ordinary** (1). **3.** Conforming to established standards ► conformist, orthodox, traditional. *See* **conventional** (1).

✦ **CORE SYNONYMS:** *standard, benchmark, criterion, gauge, measure, touchstone, yardstick.* These nouns denote a point of reference against which individuals are compared and judged: *a book that is a standard of literary excellence; a painting that is a benchmark of quality; criteria for hiring an excellent teacher; behavior that is a gauge of self-control; donations from the public, a measure of the importance of the arts; the program's success, a touchstone of cooperation in the community; farm failures, a yardstick of federal banking policy.*

---

standardize *verb*

► conform, stylize. *See* **conventionalize.**

standards *noun*
▸ morality, principles. *See* **ethics** (2).

standby *adjective*
▸ backup, reserve, supplemental. *See* **auxiliary** (2).

stand-in *noun*
▸ alternate, replacement, surrogate. *See* **substitute**.

standing *noun*
1. Positioning of one individual vis-à-vis others ▸ position, rank, situation. *See* **place** (1). **2.** An established position from which to deal with others ▸ footing, status. *See* **basis** (3). **3.** Credit or respect in the eyes of others ▸ prestige, status. *See* **face** (9).

standing *adjective*
At right angles to the horizon or to level ground ▸ on end, upright. *See* **vertical**.

standoff *noun*
An equality of scores, votes, or performances in a contest ▸ dead heat, deadlock, draw, stalemate, tie.

standoffish *adjective*
▸ aloof, chilly, impersonal. *See* **cool** (1).

standout *adjective*
Informal Beyond what is usual, normal, or customary ▸ extraordinary, outstanding, remarkable. *See* **exceptional** (1).

standpat *adjective*
Extremely or stubbornly conservative ▸ mossbacked, reactionary, rear-guard. *See* **ultraconservative**.

standpoint *noun*
▸ aspect, outlook, point of view. *See* **viewpoint**.

standstill *noun*
▸ cessation, discontinuation, tie-up. *See* **stop** (2).

star *noun*
1. The main performer in a theatrical production ▸ headliner, protagonist. *See* **lead** (1). **2.** A famous person ▸ luminary, personality, superstar. *See* **celebrity** (1).

starch *noun*
▸ might, potency, power. *See* **energy**.

staple *adjective*
▸ chief, key, main. *See* **primary** (1).

starchy *adjective*
Rigidly constrained or formal; lacking grace and spontaneity ▸ buckram, stiff, stilted, wooden. *See also* **cool, forced, prudish**.

star-crossed *adjective*
▸ ill-fated, ill-starred, luckless. *See* **unfortunate** (1).

stare *verb*
To look intently and fixedly ▸ gape, gawk, peer. *See* **gaze**. *See synonym note at* **gaze**.

stare *noun*
An intent fixed look ▸ gape, gaze. *See also* **look**.

stargaze *verb*
▸ fancy, hallucinate, imagine. *See* **dream** (1).

stargazer *noun*
▸ fantasist, romantic, theorizer. *See* **dreamer** (1).

stark *adjective*
1. Marked by cold and unpleasant conditions ▸ grim, severe. *See* **bleak** (1). **2.** Without addition, decoration, or qualification ▸ bald, unadorned. *See* **bare** (1).

3. Completely such, without qualification or exception ▸ all-out, pure, sheer. *See* **utter**[2].

starry-eyed *adjective*
1. Characterized by ideals that often conflict with practical considerations ▸ romantic, unrealistic, utopian. *See* **idealistic**. **2.** Given to daydreams or reverie ▸ fanciful, musing. *See* **dreamy** (1).

start *verb*
1. To go about the initial step in doing something ▸ approach, begin, commence, embark on (*or* upon), enter (on *or* upon), get off, inaugurate, initiate, institute, launch, lead off, open, set about, set out, set to, take on, take up, undertake. *Informal:* kick off. *Idioms:* get cracking, get going, get the ball rolling, get the show on the road, take the plunge. *See also* **cause, introduce, produce**. **2.** To set in motion ▸ activate, actuate, spark, turn on. *See also* **energize, provoke**. **3.** To move suddenly and involuntarily ▸ bolt, jump. *See also* **bump, jerk**. **4.** To come into being ▸ arise, commence. *See* **begin** (1). **5.** To bring into existence formally ▸ constitute, establish, institute. *See* **found** (1). **6.** To draw away or pull back in fear ▸ cringe, recoil, shrink. *See* **flinch**.

start out *verb*
To proceed in a specified direction ▸ head, make, set out. *See* **bear** (5).

start *noun*
1. The act of bringing or being brought into existence ▸ inception, initiation. *See* **beginning** (1). **2.** The initial stage of a developmental process ▸ genesis, inception, spring. *See* **birth** (2). *See synonym note at* **birth**. **3.** A sudden and involuntary movement ▸ bolt, jump, startle. *See also* **jerk, recoil**. **4.** A factor conducive to superiority and success ▸ head start, vantage. *See* **advantage** (1).

✦ **CORE SYNONYMS:** *start, begin, commence, initiate, inaugurate.* These verbs mean to go about the initial step in doing something. *Start, begin,* and *commence* are equivalent in meaning, though *commence* is more formal, and *start* often stresses the point where inaction turns to action: *The play begins at eight o'clock. The festivities commenced with the national anthem. We will stay on the platform until the train starts. Initiate* applies to causing the first steps in a process: *I initiated a lawsuit against the driver who hit my car. Inaugurate* often connotes a formal beginning: *"The exhibition inaugurated a new era of cultural relations"* (Serge Schmemann).

---

starter *noun*
▸ apéritif, hors d'oeuvre. *See* **appetizer**.

startle *verb*
1. To cause to experience a sudden momentary shock ▸ electrify, jolt, shock. *Idioms:* give someone a start, make someone jump, make someone's heart skip a beat (*or* stand still). *See also* **stagger**. **2.** To fill with fear ▸ horrify, scare, terrify. *See* **frighten**. *See synonym note at* **frighten**. **3.** To impress strongly by what is unexpected or unusual ▸ astonish, astound. *See* **surprise** (1).

startle *noun*
A sudden and involuntary movement ▶ bolt, jump, start. *See also* **jerk, recoil.**

start-up *or* **startup** *noun*
▶ constitution, establishment, institution. *See* **foundation** (1).

starving *adjective*
▶ famished, ravenous, voracious. *See* **hungry** (1).

stash *verb*
1. *Slang* To put or keep out of sight ▶ bury, cache, conceal. *See* **hide¹** (1). **2.** To store for future use ▶ put by, salt away, set by. *See* **save** (1).

stash *noun*
A supply stored or hidden for possible future use ▶ cache, reserve, stockpile. *See* **hoard.**

stasis *noun*
▶ counterpoise, equilibrium, equipoise. *See* **balance** (1).

state *noun*
1. An organized geopolitical unit ▶ body politic, country, land, nation, polity. **2.** A group of people who govern a political unit ▶ administration, regime. *See* **government** (2). **3.** Manner of being or form of existence ▶ situation, status. *See* **condition** (1). *See synonym note at* **condition. 4.** *Informal* A condition of excited distress ▶ fume. *Informal:* snit, sweat, swivet. *Slang:* tizzy. *See also* **distress.**

state *verb*
1. To put into words ▶ articulate, express, utter. *See* **say** (1). **2.** To utter publicly ▶ disclose, divulge, voice. *See* **air** (2). **3.** To put into words positively and with conviction ▶ avow, declare, maintain. *See* **assert** (1).

stately *adjective*
1. Impressive in size, proportion, or appearance ▶ imposing, magnificent, splendid. *See* **grand** (1). *See synonym note at* **grand. 2.** Characterized by elaborate, usually formal courtesy ▶ courtly, gallant, stately. *See* **gracious** (2). **3.** Fond of or given to ceremony ▶ courtly, formal, stately. *See* **ceremonious** (1).

statement *noun*
1. Something said ▶ saying, utterance, word. *See also* **language, speech. 2.** The act or an instance of expressing in words ▶ utterance, verbalization. *See* **expression** (1). **3.** The act of asserting positively or something so asserted ▶ claim, declaration. *See* **assertion. 4.** A recounting of past events ▶ chronicle, history, report. *See* **story** (1). **5.** Something announced or communicated ▶ announcement, declaration, notice. *See* **message** (1). **6.** A precise list of fees or charges ▶ bill, check, invoice. *Informal:* tab. *See* **account** (2).

state of mind *noun*
▶ humor, temper. *See* **mood** (1).

static *adjective*
▶ stationary, still. *See* **motionless.**

station *noun*
1. A stopping place along a route for picking up or dropping off passengers ▶ depot, stop, terminal, terminus. **2.** A center of organization, supply, or activity ▶ headquarters, installation, post. *See* **base¹** (1). **3.** Po-

sitioning of one individual vis-à-vis others ▶ position, rank, standing. *See* **place** (1).

station *verb*
To appoint and send to a particular place ▶ assign, post, set. *See also* **position.**

stationary *adjective*
1. Not moving ▶ fixed, still. *See* **motionless. 2.** Firmly in position ▶ immobile, steadfast, unmoving. *See* **fixed** (1).

statue *or* **statuette** *noun*
▶ bust, carving, figure. *See* **sculpture.**

statuesque *adjective*
▶ comely, gorgeous, stunning. *See* **beautiful.**

stature *noun*
▶ caliber, quality, value. *See* **merit** (1).

status *noun*
1. Positioning of one individual vis-à-vis others ▶ position, rank, standing. *See* **place** (1). **2.** Credit or respect in the eyes of others ▶ prestige, standing. *See* **face** (9). **3.** An established position from which to deal with others ▶ footing, standing. *See* **basis** (3). **4.** A person's high standing among others ▶ good name, reputation. *See* **honor** (2). **5.** Manner of being or form of existence ▶ mode, situation, state. *See* **condition** (1). *See synonym note at* **condition.**

statute *noun*
▶ bill, legislation. *See* **law** (2)

staunch *adjective*
▶ loyal, steadfast, true. *See* **faithful** (1). *See synonym note at* **faithful.**

stave *noun*
A fairly long straight piece of solid material used especially as a support in walking ▶ pole, staff. *See* **stick** (2).

stave off *verb*
1. To prohibit from occurring by advance planning or action ▶ anticipate, avert, obviate. *See* **prevent. 2.** To turn aside or drive away ▶ deflect, repulse, ward off. *See* **repel.**

stay¹ *verb*
1. To continue to be in a place ▶ bide, linger, tarry. *See* **remain** (1). *See synonym note at* **remain. 2.** To be in existence or in a certain state for an indefinitely long time ▶ continue, persist. *See* **endure** (2). **3.** To remain as a guest or lodger ▶ sojourn, stay. *See* **lodge** (1). **4.** To prevent the occurrence or continuation of a movement, action, or operation ▶ check, discontinue, immobilize. *See* **stop** (2). **5.** To put off until a later time ▶ delay, postpone, suspend. *See* **defer¹.** *See synonym note at* **defer¹. 6.** An act or an instance of going or coming to see another ▶ call, visitation. *See* **visit** (1). **7.** To have as one's domicile, usually for an extended period ▶ dwell, reside. *See* **live¹** (2).

stay with *verb*
To persevere in some condition, action, or belief ▶ maintain, retain, sustain. *See* **keep** (6).

stay *noun*
1. A remaining in a place as a guest or lodger ▶ sojourn, stop, stopover, visit. **2.** The act of stopping

► cessation, discontinuance, surcease. *See* **stop** (1). **3.** The act of putting off or the condition of being put off ► deferment, postponement, suspension. *See* **delay** (1). **4.** Something that limits or holds back ► check, constraint, curb. *See* **restraint** (1).

stay² *noun*
A means or device that keeps something erect, stable, or secure ► buttress, crutch, prop. *See* **support** (1).

staying power *noun*
► fortitude, stamina, toughness. *See* **endurance** (1).

stead *noun*
The function or position customarily occupied by another ► lieu, place.

steadfast *adjective*
1. Firmly in position ► stationary, steady, unmoving. *See* **fixed** (1). **2.** Capable of being depended on ► reliable, solid, trustworthy. *See* **dependable. 3.** Possessing determination or resolution ► resolute, steady, unyielding. *See* **firm¹** (3). **4.** Adhering firmly and devotedly, as to a person, cause, or duty ► loyal, staunch, true. *See* **faithful** (1). *See synonym note at* **faithful.**

steadfastness *noun*
► allegiance, faithfulness, loyalty. *See* **fidelity** (1).

steadiness *noun*
1. Reliability in withstanding pressure, force, or stress ► firmness, hardness, strength. *See* **stability. 2.** A stable emotional state ► composure, equanimity, poise. *See* **balance** (2). **3.** The condition of being without change or variation ► constancy, immutability. *See* **changelessness.**

steady *adjective*
1. Firmly in position ► stationary, steadfast, unmoving. *See* **fixed** (1). **2.** Not easily moved or shaken ► solid, stable, sure. *See* **firm¹** (2). **3.** Having no change or variation ► changeless, constant, unvarying. *See* **unchanging. 4.** Possessing determination or resolution ► resolute, steadfast, unyielding. *See* **firm¹** (3). **5.** Capable of being depended on ► stable, steadfast, steady-going. *See* **dependable. 6.** Not steep or abrupt ► gentle, moderate. *See* **gradual** (2).

steady *verb*
1. To make stronger or more resistant ► brace, reinforce, strengthen. *See* **support** (2). **2.** To put in balance ► equalize, stabilize. *See* **balance** (1).

steady *noun*
A romantic interest, especially a regular sexual partner ► paramour. *Informal:* significant other. *See* **lover** (1).

steady-going *adjective*
► reliable, solid, trustworthy. *See* **dependable.**

steal *verb*
1. To take another's property without permission ► abscond with, carry off, crib, embezzle, filch, mooch, pilfer, purloin, snatch, spirit away, thieve. *Informal:* lift, swipe. *Slang:* boost, cop, dip, heist, hook, nip, pinch, rip off, snitch. *Idioms:* make (*or* walk) off with, run off (*or* away) with. *See also* **kidnap, rob, sack², seize. 2.** To move silently and furtively ► lurk, prowl. *See* **sneak** (1).

steal *noun*
1. The crime of taking someone else's property without consent ► stealing, theft, thievery. *See* **larceny. 2.** *Slang* Something offered or bought at a low price ► bargain, find. *Informal:* buy, deal.

✦ CORE SYNONYMS: *steal, purloin, filch, snitch, pilfer, cop, hook, swipe, lift, pinch.* These verbs mean to take another's property without permission, often surreptitiously. *Steal* is the most general: *stole a car; steals research from colleagues.* To *purloin* is to make off with something, often in a breach of trust: *purloined the key to his cousin's safe-deposit box. Filch* and *snitch* often suggest that what is stolen is of little value, while *pilfer* sometimes connotes theft of or in small quantities: *filched towels from the hotel; snitch a cookie; pilfered fruit from the farmer. Cop, hook,* and *swipe* frequently connote quick, furtive snatching or seizing: *copped a necklace from the counter; planning to hook a fur coat; swiped a magazine from the rack. Lift* is to take something surreptitiously and keep it for oneself: *a pickpocket who lifts wallets on the subway. Pinch* suggests stealing something by or as if by picking it up between the thumb and the fingers: *pinched a dollar from his mother's purse.*

---

stealer *noun*
► burglar, larcenist, robber. *See* **thief.**

stealth *noun*
The act of proceeding so as to escape observation ► furtiveness, secretiveness, slinkiness, slyness, sneakiness, stealthiness, surreptitiousness. *See also* **art, secrecy.**

stealthy *adjective*
Moving or acting so as to escape observation ► catlike, feline, furtive, secretive, slinky, sly, sneaking, sneaky, surreptitious. *See also* **artful, secret, underhand.**

steam *noun*
1. A suspension in the air of tiny particles of water, dust, or smoke ► fog, mist. *See* **haze** (1). **2.** Capacity for work or vigorous activity ► might, potency, power. *See* **energy.**

steam *verb*
1. *Informal* To be or become angry ► fume, rage, seethe. *See* **anger** (2). **2.** To pass off as vapor, especially when heated ► burn off, volatilize. *See* **evaporate** (1). **3.** To feel or look hot ► roast, swelter. *See* **burn** (3).

steamroller *verb*
1. To render totally ineffective by decisive defeat ► crush, overcome, overpower, rout. *See* **overwhelm** (1). **2.** To make even, smooth, or level ► level, smooth, straighten. *See* **even** (1).

steamy *adjective*
► salacious, sensuous, sexy. *See* **erotic.**

steel *verb*
► brace, fortify, ready. *See* **gird** (1).

steep¹ *adjective*
1. Having a sharp inclination; almost perpendicular ► abrupt, bold, precipitous, sharp, sheer, sudden. *See also* **vertical. 2.** Exceeding a normal limit, especially in price ► exorbitant, extortionate, overpriced, sky-high,

stiff, stratospheric, unconscionable. *See also* **costly, excessive.**

✦ **CORE SYNONYMS:** *steep, abrupt, precipitous, sheer.* These adjectives mean so sharply inclined as to be almost perpendicular: *steep cliffs; an abrupt drop-off; precipitous hills; a sheer descent.*

steep² *verb*
To cause something to become thoroughly wet or saturated by immersion in a liquid ▶ infuse, macerate, marinate, pickle, soak, souse, suffuse. *See also* **charge, dip, wet.**

steer *verb*
1. To direct the course of carefully ▶ jockey, navigate. *See* **maneuver** (1). **2.** To show the way to ▶ direct, escort, lead. *See* **guide** (1). *See synonym note at* **guide.** **3.** To control the course of an activity ▶ direct, manage, operate. *See* **conduct** (1). *See synonym note at* **conduct. 4.** To run and control a motor vehicle ▶ chauffeur, motor, wheel. *See* **drive** (1).

steer *noun*
An item of advance or inside information given as a guide to action ▶ lead, pointer, scent. *See* **tip³** (1).

stem *verb*
1. To have as a source ▶ arise, come, derive, emanate, flow, issue, originate, proceed, rise, spring, upspring. *See also* **appear, begin. 2.** To interfere with the progress of ▶ dampen, obstruct. *See* **hinder** (1).

stem *noun*
1. The main ascending part of a plant, which supports the other parts ▶ stalk, stock, trunk. *See also* **shoot. 2.** The main part of a word to which affixes are attached ▶ root, simplex. *See* **theme** (1). **3.** A straight, rigid piece of metal or other solid material ▶ bar, shaft. *See* **rod.**

✦ **CORE SYNONYMS:** *stem, arise, derive, emanate, flow, issue, originate, proceed, rise, spring.* These verbs mean to have as a source: *customs that stem from the past; misery that arose from war; rights that derive from citizenship; disapproval that emanated from the teacher; happiness that flows from their friendship; prejudice that issues from fear; a proposal that originated in the Congress; a mistake that proceeded from carelessness; rebellion that rises in the provinces; new industries that spring up.*

stench *noun*
A strong, foul odor ▶ fetor, malodor, reek, stink. *See also* **fragrance, smell.**

✦ **CORE SYNONYMS:** *stench, fetor, malodor, reek, stink.* These nouns denote a strong, foul odor: *the stench of burning rubber; the fetor of polluted waters; the malodor of diesel fumes; the reek of stale sweat; a stink of decayed flesh.*

stentorian *adjective*
1. Marked by extremely high volume and intensity of sound ▶ booming, earsplitting, roaring. *See* **loud** (1). *See synonym note at* **loud. 2.** Offensively loud and

insistent ▶ boisterous, clamorous. *See* **vociferous.**

step *noun*
1. An action calculated to achieve an end ▶ maneuver, measure, move, procedure, tactic. **2.** A manner of walking ▶ footstep, gait, stride. *See* **walk** (2). **3.** One of the units in a course, as on an ascending or descending scale ▶ interval, level, unit. *See* **degree** (1).

step *verb*
1. To go on foot ▶ ambulate, tread. *See* **walk. 2.** To move rhythmically to music, using patterns of steps or gestures ▶ dance, foot, hoof. *See* **dance** (1).

step back *verb*
To move back or away from a point, limit, or mark ▶ ebb, retract, retreat. *See* **recede.**

step down *verb*
To withdraw or remove from business or active life ▶ pension (off), retire, superannuate. *See also* **dismiss, quit.**

step up *verb*
1. To increase the speed of ▶ hasten, quicken. *See* **speed** (1). **2.** To make or become greater or larger ▶ amplify, boost, enlarge. *See* **increase** (1). **3.** To make greater in intensity or severity ▶ deepen, enhance, heighten. *See* **intensify.**

step-by-step *adjective*
Proceeding steadily by degrees ▶ gradational, gradual, piecemeal, progressive. *Idioms:* one foot after another, one step at a time. *See also* **consecutive, methodical, slow.**

stereotype *noun*
A trite expression or idea ▶ banality, truism. *See* **cliché.**

stereotype *verb*
1. To make conventional ▶ standardize, stylize. *See* **conventionalize. 2.** To arrange or organize according to class ▶ catalog, categorize, pigeonhole. *See* **classify.**

stereotyped *adjective*
1. Without freshness or appeal because of overuse ▶ clichéd, overused, shopworn, tired. *See* **trite. 2.** Conforming to established standards ▶ conformist, orthodox, traditional. *See* **conventional** (1).

stereotypical *or* stereotypic *adjective*
▶ corny, shopworn, stock, tired. *See* **trite.**

sterile *adjective*
1. Free or freed from microorganisms ▶ antiseptic, aseptic, disinfected, germ-free, germless, hygienic, sanitary, sanitized, sterilized. *See also* **clean. 2.** Unable to produce offspring ▶ infertile, unfruitful. *See* **barren** (1). **3.** Unable to support vegetation ▶ infertile, unfruitful, unproductive. *See* **barren** (2). **4.** Lacking originality ▶ uncreative, unimaginative, uninspired, uninventive, unoriginal. *See also* **boring, trite. 5.** Lacking liveliness, charm, or surprise ▶ aseptic, colorless, pedestrian. *See* **dull** (1).

sterileness *noun*
▶ blandness, drabness, lifelessness. *See* **dullness** (1).

sterility *noun*
1. The state or condition of being free from microorganisms ▶ asepsis, germlessness, sanitization, steril-

ization. *See also* **purity. 2.** The state or condition of being unable to reproduce ▸ barrenness, fruitlessness, impotence, infertility, unfruitfulness. **3.** A lack of excitement, liveliness, or interest ▸ blandness, drabness, lifelessness. *See* **dullness** (1).

sterilization *noun*
The state or condition of being free from microorganisms ▸ asepsis, germlessness, sanitization, sterility.

sterilize *verb*
1. To render free of microorganisms ▸ decontaminate, disinfect, irradiate, sanitize. **2.** To render incapable of reproducing ▸ alter, castrate, fix, geld, neuter, spay, unsex.

sterilized *adjective*
▸ antiseptic, hygienic, sanitary. *See* **sterile** (1).

sterling *adjective*
▸ exceptional, select, superior. *See* **choice** (1).

stern¹ *adjective*
1. Rigorous and unsparing in treating others ▸ harsh, rigid, strict. *See* **severe** (1). **2.** So disagreeable as to discourage approach ▸ dour, flinty, unhospitable. *See* **forbidding** (1).

stern² *noun*
The part farthest from the front ▸ rear, tail, tail end. *See* **back.**

sternness *noun*
▸ harshness, rigidity, stringency. *See* **severity** (1).

stew *verb*
1. To cook by slow boiling or simmering ▸ boil, fricassee, simmer. *See* **cook** (1). **2.** *Informal* To focus the attention on something moodily and at length ▸ dwell, fret, worry. *See* **brood.** *See synonym note at* **brood.**

stew *noun*
Informal A state of discomposure ▸ tumult, turmoil. *Informal:* lather. *See* **agitation** (2).

steward *noun*
▸ ambassador, deputy, proxy. *See* **representative** (2).

stewardship *noun*
▸ charge, leadership, supervision. *See* **management** (1).

stewed *adjective*
Informal Stupefied, excited, or muddled with alcoholic liquor ▸ intoxicated, sodden, tipsy. *See* **drunk.**

stick *noun*
1. A short straight piece of wood ▸ baton, branch, lath, stake, switch, twig, wand. *See also* **rod. 2.** A fairly long, straight piece of solid material used especially as a support in walking ▸ cane, crook, pole, staff, stave, walking stick.

stick *verb*
1. To penetrate into a substance or place with force ▸ drive, stab, strike. *See* **plunge** (1). **2.** To become stuck or entangled ▸ hook, lodge. *See* **catch** (3). **3.** To form a tight bond ▸ cleave, cohere. *See* **bond. 4.** To put in a certain position or location ▸ locate, place, situate. *See* **position. 5.** *Informal* To put at a loss as to what to say or do ▸ confound, perplex. *Informal:* stump. *See* **baffle** (1). **6.** *Slang* To get something by deceitful

trickery ▸ bilk, defraud, swindle. *See* **cheat** (1). **7.** To penetrate with a sharp edge ▸ incise, pierce, slash. *See* **cut** (1).

stick around *verb*
Informal To continue to be in a place ▸ bide, linger, tarry. *See* **remain** (1).

stick in *verb*
To put or set into, between, or among another or other things ▸ infuse, insert, interpose. *See* **introduce** (2).

stick out *verb*
1. To be obtrusively conspicuous ▸ glare, stand out. *Idioms:* stare someone in the face, stick out like a sore thumb. **2.** To curve outward past the normal or usual limit ▸ balloon, jut, project. *See* **bulge** (1). **3.** To put up with ▸ stomach, tolerate, withstand. *See* **endure** (1).

stick to *verb*
To persevere in some condition, action, or belief ▸ retain, stay with, sustain. *See* **keep** (6).

stick up *verb*
To take property or possessions from someone unlawfully and usually forcibly ▸ hold up, mug. *See* **rob** (1).

stick with *verb*
1. To have and maintain in one's possession ▸ keep, retain. *See* **hold** (1). **2.** To persevere in some condition, action, or belief ▸ retain, stay with, sustain. *See* **keep** (6). **3.** *Informal* To force another to accept a burden ▸ charge with, inflict on (*or* upon), saddle with. *See* **impose on** (1).

sticker *noun*
▸ prick, prong, spine. *See* **spike** (1).

sticking power *noun*
▸ durability, fortitude, stamina, toughness. *See* **endurance** (1).

stick-in-the-mud *noun*
1. *Informal* An old-fashioned person who is reluctant to change or innovate ▸ fogy, fossil, fuddy-duddy. *See* **square** (2). **2.** *Informal* One who spoils the enthusiasm or fun of others ▸ spoilsport. *Informal:* wet blanket. *Slang:* party pooper. *See* **killjoy.**

stick-to-itiveness *noun*
Informal Steady attention and effort, as to one's occupation ▸ assiduousness, perseverance, pertinacity. *See* **diligence.**

stickup *noun*
Slang The crime of taking someone else's property without consent ▸ burglary, holdup, robbery. *See* **larceny.**

sticky *adjective*
1. Having the property of adhering ▸ adhesive, gluey, glutinous, gooey, gummy, mucilaginous, tacky. *See also* **viscous. 2.** Damp and warm ▸ humid, muggy, soggy, sultry. *See also* **damp, hot, rainy, wet. 3.** *Informal* Hard to deal with or get out of ▸ rough, tight, tricky. *See also* **delicate.**

sticky-fingered *adjective*
▸ light-fingered, thieving. *See* **thievish.**

stiff *adjective*
1. Rigidly constrained or formal; lacking grace and spontaneity ▸ buckram, starchy, stilted, wooden. *See also* **cool, forced, prudish.** 2. Not changing shape or bending ▸ inflexible, unbending, unyielding. *See* **rigid** (1). *See synonym note at* **rigid.** 3. Possessing determination or resolution ▸ steadfast, unyielding. *See* **firm**[1] (3). 4. Having a high concentration of the distinguishing ingredient ▸ concentrated, potent, strong. *See also* **straight.** 5. Vastly exceeding a normal limit, as in cost ▸ exorbitant, overpriced. *See* **steep**[1] (2).
stiff *noun*
1. *Slang* The physical frame of a dead person or animal ▸ corpse, relics. *See* **body** (2). 2. *Slang* A person who is habitually drunk ▸ alcoholic, dipsomaniac, tippler. *See* **drunkard.** 3. *Slang* A stingy person ▸ churl. *Informal:* penny pincher. *See* **miser.** 4. Containing alcohol ▸ intoxicative, spirituous. *See* **hard** (12).
stiffen *verb*
1. To make or become physically hard ▸ congeal, solidify. *See* **harden** (2). 2. To make or become tense ▸ tauten, tighten. *See* **tense.** 3. To change or be changed from a liquid into a soft, semisolid, or solid mass ▸ jell, set. *See* **coagulate.**
stiff-necked *adjective*
▸ bullheaded, dogged, obstinate. *See* **stubborn** (1).
stifle *verb*
1. To hold something requiring an outlet in check ▸ muffle, smother, suppress. *See* **repress.** 2. To decrease or dull the sound of ▸ deaden, mute. *See* **muffle** (1). 3. To keep from being published or transmitted ▸ ban, suppress, withhold. *See* **censor** (2). 4. To stop breathing or stop the breathing of ▸ asphyxiate, smother, suffocate. *See* **choke** (1).
stifling *adjective*
1. Lacking fresh air ▸ stuffy, suffocating. *See* **airless** (1). 2. Serving to restrain forcefully ▸ inhibitive, restraining, restrictive. *See* **repressive.**
stigma *noun*
▸ blemish, spot, taint. *See* **stain** (1). *See synonym note at* **stain.**
stigmatize *verb*
1. To cause to feel embarrassment, dishonor, and often guilt ▸ brand, mortify, reproach, shame. *Idioms:* put to shame, put to the blush. *See also* **belittle, denigrate, embarrass, humble.** 2. To bring disgrace on ▸ abase, dishonor, shame. *See* **disgrace.**
still *adjective*
1. Free from disturbance, agitation, or commotion ▸ calm, halcyon, pacific, peaceful, placid, quiet, serene, tranquil, untroubled. *See also* **calm, idyllic.** 2. Marked by, done with, or making no sound or noise ▸ noiseless, quiet. *See* **silent** (1). *See synonym note at* **silent.** 3. Not moving ▸ stationary, fixed. *See* **motionless.** 4. Lacking movement of air ▸ breezeless, windless. *See* **airless** (2).
still *noun*
The absence of sound or noise ▸ noiselessness, quiet. *See* **silence** (1).

still *adverb*
1. In spite of a preceding event or consideration ▸ all the same, anyway, however, nevertheless, nonetheless, yet. *Informal:* still and all. *Idiom:* be that as it may. 2. To a more extreme degree ▸ even, ever more so, yet. 3. In addition ▸ besides, furthermore, more. *See* **additionally.**
still *verb*
1. To cause to become silent ▸ quiet, shush. *See* **silence.** 2. To ease the anger or agitation of ▸ appease, mollify, soothe. *See* **pacify.**

✦ CORE SYNONYMS: *still, calm, peaceful, placid, serene, tranquil.* These adjectives denote absence of disturbance, agitation, or commotion: *lily pads that floated on the still waters; calm acceptance of the inevitable; a peaceful hike through the scenic hills; a soothing, placid temperament; spent a serene, restful weekend at the lake; hoped for a more tranquil life in the country.*

---

stillness *noun*
1. An absence of motion or disturbance ▸ calm, calmness, hush, lull, peace, peacefulness, placidity, placidness, quiet, quietness, serenity, tranquillity, untroubledness. 2. The absence of sound or noise ▸ noiselessness, quiet. *See* **silence** (1).
stilted *adjective*
Rigidly constrained or formal; lacking grace and spontaneity ▸ buckram, starchy, stiff, wooden. *See also* **cool, forced, prudish.**
stimulant *noun*
1. Something that causes or encourages an action or response ▸ catalyst, goad, motivation. *See* **stimulus** (1). 2. A substance that affects the central nervous system and is often addictive ▸ narcotic, opiate, psychotropic. *See* **drug** (2). 3. A medicine that restores or increases vigor ▸ energizer, restorative. *See* **tonic.**
stimulate *verb*
1. To stir to action or feeling ▸ excite, prod, trigger. *See* **provoke** (1). *See synonym note at* **provoke.** 2. To give or impart vitality and energy to someone or something ▸ invigorate, vitalize. *See* **energize.**
stimulating *adjective*
▸ bracing, energizing, exhilarating. *See* **invigorating.**
stimulation *noun*
1. Something that gives courage or confidence ▸ boost, exhortation, motivation. *See* **encouragement** (1). 2. Something that causes and encourages an action or response ▸ impulse, incentive. *See* **stimulus** (1).
stimulator *noun*
▸ fillip, impulse, inducement. *See* **stimulus** (1).
stimulus *noun*
1. Something that causes and encourages an action or response ▸ catalyst, encouragement, fillip, goad, impetus, impulse, incentive, inducement, motivation, prod, push, spur, stimulant, stimulation, stimulator. *See also* **cause, impact.** 2. Something that causes an angry or resentful response ▸ incitement, instigation. *See* **provocation** (1).

sting *verb*
1. To be painful or sore ► ache, smart. *See* **hurt** (2).
2. *Slang* To get something by deceitful trickery ► bilk, defraud, swindle. *See* **cheat** (1). 3. To penetrate with a sharp edge ► bayonet, incise, pierce, slash. *See* **cut** (1).
sting *noun*
1. A sensation of physical discomfort occurring as the result of disease or injury ► prick, smart, soreness. *See* **pain** (1). 2. A cutting quality ► incisiveness, keenness. *See* **edge** (1). 3. *Slang* A stimulating or intoxicating effect ► *Informal:* punch, wallop. *See* **kick** (1). 4. *Slang* An act of cheating ► deceit, hoax, swindle. *See* **cheat** (1).
stinging *adjective*
1. So sharp as to cause mental pain ► caustic, scathing, sharp, vitriolic. *See* **biting**. 2. Painfully intense ► brutal, harsh, severe. *See* **bitter** (2). 3. Marked by, causing, or experiencing physical pain ► achy, hurtful, sore. *See* **painful** (1).
stingy *adjective*
1. Ungenerously or pettily reluctant to spend money ► cheap, close, close-fisted, costive, hard-fisted, mean, miserly, niggard, niggardly, parsimonious, penny-pinching, penurious, petty, pinching, tight, tightfisted. *See also* **greedy**. 2. Conspicuously deficient in quantity, fullness, or extent ► puny, scant, skimpy. *See* **meager** (1).
stink *verb*
To have or give off a foul odor ► reek, smell. *Idioms:* stink (*or* smell) to high heaven.
stink *noun*
A strong, foul odor ► malodor, reek. *See* **stench**. *See synonym note at* **stench**.
stinking *adjective*
1. Having an unpleasant odor ► fetid, foul. *See* **smelly**. 2. *Slang* Stupefied, excited, or muddled with alcoholic liquor ► intoxicated, sodden, tipsy. *See* **drunk**.
stinko *adjective*
1. *Slang* Stupefied or muddled with alcoholic liquor ► intoxicated, sodden, tipsy. *See* **drunk**. 2. *Slang* Of decidedly inferior quality ► cheap, lousy. *See* **shoddy** (1).
stint *verb*
To be severely sparing in order to economize ► pinch, scrape, skimp. *See* **scrimp**.
stint *noun*
1. A piece of work that has been assigned ► chore, duty, job. *See* **task** (1). *See synonym note at* **task**. 2. A limited, often assigned period of activity, duty, or opportunity ► shift, time, watch. *See* **turn** (1).
stipend *noun*
► earnings, pay, salary. *See* **wage**.
stipple *verb*
► dapple, freckle. *See* **speckle**.
stipulate *verb*
1. To state specifically ► detail, particularize, provide, specify. *See also* **assert, describe, designate, dictate**. 2. To enter into a formal agreement ► bargain, covenant. *See* **contract** (1).
stipulation *noun*
► condition, proviso, qualification. *See* **provision** (1).

stir¹ *verb*
1. To move or cause to move slightly ► budge, move, shift. 2. To combine into one mass or mixture ► blend, fuse, intermingle. *See* **mix** (1). 3. To cease or cause to cease sleeping ► awake, rouse, waken. *See* **wake¹**. 4. To induce or elicit a reaction ► kindle, rouse, stir up. *See* **arouse** (1). *See synonym note at* **arouse**. 5. To be the cause of ► generate, induce, trigger. *See* **cause**. 6. To arouse the emotions of ► impassion, inspire, rouse. *See* **fire** (2). 7. To process ingredients by stirring ► blend, whip. *See* **beat** (6). 8. To be in a state of motion, as air or wind ► bluster, gust. *See* **blow¹** (1).
stir *noun*
1. The act or process of moving ► action, move, movement. *See* **motion** (1). 2. A condition of being agitated or disturbed ► commotion, disturbance, tumult. *See* **agitation** (1). 3. Agitated, excited activity ► bustle, flurry, fuss. *See* **agitation** (3). 4. A condition of intense public interest or excitement ► brouhaha, uproar. *See* **sensation** (2).
stir² *noun*
Slang A place for the confinement of persons in lawful detention ► brig, penitentiary, prison. *See* **jail**.
stir-fry *verb*
► fry, pan-fry, saute, sear. *See* **cook** (1).
stirring *adjective*
► impressive, moving, poignant. *See* **affecting**. *See synonym note at* **affecting**.
stitch *noun*
► prick, smart, soreness. *See* **pain** (1). *See synonym note at* **pain**.
stock *noun*
1. A supply stored or hidden for possible future use ► cache, reserve, stockpile. *See* **hoard**. 2. The main ascending part of a plant, which supports the other parts ► stalk, stem, trunk. *See also* **shoot**. 3. A group of people sharing common ancestry ► clan, kindred, lineage. *See* **family** (2). 4. One's ancestors or ancestral derivation ► blood, extraction, lineage. *See* **ancestry**. 5. A product or products bought and sold in commerce ► line, merchandise, ware. *See* **good** (2).
stock *verb*
To have for sale ► carry, deal (in), keep, offer.
stock *adjective*
1. Being of no special quality or type ► common, mediocre, standard. *See* **ordinary** (1). 2. Without freshness or appeal because of overuse ► clichéd, overused, shopworn, tired. *See* **trite**.
stockpile *noun*
A supply stored or hidden for possible future use ► cache, reserve, supply. *See* **hoard**.
stockpile *verb*
To accumulate and keep for future use ► hoard, lay in (up), store. *See* **save** (1).
stock-still *adjective*
► stationary, still. *See* **motionless**.
stocky *adjective*
Short, heavy, and solidly built ► blocky, chunky, compact, dumpy, heavyset, squat, stodgy, stubby,

stumpy, thick, thickset. *See also* **bulky, fat.**

stodginess *noun*
▸ blandness, drabness, lifelessness. *See* **dullness** (1).

stodgy *adjective*
1. Lacking liveliness, charm, or surprise ▸ aseptic, colorless, pedestrian. *See* **dull** (1). *See synonym note at* **dull. 2.** Short, heavy, and solidly built ▸ chunky, heavyset, squat. *See* **stocky.**

stoic *adjective*
▸ accepting, forbearing, resigned. *See* **patient.**

stoicism *noun*
▸ acceptance, forbearance, resignation. *See* **patience.**

stoked *adjective*
Slang Feeling a very strong emotion ▸ excited, fired up, worked up. *See* **thrilled.**

stole *noun*
A garment wrapped about a person ▸ cloak, shawl, wrap. *See also* **scarf.**

stolid *adjective*
▸ emotionless, impassive, unresponsive. *See* **cold** (2).

stolidity *or* **stolidness** *noun*
▸ disinterest, indifference, unconcern. *See* **apathy.**

stomach *noun*
A desire for food or drink ▸ hunger, taste, thirst. *See* **appetite** (1).

stomach *verb*
To put up with ▸ accept, tolerate, withstand. *See* **endure** (1).

stomp *verb*
1. To step on heavily and repeatedly so as to crush, injure, or destroy ▸ stamp, tramp, trample, tread, tromp. *See also* **crush. 2.** To walk in a laborious way ▸ stamp, tramp, trample. *See* **trudge.**

stomping ground *noun*
Slang A frequently visited place ▸ meeting place. *Slang:* hangout, stamping ground. *See* **haunt** (1).

stoned *adjective*
1. *Slang* Stupefied, excited, or muddled with alcoholic liquor ▸ intoxicated, sodden, tipsy. *See* **drunk. 2.** *Slang* Stupefied, intoxicated, or otherwise influenced by the taking of drugs ▸ high, hopped-up, lit (up). *See* **drugged.**

stonyhearted *adjective*
▸ heartless, insensitive, merciless. *See* **callous.**

stooge *noun*
▸ puppet, tool. *See* **pawn².**

stool¹ *verb*
To give incriminating information about others, especially to the authorities ▸ tip (off). *Slang:* rat, snitch. *See* **inform** (2).

stool² *noun*
Waste matter eliminated from the bowels ▸ dung, feces, waste. *See* **excrement.**

stoolie *or* **stool pigeon** *noun*
Slang One who gives incriminating information about others ▸ informant. *Slang:* snitch, squealer. *See* **informer.**

stoop *verb*
1. To bend or lower the body ▸ arch, bend (down),

bow, crouch, huddle, hump, hunch, hunker (down), scrunch, squat. *See also* **bow¹, slouch, sit. 2.** To bring oneself down to a level considered inappropriate to one's dignity ▸ deign, descend, vouchsafe. *See* **condescend** (1). *See synonym note at* **condescend.**

stop *verb*
1. To come to a cessation ▸ cease, check, desist, discontinue, halt, leave off, quit, stall, surcease. *Idioms:* come to a halt (*or* standstill *or* stop). *See also* **conclude. 2.** To prevent the occurrence or continuation of a movement, action, or operation ▸ arrest, belay, cease, check, discontinue, forbear, halt, idle, immobilize, stall, stay, surcease, tie up. *Idioms:* bring to a standstill (*or* screeching halt), call a halt to, cut short, put a stop to. *See also* **hinder, restrain, suspend. 3.** To cease trying to accomplish or continue ▸ discontinue, give up, quit. *See* **abandon** (2). **4.** To discontinue (a habit, for example) ▸ abjure, give up, leave off. *See* **break** (17). **5.** To plug up or block something, such as a hole or conduit ▸ clog, cork. *See* **fill** (2). **6.** To go to or seek out the company of in order to socialize ▸ come over, drop by, pop in, stop by (*or* in). *See* **visit** (1). **7.** To prevent or forbid authoritatively ▸ block, turn down. *See* **veto. 8.** To cease consideration or treatment of ▸ give up, relinquish, skip. *See* **drop** (7).

stop *noun*
1. The act of stopping ▸ cessation, check, cutoff, discontinuance, discontinuation, halt, idling, stay, stoppage, surcease. **2.** The condition of being stopped ▸ cease, cessation, discontinuance, discontinuation, gridlock, halt, idleness, immobilization, jam, standstill, stoppage, surcease, tie-up. *See also* **break. 3.** A concluding or terminating ▸ conclusion, ending, termination. *See* **end** (1). **4.** A stopping place along a route for picking up or dropping off passengers ▸ depot, station, terminal, terminus. **5.** Something that blocks entry or passage ▸ barrier, blockage, hindrance. *See* **bar** (1). **6.** Something used to fill a hole, space, or container ▸ cork, spigot. *See* **plug** (1). **7.** A remaining in a place as a guest or lodger ▸ sojourn, stay, stopover, visit. **8.** An act or an instance of going or coming to see another ▸ call, stay, visitation. *See* **visit** (1).

✛ **CORE SYNONYMS:** *stop, cease, desist, discontinue, halt, quit.* These verbs mean to bring or come to an end: *stop arguing; ceased crying; desist from complaining; discontinued the treatment; halting the convoy; quit laughing.*

◀ **ANTONYM:** *start*

---

stopcock *noun*
▸ fixture, spigot. *See* **faucet.**

stopgap *noun*
Something used temporarily or reluctantly when other means are not available ▸ expedient, shift. *See* **makeshift.** *See synonym note at* **makeshift.**

stopgap *adjective*
Intended, used, or present for a limited time ▸ in-

terim, provisional, short-term. *See* **temporary** (2).

stopover *noun*
A remaining in a place as a guest or lodger ▸ sojourn, stay, stop, visit.

stoppage *noun*
1. The act of stopping ▸ cessation, discontinuance, surcease. *See* **stop** (1). **2.** The condition of being stopped ▸ gridlock, jam, standstill. *See* **stop** (2). **3.** A cessation of normal activity, caused by an accident or strike, for example ▸ gridlock, immobilization, jam, tie-up.

stopper *noun*
▸ cork, stop. *See* **plug** (1).

stopping point *noun*
▸ conclusion, ending, end of the line. *See* **end** (1).

stopple *noun*
▸ cork, stop. *See* **plug** (1).

store *noun*
1. A retail establishment where merchandise is sold ▸ boutique, emporium, outlet, shop. **2.** A supply stored or hidden for possible future use ▸ cache, reserve, stockpile. *See* **hoard**. **3.** A place where something is deposited for safekeeping ▸ archive, storehouse, warehouse. *See* **depository**.

store *verb*
1. To keep for future use ▸ put by, salt away, set by. *See* **save** (1). **2.** To have or put in a customary place ▸ cache, keep, put.

storehouse *noun*
▸ archive, safe, warehouse. *See* **depository**.

storied *adjective*
▸ celebrated, famed, illustrious. *See* **famous**.

storm *noun*
1. An atmospheric disturbance characterized by strong winds and precipitation ▸ blizzard, blow, cyclone, electrical storm, gale, hurricane, ice storm, monsoon, rainstorm, snowstorm, squall, tempest, thunderstorm, typhoon. *See also* **rain**. **2.** A concentrated outpouring, as of missiles, words, or blows ▸ cannonade, fusillade, volley. *See* **barrage**.

storm *verb*
1. To manifest strong winds and precipitation ▸ blow (up), set in, squall. *See also* **rain**. **2.** To set upon with violent force ▸ assail, assault, strike. *See* **attack** (1). *See synonym note at* **attack**. **3.** To be or become angry ▸ boil over, rage, seethe. *See* **anger** (2).

stormy *adjective*
1. Violently disturbed or agitated, as by storms ▸ roily, turbulent, violent. *See* **rough** (2). **2.** Marked by unrest or disturbance ▸ tempestuous, tumultuous, turbulent. *See* **agitated** (1).

story *noun*
1. A recounting of past events ▸ account, chronicle, description, history, narration, narrative, record, report, saga, statement, version. **2.** A narrative not based on fact ▸ fable, fiction, novel, romance. **3.** The series of events and relationships forming the basis of a composition ▸ action, story line. *See* **plot** (1). **4.** A detail of news information ▸ article, feature, piece. *See*

item (1). **5.** An entertaining and often oral account of a real or fictitious occurrence ▸ anecdote, fable, tale. *See* **yarn**. **6.** An untrue declaration ▸ falsehood, fib, untruth. *See* **lie²**.

story line *noun*
▸ action, scenario. *See* **plot** (1).

storyteller *noun*
Informal One who tells lies ▸ fabulist, fibber, prevaricator. *See* **liar**.

stout *adjective*
1. Having or showing courage ▸ courageous, fearless, heroic. *See* **brave**. **2.** Capable of exerting considerable effort or of withstanding considerable stress or hardship ▸ hardy, tough. *See* **strong** (2). **3.** Having a large body, especially in girth ▸ hefty, husky. *See* **bulky** (2). **4.** Having too much flesh ▸ chubby, pudgy, tubby. *See* **fat** (1). *See synonym note at* **fat**.

stouthearted *adjective*
▸ courageous, fearless, heroic. *See* **brave**.

stoutheartedness *noun*
▸ bravery, fortitude, gallantry, valor. *See* **courage**.

stow *verb*
To store for future use ▸ put by, salt away, set by. *See* **save** (1).

strabismal *or* **strabismic** *adjective*
Marked by or affected with a squint ▸ cross-eyed, squint-eyed, squinty.

straddle *verb*
1. To sit or stand with a leg on each side of ▸ bestride, stride. **2.** To sit or lie with the limbs spread out awkwardly ▸ lounge, spread-eagle. *See* **sprawl** (1).

straggle *verb*
To grow or extend over a wide area ▸ radiate, sprawl. *See* **spread** (2).

straggler *noun*
▸ dawdler, lag, procrastinator. *See* **laggard**.

straight *adjective*
1. Not diluted or mixed with other substances ▸ fullstrength, neat, plain, pure, unblended, undiluted, unmixed. *See also* **strong**. **2.** Proceeding or lying in an uninterrupted line or course ▸ linear, straightforward. *See* **direct** (1). **3.** Having no irregularities, roughness, or indentations ▸ flush, level. *See* **even** (1). **4.** Manifesting honesty and directness ▸ candid, ingenuous, plainspoken. *See* **frank**. **5.** Conforming to established standards ▸ conformist, orthodox, traditional. *See* **conventional** (1). **6.** Marked by uprightness in principle and action ▸ honorable, righteous. *See* **honest** (1). **7.** Having or indicating an awareness of things as they really are ▸ practical, pragmatic, prosaic. *See* **realistic** (1).

straight *adverb*
1. In a direct line ▸ due, undeviatingly. *See* **directly** (1). **2.** With precision or absolute conformity ▸ exactly, precisely, squarely. *See* **directly** (3).

straightaway *adverb*
1. In a direct line ▸ straight, undeviatingly. *See* **directly** (1). **2.** Without delay ▸ forthwith, instantly, right away. *See* **immediately** (1).

straighten *verb*
1. To make even, smooth, or level ▸ level, smooth. *See* **even** (1). 2. To make or keep an area clean and orderly ▸ clean (up), neaten (up), spruce (up). *See* **tidy** (1).

straighten out *verb*
To bring something into a state of agreement or accord ▸ negotiate, set. *See* **settle** (2).

straightforward *adjective*
1. Proceeding or lying in an uninterrupted line or course ▸ linear, unswerving. *See* **direct** (1). 2. Manifesting honesty and directness ▸ candid, ingenuous, plainspoken. *See* **frank**. *See synonym note at* **frank**. 3. Clearly, fully, and emphatically expressed ▸ decided, explicit, precise. *See* **definite** (1).

straight-from-the-shoulder *adjective*
Informal Honest and direct, especially in speech; not lying or dissembling ▸ candid, ingenuous, plainspoken. *See* **frank**.

straight off *adverb*
▸ forthwith, instantly. *See* **immediately** (1).

straight-out *adjective*
▸ candid, ingenuous, plainspoken. *See* **frank**.

straight-shooting *adjective*
1. *Informal* Manifesting honesty and directness ▸ candid, ingenuous, plainspoken. *See* **frank**. 2. Marked by uprightness in principle and action ▸ honorable, righteous. *See* **honest** (1).

strain¹ *verb*
1. To exert oneself steadily, often to the point of exhaustion ▸ drive, sweat, toil. *See* **labor** (1). 2. To weigh down or place a heavy load on ▸ encumber, saddle, tax. *See* **burden¹**. 3. To remove a liquid by a steady, gradual process ▸ milk, pump. *See* **drain** (1). 4. To do, use, or stress something to excess ▸ overreach, stress. *See* **overdo**. 5. To injure a bodily part by twisting ▸ sprain, turn, twist, wrench. *See also* **hurt**.

strain *noun*
1. The use of energy to do something ▸ exertion, struggle. *See* **effort** (1). 2. An oppressive condition of distress ▸ stress, tension. *See* **pressure** (1). 3. A source of persistent worry or hardship ▸ cross, tribulation. *See* **burden¹** (1). 4. Concentrated power or force, as of effort, opinion, or emotion ▸ ferocity, fury, vehemence. *See* **intensity**.

strain² *noun*
1. An inherent, contrasting or unexpected quality, especially in a person's character ▸ streak, vein. *See synonym note at* **streak**. *See also* **disposition, inclination**. 2. A pleasing succession or arrangement of sound ▸ aria, tune. *See* **melody**.

strained *adjective*
Not natural or spontaneous ▸ contrived, effortful, forced, labored. *See also* **awkward, stiff**.

strait *noun*
▸ narrows, neck. *See* **channel**.

strait-laced *adjective*
▸ priggish, prissy, stuffy. *See* **prudish**.

straits *noun*
1. A situation requiring immediate assistance or remedial action ▸ crisis, distress, trouble. *See* **emergency**. 2. The condition of being extremely poor ▸ destitution, indigence, need. *See* **poverty** (1). 3. A difficult, often embarrassing situation or condition ▸ corner, difficulty, fix. *See* **predicament**.

strand *noun*
Something suggesting the continuousness of a filament ▸ hairline, thread. *See also* **thread**.

strange *adjective*
1. Deviating from what is conventional or customary ▸ bizarre, grotesque. *See* **eccentric**. *See synonym note at* **eccentric**. 2. Very strange or strikingly unusual ▸ fantastic, outré, unorthodox. *See* **exotic** (2). 3. Causing puzzlement; perplexing ▸ odd, peculiar. *See* **funny** (3). 4. From or characteristic of another place ▸ alien, exotic, nonresident. *See* **foreign** (1). *See synonym note at* **foreign**. 5. Of an unnatural and usually frightening nature ▸ uncanny, unearthly. *See* **weird** (1).

strangely *adverb*
▸ singularly, uncommonly, uniquely. *See* **unusually**.

stranger *noun*
▸ alien, immigrant, outsider. *See* **foreigner**.

strangle *verb*
1. To stop breathing or stop the breathing of ▸ smother, stifle, suffocate. *See* **choke** (1). 2. To hold something requiring an outlet in check ▸ smother, stifle, suppress. *See* **repress**.

strangulate *verb*
▸ smother, stifle, suffocate. *See* **choke** (1).

strap *noun*
A long narrow piece, as of material ▸ belt, girdle, sash, strop. *See* **band¹** (1).

strap *verb*
1. To punish with blows or lashes ▸ lash, thrash, whip. *See* **beat** (2). 2. To make secure ▸ bind, chain, moor. *See* **fasten** (1).

strapped *adjective*
Informal Having little or no money or wealth ▸ destitute, down-and-out, indigent. *See* **poor** (1).

strapping *adjective*
1. Full of vigor ▸ red-blooded, robust, sturdy. *See* **lusty** (1). 2. Characterized by marked muscular development ▸ brawny, robust, sturdy. *See* **muscular**.

stratagem *noun*
1. A method of deploying troops and equipment in combat ▸ battle plan, maneuver, plan of attack, strategy, tactic. 2. An indirect, usually cunning means of gaining an end ▸ deception, ploy, maneuver. *See* **trick** (1). *See synonym note at* **trick**.

strategize *verb*
▸ devise, formulate, scheme. *See* **design** (1).

strategy *noun*
1. A method of deploying troops and equipment in combat ▸ battle plan, maneuver, plan of attack, stratagem, tactic. 2. A method used for accomplishing something ▸ modus operandi, procedure, technique. *See* **approach** (1). *See synonym note at* **approach**.

stratify *verb*
▸ categorize, class, group. *See* **classify**.

stratospheric *adjective*
▸ exorbitant, overpriced, stiff. *See* **steep**[1] (2).

stratum *noun*
▸ league, rank, tier. *See* **class** (2).

straw boss *noun*
Informal Someone who directs and supervises workers ▸ foreman, manager, supervisor. *See* **boss** (1).

stray *verb*
1. To move about at random, especially over a wide area ▸ drift, meander, wander. *See* **rove**. *See synonym note at* **rove**. 2. To turn away from a prescribed course of action or conduct ▸ digress, drift. *See* **deviate** (1). *See synonym note at* **deviate**. 3. To turn aside, especially from the main subject in writing or speaking ▸ diverge, ramble, wander. *See* **digress** (1).

stray *adjective*
1. Being what remains, especially after a part has been removed ▸ extra, leftover, remaining. *Idiom:* left behind. *See also* **superfluous**. 2. Unable to find the correct way or place to go ▸ astray, disoriented. *See* **lost** (1). 3. Without a fixed or regular course ▸ devious, uncontrolled, wandering. *See* **erratic** (1). 4. Straying from a proper course or standard ▸ deviant, erring. *See* **errant** (2).

stray *noun*
A child or young animal without parents ▸ foundling, waif. *See* **orphan**.

streak *noun*
1. An inherent, contrasting or unexpected quality, especially in a person's character ▸ strain, vein. *See also* **disposition, inclination**. 2. A long narrow area that has a different color or marking from what surrounds it ▸ bar, line. *See* **stripe** (1). 3. A slight amount or indication ▸ hint, semblance, trace. *See* **shade** (2). 4. *Informal* A number of things placed or occurring one after the other ▸ order, procession, sequence. *See* **series**.

streak *verb*
To mark with a line or band, as of different color or texture ▸ band, bar, line, striate, stripe, variegate. *See also* **speckle**.

✦ CORE SYNONYMS: *streak, strain, vein*. These nouns denote an inherent, contrasting or unexpected quality, especially in a person's character: *a streak of humor; a strain of melancholy; a vein of stubbornness*.

---

stream *noun*
1. Something suggestive of running water ▸ flood, tide. *See* **flow**. *See synonym note at* **flow**. 2. A narrow line of light or other radiant energy ▸ ray, shaft. *See* **beam** (1). 3. A relatively large natural flow of water ▸ estuary, waterway. *See* **river**.

stream *verb*
1. To move freely as a liquid ▸ purl, ripple, run. *See* **flow** (1). 2. To come forth in abundance ▸ gush, pour, rush. *See* **flow** (2). 3. To move in or on the wind ▸ drift, flap. *See* **blow**[1] (2).

streamer *noun*
▸ banner, colors, pennant. *See* **flag**[1] (1).

streamline *verb*
1. To make modern in appearance or style ▸ modernize, update. *Idiom:* bring up to date. *See also* **improve, renew**. 2. To reduce in complexity or scope ▸ boil down, pare (down), simplify. *Idioms:* reduce to the basics (*or* essentials *or* bare bones). *See also* **explain**.

streamlined *adjective*
1. Acting effectively with minimal waste ▸ efficient, productive, well-oiled. *See also* **diligent, methodical**. 2. Having slender and graceful lines ▸ sleek, trim.

street *noun*
▸ path, road, route. *See* **way** (2).

street-smart *adjective*
▸ canny, knowing, perspicacious. *See* **shrewd** (1).

streetwalker *noun*
▸ sex worker, whore. *See* **prostitute**.

strength *noun*
1. The state or quality of being physically strong ▸ brawn, might, muscle, potency, power, powerfulness, sinew, thews. *See also* **endurance**. 2. Energy that overcomes resistance ▸ might, power, pressure. *See* **force** (1). 3. Reliability in withstanding pressure, force, or stress ▸ firmness, hardness, steadiness. *See* **stability**. 4. Capacity for work or vigorous activity ▸ might, potency, power. *See* **energy**. *See synonym note at* **energy**. 5. Something a person excels at ▸ specialty, strong point. *See* **forte**. *See synonym note at* **forte**. 6. A particularly good or beneficial quality ▸ asset, distinction, merit. *See* **virtue** (1).

strengthen *verb*
1. To make resistant to hardship, especially through continued exposure ▸ indurate, toughen, season. *See* **harden** (1). *See synonym note at* **harden**. 2. To prepare oneself for action ▸ fortify, ready, steel. *See* **gird** (1). 3. To add to or make whole ▸ augment, complete, enhance. *See* **supplement**. 4. To make stronger or more resistant ▸ bolster, reinforce, uphold. *See* **support** (2). 5. To make firmer in a particular conviction or habit ▸ confirm, fortify, harden, reinforce. *See also* **back, establish**.

strenuous *adjective*
1. Marked by vigorous physical exertion ▸ arduous, knockabout, tough. *See* **rough** (7). 2. Possessing, exerting, or displaying energy ▸ brisk, lively, vigorous. *See* **energetic**.

strenuously *adverb*
▸ forcefully, frantically, vigorously. *See* **hard** (1).

stress *noun*
1. Special attention given to something considered important ▸ accent, accentuation, emphasis, weight. *See synonym note at* **emphasis**. *See also* **importance**. 2. An oppressive condition of distress ▸ tautness, tension. *See* **pressure** (1). 3. A troubled or anxious state of mind ▸ distress, unease. *See* **anxiety** (1).

stress *verb*
To accord emphasis to ▸ accentuate, highlight. *See* **emphasize**.

stressor *noun*
A cause of distress or anxiety ► care, concern, trouble, worry. *See also* **anxiety, burden**[1].

stretch *verb*
1. To make or become longer ► elongate, prolong. *See* **lengthen. 2.** To move or arrange so as to cover a larger area ► extend, outstretch. *See* **spread** (1). **3.** To make or become tense ► tauten, tighten. *See* **tense. 4.** To put forward, especially an appendage ► extend, outstretch, reach, stretch out. **5.** To proceed on a certain course or for a certain distance ► lead, reach. *See* **extend** (1). **6.** To be or place oneself in a prostrate or recumbent position ► recline, repose. *See* **lie**[1] (1). **7.** To take repose, as by sleeping or lying quietly ► curl up, lie (down), recline, repose, rest. *See also* **nap, sleep. 8.** To do, use, or stress something to excess ► overreach, strain. *See* **overdo. 9.** To give an inaccurate view of by representing falsely or misleadingly ► fudge, misrepresent, pervert. *See* **distort** (1).

stretch *noun*
1. The measure of how far or long something goes in space, time, or degree ► coverage, span. *See* **extent** (1). **2.** A wide and open area, as of land, sky, or water ► extent, spread, sweep. *See* **expanse** (1). **3.** A specific length of time characterized by the occurrence of certain conditions or events ► span, term, time. *See* **period** (1). **4.** A prison term ► hitch, time. **5.** A limited, often assigned period of activity, duty, or opportunity ► stint, time, watch. *See* **turn** (1). **6.** An extent, measured or unmeasured, of linear space ► interval, length, span. *See* **distance** (1).

stretch *adjective*
Capable of being extended or expanded ► extendible, protractile, stretchable. *See* **extensible.**

stretchable *adjective*
► extendible, protractile, stretchy. *See* **extensible.**

stretching *noun*
The act of making something longer ► elongation, lengthening, prolongation, stringing out. *See* **extension** (1).

stretching *adjective*
Having great physical length ► extended, lengthy, prolonged. *See* **long**[1] (1).

stretchy *adjective*
► extendible, protractile, stretchable. *See* **extensible.**

strew *verb*
► disperse, disseminate, scatter. *See* **spread** (2).

striate *verb*
► band, line, variegate. *See* **streak.**

striation *noun*
1. A mark or shallow cut made by contact with an object ► abrasion, scrape, scratch, scuff. *See also* **cut, furrow, impression. 2.** A long narrow area that has a different color or marking from what surrounds it ► bar, line. *See* **stripe** (1).

stricken *adjective*
► ill-fated, ill-starred, luckless. *See* **unfortunate** (1).

strict *adjective*
1. Consistent with accuracy or completeness ► exact, rigorous. *See* **close** (2). **2.** Rigorous and unsparing in treating others ► harsh, stern, tough. *See* **severe** (1).

strictly *adverb*
► literally, precisely. *See* **exactly** (1).

strictness *noun*
► harshness, rigidity, stringency. *See* **severity** (1).

stricture *noun*
► check, constraint, curb. *See* **restraint** (1).

stride *verb*
1. To go on foot ► pace, tread. *See* **walk. 2.** To sit or stand with a leg on each side of ► bestride, straddle.

stride *noun*
1. Forward movement ► advancement, headway, progress. *See* **advance** (1). **2.** A manner of walking ► gait, step. *See* **walk** (2).

strident *adjective*
1. Disagreeable to the senses, especially the sense of hearing ► grating, jarring. *See* **harsh** (1). **2.** Offensively loud and insistent ► boisterous, clamorous. *See* **vociferous.** *See synonym note at* **vociferous. 3.** Marked by extremely high volume and intensity of sound ► blaring, deafening. *See* **loud** (1). *See synonym note at* **loud.**

strife *noun*
1. A state of disagreement and disharmony ► clash, difference, discord. *See* **conflict** (1). *See synonym note at* **conflict. 2.** An encounter between opposing military forces ► combat, confrontation, war. *See* **battle** (1). **3.** A vying with others for victory ► contest, rivalry, struggle. *See* **competition** (1).

strike *verb*
1. To deliver a sudden, sharp blow to ► jab, sock, whack. *See* **hit** (1). **2.** To set upon with violent force ► assail, assault, storm. *See* **attack** (1). **3.** To come together with force ► crash, impact. *See* **collide** (1). **4.** To cause great pain or suffering to ► plague, rack, torment. *See* **afflict. 5.** To try to bite something quickly or eagerly ► nip, snap, snatch. **6.** To give forth or cause to give forth a clear resonant sound ► bong, chime, peal. *See* **ring**[2] (1). **7.** To cross out or remove ► delete, erase, wipe (out). *See* **cancel** (1). **8.** To stir the emotions of ► get (to), touch. *See* **move** (1). *See synonym note at* **move. 9.** To enter a person's mind ► come to, hit, impress, occur to. *Idioms:* come (or spring) to mind, cross (or enter) one's mind, dawn on. *See also* **register. 10.** To have a sudden overwhelming effect on ► catch, seize, take. **11.** To cease working in support of demands made upon an employer ► picket, walk out. *Idioms:* go (or go out) on strike, stop work. **12.** To penetrate into a substance or place with force ► drive, stab, stick. *See* **plunge** (1).

strike back *verb*
To return like for like, especially to return an unfriendly or hostile action with a similar one ► counter, reciprocate, retort. *See* **retaliate.**

strike down *verb*
To bring down, as from a shot or blow ► floor, ground, hew. *See* **drop** (6).

strike out *verb*
1. To proceed in a specified direction ► head, make, set

out. *See* **bear** (5). **2.** To be unsuccessful ▸ fall short, founder, wash out. *See* **fail** (1).

strike *noun*
1. A cessation of work by employees in support of demands made upon their employer ▸ job action, sickout, walk-out, work stoppage, work to rule. **2.** The act of attacking ▸ onset, onslaught. *See* **attack** (1). **3.** Something that has been discovered ▸ conclusion, result. *See* **discovery.**

striking *adjective*
1. Evoking strong mental images through distinctiveness ▸ colorful, graphic, picturesque, vivid. **2.** Readily attracting notice ▸ conspicuous, outstanding, prominent. *See* **noticeable** (1). *See synonym note at* **noticeable.**

string *noun*
1. A group of people or things arranged in a row ▸ file, queue, rank. *See* **line** (1). **2.** A number of things placed or occurring one after the other ▸ order, procession, sequence. *See* **series.** *See synonym note at* **series. 3.** A band or fiber that is used to bind or tie ▸ cable, line, rope. *See* **cord. 4.** A person or group of persons whose occupation is journalism ▸ correspondent, editorialist, media. *See* **press** (1). **5.** *Informal* A restricting or modifying element ▸ condition, proviso, stipulation. *See* **provision** (1).

string *verb*
To put objects onto a thread ▸ thread.

string out *verb*
To make or become longer ▸ extend, prolongate. *See* **lengthen.**

string up *verb*
Informal To execute by suspending by the neck ▸ gibbet, hang. *Slang:* swing.

stringency *noun*
▸ harshness, rigidity, toughness. *See* **severity** (1).

stringent *adjective*
▸ harsh, stern, unyielding. *See* **severe** (1).

stringy *adjective*
Containing or consisting of fibers ▸ fibrous, sinewy, threadlike.

strip[1] *verb*
1. To remove the clothing or covering from ▸ disrobe, unclothe, undress. *See* **bare** (1). **2.** To remove the skin of ▸ pare, shuck. *See* **skin** (1). **3.** To take or keep something away from ▸ deny, withhold. *See* **deprive. 4.** To rob of goods by force, especially in time of war ▸ loot, plunder, ransack. *See* **sack**[2]. **5.** To remove the contents of ▸ clean out, evacuate. *See* **empty** (1).

strip[2] *noun*
1. A long narrow piece, as of material ▸ belt, ribbon, swath. *See* **band**[1] (1). **2.** A long narrow area that has a different color or marking from what surrounds it ▸ bar, line. *See* **stripe** (1).

stripe *noun*
1. A long narrow area that has a different color or marking from what surrounds it ▸ band, bar, line, streak, striation, strip. **2.** A long narrow piece, as of material ▸ bandeau, fillet, strip. *See* **band**[1] (1). **3.** A

class that is defined by the common attribute or attributes possessed by all its members ▸ ilk, mold, species. *See* **kind**[2].

stripe *verb*
To mark with a line or band, as of different color or texture ▸ striate, variegate. *See* **streak.**

strive *verb*
1. To exert oneself steadily, often to the point of exhaustion ▸ strain, sweat, toil. *See* **labor** (1). **2.** To make an attempt ▸ endeavor, struggle. *See* **attempt. 3.** To strive in opposition ▸ clash, combat, fight. *See* **contend** (1).

striving *noun*
1. The use of energy to do something ▸ exertion, struggle. *See* **effort** (1). **2.** A vying with others for victory ▸ contest, rivalry, striving. *See* **competition** (1).

stroke *noun*
1. A sudden heavy stroke ▸ crack, hit, swat, whack. *See* **blow**[2] (1). **2.** An act of touching ▸ feeling, palpation. *See* **touch** (1).

stroke *verb*
1. To touch or handle affectionately ▸ fondle, pat. *See* **caress.** *See synonym note at* **caress. 2.** To move over or along with pressure ▸ manipulate, work. *See* **rub** (2). **3.** To bring especially the hands or fingers into contact with ▸ handle, palpate. *See* **touch** (1).

stroll *verb*
To walk at a leisurely pace ▸ amble, perambulate, promenade, ramble, saunter, toddle, wander. *Informal:* mosey. *See also* **hike, strut, walk.**

stroll *noun*
An act of walking ▸ amble, saunter. *See* **walk** (1).

strong *adjective*
1. Having great physical strength ▸ mighty, potent, powerful. *See also* **energetic, lusty, muscular. 2.** Capable of exerting considerable effort or of withstanding considerable stress or hardship ▸ hardy, stalwart, stout, sturdy, tough. **3.** Full of or displaying force ▸ dynamic, powerful, vigorous. *See* **forceful** (1). **4.** Not easily moved or shaken ▸ solid, stable, sure. *See* **firm**[1] (2). **5.** Extreme in activity, strength, or effect ▸ fierce, furious. *See* **intense** (1). **6.** Clearly, fully, and emphatically expressed ▸ decided, emphatic, explicit. *See* **definite** (1). **7.** Resulting from or affecting one's innermost feelings ▸ heartfelt, powerful. *See* **deep** (3). **8.** Having a high concentration of the distinguishing ingredient ▸ concentrated, potent, stiff. *See also* **straight. 9.** Containing alcohol ▸ intoxicative, spirituous. *See* **hard** (12).

strong-arm *adjective*
Informal Accomplished by force ▸ coercive, forced, forcible, violent.

strong-arm *verb*
1. *Informal* To compel by threats ▸ blackjack, dragoon. *See* **coerce** (1). **2.** *Informal* To frighten into submission or compliance ▸ browbeat, bully, cow. *See* **intimidate** (1).

stronghold *noun*
▸ citadel, fortress. *See* **fort.**

strongman *noun*
▸ despot, oppressor, tyrant. *See* **dictator** (1).

strong point *or* **strong suit** *noun*
▸ specialty, strength. *See* **forte**.

strop *noun*
A long narrow piece, as of material ▸ belt, strap, strip. *See* **band¹** (1).

strop *verb*
To give a sharp edge to ▸ file, hone, whet. *See* **sharpen** (1).

structure *noun*
1. Something built, especially for human use ▸ building, construction, edifice, erection, pile. **2.** The surface arrangement of a thing ▸ configuration, design, shape. *See* **form** (1).

structure *verb*
To create by forming, combining, or altering materials ▸ build, compose, shape. *See* **make** (1).

struggle *verb*
1. To strive in opposition ▸ clash, combat, fight. *See* **contend** (1). **2.** To make an attempt ▸ endeavor, strive. *See* **attempt**. **3.** To do tedious, difficult, or menial work ▸ plod, slave. *See* **grind** (4).

struggle *noun*
1. The use of energy to do something ▸ exertion, striving. *See* **effort** (1). **2.** A vying with others for victory ▸ contest, rivalry, strife. *See* **competition** (1). **3.** An encounter between opposing military forces ▸ combat, confrontation, war. *See* **battle** (1).

strumpet *noun*
▸ call girl, courtesan. *See* **harlot**.

strut *verb*
1. To walk with pompous bearing ▸ flounce, peacock, prance, swagger, swank, swoosh. *Informal:* sashay. *See also* **hike, stroll, walk**. **2.** To make a public and usually ostentatious show of ▸ exhibit, expose, flaunt. *See* **display** (1).

stub *noun*
▸ fragment, odds and ends. *See* **end** (7).

stubborn *adjective*
1. Firmly, often unreasonably immovable in purpose or will ▸ adamant, adamantine, brassbound, bullheaded, die-hard, dogged, grim, hardheaded, headstrong, implacable, incompliant, inexorable, inflexible, intransigent, iron, mulish, obdurate, obstinate, pertinacious, perverse, pigheaded, relentless, remorseless, rigid, stiff-necked, tenacious, unbendable, unbending, uncompliant, uncompromising, unrelenting, unyielding, willful. *Idioms:* stubborn as a mule (*or* ox). **2.** Difficult to alleviate or cure ▸ obstinate, persistent, pertinacious.

✦ **CORE SYNONYMS:** *stubborn, inflexible, inexorable, adamant, obdurate, obstinate, headstrong, bullheaded, pigheaded, mulish, dogged, pertinacious.* These adjectives mean firmly, often unreasonably immovable in purpose or will. *Stubborn* pertains to innate, often perverse resoluteness or unyieldingness: *"She was very stubborn when her mind was made up"* (Samuel Butler). *Inflexible* implies unyielding adherence to fixed principles or purposes: *My boss is inflexible on many issues. Inexorable* implies lack of susceptibility to persuasion: *"Cynthia was inexorable—she would have none of him"* (Winston Churchill). It also describes things that are inevitable, relentless, and often severe in effect: *"Russia's final hour, it seemed, approached with inexorable certainty"* (W. Bruce Lincoln). *Adamant* implies imperviousness to pleas or appeals: *He is adamant about leaving right now. Obdurate* implies hard, callous resistance to tender feelings: *The child's misery would move even the most obdurate heart. Obstinate* implies unreasonable rigidity: *"Mr. Quincy labored hard with the governor to obtain his assent, but he was obstinate"* (Benjamin Franklin). One who is *headstrong* is stubbornly, often recklessly willful: *The headstrong teenager ignored school policy. Bullheaded* suggests foolish or irrational obstinacy, and *pigheaded,* stupid obstinacy: *Don't be bullheaded; see a doctor. "It's a pity pious folks are so apt to be pigheaded"* (Harriet Beecher Stowe). *Mulish* implies the obstinacy and intractability associated with a mule: *"Obstinate is no word for it, for she is mulish"* (Ouida). *Dogged* emphasizes stubborn perseverance: *dogged persistence; "two warring ideals in one dark body, whose dogged strength alone keeps it from being torn asunder"* (W.E.B. Du Bois). *Pertinacious* stresses a tenacity of purpose, opinion, or course of action that is sometimes viewed as vexatious: *The tax bill's vocal and pertinacious critics led to its defeat.*

---

stubbornness *noun*
The quality or state of being immovable in purpose or will ▸ bullheadedness, die-hardism, doggedness, grimness, hardheadedness, implacability, implacableness, incompliance, incompliancy, inexorability, inexorableness, inflexibility, inflexibleness, intransigence, intransigency, mulishness, obduracy, obdurateness, obstinacy, obstinateness, pertinaciousness, pertinacity, perverseness, perversity, pigheadedness, relentlessness, remorselessness, rigidity, rigidness, tenaciousness, tenacity, willfulness. *See also* **cruelty, decision, severity**.

stubby *adjective*
▸ chunky, heavyset, squat. *See* **stocky**.

stuck *adjective*
▸ baffled, lost, stumped. *See* **confused** (1).

stuck-up *adjective*
1. *Informal* Thinking too highly of oneself ▸ narcissistic, vain. *See* **egotistic** (1). **2.** *Informal* Characteristic of or resembling a snob ▸ *Informal:* snooty, uppity. *See* **snobbish**.

stud *noun*
1. A shaft hammered or drilled in place, used to hold together ▸ bolt, pin, spike. *See* **nail**. **2.** *Slang* A person regarded as physically attractive ▸ lovely, stunner. *See* **beauty** (1). **3.** A sturdy vertical structural support ▸ pillar, post. *See* **column** (1).

student *noun*
One who is being educated ▸ apprentice, learner, pupil, scholar, trainee. *See also* **follower**.

studied *adjective*
1. Arising from or marked by careful consideration

▸ considered, studious, thought out. *See* **deliberate** (2). **2.** Not genuine or sincere ▸ feigned, insincere. *See* **artificial** (2).

studio *noun*

1. An artist's workspace ▸ atelier, workroom, workshop. **2.** An often rented living space in a building ▸ condominium, efficiency, studio. *See* **apartment.**

studious *adjective*

1. Devoted to study or reading ▸ bookish, scholarly. *See also* **educated, intellectual, learned. 2.** Characterized by steady attention and effort ▸ assiduous, conscientious, industrious. *See* **diligent.** *See synonym note at* **diligent. 3.** Marked by careful consideration ▸ considered, studied. *See* **deliberate** (2).

studiousness *noun*

▸ assiduousness, perseverance, pertinacity. *See* **diligence.**

study *noun*

1. Careful consideration ▸ advisement, consideration, deliberation. *See also* **attention, scrutiny. 2.** The act of examining carefully or critically ▸ inspection, inquiry, scrutiny. *See* **examination** (1). **3.** The condition of being so lost in solitary thought that one is unaware of one's surroundings ▸ absent-mindedness, bemusement, reverie. *See* **trance** (1). **4.** Repetition of an action so as to develop or maintain one's skill ▸ exercise, rehearsal. *See* **practice** (1).

study *verb*

1. To apply one's mind to the acquisition of knowledge, especially when pressed for time ▸ lucubrate. *Informal:* bone up, cram, grind. **Idioms:** burn the midnight oil, hit the books. **2.** To look at or study carefully or critically ▸ investigate, peruse, scrutinize. *See* **examine** (1). **3.** To think or think about carefully and at length ▸ cogitate, deliberate, mull. *See* **ponder.**

stuff *noun*

1. That from which things are or can be made ▸ medium, substance. *See* **material** (1). **2.** The most central or essential part ▸ essence, marrow, quintessence. *See* **heart** (1). **3.** *Informal* One's portable property ▸ goods, personal effects, property. *See* **effects. 4.** A person considered to have qualities suitable for a particular activity ▸ material, timber. *See also* **comer, potential.**

stuff *verb*

To fill to capacity ▸ cram, jam, pack. *See* **fill** (1).

stuffing *noun*

▸ padding, wadding. *See* **filler** (1).

stuffy *adjective*

1. Lacking fresh air ▸ stifling, suffocating. *See* **airless** (1). **2.** Arousing no interest or curiosity ▸ dull, humdrum, monotonous. *See* **boring** (1). **3.** Marked by excessive concern for modesty or propriety ▸ priggish, prissy, strait-laced. *See* **prudish.**

stultify *verb*

▸ fatigue, tire, weary. *See* **bore²**.

stumble *verb*

1. To lose one's balance and fall or almost fall ▸ skid, slide, slip, slither, trip. **Idioms:** go flying, have one's

feet go out from under one, lose one's footing, make a false step, take a skid (*or* slide). *See also* **fall. 2.** To walk unsteadily ▸ reel, sway, totter. *See* **stagger** (1). **3.** To move heavily or clumsily ▸ clump, galumph, hulk. *See* **blunder** (1). *See synonym note at* **blunder. 4.** To proceed or perform in an unsteady, faltering manner ▸ bungle, flounder, fudge, fumble. *See* **muddle** (1). **5.** To make an error or mistake ▸ blunder, lapse, stumble. *See* **err** (1). **6.** To speak with involuntary repetitions or pauses ▸ falter, sputter, stutter. *See* **stammer.**

stumble on *or* **upon** *verb*

To find or meet by chance ▸ come across, happen on, run across. *See* **encounter** (1).

stumble *noun*

A stupid, clumsy mistake ▸ bungle, fumble. *See* **blunder.**

stumbling block *noun*

▸ complication, hardship, rigor. *See* **difficulty** (1).

stump *verb*

1. To move heavily or clumsily ▸ clump, galumph, hulk. *See* **blunder** (1). **2.** *Informal* To prevent from accomplishing a purpose ▸ foil, stymie, thwart. *See* **frustrate** (1). **3.** *Informal* To put at a loss as to what to say or do ▸ confound, perplex. *Informal:* flummox. *See* **baffle** (1).

stumpy *adjective*

▸ blocky, squat, stubby. *See* **stocky.**

stun *verb*

1. To dull the senses, as with a shock ▸ benumb, stupefy. *See* **daze** (1). *See synonym note at* **daze. 2.** To render helpless, as by emotion ▸ numb, stupefy. *See* **paralyze** (1). **3.** To overwhelm with surprise, wonder, or bewilderment ▸ dumbfound, flabbergast. *See* **stagger** (2).

stunner *noun*

1. One that evokes great surprise and admiration ▸ prodigy, sensation, wonder. *See* **marvel** (1). **2.** A person regarded as physically attractive ▸ lovely, vision. *See* **beauty** (1).

stunning *adjective*

1. So remarkable as to be hard to believe ▸ astounding, staggering, unbelievable. *See* **astonishing. 2.** Having qualities that delight the eye ▸ comely, gorgeous, ravishing. *See* **beautiful.**

stunt *noun*

A clever, dexterous act ▸ feat, trick. **Idiom:** sleight of hand. *See also* **accomplishment.**

stupefacient *adjective*

Inducing sleep or sedation ▸ narcotic, somniferous. *See* **soporific** (1).

stupefacient *noun*

Something that induces sleep or sedation ▸ narcotic, sedative. *See* **soporific.**

stupefaction *noun*

1. A stunned or bewildered condition ▸ bewilderment, stupor. *See* **daze. 2.** The emotion aroused by something awe-inspiring or astounding ▸ amazement, awe, marvel. *See* **wonder** (1).

stupefy *verb*
1. To dull the senses, as with a shock ▸ benumb, stun. *See* **daze** (1). *See synonym note at* **daze**. 2. To addle the mind, as with a narcotic or alcohol ▸ besot, impair. *See* **drug** (2). 3. To render helpless, as by emotion ▸ numb, stun. *See* **paralyze** (1).

stupendous *adjective*
1. So remarkable as to be hard to believe ▸ astounding, staggering, unbelievable. *See* **astonishing**. 2. Of extraordinary size and power ▸ behemoth, colossal, gigantic, mighty. *See* **enormous**. *See synonym note at* **enormous**.

stupendousness *noun*
▸ immensity, vastness. *See* **enormousness**.

stupid *adjective*
1. Lacking in or showing a lack of intelligence ▸ birdbrained, blockheaded, brainless, cloddish, dense, doltish, dumb, hebetudinous, idiotic, imbecilic, mindless, moronic, obtuse, softheaded, thickheaded, thick-witted, unintelligent, witless. *Informal:* boneheaded, knuckleheaded, lamebrained, muttonheaded, thick. *Slang:* dimwitted, dopey, fatheaded, half-witted, lunkheaded, pinheaded. *See also* **backward, foolish, ignorant**. 2. Lacking mental and physical alertness and activity ▸ sluggish, stuporous, torpid. *See* **lethargic** (1). 3. *Informal* Lacking worth and value ▸ drossy, good-for-nothing, valueless. *See* **worthless** (1).

stupidity *noun*
The state of being stupid ▸ brainlessness, cloddishness, density, doltishness, dumbness, idiocy, imbecility, mindlessness, obtuseness, simplicity, softheadedness, stupidness, witlessness. *Informal:* boneheadedness. *Slang:* dimwittedness, dopeness, fatheadedness, pinheadedness. *See also* **foolishness**.

stupor *noun*
1. A deficiency in mental and physical alertness and activity ▸ languor, listlessness, sluggishness. *See* **lethargy** (1). *See synonym note at* **lethargy**. 2. A stunned or bewildered condition ▸ bewilderment, perplexity, stupefaction. *See* **daze**.

stuporous *adjective*
1. Lacking physical feeling or sensitivity ▸ inert, numb, unfeeling. *See* **dead** (2). 2. Lacking mental and physical alertness and activity ▸ enervated, sluggish, torpid. *See* **lethargic** (1).

sturdiness *noun*
▸ firmness, hardness, steadiness. *See* **stability**.

sturdy *adjective*
1. Characterized by marked muscular development ▸ brawny, robust, sinewy. *See* **muscular**. 2. Capable of exerting considerable effort or of withstanding considerable stress or hardship ▸ hardy, tough. *See* **strong** (2). 3. Not easily moved or shaken ▸ solid, stable, sure. *See* **firm**¹ (2). 4. Full of vigor ▸ robust, strapping, vital. *See* **lusty** (1). 5. Having a large body, especially in girth ▸ hefty, stout. *See* **bulky** (2).

Sturm und Drang *noun*
▸ ferment, turmoil, unrest. *See* **agitation** (1).

stutter *verb*
To speak with involuntary repetitions or pauses ▸ falter, sputter. *See* **stammer**.

stutter *noun*
A way of speaking marked by involuntary repetitions and pauses ▸ stammer, stammering, stuttering.

sty *noun*
▸ corral, fold. *See* **pen**² (1).

style *noun*
1. A distinctive way of expressing oneself ▸ fashion, manner, mode, tone, vein. 2. The approach used to do something ▸ manner, mode, system. *See* **way** (1). *See synonym note at* **way**. 3. Behavior that reveals one's personality or state of mind ▸ demeanor, manner, mien. *See* **bearing** (1). 4. The current custom ▸ fad, mode, vogue. *See* **fashion** (1). *See synonym note at* **fashion**. 5. The word or words by which one is called and identified ▸ cognomen, epithet, title. *See* **name** (1). 6. The manner in which one behaves ▸ comportment, conduct, deportment. *See* **behavior** (1). 7. Refinement of manner, form, and style ▸ grace, sophistication. *Informal:* class. *See* **elegance**.

style *verb*
1. To give a name or title to ▸ christen, designate. *See* **name** (1). 2. To describe with a word or term ▸ designate, label, name. *See* **call** (4).

stylish *adjective*
▸ mod, smart, swanky. *See* **fashionable**. *See synonym note at* **fashionable**.

stylize *verb*
▸ standardize, traditionalize. *See* **conventionalize**.

stymie *verb*
▸ baffle, foil, thwart. *See* **frustrate** (1).

suave *adjective*
Gracious and tactful in social manner ▸ debonair, smooth, urbane. *See also* **courteous, cultured, glib, sophisticated**.

sub *noun*
Informal One that takes the place of another ▸ alternate, replacement, surrogate. *See* **substitute**.

sub *verb*
Informal To act as a substitute ▸ cover for, fill in. *See* **substitute** (1).

subaltern *adjective*
Below another in standing, importance, or status ▸ junior, low, secondary. *See* **minor** (1).

subaltern *noun*
One belonging to a lower class or rank ▸ inferior, junior. *See* **subordinate**.

subdivide *verb*
1. To separate into branches or branchlike parts ▸ diverge, fork. *See* **branch**. 2. To separate into parts for study ▸ break down, dissect, take apart. *See* **analyze** (1).

subdivision *noun*
1. A separate unit that belongs or contributes to a whole ▸ building block, piece, section. *See* **part** (1). 2. Something resembling or analogous to a tree branch ▸ arm, fork, offshoot. *See* **branch** (1). 3. The

separation of a whole into its parts for study ▶ break-down, dissection, reduction. *See* **analysis** (1).

subdue *verb*

1. To win a victory over, as in battle or a competition ▶ conquer, surmount, vanquish. *See* **defeat** (1). *See synonym note at* **defeat**. 2. To make or become less severe or extreme ▶ soften, tame. *See* **moderate** (1).

subdued *adjective*

1. Not irritating, strident, or loud ▶ quiet, whispery. *See* **soft** (2). 2. Not showy or obtrusive ▶ inobtrusive, quiet, unostentatious. *See* **modest** (1).

subject *noun*

1. What a speech, piece of writing, or artistic work is about ▶ argument, case, matter, point, subject matter, text, theme, topic. *See also* **heart, problem.** 2. A sphere of activity, experience, study, or interest ▶ department, domain, field. *See* **area** (1). 3. A focus of attention, thought, or action ▶ focus, recipient, target. *See* **object** (2). 4. A person owing loyalty to and entitled to the protection of a given state ▶ burgher, national. *See* **citizen.** *See synonym note at* **citizen.**

subject *adjective*

1. Subject to the authority or control of another ▶ dependent, subordinate, subservient. *See also* **auxiliary.** 2. Tending to incur ▶ prone, susceptible, vulnerable. *See* **liable** (2). 3. Depending on or containing a condition or conditions ▶ contingent, dependent, provisory. *See* **conditional.** *See synonym note at* **conditional.**

subject *verb*

1. To lay open, as to something undesirable or injurious ▶ expose, leave open. *See also* **endanger.** 2. To make subservient or subordinate ▶ dominate, subjugate. *See* **enslave.**

✦ CORE SYNONYMS: *subject, matter, topic, theme.* These nouns denote the principal idea or point of a speech, a piece of writing, or an artistic work. *Subject* is the most general: *"Well, honor is the subject of my story"* (William Shakespeare). *Matter* refers to the material that is the object of thought or discourse: *"This distinction seems to me to go to the root of the matter"* (William James). A *topic* is a subject of discussion, argument, or conversation: *"They would talk of . . . fashionable topics, such as pictures, taste, Shakespeare"* (Oliver Goldsmith). *Theme* refers especially to an idea, a point of view, or a perception that is developed and expanded on in a work of art: *"To produce a mighty book, you must choose a mighty theme"* (Herman Melville).

subjective *adjective*
▶ judgmental, personal, unscientific. *See* **arbitrary** (1).

subject matter *noun*
▶ matter, text, theme. *See* **subject** (1).

subjoin *verb*
▶ annex, append. *See* **attach** (2).

subjugate *verb*

1. To win a victory over, as in battle or a competition ▶ conquer, surmount, vanquish. *See* **defeat** (1). *See synonym note at* **defeat**. 2. To make subservient or

subordinate ▶ dominate, indenture. *See* **enslave. 3.** To seize or maintain control over by conquest ▶ capture, overrun, seize. *See* **occupy** (2).

subjugation *noun*

1. The act of conquering ▶ knockout, victory. *See* **conquest. 2.** The act of exercising controlling power or the condition of being so controlled ▶ control, dominion, reign. *See* **domination** (1). **3.** Cruel exercise of power ▶ domination, injustice, repression. *See* **oppression** (1).

subjugator *noun*
▶ master, victor. *See* **conqueror** (1).

sublet *verb*
▶ let (out), rent. *See* **lease** (1).

sublime *adjective*

1. Impressive in size, proportion, or appearance ▶ imposing, magnificent, splendid. *See* **grand** (1). **2.** Beyond what is usual, normal, or customary ▶ extraordinary, outstanding, remarkable. *See* **exceptional** (1). **3.** Being on a high intellectual or moral level ▶ elevated, noble. *See* **elevated** (4).

sublime *verb*
To pass off as vapor, especially when heated ▶ burn off, volatilize. *See* **evaporate** (1).

submerge *or* **submerse** *verb*

1. To plunge briefly in or into a liquid ▶ dunk, immerse. *See* **dip** (1). **2.** To go beneath the surface or to the bottom of a liquid ▶ founder, gravitate. *See* **sink** (1). **3.** To flow over completely ▶ engulf, inundate, overflow. *See* **flood** (1).

submission *noun*

1. The act of submitting or surrendering to the power of another ▶ capitulation, giving up, surrender. **2.** The quality or state of willingly carrying out the wishes of others ▶ compliancy, complaisance, submissiveness. *See* **obedience. 3.** Something that is put forward for consideration ▶ motion, proposition, suggestion. *See* **proposal** (1).

✦ CORE SYNONYMS: *submission, surrender, capitulation.* These nouns denote the act of giving up one's person, one's possessions, or people under one's command to the power or control of another. *Submission* stresses the subordination of the side that has yielded: *"Our cruel and unrelenting enemy leaves us only the choice of brave resistance, or the most abject submission"* (George Washington). *Surrender* is the most general: *"No terms except unconditional and immediate surrender can be accepted"* (Ulysses S. Grant). *Capitulation* implies surrender under specific prearranged conditions: *Lack of food and ammunition forced the capitulation of the rebels.*

submissive *adjective*

1. Submitting without objection or resistance ▶ acquiescent, nonresistant, resigned. *See* **passive. 2.** Willing to carry out the wishes of others ▶ complaisant, docile, supple. *See* **obedient. 3.** Marked by courteous submission or respect ▶ duteous, dutiful, obeisant. *See* **deferential.**

submissiveness *noun*
► compliancy, submission. *See* **obedience.**

submit *verb*
1. To give up in favor of another ► capitulate, give in, yield. *See* **surrender** (1). *See synonym note at* **surrender. 2.** To give in from or as if from a gradual loss of strength ► buckle, surrender. *See* **succumb** (1). **3.** To state for consideration or debate ► offer, put forward, set forth. *See* **propose** (1). *See synonym note at* **propose. 4.** To put before another for acceptance ► extend, proffer, tender. *See* **offer** (1). **5.** To conform to the will or judgment of another ► bow, defer, yield. *See also* **humor.**

subordinate *adjective*
1. Subject to the authority or control of another ► dependent, subject, subservient. *See also* **auxiliary. 2.** Below another in standing, importance, or status ► junior, low, secondary. *See* **minor** (1).

subordinate *noun*
One belonging to a lower class or rank ► inferior, junior, secondary, subaltern, underling. *Informal:* second fiddle. *See also* **assistant, pawn², slave, sycophant.**

subordinate *verb*
To make subservient or subordinate ► dominate, subjugate. *See* **enslave.**

suborn *verb*
1. To ruin morally ► debase, demoralize, deprave, warp. *See* **corrupt** (1). **2.** To buy or promise a bribe to ► fix. *Informal:* pay off. *See* **bribe.**

subpar *adjective*
► inferior, poor, substandard. *See* **bad** (1).

sub rosa *adverb*
In a secret way ► covertly, huggermugger. *See* **secretly.**

sub-rosa *adjective*
Existing or operating in a way so as to ensure complete concealment and confidentiality ► clandestine, covert, undercover. *See* **secret** (1).

subscribe *verb*
1. To give in common with others ► donate, give. *See* **contribute** (1). **2.** To respond affirmatively; receive with agreement or compliance ► agree, consent, yes. *See* **assent. 3.** To affix one's signature to ► endorse, inscribe. *See* **sign** (1). **4.** To present as a gift to a charity or cause ► bequeath, pledge. *See* **donate** (1).

subscriber *noun*
► benefactor, contributor, patron. *See* **donor.**

subscription *noun*
► benefaction, contribution, offering. *See* **donation.**

subsequent *adjective*
1. Following something else in time ► after, later, posterior, ulterior. **2.** Being or occurring in the time ahead ► coming, later. *See* **future. 3.** Occurring after another ► ensuing, next, succeeding. *See* **following** (1).

subsequently *adverb*
► afterwards, latterly, next. *See* **later.**

subservient *adjective*
1. Subject to the authority or control of another ► dependent, subject, subordinate. *See also* **auxiliary.**

2. Excessively eager to serve or obey ► obsequious, slavish. *See* **servile.**

subside *verb*
1. To become less active or intense ► abate, bate, die (away, down, off, *or* out), diminish, ease (off *or* up), ebb, fall, fall off, lapse, let up, moderate, remit, slacken, slack off, wane, wind down. *See also* **fall, depreciate. 2.** To go beneath the surface or to the bottom of a liquid ► go down, settle. *See* **sink** (1). **3.** To grow or cause to grow gradually less ► diminish, reduce. *See* **decrease.** *See synonym note at* **decrease.**

subsidence *noun*
► letup, remission, slackening. *See* **waning.**

subsidiary *adjective*
Giving or able to give help or support ► assistant, contributory, supportive. *See* **auxiliary** (1).

subsidiary *noun*
An administrative unit, as of a government or company ► affiliate, bureau, division. *See* **branch** (3).

subsidize *verb*
► back, fund. *Informal:* bankroll. *See* **finance.**

subsidy *noun*
Money or other resources granted for a particular purpose ► appropriation, budget, grant, subvention.

subsist *verb*
1. To have being or actuality ► be, exist. **2.** To have reality or life ► breathe, live. *See* **exist** (1).

subsist on *verb*
To include as part of one's diet by nature or preference ► eat, exist on, feed on, live on.

subsistence *noun*
► bread, keep, livelihood. *See* **living.**

subsisting *adjective*
► live, living, vital. *See* **alive** (1).

substance *noun*
1. That from which things are or can be made ► medium, stuff. *See* **material** (1). **2.** A basic trait or set of traits that define and establish the character of something ► nature, quintessence. *See* **essence** (1). **3.** The most central or essential part ► essence, marrow, quintessence. *See* **heart** (1). *See synonym note at* **heart. 4.** The general sense or significance, as of an action or statement ► burden, purport. *See* **import** (1). **5.** The current of thought uniting all elements of a text or discourse ► drift, intent, tenor. *See* **thrust** (1).

substance abuse *noun*
► dependence, drug abuse, fixation. *See* **addiction.**

substandard *adjective*
► inferior, low-quality, second-rate. *See* **bad** (1).

substantial *adjective*
1. Composed of or relating to things that occupy space and can be perceived by the senses ► corporeal, tangible. *See* **physical** (1). **2.** Having physical or verifiable existence ► objective, tangible. *See* **real** (1). **3.** Not easily moved or shaken ► solid, stable, sure. *See* **firm¹** (2). **4.** Characterized by abundance; as much as one needs or desires ► abundant, bounteous, plentiful. *See* **generous** (2). **5.** Having great significance ► consequential, grand, meaningful. *See* **important** (1).

6. Above average in amount, size, or scope ▸ extensive, large, sizable. *See* **big** (1).

substantiality *noun*
▸ being, entity. *See* **existence** (1).

substantially *adverb*
▸ much, quite, well. *See* **considerably.**

substantiate *verb*
1. To present evidence in support of ▸ buttress, corroborate. *See* **back** (2). **2.** To assure the certainty or validity of ▸ authenticate, corroborate, sustain, verify. *See* **confirm** (1). *See synonym note at* **confirm. 3.** To establish as true or genuine through evidence ▸ confirm, establish, validate. *See* **prove** (1). **4.** To represent (an abstraction, for example) in or as if in bodily form ▸ externalize, manifest, materialize. *See* **embody** (1).

substantiation *noun*
1. That which confirms ▸ authentication, corroboration, proof, verification. *See* **confirmation** (2). **2.** A concrete entity typifying an abstraction ▸ incarnation, manifestation, personification. *See* **embodiment** (1).

substantive *adjective*
▸ objective, solid, tangible. *See* **real** (1).

substantiveness *noun*
▸ being, entity. *See* **existence** (1).

substitute *noun*
One that can take the place of another ▸ alternate, cover, double, proxy, relief, replacement, stand-in, surrogate. *Informal:* fill-in, pinch hitter, ringer, sub. *See also* **auxiliary, counterpart.**

substitute *verb*
1. To act as a substitute ▸ cover for, fill in, function as, serve as, stand in, supply. *Informal:* pinch-hit, sub. *Idiom:* take the place of. **2.** To give up in return for something else ▸ exchange, interchange, trade. *See* **change** (3).

substitute *adjective*
Temporarily assuming the duties of another ▸ interim, provisional. *See* **temporary** (1).

substitution *noun*
▸ interchange, switch, trade. *See* **change** (2).

substratum *noun*
▸ bottom, foot, foundation. *See* **base**¹ (2).

substructure *noun*
1. The lowest or supporting part or structure ▸ footing, foundation, groundwork. *See* **base**¹ (2). **2.** A structure that supports or encloses something ▸ case, shell. *See* **frame** (1).

subsume *verb*
▸ encompass, involve, take in. *See* **contain** (1).

subterfuge *noun*
▸ deception, ploy, stratagem. *See* **trick** (1). *See synonym note at* **trick.**

subterranean *or* **subterrestrial** *adjective*
▸ belowground, buried. *See* **underground.**

subtle *adjective*
1. So slight as to be difficult to notice or appreciate ▸ precise, refined. *See* **delicate** (4). **2.** Able to make or detect effects of great precision ▸ delicate, nice, sen-

sitive. *See* **fine**¹ (8). **3.** Able to recognize small differences or draw fine distinctions ▸ astute, discerning, selective. *See* **discriminating** (1). **4.** Incapable of being apprehended by the mind or the senses ▸ imponderable, indiscernible. *See* **imperceptible** (1). **5.** Marked by treachery or deceit ▸ duplicitous, shifty, sneaky. *See* **underhand.**

subtlety *noun*
1. The ability to make or detect effects of great precision ▸ delicacy, fineness, niceness, sensitivity, subtleness. **2.** A slight variation between nearly identical entities ▸ gradation, hue. *See* **shade** (1). **3.** The ability to distinguish, especially to recognize small differences or draw fine distinctions ▸ acuteness, selectiveness, taste. *See* **discrimination** (1).

subtract *verb*
▸ abate, discount, remove. *See* **deduct** (1).

suburbs *noun*
▸ edge, environs, fringe. *See* **outskirts.**

subvent *verb*
▸ fund, subsidize. *Informal:* bankroll. *See* **finance.**

subvention *noun*
Money or other resources granted for a particular purpose ▸ appropriation, budget, grant, subsidy.

subversion *noun*
Treacherous action to defeat or do harm to an endeavor ▸ sabotage, undermining. *See also* **defeat, destruction.**

subversive *adjective*
Participating in open revolt against a government or ruling authority ▸ insurgent, mutinous, revolutionary. *See* **rebellious** (1).

subversive *noun*
A person who rebels ▸ insurrectionist, revolutionist, transgressor. *See* **rebel** (1).

subvert *verb*
1. To damage, destroy, or defeat by sabotage ▸ sabotage, undermine. *See also* **destroy, disorder. 2.** To bring about the downfall of ▸ depose, topple. *See* **overthrow** (1). *See synonym note at* **overthrow. 3.** To ruin morally ▸ debase, demoralize, deprave, warp. *See* **corrupt** (1).

succeed *verb*
1. To gain success ▸ arrive, get ahead, get on, rise. *Idioms:* go far, go places, make good, make it. **2.** To turn out well ▸ come off, go, go over, pan out, work, work out. *Slang:* click. *Idiom:* fall into place. *See also* **effect, manage. 3.** To occur after in time ▸ come next, ensue, supervene. *See* **follow** (1). *See synonym note at* **follow.**

succeeding *adjective*
▸ ensuing, next, subsequent. *See* **following** (1).

success *or* **successfulness** *noun*
▸ achievement, feat, triumph. *See* **accomplishment** (1).

successful *adjective*
1. Succeeding steadily ▸ prosperous, roaring, thriving. *See* **flourishing. 2.** Enjoying steady good fortune or

financial security ▸ comfortable, well-off, well-to-do. *See* **prosperous** (1).

succession *noun*
▸ order, procession, sequence. *See* **series**. *See synonym note at* **series**.

successive *or* **successional** *adjective*
▸ sequential, serial. *See* **consecutive**.

succinct *adjective*
1. Expressed in few words ▸ concise, short, terse. *See* **brief** (1). **2.** Precisely meaningful and tersely cogent ▸ epigrammatic, pointed. *See* **pithy** (1).

succor *noun*
1. A consoling in time of grief or pain ▸ comfort, consolation, reassurance, solace. *See also* **pity**. **2.** The act or an instance of helping ▸ aid, assistance. *See* **help** (1). **3.** Reduction of pain or distress, or a cause of that reduction ▸ ease, mitigation, palliation. *See* **relief** (2).

succor *verb*
1. To give assistance to ▸ aid, assist. *See* **help** (1). *See synonym note at* **help**. **2.** To give hope to in time of grief or pain ▸ condole, reassure, soothe. *See* **comfort**.

succorer *noun*
▸ adjutant, helper, reliever. *See* **assistant**.

succumb *verb*
1. To give in from or as if from a gradual loss of strength ▸ bow, buckle, capitulate, fold, submit, surrender, yield. **2.** To suddenly lose all health or strength ▸ crack, drop. *See* **collapse** (1). **3.** To cease living ▸ demise, expire, perish. *See* **die** (1).

suck *verb*
To draw or be drawn in so that extrication is difficult ▸ embroil, mix up, wrap up. *See* **involve** (1).

suck up *verb*
Slang To behave obsequiously or submissively ▸ grovel, kowtow. *Informal:* apple-polish. *See* **fawn**.

sucker *noun*
1. *Informal* A person who is easily deceived or victimized ▸ pushover, tool, victim. *See* **dupe** (1). **2.** A young stemlike growth arising from a plant ▸ runner, sprout. *See* **shoot** (1).

sucker *verb*
Informal To cause to accept something false, especially by trickery or misrepresentation ▸ dupe, fool, mislead, trick. *See* **deceive**.

sudden *adjective*
1. Unexpectedly sudden ▸ hurried, precipitant, precipitate. *See* **abrupt** (2). **2.** So sharply inclined as to be almost perpendicular ▸ precipitous, sharp. *See* **steep¹** (1).

sudoriferous *adjective*
Producing or covered with sweat ▸ perspiring, sweating, sweaty. *See also* **damp, sticky**.

suds *noun*
A mass of bubbles in or on the surface of a liquid ▸ froth, lather. *See* **foam**.

suds *verb*
To form or cause to form foam ▸ fizz, lather. *See* **foam** (1).

sudsy *adjective*
▸ frothy, lathery, spumy. *See* **foamy**.

sue *verb*
1. To institute or subject to legal proceedings ▸ law, litigate, prosecute. *Idioms:* bring suit, haul (*or* drag *or* hale) into court. **2.** To make an earnest or urgent request ▸ beseech, entreat, plead. *See* **appeal** (1).

suet *noun*
Adipose tissue ▸ blubber, fat, lard. *See also* **oil**.

suffer *verb*
1. To feel, show, or express grief ▸ anguish, mourn, sorrow. *See* **grieve** (1). **2.** To participate in or partake of personally ▸ go through, undergo. *See* **experience**. **3.** To put up with ▸ stomach, tolerate, withstand. *See* **endure** (1). *See synonym note at* **endure**. **4.** To neither forbid nor prevent ▸ let, tolerate. *See* **permit** (1).

sufferable *adjective*
▸ endurable, tolerable. *See* **bearable**.

sufferance *noun*
▸ resignation, tolerance. *See* **patience**.

sufferer *noun*
▸ casualty, prey, wounded. *See* **victim** (1).

suffering *noun*
A state of prolonged anguish and privation ▸ woe, wretchedness. *See* **misery** (1).

suffering *adjective*
Very uncomfortable or unhappy ▸ afflicted, wretched. *See* **miserable** (1).

suffice *verb*
▸ fill, fulfill, meet. *See* **satisfy** (1).

sufficiency *noun*
An adequate quantity ▸ adequacy, enough.

sufficient *adjective*
1. Being what is needed without being in excess ▸ adequate, ample, comfortable, competent, decent, enough, satisfactory. **2.** Adequate to satisfy a need, requirement, or standard ▸ average, decent, moderate. *See* **acceptable** (2).

✦ CORE SYNONYMS: *sufficient, adequate, enough*. These adjectives mean being what is needed without being in excess: *has sufficient income to retire comfortably; bought an adequate supply of food; drew enough water to fill the tub*.

◂ ANTONYM: *insufficient*

---

suffocate *verb*
▸ smother, stifle, strangle. *See* **choke** (1).

suffocating *adjective*
▸ stifling, stuffy. *See* **airless** (1).

suffrage *noun*
The right or chance to express an opinion or participate in a decision ▸ input, say, voice, vote. *Informal:* say-so.

suffuse *verb*
1. To cause to be filled, as with a particular mood or tone ▸ imbue, permeate. *See* **charge** (1). *See synonym note at* **charge**. **2.** To cause something to become thoroughly wet or saturated by immersion in a liquid ▸ soak, souse. *See* **steep²**.

suffusive *adjective*
Having the quality or tendency to pervade or permeate ▸ penetrating, permeating, pervading, pervasive. *See also* **general, prevailing, recurrent.**

sugar *verb*
To make superficially more acceptable or appealing ▸ honey, sugarcoat. *See* **sweeten** (1).

sugar *noun*
A person who is much loved ▸ honey, precious, sweetheart. *See* **darling** (1).

sugarcoat *verb*
1. To make superficially more acceptable or appealing ▸ candy, honey, sugar. *See* **sweeten** (1). 2. To give a deceptively attractive appearance to ▸ gild, overlay, varnish. *See* **color** (4).

sugary *adjective*
1. Having or suggesting the taste of sugar ▸ honeyed, saccharine, sweet. 2. Purposefully contrived to gain favor ▸ buttery, insinuating, saccharine. *See* **flattering** (1).

suggest *verb*
1. To cause one to remember or think of ▸ hark back, recall. *Idioms:* bring to mind, put one in mind of, take one back, remind one of. *See also* **refer, remind.** 2. To have a particular flavor or suggestion of something ▸ savor, smack, smell, taste. 3. To state for consideration or debate ▸ offer, propound, put forward, set forth. *See* **propose** (1). 4. To convey an idea by indirect, subtle means ▸ allude to, imply, insinuate. *See* **hint.** *See synonym note at* **hint.** 5. To involve by logical necessity ▸ involve, indicate, lead to, point to. *See* **imply** (1).

suggested *adjective*
▸ inferred, tacit, unspoken. *See* **implicit** (1).

suggestible *adjective*
▸ malleable, pliable, supple. *See* **flexible** (3).

suggestion *noun*
1. Something, such as a feeling or idea, associated with a specific person or thing ▸ association, connection, connotation, impression. 2. Something that is put forward for consideration ▸ motion, proposition, submission. *See* **proposal** (1). 3. A brief or indirect suggestion ▸ cue, insinuation. *See* **hint** (2). 4. An opinion as to a decision or course of action ▸ guidance, recommendation. *See* **advice** (1). *See synonym note at* **advice.** 5. A slight amount or indication ▸ hint, semblance, trace. *See* **shade** (2).

suggestive *adjective*
1. Tending to bring a memory, mood, or image, for example, subtly or indirectly to mind ▸ allusive, connotative, evocative, impressionistic, reminiscent. *See also* **designative, symbolic.** 2. Provoking a change of outlook and especially gradual doubt and suspicion ▸ implicating, insinuatory. *See* **insinuating** (1). 3. Conveying hidden or unexpressed meaning ▸ consequential, significant. *See* **pregnant** (2). 4. Concerning or arousing sexual desire ▸ amorous, lascivious, sexy. *See* **erotic.** 5. Bordering on indelicacy or impropriety ▸ provocative, risqué. *See* **racy** (1).

suggestiveness *noun*
1. The quality or condition of being sensual or being preoccupied with bodily desires ▸ sexuality, voluptuousness. *See* **sensuality** (1). 2. The quality of being erotic ▸ lasciviousness, sexuality. *See* **eroticism** (1).

suit *verb*
1. To be suitable to or in keeping with ▸ become, befit, fit, go with, match. *Idioms:* be one's cup of tea, be right down one's alley, suit one to a T. *See also* **agree.** 2. To look good on or with ▸ become, enhance, flatter. *Idiom:* put in the best light. 3. To meet a need or requirement ▸ answer, do, suffice. *See* **satisfy** (1). 4. To make or become suitable to a particular situation or use ▸ adjust, fit, reconcile. *See* **adapt.**

suit *noun*
A legal proceeding to demand justice or enforce a right ▸ action, litigation. *See* **lawsuit.**

suitability *or* **suitableness** *noun*
▸ fitness, worthiness. *See* **qualification.**

suitable *adjective*
1. Suited to one's purpose ▸ expedient, proper. *See* **convenient** (1). 2. Consistent with prevailing or accepted standards or circumstances ▸ deserved, fitting, proper. *See* **just** (2). 3. Satisfying certain requirements, as for selection ▸ fitted, qualified. *See* **eligible** (1).

suitcase *noun*
A container or piece of luggage for carrying clothing and other items ▸ bag, carryall, carryon, duffle (bag), flight bag, grip, kit, overnight bag, portmanteau, satchel, shoulder bag, valise.

suit coat *or* **suit jacket** *noun*
▸ jacket, overcoat, windbreaker. *See* **coat** (1).

suite *noun*
1. A number of things placed or occurring one after the other ▸ order, procession, sequence. *See* **series.** 2. An often rented living space in a building ▸ condominium, efficiency, studio. *See* **apartment.** 3. A group of attendants or followers ▸ entourage, train. *See* **retinue.**

suited *adjective*
▸ qualified, suitable. *See* **eligible** (1).

suitor *noun*
1. One that asks a higher authority for something, as a favor or redress ▸ appealer, appellant, petitioner. 2. One who humbly entreats ▸ beggar, petitioner, prayer, suppliant, supplicant. 3. A man who courts a woman ▸ admirer, courter. *See* **beau** (1).

sulk *verb*
To be sullenly aloof or withdrawn, as in silent resentment or protest ▸ mope, pet, pout. *See also* **brood.**

sulky *adjective*
▸ gloomy, morose, sullen. *See* **glum** (1).

sullen *adjective*
1. Broodingly and sullenly unhappy ▸ gloomy, morose, surly. *See* **glum** (1). 2. Bringing or predicting misfortune ▸ dark, lowery. *See* **fateful** (1).

sully *verb*
1. To make dirty ▸ bemire, muck up, mud. *See* **dirty**

(1). **2.** To attack the reputation or honor of ▸ besmirch, smear, tarnish. *See* **denigrate** (1). **3.** To bring disgrace on ▸ abase, dishonor, shame. *See* **disgrace.**

sultry *adjective*
1. Damp and warm ▸ humid, soggy. *See* **sticky** (2).
2. Marked by much heat ▸ blistering, boiling, burning. *See* **hot** (1).

sum *noun*
1. A number or quantity obtained as a result of addition ▸ aggregate, amount, totality. *See* **total** (1).
2. An amount or quantity from which nothing is left out or held back ▸ entirety, everything, total. *See* **whole** (1). **3.** An organized array of individual elements and parts forming and working as a unit ▸ arrangement, whole. *See* **system** (1). **4.** A review of the essential points or consequences of something: ▸ rundown, sum, wrap-up. *See* **summary.**

sum *verb*
To combine numbers to form a sum ▸ tot (up), total. *See* **add** (1).

sum up *verb*
1. To give a recapitulation of the salient facts of ▸ abstract, recapitulate, summarize. *See* **review** (1).
2. To come to in number or quantity ▸ number, reach, total. *See* **amount** (1).

summarize *verb*
▸ abstract, recapitulate, sum up. *See* **review** (1).

summary *noun*
A review of the essential points or consequences of something ▸ recap, recapitulation, rundown, run-through, sum, summation, summing-up, wrap-up. *See also* **essence, story, synopsis.**

summary *adjective*
Expressed in few words ▸ concise, short, succinct. *See* **brief** (1).

summation *noun*
1. The act or process of adding ▸ addition, totalization. *See also* **calculation. 2.** A number or quantity obtained as a result of addition ▸ amount, sum, totality. *See* **total** (1). **3.** A review of the essential points or consequences of something: ▸ rundown, wrap-up. *See* **summary.**

summer *or* **summertime** *noun*
The season occurring between spring and autumn ▸ dog days.

summing-up *noun*
▸ rundown, sum, wrap-up. *See* **summary.**

summit *noun*
1. The highest point or state ▸ apex, height, peak. *See* **climax** (1). *See synonym note at* **climax. 2.** A meeting for the exchange of views ▸ discussion, parley, seminar. *See* **conference** (1).

summon *verb*
1. To request that someone take part in or be present at a particular occasion ▸ ask, bid, invite. *Idioms:* extend an invitation to, request the presence of. *See also* **appeal, request. 2.** To bring or call together ▸ convene, convoke, muster. *See* **assemble** (1). *See synonym note at* **assemble. 3.** To bring out something

latent, hidden, or unexpressed ▸ draw (out), elicit. *See* **evoke. 4.** To give orders to ▸ charge, instruct, order. *See* **command** (1).

summons *noun*
A spoken or written request for someone to take part or be present ▸ bid, call, invitation. *Informal:* invite. *See also* **request.**

sump *noun*
▸ cesspool, gutter, sewer. *See* **pit**[1] (3).

sumptuous *adjective*
▸ lush, luxuriant, opulent. *See* **luxurious.**

sumptuousness *noun*
▸ magnificence, resplendence, sparkle. *See* **glitter** (2).

sum total *noun*
▸ amount, sum, totality. *See* **total** (1).

sunder *verb*
▸ shatter, smash, splinter. *See* **break** (1).

sundown *noun*
▸ eve, twilight. *See* **evening.**

sundries *noun*
▸ incidentals, miscellanea, oddments. *See* **odds and ends.**

sundry *adjective*
1. Consisting of a number of different kinds ▸ diverse, miscellaneous, variegated. *See* **various** (1). **2.** Consisting of a number more than two or three but less than many ▸ some, few, various. *See* **several** (1).

sunken *adjective*
▸ concave, indented. *See* **hollow** (2).

sunny *adjective*
1. Free from clouds or mist ▸ fair, fine. *See* **clear** (2).
2. Being in or showing good spirits ▸ bright, cheery, happy. *See* **cheerful** (1).

sunrise *noun*
▸ dawning, daybreak, sunup. *See* **dawn** (1).

sunset *noun*
▸ eve, twilight. *See* **evening.**

sunup *noun*
▸ dawning, daybreak, sunrise. *See* **dawn** (1).

sup *verb*
1. To take into the mouth and swallow a liquid ▸ gulp, guzzle, slurp. *See* **drink** (1). **2.** To have or take a meal ▸ breakfast, lunch. *See* **eat** (2).

sup *noun*
An act of drinking or the amount swallowed ▸ swallow, taste. *Informal:* swig. *See* **drink** (2).

super *adjective*
Informal Particularly excellent ▸ fantastic, sensational, superb. *See* **marvelous** (1).

super *adverb*
Informal Too much ▸ excessively, extremely, overly. *See* **unduly.**

superabundance *noun*
▸ exorbitance, extravagance, surfeit. *See* **excess** (1).

superabundant *adjective*
▸ exuberant, lavish, opulent. *See* **profuse** (1).

superannuate *verb*
To withdraw or remove from business or active life ▸ pension (off), retire, step down. *Idioms:* call it

quits, hang up one's spurs, put out to pasture, turn in one's badge. *See also* **dismiss, quit.**

superannuated *adjective*
▸ outdated, outmoded. *See* **obsolete.**

superb *adjective*
1. Exceptionally good of its kind ▸ first-rate, prime, splendid, tiptop. *See* **excellent. 2.** Particularly excellent ▸ divine, glorious, sensational. *See* **marvelous** (1). **3.** Impressive in size, proportion, or appearance ▸ imposing, magnificent, splendid. *See* **grand** (1).

superbness *noun*
▸ fineness, superiority. *See* **excellence.**

supercilious *adjective*
1. Overly convinced of one's own superiority and importance ▸ proud, superior. *See* **arrogant.** *See synonym note at* **arrogant. 2.** Showing scorn and disrespect toward someone or something ▸ dismissive, haughty, scornful. *See* **disdainful** (1).

superciliousness *noun*
▸ proudness, superiority. *See* **arrogance.**

supererogatory *or* **supererogative** *adjective*
1. Being more than is needed, desired, or appropriate ▸ excess, surplus. *See* **superfluous. 2.** Not required, necessary, or warranted by the circumstances of the case ▸ uncalled-for, unwarranted. *See* **wanton** (2).

superficial *adjective*
1. Lacking in intellectual depth or thoroughness ▸ cursory, naive, one-dimensional, shallow, sketchy, skin-deep, surface, uncritical. *See also* **trite. 2.** Appearing as such but not necessarily so ▸ ostensible, seeming. *See* **apparent** (2).

superficially *adverb*
▸ externally, ostensibly, seemingly. *See* **apparently.**

superfluity *noun*
1. A condition of going or being beyond what is needed, desired, or appropriate ▸ exorbitance, extravagance, surfeit. *See* **excess** (1). **2.** A thing, amount, or quantity beyond what is needed, desired, or appropriate ▸ overflow, oversupply, supernumerary. *See* **surplus.**

superfluous *adjective*
Being more than is needed, desired, or appropriate ▸ de trop, excess, extra, leftover, redundant, spare, supererogatory, supernumerary, surplus. *See also* **excessive, remaining, unnecessary.**

✚ CORE SYNONYMS: *superfluous, excess, extra, spare, supernumerary, surplus.* These adjectives mean being more than is needed, desired, or appropriate: *delete superfluous words; trying to lose excess weight; found some extra change on the dresser; sleeping in the spare room; supernumerary ornamentation; distributed surplus food to the needy.*

---

superfluousness *noun*
▸ exorbitance, extravagance, surfeit. *See* **excess** (1).

superhighway *noun*
▸ path, road, route. *See* **way** (2).

superhuman *adjective*
▸ metaphysical, transcendental. *See* **supernatural** (1).

superintend *verb*
▸ boss, oversee. *See* **supervise.** *See synonym note at* **supervise.**

superintendence *noun*
1. The act or process of managing ▸ administration, direction, supervision. *See* **management** (1). **2.** The function of watching, guarding, or overseeing ▸ charge, guardianship, supervision. *See* **care** (2).

superintendent *noun*
▸ foreman, manager, supervisor. *See* **boss** (1).

superior *adjective*
1. Of greater excellence than another ▸ better, preferable. **2.** Being at a rank or level above another ▸ greater, higher, senior, upper. **3.** Of fine quality ▸ exceptional, fine, select. *See* **choice** (1). **4.** Exceptionally good of its kind ▸ first-rate, prime, splendid, tiptop. *See* **excellent. 5.** Overly convinced of one's own superiority and importance ▸ insolent, supercilious. *See* **arrogant. 6.** Showing scorn and disrespect toward someone or something ▸ dismissive, haughty, scornful. *See* **disdainful** (1).

superior *noun*
1. One who stands above another in rank ▸ better, elder, senior. *Informal:* higher-up. *See also* **chief. 2.** Someone who directs and supervises workers ▸ foreman, manager, supervisor. *See* **boss** (1).

superiority *noun*
1. The quality of being exceptionally good of its kind ▸ superbness, transcendence. *See* **excellence. 2.** A dominating position, as in a conflict ▸ edge, upper hand, vantage. *See* **advantage** (3). **3.** The quality of being arrogant ▸ hauteur, insolence, proudness. *See* **arrogance. 4.** The right and power to command, decide, rule, or judge ▸ control, might, sovereignty. *See* **authority** (1).

superlative *adjective*
▸ optimum, unsurpassed. *See* **best** (1).

supernal *adjective*
1. Of, from, like, or being a god or God ▸ deific, heavenly, holy. *See* **divine** (1). **2.** Of or relating to the heavens ▸ cosmic, empyreal. *See* **heavenly** (2). **3.** Of or relating to heaven ▸ divine, paradisal. *See* **heavenly** (1).

supernatural *adjective*
1. Of or relating to existence outside the natural world ▸ extramundane, extrasensory, metaphysical, miraculous, mystic, mystical, numinous, otherworldly, paranormal, preternatural, spiritual, superhuman, superphysical, supersensible, transcendental, unearthly, unworldly. *See also* **divine, heavenly, immaterial, weird. 2.** Greatly exceeding or departing from the normal course of nature ▸ preternatural, unnatural. *See also* **abnormal.**

supernormal *adjective*
▸ high, raised. *See* **elevated** (2).

supernumerary *adjective*
Being more than is needed, desired, or appropriate ▸ de trop, excess, surplus. *See* **superfluous.** *See synonym note at* **superfluous.**

supernumerary *noun*
A thing, amount, or quantity beyond what is needed, desired, or appropriate ▸ overflow, oversupply, superfluity. *See* **surplus.**

superphysical *adjective*
▸ metaphysical, superhuman, supersensible. *See* **supernatural** (1).

superscribe *verb*
▸ address, direct. *See also* **ticket.**

supersede *verb*
To substitute for or fill the place of ▸ displace, replace, supplant, surrogate. *Idioms:* fill someone's shoes, take over from, take the reins from. *See synonym note at* **replace.** *See also* **substitute.**

superseded *adjective*
▸ outdated, outmoded. *See* **obsolete.**

supersensible *adjective*
▸ metaphysical, superhuman. *See* **supernatural** (1).

superstar *noun*
▸ luminary, personality, star. *See* **celebrity** (1).

superstition *noun*
▸ legend, mythology, tradition. *See* **lore** (1).

supervene *verb*
▸ come next, ensue, succeed. *See* **follow** (1). *See synonym note at* **follow.**

supervening *adjective*
▸ next, subsequent, succeeding. *See* **following** (1).

supervenient *adjective*
Not part of the real or essential nature of a thing ▸ adscititious, adventitious, incidental, inessential. *See also* **irrelevant, unnecessary.**

supervise *verb*
To direct and watch over the work and performance of others ▸ boss, monitor, overlook, oversee, superintend, watch over. *See also* **arrange, conduct.**

✦ CORE SYNONYMS: *supervise, boss, overlook, oversee, superintend.* These verbs mean to direct and watch over the work and performance of others: *supervised a team of investigators; bossed a construction crew; overlooks farm hands; overseeing plumbers and electricians; superintend a household staff.*

---

supervision *noun*
1. The act or process of managing or directing ▸ direction, leadership, management. *See* **management** (1). 2. The function of watching, guarding, or overseeing ▸ charge, guardianship, superintendence. *See* **care** (2). *See synonym note at* **care.**

supervisor *noun*
▸ foreman, manager, taskmaster. *See* **boss** (1).

supervisory *adjective*
▸ executive, managerial, organizational. *See* **administrative.**

supine *adjective*
1. Lying down ▸ horizontal, prone, prostrate. *See* **flat** (1). 2. Lacking interest ▸ indifferent, listless, uninterested. *See* **apathetic.** 3. Ignobly lacking in courage ▸ faint-hearted, pusillanimous. *Slang:* gutless. *See* **cowardly.**

supplant *verb*
1. To take the place of another against the other's will ▸ cut out, displace, usurp. *See also* **assume, occupy, seize.** 2. To substitute for or fill the place of ▸ displace, replace, supersede, surrogate. *Idioms:* fill someone's shoes, take over from, take the reins from. *See synonym note at* **replace.** *See also* **substitute.**

supple *adjective*
1. Capable of being shaped or bent ▸ bendable, ductile, plastic. *See* **malleable** (1). 2. Capable of withstanding stress without injury ▸ elastic, flexile, resilient. *See* **flexible** (1). *See synonym note at* **flexible.** 3. Easily altered or influenced ▸ malleable, pliable, suggestible. *See* **flexible** (3). 4. Capable of adapting or being adapted ▸ elastic, flexible, pliable. *See* **adaptable.** 5. Willing to carry out the wishes of others ▸ complaisant, docile, submissive. *See* **obedient.** 6. Having bodily flexibility ▸ limber, lissome, lithe. *See* **flexible** (2).

supplement *verb*
To add to or make whole ▸ accompany, augment, complement, complete, enhance, enrich, reinforce, strengthen. *See also* **increase, support.**

supplement *noun*
1. Something added to another for embellishment or completion ▸ add-on, complement, extra. *See* **enhancement** (1). 2. A subordinate element added to another entity ▸ adjunct, appendage, appurtenance. *See* **attachment** (1).

supplemental *or* **supplementary** *adjective*
1. Supplying mutual needs ▸ correlative, interrelated, reciprocal. *See* **complementary.** 2. Being an addition ▸ auxiliary, extra, more. *See* **additional.** 3. Used or held in reserve ▸ emergency, reserve, standby. *See* **auxiliary** (2).

suppleness *noun*
▸ elasticity, malleability, pliability. *See* **flexibility** (1).

supplicant *or* **suppliant** *noun*
One who humbly entreats ▸ beggar, petitioner, prayer, suitor.

supplicate *verb*
1. To offer a reverent petition to God or a god ▸ invoke, pray. 2. To make an earnest or urgent request ▸ beseech, entreat, plead. *See* **appeal** (1).

supplication *noun*
1. The act of praying ▸ benediction, invocation, prayer. 2. An earnest or urgent request ▸ imploration, plea, prayer. *See* **appeal** (1).

supplier *noun*
▸ benefactor, contributor, patron. *See* **donor.**

supply *verb*
1. To relinquish to the possession or control of another ▸ furnish, provide. *See* **give** (1). 2. To act as a substitute ▸ cover for, fill in. *See* **substitute** (1). 3. To make something readily available ▸ make available, provide. *See* **offer** (2).

supply *noun*
A supply stored or hidden for possible future use ▸ cache, reserve, stockpile. *See* **hoard.**

support *verb*
1. To aid the cause of by approving or favoring ▸ advocate, back, champion, endorse, get behind, plump for, recommend, side with, stand behind, stand by, uphold. *Idioms:* align oneself with, go to bat for, throw one's weight behind. **2.** To make stronger or more resistant ▸ bolster, brace, bracket, buoy (up), buttress, hold (up), prop (up), reinforce, shore (up), stabilize, steady, strengthen, sustain, tighten, undergird, underpin, underprop, uphold. *See also* **balance, fasten. 3.** To supply with the necessities of life ▸ keep, maintain, provide for. *Idiom:* take care of. *See also* **nourish. 4.** To act as a patron to ▸ back, patronize, sponsor. *See also* **donate, finance. 5.** To hold the weight of ▸ carry, hold (up), uphold. *See* **bear** (1). **6.** To present evidence in support of ▸ buttress, substantiate. *See* **back** (2). **7.** To put up with ▸ accept, tolerate, withstand. *See* **endure** (1).

support *noun*
1. A means or device that keeps something erect, stable, or secure ▸ brace, bracket, buttress, crutch, prop, reinforcement, shore, stay, underpinning. **2.** The act or an instance of helping ▸ aid, assistance. *See* **help** (1). **3.** An indication of commendation or approval ▸ backing, recommendation. *See* **endorsement** (1). **4.** The means needed to support life ▸ bread, keep, livelihood. *See* **living.**

✦ CORE SYNONYMS: *support, uphold, back, advocate, champion.* These verbs mean to aid the cause of by approving or favoring. *Support* is the most general: *"the policy of Cromwell, who supported the growing power of France against the declining power of Spain"* (William E.H. Lecky). To *uphold* is to maintain or affirm in the face of a challenge or strong opposition: *"The Declaration of Right upheld the principle of hereditary monarchy"* (Edmund Burke). *Back* suggests material or moral support intended to contribute to or assure success: *The important medical research was backed by the federal government. Advocate* implies verbal support, often in the form of pleading or arguing: *Scientists advocate a reduction in saturated fats in the human diet.* To *champion* is to fight for one that is under attack or is unable to act in its own behalf: *"championed the government and defended the system of taxation"* (Samuel Chew).

supportable *adjective*
▸ sufferable, tolerable. *See* **bearable.**

supporter *noun*
1. One who supports and adheres to another ▸ adherent, believer, disciple. *See* **follower** (1). **2.** One who supports or champions an activity, cause, or institution ▸ benefactor, sponsor. *See* **patron** (1). **3.** One that argues for or defends a cause ▸ champion, defender, proponent. *See* **advocate** (1).

supportive *adjective*
1. Giving or able to give help or support ▸ assistant, contributory, subsidiary. *See* **auxiliary** (1). **2.** Feeling or expressing sympathy or pity ▸ commiserative, com-

passionate, empathetic, understanding. *See* **sympathetic.**

supposable *adjective*
▸ assumptive, likely, probable. *See* **presumptive.**

suppose *verb*
1. To consider to be true without proof ▸ assume, imagine, posit, postulate, premise, presume, presuppose. *Informal:* expect, reckon. *Idioms:* take for granted (*or* as a given). *See also* **believe, infer. 2.** To oblige to do or not do by force of authority, propriety, or custom ▸ expect, oblige, obligate, require. *See also* **must. 3.** To predict or assume without sufficient information ▸ speculate, surmise. *See* **guess.**

✦ CORE SYNONYMS: *suppose, presume, presuppose, postulate, posit, assume.* These verbs signify to take something for granted or as being a fact without proof. To *suppose* often suggests that what is taken to be true is based on uncertain or tentative grounds: *Scientists suppose that dinosaurs lived in swamps.* To *presume* is to suppose that something is reasonable or possible in the absence of proof to the contrary: *"I presume you're tired after the long ride"* (Edith Wharton). *Presuppose* can mean to believe or suppose in advance: *It is unrealistic to presuppose a sophisticated knowledge of harmony in a beginning music student. Postulate* and *posit* denote the assertion of the existence, reality, necessity, or truth of something as the basis for reasoning or argument: *"We can see individuals, but we can't see providence; we have to postulate it"* (Aldous Huxley). To *assume* is to accept something as existing or being true without proof or on inconclusive grounds: *"We must never assume that which is incapable of proof"* (G.H. Lewes).

supposed *adjective*
Presumed to be true, real, or genuine, especially on inconclusive grounds ▸ alleged, conjectural, hypothetic, hypothetical, hypothesized, inferential, presumed, purported, putative, reputed, so-called, suppositional, suppositious, supposititious, suppositive. *Informal:* quote-unquote. *See also* **ambiguous, presumptive.**

✦ CORE SYNONYMS: *supposed, conjectural, hypothetical, putative, reputed, suppositious, supposititious.* These adjectives mean presumed to be true, real, or genuine, especially on inconclusive grounds: *the supposed cause of inflation; conjectural criticism; the hypothetical site of a lost culture; a foundling's putative father; the reputed author of the article; suppositious reconstructions of dead languages; supposititious hypotheses.*

supposition *noun*
1. A judgment, estimate, or opinion arrived at by guessing ▸ guess, speculation, surmise. *See* **guess. 2.** Something taken to be true without proof ▸ premise, presumption. *See* **assumption** (1).

suppositional *or* **suppositive** *adjective*
▸ hypothetical, presumptive, so-called. *See* **supposed.**

supposititious *or* **suppositious** *adjective*
1. Fraudulently or deceptively imitative ▸ fake, fraudulent, phony. *See* **counterfeit. 2.** Presumed to be

true, real, or genuine, especially on inconclusive grounds ▸ hypothetical, presumptive, suppositional. *See* **supposed.** *See synonym note at* **supposed.**

suppress *verb*

1. To overcome opposition or uprising with overwhelming force ▸ choke off, crush, extinguish, put down, quash, quell, quench, squash, squelch. *Idiom:* put the lid on. *See also* **abolish, defeat, frustrate. 2.** To keep from being published or transmitted ▸ ban, stifle, withhold. *See* **censor** (2). **3.** To hold something requiring an outlet in check ▸ muffle, smother, stifle. *See* **repress.**

suppression *noun*

1. Forceful subjugation, as against an uprising ▸ clampdown, crackdown, lockdown, repression. *See also* **oppression, restraint. 2.** The act of exercising controlling power or the condition of being so controlled ▸ control, dominion, reign. *See* **domination** (1).

suppressive *adjective*

▸ inhibitive, restraining, restrictive. *See* **repressive.**

supremacy *noun*

1. The right and power to command, decide, rule, or judge ▸ might. *Informal:* say-so, muscle. *See* **authority** (1). **2.** The condition or fact of being dominant ▸ authority, power, sway. *See* **dominance** (1).

supreme *adjective*

1. Having or arising from authority ▸ official, imperial, standard. *See* **authoritative** (1). **2.** Exercising controlling power or influence ▸ key, predominant, reigning. *See* **dominant** (1). **3.** Conforming to an ultimate form of perfection or excellence ▸ exemplary, model, perfect. *See* **ideal** (1). **4.** Surpassing all others in quality ▸ optimum, superlative, unsurpassed. *See* **best** (1).

surcease *verb*

1. To prevent the occurrence or continuation of a movement, action, or operation ▸ check, discontinue, immobilize. *See* **stop** (2). **2.** To come to a cessation ▸ discontinue, halt, quit. *See* **stop** (1).

surcease *noun*

1. The act of stopping ▸ cessation, cutoff, discontinuation. *See* **stop** (1). **2.** The condition of being stopped ▸ gridlock, standstill, tie-up. *See* **stop** (2).

sure *adjective*

1. Having no doubt ▸ assured, certain, confident, convinced, doubtless, positive, undoubting. **2.** Certain not to fail, miss, or err ▸ certain, fail-safe, foolproof, infallible, secure, unerring, unfailing. *Informal:* sure-fire. *Slang:* idiot-proof. *See also* **dependable. 3.** Established beyond a doubt ▸ inarguable, indisputable, irrefutable. *See* **certain** (2). **4.** Known positively ▸ absolute, certain. *See* **definite** (3). **5.** Bound to happen ▸ inescapable, inevitable, unavoidable. *See* **certain** (1). *See synonym note at* **certain. 6.** Not easily moved or shaken ▸ solid, stable, substantial. *See* **firm**[1] (2).

✦ **CORE SYNONYMS:** *sure, certain, confident, positive.* These adjectives mean having no doubt. *Sure* and

certain are frequently used interchangeably; *sure,* however, is the more subjective term, whereas *certain* may imply belief based on experience or evidence: *"Never teach a child anything of which you are not yourself sure"* (John Ruskin). *"In this world nothing is certain but death and taxes"* (Benjamin Franklin). *Confident* suggests assurance founded on faith or reliance in oneself or in others: *The senator is confident of reelection. Positive* suggests full, emphatic certainty: *The prosecutor had positive proof of the defendant's guilt.*

---

sure-fire *adjective*

▸ foolproof, infallible, unerring. *See* **sure** (2).

surely *adverb*

▸ certainly, definitely, unquestionably. *See* **absolutely** (1).

sureness *noun*

1. The fact or condition of being without doubt ▸ assurance, assuredness, certainty, certitude, confidence, conviction, doubtlessness, indubitability, positiveness, positivity, surety. *See also* **impudence. 2.** Reliability in withstanding pressure, force, or stress ▸ firmness, hardness, steadiness. *See* **stability.**

✦ **CORE SYNONYMS:** *sureness, certainty, certitude, assurance, conviction.* These nouns mean freedom from doubt. *Sureness* is the most general: *The jury was swayed by the sureness of the recollection of the witness. Certainty* implies a thorough consideration of evidence: *"the emphasis of a certainty that is not impaired by any shade of doubt"* (Mark Twain). *Certitude* is based more on personal belief than on objective facts: *"Certitude is not the test of certainty"* (Oliver Wendell Holmes, Jr.). *Assurance* is a feeling of confidence resulting from subjective experience: *"There is no such thing as absolute certainty, but there is assurance sufficient for the purposes of human life"* (John Stuart Mill). *Conviction* arises from the vanquishing of doubt: *"His religion . . . was substantial and concrete, made up of good, hard convictions and opinions.* (Willa Cather).

---

sure thing *noun*

▸ actuality, truth. *See* **certainty** (1).

surety *noun*

1. An assumption of responsibility, as one given by a manufacturer, for the quality, worth, or durability of a product ▸ certification, guarantee, guaranty, warrant, warranty. **2.** One who assumes financial responsibility for another ▸ guarantor, underwriter. *See* **sponsor** (1). **3.** The fact or condition of being without doubt ▸ assuredness, certainty, conviction. *See* **sureness** (1).

surface *noun*

1. An outer surface, layer, or part of an object ▸ face, facet, side. *See also* **back, bottom, front. 2.** A final coating ▸ glaze, plaster, varnish. *See* **finish** (3). **3.** An outward appearance ▸ aspect, countenance. *See* **face** (4).

surface *verb*

1. To cover with a different material ▸ clad, sheathe, side. *See* **face** (2). **2.** To apply a coating to ▸ glaze, plaster, shellac, stain, varnish. *See* **finish** (7).

surface *adjective*
Lacking in intellectual depth or thoroughness ▸ one-dimensional, shallow. *See* **superficial** (1).

surfeit *verb*
To satisfy to the full or to excess ▸ engorge, glut, sate. *See* **satiate.**

surfeit *noun*
1. Immoderate indulgence, as in food or drink ▸ intemperance, overindulgence. *See* **excess** (3). **2.** The condition of being full to or beyond satisfaction ▸ repletion, satiety. *See* **satiation. 3.** A condition of going or being beyond what is needed, desired, or appropriate ▸ exorbitance, extravagance, superfluity. *See* **excess** (1). **4.** A thing, amount, or quantity beyond what is needed, desired, or appropriate ▸ overflow, oversupply, superfluity. *See* **surplus.**

surge *verb*
1. To come forth in abundance ▸ gush, pour, rush. *See* **flow** (2). **2.** To make or become greater or larger ▸ amplify, boost, enlarge. *See* **increase** (1).

surge *noun*
1. Something suggestive of running water ▸ flood, stream, tide. *See* **flow. 2.** A sudden emergence or increase ▸ breakout, flare, outburst. *See* **eruption** (1).

surly *adjective*
1. Broodingly and sullenly unhappy ▸ gloomy, morose, sullen. *See* **glum** (1). **2.** Having or showing a bad temper ▸ cranky, grouchy, peevish. *See* **ill-tempered.**

surmise *verb*
To predict or assume without sufficient information ▸ speculate, suspect. *See* **guess.**

surmise *noun*
A judgment, estimate, or opinion arrived at by guessing ▸ guess, speculation. *See* **guess.**

surmised *adjective*
▸ unpracticed, unproved, untested. *See* **untried** (1).

surmount *verb*
1. To win a victory over, as in battle or a competition ▸ conquer, overcome, vanquish. *See* **defeat** (1). **2.** To pass by or over successfully ▸ clear, hurdle, negotiate.

surmountable *adjective*
▸ negotiable, passable, traversable. *See* **passable** (1).

surpass *verb*
1. To be greater or better than ▸ best, better, exceed, excel, outdo, outmatch, outrun, outshine, outstrip, pass, top, transcend. *Informal:* beat. **Idioms:** go beyond, go one better, one-up. *See also* **dominate. 2.** To go beyond the limits of ▸ overstep, transcend. *See* **exceed** (1).

✦ **CORE SYNONYMS:** *surpass, excel, exceed, transcend, outdo, outstrip.* These verbs mean to be greater or better than someone or something. To *surpass* another is to be superior in performance, quality, or degree: *an athlete surpassed by none. Excel* is to be preeminent (*excels at figure skating*) or to be at a level higher than another or others (*excelled her father as a lawyer*). *Exceed* can refer to being superior (*an invention that exceeds all others in ingenuity*), to being

greater than another (*a salary exceeding 70 thousand dollars a year*), and to going beyond a proper limit (*exceed one's authority*). *Transcend* often implies the attainment of a level so high that comparison is hardly possible: *Great art transcends mere rules of composition.* To *outdo* is to excel in doing or performing: *won't be outdone in generosity. Outstrip* strongly suggests leaving another behind, as in a contest: *a case of the student outstripping the teacher.*

surplus *noun*
A thing, amount, or quantity beyond what is needed, desired, or appropriate ▸ excess, extra, fat, glut, leftover, overage, overflow, overmuch, overrun, overstock, oversupply, superfluity, supernumerary, surfeit, surplusage. **Idiom:** fifth wheel. *See also* **excess.**

surplus *adjective*
Being more than is needed, desired, or appropriate ▸ excess, spare. *See* **superfluous.** *See synonym note at* **superfluous.**

surplusage *noun*
▸ overflow, oversupply, superfluity. *See* **surplus.**

surprise *verb*
1. To impress strongly by what is unexpected or unusual ▸ amaze, astonish, astound, awe, startle. **Idioms:** catch (*or* take) unawares, take aback, throw for a loop. *See also* **stagger, startle. 2.** To attack suddenly and without warning ▸ ambuscade, bushwhack, waylay. *See* **ambush** (1).

surprise *noun*
1. Something that jars the mind or emotions ▸ bombshell, jolt, trauma. *See* **shock**[1] (1). **2.** The emotion aroused by something awe-inspiring or astounding ▸ amazement, astonishment, wonderment. *See* **wonder** (1). **3.** One that evokes great surprise and admiration ▸ prodigy, phenomenon, prodigy. *See* **marvel** (1).

surprisingly *adverb*
▸ singularly, uncommonly, uniquely. *See* **unusually.**

surrender *verb*
1. To give up in favor of another ▸ acquiesce, blink, bow, capitulate, concede, give in, give up, submit, yield. **Idiom:** bend one's knee. **2.** To yield oneself unrestrainedly, as to an impulse ▸ abandon, deliver, relinquish. **Idioms:** give oneself up (*or* over). **3.** To give up or leave completely ▸ abdicate, relinquish, yield. *See* **abandon** (1). *See synonym note at* **abandon. 4.** To give in from or as if from a gradual loss of strength ▸ buckle, submit. *See* **succumb** (1).

surrender *noun*
1. The act of submitting or surrendering to the power of another ▸ capitulation, giving up, submission. *See synonym note at* **submission.** *See also* **obedience. 2.** The act of delivering or the condition of being delivered ▸ conveyance, transfer. *See* **delivery** (1). **3.** A giving up of a possession, claim, or right ▸ abdication, relinquishment, waiver. *See* **abandonment** (1).

✦ **CORE SYNONYMS:** *surrender, yield, bow, submit, capitulate.* These verbs mean to give up something in favor of something else, especially when one can no longer oppose or resist. *Surrender* and *yield* have the widest application: *The enemy troops surrendered to the victors. "The child . . . soon yielded to the drowsiness"* (Charles Dickens). *Bow* suggests giving way in defeat or through courtesy: *"Bow and accept the end/Of a love"* (Robert Frost). *Submit* implies giving way out of necessity, as after futile or unsuccessful resistance: *"obliged to submit to those laws which are imposed upon us"* (Abigail Adams). *Capitulate* implies surrender to pressure, force, compulsion, or inevitability: *"I will be conquered; I will not capitulate* [to illness]" (Samuel Johnson).

surreptitious *adjective*
▸ furtive, secretive, sneaky. *See* **stealthy.**

surrogate *noun*
One that can take the place of another ▸ replacement, stand-in. *See* **substitute.**

surrogate *verb*
To substitute for or fill the place of ▸ displace, replace, supersede, supplant. *Idioms:* fill someone's shoes, take over from, take the reins from. *See also* **substitute.**

surround *verb*
1. To shut in on all sides ▸ beset, circle, compass, embrace, encircle, encompass, environ, hedge (in), hem (in), ring. *See also* **enclose, wrap. 2.** To form a circle around ▸ circle, gird, ring. *See* **encircle** (1).

✦ CORE SYNONYMS: *surround, circle, compass, encircle, encompass, environ, ring.* These verbs mean to shut in on all sides: *Suburbs surround the city. A crown circled the king's head. Fog compassed the mountain peak. A belt encircled her waist. A lake encompassed the island. The desert environed the oases. Guests ringed the coffee table.*

---

surroundings *noun*
1. A surrounding area ▸ locale, vicinity. *See* **environment** (1). **2.** The surrounding conditions and circumstances affecting growth or development ▸ climate, milieu. *See* **environment** (2). **3.** Existing surroundings that affect an activity ▸ circumstances, context. *See* **conditions.**

surveillance *noun*
▸ monitoring, stakeout, vigil, vigilance. *See* **lookout** (1).

survey *verb*
1. To pay regular and close attention to ▸ follow, monitor, observe, watch. *Idioms:* have one's (*or* keep an) eye on, keep tabs on. **2.** To view broadly or from a height ▸ look over, overlook, scan. *See also* **look. 3.** To look at or study carefully or critically ▸ go over, inspect, review. *See* **examine** (1). **4.** To look at or on attentively or carefully ▸ eye, observe, regard. *See* **watch** (1).

survey *noun*
1. A gathering of information or opinion from a variety of sources or individuals ▸ canvass, count, poll. **2.** A general or comprehensive view or treatment ▸ overview. *See also* **synopsis. 3.** The act of examining carefully or critically ▸ analysis, investigation, study. *See* **examination** (1).

survival *noun*
▸ continuum, persistence. *See* **continuation** (1).

survive *verb*
1. To exist in spite of adversity ▸ come through, get through, last, make it, outride, persevere, persist, pull through, ride out, weather. *See also* **endure. 2.** To live, exist, or remain longer than ▸ outlast, outlive, outwear.

susceptibility *noun*
▸ endangerment, pregnability, vulnerability. *See* **exposure** (1).

susceptible *or* **susceptive** *adjective*
1. Easily imposed on or tricked ▸ dupable, naive, simple. *See* **gullible. 2.** Tending to incur ▸ prone, subject, vulnerable. *See* **liable** (2). **3.** Able to receive and respond to external stimuli ▸ impressionable, responsive. *See* **sensitive** (1). **4.** Susceptible to physical or emotional injury ▸ defenseless, helpless, unprotected. *See* **vulnerable** (1).

susceptibleness *noun*
▸ endangerment, vulnerability. *See* **exposure** (1).

suspect *verb*
1. To lack trust or confidence in ▸ disbelieve, question. *See* **distrust. 2.** To predict or assume without sufficient information ▸ speculate, surmise. *See* **guess.**

suspect *adjective*
1. Of dubious character ▸ equivocal, questionable, suspicious. *See* **shady** (1). **2.** In doubt or dispute ▸ disputable, doubtful, questionable. *See* **debatable.**

suspend *verb*
1. To stop for an indefinite period ▸ interrupt, pause. *Idiom:* put on hold. *See also* **rest. 2.** To bring an activity or relationship to an end suddenly ▸ break off, cease, discontinue, interrupt, terminate. **3.** To put off until a later time ▸ delay, postpone, remit. *See* **defer**[1]. *See synonym note at* **defer**[1]. **4.** To fasten or be fastened at one point with no support from below ▸ sling, swing. *See* **hang** (1).

suspenseful *adjective*
▸ melodramatic, sensational, spectacular. *See* **dramatic** (2).

suspension *noun*
1. The condition of being temporarily inactive ▸ dormancy, intermission, quiescence, remission. *See* **abeyance. 2.** A cessation of continuity or regularity ▸ discontinuation, disruption, interruption. *See* **break** (1). **3.** The act of putting off or the condition of being put off ▸ deferment, postponement, shelving. *See* **delay** (1).

suspicion *noun*
1. An intuitive awareness or sense of something ▸ hunch, idea, intuition. *See* **feeling** (1). **2.** Lack of trust ▸ cynicism, leeriness. *See* **distrust. 3.** A lack of conviction or certainty ▸ dubiousness, incertitude, skepticism. *See* **doubt** (1). *See synonym note at* **doubt. 4.** A subtle quality underlying or felt to underlie a situation, action, or person ▸ inkling, undercurrent. *See* **hint** (1). **5.** A slight amount or indication ▸ hint, semblance, trace. *See* **shade** (2).

suspicious *adjective*
1. Of dubious character ▸ equivocal, questionable, uncertain. *See* **shady** (1). **2.** Lacking trust or confidence ▸ doubting, skeptical, wary. *See* **distrustful** (1). **3.** Experiencing doubt ▸ hesitant, skeptical, uncertain. *See* **doubtful** (2).

suspiciously *adverb*
▸ doubtfully, questioningly. *See* **skeptically.**

sustain *verb*
1. To keep in a condition of good repair, efficiency, or use ▸ keep up, maintain, preserve. **2.** To come gradually to have ▸ acquire, form, incur. *See* **develop** (1). **3.** To hold the weight of ▸ carry, support, uphold. *See* **bear** (1). **4.** To present evidence in support of ▸ buttress, substantiate. *See* **back** (2). **5.** To assure the certainty or validity of ▸ authenticate, corroborate, verify. *See* **confirm** (1). **6.** To establish as true or genuine through evidence ▸ confirm, validate. *See* **prove** (1). **7.** To make stronger or more resistant ▸ bolster, reinforce. *See* **support** (2). **8.** To put up with ▸ stomach, tolerate, withstand. *See* **endure** (1). **9.** To help grow or develop ▸ foster, nourish. *See* **nurture.** **10.** To persevere in some condition, action, or belief ▸ retain, stick to. *See* **keep** (6).

sustained *adjective*
▸ drawn-out, overlong, protracted. *See* **long**¹ (2).

sustenance *noun*
1. Material that is fit to be eaten ▸ fare, nourishment, victuals. *See* **food. 2.** The means needed to support life ▸ bread, keep, livelihood. *See* **living. 3.** The work of keeping something in proper condition ▸ repairs, upkeep. *See* **maintenance** (1).

susurration *or* **susurrus** *noun*
▸ sigh, sough, whisper. *See* **murmur** (1).

suzerain *noun*
▸ boss, director, head, leader. *See* **chief** (1).

svelte *adjective*
▸ lean, skinny, slender, slim. *See* **thin** (1). *See synonym note at* **thin.**

swaddle *verb*
▸ envelop, roll, swathe. *See* **wrap** (1).

swag *noun*
Slang Goods or property seized unlawfully ▸ booty, loot. *See* **plunder.**

swagger *verb*
1. To walk with pompous bearing ▸ prance, strut, swank. *See* **strut** (1). **2.** To talk with excessive pride ▸ bluster, vaunt. *See* **boast** (1).

swagman *noun*
▸ nomad, roamer, vagabond. *See* **hobo.**

swain *noun*
▸ courter, suitor. *See* **beau** (1).

swale *noun*
1. A usually low-lying area of soft waterlogged ground and standing water ▸ marsh, mire, wetland. *See* **swamp. 2.** An elongated lowland between mountains or hills ▸ dale, gorge. *See* **valley.**

swallow *verb*
1. To cause to pass from the mouth into the stomach ▸ ingest, take. *See also* **drink, eat, gulp. 2.** To put up with ▸ accept, stomach, tolerate. *See* **endure** (1). **3.** To regard something as true or real ▸ accept. *Slang:* buy. *See* **believe** (1).

swallow up *verb*
To engulf completely ▸ devour, ravage, waste. *See* **consume** (1).

swallow *noun*
1. An act of swallowing ▸ gulp, ingestion, swig. **2.** A small portion of food ▸ crumb, morsel. *See* **bit**¹ (2). **3.** An act of drinking or the amount swallowed ▸ draft, taste. *Informal:* swig. *See* **drink** (2).

swamp *or* **swampland** *noun*
A usually low-lying area of soft waterlogged ground and standing water ▸ bog, fen, marsh, marshland, mire, moor, morass, muskeg, quag, quagmire, slough, swale, wetland.

swamp *verb*
To affect as if by an outpouring of water ▸ deluge, flood, inundate, overwhelm.

swank *adjective*
1. In accordance with current fashion ▸ mod, stylish, swanky. *See* **fashionable.** *See synonym note at* **fashionable. 2.** Catering to, used by, or admitting only the wealthy or socially superior ▸ chic, posh, tony. *See* **exclusive** (4).

swank *verb*
To walk with pompous bearing ▸ prance, swagger. *See* **strut** (1).

swanky *adjective*
1. In accordance with current fashion ▸ mod, smart, stylish. *See* **fashionable. 2.** Catering to, used by, or admitting only the wealthy or socially superior ▸ chic, posh, swank. *See* **exclusive** (4).

swap *verb*
1. *Informal* To give up in return for something else ▸ exchange, interchange, trade. *See* **change** (3). **2.** To give and receive mutually, as words ▸ bandy, trade. *See* **exchange** (2).

swap *noun*
Informal The act of exchanging ▸ exchange, interchange, switch. *See* **change** (2).

swarm *noun*
1. An enormous number of persons or things gathered together ▸ horde, mass, throng. *See* **crowd** (1). **2.** A number of animals considered collectively ▸ bevy, gaggle, herd, kennel. *See* **flock** (1). *See synonym note at* **flock.**

swarm *verb*
1. To move into an area or space in large numbers ▸ flood, pour, throng. *See* **crowd** (1). **2.** To be abundantly filled or richly supplied ▸ bristle, crawl, overflow. *See* **teem**¹. *See synonym note at* **teem.**

swarming *adjective*
1. Filled beyond capacity ▸ congested, teeming. *See* **overcrowded. 2.** Full of lively activity ▸ bustling, crawling, teeming. *See* **busy** (2).

swarthy *adjective*
▸ black, brunet, dusky. *See* **dark** (3).

swash *verb*

1. To make the sound of moving or disturbed water ► lap, splash, wash. *See also* **burble, swish. 2.** To hurl or scatter liquid ► bespatter, spray. *See* **splash** (1). **3.** To walk with pompous bearing ► prance, strut, swank. *See* **strut** (1).

swat *verb*

1. To deliver a sudden, sharp blow to ► jab, sock, whack. *See* **hit** (1). **2.** To hit with a sharp blow, especially of the open hand ► smack, spank, whack. *See* **slap** (1).

swat *noun*

1. A sudden heavy stroke ► crack, hit, swing, whack. *See* **blow²** (1). **2.** A sharp blow, especially with the open hand ► smack, spank, whack. *See* **slap** (1).

swatch *noun*

► ribbon, strip, swath. *See* **band¹** (1).

swath *noun*

► fillet, ribbon, strip, swatch. *See* **band¹** (1).

swathe *verb*

1. To cover completely and closely, as with clothing or bandages ► bundle, envelop. *See* **wrap** (1). **2.** To apply therapeutic materials to a wound ► bandage, bind. *See* **dress** (2).

sway *verb*

1. To move back and forth or from side to side ► fluctuate, oscillate, quake, rock, shake, swing, switch, teeter, totter, tremble, undulate, vacillate, vibrate, wag, waggle, wave, waver, weave, wobble. *See also* **shake. 2.** To have an impact on in a certain way ► affect, predispose, dispose. *See* **influence** (1). **3.** To walk unsteadily ► reel, stumble, totter. *See* **stagger** (1).

sway *noun*

1. The right and power to command, decide, rule, or judge ► control, dominion. *Informal:* say-so, muscle. *See* **authority** (1). **2.** Power to sway or affect based on prestige, wealth, ability, or position ► force, leverage, weight. *See* **influence** (1). **3.** The act of exercising controlling power or the condition of being so controlled ► control, dominion, reign. *See* **domination** (1). **4.** The condition or fact of being dominant ► authority, power, supremacy. *See* **dominance** (1).

✦ CORE SYNONYMS: *sway, swing, oscillate, rock, vibrate, fluctuate, undulate, waver.* These verbs mean to move back and forth or from side to side. *Sway* suggests the movement of something unsteady, light, or flexible: *"thousands of the little yellow blossoms all swaying to the light wind"* (W.H. Hudson). *Swing* usually applies to arclike movement of something attached at one extremity and free at the other: *The ship's lanterns swung violently in the raging storm. Oscillate* literally refers to a steady back-and-forth motion, as that of a pendulum; figuratively, it denotes vacillation, as between conflicting purposes: *"a king . . . oscillating between fear of Rome and desire of independence"* (Walter Besant). To *rock* is to swing gently or rhythmically or sway or tilt violently: *"The ruins of the ancient church seemed actually to rock and threaten to fall"* (Sir Walter Scott). *Vibrate* implies quick periodic oscillations; it can also suggest trembling, pulsating,

or quivering: *"Music, when soft voices die,/Vibrates in the memory"* (Percy Bysshe Shelley). *Fluctuate* implies fairly constant alternating change: *"Prices fluctuated violently from the irregularity of the crops"* (Lesley B. Simpson). *Undulate* refers to smooth wavelike movement: *"gleaming seaweed that curls and undulates with the tide"* (Willa Cather). *Waver* suggests unsteady, uncertain movement: *A police officer stopped the driver who was wavering from lane to lane.*

---

swear *verb*

1. To use profane or obscene language ► blaspheme, curse, damn. *Informal:* cuss. **2.** To guarantee by a solemn promise ► promise, vow. *See* **pledge** (1). *See synonym note at* **pledge. 3.** To give evidence or testimony under oath ► attest, depose, witness. *See* **testify** (1). **4.** To put into words positively and with conviction ► avow, declare, maintain. *See* **assert** (1).

swear at *verb*

To hurl strong deprecations, curses, or insults at ► *Informal:* cuss at (*or* out), mouth off at. *See also* **curse, insult, revile.**

swear off *verb*

1. *Informal* To cease trying to continue ► desist, give up, quit. *See* **abandon** (2). **2.** *Informal* To discontinue (a habit, for example) ► abjure, give up, leave off. *See* **break** (17).

swearword *noun*

A profane or obscene term ► blasphemy, curse, epithet, expletive, oath, obscenity, profanity. *Informal:* cuss. **Idioms:** bad (*or* dirty) word, four-letter word.

sweat *verb*

1. To excrete moisture through a porous skin or layer ► lather, perspire, transude. **2.** To exert oneself steadily, often to the point of exhaustion ► strain, strive, toil. *See* **labor** (1). **3.** To flow or emit something slowly ► exude, leach, seep. *See* **ooze.**

sweat out *verb*

Slang To put up with ► stomach, swallow, take. *See* **endure** (1).

sweat *noun*

1. Moisture accumulated on a surface through sweating or condensation ► condensation, lather, perspiration, transudation. **2.** *Informal* Physical exertion that is usually difficult and exhausting ► toil, travail, work. *See* **labor** (1). *See synonym note at* **labor. 3.** *Informal* A condition of excited distress ► fume. *Informal:* snit, swivet. *See* **state** (4). **4.** A difficult or tedious undertaking ► effort, grind, slog. *See* **task** (2).

sweaty *or* **sweating** *adjective*

Producing or covered with sweat ► perspiring, sudoriferous. *See also* **damp, sticky.**

sweep *verb*

1. To wield boldly and dramatically ► brandish, flourish, wave. *See* **flourish. 2.** To move freely as a liquid ► purl, run, stream. *See* **flow** (1). **3.** To be in a state of motion, as air or wind ► bluster, gust. *See* **blow¹** (1).

sweep *noun*

1. A wide and open area, as of land, sky, or water ► extent, stretch, vista. *See* **expanse** (1). **2.** An area or set of parameters within which something or some-one exists, acts, or has influence ▸ extent, realm, scope. *See* **range** (1). *See synonym note at* **range**.

sweeping *adjective*
▸ all-inclusive, broad, expansive. *See* **general** (2).

sweet *adjective*
1. Having or suggesting the taste of sugar ▸ honeyed, saccharine, sugary. **2.** Not sour or salted ▸ fresh, uncured, unsalted. **3.** Pleasing to the eye or mind ▸ enchanting, fetching, lovely, winsome. *See* **attractive** (1). **4.** Giving great pleasure or delight ▸ delectable, enchanting, heavenly. *See* **delightful**. **5.** Pleasant and friendly in disposition ▸ cordial, friendly, genial. *See* **amiable**.

sweet *noun*
A person who is much loved ▸ honey, precious, sweetheart. *See* **darling** (1).

sweeten *verb*
1. To make superficially more acceptable or appealing ▸ candy, gild, honey, sugar, sugarcoat. *See also* **moderate**. **2.** To ease the anger or agitation of ▸ appease, mollify, soothe. *See* **pacify**.

sweetheart *noun*
▸ dear, honey, precious. *See* **darling** (1).

sweetmeat *noun*
▸ morsel, treat. *See* **delicacy** (1).

sweet-sounding *adjective*
▸ euphonic, melodic, musical. *See* **melodious**.

sweet talk *noun*
Informal Excessive, ingratiating praise ▸ adulation, blandishment, oil. *Informal:* apple-polishing. *See* **flattery**.

sweet-talk *verb*
1. *Informal* To persuade or try to persuade by gentle persistent urging or flattery ▸ cajole, wheedle. *See* **coax** (1). **2.** *Informal* To compliment ingratiatingly ▸ adulate, butter up. *Informal:* soft-soap. *See* **flatter** (1).

swell *verb*
1. To expand from or as if from internal pressure ▸ balloon, bloat, blow up, bulge (out), distend, inflate, puff (up *or* out), tumefy, tumesce. *See also* **bulge**. **2.** To make or become greater or larger ▸ amplify, boost, enlarge. *See* **increase** (1). **3.** To talk with excessive pride ▸ gasconade, vaunt. *See* **boast** (1).

swell *noun*
1. The act of increasing or rising ▸ amplification, boost, escalation. *See* **increase** (1). **2.** A ridge or swell of water, or a shape suggestive of such a swell ▸ breaker, undulation. *See* **wave** (1). **3.** A man who is vain about his clothes ▸ beau, coxcomb, dandy, fop, peacock.

swell *adjective*
1. *Informal* Exceptionally good of its kind ▸ first-rate, prime, splendid, tiptop. *See* **excellent**. **2.** *Informal* Particularly excellent ▸ fantastic, sensational, superb. *See* **marvelous** (1).

swelled head *noun*
▸ self-importance. *Informal:* big head. *See* **egotism**.

swellheaded *adjective*
1. *Informal* Thinking too highly of oneself ▸ narcissistic, vain. *See* **egotistic** (1). **2.** *Informal* Overly convinced of one's own superiority and importance ▸ haughty, insolent. *See* **arrogant**.

swelling *noun*
▸ knot, lump. *See* **bump** (2).

swelter *verb*
▸ broil, roast, steam. *See* **burn** (3).

sweltering *adjective*
▸ blistering, boiling, burning. *See* **hot** (1).

swerve *verb*
1. To turn aside sharply from a straight course ▸ angle, cut, sheer, skew, slant, slue, tack, veer, zag, zig, zigzag. *See also* **bend, glance**. **2.** To turn away from a prescribed course of action or conduct ▸ digress, stray. *See* **deviate** (1). *See synonym note at* **deviate**.

swift *adjective*
1. Characterized by great speed ▸ expeditious, fleet, rapid. *See* **fast** (1). *See synonym note at* **fast**. **2.** Accomplished or experienced in very little time ▸ fast, rapid, speedy. *See* **quick** (1).

swiftly *adverb*
▸ hastily, hurriedly, quickly, rapidly. *See* **fast**.

swiftness *noun*
1. Rapidity of movement or activity ▸ expeditiousness, quickness. *See* **haste** (1). **2.** The quality of being agile ▸ dexterity, nimbleness. *See* **agility**.

swig *noun*
1. An act of swallowing ▸ gulp, ingestion, swallow. **2.** *Informal* An act of drinking or the amount swallowed ▸ draft, swallow, taste. *See* **drink** (2).

swig *verb*
Informal To take into the mouth and swallow a liquid ▸ down, sip, swill. *See* **drink** (1).

swill *verb*
1. To swallow food or drink greedily or rapidly in large amounts ▸ gobble, guzzle. *See* **gulp** (1). **2.** To take into the mouth and swallow a liquid ▸ down, sip, slurp. *See* **drink** (1).

swill *noun*
An act of drinking or the amount swallowed ▸ swallow, taste. *See* **drink** (2).

swim *verb*
1. To have the sensation of turning in circles ▸ reel, spin, swirl, whirl. *Idiom:* go round and round. **2.** To be abundantly filled or richly supplied ▸ bristle, crawl, swarm. *See* **teem**[1].

swim *noun*
The act of swimming ▸ duck, dunk. *See* **plunge** (4).

swindle *verb*
1. To get something by deceitful trickery ▸ bilk, defraud, swindle. *See* **cheat** (1). **2.** To cause to accept something false, especially by trickery or misrepresentation ▸ dupe, fool, mislead, trick. *See* **deceive**.

swindle *noun*
An act of cheating ▸ deceit, fraud, hoax. *See* **cheat** (1).

swindler *noun*
▸ cheater, rook, trickster. *See* **cheat** (2).

swing *verb*

1. To move back and forth ► oscillate, vacillate, waggle. *See* **sway** (1). *See synonym note at* **sway. 2.** To fasten or be fastened at one point with no support from below ► sling, suspend. *See* **hang** (1). **3.** To change the direction or course of ► deviate, divert, veer. *See* **turn** (2). **4.** To turn or cause to turn in place, as on a hinge or fixed point, tracing an arclike path ► pivot, slue, swivel, wheel. **5.** To shift from one attitude, interest, condition, or emotion to another ► dilly-dally, vacillate, waver. **6.** *Slang* To execute by suspending by the neck ► gibbet, hang. *Informal:* string up. **7.** *Informal* To succeed in doing ► bring off, carry out, execute. *See* **effect** (1).

swing at *verb*

To deliver a sudden, sharp blow to ► jab, sock, whack. *See* **hit** (1).

swing *noun*

1. An area or set of parameters within which something or someone exists, acts, or has influence ► extent, realm, scope. *See* **range** (1). **2.** The patterned, recurring alternation of contrasting elements, such as stressed and unstressed notes in music ► cadence, meter. *See* **rhythm. 3.** A sudden heavy stroke ► crack, hit, swat, whack. *See* **blow**² (1).

swinger *noun*

► debaucher, profligate. *See* **wanton** (1).

swipe *verb*

Informal To take another's property without permission ► purloin, snatch, thieve. *See* **steal** (1). *See synonym note at* **steal.**

swipe *noun*

1. A sudden heavy stroke ► crack, hit, swat, whack. *See* **blow**² (1). **2.** *Informal* An instance of mockery or derision ► insult, jeer, scoff. *See* **taunt** (1).

swirl *verb*

1. To move or cause to move like a rapidly rotating current of liquid ► eddy, whirl. **2.** To rotate rapidly ► spin, twirl, whirl. **3.** To have the sensation of turning in circles ► reel, spin, swim, whirl. *Idiom:* go round and round. **4.** To rotate on an axis or around a center ► twirl, whirl, wheel. *See* **turn** (1). *See synonym note at* **turn.**

swirl *noun*

1. Something with a curled or spiral shape ► curlicue, spiral, twist. *See* **curl. 2.** A circular movement around a point or about an axis ► circulation, gyration. *See* **revolution** (1). **3.** A rotating, often concave current of liquid ► eddy, vortex. *See* **whirlpool** (1).

swish *verb*

To make a sibilant sound ► fizzle, sizzle. *See* **hiss** (1).

swish *adjective*

Informal In accordance with current fashion ► mod, stylish, swanky. *See* **fashionable.**

swish *noun*

A sibilant sound ► fizzle, rustle. *See* **hiss** (1).

switch *verb*

1. To move to and fro vigorously and usually repeatedly ► wag, waggle, wave. **2.** To leave or discard for another ► change, shift. **3.** To give up in return for something else ► exchange, interchange, trade. *See* **change** (3). **4.** To change the direction or course of ► deviate, divert, veer. *See* **turn** (2). **5.** To move to and fro in short, jerky movements ► quiver, tremble, twitter. *See* **shake** (1).

switch *noun*

1. The act of exchanging ► exchange, interchange, transposition. *See* **change** (2). **2.** A short straight piece of wood ► baton, stake. *See* **stick** (1).

swivel *verb*

To turn or cause to turn in place, as on a hinge or fixed point, tracing an arclike path ► pivot, slue, swing, wheel. *See also* **turn.**

swivet *noun*

► fume. *Informal:* snit, sweat. *See* **state** (4).

swollen *adjective*

1. Expanded from or as if from internal pressure ► bloated, blown up, bulging, distended, inflated, puffed (up *or* out), tumescent. *See also* **inflated. 2.** Characterized by or given to boasting ► bombastic, cocky, vaunting. *See* **boastful.**

swoon *verb*

To suffer temporary lack of consciousness ► black out, faint, keel over, pass out. *Idioms:* drop (*or* faint *or* fall) dead away, see stars. *See also* **collapse.**

swoon *noun*

A temporary lack of consciousness ► blackout, faint, fainting spell, syncope. *See synonym note at* **faint.**

sword of Damocles *noun*

► jeopardy, menace, peril, threat. *See* **danger.**

sybarite *noun*

A person devoted to pleasure and luxury ► epicure, epicurean, hedonist, pagan, pleasure-seeker, sensualist, voluptuary.

sybaritic *adjective*

Characterized by or devoted to pleasure and luxury as a lifestyle ► epicurean, hedonic, hedonistic, voluptuary, voluptuous. *See also* **luxurious, sensual.**

sycophant *noun*

One who flatters another or behaves obsequiously in an attempt to win favor ► adulator, bootlicker, courtier, fawner, flatterer, groveler, lackey, minion, slave, toady, truckler, yes man. *Informal:* apple-polisher, brownnose, brownnoser. *See also* **follower, parasite, slave, subordinate.**

sycophantic *adjective*

► obsequious, subservient. *See* **servile.**

syllabus *noun*

► catalog, playbill, prospectus. *See* **program** (2).

symbiotic *adjective*

► correlative, interrelated, reciprocal. *See* **complementary.**

symbol *noun*

1. An object or expression associated with and serving to identify something else ► attribute, emblem, metaphor, signifier, token. *See also* **expression, term. 2.** Something visible or evident that gives grounds for believing in the existence or presence of something else ▸ evidence, indication, symptom. *See* **sign** (1). *See synonym note at* **sign. 3.** A conventional mark used in a writing system ▸ figure, sign. *See* **character** (9).

symbolic *adjective*
1. Serving as a symbol ▸ emblematic, emblematical, figurative, metaphoric, metaphorical, representational, representative, symbolical. *See also* **designative. 2.** Of or relating to representation by drawings or pictures ▸ illustrative, pictographic, pictorial. *See* **graphic** (4).

symbolize *verb*
▸ exemplify, illustrate, typify. *See* **represent** (1).

symmetrical *or* **symmetric** *adjective*
1. Characterized by or displaying symmetry, especially correspondence in scale or measure ▸ balanced, proportional, proportionate, regular. *See also* **even, parallel. 2.** Having components that are pleasingly combined ▸ balanced, concordant, congruous, harmonious.

symmetry *noun*
Satisfying arrangement marked by even distribution of elements, as in a design ▸ balance, harmony, proportion. *See synonym note at* **proportion.** *See also* **agreement.**

sympathetic *adjective*
Feeling or expressing sympathy or pity ▸ comforting, commiserative, compassionate, concerned, condolatory, empathetic, empathic, feeling, loving, pitying, softhearted, supportive, tender, understanding, warm-hearted. *See also* **attentive, generous.**

sympathize *verb*
1. To experience or express compassion ▸ ache, commiserate, condole, feel. *Idioms:* be (*or* feel) sorry, have one's heart bleed for someone, have one's heart go out to someone. *See also* **comfort, pity. 2.** To understand or be sensitive to another's feelings or ideas ▸ empathize, understand. *Idioms:* feel someone's pain, put oneself (*or* walk) in someone else's shoes. **3.** To associate or affiliate oneself closely with a person or group ▸ empathize, identify, relate. *See also* **understand.**

sympathy *noun*
1. A very close understanding between persons ▸ empathy, understanding. **2.** A relationship or an affinity between people or things in which many properties are shared ▸ harmony, synch, synchronization, synchrony. *See also* **agreement. 3.** Sympathetic, sad concern for someone in misfortune ▸ compassion, empathy. *See* **pity** (1). *See synonym note at* **pity.**

symphonic *or* **symphonious** *adjective*
▸ consonant, musical. *See* **harmonious** (2).

symphony *noun*
▸ concord, tune. *See* **harmony** (1).

symposium *noun*
▸ discussion, parley, seminar. *See* **conference** (1).

symptom *noun*
▸ evidence, indication, token. *See* **sign** (1). *See synonym note at* **sign.**

synch *noun*
A relationship or an affinity between people or things in which many properties are shared ▸ harmony, sympathy, synchronization, synchrony. *See also* **agreement.**

synchronize *verb*
To occur at the same time ▸ coincide, concur, harmonize.

synchronous *or* **synchronic** *adjective*
1. Belonging to the same period of time ▸ coexistent, concurrent. *See* **contemporary** (1). **2.** Occurring or existing at the same time ▸ accompanying, coexisting, coincident. *See* **concurrent** (1). *See synonym note at* **concurrent.**

synchronously *adverb*
At the same time ▸ concurrently, simultaneously, together. *Idioms:* all at once, all together.

synchrony *or* **synchronization** *noun*
A relationship or an affinity between people or things in which many properties are shared ▸ harmony, sympathy, synch. *See also* **agreement.**

syncope *noun*
A temporary lack of consciousness ▸ blackout, faint, fainting spell, swoon. *See synonym note at* **faint.**

syndicate *noun*
▸ cartel, pool, trust. *See* **alliance** (1).

syndrome *noun*
▸ system, tissue, web. *See* **complex** (1).

synergistic *or* **synergetic** *adjective*
▸ collective, joint. *See* **cooperative** (1).

synergy *noun*
▸ collaboration, teamwork. *See* **cooperation** (1).

synod *noun*
▸ conference, congress, convocation. *See* **convention** (1).

synopsis *noun*
A shortened version or summary ▸ abridgment, abstract, brief, condensation, digest, epitome, outline, sketch. *See also* **summary.**

synopsize *verb*
▸ abstract, recapitulate, run through, summarize. *See* **review** (1).

synthesize *verb*
▸ blend, integrate. *See* **harmonize** (2).

synthetic *adjective*
▸ manmade, simulated. *See* **artificial** (1). *See synonym note at* **artificial.**

syrupy *adjective*
▸ glutinous, mucilaginous, viscid. *See* **viscous.**

system *noun*
1. An organized array of individual elements and parts forming and working as a unit ▸ arrangement, body, entity, integral, machine, organization, sum, totality, whole. **2.** An entity composed of interconnected parts ▸ tissue, web. *See* **complex** (1). **3.** Systematic arrangement and design ▸ order, organization, scheme. *See* **method** (1). **4.** The approach used to do something ▸ manner, mode, style. *See* **way** (1). *See synonym note at* **way.**

systematic or **systematical** *adjective*
- neat, orderly, regular. *See* **methodical.** *See synonym note at* **methodical** (1).

systematization or **systemization** *noun*
- order, organization, scheme. *See* **method** (1).

systematize *verb*
- order, organize, sort. *See* **arrange** (1). *See synonym note at* **arrange.**

systemize *verb*
- order, organize, systematize. *See* **arrange** (1).

t

tab *noun*

1. *Informal* A precise list of fees or charges ► bill, check, statement. *See* **account** (2). **2.** *Informal* An amount paid or to be paid for a purchase ► charge, expense, price. *See* **cost** (1). **3.** An identifying or descriptive slip ► flag, label, tag. *See* **ticket** (1).

tabby *noun*
- gossipmonger, taleteller, whisperer. *See* **gossip** (2).

table *noun*

1. A natural, flat land elevation ► mesa, plateau. *See also* **hill. 2.** An orderly columnar display of data ► chart, tabulation. **3.** A series, as of names or words, printed or written down ► register, roster, schedule. *See* **list**[1].

table *verb*

To put off until a later time ► delay, postpone, suspend. *See* **defer**[1].

tableau *noun*
- panorama, perspective, vista. *See* **view** (2).

taboo *noun*

A refusal to allow ► prohibition, proscription. *See* **forbiddance.**

taboo *adjective*

Not allowed ► banned, outlawed, prohibited. *See* **forbidden.**

taboo *verb*

To refuse to allow ► disallow, proscribe. *See* **forbid.**

tabulate *verb*
- catalog, chronicle, write down. *See* **list**[1] (1).

tabulation *noun*

An orderly columnar display of data ► chart, table. *See also* **list**[1].

tacit *adjective*

1. Not voiced or expressed ► undeclared, unspoken. *See* **silent** (2). **2.** Conveyed indirectly without words or speech ► inferred, suggested. *See* **implicit** (1).

taciturn *adjective*

Habitually untalkative ► close, close-mouthed, incommunicable, incommunicative, laconic, quiet, reserved, reticent, silent, tightlipped, uncommunicable, uncommunicative, untalkative. *See also* **brief.**

✦ CORE SYNONYMS: *taciturn, silent, reticent, reserved, laconic, uncommunicative, tightlipped.* These adjectives describe people who habitually do not talk much. *Taciturn* implies unsociableness and a tendency to speak only when it is absolutely necessary: *"At the Council board he was taciturn; and in the House of Lords he never opened his lips"* (Thomas Macaulay). *Silent* often implies a habitual disinclination to speak or to speak out: *"The coroner was a very silent man"* (Mary Roberts Rinehart). The term may also mean refraining from speech, as out of fear or confusion: *"The person in custody must, prior to interrogation, be clearly informed that he has the right to remain silent"* (Earl Warren). *Reticent* suggests a reluctance to share one's thoughts and feelings: *"She had been shy and reticent with me, and now . . . she was telling me aloud the secrets of her inmost heart"* (W. H. Hudson). *Reserved* suggests aloofness and reticence: *"a reserved man, whose inner life was intense and sufficient to him"* (Arnold Bennett). *Laconic* denotes terseness or conciseness in expression, but when applied to people it often implies an unwillingness to use words: *"Mountain dwellers and mountain lovers are a laconic tribe. They know the futility of words"* (Edna Ferber). *Uncommunicative* suggests a disposition to withhold opinions, feelings, or knowledge from others: *an uncommunicative witness. Tightlipped* strongly implies a steadfast unwillingness to divulge information being sought: *remained tightlipped when asked about her personal life.*

---

taciturnity *noun*
- constraint, restraint, self-restraint. *See* **reserve** (2).

tack *noun*

1. An often sudden change or departure, as in a trend ► shift, turn, twist. *See also* **change, deviation. 2.** A method used for accomplishing something ► course, modus operandi, procedure, technique. *See* **approach** (1). **3.** A shaft hammered or drilled in place, used to hold together ► pin, spike, stud. *See* **nail.**

tack *verb*

1. To turn aside sharply from a straight course ► slant, veer, zigzag. *See* **swerve** (1). **2.** To make secure ► bind, chain, moor. *See* **fasten** (1).

tackle *noun*

Things needed for a task, journey, or other purpose ► equipment, gear. *See* **outfit** (1).

tackle *verb*

1. To take upon oneself ► shoulder, take on. *See* **assume** (1). **2.** To start work on vigorously ► go at, tackle. *See* **attack** (2).

tacky *adjective*
1. *Informal* Showing signs of wear and tear or neglect ▸ broken-down, dilapidated, tattered. *See* **shabby** (1).
2. *Informal* Lacking in delicacy or refinement ▸ indelicate, tasteless, unbecoming. *See* **coarse** (1). 3. *Informal* Tastelessly showy ▸ flashy, garish, vulgar. *See* **gaudy**. *See synonym note at* **gaudy**. 4. Having the property of adhering ▸ adhesive, gluey, mucilaginous. *See* **sticky** (1).

tact *noun*
The ability to say and do the right thing at the right time ▸ address, delicacy, diplomacy, discretion, savoir-faire, sensitivity, tactfulness. *See also* **consideration, decency.**

✛ CORE SYNONYMS: *tact, address, diplomacy, savoir-faire.* These nouns denote the ability to say and do the right thing at the right time with skill, sensitivity, and finesse. *Tact* implies propriety and the ability to speak or act unoffensively: *"He had . . . a tact that would preserve him from flagrant error in any society"* (Francis Parkman). *Address* suggests deftness and grace in social situations: *"With the charms of beauty she combined the address of an accomplished intriguer"* (Charles Merivale). *Diplomacy* implies adroit management of difficult situations: *Diffusing the confrontation required delicate diplomacy. Savoir-faire* involves knowing the right or graceful thing to say or do: *The hosts set the shy visitor at ease with their savoir-faire.*

tactful *adjective*
▸ diplomatic, discreet, sensitive. *See* **delicate** (2).

tactfulness *noun*
▸ diplomacy, savoir-faire, sensitivity. *See* **tact**.

tactic *noun*
1. An action calculated to achieve an end ▸ maneuver, measure, move, procedure, step. 2. A method of deploying troops and equipment in combat ▸ battle plan, maneuver, plan of attack, stratagem, strategy. 3. A method used for accomplishing something ▸ course, modus operandi, procedure, technique. *See* **approach** (1).

tactile *adjective*
1. Discernible by touch ▸ palpable, tangible, touchable. 2. Of, relating to, or arising from the sense of touch ▸ tactual.

tactility *noun*
1. The faculty or ability to perceive tactile stimulation ▸ feel, feeling, touch. *Idiom:* sense of touch. *See also* **sensation**. 2. The quality or condition of being discernible by touch ▸ corporeality, palpability, physicality. *See* **tangibility**.

taction *noun*
A coming together or touching ▸ contact, contingence, touch. *See also* **brush¹, touch**.

tactless *adjective*
Lacking sensitivity and skill in dealing with others ▸ brash, clumsy, gauche, impolitic, indelicate, insensitive, maladroit, undiplomatic, unpolitic, untactful. *See also* **abrupt, rude**.

tactlessness *noun*
▸ disregard, unthoughtfulness. *See* **thoughtlessness** (2).

tactual *adjective*
Of, relating to, or arising from the sense of touch ▸ tactile.

tad *noun*
▸ dash, drop, smidgen. *See* **bit¹** (1).

tag *verb*
1. To attach a ticket to ▸ earmark, flag, label, mark, ticket. 2. To set off by or as if by a mark indicating ownership or manufacture ▸ identify, label. *See* **mark** (1). *See synonym note at* **mark**. 3. To describe with a word or term ▸ designate, label, name. *See* **call** (4). 4. To keep another under surveillance by moving behind ▸ dog, heel, trail. *See* **follow** (3).

tag *noun*
1. An identifying or descriptive slip ▸ flag, label, tab. *See* **ticket** (1). 2. The word or words by which one is called and identified ▸ cognomen, epithet, title. *See* **name** (1).

tag end *noun*
▸ end, rear, tail. *See* **back**.

tail *noun*
1. Something that follows or is drawn along behind ▸ trail, train, wake. *See also* **stream**. 2. *Informal* An agent assigned to observe and report on another ▸ shadow, watcher. *See also* **detective**. 3. The part farthest from the front ▸ end, rear, tag end. *See* **back**. 4. *Slang* The part of the body on which one sits ▸ posterior, rump. *Slang:* fanny. *See* **buttocks**.

tail *adjective*
Bringing up the rear ▸ hindermost. *See* **last¹** (2).

tail *verb*
To keep another under surveillance by moving behind ▸ shadow, track, trail. *See* **follow** (3).

tail away *or* **off** *verb*
To become or cause to become gradually less ▸ diminish, dwindle, lessen. *See* **decrease**.

tail end *noun*
▸ end, rear, tail. *See* **back**.

tailor *verb*
1. To make or become suitable to a particular situation or use ▸ adjust, conform, fashion, fit. *See* **adapt**. *See synonym note at* **adapt**. 2. To alter or present material so as to favor a particular viewpoint ▸ doctor, slant. *See* **bias** (2).

tailored *adjective*
▸ custom-made, tailor-made. *See* **custom**.

tailor-made *adjective*
1. Made according to the specifications of the buyer ▸ custom-made, made-to-order. *See* **custom**. 2. Suitable for a particular person, condition, occasion, or place ▸ befitting, correct, right. *See* **appropriate** (1). 3. Suited to one's purpose ▸ expedient, proper, suitable. *See* **convenient** (1).

taint *verb*
1. To become or cause to become rotten or unsound ▸ deteriorate, rot, spoil, turn. *See* **decay**. 2. To ruin

morally ▸ debase, demoralize, deprave, warp. *See* **corrupt** (1). **3.** To attack the reputation or honor of ▸ besmirch, smear, tarnish. *See* **denigrate** (1). **4.** To make unclean or impure by contact or mixture ▸ adulterate, corrupt, pollute. *See* **contaminate** (1).

taint *noun*

1. A mark of discredit or disgrace ▸ blemish, spot. *See* **stain** (1). *See synonym note at* **stain**. **2.** One that contaminates ▸ impurity, poison, pollutant. *See* **contaminant**.

tainted *adjective*

▸ alloyed, combined, polluted. *See* **impure** (2).

taintlessness *noun*

▸ clarity, cleanliness, immaculacy. *See* **purity** (1).

take *verb*

1. To obtain possession or control of ▸ get, win. *Slang:* cop. *See* **capture** (1). **2.** To become affected with a disease ▸ develop, get. *See* **contract** (2). **3.** To have a sudden overwhelming effect on ▸ catch, seize, strike. **4.** To direct or impel to oneself by some quality or action ▸ appeal, draw. *See* **attract** (1). **5.** To cause to pass from the mouth into the stomach ▸ ingest, swallow. *See also* **drink, eat, gulp. 6.** To admit to one's possession, presence, or awareness ▸ accept, have, receive. *See also* **absorb. 7.** To engage in sexual relations with ▸ bed, mate. *See* **sleep with. 8.** To receive something given or offered willingly and gladly ▸ accept, embrace, take up, welcome. **9.** To lay claim to or take possession of ▸ appropriate, commandeer, usurp. *See* **seize** (1). **10.** To go aboard a means of transport ▸ board, catch. *Informal:* hop. **11.** To have as a need or prerequisite ▸ entail, involve, necessitate. *See* **demand** (2). **12.** To obtain from another source ▸ extract, receive. *See* **derive** (1). **13.** To put up with ▸ accept, stomach, tolerate, withstand. *See* **endure** (1). **14.** To act or operate in a specified way ▸ run, work. *See* **function. 15.** To perceive and recognize the meaning of ▸ apprehend, fathom, sense. *See* **understand** (1). **16.** To understand in a particular way ▸ construe, interpret, read. **17.** To cause to come along with oneself ▸ convey, fetch. *See* **bring** (1). **18.** To move something from a position occupied ▸ pick out, pluck out, take out, withdraw. *See* **remove** (1). **19.** To take away a quantity from another quantity ▸ abate, deduct, discount, rebate, subtract, take off. *Informal:* knock off. **20.** *Informal* To get something by deceitful trickery ▸ bilk, defraud, swindle. *See* **cheat** (1). **21.** To make a choice from a number of alternatives ▸ elect, pick (out), vote (for). *See* **choose** (1). **22.** To come into possession of ▸ come by, gain, procure. *See* **get** (1).

take after *verb*

To be similar especially in appearance ▸ be like, look like. *See* **resemble**.

take apart *verb*

To disassemble ▸ dismantle, dismount. *See* **disassemble**.

take away *verb*

1. To move something from a position occupied ▸ remove, take, take off, take out, withdraw. **2.** To take away a quantity from another quantity ▸ discount, subtract. *See* **deduct** (1).

take back *verb*

1. To occupy or take again ▸ reassume, reoccupy, repossess. *See* **resume** (1). **2.** To send, put, or carry back to a former location ▸ give back, restore. *See* **return** (2). **3.** To disavow something previously written or said irrevocably and usually formally ▸ abjure, recant, withdraw. *See* **retract** (1).

take down *verb*

1. To cause to descend ▸ drop, let down, sink. *See* **lower²** (1). **2.** To disassemble ▸ dismantle, dismount. *See* **disassemble**.

take in *verb*

1. To allow admittance, as to a group ▸ admit, let in, receive. *See* **accept** (3). **2.** To have as a part ▸ comprise, involve. *See* **contain** (1). *See synonym note at* **contain**. **3.** To perceive and recognize the meaning of ▸ apprehend, fathom, sense. *See* **understand** (1). **4.** To cause to accept something false, especially by trickery or misrepresentation ▸ dupe, fool, mislead, trick. *See* **deceive. 5.** To get the better of by cleverness or cunning ▸ outsmart, outthink, overreach. *See* **outwit**.

take off *verb*

1. To take from one's own person ▸ cast off, doff. *See* **remove** (6). **2.** To take away a quantity from another quantity ▸ discount, subtract. *See* **deduct** (1). **3.** To move something from a position occupied ▸ carry off, take out, withdraw. *See* **remove** (1). **4.** *Slang* To move away from a place ▸ exit, go away, retire. *See* **go** (1). **5.** *Slang* To leave hastily ▸ bolt. *Slang:* scram, vamoose. *See* **run** (3). **6.** To rise up in flight ▸ lift off.

take on *verb*

1. To take upon oneself ▸ shoulder, tackle. *See* **assume** (1). **2.** To go about the initial step in doing something ▸ enter (on), initiate, launch. *See* **start** (1). **3.** To obtain the use or services of ▸ hire, retain. *See* **employ** (1). **4.** To strive in opposition ▸ battle, fight, wrestle. *See* **contend** (1). **5.** To take and make one's own ▸ assume, embrace, espouse. *See* **adopt** (1).

take out *verb*

1. To move something from a position occupied ▸ tear out, uproot, withdraw. *See* **remove** (1). **2.** *Informal* To be with another person socially on a regular basis ▸ date, go out (with), go with, see. *Idioms:* go steady, go together. **3.** *Slang* To take the life of a person or persons unlawfully ▸ destroy, kill, slay. *See* **murder** (1).

take over *verb*

1. To free from a specific duty by acting as a substitute ▸ relieve, spell. *See also* **substitute. 2.** To seize or maintain control over by conquest ▸ capture, overrun, subjugate. *See* **occupy** (2). **3.** To take upon oneself ▸ shoulder, undertake. *See* **assume** (1).

take to *verb*

To find agreeable ▸ adore, fancy. *See* **like¹** (1).

take up *verb*

1. To move something to a higher position ▸ hoist, lift, raise. *See* **elevate** (1). **2.** To begin or go on after an interruption ▸ restart, resume. *See* **continue** (1). **3.** To be concerned with something ▸ address, consider, treat. *See* **deal** (1). **4.** To go about the initial step in doing something ▸ begin, embark, initiate. *See* **start** (1). **5.** To take in moisture or liquid ▸ absorb, soak (up), sop up. *See* **drink** (3). **6.** To take in and incorporate, especially mentally ▸ digest, imbibe, soak up. *See* **absorb** (2). **7.** To take and make one's own ▸ assume, embrace, take on. *See* **adopt** (1).

take *noun*
1. The amount of money collected as admission ▸ box office, gate, receipts. **2.** *Slang* A trying to do or make something ▸ effort, trial. *Informal:* shot. *See* **attempt** (1).

take-in *noun*
Informal An indirect, usually cunning means of gaining an end ▸ deception, ploy, stratagem. *See* **trick** (1).

takeoff *noun*
1. The act of rising in flight ▸ liftoff. **2.** A work that exposes folly by the use of humor, irony, or comic imitation ▸ burlesque, parody, spoof. *See* **satire.**

taking *adjective*
1. Pleasing to the eye or mind ▸ enchanting, fetching, lovely, winsome. *See* **attractive** (1). **2.** Capable of transmission by infection ▸ communicable, infectious, transmittable. *See* **contagious.**

tale *noun*
1. An untrue declaration ▸ falsehood, fib, untruth. *See* **lie**². **2.** An entertaining and often oral account of a real or fictitious occurrence ▸ fable, story. *See* **yarn.**

talebearer *noun*
1. A person habitually engaged in idle talk about others ▸ gossipmonger, taleteller, whisperer. *See* **gossip** (2). **2.** One who gives incriminating information about others ▸ source. *Slang:* snitch, squealer. *See* **informer.**

talebearing *noun*
Idle, often sensational and groundless talk about others ▸ hearsay, rumor, tattle. *See* **gossip** (1).

talebearing *adjective*
Inclined to gossip ▸ blabby, gossipy, taletelling.

talent *noun*
An innate capability ▸ aptitude, aptness, bent, faculty, flair, genius, gift, head, instinct, knack, turn. *See also* **ability.**

talented *adjective*
▸ endowed, natural. *See* **gifted.**

taleteller *noun*
▸ gossipmonger, snoop, whisperer. *See* **gossip** (2).

taletelling *adjective*
Inclined to gossip ▸ blabby, gossipy, talebearing.

talisman *noun*
▸ amulet, mascot. *See* **charm** (1).

talismanic *adjective*
▸ magical, witching, wizardly. *See* **magic** (1).

talk *verb*
1. To express oneself in speech ▸ speak, verbalize, vocalize. *See also* **babble, chatter. 2.** To direct speech to ▸ address, speak. **3.** To engage in spoken exchange ▸ chat, discourse. *See* **converse**¹. *See synonym note at* **converse**¹. **4.** To put into words ▸ express, state, utter. *See* **say** (1). **5.** To engage in or spread gossip ▸ rumor, whisper. *See* **gossip. 6.** To meet and exchange views to reach a decision ▸ talk. *Informal:* huddle, powwow. *See* **confer** (1). **7.** To give incriminating information about others, especially to the authorities ▸ tip (off). *Slang:* rat, snitch. *See* **inform** (2).

talk back *verb*
To utter an impertinent rejoinder ▸ talk up. *Informal:* sass, sauce. *Idiom:* give someone lip.

talk down *verb*
To represent or speak of as small or insignificant ▸ deprecate, disparage, slight. *See* **belittle.**

talk into *verb*
To succeed in causing a person to act or think in a certain way ▸ convince, prevail on. *See* **persuade** (1).

talk over *verb*
To speak together and exchange ideas and opinions about ▸ converse, debate. *Informal:* kick around. *See* **discuss.**

talk up *verb*
1. To attempt to sell or popularize by advertising or publicity ▸ ballyhoo, boost, publicize. *See* **promote** (3). **2.** To utter an impertinent rejoinder ▸ talk back. *Informal:* sass, sauce. *Idiom:* give someone lip.

talk *noun*
1. Spoken exchange ▸ dialogue, discourse, discussion. *See* **conversation** (1). **2.** The faculty, act, or product of speaking ▸ discourse, utterance. *See* **speech** (1). **3.** A usually formal spoken communication to an audience ▸ lecture, oration. *See* **speech** (2). **4.** The act or process of dealing with another to reach an agreement ▸ negotiation, parley. **5.** Idle, often sensational and groundless talk about others ▸ hearsay, rumor, tattle. *See* **gossip** (1). **6.** A formal discussion of a subject, either written or spoken ▸ dialogue, dissertation. *See* **discourse** (1).

talkative *adjective*
Given to conversation ▸ chatty, conversational, garrulous, loquacious, talky, voluble. *Slang:* gabby. *See also* **wordy.**

talker *noun*
▸ discourser, interlocutor. *See* **conversationalist.**

talkfest *noun*
Informal Spoken exchange ▸ dialogue, discourse, talk. *See* **conversation** (1).

talky *adjective*
▸ garrulous, loquacious, voluble. *See* **talkative.**

tall *adjective*
1. Not easy to do, achieve, or master ▸ arduous, laborious, tough. *See* **difficult** (1). **2.** Being of or at a relatively great height or altitude ▸ elevated, lofty. *See* **high** (1).

tall tale *noun*
1. *Informal* An entertaining and often oral account of a real or fictitious occurrence ▸ fable, story, tale. *See* **yarn. 2.** *Informal* An untrue declaration ▸ falsehood, fib, untruth. *See* **lie**². **3.** *Informal* An instance of

exaggerating ► hyperbolism, tall talk. *See* **exaggeration.**

tall talk *noun*
► hyperbolism, overstatement. *See* **exaggeration.**

tally *noun*
1. The total number of points made by a contestant, side, or team in a game or contest ► score. **2.** A noting of items one by one ► numeration, score. *See* **count** (1). **3.** A precise list of fees or charges ► bill, invoice, statement. *See* **account** (2).

tally *verb*
1. To gain a point or points in a game or contest ► post, score. *Informal:* notch. *Idioms:* make a goal (*or* point). **2.** To note items one by one in order to get a total ► numerate, score. *See* **count** (2). **3.** To be compatible or suitable ► chime, correspond, match. *See* **agree** (1).

tame *adjective*
1. Trained or bred to live with and be of use to people ► broken (in), housebroken, naturalized. *See* **domestic** (2). **2.** Easily managed or handled ► domesticated, mild, yielding. *See* **gentle** (3).

tame *verb*
1. To train to live with and be of use to people ► break in, master. *See* **domesticate.** **2.** To make an animal docile ► bust, master. *See* **gentle** (1). **3.** To make or become less severe or extreme ► soften, temper. *See* **moderate** (1).

tameness *noun*
► blandness, drabness, lifelessness. *See* **dullness** (1).

tamper *verb*
1. To prearrange the outcome of a contest ► fix, rig. *Idiom:* stack the deck. **2.** To handle something in an attempt to improve it ► fiddle, fool, mess. *See* **tinker** (1).

tang *noun*
► relish, taste, zest. *See* **flavor** (1). *See synonym note at* **flavor.**

tangent *noun*
► deviation, divergence, parenthesis. *See* **digression.**

tangential *adjective*
► long-winded, parenthetical, rambling. *See* **digressive.**

tangibility *noun*
The quality or condition of being tangible ► corporeality, palpability, physicality, tactility, tangibleness, touchableness. *See also* **matter.**

tangible *adjective*
1. Discernible by touch ► palpable, tactile, touchable. **2.** Composed of or relating to things that occupy space and can be perceived by the senses ► corporeal, substantial. *See* **physical** (1). **3.** Having physical or verifiable existence ► objective, substantial. *See* **real** (1).

tangle *noun*
1. Something that is intricately or bewilderingly complex ► cat's cradle, entanglement, imbroglio, jungle, knot, labyrinth, maze, mesh, morass, skein, snarl, web. **2.** *Informal* A discussion, often heated, in which a difference of opinion is expressed ► dispute, fight, quarrel. *See* **argument** (1).

tangle *verb*
1. To twist together so that separation is difficult ► foul, mat. *See* **entangle** (1). **2.** To make complex, intricate, or perplexing ► entangle, perplex, ravel. *See* **complicate.** **3.** To gain control of by trapping ► snare, trap. *See* **catch** (1). *See synonym note at* **catch.** **4.** *Informal* To engage in a quarrel ► dispute, fight, quarrel. *See* **argue** (1).

tangled *adjective*
► convoluted, elaborate, involved, labyrinthine. *See* **complex** (1). *See synonym note at* **complex.**

tangy *adjective*
► sharp, tart. *See* **sour** (1).

tank *noun*
► basin, cask, tub. *See* **vat.**

tanked *adjective*
Slang Stupefied, excited, or muddled with alcoholic liquor ► intoxicated, sodden, tipsy. *See* **drunk.**

tank up *verb*
► tipple. *Slang:* booze, lush. *See* **drink** (2).

tantalize *verb*
To excite by exposing something desirable while keeping it out of reach ► bait, tease. *Idiom:* make one's mouth water. *See also* **charm.**

tantalizing *adjective*
► bewitching, enticing, tempting. *See* **seductive.**

tantamount *adjective*
► identical, same. *See* **equal** (1).

tantrum *noun*
► fit, huff, passion. *See* **temper** (2).

tap[1] *verb*
1. To strike lightly or gently ► dab, flick, pat, rap. *See also* **brush**[1], **dig. 2.** To indicate time or rhythm ► beat, count. *Idioms:* keep time, mark time. **3.** To make rhythmic contractions, sounds, or movements ► pulsate, pulse, throb. *See* **beat** (5). **4.** To select for an office or position ► elect, name, nominate. *See* **appoint** (1). *See synonym note at* **appoint.**

tap *noun*
The sound made by a light blow ► knock, rap, rapping, tapping. *See also* **beat.**

tap[2] *verb*
1. To monitor telephone calls with a concealed device connected to the circuit ► bug, wiretap. **2.** To remove a liquid by a steady, gradual process ► pump, strain. *See* **drain** (1).

tap *noun*
1. A device that regulates the flow of a liquid ► fixture, spigot. *See* **faucet.** **2.** Something used to fill a hole, space, or container ► cork, stop. *See* **plug** (1).

tape *noun*
► sash, strap, strip. *See* **band**[1] (1).

taper *noun*
The act or process of decreasing ► diminishment, reduction, slash. *See* **decrease.**

taper *verb*
To become or cause to become gradually less ► abate,

dwindle, ebb, lessen, ratchet down. *See* **decrease.**

tar *noun*
▸ mariner, navigator, seafarer. *See* **sailor.**

tardily *adverb*
▸ behind, belatedly, slow. *See* **late.**

tardiness *noun*
The quality or condition of not being on time ▸ belatedness, lateness, slowness, unpunctuality.

tardy *adjective*
1. Not on time ▸ overdue, tardy. *See* **late** (1). *See synonym note at* **late. 2.** Proceeding at a rate less than usual or desired ▸ laggard, sluggish. *See* **slow** (1).

target *noun*
1. One that is fired at, attacked, or abused ▸ butt, mark. **2.** What one intends to do or achieve ▸ end, goal, objective. *See* **intention. 3.** A focus of attention, thought, or action ▸ focus, recipient, subject. *See* **object** (2).

target *verb*
1. To make a target of ▸ mark. *Idioms:* draw (*or* get) a bead on, get in one's sights. **2.** To have in mind as a goal or purpose ▸ design, plan. *See* **intend** (1).

tariff *noun*
1. A compulsory contribution that is required for the support of an authority ▸ duty, levy, tithe. *See* **tax** (1). **2.** A fixed amount of money charged for a service ▸ exaction, fee. *See* **toll**¹ (1).

tarnish *verb*
1. To spoil the soundness or perfection of ▸ flaw, impair. *See* **damage. 2.** To attack the reputation or honor of ▸ besmirch, smear, taint. *See* **denigrate** (1). **3.** To bring disgrace on ▸ abase, dishonor, shame. *See* **disgrace.**

tarnish *noun*
A mark of discredit or disgrace ▸ blemish, spot. *See* **stain** (1).

tarrier *noun*
▸ lag, procrastinator, straggler. *See* **laggard.**

tarry *verb*
1. To go or move slowly so that progress is hindered ▸ dawdle, dilly-dally, drag. *See* **delay** (2). **2.** To continue to be in a place ▸ bide, linger, wait. *See* **remain** (1). *See synonym note at* **remain.**

tart¹ *adjective*
Having a taste characteristic of that produced by acids ▸ acerbic, dry, sharp. *See* **sour** (1). *See synonym note at* **sour.**

tart² *noun*
1. A woman who engages in sex for payment ▸ courtesan, strumpet. *See* **harlot. 2.** A woman who is sexually promiscuous ▸ tramp, whore. *See* **slut.**

tartuffe *noun*
▸ dissembler, phony, poser. *See* **hypocrite.**

tartuffery *noun*
▸ phoniness, sanctimoniousness, sanctimony. *See* **hypocrisy.**

task *noun*
1. A piece of work that has been assigned ▸ assignment, chore, duty, job, office, project, stint. **2.** A

difficult or tedious undertaking ▸ chore, effort, grind, slog, sweat. *Informal:* job. *See also* **labor. 3.** The proper activity of a person or thing ▸ job, purpose, role. *See* **function** (1).

task *verb*
To force to work hard ▸ drive, push, tax, work. *Idiom:* crack the whip. *See also* **force.**

✢ **CORE SYNONYMS:** *task, job, chore, stint, assignment.* These nouns denote a piece of work that one must do. A *task* is a well-defined responsibility that is usually imposed by another and that may be burdensome: *I stayed at work late to finish the task at hand. Job* often suggests a specific short-term undertaking: *"did little jobs about the house with skill"* (W.H. Auden). *Chore* generally denotes a minor, routine, or odd job: *The farmer's morning chores included milking the cows. Stint* refers to a person's prescribed share of work: *Her stint as a lifeguard usually consumes three hours a day. Assignment* generally denotes a task allotted by a person in authority: *His homework assignment involved writing an essay.*

taskmaster *or* **taskmistress** *noun*
▸ manager, supervisor. *See* **boss** (1).

taste *verb*
1. To have a particular flavor or suggestion of something ▸ savor, smack, smell, suggest. *See also* **hint. 2.** To undergo an emotional reaction ▸ experience, feel, have, know, savor. **3.** To participate in or partake of personally ▸ feel, know. *See* **experience.**

taste *noun*
1. A liking for something ▸ fondness, partiality, preference, relish, weakness. *See also* **inclination. 2.** A limited or anticipatory experience ▸ foretaste, sample, sampling. *See also* **glance. 3.** A desire for food or drink ▸ hunger, stomach, thirst. *See* **appetite** (1). **4.** A distinctive property affecting the sense of taste ▸ smack, tang, zest. *See* **flavor** (1). *See synonym note at* **flavor. 5.** A slight amount or indication ▸ hint, semblance, trace. *See* **shade** (2). **6.** Refinement of manner, form, and style ▸ grace, refinement, sophistication. *See* **elegance. 7.** A small portion of food ▸ crumb, morsel. *See* **bit**¹ (2). **8.** An act of drinking or the amount swallowed ▸ draft, swallow. *Informal:* swig. *See* **drink** (2). **9.** The ability to distinguish, especially to recognize small differences or draw fine distinctions ▸ acuteness, selectiveness, subtlety. *See* **discrimination** (1). **10.** A small amount of liquor ▸ shot, sip, tot. *See* **drop** (8).

tasteful *adjective*
1. Showing good taste ▸ exquisite, graceful, refined. *See* **elegant** (1). **2.** Highly pleasing, especially to the sense of taste ▸ delectable, savory, scrumptious. *See* **delicious** (1). **3.** Not showy or obtrusive ▸ inobtrusive, quiet, subdued. *See* **modest** (1). **4.** Proper in appearance ▸ modest, respectable. *See* **decent** (7).

tastefulness *noun*
1. Refinement of manner, form, and style ▸ style, polish, sophistication. *See* **elegance. 2.** Lack of osten-

tation or pretension ▸ plainness, simpleness, simplicity. *See* **modesty** (2).

tasteless *adjective*
1. Lacking an appetizing flavor ▸ bland, insipid, unsavory. *See* **flat** (2). **2.** Lacking in delicacy or refinement ▸ indelicate, unbecoming, unrefined. *See* **coarse** (1).

tasty *adjective*
▸ delectable, savory, scrumptious. *See* **delicious** (1).

tatter *noun*
To wear away along the edges ▸ fray, frazzle. *See also* **erode, shred.**

tatterdemalion *noun*
A person wearing ragged or tattered clothing ▸ ragamuffin. *See also* **hobo.**

tatterdemalion *adjective*
Showing signs of wear and tear or neglect ▸ brokendown, dilapidated, shoddy. *See* **shabby** (1).

tattered *adjective*
▸ broken-down, decrepit, seedy. *See* **shabby** (1).

tatters *noun*
Torn and ragged clothing ▸ rags, shreds.

tattle *verb*
1. To engage in or spread gossip ▸ rumor, whisper. *See* **gossip.** *See synonym note at* **gossip. 2.** To give incriminating information about others, especially to the authorities ▸ tip (off). *Slang:* rat, snitch. *See* **inform** (2). **3.** To talk rapidly on trivial matters ▸ blab, jabber, prattle. *See* **chatter** (1).

tattle *noun*
1. Idle, often sensational and groundless talk about others ▸ hearsay, rumor, word. *See* **gossip** (1). **2.** Incessant and inconsequential talk ▸ drivel, patter, small talk. *See* **chatter. 3.** A person habitually engaged in idle talk about others ▸ gossipmonger, taleteller, whisperer. *See* **gossip** (2).

tattler *or* **tattletale** *noun*
1. A person habitually engaged in idle talk about others ▸ gossipmonger, taleteller, whisperer. *See* **gossip** (2). **2.** One who gives incriminating information about others ▸ informant. *Slang:* snitch, squealer. *See* **informer.**

tatty *adjective*
▸ broken-down, dilapidated, shoddy. *See* **shabby** (1).

taunt *noun*
1. An instance of mockery or derision ▸ cut, fleer, gibe, insult, jeer, scoff, twit. *Informal:* swipe. *Slang:* dig. *See also* **indignity, libel. 2.** Good-natured teasing ▸ badinage, banter, raillery. *See* **ribbing.**

taunt *verb*
1. To attack or disturb persistently ▸ harry, pester, torment. *See* **harass. 2.** To subject to ridicule ▸ jeer (at), lampoon, twit. *See* **ridicule.** *See synonym note at* **ridicule.**

taut *adjective*
1. Stretched tightly ▸ strained, tense, tight. *See also* **rigid. 2.** Characterized by an economy of artistic expression ▸ lean, spare. *See* **tight** (3). **3.** In good order or clean condition ▸ shipshape, tidy. *See* **neat** (1).

4. Feeling or exhibiting nervous tension ▸ jittery, tense. *See* **edgy.**

✦ CORE SYNONYMS: *taut, tense, tight.* These adjectives mean not slack or loose on account of being pulled or drawn out fully: *taut sails; tense piano strings; a tight shirt.*

---

tauten *verb*
▸ stiffen, stretch. *See* **tense.**

tautness *noun*
▸ strain, stress, tension. *See* **pressure** (1).

tautological *adjective*
▸ pleonastic, redundant, verbose. *See* **wordy** (1).

tavern *noun*
▸ inn, pub, saloon. *See* **bar** (2).

tawdry *adjective*
▸ flashy, garish, loud. *See* **gaudy.** *See synonym note at* **gaudy.**

tawny *adjective*
▸ brown, brunet, dusky. *See* **dark** (3).

tax *noun*
1. A compulsory contribution, usually of money, that is required for the support of an authority ▸ assessment, customs, duty, impost, levy, tariff, tithe, tribute. *See also* **toll. 2.** A source of persistent worry or hardship ▸ cross, tribulation. *See* **burden**[1] (1). **3.** A fixed amount of money charged for a service ▸ exaction, fee. *See* **toll**[1] (1).

tax *verb*
1. To force to work hard ▸ drive, push, task, work. *Idiom:* crack the whip. *See also* **force. 2.** To weigh down or place a heavy load on ▸ encumber, saddle, strain. *See* **burden**[1]. **3.** To make an accusation against ▸ charge, denounce, incriminate. *See* **accuse. 4.** To criticize for a fault or offense ▸ chide, rebuke, reprimand. *See* **chastise** (1).

tax with *verb*
To force another to accept a burden ▸ charge with, inflict on (*or* upon), saddle with. *See* **impose on** (1).

taxi *verb*
▸ chauffeur, motor, wheel. *See* **drive** (1).

taxing *adjective*
▸ backbreaking, onerous, trying. *See* **burdensome** (1).

taxpayer *noun*
▸ burgher, subject. *See* **citizen.**

tea *noun*
▸ celebration, gala, soiree. *See* **party** (1).

teach *verb*
▸ coach, discipline, instruct. *See* **educate** (1). *See synonym note at* **educate.**

teachable *adjective*
Capable of being educated ▸ docile, educable, trainable. *See also* **obedient.**

teacher *noun*
▸ instructor, trainer, tutor. *See* **educator.**

teaching *noun*
1. The act, process, or art of imparting knowledge and skill ▸ pedagogy, schooling. *See* **education** (1). **2.** A statement that is presented for acceptance, as by a

religious group ▸ dogma, tenet. *See* **doctrine.**
teaching *adjective*
Of or relating to education ▸ academic, pedagogic, scholastic. *See* **educational** (1).
team *noun*
▸ corps, squad, unit. *See* **force** (5).
teamwork *noun*
▸ collaboration, synergy. *See* **cooperation** (1).
tear¹ *verb*
1. To separate or pull apart by force ▸ rend, rip, rive, run, split. *See also* **cut, shred. 2.** To remove from a fixed position ▸ pluck, rend, wrest. *See* **pull** (2). **3.** To move swiftly ▸ dash, sprint, zip. *See* **rush.**
tear down *verb*
1. To pull down or break up so that reconstruction is impossible ▸ dismantle, level, wreck. *See* **destroy** (2). **2.** To make harmful and often untrue statements about ▸ calumniate, defame, slander. *See* **malign. 3.** To attack the reputation or honor of ▸ besmirch, smear, tarnish. *See* **denigrate** (1).
tear into *verb*
1. *Slang* To set upon with violent force ▸ assail, assault, strike. *See* **attack** (1). **2.** To criticize harshly ▸ excoriate, flay. *See* **slam** (5).
tear up *verb*
To pull or cut into many pieces ▸ grate, slice up. *See* **shred.**
tear *noun*
1. A hole made by tearing ▸ rent, rip, run. *See also* **crack. 2.** *Slang* A drinking bout ▸ brannigan, carousal, carouse, spree. *See* **bender.**

✚ **CORE SYNONYMS:** *tear, rip, rend, split.* These verbs mean to separate or pull apart by force. *Tear* involves pulling something apart or into pieces: *"She tore the letter in shreds"* (Edith Wharton). *Rip* implies rough or forcible tearing: *Carpenters ripped up the old floorboards. Rend* usually refers to violent tearing or wrenching apart: *"Come as the winds come, when/Forests are rended"* (Sir Walter Scott). To *split* is to cut or break something into parts or layers, especially along its entire length or along a natural line of division: *"They [wood stumps] warmed me twice—once while I was splitting them, and again when they were on the fire"* (Henry David Thoreau).

---

tear² *noun*
A quantity of liquid falling or resting in a spherical mass ▸ bead, droplet. *See* **drop** (1).
tear *verb*
1. To fill with tears ▸ water. **2.** To fall or let fall in drops of liquid ▸ dribble, trickle. *See* **drip.**
teardrop *noun*
▸ bead, droplet, globule. *See* **drop** (1).
tearful *adjective*
Filled with or shedding tears ▸ lachrymose, teary, weeping, weepy. *Idioms:* in tears, with tears in one's eyes. *See also* **depressed, sorrowful.**
tear-jerking *adjective*
Slang Affectedly or extravagantly emotional ▸ gushy, mawkish, soft. *See* **sentimental.**

tears *noun*
▸ blubbering, sobbing, weeping. *See* **cry** (1).
teary *adjective*
▸ weeping, weepy. *See* **tearful.**
tease *verb*
1. To arouse hope or desire without affording satisfaction ▸ bait, tantalize. *Idiom:* make one's mouth water. *See also* **charm. 2.** To attack or disturb persistently ▸ harry, pester, torment. *See* **harass.**
tease *noun*
1. A woman who is given to flirting ▸ coquette, flirt. *Informal:* vamp. *See also* **seductress. 2.** One who is habitually cruel to smaller or weaker people ▸ intimidator, tormentor. *See* **bully.**
technicality *noun*
▸ particular, specialty, technicality. *See* **detail** (1).
technique *noun*
1. A method used for accomplishing something ▸ course, modus operandi, procedure. *See* **approach** (1). **2.** Natural or acquired facility in a specific activity ▸ expertise, knack, skill. *See* **ability** (1). *See synonym note at* **ability.**
tedious *adjective*
▸ dull, humdrum, monotonous. *See* **boring** (1). *See synonym note at* **boring.**
tedium *or* **tediousness** *noun*
1. A tiresome lack of variety ▸ humdrum, sameness. *See* **monotony. 2.** The condition of being bored ▸ ennui, listlessness. *See* **boredom. 3.** A lack of excitement, liveliness, or interest ▸ blandness, drabness, lifelessness. *See* **dullness** (1).
tee-hee *verb*
To express amusement or mirth ▸ cackle, chuckle. *See* **laugh.**
tee-hee *noun*
An act of laughing ▸ cackle, chuckle, laughter. *See* **laugh** (1).
teem¹ *verb*
To be abundantly filled or richly supplied ▸ abound, bristle, crawl, flow, overflow, pullulate, roll, swarm, swim.

✚ **CORE SYNONYMS:** *teem, abound, crawl, overflow, swarm.* These verbs mean to be abundantly filled or richly supplied: *The street teemed with pedestrians. The garden abounds with flowers. The sidewalk was crawling with vendors. The house overflowed with guests. The parade route swarmed with spectators.*

---

teem² *verb*
To fall in drops of water from clouds ▸ pour, precipitate, shower. *See* **rain** (2).
teeming *adjective*
1. Filled beyond capacity ▸ congested, swarming. *See* **overcrowded. 2.** Full of lively activity ▸ bustling, crawling, swarming. *See* **busy** (2).
teen *noun*
▸ adolescent, youth. *See* **teenager.**
teenager *noun*
A young person, usually between the ages of 13 and

19 ▸ adolescent, teen, youth. *Informal:* kid, teener. *Slang:* teenybopper. *See also* **minor**.

teeny *or* **teensy** *or* **teeny-weeny** *or* **teensy-weensy** *adjective*
Informal Extremely small ▸ dwarf, miniature, minuscule. *See* **tiny**.

teenybopper *noun*
Slang A young person, usually between the ages of 13 and 19 ▸ adolescent, juvenile, youth. *See* **teenager**.

tee off *verb*
Informal To cause to feel or show anger ▸ incense, infuriate, madden. *See* **anger** (1).

teeter *verb*
1. To walk unsteadily ▸ reel, sway, totter. *See* **stagger** (1). **2.** To move back and forth ▸ swing, vacillate, waggle. *See* **sway** (1). **3.** To rest on a narrow or insecure surface ▸ poise, roost. *See* **balance** (3).

teetering *adjective*
▸ shaky, unstable, unsteady. *See* **insecure** (2).

teetotalism *noun*
▸ abstinence, sobriety. *See* **temperance** (2).

telephone *verb*
To communicate with someone by telephone ▸ buzz, call (up), dial, phone, ring (up). *Idioms:* get someone on the horn, give someone a buzz (*or* call *or* ring).

tell *verb*
1. To communicate the facts, details, or particulars of something ▸ narrate, recount, report. *See* **describe** (1). **2.** To put into words ▸ express, state, utter. *See* **say** (1). **3.** To make known ▸ disclose, divulge, transmit. *See* **communicate** (1). **4.** To disclose in a breach of confidence ▸ divulge, give away. *Informal:* spill. *See* **betray** (2). **5.** To impart information to ▸ advise, notify. *See* **inform** (1). **6.** To give orders to ▸ charge, instruct, order. *See* **command** (1). **7.** To recognize as being different ▸ differentiate, discriminate. *See* **distinguish** (1). **8.** To note items one by one in order to get a total ▸ numerate, tally. *See* **count** (2).

tell off *verb*
Informal To criticize for a fault or offense ▸ chide, rebuke, reprimand. *See* **chastise** (1).

telling *adjective*
▸ cogent, persuasive. *See* **convincing** (1).

telltale *noun*
▸ gossipmonger, taleteller, whisperer. *See* **gossip** (2).

tellurian *or* **telluric** *adjective*
▸ terrestrial, worldly. *See* **earthly** (1).

temblor *noun*
A shaking of the earth ▸ earthquake, quake, seism, tremor. *Informal:* shake.

temerarious *adjective*
▸ brash, hasty, impetuous. *See* **rash**[1]. *See synonym note at* **rash**[1].

temerity *noun*
Foolhardy boldness or disregard of danger ▸ brashness, foolhardiness, incautiousness, rashness, recklessness, temerariousness. *See also* **courage, daring**.

temper *noun*
1. A tendency to become angry or irritable ▸ bile, biliousness, cantankerousness, crankiness, disagreeability, hotheadedness, irascibility, irascibleness, irritability, orneriness, peevishness, petulance, petulancy, prickliness, spleen, temperament, testiness, tetchiness, waspishness. *Informal:* dander, meanness. *Slang:* short fuse. **Idiom:** low boiling point. *See also* **oversensitivity**. **2.** An angry outburst ▸ fit, huff, passion, tantrum. *Informal:* conniption, conniption fit, hissy, hissy fit. *See also* **state**. **3.** A prevailing quality, as of thought, behavior, or attitude ▸ climate, mood, spirit, timbre, tone. **4.** A person's customary manner of emotional response ▸ humor, nature, temperament. *See* **disposition** (1). **5.** A temporary state of mind or feeling ▸ humor, state of mind. *See* **mood** (1). *See synonym note at* **mood**.

temper *verb*
1. To make or become less severe or extreme ▸ play down, soften, tame. *See* **moderate** (1). *See synonym note at* **moderate**. **2.** To alter for proper or accurate functioning ▸ calibrate, fine-tune, regulate, tweak. *See* **adjust** (1).

temperament *noun*
1. A person's customary manner of emotional response ▸ habit, humor, nature. *See* **disposition** (1). **2.** The combination of qualities that distinguishes an individual ▸ makeup, nature, personality. *See* **character** (1). *See synonym note at* **character**. **3.** A tendency to become angry or irritable ▸ crankiness, prickliness, tetchiness. *See* **temper** (1).

temperamental *adjective*
1. Given to changeable emotional states, especially of anger or gloom ▸ moody. *See also* **testy**. **2.** Marked by whim or impulse ▸ fickle, impulsive, mercurial. *See* **capricious**.

temperance *noun*
1. Moderation or restraint of one's behavior or desires ▸ abstinence, continence, self-denial, sobriety. **2.** The practice of refraining from use of alcoholic liquors ▸ abstinence, dryness, soberness, sobriety, teetotalism. **3.** Avoidance of extremes of opinion, feeling, or personal conduct ▸ abstemiousness, sobriety. *See* **moderation** (1).

✚ CORE SYNONYMS: *temperance, sobriety, abstinence, self-denial, continence.* These nouns refer to the moderation or restraint of one's appetites or desires. *Temperance* refers to moderation and self-restraint and *sobriety* to gravity in bearing, manner, or treatment; both nouns denote moderation in or abstinence from the consumption of alcoholic liquor: *Teetotalers preach temperance for everyone.* "[T]hose moments which would come between the subsidence of actual sobriety and the commencement of intoxication" (Anthony Trollope). *Abstinence* implies the willful avoidance of pleasures, especially of food and drink, thought to be harmful or self-indulgent: "*I vainly reminded him of his protracted abstinence from food*" (Emily Brontë). *Self-denial* suggests resisting one's own desires for the achievement of a higher goal: *I practiced self-denial to provide for my family's needs.*

Continence specifically refers to abstention from sexual activity: *The nun took a vow of continence.*

temperate *adjective*
1. Free from extremes in temperature ▸ balmy, clement, mild, moderate. *See also* **pleasant**. 2. Characterized by self-restraint in appetites and behavior ▸ abstemious, continent, sober, spartan, unindulgent. *See also* **ascetic**. 3. Kept within sensible limits ▸ moderate, reasonable, restrained. *See* **conservative** (2).

tempest *noun*
1. An atmospheric disturbance characterized by strong winds and precipitation ▸ blow, gale, squall, tempest. *See* **storm** (1). 2. A condition of being agitated or disturbed ▸ ferment, turmoil, unrest. *See* **agitation** (1).

tempestuous *adjective*
1. Violently disturbed or agitated, as by storms ▸ roily, turbulent, violent. *See* **rough** (2). 2. Marked by unrest or disturbance ▸ stormy, tumultuous, turbulent. *See* **agitated** (1).

tempo *noun*
Rate of motion or performance ▸ pace, speed, velocity. *Informal:* clip.

temporal *adjective*
1. Relating to or characteristic of the earth or of human life on earth ▸ terrestrial, worldly. *See* **earthly** (1). 2. Lasting or existing only for a short time ▸ ephemeral, fleeting, temporary. *See* **transitory**. 3. Not religious in subject matter, form, or use ▸ nonecclesiastical, secular, worldly. *See* **profane** (2).

temporary *adjective*
1. Temporarily assuming the duties of another ▸ acting, ad interim, interim, pro tem, provisional, substitute. *Informal:* fill-in. 2. Intended, used, or present for a limited time ▸ ad hoc, impermanent, interim, make-do, makeshift, provisional, short-range, short-term, stopgap. 3. Lasting or existing only for a short time ▸ ephemeral, fleeting. *See* **transitory**.

✦ CORE SYNONYMS: *temporary, acting, ad interim, interim, provisional.* These adjectives mean temporarily assuming the duties of another: *a temporary chairperson; the acting dean; an ad interim admissions committee; an interim administration; a provisional mayor.*

◂ ANTONYM: *permanent*

tempt *verb*
1. To beguile or draw into a wrong or foolish course of action, especially a sexual act ▸ entice, lure. *See* **seduce**. *See synonym note at* **seduce**. 2. To behave so as to bring on danger, for example ▸ provoke, solicit. *See* **court** (1).

temptation *noun*
▸ bait, draw, enticement. *See* **lure** (1).

tempter *noun*
▸ charmer, lurer. *See* **seducer** (1).

tempting *adjective*
1. Pleasing to the eye or mind ▸ enchanting, fetching, lovely, winsome. *See* **attractive** (1). 2. Tending to seduce ▸ bewitching, enticing, tantalizing. *See* **seductive**.

temptress *noun*
▸ femme fatale, siren. *See* **seductress**.

tenable *adjective*
1. Capable of being justified ▸ defensible, excusable, justifiable. *See also* **logical, sound²**. 2. Capable of being defended against armed attack ▸ defendable, defensible. *See also* **safe**.

tenacious *adjective*
1. Persistently holding to something ▸ clinging, firm. *See* **tight** (1). 2. Firmly, often unreasonably immovable in purpose or will ▸ bullheaded, dogged, obstinate. *See* **stubborn** (1).

tenacity *or* **tenaciousness** *noun*
▸ bullheadedness, hardheadedness, rigidity. *See* **stubbornness**.

tenant *noun*
▸ denizen, occupant, resident. *See* **inhabitant**.

tend¹ *verb*
To have a tendency or inclination ▸ incline, lean, skew, slant, squint, trend. *See also* **inclined**.

tend² *verb*
1. To have the care and supervision of ▸ attend, baby-sit, care for, look after, mind, minister to, see to, watch (over). *Idioms:* keep an eye on, look out for, take care (*or* charge) of, take under one's wing. *See also* **administer, serve, supervise**. 2. To raise crops or animals ▸ cultivate, propagate. *See* **grow** (1). 3. To help grow or develop ▸ foster, nourish. *See* **nurture**.

✦ CORE SYNONYMS: *tend, attend, mind, minister to, watch.* These verbs mean to have the care or supervision of: *tended her plants; attends the sick; minded the unreliable furnace; ministered to flood victims; watched the house while the owners were away.*

tendency *noun*
1. A natural or habitual preference for something ▸ disposition, leaning, penchant. *See* **inclination** (1). 2. The current of thought uniting all elements of a text or discourse ▸ drift, intent, tenor. *See* **thrust** (1).

tendentious *adjective*
▸ partial, prejudiced, skewed. *See* **biased** (1).

tendentiousness *noun*
▸ partiality, prejudice. *See* **bias** (1).

tender¹ *adjective*
1. Of a sympathetic, considerate character ▸ kindly, softhearted, tenderhearted. *See* **gentle** (1). 2. Feeling or expressing fond feelings or affection ▸ caring, loving. *See* **affectionate**. 3. Feeling or expressing sympathy or pity ▸ compassionate, empathetic, understanding. *See* **sympathetic**. 4. Marked by, causing, or experiencing physical pain ▸ achy, hurtful, sore. *See* **painful** (1).

tender² *noun*
An act of offering or the thing offered ▸ invitation, proffer. *See* **offer** (1). *See synonym note at* **offer**.

tender *verb*
To put before another for acceptance ▸ extend, proffer. *See* **offer** (1).

tenderfoot *noun*
▸ fledgling, neophyte, novice. *See* **beginner.**

tenderhearted *adjective*
▸ kindly, softhearted, tender. *See* **gentle** (1).

tenderness *noun*
1. An intense attachment to a person or thing ▸ affection, fondness, liking. *See* **love** (1). **2.** Thoughtful attention to others ▸ concern, regard, thoughtfulness. *See* **consideration** (1). **3.** An instance of being irritated, as in a part of the body ▸ irritation, soreness. *See* **irritation** (3).

tending *adjective*
▸ disposed, prone. *See* **inclined** (1).

tendril *noun*
▸ bine, runner, sprout. *See* **shoot** (1).

tenebrific *adjective*
▸ bleak, desolate, somber. *See* **gloomy** (1).

tenet *noun*
1. A statement presented for acceptance or belief ▸ dogma, gospel, teaching. *See* **doctrine.** *See synonym note at* **doctrine. 2.** A principle governing affairs within or among political units ▸ decree, edict, institute. *See* **law** (1).

tenor *noun*
1. The general sense or significance, as of an action or statement ▸ burden, purport, substance. *See* **import** (1). **2.** The thread or current of thought uniting or occurring in all the elements of a text or discourse ▸ drift, intent, purport. *See* **thrust** (1).

tense *adjective*
1. Stretched tightly ▸ taut, tight. *See synonym note at* **taut.** *See also* **rigid. 2.** Feeling or exhibiting nervous tension ▸ jittery, nervous. *See* **edgy. 3.** Suggesting drama or a stage performance, as in emotionality or suspense ▸ melodramatic, sensational, spectacular. *See* **dramatic** (2).

tense *verb*
To make or become tense ▸ brace, stiffen, stretch, tauten, tighten.

tenseness *noun*
1. An oppressive condition of distress ▸ tautness, tension. *See* **pressure** (1). **2.** An uneasy or nervous state ▸ uneasiness, unrest. *See* **restlessness.**

tension *noun*
An oppressive condition of distress ▸ stress, tautness, tenseness. *See* **pressure** (1).

ten-strike *noun*
Informal A dazzling, often sudden instance of success ▸ sleeper. *Informal:* smash. *See* **hit** (3).

tentative *adjective*
1. Not perfected, elaborated, or completed ▸ preliminary, sketchy, unpolished. *See* **rough** (10). **2.** Depending on or containing a condition or conditions ▸ contingent, provisional, provisory. *See* **conditional. 3.** Given to or exhibiting hesitation ▸ indecisive, irresolute. *See* **hesitant** (1). **4.** Experiencing doubt ▸ hesitant, skeptical, uncertain. *See* **doubtful** (2).

tentativeness *noun*
▸ indecision, vacillation. *See* **hesitation.**

tenuous *adjective*
▸ flimsy, insubstantial, shaky, thin. *See* **implausible.**

tenure *noun*
The holding of a position ▸ incumbency, occupancy, occupation. *See also* **period.**

tepid *adjective*
Lacking warmth, interest, enthusiasm, or involvement ▸ halfhearted, Laodicean, lukewarm, unenthusiastic. *See also* **apathetic, cold, cool.**

tergiversate *verb*
1. To use evasive or deliberately vague language ▸ hedge, shuffle. *See* **equivocate** (1). **2.** To abandon one's cause or party usually to join another ▸ desert, quit, turn. *See* **defect.**

tergiversation *noun*
1. An instance of defecting from or abandoning a cause ▸ abandonment, disavowal, renouncement. *See* **defection. 2.** The use or an instance of equivocal language ▸ euphemism, prevarication. *See* **equivocation** (1). **3.** An expression or term liable to more than one interpretation ▸ double-entendre, equivocation. *See* **ambiguity** (1).

tergiversator *noun*
▸ deserter, recreant, traitor. *See* **defector.**

term *noun*
1. A sound or combination of sounds that symbolizes and communicates a meaning ▸ expression, lexical item, lexeme, locution, vocable, word. *See also* **speech. 2.** A specific length of time characterized by the occurrence of certain conditions or events ▸ span, stretch, term. *See* **period** (1). **3.** The period during which someone or something exists ▸ existence, span, time. *See* **life** (1). **4.** A restricting or modifying element ▸ condition, proviso, stipulation. *See* **provision** (1).

term *verb*
1. To describe with a word or term ▸ designate, label, name. *See* **call** (4). **2.** To give a name or title to ▸ christen, designate. *See* **name** (1).

termagant *noun*
▸ harpy, shrew. *See* **scold.**

terminal *adjective*
1. Of or relating to a terminative condition, stage, or point ▸ final, last, latter, ultimate. *See also* **climactic. 2.** Coming after all others ▸ concluding, final. *See* **last¹** (1). *See synonym note at* **last.**

terminal *noun*
1. The act or fact of coming together ▸ confluence, conflux, convergence. *See* **junction** (1). **2.** A socket connected to a power supply ▸ plug, socket. *See* **outlet** (1). **3.** A stopping place along a route for picking up or dropping off passengers ▸ depot, station, stop, terminus.

terminate *verb*
1. To bring an activity or relationship to an end suddenly ▸ break off, cease, discontinue, interrupt, suspend. **2.** To relinquish one's engagement in or

occupation with ▸ demit, leave, quit, resign. *Idioms:* hang it up, throw in the towel. *See also* **break. 3.** To bring or come to a natural or proper end ▸ close, end, finish. *See* **conclude** (1). *See synonym note at* **conclude. 4.** To end the employment or service of ▸ cashier, drop. *See* **dismiss** (1). **5.** To become void, especially through passage of time or an omission ▸ cease, run out. *See* **lapse** (1).

termination *noun*
1. A concluding or terminating ▸ cease, completion, period. *See* **end** (1). **2.** The act of dismissing or the condition of being dismissed from employment ▸ expulsion, removal. *See* **dismissal** (1). **3.** The last part ▸ closing, ending, epilogue. *See* **end** (2).

terminology *noun*
▸ jargon, lingo, patois. *See* **language** (2).

terminus *noun*
1. A stopping place along a route for picking up or dropping off passengers ▸ depot, station, stop, terminal. **2.** A concluding or terminating ▸ cease, completion, termination. *See* **end** (1).

terms *noun*
▸ footing, standing. *See* **basis** (3).

terpsichorean *noun*
A person who dances, especially professionally ▸ chorine, chorus boy, chorus girl, dancer. *Slang:* hoofer.

terrain *noun*
1. The character, natural features, and configuration of land ▸ topography. *Idiom:* the lay of the land. **2.** A sphere of activity, experience, study, or interest ▸ department, domain, field. *See* **area** (1). **3.** A particular area used for or associated with a specific individual or activity ▸ country, district, region. *See* **territory** (1). **4.** The soft part of the land surface of the world ▸ ground, soil. *See* **earth** (1).

terrene *adjective*
Relating to or characteristic of the earth or of human life on earth ▸ terrestrial, worldly. *See* **earthly** (1).

terrestrial *adjective*
1. Consisting of or resembling soil ▸ earthen, earthlike, earthy. **2.** Relating to or characteristic of the earth or of human life on earth ▸ earthbound, worldly. *See* **earthly** (1).

terrible *adjective*
1. Very bad ▸ abysmal, appalling, awful, dreadful, fearful, frightful, ghastly, horrendous, horrible, lousy, pathetic, pitiful, rotten, shocking, woebegone, wretched. *Slang:* crappy. *Idiom:* for the birds. *See also* **bad, deplorable. 2.** Causing or capable of causing fear ▸ appalling, dreadful, frightful, tremendous. *See* **fearful** (1). **3.** Extreme in activity, strength, or effect ▸ fierce, furious. *See* **intense** (1).

terrific *adjective*
1. Exceptionally good of its kind ▸ first-rate, prime, splendid, tiptop. *See* **excellent. 2.** Particularly excellent ▸ fabulous, glorious, sensational. *See* **marvelous** (1). **3.** Causing great horror ▸ hair-raising, horrific, nightmarish. *See* **horrible** (1).

terrified *adjective*
▸ fearful, frightened, scared. *See* **afraid.**

terrify *verb*
▸ horrify, scare. *Informal:* spook. *See* **frighten.** *See synonym note at* **frighten.**

territorial *adjective*
Relating to or restricted to a particular territory ▸ regional, sectional. *See also* **local.**

territory *noun*
1. A particular area used for or associated with a specific individual or activity ▸ belt, country, district, region, terrain, zone. *Slang:* turf. *See also* **environment. 2.** An area subject to rule by an outside power ▸ dependency, province. *See* **possession** (1). **3.** A sphere of activity, experience, study, or interest ▸ department, domain, field, terrain. *See* **area** (1). *See synonym note at* **area. 4.** An area regularly covered, as by a policeman or reporter ▸ round, route. *See* **beat** (2). **5.** The natural environment specific to an animal or plant ▸ habitation, range. *See* **habitat** (1). **6.** An area or set of parameters within which something or someone exists, acts, or has influence ▸ extent, realm, scope. *See* **range** (1).

terror *noun*
▸ apprehension, consternation, trepidation. *See* **fear.** *See synonym note at* **fear.**

terrorize *verb*
▸ horrify, scare, terrify. *See* **frighten.** *See synonym note at* **frighten.**

terse *adjective*
▸ concise, short, succinct. *See* **brief** (1).

test *noun*
1. A procedure that ascertains effectiveness, value, proper function, or other quality ▸ assay, dry run, essay, evaluation, experiment, experimentation, proof, shakedown, trial, tryout. *See also* **estimate. 2.** A set of questions or exercises designed to determine knowledge or skill ▸ catechism, catechization, exam, examination, quiz. *See also* **inquiry. 3.** A means by which individuals are compared and judged ▸ criterion, mark, measure. *See* **standard** (1).

test *verb*
1. To subject to a test of effectiveness, value, function, or other quality ▸ appraise, assay, check, essay, evaluate, examine, prove, try (out). *Idioms:* bring to the test, make trial of, put to the proof (*or* test). **2.** To subject to a test of knowledge or skill ▸ catechize, examine, quiz. *See also* **ask.**

test *adjective*
Serving as a tentative model for future experiment or development ▸ probative, trial. *See* **pilot.**

testament *noun*
▸ authentication, corroboration, proof, verification. *See* **confirmation** (2).

testifier *noun*
One who testifies, especially in court ▸ attestant, attester, deponent, witness.

testify *verb*
1. To give evidence or testimony under oath ▸ attest,

depone, depose, swear, witness. *Idioms:* bear witness, take the stand. **2.** To confirm formally as true, accurate, or genuine ▸ attest, verify, witness. *See* **certify** (1). **3.** To assure the certainty or validity of ▸ authenticate, corroborate, substantiate, verify. *See* **confirm** (1). **4.** To give grounds for believing in the existence or presence of ▸ attest, witness. *See* **indicate** (1). *See synonym note at* **indicate**.

testimonial *noun*
1. A statement attesting to personal qualifications, character, and dependability ▸ character, recommendation, reference. *See also* **endorsement**. **2.** A formal token of appreciation and admiration for a person's high achievements ▸ ovation, salute, salvo, tribute. *See also* **honor, memorial, toast²**. **3.** That which confirms ▸ authentication, corroboration, proof, verification. *See* **confirmation** (2).

testimony *noun*
1. A formal declaration of truth or fact given under oath ▸ affidavit, deposition, witness. **2.** That which confirms ▸ authentication, corroboration, proof, verification. *See* **confirmation** (2).

testiness *noun*
▸ crankiness, prickliness, tetchiness. *See* **temper** (1).

testy *adjective*
1. Easily moved to anger ▸ choleric, irascible, peppery, quick-tempered, short-tempered, tetchy, touchy. **2.** Having or showing a bad temper ▸ cranky, grouchy, peevish. *See* **ill-tempered**.

tetchiness *noun*
▸ crankiness, prickliness, testiness. *See* **temper** (1).

tetchy *adjective*
▸ irascible, quick-tempered, touchy. *See* **testy** (1).

tete-a-tete *noun*
▸ dialogue, discourse, talk. *See* **conversation** (1).

text *noun*
▸ matter, topic, theme. *See* **subject** (1).

texture *noun*
1. A distinctive, complex underlying pattern or structure ▸ contexture, fabric, fiber, grain, warp and woof, weave, web. *See also* **character, form, quality**. **2.** A basic trait or set of traits that define and establish the character of something ▸ nature, quintessence. *See* **essence** (1).

thalassic *adjective*
▸ maritime, sea, pelagic. *See* **marine** (1).

thankful *adjective*
1. Showing or feeling gratitude ▸ appreciative, grateful. **2.** Owing something, such as gratitude, to another ▸ beholden, indebted, obligated. *See* **obliged** (1).

thankfulness *noun*
▸ acknowledgment, gratitude, thankfulness. *See* **appreciation** (1).

thankless *adjective*
1. Not showing or feeling gratitude ▸ unappreciative, ungrateful, unthankful, unthanking. **2.** Not apt to be appreciated ▸ unappreciated, ungrateful, unthankful.

thanks *noun*
1. A short prayer said at meals ▸ benediction, blessing,

grace, thanksgiving. *See also* **prayer¹**. **2.** A being grateful ▸ gratitude, thankfulness. *See* **appreciation** (1).

thanksgiving *noun*
A short prayer said at meals ▸ benediction, blessing, grace, thanks. *See also* **prayer¹**.

thaumaturgic *or* **thaumaturgical** *adjective*
▸ magical, witching, wizardly. *See* **magic** (1).

thaumaturgy *noun*
▸ conjuration, sorcery, witchcraft. *See* **magic** (1).

thaw *verb*
▸ dissolve, liquefy, run. *See* **melt** (1).

theater *noun*
The art and occupation of an actor ▸ acting, dramatics, stage, theatrics.

theatric *or* **theatrical** *adjective*
1. Of or relating to drama or the theater ▸ histrionic, theatrical, thespian. *See* **dramatic** (1). **2.** Suggesting drama or a stage performance, as in emotionality or suspense ▸ melodramatic, sensational, spectacular. *See* **dramatic** (2).

theatricalism *or* **theatricality** *noun*
Showy mannerisms and behavior ▸ campiness, exhibitionism, staginess, theatricalness. *See also* **affectation, theatrics**.

theatricals *noun*
▸ histrionics, melodramatics, play-acting. *See* **theatrics** (2).

theatricism *noun*
▸ airs, mannerism. *See* **affectation** (1).

theatrics *noun*
1. The art and occupation of an actor ▸ acting, dramatics, stage, theater. **2.** Overemotional, exaggerated behavior calculated for effect ▸ dramatics, histrionics, melodrama, melodramatics, play-acting, theatricals. *See also* **theatricalism**.

theft *noun*
▸ pilferage, stealing, thievery. *See* **larceny**.

thematic *adjective*
Of, constituting, or relating to a theme or themes ▸ motivic, topical.

theme *noun*
1. The main part of a word to which affixes are attached ▸ base, radical, root, simplex, stem. **2.** A relatively brief discourse written especially as an exercise ▸ composition, essay, paper. **3.** What a speech, piece of writing, or artistic work is about ▸ matter, text. *See* **subject** (1). *See synonym note at* **subject**. **4.** A pleasing succession or arrangement of sound ▸ aria, tune. *See* **melody**.

theorem *noun*
1. A broad and basic rule or truth ▸ axiom, principle. *See* **law** (3). **2.** A proposition maintained by argument or empirical evidence ▸ hypothesis, thesis. *See* **theory** (2).

theoretical *or* **theoretic** *adjective*
1. Concerned primarily with theories rather than practical matters ▸ abstract, academic, armchair, conceptual, ideological, impractical, ivory-tower, moot,

speculative. *See also* **idealistic. 2.** Existing only in concept and not in reality ▸ abstract, conceptual, hypothetic, hypothetical, hypothesized, ideal, impractical, notional, postulated, virtual. *See also* **imaginary, supposed. 3.** Not tested or proved ▸ unpracticed, unproved, untested. *See* **untried** (1).

✛ **CORE SYNONYMS:** *theoretical, abstract, academic, armchair, speculative.* These adjectives mean concerned primarily with theories rather than practical matters: *theoretical linguistics; abstract reasoning; a purely academic discussion; armchair reasoning; speculative knowledge.*

---

theoretics *noun*
▸ conceptualization, philosophizing, speculation. *See* **theory** (1).

theorist *or* **theoretic** *noun*
1. A person who seeks truth by thinking ▸ philosopher, reasoner, thinker. **2.** A person inclined to be imaginative or idealistic but impractical ▸ fantasist, romantic, stargazer. *See* **dreamer** (1).

theorization *noun*
▸ conceptualization, philosophizing, speculation. *See* **theory** (1).

theorize *verb*
To formulate as a tentative explanation ▸ hypothesize, speculate. *See also* **suppose.**

theorizer *noun*
▸ fantasist, romantic, stargazer. *See* **dreamer** (1).

theory *noun*
1. Abstract reasoning, as opposed to experience ▸ conceptualization, conjecture, philosophizing, reasoning, speculating, speculation, theoretics, theorization, theorizing. *See also* **thought. 2.** A proposition maintained by argument or empirical evidence ▸ contention, hypothesis, proposal, theorem, thesis. *See also* **assumption, reason. 3.** A statement presented for acceptance, as by a religious group ▸ dogma, teaching. *See* **doctrine.**

therapeutic *adjective*
▸ remedial, restorative. *See* **curative.**

therapy *or* **therapeutics** *noun*
▸ care, doctoring, regimen, rehabilitation. *See* **treatment** (1).

thesis *noun*
1. A formal discussion of a subject ▸ dissertation, monograph. *See* **discourse** (1). **2.** A proposition maintained by argument or empirical evidence ▸ hypothesis, proposition. *See* **theory** (2). **3.** A statement presented for acceptance, as by a religious group ▸ dogma, teaching. *See* **doctrine.**

thespian *noun*
A theatrical performer ▸ actor, actress, player, trouper. *See also* **fake, lead, mimic.**

thespian *adjective*
Of or relating to drama or the theater ▸ dramaturgical, histrionic, theatrical. *See* **dramatic** (1).

theurgic *or* **theurgical** *adjective*
▸ magical, witching, wizardly. *See* **magic** (1).

theurgy *noun*
▸ conjuration, sorcery, witchcraft. *See* **magic** (1).

thick *adjective*
1. Relatively great in extent from one surface to the opposite ▸ fat. *See also* **bulky. 2.** Having all parts near to each other ▸ close, compact, compressed, consolidated, crowded, dense, packed, tight. *See also* **full. 3.** Growing profusely ▸ dense, heavy, lush, luxuriant, overgrown, profuse, rank. **4.** Short, heavy, and solidly built ▸ chunky, heavyset, squat. *See* **stocky. 5.** *Informal* Lacking in intelligence ▸ dumb, idiotic, obtuse. *See* **stupid** (1). **6.** *Informal* Very closely associated ▸ close, cozy, familiar. *See* **intimate**¹ (1). **7.** Having a heavy, gluey quality ▸ mucilaginous, viscid. *See* **viscous.**

thick *noun*
The most intensely active central part ▸ eye, midst. *See also* **center.**

thicken *verb*
To make thick or thicker, especially through evaporation or condensation ▸ condense, inspissate, reduce. *See also* **coagulate.**

thicket *noun*
▸ bushes, chaparral, undergrowth. *See* **brush**².

thickhead *noun*
▸ dummy, imbecile, numskull. *See* **dullard.**

thickheaded *adjective*
▸ dumb, idiotic, obtuse. *See* **stupid** (1).

thickness *noun*
1. The condition or degree of being dense or close together ▸ closeness, compaction, compactness, denseness, density. **2.** The physical property of being viscous ▸ glutinousness, stickiness. *See* **viscosity.**

thickset *adjective*
▸ chunky, heavyset, squat. *See* **stocky.**

thick-witted *adjective*
1. Lacking in intelligence ▸ dumb, idiotic, obtuse. *See* **stupid** (1). **2.** Having only a limited ability to learn and understand ▸ dense, dull. *See* **backward** (1).

thief *noun*
A person who steals ▸ bandit, brigand, burglar, highwayman, housebreaker, larcener, larcenist, looter, pickpocket, pilferer, purloiner, robber, stealer.

thieve *verb*
▸ carry off, purloin, snatch. *See* **steal** (1).

thievery *noun*
▸ pilferage, stealing, theft. *See* **larceny.**

thievish *or* **thieving** *adjective*
Given to committing theft ▸ larcenous, light-fingered, sticky-fingered.

thin *adjective*
1. Having little flesh or fat on the body ▸ angular, bony, fleshless, gaunt, gracile, lank, lanky, lean, meager, rawboned, scrawny, skinny, slender, slim, spare, stringy, svelte, twiggy, weedy, willowy. *Idioms:* all skin and bones, skinny as a rail (*or* post *or* beanpole). *See also* **gangling. 2.** Marked by great diffusion of component particles ▸ attenuate, attenuated, rare, rarefied. **3.** Lower than normal in strength or concentration due to admixture ▸ cut, washy. *See* **dilute.**

4. Conspicuously deficient in quantity, fullness, or extent ▸ puny, scant, skimpy. *See* **meager** (1). **5.** Not plausible or believable ▸ improbable, inconceivable. *See* **implausible. 6.** Being weak in quality or substance ▸ bloodless, pallid. *See* **pale** (2).

thin *verb*

1. To lose body weight, as by dieting ▸ slim (down), trim down. *Idioms:* get the weight off, lose weight, shed some pounds. **2.** To become diffuse ▸ attenuate, rarefy. **3.** To lessen the strength of by or as if by admixture ▸ cut, weaken. *See* **dilute.**

thin out *verb*

To disappear by or as if by rising ▸ dissipate, scatter, withdraw. *See* **lift** (4).

✤ CORE SYNONYMS: *thin, lean, spare, skinny, scrawny, lank, lanky, rawboned, gaunt.* These adjectives mean having little flesh or fat on the body. *Thin* is the most general: *clothing that only thin models could wear. Lean* emphasizes absence of fat: *fattened the lean cattle for market. Spare* sometimes suggests trimness and good muscle tone: *"an old man, very tall and spare, with an ascetic aspect"* (William H. Mallock). *Skinny* and *scrawny* imply unattractive thinness, as with undernourishment: *The child has skinny legs with prominent knees. "He* [had] *a long, scrawny neck that rose out of a very low collar"* (Winston Churchill). *Lank* describes one who is thin and tall, and *lanky* one who is thin, tall, and ungraceful: *"He was . . . exceedingly lank, with narrow shoulders"* (Washington Irving). *The boy had developed into a lanky adolescent. Rawboned* suggests a thin, bony, gangling build: *a rawboned cowhand. Gaunt* implies boniness and a haggard appearance, it may suggest illness or hardship: *a white-haired pioneer, her face gaunt from overwork.*

---

thing *noun*

1. One that exists independently ▸ being, entity, existence, existent, individual, object, something. **2.** Something having material existence ▸ article, body, item. *See* **object** (1). **3.** A small specialized mechanical device ▸ apparatus. *Informal:* widget. *Slang:* gizmo. *See* **gadget. 4.** Something done ▸ action, deed, performance. *See* **act** (1). **5.** Something to be done, considered, or dealt with ▸ affair, business, matter. *See also* **business, problem, task. 6.** Something that takes place ▸ incident, occurrence. *See* **circumstance** (1). **7.** Something significant that happens ▸ development, incident. *See* **event** (2). **8.** *Informal* An irrational preoccupation ▸ fetish, fixation, mania. *See* **obsession. 9.** *Informal* The current custom ▸ fad, mode, vogue. *See* **fashion** (1). **10.** *Slang* Something at which a person excels ▸ specialty, strong point. *See* **forte. 11.** An extravagant, short-lived romantic attachment ▸ *Informal:* crush, infatuation. *Idiom:* passing fancy. *See also* **love, obsession.**

thingamabob *or* **thingamajig** *noun*

1. *Informal* Something having material existence ▸ body, item, thing. *See* **object** (1). **2.** *Informal* A small specialized mechanical device ▸ apparatus. *Informal:*

whatsit, widget. *Slang:* gizmo. *See* **gadget.**

things *noun*

1. One's portable property ▸ goods, personal effects, property. *See* **effects. 2.** Articles too small or numerous to be specified ▸ junk, oddments, miscellanea. *See* **odds and ends.**

think *verb*

1. To use the powers of the mind, as in conceiving ideas, drawing inferences, and making judgments ▸ cerebrate, cogitate, conceptualize, deliberate, ideate, ratiocinate, reason, reflect, speculate. *Idioms:* put on one's thinking cap, use one's head. *See also* **remember. 2.** To think or think about carefully and at length ▸ cogitate, deliberate, mull. *See* **ponder. 3.** To view in a certain way ▸ believe, feel, hold, sense. *See also* **perceive, regard. 4.** To have an opinion ▸ deem, hold. *See* **believe** (3). **5.** To form mental images of ▸ envision, fantasize, visualize. *See* **imagine** (1). **6.** To predict or assume without sufficient information ▸ speculate, surmise. *See* **guess.**

think about *or of verb*

1. To receive an idea and think about it in order to form an opinion about it ▸ consider, entertain, hear of. **2.** To care enough to keep someone in mind ▸ remember. **3.** To look upon in a particular way ▸ consider, deem, view. *See* **regard** (1).

think out *or through verb*

1. To think or think about carefully and at length ▸ cogitate, deliberate, mull. *See* **ponder. 2.** To find a solution for ▸ clear up, resolve, unravel. *See* **solve** (1). *See synonym note at* **solve.**

think over *verb*

To think or think about carefully and at length ▸ cogitate, deliberate, mull. *See* **ponder.**

think up *verb*

To use ingenuity in making, developing, or achieving ▸ contrive, devise, dream up. *See* **invent** (1).

✤ CORE SYNONYMS: *think, cerebrate, cogitate, reason, reflect, speculate.* These verbs mean to use the powers of the mind, as in conceiving ideas, drawing inferences, and making judgments: *thought before answering; sat in front of the fire cerebrating; cogitates about business problems; reasons clearly; took time to reflect before deciding; speculates on what will happen.*

---

thinkable *adjective*

▸ earthly, likely, possible. *See* **conceivable.**

thinker *noun*

1. A person who seeks truth by thinking ▸ philosopher, reasoner, theorist. **2.** A person of great mental ability ▸ intellectual, mastermind. *See* **mind** (2).

thinking *adjective*

Of, characterized by, or disposed to thought ▸ contemplative, pensive, reflective. *See* **thoughtful** (1).

thinking *noun*

The act or process of thinking ▸ cogitation, deliberation, rumination. *See* **thought** (1).

third estate *noun*

▸ masses, proletariat, public. *See* **commonalty.**

thirst *verb*
To have a greedy, obsessive desire ▸ crave, hunger, itch, lust. *See also* **desire.**
thirst *noun*
1. A desire for food or drink ▸ hunger, stomach, taste. *See* **appetite** (1). 2. A strong wanting of what promises enjoyment or pleasure ▸ craving, longing, yearning. *See* **desire** (1).
thirsting *adjective*
▸ avid, bursting. *See* **eager** (1).
thirsty *adjective*
1. Needing or desiring drink ▸ dry, parched. *Idioms:* dry as a bone (*or* whistle). 2. Having little or no precipitation ▸ desert, droughty, rainless. *See* **dry** (2). 3. Intensely desirous or interested ▸ avid, bursting. *See* **eager** (1).
thistly *adjective*
▸ brambly, bristly, prickly. *See* **thorny** (1).
thong *noun*
▸ cable, line, string. *See* **cord.**
thorn *noun*
1. A sharp protuberance or projection ▸ prick, prong, spine. *See* **spike** (1). 2. Something that annoys ▸ plague, torment, trial. *See* **annoyance** (2).
thorny *adjective*
1. Covered with sharp protuberances ▸ aculeate, barbed, brambly, briery, bristled, bristly, echinate, glochidiate, muricate, prickly, pricky, spiky, spiny, thistly. 2. Full of irritating difficulties or controversies ▸ nettlesome, prickly, spiny, thorny. *See also* **complex, delicate, disturbing, troublesome.** 3. Causing discomfort ▸ comfortless, uncomforting. *See* **uncomfortable** (1).
thorough *adjective*
1. Covering all aspects with painstaking accuracy ▸ complete, exhaustive, full-dress, thoroughgoing, thoroughpaced. *See also* **diligent.** 2. Characterized by attention to detail ▸ full, particular, in-depth. *See* **detailed** (1). 3. Completely such, without qualification or exception ▸ all-out, pure, sheer. *See* **utter**[2].
thoroughbred *adjective*
1. Of pure breeding stock ▸ full-blooded, highbred, pedigreed, pureblood, pureblooded, purebred. 2. Of high birth or social position ▸ blue-blooded, elite, upper-class. *See* **noble** (1).
thoroughfare *noun*
▸ path, road, route. *See* **way** (2).
thoroughgoing *adjective*
1. Covering all aspects with painstaking accuracy ▸ exhaustive, full-dress. *See* **thorough** (1). 2. Completely such, without qualification or exception ▸ all-out, pure, sheer. *See* **utter**[2].
thoroughly *adverb*
1. To the fullest extent ▸ fully, totally, utterly. *See* **completely** (1). 2. In a painstakingly complete manner ▸ comprehensively, exhaustively, intensively. *See* **completely** (2).
thoroughness *noun*
Attentiveness to detail ▸ care, carefulness, fastidious-

ness, meticulousness, pains, painstaking, punctiliousness, scrupulousness.
thoroughpaced *adjective*
▸ exhaustive, full-dress. *See* **thorough** (1).
thought *noun*
1. The act or process of thinking ▸ brainstorming, brainwork, cerebration, cogitation, conceptualization, conceptualizing, contemplation, deliberation, excogitation, headwork, ideation, intellection, meditation, musing, pondering, reflection, rumination, speculation, thinking. *See also* **theory.** 2. That which exists in the mind as the product of careful mental activity ▸ conception, notion. *See* **idea** (1). *See synonym note at* **idea.**
thoughtful *adjective*
1. Of, characterized by, or disposed to thought ▸ cogitative, contemplative, deliberative, excogitative, meditative, pensive, reflective, ruminative, speculative, thinking. *Idiom:* in a brown study. 2. Appealing to or engaging the intellect ▸ mental, sophisticated. *See* **intellectual** (1). 3. Full of polite concern for the well-being of others ▸ courteous, respectful, solicitous. *See* **attentive** (1). *See synonym note at* **attentive.**

✣ **CORE SYNONYMS:** *thoughtful, pensive, contemplative, reflective, meditative.* These adjectives mean characterized by or disposed to thought, especially serious or deep thought. *Thoughtful* can refer to absorption in thought or to the habit of reflection and circumspection: *Thoughtful voters carefully considered the candidates. Pensive* often connotes a wistful, dreamy, or sad quality: *"while pensive poets painful vigils keep"* (Alexander Pope). *Contemplative* implies slow directed consideration, often with conscious intent of achieving better understanding or spiritual or aesthetic enrichment: *"The Contemplative Atheist is rare . . . And yet they seem to be more than they are"* (Francis Bacon). *Reflective* suggests careful analytical deliberation, as in reappraising past experience: *"Cromwell was of the active, not the reflective temper"* (John Morley). *Meditative* implies earnest sustained thought: *The scholar was reticent, aloof, and meditative.*

---

thoughtfulness *noun*
▸ concern, regard, solicitude. *See* **consideration** (1).
thoughtless *adjective*
1. Devoid of consideration for others' feelings ▸ disregardful, inconsiderate, insensitive, unthinking, unthoughtful. *See also* **rude, tactless.** 2. Lacking concern or regard ▸ heedless, inattentive, unconcerned. *See* **careless** (1). *See synonym note at* **careless.**
thoughtlessness *noun*
1. A careless, often reckless disregard for consequences ▸ abandon, blitheness, carelessness, heedlessness. *See also* **temerity.** 2. A lack of consideration for others' feelings ▸ disregard, inconsiderateness, inconsideration, insensitivity, tactlessness, unthoughtfulness. *See also* **disrespect.**
thought out *adjective*
▸ considered, studied. *See* **deliberate** (2).

thrall *or* **thralldom** *or* **thraldom** *noun*
▸ enslavement, servility, villeinage. *See* **slavery.**

thrash *verb*
1. To beat plants to separate the grain from the straw ▸ flail, thresh. 2. To swing about or strike at wildly ▸ flail, thresh, toss. *Idiom:* toss and turn. *See also* **stagger, sway.** 3. To hit heavily and repeatedly ▸ assault, batter, pummel, thresh. *See* **beat** (1). *See synonym note at* **beat.** 4. To punish with blows or lashes ▸ flog, lash, whip. *See* **beat** (2). 5. To render totally ineffective by decisive defeat ▸ crush, overcome, overpower, rout. *See* **overwhelm** (1).

thrash out *or* **over** *verb*
To speak together and exchange ideas and opinions about ▸ converse, debate. *Informal:* kick around. *See* **discuss.**

thrashing *noun*
1. A punishment dealt with blows or lashes ▸ flogging, whipping. *See* **beating** (1). 2. The act of defeating or the condition of being defeated ▸ overthrow, trouncing, vanquishment. *See* **defeat.**

thread *noun*
1. A very fine continuous strand ▸ fiber, fibril, filament, microfiber. *See also* **cord.** 2. Something suggesting the continuousness of a filament ▸ hairline, strand.

thread *verb*
To put objects onto a thread ▸ string.

threadbare *adjective*
1. Showing signs of wear and tear or neglect ▸ deteriorated, dilapidated, tattered. *See* **shabby** (1). 2. Without freshness or appeal because of overuse ▸ clichéd, overused, shopworn, tired. *See* **trite.**

threadlike *adjective*
Containing or consisting of fibers ▸ fibrous, sinewy, stringy.

threads *noun*
Slang Articles worn to cover the body ▸ apparel, clothing, garments. *See* **dress** (1).

threat *noun*
1. An expression of intent to hurt or punish another ▸ intimidation, menace. 2. Exposure to harm, loss, or injury ▸ hazard, menace, peril. *See* **danger.**

threaten *verb*
1. To give warning signs of ▸ bode, forebode, forewarn, portend. *See also* **foreshadow.** 2. To be imminent ▸ brew, hang over, hover, impend, loom, lower, menace, overhang. *Idiom:* breathe down one's neck. *See also* **approach.** 3. To frighten into submission or compliance ▸ browbeat, bully, cow. *See* **intimidate** (1). 4. To expose to possible loss or damage ▸ jeopardize, risk. *See* **endanger.**

threatening *adjective*
1. Bringing or predicting misfortune ▸ dire, foreboding, ominous. *See* **fateful** (1). 2. Involving possible risk, loss, or injury ▸ chancy, hazardous, risky. *See* **dangerous.**

three *or* **threesome** *noun*
▸ triad, trinity, triple. *See* **trio.**

thresh *verb*
1. To beat plants to separate the grain from the straw ▸ flail, thrash. 2. To swing about or strike at wildly ▸ flail, thrash, toss. *Idiom:* toss and turn. *See also* **stagger, sway.** 3. To hit heavily and repeatedly ▸ assault, batter, pound, pummel. *See* **beat** (1).

thresh out *or* **over** *verb*
To speak together and exchange ideas and opinions about ▸ converse, debate. *Informal:* kick around. *See* **discuss.**

threshold *noun*
▸ brink, fringe, margin. *See* **border** (1).

thrift *or* **thriftiness** *noun*
▸ providence, prudence. *See* **economy.**

thriftless *adjective*
▸ prodigal, profligate. *See* **extravagant** (1).

thrifty *adjective*
▸ chary, frugal, saving. *See* **economical.** *See synonym note at* **economical.**

thrill *noun*
1. A strong, pleasant feeling of excitement or stimulation ▸ lift. *Informal:* wallop. *Slang:* bang, boot, buzz, high, jollies, kick. *Idiom:* kick in the pants. 2. A nervous shaking of the body ▸ quiver, shiver, tic. *See* **tremor** (2).

thrill *verb*
1. To have a powerful emotional effect on someone ▸ electrify, transport. *See* **enrapture.** *See synonym note at* **enrapture.** 2. To give great or keen pleasure to ▸ enchant, overjoy, tickle. *See* **delight** (1).

thrilled *adjective*
Feeling strong pleasure or excitement ▸ atingle, excited, fired up, worked up. *Informal:* psyched. *Slang:* stoked, turned-on, wired. *Idiom:* pleased as punch. *See also* **elated, passionate.**

thrilling *adjective*
▸ melodramatic, sensational, spectacular. *See* **dramatic** (2).

thrive *verb*
1. To grow rapidly ▸ bloom, blossom, flourish. *See also* **increase.** 2. To do or fare well ▸ boom, flourish. *See* **prosper.**

thriving *adjective*
1. Improving, growing, or succeeding steadily ▸ prosperous, roaring, successful. *See* **flourishing.** 2. Having good health ▸ hardy, robust. *See* **healthy** (1). *See synonym note at* **healthy.**

throb *verb*
1. To make rhythmic contractions, sounds, or movements ▸ pulsate, pulse, tick. *See* **beat** (5). 2. To shine intensely and blindingly ▸ beat down, blaze, pulse. *See* **glare** (2).

throb *noun*
A rhythmic contraction or sound ▸ pulsation, pulse. *See* **beat** (3).

throbbing *adjective*
1. Marked by severe or intense pain ▸ acute, gnawing, piercing. *See* **sharp** (8). 2. Extremely or harshly bright ▸ blazing, blinding, glaring. *See* **brilliant** (2).

throe *noun*

▸ ache, pang, shoot. *See* **pain** (1). *See synonym note at* **pain.**

throes *noun*

A condition of agonizing struggle or trouble ▸ convulsion, paroxysm, spasm.

throng *noun*

An enormous number of persons or things gathered together ▸ horde, mass, swarm. *See* **crowd** (1). *See synonym note at* **crowd.**

throng *verb*

To move into an area or space in large numbers ▸ cram, pour, squeeze. *See* **crowd** (1).

throttle *verb*

1. To hold something requiring an outlet in check ▸ smother, stifle, suppress. *See* **repress. 2.** To stop breathing or stop the breathing of ▸ smother, stifle, suffocate. *See* **choke** (1).

through *adjective*

1. Having no further relationship ▸ done, finished. **2.** No longer effective, capable, or valuable ▸ done, done for, finished, washed-up. *Informal:* kaput. *Idioms:* at the end of one's line (*or* road), over the hill, past one's prime. *See also* **goner. 3.** Proceeding or lying in an uninterrupted line or course ▸ linear, straightforward. *See* **direct** (1). **4.** Having reached completion ▸ concluded, done, finished. *See* **complete** (3).

through *preposition*

By the cause of ▸ as a result of, on account of, owing to. *See* **because of.**

throw *verb*

1. To send through the air with a motion of the hand or arm ▸ bowl, cast, dart, dash, fling, heave, hurl, hurtle, launch, lob, pelt, pitch, roll, shoot, shy, sling, toss. *Informal:* chuck, fire, peg. **2.** To bring down, as from a shot or blow ▸ floor, ground, hew. *See* **drop** (6). **3.** *Informal* To cause to be unclear in mind or intent ▸ befuddle, bewilder, confound. *See* **confuse** (1). **4.** *Informal* To put at a loss as to what to say or do ▸ confound, perplex. *Informal:* stump. *See* **baffle** (1). **5.** To send out heat, light, or energy ▸ emit, radiate. *See* **shed**[1] (1). **6.** To organize and carry out an activity ▸ give, hold. *See* **have** (9).

throw away *verb*

1. To let go or get rid of as being useless or defective, for example ▸ dump, toss. *Informal:* chuck. *See* **discard. 2.** To use, consume, spend, or expend thoughtlessly or carelessly ▸ fritter away, squander, trifle away. *See* **waste** (1).

throw in *verb*

To put or set into, between, or among another or other things ▸ infuse, insert, interpose. *See* **introduce** (2).

throw off *verb*

1. To relieve a burden ▸ discharge, relieve, unburden. *See* **rid. 2.** To cast off by a natural process ▸ molt, slough. *See* **shed**[1] (2). **3.** To discharge material, as vapor or fumes, usually suddenly and violently ▸ give

forth, issue, release. *See* **emit** (1). **4.** To get away from a pursuer ▸ evade, outrun, slip. *See* **lose** (3).

throw out *verb*

1. To let go or get rid of as being useless or defective, for example ▸ dump, throw away. *Informal:* chuck. *See* **discard. 2.** To put out by force ▸ dismiss, evict. *See* **eject** (1). **3.** To displace a bone from a socket or joint ▸ dislocate, separate. *See* **slip** (7). **4.** To state for consideration or debate ▸ offer, put forward, set forth. *See* **propose** (1).

throw over *verb*

To give up or leave completely ▸ forsake, leave, quit. *See* **abandon** (1).

throw up *verb*

To eject the contents of the stomach through the mouth ▸ retch. *Informal:* puke. *See* **vomit** (1).

throw *noun*

An act of throwing ▸ bowl, cast, fling, heave, hurl, launch, lob, peg, pitch, roll, shy, sling, toss. *Informal:* chuck.

✦ CORE SYNONYMS: *throw, cast, hurl, fling, pitch, toss.* These verbs mean to send something through the air with a motion of the hand or arm. *Throw* is the least specific: *throwing a ball; threw the life preserver to the struggling swimmer. Cast* usually refers to throwing something light: *cast her fishing line into the stream. Hurl* and *fling* mean to throw with great force: *"Him the Almighty Power/Hurl'd headlong flaming from th' Ethereal Sky"* (John Milton). *He flung the tarpaulin over the boat. Pitch* often means to throw with careful aim: *"a special basket in my study . . . into which I pitch letters, circulars, pamphlets and so forth"* (H.G. Wells). *Toss* usually means to throw lightly or casually: *"Campton tossed the card away"* (Edith Wharton).

---

thrust *noun*

1. The current of thought uniting all elements of a text or discourse ▸ aim, burden, drift, gist, intent, purport, substance, tendency, tenor. *See also* **heart, meaning. 2.** An act or instance of pushing ▸ jostle, press, shove. *See* **push** (1).

thrust *verb*

1. To force to move or advance with or as if with blows or pressure ▸ butt, shove, slam. *See* **drive** (2). **2.** To penetrate into a substance or place with force ▸ drive, stab, stick. *See* **plunge** (1). **3.** To apply pressure on, against, or with ▸ press, prod, shove. *See* **push** (1).

thruway *noun*

▸ path, road, route. *See* **way** (2).

thud *verb*

To make a dull sound by or as if by striking a surface with a heavy object ▸ clomp, clump, clunk, plunk, thump, whomp. *See also* **bang.**

thud *noun*

A stroke or blow that produces a sound ▸ smack, thump. *See* **beat** (1).

thug *noun*

A person who treats others violently or roughly, especially for hire ▸ hoodlum, hooligan, mug, roughneck, rowdy, ruffian, tough. *Informal:* bruiser, toughie. *Slang:* gangsta, goon, gorilla, gunsel, hood, plug-ugly, punk. *See also* **criminal.**

thumb *verb*
▸ flip through, glance at, skim. *See* **browse** (1).

thumbs-down *noun*
▸ refusal, rejection. *See* **no** (1).

thumbs-up *noun*
▸ authorization, consent, sanction. *See* **permission.**

thump *noun*
1. A stroke or blow that produces a sound ▸ thud, whack. *See* **beat** (1). 2. A sudden heavy stroke ▸ crack, hit, swat, whack. *See* **blow²** (1).

thump *verb*
1. To strike together noisily ▸ crash, slam, whack. *See* **bang** (1). 2. To make a dull sound by or as if by striking a surface with a heavy object ▸ clunk, whomp. *See* **thud.** 3. *Informal* To hit heavily and repeatedly ▸ assault, batter, pummel, thresh. *See* **beat** (1). 4. To make rhythmic contractions, sounds, or movements ▸ pulsate, pulse, throb. *See* **beat** (5).

thunder *noun*
An explosive noise ▸ boom, crash. *See* **blast** (1).

thunder *verb*
To make an explosive noise ▸ roar, rumble. *See* **blast** (1).

thundercloud *noun*
1. An indication of impending danger or harm ▸ foreboding, forewarning, threat. 2. A phenomenon that serves as a sign of some future good or evil ▸ portent, prognostication, sign. *See* **omen.**

thunderous *adjective*
▸ booming, earsplitting, roaring. *See* **loud** (1).

thwack *verb*
1. To deliver a sudden, sharp blow to ▸ jab, sock, whack. *See* **hit** (1). 2. To strike together noisily ▸ crash, slam, whack. *See* **bang** (1).

thwack *noun*
A sudden heavy stroke ▸ crack, hit, swat, whack. *See* **blow²** (1).

thwart *verb*
To prevent from accomplishing a purpose ▸ baffle, foil, stymie. *See* **frustrate** (1).

thwart *adjective*
Situated or lying across ▸ crossways, crosswise, traverse. *See* **transverse.**

tic *noun*
▸ quake, shudder, twitch. *See* **tremor** (2).

tick *noun*
A rhythmic contraction or sound ▸ pulsation, pulse, throb. *See* **beat** (3).

tick *verb*
To make rhythmic contractions, sounds, or movements ▸ pulsate, pulse, throb. *See* **beat** (5).

tick away *verb*
To move past in time ▸ go by, slip away. *See* **elapse.**

tick off *verb*
1. To name or specify one by one ▸ list, numerate. *See* **enumerate** (1). 2. *Informal* To cause to feel or show anger ▸ incense, infuriate, madden. *See* **anger** (1).

ticker *noun*
Slang The circulatory organ of the body ▸ blood pump, heart.

ticket *noun*
1. An identifying or descriptive slip ▸ earmark, flag, label, tab, tag. 2. A list of candidates proposed or endorsed by a political party ▸ ballot, lineup, slate. 3. *Informal* A means or method of entering into or achieving something desirable ▸ formula, key, route, secret. *See also* **trick.** 4. A written or printed notification of a legal infraction ▸ citation. 5. A document that gives permission to do something ▸ permit, warrant. *See* **license** (3).

ticket *verb*
To attach a ticket to ▸ earmark, flag, label, mark, tag.

ticking *adjective*
▸ functioning, operating, working. *See* **active** (1).

tickle *verb*
▸ enchant, overjoy, thrill. *See* **delight** (1). *See synonym note at* **delight.**

tickled *adjective*
▸ agreeable, ready. *See* **willing** (1).

ticklish *adjective*
1. Marked by whim or impulse ▸ fickle, impulsive, mercurial. *See* **capricious.** 2. Requiring great tact or skill ▸ demanding, exacting, precarious. *See* **delicate** (3). 3. Quick to take offense or become angry or upset ▸ thin-skinned, ticklish. *See* **oversensitive.**

tidbit *noun*
1. Something fine and delicious, especially a food ▸ morsel, treat. *See* **delicacy** (1). 2. A small portion of food ▸ crumb, morsel. *See* **bit¹** (2).

tide *noun*
▸ flood, stream. *See* **flow.** *See synonym note at* **flow.**

tidings *noun*
▸ advice, intelligence, report. *See* **news** (1). *See synonym note at* **news.**

tidy *verb*
1. To make or keep an area clean and orderly ▸ clean (up), clear (up), neaten (up), police, spruce (up), straighten (up). 2. To make neat, trim, or presentable ▸ clean (up), freshen (up), groom, neaten (up), slick up, spruce (up), tidy up, trig (out), trim.

tidy *adjective*
1. In good order or clean condition ▸ shipshape, taut. *See* **neat** (1). *See synonym note at* **neat.** 2. *Informal* Adequate to satisfy a need, requirement, or standard ▸ average, decent, moderate. *See* **acceptable** (2). 3. *Informal* Above average in amount, size, or scope ▸ extensive, large, sizable. *See* **big** (1).

tidy sum *noun*
Informal A large sum of money ▸ mint. *Informal:* pile. *See* **fortune** (7).

tie *verb*
1. To make secure, as by means of a cord or rope ▸ bind, knot. *See* **fasten** (1). 2. To restrict the activity or free movement of ▸ fetter, handcuff, hobble. *See* **hamper¹** (1). 3. To do or make something equal to ▸ equal, match, meet.

tie up *verb*
1. To make secure, as by means of a cord or rope ▸ bind, knot. *See* **fasten** (1). 2. To prevent the occurrence or continuation of a movement, action, or operation ▸ halt, idle, immobilize. *See* **stop** (2). 3. To cause to be busy or in use ▸ engage, monopolize, occupy. *See* **absorb** (1).

tie *noun*
1. That which unites or binds ▸ ligature, link, yoke. *See* **bond** (2). 2. An equality of scores, votes, or performances in a contest ▸ dead heat, deadlock, draw, stalemate, standoff.

tie beam *noun*
▸ crossbeam, girder, timber. *See* **beam** (2).

tie-in *noun*
▸ correlation, link, relationship. *See* **relation** (1).

tier *noun*
1. A group of people or things arranged in a row ▸ file, queue, string. *See* **line** (1). 2. A division of persons or things by quality or rank ▸ league, rank, tier. *See* **class** (2).

tie-up *noun*
▸ immobilization, jam, standstill. *See* **stop** (2).

tiff *noun*
A discussion, often heated, in which a difference of opinion is expressed ▸ fight, quarrel. *See* **argument** (1).

tiff *verb*
To engage in a quarrel ▸ dispute, fight, quarrel. *See* **argue** (1).

tight *adjective*
1. Persistently holding to something ▸ clinging, fast, firm, secure, tenacious. *See also* **fixed.** 2. Stretched tightly ▸ taut, tense. *See synonym note at* **taut.** *See also* **rigid.** 3. Characterized by an economy of artistic expression ▸ lean, minimalist, spare, taut. *See also* **bare.** 4. Affording little room for movement ▸ close, confining, cramped, crowded, narrow, restrictive, snug. 5. Having all parts near to each other ▸ crowded, dense, packed. *See* **thick** (2). 6. Based on good judgment, reasoning, or evidence ▸ valid, well-founded. *See* **sound²** (1). 7. *Slang* Very closely associated ▸ close, cozy, familiar. *See* **intimate¹** (1). 8. Ungenerously or pettily reluctant to spend money ▸ close-fisted, miserly, parsimonious. *See* **stingy** (1). 9. Difficult to deal with or get out of ▸ rough, tricky. *Informal:* sticky. *See also* **delicate.** 10. Almost even ▸ nip and tuck. *Idiom:* neck and neck. 11. *Slang* Stupefied, excited, or muddled with alcoholic liquor ▸ intoxicated, sodden, tipsy. *See* **drunk.**

tighten *verb*
1. To make stronger or more resistant ▸ bolster, reinforce, strengthen. *See* **support** (2). 2. To make or become tense ▸ stiffen, stretch. *See* **tense.** 3. To make smaller or narrower by binding or squeezing ▸ compress, contract, narrow. *See* **constrict** (1).

tightfisted *adjective*
▸ close-fisted, mean, miserly, parsimonious. *See* **stingy** (1).

tightlipped *adjective*
▸ reticent, silent, uncommunicative. *See* **taciturn.** *See synonym note at* **taciturn.**

tightrope *noun*
▸ corner, difficulty, fix. *See* **predicament.**

tightwad *noun*
▸ churl, skinflint. *Informal:* penny pincher. *See* **miser.**

till *verb*
To prepare soil for the planting and raising of crops ▸ cultivate, culture, dig, fork, harrow, hoe, plow, rake, spade, turn (over), work. *See also* **fertilize, grow, plant.**

tilt *noun*
1. A competition or test of opposing wills suggesting the sport fought by mounted knights with lances ▸ joust, tournament, tourney. *See also* **battle, competition.** 2. Deviation from a particular direction ▸ grade, heel. *See* **inclination** (2).

tilt *verb*
1. To depart or cause to depart from true vertical or horizontal ▸ heel, lean. *See* **incline** (1). *See synonym note at* **incline.** 2. To strive in opposition ▸ clash, combat, fight. *See* **contend** (1).

timber *noun*
1. A person considered to have qualities suitable for a particular activity ▸ material, stuff. *See also* **comer, potential.** 2. A sturdy horizontal structural support ▸ crossbeam, girder, trestle. *See* **beam** (2).

timberland *noun*
A dense growth of trees and underbrush covering an area ▸ backwoods, forest, woodland, woods.

timbre *noun*
1. The distinct quality or character of a sound ▸ tonality, tone, tone color. 2. A prevailing quality, as of thought, behavior, or attitude ▸ mood, spirit, tone. *See* **temper** (3).

time *noun*
1. The general point at which an event occurs ▸ instant, moment. *See* **occasion** (1). 2. A rather short period ▸ interval, while. *See* **bit¹** (4). 3. A specific length of time characterized by the occurrence of certain conditions or events ▸ span, stretch, term. *See* **period** (1). 4. A particular time notable for its distinctive characteristics ▸ epoch, era, period. *See* **age** (2). 5. A prison or jail term ▸ hitch, stretch. 6. A limited, often assigned period of activity, duty, or opportunity ▸ stint, shift, watch. *See* **turn** (1). 7. The period during which someone or something exists ▸ existence, span, term. *See* **life** (1).

time *verb*
1. To set the time for an event or occasion ▸ plan, schedule, set. *See also* **arrange.** 2. To record the speed or duration of ▸ clock. *See also* **measure.**

time-honored *adjective*
1. Conforming to established practice or standards ▸ conformist, orthodox, traditional. *See* **conventional** (1). 2. Generally approved or agreed upon ▸ conventional, established, orthodox. *See* **accepted.**

time immemorial *noun*
▸ ancient history, protohistory, time immemorial. *See* **antiquity.**

timeless *adjective*
1. Existing without interruption or end ▸ constant, endless, everlasting, perpetual. *See* **continual. 2.** Existing unchanged forever ▸ ageless, eternal. *See synonym note at* **ageless.** *See also* **endless. 3.** Characterized by enduring excellence, appeal, and importance ▸ ageless, enduring. *See* **vintage** (1).

timely *adjective*
1. Occurring, acting, or performed exactly at the time appointed ▸ prompt, punctual. *Idioms:* on the dot (*or* nose), on schedule, on time. **2.** Suited for a particular purpose or occurring at a suitable time ▸ favorable, propitious, well-timed. *See* **opportune.**

time-out *noun*
1. A pause or interval, as from work or duty ▸ break, recess. *See* **rest**[1] (1). **2.** Freedom from labor, responsibility, or strain ▸ leisure, relaxation. *See* **rest**[1] (2).

timetable *noun*
▸ calendar, lineup, schedule. *See* **program** (1).

timeworn *adjective*
1. Belonging to or existing in times long past ▸ ancient, antiquated, archaic. *See* **old** (1). **2.** Without freshness or appeal because of overuse ▸ clichéd, overused, shopworn, tired. *See* **trite.**

timid *adjective*
1. Awkward or unconfident in behavior or manner ▸ bashful, demure, diffident. *See* **shy**[1] (1). **2.** Given to or exhibiting hesitation ▸ indecisive, irresolute. *See* **hesitant** (1). **3.** Filled with fear or terror ▸ fearful, frightened, scared. *See* **afraid.**

timidity *or* **timidness** *noun*
1. An awkwardness or lack of self-confidence in the presence of others ▸ bashfulness, demureness, diffidence. *See* **shyness. 2.** The act of hesitating or state of being hesitant ▸ indecision, tentativeness. *See* **hesitation.**

timorous *adjective*
▸ fearful, frightened, scared. *See* **afraid.**

tinct *noun*
▸ hue, shade, tint. *See* **color** (1).

tincture *noun*
Something that imparts color ▸ dye, paint, pigment. *See* **color** (2).

tincture *verb*
To impart color to ▸ dye, stain, tint. *See* **color** (1).

tine *noun*
▸ prick, prong, spine. *See* **spike** (1).

tinge *noun*
1. Quality of light reflected or emitted ▸ hue, shade, tint. *See* **color** (1). **2.** A slight amount or indication ▸ hint, semblance, trace. *See* **shade** (2).

tinge *verb*
To impart color to ▸ dye, stain, tint. *See* **color** (1).

tingle *noun*
A feeling of pervasive emotional warmth ▸ flush, glow.

tinker *verb*
1. To handle something in an attempt to adjust or improve it ▸ fiddle, fool, meddle, mess (around), tamper. *Informal:* monkey. *See also* **adjust, fix. 2.** To touch or handle something out of restlessness ▸ fidget, fool, play. *See* **fiddle** (1).

tinsel *adjective*
▸ flashy, garish, loud. *See* **gaudy.**

tint *noun*
Quality of light reflected or emitted ▸ hue, shade, tinge. *See* **color** (1).

tint *verb*
To impart color to ▸ dye, stain, tincture. *See* **color** (1).

tiny *adjective*
Extremely small ▸ diminutive, dwarf, Lilliputian, microscopic, midget, mini, miniature, minuscule, minute, pygmy, wee. *Informal:* peewee, pintsize, pintsized, teensy, teensy-weensy, teeny, teeny-weeny, weeny. *See also* **imperceptible, little.**

✦ CORE SYNONYMS: *tiny, diminutive, miniature, minuscule, minute, wee.* These adjectives mean extremely small: *the tiny feet of a newborn baby; diminutive in stature; a miniature camera; a minuscule amount of rain; minute errors; felt a wee bit better.*

---

tip[1] *noun*
A sharp or tapered end ▸ cusp, nib. *See* **point** (1).

tip *verb*
To put a topping on ▸ cap, crest, crown, top, top off. *See also* **cover.**

tip[2] *verb*
To depart or cause to depart from true vertical or horizontal ▸ heel, lean. *See* **incline** (1). *See synonym note at* **incline.**

tip over *verb*
1. To come to the ground from an upright position ▸ topple, tumble. *See* **fall** (2). **2.** To turn or cause to turn from a vertical or horizontal position ▸ knock over, topple. *See* **overturn** (1).

tip *noun*
Deviation from a particular direction ▸ grade, heel. *See* **inclination** (2).

tip[3] *noun*
1. An item of advance or inside information given as a guide to action ▸ clue, hint, lead, pointer, scent, steer. *Informal:* tip-off. *See also* **hint. 2.** A material favor or gift, usually money, given in return for service ▸ largess, perquisite. *See* **gratuity** (1). **3.** An opinion as to a decision or course of action ▸ guidance, recommendation. *See* **advice** (1).

tip *verb*
To give incriminating information about others, especially to the authorities ▸ talk, tattle, tip off. *Slang:* rat. *See* **inform** (2).

tip-off *noun*
Informal An item of advance or inside information given as a guide to action ▸ lead, steer. *See* **tip**[3] (1).

tipple *verb*
▸ guzzle. *Slang:* booze, lush. *See* **drink** (2).

tippler *noun*
▸ alcoholic, dipsomaniac, inebriate. *See* **drunkard.**

tipsiness *noun*
▸ inebriation, insobriety, intoxication. *See* **drunkenness.**

tipster *noun*
▸ informant. *Slang:* snitch, squealer. *See* **informer.**

tipsy *adjective*
▸ besotted, intoxicated, sodden. *See* **drunk.**

tiptop *adjective*
▸ first-rate, prime, splendid. *See* **excellent.**

tirade *noun*
A long, violent, or blustering speech, usually of censure or denunciation ▸ berating, diatribe, fulmination, harangue, jeremiad, onslaught, philippic, screed, tongue-lashing, upbraiding. *See also* **vituperation.**

tire *verb*
1. To make weary ▸ drain, exhaust, fatigue, frazzle, jade, tire out, wear down, wear out, weary. *Informal:* knock out, tucker (out). *Slang:* do in, poop (out). *Idioms:* run ragged, take it out of. *See also* **enervate.**
2. To grow weary ▸ burn out, droop, flag, give out, wear down, wear out, wilt. *Slang:* poop (out). *See also* **collapse, fade, labor. 3.** To make weary with dullness or tedium ▸ tire, weary. *See* **bore²**.

tire out *verb*
To make extremely tired ▸ exhaust, wear out. *Informal:* knock out, tucker (out). *Slang:* do in, poop (out). *Idioms:* run ragged, take it out of.

✛ **CORE SYNONYMS:** *tire, weary, fatigue, exhaust, jade.* These verbs mean to make someone weary. *Tire* often suggests a state resulting from exertion, excess, dullness, or ennui: *"When a man is tired of London, he is tired of life"* (Samuel Johnson). *Weary* often implies dissatisfaction, as that resulting from what is irksome or boring: *found the long journey wearying; soon wearied of their constant bickering. Fatigue* implies great weariness, as that caused by stress or overwork: *"fatigued by an endless rotation of thought and wild alarms"* (Mary Wollstonecraft). To *exhaust* means to wear out completely, and it connotes total draining of physical or emotional strength: *"Like all people who try to exhaust a subject, he exhausted his listeners"* (Oscar Wilde). *Jade* refers principally to dullness that most often results from overindulgence: *"Contemplation of works of art without understanding them jades the faculties and enslaves the intelligence"* (John Ruskin).

tired *adjective*
1. Depleted of energy ▸ bleary, dead, drained, exhausted, fatigued, jaded, rundown, spent, tired-out, wearied, weariful, weary, worn-down, worn-out. *Informal:* beat, bushed, knocked-out, tuckered (out). *Slang:* done in, pooped (out), wiped, wiped-out. *Idioms:* all in, ready to drop. **2.** Out of patience ▸ disgusted, fed up, sick, weary. *Idiom:* sick and tired. *See also* **angry. 3.** Without freshness or appeal because of overuse ▸ banal, clichéd, shopworn. *See* **trite.**

tiredness *noun*
▸ burnout, weariness. *See* **exhaustion.**

tired-out *adjective*
▸ exhausted, weary, worn-out. *See* **tired** (1).

tireless *adjective*
Having or showing a capacity for protracted effort, regardless of difficulty or frustration ▸ indefatigable, inexhaustible, unfailing, unflagging, untiring, unwearied, unwearying, weariless. *See also* **firm, stubborn.**

✛ **CORE SYNONYMS:** *tireless, indefatigable, unflagging, untiring, unwearied, weariless.* These adjectives mean having or showing a capacity for protracted effort, regardless of difficulty or frustration: *a tireless worker; an indefatigable advocate of human rights; unflagging pursuit of excellence; untiring energy; an unwearied researcher; a weariless defender of freedom of the press.*

tiresome *adjective*
▸ dull, humdrum, monotonous. *See* **boring** (1). *See synonym note at* **boring.**

tiring *adjective*
Causing fatigue ▸ draining, exhausting, fatiguing, wearing, wearying. *See also* **burdensome.**

tissue *noun*
▸ network, system, web. *See* **complex** (1).

titan *noun*
▸ colossus, leviathan, monster. *See* **giant.**

titanic *adjective*
▸ behemoth, colossal, gigantic, mighty. *See* **enormous.**

tit for tat *noun*
▸ counteraction, reciprocation, reprisal. *See* **retaliation.**

tithe *noun*
▸ duty, levy, tariff. *See* **tax** (1).

title *noun*
1. An issue of printed material offered for sale or distribution ▸ opus, volume, work. *See* **publication** (2). **2.** The fact of possessing or the legal right to possess something ▸ possession, proprietorship. *See* **ownership. 3.** A legitimate or asserted right to demand something as one's due ▸ pretense, pretension. *See* **claim** (1). *See synonym note at* **claim. 4.** A right or legal share in something ▸ claim, interest, portion, stake. *See also* **cut, right. 5.** The word or words by which one is called and identified ▸ cognomen, epithet, tag. *See* **name** (1).

title *verb*
1. To give a name or title to ▸ christen, designate. *See* **name** (1). **2.** To describe with a word or term ▸ designate, label, name. *See* **call** (4).

titleholder *noun*
1. One that wins a contest or competition ▸ champion, medalist, victor. *See* **winner** (1). **2.** A person who has legal title to property ▸ master, proprietor. *See* **owner.**

titter *verb*
To express amusement or mirth ▸ chuckle, giggle, snicker. *See* **laugh.**

titter *noun*
An act of laughing ▸ giggle, snicker, snigger. *See* **laugh** (1).

tittle *noun*
▸ dash, drop, smidgen. *See* **bit**[1] (1).

tittle-tattle *noun*
Idle, often sensational and groundless talk about others ▸ hearsay, rumor, tattle. *See* **gossip** (1).

tittle-tattle *verb*
To engage in or spread gossip ▸ rumor, whisper. *See* **gossip**.

tizzy *noun*
▸ fume. *Informal:* snit, sweat. *See* **state** (4).

toady *noun*
One who flatters another or behaves obsequiously in an attempt to win favor ▸ flatterer, minion, slave. *See* **sycophant**.

toady *verb*
To behave obsequiously or submissively ▸ grovel, kowtow. *Informal:* apple-polish. *See* **fawn**. *See synonym note at* **fawn**.

to-and-fro *noun*
▸ indecision, tentativeness. *See* **hesitation**.

toast[1] *verb*
To prepare food for eating by the use of heat ▸ bake, brown, griddle, grill. *See* **cook** (1).

toast *noun*
Slang One that is ruined or doomed ▸ dead duck, dead meat, goner. *See also* **through**.

toast[2] *noun*
The act of drinking to someone ▸ health, pledge.

toast *verb*
To salute by raising and drinking from a glass ▸ honor, salute. *See* **drink** (4).

today *noun*
The current time ▸ nowadays, present. *See* **now**.

today *adverb*
At the present; these days ▸ now, nowadays. *Idioms:* in our time, in this day and age.

toddle *verb*
▸ promenade, saunter, wander. *See* **stroll**.

toddler *noun*
▸ babe, infant. *See* **baby** (1).

to-do *noun*
1. *Informal* A condition of being agitated or disturbed ▸ commotion, disturbance, stir. *See* **agitation** (1). **2.** *Informal* A condition of intense public interest or excitement ▸ stir, uproar. *See* **sensation** (2).

toehold *noun*
1. A place providing support for the foot in climbing ▸ foothold, footing, perch, purchase. **2.** A factor conducive to superiority and success ▸ head start, vantage. *See* **advantage** (1).

tog *verb*
Informal To put clothes on ▸ attire, clothe, garb. *See* **dress** (1).

together *adverb*
1. In, into, or as a single body ▸ jointly. *Idioms:* as one, in one breath, in the same breath, in unison, with one accord, with one voice. **2.** At the same time ▸ concurrently, simultaneously, synchronously. *Idioms:* all at once, all together.

together *adjective*
Slang In a state of preparedness ▸ prepared, ready, set. *Informal:* go. *Idioms:* all set, in working order.

togs *noun*
▸ apparel, clothing, garments. *See* **dress** (1).

toil *verb*
1. To exert oneself steadily, often to the point of exhaustion ▸ strain, sweat, travail. *See* **labor** (1). **2.** To walk in a laborious way ▸ plod, slog, slop. *See* **trudge**.

toil *noun*
Physical exertion that is usually difficult and exhausting ▸ drudgery, travail, work. *See* **labor** (1). *See synonym note at* **labor**.

toiler *noun*
▸ menial, roustabout, worker. *See* **laborer**.

toilette *noun*
▸ garb, guise, outfit. *See* **dress** (2).

token *noun*
1. An object or expression associated with and serving to identify something else ▸ attribute, emblem, metaphor, signifier, symbol. *See also* **term**. **2.** Something visible or evident that gives grounds for believing in the existence or presence of something else ▸ evidence, indication, symptom. *See* **sign** (1). *See synonym note at* **sign**. **3.** Something that takes the place of words in communicating a thought or feeling ▸ indication, sign. *See* **expression** (2). **4.** Something given to guarantee the repayment of a loan or the fulfillment of an obligation ▸ collateral, warrant. *See* **pawn**[1]. **5.** Something that causes one to remember ▸ memento, reminder. *See* **remembrance** (1).

tolerable *adjective*
1. Capable of being tolerated ▸ endurable, sufferable. *See* **bearable**. **2.** Adequate to satisfy a need, requirement, or standard ▸ average, decent, moderate. *See* **acceptable** (2). **3.** Relating to or occupying a middle position on a scale of evaluation ▸ mediocre, fair. *See* **average** (1). *See synonym note at* **average**.

tolerance *noun*
1. Forbearing or lenient treatment ▸ charitableness, charity, forbearance, indulgence, lenience, leniency, lenity, permissiveness, toleration. *See also* **forgiveness**. **2.** The capacity of enduring hardship or inconvenience without complaint ▸ resignation, sufferance. *See* **patience**.

tolerant *adjective*
1. Not strict or severe ▸ charitable, clement, easy, forbearing, indulgent, lax, lenient, merciful, permissive, soft. **2.** Not narrow or intolerant ▸ liberal, open-minded, progressive. *See* **broad-minded**. *See synonym note at* **broad-minded**. **3.** Enduring or capable of enduring hardship or inconvenience without complaint ▸ enduring, long-suffering, resigned. *See* **patient**.

tolerate *verb*
1. To neither forbid nor prevent ▸ allow, let. *See*

permit (1). **2.** To put up with ▸ accept, stomach, withstand. *See* **endure** (1). *See synonym note at* **endure.**

toleration *noun*
▸ charity, lenience, permissiveness. *See* **tolerance** (1).

toll[1] *noun*
1. A fixed amount of money charged for a privilege or service ▸ charge, dues, exaction, exactment, fare, fee, rate, tariff, tax. *See also* **cost. 2.** The expenditure at which something is obtained ▸ cost, expense, price, sacrifice. *Informal:* damage.

toll[2] *verb*
To give forth or cause to give forth a clear resonant sound ▸ bong, chime, peal. *See* **ring**[2] (1).

tomb *noun*
▸ catacomb, crypt, mausoleum. *See* **grave**[1].

tome *noun*
▸ edition, volume. *See* **book** (1).

tomfoolery *noun*
1. Foolish behavior ▸ folly, silliness, zaniness. *See* **foolishness. 2.** Annoying yet harmless, usually playful acts ▸ diablerie, high jinks, tricks. *See* **mischief** (1). **3.** Something that does not have or make sense ▸ bunkum, drivel, garbage. *See* **nonsense** (1).

tommyrot *noun*
Informal Something that does not have or make sense ▸ bunkum, drivel, garbage. *See* **nonsense** (1).

tomorrow *noun*
Time that is yet to be ▸ by-and-by, future, futurity, hereafter. **Idiom:** time to come. *See also* **approach, possibility.**

ton *noun*
Informal An indeterminately great amount or number ▸ bunch, multiplicity. *Informal:* bushel. *See* **heap** (3).

tonality *noun*
The distinct quality or character of a sound ▸ timbre, tone, tone color.

tone *noun*
1. The distinct quality or character of a sound ▸ timbre, tonality, tone color. **2.** An expressive vocal quality ▸ accent, edge, inflection, intonation, lilt, pitch, resonance, sonority, sonorousness. **Idiom:** tone of voice. **3.** A distinctive way of expressing oneself ▸ manner, mode. *See* **style** (1). **4.** A general impression produced by a predominant quality or characteristic ▸ atmosphere, aura, mood. *See* **air** (4). **5.** A prevailing quality, as of thought, behavior, or attitude ▸ mood, spirit, timbre. *See* **temper** (3). **6.** Quality of light reflected or emitted ▸ hue, shade, tint. *See* **color** (1).

tone down *verb*
1. *Informal* To make less emphatic or obvious ▸ de-emphasize, play down, soft-pedal. *See also* **moderate. 2.** To make or become less severe or extreme ▸ soften, tame. *See* **moderate** (1).

tongue *noun*
▸ dialect, vernacular. *See* **language** (1).

tongue-lashing *noun*
▸ berating, upbraiding. *See* **tirade.**

tongueless *or* **tongue-tied** *adjective*
▸ inarticulate, voiceless. *See* **mute** (1).

tonic *noun*
An agent, such as a medecine or drink, that restores vigor or energy ▸ energizer, restorative, roborant, stimulant. *Informal:* bracer, pick-me-up. **Idiom:** shot in the arm. *See also* **cure, drug.**

tonic *adjective*
Producing or stimulating physical, mental, or emotional vigor ▸ bracing, energizing, exhilarating. *See* **invigorating.**

tony *adjective*
▸ chic, posh, swank. *See* **exclusive** (4).

too *adverb*
▸ also, besides, likewise. *See* **additionally.**

tool *noun*
1. A device used to do work or perform a task ▸ implement, instrument, utensil. *See also* **agent, device, gadget. 2.** A person used or controlled by others ▸ puppet, stooge. *See* **pawn**[2]. **3.** A person who is easily deceived or victimized ▸ butt, pushover, victim. *See* **dupe** (1).

tool *verb*
Slang To run and control a motor vehicle ▸ chauffeur, pilot, wheel. *See* **drive** (1).

✛ CORE SYNONYMS: *tool, instrument, implement, utensil.* These nouns refer to devices used to do work or perform a task. *Tool* applies broadly to a device that facilitates work; specifically it denotes a small manually operated device: *a box full of tools for bike repair. Instrument* refers especially to a relatively small precision tool used by trained professionals: *sterilized the scalpel and the other instruments. Implement* is the preferred term for tools used in agriculture and certain building trades: *rakes, hoes, and other implements. Utensil* often refers to an implement used in a household, especially in the kitchen: *cooking utensils hung by the stove.*

---

tooth *noun*
▸ prick, prong, spine. *See* **spike** (1).

toothed *adjective*
▸ notched, serrate. *See* **saw-toothed.**

toothsome *adjective*
▸ delectable, savory, scrumptious. *See* **delicious** (1). *See synonym note at* **delicious.**

top *noun*
1. Something that covers, especially to prevent contents from spilling ▸ cap, cover, covering, lid. *See also* **plug. 2.** The highest point or state ▸ apex, height, peak. *See* **climax** (1). **3.** The greatest quantity or highest degree attainable ▸ ultimate, utmost. *See* **maximum** (1). **4.** The most preferable part of something ▸ cream, elite. *See* **best** (1).

top *adjective*
1. Of, being, located at, or forming the top ▸ highest, loftiest, topmost, upmost, uppermost. *See also* **climactic. 2.** Preeminent in rank or position ▸ highest, top-drawer. **3.** Greatest in quantity or highest in degree that can be attained ▸ topmost, utmost. *See*

maximum. **4.** Exceptionally good of its kind ▸ first-rate, prime, splendid, tiptop. *See* **excellent. 5.** Most important, influential, or significant ▸ chief, key, main, principal. *See* **primary** (1). **6.** Surpassing all others in quality ▸ optimum, superlative, unsurpassed. *See* **best** (1).

top *verb*
1. To put a topping on ▸ cap, crest, crown, tip, top off. *See also* **cover. 2.** To be greater or better than ▸ exceed, excel, outshine. *See* **surpass** (1). **3.** To reach or bring to a climax ▸ culminate, peak. *See* **climax.**

top off *verb*
1. To put a topping on ▸ cap, crest, crown, tip, top. *See also* **cover. 2.** To fill to capacity ▸ charge, jam, stuff. *See* **fill** (1).

top-drawer *adjective*
▸ exceptional, select, superior. *See* **choice** (1).

toper *noun*
▸ alcoholic, dipsomaniac, tippler. *See* **drunkard.**

topflight *adjective*
Informal Exceptionally good of its kind ▸ first-rate, prime, splendid, tiptop. *See* **excellent.**

topic *noun*
▸ matter, text, theme. *See* **subject** (1). *See synonym note at* **subject.**

topical *adjective*
1. Of, constituting, or relating to a theme or themes ▸ motivic, thematic. **2.** Characteristic of recent times or informed of what is current ▸ current, modern, up-to-date. *See* **contemporary** (2).

topmost *adjective*
1. Of, being, located at, or forming the top ▸ highest, loftiest, top, upmost, uppermost. *See also* **climactic. 2.** Greatest in quantity or highest in degree that can be attainedy ▸ maximal, utmost. *See* **maximum.**

topnotch *adjective*
Informal Exceptionally good of its kind ▸ first-rate, prime, splendid, tiptop. *See* **excellent.**

topography *noun*
The character, natural features, and configuration of land ▸ terrain. *Idiom:* the lay of the land.

topple *verb*
1. To undergo capture, defeat, or ruin ▸ collapse, fall, go down, go under. *See also* **succumb, surrender. 2.** To bring about the downfall of ▸ subvert, tumble. *See* **overthrow** (1). *See synonym note at* **overthrow. 3.** To turn or cause to turn from a vertical or horizontal position ▸ knock over, upset. *See* **overturn** (1). **4.** To come to the ground from an upright position ▸ tip over, tumble. *See* **fall** (2).

top secret *noun*
▸ privileged, restricted. *See* **confidential** (3).

topsy-turviness *noun*
1. A lack of order or regular arrangement ▸ clutter, confusion, disarray. *See* **disorder** (1). **2.** The state of being messy or unkempt ▸ sloppiness, untidiness. *See* **disorderliness** (1).

topsy-turvy *adjective*
1. Characterized by physical confusion ▸ disordered,

higgledy-piggledy, upside-down. *See* **confused** (2). **2.** Turned over completely ▸ inverted, overturned. *See* **upside-down** (1).

torch *verb*
1. *Slang* To cause to burn or undergo combustion ▸ enkindle, ignite. *See* **light**[1] (1). **2.** *Slang* To undergo or cause to undergo damage by or as if by fire ▸ scorch, sear, singe. *See* **burn** (1).

torment *verb*
1. To subject another to extreme physical cruelty, as in punishing ▸ crucify, harrow, rack, torture. *Idioms:* put on the rack (*or* wheel). *See also* **punish. 2.** To come to mind continually ▸ haunt, obsess, trouble, weigh on (*or* upon). **3.** To cause great pain or suffering to ▸ agonize, plague, rack. *See* **afflict.** *See synonym note at* **afflict. 4.** To attack or disturb persistently ▸ harry, pester, worry. *See* **harass.**

torment *noun*
1. A state of physical or mental suffering ▸ affliction, misery, wretchedness. *See* **distress** (1). **2.** A place or experience of excruciating pain or punishment ▸ living hell, persecution. *See* **hell. 3.** Something that annoys ▸ bother, irritant, nuisance. *See* **annoyance** (2). **4.** Mental anguish or pain caused by loss or despair ▸ heartache, sorrow. *See* **grief.**

tormenting *adjective*
Extraordinarily painful or distressing ▸ agonizing, anguishing, atrocious, excruciating, harrowing, torturous. *See also* **bitter, terrible, unbearable.**

tormentor *noun*
▸ hector, intimidator, persecutor. *See* **bully.**

torpedo *verb*
▸ demolish, smash, wreck. *See* **destroy** (1).

torpid *adjective*
1. Lacking physical feeling or sensitivity ▸ inert, numb, unfeeling. *See* **dead** (2). **2.** Lacking mental and physical alertness and activity ▸ slothful, sluggish, stuporous. *See* **lethargic** (1). **3.** Present but not evident or active ▸ dormant, inactive, potential. *See* **latent.**

torpor *or* **torpidity** *noun*
▸ languor, listlessness, sluggishness. *See* **lethargy** (1). *See synonym note at* **lethargy.**

torrent *noun*
1. An overwhelming flow of water ▸ deluge, downpour, overflow. *See* **flood** (1). **2.** A sudden violent expression, as of emotion ▸ burst, eruption, explosion. *See* **outburst** (1). **3.** Water condensed from atmospheric vapor and falling in drops ▸ deluge, downpour, shower. *See* **rain** (2).

torrid *adjective*
1. Marked by much heat ▸ blistering, boiling, burning. *See* **hot** (1). **2.** Fired with intense feeling ▸ burning, fervent, impassioned. *See* **passionate** (1).

torridity *or* **torridness** *noun*
▸ hotness, warmth. *See* **heat** (1).

tort *noun*
▸ illegality, offense. *See* **crime** (1).

tortuous *adjective*
1. Repeatedly curving in alternate directions ▸ convo-

luted, sinuous, twisting. *See* **winding** (1). **2.** Not proceeding straight to the point or object ▸ circuitous, devious, roundabout. *See* **indirect** (1). **3.** Difficult to understand because of intricacy ▸ convoluted, elaborate, involved, labyrinthine, mystifying. *See* **complex** (1).

torture *verb*
1. To subject another to extreme physical cruelty, as in punishing ▸ crucify, harrow, rack, torment. *Idioms:* put on the rack (*or* wheel). *See also* **punish. 2.** To cause great pain or suffering to ▸ excruciate, plague, rack, torment, wound. *See* **afflict.** *See synonym note at* **afflict.**

torture *noun*
1. A place or experience of excruciating pain or punishment ▸ living hell, persecution. *See* **hell. 2.** A state of physical or mental suffering ▸ agony, misery, wretchedness. *See* **distress** (1).

torturous *adjective*
▸ excruciating, harrowing. *See* **tormenting.**

Tory *noun*
One with politically conservative views ▸ orthodox, traditionalist. *See* **conservative.**

Tory *adjective*
Favoring traditional views and values, especially as a political philosophy ▸ right-wing, traditionalist. *See* **conservative** (1).

toss *verb*
1. To move vigorously from side to side or up and down ▸ heave, pitch, rock, roll. *See also* **lurch. 2.** To swing about or strike at wildly ▸ flail, thrash, thresh. *Idiom:* toss and turn. *See also* **stagger, sway. 3.** To twist agitatedly, as in pain, struggle, or embarrassment ▸ squirm, twist, writhe. *See also* **shake. 4.** To throw a coin in order to decide something ▸ flip. *Idiom:* call heads or tails. **5.** To send through the air with a motion of the hand or arm ▸ heave, hurl, pitch. *See* **throw** (1). *See synonym note at* **throw. 6.** To impair or destroy the composure of ▸ rock, ruffle, shake (up). *See* **agitate** (2). **7.** To let go or get rid of as being useless or defective, for example ▸ dump, throw away. *Informal:* chuck. *See* **discard.**

toss around *verb*
To speak together and exchange ideas and opinions about ▸ converse, debate. *Informal:* kick around. *See* **discuss.**

toss back *or* **down** *verb*
Informal To take into the mouth and swallow (a liquid) ▸ down, sip, swill. *See* **drink** (1).

toss *noun*
An act of throwing ▸ fling, hurl, toss. *See* **throw.**

tot¹ *noun*
1. A young person between birth and puberty ▸ juvenile, youngster. *See* **child** (1). **2.** A very young child ▸ babe, infant. *See* **baby** (1). **3.** A small amount of liquor ▸ dram, shot, sip. *See* **drop** (8). **4.** An act of drinking or the amount swallowed ▸ swallow, taste. *Informal:* swig. *See* **drink** (2).

tot² *verb*
To combine numbers to form a sum ▸ sum (up), total. *See* **add** (1).

total *noun*
1. A number or quantity obtained as a result of addition ▸ aggregate, amount, sum, summation, sum total, totality. *See also* **account, count. 2.** An amount or quantity from which nothing is left out or held back ▸ entirety, everything, gross. *See* **whole** (1).

total *adjective*
1. Including every constituent or individual ▸ all, entire, whole. *See* **complete** (1). *See synonym note at* **complete. 2.** Completely such, without qualification or exception ▸ all-out, pure, sheer. *See* **utter². 3.** Concerned with, applicable to, or affecting the whole ▸ blanket, generic, universal. *See* **general** (1).

total *verb*
1. To combine numbers to form a sum ▸ sum (up), tot (up). *See* **add** (1). **2.** To come to in number or quantity ▸ number, reach, run. *See* **amount** (1). **3.** *Slang* To cause the complete ruin or wreckage of ▸ demolish, torpedo, wreck. *See* **destroy** (1). **4.** To wreck a vehicle ▸ sideswipe, wreck. *See* **crash** (1).

totalitarian *adjective*
1. Characterized by or favoring absolute obedience to authority ▸ despotic, dictatorial, tyrannic. *See* **authoritarian** (1). **2.** Having and exercising complete political power and control ▸ autocratic, despotic, dictatorial. *See* **absolute** (1).

totalitarian *noun*
1. One who imposes or favors absolute obedience to authority ▸ despot, dictator, tyrant. *See* **authoritarian** (1). **2.** An absolute ruler, especially one who is harsh and oppressive ▸ despot, tyrant. *See* **dictator** (1).

totalitarianism *noun*
1. Absolute power, especially when exercised unjustly or cruelly ▸ autocracy, despotism, dictatorship. *See* **tyranny** (1). **2.** A political doctrine advocating the principle of absolute rule ▸ authoritarianism, autocracy, despotism, dictatorship. *See* **absolutism** (1).

totality *noun*
1. The state of being entirely whole ▸ oneness, wholeness. *See* **completeness. 2.** An amount or quantity from which nothing is left out or held back ▸ entirety, everything, total. *See* **whole** (1). **3.** A number or quantity obtained as a result of addition ▸ amount, sum, summation. *See* **total** (1). **4.** An organized array of individual elements and parts forming and working as a unit ▸ arrangement, whole. *See* **system** (1).

totalization *noun*
The act or process of adding ▸ addition, summation. *See also* **calculation.**

totalize *verb*
▸ sum (up), total. *See* **add** (1).

totally *adverb*
▸ fully, thoroughly, utterly. *See* **completely** (1).

tote *verb*
Informal To move while supporting ▸ bear, haul, lug. *See* **carry** (1).

tote *nouw*
A flexible container for carrying items ▸ pouch, sack.
Chiefly Regional: poke.*See* **bag** (1).
totter *verb*
1. To move back and forth ▸ swing, vacillate, waggle.
See **sway** (1). **2.** To walk unsteadily ▸ reel, sway, teeter.
See **stagger** (1).
tottering *or* **tottery** *adjective*
▸ precarious, shaky, unsteady. *See* **insecure** (2).
touch *verb*
1. To bring especially the hands or fingers into
contact with ▸ feel, finger, handle, manipulate, palpate, press, stroke. *See also* **caress, brush**[1]**, rub. 2.** To
be contiguous or next to ▸ abut, butt, meet, neighbor.
See **adjoin** (1). **3.** To be equal or alike ▸ compare,
match, parallel. *See* **equal** (1). **4.** To stir the emotions
of ▸ get (to), strike. *See* **move** (1). *See synonym note at*
move.
touch down *verb*
To come to rest on the ground ▸ alight, light, set
down. *See* **land** (2).
touch off *verb*
1. To release or cause to release energy suddenly and
violently, especially with a loud noise ▸ burst, detonate. *See* **explode** (1). **2.** To be the cause of ▸ generate,
induce, trigger. *See* **cause.** **3.** To stir to action or
feeling ▸ excite, prod, trigger. *See* **provoke** (1). **4.** To
begin or cause to begin burning ▸ fire, ignite, kindle.
See **light**[1] (1).
touch on *or* **upon** *verb*
To call or direct attention to something ▸ advert,
allude (to), mention. *See* **refer** (1).
touch up *verb*
To improve by making minor changes or additions
▸ polish, remodel, retouch. *See also* **fix, renew.**
touch *noun*
1. An act of touching ▸ feel, feeling, manipulation,
palpation, stroke. **2.** A coming together so as to be
touching ▸ contact, contingence. **3.** The faculty or
ability to perceive tactile stimulation ▸ feel, feeling,
tactility. *Idiom:* sense of touch. *See also* **sensation.**
4. A particular sensation conveyed by means of
physical contact ▸ feel, feeling. *See also* **contact,**
brush. 5. A slight amount or indication ▸ hint, semblance, trace. *See* **shade** (2). **6.** A situation allowing
exchange of ideas or messages ▸ communication,
contact, correspondence, intercommunication. *See*
also **communication.**

✢ CORE SYNONYMS: *touch, feel, finger, handle, palpate.*
These verbs mean to bring the hands or fingers into
contact with so as to give or receive a physical
sensation: *gently touched my hand; felt the runner's*
pulse; fingered the worry beads; handle a bolt of fabric;
palpates the patient's abdomen.

---

touchable *adjective*
Discernible by touch ▸ palpable, tactile, tangible.
touchableness *noun*
▸ palpability, physicality, tactility. *See* **tangibility.**

touch-and-go *adjective*
▸ demanding, exacting, precarious. *See* **delicate** (3).
touched *adjective*
▸ crazy, lunatic, mad. *See* **insane** (1).
touching *adjective*
▸ heart-rending, moving, poignant. *See* **affecting.** *See*
synonym note at **affecting.**
touchstone *noun*
▸ criterion, mark, measure. *See* **standard** (1). *See syn-*
onym note at **standard.**
touchy *adjective*
1. Easily moved to anger ▸ irascible, quick-tempered,
tetchy. *See* **testy** (1). **2.** Requiring great tact or skill
▸ demanding, exacting, precarious. *See* **delicate** (3).
3. Quick to take offense or become angry or upset
▸ thin-skinned, ticklish. *See* **oversensitive.**
tough *adjective*
1. Physically toughened so as to have great endurance
▸ hardy, rugged. *See* **hard** (2). **2.** Capable of exerting
considerable effort or of withstanding considerable
stress or hardship ▸ hardy, sturdy. *See* **strong** (2).
3. Requiring great or extreme bodily, mental, or
spiritual strength ▸ demanding, difficult, exacting. *See*
burdensome (1). **4.** Not easy to do, achieve, or master
▸ arduous, grueling, laborious. *See* **difficult** (1).
5. Marked by vigorous physical exertion ▸ arduous,
knockabout, strenuous. *See* **rough** (7). **6.** Rigorous and
unsparing in treating others ▸ harsh, stern, strict. *See*
severe (1). **7.** Possessing determination or resolution
▸ resolute, steadfast, unyielding. *See* **firm**[1] (3). **8.** Painfully intense ▸ brutal, harsh, severe. *See* **bitter** (2).
tough *noun*
A person who treats others violently or roughly
▸ hoodlum, hooligan, ruffian. *See* **thug.**
tough out *verb*
Slang To put up with ▸ stomach, swallow, take. *See*
endure (1).
toughen *verb*
1. To make resistant to hardship, especially through
continued exposure ▸ indurate, season, strengthen.
See **harden** (1). *See synonym note at* **harden. 2.** To
make or become physically hard ▸ congeal, solidify.
See **harden** (2).
toughie *noun*
Informal A person who treats others violently or
roughly ▸ hoodlum, ruffian, tough. *See* **thug.**
tough-minded *adjective*
▸ practical, pragmatic, prosaic. *See* **realistic** (1).
toughness *noun*
1. The fact or condition of being rigorous and
unsparing ▸ harshness, rigidity, stringency. *See* **sever-**
ity (1). **2.** Unwavering firmness of character, action, or
will ▸ determination, purpose, resolve, will. *See* **deci-**
sion (2). **3.** The quality or power of withstanding
hardship or stress ▸ fortitude, stamina, staying power.
See **endurance** (1).
tour *noun*
1. A course or process that ends where it began or
repeats itself ▸ cycle, orbit. *See* **circle** (2). **2.** A journey

undertaken with a specific objective ▶ pilgrimage, voyage. *See* **expedition** (1). **3.** A limited, often assigned period of activity, duty, or opportunity ▶ stint, time, watch. *See* **turn** (1).

tour *verb*
To make or go on a journey ▶ peregrinate, travel, voyage. *See* **journey.**

tour de force *noun*
▶ exploit, feat. *See* **accomplishment** (1).

tourist *noun*
One who travels for pleasure ▶ day-tripper, excursionist, globetrotter, jet-setter, sightseer, sojourner, traveler, vacationer, visitor.

tournament *or* **tourney** *noun*
1. Any competition or test of opposing wills likened to the sport in which knights fought with lances ▶ joust, tilt. *See also* **battle. 2.** A test of skill or ability ▶ bout, match, trial. *See* **competition** (2).

tousle *verb*
To put something into a state of disarray, such as the hair or clothes ▶ disarrange, dishevel, disorder, disorganize, mess (up), muss (up), rumple. *See also* **dirty.**

tout *verb*
▶ advertise, publicize, talk up. *See* **promote** (3).

tow *verb*
To exert force so as to move something toward the source of the force ▶ drag, draw, tug. *See* **pull** (1). *See synonym note at* **pull.**

tow *noun*
The act of drawing or pulling a load ▶ drag, draw, traction. *See* **pull** (1).

toward *adjective*
▶ advantageous, favorable, helpful, propitious. *See* **beneficial.**

tower *verb*
To move from a lower to a higher position ▶ ascend, climb, soar. *See* **rise** (3). *See synonym note at* **rise.**

tower above *verb*
To rise above, especially so as to afford a view of ▶ command, overlook, overshadow. *See* **dominate** (2).

towering *adjective*
1. Being of or at a relatively great height or altitude ▶ elevated, lofty. *See* **high** (1). **2.** Beyond what is usual, normal, or customary ▶ extraordinary, outstanding, remarkable. *See* **exceptional** (1).

towheaded *adjective*
▶ blond, fair-haired. *See* **fair¹** (8).

town *noun*
▶ borough, metropolis, municipality. *See* **city.**

townsman *or* **townswoman** *noun*
▶ denizen, occupant, resident. *See* **inhabitant.**

toxic *adjective*
1. Capable of injuring or killing by poison ▶ noxious, venomous, virulent. *See* **poisonous** (1). *See synonym note at* **poisonous. 2.** Causing harm or injury ▶ deleterious, evil, injurious. *See* **harmful.**

toxicant *adjective*
Capable of injuring or killing by poison ▶ noxious, toxic, venomous. *See* **poisonous** (1).

toxicant *noun*
Anything that is injurious, destructive, or fatal ▶ canker, toxin. *See* **poison** (1).

toxin *noun*
▶ canker, contagion. *See* **poison** (1).

toy *noun*
1. An object for children to play with ▶ game, plaything. *See also* **amusement. 2.** A small showy article ▶ knickknack, trinket. *See* **novelty** (3).

toy *verb*
1. To touch or handle something out of restlessness ▶ fidget, fool, play. *Informal:* monkey. *See* **fiddle** (1). **2.** To make amorous advances without serious intentions ▶ coquet, dally, trifle. *See* **flirt** (2). **3.** To treat lightly or flippantly ▶ dally, flirt, play, trifle. *See synonym note at* **flirt.**

trace *noun*
1. A mark or remnant that indicates the former presence of something ▶ record, relic, remainder, remains, remnant, vestige. *See also* **sign. 2.** A visible sign or mark of the passage of someone or something ▶ scent, trail. *See* **track** (1). **3.** A slight amount or indication ▶ hint, tinge. *See* **shade** (2).

trace *verb*
1. To pursue and locate ▶ hunt down, nose out, run down, track down. *Idioms:* run to earth (*or* ground). **2.** To follow the traces or scent of, as in hunting ▶ track, trail.

track *noun*
1. A visible sign or mark of the passage of someone or something ▶ footmarks, footprints, marks, odor, print, scent, spoor, trace, trail. *See also* **lead, sign. 2.** A course of action to be followed regularly ▶ rote, rounds, treadmill. *See* **routine** (1).

track *verb*
1. To follow the traces or scent of, as in hunting ▶ smell out, sniff out, trace, trail. *Idiom:* be hot on the trail of. *See also* **hunt. 2.** To keep another under surveillance by moving behind ▶ shadow, trail. *Informal:* tail. *See* **follow** (3). **3.** To go or extend across ▶ pass, transit, traverse. *See* **cross** (1).

track down *verb*
To pursue and locate ▶ hunt down, run down. *See* **trace** (1).

tract¹ *noun*
1. A part of the earth's surface ▶ district, region, zone. *See* **area** (2). **2.** A piece of land ▶ acreage, patch, plot. *See* **lot** (1). **3.** A wide and open area, as of land, sky, or water ▶ extent, stretch, sweep. *See* **expanse** (1).

tract² *noun*
A formal discussion of a subject, either written or spoken ▶ disquisition, dissertation. *See* **discourse** (1).

tractability *or* **tractableness** *noun*
1. The quality or state of willingly carrying out the wishes of others ▶ compliancy, complaisance, submissiveness. *See* **obedience. 2.** The quality or state of being flexible ▶ elasticity, malleability, pliability. *See* **flexibility** (1).

tractable *adjective*
1. Willing to carry out the wishes of others ▸ complaisant, docile, submissive. *See* **obedient. 2.** Capable of being shaped or bent ▸ bendable, ductile, plastic. *See* **malleable** (1).
traction *noun*
▸ drag, draw, tow. *See* **pull** (1).
trade *noun*
1. Commercial, industrial, or professional activity in general ▸ industry, traffic. *See* **business** (1). *See synonym note at* **business. 2.** The commercial transactions of customers with a supplier ▸ business, custom. *See* **patronage** (2). **3.** A business agreement involving goods or services ▸ sale, trade, transaction. *See* **deal** (1). **4.** The act of exchanging ▸ exchange, interchange, switch. *See* **change** (2). **5.** Activity pursued as a livelihood ▸ career, employment, occupation. *See* **business** (2). **6.** Customers or patrons collectively ▸ constituency, custom. *See* **patronage** (3).
trade *verb*
1. To give up in return for something else ▸ exchange, interchange, trade. *See* **change** (3). **2.** To offer for sale ▸ handle, peddle. *See* **sell** (1). **3.** To give and receive mutually, as words ▸ interchange, swap. *See* **exchange** (2).
trademark *noun*
A name or other device placed on merchandise to signify its ownership or manufacture ▸ label, monogram. *See* **mark** (1).
trademark *verb*
To set off by or as if by a mark indicating ownership or manufacture ▸ identify, tag. *See* **mark** (1).
tradeoff *noun*
▸ arrangement, give-and-take, settlement. *See* **compromise.**
trader *or* **tradesman** *noun*
▸ merchant, tradesman. *See* **dealer** (1).
trading *noun*
▸ industry, trade. *See* **business** (1).
tradition *noun*
1. Something immaterial, as a style or philosophy, that is passed from one generation to another ▸ heritage, inheritance, legacy. *See synonym note at* **heritage. 2.** A body of traditional beliefs and notions accumulated about a particular subject ▸ folkways, legend, mythology. *See* **lore** (1). **3.** A formal act or set of acts prescribed by ritual ▸ rite, ritual, service. *See* **ceremony** (1). **4.** Behavior patterns, traits, and products considered as an expression of a certain people or period ▸ civilization, custom, ethos, society. *See* **culture** (2).
traditional *adjective*
1. Conforming to established standards ▸ conformist, orthodox. *See* **conventional** (1). **2.** Generally approved or agreed upon ▸ customary, orthodox, time-honored. *See* **accepted.**
traditionalist *noun*
One with politically conservative views ▸ orthodox, rightist. *See* **conservative.**

traditionalist *or* **traditionalistic** *adjective*
Favoring traditional views and values, especially as a political philosophy ▸ right-wing, Tory. *See* **conservative** (1).
traditionalize *verb*
▸ standardize, stylize. *See* **conventionalize.**
traduce *verb*
▸ calumniate, defame, slander. *See* **malign.** *See synonym note at* **malign.**
traducement *noun*
▸ defamation, denigration, slander. *See* **libel.**
traffic *noun*
1. Commercial, industrial, or professional activity in general ▸ industry, trade. *See* **business** (1). *See synonym note at* **business. 2.** The commercial transactions of customers with a supplier ▸ business, trade. *See* **patronage** (2).
trafficker *noun*
1. A person engaged in buying and selling ▸ merchant, tradesman. *See* **dealer** (1). **2.** A person who sells narcotics illegally ▸ dealer, peddler. *See* **pusher.**
tragedy *noun*
▸ cataclysm, holocaust, mishap. *See* **disaster** (1).
trail *verb*
1. To hang or cause to hang down and be pulled along behind ▸ drag, draggle, train. *See also* **pull. 2.** To follow the traces of, as in hunting ▸ smell out, sniff out, trace, track. *Idiom:* be hot on the trail of. *See also* **hunt. 3.** To follow closely or persistently ▸ dog, heel, tag. **4.** To keep another under surveillance by moving behind ▸ shadow, track. *Informal:* tail. *See* **follow** (3). **5.** To go or move slowly so that progress is hindered ▸ dawdle, dilly-dally, drag. *See* **delay** (2). **6.** To walk in a laborious way ▸ plod, tramp. *See* **trudge.**
trail *noun*
1. Something that follows or is drawn along behind ▸ tail, train, wake. *See also* **stream. 2.** A visible sign or mark of the passage of someone or something ▸ footprints, scent, trace. *See* **track** (1). **3.** A course affording passage from one place to another ▸ path, road, route. *See* **way** (2).
trailblazer *noun*
▸ herald, precursor. *See* **forerunner** (1).
train *noun*
1. A string of railroad cars led by a locomotive ▸ rail, railroad train, railway. *Informal:* choo-choo, choo-choo train. **2.** Something that follows or is drawn along behind ▸ tail, trail, wake. *See also* **stream. 3.** A group of attendants or followers ▸ entourage, suite. *See* **retinue. 4.** A number of things placed or occurring one after the other ▸ order, procession, sequence. *See* **series.** *See synonym note at* **series.**
train *verb*
1. To hang or cause to hang down and be pulled along behind ▸ drag, draggle, trail. *See also* **pull. 2.** To engage in activities in order to strengthen or condition ▸ drill, exercise, practice, work out. **3.** To impart knowledge and skill to ▸ discipline, instruct. *See* **educate** (1). *See synonym note at* **educate. 4.** To direct

something, often toward a target ▸ level, point, set. *See* **aim** (1). *See synonym note at* **aim**.

trainable *adjective*
Capable of being educated ▸ docile, educable, teachable. *See also* **obedient**.

trained *adjective*
▸ learned, schooled, versed. *See* **educated** (1).

trainee *noun*
▸ apprentice, pupil, scholar. *See* **student**.

trainer *noun*
▸ instructor, pedagogue, tutor. *See* **educator**.

training *noun*
1. The act, process, or art of imparting knowledge and skill ▸ pedagogy, schooling. *See* **education** (1). **2.** Repetition of an action so as to develop or maintain one's skill ▸ exercise, rehearsal. *See* **practice** (1).

traipse *verb*
▸ drift, meander, wander. *See* **rove**.

trait *noun*
▸ characteristic, feature, peculiarity. *See* **quality** (1). *See synonym note at* **quality**.

traitor *noun*
1. One who betrays ▸ Judas, snake. *Informal:* rat. *See* **betrayer**. **2.** A person who has defected ▸ deserter, recreant, renegade. *See* **defector**.

traitorous *adjective*
1. Involving or constituting treason ▸ seditious, treasonable, treasonous. **2.** Not true to duty or obligation ▸ disloyal, perfidious, treacherous. *See* **faithless** (1). *See synonym note at* **faithless**.

traitorousness *noun*
1. Willful violation of allegiance to one's country ▸ lese majesty, sedition, seditiousness, treason. **2.** Betrayal, especially of a duty or obligation ▸ falseness, perfidiousness, unfaithfulness. *See* **faithlessness** (1).

trammel *noun*
Something that physically confines the legs or arms ▸ handcuffs, hobble, irons. *See* **bond** (1).

trammel *verb*
1. To gain control of by trapping ▸ snare, trap. *See* **catch** (1). **2.** To restrict the activity or free movement of ▸ fetter, handcuff, hobble. *See* **hamper**[1] (1).

tramp *verb*
1. To travel about or journey on foot ▸ hike, backpack, march, trek. *See also* **journey, walk**. **2.** To step on heavily and repeatedly so as to crush, injure, or destroy ▸ stamp, stomp, trample, tread, tromp. *See also* **crush, trample**. **3.** To walk in a laborious way ▸ slog, stamp, stomp. *See* **trudge**. **4.** To move about at random, especially over a wide area ▸ drift, meander, wander. *See* **rove**.

tramp *noun*
1. An impoverished person ▸ beggar, insolvent, vagabond. *See* **pauper**. **2.** An act of walking ▸ ramble, stroll. *See* **walk** (1). **3.** One who wanders without a permanent home or livelihood ▸ nomad, roamer, vagabond. *See* **hobo**. **4.** A person, typically a woman, who is sexually promiscuous ▸ hussy, whore. *See* **slut**.

trample *verb*
1. To step on heavily and repeatedly so as to crush, injure, or destroy ▸ stamp, stomp, tramp, tread, tromp. *See also* **crush, trudge**. **2.** To treat arbitrarily or cruelly ▸ grind, tyrannize.

trampy *verb*
▸ fast, loose, sluttish. *See* **wanton** (1).

trance *noun*
1. The condition of being so lost in solitary thought that one is unaware of one's surroundings ▸ absentmindedness, abstraction, bemusement, brown study, daydreaming, dream, half-conscious state, hypnotic state, muse, reverie, sleepwalking, study. **2.** A stunned or bewildered condition ▸ bewilderment, perplexity, stupor. *See* **daze**.

tranquil *adjective*
1. Free from disturbance, agitation, or commotion ▸ peaceful, placid, serene. *See* **still** (1). *See synonym note at* **still**. **2.** Not excited or agitated ▸ peaceful, placid, serene. *See* **calm** (1).

tranquilize *verb*
1. To ease the anger or agitation of ▸ appease, mollify, soothe. *See* **pacify**. **2.** To administer especially a painkilling drug to someone ▸ medicate, narcotize. *See* **drug** (1).

tranquilizer *noun*
▸ narcotic, opiate, sedative. *See* **soporific**.

tranquillity *or* **tranquility** *noun*
1. An absence of motion or disturbance ▸ calmness, lull, peacefulness. *See* **stillness** (1). **2.** Lack of emotional agitation ▸ peace, serenity. *See* **calm** (1).

transact *verb*
▸ execute, prosecute. *See* **perform** (1).

transaction *noun*
1. A business agreement involving goods or services ▸ exchange, sale, trade. *See* **deal** (1). **2.** The act of beginning and carrying through to completion ▸ execution, prosecution. *See* **performance** (1).

transcend *verb*
1. To go beyond the limits of ▸ overstep, surpass. *See* **exceed** (1). **2.** To be greater or better than ▸ exceed, excel, outshine. *See* **surpass** (1). *See synonym note at* **surpass**.

transcendence *noun*
▸ superbness, superiority. *See* **excellence**.

transcendent *adjective*
▸ top, ultimate, utmost. *See* **maximum**.

transcendental *adjective*
▸ metaphysical, superhuman. *See* **supernatural** (1).

transcribe *verb*
▸ interpret, render. *See* **translate** (1).

transfer *verb*
1. To change the ownership of property by means of a legal document ▸ assign, cede, convey, deed, grant, make over, sign over, transmit. **2.** To change one's residence or place of business, for example ▸ move, relocate, remove. *Idiom:* pull up stakes. *See also* **emigrate, go**. **3.** To direct a person elsewhere for help or information ▸ refer, send, turn over. **4.** To go or

cause to go from one place to another ▶ shift, travel. *See* **move** (2). **5.** To relinquish to the possession or control of another ▶ furnish, provide. *See* **give** (1). **6.** To spread a disease to others ▶ convey, pass, transmit. *See* **communicate** (4). **7.** To serve as a conduit ▶ convey, transmit. *See* **conduct** (3).

transfer *noun*
1. The act of delivering or the condition of being delivered ▶ conveyance, transmission. *See* **delivery** (1). **2.** Legal transfer of ownership or title ▶ assignment, conveyance, transferal. *See* **grant.**

transferable *adjective*
▶ communicable, infectious. *See* **contagious.**

transferal *noun*
▶ assignment, transfer. *See* **grant.**

transfiguration *noun*
▶ change, shift, transformation. *See* **conversion** (1).

transfigure *verb*
▶ mutate, transform, transmute. *See* **convert** (1). *See synonym note at* **convert.**

transfix *verb*
1. To compel the attention, interest, or imagination of ▶ captivate, fascinate, mesmerize. *See* **grip** (1). **2.** To penetrate with a sharp edge ▶ bayonet, incise, pierce, slash. *See* **cut** (1).

transform *verb*
1. To change into a different form ▶ mutate, transfigure, transmute. *See* **convert** (1). *See synonym note at* **convert. 2.** To bring about a radical change in ▶ metamorphose, revolutionize. *See also* **change, overhaul.**

transformable *adjective*
▶ fluid, unsettled, variable. *See* **changeable** (1).

transformation *noun*
1. The process or result of changing from one use, function, or appearance to another ▶ change, mutation, transfiguration. *See* **conversion** (1). **2.** A momentous or sweeping change ▶ cataclysm, convulsion, upheaval. *See* **revolution** (3).

transfuse *verb*
▶ permeate, suffuse. *See* **charge** (1).

transgress *verb*
1. To refuse or fail to obey ▶ defy, resist. *See* **disobey. 2.** To violate a rule or law ▶ err, sin, trespass. *See* **offend** (3). **3.** To fail to fulfill a promise or conform to a regulation ▶ break, contravene, infringe. *See* **violate** (1). **4.** To go beyond the limits of ▶ overstep, surpass. *See* **exceed** (1).

transgression *noun*
1. An act of breaking a law or of nonfulfillment of an obligation ▶ infraction, infringement, violation. *See* **breach** (1). *See synonym note at* **breach. 2.** An advance beyond proper or legal limits ▶ infringement, intrusion, obtrusion. *See* **trespass** (2).

transgressor *noun*
1. One who commits a crime ▶ culprit, lawbreaker, offender. *See* **criminal. 2.** A person who rebels ▶ insurrectionist, revolutionist. *See* **rebel** (1).

transient *adjective*
1. Lasting or existing only for a short time ▶ ephem-

eral, fleeting, temporary. *See* **transitory. 2.** Moving from one habitat to another on a seasonal basis ▶ migrational, seasonal. *See* **migratory** (1).

transient *noun*
One who wanders without a permanent home or livelihood ▶ nomad, roamer, vagabond. *See* **hobo.**

transit *noun*
1. The moving of persons or goods from one place to another ▶ carriage, conveyance, transport. *See* **transportation** (1). **2.** Passage from one form, state, or stage to another ▶ change, passage, shift. *See* **transition. 3.** The act of traveling from one place to another ▶ flight, passage, progress. *See* **journey.**

transit *verb*
To go or extend across ▶ track, transit, traverse. *See* **cross** (1).

transition *noun*
Passage from one form, state, or stage to another ▶ change, flux, move, passage, progression, shift, transit, turn. *Idiom:* change of course. *See also* **change, conversion.**

transitory *adjective*
Lasting or existing only for a short time ▶ brief, ephemeral, evanescent, fleet, fleeting, fugacious, fugitive, momentary, passing, short, short-lived, temporal, temporary, transient. *See also* **temporary.**

translate *verb*
1. To express in another language ▶ construe, interpret, metaphrase, put, render, transcribe, transliterate, transpose. *See also* **convert. 2.** To express the meaning of in other, especially simpler, words ▶ rehash, reword. *See* **paraphrase. 3.** To change into a different form or substance ▶ mutate, transfigure, transform. *See* **convert** (1).

translation *noun*
1. The act or process of translating ▶ construe, crib, interpretation, metaphrase, pony, rendering, transliteration, trot. **2.** A restating of something in other, especially simpler, words ▶ restatement, version. *See* **paraphrase. 3.** The process or result of changing from one use, function, or appearance to another ▶ change, transformation. *See* **conversion** (1).

transliterate *verb*
▶ interpret, render. *See* **translate** (1).

transliteration *noun*
▶ crib, rendering. *See* **translation** (1).

translucent *adjective*
▶ crystalline, see-through, transparent. *See* **clear** (1).

transmigrant *noun*
One who emigrates ▶ emigrant, immigrant, migrant.

transmigrate *verb*
1. To leave one's native land and settle in another ▶ emigrate (from), immigrate (to), migrate, resettle. *See also* **move, settle. 2.** To change habitat seasonally ▶ migrate.

transmigration *noun*
1. Departure from one's native land to settle in another ▶ diaspora, expatriation. *See* **emigration.**

2. Settling in a country to which one is not native ▶ immigration, migration.

transmigratory *adjective*
▶ migrational, seasonal, transient. *See* **migratory** (1).

transmission *noun*
▶ conveyance, surrender, transfer. *See* **delivery** (1).

transmit *verb*
1. To cause something to be conveyed to a destination ▶ consign, dispatch. *See* **send** (1). *See synonym note at* **send**. 2. To make known ▶ disclose, divulge, impart. *See* **communicate** (1). 3. To give property to another after one's death ▶ bequeath, will. *See* **leave**[1] (1). 4. To spread a disease to others ▶ convey, pass, transfer. *See* **communicate** (4). 5. To change the ownership of property by means of a legal document ▶ deed, grant, sign over. *See* **transfer** (1). 6. To serve as a conduit ▶ convey, transfer. *See* **conduct** (3).

transmittable *adjective*
▶ communicable, infectious, tranferable. *See* **contagious**.

transmogrification *noun*
▶ change, mutation, transformation. *See* **conversion** (1).

transmogrify *verb*
▶ mutate, transform, transpose. *See* **convert** (1). *See synonym note at* **convert**.

transmutable *adjective*
▶ fluid, unsettled, variable. *See* **changeable** (1).

transmutation *noun*
▶ change, mutation, transformation. *See* **conversion** (1).

transmute *verb*
▶ mutate, transfigure, transform. *See* **convert** (1). *See synonym note at* **convert**.

transparent *adjective*
1. Free from what obscures ▶ crystal clear, see-through, translucent. *See* **clear** (1). *See synonym note at* **clear**. 2. Thin, fine, and light ▶ ethereal, gauzy, vaporous. *See* **sheer**[2] (1). *See synonym note at* **sheer**[2]. 3. Easily seen through due to a lack of subtlety ▶ blatant, overt, patent. *See* **obvious** (1).

transpire *verb*
1. To be made public ▶ break, come out, get out, out. *Informal:* leak (out). *See also* **air, announce, appear**. 2. To take place ▶ befall, come, occur. *See* **happen** (1). *See synonym note at* **happen**. 3. To flow or emit something slowly ▶ exude, leach, seep, transude. *See* **ooze**.

transplant *verb*
▶ broadcast, seed, sow. *See* **plant** (1).

transport *verb*
1. To move while supporting ▶ bear, haul, lug. *See* **carry** (1). *See synonym note at* **carry**. 2. To cause to come along with oneself ▶ convey, fetch. *See* **bring** (1). 3. To have a powerful emotional effect on someone ▶ electrify, thrill. *See* **enrapture**. *See synonym note at* **enrapture**. 4. To force to leave by official decree ▶ deport, exile, extradite. *See* **banish** (1). *See synonym note at* **banish**.

transport *noun*
1. The moving of persons or goods from one place to another ▶ carriage, conveyance, transit. *See* **transportation** (1). 2. A supremely beautiful, blissful state or experience ▶ ecstasy, paradise. *See* **heaven** (1).

transportable *adjective*
▶ moving, traveling. *See* **mobile** (1).

transportation *noun*
1. The moving of persons or goods from one place to another ▶ carriage, carrying, conveyance, conveying, freight, hauling, shipping, transit, transport. 2. Enforced removal from one's native country by official decree ▶ deportation, extradition. *See* **exile** (1).

transpose *verb*
1. To change to the opposite position, direction, or course ▶ invert, turn (about, around, over, *or* round). *See* **reverse** (1). *See synonym note at* **reverse**. 2. To change into a different form ▶ mutate, transform, transmogrify. *See* **convert** (1). 3. To give up in return for something else ▶ exchange, interchange, trade. *See* **change** (3). 4. To express in another language ▶ interpret, render. *See* **translate** (1).

transposition *noun*
1. The act of exchanging or substituting ▶ commutation, exchange, switch. *See* **change** (2). 2. The act of changing or being changed from one position, direction, or course to the opposite ▶ inversion, turnabout. *See* **reversal** (1).

transubstantiate *verb*
▶ mutate, transform, transmute. *See* **convert** (1).

transubstantiation *noun*
▶ change, transfiguration. *See* **conversion** (1).

transude *verb*
1. To excrete moisture through a porous skin or layer ▶ lather, perspire, sweat. 2. To flow or leak out or emit something slowly ▶ exude, leach, seep. *See* **ooze**.

transversal *adjective*
▶ crossways, crosswise, traverse. *See* **transverse**.

transverse *adjective*
Situated or lying across ▶ across, crossing, crossways, crosswise, thwart, transversal, traverse. *See also* **oblique**.

trap *noun*
1. A device or stratagem for catching or tricking a person or animal ▶ booby trap, deadfall, gin, noose, pit, pitfall, snare, springe, tripwire. *See also* **lure, trick**. 2. An attack or stratagem for capturing or tricking an unsuspecting person ▶ ambuscade, ambush. *See also* **deceit**. 3. *Slang* The opening in the body through which food is ingested ▶ chops, maw. *Slang:* yap. *See* **mouth** (1).

trap *verb*
To gain control of by trapping ▶ net, snare. *See* **catch** (1). *See synonym note at* **catch**.

trash *noun*
1. Items or material discarded or rejected as useless or worthless ▶ litter, rubbish, waste. *See* **garbage** (1). 2. Something that does not have or make sense ▶ bunkum, drivel, garbage. *See* **nonsense** (1). 3. A

person or group of people regarded as worthless or contemptible ▸ dregs, rabble, ragtag and bobtail. *See* **riffraff.**

trash *verb*
1. *Slang* To injure or destroy property maliciously ▸ wreck, vandalize. *See also* **destroy. 2.** *Slang* To criticize harshly and devastatingly ▸ bash, excoriate, flay. *See* **slam** (5).

trashy *adjective*
▸ cheap, lousy, poor. *See* **shoddy** (1).

trauma *noun*
1. Marked tissue damage, especially when produced by physical injury ▸ laceration, lesion, traumatism, wound. **2.** Something that jars the mind or emotions ▸ jolt, surprise. *See* **shock**[1] (1). **3.** A situation requiring immediate assistance or remedial action ▸ crisis, distress, trouble. *See* **emergency. 4.** The action or result of inflicting loss or pain ▸ detriment, injury. *See* **harm.**

traumatism *noun*
Marked tissue damage, especially when produced by physical injury ▸ laceration, lesion, trauma, wound. *See also* **harm.**

traumatize *verb*
1. To cause bodily damage to a living thing ▸ hurt, injure, wing, wound. *See also* **cut, break. 2.** To cause emotional suffering or painful sorrow to ▸ anguish, pain, wound. *See* **distress** (1).

travail *noun*
1. Physical exertion that is usually difficult and exhausting ▸ drudgery, toil, work. *See* **labor** (1). *See synonym note at* **labor. 2.** The act or process of bringing forth young ▸ childbearing, delivery, labor. *See* **birth** (1).

travail *verb*
To exert oneself steadily, often to the point of exhaustion ▸ strain, sweat, toil. *See* **labor** (1).

travel *verb*
1. To make or go on a journey ▸ peregrinate, tour, voyage. *See* **journey. 2.** To become known far and wide ▸ circulate, get around, go around, spread. *Idioms:* go (*or* make) the rounds. **3.** To go or cause to go from one place to another ▸ shift, transfer. *See* **move** (2).

travel *noun*
The act of traveling from one place to another ▸ flight, passage, progress. *See* **journey.**

traveler *noun*
▸ sightseer, vacationer, visitor. *See* **tourist.**

traveling *adjective*
1. Capable of moving or being moved from place to place ▸ moving, transportable. *See* **mobile** (1). **2.** Leading the life of a person without a fixed domicile; moving from place to place ▸ itinerant, vagabond. *See* **nomadic.**

traversable *adjective*
▸ negotiable, passable. *See* **passable** (1).

traversal *noun*
1. A refusal to grant the truth of a statement or charge ▸ disaffirmation, disclaimer, rejection. *See* **denial** (1). **2.** The act of traveling from one place to another ▸ flight, passage, progress. *See* **journey.**

traverse *verb*
1. To go or extend across ▸ pass, track, transit. *See* **cross** (1). **2.** To journey over ▸ go, cross. *See* **cover** (2). **3.** To look at or study carefully or critically ▸ investigate, peruse, scrutinize. *See* **examine** (1). **4.** To take a stand against ▸ challenge, dispute, oppose. *See* **contest** (1). **5.** To refuse to admit the truth, reality, value, or worth of ▸ contravene, disaffirm, disavow. *See* **deny** (1).

traverse *adjective*
Situated or lying across ▸ crossways, crosswise, transversal. *See* **transverse.**

travesty *noun*
A false, derisive, or impudent imitation of something ▸ caricature, farce, parody. *See* **mockery** (2).

travesty *verb*
To copy the manner or expression of another, especially in an exaggerated or mocking way ▸ caricature, mock. *See* **imitate** (1).

trawl *verb*
▸ angle, cast, troll. *See* **fish** (1).

treacherous *adjective*
1. Not true to duty or obligation ▸ disloyal, perfidious, traitorous. *See* **faithless** (1). *See synonym note at* **faithless. 2.** Involving possible risk, loss, or injury ▸ chancy, hazardous, risky. *See* **dangerous.**

treacherousness *noun*
▸ disloyalty, perfidiousness, traitorousness. *See* **faithlessness** (1).

treachery *noun*
1. Betrayal, especially of a duty or obligation ▸ disloyalty, perfidy, unfaithfulness. *See* **faithlessness** (1). **2.** An act of betraying ▸ double cross. *Slang:* sellout. *See* **betrayal** (1).

treacle *noun*
▸ bathos, maudlinism. *See* **sentimentality.**

tread *verb*
1. To step on heavily and repeatedly so as to crush, injure, or destroy ▸ stamp, stomp, tramp, trample, tromp. *See also* **crush, trudge. 2.** To go on foot ▸ step, stride. *See* **walk.**

tread *noun*
A manner of walking ▸ footfall, footstep, gait. *See* **walk** (2).

treadmill *noun*
▸ rote, rounds, track. *See* **routine** (1).

treason *noun*
1. Willful violation of allegiance to one's country ▸ lese majesty, sedition, seditiousness, traitorousness. **2.** Betrayal, especially of a duty or obligation ▸ disloyalty, perfidy, unfaithfulness. *See* **faithlessness** (1).

treasonous *or* **treasonable** *adjective*
Involving or constituting treason ▸ seditious, traitorous. *See also* **faithless.**

treasure *noun*
1. Someone or something considered exceptionally

precious ▸ find, gem, pearl, plum, prize. *Informal:* catch. *Idioms:* apple of one's eye, pride and joy. *See also* **masterpiece. 2.** A great amount of accumulated money and precious possessions ▸ fortune, pelf, riches. *See* **wealth** (1). **3.** A supply stored or hidden for possible future use ▸ cache, reserve, stockpile. *See* **hoard.**

treasure *verb*
1. To have a high opinion of or regard for ▸ cherish, esteem, prize. *See* **value** (1). *See synonym note at* **value. 2.** To keep for future use ▸ put by, salt away, set by. *See* **save** (1).

treasury *or* **treasure house** *noun*
▸ bank, storehouse, vault. *See* **depository.**

treat *verb*
1. To behave in a specified way toward someone ▸ cope with, handle. **2.** To pay for the food, drink, or entertainment of another ▸ *Informal:* set up, stand. *Slang:* blow, spring for. *Idioms:* pick up the check (*or* tab), stand treat. *See also* **amuse. 3.** To be concerned with something ▸ address, consider. *See* **deal** (1). **4.** To provide as a remedy ▸ dispense, medicate. *See* **administer** (3).

treat *noun*
1. Something fine and delicious, especially a food ▸ morsel, tidbit. *See* **delicacy** (1). **2.** Something that amuses, entertains, or pleases ▸ delight, enjoyment, pleasure. *See* **amusement. 3.** Something costly and unnecessary ▸ extravagance, frill, indulgence. *See* **luxury** (1).

treatise *noun*
▸ dialogue, dissertation, lecture. *See* **discourse** (1).

treatment *noun*
1. The systematic application of remedies to effect a cure ▸ care, doctoring, medical care, nursing, regimen, rehabilitation, therapeutics, therapy. *Informal:* rehab. *See also* **drug. 2.** An agent used to restore health ▸ elixir, medication, remedy. *See* **cure.**

treaty *noun*
A formal agreement between two or more states or nations ▸ accord, agreement, concord, concordat, convention, entente, pact. *See also* **agreement, bargain, compromise, truce.**

treble *adjective*
▸ piercing, shrill. *See* **high** (3).

trek *verb*
1. To travel about or journey on foot ▸ backpack, hike, march, tramp. *See also* **rove, walk. 2.** To make or go on a journey ▸ peregrinate, travel, voyage. *See* **journey.**

trek *noun*
A journey undertaken with a specific objective ▸ mission, odyssey, pilgrimage, tour, voyage. *See* **expedition** (1).

tremble *verb*
1. To move to and fro in short, jerky movements ▸ quiver, shudder, twitter. *See* **shake** (1). *See synonym note at* **shake. 2.** To move back and forth ▸ swing, vacillate, waggle. *See* **sway** (1).

tremble *noun*
A nervous shaking of the body ▸ quake, shudder, twitch. *See* **tremor** (2).

trembles *noun*
▸ fidgets, jumps, shivers. *See* **jitters.**

trembling *adjective*
Marked by or affected with tremors ▸ quaking, quivering, shaking. *See* **tremulous** (1).

trembling *noun*
A nervous shaking of the body ▸ quiver, shake, twitch. *See* **tremor** (2).

tremendous *adjective*
1. Of extraordinary size and power ▸ behemoth, colossal, gigantic, mighty. *See* **enormous.** *See synonym note at* **enormous. 2.** *Informal* Particularly excellent ▸ fantastic, sensational, superb. *See* **marvelous** (1).

tremendousness *noun*
▸ immensity, vastness. *See* **enormousness.**

tremor *noun*
1. A shaking of the earth ▸ earthquake, quake, seism, temblor. *Informal:* shake. **2.** A nervous shaking of the body ▸ jerk, paroxysm, quake, quaver, quiver, shake, shaking, shiver, shudder, spasm, thrill, tic, tremble, trembling, twitch, vibrating, vibration. *See also* **shake.**

tremulant *adjective*
Marked by or affected with tremors ▸ quaky, quivery, shaky. *See* **tremulous** (1).

tremulous *adjective*
1. Marked by or affected with tremors ▸ aquiver, jerky, quaking, quaky, quavering, quivering, quivery, shaky, shivering, shivery, shuddering, trembling, tremulant, twittery, vibrating. **2.** Filled with fear or terror ▸ fearful, frightened, scared. *See* **afraid.**

trench *noun*
▸ channel, ditch, rut. *See* **furrow** (1).

trenchancy *noun*
▸ corrosiveness, mordacity. *See* **sarcasm.**

trenchant *adjective*
1. Keenly perceptive or discerning ▸ incisive, keen, penetrating. *See* **critical** (2). **2.** So sharp as to cause mental pain ▸ caustic, scathing, sharp, vitriolic. *See* **biting. 3.** Expressed in few words ▸ concise, short, succinct. *See* **brief** (1).

trench coat *noun*
▸ overcoat, raincoat, slicker. *See* **coat** (1).

trend *noun*
1. A natural or habitual preference for something ▸ disposition, leaning, penchant. *See* **inclination** (1). **2.** The current custom ▸ fad, mode, vogue. *See* **fashion** (1).

trend *verb*
To have a tendency or inclination ▸ lean, skew. *See* **tend**[1].

trendy *adjective*
Informal In accordance with current fashion ▸ mod, stylish, swanky. *See* **fashionable.** *See synonym note at* **fashionable.**

trepidation *noun*
▸ apprehension, consternation, dismay. *See* **fear.** *See synonym note at* **fear.**

trespass *verb*
1. To enter forcibly or illegally ▸ break in, burglarize, invade. *See also* **rob, steal. 2.** To violate a rule or law ▸ err, sin, transgress. *See* **offend** (3). **3.** To force or come in as an improper or unwanted element ▸ cut in, horn in, interlope. *See* **intrude** (1).

trespass *noun*
1. The act of entering a building or room with the intent to commit theft ▸ break-in, breaking and entering, burglary, forced entry. *See also* **larceny. 2.** An advance beyond proper or legal limits ▸ encroachment, entrenchment, impingement, infringement, intrusion, obtrusion, overstepping, transgression. *See also* **invasion. 3.** An act of breaking a law or of nonfulfillment of an obligation ▸ infraction, violation. *See* **breach** (1). *See synonym note at* **breach.**

trestle *noun*
▸ crossbeam, girder, timber. *See* **beam** (2).

triad *noun*
▸ threesome, trine, trinity. *See* **trio.**

trial *noun*
1. A state of pain or anguish that tests one's resiliency and character ▸ affliction, crucible, ordeal, tribulation, visitation. *See also* **difficulty. 2.** The examination of evidence, charges, and claims in court ▸ court case, hearing, inquest, inquiry. *See also* **examination. 3.** An operation employed to resolve an uncertainty ▸ experiment, experimentation, test. **4.** A procedure that ascertains effectiveness, value, proper function, or other quality ▸ proof, shakedown, tryout. *See* **test** (1). **5.** A trying to do or make something ▸ effort. *Informal:* shot. *See* **attempt** (1). **6.** A source of persistent worry or hardship ▸ cross, tribulation. *See* **burden**[1] (1). *See synonym note at* **burden**[1]. **7.** Something that annoys ▸ plague, torment. *See* **annoyance** (2). **8.** A test of skill or ability ▸ bout, contest, match. *See* **competition** (2).

trial *adjective*
Serving as a tentative model for future experiment or development ▸ experimental, probative. *See* **pilot.**

✚ **CORE SYNONYMS:** *trial, affliction, crucible, ordeal, tribulation.* These nouns denote a state of pain or anguish that tests one's resiliency and character: *no consolation in their hour of trial; the affliction of a bereaved family; the crucible of revolution; the ordeal of being an innocent murder suspect; a time of relentless tribulation.*

---

tribe *noun*
▸ clan, kindred, lineage. *See* **family** (2).

tribulation *noun*
1. A source of persistent worry or hardship ▸ cross, trial. *See* **burden**[1] (1). *See synonym note at* **burden**[1]. **2.** A state of pain or anguish that tests one's resiliency and character ▸ affliction, ordeal, visitation. *See* **trial** (1). *See synonym note at* **trial.**

tribunal *noun*
▸ forum, judiciary. *See* **court** (2).

tributary *noun*
1. A relatively large natural flow of water ▸ stream, waterway. *See* **river. 2.** A small stream ▸ creek, watercourse. *See* **brook**[1]. **3.** Something analogous to a tree branch ▸ arm, fork, offshoot. *See* **branch** (1).

tribute *noun*
1. An expression of admiration ▸ commendation, praise. *See* **compliment** (1). **2.** A formal token of appreciation and admiration for a person's high achievements ▸ salute, salvo. *See* **testimonial** (2). **3.** A compulsory contribution that is required for the support of an authority ▸ duty, levy, tariff. *See* **tax** (1).

trice *noun*
▸ instant, second, wink. *See* **flash** (2).

trick *noun*
1. An indirect, usually cunning means of gaining an end ▸ artifice, deception, device, dodge, feint, gimmick, hustle, imposture, jig, maneuver, ploy, ruse, sleight, stratagem, subterfuge, wile. *Informal:* con game, fast one, shenanigan, take-in. *Slang:* snow job. *See also* **move, plot, trap. 2.** The proper method for doing, using, or handling something ▸ feel, knack. *Informal:* hang. **3.** A clever, dexterous act ▸ feat, stunt. *Idiom:* sleight of hand. *See also* **accomplishment. 4.** A mischievous act ▸ caper, joke, lark. *See* **prank**[1]. **5.** A limited, often assigned period of activity, duty, or opportunity ▸ stint, time, watch. *See* **turn** (1). **6.** *Informal* A clever, unexpected new trick or method ▸ twist. *Slang:* kick. *See* **wrinkle** (2).

trick *verb*
To cause to accept something false, especially by trickery or misrepresentation ▸ dupe, fool, mislead. *See* **deceive.**

trick out *or* **up** *verb*
Informal To dress in formal or special clothing ▸ attire, deck (out). *See* **dress up.**

trick *adjective*
So weak or defective as to be liable to fail ▸ undependable, unreliable. *See also* **defective, weak.**

✚ **CORE SYNONYMS:** *trick, wile, artifice, ruse, feint, stratagem, maneuver, dodge.* These nouns denote means for achieving an end by cunning, indirection, or deviousness. *Trick* implies willful deception: *"The . . . boys . . . had all sorts of tricks to prevent us from winning"* (W.H. Hudson). *Wile* suggests deceiving and entrapping a victim by playing on his or her weak points: *"He did not fail to see/His uncle's cunning wiles and treachery"* (William Morris). *Artifice* refers to something especially contrived to create a desired effect: *"Should the public forgive artifices used to avoid military service?"* (Godfrey Sperling). *Ruse* stresses the creation of a false impression: *Your pretended deafness was a ruse to enable you to learn our plans, wasn't it? Feint* denotes a deceptive act calculated to distract attention from one's real purpose: *One person bumped into me as a feint while the other stole my wallet. Stratagem* implies carefully planned deception used to achieve an objective: *The manager used* *ruthless stratagems to win the promotion. Maneuver* often applies to a single strategic move: *"To this day they always speak of that Reform Bill as if it had been a dishonest maneuver"* (The Standard). *Dodge* stresses shifty and ingenious deception: *"'It was all false, of course?' 'All, sir,' replied Mr. Weller, '. . . artful dodge'"* (Charles Dickens).

---

trickery *noun*
1. Lack of straightforwardness and honesty in action ▸ deviousness, slyness, underhandedness. *See* **dishonesty** (2). **2.** The act or practice of deceiving ▸ deception, duplicity, guile. *See* **deceit** (1).

trickiness *noun*
▸ craft, duplicity, shadiness, wiliness. *See* **dishonesty** (2).

trickle *verb*
To fall or let fall in drops of liquid ▸ dribble, drizzle. *See* **drip.**

trickle *noun*
The process or sound of dripping ▸ dribble, drip, drizzle, mizzle.

tricks *noun*
▸ diablerie, high jinks, tomfoolery. *See* **mischief** (1).

trickster *noun*
▸ cheater, rook, swindler. *See* **cheat** (2).

tricky *adjective*
1. Deceitfully clever ▸ sly, wily. *See* **artful** (1). **2.** Requiring great tact or skill ▸ demanding, exacting, precarious. *See* **delicate** (3).

tried *adjective*
▸ practiced, seasoned, veteran. *See* **experienced.**

trifle *noun*
1. Something or things of little importance ▸ fiddle-faddle, frippery, frivolity, froth, inconsequence, inconsequentiality, inconsequentialness, inconsiderableness, indifference, insignificance, insignificancy, levity, lightness, minutia, negligibility, negligibleness, nonsense, paltriness, pettiness, picayune, small change, smallness, triviality, trivialness, unimportance. *Informal:* small potatoes. **2.** A small showy article ▸ knickknack, trinket. *See* **novelty** (3). **3.** A tiny amount ▸ dash, drop, smidgen. *See* **bit**[1] (1).

trifle *verb*
1. To treat lightly or flippantly ▸ dally, flirt, play, toy. *See synonym note at* **flirt. 2.** To touch or handle something out of restlessness ▸ fidget, fool, play. *See* **fiddle** (1). **3.** To make amorous advances without serious intentions ▸ coquet, dally, toy. *See* **flirt** (2).

trifle away *verb*
1. To spend (time) idly or pleasantly ▸ dawdle (away), waste. *See* **idle** (2). **2.** To use, consume, spend, or expend thoughtlessly or carelessly ▸ fritter away, squander, throw away. *See* **waste** (2).

trifling *adjective*
▸ inconsequential, negligible, piddling. *See* **trivial.** *See synonym note at* **trivial.**

trig *adjective*
In good order or clean condition ▸ shipshape, tidy. *See* **neat** (1).

trig *verb*
To make neat and trim; make presentable ▸ freshen (up), slick up, trim. *See* **tidy** (2).

trigger *noun*
Something that causes an angry or resentful response ▸ incitement, stimulus. *See* **provocation** (1).

trigger *verb*
1. To be the cause of ▸ generate, induce, provoke. *See* **cause. 2.** To stir to action or feeling ▸ excite, prod, trigger. *See* **provoke** (1).

triggerman *noun*
▸ killer, massacrer, slaughterer. *See* **murderer.**

trillion *noun*
Informal An indeterminately great amount or number ▸ bunch, multiplicity. *See* **heap** (3).

trim *verb*
1. To make neat and trim; make presentable ▸ freshen (up), slick up, spruce (up). *See* **tidy** (2). **2.** To decrease, as in length or amount, by or as if by severing or excising ▸ chop, prune, truncate. *See* **cut** (3). **3.** To make a slight reduction in prices ▸ shade, shave. **4.** To furnish with decorations ▸ decorate, garnish, ornament. *See* **adorn** (1). **5.** *Informal* To punish with blows or lashes ▸ lash, thrash, whip. *See* **beat** (2). **6.** *Informal* To win a victory over, as in battle or a competition ▸ conquer, surmount, vanquish. *See* **defeat** (1). **7.** *Informal* To get something by deceitful trickery ▸ bilk, defraud, swindle. *See* **cheat** (1).

trim down *verb*
To lose body weight, as by dieting ▸ reduce, slim (down), thin (down). *Idioms:* get the weight off, lose weight, shed some pounds.

trim *noun*
1. A state of sound readiness ▸ fettle, form, order. *See* **shape** (1). **2.** Something that adorns ▸ decoration, embellishment, ornament. *See* **adornment.**

trim *adjective*
1. Having slender and graceful lines ▸ sleek, streamlined. **2.** In good order or clean condition ▸ shipshape, tidy. *See* **neat** (1). *See synonym note at* **neat.**

trimming *noun*
1. Something that adorns ▸ decoration, embellishment, ornament. *See* **adornment. 2.** *Informal* The act of defeating or the condition of being defeated ▸ overthrow, trouncing, vanquishment. *See* **defeat. 3.** *Informal* A punishment dealt with blows or lashes ▸ lashing, thrashing, whipping. *See* **beating** (1).

trine *or* **trinity** *noun*
▸ threesome, triad, troika. *See* **trio.**

trinket *noun*
▸ knickknack, whatnot. *See* **novelty** (3).

trio *noun*
A group of three individuals ▸ three, threesome, triad, trine, trinity, triple, triumvirate, triune, triunity, troika. *See also* **group.**

trip *noun*
1. A usually short journey taken for pleasure ▸ excursion, jaunt, junket, outing. *See also* **expedition. 2.** An unintentional deviation from what is correct, right,

or true ▸ inaccuracy, lapse, mistake. *See* **error** (1).
3. *Slang* A temporary concentration of interest
▸ *Slang:* kick. **4.** The act of traveling from one place to
another ▸ flight, passage, progress. *See* **journey. 5.**
Slang An experience of things or events that are not
real ▸ hallucination, phantasmagoria, phantasmagory.
trip *verb*
1. To lose one's balance and fall or almost fall ▸ skid,
slip. *See* **stumble** (1). **2.** To move in a lively way ▸ skip,
spring. *See* **bound**[1] (1). **3.** To make or go on a journey
▸ peregrinate, travel, voyage. *See* **journey.**
trip up *verb*
To make an error or mistake ▸ blunder, stumble. *See*
err (1).
triple *noun*
▸ threesome, triad, trinity. *See* **trio.**
tripping *adjective*
Slang Stupefied, intoxicated, or otherwise influenced
by the taking of drugs ▸ high, hopped-up, lit (up). *See*
drugged.
tristful *adjective*
▸ dysphoric, gloomy, melancholy, spiritless. *See* **depressed** (1).
trite *adjective*
Without freshness or appeal because of overuse
▸ banal, bromidic, clichéd, commonplace, corny,
hackneyed, musty, overused, overworked, platitudinal, platitudinous, shopworn, stale, stereotyped,
stereotypic, stereotypical, stock, threadbare, timeworn, tired, unimaginative, uninspired, unoriginal,
warmed-over, well-worn, worn-out. *See also* **boring,
dull.**
triturate *verb*
▸ atomize, grind, mill. *See* **crush** (2).
triumph *verb*
To feel or express an uplifting joy over a success or
victory ▸ glory, jubilate. *See* **exult** (1).
triumph over *verb*
To win a victory over, as in battle or a competition
▸ conquer, surmount, vanquish. *See* **defeat** (1).
triumph *noun*
1. The act of conquering ▸ knockout, victory. *See*
conquest. *See synonym note at* **conquest. 2.** Something completed or attained successfully ▸ achievement, deed, feat. *See* **accomplishment** (1). *See synonym note at* **accomplishment. 3.** The act or
condition of feeling an uplifting joy over a success or
victory ▸ jubilance, jubilation. *See* **exultation.**
triumphal *adjective*
▸ champion, triumphant, winning. *See* **victorious.**
triumphant *adjective*
1. Feeling or expressing an uplifting joy over a success
or victory ▸ exultant, gloating, jubilant. *See also*
boastful. 2. Being the winner in a contest or struggle
▸ champion, winning. *See* **victorious.**
triumvirate *noun*
▸ threesome, triad, trinity. *See* **trio.**
triune *or* **triunity** *noun*
▸ threesome, triad, trinity. *See* **trio.**

trivia *noun*
1. Something or things of little importance ▸ frivolity,
minutia, nonsense. *See* **trifle** (1). **2.** A small, often
specialized element of a whole ▸ particular, specialty,
technicality. *See* **detail** (1).
trivial *adjective*
Of little importance or seriousness ▸ fluffy, frivolous,
frothy, inconsequent, inconsequential, inconsiderable, insignificant, light, lightweight, little, negligible,
niggling, nugatory, paltry, petty, picayune, piddling,
small, small-minded, trifling, unimportant. *Slang:*
measly, rinky-dink. **Idiom:** of no account. *See also*
superficial.

✦ CORE SYNONYMS: *trivial, trifling, paltry, petty, picayune.* These adjectives all apply to what is of little
importance or seriousness. *Trivial* and *trifling* refer to
what is so insignificant as to be utterly commonplace
or unremarkable: *"I think all Christians . . . agree in
the essential articles, and that their differences are
trivial"* (Samuel Johnson). *"I regret the trifling narrow
contracted education of the females of my own country"*
(Abigail Adams). *Paltry* describes what falls so far
short of what is required or desired that it arouses
contempt: *"He . . . considered the prize too paltry for
the lives it must cost"* (John Lothrop Motley). *Petty*
can refer to what is of minor or secondary significance or size: *"Our knights are limited to petty
enterprises"* (Sir Walter Scott). What is *picayune* is of
negligible value or importance: *a picayune infraction
of the law.*

◂ ANTONYM: *important*

---

triviality *or* **trivialness** *noun*
▸ frivolity, minutia, trivia. *See* **trifle** (1).
troika *noun*
▸ threesome, triad, trinity. *See* **trio.**
troll *verb*
▸ angle, cast, trawl. *See* **fish** (1).
tromp *verb*
1. To step on heavily and repeatedly so as to crush,
injure, or destroy ▸ stamp, stomp, tramp, trample,
tread. *See also* **crush. 2.** *Informal* To walk in a laborious way ▸ stamp, tramp, trample. *See* **trudge.**
troop *noun*
1. A number of persons who have come or been
gathered together ▸ conference, group. *Informal:* get-together. *See* **assembly** (1). **2.** A group of people acting
together in a shared activity ▸ company, party. *See*
band[2] (1). *See synonym note at* **band. 3.** An enormous
number of persons or things gathered together
▸ horde, mass, throng. *See* **crowd** (1). **4.** A number of
animals considered collectively ▸ bevy, gaggle, herd.
See **flock** (1). *See synonym note at* **flock.**
troop *verb*
1. To move into an area or space in large numbers
▸ cram, press, squeeze. *See* **crowd** (1). **2.** To be with as
a companion ▸ fraternize, hobnob. *Slang:* hang out.
See **associate** (2).
trooper *noun*
1. A member of a law-enforcement agency ▸ officer.

Informal: cop. *See* **police officer. 2.** An enlisted person ► legionary, militiaman, serviceperson. *See* **soldier** (2).

trophy *noun*
1. A memento received as a symbol of excellence or victory ► accolade, award, cup, prize. *See also* **medal, reward. 2.** Something that causes one to remember ► memento, reminder. *See* **remembrance** (1). **3.** Recognition of achievement or superiority or a sign of this ► award, honor. *See* **distinction** (2).

tropical *adjective*
► sweltering, torrid. *See* **hot** (1).

trot *noun*
1. A pace faster than a walk ► jog, lope. *See* **run** (1). **2.** The act or process of translating ► crib, rendering. *See* **translation** (1).

trot *verb*
1. To move on foot at a pace faster than a walk ► lope, scamper, scurry. *See* **run** (1). **2.** To move swiftly ► dash, sprint, zip. *See* **rush** (1).

troth *noun*
The act or condition of being pledged to marry ► betrothal, engagement, espousal.

troth *verb*
To guarantee by a solemn promise ► promise, vow. *See* **pledge** (1).

troubadour *noun*
► muse, rhymer. *See* **poet.**

trouble *noun*
1. A cause of distress or anxiety ► care, concern, stressor, worry. *See also* **anxiety, burden**[1]. **2.** A situation requiring immediate assistance or remedial action ► crisis, distress, exigency. *See* **emergency. 3.** Something that obstructs progress and requires great effort to overcome ► complication, hardship, rigor. *See* **difficulty** (1). **4.** To cause inconvenience for ► discommode, incommode, put out. *See* **inconvenience. 5.** A difficult, often embarrassing situation or condition ► corner, difficulty, fix. *See* **predicament. 6.** The use of energy to do something ► exertion, striving. *See* **effort** (1). **7.** *Informal* A feeling of uncertainty about the fitness or correctness of an action ► misgiving, reservation, scruple. *See* **qualm** (1).

trouble *verb*
1. To come to mind continually ► haunt, obsess, torment, weigh on (*or* upon). **2.** To cause anxious uneasiness in ► bother, distress. *See* **worry** (1). *See synonym note at* **worry. 3.** To cause emotional suffering or painful sorrow to ► disturb, grieve, hurt. *See* **distress** (1). **4.** To cause inconvenience for ► discommode, incommode, put out. *See* **inconvenience.**

troublemaker *noun*
► instigator, malcontent, rabble-rouser. *See* **agitator.**

troubleshooter *noun*
► intermediary, mediator, middleman. *See* **go-between.**

troublesome *adjective*
1. Causing difficulty, trouble, or discomfort ► difficult, incommodious, inconvenient. **2.** Hard to treat, man-

age, or cope with ► demanding, difficult, trying, wicked. *Informal:* pesky. *Slang:* mean. *See also* **fussy, unruly. 3.** Troubling to the mind or emotions ► bothersome, irritating, unsettling. *See* **disturbing.**

troubling *or* **troublous** *adjective*
► bothersome, irritating, unsettling. *See* **disturbing.**

trough *noun*
► ditch, rut, trench. *See* **furrow** (1).

trounce *verb*
► crush, overcome, overpower, rout. *See* **overwhelm** (1).

trouncing *noun*
► overthrow, overthrow, vanquishment. *See* **defeat.**

troupe *noun*
► party, unit. *See* **band**[2] (1). *See synonym note at* **band.**

trouper *noun*
A theatrical performer ► actor, actress, player, thespian. *See also* **fake, lead, mimic.**

truancy *or* **truantry** *noun*
► cut, nonattendance. *See* **absence** (1).

truant *verb*
To fail to attend on purpose ► duck. *Slang:* skip. *Idiom:* go AWOL. *See* **cut** (8).

truant *adjective*
Not present ► away, gone, missing. *See* **absent** (1).

truce *noun*
A temporary cessation of hostilities by mutual agreement ► armistice, cease-fire, peace, white flag. *Idioms:* cooling-off period, peace agreement, suspension of hostilities. *See also* **break.**

truckle *verb*
► grovel, kowtow. *Informal:* apple-polish. *See* **fawn.** *See synonym note at* **fawn.**

truckler *noun*
► flatterer, minion, slave. *See* **sycophant.**

truculence *or* **truculency** *noun*
1. Hostile or warlike behavior or attitude ► belligerence, combativeness, pugnacity. *See* **aggression** (1). **2.** The power or will to fight ► belligerence, combativeness, pugnacity. *See* **fight** (2). **3.** The quality or condition or being cruel ► brutality, savagery. *See* **cruelty.**

truculent *adjective*
1. Inclined to act in an aggressive or hostile way ► belligerent, combative, quarrelsome. *See* **aggressive** (1). **2.** So sharp as to cause mental pain ► caustic, scathing, sharp, vitriolic. *See* **biting. 3.** Inflicting suffering or pain ► brutal, fierce, savage. *See* **cruel** (1).

trudge *verb*
To walk in a laborious way ► forge, plod, scuff, scuffle, shamble, shuffle, slog, slop, stamp, stomp, toil, trail, tramp, trample, wade. *Informal:* tromp. *Slang:* schlep. *See also* **crawl, trample, walk.**

true *adjective*
1. Occurring or existing in act or fact ► actual, existent, extant, real. *See synonym note at* **actual.** *See also* **physical. 2.** Marked by uprightness in principle and action ► good, honest, honorable, incorruptible, righteous, upright, upstanding. *Informal:* straight-

shooting. *Idioms:* on the up-and-up (*or* up and up). **3.** Being so legitimately ▸ legitimate, rightful. *See also* **lawful.** **4.** Conforming exactly to fact ▸ correct, exact, precise. *See* **accurate** (1). **5.** Free from hypocrisy or pretense ▸ honest, sincere, unaffected. *See* **genuine** (1). **6.** Not counterfeit or copied ▸ real, undoubted. *Slang:* legit, kosher. *See* **authentic** (1). *See synonym note at* **authentic. 7.** Worthy of belief, as because of precision or faithfulness to an original ▸ credible, faithful, valid. *See* **authentic** (2). **8.** Accurately representing what is depicted or described ▸ naturalistic, true-life. *See* **realistic** (2). **9.** Adhering firmly and devotedly, as to a person, cause, or duty ▸ constant, loyal, steadfast. *See* **faithful** (1). *See synonym note at* **faithful. 10.** Having or marked by uprightness in principle and action ▸ honorable, righteous. *See* **honest** (1).

true-life *adjective*
▸ factual, naturalistic, truthful. *See* **realistic** (2).

truelove *noun*
▸ dear, honey, precious. *See* **darling** (1).

truism *noun*
1. A trite expression or idea ▸ banality, platitude. *See* **cliché.** *See synonym note at* **cliché. 2.** A broad and basic rule or truth ▸ axiom, principle. *See* **law** (3).

truly *adverb*
▸ actually, genuinely, positively. *See* **really.**

trump *verb*
To outmaneuver an opponent ▸ finesse. *Informal:* one-up. *See also* **deceive, maneuver, outwit.**

trump *or* **trump card** *noun*
A key resource to be used at an opportune moment ▸ ace. *Informal:* clincher. *Idiom:* ace in the hole.

trumpet *verb*
▸ advertise, blazon, herald. *See* **announce** (1).

truncate *verb*
1. To decrease, as in length or amount, by or as if by severing or excising ▸ chop, prune, trim. *See* **cut** (3). **2.** To make short or shorter ▸ abridge, reduce. *See* **shorten.** *See synonym note at* **shorten.**

trunk *noun*
1. The human body excluding the head and limbs ▸ body, midsection, torso. **2.** The main ascending part of a plant, which supports the other parts ▸ stalk, stem, stock. *See also* **shoot.**

truss *verb*
▸ bandage, bind, swathe. *See* **dress** (2).

trust *noun*
1. Absolute certainty that a person or thing will not fail ▸ belief, confidence, dependence, faith, reliance. **2.** The function of watching, guarding, or overseeing ▸ charge, custody, guardianship, keeping. *See* **care** (2). *See synonym note at* **care. 3.** An association for a common cause or interest ▸ cartel, pool, syndicate. *See* **alliance** (1).

trust *verb*
1. To have confidence in the truthfulness of ▸ believe, credit. *Idioms:* give credence to, have faith (*or* trust *or* confidence) in, take at one's word. **2.** To place a trust upon ▸ charge, entrust. *See also* **authorize. 3.** To put in

the charge of another for care, use, or performance ▸ confide, delegate. *See* **entrust** (1). **4.** To place trust or confidence in ▸ bank on (*or* upon), count on (*or* upon), rely on (*or* upon), trust in. *See* **depend on** (1). *See synonym note at* **depend on.**

✤ CORE SYNONYMS: *trust, faith, confidence, reliance, dependence.* These nouns denote a feeling of certainty that a person or thing will not fail. *Trust* implies depth and assurance of feeling that is often based on inconclusive evidence: *The mayor vowed to justify the trust the electorate had placed in him. Faith* connotes unquestioning, often emotionally charged belief: *"Often enough our faith beforehand in an uncertified result is the only thing that makes the result come true"* (William James). *Confidence* frequently implies stronger grounds for assurance: *"Confidence is a plant of slow growth in an aged bosom: youth is the season of credulity"* (William Pitt). *Reliance* connotes a confident and trustful commitment to another: *"What reliance could they place on the protection of a prince so recently their enemy?"* (William Hickling Prescott). *Dependence* suggests reliance on another to whom one is often subordinate: *"When I had once called him in, I could not subsist without Dependence on him"* (Richard Steele).

---

trusting *adjective*
▸ dupable, naïve, susceptible. *See* **gullible.**

trustworthiness *noun*
▸ incorruptibility, integrity. *See* **honesty** (1).

trustworthy *adjective*
1. Capable of being depended on ▸ reliable, solid, steadfast. *See* **dependable.** *See synonym note at* **dependable. 2.** Worthy of belief, as because of precision or faithfulness to an original ▸ authoritative, true, valid. *See* **authentic** (2).

trusty *adjective*
▸ reliable, solid, trustworthy. *See* **dependable.**

truth *noun*
1. Correspondence with fact or actuality ▸ authenticity, correctness, validity. *See* **veracity. 2.** The quality of being honest ▸ integrity, sincerity. *See* **honesty** (1). **3.** The quality of being actual or factual ▸ actuality, fact, reality. *See* **certainty** (1).

truthful *adjective*
1. Marked by uprightness in principle and action ▸ aboveboard, veracious. *See* **honest** (1). **2.** Accurately representing what is depicted or described ▸ naturalistic, true-life. *See* **realistic** (2).

truthfully *adverb*
▸ actually, genuinely, veritably. *See* **really.**

truthfulness *noun*
▸ authenticity, correctness, validity. *See* **veracity.**

truthless *adjective*
▸ specious, spurious, untrue. *See* **false** (1).

truthlessness *noun*
▸ inveracity, perjury, untruthfulness. *See* **mendacity** (1).

try *verb*
1. To make an attempt ▸ endeavor, strive. *See* **attempt.**

2. To subject to a test of effectiveness, value, function, or other quality ▸ check, essay, evaluate, try out. *See* **test** (1). **3.** To weigh down or place a heavy load on ▸ encumber, saddle, tax. *See* **burden**[1].

try *noun*
A trying to do or make something ▸ effort, trial. *Informal:* shot. *See* **attempt** (1).

trying *adjective*
1. Requiring great bodily, mental, or spiritual strength ▸ formidable, heavy, rigorous. *See* **burdensome** (1). **2.** Hard to treat, manage, or cope with ▸ demanding, difficult, wicked. *See* **troublesome** (2).

tryout *noun*
▸ experimentation, proof, trial. *See* **test** (1).

tryst *noun*
▸ date, rendezvous. *See* **engagement** (1). *See synonym note at* **engagement.**

tub *noun*
▸ basin, cask, tank. *See* **vat.**

tubby *adjective*
▸ chubby, pudgy, stout. *See* **fat** (1).

tucker *verb*
Informal To make weary ▸ exhaust, fatigue, tucker out. *See* **tire** (1).

tuckered *adjective*
Informal Depleted of energy ▸ exhausted, weary, worn-out. *See* **tired** (1).

tug *verb*
1. To exert force so as to move something toward the source of the force ▸ drag, draw, tow. *See* **pull** (1). *See synonym note at* **pull. 2.** To exert oneself steadily, often to the point of exhaustion ▸ strain, sweat, toil. *See* **labor** (1).

tug *noun*
A sudden motion, such as a pull ▸ lurch, wrench. *See* **jerk** (1).

tug of war *noun*
▸ contest, rivalry, struggle. *See* **competition** (1).

tuition *noun*
▸ pedagogy, schooling. *See* **education** (1).

tumble *verb*
1. To bring about the downfall of ▸ bring down, overthrow, overturn, subvert, topple, unhorse. **2.** To move downward in response to gravity ▸ drop, plunge, topple. *See* **fall** (1). **3.** To come to the ground from an upright position ▸ tip over, topple. *See* **fall** (2). **4.** To become lower in value or price ▸ dive, drop, plummet. *See* **fall** (7). **5.** To put out of proper order ▸ disarrange, disrupt, jumble, muddle. *See* **disorder** (1).

tumble on *verb*
To find or meet by chance ▸ come across, run across, stumble on. *See* **encounter** (1).

tumble *noun*
1. A sudden downward motion toward the ground ▸ dive, nosedive, plunge. *See* **fall** (1). **2.** A usually swift downward trend, as in prices ▸ decline, downswing, plunge. *See* **fall** (3). **3.** A lack of order or regular arrangement ▸ clutter, confusion, disarray. *See* **disor-**

der (1). **4.** A group of things gathered haphazardly ▸ drift, mass, mound. *See* **heap** (1). **5.** A sudden drop to a lower condition or status ▸ downfall, plunge, slide. *See* **descent** (4).

tumbledown *adjective*
▸ broken-down, dilapidated, tattered. *See* **shabby** (1).

tumesce *verb*
▸ balloon, bloat, inflate. *See* **swell** (1).

tumescent *adjective*
1. Filled up with or as if with something insubstantial ▸ overblown, windy. *See* **inflated** (1). **2.** Expanded from or as if from internal pressure ▸ bloated, inflated. *See* **swollen** (1).

tumid *adjective*
▸ overblown, tumescent, windy. *See* **inflated** (1).

tumult *noun*
1. Sounds or a sound, especially when loud, confused, or disagreeable ▸ clamor, din. *See* **noise** (1). **2.** A physical conflict between two or more people ▸ free-for-all, melee. *See* **fight** (1). **3.** A condition of being agitated or disturbed ▸ commotion, disturbance, stir. *See* **agitation** (1). **4.** A state of discomposure ▸ dither, turmoil. *Informal:* lather. *See* **agitation** (2). **5.** A lack of civil order or peace ▸ anarchy, lawlessness, misrule. *See* **disorder** (2).

tumultuous *adjective*
1. Marked by unrest or disturbance ▸ stormy, tempestuous, turbulent. *See* **agitated** (1). **2.** Violently disturbed or agitated, as by storms ▸ roily, turbulent, violent. *See* **rough** (2).

tundra *noun*
▸ badlands, waste, wasteland. *See* **desert**[1].

tune *noun*
1. A pleasing succession or arrangement of sound ▸ aria, theme. *See* **melody. 2.** Pleasing agreement, as of musical sounds ▸ concord, symphony. *See* **harmony** (1). **3.** The act or state of agreeing or conforming ▸ concordance, harmony, rapport. *See* **agreement** (2). **4.** A brief composition written or adapted for singing ▸ hymn, lyrics, number. *See* **song** (1).

tune *verb*
To bring into accord ▸ conform, integrate. *See* **harmonize** (1).

tune up *verb*
To alter for proper or accurate functioning ▸ calibrate, set, tweak. *See* **adjust** (1).

tuneful *adjective*
▸ euphonic, musical, sweet-sounding. *See* **melodious.**

tunnel *noun*
1. A hollow beneath the earth's surface ▸ cavern, grotto. *See* **cave** (1). **2.** An open space allowing passage ▸ orifice, vent. *See* **hole** (2).

turbid *adjective*
1. Heavy, dark, or dense, especially with impurities ▸ hazy, murky, smoggy. *See also* **dirty. 2.** Darkened or clouded with sediment ▸ cloudy, muddy, roiled. *See* **murky** (1). **3.** Mentally uncertain ▸ confounded, perplexed, puzzled. *Informal:* mixed-up. *See* **confused** (1).

turbulence *noun*
▸ convulsion, turmoil, unrest. *See* **agitation** (1).

turbulent *adjective*
1. Violently disturbed or agitated, as by storms ▸ roily, tempestuous, violent. *See* **rough** (2). **2.** Marked by unrest or disturbance ▸ stormy, tempestuous, tumultuous. *See* **agitated** (1). **3.** Upsetting civil order or peace ▸ disruptive, unruly. *See* **disorderly** (1).

turf *noun*
1. *Slang* A sphere of activity, experience, study, or interest ▸ department, domain, field, terrain. *See* **area** (1). **2.** *Slang* A particular area used for or associated with a specific individual or activity ▸ district, region, zone. *See* **territory** (1). **3.** The soft part of the land surface of the world ▸ ground, soil. *See* **earth** (1).

turgid *adjective*
▸ overblown, tumescent, windy. *See* **inflated** (1).

turgidity *noun*
▸ fustian, grandiloquence. *See* **bombast**.

turkey *noun*
1. *Slang* A person who is deficient in judgment and good sense ▸ idiot, imbecile, nitwit. *See* **fool** (1). **2.** *Slang* An unsuccessful person or enterprise ▸ loser, washout. *See* **failure** (1). **3.** *Slang* An unpleasant, tiresome person ▸ chump. *Slang:* dip, nimrod. *See* **drip** (2).

turmoil *noun*
1. A state of discomposure ▸ fluster, tumult. *Informal:* lather. *See* **agitation** (2). **2.** A state of agitation or disturbance ▸ commotion, ferment, unrest. *See* **agitation** (1). **3.** A lack of civil order or peace ▸ anarchy, lawlessness, misrule. *See* **disorder** (2).

turn *verb*
1. To move or cause to move in circles or around an axis ▸ circle, circumvolve, go around (*or* round), gyrate, orbit, pivot, reel, revolve, rotate, spin, swirl, twirl, wheel, whirl. *See also* **incline**. **2.** To change the direction or course of ▸ avert, deflect, deviate, divert, redirect, shift, shunt, sidetrack, swing, switch, turn aside, veer. *See also* **swerve**. **3.** To change to the opposite position, direction, or course ▸ invert, reverse, transpose, turn (about, around, over, *or* round). **4.** To injure a bodily part by twisting ▸ sprain, strain, twist, wrench. *See also* **hurt**. **5.** To disturb the health or physiological functioning of ▸ derange, disorder, unsettle. *See* **upset** (1). **6.** To move or cause to move in a bent or angular direction ▸ deflect, refract. *See* **bend** (2). **7.** To deviate from a straight line in a smooth, continuous manner ▸ arch, curve. *See* **bend** (1). **8.** To make different ▸ alter, modify, vary. *See* **change** (1). **9.** To become different ▸ fluctuate, modify, turn. *See* **change** (2). **10.** To abandon one's cause or party usually to join another ▸ desert, quit, secede. *See* **defect**. **11.** To direct something, often toward a target ▸ level, point, train. *See* **aim** (1). **12.** To devote oneself or one's efforts ▸ concentrate, focus, give. *See* **apply** (1). **13.** To become or cause to become rotten or unsound ▸ deteriorate, rot, spoil. *See* **decay**. **14.** To look to when in need ▸ apply, refer, run. *See* **resort** (1).

See synonym note at **resort**. **15.** To come to be ▸ get (to be), grow (to be). *See* **become** (1). **16.** To proceed in a specified direction ▸ head, make, set out. *See* **bear** (5). **17.** To cause another to feel sure about something ▸ persuade, win over. *See* **convince** (1). **18.** To make or become less sharp-edged ▸ blunt, round. *See* **dull** (1).

turn back *verb*
1. To come back to a former condition ▸ recur, reoccur, revert. *See* **return** (1). **2.** To move back in the face of enemy attack or after a defeat ▸ fall back, pull out, withdraw. *See* **retreat** (4).

turn down *verb*
1. To be unwilling to accept, consider, or receive ▸ refuse, reject, spurn. *See* **decline** (1). **2.** To prevent or forbid authoritatively ▸ block, stop. *See* **veto**.

turn in *verb*
1. To put before another for acceptance ▸ extend, proffer, tender. *See* **offer** (1). **2.** *Informal* To go to bed ▸ bed (down). *Slang:* crash. *See* **retire** (2). **3.** To be treacherous to ▸ double-cross. *Slang:* sell out. *See* **betray** (1).

turn off *verb*
1. *Slang* To be very disagreeable to ▸ displease, repulse, upset. *See* **offend** (2). **2.** To offend the senses or feelings of ▸ appall, revolt, sicken. *See* **disgust** (1). **3.** To make distant, hostile, or unsympathetic ▸ disaffect, disunite. *See* **estrange**.

turn on *verb*
1. To set in motion ▸ activate, actuate, spark, start. *See also* **energize, provoke**. **2.** To be determined by or contingent on something unknown, uncertain, or changeable ▸ hinge on (*or* upon), rest on (*or* upon), turn upon. *See* **depend on** (2). **3.** *Slang* To arouse the interest and attention of ▸ engage, intrigue. *See* **interest** (2).

turn out *verb*
1. To supply what is needed for some activity or purpose ▸ equip, gear, outfit. *See* **furnish** (1). **2.** *Informal* To leave one's bed ▸ get up, roll out. *See* **rise** (2).

turn over *verb*
1. To direct a person elsewhere for help or information ▸ refer, send, transfer. **2.** To prepare soil for the planting of crops ▸ cultivate, plow, turn, work. *See* **till**. **3.** To turn or cause to turn from a vertical or horizontal position ▸ knock over, topple. *See* **overturn** (1). **4.** To think or think about carefully and at length ▸ cogitate, deliberate, mull. *See* **ponder**. **5.** To relinquish to the possession or control of another ▸ furnish, provide. *See* **give** (1). **6.** To put in the charge of another for care, use, or performance ▸ confide, delegate. *See* **entrust** (1).

turn up *verb*
1. To come into view ▸ issue, loom, materialize. *See* **appear** (1). **2.** To find by investigation ▸ dig (up *or* out), unearth. *See* **uncover** (1). **3.** To come to a particular place ▸ pull in, reach, show up. *See* **arrive** (1). **4.** To obtain knowledge or awareness of something not known before ▸ determine, learn, unearth. *See* **discover**.

turn *noun*
1. A limited, often assigned period of activity, duty, or opportunity ▸ bout, go, hitch, inning, shift, spell, stint, stretch, time, tour, trick, watch. *Informal:* crack, shot, whack. *See also* **opportunity, try. 2.** An often sudden change or departure, as in a trend ▸ shift, tack, twist. *See also* **change, deviation. 3.** A circular movement around a point or about an axis ▸ circulation, gyration. *See* **revolution** (1). **4.** Something bent ▸ curvature, curve, round. *See* **bend. 5.** A natural or habitual preference for something ▸ disposition, leaning, penchant. *See* **inclination** (1). **6.** An innate capability ▸ faculty, gift, knack. *See* **talent. 7.** A course or process that ends where it began or repeats itself ▸ cycle, orbit. *See* **circle** (2). **8.** Passage from one form, state, or stage to another ▸ passage, shift, transit. *See* **transition. 9.** An act of walking ▸ constitutional, stroll. *See* **walk** (1). **10.** *Informal* A trip in a motor vehicle ▸ jaunt, ride. *See* **drive** (3).

✦ CORE SYNONYMS: *turn, circle, rotate, revolve, gyrate, spin, whirl, swirl.* These verbs mean to move or cause to move in a circle. *Turn* and *circle* are the most general: *The mechanic made sure the wheels turned properly. Seagulls circled above the ocean. Rotate* refers to movement around an object's own axis or center: *Earth rotates on its axis once each day. Revolve* involves orbital movement: *Earth revolves around the sun. Gyrate* suggests revolving in or as if in a spiral course: *The top gyrated on the counter and slowly came to a stop.* To *spin* is to rotate rapidly, often within a narrow compass: *"He . . . spun round, flung up his arms, and fell on his back, shot through"* (John Galsworthy). *Whirl* applies to rapid or forceful revolution or rotation: *During the blizzard, snowflakes whirled down from the sky. Swirl* can connote a graceful undulation, spiral, or whorl: *The baker swirled the icing around the cake.*

---

turnabout *or* **turnaround** *noun*
▸ flip-flop, inversion, transposition. *See* **reversal** (1).
turncoat *noun*
▸ deserter, recreant, traitor. *See* **defector.**
turndown *noun*
A turning down of a request ▸ denial, disallowance, nonacceptance, refusal, rejection. *See also* **forbiddance.**
turned-on *adjective*
1. *Slang* Feeling a very strong emotion ▸ excited, fired up, worked up. *See* **thrilled. 2.** *Slang* Stupefied, intoxicated, or otherwise influenced by the taking of drugs ▸ high, hopped-up, lit (up). *See* **drugged.**
turning point *noun*
▸ crossroads, juncture. *See* **crisis** (1).
turnkey *noun*
A guard or keeper of a prison ▸ jailer, warden. *Slang:* screw. *See also* **guard, police officer.**
turnout *noun*
1. Things needed for a task, journey, or other purpose ▸ equipment, gear. *See* **outfit** (1). **2.** A set or style of clothing ▸ garb, guise, outfit. *See* **dress** (2).

turnpike *noun*
▸ path, road, route. *See* **way** (2).
turpitude *noun*
▸ depravity, perversion, vice. *See* **corruption** (1).
tush *noun*
Slang The part of the body on which one sits ▸ posterior, rump. *Slang:* fanny. *See* **buttocks.**
tussle *verb*
To strive in opposition ▸ grapple, scuffle, wrestle. *See* **contend** (1).
tussle *noun*
A physical conflict between two or more people ▸ free-for-all, melee. *See* **fight** (1).
tutelage *noun*
1. The act, process, or art of imparting knowledge and skill ▸ pedagogy, schooling. *See* **education** (1). **2.** The function of watching, guarding, or overseeing ▸ charge, supervision, ward. *See* **care** (2).
tutor *noun*
One who educates ▸ instructor, trainer. *See* **educator.**
tutor *verb*
To impart knowledge and skill to ▸ discipline, instruct. *See* **educate** (1).
tutoring *noun*
▸ pedagogy, schooling. *See* **education** (1).
twaddle *noun*
1. Empty or foolish talk ▸ blather, jabber, prattle. *See* **babble** (1). **2.** Something that does not have or make sense ▸ bunkum, drivel, garbage. *See* **nonsense** (1).
tweak *verb*
▸ calibrate, fine-tune, set, tune up. *See* **adjust** (1).
twelvemonth *noun*
A period of time of approximately 12 months, especially that period during which the earth completes a single revolution around the sun ▸ season cycle, year.
24-7 *adverb*
Slang ▸ endlessly, nonstop, perpetually. *See* **continually.**
twerp *noun*
1. *Slang* A totally insignificant person ▸ nobody, nothing, small fry. *See* **nonentity. 2.** *Slang* An unpleasant, tiresome person ▸ chump. *Slang:* pill, twit. *See* **drip** (2).
twiddle *verb*
▸ fidget, tinker, toy, trifle. *See* **fiddle** (1).
twig *noun*
▸ branch, stake, wand. *See* **stick** (1).
twiggy *adjective*
▸ lean, skinny, slender, slim. *See* **thin** (1). *See synonym note at* **thin.**
twilight *noun*
▸ eve, sunset. *See* **evening.**
twill *verb*
▸ braid, intertwine, twist. *See* **weave** (1).
twin *adjective*
Consisting of two identical or similar related things, parts, or elements ▸ double, dual, matched, paired. *See also* **equal.**

twin *noun*

1. One of a matched pair of things ▸ counterpart, duplicate. *See* **mate** (1). **2.** One exactly resembling another ▸ clone, second, spitting image. *See* **double** (1).

twin *verb*

To make or become twice as great ▸ double, duplicate, geminate, redouble.

twine *verb*

1. To move or proceed on a repeatedly curving course ▸ snake, spiral, weave. *See* **wind**^{2} (1). **2.** To interlace strips or strands ▸ braid, intertwine, twist. *See* **weave** (1).

twinge *noun*

A sensation of physical discomfort occurring as the result of disease or injury ▸ prick, smart, soreness. *See* **pain** (1). *See synonym note at* **pain**.

twinge *verb*

1. To be painful or sore ▸ smart, sting. *See* **hurt** (2). **2.** To cause pain, soreness, or discomfort to ▸ irritate, pain. *See* **hurt** (3).

twinkle *verb*

1. To emit light in sudden or intermittent bursts ▸ flash, glimmer, sparkle. *See* **glitter**. *See synonym note at* **glitter**. **2.** To open and close the eyes rapidly ▸ flutter, wink. *See* **blink** (1). *See synonym note at* **blink**.

twinkle *noun*

1. A sudden burst of light ▸ flicker, spark, wink. *See* **flash** (1). **2.** Sparkling, brilliant light ▸ glisten, shimmer, sparkle. *See* **glitter** (1). **3.** A very brief interval of time ▸ instant, second, wink. *See* **flash** (2).

twinkling *noun*

1. Full of bright shifting or flickering light ▸ glinting, glittering, shimmering. *See* **sparkling** (1). **2.** A very brief interval of time ▸ instant, second, wink. *See* **flash** (2).

twirl *verb*

To rotate on an axis or around a center ▸ spin, whirl, wheel. *See* **turn** (1).

twirl *noun*

A circular movement around a point or about an axis ▸ circulation, gyration. *See* **revolution** (1).

twist *verb*

1. To injure a bodily part by twisting ▸ sprain, strain, turn, wrench. *See also* **hurt**. **2.** To alter the position of by a sharp, forcible twisting or turning movement ▸ wrench, wrest, wring. **3.** To twist agitatedly, as in pain, struggle, or embarrassment ▸ squirm, toss, writhe. *See also* **shake**. **4.** To move or proceed on a repeatedly curving course ▸ snake, spiral, weave. *See* **wind**^{2} (1). **5.** To alter and spoil the natural form or appearance of ▸ disfigure, misshape, warp. *See* **deform**. *See synonym note at* **deform**. **6.** To give an inaccurate view of by representing falsely or misleadingly ▸ fudge, misrepresent, pervert. *See* **distort** (1). **7.** To interlace strips or strands ▸ braid, intertwine, twill. *See* **weave** (1).

twist *noun*

1. An often sudden change or departure, as in a trend ▸ shift, tack, turn. *See also* **change, deviation**. **2.** *Informal* A clever, unexpected new trick or method ▸ twist. *Slang:* angle, kick. *See* **wrinkle** (2). **3.** Something with a curled or spiral shape ▸ curlicue, spiral, whorl. *See* **curl**.

twisting *adjective*

1. Not proceeding straight to the point or object ▸ circuitous, devious, roundabout. *See* **indirect** (1). **2.** Repeatedly curving in alternate directions ▸ convoluted, curvy, sinuous. *See* **winding** (1).

twit *verb*

To subject to ridicule ▸ jeer (at), lampoon, taunt. *See* **ridicule**. *See synonym note at* **ridicule**.

twit *noun*

1. *Slang* A person who is deficient in judgment and good sense ▸ idiot, imbecile, nitwit. *See* **fool** (1). **2.** An instance of mockery or derision ▸ insult, jeer, scoff. *See* **taunt** (1). **3.** *Slang* An unpleasant, tiresome person ▸ chump. *Slang:* pill, twerp. *See* **drip** (2).

twitch *verb*

To move or cause to move with a sudden abrupt motion ▸ jerk, lurch, snap, wrench, yank. *See synonym note at* **jerk**. *See also* **move**.

twitch *noun*

1. A nervous shaking of the body ▸ quake, shudder, twitch. *See* **tremor** (2). **2.** A sudden motion, such as a pull ▸ tug, wrench. *See* **jerk** (1).

twitchy *adjective*

▸ jittery, nervous. *See* **edgy**.

twitter *verb*

To move to and fro in short, jerky movements ▸ quiver, tremble, vibrate. *See* **shake** (1).

twitter *noun*

A state of discomposure ▸ tumult, turmoil. *Informal:* stew. *See* **agitation** (2).

twittery *adjective*

▸ quaky, quivery, shaky. *See* **tremulous** (1).

two *noun*

▸ duet, match, pair. *See* **couple**.

two bits *noun*

1. A coin equal to one-fourth of the dollar of the United States and Canada ▸ quarter, quarter-dollar. **2.** *Slang* A small or trifling amount of money ▸ pocket money, small change. *See* **peanuts**.

two-edged *adjective*

▸ equivocal, inconclusive, nebulous, vague. *See* **ambiguous** (2).

two-faced *adjective*

1. Of or practicing hypocrisy ▸ Janus-faced, Pecksniffian, phony. **2.** Given to or marked by deliberate concealment or misrepresentation of the truth ▸ double-dealing, double-faced, insincere. *See* **dishonest** (1). *See synonym note at* **dishonest**.

two-facedness *noun*

▸ phoniness, sanctimoniousness, sanctimony. *See* **hypocrisy**.

two-fisted *adjective*

Informal Indulging in drink to an excessive degree ▸ hard, heavy.

twofold *adjective*
1. Twice as much or as large ▸ double. 2. Composed of two parts or things ▸ dual, duple, geminate. *See* **double** (2).

twosome *noun*
▸ duet, match, pair. *See* **couple.**

two-time *verb*
Informal To be sexually unfaithful to another ▸ philander. *Informal:* cheat, fool around, mess around, play around.

type *noun*
1. A class that is defined by the common attribute or attributes possessed by all its members ▸ ilk, mold, species. *See* **kind²**. 2. A concrete entity typifying an abstraction ▸ incarnation, manifestation, personification. *See* **embodiment** (1).

typic *adjective*
▸ model, prototypic, representative. *See* **typical** (1).

typical *adjective*
1. Having the nature of, constituting, or serving as a type ▸ archetypal, archetypic, archetypical, classic, classical, model, paradigmatic, prototypal, prototypic, prototypical, quintessential, representative, typic. *See also* **epitome, model.** 2. Occurring or encountered regularly ▸ commonplace, frequent, regular. *See* **common** (1). 3. Relating to, identifying, or setting apart an individual or group ▸ characteristic, individual, particular. *See* **special** (1). 4. Conforming to established standards ▸ conformist, orthodox, traditional. *See* **conventional** (1).

typically *adverb*
▸ customarily, generally, normally. *See* **usually.**

typification *noun*
▸ incarnation, manifestation, personification. *See* **embodiment** (1).

typify *verb*
▸ exemplify, illustrate, symbolize. *See* **represent** (1).

tyrannical *or* **tyrannic** *adjective*
1. Characterized by or favoring absolute obedience to authority ▸ dictatorial, totalitarian. *See* **authoritarian** (1). 2. Having and exercising complete political power and control ▸ despotic, dictatorial, totalitarian, tyrannous. *See* **absolute** (1).

tyrannize *verb*
1. To treat arbitrarily or cruelly ▸ grind, trample. 2. To command in an arrogant manner ▸ dictate, domineer, rule. *See* **boss** (1).

tyrannous *adjective*
▸ autocratic, dictatorial. *See* **absolute** (1).

tyranny *noun*
1. Absolute power, especially when exercised unjustly or cruelly ▸ authoritarianism, autocracy, despotism, dictatorship, fascism, imperiousness, oppression, totalitarianism. *Idiom:* reign of terror. *See also* **oppression.** 2. A government in which all power is vested in a single leader or party ▸ autarchy, despotism, dictatorship, monocracy. *See* **absolutism** (2).

tyrant *noun*
1. An absolute ruler, especially one who is harsh and oppressive ▸ despot, oppressor, totalitarian. *See* **dictator** (1). 2. One who imposes or favors absolute obedience to authority ▸ despot, dictator, martinet. *See* **authoritarian** (1).

tyro *noun*
▸ fledgling, neophyte, novice. *See* **beginner.**

u

ubiquitous *adjective*
Ever present in all places ▸ omnipresent, universal. *See also* **rampant.**

ugliness *noun*
1. The quality or condition of being ugly ▸ frightfulness, hideousness, homeliness, loathsomeness, monstrosity, monstrousness, odiousness, plainness, repulsiveness, unattractiveness, uncomeliness, unloveliness, unsightliness, vileness. 2. An unsightly object ▸ eyesore, monstrosity. *Informal:* fright, sight. *See* **mess** (2).

ugly *adjective*
1. Displeasing to the eye ▸ hideous, homely, ill-favored, monstrous, plain, unattractive, uncomely, unlovely, unsightly. *Idioms:* not much for looks, not much to look at, short on looks, ugly as sin. 2. So objectionable as to deserve condemnation ▸ con-temptible, disgusting, obnoxious. *See* **offensive** (1). 3. Violently disturbed or agitated, as by storms ▸ roily, turbulent, violent. *See* **rough** (2). 4. Having or showing a bad temper ▸ cranky, grouchy, peevish. *See* **ill-tempered.**

ugly *noun*
Informal An unsightly object ▸ eyesore, monstrosity. *See* **mess** (2).

✚ **CORE SYNONYMS:** *ugly, hideous, ill-favored, unsightly.* These adjectives mean displeasing or offensive to the eye: *ugly furniture; a hideous scar; an ill-favored countenance; an unsightly billboard.*

◄ **ANTONYM:** *beautiful*

---

uh-huh *adverb*
Informal It is so; as you say or ask ▸ agreed, all right, assuredly. *See* **yes.**

ulterior *adjective*

1. Lying beyond what is obvious or avowed ▸ buried, concealed, covert, hidden, obscured, undisclosed, unrevealed. *Idioms:* under cover (*or* wraps). *See also* **hidden, silent. 2.** Following something else in time ▸ after, later, posterior, subsequent. *See also* **following.**

ulteriorly *adverb*

▸ afterwards, latterly, subsequently. *See* **later.**

ultimate *adjective*

1. Of or relating to a terminative condition, stage, or point ▸ final, last, latter, terminal. *See also* **climactic. 2.** Serving the function of deciding or settling with finality ▸ decisive, determinative. *See* **definitive** (1). **3.** Of or being an irreducible element ▸ basic, essential, fundamental. *See* **elemental** (1). **4.** Greatest in quantity or highest in degree that can be attained ▸ topmost, utmost. *See* **maximum. 5.** Most distant or remote, as from a center ▸ farthest, outermost. *See* **extreme** (1). **6.** Coming after all others ▸ concluding, final. *See* **last**[1] (1). *See synonym note at* **last.**

ultimate *noun*

The greatest quantity or highest degree attainable ▸ top, utmost. *See* **maximum** (1).

ultimately *adverb*

1. After a considerable length of time, usually after a delay ▸ eventually, finally. *Idioms:* at last (*or* long last), in due course, in good (*or* due) time, in the end (*or* long run), in the fullness of time. **2.** In conclusion ▸ conclusively, finally, last, lastly. *Idioms:* at last, in the end, when all is said and done.

ultra *adjective*

Holding especially political views that deviate drastically from prevailing beliefs ▸ fanatical, radical, revolutionary. *See* **extreme** (4).

ultra *noun*

One who holds extreme views or advocates extreme measures ▸ radical, revolutionist, zealot. *See* **extremist.**

ultraconservative *adjective*

Extremely or stubbornly conservative ▸ archconservative, die-hard, mossbacked, old-line, old-school, reactionary, rear-guard, standpat. *See also* **conservative, extreme, stubborn.**

ultraconservative *noun*

One who is extremely or stubbornly conservative ▸ archconservative, die-hard, fossil, mossback, reactionary, standpatter. *See also* **extremist.**

ultraist *noun*

▸ radical, revolutionist, zealot. *See* **extremist.**

ultraliberal *adjective*

Extremely or stubbornly liberal ▸ archliberal, bleeding-heart, do-good, Jacobinical, radical. *Slang:* crunchy-granola, goo-goo, pink. *See also* **extreme, liberal.**

ultraliberal *noun*

A person who is extremely or stubbornly liberal ▸ archliberal, bleeding-heart, do-gooder, Jacobin, radical, yippie. *Informal:* tree-hugger. *Slang:* pinko. *See also* **extremist.**

ultramodern *adjective*

▸ current, modern, up-to-date. *See* **contemporary** (2).

ululate *verb*

1. To utter or emit a long, mournful, plaintive sound ▸ moan, wail, yowl. *See* **howl** (1). **2.** To feel, show, or express grief ▸ anguish, mourn, sorrow. *See* **grieve** (1).

ululation *noun*

▸ bay, wail, yowl. *See* **howl** (1).

umbra *noun*

Comparative darkness that results from the blocking of light rays ▸ penumbra, shade, shadow, shadiness. *See also* **dark, twilight.**

umbrage *noun*

▸ huff, resentment, ruffled feathers. *See* **offense** (1).

umbrageous *adjective*

▸ shaded, shadowy. *See* **shady** (2).

umpire *noun*

A person, usually appointed, who decides the issues of, decides the results of, or supervises the conduct of a competition or conflict ▸ arbiter, referee. *See* **judge** (3). *See synonym note at* **judge.**

umpire *verb*

To make a decision about (a controversy or dispute, for example) after deliberation, as in a court of law ▸ adjudicate, decide, rule. *See* **judge** (1).

umpteen *adjective*

▸ multitudinous, myriad, numerous. *See* **many.**

unabashed *adjective*

▸ bold, insolent, pert. *See* **impudent.**

unabbreviated *adjective*

▸ full-length, unabridged, uncut. *See* **complete** (2).

unable *adjective*

1. Lacking the qualities, as efficiency or skill, required to produce desired results ▸ incapable, inept, unskilled. *See* **inefficient** (1). **2.** Lacking power or strength ▸ helpless, impotent, powerless. **3.** Not capable of accomplishing anything ▸ impotent, inadequate, incapable. *See* **ineffectual** (2).

unabridged *adjective*

▸ full-length, uncensored, uncut. *See* **complete** (2).

unacceptable *adjective*

1. Arousing disapproval ▸ exceptionable, improper, undesirable. *See* **objectionable. 2.** So unpleasant or painful as not to be endured ▸ insufferable, intolerable, unendurable. *See* **unbearable.**

unaccompanied *adjective*

▸ alone, lonely, single. *See* **solitary** (1).

unaccountable *adjective*

That cannot be explained ▸ inexplicable, unexplainable. *See also* **mysterious.**

unachievable *adjective*

▸ unattainable, unworkable. *See* **impossible** (1).

unacquainted *adjective*

▸ oblivious, unfamiliar, uninformed. *See* **ignorant** (3).

unadorned *adjective*

1. Without addition, decoration, or qualification ▸ austere, plain, unvarnished. *See* **bare** (1). **2.** Of a charmingly plain, unsophisticated nature ▸ homely, homespun, natural. *See* **rustic** (1).

unadulterated *adjective*
1. Free from extraneous elements ▸ perfect, plain, unmixed. *See* **pure** (1). *See synonym note at* **pure**. 2. Produced by nature; not artificial or manmade ▸ additive-free, organic. *See* **natural** (1).

unadvantageous *adjective*
▸ antagonistic, negative, untoward. *See* **unfavorable** (1).

unaffected *adjective*
1. Lacking feeling or emotion ▸ emotionless, impassive, stolid. *See* **cold** (2). 2. Free from guile, cunning, or deceit ▸ innocent, naive, simple. *See* **artless** (1). *See synonym note at* **artless**. 3. Free from hypocrisy or pretense ▸ honest, sincere, unfeigned. *See* **genuine** (1).

unafraid *adjective*
▸ courageous, fearless, heroic. *See* **brave**.

unalterable *adjective*
1. That cannot be revoked or undone ▸ irretrievable, irreversible, irrrevocable. *Idiom:* beyond recall. *See also* **unchangeable**. 2. Incapable of changing or being modified ▸ inflexible, invariable, unchangeable. *See* **immutable** (1).

unambiguous *adjective*
1. Clearly defined; not ambiguous ▸ distinct, unmistakable. *See* **sharp** (3). 2. Having distinct limits ▸ fixed, specific. *See* **definite** (2). 3. Clearly, fully, and emphatically expressed ▸ decided, explicit, precise. *See* **definite** (1).

unambitious *adjective*
Having or expressing feelings of humility ▸ humble, lowly, meek, modest. *See also* **deferential**.

unanimity *noun*
▸ concordance, harmony, rapport. *See* **agreement** (2).

unanimous *adjective*
Being in or characterized by complete agreement ▸ accordant, agreeing, assenting, concordant, consensual, consonant, harmonious, like-minded, solid, undivided, unified, universal. *Idioms:* as one, at one, of one mind, with one voice. *See also* **agreeable, common, cooperative**.

unanimousness *noun*
▸ concordance, harmony, rapport. *See* **agreement** (2).

unanticipated *adjective*
▸ incidental, unexpected, unplanned. *See* **accidental** (1).

unapparent *adjective*
▸ covert, disguised, unseen. *See* **hidden** (1).

unappeasable *adjective*
▸ gluttonous, rapacious, ravenous. *See* **voracious** (1).

unappetizing *adjective*
▸ distasteful, inedible, uneatable, unsavory. *See* **unpalatable** (1).

unappreciated *adjective*
Not apt to be appreciated ▸ thankless, ungrateful, unthankful.

unappreciative *adjective*
1. Not apt to be appreciated ▸ thankless, unappreciated, unthankful. 2. Not showing or feeling gratitude ▸ ungrateful, unthankful. *See* **thankless** (1).

unapproachable *adjective*
1. Not friendly, sociable, or warm in manner ▸ aloof, chilly. *See* **cool** (1). 2. Unable to be reached ▸ unavailable, unreachable. *See* **inaccessible** (1).

unapt *adjective*
1. Not suited to circumstances ▸ inapt, malapropos, unbecoming. *See* **improper** (2). 2. Not likely ▸ dubious, questionable. *See* **doubtful** (1).

unassailability *noun*
▸ impenetrability, security. *See* **safety** (1).

unassailable *adjective*
1. Established beyond a doubt ▸ inarguable, indisputable, irrefutable. *See* **certain** (2). 2. Affording protection ▸ impenetrable, invulnerable, unconquerable. *See* **safe** (2).

unassuming *adjective*
1. Not showy or obtrusive ▸ inobtrusive, quiet, subdued. *See* **modest** (1). 2. Awkward or unconfident in behavior or manner ▸ bashful, demure, diffident. *See* **shy**[1] (1). 3. Not readily noticed or seen ▸ unnoticeable, unobtrusive. *See* **inconspicuous**.

unassumingness *noun*
1. Lack of vanity or self-importance ▸ humility, meekness. *See* **modesty** (1). 2. Lack of ostentation or pretension ▸ plainness, simpleness, simplicity. *See* **modesty** (2).

unattached *adjective*
▸ fancy-free, marriageable. *See* **single** (5).

unattainable *adjective*
1. Not capable of happening or being done ▸ impractical, infeasilble, unworkable. *See* **impossible** (1). 2. Unable to be reached ▸ unapproachable, unavailable. *See* **inaccessible** (1).

unattractive *adjective*
▸ homely, plain, unsightly. *See* **ugly** (1).

unattractiveness *noun*
▸ monstrosity, odiousness, unsightliness. *See* **ugliness** (1).

unavailable *adjective*
▸ unapproachable, unattainable. *See* **inaccessible** (1).

unavailing *adjective*
▸ fruitless, unsuccessful, vain. *See* **futile**. *See synonym note at* **futile**.

unavoidable *adjective*
▸ inescapable, inevitable, sure. *See* **certain** (1). *See synonym note at* **certain**.

unawake *adjective*
▸ asleep, snoozing. *See* **sleeping** (1).

unaware *adjective*
▸ oblivious, unenlightened, unknowing. *See* **ignorant** (3).

unawarely *adverb*
Without adequate preparation ▸ short, unawarely, unawares. *Idioms:* by surprise, off guard.

unawareness *noun*
▸ nescience, unconsciousness. *See* **ignorance** (2).

unawares *adverb*
Without adequate preparation ▸ aback, short, unawarely. *Idioms:* by surprise, off guard.

unbalance *verb*
To make insane ▸ dement, madden, unhinge. *See* **derange** (1).

unbalance *noun*
Serious mental illness impairing a person's capacity to function normally ▸ dementia, derangement. *See* **insanity** (1).

unbalanced *adjective*
Slang Afflicted with or exhibiting irrationality and mental unsoundness ▸ crazy, lunatic, unsound. *See* **insane** (1).

unbarred *adjective*
▸ unblocked, unobstructed. *See* **clear** (4).

unbearable *adjective*
So unpleasant or painful as not to be endured or tolerated ▸ impossible, insufferable, insupportable, intolerable, unacceptable, unendurable, unsufferable, unsupportable. *See also* **tormenting**.

unbecoming *adjective*
1. Not suited to circumstances ▸ inapt, malapropos, unseemly. *See* **improper** (2). **2.** Lacking in delicacy or refinement ▸ indelicate, tasteless, uncouth. *See* **coarse** (1). **3.** Not in keeping with conventional mores ▸ indecent, indelicate. *See* **improper** (1). *See synonym note at* **improper**.

unbecomingness *noun*
▸ inappropriateness, unseemliness. *See* **impropriety** (1).

unbefitting *adjective*
1. Not suited to circumstances ▸ inapt, malapropos, unbecoming. *See* **improper** (2). **2.** Not in keeping with conventional mores ▸ indecent, indelicate. *See* **improper** (1).

unbelief *noun*
1. The refusal or reluctance to believe ▸ incredulity, mistrust, skepticism. *See* **disbelief** (1). **2.** Lack of belief in God ▸ disbelief, impiety. *See* **atheism**.

unbelievable *adjective*
1. Not to be believed ▸ inconceivable, unthinkable. *See* **incredible** (2). **2.** Not plausible or believable ▸ improbable, inconceivable. *See* **implausible**. **3.** So remarkable as to be difficult to believe ▸ astounding, staggering, wondrous. *See* **astonishing**.

unbeliever *noun*
▸ agnostic, nonbeliever. *See* **skeptic**.

unbelieving *adjective*
▸ questioning, skeptical. *See* **incredulous**.

unbend *verb*
▸ kick back, relax, unwind. *See* **rest**[1] (1).

unbendable *adjective*
▸ bullheaded, dogged, inflexible, obstinate. *See* **stubborn** (1).

unbending *adjective*
1. Not changing shape or bending ▸ inflexible, stiff, unyielding. *See* **rigid** (1). **2.** Firmly, often unreasonably immovable in purpose or will ▸ bullheaded, dogged, obstinate. *See* **stubborn** (1). **3.** Possessing determination or resolution ▸ resolute, steadfast, unyielding. *See* **firm**[1] (3).

unbiased *adjective*
1. Free from bias in judgment ▸ impartial, just, nonpartisan, unprejudiced. *See* **fair**[1] (1). *See synonym note at* **fair**[1]. **2.** Not inclining toward or actively taking either side in a matter under dispute ▸ nonaligned, uninvolved. *See* **neutral** (1).

unbind *verb*
▸ loose, release, untie. *See* **undo** (1).

unblamable *adjective*
1. Free from guilt or blame ▸ faultless, guiltless. *See* **innocent** (2). **2.** Beyond reproach ▸ faultless, irreproachable. *See* **exemplary** (1).

unblemished *adjective*
1. Free from flaws or blemishes ▸ consummate, flawless, impeccable. *See* **perfect** (1). **2.** In excellent condition ▸ flawless, intact, sound. *See* **good** (2). **3.** Free from evil and corruption ▸ pure, uncorrupted, untainted. *See* **innocent** (1).

unblended *adjective*
▸ plain, pure, undiluted. *See* **straight** (1).

unblock *verb*
To rid of obstructions ▸ clear, free, open, remove. *See also* **rid**.

unblocked *adjective*
▸ open, unobstructed. *See* **clear** (4).

unblushing *adjective*
▸ bold, insolent, pert. *See* **impudent**. *See synonym note at* **impudent**.

unbodied *adjective*
▸ disembodied, incorporeal, nonphysical. *See* **immaterial** (1).

unbosom *verb*
To tell in confidence ▸ breathe, confide, share, whisper. *See also* **communicate, reveal, say**.

unbound *adjective*
▸ flapping, relaxed, slack. *See* **loose** (1). *See synonym note at* **loose**.

unbounded *adjective*
1. Having no ends or limits ▸ illimitable, infinite. *See* **endless** (1). **2.** Completely such, without qualification or exception ▸ all-out, pure, sheer. *See* **utter**[2].

unboundedness *noun*
▸ immeasurability, limitlessness, measurelessness. *See* **infinity** (1).

unbridled *adjective*
1. Out of control ▸ amuck, runaway, uncontrolled. *Idioms:* out of hand, running wild. **2.** Lacking in moral restraint ▸ unconstrained, uncontrolled, ungoverned. *See* **abandoned** (2). **3.** Exceeding a normal or reasonable limit ▸ extravagant, immoderate. *See* **excessive** (1). **4.** Able to move about at will without bounds or restraint ▸ liberated, unconfined, unrestrained. *See* **loose** (2).

unbroken *adjective*
1. In excellent condition ▸ flawless, intact, sound. *See* **good** (2). **2.** Not domesticated ▸ savage, undomesticated, untamed. *See* **wild** (2). **3.** Existing without interruption or end ▸ constant, endless, everlasting, perpetual. *See* **continual**.

unburden *verb*
▶ discharge, relieve, unburden. *See* **rid.**

uncalled-for *adjective*
1. Not necessary ▶ inessential, needless, unneeded. *See* **unnecessary.** 2. Not required, necessary, or warranted by the circumstances of the case ▶ supererogative, supererogatory, unwarranted. *See* **wanton** (2).

uncanny *adjective*
▶ eerie, unearthly. *See* **weird** (1). *See synonym note at* **weird.**

uncaring *adjective*
▶ heartless, merciless, unsympathetic. *See* **callous.**

unceasing *adjective*
▶ constant, endless, everlasting, perpetual. *See* **continual.**

uncensored *adjective*
▶ full-length, unabridged, uncut. *See* **complete** (2).

unceremonious *adjective*
▶ informal, casual. *Informal:* laid-back. *See* **easygoing** (1).

unceremoniousness *noun*
▶ informality, naturalness. *See* **ease** (1).

uncertain *adjective*
1. Lacking certainty or clarity ▶ dubious, indeterminate, questionable, unclear. *See* **ambiguous** (1). 2. In doubt or dispute ▶ disputable, doubtful, questionable. *See* **debatable.** 3. Liable to more than one interpretation ▶ equivocal, nebulous, vague. *See* **ambiguous** (2). 4. Of dubious character ▶ equivocal, questionable, suspicious. *See* **shady** (1). 5. Marked by lack of firm decision or commitment; of questionable outcome ▶ open, undetermined. *See* **indefinite** (2). 6. Experiencing doubt ▶ hesitant, skeptical, tentative. *See* **doubtful** (2). 7. Capable of or liable to change ▶ fluid, unsettled, variable. *See* **changeable** (1). 8. Marked by whim or impulse ▶ fickle, impulsive, mercurial. *See* **capricious.**

uncertainty *noun*
1. The quality or state of being imprecise or indefinite ▶ ambiguousness, equivocalness, unclearness. *See* **vagueness.** 2. A lack of conviction or certainty ▶ dubiousness, incertitude, skepticism. *See* **doubt** (1). *See synonym note at* **doubt.**

unchained *adjective*
▶ liberated, unconfined, unrestrained. *See* **loose** (2).

unchangeable *adjective*
▶ inflexible, invariable. *See* **immutable** (1).

unchanging *adjective*
Having no change or variation; remaining unchanged ▶ changeless, consistent, constant, equable, even, firm, fixed, flat, immutable, invariable, invariant, permanent, regular, same, set, steady, unfailing, uniform, unvarying. *Idioms:* cast (*or* etched *or* fixed *or* set) in stone. *See also* **continual, continuing, endless.**

unchaste *adjective*
1. Not chaste or moral ▶ debased, uncleanly. *See* **impure** (1). 2. Sexually unrestrained ▶ fast, loose, sluttish. *See* **wanton** (1).

unchecked *adjective*
▶ liberated, unconfined, unrestrained. *See* **loose** (2).

uncivil *adjective*
1. Lacking good manners ▶ disrespectful, impolite, unmannerly. *See* **rude** (4). 2. Causing displeasure, anger, or hurt feelings ▶ hurtful, impolite, rude. *See* **offensive** (2).

uncivility *noun*
▶ inhospitableness, uncivility, unreceptiveness. *See* **inhospitality.**

uncivilized *adjective*
1. Not civilized ▶ barbarian, barbaric, barbarous, brutish, primitive, rude, savage, uncultivated, uncultured, untamed, wild. 2. Lacking in delicacy or refinement ▶ indelicate, unbecoming, unrefined. *See* **coarse** (1).

unclad *adjective*
▶ bare, naked. *See* **nude** (1).

unclasp *verb*
▶ loose, release, untie. *See* **undo** (1).

unclean *or* **uncleanly** *adjective*
1. Covered with or stained by dirt ▶ black, filthy, muddy. *See* **dirty** (1). 2. Not chaste or moral ▶ debased, unchaste. *See* **impure** (1).

uncleanliness *or* **uncleanness** *noun*
1. The condition or state of being dirty ▶ filthiness, squalor, uncleanliness. *See* **dirtiness** (1). 2. The state of being contaminated ▶ defilement, impurity, pollution. *See* **contamination** (1).

unclear *adjective*
1. Not clearly perceptible; difficult to see clearly ▶ blear, bleary, blurry, cloudy, dim, faint, filmy, foggy, fuzzy, hazy, indefinite, indistinct, misty, obscure, shadowy, undistinct, vague. 2. Liable to more than one interpretation ▶ equivocal, nebulous, vague. *See* **ambiguous** (2). 3. Lacking certainty or clarity ▶ dubious, indeterminate, questionable. *See* **ambiguous** (1).

unclearness *noun*
▶ ambiguousness, equivocalness, nebulousness. *See* **vagueness.**

unclose *verb*
▶ free, release. *See* **open** (1).

unclothe *verb*
1. To remove the clothing or covering from ▶ disrobe, strip, undress. 2. To make visible ▶ disclose, expose, uncover. *See* **reveal** (2).

unclouded *adjective*
▶ fair, fine. *See* **clear** (2).

uncoil *verb*
▶ unreel, unravel, unroll. *See* **unwind** (1).

uncomeliness *noun*
▶ monstrosity, odiousness, unsightliness. *See* **ugliness** (1).

uncomely *adjective*
▶ homely, plain, unattractive. *See* **ugly** (1).

uncomfortable *adjective*
1. Causing discomfort ▶ comfortless, thorny, uncomforting. *Informal:* uncomfy. *See also* **disturbing, painful, tormenting.** 2. Characterized by embarrassment and discomfort ▶ constrained, uneasy. *See* **awkward** (3).

uncomfy *adjective*
Informal Causing discomfort ▸ thorny, uncomforting. *See* **uncomfortable** (1).

uncommitted *adjective*
▸ nonaligned, unbiased. *See* **neutral** (1).

uncommon *adjective*
1. Rarely occurring or appearing ▸ scarce, unusual. *See* **infrequent**. **2.** Beyond what is usual, normal, or customary ▸ extraordinary, outstanding, remarkable. *See* **exceptional** (1).

uncommonly *adverb*
1. In a manner or to a degree that is unusual ▸ singularly, strangely, uniquely. *See* **unusually**. **2.** At rare intervals ▸ rarely, seldom. *See* **infrequently**.

uncommonness *noun*
▸ oneness, singleness, singularity. *See* **uniqueness** (1).

uncommunicative *adjective*
1. Habitually untalkative ▸ reticent, silent, tightlipped. *See* **taciturn**. *See synonym note at* **taciturn**. **2.** Not friendly, sociable, or warm in manner ▸ aloof, chilly, impersonal. *See* **cool** (1).

uncommunicativeness *noun*
▸ guardedness, remoteness, reservedness. *See* **reserve** (2).

uncompassionate *adjective*
▸ heartless, merciless, unsympathetic. *See* **callous**.

uncompelled *adjective*
▸ spontaneous, unforced. *See* **voluntary** (1).

uncompensated *adjective*
▸ pro bono, unsalaried, volunteer. *See* **unpaid** (1).

uncompliant *adjective*
▸ bullheaded, dogged, obstinate. *See* **stubborn** (1).

uncomplimentary *adjective*
▸ deprecatory, derogatory, pejorative. *See* **disparaging**.

uncomprehending *adjective*
▸ obtuse, unperceptive. *See* **blind** (3).

uncomprehensible *adjective*
▸ unfathomable, unintelligible. *See* **incomprehensible**.

uncompromising *adjective*
1. Possessing determination or resolution ▸ resolute, steadfast, unyielding. *See* **firm**[1] (3). **2.** Rigorous and unsparing in treating others ▸ harsh, stern, tough. *See* **severe** (1). **3.** Firmly, often unreasonably immovable in purpose or will ▸ bullheaded, dogged, obstinate. *See* **stubborn** (1). **4.** Depicted in sharp and accurate detail ▸ explicit, realistic, vivid. *See* **graphic** (1).

unconceivable *adjective*
▸ improbable, inconceivable. *See* **implausible**.

unconcern *noun*
1. Lack of emotion or interest ▸ disinterest, indifference, uninterest. *See* **apathy**. **2.** Dissociation from one's surroundings or worldly affairs ▸ disinterest, indifference, remoteness. *See* **detachment** (2).

unconcerned *adjective*
1. Lacking interest ▸ indifferent, listless, uninterested. *See* **apathetic**. **2.** Lacking interest in one's surroundings or worldly affairs ▸ disinterested, indifferent,

uninvolved. *See* **detached** (1). **3.** Lacking concern or regard ▸ heedless, inattentive, thoughtless. *See* **careless** (1).

unconditional *adjective*
1. Without limitations or mitigating conditions ▸ absolute, full, unconditioned, unqualified, unreserved. *See also* **utter**[2]. **2.** Having no reservations ▸ absolute, unfaltering. *See* **implicit** (2).

unconditioned *adjective*
▸ full, unreserved. *See* **unconditional** (1).

unconfined *adjective*
▸ liberated, unchecked, unrestrained. *See* **loose** (2).

unconfirmed *adjective*
▸ disputable, doubtful, questionable. *See* **debatable**.

uncongenial *adjective*
1. Devoid of harmony and accord ▸ disagreeing, dissonant. *See* **inharmonious** (1). **2.** Not pleasant or agreeable ▸ bad, disagreeable, unsympathetic. *See* **unpleasant** (1).

uncongeniality *noun*
▸ inhospitableness, uncivility, uncivility. *See* **inhospitality**.

unconnected *adjective*
▸ immaterial, inapplicable, unrelated. *See* **irrelevant**.

unconquerability *noun*
▸ impenetrability, security. *See* **safety** (1).

unconquerable *adjective*
1. Incapable of being conquered or subjugated ▸ indomitable, invincible, unbeatable, undefeatable. *See also* **insuperable**. **2.** Incapable of being negotiated or overcome ▸ impassable, insuperable, insurmountable. *See also* **impossible**. **3.** Affording protection ▸ impenetrable, invulnerable, secure. *See* **safe** (2).

unconscionable *adjective*
1. Lacking scruples or principles ▸ conscienceless, unethical, unprincipled. *See* **unscrupulous** (1). **2.** Exceeding the bounds of morality, decency, or reason ▸ appalling, monstrous, shocking. *See* **outrageous**. **3.** Vastly exceeding a normal limit, as in cost ▸ exorbitant, overpriced. *See* **steep**[1] (2).

unconscious *adjective*
1. Lacking consciousness ▸ cold, comatose, insensible, out, senseless. *Idioms:* blacked out, out like a light, out cold. *See also* **dead, inanimate**. **2.** Not aware or informed ▸ oblivious, misguided, unaware. *See* **ignorant** (3).

unconsciousness *noun*
▸ nescience, unawareness. *See* **ignorance** (2).

unconsidered *adjective*
▸ brash, hasty, impetuous. *See* **rash**[1].

unconspicuous *adjective*
▸ obscure, unnoticeable, unobtrusive. *See* **inconspicuous**.

unconstrained *adjective*
▸ unbridled, uncontrolled, ungoverned. *See* **abandoned** (2).

uncontaminated *adjective*
▸ pristine, unpolluted, unspoiled. *See* **fresh** (1).

uncontrollability *or* **uncontrollableness** *noun*
▸ intractability, obstinacy, unmanageability. *See* **unruliness.**

uncontrollable *adjective*
▸ ill-behaved, obstinate, unmanageable. *See* **unruly.**

uncontrolled *adjective*
1. Out of control ▸ amuck, runaway, unbridled. *Idioms:* out of hand, running wild. *See also* **loose.** **2.** Lacking in moral restraint ▸ licentious, unbridled, ungoverned. *See* **abandoned** (2). **3.** Without a fixed or regular course ▸ stray, wandering. *See* **erratic** (1).

unconventional *adjective*
1. Not usual or ordinary ▸ atypical, novel, unordinary. *See* **unusual** (1). **2.** Deviating from what is conventional or customary ▸ bizarre, grotesque. *See* **eccentric.**

unconventionally *adverb*
▸ singularly, uncommonly, uniquely. *See* **unusually.**

unconversant *adjective*
▸ inexpert, uninitiated, unpracticed. *See* **inexperienced.**

unconvinced *adjective*
▸ questioning, skeptical. *See* **incredulous.**

unconvincing *adjective*
▸ improbable, inconceivable. *See* **implausible.**

uncooked *adjective*
Not cooked ▸ raw.

uncool *adjective*
Slang Conforming to established practice or standards ▸ conformist, orthodox, traditional. *See* **conventional** (1).

uncoordinated *adjective*
▸ gawky, graceless. *Slang:* klutzy. *See* **awkward** (1).

uncorporal *adjective*
▸ disembodied, nonphysical. *See* **immaterial** (1).

uncorrupted *adjective*
▸ pure, unblemished, untainted. *See* **innocent** (1).

uncountable *adjective*
▸ immeasurable, infinite. *See* **incalculable.**

uncouple *verb*
1. To break up the unity of something; separate into parts, sections, or branches ▸ disjoin, dissever, split up. *See* **divide** (1). **2.** To remove from association with ▸ disassociate, disengage, withdraw. *See* **detach** (1).

uncoupling *noun*
▸ disconnection, separation, withdrawal. *See* **detachment** (1).

uncouth *adjective*
▸ indelicate, unbecoming, unrefined. *See* **coarse** (1).

uncover *verb*
1. To find by investigation ▸ dig (up *or* out), disinter, exhume, turn up, unearth. *Idiom:* bring to light. *See also* **discover. 2.** To remove the clothing or covering from ▸ denude, expose, strip. *See* **bare** (1). **3.** To make visible ▸ disclose, expose. *See* **reveal** (2). **4.** To disclose in a breach of confidence ▸ divulge, give away. *Informal:* spill. *See* **betray** (2).

uncovered *adjective*
▸ revealed, spread. *See* **open** (2).

uncreative *adjective*
▸ unimaginative, uninspired, uninventive. *See* **sterile** (4).

uncritical *adjective*
▸ cursory, one-dimensional, shallow. *See* **superficial** (1).

unction *noun*
1. A substance used on the skin to soothe or heal ▸ emollient, salve. *See* **ointment. 2.** A substance that is generally slippery, combustible, and not water soluble ▸ grease, petroleum. *See* **oil** (1).

unctuous *adjective*
1. Affectedly and self-servingly earnest ▸ fulsome, oily, oleaginous, sleek, smarmy. *See also* **flattering, glib, servile. 2.** Having the qualities of fat ▸ greasy, oleaginous. *See* **fatty** (1).

✦ CORE SYNONYMS: *unctuous, fulsome, oily, oleaginous, smarmy.* These adjectives mean affectedly, self-servingly, or smugly earnest: *an unctuous toady; gave the dictator a fulsome introduction; oily praise; oleaginous hypocrisy; smarmy self-importance.*

---

uncultivated *adjective*
1. Not cultivated ▸ native, natural, rough. *See* **wild** (1). **2.** Not civilized ▸ barbarian, barbaric, rude. *See* **uncivilized** (1). **3.** Lacking in delicacy or refinement ▸ indelicate, unbecoming, unrefined. *See* **coarse** (1). **4.** Without education or knowledge ▸ lowbrow, nescient, unlearned. *See* **ignorant** (1).

uncultured *adjective*
1. Not civilized ▸ barbarian, barbaric, rude, savage. *See* **uncivilized** (1). **2.** Lacking in delicacy or refinement ▸ indelicate, unbecoming, unrefined. *See* **coarse** (1).

uncut *adjective*
▸ full-length, unabridged, uncensored. *See* **complete** (2).

undamaged *adjective*
▸ flawless, intact, sound. *See* **good** (2).

undaunted *adjective*
▸ courageous, fearless, heroic. *See* **brave.** *See synonym note at* **brave.**

undauntedness *noun*
▸ bravery, fortitude, gallantry, valor. *See* **courage.**

undeceive *verb*
▸ disenchant, disillusion. *See* **disabuse.**

undecided *adjective*
1. Marked by lack of firm decision or commitment; of questionable outcome ▸ uncertain, undetermined. *See* **indefinite** (2). **2.** Experiencing doubt ▸ hesitant, skeptical, uncertain. *See* **doubtful** (2).

undeclared *adjective*
▸ tacit, unspoken. *See* **silent** (2).

undecorated *adjective*
▸ austere, plain, unadorned. *See* **bare** (1).

undefended *adjective*
▸ ill-protected, unattended, unsafe. *See* **insecure** (1).

undefiled *adjective*
▸ pure, uncorrupted, untainted. *See* **innocent** (1).

undemanding *adjective*
Requiring little effort or exertion ▸ easy, light, moderate. *Informal:* cushy, soft.

undemonstrated *adjective*
▸ surmised, unpracticed, unproved, untested. *See* **untried** (1).

undemonstrative *adjective*
▸ aloof, chilly, impersonal. *See* **cool** (1).

undeniable *adjective*
▸ inarguable, indisputable, irrefutable. *See* **certain** (2).

undependable *adjective*
1. Not to be depended on ▸ fair-weather, irresponsible, unreliable, untrustworthy. *See also* **capricious, changeable. 2.** So weak or defective as to be liable to fail ▸ trick, unreliable. *See also* **defective, weak.**

under *adjective*
1. Not enough to meet a demand or requirement ▸ inadequate, short. *See* **insufficient** (1). **2.** Below another in standing, importance, or status ▸ junior, low, secondary. *See* **minor** (1).

underage[1] *noun*
The condition or fact of being deficient ▸ deficit, inadequacy, paucity. *See* **shortage.**

underage[2] *adjective*
Not yet a legal adult ▸ minor.

underbrush *noun*
▸ bushes, thicket, undergrowth. *See* **brush**[2].

undercover *adjective*
▸ clandestine, cloak-and-dagger, covert. *See* **secret** (1).

undercurrent *noun*
▸ inkling, suspicion. *See* **hint** (1).

underdeveloped *adjective*
▸ lagging, undeveloped. *See* **backward** (2).

underdog *noun*
▸ miserable, wretch. *See* **unfortunate.**

underestimate *verb*
▸ miscount, misjudge, misreckon. *See* **miscalculate.**

undergird *verb*
1. To provide a basis for ▸ establish, ground. *See* **base**[1] (1). **2.** To make stronger or more resistant ▸ bolster, reinforce, strengthen. *See* **support** (2).

undergo *verb*
▸ encounter, know, sample. *See* **experience.**

underground *adjective*
Located or operating beneath the earth's surface ▸ belowground, buried, hypogeal, hypogean, hypogeous, subterranean, subterrestrial.

underground *noun*
A clandestine organization of freedom fighters in an oppressed land ▸ opposition, resistance.

underhand *or* **underhanded** *adjective*
Marked by or done in a deceptive or secret manner ▸ devious, disingenuous, duplicitous, guileful, indirect, left-handed, lubricious, shifty, sneaky, subtle, unscrupulous. *See also* **artful, secret, shady, stealthy.**

underhandedness *noun*
▸ deviousness, slyness, trickery. *See* **dishonesty** (2).

underline *verb*
▸ accentuate, highlight. *See* **emphasize.**

underling *noun*
▸ inferior, junior, secondary. *See* **subordinate.**

underlying *adjective*
1. Arising from or going to the root or source ▸ basic, fundamental, primary. *See* **radical** (1). **2.** Of or being an irreducible element ▸ basic, essential, fundamental. *See* **elemental** (1).

undermanned *adjective*
Having fewer workers or participants than are needed ▸ short-handed, short-staffed, understaffed.

undermine *verb*
1. To damage, destroy, or defeat by sabotage ▸ sabotage, subvert. *See also* **destroy, disorder. 2.** To lessen or deplete the nerve, energy, or strength of ▸ debilitate, weaken. *See* **enervate.**

undermining *noun*
Treacherous action to defeat or do harm to an endeavor ▸ sabotage, subversion. *See also* **defeat, destruction.**

undermost *adjective*
▸ lowest, nethermost. *See* **bottom.**

underneath *noun*
▸ underside, undersurface. *See* **bottom** (1).

underpin *verb*
1. To provide a basis for ▸ establish, ground. *See* **base**[1] (1). **2.** To make stronger or more resistant ▸ bolster, reinforce, strengthen. *See* **support** (2).

underpinning *noun*
1. A means or device that keeps something erect, stable, or secure ▸ buttress, crutch, prop. *See* **support** (1). **2.** The lowest or supporting part or structure ▸ bottom, foot, foundation. *See* **base**[1] (2). **3.** An underlying support, as for an argument or belief ▸ cornerstone, foundation, grounds. *See* **basis** (1).

underprivileged *adjective*
Economically and socially below standard ▸ disadvantaged, impoverished. *See* **depressed** (2).

underprivileged *noun*
A person living under very unhappy circumstances ▸ miserable, wretch. *See* **unfortunate.**

underprop *verb*
▸ bolster, reinforce, strengthen. *See* **support** (2).

underscore *verb*
▸ accentuate, highlight. *See* **emphasize.**

undersexed *adjective*
▸ cold, inhibited, passionless. *See* **frigid** (3).

underside *noun*
▸ underneath, undersurface. *See* **bottom** (1).

undersign *verb*
▸ endorse, inscribe. *See* **sign** (1).

undersized *adjective*
▸ bantam, petite, smallish. *See* **little** (1).

understaffed *adjective*
Having fewer workers or participants than are needed ▸ short-handed, short-staffed, undermanned.

understand *verb*
1. To perceive and recognize the meaning of ▸ accept, apprehend, catch (on), compass, comprehend, conceive, fathom, follow, get, grasp, make out, read, see,

sense, take, take in. *Informal:* hear, savvy. *Slang:* dig. *Idioms:* get (*or* have) a handle on, get the picture. *See also* **know. 2.** To understand or be sensitive to another's feelings or ideas ► empathize, sympathize. *Idioms:* feel someone's pain, put oneself (*or* walk) in someone else's shoes. **3.** To arrive at a conclusion from evidence or reasoning ► deduce, gather. *See* **infer** (1).

✚ **CORE SYNONYMS:** *understand, comprehend, apprehend, grasp.* These verbs denote perception and recognition of the nature and meaning of something. Both *understand* and *comprehend* stress complete realization and knowledge: *"No one who has not had the responsibility can really understand what it is like to be President"* (Harry S. Truman). *"To comprehend is to know a thing as well as that thing can be known"* (John Donne). *Apprehend* denotes both mental and intuitive awareness: *"Intelligence is quickness to apprehend"* (Alfred North Whitehead). To *grasp* is to seize an idea firmly: *"We have grasped the mystery of the atom and rejected the Sermon on the Mount"* (Omar N. Bradley).

---

understandable *adjective*
1. Capable of being readily understood ► appreciable, apprehensible, coherent, comprehensible, fathomable, intelligible, knowable, lucid, unambiguous. **2.** Admitting of forgiveness or pardon ► forgivable, venial. *See* **pardonable.**

understanding *noun*
1. Intellectual hold ► apprehension, comprehension, grasp, grip, hold. *See also* **knowledge. 2.** A very close understanding between persons ► empathy, sympathy. **3.** The sum of what has been perceived, discovered, or inferred ► knowledge, lore, wisdom. *See also* **actuality. 4.** The faculty of thinking, reasoning, and applying knowledge ► aptitude, intellect. *See* **intelligence** (1). **5.** An often written acceptance of terms between parties ► accord, pact. *See* **agreement** (1).

understanding *adjective*
Feeling or expressing sympathy or pity ► commiserative, compassionate, empathetic, supportive. *See* **sympathetic.**

understood *adjective*
► inferred, tacit, unspoken. *See* **implicit** (1).

undersurface *noun*
► underneath, underside. *See* **bottom** (1).

undertake *verb*
1. To take upon oneself ► shoulder, take on. *See* **assume** (1). **2.** To assume an obligation ► engage, promise. *See* **pledge** (2). **3.** To go about the initial step in doing something ► begin, embark, take on. *See* **start** (1).

undertaking *noun*
1. Something undertaken, especially something requiring extensive planning and work ► endeavor, enterprise, project, venture. *See also* **task. 2.** An assignment one is sent to carry out ► errand, operation. *See* **mission** (1). **3.** A trying to do or make something ► effort, endeavor, trial. *See* **attempt** (1).

undertone *noun*
1. A subtle quality underlying or felt to underlie a situation, action, or person ► inkling, suspicion. *See* **hint** (1). **2.** Quality of light reflected or emitted ► hue, shade, tint. *See* **color** (1).

underwhelming *adjective*
► disheartening, sorry. *See* **disappointing.**

underwrite *verb*
► fund, subsidize. *Informal:* bankroll. *See* **finance.**

underwriter *noun*
► guarantor, surety. *See* **sponsor** (1).

undescribable *adjective*
► ineffable, inexpressible. *See* **unspeakable** (1).

undesigned *adjective*
► inadvertent, undevised, unintended. *See* **unintentional.**

undesirable *adjective*
1. Arousing disapproval ► exceptionable, improper, unacceptable. *See* **objectionable. 2.** Not welcome or wanted ► uninvited, unwanted. *See* **unwelcome** (1).

undesired *adjective*
► uninvited, unwanted. *See* **unwelcome** (1).

undetected *adjective*
Not found ► undiscovered, unexposed, unfound.

undetermined *adjective*
1. Marked by lack of firm decision or commitment; of questionable outcome ► uncertain, unsettled. *See* **indefinite** (2). **2.** Lacking precise limits ► inexact, undefined. *See* **indefinite** (1).

undeveloped *adjective*
1. Behind others in progress or development ► lagging, underdeveloped. *See* **backward** (2). **2.** Not polluted or altered by human intervention ► pristine, unpolluted, unspoiled. *See* **fresh** (1).

undeviating *adjective*
1. Proceeding in an uninterrupted line or course ► linear, straightforward, unswerving. *See* **direct** (1). **2.** Employing the very same words as another ► unvarnished, verbatim, word-for-word. *See* **literal** (1).

undevised *adjective*
► inadvertent, undesigned, unintended. *See* **unintentional.**

undiluted *adjective*
1. Free from extraneous elements ► perfect, plain, unadulterated. *See* **pure** (1). **2.** Not diluted or mixed with other substances ► pure, unblended. *See* **straight** (1).

undiplomatic *adjective*
► gauche, impolitic, maladroit. *See* **tactless.**

undirected *adjective*
► pointless, purposeless, rambling. *See* **aimless.**

undisciplined *adjective*
► ill-behaved, obstinate, unmanageable. *See* **unruly.**

undisclosed *adjective*
► concealed, covert, hidden. *See* **ulterior** (1).

undiscovered *adjective*
Not found ► undetected, unexposed, unfound.

undisputable *adjective*
► inarguable, indisputable, irrefutable. *See* **certain** (2).

undistinct *adjective*
▶ dim, faint, indefinite. *See* **unclear** (1).

undistinguished *adjective*
1. Being of no special quality or type ▶ common, mediocre, standard. *See* **ordinary** (1). **2.** Not widely known ▶ little-known, unheard-of. *See* **obscure** (2). **3.** Not readily noticed or seen ▶ unnoticeable, unassuming. *See* **inconspicuous.**

undivided *adjective*
1. Not diffused or dispersed ▶ intensive, whole. *See* **concentrated** (1). **2.** Being in or characterized by complete agreement ▶ accordant, consonant, like-minded. *See* **unanimous.**

undo *verb*
1. To free from ties or fasteners ▶ disengage, loose, loosen, release, slip, unbind, unclasp, unfasten, unloose, unloosen, untie. **2.** To become or cause to become open ▶ free, release, unclose. *See* **open** (1). **3.** To cause the complete ruin or wreckage of ▶ demolish, torpedo, wreck. *See* **destroy** (1). **4.** To lessen or deplete the nerve, energy, or strength of ▶ debilitate, weaken. *See* **enervate. 5.** To cross out or remove ▶ delete, erase, strike (out). *See* **cancel** (1).

undoing *noun*
1. The act of destroying or state of being destroyed ▶ devastation, ruin, wreck. *See* **destruction** (1). **2.** Something that causes total loss or severe impairment ▶ bane, downfall, ruination. *See* **ruin** (1).

undomesticated *adjective*
1. Not cultivated ▶ native, natural, uncultivated. *See* **wild** (1). **2.** Not tamed ▶ feral, savage, untamed. *See* **wild** (2).

undoubted *adjective*
▶ true. *Slang:* legit, kosher. *See* **authentic** (1). *See synonym note at* **authentic.**

undoubtedly *adverb*
1. Without question ▶ certainly, doubtless, doubtlessly, positively. *See* **absolutely** (1). **2.** It is so; as you say or ask ▶ agreed, all right, assuredly. *See* **yes.**

undoubting *adjective*
1. Having no doubt ▶ certain, confident, positive. *See* **sure** (1). **2.** Having no reservations ▶ unconditional, unfaltering. *See* **implicit** (2).

undress *verb*
To remove the clothing or covering from ▶ disrobe, strip, unclothe. *See* **bare** (1).

undress *noun*
The state of being without clothes ▶ nakedness, nudeness. *See* **nudity.**

undue *adjective*
▶ extravagant, immoderate. *See* **excessive** (1).

undulate *verb*
1. To have or cause to have a curved or wavy surface ▶ curl, ripple. *See* **wave** (2). **2.** To move back and forth ▶ oscillate, totter. *See* **sway** (1). *See synonym note at* **sway. 3.** To move along in a crouching or prone position ▶ creep, slither, worm. *See* **crawl** (1).

unduly *adverb*
Too much ▶ disproportionately, excessively, extrava-

gantly, extremely, inordinately, overly, overmuch. *Informal:* super.

undying *adjective*
1. Not being subject to death ▶ deathless, immortal. *See also* **endless. 2.** Existing without interruption or end ▶ constant, endless, everlasting, perpetual. *See* **continual.**

unearth *verb*
1. To find by investigation ▶ dig (up *or* out), turn up. *See* **uncover** (1). **2.** To obtain knowledge or awareness of something not known before ▶ detect, observe. *See* **discover.**

unearthly *adjective*
1. Of or relating to existence outside the natural world ▶ metaphysical, superhuman. *See* **supernatural** (1). **2.** Of an unnatural and usually frightening nature ▶ eerie, uncanny. *See* **weird** (1). *See synonym note at* **weird.**

unease *or* **uneasiness** *noun*
1. A troubled or anxious state of mind ▶ concern, distress, worriment. *See* **anxiety** (1). **2.** An uneasy or nervous state ▶ disquietude, skittishness, unrest. *See* **restlessness.**

uneasy *adjective*
1. Affording no quiet, repose, or rest ▶ restless, unquiet, unsettled. *See also* **edgy, wakeful. 2.** In a state of anxiety or uneasiness ▶ distressed, nervous, worried. *See* **anxious. 3.** Characterized by embarrassment and discomfort ▶ constrained, uncomfortable. *See* **awkward** (3).

uneatable *adjective*
▶ distasteful, unappetizing, unsavory. *See* **unpalatable** (1).

uneconomical *adjective*
▶ prodigal, profligate. *See* **extravagant** (1).

unedited *adjective*
▶ full-length, unabridged, uncut. *See* **complete** (2).

uneducated *adjective*
▶ illiterate, unlearned, untaught. *See* **ignorant** (1).

unemotional *adjective*
▶ emotionless, impassive, stolid. *See* **cold** (2).

unemployable *adjective*
▶ unserviceable, unusable, useless. *See* **unworkable** (1).

unemployed *adjective*
1. Having no job ▶ idle, jobless, unoccupied, workless. *Idioms:* out of a job (*or* employ *or* work). **2.** Marked by a lack of activity or use ▶ inert, inoperative, unused. *See* **idle** (1).

unencouraging *adjective*
▶ dim, unpromising. *See* **bleak** (2).

unending *adjective*
1. Existing without interruption or end ▶ constant, endless, everlasting, perpetual. *See* **continual. 2.** Enduring for all time ▶ ceaseless, eternal. *See* **endless** (2). **3.** Extending tediously beyond a standard duration ▶ drawn-out, overlong, protracted. *See* **long**[1] (2).

unendingly *adverb*
▶ endlessly, evermore, perpetually. *See* **forever** (1).

unendurable *adjective*
▶ insufferable, intolerable, unacceptable. *See* **unbearable.**

unenlightened *adjective*
1. Exhibiting lack of education or knowledge ▶ primitive, uninformed. *See* **ignorant** (2). **2.** Not aware or informed ▶ clueless, unacquainted, uninformed. *See* **ignorant** (3).

unenthusiastic *adjective*
Lacking warmth, interest, enthusiasm, or involvement ▶ halfhearted, Laodicean, lukewarm, tepid. *See also* **apathetic, cold, cool.**

unequal *adjective*
1. Not fair, right, or just ▶ discriminatory, inequitable, unjust. *See* **unfair. 2.** Lacking the qualities, as efficiency or skill, required to produce desired results ▶ incapable, inept, unskilled. *See* **inefficient** (1).

unequaled *adjective*
▶ incomparable, singular, unparalleled. *See* **unique** (1).

unequivocal *adjective*
1. Clearly defined; not ambiguous ▶ distinct, unambiguous. *See* **sharp** (3). **2.** Clearly, fully, and emphatically expressed ▶ decided, explicit, precise. *See* **definite** (1). **3.** Completely such, without qualification or exception ▶ all-out, pure, sheer. *See* **utter**[2].

unerring *adjective*
▶ foolproof, infallible, unfailing. *See* **sure** (2).

unessential *adjective*
▶ inessential, needless, unneeded. *See* **unnecessary.**

unethical *adjective*
▶ conscienceless, unconscionable, unprincipled. *See* **unscrupulous** (1).

uneven *adjective*
1. Lacking consistency or regularity in quality or performance ▶ erratic, inconsistent, patchy, spasmodic, spotty, unsteady, variable. *See also* **intermittent. 2.** Having a surface that is not smooth ▶ coarse, jagged, scabrous. *See* **rough** (1). *See synonym note at* **rough. 3.** Not fair, right, or just ▶ discriminatory, unequal, unjust. *See* **unfair.**

unevenness *noun*
▶ crookedness, jaggedness, unevenness. *See* **irregularity** (1).

unexampled *adjective*
▶ incomparable, singular, unparalleled. *See* **unique** (1).

unexceptionable *adjective*
▶ admissible, unobjectionable. *See* **acceptable** (1).

unexceptional *adjective*
▶ common, mediocre, standard. *See* **ordinary** (1).

unexpected *adjective*
▶ incidental, inadvertent, unanticipated. *See* **accidental** (1).

unexpectedly *adverb*
▶ singularly, uncommonly, uniquely. *See* **unusually.**

unexplainable *adjective*
That cannot be explained ▶ inexplicable, unaccountable. *See also* **mysterious.**

unexposed *adjective*
Not found ▶ undetected, undiscovered, unfound.

unexpressed *adjective*
1. Not voiced or expressed ▶ undeclared, unspoken. *See* **silent** (2). **2.** Conveyed indirectly without words or speech ▶ inferred, suggested, unspoken. *See* **implicit** (1).

unexpurgated *adjective*
▶ full-length, unabridged, uncut. *See* **complete** (2).

unfailing *adjective*
1. Remaining unchanged ▶ consistent, constant, invariable. *See* **unchanging. 2.** Existing without interruption or end ▶ constant, endless, everlasting, perpetual. *See* **continual. 3.** Having or showing a capacity for protracted effort, regardless of difficulty or frustration ▶ inexhaustible, unflagging, untiring. *See* **tireless. 4.** Certain not to fail ▶ foolproof, infallible, unerring. *See* **sure** (2).

unfair *adjective*
Not fair, right, or just ▶ dirty, discriminatory, inequitable, preferential, unequal, uneven, unjust, wrong. *See also* **biased, unscrupulous.**

unfairness *noun*
1. Lack of equality, as of opportunity, treatment, or status ▶ discrimination, inequality, unjustness. *See also* **bias. 2.** Lack of justice ▶ iniquity, unjustness, wrong. *See* **injustice** (2).

unfaithful *adjective*
▶ disloyal, traitorous, untrue. *See* **faithless** (1). *See synonym note at* **faithless.**

unfaithfulness *noun*
▶ disloyalty, infidelity, perfidy, treachery. *See* **faithlessness** (1).

unfaltering *adjective*
▶ unconditional, unreserved. *See* **implicit** (2).

unfamiliar *adjective*
1. Not aware or informed ▶ clueless, unacquainted, uninformed. *See* **ignorant** (3). **2.** Not the same as what was previously known or done ▶ fresh, novel, original. *See* **new** (1).

unfamiliarity *noun*
▶ nescience, unawareness. *See* **ignorance** (2).

unfasten *verb*
1. To free from ties or fasteners ▶ loose, release, untie. *See* **undo** (1). **2.** To become or cause to become open ▶ free, release, unclose. *See* **open** (1).

unfastened *adjective*
▶ flapping, relaxed, slack. *See* **loose** (1). *See synonym note at* **loose.**

unfathomable *adjective*
1. Incapable of being grasped by the intellect or understanding ▶ impenetrable, unintelligible. *See* **incomprehensible. 2.** Too great to be calculated ▶ immeasurable, infinite. *See* **incalculable.**

unfavorable *adjective*
1. Tending to discourage, retard, or make more difficult ▶ adverse, antagonistic, disadvantageous, negative, unadvantageous, unsatisfactory, untoward. *See also* **inhospitable. 2.** Not encouraging life or growth ▶ adverse, hostile, inhospitable. *See also* **severe. 3.** Bringing or predicting misfortune ▶ bad, evil,

ill, inauspicious. *See* **fateful** (1). **4.** Acting against or in opposition ▸ antagonistic, resistant. *See* **opposing** (1).

unfeeling *adjective*
1. Lacking physical feeling or sensitivity ▸ inert, insensible, numb. *See* **dead** (2). **2.** Lacking compassion or mercy ▸ heartless, insensitive, merciless. *See* **callous.**

unfeigned *adjective*
▸ honest, sincere, unaffected. *See* **genuine** (1).

unfettered *adjective*
▸ liberated, unconfined, unrestrained. *See* **loose** (2).

unfinished *adjective*
1. Not perfected, elaborated, or completed ▸ preliminary, sketchy, unpolished. *See* **rough** (10). **2.** Not total ▸ fragmentary, incomplete. *See* **partial** (1).

unfit *adjective*
1. Not suited to circumstances ▸ inapt, malapropos, unbecoming. *See* **improper** (2). **2.** Lacking the qualities, as efficiency or skill, required to produce desired results ▸ incapable, inept, unskilled. *See* **inefficient** (1).

unfit *verb*
To make incapable, as of doing a job ▸ disable, disqualify.

unfitness *noun*
▸ inappropriateness, unseemliness. *See* **impropriety** (1).

unflagging *adjective*
1. Having or showing a capacity for protracted effort, regardless of difficulty or frustration ▸ inexhaustible, unfailing, untiring. *See* **tireless.** *See synonym note at* **tireless.** **2.** Characterized by steady attention and effort ▸ assiduous, conscientious, industrious. *See* **diligent.** *See synonym note at* **diligent.**

unflappability *noun*
▸ imperturbability, nonchalance, sang-froid. *See* **balance** (2).

unflappable *adjective*
▸ collected, composed, cool. *See* **calm** (1).

unflawed *adjective*
▸ consummate, flawless, unblemished. *See* **perfect** (1).

unflinching *adjective*
1. Indicating or possessing determination or resolution ▸ resolute, steadfast, unyielding. *See* **firm**[1] (3). **2.** Having or showing courage ▸ courageous, fearless, heroic. *See* **brave.**

unfold *verb*
1. To move or arrange so as to cover a larger area ▸ extend, stretch. *See* **spread** (1). **2.** To be disclosed gradually ▸ disentangle, unfurl, unravel. *See* **develop** (2).

unfolding *noun*
▸ evolvement, maturation, progress. *See* **development** (1).

unforbearing *adjective*
1. Being unable or unwilling to endure irritation or opposition, for example ▸ impatient, intolerant, unindulgent. *See also* **ill-tempered, intolerant. 2.** Disposed to seek revenge ▸ avenging, spiteful, unforgiving. *See* **vindictive** (1).

unforced *adjective*
▸ spontaneous, uncompelled. *See* **voluntary** (1).

unforgivable *adjective*
▸ irremissable, unjustifiable, unpardonable. *See* **inexcusable.**

unforgiving *adjective*
▸ avenging, spiteful, vengeful. *See* **vindictive** (1).

unformed *adjective*
▸ amorphous, formless, unshaped. *See* **shapeless.** *See synonym note at* **shapeless.**

unfortunate *adjective*
1. Involving or undergoing chance misfortune ▸ hapless, hexed, ill-fated, ill-starred, jinxed, luckless, star-crossed, stricken, unhappy, unlucky, untoward. **2.** Characterized by inappropriateness and gracelessness, especially in expression ▸ awkward, ill-chosen, inappropriate, inept, infelicitous, unhappy. *See also* **improper, inconvenient, unwise. 3.** Worthy of severe disapproval ▸ disgraceful, shameful, woeful. *See* **deplorable** (1).

unfortunate *noun*
A person living under very unhappy circumstances ▸ loser, miserable, underdog, underprivileged, wretch.

✦ CORE SYNONYMS: *unfortunate, hapless, ill-fated, ill-starred, luckless, unlucky.* These adjectives mean involving or undergoing chance misfortune: *an unfortunate turn of events; a hapless victim; an ill-fated business venture; an ill-starred romance; a luckless suitor; an unlucky accident.*

◀ ANTONYM: *fortunate*

---

unfortunateness *noun*
▸ bad luck, haplessness, unluckiness. *See* **misfortune** (1).

unfound *adjective*
Not found ▸ undetected, undiscovered, unexposed.

unfounded *adjective*
▸ idle, unwarranted. *See* **baseless.** *See synonym note at* **baseless.**

unfoundedly *adverb*
Without basis or foundation in fact ▸ baselessly, groundlessly, unwarrantedly.

unfrequented *adjective*
▸ uninhabited, unpeopled, unpopulated. *See* **lonely** (1).

unfriendliness *noun*
▸ inhospitableness, uncivility, unreceptiveness. *See* **inhospitality.**

unfriendly *adjective*
Feeling or showing unfriendliness ▸ hostile, inimical. *See also* **mean**[2].

unfruitful *adjective*
1. Unable to produce offspring ▸ infertile, sterile. *See* **barren** (1). **2.** Unable to support vegetation ▸ infertile, sterile, unproductive. *See* **barren** (2).

unfurl *verb*
1. To be disclosed gradually ▸ disentangle, unfold, unravel. *See* **develop** (2). **2.** To move or arrange so as to cover a larger area ▸ extend, stretch. *See* **spread** (1).

ungainly *adjective*
1. Lacking dexterity and grace in physical movement ▸ gawky, graceless. *Slang:* klutzy. *See* **awkward** (1).
2. Difficult to manage ▸ bulky, unwieldy. *See* **awkward** (2).

ungodly *adjective*
▸ disbelieving, faithless, irreligious. *See* **atheistic.**

ungovernable *adjective*
▸ headstrong, ill-behaved, obstinate, unmanageable. *See* **unruly.**

ungovernableness *noun*
▸ intractability, obstinacy, unmanageability. *See* **unruliness.**

ungoverned *adjective*
▸ unbridled, uncontrolled, unrestrained. *See* **abandoned** (2).

ungraceful *adjective*
▸ gawky, graceless. *Slang:* klutzy. *See* **awkward** (1).

ungracious *adjective*
▸ disrespectful, impolite, uncivil. *See* **rude** (4).

ungraciousness *noun*
▸ aloofness, inhospitableness, uncivility. *See* **inhospitality.**

ungrateful *adjective*
1. Not apt to be appreciated ▸ thankless, unappreciated, unthankful. 2. Not showing or feeling gratitude ▸ unappreciative, unthankful. *See* **thankless** (1).

ungrudging *adjective*
▸ big-hearted, magnanimous, unselfish. *See* **generous** (1).

unguarded *adjective*
▸ ill-protected, undefended, unsafe. *See* **insecure** (1).

unguent *noun*
▸ emollient, salve. *See* **ointment.**

unhandy *adjective*
1. Difficult to handle or manage ▸ ungainly, unwieldy. *See* **awkward** (2). 2. Not accessible or handy ▸ inaccessible, unhandy. *Idioms:* beyond reach, out of reach, out of the way. *See also* **remote.**

unhappiness *noun*
▸ dejection, doldrums, melancholy. *See* **depression** (2).

unhappy *adjective*
1. In low spirits ▸ dysphoric, gloomy, melancholy, spiritless. *See* **depressed** (1). 2. Involving or undergoing chance misfortune ▸ ill-fated, ill-starred, luckless. *See* **unfortunate** (1). 3. Characterized by inappropriateness and gracelessness, especially in expression ▸ awkward, inept, infelicitous. *See* **unfortunate** (2).

unharmed *adjective*
1. Free from danger, injury, or the threat of harm ▸ unhurt, uninjured, unscathed. *See* **safe** (1). 2. In excellent condition ▸ flawless, intact, sound. *See* **good** (2).

unharmonious *adjective*
1. Devoid of harmony and accord ▸ conflicting, dissident, uncongenial. *See* **inharmonious** (1). 2. Characterized by unpleasant discordance of sound ▸ discordant, dissonant. *See* **inharmonious** (2).

unhealthful *adjective*
▸ unhealthy, unhygienic, unsalutary. *See* **unwholesome** (1).

unhealthy *adjective*
1. Not sustaining or promoting health ▸ insalubrious, unhygienic, unsalutary. *See* **unwholesome** (1). 2. Morally detrimental ▸ corruptive, demoralizing, perverting. *See* **unwholesome** (2). 3. Utterly reprehensible in nature or behavior ▸ depraved, miscreant, perverse. *See* **corrupt** (1). 4. Characterized by preoccupation with unwholesome thoughts or feelings ▸ sick, unwholesome. *See* **morbid** (1). 5. Suffering from or appearing to suffer from an illness ▸ ailing, indisposed, unwell. *See* **sick** (1). 6. Causing harm or injury ▸ deleterious, evil, injurious. *See* **harmful.**

unheard-of *adjective*
▸ little-known, unknown. *See* **obscure** (2).

unheeding *adjective*
▸ mindless, unthinking. *See* **careless** (1).

unhesitating *adjective*
1. Having no reservations ▸ unconditional, unfaltering. *See* **implicit** (2). 2. Committed to or unwavering in a course of action ▸ determined, fixed. *See* **intent** (1).

unhindered *adjective*
1. Free from obstructions ▸ unblocked, unobstructed. *See* **clear** (4). 2. Able to move about at will without bounds or restraint ▸ liberated, unconfined, unrestrained. *See* **loose** (2).

unhinge *verb*
▸ dement, madden, unbalance. *See* **derange** (1).

unhinged *adjective*
Informal Afflicted with or exhibiting irrationality and mental unsoundness ▸ crazy, lunatic, mad. *See* **insane** (1).

unhorse *verb*
▸ subvert, topple. *See* **overthrow** (1).

unhospitable *adjective*
▸ dour, flinty, stern. *See* **forbidding** (1).

unhurried *adjective*
Careful and slow in acting, moving, or deciding ▸ circumspect, measured, prudent. *See* **deliberate** (3).

unhurt *adjective*
1. Free from danger, injury, or the threat of harm ▸ unharmed, uninjured, unscathed. *See* **safe** (1). 2. In excellent condition ▸ flawless, intact, sound. *See* **good** (2).

unhygienic *adjective*
▸ insalubrious, unhealthy, unsalutary. *See* **unwholesome** (1).

unidentified *adjective*
▸ unacknowledged, uncredited, unnamed. *See* **anonymous.**

unification *noun*
1. A bringing together into a whole ▸ coalition, consolidation, union, unity. 2. The result of combining ▸ compound, merger, union. *See* **combination** (1).

unified *adjective*
▸ accordant, consonant, like-minded. *See* **unanimous.**

uniform *adjective*
1. Having no change or variation ▸ changeless, constant, regular. *See* **unchanging.** 2. Possessing the same or almost the same characteristics ▸ analogous, kin, similar. *See* **like².**

uniformity *noun*
1. The quality or state of being alike ▸ resemblance, similarity, uniformness. *See* **likeness** (1). 2. Logical agreement among parts ▸ congruity, consistence. *See* **consistency.** 3. The condition of being without change or variation ▸ constancy, immutability. *See* **changelessness.**

uniformness *noun*
▸ resemblance, similarity, uniformity. *See* **likeness** (1).

unify *verb*
1. To bring or come together into a united whole ▸ join, meld, unite. *See* **combine** (1). 2. To combine and adapt in order to attain a particular effect ▸ blend, integrate. *See* **harmonize** (2).

unimaginable *adjective*
1. Not to be believed ▸ unbelievable, unthinkable. *See* **incredible** (2). 2. Not capable of happening or being done ▸ impractical, unattainable, unworkable. *See* **impossible** (1).

unimaginative *adjective*
1. Lacking originality ▸ uncreative, uninventive. *See* **sterile** (4). 2. Lacking liveliness, charm, or surprise ▸ aseptic, colorless, pedestrian. *See* **dull** (1). 3. Without freshness or appeal because of overuse ▸ clichéd, overused, shopworn, tired. *See* **trite.**

unimpaired *adjective*
▸ flawless, intact, sound. *See* **good** (2).

unimpeachable *adjective*
▸ absolute, certain, sure. *See* **definite** (3).

unimpeded *adjective*
▸ unblocked, unobstructed. *See* **clear** (4).

unimportance *noun*
1. Something or things of little importance ▸ frivolity, insignificance, trivia. *See* **trifle** (1). 2. The quality or state of being little known ▸ namelessness, oblivion. *See* **obscurity** (1).

unimportant *adjective*
▸ inconsequential, negligible, trifling. *See* **trivial.**

unimpressionable *adjective*
▸ impassive, insensitive, unsusceptible. *See* **cold** (2).

unindulgent *adjective*
Being unable or unwilling to endure irritation or opposition, for example ▸ impatient, intolerant, unforbearing. *See also* **ill-tempered, intolerant.**

uninformed *adjective*
1. Exhibiting lack of education or knowledge ▸ benighted, unenlightened. *See* **ignorant** (2). 2. Not aware or informed ▸ misguided, oblivious, unaware. *See* **ignorant** (3).

uninhabited *adjective*
1. Available for use or occupation ▸ employable, operable, usable. *See* **open** (4). 2. Empty of people ▸ deserted, unpeopled, unpopulated. *See* **lonely** (1).

uninhibited *adjective*
▸ unbridled, ungoverned, unrestrained. *See* **abandoned** (2).

uninitiate *adjective*
Lacking experience and the knowledge gained from it ▸ inexpert, unpracticed. *See* **inexperienced.**

uninitiate *noun*
One lacking professional skill ▸ dilettante, layperson, nonprofessional. *See* **amateur.**

uninitiated *adjective*
▸ inexpert, unpracticed, unseasoned. *See* **inexperienced.**

uninjured *adjective*
1. Free from danger, injury, or the threat of harm ▸ unharmed, unhurt, unscathed. *See* **safe** (1). 2. In excellent condition ▸ flawless, intact, sound. *See* **good** (2).

uninspired *adjective*
1. Lacking liveliness, charm, or surprise ▸ aseptic, colorless, pedestrian. *See* **dull** (1). *See synonym note at* **dull.** 2. Lacking originality ▸ unimaginative, uninventive. *See* **sterile** (4). 3. Without freshness or appeal because of overuse ▸ clichéd, overused, shopworn, tired. *See* **trite.**

uninstructed *adjective*
▸ uneducated, unlearned, untaught. *See* **ignorant** (1).

unintelligent *adjective*
▸ dumb, idiotic, obtuse. *See* **stupid** (1).

unintelligible *adjective*
▸ impenetrable, unfathomable. *See* **incomprehensible.**

unintended *adjective*
1. Not intended ▸ inadvertent, undesigned, undevised. *See* **unintentional.** 2. Occurring unexpectedly ▸ inadvertent, serendipitous, unplanned. *See* **accidental** (1).

unintentional *adjective*
Not intended ▸ accidental, inadvertent, involuntary, undesigned, undevised, unintended, unmeant, unplanned, unthinking, unwitting.

uninterest *noun*
▸ disinterest, indifference, unconcern. *See* **apathy.**

uninterested *adjective*
1. Lacking interest ▸ indifferent, listless, unconcerned. *See* **apathetic.** 2. Lacking interest in one's surroundings or worldly affairs ▸ disinterested, indifferent, uninvolved. *See* **detached** (1).

uninteresting *adjective*
▸ dull, humdrum, monotonous. *See* **boring** (1).

uninterrupted *adjective*
▸ constant, endless, everlasting, perpetual. *See* **continual.**

uninventive *adjective*
▸ uncreative, unimaginative, uninventive. *See* **sterile** (4).

uninvited *adjective*
▸ unsought, unwanted. *See* **unwelcome** (1).

uninviting *adjective*
▸ dour, flinty, stern. *See* **forbidding** (1).

uninvolved *adjective*

1. Lacking interest in one's surroundings or worldly affairs ▸ disinterested, indifferent, remote. *See* **detached** (1). **2.** Not inclining toward or actively taking either side in a matter under dispute ▸ nonaligned, unbiased. *See* **neutral** (1).

uninvolvment *noun*

▸ disinterest, indifference. *See* **detachment** (2).

union *noun*

1. A group of people who are united in a relationship and having some interest, activity, or purpose in common ▸ association, club, confederation, congress, federation, fellowship, fraternity, guild, league, order, organization, society, sorority. *See also* **group. 2.** An identity or coincidence of interests, purposes, or sympathies among the members of a group ▸ concord, oneness, solidarity, unity. **3.** A bringing together into a whole ▸ consolidation, unity. *See* **unification** (1). **4.** The result of combining ▸ compound, merger, unification. *See* **combination** (1). **5.** An association for a common cause or interest ▸ coalition, federation, league. *See* **alliance** (1). **6.** A point or position at which two or more things are joined ▸ coupling, juncture, seam. *See* **joint** (1). **7.** The state of being married ▸ matrimony, union. *See* **marriage** (1).

uniplanar *adjective*

▸ coplanar, flat. *See* **even** (2).

unique *adjective*

1. Without equal or rival ▸ alone, incomparable, matchless, nonpareil, only, peerless, singular, unequaled, unexampled, unexcelled, unmatched, unparalleled, unrivaled, unsurpassed. *Idioms:* beyond compare, in a class by itself, second to none. *See also* **best, exceptional. 2.** Alone in a given category ▸ only, single, solitary. *See* **lone** (1). **3.** Not usual or ordinary ▸ atypical, novel, unconventional. *See* **unusual** (1).

uniquely *adverb*

▸ singularly, uncommonly, unconventionally. *See* **unusually.**

uniqueness *noun*

1. The quality or condition of being unique ▸ matchlessness, oneness, peerlessness, singleness, singularity, uncommonness. *See also* **individuality. 2.** The quality of being novel ▸ newness, originality. *See* **novelty** (1). **3.** The set of behavioral or personal characteristics by which an individual is recognizable ▸ distinctiveness, individuality, singularity. *See* **identity** (1).

unison *noun*

▸ concordance, harmony, rapport. *See* **agreement** (2).

unit *noun*

1. A group of people organized for a particular purpose ▸ corps, squad, team. *See* **force** (5). **2.** A group of people acting together in a shared activity ▸ party, troop. *See* **band**[2] (1). **3.** One of the units in a course, as on an ascending or descending scale ▸ interval, level, step. *See* **degree** (1).

unite *verb*

1. To bring or come together into a united whole ▸ connect, join, unify. *See* **combine** (1). *See synonym*

note at **combine. 2.** To form a united group ▸ join, gang. *See* **band**[2]. **3.** To come together from different directions ▸ close, converge, join, meet. **4.** To work together toward a common end ▸ concur, join. *See* **cooperate. 5.** To join or be joined in marriage ▸ espouse, wed. *See* **marry** (1).

united *adjective*

▸ collective, joint, synergistic. *See* **cooperative** (1).

unity *noun*

1. The condition of being one ▸ oneness, singleness, singularity. *See also* **completeness. 2.** An identity or coincidence of interests, purposes, or sympathies among the members of a group ▸ concord, oneness, solidarity, union. *See also* **alliance, union. 3.** The act or state of agreeing or conforming ▸ concordance, harmony, rapport. *See* **agreement** (2). **4.** A bringing together into a whole ▸ consolidation, union. *See* **unification** (1). **5.** The result of combining ▸ compound, merger, union. *See* **combination** (1).

universal *adjective*

1. So pervasive and all-inclusive as to exist in or affect the whole world ▸ catholic, cosmic, cosmopolitan, ecumenical, global, pandemic, planetary, worldwide. **2.** Ever present in all places ▸ omnipresent, ubiquitous. *See also* **rampant. 3.** Concerned with, applicable to, or affecting the whole ▸ blanket, common, generic. *See* **general** (1). *See synonym note at* **general. 4.** Being in or characterized by complete agreement ▸ accordant, consonant, like-minded. *See* **unanimous.**

universal *noun*

A broad and basic rule or truth ▸ axiom, principle. *See* **law** (3).

universe *noun*

1. The totality of all existing things ▸ cosmos, creation, macrocosm, nature, wide world, world. *Idiom:* sum of all things. *See also* **environment. 2.** Humans as a group ▸ humanity, mortals, world. *See* **humankind.**

unjudicious *adjective*

▸ indecent, indelicate. *See* **improper** (1).

unjust *adjective*

▸ discriminatory, unequal, wrong. *See* **unfair.**

unjustifiable *adjective*

▸ indefensible, unforgivable, unpardonable. *See* **inexcusable.**

unjustness *noun*

1. Lack of equality, as of opportunity, treatment, or status ▸ discrimination, inequality, unfairness. *See also* **bias. 2.** Lack of justice ▸ iniquity, unfairness, wrong. *See* **injustice** (2).

unkempt *adjective*

▸ sloppy, slovenly, untidy. *See* **messy** (1). *See synonym note at* **messy.**

unknowing *adjective*

▸ oblivious, oblivious, unaware. *See* **ignorant** (3).

unknown *adjective*

1. Not widely known ▸ little-known, unheard-of. *See* **obscure** (2). **2.** Having an unknown authorship or agency ► unacknowledged, uncredited, unnamed. *See* **anonymous.**

unlade *verb*
► discharge, relieve, unload. *See* **rid.**

unlawful *adjective*
1. Prohibited by law ► illicit, outlawed. *See* **illegal** (1). 2. Of, involving, or being a crime ► illicit, wrongful. *See* **criminal** (1). 3. Contrary to accepted, especially moral conventions ► criminal, illicit. *See also* **forbidden.** 4. Born to parents who are not married to each other ► bastard, misbegotten. *See* **illegitimate** (1).

unlawfulness *noun*
The state or quality of being illegal ► illegality, illegitimacy, illicitness, lawlessness.

unlearned *adjective*
1. Without education or knowledge ► lowbrow, uncultivated, untaught. *See* **ignorant** (1). 2. Derived from or prompted by a natural tendency or impulse ► inborn, intuitive. *See* **instinctive** (1). *See synonym note at* **instinctive.**

unlike *adjective*
► contrasting, divergent, variant. *See* **different** (1).

unlikely *adjective*
1. Not likely ► dubious, improbable, questionable. *See* **doubtful** (1). 2. Not plausible or believable ► flimsy, tenuous, unsubstantial. *See* **implausible.**

unlikeness *noun*
► contrast, discrepancy, divergence. *See* **difference** (1). *See synonym note at* **difference.**

unlimited *adjective*
1. Having no ends or limits ► illimitable, infinite. *See* **endless** (1). 2. Completely such, without qualification or exception ► all-out, pure, sheer. *See* **utter**^{2}.

unlimitedness *noun*
► immeasurability, limitlessness, measurelessness. *See* **infinity** (1).

unlit *adjective*
► inky, pitch-dark. *See* **black** (2).

unload *verb*
1. To relieve a burden ► discharge, relieve, unburden. *See* **rid.** 2. To get rid of by selling ► close out, sell off. *See* **unload.**

unloose *or* **unloosen** *verb*
► loose, release, untie. *See* **undo** (1).

unloveliness *noun*
► monstrosity, odiousness, unsightliness. *See* **ugliness** (1).

unlovely *adjective*
► homely, unattractive, unsightly. *See* **ugly** (1).

unluckiness *noun*
► adversity, bad luck, haplessness. *See* **misfortune** (1).

unlucky *adjective*
1. Involving or undergoing chance misfortune ► ill-fated, ill-starred, luckless. *See* **unfortunate** (1). 2. Bringing or predicting misfortune ► dire, ominous, portentous. *See* **fateful** (1). 3. Disturbing because of failure to measure up to a standard or produce the desired results ► discouraging, sorry, unsatisfying. *See* **disappointing.**

unmanageability *noun*
► intractability, obstinacy, uncontrollability. *See* **unruliness.**

unmanageable *adjective*
1. Difficult to manage ► ungainly, unwieldy. *See* **awkward** (2). 2. Not submitting to discipline or control ► ill-behaved, obstinate, recalcitrant. *See* **unruly.**

unmanliness *noun*
1. Ignoble lack of courage ► faint-heartedness, pusillanimity. *Slang:* gutlessness. *See* **cowardice.** 2. The quality of being effeminate ► femininity, womanishness. *See* **effeminacy.**

unmanly *adjective*
1. Ignobly lacking in courage ► faint-hearted, pusillanimous. *Slang:* gutless. *See* **cowardly.** 2. Having qualities traditionally attributed to a woman ► feminine, sissyish. *See* **effeminate.**

unmannered *or* **unmannerly** *adjective*
1. Lacking good manners ► boorish, impolite, ungracious. *See* **rude.** 2. Having or showing a lack of respect ► contemptuous, discourteous, impolite. *See* **disrespectful** (1).

unmarked *adjective*
► consummate, flawless, unblemished. *See* **perfect** (1).

unmarred *adjective*
► flawless, intact, sound. *See* **good** (2).

unmarried *adjective*
► fancy-free, marriageable. *See* **single** (5).

unmask *verb*
► disclose, expose, uncover. *See* **reveal** (2).

unmatched *adjective*
► incomparable, singular, unparalleled. *See* **unique** (1).

unmeant *adjective*
► inadvertent, undesigned, unintended. *See* **unintentional.**

unmentionable *adjective*
► eyes-only, unutterable. *See* **unspeakable** (2).

unmerciful *adjective*
► heartless, insensitive, merciless. *See* **callous.**

unmindful *adjective*
► heedless, inattentive, thoughtless. *See* **careless** (1).

unmistakable *adjective*
1. Clearly defined; not ambiguous ► distinct, unambiguous. *See* **sharp** (3). 2. Easily seen through due to a lack of subtlety ► blatant, overt, transparent. *See* **obvious** (1).

unmitigated *adjective*
► all-out, pure, sheer. *See* **utter**^{2}.

unmixed *adjective*
1. Free from extraneous elements ► perfect, plain, unadulterated. *See* **pure** (1). 2. Not diluted or mixed with other substances ► pure, unblended, undiluted. *See* **straight** (1).

unmovable *adjective*
► stationary, steadfast, unmoving. *See* **fixed** (1).

unmoved *adjective*
► emotionless, impassive, stolid. *See* **cold** (2).

unmoving *adjective*
1. Not moving ► stationary, still. *See* **motionless.**

2. Firmly in position ▸ stationary, steadfast, unmovable. *See* **fixed** (1).

unmusical *adjective*
▸ cacophonous, inharmonic, untuneful. *See* **inharmonious** (2).

unnamed *adjective*
▸ unacknowledged, uncredited, unknown. *See* **anonymous.**

unnatural *adjective*
1. Greatly exceeding or departing from the normal course of nature ▸ preternatural, supernatural. *See also* **supernatural. 2.** Deviating from what is conventional or customary ▸ bizarre, grotesque. *See* **eccentric. 3.** Departing from the normal ▸ aberrant, atypical, deviant. *See* **abnormal.**

unnaturalness *noun*
▸ anomaly, deviance, irregularity. *See* **abnormality.**

unnecessary *adjective*
Not necessary ▸ dispensable, inessential, needless, nonessential, uncalled-for, unessential, unneeded, unrequired. *See also* **extra, irrelevant.**

unneeded *adjective*
▸ inessential, needless, unessential. *See* **unnecessary.**

unnegotiable *adjective*
▸ unserviceable, unusable. *See* **unworkable** (1).

unnerve *verb*
1. To lessen or deplete the nerve, energy, or strength of ▸ debilitate, weaken. *See* **enervate. 2.** To fill with fear ▸ horrify, scare, terrify. *See* **frighten. 3.** To deprive of courage or the power to act as a result of fear, anxiety, or disgust ▸ consternate, disconcert. *See* **dismay** (1). **4.** To make less hopeful or enthusiastic ▸ dismay, dispirit. *See* **discourage** (1).

unnerving *adjective*
▸ appalling, frightening, scary. *See* **fearful** (1).

unnoticeable *adjective*
1. Not readily noticed or seen ▸ obscure, unobtrusive. *See* **inconspicuous. 2.** Incapable of being apprehended by the mind or the senses ▸ imponderable, indiscernible. *See* **imperceptible** (1). **3.** Difficult or impossible to see or distinguish ▸ covert, disguised, unseen. *See* **hidden** (1).

unobjectionable *adjective*
▸ admissible, permissible. *See* **acceptable** (1).

unobservable *adjective*
▸ imponderable, indiscernible. *See* **imperceptible** (1).

unobstructed *adjective*
▸ open, unblocked. *See* **clear** (4).

unobtainable *adjective*
1. Unable to be reached ▸ unapproachable, unavailable. *See* **inaccessible** (1). **2.** Not capable of happening or being done ▸ impractical, unattainable, unworkable. *See* **impossible** (1).

unobtrusive *adjective*
1. Not readily noticed or seen ▸ unnoticeable, unassuming. *See* **inconspicuous. 2.** Not showy or obtrusive ▸ inobtrusive, quiet, subdued. *See* **modest** (1).

unoccupied *adjective*
1. Available for use or occupation ▸ employable, operable, usable. *See* **open** (4). **2.** Marked by a lack of activity or use ▸ inert, unemployed, unused. *See* **idle** (1). **3.** Having no job ▸ idle, jobless, unemployed, workless. *Idioms:* out of (*or* a job *or* employ *or* work).

unoffensive *adjective*
▸ innocuous, safe. *See* **harmless** (1).

unordinary *adjective*
▸ atypical, novel, unconventional. *See* **unusual** (1).

unoriginal *adjective*
1. Lacking originality ▸ uncreative, unimaginative, uninventive. *See* **sterile** (4). **2.** Without freshness or appeal because of overuse ▸ clichéd, overused, shopworn, tired. *See* **trite.**

unorthodox *adjective*
1. Very strange or strikingly unusual ▸ fantastic, outré, strange. *See* **exotic** (2). **2.** Deviating from what is conventional or customary ▸ bizarre, grotesque. *See* **eccentric.**

unostentatious *adjective*
▸ plain, simple. *See* **modest** (1). *See synonym note at* **modest.**

unostentatiousness *noun*
▸ plainness, simpleness, simplicity. *See* **modesty** (2).

unpaid *adjective*
1. Contributing one's time without pay ▸ freewill, pro bono, uncompensated, unrecompensed, unremunerated, unsalaried, voluntary, volunteer. **2.** Owed as a debt ▸ collectible, payable, unsettled. *See* **due** (1).

unpalatable *adjective*
1. So unpleasant in flavor as to be inedible ▸ disgusting, distasteful, foul-tasting, inedible, nauseating, repulsive, sickening, unappetizing, uneatable, unsavory, untasteful, untasty. *Slang:* gross. *See also* **unpleasant. 2.** Difficult to accept or bear ▸ disagreeable, painful, unpleasant. *See* **bitter** (3).

unparalleled *adjective*
▸ incomparable, singular. *See* **unique** (1).

unpardonable *adjective*
▸ unforgivable, unjustifiable, unwarrantable. *See* **inexcusable.**

unpeopled *adjective*
▸ uninhabited, lonesome, unpopulated. *See* **lonely** (1).

unperceptive *adjective*
▸ obtuse, unseeing. *See* **blind** (3).

unperfected *adjective*
▸ preliminary, sketchy, unpolished. *See* **rough** (10).

unpitying *adjective*
▸ heartless, merciless, unsympathetic. *See* **callous.**

unplanned *adjective*
1. Occurring unexpectedly ▸ chance, incidental, unanticipated. *See* **accidental** (1). **2.** Not intended ▸ inadvertent, undesigned, unintended. *See* **unintentional. 3.** Having no particular pattern, purpose, organization, or structure ▸ chance, indiscriminate. *See* **random. 4.** Acting or happening without apparent forethought, prompting, or planning ▸ impulsive, involuntary. *See* **spontaneous** (1).

unpleasant *adjective*
1. Not pleasant or agreeable ▸ bad, disagreeable,

displeasing, offensive, uncongenial, unsympathetic. *Informal:* icky. *Slang:* yucky. *See also* **offensive. 2.** Difficult to accept or bear ▸ disagreeable, painful, unpalatable. *See* **bitter** (3).

unplugged *adjective*
▸ open, unblocked, unobstructed. *See* **clear** (4).

unpolished *adjective*
1. Not perfected, elaborated, or completed ▸ preliminary, sketchy, tentative. *See* **rough** (10). **2.** Lacking expert, careful craftsmanship ▸ crude, primitive, raw. *See* **rude** (1). **3.** Lacking good manners ▸ disrespectful, impolite, uncivil. *See* **rude** (4). **4.** Lacking in delicacy or refinement ▸ indelicate, unbecoming, unrefined. *See* **coarse** (1). **5.** Of a charmingly plain and unsophisticated nature ▸ homely, homespun, natural. *See* **rustic** (1). **6.** Clumsily lacking in the ability to do ▸ bumbling, clumsy, inept. *See* **unskillful** (1).

unpolitic *adjective*
▸ gauche, impolitic, undiplomatic. *See* **tactless.**

unpolluted *adjective*
▸ pristine, pure, unspoiled. *See* **fresh** (1).

unpopulated *adjective*
▸ uninhabited, unpeopled, vacant. *See* **lonely** (1).

unpracticed *adjective*
1. Not tested or proved ▸ undemonstrated, unproved, untested. *See* **untried** (1). **2.** Lacking experience and the knowledge gained from it ▸ inexpert, uninitiated. *See* **inexperienced.**

unprecedented *adjective*
1. Not the same as what was previously known or done ▸ fresh, novel, original. *See* **new** (1). **2.** Beyond what is usual, normal, or customary ▸ extraordinary, outstanding, remarkable. *See* **exceptional** (1).

unpredictable *adjective*
1. Marked by whim or impulse ▸ fickle, impulsive, mercurial. *See* **capricious. 2.** Having no particular pattern, purpose, organization, or structure ▸ chance, indiscriminate, unplanned. *See* **random.**

unprejudiced *adjective*
1. Free from bias in judgment ▸ impartial, nonpartisan, unbiased. *See* **fair**[1] (1). *See synonym note at* **fair**[1]. **2.** Not inclining toward or actively taking either side in a matter under dispute ▸ nonaligned, unbiased. *See* **neutral** (1).

unpremeditated *adjective*
▸ impulsive, involuntary. *See* **spontaneous** (1).

unpretentious *adjective*
▸ inobtrusive, quiet, subdued. *See* **modest** (1). *See synonym note at* **modest.**

unpretentiousness *noun*
1. Lack of vanity or self-importance ▸ humility, meekness. *See* **modesty** (1). **2.** Lack of ostentation or pretension ▸ plainness, simpleness, simplicity. *See* **modesty** (2).

unprincipled *adjective*
▸ unconscionable, unethical, unethical. *See* **unscrupulous** (1).

unprocessed *adjective*
1. Being in a natural state ▸ raw, unrefined. *See* **crude**

(1). **2.** Produced by nature; not artificial or manmade ▸ additive-free, unadulterated. *See* **natural** (1).

unproductive *adjective*
▸ sterile, unfruitful, waste. *See* **barren** (2).

unprofessional *adjective*
▸ nonprofessional, unskilled. *See* **amateurish.**

unprofitable *adjective*
▸ fruitless, unsuccessful, useless, vain. *See* **futile.**

unprofitableness *noun*
▸ fruitlessness, uselessness, vainness. *See* **futility.**

unprogressive *adjective*
Clinging to obsolete ideas ▸ backward, reactionary. *See also* **conservative.**

unpromising *adjective*
▸ dim, unencouraging. *See* **bleak** (2).

unpropitious *adjective*
1. Bringing or predicting misfortune ▸ bad, evil, ill, inauspicious. *See* **fateful** (1). **2.** Offering little encouragement ▸ dim, unpromising. *See* **bleak** (2).

unprotected *adjective*
1. Susceptible to physical or emotional injury ▸ defenseless, helpless. *See* **vulnerable** (1). **2.** Inadequately protected ▸ ill-protected, unsafe. *See* **insecure** (1). **3.** Not covered ▸ expanded, revealed, uncovered. *See* **open** (2).

unprotectedness *noun*
▸ endangerment, susceptibility, vulnerability. *See* **exposure** (1).

unproved *adjective*
1. Not tested or proved ▸ undemonstrated, unpracticed, untested. *See* **untried** (1). **2.** Having no basis in fact ▸ idle, unwarranted. *See* **baseless.**

unqualified *adjective*
1. Lacking the qualities, as efficiency or skill, required to produce desired results ▸ incapable, inept, unskilled. *See* **inefficient** (1). **2.** Without limitations or mitigating conditions ▸ full, unreserved. *See* **unconditional** (1). **3.** Completely such, without qualification or exception ▸ all-out, pure, sheer. *See* **utter**[2].

unquestionable *adjective*
1. Established beyond a doubt ▸ inarguable, indisputable, irrefutable. *See* **certain** (2). **2.** Without any doubt ▸ clear-cut, definite. *See* **decided** (1). **3.** Not counterfeit or copied ▸ genuine, true. *Slang:* legit, kosher. *See* **authentic** (1). *See synonym note at* **authentic.**

unquestionably *adverb*
1. It is so; as you say or ask ▸ agreed, all right, assuredly. *See* **yes. 2.** Without question ▸ certainly, definitely, surely. *See* **absolutely** (1).

unquestioned *adjective*
▸ inarguable, indisputable, irrefutable. *See* **certain** (2).

unquestioning *adjective*
▸ unconditional, unfaltering. *See* **implicit** (2).

unquiet *adjective*
Affording no quiet, repose, or rest ▸ restless, uneasy, unsettled. *See also* **edgy, wakeful.**

unravel *verb*
1. To find a solution for ▸ decipher, explain. *See* **solve** (1). **2.** To cause a line to become longer and less taut

▶ uncoil, unreel, unroll. *See* **unwind** (1). **3.** To be disclosed gradually ▶ disentangle, unfold, unfurl. *See* **develop** (2).

unreachable *adjective*
▶ unapproachable, unavailable. *See* **inaccessible** (1).

unread *adjective*
▶ illiterate, uncultivated, uninstructed. *See* **ignorant** (1).

unreal *adjective*
1. Existing only in the imagination ▶ chimerical, fanciful, notional. *See* **imaginary. 2.** Of, relating to, or in the nature of an illusion; lacking reality ▶ hallucinatory, illusory, phantasmagoric. *See* **illusive** (1).

unrealistic *adjective*
▶ romantic, starry-eyed, utopian. *See* **idealistic.**

unrealizable *adjective*
▶ impractical, unattainable, unworkable. *See* **impossible** (1).

unreasonable *adjective*
1. Not governed by or predicated on reason ▶ illogical, irrational, unreasoned. *Idioms:* out of bounds, without rhyme or reason. *See also* **fallacious, foolish. 2.** Exceeding the bounds of morality, decency, or reason ▶ appalling, monstrous, shocking. *See* **outrageous.**

unreasonableness *or* **unreason** *noun*
The absence of reason ▶ illogicality, illogicalness, irrationality. *See also* **fallacy, foolishness.**

unreasoned *adjective*
Not governed by or predicated on reason ▶ illogical, irrational, unreasonable. *Idioms:* out of bounds, without rhyme or reason. *See also* **fallacious, foolish.**

unreceptiveness *noun*
▶ aloofness, inhospitableness, uncivility. *See* **inhospitality.**

unrecompensed *adjective*
▶ uncompensated, unsalaried, volunteer. *See* **unpaid** (1).

unreel *verb*
▶ uncoil, unravel, unroll. *See* **unwind** (1).

unrefined *adjective*
1. Being in a natural state ▶ raw, unprocessed. *See* **crude** (1). *See synonym note at* **crude. 2.** Lacking in delicacy or refinement ▶ indelicate, unbecoming, uncouth. *See* **coarse** (1).

unrehearsed *adjective*
1. Spoken, performed, or composed with little or no preparation or forethought ▶ impromptu, improvised. *See* **extemporaneous.** *See synonym note at* **extemporaneous. 2.** Acting or happening without apparent forethought, prompting, or planning ▶ impulsive, involuntary. *See* **spontaneous** (1).

unrelated *adjective*
▶ extraneous, immaterial, unconnected. *See* **irrelevant.**

unrelenting *adjective*
▶ bullheaded, dogged, obstinate. *See* **stubborn** (1).

unreliable *adjective*
1. So weak or defective as to be liable to fail ▶ trick,

undependable. *See also* **defective, weak. 2.** Not to be depended on ▶ irresponsible, untrustworthy. *See* **undependable** (1).

unrelieved *adjective*
▶ all-out, pure, sheer. *See* **utter².**

unremarkable *adjective*
▶ common, mediocre, standard. *See* **ordinary** (1).

unremitting *adjective*
1. Existing without interruption or end ▶ constant, endless, everlasting, perpetual. *See* **continual. 2.** Characterized by steady attention and effort ▶ assiduous, conscientious, industrious. *See* **diligent.** *See synonym note at* **diligent.**

unremunerated *adjective*
▶ uncompensated, unsalaried, volunteer. *See* **unpaid** (1).

unrepentant *adjective*
Devoid of remorse ▶ impenitent, remorseless.

unrequired *adjective*
▶ inessential, needless, unneeded. *See* **unnecessary.**

unreserved *adjective*
1. Without limitations or mitigating conditions ▶ full, unqualified. *See* **unconditional** (1). **2.** Having no reservations ▶ unconditional, unfaltering. *See* **implicit** (2). **3.** Manifesting honesty and directness ▶ candid, ingenuous, plainspoken. *See* **frank. 4.** Disposed to be open, sociable, and talkative ▶ extroverted, gregarious. *See* **outgoing. 5.** Completely such, without qualification or exception ▶ all-out, pure, sheer. *See* **utter². 6.** Available for use ▶ employable, operable, usable. *See* **open** (4).

unresolved *adjective*
▶ uncertain, undetermined. *See* **indefinite** (2).

unresponsive *adjective*
1. Lacking physical feeling or sensitivity ▶ inert, numb, unfeeling. *See* **dead** (2). **2.** Lacking interest ▶ indifferent, listless, uninterested. *See* **apathetic. 3.** Lacking feeling or emotion ▶ emotionless, impassive, stolid. *See* **cold** (2). **4.** Deficient in or lacking sexual desire ▶ cold, undersexed. *See* **frigid** (3).

unresponsiveness *noun*
▶ disinterest, indifference, unconcern. *See* **apathy.**

unrest *noun*
1. An uneasy or nervous state ▶ disquietude, restiveness, uneasiness. *See* **restlessness. 2.** The condition of being agitated or disturbed ▶ ferment, stir, turmoil. *See* **agitation** (1). **3.** A lack of civil order or peace ▶ anarchy, lawlessness, misrule. *See* **disorder** (2).

unrestrained *adjective*
1. Able to move about at will without bounds or restraint ▶ liberated, unconfined, untrammeled. *See* **loose** (2). **2.** Lacking in moral restraint ▶ unbridled, uncontrolled, ungoverned. *See* **abandoned** (2). **3.** Unconstrained by rigid standards or ceremony ▶ informal, relaxed. *Informal:* laid-back. *See* **easygoing** (1). **4.** Exceeding a normal or reasonable limit ▶ extravagant, immoderate. *See* **excessive** (1).

unrestraint *noun*
1. A complete surrender of inhibitions ▶ inconti-

nence, wantonness, wildness. *See* **abandon** (1). **2.** Freedom from constraint, formality, embarrassment, or awkwardness ► informality, naturalness. *See* **ease** (1).

unrestricted *adjective*
► nonexclusive, public. *See* **open** (3).

unrevealed *adjective*
► concealed, covert, hidden. *See* **ulterior** (1).

unrivaled *or* **unrivalled** *adjective*
► incomparable, singular, unparalleled. *See* **unique** (1).

unroll *verb*
1. To cause a line to become longer and less taut ► uncoil, unreel, untwine. *See* **unwind** (1). **2.** To move or arrange so as to cover a larger area ► extend, stretch. *See* **spread** (1).

unromantic *adjective*
► practical, pragmatic, prosaic. *See* **realistic** (1).

unruffled *adjective*
1. Not excited or agitated ► collected, composed, cool. *See* **calm** (1). *See synonym note at* **calm. 2.** Having no irregularities, roughness, or indentations ► flush, level. *See* **even** (1).

unruliness *noun*
The quality or the condition of being unruly ► disorderliness, fractiousness, indocility, intractability, intractableness, lawlessness, obstinacy, obstinateness, obstreperousness, recalcitrance, recalcitrancy, refractoriness, uncontrollability, uncontrollableness, ungovernableness, unmanageability, untowardness, wildness. *See also* **defiance, mischief.**

unruly *adjective*
Not submitting to discipline or control ► bad, disorderly, fractious, froward, headstrong, ill-behaved, indocile, insubordinate, intractable, lawless, naughty, noncompliant, obstinate, obstreperous, recalcitrant, refractory, uncontrollable, undisciplined, ungovernable, unmanageable, untoward, wayward, wild. *Idioms:* out of control, out of line. *See also* **mischevous, rebellious.**

✚ **CORE SYNONYMS:** *unruly, intractable, refractory, recalcitrant, headstrong, wayward.* These adjectives mean not submitting to discipline or control: *Unruly* is the most general: *unruly behavior in class. Intractable* and *refractory* refer to what is obstinate and difficult to manage or control: *"the intractable ferocity of his captive"* (Edgar Allan Poe). *"The idea of ecclesiastical authority . . . woke all the refractory nerves of opposition inherited from five generations of Puritans"* (Harriet Beecher Stowe). One that is *recalcitrant* rebels against authority: *arrested the recalcitrant protestors. Headstrong* describes one obstinately bent on having his or her own way: *The headstrong senator ignored his constituency.* One who is *wayward* willfully and often perversely departs from what is desired, advised, expected, or required: *"a lively child, who had been spoilt and indulged, and therefore was sometimes wayward"* (Charlotte Brontë).

---

unsafe *adjective*
1. Inadequately protected ► ill-protected, undefended. *See* **insecure** (1). **2.** Involving possible risk, loss, or injury ► chancy, hazardous, risky. *See* **dangerous.**

unsaid *adjective*
1. Not voiced or expressed ► undeclared, unspoken. *See* **silent** (2). **2.** Conveyed indirectly without words or speech ► inferred, tacit, unspoken. *See* **implicit** (1).

unsalaried *adjective*
► uncompensated, unremunerated, volunteer. *See* **unpaid** (1).

unsalutary *adjective*
► unhealthy, unhygienic, unsalutary. *See* **unwholesome** (1).

unsatisfactory *adjective*
1. Of low or lower quality ► inadequate, poor, substandard. *See* **bad** (1). **2.** Tending to discourage, retard, or make more difficult ► antagonistic, negative, untoward. *See* **unfavorable** (1). **3.** Disturbing because of failure to measure up to a standard or produce the desired results ► discouraging, sorry, unsatisfying. *See* **disappointing.**

unsatisfied *adjective*
► collectible, payable, unpaid. *See* **due** (1).

unsatisfying *adjective*
► discouraging, disheartening, sorry. *See* **disappointing.**

unsavory *adjective*
1. Lacking an appetizing flavor ► bland, insipid, tasteless. *See* **flat** (2). **2.** So unpleasant in flavor as to be inedible ► distasteful, unappetizing, uneatable. *See* **unpalatable** (1).

unsay *adjective*
► abjure, recant, take back. *See* **retract** (1).

unscathed *adjective*
► unharmed, unhurt, uninjured. *See* **safe** (1).

unscholarly *or* **unschooled** *adjective*
► unlearned, unstudious, untaught. *See* **ignorant** (1).

unscientific *adjective*
► judgmental, personal, subjective. *See* **arbitrary** (1).

unscrupulous *adjective*
1. Lacking scruples or principles ► amoral, conscienceless, debase, degraded, ruthless, shameless, unconscionable, unethical, unprincipled. *See also* **dishonest, evil, sordid. 2.** Marked by treachery or deceit ► duplicitous, shifty, sneaky. *See* **underhand.**

unseasonable *adjective*
Not suitable for or characteristic of the season ► ill-timed, inopportune, mistimed, untimely. *Idiom:* out of season. *See also* **improper.**

unseasoned *adjective*
► inexpert, uninitiated, unpracticed. *See* **inexperienced.**

unseeing *adjective*
1. Having little or no sight ► eyeless, sightless. *See* **blind** (1). **2.** Unwilling or unable to perceive ► obtuse, unperceptive. *See* **blind** (3).

unseemliness *noun*
► inappropriateness, unsuitability. *See* **impropriety** (1).

unseemly *adjective*
1. Not in keeping with conventional mores ► indecent,

indelicate. *See* **improper** (1). *See synonym note at* **improper. 2.** Not suited to circumstances ▸ inapt, malapropos, unbecoming. *See* **improper** (2).

unseen *adjective*
▸ covert, disguised, unnoticeable. *See* **hidden** (1).

unselfish *adjective*
1. Willing to give of oneself and one's possessions ▸ big-hearted, magnanimous. *See* **generous** (1). **2.** Without concern for oneself ▸ self-denying, self-sacrificing. *See* **selfless.**

unselfishness *noun*
▸ magnanimity, munificence, openhandedness. *See* **generosity.**

unserviceable *adjective*
▸ impracticable, unusable, useless. *See* **unworkable** (1).

unsettle *verb*
1. To put out of proper order ▸ disarrange, disrupt, muddle. *See* **disorder** (1). **2.** To disturb the health or physiological functioning of ▸ derange, disorder, turn. *See* **upset** (1). **3.** To impair or destroy the composure of ▸ disturb, perturb, ruffle. *See* **agitate** (2).

unsettled *adjective*
1. Affording no quiet, repose, or rest ▸ restless, uneasy, unquiet. *See also* **edgy, wakeful. 2.** In a state of anxiety or uneasiness ▸ distressed, nervous, uneasy. *See* **anxious. 3.** Capable of or liable to change ▸ fluid, uncertain, variable. *See* **changeable** (1). **4.** Marked by lack of firm decision or commitment; of questionable outcome ▸ uncertain, undetermined. *See* **indefinite** (2). **5.** Owed as a debt ▸ collectible, payable, unpaid. *See* **due** (1). **6.** In doubt or dispute ▸ disputable, doubtful, questionable. *See* **debatable.**

unsettling *adjective*
▸ bothersome, irritating, troublesome. *See* **disturbing.**

unsex *verb*
▸ castrate, fix, spay. *See* **sterilize** (2).

unshakable *adjective*
▸ solid, stable, sure. *See* **firm**[1] (2).

unshaped *adjective*
▸ amorphous, formless, inchoate. *See* **shapeless.** *See synonym note at* **shapeless.**

unshielded *adjective*
▸ ill-protected, undefended, unsafe. *See* **insecure** (1).

unsightliness *noun*
▸ monstrosity, odiousness, unloveliness. *See* **ugliness** (1).

unsightly *adjective*
▸ homely, unattractive, unsightly. *See* **ugly** (1). *See synonym note at* **ugly.**

unsigned *adjective*
▸ unacknowledged, uncredited, unnamed. *See* **anonymous.**

unskilled *adjective*
1. Lacking the qualities, as efficiency or skill, required to produce desired results ▸ incapable, inept, unfit. *See* **inefficient** (1). **2.** Lacking the required professional skill ▸ nonprofessional, unskillful. *See* **amateurish.**

unskillful *adjective*
1. Clumsily lacking in the ability to do or perform ▸ awkward, bumbling, bungling, clumsy, floundering, fumbling, gauche, heavy-handed, inept, maladroit, unpolished. *See also* **awkward. 2.** Lacking the qualities, as efficiency or skill, required to produce desired results ▸ bungling, inexpert, unable. *See* **inefficient** (1). **3.** Lacking the required professional skill ▸ nonprofessional, unskilled. *See* **amateurish.**

unsleeping *adjective*
Not in a state of sleep or unable to sleep ▸ awake, wakeful, wide-awake. *Idiom:* tossing and turning. *See also* **restless.**

unsoiled *adjective*
▸ immaculate, spotless. *See* **clean** (1).

unsophisticated *adjective*
▸ innocent, naive, simple. *See* **artless** (1). *See synonym note at* **artless.**

unsought *adjective*
▸ uninvited, unwanted. *See* **unwelcome** (1).

unsound *adjective*
1. Not physically strong ▸ feeble, frail, insubstantial. *See* **weak** (1). **2.** Afflicted with or exhibiting irrationality and mental unsoundness ▸ derailed, off, unbalanced. *See* **insane** (1). **3.** Containing errors in reasoning ▸ false, illogical, spurious. *See* **fallacious** (1). **4.** Containing an error or errors ▸ false, inaccurate, mistaken. *See* **erroneous. 5.** Not wise ▸ ill-advised, imprudent, inadvisable. *See* **unwise.**

unsoundness *noun*
▸ decrepitude, feebleness, unsubstantiality. *See* **infirmity** (1).

unsparing *adjective*
▸ big-hearted, magnanimous, unselfish. *See* **generous** (1).

unsparingness *noun*
▸ magnanimity, munificence, unselfishness. *See* **generosity.**

unspeakable *adjective*
1. Beyond description ▸ incommunicable, indefinable, indescribable, ineffable, inexpressible, undescribable, unutterable. *Idioms:* beyond description (*or* words), defying description. *See also* **incredible. 2.** That may not be spoken of or uttered ▸ eyes-only, sacred, unmentionable, unutterable. *See also* **forbidden, holy, secret. 3.** Exceeding the bounds of morality, decency, or reason ▸ appalling, monstrous, shocking. *See* **outrageous.**

✦ CORE SYNONYMS: *unspeakable, indefinable, indescribable, ineffable, inexpressible, unutterable.* These adjectives refer to that which is beyond expression or description: *unspeakable misery; indefinable yearnings; indescribable beauty; ineffable ecstasy; inexpressible anguish; unutterable contempt.*

unspecified *adjective*
▸ uncertain, undetermined. *See* **indefinite** (2).

unspoiled *adjective*
▸ pristine, pure, unpolluted. *See* **fresh** (1).

unspoken *adjective*
1. Not voiced or expressed ▸ undeclared, unvoiced. *See* **silent** (2). 2. Conveyed indirectly without words or speech ▸ inferred, tacit, wordless. *See* **implicit** (1).

unstable *adjective*
1. Capable of or liable to change ▸ fluid, unsettled, variable. *See* **changeable** (1). 2. Marked by whim or impulse ▸ fickle, impulsive, mercurial. *See* **capricious**. 3. Lacking stability ▸ shaky, unsteady. *See* **insecure** (2). 4. Without a fixed or regular course ▸ stray, wandering. *See* **erratic** (1).

unstableness *noun*
▸ insecurity, precariousness, unsteadiness. *See* **instability**.

unstained *adjective*
▸ pure, uncorrupted, untainted. *See* **innocent** (1).

unsteadiness *noun*
1. The quality or condition of being physically unsteady ▸ ricketiness, wiggling, wobbliness, wonkiness. 2. The quality or condition of being erratic and undependable ▸ insecurity, unstableness. *See* **instability**. 3. A sensation of whirling or falling ▸ grogginess, wooziness. *See* **dizziness**.

unsteady *adjective*
1. Lacking stability ▸ shaky, tottering. *See* **insecure** (2). 2. Capable of or liable to change ▸ fluid, unsettled, variable. *See* **changeable** (1). 3. Marked by whim or impulse ▸ fickle, impulsive, mercurial. *See* **capricious**. 4. Lacking consistency or regularity in quality or performance ▸ inconsistent, patchy, variable. *See* **uneven** (1). 5. Having a sensation of whirling or falling ▸ lightheaded, reeling. *See* **dizzy** (1).

unstinting *adjective*
▸ big-hearted, magnanimous, unselfish. *See* **generous** (1).

unstudied *adjective*
▸ innocent, naive, simple. *See* **artless** (1).

unstudious *adjective*
▸ unlearned, unscholarly, untaught. *See* **ignorant** (1).

unsubstantial *adjective*
1. Having no body, form, or substance ▸ disembodied, incorporeal, nonphysical. *See* **immaterial** (1). 2. Not physically strong ▸ feeble, frail, unsound. *See* **weak** (1). 3. Not plausible or believable ▸ improbable, inconceivable. *See* **implausible**.

unsubstantiality *noun*
▸ decrepitude, feebleness, puniness. *See* **infirmity** (1).

unsubtle *adjective*
▸ clear, patent. *See* **obvious** (1).

unsuccessful *adjective*
▸ fruitless, useless, vain. *See* **futile**.

unsufferable *adjective*
▸ insufferable, intolerable, unendurable. *See* **unbearable**.

unsuitability *or* **unsuitableness** *noun*
▸ inappropriateness, unseemliness. *See* **impropriety** (1).

unsuitable *adjective*
1. Not suited to circumstances ▸ inapt, malapropos, unbecoming. *See* **improper** (2). 2. Arousing disapproval ▸ exceptionable, improper, unacceptable. *See* **objectionable**.

unsuited *adjective*
▸ inapt, malapropos, mismatched, unbecoming. *See* **improper** (2).

unsullied *adjective*
1. Free from dirt, stain, or impurities ▸ immaculate, spotless. *See* **clean** (1). 2. Free from evil and corruption ▸ pure, uncorrupted, untainted. *See* **innocent** (1).

unsupportable *adjective*
▸ insufferable, intolerable, unendurable. *See* **unbearable**.

unsure *adjective*
1. Lacking certainty or clarity ▸ dubious, indeterminate, questionable, unclear. *See* **ambiguous** (1). 2. Marked by lack of firm decision or commitment; of questionable outcome ▸ uncertain, undetermined. *See* **indefinite** (2). 3. Lacking stability ▸ shaky, unsteady. *See* **insecure** (2). 4. Experiencing doubt ▸ hesitant, skeptical, uncertain. *See* **doubtful** (2).

unsureness *noun*
▸ insecurity, unstableness, unsteadiness. *See* **instability**.

unsurpassable *adjective*
▸ top, ultimate, utmost. *See* **maximum**.

unsurpassed *adjective*
1. Surpassing all others in quality, achievement, or desirability ▸ optimum, superlative. *See* **best** (1). 2. Without equal or rival ▸ incomparable, unparalleled. *See* **unique** (1).

unsusceptibility *noun*
The capacity to withstand ▸ immunity, imperviousness, insusceptibility, resistance. *See also* **endurance**, **stability**.

unsusceptible *adjective*
1. Having the capacity to withstand ▸ immune, impervious, insusceptible. *See* **resistant** (1). 2. Lacking feeling or emotion ▸ impassive, insensitive, unaffected. *See* **cold** (2).

unswerving *adjective*
1. Not diffused or dispersed ▸ undivided, whole. *See* **concentrated** (1). 2. Proceeding or lying in an uninterrupted line or course ▸ linear, straightforward. *See* **direct** (1).

unsympathetic *adjective*
1. Lacking compassion or mercy ▸ heartless, insensitive, merciless. *See* **callous**. 2. Not pleasant or agreeable ▸ bad, disagreeable, uncongenial. *See* **unpleasant** (1).

unsystematic *adjective*
▸ disordered, topsy-turvy, upside-down. *See* **confused** (2).

untactful *adjective*
▸ gauche, impolitic, undiplomatic. *See* **tactless**.

untainted *adjective*
▸ pure, uncorrupted, virginal. *See* **innocent** (1).

untalkative *adjective*
▸ reticent, silent, uncommunicative. *See* **taciturn**.

untamed *adjective*
1. Not domesticated ▸ feral, savage, undomesticated. *See* **wild** (2). 2. Not civilized ▸ barbarian, barbaric, rude. *See* **uncivilized** (1).

untangle *verb*
1. To free from an entanglement ▸ disengage, free. *See* **extricate**. *See synonym note at* **extricate**. 2. To find a solution for ▸ clear up, resolve, unravel. *See* **solve** (1). *See synonym note at* **solve**.

untasteful *adjective*
▸ distasteful, unappetizing, untasty. *See* **unpalatable** (1).

untaught *adjective*
1. Without education or knowledge ▸ lowbrow, uncultivated, unlearned. *See* **ignorant** (1). 2. Derived from or prompted by a natural tendency or impulse ▸ inborn, intuitive. *See* **instinctive** (1). *See synonym note at* **instinctive**.

untenable *adjective*
▸ false, illogical, spurious. *See* **fallacious** (1).

untested *adjective*
▸ unpracticed, unproved. *See* **untried** (1).

unthankful *adjective*
1. Not apt to be appreciated ▸ thankless, unappreciated, ungrateful. 2. Not showing or feeling gratitude ▸ ungrateful, unthanking. *See* **thankless** (1).

unthanking *adjective*
▸ ungrateful, unthankful. *See* **thankless** (1).

unthinkable *adjective*
1. Not to be believed ▸ unbelievable, unimaginable. *See* **incredible** (2). 2. Not capable of happening or being done ▸ impractical, unattainable, unworkable. *See* **impossible** (1).

unthinking *adjective*
1. Lacking regard ▸ heedless, thoughtless, unmindful. *See* **careless** (1). 2. Devoid of consideration for others' feelings ▸ inconsiderate, insensitive, unthoughtful. *See* **thoughtless** (1). 3. Not intended ▸ inadvertent, undesigned, unintended. *See* **unintentional**.

unthoughtful *adjective*
▸ disregardful, inconsiderate, insensitive, unthinking. *See* **thoughtless** (1).

unthoughtfulness *noun*
▸ disregard, insensitivity. *See* **thoughtlessness** (2).

unthrifty *adjective*
▸ prodigal, profligate. *See* **extravagant** (1).

untidiness *noun*
▸ sloppiness, topsy-turviness. *See* **disorderliness** (1).

untidy *adjective*
▸ sloppy, slovenly, unkempt. *See* **messy** (1).

untie *verb*
1. To free from ties or fasteners ▸ loose, release, unloose. *See* **undo** (1). 2. To become or cause to become open ▸ free, unclose. *See* **open** (1).

untighten *verb*
▸ let up, loosen, slacken. *See* **ease** (1).

untimely *adjective*
1. Not occurring at a favorable time ▸ ill-timed, inconvenient, inopportune. 2. Developing, occurring,

or appearing before the expected time ▸ early, precocious, premature. 3. Not suitable for or characteristic of the season ▸ ill-timed, mistimed. *See* **unseasonable**.

untiring *adjective*
▸ inexhaustible, unflagging, unwearied. *See* **tireless**. *See synonym note at* **tireless**.

untouchable *noun*
▸ exile, pariah. *See* **outcast**.

untouched *adjective*
1. Lacking compassion or mercy ▸ heartless, merciless, unsympathetic. *See* **callous**. 2. Not polluted or altered by human intervention ▸ pristine, unpolluted, unspoiled. *See* **fresh** (1).

untoward *adjective*
1. Tending to discourage, retard, or make more difficult ▸ antagonistic, negative, unsatisfactory. *See* **unfavorable** (1). 2. Involving or undergoing chance misfortune ▸ ill-fated, ill-starred, luckless. *See* **unfortunate** (1). 3. Not submitting to discipline or control ▸ ill-behaved, obstinate, unmanageable. *See* **unruly**. 4. Not in keeping with conventional mores ▸ indecent, indelicate. *See* **improper** (1).

untowardness *noun*
1. Bad fortune ▸ bad luck, haplessness, unluckiness. *See* **misfortune** (1). 2. The quality or condition of being unruly ▸ intractability, obstinacy, recalcitrance. *See* **unruliness**.

untrameled *adjective*
▸ liberated, unconfined, unrestrained. *See* **loose** (2).

untried *adjective*
1. Not tested or proved ▸ conjectured, hypothesized, hypothetical, surmised, theoretical, theorized, undemonstrated, unestablished, unpracticed, unproved, untested. *See also* **new, pilot**. 2. Lacking experience and the knowledge gained from it ▸ inexpert, uninitiated, unpracticed. *See* **inexperienced**.

untroubled *adjective*
1. Free from disturbance, agitation, or commotion ▸ peaceful, placid, serene. *See* **still** (1). 2. Happy and free from worry or care ▸ blithe, buoyant, debonair. *See* **lighthearted** (1).

untroubledness *noun*
▸ calmness, lull, peacefulness. *See* **stillness** (1).

untrue *adjective*
1. Not true ▸ specious, spurious, wrong. *See* **false** (1). 2. Containing an error or errors ▸ false, inaccurate, mistaken. *See* **erroneous**. 3. Not true to duty or obligation ▸ false, perfidious, treacherous. *See* **faithless** (1).

untrusting *adjective*
▸ doubting, suspicious, wary. *See* **distrustful** (1).

untrustworthiness *noun*
▸ deceitfulness, mendacity. *See* **dishonesty** (1).

untrustworthy *adjective*
1. Not to be depended on ▸ irresponsible, unreliable. *See* **undependable** (1). 2. Of dubious character ▸ equivocal, questionable, suspicious. *See* **shady** (1). 3. Given to or marked by deliberate concealment or

misrepresentation of the truth ▸ duplicitous, lying, mendacious. *See* **dishonest** (1).

untruth *noun*
1. An untrue declaration ▸ falsehood, fib, misrepresentation. *See* **lie²**. 2. An erroneous or false idea ▸ error, misconception. *See* **fallacy** (1).

untruthful *adjective*
1. Not true ▸ specious, spurious, untrue. *See* **false** (1). 2. Given to or marked by deliberate concealment or misrepresentation of the truth ▸ duplicitous, lying, mendacious. *See* **dishonest** (1). *See synonym note at* **dishonest**.

untruthfulness *noun*
▸ inveracity, perjury, prevarication. *See* **mendacity** (1).

untwine *verb*
▸ uncoil, unreel, unroll. *See* **unwind** (1).

untwist *verb*
▸ uncoil, unreel, unroll. *See* **unwind** (1).

unusable *adjective*
▸ unserviceable, useless. *See* **unworkable** (1).

unused *adjective*
▸ inert, unemployed. *See* **idle** (1).

unusual *adjective*
1. Not usual or ordinary ▸ atypic, atypical, novel, unconventional, unique, unordinary, unwonted. *Slang:* offbeat. *See also* **abnormal, exotic**. 2. Rarely occurring or appearing ▸ rare, sporadic. *See* **Infrequent**. 3. Deviating from what is conventional or customary ▸ bizarre, grotesque. *See* **eccentric**. 4. Beyond what is usual, normal, or customary ▸ extraordinary, outstanding, remarkable. *See* **exceptional** (1).

unusually *adverb*
In a manner or to a degree that is unusual ▸ abnormally, atypically, bizarrely, curiously, exceptionally, extraordinarily, incredibly, oddly, peculiarly, phenomenally, remarkably, singularly, strangely, surprisingly, uncommonly, unconventionally, unexpectedly, uniquely. *See also* **absolutely, completely, considerably, really, very**.

unutterable *adjective*
1. Beyond description ▸ incommunicable, inexpressible, undescribable. *See* **unspeakable** (1). *See synonym note at* **unspeakable**. 2. That may not be spoken of or uttered ▸ eyes-only, ineffable, unmentionable. *See* **unspeakable** (2).

unuttered *adjective*
1. Not voiced or expressed ▸ undeclared, unspoken. *See* **silent** (2). 2. Conveyed indirectly without words or speech ▸ inferred, tacit, unspoken. *See* **implicit** (1).

unvarnished *adjective*
1. Without addition, decoration, or qualification ▸ plain, simple, unadorned. *See* **bare** (1). 2. Employing the very same words as another ▸ undeviating, verbatim, word-for-word. *See* **literal** (1).

unvarying *adjective*
▸ changeless, constant, uniform. *See* **unchanging**.

unveil *verb*
1. To make visible ▸ disclose, expose, uncover. *See* **reveal** (2). 2. To disclose in a breach of confidence

▸ divulge, give away. *Informal:* spill. *See* **betray** (2).

unventilated *adjective*
▸ stifling, stuffy. *See* **airless** (1).

unversed *adjective*
▸ inexpert, unpracticed. *See* **inexperienced**.

unvoiced *adjective*
▸ undeclared, unspoken. *See* **silent** (2).

unwanted *adjective*
1. Not welcome or wanted ▸ uninvited, unsought. *See* **unwelcome** (1). 2. Arousing disapproval ▸ exceptionable, improper, unacceptable. *See* **objectionable**.

unwarranted *adjective*
1. Having no basis in fact ▸ idle, unfounded. *See* **baseless**. *See synonym note at* **baseless**. 2. Not required, necessary, or warranted by the circumstances of the case ▸ supererogative, uncalled-for. *See* **wanton** (2).

unwarrantedly *adverb*
Without basis or foundation in fact ▸ baselessly, groundlessly, unfoundedly.

unwashed *adjective*
▸ common, humble, plebeian. *See* **lowly** (1).

unwavering *adjective*
▸ resolute, steadfast, unyielding. *See* **firm¹** (3).

unwearied *adjective*
▸ inexhaustible, unflagging, untiring. *See* **tireless**. *See synonym note at* **tireless**.

unwed *adjective*
▸ fancy free, marriageable. *See* **single** (5).

unwelcome *adjective*
1. Not welcome or wanted ▸ banished, excluded, rejected, undesirable, undesired, uninvited, unsought, unwanted, unwished-for. 2. Arousing disapproval ▸ exceptionable, improper, unacceptable. *See* **objectionable**.

unwelcome *or* **unwelcomeness** *noun*
Lack of cordiality and hospitableness ▸ coldness, uncongeniality, ungraciousness, unreceptiveness. *See* **inhospitality**.

unwell *adjective*
▸ ailing, indisposed, sickly. *See* **sick** (1).

unwholesome *adjective*
1. Not sustaining or promoting health ▸ insalubrious, junk, unhealthful, unhealthy, unhygienic, unsalutary. 2. Morally detrimental ▸ contaminative, corruptive, demoralizing, poisonous, unhealthy. *See also* **evil**. 3. Characterized by preoccupation with unwholesome thoughts or feelings ▸ sick, unhealthy. *See* **morbid** (1). 4. So objectionable as to deserve condemnation ▸ contemptible, disgusting, obnoxious. *See* **offensive** (1). 5. Causing harm or injury ▸ deleterious, evil, injurious. *See* **harmful**.

unwholesomeness *noun*
▸ defilement, impurity, pollution. *See* **contamination** (1).

unwieldy *adjective*
▸ bulky, ungainly. *See* **awkward** (2).

unwilling *adjective*
▸ disinclined, reluctant. *See* **indisposed** (1).

unwillingness *noun*
▸ aversion, opposition, reluctance. *See* **indisposition** (1).

unwind *verb*
1. To cause a line to become longer and less taut ▸ play out, uncoil, unravel, unreel, unroll, untwine, untwist. *See also* **extricate, undo**. 2. To take repose by ceasing work or other effort for an interval of time ▸ kick back, relax, unbend. *See* **rest**¹ (1).

unwise *adjective*
Not wise ▸ contraindicated, ill-advised, ill-considered, impolitic, impractical, imprudent, inadvisable, indiscreet, inexpedient, injudicious, unsound. *See also* **foolish, rash, unruly**.

unwished-for *adjective*
▸ uninvited, unwanted. *See* **unwelcome** (1).

unwitting *adjective*
1. Not aware or informed ▸ oblivious, misguided, unaware. *See* **ignorant** (3). 2. Not intended ▸ inadvertent, undesigned, unintended. *See* **unintentional**.

unwonted *adjective*
▸ atypical, novel, unconventional. *See* **unusual** (1).

unworkable *adjective*
1. Incapable of being used or availed of to advantage ▸ impracticable, unemployable, unnegotiable, unserviceable, unusable, useless. 2. Not capable of happening or being done ▸ impractical, unattainable, unobtainable. *See* **impossible** (1).

unworkmanlike *adjective*
▸ incapable, inept, unskilled. *See* **inefficient** (1).

unworldly *adjective*
1. Of or relating to existence outside the natural world ▸ metaphysical, superhuman. *See* **supernatural** (1). 2. Free from guile, cunning, or deceit ▸ innocent, naive, simple. *See* **artless** (1).

unwritten *adjective*
▸ spoken, verbal, vocal, voiced. *See* **oral**.

unyielding *adjective*
1. Not changing shape or bending ▸ inflexible, stiff, unbending. *See* **rigid** (1). 2. Possessing determination or resolution ▸ resolute, steadfast, unflinching. *See* **firm**¹ (3). 3. Rigorous and unsparing in treating others ▸ harsh, stern, strict. *See* **severe** (1). 4. Firmly, often unreasonably immovable in purpose or will ▸ bullheaded, dogged, obstinate. *See* **stubborn** (1).

up *adjective*
Feeling great delight and joy ▸ euphoric, overjoyed. *See* **elated**.

up *verb*
1. To increase in amount ▸ boost, hike, jack (up), jump, raise. 2. To raise in rank ▸ elevate, upgrade. *See* **promote** (1).

up-and-comer *noun*
▸ candidate, hopeful, prospect. *See* **comer** (2).

up-and-coming *adjective*
Showing great promise ▸ coming, promising. *Idiom:* on the way up.

upbeat *adjective*
▸ cheerful, sanguine. *See* **optimistic**.

upbraid *verb*
▸ chide, rebuke, reprimand. *See* **chastise** (1). *See synonym note at* **chastise**.

upbraiding *noun*
▸ berating, tongue-lashing. *See* **tirade**.

upbringing *noun*
Training in the proper forms of social and personal conduct ▸ breeding, education. *See also* **courtesy, manners**.

upchuck *verb*
▸ retch, throw up. *Informal:* puke. *See* **vomit** (1).

upcoming *adjective*
In the relatively near future ▸ approaching, coming, due, forthcoming. *Idioms:* around the corner, on the horizon. *See also* **close, imminent**.

update *verb*
To make modern in appearance or style ▸ modernize, streamline. *Idiom:* bring up to date. *See also* **improve, renew**.

upend *verb*
▸ knock over, topple. *See* **overturn** (1).

upfront *adjective*
▸ candid, ingenuous, plainspoken. *See* **frank**.

upgrade *verb*
1. To advance to a more desirable state ▸ better, enhance, meliorate. *See* **improve** (1). *See synonym note at* **improve**. 2. To raise in rank ▸ elevate, raise. *See* **promote** (1).

upgrade *noun*
1. The act of making better or the condition of being made better ▸ betterment, development, melioration. *See* **improvement** (1). 2. A progression upward in rank ▸ promotion, raise. *See* **advancement** (1).

upheaval *noun*
1. A momentous or sweeping change ▸ cataclysm, convulsion. *See* **revolution** (3). 2. The act or an example of upsetting ▸ disruption, overthrow, overturn. *See* **upset** (1).

uphill *adjective*
▸ arduous, laborious, tough. *See* **difficult** (1).

uphold *verb*
1. To move something to a higher position ▸ lift, raise. *See* **elevate** (1). 2. To make stronger or more resistant ▸ bolster, reinforce, strengthen. *See* **support** (2). 3. To hold the weight of ▸ carry, support, sustain. *See* **bear** (1). 4. To aid the cause of by approving or favoring ▸ back, endorse, stand by. *See* **support** (1). *See synonym note at* **support**. 5. To support against arguments, attack, or criticism ▸ justify, maintain, vindicate. *See* **defend** (2).

upkeep *noun*
1. The means needed to support life ▸ bread, keep, livelihood. *See* **living**. 2. The work of keeping something in proper condition ▸ preservation, repairs. *See* **maintenance** (1).

uplift *verb*
1. To move something to a higher position ▸ hoist, raise. *See* **elevate** (1). 2. To raise to a high position or status ▸ elevate, glorify, magnify. *See* **exalt** (1). 3. To

raise the spirits of ► buoy (up), exhilarate, inspire. *See* **elate** (1).

uplift *noun*
1. High spirits ► euphoria, inspiration. *See* **elation** (1). 2. An instance of lifting or being lifted ► heave, hoist. *See* **lift** (1).

upmost *adjective*
Of, being, located at, or forming the top ► highest, loftiest, top, topmost, uppermost. *See also* **climactic.**

up on *adjective*
► educated, knowledgeable. *See* **informed** (1).

upper *adjective*
Being at a rank or level above another ► greater, higher, senior, superior.

upper class *noun*
People of the highest social level ► elite, gentry, nobility. *See* **society** (1).

upper-class *adjective*
Of high birth or social position ► blue-blooded, elite, wellborn. *See* **noble** (1).

upper crust *noun*
Informal People of the highest social level ► elite, gentry, nobility. *See* **society** (1).

upper-crust *adjective*
Informal Of high birth or social position ► blue-blooded, elite, upper-class. *See* **noble** (1).

upper hand *noun*
► edge, leverage, superiority, vantage. *See* **advantage** (3).

uppermost *adjective*
Of, being, located at, or forming the top ► highest, loftiest, top, topmost, upmost. *See also* **climactic.**

uppity *or* **uppish** *adjective*
1. *Informal* Characteristic of or resembling a snob ► elitist. *Informal:* stuck-up, snooty. *See* **snobbish.** 2. *Informal* Rude and disrespectful ► bold, insolent, pert. *See* **impudent.**

uppityness *or* **uppishness** *noun*
Informal The state or quality of being impudent or arrogantly self-confident ► audacity, boldness, forwardness. *See* **impudence.**

upraise *or* **uprear** *verb*
1. To raise upright ► put up, raise. *See* **erect** (1). 2. To move something to a higher position ► take up, uphold. *See* **elevate** (1).

upraised *adjective*
1. Being in a vertical or upward-pointing position ► raised, upstanding. *See* **erect.** 2. Being positioned above a given level ► boosted, uplifted. *See* **elevated** (1).

upright *adjective*
1. At right angles to the horizon or to level ground ► on end, standing. *See* **vertical.** *See synonym note at* **vertical.** 2. Directed or pointed upward ► raised, upstanding. *See* **erect.** 3. In accordance with principles of right or good conduct ► principled, virtuous. *See* **ethical.** 4. Having or marked by uprightness in principle and action ► honorable, righteous. *See* **honest** (1).

uprightness *noun*
1. The quality or state of being morally sound ► probity, virtue. *See* **good** (1). 2. Moral or ethical strength ► integrity, principle. *See* **character** (2).

uprise *verb*
► get up, rise. *See* **stand** (1).

uprising *noun*
► mutiny, revolt, sedition. *See* **rebellion** (1).

uproar *noun*
1. A condition of intense public interest or excitement ► brouhaha, uproar. *See* **sensation** (2). 2. A condition of being agitated or disturbed ► commotion, disturbance, stir. *See* **agitation** (1). 3. Sounds or a sound, especially when loud, confused, or disagreeable ► clamor, din. *See* **noise** (1). *See synonym note at* **noise.** 4. Loud and insistent utterances or noisemaking, usually expressing disapproval ► hullabaloo, rumpus. *See* **vociferation.** 5. A lack of civil order or peace ► anarchy, lawlessness, misrule. *See* **disorder** (2).

uproarious *adjective*
► comical, humorous, laughable. *See* **funny** (1).

uproot *verb*
► eradicate, liquidate, obliterate. *See* **annihilate** (1).

upset *verb*
1. To disturb the health or physiological functioning of ► derange, disconcert, disorder, turn, unsettle. *See also* **derange.** 2. To turn or cause to turn from a vertical or horizontal position ► knock over, topple. *See* **overturn** (1). 3. To put out of proper order ► disarrange, disrupt, muddle. *See* **disorder** (1). 4. To break up the order or progress of ► interfere, obstruct. *See* **disrupt** (1). 5. To impair or destroy the composure of ► disquiet, disturb, perturb. *See* **agitate** (2). 6. To cause anger, resentment, or hurt feelings ► annoy, injure, miff. *See* **offend** (1). 7. To be very disagreeable to ► displease, repulse. *See* **offend** (2). 8. To alter the settled state or position of ► displace, disrupt. *See* **disturb** (1). 9. To bring about the downfall of ► subvert, topple. *See* **overthrow** (1). *See synonym note at* **overthrow.**

upset *noun*
1. The act or an example of upsetting ► disordering, disorganization, disruption, overthrow, overturn, upheaval. *See also* **defeat, disturbance.** 2. A state of discomposure ► tumult, turmoil. *Informal:* lather. *See* **agitation** (2).

upset *adjective*
1. Turned over completely ► inverted, overturned. *See* **upside-down** (1). 2. In a state of anxiety or uneasiness ► agitated, distressed, overwrought. *See* **anxious.**

upsetting *adjective*
► bothersome, irritating, unsettling. *See* **disturbing.**

upshot *noun*
► consequence, outcome, result. *See* **effect** (1). *See synonym note at* **effect.**

upside-down *adjective*
1. Turned over completely ► capsized, inverted, overturned, topsy-turvy, upset, upturned. *Idiom:* bottomside up. 2. Characterized by physical confusion ► dis-

ordered, topsy-turvy, unsettled. *See* **confused** (2).

upspring *verb*
▸ derive, emanate, originate. *See* **stem** (1).

upstanding *adjective*
1. Directed or pointed upward ▸ raised, upright. *See* **erect**. 2. Marked by uprightness in principle and action ▸ honorable, righteous. *See* **honest** (1).

upstandingness *noun*
▸ incorruptibility, integrity. *See* **honesty** (1).

upsurge *verb*
To make or become greater or larger ▸ amplify, boost, enlarge. *See* **increase** (1).

upsurge *noun*
The act of increasing or rising ▸ amplification, boost, escalation. *See* **increase** (1).

upswing *noun*
▸ amplification, boost, escalation. *See* **increase** (1).

uptight *adjective*
Slang Feeling or exhibiting nervous tension ▸ fidgety, jittery. *See* **edgy**.

up to *adjective*
1. Having the necessary strength or ability ▸ equal. 2. Satisfying certain requirements, as for selection ▸ equal, suitable. *See* **eligible** (1).

up-to-date *or* **up-to-the-minute** *adjective*
▸ current, modern, topical. *See* **contemporary** (2).

upturn *noun*
The act of increasing or rising ▸ amplification, boost, escalation. *See* **increase** (1).

upturn *verb*
To turn or cause to turn from a vertical or horizontal position ▸ knock over, topple. *See* **overturn** (1).

upturned *adjective*
▸ inverted, overturned. *See* **upside-down** (1).

urban *adjective*
▸ civic, local, municipal. *See* **city**.

urbane *adjective*
1. Gracious and tactful in social manner ▸ debonair, smooth, suave. *See also* **courteous, glib, sophisticated**. 2. Characterized by discriminating taste and broad knowledge as a result of development or education ▸ cultivated, educated. *See* **cultured**.

urbanity *noun*
1. Refinement of manner, form, and style ▸ grace, refinement, sophistication. *See* **elegance**. 2. Social courtesies ▸ civility, pleasantry, politeness. *See* **amenities** (2).

urchin *noun*
A mischievous youngster ▸ brat, elf, gamin, gamine, imp, juvenile delinquent, minx, scamp, whelp. *Idiom:* holy terror. *See also* **child, rascal**.

urge *verb*
To impel to action ▸ drive, exhort, induce, press. *See also* **provoke**.

urge *noun*
1. A natural or habitual preference for something ▸ disposition, leaning, penchant. *See* **inclination** (1). 2. Sexual hunger ▸ eroticism, lust, passion. *See* **desire** (2).

urgency *noun*
▸ crisis, distress, trouble. *See* **emergency**.

urgent *adjective*
1. Demanding immediate attention ▸ acute, burning, climacteric, compelling, critical, crucial, crying, desperate, dire, emergent, exigent, imperative, instant, pressing, vital. *See also* **essential, important, primary**. 2. Firm or obstinate, as in making a demand or maintaining a stand ▸ importunate, importune, insistent, persistent. *See also* **firm, stubborn**.

✚ CORE SYNONYMS: *urgent, exigent, pressing, imperative*. These adjectives mean demanding immediate attention. *Urgent* often implies that a matter takes precedence over others: *"My business is too urgent to waste time on apologies"* (John Buchan). *Exigent* and *pressing* suggest an urgency that requires prompt action: *"When once disease was introduced into the rural districts, its effects appeared more horrible, more exigent, and more difficult to cure, than in towns"* (Mary Shelley). *"The danger now became too pressing to admit of longer delay"* (James Fenimore Cooper). *Imperative* implies a need or demand whose fulfillment cannot be evaded or deferred: *The necessity for preventing war has become imperative.*

---

urging *noun*
Urgent solicitation ▸ insistence, insistency, persuasion, pressing. *See also* **demand**.

urinary *adjective*
▸ cathartic, emetic, evacuative, purgative. *See* **eliminative**.

urinate *verb*
To excrete urine ▸ make water, micturate, pass water. *Informal:* go number one, go to the bathroom, pee, peepee, powder one's nose. *See also* **eliminate**.

urination *noun*
▸ excretion. *See* **elimination** (3).

usable *adjective*
1. In a condition to be used ▸ applicable, employable, operational, serviceable, utilizable. *See also* **active, practical**. 2. Available for use ▸ employable, operable. *See* **open** (4).

usage *noun*
1. The act of consuming ▸ consumption, depletion, expenditure, use, utilization. *See also* **use**. 2. The act of putting into play ▸ employment, implementation, use. *See* **exercise** (1). 3. A habitual way of behaving ▸ form, habit, practice. *See* **custom** (1). *See synonym note at* **custom**.

usance *noun*
▸ form, habit, practice. *See* **custom** (1).

use *verb*
1. To put into action or use ▸ actuate, adopt, apply, draw on, employ, exercise, exploit, harness, implement, practice, utilize, work. *Idioms:* avail oneself of, bring into play, bring to bear, make use of, put into practice, put to use. *See also* **exercise, handle**. 2. To direct the functioning of ▸ run, work. *See* **operate** (1). 3. To treat wrongfully or harmfully ▸ exploit, ill-treat, maltreat. *See* **abuse** (1). 4. To influence or manage

shrewdly or deviously ▸ exploit, maneuver. *See* **manipulate** (1).

use up *verb*
To use all of ▸ eat up, expend, run through. *See* **exhaust** (1).

use *noun*
1. The act of consuming ▸ consumption, depletion, expenditure, usage, utilization. **2.** The quality of being suitable or adaptable to an end ▸ account, advantage, avail, benefit, merit, point, practicality, profit, usefulness, utility. *See also* **purpose**. **3.** The act of putting into play ▸ employment, implementation, usage. *See* **exercise** (1). **4.** The condition of being put to use ▸ application, service, utilization. *See* **duty** (2). **5.** A habitual way of behaving ▸ form, habit, practice. *See* **custom** (1). *See synonym note at* **custom**. **6.** Something that contributes to or increases one's well-being ▸ benefit, good, interests. *See* **interest** (1).

✦ CORE SYNONYMS: *use, employ, utilize.* These verbs mean to put into action or use. To *use* is to put into service or apply for a purpose: *uses a hearing aid; used the press secretary as spokesperson; using a stick to stir the paint. Employ* is often interchangeable with *use: She employed her education to maximum advantage.* It can also denote engaging or maintaining the services of another: *"When men are employed, they are best contented"* (Benjamin Franklin). *Utilize* is especially appropriate in the narrower sense of making something profitable or of finding new and practical uses for it: *Waterpower was once widely utilized to generate electricity.*

---

used *adjective*
1. In the habit ▸ accustomed, habituated, wont. **2.** Previously owned or made use of; not new ▸ hand-me-down, pre-owned, secondhand. *See also* **obsolete, old-fashioned**.

useful *adjective*
1. Serving or capable of serving a useful purpose ▸ functional, serviceable, utilitarian. *See* **practical** (1). **2.** Affording benefit or advantage ▸ favorable, helpful, propitious. *See* **beneficial**. **3.** Suited to one's purpose ▸ expedient, proper, suitable. *See* **convenient** (1).

usefulness *noun*
▸ benefit, profit, utility. *See* **use** (2).

useless *adjective*
1. Having no useful result ▸ fruitless, unsuccessful, vain. *See* **futile**. *See synonym note at* **futile**. **2.** Incapable of being used or availed of to advantage ▸ unserviceable, unusable. *See* **unworkable** (1). **3.** Not having the desired effect ▸ ineffective, inefficient. *See* **ineffectual** (1). **4.** Not capable of accomplishing anything ▸ impotent, inadequate, incapable. *See* **ineffectual** (2).

uselessness *noun*
1. The condition or quality of being useless or ineffective ▸ fruitlessness, unprofitableness, vainness. *See* **futility**. **2.** The condition or state of being incapable of accomplishing anything ▸ helplessness, ineffectiveness. *See* **ineffectuality**.

user *noun*
▸ customer, patron. *See* **consumer**.

usher *noun*
Something or someone that shows the way ▸ director, escort, leader. *See* **guide** (1).

usher *verb*
To show the way to ▸ direct, escort, lead. *See* **guide** (1). *See synonym note at* **guide**.

usher in *verb*
1. To make known the presence or arrival of ▸ announce, introduce. *See* **proclaim** (1). **2.** To begin something with preliminary or prefatory material ▸ lead, preface. *See* **introduce** (3).

usual *adjective*
1. Commonly practiced or used ▸ accustomed, customary, habitual, regular, wonted. **2.** Commonly encountered ▸ average, commonplace, normal. *See* **common** (1). **3.** Conforming to established standards ▸ orthodox, traditional. *See* **conventional** (1).

usual *noun*
A regular or customary matter, condition, or course of events ▸ average, commonplace, everyday, form, norm, ordinary, pattern, routine, rule.

usually *adverb*
In an expected or customary manner ▸ commonly, consistently, customarily, frequently, generally, habitually, mainly, mostly, naturally, normally, often, ordinarily, regularly, routinely, typically. *Idioms:* as usual, by and large, on the whole, per usual. *See also* **approximately, fairly**.

usualness *noun*
The quality or condition of being usual ▸ averageness, customariness, habitualness, normalcy, normality, ordinariness, prevalence, regularity, routineness.

usurp *verb*
1. To take the place of another against the other's will ▸ cut out, displace, supplant. *See also* **assume, occupy**. **2.** To lay claim to or take possession of ▸ appropriate, commandeer, preempt. *See* **seize** (1). *See synonym note at* **seize**.

usurpation *noun*
▸ expropriation, preemption, snatch. *See* **seizure** (2).

usurper *noun*
▸ despot, oppressor, tyrant. *See* **dictator** (1).

utensil *noun*
A device used to do work or perform a task ▸ implement, instrument, tool. *See synonym note at* **tool**. *See also* **agent, device, gadget**.

utilitarian *adjective*
▸ functional, practicable, useful. *See* **practical** (1).

utility *noun*
▸ benefit, profit, usefulness. *See* **use** (2).

utilizable *adjective*
1. Available for use ▸ employable, operable, usable. *See* **open** (4). **2.** In a condition to be used ▸ employable, serviceable. *See* **usable** (1).

utilization *noun*
1. The act of putting into play ▸ employment, implementation, usage. *See* **exercise** (1). **2.** The condition of

being put to use ▸ application, service, use. *See* **duty** (2). **3.** The act of consuming ▸ expenditure, use. *See* **consumption** (2).

utilize *verb*

1. To put into action or use ▸ apply, employ, harness. *See* **use** (1). *See synonym note at* **use. 2.** To direct the functioning of ▸ run, work. *See* **operate** (1).

utmost *adjective*

1. Most distant or remote, as from a center ▸ farthest, ultimate. *See* **extreme** (1). **2.** Greatest in quantity or highest in degree that can be attained ▸ topmost, ultimate. *See* **maximum.**

utmost *noun*

The greatest quantity or highest degree attainable ▸ ultimate, uttermost. *See* **maximum** (1).

utopian *adjective*

Characterized by ideals that often conflict with practical considerations ▸ romantic, unrealistic, visionary. *See* **idealistic.**

utopian *noun*

A person inclined to be imaginative or idealistic but impractical ▸ fantasist, romantic, stargazer. *See* **dreamer** (1).

utter[1] *verb*

1. To produce or make speech sounds ▸ enunciate, vocalize. *See* **pronounce. 2.** To put into words ▸ declare, express, state. *See* **say** (1).

utter[2] *adjective*

Completely such, without qualification or exception ▸ absolute, all-out, arrant, complete, consummate, crashing, damned, dead, downright, flat, full-fledged, out-and-out, outright, perfect, plain, pure, sheer, stark, thorough, thoroughgoing, total, unbounded, unequivocal, unlimited, unmitigated, unqualified, unrelieved, unreserved. *Informal:* flat out, positive. *Idiom:* out-and-out. *See also* **maximum.**

utterance *noun*

1. Something said ▸ saying, statement, word. *See also* **language. 2.** The act or an instance of expressing in words ▸ statement, verbalization. *See* **expression** (1). **3.** The use of the vocal organs to produce sound or speech ▸ enunciation, vocalization. *See* **voicing. 4.** The faculty, act, or product of speaking ▸ talk, verbalization. *See* **speech** (1).

uttered *adjective*

▸ spoken, verbal, vocal, voiced. *See* **oral.**

utterly *adverb*

▸ fully, throroughly, totally. *See* **completely** (1).

uttermost *adjective*

1. Greatest in quantity or highest in degree that can be attained ▸ topmost, ultimate. *See* **maximum. 2.** Most distant or remote, as from a center ▸ farthest, outermost, ultimate. *See* **extreme** (1).

uttermost *noun*

The greatest quantity or highest degree attainable ▸ outside, ultimate. *See* **maximum** (1).

U-turn *noun*

▸ inversion, transposition, turnabout. *See* **reversal** (1).

V

vacancy *noun*

1. Empty, unfilled space ▸ emptiness, vacuity. *See* **nothingness** (2). **2.** Total lack of ideas, meaning, or substance ▸ blankness, hollowness. *See* **emptiness** (3).

vacant *adjective*

1. Lacking intelligent thought or content ▸ blank, empty, empty-headed, impassive, inane, lifeless, unreasoning, vacuous. *See also* **absent-minded, foolish, stupid. 2.** Containing nothing ▸ bare, vacuous. *See* **empty** (1). *See synonym note at* **empty. 3.** Marked by a lack of activity or use ▸ inert, unemployed, unused. *See* **idle** (1). **4.** Lacking value, use, or substance ▸ empty, otiose. *See* **hollow** (1). **5.** Available for use ▸ operable, usable. *See* **open** (4). **6.** Empty of people ▸ uninhabited, unpeopled, unpopulated. *See* **lonely** (1).

vacate *verb*

▸ clean out, evacuate. *See* **empty** (1).

vacation *noun*

A regularly scheduled period spent away from work or duty, often in recreation ▸ furlough, holiday, leave, sabbatical. *Idioms:* time (*or* day) off. *See also* **break, trip.**

vacationer *noun*

▸ sightseer, traveler, visitor. *See* **tourist.**

vaccinate *verb*

▸ dispense, medicate, treat. *See* **administer** (3).

vacillant *adjective*

▸ indecisive, irresolute. *See* **hesitant** (1).

vacillate *verb*

1. To move back and forth ▸ swing, vibrate, waggle. *See* **sway** (1). **2.** To be irresolute in acting or doing ▸ falter, waver. *See* **hesitate.** *See synonym note at* **hesitate. 3.** To shift from one attitude, interest, condition, or emotion to another ▸ dilly-dally, swing, waver. **4.** To become different ▸ fluctuate, modify, turn. *See* **change** (2).

vacillating *adjective*

▸ hesitant, skeptical, uncertain, undecided. *See* **doubtful** (2).

vacillation *noun*

▸ indecision, tentativeness. *See* **hesitation.**

vacillatory *adjective*
▸ indecisive, irresolute. *See* **hesitant** (1).
vacuity *noun*
1. Empty, unfilled space ▸ emptiness, vacuum. *See* **nothingness** (2). 2. A space in an otherwise solid mass ▸ hollow, void. *See* **hole** (1). 3. Total lack of ideas, meaning, or substance ▸ blankness, hollowness. *See* **emptiness** (3).
vacuous *adjective*
1. Containing nothing ▸ bare, vacant. *See* **empty** (1). *See synonym note at* **empty**. 2. Lacking intelligent thought or content ▸ blank, empty, lifeless. *See* **vacant** (1).
vacuousness *noun*
▸ blankness, hollowness. *See* **emptiness** (3).
vacuum *noun*
1. Empty, unfilled space ▸ emptiness, vacuity. *See* **nothingness** (2). 2. A desolate sense of loss ▸ desolation, void. *See* **emptiness** (2).
vagabond *noun*
1. An impoverished person ▸ beggar, insolvent, tramp. *See* **pauper**. 2. One who wanders without a permanent home or livelihood ▸ nomad, roamer, vagrant. *See* **hobo**.
vagabond *adjective*
Leading the life of a person without a fixed domicile; moving from place to place ▸ traveling, vagrant. *See* **nomadic**.
vagary *noun*
▸ impulse, notion, whim. *See* **fancy** (1).
vagrant *adjective*
1. Leading the life of a person without a fixed domicile; moving from place to place ▸ traveling, vagabond. *See* **nomadic**. 2. Marked by whim or impulse ▸ arbitrary, fickle, impulsive, mercurial. *See* **capricious**.
vagrant *noun*
One who wanders without a permanent home or livelihood ▸ nomad, roamer, vagabond. *See* **hobo**.
vague *adjective*
1. Liable to more than one interpretation ▸ equivocal, nebulous, unclear. *See* **ambiguous** (2). 2. Not clearly perceptible ▸ dim, faint, indefinite. *See* **unclear** (1). 3. Marked by lack of firm decision or commitment; of questionable outcome ▸ uncertain, undetermined. *See* **indefinite** (2).
vagueness *noun*
The quality or state of being imprecise or indefinite ▸ ambiguity, ambiguousness, cloudiness, equivocalness, fuzziness, imprecision, indefiniteness, indistinctness, inexactness, looseness, nebulousness, obscureness, obscurity, uncertainty, unclearness.
vain *adjective*
1. Having no useful result ▸ fruitless, unsuccessful, useless. *See* **futile**. *See synonym note at* **futile**. 2. Lacking value, use, or substance ▸ empty, vacant. *See* **hollow** (1). *See synonym note at* **hollow**. 3. Thinking too highly of oneself ▸ conceited, narcissistic. *See* **egotistic** (1).

vainglorious *adjective*
▸ narcissistic, vain. *See* **egotistic** (1).
vainglory *noun*
▸ conceit, megalomania, narcissism, vanity. *See* **egotism**.
vainness *noun*
1. The condition or quality of being useless or ineffective ▸ fruitlessness, unprofitableness, uselessness. *See* **futility**. 2. Exaggerated love for oneself or belief in one's own importance ▸ conceit, narcissism, vanity. *See* **egotism**.
vale *noun*
▸ dale, gorge. *See* **valley**.
valediction *noun*
▸ adieu, farewell, goodbye. *See* **departure** (1).
valedictory *adjective*
▸ farewell, goodbye. *See* **parting**.
valiance *or* **valiancy** *or* **valiantness** *noun*
▸ bravery, fortitude, gallantry, valor. *See* **courage**.
valiant *adjective*
▸ courageous, fearless, heroic. *See* **brave**. *See synonym note at* **brave**.
valid *adjective*
1. Based on good judgment, reasoning, or evidence ▸ cogent, well-founded. *See* **sound**^{2} (1). *See synonym note at* **sound**^{2}. 2. Worthy of belief, as because of precision or faithfulness to an original ▸ authoritative, credible, trustworthy. *See* **authentic** (2). 3. Worthy of being believed ▸ creditable, plausible. *See* **believable**. *See synonym note at* **believable**. 4. Within, allowed by, or sanctioned by the law ▸ legal, permitted, warranted. *See* **lawful**.
validate *verb*
1. To assure the certainty or validity of ▸ authenticate, corroborate, substantiate, verify. *See* **confirm** (1). *See synonym note at* **confirm**. 2. To establish as true or genuine through evidence ▸ confirm, substantiate, verify. *See* **prove** (1).
validation *noun*
▸ authentication, corroboration, proof, verification. *See* **confirmation** (2).
validity *noun*
1. Correspondence with fact or truth ▸ authenticity, correctness, truth. *See* **veracity**. 2. The state or quality of being within the law ▸ legitimacy, licitness. *See* **legality**.
valise *noun*
▸ carryon, grip. *See* **suitcase**.
valley *noun*
An elongated lowland between mountains or hills ▸ canyon, dale, dell, glen, gorge, hollow, lowland, swale, vale.
valor *noun*
▸ bravery, fortitude, gallantry. *See* **courage**.
valorous *adjective*
▸ courageous, fearless, heroic. *See* **brave**. *See synonym note at* **brave**.
valuable *adjective*
1. Of great value or price ▸ expensive, precious. *See*

costly. **2.** Affording benefit or advantage ▸ favorable, helpful, propitious. *See* **beneficial.**

valuate *verb*
▸ assay, calculate. *See* **estimate** (1).

valuation *noun*
1. A measure of those qualities that determine merit, desirability, usefulness, or importance ▸ account, value, worth. *See also* **cost, importance. 2.** The act or result of evaluating or appraising ▸ assessment, evaluation. *See* **estimate** (1).

value *verb*
1. To have a high opinion of or regard for ▸ admire, appreciate, cherish, consider, esteem, honor, prize, regard, respect, treasure. *Idioms:* hold dear, look up to, think highly (*or* much *or* well) of, set store by. *See also* **revere, enjoy, like**[1]. **2.** To make a judgment as to the worth or value of ▸ assay, calculate. *See* **estimate** (1).

value *noun*
1. A measure of those qualities that determine merit, desirability, usefulness, or importance ▸ account, valuation, worth. *See also* **cost, importance. 2.** A level of superiority that is usually high ▸ quality, stature. *See* **merit** (1). **3.** Something that is conveyed or signified ▸ import, sense, significance. *See* **meaning** (1).

✤ CORE SYNONYMS: *value, appreciate, prize, esteem, treasure, cherish.* These verbs mean to have a highly favorable opinion of or regard for someone or something. *Value* implies high regard for the importance or worth of the object: *"In principle, the modern university values . . . the free exchange of ideas . . ."* (Eloise Salholz). *Appreciate* applies especially to high regard based on critical assessment, comparison, and judgment: *As immigrants, they appreciated their newfound freedom. Prize* often suggests pride of possession: *"the nonchalance prized by teen-agers"* (Elaine Louie). *Esteem* implies respect: *"If he had never esteemed my opinion before, he would have thought highly of me then"* (Jane Austen). *Treasure* and *cherish* stress solicitous care and affectionate regard: *We treasure our freedom. "They seek out the Salish Indian woman . . . to learn the traditions she cherishes"* (Tamara Jones).

---

valueless *adjective*
▸ drossy, good-for-nothing. *See* **worthless** (1).

vamoose *verb*
1. *Slang* To move away from a place ▸ depart, go away, retire. *See* **go** (1). **2.** *Slang* To leave hastily ▸ bolt. *Slang:* hightail, scram. *See* **run** (3).

vamp *noun*
1. *Informal* A woman who seduces or exploits men ▸ femme fatale, siren. *See* **seductress. 2.** *Informal* A woman who is given to flirting ▸ coquette, flirt, tease.

vamp *verb*
To act upon with or as if with magic ▸ enchant, mesmerize, spellbind. *See* **charm** (2).

vandalize *verb*
To injure or destroy property maliciously ▸ wreck. *Slang:* trash. *See also* **destroy.**

vanguard *noun*
1. A leading contestant or sure winner ▸ favorite, front-runner, leader, number one. *Informal:* shoo-in. **2.** The position of greatest advancement or importance ▸ cutting edge, fore, lead. *See* **forefront. 3.** One that foreshadows or prepares for something else ▸ herald, precursor. *See* **forerunner** (1).

vanilla *adjective*
▸ plain, unadorned, unvarnished. *See* **bare** (1).

vanish *verb*
▸ dissolve, fade, wane. *See* **disappear** (1). *See synonym note at* **disappear.**

vanished *adjective*
▸ mislaid, missing. *See* **lost** (2).

vanishment *noun*
▸ dissipation, expiration, waning. *See* **disappearance.**

vanity *noun*
1. Exaggerated love for oneself or belief in one's own importance ▸ conceit, narcissism. *See* **egotism.** *See synonym note at* **egotism. 2.** The condition or quality of being useless or ineffective ▸ fruitlessness, unprofitableness, uselessness, vainness. *See* **futility.**

vanquish *verb*
▸ conquer, surmount, triumph over. *See* **defeat** (1). *See synonym note at* **defeat.**

vanquisher *noun*
▸ master, victor. *See* **conqueror** (1).

vanquishing *adjective*
▸ champion, winning. *See* **victorious.**

vanquishment *noun*
▸ overthrow, trouncing, waterloo. *See* **defeat.**

vantage *noun*
1. A factor conducive to superiority and success ▸ head start, start. *See* **advantage** (1). **2.** A dominating position, as in a conflict ▸ edge, drop, upper hand. *See* **advantage** (3). **3.** The position from which something is observed or considered ▸ aspect, point of view, standpoint. *See* **viewpoint.**

vapid *adjective*
▸ bland, jejune. *See* **insipid** (1).

vapidity *or* **vapidness** *noun*
1. A lack of excitement, liveliness, or interest ▸ blandness, drabness, lifelessness. *See* **dullness** (1). **2.** The state or quality of being insipid ▸ innocuousness, wateriness. *See* **insipidity** (1).

vapor *noun*
▸ fog, mist. *See* **haze** (1).

vaporize *verb*
▸ burn off, volatilize. *See* **evaporate** (1).

vaporous *or* **vapory** *adjective*
▸ ethereal, gauzy, transparent. *See* **sheer**[2] (1). *See synonym note at* **sheer**[2].

variable *adjective*
1. Capable of or liable to change ▸ inconstant, uncertain, unstable. *See* **changeable** (1). **2.** Marked by whim or impulse ▸ fickle, impulsive, mercurial. *See* **capricious. 3.** Lacking consistency or regularity in quality or performance ▸ inconsistent, patchy, unsteady. *See* **uneven** (1).

variance *noun*
1. The condition of being unlike or dissimilar ▸ contrast, discrepancy, divergence. *See* **difference** (1). 2. A state of disagreement and disharmony ▸ clash, difference, discord. *See* **conflict** (1). *See synonym note at* **conflict**. 3. The quality of being made of many different elements, forms, kinds, or individuals ▸ diversity, heterogeneousness, variousness. *See* **variety** (1).

variant *noun*
One that is slightly different from others of the same kind or designation ▸ adaptation, permutation. *See* **variation** (1).

variant *adjective*
1. Not like another in nature, quality, amount, or form ▸ contrasting, divergent, separate. *See* **different** (1). 2. Capable of or liable to change ▸ uncertain, unsettled, variable. *See* **changeable** (1).

variation *noun*
1. One that is slightly different from others of the same kind or designation ▸ adaptation, alteration, alternative, development, form, modification, permutation, variant, variety, version. 2. The condition of being unlike or dissimilar ▸ contrast, discrepancy, divergence, variance. *See* **difference** (1). *See synonym note at* **difference**. 3. The process or result of making or becoming different ▸ alteration, modification, mutation. *See* **change** (1). 4. A departing from what is prescribed ▸ aberration, divergence. *See* **deviation** (1).

varicolored *adjective*
▸ colorful, many-hued, polychromatic. *See* **multicolored**.

varied *adjective*
▸ diverse, miscellaneous, sundry. *See* **various** (1). *See synonym note at* **various**.

variegate *verb*
▸ bar, striate, stripe. *See* **streak**.

variegated *adjective*
1. Having many different colors ▸ colorful, polychromatic. *See* **multicolored**. 2. Consisting of a number of different kinds ▸ diverse, miscellaneous, sundry. *See* **various** (1).

variegation *noun*
▸ diversity, heterogeneousness. *See* **variety** (1).

variety *noun*
1. The quality of being made of many different elements, forms, kinds, or individuals ▸ disparateness, diverseness, diversification, diversity, heterogeneity, heterogeneousness, miscellaneousness, multifariousness, multiformity, multiplicity, variance, variegation, variousness. 2. A collection of various things ▸ hodgepodge, jumble, mishmash. *See* **assortment** (1). 3. A class that is defined by the common attribute or attributes possessed by all its members ▸ ilk, mold, species. *See* **kind**². 4. One that is slightly different from others of the same kind or designation ▸ adaptation, permutation. *See* **variation** (1).

variform *adjective*
▸ crooked, nonuniform. *See* **irregular** (1).

various *adjective*
1. Consisting of a number of different kinds ▸ assorted, disparate, divers, diverse, diversified, heterogeneous, miscellaneous, mixed, motley, multifarious, multiform, sundry, varied, variegated. *See also* **complex**. 2. Not like another in nature, quality, amount, or form ▸ contrasting, divergent, separate. *See* **different** (1). 3. Consisting of a number more than two or three but less than many ▸ some, few. *See* **several** (1). 4. Having many aspects, uses, or abilities ▸ many-sided, multifaceted. *See* **versatile** (1). 5. Distinguished from others by nature or qualities ▸ individual, separate, several. *See* **distinct** (1). *See synonym note at* **distinct**.

✛ CORE SYNONYMS: *various, miscellaneous, heterogeneous, mixed, varied, assorted.* These adjectives mean consisting of a number of different kinds. *Various* is the most general: *a news program that covers various topics. Miscellaneous* implies a varied, often haphazard combination: *is selling postcards and miscellaneous novelties. Heterogeneous* emphasizes diversity and dissimilarity: *a heterogeneous urban population. Mixed* suggests a combination of differing but not necessarily conflicting elements: *a mixed program of baroque and contemporary music. Varied* stresses absence of uniformity: *"The assembly was large and varied, containing clergy and laity, men and women"* (Nicholas P.S. Wisemen). *Assorted* often suggests the purposeful arrangement of different but complementary elements: *a pretty arrangement of assorted flowers.*

variousness *noun*
▸ diversity, heterogeneousness, variegation. *See* **variety** (1).

varnish *verb*
1. To apply a coating to ▸ glaze, lacquer, shellac. *See* **finish** (7). 2. To give a bright sheen or luster to ▸ burnish, glaze, polish. *See* **gloss**¹ (1). 3. To give a deceptively attractive appearance to ▸ gild, sugarcoat, veneer. *See* **color** (4).

varnish *noun*
1. A final coating ▸ glaze, lacquer, shellac. *See* **finish** (3). 2. A surface shininess ▸ luster, polish, shine. *See* **gloss**¹ (1).

vary *verb*
1. To make different ▸ alter, modify, turn. *See* **change** (1). 2. To become different ▸ fluctuate, modify, turn. *See* **change** (2). 3. To change or fluctuate within limits ▸ range, run. *See* **go** (7). 4. To be unlike or dissimilar ▸ depart, diverge. *See* **differ** (1). *See synonym note at* **differ**. 5. To fail to be in accord ▸ contrast, disagree, discord. *See* **conflict**. 6. To turn away from a prescribed course of action or conduct ▸ digress, stray. *See* **deviate** (1).

varying *adjective*
▸ fluid, unsettled, variable. *See* **changeable** (1).

vassal *noun*
▸ serf, servant. *See* **slave** (1).

vast *adjective*
▸ behemoth, colossal, gigantic, massive, mighty. *See*

enormous. *See synonym note at* **enormous.**

vastly *adverb*
▸ exceedingly, extremely, highly. *See* **very.**

vastness *noun*
▸ hugeness, immensity, tremendousness. *See* **enormousness.**

vat *noun*
A large vessel used to hold or store liquids ▸ barrel, basin, cask, cistern, keg, tank, tub, vessel.

vatic *or* **vatical** *or* **vaticinal** *adjective*
▸ divinitory, oracular, sibylline. *See* **prophetic.**

vaticinate *verb*
▸ divine, foretell. *See* **prophesy.** *See synonym note at* **prophesy.**

vaticination *noun*
▸ oracle, soothsaying. *See* **prophecy.**

vaticinator *noun*
▸ diviner, fortuneteller, seer, soothsayer. *See* **prophet.**

vault¹ *noun*
1. A burial place or receptacle for human remains ▸ catacomb, crypt, tomb. *See* **grave¹. 2.** A place where something is deposited for safekeeping ▸ archive, storehouse, warehouse. *See* **depository.**

vault² *verb*
To move off the ground by a muscular effort of the legs and feet ▸ leap, spring. *See* **jump** (1).

vault *noun*
The act of jumping ▸ jump, pounce, leap, spring. *See also* **fall.**

vaunt *verb*
To talk with excessive pride ▸ bluster, swagger. *See* **boast** (1). *See synonym note at* **boast.**

vaunt *noun*
Boasting talk or behavior ▸ brag, gasconade. *See* **boast.**

vaunter *noun*
▸ boaster, bragger. *See* **braggart.**

vector *noun*
The compass direction in which a ship or aircraft moves ▸ bearing, course, heading. *See also* **direction.**

veer *verb*
1. To turn aside sharply from a straight course ▸ slant, zigzag. *See* **swerve** (1). **2.** To turn away from a prescribed course of action or conduct ▸ digress, stray. *See* **deviate** (1). *See synonym note at* **deviate. 3.** To change the direction or course of ▸ deviate, divert, shift. *See* **turn** (2). **4.** To turn aside, especially from the main subject in writing or speaking ▸ ramble, stray, wander. *See* **digress** (1).

vegetate *verb*
▸ loiter, lounge, slack off. *See* **idle** (1).

vegetation *noun*
The plants of an area or region ▸ flora, plant life, verdure.

vehemence *or* **vehemency** *noun*
▸ ferocity, fury, violence. *See* **intensity.**

vehement *adjective*
▸ concentrated, fierce, furious. *See* **intense** (1). *See synonym note at* **intense.**

veil *noun*
1. A covering that obscures or hides something ▸ cloak, cover, mantle, screen, shroud. *See also* **cover, façade. 2.** Clothes or other personal effects, such as makeup, worn to conceal one's identity ▸ costume, guise, mask. *See* **disguise** (1).

veil *verb*
1. To surround and cover completely so as to obscure ▸ clothe, enshroud, invest. *See* **wrap** (2). **2.** To prevent something from being known ▸ enshroud, mask. *See* **conceal** (1). **3.** To change or modify so as to prevent recognition of the true identity or character of ▸ camouflage, dissemble, mask. *See* **disguise.** *See synonym note at* **disguise.**

vein *noun*
1. An inherent, contrasting or unexpected quality, especially in a person's character ▸ strain, streak. *See synonym note at* **streak.** *See also* **disposition, vein. 2.** A temporary state of mind or feeling ▸ humor, temper. *See* **mood** (1). **3.** A distinctive way of expressing oneself ▸ manner, mode, tone. *See* **style** (1). **4.** A tube that contains a body fluid ▸ canal, duct. *See* **vessel** (2).

velocity *noun*
Rate of motion or performance ▸ pace, speed, tempo. *Informal:* clip.

venal *adjective*
▸ dishonest, mercenary, praetorian. *See* **corrupt** (2).

venality *noun*
▸ dishonesty, improbity. *Informal:* crookedness. *See* **corruption** (2).

vend *verb*
1. To offer for sale ▸ handle, peddle. *See* **sell** (1). **2.** To travel about selling goods ▸ hawk, huckster, peddle.

vendor *or* **vender** *noun*
▸ peddler, salesclerk. *See* **seller.**

veneer *noun*
A deceptive appearance ▸ guise, mask, pretense. *See* **façade** (2).

veneer *verb*
1. To cover with a different material ▸ clad, surface. *See* **face** (2). **2.** To give a deceptively attractive appearance to ▸ gild, sugarcoat, varnish. *See* **color** (4).

venerability *noun*
▸ beatitude, sanctity. *See* **holiness.**

venerable *adjective*
1. Deserving honor, respect, or admiration ▸ deserving, respectable, worthy. *See* **admirable. 2.** Belonging to, existing, or occurring in times long past ▸ ancient, antiquated, archaic. *See* **old** (1). **3.** Regarded with particular reverence or respect, especially by a religion ▸ hallowed, sacred. *See* **holy** (1). **4.** Raised to or occupying a high position or rank ▸ elevated, lofty. *See* **exalted** (1).

venerate *verb*
▸ adore, idolize, worship. *See* **revere.** *See synonym note at* **revere.**

veneration *noun*
1. The act of adoring, especially reverently ▸ adoration, idolization, reverence, worship. *See also* **devo-**

tion, praise. **2.** Great respect or high public esteem accorded as a right or as due ▸ homage, obeisance. *See* **honor** (1). *See synonym note at* **honor.**

venerational *adjective*
▸ pious, reverential, worshipful. *See* **reverent.**

vengeance *noun*
▸ counteraction, reciprocation, reprisal. *See* **retaliation.**

vengeful *adjective*
▸ avenging, spiteful, unforgiving. *See* **vindictive** (1).

vengefulness *noun*
The quality or condition of being vindictive ▸ revenge, spite, spitefulness, vindictiveness. *See also* **resentment.**

venial *adjective*
▸ forgivable, remissible. *See* **pardonable.**

venom *noun*
▸ canker, toxin. *See* **poison** (1).

venomous *adjective*
1. Capable of injuring or killing by poison ▸ noxious, toxic, virulent. *See* **poisonous** (1). *See synonym note at* **poisonous. 2.** Characterized by intense ill will or spite ▸ evil, wicked. *See* **malevolent** (1). **3.** So sharp as to cause mental pain ▸ caustic, scathing, sharp, vitriolic. *See* **biting.**

venomousness *noun*
▸ maliciousness, vindictiveness. *See* **malevolence.**

vent *noun*
An open space allowing passage ▸ orifice, tunnel. *See* **hole** (2).

vent *verb*
1. To utter publicly ▸ disclose, divulge, voice. *See* **air** (2). *See synonym note at* **air. 2.** To put into words ▸ express, state, utter. *See* **say** (1). **3.** To discharge material, as vapor or fumes, usually suddenly and violently ▸ give forth, issue, release. *See* **emit** (1).

ventilate *verb*
1. To expose to circulating air ▸ aerate, air, wind. **2.** To utter publicly ▸ disclose, divulge, voice. *See* **air** (2).

ventilated *adjective*
▸ breezy, gusty. *See* **airy** (3).

ventilation *noun*
▸ statement, utterance, verbalization. *See* **expression** (1).

venture *verb*
1. To express at the risk of rebuff or criticism ▸ adventure, brave, chance, dare, hazard, presume, pretend, risk. *Idioms:* make bold, take the liberty. **2.** To place something at risk, as in a game of chance ▸ bet, stake, wager. *See* **gamble** (2). **3.** To take a risk in the hope of gaining advantage ▸ speculate. *See* **gamble** (3).

venture *noun*
1. Something undertaken, especially something requiring extensive planning and work ▸ endeavor, enterprise, project, undertaking. *See also* **task. 2.** An exciting undertaking ▸ enterprise, odyssey. *See* **adventure. 3.** An undertaking depending on chance ▸ risk,

speculation, wager. *See* **gamble** (1). **4.** Something risked on an uncertain outcome ▸ pool, wager. *See* **bet** (1).

venture capital *noun*
▸ financing, funding, stake. *See* **capital** (1).

venturer *noun*
One who seeks adventure ▸ adventurer, daredevil, quester. *See also* **builder.**

venturesome *or* **venturous** *adjective*
1. Willing to take risks ▸ daring, enterprising. *See* **adventurous** (1). *See synonym note at* **adventurous. 2.** Involving possible risk, loss, or injury ▸ chancy, hazardous, risky. *See* **dangerous.**

venturesomeness *or* **venturousness** *noun*
▸ adventurousness, audacity, boldness, fearlessness. *See* **daring.**

veracious *adjective*
1. Marked by uprightness in principle and action ▸ aboveboard, truthful. *See* **honest** (1). **2.** Conforming exactly to fact ▸ correct, exact, precise. *See* **accurate** (1).

veracity *or* **veraciousness** *noun*
Correspondence with fact or truth ▸ accuracy, accurateness, authenticity, correctness, credibility, exactitude, exactness, faithfulness, fidelity, genuineness, realness, reliability, truth, truthfulness, validity, veridicality, verity. *See also* **certainty.**

verbal *adjective*
1. Relating to, consisting of, or having the nature of words ▸ lexical, linguistic, wordy. **2.** Expressed or produced in speech or by the voice ▸ spoken, vocal, voiced. *See* **oral. 3.** Employing the very same words as another ▸ undeviating, verbatim, word-for-word. *See* **literal** (1).

verbalism *noun*
▸ locution, phraseology, wordage. *See* **wording.**

verbalization *noun*
1. The act or an instance of expressing in words ▸ statement, utterance. *See* **expression** (1). **2.** The faculty, act, or product of speaking ▸ talk, utterance. *See* **speech** (1).

verbalize *verb*
1. To express oneself in speech ▸ speak, talk, vocalize. **2.** To put into words ▸ express, state, utter. *See* **say** (1).

verbatim *adjective*
Employing the very same words as another ▸ undeviating, unvarnished, word-for-word. *See* **literal** (1).

verbatim *adverb*
In an exact manner ▸ literally, precisely. *See* **exactly** (1).

verbiage *noun*
▸ pleonasm, redundancy. *See* **wordiness.**

verbose *adjective*
▸ long-winded, periphrastic, redundant. *See* **wordy** (1).

verbosity *or* **verboseness** *noun*
▸ pleonasm, redundancy, wordage. *See* **wordiness.**

verboten *adjective*
▸ banned, outlawed, prohibited. *See* **forbidden.**

verdict *noun*
► edict, judgment, pronouncement. *See* **ruling.**
verdure *noun*
The plants of an area or region ► flora, plant life, vegetation.
verge *noun*
A line or area where something ends or abruptly changes ► brink, fringe, margin. *See* **border** (1). *See synonym note at* **border.**
verge *verb*
1. To be contiguous or next to ► border, bound, join, meet. *See* **adjoin** (1). 2. To put or form a border on ► edge, rim. *See* **border** (1).
verge on *verb*
To attempt to equal or surpass, as in quality of amount ► approach, challenge. *See* **rival** (1).
veridical *adjective*
1. Consistently telling the truth ► truthful, veracious. 2. Conforming exactly to fact ► correct, exact, precise. *See* **accurate** (1).
veridicality *noun*
► authenticity, correctness, truth, validity. *See* **veracity.**
verification *noun*
1. That which confirms ► authentication, corroboration, proof, substantiation. *See* **confirmation** (2). 2. An act of confirming officially ► approval, ratification, sanction. *See* **confirmation** (1).
verify *verb*
1. To assure the certainty or validity of ► authenticate, corroborate, substantiate, validate. *See* **confirm** (1). *See synonym note at* **confirm.** 2. To establish as true or genuine through evidence ► confirm, substantiate, validate. *See* **prove** (1). 3. To confirm formally as true, accurate, or genuine ► attest, testify, witness. *See* **certify** (1).
verily *adverb*
► genuinely, indeed, truly. *See* **really.**
verisimilitude *noun*
Appearance of truth or authenticity ► believability, color, credibility, credibleness, creditability, creditableness, plausibility, plausibleness. *See also* **truth, veracity.**
veritable *adjective*
► genuine, true. *Slang:* kosher. *See* **authentic** (1).
veritably *adverb*
► actually, indeed, truly. *See* **really.**
verity *noun*
► correctness, truth, validity. *See* **veracity.**
vermin *noun*
► dregs, rabble, ragtag and bobtail. *See* **riffraff.**
vernacular *noun*
1. A system of terms used by a people sharing a history and culture ► dialect, tongue. *See* **language** (1). 2. A variety of a language that differs from the standard form ► jargon, lingo. *See* **dialect** (1). *See synonym note at* **dialect.** 3. Specialized expressions indigenous to a particular field, subject, trade, or subculture ► jargon, lingo, patois. *See* **language** (2).

versant *adjective*
Having good knowledge of something ► acquainted, conversant, familiar, versed. *Idiom:* up on. *See also* **accustomed, informed.**
versatile *adjective*
1. Having many aspects, uses, or abilities ► all-around, all-purpose, all-round, many-sided, multifaceted, multipurpose, multitalented, protean, various. 2. Capable of adapting or being adapted ► adaptive, flexible, malleable. *See* **adaptable.**

✦ **CORE SYNONYMS:** *versatile, all-around, many-sided, multifaceted.* These adjectives mean having many aspects, uses, or abilities: *a versatile writer; an all-around athlete; a many-sided subject; a multifaceted undertaking.*

verse *noun*
► poetry, rhyme. *See* **poem** (1).
versed *adjective*
1. Having good knowledge of something ► acquainted, conversant, familiar, versant. *Idiom:* up on. *See also* **accustomed, informed.** 2. Skilled or knowledgeable through long practice ► practiced, seasoned. *See* **experienced.** 3. Showing evidence of schooling, training, or experience ► informed, lettered, literate. *See* **educated** (1). *See synonym note at* **educated.**
versicolor *or* **versicolored** *adjective*
► colorful, polychromatic, variegated. *See* **multicolored.**
versifier *noun*
► muse, troubadour. *See* **poet.**
version *noun*
1. A recounting of past events ► account, description, report. *See* **story** (1). 2. A restating of something in other, especially simpler, words ► restatement, translation. *See* **paraphrase.** 3. One that is slightly different from others of the same kind or designation ► adaptation, permutation. *See* **variation** (1).
vertex *noun*
► apex, height, peak. *See* **climax** (1).
vertical *adjective*
At right angles to the horizon or to level ground ► on end, perpendicular, plumb, standing, upright. *See also* **erect, steep.**

✦ **CORE SYNONYMS:** *vertical, upright, perpendicular, plumb.* These adjectives mean being at right angles to the horizon or to level ground. *Vertical* and *upright* are often used to signify contrast with what is horizontal: *wallpaper with vertical stripes; an upright column. Perpendicular* and *plumb* are generally used to specify an angle of precisely 90 degrees: *a perpendicular escarpment; careful to make the doorjambs plumb.*

◄ **ANTONYM:** *horizontal*

vertiginous *adjective*
1. Producing dizziness or vertigo ► dizzy, dizzying, giddy, sickening. *See synonym note at* **giddy.** *See also* **steep.** 2. Having a sensation of whirling or falling

▸ dazed, lightheaded, reeling. *See* **dizzy** (1).

vertiginousness *noun*
▸ giddiness, unsteadiness, wooziness. *See* **dizziness.**

vertigo *noun*
▸ lightheadedness, unsteadiness, wooziness. *See* **dizziness.**

verve *noun*
1. A lively, emphatic, eager quality or manner ▸ life, vigor, vivaciousness. *See* **spirit** (1). *See synonym note at* **spirit. 2.** Passionate devotion to or interest in a cause or subject ▸ fervor, passion, zeal. *See* **enthusiasm** (1). **3.** Capacity for work or vigorous activity ▸ might, potency, power. *See* **energy.**

very *adverb*
To a high degree ▸ acutely, awfully, decidedly, dreadfully, eminently, exceedingly, exceptionally, extra, extremely, greatly, highly, hugely, intensely, most, notably, particularly, vastly. *Informal:* awful, mighty. *See also* **absolutely, completely, considerably, really, unusually.**

very *adjective*
1. Strictly distinguished from others ▸ exact, precise. **2.** Considered apart from anything else ▸ mere. **3.** Being one and not another; not different in nature or identity ▸ identical, selfsame. *See* **same** (1).

vessel *noun*
1. A conveyance that travels over water ▸ bark, barque, boat, craft, ship, watercraft. **2.** A tube that contains a body fluid ▸ artery, blood vessel, canal, capillary, duct, vein. **3.** An object, such as a carton, can, or jar, in which material is held or carried ▸ container, holder, receptacle, repository. *See also* **depository, package. 4.** A large vessel used to hold or store liquids ▸ barrel, cask, tub. *See* **vat.**

vest *verb*
▸ drape, robe. *See* **clothe** (1).

vested *adjective*
▸ deep-seated, entrenched, ingrained, inveterate. *See* **confirmed** (1).

vestige *noun*
▸ record, remains, trace. *See* **trace** (1).

vestment *noun*
Clothing worn by members of a religious order ▸ habit, robe.

vet *noun*
One who has had long experience in a given activity or capacity ▸ old hand, past master, veteran. *Informal:* old-timer. *See also* **expert.**

veteran *noun*
One who has had long experience in a given activity or capacity ▸ old hand, past master, vet. *Informal:* old-timer. *See also* **expert.**

veteran *adjective*
Skilled or knowledgeable through long practice ▸ practiced, seasoned. *See* **experienced.**

veto *verb*
To prevent or forbid authoritatively ▸ blackball, block, negative, stop, turn down. *Slang:* nix. *Idiom:* turn

thumbs down on. *See also* **abolish, decline, forbid, prevent, refuse**[1].

vex *verb*
1. To trouble the nerves or peace of mind of, especially by repeated vexations ▸ bother, irritate, nettle. *See* **annoy** (1). *See synonym note at* **annoy. 2.** To cause emotional suffering or painful sorrow to ▸ disturb, grieve, hurt. *See* **distress** (1). **3.** To make complex, intricate, or perplexing ▸ entangle, perplex, tangle. *See* **complicate.**

vexation *noun*
1. The act of annoying or the state of being annoyed ▸ bother, irritation, provocation. *See* **annoyance** (1). **2.** Something that annoys ▸ bother, irritant, nuisance. *See* **annoyance** (2). **3.** A state of physical or mental suffering ▸ agony, misery, wretchedness. *See* **distress** (1).

vexatious *or* **vexing** *adjective*
▸ bothersome, galling, irksome, troublesome. *See* **disturbing.**

viable *adjective*
▸ practicable, workable. *See* **possible** (1). *See synonym note at* **possible.**

viands *noun*
▸ bread, meat, nourishment. *See* **food.**

vibe *noun*
Slang A general impression produced by a predominant quality or characteristic ▸ atmosphere, aura, mood. *See* **air** (4).

vibrancy *noun*
▸ might, potency, power. *See* **energy.**

vibrant *adjective*
1. Very brisk, alert, and full of high spirits ▸ effervescent, high-spirited, perky. *See* **lively** (1). **2.** Having or producing a full, deep, or rich sound ▸ resounding, ringing, sonorous. *See* **resonant. 3.** Full of color ▸ bright, rich, vivid. *See* **colorful** (1).

vibrate *verb*
1. To move to and fro in short, jerky movements ▸ quiver, tremble, twitter. *See* **shake** (1). **2.** To move back and forth ▸ swing, vacillate, waggle. *See* **sway** (1). *See synonym note at* **sway. 3.** To shine intensely and blindingly ▸ blaze, throb. *See* **glare** (2).

vibrating *adjective*
Marked by or affected with tremors ▸ quaking, quivering, shaking. *See* **tremulous** (1).

vibrating *noun*
A nervous shaking of the body ▸ quiver, shake, twitch. *See* **tremor** (2).

vibration *noun*
1. *Slang* A general impression produced by a predominant quality or characteristic ▸ atmosphere, aura, mood. *See* **air** (4). **2.** A nervous shaking of the body ▸ quake, shudder, twitch. *See* **tremor** (2).

vicar *noun*
▸ ecclesiastic, minister, parson. *See* **cleric.**

vice *noun*
1. Degrading, immoral acts or habits ▸ depravity, perversion, wickedness. *See* **corruption** (1). **2.** The

quality or sate of being morally bad or objectionable ▸ iniquity, wickedness. *See* **evil** (1).

vicinity *noun*
1. A surrounding area ▸ locale, surroundings. *See* **environment** (1). 2. A particular geographic area ▸ neighborhood, place. *See* **locality** (1). 3. Approximate size or amount ▸ range. *Informal:* neighborhood.

vicious *adjective*
1. Morally objectionable ▸ immoral, sinful. *See* **evil** (1). 2. Characterized by intense ill will or spite ▸ evil, wicked. *See* **malevolent** (1). 3. Inflicting suffering or pain ▸ brutal, fierce, savage. *See* **cruel** (1). *See synonym note at* **cruel.**

viciousness *noun*
▸ venomousness, vindictiveness. *See* **malevolence.**

vicissitude *noun*
1. Something that obstructs progress and requires great effort to overcome ▸ complication, hardship, rigor. *See* **difficulty** (1). *See synonym note at* **difficulty.** 2. The process or result of making or becoming different ▸ modification, mutation, variation. *See* **change** (1).

victim *noun*
1. One that is made to suffer injury, loss, or death ▸ casualty, martyr, prey, quarry, statistic, sufferer, wounded. *See also* **fatality, scapegoat, unfortunate.** 2. A person who is easily deceived or victimized ▸ butt, pushover, tool. *See* **dupe** (1). 3. Something offered to a deity as part of a religious rite ▸ immolation, oblation. *See* **offering** (1).

victimization *noun*
▸ deceit, hoax, swindle. *See* **cheat** (1).

victimize *verb*
1. To get something by deceitful trickery ▸ bilk, defraud, swindle. *See* **cheat** (1). 2. To offer as a sacrifice ▸ immolate, sacrifice. 3. To treat wrongfully or harmfully ▸ exploit, ill-treat, maltreat. *See* **abuse** (1).

victimizer *noun*
▸ cheater, swindler, trickster. *See* **cheat** (2).

victor *noun*
1. One that conquers ▸ master, subjugator. *See* **conqueror** (1). 2. One that wins a contest or competition ▸ champion, medalist. *See* **winner** (1).

Victorian *adjective*
Marked by excessive concern for modesty or propriety ▸ priggish, prissy, strait-laced. *See* **prudish.**
Victorian *noun*
One excessively concerned with being proper, modest, or righteous ▸ Mrs. Grundy, priss, puritan. *See* **prude.**

victorious *adjective*
Being the winner in a contest or struggle ▸ champion, conquering, triumphal, triumphant, vanquishing, winning.

victory *noun*
▸ knockout, triumph, win. *See* **conquest.** *See synonym note at* **conquest.**

victuals *noun*
▸ edibles, fare, nourishment. *See* **food.**

videlicet *adverb*
▸ specifically, viz. *See* **namely.**

vie *verb*
▸ contend, race, rival. *See* **compete.** *See synonym note at* **compete.**

view *noun*
1. An act of directing the eyes on an object ▸ contemplation, look, regard, sight. *See also* **gaze, watch.** 2. That which is or can be seen ▸ landscape, lookout, outlook, panorama, perspective, picture, prospect, scene, scenery, sight, spectacle, tableau, vista. *Idiom:* field of vision. 3. The position from which something is observed or considered ▸ outlook, perspective, point of view, standpoint. *See* **viewpoint.** 4. The act of examining carefully or critically ▸ check, inspection, scrutiny. *See* **examination** (1). 5. Something thought to be true ▸ notion, persuasion, sentiment. *See* **belief** (1). *See synonym note at* **belief.** 6. What one intends to do or achieve ▸ end, goal, objective. *See* **intention.**
view *verb*
1. To direct the eyes on an object ▸ contemplate, eye. *See* **look** (1). 2. To look at or study carefully or critically ▸ investigate, peruse, scrutinize. *See* **examine** (1). 3. To look upon in a particular way ▸ consider, deem. *See* **regard** (1).

viewable *adjective*
▸ observable, perceivable, visual. *See* **visible** (1).

viewer *noun*
Someone who sees something occur ▸ audience, eyewitness, seer, witness.

viewpoint *noun*
The position from which something is observed or considered ▸ angle, aspect, eye, facet, frame of reference, hand, light, outlook, part, perspective, phase, point of view, position, regard, respect, side, slant, stand, standpoint, vantage, view. *See also* **belief, posture.**

viga *noun*
▸ crossbeam, girder, timber. *See* **beam** (2).

vigil *noun*
▸ monitoring, stakeout, vigilance. *See* **lookout** (1).

vigilance *noun*
1. The condition of being alert ▸ caution, wariness, watchfulness. *See* **alertness.** 2. The act of carefully watching ▸ monitoring, stakeout, watch. *See* **lookout** (1).

vigilant *adjective*
▸ wakeful, wide-awake. *See* **alert** (1). *See synonym note at* **alert.**

vigor *noun*
1. A lively, emphatic, eager quality or manner ▸ life, verve, vivaciousness. *See* **spirit** (1). *See synonym note at* **spirit.** 2. Passionate devotion to or interest in a cause or subject ▸ fervor, passion, zeal. *See* **enthusiasm** (1). 3. Capacity for work or vigorous activity ▸ might, potency, power. *See* **energy.**

vigorous *adjective*
1. Possessing, exerting, or displaying energy ▸ brisk, lively, strenuous. *See* **energetic.** 2. Full of vigor ▸ ro-

bust, strapping, sturdy. *See* **lusty** (1). **3.** Full of or displaying force ▶ dynamic, powerful, strong. *See* **forceful** (1). **4.** Having good health ▶ hardy, robust. *See* **healthy** (1). *See synonym note at* **healthy.**

vigorously *adverb*
▶ energetically, forcefully, powerfully. *See* **hard** (1).

vigorousness *noun*
▶ might, potency, power. *See* **energy.**

vile *adjective*
1. So objectionable as to deserve condemnation ▶ abhorrent, disgusting, loathsome. *See* **offensive** (1). **2.** Covered with or stained by dirt ▶ filthy, squalid, unclean. *See* **dirty** (1). **3.** Having or proceeding from low moral standards ▶ low, squalid. *See* **sordid.**

vileness *noun*
▶ monstrosity, odiousness, unsightliness. *See* **ugliness** (1).

vilification *noun*
▶ defamation, denigration, slander. *See* **libel.**

vilify *verb*
1. To make harmful and often untrue statements about ▶ calumniate, defame, slander. *See* **malign.** *See synonym note at* **malign. 2.** To attack with harsh, often insulting language ▶ assail, blaspheme. *See* **revile.**

villa *noun*
A house in the country ▶ chalet, cottage, country home, country house, dacha, estate, manor. *See also* **home.**

village *noun*
A small group of dwellings, usually in a rural area ▶ community, hamlet, settlement, small town. *See also* **city.**

villager *noun*
▶ denizen, occupant, resident. *See* **inhabitant.**

villain *noun*
1. A mean, worthless character in a story or play ▶ *Slang:* bad guy, heavy. **2.** One that performs evil acts ▶ scoundrel, wrongdoer. *See* **evildoer. 3.** A perversely mean, cruel, or wicked person ▶ beast, devil, monster. *See* **fiend.**

villainous *adjective*
1. Utterly reprehensible in nature or behavior ▶ depraved, miscreant, perverse. *See* **corrupt** (1). **2.** Perversely mean, cruel, or wicked ▶ devilish, diabolical, satanic. *See* **fiendish.**

villainy *or* **villainousness** *noun*
▶ depravity, perversion, vice. *See* **corruption** (1).

villeinage *noun*
▶ enslavement, servility, thrall. *See* **slavery.**

vim *noun*
1. A lively, emphatic, eager quality or manner ▶ life, verve, vivaciousness. *See* **spirit** (1). *See synonym note at* **spirit. 2.** Capacity for work or vigorous activity ▶ might, potency, power. *See* **energy.**

vincible *adjective*
▶ defenseless, helpless, unprotected. *See* **vulnerable** (1).

vinculum *noun*
▶ ligature, link, tie. *See* **bond** (2).

vindicate *verb*
1. To show to be just, right, or valid ▶ excuse, justify, rationalize. *Idiom:* make a case for. **2.** To free from a charge of guilt ▶ acquit, exonerate, purge. *See* **clear** (9). **3.** To support against arguments, attack, or criticism ▶ justify, maintain. *See* **defend** (2). **4.** To defend, maintain, or insist on the recognition of ▶ assert, demand. *See* **claim** (1). **5.** To exact revenge for or from ▶ pay off, repay. *See* **avenge.**

vindication *noun*
1. A freeing or clearing from accusation or guilt ▶ exoneration, justification. *See* **exculpation. 2.** A statement that justifies or defends something, such as a past action or policy ▶ defense, plea. *See* **apology** (1).

vindictive *adjective*
1. Disposed to seek revenge ▶ avenging, implacable, revengeful, spiteful, unforbearing, unforgiving, vengeful. *See also* **resentful. 2.** Characterized by intense ill will or spite ▶ evil, wicked. *See* **malevolent** (1).

vindictiveness *noun*
1. The quality or condition of being vindictive ▶ revenge, spite, spitefulness, vengefulness. *See also* **resentment. 2.** A desire to harm others or to see others suffer ▶ venomousness, viciousness. *See* **malevolence.**

vintage *adjective*
1. Characterized by enduring excellence, appeal, and importance ▶ ageless, antique, classic, classical, enduring, historic, timeless. *See also* **old. 2.** Relating to, identifying, or setting apart an individual or group ▶ characteristic, distinctive, particular. *See* **special** (1).

vintage *noun*
The produce harvested from the land ▶ fruit, yield. *See* **harvest** (1).

violate *verb*
1. To fail to fulfill a promise or conform to a regulation ▶ breach, break, contravene, infringe, overstep, transgress. **2.** To compel another to participate in or submit to a sexual act ▶ assault, force, molest, rape, ravish. **3.** To spoil or mar the sanctity of ▶ defile, desecrate, despoil, pollute, profane. *See also* **debase, dirty, disgrace. 4.** To refuse or fail to obey ▶ defy, transgress. *See* **disobey.**

violation *noun*
1. An act of breaking a law or of nonfulfillment of an obligation ▶ infraction, infringement. *See* **breach** (1). *See synonym note at* **breach. 2.** An act of disrespect toward something regarded as sacred ▶ blasphemy, desecration, profanation. *See* **sacrilege.**

violence *noun*
1. Energy that overcomes resistance ▶ might, power, strength. *See* **force** (1). **2.** Concentrated power or force, as of effort, opinion, or emotion ▶ ferocity, fury, vehemence. *See* **intensity.**

violent *adjective*
1. Accomplished by force ▶ coercive, forced, forcible. *Informal:* strong-arm. **2.** Extreme in activity, strength, or effect ▶ fierce, furious. *See* **intense** (1). *See synonym note at* **intense. 3.** Violently disturbed or agitated, as by storms ▶ roily, turbulent, wild. *See* **rough** (2).

violently *adverb*
With force and violence ▸ coercively, forcibly. *Idioms:* against one's will, by force, under duress.

VIP *noun*
▸ notability, personage. *Slang:* big shot. *See* **dignitary.**

virago *noun*
▸ harpy, shrew. *See* **scold.**

virgin *adjective*
1. Morally beyond reproach ▸ modest, pure, virginal. *See* **chaste. 2.** Being in a natural state ▸ raw, unrefined. *See* **crude** (1).

virgin *noun*
A pure, uncorrupted person ▸ angel, lamb. *See* **innocent** (1).

virginal *adjective*
1. Morally beyond reproach ▸ modest, pure, virgin. *See* **chaste. 2.** Free from evil and corruption ▸ pure, uncorrupted, untainted. *See* **innocent** (1).

virginity *noun*
▸ modesty, purity, virtue. *See* **chastity.**

virile *adjective*
▸ male, mannish, masculine. *See* **manly.**

virility *noun*
▸ maleness, manhood, manliness. *See* **masculinity.**

virtual *adjective*
▸ conceptual, hypothetical. *See* **theoretical** (2).

virtue *noun*
1. A particularly good or beneficial quality ▸ asset, beauty, distinction, merit, strength. *See also* **advantage, excellence, quality. 2.** The quality or state of being morally sound ▸ probity, rightness. *See* **good** (1). **3.** The condition of being chaste ▸ modesty, purity, virginity. *See* **chastity. 4.** A level of superiority that is usually high ▸ stature, value. *See* **merit** (1).

virtuoso *or* **virtuosa** *noun*
▸ musician, performer. *See* **player** (2).

virtuous *adjective*
1. In accordance with principles of right or good conduct ▸ principled, right-minded. *See* **ethical.** *See synonym note at* **ethical. 2.** Morally beyond reproach ▸ modest, pure, virginal. *See* **chaste. 3.** Regarded with particular reverence or respect, especially by a religion ▸ hallowed, sacred. *See* **holy** (1).

virtuousness *noun*
1. The quality or state of being morally sound ▸ probity, virtue. *See* **good** (1). **2.** The condition of being chaste ▸ modesty, purity, virginity. *See* **chastity.**

virulence *or* **virulency** *noun*
▸ acrimony, bitterness, rancor. *See* **resentment** (1).

virulent *adjective*
1. Capable of injuring or killing by poison ▸ noxious, toxic, venomous. *See* **poisonous** (1). *See synonym note at* **poisonous. 2.** Bitingly hostile ▸ bitter, embittered, rancorous. *See* **resentful. 3.** Capable of transmission by infection ▸ communicable, infectious, transmittable. *See* **contagious.**

virus *noun*
1. Anything that is injurious, destructive, or fatal ▸ canker, toxin. *See* **poison** (1). **2.** A tiny organism usually producing disease ▸ bug, microbe. *See* **germ** (1).

visa *noun*
▸ permit, warrant. *See* **license** (3).

visage *noun*
1. The front surface of the head ▸ countenance, features. *See* **face** (1). **2.** A disposition of the facial features that conveys meaning, feeling, or mood ▸ countenance, face, look. *See* **expression** (4). **3.** The way something or someone looks ▸ look, features, mien. *See* **appearance** (1).

vis-à-vis *noun*
One that has the same functions and characteristics as another ▸ counterpart, equivalent, opposite number.

viscera *noun*
Internal organs of the abdomen ▸ bowels, entrails, intestines. *Informal:* guts, insides.

visceral *adjective*
1. Arising from one's mental or spiritual being ▸ internal, inward. *See* **inner** (2). **2.** Derived from or prompted by a natural tendency or impulse ▸ inborn, intuitive. *See* **instinctive** (1). *See synonym note at* **instinctive.**

viscid *adjective*
▸ gelatinous, mucilaginous, viscid. *See* **viscous.**

viscidity *noun*
▸ sliminess, stickiness, thickness. *See* **viscosity.**

viscose *adjective*
▸ glutinous, mucilaginous, viscid. *See* **viscous.**

viscosity *noun*
The physical property of being viscous ▸ glutinousness, sliminess, stickiness, thickness, viscidity.

viscous *adjective*
Having a heavy, gluey quality ▸ gelatinous, glutinous, heavy, mucilaginous, syrupy, thick, viscid, viscose. *See also* **slimy, sticky.**

vise *noun*
▸ catch, clip, lock. *See* **fastener.**

visibility *noun*
The quality or degree of being visible or providing a clear view ▸ clarity, clearness, observability, perceptibility, visuality, visualness. *Idiom:* range of vision.

visible *adjective*
1. Capable of being seen ▸ discernible, observable, seeable, viewable, visual. *Idioms:* in sight (*or* view), on display (*or* view). *See also* **noticeable, perceptible. 2.** Readily seen, perceived, or understood ▸ evident, noticeable, obvious. *See* **apparent** (1).

vision *noun*
1. The faculty of seeing ▸ eye, eyesight, optics, seeing, sight. *See also* **view. 2.** Discernment or perception which is unusually competent or creative ▸ farsightedness, foreknowledge, foresight, imagination, innovation, inspiration, prescience. *Idioms:* breadth (*or* depth) of view. *See also* **brilliance, discernment, instinct, invention. 3.** An illusory mental image ▸ fancy, fantasy, illusion. *See* **dream** (1). **4.** Something that is foretold by or as if by supernatural means

▸ oracle, soothsaying. *See* **prophecy. 5.** A person regarded as physically attractive ▸ lovely, stunner. *See* **beauty** (1). **6.** A fervent hope ▸ desire, goal, wish. *See* **dream** (3).

vision *verb*
To form mental images of ▸ envision, fantasize, visualize. *See* **imagine** (1).

visionary *adjective*
1. Characterized by foresight or vision ▸ farsighted, foresighted, imaginative, inspired, insightful, intuitive, perceptive, prescient. *See also* **intelligent, inventive. 2.** Of, relating to, or in the nature of an illusion; lacking reality ▸ hallucinatory, illusory, phantasmagoric. *See* **illusive** (1). **3.** Existing only in the imagination ▸ chimerical, fanciful, unreal. *See* **imaginary. 4.** Of or relating to the foretelling of events by or as if by supernatural means ▸ divinitory, oracular, sibylline. *See* **prophetic. 5.** Given to daydreams or reverie ▸ fanciful, musing. *See* **dreamy** (1). **6.** Characterized by ideals that often conflict with practical considerations ▸ romantic, unrealistic, utopian. *See* **idealistic.**

visionary *noun*
A person inclined to be imaginative or idealistic but impractical ▸ fantasist, romantic, stargazer. *See* **dreamer** (1).

visit *verb*
1. To go to or seek out the company of someone in order to socialize ▸ call, come around, come by, come over, drop by, drop in, go by, go over, look in, look up, pop in, run in, see, stop by, stop in. *Idioms:* pay a visit (*or* a call). **2.** To remain as a guest or lodger ▸ sojourn, stay. *See* **lodge** (1). **3.** *Informal* To engage in spoken exchange ▸ discourse, talk. *See* **converse**[1]. **4.** To cause to undergo or bear (something unwelcome or damaging, for example) ▸ play, wreak. *See* **inflict.**

visit *noun*
1. An act or an instance of going or coming to see another ▸ call, get-together, look-in, social call, stay, stop, visitation. **2.** A remaining in a place as a guest or lodger ▸ sojourn, stay, stop, stopover.

visitant *noun*
1. A person or persons visiting one ▸ caller, company, guest, visitor. **2.** An immaterial supernatural being, especially the spirit of a dead person ▸ phantom, shade, specter. *See* **ghost** (1).

visitation *noun*
1. An act or an instance of going or coming to see another ▸ call, stop. *See* **visit** (1). **2.** A state of pain or anguish that tests one's resiliency and character ▸ crucible, ordeal, tribulation. *See* **trial** (1).

visitor *noun*
1. A person or persons visiting one ▸ caller, company, guest, visitant. **2.** One that arrives ▸ arrival, comer, newcomer. *See also* **addition, company. 3.** One who travels for pleasure ▸ sightseer, traveler, vacationer. *See* **tourist.**

visor *noun*
▸ brim, peak. *See* **bill**[2] (2).

vista *noun*
1. That which is or can be seen ▸ panorama, perspective. *See* **view** (2). **2.** A wide and open area, as of land, sky, or water ▸ extent, stretch, sweep. *See* **expanse** (1). **3.** A high structure or place commanding a wide view ▸ observatory, watchtower. *See* **lookout** (2).

visual *adjective*
1. Serving, resulting from, or relating to the sense of sight ▸ ocular, optic, optical, seeing. **2.** Capable of being seen ▸ perceivable, viewable. *See* **visible** (1).

visuality *noun*
▸ clarity, clearness, observability. *See* **visibility.**

visualize *verb*
▸ envision, fantasize, see. *See* **imagine** (1).

vital *adjective*
1. Having life ▸ animated, live, living. *See* **alive** (1). *See synonym note at* **alive. 2.** Full of vigor ▸ robust, strapping, sturdy. *See* **lusty** (1). **3.** Constituting or forming part of the essence of something ▸ constitutional, fundamental. *See* **essential** (2). **4.** Most important, influential, or significant ▸ chief, key, main, principal. *See* **primary** (1). **5.** Demanding immediate attention ▸ crucial, dire, pressing. *See* **urgent** (1).

vital force *noun*
▸ divine spark, soul, vitality. *See* **spirit** (2).

vitality *noun*
1. The vital principle or animating force within living beings ▸ soul, vital force. *See* **spirit** (2). **2.** Capacity for work or vigorous activity ▸ might, potency, power. *See* **energy.**

vitalize *verb*
1. To make alive ▸ animate, enliven, quicken, vivify. *See also* **elate, provoke. 2.** To give or impart vitality and energy to someone or something ▸ invigorate, stimulate. *See* **energize.**

vitalizing *adjective*
▸ bracing, energizing, exhilarating. *See* **invigorating.**

vitiate *verb*
1. To spoil the soundness or perfection of ▸ flaw, impair. *See* **damage. 2.** To ruin morally ▸ debase, demoralize, deprave, warp. *See* **corrupt** (1). *See synonym note at* **corrupt. 3.** To put an end to ▸ invalidate, negate, void. *See* **abolish** (1).

vitreous *or* **vitrescent** *adjective*
Of or resembling glass ▸ glasslike, glassy, hyaline. *See also* **translucent.**

vitriolic *adjective*
▸ caustic, scathing, sharp, truculent. *See* **biting.**

vituperate *verb*
▸ abuse, assail, execrate. *See* **revile.** *See synonym note at* **revile.**

vituperation *noun*
Sustained, harshly abusive language ▸ abuse, billingsgate, condemnation, contumely, denunciation, invective, obloquy, railing, revilement, reviling, scurrility, scurrilousness. *See also* **belittlement, curse, libel, tirade.**

vituperative *adjective*
▸ contumelious, invective, scurrilous. *See* **abusive.**

vivacious *adjective*
1. Very brisk, alert, and full of high spirits ▸ animated, chipper, perky. *See* **lively** (1). **2.** A lively, emphatic, eager quality or manner ▸ life, sparkle, verve. *See* **spirit** (1).

vivacity *or* **vivaciousness** *noun*
▸ life, verve, vivaciousness. *See* **spirit** (1).

vivid *adjective*
1. Full of color ▸ bright, rich, vibrant. *See* **colorful** (1). **2.** Evoking strong mental images through distinctiveness ▸ graphic, picturesque, striking. *See* **colorful** (1). **3.** Depicted in sharp and accurate detail ▸ explicit, realistic. *See* **graphic** (1). *See synonym note at* **graphic**. **4.** Serving to describe ▸ graphic, representative. *See* **descriptive**. **5.** Suggesting drama or a stage performance, as in emotionality or suspense ▸ melodramatic, sensational, spectacular. *See* **dramatic** (2).

vivify *verb*
To make alive ▸ animate, enliven, quicken, vitalize. *See also* **elate, energize, provoke.**

vivifying *adjective*
▸ bracing, energizing, exhilarating. *See* **invigorating.**

vixen *noun*
▸ harpy, shrew. *See* **scold.**

viz. *adverb*
▸ specifically, videlicet. *See* **namely.**

vocable *noun*
▸ expression, lexeme, word. *See* **term** (1).

vocabulary *noun*
1. All the words of a language ▸ lexicon, word-hoard. **2.** An alphabetical list of words often defined or translated ▸ dictionary, glossary, lexicon, wordbook. **3.** Specialized expressions indigenous to a particular field, subject, trade, or subculture ▸ jargon, lingo, patois. *See* **language** (2).

vocal *adjective*
1. Manifesting honesty and directness ▸ candid, plainspoken. *See* **frank. 2.** Expressed or produced in speech or by the voice ▸ spoken, verbal, voiced. *See* **oral. 3.** Characterized by, containing, or functioning as a vowel or vowels ▸ sonorant, vocalic, vowel.

vocalic *adjective*
Characterized by, containing, or functioning as a vowel or vowels ▸ sonorant, vocal, vowel.

vocalism *noun*
▸ enunciation, utterance, vocalization. *See* **voicing.**

vocalist *noun*
A person who sings ▸ singer, songster, songstress, voice. *Slang:* crooner, songbird. *See also* **player.**

vocalization *noun*
1. The faculty, act, or product of speaking ▸ talk, utterance. *See* **speech** (1). **2.** The use of the vocal organs to produce sound or speech ▸ enunciation, utterance. *See* **voicing. 3.** The act or an instance of expressing in words ▸ statement, utterance, verbalization. *See* **expression** (1).

vocalize *verb*
1. To express oneself in speech ▸ speak, talk, verbalize. **2.** To produce or make speech sounds ▸ enunciate,

sound. *See* **pronounce. 3.** To put into words ▸ express, state, utter. *See* **say** (1). **4.** To utter words or sounds in musical tones ▸ chant, warble. *See* **sing** (1).

vocation *noun*
1. An inner urge to pursue an activity or perform a service ▸ calling, mission. *See also* **dream, duty, fate. 2.** Activity pursued as a livelihood ▸ career, employment, occupation. *See* **business** (2).

vociferate *verb*
▸ bellow, holler, yell. *See* **shout.**

vociferation *noun*
Loud and insistent utterances or noisemaking, usually expressing disapproval ▸ brouhaha, clamor, hullabaloo, katzenjammer, outcry, rumpus, uproar. *Idiom:* hue and cry. *See also* **noise.**

vociferous *or* **vociferant** *adjective*
Offensively loud and insistent ▸ blatant, boisterous, clamorous, obstreperous, stentorian, strident. *Informal:* loudmouthed. *See also* **harsh, loud.**

✦ **CORE SYNONYMS:** *vociferous, blatant, boisterous, strident, clamorous.* These adjectives mean conspicuously and usually offensively loud and insistent. *Vociferous* suggests a noisy outcry, as of vehement protest: *vociferous complaints. Blatant* connotes coarse or vulgar noisiness: *"Up rose a blatant Radical"* (Walter Bagehot). *Boisterous* implies unrestrained noise, tumult, and often rowdiness: *boisterous youths. Strident* stresses offensive harshness, shrillness, or discordance: *a legislator with a strident voice.* Something *clamorous* is both vociferous and sustained: *a clamorous uproar.*

---

vogue *noun*
▸ fad, mode, trend. *See* **fashion** (1). *See synonym note at* **fashion.**

voice *noun*
1. The right or chance to express an opinion or participate in a decision ▸ input, say, suffrage, vote. *Informal:* say-so. **2.** The act or an instance of expressing in words ▸ statement, utterance, verbalization. *See* **expression** (1). **3.** A person who sings ▸ singer, songster, songstress. *See* **vocalist.**

voice *verb*
1. To put into words ▸ express, state, utter. *See* **say** (1). **2.** To utter publicly ▸ disclose, divulge, vent. *See* **air** (2). *See synonym note at* **air. 3.** To produce or make speech sounds ▸ enunciate, vocalize. *See* **pronounce.**

voiced *adjective*
▸ spoken, verbal, vocal. *See* **oral.**

voiceless *adjective*
1. Lacking the power or faculty of speech ▸ inarticulate, tongueless. *See* **mute** (1). **2.** Temporarily unable or unwilling to speak, as from shock or fear ▸ inarticulate, mute. *See* **speechless** (1).

voicing *noun*
The use of the vocal organs to produce sound or speech ▸ articulation, enunciation, pronunciation, saying, utterance, vocalism, vocalization. *See also* **speech.**

void *adjective*
1. Containing nothing ▸ bare, vacuous. *See* **empty** (1). *See synonym note at* **empty**. 2. Deprived of a quality or aspect that is desirable ▸ destitute, lacking, wanting. *See* **empty** (2).

void *noun*
1. Empty, unfilled space ▸ emptiness, vacuity. *See* **nothingness** (2). 2. A space in an otherwise solid mass ▸ hollow, vacuity. *See* **hole** (1). 3. An interval during which continuity is suspended ▸ hiatus, interim, lacuna. *See* **gap** (2). 4. A desolate sense of loss ▸ desolation, vacuum. *See* **emptiness** (2).

void *verb*
1. To remove the contents of ▸ clean out, evacuate. *See* **empty** (1). 2. To put an end to ▸ cancel, invalidate, nullify. *See* **abolish** (1). 3. To discharge wastes from the body ▸ excrete, purge. *See* **eliminate** (4).

voidance *noun*
▸ annulment, invalidation, nullification. *See* **abolition**.

volatile *adjective*
▸ fickle, impulsive, mercurial. *See* **capricious**.

volatilize *verb*
▸ burn off, vaporize. *See* **evaporate** (1).

volition *noun*
1. The mental faculty by which one deliberately chooses or decides ▸ free will, will. *See also* **spirit**. 2. The act, power, or right of choosing ▸ decision, discretion, option. *See* **choice** (1).

volitional *adjective*
▸ spontaneous, uncompelled. *See* **voluntary** (1).

volley *noun*
▸ cannonade, fusillade, storm. *See* **barrage**.

volubility *noun*
▸ articulateness, fluency, fluidity. *See* **eloquence**.

voluble *adjective*
1. Given to conversation ▸ garrulous, loquacious, talky. *See* **talkative**. 2. Fluently persuasive and forceful ▸ silver-tongued, smooth-spoken. *See* **eloquent** (1).

volume *noun*
1. A printed and bound work ▸ edition, tome. *See* **book** (1). 2. An issue of printed material offered for sale or distribution ▸ opus, title, work. *See* **publication** (2). 3. Great amount or dimension ▸ magnitude, size. *See* **bulk** (1). 4. The amount of space occupied by something ▸ extent, magnitude, proportions. *See* **size** (1).

voluminous *adjective*
1. Of full measure ▸ ample, capacious, wide. *See* **full** (3). 2. Characterized by abundance; as much as one needs or desires ▸ abundant, bounteous, plentiful. *See* **generous** (2). 3. Of large, often awkward size and weight ▸ cumbersome, heavy, oversized. *See* **bulky** (1).

voluntarily *adverb*
Of one's own free will ▸ by choice, freely, spontaneously, willfully, willingly. *Idioms:* of one's own accord, on one's own volition.

voluntary *adjective*
1. Of or relating to free exercise of the will ▸ sponta-
neous, uncompelled, unforced, volitional, willed, willful, willing. *See also* **free, independent**. 2. Contributing one's time without pay ▸ uncompensated, unsalaried, volunteer. *See* **unpaid** (1). 3. Done or said on purpose ▸ intentional, premeditated, purposeful, willful. *See* **deliberate** (1). *See synonym note at* **deliberate**.

voluntary *noun*
Someone who offers his or her services freely ▸ volunteer.

volunteer *verb*
To put before another for acceptance ▸ extend, proffer. *See* **offer** (1).

volunteer *adjective*
Contributing one's time without pay ▸ uncompensated, unsalaried, voluntary. *See* **unpaid** (1).

volunteer *noun*
Someone who offers his or her services freely ▸ voluntary.

voluptuary *noun*
A person devoted to pleasure and luxury ▸ hedonist, sensualist. *See* **sybarite**.

voluptuary *adjective*
Characterized by or devoted to pleasure and luxury as a lifestyle ▸ epicurean, hedonic, hedonistic, sybaritic, voluptuous.

voluptuous *adjective*
1. Characterized by or devoted to pleasure and luxury as a lifestyle ▸ epicurean, hedonic, hedonistic, sybaritic, voluptuary. 2. Relating to, suggestive of, or appealing to sense gratification ▸ epicurean, sensual, sensualistic, sensuous. *See synonym note at* **sensuous**. *See also* **sybaritic**. 3. Relating to the desires and appetites of the body, especially sexual desire ▸ physical, sexual, sexy. *See* **sensual** (2).

voluptuousness *noun*
1. The quality or condition of being sensuous ▸ sensualism, sensuality, sensuousness. 2. The quality or condition of being sensual or being preoccupied with bodily desires ▸ sexuality, suggestiveness. *See* **sensuality** (1).

vomit *verb*
1. To eject the contents of the stomach through the mouth ▸ heave, retch, spit up, throw up. *Informal:* puke. *Slang:* barf, boot, chuck, hurl, ralph, spew, upchuck, yack, yarf. *Idioms:* blow chunks, do the technicolor yawn, drive (*or* ride) the porcelain bus, hug the throne, worship the porcelain god. 2. To send forth confined matter violently ▸ disgorge, spew. *See* **erupt** (1).

voodoo *verb*
▸ enchant, mesmerize, spellbind. *See* **charm** (2).

voracious *adjective*
1. Having an insatiable appetite for an activity or pursuit ▸ avid, edacious, gluttonous, greedy, insatiable, obsessive, omnivorous, rapacious, ravenous, unappeasable, wolfish. *See also* **enthusiastic, greedy**. 2. Wanting to eat or drink more than one can reasonably consume ▸ greedy, ravenous. *See* **glutton-**

ous (1). **3.** Desiring or craving food ▸ ravenous, starving. *See* **hungry** (1).

✦ **CORE SYNONYMS:** *voracious, gluttonous, rapacious, ravenous.* These adjectives mean having an insatiable appetite for an activity or pursuit: *a voracious reader of history; a gluttonous consumer of fine foods; a rapacious acquirer of competing businesses; a politician ravenous for power.*

---

voracity *noun*
The quality or condition of being voracious ▸ avidity, avidness, edacity, insatiability, obsessiveness, omnivorousness, rapaciousness, rapacity, ravenousness, voraciousness. *See also* **appetite, enthusiasm, greed, lust.**

vortex *noun*
▸ maelstrom, eddy, swirl. *See* **whirlpool** (1).

votary *noun*
▸ fanatic, zealot. *See* **devotee** (1).

vote *verb*
1. To select by vote for an office ▸ elect. *See also* **choose. 2.** To cast a vote ▸ ballot, poll. *Idiom:* go to the polls. **3.** To make a choice from a number of alternatives ▸ elect, pick, vote for. *See* **choose** (1).

vote down *verb*
To keep from being admitted, included, or considered ▸ eliminate, keep out, rule out. *See* **exclude** (1).

vote *noun*
The right or chance to express an opinion or to decide ▸ input, say, suffrage, voice. *Informal:* say-so.

voter *noun*
One who votes ▸ balloter, elector. *Idiom:* member of the electorate.

vouch *verb*
1. To confirm formally as true, accurate, or genuine ▸ attest, certify, testify, vouch for, witness. *Idiom:* bear witness to. **2.** To present evidence in support of ▸ buttress, substantiate. *See* **back** (2).

vouchsafe *verb*
1. To let have as a favor, prerogative, or privilege ▸ accord, award, concede, give, grant. *See also* **yield. 2.** To bring oneself down to a level considered inappropriate to one's dignity ▸ deign, descend, stoop. *See* **condescend** (1).

vow *noun*
A declaration that one will or will not do a certain thing ▸ covenant, pledge, warrant. *See* **promise** (1).

vow *verb*
To guarantee by a solemn promise ▸ promise, troth. *See* **pledge** (1). *See synonym note at* **pledge.**

vowel *adjective*
Characterized by, containing, or functioning as a vowel or vowels ▸ sonorant, vocal, vocalic.

voyage *noun*
1. A journey undertaken with a specific objective ▸ pilgrimage, tour. *See* **expedition** (1). **2.** The act of traveling from one place to another ▸ flight, passage, progress. *See* **journey.**

voyage *verb*
To make or go on a journey ▸ peregrinate, travel, trek. *See* **journey.**

vulgar *adjective*
1. Lacking high station or birth ▸ common, humble, unwashed. *See* **lowly** (1). **2.** Lacking in delicacy or refinement ▸ indelicate, unbecoming, unrefined. *See* **coarse** (1). **3.** Offensive to accepted standards of decency ▸ bawdy, coarse, lewd, profane. *See* **obscene** (1). **4.** Tastelessly showy ▸ flashy, garish, loud. *See* **gaudy.**

vulgarian *noun*
▸ chuff, Philistine, yahoo. *See* **boor.** *See synonym note at* **boor.**

vulgarity *noun*
1. The quality or state of being obscene ▸ filthiness, profanity, smuttiness, vulgarness. *See* **obscenity** (1). **2.** Something that is offensive to accepted standards of decency ▸ dirt, sleaze, smut. *See* **obscenity** (2).

vulgarness *noun*
▸ filthiness, profanity, vulgarity. *See* **obscenity** (1).

vulnerability *or* **vulnerableness** *noun*
▸ endangerment, susceptibility, unprotectedness. *See* **exposure** (1).

vulnerable *adjective*
1. Susceptible to physical or emotional injury or attack ▸ assailable, attackable, defenseless, helpless, pregnable, susceptible, susceptive, unprotected, vincible. *Idioms:* like a sitting duck, open to attack. *See also* **insecure, open. 2.** Tending to incur ▸ prone, subject, susceptible. *See* **liable** (2).

W

wackiness *or* **whackiness** *noun*
Slang Foolish behavior ▸ folly, silliness, tomfoolery. *See* **foolishness.**

wacky *or* **whacky** *adjective*
1. *Slang* Displaying a lack of forethought and good sense ▸ daft, idiotic, ludicrous. *See* **foolish. 2.** *Slang*
Afflicted with or exhibiting irrationality and mental unsoundness ▸ daft, dotty, off. *See* **insane.**

wad *noun*
1. An irregularly shaped mass of indefinite size ▸ clod, nugget. *See* **lump**[1] (1). **2.** *Informal* An indeterminately great amount or number ▸ bunch, multiplicity.

Informal: bushel. *See* **heap** (3). **1.** *Informal* A large sum of money ▸ mint. *Informal:* pile. *See* **fortune** (7). **2.** Something used to fill a hole, space, or container ▸ cork, stop. *See* **plug** (1).

wadding *noun*
▸ padding, stuffing. *See* **filler** (1).

wade *verb*
To walk in a laborious way ▸ plod, slop, toil. *See* **trudge**.

wade in *or* **into** *verb*
To start work on vigorously ▸ dive into, go at, plunge into. *See* **attack** (2).

waffle *verb*
Informal To use evasive or deliberately vague language ▸ hedge, shuffle. *See* **equivocate** (1).

waffle *noun*
Informal The use or an instance of equivocal language ▸ euphemism, prevarication. *See* **equivocation** (1).

waft *verb*
1. To move smoothy, continuously, and effortlessly ▸ coast, drift, slip. *See* **glide** (1). **2.** To move in or on the wind ▸ drift, flap. *See* **blow¹** (2).

waft *noun*
A natural movement or current of air ▸ blast, gust, zephyr. *See* **wind¹** (1).

wag¹ *verb*
To move back and forth ▸ swing, switch, waggle. *See* **sway** (1).

wag *noun*
An expressive, meaningful bodily movement ▸ indication, signal. *See* **gesture** (1).

wag² *noun*
A person whose words or actions provoke or are intended to provoke amusement or laughter ▸ clown, comedian, jester. *See* **joker**.

wage *noun*
Payment for work done ▸ compensation, earnings, emolument, fee, hire, pay, payment, recompense, remuneration, salary, stipend.

wage *verb*
To engage in (a war or campaign, for example) ▸ carry on, carry out, conduct. *See also* **oppose**.

wage earner *noun*
▸ jobholder, staffer, worker. *See* **employee**.

wager *noun*
1. An undertaking depending on chance ▸ risk, speculation. *See* **gamble** (1). **2.** Something risked on an uncertain outcome ▸ pool, venture. *See* **bet** (1). *See synonym note at* **bet**.

wager *verb*
1. To make a bet ▸ bet, gamble, game, lay, play. *Idiom:* put one's money on something. **2.** To place something at risk, as in a game of chance ▸ bet, stake, venture. *See* **gamble** (2). **3.** To look forward to confidently ▸ await, look for. *See* **expect** (1).

wages *noun*
Informal Something justly deserved ▸ compensation, deserts, reward. *See* **due** (1).

wage slave *noun*
▸ menial, toiler, worker. *See* **laborer**.

waggish *adjective*
▸ frolicsome, impish, puckish, sportive. *See* **mischievous** (1).

waggle *verb*
1. To move back and forth ▸ swing, vacillate, wobble. *See* **sway** (1). **2.** To move the arms or wings up and down ▸ flutter, wave. *See* **flap** (1). **3.** To move along in a crouching or prone position ▸ creep, wiggle, worm. *See* **crawl** (1).

waif *noun*
▸ foundling, stray. *See* **orphan**.

wail *verb*
1. To shed tears ▸ howl, sob, weep. *See* **cry** (1). *See synonym note at* **cry**. **2.** To cry loudly, as an upset baby does ▸ holler, howl, yowl. *See* **bawl** (1). **3.** To utter or emit a long, mournful, plaintive sound ▸ moan, ululate, yowl. *See* **howl** (1). **4.** To speak or say loudly ▸ cry out, scream, yell. *See* **shout**.

wail *noun*
1. A long, mournful cry ▸ bay, ululation, yowl. *See* **howl** (1). **2.** A loud call or cry ▸ holler, scream, yell. *See* **shout**.

wailing *noun*
▸ blubbering, lamentation, sobbing, weeping. *See* **cry** (1).

wait *verb*
1. To look forward to confidently ▸ anticipate, await, wait for. *See* **expect** (1). **2.** To continue to be in a place ▸ bide, linger, tarry. *See* **remain** (1). *See synonym note at* **remain**. **3.** *Informal* To put off until a later time ▸ delay, postpone, suspend. *See* **defer¹**.

wait on *or* **upon** *verb*
1. To work and care for ▸ attend, do for, minister to, serve. *See also* **cater, help, tend², work**. **2.** To place food before someone ▸ cater, serve. *See also* **give, distribute**.

waive *verb*
1. To give up or leave completely ▸ abdicate, relinquish, surrender. *See* **abandon** (1). *See synonym note at* **abandon**. **2.** To put off until a later time ▸ delay, postpone, suspend. *See* **defer¹**.

waiver *noun*
1. A giving up of a possession, claim, or right ▸ abdication, relinquishment, resignation. *See* **abandonment** (1). **2.** The act of putting off or the condition of being put off ▸ deferment, postponement, suspension. *See* **delay** (1).

wake¹ *verb*
To cease or cause to cease sleeping ▸ arouse, awake, awaken, get up, rouse, stir, wake up, waken. *See also* **rise**.

wake *noun*
A watch over the body of a dead person before burial ▸ watch.

wake² *noun*
Something that follows or is drawn along behind ▸ tail, trail, train. *See also* **stream**.

wakeful *adjective*

1. Not in a state of sleep or unable to sleep ▶ awake, unsleeping, wide-awake. *Idiom:* tossing and turning. *See also* **restless. 2.** Marked by an absence of sleep ▶ sleepless, slumberless. **3.** Vigilantly attentive ▶ open-eyed, vigilant. *See* **alert** (1).

wakefulness *noun*

▶ caution, wariness, watchfulness. *See* **alertness.**

waken *verb*

1. To cease or cause to cease sleeping ▶ awake, rouse, stir. *See* **wake**[1]. **2.** To induce or elicit a reaction ▶ kindle, stir (up). *See* **arouse** (1).

wale *noun*

▶ blister, boil, pock. *See* **welt** (1).

walk *noun*

1. An act of walking ▶ amble, constitutional, hike, march, perambulation, promenade, ramble, saunter, stroll, tramp, turn, wander. **2.** A manner of walking ▶ footfall, footstep, gait, pace, step, stride, tread.

walk *verb*

To go on foot ▶ ambulate, foot, pace, step, stride, tread. *Slang:* hoof. *Idioms:* foot it, hoof it. *See also* **hike, rove, stroll, trudge.**

walk out *verb*

1. To cease working in support of demands made upon an employer ▶ picket, strike. *Idioms:* go (*or* go out) on strike, stop work. **2.** To abandon a former position or commitment ▶ back down, retreat, skip. *See* **renege.**

walk through *verb*

To do or perform repeatedly so as to master ▶ exercise, run through. *See* **practice** (1).

walkaway *noun*

1. An easy victory ▶ rout, walkover. *See* **runaway** (1). **2.** *Informal* An easily accomplished task ▶ pushover, snap, walkover. *See* **breeze** (2).

walking stick *noun*

▶ cane, staff, stave. *See* **stick** (2).

walk of life *noun*

▶ career, employment, occupation. *See* **business** (2).

walkout *noun*

A cessation of work by employees in support of demands made upon their employer ▶ job action, sickout, strike, work stoppage, work to rule.

walkover *noun*

1. An easy victory ▶ rout, walkaway. *See* **runaway** (1). **2.** *Informal* An easily accomplished task ▶ pushover, snap, walkaway. *See* **breeze** (2).

wall *noun*

1. A solid structure that encloses an area or separates one area from another ▶ barrier, partition. *See also* **border, screen. 2.** Something that blocks entry or passage ▶ barrier, blockage, hindrance. *See* **bar** (1).

wall *verb*

1. To separate with or as if with a wall ▶ fence, partition. **2.** To confine within a limited area ▶ box (in), cage, fence (in). *See* **enclose** (1). *See synonym note at* **enclose.**

wallop *verb*

1. *Informal* To deliver a sudden, sharp blow to ▶ jab, sock, whack. *See* **hit** (1). **2.** *Informal* To render totally ineffective by decisive defeat ▶ crush, overcome, overpower, rout. *See* **overwhelm** (1).

wallop *noun*

1. *Informal* A sudden heavy stroke ▶ crack, hit, swat, whack. *See* **blow**[2] (1). **2.** *Slang* A stimulating or intoxicating effect ▶ *Informal:* punch, sting. *See* **kick. 3.** *Informal* A strong, pleasant feeling of excitement or stimulation ▶ lift. *Slang:* bang, jollies, kick. *See* **thrill** (1).

walloping *adjective*

Informal Of extraordinary size and power ▶ behemoth, colossal, gigantic, mighty, monumental. *See* **enormous.**

wallow *verb*

1. To move about in an indolent or clumsy manner ▶ flounder, roll about, roll around, welter. **2.** To take extravagant pleasure ▶ indulge, revel, wallow. *See* **luxuriate.**

waltz *verb*

▶ coast, sail, zip. *See* **breeze.**

wampum *noun*

Informal Something, such as coins or printed bills, used as a medium of exchange ▶ currency. *Slang:* dough, moola. *See* **money** (1).

wan *adjective*

1. Appearing worn and exhausted ▶ gaunt, worn. *See* **haggard. 2.** Lacking color ▶ bloodless, lurid, sallow. *See* **pale** (1).

wan *verb*

To lose normal coloration; turn pale ▶ bleach, sallow. *See* **pale.**

wand *noun*

▶ baton, stake, switch. *See* **stick** (1).

wander *verb*

1. To move about at random, especially over a wide area ▶ drift, meander, traipse. *See* **rove.** *See synonym note at* **rove. 2.** To walk at a leisurely pace ▶ promenade, saunter. *Informal:* mosey. *See* **stroll. 3.** To turn aside, especially from the main subject in writing or speaking ▶ ramble, stray, veer. *See* **digress** (1).

wander *noun*

An act of walking ▶ ramble, stroll. *See* **walk** (1).

wanderer *noun*

▶ nomad, roamer, vagabond. *See* **hobo.**

wandering *adjective*

1. Traveling about, especially in search of adventure ▶ itinerant, roving. *See* **errant** (1). **2.** Without a fixed or regular course ▶ stray, wayward. *See* **erratic. 3.** Not proceeding straight to the point or object ▶ circuitous, devious, roundabout. *See* **indirect** (1). **4.** Without aim, purpose, or intent ▶ pointless, purposeless, rambling. *See* **aimless. 5.** Leading the life of a person without a fixed domicile; moving from place to place ▶ traveling, vagabond. *See* **nomadic.**

wane *verb*

1. To become or cause to become less active or intense

▸ die (away, down, off, *or* out), ebb, lapse. *See* **subside** (1). **2.** To become lower in quality, character, or condition ▸ atrophy, degenerate, worsen. *See* **deteriorate** (1). **3.** To become or cause to become gradually less ▸ diminish, dwindle, lessen. *See* **decrease. 4.** To lose strength or power ▸ decline, fail, weaken. *See* **fade** (1). **5.** To pass out of sight either gradually or suddenly ▸ dissolve, fade. *See* **disappear** (1).

wane *noun*
1. The process of becoming less active or intense ▸ letup, slackening. *See* **waning. 2.** Descent to a lower level or condition ▸ decadence, decline, degeneration. *See* **deterioration** (1). **3.** The act or process of decreasing ▸ diminishment, reduction, slowdown. *See* **decrease.**

wangle *verb*
Informal To use stratagems in gaining an end ▸ engineer, finesse. *See* **maneuver** (2).

waning *noun*
The process of becoming less active or intense ▸ abatement, diminishment, easing, ebb, falling off, lapsing, letup, moderation, remission, slackening, subsidence, wane. *See also* **decrease.**

wannabe *noun*
Informal One who aspires ▸ aspirant, aspirer, dreamer, hopeful, seeker.

want *verb*
1. To have a strong longing for ▸ covet, yearn. *See* **desire** (1). *See synonym note at* **desire. 2.** To be without what is needed, required, or essential ▸ lack, need, require. *See synonym note at* **lack. 3.** To have as a need or prerequisite ▸ entail, involve, necessitate. *See* **demand** (2). **4.** To have an inclination to ▸ desire, wish. *See* **choose** (2).

want *noun*
1. The condition of lacking something ▸ absence, dearth, lack. *See also* **need, shortage. 2.** The condition of being extremely poor ▸ destitution, indigence, need. *See* **poverty** (1). **3.** Something asked for or needed ▸ desire, requirement. *See* **demand** (2).

wanting *adjective*
1. Lacking an essential element ▸ inadequate, incomplete. *See* **deficient** (1). **2.** Deprived of a quality or aspect that is desirable ▸ destitute, lacking, void. *See* **empty** (2). **3.** Not enough to meet a demand or requirement ▸ inadequate, short. *See* **insufficient** (1).

wanton *adjective*
1. Sexually unrestrained ▸ easy, fast, libertine, light, loose, promiscuous, reprobate, sluttish, trampy, unchaste, whorish. **2.** Not required, necessary, or warranted by the circumstances of the case ▸ excessive, gratuitous, reckless, supererogative, supererogatory, uncalled-for, unwarranted. *See also* **careless, obscene. 3.** Lacking in moral restraint ▸ dissolute, licentious, unbridled. *See* **abandoned** (2). **4.** Exceeding the bounds of morality, decency, or reason ▸ appalling, monstrous, shocking. *See* **outrageous.**

wanton *noun*
1. An immoral or licentious person ▸ debauchee,

debaucher, gigolo, libertine, profligate, rake, rakehell, reprobate, rip, rounder. *Slang:* swinger. *See also* **lecher, philanderer. 2.** A person, typically a woman, who is sexually promiscuous ▸ tramp, whore. *See* **slut.**

wantonness *noun*
▸ incontinence, unrestraint, wildness. *See* **abandon** (1).

war *noun*
1. A vying with others for victory ▸ contest, rivalry, struggle. *See* **competition** (1). **2.** An encounter between opposing military forces ▸ combat, confrontation, warfare. *See* **battle** (1).

war *verb*
To strive in opposition ▸ clash, combat, fight. *See* **contend** (1).

warble *verb*
▸ chant, vocalize. *See* **sing** (1).

war cry *noun*
▸ call to arms, rallying cry. *See* **cry** (2).

ward *noun*
1. A person who relies on another for support ▸ charge, dependent. **2.** The state of being detained by legal authority ▸ confinement, custody, detainment. *See* **detention. 3.** The act or a means of defending ▸ protection, safeguard, shield. *See* **defense** (1). **4.** One assigned to provide protection or keep watch over someone or something ▸ guardian, protector. *See* **guard** (1). **5.** The function of watching, guarding, or overseeing ▸ guardianship, supervision, tutelage. *See* **care** (2). **6.** An area in a city or town with distinctive characteristics ▸ community, district. *See* **neighborhood** (1).

ward *verb*
1. To keep safe from danger, attack, or harm ▸ protect, safeguard, secure. *See* **defend** (1). **2.** To prohibit from occurring by advance planning or action ▸ avert, forestall, rule out, ward off. *See* **prevent.**

ward off *verb*
To turn aside or drive away ▸ deflect, repulse, stave off. *See* **repel.**

warden *noun*
A guard or keeper of a prison ▸ jailer, turnkey. *Slang:* screw. *See also* **guard, police officer.**

wardrobe *noun*
▸ garb, guise, outfit. *See* **dress** (2).

ware *noun*
▸ commodity, line, merchandise. *See* **good** (2).

warehouse *noun*
A place where something is deposited for safekeeping ▸ depot, storehouse, treasury. *See* **depository.**

warehouse *verb*
To keep for future use ▸ put by, salt away, set by. *See* **save** (1).

warfare *noun*
1. A vying with others for victory ▸ contest, rivalry, struggle. *See* **competition** (1). **2.** An encounter between opposing military forces ▸ combat, confrontation, war. *See* **battle** (1). **3.** A state of disagreement and

disharmony ▸ clash, difference, discord. *See* **conflict** (1).

wariness *noun*
1. The condition of being alert ▸ caution, wakefulness, watchfulness. *See* **alertness**. 2. Careful forethought to avoid risk ▸ care, carefulness, precaution. *See* **caution** (1). 3. Cautious attentiveness ▸ caution, heed, watchfulness. *See* **care** (1). 4. Lack of trust ▸ cynicism, leeriness. *See* **distrust**.

warlike *adjective*
1. Inclined to act in an aggressive or hostile way ▸ belligerent, combative, pugnacious. *See* **aggressive** (1). 2. Of or inclined toward war ▸ martial, militaristic. *See* **military** (1).

warlock *noun*
▸ enchanter, magician, sorcerer. *See* **wizard** (1).

warm *adjective*
1. Showing or having enthusiasm ▸ fervent, rabid, zealous. *See* **enthusiastic** (1). 2. Pleasant and friendly in disposition ▸ cordial, friendly, genial. *See* **amiable**.

warmed-over *adjective*
▸ clichéd, overused, shopworn, tired. *See* **trite**.

warm-hearted *adjective*
1. Pleasant and friendly in disposition ▸ congenial, cordial, genial. *See* **amiable**. 2. Feeling or expressing sympathy or pity ▸ commiserative, compassionate, empathetic, understanding. *See* **sympathetic**. 3. Willing to give of oneself and one's possessions ▸ bighearted, magnanimous, unselfish. *See* **generous** (1).

warmongering *noun*
Hostile or warlike behavior or attitude ▸ belligerence, combativeness, saber-rattling. *See* **aggression** (1).

warmonger *adjective*
1. Inclined to act in an aggressive or hostile way ▸ combative, hawkish, warlike. *See* **aggressive** (1). 2. Of or inclined toward war ▸ martial, militaristic. *See* **military** (1).

warmth *noun*
1. The quality of being pleasant and friendly ▸ agreeability, congeniality, pleasantness. *See* **amiability**. 2. Powerful, intense emotion ▸ fervor, fire, heat. *See* **passion** (1). 3. Warmth or degree of warmth ▸ hotness, torridity. *See* **heat** (1).

warn *verb*
To notify someone of imminent danger or risk ▸ admonish, alarm, alert, caution, forewarn. *Idioms:* put on (*or* on one's) guard. *See also* **inform, threaten**.

warning *noun*
1. Advice to beware, as of a person or thing ▸ alarum, admonishment, admonition, caution, caveat, monition. *See also* **advice**. 2. An instance that warns or discourages prospective imitators ▸ caveat, lesson. *See* **example** (2). 3. A signal that warns of imminent danger ▸ alert, red flag. *See* **alarm** (1). 4. A phenomenon that serves as a sign of some future good or evil ▸ portent, prognostication, sign. *See* **omen**.

warning *adjective*
Giving warning ▸ admonishing, admonitory, cautionary, monitory.

warp *verb*
1. To ruin morally ▸ debase, demoralize, deprave. *See* **corrupt** (1). 2. To give an inaccurate view of by representing falsely or misleadingly ▸ fudge, misrepresent, pervert. *See* **distort** (1). 3. To cause to have a prejudiced view ▸ prejudice, prepossess. *See* **bias** (1). *See synonym note at* **bias**. 4. To alter and spoil the natural form or appearance of ▸ disfigure, misshape, twist. *See* **deform**. *See synonym note at* **deform**. 5. To move or cause to move in a bent or angular direction ▸ deflect, turn. *See* **bend** (2). 6. To curve or yield under pressure ▸ buckle, sag. *See* **bend** (3).

warp and woof *noun*
▸ fabric, grain, web. *See* **texture** (1).

warped *adjective*
▸ arched, bowed, curved, rounded. *See* **bent** (1).

warrant *noun*
1. An assumption of responsibility, as one given by a manufacturer, for the quality, worth, or durability of a product ▸ certification, guarantee, guaranty, surety, warranty. 2. A justifying fact or consideration ▸ justification, reason. *See* **basis** (2). 3. That which confirms ▸ authentication, corroboration, proof, verification. *See* **confirmation** (2). 4. Something given to guarantee the repayment of a loan or the fulfillment of an obligation ▸ collateral, security, token. *See* **pawn**[1]. 5. A declaration that one will or will not do a certain thing ▸ covenant, pledge, vow. *See* **promise** (1). 6. A document that gives permission to do something ▸ permit, visa. *See* **license** (3).

warrant *verb*
1. To assure the certainty or validity of ▸ authenticate, corroborate, substantiate, verify. *See* **confirm** (1). 2. To render certain ▸ ensure, secure. *See* **guarantee** (2). 3. To assume responsibility for the quality, worth, or durability of ▸ certify, stand behind. *See* **guarantee** (1). 4. To be an appropriate occasion for ▸ call for, occasion. *See* **justify** (2). 5. To make lawful ▸ decriminalize, legitimatize. *See* **legalize**.

warranted *adjective*
▸ legal, permitted, valid. *See* **lawful**.

warranty *noun*
1. An assumption of responsibility, as one given by a manufacturer, for the quality, worth, or durability of a product ▸ certification, guarantee, guaranty, surety, warrant. 2. Something given to guarantee the repayment of a loan or the fulfillment of an obligation ▸ collateral, security, token. *See* **pawn**[1].

warrior *noun*
One who engages in a combat or struggle ▸ belligerent, combatant, fighter, soldier. *See also* **aggressor, soldier**.

wart *noun*
▸ blister, boil, pock. *See* **welt** (1).

wary *adjective*
1. Trying attentively to avoid danger, risk, or error ▸ careful, cautious, chary, circumspect, forehanded, gingerly, prudent. 2. Vigilantly attentive ▸ vigilant, wide-awake. *See* **alert** (1). 3. Lacking trust or confi-

dence ▸ doubting, suspicious, untrusting. *See* **distrustful** (1).

wash *verb*

1. To make moist ▸ bathe, dampen, moisten, wet. **2.** To flow against or along ▸ bathe, lap, lave, lip. *See also* **flow**. **3.** To make the sound of moving or disturbed water ▸ lap, splash, swash. *See also* **burble, swish. 4.** To move along with or be carried away by the action of water ▸ drift, float. **5.** To rid of dirt, stains, trash, or other impurities ▸ cleanse, launder, lave. *See* **clean** (1). **6.** To impart color to ▸ dye, stain, tint. *See* **color** (1). **7.** *Informal* To prove valid under scrutiny ▸ hold up, prove out, stand up. *Idioms:* hold water, pass muster, ring true.

wash out *verb*

1. To be unsuccessful ▸ fall short, founder, miss the mark. *See* **fail** (1). **2.** To lose normal coloration; turn pale ▸ bleach, wan. *See* **pale**.

wash up *verb*

To cause the complete ruin or wreckage of ▸ demolish, torpedo, wreck. *See* **destroy** (1).

wash *noun*

Quality of light reflected or emitted ▸ hue, shade, tint. *See* **color** (1).

washed out *adjective*

▸ colorless, faded, pallid. *See* **pale** (1).

washed-up *adjective*

▸ done, done for, finished. *See* **through** (2).

washiness *noun*

▸ innocuousness, vapidness. *See* **insipidity** (1).

washout *noun*

1. An unsuccessful person or enterprise ▸ bust, fiasco, loser. *See* **failure** (1). **2.** Something that disappoints ▸ anticlimax, bust, letdown. *See* **disappointment** (2).

washy *adjective*

1. Lower than normal in strength or concentration due to admixture ▸ adulterated, watered-down. *See* **dilute**. **2.** Lacking vigor, intensity, or bite ▸ bland, jejune. *See* **insipid** (1).

waspish *adjective*

1. Having or showing a bad temper ▸ cranky, grouchy, peevish. *See* **ill-tempered. 2.** So sharp as to cause mental pain ▸ caustic, scathing, sharp, vitriolic. *See* **biting**.

waspishness *noun*

▸ crankiness, prickliness, tetchiness. *See* **temper** (1).

waste *verb*

1. To use, consume, spend, or expend thoughtlessly or carelessly ▸ dissipate, fool away, fritter away, riot away, splurge, squander, throw away, trifle away. *Slang:* blow. *See also* **consume, give. 2.** To spend time idly or pleasantly ▸ dawdle (away), trifle away. *See* **idle** (2). **3.** To fail to take advantage of ▸ miss, pass up. *See* **lose** (2). **4.** To engulf completely ▸ devour, ravage. *See* **consume** (1). **5.** To become downcast from longing or grief ▸ ebb, shrivel. *See* **languish** (1). **6.** *Slang* To cause the death of ▸ cut down, destroy, finish (off). *See* **kill**[1] (1). **7.** *Slang* To take the life of a person or persons unlawfully ▸ destroy, kill, slay. *See* **murder** (1).

waste away *verb*

To lose strength or power ▸ decline, fail, weaken. *See* **fade** (1).

waste *noun*

1. Excessive or imprudent expenditure ▸ prodigality, profusion, squander. *See* **extravagance** (1). **2.** A desolate or unproductive region ▸ badlands, wasteland. *See* **desert**[1]. **3.** A sad or tragic deprivation ▸ loss. *See also* **deprivation. 4.** Items or material discarded or rejected as useless or worthless ▸ litter, rubbish, trash. *See* **garbage** (1). **5.** Waste matter eliminated from the bowels ▸ dung, feces, ordure. *See* **excrement**.

waste *adjective*

Unable to support vegetation ▸ sterile, unfruitful, unproductive. *See* **barren** (2).

✦ CORE SYNONYMS: *waste, blow, dissipate, fritter away, squander.* These verbs mean to use, consume, spend, or expend thoughtlessly or carelessly: *wasted my inheritance; blew a fortune at the casino; dissipated their energies in pointless argument; frittering away her entire allowance; squandered his talent on writing jingles.*

◄ ANTONYM: *save*

---

wasted *adjective*

1. Appearing worn and exhausted ▸ drawn, emaciated, gaunt. *See* **haggard. 2.** *Slang* Stupefied, intoxicated, or otherwise influenced by the taking of drugs ▸ high, hopped-up, lit (up). *See* **drugged**.

wasteful *adjective*

▸ prodigal, profligate. *See* **extravagant** (1).

wastefulness *noun*

▸ lavishness, prodigality, squander. *See* **extravagance** (1).

wasteland *noun*

▸ badlands, waste. *See* **desert**[1].

waster *noun*

▸ profligate, spendthrift. *See* **wastrel** (1).

wastrel *noun*

1. A person who spends money or resources wastefully ▸ prodigal, profligate, scattergood, spendthrift, waster. **2.** A self-indulgent person who spends time avoiding work or other useful activity ▸ bum, drone, fainéant, idler, loafer, ne'er-do-well, shirker, slacker, sluggard. *Informal:* do-little, do-nothing, good-for-nothing, layabout, lazybones, lounger, no-good, sloth, slug. *Slang:* couch potato, deadbeat, slouch, slugabed.

watch *verb*

1. To look at or on attentively or carefully ▸ eye, observe, regard, scrutinize, see, survey. *Idioms:* have one's (*or* keep an) eye on, keep tabs on. *See also* **look. 2.** To pay regular and close attention to ▸ follow, monitor, observe, survey. *Idioms:* have one's (*or* keep an) eye on, keep tabs on. **3.** To have the care and supervision of ▸ look after, mind, see to. *See* **tend**[2] (1). *See synonym note at* **tend**[2].

watch out *verb*

To be careful ▸ beware, look out, mind. *Idioms:* be on

guard, be on the lookout, keep an eye peeled, take care (*or* heed).

watch over *verb*
To direct and watch over the work and performance of others ▸ monitor, oversee. *See* **supervise**. *See synonym note at* **supervise**.

watch *noun*
1. The act of observing, often for an extended time ▸ observance, observation, scrutiny, watching. *See also* **look**. 2. The act of carefully watching ▸ monitoring, stakeout, vigilance. *See* **lookout** (1). 3. One assigned to provide protection or keep watch over someone or something ▸ guardian, protector, ward. *See* **guard** (1). 4. A limited, often assigned period of activity, duty, or opportunity ▸ stint, shift, time. *See* **turn** (1). 5. A watch over the body of a dead person before burial ▸ wake.

watchdog *noun*
▸ guardian, protector, ward. *See* **guard** (1).

watcher *noun*
1. Someone who observes ▸ beholder, bystander, gaper, gawker, looker-on, observer, onlooker, spectator. *Slang:* rubbernecker. *See also* **guard**. 2. An agent assigned to observe and report on another ▸ shadow. *Informal:* tail. *See also* **detective**.

watchful *adjective*
1. Vigilantly attentive ▸ vigilant, wide-awake. *See* **alert** (1). *See synonym note at* **alert**. 2. Cautiously attentive ▸ heedful, mindful, observant. *See* **careful** (1).

watchfulness *noun*
1. The condition of being alert ▸ caution, wakefulness, wariness. *See* **alertness**. 2. Cautious attentiveness ▸ caution, heed, wariness. *See* **care** (1).

watching *noun*
The act of observing, often for an extended time ▸ observance, observation, scrutiny, watch.

watchman *noun*
▸ guardian, protector, ward. *See* **guard** (1).

watchtower *noun*
▸ crow's nest, observatory, post. *See* **lookout** (2).

watchword *noun*
▸ call to arms, war cry. *See* **cry** (2).

water *verb*
1. To lessen the strength of by or as if by admixture ▸ attenuate, weaken, water down. *See* **dilute**. 2. To fill with tears ▸ tear.

watercourse *noun*
1. A small stream ▸ creek, rill. *See* **brook**[1]. 2. A relatively large natural flow of water ▸ stream, tributary. *See* **river**.

watercraft *noun*
A conveyance that travels over water ▸ bark, barque, boat, craft, ship, vessel.

watered-down *adjective*
▸ adulterated, thin, washy. *See* **dilute**.

wateriness *noun*
▸ innocuousness, vapidness, washiness. *See* **insipidity** (1).

watering hole *noun*
Informal A public establishment that sells alcoholic drinks and often food, often from a counter ▸ inn, pub, saloon. *See* **bar** (2).

waterish *adjective*
1. Lower than normal in strength or concentration due to admixture ▸ adulterated, watered-down. *See* **dilute**. 2. Being weak in quality or substance ▸ bloodless, pallid. *See* **pale** (2). 3. Lacking vigor, intensity, or bite ▸ bland, jejune. *See* **insipid** (1).

waterless *adjective*
▸ moistureless, sere. *See* **dry** (1).

waterlogged *adjective*
▸ drenched, soaked, soggy. *See* **wet** (1).

waterloo *noun*
1. A disastrous defeat or ruin ▸ collapse, fall, downfall. 2. The act of defeating or the condition of being defeated ▸ overthrow, trouncing, vanquishment. *See* **defeat**.

watershed *noun*
The region drained by a river system ▸ drainage basin, watershed.

watery *adjective*
1. Lower than normal in strength or concentration due to admixture ▸ adulterated, watered-down. *See* **dilute**. 2. Being weak in quality or substance ▸ bloodless, pallid. *See* **pale** (2). 3. Lacking vigor, intensity, or bite ▸ bland, jejune. *See* **insipid** (1).

wattle *verb*
▸ braid, intertwine, twist. *See* **weave** (1).

wave *verb*
1. To move back and forth ▸ swing, vacillate, waggle. *See* **sway** (1). 2. To have or cause to have a curved or wavy surface ▸ corrugate, curl, curve, ripple, undulate. *See also* **bend, fold**. 3. To move or cause to move about while being fixed at one edge ▸ flap, flutter, fly. 4. To move the arms or wings up and down ▸ flutter, waggle. *See* **flap** (1). 5. To wield boldly and dramatically ▸ brandish, flourish, sweep. *See synonym note at* **flourish**. *See also* **handle**. 6. To move in or on the wind ▸ drift, flap, flutter. *See* **blow**[1] (2). 7. To make bodily motions so as to convey an idea or complement speech ▸ gesticulate, motion, sign, signal. *See* **gesture**.

wave *noun*
1. A ridge or swell of water, or a shape suggestive of such a swell ▸ breaker, comber, ripple, roller, swell, undulation, whitecap. *Idiom:* peaks and troughs. 2. An expressive, meaningful bodily movement ▸ indication, signal. *See* **gesture** (1).

waver *verb*
1. To shift from one attitude, interest, condition, or emotion to another ▸ dilly-dally, swing, vacillate. 2. To move back and forth ▸ swing, vacillate, waggle. *See* **sway** (1). *See synonym note at* **sway**. 3. To be irresolute in acting or doing ▸ falter, vacillate. *See* **hesitate**. *See synonym note at* **hesitate**. 4. To be uncertain, disbelieving, or skeptical about ▸ disbelieve, query, wonder. *See* **doubt** (1).

wavering *adjective*
1. Experiencing doubt ▸ hesitant, skeptical, uncertain.

See **doubtful** (2). **2.** Lacking stability ▸ shaky, unstable, unsteady. *See* **insecure** (2).

wavy *adjective*
Having a curved or ridged surface ▸ corrugated, curly, curvy, rippled, sinusoidal, waggly, wiggly.

wax¹ *noun*
A final coating ▸ lacquer, polish, varnish. *See* **finish** (3).

wax *verb*
To apply a coating to ▸ lacquer, polish, varnish. *See* **finish** (7).

wax² *verb*
1. To make or become greater or larger ▸ amplify, boost, enlarge. *See* **increase** (1). **2.** To come to be ▸ get (to be), grow (to be). *See* **become** (1).

waxen *or* **waxy** *adjective*
▸ bloodless, lurid, wan. *See* **pale** (1).

way *noun*
1. The approach used to do something ▸ fashion, formula, manner, method, mode, modus operandi, path, style, system, wise. *See also* **approach. 2.** A course affording passage from one place to another ▸ alley, avenue, boulevard, canal, channel, course, drive, expressway, footpath, freeway, highway, lane, pass, passage, passageway, path, road, roadway, route, street, superhighway, thoroughfare, thruway, trail, turnpike. **3.** A habitual way of behaving ▸ form, habit, practice. *See* **custom** (1). **4.** The manner in which one behaves ▸ comportment, conduct, deportment. *See* **behavior** (1). **5.** *Informal* An extent, measured or unmeasured, of linear space ▸ interval, length, stretch. *See* **distance** (1). **6.** The spatial path along which motion or orientation is referred ▸ course, route. *See* **direction** (1).

✦ **CORE SYNONYMS:** *way, method, system, manner, fashion, mode.* These nouns refer to the approach followed to accomplish a task or attain a goal. *Way* is the most general of these terms: *"It is absurd to think that the only way to tell if a poem is lasting is to wait and see if it lasts"* (Robert Frost). *Method* implies a detailed, logically ordered plan: *"I do not know of a better method for choosing a presidential nominee"* (Harry S. Truman). *System* suggests order, regularity, and coordination of methods: *"Of generalship, of strategic system . . . there was little or none"* (John Morely). *Manner* and *fashion* emphasize personal or distinctive behavior: *a clearly articulated manner of speaking; issuing orders in an arbitrary and abrasive fashion. Mode* often denotes a manner influenced by or arising from tradition or custom: *a nomadic mode of life.*

wayfaring *noun*
▸ passage, progress. *See* **journey.**

waylay *verb*
▸ ambuscade, bushwhack, surprise. *See* **ambush** (1). *See synonym note at* **ambush.**

wayward *adjective*
1. Marked by a disposition to oppose ▸ antagonistic, contradictory, hostile. *See* **contrary** (1). **2.** Marked by whim or impulse ▸ fickle, impulsive, mercurial. *See*

capricious. **3.** Without a fixed or regular course ▸ stray, wandering. *See* **erratic** (1). **4.** Not submitting to discipline or control ▸ ill-behaved, obstinate, unmanageable. *See* **unruly.** *See synonym note at* **unruly.**

weak *adjective*
1. Not physically strong ▸ debilitated, decrepit, delicate, enervated, enfeebled, faint, feeble, flimsy, fragile, frail, infirm, insubstantial, puny, rundown, unsound, unsubstantial, weakly. *See also* **insecure, pale, sick, tired. 2.** So soft as to be barely audible ▸ faint, feeble. *See also* **soft. 3.** Lacking stability ▸ tottering, unsure. *See* **insecure** (2). **4.** Not capable of accomplishing anything ▸ impotent, inadequate, incapable. *See* **ineffectual** (2). **5.** Lower than normal in strength or concentration due to admixture ▸ adulterated, cut, watered-down. *See* **dilute. 6.** Not plausible or believable ▸ improbable, inconceivable. *See* **implausible. 7.** Being weak in quality or substance ▸ bloodless, pallid. *See* **pale** (2).

✦ **CORE SYNONYMS:** *weak, feeble, frail, fragile, infirm, decrepit, debilitated.* These adjectives mean lacking or showing a lack of strength. *Weak* is the most widely applicable: *"These poor wretches . . . were so weak they could hardly sit to their oars"* (Daniel Defoe). *Feeble* suggests pathetic or grievous physical or mental weakness or hopeless inadequacy: *a feeble intellect; a feeble effort. Frail* implies delicacy and inability to endure or withstand: *"an aged thrush, frail, gaunt, and small"* (Thomas Hardy). What is *fragile* is easily broken, damaged, or destroyed: *a fragile, expensive vase; a fragile state of mind after the accident. Infirm* implies enfeeblement: *"a poor, infirm, weak, and despis'd old man"* (William Shakespeare). *Decrepit* describes what is weakened, worn out, or broken down by hard use or the passage of time: *a decrepit building slated for demolition. Debilitated* suggests a gradual impairment of energy or strength: *a debilitated constitution that was further weakened by overwork.*

weaken *verb*
1. To moderate or change a position or course of action as a result of pressure ▸ back down (*or* off), ease off, relent, slacken, soften, yield. **Idioms:** give way (*or* ground). *See also* **assent. 2.** To lose strength or power ▸ decline, fail, languish. *See* **fade** (1). **3.** To become lower in quality, character, or condition ▸ atrophy, degenerate, worsen. *See* **deteriorate** (1). **4.** To lessen or deplete the nerve, energy, or strength of ▸ debilitate, undo. *See* **enervate. 5.** To lessen the strength of by or as if by admixture ▸ cut, thin. *See* **dilute.**

weakening *noun*
1. The sapping away of strength or energy ▸ depletion, devitalization, enfeeblement. *See* **debilitation. 2.** Descent to a lower level or condition ▸ decadence, decline, degeneration. *See* **deterioration** (1).

weak-kneed *adjective*
▸ faint-hearted, pusillanimous. *Slang:* gutless. *See* **cowardly.**

weakliness *noun*
► decrepitude, feebleness, unsubstantiality. *See* **infirmity** (1).

weakling *noun*
A weak or ineffectual person ► pushover. *Informal:* jellyfish, softy. *Slang:* cream puff, doormat, pantywaist, weenie, wimp. *See also* **baby, coward.**

weakly *adjective*
► feeble, frail, unsound. *See* **weak** (1).

weak-minded *adjective*
► dull, simple-minded. *See* **backward** (1).

weakness *noun*
1. An imperfection of character ► Achilles' heel, failing, fault, foible, frailty, infirmity, shortcoming, weak point. 2. The condition of being infirm or physically weak ► decrepitude, feebleness. *See* **infirmity** (1). 3. Something that mars the appearance or causes inadequacy or failure ► fault, glitch, imperfection. *See* **defect** (1). 4. A liking for something ► partiality, preference, relish. *See* **taste** (1).

weak point *noun*
► failing, fault, shortcoming. *See* **weakness** (1).

weal¹ *noun*
A state of health, happiness, and prospering ► prosperity, welfare, well-being. *See also* **condition, happiness.**

weal² *noun*
A ridge or bump raised on the flesh due to irritation, infection or injury ► boil, pock. *See* **welt** (1).

wealth *noun*
1. A great amount of accumulated money and precious possessions ► affluence, fortune, money, opulence, pelf, riches, treasure. *See also* **capital.** 2. Things that have economic value ► assets, capital, means. *See* **resources** (1). 3. Steady good fortune or financial security ► comfort, ease, prosperousness. *See* **prosperity** (2). 4. A great deal ► mass, profusion, world. *See* **abundance** (1).

wealthy *adjective*
► affluent, moneyed. *See* **rich** (1). *See synonym note at* **rich.**

wear *verb*
1. To reduce gradually, as by chemical reaction, weather, or friction ► consume, corrode, eat (away *or* into). *See* **erode.** 2. To make a public and usually ostentatious show of ► exhibit, expose, flaunt. *See* **display** (1). 3. To have as a visible characteristic ► display, possess. *See* **bear** (3).

wear down *or* **out** *verb*
To make weary ► drain, fatigue. *See* **tire** (1).

wearied *adjective*
► exhausted, weary, worn-out. *See* **tired** (1).

weariful *adjective*
1. Arousing no interest or curiosity ► dull, humdrum, monotonous. *See* **boring** (1). 2. Depleted of energy ► exhausted, weary, worn-out. *See* **tired** (1).

weariless *adjective*
► inexhaustible, unflagging, untiring. *See* **tireless.** *See synonym note at* **tireless.**

weariness *noun*
1. The condition of being extremely tired ► burnout, tiredness. *See* **exhaustion.** 2. A lack of excitement, liveliness, or interest ► blandness, drabness, lifelessness. *See* **dullness** (1).

wearing *adjective*
Causing fatigue ► draining, exhausting, fatiguing, tiring, wearying. *See also* **burdensome.**

wearisome *adjective*
► dull, humdrum, monotonous. *See* **boring** (1).

weary *adjective*
1. Depleted of energy ► exhausted, spent, worn-out. *See* **tired** (1). 2. Out of patience ► disgusted, fed up, sick, tired. *Idiom:* sick and tired. *See also* **angry.** 3. Arousing no interest or curiosity ► dull, humdrum, monotonous. *See* **boring** (1).

weary *verb*
1. To make weary ► drain, fatigue. *See* **tire** (1). *See synonym note at* **tire.** 2. To make weary with dullness or tedium ► fatigue, tire. *See* **bore².**

wearying *adjective*
Causing fatigue ► draining, exhausting, fatiguing, tiring, wearing. *See also* **burdensome.**

weasel *noun*
1. One who behaves in a stealthy, furtive way ► prowler, skulker, sneak, sneaker. *See also* **creep, betrayer.** 2. A repulsive, despicable, or immoral person ► *Slang:* louse, maggot. *See* **creep** (2).

weasel *verb*
To use evasive or deliberately vague language ► hedge, shuffle. *See* **equivocate** (1).

weasel word *noun*
► euphemism, prevarication. *See* **equivocation** (1).

weather *verb*
► get through, persist, pull through. *See* **survive** (1).

weave *verb*
1. To interlace strips or strands ► braid, enlace, entwine, interlace, intertwine, plait, pleach, raddle, splice, twill, twist, twine, wattle. 2. To move back and forth ► swing, vacillate, waggle. *See* **sway** (1). 3. To walk unsteadily ► reel, sway, totter. *See* **stagger** (1). 4. To move or proceed on a repeatedly curving course ► coil, snake, spiral. *See* **wind²** (1).

weave *noun*
1. An open and loosely connected structure, usually interlaced, woven, or knotted ► lattice, net, network. *See* **web** (1). 2. A distinctive, complex underlying pattern or structure ► fabric, grain, web. *See* **texture** (1).

web *noun*
1. An open and loosely connected structure, usually interlaced, woven, or knotted ► braid, lace, lacing, lattice, mesh, net, netting, network, weave. 2. Something that is intricately and often bewilderingly complex ► labyrinth, maze, skein. *See* **tangle** (1). 3. An entity composed of interconnected parts ► network, system, tissue. *See* **complex** (1). 4. A distinctive, complex underlying pattern or structure ► fabric, grain, warp and woof. *See* **texture** (1).

web *verb*
To gain control of by trapping ▸ snare, trap. *See* **catch** (1).

wed *verb*
1. To join or be joined in marriage ▸ espouse, unite. *See* **marry** (1). **2.** To bring or come together into a united whole ▸ join, unify, unite. *See* **combine** (1).

wedded *adjective*
▸ conjugal, nuptial, spousal. *See* **marital**.

wedding *noun*
The act or ceremony by which two people become husband and wife ▸ bridal, espousal, marriage, nuptials, spousals.

wedge *noun*
1. A part severed from a whole ▸ slab, sliver, slice. *See* **cut** (2). **2.** A device for supporting or holding in place ▸ dowel, grapnel, mooring. *See* **anchor** (1).

wedlock *noun*
▸ conjugality, matrimony, union. *See* **marriage** (1).

wee *adjective*
▸ dwarf, miniature, minuscule. *See* **tiny**.

weedy *adjective*
▸ lean, skinny, slender, slim. *See* **thin** (1). *See synonym note at* **thin**.

weeny *adjective*
Informal Extremely small ▸ dwarf, miniature, minuscule. *See* **tiny**.

weep *verb*
1. To shed tears ▸ howl, sob, wail. *See* **cry** (1). *See synonym note at* **cry**. **2.** To flow or emit something slowly ▸ exude, leach, seep. *See* **ooze**. **3.** To fall or let fall in drops of liquid ▸ tear, trickle. *See* **drip**.

weeping *noun*
A fit of crying ▸ blubbering, sobbing. *See* **cry** (1).

weeping *or* **weepy** *adjective*
Filled with or shedding tears ▸ lachrymose, teary. *See* **tearful**.

weigh *verb*
1. To be of significance ▸ matter, signify. *See* **count** (1). *See synonym note at* **count**. **2.** To think or think about carefully and at length ▸ cogitate, deliberate, mull. *See* **ponder**. **3.** To examine in order to note similarities and differences ▸ contrast, counterpose, juxtapose. *See* **compare** (1). **4.** To make a choice from a number of alternatives ▸ elect, pick (out), vote (for). *See* **choose** (1). **5.** To make a judgment as to the worth or value of ▸ assay, calculate. *See* **estimate** (1).

weigh down *verb*
To make sad or gloomy ▸ dishearten, dispirit, sadden. *See* **depress** (1).

weigh on *or* **upon** *verb*
To come to mind continually ▸ haunt, obsess, torment, trouble.

weight *noun*
1. The state or degree of being heavy ▸ massiveness, ponderousness. *See* **heaviness**. **2.** The greatest part or portion ▸ bulk, mass, preponderance, preponderancy. *See also* **center**. **3.** Special attention given to something considered important ▸ accent, accentuation,

emphasis, stress, weight. *See also* **importance, notice**. **4.** The quality or state of being important ▸ concernment, significance. *See* **importance**. *See synonym note at* **importance**. **5.** A source of persistent worry or hardship ▸ cross, tribulation. *See* **burden**[1] (1). **6.** Power to sway or affect based on prestige, wealth, ability, or position ▸ force, power, sway. *See* **influence** (1). **7.** The power of an argument to convince or compel agreement ▸ force, justice. *See* **cogency**. **8.** Something carried or transported ▸ freight, haul, load. *See* **burden**[1] (2).

weight *verb*
To weigh down or place a heavy load on ▸ encumber, saddle, tax. *See* **burden**[1].

weightiness *noun*
1. The condition of being grave and of involving serious consequences ▸ graveness, gravity, heaviness, momentousness, seriousness. *See also* **severity**. **2.** Intellectual penetration or range ▸ deepness, depth, profoundness, profundity. *See also* **discernment, intelligence, wisdom**. **3.** The state or degree of being heavy ▸ massiveness, ponderousness. *See* **heaviness**. **4.** The quality or state of being important ▸ concernment, significance. *See* **importance**.

weightless *adjective*
Having little weight; not heavy ▸ airy, fluffy, light, lightweight. *Idioms:* light as air (*or* a feather). *See also* **immaterial, sheer**[2].

weighty *adjective*
1. Having relatively great weight ▸ hefty, ponderous. *See* **heavy** (1). *See synonym note at* **heavy**. **2.** Having too much flesh ▸ chubby, pudgy, stout. *See* **fat** (1). **3.** Requiring great or extreme bodily, mental, or spiritual strength ▸ crushing, grueling, laborious. *See* **burdensome** (1). **4.** Having great consequence or weight ▸ serious, severe. *See* **grave**[2] (1). **5.** Having or exercising influence ▸ important, powerful. *See* **influential**. **6.** Conveying hidden or unexpressed meaning ▸ consequential, significant. *See* **pregnant** (2).

weird *adjective*
1. Of an unnatural and usually frightening nature ▸ eerie, freakish, otherworldly, strange, uncanny, unearthly. *Informal:* crawly, creepy, spooky. *See also* **mysterious, supernatural**. **2.** Deviating from what is conventional or customary ▸ bizarre, grotesque. *See* **eccentric**. **3.** Causing puzzlement; perplexing ▸ odd, peculiar. *See* **funny** (3).

✦ **CORE SYNONYMS:** *weird, eerie, uncanny, unearthly.* These adjectives refer to what is of an unnatural, mysterious, and usually frightening nature. *Weird* may suggest the operation of supernatural influences, or merely the odd or unusual: "*The person of the house gave a weird little laugh*" (Charles Dickens). "*There is a weird power in a spoken word*" (Joseph Conrad). Something *eerie* inspires fear or uneasiness and implies a sinister influence: "*At nightfall on the marshes, the thing was eerie and fantastic to behold*" (Robert Louis Stevenson). *Uncanny* refers to what is unnatural and peculiarly unsettling: "*The queer* *stumps . . . had uncanny shapes, as of monstrous creatures"* (John Galsworthy). Something *unearthly* seems so strange and unnatural as to come from or belong to another world: *"He could hear the unearthly scream of some curlew piercing the din"* (Henry Kingsley).

weirdie *or* **weirdo** *noun*
Slang A person regarded as strange, eccentric, or crazy ▶ lunatic. *Informal:* loony. *Slang:* nut, screwball. *See* **crackpot.**

weisenheimer *noun*
See **wisenheimer.**

welcome *noun*
1. An expression, in words or gestures, marking a meeting of persons ▶ hail, greeting, salutation, salute. *Informal:* hello. **2.** Favorable reception or regard ▶ approbation, approval, favor. *See* **acceptance** (2).

welcome *adjective*
Giving or affording pleasure or enjoyment ▶ agreeable, favorable, satisfying. *See* **pleasant** (1).

welcome *verb*
1. To address in a friendly and respectful way ▶ greet, hail, salute. **2.** To receive something given or offered willingly and gladly ▶ accept, embrace, take (up).

welcoming *adjective*
Easily approached ▶ accessible, approachable, responsive. *See also* **convenient.**

welfare *noun*
1. A state of health, happiness, and prospering ▶ prosperity, weal, well-being. *See also* **condition, happiness. 2.** Assistance, especially money, food, and other necessities, given to the needy or dispossessed ▶ handout, public assistance. *See* **relief** (3).

well¹ *noun*
A point of origination ▶ provenance, root, source. *See* **origin** (1).

well *verb*
To come forth in abundance ▶ gush, pour, rush. *See* **flow** (2).

well² *adverb*
1. To the fullest extent ▶ fully, totally, utterly. *See* **completely** (1). **2.** To a considerable extent ▶ much, quite, significantly. *See* **considerably.**

well *adjective*
1. Having good health ▶ fit, right. *See* **healthy** (1). *See synonym note at* **healthy. 2.** Worth doing, especially for practical reasons ▶ expedient, recommendable. *See* **advisable.**

well-being *noun*
A state of health, happiness, and prospering ▶ prosperity, weal, welfare. *See also* **condition, happiness.**

wellborn *adjective*
▶ blue-blooded, elite, upper-class. *See* **noble** (1).

well-bred *adjective*
1. Characterized by discriminating taste and broad knowledge as a result of development or education ▶ cultivated, educated. *See* **cultured. 2.** Characterized by good manners ▶ genteel, mannerly, polite. *See* **courteous** (1).

well-considered *adjective*
▶ cogent, valid, well-founded. *See* **sound²** (1).

well-defined *adjective*
▶ clear, distinct, unambiguous. *See* **sharp** (3).

well-developed *adjective*
▶ curvaceous, zaftig. *See* **shapely.**

well-fixed *adjective*
Informal Enjoying steady good fortune or financial security ▶ comfortable, well-off, well-to-do. *See* **prosperous** (1).

well-founded *adjective*
1. Proceeding from or exhibiting good judgment ▶ commonsensical, levelheaded, prudent. *See* **sensible** (1). **2.** Based on good judgment, reasoning, or evidence ▶ valid, well-grounded. *See* **sound²** (1).

well-groomed *adjective*
▶ shipshape, tidy. *See* **neat** (1).

well-grounded *adjective*
1. Proceeding from or exhibiting good judgment ▶ commonsensical, levelheaded, prudent. *See* **sensible** (1). **2.** Based on good judgment, reasoning, or evidence ▶ valid, well-founded. *See* **sound²** (1).

well-heeled *adjective*
▶ comfortable, well-off, well-to-do. *See* **prosperous** (1).

well-kept *adjective*
▶ shipshape, tidy. *See* **neat** (1).

well-known *adjective*
▶ celebrated, notorious, popular. *See* **famous.**

well-liked *adjective*
▶ fair-haired, favored, pet. *See* **favorite.**

well-mannered *adjective*
▶ genteel, mannerly, polite. *See* **courteous** (1).

wellness *noun*
▶ healthiness, soundness. *See* **health** (1).

well-off *adjective*
▶ comfortable, well-to-do. *See* **prosperous** (1).

well-ordered *adjective*
▶ shipshape, tidy. *See* **neat** (1).

well-read *adjective*
▶ informed, lettered, literate. *See* **educated** (1).

well-spoken *adjective*
1. Characterized by good manners ▶ genteel, mannerly, polite. *See* **courteous** (1). **2.** Fluently persuasive and forceful ▶ articulate, smooth-spoken. *See* **eloquent** (1).

wellspring *noun*
▶ provenance, root, source. *See* **origin** (1).

well-timed *adjective*
▶ favorable, propitious, timely. *See* **opportune.**

well-to-do *adjective*
▶ easy, well-off. *See* **prosperous** (1).

well-worn *adjective*
▶ clichéd, overused, shopworn, tired. *See* **trite.**

welt *noun*
1. A ridge or bump raised on the flesh as a result of irritation, infection, or injury ▶ blister, boil, pock, wale, wart, weal, wheal, whelk. *See also* **bump. 2.** A

sudden heavy stroke ▸ crack, hit, swat, whack. *See* **blow²** (1).

welter *verb*
To move about in an indolent or clumsy manner ▸ flounder, roll about, roll around, wallow.

wench *noun*
▸ slattern, tramp, whore. *See* **slut.**

wend *verb*
To move along a particular course ▸ go, pass, proceed, push on. *Idioms:* make (*or* wend) one's way. *See also* **advance, journey, rove.**

wet *adjective*
1. Covered with or full of liquid ▸ doused, drenched, dripping, saturated, soaked, soaking, sodden, soggy, sopping, soppy, waterlogged. *See also* **damp, sticky.** **2.** Characterized by rain or drizzle ▸ damp, misty. *See* **rainy.**

wet *verb*
1. To make thoroughly wet ▸ douse, drench, saturate, soak, sodden, sop, souse. **2.** To make moist ▸ bathe, dampen, moisten, wash.

wet blanket *noun*
Informal One who spoils the enthusiasm or fun of others ▸ spoilsport. *Informal:* stick-in-the-mud. *Slang:* party pooper. *See* **killjoy.**

wetland *noun*
▸ marsh, mire, swale. *See* **swamp.**

whack *verb*
1. To deliver a sudden, sharp blow to ▸ jab, sock, thwack. *See* **hit** (1). **2.** To hit with a sharp blow, especially of the open hand ▸ smack, spank, swat. *See* **slap** (1). **3.** To strike together noisily ▸ crash, slam, thump. *See* **bang** (1).

whack *noun*
1. A sudden heavy stroke ▸ crack, hit, swat, whop. *See* **blow²** (1). **2.** A sharp blow, especially with the open hand ▸ smack, spank, swat. *See* **slap** (1). **3.** A loud, harsh striking noise ▸ clang, smash. *See* **clash** (1). **4.** A stroke or blow that produces a sound ▸ thud, thump. *See* **beat** (1). **5.** *Informal* A brief trial ▸ crack, go, stab, try. *Informal:* fling, shot, whirl.

whack *adjective*
Slang Afflicted with or exhibiting irrationality and mental unsoundness ▸ crazy, sick, mad. *See* **insane** (1).

whackiness *adjective*
See **wackiness.**

whacky *adjective*
See **wacky.**

whale *verb*
▸ assault, batter, pummel, thresh. *See* **beat** (1).

wham *noun*
1. A forceful movement causing a loud noise ▸ bang, crash, slam, smash. **2.** A sudden heavy stroke ▸ crack, hit, swat, whack. *See* **blow²** (1).

wham *verb*
To deliver a sudden, sharp blow to ▸ jab, sock, whack. *See* **hit** (1).

whammy *noun*
Slang A denunciation invoking a wish or threat of evil or injury ▸ execration, hex, imprecation. *See* **curse** (1).

whatnot *noun*
▸ knickknack, trinket. *See* **novelty** (3).

wheal *noun*
▸ blister, boil, pock. *See* **welt** (1).

wheedle *verb*
▸ blandish, cajole. *See* **coax** (1).

wheel *noun*
1. A round closed plane shape or figure ▸ band, ring, wreath. *See* **circle** (1). **2.** A circular movement around a point or about an axis ▸ circulation, gyration. *See* **revolution** (1).

wheel *verb*
1. To turn or cause to turn in place, as on a hinge or fixed point, tracing an arclike path ▸ pivot, slue, swing, swivel. **2.** To rotate on an axis or around a center ▸ spin, twirl. *See* **turn** (1). **3.** To run and control a motor vehicle ▸ chauffeur, motor. *See* **drive** (1).

wheeze *verb*
1. To utter in a breathless or hoarse manner ▸ heave, snort. *See* **gasp** (1). **2.** To breathe hard ▸ gasp, huff. *See* **pant** (1).

whelk *noun*
▸ blister, boil, pock. *See* **welt** (1).

whelp *noun*
1. A young person between birth and puberty ▸ juvenile, tot, youngster. *See* **child** (1). **2.** A mischievous youngster ▸ brat, imp, minx. *See* **urchin.**

whereabouts *noun*
▸ location, position. *See* **bearing** (3).

wherefore *noun*
1. A basis for an action ▸ occasion, reason, why. *See* **cause** (2). **2.** A fact or circumstance that gives logical support to an assertion, claim, or proposal ▸ grounds, proof. *See* **reason** (1).

wherewithal *noun*
Things that have economic value ▸ assets, capital, means. *See* **resources** (1).

whet *verb*
▸ hone, grind, stop. *See* **sharpen** (1).

whey-faced *adjective*
▸ bloodless, lurid, wan. *See* **pale** (1).

whiff *noun*
1. A slight amount or indication ▸ hint, semblance, trace. *See* **shade** (2). **2.** A gentle wind ▸ draft, puff. *See* **breeze** (1).

whiff *verb*
To perceive with the olfactory sense ▸ scent, sniff. *See* **smell** (1).

while *noun*
1. A rather short period ▸ interval, time. *See* **bit¹** (4). **2.** The use of energy to do something ▸ exertion, striving. *See* **effort** (1).

while *verb*
To spend (time) idly or pleasantly ▸ dawdle (away), trifle away. *See* **idle** (2).

whilom *adjective*
▸ former, onetime, past. *See* **late** (2).

whim *noun*
▸ caprice, impulse, notion. *See* **fancy** (1).
whimper *verb*
1. To shed tears ▸ pule, weep, whine. *See* **cry** (1). *See synonym note at* **cry**. 2. To express feelings of pain, dissatisfaction, or resentment ▸ fuss, grouch, whine. *See* **complain**.
whimper *noun*
An expression of pain or dissatisfaction ▸ carp, fuss, whine. *See* **complaint** (1).
whimsical *adjective*
1. Showing invention or whimsy in design ▸ fanciful, fantastic, imaginative. *See also* **elaborate, ornate**.
2. Determined or marked by whim or caprice rather than reason ▸ arbitrary, capricious. 3. Marked by whim or impulse ▸ fickle, impulsive, mercurial, temperamental. *See* **capricious**. *See synonym note at* **capricious**.
whimsy *noun*
▸ impulse, notion, whim. *See* **fancy** (1).
whim-whams *noun*
Slang A state of nervous restlessness or agitation ▸ jumps, shivers, trembles. *See* **jitters**.
whine *verb*
1. To shed tears ▸ pule, weep, whimper. *See* **cry** (1).
2. To express feelings of pain, dissatisfaction, or resentment ▸ carp, fuss, grouch. *See* **complain**.
whine *noun*
An expression of pain or dissatisfaction ▸ carp, fuss, whimper. *See* **complaint** (1).
whiner *noun*
▸ complainer, grump, mutterer. *See* **grouch** (1).
whip *verb*
1. To punish with blows or lashes ▸ flog, lash, thrash. *See* **beat** (2). 2. To process ingredients by stirring ▸ blend, whisk. *See* **beat** (6). 3. To cause to move to and fro violently ▸ churn, convulse, rock. *See* **agitate** (1). *See synonym note at* **agitate**. 4. *Informal* To render totally ineffective by decisive defeat ▸ crush, overcome, overpower, rout. *See* **overwhelm** (1).
whipper-snapper *noun*
▸ nobody, nothing, small fry. *See* **nonentity**.
whipping *noun*
1. A punishment dealt with blows or lashes ▸ flogging, lashing. *See* **beating** (1). 2. *Informal* The act of defeating or the condition of being defeated ▸ overthrow, trouncing, vanquishment. *See* **defeat**.
whipping boy *noun*
▸ goat. *Slang:* fall guy. *See* **scapegoat**.
whir *verb*
To make a continuous low-pitched droning sound ▸ buzz, drone, whiz. *See* **hum**.
whir *noun*
A continuous low-pitched droning sound ▸ bumble, burr, drone. *See* **hum**.
whirl *verb*
1. To move or cause to move like a rapidly rotating current of liquid ▸ eddy, swirl. 2. To have the sensation of turning in circles ▸ reel, spin, swim, swirl.

Idiom: go round and round. 3. To rotate on an axis or around a center ▸ spin, twirl, wheel. *See* **turn** (1). *See synonym note at* **turn**. 4. To move swiftly ▸ dash, sprint, zip. *See* **rush** (1).
whirl *noun*
1. A circular movement around a point or about an axis ▸ circulation, gyration. *See* **revolution** (1). 2. Agitated, excited activity ▸ commotion, excitement, fuss. *See* **agitation** (3). 3. *Informal* A trip in a motor vehicle ▸ jaunt, ride. *See* **drive** (3). 4. *Informal* A brief trial ▸ crack, go, stab, try. *Informal:* fling, shot, whack.
whirlpool *noun*
1. A rotating, often concave current of liquid ▸ eddy, maelstrom, swirl, vortex. 2. Agitated, excited activity ▸ commotion, excitement, fuss. *See* **agitation** (3).
whisk *verb*
1. To move swiftly ▸ dash, sprint, zip. *See* **rush** (1). 2. To process ingredients by stirring ▸ blend, whip. *See* **beat** (6).
whisker *noun*
▸ hint, semblance, trace. *See* **shade** (2).
whisper *noun*
1. A low, indistinct, and often continuous sound ▸ sigh, sough, susurration. *See* **murmur** (1). 2. A slight amount or indication ▸ hint, semblance, trace. *See* **shade** (2).
whisper *verb*
1. To speak or utter indistinctly, as by lowering the voice or partially closing the mouth ▸ jabber, murmur. *See* **mutter** (1). 2. To tell in confidence ▸ breathe, confide, share, unbosom. *See also* **communicate, reveal, say**. 3. To make a low, continuous, and indistinct sound ▸ murmur, rustle, sigh, sough. *See also* **burble, hum**. 4. To engage in or spread gossip ▸ rumor, tattle. *See* **gossip**.
whisperer *noun*
▸ gossipmonger, snoop, taleteller. *See* **gossip** (2).
whispery *adjective*
▸ hushed, quiet, subdued. *See* **soft** (2).
whistleblower *noun*
▸ tattler. *Slang:* snitch, squealer. *See* **informer**.
whit *noun*
▸ dash, drop, smidgen. *See* **bit**[1] (1).
whitecap *noun*
▸ breaker, undulation. *See* **wave** (1).
white flag *noun*
▸ armistice, peace. *See* **truce**.
whiten *verb*
▸ bleach, wan. *See* **pale**.
white-tie *adjective*
▸ black-tie, full-dress. *See* **formal** (5).
whitewash *verb*
1. To give a deceptively attractive appearance to ▸ gild, sugarcoat, varnish. *See* **color** (4). 2. To conceal or make light of a fault or offense ▸ explain away, palliate, sleek over. *See* **extenuate**. *See synonym note at* **extenuate**.
whiz *verb*
1. To make a sibilant sound ▸ fizzle, swish. *See* **hiss** (1).
2. To make a continuous low-pitched droning sound

▸ buzz, drone, whir. *See* **hum. 3.** To move swiftly ▸ dash, sprint, zip. *See* **rush** (1).

whiz *noun*
1. A sibilant sound ▸ fizzle, rustle. *See* **hiss** (1). **2.** A continuous low-pitched droning sound ▸ bumble, burr, drone. *See* **hum. 3.** *Informal* A person with a high degree of knowledge or skill in a particular field ▸ ace, wizard. *See* **expert.**

whole *noun*
1. An amount or quantity from which nothing is left out or held back ▸ aggregate, all, entirety, everything, grand total, gross, sum, total, totality. *Informal:* works. **Idioms:** everything but (*or* except) the kitchen sink, lock, stock, and barrel, the lot, the whole ball of wax, the whole kit and caboodle, the whole lot, the whole megillah, the whole nine yards, the whole shebang (*or* schmeer), the works. *See also* **completeness. 2.** An organized array of individual elements and parts forming and working as a unit ▸ arrangement, totality. *See* **system** (1).

whole *adjective*
1. Including every constituent or individual ▸ all, entire, total. *See* **complete** (1). *See synonym note at* **complete. 2.** Not diffused or dispersed ▸ intensive, undivided. *See* **concentrated** (1). **3.** In excellent condition ▸ flawless, intact, sound. *See* **good** (2). **4.** Having good health ▸ fit, well. *See* **healthy** (1). **5.** No less than; at least ▸ full, good, round.

wholehearted *adjective*
▸ unconditional, unfaltering. *See* **implicit** (2).

wholeness *noun*
1. The state of being entirely whole ▸ oneness, totality. *See* **completeness. 2.** The condition of being free from defects or flaws ▸ flawlessness, intactness. *See* **soundness** (1). **3.** The condition of being physically or mentally sound ▸ healthiness, soundness. *See* **health** (1).

wholesome *adjective*
1. Promoting good health ▸ healthy, hygienic. *See* **healthful** (1). **2.** Not lewd or obscene ▸ decent, modest. *See* **clean** (5). **3.** Having good health ▸ fit, well. *See* **healthy** (1). *See synonym note at* **healthy.**

wholly *adverb*
▸ fully, totally, utterly. *See* **completely** (1).

whomp *verb*
▸ clunk, thump. *See* **thud.**

whoop *noun*
A loud cry ▸ call, holler, scream. *See* **shout.**

whoop *verb*
To speak or say in a loud cry ▸ cry out, scream, yell. *See* **shout.** *See synonym note at* **shout.**

whoosh *verb*
To make a sibilant sound ▸ fizzle, swish. *See* **hiss** (1).

whoosh *noun*
A sibilant sound ▸ fizzle, rustle, sizzling, swish. *See* **hiss** (1).

whop *verb*
To deliver a sudden, sharp blow to ▸ jab, sock, whack. *See* **hit** (1).

whop *noun*
A sudden heavy stroke ▸ crack, hit, swat, whack. *See* **blow²** (1).

whopper *noun*
1. *Slang* One that is extraordinarily large and powerful ▸ Goliath, monster, titan. *See* **giant. 2.** *Slang* An untrue declaration ▸ falsehood, fib, untruth. *See* **lie².**

whopping *adjective*
Slang Of extraordinary size and power ▸ behemoth, colossal, gigantic, mighty. *See* **enormous.**

whore *noun*
1. A person who engages in sexual intercourse for payment ▸ sex worker, streetwalker. *See* **prostitute. 2.** A person, typically a woman, who is sexually promiscuous ▸ tramp, wench. *See* **slut.**

whorish *adjective*
▸ fast, loose, sluttish. *See* **wanton** (1).

who's who *noun*
▸ elite, gentry, nobility. *See* **society** (1).

why *noun*
1. A basis for an action ▸ call, reason, wherefore. *See* **cause** (2). **2.** A fact or circumstance that gives logical support to an assertion, claim, or proposal ▸ grounds, proof, wherefore. *See* **reason** (1). **3.** What one intends to do or achieve ▸ end, goal, objective. *See* **intention.**

wicked *adjective*
1. Morally objectionable ▸ immoral, sinful. *See* **evil** (1). **2.** Characterized by intense ill will or spite ▸ evil, vicious. *See* **malevolent** (1). **3.** Hard to treat, manage, or cope with ▸ demanding, difficult, trying. *See* **troublesome** (2).

wickedness *noun*
1. The quality or sate of being morally bad or objectionable ▸ iniquity, vice. *See* **evil** (1). **2.** Degrading, immoral acts or habits ▸ depravity, perversion, vice. *See* **corruption** (1). **3.** A wicked act or wicked behavior ▸ evil, misdeed, sin. *See* **crime** (2).

wide *adjective*
1. Of large extent or expanse ▸ extended, spacious. *See* **broad** (1). **2.** Of full measure ▸ ample, capacious, voluminous. *See* **full** (3). **3.** Not closed, sealed, or fastened ▸ agape, undone, unlocked. *See* **open** (1).

wide-awake *adjective*
1. Not in a state of sleep or unable to sleep ▸ awake, unsleeping, wakeful. *See also* **restless. 2.** Vigilantly attentive ▸ vigilant, watchful. *See* **alert** (1).

widen *verb*
▸ amplify, expand, widen. *See* **broaden.**

wideness *noun*
The extent of something from side to side ▸ breadth, broadness, expanse, width. *See also* **distance.**

wide-ranging *or* **wide-reaching** *adjective*
▸ all-inclusive, broad, expansive. *See* **general** (2).

widespread *adjective*
1. Spread out over a large area ▸ far-flung. *See also* **broad. 2.** Covering a wide scope ▸ all-inclusive, broad, expansive. *See* **general** (2). **3.** Occurring or encountered regularly ▸ commonplace, frequent, regular. *See*

common (1). **4.** Most generally existing or encountered at a given time ▸ predominant, rampant. *See* **prevailing** (1).

widget *noun*
▸ contraption, contrivance. *Slang:* gizmo. *See* **gadget.**

width *noun*
The extent of something from side to side ▸ breadth, broadness, expanse, wideness. *See also* **distance.**

wield *verb*
1. To use with or as if with the hands ▸ handle, manipulate, ply. *See synonym note at* **handle. 2.** To bring to bear steadily or forcefully, as influence ▸ exercise, exert, ply. *Idiom:* throw one's weight around. **3.** To direct the functioning of ▸ run, work. *See* **operate** (1).

wife *verb*
▸ consort, mate, partner. *See* **spouse.**

wiggle *verb*
▸ creep, worm, wriggle. *See* **crawl** (1).

wiggly *adjective*
1. Lacking stability ▸ shaky, unstable, unsteady. *See* **insecure** (2). **2.** Having a curved or ridged surface ▸ corrugated, rippled. *See* **wavy.**

wild *adjective*
1. Unaltered by human intervention; not cultivated or developed ▸ native, natural, rough, uncultivated, undomesticated. **2.** Living outside of human control or intervention; not domesticated ▸ feral, savage, unbroken, undomesticated, untamed. **3.** Not civilized ▸ barbarian, barbaric, rude. *See* **uncivilized** (1). **4.** Not submitting to discipline or control ▸ ill-behaved, obstinate, unmanageable. *See* **unruly. 5.** Lacking in moral restraint ▸ dissolute, profligate, rakish. *See* **abandoned. 6.** Characterized by hurried activity and confusion or agitation ▸ delirious, frenetic, frenzied, mad. *See* **frantic. 7.** Violently disturbed or agitated, as by storms ▸ roily, turbulent, violent. *See* **rough** (2).

wild *noun*
An uninhabited region left in its natural state ▸ bush, jungle. *See* **wilderness.**

wilderness *noun*
An uninhabited region left in its natural state ▸ bush, jungle, outback, outdoors, wild, wildness, wilds. *See also* **country, desert**[1].

wildness *noun*
1. An uninhabited region left in its natural state ▸ bush, jungle. *See* **wilderness. 2.** The quality or condition of being unruly ▸ intractability, obstinacy, unmanageability. *See* **unruliness. 3.** A complete surrender of inhibitions ▸ incontinence, unrestraint, wantonness. *See* **abandon** (1).

wilds *noun*
An uninhabited region left in its natural state ▸ bush, jungle. *See* **wilderness.**

wile *noun*
An indirect, usually cunning means of gaining an end ▸ deception, ploy, stratagem. *See* **trick** (1). *See synonym note at* **trick.**

wile *verb*
To spend time idly or pleasantly ▸ fiddle away, trifle away. *See* **idle** (2).

wiliness *noun*
▸ artfulness, slyness. *See* **art** (1).

will *noun*
1. The mental faculty by which one deliberately chooses or decides ▸ free will, volition. *See also* **choice, spirit. 2.** Unrestricted freedom to choose ▸ convenience, discretion, leisure, pleasure. **3.** Unwavering firmness of character, action, or will ▸ determination, purpose, resolve. *See* **decision** (2). **4.** A desire for a particular thing or activity ▸ fancy, mind, soft spot. *See* **liking** (1).

will *verb*
1. To have an inclination to ▸ want, wish. *See* **choose** (2). **2.** To give property to another after one's death ▸ bequeath, hand down. *See* **leave**[1] (1). **3.** To make a choice from a number of alternatives ▸ elect, pick (out), vote (for). *See* **choose** (1).

willful *adjective*
1. Done or said on purpose ▸ intentional, purposeful, witting. *See* **deliberate** (1). *See synonym note at* **deliberate. 2.** Of or relating to free exercise of the will ▸ spontaneous, uncompelled. *See* **voluntary** (1). **3.** Firmly, often unreasonably immovable in purpose or will ▸ bullheaded, dogged, obstinate. *See* **stubborn** (1).

willfully *adverb*
Of one's own free will ▸ by choice, freely, spontaneously, voluntarily, willingly. *Idioms:* of one's own accord, on one's own volition.

willfulness *noun*
▸ bullheadedness, hardheadedness, rigidity. *See* **stubbornness.**

willies *noun*
Slang A state of nervous restlessness or agitation ▸ jumps, shivers, trembles. *See* **jitters.**

willing *adjective*
1. Disposed to accept, agree, or participate ▸ acquiescent, agreeable, amenable, delighted, eager, game, glad, happy, minded, pleased, ready, tickled. *See also* **obliging. 2.** Of or relating to free exercise of the will ▸ volitional, willed. *See* **voluntary** (1).

willingly *adverb*
1. Of one's own free will ▸ by choice, freely, spontaneously, voluntarily, willfully. *Idioms:* of one's own accord, on one's own volition. **2.** It is so; as you say or ask ▸ agreed, all right, assuredly. *See* **yes.**

will-o'-the-wisp *noun*
▸ hallucination, mirage, phantasma. *See* **illusion** (1).

willowy *adjective*
▸ lean, skinny, slender, slim. *See* **thin** (1). *See synonym note at* **thin.**

willpower *noun*
▸ determination, purpose, resolve, will. *See* **decision** (2).

willy-nilly *adverb*
▸ involuntarily, perforce. *See* **helplessly.**

wilt *verb*
1. To become limp, as from loss of freshness ▸ droop, flag, sag, wither. 2. To hang limply, loosely, and carelessly ▸ flop, sag. *See* **slouch** (2). 3. To grow weary ▸ droop, flag. *See* **tire** (2).

wily *adjective*
▸ cunning, scheming, sly. *See* **artful** (1).

wimp *noun*
Slang A weak or ineffectual person ▸ pushover. *Slang:* cream puff, doormat. *See* **weakling.**

wimpy *adjective*
Slang ▸ faint-hearted, pusillanimous. *Slang:* gutless. *See* **cowardly.**

win *verb*
1. To achieve victory ▸ be victorious. *Idioms:* claim the victory (*or* prize), come out on top, finish (*or* come in) first, take the laurels (*or* palm). *See also* **defeat.** 2. To acquire as a result of one's behavior or effort ▸ gain, get, merit. *See* **earn** (1). *See synonym note at* **earn.** 3. To obtain possession or control of ▸ gain, get, take. *Slang:* cop. *See* **capture** (1). 4. To come into possession of ▸ come by, gain, procure. *See* **get** (1). 5. To receive, as wages, for one's labor ▸ get, make. *See* **earn** (2).

win over *verb*
1. To cause another to feel sure about something ▸ convert, persuade. *See* **convince** (1). 2. To please greatly or irresistibly ▸ bewitch, captivate, enchant. *See* **charm** (1).

win *noun*
The act of conquering ▸ knockout, victory. *See* **conquest.**

wince *verb*
To draw away or pull back in fear ▸ cringe, recoil, shrink. *See* **flinch.**

wince *noun*
An act of drawing back in an involuntary or instinctive fashion ▸ flinch, shrink. *See* **recoil.**

wind¹ *noun*
1. A natural movement or current of air ▸ air, blast, blow, gust, waft, zephyr. *See also* **breeze.** 2. The act or process of breathing ▸ exhalation, inhalation, respiration. *See* **breath** (1).

wind *verb*
To expose to circulating air ▸ aerate, air, ventilate.

wind² *verb*
1. To move or cause to lie along a repeatedly curving path ▸ coil, corkscrew, curl, entwine, meander, snake, spiral, twine, twist, weave, wrap, wreathe. *See also* **turn.** 2. To introduce or insert by subtle and artful means ▸ infiltrate, worm. *See* **insinuate** (1).

wind up *verb*
To bring or come to a natural or proper end ▸ close, finish, terminate. *See* **conclude** (1).

wind down *verb*
To become less active or intense ▸ abate, diminish, wane. *See* **subside** (1).

windbreaker *noun*
▸ jacket, parka, slicker. *See* **coat** (1).

windiness *noun*
▸ redundancy, verboseness. *See* **wordiness.**

winding *adjective*
1. Repeatedly curving in alternate directions ▸ anfractuous, convoluted, curvy, flexuous, meandering, meandrous, serpentine, sinuous, snaky, tortuous, twisting, windy. 2. Not proceeding straight to the point or object ▸ circuitous, devious, roundabout. *See* **indirect** (1).

winding *noun*
Something with a curled or spiral shape ▸ curlicue, spiral, twist. *See* **curl.**

windless *adjective*
▸ breezeless, still. *See* **airless** (2).

window-dressing *noun*
▸ guise, mask, pretense. *See* **façade** (2).

wind-up *noun*
1. A concluding or terminating ▸ cease, completion, termination. *See* **end** (1). 2. The last part ▸ closing, ending, epilogue. *See* **end** (2).

windy *adjective*
1. Exposed to or characterized by the presence of freely circulating air ▸ breezy, gusty. *See* **airy** (3). 2. Filled up with or as if with something insubstantial ▸ overblown, tumescent. *See* **inflated** (1). 3. Repeatedly curving in alternate directions ▸ convoluted, sinuous, twisting. *See* **winding** (1).

wine bar *noun*
▸ inn, pub, saloon. *See* **bar** (2).

wing *noun*
1. A part added to a main structure ▸ annex, arm. *See* **extension** (4). 2. An administrative unit, as of a government or company ▸ agency, bureau. *See* **branch** (3).

wing *verb*
1. To move through the air ▸ flit, flutter, sail. *See* **fly** (1). 2. To move swiftly ▸ dash, sprint, zip. *See* **rush** (1). 3. To cause bodily damage to a living thing ▸ hurt, injure, traumatize, wound. *See also* **cut, break.**

wink *verb*
1. To open and close one or both eyes rapidly ▸ flutter, twinkle. *See* **blink** (1). *See synonym note at* **blink.** 2. To emit light in sudden or intermittent bursts ▸ flash, glimmer, twinkle. *See* **glitter.**

wink at *verb*
To pretend not to see ▸ disregard, ignore. *See* **blink at.**

wink *noun*
1. A brief closing of the eyes ▸ bat, flutter. *See* **blink** (1). 2. A very brief time ▸ instant, second, twinkle. *See* **flash** (2). 3. A sudden burst of light ▸ flicker, spark, twinkle. *See* **flash** (1). 4. A brief or indirect suggestion ▸ cue, suggestion. *See* **hint** (2).

winner *noun*
1. One that wins a contest or competition ▸ champion, conqueror, medalist, prizewinner, titleholder, victor. *Informal:* champ. 2. One that conquers ▸ master, victor. *See* **conqueror** (1). 3. *Informal* A dazzling, often sudden instance of success ▸ sleeper. *Informal:* smash. *See* **hit** (3).

winning *adjective*
1. Being the winner in a contest or struggle ▸ champion, triumphant. *See* **victorious.** 2. Pleasing to the eye or mind ▸ enchanting, fetching, lovely, winsome. *See* **attractive** (1).

winnow *verb*
To set apart one kind or type from others ▸ separate, sift, sort. *Idiom:* separate the sheep from the goats.

wino *noun*
Slang A person who is habitually drunk ▸ alcoholic, dipsomaniac, tippler. *See* **drunkard.**

winsome *adjective*
▸ enchanting, fetching, lovely, tempting. *See* **attractive** (1).

wintriness *noun*
▸ chilliness, frigidity, frostiness. *See* **cold.**

wintry *adjective*
▸ chill, frigid, polar. *See* **cold** (1).

wipe *verb*
To cross out or remove ▸ delete, erase, strike (out). *See* **cancel** (1).

wipe out *verb*
1. To destroy all traces of ▸ eradicate, liquidate, obliterate. *See* **annihilate** (1). 2. To kill savagely and indiscriminately ▸ annihilate, butcher, slaughter. *See* **massacre** (1). 3. To get rid of, especially by banishment or execution ▸ liquidate, purge. *See* **eliminate** (1). 4. *Slang* To take the life of a person or persons unlawfully ▸ destroy, kill, slay. *See* **murder** (1).

wiped-out *adjective*
1. *Slang* Stupefied, intoxicated, or otherwise influenced by the taking of drugs ▸ high, hopped-up, lit (up). *See* **drugged.** 2. *Slang* Depleted of energy ▸ exhausted, weary, worn-out. *See* **tired** (1).

wiretap *verb*
To monitor telephone calls with a concealed device connected to the circuit ▸ bug, tap.

wisdom *noun*
1. Deep, thorough, or mature understanding ▸ insight, intelligence, profundity, sagaciousness, sagacity, sageness, sapience. *See also* **culture, discernment, illumination, understanding.** 2. The ability to make sensible decisions ▸ judgment, reason, sense. *See* **common sense.** 3. The sum of what has been perceived, discovered, or inferred ▸ knowledge, lore, understanding. *See also* **actuality.**

wise¹ *adjective*
1. Possessing deep knowledge and understanding ▸ knowing, sagacious, sage, sapient. 2. Showing evidence of schooling, training, or experience ▸ informed, lettered, literate. *See* **educated** (1). 3. Proceeding from or exhibiting good judgment ▸ commonsensical, levelheaded, prudent. *See* **sensible** (1). 4. Having or showing a clever awareness and resourcefulness in practical matters ▸ canny, knowing, perspicacious. *See* **shrewd** (1). 5. Marked by comprehension, cognizance, and perception ▸ alive, cognizant, sentient. *See* **aware.** 6. *Slang* Rude and disrespectful ▸ bold, insolent, pert. *See* **impudent.**

wise² *noun*
The approach used to do something ▸ manner, mode, style. *See* **way** (1). *See synonym note at* **way.**

wiseacre *or* **wisecracker** *noun*
Slang One who is obnoxiously self-assertive and arrogant ▸ *Informal:* know-it-all, smarty-pants. *See* **smart aleck.**

wisecrack *noun*
Slang A flippant or sarcastic remark ▸ barb, quip. *See* **crack** (5).

wise guy *noun*
Slang One who is obnoxiously self-assertive and arrogant ▸ *Informal:* know-it-all, smarty-pants. *See* **smart aleck.**

wise man *or* **wise woman** *noun*
A person noted for wisdom, knowledge, and judgment ▸ savant, scholar. *See* **sage.**

wisenheimer *or* **weisenheimer** *noun*
Informal One who is obnoxiously self-assertive and arrogant ▸ *Informal:* know-it-all, smarty-pants. *See* **smart aleck.**

wisest *noun*
▸ recommendable, well. *See* **advisable.**

wish *noun*
1. A strong wanting of what promises enjoyment or pleasure ▸ craving, longing, yearning. *See* **desire** (1). 2. A fervent hope ▸ desire, ideal, vision. *See* **dream** (3).

wish *verb*
1. To have an inclination to ▸ desire, want. *See* **choose** (2). 2. To have a strong longing for ▸ covet, want, yearn. *See* **desire** (1). *See synonym note at* **desire.**

wishy-washiness *noun*
▸ innocuousness, vapidness, wateriness. *See* **insipidity** (1).

wishy-washy *adjective*
▸ bland, jejune. *See* **insipid** (1).

wistful *adjective*
▸ dysphoric, gloomy, melancholy, spiritless. *See* **depressed** (1).

wit *noun*
1. The faculty of thinking, reasoning, and applying knowledge ▸ intellect, mentality, understanding. *See* **intelligence** (1). *See synonym note at* **intelligence.** 2. Skill in perceiving, discriminating, or judging ▸ keenness, perceptiveness, shrewdness. *See* **discernment** (1). 3. The quality of being laughable or comical ▸ funniness, ridiculousness, wittiness. *See* **humor** (1). 4. A person whose words or actions provoke or are intended to provoke amusement or laughter ▸ clown, comedian, jester. *See* **joker.**

witch *noun*
1. A woman who practices magic ▸ enchantress, hag, lamia, sorceress. *See also* **wizard.** 2. An ugly, frightening woman, usually old ▸ beldam, crone, hag. *Slang:* battle-ax, biddy, crow. 3. *Informal* A woman who seduces or exploits men ▸ femme fatale, siren. *See* **seductress.**

witch *verb*
To act upon with or as if with magic ▸ enchant,

hypnotize, mesmerize, spellbind. *See* **charm** (2).

witchcraft *noun*
▸ conjuration, sorcery. *See* **magic** (1).

witchery *noun*
1. The use of supernatural powers to influence or predict events ▸ conjuration, sorcery, witchcraft. *See* **magic** (1). **2.** The power or quality of attracting ▸ appeal, draw, enticement, lure. *See* **attraction** (1).

witching *adjective*
1. Having, brought about by, or relating to supernatural powers or magic ▸ magical, wizardly. *See* **magic** (1). **2.** Tending to seduce ▸ bewitching, enticing, tempting. *See* **seductive**.

witching *noun*
The use of supernatural powers to influence or predict events ▸ conjuration, sorcery, witchcraft. *See* **magic** (1).

withdraw *verb*
1. To move something from a position occupied ▸ pluck out, take out, uproot. *See* **remove** (1). **2.** To pull back in ▸ draw in, retract. **3.** To move away from a place ▸ exit, go away, retire. *See* **go** (1). **4.** To move back in the face of enemy attack or after a defeat ▸ draw back, pull out, retire. *See* **retreat** (4). **5.** To remove from association with ▸ disassociate, disengage, uncouple. *See* **detach** (1). **6.** To disavow something previously written or said irrevocably and usually formally ▸ abjure, recant, take back. *See* **retract** (1). **7.** To take away a quantity from another quantity ▸ discount, subtract. *See* **deduct** (1). **8.** To disappear by or as if by rising ▸ disperse, dissipate, thin out. *See* **lift** (4).

withdrawal *noun*
1. The act of leaving ▸ embarkation, leave-taking, parting. *See* **departure** (1). **2.** The act or process of detaching ▸ disconnection, separation, uncoupling. *See* **detachment** (1). **3.** The moving back of a military force in the face of enemy attack or after a defeat ▸ fallback, pullout, retirement. *See* **retreat** (1). **4.** A formal statement of disavowal ▸ abjuration, palinode. *See* **retraction** (1).

withdrawn *adjective*
▸ aloof, chilly, solitary. *See* **cool** (1).

wither *verb*
1. To make or become no longer fresh or shapely because of loss of moisture ▸ frizzle, sear, shrivel. *See* **dry** (1). **2.** To become downcast from longing or grief ▸ ebb, shrivel. *See* **languish** (1). **3.** To render helpless, as by emotion ▸ numb, stun, stupefy. *See* **paralyze** (1). **4.** To criticize harshly and devastatingly ▸ bash, excoriate, flay. *See* **slam** (5). **5.** To spoil or destroy ▸ corrode, dash. *See* **blast** (2). **6.** To become limp, as from loss of freshness ▸ flag, sag. *See* **wilt**.

withering *adjective*
▸ caustic, scathing, sharp, vitriolic. *See* **biting**.

withhold *verb*
1. To hold oneself back ▸ forbear, hold off. *See* **refrain**. **2.** To take or keep something away from ▸ deny, rob. *See* **deprive**. **3.** To have and maintain in one's posses-

sion ▸ keep, retain. *See* **hold** (1). *See synonym note at* **hold**. **4.** To be unwilling to accept, consider, or receive ▸ refuse, reject, spurn. *See* **decline** (1). **5.** To keep from being published or transmitted ▸ ban, stifle, suppress. *See* **censor** (2).

with-it *adjective*
1. *Informal* In accordance with current fashion ▸ mod, stylish, swanky. *See* **fashionable**. **2.** *Informal* Marked by comprehension, cognizance, and perception ▸ cognizant, sensible, sentient. *See* **aware**.

withstand *verb*
1. To place in opposition or be in opposition to ▸ match, pit. *See* **oppose** (1). *See synonym note at* **oppose**. **2.** To put up with ▸ accept, stomach, tolerate. *See* **endure** (1). **3.** To turn aside or drive away ▸ deflect, repulse, ward off. *See* **repel**.

witless *adjective*
1. Displaying a lack of forethought and good sense ▸ daft, idiotic, ludicrous. *See* **foolish**. **2.** Lacking in intelligence ▸ dumb, idiotic, obtuse. *See* **stupid** (1).

witlessness *noun*
▸ idiocy, mindlessness, obtuseness. *See* **stupidity**.

witness *noun*
1. Someone who sees something occur ▸ audience, eyewitness, seer, viewer. **2.** One who testifies, especially in court ▸ attestant, attester, deponent, testifier. **3.** Something visible or evident that gives grounds for believing in the existence or presence of something else ▸ evidence, indication, symptom. *See* **sign** (1). **4.** A formal declaration of truth or fact given under oath ▸ affidavit, deposition, testimony.

witness *verb*
1. To give grounds for believing in the existence or presence of ▸ attest, testify. *See* **indicate** (1). *See synonym note at* **indicate**. **2.** To confirm formally as true, accurate, or genuine ▸ attest, testify, verify. *See* **certify** (1). **3.** To give evidence or testimony under oath ▸ attest, depose, swear. *See* **testify** (1).

wits *noun*
▸ lucidity, rationality, reason. *See* **sanity**.

witticism *noun*
▸ gag, jest, quip. *See* **joke** (1). *See synonym note at* **joke**.

wittiness *noun*
▸ funniness, ridiculousness, zaniness. *See* **humor** (1).

witting *adjective*
▸ intentional, purposeful, willful. *See* **deliberate** (1).

witty *adjective*
1. Causing laughter or amusement ▸ comical, humorous, laughable. *See* **funny** (1). **2.** Exhibiting or employing wit or originality ▸ scintillating, smart. *See* **clever** (2).

wizard *noun*
1. One who practices sorcery or magic ▸ conjurer, enchanter, magician, necromancer, prestidigitator, sorcerer, warlock. *See also* **witch**. **2.** A person with a high degree of knowledge or skill in a particular field ▸ authority, master, proficient. *See* **expert**.

wizardly *adjective*
▸ magical, witching. *See* **magic** (1).

wizardry *noun*
▸ conjuration, sorcery, witchcraft. *See* **magic** (1).

wizen *verb*
▸ sear, shrivel, wither. *See* **dry** (1).

wobble *verb*
1. To move back and forth ▸ swing, vacillate, waggle. *See* **sway** (1). 2. To walk unsteadily ▸ reel, sway, totter. *See* **stagger** (1). 3. To be irresolute in acting or doing ▸ falter, vacillate. *See* **hesitate.**

wobbliness *noun*
▸ ricketiness, wiggling. *See* **unsteadiness** (1).

wobbly *adjective*
▸ precarious, shaky, tottering. *See* **insecure** (2).

woe *noun*
1. A state of physical or mental suffering ▸ agony, misery, wretchedness. *See* **distress** (1). 2. A state of prolonged anguish and privation ▸ deprivation, wretchedness. *See* **misery** (1). 3. A cause of suffering or harm ▸ bane, scourge. *See* **curse** (3).

woebegone *adjective*
1. Very uncomfortable or unhappy ▸ suffering, wretched. *See* **miserable** (1). 2. Causing or expressing sorrow or sadness ▸ cheerless, melancholy, mournful. *See* **sorrowful** (1). *See synonym note at* **sorrowful.** 3. Very bad ▸ appalling, awful, dreadful, wretched. *See* **terrible** (1).

woeful *adjective*
1. Very uncomfortable or unhappy ▸ afflicted, wretched. *See* **miserable** (1). 2. Causing or expressing sorrow or sadness ▸ doleful, melancholy, mournful. *See* **sorrowful** (1). 3. Worthy of severe disapproval ▸ disgraceful, shameful, unfortunate. *See* **deplorable** (1).

wolf *noun*
1. A man who is given to flirting ▸ flirt. *Slang:* masher. *See also* **seducer.** 2. *Slang* A man who philanders ▸ Casanova, womanizer. *See* **philanderer.**

wolf *verb*
Informal To swallow food or drink greedily or rapidly in large amounts ▸ gobble, guzzle. *See* **gulp** (1).

womanhood *noun*
Women in general ▸ womankind, womenfolk.

womanish *adjective*
1. Relating to or characteristic of women ▸ female, feminine, womanly. 2. Having qualities traditionally attributed to a woman ▸ feminine, unmanly. *See* **effeminate.**

womanishness *noun*
▸ femininity, unmanliness. *See* **effeminacy.**

womanizer *noun*
▸ adulterer, cheater, Casanova. *See* **philanderer.**

womankind *noun*
Women in general ▸ womanhood, womenfolk.

womanliness *noun*
The quality or condition of being feminine ▸ femaleness, feminineness, femininity.

womanly *adjective*
Relating to or characteristic of women ▸ female, feminine, womanish.

womenfolk *noun*
Women in general ▸ womanhood, womankind.

wonder *noun*
1. The emotion aroused by something awe-inspiring or astounding ▸ amaze, amazement, astonishment, awe, marvel, stupefaction, surprise, wonderment. *See also* **enthusiasm, surprise.** 2. An event inexplicable by the laws of nature ▸ miracle. *Idiom:* act of God. 3. One that evokes great surprise and admiration ▸ prodigy, phenomenon, prodigy. *See* **marvel** (1). *See synonym note at* **marvel.** 4. A lack of conviction or certainty ▸ dubiousness, incertitude, skepticism. *See* **doubt** (1).

wonder *verb*
1. To have a feeling of great awe and rapt admiration ▸ admire, marvel. *Idioms:* be agog (*or* agape *or* awestruck). *See also* **gaze, stagger.** 2. To be uncertain, disbelieving, or skeptical about ▸ disbelieve, query, waver. *See* **doubt** (1).

wonderful *adjective*
1. So remarkable as to be hard to believe ▸ staggering, unbelievable. *See* **astonishing.** 2. Particularly excellent ▸ fabulous, glorious, sensational. *See* **marvelous** (1). 3. Marked by extraordinary beauty and splendor ▸ magnificent, resplendent, splendid. *See* **glorious** (1).

wonderment *noun*
1. One that evokes great surprise and admiration ▸ prodigy, sensation, wonder. *See* **marvel** (1). 2. The emotion aroused by something awe-inspiring or astounding ▸ amazement, awe, marvel. *See* **wonder** (1).

wondrous *adjective*
1. So remarkable as to be hard to believe ▸ staggering, unbelievable. *See* **astonishing.** 2. Marked by extraordinary beauty and splendor ▸ magnificent, resplendent, splendid. *See* **glorious** (1).

wonkiness *adjective*
▸ wiggling, wobbliness. *See* **unsteadiness** (1).

wont *adjective*
1. In the habit ▸ accustomed, habituated, used. 2. Having or showing a tendency or likelihood ▸ disposed, prone. *See* **inclined** (1).

wont *noun*
A habitual way of behaving ▸ form, habit, practice. *See* **custom** (1). *See synonym note at* **custom.**

wont *verb*
To make familiar through constant practice or use ▸ habituate, inure. *See* **accustom.**

wonted *adjective*
▸ commonplace, customary, regular. *See* **common** (1).

woo *verb*
▸ chase, pursue. *See* **court** (2).

wooden *adjective*
Rigidly constrained or formal; lacking grace and spontaneity ▸ buckram, starchy, stiff, stilted. *See also* **cool, forced, prudish.**

woodland *or* **woods** *noun*
A dense growth of trees and underbrush that covers

an area ▶ backwoods, forest, timberland.

wooer *noun*
▶ courter, suitor. *See* **beau** (1).

woolgather *verb*
▶ fancy, hallucinate, imagine. *See* **dream** (1).

woolgathering *adjective*
▶ daydreaming, fanciful, musing. *See* **dreamy** (1).

woolly *adjective*
1. Covered with hair ▶ furry, hirsute, shaggy. *See* **hairy** (1). **2.** Lacking certainty or clarity ▶ dubious, questionable, unclear. *See* **ambiguous** (1).

wooziness *noun*
▶ giddiness, unsteadiness, vertigo. *See* **dizziness.**

woozy *adjective*
▶ giddy, lightheaded, reeling. *See* **dizzy** (1).

word *noun*
1. A sound or combination of sounds that symbolizes and communicates a meaning ▶ lexeme, vocable. *See* **term** (1). **2.** Something said ▶ saying, statement, utterance. *See also* **language, speech. 3.** Something announced or communicated ▶ communication, notice, statement. *See* **message** (1). **4.** A declaration that one will or will not do a certain thing ▶ covenant, pledge, vow. *See* **promise** (1). **5.** An order ▶ charge, commandment, imperative. *See* **command** (1). **6.** New information, especially about recent events and happenings ▶ intelligence, report. *See* **news** (1). *See synonym note at* **news. 7.** Idle, often sensational and groundless talk about others ▶ hearsay, rumor, tattle. *See* **gossip** (1). **8.** A discussion, often heated, in which a difference of opinion is expressed ▶ quarrel. *Informal:* rhubarb, tangle. *See* **argument** (1). **9.** An expression of fact or opinion ▶ observation, reflection, remark. *See* **comment** (1).

word *verb*
To convey in language or words of a particular form ▶ express, formulate. *See* **phrase.**

wordage *noun*
1. Words or the use of words in excess of those needed for clarity or precision ▶ pleonasm, redundancy, verboseness. *See* **wordiness. 2.** Choice of words and the way in which they are used ▶ locution, phraseology, verbalism. *See* **wording.**

wordbook *noun*
An alphabetical list of words often defined or translated ▶ dictionary, glossary, lexicon, vocabulary.

word-for-word *adjective*
▶ undeviating, unvarnished, verbatim. *See* **literal** (1).

word-hoard *noun*
All the words of a language ▶ lexicon, vocabulary.

wordiness *noun*
Words or the use of words in excess of those needed for clarity or precision ▶ circumlocution, diffuseness, diffusion, long-windedness, pleonasm, prolixity, redundance, redundancy, verbiage, verboseness, verbosity, windiness, wordage. *See also* **bombast.**

wording *noun*
Choice of words and the way in which they are used ▶ diction, locution, parlance, phrase, phraseology, phrasing, verbalism, wordage. *Idioms:* turn of phrase, way of putting it. *See also* **expression.**

wordless *adjective*
1. Not voiced or expressed ▶ undeclared, unspoken. *See* **silent** (2). **2.** Conveyed indirectly without words or speech ▶ inferred, tacit, unspoken. *See* **implicit** (1). **3.** Temporarily unable or unwilling to speak, as from shock or fear ▶ inarticulate, mute. *See* **speechless** (1). **4.** Lacking the power or faculty of speech ▶ inarticulate, voiceless. *See* **mute** (1).

wordlessness *noun*
▶ muteness, speechlessness. *See* **silence** (2).

word of honor *noun*
▶ covenant, pledge, vow. *See* **promise** (1).

word-of-mouth *adjective*
▶ spoken, verbal, vocal, voiced. *See* **oral.**

words *noun*
▶ quarrel. *Informal:* rhubarb, tangle. *See* **argument** (1).

wordy *adjective*
1. Using or containing an excessive number of words ▶ circumlocutionary, circumlocutory, diffuse, long-winded, periphrastic, pleonastic, prolix, redundant, tautological, verbose. *See also* **indirect, talkative. 2.** Relating to, consisting of, or having the nature of words ▶ lexical, linguistic, wordy.

✚ **CORE SYNONYMS:** *wordy, diffuse, long-winded, prolix, verbose.* These adjectives mean using or containing an excessive number of words: *a wordy apology; a diffuse historical novel; a long-winded speaker; a prolix, tedious lecturer; verbose correspondence.*

---

work *noun*
1. Physical exertion that is usually difficult and exhausting ▶ drudgery, toil, travail. *See* **labor** (1). *See synonym note at* **labor. 2.** Activity pursued as a livelihood ▶ career, employment, occupation. *See* **business** (2). **3.** Something done ▶ action, deed, doing. *See* **act** (1). **4.** Something that is the result of creative effort ▶ piece, production, writing. *See* **composition** (1). **5.** An issue of printed material offered for sale or distribution ▶ opus, title, volume. *See* **publication** (2). **6.** The technique, style, and quality of working ▶ craft, craftsmanship, workmanship. *See also* **approach. 7.** A post of employment ▶ job, situation. *See* **position** (3). **8.** Something produced by human effort ▶ produce, product, production, manufacture. *See also* **good.**

work *verb*
1. To exert oneself steadily, often to the point of exhaustion ▶ strain, sweat, toil. *See* **labor** (1). **2.** To act in a specified way ▶ behave, operate, run. *See* **function. 3.** To turn out well ▶ go over, pan out, work out. *See* **succeed** (2). **4.** To direct the functioning of ▶ manage, run. *See* **operate** (1). **5.** To handle in a way so as to mix, form, and shape ▶ knead, manipulate, squeeze. **6.** To move over or along with pressure ▶ knead, massage, stroke. *See* **rub** (2). **7.** To introduce or insert by subtle and artful means ▶ infiltrate, worm. *See* **insinuate** (1). **8.** To prepare soil for the planting of crops ▶ cultivate, plow, turn (over). *See*

till. **9.** To force to work hard ▸ drive, push, task, tax. *Idiom:* crack the whip. *See also* **force. 10.** To put into action or use ▸ apply, employ, utilize. *See* **use** (1).

work out *verb*
1. To arrive at an answer to a mathematical problem ▸ solve, work. *Informal:* figure out. *See also* **calculate. 2.** To plan the details or arrangements of ▸ arrange, lay out, prepare, schedule. **3.** To engage in activities in order to strengthen or condition ▸ drill, exercise, practice, train. **4.** To arrive at through reasoning ▸ conclude, evolve. *See* **derive** (2). **5.** To form a strategy for ▸ devise, formulate, strategize. *See* **design** (1). **6.** To turn out well ▸ come off, go over, pan out. *See* **succeed** (2).

work over *verb*
1. To injure or damage, as by abuse or heavy wear ▸ maul, rough up. *See* **batter** (1). **2.** To prepare a new version of ▸ amend, revamp, rework. *See* **revise** (1).

work up *verb*
To stir to action or feeling ▸ excite, prod, trigger. *See* **provoke** (1).

work on *verb*
To have an impact on in a certain way ▸ incline, predispose, sway. *See* **influence** (1).

workable *adjective*
1. Capable of being shaped or bent ▸ bendable, ductile, plastic. *See* **malleable** (1). **2.** Capable of occurring or being done ▸ practicable, viable. *See* **possible** (1). *See synonym note at* **possible.**

workaday *or* **workday** *adjective*
▸ casual, quotidian. *See* **everyday** (1).

worked up *adjective*
▸ atingle, excited, fired up. *See* **thrilled.**

worker *noun*
1. One who is employed by another ▸ hireling, jobholder, staffer. *See* **employee. 2.** One who labors ▸ menial, toiler, wage slave. *See* **laborer.**

workhorse *noun*
Informal One who works or toils tirelessly ▸ grind, grub, plodder. *See* **drudge** (2).

working *adjective*
1. In action or full operation ▸ functioning, operating, running. *See* **active** (1). **2.** Having a job ▸ jobholding, retained. *See* **employed** (1). **3.** Involved in activity or work ▸ engaged, occupied. *See* **busy** (1).

working *noun*
The way in which something functions ▸ functioning, performance. *See* **behavior** (2).

working girl *noun*
1. One who labors ▸ menial, toiler, worker. *See* **laborer. 2.** *Slang* A woman who engages in sex for payment ▸ courtesan, strumpet. *See* **harlot.**

workingman *or* **workingwoman** *noun*
▸ menial, toiler, worker. *See* **laborer.**

workless *adjective*
Having no job ▸ idle, jobless, unemployed, unoccupied. *Idioms:* out of a job (*or* work).

workman *or* **workwoman** *noun*
▸ menial, toiler, worker. *See* **laborer.**

workmanship *noun*
The technique, style, and quality of working ▸ craft, craftsmanship, work. *See also* **approach.**

workout *noun*
▸ exercise, rehearsal. *See* **practice** (1).

workroom *noun*
An artist's workspace ▸ atelier, studio, workshop.

works *noun*
1. A building or complex in which an industry is located ▸ factory, mill, plant. **2.** *Informal* An amount or quantity from which nothing is left out or held back ▸ entirety, everything, total. *See* **whole** (1).

workshop *noun*
1. A meeting for the exchange of views ▸ discussion, parley, seminar. *See* **conference** (1). **2.** An artist's workspace ▸ atelier, studio, workroom.

work-up *noun*
▸ analysis, diagnosis. *See* **examination** (2).

world *noun*
1. The celestial body where humans live ▸ earth, globe, orb, planet. **2.** The totality of all existing things ▸ cosmos, creation. *See* **universe** (1). **3.** Humans as a group ▸ flesh, humanity, mortals. *See* **humankind. 4.** A sphere of activity, experience, study, or interest ▸ department, domain, field, terrain. *See* **area** (1). **5.** The surrounding conditions and circumstances affecting growth or development ▸ climate, surroundings. *See* **environment** (2). **6.** A great deal ▸ mass, profusion, wealth. *See* **abundance** (1). **7.** The ecological circumstances in which organisms live ▸ biosphere, habitat. *See* **environment** (3).

worldly *adjective*
1. Experienced in the ways of the world; lacking natural simplicity ▸ cosmopolitan, sophisticated, worldly-wise. *See also* **experienced, shrewd, suave. 2.** Not religious in subject matter, form, or use ▸ nonecclesiastical, secular, temporal. *See* **profane** (2). **3.** Relating to or characteristic of the earth or of human life on earth ▸ earthbound, terrestrial. *See* **earthly** (1).

worldly-wise *adjective*
Experienced in the ways of the world; lacking natural simplicity ▸ cosmopolitan, sophisticated, worldly. *See also* **experienced, shrewd, suave.**

world-shaking *adjective*
▸ consequential, meaningful. *See* **important** (1).

worldwide *adjective*
▸ cosmic, global. *See* **universal** (1).

worm *verb*
1. To move along in a crouching or prone position ▸ creep, slither, wriggle. *See* **crawl** (1). **2.** To introduce or insert by subtle and artful means ▸ infiltrate, work. *See* **insinuate** (1). **3.** To use stratagems in gaining an end ▸ engineer, finesse. *See* **maneuver** (2).

worm *noun*
A repulsive, despicable, or immoral person ▸ reptile. *Slang:* louse, maggot. *See* **creep** (2).

worm-eaten *or* **wormy** *adjective*
▸ decayed, putrid, rotten. *See* **bad** (2).

worn *adjective*
1. Appearing worn and exhausted ▶ gaunt, wan. *See* **haggard.** 2. Showing signs of wear and tear or neglect ▶ broken-down, dilapidated, tattered. *See* **shabby** (1).

worn-down *adjective*
▶ exhausted, weary, worn-out. *See* **tired** (1).

worn-out *adjective*
1. Without freshness or appeal because of overuse ▶ clichéd, overused, shopworn, tired. *See* **trite.** 2. Depleted of energy ▶ exhausted, fatigued, weary. *See* **tired** (1). 3. Showing signs of wear and tear or neglect ▶ broken-down, dilapidated, tattered. *See* **shabby** (1).

worried *adjective*
▶ distressed, nervous, uneasy. *See* **anxious.**

worrisome *adjective*
▶ bothersome, irritating, unsettling. *See* **disturbing.**

worry *verb*
1. To cause anxious uneasiness in ▶ ail, bother, concern, distress, trouble. 2. To attack or disturb persistently ▶ harry, pester, torment. *See* **harass.** 3. To focus the attention on something moodily and at length ▶ dwell, fret, mope. *See* **brood.** *See synonym note at* **brood.** 4. To cause to move to and fro violently ▶ churn, rock, shake. *See* **agitate** (1). *See synonym note at* **agitate.**

worry *noun*
1. A cause of distress or anxiety ▶ care, concern, stressor, trouble. *See also* **burden**[1]. 2. A troubled or anxious state of mind ▶ concern, distress, unease. *See* **anxiety** (1). *See synonym note at* **anxiety.** 3. A feeling of uncertainty about the fitness or correctness of an action ▶ misgiving, reservation, scruple. *See* **qualm** (1).

✦ CORE SYNONYMS: *worry, ail, distress, trouble.* These verbs mean to cause anxious uneasiness in: *What problems are ailing you? The bad news distressed us. Her high fever worries the doctor. His behavior troubles his parents.*

---

worrywart *noun*
▶ apocalypticist, doomsayer. *See* **pessimist** (2).

worse *noun*
Whatever is destructive or harmful ▶ bad, badness, evil, ill. *See also* **harm.**

worsen *verb*
▶ atrophy, degenerate, weaken. *See* **deteriorate** (1).

worship *noun*
1. The act of adoring, especially reverently ▶ adoration, idolization, reverence, veneration. *See also* **devotion, honor, praise.** 2. An intense attachment to a person or thing ▶ devotion, fondness, worship. *See* **love** (1).

worship *verb*
1. To feel deep devoted love for ▶ adore, love. *Idioms:* be soft (*or* stuck *or* sweet) on. 2. To regard with the deepest respect, deference, and esteem ▶ idolize, venerate. *See* **revere.** *See synonym note at* **revere.**

worshipful *adjective*
▶ pious, reverential, venerational. *See* **reverent.**

worst *verb*
▶ conquer, surmount, vanquish. *See* **defeat** (1).

worth *noun*
1. A measure of those qualities that determine merit, desirability, usefulness, or importance ▶ account, valuation, value. *See also* **cost, importance.** 2. A level of superiority that is usually high ▶ quality, value. *See* **merit** (1).

worthiness *noun*
▶ eligibility, fitness, suitability. *See* **qualification.**

worthless *adjective*
1. Lacking worth and value ▶ drossy, empty, good-for-nothing, no-good, valueless. *Informal:* dumb, no-account, nothing, rotten, stupid. *See also* **aimless, trivial.** 2. Of decidedly inferior quality ▶ cheap, lousy, poor. *See* **shoddy** (1).

worthwhile *adjective*
▶ favorable, helpful, propitious. *See* **beneficial.**

worthy *adjective*
1. Of great value or price ▶ expensive, precious, valuable. *See* **costly.** 2. Deserving honor, respect, or admiration ▶ deserving, laudable, praiseworthy. *See* **admirable.** 3. Satisfying certain requirements, as for selection ▶ equal, suitable. *See* **eligible** (1). 4. Having pleasant desirable qualities ▶ bonny, enjoyable, nice. *See* **good** (1).

worthy *noun*
An important, influential person ▶ notability, personage. *Slang:* big shot. *See* **dignitary.**

wound *noun*
1. Marked tissue damage, especially when produced by physical injury ▶ laceration, lesion, trauma, traumatism. *See also* **harm.** 2. A state of physical or mental suffering ▶ agony, misery, wretchedness. *See* **distress** (1).

wound *verb*
1. To cause bodily damage to a living thing ▶ hurt, injure, traumatize, wing. *See also* **cut, break, hurt.** 2. To inflict physical or mental injury or distress on ▶ shock, traumatize. 3. To cause emotional suffering or painful sorrow to ▶ disturb, grieve, hurt. *See* **distress** (1). 4. To cause anger, resentment, or hurt feelings ▶ annoy, injure, upset. *See* **offend** (1).

wounded *noun*
▶ casualty, quarry, sufferer. *See* **victim** (1).

wow *noun*
Informal A dazzling, often sudden instance of success ▶ sleeper. *Informal:* smash. *See* **hit** (3).

wrack *noun*
1. The remains of something destroyed, disintegrated, or decayed ▶ debris, rubble, wreckage. *See* **ruin** (2). 2. The act of destroying or state of being destroyed ▶ devastation, ruin, wreck. *See* **destruction** (1).

wrack *verb*
To cause the complete ruin or wreckage of ▶ annihilate, demolish, ravage, torpedo, wreck. *See* **destroy** (1).

wraith *noun*
▶ phantom, shade, specter. *See* **ghost** (1).

wrangle *verb*
1. To engage in a quarrel ▶ dispute, quarrel. *See* **argue** (1). *See synonym note at* **argue.** 2. To urge to move along ▶ chase, push, run. *See* **drive** (3). 3. To argue about the terms, as of a sale ▶ haggle, negotiate, palter. *See* **haggle.**

wrangle *noun*
A discussion, often heated, in which a difference of opinion is expressed ▶ dispute, fight, quarrel. *See* **argument** (1).

wrap *verb*
1. To cover completely and closely, as with clothing or bandages ▶ bundle, enfold, envelop, roll, swaddle, swathe. 2. To surround and cover completely so as to obscure ▶ cloak, clothe, enfold, enshroud, envelop, enwrap, infold, invest, shroud, veil. *See also* **conceal, cover, surround.** 3. To move or proceed on a repeatedly curving course ▶ snake, spiral, weave. *See* **wind**² (1).

wrap up *verb*
1. To put on warm clothes ▶ bundle up, wrap. 2. To bring or come to a natural or proper end ▶ close, finish, terminate. *See* **conclude** (1). 3. To draw or be drawn in so that extrication is impossible ▶ catch up, embroil, mix up. *See* **involve** (1).

wrap *noun*
1. A garment wrapped about a person ▶ cloak, shawl, stole. *See also* **scarf.** 2. The material in which something is wrapped ▶ casing, covering, packaging. *See* **wrapper.**

wrapper *or* **wrapping** *noun*
The material in which something is wrapped ▶ case, casing, cover, covering, envelope, jacket, packaging, wrap. *See also* **frame.**

wrap-up *noun*
1. A review of the essential points or consequences of something: ▶ rundown, sum. *See* **summary.** 2. A concluding or terminating ▶ cease, completion, termination. *See* **end** (1). 3. The last part ▶ closing, ending, epilogue. *See* **end** (2).

wrath *or* **wrathfulness** *noun*
▶ fury, irateness, rage. *See* **anger.** *See synonym note at* **anger.**

wrathful *adjective*
▶ furious, livid, rabid. *See* **angry.** *See synonym note at* **angry.**

wreak *verb*
▶ impose, play. *See* **inflict.**

wreath *noun*
1. Cut flowers or foliage arranged or worn for display ▶ corsage, posy. *See* **bouquet** (1). 2. A round closed plane shape or figure ▶ band, ring, wheel. *See* **circle** (1).

wreathe *verb*
▶ snake, spiral, weave. *See* **wind**² (1).

wreck *noun*
1. The act of destroying or state of being destroyed ▶ devastation, pulverization, ruin. *See* **destruction** (1). 2. A wrecking of a vehicle ▶ sideswipe, smashup. *See*

crash (2). 3. An abrupt failure ▶ crash, debacle, disaster. *See* **collapse** (2). 4. The remains of something destroyed, disintegrated, or decayed ▶ debris, rubble, wreckage. *See* **ruin** (2).

wreck *verb*
1. To damage, disable, or destroy a seacraft ▶ shipwreck, sink, run aground. 2. To injure or destroy property maliciously ▶ vandalize. *Slang:* trash. 3. To pull down or break up so that reconstruction is impossible ▶ dismantle, level, tear down. *See* **destroy** (2). *See synonym note at* **destroy.** 4. To cause the complete ruin or wreckage of ▶ demolish, torpedo, undo. *See* **destroy** (1). 5. To wreck a vehicle ▶ sideswipe, smash. *See* **crash** (1). 6. To ruin through clumsiness or ineptness ▶ blunder, foul up, spoil. *See* **botch.** 7. To spoil or destroy ▶ blight, dash. *See* **blast** (2). *See synonym note at* **blast.**

wreckage *noun*
1. Harm done to property or a person ▶ destruction, impairment, injury. *See* **damage** (1). 2. The act of destroying or state of being destroyed ▶ devastation, ruin, wreck. *See* **destruction** (1). 3. The remains of something destroyed, disintegrated, or decayed ▶ debris, rubble, wreck. *See* **ruin** (2).

wrecker *noun*
▶ bane, downfall, undoing. *See* **ruin** (1).

wrench *verb*
1. To injure a bodily part by twisting ▶ sprain, strain, turn, twist. *See also* **hurt.** 2. To move or cause to move with a sudden abrupt motion ▶ jerk, lurch, snap, twitch, yank. *See also* **move.** 3. To alter the position of by a sharp, forcible twisting or turning movement ▶ twist, wrest, wring. 4. To obtain by coercion or intimidation ▶ blackmail, squeeze. *See* **extort.** 5. To give an inaccurate view of by representing falsely or misleadingly ▶ fudge, misrepresent, pervert. *See* **distort** (1). 6. To remove from a fixed position ▶ pluck, rend, wrest. *See* **pull** (2).

wrench *noun*
A sudden motion, such as a pull ▶ tug, twitch, yank. *See* **jerk** (1). *See synonym note at* **jerk.**

wrest *verb*
1. To alter the position of by a sharp, forcible twisting or turning movement ▶ twist, wrench, wring. 2. To obtain by coercion or intimidation ▶ blackmail, squeeze. *See* **extort.** 3. To give an inaccurate view of by representing falsely or misleadingly ▶ fudge, misrepresent, pervert. *See* **distort** (1). 4. To remove from a fixed position ▶ extract, pluck, rend, wrench. *See* **pull** (2).

wrestle *verb*
▶ fight, scuffle, tussle. *See* **contend** (1).

wretch *noun*
▶ loser, miserable. *See* **unfortunate.**

wretched *adjective*
1. So objectionable as to deserve condemnation ▶ contemptible, disgusting, obnoxious. *See* **offensive** (1). 2. So unpleasant or objectionable as to cause scorn or disgust ▶ suffering, woeful. *See* **miserable** (1).

3. Worthy of severe disapproval ▸ disgraceful, shameful, unfortunate. *See* **deplorable** (1). **4.** Having lost all hope ▸ dejected, forlorn, hopeless. *See* **despondent. 5.** Very bad ▸ appalling, awful, dreadful. *See* **terrible** (1).

wretchedness *noun*
1. A state of physical or mental suffering ▸ agony, pain, torment. *See* **distress** (1). **2.** A state of prolonged anguish and privation ▸ hardship, woe. *See* **misery** (1).

wriggle *verb*
▸ creep, wiggle, worm. *See* **crawl** (1).

wring *verb*
1. To alter the position of by a sharp, forcible twisting or turning movement ▸ twist, wrench, wrest. **2.** To obtain by coercion or intimidation ▸ blackmail, squeeze. *See* **extort.**

wrinkle *noun*
1. An indentation or seam on the skin, especially on the face ▸ crease, crinkle, crow's-foot, furrow, line. **2.** *Informal* A clever, unexpected new trick or method ▸ gimmick, trick, twist. *Informal:* kicker. *Slang:* angle, kick. **3.** A line made by the doubling of one part over another ▸ crease, pleat, pucker. *See* **fold** (1).

wrinkle *verb*
1. To make irregular folds in, especially by pressing or twisting ▸ crimp, crinkle, crumple, rimple, rumple, wrinkle. **2.** To bend together or form a crease ▸ crease, crumple, rumple. *See* **fold** (1).

writ *noun*
▸ charge, commandment, imperative. *See* **command** (1).

write *verb*
1. To form letters, characters, or words on a surface with an instrument ▸ engross, indite, inscribe, pen, scribe. *Informal:* scribble. **2.** To form by artistic effort ▸ create, produce. *See* **compose** (1). **3.** To be the author of a published work or works ▸ author, compose, pen. *See* **publish** (2).

write down *verb*
1. To place on a list or in a record or book ▸ catalog, chronicle, record. *See* **list**[1] (1). **2.** To become or make less in price or value ▸ devalue, downgrade, reduce. *See* **depreciate** (1).

write off *verb*
To cease consideration or treatment of ▸ dismiss, forget. *See* **drop** (7).

write-down *noun*
▸ cheapening, markdown, reduction. *See* **depreciation** (1).

write-up *noun*
▸ feature, piece, story. *See* **item** (1).

writhe *verb*
1. To twist agitatedly, as in pain, struggle, or embar-

rassment ▸ squirm, toss, twist. *See also* **shake. 2.** To move along in a crouching or prone position ▸ creep, wiggle, worm. *See* **crawl** (1).

writing *noun*
▸ piece, production, work. *See* **composition** (1).

written *adjective*
Of or relating to representation by means of writing ▸ calligraphic, graphic, scriptural.

wrong *adjective*
1. Containing an error or errors ▸ false, inaccurate, mistaken. *See* **erroneous. 2.** Not true ▸ specious, spurious, untrue. *See* **false** (1). **3.** Morally objectionable ▸ immoral, sinful. *See* **evil** (1). **4.** Afflicted with or exhibiting irrationality and mental unsoundness ▸ crazy, lunatic, mad. *See* **insane** (1). **5.** Not fair, right, or just ▸ discriminatory, unequal, unjust. *See* **unfair.**

wrong *adverb*
Not in the right way or on the proper course ▸ afield, amiss, astray, awry.

wrong *noun*
1. A wicked act or wicked behavior ▸ evil, misdeed, sin. *See* **crime** (2). **2.** The quality or sate of being morally bad or objectionable ▸ iniquity, wickedness. *See* **evil** (1). **3.** Lack of justice ▸ iniquity, unjustness. *See* **injustice** (2). *See synonym note at* **injustice. 4.** An unjust act ▸ disservice, inequity, offense. *See* **injustice** (1).

wrong *verb*
1. To treat improperly or unjustly ▸ mistreat, oppress, persecute. *See* **abuse** (1). **2.** To cause anger, resentment, or hurt feelings ▸ annoy, injure, upset. *See* **offend** (1).

✦ **CORE SYNONYMS:** *wrong, afield, amiss, astray, awry.* These adverbs mean not in the right or expected way: *plans that went wrong; straying far afield; spoke amiss; afraid the letter would go astray; thinking awry.*

◂ **ANTONYM:** *right*

---

wrongdoer *noun*
▸ scoundrel, villain. *See* **evildoer.**

wrongdoing *noun*
1. A wicked act or wicked behavior ▸ evil, misdeed, sin. *See* **crime** (2). **2.** Improper, often rude behavior ▸ misconduct, misdoing, naughtiness. *See* **misbehavior.**

wrongful *adjective*
1. Prohibited by law ▸ illicit, outlawed, unlawful. *See* **illegal** (1). **2.** Of, involving, or being a crime ▸ illicit, unlawful. *See* **criminal** (1).

wry *adjective*
▸ satiric, scoffing, sneering. *See* **sarcastic.**

xyz

x *verb*

► delete, erase, strike (out). *See* **cancel** (1).

yahoo *noun*

► chuff, Philistine, vulgarian. *See* **boor**. *See synonym note at* **boor**.

yak *verb*

Slang To talk rapidly on trivial matters ► blab, jabber, prattle. *See* **chatter** (1).

yak *noun*

Slang Incessant and inconsequential talk ► drivel, patter, small talk. *See* **chatter**.

yammer *verb*

1. *Informal* To express feelings of pain, dissatisfaction, or resentment ► fuss, grouch, whine. *See* **complain**. **2.** *Informal* To talk rapidly and incessantly ► blabber, jabber, natter. *See* **chatter** (1).

yammer *noun*

1. *Informal* An expression of pain or dissatisfaction ► carp, whimper, whine. *See* **complaint** (1). **2.** Incessant and inconsequential talk ► drivel, patter, small talk. *See* **chatter**.

yank *verb*

1. To move or cause to move with a sudden abrupt motion ► jerk, lurch, snap, twitch, wrench. *See synonym note at* **jerk**. *See also* **move**. **2.** To exert force so as to move something toward the source of the force ► drag, draw, tug. *See* **pull** (1). **3.** To remove from a fixed position ► pluck, rend, wrest. *See* **pull** (2).

yank *noun*

1. A sudden motion, such as a pull ► tug, wrench. *See* **jerk** (1). **2.** The act of drawing or pulling a load ► drag, draw, tow. *See* **pull** (1).

yap *verb*

To utter a shrill, short cry ► squeal, yawp, yelp, yip. *See also* **cry, shout**.

yap *noun*

1. A shrill, short cry ► squeal, yawp, yelp, yip. *See also* **cry, shout**. **2.** *Slang* The opening in the body through which food is ingested ► chops. *Slang:* trap. *See* **mouth** (1).

yard *noun*

1. A roofless area partially or entirely enclosed by walls or buildings ► courtyard, enclosure, quad. *See* **court** (1). **2.** An enclosure for livestock ► corral, sty. *See* **pen²** (1).

yardstick *noun*

► criterion, mark, measure. *See* **standard** (1). *See synonym note at* **standard**.

yarn *noun*

Informal An entertaining and often oral account of a real or fictitious occurrence ► anecdote, fable, story, tale. *Informal:* tall tale.

yaw *verb*

► keel, roll, seesaw. *See* **lurch** (1).

yawn *verb*

1. To open the mouth wide with a deep breath, as when tired or bored ► gape. **2.** To open wide ► gap, gape. *See also* **open, widen**.

yawning *adjective*

Open wide ► abysmal, abyssal, cavernous, gaping. *See also* **broad, open**.

yawp *verb*

To utter a shrill, short cry ► squeal, yap, yelp, yip. *See also* **cry, shout**.

yawp *noun*

A shrill, short cry ► squeal, yap, yelp, yip. *See also* **cry, shout**.

yea *adverb*

1. It is so; as you say or ask ► agreed, all right, assuredly. *See* **yes**. **2.** Not just this but also ► indeed, moreover. *See* **even** (2).

yea *noun*

An affirmative vote or voter ► aye, yes.

yeah *adverb*

Informal It is so; as you say or ask ► agreed, all right, assuredly. *See* **yes**.

year *noun*

A period of time of approximately 12 months, especially that period during which the earth completes a single revolution around the sun ► calendar year, season cycle, twelvemonth.

yearn *verb*

► covet, want. *See* **desire** (1). *See synonym note at* **desire**.

yearning *noun*

► craving, longing, wish. *See* **desire** (1).

years *noun*

1. A long time ► eon, eternity, long. *See* **ages**. **2.** Old age ► agedness, elderliness, senescence, seniority. *See* **age** (1).

yeast *noun*

1. A mass of bubbles in or on the surface of a liquid ► lather, suds. *See* **foam**. **2.** An agent that stimulates a reaction or change ► ferment, leaven, reactant. *See* **catalyst**.

yeast *verb*

To form or cause to form foam ► fizz, lather. *See* **foam** (1).

yeasty *adjective*

► frothy, lathery, sudsy. *See* **foamy**.

yell *verb*

To speak or say in a loud cry ► call, holler, roar. *See* **shout**. *See synonym note at* **shout**.

yell *noun*

A loud cry ► call, holler, whoop. *See* **shout**.

yellow *or* **yellow-bellied** *adjective*

Slang Ignobly lacking in courage ► chickenhearted, spineless. *Slang:* gutless. *See* **cowardly**.

yellow-belly *or* **yellow streak** *noun*
Slang An ignoble, uncourageous person ▸ dastard, milksop, sissy. *See* **coward**.

yelp *verb*
To utter a shrill, short cry ▸ squeal, yap, yawp, yip. *See also* **cry, shout**.

yelp *noun*
A shrill, short cry ▸ squeal, yap, yawp, yip. *See also* **cry, shout**.

yen *noun*
▸ craving, longing, yearning. *See* **desire** (1).

yenta *noun*
Slang ▸ gossipmonger, taleteller. *See* **gossip** (2).

yep *adverb*
Informal It is so; as you say or ask ▸ agreed, all right, assuredly. *See* **yes**.

yes *adverb*
It is so; as you say or ask ▸ absolutely, affirmative, agreed, all right, assuredly, aye, gladly, indeed, indubitably, naturally, right, roger, undoubtedly, unquestionably, willingly, yea. *Informal:* OK, uh-huh, yeah, yep, yup. *Slang:* for sure, right on, ten four. *Idiom:* you got it. *See also* **actually, really**.

yes *noun*
1. An affirmative vote or voter ▸ aye, yea. 2. The act of accepting or adopting ▸ adoption, assent, consent. *See* **acceptance** (1).

yes *verb*
To respond affirmatively; receive with agreement or compliance ▸ acquiesce, subscribe. *See* **assent**.

yes man *noun*
▸ flatterer, minion, slave. *See* **sycophant**.

yesterday *or* **yesteryear** *noun*
▸ auld lang syne, yore. *See* **past** (1).

yet *adverb*
1. Up to this time ▸ heretofore, previously. *See* **earlier** (2). 2. In addition ▸ also, besides, still. *See* **additionally**. 3. To a more extreme degree ▸ even, ever more so, still. 4. In spite of a preceding event or consideration ▸ however, nevertheless. *See* **still** (1).

yield *verb*
1. To bring into existence ▸ bring forth, give, provide. *See* **produce** (1). *See synonym note at* **produce**. 2. To make as income or profit ▸ clear, gain, produce. *See* **return** (3). 3. To give up or leave completely ▸ abdicate, relinquish, surrender. *See* **abandon** (1). *See synonym note at* **abandon**. 4. To give up in favor of another ▸ capitulate, give in, submit. *See* **surrender** (1). *See synonym note at* **surrender**. 5. To give in from or as if from a gradual loss of strength ▸ buckle, submit, surrender. *See* **succumb** (1). 6. To conform to the will or judgment of another ▸ bow, defer, submit. *Idioms:* give ground, give way. *See also* **humor**. 7. To moderate or change a position or course of action as a result of pressure ▸ ease off, slacken, soften. *See* **weaken** (1).

yield *noun*
1. The amount or quantity produced ▸ garner, output, production. 2. The produce harvested from the land ▸ fruit, yield. *See* **harvest** (1).

yielding *adjective*
1. Yielding easily to pressure or weight ▸ mushy, pulpy, squashy. *See* **soft** (1). 2. Submitting without objection or resistance ▸ nonresistant, resigned. *See* **passive**. 3. Marked by courteous submission or respect ▸ dutiful, obeisant. *See* **deferential**. 4. Easily managed or handled ▸ domesticated, mild, tame. *See* **gentle** (3).

yip *noun*
A shrill, short cry ▸ squeal, yap, yawp, yelp. *See also* **cry, shout**.

yip *verb*
To utter a shrill, short cry ▸ squeal, yap, yawp, yelp. *See also* **cry, shout**.

yoke *noun*
1. Two items of the same kind together ▸ duet, match, pair. *See* **couple**. 2. That which unites or binds ▸ ligature, link, tie. *See* **bond** (2). 3. A state of subjugation to an owner or master ▸ enslavement, servility, thrall. *See* **slavery**.

yoke *verb*
To bring or come together into a united whole ▸ join, unify, unite. *See* **combine** (1).

yoke with *verb*
To force another to accept a burden ▸ charge (with), inflict (on *or* upon), saddle (with). *See* **impose on** (1).

yokel *noun*
▸ bumpkin, hick, rustic. *See* **clodhopper**.

yore *noun*
▸ auld lang syne, yesteryear. *See* **past** (1).

young *adjective*
Being in an early period of growth or development ▸ fresh, green, immature, infant, juvenile, puerile, youthful. *See also* **childish**.

young *noun*
1. Young people collectively ▸ younger generation, youth. *Informal:* kids, young'uns. 2. The offspring, as of an animal or bird, for example, that are the result of one breeding season ▸ brood, litter, spawn. *See also* **progeny**.

✛ CORE SYNONYMS: *young, youthful, immature, juvenile, puerile, green*. These adjectives mean characteristic of or being in an early period of growth or development. *Young* is the most general of the terms: *The young children took a nap after lunch. Youthful* suggests characteristics, such as enthusiasm, freshness, or energy, that are associated with youth: *The students tackled the task with youthful ardor. Immature* applies to what is not yet fully developed; it sometimes suggests that someone falls short of an expected level of maturity: *The therapist specialized in helping emotionally immature adults. Juvenile* connotes immaturity, often childishness: *The newspaper reported on the juvenile pranks of the conventioneers. Puerile* is used derogatorily to suggest silliness, foolishness, or infantilism: *It was inappropriate to tell such puerile jokes during the meeting. Green* implies lack of training or experience and sometimes callowness: *The green recruits couldn't deal with the emergency.*

---

youngster *noun*
▸ juvenile, tot. *See* **child** (1).

youth *noun*
1. The time of life between childhood and maturity ▸ adolescence, greenness, juvenescence, juvenility, puberty, pubescence, salad days, youthfulness. *Informal:* spring, springtime. *See also* **childhood. 2.** A young person, usually between the ages of 13 and 19 ▸ adolescent, teen. *See* **teenager. 3.** Young people collectively ▸ young. *Informal:* kids.

youthful *adjective*
▸ fresh, immature, juvenile. *See* **young.** *See synonym note at* **young.**

youthfulness *noun*
▸ juvenility, puberty, salad days. *See* **youth** (1).

yowl *verb*
1. To utter or emit a long, mournful, plaintive sound ▸ bay, moan, wail. *See* **howl** (1). **2.** To shed tears ▸ howl, sob, weep. *See* **cry** (1). **3.** To cry loudly, as an upset baby does ▸ howl, wail. *See* **bawl** (1).

yowl *noun*
A long, mournful cry ▸ bay, ululation, wail. *See* **howl** (1).

yucky *adjective*
Slang Not pleasant or agreeable ▸ disagreeable, uncongenial, unsympathetic. *See* **unpleasant** (1).

yuk *verb*
Informal To express amusement or mirth ▸ cackle, chuckle, guffaw. *See* **laugh.**

yuk *noun*
Informal An act of laughing ▸ cackle, guffaw, laughter. *See* **laugh** (1).

yummy *adjective*
▸ delectable, savory, scrumptious. *See* **delicious** (1). *See synonym note at* **delicious.**

yup *adverb*
Informal It is so; as you say or ask ▸ agreed, all right, assuredly. *See* **yes.**

zaftig *adjective*
1. Having too much flesh ▸ chubby, pudgy. *See* **fat** (1). **2.** Having a full, voluptuous figure ▸ curvaceous, curvy, full-bosomed. *See* **shapely.**

zaniness *noun*
1. The quality of being laughable or comical ▸ funniness, ridiculousness, wittiness. *See* **humor** (1). **2.** Foolish behavior ▸ folly, silliness, tomfoolery. *See* **foolishness.**

zany *adjective*
1. Causing laughter or amusement ▸ comical, humorous, laughable. *See* **funny** (1). **2.** Displaying a lack of good sense ▸ daft, idiotic, ludicrous. *See* **foolish.**

zany *noun*
A person whose words or actions provoke or are intended to provoke amusement or laughter ▸ clown, comedian, jester. *See* **joker.**

zap *verb*
1. *Slang* To cause the death of ▸ cut down, destroy, finish (off). *See* **kill¹** (1). **2.** *Slang* To take the life of a

person or persons unlawfully ▸ destroy, kill, slay. *See* **murder** (1).

zeal *noun*
1. Passionate devotion to or interest in a cause or subject ▸ fervor, passion, verve. *See* **enthusiasm** (1). **2.** Powerful, intense emotion ▸ ardor, fervor. *See* **passion** (1). *See synonym note at* **passion. 3.** A state of often extreme religious ardor ▸ piety, reverence. *See* **devotion** (1).

zealot *noun*
1. One zealously devoted to a religion ▸ adherent, enthusiast. *See* **devotee** (1). **2.** An ardent devotee ▸ enthusiast, fanatic, maniac. *See* **fan².** **3.** One who holds extreme views or advocates extreme measures ▸ radical, revolutionist, ultraist. *See* **extremist.**

zealous *adjective*
1. Showing or having enthusiasm ▸ fervent, rabid, warm. *See* **enthusiastic** (1). **2.** Deeply concerned with God and the beliefs and practice of religion ▸ devout, holy, religious. *See* **pious** (1). **3.** Holding especially political views that deviate drastically from prevailing beliefs ▸ fanatical, radical, revolutionary. *See* **extreme** (4).

zealousness *noun*
▸ ardor, fervor, passion. *See* **enthusiasm** (1).

zenith *noun*
▸ apex, height, peak. *See* **climax** (1). *See synonym note at* **climax.**

zephyr *noun*
1. A gentle wind ▸ draft, puff. *See* **breeze** (1). **2.** A natural movement or current of air ▸ blast, gust, waft. *See* **wind¹** (1).

zero *noun*
1. *Informal* No thing; not anything ▸ null. *Slang:* nix. *See* **nothing** (1). **2.** *Informal* A totally insignificant person ▸ nobody, nothing, small fry. *See* **nonentity.**

zero in *verb*
1. To direct something, often toward a target ▸ level, point, train. *See* **aim** (1). **2.** To direct toward a common center ▸ channel, converge, focus. *See* **concentrate** (1).

zero hour *noun*
▸ crossroads, juncture. *See* **crisis** (1).

zest *noun*
1. Spirited enjoyment ▸ gusto, relish. *See also* **enthusiasm. 2.** A distinctive property affecting the sense of taste ▸ relish, tang, taste. *See* **flavor** (1). **3.** The outer covering of a fruit ▸ peel, rind. *See* **skin** (3).

zest *verb*
To impart flavor to ▸ flavor, season, spice (up).

✦ CORE SYNONYMS: *zest, gusto, relish*. These nouns denote spirited, hearty enjoyment or pleasure: *ate with zest; telling a joke with gusto; has no relish for repetitive work.*

zesty *adjective*
▸ fiery, pungent, sharp. *See* **spicy** (1).

zigzag *verb*
To turn aside sharply from a straight course ▸ slant, veer. *See* **swerve** (1).

zigzag *adjective*
Not proceeding straight to the point or object ▸ circuitous, devious, meandering, roundabout. *See* **indirect** (1).

zilch *noun*
1. *Slang* No thing; not anything ▸ null. *Informal:* zero. *See* **nothing** (1). **2.** *Slang* A totally insignificant person ▸ nobody, nothing, small fry. *See* **nonentity**.

zillion *noun*
Informal An indeterminately great amount or number ▸ bunch, multiplicity. *Informal:* bushel. *See* **heap** (3).

zinger *noun*
Informal Words or actions intended to excite laughter or amusement ▸ jest, quip, witticism. *See* **joke** (1).

zip *noun*
1. *Informal* Capacity for work or vigorous activity ▸ might, potency, power. *See* **energy**. **2.** A lively, emphatic, eager quality or manner ▸ life, verve, vivaciousness. *See* **spirit** (1).

zip *verb*
1. *Informal* To progress quickly and effortlessly ▸ coast, sail. *See* **breeze**. **2.** To move swiftly ▸ dash, sprint, whiz. *See* **rush** (1).

zippy *adjective*
▸ brisk, lively, vigorous. *See* **energetic**.

zodiac *noun*
▸ band, ring, wheel. *See* **circle** (1).

zone *noun*
1. A part of the earth's surface ▸ district, region. *See* **area** (2). **2.** A particular area used for or associated with a specific individual or activity ▸ district, region, terrain. *See* **territory** (1).

zonk *verb*
Slang To dull the senses, as with a heavy blow, a shock, or fatigue ▸ stun, stupefy. *See* **daze** (1).

zonked *adjective*
1. *Slang* Stupefied, intoxicated, or otherwise influenced by the taking of drugs ▸ high, hopped-up, lit (up). *See* **drugged**. **2.** *Slang* Stupefied, excited, or muddled with alcoholic liquor ▸ intoxicated, sodden, tipsy. *See* **drunk**.

zoom *verb*
▸ dash, sprint, zip. *See* **rush** (1).